ENCYCLOPAEDIA
JUDAICA

ENCYCLOPAEDIA JUDAICA

SECOND EDITION

VOLUME 11
JA–KAS

FRED SKOLNIK, *Editor in Chief*
MICHAEL BERENBAUM, *Executive Editor*

MACMILLAN REFERENCE USA
An imprint of Thomson Gale, a part of The Thomson Corporation

IN ASSOCIATION WITH
KETER PUBLISHING HOUSE LTD., JERUSALEM

Detroit • New York • San Francisco • New Haven, Conn. • Waterville, Maine • London

ENCYCLOPAEDIA JUDAICA, Second Edition

Fred Skolnik, *Editor in Chief*
Michael Berenbaum, *Executive Editor*
Shlomo S. (Yosh) Gafni, *Editorial Project Manager*
Rachel Gilon, *Editorial Project Planning and Control*

Thomson Gale
Gordon Macomber, *President*
Frank Menchaca, *Senior Vice President and Publisher*
Jay Flynn, *Publisher*
Hélène Potter, *Publishing Director*

Keter Publishing House
Yiphtach Dekel, *Chief Executive Officer*
Peter Tomkins, *Executive Project Director*

Complete staff listings appear in Volume 1

For more information, contact
Macmillan Reference USA
An imprint of Thomson Gale
27500 Drake Rd.
Farmington Hills, MI 48331-3535
Or you can visit our internet site at
http://www.gale.com

LIBRARY OF CONGRESS CATALOGING-IN-PUBLICATION DATA

Encyclopaedia Judaica / Fred Skolnik, editor-in-chief ; Michael Berenbaum, executive editor. -- 2nd ed.
v. cm.
Includes bibliographical references and index.
Contents: v.1. Aa-Alp.
ISBN 0-02-865928-7 (set hardcover : alk. paper) -- ISBN 0-02-865929-5 (vol. 1 hardcover : alk. paper) -- ISBN 0-02-865930-9 (vol. 2 hardcover : alk. paper) -- ISBN 0-02-865931-7 (vol. 3 hardcover : alk. paper) -- ISBN 0-02-865932-5 (vol. 4 hardcover : alk. paper) -- ISBN 0-02-865933-3 (vol. 5 hardcover : alk. paper) -- ISBN 0-02-865934-1 (vol. 6 hardcover : alk. paper) -- ISBN 0-02-865935-X (vol. 7 hardcover : alk. paper) -- ISBN 0-02-865936-8 (vol. 8 hardcover : alk. paper) -- ISBN 0-02-865937-6 (vol. 9 hardcover : alk. paper) -- ISBN 0-02-865938-4 (vol. 10 hardcover : alk. paper) -- ISBN 0-02-865939-2 (vol. 11 hardcover : alk. paper) -- ISBN 0-02-865940-6 (vol. 12 hardcover : alk. paper) -- ISBN 0-02-865941-4 (vol. 13 hardcover : alk. paper) -- ISBN 0-02-865942-2 (vol. 14 hardcover : alk. paper) -- ISBN 0-02-865943-0 (vol. 15: alk. paper) -- ISBN 0-02-865944-9 (vol. 16: alk. paper) -- ISBN 0-02-865945-7 (vol. 17: alk. paper) -- ISBN 0-02-865946-5 (vol. 18: alk. paper) -- ISBN 0-02-865947-3 (vol. 19: alk. paper) -- ISBN 0-02-865948-1 (vol. 20: alk. paper) -- ISBN 0-02-865949-X (vol. 21: alk. paper) -- ISBN 0-02-865950-3 (vol. 22: alk. paper)
1. Jews -- Encyclopedias. I. Skolnik, Fred. II. Berenbaum, Michael, 1945-
DS102.8.E496 2007
909'.04924 -- dc22

2006020426

ISBN-13:

978-0-02-865928-2 (set)
978-0-02-865929-9 (vol. 1)
978-0-02-865930-5 (vol. 2)
978-0-02-865931-2 (vol. 3)
978-0-02-865932-9 (vol. 4)
978-0-02-865933-6 (vol. 5)
978-0-02-865934-3 (vol. 6)
978-0-02-865935-0 (vol. 7)
978-0-02-865936-7 (vol. 8)
978-0-02-865937-4 (vol. 9)
978-0-02-865938-1 (vol. 10)
978-0-02-865939-8 (vol. 11)
978-0-02-865940-4 (vol. 12)
978-0-02-865941-1 (vol. 13)
978-0-02-865942-8 (vol. 14)
978-0-02-865943-5 (vol. 15)
978-0-02-865944-2 (vol. 16)
978-0-02-865945-9 (vol. 17)
978-0-02-865946-6 (vol. 18)
978-0-02-865947-3 (vol. 19)
978-0-02-865948-0 (vol. 20)
978-0-02-865949-7 (vol. 21)
978-0-02-865950-3 (vol. 22)

This title is also available as an e-book
ISBN-10: 0-02-866097-8
ISBN-13: 978-0-02-866097-4
Contact your Thomson Gale representative for ordering information.
Printed in the United States of America

10 9 8 7 6 5 4 3 2

TABLE OF CONTENTS

Initial letter "J" of Jeremias, *at the beginning of a prologue to the Book of Haggai in a 13th-century Bible from France. Princeton University Library, Med. and Ren. Mss., Garrett no. 29, vol. II, fol. 151r.*

JA-JU

JAAZANIAH, JAAZANIAHU (**Jazaniah**, **Jazaniahu**, Heb. יַאֲזַנְיָה, יַאֲזַנְיָהוּ, יְזַנְיָהוּ, יְזַנְיָה; "YHWH hears"), name of four biblical persons in the last generation of the kingdom of Judah.

(1) Jaazaniah son of the Maacathite, officer of the troops that went to Mizpah, to *Gedaliah son of Ahikam after the Babylonian occupation of Judah (II Kings 25:23; Jer. 40:8). It is possible that he is Jezaniah son of Hoshaiah mentioned in Jeremiah 42:1. Others attribute to him the Hebrew seal inscribed "To Jaazaniah, servant of the king." On the seal is an engraving of a rooster, the only such seal ever found in Ereẓ Israel (reproduced Ahituv, 126; Hoffman, 720).

(2) Jaazaniah son of Jeremiah son of Habazziniah, a *Rechabite put to the test by the prophet Jeremiah (Jer. 35:3).

(3) Jaazaniah son of Shaphan, an elder of the house of Israel, is mentioned in Ezekiel's vision of incense to the idols (Ezek. 8:11).

(4) Jaazaniah son of Azzur was a "prince of the people" and one of the twenty-five elders of Judah who appeared in a vision to the prophet Ezekiel (Ezek. 11:1). In a Lachish ostracon there appears the name of "Jaazaniah son of Tob-Shallem" (Ahituv, 33). A certain Jaazaniahu son of Benaiyahu is found at Arad (Ahituv, 86). The name of Yedoniah, the head of the Jewish community at *Elephantine, is probably an Aramaization of the Hebrew Jaazaniah.

BIBLIOGRAPHY: Pritchard, Texts, 277; Diringer, Iscr, 181, 229; Yeivin, in *Tarbiz*, 12 (1940/41), 253ff., 258. **ADD. BIBLIOGRAPHY:** S. Ahituv, *Handbook of Ancient Hebrew Inscriptions* (1992); Y. Hoffman, *Jeremiah II* (2001).

[Yehoshua M. Grintz]

JABAL (Heb. יָבָל), first son of Lamech by Adah; culture-hero, "father" of tent dwellers who keep livestock (Gen. 4:20) in the seventh generation after Adam. He is descended from Cain and is brother to *Jubal. The name Jabal may possibly be derived from a Semitic word meaning "a ram," or a root "to bring."

BIBLIOGRAPHY: W.F. Albright, *Yahweh and the Gods of Canaan* (1968), 85 n. 119; EM, 3 (1958), 451f. **ADD. BIBLIOGRAPHY:** N. Sarna, *Genesis* (1989), 37.

JABBOK (Heb. יַבֹּק), tributary of the Jordan from the east, the first river south of the Yarmuk. The Hebrew name is derived either from the root meaning "to empty itself" or from a sound imitating the noise of water flowing over pebbles. The Jabbok is the confluent of three wadis: Wadi Amman, which rises near the city of Amman, Wadi Suwayliḥ, and Wadi al-Dhulayl. It flows at first in an easterly direction until the junction of the first two wadis, where it turns to the north. At the source of ʿAyn al-Zarqāʾ, from which the Arabic name of the river, Nahr al-Zarqāʾ, was derived, it becomes a perennial river. After joining Wadi al-Dhulayl it turns west and then southwest, watering the fertile plain of Succoth near the Jordan. It falls from approximately 2,489 ft. (758 m.) near Amman to approximately 1,684 ft. (513 m.) at Wadi al-Dhulayl and to approximately 1,149 ft. (513 m.) below sea level at the Jordan, dropping approximately 3,611 ft. (1,100 m.) in all over a total length of 43¾ mi. (70 km.). The drainage area is 1,015 sq. mi. (2600 sq. km.) and the annual discharge is 16 billion gallons (60 million cu. m.).

By cutting the mountains of Gilead into two, creating the two regions of the territory of Gilead, the Jabbok forms a natural boundary which served as a political border throughout almost all historical periods. The first biblical reference to the river occurs in connection with Jacob, who forded it on his way to meet Esau, following his departure from Haran (Gen. 32:23). His struggle with the angel took place at Peniel on a ford of the Jabbok, a place which was considered consecrated by later generations. The river is described as the northern boundary of the kingdom of Sihon the Amorite in Numbers 21:24 and Joshua 12:2. These passages apparently refer only to the lower reaches of the river, for the upper reaches were within the border of the Ammonites and were excluded from the area of the Israelite conquest (Deut. 2:37). Reuben and Gad inherited the lands of Sihon and thus the Jabbok also served as their border with Ammon (Deut. 3:16). Border disputes continued and in the time of Jephthah, the Ammonite kings claimed that the Israelite tribes had infringed upon their border (Judg. 11:13, 22). In later times the river served as the boundary of the land of the Tobiads. Eusebius describes it as the boundary of the cities of Gerasa and Philadelphia (Onom. 102:19ff.). According to a milestone placed beyond the Roman bridge built over the river, the territory of Gerasa extended slightly south of the Jabbok. In Arab times it served as the boundary between the districts of al-Balqāʾ and ʿAjlūn.

BIBLIOGRAPHY: M.G. Ionides and T.S. Blake, *Report on the Water Resources of Trans-Jordan* (1939), passim; Maisler, Untersuchungen, 41–42; Abel, Geog, 1 (1933), 174–5, 485–6; Glueck, in: AASOR, 25–28 (1951), 250–1, 313–8; EM, 3 (1965), 455–8.

[Michael Avi-Yonah]

JABÈS, EDMOND (1908–1991), French poet. Born in Egypt, Jabès settled in Paris when the Egyptians expelled him after the 1956 Sinai Campaign. Revived awareness of his Jewish identity led to the *Le livre des questions* (1963), an esoteric work mingling surrealism and Kabbalah, aphorisms and poems in the romance of two concentration camp survivors. For Jabès, writing is an act of creation, and God an enigmatic "circle of luminous lettres." *Le livre des questions* became the first of a series of seven works which consist of persistent questioning, sometimes in the form of narratives or dialogues, sometimes in the form of apocryphal talmudic discussions between imaginary rabbis or kabbalistic letter games. The condition of the Jew is for Jabès identified with that of the poet: both the creative writer and the Jew can exist only in the state of exile. The term is of course taken in a spiritual sense and has no political meaning. The title of the first volume is also the title of the whole series; the others are *Le livre de Yukel* (1964), *Le retour au livre* (1965), *Yaël* (1967), *Elya* (1969), *Aely* (1972), and *El* (1973), which is the conclusion of a search for the unity of Judaism and literary creation, and at the same time a ceaseless questioning of the relevance of language. Jabès bemoans the loss of the Word (divine inspiration) and the wandering of the People of the Book.

Le livre des ressemblances (1976), *Le livre du partage* (1987), *Le livre de l'hospitalité* (1991), *Le livre du dialogue* (1994) continued the contruction a major poetic oeuvre. *Un étranger avec, sous le bras, un livre de petit format* (1989) seeks to characterize the stranger and to describe his role. The book is also a self-portrait.

[Anny Dayan Rosenman (2nd ed.)]

JABESH-GILEAD (Heb. יָבֵשׁ גִּלְעָד), Israelite city in Gilead in the period of the Judges and the monarchy. Its inhabitants appear to have had close ties with the tribe of Benjamin as is evidenced by two biblical traditions.

(1) The people of Jabesh-Gilead did not join the expedition of the Israelite tribes against Benjamin and in punishment their city was destroyed and their maidens seized and given to the Benjamites (Judg. 21).

(2) When Jabesh-Gilead was besieged by Nahash king of Ammon, it appealed for help to Saul the Benjamite who assembled the army of Israel at Bezek, reached Jabesh-Gilead after a day's march, and routed the Ammonites (I Sam. 11). Out of gratitude the men of Jabesh-Gilead went to Beth-Shean where the bodies of Saul and his sons had been hung on its wall after their defeat at Mount Gilboa, removed the bodies, and buried them under a tamarisk in their territory (I Sam. 31:11–13; I Chron. 10:11–12). For this deed of valor and mercy they were highly praised by David (II Sam. 2:4–6).

Some scholars suggest that Elijah's surname should be read "the Jabeshite" (*ha-Yaveshi*) instead of "the Tishbite" (*ha-*

Tishbi). The name Jabesh-Gilead has been preserved in the name of Wadi Yābis, a tributary of the Jordan 3½ mi. (6 km.) south of Pella (Peḥel). Eusebius locates it 6 (Roman) miles south of Pella on the road to Gerasa (Onom. 110:11ff.). Its accepted identification is with Tell al-Maqlūb; Glueck has proposed Tell Abu Kharaz as the site of Israelite Jabesh-Gilead and Tell al-Maqbara farther down the Wadi as the Roman-Byzantine city; these identifications, however, disregard Eusebius' statement.

BIBLIOGRAPHY: Abel, Geog, 2 (1938), 352; Glueck, Explorations, 1 (1951), 213ff.; Noth, in: ZDPV, 69 (1953), 28ff.; EM, 3 (1965), 459–6; Press, Ereẓ, 2 (1948), 384–5.

[Michael Avi-Yonah]

JABEZ, 16th-century family of scholars and Hebrew printers of Spanish origin. SOLOMON (d. before 1593) and JOSEPH JABEZ set up a Hebrew press in Salonika in 1546. They were the sons of ISAAC JABEZ (d. before 1555) and grandsons of Joseph *Jabez, called "the preacher." In 1494 in Mantua, Joseph, the grandfather, wrote a homiletical work, *Ḥasdei ha-Shem*, which his son Isaac prepared for publication. An edition of Psalms with his commentary was published by his grandson Joseph in Salonika in 1571. From 1546 to 1551 Solomon and Joseph printed a number of Hebrew books there. After a short interval in Adrianople, where they printed two books (1554–55), Solomon went to Constantinople and Joseph returned to Salonika, where he was an active printer until about 1570.

A plan to print the Talmud, which had been burned and banned in Italy in 1553, was not fulfilled beyond a few tractates (1561–67). Meanwhile Solomon had begun printing in Constantinople in 1559, and his brother Joseph rejoined him there in 1570. Alone or together they printed about 40 important works, among them responsa by Elijah Mizraḥi (1559–61) and Joseph ibn Lev (3 parts, 1560?–73), the first editions of Saadiah's *Emunot ve-De'ot* (1562), and A. Zacuto's *Yuḥasin* (1566). The brothers then made a new effort to reissue the Talmud; the larger part of it appeared 1583–93. Solomon's son ISAAC JABEZ was the author of *Ḥasdei Avot* (Constantinople, 1583), a commentary on *Avot, Yafik Raẓon* (Belvedere, 1593), a commentary on *haftarot*, and *Torat Ḥesed* (Belvedere, after 1593), on Hagiographa; he was not a printer. The Jabez press in Constantinople was financed by patrons such as Solomon Abenaes. Ḥayyim *Halicz worked at the press in about 1568.

BIBLIOGRAPHY: I. Rivkind, in: KS, 1 (1924), 294ff.; A. Elmaleh, *Toledot ha-Yehudim be-Salonika* (1924), 2, 5–6, 9–10; Rosanes, Togarmah, 2 (1937–38[2]), 234ff.; R.N. Rabinowitz, *Ma'amar al Hadpasat ha-Talmud* (1952), 67ff.; A. Yaari, *Ha-Defus ha-Ivri be-Kushta* (1967), 26–30.

JABEZ, JOSEPH BEN ḤAYYIM (d. 1507), Hebrew homilist and exegete. From the prefaces to some of his works, it seems that after the expulsion from Spain in 1492, Jabez traveled to Lisbon, to Sicily, and then to northern Italy, after a brief stay in Naples, arriving in 1493 or 1494 in Mantua, one of the largest and most cultured Italian-Jewish communities. There he remained and was honorably accepted as part of that community, apparently as its official preacher. Both in his travels and in Mantua, he preached about the meaning of the catastrophe that had befallen Spanish Jewry.

Among his published works, most of which were written after the expulsion, are four theological-homiletic compositions, which treat three main questions: *Ḥasdei ha-Shem* (Constantinople, 1533), on the Diaspora and messianic expectations; *Or ha-Ḥayyim* (appended to *Ma'amar ha-Aḥdut*, Ferrara, 1554; separately Shklov, 1796), on Jewish philosophy and its influence upon the fate of Spanish Jewry; and two short treatises (published with the first edition of *Or ha-Ḥayyim*), "*Ma'amar ha-Aḥdut*" (Ferrara, 1554) and "*Yesod ha-Emunah*" (appended to *Ma'amar ha-Aḥdut*), on the *ikkarim*, the "dogmas" of Judaism.

In asserting that philosophical rationalism was to blame for the choice by so many Spanish Jews of conversion rather than exile and suffering, he expressed the feeling of many of his contemporaries. Jabez – who hated philosophy – maintained that the philosophical intellectuals did not consider the observance of the commandments as the most important aspect of religious life, and therefore were not prepared to sacrifice themselves for that observance. He did not attack *Maimonides directly, but accused Maimonides' pupils and followers of distorting his views and thus of bringing the religious catastrophe upon Spanish Jewry.

Similarly, in his treatment of the question of the *ikkarim*, Jabez opposed all his predecessors who attempted to formulate a rational basis for the dogmas of Judaism, claiming that rational proof of a dogma leaves no room for religious belief. Accordingly, he did not include the existence and unity of God – which, he maintained, can be rationally proved – among the three main dogmas he proposed, namely, the creation of the world, divine providence, and the belief in redemption and the coming of the Messiah. Although polemics against many contemporaries comprise much of his writing, *Ḥasdei ha-Shem* contains elements of hope in its description of the exile as necessary for the expiation of the people's sins, and the great Jewish sufferings in his own day as indicative of the approaching redemption.

Besides these theological works, all printed in several later editions as well, Jabez' writings include a commentary on the tractate *Avot* (Constantinople, 1533), one on Psalms (Salonika, 1571), and many other works still in manuscript.

BIBLIOGRAPHY: Ben-Sasson, in: *Zion*, 26 (1960/61), 23–64, passim; idem, in: *Sefer Yovel… Y. Baer* (1960), 216–27.

[Joseph Dan]

JABIN (Heb. יָבִין; "discerning"), king of the Canaanite city of *Hazor. Jabin headed the Canaanite alliance and is mentioned in connection with two Israelite wars at the time of the settlement – in the battle at Merom, which is attributed to Joshua (Josh. 11), and the war of *Deborah (Judg. 4–5). The king of Hazor is named in the list of defeated Canaanite kings (Josh. 12:19). There is a reference to the victory over Sisera commander of the army of Hazor in Samuel's speech (I Sam. 12:9), but the king is not mentioned; and to both Sisera and Jabin in Psalms (83:10). The Bible also refers to Jabin as the king of Canaan in the introduction and conclusion to the prose account of *Deborah's war (Judg. 4:2, 23–24). He is mentioned as allied to *Heber the Kenite (4:17) but plays no part in the body of the story. The account of Joshua 11 notes that "Hazor beforetime was the head of all those kingdoms" (Josh. 11:10). These words may be a reference to an old tradition. Excavations reveal that Hazor was the largest and most important of the cities of Israel in the days of the Hyksos (in the 18th and 16th centuries B.C.E.) and the *el-Amarna period (14th century B.C.E.). Abdi-Tirshi, king of Hazor, is unique in referring to himself as "king of" (*šar*) Hazor in a letter to Pharaoh (El Amarna Letters, no. 227). The other local Canaanite dynasts never call themselves "king" in writing to Pharaoh. According to the Bible, Jabin was killed following the battle of Merom in Joshua's day, and Hazor was totally destroyed (Josh. 11:10–13). The mention of Jabin in Deborah's battle has always puzzled biblical scholars, and several theories have been proposed:

(a) Jabin was king of Hazor and defeated by Joshua. Remnants of his family relocated to Harosheth-Goiim and produced a descendant also named Jabin, whose general Sisera engaged the forces of Barak and Deborah (Radak to Judg. 4:2).

(b) Some modern scholars claim that Hazor was rebuilt and, with Radak, say that the second Jabin is another king, possibly a descendant of the first.

(c) *Sisera of Harosheth-Goiim was in fact the chief of the Canaanite kings in Deborah's war, and that it was a later tradition which described him as Jabin's general (this theory is supported by the fact that Jabin is not mentioned in Deborah's Song).

(d) The two wars took place in the same era and that Deborah's war actually preceded the war at Merom. Thus, in Deborah's war the Israelites first succeeded in overcoming the Canaanite chariots and subsequently "the hand of the children of Israel prevailed more and more against Jabin the king of Canaan, until they had destroyed Jabin the king of Canaan" (Judg. 4:24). This last engagement is the battle at the waters of Merom, which is in the Upper Galilee not far from Hazor, and eventually came to be attributed to Joshua, as were several other battles.

None of these explanations is satisfying. The account in Joshua appears to be secondary to those in Judges and supplies far less detail. Because Joshua 10 described the hero Joshua as the conqueror of the southern kings, the late writer of Joshua 11 followed his narrative style to compose an account of Joshua's conquest of the northern kings (Ahituv). He had before him Joshua 12:19 listing Hazor as a conquest of Joshua's, as well as the verses Judges 4:2, 23–24 that Jabin was "King of Canaan." As such, he was the natural choice to head the northern coalition. The detail that Hazor alone was burned (Jos. 11:13) provides an etiology of Hazor's ruins in the days of the author.

BIBLIOGRAPHY: B. Maisler (Mazar), *Toledot Ereẓ Yisrael*, 1 (1938), 228–31; idem, in: BJPES, 11 (1944), 35–41; idem, in HUCA, 24 (1952/53), 80ff.; Y. Aharoni, *Hitnaḥalut Shivtei Yisrael ba-Galil ha-Elyon* (1957), 89ff.; Malamat, in: *Sefer Yovel… Y. Baer* (1960), 1–7; idem, in: JBL, 79 (1960), 12–19; Albright, in: JPOS, 1 (1921), 54ff.; Täubler, in: *Festschrift… L. Baeck* (1938), 9–30; Alt, in: ZAW, 60 (1944), 67–85; Alt, KI Schr, 1 (1953), 135, 267, 270; 2 (1953), 371ff.; Maas, in: ZAWB, 77 (1958), 105–17. **ADD. BIBLIOGRAPHY:** B. Halpern, in: HTR, 76 (1983), 379–401; W. Moran, *The Amarna Letters* (1992), 288–89; S. Ahituv, *Joshua* (1995).

[Yohanan Aharoni / S. David Sperling (2nd ed.)]

JABLONEC NAD NISOU (Ger. **Gablonz an der Neisse**), city in N. Bohemia, now in Czech Republic, center of the world-famous glass-jewelry industry. Jewish settlement in Jablonec, which began in 1847, was connected with the development of this industry. As the neighboring town of Smrzovka (Ger. Morchenstern), where most of the plants were situated, caused difficulties for the Jews, Jablonec became the industry's commercial center. A congregation (*Kultusverein) was founded in Jablonec in 1872, a cemetery opened in 1882, and a Moorish-style synagogue dedicated in 1892; in 1893 a community was legally established, with a substantial number of foreign citizens, representatives of foreign firms. The community statute of 1928 granted them equal voting rights. Between the world wars, the majority of the population supported German nationalistic aims; in the same period the municipality prohibited *sheḥitah* in the slaughterhouse. During the Sudeten crisis and the annexation of the area by Germany (Oct. 1938), most of the Jews left Jablonec, some reestablishing their firms in the U.S. and England. The few who remained were deported to concentration camps. On Nov. 10, 1938, the synagogue was demolished. After World War II a small congregation was reestablished, most of its members from Subcarpathian Ruthenia; in 1969 it was affiliated to *Liberec. The Jewish population in Jablonec numbered 214 in 1869, 430 in 1880, 517 in 1895, and 799 in 1930 (2% of the total population). The municipality turned the cemetery into building plots in 1969.

BIBLIOGRAPHY: Urabin, in: H. Gold (ed.), *Die Juden und Judengemeinden Boehmens in Vergangenheit und Gegenwart* (1934), 145–8; Freund, in: *Selbstwehr*, 22 (1928), no. 8 (24.2), 6–7; Pick, in: *Jews of Czechoslovakia*, 1 (1968), 399–400.

[Meir Lamed]

JABLONNA, Polish military detention camp set up in the summer of 1920 during the Red Army counteroffensive on Warsaw. The facts that Jewish officers were serving in the Red Army and Jews were prominent in the Soviet leadership created an atmosphere of suspicion toward every Jew, particularly within the army, though civil authorities urged the Jews to make every sacrifice to save Poland. Young Jews, including former officers of the Austrian army, had joined up wishing to contribute their military experience to help in the defense. However, the military authorities, with the knowledge of the war minister K. Sosnkowski, gave instructions that all Jewish volunteers, and "in particular officers," be detained in a closed camp, which had been set up in a remote village north of Lodz, on the pretext that the detainees were not yet ready for active service, although the real reason was distrust and unwillingness to appoint Jewish officers in positions commensurate with their rank and experience. Three thousand Jewish soldiers and officers, among them many with a university education, were removed from their units and subjected to physical and mental hardship in the Jablonna camp. After protests were voiced through the Jewish press and by Jewish leaders, as well as by Polish intellectuals, the authorities yielded, and on the initiative of the Socialist vice premier, J. Daszyński, the notorious camp was liquidated in September.

BIBLIOGRAPHY: *Tsaitvailiger-Jidisher-National-Rat Bericht* (1923), 18, 20; A. Ciolkosz, in: *Dzielnica Zydowska obozu w Jablonnie, Zeszyty historyczne*, 20 (1971), 178–99; A. Podlishewski, "A bletel geshihte," *Haynt*, Jubilei numer (1928) 184–85; Y. Gruenbaum, *Milkhamot Yehudei Polania* (1951), 111–12.

[Moshe Landau]

JABNEEL (Heb. יַבְנְאֵל, Yavne'el). (1) Town on the northern border of the tribe of Judah between Mount Baalah and the sea (Josh. 15:11). It is identical with the later *Jabneh-Iamnia, now Yavneh, between Jaffa and Ashdod.

(2) Town on the southern border of the tribe of Naphtali (Josh. 19:33). In the Talmud it is identified with Kefar Yamma (now Khirbat Yamma in the Jordan Valley; TJ, Meg. 1:1, 70a). The biblical town was situated at Tell al-Na'm, a small but prominent mound 1 mi. (1½ km.) to the northeast near a spring. The remains on the tell include Bronze Age and Iron Age I pottery.

[Michael Avi-Yonah]

Modern Times

(3) Village (moshavah) in Israel with municipal council status, in the Jabneel Valley of eastern Lower Galilee, 6 mi. (10 km.) east of Kinneret. Jabneel was founded in 1901 by pioneers from Russia, with the aid of the Jewish Colonization Association, on land bought by Baron Edmond de Rothschild for agriculture based on grain farming. Lack of water retarded Jabneel's growth, until rich groundwater reserves were tapped in the 1940s. Farming was then intensified and diversified. After the War of Independence (1948), a *ma'barah* was set up nearby, many of whose inhabitants (originating mainly from Yemen and North Africa) were later absorbed into Jabneel itself. Three neighboring villages were united with Jabneel in the 1950s: the moshavah Bet Gan (founded in 1904) and the moshavim Mishmar ha-Sheloshah (1937) and Semadar (1953). The moshavah's area extends over 12 sq. mi. (32 sq. km.). In 1968 Jabneel had 1,520 inhabitants. Its farming included field crops and orchards, and it had a number of small enterprises, mainly in the food and farm service branches. In 2002 the population of Jabneel was 2,580. In recent years, Braslav ḥasidim began settling in the moshavah, reaching around 400 in number.

[Efraim Orni]

BIBLIOGRAPHY: (1) Mazar, in: IEJ, 10 (1960), 67ff.; Kaplan, in: BIES, 21 (1957), 199ff.; Abel, Geog, 2 (1938), 352. (2) A. Saarisalo, *The Boundary between Issachar and Naphtali* (1927), 46ff., 116ff.; Y. Aharoni, *Hitnaḥalut Shivtei Yisrael ba-Galil ha-Elyon* (1957), 78–79.

JABNEH (**Yavneh**; Heb יַבְנָה; Ar. **Yibnā** يبنى), biblical city located on the coastal plain, S. of Jaffa. Jabneh first appears in the Bible as Jabneel, on the northern border of the tribe of Judah (Josh. 15:11). It is counted as one of the Philistine cities, together with Gath and Ashdod, whose walls were breached by Uzziah king of Judah (II Chron. 26:6). The site of the biblical city is located on the tell in the village of Jabneh, which contains Iron Age remains. Earlier remains can be found at various sites along the Sorek River (Wadi Rubin), especially at Tell al-Sultan, northwest of Jabneh. In the Middle Bronze Age, a settlement was also established on the seacoast at Jabneh-Yam, which later served as the harbor of inland Jabneh. This harbor formed a separate entity as the center of the district of Maḥoz, which is possibly mentioned as early as the time of Thutmose III in his list of conquered cities (no. 61) and in the *El-Amarna letters. The remains of the harbor city show evidence of settlement in the Early, Middle, and Late Bronze Ages down to the Byzantine period; it is surrounded by a rampart and a wall approximately 3/5 mile (1 km.) long.

In the Hellenistic period, Jabneh (called Iamnia or Jamnia; Gr. Ἰάμνια) was included in the eparchy of Idumea, but was later transferred to Paralia. During that period the traders of Jabneh-Yam dedicated inscriptions at Delos to the gods Hauran and Heracles-Melkart. A Greek inscription found in 1986 suggests that a Sidonian colony settled there by the end of the Persian period. The city was used as a base by the foreign armies for repeated attacks on Judean territory (I Macc. 5:58). At the time of the Maccabean revolt, Jabneh had a Jewish community, which was threatened with extermination by the rest of the population. As a warning, Judah Maccabee attacked the harbor and burned the ships (II Macc. 12:8–9). Jonathan the Hasmonean fought one of the decisive battles of the Maccabean revolt in the region (I Macc. 10:69ff.); another battle was fought near the city under Simeon (I Macc. 15:40). According to Josephus, Simeon captured the city (Ant., 13:215), but since the Books of Maccabees do not mention such a conquest, it is preferable to attribute it to Hyrcanus. At the accession of Alexander Yannai, Jabneh was already a Hasmonean city (Jos., Ant., 13:324) and the entire population was Jewish. Pompey attempted to revive it as a gentile town in 63 B.C.E. (*ibid.*, 14:75; Wars, 1:157), leaving the actual work of reconstruction to his deputy Gabinius (Wars, 1:166); however, the new town was short-lived as an independent unit. It was probably given to Herod at the time of his accession. He willed it to his sister Salome (Ant., 17:321; Wars, 2:98); after her death it passed to the empress Livia, and then to her son Tiberius. It was the seat of an imperial procurator (Ant., 18:158). By then, the city was purely Jewish and was a toparchy of Judea (Wars, 3:55). In the first Jewish war, it was occupied by Vespasian; Titus passed through it on his way to Jerusalem. When R. Johanan b. Zakkai left besieged Jerusalem and arrived at the Roman camp, he asked the emperor to "give him Jabneh and its scholars" (Git. 56b).

After the fall of Jerusalem, the Sanhedrin was reconstituted at Jabneh, first under R. Johanan and then under the patriarch Rabban Gamaliel II (Tosef., Ber. 2:6). The Sanhedrin met in the upper story of a house or in a vineyard near a pigeon house. In some respects, the city was now regarded as the equal of Jerusalem: there the year was intercalated and the *shofar* blown, and pilgrims from Asia visited the city three times a year (Tosef., Ḥul. 3:10; RH 29b; Shab. 11a). Among the most important decisions made at Jabneh was the arranging of the definitive canon of the Bible. Between 70 and 132 C.E., Jabneh was "the great city, the city of scholars and rabbis"; most of the *tannaim* of this period taught there and Rabban Gamaliel was buried there. The city is described as being situated near a stream of water; its wheat market was well known and cattle and poultry were raised in the vicinity.

With the outbreak of the Bar Kokhba Revolt, Jabneh ceased to be the center of Jewish life in Ereẓ Israel and the Diaspora. After the war, unsuccessful attempts were made to transfer the Sanhedrin from Galilee back to Jabneh (RH 31a–b). A strong Jewish element remained in the city, but the Samaritans constituted the majority (Tosef., Dem. 1:13). A Samaritan inscription belonging to a synagogue was discovered there. By the fifth century, the city was predominantly Christian and the bishop took part in the church councils at Nicea (325 C.E.), Chalcedon (451 C.E.), and Jerusalem (518 and 536 C.E.). The Arabs conquered the city in 634 C.E. In Crusader times it was turned into a fortress called Ybellin, a fief of the noble family of Balian that served as a base for operations against Muslim Ashkelon.

[Michael Avi-Yonah]

In Rabbinic Literature

Even before the destruction of the Second Temple, the town was a center of Torah with a well-known *bet din*, consisting of 23 members, which tried capital cases (Sanh. 11:4; Sif. Deut. 154). During the Jewish War, even before the civil war in Jerusalem, the town made its peace with Vespasian (Jos., Wars, 4:130; cf. 4:663). *Johanan b. Zakkai quickly became the leader not only of the town itself, where he displaced the "sons of *Bathyra" (RH 29b), but also of a notable section of the Jewish population of Ereẓ Israel and even of the Diaspora. He turned Jabneh into the center of halakhic study as well as the new seat of the self-governing administration of the population in place of destroyed Jerusalem (see RH 4:1–2). Jabneh's position was further consolidated with the rise of Rabban *Gamaliel II (called "of Jabneh"). The academy of Jabneh was called "the vineyard at Jabneh" (Tosef., Eduy. 1:1, Yev. 6:6; Ket. 4:6; Ber. 63b; et al.). Rabbinic literature mentions many incidents that happened in Jabneh and its scholars ("our rabbis of Jabneh" – Ber. 17a; "our rabbis in Jabneh" – Ket. 50a; "the scholars of Jabneh" – Kid. 49b; "scholars in Jabneh" – Nid. 15a; "elders in Jabneh" – Tosef., Kelim BB 5:6) are mentioned with praise: "They who went to Jabneh, to a place where disciples and scholars are numerous and love the Torah, their name became great in Torah" (ARN 14, 59). In Jabneh the new moon was proclaimed and the year intercalated, and there several important *takkanot* were made – among them formulations of the 18 blessings of the *Amidah* and the "blessing" against Christians and other heretics (see *Amidah*). At Jabneh the dispute between Bet Shammai and Bet Hillel was decided in favor of the latter (TJ, Ber. 1:7, 3b). The scholars of other academies and other localities also showed great interest in the learning at Jabneh (Tosef., Sot. 7:9, Yad. 2:16). Questions and questioners reached Jabneh from all parts of Ereẓ Israel and the Diaspora (Par. 7:6; Tosef., *ibid.* 7 (6):4, Ḥul 3:10, Mik. 4:6, Nid. 4:3, Kil. 1:3 and 4). The decisions and customs of Jabneh had their influence in the *halakhah* not only during the period of its hegemony (Tosef., Nid. 6:9), but also after its decay and even in the time of the Babylonian *amoraim* (Nid. 50b). The foundations for the editing of the *Mishnah were laid at Jabneh, and the main part of tractate **Eduyyot* was arranged there. It is referred to as the "treasure house of Jabneh" (Tosef., Dem. 1:13–14).

The outlook of the scholars of Jabneh is testified to by their saying: "I am a creature and my fellow is a creature. My work is in the town and his work is in the country. I rise early for my work and he rises early for his work. Just as he does not presume to do my work, so I do not presume to do his work. Will you say, I do much and he does little? We have learnt: Both he who does much and he who does little [do well], provided he directs his heart to heaven" (Ber. 17a). Because of the great work accomplished in Jabneh, which served as a center for the revival of the people and the *halakhah* after the destruction of the Temple, the name came to be used in the 19th century – not altogether accurately – for the idea of a spiritual center.

[Moshe David Herr]

BIBLIOGRAPHY: Abel, Geog, 2 (1938), 352–3; Avi-Yonah, Geog, index; EM, s.v.; Ben Zvi, in: BIES, 13 (1948), 166–8; Dothan, *ibid.*, 16 (1952), 37ff.; Kaplan, *ibid.*, 21 (1957), 199–207; H. Hirschensohn, in: *Yerushalayim*, 10 (1914), 311–3; G.F. Moore, *Judaism*, 1 (1927), 83ff.; M. Stein, in: *Zion*, 3 (1938), 118–22; G. Alon, *ibid.*, 183–214; S. Klein (ed.), *Sefer ha-Yishuv*, 1 (1939), 74–77; idem, *Ereẓ Yehudah* (1939), index; Baron, Social^2, 2 (1952), 120, 126; Alon, Toledot, index; Alon, Meḥkarim, 1 (1957), 219–73; E.E. Urbach, in: *Beḥinot*, 4 (1953), 61–72; J. Neusner, *Life of Rabban Yohanan ben Zakkai* (1962). **ADD. BIBLIOGRAPHY:** M. Fischer (ed.), *Yavne-Yam and its Vicinity* (1991); Y. Tsafrir, L. Di Segni, and J. Green, *Tabula Imperii Romani. Iudaea – Palaestina. Maps and Gazetteer.* (1994), 149–50; F. Vitto, "Mahoza D-Yamnin: A Mosaic Floor From the Time of Eudocia?" in: *Atiqot*, 35 (1998), 109–34; B. Isaac, "A Seleucid Inscription from Jamnia-on-the-Sea," in: IEJ, 41 (1991), 132–44; B. Bagatti, *Ancient Christian Villages of Judea and Negev* (2002), 174–75; G.S.P. Grenville, R.L. Chapman, and J.E. Taylor, *Palestine in the Fourth Century. The Onomasticon by Eusebius of Caesarea* (2003), 137.

JABOTINSKY, VLADIMIR (Ze'ev; 1880–1940), Zionist activist, soldier, orator, writer and poet; founder of the *Jewish Legion during World War I. Jabotinsky greatly influenced a large section of the Jewish people and as head of the *Betar movement was the undisputed source of inspiration to masses of Jewish youth, particularly in Eastern Europe. His accomplished oratory – in Russian, Hebrew, Yiddish, English, French, Italian, and German – characterized by compelling logic and magnetic imagery, drew large audiences around the world and was often the climactic experience of Zionist congresses. Born in Odessa into a middle-class Jewish family, Jabotinsky was educated in Russian schools. Before his bar mitzvah he took Hebrew lessons from Y *Rawnitzki, but according to his autobiography, he had "no inner contact with Judaism," and never "breathed the atmosphere of Jewish cultural tradition" during his youth. In 1898 Jabotinsky went to Berne and Rome, where he studied law and served as foreign correspondent of two Odessa dailies (often under the pen name "Altalena"). Under the influence of his professors in Rome, he became a disciple of the economic doctrine of socialism, though he rejected Marxism as a mechanistic philosophy that disregarded the individual. Later on, especially after the Bolshevik Revolution, he radically revised his attitude toward socialism as an economic conception as well. Throughout – individualism was a dominant feature of his thinking.

Jabotinsky returned to Odessa and in 1901 joined the editorial staff of *Odesskiya Novosti*, his brilliant daily feuilletons becoming widely popular. In the spring of 1903, when the danger of a pogrom in Odessa seemed imminent, he joined the initiators of a Jewish self-defense group. He then traveled the length and breadth of Russia urging self-defense on the Jewish communities. After the pogrom in Kishinev in the same year, he immersed himself in Zionist activities. As a delegate to the Sixth *Zionist Congress, he was fascinated by *Herzl's personality, but he nonetheless voted against Herzl on the *Uganda project. He became the foremost Zionist lecturer and journalist in Russia in the period before 1914. As a member of the editorial board of the Zionist journal **Raszvet*, he played a leading role in the evolution of Zionist ideology in Russia and was an architect of the *Helsingfors Program of "synthetic" Zionism (1906), which advocated both settlement in Ereẓ Israel and political and educational activities in the Diaspora. Jabotinsky also crusaded in Russia against antisemitism, Jewish assimilation, and the quasi-nationalism of the *Bund.

In 1909, after the revolution of the Young Turks, the World Zionist Organization appointed Jabotinsky editor of four publications in Constantinople (in French, Hebrew, and Ladino) and entrusted him with political work in Ottoman circles until a disagreement with David *Wolffsohn, the president of the World Zionist Organization, on questions of tactics led to his resignation. His stay in Turkey gave him a deep insight into the weaknesses of the regime.

At the outbreak of World War I, Jabotinsky was sent to Western Europe as a roving correspondent by the Moscow liberal daily *Russkiya Vedomosti*. In Turkey's declaration of war on the Allied Powers, he foresaw at once her defeat and the inevitable dismemberment of the Ottoman Empire. It was essential, he decided, that the Zionist movement should abandon its neutral stand in order to achieve its aims in Palestine at the end of the war. While in Alexandria, where thousands of Jewish deportees from Ereẓ Israel were concentrated, Jabotinsky, joined by Joseph *Trumpeldor, advanced the idea among them of raising a *Jewish Legion to join the Allies in liberating Ereẓ Israel from Ottoman rule. The British military authorities in Egypt, however, rejected the idea, explaining that Britain did not intend opening a front in Palestine at all. But the approach to the British bore unexpected fruit: the Zion Mule Corps, which took part in the Gallipoli campaign. It was led by Col. John Henry Patterson and his deputy was Trumpeldor. Jabotinsky, however, went to Rome, Paris, and London to plead before the Allied statesmen the case for a full-fledged Jewish Legion to fight in Palestine, but met with opposition on all sides. The official Zionist leadership, which insisted on remaining neutral in the war, also condemned Jabotinsky's "legionist" propaganda and actually forced him to leave the Zionist Organization. The only public figures who cooperated with him were Pinhas *Rutenberg, Meir *Grossman, and Joseph *Cowan, while Chaim *Weizmann gave him discreet support. By 1916 Jabotinsky's lonely but energetic campaign had won him substantial support in Britain, but it was only after the death in June 1916 of War Minister Kitchener, who had determinedly opposed any "eastern front," that the winds began to favor his efforts. In 1917 the British government consented to the formation of Jewish units. The first to be established was the "38th Battalion of Royal Fusiliers" under Patterson's command in England, which was joined in 1918 by the 39th (American) and 40th (Palestinian) Battalions. These were later consolidated into the "First Judean Regiment" with the *menorah* as its insignia. At the time, the British considered this an adequate solution to the problem of Jewish immigrants in East London, who were Russian nationals who could not be drafted into the British Army and refused to return to antisemitic Russia and serve in the Czar's army. Jabotinsky himself joined the 38th Battalion as a lieutenant and was decorated for heading the first company to cross the Jordan. His book *The Story of the Jewish Legion* (1945), first published in Russian (1928), is a monument to this chapter in Jewish history.

After the war, Jabotinsky insisted on the need to maintain the Jewish Legion in Palestine as a guarantee against the outbreak of Arab hostility, which was encouraged by the anti-Zionist policy of the British military administration. In spite of Patterson's efforts and Jabotinsky's unrelenting demands, Weizmann and the other official Zionist leaders ultimately accommodated themselves to the British policy, and the demobilization of the Jewish Legion took place without strong Jewish opposition. Anticipating anti-Jewish violence by Arab extremists, in the spring of 1920 Jabotinsky organized the *Haganah in Jerusalem, openly leading it to confront the incited Arab masses during the Passover riots of that year. He was immediately arrested by the British authorities, together with other members of the Haganah, and sentenced by a military court to 15 years hard labor. 19 of his young comrades were sentenced to three years each. A storm of indignation broke out in Palestine, England, and America among Jews and gentiles, and the sentences were radically reduced. In July 1920 Sir Herbert *Samuel, the newly appointed first High Commissioner for Palestine, granted amnesty to all those – Jews and Arabs alike – imprisoned in connection with the Jerusalem riots. Jabotinsky left Acre prison acclaimed a hero by all sections of the *yishuv*, including the Labor parties. Jabotinsky went to London in September 1920 and succeeded in having the whole case quashed, the sentences expunged, and a stinging rebuke handed to the Palestine judiciary by the Army's Advocate General. While in London he was urged by Weizmann to join the Board of Directors of the newly established *Keren Hayesod and, afterwards, the Zionist Executive. Together with Weizmann, he constructed a program that included demands for the restoration of the Jewish Legion and for consultation between the British government and the Zionist Organization on the appointment of the High Commissioner for Palestine. At the Twelfth Zionist Congress (1921), Jabotinsky defended the incumbent leadership against the attacks of the opposition (consisting mainly of the *Brandeis group) and was reelected to the Zionist Executive. He was a member of the first Keren Hayesod delegation to the U.S. Though he opposed Churchill's 1922 White Paper on Palestine which gave a restricted definition of the phrase "a Jewish National Home in Palestine," he did not then resign, and so formally shared with Weizmann the responsibility for the Executive's acquiescence in it.

During the 12th Zionist Congress, Jabotinsky, who was always a sympathizer of the Ukrainian national movement, met Maxim Slavinsky, the representative of *Petlyura's Ukrainian government-in-exile, which was at the time preparing to march into the Bolshevik-held Ukraine. They concluded an agreement providing for a Jewish gendarmerie to follow in the rear of Petlyura's army and protect the Jewish population against pogroms. At this juncture the Ukrainians gave up the struggle, so the project came to naught.

In the second half of 1922, Jabotinsky became increasingly critical of Herbert Samuel's rule in Palestine and of what he considered to be Zionist accommodation with Great Britain's disregard of her obligations. His urging to make public Britain's breaches of her undertaking was rejected by Weizmann. In January 1923 the combination of his acute differences with Weizmann and his other colleagues led to his resignation from the Executive and his decision to leave the Zionist Organization. For a while thereafter his sole contributions to Zionist political life were articles in the Russian weekly *Razsvet*. Later in 1923, during a lecture tour to the Baltic States, however, he met a lively response from Jewish youth and decided to form a new activist movement to revise Zionist policies. In his lectures he demanded a return to Herzl's concept of the Jewish State, the restoration of the Jewish Legion, and a widespread political offensive for the achievement of a radical change in British policy, which should have as its avowed aim facilitating a Jewish majority in Palestine – including Transjordan – by means of rapid mass immigration. Transjordan had originally been included by Britain in the projected National Home.

In 1925 a convention of his followers in Paris proclaimed the formation of the World Union of Zionist *Revisionists in which Vladimir Tiomkin was elected president. He lived in Paris and made it the headquarters of his movement until 1936, except for a brief period from 1928 through 1929 during which he lived in Jerusalem as director of the Judaea Insurance Company and editor of the daily *Do'ar ha-Yom*. In 1930, when he was on a lecture tour in South Africa, the British administration, impressed by his growing influence on the Jewish youth, prevented his return to Palestine by canceling his return visa. He resumed residence in Paris, but was constantly on the move throughout Europe, actively collaborating in dozens of publications in many languages and drawing attention to the shortcomings of Zionist political policies and economic methods in Palestine – all of which widened the chasm between him and the Zionist leadership. His relations with the Labor movement in Palestine and in the Zionist movement grew increasingly strained as they charged him with "enmity to labor," militarism, and even "fascism." The establishment of the "enlarged" *Jewish Agency in 1929, with half of the seats allocated to unelected non-Zionist "notables," and the refusal of the Seventeenth Zionist Congress (1931) to accept his proposal to define the aim of Zionism as "the establishment of the Jewish State," induced Jabotinsky to press more and more for the secession of his movement from the Zionist Organization and the formation of an independent instrument of Zionist policy and economic activity.

After Hitler's rise to power in 1933, Jabotinsky espoused the total boycott of Nazi Germany by the Jewish people and opposed the Jewish Agency's **Haavara* agreement with the Berlin regime. In the same year, he vigorously defended the two young Revisionists in Palestine, Avraham Stavski and Zevi Rosenblatt, who were accused of assassinating the labor leader Chaim *Arlosoroff. In 1934, through the mediation of Pinhas Rutenberg, Jabotinsky and David *Ben-Gurion concluded a series of agreements intended to ease internal Zionist conflicts, to regularize the relationship between the *Histadrut and the Revisionist workers, and to lead eventually to political understanding and cooperation between Labor Zionism and Revisionism. The scheme fell through, however, when the draft agreement on labor relations was rejected by the majority in a Histadrut plebiscite (1935), dominated by the far Left Ha-Shomer ha-Ẓa'ir. These events increasingly alienated Jabotinsky from the Zionist Organization. In 1935, when the Zionist General Council introduced a "discipline clause" prohibiting further "independent political activities" by the Zionist parties, a Congress in Vienna, representing 713,000 voters, mostly from Eastern Europe, founded the New Zionist Organization (NZO), with Jabotinsky as president (*nasi*) and headquarters in London. Jabotinsky's 1937 testimony before the Royal Commission on Palestine was a dramatic "*J'accuse*" against British policy and a stirring description of the "frozen stampede" of Jewish masses in Central and Eastern Europe. He simultaneously inaugurated his "policy of alliances" with European governments interested in solving the problem of their Jewish minorities through emigration. His scheme provided for an internationally sponsored ten-year plan for the "evacuation" of 1,500,000 East European Jews to Palestine. This policy was violently opposed by most sections of the Jewish public, who feared that it might be interpreted as Jewish recognition of the antisemitic contention that Jews are essentially aliens in the countries of their residence, and they refused to believe in his repeated warnings of the coming catastrophe. But Jabotinsky achieved a measure of understanding for his scheme in Polish government circles, who were prepared to exert pressure on Great Britain and defend the policy in the League of Nations. Intent on breaking the prohibitive British regulations on immigration to Palestine, Jabotinsky, starting in 1932, launched a campaign, and an organization named *Af-Al-Pi* ("in-spite-of") for "illegal" immigration, which, between 1936 and 1942, became a major activity of his movement. Jabotinsky's attitude toward Jewish defense in Palestine also underwent a transformation that paralleled his disenchantment with British rule. In the 1920s he still advanced the idea of a legion of official Jewish units serving as part of the British garrison of Palestine to prevent Arab opposition from deteriorating into anti-Jewish violence. By the end of the 1920s the hope of a resuscitation of the Legion had faded and the Zionist leadership had presided over the development of the Haganah. After the Arab riots of 1929, dissatisfaction with the political leadership of the Haganah led to a split and the creation of the Haganah "B" – which was subsequently renamed "Ha-Irgun ha-Ẓeva'i ha-Leummi" (the National Military Organization). Its members saw Jabotinsky as their inspirer and natural leader. After the Arab riots broke out in 1936, he accepted his position as the head of the Irgun, but due to his enforced absence from the country he could influence IẒL's activities only in very general terms. Differences of opinion between Jabotinsky and the IẒL leadership were ironed out in 1939 at a clandestine conference in Paris, at which David *Raziel, the commander of IẒL, unreservedly accepted Jabotinsky's authority. But opposition to Jabotinsky and his policies inside IẒL resulted in the organization's second split immediately after his death (1940), when Avraham *Stern formed his own group, *Loḥamei Ḥerut Yisrael* (Fighters for the Freedom of Israel). With the outbreak of World War II, Jabotinsky demanded the creation of a Jewish army to fight the Nazis alongside the Allied armies, and a united Jewish representation at the future peace conference. In his book *The Jewish War Front*, published in London in 1940, he formulated what he believed should be the attitude of the Jewish people to the war and its probable aftermath. His proposal for a Jewish army was rejected by British Prime Minister Chamberlain. Jabotinsky did not abandon the idea, and in February 1940 he sailed for the U.S. to enlist Jewish and non-Jewish support for a Jewish army. At the same time he urged the U.S. to join in the war against the Nazis. His stirring addresses gave rise to considerable enthusiasm, and he enlisted the support of British Ambassador Lord Lothian, who saw the value, at this critical stage of the war, of Jabotinsky's vigorous pro-British message. But on August 4, 1940, during a visit to the Betar summer camp near New York City, he died suddenly of a heart attack. In his will, written in the late 1930s, Jabotinsky said: "My remains will be transferred [to Ereẓ Israel] only on the instructions of a Jewish Government." Twenty-four years after his death, his remains, together with those of his wife, Johanna, were taken to Israel by a government decision and buried in a State funeral on Mount Herzl.

The Hebraist, Writer, and Poet

Jabotinsky took the idea of the renaissance of Hebrew as the living language of the Jewish people very seriously. Intensive study quickly made him an outstanding Hebraist. In 1910 he translated *The Raven* by Edgar Allen Poe into Hebrew and delivered his first Hebrew address in public. Before World War I he toured the Jewish communities of Russia lecturing on "The Language of Our Culture" and advocating the establishment of Hebrew day schools with Hebrew as the language of instruction in all subjects. This idea met with opposition not only in assimilationist and Yiddishist circles, but also among some Zionists, who considered it utopian. Jabotinsky's contribution to Hebrew language and literature was manifold. His translation of ten cantos of Dante's *Inferno* is a masterpiece. In 1924 he published *Targumim*, a collection of translations of French, English, and Italian poetry based on Sephardi prosody. He was the first Hebrew poet to write in Sephardi prosody. The literary "Establishment" whose poetry was conceived in Ashkenazi pronunciation finally accepted the change. Jabotinsky moreover is credited with influencing the whole gamut of modern Hebrew poetry. He collaborated with S. Perlman to edit the first Hebrew geographical atlas (1925). *Ha-Mivta ha-Ivri*, an essay on the phonetics of Hebrew, appeared in Tel Aviv in 1930. An advocate of writing modern Hebrew in Latin characters, Jabotinsky prepared a textbook of "latinized" Hebrew (*Taryag Millim*), which was published in South Africa in 1949 and in Israel in 1950. He also wrote several patriotic songs that became an inspiration for Zionist youth, particularly of the Betar movement. "*Shir Asirei Akko*" ("The Song of the Prisoners of Acre"), "*Minni Dan*," "*Kullah Shelli*," "*Shir Betar*," and "*Semol ha-Yarden*." His fragmentary autobiography *Sippur Yamai* ("The Story of My Life") is written in elegant Hebrew prose. But his main contributions to belles lettres were in Russian. Two verse plays, "*Krov*" ("Blood") and "*Ladno*" ("All Right"), were staged in 1901 and 1902 in the Odessa Municipal Theater; "*Bednaya Sharlotta*" ("Poor Charlotte": a poem about Charlotte Corday) and a masterly Russian translation of Bialik's "*Massa Nemirov*" appeared in 1904; a satirical play on Jewish life in Russia "*Chuzhbina*" ("On Foreign Soil"), written in 1908, was suppressed by Czarist censorship and published in Berlin only in 1922. Bialik's "*Songs and Poems*" in Jabotinsky's Russian translation (1910) was a best-seller (seven printings within two years), becoming a classic in its own right and making a deep impression not only on Jewish youth but on Russian intellectual circles as well. A collection of his short stories, translated from Russian into English (*A Pocket Edition of Several Stories Mostly Reactionary*) appeared in Paris in 1925.

Jabotinsky's major literary achievement, the biblical novel *Samson the Nazarite*, written and first published in Russian (1926) and later translated into Hebrew, English, and German, reflects much of his philosophy of Jewish history and life in general. Chaim Nachman Bialik described it as the only Jewish "national myth." In 1930, on his 50th birthday, his friends published a limited edition of three volumes of his poems, short stories, and essays in Russian. The novel "*Pyatero*" ("The Five"), which appeared in Russian in 1936, is a largely autobiographical picture of assimilating Jewish circles in Odessa. From the late 1920s until his death, he published articles in Yiddish almost weekly in the Warsaw Jewish press (first in *Haynt* and later in *Der Moment*) and in the New York *Jewish Morning Journal*. For years this was his only stable source of income and the chief vehicle for the propagation of his thoughts. Jabotinsky was an unusually gifted linguist, amassing a knowledge of some 20 languages. He had an intense interest in languages and a precious ability to grasp their spirit. A comprehensive, annotated collection of his writings, including speeches and letters, was published in 18 volumes in Hebrew (Tel Aviv, 1947–59) by his son Eri.

In the 1990s the Israeli Bureau of Statistics revealed that Jabotinsky was, after Herzl, the most frequently used name given to streets in Israel. The moshav Nahalat Jabotinsky, which merged with Binyaminah, and the *Ḥerut headquarters in Tel Aviv – Meẓudat Ze'ev – were named after him. The Jabotinsky Institute, located there, contains his personal archives, a comprehensive collection of manuscripts and letters as well as a museum of photographs and personal effects. His only son Eri (1910–1969), engineer and mathematician, was born in Odessa and educated mainly in Paris. In the middle and late 1930s he headed the Betar movement in Palestine and was an initiator of its aeronautic section, being himself a trained glider pilot. He was also active in the organization of "illegal" immigration from Europe on a mass scale. He was arrested several times by the British authorities and learned of his father's death while imprisoned in a detention camp. During World War II he was in the U.S. where he became a member of the Hebrew National Liberation Committee headed by Peter Bergson (Hillel Kook). The newly founded *Ḥerut party in Israel included him in its faction in the First Knesset. In 1952 Eri Jabotinsky joined the faculty of the Technion where he became, in 1967, professor of mathematics. He published mathematical studies in scientific journals in Israel and abroad and contributed also to the Revisionist and general Israel press.

[Joseph B. Schechtman]

The first volume of a digest of, and index to, the letters of Jabotinsky between the years 1904 and 1924 was published in 1972, but the project was not continued. However, the Jabotinsky Institute in Tel Aviv, together with the Zionist Library, undertook the task of publishing in Hebrew all his letters written in their various languages. Under the editorship of Professor Daniel Carpi seven volumes were published through 2005 covering the period up to 1931.

The centenary of Jabotinsky's birth was celebrated in Israel and elsewhere. A new 100-shekel banknote, the largest denomination to that date in the new currency, bearing his portrait, was issued at the time. In 2000, commemorating his 120th birthday and 60th *Yahrzeit*, symposia and lectures were organized in all of Israel's universities and by many public organizations. In a special session of the Knesset, spokesmen from all sides of the House paid tribute to his memory.

BIBLIOGRAPHY: J.B. Schechtman, *The Vladimir Jabotinsky Story*, 2 vols (1956–61); O.K. Rabinowicz, *Vladimir Jabotinsky's Conception of a Nation* (1946). **ADD. BIBLIOGRAPHY:** R. Bielsky Ben-Hur, *Every Individual a King*, (1993); Sh. Katz, *Lone Wolf*, 2 vols (1996).

JACA, city in Aragon, N.E. Spain. Jews were living in the citadel of Jaca from an early date. The community of Jaca is the oldest in Aragon. In the *fuero* (municipal charter), granted in 1062 shortly after the recapture of the city from the Muslims, they were obliged to grind their flour in the mill of the local ruler. The position of the community during the 13th century is shown by the taxes it paid, which amounted to 2,000 sólidos in 1271. For the collection of the annual tax, the community adopted the system of declaration. The poor and the invalids were exempted from paying taxes, after the example of the Barbastro community. The community of Jaca was annihilated during the *Pastoureaux massacres in 1320. Its recovery was slow and in 1350 it paid only 180 sólidos in Jaca coin to a special levy. A document from 1377 gives a list of all Jewish taxpayers in Jaca. On the basis of the list it is possible to trace the family relations of some of the local Jews. The list contains 115 Jews, usually heads of families. Compared to similar lists available, the community of Jaca seems to have been a large one. In Majorca, in 1391 there were 111 Jewish heads of family, in Barcelona 195 in 1383, in Valencia 93 in 1363. The total Jewish population in Jaca was about 450. The social division of the community is noteworthy: 10 belonged to the upper class, 24 to the middle class, and 81 to the lower class. Members of the upper class who constituted less than 9% of the taxpayers paid 70% of the total tax. The division is based totally on the amount of tax paid and had nothing to do with the family background. In 1382 Infanta Violante, the wife of Infante John, asked for the appointment of David Abembron to the position of *corredor* (financial agent) in the town. In 1383 she ordered the bailiff to uphold the laws of inheritance customary among the Jews. During the persecutions of 1391, the greater part of the Jewish quarter was burnt down and the Jews were left destitute. The impoverished condition continued until the expulsion of the Jews from Spain in 1492. On August 6, after the decree of expulsion had been issued, Infante Henry ordered the Catalonian officials to transfer to him the property of the Jews expelled from Jaca. The Jews lived in the area near the fortress, known as el Castellar. The Jewish quarter was in the streets known today as Cambras and Ferrenal, where the *Sinagoga Mayor* was. The location of another synagogue is unknown.

BIBLIOGRAPHY: Baer, Spain, index; Baer, Urkunden, index; H.C. Lea, *History of the Spanish Inquisition*, 1 (1904), 548; Lacarra, in: *Estudios de edad media de la Corona de Aragón*, 4 (1951), 139–55; M. Molho, *El Fuero de Jaca* (1964); R. del Arco, in: *Sefarad*, 14 (1954), 79–98. **ADD. BIBLIOGRAPHY:** D. Romano, in: *Sefarad*, 42 (1982), 3–39; J. Passini, in: *Minorités et marginaux en France méridionale et dans la péninsule ibérique* (*VIIe–XVIIIe siécles*, 1986), 143–55; idem, in: *Mélanges de la Casa de Velázquez*, 24 (1988), 71–97; M. Gómez de Valenzuela, in: *Argensola*, 101 (1988), 97–155.

[Haim Beinart /Yom Tov Assis (2nd ed.)]

JACHIN AND BOAZ (Heb. יָכִין, בֹּעַז), two pillars which were set up in front of the Sanctuary in Solomon's Temple in Jerusalem (I Kings 7:15–22, 41–42; II Kings 25:13, 17; Jer. 52:17, 20 ff.; II Chron. 3:15–17; 4:12–13). The form and nature of these pillars are uncertain, and many proposals have been advanced by scholars.

Description

There is a detailed description of the pillars in II Kings 7:15–22, 41–42 and II Chronicles 3:15–17; 4:12–13. The pillars were composed of two major parts: the stem, 18 cubits (c. 30 ft.) in height, five cubits (c. 8 ft.) in circumference, and one cubit in diameter; and the capital of the pillar, five cubits in height. The size of the capital was apparently altered in one of the renovations of the Temple, undertaken after the time of Solomon. Thus, in II Kings 25 the height is given as only three cubits. During the renovation all the pillars were apparently recast, which probably explains the contradiction between the description of the construction of the pillars in Kings and that in Jeremiah. According to the former, the pillars and their capitals were cast from solid copper (I Kings 7:16, 46), while according to the latter, they were hollow (Jer. 52:21).

It is more difficult to discover the nature of the capitals, as the description of their construction is filled with unclear technical terms which do not appear elsewhere (cf. Kings 7:17–20, 41–42; Jer. 52:22–23). Without going into detail, it can be said that the capitals were decorated with three varieties of ornamentation – *shushan* ("lilywork"), *sevakhah* ("meshwork") and *rimmonim* ("pomegranates"), crowned by an additional architectural design called *gullah* (גֻּלָּה). The last item is usually interpreted as a round bowl (on the basis of the parallel Akk. *gullatu* and the description of the Temple lamp in Zech. 4:2–3). The meaning of the other three terms is doubtful, and scholars usually resort to archaeological parallels for reconstructing them.

Rabbinic scholars and medieval Jewish exegetes held that the capital here is a double one (cf. I Kings 7:20). Indeed, double capitals are known from clay molds of cultic structures from Palestine and Cyprus dating to the period under consideration, i.e., the Iron Age. In these molds, as in the biblical descriptions, there is a capital of lily leaves, in the center of which is a semispherical bowl. Even more similar examples are found in ivory inlays from Palestine and Mesopotamia dating from the eighth to the sixth centuries B.C.E., which contain an additional element of a series of elongated mauve objects shaped like pomegranates hanging below a capital decorated with lilywork. Some later scholars identified this capital with the square proto-Aeolian capitals (Yadin) characteristic of the architecture of the time of Solomon, which have been discovered in various locations in Palestine (in the royal palaces in Samaria, in the fortress of Ahab in Hazor, in the governor's house in Megiddo, Ramat Rahel, Gezer, etc.). Others attempted to reconstruct the appearance of the capitals by comparison with incense stands discovered in Megiddo, Taanach, and Gezer (Smith and, following him, Albright). The closest example is that from Megiddo, which like the biblical model contains three architectural designs – a bowl, rosette work (buds of flowers and lotuses), and pomegranates. In light of recent archaeological findings it has been suggested that *sevakhah* (I Kings 7:17) should be explained as apertures in the bowl, like those found in incense stands (cf. II Kings 1:2, where *sevakhah* refers to the "window bars"). This interpretation, however, is far from the literal meaning, and what is described here is a woven net which surrounded the capitals.

Function and Significance

According to the Masoretic Version (I Kings 7:21 and II Chronicles 3:17), it appears that the pillars stood in front of the Sanctuary, inside the entrance hall. Their size, however, gives rise to doubts concerning their structural function. Thus, few scholars maintain that the pillars fulfilled any function in supporting the roof of the portico (as in temples of the Canaanite and Israelite period in Arad, Megiddo, and Tell Teinat). Most scholars tend to the opinion that these were two freestanding pillars, one on each side of the entrance, like those found in the archaeological artistic tradition of the Ancient East and in references in classical literature (Yeivin, Mazar, Albright, Smith, Roth, Watzinger, Berns, Galling, Gressmann, etc.). Thus, in the three molds from the Iron Age mentioned above, the common element is the freestanding pillars in front of the entrance. A similar phenomenon was found in three temples from the eighth century in Khorsabad in Assyria. Graphic representations of pillars standing outside the structure of a temple have been found on coins from the first century C.E. in Cyprus, Sardis, Pergamum, and Sidon. Finally, there are literary references to this type of pillar in descriptions of the temples of Herakles (Herodotus, 2:44), of the Tyrian Baal (Menader, quoted in Jos., Ant. 8:145), and of the Syrian goddess Atratah (Lucian, *De Syria Dea*, 16–27); one or two such pillars were constructed in honor of Herakles in the Tyrian settlement of Gadez (modern Cadiz) in Spain (Strabo, 3:170).

Even those scholars who agreed that these pillars played no structural role in the Temple were divided in their opinions regarding their function. One suggestion was that they had a mythological significance, as "trees of life," or cosmic pillars; or perhaps they fulfilled a ritual function as cressets or incense lamps, like those found in a drawing of a tomb in Mareshah (Smith, Albright). Another possibility is that they had only symbolic significance, symbolizing the dwelling place of God in the Temple, like the monuments found in the temple in

Shechem and the temple of Mekal in Beth-Shean (Yeivin); or perhaps they were imitations of Egyptian obelisks (Hollis).

Names

The Septuagint in one passage (I Kings 7:21 [7]) reads the Masoretic Boaz as Baaz (also Boas), and in another (II Chron. 3:17), as an adverbial phrase, Ισχύς (*be-oz*, "with strength"). The Vulgate reads it as Booz. Opinion was divided regarding the names as well. Those who maintained (Sayce, Cook, Cheyne) that what was described here is an imitation of a foreign custom maintained that the Hebrew names were a translation of the names of Babylonian or Phoenician gods. In contrast, some scholars maintained that these were predicates of the God of Israel (Klousterman). Some scholars held that these names were derived from a longer text (Sellin, Gressman). Especially well known is the suggestion by Scott that these are the first words of a literary work, similar to the biblical dynastic prophecies and royal hymns, which was engraved on the pillars. More acceptable is the opinion that the names Jachin and Boaz are proper names, like those found in other places in the Bible, representing the names of the builders or contributors (Gesenius, Ewald); or perhaps they were actually names of members of the royal household, as S. Yeivin maintains (cf. Num. 26:12; Ruth 2:1; I Chron. 24:17). Thus the pillars play a double role: they emphasize, on the one hand, the personal relationship between the Temple and the royal family and, on the other, the presence of God within the Temple.

BIBLIOGRAPHY: R.B.Y. Scott in: JBL, 58 (1939), 143–9; W.F. Albright, in: BASOR, 85 (1942), 18ff.; H.G. May, *ibid.*, 88 (1945), 19ff.; Albright, Arch Rel, 144–8; J.L. Myres, in: PEQ, 80 (1948), 22ff.; P.L. Garber, in: BA, 14 (1951), 8–10; Y. Yadin, in: Avi-Yonah (ed.), *Sefer Yerushalayim* (1956), 185; S. Yeivin, in: *Eretz-Israel*, 5 (1959), 97–104.

[Nili Shupak]

JACKAL (Heb. שׁוּעָל, *Shu'al*; AV, JPS "fox"). The jackal, *Canis aureus*, is the most prevalent beast of prey in Ereẓ Israel. Being omnivorous, it is encountered most commonly near inhabited areas, where it feeds on fruit, vegetables, offal, and carrion, whence the phrase "to become a portion for jackals" (Ps. 63:11). It also preys on small animals. The howl of packs of jackals used to pierce the night air near settlements in Israel. The damage they caused to vineyards and vegetables and the danger of their infecting dogs with rabies resulted in efforts to exterminate them by means of poisoned bait. The biblical name for a jackal is a complex problem. Given that Akkadian *zību* means jackal, it is possible that Hebrew *ze'ev* has the same sense. Most of the passages that speak of *shu'al* apparently refer to the jackal and only some of them to the *fox, which usually lives in isolated places far from human habitation. Given the oft-cited classical parallel in Ovid (Fast, 4:679ff.) that Romans sent out foxes with torches burning in their tails at the festival of Ceres, the 300 animals that Samson caught (Judg. 15:4) were probably foxes. The jackal is a cowardly nocturnal animal that usually shuns humans, being only dangerous to human beings when rabid. Hence the reference to "the bite of the *shu'al*," which is attended with grave peril (Avot 2:10). It is very closely related to the dog and sometimes the two mate. The Mishnah states that they are heterogeneous (Kil. 1:6), i.e., that it is forbidden to interbreed them. In modern Hebrew the jackal is called *tan*, but this word, mentioned several times in the Bible, refers there to an animal that inhabits deserts and ruins (Isa. 13:22; Micah 1:8); associated always with nocturnal birds, it designates a species of *owl.

BIBLIOGRAPHY: J. Feliks, *Animal World of the Bible* (1962), 36–37; idem, *Kilei Zera'im ve-Harkavah* (1967), 122–3. **ADD. BIBLIOGRAPHY:** CAD Z, 106.

[Jehdua Feliks]

JACKSON, BERNARD S. (1944–), British historian of Jewish law. Born in Liverpool, Bernard Jackson became professor of modern Jewish studies at Manchester University. He was trained as a barrister and legal historian and wrote or edited more than 20 books on the law, especially traditional Jewish law. Among his works are *Theft in Early Jewish Law* (1972), *Essays in Jewish Law and Comparative Legal History* (1975), and (as editor) *Modern Research in Jewish Law* (1980). From 1978 to 1997 he was editor of the *Jewish Law Annual.*

[William D. Rubinstein (2nd ed.)]

JACKSON, HARRY (**Jacobson**; 1836–1885), British actor and stage manager, born in London. Jackson spent his early years in Australia, acted there and in New Zealand, and went to San Francisco in 1856. In his later years he worked in England, where he appeared in variety and melodramas, and became known as a comedian in Jewish stock character roles. During the late 1870s he was the leading comedian at Drury Lane and later became stage manager there.

JACKSON, SOLOMON HENRY (d. 1847), first Jewish printer in New York City. His printing shop had both English and Hebrew type fonts, and he was thus able to print material in both languages, which he did for the various congregations of the city. His most important works were *The Form of Daily Prayers, According to the Custom of the Spanish and Portuguese Jews* (1826), a translation of the Sephardi prayer book into English, and his editorship and publication of *The Jew* (1823–25), a monthly, the first Jewish periodical in the United States. In 1827 he was active in the Ḥevrat Ḥinnukh Ne'arim, a society to promote Jewish education, and in 1837 he led a movement to settle Jews on the land.

BIBLIOGRAPHY: H.B. Grinstein, *Rise of the Jewish Community of New York 1654–1860* (1945), index.

[Hyman B. Grinstein]

JACKSONVILLE, city in northeast Florida, general population in 2005 about 800,000; Jewish population, about 13,000. Since the founding of Jacksonville in 1822, Jews have played a prominent role in the development of Florida's largest city (in land area). Jews came to Jacksonville as merchants before the Civil War and suffered the same fate as others at the hands of Union troops. Jews have served their city by defending it, holding public offices, building the economy, and contributing to the cultural arts, education and philanthropies. From the period following the Civil War until the mid-1930s, Jacksonville was the center of Florida Jewish life. Attracted by the business opportunities offered by the port, Jews migrated here via the St. Johns River and the railroad. Tourism, a lumber industry, and military bases acted as magnets to draw new residents.

The head of Florida's longest continuing documented Jewish family is Philip Dzialynski, who arrived from Prussia by 1850. He sent for his father and eight brothers and sisters. In 1857 George Dzialynski was the first known Jewish boy born in Florida, son of Philip and his wife, Ida. In that same brutal year of 1857 for Jacksonville, a yellow fever epidemic killed six members of the Dzialynski family. A Hebrew cemetery, the first in the state of Florida, was established that year. In 1867 Jacob and Morris Cohen came from Ireland and established the Cohen Bros. Department Store, the most prominent in town for more than 100 years, and Austrian-born Herman, Max, and Leopold Furchgott opened Furchgott's. The Hebrew Benevolent Society was formed in 1874 and B'nai B'rith in 1877. By 1880 there were 130 Jews, well integrated into the life of the city. The earliest known public figure is Civil War veteran Morris Dzialynski, who was the first president of Congregation Ahavath Chesed at the same time he served as mayor (1882); he was also a judge. Ahavath Chesed was the second congregation in Florida. Rabbi Israel L. Kaplan was the religious leader from 1916 to 1946 and was succeeded by Sidney Lefkowitz (through 1973), who had conducted the first Jewish service on German soil following the years of Nazi persecution.

In 1901 40 Orthodox families established B'nai Israel. Reverend Benjamin Safer was hired as the community's first *shoḥet*. Many Jews who immigrated to the U.S. in the late 19th century from Pushalotes, Lithuania, settled in Jacksonville. In 1901 a devastating fire swept through 146 blocks of Jacksonville and architect Roy Benjamin figured prominently in the rebuilding of the city. Benjamin also designed many theaters throughout Florida. This fire destroyed Ahavath Chesed. Less than a year later it was the first house of worship to be rebuilt. The congregation formed a Boy Scout Troop in 1915 and continues without interruption as the second oldest troop in Jacksonville. Henrietta Szold came to start Hadassah in 1914. The YMHA formed in 1917. Families from surrounding small communities moved to Jacksonville where they could maintain Jewish traditions and participate in Jewish life. With increasing river traffic and World War I shipyard demands, the population grew.

Benjamin Setzer came from Pushalotes in 1918 and opened his first Setzer's grocery store, which later became Food Fair. By 1961, Benjamin had started another chain, Pic N Save super drug stores. Louis Mendelson moved to Jacksonville from Live Oak and founded, in 1912, Mendelson Printing. With Morris Gelehrter, in 1924, he started *The Florida Jewish News,* which became *The Southern Jewish Weekly* in 1938, with Isadore Moscovitz as the editor for more than fifty years. Julius Hirschberg, with brother-in-law, Jacob R. Cohen, conducted the first statewide Palestine campaign just prior to World War I that raised $10,000. Morton left a generous art collection to the Cummer Museum. In 1926 B'nai Israel began to introduce Conservative Judaism practices and the Jacksonville Jewish Center was founded.

In the 1940s there were 3,095 Jews, and a Naval Air Station was built in Jacksonville, which brought tens of thousands of new faces to the city. Many of them were Jewish, married Jacksonville Jews and started families and businesses. William Katz graduated from the U.S. Air Force Officer Training School as a lieutenant in 1942. He received many medals for World War II service, after which he immigrated to Israel and later became chief pilot for El Al Airlines. Admiral Ellis Zacharias was born in Jacksonville in 1890. Following his graduation from the U.S. Naval Academy, he became chief of Naval Intelligence in World War II and assisted in breaking the Japanese code, which led to the eventual defeat of the Japanese navy.

More Jewish institutions were organized to strengthen Jewish identity and meet increasing needs: Jewish Cultural League, Jewish Community Council, Esquire Club, Council of Jewish Women, Beauclerc Country Club (1953–1984), and River Garden Hebrew Home for the Aged (1945), which is one of the outstanding institutions of its kind in the country. In 1988, the $8 million Jewish Community Alliance (JCA) opened on land that was formerly the Beauclerc Country Club.

Immigrant Morris Wolfson came in 1914, started a scrap business, and left a legacy of philanthropy to many institutions of health, education, and religion in the city through his children. In 1978 Florida had its first Triple Crown (Kentucky Derby, Preakness, Belmont Stakes) horse race winner, Affirmed, owned by Morris' son Louis E. and Patrice Wolfson. Samuel "Bud" Shorstein served Governor Bob Graham as chief of staff. When Graham was elected Florida's U.S. senator in 1987, Bud accompanied him to Washington, again as his chief of staff. Ray Ehrlich became chief justice of the Florida Supreme Court in 1988. In 1994 the National Football League awarded its 30th franchise to Jacksonville. The Jaguars, co-owned by Lawrence Dubow, began play in 1995, and Jacksonville hosted Super Bowl XXXIX in 2005.

In addition to the Jewish Federation, Jacksonville Jews also have a newspaper, seven congregations, a day school through 8th grade, a joint community Hebrew High evening program, and a full array of organizations that support a robust Jewish life. New growth is moving toward the beach areas.

[Marcia Jo Zerivitz (2nd ed.)]

JACOB (Heb. יַעֲקֹב, יַעֲקוֹב), younger twin son of *Isaac and *Rebekah, third of the *Patriarchs of the people of Israel. His father was 60 years old at the time of Jacob's birth, which occurred after 20 years of childless marriage (Gen. 25:20, 26). During a difficult pregnancy, his mother consulted an oracle and was informed by the Lord that she would deliver twins, each of whom was destined to become the founder of a great nation, and that the older would be subordinate to the younger (25:22–23). This oracle plays a vital role in the biography of Jacob, for it serves to remove completely from the realm of nature and to elevate to the level of divine will the issue of his destiny as the heir to the covenant with *Abraham and Isaac. It thus disengages the fact of Jacob's election from the morality of his subsequent actions.

The Birthright

Nothing at all is recorded of Jacob's childhood, except that he emerged from the womb grasping the heel (*akev, ʾaqev*), a play on the name Ya'akov (Yaʿaqov), of his brother *Esau (25:26). It is said that he was "a mild man who stayed in camp" (25:27), and that he was the favorite of his mother, his father showing preference for his brother (25:28). The first incident reported is Jacob's exploitation of his brother's hunger to purchase the birthright from him in exchange for lentil stew (25:29–34); the second relates to the deception he practiced upon his father to obtain his final blessing (ch. 27). At the instigation of his mother, he took advantage of his father's blindness to masquerade successfully as Esau and so to mislead Isaac into believing that he was actually blessing his older son (27:1–29). For this he earned Esau's murderous enmity (27:41), and Rebekah decided that for his safety he must flee at once to the home of her brother Laban in Haran. Another biblical tradition gives as Jacob's motivation to leave for Haran Rebekah's insistence to Isaac that their son must find a wife within the family and not among the native Hittite women (27:42–46; 28:1–4).

In connection with these two incidents, it should be noted that the disregard of primogeniture and the transference of the birthright from one son to another is proscribed in pentateuchal legislation (Deut. 21:15–17). Inasmuch as biblical law prohibits existing practices, we should not be surprised to find evidence of such practice. A document from the second millennium B.C.E. from the town of *Nuzi reads:

> Concerning my son Zirteshup, I at first annulled his relationship, but now I have restored him to sonship. He is the elder son and shall receive a double portion (E.A. Speiser, in AASOR, 10 (1930), 39).

Another document records the purchase of the birthright by a younger brother for the price of three sheep (CH Gordon, in BA, 3 (1940), 5), while a tablet from Alalakh actually deals with the prenatal conferral of the birthright (I. Mendelsohn, in BASOR, 156 (1959), p. 38–40).

His Flight

Jacob's precipitate flight from Beer-Sheba found him at sunset at a place in which he dreamed that God had appeared to him. He saw angels going up and down a stairway which spanned heaven and earth. He then heard the Lord reiterate the promises of land and numerous progeny that He had made to Abraham and Isaac. His offspring would be a source of blessing to the whole earth; he would enjoy divine protection wherever he would be, and would return one day to the land from which he was fleeing (Gen. 28:10–15). Jacob awoke from his sleep, startled to discover the presence of God in that place, which he thereupon dedicated as a sacred site, renaming it *Beth-El. He vowed to turn it into a "house of God" on his safe return and to dedicate a tithe of all his possessions (28:16–22).

His Marriages

Jacob continued his journey to Haran. A chance meeting at a well brought him face to face with his cousin *Rachel. Her father, his uncle *Laban, welcomed him into his home (29:1–15). A month later, he arranged to work for Laban for seven years as the bride-price for Rachel (29:16–20). When, however, the day of the marriage arrived, he discovered that, under the cover of darkness, Laban had substituted his older, less attractive, daughter *Leah for Rachel. Jacob was forced to agree to serve another seven years, after which period he married Rachel (29:21–30). Each of the brides received a maidservant from her father as a wedding gift, Leah's being named *Zilpah, and Rachel's, *Bilhah (29:24, 29). This practice, incidentally, is well attested in the Nuzi archives.

In relating these events at length, it may be supposed that the Scripture's intent was to indicate that the trickery practiced by Laban was the retributive counterpart, measure for measure, of the deception Jacob had perpetrated upon his father. At the same time, the unintended marriage to Leah is clearly to be understood as the determination of divine providence, for from this union issued the two great spiritual and temporal institutions of biblical Israel, the priesthood from Levi and the Davidic monarchy from Judah, both sons of Leah.

The Tribes

All in all, the 20 years that Jacob spent in the service of Laban (31:38, 41) really constituted the formative period in the development of the people of Israel, for all but one of the fathers of the twelve tribes were born during this period. The unloved Leah was blessed with four sons in succession, Reuben, Simeon, Levi, and Judah (29:31–35), whereas Rachel remained barren. Like *Sarah before her, she resorted to concubinage (see *Patriarchs) and gave to her husband her maid Bilhah, who bore Dan and Naphtali (30:1–8). Leah, who had had no children for some time, followed her sister's example, and Zilpah became Jacob's concubine, giving birth to Gad and Asher (30:9–13). Leah, herself, was delivered of Issachar, Zebulun, and a daughter, Dinah (30:14–21). Finally, after so many years of barrenness, Rachel gave birth to a son who was named Joseph (30:22–24).

The information concerning the ascription of the tribal fathers to the various wives and concubines is of considerable interest and doubtlessly reflects a very ancient layer of tribal history and interrelationships. First, all the Hebrew tribes must have originated in eastern Syria except for Benjamin, who apparently joined Joseph and the other tribes after the migration to Canaan. Secondly, the six Leah tribes must at one time have constituted a distinct fraternity, while the handmaid tribes must have had subordinate status. The primogeniture of Reuben (as later of *Manasseh) must represent an early, but lost, supremacy in the tribal confederation.

Jacob and Laban

After the birth of Joseph, Jacob decided that the time had come to return home. He struck a bargain with Laban to enable him to build up his own resources for the purpose, but, by means of a stratagem that involved the influencing of the pigmentation of the flocks through visual stimulus (see *Biology) he managed to outwit his father-in-law, and he became the prosperous owner of large, sturdy flocks, camels and asses, as well as maidservants and manservants (30:25–43).

At this point, Jacob aroused the outspoken jealousy of Laban's sons and perceived the changed attitude of Laban toward himself (31:1–2). When a divine revelation ordered him to return to Canaan (31:3; cf. 31:13), he put his case before his wives who gave their consent, stating that their father had no longer any claim to them, since he had sold them and had been paid for them in full (31:4–16). Jacob thereupon assembled his family and his possessions and, taking advantage of Laban's absence on a sheep-shearing mission, stole away. Rachel, without her husband's knowledge, used the opportunity to appropriate her father's household idols (31:17–21).

Three days later, Laban learned of the flight and set off in hot pursuit, catching up with Jacob in the hill country of Gilead. At night in a dream God warned Laban not to harm Jacob. A heated exchange took place, and Laban conducted a fruitless search for his household gods. A treaty of mutual respect was enacted, which included a provision preventing Jacob from taking any more wives. A stone mound was erected to commemorate the occasion and to mark the boundary line separating the two parties (31:22–54).

The grievance of Rachel and Leah about their own positions (Gen. 31:14–16) fits in well with what is known of the inferior position of foreign slaves in the ancient Near East. The reference to the bride-price and its fate clearly accuses Laban either of improvident disposition or embezzlement of the monetary equivalent of Jacob's years of service, rendered in lieu of the payments usually settled by the groom on the bride. The significance of the possession of the household gods (Gen. 31:19, 30–35) is unclear (see *Genesis), but the fact that a Nuzi adoption contract makes specific provision for their consignment shows that it was an issue of great importance. Finally, the restrictive marriage clause imposed upon Jacob (31:50) finds its parallels in both adoption and marriage documents.

The Return

Jacob now continued his journey homeward, encountering angels at Mahanaim (32:2–3 (1–2)). It is possible that this incident was once part of a fuller story now so truncated as to defy reconstruction. It does serve, however, to round out the cycle of events that began with the flight from Canaan, which also involved the appearance of angels (cf. 28:12).

Uncertain of the reception he would get from Esau, Jacob then made extensive preparations to mollify his brother as well as to prepare for the worst (32:4–24 (3–23)). After fording the Jabbok at Penuel, and sending his family and belongings ahead, he found himself wrestling with a mysterious stranger, a divine being, who, desperate to get away before dawn, changed Jacob's name to *Israel, but also left him with a dislocated thigh (32:25–33 (24–32)). The confrontation with Esau turned out to be cordial (33:1–16), and if Esau had any plans of luring Jacob to Seir, where he might have kept him in a somewhat inferior ("younger brother") status after all, Jacob foiled his plans by brilliant diplomatic evasion. Thus Jacob, instead of trekking southward to Seir was able to proceed southwestward to Succoth, not far from the Jordan. There he built a house and made stalls for his cattle. His next stop was well inside Canaan, at Shechem, where he purchased a plot of land and set up an altar (33:17–20).

The Rape of Dinah

Here at Shechem the rape of Jacob's daughter, *Dinah, by Shechem son of Hamor, the governor, took place. Strongly drawn to the maiden, the young man wished to enter into marriage with her. Jacob's sons, who conducted the negotiations, made the circumcision of all the male population a precondition of agreement. Shechem's fighting manhood being thereby temporarily incapacitated, Simeon and Levi avenged the outrage perpetrated on their sister by butchering the population and plundering the town; and when Jacob rebuked them for jeopardizing his relations with his neighbors, they defended their conduct on grounds of honor (Gen. 34).

This story, the only one in the Bible dealing with Dinah, contains several remarkable features: Jacob plays an unwontedly passive role; Simeon and Levi are depicted as fierce warriors acting in concert, thus reflecting a situation totally at variance with other accounts of tribal history, in which Simeon was the military partner of Judah and settled next to it in the south of Canaan, while Levi took no part in the wars of conquest, possessed no tribal territory, and no particular association with Simeon. Some scholars argue that the narrative of chapter 34 conceals a very ancient attempt on the part of some of the tribes to effect a forcible settlement in the Shechem area. At the other extreme it has been argued that the story is a late polemic directed against intermarriage or the Samaritans.

Beth-El

The next events recorded are connected with Beth-El, the site associated with a fateful moment in Jacob's life (cf. 28:10–22). At divine command, the patriarch and his retinue, after purging themselves of idolatrous emblems, made their way to the town. He built an altar there and received God's blessing renaming him Israel and promising numerous progeny, even royal descendants, as well as future possession of the land. Jacob dedicated the site of the revelation and named it Beth-El in place of Luz (35:1–15). He moved on in the direction of Ephrath, and on the way his beloved Rachel died while giving birth to Benjamin. Jacob set up a pillar over her grave (35:16–20). It is not clear whether the succeeding brief notice of Reuben's incest with Rachel's maid Bilhah, his father's concubine (35:22), is connected with this or not. It is most likely part of an originally larger account explaining the lost preeminence of the tribe of Reuben (cf. 49:3–4; Deut. 33:6; I Chron. 5:1). Jacob finally arrived at Hebron to meet his father once again. He participated with Esau in Isaac's burial here (Gen. 35:27–29), being then 120 years of age (25:26; 35:28).

Jacob and Joseph

The subsequent biography of Jacob is wholly interwoven with the life of *Joseph, his favorite son (37:3–4). He seems to have taken seriously the latter's boyish dreams of greatness even as he berated him for them (37:10–11), and his grief at Joseph's disappearance was inconsolable (37:33–35). In view of the tendency of Abraham (12:20) and Isaac (26:1) to move to Egypt in time of famine, it is of interest that Jacob chose instead to send his sons with the exception of Benjamin, to buy food there (42:1–4). The Egyptian official with whom they had to deal was, unbeknown to them, no other than Joseph, who insisted that if they came again they must bring their remaining brother with them. Very reluctantly, Jacob, under the pressure of famine and the importuning of his sons, had to agree (43:1–15).

When Joseph finally revealed his true identity and sent for his father, a divine revelation at Beer-Sheba granted the patriarch permission to migrate to Egypt and also promised to make him there into a great nation which would eventually return to the land (chapter 45; 46:1–4). Jacob thereupon traveled to Egypt with his entire family and possessions (46:5–27) and had a tearful reunion with Joseph (46:29). In an audience with Pharaoh he gave his age at this time as 130 and described his years as having been "few and hard" (47:7–10). He settled in the region of Goshen (47:6), or Rameses (47:11), where he stayed for 17 years (47:28).

As Jacob's end approached, he made Joseph swear to bury him in the ancestral vault in Canaan (47:29–31; 49:29–33). He then blessed Joseph's two sons, *Manasseh and *Ephraim, and transferred the birthright from the older to the younger (48:1–20). In his closing words to Joseph he again predicted the ultimate return to Canaan, and he bestowed on him a parting gift mysteriously described as having been "wrested from the Amorites by my sword and bow" (48:21–22), a reference to some event in the life of the patriarch not otherwise recorded.

Jacob then blessed each of his sons individually, after which he died at the age of 147 (ch. 49). He was embalmed, given a state funeral, and buried by his sons in the cave of Machpelah (50:1–13).

The Other Biblical Traditions

Surprisingly, little about Jacob is recorded outside the Genesis traditions. In the rest of the Bible he is chiefly mentioned in combination with the other two Patriarchs, particularly in reference to the covenant (e.g., Ex. 2:24; 32:13; Lev. 26:42; Deut. 29:12; II Kings 13:23). The descent to Egypt is recorded in Joshua (24:4) and Psalms (105:23). The divine love of Jacob and the rejection of Esau is stressed by Malachi (1:2–3), while Ezekiel singles out the connection between the Patriarch and the land, and refers to Jacob as God's servant (28:25; 37:25; cf. Isa. 41:8; 44:1).

The sole instance of a possible variant tradition independent of Genesis comes from *Hosea, who deprecates Jacob's attempt to supplant Esau in the womb, who places the struggle with the angel at Beth-El, before his servitude to Laban instead of at Penuel on the way home, and who has the angel weep and implore Jacob (12:4–5). He also refers to Jacob's flight and servitude (12:13). It is more likely, however, that Hosea is reinterpreting the Genesis traditions for his own didactic purposes. Similarly, it is doubtful that any independent traditions are behind such divine epithets as "the God of Jacob" (e.g., II Sam. 23:1; Isa. 2:3), "the Holy One of Jacob" (Isa. 29:23), "the King of Jacob" (Isa. 41:21), "the Mighty One of Jacob" (e.g., Gen. 49:24; Isa. 49:26), "the El of Jacob" (Ps. 146:5).

The Name

The biblical sources suggest two etymologies for the name. Genesis 25:26 treats it as a denominative verb derived from עָקֵב (*ʿaqev*; "a heel"); Genesis 27:36 involves a root עקב (*ʿqb*; "to overreach," "to supplant"; cf. Jer. 9:3; Hos. 12:4). Both clearly imply wordplays. The name, however, seems to have been widespread in the second millennium B.C.E., and it appears in one form or another in Akkadian, Old South Arabic, and Aramaic texts. A theophoric form, *Yaʿqub-ʿal*, is transcribed as *Yʿqbhr*, the name of a Hyksos prince, in a 17th-century Egyptian source, and as *Yʿqbʿr* in a 15th-century geographic list of Thutmose III. It is most likely that the Hebrew is a shortened theophoric name, perhaps meaning, originally, "may God protect."

[Nahum M. Sarna]

In the Aggadah

Since Jacob was renamed Israel (Gen. 32:28) and was destined to be the ancestor of the twelve tribes, his eventful life inevitably became, in the *aggadah*, symbolic of the later history and tribulations of the Jewish people. Likewise, Jacob's principal antagonists: Esau (Edom; cf. Gen. 25:30; 36:1), Laban "the Aramean" (Gen. 31:20), and even the angel who wrestled with Jacob (Gen. 32:24ff.), became the prototypes of the Roman (later Christian) world. The role played by Herod the Edomite "slave" (BB 3b–4a) and his family in subjecting Judea to the Roman yoke, and the close similarity of "Aramean" and "Roman" (ארמי (Aram. רַמַּאי – (ארמאי although it is also equated with רַמַּאי, a "cheat"; Gen. R. 70:19), facilitated this identification, which must be regarded as basic for the proper evaluation of the Midrash and *aggadah* on the subject.

The biblical account, which treats Esau and Laban with a certain degree of understanding, is subjected to a thorough reinterpretation, with a view to discrediting the enemies of Israel, while glorifying Jacob – regarded as virtually identical with the Jewish people. The struggle between Israel and Rome was foreshadowed before Jacob and Esau were born. Even in their mother's womb they were locked in mortal combat, and evinced different desires. Whenever Rebekah passed a synagogue or house of study, Jacob tried to break forth, but when she passed near a pagan house of worship, Esau was struggling to get out (Gen. R. 63:6; cf. Gen. 25:22). The religious contrast between Jew and gentile was thus clearly depicted as a permanent chasm between two irreconcilable civilizations. A similar contrast between Jacob and Esau was also noticeable at their birth, the former being clean, smooth, extraordinarily handsome, and born circumcised; while the latter was hairy and bearded, blood-red in color, and with all his teeth fully developed (Gen. R. 63:7–8; Targ. Ps.-Jon. on Gen. 25:25; ARN1 2:12; Tanh. Noah 5; Tanḥ. B, Gen. 32; Mid. Ps. 9:7). All this was meant to portray the contrast between the spiritual beauty of Israel and the ugliness of the pagan world – its wars and bloodshed, Rome's perennial occupation. Esau's "ruddy" color (Gen. 25:25) was indeed expressly interpreted as signifying that he (i.e., Rome) was "altogether a shedder of blood" (Gen. R. 63:8). While both brothers attended school up to the age of 13 (or, according to one version, 15) – Esau, too, thus being given the chance of studying the Torah – they parted completely once they had reached their religious majority. Jacob studied at the schools of Shem and Eber, and spent all his life in the pursuit of learning; while Esau became a dissipated idolator (Gen. R. 63:10; Yoma 28b; Tanḥ. B, Gen. 125). Here, too, the future conduct of good Jews and typical Romans was adumbrated.

Despite their explanation of how Isaac was deceived in Esau (Gen. R. 63:10), the rabbis felt that Isaac as well as Abraham who had fathered unworthy sons could not be considered equal in importance to Jacob (Pes. 56a; Gen. R. 68:11; Song. R. 3:6, no. 2) who was regarded as a model of virtue and righteousness (cf. e.g., Mak. 24a), and to whom even the mystery of the messianic redemption had been revealed (Mid. Ps. 31:7). He was, accordingly, the greatest of the patriarchs (Gen. R. 76:1), and even Abraham had been created and preserved from the fire of Nimrod's furnace only for the sake of Jacob who was destined to descend from him (*ibid.*, 63:2; Lev. R. 36:4; Sanh. 19b). Even after his death, Jacob – but not the other patriarchs – was concerned with Israel's fate, suffering with them when they were in trouble, and rejoicing with them when they were redeemed (Mid. Ps. 14:7; PR 41:5). Israel's successes in this world were entirely due to Jacob's merit (Song R. 3:6, no. 2). Hyperbolically, it was said that the entire universe had been created only for the sake of Jacob (Lev. R. 36:4) – here, as so often, a symbol of the entire people of Israel. God Himself had honored Jacob (Israel) by elevating him to a position little lower than that of the angels (Mid. Ps. 8:7), and engraving his image on the divine throne (Gen. R. 82:2).

For all that, the rabbis could not ignore the biblical account of Jacob's career, which was bound to raise moral problems. For example, his employment of devious methods to gain the birthright and the blessing of Isaac were open to criticism (cf. Hos. 12:3–4). Rabbinic apologetics, accordingly, endeavored to clear Jacob's good name, while blackening that of Esau. Accordingly, Esau had threatened to kill his mother if he was not permitted to be born first, and it was to save Rebekah that Jacob had agreed to Esau's primogeniture (Mid. Hag. to Gen. 25:22; cf. PR, 12:4). Although this is reported or hinted at only in late Midrashim, it may be an allusion to the notorious case of matricide committed by Nero, who contrived the murder of his mother Agrippina (Suetonius, Nero 34:5; Tacitus, Annals 14:1–13; Jos., Ant., 20:153; Wars, 2:250).

Jacob's desire to have the birthright was not influenced by any selfish motives, but by his wish to be privileged to offer the sacrifices, at that time the prerogative of the firstborn (Gen. R. 63:13; Num. R. 4:8). Even so, it was only because of Esau's manifest unsuitability for a spiritual office that Jacob was willing to sacrifice his life for the spiritual privileges of the birthright (*ibid.*). Hence, God Himself had assisted him to obtain blessings (Gen. R. 65:17–19; Tanh. B, Gen. 134f.). Moreover, when Jacob went in to his father, "the Garden of Eden entered with him"; but when Esau came in, "Gehenna went in with him" (Gen. R. 65:22; 67:1–3; Tanḥ. B, Gen. 141).

Isaac, too, had hesitated about conferring the blessing upon Esau, and had actually suspended the decision as to who was to be the recipient (Gen. R. 65:13). Even when he said, "Your brother came in with guile and took your blessing" (Gen. 27:35), what he really meant was that Jacob had come in with "wisdom" and "received" (i.e., was duly granted) what was due to him (Targ. Onk., and Targ. Yer., codex Neofiti I, ad loc.; Gen. R. 67:4; Tanh. B, Gen. 143). Any doubts Isaac may have had were dispelled when he learned that Esau had sold his birthright to Jacob (Gen. R. 67:2). Isaac thereupon confirmed Jacob's blessing (Gen. R. 67:12; Tanḥ. B, Gen. 143; cf. Gen. 28:1). According to another view, however, Isaac had actually sought to curse Jacob, but had been restrained by God (Gen. R. 67:1–3). Isaac had also made it clear that Jacob's supremacy was conditional on his merits (Gen. R. 67:7), and he was, therefore, sharply criticized in the Midrash (*ibid.*).

Only occasionally is Jacob criticized in rabbinic literature. Thus, Esau's "exceedingly great and bitter cry" (Gen. 27:34) had been punished in the days of Mordecai who likewise wailed "with a great and bitter cry" (Esth. 4:1; Gen. R. 67:4). Again, when Jacob rebuked Leah for aiding and abetting Laban's act of deception (cf. Gen. 29:23), she retorted, "Did not your father call you 'Esau,' and you answered him?!" (Gen. R. 70:19). Jacob is also criticized for having hidden his daughter Dinah from Esau's eyes at the time of his meeting with his brother on his return to Canaan. Jacob's fear that "this wicked man" might want to marry her is dismissed as unjustified prejudice; for he should have given her to his brother for a wife (Gen. R. 76:9). The purpose of this Midrash was apparently to encourage older brothers to give their daughters to younger brothers in marriage, thus retaining the family's property undiminished and its purity of blood unsullied.

Jacob's meeting with Esau after his return from Aram is embellished with numerous rabbinic comments, the burden of which is that Esau retained his undying hatred, so that Jacob had good reason to be afraid of him. The messengers sent by Jacob to Esau (Gen. 32:3) were in reality angels, and their huge numbers terrified Esau (Gen. R. 74:17; 75:10). Esau's reconciliation with Jacob (Gen. 33:4) was unreal. On the contrary, Esau had tried to bite his brother whose neck, however, had become like marble (Gen. R. 78:9). According to another view, however, Esau kissed Jacob "with all his heart," being temporarily compassionate (*ibid.*) Jacob's appeasement of Esau by repeatedly addressing him as "my lord" is condemned in the Midrash as humiliating to Jacob's dignity (Gen. R. 75:2, 11). The purpose of this homily was no doubt to discourage excessive cringing before the Romans.

Laban, described as "the master of deceivers" (Gen. R. 75:5), is treated in rabbinic literature with even greater disdain than Esau. He is the personification of greed, and even when he kissed and embraced Jacob (Gen. 29:13), he did so only to find out if he had any gems hidden on his body or in his mouth (Gen. R. 70:13). Jacob was well aware that Laban was a swindler (cf. *ibid.*; Meg. 13b), and took the utmost precautions in stipulating conditions with him, but all to no avail (Gen. R. 70:17). Jacob's charge that Laban had changed his wages ten times (Gen. 31:7, 41) was homiletically multiplied by the rabbis to no less than 100 deceptions (Gen. R. 74:3). Yet, despite Jacob's anger with Laban (Gen. 31:36), it never came to blows and violence, and Jacob did his best to appease Laban (Gen. R. 74:10).

An apologetic tendency is also evident in the midrashic interpretation of Jacob's relations with *Rachel. Although kissing a strange girl was considered indecent, Jacob's kissing of Rachel (Gen. 29:11) was excused as having been a permissible act, since she was his kinswoman (Gen. R. 70:12). In fact, so far from being lascivious, Jacob had never experienced nocturnal discharge (Gen. R. 79:1) and was in fact not subject to the evil impulse (BB 17a). Jacob's demand that Rachel be given to him, "so that I may cohabit with her" (Gen. 29:21), though superficially shameful "even the most dissolute does not use such language" – was nevertheless defended on the ground that Jacob's real purpose was the laudable desire to beget the 12 tribal ancestors (Gen. R. 70:18; Mid. Ag. ad loc.). Only mild criticism is leveled at Jacob for his angry outburst against Rachel when she was begging him for children (Gen. 30:1ff.): "Is that the way to answer a woman in distress?" (Gen. R. 71:7). Some slight disapproval is also voiced in the Midrash against Jacob's dislike of Leah (Gen. 29:31), who was therefore deliberately blessed with a large progeny, "so that she might be more beloved than Rachel" (Tanḥ. B, Gen. 153; Ag. Ber. 48 (49):2). A serious flaw was also seen in Jacob's marriage to two sisters (Pes. 119b); for although the Torah had not yet been promulgated, the rabbis considered the patriarchs as having had to observe the entire Law.

Jacob's favorite treatment of Joseph is condemned as a perfect example of what a father must not do – prefer one son to the others – an act which, as in Joseph's case, could lead to disastrous consequences (Shab. 10b; Meg. 16b; Gen. R. 84:8). Jacob's prolonged absence from home – during which he failed to honor his parents – was a serious offense for which he was punished by Joseph's disappearance for an equally long period (Meg. 16bff.). Conceivably, this criticism was directed primarily against young people who left their parents in Palestine and went abroad, especially to Syria and Babylonia, in search of better economic opportunities. Jacob's example was thus meant to discourage this exodus, which assumed alarming proportions during the second and third centuries C.E. More serious in the rabbinic view was Jacob's failure to intercede with God against the Egyptian enslavement of his descendants, and, worse still, his ready agreement that they should be wiped out because of their sins (Shab. 89b; cf Isa. 63:16). Finally, before his death, Jacob had sought to reveal the time of the coming of the Messiah to his sons, but at this point the Divine Presence departed from him (Pes. 56a; Gen. R. 98:2) – no doubt because Jacob's intention was considered unlawful.

For the most part, however, Jacob is depicted as a great and holy man who, among other things, introduced the daily evening prayer (Ber. 26b), and even caused the Egyptian famine to cease as soon as he arrived in Egypt (Tos., Sot. 10:9). Jacob was among those who had tasted of the Garden of Eden in their lifetime and were not subject to the power of the angel of death (BB 17a), but had died through "the kiss of death" (Rashi ad loc.). Indeed, according to one view, Jacob had never died at all (Ta'an. 5b) – evidently an allusion to the immortality of Israel.

[Moses Aberbach]

In Islam

At first, it was not clear to *Muhammad whether Yaʿqūb (Isrāʾīl) was the son of Isḥāq or his brother; he therefore adopted an ambiguous expression, "and we gave her (Sarah) the glad tidings of Isḥāq, and of Yaʿqūb after Isḥāq" (Sura 11:74). Only after his sojourn in Medina did it become evident to him that Jacob's "fathers" were Abraham, Ishmael, and Isaac and that he was the father of the Tribes (Sura 2:126–7, 130, 134). Like his ancestors, Jacob also ranks among the prophets (Sura 19:50). Of the children of Isaac, one was upright (Jacob) and the second (Esau) brought misfortune upon himself (Sura 37:113). Jacob is mentioned particularly in connection with the story of *Joseph (Sura 12). Before his death, Jacob cautioned his sons to remain faithful to "the law of Ibrahim" (Sura 2:126). On one occasion, Muhammad mentions the second name of Jacob: Isrāʾīl (Sura 3:87), when he points out that he forbade himself a certain food – probably an allusion to the sciatic nerve (Gen. 32:33). In the other places (in the *Koran) the name of Israel appears as that of the tribe, i.e., *Banū Isrāʾīl* ("the people of Israel"; e.g., Sura 2:38; 5:74; et al.). In a fragment from the Cairo **Genizah* which is attributed to al-Samawʾal, Israel is referred to as "the firstborn of the first" (cf. Ex. 4:22). According to the Arab commentators the origin of the name Isrāʾīl is derived from the fact that he fled from Esau at night.

[Haïm Z'ew Hirschberg]

In the Arts

The life and career of the patriarch Jacob provide the basis for many literary works and treatments by artists and musicians.

The episodes most favored range from Jacob's impersonation of Esau and vision at Beth-El (Gen. 27) to his final journey to Egypt at the invitation of Joseph and Pharaoh (Gen. 45–50). In literature, one of the earliest versions of the story occurs in the 12th-century *Ordo de Ysaac et Rebecca et Filiis Eorum*, an allegorical drama in which Esau represents the "pharisaical Jews" and Jacob the "faithful Christians." Another work of the Middle Ages was the 13th-century English poem *Iacob and Iosep*. Interest in the subject revived in the 16th century, particularly in England and Germany, where it inspired numerous stage productions. These include the anonymous verse play *Ein lieblich und nuetzbarlich Spil von dem Patriarchen Jacob und seinen zwelff Soenen* (Magdeburg, c. 1534); the Meistersinger Hans Sachs's *Comedia: Jacob mit seinem bruder Esaw* (1550); *Jacob und seine zwoelf Soehne* (1566), a Styrian church drama by Thomas Brunner; *A newe mery... Comedie or Enterlude... treating upon the Historie of Jacob and Esau* (London, 1568); and the *Comedie von dem Patriarchen Jakob, Joseph und seinen Bruedern* (1592) by Adam Zacharias Puschmann, an associate of Hans Sachs. A work sharply contrasting with the medieval *Ordo de Ysaac* was *The Historie of Jacob and Esau* (London, 1568; written 1557–58), a lively comedy attributed to Nicholas Udall. Here Jacob was reconfirmed as the righteous Hebrew (i.e., the true Protestant), while Esau was represented as the graceless pagan (i.e., the Catholic Antichrist). Three 17th-century treatments of the theme were the German dramatist Christian Weise's *Jacobs doppelte Heyrath* (1683); the anonymous *Comedia famosa dos successos de Iahacob e Esau* (Delft, 699), a Spanish verse play; and the Sephardi writer Isaac Cohen de *Lara's Spanish ballad, "La Fuga de Jaacob de Barsheva," which appeared with his Purim play *Aman y Mordochay* (Leiden, 1699). In the 18th century, the only writer of note to deal with the subject was the Swiss-German poet and dramatist Johann Jacob Bodmer (1698–1783) in two epics, *Jacob und Joseph* (1751) and *Jacob und Rachel* (1752).

The first modern Jewish writer who turned to the theme was the Hebrew poet Feivel Schiffer (c. 1810–1866), whose *Shirei Tiferet* (1840) retold the Bible story down to Jacob's entry into Egypt. In the late 19th century, the German Protestant playwright Wilhelm Schaefer wrote the drama *Jakob und Esau* (1896). There has been a significant revival of interest in the subject during the 20th century. The eminent German poet and playwright Gerhart Hauptmann turned to the story of Jacob in his fragmentary drama *Das Hirtenlied* (1921), as did Waldemar Jollos in his verse play *Esau und Jakob* (1919). In the first part of his unfinished David trilogy, *Jaakobs Traum; ein Vorspiel* (1918; *Jacob's Dream*, 1947), Richard *Beer-Hofmann made a dramatic attempt to justify Israel's universal mission; the play was staged in New York, and in Ereẓ Israel by Habimah in a Hebrew version. Some later works on the theme were *Jacob* (1925), a novel by the French writer Bernard *Lecache, and *Die Geschichten Jaakobs* (1933), the first part of Thomas *Mann's tetralogy *Joseph und seine Brueder* (1933–42). During World War II, Jacob Knoller published in the U.S. his four-part German drama *Verheissung, Schuld und Suehne* (1941); the U.S. writer Irving *Fineman his novel *Jacob* (1941); and the Portuguese poet José Régio his modern mystery play *Jacob e o Anjo* (1941). Laurence Housman's *Jacob's Ladder*, one of his *Old Testament Plays* (1950), sought to denigrate the Hebrew patriarch. Other postwar works include *Saint Jacob* (1954; Eng. *Jacob*, 1957), a novel by the French author Jean Cabriès; *Een ladder tegen de maan* (1957), a drama by the Dutch writer W. Barnard (Guillaume van der Graft); and *Ya'akov u-Vanav* (1958), a Hebrew novel by Ben-Zion Firer.

The life of the patriarch Jacob, packed with picturesque incident, has provided an equally rich storehouse of material for artists, who have mainly illustrated the episodes of Jacob's ladder (Gen. 28:10–22) and of Jacob and the angel (Gen. 32:24–32). There are several cycles of such episodes, the earliest being the fourth-century mosaic cycle at Santa Maria Maggiore, Rome. Scenes from the life of Jacob also figure in 12th-century mosaics at Palermo and Monreale in Sicily; and in manuscripts, including the sixth-century Vienna Genesis and the 14th-century *Sarajevo Haggadah*. The Renaissance painter Jacopo Bassano (1515–92) painted a pastoral landscape of Jacob and Esau (Vienna, Kunsthistorisches Museum). The birth of the twins (Gen. 25:24) was illustrated in 14th-century manuscripts such as the *Queen Mary Psalter* and the *Sarajevo Haggadah*, where, in an adjacent scene, Esau is shown hunting (Gen. 25:27). Their birth was also depicted by the Florentine painter Benozzo Gozzoli (1420–1497) in a fresco at the Campo Santo, Pisa. Esau selling his birthright to Jacob (Gen. 25:31–34) is illustrated in the *Vienna Genesis*, but was not popular in the Middle Ages. From the 17th century onward, there are paintings of the subject by the Spanish artist Murillo (1618–82; Harrach Gallery, Vienna), the Dutch master Hendrik Terbrugger (1587–1629; British Museum), and two ink drawings by *Rembrandt. Isaac blessing Jacob (Gen. 27:27) was also a comparatively rare subject in the Middle Ages, and commoner in the 17th century. However, it is found in fourth-century mosaics at Santa Maria Maggiore, in 13th-century frescoes at Assisi, and in medieval manuscripts, including the 12th-century *Hortus Deliciarum* and the 14th-century *Queen Mary Psalter* and *Sarajevo Haggadah*. The 17th-century Spanish painters Murillo (Hermitage, Leningrad) and Jusepe de Ribera (1588–1652; Prado) were among artists who treated the subject. Raphael (1483–1520) included a study of Isaac's halfhearted blessing of Esau (Gen. 27:39–40) in his frescoes for the Loggia in the Vatican, and there is a painting of the same subject by Rembrandt (Earl Brownlow, Grantham), which has also been thought to represent Isaac blessing Jacob.

Jacob's dream of the ladder was a favorite subject and has often been treated as a pendant to Jacob and the angel or to Moses and the burning bush. The subject first appears in the third-century frescoes of the synagogue at *Dura Europos in Mesopotamia. It is found in Byzantine and western medieval Christian manuscripts, including the *Hortus Deliciarum*, the 13th-century *St. Louis Psalter*, and the *Sarajevo Haggadah*, and also in sculpture and in the mosaics at Palermo and Monreale. In the painting by Raphael in the Loggia in the Vatican, Jacob is shown asleep at the foot of a monumental staircase which, in the grand manner of the Renaissance, replaced the simple ladder of earlier representations. There are paintings of the subject by the Spanish baroque masters Ribera (Prado) and Murillo (Hermitage) and by Rembrandt (Dresden Gallery). The English poet-painter William *Blake depicted the angels ascending and descending on a corkscrew staircase. A modern treatment is that by Marc *Chagall. In the *St. Louis Psalter* and the 15th-century *Breviary of the Duke of Bedford* (Bibliothèque Nationale) there are illuminations of Jacob anointing the stone on which he slept (Gen. 28:18).

Jacob's sojourn with his uncle Laban is illustrated by Ribera in a painting of Jacob tending Laban's flocks. His dealings with his two wives have a special significance in medieval Christian iconography, where Leah and Rachel were associated with Martha and Mary, representing the active and the contemplative life. Claude Lorrain (1600–82) painted idyllic landscapes with Jacob and Rachel (Hermitage, Leningrad) and with Jacob and Laban (Dulwich Gallery). The scene in which Jacob, on leaving Laban, divides the flocks with him (Gen. 30:32ff.) is recorded in the fourth-century mosaics at Santa Maria Maggiore, Rome, and in the sixth-century *Vienna Genesis*. Jacob's appropriation of Laban's household idols, which were taken and hidden by Rachel (Gen. 31:17ff.), appeared in Raphael's frescoes in the Vatican Loggia and was also a popular subject in the 17th century. It was treated by Murillo (Duke of Westminster collection), the Dutch genre painter Jan Steen (1626–79), and by Rembrandt's teacher, Pieter Lastman (1583–1633).

Another favorite subject was Jacob's struggle with the angel which, in the Middle Ages, received a bewildering variety of symbolic interpretations. One of the commonest was that it represented each man's fight against the forces of evil. In early Christian art it is God Himself who is shown struggling with Jacob. The theme appears in the *Vienna Genesis*, in an eighth-century fresco in Santa Maria Antica, Rome, and in an 11th-century fresco in the cathedral of Hagia Sophia, Kiev. It is found in medieval sculpture and in manuscripts such as the *St. Louis Psalter*. In the Stanza d'Eliodoro in the Vatican there is a painting of the subject by Raphael and Baldassore Peruzzi. Rembrandt produced a remarkable painting of Jacob and the angel (Berlin Museum) and Claude Lorrain made it the occasion for a poetic night landscape (Hermitage, Leningrad). The French romantic artist Eugène Delacroix (1798–1863) depicted the struggle in a fresco in the church of Saint Sulpice, Paris, and intended it to represent the artist struggling with Nature in order to wrest her secrets. In the 20th century, the sculptor Sir Jacob *Epstein showed Jacob and the angel locked in a passionate embrace, the subject being also treated by Chagall (Louvre). The reconciliation of Jacob and Esau (Gen. 33:4ff.) was illustrated in a swirling baroque composition by Rubens (Alte Pinakothek, Munich), and there is a painting by Jacopo Bassano of Jacob's return to Canaan (Doges' Palace, Venice).

In music, a "dialogo" (quasi-oratorio), *Il vecchio Isaac*, by G. Fr. Anerio (publ. 1619), treats the story of Jacob, Esau, and the birthright. The number and importance of works on the subjects of Jacob's Dream, Jacob and Rachel, and Jacob's lament over Joseph is, however, much greater. Some 16th-century motets set the text of the vision, such as *Vidit Jacob scalam* by Crecquillon (publ. 1556) or *O quam metuendus est locus iste* by Gallus (publ. 1603). One notable curiosity was the oratorio *La Vision de Jacob* which Marcel Dupré wrote in 1900 at the age of 14. For the Moscow performances of Richard Beer-Hofmann's *Jaakob's Traum* by the *Habimah Theater, music was written by M. *Milner; and the play was turned into an opera by the Israel composer Bernard Bergel. An orchestral work, *Jacob's Dream*, was written by Karol *Rathaus (1941); and in 1949 Darius *Milhaud composed a dance suite for five instruments, *Les Rêves de Jacob* (op. 294), for the Jacob's Pillow dance festival held in the Massachusetts village of that name. Arnold *Schoenberg's oratorio *Die Jakobsleiter*, with text by the composer, was begun in 1913 and remained unfinished. This is the first work in which the system of melodic manipulation, which he was to formalize soon afterwards as the "12-tone system," can be discerned. The text is a complex of philosophical ideas generated by, rather than reproducing, the vision of the ladder and Jacob's struggle with the angel (see D. Newlin, in *Yuval*, 1 (1968), 204–20). The première of the work took place in Vienna in 1961.

The story of Jacob and Rachel is treated in a motet, *Da Jakob Labans Tochter nahm*, by Joachim à Burck (1599); a "Singspiel" (comic opera), *Von Jacob doppelter Heyrath*, by Johann Philipp Krieger (1649–1725); and a duodrama, *Jakob und Rachel*, by J.E. Fuss (1800). It is also found, somewhat unexpectedly, in two Spanish polyphonic songs of the 17th century (*Siete años de pastor*, no. 18, and *Si por Rachel*, no. 62, in *Romances y letras a tres vozes*, ed. by M. Querol Gavald, 1956). For the *Ohel Theater production of *Jacob and Rachel*, the music was written by Solomon *Rosowsky, and later reworked into an orchestral suite by Julius Chajes. Jacob's word to the angel in the struggle at the Jabbok is the title-text of Bach's Cantata no. 157, *Ich lasse dich nicht, du segnest mich denn* (but with "*Mein Jesu*" added). A motet on the same text, for double choir, was written by Johann Christoph Bach (1642–1703) and formerly attributed to Johann Sebastian Bach. It was published in English in the 19th century as *I Wrestle and Pray*. Jacob's mourning over Joseph was set as a motet by many of the chief composers of the 16th century. The works begin with *Videns Jacob vestimenta Joseph* (Ger., *Da Jakob nun das Kleid ansah*) or *Lamentabatur Jacob*, and the list of composers includes Clemens non Papa, Cristobal Morales, Jacob Regnart, and Cosmas Alder (for a "Joseph play" performed at Basle). The message to Jacob that Joseph is alive appears in Orlando di Lasso's *Dixit Joseph undecim fratribus*. Other works on the theme include J.H. Rolle's oratorio *Jacobs Ankunft in Aegypten* (1746); *Jacobs Heyrath* and *Jacobs Tod und Begraebnis*, nos. 3 and 6 of Johann Kuhnau's *Biblische Sonaten* for keyboard instrument (1700); and the setting of Jacob's blessing of Judah (Gen. 49:10–42) in Heinrich Schuetz's *Geistliche Chormusik* (1648).

In Jewish folksong, Jacob appears symbolically in the many settings of *Al Tira Avdi Ya'akov* ("Fear Not, My Servant Jacob"), often with textual additions in Yiddish, such as *Amar Adonai le-Ya'akov – yo, foterl, yo* (Idelsohn, Melodien, 9 (1932), no. 485). Mordekhai *Ze'ira was the composer of the well-known Israel *horah* tune *Al Tira Avdi Ya'akov*, to a poem by Emanuel Harussi.

[Bathja Bayer]

BIBLIOGRAPHY: IN THE BIBLE: C.H. Gordon, in: BASOR, 66 (1937), 25–27; V. Maag, in: *Theologische Zeitschrift*, 6 (1957), 418–29; H.L. Ginsberg, in: JBL, 80 (1961), 339–47; W.F. Albright, *Yahweh and the Gods of Canaan* (1968), 50; N.M. Sarna, *Understanding Genesis* (1966), 181–210. For further bibl. see *Patriarchs. **ADD. BIBLIOGRAPHY:** S. Niditch, *Underdogs and Tricksters* (1987); N. Sarna, *Genesis JPS Torah Commentary* (1989). IN THE AGGADAH: Ginzberg, Legends, index; E.E. Halevy, *Sha'arei ha-Aggadah* (1963), 46–59. IN ISLAM; Tabarī, *Ta'rīkh*, 1 (1357 A.H.), 231–2; Kisā'ī, *Qiṣaṣ*, ed. by I. Eisenberg (1922), 153–4; H.Z. (J.W.) Hirschberg, *Der Dīwān des As-Samau'al ibn 'Adijā'...* (1931), 33–65; Horovitz, in: HUCA, 2 (1925), 154ff., 181; R. Firestone, "Ya'ḳūb," in: EIS², 11 (2002), 234 (incl. bibl.). IN ART: E.L. Gigas, *Esau og Jakob som dramatiske figurer* (1894).

JACOB (end of third–beginning of fourth century C.E.), Babylonian-born *amora*. Jacob was a pupil of *Judah b. Ezekiel, head of the academy of Pumbedita (Av. Zar. 28b, et al.). He transmitted teachings in the name of Ḥisda (Ber. 29b, et al.). He migrated to Ereẓ Israel where he studied under R. Johanan (Er. 80a; Suk. 12a, et al.). Jacob is frequently referred to as "a certain one of the rabbis" (see Er. 80a and Av. Zar. 28b). He was an associate of Jeremiah (Av. Zar. 13b), discussed problems with Jeremiah b. Taḥlifa and frequently explained obscure *halakhot* to him (BB 60b, et al.). It is related that the day Jacob died stars were seen at midday (MK 25b; but see Dik. Sof. ad loc.). Because there were several *amoraim* of the same name, at times it is difficult to decide to which one statements in the name of Jacob refer.

BIBLIOGRAPHY: Hyman, Toledot, s.v.; Ḥ. Albeck, *Mayo la-Talmudim* (1969), 248–9.

[Yitzhak Dov Gilat]

JACOB, BENNO (1862–1945), rabbi and Bible scholar. He studied at the rabbinical seminary and university of his native Breslau. From 1891 to 1906 he served as a rabbi in Goettingen and from 1906 to 1929 in Dortmund. In 1929 he retired from the rabbinate, settled in Hamburg, and devoted himself entirely to exegetical work. From 1939 he lived in England. His principal field of activity in biblical research was the Pentateuch. Although he was not a fundamentalist, his conclusions, as a result of his study of the text rather than on religious grounds, were a complete denial of modern Bible criticism – both textual criticism and Higher Criticism with its documentary hypothesis. He regarded the traditional text more reliable than the ancient translations. He considered the arbitrary textual emendations of Higher Criticism to be unscientific because their only purpose was to validate the latter's own assumptions. Moreover, he accused the school of Higher Criticism of antisemitic trends and of prejudices against Judaism. His opinions were propounded in *Der Pentateuch, exegetischkritische Forschungen* (1905) and *Quellenscheidung und Exegese im Pentateuch* (1916). He clarified biblical ideas and expressions which had not been properly understood in *Im Namen Gottes* (1903) and *Auge um Auge, eine Untersuchung zum Alten und Neuen Testament* (1929). He also developed a theory concerning the internal rhythm of the Bible, which is expressed by the repetition of key words in set numbers in the narratives of the Torah and its laws, in *Die Abzaehlungen in den Gesetzen der Buecher Leviticus und Numeri* (1909). His major exegetical work is *Das erste Buch der Torah: Genesis, uebersetzt und erklaert* (1934). While Jacob did not accept the Mosaic authorship of the Pentateuch nor the dogma of literal inspiration, he found in its composition so much literary unity and spiritual harmony that all search for its "sources" appeared to him an exercise in futile hypothesis. His comprehensive commentaries on Exodus and a section of Leviticus are extant in manuscript. (An excerpt from the commentary on Exodus was published in *Judaism*, 13 (1964), 3–18.) His struggle against antisemitism began during his university years; in 1886 he founded the first Jewish students' society – Viadrana – which introduced fencing duels as a method of defending the honor of Judaism when it was degraded by antisemitic students. He was active as an orator and author in the fight waged by German Jews against antisemitism mainly in the years after World War I. He opposed Zionism not only because of his belief in a Jewish-German synthesis, but also because he saw in Zionism a complete secularization of Judaism and a basis for Jewish atheism.

BIBLIOGRAPHY: Wilhelm, in: YLBI, 7 (1962), 75–94; E.I. Jacob, in: *Paul Lazarus Gedenkbuch* (1961), 93–100; idem, in: H.C. Meyer (ed.), *Aus Geschichte und Leben der Juden in Westfalen* (1962), 89–109 (includes bibl.).

[Jacob Rothschild]

JACOB, BERTHOLD (pen name of **Berthold Salomon**, 1898–1944), German-Jewish publicist between the world wars. Jacob, born in Berlin, was a volunteer in World War I. He returned a radical pacifist, and from then on unabatedly struggled against German militarism and secret rearmament. His involvement in various *causes célèbres* of the Weimar Republic led to his being summoned as a witness in various cases on a number of occasions. Together with Paul Maria Dreyfuss and Martin Sander he published *Zeit-Notizen*. An article of his in the pacifist weekly *Weltbuehne*, led to the demission of Hans von Seeckt, commander in chief of the German army. In 1932 Jacob left Germany and ran an "Independent Press Service." In 1935 he was abducted by a Nazi agent during a visit in Switzerland, but was released after six months on the intervention of the Swiss government. In 1939 he was interned by the French authorities but escaped in 1941 to Lisbon, where he was again abducted. Jacob died in 1944 in a Nazi prison. His main works are *Weltbuerger Ossietzky* (1937) and *Warum schweigt die Welt?* (1936).

BIBLIOGRAPHY: H. Cawil, *Der Fall Jacob* (1935); *Exil Literatur 1933–1945* (1967^3), index; H. Hannover and E. Hannover-Brueck, *Politische Justiz 1918–1933* (1966), index.

[Yehuda Reshef]

JACOB, BLESSING OF, a collection of poetic sayings epitomizing the traits and fortunes of the Israelite tribes, written in the guise of deathbed pronouncements by Jacob to his 12 sons (Gen. 49). "Blessing" is a misnomer since three of the tribes are in effect cursed, and others are treated with jest or satire. The sayings are cast in pseudo-prophetic form as though the patriarch foresees the destinies of his sons. In fact, most of the separate sayings appear to describe past or present tribal fortunes. The events alluded to in the sayings are highly refracted by the terse and elusive language. The Reuben saying (49:4) refers to the elder son's incest with his father's concubine (35:22), but what the event signifies in tribal terms is unknown. The Simeon-Levi saying (49:5–7) recalls the murderous attack on the Shechemites (Gen. 34), but that event is not easily connected to the wider tribal histories. The ascendancy of Judah (49:8–12) corresponds with the sudden emergence of that tribe just before the united monarchy and its political hegemony under David is almost certainly referred to in the obscure "Shiloh" passage (49:10). It is possible that the Septuagint reading of II Samuel 20:18–19 shows the Dan of verses 16–18 to be already relocated in its northern home (cf. Judg. 17–18). The animal imagery of the sayings is varied and colorful. Judah is a rapacious lion (Gen. 49:9), Issachar a lazy or stoic ass (v. 14), Dan a cunning serpent (v. 17), Naphtali a lovely hind (v. 21), and Benjamin a ravenous wolf (v. 27). Joseph, as a fruitful bough (*porat*; v. 23), breaks the series of zoological metaphors. Many interpreters prefer to read "wild ass" (*pere*) or "bull" (*parah*). The metaphors are used to focus upon some single striking feature in the tribal manner of self-defense or conquest (Judah, Dan, Benjamin), or to describe the bounteous natural setting (Naphtali, Joseph), or to explain an abject socioeconomic position (Issachar). Three of the sayings employ puns on tribal names. Dan "shall judge" (*yadin*, v. 16), Gad "shall raid" (*yagud*, v. 19), and Issachar ("man of wages" or "hired laborer") is said to have "bowed his shoulders to bear, and become a slave at forced labor" (v. 15). These literary features give the impression of being popular visualizations of tribal traits and experiences. The picturesque folkloristic motives of the sayings sharply circumscribe their direct historical value.

Critics have found it impossible to view the sayings within any single clearly delimited historical horizon. The preeminence of Reuben and the secular status of Levi suggest an early period before the rise of the monarchy. The ascendancy of Judah speaks for the late 11th century B.C.E. and verse ten strongly suggests the rule of David. The language is archaic and often obscure; it reflects ancient liturgical formulations with pronounced Canaanite influence in poetic forms, idioms, and concepts. The fullest understanding of Genesis 49 requires comparison with the similar Deuteronomy 33 and the related tribal sayings and blessings of Judges 5 and Numbers 23–24, as well as with the Ugaritic mythological texts and the Egyptian Story of Sinuhe (in: Pritchard, Texts, 18–22; COS I, 77–82). The broad milieu of the sayings is the struggle of the separate tribes to hold their own in the land against enemies and to adapt to the economies peculiar to the regions of settlement. Many realistic details of military and political combat show through the poetic embellishments. Judah has prevailed over nations and receives the homage of all the tribes (Gen. 49:8). Joseph has successfully turned back an attack or repeated attacks by archers, probably from the Canaanite cities of the plains (vs. 23–26). Dan and Gad have fought guerrilla-style actions as they harass their enemies' "heels" (vs. 17, 19). Benjamin feeds on the spoils of war (v. 27; profiting by another tribe's victory?). Distinctive features of tribal economics are noted. Judah is famed for its viticulture (vs. 11–12). Asher produces choice foods and delicacies fit for kings (v. 20). Naphtali's land is highly productive (v. 21; does "hind" refer to wild game, domesticated animals, or general agricultural bounty?). Zebulun controls shipping north of Mt. Carmel or supplies the crews for Canaanite-Phoenician ships (v. 13). Joseph dwells in the richest region in the land, full of "blessings of heaven… of the deep … of the breasts and of the womb" (v. 25). All the tribes act with commendable self-assertiveness, except that Issachar is chided for exchanging freedom for the security of a life of serfdom (v. 14; or is it being half-praised for its resourcefulness in making the most of a bad situation?). All in all, the sayings of Genesis 49 seem to have arisen separately and to have been collected secondarily in the present literary context. Their lively speech argues for oral recitation. But the purpose is uncertain. Only verses 25–26 contain a blessing proper which probably was recited at an agricultural festival. Most of the sayings have the character of scornful or admiring popular or mutual assessments of the tribes. The Judah saying has in part (v. 10) the character of a dynastic pronouncement.

Prior to the literary collection of the sayings, they probably had a cultic connection in the gathering of the tribal league to worship YHWH. This is suggested by the explicitly liturgical introduction and conclusion supplied to the similar collection of sayings in Deuteronomy 33:2–5, 26–29. It is further hinted at in the "my" of Genesis 49:6 and the "I" of 49:18 where a cultic spokesman is presupposed (in contrast to the "my" of 49:3–4 and the "I" of 49:7 which refer to the deity). Several of the sayings presuppose a feeling of belonging together among the tribes at an apparently preliterary stage (49:7b, 8, 16, 26). That the content and temper of the sayings are often secular, jocular, and satirical does not speak against an intertribal cultic context but shows rather the robustness and earthiness of early Yahwism. Whether precisely those sayings were ever cultically recited together at one time is unknown, since the literary editor may have artificially combined them from more than one source. It has been argued that at least two literary stages of collection were involved, corresponding to the early and late strands of the source J. The earliest literary version of the sayings may have concentrated on explaining why the elder sons of Jacob were not the prominent tribes in the collector's time. An estimate of the relative age of the tribal sayings in the several extant collections suggests that on the average those of Judges 5 are earliest, followed by Genesis 49, Deuteronomy 33, and Numbers 23–24 in that order.

[Norman K. Gottwald]

In the Aggadah

After his sons had assembled around his bed, Jacob warned them against dissension, since union is a precondition for Israel's redemption. Jacob wanted to reveal the exact time of the advent of the Messiah to his sons, but at that moment the *Shekhinah* ("Divine Presence") departed from him and his knowledge of this great mystery vanished (Gen. R. 98:2). Jacob thereupon became apprehensive lest one of his children was unfit and this was the cause of the departure of the *Shekhinah*. His sons, sensing his fears, exclaimed, "Hear O Israel, the Lord our God the Lord is One: Just as there is only One in thy heart, so in our heart is there only One." Jacob immediately responded: "Blessed be the name of His glorious kingdom for ever and ever" (Pes. 56a).

When Jacob rebuked his eldest, Reuben, he told him that he should have had the double heritage of his primogeniture, the priestly dignity and the royal power. However, because of his sin, the birthright was conferred upon Joseph, kingship upon Judah, and the priesthood upon Levi (Gen. R. 98:4). Simeon and Levi were next reprimanded. God fulfilled Jacob's malediction that they be dispersed in Israel by causing the Levites to be on the move requesting tithes, and the Simeonites to be wandering mendicants (Gen. R. 99:7). After he had rebuked his first three sons, the remaining ones attempted to slip away since they feared that they too would be reproached. Jacob pacified them by approaching Judah with commendatory statements, and describing the noteworthy features of the Messiah who will descend from the House of Judah (Tanḥ. Va-Yeḥi, 10).

Zebulun was blessed before his elder brother, Issachar, because Zebulun enabled Issachar to devote himself to Torah study by providing him with sustenance (Gen. R. 99:9). The fruits in Issachar's territory grew to extraordinary size due to the merits of this tribe's devotion to Torah (Gen. R. 98:12). When blessing Dan, Jacob also envisioned his descendant, Samson, and thought him to be the Messiah. However, when Jacob saw him dead, he exclaimed, "He too is dead! Then 'I wait for thy salvation, O God'" (Gen. 49:18; Gen. R. 98:14). Jacob then declared that the redemption will not be achieved by Samson the Danite, but by Elijah the Gadite, who will appear at the end of days (Gen. R. 99:11). Asher's blessing was the beauty of his women, who would be sought in marriage by kings and high priests (Gen. R. 99:12; Tanh. Va-Yeḥi, 13). In Naphtali's land all fruits would ripen quickly, and they would be given as presents to kings to gain royal favor for the givers (Gen. R. 99:12). Joseph's blessing exceeded those of all his brethren. He was particularly praised for resisting the constant attempts of the daughters of princes to entice him, and for trusting in God when slandered before Pharaoh by the magicians and wise men of Egypt (Gen. R. 8:18; Targ. Yer. to Gen. 49:22–26).

The blessing bestowed upon Benjamin contains the prophecy that this tribe would provide Israel with both its first and last biblical rulers, Saul and Esther. Likewise, Benjamin's heritage in the Holy Land contains two extremes: Jericho ripens its fruits earlier than any other region in Ereẓ Israel while Beth-El ripens them latest. Jacob also referred to the Temple service in Benjamin's blessing because the sanctuary was to be situated in Benjamin's territory (Gen. R. 99:3).

BIBLIOGRAPHY: O. Eissfeldt, *The Old Testament, an Introduction* (1965), 67, 75, 192, 196–8, 228–9; idem, in: vts, 4 (1957), 138–47; J. Coppens, *ibid.*, 97–115; E. Good, in: jbl, 32 (1963), 427–32; H.L. Ginsberg, in: *Divrei Sifrut… N.H. Tur-Sinai* (1957), 144n; A. Gunneweg, in: zaw, 76 (1964), 245–55; H.J. Kittel, *Die Stammesprueche Israels* (1959); J. Lindblom, in: VTS, 1 (1953), 78–87; E. Sellin, in: ZAW, 60 (1944), 57–67; B. Vawter, in: cbq, 17 (1955), 1–18; H.J. Zobel, *Stammesspruch und Geschichte* (1965 = bzaw, 95). **ADD. BIBLIOGRAPHY:** S. Gevirtz, in: JBL, 90 (1971), 87–98; idem, in: *Eretz Israel,* 12 (1975), 104*–112*; idem, in: HUCA, 46 (1977), 33–54; idem, in: ZAW, 93 (1981), 21–37; idem, in: HUCA, 52 (1981), 93–128; idem, in: VT, 37 (1987), 154–63; N. Sarna, *JPS Torah Commentary Genesis* (1989), 331–46.

JACOB, FRANÇOIS (1920–), French molecular biologist and Nobel laureate. Jacob was born in Nancy, attended the Lycée Carnot, and started his medical studies in Paris. With the German invasion of France in 1940 he joined the Free French Forces in exile and fought in North Africa and Normandy. He was seriously wounded and the damage to his hands destroyed his ambition to become a surgeon. He received the Croix de Guerre and the Croix de la Libération and was made a Compagnon de la Libération, one of France's highest honors. After the war he completed his medical studies (1947) and gained his D.Sc. from the Sorbonne (1954). In 1950 he joined the Pasteur Institute as assistant to Andre *Lwoff. He was appointed laboratory director (1956), head of the Department of Cell Genetics (1960), and professor of cell genetics at the College de France (1964). Jacob's research explored the relationship between bacteriophages (phage) and the bacteria these infect as a model for establishing the fundamental principles of genetic control of protein synthesis. He collaborated with many of the founding fathers of molecular biology, including Elie Wollman, Max Delbruck, Jacques Monod, and Sydney *Brenner. This work defined the operon as the control unit consisting of one or more genes encoding the messenger RNA, which dictates protein synthesis. The operon is controlled by regulatory feedback loops incorporating repressor genes which are in turn controlled by operator genes. The operon can collaborate with other operons on the chromosome and is influenced by signals coming from the cytoplasm or the environment. Thus the potential for cell function and division is determined by the nucleotide sequence in DNA which is responsive to a network of controlling signals. This framework and the supporting experimental principles have formed the basis for subsequent scientific work on gene action and regulation. He received the Nobel Prize in physiology or medicine (1965) jointly with Andre Lwoff and Jacques Monod. His many honors include the Charles Leopold Mayer Prize of the Académie des Sciences (1962) and foreign membership of the U.S. Academy of Sciences. Jacob is also a distinguished writer on the philosophy and culture of science whose highly regarded books include *The Logic of Life* (1970) and *Of Flies, Mice and Men* (1980). His cultural contributions were recognized by the award of the Lewis Thomas Prize (1994). He married the pianist Lise Bloch in 1947.

[Michael Denman (2nd ed.)]

JACOB, HEINRICH EDUARD (1889–1967), German playwright, journalist, and biographer. Born in Berlin, he became the *Berliner Tageblatt*'s Vienna correspondent. Jacob spent almost 18 months in the concentration camps of Dachau and Buchenwald before escaping to the U.S. in 1940. A versatile author, writing in an expressive and colorful style, Jacob published more than 30 books, including poetry, plays, and novels. His best-known dramas are *Beaumarchais und Sonnenfels* (1919), in which a Jew is the central character, and *Der Tulpenfrevel* (1920).

While in exile in New York, Jacob achieved distinction for his biographies of Johann Strauss (1937), Haydn (1950), and Felix Mendelssohn (1959). He also published a history of coffee, *Sage und Siegeszug des Kaffees* (1934), and *Six Thousand Years of Bread* (1944). Jacob returned to Europe in 1953 and settled in Hamburg.

BIBLIOGRAPHY: *New York Times* (Nov. 10, 1967).

JACOB, JACK FREDERICK RAPHAEL (1923–), Indian army officer. Born in Calcutta to a family of Baghdad origin, Jacob was commissioned in the Indian army in 1942 while India was part of the British Empire and served in the Middle East during World War II. He rose rapidly after India gained its independence in 1948, commanding a field regiment in 1956–57 and an artillery brigade in 1964–65. After serving as commander of the School of Artillery from 1965 to 1966 he was given command of an infantry division (1967–69). At the outbreak of the war against Pakistan in 1971, which resulted in the creation of Bangladesh, he was chief of staff, Eastern Command, with the rank of major-general. For the prominent part which he played in the campaign he was awarded the Param Vishisht Seva medal.

JACOB, MAX (1876–1944), French poet and novelist. Born in Quimper, Brittany, Jacob was the son of a tailor and descended from German Jews who immigrated to France in 1816. After an unhappy childhood, he made the first of three suicide attempts at the age of 17. For several years, he worked in a variety of occupations, including carpentry, as a lawyer's clerk, commerce, and even astrology. A gifted linguist and draftsman, Jacob eventually became an art critic in Paris, where he joined the circle of Apollinaire, Picasso, and André Salmon, centered in the Left Bank cabaret *Le Lapin agile*. At this time he evolved his basic aesthetic principles: the establishment of a "new harmony" to free men from everything which prevented them from seeing the true colors of reality (cf. his children's tales *Le Roi Kaboul et le Marmiton Gauvin* and *Le Géant du soleil*, 1904). Taking up arms against convention and prejudice, Jacob made irony his favorite device, thus providing himself with "distance" from the object and with the "patience and submission" indispensable to creativity. In 1909 he had his first vision of Jesus and wrote the *mystère* entitled *Saint Matorel* (1911) and *La Côte*, poems which later appeared in Breton. A melancholy anti-romantic, Jacob became known for his mordant humor and "surrealistic" speech: lake became suburb, valley changed to movie theater, Ibsen became Rimbaud, and Byron, Freud. The poet's yearning for love and his suffering and disillusionment combined with a second vision led to his conversion to Catholicism in 1915. The spiritual comfort which this brought him inspired a series of works characterized by a mingling of sarcasm and lyricism: *Les Oeuvres burlesques et mystiques du frère Matorel...* (1912); *Le Cornet à dés* (1917); *Le Phanérogame* (1918), a novel; *La Défense de Tartuffe*, subtitled *Extase, remords, visions, prières, poèmes et méditations d'un Juif converti* (1919); and *Le Laboratoire central* (1921). After 1921, Jacob retired to the monastery of Saint-Benoît-sur-Loire, where he wrote *Le Cabinet noir* (1922), a novel, *Le Terrain Bouchaballe* (1923), the mystical *Visions infernales* (1924), and *L'Homme de chair et l'homme reflet* (1925). During the years 1928–36, he achieved some standing as a painter in Paris, then retired once more to Saint-Beno-ît, where he wrote a book of prose poems, *Ballades* (1938). After the Nazi occupation in 1940, Jacob was arrested by the Gestapo and died in the Drancy concentration camp. Some books of verse and two volumes of correspondence appeared posthumously after World War II.

BIBLIOGRAPHY: A. Billy, *Max Jacob* (Fr., 1946); J. Rousselot, *Max Jacob au sérieux* (1958); M. Raymond, *De Baudelaire au Surréalisme* (1933), 253–62; J. Mesnil, in: E.J. Finbert (ed.), *Aspects du Génie d' Israël* (1950), 300–6; C. Lehrmann, *L'Elément juif dans la littérature française*, 2 (1961), 142–3.

[Max Bilen]

JACOB, NAOMI ELLINGTON (Naomi Ellington Gray; 1889–1964), novelist of half-Jewish parentage whose varied career is reflected in a vast output of novels. She also wrote such autobiographical books as *Me – In War-Time* (1940). In her most ambitious work, *The Gollantz Saga* (1952), she portrayed the progressive assimilation of a Jewish family. Born in Ripon, Yorkshire, and originally a schoolteacher in Middlesbrough, she lost her job for wearing trousers; thereafter, she always wore men's clothes. In 1930 she moved to Italy, where she lived for the rest of her life.

BIBLIOGRAPHY: ODNB; P. Bailey, *Three Queer Lives: An Alternative Biography of Fred Barnes, Naomi Jacob, and Arthur Marshall* (2002); E. Hamer, *Britannia's Glory: A History of Twentieth Century Lesbians* (1996).

[William D. Rubinstein (2nd ed.)]

JACOB, TESTAMENT OF, apocryphal work based on Genesis 49. Reference to an apocryphal book of Jacob is perhaps to be found in the Apostolical Constitutions 6:16 which speaks of "apocryphal books of… the three patriarchs." A testament of Jacob is to be found together with the testaments of Abraham and Isaac in Arabic, Ethiopic, and Coptic. This work is a patchwork of biblical verses, based substantially on Genesis 47:29–49:1. It was doubtless composed as a supplement to the extant testaments of Abraham and Isaac, both of which, and especially the former, contain important original material. This apocryphal work appears in a Paris Greek manuscript of the 12th century as a separate work under the title "Testament of Jacob." In Jerusalem, there is an Armenian manuscript 939, in which Gen. 47:27–50:26 precedes the Testaments of the 12 patriarchs, and under the same title as the preceding. The Testament was a common literary form in the period of the Second Temple, and doubtless the fact that Jacob is the one patriarch to whom the Bible assigns a last testament played a role in this development.

BIBLIOGRAPHY: M.R. James, *Testament of Abraham* (1892), 6, 131–61; idem, *The Lost Apocrypha of the Old Testament* (1920), 18f.; G.H. Box, *Testament of Abraham* (1927), 55–89; Stone, in: *Revue des Etudes Arméniennes*, N.S., 5 (1968), 261–70.

[Michael E. Stone]

JACOB, WALTER (1930–), U.S. Reform rabbi and university administrator. Jacob was born in Augsburg, Germany, and immigrated to the United States in 1940. He received his B.A. from Drury College (Springfield, Mo., 1950) and ordination and an M.H.L. from Hebrew Union College in 1955. He earned his D.H.L. in 1961 from HUC-JIR, which granted him an honorary D.D. in 1980. Immediately following ordination, Jacob was named assistant rabbi at Rodef Shalom Congregation in Pittsburgh, Penn., under Rabbi Solomon *Freehof, serving as well as a chaplain in the U.S. Air Force during the years 1955–57. In 1966, Jacob succeeded Freehof as senior rabbi, becoming emeritus in 1997. He was also adjunct professor at the Pittsburgh Theological Seminary (1968–74).

Jacob took an active role in helping to re-establish Reform Judaism in Germany, where he served as president of the Abraham Geiger College, the first rabbinic seminary in Central Europe since the Holocaust. Splitting his time between Berlin and Pittsburgh, he also served as president of the Solomon B. Freehof Institute for Progressive Halakhah, an international forum for Jewish law, and of the Associated American Jewish Museums, which organizes free art exhibits for synagogues and Jewish centers. Previously, Jacob served the Reform movement in the United States in several high-profile roles, including president of the *Central Conference of American Rabbis (CCAR) (1991–93). His interest and expertise in Jewish law led him to serve as chairman of the Responsa Committee of the CCAR and chairman of the International Responsa Committee of the *World Union for Progressive Judaism (WUPJ). As president of the Religious Education Association of the United States, he wrote on interfaith issues. Jacob was also an overseer of HUC-JIR, a member of the Rabbinic Cabinet of the WUPJ and chairman of the Publications Committee of Hebrew Union College Press. As CCAR president, Jacob sought to integrate a broader reinterpretation of *halakah*, in accordance with Reform theology, into the deliberations and decisions of the Reform movement.

He was made a Knight Commander of the Federal Republic of Germany in 1999 and received the Commander of the Equestrian Order of St. Gregory the Great from Pope John Paul II in 2004.

In addition to compiling several volumes of responsa on a wide variety of issues, Jacob edited, wrote, or co-authored a number of books, including *Christianity Through Jewish Eyes*, (1974); *The Healing Past: Pharmaceuticals in the Biblical World* (with Irene Jacob), (1993); and *Not By Birth Alone: Conversion to Judaism* (1997).

[Bezalel Gordon (2nd ed.)]

JACOB BEN AARON OF KARLIN (d. 1844), Lithuanian rabbi and author. Jacob b. Aaron, a grandson of *Baruch b. Jacob of Shklov, was a pupil of *Ḥayyim of Volozhin. He was first rabbi of Gorodok and later of Karlin, where he served for 30 years, until his death. Jacob was the author of the responsa *Mishkenot Ya'akov* (Vilna, 1810), many of them with Ephraim Zalman Margulies of Brod, on all sections of the Shulḥan Arukh; *Kehillat Ya'akov* (1847), novellae on a number of tractates of the orders *Zera'im* and *Mo'ed*. His halakhic works were highly esteemed by yeshivah students, by whom they were much used. Jacob's brother ISAAC, after devoting himself to business, succeeded him in the rabbinate of Karlin. Isaac, who also achieved an outstanding rabbinical reputation, was the author of *Keren Orah* (2 parts, 1852–57), on a number of tractates of the Talmud. Both brothers were noted for their struggle against the kidnapping of children for impressment into the Russian army.

BIBLIOGRAPHY: Fuenn, Keneset, 574; S. Chones, *Toledot ha-Posekim* (1910), 563f.

[Itzhak Alfassi]

JACOB BEN ABRAHAM SOLOMON (late 16th and early 17th century), Bohemian rabbi and preacher. Jacob was probably born in Poland but was active mainly in Prague. He was an acknowledged authority on the Talmud and was called *Shinena* ("the sharpminded") by his contemporaries. He wrote: (1) *Ma'aneh Lashon*, a collection of prayers and petitions mainly for mourners (first published anonymously in Prague, c. 1615; 2nd ed. Cracow, 1668; 3rd ed. Prague, 1678). A shortened form of the work accompanied by a Judeo-German translation appeared in Frankfurt in 1688. The complete text with additions, together with full translations into Judeo-German and German by Eliezer Lieberman b. Judah Loeb, appeared in Amsterdam in 1677 and was frequently reprinted (cf. Friedberg, in bibl.); (2) *Derush Na'eh*, consisting of homiletical sermons on a number of the weekly portions, as well as halakhic novellae to *Mo'ed Katan* (Prague, 1603). In addition, his decisions on questions on the laws of mourning were quoted by Moses Jekuthiel b. Avigdor Kaufmann Kohen in his *Ḥukkei Da'at*, printed as an addendum to *Yismaḥ Yisrael* (Berlin, 1699–1700) by Israel Samuel b. Solomon Rofe. Wolf and Zunz identify Jacob with the Prague *dayyan* Jacob b. Abraham who died there in 1562, while Steinschneider identifies him with Jacob b. Abraham, publisher of *Pirkei Eliyahu* (Prague, 1600). The latter appears to be more probable, as *Ma'aneh Lashon* is hardly likely to have been published anonymously around 1610 if its author had already died in 1562. Jacob's authorship of this work is acknowledged in the *Leḥem ha-Panim* (cf. Zunz, in bibl.).

BIBLIOGRAPHY: O. Muneles, *Bibliographical Survey of Jewish Prague* (1952), nos. 58, 97; Wininger, Biog, 3 (1928), 253; Friedberg, Eked, 2 (1951[2]), 646 no. 2859; Davidson, Oẓar, 2 (1929), 457 no. 4306; Zunz, Gesch, 291 no. 298 no. 225.

[Elias Katz]

JACOB BEN AḤA (end of the third and beginning of the fourth century C.E.), Palestinian *amora*. Jacob was mainly a halakhist, and his halakhic dicta are frequently mentioned in both Talmuds, but he is also known as an aggadist (Tanḥ. B., Ex. 51; PR, supplement, p. 202a; et al.). He studied under R. *Johanan (TJ, Shevu. 1:3, 33a) and frequently transmits sayings in his name (TJ, Ber. 7:2, 11b; et al.). He also frequently transmits sayings in the names of the scholars of preceding generations, such as R. *Hezekiah, the school of *Yannai, *Simeon b. Jehoẓadak (Shab. 1:1, 2d). He is mentioned as being in Sepphoris together with Hezekiah, a younger contemporary *amora* (TJ, Ber. 3:1, 6a). He was active in communal affairs, and many queries were addressed to him by leading contemporary *amoraim* (TJ, Shab. 6:2, 8a; et al.).

BIBLIOGRAPHY: Frankel, Mevo, 104b–105a; Hyman, Toledot, s.v.; Ḥ. Albeck, *Mavo la-Talmudim* (1969), 249–50.

[Shmuel Safrai]

JACOB BEN ASHER (1270?–1340), halakhic authority. Jacob was the son of *Asher b. Jehiel (the Rosh), under whom he studied. In 1303 he accompanied his father from Germany to Toledo, where he lived in great poverty, shunning rabbinical office and devoting all his time to study. In his learning, he avoided verbosity and casuistry. Typical of his style is his first halakhic work, *Sefer ha-Remazim*, in which he gave the halakhic rulings deduced from his father's work, *Ha-Asheri* (under the title *Kiẓẓur Piskei ha-Rosh*, Constantinople, 1515).

Jacob's enduring fame rests upon his major work, the *Arba'ah Turim*, as a result of which he is commonly referred to as "the Ba'al ha-Turim." Perceiving that "reasoning had become faulty, controversy had increased, opinions had multiplied, so that there is no halakhic ruling which is free from differences of opinion," he decided to compile a work to embrace all *halakhot* and customs incumbent upon the individual and the community. The work is divided into four sections (*Turim*, "rows"; first complete edition, Piove di Sacco, 1475): Part I, *Oraḥ Ḥayyim*, contains 697 chapters and deals with blessings, prayers, the Sabbath, festivals, and fasts; Part II, *Yoreh De'ah*, 403 chapters commencing with *Issur ve-Hetter*, the laws of Kashrut, such as *sheḥitah* and *terefot*, and ending with usury, idolatry, and mourning; Part III, *Even ha-Ezer*, 178 chapters on laws affecting women, particularly marriage, divorce, *ḥaliẓah*, and *ketubbah*; Part IV, *Ḥoshen Mishpat*, 427 chapters on civil law and personal relations. The arrangement of the book, its simple style, and its wealth of content, made it a basic work in Hebrew law. It opened a new era in the realm of halakhic codification (see *Codification of Law; *Shulḥan Arukh). The style and target population of each section of the *Tur* are not the same. *Ḥoshen Mishpat* and *Even ha-Ezer* are meant more for *dayyanim* (judges) than for community rabbis or laymen. *Yoreh De'ah* was meant for community rabbis, while *Oraḥ Ḥayyim* is a guidebook for both rabbis and laymen. Jacob invariably quotes the text of the Talmud and its commentaries as well as the opinions of authorities who preceded him, and then lays down the *halakhah*, mainly following *Maimonides and his own father. The *Tur* also served to apprise Spanish Jewry with the opinions of the French and German rabbinate. On questions of faith and belief, however, he does not hesitate expressly to oppose Maimonides. He was aware of the views of the Ḥasidei Ashkenaz, whose influence is discernible particularly in the *Oraḥ Ḥayyim*. The excellence of the work soon led to its dissemination throughout the Diaspora. Its authority has been recognized and accepted by all Jewish scholars throughout the generations, many of whom (including Joseph *Caro, Moses *Isserles, Isaac *Aboab, Jacob ibn *Ḥabib, Joel *Sirkes, and Ḥayyim *Benveniste) wrote commentaries on it, and made précis of it. When Caro wrote his major work, the *Beit Yosef* (published with the *Turim* ed. of Wilmersdorf, 1720–27), he decided to "base it upon the *Turim*… because it contains most of the views of the *posekim*." In writing the *Tur*, Jacob broke with the German traditions of his father. The German rabbis did not compose comprehensive halakhic codes because they did not attach universal authority to their legal responsa, viewing them as answers to individuals, and because of the numerous *minhagim* (customs) associated with each and every German Jewish community, which were often contradictory. After moving to Spain, Jacob discovered that the communities there were less learned and more centralized. These factors made the writing of a comprehensive code both necessary and easier to accomplish. Jacob prepared himself for the writing of the *Tur* by first editing his father's responsa, thus giving them universal authority, and by creating a halakhic summary of his father's talmudic commentary, *Kiẓẓur Piskei ha-Rosh*.

Jacob also wrote a comprehensive commentary on the Pentateuch (Zolkiew, 1806), containing the best expositions of the *peshat* ("literal meaning") by earlier Bible commentators, such as *Saadiah Gaon, *Rashi, Abraham *Ibn Ezra, David *Kimḥi, and others, in particular abstracting "the straightforward explanations" from the commentary of *Naḥmanides and disregarding the kabbalistic ones, since "my soul has not entered its secret" (cf. Gen. 49:6). When Jacob added his own opinions it was usually to explain the reason for a Torah law or *mitzvah*. To the beginning of each section, he added "as a little appetizer, **gematriot* and explanations of the *masorah, in order to attract the mind." Ironically, it was just these "appetizers" that were published (under the title *Perush ha-Torah le-R. Ya'akov Ba'al ha-Turim* (Constantinople, 1500 and 1514)) some three centuries before the main part of the work, and it was this portion only which was widely known for many generations. The modern edition titled, *Perush ha-Tur ha-Arokh al ha-Torah*, was published in Jerusalem in 1981.

Jacob neither served in any rabbinical post nor received any remuneration from the community but was involved in communal activities. He appended his signature to a sentence of death upon an informer (Judah b. Asher, Responsa *Zikhron Yehudah* (1846), no. 75). His ethical will to his children (first published Pressburg, 1885) reflects his high spiritual and cultural level. A late tradition, mentioned by Ḥ.J.D. *Azulai, relates that Jacob set out for Ereẓ Israel but died on the journey.

BIBLIOGRAPHY: Graetz, Hist, 4 (1894), 87–88; S.M. Chones, *Toledot ha-Posekim* (1910), 270–4; Weiss, Dor, 5 (19245), 118–28; Ḥ. Tchernowitz, *Toledot ha-Posekim*, 2 (1947), 199–220; Freimann, in: JJLG, 12 (1918), 286, 301–8; Waxman, Literature, index. **ADD. BIBLIOGRAPHY:** Y.D. Galinsky, "*Arba'a Turim ve-ha-Sifrut ha-Hilkhatit shel Sefarad be-Me'ah ha-14*" (Dissertation, 1999); Y. Shaviv, in: *Mahana'yim*, 3 (1992), 170–79; A. Ahrend in: ibid., 180–87; I. Ta-Shma, in: *Studies in Medieval Jewish History and Literature*, 3 (2000), 179–96; L. Jacobs, in: *Jewish Law Annual*, 6 (1987), 94–108; A. Steinberg, in: *Assia Jewish Medical Ethics*, 1:1 (1988), 3–4; E.E. Urbach, in: PAAJR, 46:7 (1980), 1–14.

[Ephraim Kupfer / David Derovan (2nd ed.)]

JACOB BEN BENJAMIN ZE'EV (also **Zak**; 17th century), talmudist, father of Ẓevi Hirsch *Ashkenazi (the "Ḥakham Ẓevi"). By his first marriage he was a son-in-law of Ephraim b. Jacob ha-Kohen, and by a second, of Naphtali *Kohen. He studied under Jacob of Lublin. He taught in Vilna, but he fled at the time of the Cossack uprising of 1655. He was missing for a long time and was presumed dead, but finally he reached Trebitsch (Trebic), Moravia. He was appointed rabbi of Ungarisch-Brod (Uhersky Brod) and later succeeded his father-in-law, Ephraim b. Jacob, in Budapest, where he headed a yeshivah. His pupils included David *Oppenheim. According to an opinion which has, however, been disputed, Jacob was for a time an adherent of Shabbetai Ẓevi. When Budapest was taken by storm by the Austrians in 1686, Jacob and his wife were taken by the Brandenburg army to Berlin as prisoners of war and were ransomed there. After a short stay in Altona, where his son was rabbi, he moved to Ereẓ Israel and died in Jerusalem at the age of 73.

BIBLIOGRAPHY: J. Emden, *Megillat Sefer*, ed. by D. Kahana (1897), 3–7; J. Schwarz, *Tevu'ot ha-Areẓ*, ed. by A.M. Luncz (1900), 459f.; H.A. Wagenaar, *Toledot Ya'veẓ* (1868), 1; Fuenn, Keneset, 547; idem, *Kiryah Ne'emanah* (1915²), 91f.; S. Büchler, *A zsidók története Budapesten* (1901), 148, 155, 177; D. Kaufmann, *Die Erstuermung Ofens* (1895), 17, 26f., 53ff.; J.J.(L.) Greenwald (Grunwald), *Toledot Ḥakhmei Yisrael* (1924), 3, 5, 9, 22; Frumkin-Rivlin, 2 (1928), 78–82, 152; D. Kahana, *Toledot ha-Mekubbalim ha-Shabbeta'im ve-ha-Ḥasidim*, 1 (1913), 90.

[Samuel Abba Horodezky]

JACOB BEN DUNASH BEN AKIVA (tenth century), liturgical poet. Some support for the assumption that Jacob came from North Africa can be found in the name Dunash, which is borrowed from the Berbers. A few of his *piyyutim*, discovered in the Cairo *Genizah*, have been published by various scholars. These are: a *yoẓer* for Passover, based on the Song of Songs; two *piyyutim* for the Day of Atonement, one of which was incorporated into a *kerovah* of Eleazar *Kallir for the *Musaf* of that day and is structured entirely on an analogy between the "celestial King" (God) and the "earthly king" (man); and a *piyyut* for Ḥanukkah.

BIBLIOGRAPHY: I. Davidson, in: *Festschrift Armand Kaminka* (1937), 7–14 (Heb. pt.); M. Zulai, in: *Ginzei Kaufmann*, 1 (1949), 39f.; J. Schirmann, *Shirim Ḥadashim min ha-Genizah* (1965), 42–45.

JACOB BEN ELEAZAR (12th–13th centuries), poet, grammarian, and philosopher. It has been conjectured that Jacob, who lived in Toledo, was a member of the distinguished Abenalazar family of Toledo. His Arabic work, *al-Kitāb-Kāmil* ("The Complete Book") on Hebrew grammar, called in Hebrew *Sefer ha-Shalem*, is known only from citations by a number of grammarians, e.g., David *Kimḥi in his *Mikhlol*. More important, however, is his literary contribution. At the request of the cultured philanthropist, Benveniste b. Ḥiyya Aldian, he translated and adapted in Hebrew an Arabic version of the well-known ancient Indian story, *Kalila and Dimna, in rhymed verse. A remnant of this translation was published by J. Derenbourg (see bibl.). Jacob also wrote *Sefer Pardes Rimmonei ha-Ḥokhmah va-Arugat Bosem ha-Mezimah* (Margoliouth, Cat, no. 1100/1), a philosophical work of 23 chapters in rhymed verse and prose (chapters 13–23 published by Davidson; see bibl.); and *Gan Te'udot*, on ethical and philosophical topics (Margoliouth, Cat, no. 1100/2). The most important and most interesting of his books is *Sefer ha-Meshalim* (written apparently in 1233), which comprises ten *maqāmāt* on various topics. Four of them (5, 6, 7, 9), love stories, unusual both in content and form, were published by J. Schirmann (see bibl.). This book reflects considerable Islamic and Christian influence. In addition, two *piyyutim* by him are also known.

BIBLIOGRAPHY: Davidson, Oẓar, 4 (1933), 413; idem, in: HḤY, 10 (1926), 94–105; Steinschneider, Uebersetzungen, 872–83; idem, in: ZDMG, 27 (1873), 553–60, 564f.; J. Derenbourg, *Deux versions hébraïques du livre de Kalîlâh et Dimnah* (1881), 311–88; Schirmann, Sefarad, 2 (19602), 207–37, 690; idem, in: YMḤSI, 5 (1939), 209–66; idem, in: *Etudes d'Orientalisme dédiées à la mémoire de Lévi-Provençal*, 1 (1962), 285–97.

[Abraham David]

JACOB BEN EPHRAIM NAPHTALI HIRSCH OF LUBLIN (d. 1644 or 1645), Polish rabbi. Jacob was rabbi of Brest-Litovsk (Brisk) from 1630 to 1635 and subsequently of Lublin, two of the most important Jewish communities in Poland. In

Lublin, together with his son *Joshua Hoeschel who succeeded him as rabbi there, he headed a large yeshivah and was considered the greatest teacher of Talmud study of his generation in Poland. His pupils included Ḥayyim Heika ha-Levi, rabbi of Hrubieszow, and Samuel *Koidanover. He was a member of the *Council of Four Lands. Several of Jacob's responsa have been published in the works of his contemporaries and in those of later scholars. His novellae to the Talmud and the Shulḥan Arukh have remained in manuscript. The greatest rabbis of his generation, Yom Tov Lipmann *Heller and Joel *Sirkes, quote him in their works.

BIBLIOGRAPHY: I.T. Eisenstadt and S. Wiener, *Da'at Kedoshim* (1897–98), 88f. (first pagination); S.B. Nissenbaum, *Le-Korot ha-Yehudim be-Lublin* (1899), 38f.; Fuenn, Keneset, 535; A.L. Feinstein, *Ir Tehillah* (1886), 25f., 133f., 173 etc.; Halpern, Pinkas, 67, 491f.

[Itzhak Alfassi]

JACOB BEN ḤAYYIM BEN ISAAC IBN ADONIJAH (c. 1470–c. 1538), kabbalist, talmudist, and masoretic scholar. Born in Tunis, which he left on account of persecutions early in the 16th century, Jacob went to Rome and Florence and eventually settled in Venice (c. 1520), where he worked as a proofreader and editor at the Hebrew press of Daniel *Bomberg. He converted to Christianity sometime after 1527, as had Felix Pratensis, his predecessor at the press. In the 1520s he edited books in the fields of Kabbalah, Talmud, Bible, and liturgy. He is best remembered as the editor of the second edition of the famous Rabbinic Bible *Shaar YHWH he-Ḥadash* (sic, not as often quoted: *hqdš*), "The New Gate of the Lord," based on Sephardi manuscripts. The title, taken from Jeremiah 26:10 alluded to the fact that this edition was a replacement (1524–25) for the earlier edition (1517) that had been produced by Pratensis after his conversion to Christianity, a fact that did not sit well with prospective Jewish buyers. Ben Ḥayyim provided a detailed introduction, and edited the apparatus of the masorah. These marginal notes led to Ben Ḥayyim's Bible becoming the standard "masoretic" text for centuries. The medieval rabbinic commentators chosen by Ben Ḥayyim to accompany the biblical text became "canonical" in all later editions. (In the 19th century the rabbinic Bibles based on the edition of Ben Ḥayyim acquired the name *Mikra'ot Gedolot*, "large scriptures.") The introduction was translated into Latin by Claudius Capellus (*De Mari Rabbinico Infido*, 2 (1667), ch. 4) and into English by C.D. *Ginsburg (1865). Jacob stressed the reliability of talmudic tradition and criticized Bible commentators and grammarians such as David *Kimḥi, Profiat *Duran, and Isaac *Abrabanel for not giving sufficient attention to the masorah. His work in this field was acclaimed – with reservations – by Elijah *Levita and Azariah dei *Rossi. Jacob appended extracts of the masoretic work *Darkhei ha-Nikkud ve-ha-Neginah*, ascribed to Moses ha-Nakdan, to the *Masorah Gedolah* in the Rabbinic Bible. He also wrote a dissertation on the Targum, which is prefixed to the Pentateuch editions of 1527 and 1543–44. As proofreader and reviser for Bomberg, Jacob was responsible for the *editio princeps* of many works including the Jerusalem Talmud (1523), and Maimonides' *Mishneh Torah* (1524), which he revised together with David Pizzighettone. More recently his work as a reviser has come under criticism, as his readings were not always based on manuscript evidence; his knowledge of *halakhah* and of Aramaic, particularly of the dialect used in the Palestinian Talmud, was limited, as is evident also from his dissertation on the Targum.

BIBLIOGRAPHY: Jacob ben Chajim ibn Adonijah, *Introduction to the Rabbinic Bible* (1968), prolegomenon by N.H. Snaith; C.D. Ginsburg, *Introduction to the Massoretico-Critical Edition of the Hebrew Bible* (1897), 956–74; J.N. Epstein, in: *Tarbiz*, 5 (1934), 257–72; 6 (1935), 38–55; S. Lieberman, *ibid.*, 20 (1950), 107–17; idem, in: *Sefer ha-Yovel… Ḥ. Albeck* (1963), 283–305; P. Kahle, *Cairo Geniza* (1959), 124ff; J. Penkower, in: DBI, 1:558–59; idem, in: A. Berlin and M. Brettler (eds.), *The Jewish Study Bible* (2004), 2082–83.

[S. David Sperling (2nd ed.)]

JACOB BEN ḤAYYIM TALMID (d. after 1594), leader of Egyptian Jewry. Jacob was appointed to his position by the Ottoman authorities during the second half of the 16th century. Before him, this position was held by Tajir. Jacob was a member of the renowned Talmid family which had settled in Constantinople after the Spanish Expulsion. Joseph *Sambari refers to him by the title of **nagid*. It does not, however, appear that this title was intended as the equivalent of *Ra'īs al-Yahūd*, the official title of the *nagid* during the *Mamluk period, but rather as a title of honor which was given to him by the Jewish community of Egypt. After his appointment to this position (apparently after 1560), he did not show the respect due to the most prominent of Egypt's rabbis, R. Bezalel *Ashkenazi, who, feeling insulted, issued a **ḥerem* against him. This dispute was brought before the Ottoman governor of Egypt, who ordered the banishment of Jacob and the nullification of his title of *nagid*, probably in 1584–87. From then onward, the chiefs of the community in Egypt, who were sent by the authorities in Constantinople, were referred to as *chelebi* ("gentleman [of fashion]," in Turkish). In the days of Ibrāhīm Pasha (1583–84), Jacob, together with R. Eleazar Iskandari, took the initiative for the reopening of the synagogue of the **Musta'rabim* in Cairo, which had been closed in 1545.

BIBLIOGRAPHY: Neubauer, Chronicles, 1 (1887), 116f., 157, 160; Rosanes, Togarmah, 2 (1937), 220f.; Pollack, in: *Zion*, 1 (1936), 32f.; Assaf, Mekorot, 198. **ADD BIBLIOGRAPHY:** J. Sambari, in: S. Shtober (ed.), *Divrei Yosef* (1994), 141–42, 404, 414; A. David, in: *Tarbiz*, 41 (1972), 326–29.

[Abraham David]

JACOB BEN IDI (end of the third century C.E.), Palestinian *amora*. Jacob transmitted sayings of the *amoraim* of the first generation, such as Joshua b. Levi (TJ, Kil 6:1, 30b), R. Ḥanina (TJ, Ber. 6:1, 10b), and others, but chiefly in the name of R. *Johanan, who was his main teacher. In Johanan's old age, when he was vexed that his other disciples neglected him and did not transmit his halakhic sayings, Jacob appeased him (TJ, Ber. 2:1, 46; Yev. 96b). According to the Jerusalem

Talmud (Pe'ah, 8:9, 21b), he and Isaac b. Naḥman were lay leaders of the community, apparently Tiberias. Toward the end of his life, however, he lived in Tyre or its vicinity. Jacob was regarded as one of the great scholars of his generation, and while *Zeira was still in Babylonia, he requested scholars traveling between Ereẓ Israel and Babylonia to take a circuitous route by way of Tyre in order to obtain Jacob's views on various problems (Ḥul. 98a; Er. 80a; BM 43b). R. Naḥman made a similar request to Ḥama b. Ada, "an emissary of Zion." However, when he arrived there Jacob was no longer alive (Beẓah 25b).

BIBLIOGRAPHY: Frankel, Mevo, 105a; Hyman, Toledot, 776–8; Ḥ. Albeck, *Mavo la-Talmudim* (1969), 250–2.

[Shmuel Safrai]

JACOB BEN JACOB HA-KOHEN (mid-13th century), Spanish kabbalist. Jacob was born in Soria and lived for some time in Segovia. He wandered among the Jewish communities in Spain and Provence, looking for remnants of earlier kabbalistic writings and traditions preserved by individual kabbalists. He made a prolonged stay in Provence with his younger brother *Isaac b. Jacob ha-Kohen and died in Béziers (c. 1270–80). Jacob adopted pietist ways and was strongly influenced by the mysticism of the *Ḥasidei Ashkenaz, accepting their methods in the application of numerology. He was also in contact with the last members of the kabbalist circle of the *Sefer ha-Iyyun* ("Book of Speculations"). Jacob claims to have been granted many revelations in the form of visions. These, he explains, were all associated with the function of *Metatron as the first creation and with details of the mysteries relating to this figure and its connection with the secrets of the Torah and *mitzvot*. Jacob draws a distinction between his revelation-inspired and other writings; to the latter belongs his collection of commentaries inspired by *Eleazar of Worms and material on Gnostic traditions. Jacob's principal pupil was *Moses b. Solomon b. Simeon of Burgos. Jacob was one of the main pillars of the renascent Gnostic trend in kabbalah (*ha-ma'amikim*). Neither he nor his brother was an ordained rabbi.

Jacob's works are (1) a commentary on the forms of the letters of the alphabet written in Provence around 1270 (*Madda'ei ha-Yahadut*, 2 (1927), 201–12); (2) a commentary on *Sefer *Yeẓirah* now lost, though the first part may have been preserved in a Florence manuscript (Plut. 11, Ms. 53, pp. 33–42). Abraham *Abulafia studied it and praised it as "kabbalistic"; (3) a commentary on *Merkevet Yeḥezkel* (Ezekiel's vision of the throne-chariot), incorporated anonymously in a number of manuscripts (e.g., Florence 11, 412), parts of which were published by G. Scholem in *Kitvei Yad be-Kabbalah bi-Yrushalayim* (1930), 208–13. Jacob's authorship is attested by his pupil Moses of Burgos who cites a number of passages in his master's name. The commentary blends Spanish kabbalism and pietist traditions and is partly based on Eleazar of Worms' *Sodei Rezaya*; (4) *Sefer ha-Orah* ("Book of Illumination"), a large collection of all the secrets revealed to Jacob through his visions, including speculative passages – such as the "*Perush Yedi'at ha-Bore*" ("Explanation of the Knowledge of the Creator"), explanations of the Divine Names and the alphabets in *Sefer Yeẓirah*, an explanation of certain *mitzvot* (*ẓiẓit, tefillin*, blowing the *shofar*, the red heifer) linking these precepts with the mysteries relating to Metatron, explanations of certain prayers and cosmological exegesis (*Sod ha-Levanah*, "Secret of the Moon"). The lengthy preface to *Sefer ha-Orah* is preserved in a Milan manuscript (Ambrosiana 62), which (together with Vat. 428, Vienna 258, and Schocken, Kab. 14) incorporates a large portion of this material. Three of these mysteries appearing in a Paris manuscript have been published in *Madda'ei ha-Yahadut* (2 (1927), 240–3). Collections of the traditions dealing with the powers of the *aẓilut* (*emanation) and their names and with *demonology are to be found in the writings of Jacob's brother and of his pupil Moses.

Jacob's visionary mysteries are most obscure since he veils the meaning of his words, using numerical (*gematriot*) and other combinations (*ẓerufim*). Their Kabbalah is entirely different from the theory of the *Sefirot* customarily followed by Jacob's contemporaries. The vision-inspired passages show that, long before Abraham *Abulafia, individual kabbalists had independently initiated a theosophical kabbalistic doctrine, in addition to providing a link with the Ḥasidei Ashkenaz, the kabbalists of Provence, and the exponents of later forms of "prophetic Kabbalah." *Sefer ha-Orah* was still known in the 14th century (by the name of *Sha'arei Orah*) to *Isaac b. Samuel of Acre whose *Sefer Oẓar ha-Ḥayyim* (Ms. Guenzburg 775) names *Naḥmanides, Jacob ha-Kohen, Joseph Gikatilla of Segovia, and the author of the *Zohar as the four leading kabbalists in Spain. Joseph Gikatilla in his *Ginnat Egoz* incorporates mysteries from *Sefer ha-Orah* without mentioning their source.

BIBLIOGRAPHY: G. Scholem, *Madda'ei ha-Yahadut*, 2 (1927), 163–243; idem, in: KS, 11 (1934/35), 188–9; idem, in: *Tarbiz*, 3 (1932), 258–86, 4 (1933), 122–45.

[Gershom Scholem]

JACOB BEN JUDAH (13th century), Hebrew-French poet. Jacob came from Lorraine and lived, at least temporarily, in *Troyes, where he was an eyewitness of the auto-da-fé of April 24, 1288. He wrote two lamentations on the death of Isaac Châtelain and the other 12 martyrs burned as the result of a blood libel (Vatican Ms. 327). One, *Yuẓẓa al Besari Sak va-Efer*, is composed in Hebrew (published by Bernfeld, see bibl.); the other is a free rendering of the Hebrew poem in Old French describing the *bele kedushah*, the "beautiful martyrdom" and aspiring for a wider audience. Since this gives the pronunciation of 13th-century French words in Hebrew transliteration, it has been repeatedly published with commentary and translation. Both poems have 17 strophes of four verses, but the differences are many and, in some cases, significant. Solomon Simḥah the Scribe and Meir ben Eliav also wrote laments on the same event. According to S. Einbinder, Jacob drew on sacred and secular motifs to create martyrological vignettes that bear the stamp of romance hagiographical conventions;

actually, he wrote under the constraints of two different sets of conventions. The Hebrew text contains a mosaic of biblical quotations and typologies that have particular connotations for a Jewish audience; the French text shares many traits with the hagiographical romance of the time.

BIBLIOGRAPHY: A. Darmesteter, *Deux élégies du Vatican* (1874); idem, in: REJ, 2 (1881), 199–220 (= *Reliques Scientifiques*, 1 (1890), 270–307); Renan, Rabbins, 475–82; Gross, Gal Jud, 240, 294; M. Steinschneider, *Geschichtsliteratur der Juden* (1905), 54 no. 44; E. Fleg, *Anthologie Juive*, 2 (1939), 106–8; Davidson, Oẓar, 4 (1933), 413; S. Bernfeld, *Sefer ha-Dema'ot*, 1 (1924), 343–6; Zunz, Lit Poesie, 362, 489. **ADD. BIBLIOGRAPHY:** S. Einbinder, in: *Viator*, 30 (1999), 201–30; idem, *Beautiful Death: Jewish Poetry and Martyrdom in Medieval France* (2002).

[Jefim (Hayyim) Schirmann / Angel Sáenz-Badillos (2nd ed.)]

JACOB BEN JUDAH OF LONDON (13th century), English rabbinical scholar. Either he or, more probably, his father, Judah b. R. Jacob he-Arukh (perhaps corresponding to Le Long in secular records), was *ḥazzan* of the London community. Jacob of London was the author of *Eẓ Ḥayyim* (c. 1286), a comprehensive handbook to Jewish religious law and ritual, the most ambitious work now extant by a medieval English Jew. The author's object was to supplement the *Sefer Mitzvot Gadol* of *Moses of Coucy by including such practical guiding rules as were absent from the book. To a great extent the *Eẓ Ḥayyim* follows Maimonides' *Code*, and is of some importance for establishing the correct text of that work in many passages. The author cites conditions in France, where he had presumably studied, and speaks also of Spanish usages. He quotes several Anglo-Jewish writers, including Joseph of Lincoln, Moses of London and his father Yom Tov, Berechiah of Lincoln, Elijah Menahem of London, and Isaac b. Perez of Northampton, and his work sometimes throws light on Anglo-Jewish conditions in the Middle Ages. Excerpts from the work were published by D. Kaufmann and H. Adler. The full text was edited by Israel Brodie (3 vols., 1962–67).

BIBLIOGRAPHY: H. Adler, in: *Festschrift... M. Steinschneider* (1896), 241f. (Eng., Ger. section), 186–208 (Heb. section); Kaufmann, in: JQR, 4 (1891/92), 20–63, 550–61; 5 (1892/93), 353–74; 6 (1893/94), 754–6; Marmorstein, *ibid.*, 19 (1928/29), 32–36; C. Roth, *Intellectual Activities of Medieval English Jewry* (1948), 39–43.

[Cecil Roth]

JACOB BEN KORSHAI (second century), *tanna*. References in the Mishnah to "Jacob," without a patronymic, are to be identified with Jacob b. Korshai (or Kodshai) as is shown by the same Mishnah being attributed to "Jacob" in *Avot* 4:16 and to Jacob b. Korshai in *Leviticus Rabbah* 3:1. He is mentioned in disputes with pupils of Akiva, but was a disciple of Meir, and transmits *halakhot* in his name only (Tosef., Ma'as. Sh. 2:10; Yev. 102a etc.). Apart from the statements in his name in *Avot*, Jacob is mentioned only once more by name in the Mishnah (in a Ms. of Neg. 14:10), although several well-known and fundamental laws in the Mishnah are in accordance with his opinion (BK, 9:1; cf. TJ, *ibid.*, 6d; Ohol. 12:8; Tosef., *ibid.*, 13:10). He is frequently mentioned, however, in the Tosefta and in other *beraitot* in the two Talmuds. According to the Jerusalem Talmud, Judah ha-Nasi was his outstanding disciple (TJ, Shab. 10:5, 12c; TJ, Pes. 10:1, 37b), and it is assumed that the material from Meir's Mishnah, which Judah incorporated in his Mishnah, was transmitted by Jacob, since Judah apparently did not study directly under Meir (Er. 13b).

Among his few aggadic statements are "This world is like a vestibule to the world to come – prepare yourself in the vestibule in order to enter the reception room" (Avot 4:16) and "One hour of repentance and good deeds in this world is better than all of the next world, but better is one hour of tranquility in the next world than all of this world" (Avot 4:17). According to the *aggadah* of the Babylonian Talmud, Jacob was the "*tanna*" (i.e., the teacher of *mishnayot*) in the school of R. Simeon b. Gamaliel, and once, when Jacob learned that on the following day Meir and Nathan were planning to depose Simeon from the office of *nasi* by putting questions to him on the tractate *Ukẓin* with which Simeon was not fully familiar, he proceeded immediately to teach the tractate (Hor. 13b) (but see: Goodblatt). Jacob is famous for the view that "there is no reward in this world for fulfilling *mitzvot*," interpreting the mention of tangible reward for the fulfillment of the commandments in Deuteronomy 5:16 and 22:7 as referring to the world to come (Tosef., Ḥul. 10:16). As a result of his position in this matter, the *aggadot* of both the Jerusalem Talmud (Ḥag. 77b) and the Babylonian Talmud (Ḥul. 142a; Kid. 39b) connect him indirectly with the figure of *Elisha b. Avuyah, who according to some legends became disillusioned as a result of the apparent lack of reward and punishment in this world, and so lost his faith in the Torah. In a late twist on this *aggadah* Rav Joseph even names Jacob as Elisha's grandson ("his daughter's son"), but there is no evidence, and it almost certainly reflects no more than the Babylonian Talmud's general inclination to posit family ties between characters in its aggadic narratives.

BIBLIOGRAPHY: Bacher, Tann, s.v.; Hyman, Toledot, s.v.; J.N. Epstein, *Mevo'ot le-Safrut ha-Tanna'im* (1957), 191–3. **ADD. BIBLIOGRAPHY:** D. Goodblatt, in: *Zion*, 49 (1984), 349–74 (Hebrew).

[Shmuel Safrai / Stephen G. Wald (2nd ed.)]

JACOB BEN MORDECAI OF SCHWERIN (also known as **Jacob of Fulda**; 17th century), German author. Jacob lived in Fulda which he was compelled to leave, probably during the temporary expulsion of Jews from that town in 1671, and settled in Schwerin. He was the author of *Tikkun Shalosh Mishmarot* (Frankfurt, 1691), prayers for the three vigils, chiefly from the Zohar. It was translated into Yiddish the following year, with an introduction by the author's wife, Laza (Frankfurt on the Oder, 1692). He also wrote *Shoshannat Ya'akov* (Amsterdam, 1706) on palmistry, physiognomy, and astrology, which claimed to be based on the works of seven scholars, including Aristotle who, according to Jacob, had been converted to Judaism.

BIBLIOGRAPHY: Steinschneider, Cat Bod, 462 nos. 3044, 3045, 1239 no. 5579.

[Joseph Elijah Heller]

JACOB BEN MOSES OF BAGNOLS (second half of 14th century), Provençal theologian and halakhist. Jacob, who was the grandson of David b. Samuel *Kokhavi and a student of Sen Boniac Nasi, lived in several towns of Provence, primarily in Salon and Carpentras, where he probably held the positions of judge and schoolmaster. He was the author of an untitled halakhic and philosophical work, written between 1357 and 1361, of which, apparently, there is only one manuscript extant (British Museum, Ms. Or. 2705). This work may be divided into three sections, each of which bears its own title: (1) "*Pesakim*," rules concerning that which is permitted and prohibited (*issur ve-hetter*); (2) "*Ezrat Nashim*," rules concerning marriage, *ḥaliẓah, and divorce; (3) "*Sod ha-Hashgaḥah*," which deals with several philosophical and religious problems, and pays special attention to prayers and their order. This section of the work was composed in 1357. Though more of a moralist than a philosopher, he refers to *Averroes, *Levi b. Gershom, and certain philosophical doctrines drawn from contemporary authors, some of whom have not been identified. The presence in the work of several passages in which Jacob reproaches his contemporaries for abandoning the study of Talmud for that of philosophy would seem to indicate that he had a rather negative attitude to philosophy.

BIBLIOGRAPHY: A. Neubauer, in: REJ, 9 (1884), 51–58.

[Colette Sirat]

JACOB BEN NAPHTALI (17th century), Hebrew author. Born in Gnesen (Poland), Jacob was secretary (*sofer*) of the Jewish community of that city, which he left after the persecution of 1648. In 1652 he published in Amsterdam a collection of poems under the title *Naḥalat Ya'akov Meliẓot* which, besides some of his own poems (among them an elegy on the martyrs of Nemirov), contains dirges by some of his contemporaries. In 1654, Jacob was sent to Rome as an emissary to Pope Innocent X in connection with a blood libel in Poland, and was highly recommended to the Italian communities by Moses *Zacuto.

BIBLIOGRAPHY: Steinschneider, Cat Bod, 1242, no. 5592; F. Delitzsch, *Zur Geschichte der juedischen Poesie* (1836), 84; Zunz, Lit Poesie, 435; Kaufmann, in: MGWJ, 38 (1894), 89–96; A. Heppner and J. Herzberg, *Aus Vergangenheit und Gegenwart… Posener Landen*, 1 (1909), 407.

[Jefim (Hayyim) Schirmann]

JACOB BEN NETHANEL BEN (AL-) FAYYŪMĪ (12th century), **nagid* of Yemenite Jewry, when ʿAbd al-Nabī ibn al-Mahdī, the ruler of *Yemen, decreed a forced renunciation of Judaism in about 1160. Many Jews converted to Islam and the Messiah's coming was widely awaited. R. Jacob turned for counsel to *Maimonides, who replied in the form of a letter known as *Iggeret Teiman* ("Epistle to Yemen," c. 1172) in which he sought to strengthen the faith of the Jews of the country.

BIBLIOGRAPHY: Neubauer, Chronicles, 1 (1887), 122; M. Maimonides, *Iggeret Teiman*, ed. by A.S. Halkin (1952), v–ix (introd.); A.Z. Aescoly, *Ha-Tenu'ot ha-Meshiḥiyyot be-Yisrael* (1956), 178–81; ADD. BIBLIOGRAPH: J. Kafih (ed.), *Iggerot Rabenu Moshe Ben Maimon* (1972), 9–10.

[Abraham David]

JACOB BEN NISSIM IBN SHAHIN (d. 1106/07), scholar of *Kairouan. Jacob was head of the *bet ha-midrash* in Kairouan. He is referred to under a variety of titles such as *ha-rav *alluf, rosh kallah, ha-rosh* ("chief rabbi"), etc. He had close ties with the Babylonian academies of *Sura and *Pumbedita and acted as their representative for the countries of North Africa, both with regard to the monies collected for yeshivot and transmitted through him, and in correspondence on halakhic matters. Questions from different communities in Africa were addressed to Jacob who forwarded them to the Babylonian academies, received the replies, and passed them on to the inquirers. The many responsa he received from the *geonim* of Babylon, and the praise which they bestowed on him (Mann, Texts, 1 (1931), 108) testify to his importance and status. The long historical responsum known as "The Letter of Sherira Gaon" was sent to him in 987 C.E. by *Sherira b. Ḥanina Gaon in response to Jacob's question on behalf of "the holy community of Kairouan" as to "How was the Mishnah written down?" (He sent him another responsum quoted in the *Arukh* (s.v. Abbaye) on the subject of the names of the scholars of the Talmud, which is regarded by some as part of the same responsum.) Some scholars have attributed the commentary to the weekly biblical portion of *Va-Yeẓe* mentioned in an ancient list of books (Mann, *ibid.*, 644 n. 3) to Jacob. Similarly, a commentary to the *Sefer Yeẓirah* was thought to be his; it has been proved, however, that the basis of that commentary is by Isaac b. Solomon *Israeli, and that it was apparently written by *Dunash ibn Tamim of Kairouan. His son was Rav Nissim *Gaon, who continued his father's activities and functions.

BIBLIOGRAPHY: S.D. Luzzatto, *Iggerot Shadal*, 7 (1891), 1031f.; Poznański, in: *Festschrift… A. Harkavy* (1908), Heb. pt., 204–7; idem, in: *Ha-Kedem*, 2 (1908–09), 103–5; B.M. Lewin (ed.), *Iggeret Rav Sherira Ga'on* (1921), introd. 36b; Mann, Texts, 1 (1931), 74 n. 25, 112–3, 124; V. Aptowitzer, in: *Sinai*, 12 (1943), 110 n. 14; Nissim b. Jacob, *Ḥibbur Yafeh me-ha-Yeshu'ah*, ed. by H.Z. Hirschberg (1954), introd. 23–26; Hirschberg, Afrikah, 1 (1965), 237–45 and index s.v.; Abramson, Merkazim, 42–44, 57, 77, 92, 101–3; idem, *Rav Nissim Ga'on* (1965), introd. 17–20.

[Shlomoh Zalman Havlin]

JACOB BEN REUBEN (12th century), Karaite biblical exegete, probably a native of Constantinople. He traveled to a number of countries to spread Karaism and at the same time tried to collect commentaries, mainly in Arabic, written by his Karaite predecessors. His biblical commentary *Sefer ha-Osher* is essentially a collection of excerpts from earlier Karaite authors, hence the frequent glosses in Greek and Arabic; some of these writings are otherwise unknown. His knowledge of the *Khazars and Slavs, whom he mentions, probably derives from the writings of his predecessors. Jacob mainly avails himself of the tenth-century Karaite exegete Japheth b. Ali, simply reproducing passages from his Arabic commentary. The polemics against *Saadiah Gaon and Muslim scholars are also taken from the writings of the Karaite *Salmon (Solomon) b. Jeroham. Of the works by Rabbanite authors, Jacob used those of Jonah ibn *Janāḥ and *Dunash ibn Labrat. Only his commentary on the Later Prophets (excepting Isaiah) and Hagiographa (excepting Psalms) titled *Mivḥar Yesharim* has appeared in print (Eupatoria, 1836) together with *Sefer ha-Mivḥar* by *Aaron b. Joseph (the Elder).

BIBLIOGRAPHY: S. Poznański, *Karaite Literary Opponents of Saadiah Gaon* (1908), 66–68; Mann, Texts, 2 (1935), 1275, 1415; Z. Ankori, *Karaites in Byzantium* (1959), index; M. Steinschneider, *Catalog… Leiden* (1958), 106–7, 391–2; S. Pinsker, *Likkutei Kadmoniyyot* (1860), 2nd pag., 80–86; A. Harkavy, *Zikkaron la-Rishonim…*, pt. 1 book 8 (1903), 152–5.

[Isaak Dov Ber Markon]

JACOB BEN SAMSON (early 12th century), a pupil of *Rashi, whose customs he reported. Jacob was apparently one of the teachers of Jacob *Tam. According to the tosafists, Jacob was the author of a work entitled *Seder Olam*, a chronology of the *tannaim* and *amoraim* similar to that found in the anonymous commentary to *Pirkei Avot*, in the *Maḥzor* *Vitry. Until recently Jacob was regarded as the author of this commentary, but it has now been established that it is not his, though it contains extracts from his commentary on *Avot*, as well as a number of verses with the acrostic of his name.

BIBLIOGRAPHY: A. Berliner, in: S. Hurwitz (ed.), *Maḥzor Vitry* (1923²), 184–7; Abraham b. Azriel, *Arugat ha-Bosem*, ed. by E.E. Urbach, 4 (1963), 79–80; Ta-Shma, in: KS, 42 (1966/67), 507–8.

[Israel Moses Ta-Shma]

JACOB BEN SIMEON (second half of 11th century), Karaite translator in Byzantine Greece. Jacob, who was a pupil of *Jeshua b. Judah, translated his teacher's classical Arabic treatise on the Karaite law of incest into Hebrew under the title *Sefer ha-Yashar*. His very poor Hebrew, heavily salted with Arabic and Greek constructions and loanwords, is almost unintelligible at times. Nevertheless, he and other Byzantine Karaite translators helped to make the classical Karaite literature accessible to the later European Karaites who knew no Arabic.

BIBLIOGRAPHY: Mann, Texts, 2 (1935), index; Z. Ankori, *Karaites in Byzantium* (1959), 188f., 199 n.446; L. Nemoy, *Karaite Anthology* (1952), 124.

[Leon Nemoy]

JACOB BEN SOSAS, one of the four commanders of the Idumean forces during the Jewish War (66–70/73 C.E.) who played a prominent role in the internecine struggle in Jerusalem. The other Idumean commanders were Jacob's brother John, Simeon b. Cathlas, and Phinehas b. Clusoth. Jacob may have been a member of one of the Jewish families living in Idumea, the "Jews of the south" (Klausner). He opened up Idumea to Simeon Bar Giora when sent by his countrymen to reconnoiter the strength of the latter's forces, so that Simeon was able to march into the country without bloodshed. In the defense of Jerusalem Jacob was one of the ten chiefs of the 5,000 Idumean warriors who joined forces with Simeon Bar Giora. He distinguished himself in various battles during the siege of Jerusalem. When the Idumean defenders of Jerusalem deliberated surrender after the fall of the Temple, Jacob, together with the other Idumean chiefs, was arrested by Simeon Bar Giora. Nothing else is known about him.

BIBLIOGRAPHY: Jos., Wars, 4:235, 521ff.; 5:249; 6:92, 148, 380; Klausner, Bayit Sheni, 5 (1951²), 212, 231, 239.

[Edna Elazary]

JACOB BEN YAKAR (d. 1064), German rabbi. Jacob was the principal teacher of *Rashi, who refers to him as "ha-Zaken," and also of Solomon b. Samson. Another of his pupils was the "*gaon*" quoted in the *Shitah Mekubbeẓet* to *Bava Kamma*, from chapter 7 onward. From Worms, where he was one of the earliest scholars, Jacob went to study in the yeshivah of *Gershom b. Judah in Mainz, and apparently headed the yeshivah for some time together with *Eliezer b. Isaac of Worms after Gershom's death. Later he returned to Worms, but toward the end of his life he again dwelt in Mainz, and it is there that his tombstone was found. Some regard him as the head of the Worms yeshivah and the initiator there of a method of study that differed from that of the yeshivah of Mainz, but the matter is not sufficiently clear. Jacob was Rashi's teacher in both Talmud and Scripture, and Rashi says that he learned most of his Torah from him. However, he refers to him by name only on rare occasions, where the matter was not absolutely clear to him; otherwise he quotes him without mentioning his name. Rashi refers to him as "my teacher in Scripture," excluding thereby his other teacher, *Isaac b. Judah. Joseph too quotes the comments of Jacob on Scripture. Jacob's teachings – particularly his rulings and "deeds" – are cited by Rashi and in the various books of the "School of Rashi." It is of interest that no written responsa by Jacob are extant. The *Sefer Ḥasidim* (ed. by J. Wistinetzki (1924²), 245 no. 991) relates of him that, because of great humility, he was wont "to sweep before the Holy Ark with his beard" and Rashi too emphasizes the humility of his teacher (*Maḥzor Vitry*, ed. by S. Hurwitz (1923²), 358 no. 321).

BIBLIOGRAPHY: Epstein, in: *Tarbiz*, 4 (1932/33), 11–34, 153–92; V. Aptowitzer, *Mavo le-Sefer Ravyah* (1938), 356–7; Lipschutz, in: *Sefer Rashi*, ed. by J.L. Maimon (1956), 203–4; I. Elfenbein, *Teshuvot Rashi* (1943), 403, index; Agus, in: Roth, Dark Ages, 2 (1966), 214–9.

[Israel Moses Ta-Shma]

JACOB BEN ẒEMAḤ BEN NISSIM (d. 1847), one of the wealthiest men of his time in the East. Born in Baghdad, he moved in about 1775 to India where he succeeded in amassing great wealth. Returning to Baghdad in 1831, he spent large sums on charitable purposes in various countries. Many of the Jewish religious institutions established in Baghdad in the first half of the 19th century were financed by his contributions. After his death his heirs struggled bitterly among themselves over the distribution of his estate. In 1855 a synagogue, *Midrash Ya'akov Ẓemaḥ*, was constructed in his memory in Baghdad.

BIBLIOGRAPHY: A. Ben-Jacob, *Yehudei Bavel* (1965), 140–1; D.S. Sassoon, *History of the Jews in Baghdad* (1949), 137.

JACOB DAVID BEN ISRAEL ISSAR (1808–1863), talmudist and kabbalist. Jacob was a pupil of the ḥasidic rabbi Judah Leib of Leszno and served as a rabbi in Kozienice and later in Wyszogrod. He was the author of glosses and novellae to the *Sifra*, published with the text, together with a commentary from manuscripts in Jacob's possession of Samson of Sens, under the title *Haggahot Maharid* (1866). Many of Jacob's other novellae remained unpublished.

BIBLIOGRAPHY: A. Walden, *Shem ha-Gedolim he-Ḥadash*, 1 (1864), 34a no. 208; S. Jewnin, *Naḥalat Olamim* (1882), 44, 109.

[Samuel Abba Horodezky]

JACOB HA-KATAN (i.e., "Jacob the Small"; 13th century), Hebrew translator, better known as "The Anonymous" or "The Anonymous of the 13th Century." This is due to the fact that until recently the name of this Hebrew translator of many Arabic and Latin medical works was unknown. However, the author of *Sefer ha-Yosher* (1270), a pupil of R. Nathan of Montpellier, mentions in his book a number of medical works. Among them is the *Antidotarium Nicolai* which had been translated by his brother Jacob. Furthermore, he describes Jacob as famous for his works. In the preface to the *Antidotarium*, the translator introduces himself as "Rabbi Jacob ha-Katan." The same introduction appears in the preface to the translation of Averroes' *On Diarrhea* and there he also records that he – at the suggestion of *Naḥmanides – translated other works of Averroes. It can, therefore, be assumed that Jacob ha-Katan translated other works without explicitly mentioning them by name.

BIBLIOGRAPHY: Muntner, in: *Tarbiz*, 18 (1947), 194–9; Steinschneider, Uebersetzungen, 1069–70; Benjacob, Oẓar, 220.

[Suessmann Muntner]

JACOB HA-KOHEN BAR MORDECAI, *gaon* of Sura, 797–811. A student of *Yehudai Gaon and *Ḥanina Kahana b. Huna, Jacob was held in high esteem. He is credited by some with the authorship of *Seder Tanna'im* (ed. by Z. Kahana, 1935), one of the most important works on the history and methodology of mishnaic and talmudic literature, and the first of its kind. In his decisions Jacob tended to be as lenient as possible in the interpretation of the law. One of his most important decisions concerned the talmudic rule that, whenever R. *Judah ha-Nasi's opinion is cited in opposition to only one of the sages, Judah's opinion prevails. Jacob, however, decided – in accordance with another talmudic formula – that if Judah's opponent was his father and teacher Rabban *Simeon b. Gamaliel, the latter's opinion is accepted. His responsa are written in Hebrew interspersed with Aramaic. His son Moses (Mesharsheya) was also *gaon* of Sura.

BIBLIOGRAPHY: Z.W. Wolfensohn (ed.), *Ḥemdah Genuzah* (1863), 3a no. 15; Abraham b. Isaac of Narbonne, *Sefer ha-Eshkol*, ed. by Z.B. Auerbach, 1 (1868), 91; Halevy, Dorot, 3 (1923), 241; J. Mueller, *Mafte'aḥ li-Teshuvot ha-Ge'onim* (1891), 73f.; S. Assaf, *Tekufat ha-Ge'onim ve-Sifrutah* (1955), 147f.; L. Ginzberg, *Geonica*, 2 (1909), 86.

[Meir Havazelet]

JACOBI, ABRAHAM (1830–1919), pediatrician, founder of American pediatrics. He was born in Hartum, Germany, to parents of limited means. He registered as a student of Semitic languages, but later studied medicine, graduating from Bonn University. While he was studying, the 1848 Revolution broke out in Germany, and Jacobi became a revolutionary leader. He was imprisoned but escaped in 1853 to the United States. A year later, in New York, he invented a laryngoscope, but failed to obtain a patent for his invention (before Manuel Garcia's invention in 1855).

Jacobi was appointed to lecture on children's illnesses in 1857, and in 1860 the first chair in pediatrics in New York was founded for him; he lectured for almost 25 years. His activities included the organization of the children's ward at the Mount Sinai Hospital in New York. Jacobi was one of the first to insist on the boiling of milk, and one of the first to practice intubation of the throat instead of performing a tracheotomy. In 1859 he and E. Noeggerath wrote a textbook for midwives and on children's and women's diseases.

Jacobi wrote on a large number of pediatric problems: the throat (1859), diet for children (1872), diphtheria (1876), intestinal illness (1887), the thymus gland (1889), and infant and child care (1896–1902). Jacobi also contributed three monographs to Gerhard's *Handbuch*, manual on hygiene in childbirth (1876), diphtheria (1877), and dysentery (1877). He also published important works on the history of pediatrics. His writings were published in eight volumes under the title *Collectanea Jacobi* (1898; *Dr. Jacobi's Works*, 1909).

BIBLIOGRAPHY: Garrison, in: *Science*, 50 (1919), 102–4; A. Levinson, *Pioneers of Pediatrics* (1943), 102–5.

[Joshua O. Leibowitz]

JACOBI, ERWIN REUBEN (1909–1978), musicologist and harpsichord player. Jacobi was born in Strasbourg and graduated as an engineer in 1933. In 1934 he immigrated to Ereẓ Israel where he worked in agriculture and land settlement, and later in industry. In the 1950s he turned his attention to music, studying cembalo under Frank *Pelleg (1951–52) and music theory under Paul *Ben-Haim (1952–53). In 1953 he proceeded to the United States, where he studied under Wanda *Landowska and Paul Hindemith, under whom he studied at Yale University (1952–53) and Zurich (1953–57), receiving his doctorate from him in 1957. In 1953 he moved to Zurich where he was appointed lecturer in musicology. He served as visiting professor at the School of Music of the Iowa University (1970–71) and Indiana University (1971–72). Jacobi's research centers on the theory and practice of music in the 17th and 18th centuries. He produced a complete edition of Rameau's theoretical works (*Die Entwicklung der Musiktheorie in England nach der Zeit von Jean-Phillipe Rameau*, 1971). A longtime friend of Albert Schweitzer, he has also published many articles on him. His works include "Introduction" to *J.F. Agricola: Anleitung zur Singkunst (1757) zusammen mit dem italienischen Original von Pier Francesco Tosi* (1966); *Albert Schweitzer und die Musik* (1975); *Albert Schweitzer und Richard Wagner: eine Dokumentation, Schriften der Schweizerischen Richard-Wagner-Gesellschaft*, iii (1977). His editions include *J.B. de Boismortier: Quatres suites de pièces de clavecin. op. 59, Alte Musik für verschiedene Instrumente,* (1960, 1971); *Jean Philippe Rameau: Pièces de clavecin* (1961, 1972) and *Pièces de clavecin en concerts* (1961, 1970).

BIBLIOGRAPHY: Grove online; MGG.

[Israela Stein (2nd ed.)]

JACOBI, FREDERICK (1891–1952), U.S. composer. Born in San Francisco, Jacobi studied with Rubin *Goldmark, Rafael Joseffy, Paul Juon, and Ernest *Bloch. From 1913 to 1917 he was assistant conductor at the Metropolitan Opera in New York and later taught at the Juilliard School of Music. Jacobi first attracted attention as a composer with a quartet on American Indian themes (1923). Many of his later works were on Jewish subjects or for synagogue use. *Sabbath Evening Service* (1930–31); *Six Pieces for Organ*, for use in the synagogue (1933); arrangements of Palestinian folk songs (1939–40); *Hymn* to words of Saadiah Gaon, for male choir; *Two Pieces in Sabbath Mood*, for orchestra (1946); *Ashrei ha-Ish* – arrangements of the song by Mordechai *Zeira – for mixed chorus and string orchestra (1949); and *Three Preludes*, for organ (1949).

JACOBI, GEORG (1840–1906), violinist and conductor. Born in Berlin, Jacobi worked as a violinist and conductor in Paris. In 1871 he was appointed leader of the orchestra at the Alhambra Theatre, London, where he remained for 26 years. During this period he composed or arranged the music for over 100 ballets, among them *Yolande* (1877), *The Golden Wreath*, and *Beauty and the Beast* (1898).

JACOBI, HANOCH (Heinrich; 1909–1990), Israeli composer, conductor, and string player. Born in Germany, he studied the viola and composition with Paul Hindemith at the Berlin Hochschule für Musik (1927–30). From 1930 to 1933 he played in the Grosses Orchester des Südwestdeutsche Rundfunk. In 1934 he emigrated to Ereẓ Israel and settled in Jerusalem where he joined the Jerusalem String Quartet (1934–9) and the Palestine Music Conservatory (1934–47), later the Jerusalem Academy of music, of which he became the director (1954–1958). In 1959, he moved to Tel Aviv, where he joined the Israel Philharmonic Orchestra as a violist until 1974. After leading the Herzliyah String Quartet, he founded his own quartet. Jacobi was a conservative composer although the influence of his new homeland may be felt in his works. Among his popular compositions which were considered Israeli cultural symbols are the cantata *Od Yavo Yom* ("The Day Will Come," 1944), the Suite for Strings (1946); *Kinnor Hayah le-David* ("King David's Lyre") in honor of the birth of the state of Israel (1948); and *Judean Hill Dance: Hora Variations* (1952). During his later years, he wrote pedagogical compositions for string instruments based on Jewish tunes from Mediterranean and Middle Eastern countries. He also wrote three symphonies (1944, 1955, 1960) and other orchestral works such as *Partita concertanta* (1971), *Mutatio I* (1975), *Variations* (1976), and *Mutatio II* (1977).

BIBLIOGRAPHY: Grove Music Online.

[Yohanan Boehm and Uri (Erich) Toeplitz / Israela Stein and Gila Flam (2nd ed.)]

JACOBI, KARL GUSTAV JACOB (1804–1851), German mathematician, brother of Moritz Hermann *Jacobi. Born in Potsdam, he was a child prodigy. He studied philosophy, philology, and mathematics at the University of Berlin, and in 1825 became a lecturer in mathematics. He and his brother converted to Christianity in order to remove any possible bar to government posts. His career was also helped by the famous mathematician Friedrich Gauss. A brilliant teacher, Jacobi was invited to Koenigsberg, where he became a professor at the age of 23. Overwork, together with financial difficulties caused by his father's death, brought him to a state of near collapse requiring a long convalescence. Jacobi met Sir William Rowan Hamilton, the great Irish mathematician, and, as a result of this meeting, he continued Hamilton's work in the field of dynamics. After a short and unhappy involvement in politics which cost him his royal grant, he returned to his original work. On the recommendation of Baron Alexander von Humboldt, the German naturalist, the grant was again awarded him. By 1849 Jacobi was the leading mathematician in Europe after Gauss. He died in Berlin of smallpox. Jacobi's works on differential equations and the calculus of variations serve as the mathematical basis for modern physics. His collected works, *Gesammelte Werke*, were published by the University of Berlin in eight volumes (1881–91).

BIBLIOGRAPHY: L. Koenigsberger, *Karl Gustav Jacob Jacobi* (Ger., 1904); E.T. Bell, *Men of Mathematics* (1937), index.

[Grete Leibowitz]

JACOBI, LOTTE (Johanna Alexandra; 1896–1990), U.S. photographer. Born in Thorn, West Prussia (now Torun, Poland), to a fourth-generation photographer family, Jacobi captured the heady spirit of the Weimar Republic, particularly the intellectual and artistic elite who lived in Berlin or passed through it, before she fled the Nazis in 1935. She began her photographic career at 14, documenting the world around her with a homemade pinhole camera. Her family had the most famous portrait-photography business in Germany, Atelier Jacobi, with studios in Thorn, Poznan, and Berlin. She was in her early thirties when she finished her studies and joined her parents and sister in Berlin, where the family had moved. She was equipped for the job not only by talent but by temperament. An emancipated woman with a leftist political slant, she had an inquiring approach and a knack for bringing subjects to her lens. Her aim was to capture each sitter's individuality. "In making portraits, I refuse to photograph myself," she said. "My style is the style of the people I photograph."

One of her famous subjects was Peter *Lorre. She was allowed only one image, and it turned out to be a classic, with Lorre shot as close up as possible. She captured his villainous look, but softened the angle by shooting from above. Her interest in modern dance led her to make photos of dancers in action, aided by her own quickness and new camera technology. Her photographs of an unknown Lotte Lenya holding a cigarette, the actor Emil Jannings casually peeling an apple, and the dancer Claire Bauroff captured the essence of Berlin theater life. In 1932 her leftist sympathies led her to do a series of Ernst Thalmann, the Communist candidate that year against Hitler. Then, a long trip to the Soviet Union resulted in rare and interesting shots of street scenes in Moscow and the republics of Tajikistan and Uzbekistan. But when she returned to Germany, the Nazis questioned her about her trip, her political sympathies, and her Jewish background. She finally left Germany after her father's death.

In New York, she opened a studio with her sister Ruth but struggled to find work. An important American contact was Albert *Einstein, whom she and her family had photographed in Germany. He agreed to work with her when, in 1938, *Life* magazine commissioned a photo essay on the scientist. She made several informal photographs at Einstein's home in Princeton, N.J., in conversations with his students, but *Life* felt they were too casual and decided not to publish them. However, in 1942, the magazine *U.S. Camera*, at the instigation of Edward Steichen, published a photo of a dreamy Einstein, in a rumpled leather jacket, hair askew, that became one of the most famous images of him. In the 1940s Jacobi explored the technique of photogenics, expressive abstract images made by drawing with a flashlight on photographic paper. The process had been extensively explored in the early 20th century by Man *Ray and Laszlo Moholy-Nagy.

In 1940, in New York, she married her second husband (she and her first husband had divorced), Erich Reiss, a German avant-garde publisher who was rescued from a Nazi death camp. He died in 1951. In New Hampshire, living with his son's family, she continued her interest in the forms of nature, taking pictures of snow, water, and other phenomena in the countryside. She remained active as a portrait photographer, developing a new set of subjects and friends, including the poets Robert Frost and May Sarton, the ecological activists Helen and Scott Nearing, and a fellow photographer, Paul Caponigro. She opened a gallery in Deering and served as a mentor to younger artists for 30 years. Among her other notable portraits – all in black and white – were those of the dramatist Kurt *Weill, Eleanor Roosovelt, Marc *Chagall, and the musician Pablo Casals. She bequeathed a collection of 47,000 negatives to the University of New Hampshire. Her earlier work was lost to the Nazis.

[Stewart Kampel (2nd ed.)]

JACOBI, MORITZ (Moses) HERMANN (1801–1874), German physicist and architect. Born in Potsdam, he – like his brother the mathematician Karl Gustav Jacob *Jacobi – was converted to Christianity. Jacobi practiced architecture at Koenigsberg until appointed professor of architecture at the Russian University in Dorpat, Estonia. In 1837 he was invited to St. Petersburg, where he became a member of the Russian Academy of Sciences, later state advisor, and was ennobled. In 1838 Jacobi, who was particularly interested in electricity, invented the galvano-plastic process of electrotyping. In 1839 he managed to produce molds faced with graphite which could conduct electricity. He also studied the practical use of electromagnetism for driving machinery (electrically driven boat), and experimented with the electric arc.

BIBLIOGRAPHY: E.T. Bell, *Men of Mathematics* (1937), 327–39.

[Grete Leibowitz]

JACOB ISAAC BEN SHALOM (d. 1675 or 1676), rabbi and author. Jacob served as a rabbi in Schrimm and in Lissa, Poland, where he died. Esteemed as a talmudic scholar, his opinion was frequently sought on halakhic matters. He gave his *haskamah to the *Magen Avraham* by Abraham Abele *Gombiner, his contemporary and relative. His collection of halakhic decisions, *Beit Levi*, with the subtitle *Shelom Bayit*, was never printed independently, but extracts from it were printed in *Magen Avraham* and in Jekuthiel Kaufman's *Ḥukkei Da'at*, printed as an addendum to *Yismaḥ Yisrael* by Israel Samuel b. Solomon Rofe.

BIBLIOGRAPHY: E.M. Pinner, *Maẓẓevot Kivrot ha-Rabbanim* (1861), 190; Landshuth, Ammudei, 2; Ḥ.N. Dembitzer, *Kelilat Yofi*, 2 (1893), 137b; L. Lewin, *Geschichte der Juden in Lissa* (1904), 175–6.

[Elias Katz]

JACOB ISAAC HA-ḤOZEH MI-LUBLIN (1745–1815), ḥasidic *ẓaddik* known by the epithet "Ha-Ḥozeh mi-Lublin" ("the Seer of Lublin"). Jacob Isaac was born in Lukow, the son of Abraham Eliezer ha-Levi, the rabbi of Jozefow, a descendent of Isaiah ben Abraham ha-Levi *Horowitz (Ha-Shelah). Jacob Isaac was one of the major founders of the ḥasidic movement in Poland and Galicia at the end of the 18th century and the beginning of the 19th. He was a pupil of Samuel-Shmelke *Horowitz of Nikolsburg, and *Dov Baer the Maggid of Mezhirech, as well as *Levi Isaac of Berdichev. His principal mentor, however, was *Elimelech of Lyzhansk, (1717–1786), who formulated in his court and disseminated in other communities the doctrine of the *ẓaddik* as occupying the center of ḥasidic identity. This doctrine was further circulated posthumously through his book *No'am Elimelekh* (Lemberg 1788). Jacob Isaac left his teacher and began to lead his own ḥasidic group in Elimelech's lifetime, causing much tension, anguish, and crisis in his master's court. At first active in Lancut and later in Rozwadow, during the 1790s he moved to Chekhov, a suburb of Lublin, and finally to Lublin itself. Jacob Isaac, a renowned *ẓaddik*, who was mainly responsible for making Congress Poland and Galicia into great ḥasidic centers, appears in his autobiographical writings as someone with a unique perception of himself as both a mystic and a prophet, who believed that he received divine revelations for the sake of the Jewish community. His books were written as a mixture of diaries and collections of teachings in the last two decades of the 18th century, and were published posthumously under the titles *Zot Zikaron* (1851) and *Zikaron Zot* (1869). He represented himself in his books and was represented by his contemporaries in their tales to be a miracle worker, a seer, and a prophet, beliefs responsible for the wide attraction of his court. His works reveal dialectical concepts which reflect a reappraisal of the significance of the traditional order ("awe") and the quality of the mystical religious undertaking ("love"). Significantly these concepts related to the tension between the commitment to traditional obligations and expansion of these limits through innovative mystical thought, mystical rapture, and new forms of contemplation on the meaning of religious praxis. These dialectical concepts expressed the dual meaning of the veneration of the *ẓaddik*, which included both the transcendence of existential borders ("love") and the preservation of the traditional order ("awe"). The Seer developed a new orientation of complete responsibility toward the corporeal and spiritual needs of his followers and formulated a clear distinction between the nature of divine worship insofar as it applied to the *ẓaddik* and his followers. The former was expected "to work with love," meaning to be a courageous religious innovator inspired by divine rapture, preconditioned by a high degree of self-abnegation. The *ẓaddik*, as he saw it, was someone who completely annihilates his personality and will in order to receive direct divine revelation for the benefit of his ḥasidim. Jacob Isaac engendered changes in the religious and social life of his followers as a result of these new divine revelations. These changes were much welcomed and needed because of the harsh socio-economical circumstances in Galicia and the urgent needs of the community. His followers, the ḥasidim, on the other hand, were expected by him to adhere to the normative tradition while attaching themselves to the *ẓaddik*, who took complete responsibility for all their spiritual and corporeal needs. Jacob Isaac left no direct dynastic line; however, the majority of Polish and Galician *ẓaddikim* who headed the ḥasidic movement during the first half of the 19th century were numbered among his disciples. He attracted followers from all social strata. Isaac Meir b. Israel Alter, founder of the Gur dynasty, regarded him as "everyone's rabbi" (*Me'ir Einei ha-Golah* (1928), 18).

Many of his distinguished disciples testified to his insight, his ability to discern whether a person "acted purely and honestly or conversely, God forbid," as well as to his power of predicting events. It was also reported that he could reveal the genealogy of a person's soul and discern its *tikkun* ("restitution") in each stage of reincarnation; the epithet "*ḥozeh*" ("seer") was therefore applied to him, although posthumously.

Following Elimelech of Lizhansk, Jacob Isaac emphasized the centrality of the *ẓaddik* in the life of the ḥasidic community and the "practical" work of the *ẓaddik*, stressing his duty to care for the "progeny, life, and livelihood" of his "children," the ḥasidic congregation. Believing that material abundance preceded spiritual wealth, Jacob Isaac held that in order to help a person repent it was first necessary to help the person satisfy his material needs. The *ẓaddik* ought "to extend great abundance and a comfortable living so that the people will be free to worship God." He is reported as saying that "when the body enjoys plentitude the soul too enjoys spiritual richness" (*Or la-Shamayim*, 1850, *Parashat Va-Yishlaḥ*, 15a). He particularly stressed the conduct between man and his fellow, considering social feeling to be of special significance in the secret order of the world. He perceived humility as a metaphysical element, obliging primarily the *ẓaddik* and preconditioning his mystical exaltation. He further stressed the virtue of the "love of Israel," which was one of the cherished principles of early Hasidism.

Toward the end of his life Jacob Isaac suffered a serious crisis over his conduct as a ḥasidic leader, which originated in the split in the Lublin ḥasidic center between those who emphasized the aspiration toward spiritual perfection and constant *devekut* to God and those who stressed the *ẓaddik's* need to care for the multitude of the Ḥasidim. The atmosphere of "practical" ẓaddikism, focused on the mundane needs of his followers as cultivated by Jacob Isaac, did not suit those who regarded the ḥasidic *ẓaddik* as a guide to divine worship and not as a miracle worker and social activist. Although he sensed the disappointment of his best pupils, Jacob Isaac did not change his method, believing that his exceptional spiritual capacities should be exploited first and foremost for the benefits of his followers, the ḥasidim. According to some authorities this was the background for his controversy with his most outstanding disciple, Jacob Isaac of *Przysucha, who was dissatisfied with the "practical" character of Lublin Ḥasidism. The rabbi of Przysucha attracted many disciples who regarded Ḥasidism as a spiritual-religious movement centered on pietistic measures, as well as intellectual and spiritual endeavors, while marginalizing social responsibility, aided by means of magical activity, for the improvement of material living conditions. It should be noted that academic studies concerning the socio-economic conditions of the Jews in Galicia in the last two decades of the 18th century and the first two decades of the 19th century, i.e., the period of activity of the Seer of Lublin, demonstrate the tragic urgency of the economic situation (see A. Brawer, *Galicia ve-Yehudeiha*) and explains his social and mystical position. The controversy on the hasidic mode of leadership divided Polish Ḥasidism for many years and through it the ḥasidic trend of *Przysucha-*Kotsk and Izbica evolved. While the followers of Przysucha and Kotsk resented the social, mystical total responsibility of the Seer, the Izbica ḥasidim adopted his position with enthusiasm.

Mordecai Leiner of Izbica (1800–1854) followed the teachings and practices of the Seer of Lublin and continued the mystical criticism of traditional conventions in relation to spiritual leaders, and embraced the social innovations inspired by mystical revelation. Jacob Isaac was frequently attacked by the *Mitnaggedim* both in Lublin and elsewhere, being the object of criticism of those writers of the late 18th and early 19th century among the *maskilim* and *mitnaggedim* who opposed "practical" ẓaddikism – and its consequences for the leadership in Lublin. He was also severely criticized by the rabbi of Lublin, Azriel Horowitz.

Jacob Isaac's autobiographical works, *Zot Zikaron* and *Zikaron Zot*, offer a sound historical foundation for the many stories concerning his communal work and exceptional position. Ḥasidic tradition also relates that he regarded Napoleon's march on Russia (1812), which evoked strong messianic dreams in various parts of Poland and Galicia, as the beginning of the messianic wars between *Gog and Magog and planned to join forces with other *ẓaddikim* in order to hasten redemption. However, no historical foundation is available for this contention since the Seer's writings precede the Napoleonic wars by two decades. Martin Buber wrote his novel *Gog u-Magog* on this period in the Seer's life, which, as previously noted, has no autobiographical documentation but rather left only a collection of legendary tales.

BIBLIOGRAPHY: S.B. Nissenbaum, *Le-Korot ha-Yehudim be-Lublin* (1899), 119; I. Berger, *Zekhut Yisrael… Eser Orot* (1903); E.N. Frank, *Yehudei Polin bi-Ymei Milḥemet Napoleon* (1903); Dubnow, Ḥasidut, 215–7, 287, 326–30; A.Z. Aescoly, in: *Beit Yisrael be-Polin*, 2 (1953), 86–141; A. Marcus, *Ha-Ḥasidut* (1954); A. Rubinstein, in: KS, 37 (1961/62), 123–6; M. Buber, *Gog u-Magog, Megillat Yamim* (1967). **ADD. BIBLIOGRAPHY:** R. Elior, "*Bein ha-Yesh la-Ayin – Iyyun be-Torat ha-Ẓaddik shel ha-Ḥozeh mi-Lublin*," in: I. Bartal, R. Elior, and C. Shmeruk (eds.), *Ẓadikim ve-Anshei Ma'aseh: Studies in Polish Hasidism* (1994), 167–218; R. Elior, "Between Yesh and Ayin: The Doctrine of the Zaddik in the works of Jacob Isaac the Seer of Lublin," in: A. Rapoport-Albert and S. Zipperstein (eds.), *Jewish History – Essays in Honor of Ch. Abramsky* (1988), 393–455; idem, "*Temurot ba-Maḥshavah ha-Datit be-Ḥasidut Polin*," in: *Tarbiz*, 62 (1993), 381–432.

[Avraham Rubinstein / Rachel Elior (2nd ed.)]

JACOB JOSEPH BEN ẒEVI HA-KOHEN KATZ OF POLONNOYE (D.C. 1782), rabbi and preacher; the first theoretician of Ḥasidism. Jacob Joseph, whose birthplace is unknown, became rabbi of Shargorod, the second largest community of Podolia. In 1741 he came under the influence of *Israel b. Eliezer Ba'al Shem Tov (the BeShT). A controversy with his community ensued, as a result of which he was expelled from Shargorod in about 1748. He left for Raszkow, a very small community, where he remained until 1752. In 1750/51, he hoped to go to Ereẓ Israel, but this project did not materialize. From Raszkow, he went to *Nemirov, where he remained until 1770 and openly propagated Ḥasidism. On the death of Aryeh Leib, the preacher of Polonnoye, Jacob Joseph was appointed to this position, which he held for the remainder of his life. Jacob Joseph did not succeed the Ba'al Shem Tov in the leadership of the ḥasidic movement, and this left him embittered. His son, Abraham Samson, who settled in Tiberias and Safed, was childless. He published his father's writings. His relative by marriage was Ḥayyim b. Menahem Zanzer, head of the kabbalists of the *klaus* of Brody.

Jacob Joseph's first and main work was *Toledot Ya'akov Yosef* (Korets, 1780), containing homiletics of the author, as well as the "words which I heard from my teacher," namely, the Ba'al Shem Tov. It is the first work to express the basic teachings of Ḥasidism, both in a positive formulation as well as in the bitter criticism it contains of the traditional Jewish leadership and its scale of values. The work played an important role as one of the factors which aroused opposition to Ḥasidism. Copies of it were apparently burned in Brody. Jacob Joseph's other works are *Ben Porat Yosef* (Korets, 1781), homilies mainly on Genesis; at the end, the letter sent by the Ba'al Shem Tov to his brother-in-law in 1750/51 was published for the first time; *Ẓafenat Pa'ne'aḥ* (Korets, 1782), a commentary on Exodus; and *Ketonet Passim* (Lemberg, 1866), a commentary on Leviticus and Numbers. Because of the long delay in the publication of this last work and other reasons, S. Dubnow considered it to be a forgery, but it is now regarded as authentic (see J.G. Weiss, in JJS, 9 (1958), 81–83). From various allusions, it has been assumed that Jacob Joseph also left a large work in manuscript destined to be a commentary on Deuteronomy. Jacob Joseph's homilies are traditional in structure. Their contents reveal him as leader of a community, as well as a penetrating and incisive theoretician and social critic. He viewed the preacher as the physician of the soul which he helps to cure by means of the ethical principles which he teaches. The preacher should pay due attention to the general form of the sermon, its content and method of delivery, and adapt it to the standard of his audience.

Jacob Joseph taught that the presence of God is manifest everywhere and in each and every human thought; even "when man is engaged in prayer and an alien and evil thought enters his mind, it has come to man so that he may improve and uplift it. If he does not believe in this, then his acceptance of the rule of the Kingdom of Heaven is incomplete because, Heaven forfend, he then restricts His presence" (*Ben Porat Yosef*). He proposes that man should resolve the ever-present tension created by matter which draws him to evil and by spiritual form which calls him to good through combining the joy of matter with that of form, thus achieving the perfect joy. Evil inclination will then be subdued of itself, becoming the tool of good. The ultimate purpose of man is "Thou shalt adhere to Him." This adhesion is only possible through joy, while fasting and self-affliction bring sorrow, and sorrow is the root of all evils. Prayers should be recited with a purified and concentrated mind and with joy. It is within the power of the *ẓaddik* to change an evil decree to a favorable end through his prayer, also on behalf of those who are associated with him.

The same relationship within man also exists within society. There is the "multitude" and the "scholar." The man of merit and form is the *zaddik*, while the "multitude" is matter. The *zaddik* is likened to the head or the eyes of the body, and the multitude to the feet. The congregation is thus conceived as a living organism, the *zaddik* being its life and soul in his generation. This organismic premise precludes the concept that only a few are elect. It follows that the interrelationship in this corporate body causes any failure on the part of even the lowest member – whether in matter or in spirit – to be reflected far more damagingly in the state of "the head" – the *zaddik*. None of the members can adhere truly to God, so long as only one, even if an ignoramus, is not conscious of his need to be uplifted through the head (the *zaddik*). Hence it is the duty of the *zaddik* to exert his influence over him. Moreover, for the sake of this unification with the multitude, and so as to be able to uplift it, a *zaddik* may sometimes have to descend from his own level and to sin for the good of his task. This concept of the "descent of the *zaddik*" holds an important place in Jacob Joseph's teachings. The Jew of the multitude is incapable "of studying the Torah, and as this is through no neglect of his own, God will not punish him" if he adheres to the *zaddik*. He is enjoined to believe in the *zaddik* with absolute faith, without any afterthoughts or doubts as to the *zaddik's* way of life, because all his actions are performed for the sake of Heaven.

The "man of matter" must also support the *zaddik* financially to enable him to fulfill his duty successfully and devote himself to God through Torah study and prayer. Jacob Joseph taught the importance of the communal Sabbath "third meal" for the ḥasidic congregation, saying that he who does not participate in it with his brethren "makes his Sabbath profane" (*Toledot Ya'akov Yosef*, beginning of the section on Noah). Jacob Joseph's hostility to the ordinary type of rabbi is expressed in his denunciation of them as "Jewish demons, the equivalent of the Satan and the evil inclination itself, the whole of their Torah studies being for their personal aggrandizement."

BIBLIOGRAPHY: Dubnow, Ḥasidut, 93–101; Horodezky, Ḥasidut, 1 (1951[3]), 105–32; M. Wilensky, in: *Joshua Starr Memorial Volume* (1953), 183–9; B. Dinur, *Be-Mifneh ha-Dorot* (1955), 147–55; S.H. Dresner, *The Zaddik* (1960); G. Negal, *Manhig ve-Edah* (1962); A. Rubinstein, in: *Aresheth*, 3 (1961), 193–230; S. Ettinger, *Toledot Am Yisrael ba-Et ha-Ḥadashah*, 3 (1969), 57, 59; idem, in: *Journal of World History*, 17 (1968), nos. 1–2.

[Moshe Hallamish]

JACOB JOSEPH OF OSTROG (**Yeivi**; 1738–1791), pietist preacher (*maggid*). He was the son of a *maggid* and succeeded his father in 1766, after the latter's death. Jacob Joseph's son testified that he highly esteemed the teachings of the disciples of *Israel b. Eliezer Ba'al Shem Tov, the founder of modern Ḥasidism. Jacob, who lived in poverty and privation, had a deep sense of social morality. His sermons reflected the social upheaval troubling the Jews of Eastern Europe in the 18th century. Jacob Joseph attacked perversions of justice, informing, and bribery, and took to task community leaders and rabbis who gained their appointments through their relations with the authorities instead of through Torah learning. He taught that the poor are closest to God and worthy of attaining the mystic knowledge of the Torah, but the rich are distant from Him. There exists a kind of social-spiritual division in the world in which the learned profess the unity of God above and ensure the provision of abundance below, although personally gaining only a scanty livelihood; in contrast, the ignorant collect the abundance that pours down from Heaven. Despite this distinction, Jacob insisted on the principle of internal Jewish unity, since all the Jewish people are linked with each other. The *zaddik*'s devotion to the Almighty draws all his brethren after him to holiness.

His books are *Mora Mikdash* (Korets, 1782), on order in synagogue; *Ein Mishpat* (Korets, 1782), on the prohibition on buying rabbinical office or arbitrary appointment; and *Rav Yeivi* (Slavuta, 1792), homilies.

[Avraham Rubinstein]

JACOB KOPPEL BEN AARON SASSLOWER (second half of 17th century), authority on the masoretic text and cantillation, and author of a work on the *masorah. Jacob Koppel came from Zaslavl near Ostrog (Volhynia). He was the author of *Naḥalat Ya'akov* (1686), containing the masorah for the reading of the Ten Commandments in accordance with intonation and grammar, as well as various studies on the masorah and Hebrew grammar based upon the *Si'aḥ Yizḥak* of Isaac b. Samuel ha-Levi of Posen and the *Iggeret ha-Te'amim* of Aaron Abraham b. Baruch. Jekuthiel Lazi b. Nahum Ashkenazi compiled an abridgment titled the *Kizzur Naḥalat Ya'akov* (1718) with the addition of the *kunteres Or Torah* by Menahem *Lonzano for the benefit of "those living in the countryside and in villages, who have never seen or known" the original work.

BIBLIOGRAPHY: Steinschneider, Cat Bod, 1179; Benjacob, Oẓar, 396 no. 131.

[Josef Horovitz]

JACOB KOPPEL BEN MOSES OF MEZHIRECH (d. c. 1740), Polish kabbalist. Jacob was influenced by the Shabbatean movement in Poland, and he himself influenced Ḥasidism. His main published works are: *Sha'arei Gan Eden* (Korets, 1803), a major kabbalistic treatise, dealing with all facets of kabbalistic theosophy, following the school of Isaac *Luria; and *Ha-Kol Kol Ya'akov* (Slaviuta, 1804), a formulation of the Lurianic *kavvanot* (the mystical intentions and meditations during prayer). This work served as a basis for later ḥasidic prayer books. Besides these he apparently wrote *Naḥalot Ya'akov*, an extensive commentary on the *Zohar, which has been lost. Jacob denounces the followers of *Shabbetai Ẓevi and messianic speculation in general in a few scattered remarks. However, it has been proved that he was the brother and pupil of a known Shabbatean, Ḥayyim of Ostraha (Ostrog), who influenced his writings.

A close study of the kabbalistic doctrine of Jacob proves conclusively that his works included at least one part of a "credo" of *Nathan of Gaza, the prophet of Shabbetai Ẓevi, that substantial parts of his theosophical discussions were influenced by Nathan's basic doctrines, and that his works contain many ideas and expressions similar to those of Jonathan *Eybeschuetz, another secret Shabbatean in Eastern Europe.

The Shabbatean elements in Jacob's theology are revealed in three fields. First, his theosophic doctrine, which describes the processes that led toward the creation within the Godhead itself, does not follow the orthodox Lurianic myth but uses a whole group of terms and processes introduced into the Kabbalah by Nathan of Gaza. While creating his Shabbatean theology, the latter utilized elements in the teachings of Luria's alleged pupil Israel *Sarug. Secondly, in his descriptions of development within the realm of the *Sefirot* (the divine emanations), Jacob uses a series of extremely radical sexual symbols found only in Shabbatean writings, mainly in those of Eybeschuetz. Finally, some scattered hints (which were fully developed in at least one of his works) allude to a heretical, antinomian concept of the Torah and the *mitzvot*, following the Shabbatean distinction between the laws governing the world before the coming of the messiah, Shabbetai Ẓevi, and the new laws following his appearance.

Jacob and his writings were highly praised by the early Ḥasidim, who published his works and used them extensively. A reliable ḥasidic tradition even quotes some words of praise attributed to *Israel b. Eliezer Ba'al Shem Tov. Thus Jacob's Shabbatean writings form one of the links between late East European Shabbateanism and early Ḥasidism.

BIBLIOGRAPHY: I. Tishby, *Netivei Emunah u-Minut* (1964), 197–226, 331–43.

[Joseph Dan]

JACOB NAZIR (**Jacob ben Saul of Lunel**; second half of 12th century), scholar and kabbalist in Lunel, S. France. The brother of Asher b. Saul, author of *Sefer ha-Minhagot*, Jacob was a colleague of *Abraham b. David (RABaD). Solomon Schechter (JQR 5, 1893, pp. 22–23), on the basis of statements in letters of Samuel David *Luzzatto (*Iggerot Shadal* (1882), 669), established his identity, in opposition to Zunz, who had thought him identical with Jacob b. Meshullam of Lunel. Jacob Nazir belonged to a group of hermits in Provence who carried on the mystic tradition, devoting themselves wholly to a life of contemplation. Kabbalistic tradition attributes to Jacob and Abraham b. David revelations of the prophet Elijah. Through visions and meditations they arrived at innovations in kabbalistic thought. Some of their interpretations, in which they disagreed on the details of the mystical *kavvanot* ("meditations") in certain prayers (i.e., to which *Sefirah* or quality of God should a man direct his thought in prayer?), have survived in several manuscripts (Ms. JTS New York 838 48a; British Museum 755 85b; Oxford 1646). The works that have survived contain kabbalistic terminology developed from Sefer ha-*Bahir, the *Heikhalot* literature, and a mixture of different traditions. However, there is no proof that Jacob constructed a complete and ordered system.

Jacob Nazir was the first to use the term *Malkhut* ("kingdom") to designate the last revelation of the *Sefirot*, and as a synonym for the concepts of *Kavod* ("glory") and *Shekhinah* ("Divine Presence"). According to G. Scholem this usage was derived from ibn *Tibbon's Hebrew translation of the *Kuzari*, composed in Lunel during that period (1167). One of the first kabbalists to serve as a direct link between Provence and the East, Jacob made a pilgrimage to Palestine, apparently after Saladin's capture of Jerusalem (1187). His circle transmitted traditions which he learned from R. Nehorai of Jerusalem (R. Ezra's commentary on the *aggadot*, Ms. Vatican 185; see Scholem, *Kitvei Yad be-Kabbalah* (1930), 202). Later legend of the Spanish kabbalists (c. 1300) linked his visit to the Middle East with *Maimonides' imaginary turning to Kabbalah in his old age. There is no trace of mysticism in Jacob's supplements to Rashi's commentary on Job (Ms. Oxford 295) written in 1163 or 1183. A. Jellinek's assumption that Jacob was the author of *Massekhet Aẓilut* is unfounded (*Toledot ha-Filosofyah be-Yisrael* (1921), 167).

BIBLIOGRAPHY: G. Scholem, in: *Tarbiz*, 6 (1935), 339–41; idem, *Reshit ha-Kabbalah* (1948), 70–98; idem, *Ursprung und Anfaenge der Kabbala* (1962), 201–6.

JACOB (Jakób) OF BELZYCE (16th century), scholar and physician in Poland. He took part in religious *disputations, mainly with the radical wing of Polish anti-trinitarians. Jacob's views, and even his very existence and activity, are known through the work of Marcin Czechowic: *Odpis Jakóba Żyda z Bełżyc na Dyalogi Marcina Czechowica: na ktory zas odpowiada Jakobowi Żydowi tenze Marcin Czechowic* ("The Reply of the Jew Jacob of Belzyce to the Dialogues of Marcin Czechowic: With the Reply of the Said Czechowic to the Jew Jacob") completed at Lublin on Dec. 16, 1581. This sums up – though with a Christian anti-trinitarian bias – the work that Jacob published against the Christian "dialogues" of Czechowic. In the dedication to Andrzej Lasota, Czechowic states that "you are well acquainted with this Jew with whom this dispute is being held." Czechowic also mentions that "about seven years ago" they had disputed on the nature of Jesus Christ (*ibid.*, 51) – hence about 1574 Jacob and Czechowic were already in contact. Elsewhere Czechowic mentions that "I talked to you not only through brother Marcin the tailor, but also through a Jew of Lublin, and I also informed you directly" (*ibid.*, 58). It is clear, therefore, that Jacob and his polemical work actually existed and are not a figment of Czechowic's imagination, as some scholars have thought.

BIBLIOGRAPHY: L. Szczucki, *Marcin Czechowic* (1964), index and 274–5, note 122, includes bibliography; J. Rosenthal, *Marcin Czechowic and Jacob of Belzyce; Arian-Jewish Encounters in 16th Century Poland* (1966; repr. from PAAJR, 34 (1966), 77–98).

[Haim Hillel Ben-Sasson]

JACOB OF CORBEIL (d. 1192), tosafist, pupil of Jacob b. Meir *Tam. He and his brother Judah, who were among the earliest scholars of Corbeil, are frequently mentioned in the *tosafot*. He composed *tosafot* to tractate *Pesaḥim*, and his name is mentioned in the printed *tosafot* as well as in the *Tosafot Yeshanim* to a number of other tractates. He met a martyr's death in 1192, apparently in his native town. The epithet *kadosh* ("holy"), added to his name in consequence of his martyrdom, has caused him to be confused with *Jacob of Marvège. Both Jacob of Corbeil and his brother are known to have had some connection with Kabbalah, but the only definite information on this topic is to the effect that Judah belonged to one of the circles of the *Ḥasidei Ashkenaz.

BIBLIOGRAPHY: Urbach, Tosafot, 129–30.

[Israel Moses Ta-Shma]

JACOB OF KEFAR SAKHNAYYA, Judeo-Christian disciple of *Jesus. It is related that Jacob once met *Eliezer b. Hyrcanus, to whom he reported that Jesus interpreted the verse "For of the hire of a harlot hath she gathered them and unto the hire of a harlot they shall return" (Micah 1:7), to mean that since the money originated in a place of filth, it could be applied to a place of filth; therefrom that, if the hire of a harlot had been consecrated, it could be applied to the erection of a privy for the high priest (Tosef., Ḥul. 2:24; Av. Zar. 17a; Eccles. R. 1:8, no. 3), despite the prohibition of Deuteronomy 23:19. There is no mention of such a view in Christian sources, but it is characteristic of the attitude of Jesus to fallen women (cf. Luke 7:36–50). In the family of Jesus and among his disciples there were several named Jacob, but it is not clear whether Jacob of Kefar Sakhnayya can be identified with any one of those mentioned in early Christian literature; in any case he is probably not to be identified with Jacob the brother of Jesus (as Klausner suggests). It is also unclear whether the same man is referred to in the following story (Tosef., Ḥul. 2:22–23; Av. Zar. 27b; TJ, Shab. 14:4, 14d; TJ, Av. Zar. 2:2, 40d): "It once happened that Eleazar b. Dama was bitten by a snake and Jacob of Kefar Sama (in TB, Sekhanya) came to cure him in the name of Jesus b. Pantirah, but R. Ishmael did not permit him to do so."

BIBLIOGRAPHY: J. Klausner, *Jesus of Nazareth, His Life, Times, and Teaching* (1929), 38ff., 286; Rokeah, in: *Tarbiz*, 39 (1969/70), 9–15; R.T. Herford, *Christianity in Talmud and Midrash* (1903), 137ff.; H.J. Schonfield, *History of Jewish Christianity* (1936), 73–79.

[Moshe David Herr]

JACOB OF MARVÈGE (late 12th–13th century), tosafist from Marvège, south central France. He is given the epithets *ḥasid* ("pious"), *kadosh* ("saintly"), and *mekubbal* ("the kabbalist"). He was the author of the remarkable work, *She'elot u-Teshuvot min ha-Shamayim* ("Responsa from Heaven"). He would seek answers from heaven about *halakhah*, and about what decision was to be accepted practice where the authorities differed "by means of seclusion, prayer, and uttering divine names and his questions were replied to in a dream" (Responsa Radbaz pt. 3, no. 532). In one responsum he writes: "O Supreme King, great, mighty, and revered God… command the holy angels charged with replying to questions in a dream to give a true and correct reply to the question I ask before Thy throne of Glory" (see Bibliography: Margaliot, 52). The date, 1203, of responsum 69, serves as a basis for determining his period. The replies received were cited as halakhic rulings by the great deciders who came after him. His work was first published in David ibn Zimra's responsa (pt. 5, Leghorn 1818 and subsequently in various editions; the 1895 edition has the commentary *Keset ha-Sofer* by Aaron Marcus). The first edition by R. Margaliot was published in 1926, a second edition in 1929, and a third edition, containing 89 responsa with an enlarged introduction and a corrected text from the collation of different manuscripts, in 1957.

BIBLIOGRAPHY: Guedemann, Gesch Erz, 1 (1880), 81; Gross, Gal Jud, 364–5; Marx, in: PAAJR, 4 (1933), 153; Urbach, Tosafot, 129, 202; R. Margaliot (ed.), *She'elot u-Teshuvot min ha-Shamayim* (1957[3]), 20–24; KS, 33 (1957/58), 277.

[Yehoshua Horowitz]

JACOB OF ORLEANS (d. 1189), tosafist; pupil of Jacob *Tam in Orleans. Like his fellow-student, *Yom Tov b. Isaac of Joigny, Jacob settled in England, and like him, met a martyr's death. While in England, where moneylending was the Jews' main source of livelihood, he drew up a formula for loans, whereby the prohibition against *usury could be circumvented (*Haggahot Mordekhai* to BM, 454–5). This formula gave rise to considerable perplexity in later generations. According to Meir of Rothenburg, the practice of employing a non-Jew to heat houses on the Sabbath in winter was introduced in France on Jacob's authority (Responsa, Prague (1608), 92). Jacob composed *tosafot* on a number of tractates and his name frequently occurs in the printed *tosafot*. His influence is particularly noticeable in the *tosafot* to tractates *Pesaḥim, Zevaḥim*, and *Menaḥot*. His commentary on the Pentateuch is extant in manuscript, and extracts from it are to be found in various collections of commentaries by tosafists on the Pentateuch.

BIBLIOGRAPHY: Urbach, Tosafot, 122–4.

[Israel Moses Ta-Shma]

JACOB OF PONT-SAINTE-MAXENCE (14th century), one of the leaders of French Jewry. Jacob apparently came from Pont-Sainte-Maxence, a town in the Oise department, northern France, but his name is the only indication that a Jewish community existed there. Along with *Manessier of Vesoul, he controlled the affairs of the Jews in the north, perhaps from the time of their return to France in 1359. After Jacob had quarreled with Manessier and denounced him to the authorities, Manessier was compelled to pay a heavy fine both to Jacob and to the king.

BIBLIOGRAPHY: I. Loeb, in: *Jubelschrift… H. Graetz*, 1 (1887), 54ff.; R. Anchel, *Les Juifs de France* (1946), 115ff.

[Bernhard Blumenkranz]

JACOB OF VIENNA (end of 14th–beginning of 15th century), Austrian rabbi. Known also as Jekel of Eiger, he studied under

R. Moshel of Znaim, Moravia, and was rabbi at Eiger, Krems, and Vienna. Jacob *Moellin consulted him, and Israel *Isserlein held him in high esteem. No responsa of his are extant, although almost all the great contemporary rabbis quote him. In *halakhah* he adopted an independent view, did not hesitate to disagree with his teacher and sometimes even with statements contained in *Alexander Susslin ha-Kohen's *Ha-Aguddah*. He also judged cases of mayhem (*dinei ḥabbalot*), on one occasion imposing the highest fine known in Ashkenazi Jewry for such cases. He became renowned as editor of communal decrees (Breslau, in: ZGJD, 5 (1892), 115–25). Several of his pupils are known, among them Zalman Katz, author of *Ha-Yeri'ah*. Grossberg has published from a manuscript a commentary on the Pentateuch by a Jacob of Vienna who may be identical with this Jacob of Vienna (see bibliography).

The commentary shows the influence of the German pietists and cites many other exegetes.

BIBLIOGRAPHY: I. Gastfreund, *Wiener Rabbinen* (1879), 29, 32; M. Grossberg (ed.), *Sefer Peshatim u-Ferushim al Ḥamishah Ḥumshei Torah* (1848), introd.; S. Krauss, *Wiener Geserah* (1920), index.

[Yedidya A. Dinari]

JACOBOWSKI, LUDWIG (1868–1900), German poet and author. Born in Strelno, Posen, Jacobowski spent most of his short life in Berlin. He edited the newspaper *Die Gesellschaft* and wrote several volumes of poetry including *Funken* (1891), *Satan lachte* (1898), *Aus bewegten Stunden* (1899), *Ausklang* (1901), and *Leuchtende Tage* (1901). His novel *Werther, der Jude* (1892), which expressed his inner turmoil, provoked more interest than his verse. In a second novel, *Loki, Roman eines Gottes* (1899), the eponymous figure of the lonely dark god rejected by the blond Teutonic deities symbolized the isolation of the Jew in Germanic culture. Jacobowski was also an essayist and author of a comedy, *Diyab der Narr* (1895). A significant Jewish figure in the last decade of 19th-century German literature, he conducted an interesting correspondence with many of the leading writers of his time, including Karl *Kraus, Alfred *Kerr, and Jacob *Wassermann. He was an active defender of Jewish rights in the *Verein zur Abwehr des Anti-semitismus* and entered into a controversy with Hermann *Ahlwardt, whose anti-Jewish "racial" work *Der Verzweiflungskampf der arischen Voelker mit dem Judentum* provoked Jacobowski's spirited reply, *Offene Antwort eines Juden* (1891). He also published *Der Juden Anteil in Verbrechen* (1892) and *Der christliche Staat und seine Zukunft* (1894). The works of Jacobowski reflect both his attempt to find a synthesis between Judaism and German culture and his own personal tragedy. His collected works (*Gesammelte Werke in einem Band*, ed. Alexander Mueller) appeared in one volume in 2000.

BIBLIOGRAPHY: F.B. Stern, *Ludwig Jacobowski; Persoenlichkeit und Werk eines Dichters* (1966); idem, in: BLBI, 7 (1964), 101–37. **ADD. BIBLIOGRAPHY:** H. Friedrich, *Ludwig Jacobowski. Ein modernes Dichterbild* (1901); M. Scholz (ed.), *Ludwig Jacobowski im Lichte des Lebens* (1901), *Auftakt zur Literatur des 20. Jahrhunderts. Briefe aus dem Nachlass von Ludwig Jacobowski, ed. by F.B. Stern* (1974); A. Martin, "Heinrich Mann und die 'antinaturalistische Richtung'. Bemerkungen zu einem wenig bekannten Brief des jungen Autors an Ludwig Jacobowski," in: *Heinrich-Mann-Jahrbuch*, 16 (1998), 133–144; M.M. Anderson, "*'Jewish Mimesis?' Imitation and assimilation in Thomas Mann's 'Wälsungenblut' and Ludwig Jacobowski's 'Werther, der Jude'*," in: *German life and letters*, 49 (1996), N. 2, 193–204.

JACOBS, ALETTA HENRIËTTE (1854–1929), Dutch suffragette and physician. Jacobs is primarily known for her advocacy of women's suffrage in the Netherlands. She was the daughter of Abraham Jacobs and Anna de Jongh. In 1892 she married Carel Victor Gerritsen, a businessman. Their only child died at a very young age. At the age of 16, Jacobs had corresponded with Minister J.R. Thorbecke and obtained his permission to be admitted to the University of Groningen, where she started studying medicine as the first Dutch female student in 1871. In 1879 she obtained her degree with a dissertation titled *On the Localization of Physiological and Pathological Phenomena in the Cerebrum*. Jacobs had her own medical practice and she was also involved in a number of social initiatives. She criticized the shocking housing conditions of the poor working class in the press and emphasized the difficult circumstances in which poor, illiterate, working-class women had to live. Her fight for equal rights for women led to her taking an active part in the women's movement. In 1889 she joined the recently founded Vrije Vrouwen Vereeniging (Free Women's Association), which started the separate Vereeniging voor Vrouwenkiesrecht (Association for Women's Suffrage) in 1894.

In 1903, Aletta Jacobs took over the leadership of the latter association and in this position decided to devote herself to the task of revising the Dutch constitution in order to give women the right to vote and to be elected. Thanks to the foundation of the Bond voor Vrouwenkiesrecht (League for Women's Suffrage) in 1907, this demand was brought to the international forefront. The Netherlands was neutral in World War I and therefore The Hague was chosen to hold an international women's congress on May 3, 1915. Women's rights were on the agenda as well as a potential contribution to peace. Jacobs' ardent struggle bore fruit only in September 1919, when Queen Wilhelmina finally signed the Jacobs Act, which gave Dutch women the full right to vote.

BIBLIOGRAPHY: A.H. Jacobs, *Herinneringen aan dr Aletta H. Jacobs* (1924); idem and H.N. Haenen (eds.), *Dr. Aletta H. Jacobs reist door Palestina en eet in China: fragmenten uit haar reisbrieven uit Afrika en Azië* (2004); M. Bosch, *Aletta Jacobs 1854–1929. Een onwrikbaar geloof in rechtvaardigheid* (2005); "Aletta Jacobs," at: www.iiav.nl (website of the International Information Centre and Archives for the Women's Movement in the Netherlands); W.H. Posthumus-van der Goot, in: *Biografisch Woorden-boek van Nederland*: www.inghist.nl/Onderzoek/BWN/lemmata/bwn1/jacobs.

[Monika Saelemaekers (2nd ed.)]

JACOBS, ARTHUR (**David**; 1922–1996), British music critic, author, translator, editor, and lexicographer. Born in Manchester, Jacobs received his education there and at Oxford. He was music critic of the London *Daily Express* (1947–52) and of the *Jewish Chronicle* (from 1963), as well as associate editor of the London monthly *Opera* (1961–71). He was appointed professor at the Royal Academy of Music, London, in 1964 and from 1979 to 1984 he was head of the music department at Huddersfield Polytechnic; he also taught in British Columbia (1968), Philadelphia (1970, 1971), Canada, and Australia. His many publications include *Gilbert and Sullivan* (1951), *A New Dictionary of Music* (1958, 1972 also Spanish and Swedish editions), *Choral Music* (editor, 1963), *The Pan Book of Opera/The Opera Guide* (with Stanley Sadie, 1964, 1969), *The Penguin Dictionary of Musical Performers* (1990), and *A Short History of Western Music* (1972). He translated more than 20 opera librettos from several languages, including works by Haendel, Rossini, Berlioz, Tchaikovsky, Strauss, and Berg (the complete *Lulu*), and wrote the original libretto for Nicholas Maw's *One-Man Show* (1964). Jacobs also contributed to many musical journals.

ADD. BIBLIOGRAPHY: Grove online; N. Slonimsky, *Baker's Biographical Dictionary of Musicians.*

[Max Loppert / Israela Stein (2nd ed.)

JACOBS, BERNARD B. (1916–1996), U.S. theater executive. Born in Manhattan, Jacobs graduated from New York University and Columbia University Law School. After serving in the Army in the South Pacific in World War II, Jacobs practiced law with his brother, dealing mainly with jewelry companies. It was his brother's friend, Gerald Schoenfeld, who brought him into the theater in 1958 to help him at the mighty Shubert theatrical organization, where he was chief lawyer. After J.J. Shubert died in 1963, his will turned over the bulk of his estate, including the theaters, to the Shubert Foundation, then a little-known arm of the theater company. During a bitter power struggle among irreconcilable directors, Jacobs and Schoenfeld moved to the top of the integrated organization in 1972. Although they had little theater background, the two lawyers began investing money in plays and acting as producers. By 1974 Jacobs felt that the Shubert empire was back on track with the hits *Equus, Pippin, Grease*, and *Sherlock Holmes*. The next year, *A Chorus Line* put the operation on solid footing. The two men were universally credited with taking a faltering theater concern and transforming it into a modern and financially potent enterprise. As theater owners and producers, they had more to say than anyone else about what shows opened on Broadway. They also determined what shows closed in their theaters, and when. At the end of the 20th century, "the Shuberts," as the two lawyers became known, owned and operated 16 Broadway theaters in addition to theaters in Philadelphia, Washington, Boston, and Los Angeles and other real estate property.

For years Jacobs and Schoenfeld were embroiled in suits after the state attorney general said that, as executors of the J.J. Shubert estate, they had made "grossly excessive" claims. The charges were later withdrawn. The pair also benefited from a tax ruling in 1979 that gave the Shubert Foundation an exemption to federal tax laws. This allowed Jacobs and Schoenfeld to continue as heads of both the foundation and the theater organization, the most important in the Broadway theater. By the end of the 20th century, the foundation had a value of more than $150 million and provided support to nonprofit theaters and to dance companies. Jacobs was also credited with introducing computerized methods of ticket sales, linking his box offices to computerized outlets in other cities.

In 2005, Broadway theaters owned by the Shuberts were renamed for Jacobs and Schoenfeld.

[Stewart Kampel (2nd ed.)]

JACOBS, FRANCES WISEBART (1843–1892), known as Denver's "Mother of Charities." Frances Wisebart Jacobs was born in Harrodsburg, Kentucky, on March 23, 1843. Her parents, Leon, a tailor, and Rosetta Wisebart, emigrated from Bavaria and later moved to Cincinnati, where Frances and her six siblings attended public schools. In 1859, Frances's brother Benjamin Wisebart and his friend Abraham Jacobs journeyed to the west, settling in what was soon to become Denver. Abraham Jacobs returned to Cincinnati in 1863 to marry Frances Wisebart. He and his new bride, now Frances Jacobs, made their first home in the mining town of Central City, near Denver, where Abraham operated a general store. The family relocated to Denver in 1870, where Frances was to have a profound influence on the development of benevolent charity work within both the Jewish and larger community, while Abraham became a prominent merchant and active in local politics. In 1872, Frances Wisebart Jacobs helped organize, and soon served as president of, the Hebrew Ladies' Benevolent Society, and in 1874 she helped found the nonsectarian Denver Ladies' Relief Society, primarily to aid Denver's ill and impoverished, and served as the organization's first vice president. By 1885, largely through her efforts, the first free kindergarten was opened in Denver. Frances Jacobs was also one of the three primary founders of what would become the early United Way of America, which originated in Denver in 1887 as the Community Chest.

During the last years of her life, Jacobs had been particularly attuned to the plight of tuberculosis victims, who frequently came to Denver in search of better health, without funds or medical assistance once they arrived. By the 1880s, Denver had earned the nickname of the "World's Sanitorium," and hundreds of consumptives began to pour into Colorado. The Jewish community was the first to step forward with aid, and Jacobs served as the impetus behind the founding of National Jewish Hospital for Consumptives. At the dedication of the hospital in 1899, some years after Jacobs' death from pneumonia in 1892 at the age of forty-nine, Denver's mayor observed that "out of her efforts has grown an institution national in scope and dedicated to the humane and charitable work in which during her lifetime she so earnestly engaged." In 1900, when 16 portraits of pioneers were selected to be placed in the windows of the dome of the Colorado state capitol building, Jacobs was chosen as one of the small elite group and the only woman.

Jacobs' unswerving commitment to the sick and indigent, and her amazing ability to work with men and women from a variety of ethnic and religious groups, earned her the epitaph of Denver's "Mother of Charities." Although she had no formal training, she was the prototype of the early social worker, frequently making personal visits to those who were ill and poor, freely dispensing advice, medication, and funds. The funeral of Frances Wisebart Jacobs was attended by nearly 2,000 people and served as a testimony to her impact on the development of philanthropy in early Denver.

BIBLIOGRAPHY: A. Breck, *A Centennial History of the Jews of Colorado* (1960); *Denver Republican*, July 14, 1900; S. Friedenthal. "The Jews of Denver," *Reform Advocate* (October 31, 1908); M. Hornbein, "Frances Jacobs: Denver's Mother of Charities," in: *Western States Jewish Historical Quarterly* (January 1983); *Memoirs of Frances Jacobs, 1892*; I. Uchill, *Pioneers, Peddlers, and Tsakikim* (1957).

[Jeanne Abrams (2nd ed.)]

JACOBS, GEORGE (1834–1894), rabbi. Born in Kingston, Jamaica, Jacobs came to the United States at the age of 20 and settled in Richmond, Virginia, where he studied for the rabbinate. He was ordained in 1857 and in 1869 he succeeded Isaac Lesser as rabbi of Congregation Beth Emet in Philadelphia. He was one of the founders of the Young Men's Hebrew Association (YMHA) in Philadelphia and of the Jewish Publication Society. He was a frequent contributor to the Jewish press. He revised the English version of the Szold-Jastrow Siddur. He is the author of *Catechism for Elementary Instruction in the Hebrew Faith* (1894).

[Michael Berenbaum (2nd ed.)]

JACOBS, HIRSCH (1904–1970), U.S. horseracing trainer and breeder who saddled more thoroughbred winners – 3,596 – than any other trainer in history; member of National Racing Museum and Hall of Fame. One of ten children born to an immigrant tailor in Manhattan, Jacobs began raising and racing pigeons at age eight after the family moved to Brooklyn, and by 12 could identify 100 pigeons by sight. At age 22 he bought his first thoroughbred, called Reveillon. Two years later Jacobs formed a partnership with Isadore Bieber, who served as financier and owner of horses while Jacobs did the training. Jacobs was an unusually keen observer with a phenomenal memory, especially for the ailments of other men's horses. His specialty was claiming inexpensive horses and developing them into big winners, the most famous being Stymie, which Jacobs claimed on June 2, 1943, for $1,500 and turned into one of the all-time great thoroughbreds: in 128 races Stymie won 35, was second 32 times, and third 26 times, earning $918,485, a record at the time. Stymie was also named handicap horse of the year in 1945 and was inducted into the Racing Hall of Fame in 1975.

Jacobs led all trainers in winners every year from 1933 through 1944 except 1940, when he finished second. With some of the money earned by Stymie, Bieber and Jacobs set up their own breeding farm, Stymie Manor. As a trainer, Jacobs' horses led in earnings in 1946, 1960, and 1965, and Stymie Manor led all breeders in winnings from 1964 through 1967. After suffering a stroke in 1966, Jacobs became less active and his son, John, took over much of the responsibility for training Stymie Manor's best horses. Jacobs' wife, Ethel, brothers Eugene and Sidney, son John, and daughter and son-in-law Patrice and Louis Wolfson were also long-time trainers, owners, and breeders. Jacobs' 3,596 winners earned $15,340,534, and among his best horses were Hail to Reason, the two-year-old champion in 1960; Regal Gleam, champion two-year-old filly in 1966; Straight Deal, the champion handicap mare in 1967; and Affectionately, champion sprinter in 1965. Jacobs trained six horses that raced in the Kentucky Derby, though none finished higher than third place. Pimlico Race Track in Baltimore memorialized him in 1975 with the Hirsch Jacobs Stakes. Jacobs was elected to the National Racing Hall of Fame as a trainer in 1958.

[Elli Wohlgelernter (2nd ed.)]

JACOBS, IRWIN M. (1933–), U.S. computer and communications entrepreneur. Born in New Bedford, Mass., Jacobs received an engineering degree from Cornell University and master's and doctorate degrees in electrical engineering from the Massachusetts Institute of Technology. He began his career teaching at MIT and was on the staff of the Research Laboratory of Electronics there. While at MIT, Jacobs, together with Prof. J. Wozencraft, wrote *Principles of Communication Engineering,* developing a vision of ubiquitous communications worldwide made possible by digital wireless communications. This led to the founding of his first company, Linkabit, a wellspring for most of the telecommunications industry in San Diego, Calif. Jacobs guided the growth of Linkabit from a handful of employees in 1969 to over 1,700 by 1985. Linkabit merged with M/A-Com in 1980. During most of that time, Jacobs was chairman, president, and chief executive officer of Linkabit, and executive vice president and a director of M/A. While there, Jacobs led the team that developed the first microprocessor-based, spread-spectrum satellite communication modem for military anti-jam airborne applications. He also guided the development and manufacture of the first successful video scrambling system (Videocypher), currently operating to descramble premium television transmission to millions of satellite dishes.

In 1985 Jacobs became a founder and then chairman and chief executive of Qualcomm, which develops, manufactures, licenses, delivers, and operates digital wireless communication products and services based on code-division multiple access technology (CDMA). As a pioneer in wireless communications, Qualcomm develops and supplies integrated circuits and system software for wireless voice and data communications. Its standard is used by major carriers like Sprint and Verizon Wireless. Consumers may know it best for its Eudora e-mail software. The CDMA standard was adopted as one of two digital standards for the next generation of cellular telephones in North America. In 2005 it had 7,600 employees worldwide and had revenues topping $5 billion, making Jacobs one of the wealthiest men in the United States. In 1994, Jacobs was awarded the National Medal of Technology, the highest award bestowed by the president of the United States for achievement in the commercialization of technology or the development of human resources that foster technology commercialization. Jacobs's philanthropies were diverse, with gifts to schools and museums. He and his wife gave an endowment gift to the University of California, San Diego, for an engineering college which was named the Irwin and Joan Jacobs School of Engineering. In 1992 Jacobs and his wife gave the financially troubled San Diego Symphony a $100 million endowment, then the largest ever awarded to a symphony orchestra in the United States. They have been generous to the Jewish Community Center and other Jewish charities in San Diego, but like many philanthropists, they have given their megagifts to general, not specifically Jewish causes.

In 2005, PAUL E. JACOBS (1962–) succeeded his father as chief executive of Qualcomm. Jacobs had started in his father's first company, Linkabit, in 1985 and worked at different engineering jobs at Qualcomm during his college years at the University of California, Berkeley, from which he earned a doctorate. Paul Jacobs, who formally joined the company in 1990, was president of Qualcomm's Internet and wireless group, one of the company's most important divisions. In his early years at the company, he worked on the engineering for the antenna of Qualcomm's OmniTracs system, which is used to track the routes of freight trucks. He worked on the speech compression algorithm for CDMA, and holds a patent for part of the technology, one of more than 25 Qualcomm patents that he helped develop. Paul's brother Jeff is the leader of Qualcomm's global development division.

[Stewart Kampel (2nd ed.)]

JACOBS, JAMES LESLIE (**Jimmy**, **Jim**; 1930–1988), U.S. handball champion, considered along with Vic *Hershkowitz as the greatest handball players in history; boxing manager and film historian, member of United States Handball Association Hall of Fame, World Boxing Hall of Fame, and International Boxing Hall of Fame. Jacobs was born in St. Louis, but when he was five his family moved to Los Angeles, where as a teenager he excelled as a shortstop in baseball, halfback in football, and forward at basketball, but primarily in handball. He was a remarkable all-around athlete who once ran a 9.8 100-yard dash, and was offered a tryout for the U.S. Olympic basketball team. After serving with the U.S. army in Korea – he was awarded the Purple Heart in 1951 – Jacobs developed his handball skills and became ambidextrous. As a four-wall handball player, Jacobs was the best ever, winning every match he played between 1955 and 1969. He won the Three-Wall Men's Singles three times (1959, 1960, 1961), the Four-Wall Men's Singles six times (1955, 1956, 1957, 1960, 1964, 1965, and the Men's Doubles five times (1960, 1962, 1965, 1967, 1968). Jacobs was the first to coin the "sword and the shield" theory, relying on his left hand as a shield and his right hand as his sword, and is credited as the first handball player to use the ceiling shot as a defensive weapon. He also won three AAU national titles, four YMCA national titles, and countless regional championships. He was inducted into the United States Handball Association Hall of Fame in 1972.

Jacobs was also a boxing enthusiast, and while traveling around the world to give handball exhibitions for the armed services, he began to collect films of old boxing matches not available in the United States. Jacobs became one of the world's top boxing historians. In 1961, he merged his collection with that of Bill Cayton to form the largest collection in the world, and the two worked to restore and preserve old boxing films dating to the 1890s. Their corporation, The Big Fights, Inc., produced over 1,000 boxing features, and three of their productions – *Legendary Champions*, *The Heavyweight Champions*, and *Jack Johnson* – were nominated for Academy Awards. Jacobs himself directed the 1970 documentary *AKA Cassius Clay*.

Jacobs – a nephew of boxing promoter Mike *Jacobs, who managed Joe Louis – also managed fighters together with Cayton, including three world champions: Wilfred Benitez, Edwin Rosario, and Mike Tyson. The Boxing Writers' Association of America awarded Jacobs the Al Buck Award for Manager of the Year in 1986, and he was inducted into the International Boxing Hall of Fame in 1993.

Jacobs also loved comic books from when he was a child, and his collection of 500,000 issues was said to be the largest in the world. He died at 58 after a nine-year battle with chronic lymphocytic leukemia.

[Elli Wohlgelernter (2nd ed.)]

JACOBS, JOE (**Yosef**, "**Yussel the Muscle**"; 1896–1940), U.S. boxing manager. Jacobs, the son of a tailor, was born on New York's Lower East Side to Hungarian immigrants. He was the quintessential boxing manager of the 1920s and 1930s, a cigar-chomping, fedora-wearing, streetwise, brash, combative, argumentative, and fast-talking schmoozer who "knew nothing about boxing, but he knew how to negotiate and get his man the best deal possible," in the words of his most famous fighter, Max Schmeling. Jacobs became Schmeling's manager in 1928, when the German began fighting in the United States. In Schmeling's fight for the vacant heavyweight championship on June 12, 1930, at Yankee Stadium, he was knocked down in the fourth round by a low blow from Jack Sharkey. Jacobs jumped into the ring and continued to scream "foul" until the bewildered referee disqualified Sharkey. It was the only time the heavyweight championship was decided on a foul. When the two boxers met in a rematch for the title on June 21, 1932, Sharkey won a controversial 15-round decision, leading Jacobs to utter to a national radio audience what became a classic sports quote and an entry in *Bartlett's Familiar Quotations*: "We wuz robbed!" Another *Bartlett's* quote from Jacobs that became part of the American idiom occurred when he attended the 1935 World Series in Detroit on a very cold and windy day. "I should of stood in bed," he remarked.

On March 10, 1935, Jacobs accompanied Schmeling to a fight in Hamburg, Germany, against Steve Hamas. After Schmeling knocked out Hamas, he and 25,000 fans spontaneously stood and sang the Nazi anthem with arms raised in the Sieg Heil. Jacobs – as naive about politics as he was shrewd about ring matters, and unsure what to do, according to Schmeling – then raised his right hand, with its omnipresent cigar, and joined the salute, smiling and winking at Schmeling. It bothered the Nazi brass that this Jew with cigar in hand was giving the Nazi salute, but it caused greater outrage in the United States, especially in the Jewish community, when photographs of the scene were published. "Up in the Bronx the good burghers agreed that the little man with the big cigar was no credit to their creed," wrote a *New York Daily News* reporter. Schmeling, nicknamed "The Black Uhlan of the Rhine" by Jacobs, was being touted by Germany as the paradigm of Aryan supremacy, and was under repeated pressure from the highest levels of the Nazi party to fire his Jewish manager, but he refused. Jacobs subsequently arranged for Schmeling to fight Joe Louis, whom he beat in their first fight on June 19, 1936, but he lost the rematch on June 22, 1938, in perhaps the most famous boxing bout in history.

Five months later, on November 10, 1938, *Kristallnacht*, Schmeling hid two Jewish teenage brothers, Henri and Werner Lewin, for two days in his suite at the Excelsior Hotel in Berlin, informing the front desk that he was ill and that no one be allowed to visit him. When the anti-Jewish rioting abated, the teenage brothers were transferred to another location in Berlin until they could leave Germany.

Jacobs also managed featherweight champion Andre Routis, light heavyweight champion Mike McTigue, and heavyweight contender "Two Ton" Tony Galento.

[Elli Wohlgelernter (2nd ed.)]

JACOBS, JOSEPH (1854–1916), Jewish historian, folklorist, and scholar. He was born in Sydney, Australia, studied in England, and, after graduating in history in Cambridge, went to complete his studies in Berlin where he worked under Steinschneider. On his return to England he became an author and journalist. He was an extremely prolific writer and worker. In the general sphere, he had a reputation as a folklorist and student of comparative literature, publishing large numbers of books and articles on these subjects; and he was for some years editor of the periodical *Folk-Lore*. Even as his specialized interest in folklore made him a researcher into Jewish ethnology, his interest in statistics led him to another branch of anthropology, namely the study of the "racial" characteristics of Jews. Still another anthropological interest is evident in his application of the method of comparative institutional archaeology to the Bible in his *Studies in Biblical Archaeology* (1894). But his Jewish enthusiasms were uppermost. With Lucien *Wolf he organized the Anglo-Jewish Historical Exhibition of 1887 and edited its monumental catalog and bibliography. He took the lead in organizing British public opinion at the time of the Russian Jewish pogroms in 1882 and was editor of the periodical *Darkest Russia*. He founded and edited (1896–99) the *Jewish Year Book*. His writings on medieval Anglo-Jewish history, culminating in his *Jews of Angevin England* (1893), set the study of that subject on a new basis. In 1888 he went to Spain to inquire into the Jewish historical material there, the result being his *An Enquiry into the Sources of the History of the Jews in Spain* (1894). In 1900, he was called to the U.S. as one of the editors of the *Jewish Encyclopaedia*. He not only edited, and largely wrote, the articles in the departments of anthropology and Anglo-Jewish history, but also gave direction to the whole work and wrote many articles on diverse subjects (e.g., bibliography) in emergency. At the same time, he lectured at the Jewish Theological Seminary of America, edited the *American Jewish Year Book* and the *American Hebrew*, etc. A work on *Jewish Contributions to Civilisation* was issued posthumously. He wrote a novel on the life of Jesus, *As Others Saw Him* (1895). His output was vast and generally well written, and on a very high level. It is sometimes, however, marred by carelessness and haste – a result of economic conditions – and (especially in his early work) by the inadequacy of his Hebrew knowledge.

BIBLIOGRAPHY: JHSET, 8 (1915–17), 129–52; A. Marx, *Essays in Jewish Biography* (Philadelphia, 1947), 251–4; DAB. **ADD. BIBLIOGRAPHY:** ODNB; B. Maidment, "The Literary Career of Joseph Jacobs," in: JHSET, 24 (1970–73), 101–13.

[Cecil Roth]

JACOBS, LAZARUS (c. 1709–1796), English glass manufacturer, producing the fine Bristol glass now much sought after. He was born in Frankfurt, Germany, and became head of the *Bristol Jewish community. Jacobs was responsible for the construction of the new synagogue in 1786. He was succeeded in his business by his son ISAAC JACOBS (1757 or 1758–1835) whose work, unlike that of his father, is signed, and is, therefore, more readily identifiable. He was appointed glass manufacturer to George III but ultimately met with business misfortunes. In 1809, Isaac was made a freeman of Bristol.

BIBLIOGRAPHY: Rubens, in: JHSET, 14 (1935–39), 106; C. Roth, *Rise of Provincial Jewry* (1950), 41. **ADD. BIBLIOGRAPHY:** ODNB; Z. Josephs, "Jewish Glass-Makers," in: JHSET 25 (1973–75).

[Cecil Roth]

JACOBS, LOUIS (1920–2006), English rabbi and theological writer. Born in Manchester, Jacobs received his training at the yeshivot of Manchester and Gateshead and at London University. After teaching for some time at the Golders Green Beth Hamidrash, London, he served as a rabbi of the Central Synagogue, Manchester, and at the fashionable New West End Synagogue, London, from 1954 to 1959. From 1959 to 1962 Jacobs was tutor at Jews' College, London, but he resigned when, at the retirement of I. *Epstein, Chief Rabbi I. *Brodie, as president of the college, vetoed his appointment as principal on account of his heterodox views. This led to a violent controversy within British Jewry, with the *Jewish Chronicle as Jacobs' main protagonist. Jacobs' followers created for him the post of director of a specially founded Society for the Study of Jewish Theology, for which he lectured in London and provincial centers. When in 1963 the post of minister at the New West End Synagogue became vacant, Jacobs was elected to his former post; Brodie again blocked the appointment. Thereupon, a number of the synagogue's members seceded from the *United Synagogue and founded the New London Synagogue with Jacobs as rabbi (1964); services continued to be conducted along Orthodox lines.

The controversy had its origin in Jacobs' published work, beginning with *We Have Reason to Believe* (1957, 1962²); *Jewish Values* (1960); *Principles of the Jewish Faith* (1964), an analytical study of Maimonides' Creed; and *Faith* (1968). In these the author accepted some of the methods and results of biblical Higher Criticism, denied the literal inspiration of the Pentateuch, and asserted a human element in the composition of the Bible. Jacobs also devoted several studies to Kabbalah and Ḥasidism: he translated into English Moses *Cordovero's *Palmtree of Deborah* from Hebrew (1960), adding introduction and notes; and Dov Ber Schneersohn's (of Lubavitch) *Tract on Ecstasy* (1963), with introduction and notes; he also wrote *Seeker of Unity; the Life and Works of Aaron of Starosselje* (1966). Among his other published works are *Studies in Talmudic Logic and Methodology* (1961), *Jewish Prayer* (1962³), *A Guide to Yom Kippur* (1957, 1960²), and *A Guide to Rosh Ha-Shanah* (1959, 1962²).

BIBLIOGRAPHY: S. Temkin, in: *Conservative Judaism* (Fall, 1963), 18–34; I. Maybaum, in: *Judaism*, 13 (1964), 471–7; A. Sherman, in: *Commentary*, 38 no. 10 (1964), 60–64.

JACOBS, MICHAEL STRAUSS (**"Uncle Mike"**; 1880–1953), U.S. boxing promoter, member of the International Boxing Hall of Fame and World Boxing Hall of Fame. Strauss was one of 10 children born in New York's Greenwich Village to immigrants Isaac and Rachel (Strauss). His family was poor, forcing Jacobs to work as a boy selling newspapers and candy on Coney Island excursion boats. After noticing that ticket purchases for the boats were often confusing to prospective passengers, Jacobs began scalping boat tickets, bought concession rights on all the ferries docked at the Battery, and eventually ran his own ferryboats. Jacobs then became the premier ticket scalper in New York, buying and selling theater, opera, or sports events tickets, and began sponsoring events himself, including charity balls, bike races, and circuses. Jacobs opened a legitimate ticket agency across from the Metropolitan Opera House, becoming the "standout ticket agent of New York," and also invested his money in several other successful enterprises, including real estate development, Enrico Caruso's concert tour, and a series of lectures by British suffragette Emily Pankhurst.

Jacobs began his career in boxing promotion in 1921 by working with Hall of Famer Tex Rickard, raising $100,000 in cash in just eight hours to help Rickard promote the Jack Dempsey-Georges Carpentier heavyweight championship bout. The result was the first $1 million gate in boxing history. Jacobs also helped Rickard in financing the building of the Old Madison Square Garden in 1925. But four years after Rickard's death in 1929, Jacobs formed the Twentieth Century Sporting Club with three reporters, including Damon Runyan, to compete with the Garden for the biggest boxing promotions. From 1935 until 1949, Jacobs was arguably the most powerful man in boxing, controlling practically every world title bout between Featherweights and Heavyweights, and the stretch on Manhattan's 49th Street between Broadway and Eighth Avenue was known as "Jacobs Beach." "Nobody else ever exerted such absolute dictatorship as his over any sport," wrote columnist Red Smith.

Jacobs' main attraction was heavyweight Joe Louis, whom Jacobs promoted at a time when Madison Square Garden was reticent about staging fights with blacks. Jacobs persuaded heavyweight champion Jim Braddock to break a contract with the Garden in order to fight Louis in Chicago, and Louis won. When Louis fought Max Schmeling in 1936 and 1938, some Jewish groups opposed giving Schmeling a platform, and several of them applied pressure on Jacobs to cancel the fights. Jacobs offered to donate 10 per cent of the gate to groups helping Jewish refugees. A story in the *American Hebrew* in 1946 praised Jacobs for giving Joe Louis the opportunity to strike "a terrific blow to the theory of race supremacy."

Jacobs solidified his position as a top promoter when he staged the Carnival of Champions on September 23, 1937, at the Polo Grounds in New York, featuring four world championship bouts in one night. Madison Square Garden subsequently leased the arena and the outdoor Madison Square Garden Bowl to the Twentieth Century Sporting Club. Jacobs' relationship with the Garden changed from tenant-landlord to a partnership, with Jacobs staging 320 shows there from 1937 to 1949. In 1944 he obtained the first commercial sponsorship of a television fight, featuring the Featherweight title bout between Willie Pep and Chalky Wright. Jacobs, who promoted 61 championship fights including three million-dollar bouts during his career, suffered a cerebral hemorrhage in 1946, and finally sold his empire to Madison Square Garden in 1949.

Jacobs was elected to the World Boxing Hall of Fame in 1982, and the International Boxing Hall of Fame in 1990. He was the subject of a biography by Daniel M Daniel, *The Mike Jacobs Story* (1950).

[Elli Wohlgelernter (2nd ed.)]

JACOBS, ROSE GELL (1888–1975), U.S. teacher and activist. A founding member of the Hadassah Organization in 1912, Jacobs rose through the ranks to become a prominent Zionist speaker, organizer, and national leader. She was born in New York City in 1888, educated at Columbia University, and taught in local public schools (1908–14). After marrying Edward Jacobs, an Atlanta attorney, she left teaching and became more active in Jewish affairs. She founded several Hadassah chapters in the American south and edited Hadassah's newsletter from 1920 to 1925. Jacobs held several senior posts in Hadassah and served two terms as Hadassah's national president (1930–32 and 1934–37).

With the rise of the Nazis, Jacobs pushed Hadassah to help European Jewry. It was on Jacobs' advice – and with her signature on the Jewish Agency contract in 1935 – that Hadassah officially adopted the Youth Aliyah program to rescue Jewish youth from Nazi Europe. In 1936, at great personal risk, Jacobs visited Germany to investigate the situation of the Jewish community and firm up Hadassah's role in Youth Aliyah. Over the following years, with vital support from Hadassah, Youth Aliyah rescued many thousands of youngsters from war-torn Europe.

In 1940, ignoring the dangers of wartime travel, Jacobs went to Palestine to set up the Hadassah Emergency Committee as an on-site administrative body for Hadassah's health and social welfare programs there.

Jacobs was an initiator of the building program of the Rothschild-Hadassah-University Hospital and Medical School on Mount Scopus. She also served on the executive of the Jewish Agency for Palestine from 1937 to 1946; chaired Hadassah's Committee for the Study of Arab-Jewish Relations from 1941 to 1943; and served on the board of governors of The Hebrew University. After the war, Jacobs worked with the ESCO Foundation to promote industrial development in Palestine (later Israel).

Jacobs died on August 14, 1975, in New York City.

[Erica Simmons (2nd ed.)]

JACOBS, SAMUEL WILLIAM (Wolf; 1871–1938), Canadian lawyer, politician, and Jewish community leader. Jacobs was born in Lancaster, Ontario. His family was among early East European Jewish immigrants to Canada. Educated at McGill and Laval Universities, Jacobs was called to the Quebec Bar in 1906. An expert on Canada's legal code and railway law, he was the author of *The Railway Law of Canada* (1909), co-editor, with Léon Garneau, of the *Quebec Code of Civil Procedure* (1903), and treasurer of the Montreal Bar Association, 1916–17.

Jacobs was also deeply committed to the Jewish community. In 1897, in response to the growing antisemitism in the wake of the *Dreyfus affair, Jacobs founded the *Jewish Times* with Lyon Cohen. The first continuing Canadian Jewish publication, the English-language weekly represented Montreal's middle-class Anglo-Jewish community for the next 17 years. In 1913, Jacobs and fellow lawyer Louis Fitch represented Quebec's Jewish community in the high-profile Plamondon libel case in which the accused leveled accusations of *blood libel and other outrageously calumnious accusations against Jews. Jacobs was also active in many Montreal Jewish associations serving as president of the Baron de Hirsch Institute of Montreal in 1912–14 and as life governor of Mount Sinai Sanatorium, the Young Men's Hebrew Association, and the Hebrew Free Loan Association.

Jacobs entered Liberal electoral politics in 1917 and was elected member of Parliament for the heavily Jewish riding of Montreal-Cartier, a seat he held through six consecutive elections. When first elected in 1917, he was only the second Jewish member of Parliament and the first to hold a seat in the Commons for an extended period. Jacobs was outspoken with respect to issues of importance to the Jewish community. He was particularly vocal in battling against discrimination and for Jewish immigration in an interwar period of increasingly restrictive immigration policies. While a member of Parliament he was also one of the founders of the Jewish Immigrant Aid Society (JIAS) in 1920 and served as president of the Canadian Jewish Congress from 1934 until his death in 1938.

BIBLIOGRAPHY: B. Figler, *Sam Jacobs: Member of Parliament (1871–1938)* (1959).

[Judith E. Szapor (2nd ed.)]

JACOBS, SIMEON (1832–1883), South African lawyer. Jacobs emigrated from England to South Africa in 1860 and became attorney general of British Kaffraria in the Eastern Cape Province. He was successively solicitor general and attorney general for the Eastern Districts and a judge of the Eastern Districts Supreme Court. In 1874 he was elected to the legislative assembly of Cape Colony. In 1872, as acting attorney-general, he was responsible for enacting a bill which abolished state aid to the Anglican Church.

JACOBS, SOLOMON (1777–1827), U.S. civic leader. Jacobs, who was born in Heidelberg, Pa., went to Richmond, Virginia, before 1800. He served as city recorder (1814) and acting mayor (1815), the highest public offices held by any Jew in Richmond's history. Jacobs was elected three times grand master of the Grand Lodge of Masonry in Virginia. He was a president of Beth Shalome Congregation.

[Saul Viener]

JACOBS, SOLOMON (1861–1920), rabbi. Jacobs was born in Sheffield, England. He studied at the People's College in his native town and then at Aria College in Portsmouth. He was ordained there in 1883 and received his rabbinical degree in 1886. While studying for his rabbinical degree, he served as master of the Manchester Jews School and as the minister of the congregation at Newcastle-on-Tyne. In 1886, on the recommendation of the chief rabbi, Jacobs was named minister of the United Congregation in Kingston, Jamaica. He remained there for 15 years. In addition to ministering to his congregation and supporting Jewish charities, Jacobs was also committed to non-sectarian philanthropic activities, and served as the director of the Kingston City Dispensary.

Jacobs continued to demonstrate his dual commitment to both the Jewish community and the general community when in 1901 he became minister of Holy Blossom congregation, the oldest Jewish congregation in Toronto. At Holy Blossom, Jacobs sought to maintain the traditions of Anglo-Orthodoxy even as congregational pressures mounted for Holy Blossom to join the Reform movement. In the end, Jacobs was able to steer a middle course, and it was only after his passing in 1920 that Holy Blossom formally embraced Reform.

As a native English speaker at a time when Yiddish-speaking Jews were flocking to Canada, Jacobs was often called upon to represent the Jewish community in the larger civic society. Jacobs was often a vocal protector of Jewish interests, as when he was a member of a 1906 delegation that tried to secure exemptions for Jews from the Sunday business-closing provisions of the Lord's Day Act or in his fight against missionary activities (especially the Presbyterians) targeting Jews in Toronto's immigrant neighborhood. Jacobs often wrote to the newspaper to challenge a prejudiced remark about Jews or to attack institutional anti-Jewish prejudices at universities and social clubs. A truly public-spirited individual, Jacobs served as vice president of the Associated Charities of Toronto and in 1911 was appointed a member of Toronto's first charity commission, overseeing the operation of charity organizations in the city.

Jacobs was very much an Anglophile and appreciated Great Britain's acceptance of the Jews. On numerous occasions he defended Great Britain and its Empire, and led his congregation in celebration when a monarch reached an important milestone or in expressing grief at times of loss. He was also a member of a small but important group of Anglo-Jewish Orthodox ministers which included Abraham *de Sola of Montreal and his son Meldola, and Herbert Samuel of Winnipeg, who together ministered to the early Canadian Jewish establishment. Their influence in both the Jewish and non-Jewish communities extended well beyond their small numbers.

BIBLIOGRAPHY: A.D. Hart, *The Jew in Canada* (1926), 108; S.A. Speisman, "Jacobs, Solomon," in: *Dictionary of Canadian Biography Online*, at: www.biographi.ca/EN.

[Richard Menkis (2nd ed.)]

JACOB SAMSON OF SHEPETOVKA (d. 1801), rabbi and ḥasidic leader. A celebrated talmudist, he served as rabbi of Shepetovka, Slavuta, and Bar. He was a disciple of *Dov Baer of Mezhirech and Phinehas Shapiro of *Korets. His reputation for scholarship advanced the cause of Ḥasidism among rabbis and scholars. Semilegendary stories attest the impression he left on the greatest rabbis of his generation. He helped to spread Ḥasidism by selling the books of his teacher *Jacob Joseph of Polonnoye. In later years he apparently became a follower of *Baruch b. Jehiel of Medzibezh. He went to Ereẓ Israel (1799?), settling in Tiberias where he died. Some of his halakhic works are referred to in books by contemporaries. A booklet entitled *Divrei No'am* (also other names), describing a (probably legendary) dialogue between him and R. Ezekiel *Landau of Prague, was popular among Ḥasidim.

BIBLIOGRAPHY: Horodetzky, Ḥasidut, index; Dubnow, Ḥasidut, index.

[Adin Steinsaltz]

JACOBSEN, ARNE EMIL (1902–1971), Danish architect. Jacobsen was born and educated in Copenhagen. When he was a student, neoclassicism dominated Danish architecture, but Jacobsen's meetings with Le Corbusier and Mies van der Rohe at exhibitions in Paris and Germany had an enormous effect on his work. His first houses, inspired by Le Corbusier, caused a sensation, and in 1936 he designed and built a series of housing units with staggered perspectives giving all the apartments a good view and a share of sun and light. This established him as Denmark's leading architect. After World War II the Søholme housing scheme established him internationally. He refused to specialize, and designed a wide variety of buildings, including town halls, a stadium, office blocks, and private houses. In 1959, he began to build St. Catherine's College, Oxford. During the same period he completed the famous SAS block in Copenhagen for Scandinavian Air System (1960), using glass curtain walls. In this building and in others Jacobsen designed also the furnishings and appurtenances. From 1956 he was professor of architecture at the Copenhagen Academy of Arts. His works are generally unspectacular and human in scale, and are characterized by refinement in siting, proportion, and detail, and by a sensitive use of materials.

BIBLIOGRAPHY: T. Faber, *Arne Jacobsen* (1964); J. Pedersen, *Arkitekten Arne Jacobsen* (1954).

[Julius Margolinsky]

JACOBSOHN, SIEGFRIED (1881–1926), German critic and left-wing editor. Jacobsohn began his career as the drama critic of various Berlin dailies. In 1905 he founded the theater weekly *Schaubuehne*, and until 1919 published the theater annual, *Das Jahr der Buehne*. Later he altered the direction of his periodical to give it a political character and changed its name to *Weltbuehne* in 1918. During the Weimar Republic the *Weltbuehne* reflected the outlook of independent-minded left-wing intellectuals (called by the Nazis "juedischer Kulturbolschewismus") and was vigorously attacked by the Nazis and the Communists. The periodical was, however, widely read by the German-speaking Jewish intelligentsia throughout Europe. Jacobsohn wrote two books on the Berlin theater, *Das Theater der Reichshauptstadt* (1904), which dealt with the period from 1870, and a sequel, *Max Reinhardt* (1910, 1921[5]). Though not a Zionist, Jacobsohn fought assimilation and Jewish "camouflage", and attacked Jewish journalists who worked for right-wing, antisemitic papers. The last lines he published were an attack on the *Verband nationaldeutscher Juden. His closest collaborator was Kurt *Tucholsky, the letters to whom were published in 1989, 1997[2] (*Briefe an Kurt Tucholsky 1915–1926: "Der beste Brotherr dem schlechtesten Mitarbeiter,"* ed. Richard von Soldenhoff). His collected critical essays on theatre (*Jahre der Buehne*, ed. Walter Karsch and Gerhard Koehler) appeared in 1965. From 2001 the *Jacobsohn-Journal* appeared in cooperation with the *Tucholsky-Blaetter*.

BIBLIOGRAPHY: A. Enseling, *Die Weltbuehne* (1962); J. Ruehle, *Literatur und Revolution* (1960), 185–6; I. Deak, *Weimar Germa-*

ny's Left-Wing Intellectuals (1968), index. **ADD. BIBLIOGRAPHY:** V. Otto, "Der Kampf gegen Wagner ist in Wahrheit ein Kulturkampf". Die Wagner-Rezeption in der Wochenschrift *'Die Schaubühne' / 'Die Weltbühne'* (1905–1933)," in: *Archiv für Musikwissenschaft*, 56 (1999), no. 1, 9–28; S. Oswalt, *Siegfried Jacobsohn. Ein Leben fuer die Weltbuehne. Eine Berliner Biographie* (2000); A. Weigel, "Penthesileen. Siegfried Jacobsohn, "Die Schaubühne" und die Kleist-Ehrung 1911 in Berlin," in: *Beiträge zur Kleistforschung*, 17 (2003), 164–175.

JACOBSON, ANNA (1888–1972), U.S. professor of German literature. Born in Lueneberg, Germany, Jacobson received her doctorate in German literature from the University of Bonn in 1918. Two years after immigrating to the United States in 1922, she became an instructor of German at Hunter College. She was promoted to assistant professor in 1927, associate professor in 1934, and achieved the rank of full professor in 1950. When Hunter wanted to eliminate the German department during World War II, Jacobson, who served as its acting chair from 1941–42, successfully defended the importance of continuing to teach German literature and culture at American universities; she chaired this department from 1947 until her retirement in 1956.

Anna Jacobson published books and articles in both German and English on Hermann Hesse, Franz *Werfel, Heinrich *Heine, and Richard Wagner, as well as Charles Kingsley and Walt Whitman. She became best known for her work on Thomas *Mann. Actively involved in the Modern Language Association, she served as president of Hunter College's chapter of the American Association of University Professors (1936–38) and of the New York City chapter of the American Association of Teachers of German (1949–51). Jacobson helped organize fundraising events to aid refugees from Germany, and, after 1940, she became active in the National Conference of Christians and Jews. Upon her retirement from Hunter College, Jacobson lived in Switzerland.

BIBLIOGRAPHY: Paula E. Hyman and D. Dash Moore (eds.), *Jewish Women in America*, I (1997), 686–87.

[Harriet Pass Freidenreich (2nd ed.)]

JACOBSON, DAN (1929–), South African novelist. Jacobson was born in Kimberley. After graduating from the University of Witwatersrand, he went to London, where he taught in a Jewish school. He returned to South Africa, for a short time joining the family business in Kimberley, but finally settled in England in 1954 and held a chair at University College, London. Jacobson's writing first appeared in 1953 in the American Jewish monthly, *Commentary*, and he became a frequent contributor to many leading British and American periodicals. His fiction and much of his other writing is preoccupied by two major issues: the moral implications of apartheid in South Africa, and the problem of Jewish identity in the modern world. His first two novels, *The Trap* (1955) and *A Dance in the Sun* (1956), deal with the explosive aspects of apartheid, describing dispassionately the kind of incidents which characterize day-to-day relationships between whites and blacks in the rural areas of the Republic. Both novels are dramatic and symbolic in design. *The Price of Diamonds* (1957), set in a fictional version of Kimberley, deals with the illicit diamond trade in South Africa and its impact on the life of a middle-aged Jewish wholesaler. Although it presents a brilliantly comic study in frustration, like its predecessors it is very much a moral fable. Two later works in this genre are *The Evidence of Love* (1960), the story of an interracial love affair set against a background of hatred and false liberalism, and his autobiographical novel, *The Beginners* (1966). Many of Jacobson's polished short stories also deal with Jewish or South African themes. They include the collections *A Long Way from London* (1958), *The Zulu and the Zeide* (1959), which was also the basis for a musical play, and *Beggar My Neighbor* (1964). His novel *The Rape of Tamar* (1970) was based on the biblical story of *Amnon and Tamar. Jacobson's *Evidence of Love* was published in a Russian translation, a unique achievement for an Anglo-Jewish writer. In 1973 there appeared *Inklings*, a collection of short stories, and the *Wonder-Worker*, followed in 1977 by *The Confessions of Josef Baisz* and in 1991 by *Hidden in the Heart*.

BIBLIOGRAPHY: R. Winegarten, in: *Midstream*, 12 (May 1966), 69–73.

[Michael Wade]

JACOBSON, EDWARD (Eddie; 1891–1955), U.S. businessman and longtime friend of President Harry S. Truman. Jacobson, together with Truman, operated a canteen at Fort Sill, Oklahoma, during World War I and in 1919 they opened a haberdashery in Kansas City, Missouri. While their business was initially successful, during the panic of 1921–22 the enterprise collapsed. After Truman became president, Jacobson, aware of the international plight of Jews, discussed with him the refugee and Palestine partition issues (1947). In March 1948, at a critical moment in the period preceding the establishment of the State of Israel, he persuaded the reluctant president to see Chaim *Weizmann, portraying the Zionist leader as his hero and comparing him with Truman's idol, Andrew Jackson. At Jacobson's death, Truman eulogized him for his trustworthiness, warmly recollecting their intimate association.

Jacobson's memoirs of his association with Truman were published in the *American Jewish Archives* (vol. 20 (1968), 3–15).

[Milton Plesur]

JACOBSON, HOWARD (1942–), English novelist and broadcaster. Born in Manchester, Jacobson was educated at Cambridge University, where he was strongly influenced by F.R. Leavis, the English literary critic. He then lectured in English literature at Sydney University, Australia, and, on his return to England, supervised students at Cambridge University. After a variety of jobs in publishing, teaching, and retailing, he was appointed a Lecturer in English at Wolverhampton Polytechnic. This experience was to provide the material for his first novel, *Coming from Behind*, published in 1983. Jacobson, with Wilbur Sanders, also jointly published a critical study entitled *Shakespeare's Magnanimity* (1978).

Jacobson is widely regarded as one of the most original and brilliant comic voices to have emerged in post-war England. *Coming From Behind*, a campus novel, was widely reviewed in England and quickly established Jacobson as a comic writer. According to Jacobson, the novel was meant to be "the last word in academic novels," but, instead, he found himself "writing about gentileness; about what a foreign place England is to a Jew."

Peeping Tom (1984), Jacobson's second and far more substantial novel, examines the consequences of being a culturally dispossessed Jew in a "foreign" country. In this novel, Jacobson's Jewish persona is contrasted with "peeping" Thomas Hardy and the English literary rural tradition. Jacobson, with a considerable ironic punch, then goes on to transform his persona into Hardy's reincarnation. Hardy, that is, provides the "negative" Jew with his identity.

Jacobson's distances himself from what he calls the "super-Anglicization" of many Anglo-Jewish writers in the 1980s who, with a welcome self-assurance, examine and take risks with their Jewish identity in a literary context. Jacobson, for this reason, has been compared to American-Jewish comic writers Woody Allen and Philip Roth. He has also expanded his comic talent in a series of radio broadcasts.

Jacobson's descriptions of the Anglo-Jewish community in *Roots, Schmoots* (1993) were severely criticized by some for their relentless hostility to Orthodox Judaism. Jacobson was awarded the *Jewish Quarterly* / Wingate Prize for fiction in 2001, while his semi-autobiographical novel *The Mighty Walzer* (1999) won the Bollingen Prize for the best comic novel of the year.

BIBLIOGRAPHY: *The Jewish Quarterly*, 32 (1985), 117; *Times Literary Supplement*, (May 3, 1985).

[Bryan Cheyette]

JACOBSON, ISRAEL (1768–1828), German financier and pioneer of Reform Judaism. Born in Halberstadt, Jacobson received an Orthodox education and was destined for the rabbinate. Influenced by *Mendelssohn's writings, he was early attracted to the *Haskalah movement. He did not, however, acquire a methodical secular education and thus lacked fluency in the German language. In 1786 he married Mink, the daughter of Hertz Samson, court-agent of the duchy of Brunswick. With the death of his father-in-law in 1795, he succeeded to the latter's position and titles as *Kammeragent und Landrabbiner des Weserdistrikts*. Influenced by Moses *Mendelssohn and the enlightenment Jacobson saw the best prospects for attaining Jewish emancipation in emphasizing vocational training in the secular education of Jewish children. In 1801, at his own expense, he opened in the small town of Seesen an educational institution for the children of the poor, which became known as the Religions- und Industrieschule (today Jacobson-Gymnasium). By 1805 Christian citizens of Seesen were requesting that their children be admitted to the institution. In 1804 Jacobson was granted citizenship of Brunswick. Due to his influence, the degrading *Leibzoll* (the body tax imposed on Jews) was abolished in Brunswick (1803) and in Baden (1806). He was honored with the title *Mecklenburg-Schweriner Geheimer Finanzrat* in 1806. Hesse-Darmstadt and Baden also granted him titles, and in 1807 he was awarded a Ph.D., *honoris causa*, from the University of Helmstedt. Yet in Brunswick, where he lived, Jacobson still suffered from the intrigues of the officials. His son Meir was not accepted in Brunswick's merchants' guild and his school received little attention from the authorities.

Jacobson saw *Napoleon as the emancipator of the Jews. On the occasion of the *Assembly of Jewish Notables in Paris on May 30, 1806, he addressed an enthusiastic letter to Napoleon. During the same year he published a book entitled *Les premiers pas de la nation juive vers le bonheur sous les auspices du grand monarque Napoléon*, suggesting that the emperor should organize a supreme Jewish council, which would be headed by a patriarch and whose seat would be in Paris. It is possible that Napoleon's idea of the *Sanhedrin stemmed from Jacobson's suggestion. In August 1807 Brunswick became a part of the kingdom of Westphalia, which was ruled by Napoleon's brother, Jerome. After borrowing large sums from Jacobson, Jerome was obliged to sell him state property; he thereby acquired a number of estates. On Jan. 27, 1808, to honor the emancipation of the Jews of Westphalia, Jacobson ordered a commemorative medal from the Berlin artist Abramson. The reverse side of the medal featured two angels symbolizing Judaism and Christianity united in the kingdom of Westphalia. Jacobson was instrumental in convening, in Kassel on Feb. 8, 1808, a gathering of Jewish notables, similar to the one held in Paris, to introduce reform – religious, moral, and civic – among the Jews. The majority of Westphalia's Jews, who were Orthodox, regarded Jacobson's project with suspicion. On Dec. 19, 1808, the Koeniglich Westphaelisches Konsistorium der Israeliten held its first meeting under the leadership of Jacobson rather than that of a rabbi as was the case in France. The consistory discussed questions of religion, education, culture, and the personal status of Jews. Jacobson erected the first synagogues in which services were held according to this program of religious reform. The Consistorialschule was opened in Kassel in 1809 and included a synagogue where portions of prayers were sung in German, sermons were delivered in German, and confirmation ceremonies were performed. On July 17, 1810, the "Temple" in the school of Seesen was inaugurated with a ceremony which included the ringing of a bell and the singing of hymns in German with organ accompaniment. Jacobson conducted the festivities, dressed in the robes of a Protestant clergyman.

After the fall of Napoleon and the fragmentation of the kingdom of Westphalia, Jacobson moved to Berlin, where he continued to work for religious reform. On the occasion of his son's bar mitzvah, on Shavuot 1815, he opened a Reform synagogue in his house. For lack of space the synagogue was removed to the house of the banker Jacob Hertz Beer, where

L. *Zunz and E. *Kley preached. After some eight months the government prohibited the holding of prayers in private houses. On Rosh Ha-Shanah 1817, prayers were again held in a Reform synagogue, but its existence was finally forbidden in 1823, through the influence of the leaders of the Orthodox community. During his last years, Jacobson was broken in health and spirit, and even though he continued his philanthropic activities, he ended his life an embittered and disappointed man. The majority of his ten children, the offspring of two marriages, were baptized.

BIBLIOGRAPHY: S. Bernfeld, *Toledot ha-Reformaẓyon ha-Datit be-Yisrael* (1923²), index; Lazarus, in: MGWJ, 58 (1914), 81–96; Marcus, in: CCARY, 38 (1928), 386–498, incl. bibl.; D. Philipson, *The Reform Movement in Judaism* (1967²), index; G. Ruelf, *Einiges aus der ersten Zeit und ueber den Stifter der Jacobson-Schule in Seesen* (1890); C. Seligman, *Geschichte der juedischen Reformbewegung* (1922), 170ff.; Silberstein, in: JJGL (1927), 100–9; P. Zimmermann, in: *Brunsvicensia Judaica*, 35 (1966), 23–42; H. Schnee, *Die Hoffinanz und der moderne Staat*, 2 (1954), 109–54; 5 (1965), 210–18; M. Eliav, *Ha-Ḥinnukh ha-Yehudi be-Germanyah…* (1961), 96–100, 119–26; J.J. Petuchowski, *Prayerbook Reform in Europe* (1968). **ADD. BIBLIOGRAPHY:** G. Ballin, "Ein Brief Benedict Schotts an Israel Jacobson," in: BLBI, 46–47 (1969), 205–11; J.R. Marcus, *Israel Jacobson – the Founder of the Reform Movement in Judaism* (1972); *Biographisches-Biliographisches Kirchenlexikon*, 18 (2001), 711–17.

[Jacob Rothschild]

JACOBSON, KURT (1904–1991), Portuguese biochemist. Jacobson was born in Berlin, where he received his Ph.D. at the Kaiser Wilhelm Institut under the direction of Carl Neuberg. Jacobson went to Portugal in 1929, where he was allowed to stay because of Nazi persecution in Germany and his scientific contributions. He established the country's first biochemical research unit in the Instituto Rocha Cabral in Lisbon before joining the University of Lisbon (1934), where he became professor of organic chemistry (1955) and later vice rector. His research concerned enzymology. He was president of the Centro Israelita de Portugal.

[Michael Denman (2nd ed.)]

JACOBSON, LUDVIG LEVIN (1783–1843), Danish physician, anatomist, and naturalist. He began his career as an assistant at the Academy of Surgery in Copenhagen and was a lecturer in chemistry at the Veterinary College. He began his studies in comparative anatomy and in 1809 published his discovery in mammals of an organ in the nasal cavity that is largely responsible for the sense of smell. This was known as "Jacobson's organ." Three other anatomical discoveries are associated with his name. He invented an instrument for the crushing of calculi in the bladder, "Jacobson's lithoclast," which was of great importance to surgery. For this invention, the French Academy awarded him a Prix Monthyon. Jacobson was an outstanding scientist and an excellent physician. He had been offered the post of professor of anatomy in the University of Copenhagen on condition that he convert to Christianity. However, he refused to convert. In 1816 Jacobson was appointed professor *honoris causa* by King Frederik VI of Denmark. He also refused to participate in the Scandinavian Naturalists' Congress in Christiania in 1822 because Jews were not admitted into Norway at this time.

BIBLIOGRAPHY: *Bibliotek for Laeger* (1892); *Nordisk Medicin* (1940); *Dansk biografisk Leksikon* (1937); S.R. Kagan, *Jewish Medicine* (1952), 146f.

[Julius Margolinsky]

JACOBSON, NATHAN (1916–), Australian lawyer and communal leader. Born in Kiev, he grew up in Warsaw and went to Australia in 1936. He was active in various aspects of communal and Zionist leadership, especially in promoting economic and political support for Israel. He was president of the Victorian Jewish Board of Deputies (1956–60), president of the Zionist Federation of Australia and New Zealand (1968–70), president of the United Israel Appeal of Australia (1966–69) and president of the Executive Council of Australian Jewry (1970–72 and 1974–76). He was also president of the Federation of Jewish Communities of Southeast Asia and the Far East. He was a founder of the Australian Wool Industries, Ltd., which operates a wool-processing plant in Ashdod.

BIBLIOGRAPHY: W.D. Rubinstein, Australia II, index.

JACOBSON, PAUL HENRICH (1859–1923), German organic chemist. Jacobson was born in Koenigsberg and became professor of chemistry at Heidelberg University in 1889. His considerable contribution to scientific literature dealt mainly with azocompounds. With Victor *Meyer, he wrote *Lehrbuch der organischen Chemie* (2 vols., 1893–1902), the standard textbook of its day. In 1897 he became the general secretary of the German Chemical Society and editor of its journal, *Berichte der Deutschen chemischen Gesellschaft*, considered at the time the major chemical periodical in the world. In 1911 Jacobson transferred to the society's collective literature department, and edited the third edition of Beilstein's *Handbuch der organischen Chemie*, with 5 volumes of supplements, and the first eight volumes of the fourth edition. This encyclopedia of all known chemical compounds is in continuous use in research organizations all over the world. He also edited the further editions of Richter's *Lexikon der Kohlenstoffverbindungen* and the journal *Chemisches Centralblatt*.

BIBLIOGRAPHY: H.M. Smith, *Torchbearers of Chemistry* (1949), 128; Harries, in: *Zeitschrift fuer angewandte Chemie* (1923), 209–10.

[Samuel Aaron Miller]

JACOBSON, SYDNEY, BARON (1908–1988), British editor and editorial director. Jacobson, born in South Africa, started his career as a reporter for the London *Daily Sketch* in 1928. He held various editorial positions on the paper and joined the Daily Mirror Group in 1951. The following year he became political editor of *The Daily Mirror*, the mass-circulation tabloid closely allied to the Labour Party. Ten years later, when the *Mirror* bought Odhams Press, he was appointed editor of *The Daily Herald*, the organ of the Labour Party, and in 1964 he became editor of *The Sun*, which succeeded the *Herald*. He was made editorial director in 1965 and in 1968 was named chairman of Odhams Newspapers. In June 1975 he was awarded a life peerage by the Labour government. Jacobson was a member of the British Press Council from 1968 to 1975.

[Stewart Kampel]

JACOBSON, VICTOR (**Avigdor**; 1869–1935), Zionist leader and diplomat. Born in Simferopol, Crimea, Jacobson joined *Ḥibbat Zion in his early youth and later became a member of the Russisch-Juedischer Wissenschaftlicher Verein (Berlin) and in 1897 of the newly founded Zionist organization. From 1899 he was a member of the Zionist General Council. In 1903 Jacobson strongly opposed the *Uganda Scheme and was one of the organizers of the *Kharkov Conference in opposition to *Herzl. In 1906 he became head of the Beirut office of the Anglo-Palestine Company and in 1908 of its branch in Constantinople, which was registered there as the Anglo-Levantine Banking Company. He simultaneously became the unofficial diplomatic representative of the Zionist organization in Turkey. In 1913 Jacobson was elected a member of the Zionist Executive and moved to Berlin. In this capacity, he headed during World War I the Copenhagen office of the Zionist organization, from which he maintained contact with all the branches of the movement. He issued the "Copenhagen Manifesto" (Oct. 28, 1918), which outlined postwar Jewish demands with regard to Palestine and equal rights and cultural autonomy in the Diaspora. Jacobson moved to the new seat of the Zionist headquarters in London in 1918. At the 12th Zionist Congress (1921) he and Arthur *Ruppin headed a small group that demanded close Arab-Jewish cooperation and laid the ideological foundations for *Berit Shalom (which was founded in Jerusalem in 1926). Jacobson resigned from the Executive at the Congress, and from 1925 until his death he represented the Zionist organization and the *Jewish Agency in Paris and at the the League of Nations in Geneva. He was the first Zionist "career diplomat." From 1933 he again was a member of the Zionist Executive.

During his activities in Turkey (1908–13), Jacobson acquired for the Zionist Movement the French daily *Courrier d'Orient*, which was renamed *Jeune Turc* and edited by Vladimir *Jabotinsky. In 1927 he founded and coedited (with Albert *Cohen) *La Revue Juive* in Paris. In 1928 the Comité des Amis du Sionisme, which Jacobson had formed, began publication of *La Palestine Nouvelle*.

BIBLIOGRAPHY: L. Lipsky, *A Gallery of Zionist Profiles* (1956), 94–99; R. Lichtheim, *Geschichte des deutschen Zionismus* (1954), 204–6; idem, *She'ar Yashuv, Zikhronot Ẓiyyoni mi-Germanyah* (1953), 191ff.; A. Ruppin, *Pirkei Ḥayyai*, 2–3 (1969), passim; Y. Gruenbaum, *Penei ha-Dor* (1957), 329–32; A. Boehm, *Die Geschichte der zionistischen Bewegung*, 2 vols. (1935–37), index.

[Oskar K. Rabinowicz]

JACOBSTHAL, GUSTAV (1845–1912), German musicologist. Born in Pyritz, Pomerania, Jacobsthal studied music and history at the University of Berlin (1863–70) and wrote a Ph.D. thesis on mensural notation in the 12th and 13th century. Jacobsthal was a professor of musicology at the University of Strasbourg from 1875 to 1905, the only person to hold such a post at a German university at the time. He was a pioneer in the application of historical and philological research in the study of early medieval music. Among his famous disciples were F. Genrich and P. Wagner. His writings are mainly on the music of the Middle Ages, comprising his books *Die Mensuralnotenschrift des 12. und 13. Jahrhunderts* (1871, rep. 1973) and *Die chromatische Alteration im liturgischen Gesange der abendlaendischen Kirche* (1897, rep. 1970).

BIBLIOGRAPHY: NG[2]; MGG[2]; F. Genrich, *Die Strassburger Schule fuer Musikwissenschaft* (1940).

[Amnon Shiloah (2nd ed.)]

JACOBUS APELLA VICEDOMINUS (late 11th–mid-12th century), a baptized Jew of Prague who was chief administrator of Duke Vratislav of Bohemia (1110–40). His story was first told by the Bohemian chronicler Cosmas of Prague, but the historical basis of it is hard to determine. Apparently baptized in 1096, he made a dramatic return to Judaism in 1124, defiling an altar which had been erected in a synagogue and throwing Christian relics into a sink. Prague Jewry saved him from the death penalty by paying a high ransom.

BIBLIOGRAPHY: Steinherz, in: JGGJČ, 2 (1930), 17–47.

JACOBY, JOHANN (1805–1877), Prussian politician. Born in Koenigsberg (East Prussia), Jacoby studied medicine but devoted his life to politics. As a young man, he represented the interests of his fellow Jews, publishing in 1833 a memorandum in defense of Jewish emancipation. He advocated religious reform and participated in a commission charged with revising the order of worship. Gradually his interests became concentrated on general Prussian and German matters and, without denying his Judaism, Jacoby took up the struggle for a liberal and democratic Germany. In 1848 he was elected to the Prussian Landtag, taking an active stand against the reactionary attitude of *Frederick William IV. As a member of a deputation to the king, Jacoby is alleged to have remarked that it was the former's "misfortune" that he "would not hear the truth!" In 1849 he was elected, together with six other Jews, to the German Nationalversammelung in Frankfurt. Forced into the background during the years of reaction that followed, he came to the fore again in the 1860s, with the advent of a new liberal era. In 1863 he entered the Prussian House of Representatives, linking himself with the left wing of the Progressive Party and, after a split in the party, with the Social Democratic camp. Unlike most Jewish politicians, he remained in opposition even after Germany's success in the war against France, and combated the military state and its annexationist policy. Jacoby was one of the ideologists of German democracy; his writings and speeches were published in 1872–77 and 1889.

BIBLIOGRAPHY: Adam, in: *Historische Zeitschrift*, 143 (1931), 48–76; J. Toury, *Die politischen Orientierungen der Juden in Deutschland* (1966), 39–42 and index; E. Hamburger, *Juden im oeffentlichen*

Leben Deutschlands (1968), 189–200; E. Silberner, in: *International Review of Social History*, 14 (1969), 353–411; idem, in: *Archiv fuer Sozialgeschichte*, 9 (1969).

[Reuven Michael]

JACOBY, OSWALD (1902–1984), U.S. bridge champion. Born in New York, Jacoby served in the U.S. Army in World War I and later worked as an actuary. He rapidly established himself as one of the leading U.S. bridge players and belonged to a group called "The Four Aces," which developed a new system of bidding at bridge that attracted considerable attention.

During World War II Jacoby was an officer in the U.S. Navy. During the Korean War, he was a naval commander and helped to prepare the ground for the Panmunjom armistice talks of 1951.

In 1950, he became the daily bridge columnist for Newspaper Enterprise Association. His column, which was exceptionally popular, was published in several hundred newspapers. He established a record on April 22, 1982, when his 10,000th article was printed.

Jacoby won recognition as the United States' leading bridge player and was awarded the McKenny trophy for the Bridge Player of the Year in 1959, 1961, and 1962. He pioneered many bidding concepts, such as Forcing 2 No Trump; Jacoby Transfer Bids; and Weak Jump Overcalls. An expert in backgammon as well, Jacoby captured the World Championship of Backgammon in 1973. In 1965 he was elected to the Bridge Hall of Fame, and in 1983 he was selected as Bridge Personality of the Year by the International Bridge Press Association.

Jacoby wrote many books on cards and other games, including *Oswald Jacoby on Poker* (1940, 1947²); *How to Figure the Odds* (1947); *Complete Canasta* (1950); *What's New in Bridge* (1954); *How to Win at Gin Rummy* (1959); *The Backgammon Book* (1979); *Penny Ante and Up* (1979); and *Jacoby on Card Games* (with J. Jacoby, 1989).

[Ruth Beloff (2nd ed.)]

JADASSOHN, JOSEF (1863–1936), German dermatologist. Jadassohn, who was born at Liegnitz, studied at Breslau and was professor and director of the dermatological clinic at the University of Berne, Switzerland, from 1896. From 1917 until his retirement in 1931 he was professor of dermatology at the University of Breslau and became famous for his work on skin and venereal diseases. Jadassohn devoted much of his time to research. Maculopapular erythematosa, a scaling skin affection, is known as "Jadassohn's disease" because he first identified it and his name is also associated with the Jadassohn-Bloch skin test for allergic conditions. He described the patch test and nevus sebaceus (1895). His publications include *Krankheiten der Haut und die venerischen Krankheiten* written in collaboration with Albert Neisser (1900–01) and *Allgemeine Aetologie, Pathologie, Diagnose und Therapie der Gonorrhoe* (1910). He edited *Handbuch der Haut-und Geschlechtskrankheiten* (1927–32) and coedited the *Archiv fuer Dermatologie und Syphilis*.

BIBLIOGRAPHY: S.R. Kagan, *Jewish Medicine* (1952), 423f.; *Biographisches Lexikon der hervorragenden Aerzte* (1932), 695.

[Suessmann Muntner]

JADASSOHN, SALOMON (1831–1902), composer, music theorist, and conductor. Born in Breslau, Jadassohn studied in Leipzig and then under Liszt in Weimar (1849–52). He came back to Leipzig, where he studied privately with Moritz Hauptmann and later developed and worked as a multifaceted musician. In the 1860s he conducted several groups, among them the Leipzig synagogue choir. Later he focused on composition and theory. He composed numerous works in the general style of Brahms, especially for piano, but also orchestral, vocal, and chamber music. Jadassohn is chiefly remembered as a theorist. He wrote textbooks for all major subjects of music theory, combined in the comprehensive project *Musikalische Kompositionslehre* (1883–89), including *Harmonielehre* (1883, 1903), *English Manual of Harmony* (1912), *Kontrapunkt* (1884), *Kanon und Fuge* (1884), and *Die Formen in den Werken der Tonkunst* (1889). Jadassohn's vertical theoretical orientation, his inclination to discover many modulations in chromatic passages, and the lack of almost any examples make his books difficult for the modern reader. His students include Busoni, Chadwick, Delius, and Grieg.

BIBLIOGRAPHY: NG²; MGG; B. Hiltner. *Salomon Jadassohn, Komponist – Musiktheoretiker – Pianist – Pädagoge: eine Dokumentation über einen vergessener Leipziger Musiker des 19. Jahrhunderts* (1995).

[Yossi Goldenberg (2nd ed.)]

JADDUA, high priest in the Second Temple period. Jaddua was a great-grandson of *Eliashib and commenced to minister in the priesthood c. 400 B.C.E. According to Nehemiah 12:11, his father's name was Jonathan, but many are of the opinion that the reading there should be *Johanan, as in Nehemiah 12:22. Josephus (Ant. 11:317–47) tells of a high priest called Jaddua who was a contemporary of Alexander the Great. When Alexander reached Syria, he sent envoys to the high priest requesting him to transfer his allegiance to him, but he refused because of his oath of loyalty to *Darius. This enraged Alexander, who marched against Jerusalem with his army. Jaddua prayed to God and in the night had a dream which gave him courage. He went out to welcome Alexander, clothed in his priestly garments, together with his fellow priests and all the people of Jerusalem, clad in white. When Alexander saw the high priest, he prostrated himself before him, explaining that he was bowing to the God to whom this priest ministered; that the priest had appeared to him in a dream and encouraged him to venture forth against the Persians, and assured him of victory. He subsequently acceded to Jaddua's requests on behalf of the Jews. According to Josephus, Jaddua died a short time after the death of Alexander and transmitted his office to his son Onias. Josephus also states that Manasseh, the son-in-law of Sanballat and the first priest of the Samaritan temple on Mt. Gerizim, was the brother of Jaddua. It is difficult to reconcile Josephus' statement that Jaddua lived in the time of Alexander with the account in Nehemiah, and it appears that the story is a mere legend attached to the name of Jaddua. In the Talmud a similar story is ascribed to Simeon the Just (Meg. Ta'an. 339–40; Yoma 69a).

BIBLIOGRAPHY: Guttmann, in: *Tarbiz*, 11 (1939/40), 271–94; R. Marcus, in: Loeb Classics, *Josephus*, 6 (1937), 498–511 (Appendix B); Schalit, in: *Sefer Yoḥanan Lewy* (1949), 252–72; Klausner, Bayit Sheni, 2 (1951^2), 47, 50, 96, 105.

[Uriel Rappaport]

JADĪD AL-ISLĀM, a term meaning "new Muslims," applied mainly in *Persia to Jews who were converted by force to *Islam but who, in many cases, adhered secretly to their former religion (see *Anusim). The term is associated especially with the crypto-Jewish community of *Meshed under the Kajar dynasty from 1839 onward but also with the victims of forced mass conversions in Persia in the 17th and 18th centuries, under *Abbas I and *Abbas II, and in Bukhara. Many Jadīd al-Islām fled to *Afghanistan, others settled in Ereẓ Israel in 1929–30. About 70 converted to the Bahai faith in the town of Torbat, but after a short while 67 of them returned to Judaism. A few members of the Hakimi family converted to Islam and deserted the community of Jadīd al-Islām. At the end of the 19th century the Jadīd al-Islām in Meshed lived as Jews, almost openly, and under the rule of Riza Shah (1925–41) they felt more protected, but still maintained the status of Muslims and were recognized as Jadīd al-Islām. In 1936 about 550 Jadīd al-Islām families lived in Meshed with 12 synagogues (in private buildings) and four schools. In 1954 *Oẓar ha-Torah* set up in Meshed a Jewish school for the Jadīd al-Islām. These Jews suffered from the mobs in 1946. The Sephardi chief rabbi, Ben-Zion Meir Hai *Ouziel, decided that the Jadīd al-Islām did not have any problem of *mamzerut*. The Jadīd al-Islām had many special *minhagim* in certain areas of life, especially child marriage. They had their own songs and their dead were buried in a cemetery bought by the Jadīd al-Islām. From the end of the 19th century until the 1940s most members of this community returned to Judaism. In 1973 only three Jewish families lived in Meshed and in 1995, 12 families.

BIBLIOGRAPHY: Fischel, in: *Zion*, 1 (1935), 49–74. **ADD. BIBLIOGRAPHY:** A. Neimark, *Massa be-Ereẓ ha-Kedem*, ed. A. Yaari (1947); R. Kashani, *Anusei Meshed* (1979); A. Levy, in: *Pe'amim*, 6 (1981), 57–73; D. Littman, in: *The Wiener Library Bulletin*, 32 (1979), 2–15; 35 (1988), A. Netzer, in: *Pe'amim*, 42 (1990), 127–56; B.Z. Yehoshua-Raz, *Mi-Nidaḥei Yisrael be-Afganistan le-Anusei Meshed be-Iran* (1992), 99–156; R. Patai, *Jadid al-Islam "New Muslims" of Meshed* (1997); A. Netzer, in: *Pe'amim*, 94–95 (2003), 262–67.

[Walter Joseph Fischel / Leah Bornstein-Makovetsky (2nd ed.)]

JADLOWKER, HERMANN (1878–1953), tenor. Born in Riga, Jadlowker began his operatic career in Cologne in 1889. Invited to Berlin in 1901, he sang at the Berlin State Opera for five years and in 1910 made his U.S. debut at the Metropolitan Opera, New York. Among his important roles were the Prince in the world premiere of Engelbert Humperdinck's *Koenigskinder* (1910), and Florindo in Ermanno Wolf-Ferrari's *Le Donne curiose* in its first U.S. performance in 1912. He returned to Berlin in 1913, was cantor in Riga from 1929 to 1938, and then settled in Tel Aviv as a voice teacher.

JAECKLIN, JUD (Judah b. Judah; 14th century), Ulm moneylender. Jaecklin was first mentioned in 1375 when the city of Ulm (Germany) borrowed 2,500 gulden from him. On Sept. 5, 1376, he was put under an imperial ban by *Charles IV, at the request of a feudal enemy of Ulm, for nonpayment of a debt of 4,000 gulden. When the city refused to hand him over, Charles set siege to it; however, he was forced to withdraw and to repeal the ban a year later. As revenge Charles released Duke Henry of Werdenberg, whose lands had suffered most during the siege, from his debts to Jaecklin. In 1379 Jaecklin's residence permit for Ulm was not renewed. He removed to *Constance and in 1380 requested the aid of the municipality in retrieving his property from Ulm. In 1393 Ulm complained that Jaecklin had settled in *Noerdlingen without permission and without relinquishing his citizenship, and that he was libeling the city of Ulm there. As Ulm had previously confiscated his property, it considered that it had a right to collect the debts due to him.

BIBLIOGRAPHY: E. Nuebling, *Die Judengemeinden des Mittelalters* (1896), 327–43; H. Dicker, *Die Geschichte der Juden in Ulm* (1937), 23–32; M. Stern, in ZGJD, 7 (1937), 244f.

JAEL (Heb. יָעֵל), wife of Heber the Kenite. Jael slew *Sisera in the war of *Deborah and *Barak against the Canaanites (Judg. 4–5). His army routed by Israel, Sisera fled on foot to Jael's tent, where he was offered hospitality and security, only to be slain by her while he slept (4:17–22; the details of the deed differ somewhat in Judges 5: 24–27, and permit an interpretation first voiced in rabbinic literature (below) that Jael seduced Sisera). Deborah's prophecy to Barak that the Lord would "sell Sisera into the hand of a woman" (4:9) was thus fulfilled. Jael's deed received high praise from Deborah (5:24–27). The story has political significance as well as drama. Jael's husband, "Heber the Kenite" (4:11, 17), is described as a descendant of Jethro the father-in-law of Moses. His clan had apparently been allied to *Jabin, Israel's enemy (*ibid.*), and the slaying of Sisera indicated a switch of loyalties back to Israel. It should be noted that an earlier reference to Jael in the Song of Deborah (5:6) does not seem to be to the same person. The name Jael ("wild goat") appears in Ugaritic texts as that of a man.

[Nahum M. Sarna / S. David Sperling (2nd ed.)]

In the Aggadah

Jael's action in killing Sisera teaches that a transgression performed with good intent is more meritorious than a commandment performed with no intent (Hor. 10b). But for her action, the children of the matriarchs would have been destroyed (Gen. R. 48:15). She slew Sisera with a hammer and tent pin, rather than a spear or sword, in accordance with the biblical commandment (Deut. 22:5) prohibiting the use of weapons by women (Targ. Yer., Judges 5:26). She was a descendant of Jethro, but whereas he received a redeemer (Moses) who was fleeing from the enemy (Pharaoh), Jael received an enemy (Sisera) who was fleeing from the redeemer (Barak), and killed him (Ex. R. 4:2). She was so attractive, that even her voice roused desire (Meg. 15a). Although Sisera had seven sexual relations with her on the day he fled from battle, she derived no gratification from these acts (Yev. 103a; Naz. 23b). She gave Sisera to drink of the milk of her breasts (Nid. 55b). Deborah blessed Jael and she was considered even greater than Sarah, Rebekah, Rachel, and Leah (Naz. 23b).

BIBLIOGRAPHY: EM, 3 (1958, includes bibliography), s.v.; Ginzberg, Legends, 4 (1913), 37–38, 6 (1928), 198; I. Ḥasida, *Ishei ha-Tanakh* (1964), 200–1. **ADD. BIBLIOGRAPHY:** B. Halpern, in: HTR, 76 (1983), 379–401: M. Brettler, *Judges* (2001), 61–79 (extensive history of research on Judges 4–5).

JAÉN, city in Andalusia, southern Spain. A Jewish community existed there in the Muslim period. The Ibn Shaprut family originated in Jaén, whence Isaac b. Ezra, the father of *Hisdai ibn Shaprut, moved to Córdoba. The Jews in this period engaged in all branches of commerce, and especially in tanning. In the 11th century Jews from Jaén even emigrated to Ereẓ Israel. After the murder of *Joseph ha-Nagid, the son of *Samuel ha-Nagid, when a rebellion broke out in Jaén, the Jews had to pay a heavy indemnity. At the end of the 11th century the community was headed by R. Isaac who corresponded with Isaac *Alfasi. The community was brought to an end during the *Almohad persecution.

In 1246 Jaén was conquered by Ferdinand III of Castile. It was not until 1290 that the Jews of Jaén were required to send a representative to the king to negotiate on the amount of annual tax for which the community was liable. The community became important by the middle of the 14th century when it consisted of about 300 families. The Jews in Jaén pursued the same occupations as the rest of Andalusian Jewry, cultivating vineyards and engaging in crafts and commerce. As customary in that period, many had business partnerships with Christians. The community suffered during the civil war between Pedro the Cruel and Henry of Trastamara in the 1360s. Pedro, who called the Muslims of Granada to his aid, permitted them to take the Jews of Jaén captive and sell them into slavery. The community then numbered 300 families.

No details are known about the fate of the Jews in Jaén during the persecutions of 1391, but the number of Jews who left the faith increased. In the second half of the 15th century the number of Jews in Jaén declined greatly. Throughout the area within the Kingdom of Jaén there was no *aljama* or organized community left. While the number of Jews declined, that of the Conversos rose. In 1473 riots against the *Conversos in Jaén broke out. The riots show the cruel and totalitarian policy pursued by the local authorities and the desire of the people to deprive the Conversos of their wealth. Ten years later an edict of expulsion was issued against the Jews in Jaén as in all the other Andalusian communities. In that year the Inquisition established a tribunal at Jaén, which was the third to be established in the Iberian peninsula, after Seville and Córdoba. This was surely due to the large number of Conversos who resided in Andalusia. Sources found in local archives offer ample information on the Conversos, many of whom were crypto-Jews. These sources compensate for the loss of the files of the tribunal of Jaén. We now have the many names of Conversos or crypto-Jews who were tried and condemned by the Inquisition. Apparently the tribunal did not continue to sit in Jaén but returned there in 1509 and was reconstituted as a district court. In 1526 it was amalgamated with the tribunal in Córdoba. The autos-da-fé took place in Santa María square, in front of the Cathedral.

The Conversos continued to live in what used to be the Jewish quarter, renamed Santa Cruz. The synagogue was in the street called Santa Cruz.

BIBLIOGRAPHY: H.C. Lea, *A History of the Inquisition of Spain*, 1 (1906), 548; Baer, Urkunden, index; Baer, Spain, index; Baer, Toledot, 65, 219; Ashtor, Korot, 1 (1966^2), 111, 210–1; 2 (1966), 91–92; Suárez Fernández, Documentos, 326ff. **ADD. BIBLIOGRAPHY:** L. Coronas Tejada, in: *Proceedings, 7th World Congress of Jewish Studies*, vol. 4 (1977), 141–77; idem, in: *Boletín del Instituto de Estudios Giennenses*, 97 (1978), 79–105; idem, in: *Proceedings, 8th World Congress of Jewish Studies*, vol. 2 (1982), 29–34; idem, in: *Miscelánea de estudios árabes y hebraicos*, 31:2 (1982), 101–17; idem, *Conversos and Inquisition in Jaén*, (1988).

[Haim Beinart / Yom Tov Assis (2nd ed.)]

JAFFA (Joppa; יָפוֹ), ancient port city in the central sector of the Ereẓ Israel coast. The meaning of the name Jaffa (Yaffo) is "lovely" or "pretty." The ancient city was built on a hill jutting out slightly from the coastline on the west and overlooking the open sea. At the foot of the rise on the western side extends the port, which was protected by a chain of rocks jutting out above the water; on the northern side there is a small bay that is protected from the southwest winds but open to the stormy winds from the north. Storms were probably overcome by using the mouth of the Yarkon River ("Me-Jarkon," Josh. 19:46) at a distance of 3.7 mi. (6 km.) from the northern corner, where boats took shelter in the winter. *Jonah the prophet, unwilling to fulfill his mission to Nineveh, boarded a ship at Jaffa bound for Tarshish (Jonah 1:3). Some scholars assume that the expression "the Jaffa sea," mentioned in the Bible in connection with the transport of the cedars of Lebanon to the Temple (II Chron. 2:15; Ezra 3: 7) and in Josephus in connection with the defense line built by Alexander *Yannai "from the mountainside above Antipatris to the coast at Jaffa sea" (Wars 1:99), is a reference to the jetties of the Yarkon at Tell Kadadi and Tell Qasīle. Archaeological excavations were conducted at the Jaffa tell from 1955 by Y. Kaplan on behalf of the Tel Aviv-Jaffa Antiquities Museum.

Early History

The oldest remains found are pieces of wall of sun-dried clay bricks in the eastern part of the ancient Jaffa fortress and dated from the 16th century B.C.E. Remains were also found from the 15th to the 13th centuries B.C.E., which was the period of

Egyptian rule in Jaffa. The name Jaffa is mentioned among the Canaanite cities that were conquered by Thutmosis III in 1469 B.C.E. a folktale that came into being about 200 years afterward describes the conquest of Jaffa by Thutmosis' military chief by cunning, rather than by war, through introducing soldiers into the fort in baskets. In the *El-Amarna letters, Jaffa is mentioned as an Egyptian district in which the king's stores were located. In the Anastasi Papyrus I, from the time of Ramses II (13th century B.C.E.), the Egyptian fort is described as being located on the side of the Canaanite city and containing workshops and arms stores. Excavations uncovered three stones of the fortress gate from the 13th century with inscriptions of the five titles of Ramses II.

The remains of the fortress gate (fourth level in the excavations) belong to the period of Israelite settlement, in the second half of the 13th century, and near the threshold a bronze bar that supported the corner of the left gate was uncovered. There are no written documents from this period; the description of the border of the tribe of Dan, which ran "over against Jaffa" (Josh. 19:46) is now dated by most scholars to the Davidic period. The appearance of the Sea Peoples at the beginning of the 12th century B.C.E. left its mark in the signs of destruction at the fourth level of settlement and in the few Philistine remains. However, there is basis for the supposition that the connection between the Greek legend of Perseus and Andromeda and the rocks off Jaffa is rooted in this period. It appears that Jaffa remained outside the boundary of Israelite settlement. Excavations have uncovered a part of the fortifications from the ninth century comprising a glacis covered with slabs of stone, beneath which were alternate strata of pressed earth and sun-dried clay bricks whose general width in some place reached four to five meters.

In the last third of the eighth century B.C.E., the period of the Assyrian invasions of Ereẓ Israel, Jaffa became, from what can be seen, part of the "province of Ashdod." At the end of the eighth century it was under the protection of Ashkelon, according to Sennacherib, king of Assyria, who conquered it together with Bene-Berak and Bet Dagon on his way to fight Hezekiah, king of Judah, and his Egyptian allies. In the fifth century B.C.E. the coastal cities were held by Tyre and Sidon with the support of the Persian rulers. Jaffa was under the control of Sidon according to the description of the coastal cities of Syria and Ereẓ Israel of Pseudo-Scylax (fourth century B.C.E.) and the inscription of Eshmunezer, king of Sidon, which relates that the "lord of kings" (the king of Persia) gave Sidon two cities on the Ereẓ Israel coast – Jaffa and Dor – as a sign of his gratitude. A Sidonian stone dedicatory inscription was discovered in 1892 in Jaffa and mentions the establishment of a Sidonian temple in the city. To these should be added the discovery of a part of the wall of the Sidonian fortress uncovered in excavations in Jaffa in 1955.The Hellenistic Period

After the Macedonian conquest and the death of Alexander the Great, Jaffa passed from one military commander to another until finally, in about 301 B.C.E., it fell, together with the rest of the country, to the Ptolemaic governors of Egypt. Jaffa quickly became a Greek city and its name changed to Ioppe (Ἰόππη), which is a Greek-sounding name. From the period of the Ptolemaic dynasty, which lasted a few hundred years, it is known that coins were minted in Jaffa during the reign of Ptolemy II and III bearing the name Ioppe. Another source of information on Jaffa in this period is the *Zeno Papyri (mid-third century B.C.E.). In the excavations of Jaffa in 1961, a cave of tombs built of hewn-out stones and part of a dedicatory inscription in Greek that mentions the name of Ptolemy Philopater (the IV), from the end of the third century B.C.E., were found. At the beginning of the second century B.C.E. Ereẓ Israel, and Jaffa together with it, was conquered by Antiochus III of the Seleucid dynasty.

The Roman Period

In the time of the Hasmonean revolt, Judah Maccabee attacked the city and burned the harbor in retaliation against its foreign inhabitants for drowning about 200 Jaffa Jews (II Macc. 12:3–7). Afterward, his brother Jonathan conquered the city, and following his death, Simon finally annexed it to the Jewish state, after its military governor, Jonathan b. Absalom, drove the foreigners out of the city: "And he turned aside to Joppa, and took possession of it for he had heard that they were minded to deliver the stronghold unto the men of Demetrius; and he placed a garrison there to keep it" (I Macc. 12:34). During the reign of Jonathan the Hasmonean, the Syrians again made repeated attempts to regain the income from Jaffa, but with the aid and political support of the Roman senate the city remained in Jewish hands (Jos., Ant.,13:261). Excavations have uncovered a portion of the fortress wall from the Hasmonean period that was built on the remains of an older fortress, which belongs to the end of the third century, or the beginning of the second century.

With Pompey's conquest of Ereẓ Israel (66 B.C.E.), Jaffa was separated from the Jewish state and became, as did the other coastal cities, a free city in the district given over to the authority of the Syrian commissioner. Only in 47 did Julius Caesar return the city to Judea (Jos., Ant., 14:202, 205). In 38 Herod captured Jaffa on his way to Jerusalem to establish his reign there. Afterward he built the harbor of Caesarea, which was a strong competitor to Jaffa. During the reign of Antony in the east, Jaffa, together with the other coastal cities, was given to Cleopatra, the queen of Egypt; only in the year 30 was it returned to Herod by Augustus Caesar. A part of a house that was uncovered in the excavations belongs to the Augustan period. The structure included an entrance yard, a water hole, and a wall that was part of a room with an entrance. Jaffa is mentioned in the Christian chronicles in the context of the stories of Tabitha (Dorcas) and Simon the tanner. The New Testament contains the story of the miracle of Tabitha, who was resurrected by Peter (Acts 9:36–42). While in Jaffa, Peter stayed in the house of Simon the tanner and on his roof dreamed the dream that has been interpreted to allow Christians to eat the flesh of unclean animals. It was also there that he heard the voice calling him to convert pagans, as well as Jews, to Christianity (Acts 10:9ff.). With the outbreak of war with the Romans, Cestius Gallus destroyed Jaffa, but the city was quickly rebuilt by the Jews. They stationed a fleet of ships in the sea that attacked the ships passing on the maritime route from Egypt to Syria. Prior to his arrival in Jerusalem, *Vespasian sent foot soldiers and cavalry to Jaffa, under cover of darkness, and they surprised the defenders of the city. The startled inhabitants quickly fled the city to take shelter in the boats, but, to add to the tragedy, a stormy wind broke early in the morning and dashed the boats and those in them against the rocks of the shore. The survivors were massacred by the Romans, who were waiting on the shore (Jos., Wars, 3:414–431). Vespasian then destroyed the city and built a fort on its ruins that contained a guard from the Tenth Legion. In the excavations, a piece of a tile was discovered with the seal of the Tenth Roman Legion on it.

Jaffa was rebuilt, it appears, still during the reign of Vespasian, who turned it into an autonomous city by the name of Flavia Ioppe. This is known from the coins that were minted during the reign of Heliogabalus (218–222), on which this name is mentioned. Three identical inscriptions engraved on a stone uncovered during the excavations tell of the Jewish community in Jaffa during the period between the destruction of the Second Temple and the Bar Kokhba revolt. The inscriptions contain the name "Yehudah," who was the inspector of weights and measures in the Jaffa market during the reign of Trajan. Another discovery is the floor of a cellar that belongs to the period of Trajan; above it were found many clay jars and bronze and silver coins. The Mishnah and Talmud, as well as tombstones discovered in the cemetery of Jaffa Jews in Abu-Kabir, are sources of information on Jewish Jaffa during the second to fourth centuries C.E. Among the scholars of Jaffa mentioned in the Talmud are R. Ada (Meg. 16b; Ta'an. 16b), R. Naḥman (Lev. R. 6:5), R. Yudan (Lev. R. 20:10), and others. From the tombstones it is possible to learn of the occupations and origins of the dead. It becomes clear that the Jews of Jaffa during this period lived in neighborhoods according to their country of origin. Jews from Alexandria, Cyrenaica, Cappadocia, and other places are mentioned on the stones. Among the professions were trades in cloth, perfumes, rags, fishing, etc. Jerome, who visited Jaffa in 382, expressed his surprise at the sight of "the harbor of fleeing Jonah"; he also tells that he saw the rock on which Andromeda was bound.

From this period until the Arab conquest (see below), the information about Jaffa becomes more scarce. Cyril the Holy, from Alexandria, who wrote during the first half of the fifth century, described Jaffa as an important commercial center and a port of exit for all travelers from Judea to the countries of the Mediterranean. During this period, it seems that after its Christian population grew, Jaffa became the seat of the episcopate, and thus the name of the bishop of Jaffa, Phidus, is mentioned in the list of the church council that was convened in 431 in Ephesus. The name of another bishop, Elias, who participated in the council that convened in Jerusalem in 536, is also mentioned.

Arab Period (636–1099)

In 636 Jaffa fell to the Muslims. While Ramleh flourished as the capital of the Palestine region, the importance of the port of Jaffa increased; it took over trade from Caesarea. Jaffa served as a storage center for merchant shipping and as the port of entry for Christian and Jewish pilgrims. Ahmad ibn Ṭūlūn, the ruler of Egypt and Palestine, fortified Jaffa in 878. However, its security and trade were endangered from time to time by riots and anarchy. In 1050 Ibn Baṭlān, an Arab geographer, wrote of the town "[Jaffa is] a town of starvation. There is not even a teacher for small children in it." In the early tenth century R. Joseph, the father of Saadiah Gaon, died there. A Hebrew letter dated 1071, which was found in the Cairo **Genizah*, reports the confiscation of merchandise in the port of Jaffa. A bill of divorce (*get*) written in Jaffa in 1077 proves that it had a rabbinical court at the period.

Crusader Period (1099–1268)

Jaffa was conquered by the Crusaders in the summer of 1099, prior to their conquest of Jerusalem. Genoese ships, which anchored in Jaffa harbor, brought supplies to the besiegers of Jerusalem. Jaffa also served as a base and starting point for the Crusader conquest of other coastal towns as far north as Beirut. In 1102 twenty pilgrim ships carrying Crusaders sank in the harbor during a storm. Thus "to go to Jaffa" in German acquired the connotation of "to go to Hell." In the 12th century during the first four Crusades, Jaffa was the main gateway to Jerusalem. It was the capital of the feudal kingdom of Jerusalem, which from 1157 on included Ashkelon and its surroundings. The county of Jaffa had the right to mint its own coinage. The inhabitants were a mixture of European and Oriental Christians, who mingled within a French-speaking "Palestinian nation." In 1170 Benjamin of Tudela reported that he found only one Jew in the town. In 1196 the Ayyubid ruler al-Malik al-Adil, the brother of Saladin, conquered Jaffa and destroyed it.

In the 13th century – during the latter half of the Crusades period – Jaffa failed to retain the importance it had in the preceding period; trade and shipping moved to Acre. Nonetheless, its strategic importance remained, as is evident from the fact that both Frederick II, the Holy Roman Emperor, who led the Sixth Crusade (1228), and King Louis IX of France, who led the Seventh Crusade (1248), fortified the town. During this second period the Crusaders acted with tolerance toward the Jews. The small Jewish community in Jaffa was comprised of craftsmen, potters, and glaziers (many of whom went to Europe). Their influence is noticeable in the contemporary pottery of southern France. Jaffa passed into the hands of the Khuwarizm conquerors in 1244 and to the Mongols in 1260; in 1268 it was finally conquered by the Mamluk sultan Baybars, who razed it to the ground and massacred its population.

Mamluk Period (1268–1517)

At the beginning of the *Mamluk period Jaffa was rebuilt and its port resumed operations, but in the mid-14th century, when European crusaders renewed their plans and attempts at conquest, the Mamluks destroyed the port of Jaffa and the ports of other coastal towns in order to prevent invasion by Christian warships. Jaffa was abandoned, except for occasional visits by merchant ships and pilgrims. The guards who watched over the ruins of the town would light beacons in order to warn Ramleh of the approach of a ship, but until permission to disembark was given by the authorities in Ramleh, *Gaza, or even *Cairo, pilgrims had to wait for many days on board ship, and afterward in the dark and stinking cellars of the ruins, humiliated by blows and extortion. Many died on board ship, in Jaffa, and on the way to Jerusalem. For Jews immigration via Jaffa was even more dangerous, especially in the 15th century, as a result of the decrees issued by the pope and the Venetian Republic against carrying Jews to the Holy Land. Only when the decree was revoked in 1488 did Jews openly arrive in Ereẓ Israel via Jaffa.

The Ottoman Period (1517–1831)

From the beginning of the 16th century until the mid-17th century, there was no change in the status of Jaffa. In the mid-17th century the Turks added a tower to the two existing towers, and increased the watch over the town. In 1641 the Franciscan friars, who looked after Catholic pilgrims, set up a small monastery with a church. Inhabitants and merchants of Ramleh began to gather in the town. At first, tents and booths were set up in Jaffa, but only at the end of the century were houses built there. The import and export trade gradually increased. In the early 18th century Jaffa was the manufacturing and export center of the "Jaffa soap" industry, and apparently, the first oranges in Palestine were grown in Jaffa. A quay was added to the port for the disembarkation of passengers, and hostelries and houses for trading agents and European consuls were built. Individual Jews were attracted to the town.

In 1769 Jaffa was destroyed by Uthman Pasha, the governor of *Damascus, because its inhabitants refused to be compelled into providing money for quelling the revolt of Zahir al-Amr the governor of Acre. In 1775 the town was besieged by Muhammad Bey Abu Dhahab of Egypt, who at first had assisted Zahir al-Amr but later fought for the sultan; he massacred many of Jaffa's inhabitants, among them Jews. Abu Dhahab built a monument to his victory from decapitated heads, for which the site of the monument received the name Tell al-Ruus ("hill of the heads"). In 1799 Napoleon besieged the town and conquered it in a storm.

[Joseph Braslavi (Braslavski)]

Modern Period

Jaffa suffered severely under the siege, but after it had been conquered by Napoleon's army, it recovered relatively quickly and was rebuilt by the local governor, Muhammad Abu Nabut. On his initiative, the well-planned markets of the town, as well as its central mosque (near the present-day Clocktower Square) and the water fountain on the road leading to Jerusalem (which bears his name), were built. The city wall, with its towers, and the inner citadel on top of Jaffa Hill by the sea were renewed. Hewn stones were shipped by sea from ruined ancient cities on the coast, mainly from Caesarea, for these structures.

In November 1831 Jaffa was occupied by the army of Ibrahim Pasha, stepson of the Turkish governor of Egypt, Muḥammad ʿAlī, who rebelled against the central Turkish government. During Ibrahim Pasha's eight-year rule, Jaffa progressed due to the better security situation, the improvement in the status of non-Muslim residents, and the removal of obstacles in the way of pilgrims reaching the town's port on their way to Jerusalem. Immigrants from Egypt established agricultural settlements in the vicinity, where 50 years later citrus groves were planted and were later integrated in the boundaries of either Jaffa or Tel Aviv.

After the country returned to Ottoman rule, Jaffa's growth continued slowly. Experiments in growing mulberry trees near the town to develop the silk industry were unsuccessful, but the port of Jaffa began to be visited by steamships and, beginning in the 1850s, was included in the regular shipping lines of companies from Marseilles, Trieste, and, later, Odessa. With the opening of the Suez Canal, it also came into the scope of oceangoing vessels. In about 1865 the pace of the town's and port's progress quickened: the city was connected to the telegraph network; the harbor jetty and other port installations were improved; and a lighthouse was built. The harbor entrance between the shore reefs was broadened, and a second gate was opened in the city wall. In the 1880s, these walls were entirely razed and new quarters were erected beyond Jaffa Hill. The construction of the road to Jerusalem and the wealth which came to the city with Jewish immigration and settlement; the expansion of Jerusalem; and the planting of citrus groves in the vicinity all enlivened the city's maritime commerce and contributed to its progress. Another factor was the railroad from Jaffa to Jerusalem, built in 1892, which served pilgrims and tourists. Whereas irrigated orchards could hardly be expanded before, because animal-driven well pumps could not reach deeper groundwater reserves, this became possible from 1898 onward, when small kerosene pumps were introduced. Changes took place in Jaffa's sea trade in the 50 years preceding World War I. Exports of grains and olive oil nearly ceased, but more sesame and sesame oil, watermelons, and particularly citrus fruit and soap were exported. Imports began to exceed exports in volume, as new products – petrol, building wood, cement, paints, caustic soda (as a raw material for soap production), European flour and machines – arrived. In 1885 (the first year for which reliable figures are available) goods valued at £132,579 were exported through Jaffa port, and imports amounted to £287,740. In 1913 exports came to £745,413, and imports to £1,312,695: citrus fruit (with 1,400,000 cases worth £297,000) and soap (6,250 tons worth £200,000) came first.

In 1852 a small group of Americans founded in Jaffa a small colony they called "Mount Hope," which lasted until 1858. Another unsuccessful attempt at agricultural settlement was a "model farm," which A. Isaacs, a Jewish convert to Christianity, sought to establish with the intention to do missionary work. A second attempt by Americans to settle near the city in 1866 was equally unsuccessful. In their stead came members of the German Templer community, who took over the Americans' huts, later built their own quarter (Jaffa's "German Quarter"), and became an important factor in the city's progress. They also established the agricultural colony Sarona (today the Tel Aviv "Kiryah" of government buildings) and another small urban quarter named Valhalla. All these colonies were abandoned when German males were detained by the British authorities at the beginning of World War II.

Arabs, both from Palestine and the neighboring countries, particularly Egypt, settled in Jaffa throughout the 19th and beginning of the 20th century, causing the city's population to grow from 2,500 (at most) in the early 19th century to 5,000 in the 1850s and to nearly 40,000 (with suburbs such as Tel Aviv included) in 1914. World War I brought numerous difficulties, as the port was closed, the railway to Lydda was dismantled, the town was kept under a blackout, and military objects underwent shelling. Economic life was paralyzed, and citizens were mobilized for the Turkish army. These events were followed by hunger, and a considerable part of the inhabitants abandoned the city. On Nov. 16, 1917, Jaffa was occupied by the British and for one month found itself in the front line, until the Allied armies crossed the Yarkon River and advanced north.

Under the British Mandate, Jaffa recovered, expanded, and developed. Excluding Tel Aviv, its population numbered 32,524 in 1922, 55,346 in 1931, and nearly 100,000 in the beginning of 1948. In the latter year, 70,000 were non-Jews, making Jaffa the largest Arab city in the country. Many workers were Arab immigrants coming from near and far who settled in villages of the vicinity, particularly in Salameh. Modern industry became an important foundation of Jaffa's economy, with many enterprises established by Jews and by the German Wagner, while traditional branches (olive-oil presses, soap factories) declined. Another important economic asset was the port, where modern installations, e.g., a boat anchorage protected by a breakwater dam, extended quays, and an area for wharfs and services were added in 1934–35. In 1935 608,000 tons of goods passed through Jaffa port. They amounted to LP 10,000,000, of which LP 2,300,000 were export goods. The construction of Haifa port at that time did not reduce the trade of Jaffa port, where export of citrus fruit was of great importance. The Arab riots that spread from Jaffa on April 19, 1936, and the general strike proclaimed by the Arab Higher Committee, however, paralyzed the port. When Tel Aviv's port was opened soon afterward, the port of Jaffa no longer maintained its former standing; it was closed for security reasons during World War II and could hardly recover in the years 1946–47.

The riots that broke out immediately after the UN decision to partition Palestine (Nov. 29, 1947) and soon developed into full-scale war brought large units of "volunteers" from other Arab countries to Jaffa. They established themselves as the rulers of the city and caused much suffering to its inhabitants. In the first stages of the war, the British authorities protected the city and prevented Jewish forces from occupying parts of it. On May 13, 1948, the city fell to Jewish forces, and most of its inhabitants abandoned it by sea. Large numbers of Jewish immigrants were housed in considerable parts of Jaffa, and on Oct. 4, 1949, the government of Israel decided to amalgamate Tel Aviv with Jaffa, which one year later were given the name Tel Aviv-Jaffa. For its subsequent history, see *Tel Aviv.

JEWS IN JAFFA. After North African Jews had settled in the town, the Jewish community slowly grew to number about 400 members in 1856. The Jerusalem sages gave Rabbi Judah Levy from Dubrovnik (Ragusa) the task of receiving Jewish pilgrims in Jaffa port and of aiding them on their way to Jerusalem. First beginnings in agriculture were the citrus grove of Moses Montefiore and the agricultural school of Mikveh Israel, which entertained close ties with the Jaffa community. The size of the community increased considerably with these enterprises and during the period of the First and Second Aliyah Jaffa became the center of the "new *yishuv*." Together with the opening of industrial enterprises came the creation of the organizational framework of the community, which comprised both Ashkenazim and Sephardim. Health and cultural institutions were established: e.g., the Sha'arei Zion Hospital, schools of the Alliance Israélite Universelle, and of Hovevei Zion and the Herzlia Secondary School. In 1908 the Palestine office of the Zionist organization was opened in Jaffa under Arthur Ruppin. The wholly Jewish quarters that came into being, like Neveh Zedek, Neveh Shalom, etc., later became part of Tel Aviv. In 1905 there were 4,765 Jews in Jaffa, and in 1914 their number was estimated at 15,000. After World War I more Jewish suburbs were established within its municipal boundaries, with approximately 30,000 inhabitants in 1947. These quarters theoretically belonged to Jaffa and paid taxes to its municipality, but received all services (health, education, security) from Tel Aviv, where most of their breadwinners found employment. The inner parts of Jaffa, however, were gradually deserted by Jews, following the riots of 1921, 1929, and 1936–39, and were entirely abandoned at the end of 1947. Only after the State of Israel was founded did Jewish immigrants again settle in Jaffa.

[Shlomo Aronson]

BIBLIOGRAPHY: S. Tolkowsky, *Gateway of Palestine: A History of Jaffa* (1924); Brauer, in: ZAW, 48 (1930), 75; M. Assaf, *Ha-Aravim be-Erez Yisrael* (1935); Noth, in: ZDPV, 61 (1938), 47; Ginzberg, in: AJSLL, 57 (1940), 71–74; Abel, in, JPOS, 20 (1943), 6–28; Mazar, in: *Eretz-Israel*, 1 (1951), 46; 2 (1953), 46; J. Kaplan, *Ha-Arkheologyah ve-ha-Historyah shel Tel Aviv-Yafo* (1953); Yeivin, in: *Eretz-Israel*, 3 (1954), 35; idem, in: AJA, 59 (1955), 163; Ben-Zvi, *Eretz Yisrael*, index; Kaplan, in: BJES, 20 (1956), 192–4; 24 (1960), 133–5. **ADD. BIBLIOGRAPHY:** Y. Tsafrir, L. Di Segni, and J. Green, *Tabula Imperii Romani. Iudaea – Palaestina. Maps and Gazetteer.* (1994), 152–53, s.v. Ioppe; B. Bagatti, *Ancient Christian Villages of Samaria* (2002), 213–18; G.S.P. Grenville, R.L. Chapman and J.E. Taylor, *Palestine in the Fourth Century. The Onomasticon by Eusebius of Caesarea* (2003), 138, s.v. Ioppa; M. Stern, *Greek and Latin Authors on Jews and Judaism*, vols. 1–2 (1974–80); ARAB CONQUEST TO CONQUEST OF IBRAHIM PASHA

(636–1832); *Jaffa Port in History and Legend* (1961); M. Altbauer, *Jaffa and its Port in the Travel Accounts of Christian Pilgrims from Slavic Countries* (1966); M. Assaf, *Toledot ha-Shilton ha-Aravi be-Erez Yisrael* (1935), passim; Braslavy, in: *Molad*, 18 (1960), 440–3; *Sefer ha-Yishuv* (1944), index; *Prawer, Zalbanim*, index; Runciman, *History of the Crusades* (1954), index; Hirschberg, in: *Sefer Assaf* (1953), 223–9; M. Ish-Shalom, *Masei Nozerim be-Ereẓ Yisrael* (1965), index; Doudayi, in: Ariel, no. 20 (1967), 17–32; Benvenisti, *Crusaders in the Holy Land* (1970), index.

JAFFA, German brothers who were early New Mexico settlers. HENRY N. JAFFA (1846–1901) went to the U.S. as a young man and moved out West after the Civil War, establishing stores in southern Colorado. In 1879 he opened a business in Las Vegas, New Mexico, which he extended to Albuquerque in 1882. When Albuquerque was incorporated in 1885, Jaffa became its first mayor. He organized New Mexico's first synagogue (1897) and participated in civic and fraternal affairs. NATHAN JAFFA (1863–1945) went to the U.S. from Germany in 1878, settling in Trinidad, Colorado. After brief periods in Las Vegas and Albuquerque, New Mexico (1899), Jaffa became cashier of the Bank of Roswell, NM, where he also led congregational life. From 1907 until New Mexico became a state in 1912 he was its territorial secretary by presidential appointment. Later, he served for 15 years as regent of the University of New Mexico, two years as mayor of Santa Fe, and four years as chief state tax commissioner. He became city clerk of Las Vegas, N.M. (1938) and was an active Mason.

[Edward L. Greenstein]

JAFFE, family of Hebrew printers in *Lublin in the 16th and 17th centuries. In 1557 KALONYMUS BEN MORDECAI JAFFE (d. c. 1603) was associated with *Eliezer b. Isaac and other printers in the production of a Pentateuch with *haftarot* and the Five Scrolls. Kalonymus was a second cousin of Mordecai *Jaffe, author of the *Levushim*, and married Hannah, the granddaughter of Ḥayyim *Schwartz, a well-known wandering printer. In 1559 she and her cousin Ḥayyim b. Isaac Schwarz obtained a printing privilege from Sigismund II, king of Poland. Kalonymus published two *maḥzor* editions, one in the German rite (1563), the other in the Polish (1568), and a Talmud edition (1559–77). When Eliezer b. Isaac and his son left Lublin for Constantinople in 1574, Kalonymus bought most of his type – Prague style borders and other decorations – and from then until his death he continued printing a great number and variety of works, apart from proceeding with the Talmud edition. He was soon assisted by his sons JOSEPH, ẒEVI HIRSCH, and ḤAYYIM. In 1578 he obtained a new privilege from King Stephen Bathory; in 1590 he acquired new type borders and decorations. When the plague broke out in Lublin in 1592, the family and staff took refuge in nearby Bistrowitz, where they printed a Passover *Haggadah* in 1593. Kalonymus' son Ẓevi Hirsch took up the family trade in 1604. He too issued a Talmud edition (1611–39), Samuel Edels' novellae (1617–36), and a number of other important rabbinic and nonrabbinic works. A great fire, the Chmielnicki persecutions (1648–49), and the Swedish War (1656) led to the suspension of printing activities, but in 1665 another Jaffe, SOLOMON ZALMAN (KALMANKES) of Turobin, a nephew of Kalonymus and husband of his daughter Sarah, who herself took an active part in the work, took over and continued printing, certainly until 1700, and possibly after that year. Solomon Zalman was in partnership with a certain Jacob b. Abraham and, after the latter's death, with his son Ẓevi.

BIBLIOGRAPHY: Ḥ.D. Friedberg, *Toledot ha-Defus ha-Ivri be-Polanyah* (1950), 45–60; A.M. Habermann, in: KS, 31 (1955/6), 483–500.

JAFFE, ABRAHAM B. (1924–), Hebrew literary critic and editor. Born in Beltsy, Bessarabia, he settled in Ereẓ Israel in 1940 and from 1948 lived in Tel Aviv. His articles and literary studies appeared in the Hebrew press and in periodicals from 1943. Jaffe's major work is *Avraham Shlonsky ha-Meshorer u-Zemanno* (1966), a study of the life and work of the poet Abraham *Shlonsky. He also edited *Yalkut Eshel* (1967), an anthology of Shlonsky's literary essays. His other critical writings include *Shirah u-Meẓi'ut* ("Poetry and Reality", 1951); *Charlie Chaplin* (1953, 1955); *Du-Si'aḥ Ẓarefati* ("French Dialogue," 1958), a work on modern French literature; *Sifrut ve-Ommanut* (1965), together with A. Ḥashavyah; and *Hemingway ve-"Ha-Zaken ve-ha-Yam"* ("Hemingway and 'The Old Man and the Sea,'" 1966). He edited *Al Admat Besarabyah*, vol. 2 (1962), a collection of essays on Bessarabian Jewry, and a collection of essays on S. *Ẓemaḥ (1966). From 1951, he was editor of the weekly literary supplement of the newspaper *Al ha-Mishmar*. He was also one of the editors of *Ommanut ha-Bamah be-Yisrael* ("Theater Arts in Israel," 1965). Among his other works are a memoir of Lea *Goldberg (*Pegishot im L. Goldberg*, 1984), a literary portait of the poet Shlomo Tani (1994), essays on the modern story (*Makbilot ba-Sippur ha-Moderni*, 1973), and a book on literature and art in the early years of the city Tel Aviv (1980).

BIBLIOGRAPHY: Kressel, Leksikon, 2 (1967), 95. **ADD. BIBLIOGRAPHY:** A. Ekroni, *"Bein Moreshet li-Temurah,"* in: *Moznayim* 43 (1976), 216–19.

[Getzel Kressel]

JAFFE, BEZALEL (1868–1925), Zionist leader in Russia and in Ereẓ Israel. The brother of Leib *Jaffe, he was a key figure in the Zionist movement in the area of his native Grodno. He was a member of *Benei Moshe, established a modernized *ḥeder* in his home town, and was one of the organizers of the "Grodno Courses" for the training of Hebrew teachers (1907). Jaffe took part in the first Zionist Congresses, was active in the organization of the Zionist movement in Lithuania, and in the publication of Zionist literature in Hebrew, Yiddish, and Russian. In 1909 he went to Ereẓ Israel and, upon the resignation of Meir *Dizengoff, was appointed director of the Geulah company for land purchase. Under his directorship (1910–25), this company was instrumental in extending the area of Tel Aviv and turning it into a city. He was one of the founders of Tel Aviv and a member of the town's first governing committee. Jaffe was also a member of the Va'ad Le'ummi during its early days

(1920–25). In 1912 Jaffe introduced the first modern irrigation into Petaḥ Tikvah, utilizing the waters of the Yarkon river. He was one of the few who fought to safeguard achievements of the *yishuv* during its harassment by the Turkish authorities in World War I. After 1918 he was among the organizers of the *yishuv*'s Provisional Committee and also served as president of the Jaffa-Tel Aviv Jewish community.

BIBLIOGRAPHY: *Beẓalel Jaffe* (Heb., 1960); J. Pogrebinsky, *Sefer "Ge'ullah"* (1956), 130–52, 236–7; Tidhar, 1 (1947), 269–70.

[Yehuda Slutsky]

JAFFE, ELI (1953–), Israeli conductor. Jaffe was born in Jerusalem and graduated from The Hebrew University and the Rubin Academy of Music, majoring in conducting, theory, and percussion. In 1977 he proceeded to the Royal Academy of Music in London, where he was awarded the Ernest Reed Prize for conducting in 1978. He conducted all of Israel's major orchestras as well as the London Royal Philharmonic, the Liege Philharmonic, the Baltimore Symphony, and the Prague Symphony Orchestra, which endowed him with the title, "Honorary Guest Conductor." He is artistic director of the Jerusalem School for Cantorial Art and of the Jerusalem Great Synagogue Choir, with which he has made numerous world tours. Jaffe published an encyclopedic instructional set for the entire annual cycle of Hebrew liturgy. He is also an accomplished composer. His first symphony was performed by the Israel Philharmonic, and his wind quintet was premiered by the orchestra's wind ensemble.

Jaffe conducts wearing a *kippah* (skullcap) and with his ritual fringes (*tzitzit*) protruding. His strict observance does not permit him to participate in competitions held on the Jewish Sabbath, and he does not conduct works with Christian liturgical connotations.

[Uri Toepliz and Yohanan Boehm / Yulia Kreinin (2nd ed.)]

JAFFE, ISRAEL BEN AARON (c. 1640–after 1703), kabbalist. Born in Uman (Ukraine), he fled at the age of eight to Glussk (Belorussia) on the outbreak of the *Chmielnicki persecutions (1648). He studied with *Isaac b. Abraham at Posen (*Tiferet Yisrael*, Frankfurt on the Oder (1774), 40b) and afterward continued his studies together with his friends Aryeh Loeb Epstein and Jacob Ḥayyat (*ibid.*, 35a). Later he became rabbi at Shklov (Belorussia). Jaffe, who claimed to see heavenly visions, among which were revelations of the prophet Elijah, felt himself called upon to work for the messianic redemption. He appeared in numerous communities, in order to gain adherents for his kabbalistic theories and to scourge misdeeds. For the printing of his writings he went to Frankfurt on the Oder, where his work *Or Yisrael* (1702) was published (pt. 1: interpretations of the *Zohar; pt. 2: kabbalistic commentaries on *Oraḥ Ḥayyim*; in 1702 with approbations by numerous contemporary authorities). The work roused angry feelings in rabbinic circles, since the author was suspected of Shabbatean leanings because of the repeated use of the word *ẓevi* (interpreted as referring to *Shabbetai Ẓevi) in his work. In his apology, Jaffe attributes the incriminating passages to an alien insertion; by this he contradicts the testimony of his son Aaron, who had corrected the whole work. His grandson had this apology printed at the beginning of his excerpt from his grandfather's work *Tiferet Yisrael*, in order to clear him of the accusation of Shabbateanism. Although the rabbinic authorities had, in their approval to this work, confirmed the groundlessness of these accusations against Jaffe, the suspicion was nevertheless upheld by Jacob *Emden (cf. *Torat ha-Kena'ot* (Lemberg, 1870), 145, first printed Amsterdam, 1752, and *Shevirat Luḥot ha-Aven* (Zolkiew, 1756), 53b). On the other hand, *David of Makow, who was close to the circle of *Elijah Gaon of Vilna, took Jaffe's part in his anti-ḥasidic pamphlet *Zemir Ariẓim*.

The following works of Jaffe remain unpublished: *Beit Yisrael*, additions to the Talmud; commentary on the *haftarot* and the Five Scrolls; *Yefeh Einayim; Milḥamot Adonai*; and *Tiferet Yisrael*. Excerpts from the last three works were published by his grandson and namesake (who had the appellation *Zuta* to differentiate him from his grandfather) under the title *Tiferet Yisrael* (Frankfurt on the Oder, 1774); together with them are printed *Kishut Tov* by Moses b. Menahem and an excerpt from the works of Israel Zuta himself.

BIBLIOGRAPHY: Z. Harkavy, *Mishpaḥat Maskil le-Eitan* (1953), 16–22; S.M. Chones, *Toledot ha-Posekim* (1910), 368; E. Kahan, *Kinat Soferim* (1892), 616; Fuenn, Keneset, 694–5.

[Samuel Abba Horodezky]

JAFFE, LEIB (1876–1948), Russian Zionist leader, writer, and poet. Born in Grodno, a grandson of R. Mordecai-Gimpel *Jaffe, he participated in the First Zionist Congress and in those following it and was one of the foremost Zionist propagandists in speeches, discussions, articles, and poems in both Russian and Yiddish. Jaffe was a member of the *Democratic Fraction of the Zionist movement and among the opponents of the *Uganda Scheme. At the *Helsingfors Conference, 1906, he was elected to the Zionist central committee in Russia. For a time he edited the Zionist periodicals in Russia, *Dos Yidishe Folk* and *Haolam*, in which he published articles on current and Zionist affairs. At the Eighth Zionist Congress (1907), Jaffe was elected to the Zionist General Council and he directed the regional Zionist committee for the five provinces of Lithuania. During World War I he was active on behalf of the Jewish Society for the Help of War Refugees (YEKOPO).

In 1915 Jaffe was called to Moscow to edit the monthly of the Zionist Organization, *Yevreyskaya Zhizn*. During the brief period of the February Revolution in Russia, he was at the center of Zionist propagandist and administrative work. With the consolidation of the Soviet regime, Jaffe returned to Lithuania, where he was elected president of the Zionist Organization and edited its newspaper, *Letste Nayes* (later *Di Yidishe Tsaytung*). In 1920 he went to Ereẓ Israel, where he was elected to the Va'ad ha-Ẓirim (Zionist Commission). He was an editor of the newspaper *Haaretz* (1920–21) and editor in chief 1921–22. In 1923 Jaffe joined the *Keren Hayesod and in

1926, together with A. *Hantke, became its co-director. Until his death he traveled widely in all countries of the Diaspora on public relations missions and established contacts with intellectual circles. He was killed on March 11, 1948, when a mine planted by an Arab terrorist exploded in the courtyard of the *Jewish Agency compound.

Jaffe's literary work was devoted to the renascence of the Jewish people and to the love of Ereẓ Israel. He published three collections of Jewish-Zionist literature in Russian and also two Russian anthologies of Hebrew poetry (together with the poet V. *Khodasevich, and with a foreword by M. *Gershenson), and a selection of world poetry on Jewish-national subjects. His own poetry found its best expression in Russian. In 1892 his first poem appeared in the Russian Jewish *Voskhod*. His first collection of poems, *Gryadushchee* ("The Future") appeared in Grodno in 1902 and also contains translations of Hebrew poetry. His second collection *Ogni na vysotakh* ("Fires on the Heights," 1936), appeared in Riga. Jaffe also wrote poems in Yiddish (collected in *Heymats Klangen*, 1925) and in Hebrew. A selection of his articles appeared in *Tekufot* (1948). His son Benjamin (d. 1986) edited *Ketavim, Iggerot ve-Yomanim* (1964), and *Bi-Sheliḥut Am* (1968; letters and documents 1892–1948). Jaffe edited *Sefer ha-Congress* (the book of the First Zionist Congress, 1923).

BIBLIOGRAPHY: Kressel, Leksikon, 2 (1967), 98–99; LNYL, 4 (1961), 289–91.

[Yehuda Slutsky and Melech Ravitch]

JAFFE, LEONARD (1926–), U.S. space program engineer. Born in Cleveland, Ohio, Jaffe served in the U.S. Navy (1944–46). He joined what later became the National Aeronautics and Space Administration as research engineer (1948), was the chief of the Data Systems Branch (1955), chief of communications satellites (1959), and director of the communication and navigation satellite programs of the Office of Space Science and Applications Satellites from 1963. When Jaffe was Deputy Associate Administrator for Space Applications, his office was responsible for all NASA Space Applications Satellite Projects.

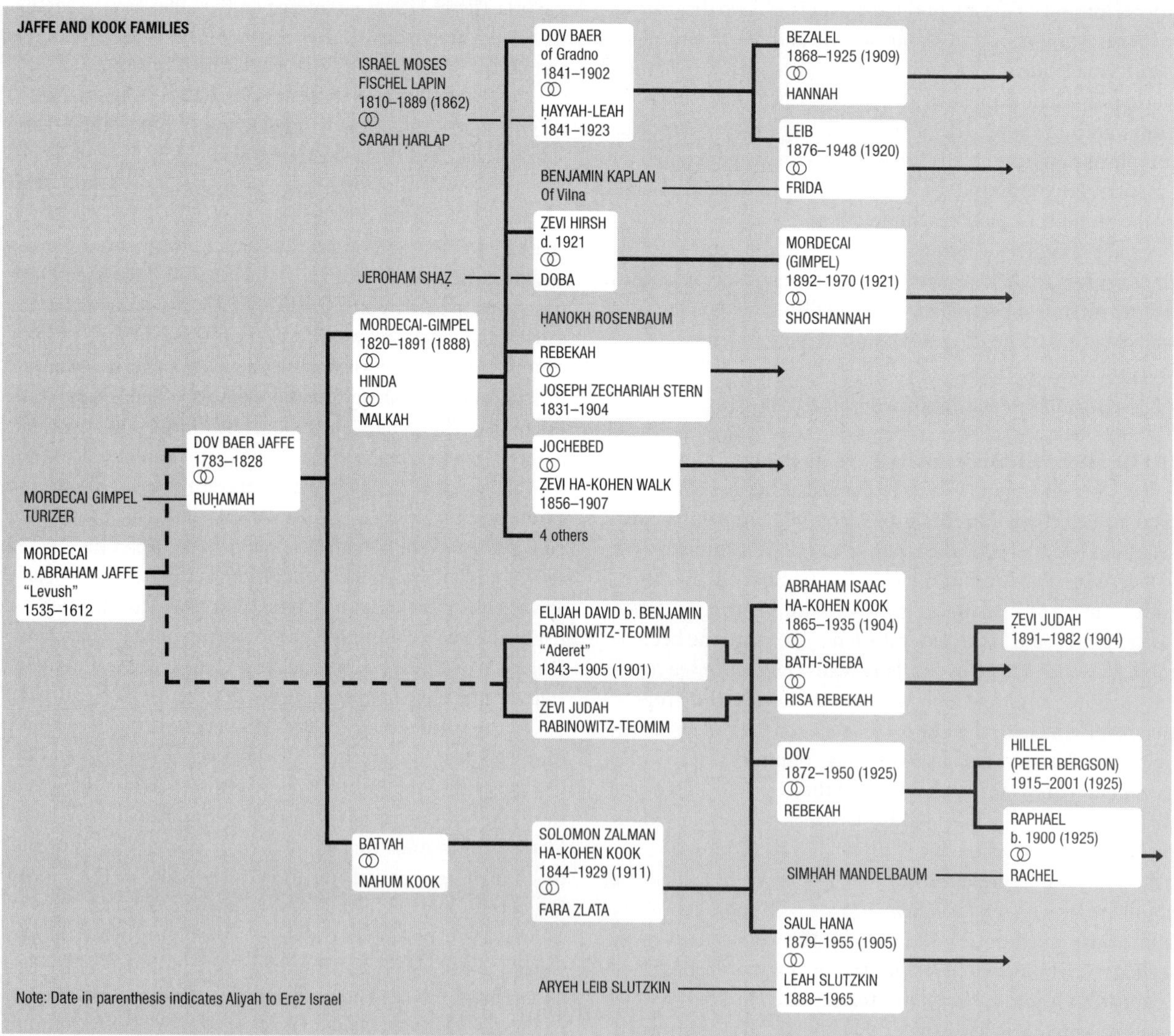

In 1979 he headed the technical team of the President's Commission on the Accident at Three Mile Island. In 1981 he joined the Computer Sciences Corp. as vice president for product management and quality assurance and later became president of their Systems Division. From 1994 to 2001 he was president and chief operating officer of the Earth Sciences Corp. He was president of the International Astronautics Federation in 1975 and 1976 and a fellow of the Institute of Electrical and Electronic Engineers (IEEE), the American Institute of Aeronautics and Astronautics (AIAA), the American Astronautical Society (AAS), and the Society of Space Professionals International (SSPI). He received numerous awards from these organizations as well as from the U.S. government.

[Bracha Rager (2nd ed.)]

JAFFE, MAURICE ABRAHAM (1917–1985), Israeli communal worker. Jaffe was born in Manchester and studied at the local yeshivah and at Manchester University, where he graduated in law (LL.B.) with honors in Public International Law. After serving as rabbi of the North Manchester Synagogue, he served as chaplain in the British army during World War II, serving inter alia as Jewish chaplain to the Allied Land Forces in Southeast Asia (1944) and senior Jewish chaplain to the British Forces in Europe (1946).

Jaffe immigrated to Israel in 1948 where he was appointed director of overseas relations of the World Mizrachi in 1949.

In 1952 he was appointed honorary executive director of the Hechal Shlomo Building Committee and became at present its executive chairman. Jaffe was chairman of the Building Committee of the Jerusalem Great Synagogue. In July 1977 he became a member of the Board of Governors of the World Jewish Congress and of the Executive of the World Zionist Organization. He received his Ph.D. from the Midwestern University, Indianapolis in 1969.

JAFFE, MEIR OF ULM (15th century), German scribe and bookbinder. Little is known about his life except that his father was probably Israel b. Meir of Heidelberg, the scribe of the Darmstadt **Haggadah*. Meir Jaffe wrote the Cincinnati *Haggadah* toward the end of the 15th century. He was also a skilled bookbinder, as a decree of the Nuremberg Council in 1468 invited *"Meyerlein, Juden von Ulm"* to come to Nuremberg to bind a Pentateuch. Signed in Hebrew "Meir Jaffe, the designer," this hand-tooled binding is in the Bavarian State Library (Cod. Hebr. 212). No other works can be ascribed to him with certainty. The itinerant scribe and bookbinder Israel son of "Mohar" of Brandenburg, who was involved in the Trent Ritual Murder trial of 1475, may have been Meir Jaffe's son.

BIBLIOGRAPHY: L.A. Mayer, *Bibliography of Jewish Art* (1967), index.

[Joseph Gutmann]

JAFFE, MORDECAI BEN ABRAHAM (c. 1535–1612), talmudist, kabbalist, and communal leader. Born in Prague, Jaffe was sent as a boy to Poland to study under Solomon *Luria and Moses *Isserles. There he devoted himself also to the study of astronomy and philosophy (apparently at the instance of Isserles). At the same time he studied Kabbalah under Mattathias b. Solomon Delacrut. After a few years he returned to Prague, where in 1553 he was appointed head of the yeshivah. Very soon he discovered that the students were not interested in mere understanding of the Talmud but preferred *"pilpul"* and "were turning the word of the living God into false, corrupt, and evil words" (Preface to his *Levush Malkhut*). Jaffe chose therefore "to minimize the time spent with these students" and applied himself to writing constructive books.

At that time Joseph *Caro's *Beit Yosef* appeared "and it was a cause for rejoicing by all who pursue the study of Torah," but Jaffe found it overly long and so began to write his *Levush Malkhut*. In this he presented the laws in abbreviated form, taking as a basis the principle followed in the *Beit Yosef* of reliance on the three "pillars of authority" (*Alfasi, *Maimonides, and *Asher b. Jehiel). While he was engaged in this work, the Jews were expelled from Bohemia in 1561. Jaffe left Prague for Italy, settling in Venice, where he resumed his writing. The appearance of Caro's Shulhan Arukh, a digest of his *Beit Yosef*, led Jaffe to consider whether he should continue writing his own work. On reflection, he concluded that there was room for it since it would contain "those laws observed by the Ashkenazi Jews of Bohemia." But word reached him that Moses Isserles "had been spurred in the same direction," and consequently he put aside his work. "Alone in a strange land without any of the friends or pupils I had in my homeland," he decided to set down in writing interpretations that he had acquired in his youth of the *Guide of the Perplexed* and the "Treatise on the Laws of the Jewish Calendar" by Maimonides and the kabbalistic Bible commentary of Menahem *Recanati.

After a stay of over ten years, Jaffe left Italy for Poland – at that time the center of Jewish learning in the Diaspora. There he was appointed *av bet din* and head of the yeshivah of Grodno in Lithuania. Later he was appointed to a similar position in Lublin, and subsequently moved to Kremeniec. In Poland, Jaffe was very active in the Council of the Four Lands, being one of the chief signatories of some of its most important *takkanot*. It seems that his many activities were motivated by his high sense of responsibility. In 1592 he returned to his birthplace, Prague, and became *av bet din* in succession to *Judah Loew b. Bezalel (the Maharal) when the latter was appointed to Posen. In 1599 Jaffe switched posts with Loew, who returned to Prague. Jaffe then remained in Posen until his death.

When the critical and supplementary notes of Isserles to the Shulḥan Arukh (called *Mappah*) appeared in Cracow in 1578, Jaffe felt that Isserles had been too brief as had Caro in the Shulḥan Arukh, and decided to resume his original work, "that will be midway between the two extremes: the lengthy *Beit Yosef* of Caro on the one hand, and on the other Caro's Shulḥan Arukh together with the *Mappah* of Isserles, which is too brief." In all, Jaffe worked on this book almost 50 years. It contains ten "attires" (*levushim*). The first five are devoted to the laws expounded in the *Beit Yosef*; the sixth, *Ha-Orah* is an elucidation of Rashi's biblical commentary; the seventh, *Simḥah ve-Sason*, contains sermons for holidays and weddings; the eighth, *Pinnat Yikrat*, is a commentary on the *Guide of the Perplexed*; the ninth, *Eder Yakar*, is a commentary on the laws of the Jewish calendar according to Maimonides and an additional commentary on Abraham b. Ḥiyya's geographical-astronomical *Ẓurat ha-Areẓ*; the last, *Even Yikrat*, is on Menahem Recanati's commentary on the Pentateuch. The last three "attires" Jaffe also termed collectively "rabbinic robes," considering that these should be learned by "every student in that order – philosophy, astronomy, and Kabbalah." Coming from a leader of 16th-century Polish and Lithuanian Jewry, these words attest to the influence of the Renaissance on Jewish scholars of that time. Jaffe regarded Kabbalah as the "crowning jewel of spirituality"; he also introduced it into the halakhic parts of the "attires" (e.g., *Levush Ḥur.*, 651:11). He was at pains, however, to point out that such confirmation of the *halakhah* from Kabbalah was not authoritative (*ibid.*, 668:1).

The *Levushim* were published between 1590 and 1604 at various presses in Lublin, Prague, and Cracow. On their appearance, they drew criticism from almost every rabbinic authority. On the other hand, Elijah Shapiro, the author of *Eliyahu Zuta* (the commentary on the first *Levush*, Prague, end of 17th century, Preface), speaks of it in the most glowing terms and testifies to its widespread acceptance.

BIBLIOGRAPHY: M. Amsel, "*Mi-Toledotav shel Rabbenu ha-Levush*" in: Mordecai Jaffe, *Levush Malkhut*, 2 (*Levush ha-Hur*; 1964); Graetz-Rabbinowitz, 7 (1899), 350–5, 429–34; S.A. Horodezky, *Le-Korot ha-Rabbanut* (1911), 145–74; S.M. Chones, *Toledot ha-Posekim* (1910), 314–8; S.B. Nissenbaum, *Le-Korot ha-Yehudim be-Lublin* (1900), 25–27; Waxman, Literature, 2 (1960), 150–2.

[Ephraim Kupfer]

JAFFE, MORDECAI-GIMPEL (1820–1891), rabbi, member of the *Ḥibbat Zion movement. Born in Utyana, Kovno district, Jaffe studied at the Volozhin yeshivah and became well known for his religious scholarship and his Hebrew and general education, the latter acquired by his own efforts. When Moses *Montefiore visited Russia in 1846, Jaffe headed a delegation to present him with a memorandum on the economic situation of the Jews of Derechin, where Jaffe served as rabbi. In the memorandum he proposed that Montefiore try to influence the Russian government to agree to the following suggestions: allotting land to Jews for farming, permitting Jews to acquire land and to settle in towns outside the *Pale of Settlement, rescinding the expulsion order to Jews settled in villages among Christian peasants, restoring the right of Jews to settle their disputes in Jewish courts, etc.

In 1855, Jaffe was appointed rabbi in the small town of Ruzhany in the Grodno district, and he remained at his post there for over 30 years. He opposed any ideas of religious reform, such as those of Moses Leib *Lilienblum. Jaffe supported the activities of the Ḥevrat Yishuv Ereẓ Israel (Central Committee for Jewish Colonization in Palestine), founded by Ẓevi Hirsch *Kalischer, and established a society of this kind in his community. He also joined the Ḥibbat Zion movement upon its establishment. When Baron Edmond de *Rothschild, urged by Samuel *Mohilewer, agreed to found an agricultural settlement in Ereẓ Israel with farmers from Russia, Jaffe aided in the *aliyah* of Jewish farmers from a village near Ruzhany.

At the end of 1888, he went to Ereẓ Israel, and after a few months in Jerusalem settled in *Yehud, near Petaḥ Tikvah, where he headed a yeshivah with eight students. During the *shemittah* controversy (1889), Jaffe demanded strict compliance with the laws of the Torah. Of his numerous writings, only his comments to the Midrash on Psalms appeared in his lifetime (1865). After his death, his son published some of his works, including the book *Zikhronot Mordekhai* (1923), in which his letters, memoranda, precepts to his sons, and his will were incorporated.

BIBLIOGRAPHY: B. Jaffe, *Ha-Rav mi-Yehud* (1957); A. Druyanow, *Ketavim le-Toledot Ḥibbat-Ẓiyyon ve-Yishuv Ereẓ-Yisrael*, 3 (1932), 888–92; Y.L. Maimon, *Sarei ha-Me'ah*, 5 (1961), 277–85; EẒD, 2 (1960), 522–38; I. Klausner, *Be-Hitorer Am* (1962), index; idem, *Mi-Katoviẓ ad Basel*, 2 (1965), index.

[Israel Klausner]

JAFFE, SIR OTTO (1846–1929), Irish industrialist and communal leader. Born in Hamburg, Germany, Otto Jaffe was a descendant of Mordecai b. Abraham *Jaffe. He was taken as a child to Belfast, where his father, Daniel Joseph Jaffe (1809–1871), founder of the Belfast Jewish community, established a linen business of considerable size. Otto Jaffe extended the firm, making it one of the chief industrial concerns in Northern Ireland and the largest linen exporter to the continent of Europe. In 1899 and 1904 he was lord mayor of Belfast and in 1901 was high sheriff of the city. He received a knighthood in 1900.

As president of the Belfast Hebrew congregation, Jaffe was instrumental in uniting the Russian immigrants and the German founder families into one community. He built a second synagogue for Belfast in 1904. Like his father before him, Jaffe made numerous benefactions to non-Jewish causes, notably to Belfast's Queen's University, and an elementary school was named after him. However, during World War I he was the object of considerable hostility because of his German origin, and he and his family left Ireland for England in 1916, never to return. His son, ARTHUR JAFFE (1880–1954), was an authority on international law and honorary secretary of the Grotius Society.

BIBLIOGRAPHY: Shillman, *Short History of the Jews in Ireland* (1945), 135f.; Carlebach, in: JHSET, 21 (1968), 261ff.; Aronsfeld, in: YLBI, 7 (1962), 317, 325. **ADD. BIBLIOGRAPHY:** D. Keogh, *Jews in Twentieth-Century Ireland* (1998), 8; L. Hyman, *The Jews of Ireland* (1972), index.

[Alexander Carlebach]

JAFFE, RONA (1932–2005), U.S. author. Born in Brooklyn and educated at Radcliffe College, Jaffe was 26 when her best-selling first novel, *The Best of Everything*, shocked many readers with its sharp-edged portrayal of "girls brought up to fulfill the image of what boys wanted" and the "rat race" to get married. Jaffe was working as an associate editor at Fawcett Publishing in the 1950s when she chronicled the lives and tortured loves of five young working women in the typing pool at a large New York publishing house. Published in 1958 and made into a movie the following year starring Joan Crawford, Hope Lange, and Suzy Parker, the book and movie were popular successes. Notorious in its time for its candor about sex, the novel was widely regarded as a cultural marker, providing a template for a gossipy genre of confessional fiction about women.

The themes in the book, Jaffe said 50 years after its publication, continued to be relevant to women: trying to balance professional success and personal happiness; pursuing an often futile search for Mr. Right; making mistakes without looking back, and finding solace in friendships with other women. Jaffe wrote the tale of ambition and lust in five months and five days, basing it loosely on her experiences as a striving 25-year-old Brooklyn innocent bent on making her way in the New York publishing world. The title became a catch phrase. The book, though dated in the details, was reissued in 2005 at a time when the television series *Sex and the City* showed women in a different light, although some critics felt that the characters, who had a compulsion to have it all, had much in common.

Jaffe, who never married or had children, wrote 16 more novels and countless magazine articles about single working women. In 1995, she began the Rona Jaffe Foundation, which gave cash grants to young women writers. The awards were the only national literary prizes that supported female writers exclusively.

[Stewart Kampel (2nd ed.)]

JAFFE, SAM (1891–1984), U.S. actor. Jaffe, born in New York, was originally a math teacher in the Bronx, New York. He began acting with the Washington Square players in 1915 and later played Jewish roles on Broadway in *The God of Vengeance* (1922), *The Main Line* (1924), *Izzy* (1925), *The Jazz Singer* (1925–28), and *The Gentle People* for the Group Theater (1939). Some of his other Broadway performances included *Mrs. Warren's Profession* (1918), *Grand Hotel* (1930), *The Eternal Road* (1937), *A Doll's House* (1937), *Café Crown* (1942), and *Mademoiselle Colombe* (1954).

He made his debut in Hollywood in the 1934 film *The Scarlet Empress*. Some of his other film work included *Lost Horizon* (1937), *Gunga Din* (1939), *Gentleman's Agreement* (1947), *The Accused* (1949), *The Asphalt Jungle* (1950), *I Can Get It for You Wholesale* (1951), *The Day the Earth Stood Still* (1951), *Ben-Hur* (1959), *The Tell-Tale Heart* (1971), *Nothing Lasts Forever* (1984), and *On the Line* (1984).

Jaffe became widely known in the 1960s for his role as Dr. Zorba in the U.S. television series *Ben Casey* (1961–65). In fact, due perhaps to his unruly hair that made him look somewhat like Albert Einstein, Jaffe was often cast in the role of a doctor or professor on television and in the movies. Some of his TV work included appearances on such shows as *The Defenders* (1962), *Tarzan* (1967), *Nanny and the Professor* (1970), *Enemies* (TV movie, 1971), *Alias Smith and Jones* (1972), *QB VII* (miniseries, 1974), *Medical Story* (1975), and *Gideon's Trumpet* (TV movie, 1980).

In 1951, Jaffe was nominated for an Academy Award for Best Supporting Actor in *The Asphalt Jungle*, and in 1962 he was up for an Emmy for his performance in *Ben Casey*.

[Ruth Beloff (2nd ed.)]

JAFFE, SAMUEL BEN ISAAC ASHKENAZI (d. late 16th century), commentator on the Midrash. Jaffe was rabbi of the Ashkenazi community of Constantinople. He studied under Joseph Leib. When Samuel reached an advanced age, his son Joseph was appointed to succeed him. Jaffe's fame rests upon his comprehensive commentary to the whole of *Midrash Rabbah*, which reveals an extensive knowledge of the relevant literature.

His works are (1) *Yefeh Mareh* (Constantinople, 1587; Venice 1590), expositions of the *aggadot* of the Jerusalem Talmud. In the preface Jaffe explains that it was his aim to interpret the *aggadot* of the Jerusalem Talmud "because they are very similar to the *aggadot* of the *Midrash Rabbah* in style and in language"; (2) *Yefeh To'ar*, commentary to the *Midrash Rabbah*: Genesis (Venice, 1597–1606); Exodus (Venice, 1597); Leviticus (Constantinople, 1648; Wilmersdorf, 1714, with a preface by his grandson); (3) *Yefeh Einayim*, pt. 1 (Venice, 1631), homiletical discourses on the weekly portions of the law; (4) *Yefeh Anaf* (Frankfurt on the Oder, 1696), a commentary on *Ruth Rabbah, Esther Rabbah*, and *Lamentations Rabbah*: (5) *Yefeh Kol* (Smyrna, 1739), a commentary on the *Song of Songs Rabbah*; (6) *Tikkun Soferim* (Leghorn, 1789), glosses on the formulas of documents of Moses *Almosnino. His responsa, *Beit Din Yafeh*, are still in manuscript.

BIBLIOGRAPHY: Azulai, 1 (1852), 175, no. 110; Benjacob, Oẓar, 228 (nos. 364, 366, 369), 668 (no. 865); Zunz, Vortraege, 99n.; S. Wiener, *Kohelet Moshe* (1893–1918), 610–2; Rosanes, Togarmah, 2 (1938), 58f.; 3 (1938), 40f.

[Yehoshua Horowitz]

JAFFEE, IRVING W. (1906–1981), U.S. speed skater, winner of two official and one unofficial Olympic gold medals, and member of the United States Skating Hall of Fame and Speedskating Hall of Fame. Jaffee was born in New York City, the middle of three children, to an immigrant family that came to the U.S. from Russia in 1896. Jaffee's father sold cotton goods from a pushcart, and Jaffee helped the modest family income by working as a newspaper delivery boy. He grew up in the Crotona Park section of the Bronx, the same neighborhood that spawned Hank *Greenberg, five years his junior, and Al *Schacht. Jaffee first became interested in speed skating at 14, cleaning the ice at the Gay Blades skating rink in midtown Manhattan because he could not afford the seventy-five cents admission. He entered the weekly speed races there and lost 22 in a row, as well as the Silver Skates competition in 1924 and

1925. Finally, in 1926 Jaffee won the Silver Skates two-mile senior championships, and the next year at Lake Placid he broke the world record for the five-mile event. He was at first denied certification for the Olympic competition in 1928, which he attributed to antisemitism. Jaffee placed fourth in the 5,000 m, the best finish ever recorded by an American at the distance. The following day, after placing seventh in the 1,500 m, Jaffee also entered the 10,000 m, beating Bernt Evensen, Norway's defending world champion. But after half a dozen races, the weather became warm melting the ice, and the remaining races were cancelled. The Norwegian referee ruled the competition no contest, a decision without precedent. His gold medal is not listed officially, but Jaffee is generally credited with winning it.

Four years later Jaffee was out of shape after taking off nine months to care for his gravely ill mother, but he qualified for the team on his final attempt. Some of his American teammates at Lake Placid made his life miserable, taunting him with antisemitic remarks, stealing his mattress and spilling water on it. When he tried to sleep at night, they shined a light in his eyes. Two days before the 5,000 m competition, a teammate goaded Jaffee into a fistfight, at the suggestion of Bill Taylor, the manager, who apparently thought he was going to take a beating. "But I had spent a lot of time around Lou Stillman's gym as a kid," Jaffee recalled, "and after two minutes I drew blood. Taylor stopped the fight immediately."

To make sure he got at least one solid night's sleep, Irving slept at the home of a friend the night before his first race. With the Winter Olympics being broadcast over radio for the first time, the U.S. audience heard Jaffee win the gold in the 5,000 m (9:40.8) and 10,000 m (19:13.6), the first American to sweep both events in one Olympics.

After a parade down Broadway, Jaffee retired from competitive skating, though he did break by five minutes a 30-year-old world record for a 25-mile marathon skate (1:26:01) on January 27, 1934, while working as the winter sports director at Grossinger's Resort in the Catskill Mountains. He also has helped train no fewer than 10 U.S. Olympic competitors.

Jaffee was elected to the U.S. Skating Hall of Fame in 1940, and the Speedskating Hall of Fame in 1967.

[Elli Wohlgelernter (2nd ed.)]

JAFFE-MARGOLIOT, ISRAEL DAVID (c. 1802–1864), Hungarian rabbi. Born in Vagszered-Sered Nadvahom, Jaffe-Margoliot was a descendant of both Mordecai Jaffe, the author of *Levush*, and Judah Loew b. Bezalel (the Maharal) of Prague. His immediate ancestors, leading members of the community in Vienna, were wealthy and on several occasions advanced loans to the royal house. For many years he studied under Moses Sofer, and several of the latter's responsa are addressed to him. After his teacher's death, Jaffe-Margoliot corresponded on *halakhah* with S.B. *Sofer, author of the responsa work *Ketav Sofer*, as well as with Moses Schick and Judah Assad. While still young, he was appointed *dayyan* of the community of Senice-Szenc in Slovakia, and in 1832, rabbi and *av bet din* of the Bazin-Pezinok community in the Bratislava (Pressburg) district. He took a prominent part in the opposition to the Reform movement which was beginning to spread at the time. At the disposal of those demanding Reform were several newspapers (*Ben-Chananja* of L. Loew, *Ha-Karmel* of Meiser) in which they propagated their views, while the Orthodox element was able to do so only from the synagogue pulpits. Jaffe's work *Meḥolat ha-Maḥanayim* (1859) was the first attempt to explain the standpoint of the observant Jews in writing. It is written in an easy, clear style and made a great impression on the moderates in the Reform camp. The author argues that innovations like moving the reading desk from the center of the synagogue to the front of the ark, the prohibition of wearing the *kittel during the High Festival services, and introduction of the organ do not justify a schism in Judaism. Nevertheless, it was as a result of these arguments that he unwittingly originated the idea of the schism of Hungarian Jewry which took place a few years later. His other works, *Yappe'aḥ la-Keẓ* (2 vols. 1862–88) and *Har Tavor* (1861), are also on the subject of moving the reading desk. His first work, *Ḥazon la-Mo'ed* (1843), in which he discusses the *Hilkhot Kiddush ha-Ḥodesh* of Maimonides' *Mishneh Torah*, reveals his knowledge of astronomy and mathematics.

BIBLIOGRAPHY: M. Stein, *Magyar Rabbik*, 3 (1907), 41–45, 138f., 144, 146–8; D. Kaufmann, *Die letzte Vertreibung der Juden aus Wien und Niederoesterreich* (1889); J.J.(L.) Greenwald (Grunwald), *Le-Toledot ha-Reformaẓyon ha-Datit be-Germanyah u-ve-Ungaryah* (1948), 85; P.Z. Schwartz, *Shem ha-Gedolim me-Ereẓ Hagar*, 1 (1914), 53b no. 278; A. Stern, *Meliẓei Esh al Ḥodshei Nisan… Tammuz* (1962^2), 118–20.

[Samuel Weingarten-Hakohen]

JAGEL, ABRAHAM (16th century), ethical writer. He was the author of *Gei Ḥizzayon*, a narrative and ethical work written in 1587, the first part of which was printed in Alexandria in 1880. Copies of *Gei Ḥizzayon*, either in manuscript or in printed form, are very rare; the complete work exists in manuscript form in the British Museum. The author has been identified with Abraham b. Ḥananiah *Jagel, but according to the data available this is not conclusive; from a passage at the beginning of *Gei Ḥizzayon*, it seems that his father's name was Jacob and not Ḥananiah. Should this interpretation be correct, then this Abraham Jagel is not the same as the one who wrote *Lekaḥ Tov*. The form and structure of *Gei Ḥizzayon* was influenced by the tradition started by Dante and followed by a number of Italian Hebrew writers. The author describes a visit to the heavenly regions guided by the spirit of his dead father. The main theme of the work is ethical: Jagel uses various literary forms to try to guide his reader toward the right moral way of life. His philosophy, deeply influenced by Renaissance concepts including a belief in astrology and predestination, at the same time posits the premise that man's actions can be motivated by ethical and religious choice, and are not only determined by fate.

Besides its direct ethical teaching, the work is a composite of three distinct literary forms:

(1) It is an autobiography in the form of narration to his father in which he tells him of his life after the latter's death. Told in prison, where he was incarcerated because of financial troubles, Jagel describes the place in detail. *Gei Ḥizzayon* is the first autobiography in Hebrew literature of an ordinary man who relates his troubles without attaching any historical, literary, or religious importance to the events in his life. The story is told sporadically and in short spurts during the first half of the work.

(2) The author uses the novella form to relate the lives of the dead for moralistic purposes. During their sojourn in the heavenly regions, Jagel and his father meet many spirits, both good and evil, who tell them the story of their lives. These prose narratives clearly belong to the Italian novella genre of the time which Jagel adapted in the form of moralistic Jewish fables. He thus introduced some of the earliest Renaissance novellae into Hebrew literature.

(3) The vision as aesthetic vehicle forms an important part of the second half of the work. Jagel, not a kabbalist in the full sense of the word, was nevertheless familiar with kabbalistic ideas. The visions described are influenced by kabbalistic concepts, though the aesthetic aspect of the vision is stressed more than the kabbalistic theological element. The influence of Dante and his followers is most pronounced in this literary aspect of *Gei Ḥizzayon*.

BIBLIOGRAPHY: M. Steinschneider, in: HB, 4 (1861), 122 no. 74; C. Roth, *The Jews in the Renaissance* (1959); *Gei Ḥizzayon* (1887), preface by A.B. Mani.

[Joseph Dan]

JAGEL, ABRAHAM BEN ḤANANIAH DEI GALICCHI (16th–17th cent.), Italian philosopher and author. He lived in Ferrara, Venice, and Sassuolo, and apparently served as private tutor to wealthy Jewish families. He was well versed in secular studies and Christian literature. Of special importance was his work *Lekaḥ Tov* (first published in Venice, 1595), which subsequently appeared in many editions and translations: Latin (London, 1679, Leipzig, 1687, Frankfurt on the Oder, 1691, Helmstedt, 1704); Yiddish (first published in Amsterdam, 1675, a freer translation in Vilna, 1884); and German (Leipzig, 1694, Brunswick, 1759). Written in the form of a dialogue between a rabbi and his disciple, and originally intended for young people, *Lekaḥ Tov* is a book of religious guidance whose main subject is ways for attaining happiness in the hereafter. Jagel sets forth faith, hope, and love (charity) as the principal foundations of religious life: faith and hope are viewed by him (as in Christianity) as "a gift given by God to our souls"; love encompasses both love of God and love of man. Jagel discusses sin and repentance and enumerates seven "principal classes of sin" and, in contrast, seven major virtues. In its form and content, this work was influenced by the Christian catechisms of Jagel's time, and especially by the writings of the Jesuit scholar, Canisius. In his listing of principles of faith, Jagel followed *Maimonides, on whose works he leaned heavily. His views on the love of man are reported in detail by his contemporary Isaiah Horowitz (1565, *Sha'ar ha-Otiyyot*, s.v. *Beri'ot*). Jagel also composed a kind of scientific encyclopedia, in four parts, entitled *Beit Ya'ar Levanon*, a few chapters of which have been published, but most of which is extant only in manuscript. Jagel's other writings deal with religious philosophy, astrology, religious tradition and law, and interpretations of astronomical works. Some modern scholars have identified Jagel with the apostate Camillo Jagel who, in 1611, was appointed by the heads of the Inquisition as book censor. This identification has been proved false since Abraham Jagel's writings, even after 1617, attest to his continuing adherence to Judaism.

BIBLIOGRAPHY: S. Maybaum, *Abraham Jagels Katechismus Lekach-tob* (1892); U. Cassuto, in: EJ, 8 (1931), 70–71.

JAGLOM, HENRY (1941–), U.S. director-actor. Born in London, England, Jaglom grew up in New York City. After graduating from the University of Pennsylvania in 1961, he studied acting, writing, and directing at the Actors' Studio and performed in off-Broadway theater. Jaglom moved to Hollywood in the late 1960s and made appearances on such television shows as *Gidget* and *The Flying Nun*. In 1967, he went to Israel to film a documentary on the Six-Day War, which never achieved wide release in the United States. Back in Hollywood, Jaglom secured his first feature-film role as a drug addict in *Psych-Out* (1968). Jaglom's work on his Six-Day War documentary earned him a spot as an editor for the Dennis Hopper film *Easy Rider* (1968), which then led to his directing *A Safe Place* (1971), a U.S. box-office disappointment that did well in Europe. In 1974, Jaglom was instrumental in bringing to the screen the Vietnam War documentary *Hearts and Minds*, which won an Oscar. With the money Jaglom earned from *Safe Place*, he was able to finance his next film, *Tracks* (1976), a tale of an Army sergeant haunted by Vietnam. In 1977, Jaglom married Patrice Townsend. Jaglom gradually began to adopt a cinema verité approach to filmmaking in which the actors under his direction were encouraged to improvise, and he increasingly drew from his own life for inspiration to make films. Following his divorce from Townsend in 1982, Jaglom directed *Always* (1985), which focused on the last days of their marriage. In *Someone to Love* (1987), the director interviews 60 friends to talk about why they are alone; the film features the final on-screen appearance of Orson Welles. Among later films, *Eating* (1991) explores women's issues with food; *Babyfever* (1994) looks at women and the biological clock; and *Going Shopping* (2005) examines women's consumerist urges.

WEBSITES: "Jaglom, Henry," in *Contemporary Authors Online* (Gale, 2002); Henry Jaglom – biography, at: www.henryjaglom.com; Henry Jaglom – IMDB, at: www.imdb.com/name/nm0415617; "'To Tell the Truth' – Henry Jaglom's Cinema of Emotional Verité Radiance," at: www.standard8media.com/rainbowfilms/radmag.htm.

[Adam Wills (2nd ed.)]

JAGLOM (née **Horesh**), **RAYA** (1919–), Zionist women's leader. Raya Jaglom was born in Bessarabia and in 1939 immigrated to Ereẓ Israel, where she studied at The Hebrew University. After her marriage in the following year to Joseph Jaglom, an industrialist, she was joined by her parents and grandmother. She first became active in *WIZO in 1941, and apart from a period of 18 months in 1947–48 when she served in the *Haganah, she has devoted the whole of her activity to this organization, visiting almost every country in the world on its behalf, including the U.S.S.R. at the invitation of the Soviet Women's Committee in Moscow. In February 1971 she headed the WIZO delegation to the World Conference on Soviet Jewry held in Brussels. She was elected chairman of the World WIZO Executive in 1963 and president in 1970, and represented WIZO on the Executive of the *Jewish Agency from 1964. She served as WIZO president for 26 years, and subsequently as honorary president. During her presidency, WIZO lent its support to the weaker groups in society, such as children and the elderly. She and her husband established a fund for students at the Hebrew and Tel Aviv universities, a club for Israel Philharmonic musicians, and a synagogue at WIZO headquarters in Tel Aviv. In addition, Raya Jaglom held many other public offices, including membership on the Board of Governors of both the Hebrew and Tel Aviv universities, membership in the Executive of the Zionist Organization, and membership on the Board of Governors of the Jewish Agency. She was also a member of the international council of the *Israel Museum and the international board of Tel Aviv Museum.

JAHAZ, JAHAZA (Heb. יַהַץ, יַהְצָה), city in Moab where Sihon the Amorite was decisively defeated by the Israelites (Num. 21:23; Deut. 2:32ff.; Judg. 11:20). Jahaz was included in the territory of the tribe of Reuben and was a levitical city of the family of Merar (Josh. 13:18; I Chron. 6:63). After being lost to Moab for a time, it was seized by Omri and later apparently by Ahab who fortified it. Mesha king of Moab recaptured the city and annexed it to Dibon (Mesha Stele, 18, 19, 20). From this time Jahaz remained a Moabite city and is mentioned as such in the Bible (Isa. 15:4; Jer. 48:34). It has been proposed to identify it with Khirbat Islandar (by Abel) or with several other sites in the vicinity of the Wadi al-Wāla, southeast of Heshbon.

BIBLIOGRAPHY: Abel, Geog, 2 (1938), 354; Glueck, in: AASOR, 18–19 (1939), 144ff.; Noth, in: ZAW, 60 (1944), 40–41, 45; EM, 3 (1965), 571–2.

[Michael Avi-Yonah]

JAHODA, MARIE (1907–2001), British social psychologist and activist. Jahoda was born in Vienna to Karl and Betty (Probst) Jahoda. Although the family could trace its Jewish roots to the 18th century, her parents, who were active social democrats, had assimilated into Austrian society and considered themselves to be without religious affiliation. Jahoda was briefly to married Paul Lazarsfeld, a young instructor at the Psychological Institute at the University of Vienna where she did her Ph.D. (they were divorced in 1934). Their only child, Lotte Lazarsfeld Bailyn, born in 1930, became a professor of management at the Massachusetts Institute of Technology. Jahoda's first book, *Die Arbeitslosen von Marienthal* (*Marienthal: The Sociography of an Unemployed Community*, 1971), written with Hans Zeisel and Lazarsfeld, was published in German in 1933 without attribution, because the publishers feared that the authors' Jewish names would attract unwanted attention. Nevertheless, most of the copies of the first edition were burned. This book is considered a classic empirical study of the psychological consequences of prolonged unemployment in a town that had been a synonym for industrial development. Jahoda, who had been a leader in the Austrian socialist youth movement since her teens, served a prison term for her political opinions in 1936–37; she was released only through the intervention of the international community on condition that she leave the country.

In 1937, Jahoda emigrated to England, where she held a variety of positions and conducted research on unemployed miners, voluntary societies, and the transition from school to work. She also became a leading member of the Austrian Socialists in Great Britain and ran the secret radio station Radio *Rotes Wien*. Near the end of World War II, Jahoda came to the United States. She worked at Columbia University with the American Jewish Committee on efforts to reduce prejudice through persuasive communications and later became a professor of social psychology at New York University and a member of its Research Center for Human Relations, a group devoted to action research. During this period, she was the senior author of a widely used book, *Research Methods in Social Relations*, published in 1951 with the sponsorship of the Society for the Psychological Study of Social Issues (SPSSI).

Throughout her life, Jahoda remained deeply committed to the use of empirical research for bettering the human condition. During her relatively brief career in the United States, she was deeply involved in the two major issues that dominated the political climate of those years, the civil rights movement and McCarthyism. She investigated the psychological effects of the suppression of political opinion by loyalty oaths, blacklisting in the entertainment industry, and the impact of security measures on the climate of thought of civil servants. Jahoda was a board member of the American Civil Liberties Union and was elected the first woman president of SPSSI in 1951; a woman was not elected again until 1971.

In 1958, Jahoda returned to Great Britain to marry Austen Albu, a Labour Member of Parliament, and became a professor of psychology at Brunel University. In 1965, she moved to Sussex University as a professor of social psychology. In the years after her 1972 retirement, she wrote two books, co-edited three others, and published 23 articles and book chapters. Her last and most prized work, *Louise Labé: Vierundzwanzig Sonette in drei Sprachen* (1997), consisted of her translations into English of the sonnets of Louise Labé, a 16th century French proto-feminist poet.

Jahoda's many honors included the Award for Distinguished Contributions to the Public Interest from the American Psychological Association in 1979 and the Kurt Lewin Memorial Award from the SPSSI. Jahoda also received awards from the British Psychological Society and the Commander of the British Empire medal, personally bestowed by Queen Elizabeth II. An academic chair in her name was established in Germany.

BIBLIOGRAPHY: *American Psychologist, 35* (1980): 74–76; S.W. Cook. "Marie Jahoda," in: A.N. O'Connell and N.F. Russo (eds.), *Women in Psychology: A Bio-Biographical Sourcebook* (1990), 207–19; "Marie Jahoda (1907–2001)," in: G. Stevens and S. Gardner, *The Women of Psychology*, vol. 2 (1982); R.K. Unger, in: *American Psychologist* 56 (2001), 1040–41.

[Rhoda K. Unger (2nd ed.)]

JAIR (Heb. יָאִיר; "who gives light").

(1) Family and head of an ancestral house in the tribe of Manasseh (Num. 32:41). According to I Chronicles (2:21–22), Jair was the son of Segub of the tribe of Judah – Segub being a son of Hezron who married a daughter of Machir – but was associated with his mother's tribe and inherited with the sons of Manasseh. According to the Chronicler's account the settlements called Havvoth-Jair resulted from peaceful expansion. According to the Pentateuch's account, however, it was after the defeat of Og, king of Bashan, and the conquest of most of the Transjordanian territory, that the family of Jair took the towns (*ḥavvot*) of the Amorites in Argob as far as the "border of the Geshurites and the Maacathites" (Deut. 3: 14), i.e., in the region north of the Yarmuk. The *ḥavvot* were a fertile strip of "fortified cities, with high walls, gates, and bars" (Deut. 3:4–5; I Kings 4:13), up to 60 in all (*ibid.*). Some have connected Hebrew *ḥavva* with Ugaritic and Arabic words for "stockade, circle of tents or houses." According to I Chronicles 2:22, the number of the cities of Jair was 23 and the rest belonged to the other sons of Manasseh (*ibid.*, 23). Some of these cities are mentioned in the *el-Amarna letters (no. 256) and among the cities taken by Thutmose III. Archaeological investigation has revealed that this region was inhabited continuously throughout the Bronze Age. In King Solomon's time this region was a part of the sixth vice-regal division (I Kings 4:13). These *Havvoth-Jair may not have been the same as the ones mentioned in Judges 10:4, which were merely small towns and not fortified cities (see below).

(2) Jair of Gilead judged Israel in the generation preceding Jephthah (Judg. 10:3–5) for 22 years. The text hyperbolizes his greatness and wealth (cf. Judg. 12:9–14), stating that he had "thirty sons that rode on thirty ass colts, and they had thirty cities..." There would seem to be some connection between these 30 cities in the land of Gilead and those in the Bashan (possibly it is to these that the text refers in I Kings 4:13). Jair was buried in Qamon, which is probably Qamm, 4 km. (c. 3 mi.) north of Tayyiba in northern Galilee.

[Yehoshua M. Grintz / S. David Sperling (2nd ed.)]

Jair Son of Manasseh in the Aggadah

Jair was born during the lifetime of Jacob and did not die until the children of Israel entered their land (BB 121b). Other sources are more specific and state that Jair was killed during the first, abortive attack on *Ai. He was in fact the only victim, the "36 men" referred to in Joshua 7:5 being a way of referring to Jair, who was "equal to the majority of the Sanhedrin [of 71]" (Lev. R. 11:7). Abraham had been told by God that all his descendants, with the single exception of Jair, would fall in the battle for the city. As a result of his prayer that this tragedy be averted (Gen. R. 39:16), the decree was reversed and Jair alone fell in the battle (Alphabet of Ben Sira, 49).

BIBLIOGRAPHY: Press, Ereẓ, 1 (1951), 36, s.v. *Argov*; 2 (1948), 255, s.v. *Ḥavvot Ya'ir*; Pritchard, Texts, 486; Bergman, in: JPOS, 16 (1936), 235–7. **ADD. BIBLIOGRAPHY:** S. Japhet, *I & II Chronicles* (1993), 80–81; J. Tigay, *JPS Torah Commentary Deuteronomy* (1996), 36; M. Cogan, *I Kings* (AB; 2000), 209; B. Levine, *Numbers 21–36* (AB; 2000), 497–98.

JAKAB, DEZSÖ (1864–1932) and **KOMOR, MARCELL** (1868–1944), Hungarian architects, designers of synagogues, nursing homes, public buildings, and private villas. Their major projects, situated outside Hungary's present borders, include the synagogue of Subotica (Szabadka), Yugoslavia, the municipality building of Tirgu Mures (Marosvásárhely), Romania, and a concert hall in Bratislava, Czechoslavakia. In partnership they built the Erkel theater in Budapest according to the plans of G. Markus (1872–1912), another Jewish architect of the Secessionist era. Komor was a victim of the Holocaust.

[Eva Kondor]

JAKOBOVITS, LORD IMMANUEL (1921–1999), rabbi. Jakobovits was born in Koenigsberg, the son of Julius Jakobovits, rabbi of the local Orthodox congregation and later *dayyan* in Berlin and London. He studied for the rabbinate at Jews' College and at the Etẓ Hayyim Yeshivah, London. After serving as minister to a number of London synagogues, in 1949 he became chief rabbi of Dublin and the Jewish communities in the Irish Republic. Jakobovits was rabbi of the Fifth Avenue Synagogue, New York, from 1958 until 1966, when he was appointed chief rabbi of the United Hebrew Congregations of the British Commonwealth, serving until his retirement in 1991. Jakobovits was appointed honorary director of the Center for Jewish Medical Ethics at Ben-Gurion University, Israel, in 1977, and a fellow of University College, London, in 1984. Knighted in 1981, Jakobovits became a peer in 1988.

His *Jewish Medical Ethics*, published in 1959 with a fourth edition in 1977, is regarded as a standard work in the field. His other publications include *Jewish Law Faces Modern Problems* (1965), *Journal of a Rabbi* (1966), *The Timely and the Timeless* (1977), and *If Only My People...Zionism in My Life* (1984). In 1991 he was awarded the Templeton Prize for Progress in Religion.

[Rohan Saxena]

JAKOBOVITS, TOBIAS (1887–1944), Prague librarian and scholar. Born of a rabbinical family in Lackenbach (Burgenland) and pupil of the yeshivot of Deutschkreuz, Szombathely, and Bratislava, he came to Prague after World War I as a teacher of religion at secondary schools and the *talmud torah*.

There he attended the German university. He reorganized the community's library, publishing a pamphlet on its history in Czech and German (*Entstehungsgeschichte der Bibliothek der israelitischen Kultusgemeinde in Prag*, 1927). Devoting himself to research on the history of the Jews in Bohemia, he published the greater number of his articles in the yearbook of the society for the history of Czechoslovakian Jewry (JGGJČ) and in *Věstnik*, the periodical of the Prague community. During the occupation of Bohemia (1939), he and Joseph Polak headed the scholarly staff of the Jewish museum, which was taken over by the Nazis in 1942 (see *Museums, Jewish). He organized a book exhibition in 1942 and wrote the major part of the museum guide. On Oct. 28, 1944, along with the rest of the museum staff, he was deported to his death in *Auschwitz.

BIBLIOGRAPHY: G. Kisch, in: HJ, 11 (1949), 112–4 (bibl.); H. Volávkov, *The Story of the Jewish Museum in Prague* (1968), passim; O. Muneles, *Bibliographical Survey of Jewish Prague* (1952), index.

[Meir Lamed]

JAKOBSON, MAX (1923–), Finnish journalist and diplomat. Born in Viborg, Jakobson worked in the Finnish News Agency and later in the Finnish department of the BBC. He was also the correspondent for *Helsingin Sanomat* and *Uusi Suomi*. He was press attaché at the Finnish embassy in Washington (1953–59) and chief of the press department of the Finnish Foreign Ministry (1962–65). In 1965 he was made permanent representative of Finland at the United Nations. He remained in the Foreign Ministry until 1974, also serving as Finland's ambassador to Sweden. He wrote *Finland in the New Europe* (1998).

JAKOBSON, ROMAN (1896–1982), philologist and literary historian. Born in Moscow, Jakobson studied and did research at Moscow University before settling in Czechoslovakia in 1921. In 1926 he was co-founder of the Cercle Linguistique de Prague, which pioneered major advances in modern linguistics. He was among the first to perceive that speech sounds are not atomic entities but complexes of a small number of universal phonetic properties ("distinctive features"). Jakobson left Czechoslovakia in 1939 and two years later reached the U.S., where he held professorships at the Ecole Libre des Hautes Etudes, NYC (1942–46), Columbia University (1946–49), Harvard (1949–67), and Massachusetts Institute of Technology (from 1960). In the 1940s Jakobson's central interest was the 12th-century Russian epic, *Slovo o polku Igoreve* ("Tale of the Host of Igor"), whose authenticity had been questioned. In a series of brilliant philological studies he fully established the medieval origin of the poem. The Igor studies renewed Jakobson's long-standing interest in the language, culture, and history of the Slavs in the Middle Ages, and the culture and language of the Jews living among the Slavs (Rus. and Eng. with commentary, in *Annuaire de l'Institut de Philologie et d'Histoire Orientale et Slave*, 8, 1948).

In general linguistics and in Slavic studies there are few areas to which Jakobson did not make fundamental contributions. Outside these disciplines, he contributed to developments in anthropology, art history, literary criticism, philosophy, and communication science. His publications include *Kindersprache, Aphasie und allgemeine Lautgesetze* (1941), *Russian Epic Studies* (with E.J. Simmons, 1949), *Fundamentals of Language* (1956), and *Selected Writings* (2 vols., 1962–66).

BIBLIOGRAPHY: *For Roman Jakobson: Essays on the Occasion of his Sixtieth Birthday* (Eng., Fr., Ger., Rus., 1956), bibl. on pp. 1–12; *To Honor Roman Jakobson: Essays on the Occasion of his Seventieth Birthday*, 3 vols. (multilingual, 1967), bibl. on pp. xi–xxxiii.

[Morris Halle]

JAKUBOWSKI, JACKIE (1951–). Born in Szczecin, Poland, Jakubowski arrived in Sweden as a political refugee in 1970. A journalist with special interest in cultural affairs, he is editor of Sweden's national Jewish magazine, *Judisk Krönika* – one of the foremost publications of its kind in Sweden. In 1986, he published his first book, *Jewish Identity in Sweden: From Mosaic Citizen to Zionist Jew*. This was followed in 1992 by *Judiska prövningar och omprövningar …* ("Jewish Problems and Considerations …") and in 2000 by *Ljudet av alef …* ("The Sound of Aleph …"). He has also coauthored works with such notable writers as Joanna Bankier and Per Ahlmark

BIBLIOGRAPHY: Megilla-Förlaget: *Svensk-judisk litteratur 1775–1994* (1995).

[Ilya Meyer (2nd ed.)]

JAMA, SAMUEL IBN (12th century), scholar of Gabès, North Africa. Samuel was the son of the *dayyan*, Jacob. Samuel himself used the Hebrew equivalent of the Arabic Jama, calling himself "Aguz" ("the store"). Jama is the author of two noteworthy works. The first is a supplement to the *Arukh*, the talmudic lexicon of *Nathan b. Jehiel. It was the first of its kind and was written about 50 years after the appearance of the original work. In it Jama supplemented the *Arukh* with words, some of which he took from the lexicon of the geonic period. He added them, together with a preface, to the copy of the *Arukh* which he himself had copied. They were first published by S. Buber in the Graetz *Jubelschrift* (1887). Jama's other book was *Hilkhot Sheḥitah* written in Arabic, which is quoted several times by *Isaac b. Abba Mari in his *Sefer ha-Ittur*. Jama appears to have lived for a time in Narbonne and in his books frequently quotes the scholars of Provence. He also frequently quotes from geonic literature, including material not known from any other source. He wrote a book on grammar that has been preserved in manuscript. Abraham *Ibn Ezra exchanged laudatory poems with him.

BIBLIOGRAPHY: S. Buber, in: *Jubelschrift… H. Graetz* (1887), 2–16 (Heb. part).

[Israel Moses Ta-Shma]

JAMAICA, an island in the Caribbean, an independent state. Christopher Columbus (Colon) visited Jamaica on his second voyage (1494) but landed there on his fourth (1503) and took it in the name of the Spanish crown. He was nominated governor of the lands he had discovered. His son, Don Diego Colon, inherited his father's titles and was nominated viceroy and admiral of the lands his father found. Upon his death (1525) Carlos V bestowed the title Marquis of St. Iago de la Vega (a Jamaican city today called Spanish Town) to his son Don Louis Colon. The title was inherited by his sister Isabella Colon who was married to a Portuguese nobleman of the house of Braganza. Under her son, Portugallo Colon, crypto-Jews from Portugal were permitted to settle in Jamaica (1530). Under their tenure the Colon-Braganza family impeded the installation of the tribunal of the Inquisition in Jamaica.

Upon the occupation of Jamaica by the English general Veneable and Admiral William Penn (1654), they were welcomed by the "Portugals."

The "Portugals" were of Jewish origin and slowly began returning to Judaism. In the new capital founded by the English, Port Royal, the Jews were joined by their brethren from Amsterdam, Bordeaux, and Bayonne. In 1662 Jews came to Jamaica from Brazil, in 1663 from England, and in 1664 from British Guiana. Their numbers were strengthened in 1673 by Jews arriving from Surinam with the English evacuees forced out by the Dutch occupation.

Jews met with immediate success in the sugar cane and cocoa plantations they founded, and in Port Royal they developed an impressive commercial center, owing to their proficiency in the Spanish language, trading with Spanish America. They formed a community and allegedly built a synagogue. Josiau Hisquiam Pardo, from a prominent family of Salonikan *hahams*, arrived from Curaçao and was hired as chief *haham*.

From the mid-17th century until the earthquake of June 7, 1692, most Jews lived in Port Royal, and though no historian mentions a synagogue there in that period, one may well have existed and been destroyed. Bryan Edwards, in his *History Civil and Commercial, of the British Colonies on the West Indies* (3 vols., London, 1793–1801), wrote, "The Jews enjoyed almost every privilege possessed by the Christian whites except…," and here he enumerated the civil disabilities still in force against them. He continued, "They have the liberty of purchasing and holding lands as freely as other people and they are likewise allowed the public exercise of their religion; and I have not heard that Jamaica has any reason to repent of her liberality towards them."

The violent earthquake of June 1692 was followed by a tidal wave that completely destroyed the city of Port Royal, and Spanish Town then became the capital. The Jews moved to it as well as to newly built Kingston, to Montego Bay, and to spots all over the island. A Spanish-Portuguese congregation was founded in Spanish Town in 1692 and the synagogue Neve Shalom was established in 1704.

One of the most important *hahams* was Jeoshua Hisquiau de Cordova who served there from 1753 to 1797. A German-English synagogue, Mikveh Israel, existed from 1796 to 1860. Of 876 white inhabitants at the end of the seventeenth century, 350 were Jewish. In 1900 Neve Shalom was abandoned.

As more Jews settled in Kingston, communities formed. In 1744 the luxurious synagogue Sha'ar ha-Shomaim was erected and in 1787 the English-German congregation founded Shaare Yosher synagogue. The two buildings were destroyed by fire in 1882. The synagogues that replaced them were toppled in the great earthquake of 1907. In 1912 The United Congregation of Israelites rebuilt Shaare Shalom, which is in service to this day. One of the main conditions for the unification of all communities in Jamaica is that "the Sephardi ritual is to be maintained except for taking out the Scrolls of the Law which will be Ashkenazi." Some of the Torah Scrolls are more than 300 years old, the synagogue's floor is covered with sand, and the hymn "Bendigamos" is sung in Spanish on Sukkot. The service is partially Conservative, partially Reform and parts are sung in English. There are 23 Jewish cemeteries dispersed all over the island.

The local government levied special taxes on the Jews. These taxes were repealed by order of King George II in 1739. The Jewish question became highly controversial in Jamaica. Citing the British Parliament's Act of 1740, the Jews demanded full political enfranchisement. The community, however, was not unanimous in the matter, and all applications for votes on the part of the Jews were refused without exception. They did, however, received full civil rights on July 13, 1831, owing to the persistent efforts of the leader Moses Delgado. As a result, in 1849 eight of the 47 members of the House of Assembly were Jewish and the House adjourned on Yom Kippur; in 1866 their number reached 13.

The number of Jews in Jamaica between 1700 and 1978 were as follows: 1700–400 Jews, out of a total of 7,000 whites; 1881–2535 out of 14,432; 1957–1,600 out of 13,000; 1978–350. In 2004 there were about 280 Jews in Jamaica.

The following are among the most prominent figures in the history of Jamaican Jewry: Daniel Lopez Laguna (1635–1730) who, after being arrested and tortured by the Inquisition, managed to escape to Jamaica where he translated the Psalms into Spanish in poetic form; Isaac Mendes Belisario (b. 1790), a brilliant artist who painted the customs of the black slave population, their culture, and folklore; the de Cordova family: grandsons of Haham de Cordova – Jacob and Joshua – founded the newspapers *The Daily Gleaner,* considered the best overseas English newspaper, and *The Texas Herald* and founded Waco, Texas; Jorge Ricardo Isaac (1837–1895), born in Colombia to a Jamaican Jewish father, wrote the novel *Maria*, Columbia's national novel, considered a masterpiece in all Latin America.

BIBLIOGRAPHY: J.A.P.M. Andrade, *A Record of the Jews in Jamaica from the English Conquest to Present Times* (1941); M. Arbell, *The Portuguese Jews of Jamaica* (2000); F. Cundall, "The Taxation of the Jews in Jamaica in the 17th Century," in *PAJHS*, 31 (1928), 243–47; S. and E. Hurwitz, "The New World Sets an Example for the Old: The Jews of Jamaica and Political Rights, 1661–1831," PAJHS, 48 (1958–59), 37–56.

[Benjamin Schlesinger / Mordechai Arbell (2nd ed.)]

JAMAL SULAYMĀN (d. 1666), a distinguished kabbalist scholar of the Jewish community of San'a in the 1660s, but not part of its formal leadership. Nothing is known about him except his central role in the *Shabbetean movement. Against the standpoint of the rabbinical court in San'a, he believed in *Shabbetai Ẓevi as the Messiah, and that he himself was assigned by Heaven to materialize the messianic vision. On the first day of Passover 1666, just after the night during which Shabbetai Ẓevi was supposed to be revealed as the Messiah, he went with his entourage of zealots to the Muslim governor of San'a and determinedly demanded from the latter to transfer to him the control of the city. The Muslim response was very harsh and, after the command of Imam Ismāʿīl (1644–1776) arrived, he was beheaded in the city market. The imam regarded the agitation among the Jews as a violation of the protection agreement (*dhimma*) of the Jews by the Muslim government and canceled all regulations protecting the Jews, which eventually entailed the expulsion to Mawzaʿ. The Jews called that year "the year of the Headgear Edict" (*shenat ha-atarot*), prohibiting the Jews from continuing to wear their fancy head coverings. According to folklore, Jamal was offered life by conversion to Islam, but he rejected the idea. His martyrdom was kept alive in the memory of Yemenite Jews and is the subject of *Leket*, an idyll by David *Shimoni.

BIBLIOGRAPHY: Y. Tobi, *Iyyunim bi-Megillat Teiman* (1986), idem, *The Jews of Yemen* (1999).

[Yosef Tobi (2nd ed.)]

JÁMBOR, FERENC-IOSEF (1899–1964), Hungarian journalist and editor. Jámbor was born in Transylvania and studied medicine at the universities of Budapest and Cluj. After serving in World War I, he settled in Cluj and turned to journalism. In 1923 he joined the staff of the Zionist daily **Uj Kelet* and was its editor from 1927 until it was closed by the Hungarian Fascist government in 1940. He was a leading member of the Hungarian Journalists' Association of Transylvania and was one of the most important Jewish publicists in Hungary between the two World Wars. Jámbor was a leader of Ha-Shomer ha-Ẓa'ir in Transylvania and from 1940 to 1941 was vice chairman of the Zionist Federation of Hungary. In 1941 he immigrated to Ereẓ Israel and joined the editorial staff of *Al ha-Mishmar*. In 1955 he was a member of the Tel Aviv municipality, representing Mapam.

Jámbor's library was transferred to kibbutz Evron near Nahariyyah after his death and housed in the cultural center named after him.

BIBLIOGRAPHY: Y. Jámbor, *Mivḥar Ketavim* (1966).

[Yehouda Marton]

JAMES, DAVID (**Belasco**; 1839–1893), British actor, born in Birmingham. James excelled in burlesque roles, such as Mercury in F.C. Burnand's extravaganza, *Ixion*, in 1863, Royalty, London. He went into management at the Vaudeville in 1870 and became famous as Perkyn Middlewick in H.J. Byron's comedy *Our Boys* which, opening in 1875, had a record run of 1,362 performances. It was revived for him in 1884, 1890, and 1892. He left much of his large fortune to Jewish charities.

ADD. BIBLIOGRAPHY: ODNB online.

JAMES, HARRY (1916–1983), trumpet player and band leader. Born in Albany, Georgia, James trained with his father, a circus band leader, and had his own orchestra at the age of 20. After two years with Benny *Goodman's band, he started his own group, concentrating on the brass section and featuring his brilliant trumpet solos. Outstanding among his popular swing arrangements and compositions in the 1940s were *Carnival of Venice, Chiribiribin, Flight of the Bumble-Bee, Two o'Clock Jump*, and *Trumpet Rhapsody*. He married the film star Betty Grable.

JAMES, SIDNEY (1913–1976), British actor. Born Sidney Joel Cohen in Johannesburg, the son of Jewish music hall entertainers, Sid James moved to London in 1946 and first acted on the London stage as a rough-hewn character in comedy roles. Subsequently, he appeared in more than 60 film productions. Among them were *The Small Back Room* (1949), *The Lavender Hill Mob* (1951), *A King in New York* (1957), *The Story of Esther Costello* (1957), and the *Carry On* series. James appeared in no fewer than 18 *Carry On* films, making him one of the most familiar character actors in the British cinema. He was also a popular figure in many radio and television programs, particularly with Tony Hancock.

BIBLIOGRAPHY: ODNB online; C. Goodwin, *Sid James: A Biography* (1995); R. Ross, *The Complete Sid James* (2000).

[William D. Rubinstein (2nd ed.)]

JAMMER, MAX (1915–), Israeli physicist. He was born in Berlin where his elementary education at the Jewish community school and secondary education gave him a grounding in classics of lasting value in his career. He studied philosophy, mathematics, and physics in Vienna (1933–35) before immigrating to Palestine where he gained a Ph.D. in molecular spectroscopy from the Hebrew University of Jerusalem (1942) preparatory to specializing in the philosophy of science. After World War II service in the British Army, he was a member of Haganah's intelligence unit during the War of Independence and was wounded during the battle for Jerusalem. He became a post-doctoral fellow and then lecturer at Harvard University (1951–57) and professor at the University of Oklahoma. He returned to Israel to establish and build a highly successful physics department specializing in solid state physics at the newly founded Bar-Ilan University in Ramat Gan. He became rector (1962) and president of the university (1967–68). Jammer's research has concerned the history and philosophy of science in the classical world, the Middle Ages and the modern era. He is especially interested in the history and philosophy of quantum mechanics. In retirement he continued his studies of the conceptual foundations of quantum mechanics, the true nature of mass (inertia), and an analysis of Einstein's philosophy of religion. His many honors include the Prize of the American Academy of Arts and Sciences (1961), the Israel Prize for the history of science (1984), and election as president of the Association for the Advancement of Science in Israel. He served as a member of many key advisory committees to the Israel government on science and higher education. He was a visiting professor at leading universities in the U.S. and New Zealand. His research and thinking are recorded in a series of very successful books, published by major universities, and translated into many languages. These include *The History of Science* (1950) and *Concepts of Space – the History of Theories of Space in Physics* (1954) which greatly interested Einstein and for which he wrote a preface. He wrote *Concepts of Force – a Study in the Foundations of Dynamics* (1957), *Concepts of Mass in Classical and Modern Physics* (1961) and *The Conceptual Development of Quantum Mechanics* (1966), the first systematic and historical account of this crucially important subject. *The Philosophy of Quantum Physics* (1968) describes the foundations of modern physics and *Concepts of Mass in Contemporary Physics and Philosophy* (2000) extends his earlier analysis of this subject. *Einstein and Religion – Physics and Theology* (2000) was named the outstanding book of the year in the field of theology and the natural sciences by the influential Center for Theology and the Natural Sciences in Berkeley, California.

[Michael Denman (2nd ed.)]

JAMMER, MOSHE (1915–), Israeli physicist. Born in Berlin, Jammer settled in Palestine in 1935. In the 1950s he began producing a series of studies on the philosophy of physics, published by the Harvard and Princeton university presses and subsequently translated into Russian, Chinese, Japanese, and Greek, among other languages. Among his other well-known books are *Development of Quantum Mechanics* and *Concept of Space* (with a foreword by Einstein). In 1959 he joined the staff of Bar-Ilan University as professor of science and head of the department of physics. In 1962 he was appointed rector of the university and acting president 1967–68. In 1984 he was awarded the Israel Prize for the history of science.

JAMPEL, SIGMUND (1874–1934), rabbi and Bible scholar. Jampel, who was born in Galicia, studied Semitics at Heidelberg University and subsequently became rabbi at Schwedt, Brandenburg in 1910. He was among the first Jewish Bible scholars who recognized the value of archaeological and epigraphical finds for establishing the antiquity of the historical accounts of the Bible and the questioning of Wellhausen's hypotheses. His work (most of which was first published in MGWJ but was also intended for the general reader) includes *Die Wiederherstellung Israels unter den Achaemeniden* (1904), dealing with the epigraphic material relative to Ezra-Nehemiah; *Das Buch Esther auf seine Geschichtlichkeit kritisch untersucht* (1907), which takes into account the archaeological excavations of Susa which authenticated the description of the royal palace in the Book of Esther; *Vorgeschichte des israelitischen Volkes und seiner Religion; mit Beruecksichtigung der neuesten inschriftlichen Ergebnisse* (1913, 1928²), a study of the importance of the western Semitic onomastic material, particularly from Mesopotamia in the Hammurapi period, for the understanding of the religion of the patriarchs; and *Die Hagada aus Aegypten* (1911, 1922²), in which he used Egyptian documents for the reconstruction of Israelite religious and social conditions in the Exodus period. He also wrote *Die neusten Papyrusfunde in Elephantine* (1911), and a number of studies on new developments in biblical research such as the two-volume *Vom Kriegsschauplatze der israelitischen Religionswissenschaft* (1909–12).

BIBLIOGRAPHY: T. Preschel, in: *Ḥokhmat Yisrael be-Ma'arav Eiropah*, 2 (1963), 146–55 incl. bibl. of Jampel's writings.

[Yehoshua M. Grintz]

JANCO, MARCEL (1895–1984), painter. Janco was born in Bucharest, Romania. In 1910–14 he exhibited at the salons in Bucharest and moved among modernist artists and poets. In 1916, while studying architecture, he was among the founders of Dada in Zurich. There he participated in the famous evenings at Café Voltaire where he was in charge of the stage and costume design. In the 1920s he was much involved in the Dada movement. He had ties with the Paris branch, participating there in an international exhibition of abstract art, and was one of the founders of the art and literature journal *Contimporanul*. In 1940, following the rise of fascism in Romania, he immigrated with his family to Ereẓ Israel. In Israel, Janco participated in many important exhibitions including those of New Horizons and the Venice Biennale. In 1953 he established the Ein Hod Artists Village and founded the Department for Art Teachers at the Oranim College. In 1967 he was awarded the Israel Prize. In 1983 he was involved in the establishment of the Janco-Dada Museum in Ein Hod.

The art style of Janco moved between the figurative and the abstract. In Israel he had many subjects: soldiers and battle situations, transit camps and immigrant types, Arabs, landscapes, and the Holocaust.

The wounded soldier virtually became the symbol of his work (*Wounded Soldier*, 1949, Israel Museum, Jerusalem). These soldiers had complex meanings. In some of the paintings they looked as if crucified, or praying, or like the figures of Picasso's *Guernica*.

Janco dealt with the theme of immigration from every possible angle. He described the crowded ships, the refugees stealing into the country sheltered by the darkness of night, particular immigrant groups like the Yemenites, tents and figures in the transit camps. In all of these paintings the expressive style seemed to be a reflection of his own experience.

Janco's arrival in Israel after many years on the world stage represented a significant contribution to Israeli art. Within weeks of his arrival, a group of gifted Israeli painters gathered around him, seeing an opportunity through him of effecting a desired change in Israel's artistic life. Janco's activism helped fulfill their expectations.

BIBLIOGRAPHY: Janco Dada Museum, Ein Hod, *In the Struggle: Marcel Janco Painting of the Forties* (1988); Tel Aviv Museum, *Marcel Janco – Retrospective* (1972).

[Ronit Steinberg (2nd ed.)]

JANKÉLÉVITCH, VLADIMIR (1903–1985), French philosopher. Born at Bourges, Jankélévitch taught at Prague, Toulouse, and Lille until he was dismissed by the Vichy government in 1940. In 1945 he became professor at Lille, and later at the Sorbonne. His first important work, *Henri Bergson* (1931), showed his sympathy for this philosopher. Jankélévitch's own views, influenced by Bergson, appeared in his dissertation, *L'Odyssée de la conscience dans la dernière philosophie de Schelling* (1933) and *La mauvaise conscience* (1966[2]). His concern was with overcoming consciousness directed to the unchangeable past. Retrospective considerations halt life's course. Irony (*L'Ironie ou la bonne conscience*, 1950[2]) does not resolve the situation. Time alone leads man on. The *Traité des vertus* (1949) and *Philosophie première* (1954) explore the metaphysics of time and the creative virtues of the instant. Other works are *La Mort* (1966) and *Le Pardon* (1967). As a musicologist, he wrote on Debussy, Fauré, and Ravel.

BIBLIOGRAPHY: Barthélemy-Madaule, in: *Revue de Métaphysique et de Morale*, 56 (1951), 406–35; 65 (1960), 511–24; C. Smith, *Contemporary French Philosophy* (1964), 181–201; *Encyclopedia of Philosophy*, 4 (1967), 249–50, incl. bibl.

[Richard H. Popkin]

JANNER, BARNETT, LORD (1892–1982), British politician and communal leader. Janner was born in Lithuania and moved with his family to Barry, South Wales, when he was six months old. He was educated at Cardiff University, became a solicitor, and was a Liberal member of Parliament for Whitechapel (1931–1935), and then a Labour member for Leicester (1945–1970). He was president of the Zionist Federation of Great Britain and Ireland (1950) and president of the Board of Deputies of British Jews (1955–1964). Janner was known in Parliament as the spokesman on Zionist matters and formed a pro-Zionist parliamentary group of which he was the secretary.

Janner was knighted in 1965 and in 1970, when he retired from the House of Commons, he was made a life peer. His son GREVILLE EWAN JANNER (1928–) became Labour member of Parliament for Leicester after his father's retirement, serving as an M.P. from 1970 to 1997. A barrister, Greville Janner also held a wide variety of communal leadership positions and was president of the Board of Deputies of British Jews from 1979 to 1985. Like his father, he was given a life peerage upon his retirement from the House of Commons, as Baron Janner of Braunstone.

BIBLIOGRAPHY: JC (July 13, 1962). **ADD. BIBLIOGRAPHY:** ODNB online; E. Janner, *Barnett Janner: A Personal Portrait* (1984).

[Getzel Kressel / William D. Rubinstein (2nd ed.)]

JANNES AND JAMBRES, two legendary Egyptian sorcerers whose names appear in various sources as the adversaries of *Moses. Jewish tradition seems to identify them with the sorcerers mentioned in Exodus 7:11ff. (cf. Targ. Jon., *ibid.*). They are also mentioned as the sons of Balaam (Targ. Jon., Num. 22:22; Yal., Ex. 168, 176) and as having played a part in the incident of the *golden calf after joining the mixed multitude that accompanied Israel in the exodus from Egypt (Tanḥ., Ki Tissa, 19). The sources of the legends surrounding the activities of Jannes and Jambres go back at least to the time of the Second Temple. They are mentioned in the "Damascus Document" (Zadokite Fragments, line 17ff.) as "Jannes and his brother" and in the New Testament (II Tim. 3:8). Mention is also made by the Church Fathers of an apocryphal book dealing with Jannes and Jambres.

The names also appear in pagan Greek and Roman literature. Both Pliny (*Natural History*, 30:11) and Apuleius (*Apologia*, 90) mention the name of Jannes only, the former including him in a list of Jewish sorcerers the first of whom is Moses, while the latter names him immediately after Moses in a list of famous magicians. Both Jannes and Jambres, however, are mentioned and discussed in detail by Numenius, the neo-Pythagorean philosopher (quoted in Eusebius, *Praeparatio Evangelica*, 9:8; cf. Origines, *Contra Celsum*, 4:51). They are described as Egyptian priests who excelled in wizardry at the period of the "expulsion" of the Jews from Egypt and as having been considered by the Egyptians capable of rescuing their country from the disasters brought upon it by Musaeus (Moses). Jannes (Iannis), with slight variations, is the most common form in which the name appears in Greek sources, as well as in the Palestinian Targum and in the main midrashic references. The Babylonian Talmud, however, gives the name as Yoḥana (cf. Yal., Ex. 235 – Yoḥane). There appears therefore to be justification for retaining the reading Johannes as it appears in the best-preserved manuscript of Apuleius.

BIBLIOGRAPHY: Schuerer, Gesch, 3 (1909[4]), 402–5; H.L. Strack and P. Billerbeck, *Kommentar zum Neuen Testament*, 3 (1926), 660ff.; F. Cumont, in: RHR, 114 (1936), 19ff.; J. Bidez and F. Cumont, *Les Mages Hellénisés*, 2 (1938), 14 no. 23; Ginzberg, Legends, 7 (1938), 251 (index); J. Guttmann, *Ha-Sifrut ha-Yehudit ha-Hellenistit*, 2 (1963), 114ff.

[Menahem Stern]

JANOAH, JANAH (Heb. יָנוֹחַ).

(1) City on the northern border of Ephraim. It is mentioned in the Bible after Taanath-Shiloh near Shechem and before Ataroth and Naarah in the Jordan Valley (Josh. 16:6–7). According to Eusebius it was situated 12 miles east of Neapolis (Eusebius, Onom. 108:20–21). It is identified with Khirbat al-Yānūn, near the village of the same name, 7½ mi. (12 km.) southeast of Shechem.

(2) City in Galilee mentioned in the Bible together with Ijon, Abel-Beth-Maacah and Kedesh among the cities conquered by the Assyrian king Tiglath-Pileser III in 733/2 B.C.E. (II Kings 15:29). Its location and identification are disputed: Vincent and Albright have proposed Tell al-Naʿam in the Huleh Valley and Kaplan has suggested Khirbat Nīḥā southwest of Kefar Giladi; others identify Janoah with the village of Yānūḥ 6 mi. (10 km.) east of Tyre; Klein and Aharoni prefer Yanoah

in Upper Galilee 2 mi. (3 km.) south of Maona-Tarshīḥā, on the supposition that part of the conquering Assyrian army advanced directly to Acre.

BIBLIOGRAPHY: Wallis, in: ZDPV, 77 (1961), 38ff.; Albright, in: AASOR, 6 (1926), 18ff.; Vincent, in: RB, 35 (1926), 470; Abel, Geog, 2 (1938), 354; EJ; Y. Aharoni, *Hitnaḥalut Shivtei Yisrael ba-Galil ha-Elyon* (1957), 97–98, 129–32; Kaplan, in: BIES, 30 (1966), 53–55.

[Michael Avi-Yonah]

JANOVSKY, SAUL JOSEPH (1864–1939), Yiddish journalist, editor, and activist. Born in Pinsk, Janovsky early became interested in the *Haskalah. After arriving in New York in 1885 he became active in the labor movement. In London in 1890, he edited a radical Yiddish weekly, *Der Arbeter Fraynd,* before returning to New York (1895). When he joined the anarchist movement, he switched from writing Russian to Yiddish, helping to found the *Pionere der Frayhayt* ("Pioneers of Freedom"), and edited anarchist Yiddish periodicals – the weekly *Di Fraye Arbeter Shtime* (1899–1919), the daily *Di Ovnt Tsaytung* (1906), and the monthly *Di Fraye Gezelshaft* (1910–11); he edited the monthly *Gerekhtigkayt*, organ of the International Ladies' Garment Workers' Union (1919–26) and also contributed to *Tsukunft* and *Forverts*. He wrote under many pseudonyms, including Y.Z., Anonymous, Bas-Kol, and Yoysef Ben Gershon. Janovsky wrote about political events and trade union problems, reviewed books and plays, and translated works by Tolstoy and others. His reviews and editorial correspondence were sharp but understanding, demonstrating a flair for recognizing talent; many Yiddish writers were discovered and first published by him.

BIBLIOGRAPHY: Rejzen, Leksikon, 1 (1926), 1219–24; LNYL, 4 (1961), 186–9; E. Shulman, *Geshikhte fun der Yidisher Literatur in Amerike* (1943); A. Gordin, *Sh. Janovsky* (1957).

[Elias Schulman / Marc Miller (2nd ed.)]

JANOWITZ, HENRY D. (1915–), U.S. gastroenterologist and a pioneer in establishing this field. He was chief of the gastrointestinal clinic at the Mount Sinai Hospital and Medical School, New York (1956–61) and professor of clinical medicine from 1967. He was assistant clinical professor of medicine at Columbia University College of Physicians and Surgeons (1960–67). He was emeritus professor of medicine at Mount Sinai Medical Center whose gastroenterology department was named in his honor. His research publications mainly concern the pathology and management of inflammatory bowel diseases. Janowitz was president of the American Gastroenterological Association and played a major role in founding the Crohn's and Colitis Foundation of America. He was a distinguished teacher with a great interest in lay education and author of the popular book *Good Food for Bad Stomachs* (1997). He was an authority on medical allusions in Shakespeare.

[Michael Denman (2nd ed.)]

JANOWITZ, MORRIS (1919–1988), U.S. sociologist. Born in Paterson, New Jersey, Janowitz worked for the U.S. government in various capacities and taught at the universities of Chicago and Michigan. He was especially interested in studies of prejudice, public opinion, and the military establishment. He published *Dynamics of Prejudice* (with Bruno Bettelheim, 1950); *The Community Press in an Urban Setting* (1952); *Reader in Public Opinion and Communication* (with Bernard R. Berelson, 1953[2]); *Comparative Study of Juvenile Correctional Institutions* (1961); *Community Political Systems* (1961); and *Social Change and Prejudice* (with Bruno Bettelheim, 1964). The prejudice studies have a bearing on the understanding of antisemitism as part of a general pattern of prejudicial attitudes. Janowitz's reputation, however, rests chiefly with his pioneering works in the analysis of the organizational structure of the military establishment. His major publications in this field are *Sociology and the Military Establishment* (1959); *The Military in the Political Development of New Nations* (1964); and especially *The Professional Soldier* (1960), in which he describes the professional life, organizational setting, and leadership of the American armed forces as it developed in the 20th century. He attempts to show how technological changes have brought about changes in the military, and that the role of the military leader must change accordingly. He concludes that devices, once designed to wage war, must now be used to ensure and maintain peace.

Later books by Janowitz include *Community Press in an Urban Setting* (1967), *Institution Building in Urban Education* (1969), *Political Conflict* (1970), *On Military Intervention* (1971), *Military Institutions and Coercion in the Developing Nations* (1977), *The Last Half-Century: Societal Change and Politics in America* (1978), *Military Conflict* (1978), *Social Control of the Welfare State* (1980), and *The Reconstruction of Patriotism* (1983).

ADD. BIBLIOGRAPHY: G. Suttles and M. Zald, *The Challenge of Social Control: Citizenship and Institution Building in Modern Society. Essays in Honor of Morris Janowitz* (1986); M. Martin, *The Military, Militarism, and the Polity: Essays in Honor of Morris Janowitz* (1984).

[Werner J. Cahnman / Ruth Beloff (2nd ed.)]

JANOW LUBELSKI (Pol. **Janów Lubelski**; Rus. **Yanov Lyubelski**), town in E. Poland. In the 16th century Jacob b. Isaac Ashkenazi, author of the *Tsenah u-Re'enah* (c. 1590), lived in Janow Lubelski. A traveler reported in 1678 that the Jews there owned especially well-built houses. In 1770 Jewish bakers and butchers were prohibited from selling bread or meat to non-Jews, and in general from trading outside the Jewish lane. There were 390 Jewish families in 1765, 1,520 persons (45.3% of the total population) in 1857, 1,447 (45.5%) in 1897, and 2,881 (44.8%) in 1921 with 13,407 (10.2%) in the whole district.

[Raphael Mahler]

Holocaust Period

In March 1941 a few hundred Jews from Vienna were deported to Janow Lubelski. A labor camp housing 1,000 Jews was set up there. In August 1942 the Jewish population was sent to the nearby towns of Zaklikow and Krasnik and were afterward deported to the death camp in Belzec.

[Stefan Krakowski]

BIBLIOGRAPHY: *Regesty i nadpisi*, 2 (1910); R. Mahler, in: *Yunger Historiker*, 2 (1929); K. Sochaniewicz, in: *Pamiętnik Lubelski* (1930); T. Brustin-Bernstein, in: *Bleter far Geshikhte*, 3 no. 1–2 (1950), 51–78. **ADD. BIBLIOGRAPHY:** J. Skarbek, "Zydzi wojewodztwa lubelskiego podcyas powstania listopadowego," in: BŻIH, 1 (1975), 93.

JANOWSKI, DAVID MARKELOVICH (1868–1927), French chess master. Born in Volkovysk, Russian Poland, Janowski settled in Paris in 1886. He attacked brilliantly but frequently failed to employ required defensive strategy. He defeated Winawer, Schowalter, and Marshall, and drew a match with Schlechter. Janowski lost twice (1901, 1910) to Emanuel *Lasker in world championship matches. For several years he was chess editor of *Le Monde Illustré*.

JANOWSKI, MAX (1912–1991), cantor, composer, conductor. A native of Berlin, Janowski was born into a musical family. His mother, Miriam, was an opera singer and his father, Chayim, led choirs and trained cantors. He studied at the Schwarenka Conservatory in Berlin. In 1933 he won a piano contest that led to his appointment in Tokyo as head of the Piano Department of the Mosashino Academy of Music – and his escape from Nazi Germany. He remained in Japan for four years before immigrating to the United States in 1937. He became the musical director of KAM Isaiah Israel Congregation in Chicago in 1938. It was to remain his home for his entire career, except for a four-year sojourn in Navy intelligence from 1942 to 1946.

As a composer he is most famous for *Avinu Malkeinu* and *Sim Shalom*. They are among the 500 compositions, which include choir and orchestra pieces, cantatas, and oratorios, that he published during his prolific career. His works are popular and moving for both the congregation and the audience. He founded Friends of Jewish Music, which was responsible for the publication of his work.

Though well-rooted in a Reform Congregation, Janowski was honored by Hebrew Union College's School of Sacred Music, the Cantor's Assembly of the Conservative Movement, and the United Synagogue of America, now called the United Synagogue of Conservative Judaism.

[Michael Berenbaum (2nd ed.)]

JANOWSKY, OSCAR ISAIAH (1900–1993), U.S. historian. Born in Poland, he was brought to the U.S. in 1910. He was appointed professor of history at New York City College in 1948. Janowsky's principal scholarly interests were recent European history and Jewish studies. He taught courses and seminars in European national minorities and imperialism, as well as in Jewish history. Among his major works are *The Jews and Minority Rights (1898–1919)* (1933); *International Aspects of German Racial Policies* (with M. Fagan, 1937); *People at Bay* (1938); and *Nationalities and National Minorities* (1945), an elucidation of "national federalism." He also wrote the following important books on U.S. Jewry: *The American Jew: a Composite Portrait* (1942); *The American Jew: A Reappraisal* (1964); *The Education of American Jewish Teachers* (1967); and on Israel, *Foundations of Israel* (1959).

An adviser to J.G. *McDonald (1935), League of Nations High Commissioner for Refugees, he helped to prepare the documentation of McDonald's *Letter of Resignation* (London, 1936). As director of the Jewish Welfare Board Survey (1946–47), he produced the *JWS Report* (1948) known also as the "Janowsky Report," which affected the orientation of Jewish community centers. As chairman of the Commission for the Study of Jewish Education in the U.S. (1952–57) he organized and, with U.Z. Engelman, directed the study (1952–55).

Janowsky's public service was extensive. He was a member of the Board of Governors of The Hebrew University of Jerusalem, and chairman of the American Friends of The Hebrew University's Academic Council (1940s–1964); and he organized and chaired the American Student Program for Study at The Hebrew University (1954–66). He was on the editorial board of the *Menorah Journal; Middle Eastern Affairs*; and *Jewish Social Studies*. He was editor of the section on Jews in historiography in the *Encyclopaedia Judaica*. In 1975 Janowsky was awarded the Lee Max Friedman Award by the American Jewish Historical Society for distinguished service in the field of American Jewish history.

[Howard L. Adelson]

JANUARIUS, a legendary Roman general. According to a story cited by R. Johanan (TJ, Av. Zar. 1:2, 39c), "The kingdoms of Egypt and Rome were at war and they proclaimed: 'How long shall we destroy one another in this war? Let us agree that the kingdom which commands its general "fall upon your sword" and he obeys – that kingdom shall rule.' The Egyptians' [general] refused, but among the Romans there was an old man by the name of Januarius [ינוברים] who had 12 sons. They said to him: 'Obey us and we will make your sons dukes, prefects, and generals.' He obeyed, and therefore they [the Romans] call it [the new year] *Calendae Ianuariae* [קלנדס ינוברים]. From the following day they mourn the 'black day' [מילני אימרא, μέλαινα ἡμέρα]." The legend thus explains why the first month is called January and also gives the alleged origins of the Roman *calendae*, and "black day" (*dies ater*) on the second of January. The story has its roots in the early Roman military practice of *devotio*, when a general would seek to sacrifice his life on the battlefield, with the understanding that the gods are thereby obliged to preserve the army. The source before Johanan claims that Janus, the king turned deity, performed this rite of *devotio*; a later Christian source (*De divisionibus temporum*, 15) describes a similar act of sacrifice attributed to Janus, and it appears that there are a number of versions to this legend.

BIBLIOGRAPHY: D. Flusser, in: *Zion*, 21 (1956), 100–2.

[Isaiah Gafni]

JAPAN, Asian state. In early medieval times Jews from Europe and the Middle East may have been involved in trade with Japan through their connection with the silk route. Later, during Japan's so-called "Christian Century" (1542–1639), some Jews participated in the limited trade initiated by the Portuguese and the Dutch. But it was not until after 1853, when Commodore Perry of the United States Navy arrived in Japan and initiated the process which was to reopen Japan to outside influences, that Jews started to settle in the country. Alexander Marks, who arrived in Yokohama in 1861, was the first Jewish resident of modern Japan. Shortly thereafter he was joined by Raphael Schoyer, an American businessman, who served as president of the municipal council of the foreign settlement from 1865 to about 1867. He was also the publisher of the *Japan Express*, one of the first foreign-language newspapers to appear in Japan. By the end of the 1860s, the city had 50 Jewish families from Poland, the United States, and England. During the next few decades Jewish communities established themselves in Nagasaki, where they were primarily involved in the import-export trade, and subsequently in Kobe and Tokyo. The community in Nagasaki may well have decided to settle here because this city, in addition to being a flourishing entrepôt, was long used by the Russian Far Eastern fleet as a base for rest and recreation. Little is known about this community, which subsequently declined, but evidence that it maintained its own cemetery has been uncovered in the post-World War II era. Nagasaki's place as a center of Jewish life in Japan was gradually taken by the rising port of *Kobe.

Jewish emigration to Japan mounted during the decade before the close of World War I. The Russian Revolution of 1905 and particularly the Bolshevik Revolution of 1917 compelled many Russian Jews to flee from Russia. Many made their way to *Manchuria and *China, while others continued on to Japan, where they were assisted by their coreligionists. Volunteer organizations, notably HIAS, played a major role in evacuating these refugees to Japan. Though some settled down permanently in *Tokyo, Yokohama, and Kobe, many others sooner or later found haven in the United States and Latin America.

For some years after World War I the Jewish community in Japan did not number more than several thousand. Despite the concentration of Jews in a few cities, they did not overly impinge upon the consciousness of the Japanese people, who for the most part remained unaware of the Jews as a distinct people and as the upholders of a distinct faith. (Even most educated Japanese long believed that the Jews were a Christian sect!) One of the first public encounters between Japan and a Jew came about during the Russo-Japanese War when the American financier *Jacob Schiff arranged a loan for Japan which in part enabled them to win the war. The role played by Schiff was well known in Japan and unprecedentedly he was invited to the Imperial Palace for lunch. A link had been established between Jews, money and power. During the 1920s signs of antisemitism began to emerge. Its purveyors were mainly soldiers who had taken part in Japan's Siberian Expedition (1918–22) and who had been infected by the tales of hatred peddled by antisemitic White Russians. These were the people who introduced the infamous Protocols of the Learned *Elders of Zion into Japan; in the following 35 years additional editions continued to be published. Still, Japanese antisemitism was not widespread. Largely "intellectual" in character and in part reflecting the growing fear of Bolshevism, with which Jews were identified, it caused Jewish residents of Japan neither embarrassment nor inconvenience. When Japan embarked upon a program of military expansion in Manchuria in 1931, the fortunes of thousands of Jews were directly and indirectly affected. Though for a while the Jewish communities in Manchuria, especially in *Harbin, were subjected to no special discriminatory actions, in time many of the erstwhile refugees from Russia, finding Japanese rule unpalatable, decided to emigrate elsewhere. Many transferred their homes and business to *Tientsin, *Shanghai, and *Hong Kong, while a few settled down in Japan. At the same time the development of closer relations with Nazi Germany resulted in a tremendous expansion of antisemitic literature in Japan. After 1937 many more antisemitic works were translated into Japanese from the German and additional works were written de novo in Japanese. But, by and large, the Japanese government and people remained indifferent to this inflammatory literature which circulated in limited circles. The most dramatic consequence of Japan's pre-war fascination with Jews and understanding of antisemitism was the so-called Fugu Plan which was a Japanese scheme elaborated by Japan's so-called Jewish experts to provide a national home for the Jewish people, in Manchuria, in exchange for the help of international and particularly American Jewry in the establishment of the Japanese Empire – the Greater East Asia Co-Prosperity Sphere. The need for such a haven had become apparent to the Japanese. A stream of Jewish refugees from Nazism poured into the Far East during the early years of World War II. Many of them, coming by sea, found temporary homes in the International Settlement at Shanghai. Others, coming overland through Siberia from Eastern Europe, stayed a while in Japan. Perhaps the best known contingent of such refugees were the members of the *Mir yeshivah in Lithuania who arrived in Japan in 1941. Though they were not permitted to remain, the Japanese government did not press them to leave until arrangements had been made for their transit to Shanghai. When shortly thereafter the International Settlement was occupied by Japanese forces, about 50,000 Jews came under Japanese military rule. Many of the refugees were placed in an internment camp for the duration of the war. Strict as this military administration was, it was a far cry from the Nazi-occupied areas of Europe.

After World War II

During the American occupation of Japan (1945–52) the number of Jews in the islands reached its highest figure, some officials of General MacArthur's regime and many GIs being Jewish. When many of these servicemen returned home after the termination of the occupation and the Korean War (1950–53), the number of Jews in Japan dwindled. Organized Jewish life in Japan during these years revolved mainly about the activities sponsored by the Jewish chaplains of the American armed forces. By 1970 the size of the Jewish community in Japan had stabilized at about 1,000, most of whom lived in Tokyo and Yokohama. Some of these local Jews had found homes for themselves in the cities of Japan before World War II; many others, however, were migrants from the United States and Europe who had settled in the islands in the postwar era. Engaging in the export-import trade, operating businesses, holding professional positions, and serving as consultants, most seemed prepared to live out their lives in Japan.

A keen general interest in Jews and Judaism began to be evident in Japan after World War II. At the time there was a growing proselytizing trend in Israel and the United States which led to "outreach" activity being initiated in Japan. Since the 1920s Jacques *Faitlovitch, the "Father" of the *Beta Israel of Ethiopia, had been interested in the possibilities presented for Jewish missionary endeavor in Japan. In 1954 Faitlovitch set off for Japan in order to set up a Jewish "outreach" center. Behind this move lurked the sense that the Japanese were thinking of converting to Judaism *en masse*. This came to nothing but speculation remained rife. The principal converts were Japanese women who married American-Jewish servicemen; ultimately many of them moved to the United States with their husbands. Among the few male converts to Judaism the best known was Setsuzo *Kotsuji, descended from a family of Shinto priests, whose quest for a faith had led him through Protestant Christianity to Judaism. With his conversion, consummated in Jerusalem in 1959, he took the name Abraham. The postwar disenchantment of the Japanese people with their traditional faiths had spurred a new interest in other religions and philosophies, including Judaism. The study of Jewish history and culture, which later drew the attention of Prince Mikasa of the imperial family, increased as never before. The Japanese Association of Jewish Studies, scholarly in orientation, undertook the publication of the journal *Yudaya-Isuraeru Kenkyu* (Studies on Jewish Life and Culture). A prime mover in the promotion of knowledge about Jewish matters was Masayuki Kobayashi, professor of history at Waseda University (Tokyo) and long a champion of Jewish studies in Japan.

The majority of Jews in Japan in the 1970s consisted of those who had come on contracts of 2 to 5 years, while the permanent Jewish population was less than 200. The Tokyo community maintained a synagogue and religious school, a Judaica and general library, a restaurant, a *mikveh*, and a *ḥevra kaddisha*. It also maintained a rich cultural, social, and recreational program. It was a member of the Federation of Jewish Communities of Southeast Asia and the Far East and had received an award from the Japanese Government for creating "mutual understanding and goodwill between the Japanese and Jewish peoples." The Jewish community served as the home of the Japan-Israel Women's Welfare Organization (JIWWO), the Japan-Israel Friendship Association (JIFA), and the Society for Old Testament Studies. The annual JIWWO Ḥanukkah bazaar, held at the community center and considered to be one of the most prestigious occasions in the Tokyo social calendar, was always attended by a member of the Japanese Imperial household. The only other active Jewish community in Japan was that of *Kobe (which consists of some 30 families), mostly of Sephardi origin. Its Ohel Shlomo synagogue was completed in 1969. The site of the synagogue built by the now defunct *Nagasaki Jewish community, confiscated as alien property during World War I and destroyed after World War II, was rediscovered, and some of the synagogue's furnishings were presented to the Tokyo synagogue in 1973. Jews and Jewish studies began to attract great interest after the publication of *Nihonjin to Yudayajin* ("The Japanese and the Jews"), which became a bestseller in Japan. Rabbi Marvin Tokayer, who was appointed rabbi of the Tokyo Jewish community in 1968, retired in 1976. In 1980 Rabbi Jonathan Maltzman became rabbi of the community. Rabbi Tokayer published three books in Japanese, including an introduction to the Talmud, a Jewish view of the Torah, and a study of Jewish humor. Books by Japanese scholars on Jewish history, mysticism, and Yiddish studies also appeared. One such scholar prepared a doctoral thesis on the Chabad Ḥasidim, and increasing interest was shown in the writings of Prof. R. Sugita, who published more than eight books on Jewish history. The Sophia Church, known as the "Christian Friends of Israel," continued to pray daily for the peace and welfare of the Jewish people. This sect built a "Beit Shalom" in both Kyoto and Tokyo where any Jew may stay and feel at home. The founder and leader of this sect is the Rev. T. Otsuke. The *Makuya sect, led by Prof. I. Teshima, believes in the possibility that the Japanese are one of the *Ten Lost Tribes. They continued to support and visit Israel. In April 1980 a statue of Anne Frank was unveiled in the compound of a church in Nichinomiya.

In 1992 approximately 1,000 Jews resided in Japan, most of them in the greater Tokyo area. The permanent Jewish population, however, was less than 200, the level at which it remained into the 21st century. About 60% came from the U.S., 25% from Israel, and the rest from all over the Jewish world. Within the community there were only a handful of Japanese converts. Most Jews residing in Japan are expatriates representing major businesses, banks, and financial institutions. There are also journalists and students. The Jewish Community Center of Japan, located in Tokyo, houses the city's only synagogue, a religious school, a Judaica and general library, a *mikveh*, *ḥevra kaddisha*, social area, and administrative offices. Religious services are held every Sabbath and on holidays. Kosher food products are imported from abroad and other religious needs and requirements are met. There are also youth programs, adult education courses, and cultural and social activities. The community is a member of the World Jewish Congress, the Asia Pacific Jewish Association, and the B'nai B'rith, and also contributes to the United Israel Appeal. The only other organized Jewish community is located in Kobe, which consists of about 35 Jewish families in Kobe itself and about 35 families in other parts of the Kansai region (Kyoto and Osaka). Jews in the American military stationed in Japan are usually serviced by two Jewish chaplains. One is stationed in Yokosuka Naval Base outside Tokyo and the other in Okinawa. There are about 100–200 Jews stationed in Japan. The Jewish Community Center continues to serve as the home for the Japan-Israel Women's Welfare Organization (JIWWO) and the Japan-Israel Friendship Association (JIFA). Especially since 1986, numerous books about Jews and Judaism have been published in Japan. Several of them have been antisemitic but have not led to any significant acts of antisemitism. The Japanese government's response has been vague and noncommittal. Jewish subjects are taught from time to time in Japanese universities. There is a Jewish Studies Section of the Institute of Social Sciences at the prestigious Waseda University. It was founded in 1976, has 16 academic members, and meets several times a year. The journal published by the Japan Society for Jewish Studies noted above, *Studies on Jewish Life and Culture*, has published several issues since 1961.

Relations with Israel

Relations between Israel and Japan have been consistently friendly. At the beginning of 1952, the governments of Japan and Israel opened negotiations on the establishment of diplomatic relations, and as the year progressed the exchange of legations was announced and the Israel legation, headed by a government minister, opened in Tokyo in December. In 1955 the Japanese minister in Ankara presented his credentials as a nonresident minister to Israel, and later the Japanese legation was headed by a resident minister. In 1963 the legations were raised to the level of embassies. In 1970 an agreement on mutual aid and the formulation of legal documents was signed.

In 1961 a delegation of Japanese anthropologists and geographers dug on the slopes of Mt. Carmel near Haifa. At the University of Tokyo, a number of Japanese students have studied biblical Hebrew and the archaeology of the Land of Israel; others have studied Hebrew in approximately a dozen other university-level institutions. Since 1965 Japanese studies have been part of the regular program of the Hebrew University, Jerusalem, and Tel Aviv University. Under the program of annual educational grants, a number of Japanese research students have studied Bible, Jewish musicology, and Jewish history in Israel and a number of Israeli students have studied in Japan. A Japanese art pavilion was opened in Haifa. The Kibbutz Society, founded in 1963 by Tezuka Nobuyoshi, numbers about 30,000 members and publishes the Kibbutz Monthly in Japanese. The moral and social values of the kibbutz serve as a source of inspiration for the members of the society, and every year three groups of Japanese youngsters (with 50–70 in each group) have spent time on kibbutzim in Israel (about 550 people participated in these visits in 1965–70). The society has even established a kibbutz in Akan, Eastern Hokkaido. The Japan-Israel Women's Welfare Society, which has a parallel organization in Israel, finances the sending of students to Israel, among other activities.

The main relationship between Japan and Israel is a commercial one. Traditionally Japan has exported steel, automobiles, processing machinery and home electronics while Israel exported diamonds, phosphates, citrus, and fashion goods. Even before the Yom Kippur War a number of leading Japanese firms boycotted Israel, but immense Arab pressure and a threat to cut off the supply of oil to Japan (which obtains over 40% of its supply from the Arab states) forced Japan in November 1973 to depart from her previous neutrality and adopt a definite pro-Arab stand. For some years Israel was one of the very few nations in the world to run a trade surplus with Japan, primarily because of booming diamond imports by the Japanese. In 1987 an economic mission from Israel, led by representatives of the Israeli Manufacturers Association, visited Japan. A return delegation of businessmen from Japan, led by representatives of the Federation of Economic Organizations of Japan (Keidanren), followed to Israel. In 1988, a conference on the Japanese economy was held in Israel and an Israeli Economy Seminar was held in Tokyo. Throughout the 1990s there were some tentative movements toward increasing trade relations with Israel by small- and medium-sized Japanese firms, but most major Japanese companies continued to adhere to the Arab economic boycott of Israel. In 1992, however, the Japanese Foreign Ministry advised Japanese companies to cease cooperating with the boycott and Japan called on Arab countries to stop the boycott. Following this declaration bilateral trade continued to grow. Since the late 1990s Japan has played an active role in such areas as the environment, economic development, and water resource management.

[Hyman Kublin, Michael J. Schudrich, Shaul Tuval, and Marvin Tokayer / Tudor Parfitt (2nd ed.)]

The Japanese government also began to take a more active political role in the Middle East, consistent with a more engaged and wide-ranging foreign policy. Japan has strongly supported the post-Oslo "peace process" and has sought to use its influence to move the process forward. In 2005 Japan pledged $100 million to the Palestinian Authority, with Prime Minister Koizumi Junichiro announcing the gift in May during a visit to Japan by PA leader Mahmoud Abbas. Japan has become one of the PA's most important sources of support, committing $860 million since the signing of the Oslo Accords in 1993. Japan also extended an invitation to Israel's prime minister Ariel Sharon to visit Japan during 2005.

Moves towards closer relations between Israel and Japan can be traced to high-level ministerial visits during the 1980s. Israel's then foreign minister, Yitzhak Shamir, visited Japan in September 1985, with the first visit by a Japanese foreign minister occurring two years later. The first visit to Japan by an Israeli head of state was made by President Chaim Herzog in February 1989 on the occasion of the funeral of Emperor Hirohito. During the post-Oslo period, Prime Minister Yitzhak Rabin visited Japan in December 1994 and Japan's Prime Minister Tomiichi Murayama traveled to Israel in September 1995. Prime Minister Binyamin Netanyahu made a visit to Japan in August 1997. There have also been visits from Israeli cabinet ministers and from other officials, including the then mayor of Jerusalem, Ehud Olmert, who visited the country in 1999.

Although knowledge in Japan about Jews and Judaism remains slight, links to the experience of the Jewish people have been strengthened through exposure to the Shoah, with the Diary of Anne Frank a part of the school curriculum and with films about the topic, such as *Life is Beautiful*, being shown on television and in cinemas. Affinities between Japan and the Jewish people have also been strengthened by the increased attention being given to the Japanese diplomat *Sugihara, who used his position in 1940 as Japan's vice consul in Lithuania to issue travel documents to Jews and thus saved many thousands of lives. The year 2000 marked the 100th anniversary of Sugihara's birth, at which time a plaque was unveiled at Japan's Ministry of Foreign Affairs at a ceremony hosted by the minister of foreign affairs in the presence of Sugihara's widow. A Sugihara Fellowship was established under the Japan Foundation for the purpose of supporting young Israeli researchers in Japanese studies. Sugihara's heroism and humanity have been further highlighted in Japan with the issue of a stamp in his honor and through his being given official recognition as one of the country's greatest figures of the 20th century.

In 1985 Sugihara became the first Japanese person to be honored by Yad Vashem as one of the *Righteous Among the Nations. Sugihara's birthplace, Yaotsu, a town in Gifu prefecture, has established memorials to him, including a museum whose exhibits and displays, including a video of his life, recreate for Japanese his courage and humanitarianism. Israel's Bar-Ilan University opened a Sugihara Center in 1994. In 2000–01 a centennial celebration in his honor, called Visas for Life, was held, with exhibits honoring Sugihara's contribution being displayed in Japan and internationally. An emissary from Israel has been based in Yaotsu to assist with the museum's educational program.

[Stephen Levine (2nd ed.)]

Jewish Discourse in Japan and the Common Origin Theory

Among the foreigners to be found in Japan in the 1870s was Norman McLeod, a Scot who started his career in the herring industry before he ended up in Japan as a missionary. In the preface to his *Epitome of the Ancient History of Japan*, which was first published in 1875, he noted that he had arrived in Japan in 1867 – the last year of the Tokugawa regime – and that he had intended to write a multi-volume work on Japan which among other things would furnish the reader with "a more detailed account of the origins of the Japanese with a description of their Jewish belongings." His "researches in Japan have satisfied him," a local newspaper reported in 1875, "that the people of this country are of Jewish family…." His notion that the Japanese people were descendants of the "Ten Lost Tribes of Israel" was set forth in several books; this contention has been repeated regularly until the present day. McLeod's ideas reached a wide international audience, including a Jewish one, and no doubt had an impact on Japanese thinking. Within a couple of decades of their publication they formed part of a half-serious discourse which circulated throughout the Western Jewish press and elsewhere.

In Japan the ideas of McLeod fell on fertile ground perhaps because of some uncertainty as to where the Japanese originated and where they belonged in the world. No doubt the multitude of theories generated in Japan linking the Jews and Japan – the so-called common origin theories – were at least in part products of the western Christian tradition of speculation on the fate of the Ten Lost Tribes of Israel. However, alongside the speculation of early western visitors, and particularly McLeod, the local reading of the Christian Bible also played an important if perhaps secondary role in the spread of the fantasy of Israelite origin. In Japan one of the first Japanese to propose a common ancestry for the Jews and the Japanese was Saeki Yoshiro (1871–1965) who published his theory as an appendix to an academic work on Nestorian Christianity in 1908. Saeki was a serious scholar of Christianity in China. He arrived at the belief that the Hata clan – a continental group which is supposed to have arrived in Japan in the fifth century and which was to be found to the west of Kyoto in a village called Uzumasa – was Jewish. He adduced in favor of this proposition a range of philological arguments: "*Uzu*," he reasoned, is a corrupt form of "*Ishu*" or Jesus and "*masa*" was the Hebrew form of Messiah. There are many other "proofs" of a similar sort. Notwithstanding the less than compelling nature of this evidence the "Uzumasa" connection was not only the linchpin of Saeki's argument but has become the basis of a great deal of subsequent common origin theorizing. In 1929 Oyabe Zen'ichiro (1867–1941), a Yale-educated Christian minister who had worked as a missionary in Hawaii, published his *Origin of Japan and the Japanese People* where he continued the arguments of Saeki. He elaborated on the contention that the Japanese emperors too were of Israelite descent. He observed: "It is well-known to Biblical scholars in the West and the world over that approximately three hundred years before the enthronement of the Emperor Jimmu (in 660 B.C.E.), two tribes of the Hebrews – Gad the most valiant and Menasseh, who were descended from the eldest son of the patriarch – fled eastward carrying the Hebrews' sacred treasures and to this day their whereabouts remain unknown. A close study of the ancient Hebrews as they are described in the Jewish scriptures reveals an extraordinary number of similarities between our two peoples. The Japanese and the Hebrews are virtually identical. These exact correspondences convince me that we are in fact one race." Underlying Oyabe's thesis was his belief that Christianity and Shinto were much the same thing and that for Shinto better to serve the Japanese nation it would do well to adapt more explicitly Christian features, including the idea of a direct line of descent from Jewish thought. Another common origin theorist was Kawamorita Eiji (1891–1960). Kawamorita, a Presbyterian minister, spent most of his life in the United States and produced a large two-volume work in Japanese – *Study of Japanese Hebrew Songs* – which argued that in Japanese folk songs were to be found traces of a Hebrew which had otherwise disappeared from Japan some thirteen hundred years before. This work continues to sustain Japanese Lost Tribes enthusiasts. Kawamorita's central idea was that Japan is a holy nation, that God is the source of all holiness and that therefore Japan's holiness must originate from God. Consequently Japan's divine emperor could only have descended from Israel – the chosen people of God. Kawamorita was led to the belief that "our Emperor is the undisputed successor to the eternal throne of the Great King David of Israel and that without the Emperor System Japan will lose its reason to exist." Israelite theories have had a striking impact on Japanese society and no doubt have contributed to the egregious Jewish discourse in Japan. The general perspective on Jews is generally more or less antisemitic but rather vague. An example is the definition of the word "Jew" in Sanseido's *New Crown English-Japanese Dictionary* (revised edition, 1964): "Jew (dzu) n. Jew: Jews covet money – consequently there are many Jewish millionaires. The word can be used in lieu of the following: 'avaricious,' 'miser,' and 'rich.'" Jewish conspiracy theories based largely on Western antisemitic ideas are rife and books peddling such ideas have achieved massive sales. Most Japanese bookstores have a "Jewish corner" where titles such as *The Jewish Plot to Control the World, The Secret of Jewish Power that Moves the World,* and so on are displayed. This interest in Jews has been present in Japan for years. In 1970 *Nihonjin to Yudayajin* ("The Japanese and the Jews") won one of Japan's most coveted literary prizes and sold well over a million copies (by 1987 it had sold three million copies), and sales of a similar order have since been achieved by *If You Understand Judea You Understand Japan, The Jewish Way of Blowing a Millionaire's Bugle, If You Understand the Jews You Understand the World: 1990 Scenario for the Final Economic War, Miracles of the Torah which Controls the World*, and others besides. The mass media frequently carry sensational stories along the same lines. A more general Japanese interest in things Jewish or Israeli is quite apparent. From the amazing popularity of *The Diary of Anne Frank* to the unprecedented commercial success of the musical *Fiddler on the Roof* a Jewish seam appears to run through Japanese society. The fascination with Israel and Jews seems endless.

In contemporary Japan perhaps the most striking legacy of the strange ideas of McLeod is to be found in the Makuya and Beit Shalom sects. Although both of them are essentially Christian sects accepting the divinity of Christ, their "Jewishness" is very visible. The Makuya are intensely nationalistic and, in some ways, are looking to the redemption of the Japanese nation, which will be modeled upon the redemption of Israel. Makuya was founded at about the same time as the State of Israel. The founder of Makuya, Avraham Ikuro Teshima (1910–1973), is said to have met and to have been influenced by Martin *Buber on a number of occasions. Over the years thousands of Makuya and Beit Shalom disciples have gone to Israel where many of them have learned Hebrew. The importance of a good knowledge of Hebrew for the Makuya can be judged by the fact that they have brought out a beautifully produced Japanese-Hebrew dictionary. Whenever the Makuya get together they sing secular and religious Hebrew songs, many of them the songs of modern Israel. They adopt Hebrew names, observe the Sabbath, and keep a form of *kashrut*: they light candles on Friday evening, break *hallah,* and read from the Jewish prayer book. Their view of the world is informed by a profound admiration for Israel and the Jewish people. Their love for Israel often finds practical expression: a Makuya volunteer was wounded in the 1967 Six-Day War and in the wake of the Israeli victory a Makuya "pilgrimage" marched through Jerusalem carrying a banner proclaiming "Congratulations on the Greater Jerusalem." To some extent their admiration for Jews derives from the Christian part of their ideology. But, in addition, it springs from the national nature of Judaism – the idea that Judaism is the religion of the Jewish people – and from Zionism.

[Tudor Parfitt (2nd ed.)]

BIBLIOGRAPHY: C. Adler, *Jacob H. Schiff: His Life and Letters*, 2 vols. (1928); I. Cohen, *Journal of a Jewish Traveller* (1925); H. Dicker, *Wanderers and Settlers in the Far East* (1962); A. Setsuzo, *From Tokyo to Jerusalem* (1964); J. Kreppel, *Juden und Judentum* (1925); H. Kublin, in: *Congress Weekly*, 23 (Oct. 22, 1956), 9–11; idem, in: *Jewish Frontier*, 25 (April 1958), 15–22; idem, in: *Congress Bi-Weekly*, 28 (Dec. 25, 1961), 13–15; A.J. Wolf, in: *Commentary*, 15 (April 1953), 352–6. **ADD. BIBLIOGRAPHY:** D.G. Goodman and M. Miyazawa, *Jews in the Japanese Mind: The History and Uses of a Cultural Stereotype* (1995); T. Parfitt, *The Thirteenth Gate* (1987); idem, *The Lost Tribes of Israel: The History of a Myth* (2002); T. Parfitt and E. Trevisan Semi, *Judaising Movements: Studies in the Margins of Judaism* (2002); M. Tokayer and M. Swartz, *The Fugu Plan: the Untold Story of the Japanese and the Jews during World War II* (1979).

[Haggai ben-Shammai (2nd ed.)]

JAPHET, ISRAEL MEYER (1818–1892), German composer and teacher. Born in Kassel, Japhet taught at Gudensberg before being appointed choir leader and teacher of the Orthodox congregation in Frankfurt in 1853, where he remained until his death. He published *Metek Sefatayim; Hebraeische Sprachlehre* (1926[3]), a Hebrew grammar in two volumes; a book on the accents of the Bible entitled *Moreh ha-Kore; Die Accente der Heiligen Schrift* (1896), with the notation of the accents according to the German-Jewish tradition; and a Passover *Haggadah* (1884) with translation and commentary in German and including four traditional tunes set for two and four voices. Japhet's most influential work was *Schire Jeschurun* ("Songs of Yeshurun," 1922[4]), a collection of 101 synagogue melodies for cantor and choir in three volumes: the first for the evening and the second for the morning services of Sabbath and festivals; the last for various occasions, such as Simhat Torah and the Sabbath. Their style shows a melodious simplicity and uncomplicated classical harmony which conforms to the general tendencies of the German synagogue of his time.

BIBLIOGRAPHY: Sendrey, nos. 2024, 3900, 6181–85, 7351–52; A. Friedmann, *Lebensbilder beruehmter Kantoren*, 3 (1927), 13–14.

[Joshua Leib Ne'eman]

JAPHETH (Heb. יֶפֶת), son of Noah, brother of *Shem and *Ham. In all the lists of Noah's sons, Japheth invariably appears in the third place (Gen. 5:32; 6:10; 7:13; 9:18; 10:1; I Chron. 1:4). However, on one occasion Ham is called the "youngest son" of Noah (Gen. 9:24). If this is not to be explained as the result of a corruption in the text, it must reflect a variant tradition, unless some principle other than chronological governs the order of the listings. Japheth was married before the *flood (7:13), which he survived, together with his family, inside the ark. When his intoxicated father lay naked in the tent, Japheth, together with Shem, displayed great modesty and delicacy in covering him up (9:23). For this act he was blessed by Noah as follows: "May God enlarge Japheth, and let him dwell in the tents of Shem; And let Canaan be a slave to them" (9:27). The full meaning of this passage is obscure, and it has been variously interpreted as referring to either a Philistine-Israelite alliance against Canaanites (perhaps in Davidic times) or the future participation of the Japhethites – perhaps the Greeks – in the religion of Israel. In the Table of Nations (see The Seventy *Nations) Japheth is assigned seven sons and seven grandsons (Gen. 10:2–4; I Chron. 1:5–7). He is thus portrayed as the eponymous ancestor of various ethnic groups living to the west and north of Israel in the Aegean and Anatolian areas, largely composed of Indo-European stock. The origin of the name Japheth is unclear. The blessing referred to above implies a folk etymology grounded in a Hebrew root meaning "to enlarge," "make spacious." It has variously been connected with the Greek Titan, Ιαπετός (cf. Javan = Ionia, Gen. 10:2), and with *Kafti*, the Egyptian name for the Eteo-Creteans.

[Nahum M. Sarna]

In the Aggadah

Although Japheth was the eldest of the three sons of Noah, he was the least endowed with wisdom, and for this reason his name is recorded last (e.g., Gen. 6:10; Sanh. 69b). In the act of covering Noah's nakedness (Gen. 9:23) the initiative was taken by Shem and Japheth merely helped him. Shem's reward was therefore greater than Japheth's in that the Temple built by his descendant (Solomon) was more holy than that built by Japheth's (Cyrus; PR 35, 160a). Nevertheless, on account of the respect he had thus shown to his father, Japheth was rewarded with a *pallium* (a cloak befitting that dignity of his Greek descendants), and by the fact that Gog, his descendant, would have the privilege of being buried in Ereẓ Israel (cf. Ez. 39:11) and would therefore enjoy the messianic era (Gen. R. 36:6). The verse "God enlarge Japheth" (Gen. 9:26ff.) is interpreted to mean that the culture ("beauty") of Japheth, particularly the Greek language, would "dwell in the tents of Shem" (Meg. 9b). In the Midrash (Gen. R. 36.8) this is made to refer particularly to the Septuagint, and the same passage also interprets it to mean that Cyrus, a descendant of Japheth, would build the Second Temple. It also taught that God blessed Japheth by making his descendants entirely white, and by giving them the desert and its fields for an inheritance (PdRE 23).

BIBLIOGRAPHY: A.H. Sayce, *Races of the Old Testament* (1891), 39–50; J. Simons, in: OTS, 10 (1954), 155–84; L. Hicks, in: IDB, 2 (1962), 802 (incl. bibl.); A. Reubeni, *Ammei Kedem* (1970), 162–84; Ginzberg, Legends, 1 (1961), 169–70; 5 (1955), 179–80, 192; 6 (1959), 459; I. Ḥasida, *Ishei ha-Tanakh*, 222.

JAPHETH (in Ar. **Al-Hasan**) **AL-BARQAMANI** (early 15th century), Karaite author, presumably living in Egypt. His only known work is the *Sefer Teshuvah*, an Arabic polemical tract against the *Rabbanites, in which he nevertheless mentioned *Maimonides with respect.

BIBLIOGRAPHY: S. Pinsker, *Likkutei Kadmoniyyot* (1860), 181, 192 (second pagination); Fuerst, Karaeertum, 2 (1865), 288f.; A. Neubauer, *Aus der Petersburger Bibliothek* (1866), 25f.

[Leon Nemoy]

JAPHETH BEN DAVID IBN ṢAGHĪR (14th century), Karaite scholar and physician in Cairo. Japheth was a pupil of Israel ha-Ma'aravi, and followed his example in rejecting the use of objective analogy (*hekkesh*) in the rules applying to matrimony and incest. He was the author of *Sefer ha-Mitzvot*, of which parts 5 to 9 have been preserved in manuscript. In it Japheth quotes many earlier Karaite scholars, including *Daniel b. Moses al-Qūmisī, as well as works of some Rabbanite authors.

BIBLIOGRAPHY: Steinschneider, Arab Lit, 244; Mann, Texts, 2 (1935), 282 n. 76.

[Isaak Dov Ber Markon]

JAPHETH BEN ELI HA-LEVI (**Yefet ben Eli; Abū ʿAlī al-Ḥasan ibn ʿAlī al-Lāwī al-Baṣrī**; second half of tenth century), Karaite scholar in Jerusalem. Details of his life are not known. He was the only Karaite who wrote biblical commentaries in Arabic, accompanied by an Arabic translation (considered very literal by some modern scholars) of the Scriptures, on the entire biblical corpus (to date Lamentations is the only biblical book on which no trace of Japheth's commentary has been identified). His commentaries are unparalleled in size and diversity of the aspects discussed in relation to the biblical text: language, *halakhah*, history, theology and much polemics against Rabbinic Judaism and also against other religions, notably Islam and Christianity. Messianic aspects of the biblical text are adduced in certain contexts, sometimes extensively. Historical facts and circumstances are mentioned or alluded to occasionally.

Japheth relied mainly on earlier Karaite authorities, whom he quotes mostly anonymously. He sometimes utilized rabbinic sources and works of Rabbanite scholars. The latter are often quoted for polemical reasons. *Saadiah Gaon is often quoted verbatim. He mastered a very wide array of sources, from which he selected in a rather sophisticated manner. Opposing interpretations are sometimes discussed at length (and ultimately rejected) when he thinks that they deserve it. His commentaries are thus a treasure house of old interpretations that often are not found in any other source.

In principle Japheth is committed to the literal meaning of the text, which nevertheless always has to be judged by reason. The result can be defined as rationalistic exegesis. Although ostensibly attacking the Muʿtazila (see *Kalam), his exegetical terminology and theological concepts are typically Muʿtazilite. Accordingly he allows for metaphorical interpretation when required by ideological-exegetical considerations (e.g. unity and integrity of the biblical corpus) or theological ones. Some scholars recently suggested that he also took into account literary considerations, and that historic-philological considerations were paramount for him, but this needs further research. While strictly conservative, Japheth's opposition to the pursuit of secular studies was somewhat milder than that of his contemporaries. His commentaries won immediate recognition among contemporary Karaite scholars and were widely used by subsequent generations of Karaite scholars. Because of their large size, some commentaries were abridged, mainly by Egyptian Karaites. Parts of his commentaries were later translated into Hebrew and thus became available to Karaites in Byzantium who had no knowledge of Arabic. The original Arabic text apparently reached Spain, which may explain the fact that interpretations of his are referred to by Abraham *Ibn Ezra.

He also wrote *Sefer ha-Mitzvot* (Book of Precepts), parts of which survived in manuscript.

Japheth's commentaries survived in many hundreds of MSS. The text seems to have developed over time in various ways and measures. Yet, only a relatively small part of Japheth's gigantic oeuvre (comprising dozens of volumes) has been published to date (mostly from the Prophets and the Writings). In recent times, however, there is an ever-increasing interest in Japheth's works, which is clearly reflected in the amount of publications (see bibl.).

BIBLIOGRAPHY: TEXTS: L. Barges (ed.), *Rabbi Yapheth ben Heli Bassorensis Karaitae in librum Psalmorum comentarii Arabici* (1846) [Psalms]; idem, *Libri Psalmorum David regis et prophetae, versio a R. Yapheth ben Heli Bassorensi Karaita* (1861) [Psalms]; idem, *Rabbi Yapheth Abou Aly … in librum Canticum Canticorum comentarium Arabicum* (1884) (Song of Songs); H. Ben-Shammai et al. (eds.), *Judaeo-Arabic Manuscripts in the Firkovitch Collections: The Commentary on Genesis by Yefet ben ʿEli* (2000) (catalogue, texts, study) (Heb.); P. Birnbaum (ed.), "The Arabic Commentary of Yefet ben Ali the Karaite on the Book of Hosea" (Ph.D. Thesis, Dropsie College, 1942); R.M. Bland (ed.), "The Arabic Commentary of Yephet ben ʿAli on the Book of Ecclesiastes, Chapters 1–6" (Ph.D. Thesis, Berkeley, 1966); S. Butbul, in: *Sefunot*, 23 (2003), 459–571 (Ruth) (Heb.); H. Hirschfeld (ed. & transl.), *Jefeth b. Ali's Arabic Commentary on Nahum* (Jews' College Publications; no. 5, 1911); O. Livne-Kafri, in: *Sefunot*, 21 (1993), 73–113 (Habakkuk) (Heb.); D.S. Margoliouth (ed. & transl.), *A Commentary on the Book of Daniel by Jephet ibn Ali, the Karaite* (1889); M. Polliack, in: *Peʿamim*, 89 (2002), 61–82 (Ovadiah, tr.) (Heb.); M. Sokolow, "The Commentary of Yefet ben Ali on Deuteronomy XXXII" (Ph.D. Thesis, Yeshiva University, 1974). STUDIES: Mann, Texts, 2 (1935), 30–33; L. Nemoy (ed.), *Karaite Anthology* (1952), 83–102; Z. Ankori, *Karaites in Byzantium* (1959), index, s.v.; H. Ben-Shammai, in: *Alei Sefer*, 2 (1976) 17–32 (Heb.); idem, "The Doctrines of Religious Thought of Abu Yusuf Yaʿqub al-Qirqisani and Yefet Ben ʿEli" (Ph.D. Thesis, Jerusalem 1977 (Heb., vol. 2 is a selection of texts)); Y. Erder, in: *Michael*, 14 (1997), 313–34 (Heb.); D. Frank, in: J. Dammen McAuliffe et al. (eds.), *With Reverence for the Word: Medieval Scriptural Exegesis in Judaism, Christianity, and Islam* (2003), 51–69; idem, *Search Scripture Well: Karaite Exegetes and the Origins of the Jewish Bible commentary in the Islamic East* (2004), index; M. Goldstein, in: G. Khan (ed.), *Exegesis and Grammar in Medieval Karaite Texts* (2001), 41–64; M. Polliack, in: G. Khan (ed.), *Exegesis and Grammar in Medieval Karaite Texts* (2001) 1–39; idem, "Major Trends in Karaite Biblical Exegesis in the Tenth and Eleventh Centuries," in: M. Polliack, *Karaite Judaism; A Guide to Its History and Literary Sources* (2003), 363–413; idem, *The Karaite Tradition of Arabic Bible Translation* (1997), index; G. Tamani, in: *Bulletin d'Etudes Karaïtes*, 1 (1983), 27–76; G. Vajda, *Deux commentaires karaïtes sur l'Ecclésiastes*, (1971); N. Wieder, *The Judean Scrolls and Karaism* (2005^2), index.

[Haggai Ben-Shammai (2nd ed.)]

JAPHIA (Heb. יָפִיעַ), city in the territory of the tribe of Zebulun between Dobrath and Gath-Hepher (Josh. 19:12). Japhia is identified with Yafa, 2 mi. (3 km.) southwest of Nazareth. It appears as Iapu in the Tell el-Amarna letters. According to Josephus, who fortified it, it was the largest village in Galilee (Life, 230; Wars, 2:573). During the siege of Jotapata Japhia was attacked, captured, and sacked by the Romans (Wars, 3:289 ff.). It remained a Jewish town however; in 1921 a synagogue lintel was found there, and in 1950 part of a synagogue paved with mosaics was excavated near the Greek Orthodox church. Its ruins include a basilical hall, 46ª49 ft. (14ª15 m.), with two rows of five columns each. The east-west orientation of the hall is unusual. The pavement contains the representation of an eagle standing on a vase whose body is shaped like a human head, tigers and dolphins, and a circle of 12 figures, of which two have been preserved. Sukenik regarded the figures as symbols of the tribes, reading the extant fragmentary inscription רים [Eph]raim; Goodenough identified them with the Zodiac, reading ריס [A]ries.

BIBLIOGRAPHY: E.L. Sukenik, in: BRF, 2 (1951), 8 ff.; Goodenough, Symbols, 1 (1953), 216–18; EM, s.v., **ADD. BIBLIOGRAPHY:** S.J. Saller, *Second Revised Catalogue of the Ancient Synagogues of the Holy Land* (1972), 84–85; Z. Ilan, *Ancient Synagogues in Israel* (1991), 213–14; Y. Tsafrir, L. Di Segni, and J. Green, *Tabula Imperii Romani. Iudaea – Palaestina. Maps and Gazetteer* (1994), 150–51; B. Bagatti, *Ancient Christian Villages of Galilee* (2001), 79–83.

[Michael Avi-Yonah]

JARBLUM, MARC (1887–1972), Zionist leader. Born in Warsaw, Jarblum was one of the founders of Poʾalei Zion in Poland and also engaged in underground activity, for which he was repeatedly jailed. He moved to Paris in 1907 and completed his law studies there. From the time of his arrival in Paris he gradually became one of the most prominent public figures in the Poʾalei Zion movement, the Zionist movement, and in French Jewry. He was especially active in the period between the two world wars. Jarblum was responsible for winning over Léon *Blum and the leaders of the Second (Socialist) International – *Jaurès, Vandervelde, and others – to the Zionist cause. For years he filled public positions – as the representative of Socialist Zionism at the Second International, as representative of the *Jewish Agency in Paris, president of the Zionist Federation and chairman of the Federation of Jewish Organizations in France, as head of the Socialist Zionist movement and editor of its organs, etc. During World War II, Jarblum lived in the unoccupied zone of France and was engaged in underground activities there and, from 1943, in Switzerland. He returned to France after the war and continued his public activities. Jarblum played a special role in securing the French vote for the UN resolution on the partition of Palestine (November 1947). Jarblum lived in Tel Aviv from 1955 and worked in the political department of the *Histadrut there. He published numerous pamphlets on current affairs in Yiddish and in French. Among his works are *The Socialist International and Zionism* (1933, with introd. by E. Vandervelde); *Le Destin de la Palestine juive de la Déclaration Balfour 1917 au Livre Blanc 1939* (1939); *Ils habiteront en sécurité* (1947); and *La Lutte des Juifs contre les Nazis* (1945).

BIBLIOGRAPHY: LNYL, 4 (1961), 223–6; *Davar* (Feb. 26, 1967); *Yiddisher Kemfer* (March 24, 1967).

[Getzel Kressel]

JARÈ, Italian family. The name is a modern transcription of the Hebrew יר"א, either implying יְרֵא ("God-fearing"), or deriving from the initials of the phrase יְהִי רְצוּי אֶחָיו ("May he be desired of his brethren"). The transcription Jarè is known only from the 19th century. Obadiah of *Bertinoro was apparently a member of the family. Others included: PETHAHIAH of Spoleto, later of Recanati (16th century), a student of Arabic, who, with his son the physician MOSES, was one of the sources of Azariah de'Rossi's knowledge of the Samaritan alphabet. BERECHIAH REUBEN (d. 1598), of Perugia and later Verona, became rabbi in Mantua, with which city the family was henceforth mainly associated. His son MORDECAI was rabbi in Mantua and edited the collection of liturgical poems *Ayyelet ha-Shaḥar* (Mantua, 1612), which also contained two of his own poems. Mordecai wrote an approbation for *Kenaf Renanim* by Joseph Jedidiah *Carmi (Venice, 1626). ISAAC was a printer in Mantua at the beginning of the 18th century. GIUSEPPE DI GRAZIADIO (1840–1915), one of the last pupils of Samuel David *Luzzatto at the rabbinical institute in Padua, was rabbi in Mantua and from 1880 in Ferrara. He published a number of studies on Italian Jewish history.

BIBLIOGRAPHY: Mortara, Indice; S. Simonsohn, *Toledot ha-Yehudim be-Dukkasut Mantovah*, 2 (1964), 499, 521f.; Zunz, Lit Poesie, 424; Milano, Bibliotheca, nos. 890–6.

[Ariel Toaff]

JARMUTH (Heb. יַרְמוּת).

(1) Canaanite royal city mentioned in a 14th-century B.C.E. Akkadian letter found at Tell al-Ḥasī as Ia-ra-mu-ti. At the time of Joshua's conquest, Piram king of Jarmuth joined the coalition led by Adoni-Zedek king of Jerusalem against Gibeon; he was defeated at Aijalon along with the others and was killed at Makkedah (Josh. 10:3, 5, 23). The king of Jarmuth is also included in the list of defeated Canaanite kings (Josh. 12:11). Jarmuth became part of Judah and at the time of the Judahite monarchy it was included in the northern Shephelah district together with Adullam, Socoh, and Azekah (as preserved in Josh. 15:35). It was resettled by Judahites in the time of Nehemiah (Neh. 11:29). Eusebius locates it ten miles from Eleutheropolis, on the way to Jerusalem (Onom. 106:24–25). It has been identified with Khirbat al-Yarmūk (Eusebius calls it Iermochus), a large and prominent mound east of Kafr Zakariyya where surveys have revealed a large city surrounded by a massive stone wall from the Early Bronze Age and a smaller but higher mound containing pottery ranging from the Late Bronze to Byzantine periods.

(2) The Jarmuth listed as a Levitical city of Issachar in Joshua 21:29 should be read Ramoth (I Chron. 6:58) or Remeth (Josh. 19:21).

BIBLIOGRAPHY: Abel, Geog, 2 (1938), 356; Albright, in: BASOR, 77 (1940), 31; EM, 3 (1965), 865–7; Aharoni, Land, index.

[Michael Avi-Yonah]

JAROSLAW (Pol. **Jarosław**), town in Rzeszow province, S.E. Poland, on the San River. Jaroslaw's development was based on the great fairs held in the 16th and 17th centuries three times yearly. The main one took place toward the fall, and Jewish traders took a prominent part. In business such as the sale of oxen, for which Jaroslaw was a market center, Jews were the main dealers. The fairs were the origin of Jaroslaw's importance in the history of Polish Jewry. They were also, to a certain extent, the origin of the unique organizational character of its Jewish intercommunal institutions. Jewish communal leaders undertook to supervise the security of Jewish merchants visiting Jaroslaw. Jewish judges for the fair (*dayyanei ha-yarid*) were appointed as was customary among Christians; and a special procedure for them was introduced. A toll was levied on each trader or wagon to defray the expenses entailed. The *Council of the Lands of Poland frequently convened at the fall fair. A temporary congregation was formed by the Jewish visitors attending the fair. One scholar described the arrangements: "It happened that we were in the city of Jaroslaw at the fair of 1608, where it was a regular custom, as at every fair, that a place was set aside as a synagogue to pray there every day. And also on the Sabbath the scholars and heads of yeshivot and leaders of the lands and many people gathered to read in the Torah as is customary in the communities. And since the town is near the congregation of Przemysl … they convey from there the Torah scroll belonging to the congregation of Przemysl" (Responsa of R. Meir of Lublin, no. 84). Few Jews were able to settle permanently in Jaroslaw after the middle of the 15th century because of the opposition of the burghers, but a settlement gradually developed during the 17th century, while the fair diminished in importance. The first local synagogue was established in the 1640s, and a synagogue of the (Four) Lands is mentioned as existing therein those years; in the synagogue of the (Four) Lands the Council's decrees of excommunication and announcements were made public. The cemetery was established in 1699. A *blood libel in 1737 led to the suicide of one of the victims subjected to torture; others were cruelly put to death. In 1738 there were approximately 100 Jewish families living in Jaroslaw. In 1813 the Jewish population numbered 2,355 (out of a total of 9,007), and in 1921, 6,577 (out of 19,973). A number of the rabbis of Jaroslaw won recognition for their learning.

[Israel Halperin]

Holocaust Period

The city was captured by the Germans on Sept. 10, 1939. Their first anti-Jewish act was to set the synagogue aflame. On Sept. 12, 1939, the Germans imposed a fine. To insure the execution of this order, some communal workers were arrested, including the prewar head of the community Mendel Reich, whose fate remains unknown. On Sept. 28, 1939, the Germans ordered the population to assemble in the Sokol sports field. Some 7,000 persons assembled and were deported across the San River to Soviet-occupied territory. At the time of deportation, the Jews had to hand over all items of value and all their belongings were stolen. On the Soviet side, their fate was that of other Jewish refugees from western Poland. They suffered from lack of proper housing conditions, difficulties in finding work, and administrative restrictions. In the summer of 1940 many were exiled into the Soviet interior. Several hundred of those exiled to Russia survived, while those in east Poland were killed by the Germans during the German-Soviet War, in the years 1941–44. The community was not reconstituted after World War II.

[Aharon Weiss]

BIBLIOGRAPHY: Halpern, Pinkas, index; M. Steinberg, *Żydzi w Jarosławiu od czasów najdawniejszych do połowy XIX wieku* (1933); idem, *Gmina żydowska w Jarosławiu od jej powstania…* (1937); W.A. Wagner, *Handel Jarosławia do połowy XVII wieku* (1929); Z. Horowitz, in: *Otsar ha-Hayyim*, 5 (1929), 203–8; N. Weinryb, in: *Khrev*, 12 (1957), 154–9.

JASIEŃSKI (Zyskind), BRUNO (1901–1939), Polish poet, novelist, and playwright. Jasieński was born in Klimentów. Together with another prominent futurist writer, Anatol *Stern, he published a celebrated pamphlet, *Nuż w bżuchu* ("A Knife in the Belly," 1921), and a collection of verse, *Ziemia na lewo* ("Land on the Left," 1924). Two volumes of his own poetry were *But w butonierce* ("The Boot in the Buttonhole," 1921) and *Pieśń o glodże* ("Song of Hunger," 1922). After emigrating to Paris in 1925, Jasieński published *Słowo o Jakubie Szeli* ("A Word about Jacob Szela," 1926), a poem in which he tried to rehabilitate the leader of an anti-feudal peasant uprising in West Galicia in 1848. Jasieński's famous novel *Palę Paryż* ("I Burn Paris," 1928), first printed in the French Communist daily *L'Humanité*, was a fantasy of the destruction of the citadel of capitalism by the international proletariat. The French government promptly expelled the author. From 1929 until his death Jasieński lived in the U.S.S.R., where he helped to organize the Union of Soviet Writers and contributed to Polish and Russian periodicals. His play *Bal manekinów* ("The Dummies' Ball," 1931) appeared in both Polish and Russian, and he also wrote short stories in Russian, and the novel *Chelovek menyayet kozhu* (1934; *Man Changes his Skin*, 1935), of which the Polish, *Człowiek zmienia skóre*, was published in 1935–37 (2 vols.). This novel dealt with the conflicts arising from Socialist reconstruction in Tadzhikistan. In 1937 Jasieński was arrested. He was sentenced to five years' imprisonment, but died later on the way to his place of exile near Vladivostok. He was officially rehabilitated by the Communists in 1956. A collected edition of his poems, edited by Anatol Stern, appeared in 1960.

BIBLIOGRAPHY: *Polski Słownik Biograficzny*, 11 (1964–65), 27–30 (incl. bibl.).

[Stanislaw Wygodzki]

JASINOWSKI, ISRAEL ISIDORE (1842–1917), Russian Zionist leader. Born in Kosov, Russia, he received a religious education and in 1874 completed his law studies at the University of Kazan, where he was awarded the degree of advocate for his thesis on "Sources of Jurisprudence in Holy Scripture and in its Oral Tradition." He then became a renowned lawyer in Warsaw, where he headed the *Ḥibbat Zion movement soon after its establishment. He was among the organizers of the *Kattowitz Conference (1884) and was elected to the Central Committee of Ḥibbat Zion. Together with Leo *Levanda and P. Loewenson, Jasinowski drafted the regulations of the "Odessa Committe" of Ḥovevei Zion, called officially the Society for Supporting Jewish Agriculturists and Artisans in Syria and Palestine, and participated in the founding meeting of the society (1890). Jasinowski joined the Zionist movement at its inception and participated in its first seven congresses. He represented the Warsaw "constituency" and his office served as the center of Zionist activities in Russian Poland. He was among those who supported the *Uganda Scheme, and, after the Seventh Zionist Congress, he joined the Jewish Territorial Organization (see *Territorialism). He was a member of its International Council and participated as its representative at the Brussels Conference on questions of Jewish migration (1906). In his last years Jasinowski became alienated from the Jewish national movement and came closer to assimilationist circles.

BIBLIOGRAPHY: A. Druyanow, *Ketavim le-Toledot Ḥibbat Ẓiyyon ve-Yishuv Ereẓ-Yisrael*, 3 vols. (1919–32), indexes; I. Klausner, *Mi-Katoviẓ ad Basel*, 2 vols. (1965), indexes.

[Yehuda Slutsky]

JASLO, town in S.E. Poland. A Jewish settlement existed there before 1463. In 1589 the town obtained the privilege *de non tolerandis Judaeis*, i.e., the right to exclude Jews, and in 1619 Jewish settlement and commerce in Jaslo were again prohibited. However, several Jewish families were living in Jaslo by 1765. In 1795, after the partition of Poland, Jaslo passed to Austria under which there were no restrictions on Jewish settlement. In 1805 six families were settled in Jaslo as farmers, and the Jewish community began to increase, in particular between 1848 and 1853. The Jewish population numbered 433 in 1880 (13.1% of the total), 934 in 1890 (20.6%), 1,524 in 1900 (23.2%), 2,262 in 1910 (22.3%), and 2,445 in 1921 (23.5%). The majority were Hasidim. Children generally received a traditional Jewish education. A number attended the local secondary school, where there were 30 Jewish pupils out of 556 in 1914. During the period between the two world wars the Jewish population was mainly occupied in light industry and crafts. In 1921, 96 Jews owned industrial enterprises employing 678 persons, of whom 76 were owners, 49 members of the family, 83 Jewish, and 470 non-Jewish workers. The only sizable enterprises owned by Jews were five chemical works, employing 35 Jewish and 420 non-Jewish workers; large or medium-sized workshops included 29 food processing, 28 clothing, eight timber, seven metallurgical, six building, three machinery, three leather, three textile, two printing, and two disinfecting.

[Nathan Michael Gelber]

Holocaust Period

In the summer of 1941, a ghetto was established in Jaslo. Refugees increased the population to around 2,300. In July and August 1942 around 650 Jews were executed in the surrounding forests. The ghetto was liquidated on August 19–20 and its inmates, with a few exceptions, were deported to Belzec and there murdered. A small number of Jews were transferred to the forced labor camp in Szebnia, which was liquidated in 1943. No Jews settled in Jaslo after World War II.

[Stefan Krakowski]

BIBLIOGRAPHY: E. Podhorizer-Sandel, in: BŻIH, 30 (1959), 87–109.

JASNY, NAUM (1883–1967), economist. Born in Kharkov, Ukraine, Jasny obtained a doctorate in law in St. Petersburg (Leningrad). Jasny practiced law for a short time, and then became director of a flour mill in Kharkov, an experience which aroused his interest in economics. After the Russian Revolution he worked on designing food policies for the Soviet government, for which he later undertook economic research in Germany. While there he joined the Business Cycle Research Institute and in 1933, with the coming of Hitler, he moved to the United States where he was appointed senior economist with the Department of Agriculture. From 1939 he was with the Food Research Institute of Stanford University where he prepared forecasts of food availability in allied and enemy countries. After World War II, he worked with the Stanford Soviet Economic Group. Jasny's main interests were agricultural statistics and economics. His estimates of grain harvests in the U.S.S.R. served for many years as the basis for the investigations into the Soviet military potential. Among Jasny's major works are *The Socialized Agriculture of the U.S.S.R.* (1949); *The Wheats of Classical Antiquity* (1944); *Soviet Industrialization 1928–52* (1961); *Soviet Planning* (1964), edited by J.T. Degras and A. Nove; and *Khrushchev's Crop Policy* (1965). His memoirs were being prepared for publication at the time of his death.

[Joachim O. Ronall]

JASON (second century B.C.E.), high priest. Jason, who adopted this Greek form of his Hebrew name Joshua, was the son of the high priest Simeon II and a brother of *Onias III. According to Josephus he was also the brother of *Menelaus, but it is almost certain, in the light of II Maccabees, that this is inaccurate. The events that occurred at the end of the high priesthood of Onias III undermined his standing in the Seleucid court. Jason exploited the ascent of Antiochus IV to the throne (176 B.C.E.) and his need of money to have his brother deposed and to obtain the high priesthood for himself (175), against the promise of large sums of money. Antiochus also granted him authority to establish in Jerusalem a Hellenist polis whose citizens were selected and registered by Jason himself. Armed with this authority, he established within Jerusalem a city-state called Antiochia, whose citizens he chose from the Hellenized aristocracy of Jerusalem, and erected a gymnasium in the capital. His actions led to a strengthening of Hellenistic culture in the city and to a weakening of the traditional way of life and of religious worship (II Macc. 4:7–15). This policy of Jason and his supporters was the chief cause of the Hasmonean revolt which broke out afterward, and which finally freed Judea from the rule of the Seleucids and gave birth to the Hasmonean dynasty. Jason sent envoys and gifts to Tyre in honor of the festivities to the Tyrean god Heracles. He also welcomed Antiochus when he visited Jerusalem in 174 B.C.E. However, three years later he was dismissed from the high priesthood by the king, and Menelaus, who offered Antiochus a larger sum of money for the office, was appointed in his stead. A few years later, in 168 B.C.E., when a false rumor spread that Antiochus was dead, he attempted to return and seize power in Jerusalem. He was unsuccessful, however, and was compelled to leave the city after instituting a slaughter of the inhabitants. For a while he was imprisoned by the Arabian king, Aretas. His last years were spent wandering from place to place, and he was not buried in the family sepulcher.

BIBLIOGRAPHY: II Macc. 4:7–29; 5:5–10; Jos., Ant., 12:238ff.; Schuerer, Hist, 24–26; A. Tcherikover, *Hellenistic Civilization and the Jews* (1959), index; S.K. Eddy, *The King Is Dead* (1961), 206–11.

[Uriel Rappaport]

JASON OF CYRENE (c. middle of second century B.C.E.), Jewish historian who wrote a work in five books on the Maccabean revolt. The work is not extant and is known only from II Maccabees, which claims to be an epitome of it (II Macc. 2:23). It opened with events in the days of Onias III and may have concluded with Judah Maccabee's victory over Nicanor or continued to a later period. From the literary character of the work, Jason was presumably a hellenized though pious Jew, who was anxious to propagate moral values and to glorify his people and God. It is difficult to assume that he was a Pharisee, and his identification with Jason, Judah Maccabee's emissary to Rome (I Macc. 8:17), is doubtful.

For further details about the work and its relation to II Maccabees, as well as for bibliography, see *Maccabees, Books of.

[Uriel Rappaport]

JASSINOWSKY, PINCHAS (1886–1954), *ḥazzan* and composer. Born at Romanovka, near Kiev, Ukraine, Jassinowsky joined the choir of Pinchas *Minkowski in Kherson, as a boy. While he was studying music in St. Petersburg, he was assistant choirmaster in a synagogue there. In 1917 he emigrated to the United States. He had a smooth and plaintive tenor voice, and his singing in synagogues and at concerts made him a celebrity. He composed a considerable body of music, including *Ve-Hayah be-Aḥarit ha-Yamim* (Isa. 2:1–4) dedicated to the new Hebrew University of Jerusalem (1926), *Aseret ha-Dibberot* ("The Ten Commandments"), *Shirat ha-Be'er* ("The Song of the Well"), *Ba-Yom ha-Hu* (Isa. 26:1–4), and music for Yiddish poems folk songs, children's songs, and songs of the High Holidays.

BIBLIOGRAPHY: Sendrey, Music, indexes; Jewish Ministers Cantors' Association of America, *Di Geshikhte fun Khazones* (1924), 140; idem, *Khazones* (1937), 227–9 (Yid. and Eng.); N. Stolnitz, *Negine in Yidishen Lebn* (1957), 125–9.

[Joshua Leib Ne'eman]

JASSY (Rom. **Iasi**), city in N.E. Romania, capital of the former principality of Moldavia from 1565. The community of Jassy was the oldest in Moldavia. Jews first settled there in the second half of the 15th century because of its position on the commercial route between Poland and Bessarabia and to the Danube port of Galati (Galatz). Their number increased when Polish Jews took refuge there during the *Chmielnicki massacres (1648/49). In 1650 and 1652 many Jews in Jassy were murdered by Cossacks. There were new disturbances in 1726 when the populace, incensed by a *blood libel, sacked the houses of the Jews in Jassy and desecrated a number of synagogues. The Jewish guild of Jassy obtained an order from the sultan to liberate the Jews who had been arrested in the blood libel case. In 1742 Prince Constantin Mavrocordat, wishing to attract Jews from Poland, exempted those who settled in the town from taxes.

At the end of the 18th century the Jews were concentrated in their own quarter. Several branches of commerce (cereals, livestock, wool, honey, cheese) were exclusively handled by Jews. By the middle of the 19th century they had taken the place of the Turks and Greeks as bankers and money changers. Many Jews were also occupied as goldsmiths, tailors, hatters, furriers, and shoemakers. A number of these crafts had their own unions, some possessing their own synagogues. When the Christian tradesmen and artisans tried to limit the activity of their Jewish counterparts, a decision was issued by the prince in favor of the Jews (1817). In 1831 Jewish merchants and artisans formed 43% of the total number of these occupations, and by 1860 their proportion had increased to 78%. The Jewish population numbered 4,396 families in 1820, 31,015 persons (47% of the total) in 1859, 39,441 (50.8%) in 1899, and 35,000 in 1910.

Persecutions

In 1835 and again in 1839 Prince Michael Sturdza initiated actions against the Jews, which were stopped only after the Jewish bankers had canceled his debts. In 1867 Jews having no legal documents of residence were declared vagrants and expelled from the country. Diplomatic representatives of England and Austria presented their protests to the Romanian government; Emperor Napoleon III of France also intervened. However the persecution intensified during the last two decades of the 19th century, in particular after the Congress of *Berlin. Despite the recommendations of the Congress of Berlin, which threatened not to recognize Romania's independence, the Romanian political class refused to grant citizenship to the Jews.

Headquarters of the Antisemitic Movement

Toward the end of the 19th century Jassy became the center of antisemitism in Romania. In 1882 and 1884 two economic congresses were held there with the aim of promoting a boycott on Jewish commerce and industry. Through the activities of a "commercial club" during this period, 196 Jewish shops were closed down in 1892, and many Jewish tradesmen were expelled from the town. A number of Jews committed suicide in consequence. The University of Jassy became the center of antisemitism in Romania, with A.C. *Cuza, who taught at the university, as its main proponent.

Internal Organization

From 1622 to 1832 the affairs of the Jewish community of Jassy were administered by the "guild of the Jews," headed by the *ḥakham bashi*, who was the chief rabbi of Moldavia and Walachia, and three *parnasim*. From the taxes on kosher meat which it levied, the synagogues, *talmud torah* institutions, shelter for transients (*hekdesh*), and cemetery were maintained. After the guild was dissolved in 1834, associations were formed according to countries of origin (Russia, Austria, Prussia).

The first modern school for boys was founded in 1852 but remained open for only five years because of opposition from Orthodox circles. In 1858 the government began to press for the closing of the traditional Jewish schools and their replacement by modern schools in an assimilationist spirit. Some steps were taken in this direction from 1860 but the schools were unable to withstand the Orthodox opposition. Modern Jewish schools were again founded in 1893, after Jewish pupils had been expelled from public schools. There were 5,000 pupils (boys and girls) attending the community schools in 1910.

In 1834 the administrators of the hospital, which was founded in 1772, took over the management of the community affairs, receiving the principal income from the tax on kosher meat. The orphanage and an old age home were founded in 1890. In 1915 the Dr. L. Gelehrter Hospital for children was founded. The Caritas Humanitas association with a membership of 2,000 was active up to the eve of World War II, providing medical assistance and aid for widows.

Zionist Movement

There had been pre-Zionist groups at Jassy even before the *Ḥibbat Zion. In 1866 the Doreshei Zion association was founded, with the aim of creating a Hebrew library. From 1878 to 1898 the Ohalei Shem association propagated the Hebrew language and Jewish culture. The Yishuv Ereẓ Israel movement also had an important center in Jassy, headed by Karpel *Lippe, who had initiated the two above-mentioned associations. The poet Naphtali Herz *Imber, author of *Ha-Tikvah*, lived in Jassy at the end of the 1870s. Inspired by the ideas of Theodor Herzl, the Jewish community of Jassy founded nine Zionist organizations, which were amalgamated in 1919.

Spiritual and Cultural Activities

Jassy had long been the spiritual center for Jews living in both Romanian principalities (Moldavia and Walachia) through the influence of important rabbis who officiated there. The first of note, Solomon b. Aroyo, a kabbalist and physician to the prince of Moldavia, lived in Jassy at the end of the 16th and beginning of the 17th centuries. Nathan Nata *Hannover and Pethahiah b. David Lida served there in the 17th century. In the 18th century Ḥasidism began to spread to Jassy and brought a number of ḥasidic leaders there, including *Abraham Joshua Heschel of Apta, who lived in Jassy at the beginning of the 19th century. In the second half of the 19th century Jassy became a center of talmudic learning with scholars like Joseph Landau of Litin and Aaron Moses b. Jacob *Taubes. Among eminent ḥasidic scholars there the most important was Isaiah Schorr. In 1897 J.I. *Niemirover began his rabbinical activity and remained in Jassy until 1911.

Hebrew books were published in Jassy from 1842 onward, among them Eliezer b. Reuben Kahana's commentary on the Five Scrolls, *Si'aḥ Sefunim*; two editions (one with Yiddish translation) of Nathan Hannover's *Sha'arei Ẓiyyon* (1843); and the *Likkutei Amarim* of Shneour Zalman (of Lubavich; publ. 1843). Hebrew printing continued into the 1880s. Some Hebrew and Yiddish periodicals were also published in Jassy. A Yiddish biweekly *Korot ha-Ittim* was published from 1855 to 1871. For a year in 1872 the first Jewish all-Romanian newspaper *Vocea apărătorului* ("Voice of the Defender") was published. The weekly *Rasaritul* ("The East") was published from 1899 to 1901 by the Zionists, who also issued two annuals. In 1914 four numbers of a literary review, *Likht* ("Light"), were published in Yiddish, with the collaboration of Jacob *Groper, Abraham L. *Zissu, Motty Rabinovici, and Jacob *Botoshansky. The illustrations were the work of the painter Reuven *Rubin.

Jassy was the cradle of the Yiddish theater. In 1876 Abraham *Goldfaden first presented his operettas in Jassy. J. *Latteiner also had his own theater company, for which he wrote 75 plays. N. Horowitz from Galicia produced his operettas with a historical setting there.

Between the Two World Wars

In 1919 the community was reorganized. In the same year elections were held for the first communal administration. The community was recognized as a public body by the Ministry of Religions in 1927. In 1939 there existed in Jassy 112 synagogues, one kindergarten, three elementary schools for boys and four for girls, four religious schools (*talmud torah*), one yeshivah, one secondary school, one general hospital, one children's hospital, two sanatoriums for invalids, an orphanage, and an old age home. A Zionist weekly *Tribuna Evreeasca* was published in Romanian at Jassy between the two world wars.

In this period also Jassy, and especially the university, continued to be the center of antisemitic activities. Under the leadership of A.C. Cuza, the "National and Christian Defense League" (LANC) was founded in 1923. The head of the youth organization, Corneliu Zelea Codreanu, founded the "Archangel Michael League" in 1927, which is also known as "All for the Fatherland" and the more familiar "Iron Guard," an extremist antisemitic organization. The continual troubles caused by the antisemitic organizations and economic persecution by the authorities led to progressive pauperization among the Jewish masses in Jassy. In consequence the Jewish population diminished from 43,500 in 1921 to 35,465 (34.4%) in 1930.

Holocaust Period and After

On Nov. 6, 1940, the Antonescu government had seized power. The persecution of the Jewish population began immediately, accompanied by arbitrary arrests, torture, extortion, confiscation of places of business, and attempts to stage trials on such charges as Communism. However, the Jewish community leaders soon managed to reach an agreement with the leaders of the Iron Guard, who promised to stop the persecution in exchange for the sum of six million lei to be paid in installments. Consequently, until the Iron Guard were forced out of the government (January 1941), there were few further antisemitic incidents in the city. The final installment of the "subsidy" was paid during the Bucharest pogrom, which occurred when the Iron Guard rebelled against Antonescu's government, and, as a result, the Jews of Jassy remained unharmed.

In the summer of 1941, on the eve of the outbreak of war against the Soviet Union, many German army units moved to Jassy. Before the first military operation in the area (on June 29, 1941) and the opening of the large-scale offensive on the southern front (July 2, 1941), antisemitic tension grew, as the result of rumors that Jews were signaling to the Russian planes bombarding the town, and had even dared to shoot at soldiers. On the eve of June 28, German and Romanian patrols, accompanied by local residents, murdered many Jews and rounded up thousands more in the courtyard of the police station, where they were shot the next day. Immediately afterward, 4,332 Jews were dispatched to internment camps, 2,205 of them suffocating en route from the terrible overcrowding in the death cars. The exact number then killed at Jassy is unknown; wartime Romanian secret police documents mention the number of 13,266 victims including 40 women and 180 children.

In 1969 there were about 2,000 Jewish families in Jassy, and 11 synagogues. Courses in Hebrew and Jewish history with about 80 participants were held. The population diminished steadily to a few hundred by the turn of the century owing to immigration to Israel and elsewhere. Those who remained were cared for through government and Jewish funds.

BIBLIOGRAPHY: I.J. Niemirower, *Ochire asupra istoriei comunității israelite din Iași* (1907); idem, *Scrieri complete*, 2 (1919), 91–105; 529–531; M.A. Halevy, *Comunitățile evreilon din Iași și Bucrueşti*, (1931); idem, in: *Almanachul Ziarului Tribuna evreească*, 2 (1938/39), 251–2; idem, in: *Studia et Acta Orientalia*, 1 (1957), 360; idem, in: *Sinai*, 1 (Bucharest, 1928), 7–10; M. Gaster, in: *Anuar pentru israeliți*, 16 (1893/95), 12, 14; A. Turcu, *ibid.*, 18 (1896/97), 184–7; W. Schwarzfeld, *ibid.*, 12 (1889/90), 21–40; 13 (1890/91), 43–66; 17 (1895/96), 50–62; idem, in: *Egalitatea*, 5 (1894), 220, 228, 236, 251, 260, 269, 299; C. Drimmer, *ibid.*, 32 (1922), 54; idem, in: *Almanachul evreesc ilustrat pentru România* (1932), 34–37; A. Hahamu, in: *Calendarul almanah evreesc* (1945), 169–71; E. Herbert, in: *Journal of Jewish Bibliography*, 2 (1940), 111f.; E. Feldman, in: Zion, 22 (1957); PK Romanyah, 141–76; M. Carp, *Cartea Neagr*, 2 (1948); M. Mircu, *Pogromul de la Iasi* (1947); I. Ludo, *Din ord-inul cui?* (1947); S.C. Cristian, *Patru ani de urgie* (1946). **ADD. BIBLIOGRAPHY:** R. Ioanid, *The Holocaust in Romania: The Destruction of Jews and Gypsies Under the Antonescu Regime, 1940–1944* (2000).

[Theodor Lavi]

JASTROW, family of scholars originating in Prussian Poland, later in the U.S. MARCUS MORDECAI JASTROW (1829–1903) was a Polish-born rabbi and lexicographer and a leader of the historical school in the United States. Jastrow was born in Rogasen, Poznania. He was ordained by Rabbis Feilchenfeld of Rogasen and Wolf Landau of Dresden. He also studied at Berlin University and took his doctorate at Halle with a thesis on the philosophy of Abraham ibn Ezra (1855). With the aid of Heinrich *Graetz he was appointed preacher of the progressive German congregation in Warsaw. There he was caught up (with other Warsaw rabbis) in the Polish insurrectionary movement of 1861–63, preaching and writing for the revolutionary cause; he was imprisoned by the Russians for three months and, being a Prussian subject, expelled from Poland. For two years he was rabbi at Worms. In this period he published *Vier Jahrhunderte aus der Geschichte der Juden* (1865), covering the period from the Babylonian Exile to the Maccabees.

In 1866 he emigrated to the United States as rabbi to Rodeph Shalom, a congregation in Philadelphia largely composed of German immigrants; he served this congregation until his retirement in 1892. His work with the congregation encountered many difficulties. He strove to hold his synagogue within the confines of tradition but he was not able to stem the tide to Reform. He introduced some reforms, such as the use of an organ and Benjamin *Szold's prayer book *Avodat Israel* (Ger., 1863), which he helped to revise and which he translated into English as *A Prayer Book for the Services of the Year...* (1885). However, in polemics in the *Hebrew Leader* and the *Jewish Times* he opposed the movement for radical Reform as expressed by I.M. *Wise, D. *Einhorn, and Samuel *Hirsch. He did not favor formation of the *Union of American Hebrew Congregations or of *Hebrew Union College. In these polemics he emerged as one of the leaders of the historical school, which developed into *Conservative Judaism.

Jastrow taught Jewish philosophy, history, and Bible at Maimonides College from 1867 until it closed in 1875. He took a prominent part in the work of the *Jewish Publication Society, served from 1895 to 1903 as editor-in-chief of its projected Bible translation, and did the translation of Job. He also edited the Talmud section of the *Jewish Encyclopedia. Jastrow was a member of the executive of the *Alliance Israélite Universelle and of *Mekiẓei Nirdamim, and served as a vice president of the American Zionist Federation.

A severe illness in 1876 forced Jastrow to restrict his communal activities, and during a prolonged convalescence he began work on his major contribution to modern Jewish scholarship, the monumental *Dictionary of the Targumim, the Talmud Babli and Yerushalmi and the Midrashic Literature* (2 vols., 1886–1903; reprs. 1926, 1943, 1950; and as *Hebrew-Aramaic-English Dictionary...*, 2 vols., 1969). Using Jacob *Levy's dictionaries and S. Kraus' *Griechische und Lateinische Lehnwoerter*, Jastrow produced an eminently serviceable dictionary for the student of rabbinics, particularly the English-speaking student. In comprehensiveness and in attention to comparative linguistics, the dictionary was a definite advance on its predecessors. Though talmudic lexicography has progressed considerably since the dictionary first appeared, Jastrow's work has retained its value as a tool for all who study rabbinic literature.

One of Marcus' sons, MORRIS JASTROW (1861–1922), was a distinguished Orientalist. He was born in Poland and was brought to the United States as a child. He took his doctorate at Leipzig in 1884 with a dissertation on Judah *Ḥayyuj (*Abu Zakarijja Jahjâ... und seine zwei grammatischen Schriften...*, 1885; *Weak and Geminative Verbs by Abu Zakariyya... Ḥayyuj*, 1897). Returning to Philadelphia, he assisted his father for a short time at Rodeph Shalom. In 1892 he began teaching Semitics at the University of Pennsylvania; he also served as librarian (from 1898) and as research professor of Assyriology there. For a time he acted as editor of the Bible department of the *Jewish Encyclopedia*, was on the board of the *International Encyclopedia*, and contributed to Hasting's *Dictionary of the Bible*, the *Encyclopedia Biblica*, and many other learned publications. His anti-Zionist attitude is evident in *Zionism and the Future of Palestine: Fallacies and Dangers of Political Zionism* (1919).

Jastrow's most important work was probably *Religion of Babylonia and Assyria* (1898; rev. ed. *Aspects of Religious Beliefs and Practice in Babylonia and Assyria*, 1969). His other works on the religious and cultural history of Assyria and Babylonia include *Fragment of the Babylonian Dibbarra Epic* (1891; now known as the II Tablet of the Era-epic); *Bildermappe... zur Religion Babyloniens und Assyriens...* (1912); an atlas of illustrations for the *Religion of Babylonia and Assyria; An Old Babylonian Version of the Gilgamesh Epic* (with A.T. Clay, 1923).

Of more immediate Jewish interest are his *Study of Religion* (1901); *Hebrew and Babylonian Tradition* (1914); *Gentle Cynic* (1919), on Ecclesiastes; *Book of Job* (1920); and *Song of Songs* (1921).

Marcus' younger son, JOSEPH JASTROW (1863–1944), was a noted psychologist. Jastrow was educated at Pennsylvania and Johns Hopkins universities. He taught psychology at Wisconsin (1888–1927), Columbia (1910), and the New School for Social Research (1927–33). In 1900 he served as president of the American Psychological Association. He made a considerable contribution to the psychology of perception and of abnormality and he popularized Freudian thought in such works as *Fact and Fable in Psychology* (1900); *Subconscious* (1906, repr. 1970); *Keeping Mentally Fit* (1928), a title Jastrow also used for a syndicated newspaper column (1928–32) and a radio series (1935–38); *The House that Freud Built* (1932; *Freud, His Dream and Sex Theories*, 1941); *Error and Eccentricity in Human Belief* (1935); *Betrayal of Intelligence* (1938); and *Story of Human Error* (ed., 1936).

BIBLIOGRAPHY: ON MARCUS: M. Davis, *Emergence of Conservative Judaism* (1963), 342–4; idem, in: *Sefer ha-Shanah li-Yhudei Amerikah*, 6 (1942), 427–39; E. Davis, *History of Rodeph Shalom Congregation* (1926), 81–104; D.W. Amram, *Memorial Address on the Tenth Anniversary of the Death of M. Jastrow* (1913); N.M. Gelber, *Juden und der polnische Aufstand* (1923), index. ON MORRIS: A.T. Clay and J.A. Montgomery, in: JAOS, 41 (1921), 337–44; T.B. Jones, *The Sumerian Problem* (1969), 62–65.

[Jacob Rothschild / Jack Reimer]

JASTRUN (Agatstein), MIECZYSLAW (1903–1983), Polish poet, essayist, and translator. Born in Korolówka, Jastrun was one of the Skamander literary group. Philosophical reflection dominated such pre-World War II collections as *Spotkanie w czasie* ("Meeting in Time," 1929), *Inna młodość* ("Another Youth," 1933), and *Strumień i milczenie* ("Stream and Silence," 1937). During the years 1945–49, he was coeditor of the literary weekly *Kuźnica*. From the end of World War II his verse reflected the period of the Holocaust, notably in *Godzina strzeżona* ("The Guarded Hour," 1944), *Rzecz ludzka* ("Human Matter," 1946), *Sezon w Alpach* ("Season in the Alps," 1948), *Rok urodzaju* ("The Fertile Year," 1950), and *Barwy ziemi* ("Colors of Earth," 1951). Jastrun also wrote three biographical novels on great Polish poets: *Mickiewicz* (1949, 1967[11]; Eng. tr. 1955; Heb. tr. 1956); *Spotkanie z Salomeą* ("Meeting with Salomea," 1951), on the poet Juliusz Slowacki; and *Poeta i dworzanin* ("The Poet and the Courtier," 1954), on the poet Jan Kochanowski. His volumes of essays include: *Dzienniki i wspomnienia* ("Diaries and Memoirs," 1955); *Wizerunki: Szkice literackie* ("Images: Literary Essays," 1956), on Polish and foreign writers; and *Mit śródziemnomorski* ("Mediterranean Myth," 1962). Selections of his verse were published in 1966 and 1968. Jastrun also edited *Poezja Młodej Polski* ("The Poetry of Young Poland," 1967), *Wolnosć Wyboru* "Freedom of Choice," essays, 1969) and *Godła pamięci* ("Memorials," poetry, 1969). Among Jastrun's outstanding translations are those from the works of Lorca, Pushkin, and Rilke. An independently minded Communist, Jastrun was one of the authors of the *Manifest trzydziestu czterech* ("Manifesto of the 34," 1964) against the cultural policy of the Polish Communist Party and government.

BIBLIOGRAPHY: J. Trznadel, *O poezji Mieczysława Jastruna* (1954); A. Sandauer, *Poeci trzech pokoleń* (1962[2]), ch. 8.

[Stanislaw Wygodzki]

JÁSZI, OSZKÁR (1875–1957), Hungarian political scientist. Born in Nagykároly (now Romania), Jászi was converted to Christianity as a child. He was editor of the radical periodical *Huszadik Század* ("Twentieth Century") from 1906 to 1919.

Jászi was particularly concerned with the problem of national minorities. In his book, *A nemzeti államok kialakulása és a nemzetiségi kérdés* ("The Evolution of the Nation States and the Nationality Problem," 1912), he argued that these minorities should be granted full cultural and social autonomy. But later he believed that the question of Russian Jewry could be resolved by the creation of a Jewish state in Palestine. He advocated that the Jews of Hungary should assimilate. In 1912 he became an assistant professor of political science at the University of Kolozsvár. In 1918, following the outbreak of revolution, he was made minister of national minorities. He recognized the right of the Jews to national self-determination and also attempted to negotiate a permanent settlement with the national minorities within the Hungarian Republic. When the Hungarian Soviet regime came to power in 1919, Jászi left Hungary for Vienna and then Munich. He published a history of the revolution in Hungary, *Magyar kálvaria – magyar föltámadás* (1920; *Revolution and Counter Revolution in Hungary*, 1924). In the following year he immigrated to the United States where he lectured at Oberon College, Ohio, and became professor of political science there in 1941. Jászi was the author of numerous works on politics and political science including *A történelmi materializmus állambölcselete* ("History of Historical Materialism," 1904), *Műyészet és erkölcs* ("Arts and Ethics," 1904), and *The Dissolution of the Habsburg Monarchy* (1929).

BIBLIOGRAPHY: *Magyar Irodalmi Lexikon*, 1 (1963), 525; *Magyar Életrajzi Lexikon*, 1 (1967), 807; UJE, 6 (1942), 46; O. Jászi, *Magyar kálvária – magyar föltámadás* (1969[2]), 7–11, introd. by I. Borsody.

[Baruch Yaron]

JÁTIVA (Xátiva), city in Valencia, E. Spain. Its community was probably second in size in the kingdom after that of the city of Valencia itself. After Játiva was captured from the Moors by James I in 1244, the quarter where Jews had lived under Muslim rule was restored to them, and the king's interpreter, Baḥye Alfaquim, received estates in the city and its vicinity. In the 13th century there were about 200 Jews living in Játiva. In 1268 James I forbade the practice of stoning the Jews on Good Friday. In 1274, a new charter exempted the community from taxes for five years in order to encourage Jewish settlement in the city. The community was governed by a council of seven members who had criminal jurisdiction. In 1283 the town council prohibited the Jews from wearing bright clothes and jewelry. A center for study of the Hebrew and Arabic languages was established in Játiva by the Dominican Order in 1291: a Jew named Yom Tov, who taught here, was exempted from taxes. In 1363 Pedro IV imposed a tax of 10,000 sólidos on the community as their contribution toward the war against Castile. John I forbade the municipal officials to prevent the Jews from setting up workshops and they were authorized to do so in any section of the town. R. Ḥayyim b. Bibas, a disciple of *Asher b. Jehiel and correspondent of *Isaac b. Sheshet (cf. resp. no. 297), was rabbi in Játiva. During the persecutions of 1391, some Jews in Játiva died as martyrs, whilst others became converted to Christianity. The Jewish settlement was renewed during the 15th century and was the only community that existed in the Kingdom of Valencia after 1391 that continued until the expulsion of the Jews from Spain in 1492. In 1482, the kabbalist Joseph *Alcastiel was living in Játiva. Other scholars who resided there were Jacob Elihahu, Amram Efrati, and Yehoshua Satabi. The paper mill at Játiva, the oldest in Christian Europe, is believed to have been a Jewish enterprise. The pioneer Spanish Hebrew printer, Solomon Zalmati (one of whose relatives was involved with the Inquisition), was a native of Játiva.

In 1941 a Hebrew inscription was discovered in the hermitage of las Santas which suggests that it was the site of the synagogue. The Jewish quarter was not far from there, in the Santas street and adjacent small streets.

BIBLIOGRAPHY: Baer, Spain, index; Baer, Urkunden, index; Cantera-Millás, Inscripciones, 361; Piles Ros, in: *Sefarad*, 20 (1960), 365, 367–9; C. Roth, *Jews in the Renaissance* (1959), 174f. **ADD. BIBLIOGRAPHY:** A. Ventura Conejero, in: *Xátiva, fira d'agost*, (1979), 29–36.

[Haim Beinart]

JATTIR, JETHIRA (Heb. יַתִּיר), Judean city situated in the southernmost hill district and mentioned together with Shamir and Socoh (Josh. 15:48). It was a levitical city of the Kohathite family (Josh. 21:14; I Chron. 6:42). Jattir was one of the cities in southern Judah to which David distributed part of the spoils taken from the Amalekites (I Sam. 30:27). Eusebius identifies it with Lether, a large village 20 Roman miles from Eleutheropolis (Bet Guvrin), inhabited only by Christians (Onom. 108:1ff.). The site of Jattir is now called Khirbat 'Attīr; its extensive ruins date from the Roman and Byzantine periods. The *Madaba map shows Jattir in the wrong place, confusing it with Ether.

BIBLIOGRAPHY: E. Mader, *Altchristliche Basiliken und Lokaltraditionen in Suedjudaea* (1918), 224; A. Alt, in: PJB, 28 (1932), 15ff.; M. Avi-Yonah, *Madaba Mosaic Map* (1954), no. 102; EM, 3 (1965), 953; B. Bagatti, in: LA, 11 (1961), 304–5.

[Michael Avi-Yonah]

JAUNIJELGAVA (Ger. **Friedrichstadt**), city in Zemgale (Courland) district, Latvia., S.E. of Riga. In the period of czarist rule it was a district capital in *Courland. Jewish artisans from the villages started to settle in Jaunijelgava under Russian rule at the beginning of the 19th century. In 1850 the Jewish community numbered 1,483, increasing to 4,128 (70% of the total population) in 1881, and 3,256 (62.5%) in 1897. Apart from petty trade and artisanship, some wealthy Jews dealt in the export of wood, hides, and bristles. During World War I, the Jews in Jaunijelgava were expelled in July 1915 into the Russian interior, but before that three prominent members of the community were arrested as hostages, to be executed if cases of treason were discovered among the Jews. The city was subsequently destroyed in the fighting between the Russian and German armies. The community did not recover after the war, and only 680 returned by 1925. The Jewish population had decreased to 561 (26% of the total population) by 1933. Despite the decline Jews dominated the town's trade, owning most of the business resources. A Yiddish school existed, and the local rabbi functioned also as deputy mayor of the town. After the Soviets took over in 1940, they nationalized businesses and liquidated Jewish public life. Germans occupied the town in the end of June 1941. The Latvian "Self-Defense" forces began killing Jews. They assembled them in the synagogue. In the beginning of August a group of young Jews was taken out to dig ditches and then was shot there. On August 7, 1941, all the Jews – 167 families – were taken there and murdered. After the war some Holocaust survivors reached the town, took care of the cemetery and the mass grave, and erected a monument to the Holocaust victims. Later they dispersed, most of them leaving for Israel. At the beginning of the 21st century no Jews lived in Jaunijelgava.

BIBLIOGRAPHY: L. Ovchinski, *Di Geshikhte fun di Yidn in Letland* (1928).

[Yehuda Slutsky / Shmuel Spector (2nd ed.)]

°JAURÈS, JEAN LÉON (1859–1914), French Socialist politician. The *Dreyfus case brought him to the forefront of the political scene. At first Jaurès sided with the Socialists, who regarded the affair as a phase in the inner struggle of the ruling class. Later, however, brushing aside political expediency, he declared himself willing to "walk the darkened road which leads to justice." In association with Georges Clemenceau and Emile *Zola, Jaurès headed a national campaign for the rehabilitation of Dreyfus. He was shot in Paris by a fanatic on the eve of World War I (July 31, 1914). Jaurès had considerable influence on Léon *Blum, who regarded himself as his disciple, and on leaders of the Zionist labor movement, in particular Berl *Katzenelson.

BIBLIOGRAPHY: M. Auclair, *La vie de Jean Jaurès* (1954); H. Goldberg, *Life of Jean Jaurès* (1962), incl. bibl.

JAVAL, French family (the origin of the name is unknown). The founder, JACQUES JAVAL (1786–1858) of Mulhouse, a banker in Paris, established one of the first printed-textile mills in Saint-Denis in 1819. He was president of the Paris *Consistoire from 1824 to 1829. His son LEOPOLD (1804–1872) participated in the July Revolution of 1830 and then joined the army, taking part in the Algerian campaign and becoming a cavalry officer. After returning to civilian life, he organized the railway network of Alsace, but he was especially interested in agricultural development. In 1857 he was elected deputy for Yonne. In the Chamber of Deputies and later at the National

Assembly, he supported a program of political and economic liberalism. From 1852 to 1871, he was the Haut-Rhin delegate to the Central Consistory. His elder son EMILE (1839–1907) was a renowned oculist and member of the Academy of Medicine. He invented an apparatus for diagnosing astigmatism and a method of teaching reading. Director of the ophthalmological laboratory of the Sorbonne from 1878 to 1900, he published a number of books and encyclopedia articles in his field. From 1885 to 1889, he too was elected deputy for Yonne. His brother ERNEST (1843–1897), an engineer, was prefect of Creuse and, from 1885, director of the National Institute for the Deaf and Dumb. Emile's elder son JEAN (1871–1915) was also elected to the Chamber of Deputies. Jean's widow, LILY JEAN-JAVAL (née Léon-Lévy; 1882–1958), wrote a number of novels; two of them, *Noémi* (1925) and *L'Inquiète* (1927), deal with Jewish subjects, and the first part of her travelogue, *Sous le charme du Portugal* (1931), is concerned with the "search for the Marranos." Emile's second son ADOLPHE (1873–1944) was a medical scholar mainly concerned with diseases of the blood, on which he published a number of works.

BIBLIOGRAPHY: S. Bloch, in: *Univers Israélite*, 37 (1872), 493–5.

[Moshe Catane]

JAVAN (Heb. יָוָן), fourth of the seven sons of Japheth, son of Noah and father of Elishah, Tarshish, Kittim, and Dodanim (or Rodanim; Gen. 10:2, 4; 1 Chron. 1:5, 7). The name Javan reflects the Greek heroic name Ion, the legendary ancestor of the Ionians, a section of the Greek people. They are mentioned only once in Homer but became important later after colonizing the central part of the west coast of Asia Minor to which they gave their name, Ionia (Ἰωνία). The rise to power of the Ionians in the mid-eighth century has implications for dating the Genesis passages. Assyrian sources of the eighth century B.C.E. call the area Jawan and Jaman. Egyptian, and Persian sources also mention the Ionians.

Through the Near East Javan came to refer to all Greece. The biblical sources mention Javanites as merchants in trade with the Phoenicians of Tyre (Ezek. 27:13, cf. 19) and as slave traders who bought Judean captives from Phoenicians and Philistines (Joel 4:6). The Javanites are also mentioned among the far-off nations who are destined to witness God's glorious deeds (Isa. 66:19). Other biblical texts seem to reflect the tensions and hopes of the Hellenistic period in which Judah and Ephraim are to take revenge on the Javanites (Zech 9:13). The Book of Daniel, which certainly refers to this period, contains an odious reference to the king of Javan (Dan. 8:23) and alludes to the power struggles of the period of the Greco-Macedonian Empire (10:20, 11:2). Javan has continued to be the Hebrew for *Greece.

BIBLIOGRAPHY: J. Skinner, *Genesis* (ICC, 1930), 196–200; C.F. Lehman-Haupt, in: *Klio*, 27 (1934), 74–83, 286–99; Albright, Arch, 143; C.H. Gordon, in: HUCA, 26 (1955), 43–108. **ADD. BIBLIOGRAPHY:** D. Baker, in: ABD, 3:650; E. Kearns, in: OCD, 763; A. Birley and S. Hornblower, *ibid.*, 764–65.

[Michael Fishbane / S. David Sperling (2nd ed.)]

JAVETZ, BARZILLAI BEN BARUCH (d. 1760), Turkish rabbi and talmudist. Barzillai served as the *av bet din* in Smyrna, where he gave rabbinic discourses in the Maḥazikei Torah Synagogue, taught in his private yeshivah, and preached in the Talmud Torah synagogue. He influenced the wealthy Joshua *Soncino to build a synagogue in his name in Smyrna and delivered a eulogy on the rabbis of Smyrna who lost their lives in the fire of 1730. Barzillai published *Leshon Limmudim* (Smyrna, 1755), on the *Turim* and *Leshon Arumim* (*ibid.*, 1749), containing homilies, annotations on Elijah Mizraḥi's supercommentary to *Rashi, comments on Maimonides, and homilies by his father.

BIBLIOGRAPHY: Fuenn, Keneset, 202; Michael, Or, 297–8, no. 643; M.D. Gaon, *Yehudei ha-Mizraḥ be-Ereẓ Yisrael*, 2 (1937), 726; Rosanes, Togarmah, 5 (1938), 63–64.

[Simon Marcus]

JAVID (Cavid) BEY, MEHMED (1875–1926), Ottoman economist and statesman. Born in *Salonica to a *Doenmeh family, he worked for the Agriculture Bank and Education Ministry after graduating from the Imperial Civil Servants School (Mülkiye) in *Istanbul in 1896, only returning to Salonica in 1902 to head the Fevziye School. There he became active in the Young Turk movement. After the 1908 Revolution, he was elected to the Ottoman parliament, where he served from 1908 to 1918. An excellent orator and able economist, he served as finance minister in five cabinets, where he was instrumental in reordering the empire's finances, securing vital foreign loans, and restoring investor confidence. The combination of his personality, ethno-religious origins, and politics made him the target of numerous accusations of corruption, espionage, even murder. His Francophile and pacifist tendencies led him to resign his post in 1914 in protest against the secret Ottoman-German alliance, although he remained a financial adviser, reassuming the ministerial post in 1917. After the war he went into hiding in Istanbul, fleeing to Switzerland after his offer to join the Nationalist Forces in Anatolia was rejected. There he lived for several years, marrying Aliye, an Ottoman princess, and returning to Istanbul in 1922. He was a member of the Ottoman delegation at Lausanne in 1921, but fell out with Ismet Inönü. After Turkey's independence, he briefly flirted with politics, but largely retired from public life. Arrested in 1926 in the wake of an attempt on Mustafa *Kemal's life, he was convicted of sedition by a military tribunal and executed, although his real offense appears to have been posing a political challenge to Mustafa Kemal. During his lifetime, he published several authoritative textbooks on economics (4 vols., 1899–1901) and statistics (1909). Along with Rıza Tevfik and Ahmet Şuayip, he wrote for and edited the influential social sciences journal *Ulum-i İktisadiye ve İçtimâiye Mecmuası* (1908–11). His voluminous memoirs, serialized in the daily *Tanin* (1943–46), are an important primary source for this period.

BIBLIOGRAPHY: *Türk Ansiklopedisi* 10:37–39; Gövsa, *Türk Meşhurları*, 78.

[Paul Bessemer (2nd ed.)]

JAVITS, JACOB KOPPEL (1904–1986), U.S. lawyer and politician. Javits was born in New York City to poor, immigrant parents. After attending Columbia University and New York University Law School, Javits formed a law partnership with his brother (1927) and for the next several years practiced as a trial lawyer, gaining fame for his work in the 1933 bankruptcy case of Kreuger and Toll. In 1932 he joined the Ivy Republican Club – the beginning of what was to be a long association for him with both politics and the Republican Party. During World War II he served with the U.S. Army in Europe and the Pacific, rising to the rank of lieutenant colonel.

Upon his return to civilian life in 1946, Javits ran for a seat in the House of Representatives from the 21st Congressional District in Manhattan and won. He remained in the House, where he became a member of the Foreign Affairs Committee, until 1954, when he was elected attorney general of New York State. In 1956 he won election to the U.S. Senate and was reelected in 1962. He was elected to the Senate again in 1968 by a margin of over a million votes. An abortive attempt to gain the 1968 Republican vice presidential nomination, however – the first time a Jew ever openly aspired to such office – never materialized. He served in the Senate until 1980, when he lost his seat and returned to his law practice. At the same time, he also served as an adjunct professor of public affairs at the School of International Affairs at Columbia University.

As a politician, Javits' strength lay in his special appeal for liberal and Jewish voters, whose sympathies in New York were more often with the Democrats, but who regarded his voting record as one of the best in Congress. He consistently supported greater public aid to education, health, urban housing, the arts, and small business, and backed civil rights and fair-labor legislation, foreign aid, tariff liberalization, and curtailment of nuclear testing.

As a senior member of the Senate, Javits served on the powerful Foreign Relations Committee from 1969. A particularly warm friend of Israel, he repeatedly argued on the Senate floor that purely American interests should dictate that the U.S. support Israel as unequivocally as the U.S.S.R. supported the Arab states. He was active in a number of Jewish organizations, including the Zionist Organization of America, B'nai B'rith, the American Jewish Committee, the Federation of Jewish Philanthropies, and the America-Israel Cultural Foundation.

He wrote *American Policy in the Near East* (1953), *Discrimination – U.S.A.* (1960), *Order of Battle: A Republican's Call to Reason* (1964), *The Defense Sector and the American Economy* (with C. Hitch and A. Burns, 1968), *Who Makes War: The President vs. Congress* (with D. Kellermann, 1973), and *Javits: The Autobiography of a Public Man* (with R. Steinberg, 1981).

Named in his honor, the Jacob K. Javits Convention Center is located in Manhattan. Built in the 1980s, it is a large exhibition venue, covering five city blocks, that hosts a variety of major trade shows and conventions.

BIBLIOGRAPHY: Viorst, in: *Esquire* (April 1966); *Time* (June 24, 1966), 25–29; Weaver, in: *New York Times Magazine* (April 4, 1965), 35ff.

[Harvard Sitkoff / Ruth Beloff (2nd ed.)]

JAWITZ, ZE'EV (1847–1924), writer and historian. Jawitz was born in Kolno to a wealthy family distinguished in lineage, scholarship, and piety. After an unsuccessful attempt at business, he devoted all his time to writing and scholarship. He contributed to Smolenskin's *Ha-Shaḥar* (in no. 11 (1882), 41–48).

Jawitz won public recognition with his article "*Migdal ha-me'ah*" ("Tower of the century," in S.P. Rabinowitz (ed.), *Keneset Yisrael*, 1 (1887); repr. in his *Toledot Yisrael*, 13 (1937), 189–250), a survey of Jewish history from the death of Mendelssohn in 1786 to the death of Montefiore in 1886. The work's originality lay in the author's command of sources in Hebrew and other languages; in the inner integrity of his approach, which was a mixture of Eastern European Judaism, the romanticism of Ḥibbat Zion, and the Judaism of Frankfurt Orthodoxy (often characterized by the phrase *Torah im derekh ereẓ*, in the sense of "Torah and secular learning"); and in his writing style, a combination of biblical and scholarly Hebrew.

Settling in Ereẓ Israel in 1888, Jawitz taught in Zikhron Ya'akov. His writings were widely published in Ereẓ Israel in such periodicals as *Haaretz, Peri ha-Areẓ* (1892), and *Ge'on ha-Areẓ* (2 vols., 1893–94). He also wrote several textbooks, including *Tal Yaldut* (1891), *Ha-Moriyyah* (1894), *Divrei ha-Yamim le-Am Benei-Yisrael* (1894), *Divrei Yemei ha-Ammim* (1893–94), and books in which he attempted to relate legends in biblical style, as in *Siḥot minni Kedem* (1887, 1927²). His popular work *Neginot minni Kedem* (1892) appeared in several editions. In Ereẓ Israel, Jawitz was active on the Va'ad ha-Lashon, the committee responsible for developing Hebrew as a modern language. He and his brother-in-law, J.M. *Pines, contributed to the development of modern Hebrew by introducing linguistic elements from the literature of the Mishnah, Talmud, and Midrash, e.g., *tarbut* ("culture") and *kevish* ("road"). Jawitz left Palestine in 1894, moving to Vilna, to Germany, and later to London. For a short while he was active in the foundation of *Mizrachi in Russia and edited the monthly journal *Ha-Mizraḥ* (1903–04). Simultaneously, Jawitz continued his major work, *Toledot Yisrael...* (14 vols., 1895–1940; the first part appeared in Warsaw, and the last five parts were published by B.M. Lewin in Tel Aviv, 1932–40). The first six parts (comprising the first section) deal with the Jews in their land, from the Patriarchal Age to the end of the period of R. Judah ha-Nasi; the next eight parts deal with the Jews among the nations of the world, from the period of the *amoraim* to Ḥibbat Zion. Although Jawitz was not a modern historian, his contribution to Jewish historiography is distinctive and valuable in that he infused his historical account with commitment to Orthodoxy and love for Ereẓ Israel.

BIBLIOGRAPHY: S. Ernst (ed.), *Sefer Jawitz... Zikkaron...* (1934); A.S. Hirschberg, in: Z. Jawitz, *Toledot Yisrael*, 14 (1940), 121–63; M.L. Lilienblum, *Kitvei...*, 3 (1912), 133–84; J. Klausner, *Yoẓerim u-Vonim*, 2 (1930), 52–61; B. Dinur, *Benei Dori* (1963), 19–22; M. Eliash, in: S.K. Mirsky (ed.), *Ishim u-Demuyyot be-Ḥokhmat Yisrael…* (1959), 155–73; Waxman, Literature, 4 (1960), 153–4, 454, 727–35.

[Benzion Dinur (Dinaburg)]

JAY, ALLAN LOUIS NEVILLE (1931–), British fencer, 1960 Olympic Silver medalist in Individual and Team Epée. Born in London, Jay attended Oxford, where he was British epée champion in 1952. He was junior sabre champion in 1953 and was named captain of the school's fencing team in 1954. In 1959, he became world foil champion, and came in second in epée, the last person to obtain two medals in the same year. Jay was also British epée champion in 1959 and 1960. He competed in the Olympics in 1952, 1956, 1960, and 1964, winning the silver medal in Team and Individual Epée in 1960. Jay was British foil champion in 1963. He also won six gold medals in foil and epée events at the 1950 and 1953 Maccabiah Games. In addition, he won the gold medal at the 1966 Commonwealth Games in the individual and team foil events.

[Elli Wohlgelernter (2nd ed.)]

JAZER (Heb. יַעְזֵר), Amorite city E. of the Jordan. After the defeat of Sihon, king of the Amorites, Moses sent spies to explore Jazer and the Israelites later captured it (Num. 21:32). The Septuagint refers to Jazer on the border of Ammon (Num. 21:24). It belonged to the territory of the tribe of Gad (Num. 32:35; Josh. 13:25) within which it was a levitical city of the family of Merari (Josh., 21:39; I Chron. 6:66). Under David a governor from among the Hebronites was installed at Jazer (I Chron. 26:31); the city's status as an administrative center is confirmed by its enumeration between Aroer and Gilead in David's census (II Sam. 24:5). In later times it fell into the possession of the Moabites (Isa. 16:8–9; Jer. 48:32). Judah Maccabee captured the city during his campaigns east of the Jordan (I Macc. 5:8). Eusebius located Jazer eight or ten Roman miles west of Philadelphia (Rabbath-Ammon; Onom. 12:3; 104:13–14). It is usually identified with Khirbat al-Ṣār, 6 mi. (10 km.) west of Amman; G.M. Landes has suggested Khirbat al-Sīra, 1¼ mi. (2 km.) northeast of Amman.

BIBLIOGRAPHY: Landes, in: BASOR, 144 (1956), 30ff.; Schmidt, in: ZDPV, 77 (1961), 46ff.; EM, s.v.

[Michael Avi-Yonah]

JAZIRAT IBN ʿUMAR, town located N. of *Mosul in northern *Iraq. During the reign of the *Abbāsid Caliphs and the Crusades, Jazīrat ibn ʿUmar was an important town which maintained close commercial ties with *Armenia. From the earliest times, a large Jewish population existed in this region which was known as "Kardu." *Benjamin of Tudela, in the second half of the 12th century, stated that there were 4,000 Jews residing there. He added that the town was located near the Ararat Mountains, where Noah's ark rested, and that ʿUmar ibn al-Khaṭṭāb made a mosque out of the ark.

BIBLIOGRAPHY: J. Obermeyer, *Die Landschaft Babylonien* (1929), index; A. Ben-Jacob, *Kehillot Yehudei Kurdistan* (1961), 22, 24–25, 30.

[Eliyahu Ashtor]

JEALOUSY. Appearing some 80 times in the Bible, the root *kna* (*qnʾ*; קנא) in its various derivatives is, in the standard translations of the Bible, most often related to the notion of "jealousy" (or "zeal"). More generally, it connotes any kind of emotional agitation resulting from a perceived threat to one's honor or sense of moral rectitude. Hence, it can be used in connection with God as well as with humans (Deut. 29:19; II Kings 19:31). It can be characterized as a grave human weakness (Prov. 14:30; Job 5:2) and also as a deep motivation for selfless acts of courage and devotion (Num. 11:29; 25:11; I Kings 19:10, 14).

Envious rivalry among men, the Bible records, is as old as the human race. Cain was distressed because the Lord paid more heed to his brother Abel's offering than to his own (Gen. 4:4), and Joseph's brothers were similarly distressed when Jacob, their father, favored Joseph (Gen. 37:4). Envy, too, was apparently behind Miriam and Aaron's speaking ill of Moses (Num. 12), as it was the motive of Korah's rebellion against Moses and Aaron (Num. 16). Interestingly enough, neither verbal forms of *qnʾ* nor its cognates are used in connection with any of these incidents, indicating that envy is not coterminous with "jealousy." Accordingly, F. Kuechler suggested that *qnʾ* primarily refers to the dark envy and suspicion arising from an erotic love relationship. In support of this view, he points to verses in the poetic books of the Bible (Prov. 6:34; 27:4; Song 8:6) and to the "ritual in cases of jealousy" described in the Book of Numbers (5:11–31). The latter is an ancient trial with some elements of the ordeal to test a wife suspected by her husband of an adulterous union (see *Ordeal of Jealousy). On the basis of these passages, Kuechler contends that the notion of God's *kinah* (*qinʾah*) is also derived from *Hosea's erotic metaphors. The relationship between God and Israel, then, is like that of a lover and his beloved. He is jealous of her affections and demands her exclusive loyalty. It is noteworthy though that the root *qnʾ* is not attested in Hosea. That divine "jealousy" is not restricted to Yahweh is shown by an Akkadian (Standard Babylonian dialect) text referring to the goddess Sarpanitum with the cognate verb *qenû*.

There is no reason to posit a late date for the epithet *el kanna* (*qannaʾ*; *kanno, qannoʾ*) which appears in early sources (Ex. 20:5; 34:14; Josh. 24:19). In fact, it seems to reflect one of the most characteristic features of the early Israelite conception of God whose presence never leaves man in repose, and who always supervenes either in moments of distress to save humans, or when humans behave as if there were no such presence. Just as the individual is jealous of his honor, so does God defend His against all who would ignore it. Since, moreover, it cannot be dissociated from His holiness, God's jealousy is manifested in a dual manner: loving concern for those who revere Him and consuming wrath toward those who set themselves against Him. It is possible for individuals, too, to be overcome by *qinʾah* in or on God's behalf, in their single-minded devotion to His covenant (Num. 25:11–13; I Kings 19:10, 14; II Kings 10:16; Ps. 119:139).

[David L. Lieber / S. David Sperling (2nd ed.)]

In Talmudic Literature

In the talmudic literature the word *kinah* is found in both the senses in which it occurs in the Bible, as jealousy and as zeal for God. Many passages speak against jealousy, such as "whoever stirs up jealousy and strife in his home is regarded by the Bible as stirring up jealousy and strife in Israel as a whole" (ARN[1] 28:85). Moses preferred to die a hundred deaths rather than to give way once to the feeling of jealousy (Deut. R. 9:9). Rabba b. Maḥasyah states in Rav's name: "A man should never single out one son among his other sons, for on account of the extra weight of two *sela'im* of silk which Jacob gave to Joseph and not to his other sons, his brothers became jealous of him, resulting in our forefathers' descent into Egypt" (Shab. 10b). R. Eleazar ha-Kappar said, "Jealousy… drives a man out of the world" (Avot 4:28), and those who do not envy are promised that their flesh will not become dust until before the resurrection (Shab. 152b). Jealousy is all-embracing, with one exception: "A person can feel jealousy and envy for everyone, except for his son and his disciple" (San. 105b). However, envy can have its positive side since it leads to emulation: "the envy of *soferim* [scholars] leads to the increase of wisdom" (BB 21a). In the same vein it is stated, "Were it not for jealousy no one would marrry or build a house" (Mid. Ps. 37:1), and had not Rachel envied the good deeds of her sister, she would not have borne children (Gen. R. 71:6). Zeal for God is highly praised: "Were it not for Abraham's zeal [*kinah*] for God, He would not have become the Possessor [*koneh*] of Heaven and Earth" (Mid. Ps. 37:1, based on Gen. 14:22). Phinehas and Elijah are singled out as exemplifying this zeal in the Bible, and Elijah is even regarded as the incarnation of Phinehas (PdRE 29, 47). According to one opinion Phinehas became priest as a reward for his zeal in slaying *Zimri (Zev. 101b). The Maccabees are later used as symbols of religious zeal: "The Holy One clothed Himself with seven garments. One was for the Greeks, as it says [Isa. 59:17],… and He was clad in zeal [*kinah*] as a cloak" – referring to the Hasmoneans (Mid. Ps. 93:1). Mattathias on his deathbed urged his sons to emulate the zeal of Phinehas and Elijah, calling Phinehas "our father" (I Macc. 2:54, 58), and Phinehas is thus regarded as the spiritual ancestor of the *Zealots (*kanna'im*). Nevertheless, Elijah is criticized for his excessive zeal, and the revelation to him at Horeb (I Kings 19:10–14) is interpreted as a censure of him for accusing instead of defending Israel (Song R. 1:6, 1). Jonah is criticized for being more zealous for the honor of Israel than for that of God (see TJ, Sanh. 11:7, 30b), but Jeremiah was praised for achieving a fine balance between the two (ARN[2] 47, 129, Mekh. to 12:1).

BIBLIOGRAPHY: F. Küchler, in: ZAW, 28 (1908), 42ff.; Pedersen, Israel, 1–2 (1926), 175, 236–7; Pritchard, Texts, 171, par. 132; N.H. Tur-Sinai, *Peshuto shel Mikra*, 1 (1962), 151; G. von Rad, *Old Testament Theology* (1963), 204; H.A. Brongers, in: VT, 13 (1963), 269–84; H. Ringgren, *Israelite Religion* (1966), 76; H. van Oyen, *Ethik des Alten Testaments* (1967), 99; T.H. Gaster, *Myth, Legend and Custom in the Old Testament* (1969), 280–300. IN TALMUDIC LITERATURE: Ginzberg, Legends, 6 (1928), 138, 158, 321. **ADD. BIBLIOGRAPHY:** CAD Q, 209–10; B. Levine, *Numbers 22–36* (AB; 2000), 289.

JEBENHAUSEN, village in Wuerttemberg, Germany. In 1777 nine Jewish families received a charter to settle and build a separate colony near the farming village. There was no restriction to the number of Jewish families, and the community, which enjoyed far-reaching autonomy, grew from 31 members in 1778 to 233 in 1804. Most families were notoriously poor at that time, seeking a livelihood from peddling. By the mid-19th century many had established themselves as merchants and factory owners, developing a flourishing textile and corset industry. There were 550 Jews living in Jebenhausen in 1845, 534 in 1854, 392 in 1862, and 151 in 1869. Between 1798 and 1870, more than 300 members of the community immigrated to America, mostly for lack of civil rights and economic prospects. After the revolution of 1848, when the larger cities in Wuerttemberg no longer refused Jews the right of residence, many left the village to settle in near-by Goeppingen, *Esslingen, or *Stuttgart. Jebenhausen was the seat of a rabbinate from 1778 to 1874, when it was transferred to Goeppingen. Only nine Jews lived in the village in 1899. The synagogue, built in 1804, was closed in 1899 and sold for demolition, and the community was formally dissolved. The members of the only remaining Jewish family were deported to *Theresienstadt in 1942 but survived. A Jewish museum was opened in Jebenhausen in 1992.

BIBLIOGRAPHY: A. Taenzer, *Die Geschichte der Juden in Jebenhausen und Goeppingen* (1927, 1988[2]); N. Bar-Giora Bamberger, *Die juedischen Friedhoefe Jebenhausen und Goeppingen* (1990); S. Rohrbacher, *Die juedische Landgemeinde im Umbruch der Zeit* (2000).

[Stephan Rohrbacher (2nd ed.)]

JEBUS, JEBUSITE (Heb. יְבוּס, יְבוּסִי), one of the peoples of Canaan. The Jebusites are mentioned in the Bible in four different connections:

(1) In the "table of nations" (Gen. 10:15–19; cf. I Chron. 1:13–14) the Jebusite appears after Sidon and Heth as the third son of *Canaan. There may be an allusion to kinship or connection between Jebus and Heth in the Book of Ezekiel (16:3): "… Jerusalem … the Amorite was your father, and your mother a *Hittite." Some (unclear) ethnic reality is reflected by this combination.

(2) The Jebusites are mentioned in the lists of the peoples of Canaan driven out by the Israelites, lists appearing in the Bible more than a score of times (e.g., Gen. 15:21; Ex. 3:8, 17) and naming from six to ten nations. Invariably the Jebusites appear at the end of each list, and in most instances immediately after the *Hivites. The Jebusites' proximity to the Hivites may be due to the fact that both groups were thought to be related to the *Hurrians. That the Jebusites are always placed last may indicate that they were the last people to appear in Canaan and, since they were only found in Jerusalem, that they may have been the smallest in number of all the ethnic groups.

(3) The Jebusites are specially mentioned as the inhabitants of *Jerusalem, e.g., "the Jebusites, the inhabitants of Jerusalem" (Josh. 15:63), "and the Jebusite – the same is Jerusalem"

(18:28). Judges 19:11, however, refers to the Jebusites without mentioning Jerusalem: "When they were by Jebus" and "this city of the Jebusites." Although the name Jebus is widely attested in biblical stories set during part of the era of settlement, it is not attested in the documents of the *el-Amarna period (first half of 14th century B.C.E.), while Jerusalem is. It is possible that the Jebusites settled in Jerusalem in the 14th and 13th centuries B.C.E., not long before the settlement of the tribes of Israel in Canaan.

(4) The Israelite capture of Jerusalem and its conversion into the capital of David's kingdom at the beginning of his reign put an end to the autonomy of the Jebusites. The capture of the city as related in II Samuel 5:6–10 is surprisingly poor with regard to details. Such as are provided, "the lame and the blind" (5:6, 8 (bis)); and the *ẓinnor* (5:8) are unclear. The parallel in I Chronicles 11:4–9 seems to be an attempt to make sense of the difficult passages in Samuel. According to Chronicles, *Joab entered Jerusalem of the Jebusites, according to one opinion, by way of the water system – if "gutter" is the sense of *ẓinnor*, which some identify with "Warren's shaft" – that leads from the pool of Siloam. But the *ẓinnor* is absent from the Chronicler's account, and Joab is absent from the Samuel account. Clearly all Jebusite inhabitants were not destroyed because David bought a threshing floor from Araunah the Jebusite in order to build an altar (II Sam. 24: 18–24), and also because David may have integrated Jebusite craftsmen and officials into his service.

The origin of the Jebusites is obscure and there are many opinions on the subject. Some scholars, on the basis of the names of the kings connected with Jerusalem, see the origin of the Jebusites in the Hurrians. The first recorded king of Jerusalem dates from the el-Amarna era and bears the name Abdi ḥeb/pa(t), "servant of ḥeb/pa(t)," a name compounded from West Semitic *ʿabdu*, "servant," "slave," and the Hurrian mother goddess ḥeb/pa(t). The second extant name, *Araunah (II Sam. 24:18–24; I Chron. 21:18–25), the Jebusite, is taken by some as a corruption of the Hurrian word for a king (*ewri*, "lord"). Another view is that the Jebusites are related to the Semitic peoples because the Jebusites are mentioned among the peoples of Canaan, and the clearly Semitic *Adoni-Zedek, king of Jerusalem, headed the Amorite alliance against Joshua (Josh. 10). Others claim that the Jebusites are Amorites because their name is similar to the name Iâbu-sum, mentioned in sources dating from the beginning of the second millennium B.C.E. and found on the northwest border of Babylonia. Research has yet to determine clearly the origin of the Jebusites and the date of their settlement in Jerusalem.

BIBLIOGRAPHY: G.A. Smith, in: *Jerusalem*, 1–2 (1907), 266–7; J. Garstang, *The Hittite Empire* (1929); H.H. Rowley, in: JBL, 58 (1939), 113–41; S. Yeivin, in: *Zion*, 9 (1944), 49ff.; O.R. Gurney, *The Hittites* (1951); J. Simons, *Jerusalem in the Old Testament* (1952), 60–61, 246–7; B. Mazar, in: M. Avi-Yonah (ed.), *Sefer Yerushalayim*, 1 (1956), 107ff.; Bright, Hist, 78–87, 178–9; H.W. Hertzberg, *Samuel* (Eng., 1964), 265–70; S. Abramsky, in: *Oz le-David Ben-Gurion* (1964), 160–4; D. Winton Thomas (ed.), *Archaeology and Old Testament Study* (1967), 3–20, 105–18, 277–95. **ADD. BIBLIOGRAPHY:** S. Reed, in: ABD, 3, 652–63; S. Japhet, *I & II Chronicles* (1993), 238–42; S. Bar-Efrat, *II Samuel* (1996), 53–55.

[Abraham Lebanon / S. David Sperling (2nd ed.)]

JEDAIAH (Heb. יְדַעְיָה; "YHWH has noted," or "YHWH has favored"), the name of two priestly ancestral houses mentioned in the list of heads of ancestral houses during the term of office of Joiakim the high priest. One is in the 17th place on the list (Neh. 12: 19) and the other in the last place (*ibid.* 21). The former is mentioned after the house of Joiarib (Jehoiarib), and it is possible that he is the one associated with Joiarib in other texts (I Chron. 9:10; 24:7); in Nehemiah 12:6 Jedaiah is listed as Joiarib's son. The other house of Jedaiah presumably includes (1) the sons of Jedaiah of the house of Jeshua, who total 973 (Ezra 2:36; Neh. 7:39), and head the list of four ancestral houses of priests that returned with Zerubbabel; and (2) Jedaiah who is last on the list of 23 heads of priestly houses that returned with Zerubbabel (Neh. 12:7); this list is, in fact, merely one of ancestral houses. However, the relationship between these two lists of priestly houses that returned with Zerubbabel is unclear.

BIBLIOGRAPHY: W. Rudolph, *Ezra und Nehemiah* (1949), s.v. **ADD. BIBLIOGRAPHY:** R. Hutton, in: ABD, 3:653–55.

[Samuel Ephraim Loewenstamm]

JEDAIAH BEN ABRAHAM BEDERSI (Ha-Penini; probably born in the 1280s and died about 1340), poet and philosopher. Possibly a native of Béziers, Jedaiah is known to have spent time in Perpignan and Montpellier. Little is known of his personal history. He may have been a physician. Jedaiah's intellectual interests were literary and philosophic, although the two spheres were not clearly separated. In his youth, he composed a poetic prayer of 1,000 words titled "*Bakkashat ha-Memim*," every word of which begins with the letter *mem* (in *Olelot ha-Boḥen*, 1808). He is also credited with a similar composition, every word of which begins with *alef*, but many believe that this latter poem was written by Jedaiah's father. In popular style he composed *Ohev Nashim* ("In Defense of Women," ed. by A. Neubauer in *Jubelschrift… L. Zunz* (1884), pt. 1, 138–40; pt. 2, 1–19). His best-known literary work is *Sefer Beḥinat Olam* ("The Book of the Examination of the World"), a lyrical, ethical monograph on the theme of the futility and vanity of this world, and the inestimably greater benefits of intellectual and religious pursuits. *Beḥinat Olam*, written in florid prose and rich in imagery, combines philosophic doctrine and religious fervor with a good measure of asceticism and pessimism.

Published originally in Mantua between 1476 and 1480, the work has been reprinted numerous times. It has been translated into English (*Beḥinat Olam or An Investigation of… Organization of the World*, London, 1806), Latin, French, German, Polish, and Yiddish, and numerous commentaries have been written on it. Jedaiah also wrote *Sefer ha-Pardes* (Constantinople, 1516; reprinted by J. Luzzatto, in *Oẓar ha-Sifrut*, 3 (1889–90), 1–18), which consists of reflections on isolation from the world, divine worship, the behavior of judges, grammar, and astronomy. The last chapters deal with rhetoric and poetry. Jedaiah was the author of commentaries on various Midrashim (Paris, Bibliotheque Nationale, Ms. 738; De Rossi, 222), as well as a commentary on *Pirkei Avot* (Escorial, Ms. G. IV, 3). He may also have written a supercommentary on *Ibn Ezra's commentary on Genesis (see Steinschneider, Cat Bod., 1283).

Jedaiah wrote a number of works which are more strictly scientific and philosophical. He was the author of explanatory notes on Avicenna's *Canon* (Bodleian Library, Ms. Mich. Add. 14, and Mich. 135), and on Averroes' commentary on Aristotle's *Physics* (Steinschneider, Uebersetzungen, 109; HB, 12 (1872) 37). A number of Jedaiah's philosophical works are found in manuscript 984 of the Hebrew manuscript collection of the Bibliothèque Nationale in Paris (see S. Munk, in *Archives Israélites* (1847), 67–72): *Ha-De'ot ba-Sekhel ha-Ḥomri* ("Theories Concerning the Material Intellect"), an epitome of Aristotle's *De Anima; Ketav ha-Da'at* ("Treatise on the Intellect"), a paraphrase of *Sefer ha-Sekhel ve-ha-Muskalot*, the Hebrew translation of al *Fārābī's *Kitāb al-'Aql wa al-Ma'aqulat* ("Treatise on the Intellect"); *Ma'amar be-Hafkhei ha-Mahalakh* ("Treatise on Opposite Motions"), in which Jedaiah criticizes the views of another scholar, whose name he never mentions, concerning *Averroes' commentary on Aristotle's *De Caelo* Bk. 1, ch. 4; and *Ketav ha-Hitaẓẓemut* ("Book of Confutation"), a refutation of the scholar's reply to Jedaiah's *Ma'amar be-Hafkhei ha-Mahalakh*. It has recently been suggested that this scholar is Levi ben Gershom (see R. Glasner, *A Fourteenth-Century Scientific-Philosophical Controversy*). This same manuscript contains a treatise titled *Ma'amar ha-Dan ba-Ẓurot ha-Peratiyyot o Ishiyyot* ("A Treatise Upon Personal or Individual Forms"), which deals with the problem of whether individuals of the same species differing in accidents also differ in their essential forms. In this latter treatise there is reference made to another essay by Jedaiah, *Midbar Kedemot*, which is a commentary on the 25 propositions with which Maimonides opens the second part of the *Guide of the Perplexed*. This treatise is no longer extant.

It has recently been suggested that Jedaiah was influenced by Christian scholasticism (see S. Pines, *Scholasticism After Thomas Aquinas and the Teachings of Ḥasdai Crescas and His Predecessors* (1967), 1–5, 52–89). Jedaiah's contention in *Ma'amar ha-Dan ba-Ẓurot ha-Peratiyyot o Ishiyyot* that individuals of the same species differ in their essential forms reflects the position of Duns Scotus and his disciples on the question of personal forms. Even his arguments are similar to those employed by the Scotists (see also John *Duns Scotus). In *Ma'amar be-Hafkhei ha-Mahalakh* and *Ketav ha-Hitaẓẓemut*, Jedaiah maintains that the mathematical concepts of number, of one, of the discrete, and the continuous, have no existence outside the soul or the intellect. This theory resembles that of the Nominalists, i.e., William of Ockham, his predecessors and disciples, more than the views of any Jewish or Arabic thinkers. While chronologically it is impossible that Jedaiah was influenced by William of Ockham himself, it appears likely that he was influenced by some of his predecessors. As yet, however, no conclusive evidence has been advanced to demonstrate this influence.

Jedaiah is also known for his *Iggeret ha-Hitnaẓẓelut* ("The Apologia," in *She'elot u-Teshuvot… Rabbenu Shelomo ben Adret* (Venice, 1545), 67a–75b; printed separately, Lemberg, 1809; reprinted Warsaw, 1882). In this epistle, addressed to Solomon b. Abraham *Adret, after the latter's pronouncement of the ban on philosophic study in Barcelona in 1305, Jedaiah attempted to exonerate the Jewish communities of Provence of the charges of heresy and disrespect to the Torah which had been leveled against them by Adret, as well as to argue the benefits of religious belief which result from the study of philosophy. Greek philosophy, Jedaiah points out, provided the scientific basis for belief in God's unity and incorporeality, and in man's free will. Adret's major accusation against the Jews of Provence was that they denied the historicity of the Torah by interpreting it entirely as an allegory. Jedaiah argued that in their allegorical interpretations these scholars were merely following the teachings of Maimonides. If they were guilty of anything it was of making these interpretations known to the masses.

BIBLIOGRAPHY: A.S. Halkin, in: A. Altmann (ed.), *Jewish Medieval and Renaissance Studies* (1967), 165–84; J. Chotzner, in: JQR, 8 (1895/96), 414–25; N.S. Doniach, *ibid.*, 23 (1932/33), 63–69; I. Davidson, *ibid.*, 349–56; S. Pines, in: *Wolfson Jubilee Volume* (1965), 187–201 (Hebrew section). **ADD. BIBLIOGRAPHY:** M. Saperstein, "Jedaiah Bedershi's Commentary on the Midrashim," in: WCJS, 8:3 (1982), 59–65); "Selected Passages from Yedaiah Bedersi's Commentary on the Midrashim," in: *Studies in Medieval Jewish History and Literature*, 2 (1984), 423–40; R. Glasner, "Yeda'ya ha-Penini's Unusual Conception of Void," in: *Science in Context*, 10 (1997), 453–70; idem, *A Fourteenth-Century Scientific-Philosophical Controversy: Jedaiah ha-Penini's Treatise on Opposite Motions and Book of Confutation* (Heb., 1998).

[Abraham Solomon Halkin / Ruth Glasner (2nd ed.)]

JEDIDIAH (Amadio) BEN MOSES OF RECANATI (or **Rimini**; 16th century), scholar and translator. Jedidiah worked as a private tutor in various Italian towns. In 1566 he made a copy (and not a translation, as Neubauer assumes) of *Sefer Piskei Halakhot* by Moses ibn Danon (Bodleian Library, Ms. Bodl. Or. 620). The other parts of this manuscript may also be Jedidiah's work (see also Bodleian Library, Ms. Mich. 259). He translated Ibn *Tibbon's Hebrew translation of *Maimonides' *Guide of the Perplexed* into Italian, under the title "Erudizione de' confusi" (Parma, De Rossi, cod. Ital. 5, Richler 1259; Berlin, Or. 4°, 487), dedicated to Immanuel (Menahem Azarijah) mi-Fano. Both manuscripts, written between 1581 and 1583, are in Hebrew script; in the introduction, Jedidiah clarifies that he intended to help the Jewish students to understand difficult works and expressions. Excerpts from this translation were published by A. Guetta (see Bibl.). Jedidiah also translated the Book of Judith from the Latin into Hebrew, adding to it a Hebrew poem in which he summarizes the contents (Schoenblum, *Catalogue de 135 manuscrits hébreux de la collection Schoenblum* (1885), 10; Ms. acquired by Kaufmann but not contained in Weiss's list). Other works by Jedidiah are: *Ketavim u-Meliẓot*, a collection of letters (Bodleian Library, Ms. Opp. Add. 8°, 38); *Turgeman*, a Hebrew-Italian glossary of the Bible (Bodleian Library, Ms. Reg. 15, dating from 1597; it is not known whether Ms. 642 of the Guenzburg collection contains the same glossary, or an Italian Bible translation); and an abridgment of Elijah Mizrahi's commentary on Rashi (Parma, De Rossi 288, Richler 669). An Oxford manuscript (Bodleian Library, Ms. Mich. Add. 67) contains a halakhic opinion by Jedidiah, and an opinion rendered by him is quoted by Shabbetai Be'er in *Be'er Esek* (Venice, 1674). A number of mathematical remarks found in the Schoenblum manuscript, mentioned above, bear Jedidiah's signature and the date 1573.

BIBLIOGRAPHY: G. Sacerdote, in: *Rendiconti della Reale Accademia dei Lincei* (1892), 308–25; D. Kaufmann, in: JQR, 11 (1898/99), 662–70; idem, in: *Archiv für Geschichte der Philosophie*, 11 (1897–98), 365–68; Kaufmann, Schriften, 2 (1910), 181–3; Steinschneider, Cat Bod, 1719, 1735; idem, *Die Handschriften-Verzeichnisse der Koeniglichen Bibliothek zu Berlin*, 1 (1878), 33; idem, in: MGWJ, 43 (1899), 33–34; Steinschneider, Uebersetzungen, 922; Neubauer, Cat, 173, 530, 749, 850; U. Cassuto, *Ha-Yehudim be-Firenze bi-Tekufat ha-Renaissance* (1967), 182. A. Guetta, in: P.C. Ioly Zorattini (ed.), *Percorsi di storia ebraica* (2005), 281–303.

[Umberto (Moses David) Cassuto / Alessandro Guetta (2nd ed.)]

JEDRZEJOW (Pol. **Jędrzejów**; Rus. **Andreyev**), town in Kielce province, S. central Poland. Jewish settlement there was prohibited until 1862, when Jewish families from the surrounding townlets and villages arrived in Jedrzejow. With the impetus given to the town's economy by the opening of the railroad station in 1884, the Jewish population rapidly increased. It numbered approximately 2,050 (45% of the total population) in 1897. The majority engaged in small-scale trading and the traditional crafts, and some were occupied in the grain and timber trade. Jews with capital established timber and flour mills and mechanical workshops. The community was organized during the 1880s. The first rabbi to hold office in Jedrzejow was Moses Mincberg. At the close of the 19th century, *Alexandrow Hasidism (Danziger dynasty) had the widest influence in the community. A Zionist committee was established in 1902, and the local *Po'alei Zion, organized in 1906. During the first weeks of Polish rule after the end of World War I there was a wave of anti-Jewish riots in the vicinity of Jedrzejow. According to the census of 1921, there were approximately 4,600 Jews living in Jedrzejow (about 40% of the total population). Between the two world wars all the Zionist organizations were active in the town, and several groups of youth immigrated to Erez Israel. During the 1930s, with the mounting antisemitism, the struggle of the Jews to retain their economic positions in Jedrzejow became increasingly severe. In 1936 five Jews were murdered in the village of Stawy, near Jedrzejow.

The Hebrew novelist Israel *Zarchi was born in Jedrzejow.

[Arthur Cygielman]

Holocaust Period

The German army entered on Sept. 4, 1939. In the spring of 1940 an "open" ghetto was established. In January 1941 about 600 Jews in the vicinity were concentrated in Jedrzejow. During the summer of 1942 another 2,000 Jews were transferred to the town from other towns nearby, increasing the Jewish population to about 6,000. The entire Jewish population was deported in an *Aktion* on Sept. 16, 1942, to *Treblinka death camp and only 200 men remained in a camp established inside the former ghetto. In February 1943 all 200 were deported or shot, and Jedrzejow was proclaimed "*Judenrein*." A number of Jews had succeeded in escaping from the ghetto before the *Aktion* took place but only a few survived in hiding; most of them were murdered by Polish gangs. After the war the Jewish community in Jedrzejow was not renewed. Organizations of former Jedrzejow residents exist in Israel, the U.S.A., Canada, and Argentina.

[Stefan Krakowski]

BIBLIOGRAPHY: B. Wasiutyński, *Ludność żydowska w Polsce…* (1930), 31, 56, 71, 76, 78; S.D. Yerushalmi (ed.), *Sefer ha-Zikkaron li-Yhudei Jedrzejow* (Heb. and Yid., 1965).

JEDUTHUN (יְדוּתוּן, יְדִיתוּן), head of a family of singers, whom David singled out from among the levites (I Chron. 25:1). His song was considered the expression of prophetic inspiration: "Jeduthun with the harp, who prophesied in giving thanks and praising the Lord" (I Chron. 25:3; cf. 6:41). He was also known as "the king's seer" (II Chron. 35:15). I Chronicles 16:42 points out that part of the family was "at the gate" of the Temple and refers to the fact that levites acted both as singers and gatekeepers. The name Ethan replaces that of Jeduthun in I Chronicles 15:17; according to one view, Jeduthun and Ethan were one person. Japhet (442–43) attributes the change of name to the homiletic purposes of the Chronicler. The link and relation between Jeduthun and the term *Jeduthun* in Psalms 39:1; 62:1; 77:1 is obscure.

BIBLIOGRAPHY: W. Rudolph, *Chronikbuecher* (1955), 122ff. **ADD. BIBLIOGRAPHY:** S. Japhet, *I & II Chronicles* (1993).

[Samuel Ephraim Loewenstamm]

°JEFFERSON, THOMAS (1743–1826), third president of the United States. The foremost advocate of religious freedom among the American founding fathers, Jefferson derived his political philosophy from the doctrine of natural law, viewing every man as endowed by nature with the same inalienable rights. As early as 1776 he sought the repeal of Virginia's law on disabilities for Dissenters and Jews. It was not until 1786, however, after having served as governor of the state, that he succeeded in passing his Bill for Establishing Religious Freedom, which served as a precedent for the freedom of religion clause passed by the Federal Constitutional Convention in 1787. A deist by conviction and strong advocate of the separation of church and state, Jefferson wrote to Jacob *De La Motta in 1820 that he was "happy in the restoration of the Jews to their social rights." In 1826, after having founded the University of Virginia, he wrote to Isaac *Harby to denounce the university for tending to exclude Jews by requiring "a course in theological reading which their consciences do not permit them to pursue."

BIBLIOGRAPHY: J.L. Blau and S.W. Baron (eds.), *The Jews of the United States, 1790–1840* (1963), 13, 704; J.R. Marcus, *Early American Jewry*, 1 (1953), 51; 2 (1953), 181, 532; Kohler, in: AJHSP, 20 (1911), 11–30.

[Aaron Lichtenstein]

JEHIEL BEN JOSEPH OF PARIS (d.c. 1265), French talmudist and tosafist. Jehiel studied at the yeshivah of *Judah b. Isaac (Sir Leon), together with Isaac b. Moses of Vienna, and succeeded Judah b. Isaac upon his death. He was renowned both for his scholarship and his upright character, and was held in esteem by Jews and non-Jews alike. Jehiel was the leading Jewish protagonist in the famous *Disputation of Paris held at the court of Louis IX, arising from charges of the apostate, Nicholas Donin, that the Talmud reviled Christianity and contained references which were in conflict with the Bible. (The account of the disputation has been preserved in "*Vikku'aḥ Rabbenu Yeḥiel mi-Paris*" (Thorn, 1873. The text with a Latin translation is included in the *Tela Ignea Satanae* of C.R. *Wagenseil (1681)). As an outcome of the disputation, copies of the Talmud were publicly burned in Paris in 1242. Jehiel continued to head the Paris academy, where students were apparently taught from memory. In about 1260 he emigrated with a large number of his disciples to Ereẓ Israel, settled in Acre, then under the rule of the Crusaders, and opened a yeshivah, which became known as the "*midrash ha-gadol*" of Paris. It was Jehiel's intention, according to *Estori ha-Parḥi, to offer in Jerusalem such sacrifices as were halakhically permissible after the destruction of the Temple (*Kaftor va-Feraḥ*, ed. A.M. Luncz (1899), 81–82). The only extant responsa of Jehiel are the few which appear in the works of his contemporaries. It is known that he compiled *tosafot* to various tractates, and there is also reference to his "*Sefer Dinim*," an adaptation of which exists in manuscript. JOSEPH, Jehiel's son, was imprisoned for some time, apparently in connection with the banning of the Talmud; he emigrated with his father to Palestine. Jehiel died in Acre.

BIBLIOGRAPHY: Baer, in *Tarbiz*, 2 (1930/31), 172–87; S.H. Kook, in: *Zion*, 5 (1933), 97–102 (included also in his *Iyyunim u-Meḥkarim*, 2 (1963), 137–41); R. Margaliot (ed.), *Vikku'aḥ Rabbenu Yeḥiel mi-Paris* (1944), 1–11 introd.; Urbach, Tosafot, 371–81; J.M. Rosenthal, in: JQR (1956/57), 58–76, 145–69; Z. Vilnay, *Maẓẓevot Kodesh be-Ereẓ Yisrael* (1963), 423.

[Israel Moses Ta-Shma]

JEHIEL MEIR (Lifschits) OF GOSTYNIN (1816–1888), rabbi and ḥasidic *ẓaddik*, known as the "Good Jew of Gostynin." Jehiel Meir was a pupil of Menahem Mendel of *Kotsk and Jacob Aryeh Gutterman of *Radzymin. After unsuccessfully engaging in trade, on the advice of Menahem Mendel of Kotsk in 1878 he became rabbi of Gostynin. His reputation for goodness and holiness was such that even in his youth he was called "one of the 36 *ẓaddikim*." The hypercritical Kotsk Ḥasidim honored him for his unsophisticated simplicity. His modest way of life gained him the love of the simple folk. He took no rewards (*pidyonot*) and gave his own money to charity. Jehiel Meir devoted much of his teaching to the Psalms and advised repeating them as the most potent form of prayer, becoming known as the "Psalm Jew" (Yid. *Der Tilim Yid*). After the death of Jacob Aryeh of Radzymin he became ḥasidic leader in Gostynin. His teachings were collected in *Merom ha-Rim* (1892) and *Mei ha-Yam* (n.d.). His son ISRAEL MOSES succeeded him in Proskurov. The personality of Jehiel Meir and his way of life left a deep impression. Shalom *Asch's historical novel *Salvation* is based upon his life.

BIBLIOGRAPHY: J.H. Goldshlag, *Merom ha-Rim* (1892, repr. 1965); A.I. Bromberg, *Mi-Gedolei ha-Ḥasidut*, 11 (1956).

[Zvi Meir Rabinowitz]

JEHIEL MICHAEL ("Michel") BEN ABRAHAM MEIR OF CIFER (d. 1844), Polish and Hungarian rabbi. After serving as rabbi in some communities of Poland, where he was born, Jehiel was appointed to Cifer near Bratislava. He was the author of *Ḥayyei Olam* (Vienna, 1830) on talmudic topics and the Shulḥan Arukh, *Yoreh De'ah*, and *Derekh Ḥayyim* (Pressburg, 1837) on the laws of Passover in the *Tur Oraḥ Ḥayyim*. The latter is in two parts – *Derekh ha-Kaẓar*, containing novellae from the responsa of the earlier authorities, and *Derekh ha-Arokh*, in which he ingeniously attempted to solve the difficulties raised by *David b. Samuel ha-Levi in his *Turei Zahav* and the *Magen Avraham* of Abraham Gombiner on the Shulḥan Arukh and *Maimonides' *Mishneh Torah*. Jehiel Michael was accused of plagiarizing the *Magen ha-Elef* of Aryeh Leib Zunz (published in the *Sar ha-Elef* (Warsaw, 1817) of Jonathan *Eybeschuetz) in his *Derekh Ḥayyim*, but his defenders point to his original contributions. In the introduction to the *Ḥayyei Olam*, he mentions two other works that have not been published.

BIBLIOGRAPHY: S. Wiener, *Kohelet Moshe* (1893–1936), 298, no. 2439; J.J.(L.) Greenwald (Grunwald), *Ha-Yehudim be-Ungarya*, 1 (1913), 79, no. 76; P.Z. Schwartz, *Shem ha-Gedolim me-Ereẓ Hagar*, 1 (1913), 45, no. 123; 3 (1915), 26, no. 39, 35, no. 18.

[Yehoshua Horowitz]

JEHIEL MICHAEL ("Michel") BEN ELIEZER (d. 1648), rabbi and kabbalist, who lived in Nemirov (the Ukraine). Jehiel's cousin Isaac praised his talmudic and kabbalistic knowledge as well as his mastery of secular sciences (introduction to *Shivrei Luḥot*). Jehiel at first regarded the *Chmielnicki persecutions as a presage of the coming messianic era. As the Cossacks came nearer to his community he exhorted its members to stay firm in their faith. During the massacre at Nemirov he and his mother were dragged to the Jewish cemetery and murdered there on the 22nd (according to others the 20th) of Sivan (1648). Jehiel's martyrdom is mentioned in the elegies composed by *Shabbetai b. Meir ha-Kohen and Yom

Tov Lipmann *Heller in memory of the 1648 persecutions. Jehiel was the author of a work on the *Al-Tikrei* interpretations of the Talmud. A large part of the manuscript has been lost; the remaining fragment was published by his nephew as *Shivrei Luḥot* (Lublin, 1680). Part of his commentary on the Pentateuch and *Al-Tikrei* interpretations were republished together with the commentary *Amarot Tehorot* by Ḥayyim Selig Goldschlag (Warsaw, 1911). Jehiel is also mentioned in *Korban Shabbat* (Dyhrenfuerth, 1691, 10b–11a) by Bezalel b. Solomon of Kobrin.

BIBLIOGRAPHY: J. Gurland, *Le-Korot ha-Gezerot al-Yisrael*, 2 (1888), 13–14; 5 (1650), 30–31; 7 (1892), 32; Graetz, Gesch, 10 (18963), 64; Fuenn, Keneset, 526; S. Bernfeld, *Sefer ha-Dema'ot*, 3 (1926), 117, 169f., 177, 204.

[Samuel Abba Horodezky]

JEHIEL MICHAEL ("Michel") BEN JUDAH LEIB HE-ḤASID (1680–1728), rabbi, known as R. Michel Ḥasid. Jehiel Michael served as rabbi of Zlotow and other Polish communities before being invited to become head of the Berlin yeshivah, and in 1714, with the approval of King Frederick William I, he was appointed to succeed his brother-in-law, Aaron b. Isaac Benjamin Wolf, as rabbi of Berlin. When Aaron died in 1721, Jehiel was also appointed to the rabbinate of Frankfurt on the Oder and its district, which had been separated from that of Berlin during Aaron's lifetime. In 1718 Frederick William I was present at the consecration of the new synagogue in Berlin and Jehiel recited a special prayer in his honor. Jehiel was attracted to Kabbalah and copied kabbalistic manuscripts. At first he favored Nehemiah *Ḥayon, one of the adherents of Shabbetai Ẓevi, but when he became aware of Ḥayon's chicanery, he became one of the strenuous opponents of Shabbateanism. At a conference of rabbis in Frankfurt on the Oder in 1726 over which he presided, he placed the Shabbateans and their suspect literature, which had made its appearance from 1666 onward, under a ban. Jehiel refrained from giving esoteric interpretations of the *aggadot* for "fear of heresy."

He wrote novellae to the tractates *Megillah* (printed in the Talmud, ed. Berlin, 1714) and *Rosh Ha-Shanah* (in the Amsterdam Talmud, 1726); glosses in the *Kol Yehudah* (Amsterdam, 1729) of Judah of Glogau and in the *Asefat Ḥakhamim* (Offenbach, 1722) of Israel Isserl; and *Yofi Mikhal*, notes and comments to Samuel Jaffe's commentary, *Yefeh Mareh* (Constantinople, 1587), on the *aggadot* of the Jerusalem Talmud (Berlin, 1725–26). These commentaries were also published in *Aggadot Yerushalmi*, part one (1863). These supplements by Jehiel to Jaffe's work were merely an extract from a larger work on that subject, but when he saw that Jaffe's commentary was very popular, he published that in full and abridged his own work.

BIBLIOGRAPHY: E.L. Landshuth, *Toledot Anshei ha-Shem*, 1 (1884), 11–19; J. Meisl, in: MGWJ, 71 (1927), 276; idem, in: *Arim ve-Immahot be-Yisrael*, 1 (1946), 100f.; idem, *Pinkas Kehillat Berlin* (1962), 515; M. Steinschneider, *Oẓerot Ḥayyim*, (1848), part on Manuscripts, nos. 329, 396, 521, 577, 591.

[Yehoshua Horowitz]

JEHIEL MICHAEL ("Michel") OF ZLOCZOW (c. 1731–1786), one of the early propagators of Ḥasidism in Galicia. He was born in Brody, the son of Isaac of Drogobych. It is related that on Jehiel's first visit to the Ba'al Shem Tov, the latter commanded that Jehiel be honored. After the death of the Ba'al Shem, Jehiel was one of the few disciples who accepted the leadership of *Dov Baer, the *maggid* of Mezhirech. He served as preacher in Brody where he was among the members of the celebrated *kloiz* (*klaus*). Later he became preacher in Zloczow, and toward the end of his life settled in Yampol, Podolia.

Jehiel was highly esteemed among the Ḥasidim and miraculous tales are related of his saintliness and asceticism, but he was strongly opposed by the *Mitnaggedim*. His distinctive spirituality is recalled by one of his disciples, who states that "it little mattered whether he had before him a *Gemara* or a kabbalistic text, for Jehiel saw in them only the means of serving God" (*Likkutei Yekarim*, 1872, 31b). In accordance with ḥasidic views, he considered the principle of **devekut* ("devotion" to God) to be of major importance and remarked that the way to attain this state was through the negation of reality (i.e., ecstasy). There are two roads to *devekut*. The positive way is to stand in fear and shame before the greatness of the Creator and hence through prayer, study, and good deeds to find the state of true love. Diligence in these practices will eventually lead to *devekut*. The negative way is through a denial of all physical desire. Jehiel Michael constantly preached on the need to uproot evil characteristics and destroy physical lusts. He knew that this way to *devekut* was difficult, for God had created man different from His own essence and therefore man could not maintain a constant state of *devekut*. Since the danger of his sinking into his physical nature was anticipated, God had imbued him with the will to achieve union with his source (i.e., God). Man's task is to conquer the material world and to view it not as the purpose of life but as a means of discovering that divinity which is reflected in the material and enlivens it. In this teaching, Jehiel Michael follows Dov Baer of Mezhirech, but he saw that this way was the most perilous for the ordinary man. He did not believe that constant *devekut* was possible for every man while he was engaged in physical activity, therefore he advised that physical acts be preceded by meditation on the Divine Creator.

When preaching he would begin his sermons: "I do not only command and admonish you but myself as well…" (*Or ha-Meir*, on *Ẓav*). The true preacher, Jehiel believed, was the man who felt that he was merely a mouthpiece of the *Shekhinah* ("Divine Presence") and not a man who spoke in his own voice. His disciple attests that he "spoke at length and explained his statements several times" (*Likkutei Yekarim*, 28b). Jehiel Michael did not leave any writings of his own. Selections from his sermons were published in the anthology *Likkutei Yekarim*, as the sermons of "the Maggid Meisharim" of Yampol. Tradition attributes many sayings to him and stories about his wondrous deeds appear in various collections. Jehiel Michael was the founder of a dynasty of *ẓaddikim* which spread throughout Galicia and the Ukraine. He had five sons:

Joseph of Yampol, Mordecai of Kremenets (teacher of *Meir of Przemyslany and father-in-law of Aaron II of *Karlin), Isaac of Radzivilov (author of *Or Yiẓḥak*, 1961), Moses of Vladimir-Volnyski, and Ze'ev Wolf of Zbarazh.

BIBLIOGRAPHY: A. Walden, *Shem ha-Gedolim he-Ḥadash* (1880), 29b–30a; M.H. Kleinmann, *Mazkeret Shem ha-Gedolim* (1908, repr. 1967), 13–32; idem, *Zikkaron la-Rishonim* (1912), 23a–41b; Dubnow, Ḥasidut, 188–91; M. Bodek, *Seder ha-Dorot he-Ḥadash* (1941, repr. 1965), 52–56; M. Buber, *Tales of the Hasidim* (1968⁴), 138–57.

[Moshe Hallamish]

JEHOAHAZ (Heb. יְהוֹאָחָז, יוֹאָחָז; "YHWH has grasped"), son of *Jehu, king of Israel c. 814–800 B.C.E. According to II Kings 13:1, Jehoahaz reigned for 17 years, while according to the synchronism made between his reign and that of Joash king of Judah, it is evident that he only reigned 14 years. It might therefore be assumed that Jehoahaz reigned together with his father Jehu during his last three years. (Another possibility is a shift in the dating system (see *Chronology). Although the writer of II Kings 13:2 classifies him as a sinner in the mold of Jeroboam son of Nebat, he observes (13:4) that Jehoahaz implored YHWH, who brought (an unnamed) savior to deliver Israel in response to the prayer of the king. This is the only story in Kings of a northern king imploring YHWH. Nonetheless, it gains credibility because something quite similar is said of Zakkur of Hamath who successfully cried out to his god Baalhamayn during a siege (Cogan and Tadmor, 143–44). He reigned during a time of decline and degradation in the kingdom of Israel. By the end of Jehu's reign, *Hazael king of Aram had occupied Transjordan, and in 813 B.C.E. (the last year of Jehu's reign and the first of Jehoahaz to reign alone) Hazael launched a military campaign which brought him as far south as Aphek on the border of Philistia (according to the addition in the Lucian version of the LXX to II Kings 13:23). At that time, or a short while later, it seems that Jehoahaz became a vassal of Aram – during the reigns of Hazael and his son *Ben-Hadad III, who exercised sovereignty over the whole of Syria and Palestine. The latter extended and imposed the authority of Aram up to the borders of Egypt. The Arameans left Jehoahaz with only "fifty horsemen, and ten chariots, and ten thousand footmen, for the king of Aram had destroyed them and made them like the dust at threshing" (II Kings 13:7). The prophecy of Amos 1:3, 13, concerning the cruelty of the Arameans and the Ammonites in the land of Gilead, probably refers to this period (cf. II Kings 8:12). The decline of Israel in the period is also evident from the series of prophetic stories concerning Elisha (II Kings 5–7), which describe the subordination of the "king of Israel" to the "king of Aram." There is no doubt that the unnamed "king of Israel" was Jehoahaz (and not Jehoram son of Ahab) and that "Ben-Hadad" (6:24) was not Ben-Hadad II (the contemporary of Ahab and Jehoram), but Ben-Hadad III, son of Hazael.

According to the prophetic story, Ben-Hadad besieged Samaria, and it was only saved after "the Lord had made the army of Aram hear the sound of chariots, and of horses, the sound of a great army, so that they said to one another, 'Behold, the king of Israel has hired against us the kings of the Hittites and the kings of Egypt to come against us.' So they fled away in the twilight and forsook their tents, their horses…" (II Kings 7:6–7); i.e., the deliverance is in this instance explained by the fear of the Arameans of an attack from the north (the kings of the Hittites, led by Hamath) or from the south (the Egyptian Pharaohs). However, the deliverance of Israel is due to the campaigns of Assyria into northern Syria of Adad-Nirari III. These campaigns began in 805 B.C.E. and continued until 802 B.C.E., their principal objective being the weakening of the Aramean supremacy in northern (the region of Arpad) and central Syria. The permanent liberation of Israel from the Aramean oppressor only came with the defeat of Ben-Hadad III by Adad-Nirari, in 796 B.C.E. during the second campaign of Adad-Nirari III into southern Syria (against Menṣuate), i.e., at the beginning of the reign of *Jehoash son of Jehoahaz. It is likely that the writer of II Kings 13:5 preferred not to name an Assyrian king as the deliverer of Israel and purposely left him anonymous. B. Mazar attributes the Samarian Ostraca to Jehoahaz' reign; he sees in them the evidence of an expansion of the kingdom of Jehoahaz, from the time when he began to liberate himself from the yoke of Aram. (For other opinions on the date of the Samarian Ostraca, see: *Samaria.)

BIBLIOGRAPHY: Bright, Hist, 236; B. Maisler (Mazar), in: JPOS, 21 (1948), 124–7; B. Mazar, in: A. Malamat (ed.), *Bi-Ymei Bayit Rishon* (1962), 149–50; H. Tadmor, *ibid.*, 166–7; idem, in: *Scripta Hierosolymitana*, 8 (1961), 241–3 (Eng.); idem, in: IEJ, 11 (1961), 149. **ADD. BIBLIOGRAPHY:** M. Cogan and H. Tadmor, *II Kings* (1988).

[Hayim Tadmor / S. David Sperling (2nd ed.)]

JEHOAHAZ (Heb. יְהוֹאָחָז, יוֹאָחָז; "YHWH has grasped"), son of *Josiah and Hamutal daughter of Jeremiah of Libnah (II Kings 23:31), king of Judah (609 B.C.E.). At first his name was Shallum (Jer. 22:11) but it was later changed to Jehoahaz, apparently when he was made king. The new name with the theophoric element referring to YHWH may be a reflection of the reforming spirit of Josiah. In the genealogical list of the descendants of David in I Chronicles 3:15, Shallum is entered as the fourth son of Josiah, whereas the first born was Johanan. It seems probable therefore that despite the Septuagint, which reads Jehoahaz instead of Johanan in I Chronicles 3:15, Jehoahaz was not the first born and that the *Am ha-Areẓ* ("People of the land") deliberately gave him precedence (II Chron. 36:1). Jehoahaz was made king, at the age of 23, in the summer of 609 B.C.E., after Josiah his father had been killed in the battle against Pharaoh *Necoh at Megiddo. It has been suggested that he was the nominee of the circles which favored the alliance with the ascending Neo-Babylonian Kingdom – bitter enemies of Assyria – who were hostile to Egypt's attempt to save Assyria from total destruction. Three months later, when Necoh returned from fighting the Babylonians and their allies – the Medes (from the district of Haran) – he deposed Jehoahaz and put his elder brother Eliakim, i.e., *Jehoiakim, in his place (II Kings 23:33–34; II Chron. 36:3–4). Accordingly,

Jehoahaz reigned from about Tammuz to Tishri of that year (609 B.C.E.). Possibly the notice that "he did evil in the eyes of YHWH" (II King 23:2) is inspired by the needs of theodicy to account for the shortness of his reign. It would seem that the tradition of II Kings 23:33, which says that Jehoahaz was deposed at Riblah in the land of Hamath, is to be preferred to that of II Chronicles 36:3, according to which he was deposed in Jerusalem. It is probable that Jehoahaz came before Necoh at Riblah, where his temporary headquarters were, in order to humble himself, but that Necoh did not accept his submission. He imposed a monetary fine of "a hundred talents of silver and a talent of gold" upon Judah (II Kings 23:33). This fine was paid by Jehoiakim, who collected it from the *Am ha-Areẓ* (*ibid.* 23:33–35). The tragic fate of Jehoahaz son of Josiah, who was exiled to Egypt and died there, served as the subject of an elegy by Jeremiah (Jer. 22: 10–12) and later by Ezekiel (Ezek. 19:4). An (unprovenanced) seal with the image of a rooster, dated paleographically to the late seventh or early sixth century B.C.E., reads: *lyhwʾḥz bn hmlk*, "belonging to Jehoahaz son of the king."

BIBLIOGRAPHY: Bright, Hist, 303; Tadmor, in: JNES, 15 (1956), 226–30; Vogt, in: VT, Supplement, 4 (1957), 92–97; S. Yeivin, in: *Tarbiz*, 14 (1941), 264–5; Malamat, in: IEJ, 18 (1968), 137–44. **ADD. BIBLIOGRAPHY:** N. Avigad, *Eretz Israel*, 9 (1969), 9; B. Cogan and H. Tadmor, *II Kings* (AB; 1988), 303–4; S. Ahituv, *Handbook of Ancient Hebrew Inscriptions* (1992), 118.

[Hayim Tadmor]

JEHOASH (Heb. יְהוֹאָשׁ, יוֹאָשׁ; "The Lord has given"), son of Jehoahaz, king of Israel (reigned 801–785 B.C.E.). Jehoash shared the throne with his father for two years or more. When the resumption of King Adad-Nirari III of Assyria's military campaigns in Syria toward the end of the eighth century B.C.E. weakened the power of *Aram, Jehoash determined to free Israel from Aramean control. The decisive stimulus for the liberation of Israel's territories to the east of the Jordan came in 796 with Adad-Nirari's campaign against Manṣuate in the Lebanon valley (*Massyas* according to Strabo 16:2, 18); at that time, the king of Assyria also attacked Damascus, defeated the Aramean armies, and exacted a heavy tribute from Ben-Hadad III, the king of Aram. The subsequent wars of Aphek (Alphikh, east of Lake Kinneret) appear to have completely broken the strength of Aram. Elisha's prophecy to Jehoash (made just before the prophet's death; II Kings 13:14–19) that the king would defeat Aram at Aphek should be interpreted against this background. It appears that Jehoash then recognized the sovereignty of Assyria, his natural ally in the war against Aram, a conjecture substantiated by an Assyrian inscription from Tel-el-Rimah in which Jehoash (written Ia'asu) of Samaria is mentioned among those paying tribute to Adad-Nirari (Cogan and Tadmor, 335). The countries subdued by the above campaign are also listed in Adad-Nirari's inscription from Calah (Nimrud). They were: Tyre, Sidon, "the land of Omri" (i.e., Israel), Edom, and Philistia (A.K. Grayson, RIMA 3, 212–13).

The relationship between Jehoash and *Amaziah, king of Judah, is not clear. Israel and Judah may have formed an alliance with the aim of conquering Edom – similar to the alliance between Jehoshaphat and Ahab – but then, for some unknown reason, the two kings quarreled. According to a late story in II Chronicles 25:6, before Amaziah went to war against Edom he hired 100,000 soldiers from Israel; but II Kings 14:8–10 relates that after the conquest of Edom, Amaziah challenged Jehoash: "Then Amaziah sent messengers to Jehoash… to say, come let us meet together." In the battle between the armies of Judah and Israel near Beth-Shemesh, Amaziah was defeated and taken prisoner. Jehoash entered Jerusalem, looted the palace and Temple treasuries, and broke down the city wall for a distance of 400 cubits "from the gate of Ephraim unto the corner gate" as a symbol of its surrender (II Kings 14:13). Shortly after his victory Jehoash died, in the 15th year of Amaziah's reign (785 B.C.E.). From the chronological data concerning the reign of his son *Jeroboam, it appears that father and son reigned jointly during Jehoash's last years.

BIBLIOGRAPHY: E.R. Thiele, *The Mysterious Numbers of the Hebrew Kings* (1951), 69; idem, in: VT, 4 (1954), 193–4; Pritchard, Texts, 281; H. Tadmor, in: *Scripta Hierosolymitana*, 8 (1961), 241–3; idem, in: *Bi-Ymei Bayit Rishon* (1961), 166–7; B. Mazar, *ibid.*, 149–50; H.L. Ginsberg, in: *Fourth World Congress of Jewish Studies*, 1 (1967), 91–93; S. Page, in: *Iraq*, 30 (1968), 139–53; idem, in: VT, 19 (1969), 483–4; A. Cazelles, in: *Comptes rendus des Académies des Inscriptions et Belles-Lettres* (1969), 106–17. **ADD. BIBLIOGRAPHY:** M. Cogan and H. Tadmor, *II Kings* (1988).

[Hayim Tadmor]

JEHOIACHIN (Heb. יְהוֹיָכִין; "YHWH will establish"; also: Joiachin, Jeconiah, Jechoniah, Coniah; in Babylonian Akkadian documents Ia-ʾ-kin), king of Judah. He ascended the throne at the height of the rebellion against Babylon, when he was 18 years old (II Kings 24:8; the version in II Chron. 36:9, which states that he was only eight at the time is difficult), and reigned for three months (II Chron. 36:9 adds another ten days). In the winter of 597 B.C.E. Nebuchadnezzar exiled him, along with his mother, family, officers, slaves, and 10,000 captives – including craftsmen and smiths – to Babylon (II Kings 24:12ff.), setting up Zedekiah in his place. It seems that Jehoiachin's mother Nehushta, daughter of Elnathan, was very influential in the palace, for she is mentioned in the Bible several times (II Kings 24:12, 15; Jer. 22:26; 29:2). The Babylonian chronicle published by D.J. Wiseman (see bibliography) describes the capture of Jerusalem and the exile of Jehoiachin in the seventh year of Nebuchadnezzar's reign, relating that the Judean king surrendered with a large part of his army shortly after Nebuchadnezzar attacked Jerusalem. Jehoiachin's surrender saved the land from destruction, but many of the people of Judah disapproved of his action; the resulting disputes between the party favoring peace and that counseling rebellion were specifically revealed in the antagonism which arose between Jeremiah and Hananiah son of Azur of Gibeon in the fourth year of Zedekiah's reign (Jer. 28). Excavations into various Judahite tells (Beth-Shemesh, Tel Bet-Mirsim, Ramat Raḥel) have disclosed the imprint of a seal reading "to Eliakim, the servant of Jochin," which Klein suggested refers to the servant of Jehoiachin, i.e., the man in charge of the property of Jehoiachin. W.F. Albright and other scholars held that these impressions belong to the reign of Zedekiah and indicate that Jehoiachin still held many estates in Judah after his exile and enjoyed the status of a king in Judah. However, subsequent study (Garfinkel) shows that the Jochin/Jochan seal impressions are from the eighth century, much earlier than previously thought, and are thus irrelevant to the biography of King Jehoiachin. Food-rationing lists belonging to the 10th to 35th years of Nebuchadnezzar's reign, found in one of the underground storerooms of his palace in Babylon, mention Jehoiachin's name four times; one such list is from 592 B.C.E. (the 13th year of Nebuchadnezzar's reign and sixth year of Jehoiachin's exile). In these lists the latter is called "king of Judah," and several documents mention distribution of food to the five sons of the king of Judah (ANET, 205; cf. I Chron. 3:17), which was given to "Hananiah." From the large quantity of oil distributed to Jehoiachin it would appear that he and his family were living together. The title given him in these documents indicates that he was considered a captive ruler, perhaps a hostage, or perhaps one who had surrendered freely and enjoyed the patronage of his captors. His family retained leadership of the Babylonian exiles (Ezek. 1:2), and his descendants were at the head of those who returned to Zion. According to the biblical account, Jehoiachin's status improved after Nebuchadnezzar's death (562 B.C.E.). His successor, Evil-Merodach, honored Jehoiachin, king of Judah (in the 37th year of his exile, on the 27th day of the 12th month), gave him new clothing and an honored seat at his own table (II Kings 25:27–30; Jer. 52:31–34). It is uncertain if the pardoning of Jehoiachin was connected with a general change in the attitude of the king of Babylon toward the exiled Jews.

[Jacob Liver]

In the Aggadah

Nebuchadnezzar's sudden attack on Jehoiachin was the result of the advice of his countrymen who warned him, "Do not rear a gentle cub of a vicious dog; much less a vicious cub of a vicious dog." Nebuchadnezzar thereupon went to Daphne (Antiocha), where he asked a deputation of the Sanhedrin to hand over Jehoiachin, in return for which he would not destroy the Temple. When Jehoiachin was informed of the request, he ascended to the roof of the Temple, and, extending the keys of the sanctuary toward heaven, exclaimed: "Lord of the Universe, since we have hitherto not proved worthy custodians for Thee, from now on these keys are Thine." A fiery hand appeared and snatched the keys (or, according to other opinions, they remained suspended between heaven and earth). Jehoiachin was then taken captive (the gate by which he left the city was thereafter called the Gate of Jeconiah; Mid. 6:2), and placed in solitary confinement. Fearing, however, that since the king was childless, the House of David would thus cease, the Sanhedrin succeeded in obtaining permission for his wife to live with him. Jehoiachin kept the laws of marital purity during this time, and as a reward was forgiven his sins (Jer. 3:22; Lev. R. 19:6). Even the decree that none of his descendants would ascend the throne (Jer. 22:30) was repealed when Zerubbabel was appointed leader of the returned exiles (cf. Sanh. 37b–38a). The exile of Zedekiah while Jehoiachin was still alive was a merciful act, since Jehoiachin could thus teach Zedekiah Torah (Git. 88a). Jehoiachin's life is illustrative of the maxim: "During prosperity a man must never forget the possibility of misfortune; nor in despair lose hope of prosperity's return." Within two days of Evil-Merodach's accession to the throne, Jehoiachin was released and accorded the highest honors (SOR. 28).

BIBLIOGRAPHY: J.W. Rothstein, *Die Genealogie des Königs Jojachin…* (1902); J. Lewy, in: *Mitteilungen der Vorderasiatisch-Ägyptischen Gesellschaft*, 29, pt. 2 (1924), 42–51; W.F. Albright, in: JBL, 51 (1932), 77ff.; idem, in: BA, 5 (1942), 49ff.; A. Malamat, in: JNES, 9 (1950), 218ff.; idem, in: IEJ, 6 (1956), 246ff.; 18 (1968), 137ff.; idem, in: Y. Aviram (ed.), *Yerushalayim le-Doroteha* (1968), 34ff.; Klausner, Bayit Sheni, 1 (1951²), 3238; F.M.T. Böhl, *Opera minora* (1953), 423–9, 525; P. Artzi, in: A. Biram (ed.), *Sefer E. Urbach* (1955), 264–5; J.P. Hyatt, in: JBL, 75 (1956), 277–82; H. Tadmor, in: JNES, 15 (1956), 226–30; D.J. Wiseman, *Chronicles of Chaldaean Kings* (626–556 B.C.E.)… (1956); E. Vogt, in: VT, Supplement, 4 (1957), 92–96; M. Noth, in: ZDPV, 74 (1958), 133ff.; E. Kutsch, in: ZAW, 71 (1959), 270ff.; J. Liver, *Toledot Beit David* (1959), 7–9, 12ff., 49ff.; Bright, Hist, index. IN THE AGGADAH: Ginzberg, Legends, index, s.v., *Jehoiakim*; I. Ḥasida, *Ishei ha-Tanakh* (1964). **ADD. BIBLIOGRAPHY:** M. Cogan and H. Tadmor, *II Kings* (1988), 310–14; Y. Garfinkel, in: BA, 53 (1990), 74–79; S. Ahituv, *Handbook of Ancient Hebrew Inscriptions* (1992), 128; J. Berridge, in: ABD, 3:661–63.

JEHOIADA (Heb. יְהוֹיָדָע; "YHWH has known," "YHWH has directed"), chief priest in the Temple in Jerusalem during the reigns of *Athaliah and *Joash of Judah. According to II Chron. 22:11, Jehoiada was married to Jehosheba (called Jehoshabath in Chronicles), the daughter of King *Jehoram and the sister of Jehoram's son *Ahaziah (II Kings 11:2; II Chron. 22:11). Jehoiada had the most important role in the return of the throne to the house of David and the introduction of new administrative procedures in the Temple in Jerusalem. After Athaliah assumed the throne and killed all the royal family (II Kings 11:1; II Chron. 22:10), it was feared that the entire house of David would be exterminated. Jehosheba succeeded in saving the year-old Joash, the youngest son of Ahaziah. She hid him and his nurse for six years in a chamber of the Temple (II Kings 11:2–3; II Chron. 22:11–12), an undertaking to which Jehoiada, as "high priest" (II Chron. 24: 6 calls him *ha-rosh*) was able to give much assistance.

As a result of the increased opposition to Athaliah and the Tyrian cult, which she had introduced in Jerusalem, Jehoiada led the resistance to the queen; the first account of a priest's involvement in the affairs of state in Judah (II Kings 11:4–12; II Chron. 23:1–11). According to Kings, the major forces against Athaliah were the priesthood and the *am ha-areẓ ("the People of the Land"), whose exact composition is debated, and the leaders of the Temple and palace guards, "the Carites and the guards" (the Carites, being foreigners, are omitted from the account of the Chronicler because he excludes foreigners from the temple). According to Chronicles, the entire people was involved in the revolt. The insurrection against Athaliah was preceded by the coronation ceremony of Joash in the temple. The young king was given the royal *nezer*, "diadem," and the *edut*. Gersonides takes this last to refer to the Torah; others to some covenant document or to an engraved amulet comparable to the priestly diadem of Ex. 23:36. He was also anointed (II Kings 11:17–20; II Chron. 23:16–21). After the ceremony Athaliah was killed outside the Temple (II Kings 11:13–16; II Chron. 23:12–15). Jehoiada then made a covenant between "YHWH, the king, and the people," and afterward, apparently between the people and the king (II Kings 11:17; II Chron. 23:16). Thus, the kingship of the Davidic dynasty was legally restored. It may be noted that an inscription carved in stone found in South Arabia, which served as a kind of constitution for the state of Qatabân, contains a similar covenant between God, the people, and the king (Pritchard, Texts, 511). The covenant of Jehoiada obligated the people to become "a people of YHWH"; i.e., to eliminate the Baal cult. Jehoiada remained the adviser teacher of the young king, but it seems that his influence was not limited to the religious sphere alone (II Chron. 24:3).

Jehoiada's other functions were mainly related to the Temple. He instituted special directions concerning the sanctification of the altar and the purification of the Temple (*ibid.* 23:18–19), which were still in effect in the generation before the destruction of the Temple (Jer. 29:26). With the cooperation of the adolescent king, Jehoiada arranged for repairs of the Temple which had been neglected during the turmoil of the previous regime. After the priests refused to set aside money from that which was brought to the Temple for repairs, as they were supposed to have done (according to the version of the story in II Chronicles 24, the priests refused to collect money in provincial cities), Jehoiada and the king agreed to designate a special box or chest (called *shofar* in the Second Temple period) in which "all the money brought to the house of the Lord" would be put (except for the purchase of guilt and sin offerings, which was kept by the priesthood). Jehoiada and the king then paid for the repairs from the money thus collected. According to Chronicles, Jehoiada lived 130 years, but this figure must be an exaggeration, especially since he died while Joash was still king. That he was much respected is attested by his burial in the city of David together with the kings (II Chron. 24:16). According to II Chronicles 24:17–22, of his sons, *Zechariah, was killed after his father's death because he rebuked Joash in harsh terms.

[Yehoshua M. Grintz / S. David Sperling (2nd ed.)]

In the Aggadah

Jehoiada's piety was such that the verse "Jehoiada was the leader of the Aaronites" (I Chron. 12:28) is explained to the effect that "Had Aaron lived in the same generation, Jehoiada would have been superior to him" (Eccl. R. 1:4, no. 4). Jehoiada and his wife, Jehosheba, preserved the young Joash by hiding him in the upper chambers of the Temple during the summer, and in the cellars during the winter (Mid. Ps. 18:23).

BIBLIOGRAPHY: Grintz, in: *Zion*, 23–24 (1958–59), 124ff.; J.A. Montgomery, *The Book of Kings* (ICC, 1951), 416ff.; Bright, Hist, 234, 237; Rudolph, in: *Bertholet-Festschrift* (1950), 473ff. IN THE AGGADAH: Ginzberg, Legends, 4 (1947), 258; 6 (1946), 354; I. Ḥasida, *Ishei ha-Tanakh* (1964), 167. **ADD. BIBLIOGRAPHY:** M. Cogan and H. Tadmor, *II Kings* (1988), 124–41; S. Japhet, *I & II Chronicles* (1993), 825–51.

JEHOIAKIM (Heb. יְהוֹיָקִים, יְהוֹיָקִם; "YHWH raises up"), king of Judah (609–598 B.C.E.). Pharaoh Neco made Jehoiakim king of Judah after he captured *Jehoahaz, Jehoiakim's younger brother, who was the choice of the *am ha-areẓ and who reigned for only three months. Jehoiakim, who was 25 when he ascended the throne (according to I Chron. 3:15 he was the second son of Josiah), was most likely selected because of his known support of a pro-Egyptian policy. Jehoiakim's original name Eliakim was changed by the Pharaoh in order to indicate the Judahite king's subservience to Egypt (II Kings 23:34; II Chron. 36:4). Egypt also imposed a heavy tax on Judah – 100 talents of silver and a talent of gold – which Jehoiakim exacted by levying a tax upon all people of the land (II Kings 23:33, 35).

During the first three years of Jehoiakim's reign Judah was a vassal of Egypt, which controlled Syria and Palestine and clashed with the Babylonian forces in the area of the Euphrates River (according to the *Babylonian Chronicle*). In 605 B.C.E. Babylon defeated Egypt at *Carchemish (II Kings 24:7; Jer. 46:2) and Babylon seized Syria and Palestine. The Babylonian army reached the borders of Judah and apparently took prisoners of war from Judah (Jos., Apion, 1:19). The following year, in the month of Kislev, *Nebuchadnezzar captured Ashkelon and exiled its king. Simultaneously, in the ninth month of the fifth year of Jehoiakim's reign, a fast day of the Lord was proclaimed in Jerusalem (Jer. 36:9). Jeremiah warned the people that the king of Babylon would destroy the land, and indeed after the fall of Ashkelon, Judah, too, came under the Babylonian yoke. According to the Bible, Jehoiakim was a vassal of Babylon for three years before he rebelled (II Kings 24:1). Although the *Babylonian Chronicle* cites neither the subjugation nor the rebellion of Judah, it does mention the campaign against Syria and Palestine, and a brief expedition against nomadic groups in the sixth year of Nebuchadnezzar's reign. Thus, although Nebuchadnezzar sent troops from Moab, Ammon, and Aram (or, according to the Peshitta, Edom; II Kings 24:2) against the border regions of Judah (cf. Jer. 35:11), Judah was able to continue its rebellion during this period. Only in the seventh year of the reign of Nebuchadnezzar (the 11th of Jehoiakim or perhaps, after his death, during the brief reign of his son Jehoiachin) did the siege of Jerusalem begin. It ended on the second day of Adar, on March 15/16, 597 B.C.E., with the surrender and exile of the new king, Jehoiachin.

The internal political and economic conditions in Judah during this period were undermined both by large-scale military movements along its border and by the incursions of robber bands from the neighboring countries. The persecutions of the prophets, whose influence had increased during the days of Josiah, also sharpened internal conflicts. The book of Jeremiah contrasts Jehoiakim with his pious forbear Hezekiah by telling how Hezekiah reacted piously to Micah's prophecy of doom. In contrast, Jehoiakim persecuted and killed the prophet Uriah the son of Shemaiah, and would have done the same to Jeremiah (Jer. 26). Similarly, Jeremiah 36 contrasts Jehoiakim's lack of contrition upon hearing Jeremiah's scroll with that of the pious *Josiah, who had torn his garments upon hearing the words of the scroll of Torah (cf. II Kings 22:11–14 with Jer. 36:23–24). According to the Book of Kings, Jehoiakim shed much innocent blood in Jerusalem (II Kings 24:4; cf. Jer. 22:17).

II Chronicles 36:6ff. relates that Nebuchadnezzar bound Jehoiakim in fetters in order to carry him to Babylon. A year later he also brought Jehoiachin to Babylon. This version not only contradicts the account given in Kings but also does not appear in the *Babylonian Chronicle*. Thus, the question remains if the Chronicles' account reflects an oral tradition that did not take into account that the king who surrendered and was exiled was not the same one who had rebelled. In II Kings 24:6 it is related that he "slept with his fathers," indicating that, at least according to this source, he died a peaceful death. Two oracles relating to Jehoiakim's death are found in Jeremiah (22:18–19; 36:30).

[Jacob Liver / S. David Sperling (2nd ed.)]

In the Aggadah

Jehoiakim is portrayed as the very incarnation of wickedness and defiant flouting of God. When he ascended the throne he said: "My predecessors did not know how to anger God." He claimed that his generation, which was in possession of the "gold of Parvaim," did not even need God to provide them with light. He therefore proceeded to flout God's word publicly by engraving the name of an idol (or according to others the name of God Himself) on his person and by the deliberate wearing of *sha'atnez*, by epistasis, and by incestuous relationships with his mother, daughter-in-law, and his father's wife. He violated women, murdered their husbands, and confiscated their wealth (Lev. R. 19:6; Sanh. 103a). He cut out from the Book of Lamentations all references to God and threw them into the fire (MK 26a). He had a dishonorable death and was even denied honorable burial. When he refused to accede to the Sanhedrin's request to surrender in order to save the Temple, he was seized and let down over the city wall to Nebuchadnezzar, according to one opinion, dying while descending. Nebuchadnezzar then either took him around the cities of Judah in a public triumph, placed him inside the carcass of an ass (cf. Jer. 22:19), or threw him piecemeal to the dogs (Lev. R., loc. cit.). His disgrace, however, did not end there. The grandfather of R. Perida found a skull at the gates of Jerusalem and recognized it as that of Jehoiakim, because the earth refused to cover it when he tried to bury it, and because it carried the inscription "This and yet another." He took it home and placed it in a cupboard. His wife found it, and thinking it to be the skull of her husband's first wife, she threw it into the fire; thus was fulfilled "this" (desecration of his body at death) and "yet another" (Sanh. 82a). Jehoiakim is still undergoing punishment for his sins. Although the Babylonian Talmud does not include him among those who have no place in the world to come (cf. Sanh. 103b), the Palestinian Talmud cites him as an example of one who has forfeited his place in heaven by publicly transgressing the law.

BIBLIOGRAPHY: Bright, Hist., 303ff.; Malamat, in: BIES, 20 (1956), 179–87; Noth, in: ZDPV, 74 (1958), 133–57; O. Eissfeldt, *The Old Testament, an Introduction* (1965), 296–7, n. 60 (extensive bibl.); EM, s.v. (includes bibliography). IN THE AGGADAH: Ginzberg, Legends, 4 (1947), 284–5; 6 (1946), 379–80; I. Ḥasida, *Ishei ha-Tanakh* (1964), 168–9. **ADD. BIBLIOGRAPHY:** M. Cogan and H. Tadmor, *II Kings* (AB; 1988), 304–8; S. Japhet, *I & II Chronicles* (1993), 1064–67; J. Berridge, in: ABD, 5:664–66.

JEHOIARIB (Heb. יְהוֹיָרִיב; "YHWH champions the cause," or "YHWH replaces"), the first of the 24 priestly divisions that served at the First Temple (I Chron. 24:7). They are not mentioned among the four major priestly families, who returned from exile and were divided into 24 divisions (as described in Ta'anit 27a–28b) for the purpose of serving at the Second Temple, the families Jedaiah, Immer, Pashhur, and Harim (Ezra 2:36–39; Neh. 7:39–42). In the Book of Nehemiah (12:1–7) 22 or 23 such divisions, including Jehoiarib, are listed (see *Jedaiah). But neither the Jehoiarib nor the Jedaiah-Jeshua houses are mentioned among the families who signed the covenant (*amanah*). Japhet (429–30) suggests that Jehoiarib is an alternative of Joiarib, who is named as the father of Jedaiah the priest in Nehemiah 11:10. The Hasmoneans descended from the Jehoiarib family, which lived at first in Jerusalem and later, possibly during the persecution of Antiochus Epiphanes, moved to Modi'in (I Macc. 2:1). A later descendant of the family was the historian *Josephus.

BIBLIOGRAPHY: EM, s.v. **ADD. BIBLIOGRAPHY:** S. Japhet, *I & II Chronicles* (1993).

[Yehoshua M. Grintz / S. David Sperling (2nd ed.)]

JEHORAM (Heb. יְהוֹרָם, יוֹרָם), the son of *Jehoshaphat, king of Judah (851–843 B.C.E.). Jehoram's wife was the Omrid princess *Athaliah. During his reign a close alliance existed between the kingdoms of Judah and Israel, ruled by his brother-in-law (or his wife's nephew) Jehoram the son of Ahab if, as may be inferred from II Chronicles 21:3, Jehoshaphat reigned jointly with Jehoram (II Chron. 21:4), – this may reflect a clash among the sons of Jehoshaphat over the succession (see: *Chronology).

At the beginning of Jehoram's reign, Edom, which had been subservient to Judah, rebelled, and Jehoram sought to subdue the rebellion. However, his war against Edom (II Kings 8:20–22) was unsuccessful, and the latter remained independent until the reign of *Amaziah. Following this military reverse, Judah, according to II Chronicles 21:16–17, was ravaged by the Philistines and others. The historicity of this account is questionable, but undoubtedly the Philistines did beset

Judah, for the statement in II Kings 8:22, "… then did Libnah revolt at the same time," can only mean that it was wrested from Judah by the Philistines. II Chronicles also says that Jehoram suffered an incurable illness, which Elijah had predicted (21:12–15, 18–19), and states that Jehoram was not buried in the tombs of the kings (*ibid.*, 21:19–20), and that the people "made no burning for him" on his death. However, II Kings 8:24 explicitly states that he was buried with his ancestors in the city of David, and it would seem that Chronicles, which dwells at length on Jehoram's wickedness and failures, drew on a folk legend about Elijah that exaggerated Jehoram's sins and represented him as one of the most evil kings of Judah because of his association with the house of Ahab. Nevertheless, it may well be that the temple of Baal mentioned in II Kings 11:18 was built (at Athaliah's instance) during the reign of Jehoram. If Israel was one of the 12 western countries (headed by Adad-Idri, i.e., Ben-Hadad, king of Damascus) which allied themselves against Shalmaneser III of Assyria in the years 849–845 B.C.E., the hypothesis (of B. Mazar) that the king of Judah also participated may be accepted. In any event, there is no doubt that in Jehoram's brief reign Judah declined rapidly from its period of glory during his father's reign. Edom's independence deprived Judah of control of the important commercial routes to Arabia and thus affected its economy negatively. The relations between the two kingdoms at this time were such that the political and economic crises that plagued Israel could not but spread to Judah (see also: *Jehoram the son of Ahab).

BIBLIOGRAPHY: Maisler (Mazar), in: *Tarbiz*, 19 (1947/48), 123–4; Yeivin, in: JNES, 7 (1941), 31; J.A. Montgomery, *The Book of Kings* (ICC, 1951), 394–8; Thiele, in: VT, 4 (1954), 186; Ginsberg, in: *Fourth World Congress of Jewish Studies*, 1 (1967), 91; EM, 3 (1965), 539–41, incl. bibl. **ADD. BIBLIOGRAPHY:** W. Thiele, in: ABD, 3:949–53.

[Hayim Tadmor]

JEHORAM (Heb. יוֹרָם, יְהוֹרָם; "YHWH is exalted"), the son of *Ahab, king of Israel from 850/1–842 B.C.E. or possibly from 853–842 B.C.E. According to II Kings 3:1, Jehoram reigned in the 18th year of the reign of *Jehoshaphat, king of Judah. However, according to II Kings 1:17 (in a prophetic story), Jehoram became king during the second year of the reign of *Jehoram the son of Jehoshaphat. The contradiction between these two synchronisms is eliminated by the assumption that Jehoram son of Jehoshaphat was co-regent with his father at the end of the latter's reign, or that the beginning of Jehoram's reign is calculated according to Jehoshaphat's years as sole ruler. Those who accept the first supposition hold that Jehoram ruled for only nine or ten years, not twelve, as recorded in II Kings 3:1. The first event related about Jehoram (II Kings 3:4–24), which should date from the beginning of his reign, is his war against King *Mesha of Moab. Aided by allies, he attempted to subdue Mesha after the latter had freed himself from Israel (II Kings 1:1) and had even raided areas of Israel north of Arnon. In this war, described in the story of the prophet *Elisha (ch. 3), the allies attacked Mesha from the south, perhaps because he had in the meantime succeeded in fortifying his northern cities. The army of Jehoram and his allies reached Kir of Moab and surrounded Mesha, but they did not succeed in conquering the city. Apparently, the Moabites, excited by the sacrifice offered by their king, defeated the army of the allies (II Kings 3:27), freeing themselves permanently from Israelite rule. It is difficult to determine the exact relations between Jehoram and *Aram. It is possible that as long as *Ben-Hadad II was alive, the alliance between Israel and Aram, known from the last years of *Ahab, remained valid. According to Assyrian annals, a coalition of the twelve kings of Hatti and the seacoast fought against Shalmaneser III in 849, 848, and 845 B.C.E. However, the records that mention these wars do not give the exact names of the allies, except for Adad-Idri (Ben-Hadad II) of Damascus and Irḥuleni of Hamath. It is a fair assumption that it was the same coalition as that of those who fought against Assyria in Qarqar in 853, mentioned in a more detailed record. King Ahab was one of the major participants in that battle. If this assumption is correct, barely two years passed during Jehoram's reign without war. With the death of Ben-Hadad in 843 and the reign of *Hazael, who founded a new dynasty, the political balance was upset. The Syrian alliance of the twelve kings was broken and Jehoram exploited this opportunity to attack Aram; he attempted to capture Ramoth-Gilead, the source of dissension between Israel and Aram – for he who held this area dominated the north of Gilead and the Bashan. Jehoram himself was wounded in battle and returned to Jezreel (9:16). While he was recovering, *Jehu, his commander in chief, rebelled against him and killed him (9:23–24).

In contrast to the struggle between the prophets and Jezebel during Ahab's reign, Jehoram permitted Elisha and the other prophets to act freely. Possibly under the influence of the prophets, Jehoram removed the pillar of the Tyrian Baal, which his father Ahab had erected (3:2), thus de-emphasizing the foreign cult of his mother Jezebel and allaying the dissatisfaction of the people. The numerous unsuccessful wars of Jehoram and the severe famine in the country at that time (4:38) formed the background to Jehu's rebellion, in which he killed Jehoram and destroyed the *Omride dynasty. Several scholars believe that Jehoram of Israel is mentioned in the Aramaic inscription attributed to Hazael that was found at Tel Dan.

[Hayim Tadmor]

In the Aggadah

Jehoshaphat's question, "Is there not here a prophet of the Lord?" (II Kings 3:11) was an allusion to Jehoram's doubt on this point (Num. R. 21:6). Nevertheless God gave victory to Jehoram in his war against Moab, because of his observance of the Sabbath (Mekh. SbY. p. 162). He was killed "between his arms" and "at his heart" (II Kings 9:24) in order to teach that he had sinned by hardening his heart and stretching out his hand to take interest from Obadiah (Ex. R. 31:4).

BIBLIOGRAPHY: Maisler (Mazar), in: *Tarbiz*, 19 (1947/48), 123–4; Liver, in: *Historyah Ẓeva'it shel Ereẓ Yisrael bi-Ymei ha-Mikra* (1964), 221ff.; Luckenbill, Records, 1 (1925), 652, 655, 659; M.F. Unger, *Israel and the Arameans of Damascus* (1957), 139ff.; Bright, Hist,228–9;

A.H. Van Zyl, *The Moabites* (1960), 136ff., 180. **ADD. BIBLIOGRAPHY:** M. Cogan and H. Tadmor, *II Kings* (AB; 1988), 98–100; W. Schniedewind, in: BASOR, 302 (1996), 75–90.

JEHOSEPH (Joseph) HA-NAGID (1035–1066), vizier of Granada, son of *Samuel ha-Nagid. In his youth he already displayed superior talents. His distinguished father supervised his education, and was particularly concerned that his son have a perfect knowledge of the Arabic language and literature. While still a little boy, Jehoseph copied and edited his father's poems. His father arranged his marriage to the daughter of his friend, the famous Rabbi Nissim from Kairouan, who came to Granada with his daughter for the wedding. His father thought that a wife from a deeply religious family would have strengthened his son religiously. Jehoseph was in his 21st year when his father died and, despite his youth, was appointed by Bādīs, king of Granada, as chief vizier of the kingdom. He did not disappoint the king's hopes. Because of his great talents he succeeded in fulfilling his assignments, of which the most important were the efficient collection of the taxes and the running of an orderly administration. Even his contemporary Muslim writers, who exhibit an attitude of hatred toward him, admit to this. He was also successful in conducting the foreign policy of the Berber kingdom of Granada in its struggle with the Arab kingdom of Seville. He established connections with other Muslim countries, also hostile to the Arab king of Seville, and gave them active support. At the same time he did not neglect his occupation with Torah, but gave instruction and composed Hebrew poems. In 1044 (according to his own testimony) he began collecting and arranging his father's poems. Fragments of Jehoseph's poems were published by A.M. Habermann (see bibl.). As in the case of his father, Jehoseph's poems record and reflect events from his stormy life. Jehoseph was arrogant and not liked. While his father's wisdom and the respect shown him sufficed to silence the dissatisfaction of the Arabic-speaking Andalusian population with the Berbers and their Jewish viziers, Jehoseph was openly censured. He surrounded himself with wealthy Jews, agents, and officers of the king, to their great benefit. He tried unsuccessfully to avert the consequences, but had the misfortune to become entangled in a harem intrigue. In 1064 the crown prince Bolougin died after having participated in a feast in the home of Jehoseph, who was then accused of poisoning him. Meanwhile, the struggle between the kings of Granada and Seville became more acute; the Berber Bādīs, fearing plots by his Arab subjects, planned to slaughter them, but Jehoseph warned the Arabs. This step harmed his relations with the king himself. Abu Isḥāq al-Ilbībī a disgruntled and fanatic Muslim theologian, composed a provocative poem against Jehoseph, in which he protested about his great wealth and the enrichment of the other Jews. There were also Muslims who accused Jehoseph of killing Bādīs secretly, since the latter avoided making any public appearance. As a consequence of this provocation he was murdered, and a bloody slaughter befell the Jews of Granada.

BIBLIOGRAPHY: Ashtor, Korot, 2 (1966), 98–117; A.M. Habermann, *ibid.*, 4 (1961), 44–58; Allony, in: *Oẓar Yehudei Sefarad*, 3 (1960), 16–22; H. Schirmann, Sefarad, 7 (1959²), 292f.; idem, *Shirim Ḥadashim min ha-Genizah* (1965), 185f., 190; idem, in: *Moznayim*, 8 (1939), 48–58; Akavya, in: *Tagim*, 1 (1969), 75; S. Katz, in: *Sinai*, 96 (1984–5), 114–34.

[Eliyahu Ashtor]

JEHOSHAPHAT (Heb. יְהוֹשָׁפָט), king of Judah, son of *Asa and Azubah, daughter of Shilhi (I Kings 22:42; II Chron. 20:31). Jehoshaphat ruled Judah for 25 years, during the second third of the ninth century B.C.E. He was a contemporary of Ahab, Ahaziah, and Jehoram, kings of Israel. A vigorous personality emerges from the biblical accounts (I Kings 22; II Kings 3; II Chron. 17:1–21:3), a vigor manifested both in foreign policy and in the internal administration of the state.

Foreign Policy

Jehoshaphat's political system was characterized by his close alliance with the kingdom of Israel, a departure from the policy of his predecessors who were not reconciled to the division of the kingdom which had been united under David and Solomon. The turning point in Jehoshaphat's relations with Israel is I Kings 22:45: "Jehoshaphat also made peace with the king of Israel." This alliance between Judah and Israel was expressed in the former's participation on the side of *Ahab in the battle against Aram which took place at Ramoth-Gilead (I Kings 22; II Chron. 18). Jehoshaphat also took part in the military operation of *Jehoram, king of Israel, against Moab (II Kings 3:4–27). The alliance was reinforced by the marriage of Athaliah, in view of her formal title "Athaliah daughter of King *Omri of Israel" (II Kings 8:26), a sister or a daughter of Ahab, to Jehoshaphat's son Jehoram (this marriage took place in Jehoshaphat's lifetime). Another aspect of the alliance was the joint venture of Jehoshaphat and Ahaziah king of Israel "in building ships to go to Tarshish, and they built the ships in Ezion-Geber" (II Chron. 20:36; cf. I Kings 22:49–50). Jehoshaphat's reconciliation with the kings of Israel stemmed from his recognition that the balance of power had shifted in Israel's favor. The kingdom of Israel, under the rule of the house of Omri, achieved great stability and became an important political, military, and economic power in the area. Jehoshaphat understood that peace with the kingdom of Israel could bring political and economic benefit to his kingdom, whereas war with Israel would be disastrous for Judah. In addition, military and political cooperation between Judah and Israel was vital in view of the strengthened position of the eastern Transjordanian states, which threatened the borders of both Israel and Judah. Moab rebelled against Israel (II Kings 1:1; 3:4–5), and Edom was waiting for an opportune time to rebel against Judah. The account in II Chronicles 20:10, 22 of an invasion of Judah by "the men of Ammon and Moab and Mount Seir" is historically improbable. Israel and Judah joined forces against Aram (I Kings 22; II Chron. 18) and against Moab (II Kings 3:4–27). Later, in an effort to repel an Assyrian invasion, Israel and Aram joined forces in the battle of Qarqar, but whether Jehoshaphat took part with his ally in this campaign is impossible to establish from the inscription of Shalmaneser III, king of Assyria, which recounts the battle.

The alliance between Israel and Judah also had economic aspects. Clearly, while Judah dominated Edom (I Kings 22:48; II Kings 3:9–27), Jehoshaphat could exploit the copper mines in the Arabah and renew maritime trade in the Red Sea utilizing the port of Ezion-Geber. In establishing a commercial fleet he needed the aid of the Phoenicians, who were expert shipbuilders and sailors. Since Tyre was allied with Israel (see *Ahab), Judah became a third partner with Tyre and Israel. The Bible indicates that the joint enterprise to establish a fleet and maritime trade was unsuccessful and that Jehoshaphat disliked Ahaziah's interference. Perhaps Ahaziah was unable to force his will on Jehoshaphat. In any event, the triple alliance of Judah-Israel-Tyre brought about great commercial and economic vitality because the three states were contiguous and extended from the Mediterranean Sea in the southwest to the desert and the Red Sea in the southeast. Jehoshaphat's domination over Edom and Ezion-Geber gave Judah the land trade routes which connected Edom and the Red Sea with the Philistine port towns. These routes were traveled by caravans which carried valuable commodities (perfumes and spices) from Arabia to the countries of eastern Asia. The tribute which the Philistines and the Arab tribes brought to Jehoshaphat (II Chron. 17:11) can be understood only against this background of power and prosperity.

Internal Affairs

The Book of Chronicles provides an idealized description of the organization of the kingdom of Judah in the days of Jehoshaphat. He reorganized the army; II Chronicles 17:13–18 lists five senior unit commanders and the size of their units. The large numbers given indicate that the figures reflect both the standing army and the reserves which could be conscripted during crisis. The regular army, equipped with chariots, was garrisoned in the fortified cities and fortresses scattered throughout Judah, including the Judean Desert and the Negev (II Chron. 17:2, 12, 19).

Some scholars believe that Jehoshaphat's administrative reorganization of the kingdom of Judah in "Ephraim" – meaning Benjamin as part of the "hill country of Ephraim" (see II Sam. 20:1, 21) – conquered by Asa (II Chron. 17:2), is reflected in the list of towns allotted to Judah in Joshua 15. A unique measure taken by Jehoshaphat in the third year of his rule is described in II Chronicles 17:7–9. The king is said to have sent a delegation of ministers, levites, and priests to visit the towns of Judah and to teach the people the "book of the law of the Lord." Those who credit the chronicler's account in detail assume "the book of the law of the Lord" in question was the Book of *Deuteronomy, not in its final form, which was established only at the time of Josiah, but in a very early stage of its formulation. This assumption is based mainly on the great similarity between Deuteronomy 16:18–20; 17:8–13, which describes the appointment of judges in rural towns and the establishment of a high court in "the place which the Lord your God will choose" (Deut. 17:8), and the description in II Chronicles 19:5–11, which tells of the appointment of judges in all the fortified cities of Judah and the establishment of a high court in Jerusalem. Amariah, the chief priest, who was in charge of "all matters of the Lord," i.e., religious law, and Zebadiah son of Ishmael, who was in charge of "all the king's matters," i.e., secular-royal law (II Chron. 19:11), were members of the high court. Establishing teaching delegations in the towns and judges in all the fortified cities and Jerusalem indicates a tendency toward the consolidation of all authoritative institutions in Judah. Jehoshaphat's religious-legal reform is regarded as an attempt to institute a single legal system in order to centralize the ruling power. The entire account may be a midrash based on the name Jehoshaphat, "YHWH Judges."

Jehoshaphat's alliance with Phoenicia and Israel did not adversely affect Judah's religious-ritualistic practices. Although Jehoshaphat did not abolish the popular practice of sacrifice (to the Lord) at local cult places, he did abolish all rituals of which the Deuteronomist disapproved (see I Kings 22:44–47). He apparently perpetuated all that his father Asa had accomplished, and the Phoenician cult established by Ahab in Samaria under the influence of Jezebel only attained some importance in Jerusalem during the reign of Athaliah, after the death of Jehoshaphat (II Kings 11:18).

BIBLIOGRAPHY: Aharoni, Ereẓ, 279ff.; idem, in: *Tarbiz*, 20 (1950), 94ff.; S. Yeivin, *Meḥkarim be-Toledot Yisrael ve-Arẓo* (1960), 213ff., 240ff.; Z. Kalai, *Gevuloteha ha-Ẓefoniyyim shel Yehudah* (1960), 23ff., 64; Noth, Hist Isr, 236ff.; Albright, in: *A. Marx Jubilee Volume* (1950), 61–82; Bright, Hist., 222–3, 228–9, 232–4; Cross and Wright, in: JBL, 75 (1956), 202–26; S. Yeivin, in: JQR, 50 (1960), 207ff.; idem, in: BIES, 25 (1961), 193–200; S. Talmon, in: *Scripta Hierosolymitana*, 8 (1961), 335–83; H.L. Ginsberg, in: *Fourth World Congress of Jewish Studies*, 1 (1967), English section 91–93. **ADD. BIBLIOGRAPHY:** M. Cogan, *I Kings* (AB; 2000), 499–501.

[Jacob Liver / Bustenay Oded]

JEHOSHAPHAT, VALLEY OF (Heb. עֵמֶק יְהוֹשָׁפָט), place mentioned in Joel 4:2, 12 where in the fullness of time God will gather all the nations to judge them. According to II Chronicles 20:26, the army of King Jehoshaphat assembled, after the defeat of his enemies, in the valley of Beracah ("Blessing") somewhere near Tekoa. Popular legend identified the Valley of Jehoshaphat with the middle section of the Kidron Valley, Jerusalem, and called the tomb-cave behind "Absalom's Tomb" the "Tomb of Jehoshaphat"; as such it is already referred to by the Bordeaux pilgrim (333 C.E.). On the Day of Judgment, according to Arab tradition, a sword will be suspended between the Temple Mount and the Mount of Olives; the righteous will pass safely along the blade but the wicked will fall into the fire of Gehenna below. In Jewish tradition the place where "God will judge" (*Yeho-Shafat*) the nations has no geographical definition (Mid. Ps. to 8:10).

[Michael Avi-Yonah]

JÉHOUDA, JOSUÉ (1892–1966), Swiss author and journalist. Born in Russia, Jéhouda settled in Switzerland, where he founded the *Revue juive de Genève*. He saw Israel's rebirth as an event of universal significance and viewed with alarm divisions between Orthodox and secular Jews, and between Israel and the Diaspora. His works include three novels, *Le royaume de Justice* (1933), *De père en fils* (1927), and *Miriam* (1928); and volumes of essays such as *La vocation d'Israël* (1947) and *Sionisme et messianisme* (1954).

JEHU (Heb. יֵהוּא), son of Hanani; a prophet during the time of Baasha, king of Israel (c. 906–883 B.C.E.), and Jehoshaphat, king of Judah (c. 867–846 B.C.E.; I Kings 16:1, 7, 12; II Chron. 19:2; 20:34). Jehu's father may have been the seer Hanani who is reported to have rebuked King Asa of Judah and been incarcerated by him (II Chron. 16:7–10; but perhaps it should read "[Jehu son of] Hanani"). Jehu foretold the destruction of the house of Baasha (I Kings 16:1ff.) and censured Jehoshaphat for joining King Ahab of Israel in the attack on Ramoth Gilead (II Chron. 19:2–3). In accordance with his theory that the Books of Samuel and Kings were written successively by the prophets who witnessed the events (cf. e.g., I Chron. 29:29; II Chron. 9:29), the Chronicler attributes to Jehu son of Hanani the portion of the Book of Kings which deals with the age of King Jehoshaphat of Judah (II Chron. 20:34).

BIBLIOGRAPHY: Noth, *Personennamen*, 143; O. Eissfeldt, *The Old Testament, an Introduction* (1965), 533. **ADD. BIBLIOGRAPHY:** M. Cogan, I *Kings* (AB; 2000), 401ff.

JEHU (Heb. יֵהוּא), son of Jehoshaphat son of Nimshi (II Kings 9–10); reigned over the Israelite kingdom at Samaria for 28 years (c. 842–814 B.C.E.). During *Ahab's reign Jehu already held a position which brought him into close contact with court circles (II Kings 9:25). During the reign of *Jehoram son of Ahab, Jehu served as commander of the garrison posted at Ramoth-Gilead, in North Transjordan. From Ramoth-Gilead he set out for Samaria and seized the throne. He established a line of kings, who ruled over Israel for nearly 100 years (II Kings 10:30; 15:12).

Internal Affairs

Most of the biblical sources on Jehu's reign concern his struggle for the throne. Jehu's way to the throne was paved with bloodshed, in the course of which the entire house of *Omri was exterminated. He killed Jehoram, king of Israel, at Jezreel, and he also put to death King *Ahaziah of Judah and his brothers (see also II Chron. 22:8–9). Then he proceeded to massacre the entire house of Ahab, including Jezebel and all members of the elite court circle that had been close to the king (II Kings 10:11). Perhaps he regarded both Judahite princes and Israelite courtiers as potential claimants to the throne as heirs to the House of Omri. The slaughter was, however, remembered with horror a long time after Jehu's death, according to the received text and traditional dating of Hosea 1:4 (but see *Hosea). Jehu was anointed king at Ramoth-Gilead by an emissary of the prophet Elisha (II Kings 9:1–10), who stood at the head of the prophetic movement that opposed the House of Omri (see *Ahab), and strove both to avenge the blood of those prophets and God-fearing men who had been persecuted and killed by Jezebel (9:7–10), and to stop the Baal worship in Israel. Accordingly, Jehu, upon ascending the throne, acted with great zeal to destroy the Tyrian cult. He executed all the Baal prophets in the temple of Baal, destroyed the temple itself with all its pillars, and according to II Kings 10:28, "Thus Jehu exterminated Baal [worship] from Israel." Jehu also had the support of the army, which was in need of a leader who might be more successful than Jehoram in the prolonged struggle for Ramoth-Gilead and the overthrow of Aramean supremacy. Along with the army and the prophetic movement, the poorer classes of the people also supported Jehu's coup; they had suffered great hardship as a result of the economic policy of the kings of the house of Omri, which had produced a large economic rift in the structure of the Israelite society. Among the poor there were those who warned against wanton luxury and stood for modest living. One such individual was Jehonadab, the son of Rechab (II Kings 10:15; see *Rechabites), who joined Jehu and helped exterminate Ahab's descendants (10:17) and eliminate the cult of the Tyrian Baal (10:22–27). Though he put an end to the cult of the Tyrian Baal that had been introduced by Ahab, Jehu did not abolish the golden calves which had been set up long before Ahab by Jeroboam son of Nebat at Dan and Beth-El, and for which there is no reason to suppose that it had been disapproved of by Elijah or Elisha. Indeed, the calves, whatever their significance, were not a foreign import. Besides, like Jeroboam son of Nebat, Jehu may have thought it politic to maintain the places of worship in Dan and Beth-El, since they served to deter the people from going up to Jerusalem (cf. I Kings 12:26), and frustrated the ambition of the kings of Judah, descendants of David's line in Jerusalem, to unite the two kingdoms once again under the throne of David.

Foreign Affairs

Jehu's coup greatly influenced the relations between the Israelite kingdom and her neighbors. The annihilation of the house of Omri, the killing of Jezebel, the murder of Ahaziah king of Judah, and the ban on the Tyrian influences all helped to loosen the ties binding the triple alliance between Tyre, Israel, and Judah and cast a shadow over Israel's relations with the other two, Judah and Tyre. Israel's resulting political isolation encouraged Aram of Damascus to increase the pressure on her northeastern border. On ascending the throne, Jehu immediately found himself surrounded by hostile states and sought to ensure his own position by expressing his loyalty to the king of Assyria. This is the background to what is related in the annals of Shalmaneser III concerning the tribute paid him by "Jehu son of Omri" (*la-u-a mār Ḫum-ri-i*) in 841 B.C.E. (COGAN AND TADMOR, 334–35). In that same year Shalmaneser III set out on a campaign against *Hazael king of Aram-Damascus, placed Damascus under siege, and thence proceeded southward with his armies to Hauran, sowing destruction among Hazael's cities. It becomes apparent from the inscription that the regions of Hauran and Bashan, as far as the Yarmuk, were under the rule of Damascus. Later in the campaign, at a place called Baal-Rosh (Mt. Carmel or some other mountain on the Phoenician coast), he collected tribute from Jehu and from the king of Tyre. In another inscription known as the Black Obelisk, a relief has been found on which "Jehu son of Omri," or his messenger, kneels before the king of Assyria while his retinue pays tribute to him. Assyria's campaigns against Hazael between 841–838 B.C.E. were invaluable to Jehu inasmuch as they prevented the Arameans from exploiting the internal confusion which beset Samaria immediately after his coup. But shortly afterward the Arameans recovered, and Hazael succeeded in penetrating deep into Israelite territory and in conquering all of Israelite Transjordan as far as the Arnon (II Kings 10:32–33). In a second campaign, which seems to have taken place in 815 (or 814) B.C.E., Hazael penetrated deep into Israelite territory west of the Jordan, even reaching as far as Gath in the northern Shephelah where he collected tribute from *Joash king of Judah (II Kings 12:18). The period of Jehu and his son Jehoahaz is considered to have been the time of the strongest military pressure from the Arameans upon Israel.

BIBLIOGRAPHY: Bright, Hist, 231ff.; J. Gray, *A History of Israel* (1960), 229–34; Morgenstern, in: HUCA, 15 (1940), 225–59; M.F. Unger, *Israel and the Arameans of Damascus* (1957), 76–78; Miller, in: VT, 17 (1967), 307–24; Ginsberg, in: *Fourth World Congress of Jewish Studies*, 1 (1967), 91–93; Pritchard, Texts, 280–1. **ADD. BIBLIOGRAPHY:** M. Cogan and H. Tadmor, *II Kings* (AB; 1988), 101–22; W. Thiel, in: ABD, 3:670–73

[Bustanay Oded]

JEITELES (Jeitteles, Geidels), prominent family first appearing in Prague. The first known Jeiteles was MOSES BEN SIMON, on record as a house owner in 1615. His son LOEB (d. 1666) was *gabbai* of the *ḥevra kaddisha* for 30 years and also of the Altschul Synagogue. BERL (Issachar Baer; d. 1685), leader of the Prague community from 1666 until his death, was imprisoned in 1664, when the community elders refused to hand over to the authorities those Jews who had attacked the witnesses against the Prague chief rabbi Simon Spira-Wedeles. He was jailed again in 1667, on a charge of instigating the shooting of the renegade informer Wenzel Wimbersky but was released in the same year. AARON BEN BAER JEITELES (d. 1777) was known as a talmudic scholar and kabbalist. His allegorical commentary on the Pentateuch, *Zera Aharon*, was published in 1797. MOSES WOLF (d. 1848), secretary of the *ḥevra kaddisha* for many years, was apparently Aaron's son. He published a compendium for the *ḥevra kaddisha* (1828) based on the *Ma'avar Yabbok* of *Aaron Berechiah b. Moses, which included a history of Prague Jewry and in which he made use of Marcus Fischer's (see Moses Fischer) allegedly medieval *Ramshak Chronicle*. He was the first to recognize the importance of gravestone inscriptions for historical research, and his notes served his son-in-law Koppelmann *Lieben in his *Gal Ed*. SIMON JEITELES was Jewish "*Vorzensor*" for the Jesuit censor, Haselbauer, in the second half of the 18th century, and ISRAEL JEITELES owned a Hebrew printing press in the 1770s.

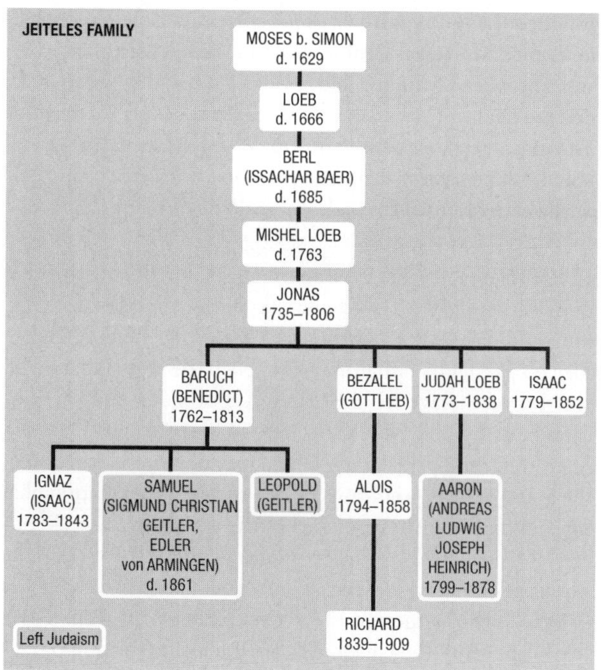

The main branch of the family were descendants of the apothecary MISHEL LOEB (d. 1763), who played a central role in spreading the Enlightenment in Prague and investing it with a characteristically Jewish national consciousness. Mishel's son JONAS (1735–1806) originally prepared for a rabbinical career in Abraham Moses Zerah *Eidlitz' yeshivah. However, he went on to study medicine at the universities of Leipzig and Halle, graduating in 1755. Settling in Prague, he later became chief physician of the Jewish community hospital (1763) and supervisor of the Jewish surgeons' board (1777), declining the offer of the post of physician to the Polish king, Stanislas II Augustus. He published articles on medical subjects and parts of his book, *Observata Quaedam Medica* (1783), were translated in early 19th-century medical textbooks. His main medical achievement, however, which was largely instrumental in earning him the name of the father of the Prague Enlightenment, was his propagation of Edward Jenner's smallpox vaccination in the face of Christian and Jewish prejudice: he inoculated his own daughter and more than 1,500 persons. In 1784 after an audience with *Joseph II, he was permitted to treat patients "without consideration of their religion." A master of ancient and modern languages, Jonas was a friend of Ezekiel *Landau. Jonas' eldest son, BARUCH (Benedict; 1762–1813), a scholar and Hebrew writer, strove for a synthesis of modern and traditional scholarship. In his youth he ran away from home to Berlin, but later returned and was reconciled with his teacher, Ezekiel Landau. He contributed poems to *Ha-Me'assef* (the journal of the *Me'assefim*) dealing with the lonely and difficult position of the enlightened intellectual in traditional society. When he eulogized Landau in his *Emek*

ha-Bakha (1793) in a wholly Orthodox and traditional manner, the radical editor of *Ha-Me'assef* attacked him. A booklet, *Sefer ha-Orev*, published allegedly in Salonika in 1795 under the pen name Phinehas Hananiah Argosi de Silva, which attacks the disrespectful attitude of the Berlin radicals to rabbinical scholars, is generally considered to be Baruch's refutation of their attacks. So, too, the pamphlet, "A Discussion between the Years 5560 and 5561" (1800 and 1801) a polemic against the Frankists in Prague, is generally attributed to him. He published four editions of Moses Mendelssohn's commentary on Maimonides' *Millot ha-Higgayon*, three of them in German translation in Hebrew type, and *Ta'am ha-Melekh* (1801), glosses to Isaac Nuñez Belmonte's novellae on Maimonides' *Sha'ar ha-Melekh*. A sermon supporting his father's vaccination campaign was published in 1805. A man of independent means, Baruch founded a yeshivah in his house and encouraged rising Hebrew authors. In 1813 he induced leaders of the Prague community to open a hospital for wounded soldiers "of all nationalities" in the Jewish quarter. He himself died of hospital fever while caring for them.

His son IGNAZ (Isaac; 1783–1843) studied law at Prague University before moving to Vienna (1810) and establishing himself there as a merchant. A prolific writer, he contributed to general and Jewish periodicals, his articles on Jewish history in **Sulamith* being of particular interest. Along with his father, he supported his grandfather's efforts toward vaccination in a pamphlet (*Die Kuhpockenimpfung*, 1804) and published *Biographie des Dr. Jonas Jeiteles* (1806). His main literary achievement was *Aesthetisches Lexikon* (2 vols., 1835–38). Ignaz was eventually estranged from Judaism. One of Baruch's other sons, SAMUEL (d. 1861), who was baptized in 1828 as Sigmund Christian Geitler, Edler von Armingen, became an outstanding industrialist and philanthropist. Baruch's youngest son, LEOPOLD, was also baptized and adopted the name Geitler (1833). JUDAH LOEB (1773–1838), another of Jonas' sons, a Hebrew writer, contributed to the *Ha-Me'assef* and to the annuals *Bikkurei ha-Ittim* and *Kerem Ḥemed*, publishing poems and biblical and halakhic articles. He was also the author of an Aramaic grammar *Mevo ha-Lashon ha-Aramit* (1813) and a collection of poems *Benei ha-Ne'urim* (1821). One of the four chairmen of the Prague community, Judah supervised its German-language school. Unlike both the radical *maskilim* and the Orthodox, he favored a school in which secular and Jewish religious education would be united. It was mainly Judah who developed the peculiar blend of Hapsburg patriotism and awareness of the Jews as one of the nations in the empire which was characteristic of the Prague Haskalah. It found its outstanding expression in his opposition to Mordecai Manuel *Noah's program for his city of refuge, Ararat (*Bikkurei ha-Ittim*, 7 (1826/27), 45–49), claiming that nobody would answer Noah's call because "they are all now living under the rule of benign and merciful kings who deal mercifully and benevolently with us, as with all the other nations who live together with us in harmony and friendship." In 1835 he published a Hebrew and Aramaic translation of the Austrian anthem (*shir tehillah me-ammei ha-araẓot*). Judah was the first to use the expression *"Haskalah" for the Enlightenment movement. For Anton von *Schmidt's fourth edition of the Bible he translated and edited several volumes. In 1830 he settled in Vienna and edited the last two volumes of *Bikkurei ha-Ittim* (nos. 11 and 12) in 1831, making it of greater interest to Jewish scholarship.

Judah's son AARON (1799–1878) was baptized in 1828 and as Andreas Ludwig Joseph Heinrich Jeiteles became professor of anatomy at Vienna University and from 1836 at Olmuetz (Olomouc). He was active in politics and in 1848 was a member of the German National Assembly in Frankfurt on the moderate left. A prolific writer on medical subjects, he published in 1832 a call to physicians to pay more attention to psychology. Under the pen name of Justus Frey he also wrote poetry, some of which was set to music by Ludwig van Beethoven. His collected poems, *Gesammelte Dichtungen*, were published in 1899. In one of his later poems he warned Jewish youth not to become renegades. Two of his sons attained some importance, one as a German philologist and the other as a geographer.

Another of Jonas' sons, ISAAC (1779–1852), also became a physician, taking over Jonas' practice and becoming head physician of the Prague Jewish hospital. He published several medical papers: of importance are those dealing with the Bohemian mineral springs. Another of Jonas' four sons, BEZALEL (Gottlieb), moved to Bruenn (Brno) where he owned a Hebrew printing press. His son, ALOIS (1794–1858), studied medicine and philosophy in Prague and Vienna, and settled as a physician in 1821 in his native Bruenn. In Vienna he was a member of the circle of Beethoven and Franz Grillparzer. In 1819 he published jointly with Ignaz (see above) a short-lived Jewish periodical, *Siona*. His cycle of poems, *An die ferne Geliebte*, was set to music by Beethoven (1816). He translated Italian and Spanish dramas into German and his parody, "*Der Schicksalsstrumpf*" (1819), achieved success. His son RICHARD (1839–1909) was a railway expert. ISAAC JEITELES (1814–1857), a popular novelist in his day, published around 100 novels under the name of Julius Seydlitz. He was baptized a few days before his death.

The Jeiteles family continued to reside in Prague through the years. Its outstanding member was BERTHOLD (Issachar Baer; 1875–1958) who had originally studied chemistry. Strictly Orthodox, he preferred to open a glove factory so that he could observe the Sabbath. The publication of his works on talmudic subjects was prevented by the Nazi rise to power (1933). After the German occupation of Prague (1939) he was deported to *Theresienstadt, where he was able to continue his studies. He was put on a transport to *Auschwitz but was returned to Theresienstadt because there had been ten too many on the transport; officially, however, he was considered dead. In 1945 he returned to Prague and found all his hidden manuscripts intact. In 1948 he moved to New York. After his death, an Institute for Publishing the Talmudic Encyclopaedia of Dr. Berthold Jeiteles was established in Manchester (England) and the first book of *Konkordanẓyah Talmudit* (1951/52) on Rav was published. Still unpublished are 45 volumes on all personalities of both Talmuds, Tosefta, and Midrash and their opinions, as well as 18 volumes of *Ẓiyyunim*, an alphabetically arranged glossary of talmudic terms and names.

BIBLIOGRAPHY: R. Kestenberg-Gladstein, *Neuere Geschichte der Juden in den boehmischen Laendern* (1969), index, bibliography; S. Hock, *Mishpeḥot Prag* (1892), 165–9; T. Jakobovits, in: JGGJČ, 7 (1935), 421; S. Kaznelson, *Die unsterbliche Geliebte* (1954), index; Zinberg, Sifrut, 6 (1960), index; G. Kirsch, in: HJ, 8 (1946), 149–80, passim; B. Jeiteles, *Konkordanẓyah Talmudit* (1951/52), prefaces.

[Henry Wasserman and Meir Lamed]

JEKABPILS (Ger. **Jakobstadt**), town in Zemgale (Courland) district, Latvia. The Jews who were present in the town despite a ban against them were expelled in 1739, and allowed to resettle there after the Russian takeover in 1795. A community was organized in 1810, and in the 1830s a yeshivah was founded by R. Joseph Ashkenazi, a disciple of Ḥayyim of *Volozhin. There were 2,567 Jews living in the town in 1835. Jews traded in grain, wood, and flax, owned two match factories, and also were artisans. Seven families (60 persons) from Jekabpils settled in agricultural colonies in Kherson province, southern Russia, in 1840. Simeon Zarḥi, rabbi of Jekabpils from 1832 to 1856, and author of *Naḥalat Shimon* (1897), settled in Ereẓ Israel. The community declined at the end of the 19th century after many of its members had emigrated to America. It numbered 2,087 (36% of the population) in 1897. Jews were expelled by the Russian army to the interior of the country in July 1915, and Jekabpils suffered severely during World War I; many Jewish houses were destroyed. Only some of the Jews returned after the war, and by 1925 they numbered 806 (14% of the total) persons. In 1935 there were 793 Jews. Between the wars they dominated town trade, owning 106 establishments out of 178 (1935). There existed a Jewish school, and Zionist youth movements were very active. Soviet rule 1940–1941 brought the liquidation of private trade and Jewish public life. On June 29, 1941, the Germans entered Jekabpils and began the persecution and forced labor of the Jews. The Jews were concentrated in synagogues, and in September 1941 they were marched outside town into a forest and murdered beside prepared ditches. About ten families returned by the end of the 1950s; they moved the Holocaust victims to the Jewish cemetery and put up a monument with a *Magen David* and a Yiddish and Russian inscription. A few years later the authorities erased the Jewish symbol and inscription. Most of the survivors left for the West and Israel. The number of Jews living in Jekabpils in 1970 was estimated at about 30.

BIBLIOGRAPHY: L. Orchinski, *Di Geshikhte fun di Yidn in Letland* (1928), 61; B. Rivkin, in: *Lite* (1951), 407–16.

[Yehuda Slutsky / Shmuel Spector (2nd ed.)]

JEKELES, widespread family of businessmen known from the end of the 16th century in *Cracow-Kazimierz. Its name is derived from the sobriquet of its founder JACOB (= Jekele) BOGATY ("the rich"), son of Moses Eberłs. Jekele, a merchant and banker during the second half of the 16th and early 17th centuries, is first mentioned in 1573 in connection with a loan of 5,000 zlotys to King Sigismund II Augustus. He took part in drawing up the *takkanot* of Cracow (1595). Sebastian *Miczynski assessed his property at between 50,000 and 80,000 zlotys. His son, ISAAC BEN JACOB (Jakubovich; Reb Eisik Reb Jekeles; d. 1653), was one of the most prominent Jewish bankers and merchants of Poland in his day. He was related by marriage to the *Nachmanovich family, and owned houses and building sites in Kazimierz and shops in Cracow. He successfully represented the Jewish community of Cracow in a lawsuit in 1608 against the municipality. From then until 1647 (with the exception of 1638), he appears to have been the leading *parnas* of the community. Between 1638 and 1644, despite opposition from the Church, he erected a magnificent synagogue in Renaissance style on one of his building plots at his own expense which still exists, known as "Reb Eisik Reb Jekeles Shul."

The second son, MOSES BEN JACOB (Jakubovich; Jekeles; d. c. 1650), was a wealthy merchant active in the community leadership. He was one of the signatories of the agreement between the community and the municipal council on Jewish commerce in Cracow in 1608–09. He built an old-age home at his own expense.

MOSES BEN ISAAC JEKELES (D. 1691), a banker and pawnbroker, succeeded his father as *parnas* of the community in 1647 for several decades. At the time of the Chmielnicki massacres (1648–49), and during and after the Swedish invasion, he represented the Jews of Cracow in negotiations with Stefan *Czarniecki, the king of Sweden Charles Gustav, the military commanders Wirtz, Wittenberg, and Georg Rákóczy, and King John II Casimir, from whom he attempted to obtain abrogation of decrees adverse to the community.

BIBLIOGRAPHY: M. Bałaban, in: JJLG, 10 (1913), 296–360; 11 (1916), 88–114; idem, *Historja Żydów w Krakowie i na Kazimierzu 1304–1868*, 2 vols. (1931–36), index; F. Wettstein, *Devarim Attikim: mi-Pinkesei ha-Kahal bi-Cracow* (1901), 14, 24; A. Landau and B. Wachstein (eds.), *Juedische Privatbriefe aus dem Jahre 1619* (1911), no. 3a; Ḥ.D. Friedberg, *Luḥot Zikkaron* (1897), 69; B.D. Weinryb, *Texts and Studies in the Communal History of Polish Jewry* (1950), index p. 109, s.v. *Isak b. Moshe R. Jekeles.*

[Arthur Cygielman]

JEKUTHIEL BEN JUDAH HA-KOHEN (first half of the 13th century), Hebrew grammarian. He was known as **YAHBI** (Heb. יה״בי; the acronym of his Hebrew name, Yekuthiel **Ha**-Kohen **Ben** Judah), by which he referred to himself. Elijah *Levita refers to him as the "Punctuator of Prague," giving rise to the supposition that he lived in Prague; from his warnings against certain exactly described pronunciations of consonants in the reading of the Torah which he expressly addressed to his pupils, it would seem, however, that he lived in the Rhineland and not in "Canaan" (Prague). These instructions are an important source of information on the pronunciation of Hebrew in his time, in Germany, Bohemia, and France. His citations of the opinions of different grammarians, the last of which is Abraham *Ibn Ezra, led to the hypothesis that he lived in about the first half of the 13th century. Little else is known about his life.

Ein ha-Kore, of which a critical edition of the first part, *The Grammar*, has been published by Rivka Yarkoni (1985), is probably his only work. According to Yarkoni, it is divided into two parts: (a) a grammatical study which also includes the above-mentioned instructions; and (b) notes on the vocalization and cantillation of the Pentateuch, the *haftarot*, and the Books of Lamentations and Esther.

The first part of *Ein ha-Kore* cannot be compared to the earlier works of grammarians of the Spanish school which attempted to present the reader with a methodical study of grammatical forms; its purpose was a practical one – to give instructions to those reading the Torah. He starts with the question: "When is a word *mille'eil* [penultimate accent; the stress being on the syllable before the last], and when *millera* [ultima accent; the stress being on the last syllable]?" This leads him to further questions on rhythm: the rule governing the *meteg*, called *gaya* in earlier literature (secondary accent; see *Masorah); and the rule of the *makkaf* (hyphen). Through his analysis of the *meteg* system, Jekuthiel became the first Hebrew grammarian in Europe to formulate the concepts of the open and closed syllables in Hebrew. He also discovered the law of the "heavy" *meteg*. His *meteg* system was published in *Mishpetei ha-Te'amim* (1801), by Wolf *Heidenheim. S. *Baer's German rendition (1869) is an attempt at a more scientific treatment of Jekuthiel's system (see bibliography). As a result of Baer's misunderstanding his *meteg* system was attributed to Aaron *Ben-Asher in works on Hebrew grammar published in other languages. W. Heidenheim also published the notes of *Ein ha-Kore* in the *Me'or Einayim* edition of the Pentateuch (1818–21) and in his edition of the Book of Esther, *Seder Yemei ha-Purim* (1822). Gumpertz published "*Sha'ar ha-Metigot*" (which is the chapter on the *meteg*), with an introduction and notes in *Leshonenu* (see bibl.).

The Orientalist P. *Kahle rejected Baer's editions of the books of the Bible which had been vocalized according to the "so-called Ben Asher system," in reality the system of Jekuthiel.

A new light was shed on Yahbi's *meteg*-rules by Aharon Dotan in his research and annotations to the newly-published authentic texts. At the end of his chapter on the *meteg*-rules, Yahbi writes expressly that, in his hundreds of examples, he decided on the use of the *meteg* neither in accordance with Ben Asher, nor with Ben Naphtali, but only on the basis of model Bible codices of Sephardi origin (of which six were in his possession), as far as their writing was in conformity with his "inspired" rules. On the basis of this statement by Jekuthiel himself all attempts to identify his punctuation with other systems are, of course, void. These rules are contained in Yahbi's statement that the majority of *metagim* were placed in words accentuated by disjunctive accents (called *melekh*), whereas no *meteg* was used in words accentuated by a conjunctive accent (*mesharet*).

The earliest Hebrew grammarians of the Tiberian school gave instructions on the use of the diacritical marks over complete words and word-blocks, and also of the *gaya* (over one syllable), adding that the *gaya* does not belong to the family of the genuine *te'amim* (cantillation accents). Only Dotan's study made it possible to fully understand the uniqueness of Jekuthiel's system. The fact that in the oldest fragments of Bibles with complete Tiberian punctuation the scarcity of (written) *gayot* is striking corresponds to the cautiousness of the Masoretic grammarians. On the other hand, the synagogal practice of the cantillating recitation – i.e., according to the *te'amim* – provokes the *gaya*, which is but the counterstress to the accented syllable of a word or word-block. Theoretically, Jekuthiel attributed this provocative power only to disjunctive accents (*melekh*), not to the conjunctive (*mesharet*). The fact that he introduced the *gaya* also into a minority of words with conjunctive accents was due, in Dotan's opinion, to his respect for the authoritative scribes from earlier generations.

A Palestinian punctuator of Ben Asher's time could not elaborate a comprehensive system because of the traditions in reading Hebrew, which was then a spoken language – and a spoken language cannot implement speech and reading according to abstract rules. Jekuthiel did not have any past connection with spoken Hebrew and, therefore, had the right to accentuate words according to the rhythmic laws which he had discovered, even when he did not find any model patterns to this accentuation. He therefore decided for himself "to follow the general rule and the opinion which was in conflict," that is to say, not only to punctuate according to the authority of Ben Asher, but also according to the opinion of an opponent such as Ben Naphtali, when the latter's opinions were in accordance with his rules. Thus he punctuated בְּיִצְחָק, לְיִשְׂרָאֵל according to the punctuation rules of Ben Asher and not לִישְׂרָאֵל, בִּיצְחָק on the basis of the spoken language as Ben Naphtali. He also punctuated הַמַּעֲשֶׂה מֵיַעֲקֹב according to his own rules, while Ben Asher and Ben Naphtali canceled the second *meteg*, because they knew from their experience of the spoken language that it is impossible to accentuate two neighboring syllables in the flow of speech.

BIBLIOGRAPHY: Elijah Baḥur, *Masoret ha-Masoret* (Venice, 1538), 71–87 (Sha'ar Shivrei Luḥot); Zunz, Gesch, 115–6; *Biblia Hebraica*, ed. by S. Baer and F. Delitzsch, 1 (1869), viii (introd.); S. Baer, in *Archiv fuer wissenschaftliche Erforschung des Alten Testaments* (1869), 55–67, 194–207; P. Kahle, *Masoreten des Westens* (1927), 19–20; Gumpertz, in: *Leshonenu*, 22 (1957/58), 36–47, 137–46; A. Dotan, in: *Textus*, 4 (1964); idem (ed.), *The diqduqé haṭṭe'amim of Aḥron ben Moše ben Ašér* (3 pts., 1967), Heb. with Eng. Introduction. **ADD. BIBLIOGRAPHY:** R. Yarkoni, "*Ein Hakore li-Yekuti'el ha-Cohen*," 1–2 (dissertation, Tel Aviv Univ., 1985); I. Eldar, in: *Leshonenu*, 40, 190–210; idem, *Masoret ha-Keri'ah ha-Kedam Ashkenzit*, 1 (1979), 191–196; idem, in: *Massorot*, 5–6, 10–16.

[Yehiel G. Gumpertz]

°**JELENSKI, JAN** (1845–1909), editor of an antisemitic Polish weekly. He was the principal opponent of Jewish assimilation to Polish society which developed in the spirit of positivism of the 1860s, mainly aiming to erode the equal rights conferred on Jews by the Wielopolski legislation. In 1870 Jelenski published a rabidly anti-Jewish pamphlet entitled *Żydzi, Niemcy i my* ("Jews, Germans and Us").

After the pogroms in *Warsaw in 1881, the climate became more propitious for propagating his ideas. In 1883 he founded a weekly, entitled *Rola*, which for 26 years continued to spread virulent anti-Jewish propaganda. Jelenski inveighed against the dangers of Jewish domination of economic and cultural life. He received support from clerical circles because of his shafts directed against Jewish assimilationist intellectuals. These, he alleged, were introducing degeneracy into the national body, and, inimical to Catholic tradition in Poland, were spreading dangerous progressive ideas. He was assisted in producing *Rola* by his friend, the notorious antisemitic author Theodor Jeske Choinski (1854–1920).

BIBLIOGRAPHY: J. Gruenbaum, *Milḥamot Yehudei Polin* (1922), 51–57; J. Shatzky, *Geshikhte fun Yidn in Varshe*, 3 (1953), 96; EG, 1 (1953), 74–78.

[Moshe Landau]

JELGAVA (Ger. **Mitau**; Rus. (until 1917) **Mitava**), city in Zemgale district (Courland), Latvia; formerly capital of *Courland. Jews lived in Jelgava from the late 17th century, but their residence was endangered with expulsion orders (that were circumvented), and Jewish trade continued to expand. In 1710 they acquired land for a cemetery. A *ḥevra kaddisha* was founded there in 1729 and a *bikkur ḥolim* society in 1770. From 1778 to 1828 the community was led by the wealthy Kalman and Samson Borkum, whose endeavors enabled the first synagogue in the city to be erected in 1784. In 1799, under Russian rule, the local Jews made up 70% of all Courland Jews. There were 642 Jewish males in the town in 1797 and altogether 5,453 Jews (21% of the total population) in 1860. Half of them traded in horses and farm products, and a third were engaged in crafts. The first historian of Courland Jewry, Reuven Joseph *Wunderbar, was active there during this period. The departure of 115 families (863 persons) from Jelgava for agricultural settlement in southern Russia in 1840, and a severe cholera epidemic in the town in 1848, brought about a decline in the community. Many also were attracted to the developing cities of *Riga and Libava (*Liepaja). The world crisis in the grain markets and the direct linkage of the agricultural areas, as well as competition from Latvians, created a decline in the economic position of the Jelgava Jews and caused about 800 families to ask for relief. According to the census of 1897, there were 5,879 Jews (16.8% of the total population). Rabbis of the community included Samuel Teomim-Ashkenazi (18th century), and Ẓevi Hirsch Nurock and his son Mordechai *Nurock (20th century). In 1910 there existed three synagogues, a *talmud torah*, a Jewish state school for boys, and three Jewish private schools. In May 1915 the Jews of Jelgava, along with the rest of the Jews in Courland, were expelled to the interior of Russia. Some returned after World War I, to find most of the houses burned down and to suffer a pogrom organized by local Germans. The community did not regain its former strength. It numbered 2,039 (6% of the population) in 1935. Levi *Ovchinski, historian of Latvian Jewry, was rabbi of Jelgava until the Holocaust. Jews maintained dominance in trade and owned, among other establishments, a large flax-processing factory. The community maintained welfare services, such as a hospital, an orphanage, and an old age home. It had a *talmud torah*, a Jewish public school, a Hebrew high school, and four synagogues. Zionist parties and youth movements were quite active. Under Soviet rule in 1940–1941 the economy was nationalized, and Jewish institutions and parties were closed. The Germans entered Jelgava on August 29, 1941. Many Jews fled with the retreating Red Army. In the first week of occupation five *Aktionen* were carried out by *Einsatzkommando* 2 and Latvian police, and many hundreds of Jews were murdered, some burned alive in the synagogues. In the beginning of September 1941 a few hundred mental patients from the town and from Liepaja were killed. In fall the town was declared by the Germans to be "free of Jews" (*judenfrei*). There were some 20 Jews living there in 1970.

BIBLIOGRAPHY: L. Ovchinski, *Toledot Yeshivat ha-Yehudim be-Kurland* (1908), 110–28; idem, *Di Geshikhte fun di Yidn in Letland* (1928), 132–68; J. Gar, in: *Algemeyne Entsiklopedye*, 6 (1963), 376, 391–2; M. Kaufmann, *Die Vernichtung der Juden Lettlands* (1947), 305–9.

[Yehuda Slutsky / Shmuel Spector (2nd ed.)]

JELINEK, ELFRIEDE (1946–), Austrian novelist and playwright. Jelinek grew up in Vienna in a working-class family. Although her father was of Czech-Jewish origin, Jelinek attended a Catholic kindergarten and then a convent school. During this time she studied organ and piano at the Vienna Conservatory and later theater and art at the University of Vienna. Jelinek started writing and publishing in the late 1960s with her first collection of poems, *Lisas Schatten* (1967). Her first works were influenced by the so-called *Wiener Gruppe* (Vienna Group) – a group that had been established by H.C. Artmann – and by Jelinek's political commitment to the *Grazer Gruppe* (Graz group). Her earliest works criticize capitalism and the consumer society. Her first novels *wir sind lockvoegel, baby!* (1970) and *Michael: Ein Jugendbuch fuer die Infantilgesellschaft* (1972) demonstrated this combination of avant-garde art and political engagement. These texts are dominated by experimental language: montage, grotesque images, simulation of nursery rhyme and imitation of pop songs. Both novels anticipate Jelinek's style of writing in her future texts. In her essay *Die endlose Schuldigkeit* (1970) Jelinek delineated the innocence and ignorance of society about cultural myths and images. Deconstructing existing myths became Jelinek's main issue in writing. In the 1980s she addressed the patriarchal society with biting criticism and aimed at deconstructing the myths of love, marriage, and family. *Die Liebhaberinnen* (1975; *Women as Lovers*, 1994) was considered Jelinek's first feminist piece of literature and applauded by the critics. Especially *Die Klavierspielerin* (1983; *The Piano Teacher*, 1988), which contains autobiographical elements, is the story of a female protagonist making her stand against her extremely protective mother. The novel became a bestseller and served as basis for a movie.

In 1989 Jelinek wrote her second bestselling novel *Lust* (Eng. 1993). As was typical in this phase of her writing, Jelinek depicts marriage as legalized prostitution and portrays the town and its inhabitants as greedy and corrupt. The protagonists in this novel are incapable of liberation because they are driven by socioeconomic forces. Their consumer ideology leads to the degradation of human beings to the status of objects.

Jelinek also wrote for the theater. Her first plays *Was geschah, nachdem Nora ihren Mann verlassen hatte; oder Stuetzen der Gesellschaft* (1978) and *Clara S. musikalische Tragoedie* (1984) show the futile attempt of her female protagonists to determine their lives independently. At the same time Jelinek wrote *Burgtheater: Posse mit Gesang* (1984), in which she used a language that illustrates and unmasks fascist ideas in daily life. Subsequent works also remained focused on the theme of lingering fascism in today's society. Her plays *Wolken Heim* (1990) and *Totenauberg* (1991), as well as the novel *Die Kinder der Toten* (1995), are thematically linked with fascism and its philosophical nationalistic roots. Especially the last-mentioned novel is a grotesque picture of zombies living their lives between suppression of history and oblivion of death.

In the 1980s her works were widely and ambivalently reviewed. Whereas some critics praised her aesthetic language, Jelinek always had to face harsh criticism in her home country of Austria. Here critics attacked Jelinek personally and limited their criticism to the explicit sexuality and abusiveness of her texts. Especially with the play *Burgtheater: Posse mit Gesang* Jelinek had to deal with personal assaults. This play is evocative of the Austrian participation in the Holocaust and the Third Reich. Jelinek was henceforth labeled a hater of Austria. Nonetheless Jelinek earned much praise from the international public and received among many others awards the Heinrich Böll Prize in 1986 and, in 1998, the prestigious Georg Büchner Prize. With this positive reception Jelinek's work was also praised in Austria. In the Burgtheater she celebrated the premiere of her play *Ein Sportstueck* (1998) which received standing ovations. Sport here is portrayed as another form of war, a mass phenomenon charged with violence. Various voices weave a texture of human behavior and contemporary social structures.

In the 1990s Jelinek's writing became more and more political. Jelinek had been a member of the Austrian Communist Party and had already criticized capitalism in her early works. Her later work concentrates mostly on the historical past of Austria and unmasks the myth of Austrian innocence during the Third Reich. Her political activism included sharp criticism of the election of Kurt Waldheim with his Nazi past, and later she protested against Joerg Haider and his right-wing party FPÖ. Haider's farewell speech, made when he stepped down from the national leadership of his nationalistic party, was transposed into the play *Das Lebewohl* (2000). The monologue can be read as a statement of a seducer yearning for power ad infinitum.

Jelinek's subsequent works were short dramas consisting of dense monologues. *Der Tod und das Maedchen I–V* (2003) depicts in five plays the death of the maiden in a male-dominated world. One of these plays, *Jackie,* was made into a radio play and received the highest recognition with the Blind War Veterans' Radio Theatre Prize.

Jelinek received the Nobel Prize for literature in 2004. In its official announcement the committee cites the "musical flow of voices and counter-voices" in her work, that "with extraordinary linguistic zeal reveals the absurdity of society's clichés and their subjugating power." Jelinek did not attend the official ceremony, as she did not feel capable of dealing with such an imposing public.

BIBLIOGRAPHY: P. Janke, *Werkverzeichnis Elfriede Jelinek* (2004); A. Johanning, *KoerperStuecke: der Koerper als Medium in den Theaterstuecken Elfriede Jelineks* (2004); Y. Hoffmann, *Elfriede Jelinek: Sprach- und Kulturkritik im Erzaehlwerk* (1999); S. Kratz, *Undichte Dichtungen: Texttheater und Theaterlektüren bei Elfriede Jelinek* (1999); M. Szczepaniak, *Dekonstruktion des Mythos in ausgewaehlten Prosawerken von Elfriede Jelinek* (1998); C. Guertler, *Gegen den schoenen Schein: Texte zu Elfriede Jelinek* (1990).

[Ann-Kristin Koch (2nd ed.)]

JELLIN, ARYEH LOEB BEN SHALOM SHAKHNA (1820–1886), Polish talmudist and halakhist. Born in Yasinovka, Jellin became rabbi of Bielsk. He was the author of *Yefeh Einayim*, on the Talmud, whose major feature is that it lists sources, parallel passages, and variant readings in the midrashic literature and in the *aggadah* of the Talmud. He maintains that as a result new light is thrown upon the subject, many obscurities becoming clear. He also draws attention to differences between the Babylonian and Jerusalem Talmuds, both in language and in the method of approach in the discussion on the explanation of the Mishnah or *baraita*. The *Yefeh Einayim* was included in the Vilna (Romm) edition of the Talmud. Jellin's fame spread as an outstanding halakhic authority, particularly on the laws of *terefot. He was the author of *Mizpeh Aryeh*, short notes on the talmudic digest of Isaac *Alfasi, and of *Kol Aryeh*, sermons appended to it, published in Johannisburg, Prussia (n.d.). The *Penei Aryeh*, a comprehensive commentary on the Palestinian Talmud, aimed at justifying the accepted text without variant readings, has not been published.

BIBLIOGRAPHY: L. Ginzberg, *Perushim ve-Ḥiddushim ha-Yerushalmi*, 1 (1941), lxi–lxii (Eng. introd.); E.P. Brawerman, *Anshei Shem* (1892), 95.

[Abram Juda Goldrat]

JELLINEK, ADOLF (**Aaron**; 1820/21–1893), Vienna preacher and scholar. He was born in a village near Uhersky Brod (Ungarisch Brod), Moravia, into a family which he believed to be of *Hussite origin. After attending the yeshivah of Menahem *Katz (Wannfried) in Prostejov (Prossnitz), in 1838 he moved to Prague where he was influenced by Solomon Judah *Rapoport, Michael Jehiel *Sachs, and Wolfgang *Wessely. Moving to Leipzig in 1842, he studied philosophy and Semitics at the university there, assisted Julius *Fuerst in editing the *Orient*, and in 1845 was appointed preacher in the new synagogue which was established under the guidance of Zacharias *Frankel. Although he opposed the radical views of his brother, Herman *Jellinek, he enthusiastically hailed the freedom resulting from the 1848 revolution. Together with Christian clergymen he then founded the Kirchlicher Verein fuer alle Religionsbekenntnisse, an association open to all religious denominations, and would have represented it at the Frankfurt German National Assembly (1848) but for the intervention of the Saxonian minister of religious affairs. He was also on the board of an association (Verein zur Wahrung der deutschen Interessen an den oestlichen Grenzen) formed to support Germans in the Slav countries. In 1857 he was appointed preacher at the new Leopoldstadt synagogue in Vienna, remaining there until he went to the Seitenstetten synagogue in 1865.

In 1862 Jellinek founded the Beit ha-Midrash Academy where public lectures were delivered by himself, Isaac Hirsch *Weiss, and Meir *Friedmann. A scholarly periodical, also called *Beit ha-Midrash*, was published under its auspices. His eldest son, GEORGE J. JELLINEK (1851–1911), a professor of public law at Basle and Heidelberg, was baptized after Jellinek's death.

Jellinek was considered the greatest preacher of his day and some 200 of his sermons were published, some were translated into Hebrew and into other languages. Their most striking characteristic was that, while related to actual problems of the day, they made brilliant and original use of *aggadah* and Midrash. Personally lenient in matters of ritual, he advocated a moderately liberal line, striving for unity in the community. Thus although he wanted to install an organ in the synagogue "to attract the indifferent," he took I.N. *Mannheimer's advice and abandoned the idea. He also opposed the omission from the prayer book of references to Zion and prayers for the restoration of sacrifices. Due to the conciliatory attitude of both Jellinek and the leader of the Orthodox group, Solomon Benjamin *Spitzer, a split in the community was avoided. Jellinek was an unsuccessful candidate for the Diet of Lower Austria in 1861. In a eulogy (1867) delivered after the execution of Emperor Maximilian of Mexico, in which he alluded to the execution of his own brother, he suggested the abolition of capital punishment for political offenses and advocated a reform of court procedures. He expressed his views on political matters regularly in the *Neuzeit*, which he edited from 1882. Jellinek was Baron Maurice de *Hirsch's trustee for his philanthropic activities in Galicia. With the rise of modern antisemitism, he turned his energies to apologetics, which he wanted to include as a subject in his Beit ha-Midrash, and he persuaded Joseph Samuel *Bloch to write his *Israel und die Voelker*. He was hostile to the emerging Jewish nationalist movement, and when Leo *Pinsker approached him he refused to back his ideas. Like many Reform rabbis of his day, he did not view Jews as a nation. They were meant to be dedicated to their European fatherland while pursuing the fulfillment of Judaism's religious goals. Thus, "Zion" became a symbol for the ultimate redemption of all mankind.

Jellinek also produced a large number of scholarly works in numerous fields. He had taken an early interest in the study of Kabbalah (one of the very few who did in that golden age of modern Jewish scholarship) and translated A. Franck's *La Cabbale* into German (1844). Jellinek's original contributions in this field were *Moses b. Schemtob de Leon und sein Verhaeltnis zum Sohar* (1851); *Auswahl kabbalistischer Mystik* (1853); *Beitraege zur Geschichte der Kabbala* (1852); *Thomas von Aquino in der juedischen Literatur* (1853); and *Philosophie und Kabbala* (1854). He also edited Abraham Abulafia's *Sefer ha-Ot* (1887), in which he showed that *Moses b. Shem Tov de Leon and not Abulafia wrote the Zohar. In his Leipzig period Jellinek also edited Menahem de Lonzano's *Ma'arikh* (1853), a dictionary of foreign words in Talmud, Midrash, and Zohar; wrote "*Sefat Ḥakhamim*" (1846–47) on talmudic idioms (in L. Benjacob, *Devarim Attikim*); and edited, with an introduction and commentary, Baḥya b. Joseph ibn Paquda's *Ḥovot ha-Levavot* (1846). In Vienna Jellinek's main scholarly effort was directed toward the publication of 99 smaller, largely unknown Midrashim (*Beit ha-Midrash*, 6 vols., 1853–78, 1938), many of which were of prime importance for the study of early Kabbalah, such as the *Heikhalot Rabbati, Nistarot R. Shimon bar Yoḥai*, etc. In a number of smaller publications (1877–84), Jellinek dealt with a variety of historical, philosophical, talmudic, and bibliographical subjects such as the persecutions during the First Crusade, the disputation of Barcelona in 1263, the Talmud commentators, those of Maimonides' *Mishneh Torah*, and others. Other publications of this period include: Simeon b. Ẓemaḥ Duran's commentary on *Avot* (1855); Judah Messer Leon's *Nofet Ẓufim* (1863); Solomon Alami's *Iggeret Musar* (1872); *Worms-Wien* (1880); and *Der juedische Stamm in nichtjuedischen Sprichwoertern* (3 vols., 1882–86).

BIBLIOGRAPHY: M. Rosenmann, *Adolf Jellinek* (Ger., 1931), incl. bibl.; A.M. Jost, *Adolf Jellinek und die Kabbala* (1852); M. Grunwald, *Vienna* (1936), index; J. Fraenkel (ed.), *Jews of Austria* (1967), index; S.W. Baron, in: PAAJR, 20 (1951), 33 n. 125; H. Tietze, *Die Juden Wiens* (1935), index; Klausner, Sifrut, 5 (1955), index; M.G. Mehrer, in: *Zeitschrift fuer die Geschichte der Juden in der Tschechoslowakei*, 3 (1932/33), 143–51; Z. Szajkowski, in: JSOS, 19 (1957), 36–38; A. Kober, *ibid.*, 10 (1948), 159–60; S.W. Baron, *ibid.*, 11 (1949), 200–1; G. Kohut, in: AJHSP, 33 (1934), 237f.; I. Schorsch, in: YLBI, 11 (1966), 42–66, passim. **ADD BIBLIOGRAPHY:** M.L. Rozenblit, in: *Leo Baeck Institute Year Book*, 35 (1990), 103–31.

[Gershom Scholem and Meir Lamed]

JELLINEK, HERMANN (1822–1848), writer, journalist, and revolutionary; younger brother of Adolf *Jellinek. While living in Prostejov (Prossnitz) and Prague, he studied independently and was taught languages by his brother. He studied in Prague and Leipzig. Jellinek first attracted attention through his lecture opposing the philosophy of Leibniz, delivered at Leipzig University on the occasion of Leibniz's 200th anniversary. Although Jellinek received a doctorate, he was expelled from Leipzig for his political activity. In reaction, he published *Das Denunciation System des saechsischen Liberalismus und das kritisch-nihilistische System Hermann Jellineks* (1847). Moving to Berlin, where he was in close contact with Bruno *Bauer, he pursued his radical revolutionary course, thereby alienating his brother Adolf. A third brother, R. Haraszti-Jellinek, owned the trolley car company of Budapest, Hungary. Expelled from Berlin for political reasons, Jellinek went to Vienna in March 1848. As a means of supporting himself, Jellinek turned to journalism, writing fiercely radical articles against the Hapsburg regime in the *Allgemeine Oesterreichische Zeitung* and later in *Der Radikale*. With the failure of the 1848 Revolution in Vienna, and with the declaration of martial law, his friends advised him to escape, but he remained and was arrested. Field Marshal Windischgraetz blamed the press for the events of the revolution and accused Jellinek and his friend A. Becher. A military tribunal sentenced both to death by hanging, but only Jellinek was executed on November 23. Adolf *Fischhof has suggested that Jellinek was selected for execution because he was a Jew and Becher, a Protestant. Jellinek's works include *Uriel Acostas Leben und Lehre* (1847) and *Die Taeuschung der aufgeklaerten Juden und ihre Faehigkeit zur Emancipation* (1847). In the latter he mocks the aspirations of Jews who attempt to attain equal rights by presenting Judaism as an enlightened religion which suits the demands of the age of Enlightenment.

BIBLIOGRAPHY: E. Lehmann, *H. Jellinek zur Erinnerung* (1848); C. Wurzbach (ed.), *Biographisches Lexikon*, 10 (1863), 157–60; ADB, 50 (1905), 649–50; J.A. Helfert, *Die Wiener Journalistik im Jahre 1848* (1877), index; *Oesterreichisches Biographisches Lexikon*, 3 (1962), 102; A. Kober, in: JSOS, 10 (1948), 133–62 passim; S.W. Baron, *ibid.*, 195–218 passim.

[Jacob Rothschild]

JELLINEK, KARL (1882–1955), German physical chemist; born in Vienna. In 1908, Jellinek joined the Technische Hochschule at Danzig; he was appointed professor of physical chemistry and director of the Institute in 1922. In 1937 the Nazis forced him out and he spent the rest of his life in London. His field of research included nitric oxide, ammonia synthesis, electrochemistry, the Nernst heat theorem, and the vapor pressure of salts. He wrote many books, including *Verstaendliche Elemente der Wellenmechanik* (2 vols., 1950–51).

JEMNICE (Ger. **Jamnitz**), town in S.W. Moravia, Czech Republic. The Jewish community in Jemnice is mentioned first in connection with its sufferings during the *Armleder massacres (1336). It is assumed that the community was one of the oldest of Moravia. A gravestone from 1362 has been preserved and in 1369 the sale of real estate by a Jew was recorded. In 1530 Jews are mentioned as house owners and throughout the 16th and 17th centuries transactions in real estate between Jews and gentiles are frequently documented. A synagogue, built in 1648, burned down in 1752. There were nine Jewish tailors in Jemnice in 1755. When the community could not meet its tax obligations in 1775, the local lord renounced his share. In 1812 a German-language elementary school was founded, which existed as a governmental school until 1918. In a fire in 1832 all 28 houses of the Jewish quarter were burned to the ground. Riots occurred in 1866 when the Jews were accused of actively supporting the Prussians.

There were 24 families living in 11 houses in 1666. In 1754 the number of permitted families was increased from 30 to 45 (see *Familiants Law) and the community increased to 263 persons (nearly 20% of the total population) in 1781, and 325 persons in 1830. Then began a steady decline, from 305 in 1857 to 200 in 1869, 102 in 1910, 84 in 1921, and 52 in 1930 (1.5% of the total). In 1942 the community was deported to the Nazi extermination camps. The synagogue ritual objects were transferred to the Central Jewish Museum in Prague.

BIBLIOGRAPHY: A. Marmorstein, in: *Mitteilungen zur juedischen Volkskunde*, 13 (1910), 28–32; R. Hruschka and B. Wachstein, in: H. Gold (ed.), *Die Juden und Judengemeinden Maehrens…* (1929), 251–66.

[Meir Lamed]

JENER, ABRAHAM NAPHTALI HIRSCH BEN MORDECAI (1805–1876), rabbi and author. Jener was appointed *dayyan* at Cracow in 1831 and in 1856, after the death of Alexander Landau, the head of the *bet din*. The extreme Orthodox element refused to elect him chief rabbi of Cracow on account of his moderation and his tolerant attitude toward the followers of the *Haskalah movement, between whom and the Orthodox he was the mediator also during the chief rabbinate of Simeon *Sofer. His approbations appear in many books, and his responsa and halakhic decisions in the works of contemporary rabbis. Several of his responsa and letters were published in Ẓevi Hirsch *Chajes' *Minḥat Kena'ot* and in Jacob Eichhorn's *Adat Ya'akov*. The most distinguished of his pupils was Solomon Zalman Ḥayyim *Halberstam. Jener wrote *Birkat Avraham*, responsa (1870), and *Ẓeluta de-Avraham*, halakhic novellae, responsa, and homilies (1868).

BIBLIOGRAPHY: Ḥ.D. Friedberg, *Luḥot Zikkaron* (1897), 79 no. 121; Busak, in: *Sefer Cracow* (1959), 97f.

[Itzhak Alfassi]

JENIN (Ar. **Janīn**), Arab town in Samaria, situated in the southern corner of the Jezreel Valley, near the junction of roads running to *Haifa, Afulah, Nazareth, and Nablus. At the end of the 19th century, Jenin's population was below 1,000, but by 1943 had increased to 3,900. In the 1967 census conducted by Israel, the town proper had 8,346 inhabitants; 4,480 more lived in a refugee camp within the municipal confines. Only 90 were Christians, all the rest Muslims. Jenin's economy is based mainly on agriculture which utilizes the abundance of springwater and the fertile soil of the vicinity. Before 1948, and again from 1967, the town's position at an important crossroads contributed to its development. It also made it an important base for the Turko-German forces in World War I, until the British Army captured Jenin in September 1918. In the 1936–39 Arab riots, Jenin lay at the apex of the aggressive Arab "triangle" (whose other two corners were Tul-Karm and Nablus) from which attacks against Jewish villages in the Jezreel Valley were launched. In the Israel *War of Independence, the Arab Liberation Army under Fawzī al-Qāwuqjī set out from Jenin to attack Mishmar ha-Emek in an effort to break through to Haifa, but was driven back. On June 2, 1948, Jewish units attacked from the north and took most of the town, but had to evacuate it again when overwhelming Iraqi forces arrived to relieve the Arab positions in the hills around. In the *Six-Day War (1967), Jenin constituted a forward Jordanian position. It fell after Israel columns entered the Dotan Valley to its rear and overcame a Jordanian counterattack (June 6, 1967). Jenin was transferred to the jurisdiction of the *Palestinian Authority following the 1995 Taba Agreement. During the so-called al-Aqsa Intifada (see *Israel, State of, under Historical Survey), Jenin was a hotbed of terrorist activity and often targeted by Israeli forces, most notably in Operation Defensive Shield in the spring of 2002. The controversial film *Jenin, Jenin* purported to document Israeli atrocities and was banned by the Israel Film Board for its distortions, a decision later overturned by Israel's Supreme Court. In 1997 the population of Jenin numbered 26,650 inhabitants, among them 50% refugees. Jenin is sometimes identified with biblical *En-Gannim.

[Efraim Orni]

°**JENKINSON, SIR (Charles) HILARY** (1882–1961), British archivist and scholar. He began his association with the Public Records Office in 1906 and became deputy keeper (director) in 1947. He built up the profession of archivist in Britain. Throughout his life he retained an early interest in medieval Anglo-Jewish history, stimulated by his discovery in the Record Office of some Jewish receipt rolls and tallies. This led, among other publications, to his editing the third volume of the Plea Rolls of the Jewish Exchequer, *Calendar of the Plea Rolls of the Exchequer of the Jews Preserved in the Records Office; Edward I 1275–1277* (1929). He modified his original view that the medieval Exchequer of the Jews was purely judicial. As president of the Jewish Historical Society of England (1953–55), he initiated the resumption of publication of medieval Anglo-Jewish records and the formation of the Anglo-Jewish Archives. Jenkinson was knighted in 1949.

BIBLIOGRAPHY: N. Bentwich, in: JHSET, 20 (1964), 257–8; *The Times* (London, March 7, 1961). **ADD. BIBLIOGRAPHY:** ODNB online; H.C. Johnson, "Biographical Memoir," in: J.C. Davies (ed.), *Studies Presented to Sir Hilary Jenkinson* (1957).

[Vivian David Lipman]

JEPHTHAH (Heb. יִפְתָּח), judge of Israel for six years and victor over the Ammonites (Judg. 11:1–12:7). According to Judges, Jephthah was the son of a harlot, and his father's name is given as Gilead. Jephthah is described as a Gileadite warrior. After the legitimate sons of his father had driven him from home, he went to live in the land of Tob, where he became the leader of a band of adventurers. The elders of Gilead recalled him to repel an Ammonite invasion (see below), and Jephthah agreed on condition that he be appointed chief of the land after the victory (11:1–11). Jephthah then proceeded to negotiate with the Ammonites, seeking in vain to convince them that Israel possessed a right to its territory and that attempts to dislodge Israel from it would be futile (11:12–28). In the course of the negotiations Jephthah acknowledged that Chemosh had given land to the Ammonites. The unexpectedly brief account of the decisive defeat of the enemy highlights Jephthah's vow to sacrifice to YHWH whatever would come out of his house to meet him on his victorious return. To Jephthah's immense grief, it was his only daughter who came first to greet him, and he felt obliged to fulfill his solemn vow. The daughter resigned herself to her fate and begged only that it be postponed for two months so that she might mourn with her companions on the mountains. At the end of this period she met her tragic fate. This serves as an etiology for the observance by Israelite women of an annual four-day mourning period (11:29–40). Jephthah's victory over the Ammonites led to a war with the Ephraimites, who resented not having been included in the call to arms. Forty-two thousand of them, caricatured as stupid in not preparing (*yakin*) to pronounce *shibbolet* correctly when their lives depended on it, are said to have been slaughtered as they attempted to cross the fords of the Jordan (12:1–6). The account exhibits clear evidence of a conflation of parallel traditional material, though the discussion among critics has not been significantly advanced since the commentaries of Moore and, especially, Burney. The latter isolated a "Moabite" narrative (10:17; 11:12–28, 30, 31, 33b, 34–40) now assimilated, albeit imperfectly, to the normative tradition in 11:1–11, 29, 32b–33a, and 12:1–6. Pivotal to any such analysis is the fact that Jephthah's messengers to the Ammonite king (11:12–28) argue Israel's case with examples from Moabite history and go so far as to suggest that Chemosh is the Ammonites' god (not Milcom or Molech as to be expected from I Kings 11:5, 7). The Ammonite invasion was prompted by a territorial dispute having its roots in the Israelite conquest of Canaan, when Israel conquered some Amorite territory in Transjordan. The Ammonites in Jephthah's time claimed that this territory had originally belonged to them and were demanding its return from Israel. The Pentateuch's account of the Mosaic conquest of the Amorite territory says nothing explicit about any of it having previously belonged to the Ammonites. In the story of the conquest of the Amorite kingdom of Sihon and the Amorite city-state of Jazer, it is mentioned that Sihon expanded his territory at the expense of the Moabites. At first apparently confined to a limited territory around Heshbon, Sihon took from the Moabites everything down to the River Arnon. In this connection a snatch of an ancient battle or taunt song celebrating Sihon's discomfiture of Moab is cited (Num. 21:23–32). The account adds that the city-state of Jazer (so read, with LXX, for "Az" in Num. 21:24) marked the border of the Ammonites and that the Israelites dispossessed its Amorite population (21:32). This, and perhaps a strip of the former kingdom of Sihon, may indeed have been formerly Ammonite territory. It is possible that only such territory was claimed by Jephthah's Ammonite contemporaries, despite Judges 11:13. The name Jephthah is apparently a shortened form of Yftaḥ-Yah or Yftaḥ-El ("God opens/may open," i.e., the womb). Jephthah appears as a place-name in Joshua 15:43, and in its fuller form in Joshua 19:14, 27.

[Harold Louis Ginsberg and Nahum M. Sarna]

In the Aggadah

Jephthah, in common with Gideon and Samson, was one of the least worthy judges of Israel. From the mention of his name together with that of Samuel in one verse (I Sam. 12:11) the rabbis deduce that "Jephthah in his generation is like Samuel in his generation, to teach that even an unworthy person, when appointed to a position of importance has to be regarded as one of the greatest" (RH 25b). He is condemned as one of the three (Ta'an. 4a) or four (Gen. R. 603) to take imprudent vows, but he was the only one who regretted his imprudence. His sinful act of immolating his daughter was due both to his ignorance and his false pride. He was unaware that he could have paid ransom to the Temple treasury in lieu of his vow, and that the high priest Phinehas could have absolved him from it. However, each refused to lower his dignity by visiting the other. Jephthah's punishment for this action was that his body was dismembered limb by limb (Gen. R. 60:3).

In the Arts

The moving and pathetic account of Jephthah and his votive sacrifice appealed to Christian writers, artists, and musicians from medieval times onward. Two of the earliest literary works based on the theme, though not written in English, were by British authors: *Jephthes si-Ve votum* (performed c. 1542), a neo-Latin drama by the Scots Protestant George Buchanan, and Ἰεφθάε (1544?; Eng. *Jephthah*, 1928), a Greek academic play by the English Catholic exile John Christopherson. The latter is a study of retributive justice with contemporary religious and political undertones and echoes of other scriptural episodes, such as the **Akedah* and the Crucifixion. At least as old is the English ballad "Jephthah Judge of Israel" quoted by Shakespeare (*Hamlet* II, ii), which Thomas Percy later included in his *Reliques of Ancient English Poetry* (1765). Among other works of the 16th century which dealt with the subject were the German *Meistersinger*, Hans Sachs's *Der Jephta und seine Tochter* (1555), and *Jephté* (1567), a French drama based largely on Buchanan's, by Florent Chrétien, a prose parody attacking the Catholic League and other enemies of Henry of Navarre. During the 17th century, the English writers Thomas Dekker and Anthony Munday staged a *Jephthah* (1602) which has not survived; the Dutch playwright Joost van den Vondel wrote the verse tragedy *Jephta* (1659); and the subject also appeared in the English *Stonyhurst Pageants*, and in *Cumplir a Dios la Palabra o la Hija de Jefte* (included in Diamante's *Comedias*, Madrid, 1670–74) by the Spanish dramatist Juan Bautista Diamante. The number of literary (largely dramatic) works about Jephthah multiplied during the 19th century, particularly in England, where they clearly appealed to Victorian sentimentality. Those in English included Lord *Byron's poem "Jephthah's Daughter" (in *Hebrew Melodies*, 1815), and William Alexander's dramatic poem *Ella, or the Prince of Gilead's Vow* (1847). Among the treatments in other languages were Karl Ludwig Kannegieser's German tragedy *Mirza, die Tochter Jephtas* (1818) and "La fille de Jephté" (in *Poèmes antiques et modernes*, 1826) by the French Romantic Alfred de Vigny; Ludwig *Robert's drama *Die Tochter Jephthas* (1813) was the first German stage production by a Jew; other works by Jewish writers included Moses Samuel Neumann's Hebrew play *Bat Yiftaḥ* (Vienna, 1805) and Leibush Lewinsohn's Hebrew novel *Neder Yiftaḥ* (1870). Modern treatments by Jewish authors include *Yiftakhs Tokhter* (1914; *Jephthah's Daughter*, 1915), a Yiddish play by Sholem *Asch; Ernst *Lissauer's drama *Das Weib des Jephta* (1928); Saul Saphire's Yiddish novel *Yiftakh un Zayn Tokhter* (1937); *Far a Nayer Velt* (1939–40), a Yiddish drama by the U.S. writer David *Ignatoff; and Lion *Feuchtwanger's last novel, *Jefta und seine Tochter* (1957; Eng. 1958).

In art, the two main subjects treated are Jephthah's meeting with his daughter on his return from battle and his sacrifice of his daughter. These, together with his battle against the Ammonites, are illustrated in the 13th-century French *St. Louis Psalter* (Bibliothèque Nationale, Paris). In a 15th-century German manuscript in the Munich State Library there is a charming miniature of Jephthah coming home in armor and greeted by his daughter, who is playing on a string instrument. Jephthah's homecoming is also the subject of paintings by Lucas van Leyden (1494–1533; private collection) and Pierre Mignard (1610–1695; Hermitage, Leningrad). Jephthah's sacrifice of his daughter is illustrated in the 14th-century English *Queen Mary Psalter* (British Museum), as well as in the *St. Louis Psalter*. The subject was again painted by Lucas van Leyden. It was popular in France in the 17th century, and was treated by Pierre Mignard (Hermitage, Leningrad), Charles Lebrun (Uffizi, Florence), and Antoine Coypel (Laon Museum). There is a painting by the French 19th-century artist Edgar Degas in Smith College, Massachusetts, U.S. Enrico *Glicenstein executed a sculpture of Jephthah's daughter. The story of Jephthah was much used for tapestries, the chief example being the series made in Tournai by Pasquier Grenier (c. 1470) for Philip the Good, duke of Burgundy.

The story also attracted the attention of oratorio composers during the formative period of the genre at the beginning of the 17th century. Some time before 1649, Giacomo Carissimi wrote his *Jephte*, which has retained a place in the musical repertory. The works which followed include G.B. Vitali's *Il Gefte overo Il zelo impudente* (1672; libretto only extant); A. Draghi's *Jefte* (1690); A. Lotti's *Il voto crudele* (*Jefta*)(1712); and *Il Sacrifizio di Jephta* by L. Vinci (1690–1730; date of composition unknown). Michel de Monteclair's "*tragédie lyrique*" *Jephté*, to a libretto by the abbé S.J. Pellegrim, was the first opera on a biblical subject licensed for stage performance in France. It had its première at the Académie Royale de Musique in 1732 and was restaged in 1733 and 1734, but it was immediately afterward forbidden by Cardinal de Noailles. The subject, with a text by Thomas Morell after an Italian prototype, was destined to inspire Handel's last work. The annotations in his manuscript score, begun on Jan. 12, 1751, and the faltering notational image, bear witness to Handel's progressing blindness. The score was finished on Aug. 30, 1751, after a slight improvement had partially restored his sight, and the first performance took place in the Covent Garden Theater, London, on Feb. 26, 1752. A reworking by Ferdinand *Hiller has remained in manuscript. Until the end of the 18th century various other settings of the subject, all oratorios, were also written. Giacomo *Meyerbeer's oratorio *Jephtas Geluebde*, written in 1812 when he was 21, has remained in manuscript. During the 19th century, the operatic potential of the story could be realized, since religious restrictions were no longer a deterrent, and the gruesome ending with a human sacrifice attracted, rather than repelled, the Romantics. Two operas were even written and performed in Spain: *Jephté* (1845) by Luis Cepeda and *La Hija de Jefté* (1876) by Ruperto Chapí. Two Jephthah cantatas figure in the list of works which won their composers the Prix de Rome of the Paris Conservatory; one by Samuel *David (1858) and another by Alexandre-Samuel Rousseau (1878). Byron's *Jephthah's Daughter* was first set to music by Isaac *Nathan and subsequently, among others, by Karl Loewe (1826, in a German translation) and Robert Schumann (in his *Drei Gesaenge*, opus 95; written 1849). Among works of the 20th century are Lucien Haudebert's *La fille de Jephté* (1929; for orchestra); Lazare *Saminsky's *The Daughter of Jephthah*, "a cantata pantomime" for solo, choir, orchestra, and dancers (publ. 1937); and Ernst *Toch's "rhapsodic poem" for orchestra, *Jephta* (1963). A.Z. *Idelsohn's *Yiftaḥ*, written in Jerusalem and published in 1922, was the first opera composed in Palestine. Idelsohn wrote the (Hebrew) text himself; the music is a singular combination of the various Jewish traditions – both Western and Eastern – which he had by then collected for his ethnomusicological studies. Modern Israel works on the subject include Mordekhai *Seter's orchestral work *Jephthah's Daughter* (publ. 1965) and several settings in the form of a pageant, created for the kibbutzim of the Gilboa region. Two dances by Amittai Ne'eman, one slow and one debkah-like and fast, both called *Bat Yiftaḥ*, and danced in succession, are in the Israel folk-dance repertory.

[Bathja Bayer]

BIBLIOGRAPHY: G.F. Moore, *Judges* (ICC, 1900), 275–310; C.F. Burney, *The Book of Judges* (1920^{2}), 293–334; R. Marcus, in: BASOR, 87 (1942), 39; J. Simon, in: PEQ, 79 (1947), 27ff.; G. Landes, in: IDB. 1 (1962), 108–14. IN THE AGGADAH: Ginzberg, Legends, 4 (1913), 43–47; 6 (1928), 202–4. IN THE ARTS: W.O. Sypherd, *Jephthah and his Daughter* (1948); M. Roston, *Biblical Drama in England* (1968), 79–82, 118, 142. **ADD. BIBLIOGRAPHY:** D. Marcus, *Jephthah and His Vow* (1986); R. Boling, in: ABD, 3:681–83, incl. bibliography; Y. Amit, *Judges* (1999), 185–212; B. Levine, *Numbers 21–36* (AB; 2000), 79–133; T. Frymer-Kensky, *Reading Women of the Bible* (2002), 102–17.

JERAHMEEL BEN SOLOMON (c. 1150), chronicler, lived in Italy. He wrote *Megillat Yeraḥme'el* (or *Meliẓat Yeraḥme'el* or *Sefer ha-Yeraḥme'eli*), a compilation of writings on history and other subjects such as grammar, music, astronomy, liturgy and more. His anthology contained also the book of *Josippon*, translation of the Aramaic chapters in the book of Daniel, and a few historical Midrashim, and it is based on both Jewish and non-Jewish sources, including selections from Strabo, Nicholas of Damascus and Philo, as well as from a few historical Midrashim and apocryphal works. It contains numerous apocalyptic legends about biblical heroes taken from unknown sources, parallel to legends in the Midrashim, in *Sefer ha-Yashar*, in Josippon, and in Christian apocalyptical works. Portions of the work were incorporated by Eleazar b. Asher ha-Levi (c. 1325) in his book *Sefer ha-Zikhronot* (Ms. Oxford). Several excerpts were published by Neubauer (JQR, 11 (1899), 364ff.). M. Gaster translated the *Megillah* into English (*The Chronicle of Jerahmeel*, 1899) and added a detailed introduction; he titled it *The Chronicles of Jerahmeel on the Hebrew Bible Historiale*. The literary works of Jerahmeel consist mostly of poems, mathematical riddles, and questions in meteorology, as well as *piyyutim*, especially *Kedushot* (Ms. Paris 646) which describe the world of creation and the holiness of the angels. Numerous rhymes and stormy rhythms are used in these *piyyutim* to imitate the sound of the enthusiasm and tumult of the angels.

BIBLIOGRAPHY: Zunz, Lit Poesie, 485f.; Neubauer, Chronicles, 1 (1887), xix–xxi, 163–78, 190f.; Neubauer, Cat, 2 (1906), 208–15; idem, in: MGWJ, 36 (1887), 505–8; idem, in: JQR, 11 (1898/99), 366–86; Halberstam, *ibid.*, 697ff.; Perles, in: *Graetz Jubelschrift* (1887), 22f.; M. Gaster, *Studies and Texts*, 1 (1925–28), 39–68; 3 (1925–28), 16–21; M. Steinschneider, *Geschichtsliteratur der Juden* (1905), 41ff., 175f.; Cohen, in: *J. Guttmann Festschrift* (1915), 173–85; Vogelstein-Rieger, 166, 186, 192; Schirmann, in: YMḤSI, 1 (1933), 97f.; Waxman, Literature, 1 (1960^{2}), 527–30; Davidson, Oẓar, 4 (1933), 425. E. Yassif, *Sefer ha-Zikhronot*, 2001; Jacobson, in: *The Studia Philonica Annual*, 9 (1997) 239–50; Schwartzbaum, Preface, in: Gaster, *The Chronicles of Jerachmiel* 2, 1971.

[Yonah David]

JEREMIAH (Heb. יִרְמְיָה, יִרְמְיָהוּ) second of the major prophets whose book is the second in the Latter Prophets section of the Bible.

This entry is arranged according to the following outline:

IN THE AGGADAH
IN ISLAM
IN THE ARTS

IN THE BIBLE

The Book of Jeremiah is the largest among the Latter Prophets and comprises the oracles of the prophet Jeremiah from the 13th year of the reign of Josiah until after the destruction of Judah by the Babylonians. It also contains biographical and autobiographical narrative concerning the prophet and his activities, as well as historical records of the destruction of Jerusalem and of subsequent events which took place in Judah and Egypt. In the prevalent masoretic editions it is placed after the Book of Isaiah. According to an old order suggested by *Bava Batra* 14b–15a, it was placed at the beginning of the Latter Prophets, before Ezekiel and Isaiah. This arrangement was followed by many Ashkenazi manuscripts. In the Septuagint it usually appears third, after the Minor Prophets and Isaiah and before Ezekiel (see *Bible, Canon). (See Table, Book of Jeremiah contents.)

BOOK OF JEREMIAH – CONTENTS

1:1–6:30	**Baruch's scroll**
1:1–19	The call of Jeremiah.
2:1–4:4	Indictment of the nation's sin.
4:5–6:30	The coming disaster "from the north."
7:1–10:25	**First editorial addition to Baruch's scroll**
7:1–8:3	Temple sermons and appended sayings.
8:4–9:21	An incorrigible people and their tragic ruin.
9:22–10:16	Miscellaneous sayings.
10:17–25	An incorrigible people and their tragic ruin.
11:1–20:18	**Second editorial addition to Baruch's scroll**
11:1–17	Preaching on the broken covenant.
11:18–12:6	Jeremiah's persecution by his relatives and fellow townsmen.
12:7–17	God expresses His sorrow for the dereliction of His people.
13:1–27	Parabolic vision of the linen waistcloth and attached sayings.
14:1–15:4	The time of drought and national emergency.
15:5–16:21	Oracles and confessions in poetry and prose.
17:1–27	Miscellany.
18:1–23	Jeremiah at the potter's house and attached sayings.
19:1–20:18	Prophetic symbolism and the persecutions; further confessions.
21:1–24:10	**Oracles concerning the House of David and the prophets.**
25:1–38	**Oracles against foreign nations**
26:1–29:32	**The biography of Jeremiah**
26:1–24	The "Temple sermon"; Jeremiah narrowly escapes death.
27:1–28:17	Events of 594 B.C.E.; the incident of the ox-yoke.
29:1–32	594 B.C.E.: Jeremiah and the exile in Babylon.
30:1–31:40	**The "Book of Consolation."**
32:1–44:30	**The biography of Jeremiah.**
32:1–33:26	Restoration of Judah and Jerusalem.
34:1–7	Words of Jeremiah as the Babylonian blockade tightens.
34:8–22	Incidents during lifting of siege.
35:1–19	Jeremiah and the Rechabites.
36:1–32	Incident of the scroll.
37:1–10	Incident during lifting of siege.
37:11–38:28	Jeremiah in prison.
39:1–40:6	Jeremiah's release from prison.
40:7–43:7	Assassination of Gedaliah and the flight to Egypt.
43:8–44:30	Jeremiah in Egypt.
45:1–5	**Baruch**
46:1–51:64	**Oracles against foreign nations**
52:1–34	**The fall of Jerusalem**

The Life and Message of Jeremiah

Despite the greater knowledge of Jeremiah's life than of any other prophet's, no biography of him can be written, for the available facts are too meager. Important background information is found in Scripture in II Kings, II Chronicles, Zephanaiah, Nahum, Habakkuk, and Obadiah. Other important sources on Jeremiah's times are the Hebrew letters from Lachish, primary documents from Egypt and Mesopotamia, and the histories of Herodotus and Josephus. It is noteworthy that II Kings, which describes events contemporary with Jeremiah in great detail, does not mention the prophet. Inasmuch as there is no direct attestation of the prophet outside the book that bears his name, scholars differ widely in their estimations of the prophet's historicity. At one extreme Holladay believes that allowing for small exceptions, the narratives and poetic sections in Jeremiah are contemporary with the prophet. They were written by Jeremiah or Baruch, and one may outline the details of Jeremiah's personality and his life by drawing on these sources. At the other extreme Carroll believes that Jeremiah is merely a literary character and there is no way of knowing whether what is narrated of him is anchored at all in historical reality. Hoffman (27–9) demonstrates the flaws of both extremes and offers his own middle-of-the-road approach, which will be, in essentials, followed here. Later generations esteemed Jeremiah greatly. According to the Chronicler (II Chr. 35:25) Jeremiah composed a lament over Josiah. His prophecies about the duration of the exile are cited in II Chronicles 36:15–21 by the author of the ninth chapter of Daniel, and probably underlie Haggai 1:2. Later writers interpolated their own compositions into his prophecies. The apocryphal Epistle of Jeremy (see *Jeremiah, Epistle of), a polemic against idolatry allegedly written by Jeremiah to the exiles in Babylonia is styled after Jeremiah 29. According to the second chapter of II Maccabees, Jeremiah secreted the ark, the tabernacle, and the altar of incense. In the New Testament, Jeremiah 31:14 (15) is quoted directly in Matthew 2:17, and his vision of the New Covenant/Testament (Jer. 31:31–34; cf. Jer. 32:38–40) is quoted in Hebrews 8:8–12 and 10:16–17. Jewish tradition identifies Jeremiah as the author of his book, of Kings, and of Lamentations (this last probably on the basis of II Chronicles 35:25).

It is known that Jeremiah's birthplace was *Anathoth (Jer. 1:1; 11:21, 23; 29:27; 32:7–9), a Benjaminite village some 4 mi. (c. 7 km.) northeast of Jerusalem. Among its inhabitants were men of priestly lineage, as shown by the reference in Jeremiah 1:1 to "the priests in Anathoth," and the appearance of Anathoth in an old list of levitical towns (Josh. 21:18). Jeremiah himself was of a priestly family of means and could spend 17 shekels on a symbolic action (cf. Jer. 32:9). He could afford to hire Baruch, son of Neriah, as a personal secretary. Jeremiah's father was a certain Hilkiah (Jer. 1:1), not to be confused with the contemporary high priest bearing the same name (II Kings 22:4ff.). It is generally assumed that Jeremiah's family was descended from David's priest *Abiathar, whom Solomon later banished to Anathoth (I Kings 2:26–27). There is much to recommend this opinion, since it is unlikely that so small a village could contain several unrelated priestly families. Jeremiah is never called a priest. He must have been born around 645 B.C.E., since he began his prophetic career in the 13th year of Josiah's reign (Jer. 1:2; 25:3), i.e., in 627 B.C.E., when he was still a very young man (1:6). He received a name whose antecedents go back to the early second millennium and, apparently quite common in biblical times, meaning "May the Lord lift up" (Heb. *yerim-yahu*), as reflected in the Greek transcription *Ieremias* as compared with the Hebrew יִרְמְיָהוּ or יִרְמְיָה. Nothing is known of Jeremiah's childhood and youth, except that he did not marry (16:1–4), which he attributed to a divine command. According to chapter 16 the divine command was due to the fact that in the coming disaster parents and their children would all perish. Jeremiah lived to see the dramatic events from the dissolution of the Assyrian Empire to the fall of the Judahite kingdom in 587 B.C.E., when the Neo-Babylonian Empire, after an interval of Judahite national independence and a few years of Egyptian supremacy, put an end to the kingdom of Judah. Jeremiah was deeply concerned with the march of events in his time, and every act of that tragic drama is reflected in his book. His words and deeds can often therefore be related to known events to a degree unparalleled by other prophets. Jeremiah's deeply personal poems, the so-called "confessions," express his reactions toward his fate and reveal his temptations and his wrestling with God. The divine compulsion was laid upon him, overruling his objections (Jer. 20:7), and Jeremiah exercised his ministry unremittingly as long as he lived.

BEGINNINGS OF PROPHECY. (See Table: Book of Jeremiah.) He began to preach in 627 with the chastening conviction that his country was under judgment. Even if Josiah's efforts for a cultic reform were already in motion, the evil legacy of Manasseh's reign in Judah and of the Assyrian occupation in the Northern provinces still encumbered the land. As a member of a monolatrous or monotheistic minority, Jeremiah could not tolerate the worship of other gods alongside of Yahweh. He thundered against it, and warned of its dire consequences, as did *Zephaniah, who was also active at the time. His precise attitude toward the reform, which reached its climax in 622 (cf. II Kings 22–23), five years after he had begun his ministry, is disputed. The most plausible supposition is that Jeremiah, though taking no direct part in its implementation, was in favor of its essential aim of reviving the ancient Mosaic covenant in which he had presumably been nurtured. Some of his oracles addressed to the Northern Kingdom even seem to indicate that he was favorable to the centralization of the cult in Jerusalem (cf. Jer. 3:14–15; 31:10–14; though some doubt these to be genuinely from Jeremiah), while others indicate a critical stance (Jer. 7:4). Jeremiah belonged by sympathy as well as by descent to the Northern Kingdom. Many of his first oracles are concerned with, and even addressed to, the remaining Israelites at Samaria. Accordingly, he is saturated with the thought and teaching of *Hosea, the finest representative of northern Israelite prophetism. The resemblance between the two prophets appears not only in the use of language and figures: it extends itself to fundamental ideas on God and His relation to Israel. Hosea seems to have been the first prophet to describe the relation of Yahweh to Israel metaphorically in terms of ancient Israelite marriage, whereby a man might be polygynous, while a woman was required to limit herself to one husband. Thus Yahweh might have two wives, Israel and Judah (cf. Ezek. 23), but neither of these could have another husband, i.e., serve another god. Using Hosea's marital image (Jer. 2:2b–3; 3:1–5, 19–25; 4:1–2), Jeremiah urges submission to the Yahweh on His own terms, expressed in the covenantal law. The Covenant required Israel to acknowledge no other god than Yahweh. Its leading principle was that Israel owed everything to the divine love which had brought it into being and without which it could not continue. The only worthy response to this free grace was a love involving submission and loyalty.

However, Israel was unfaithful to its God. Instead of repaying Him with due love, the people betrayed Him as an unfaithful wife betrays her husband for a lover (Jer. 3:20). Jeremiah therefore bids them to worship the Lord with repentance.

AFTER THE DEATH OF JOSIAH. It is a widely held view that Jeremiah was silent for a long time after the reform had been completed. The point is difficult to settle, since there is no evidence save Jeremiah's undated sayings and since almost nothing is known of Judah's internal affairs during Josiah's later years. In any case, his famous "Temple sermon" (7:2–15) is precisely dated (26:1) in Jehoiakim's accession year, i.e., the autumn of 609 or the winter of 609/8. From this address, uttered a few months after Josiah's death at Megiddo, it is clear that Jeremiah was disappointed by the results which followed the Josianic reform. Judah, by this reform, made the Temple with its sacrifices and its ritual essential to a correct relation to God. To maintain the true religion and the people's access to God, the people must only come to the one sanctuary and worship through a legitimate priesthood. Jeremiah violently rejected that vision because it not only neglected the moral principles of the Covenant, but facilitated trust in the notion that the temple cult absolved all sins, even worship of Baal (Jer. 7: 9–11; cf. Lev. 16: 30–34). This developed into a religious controversy in which the parties were sharply divided, their differences concerning the question of what does or does not constitute the essential element of the religion. The "Temple sermon" was intended to be a solemn indictment, an appeal to the national conscience. By taking this public action Jeremiah ran counter both to popular belief and official doctrine; he boldly challenged the policy of the nation's leaders, and in particular of the priests. He was also in strong antagonism with several of his fellow prophets, although he was not alone in his attitude of opposition. Another prophet, Uriah of Kiriath-Jearim, also appeared at the time, prophesying in the same terms as Jeremiah (Jer. 26:20–24). Efforts were made to silence Jeremiah and, indeed, his "Temple sermon" nearly cost him his life (Jer. 26). Authorities forbade his entrance to the Temple (36:5), and even inhabitants of his own village of Anathoth resolved to kill him if he persisted (11:18–23); members of his own family were implicated in this plot (12:6). Jeremiah's life thus entered an extremely difficult phase at the end of 609, although this did not last until his death. Nevertheless, Jeremiah continued his denunciations, without sparing the king (21:11–22:9). His message increasingly became one of stern warning of impending disaster. It was natural that he should insist that his word was the ancient word which formed the basis of Judah's religion, and that acceptance of it was essential to a correct relationship to God and, consequently, to the salvation of the nation from the impending calamity.

THE DESTRUCTION OF THE TEMPLE AND EXILE. When the Babylonian danger appeared on the horizon after the battle of Carchemish in 605 B.C.E., the prophet realized that his early prophecy of the awful "Foe from the North" (Jer. 1:13–16) was being fulfilled in the person of Nebuchadnezzar and his army; God's appointed agent of the judgment that would shortly fall upon the unrepentant people of Judah. He saw the task of announcing the imminent arrival of that danger as a leading feature of his mission to his nation and to the surrounding world. He then made a last effort to bring his country to its senses. As the priests had forbidden him to enter the Temple, he dictated to his friend and secretary *Baruch a selection of his preachings, and directed him to read the scroll in the Temple (Jer. 36). A favorable opportunity presented itself in 604 (36:9). Some high officials heard Baruch and brought the fact to the king's attention, as it also had a political bearing, the vision of the "Foe from the North" running like a red thread through the whole of Jeremiah's message. (In the ancient Near Eastern world administrators were responsible for reporting prophecies to the king. See *Mari.) Jehoiakim demanded to hear the scroll, but then snatched it from the reader's hands and threw it into the fire. He sent three men including his son to seize Jeremiah and Baruch, "but the Lord hid them" (Jer. 36:26–27). Jeremiah subsequently dictated the scroll again, with additions (36:32). The surrender of Jerusalem to the Babylonians in 597, and the deportation of King Jehoiachin and of the leading citizens seemed to confirm Jeremiah's warnings. The prophet told of the sad fate of the young king, a victim of his father's folly (Jer. 22:24–30; Cf. II Kings 23:36–24:16). At the same time, he saw in the exile of the national leaders the expression of the divine verdict. The messages he sent to the exiles reveal not only that fundamental conviction, but also his belief that the God worshiped in the Temple of Jerusalem was too great to be localized. The exiles were able to reach Him even in their new condition, far away from the soil of Israel and Judah (29:7). As well, Jeremiah told them to disregard the optimistic promises of their prophets (29:8–9). Such interventions of course brought Jeremiah into collision with the prophets who had been saying just the opposite (23:9–40; 28; 29:24–32), and with the contemporary national leaders who were making sacrifice at one shrine essential to the Judahite religion, thus tending dangerously to localize God and His grace in the sanctuary "which He chose out of all the tribes to set His name there." The contrary conviction of Jeremiah does not mean, however, that the prophet attached no specific content to the national religion. He admitted a particular relationship between Israel and God: Israel was set apart for Him as His property, His bride. This idea is already expressed in the early utterances of Jeremiah, addressed to the Northern Kingdom. Jeremiah believed that God had revealed Himself to Israel and chosen it to be His servant. Therefore he affirmed to the men of his generation the unique character of the God in whom he and they alike believed, together with the resultant uniqueness of His demands and the consequent reality of His guidance, which was not at the mercy of outward conditions or circumstances (18:3–10). The worship of the God of Israel thus could not disappear, even if His shrine and the sacrificial system disappeared, for it needed no more than prayer and obedience to His word. According to Jeremiah, everything else was an accessory. It is understandable, therefore, that after the Babylonians had destroyed the Temple and carried away the sacred vessels, Jeremiah was vindicated as the true prophet and the defender of the right religion. Jeremiah himself did not need to see these events to understand that resistance to Babylon was resistance to the Divine Will. He regarded the Babylonian army as an instrument in the Divine hands for carrying out a well-merited punishment on the guilty nation and its leaders. This conviction had arisen after the Babylonian victory at Carchemish in 605 B.C.E., but it became still stronger after the deportation of 597 B.C.E. From these historical events Jeremiah fully recognized that the power of Babylonia was irresistible and that the petty kingdom of Judah could not hope to oppose it. He concluded, therefore, that submission to Nebuchadnezzar was the will of God, who so punished the unfaithfulness of His people. The king of Babylon was the divine servant (27:6) whom the Lord was to employ for His purposes. When various vassals of Nebuchadnezzar in the West began to toy with the idea of rebellion and sent ambassadors to Jerusalem to discuss plans with King Zedekiah, Jeremiah flatly opposed such talk, appearing before the conspirators with an ox yoke on his neck and exhorting them to wear the yoke of Nebuchadnezzar (ch. 27). In the autumn of 589, when the Babylonians moved to attack Jerusalem, and later during the blockade of the city, Zedekiah sent more than once to Jeremiah asking for a word from the Lord. Yet Jeremiah gave the king no encouragement. On the contrary, he assured him that God Himself was fighting for the Babylonians (27:8). No wonder, therefore, that to Judah's leaders Jeremiah was an enemy. He was arrested, probably in the summer of 588, and remained in custody as long as the city held out. The biographical chapters 37–38 provide a circumstantial account of Jeremiah's fortunes during these tragic months. After the fall of Jerusalem in 587 B.C.E., the Babylonians allowed Jeremiah to remain with the new governor *Gedaliah at Mizpah. When Gedaliah was murdered after only a few weeks of governorship (41:1–2), his followers, fearing Babylonian reprisals, fled to Egypt, taking the prophet with them against his will (Jer. 40–43). Jeremiah was reluctant to leave the country, since he attributed the value of a sign or symbol of hope perhaps to his presence in the land. He was indeed convinced that God's purpose could not be exhausted in punishment. After 70 years of a human lifespan (Ps. 90:10; Isa. 23:15), nearly the entire sinful generation would be dead, and God, he believed, would then contract a new covenant with the new people (29:10–11; cf. 31:31–34). The refugees who had taken Jeremiah with them found asylum at Tahpanhes (Daphne), the present-day Tell Defneh, just within the Egyptian border, east of the Delta. There the last words recorded from Jeremiah were uttered (43:8–13; 44). After this, no more is heard of him. Presumably, he did not survive for long and died in his sixties. According to a later tradition recorded by Tertullian (*Adversus Gnosticos*, ch. 8, in *Patrologia Latina*, vol. 2, col. 137) and Jerome (*Adversus Jovinianum*, 2:37, *ibid.*, 23, col. 335), he was stoned. Pseudo-Epiphanius (*De vitis Prophetarium*, in *Patrologia Graeca*, vol. 43, col. 400) and Isidorus Hispalensis (*De Ortu et Obitu Patrorum*, ch. 38, in *Patrologia Latina*, vol. 83, col. 142) even affirm that this happened in Tahpanhes. The unreliability of this tradition is evident from a passage of Jerome's commentary on Isaiah, where he records another tradition according to which Jeremiah died in Egypt of a natural death.

The Composition of the Book

The Book of Jeremiah exists in two versions, one in the masoretic text, and another in the Septuagint. The latter does not place the prophecies against foreign nations at the end of the book, but after Jeremiah 23:13a. Moreover, they are not arranged there in the same order as in the masoretic text. The Septuagint version is much shorter: about one-eighth of the masoretic text is missing, mostly single verses or parts of verses, but also entire sections such as 33:14–26; 39:4–13; 51:44b–49a; and 52:27b–30. In some cases the omissions may have been made intentionally, as, for instance, where the translators omitted doublets in their second occurrence or shortened a difficult text. Other lacunae may be explained by textual criticism, as in cases of homoioteleuton, when the scribe's eye leaped over material between two sentences with similar endings (Jer. 39:4–13; 51:44b–49a). However, most of the omissions imply the existence of a shorter form of the Hebrew text. This is now clear from discoveries made at Qumran, where manuscript fragments representing both the longer and the shorter form of the text have been found (see Dead Sea *Scrolls). Thus the masoretic text and the Greek translation are based on different versions of the Hebrew text of Jeremiah. In the last pre-Christian centuries there were at least two versions of the book of Jeremiah in circulation. Both versions seem to have a relatively long history of scribal transmission behind them. However, since the Septuagint does not reveal a tendency to abbreviate plain passages, while the masoretic text seems to be an expanded one, the Hebrew archetype of the Septuagint has been considered as representing a more nearly original form to the text, superior to the late masoretic text. Some changes, however, were made in the Septuagint in the same direction as in the accepted Hebrew text. The different arrangement of some parts of the Book of Jeremiah in the masoretic text and in the Septuagint, as well as the existence of doublets, show that the book is a collection of shorter "books" plus miscellaneous material. Such "books" are explicitly mentioned in chapter 36, which gives a valuable account of Jeremiah's dictation of many of his oracles to his scribe Baruch, as well as in 25:13a; 30:2; 45:1; and 51:60. Tradition attributes the authorship of all of them to the prophet Jeremiah, but it is clear that not all the material can be derived from him. This is manifest in the case of chapter 52, which could only have been composed after 561 B.C.E. In other sections of the book, too, everything cannot come from the prophet himself (see tables in Hoffman, 62–66). This is certainly true for the narratives which use the third person in speaking of Jeremiah. In his commentary (1901), B. Duhm laid down the principle that only poetic passages can genuinely be attributed to the prophet. He held that the book consists of three types of material: Jeremiah's own words, almost exclusively poetry in *kinah* meter, comprising 280 masoretic verses; Baruch's life of Jeremiah, 220 verses; and later additions, 850 verses, which have much in common either with Deutero- and Trito- *Isaiah, or with the Deuteronomistic parts of the Former Prophets. A monograph published by S. Mowinckel in 1914 distinguished four principal sources in the Book of Jeremiah, designated as A, B, C, and D. A was Baruch's scroll, dictated by Jeremiah, with additions made by someone living in Egypt between 580 and 480 B.C.E. This collection is now contained within chapters 1–24, and is the most authentic part of the book. B was a biography of Jeremiah, based upon oral tradition written down by someone in Egypt in the same period as A; it is contained within chapters 19:1–20:6 and 26–45. C is the Deuteronomic source, composed in the fourth century B.C.E. and consisting mainly of 3:6–13; 7:1–8:3; 11:1–5, 9–14; 18:1–12; 21:1–10; 22:1–5; 25:1–11a; 29:1–23; 32:1–2, 6–16, 24–44; 34:1–22; 35:1–19; 39:15–18; 44:1–14; and ch. 45. D is the famous "Book of Comfort" or "Book of Consolation" in 30:1–31:40, dating from post-Exilic times. From the same period dates the complex of oracles concerning foreign nations (chs. 46–51), with some genuine Jeremianic elements. This collection was only later joined to Jeremiah 1–45. Mowinckel upholds the main lines of this view in his treatment of Jeremiah in the Norwegian translation issued in 1944, and, briefly, in *Prophecy and Tradition* (1946, pp. 61–65, 105–6). However, instead of sources he speaks of "traditionary circles," obviously sharing the opinion of H. Birkeland, who in 1938 introduced the views of H.S. Nyberg into criticism of the prophets and stressed the influence of the oral tradition, even when a written tradition was already in existence. According to Birkeland, the poetic sections of Jeremiah were written down earlier than the prose sermons composed in the style of Deuteronomic preaching; he thus admitted the possibility a Jeremianic nucleus in those sermons. In contrast, R.H. Pfeiffer (*Introduction to the Old Testament* (1941), 504–5) considers that Baruch combined words dictated or written by the prophet himself with his own biography of Jeremiah, revising and rewriting many of his master's sayings in his own Deuteronomistic style. Without admitting that Baruch was the author of the Deuteronomic sections (C), Mowinckel also shared this view, inasmuch as he considered Baruch to be responsible for the combination of the elements A and B. He held that around 580 B.C.E., Baruch concluded that large editorial unit with the words the prophet had addressed to him personally; this conclusion is found in Jeremiah 45, which therefore does not belong to C. Also according to Mowinckel, C was later incorporated into the "Book of Baruch" (A and B), probably when the Deuteronomistic tradition of Jeremiah was already fixed in writing. In regard to this tradition the opinion is widely held that these prose discourses represent the work of exilic authors who reconstructed the teachings of Jeremiah in terms of Deuteronomic theology, which provided an explanation of Judah's tragedy in 587 B.C.E. A stylistic approach of those "Deuteronomistic" speeches, attempted mainly by J. Bright and W.L. Holladay, led to their conclusion that the style of C is characteristic of the rhetorical prose of the late seventh and early sixth century in Judah, and that many of its typical phrases are a reshaping in prose of expressions which either are original to the genuine poetry of Jeremiah or, though not specifically Jeremianic, were employed by the prophet in his poetic oracles in an original fashion. These conclusions, if correct, suggest that the nucleus and basic content of C were authentically Jeremianic. It has also appeared in recent years that the principal literary types A, B, and C do not by themselves furnish an effective key for the study of the composition of Jeremiah. The latter is indeed not arranged according to the style of its various parts. C. Rietzschel therefore presented a new thesis regarding its composition (1966). He accepts the basic principles of classification of the literary material on the grounds of form and style, as developed mainly by S. Mowinckel, but denies that this can provide a sufficient indication of the way in which the book was composed. In particular, he holds that it cannot be assumed that poetic and prose material was handed down separately, although he links the C material with the homiletical speeches in Deuteronomistic parts of the Former Prophets. He proposes to reconstruct the process of the book's composition by an agglomeration of tradition complexes. He distinguishes in the Book of Jeremiah four main tradition blocks: (1) oracles of doom against Judah and Jerusalem (Jer. 1–24); (2) oracles of doom against foreign nations (Jer. 25; 46–51); (3) oracles of salvation for Israel and Judah (Jer. 26–35); and (4) cycle of narratives about the prophet (Jer. 36–44). He divides the first block into six complexes, namely Jeremiah 1–6, 7–10, 11–13, 14–17, 18–20, and 21–24, four of which are introduced by a Deuteronomic speech beginning with the words "the word that came to Jeremiah from the Lord" (Jer. 7:1; 11:1; 18:1; 21:1). The oracle to Baruch in Jeremiah 45 originally stood just after 20:18, so that 21–24 is an appendix to the first tradition block. Rietzschel concludes that Baruch's scroll is to be found in 1–6, and that 7–20 represents the "other words added," which are referred to in 36:32. The approach of Rietzschel has earned its place alongside earlier attempts to solve the problems of the composition of the Book of Jeremiah. The recent Hebrew commentary of Y. Hoffman argues that a stylistic study shows that most of the poetic material comes from a single source. As such, claims that the same individual could not have written both laments and hymns and prophecies of destruction and restoration is purely arbitrary. Indeed, the similarities between the poetic rebukes and the oracles to the nations show that most of the oracles to the nations can be attributed to Jeremiah, although their present form shows substantial additions. As far as the prose contents are concerned, the biographical material on the prophet and the sermons are stylistically close enough to originate in a single stream of tradition, though not in the work of a single author. With most scholars, Hoffman identifies characteristic Deuteronomic language in these sections, but argues that they often employ terminology that diverges from that of the Deuteronomic school; an indication that these sections originated in circles of disciples of Jeremiah who were influenced by the Deuteronomists but distinct from them. Hoffman identifies five stages in the book's composition: (1) the prophecies of Jeremiah before 604; (2) the prophecies both of rebuke and hope between 604 and 586; (3) post-586 psalms, narratives, and sermons with a Jeremianic core but mostly the work of transmitters of tradition who made use of the language of the Deuteronomists; (4) a second set of later additions; (5) the latest additions, which are found in the masoretic Jeremiah, but missing from the Hebrew text utilized by the Greek translators.

Whatever conclusions one reaches about the history of composition, it is plain that there were in existence oral and written sources previous to the actual blocks of material within the Book of Jeremiah. The following exposition deals first with the oracles against foreign nations (25; 46–51) and the so-called "Book of Consolation" (30–31). Then the narratives, both in the biographical and autobiographical styles, are examined. Finally Baruch's scroll (1–6) with its additions (7–20), and the oracles concerning the House of David and the prophets (21–24) are reviewed.

Oracles Against Foreign Nations

The introduction to this passage block is to be sought in 25:1–13a. This is more apparent in the Septuagint, which inserts the whole of chapters 46–51 between verses 13a and 13b, but in a different order (49:34–39; 46; 50–51; 47; 49:7–22; 49:1–6; 49:28–33; 49:23–27; 48). Jeremiah 25:13b–38 is the conclusion of that "book." It corresponds to chapters 25–32 of the Septuagint and forms a collection of prophecies concerning foreign nations, grouped together as the similar prophecies in the Books of Isaiah (Isa. 13–23) and Ezekiel (Ezek. 25–32). The Jeremianic nucleus of that block included at least chapters 46–47, which seem to date from the years 605–604; the oracle on Kedar (49:28–33), probably to be connected with the Babylonian campaign against the Arabs in the winter of 599–598; and the oracle on Elam (49:34–39), which goes back to the year 596/5, when an Elamite king, on the eve of engaging in battle against Nebuchadnezzar on the bank of the Tigris, decided to return to his land. The authentically Jeremianic collection was later expanded by the addition of the complex of oracles against Moab (48), Ammon (49:1–6), and Edom (49:7–22), the three Transjordanian kingdoms which had been entirely taken over by Arab tribes toward the end of the sixth century B.C.E. The oracles may reflect an early phase of these events, unless they allude to a campaign of Nebuchadnezzar against Moab and Ammon, dated by Josephus (Ant., 10:180–181) in the fifth year after the fall of Jerusalem, i.e., in 582 B.C.E. The prophecies concerning Moab and Edom contain numerous prose comments and enlargements, and much of their material is to be found in a substantially identical form elsewhere in the Bible, above all in Isaiah 15–16 and Obadiah 1–10. It must be assumed, therefore, that Jeremiah 48:1–49:22 consists basically of anonymous passages, commented and expanded, probably with references to historical events in 582 or later in the sixth century. Another anonymous passage, concerning Damascus and dating probably from the eighth century, was subsequently added to this collection (49:23–27). The book was most likely finished at the beginning of the fifth century. Some glosses were later added to the archetype of the masoretic text. The disposition of the material in the Septuagint reflects, on the other hand, a secondary rearrangement of the oracles. Elam, probably identified with Persia, is mentioned first; then follow the two other empires, Egypt and Babylonia. After this, the small neighboring countries are mentioned: first Philistia and Edom in southern Palestine, then Ammon, Kedar, and Damascus in the east. The long oracle against Moab closes the series.

"The Book of Consolation"

The introduction to this section appears in Jeremiah 30:1–3. It consists of the whole of chapters 30–31, which contain Jeremiah's prophecies addressed to the Northern Kingdom during Josiah's reign. These two chapters consist of a collection of originally separated passages, mostly poetic. Because they develop the theme of Israel's comfort and restoration, some scholars dated them from the Exilic period and argued that relatively few of these passages can be genuinely attributed to Jeremiah. However, they overlooked the reference to the oppressed people as "Ephraim" (31:5[6], 8[9], 17[18], 19[20]), and the mention of Samaria in 31:4[5]. The names Israel and Jacob must therefore be understood as denoting the tribes of the former kingdom of Samaria, whose territories had been liberated by Josiah and united again to Judah (cf. II Kings 23:15–20; II Chron. 34:6–7). Stylistic similarities to Deutero-Isaiah in Jeremiah 30:10 or 31:6–8 can be explained on the supposition that both prophets made use of the same conventional forms of priestly oracles. The prose passages in 30:8–9 and 31:22–33, 38–40 were probably added to the collection, but at least 31:30–33 may contain a nucleus of Jeremianic words originally addressed to the Northern Kingdom. The entire "Book of Consolation" (30–31) stands as a separate block of material in the midst of a series of chapters, mostly biographical in character (Jer. 26–29; 32–44). It was inserted after 29:32, which quotes the Lord's word alluding to "the good things that I am going to do for you." Thus the place was well suited for the insertion of the "Book of Consolation."

The "Biography" of Jeremiah

Chapters 26–29 and 32–44 are mostly biographical in character. The actual sequence of narratives reflects not only a secondary redistribution of the various episodes, but also points to a series of editors who successively handled materials from different sources. For instance, chapters 27–29 are sometimes considered as belonging to one source. The reason for deriving them from a common author is that they call the Babylonian king Nebuchadnezzar, departing from the correct spelling Nebuchadrezzar of the rest of the Book of Jeremiah, and that they speak of "Jeremiah the prophet." Yet it is noteworthy that chapters 27 and 28 differ in one cardinal point. Chapter 27 introduces Jeremiah in the first person. Chapter 28 begins in verse 1 with the first person, and then suddenly and unaccountably breaks off to speak of "Jeremiah the prophet" (verses 5 ff.). This points to a combination of the chapters by a redactor, who imperfectly joined the first and third person narratives. The slight change involved in the spelling of Nebuchadnezzar's name throughout may be due to him. The problem of the composition of the "biographical" chapters is thus rather complicated. The heterogeneous complex of chapters 27–35 has been inserted in the continuous narrative of Jeremiah 26; 36:1–37:10; 38; 39:3, with, as a conclusion, the oracle to Ebed-Melech in 39:15–18. The latter's content and position at the end of the book can be compared with those of the oracles to Baruch in Jeremiah 45, which originally ended the block of Jeremiah 1–20. This whole narrative covers the period from 609 to the liberation of Jeremiah by the Babylonians in July 587, and might have been written at the request of Ebed-Melech by Baruch, known to have been an intimate of Jeremiah from 605 (36:4, 5) until after 587 (32:12, 43:3, 6). In any case, Baruch is the most likely candidate for the authorship of these sections, which seem to come from an eyewitness. The end of 39:14 suggests that this literary unit was completed between the fall of Jerusalem and the murder of Gedaliah, i.e., in 587.

Another, shorter report of Jeremiah's imprisonment and liberation in 37:11–21; 39:11; and 40:2a, 4–6, states that Jeremiah was chained in the court of the guard (37:21). This brief account must also have been composed prior to the assassination of Gedaliah. A third narrative in 39:1–2, 4–10; 40:7–41:18; and 43:5–6b, 7a concerns Jerusalem's capture and Gedaliah's murder, in which Jeremiah played no role. This composition, too, can safely be dated in the year 587. It was used somewhat later as an historical framework by another author, who intended to expand the narrative of 37:11–21; 39:11; and 40:2a, 4–6 by telling the end of Jeremiah's career in Egypt. He composed at least all the sections of chapters 42–43, where the expression "Jeremiah the prophet" appears (42:2, 4; 43:6). The largest part of 42:1–4, 7–9a, 19; 43:2–4, and the additions in 40:2b–3 and 43:6, 7 are to be ascribed to him. This editorial unit thus included in Jeremiah 37:11–21; 39:12, 4–11; 40:2–41:18; 42:1–4, 7–9a, 19; 43:2–7a. The remaining parts of chapters 42–43 seem to reflect the same hand as chapter 44. Since the author already knew that Hophra, the king of Egypt (usually called Apries), had been given over to his enemies (44:30) and since it is known that he was overthrown and killed by Amasis in about 568 B.C.E., it can safely be concluded that this part of Jeremiah's biography was completed, probably in Egypt, a short time after this event. This is confirmed by the allusion made in 42:8–13 to the invasion of Egypt by Nebuchadnezzar in the year 568/7 (cf. Pritchard, Texts, 308). The author of that section could therefore be a somewhat younger contemporary of Jeremiah. It is uncertain whether he is also responsible for the assemblage of a larger part of the biographical chapters, and the consequent insertion of transitional verses, such as 39:13 or 40:1. These verses reveal a misunderstanding of the historical situation, since from 39:14 and 40:4 it is known that Jeremiah was not chained in order to be deported to Babylon. Several biographical passages in the tradition block inserted in Jeremiah 27–35 were originally redacted as first person narratives. To this group belong the incident of the ox yoke (27:2–22), Jeremiah's purchase of land (32:6–44), and the example of the Rechabites (35:2–19). These episodes have as common features not only the autobiographical style but also a typical content consisting of a symbolic action, explained by the prophet. Similar narratives in autobiographical style are found in other parts of the book: the wine jars (13:12–14), the potter at his work (18:2–12), the breaking of the bottle (19:1–2, 10–11a, 12a). These three passages seem to constitute an editorial unit on the common theme of pottery. The last two episodes are even connected by the catchword *yoẓer* ("potter"). They were inserted by a redactor in their actual place, probably as comments to 16:18 and 18:23. The exhortation on the observance of the Sabbath in 17:19–27 is most likely a still later insertion. All narratives of that type may have belonged to a single collection written or dictated by Jeremiah himself and reused later, with some additions, by the editors of the complexes of 11–20 and 27–35. The acted parables referred to above can be compared with the symbolic visions, also composed in autobiographical style: the almond rod (1:11–12), the bubbling pot (1:13–16), the linen waistcloth (13:1–11), the two baskets of figs (24:1–10), and the cup of wine (25:15, 17, 27–28).

Baruch's Scroll with Additions

From chapter 36 it is known that Jeremiah's utterances were first committed to writing in the fourth year of Jehoiakim's reign, i.e., in 605, when the prophet dictated them to his friend Baruch. After the scroll had been destroyed by the king, Jeremiah was directed to rewrite its contents in a second scroll, in which Baruch "wrote ... under Jeremiah's dictation everything that was in the book that Jehoiakim, king of Judah, had thrown into the fire. And, in addition to this, many further words of the same sort were added" (36:32). The conclusion of that scroll is to be found in Jeremiah 45, as shown by C. Rietzschel; "these sayings" in verse 1 refer directly to the content of the scroll. As verse 3 echoes 20:18, the catchword being *yagon* ("sorrow"), and since verse 4 alludes to Jeremiah 1:10, it can be concluded that Jeremiah 1–20 roughly corresponds to the final form of Baruch's scroll. It can be safely assumed, following C. Rietzschel, that chapters 1–6 represent the original scroll rewritten by Baruch under the prophet's dictation, while chapters 7–20 contain the successive additions to it. The scroll is introduced by the description of the prophet's call (ch. 1), which follows the usual pattern of the "call" narratives, as established by N. Habel. The literary form for the call of a divine representative was taken over from the practice reflected in Genesis 24:34–38, according to which messengers entrusted with a special mission presented their "credentials" in a specific order and manner. In so doing they not only explained the reason for their coming, but also repeated their master's commission ceremony, in which the precise words of the command were preserved, their own objections registered, and the assurance of the protective angel's presence given. In addition to this, the agent of the overlord could adduce any further evidence, such as an omen or sign, which would give added weight to his claim. By utilizing this ancient pattern, later authors and prophets emphasized the primary function of the individual who was called. The genre concerns the commissioning of messengers to God's service. Therefore, in employing its form, a prophet announces publicly that God commissioned him as His spokesman and representative. The "call" narrative of Jeremiah 1 thus provides the authentication of Jeremiah's right to speak in God's name. Since it does so in a form appropriate for public affirmation of the divine origin of his message, it was almost certainly the introduction to the scroll which Jeremiah dictated to Baruch in 605, and which he intended to be read publicly before the people in the Temple area. The "Foe from the North" constitutes a feature in which Jeremiah 4:5–6:30 advances beyond Jeremiah 2:1–4:4, so that it is reasonable to assume that 4:5–6:30 contains mostly oracles composed in 605, while 2:1–4:4 belongs to an earlier date. The Babylonian invader is mentioned, or alluded to, in 4:6–7, 13, 15–17, 21, 29; 5:6, 15–17; 6:1–6, 12, 22–25. He approached from the North to inflict on the people the judgment announced in the previous part of the scroll. The general theme of 2:1–4:4 is the nation's sin. Chapter 2 is a series of passages dealing with a single theme, the bulk of which comes from an early period of Jeremiah's ministry and was first addressed to the Northern Kingdom, but was most likely given its present form by the prophet himself in connection with the scroll of 605. The poetic material in chapters 3:1–5, 19–25; 4:1–2 forms a continuous unit which is a sample of Jeremiah's preaching prior to 622, certainly before he was launched on the stormy currents of the political and religious life of Jerusalem. This is supported by the extent to which these oracles are saturated with the fundamental ideas of Hosea. These similarities to Hosea, characteristic of the young Jeremiah, are striking not only in the dominant theme of the adulterous wife, but even in particular expressions. The poem was initially an appeal to conversion directed to the Northern Kingdom, but the piece actually concludes with a formally separate oracle of solemn warning addressed to the people of Judah and Jerusalem (Jer. 4:3–4). It prepares the theme of the "Foe from the North," developed in the following chapters, and most likely dates to the year 605. The material in 3:6–18 has a somewhat more complicated history. This section begins with a prose monologue addressed to Jeremiah by the Lord (verses 6–12a), in which the two adulterous, i.e., apostate, sisters – Israel and Judah – are compared to each other, to the immense disadvantage of the latter. The allusion in verse 8 to verses 1–5 shows that this monologue was composed in relation to the poem of 3:1–5, 19–25; 4:1–2, in order to emphasize that Judah's sin was bigger than that of Israel's. The passage probably goes back to the reign of Josiah, as verse 6 explicitly states, but dates after 622, as verse 10 brands Josiah's reform as a failure. The monologue leads to a short lyric in which the prophet summons the Northern Kingdom to return to the Lord, to worship Him on Mount Zion, and to accept the guidance of his new rulers (verses 12b–15). These verses most likely allude to Josiah's reform and to his expansionist activity in the territory of the defunct northern state; they probably date before 622. Verses 16–18, on the other hand, seem in their present form to presuppose the exile of Judah, and were in all likelihood written, or rewritten, after 587. Chapters 4:5–6:30 constitute a long editorial unit composed from a series of originally separate passages, all of which deal with the terrible disaster from the north that is about to overtake the nation (4:6; 6:1, 22; cf. 1:13–15; 10:22; 13:20; 25:9; 46:6, 24; 47:2). The entire section thus develops the theme sounded in 4:3–4. The poems are so graphic and vivid that it may be assumed, as noted above, that most of them were composed during the actual approach of Nebuchadnezzar's army in 605/4. Chapters 7–10 constitute the first editorial addition to Baruch's original scroll. The material is rather miscellaneous in character, but is dominated by two major themes: the stubborn sinfulness of the people, and the tragic fate that is about to overtake them. The section opens with the famous "Temple sermon" (7:2–15), delivered in Jehoiakim's accession year, i.e., in the autumn of 609 or in the winter of 609/8. The text is in prose and preserves the gist of what he said. Also in prose are 7:16–20, 21–28, 29–34 and 8:1–3, which, in the main, may reflect Jeremiah's preaching during Jehoiakim's reign (609–598 B.C.E.). The complexes of poems in 8:4–17 and 9:1–8 probably date to the same period. Between these passages is Jeremiah's lament over a national disaster (8:18–23), which can either refer to the defeat at Megiddo in 609 or the raids prior to the Babylonian attack in 598/7 (cf. II Kings 24:2). An oracle (Jer. 9:9–10, 16–21; 10:17–22) with dirges over the ruin of Jerusalem (9:18, 20–21; 10:19–20) follows; it was perhaps uttered on the eve of the siege and deportation of 598/7. Probably non-Jeremianic passages were later inserted, namely in 9:11–15 and 9:22–10:16. This first addition to Baruch's scroll (chapters 7–10) ends with a prayer for mercy (10:23–25). The second added complex is perhaps to be found in chapters 11–20. This unit consists basically of a series of prose passages in autobiographical style and of several series of poems. The complex begins with Jeremiah's preaching on the Covenant (11:1–17), for which he was persecuted by his own relatives and fellow townsmen (11:18–12:6). This piece is followed by a poem (12:7–13), in which God expresses His sorrow for the dereliction of His people, perhaps caused by the raids just prior to the Babylonian invasion of 598/7 (cf. II Kings 24:2). A brief prose passage seems to be a comment on that poem (Jer. 12:14–17). Chapter 13 begins with the parabolic vision of the linen waistcloth, followed by an oracle explaining its meaning (13:1–11). Connected with this, probably because it too involves a parable, is a brief passage inspired by a popular witticism concerning wine jars (13:12–14). Several short poems, apparently composed not long before the first deportation in 597, continue that section in 13:15–27; 14:5–9. One of them, addressed to Jehoiachin and the queen mother (13:18–19), was clearly uttered just prior to Jerusalem's surrender in that year. This series of poems is interrupted by a national psalm of lamentation in time of drought (14:2–9, 19–22), which is divided in two by an oracle of doom (Jer. 14:10; cf. Hos. 8:13; 9:9) and by a prose commentary in autobiographical style (Jer. 14:11–16), that ends in 15:1–4. While the psalm may be an authentic liturgical text, the prose passage of 14:11–16; 15:1–4 may be Jeremiah's genuine utterances. After one of Jeremiah's "confessions" (15:10–11, 15–18) and a "private oracle" addressed to him (15:19–21) there is another passage in autobiographical style (16:1–13), in which Jeremiah relates how he had been forbidden to marry, or even to participate in the normal joys and sorrows of his people. Attached to this composition are eight brief heterogeneous passages (16:14–15, 16–18, 19–21; 17:1–4, 5–8, 9–10, 11, 12–13) and another "confession" (17:14–18). None of these pieces can be dated, but several may confidently be ascribed to him. A Jeremianic nucleus can also be found in the prose discourse of 17:19–27, which urges the keeping of the Sabbath and is redacted in autobiographical style. There follows the autobiographical narrative of Jeremiah's visit to the potter's house (18:1–12). Since the disaster announced by the prophet is described as still avoidable (18:11), the incident is probably not later than the first years of Jehoiakim's reign. Four poetic pieces are attached to this narrative: an oracle (18:13–17) and three more "confessions" (18:18–23; 20:7–13,

14–18), separated by the complex episode of the broken bottle (19:1–2, 10–11a, 12a) and of Jeremiah's arrest by Pashhur son of Immer (19:2, 3–9, 11b, 12b–15; 20:1–6). It is noteworthy that the so-called "confessions" are redacted in the style of the psalms of lamentation. It is doubtful whether they were ever publicly proclaimed by Jeremiah. The last "confession" is immediately followed by the conclusion of chapter 45.

Oracles Concerning the House of David and the Prophets Chapters 21–24 constitute a complex of two series of oracles, one concerning the royal house (21:11–23:8) and the other the cultic prophets (23:9–40). The actual unit is introduced by two prose passages (21:1–7, 8–10), whose Jeremianic nucleus goes back to the year 589/8. Its actual form, however, dates to after the fall of Jerusalem in 587. The reason for the choice of this passage as an introduction to the oracles concerning the royal house is given by the fact that it contains an oracle of doom directed to the king Zedekiah. Chapter 24, which closes the "book," is also a prose passage from Zedekiah's time, with another oracle of doom concerning that king (verses 8–10). This pattern of inclusion shows that chapters 21–24 constitute an editorial unit. The superscriptions in 21:11 and 23:9 prove that this unit groups two older passage complexes. The first one is an important collection of prophecies containing Jeremiah's judgments on the successive rulers in his day who occupied the throne of David. The opening passage of the section (21:11–22:9), almost equally divided between poetry and prose, sets forth the principle that the Davidic monarchy is under obligation to God to establish justice in the kingdom. The sayings regarding Jehoahaz-Shallum (22:10–12) and Jehoiakim (22:13–19) follow in chronological order, and after a poem lamenting the fate of Jerusalem (22:20–23) there are two oracles concerning the young king Jehoiachin (22:24–27, 28–30). The original conclusion of the section is to be found in 23:1–2. It is followed by three brief oracles, of which the first (23:3–4) and the third (23:7–8) are in prose and presuppose the Exile. The second oracle (23:5–6) is an extract from 33:14–16, originally a solemn announcement of the enthronement of Zedekiah, here called Yozedek, according to the Septuagint. The second collection deals mainly with cultic prophets (23:9–40). The poem in verses 9–12, which consists of a soliloquy of Jeremiah, concerns them only insofar as they, like the priests, share in the general corruption (verse 11). However, the two poems in verses 13–15 and 16–22, and the piece in verses 23–32, basically in prose, deal directly with the prophets who lull the people with fallacious promises. The final passage (verses 33–40), also in prose, mentions the prophets only in passing. Since the tension between Jeremiah and the cultic prophets reached its pitch in the days of Zedekiah, most of these passages probably date to that king's reign.

[Edward Lipinski / S. David Sperling (2nd ed.)]

IN THE AGGADAH

Jeremiah was descended from Joshua and Rahab (Meg. 14b). He was born circumcised (ARN[1] 2, 12), and already showed signs of his future calling when as a newborn infant he spoke in the voice of a youth and rebuked his mother for her unfaithfulness. He explained to his astonished mother that he was really rebuking the inhabitants of Zion and Jerusalem (PR 26:129). He was related to the prophetess *Huldah. She preached to the women while Zephaniah, another contemporary prophet, was active in the synagogue and Jeremiah preached to the men in the street (PR 26:129). When the pious King *Josiah restored the worship of God, Jeremiah brought back the ten exiled tribes (Ar. 33a). Although Josiah later warred with Egypt against the prophet's advice, Jeremiah knew that the king acted out of error since he was misinformed about the piety of his generation. The fourth chapter of *Lamentations, traditionally ascribed to Jeremiah, begins with a dirge for Josiah (Lam. R. 1:18, no. 53; 4:1, no. 1). The prophet suffered under Jehoiakim and even more during the reign of Zedekiah when both the populace and the monarch opposed him. The people mocked his rebukes claiming that as a descendant of the proselyte Rahab he had no right to reprimand them (PdRK 115), and maliciously accused him of illicit relations (BK 16b). His purpose in leaving Jerusalem for Anathoth was so that he could partake of his priestly portion. The watchman who arrested him on that occasion was a grandson of the false prophet *Hananiah b. Azur. In prison, his jailer, a friend of Hananiah b. Azur called Jonathan, constantly mocked him (PR 26:130).

Jeremiah was commanded by God to go to Anathoth because his merits were so great that God could not destroy Jerusalem as long as Jeremiah was in the city. In the prophet's absence the city was conquered and the Temple set on fire. When, on his return, Jeremiah saw smoke rising from the Temple, he rejoiced, thinking that the Jews had repented and that the smoke was that of the sacrifice which they were offering. He wept bitterly when he realized his error, grieving that he had left Jerusalem to be destroyed. Jeremiah accompanied the captives as far as the Euphrates, and only then returned to comfort those who had been left behind (Jer. 40:6; PR 26:131). On the way back, he tenderly gathered together limbs of the bodies of massacred Jews, lamenting that his warnings had not been heeded by the unfortunate victims (Lam. R., Proem 34). As he approached the ruins of Jerusalem, he had a vision of a woman, clad in black, sitting on top of a mountain, weeping and exclaiming, "Who will comfort me?" After explaining that she was mother Zion, Jeremiah comforted her with the promise that God would rebuild and restore Zion (PR 26:131–132). Jeremiah remained in Egypt until Nebuchadnezzar conquered that country. He was then taken to Babylon where he rejoined his exiled brethren (SOR 26).

[Aaron Rothkoff]

IN ISLAM

Jeremiah (Ar. Irmiyā; also Armiyā and Ūrmiyā) is not mentioned in the *Koran. Some of the commentators on the Koran, however, attribute to Jeremiah, son of Hilkiah the priest, the words of *Muhammad concerning the man who passed by a city in ruins and wondered how Allah would rebuild it. Allah then put this man to death and resuscitated him one hundred years later. To the man's astonishment, it became apparent to him that he had been dead for one hundred years, but that the food and drink which were with him were nevertheless unspoiled, while the bones of his ass had been covered with skin and veins and it had been revived. He was then convinced that Allah was omnipotent (Sura 2:261). The legendary tale of *Ḥoni ha-Meʿaggel (TB, Ta'an. 23a) has been interpreted by Wahb ibn Munabbih, the celebrated traditionalist, who feels that Ḥoni was Jeremiah. Some scholars identify Jeremiah with al-Khaḍir, but other commentators believe that he was ʿUzayr (Ezra). The town which Jeremiah passed by was *Jerusalem (Beit al-Maqdis (i.e., Beit ha-Mikdash), known as Aelia Capitolina in the Byzantine period); he was comforted that it would be rebuilt.

[Haïm Z'ew Hirschberg]

IN THE ARTS

Apart from an early appearance in the medieval *Ordo Prophetarum*, where he is made to foretell the coming of the Messiah, Jeremiah was a rare figure in literary works until the 19th century. Even then, the Hungarian Protestant writer and patriot Ferenc Kölcsey was inspired more by the Book of Jeremiah than by the prophet, basing his *Hymnus* (1823), which later became the Hungarian national anthem, on the text of Jeremiah 32:21–29. The first modern author to turn to Jeremiah was Ludwig *Philippson, who wrote the tragedies *Jojachin* (1858) and *Die Entthronten* (1868), in the latter of which Gedaliah makes a rare literary appearance. Jeremiah was later also the subject of *Il profeta o La passione di un popolo* (1866–84), an Italian allegorical drama by Graziadio David *Levi. The theme has attracted much more attention in the 20th century, with works headed by Stefan *Zweig's remarkable pacifist drama *Jeremias* (1917; Eng., 1922), first staged in Zurich during World War I. Another *Jeremias*, a play by the Danish writer Knud Gjørup, appeared in 1916. These were followed by Wacław Niezabitowski's Polish tragedy *Jeremiasz* (1926), Ajzyk Ruskolękier's Yiddish drama *Yirmiyohu Hanovi* (1936), and Joseph *Kastein's biographical *Jeremias; der Bericht vom Schicksal einer Idee* (1937). The subject also attracted another leading German Jewish writer, Franz *Werfel, whose novel *Hoeret die Stimme* (1937; *Hearken unto the Voice*, 1938) was republished years later as *Jeremias* (1956). During World War II the Czech writer Jiří *Orten published a collection of poems under the title *Jeremiášův pláč* ("Jeremiah's Lament," 1941).

In premedieval Christian art, Jeremiah was regarded as a prophet of the Passion, and was thus sometimes shown holding a cross. The biblical episode in which he is cast into a pit on account of his demoralizing prophecies (Jer. 38) led to his being sometimes given the symbol of the manticore – a legendary animal living in the depths of the earth which was depicted in the bestiaries. Jeremiah is represented in ninth-century manuscripts, including the *Kosmas Indikopleustes* (Vatican Library), and in early medieval frescoes, mosaics, and sculpture. Various episodes of his life are illustrated. There is a 12th-century illumination of the calling of Jeremiah (Jer. 1:9) in the Winchester Bible (Winchester Cathedral).

Thirteenth-century sculptures of the prophet are found in the cathedrals of Amiens and Chartres. At Chartres he is shown holding a circular disc enclosing a cross. A more naturalistic representation is the sculpture by Claus Sluter (Chartreuse de Champmol, Dijon), made at the beginning of the 15th century, where the nose was originally surmounted by a pair of spectacles in gilded leather. Some outstanding works of the Renaissance were a striking sculpture by Donatello (1386–1466; Campanile, Florence); a round painting by Perugino (Nantes Museum), as well as one of *Isaiah; and Michelangelo's brooding, seated figure surmounted by nude youths (Sistine Chapel, Rome). *Rembrandt painted a picture of Jeremiah mourning over Jerusalem (painting formerly in the Stroganov collection, St. Petersburg). The same subject was treated by the German academician Eduard *Bendemann in a crowded composition (National Gallery, Berlin), while another German painter, Lesser *Ury, showed Jeremiah brooding under the night sky. There is also a sculpture of Jeremiah by Enrico *Glicenstein.

The original stage music for Stefan Zweig's *Jeremias* was written by Arno *Nadel. For the Ohel Theater's performance of the play in Palestine, the music was composed by Yedidiah *Admon. Oratorios on the theme include G.M. Schiassi's *Geremia in Egitto* (1727) and Ernst Hess's *Jeremia* (1953). Verses and sections have been set for choir, such as Heinrich Isaac's *Oratio Hieremiae* (1538), and Samuel Scheidt's *Ist nicht Ephraim mein teurer Sohn*. The lament *Quis dabit oculis meis* (Jer. 8:23), which is included in the Good Friday liturgy, also occurs in settings by many composers of the 16th century. In the Jewish musical tradition, *Ha-Ben Yakir Li Efrayim* has become a showpiece of the "artistic" *ḥazzanut* of Eastern Europe; it also appears as the text of several folk songs and ḥasidic *niggunim*. For Rachel's lament (the "voice heard in Ramah …"), see *Rachel, In the Arts. Among modern works is Leonard *Bernstein's *Jeremiah Symphony* (1944).

See also: *Lamentations, In the Arts; *Zedekiah, In the Arts.

[Bathja Bayer]

BIBLIOGRAPHY: BIBLIOGRAPHICAL REVIEWS: G. Fohrer, in: *Theologische Rundschau*, 19 (1951), 277–346; 20 (1952), 193–271, 295–361; 28 (1962), 1–75, 235–97, 301–74; E. Vogt, in: *Biblica*, 35 (1954), 357–65. WORKS ON JEREMIAH IN GENERAL: G.A. Smith, *Jeremiah* (1929^{4}); R. Calkins, *Jeremiah the Prophet* (1930); A. Gelin, *Jérémie* (1952); J.P. Hyatt, *Jeremiah, Prophet of Courage and Hope* (1958); A. Néher, *Jérémie* (1960); C. Westermann, *Jeremia* (1967). COMMENTARIES: B. Duhm, *Das Buch Jeremia* (1901); S.R. Driver, *The Book of the Prophet Jeremiah* (1906); P. Volz, *Der Prophet Jeremia* (1922); A. Weiser, *Das Buch des Propheten Jeremia* (1966^{5}); F. Nötscher, *Das Buch Jeremias* (1930); W. Rudolph, *Jeremia* (1968^{3}). FORMS OF THE TEXT: J.G. Janzen, "Studies in the Text of Jeremiah" (Ph.D. diss., Harvard, 1966); idem, in: HTR, 60 (1967), 433–47. THE COMPOSITION OF THE BOOK: S. Mowinckel, *Zur Komposition des Buches Jeremia* (1914); E. Podechard, in: RB, 37 (1928), 181–97; J. Bright, in: JBL, 70 (1951), 15–35; J.P. Hyatt, in: *Vanderbilt Studies in the Humanities*, 1 (1951),

71–95; W.L. Holladay, in: JBL, 85 (1966), 401–35; M. Kessler, in: JNES, 27 (1968), 81–88. ON STYLISTIC FORMS AND LITERARY GENRES: W. Baumgartner, *Die Klagengedichte des Jeremia* (1917); W.L. Holladay, in: JBL, 81 (1962), 44–54; N. Habel, in: ZAW, 77 (1965), 297–323. PARTICULAR QUESTIONS: J.P. Hyatt, in: JBL, 60 (1941), 381–96; idem, in: JNES, 1 (1942), 156–73; H.H. Rowley, in: *Studies in the Old Testament Prophecy* (1950), 157–74; idem, in: *Bulletin of the John Rylands Library*, 45 (1962–63), 198–234; H. Cazelles, in: *Recherches de Science Religieuse*, 38 (1951), 5–36; F. Horst, in: ZAW, 41 (1923), 94–153; J. Milgrom, in: JNES, 14 (1955), 65–69; C.F. Whitley, in: VT, 14 (1964), 467–83; G. von Rad, in: *Evangelische Theologie*, 3 (1936), 265–76; S.H. Blank, in: HUCA, 21 (1948), 331–54; J.L. Mihelic, in: *Interpretation*, 14 (1960), 45–50; H.J. Krauss, in: *Biblische Studien*, 43 (1964); O. Eissfeldt, *Kleine Schriften*, 4 (1968); M. Diman (Haran), in: BJPES, 13 (1946), 7–15; M.Z. Segal, *Be-Masoret u-Vikkoret* (1957), 145–49; Kaufmann Y., Toledot, 3 (1967[5]), 393–474. **ADD. BIBLIOGRAPHY:** R. Carroll, *Jeremiah* (1986); W. McKane, *Jeremiah 1–2* (1986–95); idem, in DBI I, 570–74; H. Thompson, *The Book of Jeremiah. An Annotated Bibliography* (1996); C. Rabin et al. (eds.), *The Book of Jeremiah* (critical edition; 1997); W. Brueggmann, *A Commentary on Jeremiah, Exile and Homecoming* (1998); W. Holladay, *Jeremiah 1–2* (1986–99); J. Lundbom, in: ABD, 3:706–21; idem, *Jeremiah 1–20* (AB; 1999); idem, *Jeremiah 21–36* (AB; 2004); Y. Hoffman, *Jeremiah 1–2* (2001); B. Sommer, in: CBQ, 66 (2004), 126–27 (review of Hoffman). IN THE AGGADAH: Ginsberg, Legends, 4 (1947[5]), 294–313; 6 (1946[3]), 384–404. IN ISLAM: Ṭabarī, *Tafsīr*, 3 (1324 A.H.), 19–20; Thaʿlabī, *Qiṣaṣ* (1356 A.H.), 188, 290–2; G. Vajda, "Irmiyā," in: EIS^2, 4 (1978), 79 (incl. bibl.).

JEREMIAH, EPISTLE OF (known in the English version as the Epistle of Jeremy), an apocryphal work, written in the form of a copy of a letter by the prophet Jeremiah "unto them which were to be led captive into Babylon by the king of the Babylonians." It was apparently composed on the basis of Jeremiah 29:1ff. (for a similar but seemingly independent tradition, cf. II Macc. 2:2, and Targ. Jon., Jer. 10:11). The work consists of a vehement polemic against idolatry, the futility of which is scorned and derided (verses 8–72). The author follows no coherent line of thought. His discourse is characterized by abrupt transitions from one idea to another, repetitions, and especially by warnings to the exiles against idolatry. Each section describing heathen gods and their worship concludes with variations on the refrain: "they are no gods: therefore fear them not," or "how should a man then think or say that they are gods?" In depicting the heathen deities the author often uses expressions which echo those in the Bible (cf. Jer. 10:9; Isa. 44:9–19; 46:1–2; Ps. 115:4–8; 135: 15–18). The author was apparently an eyewitness to certain aspects of Babylonian idolatry (see verse 31, which tells of the priests having their clothes rent, their heads and beards shaven and nothing on their heads: the ancient Sumerian priests officiated naked and shaven; see also verse 43, which apparently describes temple harlots in Babylonia). Undoubtedly he was a Babylonian Jew who wrote under the name of Jeremiah. His period may be fixed by verse 3, which probably hints at his own time, and which prophesies the return of the exiles after seven generations, that is, approximately 200 years. Reckoning from the destruction of the First Temple in 586 B.C.E. this would refer to the beginning of the fourth century B.C.E., i.e., the days of Artaxerxes II Mnemon (405–359). Scholars formerly maintained that the Epistle was written in Greek, the language in which it has been preserved, but a number of factors indicate that the original language was Hebrew, as has been conclusively shown by Ball (e.g., in verse 17, "a vessel that a man uses" (*kelei adam*) is a mistranslation of "an earthen vessel" (*kelei adamah*)). In the Vulgate the Epistle is appended to Baruch as chapter 6. A passage from the Epistle of Jeremiah (verse 5) was used by the Marranos as a theological justification of Marranism.

BIBLIOGRAPHY: J.J. Kneucker, *Das Buch Baruch*... (1879); C.T. Torrey, *The Apocryphal Literature*, 64–67; Ball, in: Charles, Apocrypha, 1 (1913), 596–611; R.R. Harewell, *Principal Versions of Baruch* (1915); Artom, in: A. Kahana, *Ha-Sefarim ha-Ḥiẓonim*, 1 (1936), 336–49; Wambacq, in: *Biblica*, 40 (1959), 463–75; 47 (1966), 574–6 (Fr.); Roth, Marranos, 170.

[Abraham Schalit]

JEREMIAH BEN ABBA (first half of the fourth century C.E.), Babylonian *amora*; usually referred to without his patronymic. Jeremiah, who was born in Babylonia, immigrated to Ereẓ Israel at the outset of his career. No discussions are extant between him and the Babylonian sages, and only in isolated instances does he quote the earliest ones. There is no reference to his emigration to Ereẓ Israel as there is to that of Babylonian sages such as Ze'eira, Abba, and others, who emigrated when they were already well-known scholars. When Abbaye and Rava, two leading Babylonian *amoraim* who were contemporaries of Jeremiah, discussed the relative worth of the sages of Babylonia and Ereẓ Israel, the former said: "One of them [in Ereẓ Israel] is worth two of us [in Babylonia]," to which Rava replied: "But when one of us immigrates there [to Ereẓ Israel], he is worth two of them. There is, for example, Jeremiah who, when he was here, did not comprehend what the sages were saying, but since immigrating there he refers to us as 'the stupid Babylonians'" (Ket. 75a). And indeed Jeremiah occupied a notable place in Ereẓ Israel, having apparently been for some time, after the death of Ammi and Assi, the head of the *bet midrash* at Tiberias. In Ereẓ Israel he studied under his Babylonian countrymen Ḥiyya b. Abba (Meg. 4a, et al.) and Ze'eira (MK 4a, et al.), as well as under Abbahu at Caesarea (TJ, Git. 9:10, 50d; et al.). With all his great devotion to study, prayer and spiritual tension in the worship of God were conspicuous factors in his outlook. Thus, when he was sitting in study before Ze'eira and the time for prayer arrived, he pressed the latter to interrupt the lesson in order to recite his prayers (Shab. 10a). When on one occasion he greatly prolonged the word "*eḥad*" in the Shema, Ze'eira checked him (Ber. 13b; TJ, Ber. 2:1, 4a.). Against the *baraita* which holds that one must not bow down "too much" in prayer, he said: "Provided one shall not do merely as a lizard does that moves its head, but pray in such a way that he fulfills (Ps. 35: 10) 'all my bones shall say: Lord, who is like unto Thee'" (TJ, Ber. 1:8, 3d). With this teaching of his there is apparently to be connected his dictum: "Great is the fear of God, for two books written by Solomon [Proverbs and Ecclesiastes] conclude with a reference to the fear of God" (Eccles. R. 3:14).

Conspicuous in his mode of study is the effort to arrive at a precise and definitive elucidation of the *halakhah*. At times, the halakhic problems that he posed are merely academic, without any application to practical life. Some of his questions and subtleties raise a smile, and most of the problems propounded by him are left unsolved in the Talmud (Shab. 38b; Suk. 33a, et al.). On the Mishnah (BB 2:6) which states that if a young pigeon is found within 50 cubits of the cote, it belongs to the owner of the cote, but if found beyond 50 cubits, it belongs to the finder, Jeremiah asked: "If its one foot is within and its other foot beyond 50 cubits, what is the *halakhah*?" For this question he was temporarily excluded from the *bet midrash* (BB 23b). (For a profound study of this characteristic of Jeremiah, see M. Silberg, in *Sinai*, 56 (1965), 13–19.)

Jeremiah came to occupy a distinguished position in both the spheres of academic and of communal service in Ereẓ Israel. He had halakhic discussions with most contemporary sages, and nearly all the leading *amoraim* of the following generation quote his statements. The Babylonian Talmud several times mentions his harsh comments on the learning of the Babylonian scholars and the Babylonian Talmud. "He hath made me to dwell in dark places…" (Lam. 3:6) – refers, according to Jeremiah, to the Babylonian Talmud (Sanh. 24a), but this did not prevent his statements from being frequently cited in it. To a question asked of him by the sages he modestly answered: "I am not worthy of having this question addressed to me, but your disciple inclines to the opinion…" (BB 165; cf. Dik. Sof., ad loc.). Avin and Dimi, who regularly went from Ereẓ Israel to Babylonia and there transmitted the teachings of Johanan and the other leading Ereẓ Israel *amoraim* of the preceding generation, included Jeremiah's statements (Pes. 60b; and see Tem. 14a, et al.). Tradition has it that anonymous opinions introduced by "They in the west say," quoted in the Babylonian Talmud, refer to Jeremiah (Sanh. 17b).

The vast majority of his statements are in the realm of *halakhah*, but a considerable number of his aggadic comments interpreting biblical passages and of his homilies have been preserved. He was the author of proems to homiletical expositions (Lev. R. 13: 1; 29: 5, et al.). Several practical decisions required in the "hall of study" (*Sidra Rabba*) were given by him (TJ, Shab. 3:7, 16c; 19:1, 16d, et al.). Like leading sages in all generations, he too traveled around to minister to and guide the inhabitants of various places, visiting the Dead Sea in the company of Ravin (Shab. 108b) and Golan on a mission for Ammi (TJ, Meg. 3:1, 73d). When the authorities imposed a heavy tax on Tiberias, he demanded, contrary to the prevailing *halakhah* exempting sages from taxation, that Jacob b. Bun, a sage, contribute his share. On the *halakhah* that one is not to pray immediately after a conversation or after being occupied in inanities, he taught: "Whoever engages in communal affairs is as one who engages in the study of the Torah" (TJ, Ber. 5:1, 8d). His fervent belief in the advent of the Messiah can be inferred from his last testament: "Clothe me in a white garment, put stockings and shoes on my feet and a staff in my hand, and lay me on my side. When the Messiah comes, I shall be ready" (TJ, Kil. 9:4, 32b).

BIBLIOGRAPHY: Frankel, Mevo, 107bff.; Bacher, Pal Amor; Weiss, Dor, 3 (1904[4]), 95ff.; Halevy, Dorot, 2 (1923), 356ff.

[Shmuel Safrai]

JEREMIAH BEN ISAAC (d. 1805), Hungarian rabbi. Jeremiah studied under Meir b. Isaac *Eisenstadt. He was rabbi of Mattersdorf (Burgenland) from 1770, and of Abaújszánto (Hungary), from about 1797. He lived for some time in Aszód (Hungary) but is not known to have held office there. He took a prominent part in 1798 in the dispute over whether the sturgeon, from which caviar is obtained, is permitted according to the dietary laws, a dispute which in its time engaged the rabbinic world. He declared it to belong to the "unclean" fish, in opposition to the view of Aaron *Chorin, his disciple, who declared it permitted. His *Moda'ah Rabbah*, supplements and comments on the *Moda'ah ve-Ones* of Ḥayyim Shabbetai, was published together with his son Joab's *Moda'ah Zuta* (*Moda'ah ve-Ones*, Zolkiew, 1795?, Lemberg, 1798).

BIBLIOGRAPHY: Joab b. Isaac, *Sha'arei Binah* (1792), introduction; L. Loew, *Gesammelte Schriften*, 2 (1890), 254; Pollak, in: IMIT, 11 (1900), 164–6; J.J. Greenwald, *Ha-Yehudim be-Ungarya* (1912), 53 no. 37; idem, *Maẓẓevat Kodesh* (1952), 118–23; D. Sofer (ed.), *Mazkeret Paks*, 1 (1962), 40–43.

[Nathaniel Katzburg]

°**JEREMIAS, ALFRED** (1864–1935), German Bible critic. He became deacon in 1890 and pastor in 1891 at the Luther-Kirche, Leipzig. From 1905 he taught at the University of Leipzig. A student of Franz Delitzsch, a Biblicist, and his son Friedrich, an Assyriologist, Jeremias was a staunch member of the Pan-Babylonian school, which maintained that the interrelationships between the cultural areas of the ancient Near East, dominated by the Babylonian civilization, decisively influenced Israel's religious development. Jeremias was the first to translate the Gilgamesh epic into German. His *Das Alte Testament im Lichte des alten Orients* (1904, 19163; Eng. tr. and enlargement from the 2nd ed. as *The Old Testament in Light of the Ancient East* (2 vols., 1911, 1916[3])) posited that the Hebrews' highly advanced cultural expression was derived from the Babylonians at the beginning of biblical history. In his *Monotheistische Strömungen innerhalb der babylonischen Religion* (1904) he argued for the existence of monotheistic faith among the Babylonians as early as the third millennium B.C.E. He wrote important works on the Sumerian-Babylonian pantheon, including his important *Handbuch der altorientalischen Geisteskultur* (1913, 1929[2]), but his comparative studies on biblical parallels are often whimsical and lacking in evidence. He is the author of *Izdubar Nimrod, eine altbabylonische Heldensage* (1891); *Im Kampfe um Babel und Bibel* (1903); *Die Panbabylonisten* (1907); *Das Alter der babylonischen Astronomie* (1909); *Allgemeine Religionsgeschichte* (1918, 1924[2]); *Die ausserbiblische Erlösererwartung* (1927).

ADD. BIBLIOGRAPHY: H. Huffmon, in: DBI I, 575–76.

[Zev Garber]

JEREZ DE LA FRONTERA, city in Andalusia, southwest Spain. No information is available on Jews under Muslim rule. Under Christian domination, it had an important Jewish community. Jerez was captured from the Muslims by Alphonso x of Castile in 1255. His register of the apportionment of property *(repartimiento)* there shows that in 1266 Jews owned 90 buildings given to them by the king. Among those who received properties, there were Jewish inhabitants of Toledo and other towns in northern Castile who had already received similar grants in *Seville. They included Todros *Abulafia, his son Joseph, and Judah b. Moses ha-Kohen. Several of the beneficiaries are described as *ballestero* ("archer," "guard," "constable"). The Jewish quarter was situated near the Calle de San Cristóbal and ran parallel to the city wall. There were two synagogues, almshouses, and a house for the rabbi. The principal occupations of the Jews were commerce and viticulture, as well as the crafts customarily pursued by Jews. In 1290, the community paid an annual tax of 5,000 gold coins, a small sum in proportion to its means. The Jews of Jerez were exempted from various customs duties and enjoyed additional privileges, which were confirmed by Ferdinand iv and Alfonso xi (1332).

The community of Jerez, which then numbered 90 families, was attacked during the persecutions of 1391. Those who survived as Jews sold part of their cemetery to the Dominican monastery. The names of 49 Jews who abandoned Judaism (see *Conversos) during that period are known. The community was, however, to regain its strength. In 1438 it paid an annual tax of 10,700 maravedis in old coin. About 1460, an accusation was brought against the Jews by the monks that they had interred a Converso within the cemetery precincts. Solomon *Ibn Verga gives a description of his relative Judah ibn *Verga, one of the last Jewish tax collectors, who saved the Jews of the town by enlisting the help of the duke of Medina Sidonia. The community still paid 1,500 maravedis in 1474 and 1482. In 1481, the Inquisition in Seville sent emissaries to confiscate the property of Conversos who had fled the town. Information that the Jews were to be expelled from Andalusia reached Jerez as early as January 1483. The *corregidor* and council requested a postponement since they considered that the decree would bring about the economic ruin of the town. The Jews began to sell their property, but the municipal authorities prohibited people from buying it. The expulsion was postponed for six months. In 1484, some Jews are still mentioned as inhabitants of the town, but by 1485 the community had ceased to exist.

Several *autos-da-fé, each lasting some days, were held in Jerez in 1491 and 1492. Some *sanbenitos* ("penitential garments") of repentant Conversos were still hanging in the parochial church of San Dionisio in the 18th century. After the Edict of Expulsion of 1492 Jews passed through Jerez on their way to exile in North Africa. In 1494, after an outbreak of plague, Christians were ordered to refuse shelter or admittance to their homes to any stranger in the town who had formerly been a Jew.

Nowadays, there is still a street called "Judería." It is near the city wall and next to where "Puerta de Sevilla" had been. The *judería* included more streets, including San Cristóbal and Alvar López.

BIBLIOGRAPHY: Baer, Spain, index; Baer, Urkunden, index; F. Fita, *España Hebrea*, 1 (1889), 32–50; A. Muñoz y Gómez, *Noticias históricas de las calles de Xerez de la Frontera* (1903); H.S. de Sopranis, in: *Sefarad*, 2 (1951), 349–70; Suárez Fernández, Documentos, 68, 81. **ADD. BIBLIOGRAPHY:** M. González Jiménez, *El libro del repartimiento de Jerez de la Frontera, studio y edición*, (1980), lx–lxv, 187–95.

[Haim Beinart]

JERICHO (Heb. יְרִיחוֹ), said to be one of the oldest fortified cities in the ancient Near East. It is identified with Tell al-Sulṭā, near the ʿAyn al-Sulṭān spring (Spring of Elisha), about 1 mi. (1½ km.) N.W. of modern Jericho (Ar. Arīḥā) and 4½ mi. (7 km.) W. of the Jordan on the road leading to Jerusalem. The tel, covering an area of about 8½ acres (34 dunams) is 65 ft. (20 m.) high and 820 ft. (250 m.) below sea level. Its warm climate and abundant waters made Jericho an oasis attracting settlers from prehistoric times. In 1868 Charles Warren excavated at the site but had a negative opinion of its archaeological potential. The first systematic examination of Jericho was conducted by E. Sellin and C. Watzinger in 1901–09. Extensive excavations were subsequently carried out by J. Garstang in 1930–36 and K. Kenyon in 1952–61. Jericho was first settled sometime during the eighth millennium B.C.E. and the material remains are of the Natufian culture. One structure has been identified as a possible cult place. The dwellings were probably huts or tents of semi-nomads. Two Neolithic subperiods are distinguished at Jericho; their main difference is the absence of pottery in the first and its appearance in the second. The pre-pottery Neolithic period (seventh millennium) is characterized by irrigation farming and the development of major communal activities represented by the building of features said to be fortifications – though whether these actually served as fortifications has recently been contested by Bar-Yosef – and curvilinear houses built of plano-convex bricks (flat with curved tops). The "fortifications" of the town consist of a stone wall, 6½ ft. (2 m.) thick, to which a stone tower was attached, 30 ft. (9 m.) high and 28 ft. (8½ m.) in diameter with an inner staircase leading to the top of the wall. For this phase radiocarbon (^{14}C) tests of organic material established a date of 6850±210 B.C.E., i.e., between 7060 and 6640 B.C.E. Following the destruction of this town, a new one was built on its ruins and also enclosed by a stone wall erected on new foundations. Rectangular-shaped houses, of elongated mud-bricks, contained plastered floors colored red or yellow and burnished to a high polish. On several were found impressions of rush mats once spread on them. Several structures from this level may have served as public buildings or perhaps temples. Eleven building phases and 22 superimposed plastered floors were distinguished in this city. Throughout its long history, the settlers had no knowledge of the art of manufacturing pottery, but they possessed a highly developed standard of sculpture making. An outstanding example of their artistic skill is a flat head modeled from clay with shells inset for eyes in a unique style. Beneath the floor of one of the houses were discovered plastered human skulls with features molded into realistic human portraits. These skulls were probably connected with some cultic practice, perhaps ancestor worship. Finds such as flint sickle blades, querns, mortars and pestles, and various types of grain indicate that the occupants of this city were agriculturists. Radiocarbon (^{14}C) tests from various levels gave dates of 6520±200 (6720–6320) and 5820±160 (5980 – 5660 B.C.E.). In the fifth millennium, newcomers seem to have arrived at Jericho. No building remains date to this time but they brought with them a new culture – the art of manufacturing pottery. The vessels of this Neolithic period pottery are handmade and coarse, but some are finer and decorated with a red, well-burnished zigzag design. The latest pottery from this period, decorated with incised herringbone patterns, parallels the Yarmukian culture of northern Ereẓ Israel. Judging from the many changes in the fortifications and the appearance of the remains, the Early Bronze Age (third millennium) was one of great upheaval for Jericho, and it was the scene of frequent wars and earthquakes. The walls were destroyed, repaired and rebuilt 17 times during this time. The thick walls, of unbaked bricks, built almost exactly over the Neolithic ones, had a semicircular tower. Round structures, whose purpose is unknown, were found, as well as a large rectangular tower, rectangular-shaped houses and tombs. Jericho flourished in this period and was destroyed by nomadic tribes which penetrated into Canaan in the Middle Bronze Age I (2100–1900 B.C.E.). The city was not rebuilt and the remains from this time are mainly a great number of tombs with weapons and pottery. In the Middle Bronze Age II (19th–17th centuries B.C.E.) the city again became prosperous, and it was defended by an imposing system of fortifications consisting of a huge glacis of beaten earth on the slopes of the tell and supported at its foot by a massive stone retaining wall 20 ft. (6 m.) high. Many tombs were found outside the city with rich offerings in alabaster and bronze, scarabs and jewelry, as well as wooden objects and reed mats and baskets which are rarely preserved in Israel. The city was probably destroyed by the Egyptians; from the period of the latter's rule of Canaan (15th–13th centuries) little remained at Jericho, but it is clear that the city was inhabited to a certain degree in the 13th century. This was the city that was said to have been encountered by the Israelites when they entered the Promised Land and whose conquest was essential for their advance into the interior of the country. Joshua sent two spies to investigate the city which the Bible describes as walled (Josh. 2:1). It was not captured in battle but by divine command: the Israelites were to encircle the city once a day for six days and seven times on the seventh day and then to the blare of trumpets, and at the sound of a great shout the wall of the city fell and it was burnt. The city and all that was in it were consecrated to the Lord and only Rahab, the harlot, who had hidden the messengers, and her household were saved (Josh. 6). However, in the excavations at Jericho, no fortification was found which could be attributed to the Canaanite city captured by Joshua (see the debate between Bienkowski and Wood for different opinions). To resolve this discrepancy, some scholars suggest that the mud-brick wall was washed away by rain and erosion during the long period that it stood in ruins. Others maintain that the Canaanite city did not possess its own wall but reused the wall of the earlier city, and still others consider the biblical tradition to be an etiological story invented to explain the destruction of the earlier city. At all events, the archaeological evidence does not help establish an exact date for the Israelite conquest of Jericho. The Bible contains many references to Jericho in the Israelite period (12th–6th centuries). The city was included in the territory of Benjamin (Josh. 18:21) and, after Joshua's conquest of the city and his curse against anyone rebuilding it (Josh. 6:26), it apparently remained uninhabited as no remains from the 12th century were found. The Bible records the capture of "the city of palm-trees" by Eglon, king of Moab (Judg. 3:13). Evidence was found of a small settlement dating to the end of the period of the Judges and the beginning of the monarchy. A large public building of four rooms which was probably a royal storehouse is attributed to the tenth century B.C.E., i.e., the time of David. On their return from the Ammonite king, David's messengers remained at Jericho until their beards grew again (II Sam. 10:5). The city was rebuilt by Hiel, the Bethelite, in the days of Ahab, and for this act he was revenged by the fulfillment of Joshua's curse (I Kings 16:34). Some building remains from this time were found. The prophets Elijah and Elisha lived there (II Kings 2:4, 18–22) and the Judahite prisoners captured by the Israelites in the time of Pekah were returned to the "city of palm-trees" (II Chron. 28:15). The city expanded considerably at the end of the Israelite period (seventh, sixth centuries) but it remained unfortified and unimportant up to its destruction by the Babylonians in 587 B.C.E. The city was resettled by 345 Babylonian exiles (Neh. 7:36) and they participated in rebuilding the wall of Jerusalem (3:2). A small settlement existed there in the post-Exilic period. Jar handles inscribed "Yehud," the Aramaic name of the province of Judea under Persian rule, indicate that Jericho was included in the Judean state. On one handle, after the name "Yehud" appears "Urio"; he was apparently the official in charge of the fiscal affairs of the state. Gabinius made it the seat of one of his councils (*synhedria*) when he reorganized Judea into five districts. Archaeological remains of the Hellenistic and Roman town of Jericho have not yet been identified, but Hasmonean and Herodian palaces have been uncovered further west at Tulūʾl Abu al-ʿAlāyiq where Wadi al-Qilt enters the Jordan Valley. Remains of imposing structures constructed by Herod were found during excavations conducted at the site by E. Netzer between 1973 and 1983. Jericho possessed vast groves of dates and persimmons. Jericho itself was destroyed during the Jewish War (66–70 C.E.) and military installations were again built there at the time of Hadrian. Jericho continued to be occupied at the time of the Bordeaux pilgrim (333 C.E.). In the Byzantine period Jericho moved about 1 m. (1½ km.) east to its present location. Near the city were remains of a seventh-century basilical-shaped synagogue. It was oriented toward Jerusalem and had a mosaic pavement decorated with a *menorah*, the inscription "peace on Israel," and a memorial inscription in Aramaic.

Jericho is mentioned in the *Onomasticon* of Eusebius (fourth century) and was depicted as a flourishing city on the Madaba Map (sixth century) where the well, which supplied the ancient city with water, is shown as a church and called the "Spring of Elisha" (τὸ τ[οῦ] ἁγι[οῦ] Ἐλισαίου). This according to tradition was the site of the story of Elisha in the Bible (II Kings 2:19–22) who was called upon to deal with the purification of the contaminated spring by casting a vessel with salt into the waters. According to Josephus, Elisha "went out to this spring and cast into the stream an earthen ware full of salt, and then, raising his righteous right hand to heaven and pouring propitious libations upon the ground, he besought the earth to mollify the stream and to open sweeter channels…" (Wars, 4:460–65). The spring is known today as Ayn al-Sulṭān. It seems that by the seventh century Jericho was again in ruins but Jewish refugees from the tribe of Banu *Nadir fled there from before Muhammad. A new synagogue arose on the site of the Byzantine one and the Masoretes mention a "Jericho Codex" existing there. With the Islamic conquest, a palace was built in 724 C.E. at Khirbat Mafjar nearby ("Hisham's Palace"). Excavations in 1935 by R.W. Hamilton brought to light beautiful mosaics and carvings there. By 891 Jericho was the district capital of the Ghauer (cleft of the lower Jordan; Yaʿkūbī, 113) and by the early Middle Ages was important for the production of indigo and sugarcane (Yākūt, 3:823, 913). It was captured by the Crusaders in 1099 and used by Raymond IV, count of Toulouse, as an encampment when his rival Godfrey de Bouillon gained Jerusalem. Queen Melisande endowed the whole of Jericho and its surrounding lands to her newly established convent of St. Lazarus (at Bethany) in 1147 and fortified Jericho with a tower. It was recaptured by Saladin without a struggle in 1187. The present Jericho is on the site of the Crusader town. Close by is the site of ancient *Dok, on the summit of which is the Byzantine Monastery of the Temptation (Qarantal) where Jesus was said to have fasted for forty days and nights (cf. Math. 4:1–5; hence its medieval name, Mons Quarantana). The Knights Templar built a fortress on the summit, called Castellum Dok, and the monastery was granted the tithes of Jericho city and the rights of the sugar mills in 1136. At the foot of the hill are the remains of three Crusader sugar mills (one nearly intact) which were referred to as early as 1116. They were driven by water systems originally built by Herod and repaired by the Crusaders. Nearby a Crusader building for boiling the sugar is in a good state of preservation. The town itself was practically uninhabited from then until the 19th century.

[Nachman Avigad / Shimon Gibson (2nd ed.)]

Modern Jericho

In the last two centuries, Jericho's population figures greatly fluctuated. In 1840 the troops of the Egyptian Governor Ibrahim Pasha razed the town before leaving the country. Jericho was again destroyed in a conflagration (1871). In 1918 Allenby secured the eastern front of the allies by the capture of Jericho from the Turks. From the beginning of the 20th century, the town expanded and in the 1940s had about 3,000 inhabitants. Included in Jordanian territory after the Israel *War of Independence (1948) the town suddenly grew when camps of Arab refugees from Israel were set up there and in the vicinity. The occupation of Jericho and the nearby Jordan banks and bridges on June 7, 1967, by Israel troops practically concluded the *Six-Day War fighting on the West Bank. Along with tropical, irrigated oasis-type farming (with date palms and pomegranates prominent, to which bananas, citrus, fodder crops, and certain tropical species, were later added), winter tourism and recreation developed, particularly from the 1950s, as an additional source of income. While shortly before the Six-Day War the Jordanian authorities estimated the population of Jericho and its surroundings at a total of 80,000, the 1967 Israel census indicated 6,837 persons in the town proper, of whom over 90% were Muslims, and less than 10% (539) Christians; within the municipal confines, 1,619 lived in a refugee camp. The surrounding area contained 2,000 inhabitants. Most refugee camps were abandoned during the fighting of June 1967 and their inhabitants crossed the Jordan River. By the end of 1967, the number of inhabitants had further decreased. In 1994 it became the first West Bank town to be handed over to the *Palestinian Authority by Israel in the framework of the Declaration of Principles (see *Israel, State of, under Historical Survey), and subsequently served as a detention area for the Palestinian prisoners released to the Authority by Israel. In 1997 the population of Jericho included 14,674 residents, among them 43.6% refugees.

Two and a half mi. (4 km.) east of Jericho a 2,000-acre farm school for refugee boys and orphans was established in 1951 and directed by the Palestinian Arab leader Mūsā al-ʿAlami. Its maintenance was aided by the Ford Foundation and other international bodies. The school utilized a method, developed before 1948 by the kibbutz *Bet ha-Aravah, of reducing the high salt content of the soil by flushing it with sweet water.

[Efraim Orni / Shaked Gilboa (2nd ed.)]

BIBLIOGRAPHY: E. Sellin and C. Watzinger, *Jericho* (1913); J. Garstang, *The Story of Jericho* (1948); Kelso and Baramki, in: AASOR, 19–30 (1955); Pritchard, *ibid.*, 32–33 (1958); H.H. Rowley, *From Joseph to Joshua* (1958); K.M. Kenyon et al., *Jericho*, 2 vols. (1960–65); Aharoni, Land, index; EM, 3 (1965), 839–60; Press, Ereẓ (1952), 459–62; EHA, 1 (1970), 243, 259; G. Le Strange, *Palestine Under the Moslems* (1940), 1855; M. Benvenisti, *The Crusaders in the Holy Land* (1970), index; S. Runciman, *History of the Crusades*, 3 vols. (1951–54). **ADD. BIBLIOGRAPHY:** K.M. Kenyon, *Digging Up Jericho* (1957); O. Bar-Yosef, "The Walls of Jericho: An Alternative Explanation," in: *Current Anthropology*, 27 (1986), 157–62; P. Bienkowski, "Jericho in the Late Bronze Age (1986); idem, "Jericho Was Destroyed in the Middle

Bronze Age Not in the Late Bronze Age," in: *Biblical Archaeology Review*, 16:5 (1990), 45–46, 69; B.G. Wood, "Dating Jericho's Destruction: Bienkowski Is Wrong on All Counts," in: *Biblical Archaeology Review*, 16:5 (1990), 45, 47–49; Z. Ilan, *Ancient Synagogues in Israel* (1991); H.J. Franken, *In Search of the Jericho Potters* (1974); P. Dorrell, "The Spring at Jericho from Early Photographs," in: *Palestine Exploration Quarterly*, 125 (1993), 95–114; E. Netzer, *The Palaces of the Hasmoneans and Herod the Great* (2001).

JEROBOAM (Heb. יָרָבְעָם), first king of post-Solomonic Israel; son of Nebat and Zeruah, from the town of Zeredah in Ephraim (I Kings 11:26). Jeroboam reigned for 22 years (14:20), approximately from 928 to 907 B.C.E. Two explanations have been offered for the meaning of his name: "[That God] will increase the number of the people"; and "he who fights the battles of the people," a name appropriate to the fact that he led the rebellion against Rehoboam. Jeroboam, a "mighty man of valor," whom King Solomon placed in charge of the corvée of Ephraim and Manasseh to fortify Jerusalem, "lifted up his hand against the king" (I Kings 11:26–28). *Ahijah the Shilonite supported Jeroboam's rebellion and promised him rule over ten tribes, as well as over people who favored political dissociation from the House of David. Details of Jeroboam's rebellion are not reported in the Books of Kings, but it appears that it took place in the second half of Solomon's reign. The Septuagint states that Jeroboam succeeded in conscripting 300 chariots and had his stronghold in the town of Zeredah (or Zererah). The rebellion failed and Jeroboam was forced to flee to Egypt, where he was sheltered by Pharaoh *Shishak (an account which also appears in I Kings 11:40 of the MT). According to the Septuagint, Shishak also gave his sister-in-law to Jeroboam in marriage and it was this union which produced a son, Abijah.

When Solomon died, Jeroboam returned from Egypt, and according to some sources he even participated in a popular meeting at Shechem and conducted, together with the elders of Israel, the negotiations with Rehoboam about the reduction of taxes (but cf. I Kings 12:20). When Rehoboam turned down their request, the leaders of the people – excluding those of Judah and Benjamin – proclaimed their political independence from the House of David, and appointed Jeroboam as their king. Immediately on ascending the throne, Jeroboam embarked on a series of moves aimed not only at countering the attempts by the king of Judah to reconquer the central and northern tribal territories but also at widening the breach between the two kingdoms. There is no record of Jeroboam's activities in the administrative and military organization of his new kingdom. It is known only that he first fortified Shechem, apparently his capital, but for unknown reasons he left Shechem and built Penuel in eastern Transjordan (I Kings 12:25), and later he possibly went to Tirzah (14:17; cf. 15:21). Jeroboam's activities in matters of ritual are described negatively in I Kings 12:25–33. He made two golden calves, placing one at Dan in the north and the other at Beth-El in the south. Calf worship was not something completely new in the ritual of Israel, but rather a reintroduction of an earlier ritualistic tradition. Dan and Beth-El were cultic holy places before the establishment of the kingdom. The *golden calf, which either served as a pedestal on which YHWH stood, or actually represented YHWH, was opposed by the writer of Exodus 32. That author composed the story of the golden calf in the wilderness (cf. I Kings 12:28 with Ex. 32:4) as a polemic against Jeroboam's cultic restoration by claiming that its origins were in ancient rebellion against YHWH (Aberbach and Smolar 1967; Sperling). It must further be observed that Ahijah, who supported the rebellion, was a prophet of YHWH. Perhaps the Shiloh tradition had no problem with the use of calves in the worship of YHWH.

In the fifth year of Jeroboam's reign, Shishak, the king of Egypt, invaded Israel. The biblical versions of Shishak's campaign (I Kings 14:25–28; II Chron. 12:2–12) recount mainly what occurred in the kingdom of Judah, but the wall engravings of the Temple of Karnak in Egypt list towns conquered by Shishak and indicate that Jeroboam's Israel suffered most in this war. Shishak invaded the southern territory of the kingdom of Israel by way of Gezer and Gibeon, penetrated the fruitful valley of Succoth, from there he turned to the Beth-Shean and Jezreel valleys, and then returned to Egypt by way of the coastal plain. Possibly Shishak intended to demonstrate Egypt's might and to reinstate its authority over Israel, but the adventure resulted not in Egyptian domination over the kingdoms in Palestine but merely in plunder. Archaeologists have discovered that many towns in the kingdom of Israel, such as Gezer, Beth-Shean, Taanach, and Megiddo, were destroyed during this campaign. *Abijah's success in conquering Jeroboam's territories in the southern part of the mountains of Ephraim (II Chron. 13:3–19) must be understood not only against the background of Jeroboam's weakness as a result of Shishak's campaign, but also in light of the increasing pressure upon Israel at Aram-Damascus in the northeast and by the Philistines in the southwest. Perhaps even by Jeroboam's time the eastern Transjordanian states had succeeded in regaining their independence by exploiting both the internal conflict between Israel and Judah and the external pressure of the Arameans and Philistines on the kingdom of Israel.

[Bustanay Oded / S. David Sperling (2nd ed.)]

In the Aggadah

Jeroboam was rewarded with royal dignity for rebuking Solomon, who closed the breaches in the walls of Jerusalem (which David had made to allow all Israel to make pilgrimages to Jerusalem on festivals.). Solomon had done this so that he could exact a toll for the benefit of Pharaoh's daughter (Sanh. 101b). When Jeroboam himself was confronted with the temptations of power (Lev. R. 12:5), his pride and his craving for predominance unbalanced him. Realizing that continued pilgrimage to Jerusalem would place Rehoboam, king of Judah, foremost in the minds of the people, he, who had once fought for free pilgrimage to Jerusalem, now erected an "iron curtain" between the people and the Temple (TJ, Av. Zar. 1:1, 39a; Sanh. 101b.). Assisted by evil men, he succeeded in setting up the golden calves in Dan and Beth-El, making use of his good reputation to obtain extra privileges from the Sanhedrin and full authority for all his actions, including idol worship. Jeroboam and his lackeys conducted a powerful propaganda campaign filled with distortions and historical misrepresentations, exalting the tolerance and forgiveness, the goodness and lovingkindness implicit in the religion of the calves, as opposed to the restrictions and severity of the Law of Moses (TJ, Av. Zar. and Sanh., loc. cit.). This propaganda did not deceive most of the people, however, so that when Jeroboam took his calves to all the tribes, none would accept them except that of Dan which had worshiped Micah's graven image in tribal times (Num. R. 2:10). No one would be appointed priest in the new shrines and Jeroboam was compelled to choose his priests from the dregs of the population (TJ, Av. Zar. loc. cit.). Since the decree prohibiting pilgrimages to Jerusalem was ignored by the people, Jeroboam posted guards on the borders and ordered all transgressors to be put to death (Tosef., Ta'an. 4:7; Sanh. 102a). Even these measures failed to put a stop to the pilgrimages and the king's son himself publicly disobeyed the order (MK 28b).

See also *Israel, Kingdom of (In the Aggadah).

[Elimelech Epstein Halevy]

BIBLIOGRAPHY: Bright, Hist, 210–9; Kittel, Gesch, 2 (1922), 387ff.; H.T. Olmstead, *History of Palestine and Syria* (1931), 150; E. Auerbach, *Wüste und gelobtes Land*, 2 (1938), 29ff.; Albright, Arch Rel, 156, 219; Albright, Stone, 228ff.; Noth, Hist Isr, index; Ginsberg, in, *Fourth World Congress of Jewish Studies, Papers*, 1 (1967), 91; IN THE AGGADAH: A.A. Halevi, *Sha'arei ha-Aggadah* (1963), 23ff. **ADD. BIBLIOGRAPHY:** M. Aberbach and L. Smolar, in: JQR, 59 (1968), 118–32.; idem, in: JBL, 86 (1967), 129–40; N. Na'aman, in: L. Handy (ed.), *The Age of Solomon* (1997), 57–80; S.D. Sperling, *The Original Torah* (1998), 91–102; M. Cogan, *I Kings* (AB; 2000), 336–83.

JEROBOAM II, son of *Joash, king of Israel (789–748 B.C.E.; see *Chronology). He was the greatest ruler of the dynasty of Jehu. It seems that his father associated him in the kingship in the last two years of his reign and that these years are included in the 41 regnal years ascribed to Jeroboam. During those two years, his father probably entrusted him with the command of the Israelite armies in their wars against *Aram-Damascus. Aram-Damascus's decline in power after the campaigns of kings Adad-Nirari III and Shalmaneser IV, the kings of Assyria, into northern and central Syria enabled Joash and his son Jeroboam not only to capture for Israel those territories which had been conquered from her near the end of the reign of Jehu and during the reign of Jehoahaz, but also to gain supremacy over non-Israelite territories which had probably come under the rule of Aram close to the time of Solomon's death. The biblical tradition relates about his war against Aram-Damascus that Jeroboam "restored the border of Israel from Lebo-Hamath unto the sea of the Arabah [i.e., the Dead Sea] in accordance with the word of the YHWH, the god of Israel … YHWH … delivered [Israel] through Jeroboam the son of Joash" (II Kings 14:25–27). Jeroboam's expansion as far as Hamath in central Syria would have required Assyrian acquiescence (Cogan and Tadmor, 163.) His victories reestablished the territorial limits attributed to *Solomon. (It is not impossible that Jeroboam's victories inspired the exaggerated claims made for Solomon). These expansionist wars probably took place in the early and middle years of Jeroboam's reign (Cogan and Tadmor, 164).

According to one opinion, the relations between Jeroboam and his other neighbors were not orderly. There is no evidence that the strained relations with Tyre, following Jehu's liquidation of the revolt of the Omri dynasty, which was allied to the kings of Tyre by marriage, ever improved. Moreover, there was no economic incentive for the renewal of relations between Tyre and Israel (see *Ahab, *Jehoshaphat, *Solomon). In addition, the relations between Israel and Judah had been complicated ever since Joash's victory over King *Amaziah of Judah on the battlefield and the destruction of a section of Jerusalem's fortifications after his victory. In the meantime Judah had gained in strength during the reign of *Uzziah, especially during the period of *Jotham's regency. It also seems that Judah conquered Rabbath Ammon and even gained control over the southern part of the King's Highway in Transjordan by which commerce was led from southern Arabia to Syria and Mesopotamia. *Pekah son of Remaliah, who was a Gileadite and governor of Transjordan under Jeroboam, had gained control of Transjordan as early as in the reign of Jeroboam. This division of Israel was desired by Aram and Judah, and they probably incited Pekah in this direction. According to other opinions, there were peaceful relations between Israel and Judah – hence the prosperity of Judah and the beginning of its political and military importance. Some argue that extensive cooperation between the two kingdoms can also be proved from the combined census carried out on the territory east of the Jordan (I Chron. 5:17). But while not chronologically impossible, the Chronicles passage is historically dubious (Japhet, 137–38). It would seem that the signs of prosperity increased with the influence over these widespread territories. The king distributed the lands among his loyal friends and favorites, and this probably spawned a wealthy class of landowners in Transjordan and other places against whom the prophet *Amos protested. According to the testimony of Amaziah the priest in Amos 7:11 (cf. Amos 7:9), the prophet prophesied (inaccurately, it turns out) that Jeroboam would die by the sword. The Book of Amos gives us an insight into the social and economic conditions during the reign of Jeroboam.

From the limited information given in the Bible, it seems that Jeroboam II was a gifted commander and an able organizer who succeeded in elevating the kingdom of Israel to a last climax before its fall. In the tradition of the Judahite redactors of the northern sources preserved in the Bible, Jeroboam is adjudged a king who "departed not from all the sins that Jeroboam, the son of Nebat, made Israel to sin" (II Kings 14:24). However, his loyalty to YHWH can be deduced not only from the name of his son Zechariah (Heb. "Remembered by YHWH") but also from the prophecies of "the prophet Jonah son of Amittai of Gath-Hepher" (*ibid.*, 14:25), who encouraged Jeroboam in his wars and prophesied his victory. It is unfortunate that these prophecies are not preserved. A stamp seal depicting a lion and reading *lšmʿ ʿbd yrbʿm*, "Property of Shema, servant of Jeroboam," was found at Megiddo (Cogan and Tadmor, pl. 12a).

BIBLIOGRAPHY: Bright, Hist, 238–9, 244–5, 252–3; E.R. Thiele, *The Mysterious Numbers of the Hebrew Kings* (1951), 69, 288ff; M. Vogelstein, *Jerobeam II* (1945); M. Noth, *Geschichte Israels* (19563), 227–8; Kittel, Gesch, 2 (1922), 346–7; E. Auerbach, *Wüste und gelobtes Land*, 2 (1936), 86ff.; Haran, in: VT, 17 (1967), 266–97. **ADD. BIBLIOGRAPHY:** M. Cogan and H. Tadmor, *II Kings* (AB; 1988); S. Japhet, *I & II Chronicles* (1993); K. Whitelam, in: ABD, 3:75–76.

JEROHAM BEN MESHULLAM (c. 1290–1350), Spanish talmudist. Born in Provence, he was a victim of the expulsion of the Jews from France in 1306, and wandered in various countries until he arrived in Toledo, Spain, where, living in utter poverty, he continued his studies under *Asher b. Jehiel (the *Rosh*), and Abraham b. Moses Ismail, a pupil of Solomon b. Abraham *Adret. In his first known work, the *Sefer Mesharim*, on civil law, Jeroham arranged the relevant laws according to their subjects, noted their sources and origins in the Talmud, and collected the decisions of many scholars. He was meticulous in arranging his work in such a way that "any man, whether a great scholar or a minor student, might easily find any law that he wished." Jeroham states, "After my friends saw its usefulness, they pressed me to compose a similar work relating to the positive and negative commandments, and I yielded to their entreaties." He then composed his second book, *Toledot Adam ve-Ḥavvah*, which he arranged according to the cycle of human life, from birth to death. The section on Adam runs from birth until marriage; the section on Eve from marriage until death. Jeroham quotes the opinions of leading scholars of France, Spain, and Provence, and transmits the customs of various communities and countries. Jeroham's works enjoyed only brief popularity, being superseded by the *Arba'ah Turim*, the superior work of his friend and contemporary, *Jacob b. Asher. Jeroham's two works were printed for the first time in Constantinople in 1516, and thereafter there was a certain revival of interest in them. The foremost legal authorities of the 16th century, Joseph *Caro, Samuel de *Medina, and others, quoted him extensively. The few editions of the book are all based upon the *editio princeps* which was printed from a very corrupt manuscript, and therefore was not much used by students. Very few commentaries were composed to it; for those that were, legend had it that either the commentator died prematurely or the commentary was lost. The *Maggid (heavenly mentor) who spoke to Joseph Caro called him Jeroham Temiri ("Jeroham the Secret"). The work entitled *Issur ve-Hetter*, published in 1882 by Jacob Abukara, was erroneously ascribed to Jeroham.

BIBLIOGRAPHY: Freimann, in: JJLG, 12 (1918), 265n., 283–5; I. Ta-Shema, in: *Sinai*, 64 (1969), 254–6.

[Israel Moses Ta-Shma]

°**JEROME** (**Eusebius Sophronius Hieronymus**; 342–420), Latin Church Father, born to Christian parents in Stridon, Dalmatia, and sent by them to study in Rome. In Gaul, where he lived a life of pleasure after completing his studies, he was overcome by thoughts of repentance; he decided to pursue an ascetic life and joined a group of ascetics in Aquileia. In 374 he decided to go to Jerusalem, but on his way he became ill in Antioch and stayed there. For three years (375–378) he lived the life of a hermit in the desert of Chalcis. There he met an apostate Jew and with his help began to learn Hebrew. He then returned to Antioch where he was ordained priest. He proceeded from there to Constantinople where he met Gregory of Nazianzus (c. 325–389) and heard his discourses on the exegesis of the Bible. From 382 to 385 he lived in Rome and served as secretary to Pope Damasus I.

During his stay in Constantinople he was engaged in translating the *Chronicon* of *Eusebius into Latin, as well as supplementing it and lengthening it to cover the period from the 20th year of Constantine to the death of Valens in 378. The adaptation is frequently slipshod and inexact. His translation of this work, which included dates of events from Abraham onward, served as the basis for all the chronography of the Middle Ages in the West and also had a direct or indirect influence upon medieval Hebrew authors. In 386 he settled in *Bethlehem, where he directed a monastery and devoted his time to study. He obtained money to found the monastery from one of his female followers in Rome, Paula, who traveled with several friends to Bethlehem, where she founded three nunneries. In Bethlehem Jerome continued his study of the Hebrew language, which he had previously studied in Syria. He had several Jewish teachers: one came from Lydda, and the second, named Bar-Ḥanina, came from Tiberias. Out of fear of the Jews, the latter was sometimes compelled, according to Jerome, to visit him at night, and at times he even sent another Jew, named Nicodemus, to take his place. At that time the Jews derided gentiles who could not pronounce the pharyngeals properly. Jerome, however, attained such a degree of proficiency in his pronunciation of Hebrew that the transcriptions of Hebrew words in his writings are important for knowledge of Hebrew pronunciation at that time.

The study of Hebrew prepared Jerome for his important work – a Latin translation of the Bible from the original (see *Bible, Latin Translations). This translation, together with his translation of the New Testament from Greek to Latin, was accepted as the official version of the Scriptures in the Catholic Church, and is known as the Vulgate from its Latin name, Vulgata. He translated the Book of Psalms three times. The first time, he translated it from the Greek, and this translation was taken into the Catholic liturgy. His second translation was included in the conventional version of the Vulgate, based on the work of Origen (c. 182–251), who had collated the Septuagint with the Hebrew version. Finally, when he translated the Bible from Hebrew, he once more translated the Book of Psalms, a translation which did not gain admission either into the official Christian text of the Scriptures or into Christian worship. Jerome also made various translations of the Books of Judith and Tobit from an Aramaic version that has since disappeared and of the additions in the Greek translation of Daniel. He did not regard as canonical works the Books of Ben Sira and Baruch, the Epistle of Jeremy, the first two Books of the Maccabees, the third and fourth Books of Ezra, and the additions to the Book of Esther in the Septuagint. The Latin translations of these works in present-day editions of the Vulgate are not from his pen.

The translation of the Bible met with complaints from conservative circles of the Catholic Church. His opponents labeled him a falsifier and a profaner of God, claiming that through his translations he had abrogated the sacred traditions of the Church and followed the Jews: among other things, they invoked the story that the Septuagint had been translated in a miraculous manner. Jerome, however, rejected the story as legend. Despite the opposition which the new translation aroused in the ancient period (an opposition also supported by Augustine), on the one hand, and the unfavorable criticism directed against it by many humanists and participants in the Reformation, on the other, the Council of Trent (16th century) declared the Vulgate to be an authentic version. This today means only that the Vulgate is authentic from the judicial, but not from the critical point of view. In addition to translating the Bible, Jerome composed commentaries on it. His commentaries were the basis of medieval Christian biblical exegesis, and even Jewish exegetes occasionally quote him. The commentaries contain much exegetic material that Jerome received from his Jewish teachers, including several Midrashim that have been lost. He makes use of both the plain meaning and homiletical exegesis in his commentaries. In his commentary to the Book of Daniel (c. 407) he rejects the claim of Porphyry (347–420) that it is not prophetic but reflects the historical situation that existed at the time of the decrees of *Antiochus. The first of Jerome's Hebrew studies appears in *Quaestiones hebraicae in Genesin* in which he collates Christian exegesis with the Hebrew text. His *Liber interpretationis nominum hebraicorum* is apparently based upon the *Onomasticon* of Origen, which has since disappeared. This dictionary of personal names occurring in the Bible and the New Testament is arranged in the order of the Holy Scriptures, and in each book the names are cited in alphabetical order. The translations of the names, however, are not always correct.

During his visits to Palestine in about 373 and in the winter of 385 and after he settled there permanently in 386, Jerome familiarized himself with the country and also learned much about it from his Jewish teachers. His major work on the topography of Palestine is *De situ et nominibus locorum hebraicorum* (c. 390), an adapted Latin translation of the Onomasticon of Eusebius. The translation supplements the source with much material that appeared in the fifth century, mainly in connection with the erection of churches in numerous holy places, such as Beth-El and Shiloh. Jerome also corrected what he viewed as inaccurate, e.g., the location of Bet Annava. Topographical material also appears in his various letters, especially in letter no. 108, a eulogy on the death of his friend Paula. In it, Jerome describes her travels in Palestine and takes advantage of the opportunity to mention many biblical sites, describing their condition at the time. The letter that he wrote after the death of Eustochium, the daughter of Paula, serves as a supplement to this description. In his comprehensive commentaries on the books of the Bible, Jerome cites many Jewish traditions concerning the location of sites mentioned in the Bible. Some of his views are erroneous, however (such as his explanation of the word *appadno* (אַפַּדְנוֹ), in Dan. 11:45, which he thought was a place-name).

Jerome was regularly in contact with Jews, but his attitude toward them and the law of Israel was the one that was prevalent among the members of the Church in his generation. He had a completely negative attitude toward the observances of both the early Christians and the Jews who converted to Christianity. This attitude was in contrast to that of Augustine, who was more tolerant in this matter, since in the eyes of Christians, the Torah preceded Christianity. The correspondence between Augustine and Jerome testifies that Augustine, as a theologian, was incapable of understanding the importance of Jerome's translations. On the other hand, Jerome was apparently incapable of original thought in the sphere of theology. One letter attributed to him (no. 19) that deals with circumcision and another (no. 149) that discusses the Jewish festivals were not compiled by him. One of Jerome's works that had a great influence on medieval Christian literature was *De viris illustribus*, which was compiled in Bethlehem in 392. Suetonius had published a book of the same name in about 113, dealing with the great Latin writers. Jerome's work dealt with 135 Christian literary personalities: he commences with Peter and ends with his own literary activity. He also discusses Philo, Josephus, and Justus of Tiberias, who were writers with both sectarian and Jewish backgrounds. The book contains errors and inaccuracies, but important information has also been preserved in it.

BIBLIOGRAPHY: D. Goldsmidt, in: *Sefer Yoḥanan Levi* (1949), 38–45; S. Krauss, in: JQR, 6 (1894), 225–38; L. Hughes, *The Christian Church in the Epistles of St. Jerome* (1923); F. Cavallera, *Saint Jérôme* (1923); P. de Labriolle, *Histoire de la littérature latine chrétienne* (1924), 445–500; G. Bardy, in: *Revue Bénédictine*, 46 (1934), 145–153; B. Blumenkranz, *Die Judenpredigt Augustins* (1946), 45–50; A. Penna, *S. Gerolamo* (1949); P. Antin, *Essai sur Saint Jérôme* (1951); F.X. Murphy (ed.), *A Monument to Saint Jerome: Essays on His Life, Work and Influence* (1952); J. Steinmann, *Saint Jérôme* (1958), 383. **ADD. BIBLIOGRAPHY:** H.F.D. Sparks, "Jerome as Biblical Scholar," in: P.R. Ackroyd and C.F. Evans (eds.), *The Cambridge History of the Bible*, vol. 1 (1970); J.N.D. Kelly, *Jerome: His Life, Writing and Controversies* (1975).

[David Flusser]

JERUSALEM

The entry is arranged according to the following outline:

HISTORY

Name

The first mention of the city of Jerusalem is in the Egyptian Execration Texts of the 19th–18th centuries B.C.E. The name is spelled wš mm and was probably pronounced "rushalimum." In the Tell el-Amarna letters of the 14th century B.C.E., it is written *Urusalim*, and in Assyrian *Ursalimmu* (Sennacherib inscription). In the Bible it is usually spelled *yrushlm* and sometimes *yrushlym* (pronounced "Yerushalayim"). The city of Salem (Gen. 14:18; Ps. 76:3) is evidently Jerusalem. The Greek *Hierosolyma* reflects the "holiness" (*hieros*, "holy") of the city. It seems that the original name was *Irusalem*, and the meaning of the two words composing it is "to found" ("*yarah*") and the name of the West Semitic god Shulmanu, or Shalim. The god may have been considered the patron of the city, which had contained a sanctuary in his honor. The popular later midrashic explanation of the name Jerusalem as "foundation of peace (*shalom*)" is associated with the poetic appellations given to the city.

The name *Jebus is that of the Jebusite people living in Jerusalem at the time of the conquest of Canaan by the Israelites, and the city was so designated until its occupation by King *David. The name Zion, whose meaning is not known, at first signified a part of the Jebusite city, probably the king's fortress – the "Stronghold of Zion" (II Sam. 5:7; I Chron. 11:5). King David called this part "David's City" ("*Ir David*"), which at first indicated the fortress (II Sam. 5:9; I Chron. 11:7). With the passage of time, both names became synonyms for the entire city. Jerusalem has many names of admiration and reverence given by the Prophets and later Hebrew poets: "The City," "God's City," the "Holy City," the "City of Justice," the "Faithful City," the "City of Peace," the "Beautiful City," etc.

Following the suppression of the Bar Kokhba revolt in 135 C.E., a new town was founded and it was renamed Aelia Capitolina after the family of Hadrian (Publius Aelius Hadrianus) and the patron gods of the city – the Capitoline triad of Jupiter, Juno, and Minerva. With the Muslim conquest in 638 C.E. the city continued to be known by its Roman-Byzantine name "Aelia," but later, from the Fatimid period onwards, the city was referred to as Bayt al-Maqdis (the "holy house," or the "temple"), and from the 10th century as al-Quds (the "holy").

[Samuel Abramsky / Shimon Gibson (2nd ed.)]

Protohistory

The earliest evidence of the existence of man in the area of Jerusalem is from the prehistoric periods. Scatters of Upper Acheulean flint implements of Lower Palaeolithic age have been found in the area of Baqa' and the Rephaim Valley (mainly handaxes and flakes) to the southwest of the city, and in Sheikh Jarrah and on Mount Scopus to the north of the city. Epi-Palaeolithic implements have also been identified in the area of the "City of David." Neolithic sites are also known from the vicinity of Jerusalem, notably at Abu Ghosh and Motza to the west. Chalcolithic pottery was discovered during excavations in the area of the "City of David" attesting to the importance of its spring of water from very early times. Chalcolithic sites are known in the vicinity of Jerusalem (e.g., Khirbet es-Sauma'a which was investigated by Nasralleh in 1936), as well as in the Judean Desert to the east and close to Bethlehem to the south, but the first proper excavation of a Chalcolithic site was made at Sataf, west of Jerusalem, in 1989.

The Bronze Age

Jerusalem emerged into the full light of history together with many other ancient cities of Canaan in the Early Bronze Age. It was one in a series of towns settled on the north-south watershed road in the central highland region. Its natural advantages were restricted; its territory probably extended over only a limited area of land. The small Early Bronze Age II settlement (a hamlet or village) was situated on the lower southwestern hill of Jerusalem, close to the spring of Gihon. Excavations have brought to light fragmentary rectangular houses and pottery. Jerusalem is mentioned as a Canaanite city-state in the Execration Texts of the 20th–19th centuries B.C.E. In the earlier group of these texts, two kings, spelled *Yqrʿm* and *Šsʿn*, are mentioned; one more ruler appears in the later group, but his name (*Ba…*) is largely illegible. More information about this period, the age of the Patriarchs, is obtained from the Bible. In Genesis 14:18, *Melchizedek, king of Salem [= Jerusalem], appears as priest of the "Most High" – in Hebrew *El Elyon*, a well-known Canaanite deity. Early Jerusalem, in common with many other cities in the Orient, was regarded as the property of a god whose vice regent on earth was its priest-king. This theocratic dynasty, the members of which bore an individual name combined with *ẓedek*, reappears in the time of Joshua, when *Adoni-Zedek was king of Jerusalem (Josh. 10: 1).

More information about Jerusalem in the Late Bronze Age is available in the El-Amarna letters of the 14th century B.C.E. Its ruler at the time was ARAD *Ḥeb/pa*; the latter (*Ḥeb/pa*) is the name of a Horite goddess and the ruler's name was pronounced either *Abdi Ḥeb/pa* or *Puti Ḥip/ba*. In one of his letters to Pharaoh, the king complains bitterly of the Egyptian garrison of Kaši (Cushite?) soldiers in the city and of the growing dangers from the *Ḥabiru (Hebrew?) invaders, with whom he and other kings loyal to Pharaoh were struggling. In the book of Joshua (10:1ff.), the king of Jerusalem was the head of the coalition of Amorite kings which fought against Joshua at Gibeon. He was defeated and killed, but his city was not conquered; although the tribe of Judah seems to have taken it temporarily (Judg. 1:8), they could not hold it. The division of Canaan into tribal lots assigned Jerusalem to Benjamin (Josh. 15:8; 18: 16) but it remained a Jebusite (not an Amorite) city until the time of David (Judg. 19:11–12), thus cutting the Israelite territory in two and separating the central tribes from the southern ones.

The topography and appearance of the Early and Late Bronze Age cities have still not been clarified, even though archaeological research has been going on in and around Jerusalem for more than a century. Scholars agree that the earliest city was situated on the eastern slope of the southeastern hill. The only spring in this area, the Gihon, was obviously the deciding factor in the location of the early city. New excavations have brought to light important fortifications from the Middle Bronze II on the eastern slope and around the Gihon Spring, including walls and towers. It appears that the hewing of tunnels to channel water had already been undertaken at this early stage. The narrow ridge in the southern part of the hill must have given Canaanite Jerusalem a good defensive position; the only weak spot was the narrow northern saddle, and it was here that the city wall was probably made strongest. In addition to walls, foundations, and water-supply installations, a series of tomb-caves, dated by their finds (mainly pottery) to the period from the Early Bronze to the Middle Bronze Age, have also been found. To the north of the city the presence of a fragment of an Egyptian stele and a libation slab may attest to the presence of Egyptians in the vicinity of Jerusalem. The appearance and size of the Late Bronze Age settlement (town or hamlet) has been much debated amongst scholars, and very few finds have been attributed to this pre-Davidic stage. One important discovery in the area of the "City of David" was that of architectural terracing (in Area G).

David and First Temple Period

CONQUEST BY DAVID. The story of David's conquest of Jerusalem is told in II Samuel 5:6ff. and I Chronicles 11:4ff. Having unified the tribes under his rule, David wanted to eliminate the foreign enclave of Jebusites that divided his own tribe of Judah from the rest of Israel. At the same time, he hoped that by taking Jerusalem – which was practically outside the various tribal areas – he would create a national capital and thus avoid inter-tribal jealousies. The capture itself was effected with surprising ease through a stratagem involving only "the king and his men," i.e., the standing forces and not the general levy of the Israelites; therefore, no one could dispute the royal possession of the conquered city. Opinions differ about both the recorded story of the Jebusites' parading their blind and lame on the walls and the stratagem that led to the conquest. It seems that the parade of the deformed may have been a magic rite, intended to arouse fear in the enemy. On the other hand, the new excavations show that a water system with tunnels was already in existence since the Middle Bronze Age, so it is not unlikely that it may have been the *ẓinnor*, or "gutter" (II Sam. 5:8), by which Joab and his men were able to scale and take the Jebusite settlement by surprise, penetrating behind its wall. David did not exterminate the vanquished locals; on the contrary, they seem to have been assigned certain administrative functions. *Araunah, who sold David the threshing floor outside the north wall of Jerusalem, where the Temple was to stand, may have been the last king of Jebusite Jerusalem (II Sam. 24:18–25). Having captured the city and defended it successfully against the Philistine assaults, David could establish it as "David's city" and the capital of the United Monarchy. By transferring the Ark of God there from its temporary abode at Kiriath-Jearim, he transformed Jerusalem from a Canaanite hamlet into a town sacred to God, the religious, as well as the political, center of Israel, the successor to Shiloh. It was due to this act that Jerusalem became the chief city of the Land of Israel (a position which neither its geographical nor its economic advantages seemed to warrant) and was frequently so throughout the ages.

According to the Bible, David's building work in Jerusalem was mainly of a utilitarian nature. He fortified the town and rebuilt the Jebusite citadel called "Zion." He may also have prepared for the extension of the city northwards by widening the saddle to the north by a massive "filling" (Millo) operation. The position of the Citadel is disputed: it may have stood at the northern and most threatened end of the City of David – some scholars believe that the stepped-stone structure uncovered in this area was connected to this citadel – or at its safest, southern end. David also built a house for his "mighty men" (his guards), probably with an armory adjoining, and prepared a dynastic tomb within the city according to royal custom (all other inhabitants were buried outside the walls). It has been claimed that rock-hewn chambers discovered on the eastern ridge in 1914 by R. Weill may have had something to do with this tomb. David inherited from the Canaanite rulers the "king's vale," a tract of fertile land close to the junction of the Kidron and Ben Hinnom Valleys, which was irrigated from the surplus water of the Gihon Spring.

UNDER SOLOMON. Under Solomon the economic advantages of Jerusalem as the center of the Israelite empire became evident. Caravans from the Euphrates to Egypt could be directed through the royal capital, while for the Phoenician trade with Elath, the Red Sea, and Ophir a passage through Jerusalem was actually the shortest route possible. Additional factors in the rapid development of the city were the establishment of the royal stores, fed by contributions from the 12 districts into which Israel was divided, as well as of the headquarters of the royal merchants. Moreover, the presence of a chariot force, foreign guards, and a sumptuous court, including a harem, also contributed to its growth. The cosmopolitan character of the city at that period was emphasized by the construction, on a hill outside the city, of sanctuaries to foreign gods, which was later accounted as one of Solomon's sins.

The construction of the First *Temple and the adjoining royal palace by Solomon gave Jerusalem a unique character, a combination of a holy city with a royal city. The Temple (erected on the summit of the eastern hill just north of the royal palace), although small in dimensions, was famous for its costly materials and technical perfection. It was included in the circuit of the city walls by an extension northward, which brought Jerusalem on the eastern hill to another saddle. It is possible that at that time the saddle was already fortified by towers, later known as the Tower of Hammeah and the Tower of Hananel (Neh. 12:39). The royal palace, the largest building in the city, occupied the entire span between the two valleys, north of David's city. Besides the throne room and the *House of the Forest of Lebanon (guard and chariotry quarters), it had an inner court of women; attached to it was the special palace on the Millo, which housed the princess of Egypt, politically Solomon's most important spouse. No archaeological remains have survived that could be interpreted as representing the First Temple or royal palace from the time of Solomon.

UNDER THE KINGS OF JUDAH. When the United Monarchy split in about 930 B.C.E., after Solomon's death, Jerusalem remained the seat of the Davidic dynasty and the capital of the smaller Kingdom of Judah. This territorial decline was accompanied by a corresponding one in economic life. *Shishak (Sheshonq), king of Egypt, did not take Jerusalem during his invasion of Judah (c. 925 B.C.E.), but the ransom paid to avoid capture further impoverished the city. Jerusalem derived one advantage from the split between Israel and Judah: many priests and levites, expelled from the Northern Kingdom by Jeroboam, returned to Judah and Jerusalem and "strengthened the Kingdom of Judah" (II Chron. 11:13–17). The situation remained unchanged until the reign of *Omri, king of Israel (ninth century B.C.E.), when peace was made with the Northern Kingdom and the trade routes opened. Foreign influence followed in the wake of the alliance with Israel; in the days of Queen Athaliah, Jerusalem was the center of a revived Baalism. The coup d'état carried out by the high priest Jehoiada (II Kings 11) put an end to such backslidings. In the reign of *Amaziah (798–785 B.C.E.), Jerusalem was captured by King *Jehoash of Israel, who broke down 400 cubits of its northern wall. *Uzziah, who remained true to the alliance with Israel, repaired the breach and strengthened the walls: "And he made in Jerusalem engines, invented by skillful men, to be on the towers and upon the corners wherewith to shoot arrows and great stones" (II Chron. 26:15). It was in the time of Uzziah that the voice of the prophet *Isaiah was heard in the city, making it the center not only of Temple worship but also of moral and social regeneration (Isa. 1:1).

Uzziah's successor, *Ahaz, attempted to curry favor with Assyria by building an altar in the Assyrian fashion and encouraging Babylonian astral cults in Jerusalem. His son *Hezekiah, counseled by Isaiah, prevailed against Assyrian influences. During his reign the Temple was purified and repaired (a prior repair was made under Joash). In anticipation of an Assyrian assault, Hezekiah reinforced the walls of Jerusalem and included in the city part of the Western Hill, the *Mishneh* (II Kings 22:14), or "second" Jerusalem, which was already settled in his time. Remains of fortifications have been uncovered on the Western Hill of Jerusalem, and some of these may represent the "other wall" built by Hezekiah (II Chron. 32:5). He also cut the famous tunnel under David's city, through which the waters of the Gihon flowed to the Pool of Solomon. The Assyrian army under *Sennacherib did indeed besiege Jerusalem in 701 B.C.E., but some kind of disaster in the Assyrian camp forced Sennacherib to agree to a treaty with Hezekiah, which left Jerusalem safe. Hezekiah was the last king buried in the Davidic tomb, in its upper passage. His son *Manasseh built, according to II Kings, altars to the "host of Heaven" and the Baalim (21: 3–5, 7). The Chronicler adds the story of Manasseh's captivity and repentance, after which he removed all the pagan altars and idols he had set up and "restored the altar of the Lord" (II Chron. 33:15–16). He was then able to add to the walls of Jerusalem and to strengthen them in many directions (II Chron. 33:14). Of the brief reign of Amon, who followed Manasseh, nothing of note for the history of Jerusalem was recorded.

Under King *Josiah, Jerusalem returned to its historical religious function. After the fall of both the Northern Kingdom of Israel and Assyria, it again became the spiritual focus of the entire remnant of the nation. After Josiah's death in the battle of Megiddo (609 B.C.E.), his weak successors vacillated between Egypt and Babylon. After the brief reign of Jehoahaz, Jehoiakim came to the throne as a tool of Egypt; compelled to submit to the Babylonians, he soon rebelled but did not live to see the subsequent events leading to the surrender of Jerusalem. As early as 597 B.C.E., when *Nebuchadnezzar, king of Babylon, approached Jerusalem, King *Jehoiachin, together with his queen, ministers, and servants, came out and surrendered; Nebuchadnezzar crowned *Zedekiah king, who was the last king of Judah. Ten years later the Babylonian army laid siege to the city and captured it after several months. The Babylonian captain Nebuzaradan exiled most of the inhabitants:

"And he burnt the house of the Lord, and the king's house, and all the houses of Jerusalem, and every great man's house burnt he with fire" (II Kings 25:9). This disaster, of which the prophets Jeremiah and Ezekiel had given ample warning, left Jerusalem desolate for over 50 years.

[Michael Avi-Yonah / Shimon Gibson (2nd ed.)]

Second Temple Period

RETURN TO ZION. The destruction of Jerusalem by the Babylonians (587/586 B.C.E.) decimated its population, and it remained desolate for five decades. Its ruins represented the decline of Judah. Nevertheless, the Jewish people remained firm in their faith in Jerusalem, which was identified with their common history and their hope for national redemption. Psalms 137:5–6, uttered in Babylonian exile, "If I forget thee, O Jerusalem, Let my right hand forget her cunning…," is a moving expression of this hope.

In 536 B.C.E., after the fall of Babylon, Cyrus, king of Persia, who became the overlord of Judah, issued his famous declaration, which allowed those desiring to return to Zion to do so and to rebuild the Temple (see *Exile, Babylonian). The resettlement of the city and the rebuilding of the Temple were effected very gradually, as the surrounding nations were hostile to this activity. Only under Darius I in 515 B.C.E. did *Zerubbabel, the governor, and Joshua, son of the high priest Jehozadak, succeed in completing the Second Temple. The city remained almost empty, however; its walls were breached and its gates were burned down. In 445 B.C.E. *Nehemiah, son of Hacaliah, an important official at the court of King *Artaxerxes, moved by reports of the miserable conditions in the Holy City, decided to leave the court and go to Jerusalem. He was appointed governor of Judah and was mainly responsible for the rebuilding of the city. He organized the inhabitants of Judah and took security precautions necessitated by the bitter opposition of its neighbors, especially the Samaritans. First he repaired the wall, following its restricted course in the period of the monarchy around David's City: "They that builded the wall and they that bore burdens laded themselves, every one with one of his hands wrought in the work, and with the other held his weapon" (Neh. 4:11). He then took steps to populate the city by commanding the nobles and one tenth of the rural population of Judah to settle there. He decreed an annual tax of a third of a shekel for the maintenance of the Temple. He suppressed the Tyrian trading market set up outside the city on the Sabbath, erected a strong fortress (the *birah*) north of the Temple, posted guards on the gates, and provided for the security of the city.

It was *Ezra the Scribe who was responsible for the restoration of the authority of the Mosaic Law and for making Jerusalem the undisputed religious center of Judaism. The rest of the Persian period is wrapped in obscurity. The many jar-handle inscriptions reading "Jerusalem" or "the city" show that it was an important administrative and fiscal center.

HELLENISTIC PERIOD. Jerusalem submitted peacefully, with the rest of Judah, to Alexander the Great (332 B.C.E.), who confirmed the privileges of the city. The visit of the king as reported by Josephus, however, seems legendary. After the death of Alexander (323 B.C.E.), the city suffered as a result of a series of wars for succession. *Ptolemy I, king of Egypt, seized it and deported a part of its population (according to a Greek historian, the conquest was made possible because the Jews would not go out to fight on the Sabbath). With the stabilization of Ptolemaic rule (301 B.C.E.), however, the relationship between Judah and Egypt improved, and a period of prosperity ensued. Judah had broad autonomy in domestic affairs and Jerusalem continued to be its administrative center. At the head of the administration were the high priests, descendants of Joshua, son of Jehozadak, and the Council of Elders, which bore the Greek name of *Gerousia*. The high priest was not only the religious head of Jerusalem and Judah but also its political and administrative leader. The *Gerousia*, despite its Greek name, was a direct continuation of the Council of Elders of the Persian times. It was composed not only of Jerusalemites, but also of heads of clans from provincial towns. The Temple was the center of the religious and social life of Jerusalem. Due to its presence, many priests (kohanim) lived there and formed a very important social class. A new class, that of the scribes (interpreters of the law), began to develop. In addition to the priestly families and the scribes, a number of noble families came into prominence. Among them was the House of Tobiah, which had extensive land holdings in Transjordan and grew rich from tax farming. These aristocratic families developed close ties with the royal court and the gentile noble families in the empire and thus came under the sway of the Hellenistic way of life.

The Seleucid conquest in 198 B.C.E. was welcomed by the Jews. They helped besiege the Egyptian garrison in the Citadel and were consequently compensated by Antiochus III. A new charter was granted confirming the right of the Jews to live by the "laws of their fathers." The population was exempted from taxes for three years, and the priests and scribes were exempted in perpetuity. In addition, the king forbade the bringing of unclean animals and even the skins thereof into the city. On the surface the situation in Jerusalem seemed to remain as it had been under the Ptolemies as far as its administration, the character of its institutions, and social conditions were concerned. In reality, however, the Hellenization of the upper strata of the society was intensified. The priests and the secular leaders came closer in their thinking and way of life to the corresponding classes among the non-Jews, and the Hellenistic influence seeped down to the lower classes. The leaders of the pro-Hellenistic movement who wanted radical changes were the houses of Tobiah and Bilgah. The traditionalists were headed by the high priest, Onias III, but even in his family there was a rift: his brother, *Jason, leaned towards the Hellenizers. The struggle became more and more polarized due to the general political situation and the financial crisis that resulted from the defeat of the Seleucid empire by Rome. The king strove to regain his power by aggrandizement of the cities in accordance with the Hellenistic tradition of the polis.

The official in charge of the Temple, Simeon of the house of Bilgah, made an effort to limit the powers of the high priest *Onias in the administration of the Temple, as well as in the economic life of the city. When his attempt failed, he turned to the Syrian governor and asked for his intervention. He pointed out that sums of money far beyond that required for ritual sacrifices were known to be in the Temple, and should, by right, be given over to the king's government. Thereupon, the king sent Heliodorus, his chief minister, to investigate. Onias opposed this move vigorously, pointing out that the monies did not belong to the Temple but were sums deposited there for safekeeping, and Heliodorus failed in his mission. Although there is no reason to believe that the king intended to harm the Temple or to intervene in religious affairs, the episode left a sediment of mistrust toward his government. Simeon continued in his attempts. There were riots in the streets of Jerusalem and Onias was compelled to ask the help of the government to maintain order.

In 175 B.C.E., with the ascent to the throne of *Antiochus IV Epiphanes, significant changes began to take place. His reign was marked by most energetic steps to Hellenize the empire. Antiochus indicated interest in the affairs of Jerusalem, and Jason seized the opportunity to convince the king to put him in the place of his brother, Onias III, as the high priest. Jason promised the king a considerable increase in taxes, as well as a large tribute, in return for his permission to make changes in the governing of the city. The two major reforms made by Jason, with the full support of the king, were the building of a gymnasium in Jerusalem and the change of the Jewish city into a Hellenistic polis (one of the many in the empire) to be known as Antioch.

The establishment under the Temple fortress of the gymnasium changed the whole spiritual and social atmosphere. It began to rival the Temple as the social center, especially among the young priests and laymen. This was a grievous blow to the traditionalists, particularly as, according to Greek tradition, the gymnasium was under the patronage of the gods Hermes and Hercules. The author of II Maccabees describes with great bitterness how, on a given signal, the priests left the Temple in order to view the games. The conversion of Jerusalem into a polis required a new census, which gave Jason and his supporters the opportunity to make changes in the register of citizens. Jason did not do away with the existing system of administration, and the traditional *Gerousia* continued to function together with the high priest. As the head of Jerusalem and Judah, he followed the line of the house of Tobiah, endeavoring to integrate the city into the general cultural and social life of the empire. Delegates from Antioch-Jerusalem were sent to Tyre to represent the city at the games in honor of Hercules.

Jason did not remain high priest for long; it seems that the king did not consider him sufficiently loyal. *Menelaus, an ardent Hellenizer of the house of Bilgah, was appointed in his place. He purchased his position for a high price, and a new chapter began in the relations between the Seleucid empire and Judah. The high priest, who had heretofore represented the interests of the Jews in the king's court, was now made an official of the administration. Menelaus was unable to fulfill his financial obligations to the king and was called to appear before him. His brother Lysimachus was left in charge and immediately availed himself of the opportunity to rob the Temple's treasury. Consequently, a revolt broke out against the rule of Menelaus in which Lysimachus was killed. The three members of the *Gerousia* who were sent to complain to the king against Menelaus were put to death, and the latter continued to enjoy the support of Antiochus.

Upon the return of the king from his first war in Egypt in 169 B.C.E., he visited the city and took away with him the golden altar, the candelabra, and other gold and silver objects found in the Temple. In the following year, when the king was again at war in Egypt, the rumor spread that Antiochus had died. At this point, the deposed Jason, at the head of a force of 1,000 men, broke into the city and gained control of all but the fortress in which Menelaus and his supporters and the permanent garrison defended themselves. On his way back from Egypt, the king seized Jerusalem, constructed a fortress, the *Acra, in a dominant position opposite the Temple, and stationed a garrison there. In 167 B.C.E. Antiochus issued decrees against the Jewish religion that were carried out with special severity in Jerusalem. The Temple was desecrated; its treasures were confiscated. Antiochus converted it into a shrine dedicated to the god Dionysus and ordered the erection of a huge temple of his favorite god, Zeus Olympius. Opponents of Antiochus' policy fled the city, while a Seleucid garrison and the Hellenizers remained in Jerusalem. All around, the countryside rebelled.

HASMONEAN PERIOD. The revolt led by *Judah Maccabee aimed at the purification of Jerusalem and the attainment of autonomy. The city was out of reach of the Jewish insurgents; however, they set up a successful blockade around the city and were able to beat back four successive attempts to relieve the Seleucid garrison. After the fourth victory of Judah in battle near Beth-Zur, they were able to reoccupy the Temple Mount, cleanse the Temple of pagan objects, rebuild the altar, and resume the sacrifices in December 164 B.C.E. Since that time Jews have observed the Feast of Dedication, or *Ḥanukkah, in memory of this occasion. After the death of Antiochus IV, his successor granted the Jews religious freedom and appointed a new high priest, Eliakim (Alkimos). The Temple walls were breached with the help of traitors, and Judah was forced to leave Jerusalem. After the death of Judah in battle (160 B.C.E.), his brothers, Jonathan and Simeon, had to operate from outside Jerusalem.

Due to the continuous conflicts and intrigues in the Seleucid empire, it became possible for the Hasmoneans to return to Jerusalem several years later. In 152 B.C.E. Jonathan was made high priest and governor of the Jews. He was allowed to reoccupy the city, with the exception of the Acra, which continued to be held by the king's garrison, and all his attempts to gain control of it failed. He therefore built a wall to cut the Acra off from the city and strengthened the wall of Jerusalem. Simeon, Jonathan's brother and successor, finally expelled the garrison and eradicated the Acra of its pagan cults. A triumphal entry into the fallen fortress was made on the 23rd of Iyyar 141 B.C.E., the date which henceforward was celebrated as the day of the final deliverance of Jerusalem. It would appear that the construction of the ("first") wall around the Western Hill was initiated by Jonathan and continued by Simeon, and that this was done for ideological reasons to renew the visible ruins of fortifications that had originally surrounded the larger city in the time of Hezekiah and to celebrate the banishment of the Seleucid Greeks.

Early in the reign of John *Hyrcanus, Jerusalem was placed by Antiochus Sidetes VII under a heavy siege, which ended in a treaty under which the city wall was breached. Evidence of this battle was unearthed during the Citadel excavations near the Jaffa Gate, consisting of scatters of ballista balls and arrowheads. For the next six decades (until 63 B.C.E.) no enemy approached the city. Jerusalem became the capital city of the Hasmonean kingdom, which included large parts of western Palestine as well as areas of Transjordan. It was the center of ever-growing political, economic, and religious activity. The Temple became the ritual and religious center of a large number of people in the Land of Israel who had not previously come under the influence of Judaism. Jews in the Diaspora, converts to Judaism, and sympathizers with Judaism contributed to the wealth of the city by paying half a *shekel, and making other contributions. The sages of Jerusalem became renowned throughout Jewry, and their influence was felt wherever Jews resided. Trades and crafts developed in the city.

The "Letter of *Aristeas" contains a description of Hasmonean Jerusalem, with its triple wall, its markets, replete with all kinds of wares, its supply of drinking water, and so forth. It was a large and prosperous city. The Hasmonean palace was built on the Western Hill, dwellings were constructed in all parts of the city, and a new rectangular esplanade was built for the Temple. Segments of the "first" wall built during Hasmonean times have been uncovered in the Jewish Quarter, the Citadel, along the western Old City wall, and around traditional Mount Zion. Hasmonean pottery, coins, and arrowheads have also been recovered during excavations. To the end of this period belong some of the splendid monuments in the Kidron Valley, such as the Tomb of the Sons of Hezir (erroneously called the Tomb of St. James), the so-called Tomb of Zechariah, and the Tomb of Jason (in the Rehavia neighborhood), which contains one of the earliest drawings of a *menorah* and a picture of a sea fight (this Jason was apparently a retired sea captain).

No external enemy menaced Jerusalem, but it was the scene of violent civil strife in the days of Alexander *Yannai (Jannaeus). His widow, *Salome Alexandra, succeeded in restoring peace to the city, but after her death conflict broke out anew. *Hyrcanus II besieged his brother *Aristobulus II in the Temple with the aid of the Nabateans, but was forced to retreat. In the end this fratricidal war profited only the Romans. In 64 B.C.E., when Pompey decided in favor of Hyrcanus, the partisans of Aristobulus shut themselves up in the Temple and defied the decision of the Roman general. Pompey was forced to undertake a siege, since the Temple was now defended by a deep rock-cut fosse on the north. In 63 B.C.E., the Temple wall was breached and the Romans broke into the Temple itself. Pompey entered the Holy of Holies, but did not touch the Temple treasuries. He left the government to Hyrcanus and his adviser *Antipater the Idumean, the father of *Herod. In 40 B.C.E. Jerusalem was seized by the Parthians, who had invaded Judea as allies of Mattathias Antigonus. Three years later (37 B.C.E.), after a prolonged siege, Herod's troops and those of his Roman allies breached the walls of Jerusalem and penetrated the city. There followed great slaughter and looting, until Herod was forced to intervene in order to save the city.

HERODIAN PERIOD. King Herod, who reigned over Judea for 33 years (37–4 B.C.E.), completely transformed the external aspect of Jerusalem. His aim was to make his hold on the city secure, knowing full well how much he was hated by its population; to satisfy his liking for ostentation and splendor; and to placate the populace by providing work. His successful financial ventures and high taxation provided the means. Herod transferred the seat of civil power from the old Hasmonean palace to a new site in the northwestern corner of the city, within the "first" wall. His palace was protected on the north by three towers: Phasael, Hippicus, and Mariamne; the base of one of these towers (probably Hippicus, though the matter is still debated), was inserted into the Hasmonean "first" wall, and this is clear from excavations inside the Citadel. The location of the other two towers is uncertain, although Josephus says that they too were built on the line of the "old" wall. Behind the three towers, to the south, extended Herod's palace, built on a podium, and protected to the west by a wall with towers through which one entered via a gate (the "gate of the Essenes"). Apparently the palace adjoined on one side the Agora or upper market. Within the wall were extensive gardens and the place which was divided into two separate blocks of buildings, called Caesareum and Agrippeum in honor of Augustus and his general Vipsanius Agrippa, respectively. The palace gardens were most likely supplied with water derived from the Mamila Pool (see Water Supply, below). A large sewer, referred to by Josephus as "Bethso," extended out of the base of the palace to the west and into the Hinnom Valley.

Herod's other projects in Jerusalem were on the eastern side of the city. He transformed the old Baris fortress into a more cohesive fortified tower-like structure dominating the Temple area, and called it Antonia, in honor of the triumvir Mark Antony. In the Temple area itself, the esplanade was enlarged, especially on its southern side, and it was given the trapezoid shape which is still preserved. The Temple Mount was surrounded by a wall built of large stone ashlars of which the *Western ("Wailing") Wall is but a section. Beneath the Temple Mount were numerous water cisterns, passages, and conduits. The Temple Mount was surrounded by a portico with columns 50 ft. (15 m.) high. The entire southern side was taken up by a two-story triple hall, the "royal basilica." Herod also entirely rebuilt the Temple itself, doubling its height and richly adorning its exterior. Various gates led into the Temple Mount.

Extant remains of Herod's building activities in Jerusalem include towers in the Citadel; fortification walls around Mount Zion; the Bethso sewage tunnel; the podium of his palace on the Western Hill with a gate to the west; the Temple Mount walls; a flight of steps built on arches (Robinson's Arch) descending from the Temple esplanade at the southwestern corner to a paved street running from north to south; the passageways of the Double and Triple gates in the southern Temple Mount walls; the rock-cut portions of Antonia with its adjacent pool, the Struthion; and the Siloam and Bethesda Pools to the south and north of the Temple Mount, respectively. Besides these, the monument of Herod's family (mentioned by Josephus) has been identified with a round structure to the north of the city. The so-called Tomb of Absalom in the Kidron Valley is also assigned to his reign; it gives an idea of the rich eclectic ornamentation of Herodian architecture current at that time.

UNDER THE ROMAN PROCURATORS. After Herod's death and the banishment of his son *Archelaus, Judea was made a province of the Roman Empire (6 C.E.). Jerusalem was ruled by Roman procurators who resided in Caesarea and thus ceased to be the capital of Judea. The procurators, however, would come to Jerusalem from time to time with their troops, especially during the three pilgrim festivals, when it was crowded with pilgrims from all over the country and from abroad. The governors would stay in Herod's old palace, which was used as a praetorium. In deference to Jewish religious sensitivity, the troops came to Jerusalem without their standards, which bore idolatrous images. The city government was in the hands of the high priest and the Sanhedrin, which fulfilled the functions of the *Gerousia* in the Hellenistic period, i.e., the municipal council. The last Jewish ruler over Jerusalem was Herod Agrippa (41–44), who began to build a new wall on the north side of the city (the "third" wall) but was stopped by order of the Romans. Under the procurators who succeeded him, sporadic riots broke out in the city, usually resulting in clashes with the Roman troops. One of the procurators, *Pontius Pilate (26–36), under whose rule the execution of *Jesus of Nazareth took place, constructed the first aqueduct which brought water to Jerusalem from the vicinity of Hebron. The small Christian community remained in Jerusalem until 66, when it retired to Pella.

Jerusalem's significance was more than that of the administrative center of a diminished Judea; it was the capital of the Jewish nation. The Temple, the Sanhedrin, and the great houses of study of the Pharisees turned it into a symbol for Jews everywhere. As Philo expressed it in his *Legatio ad Gaium*, Jerusalem was the metropolis not only of Judea, but of many lands because of its colonies. It was renowned even among non-Jews: the elder Pliny wrote that Jerusalem was the most famous among the great cities of the East. A legendary halo surrounded the city. It was the focal point of Jewish unity and attracted Jewish pilgrims and converts (e.g., Queen *Helene of Adiabene). Because of the Temple, the main priestly families resided there, as did many important aristocratic families that wished to be close to the center of affairs. Even scions of the House of Herod lived there from time to time, though their kingdoms were some distance away. Jerusalem was the center of spiritual activity. The heads of *Bet Hillel – Rabban *Gamaliel I and Rabban *Simeon son of Gamaliel – resided in Jerusalem. Houses of learning in the city attracted students from all over the country and from abroad. The city's status helped it to become an important economic center. Its area increased to one square mile and its population grew quite considerably.

One of the phenomena of Jerusalem during this period was the presence of many Jews from numerous countries, from Media and Elam in the east to Italy in the west, many of whom settled in the city. These immigrants preserved their different ways of life for long periods and congregated in distinct communities according to their lands of origin. Especially noticeable was the difference between Jews who spoke Hebrew and Aramaic and the Hellenized Jews who came from Egypt (especially from Alexandria), Cyrenaica, and Asia Minor, the latter groups having special synagogues of their own. In the last years before the destruction, social tension grew to such an extent that it affected the order and security of the city. In addition to the general enmity toward Roman rule, there were conflicts among the Jews themselves,, notably friction among different groups in the priestly oligarchy and tension brought about by the activities of the extremist fighters for freedom from the Romans (the Sicarii), who used violence and were not averse to killing their opponents. There was also an increase in the activities of visionaries and prophets who spread messianic expectations among the people and the pilgrims.

JERUSALEM AT THE END OF THE SECOND TEMPLE PERIOD. The traveler's first glimpse of Jerusalem would have been from Mount Scopus (Har ha-*Ẓofim). Crossing the Kidron Valley, he traversed the "Tombs of the Kings" (of *Helena of Adiabene), and reached the "third" wall, which stretched from the direction of the Kidron Valley to the Psephinus Tower in the northwest. Entrance to the wall was from an area of gardens and vegetable fields through the Women's Gate. Behind it was the then sparsely populated New City or Bezetha. Approaching the "second" wall, which enclosed the area known as the "Mahtesh," the commercial quarter in the upper Tyropoeon Valley, one would see (beyond this wall) the wood and sheep markets, the Pool of Bethesda (or Sheep Pool), and the Pool of the Towers (today called the Pool of Hezekiah). The Pool of Bethesda was used as a place of purification by the many

Jews who attended the festivities in the Temple. The "second" wall, which ran in a broken line from the vicinity of Herod's Palace in the Upper City to the Antonia fortress, protected the city proper. Outside it were the tombs of Alexander and John Hyrcanus; within it were the various bazaars of the city. From this residential and commercial area one could proceed through the Water Gate or the Garden Gate into the Upper City. The latter, which was the aristocratic quarter, was extensively built up and covered the whole of the Western Hill of Jerusalem. Within it stood the palaces of the high priests and of the Hasmoneans. At its northwestern extremity rose the three towers protecting Herod's palace, respectively about 135, 120, and 70 ft. high. A bridge (the remnants of which are now called Wilson's Arch in honor of the 19th-century explorer of Jerusalem) joined the Upper City to the Temple Mount.

The Upper City was protected on the east by a rocky scarp facing the Tyropoeon Valley. This valley was a popular quarter with closely set houses and was called the Lower City; it extended to the southeastern hill (the so-called Ophel), which was originally the City of David. At its southern extremity was the large, rectangular, stepped Pool of Siloam (called by Josephus the "Pool of Solomon"), which was fed with fresh water derived from the spring of Gihon. Like the Bethesda Pool, the Siloam Pool was also used for the purification of travelers who reached Jerusalem for the Jewish holidays. Stairs descended from the Upper to the Lower City and also rose from the latter to the Temple area (via Robinson's Arch).

The esplanade of the sanctuary was protected by a high, massive wall, built of typical Herodian masonry with double margins. It was surrounded by open colonnaded porticoes, of which the southern one, the "royal basilica," was the most splendid. The Temple itself stood within yet another enclosure with steps; it was very high (about 150 feet) and glittered with gold and white marble "like a snow-covered mountain." The tower of Antonia (with a height reaching about 180 feet) overlooked the esplanade from the northwest. Outside the walls, and especially to the east and the south and the west, along the Kidron and Hinnom valleys, stretched the necropolis. Among the great and imposing tombs erected in the first century C.E. were the Tombs of the Judges or of the Sanhedrin in the Upper Kidron Valley and the so-called Tomb of Absalom and Tomb of Jehoshaphat in the central Kidron Valley.

As a fortified city, Jerusalem was rendered all the stronger by its topographical position. Situated on the southern slope of a ridge issuing from the watershed line, it was protected on the west, south, and east by the Hinnom and Kidron valleys, while on the north it had three strongly reinforced walls.

The Siege of Titus. In the autumn of 66 the misrule of the procurators finally provoked the outbreak of a revolt, which soon became a full-scale war. The Roman governor of Syria, Cestius Gallus, advanced with his army to the gates of the Temple in an attempt to quell the uprising, but retreated after a disastrous defeat. For over three years, Jerusalem was free; the silver shekels (see *Coins and Currency) bearing the legend "Jerusalem the Holy" commemorate this period. However, internecine strife among the insurgents wasted the resources of the city, and only when the enemy approached in the spring of 70 did they join forces.

The Temple and the Lower City were defended by *John of Giscala, the Upper City by Simeon b. Giora. The attack was led by Titus, the son and heir of the emperor Vespasian, with an army of four legions at his disposal.

After reconnaissance and the establishment of camps in two places around the city, the Romans attacked the "third" wall near Herod's palace, hoping to penetrate the Upper City and thus end the siege in one stroke. They failed in their plan and had to content themselves with the breaching of the "third" wall and the occupation of Bezetha. Moving his camp to a place called the "Assyrian Camp" (now the Russian Compound), Titus attacked the "second" wall and scaled it after some bitter fighting in the narrow, winding bazaars. Now the siege began in earnest; attempts were made to attack by the usual methods (siege mounds with movable towers equipped with battering rams). But the besieged defenders fought with great determination, setting fire to the Roman machines of war and undermining the siege mounds reared against the Towers' Pool and the Antonia. Titus thereupon ordered the construction of a siege wall to blockade the city tightly in an attempt to weaken the population through hunger (the quantity of water in the cisterns was apparently sufficient to carry the city through the summer). After this process the attack was renewed. At the beginning of Av (August) the wall of the Antonia was finally stormed, and after a few days the Temple was set aflame (9th of Av). The Romans then spread over the Lower City and the Tyropoeon Valley, but they had to renew their siege operations against the Upper City, which only fell a month later. Most of the people in the city had either been killed or had perished from hunger; the survivors were sold into slavery or executed. The city was destroyed, except for the three towers of Herod and a portion of the western wall, which were spared to protect the camp of the Tenth Legion situated in the area of the old palace of Herod.

[Michael Avi-Yonah / Menahem Stern / Shimon Gibson (2nd ed.)]

The Roman Period

Although Jerusalem remained in ruins for 61 years, part of the inhabitants (including some members of the Christian community that left for Pella during the siege) returned and settled around the legionary camp on the Western Hill. An inscription of an officer of the Tenth Legion, Fatalis, records that he lived there with his freedwoman Ionice, and there were many others like him. Numerous rooftiles stamped with the names and symbols of the Tenth Legion have been found. Later sources state that the returning Jews had as many as seven synagogues in that area. In 130 C.E. Emperor Hadrian visited Jerusalem and decided to establish a Roman colony on the ruins of the Jewish city. The governor, Tineius Rufus, performed the ceremony of plowing along the line of the projected walls in the name of the emperor and founder.

This ceremony is represented on coins of the colony, which received the name of *Aelia Capitolina in honor of the family name of the emperor and the Capitoline triad (Jupiter, Juno, and Minerva). There is no evidence, however, that the city was captured by Bar Kokhba during the second revolt against the Romans, and Aelia Capitolina was physically only properly founded in 135 C.E. Hadrian decreed that no circumcised person should be allowed into Jerusalem and its territory under pain of death; even the Christian community was forced to change its bishop of Jewish origin for a gentile.

Aelia Capitolina was apparently built in the northern and central parts of the Old City of today, with the Roman camp of the Tenth Legion to the southwest, and with an additional quarter situated in the former Lower City, around the foot of the southwestern part of the Temple Mount. Many of the streets in the northern part of the city were originally established at this time. A forum existed at the junction of the *decumanus* (running from the Jaffa Gate area to the east) and *cardo* streets (the latter running from the Damascus Gate area to the south), with various buildings and a temple or shrine to Venus in the area of the present-day Church of the Holy Sepulcher. The other forum was situated to the northwest of the city, immediately north of the Temple Mount, with a triumphal arch (now known as the Ecce Homo arch), a shrine dedicated to Serapis and other cults, and purification pools. The location of the Capitoline Temple is debated, with some placing it in the western forum and others believing it was built on top of the ruined Antonia Fortress, overlooking the northwest forum. The Temple area (called the Quadra or "Square") was left outside the colony plan; various pagan statues were placed upon it with an equestrian statue of Hadrian in front. A large monumental inscription in Latin mentioning a "gate" has been found in the southern Temple area. Other known monuments of Aelia were a tetrapylon (four-arched gate), public baths, and steps leading to the nympheum (public fountain) outside the city, with twelve arches (the Dodekapylon), near the Pool of Siloam. The city was divided into seven wards, which for centuries bore the names of the first headmen, or amphodarchs. It did not have the rights of an Italian colony (*jus italicum*) and thus had to pay taxes on its lands. City coins were issued from the time of Hadrian to that of Valerianus (260) but are especially plentiful from the times of Antoninus Pius, Marcus Aurelius, Eleagabalus, and Trajan Decius. The 206 coin types evidence the gods worshiped in Aelia: Serapis, Tyche, the Dioscuri, Roma, Ares, Nemesis, and others are found in addition to the Capitoline triad. The worship of Serapis is confirmed by a dedicatory inscription; that of the goddess Hygieia is connected with the healing baths near the Bethesda pool.

Aelia was a quiet provincial city. The great events were imperial visits, such as that of Septimius Severus in 201, which was commemorated by an inscription discovered near the Western Wall. On this occasion the colony received the honorary title "Commodiana." Toward the end of the third century the Legio X Fretensis (still in Aelia at about 250) was transferred to Elath and replaced by a troop of Moors. In the second and third centuries, the Christian community in Jerusalem developed peacefully; one of its bishops, Narcissus, died a centenarian, after sharing the office with Alexander from Cappadocia. The latter established a famous library at Aelia. In his time Christian pilgrimages to the city began. The Jews also profited from a de facto relaxation of the prohibition against visiting Jerusalem as pilgrims.

Byzantine Jerusalem

The status of Aelia was completely revolutionized when the Christian emperor Constantine became master of Palestine in 324. At the Council of Nicaea, Macarius, the bishop of Aelia, reported to the emperor on the state of the Christian holy sites and persuaded the emperor's mother, *Helena, to visit Jerusalem (325). During her visit, the shrine or temple of Venus was destroyed and beneath it emerged a tomb identified as the Tomb of Jesus. According to slightly later Christian tradition the "True Cross" was also found at this time in a cave nearby. Constantine decided to erect a basilical martyrium at *Golgotha to mark the finding of the Tomb of Jesus. The church consisted of a forecourt leading to a basilica, a baptisterium, another court which may have contained part of the rock of Golgotha, and the Tomb of Jesus itself, which had been cut down to a cube, and which was then covered by a small building (edicule) surmounted by a dome supported on columns with silver capitals. The church was built by the architects Zenobius and Eusthatius of Constantinople, and was dedicated in 335. Another church, the Eleona, was built on the slopes of the Mount of Olives. The city then assumed a predominantly Christian character; the prohibition against the entrance of Jews into the city was renewed, with the exception of the 9th of Av, when they were allowed to lament the destruction of the Temple.

The growing importance of Jerusalem as a Christian center was temporarily interrupted by the emperor Julian the "apostate"), who reverted back to old pagan practices and favored Judaism. In 363 he ordered the reconstruction of the Temple and entrusted the task to his friend Alypius. Work went on until May 27, when an earthquake caused conflagration in the building stores. As the emperor had just started on his Persian Campaign, those responsible for the work suspended it. The death of Julian in Persia and the enthronement of the Christian emperor Jovian put an end to this project. During that time the bishop of Jerusalem was the eminent preacher Cyril, who was often exiled but always succeeded in returning (350–86). In his time Christian pilgrims of all countries, from Britain and Gaul in the west to Ethiopia, India, and Persia on the south and east, could be seen in the city.

Cyril's outstanding successor was John (396–417). During his episcopate numerous aristocratic families, led by St. *Jerome, fled from Rome to Jerusalem (385–419). Among them were noble and rich women, such as Melania and Poemenia, who erected churches and monasteries (Church of Ascension, 378, Church of Gethsemane, 390). The first hermits established themselves in the vicinity of Jerusalem at that time. The city also served as a place of refuge for fallen grandees, such as the family of the minister Rufinus. In 428 the energetic Juvenal became bishop of Jerusalem. In 438 the empress Eudocia visited Jerusalem for the first time; due to her intervention, Jews were again allowed to live in the city. After her separation from her husband, Theodosius II, she settled permanently in the Holy City (444–60), spending lavishly on churches (including the basilica of St. Stephen north of the city). She also had a new city wall constructed around Mount Zion (parts of this wall were excavated in 1895–97). Both Eudocia and Juvenal became involved in the Monophysite controversy. By successful maneuvering, the bishop succeeded in obtaining the status of patriarch and authority over the churches of Palestine and Arabia in 451. He was opposed by the Monophysite monks, however, and had to be reinstated in his see by the Byzantine army.

During the reign of *Justinian (527–65), a Samaritan revolt (529) devastated the vicinity of Jerusalem. The churches outside the town were destroyed and had to be rebuilt, and the emperor added a magnificent basilica, the "Nea" (new one), within the city in the area of the present-day Jewish Quarter. Parts of this magnificent building have been uncovered by archaeologists. The overall features of the Byzantine city at the time of Justinian are well represented in the Madaba mosaic map. Inside the north gate (Damascus Gate) was a semicircular paved plaza with a column at its center, still commemorated in the Arabic name of this gate, Bāb al-ʿAmūd. Two colonnaded streets issued from the plaza leading south. The western one passed the Church of the Holy Sepulcher and continued to the Zion Gate by way of a tetrapylon, passing the church of St. Sophia and extending as far as the Nea. On the other side of the Church of the Holy Sepulcher, the forum, the palace of the patriarchs, and the towers and monasteries near Jaffa Gate were visible. The other road (which had an offshoot to the east gate) passed a public bath and ended at another inner gate. The Western Wall was visible east of this street. The Temple area was apparently a wasteland, with one east gate (the Golden Gate) and the Church of St. James at its southeastern corner. In the southern part of the city was the Church of Mount Zion, with its Diakonikon (deacon's church) and the baths at the Siloam Pool. The Probatica pool (Sheep Pool) and large basilical church existed in the northeastern corner of the city. At the time of Justinian, two Church councils were held in Jerusalem (536 and 553), mainly in connection with the Origenist disputes. The patriarch Eustachius, like his predecessor Juvenal, had to be installed by the army.

In the course of the last Byzantine-Persian war, the Persian army of Chosroes II approached Jerusalem in 614 and besieged it with the help of its Jewish allies. The city wall was breached, many inhabitants were slain, and the patriarch Zacharias and relics of the "True Cross" were taken into exile. The Persians handed the city over to the Jews, who ruled it under a leader known only by his symbolic name, Nehemiah. The Persian conquest led to the destruction of most of the churches in Jerusalem. After some time, however, the Persians handed the city back to the Christians, who began to rebuild their holy sites under Modestus. The victories of the emperor *Heraclius led to a return of the Byzantines; on March 21, 629, he made a triumphal entry into Jerusalem, bringing back the "True Cross" relic, and the Jews were again banished from there. When the Muslim forces invaded Palestine, Jerusalem was besieged from 637 onward. As there seemed to be little hope of rescue following the decisive battle of Yarmuk (636), the patriarch Sophronius, successor to Modestus, surrendered the city to the Muslim caliph *Omar in March/April 638.

[Michael Avi-Yonah / Shimon Gibson (2nd ed.)]

Arab Period

From the time Jerusalem was conquered by the Muslims Arabs (638), it remained a provincial town and never became the seat of rich princes who had chroniclers at their court. Consequently, Arabic historiography on Jerusalem consists of only one work, *al-Uns al Jalīl fī Ta'rīkh al-Quds wa al-Khalīl* ("The honorable company on the history of Jerusalem and Hebron"), which was written by Mujīr al-Dīn al-ʿUlaymī at the end of the 15th century. The modern historian must therefore combine accounts gathered from manifold sources.

After the Arabs had invaded Ereẓ Israel in 634 (see *Israel, Land of), four years elapsed until they took Jerusalem. In those years the city, somehow isolated from its hinterland, suffered greatly, as is demonstrated by the sermons delivered by the patriarch Sophronius. The accounts of the conquest of Jerusalem differ considerably; according to the most probable version, the caliph *Omar, then at the headquarters at al-Jābiya in the Hauran, sent ʿAmr ibn al-ʿAs, a subaltern officer, to occupy the town. Some historians relate that the town surrendered under certain conditions, among which was the continued non-admission of Jews, who had not been allowed to live there under Byzantine rule. Goitein showed that this condition was probably imposed by the Umayyad Caliph Omar [the second] Ibn ʿAbd al-ʿAziz (reigned 717–720), not by "the right guided" caliph Omar b. al-Khattab. The inhabitants probably submitted under the usual conditions – that their persons, churches, and buildings would be safe as long as they paid the poll tax (*jizya*).

Omar's visit to Jerusalem shortly after the surrender has been the subject of divergent and clearly tendentious accounts. The Christian Arabic historian Eutychius, who wrote in Egypt at the beginning of the tenth century, says that Omar refused to pray in the Church of the Holy Sepulcher, whereupon Sophronius showed him the site of the Holy Rock identified with the talmudic Even ha-Shetiyyah, the site of the Temple Holy of Holies, on which the world was believed to be founded. Muslim writers, on the other hand, relate how the Christians attempted to deceive the caliph, when he asked about the site of the Rock, by bringing him to the Church of the Holy Sepulcher and to Mount Zion instead. Other sources relate that the Jewish convert *Kaʿb al-Aḥbār proposed to Omar that the Muslims should build their mosque in the north of the Rock, so they will turn towards the Rock when they turn towards the *qibla* (direction of prayer) in Mecca, but that his proposal was turned down by the caliph. It is clear from the nature of the tales that the account transmitted by Eutychius was meant to safeguard the Church of the Holy Sepulcher, whereas the story about Kaʿb's failure discloses an anti-Jewish tendency. Apparently the attempt in this instance was to show that Omar refused to turn when praying to the Holy of Holies (see *Holy Places) of the Jews and to the Kaʿba at the same time. From these tales it may be assumed that Omar ordered the Temple area to be cleaned and a place for Muslim worship established there. Herbert Busse, who devoted more than three decades to research different aspects of Jerusalem in Islam, thinks that the real conqueror of the holy city is ʿAmr ibn al-ʿĀṣ, one of the generals of caliph Omar. The rise of the city's place in Islam at the end of the seventh century caused the attribution of its conquest to a prominent person like caliph Omar instead of ʿAmr.

Various accounts confirm that Omar had Jews in his retinue who were his advisers, and that he entrusted them with keeping the area in good order. Although Omar did not accept Kaʿbs suggestion, quite rightly seeing in it a Judaizing tendency, Jewish traditions and beliefs influenced early Islam's attitude toward the holiness of the Temple Mount and its surroundings. These influences can therefore be seen as explaining why Omar did not pay attention to Sophronius' misleading information. Jewish tradition can also be recognized as the major factor in the ascription to Jerusalem of all events connected in Islam with the last judgment (see *Eschatology). In turn Muslim descriptions influenced later Jewish Midrashim (e.g., *The Book of Zerubbabel, Pirkei Mashi'aḥ, Revelations of R. Simeon bar Yoḥai*), which show an intimate knowledge of the area of the Temple Mount, the Gates of the Ḥaram (the walled area of the Muslim sanctuaries), the *Mount of Olives (see below), Mount Zion, and their surroundings. All these descriptions show that Jews lived in Jerusalem in the early Arab period. The prevailing opinion, which is based on Christian sources, that the Jews were not allowed to live in the Holy City or its surroundings during the whole Byzantine period is not confirmed by any non-Christian source. One suspects that these reports are biased in order to glorify the victory of the Church, as there is extant literary and archaeological evidence that there was a synagogue on the so-called Mt. Zion where the Cenaculum now stands. There are also extant *piyyutim* from the same time. In any event there is no doubt that during the Persian conquest (614–28) Jews lived in Jerusalem. It seems that even after the recapture of the city by Heraclius many of them remained in its vicinity. This may have caused Sophronius' request that no Jews be allowed to stay in Jerusalem. H. Busse says in this context: "The History of the Ḥaram cannot be properly understood without taking into account the Jewish activities in Jerusalem."

A document (in Judeo-Arabic) found in the Cairo **Genizah* reveals that the Jews asked Omar for permission for 200 families to settle in the town. As the patriarch opposed the action strongly, Omar fixed the number of the Jewish settlers at 70 families. The Jews were assigned the quarter southwest of the Temple area, where they lived from that time (Assaf, BJPES VII, p. 22ff.). As various texts show, they could also pray in the neighborhood of the Temple area. A late source, R. *Abraham b. Ḥiyya (12th century), mentions that they had even been allowed to build a synagogue and a *midrash* (college) on that area (Dinaburg, Zion III, 1929, p. 54ff.).

Although many Arabs came to live in Jerusalem, the great majority of the inhabitants was still Christian. The information culled from *Genizah* fragments and other Rabbanite and Karaite sources concerning the earliest Jewish inhabitants of Jerusalem during the *Umayyad period is insufficient for even a general description of historical events and the daily life of the Jewish community during Umayyad rule and the first hundred years of the *Abbasid dynasty. Even the date of such a major event as the transfer to Jerusalem of the talmudic academy from its seat in Tiberias during the late Byzantine and earliest Muslim periods is unknown.

UMAYYAD RULE. The Umayyad caliphs, who resided in *Damascus and in other towns and townlets of *Syria and Ereẓ Israel, showed a keen interest in Jerusalem, the holy city which was so near to their residence. Muʿāwiya, the founder of the dynasty, was proclaimed caliph in Jerusalem (660). He was the first who made great efforts in order to emphasize the status of Jerusalem as a holy place in Islam, collecting Jewish and Christian traditions glorifying the city and its vicinity and giving them an Islamic seal. It seems that he proceeded so as to repel the attacks of the Medinan leaders for leaving the holy cities of Hijaz, Mecca, and Medina. He probably erected the first primitive building on the place where the mosque known as al-Aqṣā (the further mosque, i.e., the furthest place reached by *Muhammad on his Night Journey) was built. The Frankish bishop Arculf, who visited Jerusalem in 670, describes this mosque as a rather ugly building whose walls consisted of simple planks, but which was able to hold 3,000 men. Above the Holy Rock the great Umayyad caliph ʿAbd al-Malik built a splendid cupola, Qubbat al-Ṣakhra (the Dome of the Rock). Its construction was finished in 72 A.H. (691), as can be seen from the inscription on it. Some Muslims believe that Muhammad placed his feet on the Rock on his Night Journey and therefore consider it holy. Both medieval Arabic writers and modern scholars, foremost I. *Goldziher, have expressed the view that ʿAbd al-Malik's purpose was to divert the pilgrimage from Mecca, where the counter-caliph *Abdallah ibn al-Zubayr resided. S.D. *Goitein has convincingly shown that the Umayyad caliph's intention was to build a magnificent Muslim house of worship in Jerusalem which would surpass the numerous churches there. A well-informed Arabic geographer explicitly said that the Dome of the Rock should be seen as a counterpart to the Church of the Holy Sepulcher (Goitein, JAOS 70, p. 104ff.). A. Elad convincingly has determined that both Goldziher and Goitein were right: the first stressed the political motives, the second, the religious side. A number of scholars saw the construction of the Dome of the Rock as a sign of ʿAbd al-Malik's desire to rebuild the Jewish Temple. The interest of the Umayyads in Jerusalem was also evinced in the many structures which they built in the vicinity of the Temple Mount. These have been uncovered by the excavations of B. Mazar and M. Ben-Dov.

A fact characteristic both of the tolerance of the Umayyads and of the role the Jews then played in Jerusalem is that ʿAbd al-Malik appointed some Jewish families as guardians and servants of the Ḥaram and decreed that they should be exempt from the poll tax (J. Raby and J. Johns (eds.), *Bayt al-Maqdis: ʿAbd al-Malik's Jerusalem* (1992)). ʿAbd al-Malik also had a government palace built in Jerusalem and the town's walls repaired. Sulaymān, one of his sons and successors, planned to make Jerusalem his residence but changed his mind and resided in Ramleh, which he had founded. From that time, Ramleh was the capital of southern Ereẓ Israel, and Jerusalem, which began to decline in importance, was neither the seat of a provincial administration nor the residence of a strong garrison which could provide work for craftsmen. The trade routes did not reach it, and the only product which could be exported from the surrounding area was olive oil. The last years of Umayyad rule were unhappy ones for the town for other reasons as well: after a revolt against the last Umayyad caliph, Marwān II, he had the town walls razed, and shortly thereafter an earthquake wrought havoc on the Dome of the Rock.

ABBASID RULE. The reign of the Abbasid caliphs, who came to power in 750, brought a long period of slow but progressive decay to Jerusalem. Ereẓ Israel was no longer at the center of the Muslim empire, and the caliphs residing in *Baghdad did not show much interest in the town. The first Abbasids continued to visit Jerusalem – al-Manṣūr in 758 and 771 and al-Mahdī in 780. Al-Mansur refused to allocate funds in order to finance the reparations. He ordered the removal of golden ornaments from al-Aqsa doors in order to coin them to pay the expenses. Al-Maʾmūn (813–33) never came to Jerusalem, although he spent some time in Syria and *Egypt, but he allotted certain sums for repairing the buildings in the Temple area. The later Abbasids showed no interest at all in the holy town. During the reign of al-Muʿtaṣim (833–42) a great disaster befell the city, when the peasants all over Ereẓ Israel rose under the leadership of a certain Abu Ḥarb, besieged Jerusalem, and sacked all its quarters, mosques, and churches; again many inhabitants fled. On the other hand, it seems that during this period the non-Muslims still enjoyed tolerance, especially the Christians, on behalf of whom Charlemagne successfully intervened with the caliph.

A new period in the history of Jerusalem began in 878, when it was annexed, with the rest of Ereẓ Israel, to the Egyptian kingdom of Aḥmad ibn Ṭūlūn. From that date the town remained under the dominion of the rulers of *Cairo, with interruptions during the Crusades (see below), until the Ottoman conquest (1516). After the downfall of the Ṭūlūnids in 905, governors appointed by the Abbasids again took over; in 941 Ereẓ Israel fell to an Egyptian dynasty, the Ikhshidids. Jerusalem itself was rarely mentioned in the chronicles of this period, because it did not play a role in the political life of the Near East. Arabic historians did not mention the town, aside from relating that the rulers of Cairo were brought to Jerusalem after their death to be buried there, a new custom which became current in this period. Christian authors, on the other hand, dwelled on the harassment and persecution of their coreligionists by the Muslims: it seems that fanaticism grew greatly in the course of the tenth century. The hatred between the various religious communities increased, as is borne out by a letter of complaint against the Jews which was sent in 932 by the Christians of Jerusalem to the Holy Roman emperor Henry I. In 938 and once more in 966 the Muslims attacked the Christians and sacked and burnt the Church of the Holy Sepulcher and other churches. On the latter occasion, when the Muslims were joined by the Jews, the patriarch was murdered and his corpse burnt.

According to *Genizah* sources, living conditions, for the most part, were difficult for Jews in Jerusalem. Aside from the tension and strife between Muslims, Christians, and Jews, the burden of various taxes and duties imposed upon the poor Jewish inhabitants was very heavy. A North African Jew describes the economic situation of the population in a letter (mid-11th century) as follows: "Meat is scarce and their cotton garments are worn out." *Solomon b. Judah served for a time as *ḥazzan* of the community, which persuaded him to accept its offer because he was a man capable of being satisfied with a small livelihood: "I accepted it and spent my time sometimes for better and sometimes for worse until this day;… but the Jerusalemites did not give me anything worth a *perutah*, because they do not have anything" (Mann, Texts, 1 (1935), 318). The majority of the community had to draw its livelihood from gifts sent from the Diaspora or offered during the pilgrimages to Jerusalem. The Karaite *Daniel b. Moses al-Qūmisī (see below) proposed a practical scheme to maintain a strong Karaite community in Jerusalem: each town (in the Diaspora) should delegate five people to dwell in the Holy City and should provide for their maintenance. Clearly, some inhabitants were also busy as merchants and in trades and handicrafts, and it seems that copying of manuscripts for the Diaspora was one of the main sources of income.

Religious Life. As mentioned, the exact date when the talmudic academy was moved from Tiberias to Jerusalem is not known. It seems that arrangements were made for the academy's head and most of its important members to divide their time between Ramleh, the Arab seat of government, and Jerusalem. A part of the western slopes of the Mount of Olives served as the main gathering place for Jewish pilgrims, and the celebrations on the festivals were held there. Among the *Genizah* fragments at Cambridge, J. Braslavi found a guide to Jerusalem written in Arabic by a contemporary Jew. The extant portion gives Hebrew and Arabic topographical names, describes sites, Jewish, Christian, and Muslim alike, and supplies a religious-historical background by references to the Bible and the Talmud. As the Jewish prayers inside the town, in the neighborhood of the Temple area, and at the Gates were gradually restricted, a place on the Mount of Olives was bought by the community for that purpose. On Hoshana Rabba, the seventh day of Sukkot, the gathering on the Mount of Olives was especially large, as the head of the academy, his deputy, or special messenger was accustomed to pronounce the fixing of the festival calendar for the following year and also to interdict the *Karaite adversaries (see below). That interdiction sometimes caused incidents and even brawls between the two parts of the community. The Karaites used their influence to get the authorities to intervene on their behalf and to make the head of the academy responsible for peaceful celebrations. Many pilgrims were accustomed to offer large sums of money for the maintenance of the academy and the payment of the many onerous taxes and duties imposed on the poor Jerusalem community.

The Karaites probably began to settle in Jerusalem during the second third of the ninth century. The report, related by a later Karaite source, that *Anan, the founder of this sect, emigrated with many followers to Jerusalem deserves no credence. *Genizah* sources confirm the information given by the Karaite *Salmon b. Jeroham (first half of the tenth century) that in the preceding century the Karaites began to build up a center in Jerusalem. They occupied a special quarter which was known as "the quarter of the Easterns," since most of its inhabitants were from *Iraq and *Persia. They called themselves *Avelei Zion ("the mourners for Zion"), as well as Shoshannim (lilies). The Karaite missionary propaganda and especially the appeals of Daniel al-Qūmisī succeeded in moving many of his fellow Karaites to spend their life in the Holy City. Sahl b. Maẓli'aḥ (a younger contemporary and colleague of Salmon) gives interesting information about life in Jerusalem. Rabbanite disciples followed many of the doctrines of Karaism, and an important Karaite center began to develop in Jerusalem.

This missionary propaganda inevitably caused friction between the two parts of the Jewish population, and it has been assumed that Karaite activities influenced the old Rabbanite community to strengthen its position in Jerusalem. The Rabbanites also moved their academy (or a part of it) to Jerusalem in an effort to diminish the power of the Karaite *nasi* ("prince," descendant of David's stock) and the head of the Karaite academy in Jerusalem (*rosh yeshivat* Ge'on Ya'akov). *Aaron Ben Meir (first half of the tenth century), the famous opponent of Saadiah Gaon and head of the Rabbanite academy, describes the clashes between the two opposite parties and mentions that one of his ancestors was killed on the Temple Mount area by the Karaites and an attempt was made to kill others. By personal intervention at the caliph's court in Baghdad and with the help of influential coreligionists in Iraq, he was successful in his endeavor to diminish the power of the Karaites, who for thirty years presided over the Jewish community in Jerusalem and represented it before the Muslim authorities. Nevertheless, even after Ben Meir's successful intervention, the spiritual power of the Karaites in Jerusalem did not decline, and they could muster an array of authors, scholars, and religious leaders like Salmon b. Jeroham, Sahl b. Maẓli'aḥ, Japheth b. Ali, Ibn Zuta, Joseph ibn Nūḥ, Ali b. Suleiman, and many others. They did important research into the Hebrew language and wrote commentaries on the Bible and the precepts, which influenced all the Karaite communities in the Diaspora. During the leadership of *Solomon b. Judah, and especially his successor Daniel b. Azariah (1051–62), both of whom resided in Jerusalem and Ramleh alternately, the relations between the Rabbanites and Karaites improved. Indeed, the general situation in Ereẓ Israel was so bad that there was no place for internal strife.

General Description. The descriptions of the Arabic geographers and other writers make it possible to conceive of what Jerusalem was like in that period. It appears that the town – called at first by the Roman name Aelia, later Bayt al-Maqdis (the "holy house," or the "temple"), and from the tenth century al-Quds (the "holy") – was larger in the first four centuries of Muslim rule than at a later time. In addition to the strong town walls, which had eight gates, it also had a moat on some sides, especially to the north and south. The Persian traveler Nasir-i-Khusrau, who visited the city in 1047, says that it had high, well-built, and clean bazaars and that all the streets were paved with stone slabs. Most Arabic authors dwell on the descriptions of the Aqṣā mosque and the Dome of the Rock. Besides these buildings and the Citadel, there was the so-called mosque of Omar, built within the southern precincts of the Church of the Holy Sepulcher in 936. The town was still predominantly non-Muslim and had a great number of splendid churches. The Jews had two quarters, one southwest of the Temple area and one west of it, near the gate of the "cave" (perhaps Warren's Gate). A letter written in the late 11th century mentions Ḥārat al-Yahūd (the Jewish Quarter) near a church (Gottheil-Worrell, Fragments p. 120 l. 30). At the end of the tenth century the Christians apparently were still the strongest element in the town. The Arabic geographer al-Maqdisī (end of the tenth century), who was a Jerusalemite, complained that there were no Muslim theologians in the town and that nobody was interested in Islamic sciences, whereas the Christians and the Jews were numerous. He also said that it was difficult to make a living. In addition, he emphasized that there were always many strangers in the city, most of whom were surely pilgrims – Christians, Jews, and Muslims – but others also came to live in it permanently, such as members of dissident Islamic sects or adepts of Muslim mysticism. The Karrāmiyya, a Muslim sect from Persia, was strongly represented, as were various currents of Sufism. Some of the founders and leaders of the Sufis came to Jerusalem, among them Bāyazīd al-Bisṭāmī, Ibrāhīm ibn Adham, Bishr al-Ḥāfī, and in the 11th century al-*Ghazālī. The information about the political situation of the Jews in Jerusalem in the tenth century is varied. According to Salmon b. Jeroham the Muslims and the Christians persecuted the Jews and tried to diminish their rights. Al-Maqdisī's assertion seems to be an exaggeration, at least in relation to the Jews.

FATIMID RULE. The *Fatimid conquest, following that of Egypt in 969, at first brought some relief to the Jewish population but ushered in a period of troubles. Whereas Egypt under the first Fatimids enjoyed security and economic prosperity, Ereẓ Israel suffered greatly from the wars between the Fatimids and their enemies, first the Qarmatians, who were accused of intending to change the *qibla* (Muslim direction of prayer) from Mecca to Jerusalem, and later the Banū Jarrāḥ, chieftains of the great Bedouin tribe of Ṭayyʾ who for 70 years tried to overthrow Fatimid rule. The coastal towns of Ereẓ Israel probably took a commensurate part in the revival of international trade in the eastern Mediterranean, but Jerusalem remained far from the trade routes. The plight of the Christians and the Jews in Jerusalem in the 11th century was especially precarious. The deranged Fatimid caliph al-Ḥākim persecuted the non-Muslims and in 1009 had the churches destroyed, among them the Church of the Holy Sepulcher. The latter was rebuilt, but once more was destroyed by an earthquake in 1034 and remained in ruins until the Byzantine emperor paid for its restoration in 1048. Only the Church of the Resurrection was rebuilt, however, and the basilica of Constantine was never restored.

The town apparently changed a great deal in those days. The decline of the old settled population – Jews, Christians, and Muslims – was only one of the changes. In 1033 the town walls were repaired, but the area within them was diminished, the entire area of Mount Zion remaining outside the walls. The decline of Ramleh in the middle of the 11th century and the increase of Christian pilgrims from European countries gave sorely afflicted Jerusalem another chance, but then, in the last third of the century it became a bone of contention between various political powers. In 1071 Jerusalem was taken by the Seljuk general Atsiz and annexed to the great empire of the sultans of Iraq and Persia. Five years later the inhabitants revolted against Atsiz, who had left to fight a war against the Fatimids, and when he returned and took the town once more, it was severely punished. Some years afterward the Seljuks appointed the Turkoman officer Urtuq prince of Jerusalem. In 1091 Urtuq left the town to his sons Suqmān and Īlghāzī, whose rule lasted no more than five years. In 1098 Jerusalem fell for a second time to the Fatimids, who held it against an attempt of the Seljuk prince Riḍwān. In 1099 Jerusalem was conquered by the crusaders.

[Eliyahu Ashtor and Haïm Z'ew Hirschberg / Shimon Gibson (2nd ed.)]

Crusader Period

The European Christian crusaders besieged Jerusalem from June 6 to July 15, 1099. When several attempts to seize the city by direct attack failed, they constructed siege towers and concentrated their forces on two weak spots: the first between the Damascus Gate and the tower in the eastern section of the northern wall and the second in the area of Mount Zion. The attack began on the night of Thursday, July 14, and was concluded the next morning. The troops of Flanders and northern France, led by Godfrey de Bouillon, scaled the walls in the northeastern sector, which was defended by both Muslims and Jews, the latter fighting to protect their own quarter nearby. At the same time, the Provençal force, led by Raymond of St. Gilles, surmounted the wall adjoining Mount Zion, while the Normans from Sicily, headed by Tancred, entered the northwest corner of the city in the vicinity of the tower (subsequently called the Tancred Tower).

The population, Muslims and Jews alike, was massacred. Many Jews perished in the synagogues that were set on fire by the conquerors; others were taken prisoner and sold into slavery in Europe, where the Jewish communities later redeemed them. Some Jewish prisoners were taken to Ashkelon (still in Muslim hands) along with the Egyptian commander of the city's fortress, who had surrendered; they were ransomed by the Jewish communities of Egypt and brought there. As a result of the massacre, the city was largely depopulated and the first period of crusader rule was a period of insecurity and economic difficulties. During the second decade of their rule, in order to repopulate the city, the crusaders transferred Christian Arab tribes from Transjordan and settled them in the former Jewish quarter, between the Damascus and Lions' Gates. In order to encourage people to settle there, the duty on food was reduced. As a matter of course, Jerusalem became the capital of the crusaders' kingdom, which was called the Kingdom of Jerusalem (*Regnum Hierusalem*), or Jerusalemite Kingdom (*Regnum Hierosolymitanorum*), or even Kingdom of David (*Regnum David*). Jerusalem was chosen to be the capital despite economic, administrative, and security problems due to its location in the crusaders' southernmost territories.

Jerusalem developed and flourished in the middle of the 12th century because of the concentration of all the government and church bodies there. The king's court, his administration, and the centers of the ecclesiastical institutions, as well as of the various monastic and military orders, were located there, providing a livelihood for a considerable number of permanent inhabitants. The most important factor in the development of Jerusalem at that period, however, was the stream of pilgrims from all countries of Christian Europe (there are records of pilgrims coming from as far as Russia, Scandinavia, and Portugal). Tens of thousands of pilgrims visited Jerusalem every year. These *pilgrimages were not only an important source of income but also added to the city's population, since a number of pilgrims remained there. Owing to its geographical position, however, it remained a consumer city, as in earlier and later periods.

THE CITY AND ITS INSTITUTIONS. Jerusalem during the crusader period was located within the walls of the previous Arab city. The basic pattern of the city remained the same, although there seems to have been an increase in the number of inhabitants. A period of construction began, the likes of which had not been seen since the time of Herod. Many of the buildings that had remained intact were used for their former purposes. First and foremost was the citadel by the western gate (Jaffa Gate), which the crusaders called Turris David (David's Tower). It housed the king's garrison, the food warehouses for the army and probably for the entire city, and the customs administration for imports, which were directed through this gate. Adjoining the citadel was the king's palace, on the site of Herod's palace and the administrative center during the Roman Byzantine periods.

At first the king and his court had their residence in the al-Aqṣā Mosque and vicinity, but when this area was given to the Templars, the king moved to the vicinity of the citadel, which was traditionally associated with the rule over the city. Just as the citadel and the palace signified the secular power, the Holy Sepulcher and its environs signified the rule of the Church and its religious ritual. Near the Holy Sepulcher, rebuilt by the crusaders and reopened in 1140, stood the palace of the patriarch of Jerusalem, and opposite its southern entrance were the monasteries of the Benedictines and the area of the Order of St. John, the Hospitalers (now the New Market). The Templars were situated in the al-Aqṣā Mosque, which the crusaders called the Temple of Solomon (*Templum Solomonis*) and which is known in Jewish tradition as *Midrash Shelomo* (Solomon's House of Study). The German-speaking order of knights, a branch of the Hospitalers, was located near the Temple Mount (in what is now the Jewish quarter); the Order of St. Lazarus, the Leper Knights, was outside the city wall, near the present New Gate.

The establishment of the crusaders' rule invigorated Christian religious life. Throughout the 12th century many Christian traditions associated with Jerusalem and its vicinity were established, particularly those pertaining to the life of Jesus. Thus the tradition of Via Dolorosa was defined. The crystallization of these traditions stimulated an unusual amount of building in the city. Many Muslim shrines were turned into churches; for example, the Dome of the Rock ("Mosque of Omar") was called the Lord's Temple (*Templum Domini*) by the crusaders. New churches were also built, among them the new Church of the Holy Sepulcher, the most important architectural endeavor of the crusaders in Jerusalem, which was dedicated in 1149, 50 years after the conquest. The crusaders concentrated a number of churches under one roof. Some were built in the Byzantine period, including the Anastasis (Church of the Resurrection), which is the traditional site of the tomb of Jesus, the Martyrion, and the chapel of Queen Helena (Church of the Holy Cross). The ancient buildings did not blend well with the new structure, and there was a lack of symmetry among the component parts: a Byzantine church in the west, a Romanesque church in the middle. The southern gates (there was only a small gate in the west) are the best examples of crusader art in architecture and sculpture of that period. Among the outstanding churches built were the Church of St. Anne, in fine Romanesque style; the renovated "Tomb of Mary" church in the Valley of Jehoshaphat; and the churches of Mount Zion.

POPULATION OF THE CITY. Most of the inhabitants of 12th century Jerusalem were of European origin, except for the Eastern Christians – the Syrians (Suriani), the Jacobites, and the Copts, who lived in the northeastern corner of the city near the church of Santa Maria Magdalena. The Armenians, who had special relations with the crusaders, having two independent Christian monarchies in the northeast Middle East, were settled in the southwestern part of Jerusalem, around the Church of St. James. There were also Georgians from Caucasia (Georgiani), whose center was the Monastery of the Cross outside the walls of the city. The majority of the population was of French descent. French was the main language (official documents were written in Latin in the 12th century and in French in the 13th). The others congregated in ethnic or linguistic communities, such as the German knights mentioned above; the Spaniards, who settled near the Damascus Gate; the Provençals, near the Zion Gate; and the Hungarians near the New Gate. These communities had their own churches and later often hostels for pilgrims from their countries of origin. Muslims and Jews were not permitted to reside in the city; however, the Muslims came into the city for business purposes and some Jews settled near the Citadel. *Benjamin of Tudela tells of a few Jewish dyers whom he met while visiting Jerusalem.

THE FALL OF CRUSADER JERUSALEM. After the battle of Hattin (July 1187) the army of *Saladin besieged Jerusalem. The patriarch of Jerusalem and the secular commanders soon agreed to surrender, on condition that they would be allowed to ransom themselves from captivity and take their possessions with them. The city surrendered in November 1187 and remained in Muslim hands until 1229. All Christians, except for the Easterners, were forbidden to reside in Jerusalem. The Easterners were allowed to take care of the Holy Sepulcher and some of the other churches. Most of the churches were either restored as Muslim shrines and mosques, like the Dome of the Rock and the al-Aqṣā Mosque, or converted into Muslim charitable or religious institutions. The Church of St. Anne became a madrasa (religious college). The Jewish community was renewed as a result of the initiative of Saladin. Jews came into the city from other towns in the country, for example, Ashkelon, which was destroyed on Saladin's orders. Prominent among these was a group of Yemenites. Others came as immigrants from the Maghreb (North Africa) and Europe. A particularly important group of immigrants were those rabbis who came from France and England (1209–11). In 1218 *Al-Harizi reported that Saladin invited the Jews to settle in Jerusalem (*Tahkemoni*, Kaminke (ed.), 214–5, 353). It seems that the Jews lived in separate communities according to their country or town of origin.

In the third decade of the 13th century, Jerusalem suffered from a systematic destruction of its fortifications by the Muslims, as in other cities which seemed likely to serve as strong points for a renewed effort of settlement by the crusaders. The attempts by the Third Crusade to capture Jerusalem failed, even though the army got very close to the city. The walls of

Jerusalem were destroyed by the Arabs in 1219. Thus Jerusalem had no wall for more than 300 years, until the Ottoman sultan Suleiman the Magnificent rebuilt it in 1537–41. What the Christians did not achieve by military action, however, they succeeded in obtaining by diplomatic negotiations. According to an agreement between al-Malik Al-Kāmil, the ruler of Egypt, and Frederick II, Holy Roman Emperor and the king of Germany, a corridor to Jaffa through Ramleh was agreed upon, and Jerusalem was divided between Christians and Muslims (Tell ʿAjjūl 1229). The Muslims received the area of the Temple Mount and freedom of worship therein; the Christians received the rest of the city, and Frederick had himself crowned King of Jerusalem in the Church of the Holy Sepulcher. During this second period of occupancy (1229–44), the crusaders tried to resettle the city, but the results were in no way comparable with their achievements during the 12th century, either in population or in economic life. In 1240 the rulers of Egypt, who were competing with Damascus for ascendancy in the area, asked for help from the hordes of the Khwarizm Turks, who attacked Jerusalem in 1244, sacked the city, massacred the Christians, and devastated the Church of the Holy Sepulcher. Only a few Christian inhabitants of the city succeeded in escaping to Jaffa. *Naḥmanides mentions in his letter (written 1267) that he found only two Jewish dyers in Jerusalem, because during the Tartar (= Khwarizim) conquest some Jews had been killed but others escaped from the city. It seems that these found shelter in Nablus, because Naḥmanides remarks that the Torah scroll which they took with them was brought back to Jerusalem, when he succeeded in establishing a synagogue (Yaari, *Iggerot*, p. 85). The city suffered greatly and did not recover until the overthrow of the Ayyubids in Egypt by the Mamluks in 1250. Jerusalem became part of the Mamluk kingdom and remained so for over 260 years.

[*Encyclopaedia Hebraica*]

Mamluk Period

After the death of al-Malik al-Ṣāliḥ Ayyūb, the sultan of Egypt, in 1249, Jerusalem was incorporated into the kingdom of al-Malik al-Nāṣir Yūsuf, ruler of *Aleppo and Damascus. While this Syrian *Ayyubid was waging war with the *Mamluks – who had taken over in Egypt – the *Mongols invaded the Near East and penetrated into Ereẓ Israel at the beginning of 1260. The inhabitants of Jerusalem fled panic-stricken when the Mongol hordes swept over the country sacking the townlets and villages. When the Mamluks succeeded in September 1260 in defeating the Mongols at ʿAyn Jālūt (ʿEin-Ḥarod), Jerusalem, with all Ereẓ Israel, was annexed to their kingdom and remained under their rule until the Ottomans conquered Syria and Egypt in 1516/17. The situation of Jerusalem in the years after the retreat of the Mongols was very depressed. *Naḥmanides reported in 1267 that only a part of the inhabitants had returned to the city and there were no more than 2,000 living there, among them 300 Christians. He persuaded some Jews who had found shelter in the villages to return and reconstitute the Jewish community.

The Mamluks did not care to fortify Jerusalem and repopulate it. Under their long rule Jerusalem became a town of theologians whose life focused on the mosques and madrasas (Muslim theological colleges). Until the last quarter of the 14th century it belonged to the province of Damascus and was administered by a low-ranking Mamluk appointed by the *nāʾib* (deputy of the Sultan) of Damascus. In 1376 al-Malik al-Ashraf Shaʿbān made Jerusalem a separate province and henceforth its head was appointed by the sultan himself. The new administrative entity was a small one, comprising the Judean hill country with Hebron, although at times Ramleh and Nablus (Shechem) were annexed to it. The promotion of its head to a higher rank, however, did not signify a great change in its status. The post was often sold to the highest bidder, who later did his best to extort from the townspeople what he had paid. The complaints of the inhabitants sometimes brought about the dismissal of the *nāʾib*, but for the most part they had to submit to his tyranny. Another very important post in the administration of Jerusalem was that of the "superintendent of the two Holy Places" (*nāẓir al-ḥaramayn*), who was in charge of the sanctuaries of Jerusalem and *Hebron. He administered the endowments and supervised the activities of the staff. Sometimes this post was also held by the deputy of the sultan himself. It seems that the administration was not very efficient, even in the field in which the Mamluks were really interested, i.e., security. Letters of Italian Jews who settled in Jerusalem during the 15th century (see below) contain reports about the lack of security in the town's surroundings, where Bedouin were roaming.

In this period Jerusalem produced soap, manufactured from the olive oil which was supplied by the villages of central Ereẓ Israel, but the Mamluk authorities encroached upon this industrial activity, e.g., by the establishment of monopolies and the forced purchase of large quantities of the raw material at high prices. The Arabic historian Mujīr al-Dīn (d. 1521) dwelled on the catastrophic consequences of these measures, and one reads in the reports of Jews who settled in the town in the 15th century about the great difficulty of making a living. Even the frequent visits by groups of pilgrims could not change the economic situation. The pilgrims only made short visits and did their utmost to escape the extortions of the authorities as soon as possible. Consequently, Jerusalem remained a very poor town. The population did not increase considerably and Western pilgrims reported that many houses were empty or had fallen into ruin. At the end of the 15th century Jerusalem probably had no more than 10,000 inhabitants. The Dominican Felix Fabri, who was in Jerusalem in 1483, says that there were 1,000 Christians. The Jewish community numbered 100–150 families.

Whereas the Mamluks did nothing for the development of Jerusalem's economy, they continued the policy and trends of the Muslims since the Crusades in underlining the religious importance of Jerusalem for Islam. Religious propaganda had found expression in the building of madrasas and *zawiyas* (convents – Ar. *zāwiya*, pl. *zawāyā*) for Sufis and the production of guidebooks for visits to the Holy Places, especially in Jerusalem and in Hebron. The Mamluk rulers generously endowed religious establishments, such as mosques and colleges. These activities corresponded well with the efforts they made to appear as the champions of orthodox Islam. The sultan Baybars had the Dome of the Rock repaired in 1261 and in 1263 he founded a hospice for pilgrims not far from the western gate of the town. Qalāʾūn (1279–90) repaired the roof of the al-Aqṣā mosque and founded another hospice. The sultans Katbughā (1294–96) and al-Malik al-Nāṣir Muhammad (d. 1341) restored the wall of the Ḥaram, and the latter also repaired the gilding of the roofs of the al-Aqṣā Mosque and the Dome of the Rock. Barsbāy (1422–38) made endowments for the upkeep of al-Aqṣā, and Jaqmaq (1438–53) repaired the roof of the Dome of the Rock once more. Tengiz, viceroy of Syria under the reign of al-Malik al-Nāṣir Muhammad, built a great madrasa in Jerusalem. Other colleges were founded in the 14th century by the emirs Ṭushtumur and Arghūn and in 1482 by the sultan Qāʾitbāy. The Mamluks also spent large sums on the restoration of the water conduits which supplied the town (or more correctly the Ḥaram), among them Tengiz in 1338 and the sultans Khushqadam and Qāʾitbāy in the second half of the century. Princes from Persia and Turkey also founded madrasas and hospices for pilgrims in Jerusalem in that period. Thus, these numerous endowments resulted in the building of a great number of religious buildings, which became the striking feature of Jerusalem. (The travelogues of Western pilgrims and other sources give one a clear picture of Jerusalem in the later Middle Ages.)

Contradictory statements as to the existence of town walls point to the fact that Jerusalem was only partly enclosed by walls. Apparently the walls were not completely razed in 1219 and parts were rebuilt in 1229. The walled-in area probably included Mount Zion in the 14th century, whereas in 15th-century descriptions it appears as being outside of the walls, thus indicating changes in the area of the city. On the other hand, there were no suburbs outside the walls. Mujīr al-Dīn mentions some small groups of houses west and northwest of the town; north and east of it there were some *zawiyas* and churches. On the southern outskirts there were also *zawiyas* and a group of houses named after the sheikh Abu Thawr, who participated in the siege of Jerusalem in 1187. The ancient Byzantine town plan had disappeared, although "David Street" (Ṭarīq Dāʾud) – the street connecting Jaffa Gate and Bāb al-Silsila, the main entrance of the Ḥaram – remained the main artery of the town. The area north and west of the al-Aqṣā Mosque was occupied by many colleges and convents of Sufi mysitcs: Mujīr al-Dīn mentions 44 madrasas and about 20 *zawiyas*. The palace of the *nāʾib* was also located northwest of the Ḥaram. The area which the Christians held in the town was reduced, and Saladin had established a convent of Sufis in the former palace of the patriarch, north of the Church of the Holy Sepulcher. The church of the Hospitalers had become a Muslim hospital, a part of the hospital itself was also handed over to Sufis, and south of the Church of the Holy Sepulcher a mosque was built. Since the number of the madrasas had increased so markedly, Jerusalem became a center of Islamic studies in the later Middle Ages. The most important schools were al-Ṣalāḥiyya al-Tengiziyya, al-Muʿazzamiyya, and al-ʿUthmāniyya, but other madrasas had students from other towns in Ereẓ Israel, and even from other countries. The theologians who taught at the madrasas were the most distinguished group in the town's population. Among them there were families which for a number of generations had held certain prominent posts in the clerical hierarchy, such as the Ibn Jamāʿa, Ibn Ghānim, al-Qarqashandī, and al-Dayrī. Some of the teachers at the madrasas of Jerusalem were well known in the Muslim world, e.g., Ibn al-Ḥāʾim (d. 1412) and Kamāl al-Dīn ibn Abī Sharīf (d. 1500), both of whom were prolific writers in various branches of Islamic theology.

In view of the fact that the Muslim theologians played so great a role in the town, one can easily understand that persecutions of the non-Muslims were frequent. The atmosphere was charged with fanaticism, and the interventions of Christian princes who tried to protect their coreligionists were not always successful. For the most part, the outbreaks of Muslim fanaticism were directed against the Latin Friars (Franciscans) who had established a monastery on Mount Zion in 1334. Several times the Friars were imprisoned and sent to Damascus or Cairo. The possession of some sites on Mount Zion, which were coveted by Christians and Muslims, and sometimes even by Jews, became a point of contention. Time and again the chapel above the grave of David's supposed tomb passed from the Christians to the Muslims and vice versa. When the Christians built a church on Mount Zion in 1452 on the site where Mary is believed to have lived for a long time, it was immediately pulled down by Muslim fanatics. At times the Muslims penetrated into the Church of the Holy Sepulcher and other churches, devastated them, and destroyed some parts completely. In 1489 the Franciscans obtained permission once again to build a church on the site where Mary had lived, but in 1490 it was pulled down.

The role of the Jews in Jerusalem was very modest. Until the end of the 15th century their number was apparently quite small. In about the middle of the 14th century there was a yeshivah in the town whose head was a rabbi named Isaac ha-Levi Asir ha-Tikvah. At the beginning of the 15th century immigration of Jews from European countries began, but the attempt of German Jews to acquire the room above the supposed tomb of David almost brought it to a halt. The Christians applied to the pope, who asked the Italian merchant republics to stop taking Jews on board their ships sailing for Ereẓ Israel; this happened in 1428. The Mamluk government also harassed the Jews, and in about 1440 it imposed a heavy tax on them to be paid yearly. Most Jews were craftsmen or petty merchants who could not afford to pay the tax and many left the town. Details on the economic situation of the Jews are given in a letter of R. Elijah of Ferrara, who settled in Jerusalem in 1438 and became rabbi of the community. R. Isaac b. Meir Latif (c. 1470) states that there were 150 Jewish families in town, whereas *Meshullam of Volterra, who visited Jerusalem in 1481, spoke of about 250, but this was probably an exaggerated figure. Even in that period the Jews suffered greatly from heavy taxation and Muslim intolerance. In 1474 the Muslims destroyed an old synagogue, but the sultan intervened and after a long lawsuit had it returned and rebuilt. R. Obadiah of *Bertinoro, who went to Jerusalem in 1488 and became the spiritual head of the community, complained about its poverty and oppression, which caused Nathan *Sholal to move from Jerusalem to Cairo, where he became *nagid* (leader) of Egyptian Jewry. Obadiah found no more than 70 Jewish families and many widows in Jerusalem, but shortly afterward a change took place. On the one hand, the government abolished the heavy tax and the Italian republics once more allowed Jews to travel on their ships to Ereẓ Israel, and on the other hand, the immigration of the Spanish exiles began. A pupil of R. Obadiah related in a letter written in 1495 that about 200 Jewish families were living in Jerusalem.

In the beginning of the 16th century there were scholars in Jerusalem who took part in the controversy which arose over the fixing of the dates of the sabbatical (*shemittah*) years. Scholars in Safed also took part in the dispute, not missing the opportunity to underline their reverence for the Jerusalemites (see *Israel, Land of, History). R. Isaac *Sholal, who was the *nagid* of Jewry in Mamluk lands and resided in Cairo, moved to Jerusalem at the end of Mamluk rule and published ordinances (*takkanot*) for the welfare and good order of the community; they are quoted in R. Moses *Basola's travel book.

[Eliyahu Ashtor / Haïm Z'ew Hirschberg]

Under Ottoman Rule (1517–1917)

SULEIMAN THE MAGNIFICENT AND HIS WORK. The present-day wall around the Old City of Jerusalem was the work of the sultan Suleiman I (1520–66), who was called al- Qānūnī ("the Lawgiver"), and in the West, the Magnificent. According to contemporary evidence, most of the wall was in ruins at the end of the Mamluk period and Suleiman, known for his widespread activities in the building of numerous mosques and public buildings in the empire, ordered that Jerusalem be surrounded by a wall in order to protect its inhabitants against marauding Bedouins. Some believe that the activities of Charles V in *Tunisia aimed against the Ottomans prompted the rebuilding of Jerusalem's wall, as a defensive measure.

The following statement was made by an anonymous contemporary "Jewish" inhabitant of Jerusalem or Hebron: "Jerusalem the Holy City has been destroyed through our sins. Nothing is left of the old structure except for a little of the foundation of the walls. Now, in 1537, they have begun to build the walls around the city by order of the king, Sultan Suleiman. They have also put a great fountain in the Temple…" (*Ha-Me'ammer*, 3, p. 211). The building of the wall made a great impression on the Jewish world, and Joseph ha-Kohen recorded it in his chronicle: "In that year 1540 [an insignificant error], God aroused the spirit of Suleiman king of Greece (= Rumelia) and Persia and he set out to build the walls of Jerusalem the holy city in the land of Judah. And he sent officials who built its walls and set up its gates as in former times and its towers as in bygone days. And his fame spread throughout the land for he wrought a great deed. And they did also extend the tunnel into the town lest the people thirst for water. May God remember him favorably" (*Sefer Divrei ha-Yamim le-Malkhei Ẓarefat u-Malkhei Beit Ottoman*, Sabionetta, 1554, 261b–262a). As is stated in the former source, the wall was rebuilt on top of its former remains, some of which dated to Second Temple times. In certain places the planner-engineer deviated from the ancient pattern, e.g., by leaving part of present-day Mount Zion outside the wall. According to tradition he was executed for this.

The construction of the wall lasted from 1537 to 1541, as is recounted in the 11 original inscriptions inserted in various parts of the wall, especially near the gates. Thus, for instance, the inscription near the Jaffa Gate (Bāb al-Khalīl, the Gate of Hebron) contains the date 945 A.H. (1538–39). The southern wall contains the Zion Gate (Bāb al-Nabī Da'ud, i.e., Gate of the "Prophet" David, since it is near "David's Tomb," which is on Mount Zion). Next is the Dung Gate (Bāb al-Maghāriba, or Moor Gate, because of its proximity to the quarter of the Maghreb Muslims). On a tablet nearby is the date 947 A.H. (1540–41). Further east along the southern wall are three gates which are closed off, dating to pre-Ottoman times: the Double Gate, the Triple Gate, and the Single Gate. Northward along the eastern wall is the Mercy Gate (which the Muslims call by the same name, Bāb al-Raḥma, or al-Dahriyya, i.e., Eternal, and the Christians call the Golden Gate). There are several legendary reasons for its being closed. Inside the area of the Temple Mount this gate has been divided into two since the early Middle Ages, one being called the Gate of Repentance (Bāb al-Tawba). In the east is the Lions' Gate (Bāb Sittna Maryam, the Gate of our Lady Mary, because of its proximity to the traditional birthplace of Mary, Jesus' mother; the Christians call it St. Stephen's Gate). On the northern side is Herod's (or the Flower) Gate (Bāb al-Zahra, a corruption of Sāhira since it leads to the plain of Sāhira (Sura 79:14) on which, as the Muslims believe, all creatures will congregate on the day of the resurrection of the dead (see *Eschatology)). The most magnificent of the gates is the Damascus Gate (Bāb al-ʿAmūd, Gate of the Pillar or Column). The seventh gate is the New Gate in the wall near the Christian Quarter (opposite the Hospice of Notre Dame), which was opened at the time of the sultan Abdul Hamid II (1876–1908) and for this reason was first called the Sultan's Gate; it was to facilitate the connection between the Christian Quarter and New Jerusalem.

Suleiman also introduced changes in the buildings on the Temple Mount. He ordered that the mosaics covering the walls of the Dome of the Rock be removed and replaced by beautiful marble tablets and facings, which adorned the building until the 1950s and were in part replaced during the repairs conducted by the Jordanian government. During Suleiman's reign four *sabīls* (public fountains) were set up in the city and one outside it near the Sultan's Pool, in order to provide water for passersby. The most beautiful of these is opposite the Chain Gate (Bāb al-Silsila) in the wall surrounding the Temple Mount. The two Jewish sources mentioned above emphasize the special attention devoted to one of the age-old problems of Jerusalem, the city's water supply, especially for the Temple Mount area. The conduits bringing water from the vicinity of Solomon's Pools (near Bethlehem) were repaired and widened by order of Suleiman and his wife Roxelana, and in 1536 the Sultan's Pool was constructed on the foundations of an ancient pool. Its water was collected by means of the dam in the Hinnom Valley (on what is the present-day road to Mt. Zion) and on it is also the fifth *sabīl.*

In order to maintain the madrasas (Muslim theological colleges) and shelters for the Sufis (*zāwiya, khanqa, tekke*) which were established in former times, many properties (*waqf*) such as lands, shops, and flour mills were dedicated, bringing a flow of money to Muslim Jerusalem. Roxelana also established a khan (inn), and especially an *ʿimāret* (a soup kitchen providing free meals for students of the madrasas, dervishes, and other poor Muslims). These institutions were supported by taxes levied on numerous villages throughout the country. Repairs, which were ordered by the sultan, were made on the fortress near David's Tower (Turk. *Qishla*, winter barracks for the soldiers). A Turkish aga encamped at this fortress together with an escort of a troop of janissaries.

THE DECLINE OF JERUSALEM. After this period of construction, however, the development of Jerusalem was halted. The authorities did nothing to preserve the show pieces of Muslim architecture and prevent their destruction through the agency of time and of man. Administratively, Jerusalem was the seat of the governor of the district, or *sanjak* (Ar. *liwāʾ*; Turk. *sanjaq*, both meaning "standard"). However, the *mīr liwāʾ* or *sanjaq bey* (i.e., the governor) was usually of a lower status than the other local regional rulers (Safed, Nablus, Gaza), since the central authorities regarded Jerusalem as no more than a town bordering on the land of the Bedouin (*Arabistan*). Jerusalem's governor was subordinate to the general governor (Turkish *wali*) of the province (*eyālet*), usually that of Damascus, but sometimes to the *wali* of Sidon (and Acre), and had no direct contact with the central authorities in Constantinople. In 1756/1169 A.H., however, Jerusalem was raised for a short time to the status of an independent provincial unit (*eyālet*), ruled by a governor (*mutaṣarrif*) bearing the standard of two *tughs* ("horsetails") – though only in the second half of the 19th century did it become an independent *mutaṣarriflik* ruled by a "two-tail" pasha – directly subordinate to the Sublime Porte in Constantinople (see below). In the city of Jerusalem the immediate control of all municipal matters was in the hands of the *qadi.* He was also the authority over all non-Muslims.

The Ottomans introduced no changes in the composition of the Muslim population of Jerusalem. During their 400-year reign only a few Turks settled in the country. The Turkish language did not take the place of Arabic, although a number of Turkish words were incorporated into the spoken Arabic. This absence of a permanently settled Turkish class facilitated the establishment of a kind of local nobility in Jerusalem, composed of the distinguished Arab families which derived their power and influence from farming taxes and duties (*iltizām*) and from their control of hereditary religious functions and, at the end of the Ottoman period, exercised administrative functions. These were the *aʿyān* (the notables, "eyes" of the community), the *effendi* (masters), e.g., the families of Khatīb, Dajjānī, Anṣārī, Khālidī, ʿAlamī, and later Nashāshībī and Ḥusaynī. Several of Jerusalem's Christian families were also well-known: Salāmeh, Tannūs, ʿAṭallah, and Katan.

One reason for the Ottoman rulers' disparaging attitude toward Jerusalem may have been its insignificance from a strategic and political point of view when there was no longer a danger of renewed Crusades. At the Ottoman conquest of Ereẓ Israel (1516) even the exact date of Jerusalem's capture was not noted. Because of its insignificance the rebels and invaders did not attempt to conquer it. The same situation existed at the time of Ẓāhir al-Omar, who in 1773 controlled the whole country except for Jerusalem. Similarly, Napoleon did not consider it necessary to conquer Jerusalem and was satisfied with the towns of the coastal strip and the plain. Another reason was the city's economic insignificance. According to the Ottoman records of land registration from the 16th century, the inhabitants of the district of Jerusalem were far fewer in number than those of Gaza, Nablus, and Safed. Accordingly, the income of Jerusalem's governor was smaller than that of the other governors. Apart from soap and Christian religious objects, almost nothing was manufactured in Jerusalem which could be exported to other districts or abroad. Nor did local trade play an important role in the city, since industry and craft did not develop in Jerusalem, which had no fertile rural areas surrounding it. Jewish, Muslim, and Christian sources were therefore justified in repeatedly emphasizing that most of the city's inhabitants were extremely impoverished. During the Ottoman Empire's period of abundance, the sultans regarded it as a duty to exempt the city's inhabitants from various taxes and even sent yearly contributions for distribution among the poor.

JEWISH JERUSALEM. Even before the Ottoman conquest there were many indications that Jewish Jerusalem was awakening from its lethargy. At the beginning of the 16th century it attracted the kabbalists who were awaiting the imminent redemption, such as Abraham b. Eliezer ha-Levi. Isaac Sholal, the *nagid* of Egypt, also settled in the city. After the conquest, and especially in light of the sympathetic attitude of Sultan Suleiman, which aroused such a positive response on the part of the Jews, it appears as if there existed, in effect, those political and social conditions which could enable Jerusalem to reassert its function as the spiritual and religious center of Judaism. David *Reuveni, a man of imagination and political courage, approached the Jews of Jerusalem. *Levi b. Ḥabib, who settled in the city and was one of the greatest scholars of his time, attacked Jacob *Berab for wanting to reestablish ordination (*semikhah*) in Safed and succeeded in foiling that plan. *David ibn Abi Zimra and, later, Bezalel *Ashkenazi taught in Jerusalem. However, the overwhelming poverty of the scholars and all the Jewish inhabitants placed the city at a disadvantage, and Safed, which attracted in the 16th century the greatest scholars and most of the immigrants, superseded Jerusalem for a time in importance as a center.

However, the communities of Egypt and Syria (especially Damascus) aided the Jerusalem community, as is attested by Moses *Trani (De Trani): "All the holy communities which send contributions to Jerusalem know that, in addition to what is distributed among the scholars and the poor, they are also used for all the fines and penalties levied on the community, for the inhabitants of Jerusalem can pay only the *kharāj* (poll tax)… and the remaining burdens… have to be met from outside contributions; for if they did not do thus, no one would want to settle in the city" (Responsa, vol. 3, no. 228). The situation of the scholars and yeshivot was especially difficult, and there are recurring and repeated complaints about this in the literature of the period.

Apparently the local rulers hindered the consolidation of the city's Jewish population. According to official censuses in 1525, 1533–39, and 1553, the number of Jews in the town ranged between approximately 1,000 and 1,500. They lived in three quarters, Sharaf, al-Maslakh ("Slaughterhouse"), and Rīsha, which are coextensive with the present-day Jewish Quarter. David ibn Abi Zimra conveys in his responsa the interesting information that the Jewish Quarter is called the "City of Zion" by the Jews and Ṣahyūn by the Arabs. He explains that in the laws pertaining to the holiness of Jerusalem a distinction is to be made between that part to which these laws pertain, called by the Arabs *Quds* (= Jerusalem), and the other part ("Zion"), which is considered outside of Jerusalem. In 1586 the authorities deprived the community of the synagogue named after Naḥmanides (restored only after the Six-Day War).

After Safed's decline at the end of the 16th century Jerusalem was built up. Bezalel Ashkenazi, who had come from Egypt, played a major role in this rebuilding. He was not content merely to act as *dayyan* but also lent his help in the organization of material assistance and even went on a mission to organize aid and save the synagogue which had been confiscated. He died in the early 1590s, however – shortly after his immigration – and was unable to carry out his activities. His initiative persisted after his death and Jewish Jerusalem continued to recover. The stream of immigrants from Turkey, North Africa, Italy, and Western Europe soon turned to Jerusalem. One of the most distinguished and famous among them was R. Isaiah *Horowitz (immigrated in 1622), author of *Shenei Luḥot ha-Berit*, whose influence was of great spiritual importance for the community. He found a population in Jerusalem composed of Sephardim, Ashkenazim, and Italians (who were considered one community), Maghrebis, and Mustaʿribs (Moriscos). There was also a small Karaite community. Shortly after his arrival the community suffered severely from the persecution of the governor Muhammad ibn Farrukh (1625), which is described in the pamphlet *Ḥorvot Yerushalayim* (published anonymously in Venice, 1636). This governor, however, was removed from his post a short while later and the community recovered.

In general, the situation improved in Jerusalem, but the tax burden and other impositions were not eased. There are various extant sources from this period, including several interesting travel descriptions (see *Travels) – among them that of R. Moses Poryat of Prague (1650) – which make it possible to achieve a faithful reconstruction of the situation. There are also descriptions from the end of the 17th century which render an exact description of the situation in Jerusalem. There were then about 300 Jewish families, with nearly 1,200 persons. This number exceeded the quota established by the Ottoman authorities for the Jews in the city, and they therefore had to be bribed so that they would not expel the "extra" ones. The extortion of monies resulting from the increased numbers of Jews caused some of the people within the community to seek to limit the number of new settlers and make them go elsewhere.

The only possibility for the economic consolidation of the community was to send emissaries abroad to seek aid. Among the Jerusalem emissaries was *Shabbetai Ẓevi, who only arrived in the city in 1662 but made such a strong personal impression that shortly thereafter he was entrusted with the task of collecting contributions in Egypt. He did, in fact, succeed in raising considerable sums but he used them for disseminating propaganda for his movement. The sages of Jerusalem, who were not convinced by his messianic claims, excommunicated him and compelled him to leave Jerusalem. This, however, led to conflict and some of the Jerusalem emissaries who went abroad engaged in Shabbatean propaganda, caused friction within the Jerusalem community, and even undermined it economically and caused its breakdown, since they hindered an effective organization of aid to the community. Spiritually, in contrast, Jerusalem flourished during the 17th century. The city inherited Safed's place in the study of the Kabbalah. R. Jacob *Ẓemaḥ settled there in the late 1630s and edited the writings of R. Ḥayyim Vital with the help of the latter's son Samuel. He himself wrote a series of books and commentaries explaining the teachings of R. Isaac Luria and Vital. Other mystics also settled in the city and, from then on, Jerusalem became the center of the kabbalists.

An important contribution to the development of the city's spiritual life was made by Jacob *Ḥagiz, who came from the Maghreb (Fez) by way of Italy, as did most of the North African immigrants of that time. With the financial assistance of an Italian family of philanthropists he established the *bet midrash* Beit Ya'akov (1658), in which leading contemporary scholars taught talented disciples. These scholars included: R. Moses *Galante, R. Samuel *Garmison, R. Solomon *Algazi, and the important *posek* R. *Hezekiah da Silva, author of *Peri Hadash*.

At the end of the 17th century the Jewish community numbered approximately 1,000 persons. According to the record of poll taxes, there were around 180 payers of the *kharāj. A quarter of them were scholars and rabbis; the remainder were craftsmen and small businessmen. Neither group belonged to the wealthy classes who paid the highest tax (*aʿlā*), only a quarter paid the intermediate (*awsaṭ*), and the great majority the lower tax (*adnā*).

Although the Shabbatean movement failed and seemed to abate at the end of the 17th century, the ferment it had aroused did not cease. A group, 500 strong, headed by Judah b. Samuel he-Ḥasid and Ḥayyim *Malakh, which contained extreme and moderate Shabbatean trends, came to Jerusalem from Poland in 1700 and settled in the courtyard which was later the site of the Ḥurvah synagogue. Before their arrival the population was around 1,200, about a sixth of whom were Ashkenazim. The group broke up quickly, however, since their behavior led to quarrels within the community, until the veteran inhabitants had to turn to Poland and Western Europe and request assistance in their battle against the newcomers. In addition, the burden of debts owed by the Ashkenazim to the Muslims became so heavy that they no longer could bear them or maneuver with the creditors. Due to disruptions on the roads in Europe, financial help did not arrive from there. On Nov. 8, 1720, the Arabs broke into the Ashkenazi synagogue and burned the Scrolls of the Law. They also seized the plot and held it until the migration of *Perushim* to Jerusalem approximately 100 years later (1816). For some time no Ashkenazi Jew could show himself in the streets of Jerusalem unless he disguised himself in Eastern dress. One of the first Ashkenazim who decided to return to Jerusalem was R. *Abraham Gershon of Kutow, brother-in-law of the Baal Shem Tov (c. 1750).

During that period of depression, the community of Constantinople had to take the Jews of Jerusalem under its wing. A "council of officials" was established in the capital of the Ottoman Empire which undertook the responsibility for clearing up the community's debts and arranging its financial affairs. The officials from Constantinople also instituted ordinances and special arrangements in order to prevent a recurrence of those events which had brought about the community's economic downfall. A special *parnas* was sent from Constantinople to supervise public affairs. Knowledge about the economic improvements resulting from these efforts became widespread and numerous immigrants again began to settle in Jerusalem, especially scholars. A special impression was made by the immigration of R. Ḥayyim b. Moses *Attar of Salé, who went with disciples from Italy and established a prominent yeshivah (1742) in a building which is still standing. According to the rule "competition among scholars increases wisdom," more yeshivot were established in Jerusalem and the sounds of study echoed in its alleys. Wealthy Jews from all parts of the Diaspora contributed to the establishment and maintenance of these yeshivot. This activity also led to the increase in written works, especially of responsa, which were published in Constantinople, Izmir, Salonika, and the towns of Italy.

At the end of the 18th century, however, there was another decline in Jerusalem's Jewish population. According to a possibly somewhat exaggerated estimate, approximately 10,000 Jews lived there in the middle of the century, but as a result of the insecurity in the southern part of the country, the decline in influence of the central authority in Constantinople, and also epidemics and natural disasters, the population at the end of the century was estimated at half that number or even less.

CHRISTIAN JERUSALEM. According to the Ottoman *defters* (lists of taxpayers) in Jerusalem, the number of Christian households increased from 119 to 303 between 1525 and 1533; if monks, clergymen, and bachelors are added, the increase was from 600 to 1,800 persons. In the villages surrounding Jerusalem – Bethlehem, Beit Jālla, Beit Ṣāḥūr – there were also Christian families. Most of them were permanent resident Syrian Christians, but all spoke Arabic. They were called "*Christiani dela centura*," i.e., the girdled Christians, referring to the *zunnār* which was their special mark of difference from the Muslims. In the course of time the sign was forgotten but the name remained. In their way of life the Christians were not different from the Muslims; their women covered their faces in the streets like the Muslim women and would not go among men. Several travelers point out that drunkenness and prostitution were widespread among the Christians: in particular, the last night of the Easter celebrations, when permission was granted to all the Christian inhabitants to congregate in the Church of the Holy Sepulcher, was believed to have been occasion for wanton immorality.

The Muslims despised the Christians and in official documents sometimes called them "infidels." They were usually subject to all the restrictions applying to the "People of the Book" in relation to the erection and maintenance of churches and other religious institutions. The authorities delayed permission for repairs, and when any attempt was made to introduce something which had not existed previously, they were forced to remove the addition. In the words of R. *Gedaliah of Siemiatycze (beginning of the 18th century): "The idol-worshipers are also in exile here – like the Jews" (Yaari, *Massaʾot*, 341). According to him (loc. cit.) their number in Jerusalem was great and exceeded the number of the Ishmaelites (Turks and Arabs). They were not allowed to marry without obtaining permission from the governor, for which they had to pay the *rusūm* tax, and the appointment of their religious leaders had to be approved by the governor or the qadi of Jerusalem.

From a religious point of view the "*Christiani dela centura*" were not a single entity but were divided into the various Eastern sects and churches, the Latins, i.e., the Catholics, being a negligible minority. Christian visitors usually counted seven to nine religious communities with an established claim to the Church of the Holy Sepulcher: Franciscans, i.e., Latin Friars of the order of St. Francis, called the "Little Brothers";

Greeks, the Orthodox Melchites, members of the Byzantine Church; Georgians; Armenians; Abyssinians, also called "Indish"; Jacobites; Syrians; Nestorians; and Copts. Each community held a certain part of the Church, to which, as well as to various honorific ceremonial functions, it claimed a prescriptive right. There were frequent conflicts among the clergy, therefore, over real or imagined encroachments, and the Muslim authorities often had to mediate and decide between the combatants (during the Ottoman period, the British Mandate; later, the keys of the Holy Sepulcher were in the hands of a Jerusalem Muslim family). The Franciscan Friars, "Custodia Terrae Sanctae," were responsible for the Christian pilgrims who came to worship at the *holy places. They would transfer to the authorities the taxes levied on the pilgrims at the gates of the city near the Church of the Holy Sepulcher, which the Muslims deprecatingly called *al-Qumāma* ("a heap of rubbish") instead of *al-Qiyāma* ("the Church of the Resurrection"). Probably only a few of the pilgrims knew that the tax collected from them was for the Muslims in the city. Conflicts periodically broke out among the Franciscans and clergymen of the other communities.

ATTITUDE OF THE EUROPEAN POWERS. No less surprising than the coolness of the Ottoman authorities toward Jerusalem (see Decline of Jerusalem, above) was the attitude of the countries of Christian Europe – first and foremost among them France, the first European power to enter into a *capitulations agreement with the Ottoman Empire. Francis I, king of France and "the most Christian of Christians," saw himself as the defender of the Christian holy places and in 1528 complained about the confiscation of the church in Jerusalem, which was made into a mosque by the Muslims. This probably referred to the Cenaculum, the Church of the Last Supper on Mount Zion. The sultan made no response to the complaint but promised that the other places in the vicinity of the mosque would remain under Christian control and would not be harmed by the Muslims.

In 1535 a capitulations agreement was reached between Francis and Suleiman the Magnificent. It contained a clause, which stated explicitly that the pope could join the agreement and enjoy all its benefits. From that time on the Christian states, especially the pope, began to appeal to the French kings to protect the interests of the Christians and Christianity in Palestine. The capitulations were intended to regulate the activities of France in key places in Palestine, especially in Jerusalem. It was reasonable to expect that a permanent French representative in Jerusalem would also be responsible for the maintenance of Christian and pilgrim holy places. However, it was only about 100 years after the first capitulation agreement and about 80 after the appointment of a French consul in Tripoli, Syria (1544), that the first French consul in Jerusalem was appointed.

The following are excerpts from the writings of the Frenchman E. Roger, who visited Palestine in 1631, as he recorded in *La Terre Sainte* (1664; 461–4):

> The third consulate is that of Jerusalem which our king, the most Christian of Christians, St. Louis [the 13th, 1610–43], blessed be his memory, established in 1621 for the protection of our monks that by means of its influence they might establish and consolidate themselves in those places and overcome the insults and injustices inflicted on them by that barbaric people.

After describing the consul's duties toward the merchants, he continued:

> The fourth and fifth clauses [of the capitulations] deal only with the holy places and the monks inhabiting them, the pilgrims who also come to visit them, and other Christian passersby who are under the protection of that consul. They need him on every occasion in order to receive assistance and support in all their dealings with the Turks; he uses his influence to convince the Turks to maintain the capitulations and to practice according to the agreements. Nevertheless, the Turks do not refrain from perpetrating their tyrannical deeds both on the monks and the Catholic Christians who are not monks. These deeds would have been a thousandfold more difficult to bear were they not curtailed by that French consul whom the king has appointed for this purpose. A constant cause for praising and blessing our king is that in all the towns in which there is a consul or vice-consul a chapel is permitted in which he usually maintains two or three of our monks from the Jerusalem community, who celebrate a holy mass daily for our king in the presence of the consul and the merchants, both those living in the towns and those at anchorage or from the ports… The reason that the attitude of the Turkish authorities to the monks and the Christian Catholics in Jerusalem is worse than in any other part of the sultan's kingdom is that there is no consul there. For the Turks, seeing that M. Jean Lempereur, whom the king sent as consul, prevents their carrying out their usual tyrannies toward the monks, made false accusations against him to the pasha in Damascus and he was taken there by a troop of Turks. However, he proved his innocence and went to Constantinople. The pashas and qadis, who have since been in Jerusalem, do everything in their power to prevent his return, since he would hinder them from filling their pockets as they do in the absence of a consul. They daily invent new means, under the pretext of administrative action, of gradually destroying us. And when we have just escaped from one matter, they raise up another, a worse one in its stead. They do this not only during our lifetime but also after our death. For it is forbidden to bring a monk or a Catholic Christian for burial unless the guardian priest has first obtained the permission of the qadi who demands 12 dinars for it, although the contents of the permit, which I wish to include here in order to show the contempt in which they hold us, reads as follows: "I Abu Suleiman, qadi of Jerusalem, permit the guardian of the Franjis to bury the cursed monk, so-and-so…"

The attempts to appoint a consul to succeed Lempereur were futile, but in 1699 a French consul was again appointed in Jerusalem. However, he fled to Bethlehem several months later because of the pasha's oppression. Another consul, the third in line, went to Jerusalem in 1713, but he too was only able to hold out for a short while. From then until 1843 no French consul was appointed in Jerusalem; the consul in Sidon would come during Easter to the Holy Sepulcher in order to maintain the splendor of the Latin ceremonies.

The most important topic which interested the European public – or at least those broad sections of the public having no direct connection with commercial dealings – in connection with the Holy Land was without doubt the assurance of the rights of the Christian faith and the protection of its holy places, especially in Jerusalem, and of its faithful who came to worship at these places. Nevertheless, no other country besides France attempted to establish a consulate or at least a consular agency in Jerusalem. All their efforts were directed toward the maintenance of representatives in the commercial centers. The Franciscan order retained the function of looking after West European pilgrims, without regard for differences in religious ritual, i.e., including Protestants, Calvinists, etc. The problem of Orthodox pilgrims coming from outside the borders of the Ottoman Empire arose only during the 19th century; until that time pilgrims from Russia were not a significant component of the general stream. The faithful of the other Eastern Churches were subjects of the Ottoman sultan.

One characteristic feature in the lives of the Christian communities of Palestine should be pointed out: their spiritual rulers and religious institutions were outside the borders of Palestine. The Latin Church had an historical and dogmatic justification for this attitude, since Rome was its cradle and focus, but this was not the case with the Eastern Churches in general and the Orthodox Church in particular. Nevertheless, the Orthodox patriarch of Jerusalem, whose church claimed priority in Christianity and thus greater rights to the Church of the Holy Sepulcher, the Church of the Nativity (in Bethlehem), and other holy places, had his seat in Constantinople. Moreover, no church concerned itself with the establishment in Palestine of an institution of higher learning and education for its priests and monks. All the Christian travelers and tourists in Palestine reported the ignorance of all the lower clergy, both those included in the monastic orders and the "secular," i.e., those outside the orders who were scattered among the smaller communities and villages. The few clergymen on a higher level sent from Rome, Athos (the important center of Greek clergy), or Constantinople were involved in controversies over prestige, real or imagined, and in intercommunal conflicts and had no time free for study or teaching.

THE CHANGE IN THE 19TH CENTURY. Beginning with the end of the 18th century there was an increase in the interest of the European powers, primarily France and England, in the Middle East, especially from an economic point of view (see *Israel). The Christian powers began to display great interest in the Christian holy places, to be concerned for their protection and welfare, and to support their traditional administrators: the Eastern and Western Christian Churches, the Orthodox and Latin orders, and the new monasteries which had sprung up. This necessitated the prolongation of the capitulations agreements and the effective protection of European citizens and stateless persons under the protection of the foreign consuls, and even the sultan's non-Muslim subjects. It is clear, however, that the international powers, which now made an appearance in Jerusalem – France, Russia, England, Austria, and Prussia – did not regard religious matters as the major and principal motive for their activities. The true intentions of the European powers became manifest when they intervened in 1840 to put an end to Muhammad Ali's revolt against Ottoman rule (see *Israel, History, Ottoman Period).

In 1835 Ibrahim Pasha, who ruled Ereẓ Israel and Syria on behalf of his father Muhammad Ali, gave the Jewish community of Jerusalem permission to "repair" its four ancient synagogues, which were in a state of disrepair, after all previous requests to the Ottoman authorities had been rejected. They now began some basic projects which were tantamount to reconstruction. It was necessary to break down weak parts of the foundations, to replace the wooden ceiling in one of the synagogues, which had been covered with mats, by a stone dome, etc. There was a danger, when these demolition works were begun, that the permission could be cancelled under pressure from Muslim circles – since this actually was new construction, which was not permitted by Muslim religious law. Furthermore, there were not sufficient funds to complete the "repairs" quickly so that they could be pointed to as a fait accompli. A special emissary was sent in order to collect contributions for these urgent needs to the "towns of the inner west" (i.e., Morocco). Nevertheless, the community incurred numerous debts. A.M. *Luncz states in *Jerusalem* (1894; p. 211 n. 3), "The community's debts increased as a result of the repairs and expansion of the R. Johanan b. Zakkai and Istambuli synagogues undertaken by the sages and rabbis of the community during the rule of Ibrahim Pasha. The former had been very small and they expanded and improved it. The latter had been covered with mats for a long time and only then did they cover it with a stone ceiling."

In the emissary's letter to Morocco five synagogues were mentioned which were suffering the ravages of time and were in need of repair, including the synagogue of R. Judah he-Ḥasid, which had become a *ḥurvah* (ruin) since the "Shiknāz," i.e., immigrants from Eastern Europe, had been forbidden to settle in Jerusalem. Great efforts were made to have this harsh decree by the Ottoman rulers abolished. In 1836 Muhammad Ali published a firman which laid down the conditions for a legal arrangement for the resumption of immigration to Jerusalem from Eastern Europe. The firman was decreed with the active support of the European powers which aimed at increasing their influence among the Jewish population of East European immigrants. The few *Perushim*, the disciples of R. Elijah the Gaon of Vilna, who were tolerated in Jerusalem, immediately seized the opportunity and started to clean out the "Ḥurvah" and erect a synagogue, called Menaḥem Ẓiyyon, which was dedicated several days after the earthquake in Safed (24th of Tevet, 1837). During the tribulations which befell Safed several times in the fourth decade, many people began to leave the town and move to Jerusalem where conditions for settlement had improved; Jerusalem became the center of the *Perushim*, who influenced the Ashkenazi community.

ESTABLISHMENT OF CONSULATES IN JERUSALEM AND INCREASED CHRISTIAN ACTIVITY. As the policy of supporting the Ottoman Empire against the rule of Muhammad Ali and his son Ibrahim Pasha came to be adopted by most of the European states, they began to pay attention to strengthening their position in the country. Thus, already in 1838 Britain made overtures toward opening a consulate in Jerusalem, the first in the city after the abolition of the French consulate more than 100 years previously. It was headed by a vice consul (1838) and later (1841) a consul (initially W.T. Young). Even before this the British consul general (whose headquarters was in Beirut) was represented in Safed and Acre by a consular agent, Moses Abraham Finzi, member of a distinguished Italian Jewish family, who was officially appointed to his position in May 1837. Since the Anglicans did not yet have their own churches in Jerusalem and no English Christians lived there, it was the British vice consul's declared function to protect the Jews – as was the function of the agent in Safed. Thus it was stated explicitly in the instructions of the Foreign Secretary Palmerston to Young on Jan. 31, 1839: "Viscount Palmerston has instructed me to signify that part of your function as British vice consul in Jerusalem will be to offer protection to the Jews in general..." He also had to take care of pilgrims and tourists from England.

Russia opened its own consulate in Jaffa in 1812 in order to assist Orthodox pilgrims who were beginning to come from Russia. It is learned from the reports made by Young during his first year in office that there was a Jewish agent in Jerusalem who represented the Russian consul and whose duty it was to take care of 40 Russian-Jewish immigrant families in Jerusalem. He maintained that the Russian consul removed one agent and appointed another in his stead, who was an Austrian subject, not a Russian.

Young also obtained possession of a letter from C.M. Basily to R. Isaiah *Bardaki. Basily had been appointed a short while previously (1839) as Russian consul for Syria and Palestine. His permanent seat was in Beirut, but in the course of time he moved to Jerusalem. Basily found it necessary to explain that Bardaki's appointment as consul of Russia had been made by his predecessor, Graf Alexander Medem. The style of the letter reflects an energetic man who already at the beginning of his career in the Middle East could control the situation. He was appointed consul general in 1844 and held important functions in guiding his country's policies in the Middle East. He had a broad range of knowledge and wrote an important work on contemporary events in Palestine and Syria.

Isaiah Bardaki, son-in-law of *Israel b. Samuel of Shklov, author of *Pe'at ha-Shulḥan*, played an important role in Jewish Jerusalem. After two or three years he became the consul of Russia and Austria and bravely combated missionary activities. Of special significance was his widespread activity in the internal matters of the *kolel* of the *Perushim*. Young expressed the fear that Isaiah Bardaki would attempt to represent all the European Jews. As a reaction to this report, he was immediately instructed by the Foreign Office in London to appoint a *wakīl* (officer-in-charge) for the English Jews in the same way that the Russian agent had been appointed. Young offered this position to David Herschell, son of Solomon *Herschell, Ashkenazi chief rabbi of England, but he refused to accept the post, as he wanted to keep out of the controversies among his brethren in Jerusalem. Another reason for his refusals, it appears, was the suspicion that the British intended to use him for purposes of intelligence.

Perhaps Herschell was also apprised of the intentions of religious circles in England to initiate missionary activities in Palestine; in fact, in 1840 an agreement was signed between Queen Victoria and Frederick William, king of Prussia, establishing an Anglican episcopacy in Jerusalem which would also supervise missionary activity in Palestine. The bishop would always be a member of the Anglican church and would be appointed alternately by the archbishop of Canterbury and the king of Prussia, while both countries would cover the costs. The first bishop who arrived in Jerusalem in 1841 was the apostate Michael Solomon *Alexander. Four years later permission was received from Istanbul for the establishment of a Protestant church in Jerusalem. Alexander immediately began his missionary activities, which were not in fact viewed with favor in the British Foreign Service since they raised many difficulties. James *Finn (1845–62), the British consul in Jerusalem who succeeded Young, was also accused of missionary intentions and was finally compelled to leave his post.

Cyril II, the Greek Orthodox patriarch for Jerusalem from 1845 to 1872, was a distinguished and, in many ways, a progressive person. He moved his abode from Istanbul, which had been used by his predecessors as the center for their activities, to Jerusalem, the official seat of the patriarchate. In 1849 he established a printing press near the Holy Sepulcher for his community's needs.

In 1843 France reopened its consulate in Jerusalem after a lapse of 130 years. This did not please the Franciscans, and they were especially disturbed by the fact that Pope Pius IX established a Latin patriarchate in Jerusalem (1847), one of whose functions was to check the increasing influence of the Orthodox and the Protestants. The Protestant clergy – Anglican, Prussian, and American – did in fact develop widespread missionary activities among the local population. Since activity among the Muslims was prohibited by the law of the land and could arouse the anger of the authorities, the missions conducted their activities among the Eastern Christian and Jewish communities. This led to the establishment of Protestant communities among the Christian Arabs of Palestine and Syria. A few Jews also converted for financial gain. There were also cases of Christians who converted to Judaism, well-known among them being the U.S. consul, Warder *Cresson, and David Classen, owners of an estate near Jaffa.

APPOINTMENT OF HAKHAM BASHI FOR JERUSALEM. In view of the rivalry for the support of the "alien" Jews of Palestine, the sultan was finally compelled to do something for his

Jewish subjects, particularly in Palestine. The firman of the beginning of Ramadan 1256 A.H. (end of October 1840), achieved by Montefiore, Crémieux, and Munk – after the blood libels in Damascus and Rhodes – for the protection of the Jews, was considered a kind of bill of rights for them, since it stated explicitly that the rights granted to all the subjects of the sultan in the Khaṭṭi sherif decree of Ghane (1839 – see *Turkey) applied to the Jews as well. The Jews of Jerusalem particularly relied on the firman in defending themselves before Muhammad Pasha, the governor of the pashalik, against the blood libel, which was propagated at the beginning of March 1847 by the Greeks in Jerusalem, with the support of their patriarch.

One direct result of the changes in the status of Jerusalem was the appointment of a *ḥakham bashi* (chief rabbi) of Palestine, whose seat was in Jerusalem. In his *Jerusalem* (1892), Luncz points out the reasons for this appointment: "In the year 1840 [!] the government saw fit to elevate the holy city Jerusalem to the status of a district town and to place in it a pasha who in the course of his duties would govern its inhabitants and the inhabitants of the towns surrounding it, and by means of this elevation in its political status the Jews gained the right to appoint a chief rabbi authorized by the government as a *ḥakham bashi*… The leaders and elders of the community then realized that for the welfare and peace of their community, which had begun to spread and increase, it was necessary that the rabbi heading it should be authorized by the exalted government, so that he might be capable of standing in the breach and legally defending the rights of his community. And through the efforts of the minister Abraham di *Camondo of blessed memory, who knew the aforementioned rabbi [Abraham Hayyim Gagin] and esteemed him greatly, this aim was realized, and shortly after his appointment he received the statement (firman) of the king confirming him for the position, and he was the first *ḥakham bashi* of Palestine" (p. 210).

The imperial authorization of appointment (*berāt humāyūn*, at the beginning and in the body of the document), which was issued in Istanbul in 1841, was of vital significance for the Jewish community of Jerusalem and Palestine. Of special significance were the rights indirectly guaranteed the community, since they indicated a legal breakthrough in the restrictions concerning the synagogues and *battei midrash*. In all versions of the *berāts* it was established that the reading of the law – i.e., reading from the *Sefer Torah* – in the house of the *ḥakham* or in other Jewish houses was in accordance with the Jewish religion, and that it was permitted to hang up curtains over the arks of the law and lamps, i.e., to set up permanent places of worship. In these *berāts* there is a certain shrewdness which permits the Covenant of *Omar – which prohibits the establishment of new synagogues and *battei midrash* – to be overlooked, and permission is given to hold public worship everywhere without running the risk of disturbances and oppression. The synagogues and their properties are protected – they may not be harmed or seized in collection of debts, which formerly occurred frequently. Each *berāt* delineated the rights and obligations of the *ḥakham bashi* and the community, and it was renewed with each new appointment to the position by the imperial authorities.

CAPITULATIONS IN THE 19TH CENTURY. The European states probably did not rely on the written promise of the *Khaṭṭi humāyūn* (i.e., the order whose beginning was written by the sultan's own hand), which was given (1856) to the sultan's subjects but not their own, and they took care to safeguard the physical and property rights of those under their protection, as well as caring for the holy places. Britain and France also sought to ease restrictions on economic expansion, to gain a liberal law that would enable their subjects to buy land, etc. Opposing them, the sultan maintained that he could not both recognize the special status of alien subjects on the basis of the capitulations and grant them complete equality with his own. If Britain and France wished to obtain economic rights for their subjects, they would have to give up their protection according to the capitulations.

Jerusalem, however, did not remain only an attraction for pilgrims. The scope of the activity of the foreign consuls widened because of the intrigues between them and the agencies and institutions for special functions, which were connected with them. Jerusalem became the residence of the various delegations, religious and secular, which were devoted to a wide range of activities in education, missionary work, medicine, and charity. The Jews were the first of the city's inhabitants to foresee this development, which involved a transformation in the status and importance of Jerusalem. The founders of the Naḥalat Shivah quarter, who left the Old City, were the pioneers and builders not only of the new Jewish Jerusalem, but of Greater Jerusalem with all its communities and nationalities.

[Haïm Z'ew Hirschberg]

THE DEVELOPMENT OF JERUSALEM, 1840–1917. Muhammad Ali's successful uprising against the central authorities in Istanbul, which had only been terminated under pressure from the European powers, had demonstrated the weakness of Ottoman rule. The growing interference of foreign powers in Ottoman affairs was particularly perceptible in Jerusalem, which was no longer off the beaten track. Improved communications with Europe, as the result of the use of steamships on regular sea routes, facilitated an increased flow of visitors and pilgrims. The Ottomans tried to improve their administration and the relative security that ensued encouraged an increase in immigration, which brought about a revolution in the composition of the population of Jerusalem within less than 40 years.

The opening of the British consulate in Jerusalem was followed within a few years by the inauguration of Russian, Prussian, Austria-Hungarian, Sardinian, Spanish, and United States consulates. In 1848 the first "bank" was opened by the *Valero family. In the absence of Ottoman postal services, the Austrians opened a post office in the same year, followed by

France, Prussia, and Italy. The press of the (Latin) Custodianship of the Holy Land was opened in 1847, followed in 1848 by the Armenian press and five years later by that of the Greek Orthodox patriarchate. The status of the Holy Places determined in an Ottoman decree of 1757 was confirmed in 1852 (the "Status quo"; see *Holy Places).

These were preceded, however, by the Hebrew press of Israel *Bak, which had been transferred from Safed after the 1837 earthquake and, in about 1841, published the first book printed in Jerusalem, Ḥ.J.D. *Azulai's *Avodat ha-Kodesh*. Apart from religious works, polemical tracts, and, later, newspapers were also printed by this press. Despite the fact that in the unanimous opinion of the visitors the Jews were the most abject and lowly of the population, changes were introduced in their lives as well. In order to free them from dependence on the missionaries, Montefiore established a clinic in Jerusalem in the early 1840s, to which he sent medications periodically and which functioned for 20 years. He also subsidized the services of a physician, Dr. Frankel, who came in 1843. The number of Jerusalem's inhabitants in 1845 has been estimated at 15,000, including 6,000 Jews.

The Crimean War, which was partly caused by struggle for control over the Holy Places, again demonstrated the weakness of the Ottoman empire vis-à-vis the European powers, whose representatives in Jerusalem became increasingly more influential – even defeated Russia increased its influence in the city. The great prestige of France was attested by the fact that in 1856 the sultan Abdul-Mejid gave the Ṣallāḥiyya building (the ancient church of St. Anne) as a gift to Napoleon III. It was renovated by its new owners and became the most impressive remnant of Crusader architecture in Palestine. Bells were installed for the first time in the Monastery of the Cross in the same year and in 1867 in the Holy Sepulcher; church bells became an integral part of the sounds of the city. In 1858–59 the Austrian hospice (now the Government Hospital on Via Dolorosa) and the hospice of the German Johanniter Order were built. Crowds gathered to gaze at the two-wheeled vehicles – surplus from the Crimean War – used in the building, for they were the first vehicles seen in the city. The filth in the city was still so great, however, that a "cleanliness society" was established under the auspices of the pasha, but to no avail. As late as the 1860s tourists were complaining about animal carcasses lying in the city's gates and streets. These carcasses, often of animals which had died during the frequent droughts, were devoured by the stray dogs depicted in many pictures of the period.

The 18-bed Rothschild Hospital was opened in 1854 and a small "rival" institution, which later became the Bikkur Ḥolim Hospital, was opened at about the same time by the *Perushim*. In 1856 a school named after the Austrian Jewish nobleman *Laemel was opened due to the efforts of L.A. *Frankl; it was the first modern school for boys in Jerusalem.

In the summer of 1859, through the initiative of the Ashkenazi community and with the aid of the "Hod" (= Holland Deutschland) *kolel*, a plot of land was bought near Mt. Zion, and by 1861 the first of the "*battei maḥaseh*" (shelter houses) were built on it. Sir Moses Montefiore, who again visited Jerusalem in 1855 and 1857, contributed more than any other single man of his generation to changing the city's face in general. In 1855 he used funds from the legacy of the American philanthropist Judah Touro to acquire a plot of land west of the walls, despite many legal difficulties, to house Jews who were living in the dark cellars of the Old City. On the plot which he had bought, he also built a windmill, which became one of the landmarks of the city and was its first "industrial" structure. Building this quarter raised difficulties, since it was supposedly too close to the Citadel, and Montefiore was only permitted to continue building after the Russians had begun building outside the city. Montefiore got the authorities to move the municipal slaughterhouse (*maslakh*) from the end of the street of the Jews, near the Zion Gate – where it had been since the Mamluk period – outside the walls. He also planned a railroad from Jaffa, the paving of interurban roads, and even afforestation, but without any practical outcome. The city's population in 1856 was estimated at 18,000.

The year 1860 marked the beginning of the growth of the "new" city and the relative decline of the Old City. Jerusalem began to emerge from behind the walls and construction started on an impressive series of buildings (inns, a cathedral, and hospitals) in the present-day Russian Compound. The buildings were erected in the Maydan area, which until then had served as a parade ground for the Turkish army and an encampment for tourists. At the same time, the building of Mishkenot Sha'ananim, the first Jewish quarter outside the walls, was completed by Montefiore (the Yemin Moshe quarter was added to it in 1894). At the same time, further northwest, the German Protestant priest Ludwig Schneller built the Syrian orphanage for orphans from the massacres of Christians in Syria. This institution expanded and became the pride of the German residents of Palestine. It burnt down in 1910 but was rebuilt. More Jewish quarters were founded: Maḥaneh Yisrael, built by Oriental Jews in 1868, and Naḥalat Shivah (1869) on the main road to Jaffa. The establishment of these quarters resulted several years later in the opening of the city gates (which had been closed at night and during the Muslim midday prayers on Fridays) 24 hours a day, and this greatly contributed to the security outside the city. Communication between the new quarters and the Old City was by paths through stony fields, which soon became roads and some of them (starting with Jaffa Road) even paved streets, although in 1917 there were still no tarred streets in the city. In the 1870s cabs and carts began to make their appearance in the streets of new Jerusalem, and on his last visit in 1875 Montefiore drove from Jaffa in a carriage. False rumors regarding a visit by the sultan in 1864 resulted in practical attempts to level the alleys of the Old City. The water supply was very poor, despite several attempts by the administration and the waqf (in 1812, in the 1850s, and 1860s) to repair the ancient conduit from ʿAyn ʿArrūb and Solomon's Pools; the stone pipes were regularly sabotaged by the fellahin.

During the frequent drought years, water was brought by animals and carriers in filthy animal-skin bags from En Rogel (Bi'r Ayyūb) and the Gihon Spring (Umm al-Daraj), through the Dung Gate and sold at high prices. However, the water supply mainly depended on the cisterns near the houses in which rainwater collected; in the 1860s there were almost a thousand of them. This water was only fit for drinking as long as it was not contaminated by sewage water (there was no sewage system), and the pollution of the drinking water brought about a severe plague in 1864, which claimed hundreds of victims and led to the city being placed in quarantine for four months. Sir Moses Montefiore came again in 1866 to help the inhabitants, Jews and non-Jews, and contributed money for improving the water supply. By 1863 two newspapers, *Ha-Levanon*, published by the *Perushim*, who set up a new press for the purpose, and *Ḥavaẓẓelet*, published by Israel Bak and the Ḥasidim, appeared in the city, competing against each other until they were closed down by the authorities. *Ḥavaẓẓelet* reappeared in 1870, followed by numerous short-lived journals. In 1868 a Jew opened the first modern bakery – a small but notable improvement in a city where many of the inhabitants had to bake their own bread. By 1865 the city was linked to the Coastal Plain by the Turkish telegraph, which contributed to security, trade, and convenience. In 1866 negotiations began for the paving of a "carriage route" to Jaffa, which was completed in 1868; it had to be repaired in preparation for a visit by the Austrian emperor Franz Josef, who was returning from the opening ceremony of the Suez Canal. Another visitor of that year was the heir to the Prussian throne (later Emperor Frederick III), who received the eastern Muristan area as a gift from the sultan in order to build a church. In the 1850s and 1860s Jerusalem attracted noted archaeologists and students of the Bible and the Ancient East, including C. Warren, W.R. Wilson, C. Schick, M. de Vog, F. de Saulcy, and other well-known scholars (see below: Archaeology).

In 1867 the German hospital was built for lepers, who until that time used to dwell near the city wall at the end of the street of the Jews. In 1868 the Germans built on a prominent site outside the city (now King George Avenue) the Talita Kumi school for Arab girls; there was already a school for Jewish girls. In the same year the magnificent building in the Latin patriarchate was built within the walls northwest of the Jaffa Gate. The French Soeurs de Sion convent was built on the Via Dolorosa. The Jewish community too was not inactive. In 1864 the first Jewish school for girls, named after Evelina de *Rothschild, opened despite the vociferous protests of the religious zealots. In the same year the magnificent Beit Ya'akov Ashkenazi synagogue was completed in the courtyard of the Ḥurvah of R. Judah he-Ḥasid. It had taken seven years to build, and shortly after its dedication, construction began on the Tiferet Yisrael (Nisan Bak) synagogue, which was completed in 1872.

In the 1860s the Jewish population in the holy city steadily grew, because of increased immigration and the reduced death rate. In the middle years of the decade the Jews became a majority in the city for the first time in 1800 years. The British consul reported in 1865 that there were approximately 18,000 residents in the city (as in 1856), of whom 8–9,000 were Jews. From that time the Jewish community continually gained in strength.

The development of Jerusalem continued in the 1870s, as testified by the establishment of a "municipal council" (*majlis baladiyya*) in 1877. The German Quarter was founded by the *Templers in 1873 and a road was built to reach it, which also served the Mishkenot Sha'ananim quarter and the eye hospital built by the Order of St. John in 1876. From this road developed the paved road to Bethlehem and Hebron. There were already two hotels in the city: one near the Damascus Gate and the other in the Christian quarter near the Pool of Hezekiah. However, the pilgrims preferred the inns of their communities and wealthy tourists still set up encampments outside the walls.

Near the road to Bethlehem the Arab Abu Tor (Ṭūr) quarter began to develop, apparently in the 1870s. Unlike the Jewish quarters, which were built as uniform blocks, usually as closed courtyards (for security reasons), the Arab and Christian quarters grew organically and slowly. Among them was Katamon which gradually grew near Saint Simon, the summer residence of the Greek patriarch. In north Jerusalem there were also signs of settlement, and Arab houses were built in Karm al-Sheikh (near the present-day Rockefeller Museum), west of it (near the present-day Herod's Gate, or Bāb al-Zahra), and to the north in Wadi Joz (Jawz). Due to this expansion, Herod's Gate was opened in 1875. Near the Damascus Gate, apparently at that time the Musrarah quarter was built. A first scientific demographic survey at that time counted 20,500 inhabitants in Jerusalem, including 10,500 Jews.

In 1871 the mosque of the Mughrabis was built in the Old City. In the Via Dolorosa the rebuilding of the church of St. John was completed (1874), followed two years later by the monastery of the White Fathers (Pères Blancs). In the course of the work many archaeological remains were discovered. Other excavations resulted in the discovery of Bethesda. Outside the city French Jewish apostates built the Ratisbonne monastery (1874). The city's expansion toward the northwest and the north was entirely due to the activities of the Jews. The Me'ah She'arim quarter was established in 1874; Even Yisrael in 1875; and shortly thereafter (1877) the Beit Ya'akov quarter, which was later assimilated into the neighboring Maḥaneh Yehudah (1887). In 1876 the traditional tomb of *Simeon the Just near the road to Nablus was bought, one of the few holy sites to come into the possession of the Jews. The Tombs of the Kings located nearby were acquired in 1878 by French Jews, who transferred them to the French government several years later (1885). The Ḥabad synagogue (Keneset Eliyahu) was dedicated in 1879.

In the 1880s Jerusalem gradually began to acquire the character of a "Western" city. Road links were established with Nablus to the north and Jericho to the east. A regular carriage service was established with Jaffa (the carriages usually left in the afternoon and, after spending the night at Sha'ar ha-Gai (Bab al-Wād), arrived in Jaffa at noontime the following day). The first modern shops were opened, as well as banking agencies. To cater to the increase in tourism, workshops were opened for woodwork, mother-of-pearl, and embroidery. Jerusalem's cosmopolitan character was recognized by the Turks, and from 1887 it became the capital of an independent sanjak, ruled by a governor holding the title of *mutaṣarrif*, who was directly responsible to Constantinople. He was advised by a *majlis idāra* (district council), as distinct from the *majlis baladiyya* headed by the mayor. Latin Orthodox, Armenians, Protestants, and Jews participated in both bodies. The Turkish garrison consisted of an entire battalion.

In 1881 the American Colony was built north of the Old City and many Swedes settled in it. On the way from the Damascus Gate to the American Quarter the British general Charles Gordon claimed to identify, in 1883, the tomb of Jesus. The place, which was named the "Garden Tomb," was bought by Protestants in 1895.

Considerable construction was carried on by the foreign powers, especially the French. In 1880 they built the convent of the Soeurs du Sainte Rosaire on Mamilla (now Agron) Street, in 1884 the convent of St. Claire (in the southern part of the city), in 1886 the monastery St. Vincent de Paul (on Mamilla Street), in 1888 the convent of the Soeurs de Reparatrice (near the New Gate), and in 1889 the St. Louis hospital. In 1881, with the aid of the French, the Armenian Catholics built the church of Our Lady of the Spasm in the Via Dolorosa. In 1886 the Germans built (on present-day Hillel Street) the Catholic Hospice and Schmidt College. In 1887 they dedicated the Leper Hospital (in Talbiyyeh). In the same year they separated themselves from their Anglican partners (since 1841) and established a separate Lutheran community, headed by an independent clergyman who built his house on the present-day Shivtei Yisrael Street. In 1888 the Russian royal court built the church of Gethsemane, with five onion-shaped towers, on the slopes of the Mt. of Olives.

In 1883 the Ohel Moshe and Mazkeret Moshe quarters (in present-day Agrippas Street) were built. At about that time the Battei Ungarn (Hungarian Houses) were constructed opposite Me'ah She'arim. In 1884 the Diskin orphanage was established. In the 1880s (apparently in 1889) Yemenite Jews settled in the village of Silwān (Kefar ha-Shilo'aḥ) – an unusual area in the history of Jewish settlement in Jerusalem (the place was abandoned by Jews in the disturbances of 1936–39). In 1887 the Maḥaneh Yehudah quarter was established with its large market, and two years later the Sha'arei Ẓedek quarter (Abu Baẓal) was built west of it. The number of Jerusalem's residents at the end of the decade was 43,000, including 28,000 Jews, 7,000 Muslims, 2,000 Latins (Catholics), 150 Greek Catholics, 50 Armenian Catholics, 4,000 Greek Orthodox, 510 Armenians, 100 Copts, 75 Abyssinians, 15 Syrians (Jacobites and Malkites), and 300 Protestants.

From the early 1890s and for many years thereafter, the French hostel of Notre-Dame de France was prominent northwest of the Old City. Its construction, claimed to be on the biblical Garev hill, began in 1887. Two other French institutions were established north of the Damascus Gate after 1892: the school of the "Frères" and the Church of St. Etienne of the well-known biblical institute (École Biblique; established 1890). The same year was marked by another important event, the completion of the railroad from Jaffa to Jerusalem, also a French enterprise. The French company bought the construction rights that had previously been granted by the sultan to a Jerusalem resident, Joseph *Navon. The width of the rails was one meter and its equipment was bought from surpluses of the Panama Canal company, which had gone bankrupt. The scheduled travel time (seldom attained) on the train, which left once a day, was two and one-half hours from Jerusalem to Jaffa and three hours from Jaffa to Jerusalem. The company had to struggle against numerous financial difficulties in the absence of extensive freight traffic.

In the fall of 1898 Jerusalem was placed in a turmoil by the impending visit of the German kaiser William II and his wife. In order to enable the visitors to enter the Old City by vehicle, the Turks filled up the moat of the Citadel and made a gap in the wall near the Jaffa Gate. The emperor's purpose was to dedicate the Erloeser Kirche (Redeemer Church) in the Muristan (on lands given to his father in 1869). The Turks gave the visitor another gift: a plot of land on Mt. Zion on which the Dormition Abbey was built. While in Jerusalem, the emperor granted an interview to Theodor *Herzl.

In the meantime the building of Jewish quarters continued: in the north the Simeon ha-Ẓaddik quarter (1891), the Bukharan quarter (also called Reḥovot; 1892), and Bet Yisrael (1894).

At the turn of the 20th century the population was estimated at 45,600, including 28,200 Jews (15,200 Ashkenazim), 8,760 Christians, and 8,600 Muslims. Evidently the number of inhabitants did not increase greatly, perhaps because of the difficulties raised for Jewish immigration. Despite this, the city continued to develop in every direction except (for geographical reasons) eastward, though the crest of the Mt. of Olives began to be covered with buildings, mainly churches and religious institutions, and a few private homes such as in the al-Ṭūr village. In 1900 the city comprised about 60 separate Jewish quarters, the spaces between which gradually became filled by new buildings and quarters. Paths became roads and later streets. Jaffa Road, near the city wall, acquired a distinctly urban character. Most of the changes in the city from now on occurred outside the Old City walls. Ha-Nevi'im (Prophets) Street became a main artery. Along it were the English Hospital, the German Hospital, the French St. Joseph monastery, the Rothschild Hospital, and the Italian Hospital (built in a medieval Florentine style). North of it the Ethiopians built their church. The German Catholic Hospice of St. Paul was completed opposite the Damascus Gate. On the road northward the Anglican Church of St. George was built. Within the walls, the Muristan market was completed (1905). Near the southern wall the Dormition Abbey was built in 1906.

The round building was constructed on the model of German castles. The Augusta Victoria convalescent home and hostel on Mt. Scopus was dedicated in grand style in 1910. In 1900 the American School of Oriental Research was established in Jerusalem.

Before the outbreak of World War I the Jewish quarters of Zikhron Moshe (1905), Sha'arei Ḥesed, Aḥavah, Even Yehoshu'a, Battei Varsha (Warsaw Houses), and Ruḥamah (all c. 1908) were built and Givat Sha'ul began to grow in the extreme west (1910). In 1906 Boris *Schatz established the *Bezalel Art School. The number of inhabitants in 1912 was estimated at more than 70,000, including 10,000 Muslims, 25,000 Christians (half of them Greek Orthodox), and 45,000 Jews. The number of Jews had increased by some 17,000 in the course of a dozen years, most of them settling in the New City, to which the center of gravity shifted. The area of the city reached about 5 sq. mi. (13 sq. km.) and the map of Jerusalem in 1914 already foreshadowed the development of the city (at least the western part) during the subsequent 50–60 years.

There are no authoritative statistics about the city's population at the beginning of World War I, but it was estimated at 80,000, including temporary residents. The development of the city came to a halt after Turkey's entry into the war at the end of 1914, and the only large building to be completed was, apparently, Zion Hall, presenting movie shows and theatrical performances from 1916.

The consuls of the Entente countries left Jerusalem during World War I, the U.S. and Spanish consuls remaining as neutral representatives to observe the action of the Turks. Epidemics, famine, arrests, and expulsions wreaked havoc among the inhabitants, whose number at the end of the war was estimated at only 55,000. Toward the end of 1917, as the British approached, the Turks had to abandon the city, and it was surrendered to the British. On Dec. 11, 1917, General *Allenby, commander in chief of the British forces, entered it, accompanied by French and Italian representatives.

[Walter Pinhas Pick]

SOCIO-INTELLECTUAL DEVELOPMENTS IN THE 19TH CENTURY. Although the Ashkenazi population of Jerusalem ceased to exist as a distinct community in 1721, the Ashkenazim continued to appear in the city either as residents or as tourists. In 1812 an epidemic broke out in Safed and some of its Jews, including the leaders of the community, R. *Israel of Shklov and R. *Menahem Mendel of Shklov, fled to Jerusalem. The latter decided to settle permanently in the Holy City and revive its Ashkenazi community. In 1816 he established his home in the city, and around him was formed a small nucleus of about a dozen disciples of Elijah of Vilna, who quickly set up a center for learning and prayer in the yeshivah of Ḥayyim b. Moshe Attar, which was placed at their disposal by the Sephardi community. The latter, which was well established, took the handful of Ashkenazim under its protection since officially its leaders served as the legitimate representatives of the Jews vis-à-vis the ruling authorities. The Ashkenazim were still persecuted by the Muslim residents, who regarded them as the inheritors of the debts from 100 years previously. Even now the Ashkenazim were compelled to don Sephardi dress so that their origin would not be recognized. Contemporary evidence shows that the Ashkenazim, and their head Menahem Mendel, prayed in the Sephardi synagogue and even had to use a Sephardi to complete their own *minyan*. This situation continued until the 1830s, when the numerous calamities suffered by Safed – epidemics, robberies, and above all the earthquake of 1837 – forced its Jews to flee to Jerusalem, and the spiritual leadership and the major center of the Ashkenazi community in Ereẓ Israel was transferred from Galilee to the Holy City.

From this period on the social, spiritual, and economic life of the Jerusalem Jewish community began to be more firmly based. The dominant figure of the Ashkenazi community of the 1860s was R. Isaiah Bardaki (see above). On the other hand the rabbi of the Sephardi community secured official recognition from the authorities in 1840, in the form of the title *ḥakham bashi* (see above). The situation of the Ashkenazi community was also eased. Its efforts and diligence bore fruit, and Muhammad Ali announced that the debts of its ancestors to the Arab creditors were void. The homogeneity of the first settlers was thus destroyed and a meaningful pluralism began. While the first nucleus was composed mainly of *Perushim*, disciples of the Vilna Gaon, the immigration to Palestine now brought additional elements, such as the members of "Hod" (Holland-Deutschland) and "Ohavei Zion" (lovers of Zion), some of whom adhered to the spirit of European culture. This immigration brought scholars, entrepreneurs, and educators such as R. Yehosef *Schwarz, Eliezer Bergman, and Isaac Prag. From 1840 the ḥasidic community began to consolidate itself in the city. Its leaders were Israel *Bak and his son Nisan, who were opposed to the leadership of the *Perushim*. This pluralism led to the emergence of separate social groups, which originated from a particular district or town and maintained independent **kolelim* that competed for independent **ḥalukkah*.

With the increasing strength of the Ashkenazim, there was growing friction between them and the Sephardim. Apart from linguistic, historical, cultural, and halakhic differences between the communities, economic and political bases of contention were added, and a fierce struggle for positions of strength within the community developed. With the aid of the foreign consuls who were interested in strengthening the position of the Ashkenazim and had them under their protection, and with the assistance of European Jewry, the Ashkenazim were released from Sephardi suzerainty. The custom of transferring heirless legacies to the treasury of the Sephardi community was abolished; the Ashkenazim set up a separate cemetery and even established independent *sheḥitah*; and they reached regular agreements with the Sephardim regarding arrangements for collecting *ḥalukkah* funds. Thus the Sephardi community lost a considerable income, although they incurred many debts as representatives of the Jewish community vis-à-vis the authorities, being responsible for handing over various taxes and other unofficial expenditures connected with the right of passage to the Western Wall, maintenance of Rachel's Tomb, etc.

However, in day-to-day life social and cultural relationships were formed between the various communities. It cannot be said that there were breakthroughs in the communal boundaries, but personal contact made its impact. This was especially the case among the younger generation, to whom the world of the East was not as strange and foreign as it was to their fathers, and some of them even tried to mingle. In the course of time mixed marriages between Ashkenazim and Sephardim began to occur. There were also reciprocal influences in language, customs, and folklore. Ashkenazim would pray in Sephardi synagogues and even wore Oriental clothing when there was no longer any need for this. Though these manifestations were not very common, they were significant in light of the deep differences between the communities.

It would be incorrect to assume, however, that the Sephardi community was entirely homogeneous. There were bitter struggles within it against attempts to break off and create separate communities. Especially well known is the struggle of the Mughrebis. Among the other communities the Georgians, and later the Bukharans, should be mentioned. In general, the power of the *ḥakham bashi* was decisive, and the authorities granted legal validity to his judgments. The *bet din* was composed of nine *ḥakhamim*. Even judgments of corporal punishment are known to have been handed down. The Ashkenazim had a separate *bet din*, which is first mentioned after the arrival of R. Samuel *Salant in Jerusalem in 1841. From that time and for many decades onward he led the community, R. Meir *Auerbach serving together with him as *av bet din* and rabbi of the community.

One of the major problems concerning the population of Jerusalem was that of education. The children and youth received their education at the *ḥeder* and the *talmud torah*, which were modeled on Eastern European institutions, or in the *kuttāb* (Ar. boys' schools), the Oriental counterpart. The older members of the community studied regularly in the *battei midrash* of their *kolelim*. The purpose of those who came to settle in the holy city was "to worship God on His holy mountain," to be free of all material concerns, and to devote themselves to purely spiritual matters. However, with the increase in the number of Jews and the growth of a young generation which had been born in Jerusalem, it was difficult for large numbers to maintain this ideal. A number of institutions and individuals – mainly outside the *yishuv* – took up the question of productivization. Efforts were made to teach young people handicrafts and even a modicum of general secular knowledge. For this purpose Montefiore, Frankl, the *Alliance Israélite Universelle, and others tried to establish boys' and girls' schools in Jerusalem, but their attempts were received with violent hostility and fierce opposition. Those who opposed these plans feared that their religious aims would be frustrated, basing their opposition on the experiences of the Haskalah in Europe.

The old *yishuv*, however, did not stagnate. With the increase in immigration and the maturing of the second generation of settlers, a new type of leader arose, public workers, scholars, and publicists such as Yosef *Rivlin, Israel Dov *Frumkin, and Abraham Moses Luncz, who were more responsive to contemporary problems. A local press was established, including *Ḥavaẓẓelet, Ha-Levanon, Yehudah vi-Yrushalayim*, and *Sha'arei Ẓiyyon*, which was considered the organ of the Sephardi community. The establishment of new neighborhoods outside the walls prepared the ground for new initiatives. Attention was given to the solution of economic problems. Mutual aid programs, which were highly developed among Jerusalem's inhabitants in the form of dozens of charitable institutions, began in certain instances to assume a character other than that of mere material assistance. Attempts were made to engage in social and cultural activities. A typical example was the Tiferet Yerushalayim company founded by ḥasidim.

The Jewish population of Jerusalem toward the end of the 19th century could be divided into three principal groups: one promoting extreme adherence to the old way of life without changing anything; the second, the moderates, practical people, tradesmen, and the like, who were devoted to religious tradition but willing to absorb new ideas; and the third, a more limited group of *maskilim* who had been educated in Palestine or abroad or new settlers such as Eliezer *Ben-Yehuda, who advocated revolutionary ideas.

[Joshua Kaniel (Mershine)]

Under British Rule (1917–1948)

In the second week of December 1917, the Turkish troops and officials began to evacuate the city. On December 9, the mayor, a member of the Husseini family, walked with a white flag to the hill overlooking Liftā (Mei-Neftoah) to surrender it to the British, but found only two privates who were looking for water. The surrender of the city was formally effected only on December 11, after a last battle with the retreating Turks near Sheikh Jarrāḥ, when General Allenby, commander in chief of the Egyptian Expeditionary Force, made his official entry. He entered the Old City on foot through the Jaffa Gate, and his proclamation, which made no mention of the *Balfour Declaration, was read from the steps of the Citadel in English, French, Italian, Arabic, and Hebrew.

In the conditions of war, especially with the normal wheat supplies from Transjordan and overseas cut off, Jerusalem was plagued by starvation, which the British military authorities tried to ameliorate by food rationing. The first military governor of Jerusalem was Ronald Storrs, until then Oriental secretary to the British residency in Cairo. No sanitary arrangements whatsoever existed in the Old City and hardly any in the newer quarters outside the walls. A British architect was brought in to report on the condition of the buildings in the Temple area, which the Turks and Muslim authorities had allowed to fall into neglect. On July 1, 1920, the military administration, officially called the Occupied Enemy Territory Administration, was replaced by a civil administration under a *high commissioner who resided in Jerusalem. The first to hold office was Sir Herbert *Samuel, whose term lasted until 1925.

Jerusalem was a conglomerate of districts and neighborhoods, each with its own character. The Old City, within the walls, contained the holy places – the Temple area with the Dome of the Rock and al-Aqṣā Mosque, the Church of the Holy Sepulcher and the Via Dolorosa, and the Western Wall. To the west new quarters had developed in the later Ottoman period along Jaffa Road to Maḥaneh Yehudah, spreading north to religious quarters around Me'ah She'arim and south to the railway station and the German (*Templer) Colony. To the east were various Christian establishments and the site of the Hebrew University on Mount Scopus; and, dotted around, various newer quarters – some Jewish, some Christian, some Muslim, and some mixed, such as Bak'a, the Greek Colony, and the Armenian Colony. The city was slowly recovering from the setback caused by World War I. The 1922 census showed a population of only 62,578, of whom 33,971 were Jews, 14,699 were Christians, 13,413 Muslims, and 495 others. The Jewish population of Jerusalem, estimated in 1910 at about 45,000 (over one-half of the Jews in Ereẓ Israel), had been reduced by the end of the war, through expulsions, disease, and maladministration, to 26,600.

The civil government soon set up administrative institutions in Jerusalem, including a Supreme Court (composed of a British chief justice, one other British judge, and four Palestinian judges). Storrs founded the Pro-Jerusalem Society (later dissolved) for the preservation and embellishment of the city and a school of music (later presented to the Jewish community). In 1922 a British-French arbitration tribunal fixed the sum payable by the Palestine government for the Jaffa-Jerusalem Railway, owned by a French concessionary, at 565,000 Egyptian pounds. In the same year houses and buildings that had been taken over by the government were restored to their previous owners. The Hebrew University on Mt. Scopus was formally opened by Lord Balfour in 1925. In 1928 the concession for the supply of electricity (within a radius of 12 mi. (20 km.) of the city) was taken over by the Jerusalem Electric and Public Services Corporation Ltd. (with British and Jewish capital).

One of the first acts of the British administration was to appoint a new municipal council consisting of two Moslems, one of whom acted as mayor, two Christians, and two Jews, one of whom, Yiẓhak Eliachar, was deputy mayor. In 1924 a new council, with three members from each community, was appointed. In 1924 the municipal council was elected for the first time – with four members from each community. In 1934, under the Municipal Councils Ordinance of that year, the city was divided into twelve constituencies, each electing one councillor. Six of the constituencies were Arab and six Jewish, although 75% of the taxpayers were Jews. The government always appointed a Muslim as mayor, despite the Jewish majority, on grounds of precedent, with one Christian Arab and one Jewish deputy. There was also a community council, *Va'ad ha-Kehillah*, representing both Ashkenazim and Sephardim, to look after specifically Jewish affairs, especially in the religious sphere. It was first elected in 1918 on the initiative of the Zionist Organization's Palestine Office. From 1932 it was elected under regulations issued by *Keneset Israel, the representative body of the *yishuv*.

The progress of the country, due partly to the ordered administration and mainly to Jewish immigration and development, was shared by Jerusalem. This was reflected in the 1931 census figures, which showed a population of 90,503, including 51,222 Jews, 19,894 Muslims, 19,335 Christians, and 52 others. The economy of Jerusalem, however, remained based on the city's being an administrative, religious, political, and educational center, industry continuing only on a small scale. Jerusalem was the seat of the Zionist Executive (later the Executive of the Jewish Agency), the Keren Hayesod and the Jewish National Fund, the Va'ad Le'ummi (national council of the *yishuv*), the Chief Rabbinate, the Muslim Supreme Council (established in 1921), and the Higher Arab Committee (1936). The residence of the high commissioner for Palestine (which included Transjordan) was in the Augusta Victoria hospital building on Mt. Scopus until it was severely damaged by the 1927 earthquake. The Russian Compound in the center of the city became an important administrative area, its buildings being taken over for police headquarters, the central prison, the law courts, and the government hospital.

Water supply to Jerusalem was a constant problem during this period. It was dependent mainly on the storage of rainwater runoff from the rooftops into cisterns dug out in the foundation rock. This system led to serious shortages in years of drought, and there were years when water had to be brought up from the coast by train (as in 1928). Matters were improved somewhat in 1918, when the army repaired the pipeline from Solomon's Pools, a short distance outside the city, to a reservoir in what is now the Romemah quarter. In 1920 this line was extended, and pumping machinery was installed at Solomon's Pools to increase the supply. Water was added from the ʿAyn Fāra springs in 1928, from the ʿAyn Fawwār springs in 1931, and from the more distant Wadi Qilt (on the way to Jericho) in 1935. It was only in that year, however, that Jerusalem's perennial dependence on the vagaries of rainfall was finally solved by the construction of a pipeline from Ra's al-ʿAyn on the Coastal Plain, replacing the old supply from five different sources and halving the cost of water.

THE DEVELOPMENT OF THE CITY. As the Jewish population increased – with a fillip due to the move from the Old City, as a result of the 1929 and 1936–39 attacks on them – new suburbs were built, some adjoining existing built-up areas and others less continuous (depending on where land could be bought). In the course of the years they formed one conurbation, including Romemah (1921); Talpiyyot (1922); Beit ha-Kerem

(1923); Mekor Ḥayyim, Mekor Barukh, Reḥavyah, Kiryat Moshe, Naḥalat Aḥim (1924); Bayit va-Gan, Maḥanayim, Sanhedriyyah (1925); Kiryat Shemu'el (1928); Ge'ullah and Kerem Avraham (1929); and Arnonah and Tel Arzah (1931). The character of these quarters was determined by the groups by or for whom they were established. Some were inhabited by Orthodox Jews, who could thus maintain undisturbed their religious practices and the quiet of the Sabbath. Others were established by professional groups or teachers, such as Beit ha-Kerem. Small workshops were concentrated in the commercial center (the center of the town) facing the Old City walls. Reḥavyah was designed for white-collar workers and people in the professions. By and large the character of each section was maintained, though, as they grew into one another, the social divisions were blurred. At the same time, the outward appearance of Jerusalem gradually changed in response to economic pressures, the increasing population, and the rising land value. Sir Ronald Storrs insisted on all buildings, private as well as public, being built of or faced with Jerusalem stone, which gives the city so much of its character. In the 1930s and 1940s, some relaxation was permitted, owing to the high cost of stone, so that in Reḥavyah, for example, some houses were built in concrete. Further afield, several kilometers from the center of Jerusalem, were Atarot (1920), Neveh Ya'akov (1924), and Ramat Raḥel (1925/26). At Atarot (Qalandiya) a small airport was built. The kibbutz of Ramat Raḥel, between Jerusalem and Bethlehem, was of special interest in its being the first attempt at combining agriculture with urban services (fruit growing with a laundry and bakery for the Jerusalem population). It also provided workmen for the city and ultimately became an extension of Talpiyyot and Arnonah.

Jerusalem was transformed from the neglected, poverty-stricken provincial town of Turkish times to a capital city. Among the public buildings erected in the years of British administration are the Pontifical (Jesuit) Biblical Institute (1927); the nearby French Consulate; the Catholic Church of All the Nations at the Garden of Gethsemane (1924); St. Andrew's Church (Scottish; 1927); the Nathan Straus Health Center (1928); the Jewish National and University Library on Mt. Scopus (1930); the Government House, later the headquarters of the UN Truce Supervision Organization, municipal offices, St. Peter in Gallicantu Church (1931); the Jewish Agency Compound (1932), the YMCA, with Jerusalem's first swimming pool (1933), the King David Hotel, the first of international standard in the city (1930); the Central Post Office; the Hadassah Hospital on Mt. Scopus; and the Rockefeller Archaeological Museum facing the northeast corner of the Old City wall (1938). Between 1938 and 1942 the al-Aqṣā Mosque on the Temple Mount was embellished with pillars of carrara marble, a gift from Mussolini. The earthquake in 1927 did considerable damage to the Augusta Victoria hospital on Mt. Scopus and to the Basilica of the Holy Sepulcher.

In 1936 the Palestine Broadcasting Service began operations, with offices and buildings in the city and the transmitting station in Ramallah. The Hebrew daily newspaper *Haaretz* appeared at first in Jerusalem but later moved to Tel Aviv. An older, established Jerusalem daily, *Do'ar ha-Yom*, had already closed down. On the other hand, the *Palestine Post* (later the *Jerusalem Post*), founded in 1931, remained in Jerusalem.

ARAB-JEWISH CLASHES. The development of the city was accompanied by disturbances that developed into violence against the Jews and the National Home provisions of the Mandate. The first outbreak occurred during Passover 1920. Despite the presence of a considerable number of British troops in the country, heavy attacks accompanied by looting were directed against Jews in Jerusalem. Before order was restored, five Jews had been killed and 211 wounded, including several women and children; four Arabs were killed and 21 wounded. The Arab mobs had been incited by rumors that the Jews intended to take hold of the Muslim holy places. The 1921 riots in Jaffa and some of the Jewish settlements did not reach Jerusalem, but the creation of the Supreme Muslim Council by government order in that year and the election of Hajj Amin al Husseini as its president promised trouble. He had earlier been appointed mufti of Jerusalem, over more moderate candidates, by the high commissioner in the vain hope that the responsibility and experience of office would moderate his violent anti-Zionist and anti-Jewish feeling. He controlled the Muslim religious endowments, the waqf, and enjoyed the right to appoint and dismiss judges and other officers of the Shariʿa courts and the patronage that went with these powers, though the salaries of the Shari'ʿa judges were paid by the government. A more moderate Arab group, the National Defense Party, controlled by the influential Nashashibi family, was also formed in Jerusalem.

Signs of trouble, however, were not wanting. In 1925 a general strike of Arabs, which extended to Jerusalem, was organized in sympathy with the Arab revolt in Syria against French rule; again in 1926 there was a strike in protest against the official visit to Jerusalem of the French high commissioner in Syria, de Jouvenel. Quiet, nevertheless, was maintained until 1928. On Sept. 23, 1928, on the eve of the Day of Atonement, Jews introduced a screen to divide the men from the women during the service held at the Western Wall, but, to preserve the "status quo," the police forcibly removed it during the following day's services. In the name of the Supreme Muslim Council, the mufti declared that "the Jews' aim is to take possession of the Mosque of al-Aqṣā gradually." A General Muslim Conference met, presided over by the mufti. In the next few months building operations were carried out near the city wall, which the Jews saw as intentional interference with their praying. The heightened tension, with demonstration and counter-demonstration at the wall, burst into flame on August 23, 1929. Attacks by Arabs on Jews throughout the country, including Jerusalem (though more seriously in Hebron and Safed), lasted until August 29, when they were put down with the aid of troops rushed in from Egypt after 133 Jews and 116 Arabs had been killed and 339 Jews and 323 Arabs wounded in Palestine (most of the Arabs by troops or police). Jewish merchants abandoned the Old City and established the new commercial center outside the walls. After a British Commission of Inquiry, chaired by Sir Walter Shaw, reported on the political background of the outburst, an international commission followed (in 1930), but no agreement regarding the Western Wall could be reached. At the end of 1931 a Muslim Conference, attended by 145 delegates from all over the Muslim world, met in Jerusalem. Its public proceedings were not political and did not lead, as had been feared, to disturbances, but they further strengthened the mufti's position.

Tension remained high. On Oct. 13, 1933, the Arabs declared a general strike. A demonstration was staged at the government offices in Jerusalem, though prohibited by the government, and was dispersed by troops. Trouble spread to other parts of the country, and on October 28 and 29 there was renewed rioting in Jerusalem, but with one profound change: whereas the 1920–1921, and 1929 riots had been directed only against the Jews, they were now aimed against the government as well.

In 1936 troubles broke out again in Jerusalem, as well as in other parts of the country. A Supreme Arab Committee (later known as the Arab Higher Committee) was established, with the mufti as president. It resolved on a general strike and the nonpayment of taxes until Jewish immigration was stopped. Arab shops were closed in Jerusalem, as elsewhere, with those Arabs who refused to join being intimidated. The strike and more active disturbances continued until the arrival in Jerusalem of the Royal Commission, with Lord Peel as chairman, on Nov. 11, 1936. An atmosphere of tension nonetheless remained. At this time the population of Jerusalem was 125,000, of whom 76,000 were Jews.

In its report the Royal Commission recommended the partition of Palestine into two separate states – Arab and Jewish – with a new Mandate covering Jerusalem and Bethlehem (over an enclave "extending from a point north of Jerusalem to a point south of Bethlehem") with access to the sea "provided by a corridor extending to the north of the main road and to the south of the railway, including the towns of Lydda and Ramleh, and terminating at Jaffa." The policy of the Balfour Declaration was not to apply to this enclave, and "the only 'official language' should be that of the Mandatory Administration." Its revenues were to be provided by customs, duties, and direct taxation, and any deficit was to be made good by the British Parliament. Arabs and Jews in Jerusalem could opt for citizenship in the Arab or the Jewish state.

The Arab campaign of sabotage, intimidation, and murder, increasingly directed against moderately inclined Arabs, continued throughout 1937, with occasional Jewish reprisals. Jewish buses were bombed, and the potash convoy from the Dead Sea to Jerusalem was attacked. For several days in October, a curfew was imposed in the municipal area of Jerusalem. There were also attacks on Jewish transport on the main road connecting Jerusalem with the coast. Jewish reprisals culminated in November in large-scale attacks on Arabs and an Arab bus in Jerusalem by the *Irgun Ẓeva'i Le'ummi (IẒL). To ensure the safety of worshipers at the Western Wall, a new road was opened through the Old City, avoiding the mainly non-Jewish quarters. Following an assassination attempt on the British inspector-general of the Palestine police force and the murder by Arab extremists of Jews and moderate Arabs, the Arab Higher Committee was declared unlawful and Hajj Amin al-Husseini was deprived of his office as president of the Supreme Muslim Council and his membership on the waqf committee. He fled to Lebanon; the Arab mayor of Jerusalem was deported to the Seychelles Islands together with other members of the Arab High Committee; and Daniel *Auster, the Jewish deputy mayor, was appointed by the government to act as mayor – the first Jew to head the Jerusalem municipality. (In the following year a new Muslim mayor was appointed.)

Conditions worsened in 1938 with an intensified campaign of murder, intimidation, and sabotage. The Arab gang warfare now gradually developed on organized and, to some extent, coordinated lines, with still only isolated Jewish reprisals. Constant attacks were made on Jewish traffic to Jerusalem from the coast and armed robberies multiplied in the surrounding Arab villages by marauding parties seeking food, money, and lodging. Uncooperative Arabs and members of the Nashashibi family and party were murdered, the party having withdrawn from the Arab Higher Committee. In October, as the Government Report for 1938 states, "the Old City, which had become the rallying point of bandits and from which acts of violence, murder and intimidation were being organized and perpetuated with impunity, was fully reoccupied by troops" in an "operation of considerable magnitude." In the same year the British government sent out the Palestine Partition Commission (known, after its chairman, as the Woodhead Commission). It produced three plans, all providing for the Jerusalem area to remain under Mandate and outside the proposed Arab and Jewish states. Jewish proposals for the inclusion of "parts of Jerusalem" (reference being to the parts of the new town outside the Old City) were rejected, and in the end none of the proposals was adopted.

WORLD WAR II AND AFTER. After the outbreak of World War II, Jerusalem became a military headquarters. The German inhabitants of the quarter known as the German Colony were interned or expelled, and their houses were taken over by civilian and military personnel, while other public buildings in the city belonging to German institutions were taken over by the government or army. Before Britain's entry into World War II, its new anti-Zionist policy, announced in the White Paper of May 1939, which severely restricted Jewish immigration and land purchase (see *White Papers), led to mass protests and to violent actions by the dissident Jewish IẒL which, in May 1939, set fire to the Department of Migration. These actions of violence continued until the outbreak of the war. In 1944 difficulties developed over the Jerusalem mayoralty, when the mayor (a Muslim) died, and the Jewish deputy mayor, who was appointed in his place, claimed full mayoralty, the population in the municipal area being estimated at 32,039 Muslims (21%), 27,849 Christians, and 92,143 Jews (61%). In the absence of agreement, the government finally appointed a Municipal Commission, all of whose members were British officials.

After 1944, when IZL and *Loḥamei Ḥerut Israel (Leḥi) renewed their anti-government violence, Jerusalem was particularly involved. Many government buildings were blown up, culminating in July 1946 in an explosion that destroyed a wing of the King David Hotel housing government and military departments, with heavy loss of life.

In November 1947, when the United Nations decided on the partition of Palestine into a Jewish and an Arab state, it also called for the internationalization of Jerusalem as a "corpus separatum." The Jewish authorities reluctantly accepted this, as well as other parts of the UN decision, but the Arabs rejected it. The Trusteeship Council of the UN appointed representatives of Australia, China, France, Mexico, the United States, and Britain to work out plans for the administration of the area, but the UN General Assembly failed to reach a decision. In the meantime, the city, nominally still under British rule, was lapsing into anarchy. The Old City, including its Jewish population, was cut off from the new, while the areas outside the walls were divided between the Jews and the Arabs in warring camps. The British forces enclosed themselves against attacks by IZL and Leḥi in barbed wire areas in the New City cleared of Jewish inhabitants (these areas were known by the Jews as "Bevingrad," after the unpopular British foreign secretary). Jewish Jerusalem was put under virtual siege by Arab attacks on supply convoys on the one road from the coast, while the British troops did little or nothing to prevent the assaults. To cope with the emergency, the Jewish Agency and the Va'ad Le'ummi established the Committee of the National Institutions for Matters Pertaining to Jerusalem (shortened to the Jerusalem Emergency Committee), headed by Dov *Joseph. In April the six Jewish members of the municipal council issued a proclamation to the Jewish citizens announcing that they had assumed the functions of a municipality for the area under Jewish control.

Arab Jerusalem did not suffer similarly as it was open to the Arab-populated parts of the country to the north, south, and east. Part of the Jewish Agency building in the center of the city was blown up by Arabs, with loss of lives, and the offices of the *Palestine Post* and a large residential and shopping block in Ben Yehudah St. were blown up, the last two almost certainly by anti-Jewish terrorists in the British Police. The nearby Jewish settlements of Atarot and Neveh Ya'akov to the north of Jerusalem, surrounded by an Arab population, were abandoned. Deir Yāsīn, an Arab village near the western outskirts of Jerusalem, from which attacks were launched on the adjoining Jewish areas, was attacked by IZL and Leḥi, with 254 of its inhabitants reported killed. A few days later a Jewish convoy taking staff to the Hadassah Hospital on Mt. Scopus was attacked and destroyed, with 78 doctors, nurses, and others killed. This occurred only some 200 yards from the British military post that was responsible for safety on the road. The water pipeline from the coastal plain at Ra's al-ʿAyn was cut. This presented the most serious threat to the Jews of Jerusalem, while it did not affect the Arabs, since a very large proportion of the Jews lived in houses built after construction of the pipeline and therefore lacked cisterns to catch the winter rains. Fortunately, a farsighted water engineer had earlier advised the Jewish authorities to make a survey of all Jewish-inhabited houses with cisterns and fill and seal them. When the pipeline was cut this supply, rationed and distributed by water trucks throughout the siege – even under continuous Arab shelling – saved Jewish Jerusalem.

Mt. Scopus with the Hebrew University and Hadassah Hospital and the adjoining Arab village, ʿIsawiyya, became a Jewish-held enclave cut off from the New City, as did the Jewish quarter of the Old City and areas to the south. Contact with these areas was occasionally possible only by troop-protected convoys. The streets dividing the Jewish and Arab areas became front lines, barbed-wired positions, with posts on the Jewish side manned by members of the Haganah, IZL, and Leḥi. Control of the Arab side passed to armed Arab groups and then to the Transjordan army, the British-officered Arab Legion, which had not been withdrawn in spite of British promises. At midnight May 14/15, 1948, when the last of the British forces and government withdrew from Jerusalem, thus ending the mandatory rule that had lasted since 1917, the Jews took control of the government buildings in the center of the town, including the general post office, the police headquarters and the broadcasting studios.

The Arab siege, however, continued for another two months, until it was broken by the construction of an alternate route through the hills from the coast (popularly called the "Burma Road") and the laying of a new water pipeline. The whole of western Jerusalem and the Mt. Scopus enclave were in Jewish hands, but Arab guns shelled the Jewish areas, killing 170 civilians and injuring a thousand. Food and water were still strictly rationed and the population was without electricity and fuel. To keep the bakeries going, oil was removed from all houses possessing central heating systems. As the Jews were cut off from the ancient cemetery on the Mt. of Olives, a temporary Jewish burial place was prepared near the Valley of the Cross, where a tiny landing strip was also set up for the occasional Piper Cub planes that flew Jewish leaders in and out.

When the Arab countries invaded Palestine, Egyptian and Iraqi troops approached the outskirts of Jerusalem, joining the Transjordanianian Arab Legion units. Ramat Raḥel changed hands several times in fierce fighting before the Arab forces were finally repelled. Meanwhile the Arab Legion closed in on the Jewish quarter of the Old City. On May 19, 1948, the Palmah breached the wall at the Zion Gate but had to withdraw. After intense fighting, with Jews and Arabs confronting one another at a distance of only a few yards and Jewish supplies of food and ammunition almost exhausted, the Jewish quarter of the Old City surrendered on May 27. Some 1,300 elderly men, women, and children, and wounded men were evacuated to the New City and others were taken prisoner. A general cease-fire for the Jerusalem area was proclaimed on June 11, 1948, leaving East Jerusalem, including the Old City, to the Arabs in Transjordanian hands and West Jerusalem in Israel hands. Jerusalem being still under siege, the Israeli Provisional Government remained for the time being in Tel Aviv.

[Semah Cecil Hyman]

The Divided City (1948–1967)

For some time the position of Jerusalem remained uncertain. The city was divided in two by a cease-fire line running roughly north-south tangentially to the western wall of the Old City, the relations between the two sides being regulated by agreement between the local commanders of the Arab Legion and the Israel Defense Forces. A resolution dealing with the temporary administration of the city had been adopted by a special subcommittee of the UN General Assembly but was not carried by the assembly itself. Egyptian troops still threatened the city from their positions in the Bethlehem area. Despite the establishment of the IDF as the new state's only armed force, IẒL and Leḥi units continued to exist in Jerusalem. On July 7 a special agreement for the demilitarization of the Scopus area was concluded between Israel and Transjordan.

During the ten days of fighting that followed the expiry of the first truce on July 7, 1948, the Israel forces broke the Egyptian lines and took Ein Karem (Ein Kerem) on the western outskirts of the city. On the night of July 16/17 the IDF nearly broke into the Old City from Mount Zion, while IẒL and Leḥi forces breached the New Gate, but they were forced to withdraw a few hours before the second truce went into effect.

Count *Bernadotte, the UN mediator, had proposed on June 27 from his headquarters in Rhodes that Jerusalem be handed over to Transjordan. The Provisional Government of Israel had categorically rejected the proposal. On July 26, two days after his arrival in the country, he proposed the demilitarization of the city, but this was also unacceptable to Israel, as it would have left the Jewish population defenseless. On August 1, to regularize the position, the Provisional Government declared Jerusalem to be under martial law and appointed Dov Joseph as military governor. Bernadotte set up the UN Truce Supervision Organization, with its seat in the former Government House. The assassination of Bernadotte on Sept. 17 impelled the government to order the disbandment of the IẒL and Leḥi units, putting all armed forces in Jerusalem under IDF command. In operation Yo'av (Oct. 15–22) the Egyptian forces in the south were isolated and withdrew, being replaced by the Arab Legion. On Dec. 13, 1948, the Transjordanian parliament confirmed the annexation of the Arab-controlled areas of Palestine and a week later the Transjordanian government appointed a new mufti of Jerusalem.

The population of the Israel-held area of Jerusalem took part in the elections to the Constituent Assembly (later called the First *Knesset) in January 1949, and at the beginning of February the provisional government announced that Jerusalem was no longer to be considered occupied territory. The Knesset held its first sessions (Feb. 14–17) in the hall at Jewish Agency headquarters, where the members took the oath, Chaim *Weizmann was elected president of the state, and the Transition Law (the "Minor Constitution") was adopted. According to article 8 of the armistice agreement with Jordan (April 3, 1949), a joint committee was to be set up to make arrangements for, inter alia, the renewal of the operations of The Hebrew University and the Hadassah Hospital on Mount Scopus and free access to the Jewish holy places in the Old City, the ancient Jewish cemetery on the Mount of Olives, and the institutions on Jordanian-held Mount Scopus. However, although these matters had been agreed upon in principle by both sides, the article remained a dead letter, as Jordan refused to cooperate.

When the Jerusalem issue was again discussed by the UN General Assembly in November 1949, the Israel government opposed the idea of internationalization but offered to sign an agreement with the United Nations guaranteeing the security of all holy places under its jurisdiction. On Dec. 10, however, the Assembly approved a resolution calling for international control over the whole city of Jerusalem and its environs and charged the Trusteeship Council to draft a statute for an international regime for the city. The Israel government reacted vigorously. On Dec. 13 it announced in the Knesset its decision to speed up the transfer of its offices to Jerusalem, proposed that the Knesset go back there, and proclaimed that Jerusalem was and would remain Israel's eternal capital. On Dec. 26 the Knesset resumed its sittings in the capital, meeting in a modest building (the Froumine building) in the center of town that had been erected for use by a bank. Both Jordan and Israel continued to oppose internationalization and the proposal was ultimately, in effect, dropped.

For a period of 19 years, Jerusalem was a divided city. In early 1948 its population was estimated at 165,000: 100,000 Jews, 40,000 Muslims, and 25,000 Christians. The city's area was about 10 sq. mi. (28 sq. km.). The battles waged in and around Jerusalem for three-quarters of a year; the UN decision to internationalize the city, the transfer of the Arab center of gravity to Amman, and the establishment of the de facto seat of the government and the legislature in Tel Aviv were the causes of a precipitous decline in population on both sides of the front. The population of the Israel side (West Jerusalem) was estimated at only about 69,000 (including 931 Christians and 28 Muslims) in 1949, and that of the Jordanian side at about 46,000 as late as 1956.

EAST JERUSALEM. In May 1948, East Jerusalem was occupied by the Arab Legion. Its first act was the destruction of the Jewish Quarter, including almost all the synagogues (Ḥurvah, Nisan Bak, etc.) and Jewish institutions (*Battei Maḥaseh*, Yeshivat Porat Yosef, etc.). The ancient cemetery on the slope of the Mount of Olives was desecrated. Jerusalem was proclaimed the "second capital" of the Hashemite Kingdom of

Jordan; it also became a district capital. East Jerusalem was entirely cut off from an approach to the Mediterranean coast, and the conversion of the former British military airfield of Qalandiya into a civil airport for the town alleviated its isolation only slightly.

East Jerusalem now turned to the east bank of the Jordan, through which all its relations with the world at large were conducted. In the 1960s a direct road to Amman, via Abdullah Bridge, was added to the old Jericho-Salt road. Traffic to the north via the Sheikh Jarrāḥ quarter was dominated by Israel forces. This situation was slightly improved by the construction of a new road that connected the Mt. Scopus area to the vicinity of the Rockefeller Museum through the upper Kidron Valley, thus diverting the daily traffic from the border region. In 1948 East Jerusalem had been completely cut off from the Bethlehem-Hebron region and a very steep and tortuous road was built through Abu-Dīs, the lower Kidron Valley, and Beit-Sāḥūr. It was only after a few years that an improved, though also steep and tortuous road, was constructed from Jerusalem to Bethlehem, via Ra's-Maqābir and Ṣūr-Bāhir. It was 10 mi. (17 km.) long, in comparison with the old 3 mi.- (5 km.-) long road through Talpiyyot, which was dominated by Israel.

The Jordanian-held part of Jerusalem had no electricity for several years until a new power station was built in Sha'fāt to replace the original one near the German Colony, which was in Israeli hands. Water supply remained very poor after the line from Ra's al-ʿAyn (Rosh ha-Ayin) was cut off, but a limited quantity was supplied by springs in the northeast of the city, and a narrow water pipe was later laid from Solomon's Pools. The economy of East Jerusalem was based almost entirely on tourism, pilgrimages, and religious and research institutions. The only large factory was the cigarette works at al-ʿAzariyya. The Jordanian government was located in Amman, and Arab Jerusalem did not wield much political influence. Due to geographical conditions (the barrier of the Kidron Valley and its extensions), the city hardly developed to the south and only a little toward the east (Silwān, Ra's-al-ʿAmūd, al-Azariyya, Abu-Dīs) and on the slopes of the Mount of Olives. On the other hand, there was much construction on the northern side, and the area between the Old City's northern wall and Wadi Joz (Jawz) became partly a shopping district (Saladin Street, Jericho Road, and their extensions) and largely a crowded residential district. The residential area of East Jerusalem, the greater part of which was not within the boundaries of the city itself, extended over a length of 7 mi. (15 km.) through Shaʿfāt, Beit Ḥanūn, and Qalandiya, almost reaching the outskirts of al-Bīra. The number of inhabitants, however, never surpassed 65,000, of whom about 25,000 lived within the walls of the Old City.

The relatively small number of luxury buildings erected in the eastern part of the city under the Jordanian administration included several large hotels, the largest of which – the Intercontinental – was built at the southern extremity of the Mount of Olives. In 1963, the "eastern" YMCA was erected on the Nablus Road. Government House was situated on Saladin Street; the St. John Hospital for eye diseases and, next to it, the French Hospital and the British consulate-general were erected in Sheikh Jarrāḥ. The Dominus Flevit Church was built on the slope of the Mount of Olives (1953). Arab refugees were rarely seen in the city itself, except for the area of the improvised buildings in the destroyed Jewish Quarter and the remains of the German Compound. Their camps were situated in the south near Bethlehem (Dahīsha) and in the north (Kafr ʿAqab) and northeast (ʿAnatā). Because of the Israel enclave on Mt. Scopus, which dominated all principal roads to the town, and the proximity of the frontier to all the important parts of the city, a sense of uneasiness hovered over East Jerusalem throughout the period. The presence of the Jordanian army was felt everywhere and there were occasional clashes between sections of the local population and the Arab Legion soldiers. The outstanding events in the city during the period included the assassination of King Abdullah (1951), the fire in the Church of the Holy Sepulcher (1953), and the visit of Pope Paul VI (1964).

WEST JERUSALEM. The cessation of hostilities and the conclusion of the armistice agreement with Jordan left the Israel sector of Jerusalem situated at the eastern extremity of a "corridor" that was almost devoid of Jewish settlements. To the north, east, and south, hostile Arab territory surrounded the city. At first the city's population was diminishing and its political future was obscure. The Jewish city began to recover quickly, however, when it was proclaimed as the seat of the Knesset and the capital of the State of Israel at the end of 1949. Water supply was resumed, at first through an emergency pipe and later through pipelines of considerable capacity, whose sources were in the corridor and the coastal plain, and an immense water reservoir was built in the southwest of the city. The electricity network was connected to the national grid. On May 1, 1949, the first train since the war arrived in the city, after Israel had gained control of the entire railway track as a result of territorial arrangements with Jordan. A landing strip for light planes was constructed in the western part of the town.

The direct highway to Tel Aviv through Arab-held Latrun remained closed, but traffic to Jerusalem was renewed along the "Road of Valor," which was constructed from Ramleh through Naḥshon to the Hartuv junction, south of the War of Independence "Burma Road." Additional approach roads were constructed from Ẓorah through Ramat Razi'el to Ein Kerem and Castel (Me'oz Zion). Another road ascended through the Elah Valley to Ẓur-Hadassah and Ein Kerem, while an emergency track was laid out along the railway line from Hartuv to the Bar-Giora junction. Hadassah's hospital and other services were housed in rented premises in the center of the city, as its buildings remained isolated in the Israel enclave on Mt. Scopus and could only be reached every fortnight by a convoy under the protection of the UN. Later on, a new Hadassah Medical Center was built on a slope overlooking Ein Kerem. In addition to the hospital, the center grew to include a medical school, a training school for nurses, a school of dentistry, and a large range of clinics. The Hebrew University and its library, which had also been compelled to leave their buildings on Mt. Scopus, resumed their activities in the city, with provisional headquarters in the Italian Terra Sancta school. In the early 1950s the construction of a new campus on Givat Ram, a hill between Reḥavyah and Beit ha-Kerem, was initiated. Campus buildings included a stadium, a synagogue, a planetarium, and the new National Library, inaugurated in 1961. On the western outskirts of the city, the Convention Center, Binyanei ha-Ummah ("National Buildings"), used for concerts, dramatic performances, exhibitions, and congresses, was built. In 1951, the 23rd Zionist Congress, the first to be held in Israel, took place there.

Immediately after the cessation of hostilities, the only border-crossing point between Israel and Jordan was opened to the United Nations in Jerusalem off the historic road leading from Damascus Gate to Nabī Samwīl (and the Coastal Plain). In time the "Mandelbaum Gate" (named after the Jewish owner of the destroyed building that had stood on the spot) became the official crossing point for tourists, with passport-control and customs offices. A second but unofficial crossing point existed for several years in the demilitarized zone around the former Government House, which had become the UN headquarters, in Ra's Maqābi.

In the late 1950s a start was made on the construction of the new government center, Ha-Kiryah, opposite the new university campus, housing the Prime Minister's Office and ministries of Finance, the Interior, and later, Labor. A compound of one-story buildings was put up for the Foreign Ministry south of Romemah. On a hill to the southeast of and above Ha-Kiryah, the large Knesset building, which was built with the contributions of the Rothschild family, was completed in 1966. To the south of the Knesset are situated the Shrine of the Book and the Israel Museum (completed 1966–67). This ensemble of impressive buildings, which links the center of the city to the western districts (Kiryat Moshe, Bet ha-Kerem, and their extensions) added to the beauty of Jerusalem and visibly symbolized its position as the capital of Israel.

Although the UN General Assembly resolution of 1949 calling for the internationalization of Jerusalem was a dead letter, it was still on the record, and most countries, including the major powers, refused to recognize Jerusalem as Israel's capital, setting up their embassies and legations in Tel Aviv or its environs. President Weizmann continued to reside in Reḥovot, but after his death in 1952, diplomats went up to Jerusalem to present their credentials to his successor, President Ben-Zvi, and visit the Foreign Ministry and the Prime Minister's Office. Gradually, too, the boycott weakened and a number of embassies moved to or were established in the capital. In 1970, out of 46 foreign missions in Israel, 22 were in Jerusalem – those of two European countries: the Netherlands and Greece; 10 African: Central African Republic, Congo Brazzaville, Congo Kinshasa, Dahomey, Gabon, Ivory Coast, Liberia, Malagasy, Niger, and Upper Volta; and 10 Latin-American: Bolivia, Chile, Colombia, Costa Rica, Dominican Republic, Ecuador, Guatemala, Panama, Venezuela, and Uruguay. In addition, 11 other countries maintained consulates or consulates-general in the city.

Besides numerous office buildings, the large Histadrut headquarters, and Heikhal Shlomo, the center of the Chief Rabbinate, were erected in the center of town. A branch of the Hebrew Union College was built near the King David Hotel, overlooking the Old City walls, and the buildings of the Academy of Sciences and Humanities were built, overlooking the south of the city from Talbiyah hill. Next to it sites of the presidential residence and the Jerusalem theater were chosen, both in advanced stages of construction at the beginning of 1971. To the southwest, the town is dominated by Mt. Herzl, renamed when Herzl's remains were reentered there in 1949. Since then, the summit of this hill has become a national cemetery where V. *Jabotinsky, J. *Sprinzak, L. *Eshkol, and others were buried. On the northern slope of Mt. Herzl is a military cemetery, and toward the west is Yad Vashem, a memorial to the victims of the Holocaust, including a research center. On the western side, the bow-shaped Jerusalem Forest encloses the town.

Many religious institutions have been established in Jerusalem since 1948. These include the Porat Yosef yeshivah, which was forced out of the Old City; the yeshivot of Belz, Netiv Meir, and Merom Zion; Yad ha-Rav Maimon and its religious college; etc. In the religious quarters an abundance of synagogues were built. New religious concentrations, resembling a second-generation Me'ah She'arim and its surroundings, were formed in the north of the city (Kiryat Mattersdorf) and in the west, at the entrance to Givat Sha'ul.

Extensive housing projects for new immigrants were erected along the armistice line in northern Jerusalem and in the northwest (Shemu'el ha-Navi St., Romemah Illit), as well as in Musrara (Morashah). The main development of the city, however, took place in the south and southwest. The southern districts, Abu-Ṭūr (Givat Ḥananyah), Bak'a (Ge'ulim), the German Colony (Refa'im), and Katamon (Gonen), which were inhabited by Christians and Arabs until 1948, became completely Jewish, while among them and next to them large new housing projects were erected (Talpiyyot, Bak'a, Katamonim, the Rassco Quarter, Givat Mordekhai, etc.). On a height overlooking the city from the southwest, Bayit va-Gan expanded, and to the south of it Kiryat ha-Yovel, Kiryat Menahem, and Ir Gannim were established and filled with a population of tens of thousands. The former Arab villages of Māliḥa (Manaḥat), Deir Yāsīn (Kefar Sha'ul), and Liftā (Mei Nefto'aḥ) were expanded and repopulated; Ein Kerem was incorporated into Jerusalem, as was part of Beit Ṣāfāfā. On Mt. Zion, the Ministry of Religious Affairs established a new religious center around the reputed tomb of David, containing the Holocaust Vault and the Temple Observation Point, as a substitute for the lost Old City. To make up for the loss of the Mount of Olives, new cemeteries were consecrated in Sanhedriyyah and on Har ha-Menuḥot.

In order to diversify the sources of livelihood in the capital, considerable efforts were made by the Israel government to develop industry. Several small and medium-sized factories for electrical and metal products, pencils, pharmaceutics, etc. were opened and a large flour mill and silo were built. Publishing houses and printing shops became important contributors to the economy. Industrial estates were built in Romemah, Mekor Barukh, Givat Sha'ul, and Talpiyyot by the Jerusalem Economic Corporation, in which about 90% of the shares were held by the government and the rest by various public bodies. Considerable impetus was also given to the tourism industry, and several large hotels were built (Kings, President, Holyland, Diplomat, etc.). After the solution of the water problem, several swimming pools were built. The University Stadium, a large sports field in the German colony, and indoor facilities in the Histadrut building, provided opportunities for sports. Beit ha-Am (where the Eichmann Trial was held in 1961) contained a hall for lectures and theatrical performances and a large municipal library. More public parks and gardens were laid out and a Biblical Zoo was opened.

A number of factors contributed to give Jerusalem a distinctive character among Israel's cities: the larger proportion of families going back several generations, newcomers from Asia and North Africa, students and university personnel, and government and other public officials among its population; the dignified public buildings and picturesque, old-established neighborhoods; the almost universal use of stone or stone facing (except in some outlying districts) in both residential and public construction; and its position as the home of the foremost university and the seat of the President, the Knesset, and the government. It was an important center for exhibitions and conventions – national, world Jewish (notably the Zionist Congresses), and international, which, even if they transacted most of their business in Tel Aviv, usually held at least their ceremonial opening sessions in the capital.

The general tone of public and cultural activity was quiet and restrained: there were no sidewalk cafes and little night life. The city was visited from time to time by the Philharmonic Orchestra and the Tel Aviv-based theater companies, which performed at Binyanei ha-Ummah, Bet ha-Am, the Histadrut's Mitchell Hall, or the distinctive Khan Theater, which had once been an Arab inn. Indigenous musical activities were provided mainly by the Broadcasting Services Orchestra and the Rubin Academy of Music. Art exhibitions were held at the Israel Museum, the Jerusalem Artists' House (which took over the premises of the *Bezalel Museum), and private galleries.

Jerusalem also became an economic and administrative center for the villages in the "Jerusalem Corridor," which connected Jerusalem with the rest of Israel (Bet Zayit, Mevasseret Yerushalayim, Me'oz Zion, Orah, Amminadav, Even Sappir, Bar Giora, Nes Harim, Mevo Betar, Ramat Razi'el, etc.), and the city was no longer threatened by isolation in a period of emergency. According to the census of 1961, its population was 166,300, including, it is estimated, several hundred Muslims and over 1,000 Christians. In 1967, the number of inhabitants was estimated at about 185,000.

SECURITY. As the border between Israel and Jordan ran through the middle of Jerusalem, there was constant vigilance on both sides. The Old City walls were hidden from view by high barriers across Jaffa Road and other streets, but from time to time Arab Legion sentries on the ramparts sniped at people in the streets of West Jerusalem and exchanges of fire developed. In April 1953, for example, the shooting went on for over 24 hours. In July 1954 it lasted for three days before a cease-fire was arranged through the UN observers. Occasionally, too, Arab infiltrators killed civilians in outlying areas. In September 1956 members of an archaeological convention examining antiquities near Ramat Raḥel were fired at from a Jordanian army post and four people were killed. There was a spate of incidents in June and July 1962, four Israelis being killed and five wounded. On the whole, however, the Jordanian authorities were not interested in making trouble and efforts were sometimes made, by informal contacts between local commanders on both sides, to reduce tension.

A constant focus of friction was the demilitarized zone on Mount Scopus. Every now and then the Jordanians would hold up the fortnightly convoy carrying replacements for the Israel police garrison that looked after the University and Hadassah buildings on the Mount, and there was tension between the garrison and the inhabitants of the Arab village of Issawiya in the Israeli part of the demilitarized zone. In January 1958 Francis Urrutia, representing the UN Secretary-General, made an unsuccessful attempt to get agreement on the implementation of Article 8 of the Israel-Jordan Armistice Agreement (see above). In May 1958, after Jordanian soldiers had opened fire on Israel patrols on the Mount, a UN officer, Col. George Flint, and four Israeli policemen were killed by Jordanian fire. This time Ralph Bunche, assistant to UN Secretary-General Dag Hammarskjöld, and then Hammarskjöld himself, visited Jerusalem and Amman in efforts to solve the problem, but without success.

MUNICIPAL AFFAIRS. After the departure of the British, an enlarged municipal committee was formed, consisting of the six Jewish councillors and representatives of the Va'ad ha-Kehillah and the Jewish quarters. In January 1949 the Ministry of the Interior nominated Daniel Auster as the head of a municipal council of similar composition and Reuven Shreibman (Shari) as deputy. In November 1950 the first municipal elections took place on the party list proportional representation system. The results reflected the fragmentation of the population on social, religious, and communal, as well as political and ideological, lines. The largest party in the new council, Mapai (Israel Labor Party), won only 25% of the votes and was closely followed by the United Religious Front (16%), General Zionists (16%), and Ḥerut (11%). The Progressives won 8% and a number of district and communal lists had 18% between them. Shlomo Zalman *Shragai (Mizrachi) was elected mayor, with the support of a coalition consisting mainly of his own party, the General Zionists, and Ḥerut. (For an account of the parties, see *Israel, State of: Political Life and Parties.) The city had difficult administrative, financial, and social problems with which to contend. The staff had been accustomed to the Oriental atmosphere of the Muslim mayoralty, and the organization of finance and services was primitive. The citizens had not been in the habit of regularly paying rates, especially in the extensive slum areas. Orthodox districts, like Me'ah She'arim, were to a large extent a law unto themselves. The new mayor was hampered in dealing with these problems by dissension inside the coalition and obstruction by the opposition. In August 1953 an inquiry commission appointed by the Ministry of the Interior produced an unfavorable report. Shragai resigned, being succeeded by Yiẓhak Kariv, of his own party. The difficulties persisted, however; in April 1955 the Ministry dissolved the municipal council and appointed a committee of officials to run the municipality until the elections. In 1955 the head of the Mapai list, Gershon *Agron, was elected mayor with the support of Agudat Israel, the Progressives, and Aḥdut ha-Avodah. When Agudat Israel withdrew from the coalition, he retained his position with the aid of a defecting member of the National Religious Party. Agron died a few days before the 1959 elections and was succeeded by Mordekhai Ish-Shalom, who held the post until 1965. In that year Teddy *Kollek, running a personal campaign on the *Rafi ticket, won 20% of the votes and formed a coalition with Gaḥal (Ḥerut-Liberal bloc) and the religious parties. During the emergency preceding the Six-Day War in 1967, the opposition was invited to share in responsibility and an all-party administration was formed. After the 1969 elections, in which Kollek headed the united Labor-Mapam Alignment list, he was reelected at the head of an all-party coalition.

The Six-Day War and After

For Jerusalem, the *Six-Day War was only a three-day war, from Monday morning (June 5, 1967) to Wednesday afternoon. The battles began with the Jordanian seizure of UN headquarters and their attempt to break through from there to the south of the city, to the accompaniment of indiscriminate shelling of the Jewish areas. The breakthrough was halted in time, and in a counterattack the Israel forces retook the UN headquarters, barred the Jerusalem-Bethlehem road, and occupied the village of Ṣur-Bāhir. At a later stage there were hard-fought battles for the occupation of the Arab Abu-Tūr quarter. The most difficult struggle, however, took place in northern Jerusalem, where Israel forces broke through to the Police School and Ammunition Hill slightly to the north of it. There was another breakthrough into Sheikh Jarrāḥ and the American Colony, and on Tuesday all of East Jerusalem north of the walls of the Old City (Bāb al-Sāhira (Zahra), Wadi Joz) was seized. Contact was also made with the Israel enclave on Mount Scopus. On Wednesday, June 1967, Israel forces broke through the Lions' Gate and took the Old City. United Jerusalem again became the capital of the nation. In the battles for the city and its surroundings about 180 Israel soldiers lost their lives, in addition to the civilians who were hit by shells, etc. As on many occasions in its history, the city was again attacked from the west and the north, although the final breakthrough came from the east.

The damage caused by the three days of fighting, which was not severe, was repaired, mines were cleared away, military positions and protective walls were destroyed, barbed-wire fences were removed, the roads between the two parts of the town were joined, and all the gates of the Old City were once more opened. The two parts of the city were officially reunited on June 28, 1967, and inhabitants from either side could visit the other for the first time in almost 20 years. East Jerusalem was connected to the Israel water supply network and the water shortage was overcome. The electricity network, however, was not united to that of Israel and continued to be operated by a Jordanian company.

The holy places of Christendom came under Israel rule. The university buildings on Mount Scopus were restored, and studies were resumed in them from the fall of 1969. A bungalow quarter was erected to accommodate students. To the west of this area, on Givat ha-Mivtar, a residential neighborhood was built, and the large Ramot Eskhol Quarter was erected between it and the Sanhedria Quarter, encompassing northern Jerusalem. A start was made on the reconstruction of the Jewish Quarter of the Old City.

One of the most important consequences of the unification of Jerusalem was the resumption of archaeological research within the Old City (in the Citadel, the Upper City, and near the western and southern walls of the Temple Mount), which, in addition to the scientific results, brought about a change in the landscape of the city. The ancient Jewish cemetery, which covers the slopes of the Mount of Olives, was restored. Efforts were made by the government of Israel and Israel public institutions to transfer their offices to Jerusalem, particularly the eastern section. Police headquarters were moved from Tel Aviv to a previously uncompleted Jordanian government building in Sheikh Jarrāḥ. Jerusalem is now distinguished by the duplication of many of its institutions, one of the last signs of the division of the town for 19 years. There are two Hadassah hospitals, two large museums, two YMCA buildings, two university campuses, many double consulates, and even two central bus stations.

Following the Six-Day War, united Jerusalem became the central attraction for tourists and many new immigrants. Thousands of Jewish students from the Diaspora, particularly from the United States, Canada, and Western Europe, enrolled at The Hebrew University, and many remained. Tourism to Jerusalem reached the peak figures of about 400,000 visitors a year (in 1968, 970,000 "nights" were registered at the hotels in the city). New immigrant centers, i.e., hostels for individuals and families were established in Katamon Tet (1968) and Mevasseret Zion on a hill west of Jerusalem (1970). The mayor of Jerusalem, Teddy Kollek, and the government encouraged the settlement of new immigrants in Jerusalem, and Israeli architects drew up a master plan for the Jerusalem of the future (in the 21st century). It did not apply, however, to the ancient parts of the city, including the Old City and a belt surrounding its walls and Mt. Scopus, the Mount of Olives, etc., which have been preserved in their traditional form.

[Walter Pinhas Pick]

REUNIFICATION: PROGRESS AND PROBLEMS. With its reunification on June 28, 1967, Jerusalem restored its traditional character as a multi-national and multi-ethnic city. The population totaled about 265,000: 199,000 Jews and 66,000 Arabs. The non-Jewish population was composed of two religious sectors: the larger Muslim community of 54,000 (83%) and the various Christian factions numbering 11,000 (including 4,000 members of the Greek Orthodox Church, 3,600 of the Latin Church, and 1,200 Greek Catholics). The Jewish community thus comprised three-quarters of the population. The fact that it was the decisive majority was not novel, as a Jewish majority had existed in the city since the last third of the 19th century.

The municipal unification of Jerusalem brought into the city's boundaries areas that had been under Jordanian municipal jurisdiction before the Six-Day War (mainly within the boundaries defined during the Mandate period), as well as a broad area that had been organized under village councils or had not enjoyed municipal status. Consequently, population groups that had never been urban were included in the city's area and in the jurisdiction of the municipality and Israel government authority. The resulting population was mostly heterogeneous, from slum dwellers and semi-nomadic Bedouin to members of the upper middle class, who had moved beyond the limits of the Jordanian city and set up magnificent suburbs to the north. The Arab population was concentrated in these areas. About 33% of it (23,000) lived inside the Old City walls; about 38% (25,000) in the northern suburbs, most of them modern; and about 26% (17,000) in the southern parts, including the villages of Silwān, Abu Ṭūr, and Ṣur Bāhir.

The rate of natural increase among the Arab population, which is slightly less than double that of the Jewish, could increase the proportion of Arabs in the city from a quarter to a third within 20 years. The Israel government, realizing the potential difficulties of this situation, expended great efforts to provide more accommodation for Jews in the city and to eradicate distinctions between the western and eastern parts. In 1967–69 there were only a handful of Jews living east of the former dividing line, but from the end of 1969, when the construction of new quarters began to be completed (e.g., Ramat Eshkol), the settlement of Jews in the eastern part of the city accelerated. In 1970 the government decided to add impetus to the establishment of Jewish quarters in the southern, northern, and northwestern parts of the Old City. As a result of these efforts, the number of Jews moving to Jerusalem reached 5,000 per year, twice as much as in the years immediately before the Six-Day War. In this way the numerical balance between Jews and non-Jews was maintained in the unified city.

During the period of the city's division, the existence of two municipalities governed by states with such differing policies, rates of development, and character resulted in the development of two different cities. So different were their economic systems and social structures that it was sometimes difficult to believe that they were both parts of the same city. West Jerusalem quickly recovered from the damage it had suffered during the War of Independence, but from 1948 to 1967 its population decreased in proportion to that of the rest of the country; whereas in 1948 it had 9.6% of the total population of the State of Israel, at the end of 1960 this ratio had decreased to 7.7%. The economy of West Jerusalem was based mainly on a constellation of public services (government, university, Jewish Agency, and Hadassah) that employed about 30% of its labor force; about 17% was employed in industry, and 14% in business and banking. Tourism, in which Jerusalem had a relative advantage, did not play a central role. Only 13% of the hotels in Israel were located there, while 32% were in Tel Aviv. One of the major obstacles to the development of the city's economy was the fact that West Jerusalem had almost no economic hinterland, while in Haifa and Tel Aviv a great part of the economic activity extended to nearby townships and settlements, and their scope of influence extended far beyond their municipal boundaries. The scope of Jerusalem's influence on the narrow underpopulated corridor that connects it with the coast was necessarily very limited.

In contrast to West Jerusalem, East Jerusalem under Jordanian rule retained its position as the largest city of the West Bank and it continued to serve as the center of a very broad economic and demographic hinterland. The city was the center of most of the financial institutions of the West Bank, as well as 85% of the tourist companies, and it also had the greatest concentration of the wholesale trade, the independent professions, and the trade in durable goods. Production per employee in East Jerusalem was 50% higher than the average in the West Bank as whole, and the average income per person was also proportionally higher. Nevertheless, the economy of East Jerusalem was based mainly on one activity: tourism. The influence of every decrease in the number of tourists would extend to the various branches of the economy and result in crisis. On the contrary, their policies of economic incentives and government aid were aimed basically at the capital, Amman, and the East Bank, as opposed to the West Bank, including Jerusalem. East Jerusalemites who wished to establish economic enterprises in their city had either to abandon their projects or implement them in Amman. Amman also received a distinct preference with regard to financial and cultural institutions. This policy led to a slowdown in the economic development of East Jerusalem and in acceleration in the development of the capital of the kingdom across the Jordan River which was implemented mainly by entrepreneurs from the West Bank, primarily from Jerusalem.

Although the economic status of East Jerusalem was more stable than that of the western half of the city, a comparison of the two reveals a formidable gap in favor of the Jewish sector of the city. On the eve of the Six-Day War, the average yearly income per person in West Jerusalem was fourfold that of the eastern part. In West Jerusalem the income per person was estimated in 1965 as IL3,400 while in the eastern part it was only IL 900. East Jerusalem contributed only 6–7% of the buying power of the unified city, in contrast to its 25% of the population. Under such circumstances it was extremely difficult to effect the economic integration of the two parts of the city and annul the effects of the war in a relatively short time. The Six-Day War resulted in a number of economic difficulties in East Jerusalem: the temporary cessation of tourism, on which the city's economy had been based; the loss of the Jordanian authorities and army as a source of economic demand; disruptions in trade between the various parts of the West Bank; the closing of the banks; the lack of liquidity; and the absence of economic stability. These brought about a serious economic crisis, which found immediate expression in mass unemployment. Four months after the war, unemployment in the eastern part covered one-third of the labor force, in contrast to 7–8% on the eve of the war. Especially affected were the building trades, transportation, and hotels. Services, such as restaurants, cafés, bakeries, and garages, which were also affected, recovered quickly due to rising demands from Israel tourists.

Within a few months, the process of economic disintegration ceased, and speedy action on the part of the authorities brought about a distinct improvement in the economic situation. The process of rehabilitation was accelerated by the huge public investments made in the city following the war, especially in construction. At the end of 1969 employment returned to its prewar level. About half of the businesses in East Jerusalem were better off than they had been on the eve of the war. The most outstanding improvement was in the situation of salaried workers. More than 5,000 workers and employees out of a labor force of about 18,000 were employed in West Jerusalem, earning salaries that were 150% higher than those they had received on the eve of the war. The recovery process had some negative manifestations, however. Price levels increased by 40–50%. About half of the businesses in East Jerusalem, especially those which could not compete with similar business in the western part of the city, were affected to varying degrees of severity.

The integration of the economic systems, and especially the implementation of the principles of a modern welfare state, brought about far-reaching changes in Arab society in East Jerusalem. The distribution of income and property became more equalized. Israel wages were paid to thousands of Arab workers, and a slow increase in the wages of Arabs employed in the Arab sector brought a general improvement in the standard of living. National Insurance, especially birth benefits and benefits to families with many children, aided in the improvement of the status of women. Nevertheless, the damage to the relative economic position of the upper middle class brought complaints of "discrimination" and "Jewish control" of certain branches, especially the import of durable goods and tourism. Because of the atmosphere of long-range political insecurity that continued to exist among the Arabs of East Jerusalem, no plan for capital investments was implemented. The closing of Arab banks continued to influence the lack of liquidity and the scarcity of sources of credit. In view of developments in 1968–70, a warning had been voiced that the integration of East Jerusalem's Arabs into the city's united economy might lead to their concentration in low-income employment requiring manual labor and might have undesirable social and inter-ethnic results.

Another unsolved problem was that of the employment of white-collar workers. With the unification of the city, many Jordanian government officials, travel agents, lawyers, etc. became unemployed. Only the Arab employees of the Jerusalem municipality and a small number of government employees (formerly Jordanian) were integrated into the institutions of the unified municipality and Israel government offices. Out of 500 people who worked in all levels of the Jordanian government on the eve of the war, only about 150 were absorbed, some of them in the military government. This problem was more of a political nature than an economic one. Some of the white-collar workers could not find employment in their professions for economic reasons; lawyers were not employed because they boycotted Israel courts. Most of them, however, especially civil servants on intermediate or senior levels, were unemployed because the functions they had fulfilled were transferred, with the change in authorities, to Israel government offices. The degree of integration of white-collar workers in the economic and administrative system became an important indicator for the reconciliation of Jerusalem's population to the new situation created by the unification of the city.

The unification of Jerusalem opened a new chapter in the complex relations between the Jewish majority and the Arab minority in the State of Israel. For the first time in its history, Israel had to absorb a developed Arab urban unit with advanced social stratification, considerable economic power, a high level of education, and a tradition of participation in the highest levels of government. Jerusalem, after its unification, became the greatest concentration of urban Arab population in the country. The percentage of high school graduates in East Jerusalem rose steadily under Jordanian rule, and in 1967, 38% of the males had completed high school and 9% had had higher education. The educational level of the Arab residents of the city was higher than that of the inhabitants of Judea and Samaria and even higher than the average of all the non-Jews in Israel, among whom the urban population was a small minority.

In contrast to the Arabs in Israel, who initially lacked an educated, stable urban class, the inhabitants of East Jerusalem lived for 20 years under independent Arab rule, during which it was the center of authority for the entire West Bank. The leadership of East Jerusalem was the major exponent of Arab-Palestinian nationalism and was integrated into the Jordanian establishment. Periodic disagreements with Amman aside, it was one of the outstanding elite groups in the Hashemite kingdom. When the city was unified, there were a considerable number of former ministers, ambassadors, members of parliament and Senate, and senior officials in East Jerusalem, in addition to an efficient and capable municipal administration. In its attitude to Israel the East Jerusalem population was one of the most extreme elements in Jordan. The Palestine Liberation Organization (see *Israel, State of: Arab Population – Arab National Movement) had great influence there, and many members of extremist parties, both right and left wing, resided in the city. As was customary in the Jordanian educational system, pupils were educated toward extreme pan-Arabism and revanche; even excerpts from the *Protocols of the Elders of Zion* were found among the teaching materials. The chauvinistic extremism stemmed, inter alia, from the fact that about 11,000 inhabitants of the city were formally refugees, i.e., the head of the family was born in an area that had been included in the State of Israel in 1948.

The Jewish population was agreeable in some respects and not agreeable in others to the improvement of relations with the Arab minority. The large number of Oriental Jews and their Israel-born children – more than 50% of the Jewish population of the city – was significant in this matter, as this group was familiar with the Arabic language and the Arab way of life and culture and could theoretically serve as a bridge between the two segments of the population. However, the immigrants from Muslim countries who had come to Israel after the War of Independence (about a quarter of the total Jewish population) were, paradoxically, a potential cause of tension. Partly because they had suffered oppression and persecution in their countries of origin, they were sometimes influenced by latent urges to revenge in their attitude to the Arab population of East Jerusalem. Other sections of the Jewish population, mainly native Israelis and immigrants from Europe and English-speaking countries, lacked familiarity with Arabs and their way of life and often misunderstood them – either regarding them in an unrealistic romantic way or suspecting them as a hostile, alien element.

The two populations, which suddenly found themselves living in one city, bore the acute psychological influences of the Six-Day War, apart from the past legacy of the Jewish-Arab conflict. The Jewish population felt a sharp sense of release from the burden of fear that existed during the prewar period and euphoria over the unification of the city and the liberation of the Western Wall and the other holy places. The Arab population was astonished by the swift conquest of their city and suffered from a deep sense of shame after their decisive defeat. On the other hand, the factor that caused the greatest surprise among the Arab population was the humane and fair treatment accorded to them by the soldiers of the Israel Defense Forces. Influenced by Arab propaganda describing Jews as murderers of women and children, the Arabs awaited the worst. Fear gave way to astonishment and feelings of gratitude.

There was an initial atmosphere of goodwill and good-neighborliness that found dramatic expression on the "day of reunification" (June 28, 1967). When the barriers were removed and free movement between the two parts of the city was allowed, the Jewish and Arab masses mingled without incident. The atmosphere of peace and harmony in the city appeared unreal to those who witnessed it. Indeed, it lasted only a few short weeks, during which these feelings slowly abated. The two sides began to adjust themselves to the new reality. Repeated incidents and the loss of lives recreated the tension within the Jewish population. The Arab population found itself subject to a rule that, although tolerant and understanding, was nonetheless foreign, with which they could not and did not wish to identify, and to whose continued existence they could not reconcile themselves. The Israel authorities quickly learned the complex problems of the Arab sector and also found ways to solve them effectively. Nevertheless, several points of friction were created by a lack of understanding and knowledge of the mentality of the Arab population. This lack of understanding stemmed mainly from an approach to the population of East Jerusalem similar to that employed to the Arab population of the State of Israel before the war, disregarding the differences between the two communities. Likewise, attempts were made immediately to put into effect the procedures of Israel administration, without allowing the inhabitants of East Jerusalem sufficient time to adapt to the ways and means unfamiliar to them.

In the course of time, the inhabitants of East Jerusalem became accustomed to these procedures, and at the same time the Israel authorities became familiar with the feelings of the inhabitants on certain matters. This mutual adaptation erased most of the points of friction, the major one being the problem of taxes. The East Jerusalemites, accustomed to the Jordanian fiscal system, which levied low taxes and in return rendered a low level of services, did not, at first, understand the principles of the Israel welfare state, demanding high taxation and providing a high level of services. Taxes connected with war and security caused additional complaints, since the inhabitants of East Jerusalem regarded their payment as "treason against the Jordanian kingdom," which was in a state of war with Israel.

In terms of their civil status, the inhabitants of East Jerusalem were Israel residents with Jordanian citizenship. (They could apply for Israel citizenship, but practically none of them did so.) This status allowed them to vote for and be elected to the Jerusalem municipality but not to the Knesset. As Jordanian citizens, they could cross the cease-fire line and visit in Jordan, while they also had the right to move freely throughout Israel, like other residents. Despite the distinct improvement in many areas of relations with the authorities and the adjustment of the inhabitants of East Jerusalem to the way of life that developed in the unified city, relations were clouded by the fact that the population of East Jerusalem avoided all political cooperation that could be interpreted as voluntary acknowledgement of the unification of Jerusalem. Members of the Arab municipal council, who were invited to join the unified city council, refused to do so; lawyers refused to appear in Israeli courts; companies refused to be registered as Israeli companies; and the Shariʿa courts refused to become part of the Muslim judicial system of Israel, despite a far-reaching compromise suggested by Israel. Nevertheless, the boundaries between political cooperation, which was regarded as "treason," and the minimal reconciliation necessary for coexistence were very elastic. Thus, for example, the mass voting by inhabitants of East Jerusalem in the municipal elections of October 1969 was not viewed as collaboration.

Political tension remained mostly latent, but it broke out a number of times and was expressed mainly in business strikes and demonstrations. Feelings of political frustration and tension were also nourished by a number of actions taken by the Israel authorities to insure the Jewish character of the city and enforce Israeli control of the eastern part. In broad areas of the eastern part Jewish dwellings began to be erected. The acts of Arab terrorists aggravated the inter-ethnic tension. After one act of terror, which claimed a number of civilian casualties in West Jerusalem (the "Night of the Grenades," August 18, 1968) young Jews attacked Arab civilians and damage was inflicted on Arab shops. Strong and unequivocal measures on the part of the Israeli government and its major leaders put an end to the hooliganism, and later acts of Arab terror (such as the explosions which in 1968–69 killed and wounded many people in a marketplace, a supermarket, the students' cafeteria in The Hebrew University, etc.) did not elicit revenge on innocent Arabs. Nevertheless, the security forces increased their supervision over the Arab residents. Membership in terrorist cells and possession of arms caches were punished, inter alia, by the destruction of several houses and the confiscation of others. All these measures resulted in alternately rising and falling tension. A major event influencing the atmosphere between the communities was the short-lived shock of the fire in the al-Aqṣā Mosque on August 21, 1969, which quickly abated when the culprit proved to be an insane Christian tourist from Australia, although the incident was blown up to major international proportions by all the Arab States.

In Jewish public opinion there were two different approaches to dealing with the Arab population. All Jews were ready to grant the Arabs full citizenship rights as individuals, but some would deny them the right of national political expression or separate representation, whereas others held that the Arabs should not only be granted individual rights but should be recognized as a national minority with legitimate aspirations of their own, entitling them to separate representation. This argument never came to a head, as the Arabs themselves refused to cooperate in any attempt at an interim arrangement and were not ready to accept any suggestion of separate representation or any kind of political organization.

By 1970 distinct progress had been made in the process of integrating the Arabs of East Jerusalem into the life of the city, and inter-ethnic relations developed and improved, despite negative forces that operated throughout the period. Nevertheless, there were still basic political differences of approach between the Jewish majority and the Arab minority with regard to the future of the city. The integration of the communities and nationalities in Jerusalem was progressively implemented, mainly in the economic sphere and in areas necessary for municipal survival. There was little social contact between the two groups, but the fact that thousands of Arab workers were employed in West Jerusalem led to significant contacts and new understanding. The deepening of reciprocal harmonious relations, however, ultimately depended upon the general solution to the Israel-Arab conflict.

[Meron Benvenisti]

The decade following 1967 was marked by the most intensive development in Jerusalem since King Herod 2,000 years before. The city tripled in size by the incorporation of East Jerusalem, under Jordanian rule from 1948 to 1967, and within seven years had the largest population of any city in Israel. Almost a third of the area of East Jerusalem – the bulk of it, rocky, non-arable hills – was expropriated for the construction of nine housing developments on clear strategic lines. Four of them – Gilo, East Talpiot, Neveh Ya'akov, and Ramot, each larger than most development towns – were cast in a wide arc around the outermost edge of the city. Five others – Ramot Eshkol, French Hill, Ma'alot Dafna, Sanhedria ha-Murḥevet, and Givat ha-Mivtar – were built across the battlefields of the Six-Day War to establish a link with Mount Scopus.

Eleven thousand apartments were built across the former border and by 1977 there were close to 40,000 Jews living in these new development areas, constituting some 15% of the city's Jewish population.

The government had succeeded in creating a physical ring around Jerusalem that would make it impossible to divide the city again. It was less successful, however, in the other major objective – reinforcing the Jewish presence demographically. The September 1967 census recorded 197,000 Jews and 71,000 non-Jews (including 3–5,000 non-Arabs, such as Armenians and other non-Arab Christians). However, in spite of the influx of immigrants and the transfer of some government offices from Tel Aviv to Jerusalem the percentage of Jews declined from 73.4 to 72.5. Ten years after the Six-Day War, Jerusalem's population had increased by more than a third, numbering 370,000, of whom 268,500 were Jews and 102,000 non-Jews, and by 1981 it was 412,000, with 295,000 Jews and 117,000 non-Jews. While the average Jewish annual increase was 3.3% – considerably higher than the national average – the non-Jewish rate was 3.8%; the Arab figure due to a higher birthrate, a substantial decrease in the mortality rate, and a halt in emigration from East Jerusalem which had prevailed throughout the Jordanian regime.

The economic boom even attracted immigration from across the Jordan River under the family reunion scheme. In addition, thousands of West Bank Arabs took up residence illegally in East Jerusalem, whose numbers are not included in the official population figures.

JEWISH-ARAB RELATIONS. The relations which developed between Arab and Jewish people in Jerusalem during the decade were shifting and ambiguous. They added up, however, to coexistence – a less satisfactory condition, perhaps, than friendship, but still infinitely superior to easily imaginable alternatives. Tranquility was achieved by a policy of liberality towards the Arabs, including open bridges and de facto control of the Temple Mount by Muslim authorities.

The West Jerusalem economy and the Arab work force grew to depend on each other. Arabs from East Jerusalem and the West Bank constituted about 15% of the 110,000-strong labor force in the Jewish economic sector, mainly in construction. More Arabs worked in the Jewish sector of Jerusalem than in the Arab sector and drew 60% higher wages than they had formerly received.

Nine thousand Arabs from East Jerusalem, including wives of 2,000 workers, joined the Histadrut, Israel's labor confederation, which assured them the same pay and benefits as Jewish workers. Arab and Jewish workers sat together on labor committees in West Jerusalem factories, and in some places Arabs were chairmen, and they participated together in social and cultural activities.

The David Yellin Teachers' College in Beit Hakerem, which had been training Jewish teachers since 1914, began accepting East Jerusalem girls in 1974. The first group of 25 graduated two years later, after completing a special course taught in Arabic. Every summer thousands of youths from both sides of the city participated in the municipality's Youth Capital day camp and periodic sports contests were held between Arab and Jewish youth clubs.

There was Arab-Jewish integration on the underworld margin of both societies. Here, Arabic-speaking Jews and East Jerusalem Arabs, sharing a common subculture, "trusted" each other enough to commit armed robberies together. The police quickly broke up these gangs, but fringe society contacts continued. West Jerusalem streetgang workers noted that their Jewish charges and their Arab counterparts were at ease in one another's company. The police were likewise integrated, engaging in joint patrols, but most of the police on the streets of East Jerusalem were local Arabs.

Nevertheless, East Jerusalem Arabs were still not reconciled to Israeli rule. The Arabs felt that Israel was altering the Arab character of East Jerusalem and endangering the Arab way of life by exposing it to an alien culture. Israeli authorities though aware that the allegiance of Jerusalem's Arabs could not be bought by higher salaries or improved services, nevertheless provided them.

The thousands of substantial houses – villas by Israeli standards – built on the hills of East Jerusalem attested to the unprecedented prosperity achieved by Jerusalem's Arabs, particularly laborers, since they came under Israeli rule. Before 1967, 41% of East Jerusalem homes had no running water and 60% had no electricity, whereas by the end of the 1970s only those living in isolated rural areas were without running water and virtually every house had electricity. The abundance of water supplied to the Old City after 1967 proved too much for the old Turkish sewer-drainage pipes which burst under the pressure, causing the inundation of building foundations and the collapse of several structures. In a massive operation expected to last decades, the municipality began gutting the alleys of the Old City in order to build a modern infrastructure. Among the utility lines being laid underground was cable television, to permit the removal of the antennas, cluttering the Old City skyline. The approaches to Damascus Gate, both from inside and outside the city walls, were completely remodeled.

The Arab Sector. Where no park or playground existed in Jerusalem under Jordanian rule, there were six a decade later. Where no kindergartens existed, there were 50. Where no lending library for adults existed, there were four, plus a mobile library serving outlying villages. Where only 73 families received welfare payments under the Jordanians, 900 families were receiving them in 1977 and 4,500 families received pension payments from Israel's National Insurance. In addition, 9,000 East Jerusalem families with three or more children received the same monthly National Insurance payments for each child as did Israeli families. These benefits were given in spite of the fact that the East Jerusalemites chose to remain Jordanian citizens and that Israel had no vested interest in promoting the Arab birth rate. A special government fund also provided more than 4,000 mortgage and business loans to East Jerusalemites whose own banks closed in 1967.

More was done to promote Arab culture in East Jerusalem after the city's unification than had ever been done under Jordanian rule. This included subsidizing their first professional theater group, expanding community centers, arranging for schoolchildren to attend an Arab play and an Arab musical performance every year, and even providing a Jewish dance teacher to launch an Arab dance troupe when no Arab teacher could be found.

Unlike the Arabs living in Israel since 1948, East Jerusalem Arabs did not sever ties with the Arab world. Besides being free to cross the Jordan River bridges in either direction, they could maintain their Jordanian citizenship while remaining official residents of Israel and citizens of an Israeli city with full voting rights in municipal elections. East Jerusalem students were originally required to study a curriculum similar to that of Israeli Arabs, but they were later granted the right to study a Jordanian curriculum (plus six hours of Hebrew and civics) and even to take examinations certified by the Jordanian Ministry of Education, so that they could proceed to universities in the Arab world.

According to Israeli experts, an increasing number of Arabs preferred an open city. This would have meant Arabs and Jews exercising sovereignty over their respective areas, with free passage from one side to the other. Although this might have seemed an ideal solution to many, Mayor Teddy Kollek strongly opposed it, warning that it would allow terrorists to turn Jerusalem into a Belfast overnight.

BUILDINGS. The texture of the city was altered physically, socially, and culturally through the 1970s. High-rise buildings, some of them exceeding 20 stories, punctured the Jerusalem skyline for the first time. Architect Moshe *Safdie pointed out that these high-rises had been approved while the city was still divided. "They could only have been conceived when you weren't thinking about what the skyline would look like from the other side."

Sixty km. of roads and 182 km. of sewage lines were built. The government channeled more than twice as much money into Jerusalem in the first five years after reunification than it had during the previous 12. In addition to the new housing developments, enormous resources were invested in the reconstruction of the Jewish Quarter of the Old City and the Hadassah Hospital and Hebrew University facilities on Mount Scopus.

Little was done, however, to strengthen the outmoded city center, groaning under the weight of the additional population it now had to serve. The plan for a Ben Yehuda street mall remained stalled, except for a small, block-long strip. The number of private offices doubled during the decade, and the government increased its floor space by a third but, with little new construction to accommodate them, the offices spilled over into Reḥaviah and other residential neighborhoods. The population in neighborhoods near the center declined substantially, while the western garden suburbs of the 1930s – Beit Hakerem and Bayit Vegan – increased their population by two-thirds in the five years after the Six-Day War. A plan for the massive redevelopment of the Mamilla district outside Jaffa Gate, which called for razing of the entire district and its replacement with modern commercial, residential, and hotel structures as well as a large underground parking lot at the entrance to the Old City, was approved in principle, but implementation was held up by shortage of funds and concern over its ambitious nature.

A proposal to build a 25,000-seat sports stadium at Shuafat in northern Jerusalem likewise encountered strong opposition, particularly from religious residents in the approaches to the stadium, who objected on account of the traffic and noise and the consequent desecration of the Sabbath. Nevertheless, earthwork began in 1979 but was subsequently halted. Sha'arei Zedek Hospital, one of the city's oldest, built a large new facility at the edge of Bayit Vegan to replace its antiquated building on Jaffa Road. The original Hadassah Hospital on Mount Scopus was restored at great expense by the Hadassah Organization to serve as a regional hospital for Jews and Arabs in northern Jerusalem.

In spite of a few blots on the landscape created by inadvisable building, the city grew more beautiful during the 10 years. The ugly antisniper walls and the ruins of no-man's land were removed. Some of the best views in Jerusalem were opened up by the demolition of the ruined buildings outside the city wall between the Jaffa and New Gates, and by renewed access to Government House Ridge and Mount Scopus.

RESTORATION. Sensitive to the city's physical heritage, the authorities attempted to restore many of its old buildings and quarters rather than subject them to urban renewal. The most notable instance was the Jewish Quarter of the Old City, where painstaking restoration was undertaken. An attempt was made to save all old buildings still structurally sound, while new construction was kept in scale. Archaeologists were given priority over the builders, even though this often meant expensive delays while excavations were carried out. Building plans were often changed to incorporate ancient remains in basement museums or leave them exposed.

There were also extensive restoration efforts outside the Old City walls. The old Turkish khan, or inn, opposite the railway station was converted into a handsome theater, while the Yemin Moshe Quarter was converted from a slum to a luxury neighborhood, The century-old structure known as Mishkenot Sha'ananim, the first building to be built outside the ancient walls, was reconstructed as a guest house for visiting artists, scholars, and writers. Preservation plans were also drawn up for neighborhoods with special character like the German Colony and Sheikh Jarrah.

PARKS AND OPEN SPACES. An elaborate open-space system was developed, including a 600-acre national park around the Old City. Apart from the creation of the new ring of housing developments, this open-space system could be the distinguishing mark made on the city during the decade. One of its most interesting sections was an Archaeological Garden incorporating ancient remains uncovered along the southern and western fringes of the Old City.

The municipality's gardening department itself almost transformed the city by creating a green matrix that softened the stony character of the desert-fringed city, On the eve of the Six-Day War, there were 23 parks in the city covering 25 acres. Ten years later there were 170 parks covering 425 acres. The six children's playgrounds that existed then grew to 78, and three "vest-pocket" parks became 150. Traffic islands were now lush with flowers. Around the fringes of the city the Jewish National Fund planted some 700 acres of forest.

A score of sculptures were installed in public places, including the last monumental work of Alexander Calder, a 12-meter high stabile installed in Holland Square at Mount Herzl.

HOUSING. Slum areas such as the Katamons were upgraded by adding rooms to cramped apartments and planting numerous gardens in the area. Housing conditions in the city improved considerably during the decade. The 30,000 apartments built or started in the Jewish sector in the ten years were almost half as many as existed in 1967 and were generally larger and better built. Four-room apartments, which constituted only 8% of the total built in 1961, constituted 40% of the units built in 1970. High-rise living, unknown in Jerusalem before 1967, became commonplace. To answer the greater demand for privacy, hundreds of terrace apartments with separate entrances were built.

In spite of vigorous efforts to expand Jerusalem's modest industrial base (non-smokestack industries) to offer a greater variety of employment opportunities, the percentage of the Jewish population employed in industry declined from 14.5 to 11.4, while employment in public services rose from 43% to 49%, The government, with 14,000 employees, remained the largest employer.

An area for heavy industry was opened in 1976 at Mishor Adumim on the Jericho Road, 15 km east of Jerusalem. The united city saw new commercial patterns developing. Tourists flooding the city preferred to sleep in West Jerusalem, where the number of hotel rooms tripled, and to shop in East Jerusalem, where the number of souvenir shops tripled. The number of bars and nightclubs increased from 12 to 28 by 1975, while the number of small kiosks selling candy and newspapers declined from 153 to 144. There was only a modest increase in personal services since 1967 – the number of doctors increased by 25% and barbers by 7% – but the number of engineers, insurance agents, and building contractors increased by 150%.

JEWISH SECTOR UNDER THE MAYORALTY OF TEDDY KOLLEK. Strenuous efforts were made to close the gap, at least the visible one, between underprivileged Jews – mostly from Arab countries – and the relatively privileged.

Nearly 1,000 indigent families were provided with apartments in the new outlying neighborhoods, Thousands of others were given subsidies to rent apartments in town or to improve their own apartments. Where physically possible, extra rooms were added onto existing apartments to enable residents to remain in the neighborhoods where they had established roots.

The municipality invested heavily in upgrading the neighborhoods into which immigrants had hastily settled during the 1950s and early 1960s. It was from these neighborhoods that the so-called Black Panthers, disaffected youths demanding a better way of life, had emerged after the Six-Day War. Parks were built to provide outdoor play areas for children of large families confined in small apartments. Schools were built, sometimes at the rate of 350 classrooms a year, roads were paved, and street lights installed.

Flowers and trees planted by the municipality and regularly uprooted overnight by local youths were, at last allowed to take root as alienation gave way to a feeling of pride in the neighborhood.

The network of youth clubs and 10 community centers, created during the decade, contributed much to social stability. Disadvantaged youths, whose older brothers had drifted into antisocial and even criminal activity, found outlet for their energies and interests in these facilities.

Neighborhood schools were eliminated in an effort to reduce social tensions through integration between children from middle-and lower-class neighborhoods. Most of the city's schools ultimately contained students from such neighborhoods at a ratio of roughly 60–40. Some educators maintained that mixing does not constitute true integration, which requires intensive efforts with disadvantaged children and their parents to close the educational gap. They have acknowledged, however, that it reduces social tension.

The most difficult social problem towards the end of the decade lay not in the slums, but in the newly built neighborhoods. Entire blocks of houses were filled with slum evacuees or with new immigrants from Georgia and Bukhara, whose cultural assimilation presented difficulties. This concentration created cores of social problems from the very start. The authorities finally came to the conclusion that it was best to disperse the slum evacuees and the immigrant families – one or two to a building – so as to promote their assimilation. In order to overcome the negative image acquired by the Neveh Ya'akov neighborhood because of settlement difficulties, the Housing Ministry offered mortgage terms so attractive that it managed to sell the apartments to young Israeli couples and other socially strong elements. Neveh Ya'akov became the first of the new neighborhoods to be filled.

A violent dispute between ultra-Orthodox and secular Jews broke out at the end of 1978 when a new road was opened to the neighborhood of Ramot. Ultra-Orthodox elements, maintaining that the road violated the sanctity of the Sabbath in religious neighborhoods it skirted, demonstrated alongside the road virtually every Sabbath and frequently threw stones at cars. Despite availability of an alternate route, the dispute has continued.

CULTURAL ACHIEVEMENTS. One of the most notable changes in the city during the past decade was in the cultural climate. The Jerusalem Symphony Orchestra, which drew about 200 persons to its weekly concerts in 1970, filled the 900-seat Jerusalem Theater almost every week seven years later. Good plays brought to Jerusalem by Tel Aviv theater groups in 1970 would perform only three or four times and then to half-empty halls. By 1977, a hit show could fill as many as 16 houses. The Jerusalem Theater's subscriptions quadrupled in four years. Two lively pocket theaters opened in the city, and the renovated khan became an active center for theater and chamber music.

Part of the reason for the new climate was a changing population. The percentage of adult Jews in Jerusalem with at least one year's post-secondary education rose from 18.7 in 1961 to 25.2 in 1972. (In East Jerusalem it rose from 5.2 to 5.5% between 1967 and 1972.) Of the 72,000 increase in the Jewish population in the decade, 20,000 were new immigrants, mostly from the Soviet Union and Western countries, with a tradition of concert and theater going.

The other major factor was Mayor Kollek, who was the prime mover in creating much of the city's cultural infrastructure – the Israel Museum, the Jerusalem Theater, and the Khan. He also initiated the Mishkenot Sha'ananim guest house. His administration began building a cultural audience for the future by arranging that every schoolchild in Jerusalem attend at least one theatrical and one musical performance a year. Violinist Isaac Stern was the initiator of the Jerusalem Music Center, just behind Mishkenot, richly endowed with videotape facilities, where some of the world's greatest musicians meet with Israeli music teachers and students in order to permit them to partake directly of the musical idiom beyond Israel's borders.

The cultural life of the city was augmented by several important new facilities. These included a museum of Islamic art dedicated to the late Hebrew University scholar L.A. Mayer and a museum portraying past life in the Jewish Quarter. A new youth wing for Arab and Jewish youth was opened by the Israel Museum in East Jerusalem to accommodate spillover from the youth wing in its main building.

Freedom of Religion. Never in history had there been such religious freedom in Jerusalem as prevailed after the reunification of the city. The Muslims were unrestricted in their religious practice and the Supreme Muslim Council had de facto control of the Temple Mount. Access by non-Muslims was permitted to general visitors through the Moghrabi Gate, except during Muslim hours for prayer. For Christians, unification meant easy access between holy places on both sides of the city and the lifting of land purchase restrictions imposed by Jordan on their side of the city.

The world still did not recognize Israeli rule over the Old City and East Jerusalem. Visiting national leaders had their national flags removed from their cars when they crossed the line which formerly divided Jerusalem in two. At Independence Day receptions, the diplomatic corps still imbibed its soft drinks just outside the walls of the Old City rather than joining the main party inside the Citadel, because that would have implied their recognition of Israeli sovereignty over the Old City. The adoption of the Jerusalem Law in 1980, officially declaring the whole of Jerusalem as Israeli territory and under Israeli rule, was condemned by the United Nations Security Council – the United States abstaining – and all the countries which had embassies in Jerusalem moved them to Tel Aviv.

The Perfection of Beauty. In spite of all the changes which had taken place in Jerusalem during the 1970s, the essential character of the city remained unchanged, Its beauty remained in the stone facing on all buildings, which gave a unifying texture to all parts of the city – in the picturesque alleys and courtyards of the older neighborhoods, in the quiet and lushly planted streets of middle-class neighborhoods, and in the sculpted hills surrounding the city.

The anniversary of the reunification of the city, the 28th day of Iyyar, was proclaimed as Yom Yerushalayim, Jerusalem Day, and was celebrated with increasing enthusiasm from year to year.

In the following decade, despite the optimistic spirit of the post-Six-Day War period, Jerusalem continued to be a city of tensions, primarily between Arabs and Jews. The initial post-1967 goal of an integrated population foundered, largely as a result of a long series of attacks (often stabbing) carried out by Arabs, sometimes evoking reprisals by Jews. In 1990, in an incident on the Temple Mount, 21 Arabs were killed and over 100 injured by Israeli forces. Tensions were also exacerbated, especially during the Shamir regime, when Jews moved into Muslim neighborhoods, including the Muslim Quarter of the Old City and the village of Silwan. In many respects the city was divided almost as much as before 1967, with little social intercourse between Jews and Arabs.

The Palestinian *intifada* brought many instances of stone-throwing by Arabs at Jewish buses and cars in East Jerusalem. There was a prolonged protest shutdown of Arab stores and a sharp fall-off in the number of Jews visiting the Arab parts of the city, including the formerly crowded marketplaces of the Old City. The Palestinians reiterated that in some form Jerusalem, or part of it, must be included in any Palestinian entity. The issue was not faced squarely in the first rounds of the peace process, but Israel refused to have Jerusalemites included in the Palestinian delegation.

The population of Jerusalem at the end of 1992 was 558,000, of whom 401,000 were Jews and 157,000 Arabs (whose percentage in the total population had risen from 25 to 28 since 1967). The growth in the Jewish population was largely due to the Russian immigration, and the new suburbs of Gilo, Neveh Ya'akov, Har Nof, Pisgat Ze'ev, and Ramot mushroomed. There was also, however, an outflow of the Jewish population as many were attracted by the favorable terms offered by settlements in the West Bank within easy commuting distance of Jerusalem.

The ultra-Orthodox (*ḥaredi*) population continued to thrive and hundreds of new yeshivot and synagogues have been built in the city since 1967. There were frequent tensions with the ultra-Orthodox, who often held demonstrations to protest Sabbath desecrations and alleged desecrations of graves by archeologists or construction workers. Their projections in the population grew constantly due to immigration and a very high fertility rate, and they ultimately constituted over 20% of the Jewish population. Jerusalem's Sabbath character took a surprising turn in the late 1980s when for the first time pubs, discotheques, and some cinemas began to open on Friday nights. In the past, ultra-Orthodox protests had managed to snuff out attempts to open entertainment facilities on Sabbath eve and young Jerusalemites who sought such outlets had to travel to Tel Aviv. In time, the Friday night life in Jerusalem became so lively that it even occasionally drew Tel Aviv youth.

A quarter-century after its unification in the 1967 Six-Day War, Jerusalem continued its dynamic transformation into a modern urban center. With the completion of most of the new housing developments launched in the wake of the 1967 war, efforts focused on providing facilities to serve the vastly increased population. In the south of the city, a 15,000-seat soccer stadium was opened in 1991, providing Jerusalem with its first major sports facility. At the insistence of its foreign donor, it was named Teddy stadium, honoring Mayor Teddy Kollek. Nearby, a 100,000-square-meter enclosed shopping mall, said to be the largest in the Middle East, was opened in 1993. Opposite Jaffa Gate, development of the new Mamilla quarter as a commercial-residential link between the Old City and West Jerusalem finally began with the construction of luxury housing, more than a decade after the previous inhabitants of the area had been evacuated. An ambitious new City Hall complex was dedicated alongside the building that had filled that role for half a century.

A major new road, Road Number One, was built to bring traffic from north Jerusalem to the city center, passing near Damascus Gate. The road's three kilometer alignment followed the line that had served as no-man's-land between Israeli and Jordanian Jerusalem before the Six-Day War. A new museum complex began to take shape alongside the Israel Museum with the dedication of the Bible Lands Museum and a science museum. The Israel Supreme Court moved in 1992 from its old quarters in the center of the city to a striking new building in the Government Center. The biblical zoo also shifted to more elaborate new quarters in the south of the city. A major expansion of the Binyanei ha-Ummah Convention Center was launched to help meet the growing demand of international congresses seeking to hold their meetings in Jerusalem. In northern Jerusalem, the last and largest of the massive post-Six-Day War housing developments, Pisgat Ze'ev, with 12,000 units, was nearing completion.

On the Temple Mount in the Old City, the gold-colored annodized aluminum dome covering the Islamic shrine, the Dome of the Rock, was replaced by a dome gilded with real gold.

Teddy Kollek, first elected mayor in 1965, served in that capacity until replaced in the 1993 elections by Ehud *Olmert.

[Abraham Rabinovich]

Since the mid-1990s the city of Jerusalem has undergone many changes – demographic, economic, social, physical, and geopolitical. The main changes took place as a result of the deterioration in relations between Israel and the Palestinian Authority. The city has been affected by relentless terrorist attacks, as a result of which there has been serious economic decline; the lack of trust between Jews and Arabs living in the city has increased; the Jewish population in its part of the city has severed its link with the Arab population; and the jewel in the crown of the fight against Palestinian terrorism has been the erection of a security fence around Jerusalem, which has had considerable economic and social consequences and implications for the city's residents, Arabs and Jews. However, despite the serious security situation, there has been no let-up in the development of new neighborhoods in the city, the upgrading of infrastructure, and the addition of many new roads.

AREA AND POPULATION. Since 1993 the municipal area of Jerusalem has not changed from around 50 sq. mi. (125 sq. km.). In this respect, Jerusalem is the largest of Israel's cities (Tel Aviv covers 20 sq. mi. (50 sq. km.) and Haifa 23 sq. mi. (60 sq km). In terms of population, too, Jerusalem is Israel's largest city. As estimated by Israel's Central Bureau of Statistics, at the end of September 2005 Jerusalem had some 716,000 residents, by comparison with 591,400 living in the city in 1995. In other words, the city's population has grown by 21% in one decade.

Jerusalem's population is made up of three main groups – the Jewish secular and traditional population, the Jewish ultra-Orthodox population, and the Arab population. The following table shows the changes that have taken place in the city over the past decade in the ratio between the two main groups.

Table 1: The population of Jerusalem by population groups 1995–2004

Year	Total	%	Jews	%	Non-Jews	%
1995	591,400	100	417,000	70.5	174,400	29.5
2004	706,400	100	469,300	66.4	237,100	33.6

Source: *Jerusalem Statistical Yearbook*, Israel Research Institute, Jerusalem 1997. For 2004 data, Israel Research Institute, Jerusalem, 2005.

A comparison of the population data of the past decade shows a continuation of the trend of decline in the relative share of the Jewish population of Jerusalem in comparison with the Arab population, from 70% in 1995 to 66% at the end of 2004. If these demographic processes continue and there is no change in the municipal boundaries of Jerusalem, by 2020 the Arab population will be 42% of the total population of the city.

The distribution of the city's population in 2004 shows that slightly more than 400,000 residents live in what is usually called East Jerusalem, that is, the area annexed to the city in 1967 when Jerusalem was reunited. Of these, around 45% (some 180,000) are Jews living in Jewish neighborhoods built since 1967. These neighborhoods include Ramat Eshkol, Givat Shapira, Givat Hamivtar, Neveh Ya'acov, Gilo, Ramot Alon, East Talpiot, Pisgat Ze'ev, the Jewish Quarter, Har Ḥomah, Ramat Shelomo, and others. In other words, almost half of all the residents living in "East Jerusalem" in 2004 were Jews.

Since 1967, when the city was reunited, the population has increased by 160%. The Jewish population has increased by 135%, while the Arab population has increased by 233%. The rapid increase of the Arab population is a result of the natural reproduction rate of this group, on the one hand, and negative migration on the part of the Jewish population, on the other. The Jewish population of the city has increased by an average of 1.1% a year, whereas the Arab population has increased by an average 3.6% a year.

Since 1995, some 163,600 people have left the city and 97,100 have moved in. Over the past decade, therefore, the city has lost 66,500 residents, or an average of approximately 6,000 people a year. Around half of those leaving moved to metropolitan Jerusalem – to the towns and communities around the city (Mevasseret Zion, Ẓur Hadassah, and Ma'aleh Adumim), but the other half moved farther away to other parts of the country. Surveys have shown that most of those who left are young people with a higher education. In recent years, the young ultra-Orthodox population is also leaving the city for Jerusalem's satellite towns such as Betar Ilit and Beit Shemesh, or the more remote communities of Kiryat Sefer and Modi'in Ilit.

CHANGES IN THE CITY'S ECONOMY. Jerusalem is the poorest of Israel's large cities. The reasons for this situation are connected to the makeup of its population, part of which does not play an active role in the work force and in the city's economy. The rate of participation in the work force in Jerusalem is low by comparison with the other large cities. In 2004 it stood at only 45%, compared with 61% in Tel Aviv and 55% in Israel as a whole. The low rate of participation in the work force is due to the social-cultural structure of the city's population. Ultra-Orthodox men, for the most part, prefer to study in yeshivah and not go out to work, and Arab women also do not play a significant part in the civil workforce. If we add to this the size of the Arab and ultra-Orthodox families in the city, and the large number of dependents per wage earner, the inevitable result is a large number of families below the poverty line.

Further evidence of the economic weakness of the city is the low per-capita income in Jerusalem by comparison with other parts of the country. In 2001, per capita income in the city was only NIS 1,961, compared with NIS 4,458 in Tel Aviv or NIS 3,485 in Haifa. Both the average monthly income and the average wage for salaried and self-employed families in the city are low by comparison with Tel Aviv, Haifa, and the country as a whole. A combination of the population characteristics and the city's employment structure contribute to the low average income in Jerusalem. The low rate of participation in the work force characteristic of the Arab population and the Jewish ultra-Orthodox population has a considerable effect on the average wage of the city's residents. In addition, the city is the national capital and the center of government, with many government offices and other national institutions in which salaries are average, by comparison with a relatively small number of people employed in the higher-paying professions such as finance, insurance, and the high-tech industries. Almost 50% of employed people in Jerusalem work in public service (public administration, education, health and welfare services, etc.), by comparison with 28% in Tel Aviv. In 2004 only 14% of all employed people in Jerusalem worked in business and financial services, as compared with 31% in Tel Aviv. The percentage of those employed in industry is also low in the city, 7% as against 10% in Tel Aviv and 17% in Israel as a whole. The relatively low level of salaries in the city affects the scope and scale of consumption by the residents, and the commercial life of the city.

In addition to the fundamental factors accompanying the economy of the city for many years, over the past decade Jerusalem has been forced to contend with serious terrorist attacks, more than any other place in the country, as Palestinian terrorism saw the city as a central target for its activities. Around 60% of all terrorist activity in the second Intifada took place in Jerusalem, exacting the heavy cost of more than 500 dead and thousands wounded. The main branches of the city's economy that were affected were commerce and tourism. Jerusalem is a tourist city of the first order. Not a tourist comes to Israel without spending a few days in Jerusalem. As a result of the terrorist attacks, tourism was seriously affected. There was a drastic reduction in the number of overnight stays in hotels in the city, from 3.4 million nights in 2000 to 1.2 million in 2002. Overnight stays by tourists from overseas dropped even more sharply, from 2.9 million in 2000 to 639,000 in 2002. Tourism, which, as mentioned, is one of the most important economic branches in the city, recovered to a certain degree in the course of 2005, with the number of overnight hotel stays in the city increasing to 1.9 million. The drop in the tourist branch hit the entire network of tourist services, including tour guides, restaurants, jewelry and souvenir shops and many other services. Many businesses closed, and others faced bankruptcy. According to the data of the municipal Chamber of Commerce, more than 1,400 businesses closed during the worst years. Hardest hit were the merchants of East Jerusalem and the Old City. Tourist traffic, especially domestic Israeli tourism, stopped coming to East Jerusalem. Even at the beginning of 2006, commerce in the city had not completely recovered, despite the fact that the relative calm of 2005 brought more and more tourists and Israelis back to Jerusalem.

An analysis of the municipal *arnona* tax data since 1995 shows that despite the bad years, there has been an increase in the number of offices and businesses in the city. In 1995 Jerusalem had 15,445 businesses and offices paying rates to the municipality, and by 2004 these had been joined by more than 3,100 new businesses. There has also been an increase in the number of factories and workshops (more than 700) during the past decade.

One of the industries that has succeeded in establishing a foothold in the city is the biotechnology industry, basing itself on Jerusalem's unique advantage: its proximity to academic institutions, research bodies, and leading medical centers. In 2005 there were some 60 biotechnology companies in the city, employing 1,500 people. Jerusalem is home to almost 25% of Israel's biotechnology industry. The city hosts important factories in this field, such as Teva, AVX, and others. Jerusalem also has the largest concentration of technology incubators, intended to support high-tech ventures. In the past decade one such incubator (the Van Leer Jerusalem Technology Incubator) accompanied the establishment of more than 50 successful start-up companies. Another incubator (JVP) dealt with more than 30 projects in the past decade, from which a number of successful companies developed.

The city has a number of successful industrial areas, including Har Ḥotzvim, which has around a quarter of a million square meters of knowledge-intensive industries such as Intel, Teva, Sigma, Phasecom, AVX, NDS, and others. Over the past decade the area has developed considerably, and houses companies such as Amdocs, Mango, Foxcom, and others.

Another technology park was established in the course of the last decade in the Malkhah neighborhood (Malkhah Technological Park), on an area of around 60,000 square meters, employing 1,400 people. Other technological parks are located at the Givat Ram campus of the university and in Pisgat Ze'ev.

In addition to the high-tech industry, which is very important to Jerusalem, the city also has other areas of employment that have developed considerably in the past decade, such as the Givat Shaul industrial zone, with a built-up area today of 350,000 square meters. Other parts of the city that have developed are the industrial zones of Talpiot and Atarot. The latter has suffered severely in the past five years as a result of its location on the northern border of Jerusalem, and many factories have abandoned it and moved out of the city.

DEVELOPMENT OF THE EDUCATION SYSTEM. The education system in Jerusalem is the largest and most complex municipal system in Israel. There are three main frameworks in the city's education system: state education, ultra-Orthodox education, and Arab education. Each of these frameworks contains secondary streams. State education includes the state and the state-religious streams; ultra-Orthodox education is divided between independent education and the *talmud torah* schools; and Arab education includes the municipal system, a private system, a church system, and the Muslim Waqf system.

The main change that has taken place in recent years is the constant increase in the number of students in the ultra-Orthodox and Arab sectors, and the gradual decrease in numbers in the state and state-religious education system. The table below shows the changes:

Table 2: Students in Jerusalem's education systems 1995 to 2005

Education system	1994/1995	2004/2005
State and state religious education	72,308 (50.1)	62,339 (33.2)
Ultra-Orthodox education	51,250 (35.5)	83,223 (44.4)
Arab education*	20,748 (14.4)	42,063 (22.4)
Total / percentage	144, 306 (100)	187,625 (100)

* Not including students in private, church, and Waqf education, representing at all times half the total number of Arab students in the city.

The great decrease over the past decade in the state and state-religious education sector, from 50% of all students in the city to only 33%, can clearly be seen. The ultra-Orthodox sector has increased by 9%, and the Arab sector by 8%.

Higher education. University education in Jerusalem has also undergone changes in the past decade. The number of students at the Hebrew University continues to decline as a percentage of all students in the country. In 1995, 20,300 students studied for all levels at the Hebrew University, at the time representing 21% of all students in Israel. In the 2003 academic year, 120,555 students studied at universities around the country, and 21,598 of these studied in Jerusalem, representing 18% of all university students in Israel.

Technological education in Jerusalem received a boost with the opening of the College of Technology. Technological education in Jerusalem includes a number of other colleges such as Hadassah College, the Lev Institute of Technology, and other institutions.

CHANGES IN HOUSING. In 1995 the Jerusalem Municipality collected residential rates from 149,400 apartments. At the end of 2004, it collected residential rates from 180,500 apartments, 144,300 of them (80%) in the Jewish sector and 36,200 (20%) in the Arab sector. Since 1995 some 31,000 apartments have been added in the city. 19,000 of these are in the Jewish sector (61%) and 12,000 in the Arab sector (39%).

New neighborhoods have been added, which has considerably increased the area used for housing. In the south of the city, between Bethlehem and Kibbutz Ramat Raḥel, the Har Ḥomah neighborhood was under construction, housing 2,000 families and slated to have a total of 6,500 housing units. Between Beit Hakerem and Bayit Vegan the new neighborhood of Ramat Beit Hakerem has been built, with 2,200 housing units. Another new neighborhood in the south of Jerusalem was being built on the land of Kibbutz Ramat Raḥel. Another was under construction on the site of the former Allenby Camp, on the road to Bethlehem and Hebron. At the southwestern edge of Jerusalem two new neighborhoods have been established: Manaḥat, close to the stadium named after Teddy Kollek, Jerusalem's legendary mayor, and Givat Masu'ah, near Moshav Orah on the fringes of Jerusalem's municipal boundaries. These two neighborhoods have around 4,200 housing units. To the north of Jerusalem (on the Shu'afat ridge) a religious ultra-Orthodox neighborhood called Ramat Shelomo was being built with 1,800 housing units. In the northeastern part of the city the Pisgat Ze'ev neighborhood, the largest of the Jewish neighborhoods built after the unification of the city in June 1967, continued to be developed. The main construction since 1995 was in the eastern and southern parts of the neighborhood, including a large commercial center at its heart. The neighborhood has also expanded northwards, joining up with Neveh Ya'acov, the northernmost Jewish neighborhood in the city.

Residential construction has naturally not passed over the older neighborhoods in the heart of Jerusalem. Many houses have been built on vacant lots in older neighborhoods such as Mekor Ḥayyim and Talpiot, additional stories have been added to existing buildings in the center of town, and in historic neighborhoods such as Rehavia, Talbieh, the German Colony, Baka, Beit Hakerem, and the ultra-Orthodox neighborhoods of Geula, Kerem Avraham, Reḥovot ha-Bukharim, Tel Arza, and Mekor Barukh, which have gradually become areas occupied by ultra-Orthodox Jewish residents.

Large-scale construction has also taken place in the Arab sector of Jerusalem, as shown by the statistics above. The form of construction in the Arab sector is different from that in the Jewish sector; there is almost no construction by public companies, most of it being private, family construction. The main concentrations of building have been in the northern Arab neighborhoods of Beit Hanina and Shu'afat, but also in the neighborhoods encircling the Old City, such as Ras el-Amud, Wadi Kadum, and A-Sheikh. In the residential areas of the Bedouin in the southeast of the city (Sawahara al-Arabia) there has also been considerable construction, as well as in A-Tur, Abu Tor, and the southern villages of Zur Baher, Umm Tuba, and Beit Safafa. The main change in the form of Arab construction in the past decade has been one of scale; from single and two-story houses to multistory buildings. In addition to Arab construction within the Jerusalem municipal area, many houses have also been constructed outside the municipal boundaries, mainly in the area of A-Ram, north of Neveh Ya'acov, where, in practice, a new town has grown up. Between Ma'aleh Adumim and Jerusalem the town of A-Zayim, established by residents of A-Tur, has also expanded considerably and considerable construction has taken place in recent years.

It can therefore be seen that the competition between the two people, Israelis and Palestinians, over Jerusalem continues unabated and each side tries to create facts on the ground to the best of its ability, capturing land by means of residential construction. This is based on the assumption that it is the spatial distribution of buildings that will determine the future borders of the state.

THE CONSTRUCTION OF INSTITUTIONS. In addition to new residential neighborhoods and increasing the density of older neighborhoods, over the past decade there has been considerable construction of public, government, and administrative institutions in the city. The Safra Municipal Complex was completed and serves all the city's residents; the Supreme Court was inaugurated at Givat Ram; and new government offices were added to the Government Campus: the Ministry of Foreign Affairs, the Ministry of Tourism, the Ministry of Trade and Industry, the Ministry of Labor, and the Israel Land Administration. The Knesset and the Israel Convention Center both have new wings. The old Sha'arei Zedek Hospital in Jaffa Road has been renovated and taken over by the management of the Israel Broadcasting Authority, and not far off, at the Western entrance to the city, a new central bus station has been built. On Mt. Herzl the Yad Vashem Museum has been built and the Herzl Museum has been renovated. Beit Shmuel in the former Mamilla neighborhood has been enlarged, and near the Yemin Moshe neighborhood the Begin Center has been constructed. New buildings have also been constructed on the Mt. Scopus University campus: the Yitzhak Rabin Jewish Sciences building, the sports center, and student hostels. Kiryat Moriah in Talpiot has been expanded, and, on the borders of the German Colony, the Hartmann Education Center has been constructed.

A number of new hotels were built during the period, completing the city's accommodation network. Three of these were built along the "seam line" of Route 1, close to the former Mandelbaum Gate; two in Herzl Blvd.; and one in King David St. as part of the Mamilla renovation. Many religious institutions and yeshivot were built, the largest being the Belz Yeshivah in Romema. The two large promenades built along the Armon Hanatziv ridge (Hass and Sherover) have been joined by the Goldman Promenade, continuing eastward to Armon Hanatziv and the new neighborhood of Nofei Zion. The Biblical zoo has also been expanded and has a new sculpture garden.

INFRASTRUCTURES AND ROADS. The past decade has seen considerable expansion of roads and infrastructures in the city. In terms of the water supply, the fourth pipeline from the coastal plain has been completed, and a big reservoir underneath the sports field of Ziv School in Beit Hakerem has been built. The effluent treatment system has been completed and a waste water purification plant has been built for the entire western and southern drainage basin in Naḥal Sorek. The supply of electricity to the city has been considerably increased, and the power substation in Emek Refaim has been renovated.

The new roads have really revolutionized the city. First and foremost, the main north–south traffic artery, Begin Blvd., was completed and a new access road to the city was developed, joining up with the Ma'aleh Beit Horon–Modi'in road (Route 443). The tunnels road southward to the Eẓyon bloc has been completed, as well as a new east–west road linking Hebron Road to the neighborhood of East Talpiot. The past decade has been characterized by the construction of new road tunnels. Five new tunnels have been constructed: the tunnels on Route 60 to the Eẓyon bloc; the Mt. Scopus tunnel toward Ma'aleh Adumim, creating a new entrance to Jerusalem from the east; the tunnel at the foot of the Old City walls under Ha-Ẓanḥanim Road, linking the Jaffa Gate to Route 1; and the Begin Blvd. tunnel under the entrance to the city. Another new road making use of bridges joins Pisgat Ze'ev and Neveh Ya'acov to the French Hill junction, encompassing the historic Ramallah Road. Another road under construction in 2006 in Emek ha-Arazim is Route 9, creating an additional entrance to the city from the west and linking the Motza junction with the Ramot junction and Begin Blvd. at the foot of Har Ḥotzvim.

In preparation for the construction of a light railway in Jerusalem, new public transport lanes have been laid along Jaffa Road, Hebron Road, Keren Hayesod St., and Herzl Blvd. Near Mt. Herzl, work started on the big parking lot which is part of the planned mass transport system.

CULTURE, ART AND ENTERTAINMENT. Jerusalem is a city with many cultural and art institutes. The city has more than 30 museums, hundreds of galleries, and other cultural institutions. Over the past decade the appearance and content of Morasha's Museum on the Seam, also known as Turgeman Post, has changed; the Underground Prisoners Museum in the Russian Compound has been renovated; and a new wing has been added to the Bernard Bloomfield Science Museum. The Menachem Begin Heritage Center, housing exhibitions and lecture halls, has been built in the area overlooking the Old City and Mt. Zion. A number of theaters have also been established in the city in the past decade, including the Laboratory Theater in the old train station, the Noah's Ark Theater, the Cylinder Theater, the Comma Theater, and the Yellow Submarine. The Ma'aleh Association for Television and Cinema Studies has also been established. A number of new bands and ensembles have been formed, including Musica Aeterna, the Ankor Choir, Arabesque, A-Capella, and others.

New entertainment districts have developed in the city, in the neighborhood of the old railway station in Emek Refaim, along with many bars and restaurants in the area of Shlomzion Hamalka St., Naḥalat Shiva, and Monbaz St. in the center of town.

POLITICAL, MUNICIPAL AND GEOPOLITICAL CHANGES. Since Teddy Kollek lost the mayoral elections in 1993 there has been a gradual revolution in Jerusalem in terms of municipal politics. The ultra-Orthodox public had a decisive weight in the upset in the 1993 election, and the weight of the ultra-Orthodox voter in the city has been gradually increasing. This may be set against the low turnout by the city's Arab population, which has never been above a few percent. In the 1998 election the Shas movement increased its hold considerably and the high rate of voting among the city's ultra-Orthodox population made United Torah Judaism the largest faction in the municipality. In January 2003 the city's mayor, Ehud Olmert, decided to take up Prime Minister Ariel Sharon's offer and join the government. As a result, elections in the city were brought forward and the candidate of the religious United Torah Judaism party, Uri *Lupoliansky, was elected with a majority of 52%. For the first time in the electoral history of Jerusalem, the religious parties achieved a majority in the City Council. In many respects this was an internal political revolution affecting the city's image, since despite the democratic elections, a situation had arisen in which representatives of one-third of the Jewish population of the city held the reins of municipal government, a situation that was not viewed with satisfaction by the secular majority, whose voter turnout at the municipal elections was lower than its numerical weight in the city.

The changes in the national geopolitical sphere are taking place against the background of an increased awakening of Palestinian nationalism, the failure of the Oslo accords, and the loss of trust between the two population groups, Jewish and Arab, in the city. The events of the first and second Intifada years and increasing Palestinian terrorism created serious tension between Jews and Arabs in Israel in general and in Jerusalem in particular. The two populations have taken a mutual step back from each other, and an ethnically polarized system has emerged in Jerusalem. The Arabs have withdrawn into their neighborhoods, and so have the Jews. Visits by Jews to the Old City and by Arabs to the Israeli city center in West Jerusalem have ceased. The security incidents and the curtailment of Palestinian movement in and around the city have deepened the economic gap between the two population groups, and exacerbated the state of public services in the eastern part of the city.

The terrorist attacks led the government of Israel, under pressure of Israeli public opinion, to take the dramatic decision to erect a physical barrier between the Palestinian and Israeli populations. Implementation of this decision in the Jerusalem area has led to a far-reaching change in the city's status, its economy, the welfare of its Arab residents, and its appearance.

THE SECURITY FENCE. Construction of the security envelope around the city is perhaps the most dramatic change to have taken place in Jerusalem since its reunification in June 1967. The route of the fence around Jerusalem was drawn up largely on the basis of security considerations, and this is also its purpose. However, it creates a new and difficult situation for a large part of the Arab population. The longer-term influence of the fence will affect the entire city, including its Jewish population. The security fence has been under construction in the Jerusalem area since 2003 and was due to be completed in 2006. In all other parts of the country, along Israel's border, the fence separates the Palestinian population from the Israeli population. In Jerusalem the situation is different. In practice, the fence separates Palestinians who are resident in the city and hold Israeli identity cards from other Palestinians resident in the West Bank and other Arab residents of Jerusalem who have moved out to live in suburbs outside the city. The fence is being erected, for the most part, along the municipal boundary and includes 230,000 Arab residents within the city. In certain areas it also deviates from the path of the municipal boundary and excludes a number of Arab Jerusalem neighborhoods. As a result of the fact that the fence cuts neighborhoods off from the city, tens of thousands of Arabs holding Israeli identity cards remain outside the fence. These people need to come into Jerusalem every morning for studies, work, medical services, to visit relatives, for prayers etc. As residents of the city, they are entitled to do so by law. Thousands of others, who also carry Israeli identity cards, have moved, over the years, to suburbs outside the city and today they find themselves outside the fence. The immediate demographic result of the situation that has arisen has been the migration of thousands of families back into the city. Their return to Jerusalem has created a serious housing problem, an increase in the cost of real estate in East Jerusalem, and a considerable worsening of residential density. All these do not enhance the socio-economic situation in Jerusalem. Furthermore, the extra Palestinian population upsets the delicate demographic balance between Jews and Arabs in Jerusalem. The economic situation of many of the city's Arabs and the residents of the surrounding villages is very poor, due to the loss of work places, the loss of consumers, and difficulties of access. The health service and education system in East Jerusalem have also been adversely affected, and many people have been cut off from their relatives.

It is still difficult to assess the full impact of the fence on the social and economic status of Jerusalem and on future relations between Arabs and Jews in the city. It is even harder to anticipate the reactions and behavior of the city's Arab residents. A large number of them have been caused personal hardship and a considerable degree of frustration and anger. In such a situation this frustration and suffering is likely to be channeled by extremists toward hostile actions.

Many questions remained unanswered, such as: What will be the future status of the security fence when peace talks with the Palestinians are renewed? To what degree will the fence affect reciprocal relations between Jerusalem and its hinterland? Does the fence not return the city to its position as a border town, similar to its situation between 1949 and 1967? Other questions relate to the future civil status of Arab residents holding Israeli identity cards who have been excluded by the fence; to the efficient functioning of passages through the fence; and to the effect that the fence will have on tourism and pilgrimage between Jerusalem and Bethlehem.

THE JERUSALEM METROPOLITAN AREA. In the past decade the Jerusalem metropolitan area, spreading from Hebron in the south to the Shilo Valley in the north and from Jericho in the east to Beit Shemesh in the west has undergone considerable change. Until the end of the 1990s, greater Jerusalem functioned as a single economic unit with economic, social, and cultural ties between the main city – Jerusalem – and the Palestinian and Israeli communities around it. Gradually, as a result of the security incidents and the government of Israel's response to them, the communities of the Palestinian area are cutting themselves off from Jerusalem. The city continues to maintain economic and cultural ties with the Israeli communities in the area, both those within the Jerusalem district to the west and the Israeli communities in Judea and Samaria; Betar Ilit, Efrat, and the Eẓyon bloc to the south of Jerusalem; Ma'aleh Adumim, Kefar Adumim, Adam, and other small communities to the east; Pesagot, Beit El, Ofra, Mikhmash, Givat Ze'ev, new Givon and Bet Horon to the north and northwest of the city.

In 1990, the entire metropolitan population (not including the city of Jerusalem) numbered 600,000 residents. Only around 17% of them (100,000) were Jews. 48% of the Jewish residents lived in the Jerusalem district within the Green Line, and 52% in the communities of Judea and Samaria. Fifteen years later, at the end of 2004, the population of this same area was estimated at 1,597,000 residents. The Jewish population was 22,000, 45% of them living in the communities of Judea and Samaria and 55% in the Jerusalem district within the Green Line. The Jewish population in the metropolitan area increased during this period by 115%, as against an increase of 27% in the Jewish population within Jerusalem. The population of the Jewish communities of Judea and Samaria increased by 90%, whereas within the Green Line the population grew at a higher rate of 145% during the same period.

The large Jewish communities in metropolitan Jerusalem today are Beit Shemesh (65,000), Ma'aleh Adumim (30,000), Betar Ilit (27,000), Mevaseret Zion (22,000), and Givat Ze'ev (11,000).

The Arab population of the same area numbered some 500,000 residents in 1990 and 1,132,000 residents in 2004, an increase of 126%. The relative weight of the Jewish population in the metropolitan area within Judea and Samaria increased slightly and stood at the end of 2004 at 20% as against 17% 15 years ago.

Metropolitan Jerusalem only partially operates as a single functional area. The majority of the metropolitan area is populated by Palestinians, who are cut off in practice from Jerusalem, a situation that will be exacerbated when the security fence around the city is completed. This fact damages the economy and the centrality of Jerusalem as a metropolitan city for all the residents of the region. It serves as a metropolitan city for only 20% of the region's population – the Jewish population.

[Israel Kimhi (2nd ed.)]

GEOGRAPHY AND ARCHAEOLOGY

Geography

Jerusalem is located on the ridge of the Judean Mountains between the mountains of Beth-El in the north and of Hebron in the south. To the west of the city are slopes of the Judean Mountains, and to the east lies the Judean desert, which descends to the Dead Sea. The geographical position of Jerusalem is linked to the morphological structure of the Judean Mountains, which appear as one solid mass unbreached by valleys, although vales and ravines are found on their western and eastern descents. This unbroken length of mountains turns the city into a fortress dominating a considerable area. Its position at the crossroads leading from north to south and from west to east enhances its importance: only by ascending to its plateau is it possible to cross the mountain. The road through the length of the mountains follows the plateau, and any deviation to east or west meets with steep ravines on one side and deep canyons on the other. This road, connecting Hebron, Bethlehem, Jerusalem, Ramallah, and Nablus (Shechem), is of the utmost consequence, and Jerusalem is located on its axis, at the very point where it crosses the road from the coast to the Jordan Valley. Jerusalem is about 9 to 10 mi. (15 to 17 km.) from the western boundary of the Judean Mountains and only about a mile (2 km.) from their eastern boundary.

THE CLIMATE. Jerusalem's climate is Mediterranean, with a rainy, temperate winter and a hot, completely dry summer; there is a high percentage of solar radiation throughout the year, especially in the summer.

The annual rainfall in Jerusalem is about 20 in. (500 mm.). The rainy season continues from September to May, and approximately 30% of the annual rain falls by December, with 40% in February and March. There are about 47 rainy days annually on the average. On most of these days there is about 0.2 in. (5 mm.) of rainfall; 1.2 in. (30 mm.) of daily rainfall occurs about five or six times during a season; and once or twice there is as much as 2 in. (50 mm.). Particularly heavy rainfalls were recorded between Nov. 5 and Nov. 9, 1938, amounting to 8 in. (200 mm.) or 30% of the precipitation of that year. In the period from Dec. 13 to Dec. 23, 1951, over 14 in. (358 mm.) fell (57% of the annual rainfall). In the 100 years during which records of rainfall were kept (1840–1950), there were two years with less than 12 in. (300 mm.) of rainfall in the entire wet season, six years with less than 16 in. (400 mm.), and three years with more than 40 in. (1000 mm.). Snow in Jerusalem is infrequent. When it does fall, it occurs mainly in January and February and can last about four or five days.

The average annual temperature in Jerusalem is 66° F (19° C). The average temperature in August, the hottest month, is 75° F (24° C) and in the coldest month, January, is 50° F (10° C). The average daily temperature from December to February is usually under 52° F (11° C). From the middle of February until the beginning of April, the temperature rises to an average of about 59° F (15° C). At the end of April it rises to about 68° F (20° C) and remains at that level until the end of July. In August it reaches 77° F (25° C), and from then until the end of October the daily average is about 68° F (20° C). The minimum temperature in the month of January goes down to 41° F (5° C). The maximum temperature during the *sharav* (heat wave) reaches 95° F (35° C). The regular wind in Jerusalem is a western one, but occasionally it is northwesterly or southwesterly. Winds do not originate in Jerusalem and its vicinity. Jerusalem is subject to heat waves during the months of May and June, as well as September and October. These periods are characterized by intensive heat and low humidity and usually last a few days. The humidity drops 30–40% below the average and the heat increases by about 27° F (15° C). The average daily humidity in Jerusalem is about 62%. The humidity drops until noon and rises toward evening. The amount of dew in Jerusalem reaches 0.8–1 in. (20–25 mm.) as an average during the 100 to 150 annual nights of dew.

FLORA. In Jerusalem, remnants of ancient trees are to be found, including the Jerusalem pine (*Pinus halepensis*, the tallest forest tree in Israel), the gall oak (*Quercus infectoria*), the common oak (*Quercus calliprinos*), the Tabor oak (*Quercus ithaburensis*), the Palestine terebinth (*Pistacia palaestina*), the mastic terebinth (*Pistacia tenticus*), the arbutus, and the wild olive. Traces of ancient vegetation were found in Tel Arzah, on Mount Scopus, on the French Hill, in the Valley of the Cross, the German Colony, Ein Kerem, Bet ha-Kerem, Talpiyyot, and Agron Street.

BOUNDARIES. The only boundary of Jerusalem that remained unchanged after the Six-Day War (1967) was its western boundary. It descends southwest from Har Ḥoẓevim to the village of Mei-Nefto'aḥ (Liftā) and west to Har ha-Menuḥot and from there to Kefar Sha'ul, Bet Zayit, Ein Kerem, the Hadassah medical center, Kefar Shalma, and Ir Gannim. The new boundaries of the city were extended north, east, and south. North of Mount Ḥoẓevim, the boundary includes the villages of Shaʿfāṭ, New Beit Ḥanīnā, and Qalandiya to the airport at Atarot, and then returns eastward to the Jerusalem-Ramallah highway, encompassing within the boundaries of the city the hilly area between Jerusalem and Atarot. The eastern boundary includes the natural mountainous framework of Jerusalem: Mount Scopus, the Mount of Olives, the village of Al-Ṭūr, the Old City, and the village of Silwān. The new boundary on the south includes the villages of Ṣūr Bāhir and Beit Ṣafāfā and continues the length of the Valley of Rephaim to the juncture with the western border. Greater Jerusalem within these borders has an area of 26,250 acres (105,000 dunams) and forms one organic unit.

TOPOGRAPHY. The watershed of the region passes through the city in a north-south direction via Mount Scopus, the Sanhedriyyah Quarter, Romemah, Maḥaneh Yehudah, Terra Sancta, the YMCA, Givat Ḥananyah, the Mandatory Government House (later the headquarters of the UN observers), Talpiyyot, and Ramat Raḥel. There are some mountain ridges branching off the watershed to the east and west. On the low eastern ridge, which descends to the river bed of Kidron, the ancient city was built. A western ridge divides the Christian and Armenian quarters of the Old City and ends on Mount Zion. It was here that the Upper City was built. A number of ridges penetrate to the west and south of Jerusalem: the ridge of Beit Yisrael, the ridge on which the Mandatory Government House stands, the ridge of Ha-Kiryah (Israel government center), the Kiryat ha-Yovel ridge, the Gonen ridge, and the ridge of Ir Gannim. The ridges and the branches of the mountains form valleys that greatly influence the structure of the city. These are divided into two groups: those facing Naḥal Kidron in the east, and those facing Naḥal Sorek in the west. Naḥal Ben Hinnom, which demarcates the southwestern boundary of historical Jerusalem, flows into Naḥal Kidron. Another tributary of the Kidron is Naḥal Egozim, which divides the Bet Yisrael Quarter from Mount Scopus. Naḥal Sorek borders Jerusalem on the north and the west. In the south the Valley of Refa'im is a tributary of Naḥal Sorek.

The topography of Jerusalem forms five main natural basins. The eastern basin includes the Old City and the drainage basin of Kidron and Ben Hinnom. The northern basin includes the Romemah, Tel Arzah, and Sanhedriyyah quarters. The southern basin includes the German and Greek colonies, Ge'ulim, Talbieh, Mekor Ḥayyim, Bet ha-Kerem, Bayit va-Gan, Kiryat ha-Yovel, Ein Kerem, and Ir Gannim. The central basin includes the government center (Ha-Kiryah), The Hebrew University, and the Israel Museum. As most of the ridges and the valleys extend in a north to south direction, only a few extending from east to west, the city has developed lengthwise. Mount Scopus is 2,700 ft. (827 m.) and the Mount of

Olives is 2,640 ft. (805 m.) high, whereas the Old City is some 200–260 ft. (60–80 m.) lower. Mount Herzl and Bayit va-Gan are 2,340 ft. (835 m.) high, whereas nearby Ein Kerem is only 2,230–2,300 ft. (650–700 m.) high.

[Elisha Efrat]

THE OLD CITY. The present-day walls of the Old City, built from 1536 under the Turkish sultan Suleiman the Magnificent, enclose a smaller area than that of the Second Temple period. The location of its seven gates (Herod's, Damascus, and New Gates in the north, Jaffa Gate in the west, Zion and Dung Gates in the south, and St. Stephen's (Lions') Gate in the east) is thought to be identical to that of the gates of antiquity.

Inside the walls of the Old City, where all the inhabitants lived until the middle of the 19th century, four quarters are distinguished: in the northwest corner, the Christian Quarter, grouped around the Church of the Holy Sepulcher; in the southwest, the Armenian Quarter; in the center and northeast, the Muslim Quarter; and, in the south, the Jewish Quarter. From St. Stephen's Gate westward to the Holy Sepulcher runs the Via Dolorosa, which passes through the Muslim Quarter and is flanked by several churches, monasteries, and Christian charitable institutions. The artificially flattened ground on Mt. Moriah, where the Jewish Temple stood, later became the site of two of the holiest shrines of Islam: the Dome of the Rock (Omar Mosque) and the Aqṣā Mosque. The Temple Area is surrounded by the colossal Herodian enclosure wall, preserved in the east, south, and west; a larger section of the Western ("Wailing") Wall, the most venerated site in Jewish tradition, was bared to view after 1967, and archaeological excavations around the southern edges of the Temple Mount have added to the knowledge of the city's structure in the Second Temple period and later. Between the Western Wall and the Armenian Quarter lies the Jewish Quarter, which had to surrender in the 1948 fighting. Under Jordanian rule, this quarter deteriorated, and all its synagogues were systematically destroyed. Following the Six-Day War (1967) reconstruction was started there.

THE NEW CITY. As a result of the gradual population rise, space between the walls of the Old City became ever more crowded, particularly in the narrow Jewish Quarter. Jews were therefore the first to found new quarters outside the walls; in 1858 Mishkenot Sha'ananim was built west of the Old City, soon followed by Yemin Moshe and by Naḥalat Shivah in the northwest. At about the same time, churches began to establish hostels and other institutions outside the walls for the benefit of the growing flow of Christian pilgrims: the buildings of the Russian Compound are notable among these.

The New City spread mainly toward the northwest along the road leading to the port of Jaffa. From this direction most goods were brought, and pilgrims, both Jewish and Christian, arrived from overseas and enlivened trade in the city. In the first Jewish quarters the houses were crowded together, primarily for security reasons; the Yemin Moshe quarter was even surrounded by a wall and its gates closed every evening. Those first quarters which the inhabitants built exclusively with their own means (e.g., Naḥalat Shivah) were shabby in appearance and lacked uniformity in style and layout. Others, where construction was partly or wholly financed by philanthropists (like Yemin Moshe, which was aided by Sir Moses Montefiore and bears his name), were better planned, generally with rows of houses of one or two stories. The Me'ah She'arim quarter took on particular importance. Founded in 1874 by pious Jews from the Old City, it has remained a stronghold of Jewish Orthodoxy.

At the end of the 19th century, the first garden suburbs made their appearance; those of non-Jews (e.g., German Colony and Greek Colony, Katamon, etc.) preceded modern Jewish quarters (Reḥavyah, Beit ha-Kerem, Talpiyyot, etc.). In all these, attempts were made to lend beauty to the individual house and surrounding garden and to plan streets, water, sewage and electricity networks along rational lines, while details were kept within the framework of the urban outline scheme.

The British Mandatory authorities aimed to preserve Jerusalem's beauty and historical treasures. All outer house walls had to be built of the fine local stone, which is both durable and in harmony with the landscape. Rules limiting the height of structures and floor space percentage covering the ground were issued, and care was taken to retain open spaces and preserve the skyline, particularly of sites of natural beauty and historical interest. An effort was made to fit the main roads to traffic densities, and a ring road was planned to connect the outer suburbs with each other. On the other hand, the authorities rejected industrialization as not befitting Jerusalem's character, and they did not encourage a rapid population growth.

CITY PLANNING (1948–1967). In the first years of the State of Israel, the most pressing tasks were repair of the damage caused in the War of Independence, absorption of new immigrants, and preparation of a new outline scheme fitting in with the border which then divided the city between Israel and Jordan; at a later stage came zoning into residential, commercial, administrative, cultural, and industrial units.

With The Hebrew University campus, the Knesset, and the Israel Museum as pivotal points, a large center of legislative, administrative, cultural, and commercial institutions was laid out. The whole area was well integrated in the general plan of the capital. Care was taken to preserve and restore sites of archaeological and historical interest, to maintain open spaces, and to develop green belts.

Jerusalem's hilly topography was taken into account: the ridges and upper slopes, which are well drained in winter and cool and agreeable in summer, were reserved for building, while valleys were earmarked for parks, gardens, and fruit orchards.

The de facto borders that surrounded Israel left the west as the only direction for Jerusalem's expansion. It was therefore decided to let the outline scheme hinge on the Binyenei ha-Ummah (Convention Center) at Romemah, the dominant height of the Jerusalem urban area which lies astride the main western entrance of the city. Accordingly, the existing commercial center was planned to expand northwestward to Romemah. The buildings of the Government ministries (Ha-Kiryah) and the new Knesset edifice, surrounded by lawns and gardens, adjoin this area to the south. Still further south lie the impressive campus of the university and the National Library, the Israel Museum, and related institutions. This whole complex is thus situated between older quarters in the east and the expansion belt of residential suburbs (Kiryat Moshe, Bet ha-Kerem, Bayit va-Gan, Kiryat ha-Yovel, etc.) in the west and southwest. The Hadassah Medical Center is the extreme point of westward expansion.

Contrary to the British view, industry is now regarded as an element indispensable to Jerusalem's economy. Owing to the city's geographical position, light industries are easiest to develop here. In addition to the enlarged existing industrial area at Tel Arza in the northwest, a second, at Givat Sha'ul in the west, was developed.

Owing to economic and security considerations, the planning authorities regarded the road system linking the capital to the rest of the State as particularly important. After the War of Independence, a single highway to Tel Aviv in the northwest was open; the railway line became usable again after border corrections in the Israel-Jordan armistice of 1949. Since then, additional roads, which converge on the city from the west and southwest, were constructed.

As elsewhere in the country, the large new suburbs in the west and southwest (Katamon, Kiryat ha-Yovel, etc.) were laid out as self-contained neighborhood units. Prior to 1967, they had to absorb many newcomers settling in Jerusalem and to aid in thinning out the overpopulated older quarters further east, some of which had been earmarked for replanning and reconstruction. In an outer circle around these suburbs spread a green belt of parks, forests, and playgrounds. Landscaping and planting of parks and lawns accentuated sites of historical interest all over the city. Although the law prescribing the facing of buildings with natural stone was relaxed in part of the city to prevent unnecessary rises in the cost of popular housing, it was retained for all representative sections of the city.

Growth And Planning After Reunification (1967). Immediately after the Six-Day War, all military installations, fences, and shell-proof concrete walls which had separated the two parts of the city were removed, and the connecting streets and roads paved and opened. Next, unseemly structures obstructing the view of the Old City wall were torn down, the wall itself and its gates painstakingly repaired, and the first gardens of a planned green peripheral belt planted in front of it. Inside the Old City, hovels were demolished close to the Western Wall. Two additional rows of its ashlars, hidden in the rubble, were uncovered and a wide square in front cleared, paved, and rendered suitable for prayer. The reconstruction of the Jewish Quarter and its historic synagogues was started and institutions of religious study moved in, their pupils forming the nucleus of the Old City's renewed Jewish community. South of the Temple Mount, archaeological excavations were started early in 1968. The slight damage caused to Christian churches and institutions during the fighting was speedily repaired and church building and renovation work (e.g., on the Holy Sepulcher), which had been in progress prior to June 1967, were resumed. Jerusalem's boundaries were redrawn, giving the capital a municipal area exceeding 100 sq. km., the largest in the country (see Boundaries, above).

One of the main problems of the Jerusalem master plan lay in reconciling the desire for a continuous built-up area with the necessity to preserve and enhance numerous historical sites, sacred to three world religions, such as the entire Old City, the Kidron and Ben Hinnom Gorges, the "City of David" to the south, Mount Scopus and the Mount of Olives, and many more. Both inside and outside the Old City walls, gardens were laid out or were planned, while other areas to the east and south were earmarked as public open spaces or sites for preservation and reconstruction.

Another difficult task, which after June 1967 assumed great urgency, lay in securing efficient traffic arteries leading through and around Jerusalem. The existent main thoroughfares had become totally inadequate, particularly Jaffa Road, which carried the bulk of both urban and interurban traffic. A network of new broad roads was blueprinted in order to provide alternative approach routes from all directions, enabling vehicular traffic to cross the municipal area to destinations beyond it (e.g., from Bethlehem directly to Ramallah) without clogging Jerusalem's main arteries. Adequate parking facilities had also to be provided throughout the city. The numerous protected historical sites and edifices and, primarily, Jerusalem's hilly terrain rendered this program highly expensive, as entire complexes of nonessential buildings would have to be demolished. In addition, earth-moving work, on a very large scale, would have to be carried out and long road tunnels excavated in the ridges.

In order to arrive at an acceptable joint solution to the traffic, social, and economic problems, planners preferred not to concentrate industry, commerce, administration, tourism, etc., each in a separate area, but rather to distribute them evenly throughout the city, thus shortening the distances between residential quarters and sites of employment and more evenly spreading traffic flow during rush hours. As more and more Government ministries and other central offices moved to the capital, an increasing need was felt to depart from the original plan of concentrating all government buildings in Ha-Kiryah but to distribute them over other sections, including East Jerusalem.

The Hebrew University saw the return of its original campus atop Mount Scopus, where, beginning with the Harry S. Truman Research Center, an intensive restoration and building program was launched in 1968, comprising lecture halls and dormitories for thousands of students. Other institutes of learning, e.g., yeshivot, Christian theological seminaries, etc., were constructed in various parts of the city.

In view of the growing need for tourist accommodation and services in Jerusalem, large sums of public and private capital were invested in hotel building, and suitable sites were earmarked for these purposes throughout the city, with an area in the south, on a ridge northwest of the former Government House, planned as the principal hotel center. The capital attracted increasing numbers of industrial enterprises, particularly in the electronics and other science-centered industries, for which new areas were set aside in the south, north, and northeast.

New housing developments called for the largest share of both space and investments. While the southwest (Kiryat ha-Yovel, etc.) continued to serve as the sector of intensive apartment building, and vacant lots elsewhere were increasingly being used for new constructions, a concentrated effort was being directed toward the favorable terrain in the north, beyond the former armistice line. New residential quarters, under construction since 1968, promised to provide accommodation for tens of thousands of citizens, both Jews and non-Jews, and to link western Jerusalem with Mount Scopus in the east and Shaʿfāṭ in the north.

[Efraim Orni]

Archaeological Research

Ever since the 19th century, when Jerusalem first became the focus of antiquarians and explorers, the complexity of studying so many superimposed ancient periods under the city, combined with the fact that so many of its important sites are inconveniently situated beneath buildings that are the focus of the three principal religions (Judaism, Christianity, and Islam), have made methodical archaeological research there a particularly difficult and challenging task. Investigation and recording of the visible ancient remains of ancient Jerusalem took place during the 19th century by many explorers: E. Robinson C. Mauss, E. Pierotti, T. Tobler, C.J.M. de-Vogüé, among others. Their work is invaluable because subsequent building activities in the city have destroyed or covered up many of the ancient remains that they recorded. Since the first proper mapping of Jerusalem in 1864 by C. Wilson during the Ordnance Survey of Jerusalem, the city has been almost continuously studied by explorers and archaeologists, with much work being undertaken in the area of the Haram al-Sharif (Temple Mount), the Southeastern Hill (the "City of David"), and the Western Hill (traditional "Mount Zion"). Important work was undertaken by C. Warren (from 1867), especially around the Temple Mount, on behalf of the British Palestine Exploration Fund. During the latter part of the 19th century and the beginning of the 20th century much work was done on the ancient topography of the city and its monuments by C.R. Conder, C. Schick, H. Vincent, and others. Important excavations were conducted by F.J. Bliss and A.C. Dickie (1894–97) on the Western Hill, by R. Weill (1913–14, 1923–24), by R.A.S. Macalister and J.G. Duncan (1923–25), by G.M. FitzGerald and J.W. Crowfoot (1927–28) on the Southeastern Hill, and by K.M. *Kenyon (1961–68) in various parts of the city.

During the 1970s and early 1980s large-scale excavations were conducted in Jerusalem by B. Mazar (1968–78) at the southern and southwestern foot of the Temple Mount, by N. Avigad (1969–83) in the Jewish Quarter, and by Y. Shiloh (1978–85) in the "City of David."

Excavations were also conducted in various areas on Mount Zion by M. Broshi (1971–78) and further remains have been uncovered in the area of the Citadel near the Jaffa Gate by H. Geva, G. Solar, and R. Sivan and others. Excavations have also been conducted by D. Bahat in the tunnels along the western Temple Mount wall.

New excavations have been undertaken in various parts of the city during the 1980s and 1990s, particularly by V. Tzaferis, S. Wulff, D. Amit, and others in the area of the Third Wall to the north of the Old City; by R. Reich, A. Meir, and others in the Mamila area to the west of Jaffa Gate; by R. Reich and E. Shukrun in the area of the Gihon Spring, along the east slope of the City of David, and in the area of the Pool of Siloam; by R. Reich and Y. Bilig in the area of Robinson's Arch; by G. Avni and Y. Baruch in the area close to Herod's Gate; and by G. Avni and J. Seligman in the Church of the Holy Sepulcher. Much work has also been conducted in the surroundings of Jerusalem with many small excavations conducted by the Israel Antiquities Authority.

BIBLICAL PERIOD. *The City and Its Fortifications.* Charles *Warren (1867–70) was the first to try to ascertain the line of the ancient fortification wall of the biblical city by the excavation of a number of pits and tunnels, especially to the southeast of the Temple Mount, with the discovery of what he identified as the wall of Ophel. Warren's work focused subsequent archaeological attention on the significance of the Southeast Hill, now known as the "City of David," as the place where the oldest parts of Jerusalem might indeed be unearthed.

Clermont-Ganneau and H. Guthe (1881) found additional wall segments that extended the line of the "Ophel wall" along the eastern slope of the City of David. At the southern end of the City of David, next to the Siloam Pool, F.J. Bliss and A.C. Dickie (1894–97) discovered a massive barrier wall that served to dam the southern end of the Tyropoeon Valley. They also discovered the continuation of this fortification wall on the slopes of the Western Hill above the Hinnom Valley. They identified in this fortification line two phases of construction and attributed the earliest phase to the time of the First Temple. Modern research cannot sustain this general attribution, with the latest phase now dated to the Byzantine period and the earliest to the Second Temple period, but it is still possible that small wall segments incorporated into the earlier phase of that wall do indeed date back to the Iron Age. M. Parker's expedition (1909–11) concentrated on digging in the area of the Gihon Spring and on the slope above it, where an additional segment of a fortification wall was discovered. (The results of Parker's expedition were eventually published by L.H. Vincent.) The southern end of the City of David was investigated by the Weill expeditions (1913–14, 1923–24), which revealed an additional build-up of fortifications.

R.A.S. Macalister and J.G. Duncan (1923–25) excavated a considerable area in the north of the City of David in the area above the Gihon Spring. They discovered segments of fortification walls, towers, and revetments whose earlier use they attributed to the biblical city. Inside the line of fortifications they uncovered a number of strata, the lowest of which they attributed to the Canaanite and Israelite cities. The J.W. Crowfoot and G.M. Fitzgerald expedition (1927–28) dug close to the area mentioned above. The results of their excavation, however, showed that most of the remnants discovered there could not be dated earlier than the Roman and Byzantine periods. They also investigated a gate (the "Gate of the Valley"), above the Tyropoeon Valley on the west side of the city (the width of the wall is approximately 28 ft. (8.5 m.), which is probably Hellenistic in date.

Various scholars subsequently published research based on these archaeological finds, namely K. Galling, G. *Dalman, J. Simons, L.H. Vincent, M. *Avi-Yonah, N. *Avigad, B. *Mazar, and others.

A difference of opinion immediately arose among these scholars regarding the topography and size of biblical Jerusalem, from the time of David and Solomon and to the destruction of the First Temple.

The excavations that were conducted by (later Dame) Kathleen Kenyon, between 1961 and 1967, opened a new page in the history of archaeological research of the city. Kenyon excavated at many locations on the Southeastern Hill, with a few areas on the Western Hill and inside the Old City (notably in the Armenian Garden). The fact that Kenyon's excavation areas were generally limited in size was eventually seen to be detrimental to the veracity of some of the important conclusions she published. However, in Kenyon's "great cut A," which was made on the slope between the line of the upper wall discovered by Macalister and Duncan in 1925 and the Gihon Spring below, the key to understanding the topography and the boundaries of the city in its earlier periods first became clear. The system of fortifications discovered by Macalister and Duncan was found to have been built on the remnants of walls and structures dating back to the beginning of the Iron Age. Hence, the line of fortifications uncovered by Macalister and Duncan had to date from the Second Temple period or later. Lower down the slope in Kenyon's "cut A," which was deepened in some places to bedrock, some 82 ft. (25 m.) above the Gihon Spring, a thick fortification wall was found built of large fieldstones which could be dated to the Middle Bronze Age. Kenyon showed that these fortifications survived until the eighth century B.C.E. and that during the reign of Hezekiah a new wall, whose width was approximately 18 ft. (5.5 m.), was built at the same place.

On the basis of a few trial excavations areas conducted on the eastern slope of the Western Hill, which did not bring to light remains from the Iron Age, Kenyon was confirmed in her opinion that there was no continuation of the Israelite city west of the Tyropoeon Valley. Her view regarding the restricted size of the Iron Age city was later contested and proven to be wrong as a result of Avigad's discovery of a fortification wall in the Jewish Quarter (see below), but Kenyon adamantly continued to insist that this enlarged city did not include the southern part of the Western Hill. Kenyon found that the narrowness of the city area on the Southeastern Hill was overcome by the construction of a series of graduated terraces filled in with stones and supported by stone walls that rose from the base of the city – the eastern wall – upslope. According to Kenyon, this system was used in Jerusalem from the 14th century B.C.E. and throughout the Iron Age period. It was identified with the "Millo," mentioned in I Kings 9:15. Kenyon demonstrated that the Canaanite city existed solely on the Southeastern Hill, and that its area approximated 15 acres (60 dunams). Ceramic evidence was adduced from the 10th century B.C.E. for the extension of the city northwards to the area of the modern-day Temple Mount. Some have speculated that this may have been where Solomon's administrative and palace buildings were situated. The total area of the Solomonic town was thought to have been approximately 120 dunams. Remnants of ashlar buildings, and the discovery of a proto-Aeolic capital by Kenyon, provided hints about splendid buildings that existed there in First Temple period Jerusalem, perhaps similar to those in Samaria and Megiddo.

While Kenyon produced important archaeological evidence concerning the early development of Jerusalem in the area of the Southeastern Hill, her results and interpretations in regard to the area of the Western Hill and in the Old City have largely been superseded by excavations carried out there by Avigad and others since 1967 (see below). Kenyon was of the opinion that there was no Iron Age settlement on the Western Hill. However, already during the excavations in the area of the Citadel by C.N. Jones (1934–40) Iron Age pottery was found, and this was confirmed during the later excavations by R. Amiran and A. Eitan (1968–69) at the same spot, with the discovery of floors and pottery. Although Iron Age pottery and walls were found by Kenyon's colleague A.D. Tushingham in the area of the Armenian Garden, these were interpreted as representing remains of activities that took place outside the city.

During N. Avigad's excavations (1969–83) in the Jewish Quarter of the Old City, fragmentary houses were found dating from the Iron Age, in addition to pottery, stamped handles, and figurines. His main find was that of a length of city wall (about 8 meters thick) running in a northeast-southwest direction across the Western Hill. Additional segments of Iron Age fortifications were discovered during subsequent excavations, all of which confirmed that the Iron Age city was very large and incorporated a large part of the Western Hill, contrary to Kenyon and others.

Archaeological excavations conducted by B. Mazar (1968–78) to the south of the Temple Mount brought to light additional remains which could be dated to the Iron Age, and some of these remains were later examined in greater detail by E. Mazar, who suggested identifying part of them as a gateway complex leading down to the Gihon Spring. Excavations by Y. Shiloh (1978–85) in the area of the City of David brought to light further remains from the Iron Age and clarified some of Kenyon's original work in regard to the terrace/stepped stone-structure (in Area G), the fortification line, and the water system associated with the Gihon Spring. Very clear signs of the Babylonian conquest of the year 586/587 B.C.E. are known from Shiloh's excavations and, together with evidence uncovered by Avigad on the Western Hill, they serve to confirm the destruction of Jerusalem at the end of the First Temple period. Later excavations by R. Reich and E. Shukrun have revealed that the first fortifications in and around the Gihon Spring were from the Middle Bronze Age, and that the Iron Age fortification system on the east slope of the City of David may very well have included a lower fortification wall close to the bottom of the slope.

Necropolises. The tombs discovered by Parker (1909–11) on the slope above the Gihon were dated by Vincent to the beginning of the Early Bronze Age. Kenyon discovered a series of tombs from the Middle Bronze Age on the Mount of Olives, in the same area where Warren had also found early tombs in the 1860s. Tombs that were rich in finds from the Middle Bronze and Late Bronze Ages were found near the Dominus Flevit Church and excavated by S. Saller (1954). Tombs with many important objects from the Late Bronze Age were also found in the Naḥalat Aḥim neighborhood (Amiran, 1961) and in the area of the UN headquarters. A series of rock-hewn tombs of the First Temple period are known east of the City of David in the area of the Silwan village, and these were studied in some detail in modern times by D. Ussishkin. Some of these tombs in Silwan were already investigated by explorers in the 19th century, notably by F. de Saulcy in 1865, who investigated the monolithic "Tomb of the Daughter of Pharaoh," and C. Clermont-Ganneau, who examined a number of tombs – among them one with the inscription " []yahu who is over the house." At the southern end of the City of David, Weill (1913–14) found monumental rock-cut chambers that he identified as the tombs of the House of David, but this identification still requires proper verification. Rock-cut tombs from the Iron Age were also investigated by Israeli scholars from the 1970s, notably by G. Barkay, A. Mazar, and others, in and around the city, notably to the north of the Old City (in the area of St. Etienne), in the Hinnom Valley, and elsewhere.

SECOND TEMPLE PERIOD. *The City and Its Fortifications.* Remains from the period of the Second Temple, and particularly from the time of King Herod (37–4 B.C.E.), served as a starting point for archaeological investigations from the 19th century. Terms and names connected with this period were obtained from the descriptions of the city as presented in the writings of the Jewish historian *Josephus. In 1867–70, C. Warren was engaged in an investigation of the Herodian enclosure walls of the Temple Mount, following on from the Ordnance Survey mapping of the Temple Mount made by C. Wilson in 1864 (published in 1865). Warren's descriptions and precise sketches of the topography of Jerusalem, particularly of the structure of Temple Mount walls, are still used by scholars. Many of the underground passages and gates of the Temple Mount studied by Wilson and Warren are now largely inaccessible to scholars. Among the structures they investigated were "Robinson's Arch" and "Wilson's Arch." Warren also uncovered a part of the foundation of the first arch of "Robinson's Arch" (later revealed in its entirety by Mazar in the 1970s) and was the first to suggest that it might have served as the base for a flight of steps leading to the valley below – a view he later abandoned but which was confirmed during Mazar's excavations. Warren also examined the vaulted areas on the southwest side of the Temple Mount, popularly known as "Solomon's Stables." He also correctly identified the site of the Antonia fortress, adjoining the northwest corner of the Temple Mount. The area was subsequently investigated by Clermont-Ganneau (1871) and Vincent and Marie-Aline de Sion (1955), but the walls and pavements which they thought belonged to the Herodian Antonia turned out to be of later Roman date (i.e., the remains shown in the convent of the Soeurs de Sion). C.N. Johns (1934–40) uncovered important remains of the northwestern corner of the "first" wall fortification system in the courtyard of the Citadel near the Jaffa Gate, dating from Hasmonean and Herodian times. This fortification line was associated with the large tower (identified as Phasael or Hippicus) which is commonly called David's Tower. (It has a preserved height of 66 ft. or 20 m.) Remnants of the "first" wall have been uncovered to the south of the Citadel, around Mt. Zion, along the edges of the Valley of Hinnom and as far as the City of David and the Kidron Valley. Fragments of this fortification line were studied by C. Schick and H. Maudsley (1871–75) in the area of the "Bishop Gobat School" on the southwest slope of traditional Mount Zion. Later, F.J. Bliss and A.C. Dickie (1895–98) uncovered substantial parts of this fortification wall around Mount Zion and as far as the Kidron Valley; Bliss and Dickie uncovered a two-phased fortification system, of which the earlier dated to the Second Temple period and the later to the Byzantine period. New evidence regarding the "first" wall was brought to light as a result of N. Avigad's excavations along the northern stretch, uncovering part of a gate (the Gennath Gate?), and M. Broshi's excavations along the western stretch, between the Citadel and the south-west angle of the Old City of today, bringing to light Hasmonean and Herodian fortifications and a gate (the Essene Gate?) that led into the city.

The line of the "second" wall has been reconstructed by scholars largely on the basis of written sources, rather than on archaeological findings. The opinions of many scholars regarding the wherabouts of this wall were heavily influenced by the study of the location of Golgotha and the Tomb of Jesus, which were supposed to have been situated outside the city walls. Established facts, however, are few. The line of the wall began at the "first" wall near the Citadel, passing to the south of the area of the Church of the Holy Sepulcher, and eventually reaching the Antonia Fortress. Conrad Schick originally found a collapsed fortification line on a rocky scarp to the southwest of the Church of the Holy Sepulcher – partly confirmed by Kenyon who dug near the Muristan Bazaar – and a fosse that may have been associated with the "second" wall, thus placing the area of Golgotha and the Tomb of Jesus outside the city. Some scholars have dated the construction of the "second" wall to the Hasmonean period, though others have attributed it to the time of the establishment of the Bezetha Quarter at the time of Herod the Great.

The course of the "third" wall, the construction of which took place at the time of Agrippa I (40–44 C.E.), has been disputed by scholars. Vincent, Simons, Kenyon, and Henessy fixed the course parallel to the line of the Ottoman wall in the northern part of the Old City of today. The opinion of E.L. *Sukenik and Mayer (1925–27), however, seemed better founded when they identifed the "third" wall with the line of the wall they uncovered – seen already by Pococke in the late 18th century and by Robinson in 1838/1852 – along a distance of approximately 1,600 ft. (500 m.) extending from the Italian Hospital to the Albright Institute of Archaeological Research. The line of wall includes towers facing north.

Excavations of this line in the 1970s by E. Netzer and S. Ben-Arieh confirmed the date of this wall and supported its identifications as the "third" wall. The wall was built carelessly and is far simpler than the other Second Temple fortification walls known in Jerusalem. The general consensus of opinion has been that this wall was first begun at the time of Agrippa I and was only completed at the time of the outbreak of the revolt in 66 C.E. in order to protect the "New City" from the Roman legions.

Significant information regarding the layout and appearance of the city during the late first century B.C.E. to 70 C.E. emerged from the excavations conducted by Mazar in the area of the southern edges of the Temple Mount, by Avigad in the Jewish Quarter excavations, and by Broshi on Mount Zion. Houses found there were first established in Hasmonean times (early first century C.E.) and were later replaced by new structures – many palatial in appearance – at the time of Herod the Great and in the first century C.E. The Herodian buildings that have been unearthed had cellars and ritual baths (*mikva'ot*) in their basements, with sumptuous rooms, many of which were adorned with wall paintings or with stucco decorations. Many artifacts from the Second Temple were uncovered: pottery, stone vessels, coins, and others.

A seven-branched *menorah – one of the oldest known examples – engraved into a plaster wall – was found in one of the houses overlooking the Temple Mount to the east. One inscription indicated that the house belonged to the priestly Bar Kathros family. The houses were violently destroyed in 70 C.E. with the capture of the city by the Romans.

The layout of the area around the southwestern corner of the Temple Mount has become clear as a result of the extensive excavations by B. Mazar and more recently by more limited work by R. Reich and Y. Bilig. Alongside the southern wall of the Temple Mount a wide street, paved with stone slabs, leading to Hulda's Gates, was discovered. A large flight of steps extended up to this gate. Nearby were ritual purification pools (*mikva'ot*). The base of "Robinson's Arch" was uncovered, which in all likelihood supported a flight of steps descending from a gate in the Temple Mount to the Lower City.

In the Second Temple period, based on the present state of archaeological research, Jerusalem expanded in the Hasmonean period (late second century B.C.E.) from the area of the small Hellenistic town on the Southeast Hill to the Western Hill, and it subsequently incorporated a very large area indeed. From the time of Herod the Great (37–4 B.C.E.) the city was substantially modified with major building operations at the sites of the Temple and palace in the Upper City, with work on improving the city fortifications as well. New fortification walls (the "second" and "third" walls) were subsequently added, and the Jerusalem that was destroyed by Titus and the Roman legions was a very large city indeed, extending over some 450 acres (1,800 dunams).

Necropolises. The cemeteries of Jerusalem during the Second Temple period extended like a belt around the city from present-day Sanhedriyyah in the northwest, through Givat ha-Mivtar, Mt. Scopus, the Mt. of Olives, and the hill of the UN headquarters, to Talpiyyot and Ramat Raḥel in the south. Almost one thousand tombs have been investigated and a catalogue of their locations and finds has been prepared by A. Kloner and B. Zissu. The internal plan of the tombs is simple, as was the custom then. On the sides of the central chambers are tunnel-like burial recesses (Heb. *kokhim*), occasionally within arched recesses (arcosolia). The dead were laid out on the benches of the central chambers or within the *kokhim*, and once the bodies had decomposed the bones were gathered into limestone ossuaries. A shrouded body of a leper (who suffered from Hansen's Disease) was discovered in a tomb in the lower Hinnom Valley. Some of the larger tombs have carved exteriors or monuments (e.g., the so-called Tomb of Absalom in the Kidron Valley) or sometimes carved interiors (e.g., a few tombs in the Akeldama area). As early as 1863 de Saulcy cleaned out the Tombs of the Kings and discovered there the decorated sarcophagi that may possibly have belonged to the family of Queen Helena of Adiabene. Clermont-Ganneau completed the excavation of those tombs. He also partially cleaned the tomb known as Absalom's Tomb (1891). In 1891 Schick published the discovery of the so-called Tomb of the Family of Herod, found near the site on which the King David Hotel was subsequently built. In 1924 N. Slouschz cleared Absalom's Tomb. From 1926 to 1940 E.L. Sukenik studied approximately 40 Jewish funerary complexes in the city (such as the tomb of the Nicanor family discovered on Mt. Scopus). Avigad investigated the various burial sites of Jerusalem, especially in the Kidron Valley (1945–47). Jason's Tomb from the Hasmonean period was excavated in Reḥavyah by L. Raḥmani (1954), who also investigated the burial sites of Sanhedriyyah (1961). In 1968 V. Tsaferis excavated several tombs at Givat ha-

Mivtar, northeast of the city. One of them contained 35 burials, including one of a young man called Yoḥanan, who had died by crucifixion. Hundreds of limestone ossuaries and simple graves were investigated on the western slope of the Mt. of Olives, near the Church of Dominus Flevit by P.B. Bagatti and J.T. Milik (1953–55). The major findings in this cemetery are from the Herodian period; however, it was used from the Hasmonean period to the Byzantine period. The subject of tombs in the vicinity of Jerusalem was investigated by A. Kloner in 1980. Numerous tombs continued to be excavated during the 1980s to 1990s, with fewer excavated since the year 2000 due to the Israeli government's agreement with the Ultra-Orthodox Jewish community in Jerusalem to disallow the excavation of human bones.

THE LATE ROMAN PERIOD. Following the destruction of the Second Temple in 70 C.E. and the suppression of the Bar Kokhba revolt (135 C.E.), a Roman city was built in its stead named Aelia Capitolina in the second century C.E. The camp of the Tenth Roman Legion (Fretensis) was situated in the area of the Citadel and Armenian Garden and is represented by the discovery of numerous rooftiles bearing the mark of the legion and with symbols of a galley and wild boar. The size and the position of the camp have been debated, and new suggestions have unsuccessfully attempted to place the camp at other locations. Kilns and other remains of the Tenth Legion have been found in the area of Givat Ram and Binyanei Ha'uma to the west of the city. Aelia was largely built up with temples, buildings, and with a western forum, and with streets and triumphal arches on the north side of the present Old City. The north gate of Aelia Capitolina was found beneath the Damascus Gate, and an inscription referring to the Roman name of the city was found chiseled upon the gate. At the beginning of the Via Dolorosa is a Roman triumphal arch, now called Ecce Homo, in the area of the Bethesda Pool which had a temple of Serapis. Clermont-Ganneau investigated the area of the Via Dolorosa in 1873–74, discovering a large pagan Roman vase with stamped decorations of gods and altars. Excavations by Kenyon (1961–67) and others in the Muristan area and around the Church of the Holy Sepulcher have shown that the area was included within the boundaries of the Roman city and that the area had been substantially filled in with the construction of numerous substructures for the superimposed buildings and temples that were built in this area (the western forum). Close to the southwest corner of the Temple Mount, Mazar uncovered a kiln, latrines, and other structures dating from this period. An inscription inscribed on stone and dating to the days of Septimius Severus (beginning of the third century C.E.) was also found. Another Latin inscription came to light in the southern area of the Temple Mount, which referred to a monumental gate that existed somewhere in the area. The southern aqueduct was duplicated in Roman times by a high-level line from Ein Etam.

THE BYZANTINE PERIOD. The city flourished during this period and it became the focal point for Christian pilgrimages. The main building changes occurred in the areas that were strongly associated with Christian tradition (for example the area of Golgotha and the Tomb of Jesus). At these places, churches, monasteries, and hospices were built. The city again spread across the Eastern and Western Hills and to the south of the Temple Mount. The excavations of Macalister and Duncan, Crowfoot and Fitzgerald, Weill, Hamilton, Kenyon, and more recently by Mazar, Shiloh, Reich, and Shukrun have brought to light remnants of streets, dwellings, and public buildings covering the south of the city. Traditional Mount Zion was also encircled by a wall. Remnants of this wall had been discovered by Warren near the Ophel (later partly excavated by Mazar), above the Hinnom Valley by Bliss and Dickie, and along the western side by Broshi. The construction of this wall is usually dated to the middle of the fifth century C.E. and is connected with the building activities of Empress Eudocia in Jerusalem. Avigad's excavations in the Jewish Quarter (1970) revealed substantial portions of the Nea Church, built by Justinian in the mid-sixth century C.E. The Church of the Holy Sepulcher has a long history of investigations spanning the work of mapping by Wilson and Schick in the 19th century, the architectural appreciation by M. Harvey in the 1930s, and the archaeological work by V. Corbo and C. Couasnon from the 1960s to the 1980s (see the summary of all the discoveries by Gibson and Taylor). The original church was founded in 325 C.E., following the destruction of pagan buildings in the area and the discovery of the Tomb of Jesus, which was undertaken by Bishop Macarius at the behest of Constantine the Great. The main portal to the basilical martyrium, contrary to the accepted form, was in the east, with the apse facing the Tomb of Jesus, which was surrounded by a circular structure (the rotunda). Excavations conducted by White Fathers (1864–67) to the northeast of the city, brought to light various remains, including remnants of a large church built above the Pool of Bethesda. Nearby were found remnants of a second Byzantine church that had been incorporated into the crusader church of St. Anne. Bliss and Dickie (1894–97) dug above the Siloam Pool and uncovered the remains of a church which they dated to the time of Eudocia. J. Germer-Durand, who dug in the eastern slope of Mt. Zion at the end of the 19th century, revealed dwellings and a church. P.G. Orfali (1909, 1919–20) excavated the remains of the Gethsemane Church in the Kidron Valley. Vincent (1959) and Corbo (1959) discovered the remains of the Church of the Ascension on the top of the Mt. of Olives. Avi-Yonah (1949) discovered remains of a church and a monastery in the area of Givat Ram. Bagatti and Milik (1953–55) uncovered a cemetery of the Byzantine period in Dominus Flevit on the Mt. of Olives. New excavations in different parts of the city during the 1980s and 1990s revealed many more architectural and artifactual remains from the Byzantine period.

The Byzantine city was destroyed at the time of the Persian conquest in 614, but there is no evidence that the Muslim conquest in 638 was destructive. Numerous structures were erected in the area of the southwest corner of the Temple

Mount at the time of the Umayyads at the beginning of the eighth century. On one of the stones in the Herodian Wall of the Temple Mount an inscription was engraved by a Jewish pilgrim (though the date of this inscription is disputed) who arrived in the city during early Islamic times. The text of the inscription was taken from Isaiah 66:14: "And when you see this your heart shall rejoice and your bones shall flourish like young grass."

[Michael Avi-Yonah / Shimon Gibson (2nd ed.)]

Water Supply

FIRST AND SECOND TEMPLE PERIODS. The location of Canaanite Jerusalem on the eastern ridge near the Kidron riverbed was related to the discovery of the only water source in the entire area on the eastern slope of the ridge. This was the Gihon Spring, which supplied 7,000–40,000 cu. ft. (200–1,100 cu. m.) daily during periods of 30–40 minutes, with interruptions of four to ten hours (according to the season). As early as the Middle Bronze Age, the inhabitants of Jerusalem dug a tunnel to assure the water supply in the event of a siege. At first they attempted to sink a shaft straight down to the water level, but did not succeed because of the hardness of the rock. They then dug an angular tunnel with stairs; at its end was a shaft ("Warren's shaft") 43 ft. (13 m.) high, which descended to the level of the spring and through which water could be drawn without the enemy's knowledge. It is possible that this system was the "gutter" (*ẓinnor*) mentioned in the account of the conquest of Jerusalem by David and his warriors (II Sam. 5:8). In addition to the tunnel, near the spring were several open canals extending southward that carried the excess spring water to the fields and gardens along the Kidron riverbed. At the end of the eighth century B.C.E., Hezekiah, king of Judah, initiated the excavation of a new 1,765 ft. (535 m.) tunnel which extended from a level of 2,086 ft. (636 m.) to 2,080 ft. (634 m.), passing in the form of two arches under the hill of the City of David. This tunnel conducted the waters of the Gihon to the Siloam (Shiloah) Pool in the valley between the two hills. The well-known *Siloam inscription recounts the excavation of the tunnel and the "day of the tunnel" in which "the stone cutters made their way toward one another ax-blow by ax-blow." The excavation of this tunnel was a considerable engineering feat, and since then the waters of the Gihon have flowed to the Siloam Pool. The pool was initially covered and hidden from enemies, as discovered in excavations.

In earliest times the inhabitants of Jerusalem had already increased the meager supply of the Gihon Spring by digging cisterns and pools. Of the two types of reservoirs, the cisterns were more difficult to make, but they were better for preserving water against evaporation. After the discovery of waterproof lime mortar, the number of cisterns in the ancient city grew equal to (if not greater than) the number of houses. Interestingly, very few cisterns have been found from the time of the First Temple. Most of those that are known date from Second Temple times. The most famous is a double cistern known as Struthion (Gr. *strouthos* – "ostrich"), located under the court of the Antonia Fortress southwest of the Temple; its maximum dimensions were 160 ft. (49m.) in length, 23 ft. (7 m.) in width, and 56 ft. (17 m.) in depth. A great number of cisterns were dug in the area of the Temple Mount (45 according to the last count), the largest among them being the Bahr el-Kabir (Ar. for the "Sea"), whose capacity was 140,000 cu. ft. (12,000 cu. m.). There were two other cisterns of 94,000 cu. ft. (8,000 cu. m.) and 60,000 cu. ft. (5,000 cu. m.) capacity.

The major pools in the area of Jerusalem are the Siloam Pool at the southern end of the central valley; the Serpents Pool (probably north of the city); the Pool of Towers (Hezekiah's Pool) north of the Fortress; and Mamilla Pool (first mentioned in the Byzantine period), located between the Jaffa Gate and the watershed line. Three of the ancient pools are not open today: the Ḥammām al-Shifāʾ Pool in the upper central valley, which may be the biblical "Upper Pool"; the Pool of Israel, which served as a ditch for the northern boundary of the Temple Mount; and the Sheep Pool, also north of the Temple Mount at some distance from it. The latter is mentioned in the New Testament (John 5:2–4), where it is called Bethesda (Beit Ḥisda), and apparently also in the Copper Scroll from the Dead Sea caves. It is a double pool and has two levels. The New Testament states that healing powers were attributed to it, and excavations of the site have revealed that a health rite took place there during the Roman period. The lower of the two pools was probably used for washing sheep, which were then sold for sacrifices at the nearby Temple.

At the end of the Second Temple period, it was clear that the growing city could not be supplied from the waters collected in the cisterns and pools, especially during mass gatherings of the three pilgrimage festivals. Pontius Pilate therefore decided to build an aqueduct from the springs of the ʿArrūb River near Hebron. It was an open canal which passed through four tunnels near Bethlehem. In order to preserve the gradient of the water level, which assured a steady flow from the springs to the Temple Mount, the aqueduct wound along the 2,574 ft. (766 m.) contour line so that, although the direct distance from the ʿArrūb River to Jerusalem is no more than 13 mi. (21 km.), the aqueduct was 42 mi. (68 km.) long. On its way southward, it also collected the water of Ein Etam (Solomon's Pools), south of Bethlehem. During the rule of Septimius Severus, a second aqueduct on a higher level was added, extending from Solomon's Pools to Jerusalem. The latter crossed the valley near Rachel's Tomb via a line of pipes operated by syphon pressure, which in many cases split the stone links.

FROM THE ROMAN PERIOD. From the Roman period to the end of the Ottoman period, Jerusalem's water supply was based mainly on rainwater collected in the city's cisterns and pools. The original Spring of Gihon had long been blocked; its location was unknown, and its waters flowed through Hezekiah's tunnel to the Siloam Pool. According to Christian tradition, these waters were used by Jesus to heal the blind man (John 9:7), and the site thus became sacred to Christians. As early as the fourth century C.E., the pilgrim of Bordeaux mentions a pool surrounded by colonnades used for bathing for healing purposes. The empress Eudocia built a church and a hospital above the pool. In the early Muslim period as well, the waters of the Siloam were regarded as having special powers, but in the course of generations the pool was neglected, and the tunnel of Hezekiah became partially blocked. The waters of the Gihon, which had ceased to flow through the tunnel, broke out to the Kidron River. Thus the Gihon Spring was rediscovered in the 14th century, and its name reappeared for the first time in a Jewish source from the 16th century. With the rediscovery of the Gihon, the site of the spring was consecrated. Christians established it as the spot where Mary had washed Jesus' swaddling clothes and therefore called it the "Virgin's Fountain." The waters of the Gihon Spring today flow again through Hezekiah's tunnel to the new Siloam Pool built in the 19th century.

During the Ottoman period the waters of the Gihon were drawn and sold in the streets of Jerusalem, but in the 19th century they became polluted from sewage water reaching the spring, and eventually they were used only for watering the flower beds of Kefar ha-Shilo'aḥ (Silwān). The Rogel Spring served Jerusalem throughout the generations as a secondary source of water. During the Ottoman period its waters, like those of the Gihon, were drawn and sold in Jerusalem, but it too primarily became a source of the water for Kefar ha-Shilo'aḥ.

A number of changes occurred in later times in the system of public pools known from the Roman period. With the concentration of Jerusalem on the western hill, the pools at the lower part of the central valley were neglected. The ancient Siloam Pool was apparently reconstructed during the Byzantine period, but was later neglected, filled with silt, and called by the Arabs the Birkat al-Ḥamrā' (Pool of the Red Earth). The pool of Ḥammām al-Shifā', near Bāb al-Silsila (the Chain Gate) of the Temple Mount, was known from medieval times but was later blocked to enable the collection of subterranean waters, which were drawn from the pool via a shaft. The pool of Beit Ḥisda (Bethesda) continued to be in use in the Byzantine period and was called the Probatike pool but was later blocked. Likewise, the Struthion pool fell into disuse.

Crusader sources mention three pools in Jerusalem: Lacus Legerii, northwest of the Damascus Gate, outside the city walls (today, Arḍ al-Birka); Lacus Germani, the ancient Snake Pool rebuilt by Germanus in 1176 (today known as Birkat al-Sultan in the Hinnom Valley); and Lacus Balneorum, the "Pool of Baths" (the ancient Pool of Towers) called Birkat Ḥammām al-Biṭrīq and Hezekiah's Pool by Christian travelers. This pool is joined by an aqueduct to the Mamilla Pool, which is at the head of the Hinnom Valley. The Mamilla Pool itself continues to be mentioned in the Umayyad period. The three latter pools were reconstructed and renovated during the Mamluk and Ottoman periods. The Arabic name Birkat al-Sultan was given because of the expansion and renovation carried out on it by Sultan Suleiman the Magnificent in 1537. Other pools in Jerusalem, the dates of whose construction are not clear, are St. Mary's pool near the eastern wall of Jerusalem and the al-Hajj pool north of the city wall, opposite the present-day location of the Rockefeller Museum. Plastered cisterns in the courtyards of houses served as a major source of water throughout all the periods. In mid-19th century, 950 cisterns were counted in the Old City, while at the end of the Ottoman period the cisterns of the entire city, including the suburbs outside the walls, numbered 6,600, with a total capacity of over 17,000,000 cu. ft. (500,000 cu. m.). In 1919 the British determined that the total capacity of the cisterns and pools of Jerusalem, including those on the Temple Mount, was approximately 53,000,000 cu. ft. (1,500,000 cu. m.).

The local sources, however, were not sufficient to meet the needs of the city, and throughout most of the periods water continued to be conducted to Jerusalem from the area of the ʿArrūb springs and Solomon's Pools. The use of the aqueduct during the Byzantine period is known from a Greek inscription that prohibits the cultivation of land at a distance of 15 cubits from the aqueduct. The reference is apparently to the aqueduct on the lower level, which was built at the time of the Second Temple and continued to be used during this period. It is reasonable to assume that this aqueduct was also in use during the Muslim and Crusader periods, and it is known that it was rebuilt during the Mamluk period, when the third pool was also built at Solomon's Pools, south of Bethlehem. Waters collected there were conducted to Jerusalem via the aqueduct. At the beginning of the Ottoman period, the lower aqueduct continued to function, and Suleiman the Magnificent even built a number of *sabīls* (public fountains) that received their waters from the aqueduct. At the beginning of the 18th century, however, a clay pipe was built into the aqueduct, and its operation entailed difficult engineering problems. The pipe was blocked and often went out of use. Various attempts to improve the aqueduct in the 19th century were unsuccessful, but at the beginning of the 20th century the clay pipe was rebuilt as far as Bethlehem, and from it a narrow iron pipe conducted a limited amount of water – about 180 cu. m. daily – to Jerusalem.

The problem of water supply was very grave at the end of the Ottoman period, to the extent that Jerusalem's inhabitants were compelled to buy water brought by train or on the backs of animals from a considerable distance. With the British conquest (1917) the need for an immediate solution to the water problem arose. The cisterns in the city were purified, and the first water project built by the British army was based on the water sources in ʿAyn ʿArrūb. The old well there was renovated, a pump was built, and an iron pipeline 15 mi. (24 km.) long was laid down to the reservoir in the Romema quarter. In 1921 Solomon's Pools were renovated, as was an ancient water project in Wadi al-Biyār which lies south of pools for collecting rainwater. Waters from this wadi and from the area of al-Khaḍr, as well as spring water in the vicinity, were collected in Solomon's Pools and pumped from there to the iron pipelines from ʿAyn ʿArrūb. In 1924 the water was conveyed from ʿAyn

Fāra in the bed of Wadi Qilt, north of Jerusalem. This project considerably increased the amount of water supplied to Jerusalem. At the same time, around 1,400 cubic meters were supplied daily from the outside, but there was still considerable use of private cisterns. With the fast growth of West Jerusalem, the water problem again became grave and the need arose for an additional abundant source of water. In 1934 the pipeline from the abundant springs at Rosh ha-Ayin (Ra's al-ʿAyn) near the coast was built, finally solving the problem of the water supply for the city until 1948. During the Israel War of Independence (1948), West Jerusalem suffered from lack of water because several pumping stations of the Rosh ha-Ayin pipeline were captured and damaged by Arab forces. Later the government of Israel built a new pipeline from the same source which supplied West Jerusalem with water. The reunified city, after the Six-Day War (1967), was supplied from the western as well as the southern and northern sources which served East Jerusalem during the Jordanian rule.

[Michael Avi-Yonah and Amihay Mazar]

Cartography

Since the beginning of mapmaking, the geographical position of Jerusalem was shown on most of the manuscript maps of the world, such as the maps at the cathedral of Herford and of the Ebstorf monastery. It appeared on the "Tabula Peutingeriana" and on all the maps of the Near East and the Holy Land. The cartographical symbols employed on these maps are of the conventional semi-pictorial design and therefore do not provide any information on particular features of the city.

PICTORIAL MAPS. The earliest topographical description of Jerusalem is the bird's-eye view of the "Holy City of Jerusalem," the central piece of a map of the Holy Land preserved on the mosaic floor of a ruined basilica at *Madaba, in Transjordan. The mosaic, dated between 560 and 565 C.E., depicts an oval-shaped city surrounded by walls, with six gates and 21 towers. It shows the "Cardo maxima," the colonnaded main thoroughfare, together with four smaller streets and 36 other features of the city – such as public squares and buildings, churches, and monasteries – and contains the oldest presentation of the Western Wall. This "map" shows Jerusalem as viewed from the west, whereas during the following centuries the city was predominantly portrayed from the east, since the view from the Mount of Olives encompassed the most important sections of the medieval town (i.e., all the parts of the Temple Mount and most of the stations of the Via Dolorosa). Typical examples of this mode of presentation are: the large map engraved by Erhard Reuwich, a Mainz woodcutter and printer, after drawings made by him on the spot in 1483; the woodcut made by Jacob Clauser for Sebastian Muenster's cosmography (published 1544 in Basle); and the copper engraving reproducing a drawing made in 1682 by Cornelis de Bruin. These productions were often copied by the many artists who were unable to paint pictures based on personal observation.

HISTORICAL MAPS. Another approach is represented in the work of the biblical scholars who, for religious reasons, intended to clarify the state of the city during different periods of biblical history, concentrating mostly on New Testament times. These mapmakers were often unfamiliar with the topography of the city and derived their knowledge from the literary sources at their disposal, i.e., the Bible, the works of Josephus and classical Greek and Latin writers, and certain passages of the Talmud. Best known among these maps are the works of the Dutch astronomer Pieter Laiksteen (dated 1544 and republished in 1573 by Benito Arias-Montano), Christian van Adrichem (Cologne, 1584), and the Rev. Thomas Fuller (London, 1650). Other maps, mostly engraved by Dutch craftsmen, appeared in many editions of the Bible and became very popular as an aid to understanding the text.

COMPARATIVE MAPS. Laiksteen opened a new chapter of cartographic development with his twin set of town maps, the first attempt to present a comparative topography of New Testament Jerusalem and the walls and buildings in the city of his own time by graphic means. The prime motive for the creation of such maps was the desire to defend the authenticity of the holy places. The correctness of their location was piously accepted by countless generations of pilgrims, but with the spread of the Reformation in 16th-century Europe, an ever growing number of pilgrims – mostly from Britain and Germany – disputed the ecclesiastical tradition promulgated by the Franciscan friars in their capacity as the officially appointed "Custodians of the Holy Land." In view of the fact that Empress Helena's Church of the Holy Sepulcher was not outside the present walls of the city, as suggested by the Gospels and Jewish tradition, an endless discussion arose, culminating in 1883 with Charles C. Gordon's identification of Jeremiah's Grotto with Mount Calvary. In order to decide this dispute, the actual course of the city walls during Roman times had to be ascertained, as the position of the Third Wall would automatically establish the location of the "True Calvary." The first map designed to solve this problem was made by the Franciscan friar Antonio degli Angelis, who lived in Jerusalem and Bethlehem from 1569 to 1577. Friar Antonio constructed a town plan based on fairly exact observations and/or actual measurements and the delineation of the course of the Third Wall. This map, published in 1578 by a monastery in Rome, was lost and is known only from a 1584 bibliographical note by Christian van Adrichem. The map was later republished and appeared in 1609 as a plate in Bernardino Amico's *Plans of the Sacred Edifices of the Holy Land*. This engraving was the work of Antonio Tempesta, but the artwork for a further edition, published in 1620, was entrusted to Jacques Callot. These two important artists added many "improvements" and embellishments, while Natale Bonifaci made a modest engraving for Johann Zuallart's travelogue (Rome, 1587). Bonifaci's version has often been copied, mainly for pilgrims interested in pictures suitable as illustrations for their reports, and has been reproduced in many 17th-century travel books of the Holy Land.

SURVEY MAPS. In 1818 an Austrian physician, Franz Wilhelm Sieber, traveled through the Near East, spending 42 days in Jerusalem. He decided to produce an exact map based on reliable measurements, because he was aware of the "mistakes and curious differences existing between all the plans published up to now" and was interested in furthering the "very important study of biblical history." He walked in and around the city and, in the disguise of a botanist or as a doctor dispensing medical advice to the population, acquainted himself with the terrain and determined the geographical position of the places he chose as points of observation. He took "approximately two hundred geometrically correct bearings, ascertained the course of the Kidron Valley, the circumference of the walls, and the position of the Temple and the mosques." His many excursions helped him fill in many smaller details, corrections and additions. His nicely engraved map appeared as an appendix to the report on his travels (Prague and Leipzig, 1823; Prague, 1826).

Until that time the Muslims placed formidable difficulties in the way of an accurate survey. In 1818 Sieber had to camouflage his work of mapmaking as Cornelis de Bruin, the Dutch landscape painter was obliged to do in 1682. During the 19th century, however, the change of political climate in the Near East provided foreign scholars with much more liberty to execute their research. The decisive point in the development of Jerusalem cartography was reached after the bombardment of Acre, when the presence of the British fleet afforded the Corps of Royal Engineers the opportunity to conduct surveys in the country. One party was dispatched to Jerusalem and, in 1841, worked openly for six weeks in and around the city without encountering any opposition. The official completion of the survey was marked by the officer in charge, Col. R.A. Alderson, personally taking the measurements of the Citadel. This was the first time that Jerusalem was mapped for nonreligious (i.e., military) considerations. Another survey, made by the Royal Engineers in 1864–65, was also conducted for purely secular reasons: it was sponsored by a benefactress eager to improve Jerusalem's water supply. This work, the Ordnance Survey, became the basis for all reliable maps of the city. Besides these British efforts, other nations (France, Germany, Italy, Netherlands, and the United States) have contributed to the mapping of the city and the topographic recording of its surrounding. These maps, while rarely offering new intelligence about fundamental facts, often serve as documentary evidence on the progress of settlement, the construction of new buildings, etc. The same information can be derived from the maps accompanying various guide books. All these maps were made by foreigners acting without any assistance from the Turkish government. No official survey of the territory was made until the British Mandatory administration established its own survey department, which prepared and printed many useful maps. After 1948 its work was taken over by the Survey of Israel, which enlarged the scope of publications considerably.

[Herrmann M.Z. Meyer]

IN JUDAISM

In the Bible

In the Pentateuch, Jerusalem is mentioned only once, incidentally, by the name of Salem (Gen. 14:18), in connection with *Melchizedek. The injunctions to worship God "in the site that He will choose" (e.g., Deut. 12:4) do not specifically refer to Jerusalem. The obscure verse "On the mount of the Lord there is vision" (*yera'eh*; Gen. 22:14), referring to the mountain in the "land of Moriah" on which Isaac was nearly sacrificed (Gen. 22), may signify an identification of the mountain with the site of the Temple; however, definite evidence for the designation of the Temple Mount by the name "Mt. Moriah" is found only in a source from the Second Temple period (II Chron. 3:1).

The uniqueness of Jerusalem as the royal city and the center of the worship of the Lord dates from the period of David (II Sam. 6–7; 24:18–25; I Chron. 21:18–22:1). During the First Temple period, when the Temple Mount was referred to as "Mt. Zion," the name "Zion" also occasionally embraced the whole of Jerusalem (cf. e.g., I Kings 8:1; Isa. 1:27). The promise of an eternal dynasty (II Sam. 7), delivered by Nathan to David in conjunction with the question of the erection of a Temple in Jerusalem, also implied eternity for Jerusalem as the royal city and the city of the Temple, although its name is not explicitly mentioned. The conception of the eternity of Jerusalem in the Bible is related to the monarchy of the House of David and must be understood as part and parcel of it.

During the reign of Solomon, the unique status of Jerusalem as the royal city was established by the erection of the Temple, which invested the monarchy, as well as the site, with an aura of holiness. In the prayer of Solomon (I Kings 8), in which the Temple is considered a house of worship, "the city" ("which Thou hast chosen") is linked with the "house." The Temple is perceived as the eternal seat of the Lord ("a place for Thee to dwell in forever"), and there is no doubt that this conception of a double eternity – that of the dynasty of David and that of the symbolic residence of the Lord – imparted sanctity to the whole city.

In Psalm 78:68 the choice of Mt. Zion symbolizes the choice of Judah after the abandonment of Ephraim and Shiloh, and the Temple on Mt. Zion is conceived as a continuation of the Tabernacle of Shiloh. In Psalm 132, which describes the bringing of the ark to the city of David, Zion is conceived not only as a city chosen by the Lord for the monarchy but also as the place and seat of the Lord – His resting place and His abode; in other verses, it is explicitly stated that the Lord has attached, or will attach, His name to Jerusalem (e.g., II Kings 21:4). Psalm 122 is a hymn of admiration and love for Jerusalem (cf. Ps. 87). Royal justice ("there thrones for judgment were set, the thrones of the House of David"; Ps. 122: 5) is particularly emphasized as the virtue of Jerusalem – possibly in the wake of the reforms of Jehoshaphat (II Chron. 17:4–11).

It is perhaps in contrast to this that Jeremiah foresees (3:17) that in the days to come "Jerusalem shall be called the throne of the Lord" – the symbol of divine righteousness and justice (cf. Ps. 89:15), a quality that is attributed to the throne of David. In the prophecy of Jeremiah (33:16), the ideal Jerusalem is also called "The Lord is our righteousness," with reference to the justice and mercy which will be dispensed in days to come by the king, upon whom this title is also conferred (23:5–6; 33:15). The expression "habitation of righteousness and holy hill" (Jer. 31:22 (23)) is also to be explained as referring to Jerusalem, even though it is seemingly applied to "the land of Judah and its cities" in general. Isaiah's "city of righteousness" (Isa. 1:26; cf. 1:21, 27) – an epithet for Jerusalem – is to be understood not as a poetic expression but as a reference to its mission to dispense justice and righteousness and to be the seat of the judges. It is not impossible that in all these appellations, there is also an echo of the name Zedek which was borne by the pre-Israelite kings of Jerusalem – Melchizedek and Adoni-Zedek (Josh. 10:1) – and which was possibly derived from an ancient name of the town.

The greatness and the splendor of Jerusalem are described in the Bible in hyperbolic poetic imagery: in Psalms – "beautiful in elevation, the joy of all the earth" (48:3 (2)), "the perfection of beauty" (50:2), and so on; in Lamentations, expressing yearning for the past – "full of people… great among the nations, princess among the cities" (1:1), "the perfection of beauty, the joy of all the earth" (2:15). In the Song of Songs (6:4), the beloved is compared to Jerusalem (and to Tirzah), the symbol of beauty and loveliness. In the "Song of Ascents" (Ps. 122, 125, and 132), the pilgrims praise Jerusalem in hyperbole; in Psalm 137, "Zion" and "Jerusalem" are symbols of the whole country, and their destruction ("the day of Jerusalem") is a symbol of the Exile.

In the Prophets and in Lamentations, the name and the concept of Jerusalem are frequently employed to represent the whole of Judah; Jerusalem embodies the conduct and the deeds of Judah and is occasionally identified with Judah, as well as with the whole of Israel, for good or ill. Sometimes, however, the parallel between "Jerusalem" or "Zion," on the one hand, and "Judah," the "cities of Judah," or "Israel," on the other, emphasizes – in praise or in disparagement – not that which is common to them but the central, independent status and the special features of the elected city. The "daughter of Jerusalem" and the "daughter of Zion" also signify both the city and the kingdom, either as an expression of affection or as a designation of the sinful city and nation. Prophetic literature reflects different trends in the historical-religious conception of Jerusalem, according to the conditions and circumstances in which the prophet waged his struggle against idolatry, and in support of the belief in the Lord. In opposition to the heathen notion that the power of the Lord of Israel over Jerusalem is not different from that of the gods of Damascus, Arpad, Hamath, and others over their respective cities, Isaiah, during the reigns of Ahaz and Hezekiah, emphasized the idea of the uniqueness of Jerusalem: as the city of the Lord of Israel, the true God, its status and fate differ from that of all other cities whose gods are no more than idols (10; 29; 30; 31; 33; 37; 38); even the mighty Assyrian conqueror shall not vanquish Jerusalem, which is assured of divine protection for the sake of the honor of His name and the name of David, His servant. It appears that, as a result of the miraculous salvation of Jerusalem from the hands of Sennacherib, in accordance with the prophecy of Isaiah, the sense of the uniqueness and the might of the city became implanted within the nation; those Psalms that stress Jerusalem's title "city of God" and God's intervention as its protector (e.g., 46; 48; 76; 87) apparently belong to this period.

Isaiah's conception was, however, given to distortion, and it turned into a belief in a quasi-magic immunity which the city, and the "Temple of the Lord" which was in it, bestowed upon its inhabitants. Jeremiah rose against this new idolatrous conception; he rejected – seemingly in contrast to Isaiah – any distinctiveness attributed to Jerusalem. He maintained that the divine protection of the city was contingent upon the people's following the ways of God; if they forsook God, Jerusalem would be abandoned to the historic fate of all the other cities which fell before the Babylonian conqueror and were destroyed (7; 17; 19; 21; 25; 27; 34, et al.). The gap between the mission of Jerusalem – to be "the faithful city… full of justice" (Isa. 1:21) – and its actual state as "… rebellious and defiled, the oppressing city" (Zeph. 3:1) preoccupies all the prophets, who react to this discrepancy in pain or in anger. For Ezekiel, this gap between the vision and the reality becomes the cornerstone of his prophecy concerning Jerusalem before its destruction. All the faults and the sins of Israel, from the time they left Egypt until the days of the prophets, are attributed to Jerusalem, which is described as having surpassed Samaria and Sodom in its corruption and wickedness. In a cruel itemization, Ezekiel enumerates the "abominations of Jerusalem" (16; 22; 23 etc.); he is the only one of the prophets from whose words it is inferred that the anticipated destruction is to be regarded as an irreversible decree.

All the prophets share the expectation of an exalted future for Jerusalem – a loftiness which includes both physical splendor and a sublime religious-spiritual significance; this anticipation refers at times to the near future and at times to the end of days. Jeremiah's vision of the rebuilt Jerusalem (30:18–19; 31:37–39) is a realistic one, and it includes a detailed demarcation of its enlarged area, the whole of which will be "sacred to the Lord." Zechariah (8:3–5) also anticipates that Jerusalem will be called "the faithful city, and the mountain of the Lord of Hosts, the holy mountain"; its streets will be filled with "old men and old women" and "boys and girls" will play there. Ezekiel raises the Holy City of the days to come above actual and historic reality; it is only indirectly implied that he is referring to Jerusalem – whose name is not mentioned at all and whose site is not indicated: "a city on the south… up on a very high mountain" (Ezek. 40:2). Its description (45:1–8; 48:8–22,

30–35) does not evoke the image of an ordinary city or even of a royal city or capital but that of a background for the Temple, a city entirely sanctified to God, the abode of the Divine Presence, whose name will be "the Lord is there." The image of Jerusalem at the close of the Book of Zechariah (14:16–21) is similar, but – unlike in Ezekiel – the sanctity of the city of the Temple is of a universal nature, which will be recognized by all the nations. The description of "the mountain of the House of the Lord" and "the House of the God of Jacob" as the place from which learning, justice, and peace will emanate to all the nations (Isa. 2:2–4; Micah 4:1–3) identifies the mountain and the house with Zion and Jerusalem. The chapters of consolation in the Book of Isaiah (40–66) contain an abundance of expression of fervent love for Zion and Jerusalem, on the one hand, and descriptions of its future greatness and splendor in a hyperbolic poetic style, on the other. When the universal character of the center of divine worship is emphasized (56:7; 66:18–21, et al.), there is no clear distinction between the Temple and the city. In the prophetic descriptions of the visionary Jerusalem and its history, there are numerous miraculous eschatological elements (Isa. 24:23; 27:13; 54: 11–12; Ezek. 47:1–12; Joel 4:2, 12–21; Zech. 12, 14).

[Samuel Abramsky and Jacob Liver]

In Halakhah

Because of its special holiness, Jerusalem is treated in the *halakhah* differently from other cities. "Jerusalem was not divided among the tribes" (i.e., there could be no permanent ownership of it), and thus even outside the field of the sacrifices and Temple services, there are several laws which do not apply to the city. In other walled cities a house which was not redeemed by the seller within one year of the sale remained in the permanent possession of the purchaser and did not revert to the seller in the Jubilee year; this law did not apply to Jerusalem (BK 82b; and see Ar. 9:6 and 32b; Z.M. Pineles, *Darkah shel Torah* (1861), p. 165). In Jerusalem it was also forbidden to rent houses to pilgrims; they were to be given lodgings gratis, and, according to Eleazar b. Simeon, it was even forbidden to rent beds (Tosef. Ma'as. Sh. 1:12; see S. Lieberman *Tosefta ki-Feshutah*, 2 (1955), 722ff.). Indeed, it was customary for the residents to vacate their homes (ARN[1] 35, 104, cf. Tosef. Suk. 2:3) for which service they received the skins of the sacrificial animals (Tosef. Ma'as. Sh. 1:13). These special laws clarify the Mishnah: "No one ever said 'The place is too confined for me to lodge in Jerusalem'" (Avot. 5:5; Yoma 21a).

The laws of the *eglah arufah* ("broken-necked heifer"), the *ir ha-niddaḥat* ("town to be destroyed for idolatry"), and "plagues in buildings" did not apply to Jerusalem (BK 82b; cf. Tosef. Neg. 6:1). The first law requires the elders of the city nearest to a murder victim to decapitate a heifer in a ceremony whose purpose is twofold: to disclaim responsibility for the crime and to expiate the defilement of their land incurred by the blood spilt (Zev. 70b). But this law does not apply to Jerusalem because its citizens do not own the city's land, and they do not belong to one tribe. A city which had gone over completely to idolatry had to be totally destroyed because the sins of the people were conceived of as being visited in their property, as was also the understanding of the phenomenon of "leprosy in buildings." Thus these laws did not apply to Jerusalem, which could not be punished for the sins of its inhabitants.

A whole series of *halakhot* were intended to remove from Jerusalem anything which would increase ritual impurity. Therefore no trash heaps were allowed which could produce insects, nor was it permissible to raise chickens which peck at trash heaps (BK 82b; but see Eduy. 6:1). Places of burial were allowed only outside the walls of Jerusalem; in addition no existing graves were maintained in Jerusalem "except for the graves of the House of David and the grave of Huldah the prophetess which have been there from the times of the early prophets" (Tosef. Neg. 6:2). When there was a funeral procession (Sem. 10), the remains of the deceased were not taken through the city (Tosef. Neg. loc. cit., and see S. Lieberman, *Tosefet Rishonim*, 3 (1939) 190). In particular, the prohibition against leaving a corpse in Jerusalem overnight was strictly enforced, except for the honor of the deceased (BK 82b; Sifra, Be-Ḥukkotai, 6:1).

During the pilgrim festivals the laws of impurity were relaxed in Jerusalem; food and drink of the *am ha-areẓ* were then considered ritually clean, and an *am ha-areẓ* was believed if he said that he had not touched an earthen vessel, for during the festivals everyone was considered a *ḥaver* (Ḥag. 26a; Yad, Metamei Mishkav u-Moshav 11:9). It seems, however, that at the end of the Second Temple period the opposition to excessive restrictions also increased: "On one occasion they found (human) bones in the wood chamber, and they desired to declare Jerusalem unclean. Whereupon R. Joshua rose to his feet and exclaimed: Is it not a shame and a disgrace that we declare the city of our fathers unclean!" (Zev. 113a; Tosef. Eduy. 3:3).

A regulation intended to enlarge the building area within Jerusalem can be seen in the *halakhah* which says of Jerusalem that "It may neither be planted nor sown nor plowed… and trees are not put in it, except for the rose garden which existed from the time of the early prophets" (Tosef. Neg. 6:2; BK 82b). The rose garden – like the graves of the House of David and Huldah the prophetess – is a remnant of a period when these *halakhot* were not in force. Possibly the same reason explains both, namely, the desire to prevent the reduction of available land for expanded housing facilities necessary to accommodate a growing population in the city and lodging places for pilgrims. According to the *halakhah* the area of the city itself may be enlarged only under special conditions: "Additions are not made to the city [of Jerusalem], or to the Temple compartments except by king, prophet, *Urim and Thummim [Oracle], a Sanhedrin of 71, two [loaves of] thanksgiving, and song; and the *bet din* walking in procession, the two loaves of thanksgiving [being borne], after them, and all Israel following behind them." (Shevu. 14a; and see Sanh. 1:5). During the Second Temple period there was no Urim and Thummim. Abba Saul relates that the area of Jerusalem was enlarged only twice

(Tosef. Sanh. 3:4; TJ, Sanh. 1:5, 19b, TB, Shevu. 16a). It is perhaps possible to explain the *halakhah* that a foreign resident is not allowed to live in Jerusalem in terms of demographic policy (Tosef. Neg., 6:2). Even if security is posited as the reason for this law, it is not, however, necessary to date it to the period of the war with Rome.

That Jerusalem, as a meeting place for pilgrims, was also a place of business, is likewise reflected in the *halakhah*. The rabbis decreed that in Jerusalem the hour must be recorded on legal documents insofar as many documents were written by one person on the same day for people who did not know each other. Thus it was important to know whose document was written first (Ket. 10:4). A location known as *"even ha-to'an"* ("depository stone," BM 28b; see Yad, Gezelah va-Avedah 13:1) was especially set aside in Jerusalem for announcing and claiming lost articles.

Jerusalem was also noted for its customs, some of which were related to its special nature as a city of pilgrims. R. Simeon b. Gamaliel said: "There was a great custom in Jerusalem: A cloth was spread over the doorway. As long as the cloth was spread the guests could enter; when the cloth was removed from the doorway the guests were not permitted to enter." According to R. Samuel b. Meir (Rashbam), this refers apparently to uninvited guests who happened to be in the city for the festival and "who knew that they could eat there and they would go there to eat" (BB 93b; see Tosef. Ber. 4:9; S. Lieberman, *Tosefta ki-Feshutah*, 1 (1955) 62f.). It is related of the dignitaries of Jerusalem themselves that "not one of them would go to a meal until he was invited, and not one of them goes to a meal until he knows who dines with him" (Lam. R. 4:4, Sanh. 23a). The different types of food were illustrated on the tablecloth "because of the fastidious people, so that none of them should eat something harmful" (Lam. R., loc. cit).

People of integrity in Jerusalem would not sign documents unless they knew who the joint signatories were. They did not sit in judgment unless they knew who sat with them (Sanh. 23a; see *ibid.*, 30a). When the Torah Scroll was removed from the ark or returned to it they would walk behind it in respect (Sof. 14:14). There was a custom in Jerusalem to educate the boys and girls to fast on fast days. When a boy was over 12 years old "they used to bring him before every priest and elder in order to bless him, to strengthen him, and to pray for him" (*ibid.*, 18:5).

R. Eleazar b. Zadok testified that in Jerusalem there were groups of people who volunteered to carry out specifically those commandments between man and his neighbor. Some attended engagement festivities, others marriage feasts, others festivities surrounding the birth of a child or circumcisions, while still others gathered bones (of the dead). "Some went to the house of celebration, others to the house of the mourner" (Tosef. Meg. 4:15). The laws concerning the festivals were prominently and elaborately observed in Jerusalem. Wherever they went on Sukkot, the people of Jerusalem did not leave their *lulavim* behind (Tosef. Suk. 2:10, Suk. 41b). They used to bind the *lulav* with chains of gold (Suk. 3:8). There was no courtyard in Jerusalem which was not lit up by the light of the water-drawing festival (*ibid.* 5:3).

Even after its destruction, Jerusalem retained its holiness, and special *halakhot* continued to be observed. The second tithe is not separated in Jerusalem since it is now forbidden to redeem it (Yad., Ma'aser Sheni 2: 1–4). When praying, one is obligated to face Jerusalem, and if he "stands in Jerusalem he should turn his heart toward the Temple" (Ber. 30a). Entrance to the Temple Mount itself is forbidden because of ritual impurity; one who comes to pray may approach only as far as the Temple Mount. The obligation of making pilgrimage to Jerusalem remained in force, but in addition one is obliged to mourn the destruction of the city. Besides the fasts and the established days of mourning, and especially the Ninth of Av, one is forbidden to eat meat or drink wine on any day in which he sees Jerusalem in its destruction (Tosef. Ned. 1:4). One who does see Jerusalem in its destruction says: "Zion has become a wilderness, Jerusalem a desolation" (Isa. 64:9) and rends his garment. One who rends his garment for Jerusalem should not rend it further for the other cities of Judah (MK 26a). One should really mourn the destruction of Jerusalem every day and in every place; it is, however, impossible to mourn too much. "The sages have therefore ordained thus. A man may whitewash his house, but he should leave a small area unfinished in remembrance of Jerusalem. A man may prepare a full-course meal, but he should leave out an item of the menu in remembrance of Jerusalem. A woman may put on all her ornaments except one or two, in remembrance of Jerusalem" (Tosef. Sot. 15: 12–14; BB 60b).

[*Encyclopaedia Hebraica*]

In the Aggadah

The many aggadic statements about Jerusalem may be divided into three classes: those dealing with the Jerusalem of historical reality from its capture by David until the destruction of the Second Temple, statements and homilies about the Jerusalem that preceded and followed this historical city, and those dealing with the "ideal" Jerusalem of the Messianic age.

THE HISTORIC CITY. Lavish are the praises of Jerusalem in the *aggadah*, which invest it with all desirable qualities and virtues. There is no beauty like that of Jerusalem (ARN[1] 28, 85). Of the ten measures of beauty that came down to the world, Jerusalem took nine (Kid. 49b). A man who has not seen Jerusalem in its splendor has never seen a beautiful city in his life (Suk. 51 b). Even Jerusalem's lack of delicious fruit and hot springs was turned into grounds for praise: "R. Isaac said: Why are there no fruits of Ginnosar in Jerusalem? So that the festival pilgrims should not say: 'Had we merely made the pilgrimage to eat the fruits of Ginnosar in Jerusalem, it would have sufficed for us,' with the result that the pilgrimage would not have been made for its own sake. Similarly R. Dostai b. Yannai said: Why are the hot springs of Tiberias not in Jerusalem? So that the festival pilgrims should not say: 'Had we merely made the pilgrimage to bathe in the hot springs of Tiberias, it would have sufficed for us,' with the result that the pilgrimage would not have been made for its own sake" (Pes. 8b; and see Sif. Num. 89).

Extravagant accounts were given of the size of Jerusalem, and the numbers of its inhabitants were magnified in order to glorify it (Lam. R. 1: 1 no.2). According to R. Hoshaiah, there were 480 synagogues in Jerusalem, each including a school for the study of the Bible and another for the study of the Mishnah (TJ, Meg. 3: 1, 73d), and in addition there were 394 *battei din* (Ket. 105a). Jerusalem was known by 70 names, all expressions of affection and esteem (Ag. Song 1:1, line 125ff.), as well as by the Name of the Holy One blessed be He (BB 75b). Among the ten miracles wrought in Jerusalem are: "No person was stricken in Jerusalem, no person ever stumbled in Jerusalem, no fire ever broke out in Jerusalem, no building ever collapsed in Jerusalem" (ARN[1] 35, 103).

The people of Jerusalem were renowned for their wisdom: "R. Yose said: Wherever a Jerusalemite went, they would spread out for him a soft seat and place him on it in order to hear his wisdom"; the Midrash tells a number of stories about Athenians who came to Jerusalem and were impressed by the wisdom of the people and about Jerusalemites who went to Athens and surprised its inhabitants by their wisdom (Lam. R. 1:1 nos. 4–14). The people of Jerusalem were of distinguished birth and those of other places sought to marry them. "A provincial who married a woman from Jerusalem gave her her weight in gold, and a Jerusalemite who married a woman from the province was given his weight in gold" (Lam. R. 1–2, no. 2). The Jerusalemites were distinguished for their beauty (BM 84a: "R. Johanan said, I am the only one remaining of Jerusalem's men of outstanding beauty"). There are many references to the pleasant customs of "the nobility of Jerusalem and of the gentle-minded in Jerusalem" (Lam. R., *loc. cit*). The inhabitants of Jerusalem were granted atonement for their sins daily (PdRK, ed. Buber, 55b).

These statements reflect the views of the sages about Jerusalem and its people during the period of the Second Temple, and in their light they considered the reason for its destruction. Some sages declared: "We find that the First Temple was destroyed because they were guilty of practicing idolatry and incest, and of shedding blood, which applied to the Second Temple too" – and this despite all the qualities for which the Jerusalemites were praised. On the other hand, Johanan b. Torta maintained "... but in the Second Temple period we know that they studied the Torah, were strictly observant of the *mitzvot* and of the tithes, and every kind of good manners was found among them, but they loved money and hated one another without cause" (TJ, Yoma 1:1, 38c; TB, Yoma 9b). As an illustration of causeless hatred there is the story of *Kamza and Bar Kamza given by R. Johanan as the cause of the destruction of Jerusalem (Git. 55b), which was also blamed explicitly on a deterioration in relations between men (BM 30b: "Jerusalem was only destroyed... because they based their judgments [strictly] on the letter of the law and did not go beyond its requirements."). This line was followed by other *amoraim* (Shab. 119b: "Jerusalem was destroyed only because the small and the great were made equal..., because they did not rebuke one another..., because scholars were despised in it..."), while others laid the blame at the door of man's transgressions toward God ("because the Sabbath was desecrated in it... because the reading of the *Shema* morning and evening was neglected"; *ibid.*). Although here proofs are deduced from biblical verses, the reference is to the destruction of Jerusalem in general and not specifically to that of the First Temple.

THE EXTRA-HISTORICAL CITY. The history of Jerusalem begins with an *aggadah* on the creation. "At the beginning of the creation of the world the Holy One blessed be He made as it were a tabernacle in Jerusalem in which He prayed: May My children do My will that I shall not destroy My house and My sanctuary" (Mid. Ps. to 76:3). Eliezer b. Jacob held that Adam offered a sacrifice "on the great altar in Jerusalem" (Gen. R. 34:9). According to one view Adam was created from a pure and holy place, the site of the Temple (PdRE 12; Gen. R. 14:8; TJ, Naz. 7:2, 56b: "he was created from the site of his atonement"), while another maintained that all the world was created from Zion (Yoma 54b).

In an extension of the vision of Isaiah (2:2) "that the mountain of the Lord's house shall be established as the top of the mountains, and shall be exalted above the hills," Jerusalem is pictured by a Diaspora Jew of the second century B.C.E. as "situated in the center of the land of Judah on a high and exalted mountain" (*Letter of Aristeas*, 83). In a *baraita*, the view of the Temple as the highest place is connected with the verse (Deut. 17:8): "Then shalt thou arise, and get thee up unto the place which the Lord thy God shall choose," which shows that the Temple is higher than the rest of Ereẓ Israel, and Ereẓ Israel than all other countries (Kid. 69a). Associated with this description of the Temple and Jerusalem is the idea that the place is also the center of the world and the *tabbur ha-areẓ* ("the navel of the earth"), a well-known Greek concept. Philo also described Jerusalem "as situated in the center of the world" (*Legatio ad Gaium*, 294), and Josephus states that Judea "stretches from the River Jordan to Jaffa. The city of Jerusalem lies at its very center, and for this reason it has sometimes, not inaptly, been called the 'navel' of the country" (Wars, 3:51–52). This idea is also found in the Midrash: "As the navel is set in the middle of a person, so is Ereẓ Israel the navel of the world, as it is said: 'That dwell in the navel of the earth' [Ezek. 38: 12]. Ereẓ Israel is located in the center of the world, Jerusalem in the center of Ereẓ Israel, the Temple in the center of Jerusalem, the *heikhal* in the center of the Temple, the ark in the center of the *heikhal*, and in front of the *heikhal* is the even *shetiyyah* ['foundation stone'] from which the world was started" (Tanḥ. B., Lev. 78; and see Sanh. 37a; Song R. 7:5 no. 3). The antiquity of this *aggadah* is attested by a parallel in the Second Book of Enoch (23:45; Cahana's edition) in which the metaphor "the navel of the earth" is connected with the site of Adam's creation ("And that Melchizedek will be priest and king in the place of Araunah saying, In the navel of the earth where Adam was created..."). These *aggadot* and others like them make Jerusalem the place where the decisive events in man's history, as recounted in the book of Genesis, occurred (see Gen. R. 22:7; PdRE 23, 31). The identification of Mount *Moriah, on which Solomon built "the house of the Lord" (II Chron. 3:1), with "one of the mountains" in the land of Moriah, on which Abraham bound Isaac on the altar, predates the special holiness of Jerusalem and its choice as the site of the Temple to before David's capture of the city, and connects this with the promise given to the patriarch Abraham. To the name by which it is first mentioned, Salem ("peace" or "perfection," Gen. 14: 18) was added *yirah* ("reverence," in Gen. 22: 14) after the *Akedah*, both combining to form the name Jerusalem (Gen. R. 56:10).

The designation, "daughter of Zion," which is often used in the Bible to refer to the people of Israel, presumes the metaphor of Jerusalem as the mother, and this is also found in the apocryphal and apocalyptic literature (IV Ezra 10:7; I Bar. 4:9; II Bar. 3:1), as well as in Midrashim (PR 26:131b; Yal. Mak. on Ps. 147:2, no. 4 in the name of the Tanh.). The term "mother" had a special significance for Hellenistic Jewry: in referring to Jerusalem as the "metropolis," they expressed the idea that the Diaspora communities were settlements founded on the initiative of the mother city, Jerusalem (Philo, *In Flaccum*, 45–46; *Legatio ad Gaium*, 281). But in the *aggadah* the term metropolis had a different connotation. Of Jerusalem, the "navel" of the earth and the light of the world (Gen. R. 59: 5), R. Johanan said that "it is destined to become the metropolis of all countries" (Ex. R. 23:10), and in the future all nations would be "daughters of Jerusalem" (Tanḥ. B. Deut. 4).

THE IDEAL JERUSALEM. The statements of the sages on the Jerusalem of the future are for the most part connected with and based on prophetic visions on this subject. Through close scrutiny of every detail of these visions and by accepting every metaphor and parable as factual, they wove fanciful and extravagant legends. Some, however, not content with inferences from biblical passages, added their own ideas. It is an aggadic tradition, said Samuel b. Nahmani, that "Jerusalem will not be rebuilt until the exiles are gathered in, and if anyone tells you that the exiles have gathered together but Jerusalem is not rebuilt, do not believe it" (Tanḥ. No'aḥ 11). In time to come God will rebuild Jerusalem and never destroy it (*ibid.*), and it will be rebuilt with fire (TJ, Ber. 4:3, 8a). In the future, said R. Johanan, the Holy One, blessed be He, will raise Jerusalem by three *parasangs* (BB 75b); "Jerusalem will be extended on all sides and the exiles will come and rest under it," and it will reach the gates of Damascus (Song R. 7:5 no. 3). Simeon b. Lakish said, "The Holy One, blessed be He, will in days to come add to Jerusalem more than a thousand gardens and a thousand towers" (BB 75b; Mid. Ps. to 48:13; and see Kohut, Arukh, 4 (1926), 24). In the future the Holy One, blessed be He, will bring forth living waters from Jerusalem and with them heal everyone who is sick (Ex. R. 15:21). The borders of Jerusalem in time to come will be full of precious stones and pearls, and Israel will come and take their jewels from them (PdRK 137a). The Holy One, blessed be He, will build Jerusalem of sapphire stone "and these stones will shine like the sun, and the nations will come and look upon the glory of Israel" (Ex. R. 15:21). Simeon b. Gamaliel declared that "all nations and all kingdoms will in time to come gather together in the midst of Jerusalem" (ARN[1] 35, 106).

Jerusalem of the future is connected with the heavenly Jerusalem. The widespread concept of the heavenly Temple, which owes its origin to Isaiah's vision (Isa. 6), is the source of the aggadic idea of a heavenly Jerusalem (*Yerushalayim shel Ma'lah*). In an homiletical interpretation of the verse: "The Holy One is in the midst of thee, and I will not enter into the city" (Hos. 11:9), R. Johanan said, "The Holy One, blessed be He, declared, 'I shall not enter the heavenly Jerusalem until I can enter the earthly Jerusalem.' Is there, then, a heavenly Jerusalem? Yes, for it is written [Ps. 122:3]: 'Jerusalem, that art builded as a city that is compact together'" (Ta'an. 5a). Another homiletical interpretation stating that the heavenly Jerusalem is located directly opposite the earthly Jerusalem is derived from the verse (Isa. 49:16): "Behold, I have graven thee upon the palms of My hands; thy walls are continually before Me" (Tanḥ., Pekudei, 1), and this Jerusalem is in the heaven known as *zevul* (Ḥag. 12b). While the heavenly Temple was fully prepared before the world was created (Tanḥ. B., Num. p. 34), the heavenly Jerusalem "was fashioned out of great love for the earthly Jerusalem" (Tanḥ., Pekudei, 1). This distinction is unknown in apocalyptic literature. In the Syriac Apocalypse of Baruch (4:3) God says that the heavenly Jerusalem is "prepared beforehand here from the time when I took counsel to make paradise."

While apocalyptic literature (IV Ezra 10) and Paul (Gal. 4:26) stress the contrast between the heavenly and the earthly Jerusalem, the *aggadah* emphasizes their affinity. Thus, in time to come, it is stated in apocalyptic literature (I Enoch 90:28–29; IV Ezra 7:26, 10:54), the heavenly Temple and the heavenly Jerusalem will descend and be established in the place of the earthly Temple and earthly Jerusalem. "For in a place where the city of the Most High was about to be revealed no building work of man could endure." This view – adopted by the Christians, who repudiated the belief in a restoration of the earthly Jerusalem – was rejected by the *aggadah*, which states that the earthly Jerusalem will extend and rise upward until it reaches the throne of Divine Majesty (PdRK 143b; and see Tanh., Ẓav, 12; PR 41: 173a). It is only in later apocalyptic literature written in Muslim countries in the Geonic period that the idea reappears of the heavenly Jerusalem coming down to earth wholly built and entire (*Nistarot de-Rabbi Shimon bar Yoḥai* in *Beit ha-Midrash*, 3 (1938), 74f., 80; *Sefer Eliyahu*, *ibid.*, 67; see also Gen. Rabbati, ed. by Ḥ. Albeck, 131).

[*Encyclopaedia Hebraica*]

In the Liturgy

STATUTORY PRAYER. In the liturgy the Jew gave full expression to the vow taken "by the rivers of Babylon" – "If I forget thee, O Jerusalem, let my right hand forget her cunning" (Ps.

137: 5). The mention of Jerusalem was obligatory in all the statutory prayers, and it is largely used (together with Zion) as a synonym for Ereẓ Israel as a whole (in point of fact, references to Ereẓ Israel are rare). The most important of the many references is the 14th blessing of the daily **Amidah*, which is entirely devoted to Jerusalem. It begins, "And to Jerusalem thy city return in mercy… rebuild it soon in our days" and concludes, "Blessed art thou, O Lord, who buildest Jerusalem." On the Ninth of Av a moving prayer of comfort to "the mourners of Zion and the mourners of Jerusalem" and for the rebuilding of the city (called *Naḥem* after its opening word) is added to this blessing in the *Amidah* of *Minḥah*, and the concluding blessing is changed to "who comfortest Zion and rebuildest Jerusalem." The first of the last three blessings (common to all the *Amidot*), an invocation for the restoration of the sacrificial system, concludes with the words "and may our eyes behold thy return in mercy to Zion. Blessed art thou, O Lord, who restorest thy Divine Presence unto Zion." The same combination of prayer for Jerusalem with the hope for the restoration of the Divine Service in the Temple is the theme of the fourth blessing of the *Musaf* on the New Moon and festivals (the Sabbath *Musaf* refers to the return to "our land"), while the **Ya'aleh ve-Yavo* prayer includes one for "the remembrance of Jerusalem thy holy city." The third benediction of the Grace after *Meals, largely devoted to Jerusalem, includes a prayer for Jerusalem, Zion, the restoration of the Davidic dynasty, and the rebuilding of the Temple. It concludes with the same benediction as the 14th blessing of the *Amidah*, with, however, the addition of the word meaning "in thy mercy."

The *Lekhah Dodi* hymn is an impressive example of the longing for Jerusalem as it found its expression in the liturgy. Designed as a hymn of welcome to "Princess Sabbath," no less than 6 of its 9 stanzas are devoted, explicitly or implicitly, to the yearning for Jerusalem.

IN PIYYUT. The theme of Jerusalem figures prominently in **piyyut*, but its implications and frame of reference are greatly extended. Whereas in the statutory prayers the theme is confined to the actual Jerusalem, in the *piyyut* Jerusalem is also the embodiment of an idea: it is a symbol of Israel's glorious past and her hopes for the future, an image of the heavenly Jerusalem whose gates directly correspond to those of the temporal Jerusalem. The various biblical names for Jerusalem are found in the *piyyut*, as well as new names suggested by the context in which Jerusalem appears in the Bible. There are hundreds of relevant *piyyutim* and many were adopted in the *maḥzorim, kinot*, and *seliḥot* of the various rites. If Jerusalem was the "chiefest joy" of Israel when it dwelt in its own land, after the Exile, the deprivation from it became the "chiefest mourning." It is thus the theme of *piyyutim* on occasions of joy, such as weddings; of sadness, as in the *kinot* of the Ninth of Av; and of solemnity, such as the *seliḥot*. One of the earliest of such *piyyutim* for marriages is the *silluk* of Eleazar *Kallir, *Ahavat Ne'urim me-Olam* (M. Zulai, in: *Sinai*, 32 (1942/43), 52–54), which contains the following stanza:

שִׂמְחוּ אֶת יְרוּשָׁלַם בְּשִׂמְחָה
וְגִילוּ בָהּ בְּהַצָּלָה וּרְוָחָה
כִּי לָעַד לֹא יַזְנִיחֶנָּהּ
וְלֹא לְעוֹלָם לָנֶצַח יַאֲנִיחֶנָּהּ

Gladden Jerusalem with gladness
And rejoice in her with deliverance and well-being,
For He shall not neglect her forever,
Nor shall He eternally abandon her to sighing.

The theme (of joy) is common to all such *piyyutim* in honor of the bridegroom. One of the best constructed *piyyutim* on Jerusalem is included in the *seliḥot* for the third day of the Ten Days of Penitence according to the Lithuanian custom. It is a 22-stanza abecedarius, beginning with the verse:

יְרוּשָׁלַיִם אֶת ה׳ הַלְלִי דָּגוּל מֵרְבָבוֹת
Jerusalem, praise the Lord, distinguished among myriads

Each strophe starts with the word Jerusalem, followed by the alphabetical acrostic word, and concludes with a biblical quotation in which the last word is Jerusalem. The *piyyutim* of **Ne'ilah* for the Day of Atonement include both the stanza from the *Avadnu me-Ereẓ Ḥemdah* of R. *Gershom b. Judah of Mainz (Davidson, Oẓar, 1 (1924), no. 86):

הָעִיר הַקּוֹדֶשׁ וְהַמְּחוֹזוֹת
הָיוּ לְחֶרְפָּה וּלְבִיזוֹת
וְכָל מַחֲמַדֶּיהָ טְבוּעוֹת וּגְנוּזוֹת

The Holy City and its environs
Have been shamed and disgraced
And all her glories engulfed and plunged into oblivion.

and the acrostic poem of *Amittai b. Shephatiah of the tenth century in Italy (*ibid*, no. 2275) beginning:

אֶזְכְּרָה אֱלֹהִים וְאֶהֱמָיָה
בִּרְאוֹתִי כָּל עִיר עַל תִּלָּהּ בְּנוּיָה
וְעִיר הָאֱלֹהִים מוּשְׁפֶּלֶת עַד שְׁאוֹל תַּחְתִּיָּה

I remember, O God, and lament
When I see every city built on its foundation
And the City of God degraded to the nethermost pit.

Almost every *paytan*, whether of Ereẓ Israel (e.g., Yannai, Kallir, *Yose b. Yose) or of the Diaspora (e.g., *Saadiah b. Joseph Gaon, Abraham *Ibn Ezra, Joseph b. Abraham *Gikatilla) composed a *piyyut* on this theme. Each expressed his praise and longing for Jerusalem. Kallir calls it "the city of strength"; Saadiah sees "the streets of the city full of rejoicing"; Ibn Ezra sings of the "beloved Zion"; a *paytan* called Isaac refers to it as "Jerusalem the Crown of Glory"; Abraham b. Menahem as "the joyous city"; while for Israel b. Moses *Najara, in his well-known Aramaic table hymn, *Yah Ribbon*, it is "the best of all cities."

In his love songs which express passionate yearning for Jerusalem, *Judah Halevi excels over all others and earned the title "the Singer of Zion." His famous *Ẓiyyon Ha-Lo Tishali*, included in the *kinot* for the Ninth of Av, gave the lead to the *kinot* which are called "Zionides" because they commence with the word Zion. In the Ashkenazi *kinot* alone there are seven such *piyyutim*, but Davidson lists some 60 (3 (1930), nos. 277–322). Jerusalem to Judah Halevi is "beautiful of elevation, the joy of the world, the capital of the great king" (*ibid.*, 2 (1929), no. 3354; all references below are to Davidson). It is "the site of the throne of the Messiah" and "the footstool of God" (*ibid.*, no. 998); the "city of the universal God" (*ibid.*, no. 3860). Ezekiel's mention of the two sisters "Oholah the elder, and Oholibah her sister" – personifications of Samaria and Jerusalem (23:4) – became a fruitful theme for the *paytanim*, often in the form of a dialogue between them (cf. Kallir, *ibid.*, 1 (1924), no. 1721 and 2 (1929), no. 789). The *piyyut* on this theme by Solomon ibn *Gabirol, *Shomeron Kol Titten* (3 (1930), no. 686) is included in the *kinot* of the eve of the Ninth of Av in the Ashkenazi rite. Jerusalem and Samaria engage in a dialogue; the former maintains that the destruction of the Temple is the cruelest possible blow; Samaria retorts that at least the descendants of Judea still exist, while hers are lost. Oholibah answers that the repeated persecutions and exiles have been worse than death. The *piyyut* ends with the prayer, "Renew our days of old, as thou didst say, 'The Lord will rebuild Jerusalem.'"

Another recurring motif is the contrast between "my departure from Egypt" (from bondage to freedom) and "my departure from Jerusalem" (from freedom to bondage). There are *piyyutim* with this refrain by, among others, David b. Samuel ha-Levi (1 (1924), no. 5634), *Ephraim b. Jacob (*ibid.*, no. 2487), and David b. Aleksandri (*ibid.*, no. 2298), and an example can be seen in the *Esh Tukad be-Kirbi* included in the *kinot* of the Ninth of Av in the Ashkenazi rite.

The poems and *piyyutim* on Jerusalem, although individual compositions, express the longings and love of the whole Jewish people. Their inclusion in the various rites clearly testifies that throughout the ages Jerusalem continued to be at the very center of the Jews' emotions and cultural heritage.

After the establishment of the State of Israel, and especially after the 1967 Six-Day War, there was a growing feeling that the *piyyutim* on Jerusalem which emphasize its utter destruction and desolation should no longer be recited. Similarly a revised version of the *Naḥem* prayer, based on variants, particularly the Palestinian version which begins *Raḥem*, composed by E.E. Urbach, is recited in some synagogues.

[Abraham Meir Habermann]

In Kabbalah

According to *Baḥya b. Asher, the dual ending of the Hebrew word for Jerusalem (*Yerushalayim*) indicates that there is a heavenly Jerusalem corresponding to the earthly Jerusalem (see Aggadah: above). It contains a "holy palace and the prince of the Presence is the high priest" (commentary on *Sefer ha-Komah*). Following the *aggadah*, the Holy Land is the center of the world and in its center is Jerusalem, whose focal point is the Holy of Holies. All the good in the world flows from heaven to Jerusalem, and all are nourished from there (Zohar, 2:157a; Joseph Gikatila, *Sha'arei Orah*, ch. 1; *Emunah u-Vittaḥon*; Naḥmanides, commentary on Gen. 14: 18, 28; 17, etc.). Jerusalem therefore symbolizes the lowest *Sefirah*, *Malkhut* ("kingdom"), which mainly rules over the world. The mystical drama behind the history of Jerusalem is expressed in various essays: Ḥayyim *Vital, for example, interpreted the war between Tyre and Jerusalem as a battle between impurity and holiness. Jerusalem is surrounded by mountains so that the forces of the *sitra aḥra* ("the left side," the demonic powers) cannot penetrate it (*Sefer ha-*Temunah*), and the angels of the *Shekhinah* are the guardians of the walls (Zohar, 2:89b, 240b). According to Naḥmanides and Baḥya, Jerusalem is therefore especially suitable for prophecy and its inhabitants have a "superior advantage," for "no curtain separates it [Jerusalem] from God" (*Reshit Ḥokhmah*) and He wishes to be worshiped there. The prayers of all Israel rise to heaven via Jerusalem, which is the gateway to the heavens (Isaiah *Horowitz, *Shenei Luḥot ha-Berit*). The walls of Jerusalem will eventually approach the Throne of Glory (Zohar, 3:56a) and then there will be complete harmony in the realm of the *Sefirot*.

As the messianic belief did not occupy a special position in Spanish Kabbalah, Jerusalem did not attain a particular status beyond the customary mystical-symbolic homiletic interpretations. After the expulsion from Spain (1492), there is evidence of a preference for Safed over Jerusalem (*Ḥesed le-Avraham* (Vilna, 1877), 25b). For a change in a later period see *Emek ha-Melekh* (Amsterdam, 1648, 116c). The Messiah will first reveal himself in Galilee and then will go up to Jerusalem. Jerusalem also appears in the following apocalyptic works: *Sefer Eliyahu, Pirkei Mashi'aḥ, Nistarot de-Rabbi Shimon bar Yoḥai* (Jellinek, *Beit ha-Midrash*, 3), and *Ma'aseh Dani'el* (*ibid.*, 5).

Until the 16th century, only a few kabbalists lived in Jerusalem. They included *Jacob Nazir of Lunel, Naḥmanides, Judah *Albotini, *Abraham b. Eliezer ha-Levi, Joseph ibn Ṣayyaḥ, Ḥayyim Vital, and scholars who bore such pseudonyms as R. Nahorai, R. Ḥanuniah, Maẓli'aḥ b. Pelatiyah, and others. However, from the 17th century on, many kabbalists were attracted to Jerusalem, including entire groups, like those around Jacob *Ẓemaḥ, Meir *Poppers, and Gedaliah Ḥayon. Shabbateans especially, such as *Rovigo, *Judah he-Ḥasid, Ḥayyim *Malakh, and others tended to look toward Jerusalem. Even the author of **Ḥemdat Yamim* wrote as if he lived in Jerusalem. Of special note is the *bet midrash*, Bet El, founded by Shalom *Sharabi, which served as a center of Kabbalah in the East for 150 years. Its students excelled in asceticism and in prayer according to Lurianic meditations (*kavvanot*).

[Moshe Hallamish]

In Modern Hebrew Literature

HASKALAH. The historical perspective with which most of the *Haskalah literature invested Jerusalem gave the city a sense of reality if not immediacy. The *maskil*, though he wanted to assimilate into European culture, also tried to preserve his historical identity; he thus not only recalled his ancient past but vivified it. The yearning for the past glory of Israel was, however, a nostalgia for the almost irretrievable. Thus one of the major trends in the Haskalah, not unlike European literature in this respect, was a harking back to a "Golden Age." This, however, was not born out of a desire to return to the Land of Israel, which was only to grow strong much later in the wake of disappointment with the Enlightenment.

Haskalah literature not only celebrated the glory of ancient Jerusalem but also lamented the Jerusalem laid waste, the bondage, and the Exile. Two of the earliest Hebrew Haskalah writers, Ephraim and Isaac *Luzzatto, celebrated the glories of Israel's past; their panegyrics were interwoven with a strain of infinite longing to be echoed later by Micah Joseph *Lebensohn (Mikhal). Jerusalem also figured prominently in the rational allegorical strain in Haskalah writings, e.g., *Emet ve-Emunah* ("Truth and Faith"; in *Kol Kitvei Adam u-Mikhal*, 3 (1895)) by A.B. *Lebensohn, where the city is the seat of wisdom. Against the symbolic landscape of Jerusalem, Micah Joseph Lebensohn wrote a number of semi-epical poems: *Shelomo ve-Kohelet, Moshe al-Har Avarim*, and *Yehudah Halevi*. In *Moshe al-Har Avarim* Moses stands on Mount Avarim and "his eye is turned toward Jerusalem." Judah Halevi is depicted as journeying to the Land of Israel, where he meets with desolation and ruin. Standing before the gates of Jerusalem the medieval poet falls into a trance and sees the host of the dead of Zion pass before his eyes. The modern poet thereby gives a kaleidoscopic view of the woeful legions of the Jews who died for Jerusalem and Zion.

Ahavat Ẓiyyon ("Love of Zion," 1853) is a colorful pageant of the ancient past. Sensitively imitating the speech of biblical Hebrew, the author captured the rhythm of life of the ancient Hebrews. Divested of any mythical analogies, symbols, or nostalgia, his graphic rendering of life in Judah, where Jews were free in their own homeland, stirred the hearts of a ghetto generation. While Jerusalem in the novel is the backdrop of the action, it is also the symbol of the Haskalah, a harmonious reconciliation between beauty and morality. Mapu also mourned the ruin of Jerusalem, which is the leitmotif of *Ayit Ẓavu'a* ("The Painted Vulture," 1857), a savage attack on Jewish obscurantism, whose butt is Lithuanian Jewry. Jerusalem, seen through the eyes of one of the characters who sits on Mount Zion contemplating its desolation, is described with an immediacy seldom found among Haskalah writers.

Judah Leib *Gordon, a later Haskalah writer, expressed his love of Zion more directly than other maskilim and in this sense is as much a writer of the renascence period as of the Haskalah. Though he never joined Ḥibbat Zion and had misgivings about the return of the Jews to their ancient homeland, 20 years before the movement's inception Gordon wrote *Al Har Ẓiyyon she-Shamam* (1862; in *Kitvei Yehudah Leib Gordon* (1953)) urging the people to rebuild Zion. Among his poems on Jerusalem are *Ahavat David u-Mikhal* ("The Love of David and Michal") and *Bein Shinnei Arayot* ("Between the Teeth of the Lions"), an epic poem on the war between Judea and Rome. The theme of the latter, a people fighting for its liberty against overwhelming odds, is exemplified through the tragic story of a Jewish warrior who fought at the gates of Jerusalem, only to be taken captive to Rome and pitted against a lion in the arena. The poet's anguish over a nation whose ancient glory is no more suffuses the poem.

RENASCENCE PERIOD (1880–1947). In late Haskalah literature there is no clear distinction between belles lettres and writings of a social and publicistic nature. This division was effected in the renascence period when issues vital to the Jewish community were in literary writing either subsumed to the aesthetic element or were so well integrated that their militancy was muted. The great poets of the time, such as Ḥ.N. Bialik and S. Tchernichowsky, excluded the Zionist issue from most of their works. Thus the Zionist poets of the renascence movement are not the literary giants of modern Hebrew literature but minor bards such as M.M. *Dolitzki, who wrote reams of poetry on Jerusalem, most of which is sentimental and trite. A minor poet, N.H. *Imber, is remembered by virtue of his poem "**Ha-Tikvah*" (about 1876).

Jerusalem features prominently in the historical dramas of the period, some of which were a continuation of the allegorical-biblical literature of the Haskalah. In J.L. *Landau's *Aḥarit Yerushalayim* ("The Last Days of Jerusalem," 1886) the protagonists expound ideas about freedom and the glory of Israel.

Major writers of the later renascence period (1920–47) returned to the theme of Jerusalem. Although some used it merely as an image, symbol, or backdrop for the development of their plot, they invested the city with a flesh and blood reality. J.Ḥ. *Brenner wrote a number of works against the background of Jerusalem, such as *Shekhol ve-Khishalon* ("Bereavement and Failure," 1920), in which he decries the Jerusalem of the *kolel* and *ḥalukkah*, and *Mi-Kan u-mi-Kan* ("From Here and There," 1911). Some of Yaakov *Cahan's historical plays, *David Melekh Yisrael* (1921), the King Solomon trilogy, and others, are set in biblical Jerusalem. In *Aggadot Elohim* ("Legends of God," 1945), a saga of the Jewish people from the time of creation to the resurrection, Cahan strikingly describes the desolation of Jerusalem which at the same time he sees as a symbol of redemption. He also edited the anthology *Yerushalayim be-Shir ve-Ḥazon*.

Dramatists of the caliber of Mattityahu *Shoham also made Jerusalem the pervading motif of some of their works. The theme of *Ẓor vi-Yrushalayim* (1933) is a culture conflict expressed through the characters: Jezebel, Elijah, and Elisha. Jezebel is associated with Zor (Tyre), the center of Phoenician culture, the seat of idolatry identified with the flesh. Elisha, at first attracted to Jezebel, dissociates himself from her. Jerusalem symbolizes the ideal society, the rule of the spirit. Elisha's self-denial and resistance to the temptations of Jezebel is in contrast to an earlier tragic emphasis in Shoham where the Jewish protagonist is overpowered. While it is a play of high dramatic quality, it is not theatrical. The characters never become flesh and blood but remain symbolic or allegorical figures. *Ha-Ḥomah* ("The Wall," 1938), a drama by Aharon Ashman, is set in the time of Ezra and Nehemiah. Jerusalem merely serves as a background for the dramatic action. Nathan (Bistritski) *Agmon's *Be-Leil Zeh* (1934), renamed *Leil Yerushalayim* ("Jerusalem Night," 1953), an impressionistic play in which the dialogue is fragmentary and the characters symbolic, dramatizes the crisis in modern Jewish history as manifested in the conflict between the conservative Jew who acquiesces in exile and the demand for redemption. While Jerusalem is the physical setting in many of these works, the city also functions as a symbolic landscape which forms the warp and woof of the play.

During this period of national revival much drama, prose, and poetry was written in which the theme of the return to Zion did not focus on Jerusalem, but rather on pioneering and the pioneer. Although the naturalistic and realistic schools did not take up Jerusalem as a motif, there were exceptions, among them Yehoshua *Bar-Yosef's *Be-Simta'ot Yerushalayim* ("In Jerusalem Alleys," 1941), a dramatization of the tragic disintegration of a family. A conflict of generations and values, whose tragic "dissolution" is in madness, unfolds against the background of the timelessness of Jerusalem.

Yehuda *Karni in his Palestine period infused the individualistic motifs of his earlier poetry with a nationalistic theme in which Jerusalem is the eternal symbol of the Jewish people and the embodiment of its destiny. He thus deviated from the realistic trend prevalent in Palestine wherein Jerusalem was a backdrop to contemporary social problems. In his book of poems, *Shirei Yerushalayim* ("Songs of Jerusalem," 1944), the hopeless stagnation and decay of 20th-century Jerusalem against the canvas of its historical continuity is portrayed as ephemeral and transient.

A lyrical and personal note runs through Ya'akov *Fichmann's poems on Jerusalem, whose wistful mood expresses an undefined longing. The poet, like a prowler, stealthily surprises the city in its most intimate moments. Onto these he projects his own moods. In the sonnet "Jerusalem," Fichmann captures Jerusalem in a moment in which all of time is gathered and in which "Dead splendor rests on furrows of new life."

Jerusalem is central to a number of Shmuel Yosef *Agnon's works, especially to his major novels: *Ore'aḥ Natah Lalun* (1940; *A Guest for the Night*, 1968), *Temol Shilshom* ("The Days Before," 1946), and *Shirah* (1971), each of which treats the Jerusalem motif differently. The action in *Ore'aḥ Natah Lalun* is set in a small Galician town to which a traveler from Jerusalem, drawn by childhood nostalgia, has come to spend the night. The two main symbols in the work, the town's *bet ha-midrash* and Jerusalem, interact on a level beyond the immediate realistic scene. They are also interwoven into the surrealistic images, often producing a sense of eeriness and unreality. On every level of the story Jerusalem functions both as a real place in time and space and as a symbol. The surrealistic atmosphere of the town and the town itself have reality by virtue of the fact that Jerusalem in *Ore'aḥ Natah Lalun* has real existence. In *Temol Shilshom* Jerusalem also functions on several different levels; most of the action takes place in the city during the period of the Second *Aliyah. *Shirah* is set in the Jerusalem of the 1930s and describes, often satirically, the life of German-Jewish and other intellectuals at The Hebrew University. Other works of Agnon in which Jerusalem is either the setting or the theme or functions as a symbol are: "*Tehillah*," *Sefer ha-Ma'asim* ("The Book of Deeds"), "*Ha-Mikhtav*" ("The Letter"), "*Iddo ve-Inam*," "*Ad Olam*" ("Forevermore"), and *Sefer ha-Medinah* ("The Book of the State"). The particular Yemenite milieu of Jerusalem has been dealt with by Ḥ. *Hazaz.

ISRAEL PERIOD. Uri Zvi *Greenberg's Jerusalem poetry belongs as much to the Mandatory period as to the period of statehood. The prophetic thunder and woeful liturgical laments are a consistent theme in his poetry. The poet, however, not only exhorts – he also dreams; and in *Mi-Sifrei Tur Malka* ("From the Books of Tur Malka") he sees the *Shekhinah* which has returned to Jerusalem and the celestial Jerusalem which comes down to the earthly city. In *Kelev Bayit* ("House Dog," 1928) Greenberg sees at the gates of Jerusalem a "miraculous horse" waiting for its rider. "Jerusalem the Dismembered," a dirge from the greater work *Yerushalayim shel Mattah*, bemoans the shame and desecration of the holy city. Despite its despair and sense of infinite loss and infinite horror, his Holocaust poetry is characterized by a leap of faith rather than a loss of faith in God. Out of the ashes he sees salvation and imagines the host of the martyred dead gathered in Jerusalem.

The theme of Jerusalem recurs less frequently in the literature of the 1950s which is concerned with the more immediate problems of the decade. At most it is a realistic landscape. Amos Elon's *Yerushalayim Lo Nafelah* ("Jerusalem Did Not Fall," 1948) is about the siege of Jerusalem in 1948 written by an eyewitness. Yet in the late 1950s a change occurred and the canvas of the dramatist as well as of the poet and prose writer extended.

Among the younger poets Yehuda *Amichai is probably the most representative. He used the Jerusalem motif in different time settings, contexts, and even mythical landscapes. The city seems to have a strong hold on him, a hold which he wants to break but cannot. In "*Ha-Kerav ba-Givah*" ("Battle for the Hill") he says he is going to fight that battle and then "I shall never return to Jerusalem" – but he does in "Jerusalem 1967." The "sea" of Jerusalem, a symbol found already in very early Hebrew poetry, is a recurring image in "Battle for the Hill" – "the sea of Jerusalem is the most terrible sea of all." Amichai's tendency to fuse historical and mythical landscapes with the present can perhaps best be seen in "If I forget thee Jerusalem" where he uses ancient themes to create new myths. His novel *Lo mi-Kan ve-Lo me-Akhshav* ("Not of This Time, Not of This Place," 1963) contains vivid descriptions of Jerusalem.

A.B. Yehoshua's Jerusalem in "*Sheloshah Yamim ve-Yeled*" ("Three Days and a Child"; in *Tishah Sippurim*, 1970) is an impressionistic yet realistic portrait of the city marked by a note of hostility which endows it with a personality as well as a landscape. The play *Laylah be-Mai* ("A Night in May," 1969) dramatizes the effect of the tension of May 1967 on a Jerusalem family; Jerusalem, however, is only incidental to the play. Another writer who has made Jerusalem the setting of many of his works is David Shahar: *Moto shel ha-Elohim ha-Katan* ("Death of the Little God," 1970), *Al ha-Ḥalomot* ("On Dreams," 1955), *Heikhal ha-Kelim ha-Shevurim* (1962), and *Maggid ha-Atidot* ("Fortune-teller," 1966), each of the four collections of short stories. Several authors have written historical novels in which Jerusalem is a central feature, such as Moshe Shamir's *Melekh Basar va-Dam* (1954; *King of Flesh and Blood*, 1958) and Aaron A. Kabak's *Ba-Mishol ha-Ẓar* (1937; *The Narrow Path*, 1968).

Other authors who have written on Jerusalem or used it as a setting include: Dov Kimḥi, *Emesh* ("Last Night," 1927) and *Beit Ḥefeẓ* (1951), novels; *Ezra Ha-Menaḥem, bein ha-Ḥomot* ("Between the Walls," 1941); Y.D. Kamson, *Yerushalayim* (1950); Aaron Reuveni, *Ad Yerushalayim* (1954) and *Leylot Yerushalayim* (1957); Efraim and Menahem Talmi, *Sefer Yerushalayim* (1956), a miscellany; H. Brandwein, *Ba-Ḥazerot Yerushalayim* (1958); Pinḥas *Sadeh, *Ha-Ḥayyim ke-Mashal* (1968²; "Life as a Parable") and *Al Maẓẓavo shel ha-Adam* ("On the Condition of Man," 1967), novels. *Mikha'el Shelli* ("My Michael," 1968), a novel by Amos Oz, is set in the Jerusalem of the period following the establishment of the State of Israel. Yiẓḥak Navon's play *Bustan Sefaradi* (1970), a dramatization of the author's childhood reminiscences, vividly portrays the Sephardi community in Jerusalem 40 years earlier. Yoram *Kaniuk tells the story of an Israeli soldier who is severely wounded during the War of Independence in his novel *Ḥimmo Melekh Yerushalayim* (*Himmo King of Jerusalem*, 1965), setting it in an old monastery transformed temporarily into a hospital. For Shulamith *Hareven, in her much-acclaimed novel *Ir Yamim Rabim* (*City of Many Days*, 1972), pre-State Jerusalem is a poetic and conceptual space in which people with different religious and cultural convictions try to shape life together. In her novel *Korot Ḥava Gottlieb* ("The Adventures of Hava Gottlieb," 1968), Miriam Schwarz sheds light on the tempestuous fate of a young woman from the Orthodox neighborhood of Me'ah She'arim who hopes to escape the fetters of strict religious life. Haim *Be'er tells of a childhood among deeply religious Jerusalemites in his novels *Noẓẓot* (1979) and *Ḥavalim* (1998). Indeed, the dichotomy between a rigid religious life and the yearning for an emancipated, liberal way of living becomes an important theme in Hebrew novels written in the 1990s, many of which portray the hermetic world of religious people in Jerusalem (e.g., in novels by Yehudit Rotem, Mira Magen, Yisrael Segal).

Jerusalem is the setting of quite a number of contemporary novels, although Tel Aviv has become a popular backdrop for many novels (e.g., by Yaakov *Shabtai, Yoram Kaniuk, Etgar Keret), and Haifa has come to play an increasingly greater role in current Hebrew literature (e.g., in prose works by Abraham B. Yehoshua, Yehudit Katzir, Zeruya Lahav). Ariella Deem wrote *Yerushalayim mesaḥeket Maḥbo'im* (1977), Reuven Bar-Yosef *Ẓohorayim bi-Yerushalaim* ("Noon in Jerusalem," 1978), and Efrat Roman-Asher tells, in *Irushalem* (2003), the story of the first baby born in the city after the Six-Day War, combining autobiographical elements with mystical undertones. Daniel Dothan tells the story of artists and dreamers in Jerusalem during the first half of the 20th century: Based upon historical and literary documents, his novel *Al Meshulash Hafukh bein Kan la-Yare'aḥ* (1993) brings together the German-Jewish poetess Else Lasker-Schüler, the sculptor Avraham Melnikov, the Hebrew poet Uri Zvi Greenberg, and others. Jerusalem is the city in which the German immigrant Bernhart tries to reorganize his life after the death of his wife, Paula, in Yoel Hoffmann's *Bernhart* (1989). The fact that Descartes' book was lost when the couple moved from the German colony to Strauss Street is no mere accident: it suggests the loss of "European" logic in a place in which the newcomers feel disoriented and forlorn. For dramatist Yehoshua *Sobol, in his controversial play *Sindrom Yerushalayim* (*The Jerusalem Syndrome*, 1987), Jerusalem becomes the quintessence of erroneous political decisions, a paradigm of Zionist ideology gone astray. More recently, Jerusalem is the backdrop for Zeruya Shalev's international bestseller *Ḥayei Ahavah* (*Love Life*, 1997). Amos Oz tells of a childhood in Jerusalem, of intellectuals and artists such as Agnon, Joseph Klausner, and Zelda, in his autobiographical novel *Sippur'al Ahavah ve-Ḥoshekh* (2002). Jerusalem as the arena of brutal terror attacks and, at the same time, a place of reconciliation and redemption, not least so in the Christian sense, is the setting for Abraham B. Yehoshua's modern Passion, his recent novel *Sheliḥuto shel ha-Memuneh al Meshabei Enosh* ("The Mission of the Human Resource Man," 2004).

[Avie Goldberg / Anat Feinberg (2nd ed.)]

IN OTHER RELIGIONS

In Christianity

Christian concern with Jerusalem involves the ancient concept of the city as a shrine of preeminent holiness, marking the physical and spiritual center of the cosmos, the spot at which history began and at which it will reach its apocalyptic consummation. The idea of an *umbilicus mundi*, a scale model, as it were, of the universe itself, at which a nation or tribe would gather periodically to renew its corporate life by the observance of the now familiar year-rites, was known to many ancient peoples, and the nations converted to Christianity had no difficulty accepting the supreme eschatological significance of Jerusalem and its Temple. The city's unique status, however, raised certain questions that have never ceased to puzzle and divide Christian theologians, namely: Just how literally are Jerusalem's claims and promises to be taken? How can the prized continuity (back to Adam) of the city's long history be maintained if Christianity is a completely new, spiritualized, beginning? How can Jerusalem be the Holy City par excellence without also being the headquarters of the Church? How can the city's prestige be exploited in the interests of a particular church or nation? These issues have all come to the fore in each of the main periods of Christian preoccupation with Jerusalem, namely: the "Golden Age" of the second and third centuries, the Imperial age from Constantine to Justinian, the Carolingian revival, the Crusades, the period of intrigues and grand designs, the time of patronage by the great powers, and the rise of Israel.

IN THE SECOND AND THIRD CENTURIES. The question of literalism was paramount in the second and third centuries; the early Christians had been Jews of the apocalyptic-chiliastic persuasion with lively visions of a literal New Jerusalem, while an educated and growing minority (also among the Jews) favored a more spiritual interpretation of the biblical promises and accused the old-school Christians of superstition and "Judaizing." The banning of Jews from the city by Hadrian gave an advantage to the gentile party, and the "Doctors of the Church" made the Hellenized or "spiritualized" image of Jerusalem the official one (e.g., St. Jerome). Still, the millennialist teachings survived beneath the surface, occasionally bursting out in sectarian enthusiasm or becoming general in times of crisis, while the "Doctors" themselves repeatedly succumbed to the enticements of a real and earthly Holy City. Hence the ambiguities of literalism versus allegory might have been minimized, were it not that the continued presence and preachings of the Jews forced the Christians in self-defense to appeal to the doctrine of a purely spiritual Jerusalem.

From Origen's time, churchmen of all sects have been one in insisting that the New Jerusalem is for Christians only, since the Jewish city can never rise again. In the absence of scriptural support for this claim, various stock arguments are used, namely, Josephus' description of the destruction of 70 C.E. with its atmosphere of gloom and finality (BJ IV, V, 3), the argument of silence in that the New Testament says nothing about a restitution of the city after Vespasian, the ominously lengthening period of time since the expulsion of the Jews, various tortured allegorical and numerological demonstrations, and the appeal to history with the ringing rhetorical challenge: "Where is your city now…?"

A favorite argument (akin to a Jewish teaching about the Diaspora) was that Jerusalem had to be destroyed so that Jews and Christians alike might be scattered throughout the world as witnesses to the fulfillment of prophecy in the new religion. Against these were arguments that never ceased to annoy: Why did the city and Temple continue to flourish for 42 years after the final pronunciation of doom, and why during that time did the Christians show every mark of reverence and respect for both? Why did Jesus weep for the destruction if it was in every sense necessary and desirable? Why do the Doctors insist that the destruction of Jerusalem by the Romans was a great crime, and yet hail it as a blessed event, saluting its perpetrators as the builders of the New Jerusalem, even though they were the chief persecutors of the Christians? If expulsion from Jerusalem is proof of divine rejection of the Jews, does the principle not also hold good for their Christian successors? How can the antichrist sit in the Temple unless the city and Temple are built again by the Jews? The standard argument, that only a total and final dissolution would be fit punishment for the supreme crime of deicide, was frustrated by the time schedule, which suggested to many that the city was destroyed to avenge the death not of Jesus but of James the Just.

But if Jerusalem was to be permanently obliterated, the Christians could only inherit it in a spiritual sense. The Church was the New Jerusalem in which all prophecy was fulfilled, the Millennium attained, and all things became new. This raised a serious question of continuity, however: Has God chosen another people? Can one preserve the meaning of the eschatological drama while changing all the characters? Can a people (the Christians) be gathered that was never scattered? And what of the Heavenly Jerusalem? The approved school solution with its inevitable rhetorical antithesis was to depict the Heavenly and the Earthly Jerusalems as opposites in all things, the one spiritual, the other carnal. Yet none of the fathers is able to rid himself of "corporeal" complications in the picture, and the two Jerusalems remain hopelessly confused, for in the end the two are actually to meet and fuse into one. Palestine was the scene of busy theological controversy on these and related mysteries when the "Golden Age" of Christian Jerusalem came to an end with the persecutions of 250.

THE IMPERIAL AGE. After the storm had passed, Constantine the Great at Rome, Nicaea, Constantinople, and elsewhere celebrated his victories over the temporal and spiritual enemies of mankind with brilliant festivals and imposing monuments. But his greatest victory trophy was "the New Jerusalem," a sacral complex of buildings presenting the old hierocentric concepts in the Imperial pagan form, with the Holy Sepulcher as the center and chief shrine of the world. Jerusalem was treated as the legitimate spoils of Christian-Roman victory over the Jews, whose entire heritage – including the Temple – accordingly passed intact into the hands of the Christians. Henceforth, there remained no objections to giving Jerusalem its full measure of honor. Continuity back to Adam was established with suspicious ease by the rapid and miraculous discovery of every relic and artifact mentioned in the Bible, and a flood of pilgrims came to rehearse, Bible in hand (the earliest pilgrims, Silvia (383) and the Bordeaux Pilgrim (333), are markedly partial to Old Testament remains), the events of each holy place and undertake weary walks and vigils in a cult strangely preoccupied with caves and rites of the dead. The patriarch Macarius, who may have contrived the convenient discoveries of holy objects with an eye to restoring Jerusalem to its former preeminence, promoted a building boom that reached a peak of great activity in the sixth and seventh centuries.

Financed at first by Imperial bounty, the building program was later supported by wealthy individuals, and especially by a line of illustrious matrons whose concern for the holy city goes back to Queen *Helena of Adiabene and whose number includes *Helena, the mother of Constantine; his mother-in-law, Eutropia; Eudocia, the wife of Theodosius II; Verina, the wife of Leo II; Sophia, the mother of St. Sabas; Paula; and Flavia, Domitilla, and Melania, rich Roman ladies and friends of St. Jerome. By the end of the fourth century, Jerusalem had more than 300 religious foundations sustained by generous infusions of outside capital, until the economic decline of the fifth century forced the government to take the initiative, culminating in Justinian's ambitious but fruitless building program. The period was one of specious brilliance in which, as J. Hubert notes, everything had to be *splendens, rutilans, nitens, micans, radians, coruscans* – i.e., brilliantly surfaced, while the actual remains of the buildings show slipshod and superficial workmanship.

Spared the barbarian depredations suffered by most of the world in the fifth and sixth centuries, Jerusalem was an island of security and easy money, where the population of all ranks was free to indulge in those factional feuds that were the blight of the Late Empire. Points of doctrine furnished stimulation and pretext for violent contests involving ambitious churchmen and their congregations, hordes of desert monks, government and military officials and their forces local and national, the ever-meddling great ladies, members of the Imperial family and their followings, and the riotous and ubiquitous factions of the games in confused and shifting combinations. The Jews of Alexandria became associated with one of these factions, which in that notoriously fickle city found itself opposed to the faction of the Emperor Phocas, who ordered his general, Bonossus, to suppress the corresponding faction in Jerusalem by converting all Jews by force. While pitched battles raged in the streets, a Persian army appeared at the gates, sent by Chosroes, the pro-Christian monarch seeking vengeance on the treacherous Phocas for the murder of his friend Mauritius. The Jews regarded this as a timely deliverance by a nation that had succored them before and sided with the Persians – an act not of treachery (as Christian writers would have it) but of war, since Phocas had already called for their extermination as a people. The Christian world was stunned when Chosroes took the cross from Jerusalem in 614 and elated when the victorious Heraclius brought it back in 628. Under the vehement urging of the monk Modestus, whom he had made patriarch and who aspired to rebuild Jerusalem as a new Macarius, Heraclius, against his better judgment, took savage reprisals on the Jews. But within ten years the city fell to Omar, who allowed the pilgrimages to continue, while making Jerusalem a great Muslim shrine by the revival of the Temple complex, which the Christians, after long and studied neglect, also now claimed as their own.

Though Christians, originally as Jews and later on church business, had always made pilgrimages to Jerusalem, the great surge of popular interest beginning in the fourth century alarmed some churchmen, who denounced the pilgrimage as wasteful of time and means, dangerous to life and morals, and a disruptive influence in the Church. Along with monasticism, with which it was closely associated, the pilgrimage to Jerusalem was an attempt to get back to the first order of the Church and retrieve the lost world of visions, martyrs, prophets, and miracles, and this implied dissatisfaction with the present order. The writings of the Church Fathers furnish abundant evidence for the basic motivation of the pilgrims, which was the desire to reassure oneself of the truth of Christianity by seeing and touching the very things the Bible told of, and experiencing contact with the other world by some overt demonstration of supernatural power (healing was the most popular). Only at Jerusalem could one receive this historical and miraculous reassurance in its fullness; only there did one have a right to expect a miracle.

The earliest holy place visited was not, as might have been supposed, the Holy Sepulcher, but the footprint of Jesus on the Mount of Olives, the spot where he was last seen by men as he passed to heaven and would first be seen on his return (Cabrol and Leclercq, Dic. 7, 231). Contact was the basic idea – contact with the biblical past and with heaven itself, of which Jerusalem was believed to be a physical fragment. Tangible pieces of the Holy City, carried to distant parts of the world, gave rise to other holy centers, which in turn sent out their tangible relics like sparks from a central fire. The Christian world was soon covered by a net of holy shrines, built in imitation of the Church of the Holy Sepulcher or the Temple and often designated by the names of Jerusalem, the Temple or the Sepulcher. Each became a pilgrimage center in its own right, and there was a graded system of holiness measured on a scale of distance in time from Jesus and in space from Jerusalem, which remained "as far above all the other cities in the world in renown and holiness as the sun is above the stars."

THE CAROLINGIAN REVIVAL. In 800, after being fought over for two centuries by Muslim dynasties, Jerusalem was placed under the protection of Charlemagne, who was doing Hārūn al-Rashīd the service of annoying his Umayyad enemies in Spain. Although Rome had come under his protection five years earlier in the same way – by the presentation of holy keys and a banner from the bishop – it was the prestige of ruling Jerusalem that warranted the change in Charlemagne's title from king to emperor. Like Constantine, Charlemagne stimulated a revival of large-scale pilgrimage to Jerusalem and a tradition of royal generosity, endowing a church, school, monastery, and library. The Jerusalem hospitals for pilgrims were a tradition going back to pre-Christian times. From Darius to Augustus and the Emperors of the West, great rulers had courted the favor of heaven by pious donations to the holy city, and this tradition of royal bounty was continued through the Middle Ages, when kings imposed Jerusalem-taxes on their subjects and monks from Jerusalem made regular fund-raising trips to Europe.

During the years of the "quasi-protectorate of the Western Emperors" over Jerusalem and the revived Byzantine control (made possible by Muslim disunity), a steadily mounting stream of pilgrims even from the remotest regions of northwestern and Slavic Europe came to bathe in the Jordan, pray at the Holy Sepulcher, and endow pious foundations. Stimulated by the end-of-the-world excitement of the year 1000, this stream "multiplied tenfold" in the 11th century, culminating in great mass pilgrimages of thousands led by eminent lords and churchmen. When the Seljuks, having defeated the Byzantine army in 1071 and occupied Jerusalem in 1075, became oppressive in their fees and controls of the holy places, Christian leadership felt obliged to "take up again the part of Charlemagne," and the armed pilgrimage led by Robert le Frison (1085–90) was hailed enthusiastically throughout Europe and viewed by pope and Byzantine emperor alike as advance reconnaissance for a crusade.

THE CRUSADES. The Crusades were the expression of a popular religious revival in which Jerusalem, restored to its full apocalyptic status (the Crusading literature has a strongly Old Testament flavor), offered a welcome door of escape to all classes from economic and social conditions that had become intolerable in Europe. The Crusades have also been described as the complete feudalization of Christianity by an ancient chivalric tradition, with Jesus as a liege lord whose injuries must be avenged and whose stronghold must be liberated. The language of the Crusading literature bears this out, as does its conscious affinity with older epic literature (reflected later in Tasso), the significant exchange of embassies, and the close resemblance of Asiatic to European arms and accoutrements, suggesting an older common "Epic Milieu" and the nature of the Crusades as a *Voelkerwanderung*.

From the fourth century the Western Church had accepted, with the Roman victory cult, the concept of world polarity, dividing the human race into the blessed (Jerusalem, Church, *ager pacatus*) and the damned (Babylon, unbelievers, *ager hosticus*), reflected in the **jihad* concept of the Muslim countercrusade. Such a concept assumed papal leadership of all crusades, giving rise to baffling questions of imperial, papal, and royal prerogative. These came to a head in the Latin Kingdom of Jerusalem, whose assizes, though the most perfect expression of a model feudal society, remained but an ideal, "a lawyers' paradise," where royalty, exploiting the city's propinquity to heaven, dramatized its own claims to divine authority with pageantry of unsurpassed splendor. This motif was developed by the military religious orders of the Hospitalers (founded by the Amalfi merchants in 1048 and open only to the nobility) and the Templars, each claiming a monopoly of the unique traditional power and glory of Jerusalem and the Temple and, hence, displaying an independence of action that in the end was its undoing.

INTRIGUES AND GRAND DESIGNS. The Crusades challenged the infidel to a formal trial-of-arms at Jerusalem to prove which side was chosen of God. The great scandal of the Crusades is accordingly not the cynical self-interest, betrayal, and compromise with the enemy that blights them from the beginning, but simply their clear-cut and humiliating failure, which dealt a mortal blow to medieval ideas of feudal and ecclesiastical dominion. With the loss of all the East, "Operation Jerusalem" adopted a new strategy of indirection, approaching its goal variously and deviously by wars against European heretics, preaching missions (through which the Franciscans held a permanent Roman bridgehead in Jerusalem), and local crusades against Jews and Muslims as steps in grand designs of global strategy. The grandiose plans of Charles VIII, Alfonso of Castile, João II, Albuquerque, and Don Sebastian all had as their ultimate objective the liberation of the Holy Sepulcher, as indeed did all of Columbus' projects (S. Madariaga, *Christopher Columbus*). A marked kabbalistic influence has been detected in these plans, and indeed the ever-living hopes of the Jews, fired by new prophecies and new messiahs, were not without effect in Catholic and Protestant circles, as appears in the career of the humanist Guillaume *Postel, who, acclaimed at the court of France for his philological researches in Jerusalem, urged the transfer of the papacy to that city and finally declared himself to be the *Shekhinah*.

Christians in the post-Crusader period continued their dream of Jerusalem, but those who did manage to obtain a foothold there were largely engaged in unseemly squabbles over minute rights in the Holy Places. The great reformers, while mildly condemning pilgrimages, placed strong emphasis on the purely spiritual nature of the New Jerusalem and the utter impossibility of the Jews ever returning to build an earthly city. This was necessary to counteract the tendency to apocalyptic excitement and renewed deference to the Jews attendant upon the Reformation's intensive preoccupation with the Bible, as various groups of enthusiasts took to building their own local New Jerusalems or preparing to migrate to Palestine for the task. Such groups flourished down through the 19th century. Protestant pilgrims to Jerusalem from the 16th to the 20th centuries have consistently condemned the "mummery" of the older pilgrimages, while indulging in their own brand of ecstatic dramatizations. Whereas the Catholic practice has been to identify archaeological remains as the very objects mentioned in the Bible, the Protestants have been no less zealous in detecting proof for the Scriptures in every type of object observed in the Holy Land. Chateaubriand's much publicized visit to Jerusalem in 1806 combined religious, literary, and intellectual interest and established a romantic appeal of the Holy Land that lasted through the century.

When Jerusalem was thrown open to the West in the 1830s by Muhammad Ali, European and American missionaries hastened to the spot with ambitious projects of converting the Jews, with an eye to the fulfillment of prophecy in the ultimate restoration of the Holy City. Even the ill-starred Anglo-Lutheran bishopric of 1841 had that in view, and Newman's denunciation of the plan as a base concession to the Jews and Protestants indicated the stand of the Roman Catholic Church, which in 1847 appointed a resident patriarch for Jerusalem. In the mounting rivalry of missions and foundations that followed, France used her offices as protector of Roman Catholics and holy places in the East (under Capitulations of Francis I, 1535, renewed in 1740) to advance her interests in the Orient, e.g., in the Damascus blood libel of 1840. When Louis Napoleon was obliged by his Catholic constituents to reactivate French claims to holy places that France had long neglected and the Russians long cherished, "the foolish affair of the Holy

Places" (as he called it) led to the Crimean War and its portentous chain of consequences.

PATRONAGE BY THE POWERS. In the second half of the 19th century, the major powers and churches were stimulated by mutual rivalry to seek commanding positions in Jerusalem through the founding of eleemosynary institutions over which they retained control. Beyond the hard facts of geography and economics, the religious significance of the city continued to exert steady pressure on the policies of all Great Powers, as when the German kaiser gratified his Catholic subjects with the gift of the "Dormition," proclaimed Protestant unity by the dedication of the great Jerusalem Church, and sought personal fulfillment in a state pilgrimage to Jerusalem and the patronage of Zionism (thwarted by his advisers). The taking of Jerusalem by Allenby in 1917 was hailed through the Christian world as the fulfillment of prophecy and deplored by the Muslims as a typical Crusade against their holy city. World War II was followed by increasing interest in Jerusalem as a center of ecumenical Christianity, though old religious and national rivalries of long standing and great variety continued to flourish. The 20th-century pilgrimages acquired a touristic air in keeping with the times, interest in Jerusalem having a more sophisticated and intellectual tone. Even the old and vexing problem of the priority of Jerusalem, "mother of Churches," over other Christian bishoprics has been approached in a spirit of mutual concession and with respect for the autonomy of the various bishoprics of Jerusalem. This liberalized attitude may be a response to what is regarded in some Christian circles as the Jewish challenge to the basic Christian thesis that only Christians can possess a New Jerusalem. While the Great Powers for over a century cautiously sought to exploit the energies of Zionism and its sympathizers, it has been openly conceded that the Jews might indeed rebuild their city – though only as potential Christians. Though some Christians are even willing to waive that proviso, the fundamental thesis is so firmly rooted that the progress of Israel is commonly viewed not as a refutation of it but as a baffling and disturbing paradox.

A NEW IMAGE OF ISRAEL. With the Israel military victories of 1948, 1956, and 1967, the Christian world was confronted by a new image of a heroic Israel. The picture was agreeable or disturbing to Christians depending on which of two main positions one chose to take, and the years of tension following the Six-Day War of June 1967 were marked by an increasing tendency among Christians everywhere to choose sides. On the one hand, the tradition of the Church Fathers and Reformers, emphasized anew by Arnold Toynbee, looked upon a Jewish Jerusalem as a hopeless anachronism and deplored any inclination to identify ancient with modern Israel. This attitude rested on the theory, developed by generations of theologians, that only Christians could be rightful heirs to the true Covenant and the Holy City. Roman Catholics continued to hold the position, propounded by Pope Pius X to Herzl in 1904, that the return of the Jews to Jerusalem was a demonstration of messianic expectations which that church considered discredited and outmoded. Those suspicious of the progress of Israel naturally chose to minimize the moral and world-historical significance of Jerusalem and to treat the problems of modern Israel as purely political. On the other hand were Bible-oriented Christians of all denominations in whom the successes of the Israelis inspired to a greater or lesser extent renewed hope and interest in the literal fulfillment of biblical prophecy. To such persons, in varying degrees, the Jewish military achievements appeared as steps toward the fulfillment of the eschatological promise to Abraham (Gen. 15:18). As interest in Jerusalem shifted from the antiquarian appeal of the 1950s to heightened eschatological allure, something of the old Christian vision of Jerusalem seemed to stir the Christian conscience.

[Hugh Nibley]

In Muslim Thought

According to orthodox Islam there are three temples in the world to which special holiness is attached: the Kaʿba in Mecca, the Mosque of Muhammad in Medina, and the Temple Mount in Jerusalem, in order of their holiness to Muslims. While researchers of past generations viewed the traditions favoring Jerusalem as originating in the period of the Umayyad caliphs who lived in Syria and had to fight against the rebels who ruled Mecca and Medina, modern researchers deny this and maintain that the adoration of Jerusalem is found in early Islam. According to Ezekiel 5:5 and 38:12, the Temple Mount and especially the **even shetiyyah* – the rock on which the Ark stood – is the hub of the universe. Muslim scientists even found corroboration for this view in their calculations that the Temple Mount is located in the center of the fourth climatic zone, the central region north of the Equator in which man can develop civilized life.

The adoration of Jerusalem in Islam, however, is primarily based on the first verse of *Sura* 17 of the Koran, which describes Muhammad's Night Journey (*isrāʾ*). Tradition states that when the "Servant" (Muhammad) was sleeping near the Kaʿba, the angel Gabriel brought him to a winged creature (*Burāq*) and they went out to the "Outer Mosque" (al-Masjid al-Aqṣā). From there they rose to heaven (*miʿrāj*). On their way through the heavens they met good and evil powers; on reaching their destination they saw Abraham, Moses, and Jesus. The "Servant" prayed among the prophets as a leader, i.e., he was recognized as the foremost among them. There are differences of opinion regarding the nature of the journey and its purpose. Some view it as a description of a dream, but the official opinion of Muslim theologians is that Muhammad made this journey while awake and actually traversed the ground. Some hold that the "furthest Mosque" is in the seventh heaven, paralleling the Kaʿba (like *Yerushalayim shel maʿlah* = Celestial Jerusalem), but the accepted opinion, at least from the second century of the *hijra*, is that this is the Temple Mount in Jerusalem (not the mosque which was built later and called *al-Masjid al-Aqṣā*). This story was probably told to Muhammad by Jews, since he was familiar with the midrashic works popular in his time, e.g., *The Book of Jubi-*

lees, *The Book of Enoch*, and *Toledot Moshe* (extant in an Arabic version), which describe Moses' journey to heaven and his visits to paradise and hell. This story and its usual interpretation greatly elevated the holiness of Jerusalem in Islam. In addition to the Temple Mount, other places in Jerusalem were also regarded as holy, e.g., the tomb of Mary where the first Umayyad caliph Muʿawiya is known to have prayed at the time of his coronation in 661.

Upon his arrival to Medina in 622, Muhammad recited the prayers facing towards Jerusalem, in order to convince the Jews of that city to adopt the new religion. He continued with this *qibla* (direction of prayer) for 16 or 18 months (Rajab or Shaʿbān of 2 A.H., i.e., January or February 624). However, failing in his attempts to attract the Jews, he changed the direction to Mecca (see Sura 2:136ff.; Tabari, *Jāmiʿ al-bayān ʿan taʾwīl āy al-Qurʾān*, III, 138 sūra 3:142).

It is noteworthy that in the Koran there is no explicit mention of Jerusalem, not by any of the names by which it was known before Islam or immediately after the appearance of the new religion. Exegesis of the Koran, which was just beginning towards the end of the first century of the *hijra*, began to ascribe to Jerusalem names and bynames which appear in the Koran. Among the rest, they mentioned *al-Masjid al-Aqsa*, the furthest mosque or the extreme one. It appears that Muhammad's Nocturnal Journey, which became one of the most important elements determining the holiness of Jerusalem for Muslims, took shape and was linked to Jerusalem no earlier than when construction began on the al-Aqṣā Mosque near the Dome of the Rock. When caliph ʿAbd al-Malik built the Dome, the identification of Jerusalem or the Temple Mount with the site of the Nocturnal Journey was neither known nor accepted, for if this were not so, the caliph would undoubtedly have utilized it to add to the holiness of the magnificent structure and the area around it. This should have found expression in the many inscriptions carved on the walls of the building. The single reference to the verse of the Nocturnal Journey is found in later additions dating from the Ottoman period.

For most Muslims the status of Jerusalem was fixed for generations: Its mosque is the third most important in Islam. However, it is not a holy site in the Muslim sense of holiness (*ḥurma*) but rather in the general sense (*qudusiyya*), for every mosque is considered a holy place. In later days, the difference between these two concepts became clouded as Muslims used the more specific (*ḥurma-ḥaram*) for Jerusalem, even though this contrasts with Islamic law, which gives the title *ḥaram* only to Mecca and Medina (I. Hasson, in J. Prawer and H. Ben-Shammai (eds.), *The History of Jerusalem, the early Muslim period* (1996), 349–85; Ibn Taymiyya, *Qāʿida fī ziyārat Bayt al-Maqdis*, in his *al-Rasāʾil al-kubra*).

Despite this change, Jerusalem retained its special holiness among the Muslims, and Muslim tradition added numerous layers to it. There are also *hadiths* (sayings attributed to Muhammad which are the basic oral law of Islam) regarding the great value of prayer said in Jerusalem. Muslim tradition relates, among other things, that the Holy Rock (*al-ṣakhra*, i.e., *even ha-shetiyyah*) is located exactly beneath Allah's throne and above a cave which is the "well of spirits," where all the souls of the dead congregate twice weekly. Due to the rock's holiness, the angels visited it 2,000 times before the creation of the first man and Noah's ark came to rest on it. It is part of paradise and all the sweet waters on earth emanate from it. These stories, mostly taken from rabbinic *aggadah*, reached the Muslims mainly from Jews converted to Islam, as indicated by the names of the narrators recorded in the tradition itself.

Muslim legend closely connects Jerusalem with the day of judgment. According to the Muslim faith, at the end of days (see *Eschatology), the angel of death, Isrāfīl, will blow the ram's horn three times while standing on the rock, which will be done after the Kaʿba comes to visit the Temple Mount. Arabic works such as *Kitāb Aḥwāl al-Qiyāma* ("Book of the Phases of Resurrection") contain detailed descriptions of the day of judgment which will then commence. All the dead will congregate on the Mount of Olives, and the angel Gabriel will move paradise to the right of Allah's Throne and hell to its left. All mankind will cross a long bridge suspended from the Mount of Olives to the Temple Mount, which will be narrower than a hair, sharper than a sword, and darker than night. Along the bridge there will be seven arches and at each arch man will be asked to account for his actions. The faithful who are found innocent will receive from Āsiya, Pharaoh's wife, and Miriam, the sister of Moses, sweet water from the rivers of paradise in the shade of a palm tree which will also be beneath the rock. Most of these stories came from midrashic literature, such as *Pirkei Moshe*, and some of them from Christian works (see "Last Judgment," in *The Encyclopaedia of the Qurʾān*; O. Liven-Kafri, in *Cathedra* 86 (1998), 23–56).

In the third *hijri* century/ninth C.E., there appeared collections of Traditions called *Faḍāʾil Bayt al-Maqdis* (the Praises of Jerusalem). The most important are *Faḍāʾil al-Bayt al-Muqaddas* of al-Wāsiṭī, *Faḍāʾil Bayt al-Maqdis wa-l-Khalil wa- Faḍāʾil al-Sham* of Abū al-Maʿālī al-Musharraf ibn al-Murajjā, and *Itḥāf al-akhiṣṣā bi-faḍāʾil al-masjid al-aqṣā* of Muĺammad ibn Shams al-Dīn al-Suyūṭī al-Minhājī.

Jerusalem also has a special place in Muslim mysticism. There is a Muslim tradition that Jerusalem is the pit of the ascetics and servants of God and that 40 righteous men live in it, thanks to whose virtues the rains fall, plagues are averted, and the world in general exists. These righteous men are called *abdāl* ("those who are replaced"), because when one dies another replaces him. Actually this tradition is apparently not an early one but reflects the importance attributed to Jerusalem by the mystics from the beginnings of the mystical trend in Islam and the growing emphasis on its sanctity from generation to generation. Even the first Muslim mystics held that living in Jerusalem or elsewhere in Ereẓ Israel purifies the soul and that eating its fruits is permitted and legal (*ḥalāl*). For this reason many of them came to Jerusalem to be close to its holiness. Apparently the adoration of Jerusalem on the part of the Muslim mystics was mainly influenced by the example of Christian asceticism, which flourished in Ereẓ Israel, and especially in the vicinity of Jerusalem, during the centuries preceding its conquest by the Muslims.

Affection for Jerusalem and its sanctuaries grew as a result of its temporary loss during the Crusades. Indeed, the reaction to the wars with the Crusaders in the 12th and 13th centuries was an important factor in the development of Arabic literature and travelogues (see *Travelers, Christian and Muslim) on Jerusalem, Hebron (al-Khalīl), and Palestine as a whole and their importance for Islam. Descriptions of the Muslim holy *places have been preserved from that time on. Some are of great historical importance, being the principal stimulus for Muslim pilgrimages to the holy places in Jerusalem.

[Eliyahu Ashtor / Isaac Hasson (2nd ed.)]

IN THE ARTS

In Literature

An immensely rich and varied treasury of literature, art, and music has been devoted to Jerusalem by both Jews and non-Jews from early medieval times onward. Many of these treatments deal with specific events, such as the return from the Babylonian captivity and the Roman siege and destruction of Jerusalem (see *Titus in the Arts). During the Middle Ages, Jewish *paytanim* composed hundreds of poems on the subject (see above; Liturgy) and parallel Christian devotional works include "Jerusalem the Golden" (from *De contemptu mundi*) by Bernard of Cluny and several other hymns of the same title. Pre-fabricated stage settings of medieval English mystery and miracle plays often represented the Holy City, and innumerable "descriptions" were written by Crusader chroniclers, Arab historians, and travelers of various periods (see *Itineraries of Ereẓ Israel; *Pilgrimages, Christian and Muslim). The major Renaissance treatment of the subject was the Italian poet Torquato Tasso's epic *Gerusalemme liberata* (1581; translated 1594 and again by Edward Fairfax as *Godfrey of Bulloigne*, 1600), an account of the Crusaders' siege and capture of Jerusalem combining the traditions of classical and medieval romance writing. Following the Reformation, many Protestant writers evoked the image of the Holy City in verse and prose, but few works were specifically devoted to the theme.

Probably as a result of the social, political, and religious ferment of the 19th century, particularly in Britain, the "New Jerusalem" became the symbol of man's yearning for a better life and a nobler form of society. This tendency had a remarkable development in the works of the English poet William *Blake (e.g., in *Jerusalem, The Emanation of the Giant Albion*, 1804), whose "Jerusalem," a poem prefacing *Milton* (1804) which was later to become a British Labour Party anthem, ends:

> I will not cease from mental fight,
> Nor shall my sword sleep in my hand,
> Till we have built Jerusalem,
> In England's green and pleasant land.

This type of idealization also characterizes John Mason Neale's "Jerusalem the Golden," one of the best-known hymns of the Victorian era. In 19th-century works ranging in tone from pious devotion to cynicism and humor, the modern city of Jerusalem was described by writers such as the Catholic Chateaubriand and the Protestant Pierre Loti in France, the Austrian Ludwig August *Frankl, and the U.S. authors Mark Twain and Herman Melville.

From the beginning of the 20th century, there was an even more pronounced literary interest in Jerusalem's present and future, especially as a result of Zionist settlement and the development of the city's new Jewish section. An outstanding Scandinavian work on the theme was Selma Lagerlöf's two-volume *Jerusalem* (1901–02; Eng. 1915), a novel about Swedish settlers in Palestine. Her fellow-countryman, Sven Anders Hedin (who was of partly Jewish descent), described his tour of the Holy Land from Damascus to Sinai in *Jerusalem* (c. 1916; *To Jerusalem*, 1917), a travel book markedly pro-German and anti-British in tone. Hedin, who was later sympathetic to the Nazis, here made many references to Jewish biblical and later history, treating Zionism in an objective manner and illustrating his text with many of his own sketches of Jewish types. A similar approach was adopted by the English Catholic G.K. Chesterton (*The New Jerusalem*, 1920) and by the French writers Jean and Jérôme Tharaud (*L'an prochain à Jérusalem!*, 1924). In most travel literature dealing with Ereẓ Israel the main stress has been on Jerusalem.

Much popular English and U.S. fiction dealt with the city and its daily life and development during the period of the British Mandate and, later, during Jerusalem's political division between Israel and Jordan (1948–67). Two books of this kind were John Brophy's novel *Julian's Way* (1949) and Muriel Spark's *The Mandelbaum Gate* (1966). However, most of the important 20th-century treatments have been the work of Jewish authors. Mainly poems, novels, and short stories, these range from evocations of bygone days in the Old City to the reunification of Jerusalem after the Six-Day War. A rare Slavonic handling of the subject was *Pesni za Erusalim* ("Songs for Jerusalem," 1924) by the Bulgarian Jewish poet Oram ben Ner (Saul Mezan, 1893–1944). Personal reflections are contained in *Das Hebraeerland* (1937), a prose work by the German poet and refugee Else *Lasker-Schueler. The Jewish people's historic return to the Western Wall forms the climax of Elie *Wiesel's novel, *Le mendiant de Jérusalem* (1968; *A Beggar in Jerusalem*, 1970). A modern collection of literature about the city is Dennis Silk's *Retrievements: A Jerusalem Anthology* (1968), and Philip Roth places the protagonist of *Operation Shylock* (1993) in Jerusalem.

In Art

Representations of Jerusalem in plastic arts combine features of the real city and signs of its symbolic meanings in the main monotheistic religions, or are purely imaginary and symbolic.

Depictions of the *Temple's implements are the earliest surviving images relating to Jerusalem. The seven-branched *menorah* was engraved on stone in the tomb of Jason (second century B.C.E.). The *menorah*, together with the showbread table, was minted on a coin of Mattathias Antigonus (ruled 40–37 B.C.E.). The Temple's menorah, table, and an altar were scratched on the plaster of a dwelling house from the Herodian period (37–4 B.C.E.). These pictures conveyed the Jewish attitude to Jerusalem as the terrestrial abode of God's Sanctuary and the foremost place of divine worship. After the destruction of the Second Temple in 70 C.E., the Temple's façade and implements of the worship and rituals became symbols of the messianic reestablishment of the Temple that would be followed by restoration of the Jewish political sovereignty in Jerusalem and Israel. An early example of this is the façade of the Temple, rendered as a classical tetrastyle, a schematic drawing of the *Ark of the Covenant in the midst of it, the *lulav* and *etrog*, and inscription "Jerusalem" on *Bar Kokhba's silver tetradrachm (133 C.E.). The *lulav* and *etrog* near the inscription "second year for freedom of Israel" on the reverse of this coin reinforce the liturgical and messianic allusions of the Temple's image: these species are used on Sukkot – the feast that marked the consecration of Solomon's Temple (I Kings 8), was celebrated by pilgrimage to the Temple (Deut. 16:16), and is the time when, at the end of days, all the peoples will assembly in Jerusalem (Zech. 14:16ff.). Creators of ancient and early medieval Jewish paintings, mosaics, and reliefs conventionally featured the Temple as a columned façade, portal, or aedicula (see *Temple: in Art), whereas the cityscape of Jerusalem did not occupy their mind.

A symbol of the whole city of Jerusalem was found in ancient Jewish jewelry: after the "war of Quietus" (early second century) some rabbis forbade brides to wear the crowns called "Jerusalem of gold" or "a city of gold," for it was a "Greek," i.e., enemy, custom (Sot. 49a–b; TJ Sot. 9:24, 3; Shab. 59a; cf. Ned. 50a). These descriptions are reminiscent of "mural crowns" designed like the walls and towers of a city and sometimes made of gold. Such a mural crown was an attribute of the goddess Tyche, whose images were widespread in the Hellenized Middle East. Purportedly, it was an act of remembrance of the destruction of Jerusalem by "putting it *al rosh simḥati*" literally "on the head of joy" (Ps. 137:6) that inspired the association of a golden mural crown on the head of a Jewish bride with an eschatological "Jerusalem of gold."

Similar symbolic modes were implemented in early images of Jerusalem in Early Christian art. An ordinary, generalized architectural setting, comprising roofed colonnades or a row of arched and crenellated city-gates behind the figures of Christ and his disciples in fourth-century Roman sarcophagi, stood for eternal, heavenly Jerusalem (e.g., sarcophagus from 380–390 in S. Ambrogio, Milan). An aedicula appeared as a *pars-pro-toto* representation of the Temple in Jerusalem in the floor mosaics from the fifth or the sixth century in Byzantine churches on Mount Nebo in Jordan and in the Latin Ashburnham Pentateuch (seventh century, Paris, BN, Lat. nouv. acq. 2334, fol. 2).

The establishment of the Sepulchrum Domini church ("Holy Sepulcher," 326–327) by Constantine the Great, along with the proliferation of churches up to the mid-sixth century, created a new Christian topography of Jerusalem. The rotunda of the Holy Sepulcher was often depicted on pilgrim's *ampullae* (vessels for consecrated liquid) that reached Christian communities in the West and East, and its round plan served as a model for many Italian churches of the second half of the fourth century. In the background of the mosaic of the Church of St. Pudenziana in Rome (384–389, 401–417), a picture of the real Constantinian complex of the Holy Sepulcher appears above the wall with 12 gates of celestial Jerusalem (two of them were later erased). This number reinforces the relation of the picture to the eschatological Jerusalem described in Revelation 21:12.

Christian religious and ideological concepts of Jerusalem were imposed on the real topography of the city. The pictorial map of Jerusalem (560–565) on the floor mosaic in the Church in Madaba (Jordan) depicts the Holy Sepulcher in the midst of the *cardo maximus* in the very center of the city, though the real church is found northwest of that point. The dominating position of the Holy Sepulcher represents the vision of mundane Jerusalem as the place of Christ's resurrection and a preview of the ideal, heavenly Jerusalem.

Since at least the ninth century, the apocalyptic vision of heavenly Jerusalem in Revelation 21:10–22:5 related patristic exegesis, and the teaching on the *Civitate Dei* by *Augustine of Hippo (354–430) inspired conventional depictions of Jerusalem in ecclesiastic art and manuscripts. The Apocalypse of Trier (North France, first quarter of the ninth century; Trier, Stadtsbibliothek, cod. 31, fols. 69–71), the earliest-known illuminated manuscript of the Book of Revelation, gives a combination of a frontal view of the fortified city wall from outside and a bird's-eye view of objects inside, with the inner side of the wall behind them. The painting creates an image of a stronghold with 12 towers (Rev. 21:12–13) enclosing in its midst churches or a lamb, a symbol of Christ, who substitutes for the Temple in the apocalyptic Jerusalem (Rev. 21:22), and the Tree of Life. Many medieval manuscripts of the Apocalypse and the commentary on it by Beatus of Liébana (d. 798) represent a geometrical scheme of heavenly Jerusalem consisting of a section of the city wall with three gates on each side of a square containing Christ and/or the lamb as an illustration of the city with the gates for the 12 *tribes of Israel (Rev. 21:12). Jerusalem in the middle of nations with its gates facing the four winds, a counterpart of the Temple in Ezekiel's vision (40:1–43:12), marks the center of the world and the prevalence of Christ's power in the cosmos. The Apocalypse of Valenciennes (Liège (?), first quarter of the ninth century; Valenciennes, Bibl. Municipale, ms. 99 fol. 38) exemplifies the circular images of heavenly Jerusalem with triple gates on the four cardinal points of the perimeter. In Romanesque cathedrals (e.g., in Aachen and Hildesheim), the monumental lamps made as a gilt hoop looking like a city wall with 12 or 24 towered gates represented heavenly Jerusalem as a luminous circular city hovering above the worshippers.

Although deviating from the definition of Jerusalem as "*civitas in quadro posita*" in Revelation 21:16, these images emphasize the idea of the city as the *umbilicus mundi* ("the navel of the world"), the concept adopted from classical thought (Philo, *Legation ad Gaium*, 294). Like the round Holy Sepulcher, a circular Jerusalem symbolized Christ's resurrection and the new life of the world. Crusader pictorial maps (e.g., Brussels, Bibl. Royale, ms. 9823–9824, fol. 157) involve frontal depictions of Christian landmarks of the mundane Jerusalem into the abstract circular scheme and stress the cruciform of the *cardo* and *decumanus* in order to give the real topography a christologic meaning. A medallion enclosing a picture of Jerusalem is the center of the map of the world, shaped as a trefoil, a symbol of the Trinity, in Heinrich Buenting's *Itinerarium Sacrae Scripturae* (Wittenberg 1587).

The symbolic approach to real Jerusalem had an effect on the Christian comprehension of the Muslim *Qubbat as-Sakhrah* (Dome of the Rock) built on the spot of the Temple in Jerusalem in 691–692. The Crusaders, who in 1141 dedicated this octagonal domed structure as the *Templum Domini* (God's Temple) church, imparted it with associations with the Temple. The *Templum Domini* and the *Sepulchrum Domini*, similarly rendered as domed towers rising behind a fortified city gate, stand for Jerusalem in the lead seal of John of Brienne, a ruler of the Crusader Kingdom of Jerusalem (1210–1225). The juxtaposition of the two edifices restates the idea that Christianity stems from both the Old and New Testaments. Ecclesiastic vessels, mainly monstrances and chalice-like ciboria containing the sacrament; reliquaries; and censers, designed as a round or equilateral domed structure, usually symbolized the *Templum Domini*, Solomon's Temple, and Jerusalem. The Dome of the Rock dominates in landscapes of biblical and real Jerusalem in European art. Erhard Reeuwich's illustration to Bernhard von Breydenbach's *Peregrination in terram sanctam* (Mainz, 1486) transforms the pilgrims' impressions of Jerusalem into a bird's-eye view of buildings around the disproportionately great Dome of the Rock. In a view of the biblical Jerusalem in Hartmann Schedel's *Liber Chronicarum* (Nuremberg, 1494), three rings of city walls enclose a great structure resembling the Dome that is explicitly labeled as the *Templum Salomonis*. Italian Renaissance painters and architects accepted the octagonal Dome in the center of Jerusalem, in the light of Vitruvius's theory locating the ideal centrally planned temple in the midst of an ideal centrally planned city. Idealized Renaissance copies of the Dome of the Rock appear in church architecture (Donato Bramante, the *Tempietto* at San Pietro in Montorio, 1502–1511, Rome) and represent the Temple in Jerusalem in paintings by Pietro Perugino (1450–1523), Raphael (1483–1520), and Vittore Carpaccio (1472–1526).

European scenery in Christian pictures of Jerusalem also stems from the Christian perception of the sacred history as ever contemporary. In Jean Fouquet's illustrations to *Jewish Antiquities* by *Josephus Flavius (1470–1475; Paris, Bibl. Nat., Ms. Fr. 247), the Temple in Jerusalem looks like a Gothic cathedral in a French city. Following the same achronical concept, the Jerusalem cityscape is painted as typically Italian in Duccio's *Entry into Jerusalem* (Maestà, verso, 1308–1311; Siena, Museo dell'Opera del Duomo), Netherlandish in Hieronymus Bosch's "*Ecce Homo*" (ca. 1485; Frankfurt am Main, Städtisches Kunstinstitut), and German in the *Stories of the Passion* by an anonymous painter from Westfalen (ca. 1480; Torun, St. Jacob Church).

The view of celestial Jerusalem as the model for the proper arrangement of Christian sacral and secular life was reflected in architecture. In religious building complexes of the Catholic West, cloisters (enclosed courtyards for religious retirement) composed of a rectangular, often square-shaped garth and surrounding arcaded passages, were paralleled to the apocalyptical square Jerusalem. In a medieval city, the same symbolism was given to the city square enclosed by arcades (e.g., the central place in Monpazier, South France, founded in 1284). Cities built on a concentric plan were related to Jerusalem as well: the verse from Isa. 51:9 inscribed above the map of concentrically planned Moscow on the title page of the printed Russian Bible from 1663 represents that city as a revived Jerusalem.

Christian architects transposed the real Jerusalem by creating local counterparts for the Golgotha, Way of the Cross ("*via Dolorosa*"), Temple Mount, Mount of Olives, Mount Zion, Jerusalem churches, etc. Within the church, cloister, or nearby, a series of sculptures, pictures, or mere inscriptions marked the "stations" of Christ on the "*via Dolorosa*" in Jerusalem. A group of connected chapels, dated to the fifth century, in the Bolognese monastery of San Stefano, also known as "*Hierusalem*," represented important Christian sanctuaries of Jerusalem. The urban or landscape copies, commonly called New Jerusalem, Calvary, or a *sacro monte*, were intended to be faithful replicas of the holy places. In practice, some of them, e.g., Kalwaria Zebzydowska (1602) in Poland, retained the mutual location and distances between original monuments in the Holy Land. The other, for instance, the *Scala Coeli* convent (ca. 1405) in Cordoba, the *sacri monti* in Varallo Sesia (1486), San Vivaldo (1499) in Italy, and the whole old city of Suzdal in Russia, established a more schematic and partial resemblance to pilgrim's topography of Jerusalem.

Paintings in Hebrew illuminated manuscripts and early printed books focus on the future Jerusalem. The *Mount of Olives, depicted as an olive tree on a hill, is the only landmark of Jerusalem beyond the Temple Mount that appears among the Temple's implements in paintings from Hebrew Bibles of the 13th to 15th centuries. The citation from Zechariah 14:4 framing the full-page painting of the Mount of Olives in the 14th-century Hebrew Bible from Saragossa (Paris, Bibl. Nat., Ms. Hebr. 31, fol. 4v) determines the symbolism of this place as the stage of God's advent in the messianic future. The vision of the city of Jerusalem is a subject of illuminated manuscripts and books of the Passover **Haggadah*. The picture of Jews lifting their hands in adoration to the Messiah waiting at the gate of heavenly Jerusalem illustrates the culminating passage: "Next year in Jerusalem" in the Birds' Head *Haggadah* of ca. 1300 from Southern Germany (Jerusalem, Israel Museum, Ms. 180/57, fol. 47r). The hovering Jerusalem is drawn as a Gothic city-gate with a section of an arcaded wall. The Messiah who rides on a donkey, preceded by Elijah the prophet, towards Jerusalem relates to the verse "Pour out Thy wrath upon the heathen." In these pictures Jerusalem looks like a fortified city with a tall tower (the Hamburg Miscellany, ca. 1427–1428, Germany; Hamburg, Staats- und Universitätsbibliothek, Cod. Hebr. 37, fol. 35v), a fortified wall with an open gate (Haggadah, 1470–1480, Italy; Munich, Bayerische Staatsbibl., Cod. Hebr. 200, fol. 24v), or a domed tower in the printed Mantua *Haggadah* (1560). A hand holding a sword above a city that is tightly embraced by a fortified wall, illustrating I Chronicles 21:16, shows divine protection over Jerusalem in the Cretan Haggadah Candia, 1583 (Paris. Bibl. Nat., 1388, fol. 11r).

Notwithstanding the fact that a polygonal domed building is at odds with the biblical and rabbinical accounts of the Temple, Jews adopted the Dome of the Rock as an image of the sanctuary in Jerusalem (Frankfurt *Mishneh Torah*, 15th century, North Italy; New York, private coll., fol. 1r). Since the mid-16th century, printers of Hebrew books in Venice and Prague used the Dome evidently labeled *Bet ha-Mikdash* ("the Temple") as their sign, and a century later, the brothers Ashkenazi used a naïve version of this building in the midst of three city walls in their books printed in Constantinople. The inscription: "The glory of this latter house shall be greater than of the former …" (Hag. 2:9) accompanying the Dome in the "printers' marks" asserts that this is a vision of the messianic Temple in the future Jerusalem, and not a picture of the historic past. In a similar way, the messianic Jerusalem has taken the Renaissance form of an octalateral city centering on the octagonal domed Temple in the Venice *Haggadah* of 1609. An image of a domed structure near lesser buildings, sometimes within a polygonal city wall, was used as a sign for remembrance of Jerusalem on 17th-century Italian Torah Ark curtains and as an eschatological symbol and a sign for the "chief joy" for Jerusalem (Ps. 137:6) at the top of the *ketubbot,* whose design followed the complex decorative program that was developed in Venice in the 1660s.

Matthaeus Merian the Elder's engraving of the biblical Jerusalem in the *Icones Biblicae* (Amsterdam, 1659) exemplifies a direct influence of Christian art on Jewish images of Jerusalem. In the 1695 Venice *Haggadah* and its numerous manuscript and printed remakes, Merian's splendid Temple of Solomon in the midst of cloister-like walled courtyards, surrounded by the city buildings and lighted up by the shining sun, was reworked for a vision of the messianic Jerusalem. Jewish artisan Eliezer Sussmann, of Brody in the Ukraine, copied later folk replicas of this picture from *Haggadot* and Grace After Meals manuscripts (also containing the plea for rebuilding of Jerusalem) into his rich wall paintings in South German synagogues in 1732–42. In these and other synagogue murals produced by East European Jewish painters of the 18th and 19th centuries, Jerusalem is represented as a conglomeration of domed and roofed buildings of different lengths, gradually increasing towards the highest domed tower or roofed palace, all rendered in the local architectural styles. In some synagogues Jerusalem as a symbol of the redemption is juxtaposed against a view of a city symbolizing the Exile: Worms in the ceiling painting (1740) by Ḥayyim ben Isaac Segal in the synagogue in Mogilev in Belorus, or Babylon in the picture of the "Rivers of Babylon" (Ps. 137) in synagogues of Predbórz (mid-18th century) and Grojec (first half of the 19th century) in Poland. In the synagogue in Kamenka-Bugskaya in the Ukraine, the picture of a burning city with wild beasts approaching its walls remind the worshippers of the fall of Jerusalem. The sorrow and remembrance for Jerusalem were expressed in a more abstract way in a Hebrew acronym שעל״ז: (שחור על לבן זכר לחרבן), "black on white, a remembrance of the Destruction [of Jerusalem]") that was painted in black paint on a white background, and in some cases located beneath a picture of Jerusalem.

Jewish pilgrims' topography of Jerusalem was cast into a pictorial form in the mid-16th century, following the spread of illustrated Hebrew descriptions of the holy places and the graves of the righteous itineraries of the Holy Land such as the *Yiḥus ha-Avot* ("Genealogy of the Patriarchs"). The local scribes traditionally alternated textual descriptions with schematic drawings of landmarks of Jerusalem but gave no general view or plan of the city. The development of this imagery in the Land of Israel led to the 18th- and 19th-century schematic "maps" depicting the holy places as almost decorative rows of flattened geometric, ornamental, or simplified architectural images, whereas the Italian and German copies of the *Yiḥus ha-Avot* rendered these patterns as classical buildings. Jewish scribes in 18th-century Italy amalgamated the landmarks from the pictorial itineraries, a cityscape of houses and towers, and a geometric plan of the ideal city into the view of the holy places in Jerusalem. Thus in the view of Jerusalem that occupies most of his scheme of holy places in the Land of Israel (first half of the 18th century; Cambridge University Library), Samuel ben Yishai of Senigallia marked the different Jewish communities in the Jewish Old City, the Tower of David within the city walls, and the so-called Tombs of Absalom and Zechariah in the Valley of Kidron. The Hebrew inscriptions identify the Dome of the Rock and the *al-Aqsa* Mosque depicted on the opposite sides of the Temple Mount as the Temple and Solomon's *bet midrash* ("house of study"), respectively. Between them, a group of cypresses rises above the western section of the wall supporting the Temple Mount. The Wailing (Western) Wall was thought to coincide with the place which, according to midrashic sources (Ex. R. 2:2; Num. R. 11:2, etc.), the Divine Presence never left, and which was the closest spot to the Holy of Holies accessible to the Jews where they mourned the destruction of the Temple. The cypresses which are seen from afar on the Temple Mount were supposedly identified with the cedars "planted in the house of the Lord" (Ps. 92:131; cf. I Kings 50:20ff.) evoking the messianic restoration of the Temple. This new composition became the most frequent pictorial sign of Jerusalem on a vast range of Jewish ritual and household objects that were sent from the Land of Israel to Jews elsewhere and on the copies of these objects made in the Diaspora. In contrast to the undying messianic hope in Jewish folk art, professional European artists of Jewish origin who converted to Christianity (e.g., Eduard Bendemann in his *Jeremiah on the Ruins of Jerusalem*, ca. 1834–1835) expressed in images of Jerusalem their despair and lack of belief in the redemption of the Jews.

In Muslim art, Jerusalem is generally symbolized by the *Qubbat as-Sakhrah* or the *Ḥaram al-Sharīf* (the Temple Mount). Admittedly, some scholars hypothetically interpret the polygonal walled city which is presented on a tray to Muhammad in a painting from a *Mi'rāj Nāmeh* manuscript (Tarbiz, ca. 1360–1370; Istanbul, Topkapi Sarayi, H. 2154, fol. 107r) as the city of Jerusalem, discerning the Dome of the Rock and *al-Aqsa* mosque among its buildings. Concurrently with the early illustrated Jewish itineraries of the Holy Land, schematic maps of the Temple Mount, like maps of Mecca and Medina, appeared in manuscript scroll guides for Muslim pilgrims (e.g., the guide from 1544–1545; Istanbul, Topkapi Sarayi, H. 1812). The site is commonly depicted as a rectangle containing the *Qubbat as-Sakhrah*, in some pictures with the rock shown inside, in the lower center; the *al-Aqsa* above; minarets; other Muslim sacred places; and also cypresses, palm trees, and mountains – all seen in profile or from above. Such maps were also depicted on the *gibla* wall in Ottoman mosques (e.g., the painting from ca. 1660–63 in the Haznedar Mosque at Sivrihisar near Ankara).

Napoleon's Egyptian campaign (1798–99) and increasing political interests of France, England, and Germany in the Holy Land prompted modern European painters to discover the real Jerusalem. With the benefit of realistic drawings from nature, Luigi Mayer (1755–1803), Henry Warren (1794–1879), David Roberts (1796–1864), and William Henry Bartlett (1809–1854) looked at Jerusalem through the traditional concept of the sacred city, giving in their pictures a distant view of the Dome of the Rock on the Temple Mount under the high sky. In due course, many artists became attracted by a closer illusionistic view of the holy places, ancient monuments, and archaeological sites as if conveying a look of an eyewitness (cf. works by Carl Friedrich Werner, 1808–1894; William Simpson, 1823–1899; Vasily Vereshchagin, 1842–1904; John Fulleylove, 1845–1908; Gustav Bauernfeind, 1848–1904; Stanley Inchbold, 1856–1921). One such subject relating to the Jewish aspect of Jerusalem was the Jews praying at the Western Wall shown at a sharp angle from the narrow court near it.

Similarly, presentations of the prayer at the Western Wall and a visionary city became subjects of pictures of Jerusalem by modern Jewish artists. Inspired by the Zionist ideas, Ephraim *Lilien in Berlin depicted Jerusalem as a promised city seen from afar, against the shining sun that stretches its rays towards a Jew suffering in the Exile (an illustration to Morris Rosenfeld's *"Der Juedische Mai," Lieder des Ghetto*, 1902). But even when the Israeli artists Reuven *Rubin (1893–1974) and Nahum *Gutman (1898–1980) observed the actual cityscape, they postulated a distance from the Temple Mount. From the 1920s, artists focused their attention on the Jewish quarters of Jerusalem, often showing them looking like a downtrodden provincial *shtetl* (e.g., Jacob *Steinhardt, 1887–1968, and Hayim Gliksberg, 1904–1970) or alleys of a European city (e.g., Ludwig *Blum, 1891–1974). The authentic sense of crude hills, poor vegetation, and rocky houses of Jerusalem feature works by Anna *Ticho (1894–1980) and Leopold *Krakauer (1890–1954). Contemporary Israeli artists take the imagery of Jerusalem in the direction of political and ideological controversies. As examples, restating the idea of the Jewish national home, Jan Rauchwerger (1942–) paints the Israeli flag streaming in fresh air over landscapes of the Judean hills near Jerusalem; David Reeb's (1952–) views of the holy places in Jerusalem supplied with a barcode evoke irony or protest against commercialism of faith and ideals; and Menashe Kadishman's (1932–) paintings of the Wailing Wall, whose stones are touched by multicolored patches of paint, question the very respect for national values.

Since 1967, the political and ideological competition over Jerusalem provoked the revival of the image of *Qubbat as-Sakhrah* in the art and visual propaganda of artists of Arab origin as a symbol of the claim for the whole of Jerusalem and Palestine. Nabil Anani (1943–), Sliman Mansour (1947–), Taleb Dweik (1952–), and others adopted the images of the ideal circular city and ethereal Jerusalem centering on the Dome of the Rock in the context of longing and struggle for the lost land. The real Jerusalem is referred to symbolically and conceptually as a place of humiliation: for instance, Kna'an Ahmed's sculpture *New Walls of Jerusalem* (ca. 2004) alludes to administrative barriers between the Eastern and Western parts of the city.

[Ilia Rodov (2nd ed.)]

In Music

In music, as in literature, there is a vast and varied body of material inspired by the theme of Jerusalem. Theoretically, the "songs of Jerusalem" include the innumerable settings of the countless biblical verses, prayers, hymns, and poems in which Jerusalem or Zion are mentioned – in art and folk music and in Jewish and Christian culture. Such a list would also have to include the Passion compositions (since their scene is Jerusalem) and works about the Crusades (including the many compositions based on Tasso's *Jerusalem Delivered*). Until the end of the 19th century, many oratorios, operas, choral works, art songs, and symphonic works dealt with the two destructions of Jerusalem by Nebuchadnezzar and Titus (the correlation with historical events is difficult to establish in most cases). However, several English and U.S. composers have turned to the "Heavenly City" subject, stimulated by the enormous success of Ewing's hymn, "Jerusalem the Golden" (see below), and also perhaps by the medieval revival. Among notable works are Ralph Vaughan Williams' oratorio, *Sancta Civitas* (1892), based on the Apocalypse, and Horatio W. Parker's *Hora novissima* (1892), based on the Latin prototype of the hymn. Works by modern Jewish composers include Lazare *Saminsky's *City of Solomon and Christ* (1932), for mixed chorus and orchestra, and Darius *Milhaud's *Les* *deux Cités* (1937), a cantata for augmented children's chorus with text by Paul Claudel (comprising "Babylone," "Élégie," and "Jérusalem").

Israel works written before 1967 dealt with certain aspects of Jerusalem, but after the Six-Day War, there was an intense preoccupation with the subject, both spontaneously and by commission. Recha *Freier organized the *Testimonium Jerusalem*, which commissioned composers in Israel and overseas to write works on the history of Jerusalem, which were played at special performances in Jerusalem. Other works composed between 1967 and 1970 include *Jerusalem Eternal*, a cantata by Haim *Alexander; *Tyre and Jerusalem*, a ballet (based on the play by Mattityahu *Shoham) by Ben-Zion *Orgad; and *Jerusalem*, a symphony for mixed chorus, brass, and strings by Mordechai *Seter.

Among the few Protestant chorales which apostrophize Jerusalem directly, the most famous is Melchior Franck's *Jerusalem, du hochgebaute Stadt* (first published 1663), of which there have been many English translations (e.g., *Jerusalem, thou city built on high*). The vision of the Apocalypse appears in a number of Latin hymns paraphrased again and again in the 19th century (J. Julian, *A Dictionary of Hymnology* (1892), S.V. *Coelestis O Jerusalem, Coelestis urbs Jerusalem, Urbs beata Jerusalem*). Outstanding among these is Alexander Ewing's music to John Mason Neale's text, "Jerusalem the Golden," which "conquered the world" after its publication in *Hymns Ancient and Modern* (1861). It draws from the section of Bernard of Cluny's *De contemptu mundi (Hora novissima)* beginning *Urbs Sion aurea/patria lactea/cive decora* (see Julian, op. cit., s.v. Neale) and the melody is in typical 19th-century hymn style; but the beautiful opening phrase C/DCFE/D-C goes back to the German Protestant chorale setting of *Nun ruhen alle Waelder.*

IN JEWISH FOLK SONG TRADITION. The following are some of the best-known Jewish folk songs on Jerusalem:

(a) Sephardi: "*De frutas sabrosas*" (M. Athias, *Romancero Sephardi* (1961², nos. 132, 133); "*Ir me quiero, madre, a Jerusalem*" (*ibid.*, no. 131), the latter often sung by families when saying farewell to a relative bound on a journey to the Holy Land.

(b) Kurdistan Jews: "*Ha-Shem vi-Yrushalayim*," for Shabbat *Naḥamu*; Aramaic, in the form of a dialogue between God and Jerusalem (Y.Y. Rivlin, *Shirat Yehudei ha-Targum*, 1959).

(c) Eastern Ashkenazi: "*In der Shtot Yerusholayim*" and *Zingt-zhe alle Yidelach* (Idelsohn, Melodien, 9 (1932), nos. 219, 225); "*Yerusholayim slavny gorod,*" with Russian words (*ibid.*, no. 438; the prototype for the later Hebrew "*Yerushalayim Ir ha-Kodesh,*" see below).

(d) Yemenite: "*Kiryah Yefehfiyyah,*" poem by Shalom *Shabbazi. The melody, already notated by A.Z. Idelsohn in his *Sefer ha-Shirim* (1911), became a Hebrew folk song and was made famous in the interpretation of Berachah *Ẓefirah.

Most of the Jerusalem songs in the Diaspora are lyrical and yearning in their texts and melodies, though some of the Eastern Ashkenazi tunes are more vigorous. Not all the Hebrew songs which mention Jerusalem are "Jerusalem songs." Even in "*Ha-Tikvah,*" the city symbolizes the whole of Ereẓ Israel – the refrain ends, in the old version: *lashuv le-ereẓ avoteinu/Ir bah David ḥanah* ("to return to the land of our fathers/ the city where David abode") and in the new version: *lihyot am ḥofshi be-arẓenu/ereẓ Ẓiyyon vi-Yrushalayim* ("to be a free people in our land/the land of Zion and Jerusalem").

Of the songs directly connected with the city, the following are the most important:

(1) J. *Engel and A. *Hameiri, *Hoi, hoi, hoi, Na'alayim*, the climax of which is: *Ḥalutz, beneh, beneh Yerushalayim* ("O pioneer, build Jerusalem!"); poem written by Hameiri in 1922 when the *Gedud ha-Avodah was working on the road to Jerusalem; setting by Engel for the *Ohel choir (1926).

(2) Adapted tune of *Yerushalayim slavny gorod* (see above); Emanuel ha-Russi *Yerushalayim Ir ha-Kodesh* (1925).

(3) M. Rapoport and A. Hameiri, "*Me-al pisgat Har ha-Ẓofim*" ("From the Summit of Mount Scopus," 1930), melody based on an Eastern Ashkenazi prototype. Rapoport later wrote another setting, but this not as popular as the first.

(4) S. Ferszko and *Ḥ. Gouri, "*Bab-el-Wad*" (1949), mourning the Jewish fighters who died during Israel's War of Independence at the "Gate of the Valley" (*Sha'ar ha-Gai*, Arabic Bab el-Wad; where the road to Jerusalem enters the mountains).

(5) E. *Amiran and R. Saporta, "*Mi va-rekhev, mi va-regel*" ("Some come by car and on foot")… *Na'aleh-na li-Yrushalayim* (1950); children's song for Independence Day, which was still in popular use for the Three-Day March to Jerusalem.

(6) Y. Ne'eman's setting of Judah Halevi, "*Yefeh Nof Mesos Tevel*" an Orientalizing melody, written for the Israel Song Festival.

(7) N. *Shemer (words and music), "*Yerushalayim shel Zahav,*" written for the 1967 Israel Song Festival, which achieved wide popularity partly because it appeared on the eve of the Six-Day War. Other Jerusalem songs written during and after the Six-Day War did not achieve the same impact.

Some Israel "Bible-verse" songs may also be considered "Jerusalem songs," e.g., *Amiran's "*Al Ḥomotayikh Yerushalayim*" (Isa. 62:6), written during the 1948 siege, "*Ki mi-Ẓiyyon Teẓe Torah*" (Isa. 2:3; c. 1942), and "*Halleluyah Kumu ve-Na'aleh Ẓiyyon*" and "*Uru Aḥim ve-Na'aleh Har Ẓiyyon*" based on Psalms (1933–36; for the Offering of the First Fruits); Y. Zarai's "*Va-Yiven Uzziyyahu*" (II Chron. 26:9; c. 1956); N.C. Melamed's "*Ve-Teḥezenah Einenu*" (c. 1950); M. *Ze'ira's "*Ashrei ha-Ish Yissa et Alumav/ Be-Ma'aleh Harei Ẓiyyon*" (c. 1942) and "*Lekhu ve-Nivneh et Ḥomot Yerushalayim*" (Neh. 2:17/ 4:15); and M. *Wilensky's "*Uri Ẓiyyon, hoi Uri, Livshi Uzzekh*" (Isa. 52:1–2).

See also *Josephus in the Arts; *Lamentations in the Arts; *Temple in the Arts; *Titus in the Arts; *Zerubabel in the Arts.

[Bathja Bayer]

BIBLIOGRAPHY: GENERAL: M. Avi-Yonah (ed.), *Sefer Yerushalayim* (1956), incl. bibl.; idem, *Jerusalem* (1960); S.W. Baron, in: *Jerusalem. City Holy and Eternal* (1954), 11–32; M. Join-Lambert, *Jerusalem* (1958); Israel Exploration Society, *Yehudah vi-Yrushalayim* (1957); idem, *Jerusalem through the Ages* (Eng. and Heb., 1968); I.S. Horowitz, *Yerushalayim be-Sifrutenu* (1964); C. Thubron, *Jerusalem* (1969); F. Maraini, *Jerusalem. Rock of Ages* (1969); M. Harel, *Zot Yerushalayim* (1969); Z. Vilnay, *Yerushalayim*, 2 vols. (1967–693), incl. bibl.; new ed., 1 (1970). **ADD. BIBLIOGRAPHY:** J. Gray, *A History of Jerusalem* (1969); M. Gilbert, *Jerusalem: Illustrated History Atlas* (1977); N. Schur, *Jerusalem in Pilgrim's Accounts: Thematic Bibliography* (1980); D.H.K. Amiran and A. Sachar, *Atlas of Jerusalem* (1973); K. Prag, *Blue Guide: Jerusalem* (1989); K.J. Asali (ed.), *Jerusalem in History* (1989); D. Bahat, *The Illustrated Atlas of Jerusalem* (1990); K. Bieberstein and H. Bloedhorn, *Grundzuege der Baugeschichte vom Chalkolithikum bis zur Frühzeit der osmanischen Herrrschaft*, vols. 1–3 (1994); H. Shanks, *Jerusalem, An Archaeological Biography* (1995); M. Ben-Dov, *Historical Atlas of Jerusalem* (2002; see critical review by J. Magness in: BASOR 330 (2003), 94–96); E. Baruch and A. Faust (eds.), *New Studies on Jerusalem*. Vols. 1–10 (1995–2004) GEOGRAPHY: L.H. Vincent, *Les Noms de Jérusalem* (1911); H. Kendall, *Jerusalem – the City Plan* (1948); *Jerusalem – the Saga of the Holy City* (1954); J. Scofield, in: *National Geographic Magazine*, 115 (1959), 492–531; E. Orni and E. Efrat, *Geography of Israel* (1971³); J. Dash and E. Efrat, *The Israel Physical Master Plan* (1964); D. Ashbel, *Ha-Aklim ha-Menonar shel Yerushalayim* (1965), with Eng. summary; E. Efrat, *Yerushalayim ve-ha-Perozedor* (1967). **ADD. BIBLIOGRAPHY:** I.W.J. Hopkins, *Jerusalem: A Study in Urban Geography* (1970). BIBLICAL PERIOD: G.A. Smith, *Jerusalem… from the earliest times to A.D. 70*, 2 vols. (1907–08); Galling, Reallexikon, 297ff.; L. Mayer and M. Avi-Yonah, in: QDAP, 1 (1932), 163ff.; J.J. Simons, *Jerusalem in the Old Testament* (1952); L.H. Vincent, *Jérusalem de l'Ancien Testament*, 3 vols. in 2 (1954–56); M. Avi-Yonah, in: IEJ, 4 (1954), 239ff.; idem, in: *Ereẓ Yisrael*, 9 (1969), 175ff.; B. Mazar, *ibid.*, 161ff.; EM, 3 (1965), 793–837, incl. bibl.; D.R. Ap-Thomas, in: D. Winston Thomas (ed.), *Archaeology and Old Testament Study* (1967), 277–95; S. Abramsky, *Yerushalayim bi-Ymei ha-Mikra* (1968); *Qadmoniot*, 1–2 (1968). **ADD. BIBLIOGRAPHY:** G. Barkay, *Northern and Western Jerusalem in the End of the Iron Age* (1985); S. Ahituv and A. Mazar (eds.), *The History of Jerusalem. The Biblical Period* (2000); A.G. Vaughn and A.E. Killebrew (eds.), *Jerusalem in Bible and Archaeology: The First Temple Period* (2003); O. Lipschits, *Jerusalem Between Destruction and Restoration: Judah Under Babylonian Rule* (2004). SECOND TEMPLE: E. Bevan, *Jerusalem under the High-Priests* (1904; repr. 1948); S. Safrai, *Ha-Aliyyah la-Regel bi-Ymei Bayit Sheni* (1965); S. Abramsky, *Yerushalayim bi-Ymei Bayit Sheni* (1968); J. Jeremias, *Jerusalem in the Time of Jesus* (1969); H.H. Ben-Sasson (ed.), *Toledot Am Yisrael*, 1 (1969), index (also incl. bibl.). **ADD. BIBLIOGRAPHY:** N. Avigad, *Ancient Monuments in the Kidron Valley* (1954); F.J. Hollis, *The Archaeology of Herod's Temple* (1934); R. Furneaux, *The Roman Siege of Jerusalem* (1973); J. Wilkinson, *Jerusalem as Jesus Knew It: Archaeology as Evidence* (1978); A. Roitman, *Envisioning the Temple* (2003); A. Kloner and B. Zissu, *The Necropolis of Jerusalem in the Second Temple Period* (2003); A.S. Kaufman, *The Temple Mount. Where is the Holy of Holies?* (2004). ROMAN AND BYZANTINE PERIODS: C.W. Wilson, in: PEFQS, 37 (1905), 138–44; R. Harris, in: HTR, 19 (1926), 199–206; C. Kuhl in: PJB, 24 (1928), 113–40; idem and W. Meinhold, *ibid.*, 25 (1929), 95–124; A. Alt, *ibid.*, 124–6; S. Krauss, in: BJPES, 4 (1936), 52–60; E.L. Sukenik, in: JQR, 38 (1947), 157ff.; R.W. Hamilton, in: PEQ, 84 (1952), 83–90; J. Meyshan, *ibid.*, 90 (1958), 19–26; idem, in: IEJ, 9 (1959), 262–3; L. Kadman, *Coins of Aelia Capitolina* (1956); A. Spijkerman, in: LA, 7 (1957), 145–64; R. Beauvery, in: RB, 64 (1957), 72–101. **ADD. BIBLIOGRAPHY:** Y. Tsafrir and S. Safrai (eds.), *The History of Jerusalem. The Roman and Byzantine Periods* (1999). ARAB PERIOD: M. Assaf, *Toledot ha-Shilton ha-Aravi be-Ereẓ Yisrael* (1935); I. Lichtenstadter, in: HJ, 5 (1943), 39–45; J. Prawer, in: *Zion*, 12 (1947), 136–48; S.D. Goitein, *Mediterranean Society*, 1 (1967), index; idem, in: JAOS, 70 (1950), 104–8; idem, in: *Melilah*, 3 (1950), 156–65; idem, in: *Yerushalayim*, 4 (1953), 82–103. **ADD. BIBLIOGRAPHY:** H. Nicholson and N. David, *God's warriors: Crusaders, Saracens and the Battle for Jerusalem* (2005); R.W. Hamilton, *A Structural History of the Aqsa Mosque: A Record of Archaeological Gleanings From the Repairs of 1938–1942* (1949); J. Prawer, *Ha-Ẓalbanim Deyuqanah shel Ḥevra Kolonyalit*, (1975), 49–59 and index (incl. bibl.); B.Z. Kedar and Z. Baras (eds.), *Perakim be-Toledot Yerushalayim bi-Ymei ha-Benayim* (1979); M. Rosen-Ayalon, *The Early Islamic Monuments of Haram al-Sharif*, in: *Qedem*, 28 (1989); M. Gil, *A History of Palestine, 634–1099*, (1992); J. Prawer and H. Ben-Shammai (eds.), *The History of Jerusalem. The Early Islamic Period, 638–1099* (1996); M.F. Abu-Khalaf, *Islamic Art Through the Ages; Masterpieces of the Islamic Museum of al-Haram al-Sharif (al-Aqsa Mosque), Jerusalem* (1998); S.D. Goitein, "Contemporary letters on the Capture of Jerusalem by the Crusaders," in: JJS, 3:175ff. CRUSADES: S. Runciman, *History of the Crusades*, 2 (1952; repr. 1965), incl. bibl.; Prawer, Ẓalbanim, 1 (1963), 134–48, 549–61; 2 (1963), 386–405 and index (incl. bibl.); idem, *Mamlekhet Yerushalayim ha-Ẓalbanit* (1947); idem, in: *Zion*, 11 (1946), 38–82; S.D. Goitein, *ibid.*, 17 (1952), 47–129; Dinur, Golah, 2 pt. 1 (1965²), 1–127, 398–551; M. Benvenisti, *The Crusaders in the Holy Land* (1970), index. **ADD. BIBLIOGRAPHY:** J. Prawer, "Jerusalem in the Christian and Jewish Perspectives of the Early Middle Ages," in: *Settimone di studio Centro italiano di studi suli'alto medioevo*, 26 (1980), 739–95; idem, *The History of the Jews in the Latin Kingdom of Jerusalem* (1988); J. Prawer and H. Ben-Shammai (eds.), *The History of Jerusalem. Crusaders and Ayyubids (1099–1250)* (1991). MAMLUK AND OTTOMAN PERIODS: Ben-Zvi, Ereẓ Yisrael, index; idem, *She'ar Yashuv* (1965²), index; B. Lewis, *Notes and Documents from the Turkish Archives* (1952), index; D. Tamar, *Meḥkarim be-Toledot ha-Yehudim be-Ereẓ Yisrael u-ve-Italyah* (1970), index; Ashtor, Toledot, 3 (1970), index; idem, in: *Yerushalayim*, 5 (1955), 71–116; J. Prawer, *ibid*, 1 (1948), 139–59; C. Roth, in: JHSEM, 2 (1935), 99–104; M. Benayahu, in HUCA, 21 (1948), 1–28 (Heb. section); J.W. Hirschberg, in: IEJ, 2 (1952), 237–48. **ADD. BIBLIOGRAPHY:** A. Cohen, *Ottoman Documents on the Jewish Community of Jerusalem in the Sixteenth Century* (1976); A.G. Walls and A. Abul-Hajj, *Arabic Inscriptions in Jerusalem: A Handlist and Maps* (1980); H. Lutfi, *Al Quds al-Mamlukiyya* (1985); M.H. Burgoyne and D.S. Richards, *Mamluk Jerusalem: An Architectural Study* (1987); R. Hillenbrand, *The Architecture of Ottoman Jerusalem: An Introduction* (2002); A. Cohen (ed.), *Perakim be-Toledot Yerushalayim be-Reshit ha-Tekufah ha-Uthmanit*, (1979); J. Rood Mendelsohn, *Sacred Law in the Holy City: the Khedival Challenge to the Ottomans as Seen from Jerusalem 1829–1842* (2004); Kh. I. Salameh, *Aspects of the sijills of the Shar'i court in Jerusalem* (2003). MODERN PERIOD TO 1948; THE NEW CITY: J. Finn, *Stirring Times*, 2 vols. (1878); Pro-Jerusalem Society, *Jerusalem 1918–20* (1921); *Jerusalem 1920–22* (1924), ed. by C.R. Ashbee; A.M. Hyamson (ed.), *The British Consulate in Jerusalem*, 2 vols. (1939–41); J. Rivlin, *Reshit ha-Yishuv mi-Ḥuẓ le-Ḥomat Yerushalayim* (1939); P. Grajewsky, *Toledot Battei ha-Defus ha-Ivrim be… Yerushalayim* (1939); A. Furst, *Yerushalayim ha-Ḥadashah* (1946); I. Shapira, *Yerushalayim mi-Ḥuẓ la-Ḥomah* (1947); J. Gelles, *Shekhunot bi-Yrushalayim* (1962); H. Luncz, *Avraham Moshe Luncz ve-Doro* (1963); E. Porush, *Zikhronot Rishonim* (1963); B.-Z. Gat, *Ha-Yishuv ha-Yehudi be-Ereẓ Yisrael ba-Shanim 1840–1881* (1963); A.B. Rivlin,

Yerushalayim; Toledot ha-Yishuv ha-Ivri ba-Me'ah ha-19 (1966); Y.Y. Yellin, *Avoteinu* (1966); E. Cohen, *Mi-Zikhronot Ish Yerushalayim* (1967²); B.-Z. Yadler, *Be-Tuv Yerushalayim… Zikhronot me-Ḥayyei Yerushalayim u-Gedoleha ba-Me'ah ha-Aḥaronah* (1967); M. Eliav, *Ahavat Ẓiyyon ve-Anshei Hod* (1970), index; E. Samuel, *Lifetime in Jerusalem* (1970); M. Vereté, in: *English Historical Review*, 85 (1970), 316–45. **ADD. BIBLIOGRAPHY:** Y. Ben-Arieh, *Jerusalem in the Nineteenth Century: Emergence of the New City* (1986); idem, *Ir bi-Re'i Tekufah, Yerushalayim ba-Me'ah ha-Tesha Esre, ha-Ir ha-Atiqah* (1977); idem, *Ir bi-Re'I Tekufah, Yerushalayim ha-Ḥadashah be-Reshitah* (1979); idem, *ErezYisrael ba-Me'ah ha-Yud-Tet, Gilluyah me-Ḥadash* (1970); idem, "Ha-Shekhunot ha-Yehudiyyot she-Nivnu bi-Yrushalayim she-mi-Ḥuẓ la-Ḥomot bi-Shnot ha-Shmonim shel ha-Me'ah ha-Yud-Tet, *Cathedra*, 2 (1977), 20–58; idem, *Šayyareha we-Ẓiyyureha shel Erez Yisrael ba-Me'ah ha-Tesha Esre* (1993), index. MODERN PERIOD 1948–2005: I.A. Abbady (ed.), *Jerusalem Economy* (1950); H. Levin, *I Saw the Battle of Jerusalem* (1950); D. Joseph, *The Faithful City, the Siege of Jerusalem 1948* (1960); *Mifkad ha-Ukhlusin ve-ha-Diyyur* (1961); *Mifkad… Mizrah Yerushalayim* (Heb. and Eng., 1968); G. Golani, *Urban Survey of Existing Residential Quarters in Jerusalem* (Eng. and Heb., 1966); B.J. Bell, *Besieged* (1966), 201–43; M. Roman, *Seker Kalkali-Ḥevrati al Yerushalayim ha-Shelemah* (1967); E. Lauterpacht, *Jerusalem and the Holy Places* (1968); R. Westmacott, *Jerusalem; a New Era for a Capital City* (1968); E. Landau, *Jerusalem the Eternal; the Paratroopers' Battle for the City of David* (1968); M. Tokolovaski, *Shiḥrur Yerushalayim* (1968); M. Natan, *Ha-Milḥamah al Yerushalayim* (1969⁸). **ADD. BIBLIOGRAPHY:** O. Aḥimeir and M. Levin (eds.), *Adrikhalut Monumentalit bi-Yrushalaym,* (1984); R. Gonen and D. Kroyanker, *To Live in Jerusalem* (1993); D. Kroyanker, *Jerusalem Architecture Periods and Styles, Jewish Quarters and Public Buildings Outside the Old City Walls 1860–1914,* (1983); idem, *The Rothschild Compound Story* (Eng. and Heb.; 2001); idem, *Jerusalem Architecture* (2002); R. Hillenbrand, *The Architecture of Ottoman Jerusalem: An Introduction* (2002); M. Benvinisti, *Jerusalem, the Torn City* (1976); K. Kahvedjian, *Jerusalem Through My Fathers's Eyes* (1998). OLD CITY: H. Bar-Deromah, *Yerushalayim, ha-Topografyah shel ha-Ir ha-Attikah* (1935); I. Shapira, *Yerushalayim, ha-Ir ha-Attikah* (1945); M. Avi-Yonah, *Yerushalayim ha-Attikah* (1948); S.H. Steckoll, *Gates of Jerusalem* (1968). **ADD. BIBLIOGRAPHY:** C.W. Wilson, *Ordnance Survey of Jerusalem* (1865); C.R. Conder and C.W. Warren, *The Survey of Western Palestine. Jerusalem Volume* (1884); R. Sivan, *David's Tower Rediscovered* (1983); Y. Ben-Arieh, *Jerusalem in the Nineteenth Century: The Old City* (1984); S. Gibson, *Jerusalem in Original Photographs, 1850–1920* (2003); R. Rubin, *Image and Reality: Jerusalem in Maps and Views* (1999); D. Kroyanker, *Jerusalem Architecture* (2002²); S. Nusaibeh and O. Grabar, *The Dome of the Rock* (1996). WATER SUPPLY: M. Hecker, in: BJPES, 4 (1937), 95–98; 5 (1937), 10–14; 6 (1938), 8–15; Press, Ereẓ, 2 (1948), 430–1; A. Comay, *Goremim ha-Mashpi'im al Bikkush ha-Mayim be-Yisrael* (1969). ARCHAEOLOGY: C.W. Wilson, *Recovery of Jerusalem* (1871); C. Warren, *Underground Jerusalem* (1876); G. Saint Clair, *The Buried City of Jerusalem* (1887); F.J. Bliss, *Excavations at Jerusalem 1894–1897* (1898); L.H. Vincent, *Jérusalem; recherches de topographie, d'archéologie et d'histoire*, 2 vols. (1912–26); Z. Vilnay, *Mazzevot Kodesh be-Ereẓ Yisrael* (1963), index; K.M. Kenyon, *Jerusalem; Excavating 3000 Years of History* (1967), incl. bibl. **ADD. BIBLIOGRAPHY:** R.A.S. Macalister and J.G. Duncan, *Excavations on the Hill of Ophel, 1923–25* (1926); J.W. Crowfoot and G.M. Fitzgerald, *Excavations in the Tyropeon Valley, Jerusalem, 1927* (1929); K.M.Kenyon, *Digging Up Jerusalem* (1974); Y. Yadin (ed.), *Jerusalem Revealed: Archaeology in the Holy City, 1968–1974* (1975); N. Avigad, *Discovering Jerusalem* (1983); Y. Shiloh et al., *Excavations at the City of David*. Qedem, vols. 1–6 (1984–2000); A.D. Tushingham, *Excavations in Jerusalem, 1961–1967* (1985; see critical review by S. Gibson in: PEQ 119 (1987), 81–96); M. Ben-Dov, *In the Shadow of the Temple: The Discovery of Ancient Jerusalem* (1985); B. Mazar and E. Mazar, *Excavations in the South of the Temple Mount*. Qedem 29 (1989); G.J. Wightman, *The Damascus Gate, Jerusalem* (1989); D. Ussishkin, *The Village of Silwan: The Necropolis From the Period of the Judean Kingdom* (1993); G.J. Wightman, *The Walls of Jerusalem From the Canaanites to the Mamluks* (1993); H. Geva, *Jewish Quarter Excavations in the Old City of Jerusalem: Architecture and Stratigraphy* (2002); H. Geva (ed.), *Ancient Jerusalem Revealed* (1994; expanded ed. 2000); S. Gibson and J.E. Taylor, *Beneath the Church of the Holy Sepulchre, Jerusalem: The Archaeology and Early History of Traditional Golgotha* (1994); G. Avni and Z. Greenhut, *The Akeldama Tombs* (1996); S. Gibson and D.M. Jacobson, *Below the Temple Mount in Jerusalem: A Sourcebook on the Cisterns, Subterranean Chambers and Conduits of the Haram al-Sharif* (1996); R. Reich, G. Avni, and T. Winter, *The Jerusalem Archaeological Park* (1999); E. Mazar, *The Complete Guide to the Temple Mount Excavations* (2000); H. Geva (ed.), *Jewish Quarter Excavations in the Old City of Jerusalem*, vols. 1–2 (2000, 2003); E. Mazar, *The Temple Mount Excavations in Jerusalem 1968–1978 Directed by Benjamin Mazar,* Qedem 43 (2003; see critical review by J. Magness in: BASOR 337 (2005), 104–6 and J. Murphy O'Connor, in: RB 112 (2005), 126–30). IN HALAKHAH AND AGGADAH: A. Buechler, in: JQR, 20 (1908), 798–811; idem, in: REJ, 62 (1911), 201–15; 63 (1912), 30–50; S. Krauss, *Kadmoniyyot ha-Talmud*, 1 (1924), 92–113; A. Aptowitzer, in: *Tarbiz*, 2 (1930/31), 266–72; S. Bialoblocki, in: *Alei Ayin, Minḥat Devarim li-Shelomo Zalman Schocken* (1948–52), 25–74; L. Finkelstein, in: *Sefer ha-Yovel… Alexander Marx* (1950), 351–69; B. Dinaburg, in: *Zion*, 16 (1951), 1–17; M. Ha-Kohen, in: *Maḥanayim*, 58 (1961), 60–68 (Eng. summary in I. Jakobovits, *Jewish Law Faces Modern Problems* (1965), 128–31); J. Zahavi (ed.), *Midreshei Ẓiyyon vi-Yrushalayim* (1963); D. Noy, in: *Ve-li-Yrushalayim* (1968), 360–94; A. Newman, in: *Jewish Life* (Jan./Feb., 1968), 24–27. IN MODERN HEBREW LITERATURE: S. Ben-Barukh, *Yerushalayim be-Shiratenu ha-Ḥadashah* (1955); B. Kurzweil, *Massot al Sippurei S.Y. Agnon* (1962), 301–10; S.Y. Penueli and A. Ukhmani (eds.), *Anthology of Modern Hebrew Poetry*, 2 vols. (1966); I. Rabinovich, *Major Trends in Modern Hebrew Fiction* (1968); D. Silk (ed.), *Retrievements: A Jerusalem Anthology* (1968); S. Halkin, *Modern Hebrew Literature* (1970²). **ADD. BIBLIOGRAPHY:** H. Hamiel, "*Yerushalayim ba-Shirah ha-Ivrit*," in: *Mabu'a*, 14 (1982), 158–63; Z. Ben-Porat, "History in Representations of Jerusalem in Modern Hebrew Poetry," in: *Neohelicon*, 14:2 (1987), 353–58; N. Govrin, "Jerusalem and Tel Aviv as Metaphors in Hebrew Literature," in: *Modern Hebrew Literature*, 2 (1989), 23–27; S. Werses, "Yerushalayim shel Agnon," in: *Alon la-Moreh le-Sifrut*, 14 (1993), 168–75; M.J. Meinster, "A Short Study of the Image of Jerusalem in Selected Arabic and Hebrew Poems," in: *Journal of Semitics*, 5:2 (1993), 200–22; D. Miron, "Depicitons of Hebrew Poetry on Jerusalem," in: *City of the Great King* (1996), 241–87; 515–16; G. Shaked, "Yerushalayim ba-Sifrut ha-Ivrit," in: *Mada'ei ha-Yahadut*, 38 (1998), 15–32; T. Cohen, "*Ha-Ir Roveẓet al Ḥayei: Yerushalayim u-Migdar ba-Shirah ha-Ivrit*," in: *Ishah bi-Yerushalayim* (2002), 192–229; E. Bar-Eshel, "*Ḥovot shel Zeman: Yerushalayim kemerḥav Poeti ve-ideii bi-Yezirot S. Hareven*," in: *Alei Si'aḥ*, 48 (2002), 64–76; Y. Berlovitz, "*Likro et Yerushalayim ke-Tekst Nashi*," in: *Ishah bi-Yerushalayim* (2002), 158–91; A. Holtzman, "*Yerushalayim ha-Mandatorit ba-Sifrut ha-Ivrit*," in: *Yerushalayim bi-Tekufat ha-Mandat* (2003), 370–92; D. Grossberg, "Yehuda Amichai´s Jerusalem," in: *Midstream* 50, 4 (2004), 38–40. IN CHRISTIANITY; CHRISTIAN HOLY PLACES: L.H. Vincent and F.M. Abel, *Jerusalem*, 2 (1914–26); F. Cabrol and H. Leclercq, *Dic-*

tionnaire d'Archéologie chrétienne et de Liturgie, 7 (1926), 2304–93; J.W. Crowfoot, *Early Churches in Palestine* (1941); *New Schaff-Herzog Encyclopedia of Religious Knowledge*, 6 (1950), 134–7; S.G.F. Brandon, *The Fall of Jerusalem and the Christian Church* (1951); D. Baldi, *Enchiridion locorum sanctorum* (1955); A. Potthast, *Wegweiser durch die Geschichtswerke des europaeischen Mittelalters*, 2 (1957), 1734; *Lexikon fuer Theologie und Kirche*, 5 (1960), 367, 905–10; E.A. Moore, *Ancient Churches of Old Jerusalem* (1961); D. Attwater, *Christian Churches of the East*, 2 vols. (1961–62); C. Kopp, *Holy Places of the Gospels* (1963); M. Ish-Shalom, *Masei Noẓerim le-Ereẓ Yisrael* (1965), index; *New Catholic Encyclopedia*, 7 (1967), 881 ff.; C. Hollis, *Holy Places* (1969). **ADD. BIBLIOGRAPHY:** B. Bagatti et al., *New Discoveries at the Tomb of the Virgin Mary in Gethsemane* (1975); C. Coüasnon, *The Church of the Holy Sepulchre, Jerusalem* (1974); V.C. Corbo, *Il Santo Seolcro di Gerusalemme*, 3 vols. (1981–82); A. Rock, *The Status Quo in the Holy Places* (1989); M. Biddle, *The Tomb of Christ* (1999). IN ISLAM: EIS, S.V. *Al-Kuds*; C.D. Matthews, *Palestine – Mohammedan Holy Land* (1949); J.W. Hirschberg, *Sources of Moslem Traditions Concerning Jerusalem* (1952); A. Guillaume, in: *Al-Andalus*, 18 (1953), 323–36; S.D. Goitein, *Studies in Islamic History and Institutions* (1966), 135–48; idem, in: *Bulletin of the Jewish Palestine Exploration Society*, 12 (1946), 120–6; idem, in: *Minḥah li-Yhudah… Zlotnick* (1950), 62–66; E. Sivan, in: *Studia Islamica*, 27 (1967), 149–82; H. Busse, in: *Judaism*, 17 (1968), 441–68; M.J. Kister, in: *Le Museon*, 82 (1969), 173–96; **ADD. BIBLIOGRAPHY:** Y. Reiter (ed.), in *Ribbonut ha'el we-ha-adam, Qedusha wu-merkaziyut politit be-har ha-bayit* (2001); H. Busse, in: JSAI, 5 (1984), 73–119; idem, in: JSAI, 8 (1986), 149–68; idem, in: JSAI, 9 (1987), 279–89; idem, in: JSAI, 14 (1991), 1–40; idem, in: JSAI, 17 (1994), 142–65; idem, in: JSAI, 20 (1996), 1–17; idem, in: JSAI, 22 (1998), 1–17; S. Bashear, in: BSOAS, 52 (1989), 217–38; idem, in *Der Islam*, 67 (1990), 243–77. IN MUSLIM LITERATURE OF THE PRAISES OF JERUSALEM: E. Sivan, in: IOS, 1 (1971), 263–71; I. Hasson, *The Jerusalem Cathedra*, 2 (1981), 167–84; O. Livne, "Kafri," in: JSAI, 14 (1991), 71–83; idem, in: *Iyyunim be-Ma'amadah shel Yerushalayim ba-Islam ha-Kadum*, (2000); A. Elad, in: *JSAI*, 14 (1991), 41–70; M. Sharon, in: *Bibliotheca Orientalis*, 49 (1992), 55–67; F.E. Peters, *Jerusalem and Mecca: the Topology of the Holy City in the Near East* (1986); R. Firston, *Journeys in the Holy Land: the Evolution of the Abraham –Ishmael Legends in Islamic Exegesis* (1990); O. Grabar, *The shape of the Holy: Jerusalem 600–1990*; Abū Bakr al-Wāsiī, *Faḍā'il al-Bayt al-Muqaddas*, ed. I. Hasson (1979). IN LITERATURE, ART, AND MUSIC: L.A. Mayer, *Bibliography of Jewish Art* (1967), index; Y. Cohen, *Yerushalayim be-Shir ve-Ḥazon* (1938); M.S. Geshuri, *Yerushalayim Ir ha-Musikah mi-Tekufat Bayit Sheni* (1968), includes bibliography. **ADD. BIBLIOGRAPHY:** M. Grindea (ed.), *Jerusalem: The Holy City in Literature* (1968); G. Perer and M. Luisa (eds.), *La Gerusalemme celeste* (1983); B. Kuehnel, *From the Earthly to the Heavenly Jerusalem: Representations of the Holy City in Christian Art of the First Millennium (1987); S. Kobelius, Niebiańska Jerozolima: od sacrum miejsca do sacrum modelu* (1989); A. Batalov and A. Lidov (eds.), *Ierusalim v russkoy culture* (1994); H. Budde and A. Nachama (eds.), *Die Reise nach Jerusalem: eine kulturhistorische Exkursion in die Stadt der Städte. 3000 Jahre Davidsstadt* (1996); D. Bahat and S. Sabar, *Jerusalem – Stone and Spirit* (Heb., 1997); P. Paszkiewicz and T. Zadrożny (eds.), *Jerozolima w kulturze europejskiej* (1997); B. Kuehnel (ed.), *The Real and Ideal Jerusalem in Jewish, Christian and Islamic Art*, in: *Jewish Art* 23–24 (1997–98); G. Elkoshi et al. (eds.), *Ve-li-Yrushalayim Divrei Sifrut ve-Hagut* (1968).

JERUSALEM, KARL WILHELM (1747–1772), German philosopher. Jerusalem was the son of a well-known court preacher in Brunswick, Germany, who was probably of Dutch Jewish origin. Jerusalem studied law at Leipzig and Goettingen, and became a functionary of the legation at Wetzlar. He knew *Goethe and was a friend of G.E. *Lessing. Unhappy about his life and about a love affair, Jerusalem shot himself. Goethe was shocked by Jerusalem's suicide and immortalized him in *Die Leiden des jungen Werthers* (1774) and for a while Jerusalem's grave became a place of pilgrimage. Lessing, concerned about Goethe's picture of Jerusalem, published Jerusalem's writings under the title *Philosophische Aufsaetze* (1776; ed. by P. Beer, 1900) to show Jerusalem's intellectual side. Jerusalem was a minor Enlightenment thinker. His brief writings deal with the origins of language, the nature and origin of general and abstract concepts, freedom, Mendelssohn's views, and the nature of experience. Jerusalem was a determinist, and Lessing's preface to the *Aufsaetze* is one of the important statements of his own determinism. Jerusalem's *Aufsaetze und Briefe* were published in 1925 by H. Schneider.

BIBLIOGRAPHY: R. Kaulitz-Niedeck, *Goethe und Jerusalem* (1908).

[Richard H. Popkin]

JERUSALEM, LEGAL ASPECTS.

Introduction

At least in three respects Jerusalem differs from most other places: the city is holy to adherents of three religions, it is the subject of conflicting national claims by two peoples, and its population is heterogeneous to a considerable degree. These characteristics require some elaboration.

In the city one finds Holy Places of Christianity, since according to Christian tradition Jesus lived and was active in various locations in Jerusalem. Under the Islamic tradition, the al-Aksa Mosque and the Dome of the Rock as well as the Temple Mount on which they are situated are Holy Places, due to Muhammad's nocturnal visit, and for the Jewish people the whole city is holy, in particular the Temple Mount, because of the divine presence (the *Shekhinah*).

It has been argued that some of the events which are associated by the various religions with Jerusalem could not, from a historical point of view, have actually occurred. However, religious faith deserves respect and historical accuracy is not relevant. Religious belief in the sanctity of certain sites in Jerusalem has been exploited by various individuals, states, and institutions in order to achieve political goals.

As for the national aspect, according to Israeli law united Jerusalem is the capital of the State of Israel, but the Palestinians also have claims on the city, at least on the eastern part thereof, and seek to make it their capital.

Turning to the heterogeneous nature of the population, it is sufficient to stroll through the streets of the city to realize that it indeed consists of a mosaic of many and various communities. Thus, for example, adherents of some 40 different religions or ethnic communities live in Jerusalem.

These features may explain why there are so many different opinions concerning the legal status of the city, and why it is such a thorny problem in the peace process.

Opinions on the Legal Status of Jerusalem

Many statesmen as well as experts in international law have expressed their opinion on the status of Jerusalem.[1] In the framework of this article only the most representative ones can be reviewed, and the opinions will be stated without analyzing the controversies they have engendered. As the western parts of the city have not undergone a considerable change since 1949, opinions on their status can be analyzed without a temporal division. However, the eastern sectors changed hands in 1967, and therefore it may be useful to divide the discussion accordingly.

With regard to west Jerusalem, there are four basic opinions. According to the first, mainly developed by Sir Elihu Lauterpacht, Israel lawfully acquired sovereignty in 1948. When Britain left the area, a vacuum of sovereignty ensued. This vacuum could validly be filled only by a lawful action. Since Israel acquired control of west Jerusalem in 1948 by a lawful act of self-defense, she was entitled to fill that vacuum and thus became the lawful sovereign.[2]

Prince Hassan bin Talal of Jordan has expressed the opinion that sovereignty over Jerusalem is suspended until a comprehensive settlement is agreed upon.[3]

According to Henry Cattan, the Palestinian Arab people has had and still has "legal sovereignty" over the whole of Palestine including Jerusalem since the mandatory period.[4]

Others maintain that the status of Jerusalem is subject to the UN General Assembly resolution of 1947 which recommended the establishment of a *corpus separatum* under a special international regime and administered by the United Nations.[5]

Most foreign states have not adopted a clear-cut stand on the status of west Jerusalem.[6] Although there are differences among various states, one can discern certain similarities with regard to the basic questions. Apparently foreign states were not prepared to recognize the legality of Jordanian or Israeli rule over the respective zones of the city under their control. Thus, for example, the foreign consuls stationed in the city refused and still refuse (in 2005) to apply to Jordan (in the past) or Israel (as the case may be) for the granting of *exequatur*, i.e., permission to carry out their functions in the city. The refusal to recognize Israeli rule over the western sector was apparent, for example, in the 1952 case of the *Heirs of Shababo v. Roger Heilen, the Consulate General of Belgium and the Consul General of Belgium in Jerusalem*: the driver of the Belgian Consulate had been involved in a fatal road accident that caused the death of Mr. Shababo. The family members of the deceased sued the driver, the Consulate and the Consul General, and claimed damages. The incident was the subject of several judgments of the Jerusalem District Court.[7] Of particular interest for the present discussion is the first deliberation, where the driver and his principals denied the jurisdiction of the Israeli courts over the accident since it had taken place in Jerusalem. That argument was dismissed by the court.

It seems, however, that despite this non-recognition of Israeli sovereignty, most states have nevertheless accepted the *de facto* applicability of Israeli law,[8] and none has so far demanded that the laws of occupation including the 1949 Fourth Geneva Convention Relative to the Protection of Civilian Persons in Time of War be applied to west Jerusalem.[9]

East Jerusalem during the period 1949–67 was under Jordanian rule. According to Sir Elihu Lauterpacht, during that time the area was under a vacuum of sovereignty: Britain had abandoned sovereignty, but Jordan could not fill this gap because it had occupied east Jerusalem by an illegal act of aggression.[10]

Under Henry Cattan's theory – similar to the parallel one concerning west Jerusalem – the Palestinian Arab people has had and still has title to "legal sovereignty" over the whole of Palestine, including east and west Jerusalem.[11]

A third opinion, represented by Yoram Dinstein, recognized Jordanian sovereignty over east Jerusalem, derived from the exercise of the right of self-determination by the inhabitants, i.e., the resolution adopted by the notables in Jericho in 1949, requesting the annexation of the West Bank to Jordan.[12]

Lastly, with regard to east Jerusalem, like the western parts, certain writers claim that the *corpus separatum* solution is still valid.[13]

How were these opinions influenced by the changes that occurred in 1967? According to Sir Elihu Lauterpacht, the vacuum of sovereignty existed until Israel occupied east Jerusalem by a lawful act of self-defense and thus was entitled to fill the gap.[14] A similar conclusion was reached by other writers who based Israel's sovereignty on the idea that Israel has the strongest relative title to the area in the absence of a lawful "sovereign reversioner" due to Jordan's lack of a valid claim to sovereignty.[15]

The opinion held by Henry Cattan under which the Palestinian Arab people has "legal sovereignty" over the whole of Palestine irrespective of the factual situation, did not have to change as a result of the Six-Day War.[16]

Yoram Dinstein who recognized Jordanian sovereignty in east Jerusalem expressed the opinion that this sovereignty survived the 1967 war, but that Israel is a lawful occupant of those areas since she occupied them in a war of self-defense.[17]

The *corpus separatum* theory was not affected by the war.[18]

As to the practical attitude of the international community: as mentioned, neither before nor after 1967 did the foreign consuls request an *exequatur* from Jordan or from Israel, which means that neither the sovereignty of the one nor of the other was recognized. Moreover, since 1967 the UN organs, including the Security Council, have repeatedly stated that east Jerusalem is occupied territory subject to the Fourth 1949 Geneva Convention.[19]

The attitude of the United States has been expressed inter alia in a letter sent by President Carter to Egypt and Israel in the context of the 1978 Camp David accords.[20] The president wrote that the position of the U.S. remained as stated by Ambassador Goldberg at the UN General Assembly in 1967 and subsequently by Ambassador Yost in the Security Council in 1969. There is, however, a difference between the speeches of the two ambassadors. While they both stressed that the actions of Israel in the city were merely provisional and that the problem of Jerusalem's future should be settled by negotiations, Ambassador Yost added that east Jerusalem was occupied territory to which the Fourth 1949 Geneva Convention Relative to the Protection of Civilian Persons in Time of War applied.[21] This attitude, however, did not prevent the U.S. administration from requesting Israel to extradite to the U.S. a person who lived in the eastern sector of the city.[22] However, in 1995 the U.S. Congress passed a bill that calls for the recognition of united Jerusalem as the capital of Israel. The bill also required that the U.S. Embassy be moved from Tel Aviv to Jerusalem by 1999. As of 2006 this move has not yet taken place, due to a provision in the bill that authorizes the president to postpone its implementation if the security of the United States requires it.

As to the European Community, it adopted in 1980 a declaration (the Venice Declaration) on the Middle East which included a paragraph on Jerusalem:

> The Nine recognize the special importance of the role played by the question of Jerusalem for all the parties concerned. The Nine stress that they will not accept any unilateral initiative designed to change the status of Jerusalem and that any agreement on the city's status should guarantee freedom of access for everyone to the Holy Places.[23]

In 1993, the ambassador of Germany in Israel sent a diplomatic note to Israel in the name of the European Union. According to the communication he "reaffirmed" the position of the EU, stating that the status of Jerusalem is still the corpus separatum one.

The International Court of Justice, in its Advisory Opinion on the "Legal Consequences of the Construction of a Wall in the Occupied Palestine Territory" (2004), spoke of East Jerusalem as occupied Palestinian territory.

Two internationally relevant developments concerning Jerusalem occurred in the 1980s. In 1981 the Old City and its walls were registered by Jordan in the World Heritage List established under the 1972 UNESCO Convention for the Protection of the World Cultural and Natural Heritage, and in 1982 it was included in the list of sites in danger.

The second event to be mentioned is the declaration of King Hussein of Jordan in 1988 that Jordan was detaching itself from the West Bank.

Thus far, we have reviewed the opinions on the legal status of Jerusalem under international law. But what is its status under Israeli law? Jerusalem was not mentioned in the Declaration of the Establishment of the State of May 14, 1948.[24]

The application of Israeli law to the western sector of Jerusalem was ensured by a proclamation made by the minister of defense in 1948,[25] and by the Area of Jurisdiction and Powers Ordinance of 1948.[26] That ordinance provided that the law in force in the State of Israel should also apply to any part of Palestine which the minister of defense would designate by proclamation to be under occupation of the Israel Defense Forces.

At the end of 1949, following the renewed debate on Jerusalem in the UN General Assembly, Israel's Prime Minister David Ben-Gurion announced in the Knesset (Israel's parliament) that Jerusalem was an inseparable part of the State of Israel and its eternal capital[27]; this position was approved by the Knesset.[28]

After the Six-Day War (1967), various measures were taken in order to include areas east of Jerusalem in Israel's jurisdiction: the Knesset passed the Law and Administration Ordinance (Amendment No. 11) Law of 1967,[29] authorizing the Government to apply the law, jurisdiction and administration of Israel to any area which was formerly part of Mandatory Palestine. Likewise the Municipalities Ordinance was amended so as to allow for the extension of the bounds of a municipality where a decision has been made as to the application of Israel's jurisdiction to a certain area, as referred to above.[30] And indeed, the Government issued an appropriate order as a result of which Israeli law was made to apply to the eastern sector of Jerusalem,[31] which was also included within the jurisdiction of the Jerusalem municipality.

In several respects Israeli law granted east Jerusalemites certain facilities, by laying down special arrangements for them, as embodied in the Legal and Administrative Matters (Regulation) Law [Consolidated Version] of 1970.[32] This law dealt, for example, with the registration of companies and with the citizenship of policemen. The most conspicuous examples of the differences between the law as applied to Israel on the one hand and to east Jerusalem on the other hand not mentioned in that law, are the system of education, and rules on foreign currency: in the eastern neighborhoods the Jordanian and later the Palestinian school curriculum has been taught, and the Jordanian dinar is used in parallel with the Israeli shekel.

As to the status of Palestinian inhabitants of East Jerusalem, they have been recognized as permanent residents of Israel, holding an Israeli identity card and having Israeli social rights, i.e., social security and medical insurance. They may also vote in municipal elections.

Israel has not imposed its citizenship on the East Jerusalemites, but they may of course apply for naturalization. So far not many have applied for Israeli citizenship.

Israel has increased the municipal boundaries of Jerusalem, and they were fixed as extending from Atarot in the north almost to Rachel's Tomb in the south, and from Ein Kerem in the west to the eastern slopes of Mount Scopus. (A further extension to the west, i.e., into Israel proper, was effected in 1993.)

The application of Israeli law to East Jerusalem was met with fierce criticism from various UN bodies.[33]

The question arose at the time as to whether these acts constituted annexation of the eastern parts of Jerusalem. The then minister of foreign affairs, Abba Eban, informed the UN Secretary General in writing in July 1967[34] that they did not constitute annexation, but administrative and municipal integration. On the other hand, from the point of view of Israeli law, it was held in a number of decisions of the Supreme Court that the eastern sectors of Jerusalem had become a part of the State of Israel.

One of the earlier cases on this question is *Ruidi and Maches v. Military Court of Hebron.*[35] This case involved an antiquities dealer from Hebron who transferred antiquities from Hebron to East Jerusalem, without first obtaining an export license as required by the Jordanian antiquities law which applies on the West Bank. The dealer pleaded in his defense that at the critical time East Jerusalem was not foreign territory in relation to the West Bank, so that he could not be charged with exporting without a license. However, the Supreme Court did not accept this argument since it considered that the eastern sectors of Jerusalem had already become part of Israel.

In 1980 the Knesset adopted a new law concerning Jerusalem – the Basic Law: Jerusalem Capital of Israel.[36] This law states that "Jerusalem, complete and united, is the capital of Israel," that it is "the seat of the President of the State, the Knesset, the Government, and the Supreme Court," that the Holy Places shall be protected, and that the Government has to provide for the development and prosperity of Jerusalem. Its adoption aroused resentment in the international community and was considered by the Security Council to be "a violation of international law."[37] The Council called upon member States with embassies situated in Jerusalem to withdraw them from the city, and, indeed, the embassies, 13 in number, left the city following the resolution. In 1982 the Embassy of Costa Rica returned to West Jerusalem, and was followed by that of El Salvador. In 2000 Basic Law: Jerusalem Capital of Israel was amended. Two new provisions were added. The transfer of any powers, whether permanently or provisionally, concerning Jerusalem in its 1967 boundaries requires the consent of the majority of the Knesset (namely 61 votes). This provision relates to any powers vested by Israeli law in the government or in the municipality of Jerusalem.

Perhaps the most comprehensive discussion of the status of Jerusalem under Israel law as well as under Jewish law is included in Justice M. Elon's judgment in the case of *The Temple Mount Faithful Association et al. v. The Attorney General et al.*, decided in 1993.[38] In this case the petitioners requested the High Court of Justice to order the Attorney-General and various other Israeli authorities to prosecute the Muslim Waqf for having undertaken on the Temple Mount certain works without the necessary permit. The High Court decided not to interfere in the discretion of the relevant authorities. In reaching its conclusion, the Court emphasized that the Temple Mount is part of the territory of the State of Israel and that the sovereignty of the State extends over unified Jerusalem in general and over the Temple Mount in particular. Hence all the laws of Israel, including the laws which guarantee freedom of worship at, the right of access to, and the protection of the Holy Places against desecration apply also to the Temple Mount. However, in several cases the Supreme Court has not applied the law to its full extent in matters relating to the Temple Mount.

The attitude of the Palestinians was expressed inter alia in 1988 and 2002. When the Palestine Liberation Organization proclaimed in 1988 the establishment of a Palestinian state, it asserted that Jerusalem was its capital. In 2002 the Palestinian Legislative Council adopted the Law of the Capital, which stipulated that Jerusalem was the capital of the Palestinian State, the main seat of its three branches of government. The State of Palestine is the sovereign of Jerusalem and of its holy places. Any statutes or agreement that diminishes the rights of the Palestinian State in Jerusalem is invalid. This statute can be changed only with the consent of two-thirds of the members of the Legislative Council.

Jerusalem and the Peace Process

One could argue over the question as to when the present peace process began. For practical purposes, the adoption of Security Council Resolution 242 of November 1967 can be chosen as the starting point, since this text is referred to in many of the agreements which have so far been reached. Resolution 242 does not include any express reference to Jerusalem. This Resolution, adopted in the wake of the Six-Day War, laid down the basic principles upon which peace should be founded.[39] Similarly, Security Council Resolution 338 adopted after the 1973 October War does not deal with Jerusalem. Neither do the Camp David accords of 1978[40] include provisions on Jerusalem, but the parties expressed their differing opinions on the subject in accompanying letters: Israeli Prime Minister Menachem Begin stated that in accordance with legislation of 1967, "Jerusalem is one city, indivisible, the Capital of the State of Israel," whereas Egypt's President, Anwar el-Sadat, stated that "Arab Jerusalem is an integral part of the West Bank," and "should be under Arab sovereignty." At the same time he determined that "essential functions in the City should be undivided," and that "a joint municipal council composed of an equal number of Arab and Israeli members can supervise the carrying out of those functions." He added that "in this way, the city shall be undivided."[41]

There was no reference to Jerusalem in the Peace Treaty concluded in 1979 by Egypt and Israel.[42]

In October 1991 the Madrid Conference for Peace in the Middle East was convened by the United States and the Soviet Union.[43] After the Conference, bilateral negotiations took place. The question of Jerusalem was especially relevant to the negotiations between Israel and the Palestinians who attended the Conference as part of a joint Jordanian-Palestinian delegation.

According to the invitation from the U.S. and the Soviet Union, the negotiations with the Palestinians were to deal at the first stage with the establishment of interim self-government arrangements in the West Bank and Gaza for a period of five years, while in the third year after the setting up of that regime, negotiations on the permanent status of these areas would start. Although the text of the invitation to the Conference does not refer to Jerusalem, the city played an important role in the negotiations that preceded the Conference and in the letters of assurances from the United States to the Palestinians.

The U.S. promised that the composition of the delegation would not affect the claims of the Palestinians to Jerusalem. It expressed the view that the city should never again be divided, and that its final status should be determined by negotiations. The U.S. also stated that it did not recognize the annexation of east Jerusalem by Israel nor the extension of the municipal boundaries. It was the view of the U.S. that "Palestinians of east Jerusalem should be able to participate by voting in the elections for an interim self-governing authority," and that the Palestinians have the right "to bring any issue, including east Jerusalem, to the table." The U.S. did not specify whether Jerusalem could be brought "to the table" of the negotiations on the interim arrangements, or of the later permanent status negotiations.[44] The letters of assurances were issued by the United States in order to prod the parties to participate in the Conference.

While the post-Madrid bilateral meetings took place between Israel and a Palestinian delegation which, upon Israel's demand, formally did not include representatives of the PLO, the latter and Israel conducted secret negotiations in Oslo with the good offices of Norway's Minister of Foreign Affairs. As a result, three letters were exchanged and a Declaration of Principles was initialed in Oslo and signed in Washington, D.C., on September 13, 1993.[45] This text was a turning point in the attitude of the two parties on the question of Jerusalem: it was agreed that Jerusalem would not be included in the interim self-government arrangements to be agreed upon – a concession by the Palestinians, and, on the other hand, Israel conceded that Jerusalem would be one of the subjects to be dealt with in the framework of the negotiations on the "permanent status" to start in 1996.[46] In addition, it was agreed that "Palestinians of Jerusalem who live there will have the right to participate in the election process" for the Interim Self-Government Authority for the West Bank and Gaza.[47] The parties disagreed on the question whether the Palestinians of Jerusalem have only the active right to vote, or also the right to be elected.

Israel's insistence on denying the right to be elected stemmed from the fear that the granting of such a right would be incompatible with Israeli sovereignty over the entire city. In addition, there was disagreement on the question, where the Jerusalemites should vote.

These matters were solved, at least partly, in the Israeli-Palestinian Interim Agreement on the West Bank and the Gaza Strip, of September 28, 1995.[48] As to the passive right to be elected, it was agreed that only a Jerusalemite who has an additional address in the West Bank or Gaza may be elected, and he is to represent the other area, namely, not the city of Jerusalem (Article III (1)(b) of Annex II to the Interim Agreement). With regard to the physical location where Jerusalemites were actually to vote, it was agreed that most of the residents of Jerusalem would cast their vote in the Palestinian Jerusalem constituency beyond the municipal boundaries of the city. This solution was possible since the Jerusalem constituency according to the Palestinians is much larger than the city. In fact, on election day (January 20, 1996) most of the residents voted in Abu Dees – an Arab village just beyond the confines of the city. Only a small number of Palestinians – about 4,500 persons – were permitted to vote in post offices within the boundaries of the municipality proper (Article VI (2)(a) of Annex II). Voting at the post offices was procedurally somewhat different from voting at a regular polling station, to emphasize that Jerusalem is not part of the areas under the jurisdiction of the Palestinian Council.

About a month after the signing of the Declaration of Principles, in October 1993, Israeli Foreign Minister Shimon Peres sent a letter concerning Palestinian institutions in East Jerusalem to the foreign minister of Norway, Johan Jurgen Holst.[49] The letter was kept secret for some time, and its discovery aroused much criticism in Israel. According to this letter, "all the Palestinian institutions of East Jerusalem, including the economic, social, educational, cultural, and the holy Christian and Moslem places, are performing an essential task for the Palestinian population ..." and "will be preserved...." The meaning of this text and its effect raise difficult questions of interpretation.[50]

Once the ice was broken between Israel and the Palestinians, the road was open for progress in the negotiations between Israel and Jordan. First a "Common Agenda" was agreed upon (September 14, 1993), then a joint declaration was adopted (July 25, 1994) and on October 26, 1994, a Peace Treaty was concluded.[51] This Treaty includes, inter alia, a promise by Israel "to respect the present special role of Jordan in Muslim Holy Shrines in Jerusalem," and, "when negotiations on the permanent status will take place, Israel will give high priority to the Jordanian historic role in these shrines."[52]

According to some press reports, in 1996 Jordan promised to transfer the custody of the Holy Places to the Palestinians once the latter acquire control of the city in the framework of the permanent status to be negotiated later.[53] However, the status of the Muslim Holy Shrines in Jerusalem is of interest and concern not only to Jordan, the Palestinians, and Israeli Muslims.

In the wake of the improved relations with the Palestinians and with Jordan, several other countries have established or re-established diplomatic relations with Israel. Of particular interest in this regard is the normalization of relations between Israel and the Holy See, foreseen by the Fundamental Agreement of December 30, 1993.[54] This document does not deal expressly with Jerusalem, but some of its provisions are relevant to the city, e.g., the commitment to favor Christian pilgrimages to the Holy Land, and the right of the Catholic Church to establish schools and to carry out its charitable functions. The parties affirmed their "continuing commitment to maintain and respect the 'status quo' in the Christian Holy Places to which it applies …" – a reference to the *status quo* established in the 18th and 19th centuries by the Ottoman Empire in order to regulate the rights of various competing Christian churches at certain Holy Places in Jerusalem and in Bethlehem.[55]

The negotiations on the permanent status started in May 1996, but were suspended after a few hours. They were resumed in 1999 and led to the July 2000 Camp David Summit. These intensive negotiations failed, to a large extent because of disagreement over the future of Jerusalem, in particular over the Old City and the Temple Mount. Some of the Palestinian leaders, including Arafat, even claimed that there had never been a Jewish Temple on the Temple Mount. Neither did the January 2001 meeting in Taba lead to a breakthrough.

Since then, several proposals have been drafted concerning the search for a resolution to the Israel-Palestinian dispute including Jerusalem (e.g., President Clinton, 2000; Ayalon-Nusseibeh, 2002; the Arab States Peace Initiative, 2002; Beilin-Abd Rabbo Geneva Initiative, 2003), but so far (2006) none has been adopted by the parties. On the other hand, the 2003 Road Map, sponsored by the U.S., Russia, the UN, and the EU (the Quartet), has been accepted by the parties. According to this text, the conflict should be resolved in stages. With regard to Jerusalem, it states that in the third stage, the parties should negotiate and reach an agreement that includes a resolution of the status of Jerusalem that takes into account the political and religious concerns of both sides, and protects the religious interests of Jews, Christians, and Muslims worldwide

Conclusion

The status of West and East Jerusalem has been the subject of very differing opinions of various writers. So far foreign states have not recognized any sovereignty over Jerusalem, but have acquiesced in Israeli *de facto* control over western Jerusalem, while claiming that East Jerusalem is occupied territory. For the Israeli authorities, the whole of Jerusalem is part of the State of Israel.

In some of the agreements so far reached there are timid references to Jerusalem and the Holy Places: in the 1993 Declaration of Principles it was agreed that Jerusalem (without definition of its contours) would not be discussed in the negotiations on the interim self-government arrangements (a concession by the PLO), but that it would be included in the negotiations on the permanent status (a concession by Israel). The Declaration of Principles also foresees the participation of East Jerusalemites in the elections for the self-government authority.

In the 1994 Israel-Jordan Treaty of Peace Israel promised to respect Jordan's present role in Muslim Holy Shrines in Jerusalem, and also undertook to give high priority to Jordan's historic role at those shrines when negotiating on the "permanent status."

The difficulties concerning these early provisions were but a foretaste of the diplomatic battle over Jerusalem in the negotiations on the permanent status. Disagreement has encompassed many thorny questions, e.g., matters related to sovereignty; jurisdiction and powers, in particular in the sphere of security, transportation and access roads, town planning; Holy Places (foremost those that are holy to two or more denominations) such as the Temple Mount; and municipal matters. There is hardly any subject which could not lead to conflict, but where there is a will there is a way and if both parties are sincerely looking for a compromise, it may be hoped that they will find one.

Notes

1. For a concise overview of the various opinions, see Moshe Hirsch in Ruth Lapidoth and Moshe Hirsch, *Jerusalem – Political and Legal Aspects* (The Jerusalem Institute for Israel Studies, 1994), 11–15 (in Hebrew), and in Moshe Hirsch, Debra Housen-Couriel, and Ruth Lapidoth, *Whither Jerusalem? Proposals and Positions Concerning the Future of Jerusalem* (The Hague, Kluwer Law International, in Collaboration with The Jerusalem Institute for Israel Studies, 1995), 15–24.
   In the present article only opinions on the *lex lata* are reproduced. For a summary of the various proposals *de lege ferenda*; see M. Hirsch, D. Housen-Couriel, and R. Lapidoth, *op. cit.*, 25–125 and Naomi Chazan, *Negotiating the Non-Negotiable: Jerusalem in the Framework of an Israeli-Palestinian Settlement* (International Security Studies Program, American Academy of Arts and Sciences, Cambridge, MA, Occasional Paper No. 7, March 1991). Gershon Baskin, *Jerusalem of Peace – Sovereignty and Territory in Jerusalem's Future* (Jerusalem, Israel/Palestine Center for Research and Information, 1994); Dore Gold, *Jerusalem – Final Status Issues: Israel-Palestinians*, Study No. 7 (Tel Aviv, The Jaffee Center for Strategic Studies, Tel Aviv University, 1995): proposal prepared by the Arab Studies Society in 1995 (a summary in Hebrew was published in the Jerusalem weekly *Kol Ha-Ir* of October 20, 1995; President Clinton's proposals of 2000, the Arab States proposal of 2003, Sari Nusseibeh-Ami Ayalon principles of 2002, and the Yossi Beilin-Yassir Abd Rabbo Geneva Initiative of 2003
2. See e.g., Elihu Lauterpacht, *Jerusalem and the Holy Places* (London, The Anglo-Israel Association, 1968, reprinted 1980); Julius Stone, *Israel and Palestine – Assault on the Law of Nations* (Baltimore, The Johns Hopkins University Press, 1981), 116–118; Stephen Schwebel, "What Weight to Conquest?" *American Journal of International Law*, 64 (1970), p. 344. For a similar but not quite identical opinion, see M.I. Gruhin, "Jerusalem: Legal and Political Dimensions in a Search for Peace," *Case Western Journal of International Law*, 12 (1980), p. 169.
3. HRH Crown Prince Hassan bin Talal, *A Study on Jerusalem* (London, Longman, 1979), 24–27. See also G.I.A.D. Draper, "The Status of Jerusalem as a Question of International Law," in: Hans Koechler (ed.), "The Legal Aspects of the Palestine Problem with Special Regard to the Question of Jerusalem," *Studies in International Relations*, 4 (Wien, Braumueller, 1981), 154–163.
4. Henry Cattan, *Jerusalem* (New York, St. Martin's Press, 1981), 104 and 107; idem, *Palestine and International Law*, 2nd ed. (London,

Longman, 1976), 112–121; idem, *The Palestine Question* (London, Longman, 1988), 324–326.

5. *The Status of Jerusalem* (New York, United Nations, 1979), prepared for the Committee on the Exercise of the Inalienable Rights of the Palestinian People; Sally V. Mallison and W. Thomas Mallison, "The Jerusalem Problem in Public International Law: Juridical Status and a Start Towards Solution," in Hans Koechler, ed., supra note 3, 98–119, at p.107; Antonio Cassese, "Legal Considerations on the International Status of Jerusalem," *ibid.*, 144–153, 149 and 151. For the text of the Resolution, see Official Records of the second session of the UN General Assembly, Supplement No. 11, Volumes I–IV. It has been reproduced inter alia in Ruth Lapidoth and Moshe Hirsch (eds.), *The Arab-Israel Conflict and its Resolution: Selected Documents* (Dordrecht, Martinus Nijhoff, 1992), 33–54 (henceforth: *The Arab-Israel Conflict – Documents*).
6. For a comprehensive analysis of the attitude of the United States, see Shlomo Slonim, "The United States and the Status of Jerusalem, 1947–1984," *Israel Law Review*, 19 (1985), p. 179.
7. Civil Case Jerusalem 208/52, Pesaquim Mehoziyyim, 8 (1952/1953), p. 455; Pesaquim Mehoziyyim, 16 (1958), p. 20; Execution Case Jerusalem 157/53, Pesaquim Mehoziyyim, 9 (1953/1954), p. 502. For an English overview of the various decisions, see *International Law Reports*, 20, 1953 (1as7), 391–405.
8. See, e.g., Statement by the Minister of State of the United Kingdom in the House of Commons, April 27, 1950, reproduced in Ruth Lapidoth and Moshe Hirsch (eds.), *The Jerusalem Question and its Resolution: Selected Documents* (Dordrecht, Martinus Nijhoff, in cooperation with The Jerusalem Institute for Israel Studies, 1994), 147–148 (henceforth: *Jerusalem – Selected Documents*); letters by Janet G. Mullins, United States Assistant Secretary of State for Legislative Affairs, to Lee H. Hamilton, Chairman of the Subcommittee on Europe and the Middle East, U.S. House of Representatives, of 29 June and 6 September 1989, reproduced *ibid.*, 447–449.
9. See, e.g., *ibid.*, p.449.
10. For references, see supra note 2.
11. For references, see supra note 4. For somewhat similar opinions, see Michael Van Dusen, "Jerusalem, the Occupied Territories and the Refugees," in Majid Khadduri (ed.), *Major Middle Eastern Problems in International Law* (Washington DC, American Enterprise Institute, 1978), p. 51; John Quigley, "Old Jerusalem: Whose to Govern," *Denver Journal of International Law and Policy*, 20 (1991), 145, 164–166.
12. Yoram Dinstein, "Autonomy," in Y. Dinstein (ed.), *Models of Autonomy* (New Brunswick, Transaction Books, 1981), 291–303, p. 300. On the Jericho meeting, see *Jerusalem – Selected Documents*, 145–148. It is not known whether Dinstein has changed his opinion on the question of sovereignty due to Jordan's disengagement from the West Bank in 1988. For the text of this statement concerning disengagement, see *International Legal Materials*, 27 (1988), p. 1637, reproduced in *The Arab-Israel Conflict – Documents*, p. 339.
13. For references, see supra note 5.
14. For references, see supra note 2.
15. Yehuda Z. Blum, *The Juridical Status of Jerusalem* (Jerusalem, The Leonard Davis Institute for International Relations, 1974); idem, "The Missing Reversioner: Reflections on the Status of Judea and Samaria," *Israel Law Review*, 3 (1968), 279–301.
16. For references, see supra note 4.
17. For references, see supra note 12.
18. Supra, note 5.
19. E.g., Security Council Resolution 465, of March 1, 1980, SCOR, 35th Year, 1980, Resolutions, p. 5, UN Doc. S/INF/36; Security Council resolution 478, of August 20, 1980, SCOR, 35th Year, 1980, Resolutions, p. 14, both reproduced in *Jerusalem – Selected Documents*, 311 and 351.
20. *Jerusalem – Selected Documents*, p. 300.
21. For the Statement made by Ambassador Goldberg, see GAOR, 5th Emergency Special Sess. (Plenary Meetings), 1554th meeting, July 14, 1967, 9–11. For Ambassador Yost's Statement, see SCOR, 24th year, 1969, 148th meeting, July 1, 1969. 11–12; both are reproduced in *Jerusalem – Selected Documents*, 174–177 and 236–238.
22. Attorney General v. Yoel Davis, Pesaquim Mehoziyyim, 3 (1988/1989) (3), 336–342. For a summary in English, see *Jerusalem – Selected Documents*, 535–539.
23. Bulletin of the European Communities, 6 – 1980, p. 10, reproduced in *Jerusalem – Selected Documents*, 314–315.
24. *Laws of the State of Israel, Authorized Translation* (henceforth: LSI), vol. 1, 5708 – 1948, p. 3, reproduced in *The Arab-Israel Conflict – Documents*, p. 61.
25. English translation published in *Jerusalem – Selected Documents*, 27–29.
26. LSI, 5708 – 1948, p. 64.
27. English translation in Meron Medzini (ed.), *Israel's Foreign Relations: Selected Documents 1947–1974* (Ministry of Foreign Affairs, Jerusalem, 1976), 223–226, reproduced in *Jerusalem –Selected Documents*, 81–84.
28. *Ibid.*
29. LSI, vol. 21, 5727 – 1966/67, p. 75, reproduced in: *Jerusalem – Selected Documents*, p. 167.
30. LSI, *ibid.*, p. 75; *The Arab-Israel Conflict – Documents*, p. 130.
31. Law and Administration (No. 1) Order, of 28 June 1967, Collection of Subsidiary Legislation (*Kovets Ha-Takanot*), 5727 (1966/67), p. 2690. Another important law that was adopted in 1967 and which is relevant to Jerusalem is the Protection of the Holy Places Law, 5727 – 1967, LSI, Vol. 21, 5727 – 1966/67, p. 76, reproduced in: *The Arab-Israel Conflict – Documents*, p. 132.
32. LSI, Vol. 24, 5730 – 1969/70, 144–152, reproduced in *Jerusalem – Selected Documents*, 242–251.
33. See e.g., General Assembly Resolution 2253 (ES-V), of July 4, 1967, GAOR, 5th Emergency Special Session, 1967, Resolutions, Su 1 (A/6978), p. 4, reproduced in *Jerusalem – Selected Documents*, p. 170.
34. Letter of July 10, 1967, GAOR, 5th Emergency Special Sess., 1967, p. 1 (A/6753–S/8052), reproduced in *Jerusalem – Selected Documents*, 171–173.
35. 24 (2) Piske Din (1970), p. 419. For a summary in English, see *Jerusalem – Selected Documents*, 502–506.
36. LSI, Vol. 34, 5740 – 1979/80, p. 209, reproduced in *Jerusalem – Selected Documents*, p. 322.
37. Security Council resolution 478, of August 20, 1980, SCOR, 35th year, 1980, Resolutions, p. 14, reproduced in *Jerusalem – Selected Documents*, p. 351.
38. 47 (5) Piske-Din (1993), 221–288.
39. SCOR, 22nd year, Resolutions and Decisions, 8–9, reproduced in *The Arab-Israel Conflict – Documents*, p. 134. This resolution has been the subject of differing interpretations by the parties, and of a great number of scholarly articles. Among the more recent ones are: Adnan Abu Odeh, Nabil Elaraby, Meir Rosenne, Dennis Ross, Eugene Rostow, Vernon Turner, *UN Security Council Resolution 242: The Building Block of Peacemaking* (The Washington Institute for Near East Policy, 1993); Ruth Lapidoth, "Security Coun-

cil Resolution 242 at Twenty Five," *Israel Law Review*, 26 (1992), 295–318.

40. United Nations Treaty Series, vol. 1138, 39–56, reproduced in *The Arab-Israel Conflict – Documents*, 195–201.
41. *Jerusalem – Selected Documents*, 299–300.
42. United Nations Treaty Series, Vol. 1138, No. 17855, 72–163, reproduced in *The Arab-Israel Conflict – Documents*, 218–242.
43. Text of the letter of invitation reproduced in *The Arab-Israel Conflict – Documents*, 384–386.
44. Letter of October 18, 1991, reproduced in *The Jerusalem Post*, October 31, 1991.
45. UN Doc. A/48/486 – S/26560 (Annex), of October 11, 1993; *International Legal Materials*, 32 (1993), 1525–1544. On the Declaration of Principles, see Joel Singer, "The Declaration of Principles on Interim Self-Government Arrangements," *Justice*, no. 1, February 1994, 4–21; Eyal Benvenisti, "The Israel-Palestinian Declaration of Principles: A Framework for Future Settlement," *European Journal of International Law*, 4 (1993), 542–554; Antonio Cassese, "The Israel-PLO Agreement and Self-Determination," *ibid.*, 5564 – 571; Raja Shihadeh, "Can the Declaration of Principles Bring About a 'Just and Lasting Peace'?," *ibid.*, 555–563.
46. Articles IV and V (3), and Agreed Minutes.
47. Annex I, para 1.
48. Published by the Ministry of Foreign Affairs, Jerusalem.
49. Reproduced in the *Jerusalem Post*, June 7, 1994.
50. For an analysis of these questions, see Ruth Lapidoth, "Jerusalem and the Peace Process," *Israel Law Review*, 28 (1994), 402–434, 428–430.
51. International Legal Materials (1995), p. 43.
52. Article 9 of the Treaty of Peace.
53. *Ha'aretz*, November 6, 1994, p. A–4; *Ha'aretz*, November 13, 1994, p. A–10.
54. *International Legal Materials*, 33 (1994), p. 153.
55. On the *status quo*, see Shmuel Berkovitz, "The Legal Status of the Holy Places in Israel," Thesis submitted for the degree of Ph.D. to the Hebrew University, March 1978, 35–45; L.G.A. Cust, *The Status Quo in the Holy Places* (1929, reproduced in 1980 by Ariel Publishing House, Jerusalem).

[Ruth Lapidoth (2nd ed.)]

JERUSALEM, WILHELM (1854–1923), Austrian philosopher and psychologist. Jerusalem, who was born in Drenic, Bohemia, was a schoolteacher for several years after completing his university studies in philology. During this time he became interested in the psychology of speech and the education of blind deaf-mutes, and in 1890 wrote a book on the American blind deaf-mute, Laura Bridgman. In 1891 he began lecturing in philosophy at the University of Vienna, and in 1903 in pedagogics, but it was not until 1920 that he received a professorship in these two subjects. Between 1894 and 1902 he also taught at the Juedisch-Theologische Lehranstalt in Vienna. Jerusalem's general philosophical view was empirical, employing the genetic method, and biological and social ways of interpreting the mind. He was influenced by H. Spencer, E. Mach, and W. James, whose *Pragmatism* he translated into German. Jerusalem opposed neo-Kantianism and E. *Husserl's pure logic as merely intellectual and unrelated to life. He saw no need for a conflict between religion and philosophy, as long as the fundamental principles of science are utilized to erect structures of faith, interpreting the spiritual nature of man and developing a world view that can "inspire human life with incentive, purpose and direction." He wrote on the sociological in *Der Krieg im Lichte de Gesellschaftslehre* (1915) and *Moralische Richtlinien nach dem Kriege* (1918). Among Jerusalem's major works were *Einleitung in die Philosophie* (1899; *Introduction to Philosophy*, 1910), *Gedanken und Denker* (1905), *Der Krittische Idealismus und die reine Logik* (1905), and *Einfuehrung in die Soziologie* (1926).

BIBLIOGRAPHY: W. Eckstein, *Wilhelm Jerusalem, sein Leben und Wirken* (1935); M. Schloemann, *Die Denksoziologie Wilhelm Jerusalems* (1953); *Festschrift fuer Wilhelm Jerusalem …* (1915); E. Jerusalem, *Verzeichnis der Veroeffentlichungen Wilhelm Jerusalems* (1925); W. Jerusalem, in: *Die Philosophie der Gegenwart in Sebstdarstellungen*, 3 (1922), 53–98; Winiger, Biog, 3 (1928).

[Richard H. Popkin]

JERUSALEM INSTITUTE FOR ISRAEL STUDIES (JIIS), an Israeli policy research center, established in 1978 as an independent, non-profit organization. Its mission is to provide policy makers and the public with accurate, relevant data, in-depth background materials, and up-to-date analyses of critical trends and strategic options on subjects of national importance. JIIS research and analysis is designed to consider key issues facing Israel, to place them on the agenda of public debate, and to promote long-term planning and public involvement in the civic process. Materials are prepared by leading scholars as well as experienced practitioners in relevant fields. JIIS has particular expertise in issues related to the capital city of Jerusalem, the management of the Israeli-Palestinian conflict, and the status of the environment in Israel. Its work in these areas is organized in four study areas: The Center for Jerusalem – The Teddy Kollek Center, The Center for Joint Israeli-Palestinian Studies, The Environmental Policy Center, and the Center for Industrial Technological Policy. JIIS background papers and perspectives on the future of Jerusalem were central to the 1999–2000 peace negotiations led by Prime Minister Ehud Barak.

The institute was founded by Teddy Kollek, mayor of Jerusalem from 1965 to 1993, and chaired successively by scholars David Amiran (1978–1985), Amiram Gonen (1985–1989), and Abraham Friedman (1989–2002). Since 2002, it has been chaired by Yaacov Bar Siman Tov. From 1981, JIIS worked in close partnership with the Charles H. Revson Foundation in New York, which supports its initiatives and major projects. JIIS published approximately 20 books and reports a year; presented about 60 annual conferences and seminars; held press conferences to promote public awareness of key issues; and posted its data and selected policy research on its web site. Publications include *The Statistical Yearbook of Jerusalem* (edited by Maya Choshen), *Jerusalem and the Peace Process* (a series edited by Ruth Lapidoth and colleagues), *The Jerusalem Lexicon* (edited by Amnon Ramon), *Jerusalem's Architecture* (a series by David Kroyanker), and *The War Over the Holy Places* (by Shmuel Berkowitz).

[Ora Ahimeir (2nd ed.)]

JERUSALEM POST (until 1950 *The Palestine Post*), independent English-language daily newspaper published in Jerusalem. It was founded in December 1932 (after having purchased and incorporated the *Palestine Bulletin*, which had appeared since 1925) by Gershon Agronsky (*Agron), with the assistance of Ted R. *Lurie, who became editor when Agron was elected major of Jerusalem in 1955. The paper covers local news of both Jewish and Arab interest as well as world affairs, with special attention to developments in the Middle East. During the British Mandate, the *Post's* defense of Jewish interests and criticism of the Mandatory government, such as over the White Paper and its consequences, led to frequent disagreements with the British administration, especially the political censorship resulting from this policy. In February 1948, its offices and press were blown up by a bomb planted in a British-Arab conspiracy, as a reprisal against Jewish terrorism. Lurie died in 1974. In 1975 Ari Rath and Erwin Frenkel were appointed joint editors. The *Post* gave general support to the Labor movement, and, after 1948, to the government of Israel, while criticizing them on points of detail, particularly on economic and social policy. Following the election of the *Likud in 1977, the paper criticized or supported government policy on an issue-by-issue basis. The paper was owned by the *Histadrut. Unable to cover the paper's expenses, it sold the paper to the Canadian newspaper chain Hollinger. With the appointment by Hollinger of Yehudah Levy as the local publisher, the paper took a right-wing turn. Twenty-eight journalists initiated a labor dispute and were subsequently fired; Rath retired, and Frenkel resigned. The period since 1990 was characterized by organizational and financial instability, including seven editors-in-chief and a rapid turnover of editorial and printing personnel. On the issue of defense, the paper moved editorially in the post-1990 years between a centrist position under David Macovsky (1999–2000) and David Horowitz (2004–) as editors, and a right-wing position under David *Bar-Illan (1990–96) and Brett Stephens (2002–4). A neo-liberal capitalist outlook on economic and financial affairs replaced the socialist outlook of earlier years. Organizational and financial instability intensified after Tom Rose was appointed publisher in 1998. Despite its financial success, the newspaper's commercial printing press was closed down. By 2005 the *Jerusalem Post's* circulation had dropped to 12,000 daily and 28,000 on weekends, a decline from a high of 33,000 and 50,000, respectively, in 1967. Its readers comprised mostly immigrants from Anglo-Saxon countries, foreign diplomats, foreign correspondents, and to a limited extent the Palestinian population. The *Post's* monopoly as Israel's English-language daily was challenged with the appearance in 1997 of an English daily edition of *Haaretz*. In 2004 the paper was bought by an Israeli company, the Mirka'ei Tikshoret group, and the Canadian media group CanWest Global Communications.

In 1959 the paper founded an international weekly edition, based entirely upon copy from the local daily edition; though highly remunerative, its circulation fell from 70,000 in its early years to 28,000. Circulation of a weekly French-language version of the paper begun in 1991 – and sold in France, Canada, and Israel – remained low at 4,000 copies weekly. In 1995 the newspaper launched a successful Internet edition, www.jpost.com, drawing upon the daily newspaper's reporting. In 2004, the site had 14 million page views per month, one million general users monthly, and 385,000 registered users, according to the newspaper, and its yearly profits from advertising were over $1 million.

BIBLIOGRAPHY: E. Frenkel, *The Press & Politics in Israel: The Jerusalem Post from 1932 to the Present* (1993); A. Zvielli, "Reflections on the 60-Year History of 'The Jerusalem Post,'" in: *Kesher*, no. 12 (Nov. 1992).

[Yoel Cohen (2nd ed.)]

JERUSALEM PUBLISHING HOUSE, THE, Israeli publisher. Founded in 1966 by Shlomo S. (Yosh) Gafni, the company has as its aim the publication of books in foreign languages on Jewish and general subjects. Over the years the publishing house has specialized in producing encyclopedias. The first editor in chief of The Jerusalem Publishing House was Geoffrey *Wigoder. Its bestselling title, *The Illustrated Dictionary and Concordance of the Bible,* sold over one million copies. Other works dealing with the Bible include *Almanac of the Bible, The Glory of the Old Testament, The Glory of the New Testament, Archaeological Encyclopedia of the Holy Land,* and *The History of Israel and the Holy Land.*

The prize-winning *Encyclopedia of Judaism,* published in a second edition in 2002 as *The New Encyclopedia of Judaism* and in a youth edition as *The Student's Encyclopedia of Judaism* (2004), is a standard reference work in several languages. The *Political Encyclopedia of the Middle East* is an objective survey of the conflicts in the region. Series of richly illustrated encyclopedias covering the most important cultural events in Western civilization are *Peoples of the World* with an edition for young adults (10 vols.), *Encyclopedia of the Classical World, Renaissance, Medieval Civilization, Encyclopedia of International Boundaries*, etc.

From the late 1990s The Jerusalem Publishing House has co-published with *Yad Vashem encyclopedias on the subject of the Holocaust for general and educational purposes. These include such seminal works as *The Encyclopedia of Jewish Life Before and During the Holocaust* (3 vols.) and the ongoing *Encyclopedia of the Righteous Among the Nations* (6 vols. through 2005).

The biggest project of The Jerusalem Publishing House is the publication of the 21-volume second edition of the *Encyclopaedia Judaica* in cooperation with the *Keter Publishing House in Jerusalem and Thomson Gale (Macmillan) in the U.S. Fred Skolnik, editor-in-chief of The Jerusalem Publishing House, is also editor-in-chief of the *Encyclopaedia*, while Michael *Berenbaum of the U.S. is executive editor.

Founder Gafni remains president of the company and Rachel E. Gilon is the general manager.

JERUSALEM REPORT, international Jewish magazine published in Jerusalem. Founded in 1990 and appearing first as a weekly and later fortnightly, the news magazine covers political, social, economic, and cultural developments and trends in Israel, the Jewish world, and the Middle East. Its founding editor, Hirsh Goodman, formerly the *Jerusalem Post*'s military correspondent, conceived of the magazine as providing a mutual mirror for Diaspora Jews and Israelis to learn about one another. In 1998 David Horovitz became editor and in 2004 Sharon Ashley. The focus of its coverage is Israel. It drew together a circle of skilled journalists including Leslie Susser, Ehud Ya'ari, Stuart Schoffman, Netty Gross, Isabel Kirshner, and Zeev Chafetz. Its coverage of the Arab world is eclectic, and not limited to Arab developments relating to Israel. It maintains correspondents in Arab capitals as well as in different centers of the Jewish world. While its Jewish world coverage improved over the years, it mainly describes developments within individual Jewish communities rather than dealing with trends in the Jewish world at large. It has a large following in the Jewish world, with many Jewish communal and other decision makers among its readers, but has made less impact inside Israel. Its circulation is 50,000, four-fifths of which is in North America. The magazine sells 3,000 copies inside Israel and the remainder mostly in Britain and other English-speaking countries. Funded initially by five Jewish philanthropists, the magazine was sold in 1998 to the Hollinger newspaper chain, which included the *Jerusalem Post*. It was subsequently acquired by CanWest Global Communications and Mirka'ei Tikshoret in 2004. Apart from a brief period, it has been unprofitable. In 2004 it won the American Joint Distribution Committee's Boris Smolar award for coverage of the Jewish World. *The Report*'s staff published a biography of Yitzhak Rabin, *Shalom, Friend* (1996).

[Yoel Cohen (2nd ed.)]

JERUSALIMSKI, MOSES NAḤUM BEN BENJAMIN (1855–1914), rabbi and author. Jerusalimski served as rabbi of Kamenka in 1880, of Ostroleka in 1901, and in 1902 was appointed rabbi of Kielce. While still a young man, he corresponded with S.Z.H. *Halberstam of Sandec and J.S. *Nathanson of Lemberg. Although he never openly joined the Zionist movement, he was among the first Polish rabbis to support the Ḥovevei Zion. He also occupied himself with ramified communal activitiy and participated in the St. Petersburg conference of rabbis of 1909. He was the author of *Minchat Moshe* (1882) responsa, published together with *Hukkei ha-Shem* on the writing of names in bills of divorce; *Be'er Moshe* (1901), responsa and eulogies; *Leshad ha-Shemen* (1881), on Maimonides' *Mishneh Torah; Birkat Moshe* (1886), responsa, novellae, and the laws of *sheḥitah. Extracts from his diary during World War I were published in the *Sefer Kilz [Kielce]* (1957, pp. 273–93).

BIBLIOGRAPHY: B. Eisenstadt, *Dor, Rabbanav ve-Soferav*, 1 (1895), 32; S.N. Gottlieb, *Ohelei Shem* (1912), 180f.

[Itzhak Alfassi]

JESCHURUN, name of several Hebrew and German or German-Hebrew periodicals. The best known were:

(1) An Orthodox monthly published in German by Samson Raphael *Hirsch at Frankfurt (16 vols., 1854–70), and later issued as a weekly by his son Isaac Hirsch at Hanover (1883–88). Hirsch's famous polemics against Z. *Frankel and H. *Graetz first appeared in this *Jeschurun*.

(2) A less polemical and more scholarly periodical of moderate Conservative tendencies published by Joseph I. Kobak. This appeared with interruptions between 1856 and 1878 (nine volumes) at Lemberg, Breslau, Fuerth, and Bamberg. The first volume was in Hebrew only, the remainder in Hebrew and German. The contributors included L. *Dukes, S.D. *Luzzatto, S.J. *Rapoport, J. *Reifmann, M. *Steinschneider, and D. *Cassel.

(3) An Orthodox German-language monthly published by J. *Wohlgemuth during the years 1914–30 (17 volumes). It represented the ideology of the Berlin Rabbinical Seminary and published scholarly contributions written mainly by its teachers and pupils. Volumes 7–13 also contained a Hebrew section.

BIBLIOGRAPHY: E. Ben-Reshef, in: S. Federbush (ed.), *Ḥokhmat Yisrael be-Ma'arav Eiropah*, 1 (1958), 560–2; I. Grunfeld, in: S.R. Hirsch, *Judaism Eternal*, 1 (1956), xliv, liii–lx; Posner, in: *Shai li-Yshayahu* (1955), 73–78.

JESHUA (Heb. יֵשׁוּעַ, יְהוֹשֻׁעַ), high priest, son of Jehozadak (Jozadak; Ezra 3:2; 10:18) and a grandson of Seraiah the last high priest in the First Temple (1 Chron. 5:40). Together with *Zerubbabel, Jeshua organized the return to Zion (Ezra 2:2; Neh. 7:7) and was active in the rebuilding of the Temple and the state. He headed the priestly family of Jedaiah which returned to Judah, and it was thereafter known by his name (Ezra 2:36; 10:18). He and Zerubbabel established the order of sacrifices and planned the reconstruction of the Temple. They rejected the offer of the Samaritans to help in the labor, and when, after an interval of years, at the beginning of the reign of Darius I, *Haggai and *Zechariah aroused the people to renewed labor, they again headed the project. Jeshua's importance in this "condominium," or "diarchy," is a change from the pre-exilic situation in which the priesthood was subservient to royalty, and is approved by the contemporary prophets. Haggai almost always joins Jeshua's name to that of Zerubbabel (1:1, 14; 2:2, 4), and he is the central figure in Zechariah's earlier visions (Zech. 3–6). These visions, most of which, despite various interpretations, are obscure, in the main defy interpretation; Jeshua and his men are considered "men who are a token" (Zech. 3:8). In one vision, Satan stands at Jeshua's right, and the angel of the Lord rebukes him: "May the Lord who chose Jerusalem rebuke you! Why, this is a brand plucked out of the fire." (Jeshua's grandfather Seraiah was killed by Nebuchadnezzar and his children barely escaped; Zech. 3:2) The angel then commands those in attendance to dress Jeshua in robes and to place a pure miter on his head, symbolic of cleansing from sin – evidently the "iniquity of the land" (Zech. 3:9) – in line with the concept of the righteous being prosecuted for the sins of the generation. (The Talmud (Sanh. 93a) says this refers to the sin of intermarriage – Ezra 10:18 – but this was in a later generation.) Jeshua and Zerubbabel are called "the two sons of pure oil (*yiẓhar*) who wait upon the Lord of all the land" (Zech. 4:14). In Zechariah the prophet takes silver and gold brought by the exiles and has it made into crowns, one of them for Jeshua (Zech. 6:9ff.). These crowns were later kept in the Temple (Mid. 3:5). The form Jeshua, as opposed to the earlier Joshua, underlies the Greek that produced English "Jesus."

ADD. BIBLIOGRAPHY: T. Eshkenazi, in: ABD, 3:769–71; T. Eshkanazi, in: R. Albertz and B. Becking (eds.), *Yahwism after the Exile* (2002), 1–17. (See also Bibliography in *Haggai.)

[Menahem Stern]

JESHUA BEN JOSEPH HA-LEVI (15th century), talmudist. Following the persecutions of Jews in *Algiers in 1467, he fled from his native town Tlemcen and went to Castile, settling in Toledo, where he was supported by Don Vidal b. Lavi. At the latter's insistent request he wrote his talmudic methodology, *Halikhot Olam* (printed c. 1490). The work is divided into five sections dealing with the composition of the Mishnah and the *Gemara*, the methodology of the *Gemara*, and the manner in which the *halakhah* is determined. As the basis of his work, Jeshua made use of *Sefer Keritot* by *Samson b. Isaac of Chinon. The work appeared in several editions and served as the basis for Joseph *Caro's *Kelalei ha-Gemara*, which contains notes and supplements to the *Halikhot Olam* and for Solomon *Algazi's *Yavin Shemu'ah*. Both commentaries were published together with *Halikhot Olam* (Venice edition, 1639). David b. Raphael *Meldola's pamphlets *Limmud ha-Talmidim* and *Hanhagat ha-Talmidim* (appended to the Amsterdam edition, 1754) are also based on Jeshua's work. A Latin translation by D.C. l'Empereur was appended to the Leiden 1634 and Hanau 1714 editions; the latter contained notes by H.J. *Bashuysen. Jeshua also compiled *shitot* on the Talmud. It has been shown that he was the author of a *shitah* on *Bava Kamma* which is frequently mentioned in the *Shitah Mekubbeẓet*, although Bezalel *Ashkenazi was not aware of the identity of its author.

BIBLIOGRAPHY: Conforte, Kore, 27b; Weiss, Dor, 5 (1904[4]), 236; H.L. Strack, *Introduction to the Talmud and Midrash* (1931), 136; Finkelstein, in: KS, 12 (1935–36), 368f.

[Yehoshua Horowitz]

JESHUA BEN JUDAH (sometimes erroneously called **Joshua ben Judah**; his Arabic name was **Abū al-Faraj Furqān ibn Asad**; second half of the 11th century), Karaite scholar who lived in Jerusalem. A worthy pupil of his distinguished teacher Yūsuf al-*Baṣīr (Joseph ha-Ro'eh), he was regarded by the Karaites as one of the outstanding savants of his century, although in later times his philosophical and exegetical works tended to be neglected. Jeshua's greatest contribution, however, was his decisive opposition to the so-called catenary theory (in Hebrew *rikkuv*, literally "compounding") of incest, which had the support of the majority of earlier Karaite jurists, from *Anan downward, which severely limited the circle of women whom a Karaite man could lawfully marry. Jeshua was not the first to oppose this theory – his teacher Yūsuf al-Baṣīr is said also to have been an opponent of it, as was an earlier authority, *David b. Boaz (second half of the tenth century). However, Jeshua's tract on the law of incest dealt with it incisively and in great detail, and since it was subsequently translated from its original Arabic into Hebrew (*Sefer ha-Yashar* (1908); extracts in Leon Nemoy's *Karaite Anthology* (1952), 127–32; cf. Steinschneider, Arab Lit, 91–94), it remained accessible to later Karaite scholars who knew no Arabic and thus retained its influence upon them. In order to loosen the ever tightening noose fastened by the catenary theory upon the physical survival of the Karaite group, Jeshua established the following principles:

(1) The biblical dictum that man and wife become "one flesh" (Gen. 2:24) does not mean that all close relatives of the wife automatically become equally close to the husband, but merely refers to the couple's mutual affection and intimacy;

(2) The biblical identification of the wife's "nakedness" with the husband's "nakedness" similarly has nothing to do with incest, but merely refers to the husband's duty to guard his wife's chastity, the violation of which is as much an injury to him as to her;

(3) The biblical use of terms like "sister" or "aunt" with reference to distant or adopted relatives is merely figurative;

(4) The forbidden degrees of relationship are those listed in Scripture, their blood relatives, and those derived from them by analogy used only once – piling analogy upon analogy (as was done by the adherents of the catenary theory) is both unlawful and absurd, since it has no definable limit. Jeshua's definition of incest became the rule in later codes of Karaite law, down to and including Elijah *Bashyazi's authoritative code.

Although Karaite limitations on permissible marriages remain more stringent than the Rabbanite ones, Jeshua is responsible for one of the very few radical reforms ever introduced in Karaite jurisprudence. Jeshua's other works comprise an Arabic translation of the Pentateuch with a longer and shorter philosophical commentary, and comments on Genesis and on the Decalogue, extant mostly in fragments. A short Hebrew tract on the law of incest (*Iggeret ha-Teshuvah* or *Teshuvat ha-Ikkar*, Eupatoria, 1834) was printed under his name, but his authorship of it seems uncertain. Two philosophical tracts are also ascribed to him. Like his teacher, Jeshua follows in the footsteps of the Muʿtazilite (see *Kalam) school of Arab philosophers. He agrees with al-Baṣīr that certain knowledge of the creation of the world and the existence of God cannot be derived from the Bible alone but must come originally from rational speculation. Like al-Baṣīr he regards as the cornerstone of his religious philosophy the proof that the world was created in time. He also maintains that the Creator is not a "cause," i.e., an impersonal entity which by necessity produces other things from itself, but an "agent," i.e., one acting with will and choice. Jeshua offers several proofs for God's incorporeality. He likewise agrees with al-Baṣīr in regarding the nature of good and evil as absolute, not relative, and as binding upon God as well. God can do evil as well as good, but prefers to do good. Besides, all evildoing is the result of some need, but God has no needs, being self-sufficient; hence He does not do evil. God's purpose in creating the world cannot have been selfish, since God is without need, and must therefore have been the well-being of His creatures. Among Jeshua's pupils were the Byzantine scholars *Tobiah b. Moses and *Jacob b. Simeon, both translators of important Karaite works from the Arabic into Hebrew, and Ibn *al-Tarās, a Karaite who engaged in vigorous missionary activity among Rabbanites in his native Spain.

BIBLIOGRAPHY: M. Schreiner, *Studien ueber Jeschua ben Jehuda* (1900); S. Poznański, *The Karaite Literary Opponents of Saadiah Gaon* (1908), 48–53, 103; Husik, Philosophy, 55–58; Guttmann, Philosophies, 78–81.

[Leon Nemoy]

JESHURUN (Heb. יְשֻׁרוּן), poetic name of Israel, which occurs four times in the Bible (Deut. 32:15; 33:5, 26; Isa. 44:2; cf. Ecclus. 37:29, Heb. version). Its form and meaning are not clear. The Septuagint takes it as an adjective meaning "beloved," as does the Vulgate, in Deuteronomy 32:15. Elsewhere, however, the Vulgate translated it as *rectissimus*, "the most righteous." Aquila, Theodotion, and Symmachus render it as *euthús*, "straight, direct," suggesting the root ישר, "straight, righteous."

Many early and modern scholars follow this etymology. According to W. Bacher, the name Jeshurun is formed on the pattern of Zebulun and is intended to express the uprightness of Israel, in contrast to the appellation Jacob, which hints at his deceitfulness. The analogy to Zebulun has been abandoned, because the appearance of Jeshurun in Deuteronomy 32–33 means that it cannot be considered as a late artificial form of Israel.

The theophorus element *išar* is common in Akkadian names, and occurs also with *s* in Amorite names (*isar*). Jeshurun can then be compared to names such as *I-šar-be-li, I-šar-li-im, I-ša-rum*, and *Ya-sa-rum* (cf. Gadd, and Huffmon in bibl.).

BIBLIOGRAPHY: W. Bacher, in: ZAW, 5 (1885), 161–3; M. Naor, *ibid.*, 49 (1931), 318; J.C. Gadd, in: *Iraq*, 7 (1940), 38–39; J.S. Licht, in: EM, 3 (1958), 937–8; H.B. Huffmon, *Amorite Personal Names in the Mari Texts* (1965), 212, 216. **ADD. BIBLIOGRAPHY:** S. Jeansonne, in: ABD, 3, 771–72.

JESI, SAMUEL (1788–1853), Italian copper engraver and lithographer. Born at Corregio, he was trained to engrave copies of paintings, much in demand as a means of reproduction. Jesi specialized in translating the works of the Renaissance painters into the black and white medium of the copper engraving and achieved high recognition for his prints. In 1821 Jesi received the prize of the Milan Academy for his engraving *Abraham Dismissing Hagar* after Guercino. In 1842 Jesi became a correspondent of the French Academy. The Academies of Florence, Genoa, and St. Petersburg made him an honorary member. He died in Florence.

BIBLIOGRAPHY: A. Balletti, *Gli Ebrei e gli Estensi* (1930), 249–50.

[Elisheva Cohen]

JESSE (Heb. יִשַׁי, אִישַׁי), father of King *David. According to the Book of Ruth (4:17–22), Jesse was the grandson of Boaz and Ruth and was listed among the descendants of Pereẓ, son of Judah, who lived in Beth-Lehem. When *Samuel anointed David, he invited Jesse and his sons to a feast in their honor, which was a natural thing to do, in order to avoid arousing Saul's suspicions (I Sam. 16:1–5). It is possible that it is his social position that is indicated in the Hebrew text of I Samuel 17:12, which says of Jesse that he "was an old man… who entered among men (of standing)" (Heb. *ba-anashim*). The word "men" in this context has been compared with its semantic parallel, Akkadian *awēlu*, which in Mesopotamian society refers to men of the upper stratum, namely the elders and chiefs of the community. The stories concerning David mention Jesse's flocks, but his standing and his descent from Boaz suggest that he was also a landowner. It must be noted that both the Greek Septuagint and the Syriac Peshitta (see *Bible: Translations) presuppose a Hebrew: *ba ba-shanim*, "entered into years," i.e. "old."

[Samuel Ephraim Loewenstamm / S. David Sperling (2nd ed.)]

In the Aggadah

Jesse merited to be the ancestor of the royal house by virtue of his own good deeds. He expounded Torah to a multitude of 60 myriads (Yev. 76b). His father-in-law Ithra, an Ishmaelite, converted to Judaism and gave Jesse his daughter in marriage, when he heard him recite Isaiah 45:22 "Look unto Me and be saved, all the ends of the earth" (TJ, Yev. 8:3, 9b). After the birth of his sixth son, Jesse separated from his wife for three years but on one occasion attempted to seduce one of his female slaves. His wife, however, disguised herself as the slave girl (on the latter's advice), and it was thus that David was conceived (Yal. Mak. to Ps. 118:28). It was Jesse who encouraged David to slay Goliath and thus protect King Saul, seeing in it a continuation of the protection which Judah (David's ancestor) had afforded to Benjamin (Saul's ancestor) in Egypt (Tanḥ. B., Gen. 104). David's cruelty toward the Moabites (II Sam. 8:2) is justified by the fact that it was they who had treacherously killed Jesse after David had entrusted him to their care while he fled from Saul (cf. I Sam. 22:3; Num. R. 14:1). It is also stated, however, that Jesse was one of the four persons who were untainted by sin and died merely because death was decreed upon all mankind, as a result of the serpent's seduction of Eve. It is for this reason that Abigail, who was really Jesse's daughter, is referred to by Scripture (II Sam. 17:25) as "the daughter of Nahash" ("serpent"; BB 17a). Jesse is one of the eight "messianic princes among men" referred to in Micah 5:4 (Suk. 52b).

BIBLIOGRAPHY: IN THE AGGADAH: Ginzberg, Legends, 4 (1954), 81, 86; 6 (1959), 245, 249–53; I. Ḥasida, *Ishei ha-Tanakh* (1964), 239–40. **ADD. BIBLIOGRAPHY:** S. Bar-Efrat, *I Samuel* (1996), 225.

JESSE BEN HEZEKIAH (13th century), "exilarch of all the Diasporas of Israel" in *Damascus. Jesse is known for his participation in the controversy over the writings of *Maimonides, which broke out during the 1290s as a result of the activities of Solomon Petit, the leader of the kabbalists in *Acre. He signed the ban against the opponents of Maimonides in 1286. He was possibly a descendant of Josiah (Hassan), the brother of the exilarch *David ben Zakkai, a contemporary of Saadiah Gaon.

BIBLIOGRAPHY: S. Poznański, *Babylonische Geonim im nachgaonaeischen Zeitalter* (1914), 123f.; Mann, in: *Sefer Zikkaron… S.A. Poznański* (1927), 29; Ashtor, Toledot, 1 (1944), 132, 260f.

[Eliyahu Ashtor]

JESSEL, SIR GEORGE (1824–1883), English jurist, one of the country's great lawmaking judges. Born in London, the son of a diamond merchant, Jessel was called to the bar in 1847, and became a Queen's Counsel in 1865. He entered Parliament as Liberal member for Dover in 1868 and was appointed solicitor general in 1871, being the first Jew to hold ministerial office in England. In 1873 he became master of the rolls. Jessel's tenure of the office was marked by a succession of judgments which became notable precedents, and his contribution to the evolution of law and the development of the principles of equity was considerable. His judgments were short and clear and were hardly ever reversed on appeal. Jessel was the organizer of the Court of Chancery in its modern form. A member of the council of Jews' College from its inception in 1855 until 1863, Jessel helped to draft its original constitution. He was also vice president of the Anglo-Jewish Association. After Jessel's death, a baronetcy was conferred on his son SIR CHARLES JAMES JESSEL (1860–1928) in recognition of his father's services. The second son, HERBERT MERTON JESSEL (1866–1950), was active in Conservative politics and was raised to the peerage as Lord Jessel in 1924. FREDERICK HENRY JESSEL (1859–1934), nephew of Sir George Jessel, compiled the standard English bibliography on playing cards (1905) and left his comprehensive collection on the subject to the Bodleian Library, Oxford. RICHARD FREDERICK JESSEL (1902–1988), a great-nephew of Sir George Jessel, was among the British naval heroes of World War II. Frederick's son Toby Jessel (1934–) was a Conservative member of Parliament from 1970 to 1997. The connection of the family with the Jewish community became very slight.

BIBLIOGRAPHY: I. Finestein, in: JHSET, 18 (1958), 243–83; C. Roth, Mag Bibl, 132; Lehmann, Nova Bibl, 101, 109; P.H. Emden, *Jews of Britain* (1943), index. **ADD. BIBLIOGRAPHY:** ODNB online; Jolles, *Distinguished British Jews*, index.

[Israel Finestein]

JESSEL, GEORGE ALBERT (1898–1981), U.S. entertainer. Born in New York, Jessel began his career as a boy singer in vaudeville, and at the age of ten was teamed with Eddie *Cantor. He went to London as a comedian in 1914, appeared at the Victoria Palace theater and, returning to New York in 1919, acted in revue. He developed a one-man act, and then turned to more serious work. He had his greatest success in 1925 on Broadway in *The Jazz Singer*, a play by Samson Raphaelson based on a short story "The Day of Atonement." Jessel played the role more than a thousand times. He participated in the writing of several plays in which he appeared, such as *The War Song* (1928) and *High Kickers* (1942). Some of his other Broadway performances included *Helen of Troy, New York* (1923); *Joseph* (1930); *Sweet and Low* (1930); and *Show Time* (1942).

Jessel was New York's official toastmaster from 1925 and appeared at banquets, army entertainments, and was particularly active at fundraising events for Jewish charities and on behalf of Israel. Because of his frequent role as master of ceremonies at so many entertainment and political gatherings, he was nicknamed "Toastmaster General of the United States."

Having starred in several silent films for Warner Brothers during the 1920s, Jessel was offered the lead in their history-making first talkie, *The Jazz Singer*. Jessel and the studio could not agree on Jessel's salary, and the role ultimately went to Al Jolson. Jessel often lamented that it was the biggest professional mistake he ever made. In addition to producing more than a dozen movies (*When My Baby Smiles at Me, Dancing in the Dark, Bloodhounds of Broadway, Tonight We Sing*) between 1945 and 1953, Jessel appeared in such films as *Private Izzy Murphy* (1926), *Ginsberg the Great* (1927), *Sailor Izzy Murphy* (1927), *George Washington Cohen* (1928), *Lucky Boy* (1929), *Love, Live, and Laugh* (1929), *It Might Be Worse* (1931), and had small roles in *The Busy Body* (1967), *Valley of the Dolls* (1967), *and Reds* (1981).

In 1970 Jessel received the Jean Hersholt Humanitarian Award at the Academy Awards.

No stranger to television audiences, Jessel appeared on many variety shows, as well as hosting a few of his own, namely *Four-Star Revue* (1952–53), *The Comeback Show* (1953), and *The George Jessel Show* (1953–54).

Jessel wrote several books, including an autobiography *So Help Me* (1944); a sequel, *This Way, Miss*; (1955); an instructive *You Too Can Make a Speech* (1956); a toastmaster's handbook, *Jessel, Anyone?* (1960); a book of poems, *Elegy in Manhattan* (1961); a whimsical *Halo over Hollywood* (1963); another autobiographical work, *The World I Lived In* (with J. Austin, 1975); and *The Toastmaster General's Favorite Jokes: Openings and Closings for Speechmakers* (1978).

BIBLIOGRAPHY: B. Treadwell, *Fifty Years of American Comedy* (1951), 109–12; L. Wilde, *Great Comedians Talk About Comedy* (1968), 281–303.

[Barth Healey / Ruth Beloff (2nd ed.)]

JESSELSON, LUDWIG (1910–1993), U.S. businessman and philanthropist. Jesselson was born in Neckarbischoffsheim, Germany, where he began a career in business at a young age. In 1934 he left Germany, and after three years in Holland he arrived in New York (1937), joining the firm of Philipp Brothers, which specializes in oil, metal, and chemicals, eventually becoming president and chairman. Jesselson collected Judaica and Hebraica and was highly active in Jewish life, concentrating on Orthodox and educational institutions. He was a trustee of Yeshiva University, was a founder of the Albert Einstein College of Medicine, and was a director of the American Committee for the Weizmann Institute. In 1973 he and his wife, Erica, founded the Yeshiva University Museum. In Israel he was a member of the boards of Bar-Ilan University, the Haifa Technion, and the Shaare Zedek Hospital. He was also involved with the Jewish National Library of The Hebrew University and the Israel Museum and Bezalel School of Art.

To encourage originality and excellence in Judaica design, Jesselson and his wife established the Jesselson Prize for Contemporary Judaica Design, awarded by the Israel Museum to an outstanding Judaica artist. They also purchased the Steiglitz Collection. The largest private collection of high-quality Judaica, it constitutes almost the entire Judaica section of the Israel Museum in Jerusalem.

The Ludwig and Erica Jesselson Institute for Advanced Torah Studies at Bar-Ilan University is dedicated to advancing a synthesis of Torah and academic study. Made up of the Institute for Men and the Midrasha for Women, it provides students the opportunity to engage in traditional talmudic and Judaic studies, combined with full university degree programs.

[Ruth Beloff (2nd ed.)]

°**JESSEY (Jacie), HENRY** (1601–1663), English philo-Semite and Baptist divine. Jessey was inclined to literal observance of biblical precepts (including the seventh-day Sabbath, i.e., on Saturday). He corresponded with *Manasseh Ben Israel in Amsterdam about the Lost Ten Tribes and dedicated to him his *Glory of Jehudah and Israel* (London, 1653). Jessey was among those who participated in 1655 in the Whitehall Conference (see *England), and later published an account of its proceedings. He subsequently collected £300 from English Christians to send to R. Nathan *Spira in Amsterdam for distressed Jews in Jerusalem, whose suffering he described in the anonymous *An Information, Concerning the Present State of the Jewish Nation in Europe and Judea* (London, 1658).

BIBLIOGRAPHY: C. Roth, *Life of Menasseh Ben Israel* (1934), index; N. Sokolow, *History of Zionism*, 2 (1919), 212–5; Roth, Mag Bibl, index; JHSEM, 2 (1935), 99–104. **ADD. BIBLIOGRAPHY:** ODNB online; E.G. van der Wall, "A Philo-Semitic Millenarian on the Reconciliation of Jews and Christians," in: D.S. Katz and J.I. Israel (eds.), *Sceptics, Millenarians, and Jews* (1990).

[Cecil Roth]

JESSNER, LEOPOLD (1878–1945), German theatrical director and manager. Starting as an actor, Jessner was director at the Thalia Theater in Hamburg (1904–15). He later directed the Neues Schauspielhaus in his birthplace Koenigsberg (1915–19). From 1919 to 1930 he was director and manager (*Intendant*) of the Staatstheater Berlin. In this period he was the most influential theatrical director in the German-speaking world. His theatrical style, often called "expressionist," came to the fore in the plays of classical authors such as Schiller (*Wilhelm Tell, Wallenstein*) and Shakespeare (*Richard III, Othello, Hamlet*), and also modern writers such as Wedekind (*Marquis von Keith*). His aim was to develop the central ideas of each play with a point of view focused on actual political and social developments. His leading actor was Fritz *Kortner. As a Social Democrat and a professing Jew (he was an executive member of the *Central-Verein), he was a target of political and antisemitic attacks from the beginning of his work in Berlin. As a result he was forced to resign as early as 1930. Before settling in Los Angeles, he served as a guest director of Habimah in Ereẓ Israel (1936–37).

BIBLIOGRAPHY: L. Jessner, *Schriften* (1979); M. Heilmann, *Leopold Jessner –Intendant der Republik* (2005).

[Jens Malte Fischer (2nd ed.)]

JESUITS (or **Society of Jesus**), Roman Catholic religious order established in 1534. Its founder, the Spaniard Ignatius of Loyola, in his youth had been on pilgrimage to Jerusalem and was mainly responsible for the establishment of the House of *Catechumens, a home for converted Jews, in Rome in 1543. However, the object of the new order was not propaganda among the Jews but counter-propaganda in the Christian world to confront the growing danger from Protestantism. A problem with which the order had to deal from its earliest days was whether persons of Jewish origin should be admitted – in particular *Conversos or *New Christians in Spain, where the order was soon strongly entrenched. In the face of considerable opposition from his colleagues, Loyola himself insisted on disregarding the racial principle. Giovanni Battista *Eliano (Solomon Romano), the converted grandson of Elijah *Levita, became a member of the order as early as 1552. Loyola's secretary Juan Alfonso de Polanco and his principal coadjutor, Diego (Jaime) Lainez notoriously belonged to New Christian stock; the latter was elected in 1558 as Loyola's successor, serving as general of the order from 1558 to 1565. The more narrow view nevertheless gathered weight. In 1573, Polanco was not elected as general mainly because of his New Christian origin. In 1593, all descendants of Jews and Moors were debarred from membership of the order, and in 1608 this provision was confirmed in less explicit terms by the sixth general congregation. In its zeal for the propagation of the Catholic faith the Jesuits not infrequently spearheaded the onslaught on the Jews and Judaism, as was the case especially in *Poland in the 18th century. On the other hand, the attempt to curb the excesses of the Portuguese Inquisition in the second half of the 17th century was led by the Jesuit scholar Antonio Vieira, who was strenuously supported by his order. Jesuits, such as Augustine, Cardinal *Bea, have played an important role in the evolution of the post-World War II Catholic attitude to the Jews.

BIBLIOGRAPHY: Baron, Social[2], 14 (1970), 9–17, 306–9, 306 n. 12, 308 n. 16.

JESURUN (Jessurun, Yeshurun), descendants of a Marrano family who fled the Spanish Inquisition and settled mainly in Amsterdam and Hamburg. The Hamburg branch is best known for Isaac b. Abraham Ḥayyim *Jesurun (d. 1655), rabbi of Hamburg's Portuguese community. He was succeeded by ISAAC JESURUN, formerly of Venice, who was installed as *ḥakham* in the fall of 1656. During the same period JOSEPH JESURUN (d. 1660) headed Hamburg's Talmud Torah congregation. Joseph was the brother of ISAAC JESURUN of Ragusa (see *Dubrovnik), who was sentenced in the *blood libel of 1622 and freed when several of the judges who had condemned him died suddenly. SARAH (b. c. 1602), daughter of Amsterdam's renowned Reuel *Jesurun, married Moses Gideon Abudiente of Lisbon and lived in Hamburg. The name DAVID JESURUN appears on a list of Judaizers residing in Hamburg, which a spy for the Lisbon Inquisition drew up in 1644.

BIBLIOGRAPHY: Roth, Marranos, 313; idem, in: ZGJD, 2 (1930), 228–36; H. Kellenbenz, *Sephardim an der unteren Elbe* (1958), index s.v. *Jessurun*.

[Aaron Lichtenstein]

JESURUN (Jessurun), ISAAC BEN ABRAHAM ḤAYYIM (d. 1655), *ḥakham* of the Portuguese community of Hamburg, Germany. His *Panim Ḥadashot* (Venice, 1651) deals with halakhic rulings following Joseph *Caro, and provides a detailed guide to *halakhot* in the Mishnah and the Talmud, and the rulings of the *posekim*. His *Livro da Providência Divina* ("Book on Divine Providence") appeared in Amsterdam in 1663. He published or edited *Sefer ha-Zikhronot* attributed to Samuel Aboab (Steinschneider, Cat Bod, 1128).

BIBLIOGRAPHY: Kayserling, Bibl., 53; H. Kellenbenz, *Sephardim an der unteren Elbe* (1958), index.

JESURUN, REUEL (formerly **Paulo de Pina**; c. 1575–1634), Portuguese Marrano. Born in Lisbon of a *New Christian family, Paulo set out for Rome in 1599, intending to join a Christian order there. En route he called on the Marrano physician Elijah Montalto, a friend of his family residing at Leghorn, Italy. After Montalto had persuaded him to return to Judaism, Paulo went back to Lisbon, embarking for Brazil in 1601 in the company of the confirmed Judaizer Diego Gomez (Abraham Cohen) *Lobato. Moving to *Amsterdam in 1604, he openly espoused Judaism, taking the biblical name Reuel Jesurun. Devoting himself to the Beth Jacob congregation, he served as administrator of the Talmud Torah rabbinical school during 1616. A man of considerable literary talent, he composed *Diálogo dos montes* (published in 1767), a dramatic poem in praise of Judaism which was first read in the Beth Jacob synagogue on Shavuot 5384 (1624). The poem was translated from Portuguese to English by Philip Polack and appeared in *The American Sephardi*, vol. 4, nos. 1–2 (Autumn, 1970), 48–88. The Beth Jacob archive contains Jesurun's initial account of Amsterdam's historic Jewish cemetery, which he helped to establish. There he interred his benefactor Elijah Montalto, who had died in 1616 in France and been embalmed by his royal patrons. Jesurun himself died in Altona.

BIBLIOGRAPHY: Roth, Marranos, 313–6; J. Meijer, in: ESN, s.v. *Parnassim*; W.C. Pieterse, *Livro de Bet Haim do Kahal Kados de Bet Yahacob* (1970).

JESUS (d. 30 C.E.), whom Christianity sees as its founder and object of faith, was a Jew who lived toward the end of the Second Commonwealth period. The martyrdom of his brother James is narrated by Josephus (Ant. 20:200–3), but the passage in the same work (18:63–64) speaking about the life and death of Jesus was either rewritten by a Christian or represents a Christian interpolation. The first Roman authors to mention Jesus are Tacitus and Suetonius. The historicity of Jesus is proved by the very nature of the records in the New Testament, especially the four Gospels: Matthew, Mark, Luke, and John. The Gospels are records about the life of Jesus. John's Gospel is more a treatise reflecting the theology of its author than a biography of Jesus, but Matthew, Mark, and Luke present a reasonably faithful picture of Jesus as a Jew of his time. The picture of Jesus contained in them is not so much of a redeemer of mankind as of a Jewish miracle maker and preacher. The Jesus portrayed in these three Gospels is, therefore, the historical Jesus.

The Gospels

The precise date of the composition of the Gospels is not known, but all four were written before 100 C.E. and it is certain that Matthew, Mark, and Luke are interdependent. Scholars call these three the Synoptic Gospels because they can be written in parallel columns, such form being called synopsis. It is generally accepted that the main substance of the Synoptic Gospels comes from two sources: an old account of the life of Jesus which is reproduced by Mark, and a collection of Jesus' sayings used in conjuction with the old account by Matthew and Luke. Most scholars today identify the old account that lies behind Mark with the known Gospel of Mark, but a serious analysis, based especially upon the supposed Hebrew original, shows that Mark had entirely rewritten the material. It may be assumed, therefore, that the old account, and not the revision, was known to both Luke and Matthew. According to R. Lindsey (see bibliography), Matthew and Luke, besides drawing upon the sayings, also drew directly upon the old account; the editor of Mark used Luke for his version, and Matthew, besides using the old account, often drew also upon Mark. Lindsey's conclusions are also supported by other arguments.

Both of the chief sources of the Synoptic Gospels, the old account, and the collection of Jesus' sayings, were produced in the primitive Christian congregation in Jerusalem, and were translated into Greek from Aramaic or Hebrew. They contained the picture of Jesus as seen by the disciples who knew him. The present Gospels are redactions of these two sources, which were often changed as a result of ecclesiastical tendentiousness. This becomes especially clear in the description of

Jesus' trial and crucifixion in which all Gospel writers to some degree exaggerate Jewish "guilt" and minimize Pilate's involvement. As the tension between the *Church and the Synagogue grew, Christians were not interested in stressing the fact that the founder of their faith was executed by a Roman magistrate. But even in the case of Jesus' trial, as in other instances, advance toward historical reality can be made by comparing the sources according to principles of literary criticism and in conjunction with the study of the Judaism of the time.

The Name, Birth, and Death Date of Jesus

Jesus is the common Greek form of the Hebrew name Joshua. Jesus' father, Joseph, his mother, Mary (in Heb. Miriam), and his brothers, James (in Heb., Jacob), Joses (Joseph), Judah, and Simon (Mark. 6:3) likewise bore very popular Hebrew names. Jesus also had sisters, but their number and names are unknown. Jesus Christ means "Jesus the Messiah" and according to Jewish belief, the Messiah was to be a descendant of David. Both Matthew (1:2–16) and Luke (3:23–38) provide a genealogy leading back to David, but the two genealogies agree only from Abraham down to David. Thus, it is evident that both genealogies were constructed to show Jesus' Davidic descent, because the early Christian community believed that he was the Messiah. Matthew and Luke set Jesus' birth in *Bethlehem, the city of David's birth. This motif is made comprehensible if it is assumed that many believed the Messiah would also be born in Bethlehem, an assumption clearly seen in John 7:41–42, which, telling of some who denied that Jesus is the Messiah, says: "Is the Christ (Messiah) to come from Galilee? Has not the Scripture said that the Christ is descended from David, and comes from Bethlehem, the village where David was?" John therefore knew neither that Jesus had been born in Bethlehem nor that he was descended from David. The home of Jesus and his family was *Nazareth in Galilee and it is possible that he was born there.

The story of Jesus' birth from the Virgin Mary and the Holy Spirit without an earthly father exists in the two independent literary versions of Matthew and Luke. It is not to be found in Mark or John, who both begin their Gospel with Jesus' baptism by *John the Baptist. Jesus' virgin birth is not presupposed in other parts of the *New Testament. Apart from Matthew and Luke, the first to mention the virgin birth is Ignatius of Antiochia (d. 107). According to Luke's data, Jesus was baptized by John the Baptist either in 27/28 or 28/29 C.E., when he was about the age of 30. On the evidence in the first three Gospels, the period between his baptism and crucifixion comprised no more than one year; although according to John it ran to two or even three years. It seems that on the point of the duration of Jesus' public ministry the Synoptic Gospels are to be trusted. Most probably, then, Jesus was baptized in 28/29 and died in the year 30 C.E.

Jesus' Family and Circle

Jesus's father, Joseph, was a carpenter in Nazareth and it is almost certain that he died before Jesus was baptized. All the Gospels state that there was a tension between Jesus and his family, although after Jesus' death his family overcame their disbelief and took an honorable place in the young Jewish-Christian community. Jesus' brother, James, became the head of the Christian congregation in Jerusalem and when he was murdered by a Sadducean high priest (62 C.E.) for the faith in his brother, he was succeeded by Simon, a cousin of Jesus. Grandsons of Jesus' brother, Judah, lived until the reign of Trajan and were leaders of Christian churches apparently in Galilee.

John the Baptist, who baptized Jesus in the river Jordan, was an important religious Jewish personality; he is recorded in Josephus (Ant. 18:116–9) as well as the New Testament. From Josephus it is seen that John's baptismal theology was identical with that of the *Essenes. According to the Gospels, in the moment of Jesus' baptism, the Holy Spirit descended upon him and a voice from heaven proclaimed his election. When he left John the Baptist, Jesus did not return to Nazareth, but preached in the area northwest of the Sea of Galilee. Later, after his unsuccessful visit to his native Nazareth, he returned again to the district around *Capernaum, performed miraculous healings, and proclaimed the Kingdom of Heaven. From his closest disciples he appointed 12 *apostles to be, at the Last Judgment, judges of the 12 tribes of Israel. After the death of Jesus the 12 apostles provided the leadership for the Jerusalem Church.

The Arrest of Jesus

Meanwhile, Herod Antipas, who had beheaded John the Baptist, also wanted to kill Jesus, whom he saw as the heir of the Baptist, but Jesus wanted to die in Jerusalem, which was reputed for "killing the prophets" (Luke 13:34). With Passover drawing near, Jesus decided to make a pilgrimage to the Temple at Jerusalem. There he openly predicted the future destruction of the Temple and the overthrow of the Temple hierarchy. According to the sources, he even tried to drive out the traders from the precincts of the Temple, saying, "It is written, 'My house shall be called a house of prayer,' but you have made it a den of robbers" (Luke 19:45–6). These actions precipitated the catastrophe. The Sadducean priesthood, despised by everyone, found its one support in the Temple, and Jesus not only attacked them but even publicly predicted the destruction of their Temple. The first three Gospels indicate that Jesus' last supper was the paschal meal. When night had fallen he reclined at the table with the 12 apostles and said: "With all my heart I have longed to eat this paschal lamb with you before I die, for I tell you: I will never eat it again until I eat it anew in the Kingdom of God." He took a cup of wine, recited the benediction over it and said: "take it and share it among you; for I tell you, I will not again drink of the fruit of the vine until I drink it new in the Kingdom of God." He took bread, recited the blessing over it and said: "This is my body" (cf. Luke 22:15–19). Thus Jesus' Passover meal under the shadow of death became the origin of the Christian sacrament of the Eucharist.

After the festive meal, Jesus left the city together with his disciples and went to the nearby Mount of Olives, to the garden of Gethsemane. There, although he had foreseen the danger of his death, he prayed for his life (Luke 22:39–46). One of the 12 apostles, Judas Iscariot, had already betrayed him from unknown motives. Judas had gone to the high priests and told them he would deliver Jesus to them and they had promised to give him money (Mark 14:10–11). The Temple guard, accompanied by Judas Iscariot, arrested Jesus and took him to the high priest.

The "Trial" and Crucifixion

The Gospels in their present form contain descriptions of the so-called "trial" of Jesus rewritten in a way making them improbable from the historical point of view. Nevertheless, a literary analysis of the sources is capable of revealing a closer approximation of the reality. In the first three Gospels, the Pharisees are not mentioned in connection with the trial, and in John, only once (18:3). Luke (22:66) and Matthew (26:59) explicitly mention the Sanhedrin once, and Mark mentions it twice (14:55; 15:1). In the whole of Luke – not just in his description of the Passion – there is no mention of the Sanhedrin's verdict against Jesus, and John records nothing about an assembly of the Sanhedrin before which Jesus appeared. Thus it seems very probable that no session of the Sanhedrin took place in the house of the high priest where Jesus was in custody and that the "chief priests and elders and scribes" who assembled there were members of the Temple committee (see also Luke 20:1): the elders were apparently the elders of the Temple and the scribes were the Temple secretaries. The deliverance of Jesus into the hands of the Romans was, it seems, the work of the Sadducean "high priests," who are often mentioned alone in the story. A man suspected of being a messianic pretender could be delivered to the Romans without a verdict of the Jewish high court. In addition, the high priests were interested in getting rid of Jesus, who had spoken against them and had predicted the destruction of the Temple. The Roman governor *Pontius Pilate ultimately had Jesus executed in the Roman way, by crucifixion. All the Gospels indicate that on the third day after the crucifixion Jesus' tomb was found empty. According to Mark an angel announced that Jesus had risen, and the other Gospels state that Jesus appeared before his believers after his death.

Jesus and the Jewish Background

The tension between the Church and the Synagogue often caused the Gospels, by means of new interpretations and later emendations, to evoke the impression that there was a necessary rift between Jesus and the Jewish way of life under the law. The first three Gospels, however, portray Jesus as a Jew who was faithful to the current practice of the law. On the matter of washing hands (Mark 7:5) and plucking ears of corn on the Sabbath (Mark 2:23ff.), it was the disciples, not the master, who were less strict in their observance of the law. According to the Synoptic Gospels, Jesus did not heal by physical means on the Sabbath but only by words, healing through speech having always been permitted on the Sabbath, even when the illness was not dangerous. The Gospels provide sufficient evidence to the effect that Jesus did not oppose any prescription of the Written or Oral Mosaic Law, and that he even performed Jewish religious commandments. On all of the foregoing points the less historical John differs from the first three Gospels.

The wording of the Gospels exaggerates the clashes between Jesus and the *Pharisees. This becomes evident after an analysis of Jesus' sayings which are a more faithful preservation than are the tendentious descriptions of the situation in which the sayings were uttered. Jesus' major polemical sayings against the Pharisees describe them as hypocrites, an accusation occurring not only in the Essene Dead Sea Scrolls and, indirectly, in a saying of the Sadducean king, Alexander Yannai, but also in rabbinic literature, which is an expression of true Pharisaism. In general, Jesus' polemical sayings against the Pharisees were far meeker than the Essene attacks and not sharper than similar utterances in the talmudic sources. Jesus was sufficiently Pharisaic in general outlook to consider the Pharisees as true heirs and successors of Moses. Although Jesus would probably not have defined himself as a Pharisee, his beliefs, especially his moral beliefs, are similar to the Pharisaic school of Hillel which stresses the love of God and neighbor. Jesus, however, pushed this precept much further than did the Jews of his time and taught that a man must love even his enemies. Others preached mutual love and blessing one's persecutors, but the command to love one's enemies is uniquely characteristic of Jesus and he is in fact the only one to utter this commandment in the whole of the New Testament.

The liberal Pharisaic school of Hillel was not unhappy to see gentiles become Jews. In contrast, the school of Shammai made conversion as difficult as possible because it had grave reservations about proselytism, most of which Jesus shared (Matt. 23:15). As a rule he even did not heal non-Jews. It should be noted that none of the rabbinical documents says that one should not heal a non-Jew.

In beliefs and way of life, Jesus was closer to the Pharisees than to the *Essenes. He accepted, however, a part of the Essene social outlook. Although Jesus was not a social revolutionary, the social implications of his message are stronger than that of the rabbis. Like the Essenes, Jesus also regarded all possessions as a threat to true piety and held poverty, humility, purity of heart, and simplicity to be the essential religious virtues. Jesus, as did the Essenes, had an awareness of and affection for the social outcast and the oppressed. The Essene author of the *Thanksgiving Scroll (18:14–15) promises salvation to the humble, to the oppressed in spirit, and to those who mourn, while Jesus in the first three beatitudes of the Sermon on the Mount promises the Kingdom of Heaven to "the poor in spirit" to "those who mourn," and to "the meek" (Matt. 5:3–5). Moreover, Jesus' rule "Do not resist one who is evil" (Matt. 5:39) has clear parallels in the Essene Dead Sea Scrolls.

Jesus as the Messiah

The early Christian Church believed Jesus to be the expected *Messiah of Israel, and he is described as such in the New Testament; but whether Jesus thought himself to be the Messiah is by no means clear. Throughout the New Testament there are indications that Jesus had seen himself as a prophet. The Ebionites and Nazarenes, *Jewish Christian sects, both ranked Jesus among the prophets and stressed his prophetic role. Jesus himself apparently never used the word "Messiah," and always spoke of the "*Son of Man" in the third person, as though he himself were not identical with that person. The "Son of Man" originally appears in the Book of Daniel (7:9–14) as the man-like judge of the Last Days. Jesus based his account of the "Son of Man" on the original biblical description of a superhuman, heavenly sublimity, who, seated upon the throne of God, will judge the whole human race. In Jewish literature of the Second Commonwealth, the "Son of Man" is frequently identified with the Messiah and it is probable that Jesus used the phrase in this way too. In his own lifetime, it is certain that Jesus became accepted by many as the Messiah. The substance of many sayings make it obvious that Jesus did not always refer to the coming "Son of Man" in the third person simply to conceal his identity, but because Jesus actually did not believe himself to be the Messiah. Yet other apparently authentic sayings of Jesus can be understood only if it is assumed that Jesus thought himself to be the "Son of Man." Thus Jesus' understanding of himself as the Messiah was probably inconsistent, or at first he was waiting for the Messiah, but at the end, he held the conviction that he himself was the Messiah.

In the faith of the Church, Jesus, the Jewish prophet from Galilee, became the object of a drama which could bring salvation to pious spectators. This drama developed from two roots: Jesus' conception of himself as being uniquely near to his Heavenly Father, his message about the coming of the "Son of Man," and other Jewish mythical and messianic doctrines; the other root was Jesus' tragic death, interpreted in terms of Jewish concepts about the expiatory power of martyrdom. If, as Christians believe, the martyr was at the same time the Messiah, then his death has a cosmic importance. Through the teachings of Jesus, as well as through other channels, the Jewish moral message entered Christianity. Thus the historical Jesus has served as a bridge between Judaism and Christianity, as well as one of the causes for their separation.

[David Flusser]

In Talmud and Midrash

Statements in rabbinic literature that explicitly mention Jesus by name or that allude to him and to his actions are few. Nothing has been transmitted in the names of the rabbis from the early half of the first century. Even those statements dating from the second century are to be regarded as reflecting the knowledge and views of Jews of that time about Christians and Jesus, which derived in part from contemporary Christian sources. They were partly a reaction to the image of Jesus as it had crystallized in the Christian tradition. Apparently, the beginnings of Christianity attracted no greater attention than did the many other sects that sprang up toward the close of the Temple period, and it is certain that the incidents connected with its founder were not at the center of events of the time, as the Gospels would lead one to believe.

Beginning with the Basle edition of the Talmud (1578–80), those passages in which Jesus was mentioned, as well as other statements alluding to Christianity, were deleted from most editions of the Babylonian Talmud by the Christian censors or even by internal Jewish censorship. These deletions were later collected in special compilations and in manuscripts (cf. R.N.N. Rabbinowicz, *Ma'amar al Hadpasat ha-Talmud* (1952), 28n.26). From the stories about Jesus in the Babylonian Talmud, it is evident that he was regarded as a rabbinical student who had strayed into evil ways: "May we produce no son or pupil who disgraces himself like Jesus the Nazarene" (Ber. 17b; Sanh. 103a; cf. Dik. Sof. ad loc.). The rabbis were not certain of his time or his activities. Thus he is described as a pupil of *Joshua b. Peraḥyah (Sanh. 107b; see Dik. Sof. ad loc.).

In the Middle Ages, *Jehiel of Paris claimed that there was no connection between Jesus, the pupil of Joshua b. Peraḥyah and Jesus the Nazarene (*Vikku'aḥ*, ed. by R. Margaliot (1928), 16f.). In one *baraita* Jesus appears as a sorcerer and enticer who led people astray. "They hanged Jesus on the eve of Passover. Forty days earlier a proclamation was issued that he was to be stoned for practicing sorcery and for enticing and leading Israel astray." "Let anyone who can speak in his favor come forward." "Nothing in his favor was discovered and they hanged him on the eve of Passover." The date given for the hanging, the 14th of Nisan, agrees with the date given in John 19:14. (In the Gospels the date given is the first day of the festival which is the 15th day of Nisan.) In conformity with the *halakhah* (Sanh. 7:4) he was sentenced to stoning, the penalty for enticing, leading astray, or practicing sorcery. After the stoning he was hanged, since all who are put to death by stoning are subsequently hanged, according to R. Eliezer who often transmits ancient *halakhah* (Sanh. 6:4). Jesus was crucified, i.e., hanged alive, "as is done by the non-Jewish government" (Sif. Deut. 221). In the talmudic account, however, his death conforms with the death penalty of the *bet din* as prescribed by the *halakhah* (see *Crucifixion).

Later conditions are reflected in the story of *Onkelos the proselyte who raised Titus, Balaam, and Jesus from the dead to ask their advice whether he should become a proselyte. Whereas Balaam said, "Thou shalt not seek their peace nor their prosperity all their days forever" (Deut. 23:7), Jesus answered, "Seek their peace, seek not their evil, whoever hurts them is as if hurting the pupil of his eye." The Talmud itself emphasizes the difference between Jesus and Balaam by adding, "Come and see the difference between infidel Israelites and the idol-worshiping gentile prophets" (Git. 57a, in uncensored editions). The purpose of the story is to show that

Jesus warned against persecuting Jews and forbade their oppression. It can only be understood in the context of an era in which such a warning was already important, namely the fourth century.

These are all the stories about Jesus in the Talmud. Whenever his name is mentioned elsewhere, it is in connection with his disciples. It speaks about "Jesus the Nazarene having had five disciples, Matthew, Nakai, Nazar, Boneh, and Thodah," all of whom were put to death. For each of them a verse is cited in which his name is mentioned and his execution hinted at (Sanh. 43a; Dik. Sof. ad loc.; Yal. Mak. to Isa. 11:1). Only two of them, Matthew and Tadi (Thaddaeus) can be identified with certainty as the apostles. Besides these there is mention of Jacob of Kefar Sama who came in the name of Jesus b. Pantira to cure *Eleazar b. Dama of a snake bite but was prevented by Ishmael (Tosef., Ḥul. 2:22; TJ, Shab. 14:4, 14d; TJ, Av. Zar. 2:2, 40d). Since this Jacob was a contemporary of Ishmael, he could not be a disciple of Jesus but at the most a disciple of his disciple. It is also very doubtful whether he can be identified with Jacob of Kefar Sakhnayya of whom Eliezer told Akiva that he had transmitted to him a sectarian teaching in the name of Jesus (Tosef., Ḥul. 2:24; Av. Zar. 17a; Eccles. R. 1:8, no. 3). This Jacob, too, merely transmitted a teaching he had heard in the name of Jesus and one cannot assume that he knew him. He certainly cannot be identified with Jacob, the brother of Jesus.

In both accounts the father of Jesus is called Pantira. Epiphanius reports that Pantira was another name of Jacob, the father of Joseph, father of Jesus (*Adversus Haereses* 3:78, 7). It is possible that this statement should be regarded as an answer to the assertion of the Jews which is also mentioned by Origen. He mentions that Celsus heard from a Jew that Miriam had been divorced by her husband who suspected her of adultery, and that Jesus was born as the result of her secret affair with a Roman soldier, Panthera (Πανθηρα; *Contra Celsum* 1:28, 32). In the Tosefta there is no suggestion of anything disparaging in the name Pantira, but it is found in the statement of a third-century Babylonian *amora*, a young contemporary of Celsus, where it is connected with the name *Ben Stada. Ben Stada is mentioned in the Tosefta (Shab. 11:15) and in the Babylonian Talmud (Sanh. 67a; Dik. Sof. ad loc.). The reading is "And thus they did to Ben Stada in Lydda and hanged him on the eve of Passover." This reading has been taken to refer to Jesus, but there is no basis in tannaitic literature for this indentification. When Eliezer referred to Jesus he called him by name.

Since the time of Geiger (JZWL, 6 (1868), 31–37) various scholars have tried to view the name Balaam, occurring in many *aggadot*, as a pseudonym for Jesus. They find their proof in the passage: "A certain sectarian said to Ḥanina 'Have you heard how old Balaam was?' He replied 'It is not actually stated, but since it is written "Bloody and deceitful men shall not live out half their days" [Ps. 55:24] he must have been 33 or 34'. He rejoined 'You have spoken correctly; I personally have seen Balaam's Chronicle, in which it is stated, "Balaam the lame was 33 years of age when Phinehas the robber killed him" [Sanh. 106b].'" On the basis that Jesus lived about 33 years and is called a sectarian, it was maintained that Balaam's Chronicle is none other than the Gospels and "Phinehas the robber" Pontius Pilate. However, it is impossible to imagine that a Christian would ask a Jew how old Jesus was, and call the Gospel Balaam's Chronicle or that Pontius Pilate, who is not mentioned even once in the whole of rabbinic literature, should be referred to as Phinehas the robber. The sectarian referred to was merely a member of a Gnostic sect who was testing whether Ḥanina could answer a question which is not answered in the Torah. Balaam's Chronicle was an apocryphal book on Balaam. These books often adopted an unfavorable attitude to the patriarchs and the prophets and it was possible that Phinehas of the Bible was called in them Phinehas the robber. Efforts to find allusions to Jesus and his disciples in the Mishnah (Sanh. 10:2; Avot 5:19) have no basis at all in the sources. Nor can one justify the conjecture that the word "Such a one" (Heb. *peloni*) used by Ben Azzai (Yev. 4:13) refers to Jesus. The *tannaim* did not ascribe an illegitimate birth to Jesus and had they done so they had no reason to conceal it, any more than the *amoraim* later did. Similarly one cannot say that the pupils of Eliezer had Jesus in mind when they asked their master the cryptic questions, "Has such a one a portion in the world to come? Has a bastard a portion in the world to come?" (Yoma 86b).

Polemics directed against the Christian dogmas that Jesus was the Messiah, the son of God, and God, are found in homilies and sayings of *amoraim* in the third and fourth centuries. Some of these homilies are merely a reply to the Christological interpretations of the *Church Fathers, who sought to find proof and supports for their teachings in the Scriptures. The words of Ḥiyya b. Abba, "If the son of the harlot says to you there are two gods, say to him 'I am He of the Red Sea; I am He of Sinai'" (PR 21:100), are directed against Christian dualism (the doctrine of the Trinity not yet having been accepted in the third century). The expression "son of a harlot" has a dual meaning, referring to Jesus in person, and to his heretical teaching, i.e., "son of heresy." Simeon b. Lakish, a contemporary of Origen, explained the verse "Alas who shall live after God hath appointed him" (Num. 24:23) to mean "Woe for him who resurrects himself with the title god" (Sanh. 106a). *Abbahu, who lived in Caesarea and had many disputes with heretics, explained Balaam's words, "God is not a man that He should lie; Neither the son of man that He should repent" (Num. 23:19) in a way that left no doubt about whom it was directed against, "If a man says to you, I am god, he lies; [if he says] I am the son of man, he shall regret it; [if he says] I shall rise to heaven, he says but he shall not fulfill it" (TJ, Ta'an. 2:1, 65b; Sanh. 106a; Dik. Sof. ad loc.). In this interpretation, Abbahu represents Balaam as rebuking and warning the gentiles not to be ensnared by the new religion, in the same way as his fellow citizen, the Church Father Origen, puts Christological teachings into Balaam's mouth (see his commentary on Num. 15:4). These teachings are also contradicted by Balaam in a homily to Eleazar ha-Kappar (Yal. Num., ed. Salonika, 765, from where it was published in Jellinek's *Beit ha-Midrash*, 5 (1967^3), 208). Most of it, however, is by a fourth-century preacher who had already witnessed the spread of Christianity in Caesarea.

A polemic of the amoraic era is also found in the story of Rabban Gamaliel and his sister *Imma Shalom (Shab. 116aff.), but it cannot be regarded as authentic. It contains no quotation from any early version of "the words of Jesus," but parodies the words of Matthew. The *tanna* and his wife ridicule their neighbor, the "philosopher" – who is simply a Christian teacher – criticizing the contradictions in the teaching of Jesus, which on the one hand appears as a different law, while on the other Jesus himself says, "I have come neither to diminish the law of Moses, nor to add to it" (cf. Matt. 5:17, "think not that I am come to destroy but to fulfill"). As an example of "another Torah," a quotation is brought from the *Avon Gilyon* ("sinful margin," a disparaging name for *Evangelion*, Gospel in Greek): "Son and daughter inherit alike." No such statement occurs in the Gospels. It is possible that the statement of the philosopher that a daughter does not inherit was intended to cast doubt on the messianic status of Jesus, whose claim to be the Messiah was dependent on his Davidic descent. If he was of virgin birth, that descent could only have been on his mother's side.

[*Encyclopaedia Hebraica*]

BIBLIOGRAPHY: A. Schweitzer, *Quest of the Historical Jesus* (19543); J. Klausner, *Jesus of Nazareth* (1957) containing details and descriptions of Jewish scholarship on the subject of Jesus; M. Hooker, *Jesus and the Servant* (1959); G. Bornkamm, *Jesus of Nazareth* (1960); S. Pines, *Jewish Christians of the Early Centuries of Christianity According to a New Source* (1966); H. Cohn, *The Death of Jesus* (1971); D. Flusser, *Jesus* (1969); R.L. Lindsey, *Hebrew Translation of the Gospel of Mark* (1969); S. Sandmel, *We Jews and Jesus* (1965); S. Zeitlin, *Who Crucified Jesus?* (1964^4); S.G.F. Brandon, *The Trial of Jesus of Nazareth* (1968); J. Carmichael, *The Death of Jesus* (1962). IN TALMUD AND MIDRASH: M. Guedemann, *Religionsgeschichtliche Studien* (1876), 65–97; D. Chwolson, *Das lezte Passahmahl Christi* (1892), 85–125; H. Laible, *Jesus Christus im Thalmud* (19002); S. Krauss, *Das Leben Jesu nach juedischen Quellen* (1902), 181–94; R.T. Herford, *Christianity in Talmud and Midrash* (1903); H.L. Strack, *Jesus, die Haeretiker und die Christen…* (1910); Z.P. Chajes in: *Ha-Goren*, 4 (1923), 33–37; Kaminetzki, in: *Ha-Tekufah*, 18 (1923), 509–15; Guttmann, in: MGWJ, 75 (1931), 250–57; J.Z. Lauterbach, *Rabbinic Essays* (1951), 473–570; E.E. Urbach, in: *Tarbiz*, 25 (1956), 272–89; idem, *Ḥazal, Pirkei Emunot ve-De'ot* (1969), index. **ADD. BIBLIOGRAPHY:** D. Flusser, *Jesus* (1969); G. Vermes, *Jesus the Jew* (1973); I. Wilson, *Jesus: The Evidence* (1984); J.D. Crossan, *The Historical Jesus: The Life of a Mediterranean Jewish Peasant* (1991); J.H. Charlesworth (ed.), *Jesus and the Dead Sea Scrolls* (1992); E.P. Sanders, *The Historical Figure of Jesus* (1993); G. Vermes, *The Changing Faces of Jesus* (2000); T. Khalidi, *The Muslim Jesus: Sayings and Stories in Islamic Literature* (2001); J.D. Crossan and J.L. Reed, *Excavating Jesus* (2001); J. Efron, *The Origins of Christianity and Apocalyptism* (2004).

JETHRO (Heb. יֶתֶר, יִתְרוֹ), Midianite priest and father-in-law of *Moses. Jethro had seven daughters who served as his shepherdesses. When Moses fled from Egypt he came to the well in Midian where he witnessed local shepherds mistreating the girls. He saved them and watered their flocks for them. In return, Jethro welcomed Moses into his home and gave him one of his daughters, *Zipporah, as a wife. He also appointed Moses as shepherd of his flocks (Ex. 2:16–21; 3:1). Jethro is next mentioned after the incident of the burning bush when Moses, having decided to return to Egypt, asked and received his father-in-law's permission to do so (4:18).

After the Exodus from Egypt, when the Israelites had arrived in the vicinity of Sinai, Jethro brought Zipporah, whom Moses had divorced, along with her two sons to Moses. Although no mention is made of Moses' reconciliation with his wife, we learn that Jethro received a most honorable welcome. He expressed his delight at the deliverance of Israel, blessed YHWH and praised Him as "greater than all gods," and brought sacrifices to Him, afterward partaking of a meal with Aaron and all the elders of Israel (18:1–12). The following day, Jethro advised Moses on the reorganization of the judicial system and returned to his own land (18:13–23, 27). The narratives about Jethro have raised many problems. He is given this name in Exodus 3:1; 4:18; 18:1–2, 5–6, 12. However, he is called Reuel in Exodus 2:18 and in Numbers 10:29 as well, while Judges 4:11 refers to Hobab as the father-in-law of Moses. In the former passage, Moses asked Hobab to act as a guide for the Israelites through the wilderness. His final reply is not given there, but from Judges 4:11 it would seem that he allowed himself to be persuaded. Another difficulty lies in the fact that the Pentateuch describes Moses' father-in-law as a Midianite, whereas he is elsewhere termed a Kenite (Judg. 1:16; 4:11).

Varying solutions have been suggested to account for the conflicting data (for traditional account see below). Some modern scholars assign Hobab to the J source and Jethro to the E document. "Reuel their father" in Exodus 2:18 would then either be a misunderstanding of Numbers 10:29 or refer to the grandfather of the shepherdesses. Others take Jethro and Reuel to be one and the same person and regard Hobab as the son, a solution that requires the emendation of Judges 4:11. In the opinion of W.F. Albright, the Jethro-Reuel-Hobab traditions are quite homogeneous. The roles of Jethro and Hobab are so different as to preclude identity. The former is an old man who already had seven grown daughters when Moses arrived in Midian and who gave Moses in the wilderness the kind of advice that could only be the product of mature wisdom. Hobab is a young, vigorous man who could withstand the rigors of acting as a guide in the wilderness wanderings. He is, therefore, not the father-in-law, but the son-in-law of Moses, and *ḥoten* in Numbers 10:29 and Judges 4:11 should be read *ḥatan*. Reuel is the name of the clan to which both Jethro and Hobab belonged (cf. Gen. 36:10, 13; I Chron. 1:35, 37), and Exodus 2:18 should read, "they returned to Jethro, son of Reuel (i.e., the Reuelite), their father." Finally, the epithet "Kenite" is not in contradiction to Midianite, since it is an occupational, not an ethnic, term meaning a "metalworker, smith," as in Aramaic and Arabic (cf. Gen. 4:22). But the solution appears contrived, and it is probably wisest to assume a conflation of different traditions.

Beginning with the hint that Jethro was a priest, some scholars have credited the Midianites with introducing the god YHWH to the Hebrews, a theory known as the Midianite or Kenite hypothesis (see van der Toorn). These scholars note Jethro's blessing of YHWH in Exodus 18:10 and his provision of sacrifices and his participation in the cultic meal "before God" (Ex. 18:12). While this is intriguing, the exact role of Jethro in the development of Israelite religion cannot be determined, in the absence of any data about the nature of the religion of Midian. The attribution of the organization of the judicial system in Israel to the advice of a Midianite priest is itself, however, eloquent testimony to the antiquity and reliability of the Exodus tradition. Significantly, the account in Deuteronomy 1:9–17 completely obscures the role of Jethro.

In like manner, 11:11–12, 16–18, 24–30 omits mention of Jethro in the judicial reform, attributing it to YHWH's response to a complaint by Moses. The name Jethro itself (shortened to Jether in Exodus 4:18) may be abbreviated from a theophoric form. The basic element, which probably means "excellence" or "abundance" (cf. Gen. 49:3), appears as a component of many west Semitic names. Cf. Akkadian Atra-ḫasīs, "Exceeding-Wise," the name of an Old Babylonian flood hero of the Noah type.

[Nahum M. Sarna / S. David Sperling (2nd ed.)]

In the Aggadah

Jethro was one of Pharaoh's counselors. According to one account, he – together with Amalek – "gave the evil counsel" (to throw the male Israelite children into the river) to Pharaoh, but later repented (Ex. R. 27:6). According to another tradition, his fellow counselors were Balaam and Job. Balaam advocated the destruction of the children, Job remained silent, and Jethro fled to Midian (Sanh. 106a). He became a genuine convert to Judaism. His title as the "priest of Midian" (Ex. 18:1) means either that he was its pagan priest or its prince (Mekh., Yitro, 1). The sages had an ambivalent attitude toward Jethro. Some regarded him as an arch-idolator, and as such he was able to testify to the supremacy of God, nonetheless still holding that the idols possessed some divine powers (Yal., Ex. 269; cf. Ex. 18:11). Jethro early realized the worthlessness of idol worship and repented even before Moses fled to Midian. Jethro's neighbors excommunicated him for renouncing their idolatrous beliefs, and it was because of this ban that his daughters had to tend the sheep (Ex. R. 1:32). A competing tradition claims that Jethro was still so steeped in idolatry at this time that he only permitted Zipporah to marry Moses on condition that their first son be raised to worship idols (Mekh., Yitro, 1).

Jethro's reaction to the miracles performed by God for Israel is likewise interpreted in two contrasting fashions. "And Jethro rejoiced" (וַיִּחַדְּ יִתְרוֹ, *va-yiḥadd Yitro*; Ex. 18:9) either means that he now accepted monotheism (*Yiḥed shemo shel ha-Kadosh Barukh Hu*; Tanh. B., Ex. 71) or that his skin developed gooseflesh (*na'asah kol besaro ḥidudin ḥidudin*) in sympathy for the tribulations of the Egyptians (Sanh. 94a). Jethro was the first to utter a benediction to God for the wonders performed for the Israelites. It was a reproach to Moses and the 600,000 Israelites that they did not bless the Lord until Jethro came and did so (*ibid.*). When Jethro arrived at the camp of Israel, he wrote a letter and with an arrow shot it into the camp (Tanḥ. B., Ex. 73). Moses immediately went out to meet his father-in-law, accompanied by Aaron, Nadab, Abihu, and the 70 elders of Israel. It is even stated that the *Shekhinah* also greeted Jethro (Mekh., Yitro, 1). Moses finally sent Jethro away (Ex. 18:27), since he did not want a stranger present at the revelation on Mount Sinai (Tanḥ. B., Ex. 75). According to another tradition, Jethro left to spread the knowledge of the true God among his brethren in Midian (Tanḥ. B., Ex. 73).

Jethro had seven different names which reflect his virtues. He was called Jether (Ex. 4:18) because he was responsible for the "addition" of a passage to the Pentateuch; Jethro (Ex. 3:1), because he "overflowed" with good deeds; Hobab (Num. 10:29), the "beloved" son of God; Reuel (Ex. 2:18), the "friend of God"; Heber (Judg. 4:11), the "associate" of God; Putiel (Ex. 6:25), because he had renounced idolatry (*niftar*; another interpretation, however, is that "he fattened calves" (*pittem*) for idolatrous sacrifice: BB 109b); and Keni (Judg. 1:16) in that he was "zealous" for God and "acquired" the Torah (Mekh. Yitro, 1).

[Aaron Rothkoff]

In Islam

The commentators of the Koran identify Shuʿayb with the father-in-law of Moses (Jethro), whom Muhammad mentions as living in Midian (Sura 28:21–27). In another sura (26:176–89) it is related that Shuʿayb was sent as a prophet and that he rebuked the inhabitants of al-Ayka ("the people of the thicket"), while in other suras he rebuked his fellow Midianites (7:83–91; 11:85–98). Their attitude toward him was a negative one, just as that of other tribes toward the prophets who were sent to them (Sura 11:93). The legends of the prophets relate many more details about the sojourn of Moses in the house of his father-in-law, his marriage with Zipporah, etc.

The Druze, the most extreme of the Ismāʿīliyya sects, hold Shuʿayb in the highest esteem. He is one of the early incarnations of the *ḥudūd*, the emanations from the light of the Creator (*al-bāriʾ*). These incarnations, the Imāms, were the leaders of their respective generations. Shuʿayb was considered one of these incarnations during the days of Moses. His traditional grave at Kefar Ḥittin (near Tiberias) is the site of the Druze pilgrimage (*ziyāra*) between April 23 and 25.

[Haïm Z'ew Hirschberg]

BIBLIOGRAPHY: H. Gressmann, *Mose und seine Zeit* (1913), 161–80; M. Buber, *Moses* (1946), 94–100; H.H. Rowley, *From Joseph to Joshua* (1950), 19ff.; W.F. Albright, in: CBQ, 25 (1963), 3–9; idem, *Yahweh and the Gods of Canaan* (1968), 33–42. IN THE AGGADAH: Ginzberg, Legends, 2 (1910), 289–96, 327f., 3 (1911), 63–77, 380, 388f., 5 (1925), 410–2, 6 (1928), 26–29, 122, 134, 232. IN ISLAM: Thaʿlabī, *Qiṣaṣ* (1356 AH), 146–8; Kisāʾī, *Qiṣaṣ*, ed. by I. Eisenberg (1922), 190–4; H.

Speyer, *Biblische Erzaehlungen…* (1961), 251–4; H.Z.(J.W.) Hirschberg, *Religion in the Middle East*, 2 (1969), 350 and passim. **ADD. BIBLIOGRAPHY:** K. van der Toorn, in: DDD, 910–19; W. Propp, *Exodus 1–18* (AB; 1998), 630; A. Rippin, "Shuʿayb," in: EIS², 9 (1997), 491 (incl. bibl.).

JEVICKO (Czech **Jevičko**; Ger. **Gewitsch**), town in W. Moravia, Czech Republic. It is thought that the Jewish community was founded in the 14th century, but the first documentary mention dates from 1566. In 1657 there were 16 Jewish households in the town. A prayer room was opened in 1620, but a synagogue was not built until 1784. A fire in 1869, which destroyed the main part of the Jewish quarter, made many Jews leave the town. The Jevicko community was one of the political communities (see *politische Gemeinden). Between 1798 and 1848 there were 138 permitted families in Jevicko (see *Familiants Laws). The Jewish population fluctuated from 776 persons in 1830 to 989 in 1848, 462 in 1869, and 286 in 1890. On the territory of the political community there were 184 Jews and 33 Christians living in 1880 and 93 Jews and 75 Christians in 1900. In 1930 there were 86 Jews in Jevicko (3.1% of the total population). The community was deported to Nazi extermination camps in 1942 and the synagogue equipment sent to the Central Jewish Museum in Prague. The building is used by the Hussite church and the Czech Brethern Protestant church.

BIBLIOGRAPHY: M. Tauber, in: H. Gold (ed.), *Juden und Judengemeinden Maehrens in Vergangenheit und Gegenwart* (1929); B. Bretholz, in: JGGJČ, 2 (1930), 184–241. **ADD. BIBLIOGRAPHY:** J. Fiedler, *Jewish Sights of Bohemia and Moravia* (1991), 84–85.

[Meir Lamed]

JEW (Heb. יְהוּדִי, *Yehudi*).

Semantics

The word "Jew" passed into the English language from the Greek (*Ioudaios*) by way of the Latin (*Judaeus*), and is found in early English (from about the year 1000) in a variety of forms: *Iudea, Gyu, Giu, Iuu, Iuw, Iew* which developed into "Jew." The word "Jew," therefore, is ultimately traced to the Hebrew *Yehudi*, a term which originally applied to members of the tribe of Judah, the fourth son of the patriarch, Jacob. The term was also utilized for those who dwelt in the area of the tribe of Judah and thus later, during the seven years that David reigned in Hebron, his territory was called the Kingdom of Judah (II Sam. 5:5). Later still, with the split of the kingdom during the reign of Rehoboam, the Northern Kingdom was called Israel and the Southern was called Judah, although it also encompassed the territory of the tribe of Benjamin (I Kings 12:16–21). From that time on the term "*Yehudi*" applied to all residents of the Southern Kingdom, irrespective of their tribal status. After the destruction of Israel only Judah remained, and the term "*Yehudi*," or "Jew," then lost its specific connection with the Southern Kingdom. This is strikingly illustrated in Esther 2:5, 5:13, where Mordecai, although belonging to the tribe of Benjamin, is called a *Yehudi*. This term was also utilized at that time for the Jewish religion since it is related that, after Haman's downfall, many from among the people of the land converted to Judaism (*mityahadim*, Esth. 8:17). The term "Jew" connoted by this time a religious, political, and national entity, without differentiation between these categories. "Jew," however, was mainly used outside the Land of Israel by Jews and non-Jews and in languages other than Hebrew. Thus Nehemiah, who was an official at the Persian court, refers to "Jews" in his personal "diary," and the Book of Esther (see above) was almost certainly written by someone close to court circles. From the Persian and Aramaic, the word passed into Greek and from there into Latin. However, while the name "Jew" became common usage outside the Land of Israel, the Hebrew-speaking Jews within the land were particular to call themselves "Israel" (*Yisrael*: "Israelites"). It seems that this was a deliberate reaction parallel to the general intensification of ancient religious and literary values and aimed at strengthening the identification with the nation's early history. Thus Ezra, as opposed to Nehemiah, uses the name Israel throughout, and even in the Aramaic letter given to him by the Persian king. From that period on the name "Israel" is used in all Hebrew literature: in the Hebrew books of the Apocrypha (Judith, Tobit, I Maccabees, etc.); in the Judean Desert Scrolls; in the Mishnah and the Hebrew parts of the Talmud; and on the coins of the 70 C.E. revolt and of that of Bar Kokhba ("the redemption of Israel"; "the freedom of Israel"). Exceptions such as "Prince of the Jews" on the copper column erected on Mt. Zion in honor of Simeon the Maccabee (I Macc. 14:47, also 37 and 40) and "Group of the Jews" on the coins of his son, Johanan, are to be explained by the political designation, Judea, by which the gentile world knew the limited territory of the Jewish State. When, indeed, that territory was enlarged, the name "Land of Israel" came once more into use. This difference in usage is strikingly illustrated in the Gospels: the Jews are recorded as having referred (mockingly) to Jesus as "king of Israel," whereas the Roman, Pilate, and his soldiers refer to him – both verbally and in writing – as "king of the Jews" (Mark 15:32, 2, 9, 18, 26). For Christians, the word "*Judaeus*" was early conflated with the name of the villain of the gospel story, Judas Iscariot, who was considered the typical Jew. Judas was linked with the devil (Luke 22:3), and the result was an evil triangle of devil-Jew-Judas. This relationship helped to establish the pejorative meaning of the word "Jew" in popular usage. The noun could mean "extortionate usurer, driver of hard bargains," while the verb was defined as "to cheat by sharp business practices, to overreach." Many attempts to root out these derogatory meanings by having the dictionary definitions revised have been made in the United States, England, and Europe; they have, however, met with little success, since the problem is not one of ill-will on the part of the lexicographers, but rather of semantics and popular usage. In order to avoid the unwelcome associations and connotations of the word, Jews began in the 19th century to call themselves "Hebrews" and "Israelites" (e.g., Alliance Israélite *Universelle, founded 1860). Nevertheless, these new names quickly took on the same pejorative associations as "Jew," as scores of 19th century novels testify. Recently, there has been a gradual change in the usage of the word. The brutal murder of a great part of the Jewish people during the *Holocaust has limited subsequent degrading usage of the term. Since the conclusion of the war, antisemitism is under legal scrutiny in many countries, and this covers the use of "Jew" in the pejorative sense, along with "Yid," "Sheeny," "Ikey" and the like.

[Yehoshua M. Grintz]

Halakhic Definition

Both a child born of Jewish parents and a convert to Judaism are considered Jews, possessing both the sanctity of the Jewish people (Ex. 19:6) and the obligation to observe the commandments. The status of children from intermarriage is designated by the Mishnah and Talmud as following that of the mother (Kid. 3:12; Yad, Issurei Bi'ah 15:3–4). "Thy son by an Israelite woman is called thy son, but thy son by a heathen woman is not called thy son" (Kid. 68b). A child born of a non-Jewish mother must therefore undergo ritual conversion, even though his father is Jewish (see *Proselytes). This halakhic definition was accepted for centuries. However, in modern times and particularly since the establishment of the State of Israel, the definition has been more and more questioned. The act of conversion is of course a religious act, and thus any candidate for conversion is required to subscribe to the principles of Judaism (or dogma; see Articles of *Faith) and to practice all the *mitzvot, something which the majority of born Jews do not do. Thus it is felt in wide circles that identification with the Jewish people and its fate should constitute sufficient grounds for being considered a Jew, particularly since during the Holocaust tens – even hundreds – of thousands of Jews, who were not halakhically so considered, perished because the Nazis had considered them Jews. This problem has been especially grave in the State of Israel where the children of mixed marriages (in which the wife is not Jewish), who speak Hebrew, are educated in the spirit of Jewish history, subscribe to Israeli nationalism and serve in the army to defend it, feel discriminated against in that they are not considered Jews and are not registered as Jews in the identity cards which they are, by law, required to carry at all times. In fact, what they are campaigning for is a secular definition of Jew (see *Judaism) which is, understandably, vigorously opposed by the Rabbinate of Israel and the religious political parties. In 1958 a cabinet crisis came about over the problem of the registration of *le'om* in the identity card. This word means "nationality" or "nationhood" but its exact definition is a matter of debate. The secular Israeli political parties contended that an affirmation of national identification with the Jewish people should suffice for such registration, whereas the religious parties demanded that the halakhic guidelines be retained. David Ben-Gurion, then prime minister, elicited responsa to this question from rabbinical leaders and Jewish scholars in Israel and throughout the Diaspora; the overwhelming majority of the respondents indicated that the State of Israel should follow the *halakhah* in this issue, and the final directives issued to the registering officers required that there must be a bona fide conversion before the applicant could be registered as Jewish. The situation reached a kind of climax in 1968 when a lieutenant commander in the Israel navy, Benjamin Shalit, requested that his two children born of a non-Jewish mother be registered on their identity cards as Jews. When the Ministry of the Interior refused to accede to this request, Shalit petitioned the Supreme Court to order the ministry to show cause why they should not so register the children. The Supreme Court, sitting for the first time in its history in a complement of nine judges, suspended the hearing in order to make a recommendation to the government to change the law requiring the entry *le'om* and thus solve the problem. The government refused to accept the recommendation and subsequently the court decided (on Jan. 23, 1970; case no. HC 58/68) by a majority of five to four that the registrar had no right to question a statement made in good faith by the applicant but was duty bound to register what he was told. Each of the judges wrote his own opinion and some stated that, to their mind, the term *le'om* admitted a secular definition. It was pointed out that the decision was only with regard to registration and had no implications as far as personal status was concerned, which would continue to be governed by the courts in whose jurisdiction it lay. Thus for matters of marriage and divorce, which are in the jurisdiction of the rabbinical courts, the Shalit children would be considered non-Jews. The decision raised a strong public protest and the law was subsequently changed to accept only those born of Jewish mothers or converted. However, it was not specified that the conversions have to be by Orthodox rabbis and thus non-Orthodox conversions performed outside the State of Israel would be admitted as sufficient for registration as a Jew. It was also legislated at that time that non-Jewish spouses or children and grandchildren of Jews arriving in Israel with their Jewish spouse or parent would be granted all the privileges of the Law of Return, including the right to automatic Israel citizenship. In a previous decision the Supreme Court decided in the case of Oswald Rufeisen, a born Jew who converted to Catholicism and joined the Carmelite order (for a full treatment of that case see *Apostasy) that, although in the opinion of the court the appellant might be a Jew halakhically, for the purpose of the Law of Return he could not be so considered. Throughout the ages the rabbinical authorities have been concerned with the problem of a person who is technically a Jew but subscribes to another religion. When a Jew merely does not subscribe to Judaism, the problem is of a lesser degree since such a person can be considered a "relapsed" Jew to whom all the laws apply. However, when that person has no connection whatsoever with Judaism and indeed considers himself to be a member of another religion, the problem is most severe. In the Middle Ages the question arose as to whether a Jew is allowed to lend money to such a person on interest or borrow from him on interest (see *Usury), something which is forbidden between two Jews. In the discussion of this problem there were opinions that it is permitted since such a person cannot be considered a Jew at all (*Shibbolei ha-Leket*, Ha-Segullah ed., ch. 46). However, the majority of the decisors have always felt that such a person must halakhically be considered a Jew.

With regard to conversion, the strict law has been that converts should be accepted only when they come out of altruistic reasons, i.e., because they have realized the superiority of the Jewish religion. However, when they wish to convert in order to marry a Jew or for some other reason, they should not be accepted in the first instance; but if they were accepted and have undergone the full ceremony of conversion, they are, post facto, considered to be valid converts. The full ceremony of conversion as pointed out above involves the acceptance of the *mitzvot*, and the general opinion has been that without such acceptance and performance the conversion is invalid even post facto. Since the majority of conversions are not for altruistic reasons, this matter has been very problematic. Moses Feinstein in his *Iggerot Moshe* (YD (1959), no. 160) has suggested that such conversions might be valid since the lack of knowledge of the *mitzvot* does not invalidate a conversion; what would invalidate it is the nonacceptance or lack of observance of the *mitzvot* which are known to the convert. Rather ingeniously he has pointed out that, although the religious court performing the conversion told the convert the more important of the *mitzvot*, and although the convert at least verbally accepts what he or she is told, in fact the convert knows that the overwhelming majority of Jews do not observe these *mitzvot* and believes that the court's standards of observance are in fact unrealistic and not absolutely essential; for otherwise why do the Jews themselves not adhere to these standards. Thus Feinstein sees the lack of observance as a sort of lack of knowledge and, post facto, tends to accept such converts. This, of course, is quite a revolutionary step in that it is accepting – albeit post facto – the standards of Judaism as practiced in preference to the standards of Judaism as codified. It must be pointed out, however, that Feinstein's position is not one which is accepted by the majority of rabbinical authorities. With the immigration from Eastern European countries, the problem of mixed marriages has become a most serious one in the State of Israel, and efforts are being made to facilitate the speedy conversion of the non-Jewish partner and children in order to avoid problems of personal status later on. It can be said that the rabbinical courts are being more permissive in this matter than hitherto, perhaps because of the enormous social and human pressures being brought to bear and the fact that the converts will grow up in a Jewish milieu.

[Raphael Posner]

BIBLIOGRAPHY: Y.M. Grintz, in: *Eshkolot*, 3 (1959), 125–44; S. Zeitlin, in: JQR, 49 (1958/59), 241–70; B. Litvin and S.B. Hoenig (eds.), *Jewish Identity* (1965).

"JEW BILL" CONTROVERSY, ENGLAND, term used to refer to the agitation which arose in England in 1753 after the passage of the Jewish Naturalisation Act. Foreign-born persons desiring naturalization as British subjects had, as part of the process, to receive the sacrament at Anglican Holy Communion. Jews wishing to be naturalized, mainly wealthy Sephardi merchants in London, could be exempted from this requirement, although in so doing they would be granted only what was termed "endenization" rather than full citizenship, which carried with it fewer rights. In 1753 the Whig government, which was close to the Jewish commercial community, passed a bill through Parliament allowing Jews to be naturalized without participating in an Anglican service. It had no other effect on the status of British Jews and had no effect on any other group. This Act easily passed through both Houses of Parliament in May 1753. Immediately, however, great antisemitic agitation blew up which forced the government to repeal the Act in December 1753. Propaganda appeared accusing the Jews of ritual murder, of planning to turn St. Paul's Cathedral into a synagogue, and of wanting to force all British males to be circumcised, together with large numbers of broadsides and ballads aimed at the Jews. Although no violence against Jews or Jewish property occurred, several prominent Jews were hissed by crowds when they appeared in public.

The "Jew Bill" agitation had no real precedent and, significantly, no continuation, and no subsequent antisemitic agitation of any kind can be seen in Britain for many decades. It has been linked by historians with popular demagoguery by the Tory opposition just before a general election, as well as with economic fears by poorly paid Anglican clergymen, but remains a genuine puzzle to those historians who have examined it. It seems clear, however, that traditional Christian antisemitic stereotypes had little lasting resonance in Britain by the mid-18th century.

BIBLIOGRAPHY: Katz, England, 240–53; T.W. Perry, *Public Opinion, Propaganda and Politics in Eighteenth-Century England: A Study of the Jew Bill of 1753* (1962); Endelman, *Jews of Georgian England,* index; F. Felsenstein, *Anti-Semitic Stereotypes: A Paradigm of Otherness in English Popular Culture, 1660–1830* (1995), 187–214; W.D. Rubinstein, *Jews in Great Britain,* 55–56; Cecil Roth, *A History of the Jews in England* (1964), index.

[William D. Rubinstein (2nd ed.)]

JEWESS OF TOLEDO, the central figure in a legendary love affair of King Alfonso VIII of Castile (1155–1214), which has furnished material for innumerable plays, poems, and novels in Spanish and other languages. The essential story is that Alfonso falls in love with Fermosa (Span. *hermosa*), a beautiful Jewish girl of Toledo, and as a result of his infatuation is accused of neglecting his royal duties. To remove this "nefarious" influence, Alfonso's nobles (in some versions, urged on by the queen) conspire together and murder the unfortunate Jewess. The story must be considered legendary, since the earliest references to it (in reworkings of Alfonso X's *Crónica general* and of the *Castigos é documentos para bien vivir* attributed to Sancho IV) are several generations removed from Alphonso VIII.

The earliest purely literary work dealing with the theme is a ballad by Lorenzo de Sepúlveda (1551). Lope de Vega, whose treatment of the Jews was almost invariably hostile, first mentions the Jewess in his long poem *Jerusalén Conquistada* (Madrid, 1609). He later developed the theme in his play *Las paces de los reyes y judía de Toledo* (1617; ed. by J.A. Castañeda, 1962 Madrid). This work is loosely constructed and the characters are shallow. Though a woman of lax morals, Raquel, as the Jewess is now called, sincerely loves the king and, in her dying words, confesses her belief in Christianity – undoubtedly an attempt by the author to gain more sympathy for her. The nobles who kill her are presented as vicious murderers. The next dramatic treatments are Antonio Mira de Amescua's *La desdichada Raquel* (1635; published Amsterdam, 1726); and *La Judía de Toledo* (Madrid, 1667), a reworking of Amescua's play by Juan Bautista Diamante. In the former, Raquel is presented as an ambitious woman and the character Rubén, her mentor, is a scheming rabbi. Diamante, on the other hand, makes Raquel almost a second Esther and he also presents her father in a favorable light. Other treatments in the 17th century were poems by Paravicino and Luis de Ulloa.

The verse tragedy *La Raquel* (1778, published 1814), by Vicente García de la Huerta (1734–1787) was the only really successful and popular theatrical work of 18th-century Spanish neoclassicism. Raquel is here a more complex character, astute and proud, but in love with the king. The villain is Rubén; perfidious and cowardly, he kills Raquel in an attempt to save his own life. Various works in the 19th century indicate that the theme was still popular, but the treatment betrays a decadence in artistic technique.

From Spain the legend passed to other countries. A French version was Jacques Cazotte's short story *Rachel ou la belle juive* (in *Oeuvres badines et moules*, 1776–88), which radically modified the traditional elements of the story. The tale was more popular in Germany. The earliest German version was the three-act drama, *Rahel, die schoene Juedin* (1789), by Johann Christian Brandes (1735–1799) who imitated Huerta's work. Gottlieb Konrad Pfeffel treated the theme poetically in *Alphons und Rahel* (1799). The most famous version of the legend in German is that by the Austrian playwright Franz Grillparzer, *Die Juedin von Toledo* (1873). Here Raquel is impetuous and flighty and her father unscrupulously seeks advancement through his daughter's beauty. The main character is the king, and the real interest of the play lies in his inner conflict between love and duty – always the dramatic situation in Grillparzer's works – but the most sympathetic and noble character is Raquel's sister, Esther. That the theme has retained vitality is clear from its reappearance in Lion *Feuchtwanger's historical novel *Spanische Ballade* (1955; *Raquel, the Jewess of Toledo*, 1956). This is the most sympathetic treatment of Raquel and the Jews. She is portrayed as a devoted and loving woman and her father is presented as a man of heroism and integrity. The Spanish composer Tómas Bretón used Grillparzer's drama as the basis for his opera *Raquel*, first performed in Madrid in 1900.

BIBLIOGRAPHY: S. Aschner, in: *Euphorion*, 19 (1912), 297ff.; E. Lambert, in: *Jahrbuch der Grillparzer Gesellschaft*, 19 (1910), 61–84; *Enciclopedia Universal Ilustrada*, 62 (1928), 415–6.

[Kenneth R. Scholberg]

JEWISH AGENCY (Heb. הַסּוֹכְנוּת הַיְהוּדִית לְאֶרֶץ יִשְׂרָאֵל, *Ha-Sokhenut ha-Yehudit le-Ereẓ Israel*), international, nongovernment body, centered in Jerusalem, which is the executive and representative of the *World Zionist Organization, whose aims are to assist and encourage Jews throughout the world to help in the development and settlement of Ereẓ Israel. The term "Jewish Agency" first appeared in Article Four of the League of Nations Mandate for Palestine, which stipulated that "an appropriate Jewish agency shall be recognized as a public body for the purpose of advising and cooperating with the administration of Palestine in such economic, social, and other matters as may affect the establishment of the Jewish National Home and the interests of the Jewish population in Palestine." The article went on to recognize the Zionist Organization as such an agency "so long as its organization and constitution are in the opinion of the Mandatory appropriate." Indeed the two were coterminous from the time that the Mandate was ratified by the League Council in July 1922 until the enlarged Jewish Agency came into being in August 1929. From that date until the establishment of the State of Israel, this body played the principal role in the relations between the National Home and world Jewry on the one hand and the Mandatory and other powers on the other. In May 1948 the Jewish Agency relinquished many of its functions to the newly created government of Israel, but continued to be responsible for immigration, land settlement, youth work, and other activities financed by voluntary Jewish contributions from abroad.

Early History

Even before the Mandate became effective, discussions had begun in a joint committee of the Zionist Organization and the *Board of Deputies of British Jews with a view to broadening the base of the Jewish Agency by forming a new body representing both Zionists and non-Zionists. It had become clear that the Zionist Organization alone could not command the resources required for building the National Home. As a symbol of Jewish nationalism, it was unacceptable to the non-Zionists whose support was being sought. The appeals to them by the Foundation Fund, established in 1921 as its fund-raising organization, had proved ineffectual. There was also the hope that a more representative body would have greater authority in its dealings with the British government and the Palestine administration, neither of which had sought the advice and cooperation of the Zionist Organization to any large extent.

In 1923, Chaim *Weizmann, the president of the Zionist Organization, was authorized by its general council to set up such a representative body. Weizmann found in Louis *Marshall, long-time president of the *American Jewish Committee, a willing counterpart, but it took six years of intermittent negotiation before the new body came into being. While both the principals strove single-mindedly toward their goal, others were not easily convinced that the two parties could work together. The Zionists resented the tendency of the other side to see in the National Home merely a philanthropic enterprise. The non-Zionists were skeptical of the Zionists' capacity to subordinate their organization and its nationalist aims to a new body more representative of world Jewish opinion. Marshall had pointedly announced the American Jewish Committee's intention to "cooperate for certain specific purposes which do not include the establishment of an independent Jewish state or commonwealth." At one time, the negotiations nearly foundered over the American *Joint Distribution Committee's sponsorship of the project for the resettlement in the Crimea of Russian Jews displaced by the Revolution. The project was bitterly opposed by the Zionists, both for ideological reasons and because it threatened to divert funds from Palestine.

After this controversy died down, much of the residual anti-Agency feeling in Zionist ranks was overcome by economic necessity: the National Home was sorely in need of greater financial support. The 15th Zionist Congress meeting in 1927 set up a Joint Survey Commission, under Sir Alfred Mond (later Lord *Melchett), to formulate a concrete program for cooperation. After a survey in Palestine, its report was submitted in October 1928. The 16th Congress, meeting in Zurich in August 1929, endorsed the proposals by a vote of 230 to 30. There followed the constituent meeting of the council of the enlarged Jewish Agency: a body described by Marshall as "coextensive with the Jewish people everywhere." Among the non-Zionist delegates (40% of whom were Americans) were such figures as Albert *Einstein, Sholem *Asch, Leon *Blum, Sir Herbert (later the first Viscount) *Samuel, and Lord Melchett.

The Agency's constitution provided for parity between Zionists and non-Zionists on its three governing bodies: the 224-member council, the administrative committee, and the executive. The president of the World Zionist Organization was to serve as president of the Jewish Agency unless three-quarters of the council voted otherwise. Officers elected at the first council meeting were Chaim Weizmann, president, Louis Marshall, chairman of the executive, Lord Melchett, associate chairman, Baron Edmond de *Rothschild, honorary chairman, and Felix *Warburg, chairman of the administrative committee.

Subsequent Developments

Notwithstanding its founders' hopes, the Jewish Agency never succeeded in functioning independently of the World Zionist Organization. The parity principle proved unrealistic. Non-Zionists in the Diaspora, without organizational backing (the American Jewish Committee was determined to stay out of the Agency structure even though its officers filled the most important posts), had difficulty in recruiting their quota for council meetings. The "non-Zionists" in Palestine were really Zionist in all but formal affiliation. The Zionists later sought to have the parity provision abolished, and this led to some ill feeling. The deaths of Louis Marshall and Lord Melchett shortly after the founding meeting removed much of the motive power behind the Jewish Agency idea in their respective communities, and the worldwide depression impeded the raising of additional money for Palestine.

At the same time, Arab apprehensions were aroused by the apparent reinforcement of Zionist power, and the 1929 riots in Palestine accelerated the Mandatory disinclination to foster the Jewish National Home. Following the inquiry by the Shaw Commission into the causes of the 1929 disturbances, the British government, through its secretary of state for the colonies, Lord Passfield, issued a *White Paper which called for severe limitations on Jewish immigration and settlement in Palestine. Pressure by the Jewish Agency, including the resignations of Weizmann and Warburg, led Prime Minister Ramsay MacDonald to provide assurances which virtually nullified the White Paper.

Functions

The Jewish Agency maintained an executive in Jerusalem and another in London (a New York branch superseded the latter when the center of diplomatic and Jewish activity shifted to the U.S. after World War II). The Jerusalem executive organized the movement and absorption of immigrants, fostered settlement on the land, took part in the development of the Jewish economy, and promoted educational and social services in cooperation with the *Va'ad Le'ummi (National Council of the Jews of Palestine). The Agency's political department in Jerusalem negotiated with the Palestine administration, while the London executive maintained contact with the colonial and foreign offices. The Agency was represented at the sessions of the Permanent Mandates Commission of the League of Nations when Palestine was being discussed. Together with the Va'ad Le'ummi, the Agency supervised the *Haganah, the clandestine Jewish defense force.

The major political effort of the Jewish Agency was concentrated on inducing the Palestine administration to interpret liberally the "economic absorptive capacity" by which Jewish immigration was regulated. With the rise of Hitler, its exertions resulted in the legal immigration of 62,000 persons in a single year, 1935. Under the **Haavara* ("transfer") agreement with the German government, some $25 million in German Jewish assets were transferred to Palestine. During the same period, the Agency assumed responsibility for the *Youth Aliyah program designed to bring children to Palestine from Nazi Germany.

These developments kept the Jewish Agency structure together for nearly a decade in spite of internal stresses. But the arrangement barely withstood the strains generated by the recommendations of the Peel Commission (sent in 1936 to investigate the causes of the disturbances) to partition Palestine into Jewish and Arab states. While the 20th Zionist Congress, meeting in Lausanne in August 1937, endorsed the principle of partition by a narrow margin, the non-Zionist section of the Jewish Agency council, which subsequently convened in the same city, strongly opposed it. But the partition proposal was carried by the Zionists instructed to vote en bloc, and Felix Warburg, who had succeeded Marshall as the senior American member of the executive, died while negotiating a compromise.

The Arabs also opposed partition, and Britain reversed its position in the wake of still another committee of inquiry (the Woodhead Commission). Following the failure of a round-table conference called by the British government as a last attempt to reconcile Jewish and Arab views, the MacDonald White Paper was issued in May 1939. This temporarily restored unity of action in the Agency. The American non-Zionists now submitted a plan to Weizmann for its reorganization, but the crisis leading to World War II prevented the convening of its council in Europe, and no further joint meetings were held.

World War II and the Struggle for the State

With the adoption by the Zionists in May 1942 of the *Biltmore Program calling for a Jewish commonwealth in Palestine, effective non-Zionist participation in the Jewish Agency came to an end, and it once more became identified with the World Zionist Organization. As such it fought the White Paper restrictions on land purchase and immigration, mainly by organizing "illegal" immigration of survivors from Europe in the face of determined British opposition, throughout the war and until the eve of statehood. At the same time, the Agency took the lead in mobilizing the resources of the *yishuv* on behalf of the Allied war effort. David *Ben-Gurion, chairman of the executive from 1935, called on the *yishuv* "to fight the White Paper as though there were no war and to fight the war as though there were no White Paper."

The defeat of the Axis and the disclosure of the Nazi Holocaust in Europe brought the Agency to the forefront of the struggle for statehood. Its defiance of the British authorities led to the arrest of members of the executive, along with other leading figures in the *yishuv*, on June 29, 1946. On the diplomatic front, the arena shifted from Palestine (where the executive stated the Jewish case first to the Anglo-American Commission of Inquiry of 1946 and later to the United Nations Special Committee on Palestine) to London, and to New York where Moshe *Sharett and Rabbi Abba Hillel *Silver were the chief Jewish Agency spokesmen in the deliberations leading to the UN General Assembly's partition resolution of November 29, 1947. In the interim period until the declaration of independence, the Agency and the Va'ad Le'ummi set up a National Council of 37 and a National Administration of 13, which, on the declaration of independence, became the State of Israel's provisional legislature and government. With the creation of the state, the Jewish Agency transferred its political functions to the provisional government and leading members of the Jerusalem executive, led by Ben-Gurion and Sharett, moved over to the Cabinet.

The Jewish Agency after 1948

The Zionist General Council decided in August 1948 that the Agency should continue to deal with immigration to Israel, absorption of immigrants, land settlement, and the channeling of world Jewry's support to the state. This decision was approved by the Zionist Congress in Jerusalem in 1951, which adopted the "Jerusalem Program" and was incorporated in the World Zionist Organization-Jewish Agency (Status) Law adopted by the Knesset on November 24, 1952. (The law considered the World Zionist Organization and the Jewish Agency to be identical.) On July 26, 1954 a formal covenant was signed between the Israel government and the World Zionist Organization-Jewish Agency, recognizing the latter as the representative of world Jewry in relation to the functions cited above. These were carried out through the following departments: immigration, absorption, agricultural settlement, Youth Aliyah, economic, organization, information, external relations, youth and He-Ḥalutz, education and culture in the Diaspora, and later Torah education and culture in the Diaspora. The members of the executive, elected by the Zionist Congress along party lines, headed the departments.

The first five of these departments played key roles in the settlement of the immigrants. The immigration department operated a network of facilities in Europe and elsewhere for processing the migrants at points of origin and in transit. It arranged for medical examinations and other formalities and supplied transport, at times chartering ships and aircraft. The department of absorption received the newcomer on arrival, provided initial grants of cash and household goods, sent him to a camp, village or town, and allotted him housing accommodation. It also provided Hebrew instruction in its **ulpanim*, offered vocational training courses and, with the economic department, made loans to artisans and small businessmen. It provided health insurance and welfare services during the first few months in the country, operated hostels for professionals, and planned the rehabilitation of hard-core social cases. For some years, the Agency shared with the government the cost of housing construction in immigrant areas.

The Youth Aliyah program, originally conceived to care for orphaned or unaccompanied youngsters from Nazi-dominated Europe and elsewhere, adapted itself to the new conditions by also providing for children of immigrant families unable to give them a decent home and education. Where previously the great majority of the children had come from Europe, in later years about 80% of the 12,000 youngsters under Youth Aliyah care at any one time were of non-European origin. As in the past, most were placed in kibbutzim or in children's villages where they divided their time between schooling and agricultural training. Foster care and occupational training in trades other than agriculture were also provided.

In 1949, the Department for Education and Culture in the Diaspora was established to help replace the loss of centers of Jewish learning destroyed in the Holocaust. At its Ḥayyim Greenberg Teachers' Seminary in Jerusalem, Diaspora Jewish youth, mainly from Latin America, were trained as Hebrew teachers, while Israelis were sent abroad to supplement local personnel in schools, camps, and youth organizations. This activity was stepped up considerably after the events of 1967 called for development of greater Jewish consciousness as well as Hebrew study in the Diaspora. Furthermore, advice and literature were sent to Hebrew-teaching schools, and seminars were organized in Israel for high-school age students of Hebrew.

A parallel Department of Torah Education and Culture in the Diaspora was established in 1951 which promoted similar activities along Orthodox lines, and also provided for the training of *shoḥatim, mohalim*, and *ḥazzanim* from the Diaspora. Its principal educational center in Israel is the Rabbi Gold Teachers Seminary in Jerusalem. Israeli teachers were trained for work abroad at Bar-Ilan University. The department also sent emissaries and textbooks abroad.

The Youth and He-Ḥalutz Department was established in 1940 and in 1946 the Institute for Youth Instructors from Abroad was founded in Jerusalem. Many kibbutzim cooperated in its schemes in providing work and instruction as part of the course. Between 1946 and 1967 more than 3,500 instructors studied there. The department was thoroughly reorganized in 1968 to meet the influx of youth from the West after the Six-Day War. Four sections were established for the training of youth in North America, Latin America, Europe, and "English-speaking" countries by means of emissaries. As part of this project the Arad and Emissaries Institutes were established in Israel. A students' division was also added to the department to cope with the 1967 volunteers who remained in Israel to study at the institutes of higher learning. The department developed a wide range of summer programs in Israel for youngsters from abroad.

Foremost in annual budget and personnel was the Department of Agricultural Settlement, with a staff of some 1,500 at the peak period and expenditure of as much as $50 million in a single year. It established 480 new villages after 1948, comprising some 32,000 farm units, furnishing them with equipment, livestock, and irrigation installations, as well as expert instruction. Their aggregate production in the late 1960s constituted 70% of the country's total agricultural output.

During the first years of the state, the Agency performed the tasks connected with mass immigration creditably, at times brilliantly. It succeeded in accommodating the record number of 239,000 immigrants who came in 1949, so that none remained without a roof over his head for a single night. In 1950, some 169,000 newcomers arrived and 174,000 in 1951. Among the earlier waves were the inmates of the European DP camps and those forcibly detained in Cyprus, Yemenite Jews ferried to Israel in "Operation Magic Carpet," and hundreds of thousands from Eastern Europe and North Africa. In 1951, Iraqi Jews were evacuated in "Operation Ezra and Nehemiah." Nearly the whole of Bulgarian Jewry, more than half the Jews of Yugoslavia, as well as 40,000 from Turkey and 18,000 from Iran, went to Israel during those first three years. The Agency accommodated the mass influx first by utilizing abandoned Arab housing, then setting up tented camps in various parts of the country, later superseded by *ma'barot* ("transit camps") consisting of one-room shacks. While the tent dwellers were wholly supported by the Jewish Agency, the *ma'barot* were located near towns where the newcomers eventually found jobs and could thus dispense with direct Jewish Agency support. In 1951, the 123 *ma'barot* had a population of 227,000.

By the time the World Zionist Organization-Jewish Agency Status Law was enacted, however, immigration had dwindled, and the Jewish Agency's future was being widely questioned. The expectation that the World Zionist Organization would become the principal link between Israel and the Diaspora proved unrealistic. Non-Zionist groups maintained their primacy there, especially in the United States. Israel, moreover, was also anxious for immigration from the free lands of the West, and the Agency did not succeed in creating such a movement on an appreciable scale. Prime Minister David Ben-Gurion took the Zionist movement to task on these and other counts, and his sallies damaged its prestige. Differences of opinion over foreign policy with the Jewish Agency chairman and World Zionist Organization president, Nahum *Goldmann, widened the rift between Israel's political leaders and the Zionist movement. However, the Agency successfully coped with the resumption of immigration from Eastern Europe and North Africa in 1955–57 and 1961–64. It evolved the ship-to-settlement plan bringing immigrants directly to permanent homes in villages or development towns. The rural settlement area of Lachish, with its cluster of villages built around an urban industrial and administrative center, won renown as a model of integrated planning.

The election of Moshe *Sharett to the chairmanship of the Jewish Agency Executive in 1960 marked the beginning of an effort to instill new vigor into the Jewish Agency by broadening its base. Both he and Goldmann, who continued as president, wished to see non-Zionists co-opted to the executive and to break the exclusive hold of the Zionist parties. In 1960, a new constitution was adopted which opened membership to territorial or interterritorial Zionist organizations, as well as to national and international Jewish bodies accepting the Jerusalem Program. Although associated groups from seven countries were represented at the 25th Congress in 1960, the constitutional reform had little practical effect. The 26th Congress in 1965 went further by resolving to co-opt several prominent non-Zionists as members of the executive without portfolio. Thus the executive reverted toward its former composition, but without the underpinning of non-Zionist representation in the constituent bodies. The question of non-Zionist participation meanwhile had come up on another level. In 1960, an American body was created to supervise disbursement in Israel of funds raised by the *United Jewish Appeal, in compliance with U.S. government regulations on tax-deductible gifts to charitable organizations. The new body was named the Jewish Agency for Israel, Inc. (changed to United Israel Appeal, Inc. in 1966). Its board of directors was composed in equal parts of organized Zionists, non-Zionists, and persons drawn from both camps who were active in fundraising. The Jerusalem executive of the Agency was appointed by this body as its official agent for implementing the programs for which American funds were allocated. To monitor these expenditures, it maintained an office in Israel.

Department in U.S.

The Jerusalem Executive, in turn, was represented in America by a body known as The Jewish Agency – American Section, Inc., which consisted of those members of the Executive who resided in the United States. These included Zionist leaders elected to the Executive along party lines as well as nonparty members co-opted in accordance with the decision of the 26th Zionist Congress. Unlike their colleagues in Jerusalem, the American members of the Executive did not head Agency departments, but some of them were responsible for the activities of certain departments in the Western Hemisphere. As an agent of the Jewish Agency, Jerusalem, The Jewish Agency – American Section, Inc. was required to register with the U.S. Department of Justice under the Foreign Agents Registration Act of 1938.

Finances

The following is a summary of income of the Jewish Agency for the period from Oct. 1, 1948 to Mar. 31, 1963: Gift funds, $653.6 million (54.1%), German Reparations, $173.1 million (14.3%), income from assets, + sundries, $53.9 million (4.5%), allocations from public bodies, $32.1 million (2.7%), Israel Government participation $169.6 million (14.0%) and earmarked contributions, $124.9 million (10.4%).

Of the gift funds, about 80% came from the United States. Assets on March 31, 1963 (registered in the name of *Keren Hayesod) were put at $307 million, liabilities at $201 million. The Agency's income from donations by world Jewry increased dramatically after the Six-Day War, enabling it to finance costs of welfare and other services on behalf of immigrants, hitherto borne by the Israel government.

New Directions

In the second half of the 1960s, proposals were heard from within the movement to separate the Jewish Agency once more from the World Zionist Organization structure. The reason this time was not related to non-Zionist participation. The proponents of separation felt that the mixture of practical tasks with ideology was detrimental to both; that by leaving the concrete tasks of immigration resettlement to the Agency the Zionist Organization could concentrate on winning the Diaspora to its ideology. However, the 27th Congress (June 1968) did not adopt these proposals. Instead, it approved reforms proposed by Louis *Pincus (who had become chairman upon Moshe Sharett's death in 1965), which consolidated the various departments in the interests of efficiency and reduced the membership of the executive. Nahum Goldmann was not reelected as WZO president, and the office remained vacant. The Congress also adopted a new, more outspokenly Zionist, Jerusalem Program, and decided to set up a nonparty *aliyah* movement.

While the 27th Congress was in session, the Israel government announced the creation of a new Ministry of Immigrant Absorption thus assuming direct responsibility in this sphere. The Jewish Agency's department of immigration and absorption continued to register and bring over the immigrants, look after *ulpanim* and reception centers, and care for needy newcomers. A joint government-Jewish Agency authority was charged with delineating the respective areas of competence, and the modus vivendi agreed upon provided for continued Jewish Agency responsibility primarily for immigration abroad, with the ministry dealing with most areas of absorption in Israel itself. The government, however, stopped short of a complete takeover in this area with the knowledge that the financial contributions of world Jewry, and of American Jews in particular, must be disbursed by nongovernmental bodies in order to be entitled to exemption from income taxes. At the same time, a renewed effort was made to give the Jewish Agency fresh vigor and legitimacy by broadening its base and by giving, in the words of its chairman, Louis Pincus, "world Jewry, which raises the funds for Israel, a direct say in the way the funds are spent." Under a plan approved by the Zionist General Council in July 1969, the structure and functions of the Jewish Agency and World Zionist Organization were to be separated in much the same manner as provided for by the 1929 agreement to set up the enlarged Jewish Agency: the Jewish Agency was to deal with "practical" work in Israel and the World Zionist Organization with Zionist, educational, and organizational tasks in the Diaspora. Like its predecessor, the reconstituted Jewish Agency was to consist of three parts – an assembly, a board of governors, and an executive – and once again 50% of the members of the assembly were to be designated by the World Zionist Organization. A vexing problem that had plagued the original Jewish Agency, namely the designation of non-Zionist members, was to be obviated by having the second 50% of the membership designated by the principal fund-raising organizations functioning in the Diaspora on behalf of Israel. This plan was finalized in 1970 and thus after 40 years of activity, the Jewish Agency in effect reverted, in its organizational form, to the ideas that first created it.

[Ernest Stock]

Into the 1990s and Beyond

Since the mid-1980s, the Jewish Agency (JA) and World Zionist Organization (WZO) have sought ways to redefine many of their traditional programs and modes of operation as well as to effect a new division between them. This process emerged in response to changes in Israel-Diaspora relations, but it was also shaped by ongoing tensions and differences in the relative strength of the constituent groups of these bodies. As a result, major transformations occurred.

Far-reaching programmatic and operational modifications have been made in an effort to streamline bureaucracy and bring about cost efficiency. In 1988 alone, 559 budgeted personnel positions were terminated in the JA. By 1990, one third of all JA employees had been made redundant. Traditional Agency departments: Aliyah, Youth Aliyah, Rural Settlement, and Project Renewal were restructured. Another three departments, Torah Education & Culture, General Education & Culture, and Youth & He-Ḥalutz, formerly solely in the domain of the WZO, have come under the budgetary and programmatic aegis of a newly created JA/WZO Authority for Jewish Zionist Education. Initially it was envisaged that the budget of the Authority would be about $50 million a year approximating the aggregate of the separate departments, but the 1993 budget allocated only $33.9 million.

In 1993, the departments of Rural Settlement and Renewal & Development were merged into a combined Department for Rural and Urban Development. This culminated a process which began at the June 1991 Assembly. The new department was mandated to operate on a time and resource limited project base.

Budgetary constraints also forced a gradual reduction in the total number of youngsters in the care of the Youth Aliyah Department from 19,000 in the fiscal year 1986/87 to 14,000 in 1992/93. This cutback was made despite the massive inflow of immigrants and the deteriorating economic state of broad sections of Israeli society. Here, as in the case of rural settlement and urban renewal, the economies of scale followed on studies conducted by consultants appointed by the JA Board of Governors.

Several catalysts together generated the changes. Among these were an extended world business slump, demands that funds raised in the Diaspora be used domestically, and the unforeseen enormous costs of financing *aliyah* from the former Soviet Union and Ethiopia. The personalities of the leaders of the WZO and the JA, and the divergent political, public, and business cultures from which they hailed also contributed to the shifts. Overriding all these components was the difficult structural and philosophic interface between two systems – the political WZO and the philanthropic/communal JA.

Almost all the leadership elites of the JA reside overseas and are appointed to their positions, whereas the majority of WZO officials live in Israel and are elected through political parties.

Jewish communal life in the Diaspora revolves around the maintenance of educational systems, welfare institutions, synagogues and other functions, all of which require funding; this calls for a highly complex fundraising capacity. Lacking the means to levy taxes, the compelling issue facing those structures is the mobilization of funds. Since fundraising is not a democratic activity, cost efficiency is arguably at the top of campaign considerations. The role of major contributors is thus perpetuated, which in turn coalesces into an oligarchy.

In the WZO, leadership is by demonstrated electability. While Zionists are critical of what they term dominance by people of wealth, community leaders in the Diaspora are equally critical about what they term the exaggerated politicizing of Israeli-Zionist leadership and the attendant political coloration of policy.

In 1971, the Reconstituted Jewish Agency was composed of representatives of institutional Jewish life in the Diaspora, e.g., the communal federation system and the fund-raising community, who joined the existing structure – which had been made up exclusively of Zionists – in a fifty-fifty partnership. Subsequently, the creation of JA governing bodies – an Executive, a Board of Governors, and an Assembly – separated the JA from the WZO's governing bodies – an Executive, the Zionist General Council, and Zionist Congress. (By statute, however, certain positions, particularly those of the chairman and the treasurer of the Executive, remained common to both.) The result was that the JA became an autonomous organization in which the leadership of Diaspora communities initially acquired equal responsibility, and later supremacy in determining policy and budget.

Until February 1988, the Jewish Agency Executive, like that of the WZO, worked both ideologically and operationally as a collective. This meant that the chairman functioned as the "first among equals," with decisions taken as a group. In response to the demand by Diaspora members of the Board of Governors, particularly the Americans, to institute a corporate managerial style, each head of department within the JA tacitly agreed in 1992 that the chairman of the Executive may operate, when necessary, with decision-making authority. In addition, prior to February 1988, the director-general of the JA merely had a coordinating role. Subsequently, all department directors-general, and the secretary-general of the JA, are professionally responsible to the director-general.

Certain checks-and-balances were incorporated into the JA system. Fifty percent of the representatives in the 398-member Assembly of the JA (convened annually) are elected for a four-year term by the Zionist General Council. The remaining members are appointed by the United Jewish Appeal (30%) for a one-year term, while Keren ha-Yesod (20%) appoints representatives for a four-year period. The chairman of the WZO Executive also serves as chairman of the Assembly which determines basic policy and goals, reviews and acts upon budgets, determines priorities and directions of future budgets, adopts resolutions and elects the Board of Governors. The 75-member Board of Governors, which meets in between Assemblies to determine policy, manage, supervise, control, and direct operations and activities, is composed according to the same key as the JA Assembly.

The challenges met during the 1980s and 1990s by the JA have been its greatest since the early days of the State of Israel. The twin chapters of immigration from the former Soviet Union and from Ethiopia appear to have had an exhilarating effect on Jews around the world, effecting a great increase in fundraising and wrenching it out of the doldrums of eroding incomes. In the first years of the 21st century it was operating in nearly 80 countries through over 450 emissaries with a budget of around $400 million. Avraham *Burg served as chairman of the Executive from 1995 to 1999, succeeded by Sallai Meridor (1999) and Zeev Bielski (2005).

[Amnon Hadary]

BIBLIOGRAPHY: Non-Zionist Conference Concerning Palestine, *Verbatim Report of the Proceedings, October 20, 21, 1928* (1928); Jewish Agency for Palestine, *Constituent Meeting of the Council held at Zurich, August 11–14, 1929* (1930); idem, *Pact of Glory* (1929); C. Weizmann, *Trial and Error* (1949); C. Reznikoff (ed.), *Louis Marshall, Champion of Liberty, Selected Papers and Addresses*, 2 vols. (1957); Zionist Organization and Jewish Agency Executives, *Reports to the Zionist Congresses 17th ff.* (1931ff.), and *Sessions of Council*, 2–6 (1931–39); I. Cohen, *The Zionist Movement* (1945); Esco Foundation, *Palestine: A Study of Jewish, Arab and British Policies*, 2 vols. (1947); B. Halpern, *Idea of the Jewish State* (1961), passim; Jewish Agency, *Jewish Case before the Anglo-American Committee of Inquiry on Palestine* (1947); S.Z. Chinitz, *The Jewish Agency and the Jewish Community in the United States* (unpublished Master's Essay, Columbia University, 1957); Jewish Agency, American Section, *Story of the Jewish Agency for Israel* (1964). **WEBSITE:** www.jafi.org.il.

JEWISH AGRICULTURAL (and Industrial Aid) SOCIETY, organization chartered in New York in 1900 to provide East European immigrants with training "as free farmers on their own soil…" A subsidiary of the *Baron de Hirsch Fund, the society emphasized self-supporting agricultural activities, with rural industry to supplement farm incomes. Its *Industrial Removal Office, autonomous after 1907, relocated thousands of immigrant workers from the cities. Among the society's continued functions was the extension of loans on generous terms to farm cooperatives as well as individuals. It offered placement services and advice to potential agriculturists. A Yiddish and English-language monthly, *The Jewish Farmer*, was a vital channel of communication. While its extension specialists fostered agrarian innovations, the Bureau of Educational Activities stimulated cultural life, especially in the established rural communities of southern New Jersey and Connecticut. The society's officers included Eugene S. Benjamin, Cyrus L. Sulzberger, Jacob G. Lipman, Henry Morgenthau, Jr., and Lewis L. Strauss. An early shift from group colonization to assisting individual enterprise became the basis of most of the society's operations. Its diversified programs for self-help, whether in New Jersey, New York, New England, or California, were extended to thousands of displaced persons in the post-World War II era.

BIBLIOGRAPHY: G. Davidson, *Our Jewish Farmers and the Story of the Jewish Agricultural Society* (1943).

[Joseph Brandes]

JEWISH AND ISLAMIC LAW, A COMPARATIVE REVIEW.

The Relationship between Jewish and Islamic Law

Comparative studies in the field of Jewish and Islamic Law began more than 150 years ago with the publication of Abraham Geiger's *Was hat Mohammed aus dem Judenthum aufgenommen* (1833, rev. 1902). That study, and those that followed, concentrated primarily on the attempt to pinpoint cases in which Jewish law influenced Islamic law in the latter's early stages, against the background of the close physical and geographical proximity of Jews, Arabs, and Muslims – sometimes as actual neighbors – around the time of Islam's birth and later, creating what scholars have called "a state of symbiosis." Scholars were also mindful of the overall similarity of the two legal systems, both being casuistic, formal, personal, relevant to all areas of human behavior, developed mainly by the efforts of legal scholars rather than by judicial precedent; both do not distinguish between state and religion, since both give religious law precedence over the state; both distinguish between areas associated with religious ritual (*issur ve-hetter* in Judaism, *ʿibādāt*) and those relating to private law (*dinei mamonot, muʿāmalāt*), between matters concerning man and God (*bein adam la-makom, ḥaqq Allāh*) and matters concerning interpersonal relations (*bein adam la-ḥavero, ḥaqq ādamī*). In both systems, a system of punishment evolved alongside that prescribed by the Bible (rabbinically ordained flogging) or by the Qurʾān (Koran; *taʿzīr* punishments based on the late principle of *siyāsa sharʿiyya* – administrative justice within the limits of the *Sharīʿa*).

Despite the similarities in the main characteristics of the two legal systems, the differences are clearly visible. Thus, although both were developed by legal scholars, the Muslim magistrate, the *qāḍī*, generally appointed by the ruler, is not necessarily well versed in the law but must consult with legal scholars, his main task being the administration of the law in practice; neither can his judgment be appealed in a higher court. In Jewish law, however, the court generally comprises several judges (3, 23, or 71) who must be learned in the law; litigants often having the option of appealing to a higher court.

Quite naturally, early comparative studies of Jewish and Islamic law focused mainly on the influence of Jewish law in ritual matters (*ʿibādāt*), such as prayer, fasting, charity, ritual fitness of foods, etc., and less on other areas of law. In time, particularly in recent years, attention has also focused on the influence of Islamic law on Jewish law. Any discussion of the relationship between the two systems must therefore concern itself with two phases: (1) the early history of Islam, characterized mainly by Jewish influence on Islamic law; and (2) greater influence of Islamic on Jewish law as Islam consolidated its political power and evolved its own legal principles, from the 8th to the 12th centuries. Muslim influence, however, never actually reached the proportions of "legal transplants," but was rather limited, primarily affecting a few topics of legal theory, private law (*muʿāmalāt*), and, to a certain degree, genres of legal literature.

The comparative study of Jewish and Islamic law is meaningful not only in areas of mutual influence, but also as regards differences and parallels owing to social and economic factors (representing the human age in their background), to the possible influence on both of a third legal system, or to early traditions in the environment in which each evolved (the so-called "juristic *koiné*"). A major object of study is thus the characterization of each system and its particular trends of development. In the following discussion, the specific characteristics of each system and the relationship between the two systems in both phases will be reviewed, as well as parallels that were not necessarily the result of mutual influence.

FIRST PHASE. The earliest evidence in the first phase is of local Jewish customs that influenced the Arabs in pre-Islamic times, as attested by various Arab traditions, such as ablution before prayer: "For we have Jewish neighbors and they are accustomed to wash their lower parts of excreta, and we washed as they did" (Kister, "On the Jews of Arabia," p. 231). These traditions persisted after the birth of Islam: "'We washed with water during the *jāhiliyya* and did not abandon [the practice] when Islam appeared,' he [Muḥammad] said, 'do not abandon it'" (Kister, *ibid.*). Such influence finds expression in the Qur'ān, which in several cases notes that it is sometimes guided by earlier books or laws (as in IV, 31; V, 52; etc.). Some *sūras* in the Qur'ān clearly echo biblical or mishnaic texts. For example, V, 45 reads: "And therein [= in the Torah] We prescribed for them: 'A life for a life, an eye for an eye, a nose for a nose, an ear for an ear, a tooth for a tooth, and for wounds retaliation'; but whosoever forgoes it as a freewill offering, that shall be for him an expiation." This is a close parallel of the biblical verses Ex. 21, 23–24 and Deut. 19, 21. Another example (*ibid.*, 32) is: "Therefore We prescribed for the Children of Israel that whoso slays a soul not to retaliate for a soul slain, nor for corruption done in the land, shall be as if he had slain mankind altogether; and whoso gives life to a soul, shall be as if he had given life to mankind altogether," echoing the well-known mishnaic adage "Whosoever destroys a single soul of Israel, Scripture imputes [guilt] to him as though he had destroyed a complete world; and whosoever preserves a single soul of Israel, Scripture ascribes [merit] to him as though he had preserved a complete world" (San. 4, 5). The verse prescribing the beginning of the fast of Ramadan (II, 187), "Eat and drink, until the white thread shows clearly to you from the black thread at the dawn…," recalls the definition of the earliest time for reciting the *Shema'* in the Mishnah (Berakhot 1.2): "From what time may one recite the *Shema'* in the morning? From the time that one can distinguish between blue and white. R. Eliezer says: Between blue and green." There is also evidence in the Qur'ān, albeit not explicit, for a link between the Muslim fast of Ramadan and the Jewish Day of Atonement: "O believers, prescribed for you is the Fast, even as it was prescribed for those that were before you" (II, 183). Muslim tradition refers to an indirect link between the Muslim Friday (LXII, 9) and the Jewish Sabbath; it was this link that inspired the people of Medina to request Friday as a day of prayer, when they complained: "The Jews have a day on which, once in seven days, they gather together, and the Christians similarly. Let us establish a day in which we will congregate, speak of Allah, pray, and thank Him" (Kister, *ibid.*, p. 245). It has been argued that some of the Ten Commandments are represented in the Qur'ān, though in Muslim guise. The list of marriages that are prohibited because of a blood relationship (IV, 22) is largely parallel to the list in Lev. 18: 6–20. Some scholars believe that the prohibition of usury in the Qur'ān (II, 287–288; IV, 33) was also influenced by the Jewish prohibition (Lev. 25:36; Deut. 23:20–21).

It is evident from these examples that the early Muslims were acquainted with Jewish sources not only by observation of their Jewish neighbors, but also, and perhaps primarily, thanks to Jews who had converted to Islam and brought their Jewish traditions with them. This was at first an oral process, with such converts presumably reading the Torah and translating it; the earliest documented Arabic translations of the Torah, however, date to a later period. An early collection of Muslim *ḥadīths* (al-Bukhari's *Ṣaḥīḥ*) reports that the Jews used to read the Torah in Hebrew and translate or interpret it for Muslims in their own language. Another tradition relates that Muḥammad permitted his followers to read the Torah and tell stories of the Children of Israel from Jewish sources, provided that they did not obey its commandments (Kister, *Ḥaddīthū*, p. 234). According to one tradition, Muḥammad actually judged Jews who had been accused of adultery, sentencing them to be stoned after he had consulted the Torah itself to determine their punishment; Muslim tradition has it that as a result a verse prescribing stoning, not originally in the Qur'ān, was revealed (J. Burton, *The Sources of Islamic Law*, 1990, pp. 129–132).

Because of the eclectic nature of the Qur'ān, some Qur'ānic verses, among other things (see below), actually contradict biblical or talmudic law. One example is the prohibition on marriage with one's niece (IV, 22), which talmudic law permits and in fact considers a meritorious act (Tosefta, Kid. 1. 5; Yev. 62b). Similarly, divorce as prescribed in the Qur'ān deviates in two respects from biblical law. First, divorce is effected, according to the Bible, by means of a document handed to the woman (Deut. 24:1–4), whereas a Muslim may divorce his wife by a unilateral announcement; second, the Qur'ān permits a divorced woman who has remarried to return to her first husband (II, 230), while biblical law forbids such a marriage (Deut. *ibid.*). There are also differences in inheritance laws: The Qur'ān allows female relatives to bequeath property or inherit it (II, 7–12), whereas biblical law gives preferential treatment to men in the context of inheritance (Num. 36:1–4). In addition, there are differences pertaining to marriage, dowry, and procedure.

Besides the aforesaid eclectic nature of the Qur'ān, some of the differences between Jewish and Islamic law may also be attributed to the early Muslims' contact with sectarian Jews, who rejected rabbinic *halakhah*, such as the prohibition of marriage with one's niece. Other differences stem from the particular social and economic structure of Jewish society, which was largely agricultural, as against Muslim society, which was primarily mercantile. These differences might explain the nature of Jewish inheritance law, which tended to preserve the integrity of large properties, whereas Islamic law permitted the distribution of small shares to several heirs.

Similarly, Jewish law, characteristically for an agricultural society, impeded the transfer of property by requiring an act of acquisition, whereas the largely mercantile Muslim society was content with oral agreements, which imposed fewer restrictions on commercial life. Some of the differences may be attributed to Muḥammad's tendency to distance himself from the more rigorous aspects of Jewish law, as implied in the Qur'ān (II, 286): "Our Lord, do Thou not burden us beyond what we have the strength to bear." This tendency was implicit in a later interpretive principle of Islamic law known as *rikhṣa* (permission, alleviation), as against Jewish law, which, as Goitein pointed out in a well-known article, is referred to as *azīma* (stern, rigid).

Muslim jurists differed as to the status of provisions of Jewish law incorporated in the Qur'ān and in the *Sunna*. In one view, pre-Islamic law was an integral part of the Islamic system unless explicitly abrogated. This was the case with respect to various laws derived from Qur'ānic verses that had originated in the Bible, such as the verse concerning suretyship (XII, 71–78), of which the Ḥanafi jurist Sarakhsī (d. 1099) wrote: "The law that preceded us is our law as long as it has not been abrogated." Muslim jurists also applied the principle in the areas of dowry and hiring. Other Muslim scholars, however, preferring to distance themselves from Jewish influence, entirely rejected the possibility of Islamic law assimilating laws from the Jewish system.

SECOND PHASE. The second phase, comprising the period of the *geonim* (8th to 11th centuries), was marked by a change in the patterns of influence, in that it was primarily Islamic law that began to influence the practice of Jewish law in the Jewish communities of the East; the latter, as a minority group, were influenced by legal practice as determined by the ruling majority, in several areas: legal theory, rules of inference, linguistic terminology, and literary creation. Patterns of Muslim legal literature also influenced the writings of leading Jewish legal authorities. Muslim influence was not without its effect on the lower echelons of Jewish society, which sometimes adopted customs from the environment that reflected Islamic law.

Several factors combined to influence patterns of influence in the second phase. First, the *geonim* were familiar with Islam and its law, which often provided the background to their own rulings. For example, one geonic responsum, discussing the question of whether a convert forfeits inheritance rights, writes: "…these Muslims… for in the religion of Ishmael they do not permit a convert to inherit the property of his father." R. Saadiah Gaon is familiar with the legal terms relating to Muslim deeds: "I would like to know, concerning a scribe among the Muslims who knows ten formulations from the books of deeds by heart, what would his position be among them? Would he thereby become a sage, or a legal scholar, or a jurist, or a judge?" (all terms taken from Islamic law). In connection with the administration of oaths, R. Hai Gaon rules "that the oath sworn by the Ishmaelites, saying, 'There is no God but Allah,' is a major oath." Elsewhere, he notes: "Thus we see that in this city in which we now live, that is, Baghdad, the non-Jewish courts admit evidence only from competent witnesses, adult and rich, of whom there has been no breath of theft, falsehood or vanity, who are specified in their religion and called *al-mu'addilīn*." Islamic law is sometimes reflected in the formulation of questions, as in the case when Rav Natronai of Sura was asked: "In our locality it is customary that if a person frees his slave and that slave dies without sons, then his master inherits him" – as in Islamic law, where a master can inherit from a slave. On the other hand, one also finds negative reactions to Islamic law. Thus, R. Yehudai Gaon expresses disapproval of the practice of handing down a legal opinion to one of the litigants: "It is forbidden to discuss the law with him or tell him anything about the law. For that is the practice of the courts of the Cutheans [= non-Jews], that one requests a legal opinion in advance." And Rav Hai criticizes the Muslim version of the lunar calendar, whose festivals do not occur in the same season every year: "…[the Muslims' festivals] move around [from season to season], for their months are the months of the [lunar] year and they have no intercalation."

Another factor that figured in the flow of influence was the frequency of Jewish contact with Muslims and with the Muslim authorities, fear of which inspired the *geonim* to adopt a generally moderate attitude to Muslim religion, Islamic law, Muslim rulers, and their subjects. The *geonim* applied the principle of *dina de-malkhuta dina* ("the law of the state [lit.: kingdom] is law"), on the assumption that Muslim rule was a result of divine providence. Jewish legal authorities therefore acquiesced in the laws promulgated by the Muslim authorities, recognizing deeds issued or approved by Muslim courts, although explicit mention of *dina de-malkhuta* is fairly rare; their attitude to the Muslim authorities was generally positive: "These Muslims are most solicitous for us and most protective toward us." This may be an appreciation of their judicial autonomy under Muslim rule. However, they also complain of "a cruel and harsh government," implying apprehension of the ruling authorities and the need to make allowance for the imposition of Islamic law in certain areas, as in their ruling that it is permissible administer an oath to a non-Jewish partner, contrary to talmudic law (Sanh. 63b). Because of the prohibition of usury in Islamic law, Rav Hai prohibits loans at interest to Muslims, although the biblical injunction against usury does not apply to non-Jews: "It is not permitted to charge a non-Jew interest save in the case of non-Jews for whom this is proper; that is, who themselves lend and borrow at interest. But as for these Ishmaelites, who forbid this in their religion, it is forbidden to lend them at interest – even learned scholars, for that would involve desecration of God's name." Significantly, they do not consider Muslim wine as "libated wine," not categorizing Muslims as idolaters. There are many other cases of similar import.

A third factor influencing the absorption of Muslim usages was the lenience of Islamic law in certain areas, in regard to both substance and procedure, compared to the corresponding provisions of Jewish law – especially since Muslim courts possessed powers of coercion. Accordingly, there was a growing tendency among Jews to turn to Muslim courts, furthering an appreciation among Jews of the Muslim court system and its regulations. There is ample evidence, for example, of women in the category known as "rebellious wife" (*ishah moredet*) appealing to Muslim courts in order to circumvent Jewish law, which would not readily grant them a divorce; in such cases the *geonim* felt it necessary to deviate from talmudic law, in order to keep such women in the frame of Jewish courts.

A fourth factor furthering Muslim influence was the occasional encouragement of Jews to have recourse to Muslim courts, in the hope that such Jews might be persuaded to convert to Islam. This was done in two mutually complementary ways. First was the ruling in most areas of civil law, sometimes also in connection with personal status, such as marriage money, that there should be no difference in the treatment of Muslims and members of the "protected peoples" (*dhimmi*), including Jews; second, most Muslim jurists ruled that Islamic law would apply even in cases in which only one litigant had appealed to the court.

The above factors explain several innovatory halakhic rulings of the geonic period, as well as the assimilation of various Muslim legal norms in the legal literature, sometimes through the instrument of custom, at other times almost secretively, without any special indication. Customs taken over by the *geonim* from Muslim practice without change may be called "borrowed" customs, whereas others, constituting only a response to Muslim norms but not necessarily imitating them, may be termed "responsive" customs. Some adopted customs were intended to prevent recourse to Muslim courts, reflecting the fear of the *geonim* that the more lenient Islamic law might encourage conversion to Islam. Thus, the *geonim* created a *takkanah* (enactment) that a "rebellious wife" could obtain a divorce immediately, rather than wait the extensive time required by rabbinic law, without forfeiting the statutory value of her *ketubbah* (marriage contract). Recognition was accorded to the institution of "estimated" *mahr* (marriage money), according to which a woman who had lost her *ketubbah* was entitled to a sum of money as befitted a woman of her position, based on criteria taken from Islamic law. In connection with bankruptcy, they established various procedures at variance with talmudic law: they instituted a new oath of destitution, "I have no means," as practiced in Islamic law (*yamīn al-adam*); pronounced a ban on recalcitrant debtors as a substitute for the Muslim measure of imprisonment for debt; made arrangements for the needs of a debtor's wife and children when his property was taken over, as was customary in Islamic law but contrary to the ruling of the Talmud. Similarly, we find instances of the *geonim* permitting husbands to give their adult daughters in marriage without the daughters' explicit agreement, as permitted by some schools of Islamic law but contrary to talmudic law; this was done by creating a legal construct that brought the practice in line with the latter. Many examples of Muslim influence may be found in the realm of commercial law, one of the most prominent being the *suftaja* (bill of exchange; *diokni* in talmudic phraseology), in relation to which one geonic responsum states: "Our laws, strictly speaking, do not permit the sending of *suftaja*, since our Sages said, 'It is forbidden to send money by *diokni*' [TB BK 104b].... However, since we have seen that people use it, we have begun to sanction it, so that transactions among people should not be voided. So we have agreed to sanction it in accordance with the traders' law, no more and no less."

An example of a "responsive custom" is the institution of the "anonymous ban" (*ḥerem setam*), which was devised as a substitute for the administration of oaths to litigants during a judicial procedure, when an actual oath was not sanctioned by talmudic law. The *geonim* thus created a parallel to the Muslim system of oaths, according to which, in cases of doubt, a litigant could be required to take an oath even in the course of a judicial procedure, not only at its end.

A striking feature of geonic assimilation of Islamic practices is the frequent use of accepted custom to that end; in fact, that was preferred over the talmudic principle of *dina de-malkhuta*, of which (as already mentioned) they made very little use, perhaps out of reluctance to admit the influence of an external source. They used custom, a well-proved legal source of Jewish law, as a kind of signpost indicating what might be an ad hoc measure, a step in the development of Jewish law according to the needs of time and place. Many such customs associated with the constraints of time and place disappeared later, when the constraints were no longer relevant, and were replaced by a return to talmudic law.

However, as stated previously, Islamic law also made its way into geonic *halakhah* by channels other than custom; only careful examination of Muslim legal literature can reveal the Muslim source, which is not obvious at first sight. Such examination will reveal the Muslim background prominent in monographs written by the *geonim* on practical legal topics, such as the laws of abutters' rights or the laws of suretyship (which receive only sparse treatment in the Talmud), as well as on family law and matters of personal status.

Thus, there are clear-cut parallels between the "Book of Abutters' Rights" (*Kitāb al-shuf'a*) by Rav Ḥofni b. Samuel (d. 1013) and Muslim works, not only in structure, but also in relation to specific laws that the author seems to have borrowed from Islamic law. A few examples, among many, will suffice: conferral of abutters' rights to land acquired by barter; the right of rescission (*khiyār*); the existence of abutters' rights in voidable sales; division of a property among abutters on the basis of their number rather than their proprietary rights in the abutting property; establishment of a hierarchy among parties with proprietary rights to the property itself (*nafs al-mubay'*), parties with various non-proprietary rights pertaining to the property (such as right of way; *ḥuqūq al-mubay'*), and abutters proper (i.e., owners of adjoining properties; *jār al-mulāṣaq*); abutters' rights in the sale of a well or spring in another's property; real-estate transactions that do not confer abutters' rights, such as leasing, bailment, borrowing, or endowment. Moreover, the procedure in pleas concerning abutters' rights largely emulates that customary in Muslim courts. It is especially worthy of note that, even where R. Samuel b. Ḥofni adheres to talmudic law, his formulation is in the style of Muslim legal texts.

Similar links may be observed in R. Samuel b. Ḥofni's treatise on suretyship and hiring (*Kitāb al-ḍamān wa'l-kafāla*), many of whose provisions, in addition to the structure of the work and its division into chapters, are taken from the parallel Muslim literature or from the prevalent practice of the *milieu*. Thus, he devotes separate chapters to various types of suretyship. One chapter deals with suretyship for the obligee's person where the surety's only commitment is to bring the debtor to court. Another chapter deals with a surety who is also committed to defraying the debt in case he fails to present the obligee. There are chapters on the case of a surety who defrayed the debt before he himself or the obligee was sued by the principal, and on suretyship for an unknown sum. Sometimes, Muslim usage in matters of suretyship is cited in a geonic responsum rather than in a special treatise, as in a responsum by R. Sherira Gaon on suretyship. Another work parallel to Islamic law in several aspects is R. Samuel b. Ḥofni's treatise on divorce. Rav Hai's great work *Mishpetei Shevu'ot* is marked in part by echoes of Islamic law, such as making arrangement for the assets of a bankrupt debtor, as well as the oath of destitution, already mentioned previously.

At this point it should be noted that some of the parallels cited above may well reflect the influence of a third legal system from which both Jewish and Islamic law borrowed, or from an earlier legal tradition (juristic *koiné*). This may indeed be the case in such areas as abutters' rights and suretyship; alternatively, Islamic law may have been merely the channel through which they reached Jewish law. Some of the parallels and similarities may be explained on the basis of S.D. Goitein's theory of feedback or "full circle," according to which an idea was adopted by Islam, transformed and reshaped, and subsequently, in a new guise, "came round full circle" and impacted Jewish law. Examples of this process are the Muslim *mahr* (marriage money, dowry) and suretyship for person, both already found in biblical law (in the latter case, some Muslim jurists admit this origin). Both institutions experienced further development in Islamic law, finally returning in a new figuration to influence Jewish law.

Links with Islamic law may also be identified in the area of legal theory (*uṣūl al-fiqh*), especially in the writings of R. Saadiah Gaon and R. Samuel b. Ḥofni. As shown by M. Zucker and later scholars, Muslim writings are the source not only of the metaphorical terminology of "roots" and "branches" (*uṣūl, furū'*) in relation to legal analogy (*qiyās*), but also of some of the basic conceptions of *qiyās* and its practical application, especially as formulated in the writings of Saadya and Samuel b. Ḥofni, who were apparently influenced mainly by *Mu'tazila* scholars. Such is the case, e.g., in regard to the question of whether analogy produces certain knowledge or only plausibility, or even in regard to the actual use of analogy as a source of law. The first signs of the use of consensus as a source of law in geonic works, including its definition and relationship to tradition, attest to the influence of the Muslim concept of *ijmā'*. The same is true of the use of interpretive tools taken over from commentaries on the Qur'ān, such as the terms *maḥkamāt* (univocal expressions) and *mutashābāhāt* (equivocal expressions), which were employed by both *geonim* and Muslims, among other resources, to explain contradictory verses in the Bible.

The primary genre of legal literature used by the *geonim* at this time, the halakhic monograph, dates back to R. Saadya Gaon, continuing in the later period of R. Samuel b. Ḥofni and Rav Hai. These authors' formularies (manuals of deeds, *shurūṭ, wathā'iq*) and dozens of other works, which later provided the basis for Maimonides' great work of codification, were written along the lines of the Muslim model.

After the geonic period, one finds less frequent instances of the influence of Muslim sources or of responsa written against the background of Islamic law or religious practice. An underpinning of Islamic law may be detected only rarely in the works of R. Joseph ibn Migash or R. Isaac Alfasi, both of whom, used concepts borrowed from the Muslim world, such as substance and accident (*jawhar, 'arḍ*), in connection with obligations concerning tangibles and intangibles. At times, Alfasi also employs Islamic legal terms, such as *naẓar, dalīl*, and *istidlāl*, in his talmudic discourse. Maimonides, however, betrays Islamic influence more frequently in his wording, in legal formulas, in methods of interpretation (*tāwīl, ẓāhir*, and *bāṭin*), and in actual laws and legal institutions; but it is not always possible to determine whether he was influenced directly by Muslim sources and practice or, indirectly, by geonic rulings and terminology, themselves reflecting the influence of Islamic law. Particularly prominent in Maimonides' code are certain provisions in the area of public law, in his "Laws concerning Kings," which reflect Muslim thought and parallel elements of Islamic law. This is especially apparent where he rules, for example, that a Jewish king is not bound by normative penal law and procedure – recalling the Muslim institution of *al-naẓar fi'l-maẓālim* ("investigation of complaints concerning injustice"). In regard to the supervision of public morals, Maimonides' treatment recalls the Muslim institution of *muḥtasib*. In family law and personal status he employs norms and practices borrowed from Islamic society and law: restrictions on women's freedom of movement, the husband's right to beat a wife who ignores her wifely duties, and so on. In private law (suretyship and abutters' rights) he lists a series of laws which, both in general and in particular, may well have been taken over from the Muslim legal literature. In legal theory he applies some aspects of analogy (*qiyās*) according to the Muslim model, makes frequent use of consensus (*ijmā'*) both in his code and in the *Guide of the Perplexed*, and divides human behavior into five "legal qualifications" (*aḥkām al-khamsa*), a common pattern in Muslim legal literature. The very structure of his code *Mishneh Torah* resembles in some respects the style of the parallel Muslim literature (*fiqh*). Maimonides' usage in the area of legal theory and positive law shows at times the influence both of the Shi'a Isma'ili sect and of the Sunni Shafi'i school. These schools were particularly active in Egypt, which was also the locale of Maimonides' halakhic activity, and they most probably contributed to the consolidation of his legal theory. As is well known, Maimonides followed several *geonim* in ruling that Muslims were not to be considered as idolaters, and this ruling may have influenced his attitude to some of their practices and customs.

Where Islamic law contradicts Jewish law, however, Maimonides will often use rhetorical or polemical tools to reject it. Thus, he rules against imprisoning a debtor who pleads destitution or even against administrating an oath to such a debtor; he stresses the halakhic requirement that divorce be effected by a written document, pointing out the danger of oral divorce as in Islam; he upholds the need for the public nature of the marriage ceremony; and in the area of commerce, he rules that a sale cannot be effected by oral means alone as in Islamic usage.

An acquaintance with Islamic law is also evident in the writings of Maimonides' son Abraham b. Maimon, and its influence may sometimes be detected. In one responsum (*Resp. R. Abraham ben ha-Rambam*, Jerusalem 1938, #97), he writes that the laws of abutters' rights are also practiced "by people other than our coreligionists," clearly referring to the Muslims. In another (*ibid.*, #66), he employs the phrase "the gate of investigation and analogy is not closed," echoing a dispute among Muslim scholars as to whether the "gates of *ijtihād*" were closed; and in his *Sefer ha-Maspik le-'Ovedei ha-Shem* he discusses the relationship between written law, analogy, and custom in terms that recall the Muslim approach: "Custom is not the main thing that should govern our conduct, but written material or analogy, or both together." Abraham b. Maimon is also known to have been influenced by Islam in synagogue procedures, such as ablution, prostration, and seating arrangements, among others.

Later Spanish-rabbinical authorities, such as R. Asher b. Jehiel, R. Solomon b. Adret, R. Simeon b. Ẓemaḥ Duran, and R. Solomon b. Simeon Duran, show only isolated instances of the influence of Islamic law. Such instances may be found in the area of marriage law, such as R. Simeon b. Ẓemaḥ Duran's discussion of polygamy, where he recommends the egalitarian treatment of polygamous wives, or the connection made by R. Simeon b. Ẓemaḥ, R. Isaac bar Sheshet, and R. Solomon b. Simeon Duran between the Jewish *ketubbah* and the Islamic *mahr* (*ṣadāq*). Islamic influence is also felt in the treatment by several authorities of the arrangement for payment of *ketubbah* money where a woman has lost her *ketubbah*. Further reference to Islamic law in these sources revolves around the question of the desirable Jewish attitude to Islamic religious customs and to the usage of the Muslim environment, such as the obligation of a witness to take an oath as to the truth of his testimony, cutting the hair, eating flesh of animals slaughtered according to Muslim custom or in the direction of Mecca, taking off one's shoes upon entering the synagogue, hanging a mat with an illustration of the *Ka'ba* in the synagogue, and other subjects (R. Asher b. Jehiel and others).

Sources of the Law in Jewish and Islamic Tradition

The *Sharīʿa* recognizes four sources: The Qur'ān, *Sunna*, *ijma'* (consensus), and *qiyās* (legal analogy). The first two, Qur'ān and *Sunna*, are written sources (*naṣṣ*), whereas the last two, *ijmā'* and *qiyās*, are unwritten methodological legal sources. Islamic law does not recognize laws of equity or any equivalent of the halakhic principle of *lifnim mi-shurat ha-din* ("beyond the strict letter of the law"). The principle of *istiḥsān* (public welfare), which seemingly allows for deviation from legal analogy where necessary for the public good, is not generally perceived as a rule of equity; it has been described by some authorities as a kind of hidden analogy, the basic idea being that the *ratio* of a legal rule from which inferences are to be made as to a new rule is not immediately obvious. By contrast, Jewish law recognizes a broad spectrum of legal sources, including midrashic exposition, enactment (*takkanah*), custom, reason (*sevara*), and precedent. In addition, there are valid rules of equity, such as the aforementioned *lifnim mi-shurat ha-din* or the rule based on the biblical verse "Do what is right and good" (Deut. 6:18).

Underlying the differences between the sources recognized in each system are their conflicting attitudes to the law in general. Common to the four Muslim sources, as emerges from the legal literature, is the tendency to leave the law and its sources in the province of divine revelation, and to restrict as far as possible – if not absolutely to avoid – human involvement in the development of law and the establishment of legal norms. Thus, the verses of the Qur'ān are not readily interpreted in any sense other than the literal; any law in the *Sunna* must be supported by a *ḥadīth* consisting of the *matn*, the body of the tradition, and the *isnād*, a chain of transmitters traced back to Muḥammad or his companions and thereby endowed with an indelible prophetic stamp of approval. Consensus (*ijmā'*) is intended mainly to approve (a posteriori) norms upon which Muslims have agreed, such agreement attesting to their truth and divine origin; consensual norms are therefore almost inviolable, although consensus by itself cannot be used to establish future legal norms. The task of analogy (*qiyās*) is the expansion of existing law from a written source, but never the creation of new legal norms. Other principles accepted by Islamic law as tools to effect legal changes, such as the aforementioned *istiḥsān* (the principle of public welfare) and *ijtihād*, "effort," i.e., the use of individual reasoning or exegesis to decide the law, caused no significant change in the theological perception of law as based invariably on a divine source. We have already pointed out that *istiḥsān* was not seen as a channel of equity but as a kind of hidden analogy. In effect, therefore, Islamic law always remained "in heaven," the sole task of the jurist being to reveal it, with no freedom to exercise discretion in laying down the law.

In Jewish law, by contrast, the recognized sources grant halakhists extensive authority to develop legal creativity, on the basis of the biblical verse "It is not in heaven" [Deut. 30:12], as established in a celebrated dispute between R. Eliezer b. Hyrcanus and the Sages concerning the ritual purity of the "oven of Akhnai" (BM 59b). The difference between Jewish and Islamic law, in consequence of their different theological perceptions of the sources of law and the authority of legal scholars had implications in many areas of the law, determining the specific character of each. Islamic law, lacking suitable tools of jurisprudence, remained basically static, whereas Jewish law, by virtue of its sources of law, was more dynamic and enabled halakhists to cope more easily with changing realities.

These differences can be demonstrated in areas where the original legal nucleus of both systems was the same or similar, but because of the different nature of their legal sources, Islamic law remained relatively static, whereas Jewish law was capable of adapting itself to new conditions. Thus, for example, there was at first no basic difference between the Muslim *mahr* and the Jewish *ketubbah* (in the sense of a statutory payment). The biblical *mohar* (bride-price), originally a matter of oral agreement as to the payment made to the bride's family at the time of the marriage, as was customary in Islamic law, gradually evolved into the written document known as the *ketubbah*. Rabbinic sources attribute this development to R. Simeon b. Shetaḥ, who "ordained that all the property of a husband is pledged for the *ketubbah* of his wife" (Ket. 82b); consequently, the payment, instead of being made before marriage, became a debt payable to the wife at a later date in the event of her being divorced or widowed. This revolutionary development created a major gap between the two systems, which might otherwise have remained very similar in this respect.

There are other aspects of divorce laws in which Jewish and Islamic law were at first largely in agreement, but later drew apart owing to the dynamic and adaptive nature of Jewish law. Thus, in Jewish law as represented by the Mishnah (Yev. 14:1), later also accepted by the *geonim* in Iraq, "While a woman may be divorced of her own free will or against her will, a man can give divorce only of his own free will." Even more extreme was the attitude of R. Akiva, who taught that a husband may divorce his wife virtually at will, "even if he finds another woman more beautiful than she is" (Mishnah, Gitt. 9:10). The divorce procedure, too, is a private affair, with no involvement of the religious court. These aspects also exist in Islamic law as practiced (except for the halakhic requirement that the writ of divorce be handed to the woman, for which there is no parallel in Islamic law, and the biblical prohibition of remarrying one's divorced wife if she herself had remarried in the meantime). Jewish law, however, as practiced by Ashkenazic Jews, was radically altered by an enactment, attributed to R. Gershom Me'or ha-Golah (Germany, 11th century), forbidding a husband to divorce his wife against her will. Another gap was thus formed between (Ashkenazic) Jewish law and Islamic law.

Another example of this pattern is the question of the lineage of a child of a mixed marriage, which in the Bible, according to critical consensus, was based on patrilineal descent, whether in marriages between Jews or between a Jew and a non-Jew. This principle was later superseded by that of matrilineal descent, based on a midrashic exposition of Scripture, in response to changing realities. The Mishnah reports the final stage in a process of halakhic change that had presumably begun beforehand, which ultimately became the halakhic norm: "Whatever [woman] cannot be betrothed to that particular person or with others, the issue follows her status; this is the case with the issue of a bondmaid or a gentile woman" (Kid. 3:12). Islamic law, however, maintained the principle of patrilineal descent (probably because Islamic law permits a Muslim man to marry a non-Muslim woman).

At times, the change in Jewish law can be attributed to changed values in the rabbinic world, such as the midrashic redefinition of the term *na'arah* (unmarried girl), previously understood as designating status (as in the Bible): the Midrash redefines the term as denoting a young girl between certain age limits, so that a woman beyond those limits was considered independent. By contrast, in some schools of Islamic law, the cognate term continued to designate status, the girl remaining under her father's authority irrespective of her age. Similarly, the rabbinic interpretation of the scriptural verse "an eye for an eye" as referring not to physical retribution but to monetary compensation, has no parallel in Islamic law, which has retained the literal meaning of the phrase.

Both Islamic and Jewish law recognized the legitimacy of disagreement and legal pluralism, epitomized in the latter by the talmudic saying, "Both [conflicting opinions] represent the words of the living God." In Islamic law, however, this principle received prominent normative significance, in the sense that it granted equal status to different legal schools. This situation made adjustment to changing realities possible by transferring the focus of legal development from the text to the personality at the head of a particular school. A diversity of opinions was thus generated, making for a more flexible machinery of legal decision and somewhat compensating for the lack of dynamic sources of the law. Jewish law, however, from the start, adopted a rigid system of decision rules, unparalleled in Islamic law, meant to guide the halakhic decisor in dealing with differences of opinion. This somewhat limited the Halakhist's freedom to deviate from the halakhic text.

Legal Literature in Jewish and Islamic Law

The legal bases of the two systems, stemming as they did from diverse theological differences, affected their respective genres of literary creativity, as well as the nature and function of those genres. A basic similarity between the Bible and the Qur'ān is that both laid the normative groundwork for their respective legal systems, transforming in part earlier practices. In both, the legal material occupies only part of the text, which also includes a good measure of narrative. The Muslims evolved a special literary genre for the legal material of the Qur'ān, known as *Aḥkām al-Qur'ān*, "Laws of the Qur'ān," reminiscent of the contemporary Jewish genre of *Sefer ha-Mitzvot*.

Yet, the differences between the two systems outweigh the similarities. Primary is the difference in their mode of revelation. The theophany at Sinai was the sole source of the Torah, whereas the Qur'ān, according to Muslim tradition, was "brought down" from heaven, chapter by chapter, over 20 years. This gave rise to contradictions between different sections, leading to a criterion of "early" and "late" – later verses that repealed earlier ones – and as a result generated a genre specific to Islamic law to resolve such contradictions (*Kitāb al-nāsikh wa'l-mansūkh*). In Jewish law, however, the ruling principle was that no differentiation could be made between "early" and "late" material, and there was no need of such a genre. Instead, what emerged was recognition of an Oral Law accompanying the Written Law.

A special feature of Jewish legal tradition was the development, especially in the late Second Temple period and for some time afterwards, of literary genres designed to "prove" the Oral Law as being embodied in the Written. These "proofs" formed the basis for the compilations known collectively as "Halakhic Midrash," as edited in the rival schools of R. Akiva and R. Ishmael. Both schools evolved a system of hermeneutical rules for the presentation of the Oral Law as embodied in Scripture. Tradition makes Hillel the Elder the expounder of seven such rules, expanded later by R. Ishmael to 13. Among the more familiar of these rules are *kal va-ḥomer* (argument a forteriori), *gezerah shavah* (comparison of similar expressions), *binyan av* (inference from a particular case), *davar ha-lamed me-inyano* (argument from context). Two general rules of scriptural interpretation, outside the realm of hermeneutics, are the principles: "The Torah speaks in human language" and "The Torah speaks of the present [situation]" (both enunciated by the school of R. Ishmael). These rules, instrumental in the confirmation of Oral Law, are unparalleled in the Muslim legal literature.

The two systems differ in other branches of legal creativity, some deriving from theological reasons, others from the particular practical needs of each system. Exceptions are certain literary genres in which Jewish literary creation emulated its Muslim counterpart, in view of similar needs – such as the appearance of halakhic monographs on a variety of topics. Sometimes, despite a superficial similarity of literary function, the structure of the work is quite different. Thus, while both systems in time committed their oral traditions to writing – though both had originally forbidden such a procedure – there are still fundamental, theologically based, differences in the methods of transmission, the level of authenticity of a tradition, and its sources. In Jewish law, the main sources of the Oral Law are the Mishnah, the Tosefta, and the Halakhic Midrashim. The transmission tradition that establishes the validity of the Oral Law was enunciated at the beginning of Tractate *Avot* of the Mishnah: "Moses received the Torah at Sinai and transmitted it to Joshua, and Joshua transmitted it to the Elders, and the Elders to the Prophets, and the Prophets transmitted it to the men of the Great Synagogue…" Thus, the Oral Law (tradition) is firmly rooted in a divine source and is the basis of the authority of the editor of the Mishnah, R. Judah ha-Nasi. Muslim oral law, the *Sunna*, however, consisted of diverse collections of traditions, all endowed with canonical status; these were also based on chains of transmitters, but there the similarity ends: The *isnād* (chain of transmitters) is personal rather than institutional, extending from the last authority in the chain to the first, who is closest in time to Muḥammad or his companions; each law needs its own *isnād* as proof of its truth and authenticity. While rabbinic literature sometimes presents a similar concept of a chain of transmission, it is generally shorter and not necessarily based on names (such as the Mishnah, *Eduyot* 8:7; see Cook, "Opponents of the Writing of Tradition," pp. 510–11), though at times a chain of tradition combines both personalities and institutions (as in the Mishnah, *Pe'ah* 2:6). Some scholars believe that such chains were the model for the Muslim concept, which in turn had its influence on Jewish chains of tradition in later literature, in a kind of feedback effect; in the Mishnah and the Talmud, however, they were not a precondition for the validity of a law or a criterion of its authenticity. Because of this feature of Islamic law, there was a phenomenon of artificial chains as well as attempts to attribute late laws to the prophet himself. A similar phenomenon of attribution to prestigious authorities may also be found in geonic literature.

Around the same time as the consolidation and redaction of *Sunna* collections in Islamic law – a process that took more than 200 years, from the 9th to the mid-11th century – the genre of halakhic responsa evolved in Jewish law, to meet the needs of Jewish communities throughout the East. This genre made an inestimable contribution to the development of Jewish law and is unparalleled in contemporary Islamic law.

The different contemporary developments – emergence of the *Sunna* in Islam and of responsa literature in Judaism – reflect the different legal and historical needs of the two systems. Islam focused on the consolidation of a legal tradition and its attribution to Muḥammad, through the existence of independent legal centers in the Muslim world, which obviated the need to appeal to a single center. Jewish law, in contrast, was based on the already consolidated Oral Law; thus the leading legal center of authority in Iraq strove to decide questions of law generally, throughout the Jewish Diaspora, and with the institution of the responsum maintained its central position in the world of Jewish law. The responsa literature also served as a kind of corpus of legal precedents, again a phenomenon with no parallel in contemporary Muslim legal literature.

A further literary genre characteristic of Islamic law, but with no counterpart in Jewish law was that concerned with the "roots" of Islamic law, *Uṣūl al-fiqh*, that is, defining the legal sources of Islamic law, its theoretical bases, and rules for the derivation of rules from the "roots." This genre was necessary because of the confrontation between the supporters of tradition (*ahl al-ḥadīth*) and the supporters of legal theory (*ahl al-ra'y*). The quite intense tension between these two groups required tools to define legal theory and the limits and rules of legal methodology. These tensions hardly existed in the rabbinical world of *halakhah*, where a separate branch of legal theory was not necessary. Such topics were nevertheless taken up on the periphery of legal writing, as in the works of R. Saadia Gaon and R. Samuel b. Ḥofni on scriptural exegesis, or in specialized works such as those written by Karaites in the same period; these works, however, did not constitute an independent halakhic genre.

Yet another specifically Islamic creation was the literature of legal devices or evasions (*ḥiyal*). Certain topics elaborated in Islamic legal theory resulted in significant discrepancies between what was taught in the law schools and the reality of practice, such as the prohibition of usury. The *ḥiyal* literature tried to bridge this gap between theory and practice by way of various legal devices or fictions (such as the "double sale" of property in order to circumvent the prohibition of usury). While Jewish law also makes use of legal fictions (in the geonic period – perhaps owing to Muslim literature), this never reached proportions that dictated the composition of specialized works on the subject, especially since the legal substrate available to Jewish law, as described above, obviated the need for such works.

The literature of "disagreements" (*ikhtilāf*), which concerned itself with disagreements between Muslim jurists over a broad spectrum of subjects, is not characteristic specifically of Islamic law. Indeed, a similar genre existed in pre-Islamic Jewish law – the literature of *ḥillukim*. Again, however, the difference was significant: the Muslim genre had to cope with the existence of multiple legal opinions so as to ensure the equal status of the different legal schools; no such need existed in contemporary Jewish law. The Muslim formularies (*shurūṭ*) also aimed to harmonize the rulings of the different legal schools.

The one field in which the *geonim* clearly took Muslim literature as a model was the writing of halakhic monographs, frequently on the very same topics. We thus have works on the duties of judges and formularies, among dozens of works on a variety of subjects. In this area the *fuqahā'* (religious lawyers of Islam) and the *geonim* had a similar goal: to help their contemporaries conduct themselves in accordance with the law and to inculcate a common vocabulary (*lingua franca*) of terms and concepts. The *geonim* made use of such works, written in Arabic, and their legal terminology, which they used as a contemporary frame of legal composition. The flourishing legal literature of the geonic period was made possible thanks to the Muslim authorities, who granted their non-Muslim "protected" subjects, the *dhimmīs*, including the Jews, legal autonomy, spurring the growth of a ramified legal literature in a contemporary legal form.

There was nevertheless a significant difference in the writing of legal monographs in both systems: The Muslims would write comprehensive works on the totality of legal topics, whereas the *geonim* as a rule devoted a separate work to each topic. Later, however, it was these specialized works that provided the basis for the great comprehensive work of codification, in particular, for Maimonides' *Mishneh Torah*. Such codificatory activity was made possible by the existence of the rules of decision of Jewish law, which provided the backbone for these literary efforts. In Islamic law, however, with its pluralistic nature and the absence of an agreed system of rules of decision, the codificatory nature of the Muslim legal monographs was less obvious. The phenomenon of codification, which was unique to Jewish legal creativity under Islam (including R. Jacob b. Asher and his *Arba'ah Turim*, R. Joseph Caro and his *Shulḥan 'Arukh*), created a gap between the Spanish and Middle-Eastern works of *halakhah* and contemporary writing in Franco-Germany, where there was no such codificatory activity. This, then, is yet another example of the way Islamic law influenced the development of Jewish law in Eastern countries, sometimes leading to a veritable division between the Spanish and Middle-Eastern variety of Jewish law and that current in Franco-Germany (Ashkenaz), a division sometimes evident even in the actual content of specific laws.

BIBLIOGRAPHY: M. Cook, "The Opponents of the Writing of Tradition in Early Islam," in: idem, *Studies in the Origins of Early Islamic Culture and Tradition* (2004); R. Drory, *Models and Contacts: Arabic Literature and its Impact on Medieval Jewish Culture* (2000); A. Geiger, *Was hat Mohammed aus dem Judenthum aufgenommen*, rev. ed. (1902); S.D. Goitein, "The Interplay of Jewish Law and Islamic Law," in: B.S. Jackon (ed.), *International Conference on Jewish Law in Legal History and the Modern World* (1980), 61–77 [= R. Link-Salinger (Hyman) (ed.), *Jewish Law in Our Time* (1982), 55–76]; idem, "The Stern Religion: Some Comments on the Portrayal of Judaism in Early Muslim Literature," in: M. Schwabe et al. (eds.), *Dinaburg Jubilee Volume* (1949), 151–64, 423 (Heb.); M.J. and M. Kister, "On the Jews of Arabia; Some Notes," in: *Tarbiz*, 48 (1979), 231–47 (Heb.); M.J. Kister, "*Ḥaddithu 'an Bani Isra'il wa-la ḥaraja*: A Study of an Early Tradition," in: *Studies in Jahiliyya and Early Islam* (1980), 215–39; J. Kraemer, "The Influence of Islamic Law on Maimonides: The Case of the Five Qualifications," in: *Te'udah*, 10 (1996), 225–44 (Heb.); H. Lazarus-Yafeh, "Some Halakhic Differences between Judaism and Islam," *Tarbiz*, 51 (1982), 207–22 (Heb.); G. Libson, *Jewish and Islamic Law: A Comparative Study of Custom During the Geonic Period* (2003). idem, "Islamic Influence on Medieval Jewish Law?" *Sefer Ha'arevuth* (Book of Surety) of Rav Shmuel ben Ḥofni Gaon and Its Relationship to Islamic Law," in: *Studia Islamica*, 73 (1991), 5–23; idem, "More on the Relationship of Rav Shmuel ben Ḥofni Gaon's *Sefer Hamatzranot* to Islamic Law," in: D. Boyarin et al. (eds.), *'Atara L'Ḥaim in Honor of Professor H.Z. Dimitrovsky* (2000), 371–409; J.R. Wegner, "Islamic and Talmudic Jurisprudence: The Four Roots of Islamic Law and Their Talmudic Counterparts," in: *The American Journal of Legal History* (1982), 25–69; M.R. Zucker, *Saadya's Commentary on Genesis* (1984), 11–69; A. Zysow, *Ṣadaka*, in: EI² (1995), 8, 708–15.

[Gideon Libson (2nd ed.)]

JEWISH BOOK COUNCIL, THE, the literary arm of the organized Jewish community. The Council was established in 1946 in North America and became an international organization in 2005 with the establishment of the Jewish Book Council in Israel. The renaissance of Jewish books in the English-speaking world served as catalyst to expand its boundaries. The world-wide mission is to promote the reading, writing and publishing of quality English language books of Jewish interest.

Among its most prominent activities to advance these goals are sponsorship of the National Jewish Book Awards, now in its 55th year, and sponsorship of Jewish Book Month, which runs annually 30 days before Ḥanukkah.

Among its publications are *Jewish Book Annual* and *Jewish Book World: the Publishers Weekly of the Jewish World.* It also features Jewish Book NETWORK, a membership organization to promote Jewish book fairs in North America and Israel, and participates in major conferences, including the Jerusalem Book Fair, to promote Jewish books. The Council sponsors combined author programs between Israeli and American writers, and it serves as a resource for information on Jewish literature.

[Carolyn Hessel (2nd ed.)]

JEWISH BRIGADE GROUP, the only military unit to serve in World War II in the British army – and in fact in all the Allied forces – as an independent, national Jewish military formation. It was made up mainly of Jews from Palestine. The brigade had its own emblem, a gold Magen David on a background of blue-white-blue stripes and bearing the inscription "חי״ל [the initials of the Hebrew name חֲטִיבָה יְהוּדִית לוֹחֶמֶת – Jewish Fighting Brigade] – Jewish Brigade Group." It saw service in Egypt, on the north Italian front, and in northwest Europe, in the years 1944–46.

The establishment of the brigade was the final result of prolonged efforts by the *yishuv* and the Zionist movement to achieve recognized participation and representation of the Jewish people in the war against the Nazis, to lift the mantle of anonymity from the war effort made by the *yishuv* with its tens of thousands of volunteers, and to reinforce the *yishuv*'s political standing and promote the aims of Zionism. The British authorities, opposed as they were to these aims, were reluctant to have Jews serving in fully fighting units and confined them to auxiliary corps, while the infantry was largely employed on guard duties in Palestine. These obstacles were overcome only after a sustained and unrelenting campaign, headed by Chaim *Weizmann in London and by Moshe Shertok (*Sharett), head of the *Jewish Agency Political Department, in Jerusalem.

In 1940 the Jews of Palestine were permitted to enlist in Jewish companies attached to the East Kent Regiment (the "Buffs"), and 15 such companies came into being. In 1942–43 these companies were formed into three infantry battalions of a newly established "Palestine Regiment"; the battalions, whose men had previously served only in Palestine, were moved to Cyrenaica and Egypt, but there, too, as in Palestine, they did not receive their full equipment and continued to be engaged primarily in guard duties. The Jewish soldiers stepped up their demands for participation in the fighting and for the right to display the Jewish flag. It was not until September 1944, however, that the British government agreed to the establishment of a "reinforced brigade" which would be fully trained and then join the troops at the front. The brigade was composed of the three infantry battalions of the "Palestine Regiment," a field artillery regiment, and various other service and auxiliary units, largely made up of the Palestine Jewish units – particularly of the Royal Army Service Corps, which had seen service in North Africa. Brigadier Ernest Frank *Benjamin, a Canadian-born Jew serving in the Royal Engineers, was appointed brigade commander; the battalion commanders were British, while the company commanders were mostly Jewish. Some refugees and "illegal" immigrants also joined the brigade, and some Jews serving in British units were transferred to it. The total strength of the brigade was approximately 5,000.

After a period of training in Egypt, the brigade was moved to Italy, where it joined the Eighth Army and continued its training until the end of February 1945. It then took up positions on the Alfonsini sector of the front, where it soon engaged in the fighting, initiating two attacks (March 19–20, 1945), and took prisoners. Moving to another sector of the front, on the Senio River, the brigade found itself facing a German parachute division. In the course of further operations, the three battalions crossed the Senio on April 9, establishing a bridgehead which they broadened the following day. The brigade's casualties consisted of 30 killed and 70 wounded; 21 of its men were awarded military distinctions and 78 were mentioned in despatches.

In May 1945 the brigade was moved to northeast Italy, and it was there that it met for the first time with survivors of the Holocaust. Rescue committees were established in the brigade units to care for the Jewish refugees, while maintaining secret contact with the Jewish authorities' Merkaz la-Golah ("Diaspora Center"; see *Beriḥah). The brigade thus became a major factor in the care of the Jewish survivors of the ghettos and concentration camps. Without neglecting their military duties, the Jewish soldiers extended systematic aid to the refugees, provided them with clothes and educational facilities for their children, guided them across the frontiers, and smuggled them into Palestine. These activities continued when the brigade was moved to Holland and Belgium in July 1945. Some members of the brigade were attached to the tracing service of the occupation authorities and in their search for surviving Jews got as far as Poland and Czechoslovakia.

In the summer of 1946, in the wake of the increasing tension between Britain and the *yishuv*, the authorities decided on the disbandment of the brigade; most of its men were returned to Palestine and discharged there. Apart from its contribution to the war effort against Nazi Germany, the brigade fulfilled two historic functions: it was a decisive factor in strengthening the staying power of the Jewish survivors and refugees in Europe, and the experience it gained in military organization and in battle subsequently became one of the foundations of the Israel Defense Forces. Many of the officers of the Israel army, among them two chiefs of staff, M. Makleff and Ḥ. Laskov, had seen previous service in the Jewish Brigade.

See also *Israel, State of: Historical Survey (1880–1948); Israel, State of: Defense (Ottoman and Mandatory Period); *Zionism: Zionist Policy.

BIBLIOGRAPHY: L. Rabinowitz, *Soldiers from Judea* (1945²); Esco Foundation for Palestine, *A Study of Jewish, Arab and British Policies*, 2 (1947), 1020–35; Y. Lifshitz, *Sefer ha-Berigadah ha-Yehudit* (1947); D. Ever-Hadani, *Am be-Milḥamto* (1954³); Y. Bauer, *Flight and Rescue: Brichah* (1970), index; idem, *From Diplomacy to Resistance* (1970), index; B.M. Casper, *With the Jewish Brigade* (1947); Z. Shefer, *Sefer ha-Hitnaddevut* (1949); Y. Allon, *Shield of David* (1970).

JEWISH CAMPING, the collective term for the various forms in which the organized Jewish community and private Jewish entrepreneurs in North America have adapted the classic American summer *organized camping* format to meet the needs or desires of Jewish parents and/or the objectives of leaders of Jewish organizations and movements. A publication of the American Camping Association defines *organized camping* as "a sustained experience which provides a creative, recreational, and educational opportunity in group living in the out-of-doors. It utilizes trained leadership and the resources of natural surroundings to contribute to each camper's mental, physical, social, and spiritual growth." Jewish camping differs from Jewish youth movement activity (e.g., the Israeli *tenuot no'ar* or North American Jewish youth organizations) in that it refers to a program of varied activities which are focused at a permanent campsite which may be leased, though usually is owned by a sponsoring organization or in the cases of for-profit camps, by the camp's owner(s).

A census of the Jewish camp world, done by Amy Sales, Leonard Saxe, and their staff at Brandeis University, in the year 2000, counted 191 "mainstream" residential Jewish Camps in the United States, each summer serving approximately 83,000 Jewish children and teenagers, and also involving 18,000 Jewish adults who serve on their staffs. Many of the latter are college students working as bunk counselors who are also regarded by the camp administration, in most of the camps, as targets of the educational program. This is especially true in the camps under denominational or organizational auspices

Camps were included in the census of Jewish camps done by Sales and Saxe if they met the following three conditions: "(1) The camp has Jewish owners or is sponsored by a Jewish organization; (2) at least half of the campers are Jewish; and (3) the camp identifies itself as a Jewish camp." They suggest the usefulness of categorizing these 191 Jewish camps by their sponsorship and identify seven types of Jewish camps, which they divide into three major categories:

Community	
Jewish federation/Jewish community center	35
Agency/organization	32
Movement	
Zionist	15
Denominational	18
Private	
Non-Orthodox for-profit	64
Foundation/independent nonprofit	15
Orthodox for-profit	12
Total	191

The extent to which Jewishness is reflected in the programs of these camps varies greatly. It can be charted along a continuum ranging from camps which simply meet the above three basic identification criteria but offer virtually no Jewish content programming, to camps in which the Jewishness is the primary factor controlling much or most of the content of the camp program.

The earliest Jewish-sponsored camps were camps that were sponsored by settlement houses, as then existed on Manhattan's Lower East Side, with the purpose of taking the children of poor families out of the teeming city for a healthful fresh air experience in the country around the end of the 19th century. In 1893 the Jewish Working Girls Vacation Society of New York City opened Camp Lehman (eventually renamed Camp Isabella Friedman). This camp invigorated over the course of the years by the addition of a center for environmental education and a program for seniors was still operating in 2005. Another such camp, now known as Surprise Lake Camp, in Cold Spring, New York, was founded in 1901. In the 20th century as the *Settlement House movement declined, the Jewish "Y" movement and Jewish Center movement grew, camping was seen as an intrinsic part of the program of these institutions, and many of the Centers built and established camping programs. In 2004, the Jewish Community Center Association reports that its affiliates sponsor 35 resident camps and some 200 day camps (see below). Under the sponsorship of UJA-Federation of Greater New York, Surprise Lake Camp serves as the official camping program for five JCC's throughout New York City, and five more in the surrounding suburban counties. Other Y's and JCC's have operated their own resident camps.

Directed as they often were by social workers, many of whom lacked significant Jewish backgrounds, the programmatic emphasis in the "Y" and JCC camps was laid upon recreational programming and especially upon the democratic values of group living emphasized in American schools of social work. The specifically Jewish aspect of the programs of these camps, if such existed, consisted of a brief religious service for the camp community on Friday evening or Saturday morning. In the last half of the 20th century, however, as Jewish community centers were pressed to intensify the Judaic content of their programs, so too, the summer camps affiliated with the centers intensified the Jewish content of their programs, including the importation of counseling staff from Israel, and observing the laws of *kashrut* in their kitchens.

In the 1920s and 1930s a recognition began to arise that the summer camp might play a significant role in Jewish education and the socialization of the Jewish child into Judaism. Samson Benderly, the first director of New York's Bureau of

Jewish Education, was the first to recognize the unique opportunity that the summer camp offered for teaching modern Hebrew and other traditional Jewish values, through immersing children in a Hebrew and Judaic environment. In 1927 he opened Camp Achvah, the first Hebrew-speaking camp in Arverne, on New York City's Rockaway peninsula. In 1932, he sought to expand the program and purchased a campsite in a rural setting in upstate Godeffroy, New York. The expanded program retained the intensive Judaic program but was not Hebrew speaking, as had been the program at the Arverne site.

A.P. Schoolman, the director of the Central Jewish Institute, a *talmud torah* on Manhattan's upper East Side, saw the potential for creating a camp, conducted in English, which, along with its recreational program, would offer all kinds of activities with a Jewish content to them. Originally created in 1919 to complement the program of the CJI Hebrew school, the camp, located in Port Jervis, NY, grew to become the most significant non-Hebrew Jewish cultural camp. In later years, Schoolman's Camp Cejwin grew to accommodate some thousand children each summer. As an indication of its stature, each summer it hosted the noted scholar, Rabbi Mordecai Kaplan, the founder of Reconstructionist Judaism. Schoolman was long regarded as the "dean" of Jewish camping in North America.

Surprisingly, the years of World War II (1941–45) proved to be a very fertile period for the foundation of camps that were intensively Jewish. Jonathan Sarna refers to the 1940s as the "crucial decade in Jewish camping." This occurred despite the difficulties which wartime and the postwar period presented as regards to obtaining staff, obtaining building materials, purchasing foodstuffs, providing transportation, etc. The year 1941 in which the United States entered the war saw the birth year of Camp Massad, the most significant of the Hebrew camps. It was founded by a group of distinguished Jewish educators in New York City at the initiative of Hanoar Haivri – the Hebrew culture organization for Jewish youth, under the leadership of Shlomo Shulsinger who remained its director until he departed for Israel in 1977. That first summer, Massad opened as a day camp in the Far Rockaway section of New York City (not far from where Benderly had opened his first camp). The next summer, 1942, the camp operated at a leased campsite within an established Orthodox camp in the Catskill resort area. The following summer, 1943, the camp opened at its own site that it had purchased in Tannersville Pennsylvania, in the Pocono Mountains. Alumni of the Massad Camps speak glowingly of the Massad experience and point to the many distinguished Massad alumni. Shulsinger demanded that Hebrew alone be spoken at all times in the camp and gave awards to campers who achieved this goal.

Significantly, the Massad camps (at the zenith of their popularity there were three of them) and Camp Cejwin faded away toward the end of the 20th century, as the denominational camps (see below) flourished and grew in number. A number of reasons have been suggested for this development. Probably most crucial was the factor that these camps, as they developed and flourished over time, became independent of any organizational or institutional base. The denominational camps could depend upon the support of nationwide movements made up of many hundreds of synagogues. In addition Massad and Cejwin were the products of charismatic individuals (Shulsinger and Schoolman) who remained as long time camp directors. When they retired from the scene without leaving behind equally talented successors, the camps floundered and then withered away. In the case of Massad, there was also the growing weakness of the centrist Orthodox community which had for decades provided the bulk of the camper populations, especially from the students of the Ramaz and Flatbush Yeshivot – the first in Manhattan and the second in Brooklyn. The availability of a trip to Israel as a summer option for students as well as the acquisition of summer homes by parents offered other options for a summer away from the hot city.

In 1943 steps were taken by Louis Hurwich, president of the Boston Hebrew College, to found a Hebrew-speaking camp, Camp Yavneh, which would carry on in the summer its work of preparing students in the college to be teachers for Jewish schools. It was also at this time that the College of Jewish Studies in Chicago undertook the founding of Camps Sharon and Avodah in Buchanan, Michigan – Sharon, a Hebrew teachers training camp, and Avodah, a farm camp for Chicago teenagers who volunteered to attend camp in order to replace farm hands who had been called up to military service. In 1944, the Cleveland College of Jewish Studies opened a children's camp, Camp Galil. Of these camps sponsored by the Hebrew Colleges, only Camp Yavneh survived into the 21st century.

Most notable in the immediate postwar period, because of their long-range impact, were the founding of the Conservative Ramah camping movement and the Reform UAHC (later URJ) Camp-Institutes movement. Both began with single camps serving the Chicago and broader Midwest area: the first Ramah Camp in Conover, Wisconsin (1947) and the first UAHC Camp-Institute in Oconomowoc, Wisconsin (1950). Attached as they were to well organized national synagogue movements, the Conservative movement's United Synagogue (now known as the United Synagogue of Conservative Judaism) and the Reform movement (now known as the Union for Reform Judaism), within a decade, camps were established throughout North America to serve the various geographical concentrations of North American Jews affiliated with the movements. The initiative and long-time supervision of the Conservative camps was vested in the Teachers' Institute of the Jewish Theological Seminary, the institution that trained Conservative rabbis and educators. Supervision of the Reform camps was vested in the Camping and Youth Department of the UAHC. While there are individual notable Orthodox educational camps, such as Camp Morasha in Lake Como, Pennsylvania, and the camps of the Bnei Akiva religious Zionist youth movement, the divisions within American Orthodoxy seem to have precluded the establishment of a national Orthodox camping movement, along the lines of the Ramah or URJ camps.

In the year 2004, there are 7 Ramah resident camps (in California, Ontario Canada, Georgia, Massachusetts, New York, Pennsylvania, and Wisconsin) serving 6,500 children and youth each summer. There are 13 URJ Camp-Institutes (in New York, Massachusetts (2), Ontario Canada, Pennsylvania, Georgia, California (2), Wisconsin, Indiana, Mississippi and Texas) serving a total of 10,000 children and youth each summer. An additional camp is under construction in the state of Washington. In addition there are 4 Reform camps sponsored by individual temples.

The programs of these two denominational camping networks lay emphasis on classes, religious services and observances, and a creative mix of activities planned in the spirit of the philosophy of the sponsoring movement. At the same time the camps offer programs rich in the classic recreational areas: sports, aquatics, arts and crafts, drama, dance, music, nature and camping. In the Ramah Camps, from the start, Hebrew was the official language; in the UAHC Camps, there are Hebrew-speaking units in each camp. There is no doubt that both these denominations attracted their future leadership from the summer camping experience.

While on the surface, Jewish camps which offer intensive educational programs appear to be recreational enterprises, resembling as they do their non-Jewish counterparts which in the summer provide children and youth with an enjoyable alternative to the school-burdened fall, winter and spring, they have turned out to be much more than that. The founders of the Reform and Conservative camping movements early on proclaimed the goal of offering an intensive educational program to supplement the classes offered in synagogue and temple religious schools. Moreover they had declared the goal of making their camps "hothouses" for the production of layman and professionals who would assume roles of knowledgeable leaders in the movements. An examination of the backgrounds of rabbis, cantors, educational directors, and teachers affiliated with these movements documents the achievement of this later goal. Further, in many ways, the educational programs offered in the camps served as a testing ground and a stimulus for educational activity within their movements, beyond the summer, among them: (1) the use of informal education techniques as an educational tool; (2) as a means of strengthening year-round youth movements; (3) as an opportunity to explore new curricular areas (notable work was done in the camps on teaching about the contemporary State of Israel, the Holocaust, and Soviet Jewry, all later replicated in the year-round schools); (4) as a location for offering innovative types of Jewish education for adolescents with developmental disabilities; (5) providing college students with training in educational techniques; and (6) encouraging the study of Judaica at the college and graduate level.

The camps played a unique and fruitful role in educating Jewish youth about the role of Israel in Jewish life through injecting Israeli and Zionist themes throughout all aspects of the camp programs, by cooperating with the Jewish Agency in bringing Israeli counselors and specialists to serve on the camp staffs, and by integrating summer trips to Israel for the oldest campers into the range of camp experiences offered under the camp's sponsorship.

While Jewish camping is largely an American phenomena, Jewish camps on the American model are to be found in other countries. A few camps representing each of the major categories have been established in Canada: i.e., Reform, Conservative, Hebrew, Zionist, community center, and private for-profit. Notable are the Jewish institutional camps in South America and in Eastern Europe. When the Seminario Rabinico Latinamericano was established by the American Conservative movement in Buenos Aires, a Ramah camp was also established. As rabbis were ordained by the Seminario, and took pulpits in other South American countries, they took the idea of the Jewish educational camp with them, and established camps in those locales. When the Masorti movement (the Israeli Conservative movement) sought a means to provide Jewish educational programs for the culturally and religiously deprived Jews of Eastern Europe, the American-born rabbis who were leaders of Masorti embraced the idea of establishing camps on the Ramah model which they established for short periods on leased premises in various Eastern European countries.

The Ronald S. Lauder Foundation has made notable use of camping as a tool of Jewish education in Eastern Europe to help realize its commitment to rebuilding Jewish life in that part of Europe where the destruction of the Holocaust was followed by the oppression of Communist rule. Especially notable is the large permanent campsite it has established at Szarvas, Hungary, operated in partnership with the American Jewish Joint Distribution Committee, which each summer offers intensive Jewish camping experiences to more than 1,000 youths from more than 20 countries. The Szarvas campers dance, swim, sing, and canoe, and they also attend daily prayer and learn what it means to observe Passover, Purim, and Ḥanukkah, which the staff recreates with them. The language of the camp is English, which also attracts campers anxious to become part of the global elite,

Ever since the 1950s, there has been much praise (especially in non-Orthodox circles) for the efficacy of the Jewish educational camps in socializing and educating young Jews into Jewish life. Based on Sherif's research, Sales and Saxe identify the factors which make the summer camp such an effective medium for Jewish socialization of children and youth, as follows: "camp is an intense, enclosed setting," "camp activities are absorbing," camps "provide a framework for profound social learning," camp "provides the luxury of extended time with participants," "camp offers continuous interaction among campers and between campers and staff," and "[c]amp emphasizes learning through doing."

While there is a positive attitude toward camping in the Orthodox community, it seems to be mainly embraced as a summer recreational setting for the child. Because of the intensive socializing role of the Jewish home and the synagogue, and the intensive program of Jewish studies which most Orthodox children pursue in the day school, parents feel less need to utilize the summer for the intensive education, such as do parents of children enrolled in the Conservative and Reform camps. Among the Orthodox only the Chabad, who utilize camping to teach Judaism to children from non-religious families, emphasize the educational potential of camping.

Two other types of camps which have played a significant role in the history of Jewish camping are the Yiddishist camps and the Zionist camps. The first Zionist camps, intended for the youth affiliated with the various Zionist youth movements, were built in the 1930s. Today, with the exception of the Young Judea camps, sponsored by the Hadassah Women's Zionist Organization, the others are sponsored by the American affiliates of Israeli political parties. These camps are essentially the summer "homes" of the year-round Zionist youth movements. Isaacman reports that in 1945 there were 30 Zionist-sponsored camps in North America, while in 2000 Sales and Saxe report the existence of 15 such camps. The major groupings of Zionist camps are the Bnei Akiva camps, the Habonim-Dror camps, and the Young Judea camps. The decline in the number of such camps mirrors the decline in youth affiliated with the Zionist youth organizations.

As for the Yiddish camps, Isaacman writes, in 1970, "There are five camps in our study that bear the identification of "Yiddish" camps… these camps are misnamed, since the Yiddish language does not play a significant role in all of the camps but one." This statement describes the character of these camps 35 years later. The designation of the camps as Yiddish pretty much reflects the goals of the organizations that sponsor these camps and not the camp programs. The 2005 website of Camp Kinder Ring, sponsored by the Workman's Circle states, "Many years ago all campers and counselors at Camp Kinder Ring spoke Yiddish … American Jews have not kept up with the language of our grandparents … we still have an appreciation for our *mamaloshn*… and we share this with our campers through the many Yiddish songs we sing."

There are also a significant number of Jewish day camps (some 200 under the sponsorship of Jewish Community Centers) in North America, which meet during the summer months, on Monday through Friday, usually from 9:00 A.M. through 4:00 P.M. These day camps replicate in their programs many of the types of activities offered by the overnight camps. Day campers live at home and are bussed to the campsite each morning. As a rule, a center that sponsors a resident camp will sponsor one or more day camps. The Conservative and Reform movements each sponsor a small number of day camps that serve as feeders to the overnight camps.

There have been a number of attempts to bring together the Jewish camping community over the years. Most often the effort was made to bring together the directors of the Jewish camps for annual meetings. Unfortunately, these efforts were poorly funded and rarely achieved more than holding an annual conference and publishing its proceedings. In 1998, Robert and Elisa Bildner, parents of camp-aged children who were pleased with what the Ramah camping experience had done for them and their children, made a contribution of one million dollars as seed money to establish The Foundation for Jewish Camping, headquartered in New York City. "The Foundation advocates for Jewish camping, encourages growth of the camp system, helps camps recruit staff, makes grants to promote programmatic excellence, champions the growth of camp scholarships, and offers information resources to parents, camps and the Jewish community." The Foundation has been successful in eliciting additional funding for its programs from groups such as the Avi Chai Foundation.

BIBLIOGRAPHY: *Adventure in Pioneering: The Story of 25 Years of Habonim Camping* (1957); B. Chazan, S.M. Cohen, and S. Wall, *Youth Trips to Israel:: Rationale and Realization* (1994); E. Eels, *Eleanor Eels' History of Organized Camping: The First 100 Years* (1986); S. Ettenberg and G. Rosenfield (eds.), *The Ramah Experience: Community and Commitment* (1989); S. Dorph (ed.), *Forward from Fifty: Ramah Reflections at Fifty* (1999); M. Havatzelet (ed.), *Kovetz Massad: Essays in Hebrew Literature and Thought by Friends of Massad Camps* (Heb., 1978); D. Isaacman, "Jewish Summer Camps in the United States and Canada 1900–1969" (unpublished Ph.D. Dissertation, Dropsie University, 1970); M. Lorge and G. Zola, Gary (eds.), *Summer in Oconomowoc: The Rise of Reform Jewish Camping* (forthcoming 2006); A.L. Sales and L. Saxe, *How Goodly Are Thy Tents: Summer Camps as Jewish Socializing Experiences* (2004); A. Shapiro and B. Cohen (eds.), *Studies in Jewish Education and Judaica in Honor of Louis Newman* (1984); Sh. Shulinsinger-Shear Yashuv (ed.), *Kovetz Massad Volume II: Hebrew Camping in North America* (1989).

[Burton I. Cohen (2nd ed.)]

JEWISH-CHRISTIAN RELATIONS. Christian-Jewish contacts have progressed significantly at the initiative of the major international Church organizations and of national and regional church bodies. Of special importance are the contacts with the main Church organizations: the Roman Catholic Church and the World Council of Churches, the latter being a federation embracing the majority of non-Catholic Churches, but representing mainly the interests and views of the Protestant Churches. Direct contacts with the Orthodox Churches, outside the framework of the WCC, are at a very initial stage. The political situation prevailing in countries with orthodox populations evidently does not encourage interreligious dialogue.

Contacts with the Roman Catholic Church

Since the historic declaration *Nostra Aetate* on the relationship of the Church to the non-Christian religions (No. 4), issued by the Second Vatican Council on Oct. 28, 1965 (for text see *Church Councils), the implementation of the Vatican Council's decision was entrusted to the Secretariat for promoting Christian unity, headed by Cardinal Johannes Willebrands, and a special office within the Secretariat maintained contact with representatives of Judaism until October 1974. The aims of this office are: combating antisemitism and racial prejudices, the solution of the problems of human rights, and in general the desire to start an interreligious dialogue.

On Oct. 23, 1974, Pope Paul VI established a special commission with the aim of advancing and stimulating religious relations between Christians and Jews. The commission, having the status of an independent organism, is linked with the Secretariat for promoting Christian unity and is headed by Cardinal Willebrands. On Jan. 31, 1976, Pope Paul named eight consultants to the commission.

It is noteworthy that whereas the commission dealing with contacts with Judaism is linked with the Secretariat for Christian unity, a similar commission concerned with relations with Islam is linked with the Secretariat for non-Christian religions. The special relationship of Christianity with Judaism is thus also emphasized administratively. At a preliminary Catholic-Jewish consultation held in Rome in December 1970, it was recommended that an annual meeting of an international Catholic-Jewish Liaison Committee be held for the purpose of fostering mutual understanding between the two faiths and encouraging exchange of information and cooperation in areas of common concern and responsibility.

The first meeting took place in Paris in December 1971. Its five Catholic members, consisting of clergymen specializing in Jewish contacts, were appointed by Cardinal Willebrands, with the approval of Pope Paul VI. The six Jewish members represented the International Jewish Committee on Interreligious Consultations (IJCIC), comprising leading figures from the following Jewish organizations: the Union of American Hebrew Congregations, the World Jewish Congress, the Anti-Defamation League of B'nai B'rith, the Synagogue Council of America, the American Jewish Committee and the Jewish Council for Interreligious Consultations in Israel.

The second meeting was held in Marseilles in December 1972, at which preliminary papers on "Religious Community, People and Land in Jewish and Christian Traditions" were discussed. Information and views on subjects of common interest were also exchanged. The third annual meeting was held in Antwerp in December 1973, at which two papers on "People, Nation and Land" were submitted by Jewish and Catholic experts. The Committee also decided to initiate research on the moral and spiritual basis of human rights and religious liberty, according to the religious traditions of the two faiths.

The fourth meeting was held in Rome in January 1974, a month after the publication of the *Guidelines* by the Commission of the Catholic Church on Religious Relations with the Jews. The *Guidelines* and suggestions for implementing the Second Vatican Council declaration *Nostra Aetate* is a most important document. It was signed by Cardinal Willebrands, president of the commission, and by its newly appointed secretary Pierre Marie de Contenson O.P., and was issued with the aim of guiding Catholics in their attitude to Jews. It was expressly directed to the bishops and to the commissions or secretariats episcopally appointed for that purpose. The introduction to the document recalls the principal decision of Vatican Council II, condemning antisemitism and all forms of discrimination and imposing the obligation of reciprocal understanding and esteem. It advocates a better knowledge on the part of Christians of the essence of Jewish religious tradition and self-identification. The text contains a series of concrete suggestions. One section calls for fraternal dialogue and for the establishment of in-depth doctrinal research and recommends joint prayer meetings.

Mention is made of the links between Christian and Jewish liturgy and the caution needed in dealing with biblical commentaries, and with liturgical explanations and translations. The section dealing with teaching and education clarifies the nexus between the two Testaments. The question of the trial and death of Jesus is touched upon and stress laid on the note of expectation which characterizes both Judaism and Christianity. Specialists are invited to engage in serious research, and the establishment of university chairs of Hebrew studies is encouraged as well as collaboration with Jewish scholars. The final section deals with the possibilities of shared social action in the quest for social justice and peace. The *Guidelines* conclude with an allusion to the ecumenical aspect of relations with Judaism, the initiatives on the part of local Churches, and the essential lines of the work of the new commission set up by the Holy See.

The International Jewish Committee for Interreligious Consultation (IJCIC) welcomed the *Guidelines* at the annual meeting held in January 1974. Reservations were, however, made concerning the lack of reference to the central role of the Land of Israel in Jewish religious thought and what in its view were the concealed conversionist aims of the document and certain of its proposed interreligious activities.

In January 1975 the members of the Liaison Committee had an audience with Pope Paul VI who mentioned the difficulties and the confrontations that had marked contacts between Christians and Jews over the past two millennia. He expressed the hope that the dialogue, carried out in mutual respect, would help both sides to become better acquainted with one another.

The fifth meeting of the Liaison Committee took place in Jerusalem in March 1976 and it was regarded of special significance that for the first time the meeting was held in the capital of Israel. The main subject of this consultation was a joint assessment of major developments in Catholic-Jewish relations since the publication of the *Nostra Aetate*.

At the sixth annual meeting held in Venice in March 1977, the main item on the agenda was a study paper on "Mission and Witness of the Church." The paper, delivered by Professor Tommaso Federici, claimed that the Catholic Church clearly rejects every form of proselytism affecting the Jews, including any sort of witness and preaching which constitutes physical, moral, psychological or cultural constraint on the Jews, whether individuals or communities, which might destroy or even simply reduce their personal judgment, free will and full autonomy of decision. Rabbi Siegman, a member of the IJCIC, observed that the paper was a Catholic document dealing with theological issues, and as such its unqualified condemnation of proselytism among the Jews represented a notable advance in the Catholic Church which is bound to make for a deeper understanding between the two faiths. At this meeting the Catholic chairman introduced the newly appointed secretary, Reverend Jorge Mejia, who succeeded Father Contenson, who passed away in July 1976.

The seventh annual meeting was held in Madrid in April 1978. The opening session was held in the historic El Transito Church, formerly a *synagogue, which was returned to the Jewish community a few years earlier. The main topic of the meeting was "The image of Judaism in Christian education and the image of Christianity in Jewish education." Both sides noted significant progress in Catholic teaching on Judaism and Jewish teaching on Christianity. Information was exchanged on the recent Israeli law on conversion, the human rights situation in different countries, the resurgence of antisemitism, the Catholic-Muslim dialogue and contacts between Muslims and Jews. The discussions took place in an atmosphere of frankness and cordiality and were seen by both delegations as an important contribution to better mutual understanding. The members of the two delegations were, however, aware that there did not exist a perfect parallelism between the stand of the two sides because Judaism, unlike Christianity, links religion with peoplehood and land.

The eighth annual meeting took place in Regensurg (Bavaria) in October 1979. The significance of the meeting's being held in Germany was underlined in a telegram from Chancellor Helmut Schmidt. The two main subjects discussed at the encounter were: Religious Freedom, and Education for Dialogue in a Pluralistic Society.

Political Aspects of the Christian-Jewish Relationship

The influence of the political factor is particularly evident in the case of the Roman Catholic Church, since it is both a worldwide religion and a sovereign state. Although no formal diplomatic relations exist between the Vatican and the State of Israel, contacts have steadily improved during the past few years. Foreign ministers and high ranking Israeli officials met Pope Paul VI, his two predecessors, and dignitaries of the Vatican Secretariat. Highly significant was the audience granted by Pope Paul VI in January 1973 to Golda Meir, then Israel's prime minister. According to a joint statement released after the meeting, the Pontiff referred both to the sufferings of the Jewish people and to his humanitarian concern for the plight of the Arab refugees, He also expressed his concern regarding a solution to the problem of the status of the holy places and the maintenance of Jerusalem's universal character. The same solicitude for the Holy City was expressed by the pope during the audience granted in January 1977 to the late Foreign Minister Moshe Dayan. The late Pontiff showed his concern on a number of occasions in his speeches and meetings for the events taking place in the Holy Land and never discarded his proposal for the internationalization of Jerusalem, although he did not exclude other possibilities.

There is ample evidence of progress in the relationship between the State of Israel and the Holy See. Israeli official delegations were invited to the opening and closing sessions of the Vatican Council. Israeli official representatives were likewise invited to the funerals of deceased popes and to coronation ceremonies of the newly elected popes. Friendly messages were exchanged between presidents of Israel and Pope Paul VI, as well as his successors Pope John Paul I and Pope John Paul II. Since his election in October 1978, Pope John Paul II has granted private audiences to several Israeli representatives, among them the director general of the Foreign Ministry Yoseph Cjechanover and Ambassador Moshe Alon.

Political considerations have also influenced the attitude of the WCC toward Judaism and the people in Israel. The Arab Christian Churches, which are members of the WCC, have made their negative influence increasingly felt on the decisions of the prestigious Council, and in August 1980 the Council adopted a strong anti-Israel resolution at its conference held in Geneva, which *inter alia* urged member churches to "exert pressure on Israel through their respective governments to withhold any action on Jerusalem, the future of which should be included in negotiations on self-determination involving Israel and the Palestinian people." The WCC's Committee on the Church and the Jewish People stands, however, firmly for a relationship toward Judaism, uninfluenced by hostile political influence.

Contacts with the World Council of Churches

The relations of the WCC with Judaism have progressed in recent years and have become firmly established. It has its seat in Geneva and is an umbrella organization, the membership of which in the early 1970s was composed of 250 Churches from more than 80 countries, among them the majority of the Protestant Churches, the Anglican Church, the autocephalous Orthodox Churches, and Monophysite Churches.

The progress found its organizational expression in the inclusion of Judaism in the work of the sub-unit for Dialogue with People of Living Faith and Ideologies (Committee on the Church and the Jewish People), whereas previously the Committee functioned as a commission of the Division on Mission and Evangelism. This change in the administrative structure was carried out in conformity with the recommendations at the meeting in Addis Ababa of January 1971.The first joint meeting, opened by Dr. Eugene Blake, secretary general of the WCC, was held in June 1968. A further consultation was held in Locarno in October 1970.

A meeting cosponsored by the WCC and the IJCIC was held in Geneva in December 1972, the Jewish delegation consisting of representatives of the same bodies which met with the Catholic delegation. The principal theme of the meeting was "The Quest for World Community: Jewish and Christian Perspectives." Christian and Jewish scholars presented a series of papers, essaying to clarify common as well as divergent concepts and approaches to the organization of the world community as a "community of the communities." It likewise provided an opportunity for an exchange of views of the following subjects: the problem of violence; racism in South Africa; human rights in the Soviet Union; the Middle East conflict; the Bible and social justice; and Christian-Jewish cooperation in relation to international organizations for the advancement of human rights. At the initiative of the WCC a consultation was held at Cartigny, near Geneva, in January 1974, which was attended by some 30 Christians from various theological traditions and from different countries. The main topics were the Middle East conflict and the impact of the Bible on the present situation in the Holy Land.

A multilateral dialogue, sponsored by the WCC's Department for Dialogue with People of Living Faiths and Ideologies, took place at Colombo, Sri Lanka, Ceylon, in April 1974, and was attended by 50 participants from 22 countries and 5 living traditions: Hindu, Buddhist, Jewish, Christian, and Muslim. They discussed their resources and responsibilities toward the world community.

A meeting of representatives of the WCC and of the IJCIC was held in London in January 1975 to discuss the concept of power in Jewish and Christian tradition, its application to the contemporary social order and its bearing on joint search for world community.

On Apr. 1, 1975, Dr. Franz von Hammerstein succeeded Rev. Johan M. Snoek as secretary of the Council's agency for Consultation of the Church and the Jewish People (CCJP). Both were well acquainted with Jewish aspirations and needs, having resided in Israel for many years.

The next meeting between representatives of the WCC and the IJCIC was held in Jerusalem in February 1976 and opened with a report on the WCC Nairobi conference and a discussion on its resolution on the Middle East and the status of Jerusalem. In a preliminary debate on "Relations between Churches and the Jewish People in the Wider Context of the Human Community," regret was expressed that the WCC had not paralleled the Vatican in issuing guidelines on Christian-Jewish relations. It was, however, plain that publication of such a document would have to be ratified by a plenary session of the Council and such an attempt might be doomed to failure, in view of the composite structure of the Council.

A planning meeting held in Geneva in October 1976 was followed by a Christian-Jewish Consultation in Zurich in February 1977, under the auspices of WCC and the IJCIC. A number of papers were submitted on the "Jewish and Christian Traditions concerning Nature, Science and Technology."

At a meeting held in Jerusalem in June 1977, representatives of the CCJP began work on a draft of the WCC's guidelines for the Christian-Jewish dialogue. The IJCIC was invited to submit comments on the draft, and did so at a Liaison and Planning Committee (LPC) meeting in Geneva in February 1979. An Ad Hoc Committee of the CCJP gave further attention to the draft in March 1980.

In September 1979 Rev. Allan R. Brockway succeeded Dr. Franz von Hammerstein as secretary of the council's agency for the CCJP.

A meeting on "Science and Faith" took place in July 1979 at the Massachusetts Institute of Technology (MIT).

A conference, cosponsored by the IJCIC and the WCC, was held in Toronto, Canada, in August 1980, the theme being "Religion and the Crisis of Modernity."

Contacts with Representatives of the Orthodox Churches

In March 1977, under the aegis of the Lucerne University's Department of Theology, an unprecedented academic dialogue was conducted between Jewish leaders and the representatives of the Greek Orthodox Church. This initial meeting was followed by a much larger forum held in Bucharest, Romania, in October 1979, with representatives of the IJCIC meeting with Orthodox theologians from Bulgaria, Cyprus, France, Greece, Romania, Switzerland, and the United States. Following the presentation of papers, the discussions centered on the interpretation of scripture in tradition,

Contacts with National Churches

In February 1979, a two-day meeting took place in Berlin between representatives of the IJCIC and the European Lutheran Commission on the Church and the Jewish People. A decision was taken to appoint a committee of two members from each organization to ensure the maintenance of contact between them.

A meeting between the IJCIC and Consultants of the Anglican Church on Interfaith Consultations was held at Amport House, Andover, Hants in November 1980. The theme discussed was "Law and Religion in Contemporary Society."

Societies for Christian-Jewish Cooperation

In addition to the important Church bodies referred to, there exist in various European and American countries local organizations interested in fostering good relations between Christians and Jews and in combating antisemitism. Most of these societies were established during the Nazi period or immediately afterwards, in consequence of the shock produced by the terrible consequences of antisemitism. Both Catholic and Protestant Church leaders were active in such organizations. Among these societies are the Council of Christians and Jews in Great Britain, which publishes the quarterly *Common Ground*, and the National Conference of Christians and Jews in the U.S.A. of which Bernard J. Lasker was elected cochairman in March 1978. The other two cochairmen were William F. May representing the Protestant Church and Nicholas V. Petrov, the Eastern Orthodox. This body is 50 years old and has many branches with a considerable budget at its disposal. In 1947 these two societies convened an Emergency Conference at Seelisberg in Switzerland, and the "Ten Points" adopted then have served in the period under review as an important guide for the Protestant Churches in their attitude to Judaism.

Other important societies are the German Council for Jewish-Christian Cooperation, which has branches in many towns in Germany and publishes the bi-monthly *Emunah* ("Faith"); the Jewish-Christian Brotherhood in France which publishes the quarterly *Sens*; the Christian-Jewish Cooperation in Switzerland which publishes the magazine *Christlich-jüdisches Forum*; the Action against Antisemitism in Austria; the Christian-Jewish Fraternity of Brazil, which publishes *Encontro*; the Council of Christians and Jews in Canada; and the Swedish Association for Cooperation among Jews and Christians.

Recently the national societies interested in fostering Christian-Jewish friendship held joint consultations, in order to extend their activities and influence, in view of the recrudescence of antisemitism in many parts of the world. As a result, there was established the International Council of Christians and Jews (ICCJ), a federation of the various national brotherhoods with an annual rotating chairman. Meetings of the ICCJ have taken place in Vienna (1973); in Basel (1974); in Cologne (1974); in Hamburg (1975); in Jerusalem (1976); in Southampton (1977); in Luxembourg (1977); in Vienna (1978); in New York (1979); and in Sigtuna, Sweden (1980). An ICCJ International Youth Conference was held in Jerusalem in August 1980.

Declaration by National Churches and Other Ecclesiastical Organizations

Most important on the national level was the Declaration of the French Episcopal Committee, headed by Mgr. Elchinger, Bishop of Strasbourg. The Declaration, issued on the eve of Passover 1973, referred to the Jewish document adopted by the Vatican Council, and emphasized that the new approach to Judaism should be considered a beginning rather than an end. Of momentous weight were the references of the Declaration to the ingathering of the Jewish people in the Land of the Bible and the statement that the conscience of mankind cannot deny the Jewish people, which has undergone so many vicissitudes in the course of its history, the right and the means for its own political existence among the nations.

Of special importance also was the manifesto "Christians and Jews," issued by the German Evangelical Church in 1975. It emphasized the Jewish origins of the Christian Church, and examined Christian-Jewish relationships from a theological perspective. The manifesto also recognized that full realization of Jewish life has been bound up with the Land of Israel in all ages, and therefore the present State of Israel, albeit a political entity, must also be understood in the historical context of the Chosen People.

Consultations were held by the Lutheran World Federation, the American Lutheran Church, the Baptist Convention, the General Conference of the United Methodists, the Reformed Church of Holland, and the European Mennonites. In an address given in July 1977 to the Jewish Board of Deputies, the Archbishop of Canterbury said that love, not power, should rule the world and stressed his strong opposition to any sort of racial discrimination.

The Interconfessional Dialogue in Israel

The interconfessional dialogue in Israel has been fostered on the initiative of selected groups of Jewish and Christian scholars. Prominent in the interconfessional exchange is the "Rainbow Group," composed of Christian theologians and Jewish scholars, mainly professors of Bible and of comparative religion. The members of the group meet periodically to examine, compare, and evaluate their respective religious traditions and tenets.

Another interconfessional group is the Interfaith Committee, the aims of which are practical rather than scholarly. The committee has taken upon itself to guarantee that proper respect be shown to all creeds represented in the Holy Land. The Christian Fraternity of Theological Research, besides deepening ecumenical relations among Christian denominations, regards its task as the study of the attitude of those denominations toward Judaism. Active in the field of interconfessional dialogue are also the American Jewish Committee's office in Jerusalem, the Ecumenical Institute in Tantur near Jerusalem, the Ecumenical Discussion Center for Students in Jerusalem, and the Interreligious Group in Tel Aviv.

Whereas an interconfessional dialogue conducted between equals is considered positively by the majority of the Jews in Israel, all forms of Christian proselytizing activity among the Jews is deeply resented, and the main Christian Churches, aware of this, generally abstain from missionary activity, In practice, such activity is carried out mainly by some small Protestant sects, with little success. The mission problem, which from time to time agitates public opinion in Israel, became more acute with the appearance on the Israeli scene of the "Jews for Jesus Movement." Jewish religious quarters, which had always advocated antimissionary legislation, took the opportunity given by a change in the political constellation to pass in the Knesset a Penal Code Amendment which outlaws the use of bribery for religious conversion. The Amendment (enticement to change religion), enacted in December 1977, aroused concern in Christian and interfaith circles in Israel and abroad.

[Saul Paul Colbi]

Later Developments

Throughout the years since World War II, and under the impact of the revelation of the facts of the Holocaust and the establishment of the State of Israel, Christians individually and collectively have felt themselves impelled to reassess their relationships with Jews and Judaism, and at the very least to repudiate traditional antisemitism and the "teaching of contempt." This movement has been expressed in Church documents, in theological writings, and in dialogue with Jews. By 1985 the main lines had been drawn, and the last years of the 1980s were essentially a period of consolidation, and of educational initiatives to ensure that the guidelines of Churches would be absorbed into teaching and preaching. At the same time, however, a number of "sticking points" in the dialogue emerged clearly, and a series of incidents created tensions.

The Church of Rome

High level dialogue between the Roman Catholic Church and the Jewish people is undertaken by the International Catholic-Jewish Liaison Committee (ILC). On the Catholic side, this consists of representatives of the Holy See's Commission on Religious Relations with the Jews, an office within the secretariat for Promoting Christian Unity. On the Jewish side, the representative body is the International Jewish Committee on Interreligious Consultations (IJCIC), composed of the World Jewish Congress, the Synagogue Council of America, the American Jewish Committee, B'nai B'rith International-Anti-Defamation League, and the Israel Jewish Council for Interreligious Relations.

The 1985 meeting of the ILC took place on October 28–30 in Rome, and was a major commemoration and reassessment of the publication 20 years previously of *Nostra Aetate* no. 4, part of the "Declaration on the Relationship of the Church to non-Christian Religions," the Second Vatican Council document which paved the way for the subsequent development of Catholic attitudes to Jews and Judaism. The progress which had taken place in the intervening years was evaluated, a program for the future outlined, and the importance attached by the Church to the proceedings emphasized by an audience with Pope John Paul II. An added touch to all of the foregoing activity was the recognition, by a special lecture, of the 850th anniversary of the death of Maimonides.

The most substantial discussions at the Rome meeting, however, were in connection with the newly prepared Vatican document, "Notes on the correct way to present the Jews and Judaism in preaching and catechesis in the Roman Catholic Church." This "internal" Church document, intended to develop the teaching of *Nostra Aetate* and to help integrate it into the everyday life of the Church, met with a mixed response from the Jewish delegation. On the positive side, the State of Israel was for the first time mentioned in a Vatican document, Jewish suffering in the Holocaust recognized, the "ongoing spiritual vitality of Judaism" to modern times appreciated, and guidance given on how to interpret New Testament texts without deriving antisemitism from them. On the other hand, Jews were upset that they had not been fully consulted in preparing the document, felt that treatment of the Holocaust failed to acknowledge any Christian guilt, were dissatisfied with the lack of a positive theological evaluation of Israel, and detected inconsistencies in the theological sections, including remnants of typology and "replacement theology."

On Sunday April 13, 1986, Pope John Paul II made a historic visit across the Tiber to the Synagogue in Rome, where he was welcomed by Chief Rabbi Elio Toaff. The president of the Jewish community, Professor Giacomo Saban, reminded the pope of the illustrious history of the Roman Jewish community, extending back to pre-Christian times. Generally, the visit was welcomed by Catholic and Jewish leaders as a signal of the pope's personal commitment to carrying forward the initiative of *Nostra Aetate*; indeed, the pope lost no opportunity to address Jewish communities in the numerous cities he visited around the world, frequently welcomed visiting Jewish dignitaries at the Vatican, and used these occasions repeatedly to denounce antisemitism and to recognize Jewish sufferings in the "Shoah," as he consistently called the Holocaust.

It was at about this time that the *Auschwitz Convent controversy erupted (the Cracow Church's approval for the project had been given on September 30, 1984, without attracting attention), and plans for a major Consultation of the ILC on the subject of the Holocaust were postponed indefinitely. Relations were further exacerbated when the World Jewish Congress, in the form of a letter from its president, Edgar Bronfman, dated December 4, 1986, while declaring that its commitment to improving relations with the Catholic Church had never been stronger, launched a "global campaign" to force the Holy See to "recognize" Israel. Although the steering committee of the ILC continued to meet, no full Consultation took place until that in Prague in September 1990. One of the effects of this postponement was delay in producing a comprehensive Vatican statement on the Holocaust. Archbishop Edward (later Cardinal) Cassidy, who led the Catholic delegation at Prague in his capacity as president of the Commission on Religious Relations with the Jews in succession to Cardinal Willebrands, declared in his opening remarks "that antisemitism has found a place in Christian thought and practice calls for an act of *Teshuvah* (repentance) and of reconciliation on our part as we gather here in this city which is a testimony to our failure to be authentic witnesses to our faith at times in the past." The statement issued from the Prague meeting cited these words and was the first document with Vatican authority to acknowledge, if somewhat obliquely, Catholic guilt in relation to the Holocaust. The statement also stressed the educational task in Jewish-Christian relations, and the opportunities for common social work and spiritual witness. The statement was endorsed by John Paul II when he received the ILC on the occasion of the 25th anniversary of *Nostra Aetate* in December 1990.

Relations moved further ahead as a result of a Conference of the ILC in Baltimore in 1992 when the Vatican participants proposed the establishment of joint Catholic-Jewish delegations to appear before international bodies on matters of mutual concern. They also undertook to extend to other countries the initiative of the Italian bishops who had declared that one day a year in their dioceses would be devoted to the study of Judaism and the Jewish people. In the summer of 1992, the Vatican announced the opening of discussions with Israel for the normalization of relations between the two countries toward the establishment of diplomatic ties, which was finally achieved at the end of 1993. (See *Vatican for further developments.)

The World Council of Churches and Protestant Churches

The World Council of Churches (WCC), while unrelenting in its opposition to antisemitism, has progressed only slowly in dialogue in the period under review. This is thought to be partly because of political pressure from the Middle East Council of Churches, and partly because of the reluctance of some member Churches to abandon an actively evangelical approach toward non-Christians including Jews. Moreover, whereas the Catholic Church has several times stated that relations with Jews and Judaism are at the center of Christian concern, the World Council tends to place the matter lower on its scale of priorities. The World Council is an amorphous federation rather than a hierarchical structure like the Roman Church; it cannot determine standards from the top down, but must work on the basis of consensus.

Some progress was made at the "Consultation on the Church and the Jewish People" in Arnoldshain, West Germany, February 10–14, 1986, but the most significant advance was the document formulated at the November 1988 meeting at Sigtuna, Sweden, of the WCC's Committee on the Church and the Jewish People. This document recognizes the lack of consensus among its members on mission and on the significance of the Land of Israel, but claimed wide agreement for the following:

1. The covenant of God with the Jewish people remains valid.

2. Antisemitism and all forms of the teaching of contempt for Judaism are to be repudiated.

3. The living tradition of Judaism is a gift of God.

4. Coercive proselytism directed toward Jews is incompatible with Christian faith.

5. Jews and Christians bear a common responsibility as witnesses to God's righteousness and peace in the world.

In addition, it agreed nine affirmations, which recognized Israel's call, acknowledged the spiritual treasures shared by Jews and Christians, made clear that Jews should not be blamed for Jesus' passion, and expressed sorrow at the Christian share of responsibility for Jewish suffering, culminating in the Holocaust.

Like the Vatican, the WCC engages in dialogue at the highest level with IJCIC. One of their most notable joint ventures was an African Christian-Jewish Consultation which took place in Nairobi, Kenya, from November 10–13, 1986; the emphasis here was on the shared concern of Jews and African Christians with tradition and its relationship with Scripture. As was aptly remarked, "Scripture is not a European creation."

Since the WCC can work only by consensus, the statements of its individual constituent Churches are of significance.

The Anglican Communion held its own Consultation with IJCIC at Shallowford House, Stafford (England), in 1986, focusing on two issues of common concern to Jews and Anglicans, AIDS and inner city deprivation, though few who were present would deny that the high point of that Consultation was Dr. Gerhart Riegner's spontaneous and moving narration of the events of 1942 when, from his Geneva office, he had battled against immense resistance to inform the unbelieving world of the implementation of the "Final Solution."

This Consultation undoubtedly fed into the 1988 Lambeth Conference, the 10-yearly gathering of Anglican Bishops from around the world. For the first time in their history they devoted attention to Christian-Jewish relations, and produced and unanimously commended a document "Jews, Christians and Muslims: the Way of Dialogue." This, from assimilating the relationship with Judaism to that with all monotheists, clearly spelled out its special nature and obligations, Christian guilt for the "teaching of contempt" which provided the soil in which Nazism could thrive, and the nature of Judaism as a living religion not to be confused with a literal reading of the Old Testament.

The Lutheran Churches in Germany and elsewhere were among the first and most copious in the production of documents. The Lutheran European Commission "Church and the Jewish People," in its May 8, 1990, "Statement on the Encounter between Lutheran Christians and Jews" (Driebergen, Netherlands), recognizes that a prerequisite to a new, more tolerant relationship with the Jewish faith is "a partial renunciation of the requirement for evangelization of Jews, as well as the call for a self-critical analysis of the Lutherans' own theology."

Excellent statements and guidelines have emanated from other church groups within the WCC, such as Methodists and Presbyterians – and even from those outside the WCC, such as the Unification Church.

Special mention should be made of the June 12, 1990, "Statement by the Synod of the Reformed Church in Hungary on its Relations with the Jews," perhaps the first document of this nature to emanate from a non-Catholic Church in Central Europe since the imposition of communism, yet able to confess repentance in the words of a 1946 statement of its Reformed Free Council: "Under the responsibility resting upon us because of sins committed against the Jews, however late, we now ask the Hungarian Jews before God to forgive us."

The International Council of Christians and Jews and National CCJ's

Much of the dialogue at "grassroots" level is undertaken through local branches of the national Councils of Christians and Jews (CCJ's). The national councils are members of the International Council of Christians and Jews (ICCJ). With the admission in 1990 of CCJ's in Poland, Czechoslovakia, Hungary, and New Zealand, there are now 23 national groups.

Members of the national CCJ's are able to meet at the ICCJ's International Colloquium, held each year in a different country. In the period under consideration they have met in Dublin (1985), Salamanca (1986), Fribourg (1978), Montreal (1988), Lille (1989), and Prague (1990). The Salamanca meeting was notable for its strong Muslim participation, and some element of this has been maintained. At the Prague meeting, delegates from Central and East European countries outlined their local situations and problems. Each colloquium is combined with a women's symposium and a young leadership conference, though in 1990 the young leadership conference took place separately, in Israel.

ICCJ had sponsored other major meetings and initiatives, including "Identity and Commitment in the Religious Encounter," Jerusalem, December 1986. It had a first conference in Eastern Europe with its 1985 meeting in Budapest (see below). This was followed, in September 1987, with a second "Seminar of Jews and Christians from the East and the West" in Buckow, then East Germany – an occasion remarkable for the presence of 12 Israeli scholars. Together with the Konrad Adenauer Stiftung it held a Symposium of Jews, Christians and Muslims from May 29–June 2, 1988, in Sankt Augustin, near Bonn, where there was much discussion of the stereotypes which hinder mutual understanding.

The largest popular gathering in Christian-Jewish relations is the National Workshop of the NCCJ in the United States. Such workshops attract well in excess of a thousand participants.

Opening up the East

THE DIALOGUE. Long before the demise of communism in Central Europe in 1989, contact had been established with the Churches and with the small remaining Jewish communities and the foundations laid for a positive development in Jewish-Christian relations. At that time the Churches themselves were struggling to exist in the face of a hostile regime. This gave them a sense of solidarity with the Jewish minority, but as against this was the lack of familiarity with Western developments in Christian theology, lack of knowledge of Judaism, and lack of local Jews with knowledge of their own faith.

In November 1985 the International Council of Christians and Jews, together with the Interchurch Peace Council in Hungary, sponsored a four-day conference on "Jewish-Christian Dialogue and its Contribution to Peace." Hungary has not only a substantial Jewish community but also several native Jewish scholars. Mention has already been made of the September 1987 "Seminar of Jews and Christians from the East and the West" which took place in East Germany.

In Poland there had been, through much of the communist era, a fascination with Jewish culture, as manifested for instance in the continuation of the Yiddish theater, but only in the 1980s did a serious attempt at critical reassessment of the past commence. The pope, in his 1979 visit to Auschwitz, had perhaps initiated the process by referring there to "the great sufferings of the Jewish people." A highly significant series of articles appeared in the Catholic journals *ZNAK* and *Tygodnik Powszechny*, commencing in 1983; Jan Blonski's challenging 1987 article "The Poor Poles Look at the Ghetto" deserves special mention. In May 1986 the Polish Bishops' Conference set up a sub-commission (later upgraded to a full commission) to examine, in a Polish context, relationships with Jews and Judaism, and under its chairman, Bishop Henrik Muszynski of Wloclawek, this group has led the Polish church to take seriously the new attitudes to Jews and Judaism emanating from Rome, and in 1990 published a book of recent Catholic documentation on Judaism and the Jews. Since the beginning of the decade there have been large international scholarly gatherings on the history and culture of Polish Jews; the Jagellonian University at Cracow has a special department for these subjects. International conferences on Jewish-Christian relations have also taken place, including one arranged by the Bishops' Commission together with the Anti-Defamation League of B'nai B'rith (Tyniec, 1987), and another at Cracow in November 1989, at which the Catholic sponsors were the KIK (Catholic Intellectuals' Club) of Cracow, which has all along taken a leading part in these matters. Educational work has proceeded apace; 22 Polish seminary professors spent seven weeks in Chicago in 1989 studying together with rabbis and other Jewish scholars, and in April 1990 a British scholar, Rabbi Norman Solomon, lectured at the Academy of Catholic Theology in Warsaw.

THE CHURCHES AND THE RESURGENCE OF ANTISEMITISM. On the downside of the 1989 Central European rejection of communism has been a resurgence of antisemitism, coinciding with similar phenomena in Western Europe. It is difficult to know how much of this arises from Church influence, and how much from nationalist sentiment, but it has been interesting to observe the reactions of the Churches which, far from encouraging such attitudes, have been strongly condemnatory. In his letter of August 8, 1990, Dr. Emilio Castro, the general secretary of the World Council of Churches, reaffirmed the council's 1948 pronouncement that "antisemitism is a sin against God and man," reminded Christians of their special responsibility for antisemitism, and called upon them not to fail in resolute action against it. Responses from the Vatican and from the Lutheran World Federation were equally strong, and have been followed by declarations from numerous church bodies and leaders worldwide. The real interest focused on the Orthodox Churches which, though members of the World Council, have not previously evinced much interest in dialogue. They are dominant in many of the countries in which incidents have occurred; it was therefore reassuring that Archbishop Kirill, of the Russian Orthodox Church, unambiguously condemned, with the authority of January 30–31, 1990, meeting of his episcopal synod, "any teaching of hatred, violence or national exclusivity," though it remains to be seen to what extent this condemnation will influence the behavior of Russian Christians.

The problem is that although the Churches do indeed condemn antisemitism, they will continue to foster it unintentionally unless they can achieve the reinterpretation of basic Christian teachings in the light of the new theology, thus abandoning "replacement theology" and the "teaching of contempt." One should not underestimate the magnitude of such a task especially in countries where clergy training is minimal and old habits of thought persistent.

Latin America and the Theology of Liberation

Whereas for Europeans and North Americans the Holocaust casts its shadow over contemporary theology, the burning issue in South American and much third-world theology has been liberation from the centuries of bondage and oppression, even genocide, imposed by European Christian colonists, and from the grinding poverty and deprivation suffered by the masses still today. The biblical Exodus is the great paradigm for the theology of liberation, though too few liberation theologians have perceived its relevance to the story of the modern Jewish liberation from the bondage of European oppression and Nazism to the freedom of independent statehood in Israel. Still, the return through Exodus to the "Jewish Old Testament," and the emphasis of the new theology on "praxis" rather than theory, have combined with some influx of the new Catholic outlook on Jews and Judaism to enable serious Jewish-Christian dialogue to get under way.

The first Pan-American Conference on Catholic-Jewish Relations, jointly arranged by the American Jewish committee and the National Conference of Brazilian Bishops, São Paulo, Brazil, took place on November 3–5, 1985. The most recent major gathering was the November 1990 25th anniversary commemoration of *Nostra Aetate*, attended by Archbishop Cassidy, who agreed to transmit back to Rome a number of resolutions of the Brazilian National Commission on Catholic-Jewish Religious Dialogue, including a protest against the proposed canonization of Queen Isabella, and a denunciation of anti-Zionism as a current form of antisemitism.

Obstacles and Irritants

Incidents apart, there are two themes which constantly give rise to friction within the dialogue.

The first of these is the Christian commitment to evangelization. While the Roman Catholic Church and many other major Churches no longer target Jews, only a few Christians, whether because of the Holocaust or for more fundamental theological reasons, would demand the positive exclusion of Jews from evangelization. All nowadays reject coercive or deceitful evangelization, though definitions differ. However, a recent feature of Christian life has been the rise of small, independent evangelical sects who are beyond the control of the major Churches; some such groups do target Jews. Moreover, the 1990s were declared a "decade of evangelism," and a fine balance would have to be struck between mission and dialogue. The 1980s saw a strong growth of Jewish anti-missionary groups, and it is difficult for mainstream Jews and Christians engaged in serious dialogue to remain indifferent to the snapping at their heels on both sides. The second major topic of friction is Israel, and this has both a political and a theological dimension. On the political level, both Jews and many Catholics found it hard during the period under review to accept the failure of the Holy See to establish normal diplomatic relations with the State of Israel. Of course, only the Roman church had this problem, as other churches do not claim to be sovereign territories. What is often overlooked is the extent to which documents from the non-Roman Churches affirm the existence of Israel. For instance, the World Council of Churches, in the Statement on the Middle East it adopted at its Sixth Assembly in Vancouver in 1983 and upheld subsequently, unambiguously affirmed "the right of all states, including Israel and Arab states, to live in peace with secure and recognized boundaries," reflecting the terminology of United Nations Security Council Resolution 242. The Lambeth Conference Resolutions of 1988 were similarly forthright, though few churches have gone as far as the Hungarian Reformed Church which declared, in the document cited above, "We express our joy over the fact that our country established diplomatic relations with Israel."

Theological views differ. Conservative Evangelicals are often the strongest supporters of Israel, because they see the state as the fulfillment of prophecy, heralding the second coming of Jesus – and the conversion of any remaining Jews! The Roman Catholic Church made clear in the 1985 Notes that, while it understands the Jewish religious attachment to the Land, the Church itself related to the State of Israel solely on the basis of international law; Church spokesmen strongly denied that there was any theological impediment to full diplomatic relations. Others steer a middle course, seeing the restoration of the Jews to Israel as a significant divine act, but without commitment to literal interpretation of prophecy.

There are several irritants which one hopes will prove temporary rather than permanent sources of friction within the dialogue. The Auschwitz convent has been one of them, and the beatifications of Edith Stein and Maximilian Kolbe another. Requests for the beatification of Queen Isabella in 1992 have been formulated in certain Spanish Catholic circles. Several actions of the pope – his reception of Yasser Arafat and of Kurt Waldheim, some unfortunate Easter sermons – have been irksome. In the non-Catholic world Passion Plays, such as that at Oberammergau (greatly improved in 1990), have strained the Jewish-Christian relationship.

Conclusion

The 1980s saw a proliferation of writing in Jewish-Christian relations. Scholarly and deeply sensitive works appeared by Protestant scholars such as Hans-Joachim Krauss, Roy Eckardt, and Paul van Buren, and Catholics such as Franz Mussner, John Pawlikowski, and Eberhard Bethge. Churches of many denominations and in many countries produced statements and guidelines. Serious consideration has been given to the reinterpretation of fundamental Christian beliefs in the light of the new understanding of Jews and Judaism.

The Jewish-Christian dialogue reached a stage of maturity. It is not without problems and is not yet firmly rooted in either of the religious communities involved. The main task, however, remains that of education, of ensuring that the new insights of the Churches and their theologians actually become part of normal Christian teaching and preaching, not only in the better educated West, but amongst Christians in all lands.

For Vatican II and subsequent developments, see *Church, Catholic; *Church Councils.

Bibliographical Information

Christian-Jewish Relations, a quarterly published by the Institute of Jewish Affairs, London, in conjunction with the World Jewish Congress, published not only academic articles on the important themes, but the major documents and reports on events, including those in Israel. It ceased to appear in 1993. *Immanuel*, published by the Ecumenical Research Fraternity in Jerusalem, carries high-caliber theological and historical articles, many of them translations of Hebrew articles. Other journals carrying documentary and original material are the SIDIC newsletter published in Rome by the Sisters of Sion and *El Olivo*, published in Madrid by the Centro de Estudios Judeo-Cristianos.

The last years of the 1980s saw a proliferation of books summing up the dialogue so far. In 1988 the International Catholic-Jewish Liaison Committee published its account of "Fifteen Years of Catholic-Jewish Dialogue 1970–1985" through the official Vatican publishers. In the same year the World Council of Churches published its documents and those of member churches, with an illuminating commentary by Allan Brockway and others, and an authoritative Jewish account of the dialogue, *Jewish-Christian Relations since the Second World War* by Geoffrey Wigoder, also appeared in 1988. David Novak's *Jewish-Christian Dialogue: A Jewish Justification* was published in 1989. One of the most sensitive and balanced Christian accounts is Marcus Braybrooke's *Time to Meet: Towards a Deeper Relationship between Jews and Christians* (1990).

Of the documentary collections the most comprehensive (though there are lacunae) is Rolf Rendtorff and Hans Hermann Henrix's *Die Kirchen und das Judentum: Dokumente von 1945–1985*. For English readers, the two volumes of *Stepping Stones* edited by Helga Croner (1977 and 1985) are the most useful.

[Normon Solomon]

JEWISH CHRONICLE, English newspaper and the oldest Jewish periodical in existence. It first appeared on Nov. 12. 1841 under the editorship of D. *Meldola and M. *Angel and was issued subsequently as a weekly, until publication was suspended in May 1842. Publication was resumed in October 1844 as a fortnightly, with Joseph Mitchell as its editor, but in 1847 it became a weekly newspaper again and has remained so ever since. Mitchell was editor of the *Jewish Chronicle* until 1854, when he was succeeded by M.H. Bresslau. In the following year A. *Benisch became proprietor and editor and edited the newspaper until his death in 1878, save for the years 1869 to 1875 when Michael *Henry was editor. Benisch bequeathed the *Chronicle* to the *Anglo-Jewish Association who sold it to Asher I. *Myers, its new editor, Sydney M. *Samuel, and Israel David. Later it passed into the control of a limited company, where it has since remained. The *Jewish Chronicle* rapidly established itself as the leading journal of Anglo-Jewry. Its efficient news service and near monopoly of personal advertising of family events made its position unchallengeable, and it swallowed its principal competitors, the *Hebrew Observer* and the *Jewish World*. The *Chronicle* also prided itself on being a quality newspaper. Under the editorship of Asher Myers, lavish literary and historic articles appeared and for many years Israel *Abrahams edited a literary page. A supplement in modern Hebrew first came out in 1906 and a monthly literary supplement was brought out during the interwar years. Shortly before the outbreak of World War II, the *Jewish Chronicle* underwent considerable changes in format. After the war the newspaper steadily grew in size and by 1960 boasted a circulation of over 60,000 – more than three times the pre-war figure. At the same time the scope of the newspaper was considerably broadened. Events in Israel occupied increasingly more space, and the *Jewish Chronicle* also expanded its service of provincial, sports, and financial news and provided separate columns for women, children, teenagers, and students, thereby making it of interest to a wide cross section of Anglo-Jewry. It also ran an international Jewish news and feature service. From its inception, the *Jewish Chronicle* reflected Anglo-Jewry's desire for political and social equality in Britain and set out to arouse public opinion to the plight of Jews in Russia and later Romania. From 1891 to 1892 a monthly supplement called "Darkest Russia" was published, which gave detailed reports of the persecution of Russian Jews. The *Chronicle* was one of the first journals to inform the world of Nazi atrocities during World War II and later reported on outbreaks of antisemitism in the Soviet Union, Eastern Europe, and South America. Its viewpoint on domestic issues generally reflected that of the Anglo-Jewish establishment and upheld the authority of the chief rabbi and the Beth-Din. For many years the *Chronicle* was hostile to the Reform and Liberal movements, particularly during the editorship of Leopold *Greenberg, but the trend away from Orthodoxy in Anglo-Jewry led to a change in the newspaper's policy, and more space was given to developments in Progressive Judaism. At the same time the *Chronicle* became increasingly critical of the Orthodox position on halakhic issues, which it regarded as too rigid. When Rabbi Louis *Jacobs was passed over for the position as principal of Jews' College and later prevented from acting as minister of the New West Synagogue, the *Jewish Chronicle* – under the editorship of William Frankel – championed his cause against the authority of the chief rabbi, Beth-Din, and United Synagogue. The *Jewish Chronicle* consistently devoted considerable space to Israel and Zionism, and one of its first editors, Abraham Benisch, published news from Jerusalem, Tiberias, Safed, and Hebron. However, under the ownership of Asher Myers and Israel Davis, the paper was hostile to Zionism in line with the official line of the religious and lay leaders of the community. Nevertheless, on Jan. 17, 1896, the *Chronicle* published Herzl's first article "A Solution to the Jewish Problem," which appeared a month before *Der Judenstaat*, and with its editorial, "A Dream of a Jewish State" opened the readers' columns to a discussion of Herzl's plan. At the end of 1906 Israel David offered the *Jewish Chronicle* to Leopold J. Greenberg who, together with David *Wolffsohn, Joseph *Cowen, Jacobus H. *Kahn, and Leopold *Kessler, bought the shares. Greenberg became its editor in January 1907. He made the paper strongly Zionist. In 1917 the British government postponed publication of the Balfour Declaration for a week in order to allow the *Chronicle* to print the news at the same time as the rest of the press. The

Chronicle supported the formation of the Jewish Legion under Vladimir *Jabotinsky and, after the Palestine Mandate was allotted to Great Britain, the *Jewish Chronicle* remained firmly Zionist until Greenberg's death in 1931. In that year, Leopold Kessler became chairman of the board of directors, and the paper resumed a lukewarm Zionist line. In 1946 Ivan Greenberg was removed from editorship because of his support for Revisionism and John *Shaftesley was appointed in his place. In 1958 William Frankel became editor. David F. *Kessler, the son of Leopold Kessler, became the chairman and managing director of the Jewish Chronicle Ltd. Kessler remained editor until 1977, when he was succeeded by Geoffrey Paul (b. 1929), from 1977–90, and then by Edward J. Temko (b. 1952), from 1991. After the creation of the State of Israel it consistently maintained a sympathetic, though not always uncritical, attitude to the Jewish state, and is internationally known for its wide and intelligent range of opinion.

BIBLIOGRAPHY: C. Roth, *The Jewish Chronicle 1841–1941* (1949). **ADD. BIBLIOGRAPHY:** D. Cesarani, *The Jewish Chronicle and Anglo-Jewry, 1841–1991* (1994).

[Cecil Roth and Josef Fraenkel]

JEWISH COLONIAL TRUST, the first Zionist bank. The Jewish Colonial Trust (Juedische Colonial Bank) Ltd. was incorporated in London on March 20, 1899, in accordance with the decisions of the First and Second Zionist Congresses. Theodor *Herzl had been the leading proponent of this decision, as from the beginning he had foreseen the need for a powerful financial instrument for the political and economic realization of Zionism. In *Der Judenstaat* he had proposed the establishment of the "Jewish Company" for the orderly liquidation and transfer of the immigrants' capital; in his *Diaries* Herzl repeatedly spoke of the need for a strong financial instrument able to offer aid to Turkey in return for the granting of the desired "charter." Herzl's vision was of an organization like the East India Company, which had achieved a para-governmental status. The various aims of the institution are reflected in the Trust's Objectives, as set out in its statutes:

> To promote, develop, work and carry on industries, undertakings and colonization schemes… migration from or immigration into any country or countries… and in particular of persons of the Jewish race into Palestine, Syria and other countries in the East… To carry on the business of banking so far as… considered expedient incidentally to any other business of the company… To *acquire from any state* or other authority in any part of the world any *concessions, grants, decrees, rights and privileges whatsoever*… to seek and obtain openings for the employment of capital in Palestine, Syria and in any part of the world, and, with a view thereto, to prospect, examine, explore, test and develop any mining, landed, agricultural and other properties, and to dispatch and employ expeditions, agents and others.

The political-economic character of the Trust made it necessary to vest control over it, by way of Founder Shares, in the bodies of the Zionist Organization. The Trust's authorized capital was £2,000,000 in shares of £1 each, but it took three years (until 1902) before the statutory minimum of £250,000 that permitted it to commence operations was paid up. In that year in London the Trust incorporated the Anglo-Palestine Company, now Bank Leumi le-Israel BM, as its subsidiary for operations in Ereẓ Israel. Banking, considered an incidental business in the Trust's Objectives, became its main activity. Although the JCT planned to open branches and agencies in various Jewish centers, such as New York and Odessa, only one branch, in Whitechapel, was actually opened in 1905. The various Balkan wars slowed down the development of business in its early years, and the Trust suffered considerable losses in Russia during World War I. With the advent of the British Mandate, the Trust invested in new ventures in Palestine, such as the General Mortgage Bank, the Workers' Bank (Bank ha-Po'alim), the Palestine Electric Corporation etc., and became deeply involved in some Jewish banking ventures in Eastern Europe, such as the Lodz Deposit Bank and the Jewish Central Bank, Kovno. In consequence of the economic depression, most of these latter assets, exceeding £550,000, became frozen or doubtful. Thus a reorganization of the Trust became necessary in 1933, and as of Jan. 1, 1934, the Trust handed over its banking business and investments in Palestine to the Anglo-Palestine Bank (formerly Anglo-Palestine Company). Profits on a share issue of the latter enabled the Trust to recover its share capital of £395,000 and £95,000 of its reserves. Since then the Trust has been solely the holding company for Anglo-Palestine Bank (Bank Leumi) shares.

In 1955 the Trust was converted into an Israel company under its original Hebrew name of Oẓar Hityashevut ha-Yehudim. Its share capital in 1969 was increased from IL. 7,000,000 to IL. 10,000,000 by issue of bonus shares, and a 12% dividend was declared for 1968. The Trust holds 23.5% of Bank Leumi's outstanding share capital, but 88.3% of the (controlling) ordinary shares (as of March 31, 1969).

[Kurt Grunwald]

JEWISH COLONIZATION ASSOCIATION (ICA), philanthropic association to assist Jews in depressed economic circumstances or countries of persecution to emigrate and settle elsewhere in productive employment, founded by Baron Maurice de *Hirsch in 1891. It was incorporated in London as a joint-stock company whose other shareholders were Baron Edmond de *Rothschild, J. *Goldsmid, Sir Ernest Joseph *Cassel, F.D. *Mocatta, Benjamin S. Cohen, S.H. Goldschmidt, and Salomon *Reinach. In 1893 de Hirsch's shares were distributed between the *Anglo-Jewish Association, and the Jewish communities of Brussels, Berlin, and Frankfurt. The basic endowment was later increased to £8,000,000. The association's offices were located in Paris until transferred to London in 1949. De Hirsch was president until his death in 1896. He was succeeded by Salomon Goldsmid (1896), Narcisse *Leven (1896–1919), Franz *Philippson (1919–29), Lionel Leonard *Cohen (1929–34), Sir Osmond d'Avigdor *Goldsmid (1934–40), Leonard Montefiore (1940–47), and Sir Henry Joseph d'Avigdor *Goldsmid (1947–). De Hirsch's immediate plan envisaged a mass emigration of the Jews from countries in Europe, where they were persecuted, to *Argentina, though circumstances forced ICA to give priority to the various needs of Jews in Europe.

EMIGRATION

Emigration was the cornerstone of ICA's activity throughout its history. From 1904 to 1914 ICA established 507 emigration committees in Russia, and a central office in St. Petersburg, with the approval of the Russian government. In New York the Hirsch Fund established a trade school in 1891 in order to prepare new immigrants for the task of earning a living. The large-scale immigration into America in the early 20th century led ICA and the Jewish Agricultural and Industrial Aid Society jointly to establish the Removal Committee. This organization linked immigrants in America with their relatives remaining in Europe. Information bureaus sprang up all over Europe, and by 1912 the Removal Committee had helped over 70,000 immigrants. In 1922 this organization was dissolved. After World War I many countries closed their doors to immigration, and new conditions demanded a new machinery. ICA's initiative led to the creation of immigration societies in Canada, Argentina, and Brazil. In 1921 ICA called a conference in Brussels and in 1922 in Paris for the establishment of a united emigration association. The conferences failed, but in 1925 the United Evacuation Committee was formed by ICA jointly with Emigdirekt and the *American Jewish Joint Distribution Committee (JDC). In 1927 *Hias (Hebrew Sheltering and Immigrant Aid Society), ICA, and Emigdirekt founded a new association, *Hicem, which had established 57 committees in 21 countries by 1937. In 1928 ICA formed an emigration bureau in Moscow to supervise emigration from Russia, and at the instigation of ICA all the private organizations dealing with emigrants jointly set up a committee for their protection, with its seat in Geneva. From 1933 to 1939 ICA spent £800,000 on the emigration of Jews from Germany.

AID AND SETTLEMENT

Eastern Europe

AGRICULTURE. In 1898 ICA began a detailed investigation into the position of the Jews in Russia and published the results in 1904 in the *Recueil des matériaux sur la situation économique des israélites de Russie*. In the different areas of Jewish settlement there, ICA officials worked to improve local farming methods, introduce new crops, and establish cooperatives, with the result that output rose considerably. During World War I the agricultural population in Russia was reduced by one-quarter. By 1930, due to ICA's efforts, 43 of the former colonies had been reestablished and supported a population of over 30,000. In the late 1920s ICA also successfully established a few thousand families on 50 new colonies founded on land provided by the government in south Ukraine.

In Poland ICA founded and supported eight agricultural cooperatives, and by 1930 had purchased some 2,500 hectares of land for the enlargement of existing small holdings. In Romania, ICA repaired the wartime damage and in 1930 established a new colony in southern Bessarabia.

EDUCATION. By 1914 ICA had established or supported some 40 technical and agricultural schools in Russia, ran adult education courses, and subsidized Jewish primary education. After the war ICA restored the majority of these schools to their prewar position, supporting them until they could exist independently. In Romania, ICA was subsidizing approximately 46 schools by 1914. In Galicia a number of technical and agricultural schools were founded, the most well-known being the agricultural school in Slobodka-Lesna, established on land acquired by ICA in 1900. The school flourished until it was damaged and closed during World War I. In postwar Poland ICA also reorganized the school system and introduced institutions for adult education in the centers of Jewish population.

COOPERATIVE LOAN AND SAVINGS BANKS. ICA established a network of cooperative loan and savings banks in Russia for farmers and artisans. From 1905 the Russian government allowed their unrestricted development and they spread rapidly, flourishing until World War I. By 1914, 680 such funds with over 450,000 members, and covering a sum of 40,000,000 roubles, had been organized and financed by ICA, a pioneer in this field. ICA resumed this work in 1922, in conjunction with the American Jewish Joint Distribution Committee, creating in 1924 the American Joint Reconstruction Foundation (AJRF). Its main aim was to continue the prewar work by supporting existing credit funds and creating new ones. In 1924 there were 322 such institutions in the 12 countries where the foundation worked. By 1930 the AJRF was supporting 760 loan banks with 325,000 members and a capital of 3,555,000 dollars. The association also established commercial banks for middle-class clients from 1930, supported workers' cooperatives, and rebuilt housing destroyed during the war. World War II ended all this activity, and in 1951 the AJRF was liquidated.

Argentina

In 1889 ICA aided Jewish immigrants in Argentina who purchased approximately 100,000 hectares of land in Santa Fé. They established the colony of Moisésville, and created a number of new settlements in the provinces of Santa Fé, Entre Ríos, La Pampa, and Buenos Aires, mainly before World War I. The colonists were given equipment, instruction, and credit, and a network of schools was established. By 1930, the peak of ICA settlement in Argentina, over 20,000 colonists farmed approximately 500,000 hectares of land, nearly half of which was owned by settlers who became independent. Progress was hampered by insufficient land for extensive cultivation and the unfavorable location of many of the colonies. The settlers attacked a system which permitted the repayment of debts and independence only over a long period of time; cooperatives also led a struggle against the ICA bureaucracy. During the 1930s several hundred families from Germany were settled on the land, but town life attracted many, and by 1966 only 8,000 Jews remained in the ICA colonies, the population there being largely non-Jewish. Nearly all of the settlers by then owned their land and ICA's role in Argentina was rapidly diminishing.

Brazil

In 1904 ICA acquired land in the Rio Grande do Sul area, and a small colony was established for settlers from Bessarabia. The colony did not prosper and in 1928 was virtually liquidated. A further colony of 93,000 hectares was established in 1909 in Quatro Irmãos, but disintegration began before World War I. ICA tried to revive the colony by resettlement, but political troubles combined with mismanagement led to its liquidation in 1965. One further attempt at Brazilian settlement failed in the 1930s when ICA selected families in Germany for settlement on 2,000 hectares purchased in the State of Rio de Janeiro. From 1953 the Brazilian government followed a more liberal immigration policy, but potential settlers were lacking. By 1960 large areas of land held by ICA had been liquidated. Meanwhile ICA had established educational institutions and credit facilities in the main centers of Jewish settlement and from 1954 onward continued to support the latter in conjunction with the American Joint Distribution Committee.

United States

In 1891 Baron de Hirsch established the Baron de Hirsch *Fund with the aim of aiding Jewish immigrants to the United States and promoting the establishment of rural centers there. The fund founded the agricultural school of Woodbine in New Jersey and several others, and became the main organ used by ICA for its own work in the U.S. In 1900 the two organizations jointly established the Jewish Agricultural and Industrial Aid Society (later the *Jewish Agricultural Society), which acquired land in New York, New Jersey, Pennsylvania, and Connecticut in order to settle Jewish immigrants on the land. By World War I, 78 farms had been established. The main work of ICA in the United States was not, however, this small-scale colonization but the provision of credit facilities for the immigrants. By 1930, ICA had distributed over 10,000 loans. Work in the educational field was less successful, and Woodbine was closed down during the interwar years. By the outbreak of World War II ICA's activities in the United States had virtually ceased.

Canada

In 1892 ICA established the colony Hirsch in the province of *Saskatchewan in *Canada, where some Jewish families had already settled in the 1880s, and aided individual immigrants arriving from Russia in the early 20th century. Until 1903 the Jewish Agricultural Society of New York managed ICA's colonization work in Canada and several new colonies were established in *Manitoba and Saskatchewan. In 1909 their supervision passed to a Canadian committee formed for this purpose. By 1910 ICA had founded or aided five main colonies with a population of 777 on an area of 49,914 acres, and a few smaller centers. The Canadian government refused to sell larger expanses of land, blocking the way to a more extensive settlement. The economic position after World War I led to the disintegration of the smaller centers. ICA tried to expand the more successful colonies, establishing 40 farms for new immigrants by 1930. After World War II, ICA settled a number of people from displaced persons' camps in the fertile Niagara peninsula and south Ontario, and by 1960 approximately 120 families were farming under the auspices of ICA.

Ereẓ Israel

From 1896 ICA provided financial aid for independent colonists in Gederah, Ḥaderah, Nes Ẓiyyonah, and Mishmar ha-Yarden. In 1899 Baron Edmond de Rothschild transferred to ICA the colonies under his care, and those he himself had founded, providing 15,000,000 francs to finance their further development. He presided over an administrative body, the Palestine Commission, formed in Paris. In the Rothschild colonies ICA introduced new forms of cultivation and other reforms. ICA also continued its previous independent work and purchased land in Lower Galilee in order to found new settlements, Jabneel (Yemma), Bet Gan, Mesḥa (Kefar Tavor), Sejerah (Ilaniyyah), and others. Despite progress, ICA's work was continuously attacked by Zionist opponents who accused it of inept management, wasted funds, and diverse aims. During World War I Rothschild realized that impending political changes necessitated the formation of a stronger organization and established the Palestine Jewish Colonization Association (*PICA) in 1923. This returned the colonies to a direct Rothschild administration. ICA resumed work in Palestine after the 1929 riots, establishing Emica jointly with the Emergency Fund. Plans for draining the Ḥuleh swamps were stopped by the outbreak of war, but Emica reconstructed Be'er Toviyyah and founded other settlements: Kefar Warburg, and later Nir Banim, Sedeh Moshe, Kefar Maimon, and Lachish. In 1955 Emica became "ICA in Israel," as Israel became the main field of activity. Jointly with the Jewish Agency, ICA participated in the development of Upper Galilee and in a project to assist some 30 immigrant settlements. In addition to credit facilities for agriculture, ICA provides extensive grants for educational institutions in Israel, among them Mikveh Israel, ORT, and the agricultural faculty of the Hebrew University.

Cyprus and Turkey

In 1897, at the request of the British government, ICA transferred 33 Russian refugee families from England to Cyprus, establishing three small colonies there. This venture failed and after a few years the settlers re-emigrated. In 1891 ICA bought land near Smyrna in Turkey, and established an agricultural training center, Or Yehudah, on an area totaling 3,000 hectares by 1902. Owing to numerous difficulties the center was closed in 1926. A group of Romanian Jews in Anatolia were assisted by ICA in the early 20th century, and a small-scale Russian immigration led ICA to establish an immigration bureau in Constantinople in 1910. ICA also bought land in Anatolia and Thrace, and founded Mesillah Ḥadashah and two other agricultural settlements for several hundred families. During

World War I the settlers were forced to leave, and in 1928 the colonies were practically liquidated, only the immigration bureau remaining to assist migrants in transit for Ereẓ Israel.

WORLD WAR II AND AFTER

ICA found new fields of work as older ones dwindled in importance, Israel becoming the major concern. ICA also began to help North African Jewry, developing credit facilities in Tunisia and Morocco, in conjunction with the JDC, and founding an agricultural training center in Morocco. In 1952 ICA and the Alliance Israélite Universelle jointly founded the Société Agricole pour les Israélites Marocains. From 1965 ICA cooperated with the United Hias Service, contributing substantially to the "Special Rescue Program" for the transportation of emigrants from Eastern Europe and North Africa to Australia, Canada, and France. There ICA organizes mortgage facilities, and in Kenya provides loans for agriculture. Miscellaneous Jewish institutions in Britain, France, Belgium, Israel, Argentina, and Brazil receive financial assistance as in the past, special attention being paid to education and culture.

BIBLIOGRAPHY: *Rapport de l'administration centrale au conseil d'administration* (1898–1931); *Atlas des colonies et domaines de la Jewish Colonization Association en République Argentine et au Brésil* (1914); *Le Baron Maurice de Hirsch et la Jewish Colonization Association; à l'occasion du centenaire de la naissance du Baron de Hirsch* (1932); *Jewish Colonization Association; Its Work in the Argentine Republic, 1891–1941* (1942); M.D. Winsberg, *Colonia Barón Hirsch; A Jewish Agricultural Colony in Argentina* (1964); K. Grunwald, *Tuerkenhirsch* (1966).

[Ann Ussishkin]

JEWISH COMMUNAL SERVICE ASSOCIATION OF NORTH AMERICA, THE (JCSA). The JCSA was founded in 1899 as the Conference of Jewish Charities. JCSA links together highly skilled and knowledgeable professional Jewish leadership in pursuit of the shared goals of advancing the Jewish community and enhancing professional development. JCSA assists local, regional, national and international efforts to enhance professional knowledge, research, education, and networking through:

(a) promoting and sustaining professional standards for the field;

(b) supporting and connecting the independent activities of local groups of Jewish communal professionals in Atlanta, Baltimore, Boston, Chicago, Cleveland, Los Angeles, Miami, New Orleans, New York, New Jersey, Philadelphia, and St. Louis;

(c) supporting and connecting the independent activities of affiliated professional associations such as the Association of Jewish Aging Services, the Association of Jewish Center Professionals, the Association of Jewish Community Organization Professionals, the International Association of Jewish Vocational Services, the Jewish Social Services Professionals, the North American Association of Synagogue Executives, and the World Council of Jewish Communal Service;

(d) providing special courses and seminars designed to advance the careers of professionals and to enhance their ability to serve the Jewish community, including an annual program meeting;

(e) advocating for family friendly work policies and gender equity through such sponsored activities as JCSA Networking Parents;

(f) promoting the recruitment and retention of personnel through Networking Express, the JCSA Graduate Students Network, and the Young Professional of the Year Award;

(g) offering group retirement, insurance policies, and other personnel benefits through the JCSA Benefits Program;

(h) Publishing the *Journal of Jewish Communal Service*, a quarterly review of professional trends and developments, and a monthly e-newsletter.

JCSA's website address is www.jcsana.org and inquiries can be sent to info@jcsana.org.

[Brenda Gevertz (2nd ed.)]

JEWISH COUNCIL ON PUBLIC AFFAIRS (JCPA; formerly, **The National Jewish Community Relations Advisory Council**). The JCPA was formally established as the National Community Relations Advisory Council (NCRAC) in 1944 by the Council of Jewish Federations, with the object of formulating policy and coordinating the work of national and local Jewish agencies in the field of community relations in the United States. NCRAC was designed to be the public affairs branch of the organized Jewish community; its name has been changed twice. The first time, in 1968, just after the June 1967 War, the word Jewish was added to make it the National Jewish Community Relations Advisory Council and emphasize a fact that had previously not been manifest – that this was a Jewish organization – and a second time, in 1997, it was changed to the Jewish Council for Public Affairs to more accurately reflect its mission.

Before 1944, as organized antisemitic activity became a serious problem in the United States, there was much overlapping and competition among the Jewish organizations seeking to combat it. The Jewish Welfare Funds, beset with claims for support, exercised pressure for the coordination of activities, and the result was the establishment of the Council. It was composed initially of four national organizations and 14 local community relations councils. The purpose was to enable member agencies to exchange views and to work together voluntarily, while each member retained full autonomy.

While the Council secured a measure of coordination, competitive activity and jurisdictional conflicts remained, and in 1950, at the insistence of the larger welfare funds, the Council instituted a study of Jewish community relations work. The result was the R.M. MacIver Report, under which the authority and responsibilities of the Council would have been enlarged considerably and separate spheres of activity allotted to its member agencies. The Council generally favored these proposals, but the result was the withdrawal from membership of its two most active constituents, the American Jewish

Committee and the B'nai B'rith (1952). The latter returned to membership in 1965 and the Committee in the following year on terms which emphasized the autonomy of the member organizations. In 1968 the membership of the Council consisted of nine national organizations and 81 state or local community relations councils.

The Jewish Council for Public Affairs (JCPA) serves as the representative voice of the organized American Jewish community in addressing the mandate of the Jewish community relations field. The mandate is expressed in two, interrelated goals: (1) to safeguard the rights of Jews in the U.S., in Israel, and around the world; and, in order to accomplish that, (2) to protect, preserve, and promote a just American society, one that is democratic and pluralistic.

These goals are pursued in a non-partisan manner informed by Jewish values. The Council's dual goals link the safety and security of Jewish interests with the protection of American democratic traditions and social justice at home. The Jewish community, it believes, has a direct stake – along with an ethical imperative– in assuring that America remains a country wedded to the Bill of Rights and committed to the rule of law, whose institutions continue to function as a public trust.

The JCPA reflects a unique and inclusive partnership of national member agencies, local community relations councils and committees, and the federations of which they are a component part or affiliated agency. It convenes the "common table" around which member agencies, through an open, representative, inclusive and consensus-driven process, meet to identify issues, articulate positions, and develop strategies, programs, and approaches designed to advance the public affairs, goals and objectives of the organized Jewish community.

The work of the JCPA, especially in matters relating to democratic pluralism and social justice, reflects the organizations emphasis on the Jewish value of *tikkun olam*, the repair of the world. It expresses the conviction of the organized Jewish community that it must be active in the effort to build a just society. The JCPA has the responsibility to enhance the capacity of member agencies to effectively pursue the public affairs agenda. This responsibility requires the JCPA to provide coordination, support, and guidance for public affairs initiatives undertaken by national and local member agencies, to advocate on behalf of the public affairs policies of the organized Jewish community, and to respond to those member-identified needs which strengthen their individual and collaborative capacity to advance the communal public affairs agenda.

Among the national organizations that constitute JCPA are each of the major Jewish defense agencies, ADL, *American Jewish Committee and *American Jewish Congress (aside from the *Simon Wiesenthal Center), the major religious denominations, *Hadassah, and the *Jewish Labor Committee, the *Jewish War Veterans, *National Council of Jewish Women as well as 122 local equal and independent partner agencies. The JCPA serves as a catalyst that heightens community awareness, encourages civic and social involvement, and deliberates key issues of importance to the Jewish community.

[Michael Berenbaum (2nd ed.)]

JEWISH CULTURAL RECONSTRUCTION, INC. (JCR), organization established in 1947 to deal with the collection and redistribution of heirless Jewish cultural property in the American Zone of Germany, centered in Offenbach and later in Wiesbaden. Its headquarters were in New York and its logistical and financial support came from the Jewish Restitution Successor Organization (JRSO). Its leadership was comprised of some of the foremost Jewish intellectuals of the day: Salo *Baron was its executive director; Joshua *Starr and later Hannah *Arendt served as executive secretaries. Gershom *Scholem, Shlomo Shunami, Bernard Heller, Mordechai *Narkiss, and E.G. Lowenthal were among those working in conjunction with JCR in Europe. Under the American Restitution Law (no. 59), JCR functioned as a trustee for those Jewish cultural items whose owners or heirs could not be located. By the end of its operations in 1951–52, JCR had redistributed hundreds of thousands of books and thousands of Torah scrolls and other ritual objects to major libraries and museums, including the Library of Congress and Bezalel in Jerusalem, as well as to institutions of higher learning such as the Jewish Theological Seminary in New York. A total of 85% of the cultural property was sent to Israel and the United States; 8% was allocated to Western European countries (with half going to Britain) and the remaining 7% was distributed to South Africa, Argentina, Brazil, Australia, Canada, and West Germany. Although it had no international standing, the organization encouraged the establishment of similar bodies in the British and French Zones of Occupation.

BIBLIOGRAPHY: B. Heller, "Operation Salvage," in: *The Jewish Horizon*, 6 (Feb. 1950), 12–14; M.Kurtz, "Resolving a Dilemma: The Inheritance of Jewish Property," in: *Cardozo Law Review*, 20, no. 2 (1998–99), 625–55; *Scopus*, 13, no. 2 (1959), 5f.; R. Waite, "The Return of Jewish Cultural Property: Handling of Books Looted by the Nazis in the American Zone of Occupation," in: *Libraries and Culture* (July 2002), 213–28.

[Dana Herman (2nd ed.)]

JEWISH DAILY FORWARD (Yid. **Forverts**), U.S. Yiddish newspaper. Established in New York in 1897 as a more moderate offshoot of the militantly left-wing *Abendblatt* the *Forward* was in its heyday the wealthiest and most widely read Yiddish newspaper in the United States, with 11 local and regional editions reaching as far west as Chicago. Under the editorship of Abraham *Cahan, who ruled the paper for nearly half a century, from 1903 to 1951, for much of the time with the assistance of general manager Baruch Charney *Vladeck, the *Forward* combined conscientious journalism with a partisan commitment to democratic socialism and the Jewish labor movement. It published stories and serialized novels by such authors as Sholem *Asch, Jonah *Rosenfeld, Zalman *Shneour,

Abraham *Reisin, Israel Joshua *Singer and his brother Isaac *Bashevis Singer, gave lessons in English and other subjects for old and new immigrants, and counseled and consoled several generations of readers with its famous advice column, the *Bintel Brif* ("Bundle of Letters"). Its *Forward* building, completed in 1908, was from the first a landmark on New York's Lower East Side, where it housed the headquarters of the United Hebrew Trades, the Workmen's Circle, the Jewish Socialist Federation, and other organizations, and served as a center for the Jewish labor movement in the United States. The paper's peak circulation of nearly 200,000 was reached during World War I, when the intervention of Louis *Marshall barely saved it from being shut down by the U.S. government for its pro-German sympathies; thereafter its readership declined steadily, like that of the rest of the Yiddish press, though increased advertising revenues in the 1920s and 1930s cushioned it financially and even enabled it to launch its own Yiddish radio station, WEVD. At the time of Cahan's death in 1951 the *Forward*'s circulation had fallen to 80,000, while in 1970 it was officially put at 44,000. In 1983, it was forced to become a weekly. Editors after Cahan were Hillel *Rogoff (1951–62), Lazar Fogelman (1962–68), Morris Crystal (1968–70), Simon Weber (1970–87), and Mordechai Strigler (1988–98).

From 1990, it published the weekly *Forward* in English as well as the Yiddish *Forverts*. The English *Forward* was edited by Seth Lipsky, who was replaced in July 2000 by J.J. Goldberg. In 1995–2005 the Forward Association also published the Russian *Forverts*. In 1998, the Yiddish prose-writer Boris Sandler (born in 1950 in Soviet Moldova), was appointed as editor of the Yiddish *Forverts*.

BIBLIOGRAPHY: R. Sanders, in: *Midstream*, 4 (1962), 79–94; J. Chaikin, *Yidishe Bleter in Amerike* (1946), index; H. Rogoff, *Der Gayst fun Forverts* (1954); A. Cahan, *Bleter fun Mayn Lebn*, 3 (1926), 4 (1928), 5 (1931), index; J. Teller, *Strangers and Natives* (1968), index. **ADD. BIBLIOGRAPHY:** J.C. Rich, *The Jewish Daily Forward* (1967); I. Metzker, *A Bintel Brief* (1981).

[Hillel Halkin / Gennady Estraikh (2nd ed.)]

JEWISH DAY (Yid. *Der Yidishe Tog*), U.S. Yiddish daily. Founded in 1914 by a group of New York City intellectuals and businessmen led by Judah *Magnes and Morris Weinberg, *The Day* aspired from the first to be a nonpartisan, liberal newspaper of high literary and journalistic standards that would enable it to live up to the slogan on its masthead, "The newspaper of the Yiddish intelligentsia." Under the editorship of William Edlin, it assembled a gifted staff that included critic Samuel *Niger; playwright David *Pinski; poet and essayist Aaron *Glanz; and reporters Joel Slonim, Peretz *Hirshbein, and Abraham *Coralnik. Its regular contributors included such outstanding figures as the novelist Joseph *Opatoshu and the poet *Yehoash. *The Day* reached a peak circulation of 81,000 in 1916. Thereafter, in common with the rest of the Yiddish press, and despite its absorption of Louis Miller's *Die Warheit* in 1919, its circulation declined. Throughout the 1930s, the paper was ridden by feuding between a politically conservative faction led by editor Samuel *Margoshes and a left-wing element headed by the Yiddish journalist and author B.Z. *Goldberg. The conflict contributed to a bitter six-month strike in 1941 that almost led to the *Day*'s extinction. However, the paper survived to merge with the **Jewish Morning Journal* in 1953. In 1970 the circulation of the combined *Day-Morning Journal* was estimated at 50,000. In 1971 the paper ceased publication.

BIBLIOGRAPHY: J. Chaikin, *Yidishe Bleter in Amerike* (1946), index; J. Teller, *Strangers and Natives* (1968), 32–36.

[Hillel Halkin]

JEWISH EDUCATION SERVICE OF NORTH AMERICA (JESNA). The Jewish Education Service of North America (JESNA) formally came into being on July 1, 1981 as the successor agency to the *American Association for Jewish Education (AAJE) founded in 1939.

In 1978, AAJE and the *Council of Jewish Federations (CJF) jointly appointed a "Committee to Consider Future Directions of the AAJE" which affirmed the need for a continental instrument for Jewish educational planning and services for the federation system. An Implementation Committee supervised the restructuring of the agency into JESNA and put in place a new governance in accordance with the recommendation of the Study Committee.

JESNA's goal is to make engaging, inspiring, high quality Jewish education available to every Jew in North America. Operating as a national resource, a community partner, a catalyst and a consultant, an innovator and a guarantor of quality, JESNA helps to recruit and prepare new generations of talented, committed Jewish educators; create and identify models of excellence in educational practice; and assist communities and front-line institutions in improving their programs and performance.

JESNA partners with local Jewish communities and with a dynamic and a growing group of individuals, organizations, institutions, and foundations to create consistent excellence in Jewish education. In addition, JESNA works closely with the central agencies for Jewish education that operate in more than 60 communities, and the Jewish federations in more than 150 communities, throughout North America.

JESNA has become a leading force promoting consistent excellence in Jewish education through a combination of high-quality community services and innovative initiatives that address Jewish education's foremost challenges. JESNA is responsive to the evolving needs of the community, which in the early 21st century focused on three overarching areas of activity:

a) People: Recruiting talented educators and creating the conditions that will enable them to thrive;

b) Best Practice: Identifying and disseminating models of excellence in educational practice; and

c) Innovative Solutions: Developing creative new approaches to expand the impact of Jewish education.

JESNA works to significantly improve Jewish educator

recruitment and retention and to mobilize a coalition of communal leaders – both lay and professional – who will make this vision a reality. Teaching in Jewish schools was often a secondary career for those teaching elsewhere and in need of earning additional funds, or a way station for Israelis en route to Americanization. With the expanding day school movement in the United States there was a great need for initiatives to achieve three primary goals: attracting talented people into the field of Jewish education; creating a culture of support for Jewish educators within Jewish institutions; and developing meaningful career paths to allow people to grow and advance as Jewish educators throughout their lives. JERRI, the Jewish Educator Recruitment and Retention Initiative, was created to harness ideas, expertise, and resources from throughout the community to re-create Jewish education as an honored, joyous and sacred profession. JERRI is convening a broad consortium of partners to experiment with ideas and to implement programs that will catalyze the changes needed to imprint this vision onto reality.

JESNA works to identify and disseminate models of excellence in educational practice by providing expertise, resources, research and evaluation, and training. JESNA's Mandell L. Berman Jewish Heritage Center for Research and Evaluation in Jewish Education is uniquely placed to develop this combination of expertise, information, and communication that has the potential to effect major change in the Jewish world. With years of hands-on experience evaluating Jewish education programs, curricula, and innovative ventures, the Center has a talented and experienced staff, an extensive body of research, and strong relationships within the Jewish education community.

The Center's métier is evaluation, and in the world of Jewish education, it has a twofold effect. On the local level, evaluation enhances Jewish education programs, materials, and initiatives by assessing their impact and advising changes that improve quality and effectiveness. More globally, each evaluation contributes to a broader understanding of what works and what does not throughout Jewish education. Using findings from the nearly 80 evaluations of Jewish education programs and studies of Jewish education issues that it has completed since 1992, the Berman Center possesses the beginnings of a database of best practices and solid research that can be disseminated throughout the Jewish world.

The Berman Center seeks to increase and improve the utilization of evaluation to improve the quality of Jewish educational programs in North America; to raise the prominence and support the field of Jewish educational research; and to achieve a greater understanding of factors leading to Jewish identity, educational change, and improvement.

In addition to working to improve existing programs, JESNA develops creative new approaches to expand the impact of Jewish education. JESNA's Lippman Kanfer Institute is an action-oriented think tank for innovation in Jewish learning and engagement, focusing on designing and infusing the educational system with new ideas and approaches that enable Jewish education to respond effectively to a rapidly changing world.

JESNA uses its three-pronged strategy to strengthen and improve key educational domains such as congregational education (through its Center for Excellence in Congregational Education) and youth (through its Youth Initiatives Program).

JESNA works closely with central agencies for Jewish education and federations in more than 150 communities throughout North America.

[Donald J. Sylvan (2nd ed.)]

JEWISH HISTORICAL INSTITUTE, WARSAW, institution devoted to the study of Polish Jewish history. The Central Jewish Commitee in Poland (CKZ) came alive in summer 1944 simultaneously with the liberation of Poland by the Soviet and Polish armies. The CKZ established a Jewish Historical Commission in August 1944 and, from December 28, a Central Jewish Historical Commission (CJHK) in Lublin headed by the historian Philip Friedman. The CJHK moved to Lodz (1945) and Warsaw and established branches in 25 places, including Cracow, Katowice, Wroclaw, Bialystok, Tarnow, and Lublin. Its main task was to preserve a record of the gruesome events of the Holocaust by research, documentation, collection of evidence, and publications..The CJHK provided a framework for researchers, publishing methodical instructions for collecting materials and organizing proper archives, and libraries.They also established contacts with Jewish organizations abroad and with the Polish Academy of Sciences (PAN = Polska Akademia Nauk). The CJHK issued its first bulletin, *Yedies*, in November 1949 (in Yiddish, quarterly publication, *Biuletyn Żydowskiego Instytutu Historycznego* (1950–) in Polish (with summaries in English), and an annual in Yiddish, *Bleter far Geshikhte* (1948–). These activities were financed mainly by a grant from the Polish Academy of Sciences (PAN), and by the *American Jewish Joint Distribution Committee. In 1968 the official antisemitic campaign in Poland induced almost all the workers of the Institute to emigrate, and the publication of the quarterly was impaired. Among the major works inspired by the Institute were collections of documents on the German occupation of Poland, including various reports from the ghettos and concerning underground activities in the ghettos and camps (1946); *i Geshikhte fun Yidn in Poyln* ("History of the Jews in Poland," 1951), by Bernard (Berl) *Mark, of which only one volume (until the 17th century) appeared in print (Yiddish); and *Hitlerowska Polityka Zaglady Żydów* ("Hitler's Policies of Extermination of the Jews," 1961) by A. Eisenbach. The number of other publications runs into several scores, dealing mainly with the Holocaust period.

BIBLIOGRAPHY: *35 lat dzialalnosci Zydowskiego Instytutu Historycznego w Polsce ludowej* (1980); *Żydowski Instytut Historyczny – 50 lat dzialalnosci* (1996); S. Netzer, "The Holocaust of Polish Jewry in Jewish Historiography," in: Y. Gutman and al. (eds.), *Historiography of the Holocaust Period* (1988), 133–40.

[Shlomo Netzer (2nd ed.)]

JEWISH HISTORICAL SOCIETY OF ENGLAND, English learned society. First projected in 1859, a serious attempt at its foundation was made in 1885–86 by Lucien Wolf and Alfred Newman. After the Anglo-Jewish Historical Exhibition of 1887, the plan was again brought forward, but the scheme became an actuality only in 1893, Lucien Wolf serving as first president. In recent times the Society held about ten meetings a year, at which a paper was presented by an expert speaker, and established branches in Birmingham, Manchester, Essex, and other places which also held periodic meetings. Through 2004, it published 39 volumes of its *Transactions* (renamed *Jewish Historical Studies* in 2000) and other miscellaneous material, especially on medieval Anglo-Jewry. It is probably the oldest existing Jewish historical society in the world and in the early years of the 21st century had about 800 members. Among its many distinguished presidents were Cecil *Roth, Albert M. *Hyamson, and Sir Isaiah *Berlin.

[Cecil Roth / William D. Rubinstein (2nd ed.)]

JEWISH IDENTITY. Through the ages Jewish identity has been determined by two forces: the consensus of thinking or feeling within the existing Jewish community in each age and the force of outside, often anti-Jewish, pressure, which continued to define and to treat as Jewish even such groups which had in their own consciousness and that of the Jews already severed all ties with Jewry. The most enduring definition of Jewish identity has been that of the *halakhah*, but it was not the first definition and it was not the only one, at least in some minority opinions, even during the many centuries when it was the dominant view. Among gentiles, hatred of Jews has generally dominated from age to age among those forces which have fashioned far more inclusive definitions of Jewish identity than Jews themselves would accept.

Biblical Period

In the biblical period Jewish identity meant belonging to the Jewish community as a religio-national entity. The "stranger" (*ger*) would become naturalized into this community by choosing to live its life. At the very beginning of Jewish history, in the Exodus from Egypt, a substantial number of strangers chose to accompany the Jews into the desert (Ex. 12:48; Lev. 24:10). During the conquest of Canaan, remnants of the earlier inhabitants of the land of Canaan remained resident among the Jews (I Kings 9:20–21) and from time to time, some refugees from nearby peoples also came into the Land of Israel (Isa. 16:4; 24:14–15). These strangers were not treated as slaves and it was regarded as a religious obligation, oft repeated, to treat them fairly (Lev. 19:33:34; Mal. 3:5). However, they were not given land among the tribes of Israel, even though Ezekiel commanded even this (47:22). Marriage with *gerim* was expressly permitted, with the exception of those who descended from Ammonites and Moabites, and for three generations, those who descended from Edomites and Egyptians (Deut. 23:4–9). In ritual matters the obligations and the privileges of such resident aliens were not markedly different from those of native Jews, especially if such strangers had undergone circumcision (see Ex. 12:48 and Lev. 17:8–14). There are some counterthemes in the Bible suggesting that the stranger remained not quite fully accepted religiously (in Deut. 14:21 he is the one who is permitted to eat *nevelah*, i.e., the flesh of a permitted animal which is, for one reason or another, not *kasher*). Nonetheless the situation in the Bible is such that a worthy such as *Naaman takes back with him to his own land soil from the land of the God of Israel and proclaims his reverence for that deity, without becoming a Jew (II Kings 5:17). It is the alien who chooses to live permanently within the Jewish polity (*ger toshav*) who is in the course of time assimilated into and accepted within Jewry.

The first important change in these attitudes occurred after the Babylonian Exile. The handful of Jews who returned under Zerubbabel and Ezra in the 6th and 5th centuries B.C.E. were now an embattled minority, even in the very heart of their own settlement, in Jerusalem and the land nearby. They found that those Jews who had remained during the period of the Exile had intermarried with the tribes whom the Assyrians had brought to dwell in the land. Formal religious conversion had not yet been devised, and even had it been thought of then, as there is some contemporary evidence that it was (Neh. 10:29), mass conversion could not have solved the national problem of the feared dissolution of the returning Jews into some syncretism containing elements of their own faith and culture along with foreign elements (such as the practices of the Samaritans nearby). In this situation Ezra chose the uncompromising path of ordering all of those who wanted to remain faithful as Jews to put away their foreign wives (Ezra 9–10). A minority community, which remained, even after the rebuilding of the Temple, semi-autonomous but not nationally sovereign, could not return to the biblical practice of accepting any who chose to live within it. A community becoming a theocracy had now to conceive of its identity as primarily religious and to accept within itself only those who underwent formal acts of religious assent.

Such religious assent was not yet halakhic, in large measure, of course, because the rabbinic *halakhah* itself was yet in the process of being created. The *Samaritans, who were being separated from the main body of Jewry in the centuries that followed immediately after their quarrel with Ezra, were indeed defined by the *halakhah* as very nearly Jews, for they were regarded in rabbinic law as trustworthy with respect to all the commandments which they were known to keep (Kid. 76a). What divided them from Jews was that they refused to accept the centrality of the Temple in Jerusalem and thus chose a separate communal destiny, and the rabbis held that they could be received as Jews only after they renounced Mount Gerizim (Kuthim, end.). In later ages the Samaritans themselves were quite eclectic in their sense of identity. They chose to be regarded as Jews in those periods when such definition brought them practical advantage. In the course of time the leniency of the *halakhah* toward the Samaritans evaporated; they were regarded as the classic example of what happens to some Jews who intermarry, adopt syncretistic religious practices, and live as a separate community, but this process of divergence, despite Ezra's anathemas, took generations.

Hellenistic and Early Christian Periods

The encounter of Jews with the Hellenistic world began with the presumption that the first few individuals who were acceptably learned in Greek language and ways could be regarded as both Jews and Greeks. There is a story, probably apocryphal, told by Clearchus, the disciple of Aristotle, that his master met a pious Jew whom, after conversation, he called "a Greek man both in language and in spirit." This openness soon became problematic. Hellenistic culture necessitated involvement of all those who wished to be part of it in activities which required formal worship of the pagan gods. There was much Jewish syncretism with the prevailing culture, as is proved by the fact that the Maccabeans revolted, in the first instance, against the Hellenistic party within Judea itself. Nonetheless, most Jews were not "good citizens" in their widespread Diaspora or in their own land, when it was dominated by the foreigners. They were exempt from military service, because it interfered with the observance of the Sabbath and the festivals, and they did not take part in the liturgies, the physical service that all citizens gave in working on such tasks as road repair, and the contributions for the upkeep of the gymnasia. There continued to be Jews who wanted to be accepted as Hellenes, but even they were soon rejected. In Alexandria in 41 C.E. the local Greek community fought bitterly against the desire of some Jews to be admitted to the local gymnasium, the usual first step in attaining complete Greek citizenship. In this quarrel the Alexandrian Greeks were upheld by the Emperor Claudius, who made it clear in the text of his decree that he regarded the Jews as a separate and unique entity within his realms. By that time the attitude of the Hellenistic world had crystallized with substantial clarity: anyone who still belonged to Jewry, by any kind of religious affiliation, such as contributing to the support of the Temple in Jerusalem, even if he were culturally Hellenized, remained a Jew in the eyes of the pagan world; only complete conversion to Hellenistic paganism, the step taken by a figure such as Tiberius Alexander, the nephew of Philo, the outstanding figure of Hellenistic Jewry, could make an end of Jewish identity, as perceived by the gentiles. It was almost as completely agreed, as a number of haters of Jews had been saying for two centuries before the embittered battles between Greeks and Jews in Alexandria in the middle of the first century, that the peculiar practices and religion of the Jews represented an attack on the rest of society (see *Antisemitism).

The issues between Jews and Greeks had been sharpened by the Maccabean revolt. Greek writers had known as early as Herodotus that Jews were somewhat strange but there was no major venom in these encounters until the Maccabeans raised the standard not merely of national independence but of the need to purify the national religion. Hellenistic paganism could not be accepted on any terms for the sake of civil peace; it was idolatry which had to be destroyed. In the century before the Maccabean revolt there had appeared Jewish writers in Greek who claimed that all Greek and Egyptian wisdom had descended from Jewish biblical teachers. The inevitable angry answer was that Jews had been inferior disciples of the Egyptians. *Manetho, a Hellenized Egyptian priest who wrote, in the third pre-Christian century, the first serious attack on Jews, accused them of having been at the time of the Exodus from Egypt a group of lepers who were thrown out for the sake of the health of the country, and such attacks became frequent in the next century. In such an atmosphere sharp choices had to be made. There is some evidence that the Hellenistic party in Palestine totally left the Jewish community after the Maccabean victory. There is more convincing evidence that, at least for the next couple of centuries, Greek-speaking Jewry in the Diaspora had a very low rate of *apostasy, regardless of changing and often lessening factors of inner Jewish cohesion. Here the causative factor of Jewish cohesion was primarily external, the pressure of their enemies on Jews whose religion was becoming more and more syncretistic and ever more condemned by the rabbis.

The attitude within Jewry itself toward Jewish identity was being changed and new formulations arose because of the remarkable success that Jews were having in a variety of areas in converting others. The Hasmoneans forced Idumeans and a number of other border communities to convert to Judaism, and it is not entirely clear whether this conversion was conducted with more formality than those of the ancient biblical *gerim*, who were merely added to the life and fate of the Jewish polity. In the Diaspora there was an increasing number, perhaps millions by the first century, of *sebomenoi* (*metuentes, yereim* – God fearers), gentiles who had not gone the whole route toward conversion. There were some gentiles both in the Diaspora and in Ereẓ Israel who did just that, among them even some of the great figures of Pharisaic history, such as the ancestors of Shemaiah and *Avtalyon among the early leaders and the translator of the Bible into Aramaic, *Onkelos. Most half-judaized gentiles remained in that estate, and were regarded not as Jews but as sympathizers, for Jewish identity had assumed, in the minds of most Jews, halakhic definitions, certainly by Hasmonean times. The gentile world, contemplating these *sebomenoi*, continued to regard them, even after many of them turned Christian, as people who harbored strange, unworthy private opinions, not far different in quality from the many others who had taken up Oriental mystery religions. This did not confer upon these believers any new legal status, such as exemption on the grounds of belief from civic duties. Late Hellenistic paganism regarded the *sebomenoi* not as Jews or as half-Jews but as suspiciously aberrant pagans.

The forces both of Jewish acceptance and of definition by gentiles were more nearly univocal in the case of nascent *Christianity. The earliest Pauline Christians, those gentile converts to the new religion who had not first become Jews according to the Law, were not regarded by anyone as Jews. The Jewish Christians, especially the circle in Jerusalem and the Holy Land in the first century, were much more of a problem. Whatever may have been the exact beliefs of these Ebionites, their exclusion from the Jewish community did not occur primarily for halakhic reasons. By their own choice these Jewish Christians left Jerusalem and emigrated to Pella at the beginning of the war of 66–70, and they thus separated themselves from the national destiny of the Jews. Despite the fact that the Pharisaic leadership of that time was opposed to the war, this action by the Christians set the seal upon tensions which had originated in dislike of the beliefs of the new sect. Within a generation, by the end of the first century, the rabbis included a new prayer in the *Amidah*, "And for the *minim* let there be no hope" (cf. **Birkat ha-Minim*). By that time the Roman Imperial authorities were recognizing Christianity officially as a new religion, because the emperor Nerva (96–98) exempted the Christians from the *fiscus judaicus*.

The Jewish Christian group remained nonetheless for some years in an intermediate position, but this stance ended during the Bar Kokhba revolt (132–5) and its immediate aftermath. Those who did not participate in that glorious tragedy could no longer lay any claim on being Jewish. Official Christianity was by then largely gentile and it was systematically excluding all traces of the preeminence of Jews in the new religion. The animosity between the two groups was quite pronounced by the middle of the second century, and in the next century, when Christianity was declared an illegal religion, Judaism retained its status as a *religio licita*. Even in a religious convulsion of the most profound kind it was not ultimately theological formulation or even halakhic norms which were decisive for the separating definitions of Jewish and Christian identity. Matters of belief might have remained a family quarrel within Jewry. What ultimately separated the two communities was the choice of the Christians to live out a separate historic destiny – and the agreement of the Romans to permit them this choice.

Middle Ages to the 19th Century

The *Karaite heresy through its various permutations from its origin 12 centuries ago was, for the most part, regarded as part of the Jewish community even though, paradoxically, the weight of halakhic opinion was that their legal practices, especially in relation to the marriage law, had excluded them from Jewry. Marriages between Karaites and Rabbanites continued well into the Middle Ages and did not cease entirely until the 15th and 16th centuries. Karaites were petitioned along with Rabbanites in Egypt, in the 11th century, and no doubt earlier and later, to help ransom captives from both communities; Karaite elders were at that time prominent in Fostat in the affairs of the largely Rabbanite community. All of this existed immediately after Saadiah's leadership in both Palestine and Egypt, with all of his anathemas against the Karaites, the practice of pronouncing an excommunication each year on the Mt. of Olives by the Rabbanites against the Karaites, and the bitter Karaite continuing counter-polemics. Under Islam, the Karaites refused to accept the authority of the *geonim* and the Exilarchs, who were Rabbanites. Nonetheless both groups continued to await the same national and messianic redemption; they shared the same destiny as Jews and they regarded each other as such and were so regarded by the gentile majority. All over the world, both Moslem and Christian, wherever both Rabbanites and Karaites were represented, they were treated throughout the centuries as belonging to the same community. The only exception occurred after 1795 in Czarist Russia when the legal discriminations against Jews were lifted entirely from Karaites, in the ensuing half-century, with the result that Karaites and Jews no longer regarded themselves as members of the same community.

The most complicated example of interweaving of internal and external forces was that of Marranism (see **Anusim*; *Marranos). On occasion both Islam and Christianity forced Jews to apostasize, in such places as Yemen and North Africa, in the early centuries of Islam, and from late antiquity throughout the Middle Ages in the Iberian Peninsula, in the case of Christianity. The historic destinies of these various Marrano groups were not always the same. Under Islam forced apostates were usually allowed to return to Judaism within one generation. Those who chose not to do so usually rapidly assimilated. Under Christianity the situation was different. The majority which had forced the conversions looked upon the newcomers with suspicion for many generations. This "anti-semitism" always lasted longer than any intensity of Jewish feeling or affirmation among the Marranos themselves, for, especially wherever there was some opportunity to escape, those who chose to remain Marranos had, in one or two generations, little Jewish loyalty and even less secret Jewish practice than they were suspected of harboring. Remaining Jewish loyalties were revoked into new vigor in Spain of the 16th century not so much by memories of the past as by persecution by the Inquisition. The attacks continued in the 17th and 18th centuries in the name of the doctrine of **limpieza de sangre* ("purity of blood"), under which *New Christians of even partial Jewish ancestry were barred from the highest offices of state and Church; there was therefore new reason for people who had ceased to be Jewish except by accident of birth to reinvent a kind of Judaism which was really their Christian upbringing, with the subtraction of its specifically Christian elements. For such figures, e.g., Uriel da *Costa, their return to a Jewish community which was actually living normative Judaism, such as the one in Amsterdam in the 17th century, was a difficult and sometimes tragic journey into a strange and constricting world.

The Jewish community to which the escaping Marranos were returning was in theory defining its attitude toward them in terms of the *halakhah*. The basic view in all versions, both Franco-German and Spanish, of the legal tradition was that a Marrano, or any other kind of forced convert, remained a Jew and was to be welcomed back as such upon his return; indeed, in law, he was regarded as a Jew in a state of grave transgression. This definition was completely unproblematic so long as it was confronted either by forced apostates who threw off their apostasy at the earliest possible moment or by apostates by choice who never looked back over their shoulder at what the Jewish community might be saying about their halakhic identity. It ran into difficulties when confronted by all the ambiguities and indefiniteness of Marranism, where the apostasy as such was not always forced but rather, as in Spain in 1492, largely the choice of many of the wealthy not to leave their property and to accept Christianity in the hope that some change might soon happen. Opportunities occurred in many situations, especially in Christian Spain in the 15th and 16th centuries, to escape, but the choice was most often not taken. Nonetheless some family ties remained, and were remembered, with Jews elsewhere; some inner cohesion, if only of evaporating sentiment, was still felt; and those who did escape, often the children or grandchildren of marriages that were questionable from the Jewish point of view, laid claim to Jewish identity and to full acceptance. The rabbinic authorities who dealt with this question were divided, the most liberal, Ẓemaḥ Duran, maintaining that even if the Marranos were to be regarded as true apostates they must nonetheless be accepted as Jews on purely halakhic grounds. On the other hand, Jacob Berab, who had himself fled from Spain, took a much harder line against those who had remained and ruled that the Marranos were gentiles in every respect except for the laws of marriage and divorce.

In actual fact these halakhic definitions were not ultimately determinant of the attitude of the Jewish community toward Marranos. The overwhelming evidence is that wherever they turned up, from the 15th to the 16th centuries, be it Venice, or Bordeaux, or Hamburg, and declared themselves to be Jews, the males were soon circumcised, the marriages were resolemnized, and no barriers were put in the way of their joining the existing Jewish communities. No serious questions were asked about the validity of the marriages of their Marrano ancestors. To be sure, there was halakhic warrant for this attitude, because in talmudic law in the absence of any evidence to the contrary a Jew is believed in any declaration that he makes about his personal status, and certainly about whether he is a Jew. It is also true that these returning Marranos formally accepted upon themselves all of the commandments of rabbinic Judaism. Nonetheless the determining act was their willingness to become part of the Jewish community, and all the halakhic doubts of rabbinic authorities remained theoretical in the face of acts of return.

A more curious case was that of the *Doenmeh, those followers of the false messiah Shabbetai Ẓevi who emulated their master and converted to Islam in 1686 or 1687. Their separation from the main body of Jewry was not complete for centuries. Even the rabbis spoke of them as "Jewish sinners" and not as "people uprooted and separated from Israel, who have no part in it." Halakhic considerations were here operative, for it had long been held, at least since Maimonides, that conversion to Islam was not a denial of the unity of God or a form of idolatry. Nonetheless these were not forced converts and, what is more, they held messianic ideas which had been declared heretical in the most violent terms. On the other hand, the Doenmeh were never trusted by the Muslim majority and, at least in the early years during the persecution by the Pasha Hassan (1722), they were made to suffer as Jews. Until the middle of the 19th century, the Doenmeh studied Talmud with Jewish scholars and they discontinued this in 1859, along with making some other of their Jewish practices even more secret, only under investigation by Muslim authorities. The identity of the Doenmeh was still sufficiently separate, and separated, in the social sense for it to have been noted that young men of this origin were particularly prominent in the Young Turk Revolution of 1908. It is even still rumored that Kemal Ataturk belonged to the Doenmeh. The Doenmeh experience paralleled that of the Christian Marranos. After conversion something of their Jewish identity was maintained in secret by choice; persecution made the content of this identity ever harder to preserve, but it kept alive a pained sense of alienness for many generations.

The Modern Era

At the dawn of the modern era the definition of Jewish identity was no problem almost everywhere in the world. The trickle of Marranos coming out of the Iberian Peninsula ceased almost completely by 1800 and the Inquisition came to its effective end soon thereafter. On the European stage a Jew was someone defined by *halakhah*, that is one who was born of a Jewish mother (or who converted to Judaism) and who in actual practice regarded himself and was regarded as belonging to the Jewish community. This had legal relevance, for the Jew was structurally part of systems of law, both his own and of the governing powers, which depended on his identity's being clear cut. The only way that he could change was by conversion to another religion, which in actual practice in Europe meant some form of Christianity. Halakhically even this may not yet have excluded him from Jewry, but it did everywhere admit him to legal rights and status within the majority. So long as this was the action of a relative few, followed in due course by intermarriage with people not of Jewish stock (see *Mixed Marriage), some social discrimination might remain, but conversion effectively ended Jewish identity in most cases. Indeed in the aftermath of the Jacob *Frank episode in the 1770s his followers who converted to the Catholic faith quickly intermarried with Polish nobility, and the Jewish origins of their descendants were not widely remembered.

With the era of the *emancipation the whole question of Jewish identity appears in new forms. The structure of law which enshrined a precise definition of who was a Jew came to an end wherever any version of the modern secular state was created. Before the law religion became a matter of indifference and the choice to uphold one's own became purely voluntaristic. The law protected the right to private opinion and free association for worship, provided the specific practices of a religion were not flagrantly in conflict with public order as conceived by the state. This formulation had Christianity in mind, for it defined religion as containing dogma about God and the world to come and as acting in specific forms of worship. These premises were accepted by the founders of *Reform Judaism both in Germany and in the United States, who constructed a modern definition of Jewish identity as that of individuals who belonged to the Jewish religious faith, now conceived as containing primarily ethical content and personal edification. This non-national definition of Judaism and Jewry was shared in many senses by the *neo-Orthodoxy that arose in Western and Central Europe under the leadership of Samson Raphael *Hirsch. Here too, the general culture was accepted and patriotic identification was made with the state. What was different was that neo-Orthodoxy identified the content of Jewish religion with every aspect of the inherited law, meticulously observed as divine commandment, but whatever was national in Judaism was relegated to far-off, apocalyptic days and thus made largely irrelevant. Both of these versions of Jewish identity could not utterly deny the obvious, that they were addressing themselves to the biological descendants of Jews, and that, regardless of their self-definitions, they were inevitably involved with all sorts of Jews, both in their own countries and all over the world. Many of those who thus began with definitions of Judaism, but wanted no identification with the Jewish people, moved into a general ethical humanism and entirely out of Jewry.

To be sure, in a number of European states the institutions of the Jewish religion were in some sense still "established" even after the emancipation, and in some jurisdictions, such as Hapsburg Austria and its successor republic and in Prussia, a Jew could cease paying some fractional tax to the Jewish community only by declaring himself "without religion." It was, of course, an open secret that such people were, in the overwhelming majority, Jews, and some social discrimination was directed against them. Nonetheless at the height of 19th-century liberalism in Europe and America, it was possible for some Jews to "pass" without doing anything more than simply ceasing to function in any Jewish association of any kind. On the other hand, it was possible for Jews to feel a strong sense of Jewish identity on the basis of minimal or no association, even after every vestige of religious faith and practice had evaporated. Increasingly there arose the institutions of the voluntaristic Jewish *community of the modern era, which accepted this situation. These bodies regarded it as their task to serve any who claimed to be Jews, especially at moments of danger or when such people needed social services. Indeed, these very voluntaristic associations to alleviate suffering became increasingly the overarching Jewish community organization. This modern pattern had been forecast, when the delegates of the Portuguese Jews returned in February 1790 from Paris to Bordeaux with the news that their community had been granted equality. It was decided that very day to make an end of the historic "Spanish-Portuguese Jewish nation" and to reorganize the community as a welfare committee.

However, the majority community did not easily accept these various new forms of Jewish identity, especially as ever greater numbers of Jews moved in the direction of appearing to be, and even feeling that they were, undifferentiated westerners, and so the marginal Jew appeared, marginal both to his own earlier identity and to the one that he was trying to acquire. Such figures had appeared at the very dawn of the era of the emancipation, in Isaac de Pinto, the Franco-Dutch Sephardi who debated with Voltaire, and David Friedlaender, the disciple of Mendelssohn. Men such as these, and their equivalents (e.g., Heine, Bernard Berenson) were to occur in every generation of the modern era, especially wherever the Jews were a minority fighting for equality. Some were ambivalent about their Jewishness and spent their lives in emotional torment, but most believed that Jews would achieve equality only by total assimilation to the way of life and outlook of the majority. An element of such a vision was an assumption of responsibility on the part of Jews for helping to create the kind of society which would live up to its most spacious new vision of equality for mankind. Inevitably the moral commandments of this doctrine moved Jews to turn away from specific concerns for their own community to the concerns of the general community, and the battle for Jewish rights itself could, and often was, identified with the struggle for the rights of all oppressed individuals and minorities. Since men do not easily jump out of their skins, this basic position was often identified as messianic, arising out of Jewish prophetic teaching and carrying it to the ultimate conclusion of the dissolution of Jewish specificity as the climactic act in the historic drama of Jewish existence.

The appearance of Jews in the revolutionary movements of the modern age was, in terms of Jewish identity, motivated by considerations comparable to those given just above which inspired their immediate Jewish predecessors in modernity, who did battle for the rights of Jews in the liberal era. Here there was already an awareness that bourgeois society was not living up to the promises of the middle-class revolutions and that from the perspective of all the oppressed, and certainly from that of the Jews, the only hope for real human equality was to uproot the past and to begin all over again in some new dispensation in which all men were equally cofounders. The more apocalyptic was the vision of a heaven on this earth, the more, either explicitly or in subterranean ways, did the allegiance of Jews to revolutionary movements represent both a conscious denial of specifically Jewish identity and an expression of certain aspects of that very identity. Here the battle against antisemitism and reechoes of Jewish prophetic messianism fused to create the post-Jewish revolutionary. So prominent have Jews been in modern movements of social reform, political revolution, new literary and art forms, and new modes of human self-understanding, that their enemies generally identified the hated and upsetting newness of things and thoughts with Jews. In many western countries during the last century the literary and intellectual community was heavily penetrated by Jews; and such subcultures as a whole, although Jews were often under attack within them, became identified as "Jewish," even though the

Jews within these circles did not, except sometimes in crisis, function as Jews.

If inner Jewish commitment had become functional and diverse in the modern era, so had the outside world in which Jews were attempting to live. Before the middle of the 19th century the vision of the Enlightenment, an all-human society to which all regenerated men would belong, had been joined, both as ideal and as political doctrine in Europe, by nationalism. The question was therefore raised again whether Jews could ever participate in a national culture and society with historic roots in a distant past in which they did not share. More important, antisemitism was not in the process of coming to an end, not even among the most modern and revolutionary groups. On the contrary, to the older religious and economic rationales for hatred of Jews among some of the makers of modernity, such as Voltaire in the 18th century and some of the founders of socialism (Proudhon and Fourier) in the 19th, new anti-Jewish arguments were added about the ineradicable cultural alienness of even the most assimilated Jews. The racial theorists who followed after Gobineau defined Jews as a biologically alien race. Even non-socialists who were not anti-Jewish, such as Werner Sombart and Max Weber, elaborated on the essay (*Zur Judenfrage*) of the young Karl Marx, agreeing that the Jews had a very special, middleman and capitalist, role in the economy from the very beginning of their existence and that they were, if not by their very nature at least by long historical experience, removed from primary production and agriculture and thus unassimilable into all the healthy pursuits of a normal economy. From a variety of perspectives the Jew who wanted to become part of the contemporary world was thus faced with ever more complicated dilemmas. He could choose to remake himself even more thoroughly than he had imagined and get rid of every trace of his supposed past nature. He would nonetheless remain confronted by some, such as the German historian Treitschke, who would continue to insist that the most dejudaized of Jews had not yet become German. A future therefore had to be fashioned by the modern Jew in another direction: the creation of some realm of his own within which he could enter the contemporary world free of the intellectual and physical pressure of his enemies. This was all the more necessary for the westernizing Jewish intelligentsia that arose in the modern era, precisely because they were themselves part of all the secular and secularizing movements and states of mind to which their relationship was increasingly ambiguous.

All of this, especially as antisemitism became ever more virulent in the last third of the 19th century, led away from both reformed religious definitions of Jewish identity, or various modes of acculturation, to national definitions of what the contemporary Jew was or could become.

Its essential affirmation was that the Jews are a people, an organically developing historic community among many such communities which together make up human society. The Zionist version of this definition is not the only one, and it indeed arose somewhat later than most of the others. From this perspective the Jewish people is unlike most others in the extent of its dispersion, its persistence for many centuries without a land of its own, and a number of other differences from the prevailing norms of modern national identity. Despite the fact that this was a people which harbored a particular religion, belonging to this people, from the beginning and certainly in the modern, secular era, was defined as a national sentiment rather than a matter of religious assent. Just as it was possible in the modern age of doubt to cease being Anglican and remain English, so it was possible to cease believing in Judaism and remain Jewish. At least in theory, such secularization solved the problem of Jewish identity and continuity in the modern age, but those who accepted these new premises remained confronted by two questions: why should an individual prefer one secular culture over another, unless his own is always demonstrably higher? In what sense can a secular culture lay moral onus on those who abandon it? Questions such as these led such theoreticians of Diaspora nationalism as Simon *Dubnow to opt for Jewish communal organization, an international Jewish parliament, and national institutions of culture and education to maintain the national ethos. Others, such as the Yiddishist movement which arose at the beginning of the 20th century, laid the accent on Yiddish as the spoken and living language of the vast majority of world Jewry, at least before 1939, and aimed at preserving a secular national culture in that language.

Even before the Nazi Holocaust, the Zionist criticism of Diaspora nationalism was its unrealism. It was argued that national identity would be abandoned by Jews in the Diaspora, at the very least because of economic and social demands made upon the individual Jew by his quest for personal economic success. Some sentiment might remain, but inner Jewish content would inevitably evaporate in any post-ghetto society, even in one such as Poland between the two world wars, where bitter discrimination continued to exist in many areas. Zionism held that a continuing secular Jewish identity was, as a matter of social fact, possible only where Jews had achieved territorial concentration. Moreover, to be historically valid, a nation had to be involved in its own land, the soil of its ancestors, not in some new arrangements in new places, and the people had to revive its capacity to speak its own classic language, Hebrew. This was not only valid historic identity, but also the preservation in the secular, modern context of the best resonances of the religio-national past.

In contemporary Israel, therefore, the question of Jewish identity revolves around the interpenetration between the older, religious and halakhic definitions of who is a Jew and the both more contemporary, and far older communal-national emphases. Very small elements within the whole of Israel would go so far as to declare themselves to be Jewish Canaanites; however, many are in sympathy with the idea that the strictest of religious tests cannot be applied to those non-Jews by birth who have chosen to identify themselves in Israel with its Jewry. On the other hand, in circles far wider than those of the officially Orthodox, there is continuing and even increasing concern about returning to a sense of tradition which is beyond the purely secular. Indeed, one of the recurring problems studied by Israel sociologists is whether its population, and especially its younger population of Jews, regard themselves as primarily Israelis or primarily Jews. By all of the usually established criteria, from religious observance to involvement in the destiny of world Jewry, the Orthodox and most of the non-Sabras of all persuasions rank as "Jews." The non-Orthodox Sabras consider themselves "Israelis" on all counts except that they feel strongly about their connection to the Jews of all the world and their involvement in this international destiny.

In recent years the question of what is contemporary Jewish identity has been a matter of considerable political and social concern for the State of Israel. Under its Law of Return all Jews have a right to automatic admission and immediate citizenship in Israel. For this purpose non-Jewish spouses and the often halakhically non-Jewish children (of gentile mothers) have been allowed to accompany the Jewish member of the family who emigrated to the land of his ancestors. Many of the problems which have thus arisen have been solved individually by ritual conversion, but the question of definition was inevitably tested further by a Jew by birth who had become Christian (the Brother Daniel Case before the Supreme Court of Israel in 1966, see *Apostasy), and by intermarried nonbelievers who refused to allow their children to undergo ritual conversion (the Shalit Case of 1970). The Supreme Court of Israel decided against Brother Daniel, despite his valid halakhic claims to Jewish status, on the ground that he had chosen to remove himself by conversion from the history and destiny of the Jewish community. In the Shalit case, the court ruled that the technically non-Jewish children of this intermarried couple should be registered as Jews because they were growing up within the Jewish community of Israel as indissolubly bound to its destiny. Such registration, however, would have no bearing in matters of marriage and divorce. This emerging consensus was inevitably involved with concern about what such new, legal definitions of what is a Jew would do to the unity of world Jewry, where, in theory, the halakhic definition prevailed. Considerations such as these were important in the overturn by the Israeli Knesset of the Supreme Court's decision in the Shalit case, by reaffirming the halakhic definition. Years earlier, in 1958, after a governmental decision that anyone who declared himself to be Jewish would be registered as such, the then prime minister, David Ben-Gurion, wrote to a wide variety of Jewish religious, intellectual, and legal figures both in Israel and in the Diaspora. The answers that he received ranged from reaffirmation of the *halakhah* to acceptance of inner emotional choice and labeling by the outside world as valid forms of Jewish identity.

The social situation of world Jewry outside Israel more nearly approximates the second rather than the first definition. In the major center of the Jewish Diaspora, the United States, the rate of intermarriage is now generally held to be at least one in two. It is estimated that many thousands of conversions to Judaism are taking place every year, the largest number under Reform auspices, and thus not halakhically satisfactory. There are even a number of Jewish clergy in the U.S. who are officiating at intermarriages even without conversion. All of these non-Jews are coming into some relationship with the Jewish community, and even the many who live entirely outside it are affected in some degree, even in those cases where their spouses are substantially dejudaized. Among those born and raised as Jews, the whole corpus of contemporary American Jewish sociology has had as its major subject in this generation repeated study of such questions as the rapid evaporation of Jewish ritual observance and intensive Jewish learning, the negligible rate of regular synagogue attendance, and the erosion of opposition to associating or marrying outside the Jewish group. On the other hand, these same studies have proved a very high rate of almost exclusive association of Jews each with the other even among those younger Jews who affirm little or nothing of the content of the Jewish tradition and an ongoing sense of at least passive involvement in what happens to Jews all over the world. To be sure, there are small, though notable, circles of younger Jewish intellectuals in all of the extreme revolutionary groups, and Jews also figure prominently among those who are dropping out of society in the name of highly personalist, often mystic, fulfillment. Even among these, some Jewish consciousness is still present, and it certainly does exist among the vast majority of their less radical contemporaries. This emerging, or eroding, Jewish identity is historic, in a very muted way, and situational.

The fate of Jewish identity in Eastern Europe, particularly after World War I, evolved under far different circumstances. The fundamental fact underlying this development is the unchanging concept, shared there by Jews and non-Jews alike, that the Jews are a historic, ethnic unit, i.e., a people, a "nationality" or even a "nation," into which a person is born and to which he belongs, whether he lives up to it in his linguistic, cultural, and religious habits or not. Out of this concept emerged for some periods and under favorable political circumstances, certain forms of official Jewish autonomy, mainly in educational and cultural facilities (as, e.g., in Poland, the Baltic states, and also in the Soviet Union in its first decades, where even an unsuccessful experiment of Jewish territorial autonomy in *Birobidzhan was made). Ultimately, however, particularly from the 1950s, Jewish identity in the Soviet Union became trapped into an unprecedented cruel paradox. The obligatory registration of each individual born of Jewish parents as being of Jewish nationality, even when he is a declared atheist or even a convert, remained in force, though all traces of the Jewish historical heritage and of Jewish educational or cultural facilities were eradicated, thus transforming the Jewish population into a kind of a "ghost nation." In other East European countries, the registration of the Jewish nationality was optional, and not obligatory; but eventually this formality did not lead to the obliteration of Jewish identity through the assimilation of a sizable number of Jews into the majority nation, but rather to mass emigration, to Israel or to other countries, since the formal option did not change the traditional concept of the Jew, sometimes even people of partly Jewish descent, as being ethnically different and "alien." This fact was often exploited in antisemitic campaigns for political purposes, as, e.g., in Poland in 1968–70. In the U.S.S.R. the paradox of the obligatory registration of the Jewish nationality, though devoid of any historical or cultural content, caused a growing manifestation of Jewish identity and even identification with the independent Jewish nation in Israel, mainly among the younger generation, including spontaneous efforts of small groups to study Hebrew and Jewish history and to congregate en masse in and around the synagogues in the great cities. The tension engendered by it transformed the solution of the problem of Jewish identity in the Soviet Union gradually into an international moral issue of major magnitude (see *Antisemitism, in the Soviet Bloc, *Assimilation, in the Soviet Union, *Russia).

In the last third of the 20th century there were many Jews, especially that worldwide, intensely Jewish, religiously traditionalist minority, for whom the question of Jewish identity was decided by the *halakhah*. The overarching institutions of world Jewry, while paying respect to this view, determine their policy by broader and more amorphous considerations of history and situation. So, when the last remaining, completely dejudaized, almost entirely intermarried communists of Jewish parentage in Poland were purged in 1968, the Israeli government provided them with the necessary exit passports, even though few were going to Israel; the world Jewish social service budget took care of the overwhelming majority who opted to go to other countries. Those who suffer as Jews, regardless of their own perception of that suffering, and those whose Jewish consciousness might one day be rekindled, remain part of world Jewish concern. In the broadest sense, significant elements of world Jewry in the modern era have defined, and are defining, Jewish identity as a community of history and destiny of those who still feel their involvement in this community or about whom others feel strongly that these people belong to Jewry.

[Arthur Hertzberg]

In the last third of the 20st century significant developments occurred in the three largest centers of Jewish life – the Soviet Union, the United States, and Israel. In the Soviet Union, the upsurge of Jewish feeling triggered by Israel's Six-Day War created steady pressure for immigration to Israel and the accompanying phenomenon of the *"refusenik," denied an exit visa by the Soviet authorities, as well as open celebration of Jewish holidays in the streets of Russian cities. With the collapse of the Communist system the mass emigration of Soviet Jewry commenced, most arriving in Israel, where it may be said that for most a process of "Israelification" set in which, though it involves sets of identities tied to the everydayness of life in a modern Western society, also bears the powerful imprint of the country's Jewish identity. In the former Soviet Union itself, Jewish communal life has also revived, centered on synagogues, community centers, and an extensive Jewish educational system, often under the auspices of Chabad rabbis but also with the support of the Jewish Agency and other international organizations. In the United States all the disturbing demographic trends noticeable since World War II continued, but here too Jewish identity was fortified among identifying Jews, partly as a result of the emotions generated by the Six-Day War and partly as part of the general upsurge of ethnic pride in the United States in which blacks and Alex Haley's *Roots* played a pioneering role. However, the precise nature of this Jewish identity, which seeks to affirm Diaspora life as a legitimate variety of Jewish experience, no less valid than a Jewish experience centered in a Jewish state, remains problematic, if only for demographic reasons. In the last analysis, the Jewishness of this identity does not prevent Jews from drifting away from Judaism, even if Judaism is perceived as no more than a cultural identity or intellectualized under the rubric of a Diaspora multiculturalism that seeks "to create a community of communities and a culture of cultures," as the editors of *Insider/Outsider* put it.

In Israel, Jewishness permeates everyday life. How one defines oneself – as a Jew, Israeli, human being, or professional person – does not alter the context of this daily life, which is life in a Jewish state whose symbols, ceremonies, aspirations, and commonality are rooted in palpable Jewish experience. In Israel one may be Jewish in spite of oneself. This is its saving grace, and the meaning of the Jewish state. It cements the Jewish identity and, like the strictest Orthodoxy, ensures its survival.

[Fred Skolnik (2nd ed.)]

BIBLIOGRAPHY: S.N. Herman, *Israelis and Jews: The Continuity of an Identity* (1971); Y. Kaufmann, *Golah ve-Nekhar*, 1 pt. 1 and 2 (1929); Kaufmann, Y., Toledot, 4 pt. 1 (1956), 501–3; B. Ringer, *The Edge of Friendliness, A Study of Jewish-Gentile Relations* (1967); M. Sklare, *Jewish Identity on the Suburban Frontier* (1967); L. Fein, *Studying Jewish Identity – Observation and Bibliography* (1966); E. Rosenthal, in: AJYB, 64 (1963), 3–53; 68 (1967), 243–64; M.H. Stern, *Americans of Jewish Descent* (1960); R. Lowe, in: JSS, 7 (1965), 153–75; E. Schoenfeld, *Small-town Jews, A Study in Identity and Integration* (1967); S.N. Eisenstadt, *Israeli Society* (1967); B. Netanyahu, *The Marranos of Spain* (1966); B. Litvin and S.B. Hoenig (eds.), *Jewish Identity: Modern Responsa and Opinions on the Registration of Children of Mixed Marriages* (1965); W.G. Braude, *Jewish Proselyting in the First Five Centuries of the Common Era…* (1940); B.J. Bamberger, *Proselytism in the Talmudic Period* (1968²), J.A. Montgomery, *The Samaritans, the Earliest Jewish Sect…* (1968); A.I. Gordon, *Intermarriage, Interfaith, Interracial, Interethnic* (1964); S.W. Baron, *Russian Jews under Tsars and Soviets* (1964); G. Friedmann, *The End of the Jewish People?* (1968).

JEWISH IMMIGRANT AID SERVICES OF CANADA

(JIAS), one of the oldest chartered nonprofit settlement organizations in Canada. For over 80 years JIAS has been the voice of the Canadian Jewish community on issues of integration and resettlement in Canada and has helped in the settlement of hundreds of thousands of Jewish immigrants to Canada. The agency continues to champion the cause of new immigrants and refugees by positively influencing Canadian immigration laws, policies, and practices, and by ensuring that they are humane in nature and responsive to the needs of new arrivals to Canada. JIAS also assists individuals to navigate the Canadian immigration process and works for the integration of Jewish immigrants into local communities across Canada.

JIAS was founded in the wake of World War I. In 1919, the Canadian Jewish Congress (CJC) was formed. At its plenary, the delegates, moved by the plight of Jewish refugees in Europe, called upon the government of Canada to maintain an open door policy and reject restrictionist pressure to exclude a "whole race or nation." But CJC was weak, and its leaders, including Lyon *Cohen and Sam *Jacobs, realized that a separate organization was needed to deal with issues of immigration. The Jewish Immigrant Aid Society was established in 1920, and incorporated in 1922. JIAS opened an office in Montreal and was soon lobbying government on immigration issues and assisting individual Jews in dealing with immigration authorities. As a community agency, JIAS also became the center for the sponsorship and transportation of immigrants, challenging the fixers, agents, and lawyers who sought to profit from the immigration process.

JIAS was arguably the most active Jewish communal organization in the 1920s. In its early years JIAS was active in assisting Russian refugees trapped in Romania and immigrants detained at Canadian ports of arrival. While the agency suffered under the weight of serious financial strains and an increasingly restrictionist Canadian immigration policy, it succeeded in intervening with the government to allow the arrival of several thousand Jewish refugees and the release of most of the detainees. While its financial situation remained difficult, JIAS soon earned the respect of the government and the Jewish community for its efforts on behalf of Jewish immigration.

With the Nazi seizure of power in Germany, the situation for European Jewry became more precarious. CJC was revitalized and, in partnership with JIAS, turned to the challenge of dealing with the policies of a government determined to restrict immigration and that of Jews in particular. Jewish delegations met with government immigration authorities, but their lobbying efforts were rebuffed. Only after World War II and a reopening of immigration was JIAS able to turn its efforts to the rescue, resettlement, and rehabilitation of Jews. Notably, in the aftermath of the Holocaust, JIAS, together with the Jewish Labour Committee and the Canadian Jewish Congress, successfully lobbied the government to allow the entry of orphans and workers. In all, some 35,000 Holocaust survivors and their children settled in Canada between 1947 and 1957. Servicing so large and sudden an inflow of immigrants strained JIAS resources and led to a duplication of services by other Jewish agencies. In 1947 Joseph *Kage was appointed executive national vice president and, with Canada now a major immigrant-receiving country, Kage was instrumental in restructuring JIAS so as to assist in the immigration and integration of Holocaust survivors and other Jewish immigrants.

In 1956 JIAS was in the lead helping with the resettlement of Hungarian Jews fleeing the failed Hungarian Revolution, and the wave of Jewish immigrants arriving in Canada from North Africa. In 1968, a purge of "Zionist elements" in Poland led to the emigration of most of the Jewish community. JIAS helped in the resettlement of some in Canada. JIAS' largest postwar challenge was assisting in the transport and integration of Soviet Jewry. Beginning in the 1970s, their migration to Canada grew until it reached some 30,000 arrivals. JIAS has helped not only with their resettlement but with their integration into Jewish life. Since the 1980s, JIAS has helped in the resettlement of Jews from Syria, the former Yugoslavia, and Argentina.

By the beginning of the 21st century there was an organizational restructuring of JIAS, so that there are three separate Jewish immigrant service provider agencies. Jewish Immigrant Aid Services of Canada, funded by UIA, with its head office located in Toronto assists Jewish newcomers to immigrate and settle in Canada. It also provides information and support to Jewish Family Service agencies serving new immigrants across the country. JIAS Toronto, located in Toronto, is a charitable organization (under the laws of Canada) funded jointly by the Jewish community and federal and provincial governments. Serving more than half of all Jewish immigrants arriving in Canada, JIAS Toronto assists newcomers to become part of the Toronto community. Similarly JIAS Montreal, located in Montreal, is also a charitable organization (under the laws of Quebec), funded jointly by the Jewish community and government to assist new immigrants to become part of the Montreal/Quebec society.

[Frank Bialystok (2nd ed.)]

JEWISH LABOR COMMITTEE, a Jewish communal agency linking the organized Jewish community and the Labor movement. Representatives from a number of trade unions and other organizations traditionally identified with the Jewish labor movement assembled at a conference in New York City in 1934 and launched the Jewish Labor Committee, charging it with the following tasks: (1) support of Jewish labor institutions in European countries; (2) assistance to the anti-Hitler underground movement; (3) aid to the victims of Nazism; (4) cooperation with American organized labor in fighting anti-democratic forces; (5) combating antisemitism and other evil effects of Fascism and Nazism upon American life.

During the first five years of its existence, the Jewish Labor Committee concentrated mainly on supporting anti-Nazi labor forces in Europe and sending relief to Jewish labor institutions there, especially those maintained by the *Jewish Labor Bund and the "left" Labor Zionist movement (the "right" Labor Zionists organized their own relief and rehabilitation committee), and encouraging and strengthening U.S. and Canadian opposition to the Nazis, in the labor and democratic left, as well as in the community-at-large. At the same time it organized mass anti-Nazi demonstrations; in 1936, with the American Jewish Congress, through the Joint

Boycott Council, it conducted a boycott on German goods and services.

After the outbreak of World War II, the emphasis shifted to efforts to save Jewish cultural and political figures, as well as Jewish and non-Jewish labor and socialist leaders facing certain death at the hands of the Nazis. With powerful help from the American Federation of Labor, the Committee succeeded in bringing over a thousand such individuals to the United States, or to temporary shelter elsewhere.

Beginning in the late 1930s, the Committee became increasingly concerned with Jewish defense work and community relations in the United States. It was one of the four founders of the short-lived General Jewish Council and helped organize the National Community Relations Advisory Council [re-named the National Jewish Community Relations Advisory Council in 1968 and Jewish Council for Public Affairs in the 1997], of which it is still an active member. Unlike other community relations agencies, the JLC has its sphere of action clearly delineated: it strives to represent Jewish interests in the American labor movement, and labor interests in the Jewish community. Working with the American Federation of Labor–Congress of Industrial Organization since the federation's formation in 1956, the JLC works with and has the support of a wide range of unions and their associated organizations, locally as well as nationally. Comprising diverse organizations and a variety of ideological groups, the Committee has been guided in its work by pragmatic policies rather than by a clear Jewish philosophy. While Bundist influence was significant in the organization, particularly in the early period, the organization has had a positive position on the State of Israel since 1948.

The JLC is a member of the Conference of Presidents of Major Jewish Organizations, the Memorial Foundation for Jewish Culture, as well as the Conference on Jewish Material Claims Against Germany and the National Conference on Soviet Jewry. The JLC holds both national conventions of delegates and committee meetings of its executive committee and national board. In 2005, the organization, with headquarters in New York, had staffed field offices in Boston, New York, Philadelphia, Detroit and Los Angeles, and lay-led groups in Washington, D.C.; Cleveland, Ohio; Phoenix, Arizona; and Seattle, Washington. Its funding comes from independent campaigns, contributions from trade unions, allocations from welfare funds, and grants from foundations. Originally a body of organizations and unions, the Committee has also had individual members since the mid-1960s.

BIBLIOGRAPHY: Jewish Labor Committee, *Jewish Labor Committee in Action* (1948); idem, *The Time is Now…* (1951); idem, *Finf un Tsvantsik Yor…* (1960); idem, The Jewish Labor Committee Story (2004); W. Herberg, "The Jewish Labor Movement in the United States," in: AJYB, 53 (1952), 3–74; I. Knox, *Jewish Labor Movements in America* (1958). **ADD. BIBLIOGRAPHY:** G. Malmgreen, "Labor and the Holocaust: The Jewish Labor Committee and the Anti-Nazi Struggle," in: *Labor's Heritage* (October 1991).

[Charles Bezalel Sherman / Arieh Lebowitz (2nd ed.)]

JEWISH LANGUAGES.

History

The linguistic history of the Jews accurately mirrors their dispersion over the world. The prehistory of the Hebrews took place in the Aramaic sphere, and the impact of that tongue on the first "Jewish" language, Hebrew, was so strong that it has been called a fusion of Canaanite and Aramaic. The lifespan of Hebrew covers roughly the period of the political independence of those speaking it. It does not, however, coincide with the era in which they inhabited Ereẓ Israel because, some centuries before the Christian era, Hebrew had started giving way to Aramaic, which had been spreading over wide areas of western Asia, including Palestine. Different branches developed which had their parallels in Judeo-Aramaic (i.e., the Jewish forms of Aramaic). Both language groups survived until the seventh century C.E. Two branches, however, are still alive – in far developed forms – the larger one in a few small communities in Kurdistan, Christian as well as Jewish. The language of the Jews there is known as Jabali.

Long before the end of the Second Temple period the Greek Koinē had been adopted by the Jews of the Hellenistic world – in the Balkans, Cyprus, southern Italy (Graecia Magna), the Black Sea region, and Egypt. The other great language of European classical antiquity, Latin, played a certain role in Jewish linguistic history. However, Blondheim's theory according to which the Judeo-Romance languages sprang from a common Judeo-Latin stock proved to be farfetched. The Jewish communities of Late Antiquity were Greek-speaking even after they settled in Rome and in the western provinces of the Empire. The crystallization of a specifically Jewish counterpart of the various Romance vulgars goes back to a far later period. Moreover not every scholar of Jewish languages would add the determiner "Judeo-" to the Romance languages spoken by Medieval Jews in the Romance country. The Old French used by Rashi in 11th-century France and the Old Spanish used by Iberian Jews before the expulsion do not seem to have differed from the languages of the Christian surroundings. Indeed, the use of Hebrew letters in order to commit the Romance vernaculars to writ does not constitute a sufficient criterion to consider a Jewish variety of Romance vulgar (*la'az*) a full-fledged Judeo-Language.

To the east of the Romance territory, Germanic has given rise to only one Jewish language: *Yiddish. This originated among Romance-speaking Jews who either immigrated to a German-speaking region or else inhabited a Romance area that had been taken over by a Germanic tribe. Nothing is known about the Jews in Germany between Roman times and the Carolingian period, so that Jewish history there effectively begins in the ninth century C.E. It is thought that *Yiddish did not evolve as a separate language before the 13th century, that is, at the stage of Middle German. The process of koineization that led to the crystallization of Proto-Yiddish is bound up with the beginning of the emigration of the German Jews eastwards, following the growing hostility of the Gentile surroundings. The components of this koiné are not always easy to identify. Several theories compete. The first one sees Rhineland as the cradle of Yiddish. The second one associates the nucleus of Yiddish with Central dialects like Thuringian or East-Franconian. Besides, some features from such Southern dialects as Bavarian are recognizable in the koiné on which Yiddish is based.

A small element of Romance origin still survives in present-day Yiddish. But the most important external influence exerted upon Yiddish was that of the Slavic languages. When Yiddish- or Proto-Yiddish- speaking Jews still lived in Germany, they may have been in contact with Czech. Later on, after their migration to Eastern Central and Eastern Europe, Polish played a crucial role in the process of Slavization of Yiddish. Before WW II, Yiddish-speaking Jews comprised three-quarters of the entire Jewish people.

In the seventh century C.E. an important language change took place in the Orient. When the Arabs conquered much of western Asia, their new religion, Islam, was adopted by the inhabitants of wide areas in that region, and, with it, the Arabic language and alphabet. The Jews, too, adopted Arabic, although they did not abandon their religion and their alphabet. Their tongue, Judeo-Arabic, was like Arabic spoken over far too wide an area to remain uniform. Its most divergent branches are the Maghrebi ones of northwestern Africa, parallels to the local dialects of the Muslims (see *Judeo-Arabic/Judeo-Berber).

However, not all the areas that embraced Islam adopted Arabic. The most important exception was Persia, although here the Arabic alphabet was taken over, many Persian scholars and poets writing in Arabic and the Persian language itself being strongly influenced by that tongue. Thus, in the Iranian lands the Jews developed a Jewish variety of Farsi usually called *Judeo-Persian; in Central Asia, the Jews of Uzbekistan developed a Jewish variety of Tadjik; in Daghestan, the Dagh Churfut ("Mountain Jews") speak *Judeo-Tatic, an archaic variety of Farsi enriched with Hebrew words. In the southern Caucasus, in Georgia, we come across a non-Semitic, non-Indo-European Jewish language, Judeo-Georgian, which hardly differs from the Georgian spoken by the non-Jewish surrounding. To the west, there arose another language of neither Semitic nor Indo-European stock: Crimchak, spoken by the Crimean Jews and belonging to the Turkic language family (see *Krimchaks).

The languages of the Karaites form a group of their own; Karay in Lithuania and Poland; and Chaltay in the Crimea. Both of the latter go back to a common origin (in the Turkic family), but diverged widely.

The inroads of secularization in the 19th and 20th centuries have affected all the Jewish languages. Since statistics are not available, we do not know to what extent the number of speakers in each group has decreased.

Causes

New languages have perpetually come into being in the course of history. The causes are common to all linguistic development: migration, involving separation from the original language territory; divergence, through the growth of different political centers; and intermingling of populations, through conquest or pacific interpenetration. Of these causes only one has played a role in Jewish linguistic history – migration, i.e., the dispersion of the Jews over Asia and Europe during the centuries around the beginning of the Christian era. However, once the dispersion had, in the main, been completed, migration only rarely accounted for linguistic evolution, as in the development of East Yiddish and Judeo-Spanish. Language is a function of group life. The Jewish group is a creation of the Jewish religion, and that this is true of the past is beyond doubt. Hence the Jewish languages are creations of the group-forming factor of religion. This basic cause is reflected in features common to all of them: (1) they contain an element of Hebrew and Aramaic; (2) they are written in the Hebrew alphabet; and (3) the origin of their respective spelling systems is talmudic orthography.

Name

The correct designation for the various linguistic structures of the Jews is Jewish languages. All other names make no sense in modern linguistic scholarship; the terms "dialects," "jargons," "mixed languages," "corrupted languages," "Creolized languages," "Judeo-...," etc. are to be rejected for the following reasons. Jewish languages are not jargons, because a jargon is the restricted vocabulary used by those engaged in a particular occupation, but does not form the general vehicle of communication among its members. The Jewish languages are not more mixed than many other tongues, ranging from English and German to Persian and Turkish. They are not corruptions, because they obviously fulfill their function. The individuals within the Jewish groups in question communicate with each other through the medium of the particular language. When a linguistic structure fulfills this function, it is not "corrupted." There is much less justification for calling these Jewish tongues "Creolized" languages than there would be for classifying French or Spanish as "Creolized Latin."

The Hebrew and Aramaic Elements

In the Jewish languages, Hebrew and Aramaic elements form part of an uninterrupted development in speech and writing: they represent the present linguistic stage of a continuous process, previous stages of which crystallized into the languages of the Bible, Mishnah, *Gemara*, Midrash, liturgy, etc. In other words, they are connected with the sphere of religion, Judaism. This does not mean that the words in question are exclusively religious terms. Only a small minority can be so described. Moreover, these elements are to be found not only in the vocabularies of the Jewish languages, but also in their morphology and syntax, which cannot have any connection with religion.

Script

The Hebrew script is not included as part of the Hebrew and Aramaic elements, because language and script are independent of each other. Thus the script constitutes evidence of its own for the religious basis of the Jewish languages. It is a fact that the alphabet in which a language is written is, broadly speaking, decided by the religion of those speaking it. Maltese, for example, materially an Arabic language, is written in Latin characters because the Maltese are a Christian people belonging to the Western (Roman Catholic) Church. The same is true of the Croats, who, therefore, use the Latin alphabet for Croatian; while Serbian, for all practical purposes the exact same language, is written in the Cyrillic characters employed by the Eastern (Orthodox) Churches of Europe (apart from the Greek). The Arabic alphabet is used by the most heterogeneous languages and language-families (Persian, Urdu, Kurdish, Ottoman Turkish, Chagatay, Indonesian, Malay, Swahili, Malayalam, Haussa, Nubian, Fula, etc.), because those speaking them are Muslims. Cases where the religious factor has not been the historical cause for the use of a script appear to be very rare.

BIBLIOGRAPHY: H. Loewe, *Die Sprachen der Juden* (1911); S.A. Birnbaum, in: *Essays Presented to Dr. J.H. Hertz* (1943), 51–67; Idem, in: *Slavonic and East European Review*, 29 (1951), 42–443. **ADD. BIBLIOGRAPHY:** H.H. Paper (ed.), *Jewish Languages, Themes and Variations (Proceedings of Regional Conferences of the Association for Jewish Studies Held at The University of Michigan and New York University in March–April 1975)* (1978); J.A. Fishman (ed.), *Readings in the Sociology of Jewish Languages* (1985); S. Morag, M. Bar Asher, and M. Meyer Modena (eds.), *Vena Hebraica in Judæorum Linguis. Proceedings of the 2nd International Conference on the Hebrew and Aramaic Elements in Jewish Languages (Milan, October 23–26, 1995)* (1999).

[Solomon Asher Birnbaum / Cyril Aslanov (2nd ed.)]

JEWISH LEGION, military formation of Jewish volunteers in World War I who fought in the British army for the liberation of Ereẓ Israel from Turkish rule. When Turkey entered the war on the side of the Central Powers (Oct. 30, 1914), two different concepts of the Jewish role in the world conflict emerged among Zionists. In November David *Ben-Gurion and Yiẓḥak *Ben-Zvi submitted to the Turkish commander in Jerusalem a proposal to raise a Jewish Legion attached to the Turkish army. The project was approved by the Turkish military council in Jerusalem, and the first 40 Jewish volunteers began their training. Authorization, however, was soon canceled by Jamal Pasha, the supreme commander of the Turkish army in Palestine and Syria, who instigated severe persecutions of Zionists. Many were imprisoned; others, among them Ben-Zvi and Ben-Gurion, were deported. Of the 18,000 Jewish deportees and refugees, some 12,000 landed in Alexandria, Egypt.

The Zion Mule Corps

Vladimir Jabotinsky advanced a diametrically opposite concept. In December 1914, while a roving correspondent of a Moscow daily, he arrived in Alexandria and expounded to the Palestine deportees the idea of raising a Jewish Legion to fight with the Allies in order to liberate Palestine from the Turks. Joseph *Trumpeldor, one of the deportees, fully embraced Jabotinsky's idea. It was also endorsed by the majority of the Palestine Refugees' Committee. On March 22, 1915, about half of the 200 people present signed a seven-line resolution in Hebrew "to form a Jewish Legion and propose to England its utilization in Palestine." Within a few days about 500 enlisted, and training started immediately. Nonetheless, General Maxwell, commander of the British force in Egypt, told a delegation of the volunteers that an offensive on the Palestine front was doubtful and that regulations prohibited the admission of foreign nationals into the British army. He suggested that the volunteers serve as a detachment for mule transport on some other sector of the Turkish front. His proposal was rejected by most members of the Legion Committee, including Jabotinsky, but Trumpeldor's position was that any anti-Turkish front would "lead to Zion."

Together with Lieutenant Colonel John Henry *Patterson, delegated by the British military authorities, Trumpeldor succeeded in forming the 650-strong Zion Mule Corps; 562 of its members were sent to the Gallipoli front under Patterson, with Trumpeldor as second in command. The Zion Mule Corps' services were highly appreciated by General Ian Hamilton, commander of the Gallipoli Expeditionary Force, who wrote to Jabotinsky on Nov. 17, 1915: "The men have done extremely well, working their mules calmly under heavy shell and rifle fire, and thus showing a more difficult type of bravery than the men in the front line who had the excitement of combat to keep them going." The unit, however, posed severe disciplinary problems, and punishments such as public flogging had to be meted out. In addition, the differences between the idealists and those who had joined only in order to escape from the misery of the refugee camps resulted in clashes between Trumpeldor, the "Russian", and the Sephardi Jews. It was Patterson's goodwill and patience, coupled with Trumpeldor's devotion, that held the unit together throughout the Gallipoli campaign. Six legionnaires were killed, 25 were wounded, three received military honors, and one was decorated with a Distinguished Conduct Medal. The Corps was disbanded after the withdrawal of the ill-fated Gallipoli expedition early in 1916.

The Royal Fusiliers

Pursuing his project of a Jewish Legion for the Palestine front, throughout 1915–16 Jabotinsky had been trying unsuccessfully to win understanding and support in Rome (together with Pinḥas *Rutenberg), Paris, and London. In London he was ignored by the War Office and met with active disapproval on the part of Jewish assimilationist circles, as well as most of the Zionist leadership; an exception was Chaim *Weizmann, who promised assistance. Among the few active supporters were also Meir *Grossman, Jacob *Landau, Joseph *Cowen, and Montagu *Eder. In 1915–17 Grossman was publishing a Yiddish biweekly, *Di Tribune*, in Copenhagen and promoted the Legion idea. Zionists in Russia, which Jabotinsky visited in 1915, were almost unanimous in their condemnation of the idea. Appeals to the Jewish youth in London's East End were frustrated by apathy, which frequently erupted into open hostility, fanned by anarchist and communist émigrés. Public meetings, at which Jabotinsky, Trumpeldor, and Grossman tried to plead the Legion cause, were the scene of obstruction and abuse. Only about 300 signatures of men of military age were collected under the declaration: "Should the Government create a Jewish Regiment to be utilized exclusively for Home Defense or for operation on the Palestine front – I undertake to join such a Regiment."

At the end of 1916, when 120 former Zion Mule Corps soldiers, who again volunteered into the British army, had arrived in London, the tide began to turn. Assigned as a unit to the 20th London Battalion, they formed the nucleus of the Legion. Jabotinsky enlisted as a private in this battalion and, together with Trumpeldor, submitted to the British government a petition proposing the formation of a Jewish Legion for Palestine. Public opinion in Britain had been roused against the Russian Jews as "foreigners" who were earning their bread in the country and contributing nothing toward its defense. It was in this atmosphere that the British government decided to enlist the "foreigners." This decision, coupled with the revolution in Russia, weakened opposition to the Legion idea among Whitechapel's Jews. In July 1917, Patterson was ordered by the War Office to commence the organization of the Jewish regiment, and Jabotinsky was put in charge of recruitment. On August 23, when the British cabinet was already preparing the Balfour *Declaration, the formation of a Jewish regiment was officially announced in the London *Gazette*. Initially, assurances were given that the unit would be unequivocally Jewish in character and would be provided with Jewish emblems. The efforts of anti-Zionist Jews, however, succeeded in frustrating these achievements, and the unit was designated as the "38th Battalion of the Royal Fusiliers." It was promised that when it had proved its mettle in action, it would be granted both a Jewish name and Jewish insignia. About 50% of the battalion were British-born or naturalized; the remainder included members of the former Zion Mule Corps, a large number of Russian Jews, and a curious mélange from several Allied and neutral countries. On Feb. 2, 1918, the battalion marched through the City of London with fixed bayonets, a special privilege granted by the Lord Mayor, and on the following day it embarked for Egypt, where it continued training. Late in April it was joined by the 39th Battalion of Royal Fusiliers, over 50% of which was American volunteers, commanded by Lieutenant Colonel Eliezer *Margolin.

Transferred to Palestine in June 1918, the 38th Battalion was assigned front positions some 20 miles north of Jerusalem on the hills facing a Turkish encampment. There, Patterson later related, it "at once assumed a vigorous offensive policy" that "thoroughly scared the Turks, so much so that they never once attempted to come anywhere near our front." Afterward, the battalion spent seven weeks in the tropical Jordan Valley, where malaria took a heavy toll of the unit. Of 800 men, no more than 150, and only half of its 30 officers, remained in active service at the end of this ordeal. Over 20 were killed, wounded, or captured; the rest were stricken with malaria, of whom more than 30 died. On September 19, the 38th Battalion and two companies of Margolin's 39th Battalion were assigned the task of capturing both sides of the Umm Shart ford across the Jordan River and advancing east beyond the Jordan. After the first attempt to gain the ford failed, Jabotinsky's company "was ordered to make the second attempt … and achieve the purpose at all costs." The operation was successful. Margolin's two companies of American volunteers crossed the Jordan and marched to al Ṣalt, where Margolin was appointed commander of the town. General Chaytor, commander of Allenby's right wing, told the Legionnaires: "By forcing the Jordan fords you helped in no small measure to win the great victory gained at Damascus."

The Palestinian Volunteers

Early in 1918 a strong movement for the formation of a Palestinian Jewish Legion developed among the 18,000–20,000 Jews in the part of the country (Jerusalem, Tel Aviv, Jaffa, the settlements in Judea) by then occupied by the British army. The British forces were received as deliverers, and the call for volunteers, first made by General Hill, the British commander of the Jaffa-Tel Aviv area, received a response among the workers, the students of the Hebrew High School in Tel Aviv, and a few farmers, led by Moshe Smilansky. At a conference held in Jaffa on Feb. 15–16, 1918, the volunteers drafted their aims and chose a committee, and a mass meeting in Reḥovot, attended by about 1,000 volunteers, was addressed by Jabotinsky. These volunteers encountered great difficulties in their desire to enlist, as there was much hesitation on the part of the British, and some influential circles in the *yishuv* also opposed the idea. In 1920 the British foreign office related that the initiative had come from "the Jewish population itself, rather than from any desire or even encouragement from the British authorities." A petition with several hundred signatures was submitted to the military authorities in January 1918 but the authorization for recruitment was not given before May. According to the Foreign Office, "practically the whole available Jewish youth, whatever their national status," had enlisted. The Jaffa area supplied 457 recruits (10% of its Jewish population) and Jerusalem supplied 350. Within the first few weeks, more than 1,000 men volunteered. Most of them were Ottoman subjects and, if captured by the Turks, would have been hanged. With the advancement of Allenby's army, more volunteers were coming forward from the areas in the north; permission to join was given to 92 Turkish Jews who were prisoners of war in Egypt. In August a recruiting office was opened in Cairo and attracted some 200 volunteers. Many Palestinian recruits were highly educated, with a thorough knowledge of the country; they spoke Arabic fluently, and were expert shots and horsemen. They were formed into the 40th Battalion of Royal Fusiliers, under the command of Colonel M.F. Scott, and were sent for training to the Tell al Kabīr camp in Egypt, where they were kept for an unduly long time, so that they missed the decisive offensive in September 1918.

The American Volunteers

In America, enlisting for the Jewish Legion started practically in 1917, after the publication of the Balfour Declaration. Most of the volunteers were aliens or holders of first naturalization papers and thus not eligible for the U.S. draft; some American-born citizens below the draft age of 21 deliberately misstated their age to join the Legion, and those eligible for the U.S. draft received transfers to the Legion-in-formation without difficulty. One of the prime movers of the idea was the Po'alei Zion Party led by Ben-Gurion and Ben-Zvi. The Zionist Organization of America, which had been opposed to the Legion project, now decided – largely due to Justice *Brandeis' influence – that "the Jewish Legion is one of the most important factors in the realization of the aims of political Zionism." In February 1918 the first group of 150 volunteers left New York for military training in Windsor, Canada; further contingents were leaving the United States at regular intervals of three weeks, and a total of 2,700 were ultimately accepted. Among them were some 200 Palestinian exiles in America, and 150 more were drawn from the local pioneer groups; Ben-Gurion and Ben-Zvi themselves enlisted on April 26, 1918. When a train carrying a group of volunteers passed through Bangor, Maine, it was flagged down to enable a crowd lining the tracks to see and embrace the Legionnares. The volunteers wore the *Magen David* on their khaki uniforms and had their own blue-white banner with the inscription, "If I forget thee, O Jerusalem." In August 1918 they sailed with the Canadians for further training, first to Camp Eggbuckland in Plymouth, England, and then to the Tell-al-Kabīr camp in Egypt, where they joined the 39th Battalion. There was considerable dissatisfaction among them with the protracted training period, which lasted so long that the American volunteers did not see action in Palestine, for they arrived when the war had already ended.

After the War

When the armistice with Turkey was signed on October 31, the entire territory of Palestine was liberated from the Turks. The battered remnant of Patterson's 38th Battalion (predominantly "English" with an admixture of "Americans") took over the "line of communication" duty. It was soon joined by Margolin's 39th Battalion (mostly American volunteers). Early in December 1918, the 40th Battalion (Palestinians only), which was deliberately kept in reserve in Egypt – allegedly for further training – also succeeded in being transferred to Palestine. By the beginning of 1919, the three battalions numbered over 5,000 men, about one-sixth of the entire British army of occupation, one-quarter of the infantry, and almost one-half of the white infantry regiments. While a large portion of the British contingent was transferred to Syria and southern Anatolia and another was sent to Egypt in the spring of 1919, the Legion's strength had increased threefold from 1918, when only 1,500 were able to actually take part in the military operations. The major component constituted the volunteers from the United States (34%), followed by the Palestinians (30%), volunteers from England (28%), Canada (6%), Argentina (1%), and Turkish war prisoners (1%). After the victorious end of the Palestine campaign, the name "Royal Fusiliers" was changed, as promised, to "Judean Regiment"; its insignia became a *menorah* with the Hebrew word "*kadimah*" (before that, all officers and men at the front wore a *Magen David* on their sleeves: one battalion red, the second blue, and the third violet). The actual strength of the Legion could have been more than twice as large. Applications for enlistment came from several countries; 1,500 volunteered in Salonika; in Italy, 2,000 Transylvanian prisoners of war applied to be enlisted; the "Mountain Jews" from Dagestan in the Caucausus sent emissaries offering all their youth. The number of those who had actually enlisted – in addition to the 5,000 in active service – by Armistice Day (Nov. 11, 1918) was 5,600 (mostly Americans, with a sprinkling from Canada); however, it was not considered worthwhile to send them to the Palestine front. They were demobilized directly from the original Legion base at Plymouth, where they had gone through their training under the command of Colonel J.S. Miller, a Jew.

At an early stage, there was a definite plan to convert the Legion into a full-fledged brigade, comprising four battalions. Sir Nevil Macready, adjutant general of the British War Office, told Patterson that his aim was the formation of a complete Jewish Brigade. Allenby opposed such a project at the outset but later wrote to Patterson that he would "form a provisional Brigade of the Jewish battalions until a complete Jewish Brigade can be formed." This plan was never fulfilled. "Instead," relates Patterson, "we were pushed around from brigade to brigade and from division to division; in the space of three months we found ourselves attached to not less than 12 different formations of the British Army." British military authorities openly discriminated against the Legion. Jerusalem was placed out of bounds for Jewish soldiers. They were often so molested by the military police that, according to Patterson, the only way they could enjoy a peaceful walk outside the camp limits was by removing their distinctive badges. There were cases of disobedience and mutiny among the frustrated Legionnaires. 55 Canadian and U.S. volunteers in the 38th Battalion were sentenced by court martial to various terms of penal servitude, ranging from seven years downward (they were amnestied four months later), and 44 Legionnaires of the 39th Battalion received sentences of two to seven years (for most of them the term was reduced to one year; actually, they served six months).

The Demobilization

As long as the Legion remained in full strength, occupying strategically crucial positions, there was peace and order in the country. The situation began to deteriorate with the progressive whittling down of the Judeans. The anti-Zionist military administration was eager to promote their demobilization at the earliest possible date. When the formation of a standing army of occupation was announced, several hundred overseas (predominantly American) volunteers offered their services, but British headquarters sabotaged their reenlistment. Jabotinsky, who was urging the volunteers to stay on and who had himself registered for further service, was forcibly demobilized in August 1919. Largely as a result of this official attitude, an ever-growing eagerness to be discharged and repatriated emerged among the American volunteers. Appeals to hold on in order to safeguard the security of the Palestine Jewish community were of little avail: very few believed that there was any real danger of Arab violence. A marked tendency toward speedy repatriation also developed among the Legionnaires from England. There were among them both volunteers and conscripts; the latter were predominantly tailors from the London East End, and only a few of them held Zionist convictions. The "tailors," however, remained in Palestine longer than any other group of overseas Jewish soldiers and were among the last to be discharged. The urge for demobilization that developed among the Palestinian volunteers was largely motivated by eagerness to resume work or to join a kevuẓah. Yet several hundred of them clung to the belief that the upbuilding of Ereẓ Israel required protection, and they fought strenuously against demobilization. When their period of engagement ended, they contrived to have it extended for three months and then for another three months. Nonetheless, the whittling down of the Legion proceeded. In the second part of 1919, only two of the three battalions were still in existence, then one (the Palestinian unit), and then only part of that. In the spring of 1920 a mere 300 to 400 men remained.

During the Riots of 1920–21

In 1920, when the first anti-Jewish riots broke out in Jerusalem, the remnants of the Jewish Legion were confined to barracks. Two companies of a self-defense corps (Haganah), organized by Jabotinsky and trained by demobilized Legionnaires, marched to the Jaffa and Damascus Gates of the Old City of Jerusalem, but found them closed and guarded by British troops. Jabotinsky and 19 others, mostly former Legionnaires, were subsequently arrested and sentenced to penal servitude by a British military tribunal (they were later amnestied). Sir Herbert *Samuel, the first high commissioner of Palestine, created a mixed Arab-Jewish militia, based on voluntary enlistment. The last 400 Palestinian Legionnaires joined this formation, and Margolin was appointed commander of its Jewish half. On May 1, 1921, when anti-Jewish riots broke out in Jaffa, leaving behind 13 massacred Jews, Margolin entered the town with his men fully armed, without asking permission from the military authorities. Accused of breach of discipline, he was forced to resign.

In 1921 the Executive of the World Zionist Organization requested of the British government that the 38th–40th Royal Fusiliers ("Judeans"), as established in 1917–18, should "continue to form part of the British Forces in Palestine"; recruiting of Jewish volunteers should be reinstituted until their number reached at least one-half of the proposed total strength (7,700) of the British garrison in Palestine. This demand was subsequently endorsed by the Zionist General Council and by the 12th Zionist Congress at Carlsbad (August 1921). The initial program of the *Revisionist movement, voted upon at its first world conference (April 1925), included as its central plank the demand that the Jewish regiment be "restored as an integral part of the British garrison in Palestine." At the 14th Zionist Congress (Vienna, August 1925), however, Weizmann reversed his previous stand and declared that under the existing circumstances the demand for a Jewish Legion was "not only useless but even harmful." Faced with the decision of the Mandatory administration to set up an Arab military unit for service in western Palestine and a Circassian one to serve on the borders of Transjordan, in October 1926 the *Va'ad Le'ummi urged the administration to establish a purely Jewish military unit within the Transjordan Frontier Force. The demand remained unheeded, though individual Jews were accepted for service in it. The Palestine government promised to facilitate the settlement of demobilized Legionnaires on government land, but the promise was not honored, as areas offered by the government were not suitable for agricultural settlement. In 1932, 60 former Judeans from the United States, Canada, and Argentina founded a moshav ovdim, *Aviḥayil, north of Netanyah. Continuing the tradition of the Legion, 65 men, out of its population of 345, volunteered for military service during World War II. In 1961 a cultural center (Legion's House) and Museum of the Legion was inaugurated there.

[Joseph B. Schechtman]

History

A definitive history of the Jewish Legion was published in Hebrew by Yigal Elam, under the title *Ha-Gedudim ha-Ivri'im be-Milḥemet ha-Olam ha-Rishonah* (1973).

BIBLIOGRAPHY: V. Jabotinsky, *The Story of the Jewish Legion* (1945); J.H. Patterson, *With the Zionists in Gallipoli* (1916); idem, *With the Judeans in the Palestine Campaign* (1922); E. Gilmor, *War and Hope – A History of the Jewish Legion* (1969); Dinur, Haganah, 1 (1954–56), 425–532, 641–4, 748–68, 868–90, and indexes; *Me-Ḥayyei Y. Trumpeldor, Koveẓ Mikhtavim ve-Kitei Reshimot* (1945), 115–314, 355–60; E. Golomb, *Ḥevyon Oz*, 1 (1953), 141–202, 353–70; D. Ever ha-Dani, *Am be-Milḥamto* (1948), 7–181; Mifleget Po'alei Zion be-E.I., *Al ha-Saf* (1918); M. Smilansky, *Be-Ẓel ha-Pardesim* (1952).

JEWISH MESSENGER, THE, New York weekly. Issued first in 1857 as a semimonthly produced by the pupils of the school conducted by the Rev. S.M. *Isaacs, *The Jewish Messenger* soon became a weekly, edited by Isaacs till his death in 1878. It took a traditionalist, anti-Reform position in religious matters and identified itself closely with the Board of Delegates of American Israelites. Before and during the Civil War it was strongly Abolitionist in viewpoint. On the death of S.M. Isaacs, the paper was taken over by his son Myer S. *Isaacs. Under his direction, its outlook became more favorable to Reform Judaism. *The Jewish Messenger* was absorbed by the *American Hebrew* in 1903.

JEWISH MORNING JOURNAL (Yid. **Der Morgen Zhornal**), U.S. Yiddish daily. Founded in 1901 by the politically conservative and religiously Orthodox publisher Jacob Saphirstein, and edited by Peter Wiernik, the *Morning Journal* was for years New York City's only morning Yiddish paper. This resulted in it doing a highly profitable business in want ads. It was also unique in its support of the Republican Party. In 1916 it reached its peak circulation of 111,000. The same year Jacob *Fishman was appointed editor, and under his direction (1916–38) the paper took on a more liberal, intellectual tone. Among some of the prominent writers on Fishman's staff were the critics Bernard *Gorin and A. *Mukdoni, the poet Jacob *Glatstein, city editor Jacob *Magidov, and Gedaliah *Bublick, formerly editor of the *Yidishes Tagblat*. In common with the rest of the Yiddish press, the *Morning Journal's* readership declined steadily after World War I. In 1928 it absorbed the *Yidishes Tagblat* and in 1953 it merged with the *Jewish Day. In 1970 the circulation of *The Day-Morning Journal* was put at 50,000. It ceased publication in 1971.

BIBLIOGRAPHY: J. Chaikin, *Yidishe Bleter in Amerike* (1946), index; J.L. Teller, *Strangers and Natives* (1968), index.

[Hillel Halkin]

JEWISH MUSEUM. The Jewish Museum in New York City is widely admired for its exhibitions and educational programs that inspire people of all backgrounds; it is the preeminent United States institution of its kind exploring 4,000 years of art and Jewish culture.

The Jewish Museum was established on January 20, 1904, when Judge Mayer Sulzberger donated 26 objects to The Jewish Theological Seminary of America as the core of a museum collection. The museum was the first institution of its kind in the United States and one of the very few in the world when it was established. The incorporation of several major collections – the H. Ephraim and Mordecai Benguiat Collection of objects from Smyrna, Turkey in 1924; the Danzig (then Germany and now Gdansk, Poland) Jewish Community Collection in 1939; the Benjamin and Rose Mintz Collection from Warsaw, Poland, in 1947; and ceremonial objects, looted by the Nazis and recovered by the United States Military Government in Germany, presented to the museum by the Jewish Cultural Reconstruction in 1952 – transformed the original holdings into a significant museum collection. A collection of numismatics was established through gifts of Samuel J. Friedenberg and his son, Daniel, for over 50 years beginning in 1948. Dr. Harry G. Friedman was a major donor, from 1941 until his death in 1965, who purchased for the museum over several thousand works in all media from Europe, North Africa, and the Middle East.

The collection was installed in the new Jacob H. Schiff Library of The Jewish Theological Seminary as The Museum of Jewish Ceremonial Objects in 1931. In 1944, Frieda Schiff Warburg gave the seminary her family residence at 1109 Fifth Avenue and 92nd Street to house the Museum. The Jewish Museum opened at its current location in the former Warburg mansion in 1947.

This led to a new emphasis on temporary exhibitions of objects of various media. A fine arts collection was developed that encompassed not only paintings and sculpture, but also prints, photographs, and drawings. In 1956, the Tobe Pascher Workshop was established for the creation of Jewish ceremonial art in a modern style. In the late 1960s, The Jewish Museum began collecting and exhibiting archaeological artifacts from Israel and the ancient Jewish Diaspora. There was an added impetus in the 1980s to collect the works of Israeli artists and contemporary art by American artists, spurred by research related to several exhibitions. Established in 1981, the National Jewish Archive of Broadcasting has since become the largest and most comprehensive body of television and radio programs on 20th-century Jewish culture in the United States. In the late 1990s, collecting contemporary ceremonial art and photography received greater emphasis.

The museum reopened in dramatically expanded and renovated quarters at the Fifth Avenue mansion in 1993. In 2005 The Jewish Museum maintained an important collection of 25,000 objects – paintings, sculpture, works on paper, photographs, archeological artifacts, ceremonial objects, decorative arts, and broadcast media.

Culture and Continuity: The Jewish Journey, originally mounted in 1993 and reinstalled in two stages in 2000 and 2003, explores the dynamic interaction between continuity and change within Jewish culture and history that was important for Jewish survival over 4,000 years. Highlights include paintings by such artists as Max *Weber, Moritz Daniel *Oppenheim, Isidor *Kaufmann, Morris *Louis, Ken Aptekar, and Deborah Kass; prints by Ben *Shahn and El *Lissitzky; and sculptures by Chana *Orloff and Hannah Wilke. Displays of Torah ornaments and Hanukkah lamps allow the viewer to compare artistic styles from different parts of the world. Leonard Baskin's 1977 sculpture, *The Altar* (based on the biblical story of the sacrifice of Isaac), considered the artist's greatest carving, is on view as is George *Segal's 1982 work, *The Holocaust*. Featured television excerpts range from David Ben-Gurion declaring the independence of the State of Israel in 1948 to Abraham Joshua Heschel and Martin Luther King, Jr. in Alabama in 1965 to Adam *Sandler singing part of *The Hanukkah Song*.

The Jewish Museum has been host to some groundbreaking temporary exhibitions. Among them were *Artists of the New York School: Second Generation* (1957), featuring works by 23 emerging artists, including Helen *Frankenthaler, Jasper Johns, Robert Rauschenberg, and George Segal; *Primary Structures* (1966), the landmark exhibition that defined the Minimalist movement; *Lower East Side: Portal to American Life* (1966); *Masada: Struggle for Freedom* (1967); *Software* (1970), a pioneering exhibition about information technology and interactive art; *The Precious Legacy: Judaic Treasures from the Czechoslovak State Collections* (1984) which brought to the United States treasures from the State Jewish Museum in Prague, the bulk of which had been confiscated from the Jews of Bohemia and Moravia by the Nazis for a proposed museum to an extinct race; *Gardens and Ghettos: The Art of Jewish Life in Italy* (1986); *The Dreyfus Affair: Art, Truth and Justice* (1987), an acclaimed exhibition integrating the visual arts and social history; *Too Jewish? Challenging Traditional Identities*

(1996), which explored how ethnic consciousness had a profound effect on many Jewish artists; *Marc Chagall: 1907–1917* (1996); *An Expressionist in Paris: The Paintings of Chaim Soutine* (1998); *New York: Capital of Photography* (2002); *Schoenberg, Kandinsky, and the Blue Rider* (2003); *Modigliani: Beyond the Myth* (2004); *The Power of Conversation: Jewish Women and Their Salons* (2005); and *Sarah Bernhardt: The Art of High Drama* (2005).

[Jewish Museum Staff (2nd ed.)]

JEWISH NATIONAL FUND (Heb. קֶרֶן קַיֶּמֶת לְיִשְׂרָאֵל - (קק"ל), **Keren Kayemeth Leisrael**), the land purchase and development fund of the Zionist Organization. It was founded on December 29, 1901 at the Fifth Zionist Congress at Basle, which resolved: "The JNF shall be the eternal possession of the Jewish people. Its funds shall not be used except for the purchase of lands in Palestine and Syria." The Hebrew name comes from the talmudic dictum about good deeds "the fruits of which a man enjoys in this world, while the capital abides (*ha-keren kayyemet*) for him in the world to come" (Pe'ah 1:1). A land fund was first suggested by Judah *Alkalai in 1847. It was proposed by Hermann *Schapira at the *Katowice Conference in 1884 and again at the First Zionist Congress in 1897. Schapira based his idea of public ownership of land on the biblical injunction "The land shall not be sold forever for the land is Mine," and on the institution of the Jubilee Year, which stipulates that all holdings which have changed hands revert to their original owners in the 50th year (Lev. 25:10, 23–24).

JNF leasehold contracts run for 49 years and can be prolonged by the lessee or his heirs as long as they serve the purpose specified; holdings may neither be united with other domains nor divided among several heirs; the lessee needs the lessor's consent if he wishes to use his holding for a purpose other than that stipulated in the contract; on rural tracts, the lessee must cultivate his own soil; ground rents are to be kept as low as possible, whether the land serves farming, industry, housing, or other purposes.

Early Activities

Between 1902 and 1907, the JNF had its administration in Vienna, where Johann *Kremenezki created a worldwide organization for fund raising by means of JNF stamps, the Blue Box, a small tin collection box, and the Golden Book for honoring a person by donating a large contribution in his name which is inscribed in the book, which soon became popular Zionist symbols. In 1907 the head office was transferred to Cologne, with Max *Bodenheimer as chairman of the board of directors, and the JNF was incorporated in London as an "association limited by guarantee." The first tract of land acquired was that of Kefar Ḥittim in Lower Galilee (1904), followed in 1908 by Ben Shemen and Ḥuldah in Judea, and Kinneret-Deganyah near Lake Kinneret. The JNF made its first experiments in tree planting in 1908 with the Herzl Forest, financed by its Olive Tree Fund. It aided urban development by long-term loans to the founders of Tel Aviv and by acquiring the building of the *Bezalel Art School in Jerusalem, land for the Herzlia High School in Tel Aviv, and the *Technion in Haifa. It also financed the activities of the Palestine Office of the Zionist Organization. In 1914, with the outbreak of World War I, the head office was transferred to The Hague in neutral Holland under Nehemia de *Lieme. In July 1920, the London Conference of the Zionist Organization, which established an additional fund, the *Keren Hayesod, declared the JNF to be "the instrument of the urban and rural land policy of the Jewish people," devoted exclusively to land acquisition and improvement.

Under the Mandate

The first large settlement area was acquired in 1921 in the Jezreel Valley ("The Emek"), increasing JNF land property from 4,000 to almost 15,000 acres (16,000 to 59,000 dunams) after a violent debate with Zionist leaders who preferred the acquisition of urban holdings. In 1922, the head office was transferred to Jerusalem, and Menahem *Ussishkin became its president. During the later 1920s, it acquired the Emek Ḥefer, creating a continuous chain of Jewish settlement in the coastal plain, with the Plain of Zebulun as hinterland to Haifa port. The Arab riots of 1936–39, and the Peel Commission's partition plan (1937–38) lent increased political importance to JNF land acquisition. Jewish holdings and "*stockade and watchtower" settlements were rapidly extended to new regions (Beth-Shean and Ḥuleh valleys, Manasseh Hills, Western Galilee, southern Coastal Plain). During World War II, the JNF sought intricate legal expedients to overcome the severe restrictions imposed in February 1940 by the land regulations issued under the British White Paper, and stepped up land acquisition even further. Opening up the northern Negev for Jewish settlement and strengthening positions in Galilee, it brought its possessions in 1947 to 234,000 acres (936,000 dunams), more than half the total Jewish holdings in Palestine. After Ussishkin's death in 1941, a committee of three – Berl *Katzenelson, Rabbi Meir *Bar-Ilan (Berlin), and Abraham *Granott – headed the JNF board of directors. In 1945, Granott took over as chairman and on his death in 1960 was succeeded by Jacob *Tsur.

In Independent Israel

With the founding of the State of Israel, the emphasis of JNF activity shifted from land purchase to land improvement and development as well as afforestation, headed by Joseph *Weitz from the early 1920s. Besides swamp drainage (Jezreel Valley, Ḥefer and Zebulun plains, etc.), much was done for hill reclamation through stone clearing and terracing, principally along the 1949 armistice borders, opening new areas for settlement. In the Negev contour-line plowing, planting of shelter belts around fields, and leveling of eroded terrain have won new areas for farming. The JNF's most important swamp draining enterprise was that of the Ḥuleh Valley (1952–58). By 1967 the JNF had reclaimed a total of 120,000 acres (480,000 dunams) and another 125,000 acres (500,000 dunams) approximately through swamp draining, together totaling about a quarter of the 1.05 million acres of cultivated land inside Israel's 1966 borders. Up to 1947, the JNF planted 5,280,000 forest trees on approximately 5,000 acres. Annual planting equaled or exceeded these figures since 1948, bringing the total in 1967 to more than 90,000,000 trees and 100,000 acres, in addition to thousands of acres of degenerated natural brush rehabilitated by adequate care. The JNF serves tourism by installing camping and picnic grounds in its forests, and participates in landscaping national parks and nature reserves. As part of its reclamation and afforestation programs, it has paved over c. 1200 miles (2,000 kilometers) of roads, particularly in border areas. It also constructs storage dams to make storm-flood water available for irrigation. The JNF has aided immigrant absorption by setting up "work villages" and providing work for newcomers, especially during periods of unemployment. Since the mid-1950s, the JNF has embarked on comprehensive regional development projects (the Adullam, Adoraim, Yatir regions in southern Judea, the Modi'in region in northern Judea, the Iron Hills and Mount Gilboa in Samaria, the Chorazim region north of Lake Kinneret, and, from 1963, Central Galilee bordering on Lebanon). In the 1960s, the JNF started building *Naḥal outpost villages in reclaimed border areas.

In July, 1960, the Knesset passed a fundamental law on Israel land holdings, followed by the Israel Land Administration Law. An agreement between the JNF and the government, signed on August 1, 1960, set up an Israel Land Authority for the administration of all government and JNF holdings, with a council of seven government and six JNF representatives, and a Land Development Authority functioning in the JNF framework, with seven JNF and six government representatives on its council. The latter is responsible for land development and afforestation of all public land. In 1967, JNF land holdings totaled more than 637,000 acres (2,549,000 dunams), including 332,500 acres (1,330,000 dunams) which the JNF acquired from the state after 1948. In 1967, the government approved a concession to the JNF for the development of state domain land totaling 125,000 acres (500,000 dunams).

The JNF derives its budget largely from contributions from world Jewry, which in the 1960s averaged IL24,000,000 per year; the balance of the IL56,000,000 budget comes from leasehold fees and other sources. It operates in approximately 40 countries. It engages in Zionist education in schools and youth movements both in Israel and abroad; a JNF teachers' council is active in Israel, as well as in a number of Diaspora countries. The JNF is headed by a board of directors consisting of 26 members elected by the Zionist General Council and up to three governors nominated by the Zionist Executive.

After the Six-Day War the JNF reclaimed 11,000 acres of land and helped establish new settlements in both the Rafiah area and the Aravah. In afforestation work, JNF trees reached the 100 million mark. During the 1980s a quarter of the JNF's trees were planted in the Negev, bringing its afforested area up to 45,000 acres. The JNF built dams and reservoirs to combat Israel's chronic water shortage, and in the 1990s started to rehabilitate the Hula Valley in order to prevent the flow of pollutants to the Sea of Galilee and restore the fertility of agricultural lands. It also provided the infrastructure for housing the massive waves of immigrants during the decade.

In the hundred years since it was founded, the JNF has planted more than 240 million trees, built more than 180 dams and reservoirs, developed more than 250,000 acres of land, and created more than 1,000 parks throughout Israel. It ensured that Israel was the only nation in the world to end the 20th century with more trees than it had at the beginning.

BIBLIOGRAPHY: A. Boehm and A. Pollak, *Jewish National Fund* (1939); A. Granott, *Agrarian Reform and the Record of Israel* (1956); J. Tsur, *Old Concepts and New Realities* (1962); J. Weitz, *Activities and Tasks of the Jewish National Fund* (1933); idem, *Afforestation Policy in Israel* (1950); idem, *Struggle for the Land* (1950); *Reports of Keren Kayemeth Leisrael to the Zionist Congresses*, beginning from the Sixth Congress (1903–). **WEBSITE:** www.kkl.org.il.

[Jacob Tsur]

JEWISH PUBLICATION SOCIETY, THE (JPS), a nonprofit, non-denominational association established to disseminate works of Jewish content in English, founded on June 3, 1888, as a membership organization and publisher. Two earlier attempts to establish an "American Jewish Publication Society" failed: the first founded by Isaac *Leeser in Philadelphia in 1845 and discontinued in 1851; the second founded by a New York group and lasting from 1873 to 1875. The third such body, The Jewish Publication Society of America, succeeded and has been in continuous operation since 1888. The organizational meeting was called in Philadelphia, then still considered the cultural capital of the United States, by Rabbi Joseph *Krauskopf and Dr. Solomon *Solis-Cohen. In the 1990s, the Society dropped "of America" from its name, and broadened its original mission statement to encompass secular as well as religious works, for non-Jewish as well as Jewish readers throughout the world.

The Society functions through a board of trustees, whose membership reflects geographic, professional, and religious diversity. The first president was Morris Newburger; his successors have included leaders in business, law, education, and medicine. The editorial committee, consisting of scholars and learned laypeople and originally known as the publication committee, advises the professional staff and board of trustees on acquisitions. Committee chairs have included Mayer *Sulzberger, Cyrus *Adler, Jacob R. *Marcus, Gerson D. Cohen, Yosef Yerushalmi, and Chaim Potok. From 1919 to 1950 the Society also operated a Hebrew-English press, established through the gifts of Jacob H. *Schiff.

The Society's first book was Lady Kate Magnus's *Outline of Jewish History* (1890). In 1891 it began publication of Graetz's six volume *History of the Jews* (1891–98). Among the many authors on the Society's list are Solomon Schechter, Louis Ginzberg (*Legends of the Jews*, 7 vols., 1909–38), S.M. Dubnow, Leo Baeck, Cecil Roth, Jacob R. Marcus, Louis Finkelstein, S.W. Baron, Martin Buber, Mordecai Kaplan, S.Y. Agnon, Joseph Soloveitchik, Yehudah Amichai, and Avivah Zornberg.

JPS has published works covering every aspect of Jewish life. During its first few decades when it was the only North American publisher of Jewish books in English, the Society's list spanned the full spectrum of Jewish literature: history, Bible, rabbinics, textual commentary, biography and memoir, belles-lettres, politics and social science, folklore, intellectual history, contemporary thought, and children's books. After other presses – organizational, commercial, academic, and Jewish – began publishing Judaica in English beginning in the 1920s and expanding after World War II, the Society began to focus its publishing program. In recent times, it has moved away from scholarly monographs, belles-lettres, and overly commercial books, concentrating on Bible and commentary, classic texts in translation, reference and resources for adult Jewish learners and lay readers, and children's books for middle readers.

The Society has also published a number of series: the Schiff Classics (9 titles, 16 volumes); histories of Jewish communities (8 volumes); critical Bible commentaries (9 volumes, ongoing); and a series of biographies for young people. *The American Jewish Yearbook* (AJYB) was initiated by JPS in 1899, and was later published jointly by the Society and the American Jewish Committee from 1908 to 1995, after which AJC continued as sole publisher. Occasionally the Society publishes works jointly with other institutions and publishers. The annual number of volumes has varied between two and eighteen; in recent years, its annual list has averaged twelve new publications per year.

Among the Society's major undertakings have been two translations of the Hebrew Bible in English. The first translation, adapted from the Protestant Revised Standard Version in light of Jewish interpretive tradition, appeared in 1917 as *The Holy Scriptures;* a Hebrew–English edition appeared in 1955. That same year the Society began a second translation, this time based on the Hebrew Masoretic text rather than on earlier English translations, with the twin goals of incorporating the latest scientific research in philology, Comparative Semitics, and archaeology; and of making the Bible more comprehensible to modern readers. First appearing in three separate volumes – *Torah* (1962), *Prophets* (1978), and *Writings* (1982), the final one-volume *JPS TANAKH* was published in 1985. A Hebrew-English edition was published in 1999.

The Society's first editor was Henrietta *Szold, although she was never accorded the formal title. From 1892 to 1916, she served as secretary of the publication committee, and also performed the functions of editor, proofreader, sometime translator, and production manager. Later editors have included Isaac *Husik (1924–39); Solomon *Grayzel (1939–66); Chaim Potok (1966–74); and Ellen Frankel from 1981.

BIBLIOGRAPHY: AJYB (1899–), report of JPS; *Jewish Publication Society of America, 25th Anniversary* (1913); J. Bloch, *Of Making Many Books* (1953); Grayzel, in: JPS, *Bookmark*, 10 no. 4 (1963), 4–7; J. Sarna, *JPS: The Americanization of Jewish Culture, 1888–1988.*

JEWISH QUARTER. The existence of separate Jewish streets or quarters (Lat. Platea Judaeorum; Sp. Judería; Fr. Juiverie; It. Giudecca; Eng. Jewry; Ger. Judengasse, Pol. Ulica Żydowska) originated in the voluntary preference of the Jewish community to live in a way that would enable it to keep to its laws and customs and defend itself from hostile attacks if need be. The nature and character of Jewish life, entailing observance of the precepts, the necessity of maintaining a quorum for prayers, a cemetery, and *mikveh*, the need for providing mutual assistance as a persecuted and degraded minority as well as insecurity from attack by strangers and enemies – all combined to make Jews concentrate in a particular street or neighborhood in all the countries of Europe. At times, non-Jews also lived in the Jewish district, while Jews also lived outside it. These quarters were generally closed off by a wall and gates. Occasionally, they were even in the center of the city or in its main street. According to Benjamin of *Tudela, the Jews of *Constantinople had their separate quarter at the end of the 12th century. In several Spanish cities, such as *Toledo, *Seville, and *Saragossa, the Jewish quarter constituted a separate townlet, surrounded by a wall and even fortified. The right to live in a separate quarter surrounded by a wall was granted to the Jews of *Speyer in 1084 by the bishop, at the express request of the Jews themselves; similar privileges permitting fortified "Jewish quarters" were granted to Jews in Christian Spain during the Reconquest. This changed as the status of the Jews deteriorated and the image of the Jew was even more viciously blackened.

Establishment of the Ghetto

From the beginning of the 16th century, the name given in Italy to the Jewish quarter, which was separated and closed off by law from the other parts of the town by a wall and gates, was "*ghetto." From then on, the word ghetto has also been used to designate Jewish quarters which were officially set aside in other countries. Figuratively and erroneously, this name has also been regularly applied to quarters, neighborhoods, and areas throughout the Diaspora, which became places of residence for numerous Jews.

The root of the word ghetto has been sought in Hebrew (*get* – "bill of divorcement"), in Yiddish, Latin, Greek, and Gothic. There is, however, no doubt that the origin is *geto nuovo* ("the new foundry"), the site of the first separate Jewish quarter in *Venice from 1516. The Jews of Italy occasionally referred to the ghetto in their dialect as *get*, but the usual appellation was "courtyard." In the towns of southern France under papal rule where ghettos were established after the Italian model, they were named *carrière* in French and *mesillah* ("road") in Hebrew.

The idea of the ghetto in its restricted sense resulted from the tendency implanted in Christianity from the fourth to fifth centuries to isolate the Jews and humiliate them. It first appears in the West in the proceedings of the Church *councils of the Middle Ages, especially at the third Lateran council (1179), where Jews and Christians were prohibited from living together. Initially, this prohibition was enforced in a few places, as in London from 1276. From the beginning of the 15th century it was included – in conjunction with the prohibition on moneylending against interest and the order concerning the Jewish *badge – in the anti-Jewish program of the Christian religious orders, especially in Italy; it was thus applied, for example, in Bologna from 1417 and in Turin from 1425. However, the ghetto did not appear as a permanent institution until its introduction in Venice in 1516. Then Jews who sought refuge in the city, from which they had been banned over a lengthy period, were admitted on condition that they live in the *geto nuovo* quarter, an isolated island among the canals of Venice which could easily be completely cut off from its surroundings by a wall, gates, and drawbridges. In 1541, the *geto vecchio* ("the old foundry") quarter was added for the integration of Jews from Oriental countries, and the whole area was from then on known as the "ghetto."

In 1555, Pope Paul *IV in his bull *Cum nimis absurdum* ordered that the anti-Jewish program of the monks should be applied in Rome and the Papal States (see also Bulls, *papal). On July 26, 1555, which fell on the Ninth of Av, the Jews of Rome were compelled to move to the new quarter on the left bank of the Tiber River; the area was immediately surrounded by a wall to isolate it from the city. After a short while, this innovation was also introduced in the other towns of the Papal States, and from 1562 the new institution became known, even officially, by the name of the Jewish quarter of Venice – "ghetto."

Pressure was also exerted on the other rulers of the Italian states to introduce the ghetto (in Tuscany in 1570–71; in Padua in 1601–03; in Verona in 1599; in the duchy of Mantua in 1612; etc.) so that the ghetto institution was finally established throughout Italy, with the exception of *Leghorn.

The ghetto introduced by Christians was accompanied by imposition of the badge, compulsory attendance of Jews at conversionary sermons, restriction of the professions they were authorized to practice, and other humiliations. Generally, the authorities did not allow extension of the ghetto boundaries, even when the population had increased; the ghettos were therefore crowded and unsanitary. For the same reason, additional stories were continually built onto the existing houses and the buildings were in constant danger of collapse; misfortunes occasionally occurred, and when fires broke out, severe damage was caused to the ghettos.

According to papal decree, when a ghetto was established it was to have one gate only. In fact, however, it usually had two or three gates. These were guarded by Christian gatekeepers, whose salaries the Jews were compelled to pay; they were closed at night and on all important Christian festivals, including the Easter period, from the Thursday until the Sunday of Holy Week. At night and during Christian festivals, no Jew was permitted to leave the ghetto. In several smaller localities, all the houses in the ghetto were connected to each other by passages and doors to facilitate movement in times of emergency. Non-Jewish landlords were not permitted to raise the rents, and the rights of Jewish tenants were protected by *ḥazakah* ("established claim"), an ancient institution recognized by Italian law (under the name *jus gazaga*). Although Jews were not allowed to acquire the houses in which they lived, the right of *ḥazakah* could be sold, purchased, or bequeathed, as though it were an actual property right. The ghetto, as all Jewish quarters in all periods, was an almost autonomous town and the institutions of the Jewish community operated within its boundaries; at times, the communal life of the ghetto was better organized than that of the Christian town in which it was situated. There were even Jews who did not ignore the positive aspects of the ghetto. In Verona and Mantua it was customary to commemorate the anniversary of its establishment by a special prayer in the synagogue.

Toward the close of the 18th century, the severity of the ghetto regime was somewhat alleviated in several of the Italian states. In 1796 the armies of the French Republic tore down the ghetto walls of all the Italian towns. However, the ghettos were reestablished after the fall of Napoleon in 1815, but not with the same measure of stringency. The ghetto walls were only rebuilt in Rome, Modena, and a few other towns. With the consolidation of the liberal regime in Italy during the 19th century, the ghetto was again abolished, although there were still some occasional periods of reaction here and there. The gates of the Rome ghetto were destroyed in 1848; the right of residence of the Jews was, however, officially restricted to a special quarter until the fall of the papal regime in 1870. Outside Italy, the ghetto – in the original sense of the Italian term – was only enforced in the provinces under papal rule in southern France, in several German towns, and in a few places in eastern Europe. In detail, there were always considerable differences between them.

For Holocaust period, see *Ghetto.

[Cecil Roth]

In Muslim Countries

Well before the advent of *Islam the preference of religious and ethnic groups to live together in their own streets was commonly known in the Orient. These streets finally became distinct quarters. The quarters in which the majority of the population was Jewish were usually given the name of *ḥārat al-yahūd*, which literally translated from the Arabic means "Jewish Quarter," or simply *al-ḥāra*, as in *Tunisia, *Algeria, and *Tripolitania. In *Persia they were known as *maḥallat al-Yahūd*, in the Balkans as *maḥalla*, while in *Yemen they were named *qāʿat al-Yahūd*; the term *masbata* (namely, the place where those who observe the Sabbath live) was also employed. The Jews themselves sometimes called their quarters *shekhunat ha-Yehudim*, the Hebrew equivalent of the various above-mentioned names. Barring a few exceptions, the Jewish quarters of Muslim countries had nothing in common with the ghettos of Christian countries. These quarters were not surrounded by a wall and did not have a gate which was closed at night, on the Sabbath, or on the Festivals. When such a wall existed, it was often because the whole town was divided into several separate quarters which were partitioned off from each other by a wall which contained one or two gates; the gates were closed from dusk to dawn for security reasons or upon the order of the police. In the *Ottoman Empire the Jews were not compelled to live separately from the other inhabitants. The sole exception to this practice was in Yemen. Even when there were Jewish quarters, some Jewish families lived alone or in groups in the other quarters, dispersed among the Muslims. As early as the Middle Ages many Jews of *Baghdad lived in houses situated beyond the two quarters of the town where most of them had their dwellings. During the 12th century most of the Jews of *Fez lived in the north of the city, in a quarter which had been given to them when the town was founded at the beginning of the ninth century. There were, however, many others who lived in the center of the town, well inside the Muslim quarter. Those whose houses were directly adjacent to the Great Mosque were dispossessed when it was decided to enlarge the structure. They were indemnified for their losses and left the site. During the era of its splendor, *Kairouan had a Jewish quarter, but it appears to have been a common occurrence for Jews to live outside this quarter. In Muslim *Spain the Jews often lived among the other inhabitants. The fortified Jewish quarters did not become the general rule until the country was reconquered by the Christian Spaniards. During that period, however, there were also Muslims who lived in quarters with a Jewish majority. Muslims were never forbidden to live in the Jewish quarters. Any difficulties, rather, arose from rabbinic laws which disapproved of the sale or rental of dwellings in the Jewish street to a gentile and granted priority rights over these dwellings to any Jew from the neighborhood. On the other hand, private houses belonging to Jews and Christians were to be found in all the quarters of the town. For this reason the Muslim religious authorities would not allow these houses to be higher than the neighboring mosque or the houses of the "believers."

In Muslim countries, the Covenant of *Omar did not stipulate the physical separation of the Jews from the "faithful" (the Muslims), neither in towns nor in villages. On the contrary, in order to propagate their religion, the early Muslim theologians recommended that the "unbelievers" (Jews and Christians) be encouraged to live in all the quarters of the large towns. They said that they would thus become acquainted with the religion of the Prophet Muhammad by observing the lives of its believers at every moment. There were only a few Muslim jurists of the later periods who advised that non-Muslims be confined to separate quarters. Until the beginning of the 15th century, however, the orthodox Muslim rulers or their representatives had never officially prescribed the establishment of special quarters for the members of other religions. It was only in *Egypt, and then only for a short while at the beginning of the 11th century, that the Fatimid caliph al-Ḥākim, who had suddenly become insane, confined all the Jews of *Cairo to the Bāb-Zuwayla quarter. In the eastern part of the Muslim world, in the countries dominated by the Shiʿites (non-orthodox Muslims), the Jew were compelled to live in special quarters which resembled the European ghettos. In Persia, as in *Afghanistan and the surrounding regions, the Jewish quarter was not only isolated behind a high wall but its inhabitants were also not authorized to own any shops beyond it. The Jews of Persia remained in their ghettos until recently, even though there was no law which forced them to do so.

In *Morocco the term mellah, which designates the Jewish quarter, was originally the name of the site to the south of Fez-Jaīd on which the first special quarter for Jews in Morocco was actually established (probably in 1438). This mellah was and has since remained a special quarter surrounded by a wall and distinctly separated from the surrounding quarters. The segregation of all the Jews of Fez into its area was ordered. It was thus a ghetto, the first and, for a long time, the only one in Morocco. It was not until 1557 that a second ghetto was established in the country, in *Marrakesh. Approximately 125 years later a third mellah was created in *Meknès, and in 1808 four new ghettos were simultaneously erected in the principal ports of Morocco, in *Tetuán, *Salé, *Rabat, and *Mogador. The sharif granted the Jews of these towns one year in which they could sell their houses in the different quarters and build new ones in the mellah. The only exception made was for some 20 eminent families of Mogador, who continued to occupy their luxurious houses in the same residential quarter as that of the Muslim and Christian notables. In 1808 the Jews of Tetuán were compelled to move into a mellah because the sultan wished to erect a mosque in a street which was inhabited by them. At the same time, the sultan exploited the proximity of the Jewish houses to the mosque of Salé as a pretext to order the Jews of this town to live in a special quarter. The Jews of Morocco considered the creation of each mellah as a catastrophe; they therefore hastily abandoned it as soon as they had the means or the possibility. From the beginning of the 20th century, only the poor Jews continued to live in the mellahs. The name mellah was at first given, after Fez, to the few ghettos mentioned above and then to a few other quarters in other towns which were inhabited by the Jewish masses. The mellah of *Casablanca, for example, did not have the characteristics of a ghetto. The decline of Muslim power generally resulted in the impoverishment of the Jewish communities, whose quarters reflected this situation. These quarters were often overpopulated. These ghettos, however, always contained a few well-kept streets with very large and beautiful houses, the properties of wealthy citizens, as was the case in Fez and Marrakesh.

In 1728 and 1731 the Ottoman authorities ordered the Jews of *Istanbul (Constantinople) to leave the quarters where they lived, under the pretext that their presence in these quarters profaned the sanctity of the neighboring mosques; but the Jews were not enclosed in a ghetto, they merely went to live in other quarters. In 1679 the Jews of Yemen were expelled from the towns in which they had lived until then, and they were only authorized to establish themselves outside these cities, in special quarters. In the Islamic countries the two holy cities Mecca and *Medina, as also the whole of the *Hejaz, are prohibited to non-Muslims. Between the 13th and 15th centuries, for example, such Maghreb towns as Bougie, Gafsa, and Tebessa were, with intermissions, forbidden to non-Muslims. From the ninth century until the present the town of Moulay Idris, in Morocco, could not be visited by the "unbelievers." Kairouan, once a great Jewish center, remained out of bounds to non-Muslims from the 13th century until the end of the 19th century. On the other hand, some towns were exclusively, or in their majority, inhabited by Jews. This was the case with Lucena in Muslim Spain, Aghmat-Ailan (near Marrakesh) in Morocco, and Tamentit in the Algerian Sahara until 1492. Many other examples exist.

[David Corcos]

BIBLIOGRAPHY: D. Philipson, *Old European Jewries* (1894), L. Wirth, *The Ghetto* (1928; repr. 1956); A. Pinthus, *Die Judensiedlungen der deutschen Staedte* (1931); I. Abrahams, *Jewish Life in the Middle Ages* (1932²), index, s.v. *Ghetto*; R. Giacomelli, in: *Archivum romanicum*, 16 (1932), 556–63; 17 (1933), 415–44; Roth, Italy, index; idem, in: *Romania*, 60 (1934), 67–74; J.R. Marcus, *Jews in the Medieval World* (1938), index, s.v. *Ghetto*; R. Anchel, in: JSOS, 2 (1940), 45–60; Baron, Community, index, s.v. *Quarters, Jewish*; Baron, Social², index, s.v. *Ghetto*; 9 (1965), 32–36; 11 (1967), 87–96; I. Cohen, *Travels in Jewry* (1952), index, s.v. *Ghetto*. JEWISH QUARTERS IN MUSLIM COUNTRIES: H.Z. Hirschberg, in: *Eretz-Israel*, 4 (1956), 226–30; idem, in: A.J. Arberry (ed.), *Religion in the Middle East*, 1 (1969), 130, 154–5; R. Brunschvig, *Berbérie orientale sous les Ḥafṣides*, 1 (1940), 415–6; M. Gaudefroy-Demombynes, in: JA, 2 (1914), 651–8; S.D. Goitein, *Jews and Arabs* (1964), 74–75 and passim.

JEWISH QUARTERLY REVIEW (JQR), learned journal published first in London and subsequently in Philadelphia. The *Jewish Quarterly Review* was established in 1889 by I. Abrahams and C.G. Montefiore, who acted as editors. The detailed editorial work was undertaken by Abrahams; Montefiore bore the expenses. Modeled on the scholarly journals published in Europe, the JQR attracted articles from the great savants of the day, and much original scholarship (e.g., Schechter's *genizah* discoveries) first appeared in its pages. But the JQR differed by giving space to more ephemeral topics, as well as including theological controversies. At the beginning of volume 20, the editors announced their intention to discontinue the "quarterly," stating that their hope that it "might be the medium for a living theology" had been disappointed, and that Abrahams was finding his editorial duties too onerous.

Cyrus *Adler, president of the newly established Dropsie College in Philadelphia, offered to take over the JQR, and a new series, published by Dropsie College and edited by Cyrus Adler and Solomon *Schechter, began in July 1910. At the outset of their regime, the editors observed that "the fact that the *Review* has passed from the hands of private individuals into those of a learned institution with a strict academic character… will necessitate the exclusion of all matter not falling within the province of Jewish history, literature, philology and archaeology…." Volumes 1–6 of the new series were edited by Adler and Schechter and volumes 7–30 by Adler alone. A.A. Neuman and Solomon *Zeitlin edited volumes 31–57, while Zeitlin was sole editor from volume 58 onward. After the discovery of the Dead Sea Scrolls, a considerable proportion of the space of the JQR was devoted to Zeitlin's views as to their authenticity.

The *Jewish Quarterly Review* is now published at the University of Pennsylvania for its Center for Advanced Judaic Studies. Considered to be the oldest English-language journal in the field of Jewish studies, the JQR strives to preserve the attention to textual detail that has always been characteristic of the journal, while attempting to reach a wider and more diverse audience.

BIBLIOGRAPHY: A.A. Neuman and S. Zeitlin (eds.), *Jewish Quarterly Review, Seventy-Fifth Anniversary Volume* (1967), 60–68.

[Sefton D. Temkin]

JEWISH SOCIAL DEMOCRATIC PARTY (or ŻPS, the initials of the party's name in Polish), party existing in Galicia from 1905 to 1920, the equivalent there of the *Bund. In the early 1890s attempts were made in Galicia to establish a Jewish workers' party to be federatively joined to Polish and Ukrainian workers' parties. The reorganization of the Austrian Social Democratic Party on a federative basis in 1897, as well as the stress on the Polish character of the Social Democratic Party of Galicia (from 1897 the Polish Social Democratic Party of Galicia and of Cieszyn (Teschen) Silesia, the PPSD), gave rise to a movement among Jews for an autonomous Jewish workers' organization within the PPSD. The party leadership, and particularly its Jewish assimilationist members like H. *Diamand and Emil Haecker, opposed this project. However, the chauvinist Polish note of this opposition, the practical needs of organization and propaganda among Jewish workers, and the example of the Bund in Russia (which refused to extend direct help) led to the establishment of an initiating committee in Lvov in 1902, and of an organizing committee (August 1904) for the establishment of an independent Jewish Social Democratic Party. In October 1904 the PPSD convention, 40% of whose delegates were Jewish, rejected the idea. Subsequently, in a manifesto issued on May 1, 1905, the establishment of a Jewish Social Democratic Party (JSDP) was announced. The manifesto rejected the discriminatory Polonization tendency and pointed out that Jews, like the other nationalities, needed their own workers' organization. The leaders of the party included H. Grossman, its principal theoretician (after World War I an economist and communist in Germany), K. *Einaeugler, R. Birnbaum, L. Landau, S. Blum, A. Mosler, L. Feiner, H. Schreiber, and J. *Bross, and later also J. Kissman. Membership in the party was collective through the trade unions, while intellectuals joined individually. There were 2,500 organized workers in the party in 1905, 3,500 in 1908, and 4,200 in 1910. The PPSD opposed the JSDP as "separationist" and "Zionist," although the JSDP contended against the *Po'alei Zion. All the same, in 1906 the PPSD had to establish its own Jewish section. The leaders of the Austrian Social Democrats also denigrated the JSDP. Nathan *Birnbaum supported the party in Jewish circles. The second JSDP convention, held in Lemberg in May 1906, put forward the claim for "national-cultural autonomy," rejecting the slogan of "national curiae" in the electoral system. The establishment of the party and its national program prompted O. *Bauer to formulate his assimilationist conception in his *Die Nationalitaetenfrage und die Sozialdemokratie* ("The Problem of Nationalities and Social Democracy," 1907). The fourth party convention in Lemberg, October 1910, demanded the establishment of state schools providing instruction in Yiddish, as well as recognition of Yiddish as a spoken language in the population census. It was supported in this matter by the Po'alei Zion. The Jewish section of the PPSD subsequently altered its policy and approved the principle of recognition of the Jewish nation (1907). In May 1911 an amalgamation agreement was signed between the JSDP and the section, represented by N. Korkes, M. Zeterbaum, D. Salamander, and R. Buber. In view of the elections to the Austrian parliament, the PPSD agreed to amalgamation, but carried through omission of the article regarding national autonomy from the platform of the united party. The capitulation of the JSDP on this point aroused strong opposition from within. The demand was raised again only in 1917. Meanwhile the struggle of the PPSD for hegemony provoked new dissensions and a rift (1913). The Jewish Social Democrats in Bukovina, headed by J. Pistiner, joined the JSDP. At the end of World War I the party cooperated with other Jewish parties in the "national councils." In 1920 the JSDP joined the Polish Bund.

BIBLIOGRAPHY: J. Kissman, in: *Di Geshikhte fun Bund*, 3 (1966), 337–480; I.M. Horn, *Meḥkarim* (1951), 143–86; J. Bross, in: *YIVO Historishe Shriftn*, 5 (1950), 50–84; 3 (1939), 484–511; K. Einaeugler, *ibid.*, 512–9; S. Blum, *ibid.*, 520–6; N. Buxbaum, *Yidisher Arbeter Pinkes* (1927), 500–8. **ADD. BIBLIOGRAPHY:** H. Piasecki, *Sekcja żydowska PPSD i Żydowska partia socjalno demokratyczna* (1983).

[Moshe Mishkinsky]

JEWISH SOCIALIST VERBAND, U.S. organization devoted to the promotion of democratic socialism and the strengthening of Jewish group life on the basis of modern Yiddish culture. The Jewish Socialist Verband [JSV] was founded in 1921 by a minority group of Yiddish-speaking activists who split off from the leftist Jewish Socialist Federation (itself founded in 1912), when the latter voted in a hotly contested decision to sever its relationship with the Socialist Party, and a majority of the JSF embraced Communism (in 1922 it was absorbed into what became the Communist Party USA).

Small numerically, and led by such individuals as *Jewish Daily Forward* editor Abraham Cahan and the Workmen's Circle's Nathan Chanin, it had a close identification with the Jewish leaders of the needle-trade unions, the Workmen's Circle, and the *Forward*. The JSV struggled to spread the gospel of social democracy and trade unionism, and combat Communist influence in the Jewish community.

The support it received from the *Forward* and the Workmen's Circle enhanced its status in the Jewish community and enabled it to play a role in the field of Yiddish culture. The JSV published *Der Wecker*, beginning in September 1922 and continuing until the 1980s, and operated Farlag Wecker, a publishing house.

While the JSV's approach to Jewish problems reflected the Bundist training and orientation of its leaders, as with much of the mainstream of the American Jewish labor movement, it gradually veered away from Bundist anti-Zionism; at a national convention in November 1967, for instance, it formally adopted a pro-Israel declaration.

The JSV was among the organizers of the Jewish Labor Committee and the World Congress for Jewish Culture. In the early 1970s, as part of a reorganization of socialist parties and non-party organizations in the United States, the JSV combined with a small group, the Union of Democratic Socialists, forming the JSV-UDS, which went on to merge with the Socialist Party of America in 1972. With the Socialist Party's disintegration a year later, the JSV began a relationship with the fervently anti-Communist Social Democrats, USA.

BIBLIOGRAPHY: J.S. Hertz, *Yidishe Sotsialistishe Bavegung in Amerike* (1954). **ADD. BIBLIOGRAPHY:** *American Jewish Year Book* (1987); anon., *Old American Jewish Red Groups* [website] (2005); M. Epstein, *Jewish Labor in the U.S.A.*, 2 vols. (1969); J. Holmes and A. Lebowitz, "Jewish Socialist Federation," in: *Encyclopedia of the American Left* (1998[2]); A. Menes, "The Jewish Labor Movement," in: *The Jewish People Past and Present*, vol. 4 (1955).

[Charles Bezalel Sherman / Arieh Lebowitz (2nd ed.)]

JEWISH SOCIALIST WORKERS' PARTY (also known as **Sejmists**, or **J.S.** = Jewish Socialists; Rus. abbrev., **SERP** = Sotsialisticheskaya Yevreyskaya Rabochaya Partiya), party based on a synthesis of national and socialist ideas, founded at a conference in Kiev in April 1906. Its leaders were M. *Silberfarb, *Ben-Adir, M. *Ratner, N. *Shtib, J. Novakovski, I. *Yefroykin, Z.H. *Kalmanovich, M. Levkovski, V. Fabrikant, and B. Friedland. The party published an organ in Yiddish, *Folksshtime* (1907), a collection, *Shtime* (2 vols., 1908), and a social-political organ in Russian, *Serp* ("Sickle," 1907–08). The party evolved from differences within the *Po'alei Zion movement and was the successor of the *Vozrozhdeniye group. In general matters the Jewish Socialist Workers' Party regarded itself as part of the international socialist movement, but claimed that the manifold national pressures from all sides confronted the Jewish proletariat and the Jewish people in general first and foremost with the national question. According to the party platform, autonomy was an essential principle for the multinational states. Hence the party demanded the assurance of a special legal status for the Jews as a national group to be embodied in an extraterritorial "national personal autonomy" (*Autonomism). The theoretical foundation for this claim also rested on the vital continuity of the historic trend in Jewry to preserve its specific forms of existence and creativity in all spheres of life.

The Sejmists derived their ideological inspiration from C. *Zhitlovsky, who had already advocated socialist autonomism in the 1890s. They were also influenced by S. *Dubnow and trends in Austrian Social Democracy. The party claimed that the basis for Jewish autonomy should be the Jewish community, and its supreme institution, to be endowed with binding authority, a Jewish national Sejm (parliament). The Sejm would represent the collective affairs of the whole of Jewry. Its functions, whose details would be defined by a Jewish constituent assembly, would include cultural and educational matters, medical and health concerns, mutual aid, assistance in work, agricultural training, statistics, organization of emigration, and the settlement of emigrants in a "free, unsettled territory." The acquisition of autonomy was a prerequisite for a Jewish territorial center to be established "anywhere" which would have an impact on all aspects of Jewish life in the Diaspora. But the realization of the project was put off to "some time" in the distant future.

Unlike the *Zionist Socialist Workers' Party (SS) and the Po'alei Zion, the Jewish Socialist Workers' Party did not adhere to Marxism. On the agrarian question the party identified with the Social Revolutionaries who were also more inclined than the Social Democrats to support federalist and autonomist solutions to the national question. The Jewish Socialist Workers' Party was represented at the congresses of the Socialist International as a subsection of the Social Revolutionaries. In conjunction with the Social Revolutionaries, the Sejmists convened a conference of national socialist parties in Russia to discuss the national question in 1907.

The main stronghold of the Jewish Socialist Workers' Party was in the Ukraine, with some adherents in Lithuania and none at all in Poland. It took part in the revolutionary events of 1905–06: in the series of strikes and in the "self-defense" organized by socialist parties against pogroms. In Yekaterinoslav (*Dnepropetrovsk) the Sejmists established a Jewish Council of workers' delegates. They upheld the principle of inter-party solidarity within united trade unions. The party boycotted the elections for the First *Duma, while for the second it nominated candidates in six districts (Zhitlovsky was the candidate for Vitebsk). In other places it supported the Social Revolutionaries in preference to the Social Democrats, and the *Bund in preference to the Zionist Socialist Workers' Party.

During the reaction that followed the 1905 Revolution the party became limited mainly to intelligentsia circles. Some of its active members went over to the Folkists (Folkspartei) while the SERP group, headed by Zhitlovsky, was also active in the United States. In 1909 it united with Po'alei Zion and the Socialist-Territorialists. The Jewish Socialist Workers' Party cooperated with the world organization of Po'alei Zion and the Zionist Socialists toward the establishment of a Jewish section in the Socialist International. After the 1917 Revolution the Jewish Socialists united with the Zionist Socialists and established the *United Jewish Socialist Workers' Party.

BIBLIOGRAPHY: N.A. Buchbinder, *Geshikhte fun der Yidisher Arbeter-Bavegung in Rusland* (1931), 398–402; O.I. Yanowsky, *Jews and Minority Rights* (1933), index s.v. *Seymists; Sotsialistisher Teritorializm* (1934), 51–78; A.L. Patkin, *The Origins of the Russian-Jewish Labor Movement* (1947), 237–41; A. Menes (ed.), *Yidisher Gedank in der Nayer Tsayt* (1957), 172–5; B. Borochov, *Ketavim*, 1 (1955), 383, 488–9; 2 (1956), 543–4; Y. Maor, *She'elat ha-Yehudim ba-Tenu'ah ha-Liberalit ve-ha-Mahpekhanit be-Rusyah* (1964), 221–7.

[Moshe Mishkinsky]

JEWISH SOCIETY FOR HISTORY AND ETHNOGRAPHY (Russ., **Yevreyskoye Istoriko-Etnograficheskoye Obshchestvo**), Jewish scholarly society in Russia. The society was established at the end of 1908 in St. Petersburg as a continuation of the Jewish Historical Ethnographical Committee of the *Society for the Promotion of Culture Among the Jews of Russia, which had been founded in 1892 on the initiative of Simon *Dubnow. The officers elected to the first committee of the new society were S. Dubnow, M. *Vinaver, and M. *Kulisher. It had a total membership of 774 in 1915. The society held lectures on Jewish history, especially Jewish history in Russia and Poland, and established archives, a museum, and a library. It assisted S. *An-Ski on a project to conduct ethnographic research in towns of the Pale of Settlement and awarded prizes for Jewish historical research.

Publication of documents relating to the history of the Jews in Russia, *Regesty i Nadpisi* (vols. 2–3, 1910–14), was continued by the society. Its major undertaking was the publication of a historical quarterly *Yevreyskaya Starina* ("Jewish Antiquities"), of which ten volumes (1909–18) were edited by Dubnow, and the last three (1924–30) by a collective editorship. The journal published studies, memoirs, and documents. After the 1917 Revolution the society published two volumes of documents on the origins of the pogroms of 1881 and 1903 in Russia. In the early years of the Soviet regime the activities of the society were permitted, although reduced. After Dubnow left Russia in 1922, a small group faithfully continued the work, which was sharply criticized by Jewish Communists of the *Yevsektsiya. At the end of 1929 the society dissolved. The last volume of *Yevreyskaya Starina* was edited by I. *Zinberg and published after the society's dissolution. Its museum and archives became the property of Soviet-Jewish institutions, including the Jewish Cultural Institute in Kiev.

BIBLIOGRAPHY: S. Dubnow, in: *Literarishe Bleter*, 1 (1930), 80–83, 114–5; idem, *Kniga zhizni*, 2 (1935), index; A.G. Duker, in: HUCA, 8–9 (1931–32), 525–603 (a bibliography); A. Greenbaum, *Jewish Scholarship in the Soviet Union* (1959), 8–17.

[Yehuda Slutsky]

JEWISH STATE PARTY, Zionist political party formed by dissidents from the *Revisionist movement after the final split between Vladimir *Jabotinsky and most of his colleagues in the leadership of the world movement (at its session in Katowice, April 1933). The new party comprised a number of veteran leaders, including Meir *Grossman, the Hebrew poet Yaakov *Cahan, Richard *Lichtheim, Selig *Soskin, Robert *Stricker, and Jonah Machover, Herzl Rosenblum, and Baruch Weinstein, but only a fraction of the rank and file Revisionists and even less of the membership of the *Betar youth movement, who remained faithful to Jabotinsky. The point over which the members of the Jewish State Party (or the "Grossmanites," as they were popularly called) departed from Jabotinsky and the Revisionist majority was the attitude to the World Zionist Organization (WZO). Whereas Jabotinsky refused to recognize it as the only body representing the Zionist movement, wanted to act independently of it in the international field, and eventually secede from it, Grossman and his colleagues and followers unreservedly recognized the sovereignty and binding political discipline of the WZO. The group first appeared on the Zionist scene immediately after the 1933 split, when it contested the elections to the 18th Zionist Congress in 13 countries and received 11,821 votes, gaining three mandates. During the 18th Zionist Congress, a conference of dissident Revisionists from Austria, England, France, Latvia, Lithuania, Palestine, Poland, Romania, and South Africa officially formed the Jewish State Party. It was recognized by the WZO as a *Sonderverband* (see *Zionism: Zionist Organization, Organizational Structure) and granted representation on the Board of Directors of the *Jewish National Fund and the *Keren Hayesed. In the elections to the 19th Zionist Congress in 1935, the party received 24,322 votes in 16 countries, gaining nine mandates.

In 1937 the party convoked its first regular conference in Paris. Its rejection of the proposal of the British Royal Commission to partition Palestine led to Lichtheim and Soskin's resignation. In the elections to the Zionist Congress, it received 6,705 votes, gaining only six mandates. In the pre-World War II period, the party numbered some 8,000 registered members, mostly in Poland, Lithuania, and Austria. Following the split in the Revisionist movement in 1933, a group of dissidents from Betar formed a youth movement of the Jewish State Party called Berit ha-Kanna'im (Zealots' Union), with affiliates in Austria, Czechoslovakia, Germany, Palestine, and Poland. The first conference of the organization convoked in Lucerne in 1935 elected a high command (*mifkadah elyonah*) consisting of R. Feldschuh Ben-Shem, N. Netaneli-Rothman, and F. Richter; Y. Cahan was elected its leader (*av Berit ha-Kanna'im*). In 1930 Weinstein was elected to the *Asefat ha-Nivḥarim* on the Revisionist slate; after he left the Revisionist fraction in April 1933, he was recognized representative of the Jewish State Party. At the outbreak of World War II the party's activities were paralyzed, and in 1946 it officially ceased to exist by merging with the Union of Zionist Revisionists, which had meanwhile rejoined the WZO under the name United Zionist Revisionists. Many of its leaders and members, however, including M. Grossman, later joined the *General Zionists. The publications of the party were: *Unzer Velt*, a weekly (Yid., Warsaw, 1936–39); *Die Neue Welt*, a weekly (Ger., Vienna, 1927–48), superseded by *Neue Welt und Judenstaat* (Ger., Vienna, 1948–52); and *Ha-Mattarah* (Heb., Tel Aviv, 1933).

[Yehuda Benari]

JEWISH STUDIES. Jewish studies, or often Judaic studies, refers here to the academic teaching of aspects of Jewish religion, history, philosophy, and culture, and associated languages and literatures, at the undergraduate and graduate level in institutions of higher education. Jewish studies scholarship and teaching is non-doctrinal, non-parochial, and non-denominational. At its best, it represents a mode of intellectual exploration that is open to all interested students regardless of their religious or ethnic backgrounds. Jewish studies include scholars and students who make use of a broad range of disciplinary methodologies from the full range of academic fields in the humanities and social studies. What defines this diverse and interdisciplinary area of inquiry is the object of its study – Jewish experience in its widest sense – rather than any specific analytical approach.

Jewish Studies in American Universities

The significant expansion of Jewish studies in American universities is a recent phenomenon. Nevertheless there are antecedents to this development which should be noted. In the 17th and 18th centuries, the Hebrew language was included in the curriculum of several of the earliest colleges to be established on the North American continent. The subject was taught as part of a theologically oriented curriculum designed to assist potential Christian clergymen in understanding their Christian heritage. The disappearance of the last vestiges of Hebrew from the curriculum in the early decades of the 19th century was the result of changing vogues in Protestant theology and in the dynamics of Christian denominationalism in the United States and was totally unrelated to any concern for Jews or Judaism.

More relevant was the growth of modern Jewish scholarship (as distinguished from traditional Jewish study of sacred texts) which emerged with the development of the *Wissenschaft des Judentums movement in Central Europe in the 1820s and thereafter. The researches of the Wissenschaft scholars created a body of knowledge, a literature and a method of research which made it possible to conceive of a Jewish cultural tradition which was the ongoing expression of a people and which was subject to the same methods of academically disciplined study as that of other peoples. While most early Jewish scholars viewed this tradition as essentially religious, it was nonetheless studied in its literary, philosophical and historical as well as its theological aspects.

This development of Jewish critical scholarship led to the hope that the study of Judaic culture would find a place in the developing world of the secular university. As early as 1838, Abraham *Geiger proposed the establishment of a "Jewish theological faculty" in a German university. For a variety of reasons, social and political as well as academic, this proposal and subsequent suggestions which were broached never came to fruition. Jewish scholarship remained a solitary and unremunerative occupation pursued by dedicated individuals. When such scholarship succeeded in finding a place in an academic setting, it was consigned to the modern theological seminaries which emerged in Central Europe in the last third of the 19th century. Some scholars, like Moritz *Steinschneider, denigrated the development of such seminaries as a "new ghetto of Jewish learning" which could not transcend "scholarly immaturity." However, nothing came of Steinschneider's hope that European governments could somehow be induced to "establish professorships," and the seminaries remained the only academic institutions in which at least some aspects of modern Jewish scholarship found a place.

In America the openness and diversity of the society and the participation of the Jews in the general culture generated more ambitious aspirations. The desirability of creating a faculty of Jewish studies was broached as early as 1818. Since higher education in 19th century America was almost exclusively sponsored by various religious denominations, Mordecai Manuel *Noah proposed that American Jewry emulate other sects and establish its own college in which Jewish studies would constitute a central element of the curriculum. The proposal was never implemented, not for lack of opportunity, but rather for lack of interest and intellectual resources on the part of the numerically small American Jewish community of that time.

In the 1840s and 50s suggestions for Jewish-sponsored colleges were revived by Isaac *Leeser and Isaac Mayer *Wise, both immigrants from Central Europe. A number of abortive efforts to organize such colleges were undertaken and in 1855 Wise actually announced the establishment of an institution known as Zion College in Cincinnati. This and subsequent efforts failed, again because of lack of support from the growing American Jewish community which was fragmented and was more concerned with integrating itself into the general culture than in fostering its own intellectual distinctiveness. When, in 1875, Wise finally succeeded in forming an academic institution, it was, like its European counterparts, a rabbinic seminary and not, as originally intended, a general college in which a Judaic faculty was a part of a larger academic enterprise. The original concept survived only in the name of the Reform movement rabbinical seminary which Wise called *Hebrew Union College.

Toward the end of the 19th century, chairs in "Semitics" were established in a handful of American universities: Columbia, Johns Hopkins, the University of Pennsylvania, and the University of Chicago. These positions reflected the contemporary interest in "scientific" biblical studies as well as the attainment of financial prominence by some Jews and of modest scholarly credentials by others. The chairs were initially held by Jews whose teaching was primarily related to Semitic philology rather than to the broader aspects of Jewish culture. There is little evidence of academic concern with the total Jewish experience, especially with the content of Jewish culture and history in the centuries following the separation of Christianity from its Jewish source.

In 1896 William Rosenau, a Baltimore Reform rabbi who taught "Semitics" at Johns Hopkins, wrote an article extolling the desirability of "Semitic studies in American Universities." None of the benefits which he mentioned related to Jewish literature or Judaism. It is therefore a matter of judgment whether or not the inception of Jewish studies in American universities can properly be dated from the establishment of these academic posts. At best, the number of positions remained small and the treatment of the totality of the Jewish tradition as an area of study of intrinsic worth without regard to its relationship to the predominant culture was negligible.

In the following decades, the development of Jewish scholarship in the United States was primarily centered in the theological seminaries and in institutions which were under Jewish sponsorship and were devoted solely to Jewish studies, such as Dropsie College in Philadelphia and a handful of communal Hebrew teachers colleges. The rise of Hitler and the destruction of Jewish institutions in Central and Eastern Europe led to an influx of distinguished Jewish scholars to the United States. These men assumed leading positions in Jewish institutions of higher learning and greatly enhanced the cultural resources of American Jewry. Despite their credentials, few found places in secular universities.

Prior to 1940 a few chairs of Judaica had been established in major universities, almost always due to the philanthropy of local Jewish communities. Some of these were occupied by outstanding scholars, most notably Salo W. *Baron in the department of history at Columbia and Harry A. *Wolfson in the department of Near Eastern languages at Harvard. In the late 1930s modest programs in the teaching of modern Hebrew had been established in universities in New York City, primarily as a result of the introduction of Hebrew language instruction into the curriculum of New York City public high schools and the need to certify teachers for positions. However, as late as 1945, no more than 12 full-time positions in Jewish studies existed in ten American universities. When, in 1943, Ismar Elbogen surveyed "American Jewish Scholarship," his review dealt with the work of individual scholars and made no mention of Judaic studies in universities. These circumstances led Alfred Jospe to conclude that "it was only after the end of World War II that we find a growing awareness and recognition that Jews and Judaism are legitimate subjects of academic study and inquiry."

Since that time the development of Judaic studies in American universities has been striking. By 1966, when Arnold Band of the University of California at Los Angeles completed his survey of "Jewish Studies in American Colleges and Universities" (AJYB, 1966), the number of institutions offering one or more aspects of Jewish studies had grown sevenfold. Band listed 61 full-time positions in the area of Jewish studies and estimated that approximately 40 accredited colleges and universities offered "fairly adequate training in undergraduate Judaic studies" and at least 25 others offered a "variety of courses, but no undergraduate major."

In addition, by 1966, the number of universities offering graduate programs had grown from six to more than 20. Important new concentrations of Judaic teaching and scholarships had emerged in such disparate institutions as Brandeis University – a Jewish sponsored non-sectarian private university – and the state-sponsored University of California in both its Los Angeles and Berkeley branches. The Jewish cultural heritage was on the agenda of the American academic enterprise.

Band's survey also revealed the growing maturity of American Jewry in providing its own intellectual leadership. Over one half of the faculty members engaged in the Jewish programs were either born in the United States or arrived as children. Even more significant, over 80% had received their graduate training in American universities. In almost every case, a period of study at a university in Israel provided essential supplementation; frequently the early doctoral graduates in Judaica relied heavily on training outside the university framework, especially in seminaries and yeshivot. Whatever the obstacles and lacunae, it was clear that, by 1966, the dependence of American Jewry on scholars imported from abroad was waning. A generation of American-born and trained scholars and teachers was emerging; resources of American universities to provide Judaic training were growing.

This development cannot be described as a "movement" since it was neither anticipated nor actively fostered by the organized Jewish community or by any other group. Indeed, there are indications that American Jewry was hardly aware of the growth taking place in its midst. In *The American Jew: A Reappraisal* (1964), edited by Oscar Janowsky, only one brief paragraph in 568 pages is devoted to Jewish studies in universities. The initial expansion was generated by changing circumstances within both the Jewish and the academic communities and not by deliberate design.

Since 1966 proliferation of Jewish studies throughout the North American continent has accelerated and shows no signs of abating, despite the general retrenchment currently taking place in American universities. Growth has continued not only in the number of institutions offering courses, but in the number and variety of subjects taught and in the size of Judaic faculties within universities, in the quality of the programs and in the number of students enrolled and majoring on both the undergraduate and graduate levels. Important new concentrations have developed in such state universities as Ohio State and the State University of New York, in prestigious private institutions such as Brown University, and in a number of Canadian universities. More recently, the major rabbinical seminaries have placed new emphasis on Ph.D. programs designed to train scholars to teach in secular universities.

The growth of the field was rapid. A 1973 survey by the Institute for Jewish Policy Analysis estimated that "over 350 institutions now offer one or more courses in Judaica" and observed that "Jewish studies programs have opened new teaching and research opportunities to Jewish scholars, increased the prestige and influence of professors in these areas, and encouraged graduate students to enter this field of study." By 2005, over 70 institutions had Jewish studies degree-granting programs of one kind or another.

The establishment the *Association for Jewish Studies (AJS) in 1969 to provide for regular communication among scholars teaching in the field was another indication of the growth of Jewish studies in the last third of the 20th century. By 2005, this organization had over 1,500 members, most of whom were faculty teaching some area of Jewish studies in an institution of higher education. 20% of the membership consisted of graduate students, representing the future of Jewish studies in North America. In recent decades, several regional organizations, including the Midwestern Jewish Studies Association and the Western Jewish Studies Association have also been formed. These groups hold annual meetings. The Women's Caucus of the AJS, which was founded in 1986, meets in the context of the AJS annual conference.

Many factors contributed to the development of Jewish studies in North America. Perhaps the most basic was the recognition which emerged only after the creation of the State of Israel: that the Jewish people was a living and developing nation whose rich past was related to a vital present and whose historic and continuing experience was worthy of study. In addition, the dynamic development of Jewish culture within Israel society and of Jewish scholarship within Israel universities, provided a focal point for serious study, a body of literature, and a cadre of distinguished teachers who provided a significant impetus for the awakening of both the Jewish and the university worlds to the dimensions of Jewish culture and history and the quality of serious Jewish scholarship. Since American universities in the post-World War II period were broadening their areas of study to accommodate a variety of cultures and experiences outside the framework of the classical humanistic curriculum, Jewish studies were readily accepted and frequently encouraged in departments of religion, of modern and ancient Near Eastern studies, of history, and of comparative literature. In a few instances – most notably Brandeis University, Rutgers, and the University of Wisconsin – separate departments of Jewish studies were established. In a variety of settings, the American university was open to the entry of the diverse elements of Jewish studies.

At the same time, the growing self-consciousness and self-confidence of American Jewry in recent decades created a demand for Jewish studies and a desire to take advantage of the opportunities for learning. American Jewry's awareness of itself was nourished by the reaction to the Holocaust and the rise of the State of Israel. The trauma of the Six Day War in 1967 and the Yom Kippur War of 1973 provided added incentives for study of the Jewish past and present, which frequently accompanied a desire for renewal of identity and identification. The unprecedented number of Jewish "baby boomers" who descended on college campuses beginning in the mid-1960s obviously played a role as well, as did the growing number of Jews in the professoriate at this time.

Perhaps the final factor which contributed to the rapid growth of Jewish studies in the 1960s and 1970s was the assertiveness of other ethnic groups on the American campus, including African-Americans and Latinos, in advocating for academic courses that explored and analyzed their particular historical and cultural experiences. Another parallel was the growing interest in women's and gender studies. Large numbers of Jewish students and faculty rediscovered the richness of their own tradition. They requested, and occasionally even demanded, that universities provide them with the same opportunity to study this tradition with the high level of critical examination and seriousness of purpose as were applied to all other academic pursuits. For the first time in American Jewish history large numbers of mature Jewish students outside of the yeshivot and theological seminaries had the opportunity to devote themselves to serious Jewish study.

The actual framework for such studies varied from institution to institution. In a few instances Jewish studies were taught in a separate department (as at Brandeis). More often they were concentrated in departments of history (as at Columbia), religion (as at Brown), Near Eastern Languages (as at Harvard), Comparative Literature (as at UCLA), Oriental Studies (as at University of Pennsylvania), or Philosophy (as at Washington University). Increasingly, interdepartmental concentrations in Jewish studies were organized, with various faculty members holding appointments in departments according to their scholarly disciplines (as in Ohio State University). In recent years, the free-standing Jewish or Judaic studies program that awards undergraduate degrees in Jewish/Judaic studies, and offers courses taught by faculty with appointments in regular academic departments, has become more common. Often donor endowments support the hiring of a faculty director and the operations of the program itself. This variety of organizational and structural approaches in the teaching of Jewish studies, depending on individual circumstance in any given institution, has remained a constant into the 21st century.

A significant number of Jewish studies programs requires Hebrew language and literature study for undergraduate majors and for graduate students. In some cases students must study Classical Hebrew language and texts; in others Modern Hebrew is required. The result has been a proliferation of Hebrew language study across North American institutions of higher education to a degree that would certainly not have occurred without the linkage of Hebrew to Jewish Studies. Several Jewish studies programs also offer instruction in Yiddish language and literature.

Prior to the 1970s most scholars and teachers of Jewish studies in North America were men, many of whom had moved into the academic world after completing rabbinic training. A noteworthy change in Jewish studies in North America in the decades between 1975 and 2005 is the number of women who have entered the field and climbed the academic ladder from graduate students to professors in every area of Jewish studies scholarship. Women have also assumed leadership roles in Jewish studies professional organizations, including the Association for Jewish Studies. This phenomenon reflects a larger sea change in the academic world in general as a result of the feminist movement of the last third of the 20th century and the changes it has wrought in expanding women's personal and professional opportunities. Concurrently, Jewish Studies teaching and scholarship has become more aware of gender as an intellectual category of analysis and of the necessity to consider the constructions and consequences of gender in explicating the Jewish experience. While some Jewish studies courses integrate female experience into a general curriculum, other courses have been created that focus entirely on women in specific historical eras, bodies of literature, or from particular disciplinary perspectives.

The teaching of Jewish subject matter in secular universities cannot be considered as "Jewish education" in the sense of religious education. As Alfred Jospe commented, "the purpose of Jewish studies in the university is the study of Judaism and the Jewish people and not the Judaization of young Jews, the stimulation of their Jewish commitment, or the strengthening of their Jewish identification." At the same time, Jewish studies programs have provided significant new "Jewish presences" on college campuses, as well as new resources for the entire university community that offer familiarity with Jewish culture and history and a new respect for the quality of Jewish creativity in the past and in the present.

[Leon A. Jick / Judith R. Baskin (2nd ed.)]

JEWISH STUDIES IN NORTH AMERICAN HIGHER EDUCATION: THE VANTAGE POINT FROM 2006. From the 1970s, Jewish/Judaic studies continued to thrive and expand in a variety of North American institutions of higher learning, in significant part though the philanthropy of individual donors. The growth of personal wealth in this era, together with increasing communal concern about strengthening of Jewish identity at a formative period in young people's lives, have led to a proliferation of endowed faculty positions, programs, and Jewish/Judaic studies centers, both at public and private research universities offering graduate degrees and at institutions with a primary focus on undergraduate education. Information from Jewish population surveys which shows that as many as 40% of Jewish students in North America take at least one course in Jewish Studies during their undergraduate careers has added further impetus to such initiatives. Although, definitive data as to the number of such positions, programs, and departments were not available in 2006, an unofficial directory of directors and chairs of Jewish studies entities of one kind or another listed over 70 individuals. Although not all positions in Jewish Studies in North America are dependent on this kind of outside funding, the investment of philanthropic resources to fund Jewish Studies has been a wonderful boon for colleges and universities and for the field itself. However, such dependence on donor generosity has also raised challenging issues of academic objectivity versus parochial communal agendas; questions of undue dependence on donors' particular interests and propensities; and concern over the increasing amounts of faculty time and effort devoted to fundraising activities. Moreover, additional donor-driven funding for lecture series, visiting scholars, student scholarships, etc., has often placed Jewish studies programs in a privileged position in relation to other older and larger academic departments as well as to newer, struggling academic entities. In the best circumstances, Jewish studies directors have found ways to create intellectual and interdisciplinary partnerships with less well-endowed academic departments and programs in endeavors of mutual interest.

While many donors to Jewish studies programs at colleges and universities with significant Jewish student bodies have expressed particularistic concerns about educating Jewish students as a way to strengthen Jewish identity formation, others have chosen to endow Jewish Studies positions and programs at institutions, both public and private, that do not have a critical mass of Jewish students, including colleges and universities in parts of North America with small Jewish populations and at institutions linked to the Roman Catholic Church and various Protestant denominations. These donors, some of whom were also interested in supporting local institutions, argued that Jewish studies should be integrated into the academic curriculum of all institutions of higher education; they hoped, as well, that exposing diverse groups of students to academic study of aspects of the Jewish experience would increase understanding and tolerance in the larger North American society.

Changing demographics in the early 21st century make clear that the absolute numbers of Jews in the larger population, including student populations, is in steady decline. The future of Jewish Studies in North American universities will depend on the field's appeal to a larger constituency. Most Jewish Studies programs design their curriculum and courses to appeal to the broadest possible student audiences, in part by ensuring that their courses fulfill university "general education" and "diversity" requirements. Already in 2006, more and more students who take courses and choose undergraduate majors and graduate training in Jewish Studies are non-Jews who come to the field out of intellectual curiosity, not out of interest in their own religious or ethnic heritage. Similarly, increasing numbers of scholars and faculty members who work in Jewish Studies are not themselves Jews. This phenomenon is indicative of the increasing integration of Jewish Studies as the field has moved beyond being an academic venture "about Jews, by Jews, and for Jews." While this "normalization" of Jewish studies within the university is desirable from a scholarly point of view, it also points to potential future conflict between academic Jewish studies programs and the concerns of the Jewish communities and donors who have thus far been absolutely essential to the presence and success of Jewish Studies at many North American institutions. Communal funding of positions in Israel studies is one area which has proved particularly contentious when scholars who are supported by endowment funds voice views that do not accord with some local opinions about Israeli history, society, and politics.

Jewish studies programs and departments in North America have consistently encouraged their students, undergraduate and graduate, to study in Israel. Many programs have also welcomed academic colleagues from Israel into their midst as speakers and visiting scholars. These ties have been strengthened for many by participation in the World Union of Jewish Studies (centered at The Hebrew University), which holds conferences every four years in Jerusalem. Recent decades have also seen the growth of Jewish studies organizations in Western Europe and in Eastern Europe and the former Soviet Union. Among these are the European Association for Jewish Studies (EAJS), founded in 1981, with offices in Oxford, UK, which encourages and supports the teaching of Jewish studies at the university level in Europe and furthers an understanding of the importance of Jewish culture and civilization and of the impact it has had on European cultures over many centuries. In Russia, SEFER, housed at the Moscow Center for University Teaching of Jewish Civilization, is an umbrella organization for university Jewish Studies in the CIS (Commonwealth of Independent States) and the Baltic States. It seems likely that, in the future, Jewish studies professionals from North America will play a growing role in an increasingly vibrant and active international community of students and scholars.

[Judith R. Baskin (2nd ed.)]

In the U.S.S.R., 1950–1990

In the year 1950 Jewish studies in the Soviet Union reached a low point. Research under independent Jewish auspices had ended by fiat in 1930. Jewish departments at Soviet academic institutions, which published their studies in Yiddish – the official Jewish language – had been in decline even before World War II; the Office for the Study of Soviet Jewish Literature, Language, and Folklore at the Ukrainian Academy of Sciences was the only such body which still existed after the war, but it was closed early in 1949 as part of the secret Stalin purge of Jewish culture. Its head, the Yiddish linguist Elijah Spivak, perished in prison in 1950. It has been surmised that the closing at the time of the Chair of Assyriology-Hebrew Studies at Leningrad University was politically motivated. The low esteem in which the Jews and their culture were then held by the Soviet establishment can be seen in the short and prejudiced entry "Evrei" ("Jews") in the second edition of the *Bol'shaia sovetskaia entsiklopediia* ("Large Soviet Encyclopedia"), which went to press in 1952.

After Stalin's death in 1953 there were slow but perceptible changes. Translations from the Yiddish began to appear, followed in 1959 by the resumption of Yiddish publishing and from 1961 by the appearance of the still existing Yiddish journal *Sovetish Heymland*. But these concessions did not include a revival of the scholarship under academic auspices which had been a part of Soviet minority policy between the wars. For a considerable time the only outlet was the traditional one of Jewish studies under the broader aegis of Near Eastern studies. These themselves were then being reorganized, with the "Institut vostokovedeniia" (Institute of Oriental Studies) temporarily renamed "Institut narodov Azii" (Institute of the Peoples of Asia). The Institute of Oriental Studies, being attached to the Soviet Academy of Sciences, was in Moscow but maintained a Leningrad (St. Petersburg) branch, at which Semitics were more actively cultivated. At the same time Leningrad University remained the instructional center for this branch of learning, continuing a tradition dating back to czarist times.

Around 1951 the "Russian Palestine Society," moribund since 1930, was revived as an affiliate of the Soviet Academy of Sciences. In czarist days this organization, known then as the "Pravoslavic Palestine Society," had been more missionary than scholarly. Its reappearance, and the revival in 1954 of its publication *Palestinskii sbornik* ("Palestine collection"), raised eyebrows and was seen by some as directed against the new State of Israel. It seems more likely that it was part of the wave of Russian patriotism then encouraged by Stalin and was intended to point out the continuing Russian interest in the Near East and its emerging states – while for political reasons avoiding all mention of the State of Israel and indeed the modern Jewish settlement in Palestine. However, this taboo was not extended to ancient Israel or medieval Jewry, so that, beginning with volume 2 (1956), Jewish studies have a modest place in *Palestinskii sbornik* alongside a plethora of articles on Arabic studies, Persian studies, Egyptology, and related fields. Circumspection demanded that studies on biblical and talmudic themes avoid the words "Bible" and "Talmud" in the title of the article; thus, in an article comparing the Samaritan Pentateuch with biblical citations in the Jerusalem Talmud, the latter is called a "Palestinian oral tradition" (v. 15, 1966). The author, Isaac Vinnikov (1897–1973), a veteran Arabist, Aramist, and talmudist, had been the last incumbent of the Chair of Assyriology-Hebrew Studies at Leningrad University, and contributed regularly to *Palestinskii sbornik* until his death. His major contribution was a dictionary of Aramaic inscriptions extending over a number of issues. Vinnikov called on the Judaic scholars of the world to produce dictionaries and concordances of talmudic and targumic literature which would take into account recent research; and as a sample published his material on the letter g (v. 5, 1960).

Another talmudist who wrote in this period but did his most important work earlier was Judah Solodukho (1877–1963), whose studies of the social history of "Iraq" in the first centuries of the Christian era were actually studies of the Babylonian Talmud.

A contributor to *Palestinskii sbornik* was Joel Weinberg, or Veinberg in his Russian-language articles. Weinberg, born in 1922 in what was then independent Latvia, was a professor of ancient history at the University of Daugavpils (Dvinsk), and his interests included the biblical period. In the 1960s he published two books in Latvian on the Bible and its setting. Like many other scholars in this era of more open communication, he wrote frequently for academic journals in the West. Contributors to *Palestinskii sbornik* also included the Hebrew linguist Anatolii Gazov-Ginzberg, the Qumran (Dead Sea community) scholar Klavdiia Starkova, and the versatile Semitist Elijah Shifman. Gazov-Ginzberg (b. 1929) changed his name to Amnon Ginzay and was a translator and editor in Israel. Starkova (b. 1915) had a book on the Qumran scrolls accepted in the journal's monograph series (v. 24, 1973). She was also one of Russia's few experts on medieval Hebrew literature and had written on the poetry of Judah Halevi. Among the many writings of Shifman (1930–1990), a specialist on Phoenician civilization, was *Vetkhii Zavet i ego mira* ("The Old Testament and its World," 1987) – published at a time when the Bible had again become a legitimate part of world literature for the Soviet reader.

Palestinskii sbornik, which over the years had become more hospitable to Jewish studies, began to include reviews of recent Judaica in its book review section in the 1970s. In the 1980s, however, the journal became more overtly political and published articles on the Palestine problem which depicted Israel as the main obstacle to peace in the area.

The Soviet reorganization of Semitic and Near Eastern studies at the beginning of the 1950s left the journal *Vestnik drevnei istorii* ("Bulletin of Ancient History") untouched. Among its regular contributors was Joseph *Amusin (1910–1984), a Bible scholar whom Soviet writers and intellectuals used to consult on the subject. Amusin became the Soviet Union's leading expert on the Dead Sea scrolls after these were discovered and wrote both popular and scholarly books on the topic, including shortly before his death, *Kumranskaia obshchina* ("The Qumran Community," 1983). In 1971 a translation of the scrolls into Russian under his editorship produced its first volume.

In general, however, book-length studies on Judaic topics in the period covered by this survey were few. Some relatively early examples are: Nikita Meshcherskii's edition of the Slavonic Josephus (1958): and Mikhail Artamonov, *Istoriia khazar* ("The History of the Khazars," 1962). The latter book, by a non-specialist, was considered antisemitic by the Israeli historian Shemuel Ettinger, since Artamonov not only rejected the idea of a Khazar heritage in Russian history – an idea generally accepted – but even considered the conversion of the Khazar royal court to Judaism as a negative factor in and of itself (see Ettinger's review in *Kiryat Sefer*, v. 39, pp. 501–504).

Starkova and Meshcherskii (b. 1906, an expert on translations of old Hebrew classics into Slavic) belonged to the small group of Russians with an interest in classical Hebrew. So did Igor Diakonov (b. 1915), the elder of Soviet Near Eastern studies, whose works on the languages of the ancient East include Hebrew and who has translated biblical poetry into Russian. In this connection we also take note of an outstanding Russian Semitist from an earlier generation, Pavel Kokovtsov (1861–1942), who taught Meshcherskii, Vinnikov, and many others in the interwar period; in Hebraic studies ("gebraistika" in Russian) he is best known for his edition of the correspondence between the Spanish Jewish courtier Hasdai ibn Shaprut and the king of the Khazars (*Evereisko-khazarskaia perepiska v X veke*, 1932).

In the "First Conference on Semitic Languages" held in Tbilisi (Tiflis), Georgia, in 1964, Hebrew had a prominent place, and even modern Hebrew entered the discussions. The editor of the conference proceedings – published in 1965 as volume 2 of *Semitskie iazyki* ("Semitic Languages") – noted in the introduction that "Hebraistics were one of the most important and oldest areas of Semitology," and singled out the then new Hebrew-Russian dictionary (*Ivrit-russkii slovar'*) by Feliks (Faitl) Shapiro (1876–1961), edited by Benzion Grande (1891–1974) and published in 1963. The Iranist Michael Zand (b. 1927), subsequently a professor at The Hebrew University, dealt with Yiddish as a substratum of Hebrew, and the Semitist Meir Zislin (b. 1916) wrote on some medieval Hebrew grammars. The participants also included the leading Georgian Aramaist Konstantin Tsereteli (b. 1921), who helped make the University of Tbilisi a center of Semitic studies alongside the better known institutions in Leningrad and Moscow.

As usual the atmosphere in Georgia was freer than the one found in the north, and Hebrew was not neglected in the work being carried on in Tbilisi. In 1975, Tbilisi University published a Karaite Hebrew grammar, *Ma'or Ayin*, edited by Zislin, while under the patronage of the Georgian Academy of Sciences Nisan Babalikashvili edited a collection of local Hebrew inscriptions, largely from tombstones: *Evreiskie nadpisi v Gruzii, XVIII–XIX vv.* ("Hebrew Inscriptions in Georgia, 18th to 19th Centuries," 1971). Babalikashvili (1938–1986), the son of the rabbi of Tbilisi, unfortunately died at a young age. So did the talented young Georgian Jewish Hebraist Boris (Dov) Gaponov (1934–1972), whose translation of the Georgian national epic, Shota Rostaveli's "The Man in the Panther's Skin," was published in Israel with the collaboration of the Georgian Academy of Sciences (Oteh or ha-namer, 1969). Gaponov's first-rate translation, which made a strong impression, became the subject of a dissertation submitted in 1985 to the University of Tbilisi by a young Hebraist Manana Gotsiridze. Earlier, in 1982, Yurii Kornienko had defended his dissertation at the same university on the morphology of word formation and word change in contemporary Hebrew.

At the 1964 conference we see the use of the word "Ivrit" in Russian to designate Hebrew in place of the earlier "drevneevreiskii iazyk" ("Old Jewish language"). By the time the third edition of the Large Soviet Encyclopedia appeared in the 1970s, "Ivrit" had become the standard term for the language; the entry "Ivrit" was written by the Soviet Semitist-Hamitist Aaron Dolgoposkii (b. 1930), subsequently teaching at the University of Haifa. In this connection we note that the abovementioned Hebrew-Russian dictionary, the life work of the educational specialist Feliks Shapiro, was scheduled for publication in the 1950s but was withdrawn – whereupon the author turned to the highest party circles in an attempt to prove the work's importance for Soviet Semitology (see the Russian commemorative volume *Feliks L'vovich Shapiro*, edited in Israel by his daughter Leah Prestin, 1983). The dictionary, which finally appeared after its author's death, served Soviet academic institutions as well as the young Jews studying their ancestral tongue more or less surreptitiously.

However, the official language of Soviet Jewry remained Yiddish, and the veteran Yiddish grammarian Emanuel Falkovich (1898?–1982?), who also wrote the entry "Yiddish" for the above-mentioned encyclopedia, contributed a chapter on the language to the linguistic collection *Iazyki narodov SSSR*, v. 1 ("Languages of the People of the U.S.S.R.," 1966). Dolgopolskii and Falkovich together produced the article on Hebrew scripts ("Evreiskoe pis'mo") for the encyclopedia. Falkovich also took an active part in the efforts of the journal *Sovetish Heymland* to teach Yiddish to Soviet Jews, although his silence on the future prospects of the language in the 1966 article makes it seem likely that he was pessimistic on the subject.

This brings us to Jewish studies in Yiddish. As noted, the Soviet authorities did not revive the interwar institutional structure to which we owe a number of studies in Yiddish on Jewish history, demography, Yiddish linguistics, Yiddish literary research, and bibliography. The older generation of scholars who had carried on this work was passing on in any case, and the absence of Yiddish schools made the problem of succession insoluble. In addition, the rapid linguistic assimilation of Soviet Jewry made the audience for what was left of Yiddish-language scholarship very small.

Yet even now some work was done. A number of scholars who had been associated with the Jewish subdivisions of the Ukrainian Academy during the 1928–1949 period were released from prisons and camps in the mid-1950s. Among them was the outstanding music folklorist Moses Beregovskii (1892–1961), who was, exceptionally, able to put together a book, posthumously published as *Evreiskii narodnye pesni* ("Yiddish Folk Songs," 1962). Many of Beregovskii's writings are now available in Mark Slobin's English edition (*Old Jewish Folk Music*, 1982).

The main outlet for Yiddish-language studies was naturally the standard-bearing monthly *Sovetish Heymland*. Because of its nature as a literary journal it tended to restrict research to the history of Yiddish literature and related topics. Among the more important literary scholars was Hersh Remenik (1905–1981). Two surviving Soviet Jewish historians, Hillel Aleksandrov (1891?–1972) and Asher Margolis (1891–1976) – the former after 20 years of imprisonment for "Trotskyism" – contributed occasional articles on the borderline of history and literature. Oldtime linguists writing in the journal included Reuben Lerner (1902?–1972), Khaim Loytsker (1898–1970), Moses Maydanski (1900?–1973), and Moses Shapiro (d. 1974). Shapiro, together with the Stalin victim Elijah Spivak (mentioned above), had been working for many years on a Russian-Yiddish dictionary, which finally appeared long after their deaths (*Russko-evreiskii (idish) slovar'*, 1984).

Two other veteran scholars, the historian Israel Sosis (1878–1967?) and the demographer Jacob Kantor (1886–1964) found no outlet in Russia during this period and published occasionally in the Warsaw Yiddish newspaper *Folksshtime*, where Kantor took on the then taboo topic of Jewish participation in the Red Army. Kantor also published his last demographic study, in which he analyzed Jewish data from the 1959 census, in the Warsaw Jewish historical journal *Bleter far geshikhte* (v. 15, 1962/63, translated and annotated by the present writer in *Studies... in Honor of I. Edward Kiev*, 1971). Sosis' unpublished "History of the Jews in Russia" was said to be in the possession of *Sovetish Heymland*.

As time went on *Sovetish Heymland* became more hospitable to studies not connected with Yiddish literature. Especially noteworthy among these are the articles by Leyb Vilsker (1919–1988), for a number of years head of the Jewish Department of the Leningrad Public Library. Vilsker was *inter alia* an expert on the Samaritan language and literature, and published *Samaritianskii iazyk* ("The Samaritan Language") in 1974. His most important contributions to the Yiddish monthly were previously unpublished Hebrew texts, such as poems of the famous medieval poet Judah Halevi (*Sovetish Heymland*, 1982, no. 2). Vilsker and his wife, Gita Gluskina (b. 1922) – a Hebraist in her own right – also contributed to *Palestinskii sbornik*. Gluskina, daughter of the Leningrad rabbi Mendel Gluskin, worked on medieval Hebrew texts and is best known for her edition of the mathematical treatise *Meyasher Akov* ("Straightening the Crooked," 1983) by Abner of Burgos. Later she moved to Jerusalem.

In the period we are dealing with, the absence of formal Jewish institutions other than synagogues did not stop young Jews from searching for their roots, and this became especially marked after the Six-Day War in 1967. The growing Soviet phenomenon of "samizdat" (private, unauthorized publishing) had a Jewish counterpart, where attempts were made to provide anthologies of Jewish literature in Russian. In 1976 the physicist Benjamin Fain (b. 1930), who later emigrated to Israel, decided to conduct a sociological survey of Jewish self-identification under "samizdat" conditions. About 1,500 Soviet Jews served as his sample, and the results are now available in English in an Israeli publication (*Jewishness in the Soviet Union*, 1984). Fain also organized a cultural symposium in Moscow at the end of 1976, to which the police put a quick end.

In the 1980s growing interest in Russian Jewish history made itself felt both inside and outside "samizdat" circles. In one of the major publications of Jewish "samizdat," *Leningradskii evreiskii al'manakh* ("Leningrad Jewish almanac," 1982–1989) Michael Beizer (b. 1950) published articles on the Jews of St. Petersburg, as the old capital used to be called. These resulted in 1986 in the "samizdat" book *Evrei v Peterburge* (published in 1990 in English translation as *The Jews of St. Petersburg* after Beizer emigrated to Israel). In the 1980s the official *Sovetish Heymland* became more receptive to articles on Jewish historical topics; the editors made a concerted effort in 1986 to print young writers and rejuvenate the journal, even if it meant translating from Russian writers who knew no Yiddish. One such, and probably the most talented of the younger historians, was Mark Kupovetskii (b. 1955), who was engaged in what in the Soviet Union was called "ethnography." Kupovetskii published in *Sovetish Heymland* short but up-to-date demographic studies on the Jews of Moscow, the Ukraine, and the Baltic republics; a longer version of his article on the Jews of Moscow appeared in *Etnodispersnye gruppy v gorodakh evropeiskoi chasti SSSR*, 1987. Kupovetskii's colleague and fellow Muscovite, Igor Krupnik (b. 1951), contributed a survey of recent accomplishments in Jewish studies to the journal (1986, no. 11 – for an annotated English translation see the bibliography). The author emphasized the youth of many scholars, and the fact that they had no "firm academic tradition" to rely upon and had to prepare themselves through their own efforts. Krupnik devotes much attention to the work being done in Georgia; in the Russian Republic he notes among others the Moscow linguist Aleksandra Eikhenvald (b. 1957), who herself published an article on the formation of modern Hebrew in *Sovetish Heymland* (1986, no. 7 – strongly criticized by Vilsker in issue no. 11 of that year). A Leningrad scholar and bibliographer mentioned by Krupnik was Simon Yakerson (b. 1956), who also contributed to the journal on occasion. Yakerson made a name for himself by his descriptive catalogues of Hebrew incunabula found in Leningrad and Moscow libraries; these catalogues appeared in 1985 and 1988 after Soviet bibliography had neglected Hebraica for almost 50 years.

In 1987, and even more in 1988, the effects of "perestroika" made themselves felt in the field of Jewish culture and scholarship. The very conservative Yiddish monthly now turned course and began to explore a long taboo topic: the fate of Jewish writers and cultural activities in the "black years" of 1948–1952. For the first time survivors of Stalin camps published memoirs of those days in *Sovetish Heymland*. "Samizdat" now became private rather than underground publishing, but tolerance did not mean support, and the contrast between official and unofficial publications remained striking. Scholarship played a relatively minor part in the plethora of Jewish cultural associations which sprang up in the Soviet Union, but efforts were made, often imitating earlier models. In Moscow a Jewish Historical Society now existed; it was instrumental in convening there an unprecedented international conference on Jewish studies (December, 1989) and planned to publish the proceedings. In Leningrad there was a "Jewish People's University" in apparent imitation of the one which existed in the early Soviet regime. This institution organized expeditions to places of Jewish interest and tried to document the Jewish past in Russia while there was still time. The chairman of the Historical Society was Valerii Engel, while the People's University was led by Elijah Dvorkin – both men in their thirties.

Yet it must be said that the massive emigration of Jews from the country, which assumed the proportions of flight, worked against the cultural and scholarly revival. Thus, the continued existence of Moscow's *Evreiskii istoricheskii al'manakh* ("Jewish Historical Almanac," 1987–1988), a "samizdat" publication, became questionable because both of its editors, Aleksandr Razgon (b. 1949) and Vladimir (Velvl) Chernin (b. 1958), left for Israel. Chernin, a Yiddish poet and folklorist, also wrote for official publications and tried to bridge the gap between the two spheres.

On the more hopeful side we see that modern Jewish topics, spurned for such a long time by Soviet academic editors and university administrators, were now acceptable for articles and dissertations. This was particularly true in the field of ethnography, for example, a joint article by Kupovetskii and Krupnik on the Kurdish Jews of the U.S.S.R. appeared in *Sovetskaia etnografiia* (1988, no. 2) after being reportedly rejected some years previously. Michael Chlenov (b. 1940), who had emerged as the leader of the Vaad (Board of Deputies) of the organized Jewish communities, was himself an ethnographer. Much help was given to younger scholars by the veteran Leningrad ethnographer Natalia Yukhneva, who, although not Jewish, supported Jewish ethnographic work and was actively engaged in the battle against Soviet antisemitism. Yukhneva and others mentioned here were able to visit Israel and were in contact with Israeli academic institutions.

With the breakup of the Soviet Union, Jewish Studies at the institutional level, like Jewish communal life in general, has burgeoned, largely through the Federation of Jewish Communities of the Former Soviet Union, which operates five Jewish universities, and various foreign Jewish organizations and agencies.

[Avraham Greenbaum]

Jewish Studies in France

The academic field of Jewish studies was founded in France at the end of the 19th century with the creation of the *Société des études juives, which then began to publish – and still does – a learned periodical, **Revue des Etudes Juives*, and directed the publication of the classic works of Henrich *Gross (*Gallia Judaica*, 1897) and Theodore *Reinach.

During the 20th century the pioneering works of Bernhard *Blumenkranz on medieval Jewish History, Léon *Poliakov on antisemitism, and Georges *Vajda, Charles *Touati, and Haim *Zafrani on Jewish mysticism were the most notable achievements in the field of Jewish studies in post-World War II France and provided the basis for further development. With their guidance, a process began which allowed Jewish history and Jewish studies eventually to acquire a more respected place in the French academic world, illustrated by the enrollment of researchers on Jewish themes at the National Center for Scientific Research (CNRS) and the running of programs on Jewish themes – like the New Gallia Judaica, headed by Danièle Iancu-Agou in 2005 – and their introduction into the curriculum of the universities. Despite the upheaval of World War II and the discontinuity of organized Jewish life, some scholars managed to preserve the spirit of the past and to transmit the skills of Jewish scholarship to the younger generation. But the goals changed and new horizons were sought by the new researchers.

Reflecting the revival of Jewish cultural life in France, the field of Jewish Studies grew constantly in France during the second part of the 20th century and, more specifically, in its last decades. The traditional chairs at the Ecole Pratique des hautes études (EPHE) were challenged by the development of many courses and research centers located in universities, at the École des hautes études en sciences sociales (EHESS), and also in community institutions. With courses on Jewish civilization (history, philosophy, Jewish thought, and Jewish languages, the last mainly at Paris VIII and the Institut des Langues orientales INALCO, etc.,), Jewish Studies grew out of almost nothing to become an active area of learning in almost all the main French universities (Aix-en-Provence, Lille, Lyon, Montpellier, Strasbourg, Toulouse, etc). This evolution toward recognition of the particularity of Jewish existence during the past centuries is linked to a cultural phenomenon that brought forth on the one hand a general trend toward a quest for singular roots, and on the other hand a renewed dialogue between religions in the aftermath of World War II. It also owes much to the transformations that occurred within French Jewry: the transformation of attitudes and outlooks in the aftermath of the Six-Day War of 1967 between Israel and its Arab neighbors, and last, to the mass immigration of North African Jews to France. Simultaneously there was a significant expansion in the treatment of Jewish subjects in the press, and from the late 1980s new Jewish periodicals providing information and articles on traditional, modern, or contemporary Jewish issues (*Traces, Pardes, Cahiers du Judaïsme, La Revue d'histoire de la Shoah, Le Monde juif*) or scholarly research. In 1989 the *Alliance Israélite Universelle opened a renewed library which is now the largest Jewish library in Europe, and recently, the three major Jewish libraries (Medem, Séminaire rabbinique, and AIU) joined hands to create a common network. It also has created a College of Jewish Studies focusing its activities on the in-depth study of Jewish thought in its various manifestations, headed by Shmuel *Trigano. Deserving of mention is also the significant push given to the renewal of studies on World War II by the Institut d'histoire du temps présent (IHTP), which also administers a library, founded in 1980 and directed (1994–2005) by Henry Rousso, where a new generation of researchers is at work. The *Centre de la documentation juive contemporaine (CDJC) was initially founded in 1943 by Isaac *Schneersohn to gather all the documents related to the fate of the French Jews during the war, to bear witness, and to prosecute war criminals. In the early 1950s the tomb of the unknown Jewish martyr was dedicated at the CDJC, and it became the central memorial and symbol of Jewish memory and serves as the venue for Holocaust commemorations. In January 2005 the CDJC opened a new site under the auspices of the Memorial of the Shoah, which offers to the public a large research library and an active publication program. The CDJC organizes permanent and traveling exhibitions, conducts wide-ranging educational programs, and provides pedagogic courses for teachers and children. Community organizations, like Centre Rachi, and recently the Institut Elie Wiesel, also began to supply courses and diplomas to promote these studies and give students the opportunity to learn something about Judaism during their studies. A new generation of scholars born or educated in France has emerged who devote themselves to particular areas of Jewish scholarship. Generally speaking, they range from the translation and interpretation of the traditional texts of Jewish thought to the study of contemporary Jewish issues. Their work falls into a number of broad areas. The first is concerned with the Jewish world as seen from within: Jewish Thought and Philosophy, Sciences, Jewish History. A second area is Textual and Classical Studies and Archaeology. A third deals with the relations of Jews with Israel and France as well as to the Holocaust. One can also distinguish between scholars born before and after World War II. The former were obviously more involved in classical and textual studies, while the latter tended to scrutinize the past to better understand the present. This change signals the passage from learned and scholarly academic work to the much more public sphere of the media. The tendency to secularize traditional teaching and endow it with the flavor of the sciences, inherited from the *Wissenschaft des Judentums, is also less and less felt, since there is an increasing demand for purely religious studies outside rabbinical and consistory circles. It is thus difficult to determine the direction of future Jewish studies.

Among the many active Jewish scholars, we shall only mention those who have published extensively. In the field of Jewish Thought and Philosophy, Charles *Mopsik (1956–2003) was one of the outstanding figures. He worked mainly on the editing and publication of original Kabbalah manuscripts in French, which were subsequently translated into other languages, such as Hebrew, Italian, Spanish, Russian, and English: *Les grands textes de la cabale: les rites qui font Dieu* (1993); *Cabale et cabalistes* (1997); *R. Moses de Leon's Sefer Shekel ha-Kodesh*, (Heb., 1996), *Sex of the Soul: the Vicissitudes of Sexual Difference in Kabbalah* (2005).

Paul B. Fenton (1951–), a disciple of the late Georges Vajda, was the head of Jewish Studies at Paris IV (Sorbonne). He focused on Judeo-Arabic philosophy and thought: *The Treatise of the Pool of Obadyah Ben Abraham Ben Moses Maimonides* (1981); *Philosophie et exégèse dans le Jardin de la métaphore de Moïse Ibn Ezra, philosophe et poète andalou du XIII siècle* (1997); *Joseph b. Abraham Ibn Waqar: Principles of the Qabbalah* (2004); he also edited Georges Vajda's *Le commentaire sur le "Livre de la création de Dunas ben Tamim de Kairouan (Xe siecle)* (2002). He succeeded emeritus Roland Goestchel (1930–), who worked mainly on Kabbalah and medieval philosophy: *La Kabbale* (1985); *Isaac Abarbanel: conseiller des princes et philosophe* (1996).

Dominique Bourel (1951–), a researcher at the CNRS, was the director of the Centre de la recherche française à Jérusalem (CRFJ) between 1994 and 2004. Working on German Jewish philosophers, he published *Moses Mendelssohn, la naissance du judaïsme moderne* (2004) and edited many books, such *Max Nordau: critique de la dégénérescence, médiateur franco-allemand, père fondateur du sionisme* (1996), with Delphine Bechtel (1958–), an associate professor at Paris IV, who focused on German Jewish literature and published *La renaissance culturelle juive en Europe centrale et orientale, 1897–1930* (2002). Bourel translated Martin *Buber's letters in *Lettres choisies de Martin Buber, 1899–1965* (2004) with Florence Heymann (1948–), a researcher at the CFRJ who wrote *Le crépuscule des lieux, identités juives de Czernowitz* (2003) and had previously published *L'historiographie israélienne aujourd'hui* (1998) with Michel Abitbol.

Shmuel Trigano, born in Algeria (1948–), a sociologist and philosopher, is a professor at Paris X. A prolific writer, he published, among many other books, *Le récit de la disparue: essai sur l'identité juive* (1977); the five-volume *La Société juive à travers l'histoire* (1992); and *Les frontières d'Auschwitz: les ravages du devoir de mémoire* (2005).

On the history of science and philosophy, Gad Freudenthal (1944–), also from the CNRS, published *Science in the Medieval Hebrew and Arabic Traditions* (2005). He edited *Studies on Gersonides: A Fourteenth-Century Jewish Philosopher-Scientist* (1992); and with Samuel Kottek and P.B. Fenton, published *Mélanges d'histoire de la médecine hébraïque* (2003).

In the field of Jewish history, Gérard *Nahon (1931–), emeritus professor at the EPHE, wrote both on medieval France and Sephardi history. He headed the Nouvelle Gallia Judaica from 1981 to 1992, directed the *Revue des Études Juives* (1972–96), and was president of the Société des Études juives. Among his books are *Inscriptions hébraïques et juives de France médiévale* (1986); *Menasseh Ben Israël, The Hope of Israel*, published with Henry Mechoulan (1987; Fr. 1979); *Métropoles et périphéries séfarades d'Occident* (1994); *Juifs et judaïsme à Bordeaux* (2003).

Gilbert Dahan (1943–) a researcher at the CNRS and professor at the EPHE, continued and deepened the work of Blumenkranz on medieval France: *Les intellectuels chrétiens et les juifs au Moyen Age*, (1990); *The Christian Polemic against the Jews in the Middle Ages* (1998, Fr. 1991), and edited *Les Juifs au regard de l'histoire: mélanges en l'honneur de Bernhard Blumenkranz* (1985).

Danièle Iancu-Agou (1945–), a researcher at the CNRS in Montpellier, also published on France: *Les Juifs en Provence (1475–1501), De l'insertion à l'expulsion* (1981); *Les juifs du Midi: une histoire millénaire* (1995); *Juifs et néophytes en Provence: l'exemple d'Aix à travers le destin de Régine Abram de Draguignan* (2000).

Simon Schwarzfuchs (1927–), professor emeritus at Bar-Ilan University, who settled in Israel, published among other works *Napoleon, the Jews and the Sanhedrin* (1979); *A Concise History of the Rabbinate* (1993); and *A History of the Jews in Medieval France* (2001).

On other themes, Jean Baumgarten (1950–) a researcher at the CNRS, participated in the creation and publication of the main Jewish French periodicals and engaged in the study of Yiddish literature: *Introduction to Old Yiddish Literature*, (2005; Fr. 1993); *Récits hagiographiques juifs* (2001); *La Naissance du Hassidisme. Mystique, rituel et société* (2006).

Sylvie Anne Goldberg (1953–), at the EHESS, works

on the cultural history of traditional Judaism. She published *Crossing the Jabbok, Illness and Death in Ashkenazi Judaism in Sixteenth through Nineteenth Century Prague* (1996; Fr. 1989) and two volumes on the Jewish uses of time: *La Clepsydre. Essai sur la pluralité des temps dans le Judaïsme* (2000); *La Clepsydre II, Temps de Jérusalem, temps de Babylone* (2004).

Maurice Kriegel (1949–) headed the Centre d'études juives at the EHESS and was editor of a series on Judaism. He published *Les Juifs à la fin du Moyen âge, dans l'Europe méditerranéenne* (1979).

Daniel Tollet (1945–), at the Paris IV Sorbonne, focused on the history of the Jews in Poland, and edited a series on Jewish Studies. He published *Histoire des juifs en Pologne: du XVIe siecle à nos jours* (1992); *Accuser pour convertir: du bon usage de l'accusation de crime rituel dans la Pologne catholique* (2000); and *Marchands et hommes d'affaires juifs dans la Pologne des Wasa* (1588–1668) (2001).

In the field of textual studies, Judith Olszowy-Schlanger (1967–), born in Poland and trained in England, was a professor of codicology and paleography at the EPHE. She published *Karaite Marriage Documents from the Cairo Geniza. Legal Tradition and Community Life in Mediaeval Egypt and Palestine* (1998); *Les manuscrits hébreux dans l'Angleterre médievale: étude historique et paléographique* (2003); and with Geoffrey Khan and María Ángeles Gallego, *Abu al-Faraj Harun ibn al-Faraj, The Karaite Tradition of Hebrew Grammatical Thought in its Classical Form, a Critical Edition and Translation* (2003). She succeeded professor emeritus Colette Sirat (1934–), who moved to Israel after pioneering the field in France. Sirat published, among other books, *Les papyrus en caractères Hébraïques trouvés en Égypte* (1985); *Hebrew Manuscripts of the Middle Ages* (2002; Fr. 1994); and *A History of Jewish Philosophy in the Middle Ages*, 1993 (French 1983).

Classical studies are represented by Mireille Hadas-Lebel (1940–), former professor at INALCO, now at Paris IV Sorbonne. She published several books on Hebrew language and later focused on Jewish Greek and Latin authors: *Philon d'Alexandrie: un penseur en diaspora* (2003); *Flavius Josephus: Eyewitness to Rome's First-Century Conquest of Judea* (1993; Fr. 1989); and *Jerusalem against Rome* (2005; Fr. 1990).

Archaeology and Qumran studies are also well represented by André *Caquot (1923–2004), who taught at the Collège de France: *Ugarit-Forschungen, 35* (2003–4): *Festschrift André Caquot*, edited by Manfried Dietrich and Oswald Loretz. Caquot published with René Labat *Les Religions du Proche-Orient asiatique: textes babyloniens, ougaritiques, hittites* (1970) and, with Maurice Sznycer, *Ugaritic Religion* (1980; Fr. 1974).

André Lemaire, (1942–), archaeologist and a professor at the EPHE, whose works deals with Aramean and Hebrew epigraphy, published *Les écoles et la formation de la Bible dans l'ancien Israël* (1981) and *Naissance du monothéisme: point de vue d'un historien* (2003)

Joseph Mélèze-Modrzejewski (1930–), born in Poland, was a professor at Paris I and a scholar in Greek and Egyptian papyri, focusing his research on ancient legal history: *The Jews of Egypt: from Rameses II to Emperor Hadrian* (1995; Fr. 1991); *Droit impérial et traditions locales dans l'Égypte romaine* (1990).

On contemporary France, Pierre Birnbaum (1940–), professor of political science and sociology at the University of Paris I (Sorbonne), director of *Les cahiers du judaïsme*, opened a new vista on the relationship between Jews and the French Republic. He is the author of numerous books, several of which have been translated into English: *Anti-Semitism in France: a Political History from Leon Blum to the Present* (1992; Fr. 1988); *The Jews of the Republic: A Political History of State Jews in France from Gambetta to Vichy* (1996; Fr. 1992); and *The Anti-Semitic Moment: A Tour of France in 1898* (2003; Fr. 1998).

On the history of World War II France, Anne Grynberg (1951–), who was active in the AIU and editor of *Les cahiers du judaisme*, wrote *Les camps de la honte: les internés juifs des camps français, 1939–1944* (1991). And, although living in Israel, Renée Poznanski (1948–) contributed as well with her *Jews in France during World War II* (2001; Fr. 1994).

The field of Holocaust studies developed relatively late in France, initiated with a literary approach by Rachel *Ertel (1939–), professor at Paris VII, who wrote *Le shtetl, la bourgade juive de Pologne* (1982); *Dans la langue de personne* (1993); and *Brasier de mots* (2003).

Annette *Wieviorka (1948–), a researcher at the CNRS, began with the problematics of remembrance, publishing with Itzhok Niborski (b. 1947 in Buenos Aires and a scholar in Yiddish) *Les Livres du souvenir: mémoriaux juifs de Pologne* (1983). Later she wrote *Déportation et génocide, Entre la mémoire et l'oubli* (1992), *The Era of the Witness* (2006; Fr. 1998), and *Auschwitz, 60 ans après*, (2005).

On Israel, Alain Dieckhoff (1958–) published *Les espaces d'Israël: essai sur la stratégie territoriale israélienne* (1987) and *The Invention of a Nation: Zionist Thought and the Making of Modern Israel* (2003; Fr. 1993).

Esther Benbassa (1950–) and Jean-Christophe Attias (1958–), professors at the EPHE; both moved from history to more polemical essays on Jewishness and the State of Israel, writing together: *Israel, the Impossible Land* (2003; Fr. 1998) and *Jews and Their Future: A Conversation on Judaism and Jewish Identities* (2004; Fr. 2001). Previously Benbassa had published, among other books, *The Jews of the Balkans: The Judeo-Spanish community, 15th to 20th centuries*, with Aron Rodrigue (1995; Fr. 1993); and *The Jews of France. A History from Antiquity to the Present* (1999; Fr. 1997). Attias published works on Karaism: *Abraham Aboulafia, L'Épître des sept voies* (1985); *Le Commentaire biblique. Mordekhai Komtino ou l'herméneutique du dialogue* (1991); and *Isaac Abravanel, la mémoire et l'espérance* (1992).

[Sylvie Anne Goldberg (2nd ed.)]

BIBLIOGRAPHY: J. Baskin and S. Tenenbaum (eds.), *Gender and Jewish Studies: A Curriculum Guide* (1994); D. Biale, M. Galchinsky, and S. Heschel, *Insider/Outsider: American Jews and Multiculturalism* (1998); L. Davidman and S. Tenenbaum (eds.), *Feminist Perspec-*

tives on Jewish Studies (1994); Z. Garber (ed.), *Academic Approaches to Teaching Jewish Studies* (2000); P. Ritterband and H.S. Wechsler, *Jewish Learning in American Universities: The First Century* (1994).

JEWISH SUCCESSOR ORGANIZATIONS in Germany, organizations for tracing and recovering heirless Jewish property of those Jews who were victims of the Nazis.

Jewish Restitution Successor Organization (JRSO)

The Americans were foremost in setting up a framework, and the first Jewish body for claims in the American Zone, the Jewish Restitution Successor Organization (JRSO), was established in 1948 with offices in Nuremberg. In 1950 a similar body, the Jewish Trust Corporation (JTC), was established in the former British Zone (northwest Germany) with the approval of the British government. Later a separate branch was established in the French Zone. A joint office was created by them for the three sectors of West Berlin.

Where the former Jewish property owner within the American Zone had died without an heir, or where no claim was made, the JRSO was empowered to file claims and apply the proceeds to the relief of needy refugees anywhere in the world. The JRSO also claimed restitution of Jewish communal property. The proceeds served primarily the religious and cultural needs of the surviving communities in West Germany and were then handed over to the general refugee funds. Where an individual claimant subsequently appeared too late to lodge his own claim application, the JRSO, as well as the JTC, adopted an equity procedure for settlement up until Dec. 31, 1958. The American organization recovered by the end of 1967 nearly 200,000,000 DM ($50,000,000) in addition to the immovable property restored to the communities, and the operation was not yet completed. The amount recovered includes the value of property in West Berlin. The overwhelming part of the fund was obtained by a global settlement made with the authorities of the German Laender and of West Berlin, in the areas in which the property was situated or had been confiscated. The authorities were asked to pay a lump sum and, in return, were subrogated to the remainder of the unsettled claims of the organization against German individuals who had acquired the immovable property. The authorities could then make their settlement with the German owner.

[Norman Bentwich]

Jewish Trust Corporation (JTC).

The primary task of the JTC was to locate within an 18-month time limit property that remained unclaimed after June 30, 1950, the deadline established by the Restitution Law for the British Zone for claims by the original owners or their heirs. The declaration of former Jewish property by those who had acquired it under the Nazi regime proved unreliable and incomplete, so that 70% of JTC's claims for landed property resulted from its own search activities. Not a single item of former communal and organizational property remained undiscovered, and in only a very few cases did former individual property come belatedly to the notice of the JTC. The JTC enforced proceedings before restitution courts for the recovery *in natura* of property claimed by it, or arrived at cash settlements with those who had acquired it under the Nazi regime. Certain claims (those resulting from mass confiscatory measures of the Third Reich) were settled in bulk with the Federal German Republic and other claims (damage to former Jewish communal organizational property) with the Laender, or with Hamburg and Berlin. By the end of 1967, the JTC had recovered a total of 169,500,000 DM (approx. $42,375,000). The Corporation by that time almost reached the end of its operations, but it was expected that about four million DM (approx. U.S. $1,100,000) might still accrue to its funds. The major recipients of JTC funds were the Jewish Agency for Israel, for Youth Aliyah work; the American Jewish Joint Distribution Committee for *Malben work; the Central British Fund for assistance to Nazi victims in the U.K.; the Leo Baeck Charitable Trust, for assistance to Nazi victims in various countries; equity claimants; Jewish communities in Germany and their organizations; organizations for the building of synagogues and maintenance of yeshivot in Israel; and the *Hebrew University of Jerusalem.

Branche française de la Jewish Trust Corporation for Germany

In the French Zone of occupation the right to heirless and unclaimed Jewish property was originally vested by the French authorities in the Laender governments, and the proceeds were used for general indemnification purposes. In September 1951 the rights of the Laender were abrogated. In March 1952 the French Haut Commissaire for Germany appointed a specially created department of JTC, the so-called Branche Française, as the Jewish successor organization for the French Zone. The branch was fully autonomous. It had its seat in Paris and was directed by its own Conseil d'Administration. The operational office was in Mainz. The claiming period accorded to the branch ended on April 30, 1953, and the branch was limited to claims on such property as had not already been adjudicated with the Laender governments. The total amount recovered by the end of 1967 was 27,550,000 DM (approx. $6,888,000).

After the 1960s the role of the Jewish Successor Organizations diminished. All activities ended in the 1970s.

[Charles I. Kapralik]

JEWISH TEACHERS' SEMINARY AND PEOPLE'S UNIVERSITY, the only Yiddish teachers' training college and school for advanced Yiddish studies in North America. It was founded in 1918 under the auspices of the Labor Zionist movement by Joel *Entin and Judah *Even Shemuel (Kaufman), who headed it during its formative years and provided opportunities for adult education in both secular and Jewish studies on the model of the European "Folks-Universitet." In 1935 it was incorporated by an act of legislature of the State of New York with the right to grant degrees. A Jewish Music Division was inaugurated in 1964 and in 1965 it merged with the *Herzliah Hebrew Teachers' Institute. It acquired new premises in 1970 and had a library of 40,000 volumes, in Yiddish and Hebrew.

The Seminary provided teachers for all the groups in the Yiddish school movement, except for the Communists. Its program emphasized "the historic and religious values and institutions, the cultural heritage of Yiddish and Hebrew … the national renaissance in the Land of Israel, the ideas of the Jewish labor movement, and the American democratic way of life." Its graduate program offers study and research in Yiddish Language and Literature, Hebrew Language and Literature, and Jewish Social Studies (the last embracing Education, History, Philosophy, and Sociology). The institute was governed by an independent board of trustees which includes representatives of the Labor Zionist Movement, the Workmen's Circle, and the Zionist Organization of America. The Seminary published a scholarly Yiddish-English quarterly *Kultur un Leben* in the 1940s.

With American Jewish education evolving along religious denominational lines in the post-World War II period, and with the Yiddish secular movement failing to rally behind its own institute of higher learning, the Seminary could not keep pace with developments in the Jewish community. A similar situation in the Hebraist Herzliah Hebrew Teachers' Institute was the cause of their merger. In spite of the centrality of Yiddish in the Seminary as against the formerly exclusive emphasis upon Hebrew in the Herzliah curriculum, the common ideological commitment to modern Jewish education within a national-cultural frame of reference allowed for parallel continuation of each program in accordance with differing linguistic commitments. The merger of the two hitherto weakened institutions prolonged the life of both for a time but was ultimately unsuccessful, and the school closed.

[Gershon Winer]

JEWISH TELEGRAPHIC AGENCY (JTA), bureau for the gathering and distribution of Jewish news. Established by Jacob *Landau in the Hague in 1914 as the Jewish Correspondence Bureau, the Jewish Telegraphic Agency was reestablished in London by Landau in collaboration with Meir *Grossman in 1919. In 1922 its headquarters was moved to New York. Under a 1950 reorganization, Landau divested himself of his stock and control passed nominally to an independent board of directors although the operating deficit on operations was being met by the *Jewish Agency. From 1960 the stock was vested in the American Jewish News Foundation. The debts due to the Jewish Agency were canceled, and the JTA became eligible to receive subventions from Jewish Welfare Funds which were essential to its survival, since less than one-third of its income came from subscriptions to its publications and the sale of its services to the press. Apart from its wire services, the JTA has published the *Jewish Daily Bulletin* from 1924. In 1962 it began a weekly bulletin, *Community News*. Boris Smolar was editor-in-chief from 1924 to 1968. Subsequently it continued to operate as a global news agency covering Jewish affairs around the world with correspondents in more than 30 cities.

WEBSITE: jta.org.

JEWISH THEOLOGICAL SEMINARY (JTS). JTS is the primary educational and religious center of *Conservative Judaism and a leading institution for the academic study of Judaism. With its main campus in New York City, JTS is currently comprised of a rabbinical school, a cantorial school, a graduate school of Jewish Studies, a graduate school of Jewish Education, an undergraduate school, a supplemental religious high school, and several research institutes. It houses a world-class Judaica library on campus; its museum, now called the *Jewish Museum, occupies another Manhattan site.

Inception and Early History

JTS arose from the debate within the ranks of 19th century American Jewish leaders concerning the scope of religious reform. Its founders, a diverse group of religious centrists, with both traditionalist and modernist leanings, nonetheless shared the consensus that Reform was breaking too radically with Jewish norms. Responding to the highly-publicized banquet celebrating the ordination of the first class of rabbinical students at the Reform *Hebrew Union College, featuring a variety of non-kosher foods, and to the promulgation of the Reform movement's 1885 Pittsburgh Platform, dismissing biblical and rabbinic rituals regulating diet and dress as anachronisms, moderate rabbis and scholars, principally Sabato *Morais, Henry Pereira *Mendes, Alexander *Kohut, and Cyrus *Adler, organized support for the establishment of a new and more traditional rabbinical seminary. At the same time, the new academy was intended to reflect the 19th century Historical School's conception of Judaism as a developing religion. By January 1887, the Jewish Theological Seminary Association opened in New York City, with the mandate to preserve "the knowledge and practice of historical Judaism." The new school modeled its curriculum after the *Juedisch-Theologisches Seminar, Breslau, stressing biblical, historical and philosophical subjects in addition to the traditional Ashkenazi focus on rabbinics. As a self-consciously American institution, the Seminary Association sought to acculturate its largely immigrant student body to life in their new country. Despite initiatives in Jewish educational outreach and community organizing, however, Seminary Association leaders were not successful in creating a congregational base to sustain their school. Without significant congregational support, the school struggled financially during its first fifteen years and was at the point of closing in 1902. In this first phase of its existence, the Seminary Association graduated 14 rabbis and three *hazzanim*, including Joseph H. *Hertz, who became chief rabbi of the British Empire, and Mordecai M. *Kaplan, theologian, long-time faculty member at the Jewish Theological Seminary, and founder of *Reconstructionist Judaism.

Reorganization and Growth

While revered as the first president of the Seminary, Morais, occupied with his congregational duties, had never been able to attend to the school on a full-time basis. As early as 1890, lay leaders of the Seminary began circulating the idea of approaching Solomon *Schechter, and months before Morais' death in 1897 members of the Seminary Association board offered Schechter the presidency of their school. Fluent in traditional Jewish disciplines of study and loyal to norms of ritual behavior, and yet also a leading critical-academic Rabbinics scholar and a gifted popularizer of Jewish scholarship for an English-speaking audience, Schechter exemplified the kind of religious leader the Seminary backers hoped their school would train. As Adler and the financial supporters of the Seminary Association, Louis *Marshall, Jacob *Schiff, and Judge Mayer *Sulzberger, concluded that the school needed reorganization, they invited Schechter to become the president of the faculty of the new entity, The Jewish Theological Seminary of America (JTS), completing the transition in March 1902.

Schechter saw Judaica scholarship as an instrument for strengthening Jewish life, and thus embraced the vision that JTS would provide leadership for American Jewry by training religiously observant and intellectually open-minded rabbis. To accomplish that goal, he focused on raising the level of scholarship practiced and taught within the school. Schechter engaged a faculty of young, promising academicians, including the literary scholar Israel *Davidson, the biblical scholar Israel *Friedlander, the talmudist Louis *Ginzberg, and the historian Alexander *Marx. Schechter and Marx oversaw the creation of what would ultimately become the largest Judaica library in America. Schechter transformed rabbinical training into a graduate-level course of study.

As regards undergraduate students, a 1908 New York City police report about Jewish criminality spurred Schechter to overcome earlier ambivalence on the part of the Seminary board and to extend the mission of JTS to include training teachers. This was meant to create an additional channel for providing beneficial spiritual influences to the "downtown" immigrant population. In 1909, he appointed Mordecai Kaplan as principal of the Teacher's Institute. Over time, Kaplan broadened the scope of that school's activities to include general academic undergraduate courses, and in 1931, he became the dean of the Seminary College of Jewish Studies. Under Kaplan's direction, the Teacher's Institute/Seminary College imbued JTS students with the values of cultural Zionism, Hebraism, and consciousness of Jewish community – in short, with a Kaplanian interpretation of Judaism as a religious civilization.

Schechter did not envision that JTS would become the fountainhead of a new denomination, Conservative Judaism, but rather that it would offer an Americanized and enlightened traditionalist alternative to Reform. After Schechter's death in 1915, his successor at JTS, Cyrus Adler (temporary president, 1915–24; president, 1924–40), maintained the school's ideological posture and social program, resisting calls to formulate partisan ideological platforms. Rather, he focused on the Seminary's institutional growth. During his tenure, JTS graduated 236 rabbis and 364 teachers. Working with the *Rabbinical Assembly, the successor organization to the JTS Rabbinical School alumni association, Adler began the process of professionalizing the placement of graduates in pulpits. Drawing on his experience as an administrator at the Smithsonian Institute and *Dropsie College, Adler systematized the Seminary's administrative procedures and, in 1925, amassed the core collection of its Jewish Museum. He presided over the construction of the Seminary's new campus at its current location in Manhattan. He labored to stabilize its financial condition and guided it through the difficulties of the Great Depression, while nonetheless adding to its library and hiring additional faculty members, including the Bible scholars H.L.*Ginsberg and Robert *Gordis.

The most consequential of those additions to the faculty was the hiring of Louis *Finkelstein in 1925 as a lecturer in theology. With an eye to an orderly succession, Adler promoted him steadily. By the time of Adler's final illness (1939–40), Finkelstein was the school's actual administrator and, in May 1940, became its president.

The tenure of Louis Finkelstein (1940–72), a JTS alumnus himself, represents a coming of age of the institution. By these decades, JTS was growing rapidly, and to staff its expanded programs, Finkelstein recruited administrators from the ranks of the Seminary's own graduates, notably Max *Arzt, Moshe *Davis, Simon *Greenberg, and Bernard *Mandelbaum. As part of the restructuring of administrative responsibilities, Finkelstein became chancellor, rather than president, in 1951.

While maintaining the largely traditionalist religious outlook of Schechter and Adler, Finkelstein dramatically revised the role of the Seminary. In the post-war and post-Holocaust era, JTS was to be the leader of the effort to save American Jewry from assimilation and to inculcate in society at large the values of toleration, democracy, and respect for Judaism. Among the many programs he fostered, in support of the goal of having JTS influence American Jewry and the broader American society, Finkelstein created ecumenical institutes, notably the Institute for Religious and Social Studies, and expanded JTS educational outreach to include radio and television programming. The post-war Jewish reckoning, in which JTS would help remedy the huge void in Jewish knowledge caused by the Holocaust, also figured in the reasoning behind the Seminary's opening a Cantorial School in 1952.

The expansion of the role to be played by JTS included cooperative work with the neighboring Columbia University. In 1953, the two schools opened a dual degree program for undergraduates.

Moreover, JTS moved into pre-undergraduate education. In 1945, JTS sponsored a youth leadership program, the Leaders' Training Fellowship, and three years later, it embraced the recently-opened Ramah educational summer camps. In a similar vein, in 1951, JTS opened the Prozdor, an honors-level Hebrew High School, and the Melton Research Center for Jewish Education in 1960. The Leader's Training

Fellowship initiative waned by the 1970s, but the others have flourished.

Finkelstein also presided over the geographical expansion of JTS, opening a West Coast affiliate, the *University of Judaism, in 1947, and a Seminary Center in Israel in 1962. All these activities succeeded in raising the profile of JTS dramatically.

There were tensions at JTS in the Finkelstein era. The revolutionary turbulence of the 1960s, which rocked many college campuses, also impacted on JTS. Students lobbied for greater recognition from their teachers and administrators in the conduct of seminary life and learning, and also sought to synthesize their political views with their Jewish studies. They rallied around the theologian Abraham Joshua *Heschel, who broke ranks with the apolitical profile of JTS by marching in the Civil Rights movement, working in the Soviet Jewry movement, and most controversial of all, voicing opposition to the Vietnam War.

Tension also mounted in the relationship between JTS and the Conservative Movement. In matters of religious practice, the school was frequently more traditional than the denomination as a whole, as in the maintenance of separate seating, rather than mixed seating, in the JTS synagogue. The faculty appointment of the talmudist Saul *Lieberman in 1940, and his designation as rector of JTS in 1958, decisively reconfirmed the traditionalist atmosphere at JTS for the duration of the Finkelstein administration. Finkelstein's critics, notably the leading Conservative rabbi Solomon *Goldman, criticized JTS for refusing to position itself unambiguously as a denominational school and building up the institutions of the denomination. In fact, Finkelstein's focus on affecting all of American or even world Jewry was at cross-purposes with the agenda of denominational service.

The price of engagement of a broader public affected JTS as well as the development of the Conservative Jewish denomination. During the Finkelstein era, JTS successfully sought to train a group of rabbi-scholars who were to occupy academic chairs in the expanding field of Judaic Studies. Several of the most eminent of these JTS alumni were honored at the 100th anniversary of JTS, including Robert L. Chazan, Naomi Wiener Cohen, Seymour Feldman, Jonathan Goldstein, David Weiss *Halivni, Arthur *Hertzberg, Arthur Hyman, Baruch Levine, Samuel Morell, and Jacob *Neusner. While these scholars have enriched their Judaic Studies disciplines, most of them did not work in the schools or synagogues of the Conservative Movement. Moreover, by serving other schools of higher education, they advanced a decentralization of Jewish learning that denied JTS the exclusivity that it once enjoyed.

Recent History

During the tenure of Finkelstein's successor, Gerson D. *Cohen (1972–86), the tensions between school and denomination came to a head, precipitated by the debate over the ordination of women as Conservative rabbis. The influence of the feminist movement of the 1960s and 1970s had led to the ordination of women in the Reform and Reconstructionist seminaries, and a growing number of Conservative rabbis and laity called for JTS to admit qualified women to its Rabbinical School. Although initially opposed to that change, in the course of a movement-wide study process, Cohen became an ardent proponent of women's ordination. To his traditionalist critics, he insisted that women's ordination was fully within the parameters of Conservative Judaism. As custodian of his institution, Cohen also argued that JTS risked forfeiting its leadership position within the denomination if it failed to ordain women rabbis, seeing that the Rabbinical Assembly was moving closer to admitting women candidates ordained elsewhere. In 1983, four years after the JTS faculty rejected his first attempt to revise school policy, Cohen succeeded in gaining approval for the proposed reform. In the aftermath of that decision, with some movement traditionalists abandoning the Conservative denomination, the renowned talmudist, Weiss Halivni, resigned from the JTS faculty. Weiss Halivni, whom Cohen had not appointed rector to succeed Lieberman, became the leading scholar at the rabbinical seminary of the break-away group, the Union for Traditional Judaism.

The evolution of JTS policy on women's ordination reveals that, by the end of Cohen's tenure, the school having decisively embraced its identity as a Conservative Jewish institution, it thereby abandoned its earlier hopes to provide a non-denominational unifier for traditional and moderate American Jews. Consistent with this development, JTS opened its Ratner Archives for the Study of Conservative Judaism in 1985. Cohen likewise aligned JTS more vigorously with the development of Conservative (Masorti) Judaism in Israel. Cohen involved JTS in several educational initiatives in Israel, requiring all JTS rabbinical students to live and study for a period at the school's expanded Jerusalem campus, Neve Schechter, creating Midreshet Yerushalayim, a Conservative yeshivah program there, and, in 1984, opening a Masorti rabbinical school in Israel, the Beit ha-Midrash le-Limudei ha-Yahadut.

Cohen implemented changes in JTS governance and presided over a process of curricular revision. He established a faculty senate, unifying the faculty of the Seminary's several schools and organizing them by academic departments, and revamped the rabbinic training program to take cognizance of the diminished level of Jewish knowledge and practice among entering students, as compared to students of earlier days. He consolidated the undergraduate programs of JTS, merging the Seminary College of Jewish Studies with the Teacher's Institute. This further curtailed the Teacher's Institute's autonomy, which had begun to wane with Kaplan's retirement in 1945.

Extending Finkelstein's program of reaching audiences beyond JTS, Cohen focused on influencing the study of Judaism on the secular college campus. In 1974, Cohen replaced the underperforming JTS graduate program, the Institute for Advanced Studies in the Humanities, with a non-sectarian graduate school encompassing all non-theological graduate training. Under Cohen's aegis, the JTS graduate school became the largest institution of its kind in the Diaspora, training many of the scholars filling Judaic Studies chairs in North American universities in the late 20th century.

The desire to remain in close contact with other institutions of high learning influenced the 1973 JTS decision to remain in its Morningside Heights, Manhattan, location, despite rising crime in that neighborhood. Having decided not to relocate, JTS intensified its collaborative work with the neighboring Columbia University and Union Theological Seminary. Cohen also presided over a major enhancement of the Seminary's physical campus, building a new library to replace the structure damaged in the Seminary's disastrous library fire of 1966, and dedicating the new library in 1983. The library has grown to over 340,000 volumes and houses the most complete collection of Judaica in the Western Hemisphere. Thirty years after the fire, JTS refurbished its historic library tower, part of the continuing expansion of its physical plant. These building projects have strained the school financially but enhanced its capabilities.

When Cohen resigned in 1986, for health reasons, the JTS board appointed as his successor its provost, Ismar *Schorsch (to retire in 2006). During his tenure, JTS has built upon the developments of Cohen's era, opening a graduate school of Jewish education in 1996 and strengthening the Seminary's Israel campus. It has also embarked on new initiatives: In 1991, JTS, YIVO and the Russian State University for the Humanities opened Project Judaica, a Jewish studies training program in Moscow aimed at fostering the revival of Jewish life and learning in Russia.

As JTS chancellor, Schorsch emerged as an outspoken advocate for Conservative Judaism, publishing a monograph outlining its fundamental tenets, speaking out against discrimination faced by Masorti Jews in Israel, and opening the Schechter Institute of Jewish Studies in Jerusalem. He also brought JTS into closer relationship with the Conservative movement's network of Solomon Schechter Hebrew Day Schools. Schorsch disseminated a Conservative perspective to a wide readership, addressing the public directly in his weekly Torah commentary. On certain contemporary issues affecting JTS, however, notably the debate over the acceptance of avowed homosexuals as rabbinical candidates, Schorsch's traditionalist position was challenged within the denomination. Moreover, as the leading spokesman for his denomination, Schorsch was also criticized for the declining percentage of American Jews who self-identity as Conservative.

The American Jewish community having decentralized, JTS is no longer the sole Conservative Jewish center of higher learning and rabbinic training. In 1996, the University of Judaism opened its own Ziegler School of Rabbinic Studies. A harsh reaction by the mother institution led to a formal separation of the two institutions. Nonetheless, JTS remains the most influential Conservative higher-educational institution in the world.

BIBLIOGRAPHY: N.B. Cardin and D.W. Silverman (eds.), *The Seminary at 100*; M. Davis, *The Emergence of Conservative Judaism*; E. Dorff, *Conservative Judaism*; R. Fierstien, *A Different Spirit*; idem, *A Century of Commitment*; idem (ed.), *Solomon Schechter in America*; N. Gillman, *Conservative Judaism*; M. Greenbaum, *Louis Finkelstein and the Conservative Movement*; P. Nadell, *Conservative Judaism in America*; *Proceedings of the Rabbinical Assembly*; J. Sarna, *American Judaism*; M. Sklare, *Conservative Judaism* (1972); M. Waxman, ed., *Tradition and Change*; J. Wertheimer, *A People Divided*; idem., *Conservative Synagogues and Their Members*; idem (ed.), *Tradition Renewed.*

[Michael Panitz (2nd ed.)]

JEWISH WAR VETERANS OF THE U.S.A. (JWV), active war veterans organization in the United States. From the beginning of Jewish life in America, there has been a strong tradition of military service; dating back to 1654, when Jewish settlers in New Amsterdam demanded the right to help stand guard at the stockade. The JWV has more than 300 branches in all parts of the country. Organized on March 15, 1896, in New York City by Jewish veterans of the American Civil War, it was first known as the Hebrew Union Veterans Organization. In 1917 it amalgamated with the Hebrew Veterans of the War with Spain, and in 1918 changed it name to Hebrew Veterans of the Wars of the Republic. In 1923 the word "Jewish" was substituted for "Hebrew." The present name was adopted in 1929. In 1954 the national headquarters moved from New York City to Washington, D.C. In its headquarters building the JWV maintains a National Shrine to the Jewish War Dead, consisting of a chapel, museum, library, record rooms, and a Hall of Heroes. The JWV maintains veterans service offices in 14 of the largest American cities. The JWV and its women's auxiliary carry on an active program on behalf of the war wounded and those who are patients in Veterans Administration hospitals. The group also participates in and organizes several Jewish as well as patriotic programs across the country. During the past 100 years JWV has stood for a strong national defense and for just recognition and compensation for veterans. JWV supports the rights of veterans in promoting American democratic principles, in defending universal Jewish causes, and in vigorously opposing bigotry, antisemitism, and terrorism – in the U.S. and abroad. The Jewish War Veterans cooperates with other veteran groups and is a visible reminder of American Jewish patriotism and of the fact that Jews have served in the armed forces and paid the ultimate price for that service.

[David Max Eichhorn / Ben Paul (2nd ed.)]

JEWISH WOMAN, THE, a quarterly journal that began as the in-house newsletter of the *National Council of Jewish Women (NCJW) in 1921. By the time it ceased publication in 1931, *The Jewish Woman* had reached out to a wide audience of American Jewish women through its articles and its advocacy of social issues and programs. To a great extent, the forward-looking agenda of NCJW during a crucial period of growth and redefinition in the 1920s can be gleaned by reading its journal.

Founding editor Estelle Sternberger of Cincinnati was a leading force behind *The Jewish Woman*'s two-pronged approach to its mission (and, by proxy, to NCJW's mission). The publication's first stated goal was to inform the public about issues and projects of importance to NCJW. Its second, and loftier, aim was to provide a platform for "the ideals and aspirations of Jewish womanhood in every field of endeavor." Subjects addressed in editorials and articles included the rise of antisemitism in America, anti-immigration legislation in Congress (which the magazine vehemently criticized), and the separation of church and state in public education.

Articles in *The Jewish Woman*, including those written by NCJW officers, sometimes demonstrated ambivalence with regard to the social role of NCJW members. In particular, a careful balance was maintained with regard to the organization's relationship to Jewish women who were recent immigrants to America. Pride in such developments as the opening of a Jewish School of Social Work, which the magazine's writers felt would offer opportunities for positive growth to immigrant women, was tempered by an oft-voiced concern that outsiders might perceive the Jewish community in America to be mostly foreign-born "aliens." This occasional discomfort reflected debates raging in the U.S. Congress and the public square over the increasingly restrictive quotas placed on immigration in 1921 and 1924. Journal articles that lauded pacifism, meanwhile, were indicative of a popular antiwar sentiment following U.S. involvement in World War I.

In its later years, *The Jewish Woman* embodied something of a paradox: while increasing coverage of general issues in order to appeal to women outside NCJW, the magazine showed signs of losing its audience even within its sponsoring organization. The number of articles in each issue was pared down, and attempts to institute a subscription price failed. After its October 1931 issue, the journal ceased publication. In succeeding decades, NCJW's mission and activities were represented by other magazines; first, the *Council Woman* in the 1940s and 1950s, and then the *Council Journal*.

BIBLIOGRAPHY: J. Bolton-Fasman. "*Jewish Woman, The*," in: P.E. Hyman and D.D. Moore (eds.), in: *Jewish Women in America*, vol. 1 (1997), 698–700; F. Rogow, *Gone to Another Meeting* (1993).

[Lauren B. Strauss (2nd ed.)]

JEWISH WORLD, English Jewish weekly newspaper published in London from 1873 to 1934. It was founded by George Lewis Lyon, a financial journalist (1828–1904), and its first editor was Myer Davis (1830–1912). Among other editors were S.L. *Bensusan, Jacob de *Haas, John Raphael, Lucien *Wolf, Stanley Fay, M.J. Landa, and David Spiro. For a time it published a Yiddish supplement, edited by Jacob *Hodess. In its time the *Jewish World* filled a position of some importance in Anglo-Jewish life, publishing articles by various Zionist leaders, as well as by non-Jewish precursors of Zionism such as Henry Wentworth Monk, and Holman Hunt, the painter. It was taken over in 1913 by the **Jewish *Chronicle*, with which it was merged in 1934.

BIBLIOGRAPHY: *The Jewish Chronicle, 1841–1941 – A Century of Newspaper History* (1949). **ADD. BIBLIOGRAPHY:** D. Cesarani, *The Jewish Chronicle and Anglo-Jewry, 1841–1991* (1994).

[Josef Fraenkel]

JEWNIN, ABRAHAM JONAH (1813–1848), Russian talmudist, born in Parichi, province of Minsk. Abraham settled in Grodno, where he remained until his death. Despite his premature death he achieved renown as an outstanding scholar. He wrote novellae on the *Sefer ha-Mitzvot* of Maimonides under the title *Makhshevet Moshe*, part of which appears in the Vilna 1866 edition of the *Sefer ha-Mitzvot*, and other parts in the Warsaw 1882 edition of the *Mishneh Torah*. Abraham had three sons: NATHAN, author of *Nitei Or* (1900), novellae on the Talmud, and *Binyan Yerushalayim* on the Passover *Haggadah* (1914); SAMUEL, author of *Divrei Ḥefeẓ* on the Torah (1873); and BEZALEL, who became renowned in America as a preacher.

BIBLIOGRAPHY: S.E. Friedenstein, *Ir Gibborim* (1880), 85; *Yahadut Lita*, 3 (1967), 53.

JEWS' COLLEGE, rabbinical seminary in London. Jews' College was founded in 1855 by the Ashkenazi chief rabbi, Nathan Marcus *Adler (but with support from the Sephardi community). It had two objectives: to train English-speaking ministers and laymen in Jewish and secular subjects; and to educate boys in a Jewish secondary school. The secondary school was closed in 1879, as middle-class pupils increasingly entered secular schools, but the college continued to train ministers, readers, and teachers for the English-speaking world. From 1883 onward its pupils normally graduated at London University. The first principal, Louis Loewe (who resigned in 1858), was succeeded by Barnett Abrahams. Continental standards of scholarship were upheld by Michael *Friedlaender (1865–1907) and especially Adolph *Buechler (1907–39). He was succeeded by Isidore *Epstein (1945–61), a former student, who developed the college's activities, including a teachers training faculty, a cantors' institute, and extension lectures. On his retirement a controversy arose over the refusal of Chief Rabbi Israel *Brodie, the college president, to confirm the appointment of its tutor, Louis *Jacobs, as principal. Eventually, H.J. *Zimmels was appointed principal. Subsequent principals were Nahum Rabinovitch (1971–83), Jonathan Sacks (1984–90), Irving Jacobs (1990–93), and Daniel Sinclair (1994–). Among those who lectured at the college were such distinguished scholars as Israel Abrahams, S.A. Hirsch, H. Hirschfeld, A. Marmorstein, Samuel Daiches, and C. Roth.

Despite the distinction attained by staff and graduates, attendance at Jews' College was never high. Between 1883 and 1967, 91 qualified as ministers with a university degree, and between 1896 and 1967, 65 obtained the rabbinical diploma (47 from the course instituted by I. Epstein and conducted by K. Kahana). Twenty-two rabbis graduated between 1971 and 1995 (15 of them since 1989). The college has not always found it easy to be both a committed seminary for Orthodox ministers and a college in the liberal academic tradition. Since 1989, the college has seen a resurgence of interest never experienced before in Anglo-Jewry. The College is an Associate Institution of the University of London. The 1995 student population of the college was 140. The college offers B.A. (Honours) degrees in Jewish Studies and an M.A. in Hebrew and Jewish Studies. Both degrees are accredited by the University of London. The college offers facilities leading to M.Phil. and Ph.D. degrees of the University of London in areas within the research interest of its staff.

In addition to the rabbinate, many of those who graduate with a university degree enter into the burgeoning educational field or serve the Social Services in Great Britain and lately also in Israel.

The college publishes a biannual magazine, *Le'ela*, which contains both scholarly articles and review of books of Judaic interest. The series of *Jews' College Publications* comprises a number of important contributions to Jewish scholarship. In 1995 the library, founded in 1860, contained 80,000 printed books, 30,000 pamphlets, and 700 manuscripts (including the Montefiore collection).

[Vivian David Lipman]

BIBLIOGRAPHY: I. Harris, in: *Jews' College Jubilee Volume* (1906), 3–182; A.M. Hyamson, *Jews' College, London, 1855–1955* (1955) I. Epstein, *Contribution of Jews' College to Jewish Learning* (1960).

JEWS' TEMPORARY SHELTER, charitable institution in London. In 1885 Simon Cohen, a baker, opened a refuge for East European immigrants who had been arriving in England in large numbers since 1881. It was maintained by Cohen himself and by other immigrants; the Jewish communal authorities, opposing it as encouraging immigration, succeeded in having it closed as unsanitary. Following protests, a new Poor Jews' Temporary Shelter was opened in October of the same year by communal leaders, including Samuel *Montagu and Herman Landau, O.B.E. (1849–1921), an immigrant teacher who became a prosperous stockbroker and communal leader in Jewish religious and charitable work. The Shelter, located in Leman Street, in the East End of London, arranged for immigrants to be met at the docks and provided accommodation for a maximum period of 14 days.

After some difficulties, the Shelter established a modus vivendi with the London Jewish Board of Guardians, the main charitable body of the community, which was anxious not to encourage immigrants, although it later realized that conditions in Eastern Europe made immigration inevitable. It was largely due to the Board's influence that the Shelter prohibited a long stay and did not give cash doles to immigrants. Finally, in 1900, the problem of immigrants from Romania (the *fussgayer* movement) led to a formal agreement between the two bodies. Until 1914, between 1,000 and 4,000 immigrants and transmigrants a year stayed there.

After the main Russo-Polish immigration ended with the outbreak of World War I in 1914, the Shelter continued to receive immigrants from other countries, although separate arrangements were made for some 9,000 Belgian refugees. During the war the Shelter moved temporarily to Poland Street, in the West Central district of London, but later returned to East London, first to Leman Street and then, in 1930, to Mansell Street.

It was estimated that from 1885 to 1937 the Shelter had been responsible for meeting 1,180,000 immigrants at the docks and that 126,000 had stayed at the Shelter. During the 20th century, the Shelter was associated especially with the brothers Otto M. (1875–1952) and Ernst Schiff (1881–1931). Born in Frankfurt on the Main into the famous Schiff banking family, they settled in London and became members of the Stock Exchange. They were active communal leaders, especially in religious, charitable, and educational work. Ernst Schiff became president of the London Jewish Religious Education Board and warden of the Great Synagogue. Coming under the influence of Herman Landau, the two brothers were active on behalf of refugees, first the Belgian immigrants in World War I and then Jewish refugees in general. Otto Schiff was president of the Shelter in 1922–48, then life president. Both were honored for this work, Ernst Schiff being appointed M.B.E., and Otto Schiff first O.B.E. for his work for Belgian refugees and C.B.E. for his services to German refugees.

After World War II, the Shelter continued to help immigrants, especially refugees from Hungary and from the Middle East (Aden, Egypt, and other countries), India, and Pakistan. In 1973, it moved from East London to Willesden, an area in North-West London with a considerable Jewish population.

BIBLIOGRAPHY: L.P. Gartner, *The Jewish Immigrant in England* (1973[2]); V.D. Lipman, *A Century of Social Service* (1959); S. Zweig, *House of a Thousand Destinies* (n.d. 1937?); *Jewish Chronicle* (Jan. 1, 1932; Oct. 15, 1952; Dec. 28, 1973).

[Vivian David Lipman]

JEZEBEL (Heb. אִיזֶבֶל, perhaps from זבל, "the exalted one" with the prefix [*i*;] meaning "Where is the Exalted One / Prince?" (cf. Ichabod, "Where is the Divine Presence?). Another possibility is "The Prince Lives," by assimilation from **ʾš zbl > yzbl > ʾyzbl* and the addition of prothetic *aleph*; see Cogan, 420). "Prince" should be connected to an attested epithet of Baal. Jezebel's father's name, Ethbaal, would indicate devotion to Baal going back at least two generations, and presage her own Baalistic enthusiasm. Jezebel was the daughter of Ethbaal king of the Sidonians, wife of *Ahab king of Israel, and mother of *Ahaziah and *Jehoram (Joram), sons and successors of Ahab (note their Yahwistic names). Jezebel was born about the end of the first decade of the ninth century and was killed in the insurrection of Jehu in 841 B.C.E. Her marriage to Ahab, arranged evidently by Ahab himself (I Kings 16:31), sealed a mutually advantageous alliance between Israel and the Tyrian Empire. She instituted the worship of the Tyrian Baal in Israel, and for her sake Ahab built a temple to Baal in Samaria that not only served the court of the queen and the Tyrian merchants, artists, and craftsmen, but deeply influenced the aristocracy of Israel. In the stories about *Elijah, Jezebel is the prototype of the enemies of the god of Israel and his prophets. She is depicted as a zealot for the deities of her homeland, who slaughtered the prophets of YHWH (I Kings 18:4) and supported the prophets of Baal and Asherah (I Kings 18:19). Jezebel is a vigorous character with a strong will. She is also literate (I Kings 21:8). The addition in the Septuagint (to I Kings 19:2), "As you are Elijah, and I am Jezebel," emphasized her position as the true enemy of the prophet. When Naboth defied Ahab by refusing to sell his vineyard, Jezebel instigated a judicial murder (I Kings 21) of Naboth, a deed regarded with great reprobation in Israel. The story depicts Ahab as a weakling dominated by his wife. It must be observed that the account of the misappropriation of Naboth's vineyard in I Kings 21 differs from II Kings 9, and, significantly, omits a reference to judicial murder. After Jehu's murder of her son Jehoram, Jezebel adorned herself as a queen, perhaps as a gesture of defiance to Jehu, and Jehu ordered her thrown out of the window. Still he saw to it that she was buried, because she was "a king's daughter" (II Kings 9:34). Jehu's baiting of Joram by referring to Jezebel's harlotries and sorceries (II Kings 9:22) may be the rhetoric of hostility: "Your mother is a whore and a witch." It is noteworthy that rivalries at the court of the Hittite kings Murshili II (mid-14th century B.C.E.) led to similar accusations against the queen mother (Cogan and Tadmor, 110).

In 1964 Avigad published a seal from the ninth or eighth century B.C.E., which reads *yzbl*, but it is doubtful whether one can identify this name with the name of the queen.

[H. Jacob Katzenstein / S. David Sperling (2nd ed.)]

In the Aggadah

Jezebel was the instigator of the sins of her husband, Ahab (TJ, Sanh. 10:2, 28b). When R. Levi expounded the verse "But there was none like unto Ahab, which did sell himself to work of wickedness in the sight of the Lord, whom Jezebel his wife stirred up" (I Kings 22:25), Ahab appeared to him in a dream and reproved him for dwelling overmuch on the first part of the verse. He thereupon spent two months demonstrating that Jezebel was the instigator of the sins of her husband (TJ, Sanh. 10:2, 28b). Every day she used to weigh out golden shekels for idol worship (Sanh. 102b). She also placed portraits of harlots in Ahab's chariot in order to excite him, and it was these which were smeared with his blood (cf. I Kings 22:38) when he was killed (Sanh. 39b). However, she was not without virtue. Whenever a funeral passed her residence, she would join in the mourning by clapping her hands, say words of praise for the deceased, and follow the cortege for ten steps. As a reward her palms, skull, and feet were not consumed by the dogs when the prophecy of Elijah was fulfilled (PdRE 17).

In Christianity

In the New Testament (Rev. 2:20–23) the church at Thyatira is admonished "because you allow that woman Jezebel who calls herself a prophetess to teach and seduce my servants to commit sexual immorality and eat things sacrificed to idols." While Jezebel was probably an epithet rather than the woman's name, this passage based on the accounts in the Hebrew Bible served to immortalize the name Jezebel as a byword for an utterly wicked woman.

[S. David Sperling (2nd ed.)]

BIBLIOGRAPHY: Peake, in: BJRL, 11 (1927), 296ff.; Albright, in: JPOS, 16 (1936), 17ff.; Avigad, in: IEJ, 14 (1964), 274ff.; Cross, in: BASOR, 184 (1966), 9 n.17; Eissfeldt, in: VT *Supplement*, 16 (1967), 65ff.; Bright, Hist, index; EM, 1 (1965), 257–8. **IN THE AGGADAH:** Ginzberg, Legends, 4 (1947), 188–9; 6 (1946), 313; I. Ḥasida, *Ishei ha-Tanakh* (1964), 60–61. **ADD. BIBLIOGRAPHY:** A. Rofé, in: VT, 38 (1988), 89–104; M. Cogan and H. Tadmor, *II Kings* (AB; 1988); M. White, in: VT, 44 (1994), 66–76; G. Yee, ABD, 3:848–49; M. Cogan, *I Kings* (AB; 2000).

JEZREEL (Heb. יִזְרְעֶאל), city in ancient Israel. The city of Jezreel (in Heb. *Yizre'el*, "May God give seed") was founded by Israelites of the tribe of Issachar south of Shunem (abandoned in the El-Amarna period, cf. Josh. 19:18). With the decline of Beth-Shean in the Iron Age, Jezreel became the head of a district in Saul's kingdom (II Sam. 2:9). It served as the base for Saul and his army before the disastrous battle with the Philistines at Mt. Gilboa; they camped by the spring in Jezreel (I Sam. 29:1). Under Solomon it was excluded from the main Jezreel Valley district and was evidently assigned to the tenth district of Issachar, administered by Jehoshaphat, the son of Paruah (I Kings 4:12, 17). Omri chose it to be the winter capital of the Israelite kingdom and all the kings of his dynasty, down to Joram, resided there. The royal palace at Jezreel was provided with a tower from which the whole vicinity could be surveyed (II Kings 9:17). The palace bordered on the vineyard of Naboth, whose property passed to Ahab through fraud and a perversion of justice (I Kings 21); according to the biblical tradition the dynasty of Ahab was exterminated at Jezreel in retribution for this deed – Jezebel was thrown to the dogs from the palace window and Joram was killed there along with his courtiers (II Kings 10:11). According to the Bible, Jezreel at that time contained a wall and a gate and was administered by a council of elders and nobles (*ibid.*, 10:1, 8). After the downfall of the Omri dynasty, Jezreel declined. It appears in Judith in connection with its plain, as Esdraelon (1:8). Eusebius speaks of it as a village between Scythopolis and Legio (Onom. 108; 13ff.); the Bordeaux pilgrim (333 C.E.) calls it Stradela (19:20). The Crusaders called it "le Petit Gerin" to distinguish it from "le Grand Gerin" (Jenin) and built a church there. The ancient remains of the city are located at the site of the kibbutz with the same name (Zarīn in Ar.; see *Yizre'el), 1½ mi. (7 km.) south of Afulah; they include Iron Age and Roman pottery.

Excavations at the tel were conducted by Tel Aviv University and the British School of Archaeology between 1990 and 1995 by D. Ussishkin and J. Woodhead. Although Early Bronze Age and Iron Age I pottery was found at the site, the first archaeological finds of significance date from the ninth century B.C.E. It appears to have served as a royal center of some importance during the Omride Dynasty (882–42 B.C.E.) and a large rectangular enclosure (332 × 184 m.) was uncovered, surrounded by a casemate wall with projecting towers at the corners and with an outer rock-cut moat. The site was briefly in use during the eighth century B.C.E. and strata from the Persian, Hellenistic, Roman, Byzantine, and Early Islamic periods were also uncovered.

BIBLIOGRAPHY: Alt, Kl Schr, 1 (1953), 116, 123, 267; 2 (1953), 388ff.; EM, s.v.; G.A. Smith, *Historical Geography* (193125), 379ff. **ADD. BIBLIOGRAPHY:** D. Ussishkin and J. Woodhead, "Excavations at Tel Jezreel, 1990–1991: Preliminary Report," in: *Tel Aviv*, 19 (1992), 3–56; idem, "Excavations at Tel Jezreel, 1992–1993: Preliminary Report," in: *Levant*, 26 (1994), 1–48; H.G.M. Williamson, "Jezreel in the Biblical Texts," in: *Levant*, 18 (1991), 72–92.

[Michael Avi-Yonah / Shimon Gibson (2nd ed.)]

JEZREEL, VALLEY OF (also known as the "Plain of Esdraelon"; (Heb. עֵמֶק יִזְרְעֶאל), *Emek Yizre'el*, named after the city of *Jezreel), the largest of the inland valleys of Israel, after the Jordan Valley. It consists of the alluvial plain of the Kishon River, forming a rough equilateral triangle with its base at the Carmel range and its continuation and its apex at Mount Tabor. Each side is about 20 mi. (33 km.) long and the total area about 96.5 sq. mi. (250 sq. km.). Whether the valley of the Naḥal Ḥarod (the Ḥarod Valley), its southeastern extension in the direction of the Beth-Shean Valley, should be included in the Jezreel Valley is disputed. The first mention of the "Valley of Jezreel" occurs in Joshua 17:16 where it appears together with the region of Beth-Shean as an area dominated by the iron chariots of the Canaanites and therefore outside the control of the tribe of Manasseh of the House of Joseph (cf. also Josh. 17:11–12; Judg. 1:27). When Manasseh became stronger, however, it put the cities in the Valley of Jezreel to tribute and Issachar was able to establish a foothold at the city of Jezreel itself. As a result of the battle Deborah and Sisera fought in the Kishon Valley, the northern slopes of the valley became Israelite. In their thrust westward the Midianites passed into the valley and camped in its eastern part near Gibeath-Moreh (Jebel al-Daḥī), while Gideon camped opposite them at En-Harod (Judg. 7:1). Gideon's victory secured the valley from the east. The Philistines advanced against Saul through the valley where they had bases at Shunem and Beth-Shean and tried to split his kingdom in two; however, even after Saul's defeat the district of Jezreel remained in Israelite hands (II Sam. 2:9). David eliminated the foreign enclaves in the valley and secured it for Israel. The establishment at Jezreel of the winter capital of the kingdom of Israel strengthened its hold on the region, especially as the kings were interested in creating a royal estate in its fertile lands – an activity of which the dispossession of Naboth was but one instance. Subsequently the main part of the valley remained a royal estate of whatever power dominated the country. When Tiglath-Pileser III reduced Israel to the mountains of Ephraim, he made Megiddo the capital of an Assyrian province. After the fall of Assyria, Josiah, king of Judah, who expanded his kingdom northward, tried to bar the passage of the valley to Pharaoh Necoh at Megiddo, but lost the battle as well as his life (609 B.C.E.).

The status of the valley is not clear under Babylonian and Persian rule. In Hellenistic times it was administered from the royal fortress of Itabyrion (Tabor). In I Maccabees 12:49 and in the writings of Josephus it is called "the great plain." Its position between Galilee and Samaria is not clearly defined: Galilee ended at Exaloth (I'ksol) at the foot of Mount Tabor and Samaria began at Ginae (Jenin; Jos., Wars, 3:39, 48). The villages in the plain were the property of the Hasmonean dynasty; they were taken from the Jews by Pompey but restored to Hyrcanus II by Julius Caesar (Ant., 14:207), and the valley later belonged to the Herodian dynasty. Queen Berenice had her grain stored at Besara (Bet She'arim) on the northern side of the plain. With the extinction of the Herodian dynasty the plain passed to the emperor. When the Legio VI Ferrata was posted near Megiddo at Caparcotnei (whence the place was called Legio, in Arabic Lajjūn), it was given the Jezreel Valley which was thus known in late Roman and Byzantine sources as Campus Maximus Legionis. It formed the territory of the city known as Legio-Maximianupolis in later times. The northern slopes of the valley belonged to Sepphoris from which they were separated in the fifth century and formed into the territory of Naim, which included the Plain of Exaloth (Bikat Iksalo of the Midrash; Gen. R. 98:17). In the Middle Ages the valley of Jezreel was known as the Campus Fabae ("Plain of the Bean") after the castle called La Fève. In Mamluk times it was called Merj Bani Amir after the Bedouin tribe who had occupied it. After the Crusader period the valley developed into a marshy plain, abandoned to the nomads; the swamps bred malaria which made settlement impossible. In 1799 a battle between the French army under Napoleon and the Turks was fought at Afulah. In 1918 the swift passage of Australian cavalry across the plain decided Allenby's victory. Soon after the establishment of the British Mandate, large tracts of the valley were acquired by the *Jewish National Fund (following the founding of a pioneer settlement at Merḥavyah in 1911). In the 1920s the valley was drained and settled, making it the showpiece of Zionist pioneering and progressive regional development. In 1948, after the establishment of the State of Israel, an additional 19 rural settlements were founded as well as two urban settlements – Migdal ha-Emek and Nazareth. The present-day Jezreel Valley maintains its rural character, while the major urban settlement is Afulah, also known as the "Jezreel valley capital." Kibbutz Yifat houses the Museum of the Beginning of Settlement, exhibiting items and photos of the pioneer settlement in Israel. In 2003 the Jezreel Valley numbered 412,600 inhabitants.

BIBLIOGRAPHY: G.A. Smith, *Historical Geography* (1931[25]), 379ff.; Abel, Geog, 1 (1933), 91–92, 411ff.; Avi-Yonah, Geog, index; EM, s.v.; Y. Aharoni, et al., *Me-Ereẓ Kishon…*, ed. by N. Tardion (1967), 107ff. **ADD. BIBLIOGRAPHY:** A. Turai, *The Emek Jezreel and the Beisan Valley*. Palestine Pioneer Library No. 5 (1947); Y. Tsafrir, L. Di Segni, and J. Green, *Tabula Imperii Romani. Iudaea – Palaestina. Maps and Gazetteer* (1994), 182, s.v. Mega Pedion, Campus Maximus

[Michael Avi-Yonah / Shaked Gilboa (2nd ed.)]

JHABVALA, RUTH PRAWER (1927–), novelist and screenwriter. Ruth Prawer Jhabvala was born in Cologne and emigrated with her family to England in 1939. There she married an Indian architect, C.S.H. Jhabvala, and moved to Delhi, where she made her home.

Her experience as a refugee is a dark, albeit not a dominant, theme in her work. In the best of her stories of India there appears, invariably, the misplaced European, a tragic wanderer of middle age and older, a person of no means and no occupation, without a place in his adopted society, living on sufferance. The story, "A Birthday in London," depicts a gathering of German-Jewish refugees in London, long after the war, where they recall the first bitterness of their exile.

The dominant theme of Mrs. Jhabvala's work, however, is that of caste and class in India. She is a satirist, and the object of her satire is the particular element in Indian society which she knows well, that of the progressive-minded, the upper-mobile, and the culture-hungry. The world of her novels and short stories is peopled with prim Indian civil servants and their faintly dissatisfied young wives, with dreamers and faded beauties of waspish temper. To these are added the forlorn Europeans, who yearn to discover the true India, to merge with it, but who forever remain inveterately European.

Her first novel *To Whom She Will* (1955) was followed by *The Nature of Passion* (1956), *Esmond In India* (1958), *The Householder* (1960), *Get Ready For Battle* (1962), and *A Backward Place* (1965). *Travelers* (1973; published in England under the title *A New Dominion*, 1972) was acclaimed for its wit, its deft parody, and its assault on the spiritual humbug of the *gurus* and their devotees, both Indian and European. Her novel *Heat and Dust* (1975) won the 1975 Booker Prize for fiction.

Jhabvala has also published three collections of short stories, *Like Birds, Like Fishes* (1964), *A Stronger Climate* (1968), and *An Experience of India* (1971), and wrote the script of three films, *Shakespeare-Wallah* (1965), *The Guru* (1959), and *Bombay Talkie* (1971).

Jhabvala achieved worldwide fame in the 1980s through her collaboration with the film production-direction team of Ishmael Merchant and James Ivory, for whom she scripted several highly successful films, including adaptations of E.M. Forster's novels *A Room with a View* (1986) and *Howards End* (1992). Both earned Jhabvala Academy Awards for best screenplay, while the 1993 Merchant-Ivory Production *The Remains of the Day* was nominated for the same honor. More recent screenplays include *Surviving Picasso* (1996), *The Golden Bowl* (2000), and *Le Divorce* (2003).

BIBLIOGRAPHY: V.A. Shahane, *Ruth Prawer Jhabvala* (1976).

[Dorothy Rabinowitz and Rohan Saxena]

JIHĀD, "struggle or striving, but often understood both within Muslim tradition and beyond it as warfare against infidels" (*Enc. of the Qur'ān*, s.v. *Jihād*); in other words, the Holy War. During the period of *Muhammad's stay in *Medina some of his revelations deal with the problem of the *jihād*, the holy war to be waged against Allah's enemies and the infidels (e.g., Sura 2:186–90, 212–15, 245, 247). Those who fight according to Allah's way may hope for His mercy. Muhammad promises that everyone who is killed while fighting in Allah's way will win the highest reward (Sura 4:76). Such a man is a *shahīd*, a martyr.

According to Muslim religious law, the caliph is obliged to lead the *jihād* against the inhabitants of those countries which did not adopt *Islam. These countries are called *dār al-ḥarb* ("war territory"), while the countries under Islamic rule are referred to as *dār al-Islām* ("territory of Islam") – Jews and Christians could live there only as **dhimmī* ("protected people") and have to pay a poll tax (*jizya*), thereby recognizing the superiority of Islam. In practice, this bipartite division of the world was only able to last a short time during the first hundred years of Arab-Muslim expansion. For the later period the Muslim constitutional-religious law was obliged to create a third category, the *dār al-ṣulḥ* or *dār al-ʿahd* ("territory of treaty") of non-Muslim countries not subject to Muslim sovereignty but connected with the *dār al-Islām* by temporary treaties; this sometimes involved the payment of a token tribute. The main cause for the creation of this compromise category was that many non-Muslim governments were considered too strong, or too far away from the center of Muslim power, to be overthrown by force. In the modern Muslim national movements and states there does not seem to be a place for the idea of a holy war against infidels. Nevertheless, it still plays a very important role among the masses. They can easily be incited by the fanaticism of leaders, preaching in the name of the *Koran and Muhammad, to initiate riots against unbelievers inside the country and at least plan a war against infidels outside the Muslim state.

The last proclamation of a *jihād* occurred during World War I when the Turkish sultan proclaimed it against his enemies, the Entente powers. This proclamation, however, proved a failure, particularly in view of the pro-British Arab revolt which started in the holy cities of *Hejaz, and also because the Sultan himself was allied with Germany, a Christian power. When some Muslim authorities later tried to proclaim their struggle against Israel as a *jihād*, they were equally unsuccessful mainly because of the Arab nationalist character of the anti-Israel campaign, which included many non-Muslims. This was the case also in many inter-Muslim wars in the second half of the 20th century, when the leaders of both sides declared the *jihād* (*Yemen-*Egypt, *Iraq-*Iran, *Algeria, and al-Qāʿida-*Saudi Arabia); but after the establishment of a Communist regime in *Afghanistan and the Soviet invasion, the declaration of *jihād* attracted Muslims from different countries who fought there for years. Some of them formed groups of warriors who were ready to take part in the wars of different Muslim minorities or states (Bosnia-Herzegovina, Chechnya and Iraq), seeing them as *jihād*. Those *jihadists* claimed that "Muslims who interpret their faith differently are infidels and therefore legitimate targets of *jihād*. Today, *jihād* is the world's foremost source of terrorism, inspiring a worldwide campaign of violence by self-proclaimed jihadist groups" (D. Pipes, *N.Y. Post*, December 31, 2002).

The idea of the *jihād* has certain analogies to *milḥemet ḥovah* ("the prescribed [by the Torah] war") as it is discussed in the Talmud (Sot. 44b; TJ, Sot. 8:10, 23a) and in some aspects of *kiddush ha-Shem* (the sanctification of God's name).

BIBLIOGRAPHY: M.J. Kister, "*An yadin* (Koran IX/29), an Attempt at Interpretation," in: *Arabica*, 11 (1964); R. Peters, *Islam and Colonialism. The Doctrine of Jihād in Modern History* (1976); A. Morabia, *Le Jihād dans l'Islam médiéval. Le "combat sacré" des origines aux XII*e *siècle*, (1986); R. Firestone, *Jihād. The Origin of Holy War in Islam* (1999); E. Landau, *The Encyclopaedia of the Qur'ān*, 3, 35–42, s.v. *Jihād*.

[Haïm Z'ew Hirschberg / Isaac Hasson (2nd ed.)]

JIHLAVA (Ger. **Iglau**), city in W. Moravia, Czech Republic. Jews are first mentioned in Jihlava in 1249. In 1345 *Charles IV induced the municipality to invite Jews to settle there and promised to grant them an exceptional status. After a fire in 1353 the Jews, like the rest of the citizens, were released from paying taxes. City records covering the years from 1359 to 1420 note 2,700 financial transactions between Jews and gentiles. In 1426 *Albert V expelled the Jews because of their alleged support of the *Hussites. They settled in nearby Puklice (Puklitz), Pulice (Pullitz), Pyrnice (Pirnitz), and *Trest (Triesch). The synagogue was converted into a church in 1511. Between 1708 and 1782, Jews were admitted to the town for business purposes on payment of a special tax. In 1837, 17 Jews lived in Jihlava legally, but more were present illegally. After 1848 a community grew rapidly, opening a prayer room in 1856, a synagogue in 1863, and a cemetery in 1869. Jews were instrumental in developing industry. The community numbered 1,179 persons in 1869, 1,180 in 1921, and in 1930, 1,025 (3.3% of the total population), 327 of whom declared themselves as Jewish by nationality as well as religion. After the Sudeten crisis (1938) many Jews sought refuge in Jihlava. On Nov. 10, 1938, the synagogue was burned down, and Jewish shops were demolished on April 28, 1939. In 1940 the remaining Jews were compelled to move to the villages where Jews had lived previously. They were deported to the Nazi extermination camps in 1942. The synagogue equipment was sent to the Central Jewish Museum in Prague (see *Museums, Jewish). The congregation was revived briefly after the liberation in 1945. The cemetery is still in use. Jihlava was the birthplace of the composer Gustav *Mahler, and of Theodor Herzl's collaborator, Siegmund *Werner. The parents of Gustav Mahler and his two siblings are buried there.

BIBLIOGRAPHY: B. Bretholz, *Geschichte der Juden in Maehren…*, 1 (1934), index; idem, *Quellen zur Geschichte der Juden in Maehren* (1935), xxxiv–lxvi and index; H. Gold (ed.), *Juden und Judengemeinden Maehrens…* (1929), 243–50. **ADD. BIBLIOGRAPHY:** J. Fiedler, *Jewish Sights of Bohemia and Moravia* (1991), 87–88.

[Oskar K. Rabinowicz]

JINDRICHUV HRADEC (Czech **Jindřichův Hradec**; Ger. **Neuhaus**), town in S. Bohemia, Czech Republic. In 1294 the local lord asked permission to settle eight Jews in the town and receive royal prerogatives over them. The Jews built a small hut outside the city walls in 1315 to shelter those who arrived after dark or those visiting the town. A settlement of Jews is noted in 1389. At the request of the burghers, in the 15th century the number of Jewish families in Jindrichuv was reduced to four and its economic activities were restricted. Among the permitted occupations was that of glazier. Of the six families (31 persons) recorded in 1682, one was expelled as exceeding the limit; at that time the Jews mainly traded in textiles. Jews expelled from Prague settled in Jindrichuv in 1745. The synagogue and Jewish houses were burned down in a fire in 1801. The cemetery, consecrated around 1400, was extended in 1576. Samuel Judah b. David *Kauder served as rabbi in the town from 1822 to 1834.

Severe anti-Jewish excesses occurred in Jindrichuv in 1859, when the Jews were suspected of opposing the Hapsburgs, and again during World War I, when they were accused of being pro-Hapsburg. Jewish shops were plundered in 1919. The pro-Czech Jewish movement (*Cechů židů), led by Eduard (Leda) *Lederer, was very active in Jindrichuv. In 1905 it had the Jewish German-language school in the town closed down. There were 791 Jews in the district in 1869 and 617 in 1880; the community had 339 members in 1902 and 234 (2.5% of the total population) in 1930, eight of them of declared Jewish nationality.

The remainder of the community who had not left by 1942 was deported to the Nazi death camps. The community was not reestablished after World War II. The synagogue equipment was sent to the Central Jewish Museum in Prague. The synagogue was used from 1952 by the Hussite church. The cemetery was also used after World War II.

BIBLIOGRAPHY: M. Rachmuth, in JGGJČ, 3 (1931), 185–216; 4 (1932), 183–252; idem, in: M. Gold, *Die Juden und Judengemeinden Boehmens in Vergangenheit und Gegenwart* (1934), 447–51; Germ Jud, 2 (1968), 576. **ADD. BIBLIOGRAPHY:** J. Fiedler, *Jewish Sights of Bohemia and Moravia* (1991), 88–89.

[Meir Lamed]

°**JIRKU, ANTON** (1885–1972), German Bible scholar. Born in Birnbaum, Moravia, Jirku was a pupil of Ernst *Sellin and the Assyriologist Friedrich *Delitzsch. From 1914 he taught at Kiel University and then held professorships at Breslau (1922), Greifswald (1934), and Bonn (1935–45). The basic trend in his work, prolific and often forced in its scholarly presentation (see his collected works *Von Jerusalem nach Ugarit*, 1966), is the attempt to understand biblical phenomena by comparing them with their ancient Oriental environment. His early works are mainly concerned with the popular religion of ancient Israel, in particular with its miraculous and magical elements (*Die Daemonen und ihre Abwehr im Alten Testament*, 1912; *Mantik in Altisrael*, 1913; *Materialien zur Volksreligion Israels*, 1914). He collected ancient Near Eastern parallels to the separate books of the Bible in his *Altorientalischer Kommentar zum Alten Testament* (1923). Numerous single studies led up to his *Geschichte des Volkes Israel* (1931), and *Geschichte Palästina-Syriens im orientalischen Altertum* (1963). The point of departure in his later works was mainly Ugaritic texts, a selection of which he translated (*Kanaanäische Mythen und Epen aus Ras Schamra-Ugarit*, 1962). Jirku was generally conservative with regard to the Bible's historicity, accepting the biblical account of the invasion of Canaan and the attribution of the Decalogue to Moses.

ADD. BIBLIOGRAPHY: W. Thiel, in: DBI, 1, 585–86.

[Rudolf Smend / S. David Sperling (2nd ed.)]

JITTA, DANIEL JOSEPHUS (1854–1925), Dutch expert in private international law. Jitta believed in an international world order and he considered the creation of something like the United States of Europe a possibility. He also believed in world peace, even after World War I. People had to understand that they were not only citizens of nations, but also members of the human race, citizens of the world. He was not naive, he used to say, because he would not live to see the day.

Born in Amsterdam, Jitta was the third generation of a family which originated in Bamberg in Germany. His father was a jeweler in the family business, which was the official purveyor of jewelry to the Dutch queens Sophie and Emma, the French princess Mathilde, and the Duke of Saxen Coburg-Gotha. Aged three Jitta moved to the Belgian capital of Brussels because of his mother's health problems. Being a very bright boy he finished the Royal Athenee when he was only 16 and went to university to read law. After graduation four years later he returned to the Netherlands, where his Belgian diploma turned out to be invalid. He went back to university in Leyden, graduated in 1880, and became a lawyer.

He began to publish on international private law. One of his earliest publications, *La Méthode du Droit International Privé* (1890), is still considered one of his most important and influential works. In 1894 he succeeded T.M.C. Asser as professor of commercial and private international law at Amsterdam University. Nine years later he succeeded Asser again, this time as member of the Netherlands Council of State.

Jitta also had a political career. From 1884 to 1894 he was a member of the Amsterdam city council for the liberals of Burgerpligt, like his father-in-law, banker and philanthropist A.C. Wertheim, and his uncle Simon Josephus Jitta (1818–1897), director of the Amsterdamsche Kanaalmaatschappij, which built the North Sea Channel.

As a student Jitta was a passionate rower and later he was one of the driving forces behind gymnastics and public swimming pools in the Netherlands. He was also a firm believer in hygiene, probably influenced by his younger brother Nicolaas (1858–1940), an eye doctor who later became chairman of the League of Nation's International Office for Public Hygiene and belonged to the Hygiënisten (Hygienists), a group of medical doctors who used statistics to stimulate more care for public health. For hygienic reasons Jitta and his younger brother, unlike their parents and elder brother and sister, wished to be cremated after their death. Although no longer a religious Jew, Jitta was still affiliated with Jewish institutions. He was a member of the board of the Jewish orphanage and mental home in Amsterdam.

BIBLIOGRAPHY: W. van Italie van Embden, in: *Sprekende Portretten* (1925) 136–46; W.M. Petelier, in: *Biografisch Woordenboek van Nederland*, 2 (1985), 269; P. Hofland, *Leden van de raad. De Amsterdamse gemeenteraad 1814–1941* (1998); T. Toebosch, *Van Keizersgracht naar Prinsengracht, geschiedenis van de Jitta's* (working title, forthcoming).

[Theo Toebosch (2nd ed.)]

JIZFĀN, JUDAH BEN JOSEPH (d. 1837), Yemenite author of scholarly books on biblical themes and scribe. Jizfān was known for two works (both still extant in manuscript): *Minḥat Yehudah*, a voluminous collection of commentaries on the Pentateuch based on some 300 printed works and manuscripts, and quoting a large number of sources; and *Panim Ḥadashot*, containing original comments on the Pentateuch by the author. Jizfān also composed threnodies on several events that took place in his lifetime, such as the drought of 1808 and the pillaging of the Jewish quarter of *San'a on Passover night in 1818. Both he and his sons Joseph and Solomon were known as gifted scribes of *Tājs* ("Torah scrolls"), prayer books and collections of Yemenite songs. Jizfān edited Yemenite songs and wrote an introduction to the poems of R. Shalem *Shabazi; this introduction, as well as his writings on biblical subjects, indicate that Jizfān was a kabbalist.

BIBLIOGRAPHY: Ratzaby, in: *Minḥah li-Yhudah* (1950), 274–5; idem, in: *Afikim*, 17 (1966), 8; Y.L. Naḥum, *ibid.*, 18 (1967), 11; Y. Tobi, *ibid.*, 19 (1967), 10–11.

[Yehuda Ratzaby]

JOAB (Heb. יוֹאָב; "YHWH is father"), David's commander in chief; son of Zeruiah, one of David's sisters (I Chron. 2:16). Although Joab's kinship with David no doubt helped him to attain the high post of Israelite commander in chief, his bravery on the battlefield, his powers of leadership in war, and his loyalty to David all proved him fully worthy of occupying a position of eminence in the apparatus of state government established by David. Joab first appears in David's service in the armed encounter at the pool of Gibeon between the servants of David and the followers of *Abner son of Ner. At that time Joab was already the leader of David's armed force and was empowered to muster all the men of Judah for war (II Sam. 2:28). However, from the mention of Joab's brothers, Asahel and Abishai, in the list of David's captains (which is most probably from the early days of David's reign in Hebron), it would appear that Joab occupied a leading position in David's band of warriors even before David was proclaimed king in Hebron. In the stories about the period of David's reign in Hebron, Joab appears as the leader of David's force; but in the account of the capture of Jerusalem given in I Chronicles 11:6, one finds: "And David said, 'Whoever shall smite the Jebusites first shall be chief and commander.' And Joab the son of Zeruiah went up first, so he became chief." According to this verse, Joab was appointed commander in chief only after the capture of Jerusalem, i.e., at the end of David's reign in Hebron.

Joab's successes in the wars against the supporters of Ish-Bosheth, son of the slain Saul, and the heroism that he displayed in the conquest of Jerusalem, confirmed David's confidence in his fitness to be the commander of the whole Israelite army, both in peace and in war. David demonstrated his trust in Joab in the wars in which the latter commanded the army in the field, while David himself remained in Jerusalem. When Hanun son of Nahash, the Ammonite, deliberately provoked David, the Israelite king sent Joab to wage war against the Ammonites and their allies (II Sam. 10; I Chron. 19). In this battle Joab showed his military resourcefulness and his ability to inspire his soldiers with enthusiasm and confidence (II Sam. 10:9–12). He also played a leading role in the defeat of the Edomites (II Sam. 8:13–14; I Kings 11:16; Ps. 60:2).

Despite his personal desire for honor and power, Joab displayed extraordinary loyalty to David, never attempting to diminish the respect due to his royal master. When Joab was about to reduce the besieged city of Rabbath-Ammon, he did not hurry to claim the credit of the victory for himself, but called on David to come and complete the conquest, "lest I take the city, and it be called by my name" (II Sam. 12:28). As the king's confidant and right-hand man, Joab performed various important functions in the consolidation of David's kingdom (II Sam. 24; I Chron. 11:8) and took the lead in the suppression of the revolts which threatened it from within, such as the revolts of Sheba son of Bichri (II Sam. 20:7–23) and that of Absalom (II Sam. 15–18). Joab's handling of the affair of Absalom shows his deep understanding of his royal master's nature. Knowing the king's yearning for his son, he found a way to make the king decide to bring Absalom back to Jerusalem (II Sam. 14:1–23). At the same time, Joab's concern for his own position and for the stability of David's kingdom led to his acting, in many matters, on his own initiative. Thus, he murdered Abner, after the latter had made a covenant with David and promised to bring the supporters of the house of Saul over to him. Joab's ostensible reason for killing Abner was that he was a spy (II Sam. 3:25); but, at the same time, the murder enabled Joab to take revenge for Abner's slaying of his brother, Asahel (II Sam. 2:23; 3:26–27), and also to remove from his path an obvious rival for the post of commander in chief.

Although David cursed Joab for the murder, he was too well aware of the power wielded by the sons of Zeruiah to dare to dismiss him (II Sam. 3:39). Again, Joab ordered Absalom to be killed, even though the king had urgently commanded that his son's life be spared. In this case Joab's decision was probably wise, if unsentimental. Similarly, Joab displayed political acumen by rebuking David for mourning his son, urging him instead to express gratitude to his supporters who had enabled him to defeat Absalom (II Sam. 19:6–8). Some acts performed by Joab aroused the king's anger against his commander in chief and eventually led to his tiring of him. When David promised to appoint Amasa in Joab's place (II Sam. 19:14) as the price of his leading Judah to welcome him back from his flight to Transjordan, Joab took the first opportunity to murder Amasa (*ibid.*, 20:9–11). Though expressing his disgust at Joab's murders (I Kings 2:5), David never penalized Joab even when his reign was well established. Toward the end of David's life, Joab tried to maintain his position of power in the royal court by taking an active part in the intrigues that developed in connection with the succession to the throne, giving his support to Adonijah (I Kings 1:7). In so doing, Joab sealed his own fate, since by supporting Adonijah he was outmaneuvered by the pro-Solomon party, which moved quickly to eliminate him. According to I Kings 2:5–6, David ordered Solomon to take vengeance on Joab for the murders he had committed, and "not let his head go down to Sheol (the netherworld) in peace." When Joab realized that his life was in danger, he fled to the Tent of the Lord and seized hold of the horns of the altar. Nevertheless, Solomon ordered Benaiah son of Jehoiada to strike Joab down, justifying the action on the grounds that he was determined to carry out his father's dying injunction to remove "from me and from my father's house the guilt for the blood which Joab shed without cause" (I Kings 2:31).

[Bustanay Oded / S. David Sperling (2nd ed.)]

In the Aggadah

When David fought against the Jebusites, the inhabitants of Jerusalem, Joab the son of Zeruiah was the first to go up on the wall. David bent down the top of a young cypress growing near the wall, and Joab, climbing onto David's head, grasped the tree which, when released, enabled him to jump onto the wall (Mid. Ps. to 18:24, a story reminiscent of Sinis, "the pine bender," see Apollodorus, *Bibliotheca*, 3:9, 2). Although Joab was loyal to David throughout his life, the latter before his death commanded that he be brought to trial for having killed Abner and Amasa (I Kings 2:5). Joab was acquitted for the murder of Abner since he had thereby avenged the blood of his brother Asahel whom Abner had killed, but his defense that he was justified in killing Amasa, since he had been guilty of treason in delaying to fulfill David's command (II Sam. 20:4), was not accepted. Joab was himself accused of treason by Solomon (Sanh. 49a).

[Elimelech Epstein Halevy]

BIBLIOGRAPHY: Bright, Hist., 176–93, passim; de Vaux, Anc Isr, index; Yadin, in: JPOS, 21 (1943), 110–6; idem, in: *Biblica*, 36 (1955), 332 ff. (Eng.); idem, in: Y. Liver (ed.), *Historyah Ẓeva'it shel Ereẓ Yisrael…* (1964), 351–5; Maisler (Mazar), in: BJPES, 15 (1950), 85. IN THE AGGADAH: Ginzberg, Legends, index. **ADD. BIBLIOGRAPHY:** D. Schley, in: ABD, 3:853–54; M. Cogan, *II Kings* (AB; 2000), 173.

JOAB BEN JEREMIAH (d. 1810), Hungarian rabbi. Joab's father went to Hungary from Oswiecim (Auschwitz), Poland, and was *av bet din* and head of a yeshivah in Mattersdorf, one of the "seven Hungarian communities," and later in Santov (Abaujszanto). Through the efforts of Aaron Chorin, a former pupil of his father's yeshivah who then lived in Nemetkeresztur-Deutschkreutz, Joab was appointed rabbi of that community; he was subsequently appointed rabbi of Hunsdorf (Huncovce-Hunfalu) and, on the death of his father in

1806, was appointed his successor in Santov. He was one of the outstanding talmudists of his time and was eulogized as a great scholar and saint by Moses Sofer. Well-known is his work *Moda'ah Zuta*, a commentary on the work *Moda'ah ve-Ones*, which he published together with his father. His other works are *Sha'arei Binah*, on the *Sha'arei Shevu'ot* of Isaac ben Reuben *al-Bargeloni; *Ḥen Tov ve-Zeved Tov* (Zolkiew, 1806), on chapter 17 of the Shulḥan Arukh *Even ha-Ezer*; and *Imrei No'am*.

[Samuel Weingarten-Hakohen]

JOAB THE GREEK (**Ha-Yevani**; c. 1400), liturgical poet. His Arabic surname Shuau (Heb. שעאע) and the fact that his poems are known only from manuscripts and the printed texts of the Aleppo rite, indicate that he must have lived in the Near East, apparently in Aleppo. In a religious poem Joab expressly mentions the Jewish community of this city. The surname ha-Yevani may indicate that he was born in Greece or was the son of Greek parents. In the acrostics of his 12 poems he always introduces his Arabic surname. It is possible that he may be identical with the אבן שעאע, a fragment of whose Arabic translation of Samuel ha-Nagid's *Ben Kohelet* is extant.

BIBLIOGRAPHY: Zunz, Lit Poesie, 517; S. Krauss, *Studien zur Byzantinisch-juedischen Geschichte* (1914), 139; Davidson, Oẓar, 4 (1933), 397; Margoliouth, Cat, 3 (1965), 236f.; Allony, in: *Tarbiz*, 17 (1945/46), 74–86; S. Poznański, in: REJ, 65 (1913), 157.

[Jefim (Hayyim) Schirmann]

JOACHIM, JOSEPH (1831–1907), violinist. Born in Kittsee (Kopczeny), Joachim moved with his family to Budapest where his musical education began at the age of five. He gave his first concert at seven and at nine he was taken to Vienna to study with Hellmesberger and Boehm. At 12 he went on to Leipzig, where his studies were supervised and fostered by Felix *Mendelssohn, Ferdinand *David, and Moritz Hauptmann. From 1849 to 1854 he was concertmaster of Liszt's orchestra at Weimar, and from 1854 to 1864, concertmaster and conductor of the Royal Hanoverian Orchestra. He finally settled in Berlin in 1866 as director of the newly founded Hochschule fuer Musik. There he also founded the Joachim Quartet which became the leading quartet in Europe. His pedagogical talent attracted a great number of pupils, among whom were Leopold *Auer, Jenő Hubay, and Tivadar *Nachez.

Joachim's concert activity in Europe and England continued steadily throughout his career. Although he eschewed the character and role of a "traveling virtuoso," he became, at an early age, the most notable violinist of his generation (and its most distinguished teacher): an artist in whom technique, taste, intellect, and emotion were combined to a rare degree. His interpretation of the Beethoven Violin Concerto, for example, was considered definitive. He also re-edited Mendelssohn's Violin Concerto in conformity with the original manuscript; revived the works of Tartini; and established in the repertoire Bach's works for solo violin in their original form, without the accompaniments added by 19th-century "improvers." Joachim's friendships with the great composers and performers of his time are an important factor in the history of music in the 19th century, especially his association with Mendelssohn, Liszt, Robert Schumann, Clara Schumann, and Brahms. Joachim introduced the young Brahms to Liszt, and arranged the fateful meeting between Schumann and Brahms in 1853. Of his own compositions, which include works for violin and orchestra, violin and piano, and songs, only the Violin Concerto op. 11 ("Hungarian") survived. His cadenzas for the Beethoven and Brahms concertos, however, are still performed. He also wrote a violin method with A. Moser. Although Joachim had converted to Protestantism in 1855, his decision to resign from the Hanoverian service was finally brought about in 1864, when the violinist J.M. Gruen was refused tenure as a Jew (a principle which had not been observed in Joachim's case). Joachim tendered his resignation on the grounds that he "would never be able to surmount the purely personal feeling of having been enabled through my earlier conversion… to enjoy worldly advantages in the Royal Hanoverian Orchestra while the members of my race occupy a humiliating position there." His *Hebraeische Melodien* for viola and piano, op. 9 (1854), were inspired mainly by Schumann's enthusiasm for Byron's poems. Although Wagner thought that Joachim's break from the Liszt-Wagner circle in 1857 was due to the republication at that time of *Das Judentum in der Musik* in Wagner's name (it had first been published anonymously in 1850), the break was undoubtedly caused by musical considerations.

Hundreds of works were dedicated to Joachim, including the Schumann, Brahms, Dvorak and Bruch (nos. 1 and 3) violin concertos, Liszt's *Hungarian Rhapsody* no. 12, and Schumann's Fourth Symphony (second version, 1853).

Joachim's grandnieces, the sisters Adila Fachiri (d'Aranyi, 1888–1962) and Jelly E. d'Aranyi (1895–1966), were well-known violinists.

BIBLIOGRAPHY: A. Moser, *Joseph Joachim* (Ger., 1904[3]); J. Joachim and A. Moser (eds.), *Briefe von und an Joseph Joachim*, 3 vols. (1911–13); MGG, incl. bibl.; Riemann-Gurlitt, incl. bibl.; Baker, Biog Dict, incl. bibl.; Grove, Dict, incl. bibl.

[Bathja Bayer]

JOACHIMSEN, PHILIP J. (1817–1890), U.S. jurist and communal worker. Joachimsen, who was born in Breslau, Germany, was taken to New York in 1827. He was admitted to the bar in 1840, and held several municipal attorneyships. Joachimsen was made brevet brigadier general for his service in the Civil War as organizer and commander of the 59th New York regiment. He served as judge of the Marine Court of New York from 1870 to 1876. Joachimsen was a leading figure in New York Jewry. He was president of the Hebrew Benevolent Society (1855), first president of the Hebrew Orphan Asylum (1859), and organizer of the Hebrew Sheltering Guardian Society for Children in New York (1879).

[Edward L. Greenstein]

JOASH (Heb. יְהוֹאָשׁ, יוֹאָשׁ; "YHWH has given"), son of Ahaziah, king of Judah (835–798 B.C.E.). Joash ascended the throne in the seventh year of the reign of Jehu, king of Israel (II Kings 12:2), and ruled until the second year of the reign of Joash (Jehoash) of Israel (*ibid.*, 14:1). According to II Kings 11, he was the youngest of the sons of *Ahaziah. After the death of Ahaziah, the king's mother *Athaliah had all his sons murdered; but the infant Joash was saved by Jehosheba, sister of Ahaziah and wife of *Jehoiada, the high priest (II Chron. 22:11). Joash was hidden in the Temple for six years; in the seventh year Jehoiada plotted against Athaliah, then regent, to have him crowned. He was supported in this carefully planned plot by the captains, the messengers, and the citizens. Athaliah was killed, and Joash was appointed in the Temple in a festive ceremony. (The first mention of the decisive role of the citizens (*am ha-areẓ) in the choice of the kings appears in this connection.)

The ceremony seems to have been in the nature of a renewal of the dynasty (cf. the display of King David's armament emblems and spear, II Kings 11:10; II Chron. 23:9). Accordingly, it was augmented by a joint covenant between the king and the people, in which the royal privileges and responsibilities were reestablished, and by a covenant between God, the king, and the people against the worship of Baal, which marked the beginning of religious reform in Judah. The city was cleansed of the Tyrian cult, which had taken root during Jehoram's reign and flourished during Athaliah's reign, and Mattan, the priest of Baal, was killed. It is not known if the "high places" in Judah were destroyed, but it is clear that the Temple in Jerusalem and the priesthood headed by Jehoiada gained in importance and achieved decisive influence in national affairs for the first time in the history of Judah. Later, the Temple was repaired (II Kings 12:7–17; II Chron. 24:4–14 is a later version with variations in details); the work was completed in the 23rd year of Joash's reign. (The role of the king in building and maintaining temples figures prominently in ancient royal inscriptions from Egypt and Mesopotamia.) In that same year Hazael, king of Aram, attacked Israel, reached Aphek in the Sharon Plain and *Gath, and prepared to attack Jerusalem. Joash was forced to yield to Hazael; and according to II Kings 12:19, he gave him all the gold that was found in the treasuries of the Temple and the palace, and all the votive gifts that the preceding kings had dedicated to the Temple. After this surrender, Judah entered a period of political decline. The Philistines attacked the western boundaries of Judah, and Edom attacked it from the south. (Evidently, the prophecy of Amos 1:6 refers to these events.) After the death of Jehoiada during the last years of Joash's reign, the king came into conflict with the priests. As a climax to this quarrel, according to the late narrative in II Chronicles 24, Joash commanded that Zechariah, the son of Jehoiada, be stoned in the Temple courtyard. II Chronicles 24:23–24 also relates that one year later the Arameans attacked and despoiled Judah "and destroyed all the princes of the people from among the people, and sent all the spoil of them unto the king of Damascus." However, the credibility of this story is very doubtful. Joash died a violent death in a conspiracy, the circumstances of which are unknown and which seems to have gained considerable support. His murderers – Jozakar (var. Jozabad), the son of Shimeath and Jehozabad, the son of Shomer (II Kings 12:21–22 [but cf. II Chronicles 24:26]) – were apparently high state officials (i.e., royal "servants"). It is of significance that they were not punished immediately. Only when *Amaziah, son of Joash, felt that he was firm on his throne did he put to death the murderers of his father. Years later, however, he too was killed in a court conspiracy (II Kings 14:19). According to II Kings 12:1 Joash reigned 40 years. But, to judge from other chronological evidence in II Kings, his reign could not have exceeded 37 or 38 years. It is still debated whether Athaliah's 6 (or 7) year usurpation of the Davidic dynasty was retroactively included by Joash in his regnal years (i.e., Joash's first regnal year was regarded in his official reckoning as his seventh). However, the synchronisms between the contemporary kings of Israel and Judah make it clear that the editor of the chronological framework of the Book of Kings regarded Athaliah's regency as an independent reign, not counting it within Joash's "40" years. Na'aman argued that the account of the temple repairs (II Kings 12) was probably based on a royal inscription. An unprovenanced tablet purporting to be the very inscription hypothesized by Na'aman, and widely publicized in the media in 2003, was shown to be a forgery (Cross).

BIBLIOGRAPHY: Bright, Hist, 234, 236–7; H. Tadmor, in H.H. Ben-Sasson (ed.), *Toledot Am-Yisrael bi-Ymei Kedem*, 1 (1969), 125–6; S. Mowinckel, *Acta Orientalia*, 10 (1932), 236; B. Maisler (Mazar), in *Sefer Assaf* (1953), 351–6; idem, in: JPOS, 21 (1948), 125–6; Torrey, in: JNES, 3 (1943), 30; Oppenheim, *ibid.*, 6 (1947), 117–8; W. Rudolph, in: *Festschrift... A. Bertholet* (1950), 473–8; S. Yeivin, in: *Tarbiz*, 12 (1940/41), 242–6; H.L. Ginsberg, in: *Fourth World Congress of Jewish Studies*, 1 (1967), 91–93; idem, in: JBL, 80 (1961), 339–47; H. Tadmor, in: EM, 4 (1962), 281ff. **ADD. BIBLIOGRAPHY:** M. Cogan and H. Tadmor, *II Kings* (AB; 1988), 135–41; N. Na'aman, in: VT, 48 (1998), 333–49; F. Cross, in: IEJ, 53 (2003), 119–23.

[Hayim Tadmor /S. David Sperling (2nd ed.)]

JOB, BOOK OF (named for its hero (Heb. אִיּוֹב), ancient South Arabian and Thamudic *y'b*; Old Babylonian *Ayyābum*, Tell el-Amarna tablet, no. 256, line 6, *A-ia-ab*; either from *y'b*, "to bear ill-will" or compounded of *ay* "where?" and *'ab*"[divine] father"), one of the Hagiographa, Hebrew *Ketuvim*, which constitute the third division of the Hebrew Canon.

Position within the Hagiographa

In most printed Hebrew Bibles the first three books of *Ketuvim* are Psalms, Proverbs, Job; in BH^3 and BH^5 however (which are based on the Leningrad manuscript of 1008 C.E.), they are Psalms, Job, Proverbs. The latter sequence is the one prescribed by the famous *baraita* in *Bava Batra* 14b. As in the case of the Prophets (*Nevi'im*), the *baraita* requires that the nonhistorical books constitute a solid block arranged according to descending numbers of *sedarim*. Proverbs contains the same number of *sedarim* (eight) as Job; the deciding factor in its being placed after it, however, was not that it contains fewer verses but that it shares with the book which has the next highest number of *sedarim* (four) in the group, namely Ecclesiastes, the attribution to Solomonic authorship in its superscription. The proof is the sequence of the remaining two books in the group: although the Song of Songs has fewer verses than Lamentations, the circumstance that it has the same number of *sedarim* (neither book being divided into *sedarim*) left the arranger free to place it first, so that it might stand next to its Solomonic fellow Ecclesiastes. So, too, Ezekiel has fewer verses than Isaiah (1,273 as against 1,291), but the *baraita* gives it the precedence because it has more *sedarim* (29 as against 26). The *baraita*, however, separates the historical book Ruth from the body of historical Hagiographa that follow the non-historical block and places it before this block – in order that David-authored Psalms may be preceded by the Davidic genealogy at the end of Ruth. The foregoing is a refinement of L. Blau, in: JE, 3 (1902), 143–4 (following H.L. Strack).

CRITICAL ANALYSIS

The Framework and the Poem: Job the Patient and Job the Impatient

It is customary to speak of Job as a wisdom book. But it is so much more sophisticated, not only in its message but also in its technique, than Proverbs, Ecclesiastes, or even the extra-canonical book of *Ben Sira, that it is really in a class by itself. To begin with, it exhibits the striking feature of consisting of a narrative prose framework – the Prologue, chapters 1–2, and the Epilogue, 42:7–17 – and a poetic disputation, 3:1–42:6. The Prologue is easy to follow, and the transition from it to the Poem is natural. The Epilogue, taken by itself, is also fairly easy to follow, except that 42:11–17 seems to come much too late (see below). Puzzling, however, is the logic of such an Epilogue, especially verses 7–10 thereof, to such a Poem.

THE STORY OF THE PROLOGUE. (Chapter 1). Job was an inhabitant of the land of *Uz. This location places Job within the territory of Edom (see Lam. 4:21), the nation to which Job's three friends also belong (see below). Moreover, it clearly places the mortal protagonists, with the possible exception of Elihu, in the land whose wisdom was proverbial (see Jer. 49:7; Obad. 1:8).

His wealth, consisting (like that of the Patriarchs in Genesis) primarily of livestock and slaves, exceeded that of any other man among the *Kedemites. He also had seven sons and three daughters. After the children's (annual?) week of feasting, he used to offer burnt offerings for all of them to make expiation for any irreverent thought they might have admitted into their hearts when their consciences were dulled by wine. The *Satan (accusing angel), however, argued with the Lord that piety coupled with such wealth could not be termed disinterested. Let the Lord try depriving Job of it, and he would surely denounce the Lord to his face. So Job in a series of calamities lost all his property, and his sons and daughters, all in one day. Job learned of these disasters from four successive messengers. On hearing the message of the last one, he performed the usual acts of mourning (1:20), but never a disparaging word about God crossed his lips. On the contrary, he declared: "Naked I came out of my mother's womb,/ And naked again I will depart.// The Lord has taken what the Lord gave:/ The name of the Lord be blessed."// The resourceful Satan now argued that after all the true test of disinterested piety was bodily suffering. With God's permission, he struck Job with a terrible inflammation of the skin from head to foot, and Job sat in the dust scratching himself with a sherd. But still Job did not "sin with his lips." On the contrary, to his wife's suggestion that he denounce the God who had requited his loyalty so shabbily, he retorted indignantly, "You talk like a base woman! Can we both accept the good from God and not accept the bad?" Job had three friends in three different parts of the Kedemite world: Eliphaz the Temanite, Bildad the Shuhite, and Zophar the Naamathite. These, on learning of Job's misfortunes, met, and journeyed together to the home of Job in order to condole with him and comfort him. This is stated explicitly, and their reaction to the spectacle of his misery (2:12–13) leaves no doubt about the sincerity of their friendship.

THE EPILOGUE. Not everybody can be a Job, and if the foregoing were followed by an account of how, moved as was Job's wife by their grief for him but equipped with more education and eloquence, the friends declared that the God who requited Job's loyalty so shabbily was unworthy of it and delivered themselves of some critical reflections on God's conduct of the world – and how Job again demonstrated his unique steadfastness, and not only by not heeding these suggestions but by replying to them forcefully – nobody would be surprised. Indeed, some scholars have suggested that the first three verses of the Epilogue presuppose just such an exchange between Eliphaz and his two companions, on the one hand, and Job, on the other. However, it is primarily on the Prologue and the Epilogue that the traditional picture of Job as a patient sufferer (in English, the King James Version of Epistle of James 5:11 has made "the patience of Job" a household word) is based, for in the Poem, Job is for the most part a critic of Providence. In fact some moderns deny that 42:7–10 does presuppose a conventionally saintly Job and claim that it wishes to teach that God approves just of honest critics like the Job of chapters 3ff. and is mildly contemptuous of apologists like the friends of chapters 4ff. Proponents of this view argue (1) that if the Lord rebuked the friends for speaking as Job's wife had spoken, he might be expected to rebuke Job's wife too, and (2) that 13:7–10 actually predicts that God is going to rebuke the friends for "speaking falsely for God." These arguments are easily disposed of. With regard to the former, the Bible does not place women wholly on a par with men. The limited influence of Job's wife as a woman – and one not even distinguished enough for her name to be recorded – made her expression of objectionable views a less serious matter than that of the friends. Besides, she was not fully a person in her own right, but largely an extension of her husband. Thus in 31:9–10 Job thinks that if he were guilty of adultery it would be a fitting punishment for him if another man enjoyed his wife; how she might feel about it does not concern him; much worse are Deuteronomy 28:30a; Amos 7:17a; etc. To the second argument, all that Job says in 13:3ff. is that God will rebuke his friends if they butt in with their stupid apologetics while he is addressing his indictment to God, for then they would be speaking falsehood directly to – not for – God. Since therefore, the friends do hold their peace until Job has finished his arraignment of God, 42:7–10 is not a fulfillment of 13:10. The author of the bulk of 3:1–42:6 was indeed of the opinion that the facts of life are as Job presents them rather than as Eliphaz and his friends do; but their honest error (it is not the monstrous one that is commonly imputed to them; see below 3 (A) (i)) is a less serious offense in his estimation than Job's presumptuous demand of an explanation from God. He represents God as rebuking Job, not his friends, 38: 1–42:6, and Job as humbly and contritely admitting his fault – twice, 40:3–5 and 42: 1–2, 3*ab*–b, 5–6 (42:3*aa* and 4 are out of place). It simply cannot be denied that "the prose framework" presupposes between Prologue and Epilogue a very different disputation from chapters 3–26; 29–31; 38:1–42:6. Fortunately, a large fragment of this very different disputation has been preserved. H. Fine has demonstrated that chapters 27–28 are a reply by Job as known from chapters l–2 – we shall call him "Job the Patient" – to people whom he addresses in the masculine plural and accuses of having urged him to "stop being a sucker" who "does not sin with his lips" and, as the Lord has noted approvingly after the first trial (2:3) and Job's wife uncomprehendingly after the second (2:9), "still holds fast to his integrity" instead of denouncing God. That this is the case with most of 27:2–6 had already been seen, though Fine was unaware of it, 30 years before by F. Buhl, and one can only marvel that Buhl had failed to see that the following is the only natural and honest interpretation of all of 27:2–6: "(2) Witness God who denies me redress,/ Shaddai who has made me wretched!// (3) So long as my breath is in me,/ The life-breath from God in my nostrils,// (4) My lips shall never speak godlessness,/ My tongue never utter impiety. // (5) Far be it from me to declare you right!/ I will not give up my integrity until I die.// (6b) Never in my life has even my heart blasphemed./(6a) I have held fast to my righteousness and I will not let go of it."// (Notes: *On 5b.* In an attempt to harmonize this line with chapters 3–26, most writers interpret it to mean, "I will never give up my assertion of my integrity." But such a forced meaning could at most be justified if the friends in 3–26 disputed Job's claim to be a good man or if Job himself in those chapters claimed to be without sin; neither is the case, as will be demonstrated further on. *On 6a.* Since, therefore, 5b can only mean what it says, *we-lo' a'rpeha* must be given its natural future meaning – in 6a, idiom sanctions the imperfect before *mi-yamai*, as can be seen from I Sam. 25:28.)

There can be no doubt but that just as the rebuke of the traditional saint Job to his friends who had fallen into error is many times longer and more detailed than his rebuke to his wife for the rash suggestion she made under stress, so the friends had expressed their view in a many times longer and more elaborate speech than Job's wife. For the unmistakable implication of 27:7ff. is that the friends had argued that very often just the wicked fare best on earth – exactly as the unconventional Job (Job the Impatient (JIP) does in chapter 21. And conventional Job opposes this view in 27:7ff. with no less warmth than the unconventional Job's conventional opponents do in 15:20ff., 18:5ff, or 20:4ff. As for chapter 28, N.H. Tur-Sinai's rearrangement appears correct, as does his interpretation in the main. Its theme is: Wisdom is God's, and He has taught man that it is wise to be godly. The concluding and climactic sentence, "Behold, wisdom is to revere my Lord (perhaps to be emended to *'Elohim*, "God," cf. 1:1, 8; 2:3), understanding is to shun evil," is unmistakably intended to recall the description of Job the Patient in 1:1, 8; 2:3, and to imply that the smartest thing a man can do is emulate Job the Patient. For chapters 27–28 constitute a single speech by this very Job the Patient, and it is to this that 42: 7–8 refers when it says, twice, that "my servant Job" (cf. 1:8; 2:3) "spoke properly" about YHWH. Only the speech in which Eliphaz and his companions "did not speak properly" about God has not been preserved, though it is unmistakably presupposed by chapter 27. The original book of Job the Patient (JP), then, was made up as follows: (i) 1:1–2:8, Job's disinterested piety. Put to much crueler tests than the one by which Abraham (Gen. 22) proved that he was a true *yere' 'Elohim* (Gen. 22:12) or god-fearing, i.e., pious, man, Job proved that he was a *yare' 'Elohim ḥinnam* (cf. Job 1:9), i.e., was unconditionally god-fearing or pious. (ii) 2:9–10. Job defends, against his wife, the view that men must remain devoted to God under all circumstances. (iii) 2:11–13. Arrival of Job's three friends. (iv) Now missing: the urging of the friends that Job repudiate the God who has so shamefully failed him. (v) Chapters 27–28. Job's emphatic refusal (27:2–6), citing the unwisdom of wickedness (27:7ff.) and the wisdom of godliness (chapter 28). (vi) A second missing passage, in which God assured Job that he would reward his steadfastness (cf. Gen. 22:16). It is far more likely that 42:7a is an integral part of JP and refers to such a revelation of approval and promise than that it was written by an editor or – even less likely – by the author of the book of Job the Impatient (JIP) for the purpose of connecting 38:1–42:6 with 42:7bff. For in the former God intimates to Job in no uncertain terms that he has spoken improperly about Him, and Job contritely admits it, twice: 40:3–4 and 42:2, 3*ab*–b, 5–6 (verses 3*aa* and 4 are variants of 38:2–3). (vii) 42:7b–17. God's rebuke to the friends for their aberration and reward to Job for his constancy.

[Harold Louis Ginsberg]

Against the Buhl-Fine-Ginsberg theory of two books of Job – JP and JIP – Gordis (1978, p. 578) argues that "the existence of one book of Job is a *datum*, while the theory of two books of Job is a *hypothesis*. Thus the burden of proof rests upon the proponent of the new theory. Its power to persuade depends upon the degree to which it is free from difficulties of its own." In fact, Gordis (1978, pp. 287–311) endeavors to work around the canonical Book of Job's bracketing chapters 27–28 with the expression "Job again took up his discourse, saying" in 27:1 and 29:1. The demonstration by Buhl, Fine, and Ginsberg that chapters 27–28 can and should be read as a document distinct from chapters 3–26 and 29:1–42:6 accounts for the bracketing of these chapters in the canonical Book of Job. Moreover, the Buhl-Fine-Ginsberg theory accounts for chapter 28 as a long and involved rhetorical question posed by Job, "As for wisdom where may it be found?" (28:12) culminating in Job's answer to his impious friends, "To humankind He [God] said, 'Behold: piety [lit., fearing of God] is wisdom, and ethical behavior [lit., shunning of evil] is discernment'" (28:28). The latter assertion is reminiscent of the description of Job in 1:1, 8 and 2:3 as indeed "fearing God and shunning evil." Gordis's, albeit more conventional (in terms of the trends in 19th- and 20th-century biblical studies) theory, no less than the Buhl-Fine-Ginsberg theory, also ignores the datum of a single book of Job. Indeed, Gordis treats chapter 28 as a separate composition, which he calls "The Hymn to Wisdom," and which he describes as "clearly an independent lyrical poem." In fact, it is not a "Hymn to Wisdom," but a declaration that the fear of God is the true wisdom. Moreover, again ignoring the bracketing of chapters 27–28 as a unitary entity within the canonical Book of Job, Gordis (with a majority of modern commentators) assigns 27:13–23 to Zophar while he combines 27:1–8 with 26:1–4 to create an enigmatic reply of Job to Bildad. In reconstructing Bildad's speech in this manner, Gordis (and even Tur-Sinai 1967, p. 378) ignore one of Gordis's monumental contributions to the understanding of the Book of Job (Gordis 1965, p. 187): Job always addresses his friends in the plural so that when as in chapter 12:7–8 "the use of the singular verb and suffixes 'ask thou,' 'will teach thee,' 'to thee,' 'speak thou'" indicates "a restatement by Job of the Friends' admonition to him." Gruber (*Jewish Study Bible*, 2003) solves this problem by going beyond Tur-Sinai's and Ginsberg's reassigning 25:2–6 to Job and assigning 26:2–14 to Bildad. All that is required is to understand that the headings of the two chapters were mistakenly reversed in antiquity.

[Mayer I. Gruber (2nd ed.)]

Job the Impatient (JIP)

CHAPTERS 3–26; (B) 29:1–42:6. All this has been grafted onto the foregoing. Its two constituent blocks may be titled:

(a) Job and the Three Friends; (b) Job, the Intruder Elihu, and God and Job.

JOB AND THE THREE FRIENDS, CHAPTERS 3–26. If one thing is obvious, it is that here, far from being a conventional saint, Job strongly criticizes providence while the friends defend it. In chapter 3, Job terminates the seven days' leaden silence of himself and his visitors (2:13) with a bitter outcry against the unreasonableness of allowing men to be born who were fated, like himself, to have such a life that they can only wish for death. Thereupon, in the order in which they have been introduced, each of the friends tries to reason with him but is rebutted (chapters 4–14). The cycle is repeated (chapters 15–21). A third cycle is begun, but at least in the book as it has come down to us it remains incomplete. There is a complete speech by Eliphaz (22) and there is a complete reply by Job (23–24), but after that there is only a fragmentary speech which is attributed (with questionable propriety) to Bildad (25) and a fragmentary speech by Job (26).

The First Cycle (chapters 4–14). Job's friends try hard to comfort him. Things are bound to end up well for Job, says Eliphaz, since he is a good man and only the wicked end badly (4:6–7). Since no human being is impeccable, a good man sometimes incurs chastisement, which redounds to his own benefit, 5:17ff. Segal rightly argues that Job 5:17, "Nay, happy is the man whom God reproves! – Do not reject Shaddai's discipline," can only be a modification of Proverbs 3:11, "My son, do not reject the Lord's discipline; Do not spurn his reproof," since it destroys the parallelism of the latter and does it by substituting in the first hemistich for the negative imperative of Proverbs 3:11 the "happy is the man" construction of Proverbs 3:13. Thus Eliphaz utilizes the very passage in classical wisdom literature which is incompatible with a view that Job's misfortunes prove that he is a moral degenerate. That the classical doctrine of retribution requires such a conclusion and that the friends draw it (then why don't they curse him and walk away in disgust?) is itself a dogma of current Job exegesis. To be sure, Eliphaz is of the opinion that it is dangerous for Job to disregard the teachings of wisdom, for a man may ruin his own and his children's future not only by wickedness but also by folly: 5:1–5; 4:21; 5:6–7 (see Ginsberg, 1969, 95–96). But if Job will do what wisdom prescribes for cases like his – namely, turn to God in humble repentance and, where possible, make restitution for the wrongs he had done – it is absolutely certain that his latter estate will be even more enviable than his former one (5:8–27). Like Eliphaz, Bildad and Zophar conclude their perorations with this assurance, and they add to it at the very end: Such are your prospects, Job, the diametrical opposite of those of the wicked (8:20–22; 11:16–20). In the case of Zophar (chapter 11), this exuberant conclusion might seem to be at variance with 11:5–6. But if it were, the former would prove that Zophar did not mean the latter seriously, not the other way around. In fact, the latter passage is nothing more scathing than an assertion that Job's impression that the sum total of his guilt is too insignificant to warrant even benevolent chastisement, and merely illustrates the truism that human memories cannot compare in retentiveness with God's memory. Job, however, has no patience with his friends' well meaning defense of God and advice to himself. In his first and second replies, he maintains that it is unreasonable of God to be so harsh with a human being like Job – whose years are so short; who, whatever his sins, represents no threat to God (chapter 7); and who, after all, is God's handiwork, for which He might be expected to have some positive sentiments (chapter 10). As for the friends, Job accuses them of lack of feeling. In his third reply, finally, Job contemptuously dismisses his friends' competence to judge his case and rudely asks them to shut up while he formally arraigns God. And whereas in chapter 7 Job merely complained to God (see 7:11) and in 9:33–35a; 10:1*ab* he merely indulged in the fancy of how he would indict God if he could plead with Him on equal terms, he now takes his life in his hands (13:13–14) and does challenge God to justify his spiteful treatment of him. What sort of sadism (13:25) he demands, is this, requiring purity of that which is impure by its very nature (14:4), showing not the slightest magnanimity in view of man's helplessness (13:25) and his pitifully short span of life (14:5–12), but jealously guarding Job's guilt (14:21) as a usurer might guard the proofs of his debtors' indebtedness? Contrary to the prevailing belief, 13:7–10 does not mean that God will under all circumstances take the friends to task for painting a false picture of a just world order, but only if they do so while Job is formally indicting God; since, therefore, Eliphaz and his two companions hold their peace until Job has finished indicting God, our passage does not anticipate 42:7–8. But Job has both questioned their sincerity (for the first cycle, this must be admitted) and made hash of their wisdom.

The Second Cycle (chapters 15–21). Between that and his daring arraignment of God, no wonder that in the second cycle (chapters 15–21) the tone of the three sages is notably chillier than in the first. Of course they do not, any more than in the first cycle, declare that Job is a scoundrel, for that would be contrary to their innermost convictions. Eliphaz, in fact, again (as in 4:6) alludes to Job's proverbial piety (15:4: Or would you, of all people, offend against piety/ And eavesdrop on God's deliberations?) Nor do they deny that Job may still have a glorious future, because that too would be contrary to their belief. Instead, Eliphaz repeats his original warning of the evil consequences of forsaking the teachings of the wise (15:19: To them alone (i.e., to the sages – not the ancients – of verse 18) has earth been given;/ No outsiders have shared it with them.), and all three of the friends subtly indicate their pique by dwelling only on the negative aspect of the law of retribution – the unenviable fate of the wicked – leaving its complementary aspect, the happy fate of the just, only to be inferred. And Job? With consummate art the author makes him soften his tone toward the three others just in face of their hardened tone toward him. By beginning his response to Eliphaz' admonition with (16:2) "I have heard such talk countless times./You are all illusory comforters,"// he admits that at any rate their intention is to comfort him, and he immediately adds that he realizes that they are not aware that their consolations are illusory: "If (16:4) you were in my place,/ I would be talking just as you are// I would speak to you words of condolence/ And shake my head in commiseration.// (5) With my mouth I would brace you,/ Sympathy from my lips would give you strength (for *yḥsk*, which arose through contamination by verse 6, read *yḥzqkm* after 4:3)."// To be supplied mentally at this point is: "As Eliphaz remarked at the beginning of the discussion, that is exactly what I used to do formerly (4:3–4)." Eliphaz, however, had added an expression of his surprise that Job should be helpless (verb *l'y*) now to render to himself the same service that he used to render to others in misfortune. In obvious allusion to this, Job continues: "(16:7) Alas, now God's enmity has made me helpless,/ His hostility (8) has overpowered me./ / He has arisen against me as an accuser;/ It is his vexing (read כעשו, cf. 10:17) that testifies against me." // Job then enlarges in sundry figures of speech on God's persecution of him, and then repeats:(16:19)/ "Truly, now my opponent is in heaven,/my adversary is on high."// In his second speech (chapter 19), Job tearfully begs his friends not to address him harshly but rather (19:21), "Oh, pity, pity me, at least you, my friends, / For I have been struck by the hand of God." // And in his last speech in this cycle (chapter 21), Job takes up the theme on which they have all harped in order to comfort him, of villains always getting their deserts. Significantly enough, he begins with "Just listen to my statement,/ And see what becomes of your comfortings"// (21:2) and ends with "So alas, you comfort me with futilities,/ Your arguments remain illusory" (21:34, reading *'ml* as in 16:2.) // What he says in between is naturally that the facts are the opposite of what they claim (21:7–16). Actually, he demands, how often does calamity overtake the wicked (21:17–18)? And Job refuses to be comforted by the assurance that if retribution fails to overtake the reprobate it will yet overtake his children: what does the scoundrel care about what happens to his household after his death (21:19–21)? After verse 22, which is not clear, the same thought is repeated to the end of the chapter. All this is said not in anger but in sorrow, and Job's listeners would be the hyenas that the prevailing exegesis makes them out to be if they did not respond accordingly. But they do.

The Third Cycle (chapter 22). The third cycle is a torso, and only one friend's speech, that of Eliphaz, has been preserved; but it is enough. Like all of the friends' speeches in the first cycle, so the one preserved in the third (chapter 22) concludes with an assurance that as soon as Job makes his peace with God, God will restore him to greater bliss than ever, because (22:30) "God (read *El*, apparently) saves the blameless;/For your innocence you shall be saved." // As in the case of the first speech of Zophar (chapter 11, paragraph i above), the concluding reassurance seems to be at odds with the opening. But as in that case, in the first place, the conclusion is, by definition, the speaker's final word and, in the second place, the opening does not mean what it seems to mean at a superficial glance. Job 22:4 means, "Does he fear you that he should arraign you, enter into a lawsuit with you?"; 22:5–7, 9–11 "are a tongue-in-cheek parody of the sort of bill of particulars of his offenses that Job has been demanding of God (12:18ff.); Eliphaz does not wish to imply that Job is such a monster"; and 22:12 means, "You surely cannot expect God to deign to take the trouble to oblige you with such a bill of particulars." Job's reply (chapters 23–24) to Eliphaz is much in the spirit of his replies in the second cycle, except that he says nothing about the friends. For he expresses perplexity rather than bitterness about his own fate and the world order generally, and he expresses the wish rather than a demand to be able to talk it over with God (chapter 23). Chapters 25 and 26 are but fragments – probably the former (despite its superscription) as well as the latter from a speech or speeches of Job – and nothing more has been preserved of the third round of speeches. That a large block of material from "Job the Patient," namely chapters 27–28, should be preserved just where a large block of "Job the Impatient" is missing are two facts which it seems must somehow be connected, but just how cannot be considered here.

[Harold Louis Ginsberg]

Concerning the reassignment of 25:2–6 to Job (so already Tur-Sinai and Ginsberg) and the reassignment of 26:2–14 to Bildad see above at the end of the discussion of Ginsberg's theory of two books of Job, JP and JIP. For the reasons for assigning 25:2–6 to Job see below concerning the place of the dream vision in the ideology of Job.

As for the common perception that the third cycle has undergone significant damage, this perception is fostered by the notion that one is meant to reconstruct the speeches of Bildad and Zophar from 27. Once, however, one recognizes (a) that 27–28 represent an alternative response of Job to a different set of challenges than those posed in JIP; and (b) that by reversing 25:1 and 26:1 one has rediscovered the missing speeches of Job and Bildad, it is plausible to accept the contention of Mayan Ganim (12th century) and S.R. Driver that Zophar had simply said everything he had to say in the first and second cycles, and that little if anything was lost from the third cycle.

[Mayer I. Gruber (2nd ed.)]

JOB; ELIHU THE INTRUDER; GOD AND JOB. CHAPTERS 29:1–42:6. *Job (chapters 29–30).* In his classic study of the Book of Job in the 1971 EJ Ginsberg writes: "No longer arguing with his visitors, Job first laments his appalling change of fortune (29–30). He was once fabulously prosperous (expressed figuratively in 29:6) and influential: even the oldest and most honored and revered deferred to him, for he was friend, champion, and benefactor of the poor, the weak and the unfortunate. And he was confident that he would live long in undiminished vigor and power (29:18–20). Now, alas, he is despised and abused even by the children of outcasts (30:1–15). His grief is so intense that he suffers physically; he feels that God is implacably pursuing him and that his days are numbered (30:16ff., 25–26 belong in chapter 31, e.g., after 31:20). Then in chapter 31, Job utters an elaborate declaration of innocence: he has lived up to the highest ethical standards, and has not even strayed from the path of strict monotheism (31:26–28). (31:37–40 are properly the conclusion of verse 8, and verse 1 a preface to verses 9ff.) The conclusion is: (31:35–37) This is my case; I desire nothing so much as a statement of God's case." By stating, "His grief is so intense that he suffers physically," Ginsberg reflects the conventional view in modern biblical scholarship, which ignores the presentation in chapters 1–2 of the circumstances that brought Job to curse the day on which he was born (2:1), and which brought his three friends – Eliphaz, Bildad, and Zophar – to visit him. In fact, 2:7b records that, with God's permission, the Adversary "afflicted Job with a foul pox from head to toe" while 2:12 records that – apparently because of the debilitating effect of the aforementioned dermatological affliction – when the friends saw Job in the distance on their way to his home, "they could not recognize him." Job himself refers to his diseased condition in the so-called dialogue or symposium (chapters 3–26). For example, in 19:17, Job declares, "My breath is offensive to my wife// my stench to my own children" (so Pope), and in 19:20 he declares, "My bones stick to my skin and flesh// I escape with the skin of my teeth" (NJV), and in 19:21 he pleads with his three friends, "Pity me, Pity me, you [who are supposed to be] my friends, for a plague [Hebrew idiom known also from Ugaritic and Akkadian; the literal meaning is 'a divine hand'] has struck me." So it is not that overreacting, as it were, to the death of Job's seven sons and three daughters that made Job sick and possibly in need of psychological counseling. Rather, it is the fact, as often happens, Job's debilitating illness struck him precisely when he was in mourning over the sudden and untimely death of his sons and daughters. Job's friends, as it is reported in 2:11, set out "to comfort him and console him." The Hebrew *lanud* commonly translated "to comfort" (see again in 42:11) is a gesture-derived expression referring originally to shaking one's head in sympathy for a sick or bereft individual (see also Jer. 15:5; 18:16; and see the extensive discussion in Gruber, *Aspects*, pp. 406–7). Indeed, the prologue relates that when Job's three friends saw his debilitated physical condition, they expressed complete empathy by crying and by throwing dust upon their heads and sitting on the ground with Job for seven days and seven nights without saying a word to Job. However, when Job himself finally speaks up at the end of those seven days and seven nights and says, "I wish I were dead, or, better yet, that I had never been born, or at least that I might have died at birth," his highly educated and well-meaning friends do not simply respond with, "We hear you; tell us more about how you feel" (see Gitay; and see Gruber 1998). Instead, similar to what takes place nowadays during many a hospital visit and in many a house of mourning, Job's three friends get carried away with themselves, and suggest again and again that people who suffer death, bereavement, and disease have it coming to them (Eliphaz in 4:7–8: "Think now, what innocent man ever perished? Where have the upright been destroyed? As I have seen, those who plow evil and so mischief reap them" (so NJV); Bildad in 8:4: "If your sons sinned against Him, He dispatched them for their transgression"). Zophar even suggests that the reason that Job declares, "I have been innocent" (Zophar quoting Job in 11:4; precisely what the reader is supposed to remember from the prologue, chapters 1–2) is that Job is the victim of a divinely bestowed loss of memory: "God made you forget your sin" (Zophar to Job in 11:6c; translation following Tur-Sinai 1967).

Indeed, the Book of Job is a complex and profound literary work that may not be reduced to a single message.

However, a major theme of both the prose and the poetry of the Book of Job, from beginning to end, is the failure of Job's friends to provide him with moral support. Instead they argue with Job and blame him for his suffering. As the dialogue in the Book of Job indicates, the well-intentioned comforters insult the mourner. They tell him that he talks too much (8:2; 11:2–3; 15:2–3; 18:2). Job takes note and quotes their having said this in 16:3 where the 2d person singular pronominal suffixes prove that it is Job rather than the friends, who are being addressed (see below on the use of 2d person singular and plural as keys for when Job and the friends, respectively, are addressed). Job, in contrast, continually has to remind his friends that they are supposed to console/condole rather than insult him (6:14–30; 13:4–12; 16–2, 4; 19:1–5: "How long will you [plural, clearly addressing the three friends] grieve my spirit and crush me with words? Ten times you have humiliated me, And are not ashamed to abuse me. If indeed I have sinned, My error remains with me. But, in fact, you are overbearing toward me, reproaching me with my disgrace" (cf. NJV). In 21:2 Job has the daring to say, "Listen well to what I say, and let that [i.e., just being quiet long enough to give a fair hearing to what I have to say] be your consolation" (so Rashi!).

Unfortunately, many of the modern commentators seldom remind the reader that both Job (chapter 13) and God (chapter 42) tell us that persons who insult the mourner or the victim of illness must be called to account and must seek expiation for their sin (see Gruber 2003). In contrast, the talmudic rabbis (MK 28b) and the halakhic codes (e.g., Sh. Ar., *Yoreh De'ah* 376:1) took to heart Job's repeated suggestion that the best his friends might have done would have been to maintain their silence. They derive from the initial silence of Job's friends in 2:13 the profound lesson that would-be comforters should not say a word to the mourner unless and until she/he indicates verbally or nonverbally a willingness to listen. In fact, in the Shulḥan Arukh, *Yoreh De'ah*, the *halakhah* provides two concise and profound manuals of pastoral care. One of these manuals is called "Laws of Visiting the Sick" (chapter 335), and the other is called "Behavior of Comforters" (chapter 376). Perhaps, the Book of Job is underutilized in the literature of pastoral care because the Book of Job itself was damaged in the early Middle Ages after Yannai had already utilized the original Book of Job in which the dream vision was properly assigned to Job and not to Eliphaz, in whose mouth the dream vision seems to justify blaming the victim (in fact, the latter interpretation is embodied in Maimonides, *Guide for the Perplexed*. Book 3, chapter 25).

[Mayer I. Gruber (2nd ed.)]

Elihu (chapters 32–37). This is a famous enigma. If not for 32:1–5, one would have had the distinct impression that Job's three visitors were no longer with him when he spoke chapters 29–31, especially as God himself answers Job, chapters 38 ff. – hardly after letting a mortal speak first. Now we suddenly learn that not only they but still a fourth visitor, who has not been mentioned before, is still present: Elihu. As a younger man, he has waited while they conversed with Job (read *ḥikkah be-dabberam ʾet ʾIyyov*), but when they fail to respond to Job's last utterance he feels that the duty of justifying God has devolved upon him. Y. Kaufmann has well summarized Elihu's pronouncement. Elihu's purpose is to refute Job's denial of providence. He seeks to do so by citing alternately examples from what occurs occasionally and from what occurs constantly or regularly, three of each. First (32:6–22) he explains to the three friends why he is intruding: his elders have failed to refute Job, which goes to show that wisdom is a matter not of age but of genius; therefore his urge to say what they ought to have is irrepressible. Here his conceit makes his bombast somewhat amusing, after that the latter is merely irritating. Then (33:1–13) he turns to Job, "You claim you could prove you are in the right but a tyrannical God refuses to talk to you. Well, I am no god; if you do not win against me, it is because your case is without merit." *Example no. 1 from the occasional*, 33:14–33. God does so communicate with men, and in more ways than one. You cannot deny that he sometimes warns a man to mend his ways by means of a dream or an illness; the man "gets the message," acts accordingly and his life is spared. *Example no. 1 from the permanent.* This time the preface is addressed to the wise (34:1–12): Job, by asserting that God has wronged him, has associated himself with rogues and villains. *The proof itself* (34:13–14): Every living creature exists only by God's kindness; if he withdrew the breath of life from it, it would perish forthwith. *Example no. 2 from the occasional*, 34:16–37. Potentates are often overthrown suddenly. By whom but by God? For what but for misrule, oppression, and injustice? *Example no. 2 from the permanent*, chapter 35. God has distinguished man from the beasts by endowing him with a conscience. Surely, he to whom we owe our sense of right and wrong does not do wrong. *Example no. 3 from the occasional*, 36:2–21. It is a variant of no. 1. Besides illness other forms of suffering may serve as a warning from God, and a man may determine his own fate by heeding or ignoring it. *Example no. 3 from the permanent.* 36:22–37:24 is not a mere introduction to the third example, which is itself chapter 28 (so Kaufmann). Chapter 28 quite rightly follows directly on chapter 27, and the character of chapters 27–28 has already been elucidated under 2 (b). 36:22–37:24 itself is Elihu's example no. 3 from the permanent: the rain by means of which God supplies the food needs of nations (36:27–31) and (chapter 37) the majesty and terrors of thunder and tempest, of snow and rain and cold, by which God may either benefit or castigate (37:12–13), as also the wonders of the firm dome of heaven, which God can utterly darken with clouds and then clear up again (37:15–22). Wise people cannot but revere such a God. But 38:22–35 says the same thing as Elihu's example no. 3 from the permanent, and says it lucidly and succinctly instead of turgidly and long-windedly. The effort to understand the Elihu speeches is often great, all out of proportion to the profundity of the thought; and since the gem chapter 28, as has been said, is no part of them and so cannot be regarded as redeeming these shortcomings, Kaufmann's view that the Elihu chapters are, and were from the start, integral to what we have called "Job the Impatient" is untenable. More plausible is R. Gordis's view that the author added them in his old age, since the styles of good writers have been known to deteriorate in old age (but to such an extent?). But the more widely held view of Pope that they are by a later hand is at least equally plausible.

[Harold Louis Ginsberg]

Greenstein, in "Job's Initial Speech," in *Studies in Honor of Menahem Cohen*, ed. S. Vargon et al. (2005), pp. 256–58, demonstrates that Elihu's reference to the description of a dream in 33:15 supports the Tur-Sinai-Ginsberg thesis that assigns 4:12–21 to Job rather than Eliphaz (see above and below).

[Mayer I. Gruber (2nd ed.)].

God and Job (chapters 38:1–42:6). Twice God answers Job "out of the storm," 38:1 and 40:6. The original opening formula of the second reply has been superseded by a verse (40:7) from the opening of the first (38:3), but it has been preserved, telescoped into Job's second acknowledgment of defeat, as 42:3a*a*, 4. Since, however, God's first attack has already elicited from Job the abject surrender: "(40:4) Behold, I am worthless – / What can I say in reply? // I put my hand to my mouth. (5) I spoke once – I shall not a second time;/twice, but I shall not again," // the need for a second attack is not obvious, and many claim that the second one is also inferior from an artistic point of view and is a later interpolation. Neither speech can be said to offer a direct answer to Job's questions about the reasons for his own suffering and about the general lack of any discoverable relationship between men's characters and their fortunes. The first, the more sparkling and pointed of God's two replies, may be summarized and paraphrased as follows: You did not even exist when the world was created, you haven't even seen more than a fraction of it, and the idea of your running it is grotesque. Pity the world if it had to depend on you to make the sun rise and set, the gazelle drop her young at the proper season and the young scramble to their legs and grow up all without any help, etc.! In the context of the book, this can only mean that for such an insignificant being as man to ask the Lord of the Universe for an explanation is "to darken/obscure counsel ignorantly with words" (38:2; 42:3a*a*); and whatever those words may mean exactly, the implication is that one must serve God not only in spite of all adversity but without even the expectation of an explanation.

[Harold Louis Ginsberg]

Israel Knohl, *The Divine Symphony* (2003), p. 116, asks what it is about God's description of the wonders of Creation in chapters 38–41 that prompts Job to declare: "I had heard You with my ears, but now I see You with my eyes. Therefore, I recant and relent, being [that I am] only dirt and dust" (42:5). The answer to Knohl's question is to be found through careful attention to what Job asks of God throughout the cycle of speeches in chapters 3–26. Indeed, Job and his friends have been arguing as to whether or not the friends know how to provide comfort. Likewise, Job and his friends have been arguing as to whether or not Job, the paradigmatic sufferer, has it coming to him. On both of these counts, Job, in chapter 42:7 is vindicated while the friends are asked to seek forgiveness and to ask that Job intervene on their behalf with God. There is, however, a third issue that appears in Job's speeches in chapters 3–26 when he addresses God in the second person singular. He asks that God acknowledge that Job has asked to have a dialogue with him (13:18–28; 23). In so doing, it is Job who brings up the subject of the personified sea (Hebrew and Ugaritic *yam*; 7:12), who is also called *Leviathan. The latter entity is commonly understood to be a mythological monster. This monster, in turn, is commonly understood to be a personification (in Israel's Canaanite heritage best known from the epic poetry of *Ugarit) of the yearly struggle for dominion over the cosmos between the deified storm and rain (*Baal) the pair Sea/River [e.g., Ps. 114:3, 5], and the deified summer drought. Concerning the interpretation of references to the Sea personified as Leviathan or Serpent (Heb. *tannin*; see in Job 7:12) or Rahab or the Elusive Serpent (Job 26:13) or the Twisting Serpent (Isa. 27:1) as reflections of the aforementioned seasonal pattern, see T.H. Gaster, *Thespis* (1961), especially pp. 141–48. Two of the most prominent Jewish interpreters of Job in the 20th century – M. Buttenwieser (*Job*, 1925) and Gordis – argued, on the other hand, that Leviathan in the Book of Job is simply the crocodile. For the demonstration that Heb. *tannin* refers to the crocodile only in Ezekiel 29:3 and 32:2 see C. Cohen in *Studies in Honor of H.M.Y. Gevaryahu*, vol. 2 (1991), pp. 75–81.

In fact, the seasonal pattern posited by Gaster is not a feature of life in the southern Levant. Moreover, the treatment of references to a battle between either the God of Israel or the Canaanite Baal as mythology (from Greek *mythos* meaning "lie") suggests that the idea that there was at some time in the remote past a battle between God and the personified Sea, which seriously challenged God's omnipotence is a kind of collective false memory. In fact, the record of destructive tidal waves generated by earthquakes far out at sea, which killed thousands and even hundreds of thousands of people, seems to belong more to collective repressed memory than to collective false memory because it is virtually unmentioned in history books. When just such a tidal wave – now commonly known by the Japanese term tsu-nami – killed more than 100,000 people in Southeast Asia in December 2004, suddenly the newspapers recovered from humankind's repressed memory the distinct possibility that such a tidal wave had put an end to the Minoan Civilization in 1628 B.C.E. and the fact that, inter alia, such a tidal wave had destroyed the city of *Acre in 1303 C.E.

Now it is precisely this natural force – the sea or tidal wave described as a monster or serpent – that Job mentions in 7:12 when he asks God, "Am I the sea or the Dragon [*tannin*] that You have set a watch over me?" Bildad (in Gruber's reassignment of 26:2–14) brings up this monstrous entity again in 26:12–13: "By His power He stilled the sea; By His skill He struck down Rahab. By His wind the heavens were calmed;

His hand pierced the Elusive Serpent." And so, Job has every reason to be satisfied that in finally acceding to his oft-repeated request that God only show that He is listening to Job's entreaties. God responds and indeed refers to the monstrous Leviathan, the personification of the forces from beneath the depths of the sea that wreak havoc. And here God does not engage in theodicy, confirming Eliphaz's, Bildad's, and Zophar's contention that people suffer because they have it coming to them. On the contrary, he intimates that in his own home suffering from his undeserved illness and his undeserved bereavement Job should have been the center of a universe in miniature and should have merited the empathy of Eliphaz, Bildad, and Zophar. However, in the larger world out there God has endowed with a measure of free choice not only humans but also other entities including the tsu-nami, a.k.a., the Leviathan. In this grand scheme of things, Job's debilitating case of what appears to be a not uncommon, life-threatening form of psoriasis assumes vastly less cosmic significance. In the end, however, God as portrayed in the Book of Job does, as it were, take out time from dealing with the monstrous tsu-nami to address Job directly and not, as many a modern mortal potentate might be wont to do, by way of some minor official. In so doing, God suggests that at least for the readers of Job – humans, who have not yet harnessed the forces of destruction from beneath the sea – the abiding challenge is to learn how to speak and, better still, how to keep silence in the face of our friends and neighbors, who have a right to cry out in their physical and emotional pain. Indeed, all people can learn to simply nod their head in empathy (Heb. *lanud*). After all, even God listens and even answers with empathy, even if only in chapter 38 of one of the Bible's longest books.

In Job 40:9–14, in God's second speech out of the whirlwind, which conventional biblical scholarship (see Ginsberg above) has found wanting, God challenges Job, "Have you an arm like God's? Can you thunder with a voice like His? ... See every proud man and humble him, And bring them down where they stand. Bury them all in the earth; Hide their faces in obscurity. Then even I would praise you for the triumph your right hand won you." Harold S. Kushner, *When Bad Things Happen to Good People* (1981), argues that the profound message of this passage is that although God would like us to have all the happiness we deserve, He cannot or will not save innocent victims from cruelty or chaos. A century before Kushner, Benjamin Szold (*Job* 1886; in Hebrew) warned against expecting to find in God's speeches from out of the whirlwind in Job 38–41 an answer to the question as to *why* bad things happen to good people. After all, argued Szold, the book was not written by God; it was written by a theologian. At the end of the day, therefore, the best that this theologian can offer us is not a theodicy but an anthropodicy. And this, no less than the beautiful Hebrew poetry of the Book of Job, is one of the abiding messages of this great book of Scripture (see below).

C. Newsom (*Job* 2003, pp.234–58) points out, "Almost every commentator notes that the divine speeches refuse to engage Job's arguments on his terms." This fact prompts Newsom to compose a brilliant essay, which almost rivals Job 38–41 in its literary artistry and intellectual sophistication. Nevertheless, it appears that "almost every commentator" has failed to heed not only Szold's sound advice that the Book of Job cannot be expected to supply an answer to the question as to why bad things happen to good people but also to heed the simple fact that while Jeremiah may have asked, "why do the wicked prosper," Job, strange to relate, does not ask, "Why do the innocent suffer bereavement and disease?" Consequently, the author of the divine speeches cannot and should not be faulted for not providing an answer to the question Job does not ask. All the more, no holistic reading of the Book of Job, can fault the divine speeches for not repeating the answer given to Job's own particular suffering in chapters 1–2. There it is related that Job was, like the proverbial albino mouse in the proverbial laboratory maze, the subject of a highly successful experiment. In this experiment, Job did not curse God. A highly sophisticated theory as to how each and every individual is duly rewarded in good measure for virtuous behavior and duly punished for misbehavior is set forth, in fact, in Moses' Naḥmanides, *The Gate of Reward,* which includes a short commentary on the Book of Job. Indeed, Naḥmanides may have been inspired to work out a veritable higher mathematics of reward and punishment precisely because neither JP or JIP offers an adequate explanation of the brilliant question, which Job does not actually ask in the canonical Book of Job. This question is, "Just how are people rewarded for their virtue and punished for their misdeeds?" After all, much human experience often seems aptly described by Job 9:22: "It is all one; therefore I say, 'He [God] destroys the blameless and the guilty'"; and Job 21:30: "For the evil man is spared on the day of calamity, on the day when wrath is led forth."

What does Job actually ask, and what precisely does God reply? In fact, the Book of Job contains altogether 16 questions introduced by the interrogative particles *lammah* (9), *maddu'a* (6), *and mah* (1). None of these 16 questions is, "Why do good people suffer?" On the other hand, Job does ask three times in chapter 3 (v. 11, 12, 30) and once more in 10:20, "Why was I born?" This rhetorical question seems to mean simply, "I wish I had not been born." In 18:3 it is Bildad who asks Job why he thinks that Bildad and his two friends are foolish while in 19:22; 21:4; 27:12 Job addresses "why" questions to his three friends. In 33:13 it is Elihu who asks Job why he can possibly call God to account for not replying to people when, in fact, God does respond to people in dreams. Elihu supports his argument by quoting almost verbatim from Job's account of a dreadful dream (Elihu in 33:15ff. referring back to 4:13, on which see above).

In 7:20 Job asks, "Why [*lammah*] do you make *me* your target?" The holistic reading of the canonical Book of Job does not require an answer for this, which was provided in chapters 1–2. This answer, that Job was being tested and did not deserve to suffer, is confirmed in 42:7: "You [Eliphaz and your two friends] did not speak right about me as did my servant Job." In 7:21 Job asks, "Why [*mah*] do you not forgive my transgression and forgive my iniquity?" The latter question is certainly not about why bad things happen to good people. Indeed, in 9:29; 21:7, and 24:1 Job does echo Jeremiah in asking, "Why do the wicked prosper?" Asking the question is itself a challenge to the contention of Eliphaz (4:7), Bildad (8:12–22), and Zophar (20) that the wicked are punished and the just rewarded.

This search for the "why" question, which, scholars often contend, the divine speeches ought to answer, leaves us with only two more candidates: 30:2 and 13:24. The first of these, 30:2, "What can I gain from the strength of their hands, from men whose vigor is spent?" is most assuredly not addressed to God. It is, as Gordis (1978, p. 330) explains, a virtual quotation, explaining why Job did not employ as shepherds the fathers of the young men, who now scorn him. This leaves us with only 13:24 where Job asks God, "Why do you hide your face?" And this is precisely the question, which the divine speeches answer most directly in 38:1 and again in 40:1: "the LORD answered Job from out of the whirlwind." In fact, God even responds directly to Job's challenge in 9:19, 13:8, 31:35 that God please grant him a day in court to bring a veritable lawsuit against God. This response is stated in 40:2 in the form of a rhetorical question: "Will the reprover contend with Shaddai// Will He [God] provide an answer to one who seeks to reprove God?" (cf. Tur-Sinai 1967, p. 554) God's question seems to mean, "Job, you summoned God into the courtroom. Are you certain that you want to go through with this lawsuit?" What could be a more appropriate response to Job's having asked for a day in court? Moreover 42:5, in which Job says, in response to the last of the God speeches, "I have heard about you with my ears, but now I see you with my eyes," Job acknowledges that God has indeed granted Job's wish, expressed in 19:25–27 (in NJV): "But I know that my Vindicator lives; In the end He will testify on earth – This, after my skin will have been peeled off. But I would behold God while still in my flesh, I myself, not another, would behold Him; would see with my own eyes."

So – in the end – the circle is closed. God meets Job in court, and He confirms to Job's friends and to all readers of the Book of Job (42:7) that indeed bad things do happen to good people and that victims should not be insulted by would-be comforters – quite a profound lesson in anthropodicy, albeit it not the theodicy we might have expected from a theophany. For such a theodicy one must look instead to Maimonides' and Naḥmanides' demonstrations that bad things do not really happen to impeccable people or to the promise in the Book of Daniel (12) that in the long run those who sleep in the dust – the good and the bad (cf. Job 3:13) – will all receive their appropriate eternal rewards. In the interim, the abiding message of God to Job's would-be comforters is enshrined in *halakhah*. And that is no small achievement of the book's author and of the faith community that preserved and cherished the Book of Job.

[Mayer I. Gruber (2nd ed.)]

The Origin and the Literary Evolution and Character of the Book of Job

Ezekiel 14:12–20 reveals an acquaintance on the part of a writer of the early sixth century B.C.E. with a tradition about a saint of old by the name of Job who was presumably identical with the hero of the canonical book of that name. Of the two saints whom Ezekiel names together with Job, namely, Noah and Daniel, the former is the well known hero of the Flood. For Daniel, he is apparently the one who is also known from Ugaritic literature, see *Daniel. Details about Job are known only from the Book of Job. It is held that in this book a later composition, "Job the Impatient" (JIP), has been grafted onto an older one, "Job the Patient" (JP), and it stands to reason that the latter is closer to the original tradition about Job than the former. But JP itself consists of more than one stratum. Observations made by writers like W.L. Batten, A. Alt, and H.A. Fine point to the following stratification: (a) JPa, 1:1–5, 13–22; 42:11–17. These 22 verses constitute a simple but complete story, which knows nothing about any role of Satan; for (1) in 1:13, "his sons" refers back to the "Job" in verse 5b, not to "the Satan" in verse 12b; (2) the text does not say that the calamities of 1:13–19 were caused by the Satan (contrast 2:7), and in 42:11 we read that the friends comforted Job "for all the misfortune that God had inflicted upon him"; and finally (3) the blessing of God in 42:12–13 presupposes the previous loss of his property and his children in 1:13–19 but not the inflicting of an unbearable dermatitis in 2:7–8, 13. (b) JPb, 1:6–12; chapter 2; chapters 27–28; 42:7–10 plus some lost sections on which see the last part of section 2. The author of JPb was a writer of high quality. Finding in JPa that Job lived in the Kedemite region of Uz (see above, Sec. 2a) he furnished him with friends from three other Kedemite tribes or localities. He obviously created Eliphaz the Temanite out of two of the names in Genesis 36:11, and it is probable that he spun Zophar the Naamathite out of two other names in the same verse. Some texts of the Septuagint actually have Zophar there for Zepho, and the writer either had an aberrant reading *nʿmt* for *gʿtm* or was bold enough to modify *gʿtm* to *nʿmt* for his purpose. How he arrived at the name Bildad is uncertain (perhaps he thus modified Bedad, Gen. 36:35), but the gentilic Shuhite was obviously suggested to him by the last name in Genesis 25:2. Remembering that his characters are non-Israelite (and probably pre-Mosaic) he has them employ the divine names El, Eloah, and Shaddai, but never YHWH. He is the author of the lovely poem which is chapter 28. By introducing the Satan, an angel with the permanent office of accuser, he reveals that he dates from the Persian period, since the earliest datable passage in which he occurs with this role is Zechariah 3:1ff. JPa may possibly be of late pre-Exilic authorship, though one has the feeling that it too is post-Exilic. The real genius of the Book of Job is, of course, the author of JIP (whether or not it originally included the Elihu chapters and the second God-Job exchange, see end of 3). He not only changed Job from a conventional saint to a negator of retribution and providence, but he built up a structure of consummate literary art. To the limiting of their speech to pre-Yahwistic divine names, he adds a Kedemite linguistic coloring. Kedem, the cradle of the Kedemite stock, is primarily the Middle Euphrates region (those Kedemites who lived farther south were believed to be descendents of Abraham and Lot, both of whom migrated from the original Kedem). Now, Kedem in this sense stands in synonymous parallelism with Aram in Numbers 23:7, and a famous native of this region is styled Laban the Aramean and represented as speaking Aramaic, Genesis 31:24, 47. It is therefore for the sake of local color that this writer, whose knowledge of Hebrew (and of Hebrew Scriptures) was excellent, not only makes his characters keep using the noun *millin* ("words," infrequent in Hebrew) and interlard their speech with such hair-raising Aramaisms as *sahed* (the classical parallel synonym of *ʿed* "witness" is *yafeaḥ*, and he surely knew it) and *geled* ("skin"), and such forms as *minhem* ("from them," Heb. *mehem*). The subtle devices by which he makes the friends express their pique in the second round by dwelling only on the punishment of the wicked, or Job employ against his opponents telling allusions to words previously spoken by one of them, have already been pointed out. A serious hindrance to the modern reader's appreciation of his art are, apart from minor corruptions, the many displacements of lines. Both are particularly liable to occur in lyrical texts, where the logic of the story and of prose syntax, which are such an effective check on corruption in prose narrative, are totally wanting. Torczyner (Tur-Sinai) observed that a principal reason why the characters often seem to be speaking pointlessly or even arguing against themselves is that in the received text 4:12–19 stands in a speech of Eliphaz. The critics never tire of deprecating the complacency of Eliphaz and his friends. Yet here he cites a terrifying nightmare in which he was told that God accounts no man righteous because He is an impossible tyrant even with the angels. On the other hand it is Job who has just said: I wish I were dead because there I would have calm and rest and I would not have trouble. As it is (3:26) I have no calm, no tranquility, and no rest, and trouble has come upon me (3:25) For I had a dread and it has come true, just what I feared has come to pass. It is in 4:13–16, 12, 17–20 that Job goes on to tell what that premonition of disaster was: a dream in which an angel informed him obliquely that he was living in a fool's paradise if he imagined that his righteousness was a guarantee against ruin: God, who found fault with his angels, certainly did not recognize any such category as righteous men. This, so far from being the view of Eliphaz, is so repugnant to him that in chapter 15, in verses 14–16 of which he cites it as Job's view, he berates him for it mercilessly. On the other hand, it is Job who says in 6:10 end, "I have not withheld the words of a holy being," and who throughout the discussion keeps complaining that God is unreasonable. This insight of Torczyner's (Tur-Sinai's) makes many other things in the disputation fall into place. Grafted onto JPb, JIP must be younger than JPb. In effect, Segal has shown that it abounds in parallels to other books of the Bible, and that in all but a small fraction of cases Job is either demonstrably or probably dependent on those other books. The clear case of Proverbs 3:11–13 > Job 5:17 has already been cited (in 3, a, i), but since the age of Proverbs 1–9 is controversial this observation is of little help in arriving at a terminus post quem for JIP. A decisive case, however, is Isaiah 44:24b > Job 9:8. Not only has the former perfect parallelism and the later none, in the former *levaddi*, "I alone," is just the point: God made everything, no one else had any part in the creation of either the sky or the earth. In the latter, on the other hand, the only reason why the author added *levaddo*, "all alone," after *noṭeh shamayim* was that he found *levaddi* after *noṭeh shamayim* in the former, which served him as model. (It follows that the parallelism is also due to borrowing on the part of Job in the case of Isa. 41:20 > Job 12:9; Isa. 50:9 > Job 13:28; Isa. 59:4 > Job 15:35; et al.). On these grounds Segal dates Job (i.e., JIP) after Deutero-Isaiah, that is, after the third quarter of the sixth century B.C.E. (That JIP, in borrowing the phrase in question, assigned to the word *noṭeh* a different meaning from the one it has in its original context is an observation for which see Ginsberg, 1968.)

[Harold Louis Ginsberg]

The Name Eliphaz

As the name of the leader of the three wise men who enter the house of the bereft and infirm Job, and, despite their initial good intentions, insult him and blame his dead children for their own untimely death, the name *Eliphaz is most appropriate. According to Genesis 36:10 Eliphaz was the first born son of Esau. Esau, according to Gen. 25:30 and 36:1, is the progenitor of Edom, the nation depicted as Israel's arch-enemy in Malachi 1:2–4. Moreover, Eliphaz, the son of Esau is identified as the father of Amalek in Genesis 36:10. Amalek, of course, is the enemy of Israel, who is described in Deuteronomy 25:18 as follows: "undeterred by fear of God [the foremost quality of Job in 1–2; and the essence of true wisdom in Job 28:28], he surprised you on the march, when you were famished and weary, and cut down all the stragglers in your rear." Other than to ascend a ladder and hold up a sign as to who is the hero and who is the villain in Job 3–26, the author of the canonical Book of Job, could not have done more than naming that villain Eliphaz to suggest that the anti-hero of the Book of Job is the wise person who comes to a house of mourning and insults both the mourner(s) and the mourned by saying that they had it coming to them. This author has done his/her very best by suggesting that as Isaac is the link between Abraham and Jacob so is Eliphaz the link between Esau and Amalek. Yet, most of the standard commentaries attach no special meaning to the deliberate choice of the name Eliphaz for one who, like his son Amalek, hits the book's real hero when he is down. Acutely aware of the not so subtle message of calling Job's protagonist by the name of the son of Esau and the father of Amalek, a number of midrashim quoted in Ginzberg's *Legends*, 1, p. 422 suggest that when Job reminded Eliphaz that he was, after all, the son of Esau, Eliphaz replied, "I have nothing to do with him; 'a child shall not bear the iniquity of one's parent'" (Ezek. 18:20). Another midrash quoted in Ginzberg's

Legends, 5, 322 accounts for Amalek's reprehensible behavior not as something he might have learned from his parents but as the kind of behavior that results when a great prophet neglects the education of her/his children because of excessive involvement in the public domain! Obviously, both of these midrashim seek to tone down the biblical author's message that people who insult the bereaved and the infirm belong to the enemies of Israel.

Why Kedemites?

Gruber 1998 noted that the characterization of Job as "greater than all the Kedemites" (1:3) ought to remind one of King Solomon, whose "wisdom was greater than the wisdom of all the Kedemites ..." (1 Kings. 5:10). Here again as in the choice of the name Eliphaz (son of Esau and father of Amalek) for the anti-hero the author of the canonical Book of Job already intimates that the true wisdom is not with Eliphaz and his friends but with Job as Job will argue in 12–14 and as God will concur in 42:7 where again God, not fortuitously, addresses specifically Eliphaz and says, "you and your two friends" (i.e., Bildad and Zophar). And yet, perhaps part of the greatness of the artistry of the Book of Job is that despite all the not so subtle hints scattered all over the book, readers must rediscover who spoke rightly and who did not. Ultimately, the difficulty lies not in the difficult vocabulary that requires years of study of ancient languages but in the unpleasant realization that if bad things really do happen to good people on a regular basis (as is suggested in the talmudic dictum in Bava Batra 15a, which sees Job not as a one-time historical personage but as a paradigm (Heb. *mashal*) of all innocent victims), then it could happen to anyone of the innocent readers of the Book of Job. Just as some persons go into what psychologists call denial when they receive a death sentence from a cardiologist or oncologist, so do many readers and commentators on the Book of Job go into denial when they face up to the fact that the Book of Job says a great deal about the fact that bad things happen to good people and as little as possible about why this happens.

The Dream Vision in the Book of Job and Beyond

In the 1960s Tur-Sinai and Ginsberg were alone in construing the teaching revealed in the dream vision (chapter 4:12–19; and referred to again by Job in 6:10 ("I have not withheld the words of a holy being"; see Ginsberg 1967, p. 99) and in 9:1 ("Indeed, I know that it is so: 'how can a human be vindicated before God'?") and clearly mocked by Eliphaz in 5:1, 8 ("Just call – see if anyone answers you! To whom of the 'holy' beings can you turn? I [Eliphaz], on the other hand, resort to God, to God do I address my plea"; Ginsberg 1967, p. 99) and again in 15:11–19:

> Do these comfortings [by Eliphaz, Bildad, and Zophar] fail to satisfy you
> Because you know some word that reached you by stealth?
> What sinful haughtiness!
> What monstrous pride!
> To blow your wind at these men
> And to belch forth such words:
> "How can a mortal be judged righteous
> a human born of a woman accounted just?
> If he [God] disapproves of his sacred abode [the sky]
> If the very skies [whose purity is described in Exod. 24:10]
> are not pure in His sight,
> How much less a thing loathed and detested,
> a human, who drinks godlessness like water!"
> Listen [says Eliphaz to Job], and let me [Eliphaz] tell you [Job],
> relate what I have seen ...
> (translation from Ginsberg 1967, pp. 100–2 with modifications for the sake of greater clarity)

On the basis of the clear evidence that Job saw in the dream vision a vindication of his own position that his suffering is not the cause of some heinous sin since, as is revealed in the vision, even the sky and the stars and moon therein would not pass muster if summoned to account before the divine Judge, Tur-Sinai and Ginsberg assign also chapter 25, vv. 2–6 to Job:

> Dominion and dread are His;
> He imposes peace in his heights [Heb. *oseh shalom bi-meromav*; the source of the first
> clause of the final line of the Kaddish!; see below]
> Can His troops be numbered?
> On whom does His light not shine?
> How can a human be in the right before God?
> How can one born of a woman be cleared of guilt?
> Even the moon is not bright,
> And the stars are not pure in His sight.

By the end of the 20th century numerous other scholars adopted and elaborated upon the Tur-Sinai-Ginsberg thesis with respect to the place of the dream vision in the Book of Job. These scholars include G.V. Smith, in: VT, 40 (1990); Margaret B. Crook, *The Cruel God* (1959); J.C.L. Gibson, in: *Scottish Journal of Theology*, 28 (1975), Y. Gitay, in: JNWSL, 25 (1999), and especially E.L. Greenstein in numerous publications including the commentary on Job in the Hebrew Commentary Series *Mikra LeYisrael* (2006). Gruber (1998; 2003) demonstrated that, in fact, the treatment of the dream vision as a defense of the individual who must give an account of himself before the divine Judge rather than an attack by Eliphaz upon Job's claim of integrity is reflected in a series of Jewish liturgical poems associated with the penitential season that precedes the Jewish New Year (Rosh Ha-Shanah) and culminates in the Day of Atonement. Moreover, he suggested that rather than attributing to the sixth century C.E. liturgical poet *Yannai a radical rearrangement of the Book of Job, anticipating Tur-Sinai, Ginsberg, and Greenstein, one can assume the following: at least the earliest of the synagogal poets who elaborated upon the dream vision as a defense of humankind standing before the divine tribunal on Rosh Ha-Shanah and the Day of Atonement read Job in its original form before the unfortunate series of displacements in the current Hebrew text, which the aforementioned modern scholars recognized. Gruber was able to buttress this claim by pointing to various biblical texts recovered from *Qumran in which the order of verses, pericopes, and even chapters differs radically from the standard Hebrew text of Hebrew Scripture. For additional data as to how blocks of text were displaced in the copying of ancient manuscripts, see Greenstein 2005, pp. 260–62.

Holistic Interpretation of the Book of Job: Beyond Ginsberg and Gordis

One of the most important trends in late 20th century and early 21st century biblical scholarship is holistic interpretation. Holistic medicine, which developed during the same era, utilizes the data and techniques developed in treating specific maladies of specific organs and tissues to treat the entire person far more effectively than either the new techniques alone or the old-fashioned family physician. By the same token, holistic biblical interpretation seeks to utilize the data garnered by classic 19th and 20th century atomistic exegesis in order to fully understand not only individual units but also entire books as they appear in the ancient Hebrew and Greek versions of the Jewish Bible. Two of the important exponents of holistic interpretation, who have contributed immensely to improved understanding of the Book of Job, are E.L. Greenstein and Carol Newsom.

Following up on Gordis's argument that the canonical Book of Job is a datum while its division into previous compositions is only a theory, holistic interpretation tends to see 42:7b–17 not only as the fitting rebuke of Job's friends for having urged him to curse God and the fitting laudation of Job for having rebuked his friends in 27–28 but as the equally fitting conclusion to the canonical Book of Job, which has privileged the infinitely more profound work which Ginsberg calls JIP. In 42:7b–8 it is stated, "And the LORD said to Eliphaz the Temanite, 'I am angry at you and your two friends because you did not speak rightly about me as did my devotee Job. Now take for yourselves seven bulls and seven rams and go to my devotee Job and offer a burnt offering for yourselves. And let Job, my devotee, pray for you; for him will I accept and not treat you badly, since you have not spoken rightly about me as did my devotee Job.'"

Significantly, in this passage God employs the expression "show deference" (literally, "lift up someone else's face") for precisely the generally forbidden activity (see e.g., Lev. 19:15) of which Job, himself accused Eliphaz and his friends in 13:6–10:

> Will you tell lies on behalf of God
> speak falsehoods on his behalf?
> Will you show bias in his favor,
> play the advocate for God?
> Will it be pleasant when he takes you to task?
> Can you mock him as you mock mortals?
> And accuse you he surely will
> If you show partiality in the dispute.
> (Translation adapted from Ginsberg 1967, p. 98.)

Thus it turns out that Job in the very heart of his debate with Eliphaz, Bildad, and Zophar has accused these friends of showing partiality in a dispute in order to justify God in the face of Job's undeserved suffering. What the reader of the canonical book is meant to know from chapters 1–2 is that, in fact, Job is totally innocent. He is the subject of an experiment. Job does not know this, nor do the friends. Job proves that God was correct and "the Adversary" mistaken. Contrary to the dire prediction of "the Adversary" in 1:10 and 2:5, Job does not curse God. He insists again and again that (a) he has done nothing to deserve the untimely tragic death of his seven sons and three daughters; (b) his three friends who have come to visit a bereft and infirm individual have misbehaved by blaming the victim rather than sitting silently and nodding their heads; and (c) all he wants from God is that God should dialogue with him and acknowledge him.

Consequently, when God rebukes the friends in 42:7–8, he confirms the correctness of what Job has insisted throughout his speeches in chapters 3–26; 29–31. Moreover, when God does address Job in 38–41 he has acceded to Job's simple request uttered in 9:32–35: "For God is not a man, like me, whom I could answer when we came to trial together. If only there were an arbiter between us, who would lay his hand upon us both, who would remove God's rod from me so that my dread of Him would not terrify me. Then I would speak, and not fear Him, for He is far from just to me." And, in fact, at the end of the book, God does address Job (see below concerning the God speeches). Moreover, by God's saying that Job has spoken rightly and the friends not, God has vindicated Job both in his complaint that his friends do not know how to comfort a bereft and infirm individual and in his conviction that his suffering is totally undeserved.

[Mayer I. Gruber (2nd ed.)]

The Message and Meaning of Job

The problem of the final meaning and message of the book, no less than that of its provenance and composition, has elicited over the centuries a wide variety of responses. To some sages of the Talmud and Midrash, Job is to be regarded as one of the few truly God-fearing men of the Bible (Mid. Lekaḥ Tov to Gen. 47:12), the most pious gentile that ever lived (Deut. R. 2:4), exceeding even Abraham in this regard (BB 14b). To others, he was a blasphemer (*ibid.*). According to R. Joshua b. Hananiah (second century), Job served God out of love, the highest possible motivation; according to R. Johanan b. Zakkai (first century), it was only fear that prompted Job to serve God (Sotah 5:5). Maimonides (*Guide*, 3:22–23) attributes Job's defiant questioning of God's justice to his defective knowledge of God; defective, since it was based on the mere acceptance of authority. However, when Job attained a true, philosophical knowledge of God (after the theophany from the whirlwind), he realized that it alone constitutes true happiness. No misfortune, however grave, can trouble a man once he is in possession of a truly philosophical knowledge of God gained through revelation. The latter instructs him that God's knowledge, rule of the world, and providence are in no wise to be compared to man's conception of these matters. "If a man knows this, every misfortune will be borne lightly by him."

Modern commentators are sharply divided as to what the author of Job meant to teach his readers. The problem arises from the fact that in the speeches of God from the whirlwind (Job 38–42), God majestically ignores the issue as Job has posed it. Instead of giving an explanation of Job's sufferings, God confronts Job with a series of seemingly irrelevant, ironic questions intended to convince him of the paltriness of human knowledge and power. The rhetorical questions, encompassing the unfathomable wonders of creation, the immensity of its expanse, and the marvels of nature, in whose presence man's understanding and power are as nought, seem to imply that it is presumptuous of man to question God's justice. This reading appears to be borne out by God's challenge: "Wilt thou even make void My judgment? Wilt thou condemn me that mayest be justified?" (40:8). Even more, Job acknowledges (40:4) that he is "of small account" and that in view of God's unanswerable questions, he will "proceed no further" (*ibid.*) with his questioning of God's justice. Indeed, Job is mildly rebuked by God for speaking out of ignorance and of "darkening counsel" (38:2). Yet, the friends are even more sharply rebuffed by God, since by their words they have enkindled his wrath: "For ye have not spoken of me the thing that is right, as My servant Job hath" (42:7). Taken at face value, the implication is that Job's repeated assertion of the lack of a visible correlation between his life of rectitude and the dreadful fate visited upon him disproves the friends' contention that suffering is proof of sin. If one were to employ the argument from silence, then the absence of any charge of guilt against Job in God's reply would constitute divine vindication of both Job's innocence and his argument. In sum, the book would teach (Terrien): (1) that the old doctrine of a causal connection between suffering and moral evil is untenable; (2) that the splendors of creation and their marvelous sustainment (38:39, 40), phenomena beyond the capacities of man, are proof of the justice of God; and (3) that the question of man's actual lot as contrasted with his rightful deserts is one on which God prefers to maintain silence. Moreover, in the face of an awareness of the divine power, as expressed in God's series of questions to Job (38:4–39; 40:9–32), Job's question becomes irrelevant. Conceivably, the thought is implied that if man could match God's power and wisdom, only then could he grasp the workings of God's providence. Job admits the total impossibility of such a feat (42:3) and concludes by abhorring his words and repenting, "Seeing I am but dust and ashes" (42:6).

The enigmatic character and dubious relevance of God's reply to Job have suggested an interpretation that, in the first instance, denies that the book was written as an attempt to solve the mystery of the suffering of the innocent. Neither the colloquy nor the theophany penetrate to the reason for Job's suffering. That reason, however, emerges quite clearly from the prologue and epilogue. Job's suffering is merely a divine test of his piety. In addition to controverting the conventional view that suffering is punishment for sin, the book proposes not an answer but an experience. The message of Job is neither theological nor philosophical. It is profoundly religious. Its origin is to be sought in the biblical concept of the consequence of sin as isolation from God (Gen. 4:14). In his agony, Job feels not only isolated from God but that God has become his implacable enemy (7:20; 9:16–18; 13:21, 25; 16:9, 12:19:6–9; 30:20) and has hidden his face from him (13:24). He insists that death would be preferable to his life of unmitigated woe (3:17) and that never to have seen the light of day would have been an even more desirable fate (3:11, 12), since in either case he would have been beyond God's hostile power. No isolation from God could be more total than this. God's reply from the whirlwind is tantamount to the assurance that suffering need not spell isolation from God. The divine revelation is itself an act of grace, so much so that in its presence, Job does not ask to be delivered from his suffering. Even more, he admits that whereas heretofore he "had heard of Thee by the hearing of the ear; But now mine eye seeth Thee" (42:5). God's presence is more than enough to sustain him. "It may be good to understand the cause (of suffering); but it is better to be sustained to endure" (H.H. Rowley). Unknowingly, then, Job in his suffering was vindicating God's trust in him and thus honoring God.

Georg Fohrer's interpretation is a nuance of the foregoing. The essential question the book sets out to answer is: what is the conduct proper to suffering man? The final reply of Job (40:2, 3; 42:5) is the answer to the question, conceptualized by Fohrer in the following: "In his unreserved devotion to God and in his personal fellowship with him, Job bears and endures his fate.… This is the true understanding and appropriate attitude for man towards suffering; the humble and reverential silence sustained by repose in God." Marcus sees Job as the "first existentialist." Basing himself on 40:7–14, he sums up the book's message: "Just as God exerts his heroic will to subdue the demonic elements of the universe and to sustain his creation by bringing light to the stars, rain to the sea and land, and food to all living creatures, so man must exert his will to subdue evil and overcome frustration." Thus, the book is "an exhortation to emulate God's unconquerable will." Freehof, after reviewing the various theories of the reason for suffering as put forth in the book (Prologue: suffering is a divine test; the Friends: suffering is divine punishment for sin acknowledged or unacknowledged; Job: a denial of the latter; Elihu: suffering is a divine warning and is educative), interprets the denouement as bearing a twofold meaning: (1) If God's mysterious power and wisdom fill the universe, it should not be unendurable to accept one more expression of it, human innocent suffering; (2) the very divine power manifest in creation should by implication serve man as a mandate to extend human control over nature as a means of conquering much human suffering. Gordis regards the book as aiming at two central conclusions. Since the world contains so much that is not intended for man's use and that is beyond his sway, neither the universe nor its Creator can be judged from the limited human perspective. There is implied acknowledgment on the part of God that much in the world order is imperfect. But, then, could Job, if he were to mount God's throne, do much better; could he humble the arrogant and crush the evildoers? Again, the order and harmony that pervade the natural world though faintly grasped by man is, by analogy, evidence of order and meaning in the moral sphere, though the latter, too, is often incomprehensible to man. Though the book offers no justification for suffering from the human viewpoint, it does demonstrate that "it is possible for men to bear the shafts of evil that threaten their existence if they cultivate a sense of reverence for the mystery and miracle of life … and strive to discern intimations of meaning in its beauty."

[Theodore Friedman]

Spiegel shows that the prose tale of Job "revolves around the question, "Is there such a thing as unselfish virtue." The prose tale of Job provides an affirmative answer to this question. In addition, Spiegel shows that the poem of Job "boldly assails the dogma of retribution as both untrue and unfair." Consequently, anticipating by more than half a century the post-modern holistic interpretations, Spiegel reads 42:7, "for you [Eliphaz, Bildad, and Zophar] have not spoken the truth about me as did my servant Job," as both the conclusion of the prose tale and as the conclusion of the poem [Ginsberg's JIP]. This, Spiegel explains, means that Job 42:7 constitutes "the disavowal [by God] of the doctrine of individual retribution."

[Mayer I. Gruber (2nd ed.)]

The most radical interpretation is that offered by Tsevat. According to him the book maintains that there is no principle of divine retribution in the world. "The assertion of punishment of the wicked and reward of the righteous is without foundation.… Justice is not woven into the stuff of the universe nor is God occupied with its administration." Justice is simply a human ideal. "He who speaks to man in the Book of Job is neither a just god nor an unjust god but God." Hence, Job's denial of the notion that his suffering is evidence of his sin is closer to the final truth as enunciated in God's reply from the whirlwind than the conventional doctrine put forth by the friends.

This summary of diverse current interpretations underlines the problematic character of the book no less that its endless fascination for those who ponder the "impossible problem of reconciling infinite benevolence and justice with infinite power in the creator of such a world as this" (J.S. Mill). In the words of the sages (Avot 4:15), "It is beyond our power to understand why the wicked are at ease, or why the righteous suffer."

[Theodore Friedman]

The Book of Job as Anthropodicy Rather than Theodicy

In 1710 Baron Gottfried Wilhelm von Leibniz (1646–1716) published his book, *Théodicée*, "the vindication of the divine attributes, especially justice and holiness with respect to the existence of evil." The English form of the French term *théodicée*, i.e., "theodicy," is first attested in 1797. The term invented by Leibniz is based upon the Greek noun *theos*, "God," 'and the Greek infinitive *dikein*, "to justify." Consequently, the term theodicy is a close semantic equivalent of the Hebrew term *ẓidduk ha-din*, "justification of the [divine] decree," which is the name of the central liturgical poem recited at the Jewish funeral service since Late Antiquity. Numerous common interpretations of the Book of Job see this book as a treatise on theodicy. Notable exceptions are the interpretations of Spiegel, Tsevat, and Kushner (see above). The Book of Job and the God who speaks to Job from the whirlwind and ultimately defends Job and castigates his friends cannot or will not justify God with respect to Job's suffering from the undeserved, untimely death of his sons and daughters. Nor does this book or the God who is represented as speaking through this book justify Job's being afflicted with a severely debilitating disease. Consequently, neither the book as a whole nor the God speeches can be construed as a treatise or treatises on theodicy. In fact, the canonical Book of Job three times skirts the entire issue of theodicy. The first time that the Book of Job skirts the issue of theodicy is by telling the readers in chapters 1–2 that, in fact, Job's suffering is totally undeserved; it is simply an experiment designed to vindicate God's trust in Job's virtue despite the charges leveled against Job by "The Adversary." The second time that the issue of theodicy is skirted is in the God speeches. Tsevat and Kushner have simply made explicit to large audiences of biblical scholars and laypersons respectively the rather unpleasant ideas, which the author of Job left to the imagination of those learned enough to plumb the depths of the author's high register Hebrew poetry. The third time that the canonical Book of Job skirts the issue of theodicy is in 42:13, "He also had seven sons and three daughters." The latter verse does not assert, God forbid, that there were born to Job seven sons and three daughters as stated in 1:2. To have said that would imply that while in the course of God's performing an experiment on an unwitting human victim God had the original children killed. Thereafter, as it were, God simply replaced them with new children. This would not be justification of God but condemnation of God. Instead, as Gordis often explained orally in his classes (but not in his published commentary), in the fairy-tale like epilogue of the book, Job's original children were restored to him just as in the Ugaritic Epic of Danel (paired with Job and Noah in Ezekiel 14:14, 20; cf. Gordis 1965, p. 68), the son Aqhat is brought back to life as a reward for the virtue of his parents and in response to his sister Pughat's eloquent and heartfelt prayers.

The Book of Job does not justify God in the face of human suffering, be it the suffering of a person who is being experimented upon as is described in chapters 1–2 or in the face of tidal waves (tsu-nami or Leviathan) that kill as many people as did the Americans at Hiroshima in 1945. Consequently, the Book of Job is not a work of theodicy. Most of the Book of Job, however, is devoted to Job's defending himself in the face of the charge reiterated again and again by his friends that people (such as Job and his children) suffer because they have it coming to them. Since, the book portrays God as vindicating Job's claim to innocence and condemning his friends for suggesting that he had it coming to him, the book may best be described not as theodicy but anthropodicy. If theodicy is the justification of God, then *anthropodicy* (from Greek *anthropos*, "human," and Greek *dikein*, "to justify") is the justification of suffering humans in the face of people, who add insult to injury by blaming the victim, including the bereaved and the infirm. James Moore, *Post-Shoah Dialogues* (2004, p. 232) previously used this same term to mean "evil [committed] by man." The essay on pastoral care by Rabbi Myriam Klotz (see Bibliography) is a rare example of the utilization of the Book of Job in a handbook on pastoral care. To be more precise, the Book of Job is not about the vocation of rabbis and other clergy that includes visiting the sick and the bereaved. In fact, most of the Book of Job deals with the question of how *not* to behave when attempting to carry out the two most ubiquitous *mitzvot*, i.e., holy obligations, which the Jewish religion regards as incumbent upon all people – regardless of their vocation – with respect to the sick and the bereaved among us. It would seem to be very simple: one needs no *shofar*, no *lulav* and no *mazzah*, not even a prayerbook. One needs only to know when to keep one's mouth shut. This was a lesson, which some of the greatest of the sages of antiquity – Eliphaz, Bildad, and Zophar – learned only after God Almighty emerged from the whirlwind to rebuke them for the untoward consequences of their very, very good intentions.

In Halakhah and Liturgy

Mishnah, *Bava Meẓia* 4:10 asserts that just as there is defrauding (and some translate overreaching; the Hebrew term is *hona'ah* or *ona'ah*) in commerce so is there defrauding in speech. Tosefta, *Bava Meẓia* 3:25, followed by Babylonian Talmud, *Bava Meẓia* 58b, explains that defrauding in speech is exemplified by a person who in response to someone else's suffering, becoming sick, and/or having the misfortune of having his children predecease her/him says to that person as did Job's friends, "Is not your piety your confidence, Your integrity your hope? Think now, what innocent person ever perished," quoting Eliphaz to Job in 4:6–7. The *halakhah* thus canonizes the view of Job and of God as portrayed in 42:7 that such despicable verbal behavior is an offense against the Torah.

As noted above, the initial silence of the friends of Job recorded in 2:13 until Job himself had spoken in 3:1–16 is cited as the inspiration for the rule set forth in TB, *Mo'ed Katan* 28b and canonized in Shulḥan Arukh, *Yoreh De'ah* 376:1 that would-be comforters not address the mourner until the mourner indicates either verbally or nonverbally that she/he would like to be addressed.

Shulḥan Arukh, *Oraḥ Ḥayyim* 492 canonizes a medieval practice of observing three successive fasts on the first Monday-Thursday-Monday following the New Moon of Marheshvan in order to atone for any minor sin committed during the jolly festival of Sukkot (Tabernacles) and a similar three successive fasts on the first Monday-Thursday-Monday following the New Moon of Iyyar to atone for any minor sin committed during the jolly festival of Passover. The two series of three fasts are called *behab* (בה"ב) following the Hebrew numerals designating Monday-Thursday-Monday. The inspiration for these fasts of atonement is Job's offering sacrifice at the end of each of his children's series of parties, for "perhaps my children have sinned and blasphemed God in their thoughts" (1:5); see J.D. Eisenstein, *Digest of Laws and Customs* (Heb., 1917), pp. 35–36.

The daily service in the synagogue begins with the benediction, Praised are You, O Lord, our God, king of the world, who gave the rooster the discernment to distinguish between day and night. According to TB, *Berakhot* 60b this benediction is to be recited upon hearing the sound of the rooster at dawn. This benediction is based upon Job 38:36 where God addresses to Job the rhetorical question, "Who gave wisdom to the ibis//or who gave discernment to the rooster?" (See extensive discussion in Gordis 1978, pp. 452–453.)

Just as the daily service in the synagogue begins with a quotation from the Book of Job so does virtually every service conclude with the Mourner's Kaddish, whose last line quotes Job 25:2b, "He establishes peace in the heavens." The very same utterance, with which the Mourner's Kaddish invokes Job 25, namely, "May He who establishes peace in the heavens establish peace among us and upon all Israel, and say, 'Amen,'" is recited silently by individuals at the conclusion of the *Amidah, and it is recited also at the close of the *Grace After Meals.

[Mayer I. Gruber (2nd ed.)]

In the Aggadah

The rabbis were fascinated and troubled by Job, as is evident in the large number of *aggadot* about him. A primary concern is when Job lived. Opinions expressed in Bava Batra 14b–16b include the time of Abraham, the time of the tribes (when he married Jacob's daughter Dinah), the time of the Exodus, the period of the Judges, and the return of the exiles from Babylon. He is said to have been contemporaneous with both the Queen of Sheba and Ahasuerus. Some said Job never existed and his story is an allegory. The most widespread rabbinic view is that Job lived in the time of Moses and served as an advisor to Pharaoh (see below).

A closely linked question is whether Job was a Jew or a gentile. Some say that he was "a righteous proselyte" and "one of the seven gentile prophets," others that "he was an Israelite" and that *halakhah* can even be deduced from him. Most rabbinic opinion presents Job as a righteous gentile and sages praise his positive qualities, including modesty and hospitality. Nevertheless, this admirable non-Jew falls short in comparisons to Abraham (ARN², 7; BB 16a). Abraham is said to have served God out of love while Job served God only out of fear of losing his reward (TJ, Ber. 14b), although others disagree (Mish. Sot. 5:5 and TJ, Sot. 20c). Resolution is achieved in Sotah 31a, where a tradition attributed to R. Meir equates "fearing God" with "loving God" for both Abraham and Job.

Job's sufferings are explained variously. According to TB, Sotah 11a, Job joined Balaam and Jethro in advising Pharaoh on how to deal with the enslaved children of Israel. Balaam, who advised slaying male children, was himself slain. Job, who remained silent, was sentenced to suffering. Jethro, who fled, became a proselyte to Judaism (similarly TB, Sanh.106a; Exod. R. 27:3). Job is also accused of questioning divine justice in his heart, even before his actual afflictions began (TB, BB 16a–b).

Rabbinic ambivalence towards Job is based not only on the difficulties of the book of Job, itself, but on the predominant identification of Job as a gentile. Job's complaints during his suffering are frequently compared unfavorably to the endurance of the patriarchs, kings, and prophets of Israel who faced far greater trials (Deut. R. 2:4; Pes. R. 47). Some sages explain Job's restoration with the claim that "the Holy One doubled his reward in this world in order to banish him from the world to come" (TB, BB 15b). Conversely, *Pesikta Rabbati* links Job's punishments and redemption with the chastisements and ultimate consolation of the Jewish people (26:7, 29/30).

There may be an element of anti-Christian polemic in rabbinic efforts to denigrate Job, or in contrast, to claim him as a Jew. Such approaches, already in tannaitic sources, may be responding to Christian portrayals of Job as a patient sufferer and to Job's inclusion in Christian constructions of a pre-existent community of gentile priests outside the nation of Israel. Evidence of disputes over Job's identity appears in one of the letters of the Church Father *Jerome, where he identifies Job as descended from Esau and not Levi, "although the Hebrews declare the contrary" (Lt. 73).

[Judith R. Baskin (2nd ed.)]

In Islam

Ayyūb (Job) is briefly mentioned in several suras as the servant of Allah who underwent hardship (4:161; 21:83–84; 38:40–43); Allah therefore restored all of the fortune which he had lost. Post-Koranic literature greatly enlarges on the descriptions taken from the Bible and the Midrashim. As in Jewish literature, there are various opinions as to Ayyūb's origin and the period during which he lived. Some believe that he was a *Rūmī*, that is, an Edomite, and that he lived during the days of Lot, Abraham, Jacob, or Ephraim son of Joseph. His wife was Leah(!), the daughter (!) of Jacob (Gen. R. 57:4, Dinah, the daughter of Jacob was the wife of Job). Ayyūb died at the age of 93. His son Bishr succeeded him as prophet and was known as Dhū al-Kifl. It is interesting that many of the legends about Ayyūb are connected with the immediate environs of Jerusalem, Transjordan, and Hauran, and the vicinity of Damascus.

[Haïm Z'ew Hirschberg]

In the Arts

IN LITERATURE. The sorely tried Job, canonized by the medieval Church, has inspired far more literary, artistic, and musical work by Christians than by Jews. Two of the earliest treatments in literature were the *Mystère de Job* (part of the famous *Mistère du Viel Testament*, 1478?) and *L'Hystore Job*, a French verse adaptation of the *Compendium in Job* by Pierre de Blois. The Book of Job contains all the stuff of drama – man's struggle to understand the reason for injustice in the world – which should have made it a natural choice for Protestant writers of the 16th and 17th centuries. However, Job's very perfection and his daring and blasphemous questioning of God led to widespread neglect of the theme. Among the very few works on the subject to appear in the 16th century were the *Meistersinger* Hans Sachs's play *Der Hiob* (1547); Ralph (Robert) Radcliffe's biblical drama *Job's Afflictions* (c. 1550); and Robert Greene's *The Historie of Job* (1594). *Job*, a drama of the same period, is one of the few surviving literary works in Romansch (Rhaeto-Romance) and was published in 1896. Rather more interest was shown in the theme during the 17th century. In Spain, the Marrano playwright Felipe *Godínez published *La gran Comedia de los trabajos de Job* (1638) and Pedro Calderón de la Barca devoted one of his *autos sacramentales* to the subject.

The subject acquired more significance in literature from the early 19th century onward. Works based directly on the theme include *Az ember tragédiája* ("The Tragedy of Man," 1862) by the Hungarian writer Imre Madách; *Hiob* (1866), a drama by Johann Adolf Philipp Zapf; *Giobbe* (1872), a five-act Italian tragedy by Marco Wahltuch; and a dramatic poem (1898) by the Romanian author G. Gârbea. One outcome of the controversy roused by the biblical criticism of Ernest *Renan was a curious work by the French Socialist philosopher Pierre-Henri Leroux – *Job, drame en cinq actes… par le Prophète Isaie, retrouvé, rétabli dans son intégrité, et traduit littéralement sur le texte hébreu …* (1886). During the first decade of the 20th century there were some interesting treatments in German: *Geschichte des Heimkehrenden (Das Buch Joram*; 1905), a pastiche by Rudolf Borchardt; *Sphinx und Strohmann* (1907) reissued as *Hiob* (1917), a drama by the painter and author Oskar Kokoschka; and *Der Blumenhiob* (1909), a novel by Hans Kyser. In Germany, works on the theme included Fritz Weege's modern miracle play, *Das Spiel Hiob* (1926) and Bartholomaeus Ponholzer's religious drama, *Job, der fromme Idealist* (1927). Three other modern interpretations were the Swedish writer Karin Maria Boye's unfinished cantata, *De sju dödssynderna* ("The Seven Deadly Sins," 1941), on the theodicy issue; H. de Bruin's Dutch epic, *Job* (1944); and Giovanni Battista Angioletti's Italian dialogue drama, *Giobbe, uomo solo* (1955). Two of the most original and interesting modern treatments were those by the U.S. writers Robert Frost and Archibald MacLeish. Frost's *A Masque of Reason* (1945), a poetic drama in the guise of an apocryphal chapter of the Book of Job, humanized the story without robbing it of essential dignity. MacLeish's *J.B.* (1958), a verse play that won the Pulitzer Prize, made the hero a prosperous businessman whose life is shattered by a series of disasters. Reversing the arguments in the Bible, MacLeish has J.B.'s plausible comforters (a clergyman, a scientist, and a Marxist) exonerate him, while he insists on condemning himself. Among the very few Jewish writers who turned to the subject were the Austrian novelist Joseph *Roth, author of *Hiob* (1930; *Job: The Story of a Simple Man*, 1931); the Egyptian Karaite Murād *Faraj, whose *Ayyūb* (1950) was a prose version in rhymed Arabic; the Yiddish writer H.

*Leivick, who published the dramatic poem *In di Teg fun Iyov* (c. 1953); and the French author Henri *Hertz, whose short story "Ceux de Job" (in *Tragedies des temps volages*, 1955) describes the grandeur and despair of the Jewish experience.

IN ART. In art, Job has been a popular subject since early Christian times. In the Middle Ages he was regarded as the type of the suffering Jesus, the persecuted Church, or of the Christian soul's endurance. He was portrayed sitting covered with boils, half-naked on a "dungheap," as the Septuagint picturesquely mistranslated "ashes" (Job 2:8). Sometimes Job sat on a tortoise, the symbol of patience. He was afflicted by Satan with sore boils (Job 2:7), reproached by his wife (Job 2:9–10), and visited by Three Friends (Job 2:11). All these events are represented in illustrations of Job's ordeal. The reproaches of his wife were expanded in medieval pious literature and miracle plays, with the result that she came to be depicted as a shrew; and Job's Three Friends were sometimes shown mocking him by playing musical instruments (see below). Cycles of paintings or sculpture illustrating the trials of Job include 13th-century carvings from Chartres and Rheims and *The Story of Job* (1480–83), a 15th-century painting by the Master of the Legend of St. Barbara (Cologne Museum). The subject was treated in an altarpiece by Rubens for the Church of St. Nicholas, Brussels, and in a series of watercolors and engravings by the English poet and painter William *Blake which include *Job Laughed to Scorn* (Job 30). The destruction of Job's children (Job 1:18–19) is shown in a crowded painting by Bernart van Orley (c. 1491–1542; Brussels Museum). Figures of the suffering Job, alone or accompanied by his wife and friends, or afflicted by the Devil, are found in early Christian frescoes from the Roman catacombs and from the graveyard of St. Peter and St. Marcellino; and on Roman sarcophagi. From the ninth century onward, other figures appear in Byzantine and European manuscripts, including the 12th-century Admont Bible (Vienna State Library) and the *Hortus Deliciarum*. At Chartres, there is a 13th-century carving of the ulcerated Job sitting on his dungheap and watched by his family. A demon places his right hand on Job's bald head and his left hand under his foot, in accordance with the biblical description: "So Satan went forth from the presence of the Lord, and smote Job with sore boils from the sole of his foot even unto his crown" (Job 2:7). There is also a 13th-century bas-relief at Notre Dame, Paris. From the 15th century onward there are impressive German woodcarvings and an illumination by Jean Fouquet to the *Hours* of Etienne Chevalier (Musée Condé, Chantilly). During the Renaissance, the subject was mainly popular in northern Europe. It was represented in the wings of the Jabach altarpiece by Duerer (Staedel Institute, Frankfurt, and Cologne Museum), in which Job's wife is shown dousing her husband with a pail of water. It also appears in the work of Dutch and Flemish painters, in carved choirstalls at Amiens, and in French *Books of Hours*. In the 17th century, the subject was treated by the Spanish masters Murillo and Ribera (both paintings are in the Parma Pinacotheca); by Georges de La Tour in a characteristic night scene also thought to represent St. Peter released from prison by an angel; and by *Rembrandt in a pen and ink drawing. Modern representations of Job include those by Max *Liebermann and Yehuda Epstein.

IN MUSIC. Among the saintly patrons of music and the professional musician, "Saint Job" appeared – suddenly, but prominently – during the 14th–18th centuries in France, Germany, and England, and especially in Holland and Belgium. The tradition is thought to derive from an interpretation of Job's complaint: "Therefore is my harp (*kinnor*) turned to mourning, and my pipe (*uggav*) into the voice of them that weep" (Job 30:31); another possible source lies in the Job mystery plays, which were themselves largely based on the apocryphal *Testament of Job*. All these traditions are reflected in the many paintings and illustrations which show Job being consoled (and sometimes also mocked – cf. Job 30: 1, 7, 9, 14) by musicians, mostly wind-instrument players. Where the musicians were three in number, a conflation with the motif of the Three Friends is sometimes noticeable (for a survey of the subject see: V. Denis, in MGG, 6 (1957), 458–60). Motet collections of the first half of the 16th century include a number of settings from the Book of Job (by C. de Sermisy, P. de La Rue, L. Senfl, L. Morales, T. Crecquillon, and J. Clemens non Papa), mainly of the sadder verses, a symptom of the early Baroque period's emphasis on demonstrative repentance scenes. These treatments culminate in Orlando di Lasso's two extended settings: *Sacrae lectiones novem ex propheta Hiob* (1565, repr. 10 times by 1587), for four voices; and *Lectiones sacrae ex libris Hiob excerptae musicis numeris* (1582), also for four voices. The first setting is extremely pathetic, the second more restrained. Further settings of the period were those by Jacobus Gallus (Handl) and Joachim à Burck (1610).

From about the turn of the century, Protestant composers increasingly favored the half-verse "I know that my Redeemer liveth" (Job 19:25), of which there are two settings by Heinrich Schuetz. The rise of the oratorio form had meanwhile produced several works on the subject (by G. Carissimi and P. d'Albergatti). The authenticity of Bach's Cantata no. 160, *Ich weiss dass mein Erloeser lebt*, has sometimes been doubted. The most famous setting of this text is the contralto aria, *I know that my Redeemer liveth*, in G.F. Handel's *Messiah* (1742); its opening is engraved on the scroll held by Roubillac's statue of Handel on the composer's grave in Westminster Abbey. There were a few oratorios on the theme in the 19th century. Frederick Shepherd Converse's *Job* (performed in Worcester, 1907; and Hamburg, 1908) was one of the first works by a U.S. composer to be presented in Europe. There has been a marked predilection for the subject in the 20th century, probably because of its philosophical connotations. Ralph Vaughan Williams' *Job; a masque for dancing* (1927–30), based on a libretto by Sir Geoffrey Keynes and Gwen Raverat, was composed for the Ballet Rambert and here the decor and the dancers' movements follow Blake's illustrations. Vaughan Williams later adapted a suite for orchestra and "The Voice out of the Whirlwind," for choir and organ, from this work. For Nicolas Nabokov's oratorio *Job* (1932), Jacques *Maritain adapted the text from the Bible. Other modern works include György Kósa's *Hiob* (cantata, 1933); Hugo Chaim *Adler's *Hiob* (oratorio, 1933); Lehman Engel's *Four Excerpts from "Job"* (for voice and piano, 1932); and Luigi Dallapiccola's *Giobbe* (oratorio – also for scenic performance – 1949).

[Bathja Bayer]

ADD. BIBLIOGRAPHY: ARAMAIC VERSIONS (TARGUM): *Le Targum de Job de la Grotte XI de Qumran* (1971); *The Targum to Job from Qumran Cave XI*, ed. M. Sokoloff (1974); D.M. Stec, *The Text of the Targum of Job: An Introduction and Critical Edition* 1994); D. Shepherd, *Targum and Translation* (2004). COMMENTARIES: MEDIEVAL: Rashi; Ibn Ezra; and Ralbag (in the standard Rabbinic Bible). **ADD. BIBLIOGRAPHY:** Saadiah ben Joseph (892–942 C.E.), *The Book of Theodicy: Commentary on the Book of Job*, trans. L.E. Goodman (1988); *El Commentario de Abraham ibn Ezra al Libro de Job*, ed. M.G. Aranda (2004); *The Book of Job with the Commentaries of Rashi, Rabbenu Jacob ben Meir Tam, and a Disciple of Rashi*, ed. A. Shoshana (Heb., 1990); *The Commentary of Rabbi Samuel Ben Meir (Rashbam) on the Book of Job*, ed. S. Japhet (Heb., 2000), includes extensive bibliography; *Le commentaire sur Job de Rabbi Yoseph Qara* (1978); *A Commentary on the Book of Job: From a Hebrew Manuscript in the University Library, Cambridge*, ed. W.A. Wright (1906); *Commentary Eines Anonymous zu Buche Hiob*, ed. A. Sulzbach (1911); and see R. Harris in JQR, 96 (2005), 163–81; Samuel ben Nissim Masnuth, *Majan-Gannim: Commentary on the Book of Job*, ed. S. Buber (Heb., 1889); Commentary on Job by Ramban (= Moses Naḥmanides; 1194–1270) edited from manuscripts with supercommentary in *Collected Works of Nahmanides*, vol. 1, ed. C. Chavel (1963), 9–128 (Heb.; 1963); idem, *The Gate of Reward*, trans. and annotated by C.B. Chavel (1983); *The Commentary of Levi ben Gerson on the Book of Job*, trans. A.L. Lassen (1946). AFTER 1920: S.R. Driver and G.B. Gray (ICC, 1921, 1950); E.J. Kissane (Eng., 1946^2); S.L. Terrien (Eng., 1954); N.H. Tur-Sinai (Heb., 1952; Eng., 1967); G. Fohrer (Ger., 1963); A. Hakham (Heb., 1970); M.H. Pope (Eng., 1973^3), includes bibliography; R. Gordis (Eng., 1978), includes bibliography. **ADD. BIBLIOGRAPHY:** N.C. Habel (Eng., 1985); J.C. Hartley (Eng., 1988); J. Klein et al. (Heb., 1993); E. Dhorme (Eng., 1967); D.J.A. Clines (Eng., 1989); M.I. Gruber, in: A. Berlin and M.Z. Bretler (eds.), *Jewish Study Bible* (2003). STUDIES: N.H. Torczyner (Tur-Sinai), *Das Buch Hiob* (1920); F. Buhl, in: BZAW, 41 (1925), 52–61; W.L. Batten, in: *Anglican Theological Review*, 15 (1933), 125–8; A. Alt, in: ZAW, 55 (1937), 265–8; S. Spiegel, in: *L. Ginzberg Jubilee Volume* (1945), 323–36 (Eng. section); W.B. Stevenson, *The Poem of Job* (1948^2); M.H. Segal, in: *Tarbiz*, 20 (1950), 35–48; H.A. Fine, in: JBL, 14 (1955), 28–32; N.M. Sarna, in: JBL, 76 (1957), 13–25; H.L. Ginsberg, in: *Leshonenu*, 21 (1957), 259–64; idem, in: *Conservative Judaism*, 21 (1967), 12–28; idem, in: VTS, 17 (1969), 88–111; idem, in: *Ereẓ-Israel*, 9 (1969), 49–50, 220. **ADD. BIBLIOGRAPHY:** Y. Hoffman, *Blemished Perfection* (1996); M. Weiss, *The Story of Job's Beginnings* (an innovative study of the prose prologue of the Book of Job; 1983 in Hebrew); E.L. Greenstein, in: L. Mazor (ed.), *Job in the Bible, Philosophy and Art* (Hebrew, 1995), 43–53; idem, in: M.V. Fox et al. (ed.), *Texts, Temples, and Traditions* (1996), 241–58; idem, in: JBL, 122 (2003), 651–66; idem, in: E. van Wolde (ed.), *Job 28: Cognition in Context* (2003), 253–80; idem, in: S. Vargon et al. (ed.), *Studies in Bible and Exegesis in honor of Menahem Cohen* (2005), 245–62; C. Newsom, *The Book of Job* (2003). THE MESSAGE AND MEANING: S.B. Freehof, *The Book of Job* (1958); R. Gordis, *The Book of God and Man* (1965); R. Marcus, in: *Review of Religion*, 14 (1949–50), 5–29; M. Buber, *The Prophetic Faith* (1949), 94ff.; H.H. Rowley, *From Moses to Qumran* (1963), 141–83; M. Tsevat, in: HUCA, 37 (1966), 73–103; S. Terrien, *Job, Poet of Existence* (1957); **ADD. BIBLIOGRAPHY:** R.P. Scheindlin, *The Book of Job* (1998); N.M. Glatzer, *The Dimensions of Job: A Study and Selected Readings* (1969); *The Book of Job: A New Translation* with introductions by M. Greenberg; J.C. Greenfield; and N.M. Sarna (1980); M.I. Gruber, in: M. Lubetski et al. (ed.), *Boundaries of the Ancient Near Eastern World* (1998), 88–102; idem, in: *Journal of Psychology and Judaism*, 22 (1998), 51–64. IN RABBINIC LITERATURE: Ginzberg, Legends, 2 (1910) 223–42; 5 (1925), 381–90; and see especially TB, *Bava Batra* 14a–16b. **ADD. BIBLIOGRAPHY:** J.R. Baskin, in: L.G. Perdue and W. Clark Gilpin (ed.), *The Voice from the Whirlwind* (1992); idem, *Pharaoh's Counsellors: Job, Jethro and Balaam in Rabbinic and Patristic Tradition* (1983); H. Mack, *Job and the Book of Job in Rabbinic Literature* (2004; Heb.). IN JEWISH LITURGY: **ADD. BIBLIOGRAPHY:** M.I. Gruber, in: *Review of Rabbinic Judaism*, 6 (2003), 87–100. IN THE AGGADAH: **ADD. BIBLIOGRAPHY:** J.R. Baskin. *Pharaoh's Counsellors* (1983). ANCIENT NEAR EASTERN PARALLELS: **ADD. BIBLIOGRAPHY:** W.G. Lambert, *Babylonian Wisdom Literature* (1960); S.N. Kramer, in: VTS, 3, 170–82; J. Nougayrol, in: RB, 59 (1952), 239–250; M. Weinfeld, "Job and Its Mesopotamian Parallels," in: W. Classen (ed.), *Text and Context* (1988), 217–218; G. von Rad, in: *The Problem of the Hexateuch* (1966), 281–91; Newsom, 72–89. IN PASTORAL CARE: **ADD. BIBLIOGRAPHY:** M. Klotz, "Wrestling Blessings: A Pastoral Response to Suffering," in: D.A. Friedman (ed.), *Jewish Pastoral Care* (2001), 35–59. JOB'S MOTHER: I. Pardes, in: C. Meyers, T. Craven, and R.S. Kraemer (ed.), *Women in Scripture* (2002), 292. JOB'S SISTER AND MOTHER AND FATHER: C. Meyers, in: *ibid.*, 294. JOB'S SISTERS AND BROTHERS: C. Meyers, in: *ibid.*, 296. JOB'S WIFE: E.L. Greenstein, in *Beit Mikra*, 49 (2004), 19–31 (in Hebrew); M.I. Gruber, in: *Scriptura*, 87 (2004), 261–66; I. Pardes, in: C. Meyers, T. Craven, and R.S. Kraemer (ed.), *Women in Scripture* (2002), 292. JOB'S DAUGHTERS: I. Pardes, in: *ibid.*, (2002), 99–100, 107, 108, 292; Z. Ben-Barak, *Inheritance by Daughters in Israel and the Ancient Near East* (Heb.; 2003). JOB'S SERVING GIRLS AND MALE SERVANTS: C. Meyers, in: *Women in Scripture*, 294. GESTURE LANGUAGE IN THE BOOK OF JOB: M.I. Gruber, *Aspects of Nonverbal Communication in the Ancient Near East* (2 vols.; 1980); idem, *The Motherhood of God and Other Studies* (1992). IN ISLAM: Tabarī, *Ta'rīkh* (1357 AH), 226–8; Thaʿlabī, *Qiṣaṣ* (1356 AH), 128–37; Kisa'ī, *Qiṣaṣ*, ed. by I. Eisenberg (1922), 179–89; Yāqūt, *Muʿjam al-Buldān* (1323 AH), s.v. Dayr Ayyūb; M. Gruenbaum, *Neue Beitraege zur semitischen Sagenkunde* (1893), 262ff.; H. Speyer, *Biblische Erzaehlungen…* (1961), 410–2; D. Sidersky, *Origines des légendes musulmanes* (1933), 69–72; EI; Maqdisī, in: *Bibliotheca Geographorum Arabicorum*, 3 (1906), 171. **ADD. BIBLIOGRAPHY:** A. Jeffrey, "Ayyūb," in: EIS^2, 1 (1960), 795–96 (incl. bibl.). IN LITERATURE: **ADD. BIBLIOGRAPHY:** H.M. Kallen, *The Book of Job as a Greek Tragedy* (1918; 1959^2); E. Weitzner, *The Book of Job: A Paraphrase* (1960).

JOB, TESTAMENT OF (Gr. Διαθήκη τοῦ Ιωβ), Greek pseudepigraphon purporting to reveal the secrets and last wishes of *Job. In its present form the Testament of Job is closely linked with the Greco-Jewish historian *Aristeas, who flourished about 100 B.C.E., and with the Greek version of Job. It is likely, however, that a Hebrew or Aramaic model was known to the author(s) of the Testament of Job. This explains the Palestinian background of certain terms as well as the kinship with such works as the Testaments of the Twelve *Patriarchs and *Jubilees.

The author(s) of the Testament of Job aimed to present a Job who would conform to the stringent ideals of the pietistic sects more than the canonical figure. Omitting the lengthy discourses, they are a richer narrative than found in Scripture. By making Job the narrator and by introducing hymns and a chorus, the work frequently resembles a Greek tragedy. The integrity of the work, however, has been compromised by later additions. The double self-identifications, first as Job and afterward as Jobab (Gen. 36:33), and the allusions to missing sections suggest that parts of the book are abridgments of a larger pseudepigraphon. The view that a Christian retouched this book is to be rejected since no Christian would have invented a Jesus-like Job. More likely is the link of the original version of the Testament of Job with the Qumran sect, and the present Greek text with the *Therapeutae of Alexandria. The Palestinian version was probably the source of the talmudic traditions about Job.

Despite the unsatisfactory state of the text, the Testament of Job tells a moving story. Jobab (Job) the son of Esau, the king of Edom, reveals his secrets to his seven sons and three daughters by his second wife Dinah, Jacob's daughter. It is God who instigates the antagonism between Job and Satan. An archangel tells Job that the Lord wishes him to destroy the popular shrine where the people worshiped Satan's image. Job is forewarned that Satan will avenge the wrong done to him, but he is also promised that, if he endures Satan's trials, his final exaltation is assured. Job now assumes an even higher role than that ascribed to Abraham. He becomes a protagonist in God's struggle against evil. Describing his own remarkable deeds of charity and hospitality, Job relates how Satan disguised himself as a beggar to gain entrance into his home. Failing in his purpose, Satan succeeds in persuading the king of Persia to besiege Job's city. Job's fellow citizens pillage his palace, killing his ten children by his first wife, Sitis. Again with God's permission, Satan, appearing in the form of a whirlwind, smites Job with a plague, ulcers, and worms (cf. Genesis Apocryphon, 20:16ff.). The hero's patience is exemplified by his putting back on his body every single worm that crawled off. Suffering from hunger, Sitis (etymologically related perhaps to Satan or *sotah*, "unfaithful wife") unknowingly barters her hair to Satan for three loaves of bread, whereupon she addresses Job: "The feebleness of my heart has crushed my bones, rise then and take these loaves of bread and enjoy them, and speak some word against the Lord and die" (Job 2:9). Job realizes that it is Satan who is speaking through Sitis' mouth. After selling herself into slavery, Sitis reappears momentarily as Jobab's royal friends come to visit him. She begs them to dig up her ten sons from the ruins, but Job refuses permission, saying that they are now in the presence of God. When Sitis dies in her master's stable, Satan speaks through Elihu, who unjustifiably upbraids Job for his overbearing pride and boasting. The evil Elihu is thereupon damned in a long hymn led by Eliphaz. In the last part of the book (which may be an addition by another hand), the angels come to take Job's soul. He divides his possessions among his sons, but to his daughters he offers miraculous belts which would enable them to bless the approaching angels. Although it was quoted in James 5:11, Pope Gelasius I (492–496) removed the Testament of Job from the apocrypha, as a result of which it was lost, and recovered only in the 19th century. Its novel characterization of the antagonists, its lively use of dialogue, and deep understanding of human feeling make the Testament of Job a classic among the perennial attempts to reinterpret the meaning of the most tragic of biblical figures.

BIBLIOGRAPHY: M.R. James, *Apocrypha Anecdota*, Series 2 (1897), lxxii–cii, 104–37; R.H. Pfeiffer, *History of New Testament Times* (1949), 70–72; M. Philonenko, in: *Semitica*, 8 (1958), 41–53; EM, 5 (1968), 1119.

[Ben Zion Wacholder]

JOCHEBED (Heb. יוֹכֶבֶד), wife of Amram and mother of Moses, Aaron, and Miriam (Num. 26:59). Exodus 2, which describes the birth of Moses, does not name her, or, for that matter, the father or sister of Moses. She is described as the daughter of Levi, born to him in Egypt (Num. 26:59; cf. Ex. 2:1), and thus was Amram's paternal aunt (Ex. 6:20). Marriage with an aunt violates the law of Leviticus 18: 12. This is in keeping with biblical traditions that trace the birth or ancestry of important figures to sexual relations generally prohibited: Abraham and Sarah, his half-sister (Lev. 18:9); Judah and Tamar, his daughter-in-law (Lev. 15:15); Jacob and the two sisters Rachel and Leah (Lev. 18:18); and the marriage of the Moabite Ruth to Boaz (Deut. 23:4). The meaning of the name is problematic. No personal name formed with the component *yo* (Heb. יוֹ) is otherwise attested before the time of Moses.

[Nahum M. Sarna / S. David Sperling (2nd ed.)]

In the Aggadah

Jochebed was so called because her face was like the *ziv hakavod* ("splendor of glory"; Mid. Hag. Gen. 23:1). She was born during the journey of the children of Israel to Egypt (Gen. R. 94:9). She was therefore 130 when she gave birth to Moses. Despite this she is called the "daughter" of Levi (Ex. 2:1) because her youth returned to her, her skin becoming smooth and the wrinkles of age disappearing (Gen. R. 94:9). She gave birth to Moses after she had remarried her husband who had divorced her because of the decree that all male children be killed. Her second marriage was as happy as her first; Amram placed her in a palanquin and Aaron and Miriam danced before her (Sot. 12b). Due to her righteousness, the birth of Moses was a painless one, indicating that she had been excluded from the decree against the descendants of Eve (cf. Gen. 3:16; Sot. 12b).

Jochebed is identified with *Shiphrah (Ex. 1:15), because the Israelites were fruitful – *she-peru* – in her days (Sot. 11b), and with Jehudijah the Jewess (I Chron. 4:18), because she brought Jews into the world (Lev. R. 1:13). The "houses" given to the two Hebrew midwives (Ex. 1:21) means that she was destined to become the ancestress of the priestly family (Ex. R.

1:17). She survived all her children and was permitted to enter Ereẓ Israel with Joshua when she was 250 (SOR 9).

BIBLIOGRAPHY: Noth, *Personennamen*, 111; H. Bauer, in: ZAW, 51 (1933), 92ff.; J.J. Stamm, *Die akkadische Namengebung* (1939), 135; H.H. Rowley, *From Joseph to Joshua* (1948), 71, 73, 136, 159ff. IN THE AGGADAH: Ginzberg, Legends, index; I. Ḥasida, *Ishei ha-Tanakh* (1964), 183. **ADD. BIBLIOGRAPHY:** R. Burns, in: ABD, 3:871–72; W. Propp, *Exodus 1–18* (AB; 1998), 276–78.

JOCHELSON, VLADIMIR (Waldemar; 1855–1937), Russian anthropologist. Born and educated in the Rabbinical Institute in Vilna, together with Zundelevich and Liberman he organized there in 1872 a group to study revolutionary literature. In 1879 Jochelson became involved in the revolutionary movement of "Narodnia Volia," working in the underground laboratory which prepared dynamite and false passports. In 1880 he immigrated to Switzerland, where he headed the movement's printing shop in Geneva. In 1885 he tried to cross the border back to Russia, but he was arrested and sentenced to three years imprisonment and then ten years of exile in Siberia. Here Jochelson became interested in the study of the native peoples of the region and in scientific ethnography, as did his fellow prisoners Vladimir *Bogoraz and Lev *Sternberg with whom he was to be associated in a lifetime of work in this discipline. Their articles on the nomadic tribes in the area began to attract attention. By special permission Jochelson and Bogoraz were attached to the Yakut expedition organized by the Russian Geographic Society (1894–97) and studied the ethnology of the northern districts of the Yakut provinces of Verkhoyansky and Kolyma. After the Bolshevik revolution Jochelson became professor of ethnology at the University of Leningrad.

Jochelson participated in the Jesup North Pacific expedition under the auspices of the American Museum of Natural History and engaged in an investigation of the Koryak of the Sea of Okhotsk and Yukaghir of the Kolyma district. Jochelson prepared studies on the Yukaghir, the natives of the Kolymsk and Virkhoian regions, which were published in *Izvestia* on his return to St. Petersburg. Subsequently he participated in expeditions to Kamtchatka and later to other sites in East Asia and Alaska. Later he left Russia and spent his last years in the United States working for the American Museum of Natural History, endeavoring to complete his work on the Yukaghir ethnology. His stance in ethnology, like that of his associate Bogoraz, was that of a positivist and naturalist.

BIBLIOGRAPHY: Krader, in: L-ESS, 2 (1968), 116–9.

[Ephraim Fischoff / Shmuel Spector (2nd ed.)]

JOCHSBERGER, TZIPORA (1920–), composer, musicologist, and educator; founder of the Israel Musical Heritage Project. Born in Leuterhausen, Germany, Jochsberger entered the Palestine Academy of Music, now the Rubin Academy for Music and Dance, in 1939, where she studied piano and trained as a music teacher. She later earned an M.A. (1959) and Ph.D. (1972) in Jewish music from the Jewish Theological Seminary. Her many books include *Bekol Zimra: A Collection of Jewish Choral Music* (1966) and *A Harvest of Jewish Song* (1980). Jochsberger hosted and produced three 13-part television series, *Music of the Jewish People* (1976); *Experiences in Jewish Music* (1977); and *A Kaleidoscope of Jewish Music* (1978). She was also executive producer of an 11-part documentary video series, *A People and Its Music* (from 1991), devoted to the musical traditions of a variety of Jewish communities. Her published musical compositions include *Four Hebrew Madrigals* and *A Call to Remember: Sacred Songs of the High Holidays.*

BIBLIOGRAPHY: M.B. Edelman. "Jochsberger, Tzipora," in: P.E. Hyman and D.D. Moore (eds.), *Jewish Women in America*, vol. 1 (1997), 701–2.

[Judith R. Baskin (2nd ed.)]

JOEL (Heb. יוֹאֵל; "YHWH is God"), the second book in the *Minor Prophets. The superscription of the book names the prophet Joel son of Pethuel as the author. No indication of the author's life, time, or place of residence is given, and the name of the prophet is not mentioned again either within the book itself or anywhere else in the Bible.

The four chapters of the book fall into two distinct parts:

(1) Chapters 1 and 2 give a vivid, graphic description of a plague of locusts of unprecedented severity which strikes the land like a marauding enemy, leaving in its wake ravished fields and vineyards, depriving the people of food and the sanctuary of its grain and wine offerings. Though most of the work is couched in literary images, the locusts are described realistically – even to their various forms, apparently stages in their development: there is the cutting insect (*gazam*), the swarming one (*ʾarbeh*), the hopping one (*yelek*, *yeleq*), and the destroying one (*ḥasil*) (1:4). The prophet exhorts the priests, the elders, and all the people to seek the Lord's mercy through repentance, fasting, and prayer. He promises that the Lord will have pity on His people, bringing an end to the plague, rains in their season, new blossoming and abundant harvests, and a time of fruitfulness and peace.

(2) Chapters 3 and 4 consist of a prophecy of the end of days, "of the great and awesome *Day of the Lord." Then the spirit of the Lord, the gift of prophecy and vision, will be poured out on all flesh, and awesome signs will be seen in the heavens and on earth. Only those "who call on the name of the Lord," the remnant of Israel who had remained true to Zion and Jerusalem, will escape total destruction. The Lord will gather all the nations into the valley of Jehoshaphat and deliver judgment on those who drove the people of Israel into exile, scattering them among the nations, on those who divided the land of the Lord among themselves; the land of the inhabitants of Tyre and Sidon and the regions of Philistia are singled out as those who sold the people of Judah and Jerusalem to the Greeks. The nations will be destroyed on the day of judgment; God will restore His exiled people, fructify His land, and avenge the blood spilled by Egypt and Edom.

Early and later commentators alike disagree on the connection between the two parts of the book, which, though remote from one another in content, are close in vocabulary and imagery – notably in the use of the phrase "the day of the Lord" (1: 15; 2:11 and 3:4; 4:14) and in the description of changes in the order of nature (2:2, 10 and 3:4; 4:15, 16). Among earlier scholars, Rothstein, Duhm, and Hölscher maintain that only chapters 1 and 2 can be attributed to the early Joel, while chapters 3 and 4 are the work of a post-exilic seer, and they include in this later composition even those verses from the first two chapters which deal with "the day of the Lord." Another opinion (held by Y. Kaufmann among others) holds that the entire book is an eschatological unity and the plague of locusts is a symbol heralding the day of judgment of the Lord, a view already found in the Aramaic Targum Jonathan. A third group of scholars (J. Wellhausen and K. Marti) believes that Joel composed the book after an actual plague of locusts, which he saw as a first sign of the approach of the end of days. It would therefore seem that "the day of the Lord" was not used with the same meaning in the first part of the book as in the second: in the first part it is simply a general name for the day of upheaval, while in the second it is the day when the nations shall be punished, the herald for Israel of the time to come (U. Cassuto). To come to some conclusion in this argument it is necessary to take account of the similarity of the imagery in both sections, which would appear to be convincing evidence of the unity of the book. There is no reason categorically to assume that a prophet who could give a realistic description of a plague of locusts could not on another occasion prophesy in a different spirit concerning the day of judgment and the end of days. More recently, Woolf analyzed Joel from a form-critical perspective and concluded that it is the work of a single author, with some later additions. On the basis of historical allusions, Cogan suggests a date in late 6th–early 5th century. The destruction and exile are fresh in memory (4:2); the temple is standing and there is no mention of royalty, only the priesthood. Cogan also demonstrates the familiarity of Joel with earlier biblical literature, as well as his artful use of the work of his predecessors (Cogan, 6–8), an indication of relative lateness.

The role of Greeks as buyers of slaves from the Sidonians and Philistines points in the same direction. The date of the Book of Joel still cannot be determined with certainty, and scholars differ by centuries in their estimations. Nonetheless, it is probably safe to accept Cogan's dating of the bulk of the book and to view Joel 4:4–8 as a fourth century interpolation.

In the Arts

The prophecies of Joel inspired some medieval artists and Renaissance composers, though scarcely any works of importance in literature. Joel announced an invasion of locusts, described as a people with lions' teeth (Joel 1: 1–6), which stripped the land of vegetation; later, however, there would be a period of abundance. His attributes in art are therefore a lion, a swarm of locusts, and a cornucopia. In another passage (Joel 2:1–12), he announced the day of the Lord and was therefore sometimes shown blowing a trumpet of judgment. The passage in which the prophet said that God would pour out His Spirit upon all flesh (Joel 3:1–2) caused him to figure in representations of the Pentecost. A mosaic in St. Mark's, Venice, and a fresco by Pinturiccio (1434–1513) in the Vatican show Joel holding 12 scrolls, representing the gospel preached by the 12 apostles in 12 languages, as a manifestation of the outpouring of the Spirit. The prophet was chiefly represented during the Middle Ages. He appears in medieval manuscripts, including the 12th-century *Hortus Deliciarum* (Strasbourg University Library), the Admont Bible (Vienna State Library), and the 14th-century French Bible of Robert de Bylling, illustrated by Jean Pucelle (Bibliothèque Nationale). Other representations include a statuette from the 12th-century Shrine of the Three Magi (Cologne Cathedral) and 13th-century carvings and stained glass. In the 16th century, Joel is represented by Michelangelo on the Sistine Chapel ceiling. He is shown seated, reading a scroll. In music there are several late 16th- and early 17th-century settings of *Canite tuba in Syon* (Joel 2:1). These catered for the predilection for festive compositions allowing "trumpet fanfare" imitations by the choir, and include motets by Regnart (printed 1568); and by Palestrina and Ingegneri (both printed in the collection *Corollarium Cantionum Sacrarum*, Nuremberg, 1590).

BIBLIOGRAPHY: A. Merx, *Die Prophetie des Joel und ihre Ausleger* (1879); S.R. Driver, *An Introduction to the Literature of the Old Testament* (19139), 307–19; J. Schmalohr, *Das Buch des Propheten Joel* (1922); G. Amon, *Die Abfassungszeit des Buches Joel* (1942); A.S. Kapelrud, *Joel Studies* (1948); T.H. Robinson, *Die Zwölf kleinen Propheten* (1954); Kaufmann Y., Toledot, 3 (1960) 334–47; W.O. Oesterley and T.H. Robinson, *An Introduction to the Books of the Old Testament* (19656), 355–63. **ADD. BIBLIOGRAPHY:** H.W. Woolf, *Joel and Amos* (1977); D. Stuart, *Hosea –Jonah* (Word Biblical Commentary; 1987), 222–71, extensive bibl.; T. Hiebert, in: ABD, 3:873–80, incl. bibl.; M. Cogan, in: *Joel and Amos* (1994; bibl. 11–15); K. Nash, in: DBI, 1:599–602, incl. bibl.

[*Encyclopaedia Hebraica* / S. David Sperling (2nd ed.)]

JOEL, SIR ASHER (1912–2004), Australian businessman and politician. Born in Sydney, Sir Asher Joel became a journalist and then a public relations consultant. He organized New South Wales's ceremonials for the coronation of King George VI in 1937 and, after the World War II (in which he was decorated) many public events in Sydney, including the opening of the Sydney Opera House in 1973. Joel served as an Independent and, later, a Country party member of the New South Wales Legislative Council from 1957 to 1978. He was knighted in 1974. Joel served on a wide variety of Jewish and pro-Israeli bodies in Sydney.

BIBLIOGRAPHY: W.D. Rubinstein, Australia II, 307.

[William D. Rubinstein (2nd ed.)]

JOEL, BILLY (1949–), U.S. singer and songwriter. Born in the Bronx, New York, Joel grew up in Levittown and went to high school in nearby Hicksville. The son of a Holocaust survivor who came to New York by way of Cuba, Joel first climbed the music charts with his self-confessed autobiographical sketch "Piano Man" (1976). This was followed by a series of eclectic hit singles such as "Just the Way You Are" (1977), "She's Always a Woman to Me" (1978), "It's Still Rock and Roll to Me" (1979), and "Allentown" (1981). Other popular songs of Joel's include "Honesty," "The Longest Time," "New York State of Mind," "Tell Her About It," "Uptown Girl," and "We Didn't Start the Fire." His albums were so successful, that by 1994 he was the only artist to have four albums at the septupleplatinum (7 million units) mark.

A musical based on Joel's music, called *Movin' Out*, debuted in Chicago in 2002 and then moved to Broadway. In 2003 it received 10 Tony nominations. Joel, who wrote the music, the lyrics, and did the orchestration, won a Tony for Best Orchestrations. Joel has won five Grammy Awards for his music, as well as receiving the Grammy Legend Award in 1990.

Joel went to Cuba in 1979 for a historic three-day musical event, Havana Jam, at the Karl Marx Theater in the Cuban capital. Then, in the summer of 1987, he made a significant cultural breakthrough by performing in Moscow and Leningrad, becoming the first American pop star to bring a fully staged rock production to the Soviet Union.

Joel has performed in many benefit concerts in support of a variety of causes, such as AIDS, the rainforest, earthquake relief, and the environment. In 1985 he headlined a benefit concert for the Long Island-based organization Charity Begins at Home; that year he also participated in the star-studded "We Are the World" recording; in 2001 he performed at the benefit Concert for New York City after 9/11. In 2002 he was named Music Cares' Person of the Year.

Among his other awards and accolades, Joel was inducted in the Songwriters Hall of Fame 1992. In 1994 he was awarded the Billboard Century Music Award. In 1997 he received ASCAP's Founder's Award for lifetime achievement. He was inducted into the Rock and Roll Hall of Fame in 1999 and, in the same year, received the Award of Merit from the American Music Awards. In 2000 he was presented with the Smithsonian Institution's James Smithson Bicentennial Medal. In 2001, the Songwriter's Hall of Fame bestowed on him its highest honor, the Johnny Mercer Award.

BIBLIOGRAPHY: M. McKenzie, *Billy Joel* (1985); J. Tamarkin, *Billy Joel: From Hicksville to Hitsville* (1984); P. Gambaccini, *Billy Joel: A Personal File* (1979).

[Ruth Beloff (2nd ed.)]

JOEL, DAVID HEYMANN (1815–1882), rabbi and scholar. Born in Inowroclaw (Poznan province), Joel studied under his father, a rabbi, and under R. Akiva *Eger. In 1836 he went to Berlin to continue his studies and took courses at the university. In 1842 he was ordained as a rabbi and in 1843 was appointed rabbi in Swarzedz (Poznan region). There he wrote his major work: *Midrash ha-Zohar: Die Religionsphilosophie des Sohar und ihr Verhaeltnis zur allgemeinen juedischen Theologie* (Leipzig, 1849). This book was one of the first Jewish studies which made a serious, scholarly approach to Kabbalah. Joel criticizes the work of A. Frank on Kabbalah and attempts to prove that there is no essential difference between Kabbalah as formulated in the Zohar and the Jewish theology current in the Middle Ages, the differences amounting only to the choice of daring metaphors in Kabbalah. Joel denies the decisive influence of Persian religion, Platonism or neoplatonism, Christianity, or Gnosis on the Kabbalah, which he regards as an original Jewish creation. From 1859 to 1879 Joel served as rabbi in Krostoszy, and from 1880 until his death was teacher of Talmud and rabbinic literature in the Jewish Theological Seminary of Breslau. There he wrote his valuable work, *Der Aberglaube und die Stellung des Judentums zu demselben*, of which only two parts were published (Breslau, 1881–83).

BIBLIOGRAPHY: A. Heppner-J. Herzberg, *Aus Vergangenheit und Gegenwart der Juden in Hohensalza* (1907), 58; idem, *Aus Vergangenheit und Gegenwart der Juden und der Juedischen Gemeinden in den Posener Landen* (1909), 481–2; M. Brann, *Geschichte des Juedischen Theologischen Seminars in Breslau* (1904), 108–9; B. Ziemlich, in: *Ost und West*, no. 2 (1904), 775–6; Ch. D. Lippe, *Bibliographisches Lexicon*, 1 (1881), 211; 2 (1887), 120; G. Scholem, *Bibliographia Kabbalistica* (1933), 78 no. 613.

[Gershom Scholem]

JOEL, KARL (1864–1934), philosopher. His father R. Herman Joel, had been a pupil of Schelling and apparently had a great influence on his son's attitude toward philosophy. He was born in Hirschberg, studied in Leipzig, and spent some time in Berlin (1887–92), where he became a friend of Georg *Simmel. In 1897 he was appointed to the University of Basle, where he taught until his death. Joel called his philosophical system "New Idealism." He defended the completeness of philosophy against the attempts to divide it up into "specialized" branches and compartments, and he emphasized the necessity of a comprehensive outlook. He opposed methodological positivism and metaphysical naturalism and sought to ridicule those who claimed "objectivity" in the study of reality, that is, spiritual activity deprived of all subjective and emotional ingredients. His main works include *Nietzsche und die Romantik* (1905), *Der Ursprung der Naturphilosophie aus dem Geiste der Mystik* (1906), *Seele und Welt* (1912), and *Die philosophische Krisis der Gegenwart* (1914). An autobiographical sketch appeared in *Die deutsche Philosophie der Gegenwart in Selbstdarstellungen*, 1 (1921), 71–90. He was a nephew of Manuel *Joel.

BIBLIOGRAPHY: *Festschrift... Karl Joel* (1934); Schenk, in: *Basler Nachrichten* (July 24, 1934).

[Aaron Gruenhut]

JOEL, MANUEL (1826–1890), rabbi and scholar. Joel, who was born in Birnbaum, Poznan province, was the son of the local rabbi. He studied classics and philosophy at Berlin and obtained a doctorate at Halle. In Berlin he came under the influence of Leopold *Zunz and M. *Sachs. Joining the staff of the *Juedisch-Theologisches Seminar in Breslau on its foundation in 1854, he taught classical languages, religious philosophy, and homiletics there. In 1864 he was appointed rabbi of the Breslau community, succeeding A. *Geiger. At the *rabbinical assemblies of Kassel (1868) and Leipzig (1869), he defended moderation in Reform against Geiger's radicalism and stressed the need for preserving the Jewish character of synagogue worship and respect for the historical past. He also expressed these views in a number of publications, particularly in his prayer book (1872) and his sermons (1867, 1893–98), which were highly influential.

Joel's scholarly importance lies mainly in the field of religious philosophy. He wrote on Ibn Gabirol, Maimonides, Crescas, and Levi b. Gershom, investigating their Greek and Arabic sources, and their influence, in turn, on Christian scholasticism and Spinoza. These essays were collected in his two-volume *Beitraege zur Geschichte der Philosophie* (1876). His two-volume *Blicke in die Religionsgeschichte...* (1880–83) was an important and influential contribution to comparative religion. Joel presented (apart from his sermons) his own religious philosophy, based on Kant and also on Schleiermacher's religion of emotion, in his *Religionsphilosophische Zeitfragen* (1876) and in a posthumously published article "Mosaismus und Heidentum" (in JJGL, 7 (1904), 35ff.), as a belief in revelation as the "thinking of the heart."

BIBLIOGRAPHY: I. Heinemann, *Manuel Joels wissenschaftliches Lebenswerk* (1927); idem, in: G. Kisch (ed.), *Breslau Seminary* (1963), 255ff.; M. Brann, *Geschichte des juedisch-theologischen Seminars in Breslau* (1904), 86ff., 126f. (bibl.).

[*Encyclopaedia Judaica* (Germany)]

JOEL, OTTO J. (1856–1916), Italian banker of German origin. Joel was born in Danzig, East Prussia, the son of a lottery collector. As a young man he was sent to Italy for his health, stayed there, and became a successful banker and completely revamped the financial and industrial Italian life. Together with Federico Weil (1854–1919), and with the cooperation of German banks, he formed the Banca Commerciale Italiana in 1894. In 1908 he became its central manager, and eventually its managing director. Despite the fact that he had become an Italian citizen several years before World War I, Joel had to resign from active work at the bank in 1915 on account of his German descent, and a year later, although he remained a vice president, was forced to withdraw from the board of directors. Otto Joel's son, ALESSANDRO (1891–?), joined the Banca Commerciale Italiana in 1920. He became manager of the London branch, but severed his connections with the bank in 1932.

[Joachim O. Ronall]

ADD. BIBLIOGRAPHY: R. Garruccio, *Minoranze in affari. La formazione di un banchiere: Otto Joel* (1997).

JOEL, RAPHAEL (1762–1827), the first Jewish advocate in the Hapsburg Empire. Born in Volyne, western Bohemia, Joel availed himself of the rights granted by the patents of toleration of the emperor *Joseph II and studied law at Prague University. When in 1790 he was about to be awarded a doctorate, Prague advocates petitioned the emperor Leopold II, claiming that there was no precedent at any university for such an award to a Jew. They contended that a rescript of 1731 prevented Jews from representing Christians, and that notwithstanding the patents of toleration Jews were still considered doubtful witnesses at law and should certainly not deal with canon law. The archbishop, as chancellor of the university, supported the advocates' opposition, but the academic authorities were adamant, and the emperor Leopold II decided that Jews could become doctors of civil though not of canon law, and could represent both Jews and Christians. Joel was awarded his doctorate. In 1798, however, he was baptized in Vienna, adopted the name Carl after divorcing his wife, a daughter of the physician Abraham *Kisch, who refused to follow him. In 1817 he was ennobled as "von Joelson." His offspring became high-ranking army officers.

BIBLIOGRAPHY: P.J. Diamant, in: *Zeitschrift fuer die Geschichte der Juden in der Tschechoslowakei*, 4 (1934), 10–17; G. Kisch in: JGGJČ, 6 (1934), 55–60; L. Singer, *ibid.*, 229–32; A.F. Pribram, (ed.), in: *Urkunden und Akten zur Geschichte der Juden in Wien* 2 (1918), 3–9.

JOEL, RICHARD M. (1950–), U.S. lawyer, educator, administrator, and president of Yeshiva University. Born in New York City in 1950, Joel grew up in a modern Orthodox family in Yonkers, New York, the only child of Avery and Annette Joel. His father had immigrated to Cape Town, South Africa, from Vilna, Lithuania prior to moving to the U.S. Raised in a musical home steeped in Jewish tradition and values, Joel spent a formative year with his parents in South Africa during the 1950s. His father tragically passed away in 1964 a few months after the Bar Mitzvah of his only child.

Joel graduated from Yeshiva University High School (1968), New York University (1972), and New York University Law School (1975). He spent three years as an assistant district attorney in the Bronx, prosecuting violent criminal behavior during some of the borough's most challenging years. Joel joined the Yeshiva University (YU) administration full-time beginning in 1978, first as director of Alumni Affairs and then as associate dean and professor of law at Benjamin N. Cardozo School of Law. In 1988, Joel interviewed for the top post in *Hillel, the oldest and largest organization in the Jewish world serving college and university students, and received an offer to head the organization, a position traditionally held by experienced Hillel professionals and rabbis.

Joel dramatically transformed Hillel during his 14-year tenure. Articulating a vision of a revitalized Hillel able "to provoke" a Jewish renaissance in America, Joel jettisoned the synagogue on campus model to promote a vision of campus communities supporting a wide range of Jewish organizations and interest groups. He set aside rabbinic ordination as the *sine qua non* of Hillel employment by expanding and diversifying the ranks of Hillel professionals. He encouraged Hillels to eliminate student membership and dues and championed open-architecture participation over more traditional affiliation models. He inspired Hillels to become less building-centered, even as more and newer buildings opened each year, to connect with Jewish students in multiple campus and community settings. He attracted major financial support from key Jewish philanthropists and foundations, including Edgar Bronfman, Michael Steinhardt, and Lynn Schusterman. He engineered Hillel's independence from B'nai B'rith and deepened the partnership with a Jewish Federation system alarmed by the implications of the 1990 National Jewish Population Survey (NJPS). He increased Hillel's global presence by adding affiliates in the former Soviet Union and Latin America.

Following the announced retirement of Yeshiva University President Rabbi Norman Lamm, the YU Board of Trustees, unable to find a suitable rabbinic candidate to replace Lamm, became deeply interested in Joel.

Inaugurated as the fourth president of Yeshiva University in 2003, Joel would break new ground – though not without some initial opposition – in becoming the first non-rabbinic-scholar to head Yeshiva University in its 117-year-history.

[Jay L. Rubin (2nd ed.)]

JOEL, SOLOMON BARNATO (1865–1931), South African mining magnate and financier. He was one of three brothers, sons of a Whitechapel shopkeeper and nephews of Barney *Barnato. They succeeded to Barnato's financial empire after his suicide in 1897. Joel (who was known as "Solly Joel") and his two brothers had joined their uncle on the Kimberley diamond fields in South Africa and were the earliest to reach the Rand after the discovery of gold. Joel faced his biggest challenge when the gold market was shaken by the aftermath of the Jameson Raid in 1896, when he was arrested but freed. This was followed by his uncle's suicide and the death of his brother Woolf, who was shot and killed in his Johannesburg office. Joel succeeded Barnato as a director of De Beers and chairman of the Johannesburg Consolidated Investment Company and other companies. Despite criticism, he successfully followed a policy of restricting diamond output to keep pace with demand and became one of the richest men of his time.

Solly Joel, who had a different suit for each day of the year, came to typify the new generation of millionaires produced by South Africa at the turn of the century, who were well known in London as well. He was a sportsman and a lavish host, a patron of the theater, and owned yachts, racing stables, and the Maiden Erleigh stud farm. In 1915 his horse won the Derby and the St. Leger and in 1921 he headed the list of winning owners. The career of his brother ISAAC BARNATO "JACK" JOEL (1862–1940) resembled, in part, that of Solly, whom he succeeded as chairman of the Johannesburg Consolidated Investment Company. He was also prominent on the English turf, won the Derby twice (1911, 1921) and three times headed the list of winning owners (1908, 1913, and 1914). Jack Joel left a fortune of £3,684,000 at his death.

BIBLIOGRAPHY: G. Saron and L. Hotz (eds.), *Jews in South Africa* (1955), 113f.; P.H. Emden, *Randlords* (1935), index. **ADD. BIBLIOGRAPHY:** ODNB online; Dictionary of South African Biography; S. Joel, *Ace of Diamonds: The Story of Solomon Barnato Joel* (1958); G. Wheatcroft, *The Randlords* (1986).

[Lewis Sowden]

JOEL BEN ISAAC HA-LEVI (1115?–1200), one of the eminent talmudic scholars of Mainz. Little is known about his life. He was related on his maternal side to some of the most distinguished families of the generation, including that of *Samuel b. Natronai (his cousin, or uncle, later his brother-in-law) and *Eliezer b. Nathan (his father-in-law). He himself founded a family of talmudic scholars, beginning with his son *Eliezer, and leading to *Mordecai b. Hillel, five generations later. He acquired the foundation of his learning at Regensburg and is known to have spent some time in Wuerzburg, and also lived for a period in Cologne; but his place of residence was Bonn and he is referred to in literary sources as R. Joel of Bonn (*Sefer ha-Terumah*, 130 et al.). His teachers in Regensburg were *Isaac b. Mordecai, *Ephraim b. Isaac, and Moses b. Joel. With Ephraim b. Isaac he had a sharp exchange of views concerning the eating of abdominal fat, a custom which he permitted contrary to the opinion of Ephraim. Although as head of a yeshivah he had many pupils, only *Ephraim of Bonn is known, apart from his son Eliezer. Quotations from his works have survived in the *Sefer ha-Ravyah* of his son Eliezer and in the works of many contemporary scholars with whom he carried on a correspondence, particularly in the *Raban* of Eliezer b. Nathan, and a little in the *Yiḥusei Tanna'im va-Amora'im* of *Judah b. Kalonymus; from there it is known that Joel was the author of talmudic novellae and decisions of *tosafot* to many tractates, and of numerous responsa. Several of his liturgical hymns, reflecting the horrors of the Second Crusade, are also known. He was held in great esteem by all his contemporary German and French scholars, and Isaac b. Samuel, the most distinguished French scholar of his time, refers to him with great admiration (*Ravyah*, 933). Joel's gentle nature is evidenced in the above-mentioned exchange of letters between himself and R. Ephraim, and in his decision on the proselyte of Wuerzburg (*Ravyah* 2,253–6), whom Joel not only befriended but even permitted to conduct prayers, contrary to the opinion of other scholars.

BIBLIOGRAPHY: Davidson, Oẓar, index s. v. *Yo'el ha-Levi mi-Bonn (ben Yiẓḥak)*; V. Aptowitzer, *Mavo le-Sefer Ravyah* (1938), 37–48, 164–87; Urbach, Tosafot, 171–4, 179–81.

[Israel Moses Ta-Shma]

JOEL BEN MOSES GAD (17th century), Polish talmudist. Joel was the author of *Meginnei Zahav*, in which he defended the *Turei Zahav*, the commentary on the Shulḥan Arukh by his grandfather, *David b. Samuel ha-Levi, against the strictures of *Shabbetai b. Meir ha-Kohen in his *Nekuddot ha-Kesef.* Joel was supported by leading talmudists, who praised his work and, at an "assembly at the Fair at Gremnitz" in 1683, resolved that the views of the author of the *Turei Zahav* were not to be rejected on account of Shabbetai's criticism. However, fortune frowned upon the *Meginnei Zahav.* Most of the manuscript was lost. In 1720 part of it was published by the author's grandson, but it was defective and badly printed (Prague, 1720). Primarily for this reason, Joel's views were not quoted and discussed by later commentators on the Shulḥan

Arukh. However, it was largely the favorable opinion engendered by his work which caused the author of *Turei Zahav* to be accepted without demur as a halakhist of the first rank. Joel also wrote novellae to a number of talmudic tractates (Altona, 1736). JOEL B. MOSES GAD, his grandson, prepared for publication the manuscript of the *Turei Zahav* to *Evenha-Ezer*, but died before seeing it through the press. It was published by his son Gad (Zolkiew, 1754).

BIBLIOGRAPHY: H.N. Dembitzer, *Kelilat Yofi*, 1 (1888), 59b–60a.

[Abram Juda Goldrat]

JOEL BEN SIMEON (called **Feibush Ashkenazi**), scribe and illuminator active in Germany and Italy in the second half of the 15th century. Of German origin, probably from Cologne or Bonn, he established a workshop in northern Italy. In his signed manuscripts he referred to himself as a *sofer* ("scribe"), *lavlar* ("scrivener"), and a *ẓayyar* ("painter"). Probably he himself was not the copyist and illuminator of all the manuscripts signed by him, but he was head of an atelier which moved from town to town, with several craftsmen in his service. In style and iconography his workshop combined Ashkenazi and Italian art.

Of the 11 surviving manuscripts signed by him, only six are dated; several others are attributed to him on stylistic grounds, both in script and illumination.

Dated Manuscripts

1. The *Parma Siddur* of 1449. Parma, Biblioteca Palatina, Ms. 3144 (De'Rossi) 1274, signed by the "scribe Joel ben Simeon, called Feibush of Bonn." Decorated. 2. *Maḥzor Cremona* of 1452. Formerly Turin, Royal Library Ms. 63; destroyed by fire. Signed by "Joel ben Simeon… Feibush of Bonn." 3. *The Second New York Haggadah* of 1454. N.Y., Jewish Theological Seminary, Mic. 8279. Signed by the "scrivener Joel ben Simeon, called Feibush Ashkenazi of Cologne on the Rhine who wrote, punctuated and painted it." Illustrated. 4. *The Lady's Maḥzor* of 1469. London, British Museum, Add. Ms. 26957. Signed by the "scrivener Joel ben Simeon." Illustrated. 5. *Washington Haggadah* of 1478. Library of Congress. Signed by "the humblest of scribes Joel ben Simeon." Illustrated. 6. *Commentary on the Psalms*. Modena, 1485. Parma, Biblioteca Palatina, Ms. 2841. Signed by "the scrivener Joel ben Simeon Ashkenazi, for Manuel ben Isaac of Modena." Not illuminated.

UNDATED MANUSCRIPTS. 7. *The First Nuremberg Haggadah*, Jerusalem, Schocken Library (formerly Nuremberg, National Museum, Ms. 2170b). Signed by "the scribe Joel ben Simeon." Illustrated. The manuscript was incorrectly dated to 1492 by Mueller, to 1410 by Fooner, to 1400 by Landsberger, and to after 1454 by Italiener (the last by interpreting the name Proyna mentioned in the manuscript, as Bruenn, from where the Jews were expelled in 1454.) It should be noticed that Joel was already in Cremona by 1452 and elsewhere in Italy by 1449. 8. *The British Museum Haggadah*. Add. Ms. 14762. Signed "Feibush called Joel, [who] painted it." Illustrated. 9. *The First New York Haggadah*. New York, Jewish Theological Seminary, MS. 75048. Signed by the "scribe Joel ben Simeon." Illustrated. 10. *Implements of the Temple*, six leaves. *Ibid.*, Ms. 0822. Signed by "Joel the painter called Feibush." Illustrated. 11. *The Dyson-Perrins Haggadah*. Cologne and Geneva, Martin Bodmer Collection (formerly: Malvern, Dyson-Perrins Collection Ms. 124). Signed by the "scribe Joel ben Simeon called Feibush Ashkenazi of Cologne on the Rhine." Illustrated.

Attributed Manuscripts

12. *Haggadah*. Parma, Biblioteca Palatina, Ms. 2998 (Ms. De'Rossi 111). Illustrated. 13. *Haggadah*. Stuttgart, Württembergische Landesbibliothek, Cod. Or. 4°, I. Illustrated. 14. *The Murphy Haggadah*: Yale Univ., Heb. Ms. +143. Illustrated.

Most of the manuscripts signed by Joel ben Simeon are illustrated, but some are merely decorated. The illuminations are primarily initial-word panels and marginal text illustrations, typically Ashkenazi. The only full-page illuminations are the six leaves of Temple Implements which may have been used as models in his workshop.

Most of Joel's illuminations consist of colored-pen drawings in Florentine style. The best example is the expressively drawn *Washington Haggadah* of 1478, which has more illustrations than any of his other signed *Haggadot*. Two undated and signed *Haggadot* are problematic because of their German stylistic elements. The *First Nuremberg Haggadah*, now in the Schocken Library, Jerusalem, must be one of the earliest manuscripts which Joel executed in Italy; the style of the illumination, painted in sepia, is still essentially German, though at times quite Italianized. It is related in style to the *First New York Haggadah*. The *British Museum Haggadah* was painted by at least three different artists, two definitely German and one Italian, though in his colophon Joel claims to be the one painter. As the *Parma Maḥzor* of 1449 was decorated in Italian style, the *British Museum Haggadah, The First New York Haggadah*, and the *First Nuremberg Haggadah*, may have belonged to a transition period around 1450.

See also Hebrew *Illuminated Manuscripts; Illuminated *Haggadot*; and Illuminated *Maḥzorim*.

BIBLIOGRAPHY: L.A. Mayer, *Bibliography of Jewish Art* (1967), nos. 265, 723, 1147, 1431, 1433, 1435, 1662–63, 1760, 1792, 2074, 2193, 2981; *Monumenta Judaica*, 1 (1963), nos. D68–70; M. Geisberg, *Der Meister E.S. und Israel von Meckenem* (1924); G. Tamieni, in: *La Bibliofilia*, 70 (1968), 38–137; A. and W. Cahn, in: *Yale University Library Gazette*, 41 (1967), no. 4; B. Narkiss, *Hebrew Illuminated Manuscripts* (1969), 39, 114, 124, 140, 171–2; J. Gutmann, in: *Studies in Bibliography and Booklore*, 9, no. 2–3 (1970), 76–95.

[Bezalel Narkiss]

JOEZER, SON OF BOETHUS, high priest (23–5 B.C.E.), appointed shortly before *Herod's death, as successor to *Mattathias b. Theophilus. The latter had been deposed for his part in tearing down the golden eagle which Herod had ordered to be placed over the Temple gate. He was a brother of Mariamne, Herod's wife, and of Eleazar, who also served as high priest. Joezer played an important role in pacifying the people when they resisted the attempts of *Quirinius, governor of Syria, to conduct a census in Judea, after the deposition of Archelaus in 6 C.E. Though Joezer ensured the cooperation of the people, Quirinius nevertheless deposed him soon after.

BIBLIOGRAPHY: Jos., Ant., 17:164; 18:3, 26; Schuerer, Gesch, 1 (1901[4]), 468, 541f.; 2 (1907[4]), 270.

[Lea Roth]

JOFFE, ABRAHAM FEODOROVICH (1880–1960), Russian physicist. Joffe was born in Romny, Ukraine. Between 1907 and 1913, he conducted intensive research on the quantum theory of light. In 1913 he was appointed professor extraordinary of physics at the Polytechnic Institute, an appointment only open to baptized Jews. In 1915, the Institute made him a full professor, and he received the prize of the Academy of Sciences. After the Bolshevik revolution, he and M. Nemnov founded the Roentgenological and Radiological Institute, out of which was born the Physical-Technical Institute of the Soviet Academy of Sciences. In 1919, Joffe opened and became dean of a Physical-Mechanics department. In 1921, while visiting Berlin, he met Einstein, who was sympathetic to Zionism. In their discussion, Joffe favored assimilation as the solution to the Jewish problem.

In 1932, Joffe initiated the opening of an Institute for Metal Physics in the Urals, and founded an Agrophysics Institute in Leningrad. In 1933, he helped to found a Physical-Technical Institute at Dnepropetrovsk, with a large laboratory for technical radiological examinations. Joffe edited several scientific journals and in 1958 founded the journal of the physics of solids.

Joffe's main scientific work belongs to three fields: the mechanical properties of crystals; the electrical properties of dielectric crystals; and semiconductors. His most important works are *Fizika poluprovodnikov* (1957[2]; *The Physics of Semi-Conductors*, 1960), which was translated into many languages, and *Osnovnye predstavleniya sovremennoy fiziki* ("Basic Concepts of Modern Physics," 1949). Joffe received many honors including election to the presidium of the Academy of Sciences of the Soviet Union. In 1942 he joined the Communist Party.

[Isaac Kalugai]

JOFFE, ADOLPH ABRAMOVICH (1883–1927), Russian revolutionary and diplomat. Born in Simferopol to a very rich merchant, he studied medicine at the universities of Berlin and Vienna. Joffe joined the Mensheviks in 1903, lived abroad, and was a member of the committee of the RSDRP (Russian Social Democratic Workars Party.) In 1908, after meeting *Trotsky, by whom he was greatly impressed, he became coeditor and contributor to the Bolshevik periodical *Pravda* in Vienna. He organized the smuggling of *Pravda* into Russia and was arrested while trying to get into Russia, and imprisoned by the Czarist authorities in 1912. Joffe was released by the Kerensky government following the February revolution of 1917 and in July of that year joined the Bolsheviks, and was elected a member of the Central Committee of the party. After the October revolution, he led the Soviet delegation to the peace talks with Germany at Brest-Litovsk, but as he was in favor of continuing the war he was replaced by Trotsky, but remained there as adviser. He was made ambassador to Germany in the following year. In 1920 he headed the Russian delegation at the peace talks with Poland and the Baltic republics, and subsequently was Soviet ambassador to Peking (Beijing) (1922–23), Vienna (1923–24), and Tokyo (1924–25). In the years 1925–27 he was one of the leaders of the left (Trotskyist) opposition. As a supporter of Trotsky, Joffe was not favored by *Stalin when the latter came to power, and he was relegated to professor at the Oriental Institute at Moscow. After Trotsky's expulsion from the Communist Party, Joffe committed suicide. A letter he left for Trotsky giving the reason for his suicide was considered an important document in the history of the Soviet Union.

His wife, MARIA JOFFE, was a member of the Bolshevik party from 1917 and worked as a journalist and editor in the Soviet press. In a meeting in 1929 she protested against the expulsion of Trotsky and the attacks on him in the press. She was arrested in the same year and spent 28 years in camps and exile. From 1975 she lived in Israel, where she published her memoirs (1977).

BIBLIOGRAPHY: L. Trotsky, *My Life* (1930), passim; *The Last Words of Adolf Joffe, a Letter to Leon Trotsky*, tr. by Max Eastman (1950).

[Shmuel Spector (2nd ed.)]

JOFFE, ELIEZER LIPA (1882–1944), Ereẓ Israel pioneer; father of the idea of the moshav *ovedim. Joffe was born in Yanovka (Ivanovka), Bessarabia, and in 1902 published a call to young Jews to settle in Ereẓ Israel (in the Hebrew daily, *Ha-Meliẓ*). He went to the United States in 1904 to study advanced agricultural techniques in preparation for his own settlement in Ereẓ Israel. In 1905 Joffe founded the Ha-Ikkar ha-Ẓa'ir ("Young Farmer") association for *aliyah* to Ereẓ Israel in Woodbine, New Jersey, whose members were students at the agricultural school there. He also published *Ha-Ikkar ha-Ẓa'ir*, which advocated agricultural training and preparation for life in Ereẓ Israel. At the same time, he founded *He-Ḥalutz in New York City. In 1910 he settled in Ereẓ Israel, establishing an experimental farm at *Ein Gannim near Petaḥ Tikvah. He settled in Galilee in 1911 and in 1913 organized American pioneers in the Ha-Ikkar ha-Ẓa'ir group for the autonomous cultivation of the *Kinneret farm. Joffe expounded his idea of the moshav ovedim in a brochure, *Yissud Moshevei Ovedim* ("Establishment of Agricultural Smallholder's Cooperatives," 1918) and in 1921 was one of the founders of *Nahalal, the first moshav ovedim, based on the principles he had formulated. In 1928 he became a founder of Tenuvah (the largest marketing cooperative in Israel), serving as its director until 1936.

A leader of the Ha-Po'el ha-Ẓa'ir party, Joffe served as its representative at Zionist Congresses. He published books on agricultural subjects and was the first editor of *Ha-Sadeh* ("The Field"), a monthly agricultural magazine. His works,

Kitvei Eliezer Joffe, were published in six volumes, together with a biography, in 1956.

BIBLIOGRAPHY: B. Ḥabas (ed.), *Sefer ha-Aliyyah ha-Sheniyyah* (1947), index; J. Burtniker, *Bibliografiyah shel E.L. Joffe* (1950); M. Smilansky, *Mishpaḥat ha-Adamah*, 4 (1953), 35–46; B. Katznelson, *Be-Ḥevlei Adam* (1950), 140–52.

[Yosef Shapiro]

JOFFE, HILLEL (1864–1936), Ereẓ Israel pioneer, doctor, and specialist in malaria. Born in Bristovka, Ukraine, he was educated at a Russian high school in Berdyansk. Under the influence of his brother-in-law, the writer M. Ben-Ami, he became an adherent of Ḥibbat Zion. Upon completing his medical studies in Geneva in 1891 Joffe went to Ereẓ Israel and served as doctor of the Jewish community in Tiberias. Two years later he accepted the invitation of Baron Rothschild's officials to practice in Zikhron Ya'akov. He treated malaria victims in Ḥaderah and Athlit and, on his advice, a forest of eucalyptus trees was planted in the Ḥaderah swamps. From 1895 to 1905 he served as chairman of the Ḥovevei Zion executive committee. In 1898 Joffe accompanied Herzl on his tour of the settlements in Judea, and, in 1903, was a member of the Zionist commission which examined possibilities for Jewish settlement in *El-Arish. In 1907 he returned to Zikhron Ya'akov to establish a hospital and medical center for Galilee and Samaria, also organizing an anti-malarial service there. Joffe devoted particular attention to the health problems of the Jewish workers in the settlements and wrote many papers on preventive medicine. In 1919 he moved to Haifa where he practiced medicine and remained active in public life until his death. His reminiscences, letters and diaries appeared as a book, *Dor Ma'pilim* ("Generation of First Pioneers," 1939). The moshav Bet-Hillel and a hospital in Ḥaderah are named for him.

BIBLIOGRAPHY: J. Yaari-Poleskin, *Ḥolemim ve-Loḥamim* (1950), 141–5; M. Smilansky, *Mishpaḥat ha-Adamah*, 2 (1954²), 166–72; Tidhar, 3 (1958²), 1141–4; B. Ḥabas (ed.), *Sefer ha-Aliyyah ha-Sheniyyah* (1947), index.

[Yehuda Slutsky]

JOFFE, JUDAH ACHILLES (1873–1966), Yiddish philologist. Born in Bakhmut (southern Russia), Joffe excelled from earliest youth in his linguistic abilities. As a musicologist and expert on Slavic languages, he was a contributor to such publications as *New International Encyclopedia* (1902), *International Yearbook* (1900, 1901, 1902), and *Nelson's Looseleaf Encyclopedia* (1910). His main interest, however, was Yiddish philology, for the purpose of which he built up a large library which included many rare early Yiddish texts. Prominent among his achievements is the critical edition (1949) of the *Bove-Bukh* ("Bove Book," 1541) by Elijah Baḥur *Levita, which was intended to be the first in a three-volume series of that noted scholar's Yiddish literary works. Also noteworthy are Joffe's studies of the Slavic component in Yiddish (in: *Pinkes*, 1 (1927/28), 235–56, 296–312), of Yiddish in America (in: *YIVO Bleter*, 10 (1936), 127–45), of Yiddish deluxe editions since 1534 (in: *YIVO Bleter*, 16 (1940), 45–58), as well as various etymological issues. Joffe translated and edited books from several languages including Yiddish, English, and French. He assisted editorially with the *Psychiatric Dictionary* (1940) by L.H. Hensie and J. Shatzky (1940), and the *Groyser Verterbukh fun der Yidisher Shprakh* ("Great Dictionary of the Yiddish Language," 1961–), the first volume of which he edited jointly with Yudel *Mark. Joffe was a pioneer of Yiddish orthographic reform and a man with controversial linguistic ideas. For his 85th birthday, *YIVO published the Yiddish *Yuda A. Yofe-bukh*, edited by Yudel Mark (1958, includes bibl.).

BIBLIOGRAPHY: LNYL, 4 (1961), 204–8.

[Mordkhe Schaechter]

JOFFEN, ABRAHAM (1887–1970), *rosh yeshivah* and leading exponent of the Novogrudok school of *Musar, Joffen was born near Pinsk and studied under Rabbis Zalman Sender Shapiro in Krinki and Joseph Horowitz in Novogrudok (whose daughter he married in 1913). He became an ardent follower of Horowitz's dynamic approach to *musar*. Joffen was appointed *rosh yeshivah* in the Novogrudok yeshivah and assisted his father-in-law in administering the branches of this school. Upon the latter's death (1920) Joffen succeeded him as head of the movement. In 1921 he and ten of his students were imprisoned by the Communists on suspicion of disloyalty to the new regime. After their release, they escaped to Poland, where Joffen reorganized the central Novogrudok yeshivah in Bialystok. In 1929 he visited Ereẓ Israel, where he aided in the organization of the "Novogrudok Bet Joseph" yeshivah in Tel Aviv. After the outbreak of World War II, Joffen emigrated to the United States, where he reestablished the central Novohrodok (= Novogrudok) yeshivah in Brooklyn. In 1964 he settled in Jerusalem where he continued to guide the various Novogrudok yeshivot. Joffen's reputation as a leading talmudic scholar gained acceptance for his school in the Lithuanian yeshivah world and nullified the criticism previously leveled against the Novogrudok yeshivot that they stressed the study of *musar* instead of Talmud. Joffen's talmudic lectures on *Ḥullin* and *Bava Meẓia* were published under the title *Derekh Eitan* (1958), and his *musar* discourses under the title *Sefer ha-Musar ve-ha-Da'at* (1957).

BIBLIOGRAPHY: S.K. Mirsky (ed.), *Mosedot Torah be-Eiropah* (1956), 247–90; D. Katz, *Tenu'at ha-Musar*, 4 (1963), index.

JOGICHES, LEON (**Jan Tyszka**; 1867–1919), socialist leader in Poland and Germany. Born in Vilna, Jogiches in 1885 became a member of the revolutionary party Narodnaya Volya. He was a leading member of the Vilna group and was connected with its terrorist organization. He was later arrested by the Czarist authorities. On his release he emigrated to Switzerland and from 1890 to 1893 worked with Plekhanov's Marxist group Osvobozhdeniye Truda ("Emancipation of Labor"). Jogiches was a founder and leader of the Social Democratic Party of Poland and Lithuania and considerably influenced Rosa *Luxemburg, with whom he was in close personal contact. He edited the party organ *Sprawa Robotnicza*

("The Workers' Cause") with Rosa Luxemburg and others and later edited four other periodicals: *Czerwony Sztandar* ("Red Banner"); *Przegląd Socjaldemokratyczny* ("Social-Democratic Review"); *Trybuna Ludowa* ("People's Tribune") and *Trybuna*. Jogiches returned to Poland on the outbreak of the Russian revolution in 1905 and organized the Warsaw workers' strikes of December 1905. He was arrested in 1906 and sentenced to eight years hard labor. In 1907, however, he escaped to Germany where he became active in the Polish, Russian, and German Socialist movements. During World War I, Jogiches was a leading figure in the left-wing groups Internationale and Spartacus until his arrest in 1918. After the revolution in Germany (Nov. 1918) he joined Rosa Luxemburg and Karl Liebknecht in forming the German Communist Party (KPD), but early in 1919 was rearrested and murdered in prison.

BIBLIOGRAPHY: J. Krasny, *J. Tyszka, zarys życia i dziaxalności* (Moscow, 1925); *Polski Słownik Biograficzny*, 11 (1964–65), 260–2 (incl. bibl.).

[Abraham Wein]

JOHANAN (Heb. יוֹחָנָן; "YHWH has been gracious"), the son of Kareah, the principal military officer in the entourage of *Gedaliah the son of Ahikam at Mizpah. After Gedaliah's assassination he led Jeremiah and other Jews down to Egypt (Jer. 40:8, 13–16; 41:11–16; 42:1,8:43: 2–5).

JOHANAN BEN BEROKA (beginning of the second century C.E.), *tanna*. Johanan's halakhic opinions are cited ten times in the Mishnah and as often in the Tosefta. He was an associate of *Eleazar Ḥisma. Although he considered himself a pupil of *Joshua b. Hananiah, whom he visited in his home in Peki'in (Tosef., Sot. 7:9), he came chiefly under the influence of *Johanan b. Nuri, whom he also visited in his home in Bet She'arim (Tosef., Ter. 7:14), and whose customs he followed (Tosef., RH ed. by Lieberman 316–7).

BIBLIOGRAPHY: Hyman, Toledot, s.v.

[Zvi Kaplan]

JOHANAN BEN GUDGADA (first–early second centuries C.E.), *tanna*. According to the Tosefta Johanan served in the Temple, where it was his duty to see to the closing of the Temple gates (Tosef. Shek. 2:14). It was his custom to eat food "in the ritual purity required for sacred food" throughout his life (Ḥag. 2:7). He testified with regard to a number of *halakhot* (Git. 5:5). His children were deaf-mutes (Tosef. Ter. 1:1), and according to the Talmud his daughter's sons, who were dumb but not deaf, studied in the academy of Judah ha-Nasi. Judah prayed for them and they were healed, and it was found that they had complete knowledge of the whole Torah (Ḥag. 3a). It is striking that one of his testimonies (Git. 5:5) concerned a deaf-mute given in marriage by her father, to the effect that she could be divorced by a bill of divorce.

BIBLIOGRAPHY: Hyman, Toledot, s.v.

[Zvi Kaplan / Stephen G. Wald (2nd ed.)]

JOHANAN BEN HA-ḤORANIT (also ha-Huranit, ha-Horoni, or ha-Hurni; mid-first century B.C.E.), *tanna*. A contemporary of *Shammai and *Hillel, he was probably named after his place of origin, the *Hauran region south of Damascus. He is only mentioned once in the Mishnah (Suk. 2:7) as having been visited in his *sukkah* by the elders of the academies of Shammai and of Hillel, who found him observing the *sukkah* ritual according to the rules of Hillel, though he is generally regarded as a disciple of Shammai (Tosef. Suk. 2:3). This is also reflected in the story that he refused once, during a famine, to eat moist olives until he was assured that, according to the rules of Hillel, they were ritually clean (*ibid.*). His most famous disciple was the *tanna* *Eliezer b. Zadok (*ibid.*).

BIBLIOGRAPHY: Hyman, Toledot, 674.

JOHANAN BEN JEHOIADA, (fifth century B.C.E.), high priest. Opinions differ as to the name of Johanan's father. In a number of places he is called Eliashib (Ezra 10:6; Neh. 12:23), whereas Josephus refers to him as "the son of Joiada and grandson of Eliashib" (cf. also Neh. 12:22 and 5:11; reading Johanan instead of Jonathan). In the opinion of A. Schalit Johanan was a nephew of *Manasseh. Johanan served as high priest after the reforms of Ezra and Nehemiah and is mentioned in one of the *Elephantine papyri of 408 B.C.E. According to this papyrus (Cowley, Aramaic 108–19, no. 30), he opposed the construction by the Jews of the Elephantine Temple and did not reply to a letter which they addressed to him on the subject. Johanan murdered his brother Jeshua in the course of a dispute with him in the Temple area. In consequence of this crime, the Jews were punished by Bagoas (*Bagohi), the Persian governor. These events are better understood in light of the fact that Johanan was a supporter of Ezra and Nehemiah (Jos., Ant. 11:297–301), whereas the connections between Jeshua and Bagoas, and between the latter and the Samaritans, suggest that Jeshua favored closer relations with the Samaritans.

BIBLIOGRAPHY: Schalit, in: *Sefer Yoḥanan Levi* (1949), 252–72; Klausner, Bayit Sheni, 1 (1951^2), 226–303; 2 (1951^2), 11–12, 19–20; E. Meyer, *Der Papyrusfund von Elephantine* (1912), 70 ff; Schuerer, Gesch, 3 (1909^4), 7, 26–27.

[Uriel Rappaport]

JOHANAN BEN JOSHUA HA-KOHEN (c. ninth or tenth century), liturgical poet. *Zunz assumed, with reservations, that Johanan, one of the principal representatives of the older *piyyut*, lived in the period after Eleazar *Kallir, and was of Greek extraction. The discovery of Johanan's poems among the *Genizah* fragments in Cairo, and the new light on synagogal poetry that has been acquired over the past century indicate that Johanan lived in Palestine, and that although it is difficult to determine his dates he may have lived before the Muslim conquest. Johanan composed three lengthy *piyyutim*: (1) a *kerovah* for Shavuot (found in a number of manuscripts of the Greek ritual); (2) a *kerovah* for *Musaf* of the Day of Atonement (printed in two different versions in the *Maḥzor*

Romania (see *Romaniot and Roman rituals); (3) an **Avodah* for the day of Atonement (which figures in the Roman ritual). Other *piyyutim* by Johanan are found in manuscript form, notably in the *Genizah* texts.

BIBLIOGRAPHY: Dukes, Poesie, 49, 143; Zunz, Poesie, 81, 108; Zunz, Ritus, 81f.; Zunz, Lit Poesie, 98–100; Landshuth, Ammudei, 82f.; I. Elbogen, *Studien zur Geschichte des Juedischen Gottesdienstes* (1907), 84f.; Davidson, Oẓar, 4 (1933), 398; M. Zulay, in: YMḤSI, 2 (1936), 324–5, 347, 358; 5 (1939), 155–7. **ADD. BIBLIOGRAPHY:** E. Fleischer, *Hebrew Liturgcal Poetry in the Middle Ages* (1975), 118 (Heb.).

[Jefim (Hayyim) Schirmann]

JOHANAN BEN NAPPAḤA (c. 180–c. 279), one of the most prominent Palestinian *amoraim* of the second generation whose teachings comprise a major portion of the Jerusalem Talmud (TJ), and a significant portion of the Babylonian Talmud as well. The fact that R. Johanan's name is more frequently mentioned in the Jerusalem Talmud than that of any other *amora* led Maimonides to ascribe to him the compilation of this Talmud (Intro. to Yad), though R. Johanan certainly could not himself have served as the final redactor of the Jerusalem Talmud as we possess it today (see Jerusalem *Talmud). His cognomen "bar Nappaḥa," which is found in this Aramaic form throughout the Babylonian Talmud (see Rashi, Sanh. 96a) is usually understood to mean "the son of a smith" (cf. the parallel Hebrew form "*ben ha-nappaḥ*" found in TJ, RH 2:7, 58a, Sanh. 1:2, 18c), and it has even been understood as a reference to R. Johanan's extraordinary physical beauty (Rashi ad. loc., presumably interpreting *bar nappaḥa* to mean "capable of inflaming [one's desires]"; cf. TB, BM 84a, Ber. 20a, 5b). It is nevertheless quite likely that it originally refers to his home town, the village of "*nappaḥ*" (Epstein, *Introduction*, 238). He is generally cited as "R. Johanan," sometimes by his cognomen only (e.g., Mak. 5b), but never by both together.

Like many of the *tannaim* and like many other prominent *amoraim*, R. Johanan's life quickly became the subject of numerous *aggadot*, which developed and changed as the stories were told and retold, each time in accordance with the literary and theological aims of the different storytellers. As a result it is difficult to give a precise account even of those few events from R. Johanan's life which are actually related in talmudic sources, since they are often reported in various ways in different versions of the same story. Similarly, R. Johanan's own halakhic and aggadic teachings were subjected to intense scrutiny, not only by his immediate disciples, but also by virtually all subsequent scholars. This process of study and analysis gave rise to varying and often conflicting interpretations of his words. These differing interpretations in turn were formulated as independent and sometimes contradictory statements, and then disseminated under R. Johanan's name (see, for example, Wald, *Pesaḥim III*, 59–65). This problem is further compounded by the fact that in the eyes of the Babylonian Talmud virtually any authoritative tradition deriving from the Land of Israel may come to be ascribed to R. Johanan, whether he was the original author of the statement or not. For example, the halakhic statement ascribed to R. Johanan in TB, Shabbat 73b top, is virtually identical to the anonymous tannaitic statement found in Tosefta Shab. 8:3 (see Wald, *Shabbat VII*, sugya 11). Similarly, the famous aggadic statement ascribed to R. Johanan in TB, Git. 56a, "The humility of R. Zekharia b. Avkulas destroyed our Temple, burned our Holy of Holies, and exiled us from our land," is in fact a slightly expanded version of the statement of the *tanna* R. Yose found in Tosefta Shab. 16:7 (see *Five Sugyot*, 106–111). After describing in outline the life and career of R. Johanan as it is reflected in talmudic sources, we will examine a few of the problems involved in the critical evaluation of these traditions, using one halakhic tradition and one aggadic tradition as examples.

Apparently born at Sepphoris, Johanan was said to be descended from the tribe of Joseph (Ber. 20a). According to the Babylonian Talmud, his father died before his birth and his mother in childbirth (Kid. 31b), and according to the Jerusalem Talmud R. Johanan was raised by his grandfather (TJ, Ma'as. 1:2, 48d). One tradition relates that R. Johanan inherited fields and vineyards from his parents, all of which he sold to support himself during his student years, claiming that he was disposing of objects created in six days to acquire the Torah, which was given in 40 days (Song R. 8:7). While this source represents him as having chosen poverty voluntarily, another mentions his poverty without any such qualification (Ta'anit 21a). These representations of R. Yohanan as a struggling scholar are consistent with his view – quoted by R. Abbahu – that a *talmid hakham* is one who neglects his business for study (TJ, Moed Katan 3:7, 83b). According to the Babylonian Talmud, R. Johanan's family life was marred by tragedy, and during his lifetime he buried ten of his sons. He is said to have retained a "bone" (according to the commentaries "a tooth") of the last of his sons, showing it to people in mourning to induce in them a spirit of resignation such as he himself had found in his successive bereavements (Ber. 5b; Arukh ad. loc.). In a parallel version of this *aggadah* (Song R. 2), however, there is no mention either of this tragedy or of this particular practice, and in another source reference is made to the marriage of a daughter who survived (Kid. 71b).

The Babylonian Talmud states that in his youth he studied with *Judah ha-Nasi for a short time, although R. Johanan apparently could not then comprehend his master's teachings (Ḥul. 137b). Nevertheless, according to this *aggadah*, Judah recognized Johanan's talents and predicted that he would be a leading teacher in Israel (Pes. 3b; cf. Yoma 82b). His primary teachers were R. *Yannai (BB 154b; TJ, Ket. 9:5, 33b), and *Oshaiah Rabbah (Eruv. 53a; TJ, Ter. 10:3, 47a). From Ḥanina b. Hama, he apparently received homiletic traditions on almost all the biblical books, as we are told that Ḥanina once noticed unusually large crowds hurrying by to hear R. Johanan's lectures on the *aggadah*; whereupon Ḥanina thanked God for permitting him to see his life's work bearing such blessed fruit (TJ, Hor. 3:7, 48b). Johanan also is described as having mastered the mystical traditions of the *Merkabah* (Ḥag. 13a), the science of intercalating months (TJ, RH 2:6, 58a, b), and medicine (Shab. 109b; 110b).

R. Johanan began teaching in his native city, Sepphoris, in the yeshivah of R. Bana'ah, and his classes became very popular. Later, R. Johanan opened his own academy in Tiberias (TJ, Beẓah 1:1, 60a) which soon attracted the most gifted students of his generation, among whom were Abbahu, Ammi, Assi II, Eleazar b. Pedat, Ḥiyya b. Abba, Yose b. Ḥaninah, and Simeon b. Abba. His disciples spread his teachings, and R. Johanan also visited other localities, deciding questions of law there (Ket. 7a; Yev. 64b). His fame spread afar, and in certain circles in the Diaspora the impact of his teaching was felt almost as strongly as in his native land (Z.M. Dor).

According to a tradition in the Babylonian Talmud, R. Johanan recognized no authority outside Ereẓ Israel except for *Rav, with whom he corresponded, addressing him as "our master in Babylon." After Rav's death, R. Johanan addressed his colleague, Samuel, as "our colleague in Babylon." However, after Samuel had sent him his calendar calculations and responsa concerning *terefah*, R. Johanan reportedly exclaimed that Samuel was also his master. He therefore resolved to visit Samuel, but to spare him from the hardships of the long journey to Babylon, "God caused him incorrectly to believe that Samuel had in the meantime died" (Ḥul. 95b).

R. Johanan is represented not only as authoritative among other rabbis (cf. TJ, Ber. 8:1, 12a), but also outside of rabbinic circles. A litigant in Antioch is said to have agreed in advance of adjudication to abide by whatever R. Johanan decided (TJ, Sanh. 3:2, 21a), while another source stresses his popularity as a preacher (TJ, Hor. 3:7, 48b; TJ, BM 2:11, 8d). R. Johanan is also described as giving orders to the Kifra synagogue (TJ, RH 4:4, 59c) and to midwives (TJ, Shab 9:3, 12a), descriptions which presuppose some degree of receptivity on the part of the persons and communities in question.

R. Johanan is also represented as a man of affairs. He is described as having enjoyed the regard of the archon of Sepphoris (TJ, Ber. 5:1, 9a), and he is also represented as having regard for the honor of the patriarchate (e.g., Gen R. 97:48, Theodor-Albeck, p. 1245). R. Johanan reportedly felt that there should only be one leader in a generation (Sanhedrin 8a) – presumably the patriarch – whom he is also represented as urging to dress in a manner more appropriate to his office (TJ, Sanh. 2:5, 20c). On one occasion when the patriarchal house was late in informing R. Johanan and Resh Lakish of the proclamation of a public fast, R. Johanan insisted that they nevertheless had to observe it, since – presumably as the patriarch's subjects – they were legally presumed to have accepted the fast when it was proclaimed (Ta'an. 24a). R. Johanan also reportedly made a journey to perform a service on behalf of the patriarch (TJ, Av. Zar. 2:4, 41b). Descriptions of R. Johanan's willingness to submit to the authority of the patriarch may be connected to the accounts of how he was able to mediate between the patriarch and Resh Lakish (TJ, Sanh. 2:1, 19d–20a; TJ, Hor. 3:2, 47a), and how he had the stature to intervene in a conflict involving two of the most prominent families in Sepphoris (TJ, Shab. 12:3, 13c). R. Johanan also reportedly used his connections with the patriarchate in order to begin integrating rabbinic scholars into the patriarchal bureaucracy, as well as into positions of communal leadership. R. Johanan's students continued his policy of appointing scholars for such posts. This expansion of R. Johanan's influence into the political realm may account at least in part for his influence over Palestinian rabbinism overall. The Talmud also ascribes to R. Johanan's an almost unbounded respect for the previous generations of scholars, quoting him as saying that "the hearts of the ancients were like the larger outer door to the Temple [*ulam*], but that of the later generations is like the smaller inner door [*heikhal*], while ours is like the eye of a fine needle" (Er. 53a), and that "the fingernail of the earlier generations is better than the whole body of the later generations" (Yoma 9b).

In addition to his numerous halakhic and aggadic statements (*memrot*), which touch on virtually every aspect of talmudic law and lore, the Babylonian Talmud also ascribes to R. Johanan a number of general rules which were accepted as authoritative in determining the *halakhah*. (e.g., Sanh. 31a, Er. 46b). One notable example of this sort of statement is the widely quoted (cf. the list in the margin of Shab. 46a) principle that "the *halakhah* is in accordance with an anonymous Mishnah." Nevertheless, it is difficult to accept the accuracy of this tradition on face value. In every case where this statement is quoted in the Babylonian Talmud, it is contradicted by another explicit statement of R. Johanan in which he decides the *halakhah* in opposition to the view of an anonymous Mishnah. In many cases the Talmud manages to "resolve" these contradictions, but some of these resolutions require textual emendations (Shab. 147b, 157b), some involve explicitly forced interpretations (Shab. 46a, 112b), and some remain unresolved (Yev. 16b, Nid. 56b).

The source of this problematic tradition can be traced to a passage in the Jerusalem Talmud, (Yev. 4:11, 6b; cf. TB, Yev. 42b–43a, and TJ, Ta'an. 2:14, 66a; Meg. 1:4, 70d), where R. Johanan decided the *halakhah* in favor of the position of R. Jose, and in opposition to an anonymous halakhic position, both of which are brought in Mishnah Yev. 4:11. The Jerusalem Talmud explains that R. Johanan did not consider an anonymous halakhah binding unless it represented the position of the majority of scholars, whereas in this case the anonymous *halakhah* was only the opinion of R. Meir. Further on the Jerusalem Talmud indeed quotes a tradition in the name of R. Eleazar, according to which the *halakhah* always follows the anonymous position of the Mishnah, even when it is only the view of an individual *tanna*. It is clear, however, that this is not the view of R. Johanan himself, but rather only of his disciple R. Eleazar.

Why then was this tradition ascribed to R. Johanan in the Babylonian Talmud? The answer to this question can be found in another statement by R. Johanan in the Jerusalem Talmud there (TJ, Yev. 4:11, 6b): "R. Johanan said: Any place where [Rabbi] taught an anonymous Mishnah, that [anonymous Mishnah] is [presumed to represent] the majority position, until one receives explicit information from one's teacher [to the contrary]." Assuming that the *halakhah* is generally in accordance with the majority opinion, one could summarize R. Johanan's rather convoluted statement in the following way: "The *halakhah* is in accordance with an anonymous Mishnah" – but only if one recalls that R. Johanan's statement is not a universal and binding legal rule, but rather a generalization, which may serve as a legal presumption, so long as it has not been contradicted by other evidence. When this simplified, but still correct, version of this tradition was transmitted to Babylonia, however, these qualifications were blurred or lost altogether, and it was interpreted as a universal and binding legal rule: "the *halakhah* is [always] in accordance with an anonymous Mishnah" – as if R. Johanan himself agreed with the position of his disciple R. Eleazar! As a result of the conflation of these two traditions, a contradiction arose between this tradition (as understood by the Babylonian Talmud) and more than 20 other explicit rulings ascribed in the Babylonian Talmud to R. Johanan, in which he decided the *halakhah* in opposition to the position of an anonymous Mishnah.

Similar problems arise when one tries to trace the origin and to verify the authenticity of aggadic traditions relating to R. Johanan. Talmudic storytellers frequently elaborated and reformulated historical traditions, transferred stories from one narrative to another, and even from one historical figure to another. For example, the Talmud In TB, BM 84a provides a detailed account of the manner in which R. Johanan first met his life-long study partner, R. *Simeon b. Lakish (Resh Lakish), and of the tragic events surrounding their deaths. We are told there that R. Johanan was once bathing in the Jordan, when Resh Lakish, who at that time was a highway robber by profession, passed by. Resh Lakish was so impressed with R. Johanan's beauty that he "jumped over the Jordan" to get a better look. R. Johanan was so impressed by Resh Lakish's physical strength that he said to him: "Your strength should be devoted to the study of Torah." Resh Lakish replied: "Your beauty should be devoted to women." Johanan responded: "If you come back with me [to study Torah], I will give you my sister [in marriage], who is even more beautiful than I am." As soon as Resh Lakish agreed to return and study Torah, he lost all his physical strength, and was unable to jump back across the Jordan in order to bring his things. The story then breaks off and picks up some years later, with R. Johanan and Resh Lakish engaged in a dispute over the halakhic status of various weapons – "The sword, the dagger," etc. – in which Resh Lakish disagreed with R. Johanan's view as to when such weapons are considered finished and ready for use. R. Johanan quipped that Resh Lakish's apparent expertise in this matter would seem to be due to his former occupation as a highway robber. Resh Lakish was taken aback by this insensitive reference to his former life of crime, became despondent and eventually died. R. Johanan, in turn, also became increasingly despondent, not so much because he had caused the death of his lifelong friend, but rather because he was unable to learn Torah effectively without the assistance of an aggressive study partner like Resh Lakish, who was always both willing and able to challenge him on every point. R. Johanan's mental state eventually deteriorated into insanity, whereupon R. Johanan's colleagues prayed for him that he might find peace – and so he died.

This story is fascinating in many respects, but it is also highly suspect as a report of events that supposedly occurred in the lives of these two scholars. The opening scenario is remarkably similar to another story found in Song R. 2, in which a member of Rabban Gamaliel's household, who is described as possessing superhuman strength, becomes enfeebled as soon as he begins to learn Torah. Even R. Johanan's comment to Resh Lakish in the Babylonian Talmud is remarkably similar to Rabban Gamaliel's words there: "You have all this great strength (*ḥela*), and you do not learn Torah (*oraita*)?" (Song R.) = "Your strength (*ḥelakh*), should be devoted to the study of Torah (*l-oraita*)." Also, the story of R. Johanan's pathetic inability to study Torah in the absence of Resh Lakish is the subject of another, very different, *aggadah* found in Yerushalmi Sanh. 2, 19d and Hor. 3, 47a (see Friedman, Rav Kahana, 265–67). Moreover, the entire halakhic discussion between R. Johanan and Resh Lakish in this story seems artificial and somewhat improbable (cf. Tosefot BM 84b bottom). Finally, the striking description of R. Johanan's insanity and resulting death are not reflected in any parallel description of R. Johanan's death (cf. MK 25b; TJ, Kil. 9:3, 32b, Ket. 12:3, 35a; Gen. R. 100:2, Theodor-Albeck 1285).

The lives of great figures such as R. Johanan inevitably become enmeshed in a web of legend, as their teachings are subjected to reinterpretation and reformulation. It is often difficult, if not impossible, to disentangle the more original elements of these traditions from later accretions and elaborations. Notwithstanding these difficulties, these traditions bear clear witness to the enormity of the achievement and legacy which R. Johanan left to posterity.

BIBLIOGRAPHY: Bacher, Pal Amor; Halevi, Dorot, 2 (1923), 298–332; Weiss, Dor, 3 (1904), 62–71; J.S. Zuri, *Rabbi Jochanan* (Ger., 1918); H.L. Strack, *Introduction to the Talmud and Midrash* (1945), 65, 319; S.A. Jordan, *Rabbi Jochanan Bar Nappacha* (Ger., 1895). **ADD. BIBLIOGRAPHY:** Z.M. Dor, *The Teachings of Eretz Israel in Babylon* (1971); P.E. Hayman, "Development and Change in the Teachings of Rabbi Yohanan ben Nafha" (Hebrew), (Dissertation, 1990); S. Wald, *BT Pesaḥim III* (Hebrew, 2000); idem, *BT Shabbat VII* (Hebrew) (forthcoming); S. Friedman (ed.), *Five Sugyot from the Babylonian Talmud* (Hebrew, 2002); S. Friedman, "The Further Adventures of Rav Kahana," in: P. Schaefer (ed.), *The Talmud Yerushalmi and Graeco-Roman Culture III* (2002), 247–71; R. Kimelman, in: SBLSP, 2 (1979) 35–42; idem, in: HTR, 73:3–4 (1980), 567–95.

[Stephen G. Wald and Alyssia Gray (2nd ed.)]

JOHANAN BEN NURI (first half of the second century), *tanna*. Johanan lived in Bet She'arim (Tosef., Ter. 7:14; *ibid.*, Suk. 2:2) and was also in Ginnegar and Sepphoris. His teacher was apparently *Eliezer b. Hyrcanus, since he transmits several sayings in his name and engaged in discussions in his presence (Tosef., Kelim, BK 6:3; et al.). During the war of Lucius *Quietus (115–17 C.E.), Johanan was in Sepphoris in the company of outstanding scholars (Tosef., Kelim, BB 2:2). He had great influence in molding the laws and customs of the Jews of Galilee, who followed his rulings, in contrast to Judea where they followed *Akiva (TJ, RH 4:6). Despite the fact that *Joshua b. Hananiah praised him for his great knowledge and as one who "was able to estimate the number of drops of water in the sea," he was extremely poor and "went out with the last of the gleaners to bring home his living for the whole year" (TJ, Pe'ah 8:1). Even after Rabban *Gamaliel appointed him a member of the Sanhedrin, he continued to behave with simplicity: "It happened that Rabban Gamaliel promoted Johanan b. Nuri and Eleazer b. Ḥisma, and the disciples did not recognize them. In the evening they took their place among the disciples… [Rabban Gamaliel] entered and found them sitting among the pupils. He said to them: 'You have already shown publicly that you deserve no position of authority. In the past you were your own masters, henceforth you are servants subject to the community'" (Sif. Deut. 16; and cf. Hor. 10a). He is frequently mentioned in the Mishnah, chiefly in discussions with Akiva with whom he was intimate. Johanan b. Nuri said: "I call heaven and earth as witnesses that on more than five occasions Akiva was criticized because of me before Gamaliel in Jabneh, because I complained about him and Gamaliel rebuked him, but despite that I know that his affection for me grew" (Sif. Deut. 1). He is frequently mentioned as conveying the teaching of the scholars of Jabneh to the older scholars of Galilee (Tosef., BB 2:10; *ibid.*, Oho. 5:8; et al.). His *halakhot* are frequently mentioned in the Mishnah and *baraita* and he was called "a basket of *halakhot*" (ARN[1] 18–68). Johanan b. Beroka is referred to as one of his pupils (Tosef. Ter. 7:14), and Yose transmitted *halakhot* in his name (Ket. 1:10; et al.). He was still alive after the *Bar Kokhba war and the fall of Bethar (Yev. 14:2–15:1), and Judah ha-Nasi still went to visit him in Bet She'arim (Tosef. Suk. 2:2; see Lieberman, *Tosefta ki-Feshutah*, 4, 850/51).

BIBLIOGRAPHY: Frankel, Mishnah (1923), 130–2; J. Brill, *Mevo ha-Mishnah*, 1 (1876), 122–5; Hyman, Toledot, s.v.; L.A. Rosenthal, in: *Hoffmann-Festschrift* (1914), 234–40.

[Shmuel Safrai]

JOHANAN BEN TORTA (first half of the second century), *tanna*, a contemporary of *Akiva. Only one statement by him is known, in which he gives the reasons for the destruction of the Temple. "Why was Shiloh destroyed? Because of the contempt in which the sacred objects there were held. Why was the first Temple destroyed? Because of three evil things which prevailed then – idolatry, immorality, and bloodshed. But in the period of the Second Temple we know that they labored in Torah and were careful to give tithes; why then were they exiled? Because they loved wealth and hated one another. This is to teach thee that hatred of one's fellow men is considered by God as grave as idolatry, immorality, and bloodshed" (Tosef. Men. 13:22, cf. Yoma 9a, b). Johanan b. Torta vigorously opposed Akiva's acceptance of Bar Kokhba as the Messiah, saying to him, "Akiva! Grass shall grow from your jaws before the son of David appears" (TJ, Ta'an. 4:8, 68d). According to a late *aggadah*, Johanan was a proselyte who became converted when he saw that the cow he bought from a Jew refused to work on the Sabbath (PR, Parah, 56b–57a). This, however, would appear to be merely a homiletical interpretation based on his name (*torta*, "cow") which, in fact, refers to his birthplace.

BIBLIOGRAPHY: Bacher, Tann.; Alon, Toledot, 2 (1957), 42.

[Shmuel Safrai]

JOHANAN BEN ZAKKAI (first century C.E.), *tanna*, considered in talmudic tradition the leading sage at the end of the Second Temple period and the years immediately following the destruction of the Temple. Johanan b. Zakkai's personality and work are depicted in a blend of fact and legend, neither of which gives information concerning his family or place of origin. Compared to Moses and *Hillel before and to *Akiva after him, Johanan is said to have lived 120 years, divided into three periods: "For 40 years he was in business, 40 years he studied, and 40 years he taught" (Sif. Deut. 357; RH 31b; Sanh. 41a). In the chain of the tradition of the Oral Law it is mentioned in general terms that he received the tradition from Hillel and *Shammai (Avot 2:8). Other statements, however, refer to him only as the pupil of Hillel, although these too contain no direct evidence of any discussions between them. According to a talmudic *aggadah* (TJ, Ned. 5:6, 39b, TB, Suk. 28a, BB 134a; ARN[1] 14, ARN[b] 28), Johanan was the least among Hillel's many pupils, 80 according to some traditions, 160 according to others. Nevertheless, Hillel (according to TJ and ARN[2]) singled Johanan out on his deathbed, calling him "father of wisdom and father of the generations," and according to another tradition (TB; cf. ARN[1]) "it was said of him that he did not leave unstudied the Bible and Mishnah, Talmud, *halakhah*, and *aggadah*, exegetical details of the Torah and of the Scribes, inferences *a minori ad majus* and analogies, calendrical computations and *gematriot*, the speech of the ministering angels, of spirits, and of palm-trees, fullers' parables and fox fables, and any matter great and small, 'great' meaning: *ma'aseh merkavah* (mystical speculation); 'small' meaning: the discussions of Abbaye and Rava."

Very little is known of Johanan's activity as scholar or teacher in Jerusalem before the destruction. One talmudic *aggadah* states that for 40 years before the destruction of the Second Temple the doors of the *heikhal* (front part of the Temple building) were locked at night and in the early morning were found open. Johanan b. Zakkai said to it: "*Heikhal*, why do you agitate us? We know that you will eventually be destroyed, as it is said [Zech. 11:1]: 'Open thy doors, O Lebanon, that the fire may devour thy cedars'" (TJ, Yoma, 6:3, 43c; TB, Yoma 39b; and see Jos., Wars, 6:293). Another tradition (see Mid. Tan. on Deut. 26:13), tells of his relations with Rabban *Simeon b. Gamaliel, indicating that he occupied a special place among the sages and filled a role – either with or without any particular title – alongside the *nasi.*

Johanan and the Temple

According to tradition Johanan expounded and taught "in the shadow of the Temple" (TJ, Av. Zar. 3:13, 43b; Pes. 26a), and it may be there that he came into contact with "the sons of high priests" mentioned in Ket. 13:2. On the other hand Johanan's dispute there with Dosa ben Hyrcanus over the words of "the sons of high priests" may reflect a later stage in the development of this *halakhah* which occurred after the destruction. Tannaitic sources report a number of explicit disputes between Johanan and the Sadducees. In one, Johanan clashed openly with one of them and was able to give practical expression to the Pharisaic view (Tosef., Par. 3:8; and see Mish., Par. 3:7). The Mishnah also records a controversy between Johanan and the Sadducees on whether the Holy Scriptures "render the hands unclean" (Yad. 4:6). The other accounts of his disputes with them (BB 115b; and see Men. 65a; Meg. Ta'an. 338) are legendary in character. These accounts were apparently composed when the Sadducees had ceased to exist. By his active opposition to them Johanan undoubtedly sought to curtail their influence in the Temple and in its service. He was also opposed to the special privileges which the priests had arrogated to themselves, such as exempting themselves from paying the half shekel. Johanan declared against them: "Any priest who does not pay the shekel is guilty of a sin …" (Shek. 1:4; and see Maimonides' Mishnah commentary, ad loc.). It was however clear to him that the sages were powerless to impose their views fully on the priests (Eduy. 8:3, 7). Nevertheless he may have succeeded in increasing the number of Pharisaic priests who accepted his decisions (see Tosef., Oho. 16:8; Tosef., Par. 10:2) and in influencing their ways and the order of the Temple service.

No information is extant of the regulations issued by Johanan before the destruction of the Temple. The Mishnah (Sot. 9:9) does indeed declare that he discontinued the ceremony of the ordeal of the bitter water which the woman suspected of adultery had to drink, but the passage "Rabban Johanan b. Zakkai discontinued it" was apparently not part of the original Mishnah, he having merely testified to its discontinuance on account of prevailing circumstances, as stated in the Tosefta (Sot. 14:1–2): "R. Johanan b. Zakkai said: With the increase in the number of murderers an end was put to the ceremony of breaking the heifer's neck [Deut. 21:1ff.], for the ceremony of breaking the heifer's neck applies only to a doubtful case, whereas now they murder openly. With the increase in the number of adulterers, an end was put to the ceremony of the bitter water, for the ceremony of the bitter water applies only to a doubtful case, whereas now there have already increased those who are openly guilty of it."

As a Teacher

Johanan's chief activity was directed to spreading the knowledge of the Torah (RH 18a; Yev. 105a); but while regarding its study as the aim of man's life, he warned that this did not justify claiming any credit for oneself: "If you have learnt much Torah, do not ascribe any merit to yourself, since it was for this that you were created" (Avot 2:8). Five of his pupils are mentioned by name: Eliezer b. Hyrcanus, Joshua b. Hananiah, Yose ha-Kohen, Simeon b. Nethanel, and Eleazar b. Arakh (*ibid.*), but frequently reference is made to his pupils without mentioning their names. He used the dialogue as his method of instruction. He asked questions of his pupils, probed their answers, and praised the correct reply (Avot 2:9). The earliest tannaitic sources describe him as teaching *halakhah* and *aggadah*, ethics and the reasons for the commandments, and mysticism as well – *ma'aseh bereshit* and *ma'aseh merkavah* (see below). His tendency to base *halakhot* on biblical texts is evidenced by his fear that "another generation is destined to pronounce clean a loaf that is unclean in the third degree on the ground that no text in the Torah declares it to be unclean" (Sot. 5:2). A *baraita* (Tosef., BK 7:3ff.) enumerates five things which R. Johanan b. Zakkai interpreted "as a kind of *ḥomer*," an expression that has not been satisfactorily explained. This *baraita* contains allegorical interpretations and homilies based on analogy, on an inference from a similarity of biblical phrases, and on a conclusion *a minori ad majus*. Their common feature is that they give reasons for biblical statements: "Why, of all the organs of his body, was it specifically the ear of the Hebrew servant who, although able to go free after six years' service yet chose to continue serving his master, which was pierced? [Ex. 21:2–6]. Because the ear was the organ that heard at Mt. Sinai 'for unto Me the children of Israel are servants' [Lev. 25:55] but this one elected to serve a human master. Therefore, declares the Bible, let his ear be perforated … The Bible says [Deut. 27:5]: 'And there shalt thou build … an altar of stones; thou shalt lift up no iron tool upon them.' For fashioning the stones of the altar, which symbolizes atonement, iron is not to be used, since from it the sword, symbolizing calamity, is manufactured. If this applies to the altar which makes atonement between Israel and their Father in heaven, by a conclusion *a minori ad majus*, students of the Torah, who are the atonement of the world, should not be touched by any one of all the harmful agents" (Tosef., BK loc. cit.).

Johanan's method of minutely studying a biblical passage, inquiring into its motivation, and finding the grounds for some detail which he then converts into a universal idea transcending the specific context of the passage, is evident also in his other expositions not designated "as a kind of *ḥomer*." On the verse (Ex. 21:37: "he shall pay five oxen for an ox, and four sheep for a sheep," he said: "Come and see to what extent God shows consideration for the dignity of human beings. For an ox, which walks with its legs, the thief pays fivefold; for a sheep, since he carries it, he pays only fourfold" (Tosef., BK 7:10; Mekh., ed. Horowitz-Rabin, *Nezikin*, 12). In later sources mention is made of questions addressed to Johanan in the presence of his pupils by a Roman general who in the main posed problems raised by contradictory biblical passages (see Bek. 5a; TJ, Sanh. 1:7, 19 c–d; Num. R. 4:9). At times Johanan gave him an evasive answer, which failed to satisfy his pupils.

On one occasion when "he saw his disciples looking at one another, he said to them, 'You are doubtless surprised that I should have dismissed him with a vague reply ...'" (Ḥul. 27b, and see Tos., ad loc.). On another occasion his pupils said to him: "Him you have dismissed with a vague reply, but to us what answer do you give?" (TJ, Sanh. 1:3, 19b). According to another tradition, a certain non-Jew once asked Johanan about the ceremony of the red heifer which "seems like sorcery." In this story, too, it is said that Johanan's answer to the general failed to satisfy his pupils "who, when he left, said, 'Our master, him you have dismissed with a trivial reply. What answer do you give us?' He said to them, 'By your life, a corpse does not defile nor does water make levitically clean, but it is the decree of the Holy One Blessed Be He who declared, I have issued an ordinance and enacted a decree, and you are not permitted to question My decree'" (PdRK 71; Tanh., Ḥukkat, 8).

Johanan is the first sage explicitly mentioned in tannaitic sources as having engaged in mysticism – standing at the head of a chain, as it were, of sages who engaged in the subject, given by Yose b. Judah of the latter half of the second century C.E. (Tosef., Ḥag. 2:2). Recent studies, however, have raised questions about the historical foundations of these traditions. They may have originated in an attempt of later *tannaim* to use the figure of Eleazar b. Arakh (otherwise largely ignored in tannaitic sources) as a prototype for the "sage who is able to achieve understanding though his own abilities" (Ḥag. 2:1), but nevertheless remains in need of the approval and supervision of his master in order successfully to engage in mystical speculation (Goshen-Gottstein; Wald). Similarly, the traditions concerning the "chain of mystical tradition" may have arisen out of a need to explain Akiva's unique success in the mystical ascent to the *pardes* (Tosef. Ḥag. 2:3–4), leading the Tosefta to connect Akiva through R. Joshua to an officially sanctioned rabbinic mystical tradition (Rabban Johanan b. Zakkai), to which the other three – all of whom were harmed in one way or another during the mystical ascent – were not privy. All the same, these traditions concerning Johanan's close connection with the origins of tannaitic mysticism are firmly rooted in the earliest sources, and they are progressively expanded and elaborated in later talmudic sources (Neusner, *Development of a Legend*, 247–52; Wald). Closely connected to these traditions are two statements ascribed to Johanan, the one describing the entrance to Gehinnom (Suk. 32b) and the other the size of the world (Ḥag. 13a; and see Pes. 94 a–b). Only very few of *halakhot* (Kelim 2:2, 17:16) report Johanan's own wording. Remnants of his teaching have apparently been preserved in tractate *Sotah*, too, particularly in chapters 8 and 9, in which there are many references to *tannaim* of the end of the Second Temple period.

Aggadot of the Destruction

Nothing is clearly known concerning Johanan's attitude to the events that took place in Jerusalem during the tempestuous years preceding the destruction of the Second Temple. There is certainly no reason to believe that he belonged to the party of the Zealots. Statements ascribed to him concerning the establishment of peace "between nation and nation, between government and government, between family and family" (Mekh., Ba-Ḥodesh, 11) were certainly intended to promote peace for everyone, even for a heathen in the street (Ber. 17a), this being borne out by his admonition: "Do not be precipitate in tearing down the high places of the non-Jews, that you shall not rebuild them with your hands, that you shall not tear down those of bricks and they will tell you to make them of stones, those of stones and they will tell you to make them of wood" (Mid. Tan. on Deut. 12:2). Johanan may have expected a peaceful issue of the conflict and the preservation of Jerusalem. According to amoraic and post-amoraic tradition, he even worked to this end, and only after becoming convinced that all hope was lost decided to leave the city. This aggadah has been preserved in four versions (ARN[1] 4, 22–24, ARN[2], 19; Lam. R. 1:5, no. 31; Git. 56a–b), in which there are not a few substantial differences and variants. Various editorial interpolations reflecting the spirit of the narrator's outlook can be discerned in the different versions of this story, such as Johanan's prophecy to Vespasian that the latter was destined to become emperor, ascribed by Josephus to himself (Wars, 3:399ff.), as well as the motif emphasizing Johanan's wisdom in the eyes of the non-Jews. All these sources agree that he succeeded in outwitting the extremists, left the besieged city, and arrived at Vespasian's camp, probably in 68 C.E. Scholars have offered radically differing evaluations of the historical reliability of these traditions. Based on an analysis of extra-talmudic evidence, G. Alon rejected much of these traditions, while favoring certain elements – Johanan's requests to the emperor – found only in Lam. R., largely because they fit well with his historical reconstruction. Others hold that the most probable tradition concerning his requests to the emperor is that preserved in the Babylonian Talmud, according to which he asked only that the sages of the generation be saved – Jabneh with its sages, the dynasty of Rabban Gamaliel, and R. Zadok – requests that were personal and circumscribed in character. Another, totally different approach to these traditions was begun with Neusner's groundbreaking synoptic studies in his *Development of a Legend* (228–34), in which he argued that the version in Lam. R. is literarily dependent on the version in the Babylonian Talmud, thus negating its value as an independent source of reliable historical information. In general, Neusner's literary and synoptic approach has led to a general reevaluation of the use of talmudic *aggadah* in the writing of history, with the emphasis moving away from the reconstruction of actual concrete events – which are rarely the concern of the later amoraic and post-amoraic *aggadah* – toward the analysis of the development of talmudic legends themselves and the changing perspectives and agendas of the different later talmudic storytellers. While a recent study has tried to show that the differing versions found in ARN manuscripts preserve a number of relatively early fragmentary traditions (Kister), this in no way affects the evaluation of the historical reliability of these works as a whole.

According to the legend, the destruction of the Temple, which he foresaw, stunned Johanan no less than his contemporaries, and his immediate reaction was one of profound grief: "Rabban Johanan sat and watched in the direction of the wall of Jerusalem to learn what was happening there, even as Eli sat upon his seat by the wayside watching [I Sam. 4:13]. When R. Johanan b. Zakkai saw that the Temple was destroyed and the *heikhal* burnt, he stood and rent his garments, took off his *tefillin*, and sat weeping, as did his pupils with him" (ARN[2] 7, 21). The cessation of the Temple service, one of the three things on which the world is based (Avot 1:2), led to a movement of excessive abstinence (Tosef., Sot. 15:11) and to a despair of the possibility of atoning for sins. Johanan took it upon himself to give guidance to the bewildered: "Once when R. Johanan b. Zakkai was leaving Jerusalem, R. Joshua was walking behind him and saw the Temple in ruins. R. Joshua said, 'Woe is us that this has been destroyed, the place where atonement was made for the sins of Israel.' 'No, my son, do you not know that we have a means of making atonement that is like it? And what is it? It is deeds of love, as it is said [Hos. 6:6]: "For I desire kindness, and not sacrifice"'" (ARN[1] 4, 21).

According to the aggadah, Johanan ascribed the destruction of the Temple to Israel's failure to perform the will of God; but the aggadists were also witness to the consequences of the Jewish people having been delivered "into the hands of a low people" (Ket. 66b). This led to differing attitudes toward the charitable acts of the non-Jews. Thus, according to one tradition, Johanan said: "Just as the sin and guilt offerings make atonement for Israel, so charity and kindness make atonement for the nations of the world" (BB 10b; see Dik. Sof., ad loc.). But, according to another post-talmudic tradition, Johanan praised his pupil Eleazar b. Arakh's exposition of the verse (Prov. 14:34): "Righteousness exalteth a nation, but the kindness of the peoples is sin," saying to his pupils, "I approve the words of Eleazar b. Arakh rather than yours, for he assigns charity and kindness to Israel and sins to the nations of the world" (PdRK 21). According to this view, after the destruction of the Temple the atonement of sins was denied not to Israel but to those who had destroyed it.

Johanan at Jabneh

According to these traditions, Johanan was not content merely with such expressions of consolation, but took concrete steps toward the renewal of the nation's religious and national leadership by raising the prestige of the *bet din* at Jabneh. The tannaitic traditions preserve a number of decrees established by Johanan, concerning the blowing of the *shofar* on Shabbat, the "day of waving," the taking of the *lulav* outside of the Temple, the acceptance of testimony concerning the new moon (Neusner, *Development of a Legend*, 206–9). These decrees all reflect the need to bring accepted *halakhah* in line with the changed circumstances after the destruction of the Temple. However, only one of these decrees is linked explicitly to Jabneh, and then only according to one version of the tradition (RH 4:1). Johanan is mentioned once in the context of a halakhic debate at Jabneh, but he is not explicitly described as playing any official role (Shek. 1:4). On the other hand, the Mishnah (Shab. 16:7; 22:3) quotes two decisions which Johanan gave in Arav in Lower Galilee, and according to the *amora* Ulla, he lived there for 18 years, during which time these were the only two incidents which came before him – hence the statement ascribed to him complaining of the hatred of the Torah in Galilee (TJ, Shab. 16:7, 15d). Johanan's name is connected in a tannaitic source (Tosef, Ma'as. 2:1) to another location – the village Beror Ḥayil – and a later talmudic tradition (TB, Sanh. 32b) even describes Johanan as having had a "yeshivah" there. All this stands in sharp contrast to Rabban Gamaliel, who is regularly described as playing an official leading role in the *bet din* at Jabneh (RH 2:8–9; Kelim 5:4; Tosef. Demai 2:6; Tosef. RH 2:11; Tosef. Sanh. 8:1).

These facts have fueled a sharp scholarly debate over the question whether Johanan ever occupied the position of *nasi*, and if so, whether he was universally recognized or exercised full authority (see Frankel, Brüell, Halevy, Alon, Safrai). A moderate view of events might suggest that Johanan helped to prepare the groundwork for the eventual reestablishment of the office of *nasi*, under Rabban Gamaliel, who was accorded the recognition due to him as the legitimate heir of that office. The date of Johanan's death is unknown, but the esteem of the generations for his image and work was expressed in the mishnaic statement (Sot. 9:15) that "when R. Johanan b. Zakkai died, the luster of wisdom ceased."

The *aggadah* of the Bavli provides this moving account of his death: "When he fell ill, his disciples went to visit him. When R. Johanan b. Zakkai saw them, he began to weep. His disciples said to him: 'Light of Israel, pillar of the right hand, mighty hammer! Why do you weep?' He replied: 'If I were being taken today before a human king who is here today and tomorrow in the grave, whose anger – if he is angry with me – does not last forever, who if he imprisons me does not imprison me forever, and who if he puts me to death does not put me to everlasting death, and whom I can persuade with words and bribe with money, even so I would weep. Now that I am being taken before the supreme King of Kings, who lives and endures for ever and ever, whose anger is an everlasting anger, who if He imprisons me imprisons me forever, who if He puts me to death puts me to death forever, and whom I cannot persuade with words or bribe with money – nay more, when there are two ways before me, one leading to Paradise and the other to Gehinnom, and I do not know by which I shall be taken, shall I not weep?'" It is possible that the reference to appearing before an earthly king may be connected with his appearance before Vespasian. At the moment of his death, he said to his disciples: "Remove the vessels so that they shall not become unclean, and prepare a throne for Hezekiah the king of Judah who is coming to accompany me into the next world" (Ber. 28b).

BIBLIOGRAPHY: J. Neusner, *A Life of Rabban Yoḥanan ben Zakkai* (1962, second revised edition 1970); idem, *The Development of a Legend: Studies on the Traditions Concerning Yoḥanan ben Zakkai*

(1970); Hyman, Toledot, 674–82; Landau, in: MGWJ, 1 (1852), 163–76; Frankel, Mishnah, 66–68; J. Spitz, *Rabban Jochanan ben Sakkai* (Ger., 1883); A. Schlatter, *Jochanan ben Zakkai, der Zeitgenosse der Apostel*, in: *Beitraege zur Foerderung christlicher Theologie*, 24 (1899; = *Synagoge und Kirche bis zum Barkochba-Aufstand* (1966), 175–236); Halevy, Dorot, 1 pt. 5 (1923), 41–71; Blau, in: MGWJ, 43 (1899), 548–61; Bacher, Tann; A. Buechler, in: *Tanulmányok Blau L.* (1938), 157–69 (Heb. pt.; = *Studies in Jewish History* (1956), 1–14 (Heb. pt.); Alon, Toledot, 1 (19593), 53–71; Alon, Meḥkarim, 1 (1957), 219–73; E.E. Urbach, *Ḥazal* (1969), index; idem, in: *Zion*, 16 (1951), pt. 3–4, 1–7; idem, in: *Beḥinot*, 4 (1953), 62–66; Epstein, Tannaim, 40–43, 400–3; Daube, in: JTS, 11 (1960), 53–62; Halevy, in: *Molad*, 21 (1963), 215–8; Y. Gilat, *Mishnato shel R. Eliezer b. Horkanos* (1968), 317–20; I. Konovitz, *Ma'arakhot Tanna'im*, 3 (1968), 80–97. **ADD. BIBLIOGRAPHY:** S. Safrai, in: Z. Baras, S. Safrai, M. Stern, Y. Tsafrir (eds.), *Ereẓ Israel from the Destruction of the Second Temple to the Moslem Conquest* (Hebrew), vol. 1 (1982), 18–30; M. Kister, in: *Tarbiz*, 67 (1998), 483–529; A. Goshen-Gottstein, *The Sinner and the Amnesiac* (2000), 233–65; S. Wald. "The Mystical Discourse of R. Eleazar ben Arach" (Hebrew), in: *JSIJ* (forthcoming).

[*Encyclopaedia Hebraica* / Stephen G. Wald (2nd ed.)]

JOHANAN HA-SANDELAR (first half of the second century C.E.), *tanna*, one of the last pupils of *Akiva (Ber. 22a; Gen. R. 61:3). Johanan's surname may mean "the sandal-maker," though it has been suggested that his surname reflects his place of origin ("of Alexandria") and not his profession (TJ, Ḥag. 3:1). Johanan is mentioned a number of times in the Mishnah and in the Tosefta, mainly discussing *halakhah* with the pupils of Akiva or transmitting it in his name. He is also mentioned in a tannaitic story, together with Eleazar b. Shammua, which relates that they "were on the way to Nisibis to Judah b. Bathyra to learn Torah from him, but when they reached Sidon and remembered the land of Israel, they raised their eyes, their tears flowed down, and they rent their garments … and said: dwelling in Ereẓ Israel is equal to all the precepts of the Torah, and so returned to their own place" (Sif. Deut. 80). The *aggadah* tells that when Akiva was imprisoned after the Bar Kokhba War for teaching Torah, the sages sent Johanan to him to obtain an answer to a problem arising from the harsh realities of those days – as to whether **ḥaliẓah* is valid if not executed before the *bet din*. Johanan pretended to be a peddler and by this ruse was able to bring the answer from the prison that it was valid (TJ, Yev. 12:5). Similarly, Johanan is enumerated among the scholars who convened in the valley of Bet Rimmon in order to revive the study of Torah and communal life after the persecutions had abated (TJ, Ḥag. 3:1). His favorite maxim was: "Every assembly which is for the sake of Heaven will in the end be established, and every assembly which is not for the sake of Heaven will not in the end be established" (Avot 4:11).

BIBLIOGRAPHY: Bacher, Tann, 2; Hyman, Toledot, s.v.

[Shmuel Safrai / Stephen G. Wald (2nd ed.)]

JOHANAN THE HASMONEAN (d. 161 B.C.E.), son of *Mattathias the Hasmonean and brother of Judah Maccabee, Jonathan, Simeon, and Eleazar. If their names in I Maccabees 2:2–5 are given in the order of their ages, he was the oldest son of Mattathias. His cognomen was "Gaddi" (alternate form "Gaddis" or "Gaddim"), the exact meaning of which is uncertain. The name Gaddi occurs in the Bible (Num. 13:11); some connect it with *gad*, "fortune," and others with "grain" (or "produce"). Johanan did not play an important role in the Hasmonean wars. He appears only in the difficult period following the death of Judah (160 B.C.E.), when he and his brothers were pursued by *Bacchides. He is referred to as "a leader of the multitude" (I Macc. 9:35), an office whose meaning is unknown. He was sent by his brother Jonathan to the Nabateans to deposit a large quantity of baggage with them. On the way he was attacked by the sons of Ambri (in Jos., Ant. 13:11 *Amaraios*) who dwelt in Madeba on the eastern bank of the Jordan but whose identity is not clear. They plundered the goods and killed Johanan and his men (I Macc. 9:36ff.; Jos., *ibid.*, 11ff.). Subsequently, Jonathan and Simeon made a surprise attack on the sons of Ambri while they were celebrating a wedding and avenged the blood of their brother by a mass slaughter (I Macc. 9:37–42.).

BIBLIOGRAPHY: Schuerer, Gesch, 1 (1901), 223–4.

[Uriel Rappaport]

JOHANNESBURG, largest city in the Republic of *South Africa; center of the world's most important gold producing industry. The city was founded in 1886, when gold was discovered on the Witwatersrand. The first Jewish inhabitants came mainly from Britain and Central Europe, but they were soon followed by immigrants from Eastern Europe, chiefly Lithuania, who later formed the bulk of the city's Jewish population. Some leading Jews – most of them not recent East European immigrants – were prominent among the "Uitlanders" whose demands for greater rights precipitated the South African War of 1899–1902. In 1896 there were 6,253 Jews in the city, more than half of them from Eastern Europe. By 1899 the Jewish population had risen to between 10,000 and 12,000. After the South African War ended the number increased rapidly, making the Johannesburg Jewish community the largest in South Africa, with half the country's total Jewish population. In 2001 Jews numbered approximately 48,000, about 66 percent of all Jews in South Africa. The vast majority live in the northern and northeastern suburbs.

Jews have been prominent in Johannesburg life from its earliest days. They were among the leaders of the gold mining industry and helped build up the city as South Africa's commercial, industrial, and financial center. Prominent among the Jewish "Randlords" were the colorful Barney *Barnato, Solly *Joel, and Samuel *Marks. From the earliest days of local government Jews were members of the municipal councils and Johannesburg had a long line of Jewish mayors, first of whom was Harry Graumann (1910). Jewish contributions to all aspects of cultural life have been considerable. Between the World Wars there was an active Yiddish theater with Sarah Sylvia as the leading actress. Four weekly Jewish newspapers (one in Yiddish, others in English) were published in Johannesburg and three monthly journals – one in English and the others in Yiddish and Hebrew. Jews are well represented in the teaching staff and student body of the Witwatersrand University and in the professions.

Communal Life

The first congregation in Johannesburg (the Witwatersrand Old Hebrew Congregation) was formed in 1887 and the first synagogue built in 1888. In 1892 the Johannesburg Hebrew Congregation built the Park Synagogue, which was opened by President Paul Kruger and served the community until the Great (Wolmarans Street) Synagogue was built. J.H. *Hertz was rabbi of the Old Hebrew Congregation (1898–1912); J.L. *Landau became rabbi of the Johannesburg Hebrew Congregation in 1903 and chief rabbi of the United Hebrew Congregation in 1915. He was succeeded from 1945 to 1961 by L.I. *Rabinowitz and by B.M. *Casper in 1963. C.K. *Harris became chief rabbi of the whole of South Africa in 1988, a position he held until the end of 2004 when he was replaced by W. Goldstein. After its foundation in 1892, the Johannesburg Orthodox Hebrew Congregation, whose members were primarily Eastern European immigrants, opened a synagogue the following year and moved to new premises (Beth Hamedrash Hagodal) in 1931. The first minister was Moshal Friedman and later incumbents were Isaac Kossowsky (1877–1951), who came to South Africa in 1933, and his son Michel (1908–1964). The growth of Johannesburg's suburban areas led to the establishment of many new congregations and synagogues. They numbered 55 in 1969, including three Reform temples, whose chief ministers have included rabbis Moses Cyrus Weiler (d. 2000) and Arthur Saul Super (d. 1979) and one Masorti congregation. There are 33 Orthodox synagogues, three Reform temples, and one Independent temple, affiliated to the Conservative movement. There has been a large growth in the *ba'al teshuvah* movement (returnees to Judaism), and 27 small *shtieblach* (synagogues) function in and around Johannesburg. The Lubavitch movement has made inroads into the community since its establishment in 1972. Ohr Somayach, Aish HaTorah, and Bnei Akiva also run highly successful programs. Bnei Akiva inaugurated a synagogue at its headquarters.

Johannesburg has a number of educational institutions set up or supervised by the South African Board of Jewish Education: a seminary for training teachers; three King David primary and two high schools (with a total enrollment in 2001 of 3,300). There are 18 Hebrew nursery schools. More intensive religious Jewish education is provided for approximately 2,000 pupils by Yeshiva College, the Torah Academy of the Lubavitch Foundation, the Bais Yaakov Girls' School, the Sha'arei Torah Primary School, Yeshivas Toras Emes, Yeshiva Maharsha, the Johannesburg Cheder and Hirsch Lyons. Yeshiva College, the largest of these schools, began as a part-time yeshivah in 1951 and became a full-time day school in 1958. The Menorah School (later called the Laila Bronner School) for girls was added in 1969. In 2004, Yeshiva College had a total of 850 students from nursery age to matriculation.

The United Hebrew Schools of Johannesburg provides Jewish education for pupils attending the government schools. Two religion schools are maintained by the S.A. United for Progressive Judaism in Johannesburg. There is a department of Hebrew with a full-time chair at the University of the Witwatersrand.

The Johannesburg Jewish Helping and Burial Society (Chevra Kaddisha) is the most important welfare institution in Johannesburg. Founded in 1887, in 2004 it incorporated a number of other important welfare institutions under its umbrella, amongst them the Jewish Women's Benevolent Society, Jewish Community Services, the Arcadia Jewish Orphanage, and the two Jewish aged homes – Sandringham Gardens and Our Parents Home. Other important welfare institutions include the free-loan societies the Witwatersrand Hebrew Benevolent Association (founded 1893) and the more recent Rambam Trust, the Selwyn Segal Home for Jewish Handicapped (1959), Yad Aharon, Hatzollah (medical rescue), Kadimah Occupational Centre, B'nai B'rith, and Nechama (bereavement counselling).

Zionism took early root in Johannesburg. The South African Zionist Federation was formed there in 1898, and the Zionist Center built in 1958 became an important cultural center until it was eventually sold in 1999. The headquarters of all Jewish national and many semi-national institutions are situated in Johannesburg. In addition to the three major organizations – the South African Jewish Board of Deputies (SAJBD), the South African Zionist Federation (SAZF), and the South African Board of Jewish Education – a large number of other institutions have their head offices in the city. In 2000, the SAJBD, SAZF, Union of Jewish Women, Israel United Appeal-United Communal Fund and a number of smaller organizations moved into single, shared premises, known as Beyachad. A range of welfare institutions, including the Chevra Kadisha and the South African Union of Jewish Students are affiliated to the SAJBD. The Jewish community is not to be measured merely in terms of its numerical strength. The intensity of Jewish life and identity and its strong Zionist devotion is to many a model for community organization.

BIBLIOGRAPHY: L. Herrman, *History of the Jews in South Africa* (1935), 238–40; P.H. Emden, *Randlords* (1935), passim; G. Saron and L. Hotz, *Jews in South Africa* (1955), index; L. Feldman, *Yidn in Johannesburg* (Yid., 1956); Bernstein, in: *South Africa Jewish Year Book* (1956), 29–39; M. Gitlin, *The Vision Amazing* (1950), index. **ADD. BIBLIOGRAPHY:** M. Kaplan and M Robertson (eds.), *Founders and Followers – Johannesburg Jewry, 1887–1915* (1991).

[Louis Hotz and Gustav Saron / David Saks (2nd ed.)]

°JOHN, kings of Portugal.

JOHN II (1455–1495), king of Portugal from 1481; one of the most distinguished Portuguese kings, he succeeded his father Alfonso V and became a most capable, but tyrannical ruler. He harshly repressed the feudal nobility, strengthened the monarchy, and promoted his country to greatness. John captured Tangier from the Moors, and the Portuguese exploration of Africa was extended during his reign. Two years after John succeeded to the throne, Don Isaac *Abrabanel had to flee Portugal because of his relations with the duke of Braganza, who was executed by John with several other members of the nobility in 1483. After the expulsion of the Jews from Spain in 1492, John authorized many refugees to settle temporarily in Portugal, mainly out of financial considerations. About 120,000 Jews then moved from Spain to Portugal, among them 600 wealthy families whom the king allowed to settle in his realm against payment of 100 ducats per head. Among the newcomers there was also Abraham *Zacuto who was appointed physician and astronomer to the king. John further allowed numerous refugees to stay in Portugal for eight months on payment of eight gold cruzados each; those who remained after that period were to be considered slaves. This proviso was effectively implemented in 1493, when he ordered those exiles from Spain who had stayed on in Portugal to be sold as slaves. Their children were removed and many of them sent to the Santo Tomé islands off the African coast, where they died because of the harsh conditions.

JOHN III (1502–1557), king of Portugal from 1521; son of Emanuel I, grandson of Ferdinand and Isabella, the Spanish monarchs, and brother-in-law of Emperor Charles V. In 1525 David *Reuveni arrived in Portugal and succeeded in rousing the king's interest in his fantastic projects. That year John asked the pope for permission to establish the Inquisition in Portugal, but this was delayed through negotiations by the *Marranos and their supporters with the pope. However, in 1531 the king appointed the monk, Diego da Silva, head of the Inquisition in Portugal without waiting for papal authorization, which was given in 1536. In that year a tribunal of the Inquisition began activities in *Évora against the Marranos there. In 1547, after numerous Marranos had fled from Portugal, John revived the law enacted in 1499 prohibiting the Marranos from leaving the country.

BIBLIOGRAPHY: M. Kayserling, *Geschichte der Juden in Portugal* (1876), index s.v. *João*; J. Mendes dos Remedios, *Os Judeus em Portugal* (1895), passim; N. Slouschz, *Ha-Anusim be-Portugal* (1932), passim; Roth, Marranos, index; Baron, Social[2], 11 (1967), 245–6; 13 (1969), 47ff.

°JOHN II (**"The Good"**; 1319–1364), king of France from 1350. His son *Charles V, who assumed the regency while John was in captivity in England, authorized the return of the Jews to France in 1359; it was largely due to their financial contributions that John's ransom could be paid to the English. This was probably the kernel of truth on which Gionnino Guccio of Siena, an impostor who claimed to be John I of France, based the story related in his memoirs, that he had received considerable sums from a Venetian Jew, Daniel, in return for promising to grant the Jews freedom of residence in France, once he was restored to the throne. Although John II confirmed his son's decree concerning the return of the Jews, he renewed the obligation to wear the Jewish *badge in 1363. A draft ordinance, which apparently was never promulgated, ordered the strict isolation of the Jews, prohibited theological disputations with Christians and possession of any books except the Bible, and, finally, ordered that circumcision should be delayed until children were able to answer questions concerning their faith.

BIBLIOGRAPHY: U. Robert, in: REJ, 6 (1882), 83; M. Jusselin, *ibid.*, 54 (1907), 142f.; E.G. Leonard, *Les Angevins de Naples* (1954), 390.

[Bernhard Blumenkranz]

°JOHN XXII (**Jacques Duèse**; b. c. 1245), pope at Avignon, 1316–34. Pragmatically adapting his attitude to suit the current situation, John XXII could be called neither benevolent nor severe in his dealings with the Jews. He wished to encourage the conversion of the Jews and advised employing a convert with a perfect knowledge of Hebrew and Aramaic to teach these languages to Christians (1319); he also allowed converts to keep their possessions (1320). In 1320 he intervened on at least five occasions to protect the Jews from the *Pastoureaux. However, in this same year, he once more determined to seize the Talmud and other Jewish books and considered expelling the Jews from Church lands. Although the expulsion order was revoked on the payment of large sums by a delegation of Jews from Rome, John XXII nevertheless proceeded to burn the Talmud in 1322, at the same time instituting local expulsion orders. He confirmed the jurisdiction of the Inquisition over converts who, suspected of Judaizing practices, had found refuge in monasteries (1317; 1322); only when Church revenue from the Jews was endangered, as in Apulia in 1328, did John take back from the Inquisition, for a temporary period, the jurisdiction over the Jews.

BIBLIOGRAPHY: Milano, Italia, 148; P. Browe, *Judenmission im Mittelalter* (1942), 208, 259; S. Grayzel, in: HUCA, 23 (1950/51), 37–80.

[Bernhard Blumenkranz]

°JOHN XXIII (1881–1963), pope 1958–63. Born Angelo Giuseppe Roncalli, he convened the Second Vatican Council (1962–65) and raised the papacy to new popularity with his warm, friendly style after the severe formality of his predecessor, *Pius XII. He served as a parish priest and seminary professor from 1904 to 1925 in Bergamo, Italy, and was appointed archbishop and papal nuncio to Bulgaria and later apostolic delegate to Turkey by Pope Pius XI (1922–39). While serving as nuncio in Istanbul, Turkey, during World War II, Roncalli distributed quasi-official-looking documents and other papers for Jewish refugees seeking to enter Palestine, sending thousands of such documents also to the papal nuncio in Budapest, Angelo Ratti, who was working closely with Raoul *Wallenberg and other neutral diplomats to save tens of thousands of Jewish lives. Roncalli intervened personally with the Queen of Bulgaria, a Catholic, eliciting her help in convincing her husband to protect the Jews of that country.

In 1944, he received the key post of France. When he saw a newsreel of the liberation of the death camp at Bergen-Belson, he is reported to have said: "*This* is the mystical body of Christ!" (a reference to Pope Pius XII's encyclical on the nature of the Church). Roncalli was made primate of Venice and a cardinal in 1953. When Pius XII died in 1958 after a long pontificate that began in 1939, the College of Cardinals looked for a candidate with a fresh touch and appeal, but who would not make any radical changes. Roncalli, popular with both the Italian and French cardinals (then the two largest groups) and 77 years old, seemed to fit the bill. In Venice, he was strict with his priests with regard to personal morality. He appeared decisive in making decisions quickly, relying on his faith in the Holy Spirit to guide him. Closer to the earth and the working community than his aristocratic predecessor, John did not see the world simply divided into simple good and evil (free world and communist), but was willing to work across the lines of division of the times, politically and theologically, startling many with his *apertismo* (policy of openness). He granted some 120 private audiences to Jewish individuals and groups, including representatives of the government of Israel, who were accorded the dignities of a state visit.

In an early act of his papacy, in March 1959, John XXIII suppressed the term "perfidious" from the Good Friday prayer, turning it into a "prayer for the Jews," though it was not until after the Council that it ceased to be a prayer for their conversion. That same year, he ordered an end to an annual pilgrimage to the shrine in *Deggendorf, Bavaria, where thousands of pilgrims came annually to "celebrate" the massacre in 1338 of the town's Jewish community. Also in 1959, he deleted from the Mass a petition made during the consecration referring to "the blood called upon (the Jews) of old," and from the rite of baptism the formula in which the baptized were to "abhor Jewish unbelief and reject the Hebrew error."

Finally in 1959, inspired, he said, by the Holy Spirit, John called for a world-wide synod of bishops, or Ecumenical Council. The Council he called was to be distinctive. It was not to condemn errors but to "open the windows" of the Church to the world and to other religions, an "*aggiornamento*" (updating) of the whole life of the Church. John's encyclicals, *Mater et Magistra* (1961) and *Pacem in Terris* (1963), established the spirit of the Council, just as Pope Pius XII's *Divino Afflante Spiritu* and *Mystici Corporis* (both in 1943) established its theological foundations by mandating the use of modern biblical scholarship in the former and offering a vision of the Church not as a hierarchy but a spiritual community.

In 1960, receiving a delegation of American Jewish leaders, he was presented with a Torah scroll to express gratitude for the Jewish lives he had saved during the Holocaust, and replied: "We are all sons of the same heavenly Father. Among us there must ever be the brightness of love and its practice." He concluded: "I am Joseph, your brother" (Genesis 45:4). In using his baptismal name, the pope was not only quoting the biblical self-revelation of Joseph to his brothers in Egypt, he was also making an unprecedented gesture of filial warmth toward all Jews, who he considered deserved their full dignity as descendants of the Patriarchs of the Bible. It was a statement pregnant with theological implications.

In October of 1960, John XXIII received French scholar Jules *Isaac, whose personal family losses during the Holocaust had caused him to study the origins of antisemitism in Christianity's ancient "teaching of contempt" against Judaism. He responded positively, placing the issue on the Council's agenda, and assigning Cardinal Augustine *Bea, S.J., a German biblical scholar and the pope's own confessor. Indeed, the first formal request by Catholics that the Council consider directly the bond between the Church and the Jewish People came on April 24, 1960, when the Pontifical Biblical Institute of Rome presented its formal *petitio*. It argued on the basis of the Pauline epistles and the Council of Trent that it was part of "the deposit of faith" that the Jews could not be seen as "rejected" by God or collectively guilty of the death of Jesus, despite the "erroneous interpretation of certain New Testament citations" over the centuries. After many adventures and the Pope's death, the statement, *Nostra Aetate*, was overwhelmingly approved by the Council Fathers on October 28, 1965. In just 15 Latin sentences, the document rejected the charge of Jewish guilt for the death of Jesus, established a new, positive understanding of the Jewish People in covenant with God, and called on the Church to engage Jews in a "dialogue of mutual esteem."

BIBLIOGRAPHY: P. Hebblethwaite, *Pope John XXIII: Shepherd of the Modern World* (1985); P. Lapide, *Three Popes and the Jews* (1967).

[Michael Berenbaum (2nd ed.)]

JOHN THE BAPTIST, the forerunner (*prodromus*) of Christ. There are two main sources of data regarding the life of John: the Gospels, the earliest of which were in circulation during the latter part of the first century, and Josephus' *Jewish Antiquities*, written following the fall of Jerusalem in 70 C.E. In addition there are apocryphal texts, such as the *Protevangelium of James*, from the mid-second century. If one accepts the infancy narrative in Luke 1:5–80 as based on factual biographical information, then John was born to parents (Zacharias and Elizabeth) from a priestly background. The OT allusions underline John the Baptist's role as ushering in the NT and his birth to the elderly Zechariah and his barren wife Elizabeth (a parallel to Abraham and Sarah) served to indicate the divine origin of his conception. His relation to Jesus is emphasized even before they were born: when Elizabeth heard Mary's greeting, her baby leaped in her womb (Luke 1:41). Even John's name (meaning "God shows grace") was given to him by the angel Gabriel. John's mother and Mary, mother of Jesus, are assumed to be cousins, but the Greek word in Luke 1:36 is not very specific and indicates only that they were kinswomen. The house of Zacharias was situated in a "city of Judah" in the hilly country, presumably at *Bet Cherem west of Jerusalem, identified at En Kerem. The apocryphal *Protevangelium of James* has Elizabeth fleeing with her baby from Herod's soldiers and hiding in a cave in the hilly country. Luke 1:80 suggests that the child John grew up in "wilderness places" before he came of age. It is unlikely that the child John would have been able to survive for very long in the inhospitable Judean Desert all by himself. Hence, there is nothing to support an oft-quoted theory that John was brought up by the *Essenes. Indeed, the Greek word *eremos* means a desolate or lonely region, i.e., a place that could be frequented by an occasional shepherd. Hence, there is no need to seek a childhood for John in a barren desert. John may have been brought up as a shepherd boy and as such would by necessity have spent spells of time by himself away from his parent's home (or from the house of the extended family if his parents had died). John wore an outer garment (an *adderet*) made of camel's skin and a leather girdle (Matthew 3:4; Mark 1:6), echoing the appearance of the Prophet Elijah (II Kings 1:8). There is no evidence that John was a Nazarite (cf. Num 6:1–4) or that he led an ascetic life. The reference to John not eating bread or wine probably indicates that John preferred to eat foods that had not been processed by human hands and would not therefore be susceptible to impurity. For this same reason John was said to have eaten locusts and honey (Matt. 3:4), both of which were regarded by his fellow Jews as pure items of food.

In terms of chronology, it would appear that John was born before the death of *Herod the Great (i.e., in 4 B.C.E. at the latest) and that he was called on his mission to the Jordan River in the 15th year of Tiberius Caesar (Luke 3:1–2), which would have been in 28 or 26 C.E. if one counts from the time of Tiberius' co-regency. It would appear therefore that we know nothing whatsoever about the events in John's life between the ages of 12, the time of his "shewing unto Israel" (Luke 1:80), and until he was about 30 and began his baptisms at the Jordan River. John evidently was attracted to the Jordan River because of its associations with the Prophet Elijah and his message was "repent, for the kingdom of heaven is at hand" (Matt. 3:2).

John baptized his followers to signify the drowning of their old life and their emergence from the water into a new life. Significantly, John is mentioned particularly as baptizing in the Jordan River, through which the 12 tribes of Israel passed into the promised land. John, like *Jesus later, immediately ran into conflict with the *Pharisees and *Sadducees for whom he had sharp words (Matt. 3:7–12). The Gospel of John relates that they asked him who he was; when John answered that he was neither the Christ nor the prophet Elijah, they queried his baptizing activities. John replied that he was baptizing in water only ("unto repentance," Matt. 3:11), but that he was to be followed by one who would baptize with the Holy Spirit and fire (that is, eternal punishment, cf. Matt. 3:11–12; John 1:19–28). According to the Gospels when John saw Jesus, he proclaimed him "the Lamb of God who takes away the sin of the world" and testified that he saw the Spirit descending as a dove out of heaven and abiding in him (at Jesus' baptism) going so far as to declare that "this is the Son of God" (John 1:29–34).

Jesus himself appraised his forerunner in Matthew 11:7–15: John was much more than a prophet, surpassing his predecessors in greatness and comparable to Elijah. Nevertheless, John's generation did not accept him, alleging instead that he was demon-possessed (Matt. 11:17–18), as was later said of Jesus himself. John was beheaded at Machaerus by the tetrarch Herod Antipas, who imprisoned him in revenge for John's condemnation of his incestuous marriage to his brother's wife, Herodias (Luke 3:19–20). Herodias' daughter danced for Herod, who rewarded her by offering her whatever she wished. On the advice of her mother, she requested the head of John the Baptist on a platter. Herod, who enjoyed listening to John (Mark 6:20), was grieved at being required to execute him; but having given his oath before witnesses, he commanded that it be done (Matt. 14:1–13; Mark 6:14–29). Luke 9:7–9 relates that when Herod later heard that Jesus was being identified with the resurrected John, he became curious about the subject of the rumor.

Recent archaeological work is shedding new light on John's early baptism activities in the "wilderness places" (Luke 1:80) and prior to his mission at the Jordan River. A cave was uncovered in 2000 at Suba/Tzova close to his traditional hometown at En Kerem (see *Bet Cherem) that was used in the early first century C.E. for ritual immersions in water, remarkably resembling John's baptism procedures at the Jordan River as described in the Gospels. The cave at Suba brought to light cultic installations and a foot-anointing stone. The cave was used later in the Byzantine period as a memorial cave and drawings of John the Baptist and symbols of his relic head and arms were found inscribed on the walls.

New archaeological work on the banks of the lower Jordan River has revealed churches of the Byzantine period, as well as sparse remains from the Roman period, associated with the traditional baptism spot.

BIBLIOGRAPHY: D. Flusser, *Tevilat Yeshu ve-Kat Midbar Yehudah* (1961); M. Dibelius, *Die urchristliche Ueberlieferung von Johannes dem Taeufer* (1911); E. Lohmeyer, *Das Urchristentum, vol. 1: Johannes der Taeufer* (1932); C.H. Kraeling, *John the Baptist* (1951); I. Steinmann, *Saint Jean-Baptiste et la spiritualité du désert* (1955); M. Goguel, *Au seuil de l'Evangile: Jean Baptiste* (1958²). **ADD. BIBLIOGRAPHY:** J. Bergeaud, *Saint Jean-Baptiste* (1961); D. Baldi, *Enchiridion Locorum Sanctorum: Documenta S. Evangelii Loca Respicientia* (1982); D. Baldi, and B. Bagatti, *Saint Jean-Baptiste: Dans Les Souvenirs de sa Patrie* (1980); O. Cullman, *Baptism in the New Testament*, Studies in Biblical Theology (1950); W.R. Farmer, "John the Baptist," in: G.A. Buttrick, *The Interpreter's Dictionary of the Bible* (1962), 955–62; P.W. Hollenbach, "John the Baptist," in: D.N. Freedman, *Anchor Bible Dictionary*, vol. 3 (1992), 887–99; C.H. Kraeling, *John the Baptist* (1951); H. Leclercq, "Jean-Baptiste (Saint)," in: F. Cabrol, and H. Leclercq, *Dictionnaire D'Archéologie Chrétienne et de Liturgie*, vol. 7 (1927), 2167–184; J. Murphy-O'Connor, "John the Baptist and Jesus: History and Hypotheses," in: *New Testament Studies*, 36 (1990), 359–74; H.C. Scobie, *John the Baptist* (1964); W.B. Tatum, *John the Baptist and Jesus: A Report of the Jesus Seminar* (1994); J.E. Taylor, *John the Baptist Within Second Temple Judaism* (1997); R.L. Webb, *John the Baptizer and Prophet: A Socio-Historical Study* (1991); W. Wink, *John the Baptist in the Gospel Tradition*

(1968, reprinted in 2000); S. Gibson, *The Cave of John the Baptist* (2004).

[Shimon Gibson (2nd ed.)]

°**JOHN CHRYSOSTOM** (354–407), most distinguished *Church Father of the East and one of the most virulently anti-Jewish preachers. Born in Antioch, the son of pagan parents, he was baptized in 373 and ordained a priest in 384. His eight sermons (homilies) against the Jews were delivered during his first two years of preaching activity in Antioch (386–387). They were written down verbatim by his audience and subsequently circulated. Thus their great anti-Jewish influence was felt beyond the period in which they were written. Chrysostom attacks not only the teachings of Judaism, but more especially the way of life and the views of contemporary Jews (incidentally, thereby giving valuable information on the life of Antioch Jewry in the fourth century and on the influence they exerted on their non-Jewish environment), accusing them of missionary activity, which dangerously competed with that of the Christians. The defeated and dispersed Jews, he ironically adds, were becoming the teachers of the whole world. He criticized those Christians in Antioch who cooperated with Jews in religious matters, kept the Sabbath, the "great fast," and other Jewish festivals; they even submitted to circumcision and participated in pilgrimages to Jewish holy places. Chrysostom claimed that on the Sabbaths and festivals the Jewish synagogue was full of Christians, especially Christian women, who loved the solemnity of the Jewish liturgy, enjoyed listening to the *shofar* on Rosh Ha-Shanah, and applauded famous preachers (according to contemporary custom). Chrysostom attempted to defame the synagogue, which he compared to a pagan temple and which he represented to his audience as the source of all vices and heresies. In this connection he reported that actors appeared in the synagogues on Jewish festivals. His claim that among the Jews the priesthood may be purchased and sold for money is specified by his biographer, Palladius, who writes that "the patriarch – as well as the head of the synagogue – is changed every year so as to replenish the cash-boxes." In other respects as well, Chrysostom, the pioneer of ascetic monkish life, criticized the Jews for their avarice and viciousness. He also testified to the Jewish influence on the judiciary of Antioch by reporting that Christians often took refuge in Jewish law courts and, when on oath, often used the Jewish oath formula. Even his sermons on the Maccabees were not in praise of the Jews, but in order to emphasize the difference between Jews and Christians, and it is not a mere coincidence that the destruction of the synagogue of Callinicon (also in Syria, cf. *Ambrose of Milan) took place immediately after a series of anti-Jewish sermons on the occasion of a procession in honor of the Maccabees in 388.

After a short period of activity in Constantinople, Chrysostom fell victim to court intrigues and was deposed by Emperor Arcadius. He then admitted that Jews, heretics, and pagans felt sorry for him, but Christians closed their hearts. Whether this "confession" was only a rhetoric paradox, or whether there were really Jews in Constantinople who behaved to him in a friendly manner, is hard to determine. Nor is it possible to decide if his downfall was not engineered by some influential Jews at Arcadius' court.

Like the writings of other Church Fathers, Chrysostom's books contain various exegetical commentaries that concur with talmudic *aggadah*.

BIBLIOGRAPHY: F. Perles, in: *Ben Chananja*, 3 (1860), 569–71; Graetz, Hist, 2 (1893), 613–4; H. Lucas, *Zur Geschichte der Juden im vierten Jahrhundert* (1910), 7–11; H. Usener, *Religionsgeschichtliche Untersuchungen* (1911), 235–47; Juster, Juifs, 1 (1914), 62–63; 2 (1914), 114, 125; B. Koetting, in: *Kirche und Synagoge* (1968), 158–65.

[Yohanan (Hans) Lewy]

JOHN (Johannan) THE ESSENE (d. 66 C.E.), patriot and leader, described by Josephus as a man of outstanding courage and sagacity. Already recognized for his ability at the beginning of the revolt against the Romans, he was placed in command of the province of Thamna by the revolutionary government. Shortly afterward, in association with Niger of Perea, the deputy governor of Idumea, and Silas the Babylonian, a trained soldier formerly in the service of King Agrippa (both of whom had distinguished themselves in the victory over *Cestius), he was put in charge of the disastrous expedition against Ashkelon.

He and Silas were killed in the first attack. It is doubtful if "the Essene" implies that he belonged to that body. It may mean "a man of Esse," i.e., Gerasa in Transjordan.

BIBLIOGRAPHY: Jos., Wars, 2:567; 3:19; Klausner, Bayit Sheni, 5 (1951^2), 309, index.

[Cecil Roth]

JOHN OF CAPUA (Johannes de Capua; 13th century), Italian translator who lived in Rome during the pontificate of Bonifacius VIII (1294–1303). Probably born in Capua before 1250, John of Capua, an apostate, is known for his translation of *Kalila and Dimna* from Hebrew into Latin. John translated this famous collection of tales, working on the basis of a previous Hebrew version done from Arabic in the 12th century by a Jew named Joel. He worked on this Latin translation between 1263 and 1278 and dedicated it to Cardinal Matteo Orsini. The work was thereafter widely known under its Latin name, *Directorium humanae vitae, alias parabolae antiquorum sapientium* ("The Guide of Human Life, or Proverbs of the Ancient Sages"). The influence of the *Directorium* on the writers and collectors of fables with an ethical-didactic purpose was immense, and eminent writers and novelists dealt with this work until the 17th century. The *Directorium* was first published between 1484 and 1493; a critical edition was established by F. Geissler only in 1960. John of Capua also translated – always from the Hebrew translations of the Arabic – treatises dealing with medicine, including the *al-Taysīr* ("The Facilitation"), a treaty on pathology and therapeutics by Abu Marwan ibn Zuhr (1090–1162); several medical texts by Maimonides: "On

Hygiene" (*De regimine sanitatis*) dedicated to Bonifacius VIII, "On the Causes of Accidents" (*De causis accidentium*), *De haemorroidibus*, on the initiative of one of the papal physicians and possibly also *De coitu*.

BIBLIOGRAPHY: Steinschneider, Uebersetzungen, 2 (1893), 748, 772, 875–6, 981. **ADD. BIBLIOGRAPHY:** F. Geissler, in: *Mitteilungen des Instituts fuer Orientforschung*, 9 (1963), 433–61; M. Zonta, in: *Dizionario Biografico degli Italiani*, vol. 55 (2000), 760–61.

[Joseph Baruch Sermoneta / Alessandro Guetta (2nd ed.)]

JOHN OF GISCALA (Johanan ben Levi), a leader of the revolt against Rome (66–70 C.E.). John was a native of *Giscala (Gush Ḥalav) in Galilee. Little is known of him before the war. When the inhabitants of Tyre, Gadara, and others sacked and burned his native town, he rebuilt it and took revenge on the invaders. His realization that the Romans had stood by and even encouraged the invaders to attack Jews made him alter his former attitude of loyalty toward the Romans, and he began to prepare Galilee for the coming struggle. In the spring of 66, *Josephus arrived as commander of Galilee and was soon involved with John in a conflict which developed into a lasting and bitter struggle. Josephus' account is prejudiced by his personal animosity toward John, but he nevertheless gives credit to John's efforts in preparing for the struggle. John suggested to Josephus that funds be provided from the sale of grain belonging to the Romans, and from olive oil sold to Jews in Syria. He presumably needed these funds for defense, although Josephus accuses him of desiring to use them for personal purposes. Open conflict erupted between them at Tiberias when John learned that Josephus intended to restore the property plundered from the steward of King Agrippa, who was considered a Roman sympathizer. John's supporters included many Galileans; fugitives from Tyre; men of Gabara, including their leader, Simon; Justus of Tiberias and his father Pistus; and the archon of Tiberias, *Joshua (Jesus) son of Sapphas. John dispatched a delegation to Jerusalem, demanding that Josephus be dismissed from his position for failing to fulfill his tasks loyally. This request was acceded to, according to Josephus, as a result of John's bribery and exploitation of his friendship with *Simeon b. Gamaliel. Emissaries were sent to dismiss Josephus from his command and advise the citizens of Galilee to support John. Josephus ignored all this and went so far as to threaten John's supporters. Josephus claims that he succeeded in weaning most of John's followers away from him. John's efforts to organize Galilee for war were unsuccessful and, with the exception of his native city, the whole province fell to the Romans. In the winter of 67, when Titus was at the gates of Giscala and offered terms of surrender, John seized on the intervening Sabbath as a pretext for delaying negotiations and escaped to Jerusalem.

John in Jerusalem

John encouraged the insurgents in Jerusalem to continue the war against Rome. At first he cooperated with *Anan b. Anan and members of the government. Relations between the Zealots and the government, however, steadily deteriorated and reached a crisis when *Phinehas (Phanni) b. Samuel, the high priest, was selected by lot. In the ensuing struggle the priestly circles aroused the people against the Zealots; John tried to serve as mediator. Josephus accused him of betraying the trust placed in him, but it seems that John became convinced that it was impossible to bridge the gulf between the two camps and went over to the side of the Zealots. He may possibly have been influenced by rumors that the moderate elements were thinking of surrendering the city to the Romans. On his advice, the Zealots, who had fortified themselves in the Temple, made common cause with the Idumeans and together overcame the moderates. The government of Jerusalem was thus concentrated in John's hands, causing division for a time among the Zealots, as those in Jerusalem disapproved of the supremacy of the Galilean, and one of their leaders, *Eleazar b. Simeon, actually opposed John for a time. John gradually prevailed and the Jerusalem Zealots joined his camp. Josephus portrays the period of John's rule in Jerusalem in the most somber terms, depicting complete anarchy and lack of regard for human life. Even if it is conceded that the Zealots avenged themselves on their opponents with scant regard for judicial procedure, John's positive efforts to fortify the city and properly equip it against the coming siege cannot be overlooked. His opponents, however, would not reconcile themselves to his victory and invited *Simeon Bar Giora to the city to head the opposing forces. Incessant internecine strife between the two leaders was checked in part, but not entirely, only when Titus appeared at the gates of the city. As the siege intensified, John did not hesitate to melt down the vessels of the Temple to provide weapons and used the Temple's supplies set aside for ritual purposes to ease the famine. With the city's capture, John was among the prisoners taken to Rome and included in Titus' triumphal victory procession. Simeon Bar Giora was apparently regarded by the Romans as the Jewish commander in chief and was executed, while John was sentenced to life imprisonment.

BIBLIOGRAPHY: Schuerer, Hist, 251f., 257f., 260, 262–73; Klausner, Bayit Sheni (1951²), index s.v. *Yoḥanan b. Levi*; Josephus, index; C. Roth, *Dead Sea Scrolls* (1965), index.

[Lea Roth]

°**JOHN PAUL II** (1920–2005), pope from 1978 to 2005. Born Karol Wojtyla in Wadowice, Poland, he was a student in the University of Cracow when the Germans invaded Poland, effectively closing the university. Under the occupation he worked in a stone quarry, continuing his involvement with theatrical and literary circles that engaged in anti-Nazi resistance, and possibly helping Jews escape, while studying in an "underground" seminary. He established early and lasting friendships with Jews. Ordained a priest in 1946, Wojtla was sent to Rome, where he earned a doctorate of theology, with a thesis on St. John of the Cross. He then took a doctorate in philosophy at the Jagellonian University, with a dissertation on Max Scheler. He published numerous theological and philosophical articles and books of poetry, the latter often under the name "Jawien."

Consecrated auxiliary bishop of Cracow in 1958, he participated in the Second Vatican Council, where he was credited with the compromise that led to the document "The Church in the Modern World" (*Gaudium et Spes*). He became archbishop of Cracow in 1964 and cardinal in 1967.

As pope, he continued the theological renewal begun by the Council, although his approaches were not without controversy, and wrote numerous encyclicals on Christ, human dignity, and various social issues. His support for the Polish labor movement, Solidarity, and other such groups in Eastern Europe, even while maintaining a diplomatic *Ostpolitik*, is credited as one of the factors leading to the collapse of Soviet hegemony. He traveled more widely throughout the world than any of his predecessors, invariably meeting with Christian, Jewish, and other leaders of major world religions, many of whom he brought together in prayer in late 1986 in Assisi, Italy. In 1981 he survived an assassin's bullet. He worked assiduously for the cause of world peace.

John Paul was the first pope to visit a death camp, *Auschwitz, in 1979. The Communist monument there, as at *Babi Yar, intentionally obscured the Jewish and Polish specificities of the camp, making it a memorial to humanity in general. Stones in different languages were set up representing the countries from which the victims came. The pope stopped and prayed at only two: first the Hebrew inscription, and then the Polish, subtly rebuking the memorial's ideology.

In 1986 the pope again made history by being the first since St. Peter to visit and pray in a synagogue, the Great Synagogue of Rome. He had condemned antisemitism as "sinful" earlier that year in Austria. At the synagogue, he affirmed the validity of Jewish faith and God's covenant with the Jews: "The Jewish religion is not extrinsic to us, but in a certain way intrinsic to our own religion. With Judaism, therefore, we have a relationship, which we do not have with any other religion. You are our dearly beloved brothers and, in a certain way, it can be said that you are our elder brothers." Though some Jews thought this referred to Jacob usurping the divine promise from his elder brother, Esau, the reference was most likely to the parable of the prodigal son, in which the father reassures the elder son: "My son, you are here with me always; everything I have is yours" (Luke 15:31).

In 1987 the pope met with the Jewish leadership of both Poland, which had the world's largest Jewish community before World War II, and the United States. In Warsaw, he called Jewish witness to the *Shoah* a prophetic "warning voice for all humanity." In the U.S. that same year, the pope called for the integration of Holocaust education on every level of Catholic education and for the world to recognize the right of the Jews "to a homeland," an important point in view of the infamous United Nations resolution attacking Zionism as "racism."

When the newly reunited Germany sent its first ambassador to the Vatican in 1990, the pope for the first time spoke of "the heavy burden of guilt for the murder of the Jewish people" that for Christians "must be an enduring call to repentance." In December 1993 the Vatican and Israel entered into a "Fundamental Agreement," exchanging ambassadors the next summer. In 1994, too, the pope presided over a Shoah Day concert within the Vatican itself, yet another "first."

Controversies, many of them centered on Holocaust issues, also marked John Paul's long pontificate. The longest-running, the Auschwitz Convent controversy, began in early 1986 and was not resolved until 1993 when the pope personally sent a letter to the Carmelite nuns to move to the new property a short distance away which had been built for them. They left, however, the large cross that had been in their garden, which came to be surrounded by numerous smaller crosses erected by some Polish Catholics. These were removed by the government on the eve of the pope's eighth trip to Poland in 1999, though the large cross remains.

In summer 1987, only weeks before the Pope was to meet with representatives of the U.S. Jewish community, the world's largest, a papal audience was arranged for the president of Austria, Kurt Waldheim, who had just been revealed to have been a member of the Nazi Party during World War II, creating a crisis that was resolved only by a meeting of Jewish leaders with the Pope at Castel Gandalfo ten days before the scheduled Miami meeting.

Controversies have also revolved around candidates for sainthood, such as Edith Stein (a Roman Catholic nun who was a Jewish convert to Catholicism and died in Auschwitz because she was defined by the Nazis as a Jew), *Pius XI (who raised in his household as a Catholic a Jewish boy forcibly taken from his parents on the word of a family maid that she had baptized him), Catherine Emmerich (a 19th century nun whose reputed visions of Jesus' death typified and intensified anti-Jewish elements found in passion plays in the period), Queen Isabella (see *Ferdinand and Isabella) of Spain (who ordered the expulsion of the Jews in 1492 and institutionalized the Inquisition), and *Pius XII (who served as pope during World War II).

In February of 2000, the pope led a Liturgy of Repentance in which he articulated the Church's repentance for the sins against Jews by Catholics over the centuries. Later that month the pope went to Israel. His predecessor, *Paul VI, had very briefly come to Jerusalem in 1964, entering Jerusalem without acknowledging the borders of the State of Israel, but this was the first extensive visit by a pope to the Jewish state. As was his custom, the pope kissed the soil of the land. The pope visited *Yad Vashem, Israel's memorial to the victims of the Holocaust, meeting there with a group of survivors. Finally, he went to the Western Wall, the last remnant of the Jerusalem Temple. There, he placed a prayer of petition to the God of Israel.

> God of our fathers,
> you chose Abraham and his descendants
> to bring Your name to the nations:
> we are deeply saddened
> by the behavior of those
> who in the course of history

have caused these children of Yours to suffer
and asking Your forgiveness
we wish to commit ourselves
to genuine brotherhood
with the people of the Covenant

John Paul died on April 2, 2005. He was succeeded by Pope Benedict XVI.

BIBLIOGRAPHY: E. Fisher & L. Klenicki (ed.), *Spiritual Pilgrimage: Pope John Paul II on Jews and Judaism 1979–1995* (1995); *New Catholic Encyclopedia Jubilee Volume: The Wojtyla Years* (2001).

[Eugene J. Fisher (2nd ed.)]

°JOHNSON, LYNDON BAINES (1908–1973), 36th president of the United States. As Democratic floor leader, he opposed President Eisenhower's plan for sanctions against Israel after the 1956 Arab-Israel war.

As president, Johnson was extremely effective in pushing through Congress significant and far-reaching liberal measures which were strongly welcomed by Jews and other American minority groups to whom they were of obvious benefit. These "Great Society" programs sought to remove poverty, discrimination, and ignorance, and included important welfare, civil rights, tax reduction, education, and employment legislation. As a result, the customary strong affinity of American Jews for the Democratic Party, especially its liberal wing, continued under the Johnson administration. In the Middle East Johnson proved a friend to Israel. In addition to providing political and economic support, he was instrumental in creating a joint U.S.-Israeli study program for a large water desalinization project to meet Israel's pressing need for more fresh water. In 1966 he met with President Shazar of Israel who was on an unofficial visit to the U.S. At the time of the 1967 Six-Day War, he worked closely with the Soviet Union to prevent a major power confrontation, while at the same time firmly upholding Israel's basic rights. Subsequently he withstood various pressures and continued to uphold Israel's right to have "secure and agreed frontiers" as a precondition to her evacuating territories occupied as a result of the Six-Day War. In 1968 he received the Israel premier Levi *Eshkol. Later that year Johnson announced that he had acceded to Eshkol's request to supply Israel with Phantom jet planes. One of Johnson's close associates was the Texas businessman J. *Novy.

[Stanley L. Falk]

JOIGNY (Heb. יואני), town in the Yonne department, central France. The present Rue des Juifs is a reminder of the medieval Jewish community, known only through the scholars who originated there. Most important of these were the tosafists and exegetes Menahem b. Perez of Joigny (12th century) and *Yom Tov b. Isaac of Joigny (martyred at *York in 1190), a tosafist named Joseph, and an exegete, Samson.

BIBLIOGRAPHY: Gross, Gal Jud, 250–3; Urbach, Tosafot, index s.v. the various tosafists.

[Bernhard Blumenkranz]

JOKNEAM (Heb. יָקְנְעָם), royal Canaanite city near Mount Carmel. Jokneam appears in the list of Canaanite kings defeated by Joshua (Josh. 12:22) and is already mentioned in the list of conquests of Thutmosis III in about 1469 B.C.E. (no. 113: ʿn qnʿm, "the spring of [Jo]kneam"). It was a levitical city of the Merari family (Josh. 21:34) in the territory of the tribe of Zebulun, whose boundaries reached as far as the "brook that is before Jokneam" (Josh. 19:11). Some scholars maintain that Solomon's fifth district extended "as far as beyond" Jokneam, but the city Jokneam is in fact mentioned in this connection (I Kings 4:12; cf. I Chron. 6:53). It was apparently destroyed by the Assyrian Tiglath-Pileser III in 733/2 B.C.E. and does not appear in later sources. Eusebius called it Kammona, a village six Roman miles north of Legio (Lajjun – the mishnaic Kefar Otnay). It was called Caimont in Crusader times, when it was a fief of the royal domain with its own court of burgesses. Jokneam is identified with Tell Qamūn (today Tel Jokneam near the village of the same name), a prominent mound of 23½ dunams which contains pottery from the Canaanite and Israelite periods.

[Michael Avi-Yonah]

Contemporary Period

Modern Jokneam is a semi-urban community and moshav on the southwestern rim of the Jezreel Valley. Jokneam was founded as a village in 1935 by settlers from various countries, Holland, Yemen, and Eastern Europe. After World War II, demobilized soldiers joined the first settlers. Jokneam then adopted the form of a *kefar shittufi*, similar to a moshav, and later became affiliated with Ha-Mo'aẓah ha-Ḥakla'it. The inhabitants mainly engaged in farming intensive field, fruit (including melon), and garden crops, as well as raising livestock. In 1968 the moshav had 440 inhabitants and at the end of 2002 it numbered 1,020 residents. In the first years of statehood, new immigrants received temporary, and later permanent housing at Jokneam. The local labor force, which in the initial years had to rely mainly on public works, was eventually absorbed in metal and other industries. In 1967 the semi-urban settlement was separated from the moshav and in 1968 given municipal council status, at which time it had 3,640 inhabitants. By the end of 2002 the population had grown to 16,700. The municipality's jurisdiction includes 3 sq. mi. (8 sq. km.).

[Efraim Orni / Shaked Gilboa (2nd ed.)]

BIBLIOGRAPHY: Abel, Geog, 2 (1938), 365–6; Albright, in: JBL, 58 (1939), 184; EM, s.v.

JOKTAN (Heb. יָקְטָן), younger son of Eber and brother of Peleg in the line of *Shem (Gen. 10:25; I Chron. 1:19). He fathered 13 sons or nations (Gen. 10:26–29; I Chron. 1:20–23), the names of most of which can be identified with Arabian tribes or place-names. Indeed, their settlements are said to have extended from Mesha which is in the north of Arabia to Sephar, the hill country to the east (Gen. 10:30). The origin of the name is uncertain.

BIBLIOGRAPHY: A. Reuveni, *Shem, Ḥam, ve-Yafet* (1932), index; J.A. Montgomery, *Arabia and the Bible* (1934), 37ff.; B. Maisler, in: *Zion*, 11 (1946), 13; H.Z. Hirschberg, *Yisrael ba-Arav* (1946), 30–32; M.D. Cassuto, *Commentary on Genesis*, 2 (1964), 221. **ADD. BIBLIOGRAPHY:** R. Hess, in: ABD, 3:935.

JOLLES, JACOB ẒEVI BEN NAPHTALI (c. 1778–1825), Galician talmudic scholar and kabbalist. Born in Przemysl, he served as rabbi in Glogow and Dinow. He leaned toward Ḥasidism, and was among the disciples of Jacob Isaac ha-Ḥozeh of Lublin. His most famous work was *Melo ha-Ro'im* (Zolkiew, 1838), an encyclopedic work on the rules and principles of rabbinic law which made a great impression and was reprinted several times. His other published works are *Ḥinnukh Beit Yehudah*, a homiletic work in philosophic style (Warsaw, 1869); *Kehillat Ya'akov*, an encyclopedic treatment of kabbalistic topics (Lemberg, 1870); *Emet le-Ya'akov*, a homiletic work in ḥasidic style (Lemberg, 1884); *Beit Va'ad le-Ḥakhamim*, a directory of talmudic sages (Cracow, 1884); *Parashat Derakhim Zuta*, homiletic discourses (Cracow, 1885); *Zikhron Ya'akov vi-Yhudah* also consisting of homiletic discourses (Munkacz, 1928); and *Yashresh Ya'akov*, on Kabbalah (New York, 1945). His notes and novellae on the Talmud are printed in the Vilna edition. Jolles composed many other books (27 are referred to in his foreword to *Melo ha-Ro'im*), but most of them have disappeared.

BIBLIOGRAPHY: A. Walden, *Shem ha-Gedolim he-Ḥadash*, 1 (1864), s.v.; Fuenn, Keneset, s.v.

[Aryeh-Leib Kalish]

JOLLES, ZECHARIAH ISAIAH (1816–1852), talmudic scholar and *maskil*. Jolles was born in Lemberg. He corresponded with the great contemporary rabbis including Akiva *Eger and Z.H. *Chajes on halakhic topics, and with *maskilim* (such as Ḥ.Z. *Slonimski, I.H. Jost, and others) on Jewish scholarship. He was critical of "talmudists without secular scholarship" and of scholars "who had forgotten Torah." In his youth he published two pamphlets: *Dover Meisharim* (Lemberg, 1831) in which he established that the *Haggahot ha-Shas* attributed to Mordecai *Jaffe was not by him; and *Et Ledabber* (*ibid.*, 1834), a kind of letter of moral advice to a younger rabbi in the spirit of moderate *Haskalah. Jolles welcomed the plans of Uvarov, the Russian minister of education, to establish Jewish schools and was one of Max *Lilienthal's supporters when the latter came to Minsk in 1842. After his death in Minsk, his son Sussman Jolles published his writings: *Zekher Yeshayahu* (2 vols., 1882), novellae on Maimonides' *Mishneh Torah* and responsa; *Sefer ha-Torah ve-ha-Ḥokhmah* (1913), containing his other writings including letters and poems. These writings are interesting, as they reveal the intermediate position of one who lived during the transition between the traditional rabbinic outlook and Haskalah.

BIBLIOGRAPHY: Z.I. Jolles, *Sefer ha-Torah ve-ha-Ḥokhmah* (1913), introduction; B.Z. Eisenstadt, *Rabbanei Minsk ve-Ḥakhameha* (1898), 29–31, 46.

JOLLES, ZVI ENRICO (1902–1971), organic chemist. Born in Lemberg, Jolles was a pioneer in Ereẓ Israel in 1920 and worked on the land until 1924. He immigrated to Italy and studied at the University of Florence, where he subsequently became associate professor of applied chemistry and was consultant to the Italian Directorate of Naval Armaments (1931–34). In 1938, when the Fascists applied racial laws in Italy, he was dismissed from all appointments. He found refuge in London, joining the biochemical department of the Lister Institute. In 1940 Jolles joined the dyestuffs division of Imperial Chemical Industries in Manchester, where he pioneered novel dyestuffs applications, in particular fiber-reactive dyes. In 1955 he was appointed research director of two commercial firms, where he established a successful range of flame-retardants and other additives for polymers. On retiring he became adviser to the national Council for Research and Development of Israel. He contributed numerous papers, mainly in the field of nitrogen compounds. He was the author of more than 30 patents in fields of applied chemistry. He edited and contributed to *Bromine and its Compounds* (1966).

[Samuel Aaron Miller]

JOLOWICZ, HERBERT FELIX (1890–1954), British legal scholar. Probably Britain's foremost scholar of Roman law, Jolowicz was born in London and educated at St. Pauls School, Cambridge University, and in Germany. After service in World War I, Jolowicz became a barrister and, in turn, reader in Roman Law at University College, London, and then, from 1948, Regius Professor of Civil Law at Oxford. Because of England's common law system, Roman law had been relatively neglected by scholars. Jolowicz established an international reputation with such works as his *Historical Introduction to the Study of Roman Law* (1932) and his posthumously published *Roman Foundations of Modern Law*. He was noted for the excellence of his classroom teaching.

BIBLIOGRAPHY: ODNB online.

[William D. Rubinstein (2nd ed.)]

JOLSON, AL (**Asa Yoelson**; 1886–1950), U.S. singer, vaudeville and film star. Born in Srednik, Lithuania, the son of a cantor, Jolson worked for some years in circuses, minstrel shows, and vaudeville houses in the U.S. In 1911 he was an instant success in his first Broadway appearance, *La Belle Paree*. Then came a long succession of starring roles in musicals, including *Vera Violetta* (1911); *The Whirl of Society* (1912); *The Honeymoon Express* (1913); *Sinbad* (1918), which had a two-year run; *Bombo* (1921), at Jolson's 59th Street Theater (named in his honor by the Shuberts); *Big Boy* (1925); *Ziegfeld Follies* (1927); and *Wonder Bar* (1931). Known in show business as "the world's greatest entertainer," Jolson had a dynamic personality. He received unparalleled rave reviews; and his adoring fans would explode with enthusiasm when he came on stage, often holding up the progress of the show with their unbridled cheers and applause.

In 1927 Jolson made screen history in *The Jazz Singer*, the first full-length talking film made in America. This was followed by *The Singing Fool*. Jolson's hearty, exuberant style was particularly well suited to early "talkie" technique. His other films, mainly musicals, included *Say It with Songs* (1929), *Mammy* (1930), *Big Boy* (1930), *Hallelujah I'm a Bum* (1933), *Wonder Bar* (1934), *Go into Your Dance* (1935), *The Singing Kid* (1936), *Rose of Washington Square* (1939), and *Swanee River* (1939).

Some of the songs that Jolson is credited to have co-written are "California, Here I Come," "Me and My Shadow," and "Sonny Boy."

The film *The Jolson Story* (1946) was based on his career and starred Larry Parks in the title role, using Jolson's dubbed voice. It was such a success that a second film followed three years later, entitled *Jolson Sings Again* (1949). To date, it is the only biography sequel in film history.

In 1948, Jolson was voted Most Popular Male Vocalist by a *Variety* poll, superseding such top singing stars of the time as Frank Sinatra, Bing Crosby, and Perry Como.

Jolson died shortly after returning from Korea, where he had gone to entertain the UN troops. He was awarded the Medal of Merit posthumously. His will divided more than $4,000,000 equally among Jewish, Protestant, and Catholic charities and established scholarships for undergraduates.

BIBLIOGRAPHY: P. Sieben, *The Immortal Jolson, His Life and Times* (1963). **ADD. BIBLIOGRAPHY:** H. Goldman, *Jolson: The Legend Comes to Life* (1988); D. McLelland, *Blackface to Blacklist* (1987); R. Oberfirst, *Al Jolson: You Ain't Heard Nothin' Yet* (1982); B. Anderton, *Sonny Boy: The World of Al Jolson* (1975); M. Freedland, *Jolson* (1973).

[Jo Ranson / Ruth Beloff (2nd ed.)]

JONA, GIOVANNI BATTISTA (1588–1668), apostate scholar. Jona was born Judah Jona at Safed in Galilee and for that reason was known also as Galileo. After a life of wandering, apparently as a teacher and, according to his own account, as a rabbi, in Italy, Holland, and Germany, he, his wife, and children converted to Christianity in Warsaw in 1625. The kings of Poland and Sweden were among their godparents. Contrary to normal practice, he retained his previous Jewish surname. After further wanderings he arrived in Rome in 1638, where he became a reader in Hebrew at the College of *Propaganda Fide*. Among his publications are Hebrew translations of the Christian catechism, *Limmud ha-Meshiḥim* (Rome, 1658), and of the New Testament (1668), which he dedicated to Pope Clement IX. Extant in manuscript are a dictionary of talmudic idioms and a work on Targum variants which was completed by Guilio Morosini.

BIBLIOGRAPHY: P.S. Medici, *Catalogo de' Neofiti Illustri* (Florence, 1701), 24ff.; Vogelstein-Rieger, 2 (1896), 256f.

JONAH (mid-fourth century C.E.), Palestinian *amora*. Jonah and his associate Yose (Yosi) were the heads of the "Beit Va'ad" (the Sanhedrin) in Tiberias. The Jerusalem Talmud is replete with the halakhic discussions of these two scholars; there is not a single tractate in which they are not mentioned. However, whereas Jonah is frequently referred to in the order *Zera'im* and progressively less and less in the succeeding orders until in *Nashim* and *Nezikin* he is hardly talked of at all, his associate Yose, who outlived him (TJ, Ma'as. Sh. 4:9, 55b), is consistently mentioned throughout. Jonah, a pupil of Johanan's pupils, such as Ilai and Ze'ira, established original principles for the study of the Talmud and the understanding of the Mishnah. For instance, he established that the minimum quantities given by the Talmud, such as an olive's bulk or that of an egg, are of rabbinic and not biblical origin (TJ, Pe'ah 1:1, 15a); that when the Mishnah introduces a law with the comprehensive word "all" or "these," it does not imply that the laws referred to are of permanent validity (TJ, Yev. 2:5, 12d), and that many incidents related in the Bible and the Mishnah are given not in order to establish the *halakhah* for future generations, but mainly to provide information about how they were practiced in earlier generations (TJ, Shev. 1:7, 33a). In many cases he rejects the formula of the Mishnah and the order of its statements, preferring that of the Tosefta. He emends the Mishnah in various ways and asserts that it should be taught accordingly, in contrast to Yose who endeavors to justify the text of the accepted Mishnah (TJ, RH 2:1, 57d; Pes. 1:2, 27c). One of his novel interpretations is in the story told of him that he gave his *tithes to Aḥa b. Ulla, not because he was a priest but because he was occupied with study (TJ, Ma'as. Sh. 5:5, 56b). Many of the *amoraim* of the succeeding generation, including some of the "scholars of the south," were his pupils.

Jonah is also mentioned several times in the Babylonian Talmud, and in one place is referred to as one of "the resolute men of Palestine" who are "more saintly than the pious of Babylon" (Ta'an. 23b). Jonah, like Yose, was not only the head of the Sanhedrin, preaching in public and teaching *halakhah*, but was also politically active. During their time, the rebellion of Gallus broke out (351) and some of their halakhic rulings are connected with this event. While the Roman armies were stationed in the country they both permitted the Jews of Galilee to bake bread for the army of Ursicinus on the Sabbath because, in demanding this, "the aim [of the soldiers] was not to apostatize, but merely the desire for fresh bread" (TJ, Shev. 4:2, 35a). They forbade the inhabitants of Sennabris, whose *Sefer Torah* had been burnt by Ursicinus, to use a defective scroll. The Talmud adds that they gave this ruling not because it was the *halakhah*, but so that the people of the locality should purchase another scroll (TJ, Meg. 3:1, 74a). Another tradition tells of their journey to Antioch, their meeting with Ursicinus, and the great honor he showed them (TJ, Ber. 5:1, 9a). It is possible that this visit was not during the revolt but during Ursicinus' second journey to Syria in 361 for the Parthian war (but see Lieberman, in JQR, 36 (1946), 341 n. 89). Very little of Jonah's *aggadah* has been preserved, but accounts of many of his pious deeds have been transmitted, particularly his deeds of charity. When a person of good family became impoverished he said to him: "My son, I have heard that you have been left a legacy, take this money; you can repay it when you receive the legacy." When he had taken it he would say: "Let it be a gift"

(TJ, Pe'ah 8:9, 21b). He was succeeded by his son Mani *II as head of the council of the Tiberias community.

BIBLIOGRAPHY: Frankel, Mevo 98–99; Graetz, Gesch, 4 (1908), 304ff.; Weiss, Dor, 3 (19044), 98–100; Z.W. Rabinowitz, *Sha'arei Torat Bavel* (1961), 433, 435; Epstein, Mishnah, 395–9.

[Shmuel Safrai]

JONAH, BOOK OF (Heb. יוֹנָה), the fifth in the collection of the 12 short prophetic books (*Minor Prophets). Unlike the other books of this collection the Book of Jonah contains a prophecy of only five words (3:4); the rest of the book is a story about Jonah son of Amittai. The book was added to the prophetic books, probably because a prophet of this name was known from the time of Jeroboam II (II Kings 14:25.) and because the book deals with the problem of a man whose task it was to bring the word of God to Nineveh.

Outline of Contents

Jonah son of Amittai is ordered by YHWH to go to Nineveh and proclaim judgment upon its people for their wickedness. Jonah refuses to fulfill the mission and tries to escape. At Jaffa he boards a ship bound for Tarshish, a direction precisely opposite to Nineveh. YHWH brings on a great storm. The sailors try to avert the danger by praying to their gods and jettisoning the cargo. Jonah, who has gone to sleep, is awakened by the captain who asks him to pray to his God, in the hope that He may prove responsive. The sailors then decide to find out by casting lots on whose account the misfortune has come upon them. The lot falls on Jonah, and they try to find out what wrong he has done. Jonah discloses that he is fleeing from a mission of his god, YHWH, and that the only way they can make the storm abate is by heaving him overboard. The sailors first try to row back to land, but this proves futile, so they throw Jonah overboard and pray to the Lord not to hold them guilty for his murder, since it was He who has left them no other way of saving themselves. The storm subsides at once and the sailors, who now fear YHWH, offer sacrifices and make vows (Jonah 1). Jonah himself is swallowed by a great fish, from inside of which he prays to YHWH, and after three days and nights in the fish's belly he is spewed out on dry land (Jonah 2).

Jonah is called by YHWH a second time to bring His message to Nineveh. This time Jonah does go to Nineveh, a huge city. He proclaims that in 40 days Nineveh will be overthrown. The people of Nineveh believe God, proclaim a fast, and put on sackcloth. The king of Nineveh too takes part in the acts of repentance and orders all the inhabitants to pray to God and to repent of their evil ways: "God may turn and relent" (3:9). As a result of Nineveh's repentance, God renounces the punishment He had planned to bring upon it (Jonah 3). Jonah is greatly displeased by this mercy and complains of it to YHWH: he had tried to escape his mission in the final place for fear that YHWH would be moved to renounce His punishment out of mercy. In his vexation Jonah asks YHWH to take his life. At this time Jonah is outside Nineveh sitting in the shade of a booth waiting to see what will happen to the city. The Lord causes a ricinus plant (see *castor oil plant) to grow unexpectedly over Jonah to provide shade over his head, to his great relief. On the following day, however, the Lord provides a worm, which attacks the plant causing it to wither. When the sun rises, the Lord causes a sultry east wind to beat down on Jonah's head. Jonah becomes faint and asks for death. Then the Lord says: "You cared about the plant, which you did not work for and which you did not grow, which appeared overnight and perished overnight. And should I not care about Nineveh, that great city, in which there are more than a hundred and twenty thousand persons who do not yet know their right hand from their left, and many beasts as well?" (4:10–11).

The Unity of the Book

The Book of Jonah raises exegetical problems, such as the question why the king had to order the people (and the cattle too!) to wear sackcloth and to fast, after they had already done so on their own initiative (3:5–8), or why Jonah needed the ricinus plant while he sat in the shade of the booth (4:5–6). Some scholars have tried to solve these problems by the application of the source-theory. However, some 20th century scholars argued for the unitary authorship of the book while allowing for the possibility of later additions. Some scholars regard verse 4:5, which seems out of place, as one of these additions. Others place this verse after 3:4. The Psalm of Jonah (2:3–10) is regarded by many scholars as an interpolation, particularly because it is neither an expression of penitence nor a plea for deliverance, but is a thanksgiving psalm. The conditions referred to in the psalm also have nothing to do with the distress experienced in a fish's belly. The psalm could, therefore, have been added to the book later. However, it has been shown that the psalm is probably an integral part of the book. Some of the main expressions in the psalm relate directly to the language used in the previous chapter (cf. 1:2, 6 with 2:3; 1:16 with 2:10) and apparently came to determine the choice of psalms by narrative authors at an early date; cf. the choice of "Hannah's psalm" solely on account of I Sam. 2:5b (Y. Kaufmann). Besides, the removal of the psalm from the book would unbalance the symmetry of the two major parts (G.H. Cohen, G.M. Landes). It may therefore be assumed that the psalm – though perhaps borrowed or compiled from another source – was always part of the book.

Special attention should be given to the changes in the use of God's names. YHWH ("the Lord") is His name as the God of the "Hebrew" (1:9) Jonah. In connection with the non-Israelite people of Nineveh He is *Elohim*, "God." The sin for which Nineveh is judged is not idolatry but lawlessness (3:8). Jonah objects to God's habit of renouncing a punishment which was merited and has already been decreed, but God's purpose in sending prophets to announce His punishments is precisely to make them unnecessary. For He has precisely the "sentimental" attachment which Job 10:3a, 8ff. accuses Him of lacking; and besides there are always the innocent children and dumb beasts (Jonah 4:10–11).

The Motifs of the Book

The main motifs of the book are similar to those found in the literature of other cultures. Many stories tell about a person's being swallowed by a great fish and rescued thereafter (Heracles the Hesione, Perseus and Andromeda, etc.). However, only in the Book of Jonah is the man in the fish rescued not by force (fire from inside or sword from outside) but by prayer, his salvation thus resulting from the combined action of God and humans. It should also be noted that in the Jonah story the fish and the man remain unharmed. Thus the story of Jonah – despite its similarities to other stories – has a unique biblical character. Basically, the same situation of the Book of Jonah is found in the story of Daniel's rescue from the lion-pit and the salvation of the three boys from the fiery furnace (Dan. 3 and 6). In all these stories the motif of swallowing becomes a symbol for the act of faith between God and humanity.

The common factor in all parts of the story is the acceptance of God's commands. Jonah tries to escape God's will but he learns that this cannot be accomplished. Even the sea and the great fish, which according to myth are great independent powers in the universe (cf. Isa. 51:9–10; Ps. 74:13–15; 89:10–11; Job 26:12), have to obey the orders of God. The sea becomes stormy and calm according to the wish of God (1:3, 15); the fish swallows and spews out according to God's order (2:1, 11); the castor-oil plant, the worm, and the east wind are all obedient servants of God (4:6–8).

The Teaching of the Book

The purpose of the book has been explained in various ways. According to many scholars the book is to be understood in its historical context. The best-known opinion connects the book with the times of Ezra and Nehemiah and assumes that it is the expression of universalistic opposition to the particularistic ideas of that time. This has been challenged by the observation that a book which uses Nineveh as the symbol of the repenting city and which does not mention the name Israel even once has such an historic tendency.

The book has also been regarded as an essay dealing with the profession of the prophet. The prophet cannot escape his mission and he should not regard it as weakness or failure if his prophecy is not fulfilled. However, since the book does not speak explicitly about prophets and prophecy (the word is not mentioned even once) and since Jonah's argumentation contains no aspects of his personal life, this explanation seems improbable too. In addition, the whole point of classical biblical prophecy is to bring sinners to repent so that they may avoid destruction. In that case any successful prophet of rebuke would fail the test of prophecy (e.g., Ezek. 3:18).

The Book of Jonah has to be understood as a lesson in divine governance, forgiveness and mercy. Jonah tries to escape his mission, explaining to God that he had fled because he knows that God often relents after having decreed punishment (Jonah 4:2; cf. Joel 4:13). Indeed, God renounces his punishment after the repentance of the city out of mercy for the inhabitants.

As pointed out by Simon, underlying Jonah's complaint is the notion that divine forgiveness should not wipe out all penalty (cf. Jonah 4:2 with Exod. 34:6–7), the threat of penalty serving as a deterrent. But whereas human rulers require deterrence in order to maintain the social order, God does not require it. As the story shows, God has the power to intervene at anytime. He sends the storm (1:4); "appoints" the fish to swallow Jonah (2:1); commands the fish to spew him out (2:11); "appoints" the plant (4:6); and the worm that makes it wither (4:7). The book begins and ends with the word of God, an assertion of God's absolute power over all creation, the sea and the dry land (1:9). The greatest theological challenge facing the author was the identity of the god in whose name Jonah's prophecy (3:4) was delivered. To use the specifically Israelite name Yahweh as the source of Jonah's words would have implied conversion of the Ninevites. In contrast, to have had the Ninevites turning to their native gods, Asshur and Ishtar for example, would have been a theological enormity for a Hebrew writer. Accordingly, the neutral *elohim* (3:5) was employed.

The Date of Origin

Opinions vary greatly concerning the date of the book's composition. Some date it as early as the eighth century B.C.E. and accept it as a story told about Jonah the prophet who lived in the time of Jeroboam II similar to stories about Elijah and Elisha (cf. II Kings 8:4). Others date it as late as the third century B.C.E. As the book is mentioned by Ben Sira (49:10) it cannot have been written later than his time.

The main points for fixing the date are the following:

(1) The language: Some words seem to be late like the relative pronoun *she* and the Aramaisms *mallaḥ* (1:5); *yitʿashet* (1:6); *taʿam* (3:7); and *ribbo* (4:11). However, *she* is attested very early in northern Israel (Jud. 5:7; 6:17) and, for geographical reasons, Aramaisms may likewise have penetrated there at an early date. The presence of many Aramaisms however, suggests a relatively late date.

(2) Reference to Nineveh: It is said about Nineveh that it "was an enormously large city" (3:3) and it seems therefore that the book was written after the destruction of this famous city (612 B.C.E.). In contrast, it has been pointed out that the past tense can also be used to describe a continuous existing situation (cf. Jer. 1:18). This, however, does not account for the unhistorical title "king of Nineveh" and the legendary size of the city.

(3) The identity of the prophet: The question of the date of the book is related to the time of the prophet, who, apparently, was a historical figure (II Kings 14:25). However, if the prophet's name was chosen only to give a later book more authority, the prophet's identity cannot be helpful in fixing the date of the book's composition, especially since it is possible that the story is connected with a historical prophet, but the book itself was written much later.

(4) Parallels to other books: The Book of Jonah contains parallels to the stories about Elijah (cf. Jonah 4:3 with I Kings

19:4); to the prophecies of Jeremiah (cf. Jonah 3:8–10 with Jer. 18:7–8); and particularly to the Book of Joel (cf. Jonah 3:9 with Joel 2:14; Jonah 4:2 with Joel 2:13). It is, however, impossible to prove if and in which way these sources influenced the Book of Jonah or were influenced by it.

It is quite probable that the book recounts an early story, since the people of Nineveh are worshiping idols, but the prophet only speaks, as in early times, against their moral sins. The lack of any national aspect has also been cited in favor of an early date of the story, which was perhaps first told orally and written down only at a later date.

The Book of Jonah aroused special interest throughout the ages not only because of its dramatic content and literary devices but also because of its important role in the religious world. The book of Jonah is read in the synagogue at the Day of Atonement afternoon service (Meg. 31a).

[Gabriel H. Cohn / S. David Sperling (2nd ed.)]

In the Aggadah

When sent to prophesy against Nineveh, Jonah suppressed his prophecy, although liable to suffer death at the hands of Heaven for doing so (Sanh. 11:5), and did not go, preferring rather to honor the son (the people of Israel) than the Father (the Almighty). For were he to go to Nineveh, Jonah argued, its people would immediately repent, with the result that the Almighty would have mercy on them and hold Israel blameworthy, declaring that, unlike the gentiles, they became stubborn whenever He sent His prophets to them (cf. Matt. 12:41). Jonah tried to flee abroad to a gentile country "where the Divine Presence neither dwells nor appears." First the sailors plunged him in the sea up to his knees and then up to his neck, each time the sea became calm but grew stormy again when they lifted him back on deck. Thereupon they hurled Jonah into the sea, which immediately stopped its raging (Mekh., Bo, Introduction: Tanh., Lev., 8; PdRE 10).

[Elimelech Epstein Halevy]

In Christianity

Jonah is regarded in Christianity as the proof of the capacity of the gentiles for salvation and the design of God to make them partake of it. This is the "sign of Jonas" referred to in Luke 11: 29–30. In the same passage he is referred to, as are many of the prophets, as a forerunner of Jesus. "The men of Nineveh … repented at the preaching of Jonas; and behold, one greater than Jonas is here" (*ibid.*, v. 32). Similarly the three days and three nights which he spent in the whale's belly are seen as a prefiguration of the three days and three nights he would be "in the heart of the earth" (Matt. 12:40).

In Islam

Yūnus (Jonah) the prophet, "the man of the fish," was one of the most prominent descendants of Abraham. He was one of the apostles of Allah, even though he fled from his mission because he thought that Allah did not control him (Sura 6:86; 22:87). Sura 10 of the *Koran is named after him. In Sura 37:139–49, *Muhammad relates how Jonah hid in a ship loaded with freight. His fate, however, designated him for destruction. Had he not praised Allah, he would have remained in the belly of the fish until the day of the resurrection of the dead. The myriads who were warned by Jonah believed in Allah and continued to enjoy His mercies for a time (Sura 10:96–98). Umayya ibn Abi al-Ṣalt (Schulthess, 32:21) knew that Jonah had stayed only a few days in the belly of the fish. The story of Jonah was a favorite subject in Islamic legend; several motifs worthy of adaptation are found in it: the repentance of the inhabitants of Nineveh on the day of *ʿāshūraʾ*: the sojourn of Jonah in the belly of the fish; his prayer, etc.

[Haïm Z'ew Hirschberg]

In the Arts

The allegorical nature of the Book of Jonah and the colorful episodes which it contains have inspired writers, artists and musicians throughout the ages. One of the earliest literary works based on Jonah was *Patience*, an anonymous English adaptation in verse probably dating from the mid-14th century. The theme of the punishment awaiting the "sinful city" was exploited by English puritanical writers of the 16th and 17th centuries. Thus, *A Looking Glasse for London and England* (London, 1594), a play by Robert Greene and Thomas Lodge, weaves the story of Jonah into a dramatic account of the kingdom of Israel after the overthrow of Jeroboam. In their comparison of Nineveh with vice-ridden London, the playwrights mingled Elizabethan satire with biblical and moralistic elements in the spirit of the Reformation. The subject also inspired *A Feaste for Wormes* (1620), a paraphrase of Jonah by the English royalist writer Francis Quarles, in whose *Divine Poems* (1630) the story later reappeared. Two other works of the 17th century were the anonymous English tragicomedy *Nineveh's Repentance* (c. 1656) and *Jonas* by the German Protestant poet Martin Opitz. The subject fell into comparative neglect until the second half of the 19th century, when the *Historie of Jonah*, a dramatic poem, appeared in Zachary Boyd's *Four Poems from "Zion's Flowers"* (1855). This was followed by John Ritchie's dramatic poem *The Prophet Jonah* (1860), John T. Beer's play *The Prophet of Nineveh* (1877), and *Profeta-lomb* ("The Prophet Bough," 1877), a work by the Hungarian writer János Arany.

There was a revival of interest in the theme among writers of the 20th century. A.P. Herbert's *The Book of Jonah (As almost any modern Irishman would have written it)* (1921) was a novel, comic dramatization of the biblical story written in a broad Irish brogue. Behind the superficial frivolity of the Scots playwright James Bridie's *Jonah and the Whale* (1932; revised as *Jonah 3* in *Plays for Plain People*, 1944) lies a more serious and sympathetic approach to the central issue. This contrasts with Laurence Housman's playlet *The Burden of Nineveh* (in *Old Testament Plays*, 1950), an attempt to debunk the Bible. Two other works in English were *A Masque of Mercy* (1947), a play in blank verse by the U.S. poet Robert Frost presenting the theme of man's relationship with God in Christian terms; and the English novelist and critic Aldous Huxley's poem "Jonah" (in *The Cherry Tree*, 1959). *Der Mann in Fisch* (1963) was a novel about Jonah by the German religious writer Stefan Andres. Perhaps because of its nautical interest, the subject has also inspired works by several Scandinavian authors, notably Haakon B. Mahrt's Norwegian novel *Jonas* (1935), Harald Tandrup's Danish novel *Profeten Jonas privat* (1937; *Jonah and the Voice*, 1937), and Olov Hartman's modern Swedish miracle play *Profet och timmerman* (1954). Works about Jonah by 20th-century Jewish writers include the U.S. novelist Robert *Nathan's *Jonah; or the Withering Vine* (1925; published in Britain as *Son of Amittai*, 1925); M.C. Lichtenstein's Yiddish novel *Yonah ben Amittai* (1929); a Hebrew play of the same title by Meir Foner (1930); and *It Should Happen to a Dog* (1956), a one-act play by Wolf *Mankowitz utilizing the humor and idiom of London's Jewish East End.

In art, there are no less than 57 examples in catacombs in Rome and on numerous sarcophagi, from the second to the first centuries, some of which may possibly be Jewish. The four scenes are: the storm, the swallowing and spewing forth by the whale, and Jonah chiding God. In specifically Christian typology, the story has three parts, the parallelism between Jonah and the whale and the visit to Limbo by Jesus being paramount. The Jewish tradition appears fully in the four-part Jonah sarcophagus of the British Museum. The Jonah cycle may well be older than its Christological interpretation, and the sarcophagus would thus afford an indication of a lost Jewish pictorial prototype.

[Helen Rosenau]

Individual representations of Jonah are rare. The two major examples are the figure by Michelangelo in the Sistine Chapel, Rome, and the marble statue designed by Raphael and executed by his pupil Lorenzetto di Ludovico Lotto(?) in the church of Santa Maria del Popolo, Rome. The prophet, who is generally represented as bald, is here shown as a nude youth with curly hair. The story of Jonah and the fish as a prefiguration of the Entombment and Resurrection and the resurrection of the individual soul and the hope of life hereafter accounts for its extraordinary popularity in the funerary art of the early Christians. An interesting fourth-century ivory relief of the subject is found on the Lipsanoteca in the Museo Civico Cristiano at Brescia.

Jonah was also a popular subject in Byzantine manuscripts of the 6th–11th centuries, including the sixth-century Rabula Codex, the Topography of Kosmas Indikopleustès (Vatican), the ninth-century Homilies of Gregory of Nazianz, and the 11th-century Khlyudov Psalter (Moscow). In these, new episodes are illustrated, such as the "calling" of Jonah (Jonah 1:2), his embarkation at Joppa (Jonah 1:3), and his preaching before the king of Nineveh (Jonah 3:4ff.). The theme was less popular in the Middle Ages, but survived as one of the types of the Resurrection. Some notable medieval examples are the early 13th-century sculpture at Bamburg showing the bald Jonah engaged in animated conversation with the prophet Hosea; and the delightful illuminations in the 12th-century *Hortus Deliciarum* (University Library, Strasbourg) and Admont Bible (National Library, Vienna). In both manuscripts, Jonah is shown emerging from a fish, in the latter case with a rhetorical gesture, as if about to make a speech. Illuminations of Jonah were also included in medieval Hebrew Manuscripts, such as the Spanish Cervera Bible (1300; Lisbon National Library) and the Kennicott Bible (1476; Bodleian Library, Oxford). In an early 15-century German *maḥzor* (Academy of Sciences, Budapest), there is a casual, but vivid, sketch of a bald and mustachioed Jonah sitting under the gourd (Jonah 4:6).

After the Middle Ages, the subject was comparatively rare. Rubens included a painting of Jonah thrown into the sea as the predella of a triptych of the miraculous draught of fishes ordered by the Malines Fishmongers Corporation in 1618; and there is a stormy landscape of the same subject by Gaspard Poussin at Windsor Castle, England. In Italy, Salvator Rosa painted a picture of Jonah preaching to the Ninevites. The Israel wood-engraver Jacob *Steinhardt illustrated the Book of Jonah in 1953.

Musical compositions on the Jonah theme are less abundant. One of the early masters of the oratorio, Giacomo Carissimi (1605–1674), wrote an oratorio, *Jona* (of which a 19th-century revision by Ferdinand *Hiller has remained in manuscript); two notable oratorios dating from 1689 are G.B. Bassani's *Giona*, which has an opening instrumental "Sea Symphony," and the *Giona* of G.B. Vitali. In the 18th century P. Anfossi (1727–1797) composed *Ninive conversa* and, in the 19th century, the subject was represented, like most biblical stories, in the English festival-oratorio production. Some increase in musical interest has been noticeable in the 20th century, with Hugo Chaim *Adler's cantata *Jonah* (1943) and oratorios by Lennox Berkeley (*Jonah*, 1935), Mario *Castelnuovo-Tedesco (*Jonah*, 1951), and Vladimir *Voegel (*Jonah ging doch nach Ninive*, for speaker, baritone solo, speaking-choir, mixed choir, and orchestra, 1958).

[Bathja Bayer]

BIBLIOGRAPHY: INTRODUCTIONS: S.R. Driver, *Introduction to the Literature of the Old Testament* (1913), 321–32; R. Pfeiffer, *Introduction to the Old Testament* (1948), 586–9; A. Bentzen, *Introduction to the Old Testament* (1952), 144–7; O. Eissfeldt, *The Old Testament, An Introduction* (1965), 403–6; H.L. Ginsburg, *The Five Megilloth and Jonah* (1969). COMMENTARIES AND SPECIAL STUDIES: H. Schmidt, *Jona, Eine Untersuchung zur vergleichenden Religionsgeschichte* (1907); S.D. Goitein, in: JPOS, 17 (1937), 63–77; A. Feuillet, in: RB, 54 (1947), 161–86; G. Ch. Aalders, *The Problem of the Book of Jonah* (1948); H. Rosin, *The Lord Is God* (1955), 6–54; Kaufmann Y., Toledot, 2 (1960), 279–87; N. Lohfink, in: BZ, 5 (1961), 185–203; H.W. Wolff, *Studien zum Jonabuch* (1965); G.M. Landes, in: *Interpretation*, 21 (1967), 3–31; E.J. Bickerman, *Four Strange Books of the Bible* (1967), 1–49; L. Frankel, in: *Ma'yanot*, 9 (1967), 193–207; G.H. Cohn, *Das Buch Jona* (1969). IN THE AGGADAH: Ginzberg, Legends, 7 (1938), 261 (index); Urbach, in: *Tarbiz*, 20 (1950), 118–22. IN ISLAM: D. Sidersky, *Les origines des légendes musulmanes dans le Coran et dans les vies des Prophètes* (1933), 130; H.Z. (J.W.) Hirschberg, *Juedische und christliche Lehren im vor- und fruehislamischen Arabien* (1939), 63–64; Umayya ibn Abi al-Ṣalt, *Umajja ibn Abi's Salt; die unter seinem Namen ueberlieferten Gedichtfragmente*, tr.by F. Schulthess (1911); H.A.R. Gibb and J.H. Kramers (eds.), *Shorter Encyclopaedia of Islam* (1953), s.v. *Yūnus b. Mattai*, incl.

bibl. **ADD. BIBLIOGRAPHY:** "*Yūnus*," in: EIS[2], 11 (2002), 347–49 (incl. bibl.). IN THE ARTS: H. Rosenau, in: *Journal of the British Archaeological Association*, 3rd Series, 24 (1961), 60 ff.; U. Steffen, *Das Mysterium von Tod und Auferstehung: Formen und Wandlungen des Jona-Motivs* (1963); G. Landes, in: *Eretz Israel*, 16 (1982), 147*–70; J. Magonet, in: ABD, 3:936–42 (with bibliography); idem, in: DBI, 1:620–22; U. Simon, *The JPS Commentary Jonah* (1999); D. Marcus, *Review of Biblical Literature* 10/30 (electronic review of Simon; 2000).

JONAH, MOSES (16th century), kabbalist and one of the most important disciples of Isaac *Luria. Ḥayyim *Vital places him in the second group of Luria's pupils (*Sha'ar ha-Gilgulim*) and states that this is his first transmigration as a human being, and therefore he is a great jester and his conduct is not seemly (*Sefer ha-Gilgulim*, "The Book of Transmigrations," 1875, 66). These remarks attest to some personal tension between the two kabbalists, which is also borne out by the story quoted in Menahem *Lonzano's book, *Omer Man*, on Luria's last words before his death. According to this story, Jonah asked Luria if Vital understood his doctrine and Luria answered "A little." Jonah headed a yeshivah in Safed for a time and also spent some time in Egypt and Constantinople. His signature occasionally appears (c. 1590) on letters sent from Safed to Worms. His fragmentary notes on Luria's Kabbalah (of 1586) are in an autograph in the Schocken collection. However, several years earlier, apparently in the 1570s, he had written a systematic treatise on his teacher's Kabbalah. In 1582 he himself copied this book, called *Kanfei Yonah* in the complete manuscripts, and dedicated it to one of the rich men of Constantinople. The bulk of this copy is preserved in Sassoon Ms. 993. This work is clear and well arranged and is superior in several respects to Vital's different editions of *Eẓ Ḥayyim*. Menahem Azariah da *Fano compiled extracts from this book in five parts, 1–4 (1785) and 5 (1899); manuscripts of the original book also circulated widely (Ms. Ben Zvi Institute, 2218). Jonah taught Jacob Schweinfurt, who brought some of his kabbalistic traditions to Germany in 1613. A summary of Jonah's major work in 13 chapters was printed under the title *Sha'ar ha-Kelalim* at the beginning of the published editions of *Eẓ Ḥayyim*. It is said in many manuscripts that this summary was written by three kabbalists: Moses *Najara, Jonah, and Joseph *Arzin.

BIBLIOGRAPHY: Yaari, Sheluḥei, 153; Kaufmann, in: mgwj, 42 (1898), 96; M. Ḥagiz, *Magen David of David b. Zimra* (1713), preface; J. Hahn, *Yosif Omeẓ* (1928), 271.

[Gershom Scholem]

JONAH BEN ABRAHAM GERONDI (c. 1200–1263), Spanish rabbi, author, and moralist. In his youth Gerondi studied in the French yeshivot under Moses b. Shneur and his brother *Samuel of Evreux, and later under *Solomon b. Abraham of Montpellier. When in 1232 the latter began his campaign against Maimonides' philosophical works, Jonah followed his teacher and became one of his most devoted assistants in the conflict, which ended, according to tradition, in the burning of these books by the Inquisition. A few years later, in 1240, in the same square in which Maimonides' books had been burnt, tractates of the Talmud were burnt and Jonah saw this as divine retribution. Tradition has it that he repented, proclaiming in the synagogues: "I undertake to prostrate myself at Maimonides' grave and to confess that I spoke and sinned against his books" (letter of Hillel of Verona). Consequently, Jonah devoted himself to the study of Maimonides' works. Legend tells that Jonah tried to travel to Ereẓ Israel to ask forgiveness at Maimonides' grave, but was delayed in Toledo, where he later died violently. Modern scholars disagree as to the veracity of this account. Everyone is in agreement that Jonah reversed his opinion of Maimonides in the latter part of his life. Gerondi was in contact with *Isaac the Blind, son of *Abraham b. David of Posquières, concerning Kabbalah. Naḥmanides was his cousin and in-law. Jonah returned from France to his birthplace, Gerona, and began to preach publicly his *torat ha-musar* (doctrine of ethics and morality) – a subject which was near to his heart all his life. Later he left Gerona and settled in Barcelona, where pupils from Spain and elsewhere flocked to him. These included some of the outstanding rabbis of the next generation, such as Solomon b. Abraham *Adret and *Hillel b. Samuel of Verona. Years later, he left for Ereẓ Israel, but on passing through Toledo, the Spanish community approached him and importuned him to stay in the city for a year or two. He consented to remain and established a large yeshivah there, and there he died.

Jonah was famous not only as a scholar, but as "father of the virtues" of piety, humility, and ascetism. He acquired enduring fame through his ethical books. In these books he protested forcefully against the many Spanish Jews who disregarded the *mitzvot* and against widespread sexual immorality. He proclaimed a "ban on concubines" and reacted sharply to the failure of society to keep the *mitzvot* governing the relations of man and his neighbor. Among the "ten gravest sins of the generation" which he specified, were: "disregarding the poor, slander, senseless hatred, confusion of the heart, and causing others to fear." Jonah condemned the actions of despots and tyrants, warning the large estate owners among the Jews of Spain against using force to evict small landowners from their plots. Not content with warnings, Jonah called for action and suggested that instead of strong community leaders who strike fear into the hearts of the public, "in every town volunteers should be ready to take action whenever a Jewish man or woman is in trouble" (*ibid.*). According to Jonah, communal activities should be incumbent on every Jew and not confined to communal leaders (*ibid.*). Even prayer in time of public or private sorrow and even the formulation of prayers are not matters for the pious or sages alone; it is the duty of every man to pray "every day, in accordance with his ability, on behalf of all the sick among the Holy People … and for the release of all prisoners…."

Jonah was doubtless familiar with the teachings of the *Ḥasidei Ashkenaz, but his ethical doctrine differed fundamentally from theirs. It was not based upon mystical speculation but on the *halakhah* and the popular *aggadah*. His ethical works were widely read. His repeated emphasis on the practice of social justice and social ethics undoubtedly contributed to their popularity throughout the Jewish world and to the influence they exercised upon the socio-religious thinking of later generations.

Jonah's works include: (1) Commentary on Proverbs (1910); (2) Commentary on *Avot* (Berlin-Altona, 1848, and compared to Mss., 1966); (3) novellae to tractate *Bava Batra: "Aliyyot de-Rabbenu Yonah"* up to page 77b (1966), and to *Sanhedrin* (in: *Sam Ḥayyim*, Leghorn, 1803); (4) Commentary on Alfasi to *Berakhot*, and printed with it, the commentary was compiled by his pupils; (5) Laws of examining the knife and lungs during *sheḥitah* (at the end of the *Teshuvot ha-Ge'onim*, 1871); (6) *Iggeret Teshuvah* (Constantinople, 1548); (7) *Sefer ha-Yirah* (Fano, c. 1505; Salonika, 1529; Yiddish translation Freiburg, 1583); (8) *Sha'arei Teshuvah* (Fano, 1505; Constantinople, 1511); a chapter out of this work, by name *"Sha'arei ha-Avodah,"* which was known as lost, was printed in 1967 from an unknown manuscript but there are still grave doubts whether it is really his; (9) Novellae of Rabbenu Jonah's pupils on tractate *Avodah Zarah* (1955); (10) Sermon and explanation on the Torah, *Sefer Derashot u-Perushei Rabbenu Yonah Gerondi le-Hamishah Humshei Torah*, were published from manuscript in 1980; (11) Novellae on the laws of the Passover *Seder* were published from manuscript in 2001.

In addition to these works, there is reference in medieval rabbinic works to his novellae on *Pesaḥim, Megillat Setarim*, laws of Ḥanukkah, and sermons.

BIBLIOGRAPHY: Michael, Or, no. 1038; A. Loewenthal, *R. Jonah Gerundi und sein ethischer Kommentar zu den Proverbien* (1910), 3–36 (introd.); A.T. Shrock, *R. Jonah b. Abraham of Gerona* (1948); H. Zarkowski (ed.), *Ḥiddushei Talmidei Rabbeinu Yonah le-Massekhet Avodah Zarah* (1955), introd.; Scholem, in: *Sefer Bialik* (1934), 141–55; Bronznick, in: *Hadorom*, 28 (1969), 238–42; J.M. Toledano, in: *Ha-Ẓofeh le-Ḥokhmat Yisrael*, 11 (1927), 239; I. Tishby, *Mishnat ha-Zohar*, 2 (1961), 67–8 n. 12. **ADD. BIBLIOGRAPHY:** I. Ta-Shma, in: *Exile and Diaspora: Studies Presented to Prof. Haim Beinart* (1988), 165–94; idem, in: *Jewish Mystical Leaders and Leadership in the 13th Century* (1998), 155–77.

[Ephraim Kupfer / David Derovan (2nd ed.)]

JONAS, EMILE (1827–1905), French composer, conductor, and cantor. He studied at the Paris Conservatoire where he received a second prize for harmony (1847). Jonas was professor of solfège at the Paris Conservatoire from 1847 until 1866. He composed several light operas in the style of *Offenbach and enjoyed success abroad as well as in France. He was music director at the Portuguese synagogue in Paris, for which he wrote two collections of songs, *Shirot Yisrael* (1854) and *Shirei Yisrael* (1886).

BIBLIOGRAPHY: NG2; MGG2.

[Amnon Shiloah (2nd ed.)]

JONAS, HANS (1903–1993), philosopher. Jonas studied with Martin Heidegger and Rudolf Bultmann in Marburg. Adhering to Zionist convictions since his youth, he left Nazi Germany in 1933 for Jerusalem, where he was a lecturer at the Hebrew University before World War II. During the war he served in the British Army (in the *Jewish Brigade Group) in the Middle East, taught in Palestine, and was a lieutenant in the Israeli Army 1948–49. In 1949 he went to McGill University in Montreal, in 1950 to Carleton College, Ottawa, and from 1951 was professor of philosophy at the New School for Social Research in New York.

Jonas' original work was on philosophy and religion in late antiquity and early Christianity, writing on *Augustin und das paulinische Freiheitsproblem* (1930), and *Gnosis und spaetantiker Geist* (2 vols., 1934–54; partial Eng. tr., *The Gnostic Religion*, 1958). His revolutionary study on Gnosticism initiated the movement to understand religions by demythologizing them and revealing their existential meaning. The Nazi's abandonment of all that is human as well as the confrontation with Heidegger's affinity to Nazism inspired Jonas to set forth a counterphilosophy to modern nihilism. He wrote on phenomenology and existentialism (*Zwischen Nichts und Ewigkeit*, 1963) and on philosophical biology (*The Phenomenon of Life*, 1966), offering an anti-dualistic understanding of organic life that interprets human existence as part of a nature that is meaningful in itself. In his *The Imperative of Responsibility* (1984), Jonas explored the ethical consequences of his speculative ontology for a world dominated by the dangers inherent in science and technology, especially genetic engineering, suggesting strategies of human self-limitation and respect for the integrity of life. In his essay *The Concept of God after Auschwitz* (1987), Jonas radically transformed the question of theodicy into the question of the justification of man and rejected the notion of God's power in history; stimulated by ideas of Lurianic Kabbalah, he employed a speculative myth to unfold a process of theogony and cosmology in which God, in the course of evolution, withdraws completely back into Himself, relinquishes His omnipotence, and makes the world subject to human responsibility.

ADD. BIBLIOGRAPHY: T. Schieder, *Weltabenteuer Gottes: Die Gottesfrage bei Hans Jonas* (1998); D.J. Levy, *Hans Jonas: The Integrity of Thinking* (2003); C. Wiese, *Hans Jonas. Zusammen Philosoph und Jude* (2003); C. Wiese & E. Jacobson (eds.), *Weiterwohnlichkeit der Welt. Zur Aktualitaet von Hans Jonas* (2003); W.E. Müller (ed.), *Von der Gnosisforschung zur Verantwortungsethik* (2003).

[Richard H. Popkin / Christian Wiese (2nd ed.)]

JONAS, JOSEPH (1792–1869), English-born jeweler who was Ohio's earliest permanent Jewish settler. Jonas arrived at Cincinnati in 1817 and in 1824 became president of the newly founded Bene Israel Congregation, the first in Ohio. He and his brother Abraham both married daughters of Gershom Mendes Seixas. Some years after Rachel Seixas' death, Jonas married Martha Oppenheim. Jonas wrote "The Jews of Ohio" for Isaac Leeser's *Occident* in 1842. He was a leading freemason and politician and helped organize Cincinnati's Democratic Party. While serving in the Ohio legislature in 1860–61, he advocated compromise with the South. Jonas moved to Alabama in 1867. His brother ABRAHAM (1801–1864) arrived in Cincinnati several years after Joseph. He then moved to Kentucky where he was several times elected to the state legislature, and was also prominent in the Masonic lodge. He later moved to Illinois, where he was active in the Republican party as a supporter and friend of Abraham Lincoln. Abraham's son, BENJAMIN FRANKLIN (1834–1911), moved to New Orleans where he was active in the Democratic party, served in the Louisiana state legislature, and was elected U.S. senator (1879–85).

BIBLIOGRAPHY: JOSEPH: Jonas, in: *Occident*, 1 (1843–44), 547–50; 2 (1844–45), 29–31, 143–7, 244–7; D. Philipson, in: AJHSP, 8 (1900), 44–57; B. Koln, *American Jewry and the Civil War* (1951, paperback 1961), 189. ABRAHAM: E. Hertz, in: *American Hebrew* (Aug. 8, 1927), 327, 342; A. Harkens, in: AJHSP, 17 (1909), 123ff. BENJAMIN FRANKLIN: D. Philipson, in: AJHSP, 8 (1900), 53; I. Harkens, *ibid.*, 17 (1909), 127; AJBY, 2 (1900/01), 518–9.

[Stanley F. Chyet]

JONAS, NATHAN S. (1868–1943), U.S. banker and philanthropist. Jonas was born in Montgomery, Alabama, and was raised in Brooklyn, N.Y. Starting work at the age of 13 as an errand boy, Jonas became a traveling salesman and then went into the insurance business. In 1905 he was made president of a new bank, which later became the Manufacturers Trust Company, and led it until 1931, when its total resources were $327 million, with 45 unit offices. Active in civic and philanthropic affairs, Jonas was a founder and president of the Brooklyn Jewish Hospital, organizer and first president of the Brooklyn Federation of Jewish Charities, and a member of the New York City Board of Education during 1902–09. He wrote an autobiography, *Through the Years* (1940).

BIBLIOGRAPHY: *New York Times* (Oct. 18, 1943), 15.

[Morton Rosenstock]

JONAS, REGINA (1902–1944), German rabbi and Holocaust victim. Born in Berlin in 1902, Regina Jonas completed her secondary education, receiving a license to teach in girls' schools in 1924. Shortly afterwards, she began studying at the Berlin rabbinical seminary, the *Hochschule fuer die Wissenschaft des Judentums (College of Jewish Studies). Ordinarily the Hochschule awarded female students a diploma certifying them as Academic Teachers of Religion. Jonas, however, desired rabbinic ordination. In 1930, she completed her thesis, "Can a Woman Hold Rabbinical Office?" in which she argued that Jewish law permitted female ordination. Although the distinguished scholar Professor Eduard Baneth accepted her thesis, he died before he could administer the oral exam in Jewish law required of all rabbinical candidates. Whether or not Baneth would have ordained her is not known. His successor believed Jewish law forbade women's ordination, and would not ordain Jonas. Instead she received a special transcript noting that she was becoming a skilled preacher.

In the years immediately following her graduation from the Hochschule, Jonas indeed found opportunities to preach. In 1935 Rabbi Max *Dienemann, one of the leaders of German Liberal Judaism, examined her and privately ordained her. She thus became the first woman rabbi, and from then until her death, many knew her as Fräulein Rabbiner Jonas. In 1937 the Jewish community of Berlin hired her to teach and also to provide rabbinical spiritual care for the elderly and the ill. As Nazism intensified its anti-Jewish persecution, Jonas was an active community presence, serving congregations whose rabbis had emigrated or been arrested. In late 1942, she was deported to Theresienstadt. Her work there included meeting new arrivals at the train station, trying to alleviate their horror as they confronted this terrible ghetto. She also lectured on biblical, talmudic, and religious themes for the ghetto's cultural programs. From there, Fräulein Rabbiner Jonas made her final journey. Sharing the fate of her people, the first woman rabbi was murdered in Auschwitz.

BIBLIOGRAPHY: K. von Kellenbach. "'God Does Not Oppress Any Human Being': The Life and Thought of Rabbi Regina Jonas," in: *Leo Baeck Institute Year Book* 39 (1994), 213–25; P.S. Nadell. *Women Who Would Be Rabbis: A History of Women's Ordination* (1998), 85–87, 112–16; E. Klapheck, *Fräulein Rabbiner Jonas: The Story of the First Woman Rabbi* (2004).

[Pamela S. Nadell (2nd ed.)]

JONATHAN (Heb. יוֹנָתָן, יְהוֹנָתָן; "YHWH has given"), name of several biblical characters.

(1) Son of Gershom, son of Moses (Judg. 18:30; MT, "Manasseh" written with suspended *nun*, apparently a scribal insertion in deference to Moses). He is apparently to be identified with the levite from Beth-Lehem in Judah who was taken into the service of Micah the Ephraimite as "father and priest" (Judg. 17:10) in the sanctuary which Micah had founded. Not long after he had taken up residence there, 600 Danites, on their way northward to find a more suitable homestead, induced Jonathan to leave Micah and to assume the more honorable position of priest to the tribe of Dan (Judg. 17–18). The family of Jonathan served as priests to the tribe of Dan until the captivity (Judg. 18:30).

(2) Son of *Saul.

(3) Uncle of David, a counselor, wise man, and scribe (I Chron. 27:32).

(4) Son of Shimea (or Shimei), David's brother. He slew a Philistine giant who taunted Israel at Gath (II Sam. 21:20–21; I Chron. 20:6–7).

(5) One of David's "valiant men" known as the "Thirty" (II Sam. 23:32–33; I Chron. 11:34).

(6) Son of Uzziah. He was in charge of the royal treasuries of David in the cities, villages, and towers outside the capital (I Chron. 27:25).

(7) Son of Abiathar, descendant of Eli, a priest in the time of David. During his flight from Absalom, David was joined by Jonathan who was, however, sent with *Zadok, *Abiathar, and *Ahimaaz, to spy on Absalom. Jonathan and Ahimaaz were appointed runners for the purpose of transmitting information from Jerusalem to the fleeing David (II Sam. 15:36). The two men hid at En Rogel, where a lad eventually discovered and betrayed them. Fleeing from Absalom's forces, both runners arrived at Baḥurim, where they were saved by a woman

who hid them in a well. Before morning, however, the runners reached David, bringing the information which permitted the king and his people to cross the Jordan in time to avoid a premature clash with Absalom's army (II Sam. 17:15–22). During Solomon's struggle for the throne (I Kings 1) Jonathan had, like his father Abiathar the priest, supported Adonijah as king. It was Jonathan who came to Adonijah at the stone of Zoheleth to inform him that Solomon had been anointed king (I Kings 1:9, 42–48). After Solomon's accession to the throne, nothing more is said about Jonathan who, together with his father, probably fell into disgrace and was sent to Anathoth (I Kings 2:26–27).

(8) A levite during the reign of Jehoshaphat (II Chron. 17:8).

(9) The scribe whose house was converted into a prison in which Jeremiah was confined on an alleged charge of desertion during the siege of Jerusalem (Jer. 37:15, 20; 38:26).

(10) Son of Kareah, an officer who joined Gedaliah at Mizpah, and the brother of Johanan (Jer. 40:8). The name Jonathan is omitted in some Hebrew manuscripts, in the Greek, and in the parallel passage in II Kings 25:23, and may have resulted from a dittography of Johanan.

(11) A son of Jerahmeel (I Chron. 2:32–33).

(12) A priest from the family of Shemaiah in the days of Joiakim the high priest (Neh. 12:18).

(13) Father of Ebed, who was head of the family of Adin. He joined Ezra in his journey to Jerusalem (Ezra 8:6).

(14) Son of Asahel, who, it seems, opposed Ezra in the matter of the foreign marriages (Ezra 10:15).

(15) Father of the priest Zechariah, who took part in the dedication of the walls of Jerusalem during the days of Nehemiah (Neh. 12:35).

(16) Son of Joiada, one of the high priests of the post-Exilic period (Neh. 12:11). However, Jonathan here appears to be a corruption of Johanan, by which name he is known in Ezra 10:6 and Nehemiah 12:22–23.

[Shlomo Balter]

JONATHAN (Heb. יוֹנָתָן, יְהוֹנָתָן), eldest son of *Saul, the first king of Israel (I Sam. 14:1). At the beginning of Saul's reign, during the revolt against the Philistines, Jonathan already was the commander of a part of the army (I Sam. chs. 13–14). He was a constant friend and companion of *David and assisted him when David was forced to escape Saul's wrath (I Sam., chs. 18, 19, 20, 23). Jonathan died together with his father and two of his brothers in the battle with the Philistines at Mount Gilboa (ch. 31). Their corpses were despoiled by the Philistines and exposed on the wall of Beth-Shean (I Sam. 31:12). David lamented their death in a moving elegy (II Sam. 1:17–27).

In the stories of the Book of Samuel the character of Jonathan is idealized, with no contrasting bad qualities. He is portrayed as the intrepid and heroic son of the king, a loyal comrade to the end. In the biblical account he stands in sharp contrast to Saul, whom God had rejected as king, and who was obsessed by an evil spirit. In the portrayal of Jonathan pure literary motifs are employed: the heroic son of the king leads an assault on the enemy with only his armor-bearer; he unwittingly transgresses the king's adjuration and faces all the danger resulting from such an action (ch. 14), and he becomes a faithful friend of the very man who is destined to deprive his father's house of its royal inheritance. In the story as a whole, there is a marked tendency to show Jonathan on the one hand as the war hero who played a decisive role in the struggle for freedom from the Philistine yoke, and on the other hand as David's faithful friend who recognized fully that even though he was himself heir to the throne, David would succeed Saul as king. (Jonathan's recognition of David's ultimate rule is displayed with some subtlety. Jonathan takes off his robe and gives it to David, along with his armor, sword, bow, and belt (I Sam. 18:3). Jonathan expresses the hope, "May YHWH be with David as he was with my father" (I Sam. 20:13)). Apparently these two elements became intertwined from the very outset in the book of Samuel, and in David's lament over Saul and Jonathan the two themes are combined (II Sam. 1:17–27). Both themes are based on reality, and there is no reason to doubt the tradition of the pact of friendship between David and Jonathan, even though these events occur in the context of stories designed to justify David's right to the kingdom. Indeed, Morgenstern raised the possibility that in early Israel the son-in-law of the king might have had a greater presumptive right to the throne than his son, and so a pact between Jonathan and David would have been appropriate. Even after Jonathan's death, David was careful to honor this pact and dealt very kindly with Jonathan's son *Mephibosheth (II Sam. 9:1ff.). In the list of Saul's descendants, which is included in the genealogical lists of families of the tribe of Benjamin in I Chronicles 8:33ff., ten generations are mentioned after Jonathan through Merib-Baal (that is Mephibosheth). It would seem that the object of this list is to illustrate the maintenance of the pact between the house of David and the house of Jonathan.

[Jacob Liver / S. David Sperling (2nd ed.)]

In the Aggadah

The Midrash applies the verse "For love is strong as death" to the love that Jonathan bore for David (Song R. 8:6, 4). Because of that great love, he risked his life for him (Ar. 16b), when he said to his father, "Wherefore should he (David) be put to death? What hath he done?" (I Sam. 20:32). His humility is revealed in his statement to David "Thou shalt be king over Israel and I shall be next to thee" (I Sam. 23:17). But the opinion is also expressed that he said this only because he saw that the people were flocking to David (BM 85a), and that "even the women behind the beams of the olive press knew that David was destined to be king" (TJ, Pes. 6:1, 33a). Jonathan, however, committed an inadvertent transgression which was regarded as reprehensible as though it had been deliberate, in that he failed to provide David with food when he advised him to flee (I Sam. 20:42), "for had Jonathan given David two loaves of bread for his travels, the priests of Nob would not have been massacred, nor would Saul and his three sons have been killed" (Sanh. 103b–104a). The love of David and Jonathan did not depend upon any material cause, and it is taken as the prototype of disinterested love which never passes away (Avot 5:16). This distinction between two types of love is also made by Greek scholars (Aristotle, *Magna Moralia*, 1209b; *Nichomachean Ethics*, 1156a).

[Elimelech Epstein Halevy]

BIBLIOGRAPHY: De Vaux, Anc Isr, index; Kallai, in: J. Liver (ed.), *Historyah Ẓeva'it…* (1965), 134, 136–7, 144; Noth, Personennamen, index; EM, 3 (1965), 533–5. IN THE AGGADAH: Ginzberg, Legends, index. **ADD. BIBLIOGRAPHY:** J. Morgenstern, in: JBL, 78 (1959), 322–25; J. Thompson, in: VT, 24 (1974), 334–38; D. Edelman, in: ABD, 3:944–46; S. Bar-Efrat, *I Samuel* (1996), 235–36.

JONATHAN, second-century *tanna*. Although his patronymic is never given when he is mentioned, as he most frequently is, with his colleague *Josiah, he is identical with the Jonathan b. Joseph and Nathan b. Joseph mentioned elsewhere in rabbinical literature. Like his colleague, he was a disciple of R. Ishmael b. Elisha and followed his system of hermeneutics, the main feature of which is the interpretation of scriptural verses according to the rules laid down by him in order to establish the *halakhah*, in oppositon to the system of R. Akiva (see *Midreshei Halakhah), and his exegesis is largely confined to this. His statements therefore appear mostly in the halakhic Midrashim which emanate from the school of R. Ishmael, the *Mekhilta of R. Ishmael* and the *Sifre* to Numbers (but see also TB Yoma 57–58 and TB Sotah 74–75). Apart from one Mishnah in his name in Avot 4:9, "Whosoever observes the Torah in poverty shall be vouchsafed to observe it in affluence, and he who neglects its observance in affluence will live to neglect it because of poverty" (Chap. 4), like his colleague, he is not mentioned in the Mishnah, and it has been assumed that this was due to the fact that Rabbi Judah ha-Nasi, the compiler of the Mishnah, based himself on the Mishnah of R. Meir.

After the death of his master he seems to have adopted part of the system of R. Akiva (see TJ Ma'as 51b).

Jonathan is the author of the rule that the saving of human life transcends the Sabbath (TB Yoma 85b). After the Hadrianic persecution, like his colleague, he decided to leave Ereẓ Israel. Whereas, however, Josiah emigrated to Nisibis in Babylonia, Jonathan relented. Together with Mattiah ben Ḥeresh, Ḥananiah, the nephew of R. Joshua, and R. Judah b. Hai, he set out, but when they reached the frontiers of Israel, their love for the Land of Israel prompted them to relinquish their plan and they returned (Sifre, Deut. 80).

BIBLIOGRAPHY: Bacher, Tann 2, 351; Frankel, Mishnah, 146; Hyman, Toledot, 697–700.

JONATHAN BEN ABRAHAM ISAAC (Abelman; 1854–1903), rabbi and talmudist. Born in the Kovno province, Jonathan went at the age of 15 to study under R. Israel *Lipkin in Vilna, where he later married the daughter of Abba Levinsohn, his teacher's brother-in-law. In 1877 he accepted the position of rabbi in the small town of Choroszcz, where he stayed until 1883. That year he was appointed a member of the *bet din* in Bialystok and became its *av bet din* when Samuel *Mohilever was chief rabbi of the community. Jonathan held the position until his death. His works include *Torat Yehonatan* (1889), dealing with the question of *shemittah*, which became particularly relevant as a result of the newly established agricultural settlements in Ereẓ Israel. He also wrote *Zikhron Yehonatan*, published after his death by his son (1905), consisting of novellae on parts of the Shulḥan Arukh. Some of his responsa are included in David Kempner's *Le-Matteh Yehudah* (1892).

BIBLIOGRAPHY: B. Eisenstadt, *Dor Rabbanav ve-Soferav*, 1 (1895), 7.

JONATHAN BEN AMRAM (late second and early third century), sage of the transitional period between the **tannaim* and the **amoraim* and a pupil of *Judah ha-Nasi. He is rarely mentioned in the Talmud (some two or three times). The Talmud relates that once, during a period of famine, when Judah ha-Nasi opened a house of food to scholars only, he failed to recognize Jonathan, who, too humble to proclaim himself a scholar, asked to be fed "as a dog is fed." When Judah later learned Jonathan's true identity, he decided to distribute food to everyone, without distinction (BB 8a). The few *halakhot* quoted by him (Ḥag. 20a; Av. Zar. 36b) center around details of the laws of levitical cleanness, and he was apparently one of those who observed, even for ordinary meals, all the prescriptions attaching to the eating of *terumah* (the Priestly Portion), which had to be eaten in a state of ritual cleanness.

BIBLIOGRAPHY: Hyman, Toledot, 703.

[Israel Moses Ta-Shma]

JONATHAN BEN ANAN, high priest in 36–37 C.E. Jonathan was appointed high priest by Vitellius, governor of *Syria, succeeding Joseph *Caiaphas (Jos., Ant., 18:95). After a year he vacated the office in favor of his brother, Theophilus (*ibid.*, 123). When Agrippa I wished to reappoint him, he declined, and another brother, Matthias, was appointed (*ibid.*, 19:313–6). Jonathan was apparently greatly respected and occupied an important place in the community even after his removal from the high priesthood, as is evidenced by the events during the final days of the governorship of Cumanus (52 C.E.). When disturbances broke out following the murder of a Galilean pilgrim by the Samaritans, Jonathan b. Anan complained to Quadratus, governor of Syria, pointing to Cumanus as the chief culprit. Quadratus, after severely punishing those responsible for the disturbance, sent the former high priests, Jonathan and Hananiah, as well as the latter's son, Anan, and a number of Jerusalem notables to Rome for trial before the emperor Claudius. The decision was in favor of the Jews, and at the request of Jonathan, Cumanus was dismissed and exiled (Jos., Wars, 2:232–47; Ant., 20:162). Felix, appointed to succeed Cumanus, hated the former high priest, who rebuked him for the cruelty of his rule. Felix suborned a certain Doras, a native of Jerusalem, to hire assassins who mingled with the crowd ascending to the Temple and murdered Jonathan. This, according to Josephus, was the precedent for many other murders by *Sicarii (Jos., Ant., 20:162–6; Wars, 2:256).

[Abraham Schalit]

JONATHAN BEN DAVID HA-KOHEN OF LUNEL (c. 1135–after 1210), talmudic scholar of Provence, the leading rabbi of Lunel after the death of *Meshullam b. Jacob. He was a pupil of Moses b. Joseph Merwan in Narbonne and possibly of Meir ibn Migash – the son of Joseph ibn *Migash – in Spain, a fellow student of Zerahiah ha-Levi *Gerondi, and a pupil-colleague of *Abraham b. David of Posquières.

Jonathan was in the vanguard of the defenders of Maimonides in the controversy stirred up against him by Meir *Abulafia. In his reply (signed, however, by *Aaron b. Meshullam of Lunel) to Meir's letter to the sages of Provence, Jonathan strenuously countered Meir's accusation, at the same time highly praising Maimonides and his work. Jonathan's correspondence with Maimonides, which in the course of time created strong bonds of mutual affection and admiration, originated from a copy of Maimonides' *Letter to Yemen*, which found its way into his hands. Greatly impressed by its contents and the writer's wide vision, he sent him a letter full of praise, containing questions on the authenticity of astrology and the possibility of guarding against its prognostications. In his reply, delayed for several years, Maimonides referred Jonathan to his *Yad ha-Ḥazakah*, enclosing a copy with his reply. There followed a halakhic correspondence in which Jonathan submitted to Maimonides questions and strictures on the work by himself and the other scholars of Lunel. Maimonides was thus made aware of the vast talmudic knowledge of the Lunel scholars, and his replies were phrased in terms of great esteem. The whole exchange, permeated with a spirit of humility and reverence, is among the finest in the literature of Hebrew correspondence. In the course of it, Jonathan also requested Maimonides to send him his *Guide of the Perplexed*, which he thereafter submitted to Samuel ibn *Tibbon for translation into Hebrew. Jonathan was among the leaders of the "300 French and English rabbis" who emigrated in 1210 to Ereẓ Israel, and there he died.

Jonathan wrote commentaries on the Mishnah, Talmud, and Alfasi, embracing most of the Talmud. Much of his work, hitherto in manuscript, has recently been published. It includes commentaries on the tractates *Megillah, Mo'ed Katan* (1956), *Berakhot* (1957), *Shabbat, Pesaḥim, Beẓah, Ḥagigah, Ketubbot, Bava Kamma* (critical edition ed. S. Friedman, 1969), *Bava Meẓia, Sanhedrin, Makkot, Avodah Zarah*, and on *Halakhot Ketannot* and laws of ritual uncleanness (in *El ha-Mekorot* – Pardes ed. of the Talmud, 1959–63); *Eruvin* (standard editions of Alfasi); *Rosh Ha-Shanah, Yoma, Ta'anit Sukkah* (in *Ginzei Rishonim*, 1962–63); *Horayot* (in *Ḥizzei Menasheh*, 1901); *Ḥullin* (in *Avodat ha-Leviyyim*, 1871). It is possible that he also wrote a treatise resolving David of Posquières' strictures on Maimonides (A. Neubauer, *Sefer ha-Ḥakhamim*, 2 (1891), 232, etc.). Numerous quotations from his teachings are to be found in the statements of other *rishonim*.

BIBLIOGRAPHY: Marx, in: HUCA, 3 (1926), 328ff.; idem, in: JQR, 25 (1935), 408; Assaf, in: KS, 1 (1924), 61; idem, in: *Tarbiz*, 3 (1931/32), 27–32; idem, in: *Minḥah li-Yhudah* (1950), 162–9; Wieder, in: *Meẓudah*, 2 (1943), 126ff.; Stern, in: *Zion*, 16 (1951), 18–29; S.K. Mirsky, in: *Sura*, 2 (1955/56), 242–66; M. Hakohen, in: *Sinai*, 40 (1956/57), 408–13; I. Twersky, *Rabad of Posquières* (1962); S. Friedman (ed.), *Perush R. Yonatan me-Lunel le-Bava Kamma* (1969), introd., 1–62.

[Israel Moses Ta-Shma]

JONATHAN BEN ELEAZAR (beginning of the third century C.E.), *amora*. He is the R. Jonathan mentioned in the Talmud and Midrash without patronymic. Jonathan was of Babylonian origin but went to Ereẓ Israel in his youth and *Johanan Nappaḥa referred to him as "our Babylonian colleague" (Git. 78b). He was a pupil of Simeon b. Yose b. Lakunya in whose name he frequently transmits dicta. He was the teacher of *Samuel b. Naḥman and one of the associates of *Ḥanina b. Ḥama. Jonathan lived in Sepphoris and was called *Sar ha-Birah* ("the prince of the city") – a designation whose exact connotation is unknown. He belonged to the intimate circle of the *nasi and together with Johanan went to the "south" (Lydda) on his mission, apparently, of "peacemaking" (TJ, Ber. 9:1, 12d; the reading there is not clear). He once paid a visit to Jerusalem to see the ruins of the Temple (TJ, Ma'as. Sh. 3:3) and to Tiberias to bathe in the hot springs (TJ, Er. 6:4, 23c). Several scholars, including Johanan, transmit statements in Jonathan's name.

Jonathan is hardly referred to in the *halakhah*. On the other hand he is regarded as one of the great aggadists. His well-known defense of such biblical personalities as Reuben, the sons of Eli, the sons of Samuel, David, Solomon, and others (despite the explicit reference in the Bible to their transgressions) begins with the words: "Whoever maintains that so-and-so sinned is in error!" (Shab. 55b–56a). He also engaged to a considerable extent in polemics with heretics. He comments, for instance, on Genesis 1:26, "let us make man in our image": "When writing the Torah, Moses wrote down the acts of creation of each day. When he came to this verse, 'let us make man in our image after our likeness,' he said to God, 'Sovereign of the universe! Why dost Thou provide an opening for heretics? [since the plural form of the verse suggest dualism].' Replied [the Almighty] 'whoever wishes to err, let him err. From this man that I have created, great and small men shall spring. If the great man should say, "why do I need to request permission from one of less importance than I," they will answer him: Learn from thy Creator who created all that is above and below, yet when He came to create man, He took counsel with the ministering angels'" (Gen. R. 8:8).

BIBLIOGRAPHY: Bacher, Pal Amor; Z.W. Rabinowitz, *Sha'arei Torat Ereẓ Yisrael* (1961), 436f.; Ḥ. Albeck, *Mavo la-Talmudim* (1969), 167f.

[Israel Moses Ta-Shma]

JONATHAN BEN JACOB (17th century), Hungarian rabbi. Jonathan was born in Ofen, Hungary, where, according to the testimony of David Oppenheim, he was one of the leaders of the community. When Ofen was captured from the Turks by the Austrian emperor Leopold I in 1686, Jonathan was taken captive and was ransomed by the Jews of Nikolsburg. He dwelt for a time in the home of Simḥah Ephraim b. Gershon ha-Kohen *Freudemann in Belgrade and transmitted various customs in his name. Jonathan became known through his *Keset Yehonatan* (Dyrhenfurth, 1697), a collection of the laws of prayer and moral sayings garnered from the *Sefer Ḥasidim* and the *Shenei Luḥot ha-Berit* of Isaiah Horowitz. He also compiled the *Neu Maaseh Buch* (*ibid.*, 1697), a collection of stories in Yiddish.

BIBLIOGRAPHY: M. Brann, in: MGWJ, 30 (1881), 543 n. 2; J.J.(L.) Greenwald (Grunwald), *Ha-Yehudim be-Ungarya* (1913), 27; P.Z. Schwarz, *Shem ha-Gedolim me-Ereẓ Hagar*, 1 (1913), 81 no. 25; 3 (1915), 326 no. 25.

[Yehoshua Horowitz]

JONATHAN BEN JOSEPH OF RUZHANY (late 17th–early 18th century), talmudist and astronomer. Jonathan was born in Ruzhany (Grodno province) and in his youth acquired an extensive knowledge of mathematics and astronomy in addition to that of Talmud. When a plague broke out in his native town in 1710, he vowed that, should he be spared, he would spread the knowledge of astronomy among Jews. In fulfillment of this vow, he proceeded to Germany, although already blind, and finally settled in Frankfurt. There he wrote *Yeshu'ah be-Yisrael*, a commentary on *Kiddush ha-Ḥodesh* (the laws concerning the blessing of the New Moon) of Maimonides' *Mishneh Torah* (Frankfurt, 1720). He also wrote a commentary on *Abraham b. Ḥiyya's astronomical work *Ẓurat ha-Areẓ*, and glosses to the translation of Sacroboscos' *Sphaera Mundi* (entitled *Mareh ha-Ofannim* or *Asferah ha-Gadol* by its translator Solomon b. Abraham Avigdor) and to another Hebrew translation of the same work, entitled *Sefer ha-Galgal*. These three works were published by Jonathan with his own commentaries, and others by Perez Nasi, Mordecai b. Abraham *Jaffe, Mattathias b. Solomon *Delacrut, and Shemariah Manoah Hahndel (Offenbach, 1720). In 1725 Jonathan made the acquaintance of the Christian bibliographer and Hebraist, Johann Christoph *Wolf, in Hamburg.

BIBLIOGRAPHY: Fuenn, Keneset, 428f.; Steinschneider, Uebersetzungen, 644, 646.

[Moshe Nahum Zobel]

JONATHAN BEN UZZIEL (first century B.C.E.–first century C.E.), translator of the Prophets into Aramaic (see *Bible: Translations) Jonathan is mentioned as the outstanding pupil of *Hillel (BB 134a; Suk. 28a). All that is recorded of him, however, is that he translated the prophetical books into Aramaic "from the mouth of Haggai, Zechariah, and Malachi" (an anachronistic statement meant to claim unbroken continuity between the latest prophets and the Aramaic translation), and that the translation evoked a storm of criticism, "rocking Ereẓ Israel over an area of 400 parasangs by 400 parasangs." The same account continues that a Heavenly Voice came forth, demanding to know who it was that had revealed divine mysteries to humans, and Jonathan replied that he had done so, not for the sake of personal honor "... but in order that disputes should not multiply in Israel" (Meg. 3a). It would appear that the translation was midrashic, and it is possible that it contained eschatological elements. In the same passage it is stated that Jonathan was desirous of translating the Hagiographa also, but a Heavenly Voice deterred him, saying "Enough." It has been suggested that the Targum to Job, which Gamaliel the Elder ordered to be hidden away (Shab. 115a), was the work of Jonathan, and that the ensuing furor deterred him from continuing with his self-appointed task. The extent to which the existing Aramaic translation of the Prophets is derived from the Targum attributed by the Talmud to Jonathan is difficult to say. Yet, it is clear that there is no connection between Jonathan and the Aramaic translation of the Pentateuch at first called *Targum Ereẓ Yisrael* and later *Targum Yerushalmi*. It was erroneously attributed from the 14th century to Jonathan, because the initials ת"י were taken to refer to Targum Jonathan instead of *Targum Yerushalmi* (Palestinian Targum).

BIBLIOGRAPHY: Bacher, Tann; Zunz-Albeck, Derashot, 35–41; Hyman, Toledot, s.v. **ADD. BIBLIOGRAPHY:** B. Chilton, in: DBI, 1:531–34.

[Yehoshua M. Grintz / S. David Sperling (2nd ed.)]

JONATHAN THE HASMONEAN (also called **Apphus**; d. 143 B.C.E.), head of the Jewish state (160–143); youngest son of *Mattathias. Jonathan fought, together with his brother Judah Maccabee, in the first battles at the beginning of the Hasmonean revolt and took over the command after the latter's death. In the disastrous encounter at Elasa (160 B.C.E.) Jonathan assumed the command and took refuge with his followers in the wilderness of Tekoa. Here he was ineffectually attacked by *Bacchides, the Syrian commander, and succeeded in inflicting serious losses on the enemy. Bacchides thereupon returned to Judea. After the death of the high priest *Alcimus, Bacchides went back to Syria, but was persuaded by the Hellenists to return in the hope of attacking Jonathan by surprise. When the plan failed, Bacchides turned against those who had urged his return, while Jonathan seized the opportunity to proffer a peace pact. This was agreed upon and Jonathan returned the prisoners in his hands. From about 158–157 Jonathan resided at Michmash as the *de facto* leader of the Jewish people, without any official status. In the civil war between *Alexander Balas and *Demetrius I for the Syrian throne Jonathan supported the latter, and after receiving various concessions removed his headquarters to Jerusalem (153). The hostages in the *Acra citadel were released and, to the dismay of the Hellenists, Jonathan was permitted to recruit an army. His first act was to fortify Jerusalem. Alexander Balas, equally anxious to secure Jonathan's support, offered him even more attractive terms than Demetrius, including appointment as high priest. Jonathan accepted, and took up his duties as high priest on the festival of Tabernacles in 153. He remained loyal to his patron despite further extravagant offers from Demetrius. After Demetrius was killed in battle (150), Balas invited Jonathan to the celebration of his marriage to Cleopatra, daughter of Ptolemy Philometor. Jonathan was royally received and was appointed *strategus* and *meridarch*, thus acquiring both military and civil authority. During the ensuing struggle against Demetrius II for the Syrian throne, Jonathan remained loyal to Balas, who rewarded Jonathan with the city of Ekron and its environs for his defeat of the army of Appolonius in a campaign along the coast. After the death of both Balas and Ptolemy Philometor, Demetrius II emerged victorious from the struggle. When Jonathan sought to extend his authority in Judea by besieging the Acra citadel, the irate monarch summoned him to an audience at Acre. Although he did not raise the siege, Jonathan went laden with presents, and an agreement was reached whereby the Samaritan districts of Lydda, Aphaerema (Ephraim), and Ramathaim were added to Judea, the whole of which was exempted from taxes. Jonathan's status as high priest and leader was confirmed. In matters of domestic policy he took care not to appear as the sole ruler, and the "elders of the nation" are always mentioned as supplementing his authority. The internal struggle in Syria flared up again when *Tryphon sought to wrest the crown from Demetrius II. Jonathan at first gave his support to Demetrius, sending an army to help suppress the rebellion against him in Antioch, but he went over to Tryphon's camp when Demetrius reneged on his agreement to hand over the Acra citadel to him. Uneasy over his ally's strength, Tryphon persuaded him to disband most of his army, promising to award him Acre and other cities. When Jonathan arrived at Acre, Tryphon ordered him seized and his companions put to death. In addition, he took two of Jonathan's sons hostage and extorted large sums of money. In frustration at the failure of his assault upon Jerusalem, Tryphon put Jonathan to death. The fate of his sons is unknown. Jonathan was succeeded by his last surviving brother *Simeon. Josephus (*Life*, 4) claimed descent from a daughter of Jonathan. Notwithstanding his tragic end, Jonathan may be regarded as the true founder of the Hasmonean state.

BIBLIOGRAPHY: I Macc. 9:31–12:53; Jos., Ant., 13:1–212; V. Tcherikover, *Hellenistic Civilisation and the Jews* (1959), 231–4, 236–53; S. Zeitlin, *The Rise and Fall of the Judean State* (1962), index.

[Lea Roth]

JONATHAN SON OF ABSALOM, one of the army commanders of *Simeon the Hasmonean. Jonathan was sent to Jaffa in 135 B.C.E. by Simeon, who feared that the local population might surrender to *Tryphon. Jonathan succeeded in holding the city after having driven out the gentile population. Some identify him with Mattathias b. Absalom, but it seems more likely that Jonathan and Mattathias were brothers who belonged to the Hasmonean family.

BIBLIOGRAPHY: Jos., Ant., 13:202; I Macc. 13:11; Klausner, Bayit Sheni, 3 (1950^2), 65.

[Edna Elazary]

JONAVA (Rus. **Janovo**), town in Lithuania, northeast of Kovno. Jews were invited to settle there when the town was founded in 1775. They numbered 813 in 1847. Jonava developed through its position at the junction of the routes to the Baltic Sea (Viliya River, the Romny–Libava railroad) and on the St Petersburg–Warsaw road. The surrounding forests supplied timber for the local industry (carpentry, furniture, matches) and for export. There were 3,975 Jews living in Jonava (80% of the total population) in 1897. The town was destroyed by fire in 1905 but was quickly rebuilt. In the spring of 1915 the Jews in Jonava were expelled to the Russian interior, and only part of them returned. The community numbered 1,800 in 1921 and 3,000 (60% of the total population) on the eve of the Holocaust. The Germans occupied the town on June 22, 1941. On June 29, 2,108 Jews were executed in the woods outside the town.

Jonava was the birthplace of the poet Morris *Vinchevski and the scholar Israel *Davidson.

BIBLIOGRAPHY: *Yahadut Lita*, 3 (1967), 319–20; Z.A. Brown and D. Levin, *Toledoteha shel Maḥteret* (1962), index.

[Yehuda Slutsky]

JONG, ERICA (1942–), U.S. novelist and poet. Born Erica Mann in New York, where she was educated and began to write poetry, she lived in Heidelberg, Germany, from 1966 to 1969, where her husband (from whom she was later divorced) was serving in the U.S. Army. Her experiences there were featured in the autobiographical novel *Fear of Flying* (1973). In Germany she continued to write poetry which began to evolve a feminist outlook. In 1971, she published her first collection of poetry, *Fruits and Vegetables*, much of which explored the position of women as artists. Her second volume of poetry, *Half-Lives* (1973), continued to explore feminist and psychological issues.

The publication of *Fear of Flying* established her popularity as a novelist. The novel, which describes the search for self-identity and analyses the upbringing, neuroses, and sexuality of its heroine, Isadora Wing, mirrored much of Jong's own intellectual background and Jewish upbringing. It includes a chapter describing her life in Germany and its effect on her Jewish consciousness. The novel's sexual frankness sparked much controversy.

In 1977, she published her second novel, *How to Save Your Own Life*, a sequel to *Fear of Flying*, which explored Isadora Wing's experiences with fame, divorce, and new relationships. This was followed in 1980 by *Fanny: Being the True History of the Adventures of Fanny Hackabout-Jones*, a contemporary "18th-century novel" describing the adventures of a female Tom Jones.

Jong has also published volumes of poetry, *Loveroot* (1975) and *At the Edge of the Body* (1979). Numerous novels and books of poetry followed. In 1994 Jong published her autobiography, *Fear of Fifty*, followed in 2006 by *Seducing the Demon* on the writing life. In 1982 she was awarded title of Mother of the Year, while she served as president of the Authors Guild of the United States between 1991 and 1993. In 1998 she published a collection of essays. *What Do Women Want?* She is regarded as one of the most significant authors to have been produced by the feminist movement.

ADD. BIBLIOGRAPHY: C. Templin (ed.), *Conversations with Erica Jong* (2002).

[Susan Strul / Rohan Saxena (2nd ed.)]

JONG, LOUIS (Loe) DE (1914–2005), Dutch historian. Born in Amsterdam into a secular socialist family, De Jong studied history in Amsterdam and started his career in 1938 as foreign editor of the anti-Nazi weekly *De Groene Amsterdammer.* Upon the German invasion in May 1940 De Jong and his wife managed to flee the European mainland, leaving behind his parents, sister, and twin brother – none of whom survived the war. De Jong spent the war years in London, working for Radio Oranje, the voice of the Dutch government-in-exile. He also wrote four volumes on the events in the occupied Netherlands.

In September 1945 De Jong was appointed head of the Netherlands State Institute for War Documentation, which had been founded in Amsterdam immediately after the liberation. In 1953 he earned his doctorate with a study of the German fifth column. In 1955 he was commissioned by the government to write the history of the Netherlands in World War II. Between 1969 and 1991 *Het Koninkrijk der Nederlanden in de Tweede Wereldoorlog* ("The Kingdom of the Netherlands in World War II") was published in 14 volumes.

Aside from his position as head of the RIOD, De Jong also gained recognition and respect in television appearances. He worked as a commentator on international current affairs and from 1960 to 1965 presented a series on the Netherlands during World War II.

He always remained an assimilated, secular Jew. During the Six-Day War (1967), however, he identified with the Israeli cause. De Jong became more and more a conscious Dutch Jew rather than a Dutchman of Jewish descent.

BIBLIOGRAPHY: C. Kristel, *Geschiedschrijving als opdracht. Abel Herzberg, Jacques Presser en Loe de Jong over de jodenvervolging* (1998).

[Conny Kristel (2nd ed.)]

JORDAN (Heb. (הַ)יַּרְדֵּן), river flowing from the Anti-Lebanon mountains south through Lake Kinneret and emptying into the Dead Sea. The name Jordan is first attested in the 13th-century B.C.E. Papyrus Anastasi I (13:1). In the Septuagint the Hebrew form Yarden is transliterated Yordanes or Yordanos. Some scholars argue that the name is derived from an Indo-European root such as the Persian *yar* ("year") and *dan* ("river"), i.e., a river that flows the year round; others note similarly named rivers in Crete, Greece, and Asia Minor. The majority view, however, is that the name Jordan is connected with the Semitic root *yarod* ("to descend") or the Arabic *warad* ("to come to the water to drink"). The alternative Arabic name of the Jordan – Nahr al-Sharī'a ("the water trough") – sometimes

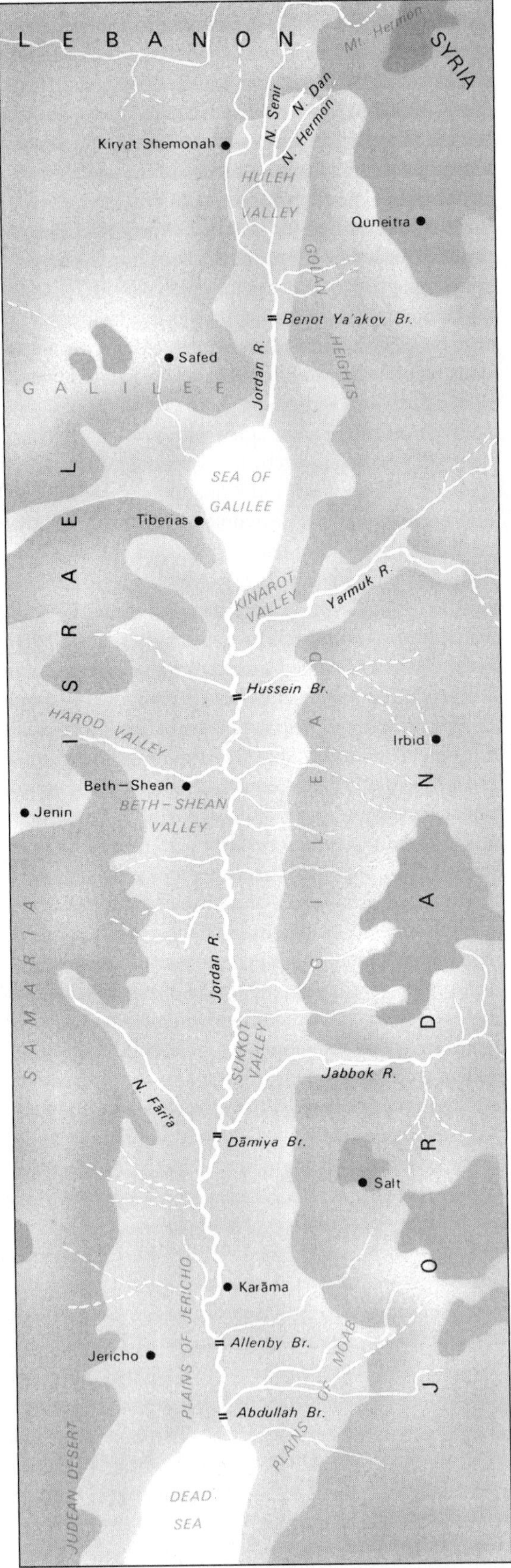

The Jordan River and Valley.

used with the addition *al-kabīr* ("the great") – has the same meaning. The talmudic interpretation (Bek. 55a) of the name Jordan as a combination of *ye'or* ("river"; actually an Egyptian word) and *Dan*, i.e., the "river that descends from Dan" was generally accepted in the Byzantine period and the Middle Ages but it is no longer regarded as valid. The Jordan has its source in three headstreams whose waters are drawn mainly from the precipitation on top of Mount *Hermon and also from scores of springs. Near Sedeh Neḥemyah in the *Ḥuleh Valley they unite into a single watercourse to form the river Jordan. The three streams are Naḥal Senir, issuing from the foot of the Hermon or its western side opposite the Lebanese village Ḥaṣbiyyā and hence called Nahr al-Ḥaṣbānī in Arabic; Naḥal Hermon emerging from the Paneas cave in the village of *Banias, and thus called Nahr al-Bāniyās in Arabic; and Naḥal Dan (Ar. al-Liddhān) rising at the foot of the ancient Tell Dan (Ar. Tell al-Qāḍī), near kibbutz Dan. The Senir is the longest of the sources. From its start until it empties into the *Dead Sea, the Jordan covers a distance of c. 127 mi. (205 km.) and its meanderings between the Sea of Galilee and the Dead Sea increase its length to c. 186 mi. (300 km.). The Senir in its upper course is an intermittent stream (called Wadi al-Taym) which covers a distance of c. 15½ mi. (25 km.) before reaching the Ḥaṣbiyyā spring. During heavy rainstorms it receives much surface runoff. The Senir discharges an annual average of c. 152 million cu. m. of water into the Jordan of which about 37% is runoff; its seasonal and annual variations are considerable. Naḥal Hermon (Banias) provides c. 123 million cu. m. of which 12.5% is runoff and Naḥal Dan discharges c. 240 million cu. m., almost all from springs and with little fluctuation.

The drainage area of the Jordan is 6,380 sq. mi. (16,335 sq. km.), 5,312 sq. mi. (13,600 sq. km.) south of Lake *Kinneret (the Sea of Galilee) – 4,531 sq. mi. (11,600 sq. km.) to the east, and 781 sq. mi. (2,000 sq. km.) to the west. The water network of the Jordan is asymmetrical; the watershed between the Jordan and the Mediterranean streams is close to the Jordan while the watershed of the desert streams east of it is farther away. Since the drainage of the Ḥuleh Valley, the water flows through two canals, one to the west c. 12 mi. (19.5 km.) long, and one to the east c. 10 mi. (16 km.) long, with a lateral canal connecting them. In the area of the drained Ḥuleh Lake the tributaries unite into a single stream and flow through the old riverbed which has been deepened to provide an exit for the waters of the lake and the marshes. In descending the 10 mi. (16 km.) between the drained area and Lake Kinneret, the Jordan falls from approximately 197 ft. (60 m.) above sea level to 695 ft. (212 m.) below it. The point of sea level is reached about 7.5 mi. (12 km.) north of Lake Kinneret. Before emptying in Lake Kinneret, the Jordan creates a small delta. Between its entrance and outlet from Lake Kinneret (c. 13 mi.; 21 km.), much of the water of the Jordan is carried off by evaporation but it is replenished from streams and springs, both above and below the water level. Some contain salts, especially chlorides, and the water is much more suitable for irrigation before reaching Lake Kinneret than after leaving it. For political reasons the pumps for the National Water Carrier had to be installed, in the 1960s prior to the Six-Day War, at Lake Kinneret and not in the Ḥuleh Valley. The amount of water flowing out of Lake Kinneret is now regulated, according to the requirements of irrigation, by sluice gates installed at Deganyah Alef. Before that, a maximum of 915.2 million cu. m. was recorded for the year 1929 and a minimum of 466 million cu. m. the previous year. A monthly maximum of 227 million cu. m. was once registered for March and a minimum of 29 million cu. m. for August. The *Yarmuk, the Jordan's largest tributary, empties into it 5 mi. (8.5 km.) south of Lake Kinneret. It carries an average of c. 450 million cu. m. a year, mostly runoff water. Its annual maximum was 893 million cu. m. in 1929 and its minimum, 268.5 million cu. m. the previous year. Exploiting the floodwaters of the Yarmuk is possible only by diverting the river to Lake Kinneret or by constructing a high dam of 558 ft. (170 m.) or more in its gorge. The Jordan discharges c. 875 million cu. m. into the Dead Sea a year; its yearly fluctuations are great and are caused mainly by the Yarmuk: in 1933, 287 million cu. m. and in 1935, 1,313 million cu. m. On its way to the Dead Sea the Jordan loses a great quantity of water through evaporation – up to 1,900 m. a year near the Dead Sea – and through seepage. Only some 18% of the rainfall in its drainage area reaches the Dead Sea through the Jordan's channel. Between Lake Kinneret and the Dead Sea the Jordan constitutes a geologically recent river. In the Upper Pliocene period, Lake Kinneret possessed an outlet to the Mediterranean when the Jordan together with the Yarmuk apparently flowed to the Harod Valley and the Kishon River. In the Middle Pleistocene, Lake Kinneret and the Dead Sea formed a single saline lake which deposited thick strata of Lisan marl. At the end of the Middle Pleistocene the two lakes separated and a channel was created through which the water flowed from the upper to the lower lake. As the two lakes shrank in size, the channel became longer and deeper. The bed of the ancient lake is the *kikkar* of the Jordan on both sides, called Ghawr in Arabic. Within the *kikkar* (central part of the Jordan Valley) is a broad plain 1–2 mi. (2–3 km.) wide through which runs the narrow channel of the Jordan. Only when the river floods do its waters inundate the broad plain, called *ge'on ha-Yarden* (Ar. *al-Zawr*). Because of the great heat and humidity in the *ge'on ha-Yarden* a dense vegetation covers both banks of the river. The Jordan weaves its course through the soft marl strata which are 164 ft. (50 m.) thick in the northern part of the *kikkar* and up to 492 ft. (150 m.) thick in the south. Because of the great quantity of eroded material which the Jordan carries and deposits in its channel, forming sandbars, and because the high steep banks of the plain occasionally collapse, fall into its bed, and dam it, the path of the Jordan leaves its channel. Sometimes in its meanderings it cuts through a serpentine loop shortening the course and many oxbows thus remain which are clearly seen in air-photos. In flood times the water also reaches these abandoned channels. South of the *Jabbok's outlet into the Jordan (25 mi. (38 km.) north of the Dead Sea) are the remains of a bridge above an abandoned channel. The outlet of the Jordan into the Dead Sea is a delta of 5.8 sq. mi. (15 sq. km.). The river splits into two arms, a western one and a shorter eastern one, c. 4,100 ft. (1,250 m.) apart. From the coarse sediment the western arm forms a shoal strip c. 5,900 ft. (1,800 m.) long. West of this strip extends a lagoon, 11,480 ft. (3,500 m.) long and c. 1,640 ft. (500 m.) wide, a tongue c. 330–660 ft. (100–200 m.) wide separates the lagoon from the open waters of the Dead Sea which in the winter of 1954 dropped to a low of c. 1,300 ft. (398 m.) below the level of the Mediterranean. At present the Jordan falls c. 3,018 ft. (920 m.) from the springs of the Senir to the Dead Sea. The delta below the surface of the Dead Sea is small even when compared with several small streams in the Judean Desert because of the sharp declivity of its bottom. The light muddy waters of the Jordan spread like a fan with a radius of several miles over the heavy waters of the Dead Sea. The influence of the Jordan on the upper level of the Dead Sea is evident for c. 31 mi. (50 km.) to the south. The Jordan is not navigable; only with great difficulty can small flat boats sail between Lake Kinneret and the Dead Sea and they must be towed over the sandbars.

History

In the Bible the Jordan is associated in particular with *Jericho and is frequently mentioned with that city in whose vicinity the Israelites crossed the Jordan (Num. 22:1, et al.). Other biblical terms connected specifically with the Jordan are the *kikkar* (usually translated "plain of the Jordan," Gen. 13:10, et al.) which refers to the cultivable middle section of the three terraces composing the Jordan Valley. (It was this part of the valley whose fertility attracted Lot recalling "the garden of the Lord, like the land of Egypt.") The upper lands of the Jordan Valley are called *gelilot ha-Yarden* (the "region about the Jordan"; Josh. 22:10). The lowest terrace, bordering on the river itself and densely wooded, is called *ge'on ha-Yarden* ("thickets of the Jordan"; Jer. 49:19); there the "sons of the prophets" went to cut wood (II Kings 6:4); it was the haunt of dangerous beasts, even lions (Jer. 49:19, et al.) and is cited as the opposite of lands where man is safe.

In biblical times the Jordan was crossed by means of its fords; Jacob passed over it with a staff on his way from Beth-El to Haran (Gen. 32:10[11]) and in returning recrossed it into Canaan near Succoth. The most famous passage of the Jordan was that of the Israelites opposite Jericho, as related in Joshua 3. As it was very difficult to ford the river at that place and in that season the sudden cessation of the Jordan's flow was regarded as miraculous. Such occasions, however, have actually been recorded several times in history: in 1267 the Jordan ceased flowing for eight hours; in 1546, for two whole days; and in 1927 for 21½ hours. In all three cases the cessation was the result of earthquakes which caused the high banks to collapse blocking the river bed and stopping its flow. The crossing of the Jordan is recorded as one of the great miracles of the Lord (Ps. 114:3ff.) and was remembered as such in later times. The river thus acquired a sacred character; its waters were expected to heal Naaman (II Kings 5:10–14). Other miraculous crossings were made by Elijah before he was taken up to heaven near the Jordan and by Elisha, both accomplished with Elijah's mantle. As a serious obstacle to movement the Jordan played an important part in Israel's military history. The occupation of the fords was generally intended to complete the discomfiture of a retreating army or to prevent an attack. Thus the fords were taken by Ehud after the assassination of Eglon king of Moab (Judg. 3:28) and by Gideon to deny passage to the Midianites and the Ephraimites (*ibid.* 7:24; 12:5–6). The Jordan was crossed mostly on foot or on animals but David and his army may have used a ferryboat (II Sam. 19:19). In prebiblical times the Jordan was not only a military obstacle but also a political boundary. With the decline of settlement east of the river in the Middle Bronze Age, the limits of the Egyptian province of Canaan – as recorded in the biblical description of the boundaries of the Promised Land (Num. 34) – extended along the Jordan from the Sea of Chinnereth to the Dead Sea (*ibid.* 34:12). After the establishment of the kingdoms east of the Jordan, the river formed the boundary of the kingdoms of Sihon the Amorite and of Og king of Bashan. Their territories were allotted to the tribes of Reuben, Gad, half of the tribe of Manasseh. Thus from an interstate boundary, the Jordan became a tribal one. Its function as the eastern border of Canaan, however, was well remembered and it was the eastern tribes who were anxious not to lose contact with their western brethren (Josh. 22). Throughout Israelite history its people held lands on both sides of the river, although its main territory was west of it. In later times it was usually the weaker party which retired east of the Jordan – as did Abner with Ish-Bosheth the son of Saul after the defeat at Mount Gilboa (II Sam. 2:8) and David after the initial success of Absalom's rebellion (*ibid.*, 17:22). In post-biblical times the Jordan formed the eastern boundary of the Persian and Hellenistic province of Judea, although the land of the Tobiads east of the Jordan was also Jewish territory. The Hasmoneans freely crossed the river to fight on both banks; Jonathan made one such passage against the army of Bacchides who tried to use the Jordan as a tactical barrier (I Macc. 9:43). Alexander Yannai retired beyond the Jordan from the army of Ptolemy, king of Cyprus, but throughout the Hasmonean period, its kingdom extended on both sides of the river. Even under Roman domination the Jewish district of the Perea ("the land beyond" [the Jordan]) remained part of Judea. In the Hellenistic and Herodian periods the digging of irrigation channels in the Jordan Valley led to its economic development and it became one of the most fertile areas of Ereẓ Israel. In March 68 C.E. during the Jewish War, the Jews retreating from Bethennabris across the Jordan fords were surprised by a sudden rise of the river's level; they were partly drowned and partly destroyed by the enemy (Jos., Wars, 4:432–436). Jewish villages continued to exist on both banks of the lower Jordan up to the Byzantine period. In the Talmud the Jordan is mentioned as one of the four rivers of the Holy Land (TJ, Kil. 9:5, 32d; BB 74b) and the word is regarded as derived from *Yored Dan* (Bek. 55a). According to the same source, the Jordan issues from a cave at Paneas, traverses the seas of Samkho (Ḥuleh), Tiberias, and Sodom (Dead Sea), and falls into the Mediterranean (!). It is called the Jordan only from Bet Yeraḥ and below (the standard version has "Bet Jericho"). In Roman and Byzantine times the Jordan did not form a boundary; the provinces of Palaestina prima and secunda both overlapped it. The first three attempts to bridge the river were apparently made then: one at the Ford of Jacob's Daughters (Gesher Benot Ya'akov) and two below the Sea of Galilee at Sinnabra-Bet Yeraḥ and Gesher Naharayim (Jisr al-Mujāmiʿ). Two ferries are marked on the Jordan on the Madaba Map, one at Aenon below Beth-Shean, and the other near Archelais (Khirbat ʿAwja al-Taḥtā). The waters of the Jordan became sacred in Christian eyes because on its banks John the Baptist performed baptisms and there too Jesus was baptized. The exact location of his baptism is in doubt: the usual assumption, based on Matthew 3 and Mark 1:5ff., is near Jericho, but another tradition, based on John 3:23, places it at Aenon near Salim in the vicinity of Beth-Shean.

After the Arab conquest the Jordan continued to separate the province of Filasṭīn (formerly Palaestina prima) from Palaestina secunda, now called al-Urdunn ("the Jordan") after the river itself. In Crusader times a series of bridges were built or repaired across the river which then did not form a boundary; one at the Ford of Jacob's Daughters (end of the 13th century); one known as the Bridge of Sinnabra (12th century), one at Naharayim (before 1300) and one at Dāmiya, built by Baybars in 1266/67. During the construction of the last, the waters of the Jordan stopped flowing on December 7/8 because of a landslide. During the Mamluk and Turkish periods the Jordan Valley was first included in the *mamlaka* ("province") of Damascus, and later in the sanjak of Nablus. It was only in 1921 with the setting up of the Emirate of Transjordan that most of the Jordan again became a political frontier, remaining so through the Mandate period up to 1948. In the War of Independence the Arab Legion of Transjordan occupied the mountains of Nablus and Hebron west of the river. Syrian attempts to cross the Jordan at Deganiyah were foiled; the Syrian bridgehead at Mishmar ha-Yarden was evacuated after the armistice in 1949. From 1948 to 1967 the upper course of the Jordan was inside the territory of Israel and the lower course in the Kingdom of Jordan. In 1953 Israel started work south of the Ḥuleh Lake, in the demilitarized zone at the Syrian border, on its project to channel part of the Jordan waters to the Negev. This project evolved into an international issue debated at the UN Security Council. In 1955 Israel accepted the so-called Johnston plan, initiated by the United States government, for the utilization of the Jordan and Yarmuk waters by dividing them among Israel, Syria, Lebanon, and the Kingdom of Jordan, but the Arab League rejected the plan. Israel then decided to implement its part of the Johnston plan by diverting water from Lake Kinneret to the Negev through the construction of the National Water Carrier. In 1964 the Arab States tried to frustrate Israel's plans by diverting the headwaters of the River Jordan into Arab territories, but in 1965 Israel took military action against Syrian preliminary works at the headwaters, and Israel's water carrier to the Negev was completed without further interference.

After the Six-Day War of 1967 the Jordan from Gesher southward to the Dead Sea formed the ceasefire line between Israel and Jordan; communications between the two banks were kept open by the Israel Defense Forces. The Senir (Ḥaṣbiyyā) source of the Jordan was in Lebanese territory and the Hermon (Bāniyās) and Dan sources were held by Israel.

BIBLIOGRAPHY: N. Glueck, *The River Jordan* (1946); Abel, Geog, 1 (1933), 161ff.; J. Braslawsky, *Le-Ḥeker Arẓenu* (1954), 231–3; EM, s.v.; Neubauer, Geog, 29–31; Schattner, in: *Scripta Hierosolymitana*, 11 (1962); idem, in: bies, 28 (1964), 3ff.

[Abraham J. Brawer and Michael Avi-Yonah]

JORDAN, CHARLES HAROLD (1908–1967), U.S. social worker. Jordan was born in Philadelphia and educated in Germany. He joined the *American Jewish Joint Distribution Committee (JDC) in 1941 as a social worker in Cuba. After service in the U.S. Navy during World War II, Jordan became JDC director in Shanghai, responsible for the care and emigration of Jewish refugees. After serving as head of the JDC Emigration Department in Paris from 1948, Jordan became JDC assistant director general, and in 1955 director general in Europe. In these capacities Jordan was a key figure in the mass migration of Jews to Israel from Europe and the consequent closing of the displaced person camps in Europe. He sponsored the development of *Malben in Israel for immigrant social care, and the work of the JDC in North Africa. In 1965 he became executive vice chairman of the JDC. As chairman of the Governing Board of the International Council of Voluntary Agencies from 1962, Jordan gained recognition as an international expert in his field. In 1967 he became chairman of the American Council of Voluntary Agencies for Foreign Service, and interested himself especially in world refugee problems. On August 16, 1967, he was mysteriously murdered in Prague.

[Yehuda Bauer]

New light has since been thrown on Jordan's death. His body was found floating in the Vltava River in Prague, and the Czechoslovak government issued a terse statement that he had committed suicide.

According to Josef Frolik, who for 17 years worked for Czechoslovak intelligence and later defected to the United States, Jordan was suspected by the Arabs of being an Israeli spy and was kidnapped after leaving his hotel to buy cigarettes. He was brought to the Egyptian embassy for interrogation, during which he was killed by three Palestinians. Early the next morning his body was carried out to a car by four men and thrown into the river. The Czech authorities were aware of the facts but decided not to inform the American embassy of the fate of Jordan. Three days after the body was found the First Secretary at the Egyptian embassy at Prague left the country at the government's request, and the three Palestinians left a week later.

BIBLIOGRAPHY: *New York Times* (Feb. 3, 1974).

JORDAN, HASHEMITE KINGDOM OF (Ar. **al-mamlaka al-Urdunniyya al-Hashimiyya**), an independent state in W. Asia, bordering on Israel and the West Bank of the Jordan River in the west, *Saudi Arabia in the south and southeast, *Iraq in the east, and *Syria in the north. Transjordania, the territory east of the Jordan River – including the biblical *Bashan and *Gilead – was an important center of Israelite and Jewish life in biblical times and until well after the destruction of the Second Temple. Under Byzantine rule the Jewish population declined rapidly, and after the Muslim conquest there were only occasional cases of Jews living there, though "the Land of Gilead" played no small part in Zionist dreaming and planning.

Transjordania was included in the area of the British *Mandate for Palestine, but in 1921 *Abdullah, a son of the sharif Hussein of Mecca, who had moved into the territory with a band of Arab guerrillas, was recognized by Winston *Churchill, then British colonial secretary, as emir of Transjordan, and the emirate was later excluded from the applicability of the articles in the Palestine Mandate relating to the Jewish National Home. At the time it had a population of some 200,000, mostly Bedouin. In 1946 Abdullah was crowned king of Transjordan, and its independence was recognized by the British.

In the Arab-Israel war of 1948 and its aftermath, the Jordanian Arab Legion occupied East Jerusalem and the Arab-inhabited areas of Judea and Samaria on the west bank of the river, which were finally unified with the east bank under the name of the Hashemite Kingdom of Jordan in April 1950. Israel and most Arab states defined this step as a unilateral act of annexation, though it was recognized by Britain. The influx of Palestinians enormously swelled Jordan's population, which in 1965 totaled some 2,000,000, of whom about 900,000 lived on the West Bank.

In the *Six-Day War of 1967 Israel occupied Judea and Samaria, leaving Jordan in control of the area of the old emirate, apart from adjustments (in 1965) of the frontier with Saudi Arabia. The area of Jordan thereafter was about 34,500 sq. mi. (about 86,000 sq. km.) and its population was estimated at 1,500,000, including a net influx of some 250,000 persons from the West Bank after the 1967 War. *Amman, the capital, has grown within fifty years from an inconsiderable village into a sprawling city of over 400,000 inhabitants. At the turn of the 21st century Jordan's population exceeded five million, over 40% of which lived in the greater Amman-Zarqa area.

Geography

The country is divided into three main zones, all running north-south: the Jordan river depression, the hill country, and the arid plateau sloping east toward the Euphrates and the Persian Gulf. The first two zones are cut laterally by steep-walled valleys opening into the Jordan depression, the Dead Sea and the Aravah, making north-south communication difficult except by detours through the desert in the east. Only the second zone is suited by nature to settlement on a considerable scale, possessing a bracing climate, good soil, and relatively abundant winter rain; here a settled, grain-growing population provided the country with its main sources of livelihood until the revolutionary changes from the late 1940s on. The east-west historical and administrative differentiation of these zones is parallel to the geographical division. From the Syrian border (the *Yarmuk River) to the biblical Yabok River (Wadi Zarka): the Ajlun area (biblical *Gilead); from the Yabuk to the *Arnon River (Wadi Mujib): the Amman and Balqa area (biblical *Ammon); from the Arnon to *Zered River (Wadi Hasa): the Karak area (biblical Moab) and from there to the Red Sea: the Ma'an area (biblical *Edom). The population speaks Arabic, except for the elder generation of some 15,000 Circassians, who cling to their Caucasian tongue. Sunni *Islam is the prevailing religion. Christians, mostly Greek Orthodox, number 5–10%. There are probably less than 50,000 true nomads or Bedouin, though a far greater number are still tribally organized.

Economy

The economy of Jordan has always rested on heavy subsidies from abroad. These were provided in the main by Britain till 1957, then by the United States, and after the Six-Day War by the oil-rich Arab states of Saudi Arabia, *Kuwait, and *Libya. Another important item in the balance of payments is money transfers from Jordanians abroad. Jordan's international trade has always been unbalanced, exports paying in 1966 for only about one-eighth of imports; the picture has grown even darker since, and the tourist trade suffered disastrously after 1967. Main exports are phosphates, Dead Sea minerals, and agricultural produce. Akaba, Jordan's only port, is distant from the center and suffered from the closure of the Suez Canal. The outlet via *Beirut was hampered by the chronic political tension with Syria. The outsized army provided the livelihood of an important sector of the population. In the early 1980s the Jordanian economy showed an impressive recovery, but from the second half of the 1980s it again plummeted, owing to the termination of the Iran-Iraq war (from which Jordan had benefited considerably), the *intifada*, and the Iraqi invasion of Kuwait. In the early 2000s Jordan's economy suffered mainly from an unemployment rate of over 20% and from an external debt of over $7 billion. King Abdallah II has invested most of his time and energy in economic affairs.

Governance

Jordan's constitution (1952, with later amendments) describes the country's government as "a hereditary monarchy, parliamentary in form." There are two houses: the Senate, appointed by the king, and the Chamber of Deputies, elected on the basis of general (in practice male) franchise. The Council of Ministers is responsible to the Chamber of Deputies. In reality, however, the king has always exerted much greater influence than the constitution would suggest. Their unpopularity with a majority of their subjects – especially Palestinians – compelled Abdullah first, and later his grandson *Hussein, to set aside "the will of the people" to a considerable extent. Their rule was maintained, despite internal disaffection and calls from *Cairo, *Damascus, and *Baghdad for Hussein's destruction as a "tool of imperialism," by favors proffered and withheld, press supervision, and directed elections, while coercion – from martial law and the suspension of parliament to the wholesale imprisonment and exile of malcontents – played a prominent part. The army, recruited as far as possible from the East Bank and preferably from Bedouin, was considered the main prop of the regime, its senior officers being handpicked for their loyalty. Shortly before the 1967 war, a new press law forced all newspapers to close down, and carefully circumscribed the conditions under which new ones might appear.

Although the Six-Day War improved Hussein's relations with the Arab world, his position within his own country soon started to deteriorate. Numerous organizations for "the liberation of Palestine" succeeded in constituting themselves as "kingdoms in themselves," first in and near the Jordan Valley, and then in mounting measure in the interior. Various agreements to coexist failed, mainly because the Palestinian leaders would not, or could not, coerce their followers. By the summer of 1970 the sovereignty of the state had become nonexistent. In the first half of September, when an attempt on Hussein's life by one of the Palestinian organizations (The Democratic Front for the Liberation of Palestine) was followed by a virtual siege laid on Hussein's residence, the king realized the inevitability of armed confrontation. A week's warfare, mainly in and about Amman, went in favor of the army. By July 1971 the Palestinian organizations had been by and large liquidated in Jordan and subsequently moved mostly to *Lebanon.

Jordan sat out the 1973 war with Israel. After Anwar *Sadat's visit to Jerusalem in 1977, Jordan–PLO relations improved.

King Hussein's historic decision to give up Jordan's claim to the West Bank of the Jordan River in 1988 and food riots in southern Jordan in 1989 paved the way for a democratization process in Jordan's political life. General elections (the first since 1967) were held in 1989. A new Chamber of Deputies was democratically elected by the inhabitants of the East Bank only. Political parties were formed and political freedoms were restored. The democratic process was somewhat slowed down in the late 1990s, out of fear that more political reforms (as demanded by the opposition, whose backbone was the Islamic movement) might challenge the authority of the monarch.

In 1994 Hussein became the second Arab head of state, after Sadat of Egypt, to sign a peace treaty with Israel. During the *Rabin years relations between the two countries were warm, but cooled off somewhat with the Likud in power under Binyamin *Netanyahu and with the second intifada.

When King Abdullah II came to the throne in 1999 after the demise of his father, King Hussein, the democratization process had almost completely stopped, as the cross-purposes of democracy and survival of the regime seemed unbridgeable. From 2003 there have been more than a few indications that Abdullah had decided to return to the democratization path.

BIBLIOGRAPHY: C. Bailey, *The Participation of the Palestinians in the Politics of Jordan* (1970); Māḍī & Mūsā, *Ta'rīkh al-Urdunn fi-al-Qarn al-ʿIshrīn* ("History of Jordan in the Twentieth Century," Amman, 1959). F.G. Peake, *History of Jordan and its Tribes* (1958); B. Shwadran, *Jordan, A State of Tension* (1959); P.J. Vatikiotis, *Politics and the Military in Jordan* (1967). **ADD. BIBLIOGRAPHY:** M. Sulayman, *Ta'rikh al-Urdunn fi al Qarn al-Ishrin, al-juz' al-Thani 1958–1995* (Amman, 1995); K. Salibi *The Modern History of Jordan* (1993).

[Uriel Dann / Joseph Nevo (2nd ed.)]

JORTNER, JOSHUA (1933–), Israeli physical chemist. He was born in Tarnow, Poland and gained his Ph.D. from the Hebrew University of Jerusalem (1960). He joined the staff of the university's department of physical chemistry (1961–65) before moving to the department of chemistry at Tel Aviv University (1964) where he became professor (1966), head of the school of chemistry (1966–72) and deputy rector (1966–69), acting rector, and vice president of Tel Aviv University (1970–72). He was research associate and then visiting professor at the University of Chicago (1962–71) among many visiting distinctions. His initial research concerned energy dynamics and transfer in materials and between molecules. Later he studied order and oscillations in molecules and nanosystems including femtosecond chemistry which concerns very fast chemical reactions and biological processes such as protein folding and conformational changes. His later research concerned the fragmentation on molecular structure induced by ions and had fundamentally important implications for understanding stability in physical and biological systems and perturbing influences such as radiation effects. He continued to work actively in this field. Jortner had a major and continuing influence on the development of science and technology and on scientific education in Tel Aviv University, Israel, and the wider world. He consistently emphasized the importance of inter-disciplinary research. He served on the National Council for Higher Education and the National Council for Research and Development; he was scientific adviser to three Israeli prime ministers. He was also president of the International Union of Pure and Applied Chemistry which represents sixty member states (1998–99). His many honors include the Weizmann prize (1973), the Rothschild Prize (1976), the Israel Prize in chemistry (1982) the Wolf Prize in chemistry (1982), and the RS Mulliken Medal (1998). He was a foreign associate of the U.S. Academy of Sciences and was elected to the Israel Academy of Sciences and Humanities of which he was vice president (1980–86) and president (1986–95).

[Michael Denman (2nd ed.)]

JOSCE OF YORK (d. 1190), English financier and martyr. He was a leading agent of *Aaron of Lincoln and one of the

Jewish representatives at the coronation of Richard I (1189), but escaped when the mob attacked the Jews. He survived the first attack on *York Jewry in March 1190 and led those who took refuge in the castle keep. When the keep was attacked, he died in the act of mass self-destruction, reputedly at the hand of R. *Yom Tov of Joigny. He is admiringly described as a patron of learning in the elegy on the York martyrs by *Joseph b. Asher of Chartres.

BIBLIOGRAPHY: Roth, England, 22f.; M. Adler, *Jews of Medieval England* (1939), 128–31; JHSET, 16 (1952), 213–20.

[Vivian David Lipman]

JOSELEWICZ, BEREK (Berek, son of Yosel; c. 1770–1809), colonel of the Polish armed forces, participant in the *Kosciuszko rising and the Napoleonic Wars. Born in Kretinga, Lithuania, he later became court factor to Bishop Massalski of Vilna. In the course of his assignments abroad on behalf of the bishop, he visited Paris on the eve of the revolution and there came into contact with revolutionary ideas. Later Berek and his wife Rebekah settled in Praga, a suburb of Warsaw. The vociferous debate on the status of the Jews then in progress in the Sejm (1788–92) and the movement toward Jewish *emancipation led some Jews to identify with the Polish struggle against the partition of Poland-Lithuania. At first their number was small, but when the insurrection led by Thaddeus Kosciuszko broke out in 1794, numerous groups of Jews joined in the uprising. During the siege of Warsaw, Jewish inhabitants fought alongside the Polish population of the capital against the Russian army. Berek appealed to the Jewish population to join the struggle and fight "like lions and leopards." On September 17, the official *Gazeta Rządowa* announced that two Jews, Berek Joselewicz and Jozef Aronowicz, had requested permission to create a separate Jewish light-cavalry regiment. Warmly praising this initiative, Kosciuszko granted the request, and a regiment of 500 Jews was organized, some of them volunteers.

After the defeat of the insurrection, Berek fled to Austria and later reached France, where he established contact with Polish emigrés. Joining the French army, he served in the cavalry of Napoleon's Polish Legion. In 1801 his unit crossed the Alps. He was promoted to the rank of captain of a dragoon regiment in the French army and was awarded the cross of the Légion d'Honneur. After the establishment of the grand duchy of Warsaw (1807), his detachment was incorporated into the regular Polish army; becoming a squadron leader, he received the order *Virtuti Militari*. Berek's military career was greatly hampered by the antisemitism prevailing in army circles, but he was respected by the Polish liberals of his day and was admitted to the aristocratic Masonic lodge Bracia Polscy Zjednoczeni ("United Polish Brethren"). During the Austrian campaign in 1809, he commanded two squadrons of Prince Jozef Poniatowski's army. After fierce resistance against the numerically superior Austrian forces, Berek was killed at Kock in May 1809. He became a hero and was often cited in apologetics in support of assimilation in Poland.

His son Joseph *Berkowicz was also an army officer.

BIBLIOGRAPHY: Mstislavskaya, in: *Yevreyskaya Starina*, 3 (1910), 61–80, 235–52; E. Luniński, *Berek Joselewicz i jego syn* (1909); *Heroische Gestalten juedischen Stammes* (1937), 23–40; E. Ringelblum, *Żydzi w powstaniu Kościuszkowskim* (1938); Kermish, in: *Sefer ha-Yovel… N.M. Gelber* (1963), 221–9; N.M. Gelber, *Aus zwei Jahrhunderten* (1924), 9–13; A. Lewinson, *Toledot Yehudei Varsha* (1953), 94–95. **ADD. BIBLIOGRAPHY:** M. Balaban (ed.), *Album pamiatkowy ku czci Berka Joselewicza* (1934).

[Nathan Michael Gelber]

JOSEPH (Heb. יוֹסֵף, יְהוֹסֵף), son of *Jacob and Rachel. He was born in Paddan-Aram after his mother had been barren for seven years (Gen. 29:20, 30; 30:22–24, 25; 31:41). Nothing is related of his childhood.

Joseph and His Brothers

At the age of 17 Joseph tended his father's sheep in the land of Canaan. He became completely alienated from his brothers because he used to report their misdeeds to their father, because Jacob showed obvious favoritism toward him even to the extent of presenting him with a ceremonial robe, and because of a series of dreams in which he, Joseph, was the object of his brothers' adoration (37:1–11). On one occasion Jacob sent Joseph to visit his brothers and to report back on their welfare. The road led from Hebron to Shechem and on to Dothan, a route which corresponds to the ancient north-south road west of the Jordan which traversed the central hill country along the entire length of the Palestinian watershed. Each of the cities mentioned was an important site, whose mention would have resonated with the ancient audiences. When the brothers saw Joseph from a distance their hatred and hostility welled up into a desire to murder him. The present story combines different traditions about which brother attempted to save Joseph. According to Genesis 37:22, Reuben suggested it would be better to throw him into a nearby pit. He secretly hoped, thereby, to save Joseph's life and to take him back home. When Joseph approached, the brothers stripped him of his robe and cast him into the pit.

While they were partaking of a meal, and in Reuben's absence, a caravan of traders from Gilead bearing gum, balm, and laudanum passed by on its way to Egypt (cf. Jer. 8:22; 46:11). These items played an important role in the life and economy of ancient Egypt, and such a caravan would have come from Gilead by way of the *Beth-Shean Valley and would indeed have passed through Dothan in order to join the road leading to Egypt. At this point a different tradition surfaces, according to which Judah suggested selling Joseph to the traders who bought him for 20 pieces of silver (Gen. 37:25–6). The conflation of the two traditions is most obvious in Gen. 37:29–30, describing Reuben's discovery that Joseph was gone. At this point the story proceeds to describe how the brothers sought to deceive their father about Joseph's fate. They dipped the robe in the blood of a slaughtered kid and brought it to Jacob for identification. The patriarch recognized it, convinced that his son had been torn to pieces by a savage beast. He mourned for Joseph many days and his grief was inconsolable (Gen. 37:12–35).

Joseph in Potiphar's House

Meanwhile, Joseph was sold in Egypt to Potiphar, a courtier and chief steward of Pharaoh (37:36; 39:1). The sale into slavery in this manner accords with what is known from 18th-century B.C.E. and later slave inventories which well document the commercial traffic in human misery between Canaan and Egypt. Another authentic background note is the name and title of Joseph's master. "Potiphar" (*ibid.*) is generally regarded as an abbreviated form of "Poti-Phera," the name of Joseph's father-in-law (41:45), which appears in Egyptian sources as *Pa-di-pa-reʿ*, "He whom Re (the sun-god) had given." The first two syllables are quite common in Egyptian personal names. The title "chief steward," literally "chief cook," corresponds to the title *wdpw*, "cuisinier," which came to designate those who served as superintendents and judicial functionaries in pharaonic court, although it has parallels in Neo-Assyrian usage as well.

In his new situation, Joseph soon earned the confidence of his master, who promoted him to be his personal attendant and overseer of his estate (39:2–6), a function conforming to that frequently encountered in Egyptian texts as *mer-per*, or comptroller. Joseph's favorable turn of fortune did not last long, for after a while Potiphar's wife – unnamed in the text – attempted to seduce him. Notwithstanding her repeated blandishments, he resisted the temptation. In revenge, she slandered him before her husband, who had Joseph thrown into the prison where prisoners of the king were confined (39:7–20).

This episode in Joseph's life has aroused special interest on account of the presence of the same motif in an Egyptian narrative known as the "Tale of Two Brothers," which has been preserved in late sources, but which is undoubtedly more ancient. It tells of an unsuccessful attempt to seduce a bachelor brother-in-law, whose honor is then impugned by the temptress. The story provides local coloration for the biblical account, and if it were a popular piece of Egyptian fiction it could well have influenced the artistic form in which the biblical narrative has been presented; its moral climate is far different in that Joseph stresses the sin against God involved in the proposed act of treachery and adultery (39:9).

The focus of attention in the Genesis narrative is the nobility of Joseph's character and the salvation that came through suffering, placing the incident in the concatenation of events that led eventually to the migration of the Israelites to Egypt, their enslavement and redemption. It was precisely as a result of Joseph's innocent suffering that he was enabled to rise to power.

Joseph in Prison

During his incarceration, Joseph won the trust of the chief jailer who placed him in charge of his fellow prisoners. Among these were the chief *cupbearer, a title with Assyrian parallels, and the chief baker to Pharaoh (39:21–40:4). One night the two experienced disturbing dreams. That of the cupbearer was favorably interpreted by Joseph to mean that in three days' time a royal amnesty would restore him to his former position. The baker's anxiety, however, was not relieved; impalement awaited him.

Joseph then took the opportunity to beg the cupbearer to use his regained influence in order to get him freed from his undeserved imprisonment. The predictions were indeed fulfilled, but the cupbearer soon forgot Joseph (40:5–23). In this connection it must be remembered that the office of chief cupbearer carried with it far more than the name implies.

Pharaoh's Dreams

Some two years later, the fateful role played by dreams in Joseph's life manifested itself again. The inability of Pharaoh's magicians and sages to interpret his dreams reminded the chief cupbearer of his own experience in prison. Joseph was brought to the palace and Pharaoh related his dreams, which the Hebrew slave proceeded to explain as portending seven years of great abundance in Egypt to be followed by a similar period of famine. Joseph then offered some unsolicited advice on how to deal with the situation. He proposed the appointment of a supreme commissioner of supplies to be aided by overseers, and the organization of a reserve bank of food during the years of plenty (41:1–36).

It should be noted that on none of the occasions in which Joseph is involved with dreams does God figure explicitly. Nevertheless, it is naturally assumed that He is the ultimate source of the message being conveyed. Since throughout the ancient Near East, including Israel, dreams were recognized as a means of divine communication (cf. 20:3; 28:12–15; 31:11–13, 24), it is not surprising that they were productive of anxiety, heightened in this instance by their duplication. The science of dream interpretation was especially well developed in Egypt and in the rest of the ancient Near East. Neither Joseph nor his brothers needed the services of an interpreter and Joseph himself was careful to disclaim any innate ability, simply ascribing all to God (40:8; 41:16).

Further local background in the narrative of Pharaoh's dreams is provided by both the imagery and vocabulary employed. It is not an accident that the king saw cows rather than sheep, for the latter played a very minor role in the Egyptian economy while cows were abundant and important. Moreover, the motif of seven cows is attested in the literature. At the same time, the Hebrew terms used for the Nile (*ye'or*, 41:17) and for the reedgrass (*'aḥu*, 41:18) are borrowed from Egyptian. As for the predicted seven year cycles, this, too, is a very common motif in ancient Near Eastern sources. A special Egyptian twist is given to the famine cycle through a text dealing with the reign of the Third Dynasty king Djoser (c. 28th century B.C.E.), which reports on a severe famine attributed to the failure of the Nile to rise for seven years.

Joseph's Elevation

Joseph's advice to Pharaoh struck a responsive chord. The king was impressed by the man's mature wisdom, at once adopted his suggestions, and appointed him, then aged 30 (41:46), to be in charge of their practical application (41:37–40).

The possibility of the rise of a foreigner to high station in the Egyptian court and administration is well substantiated. A Semite named Yanḥamu was Egyptian commissioner for Canaan and Syria in the time of Akhenaten (14th century B.C.E.), and a certain Ben-Ozen from northern Canaan rose to the position of marshal at the court of Merneptah (13th century B.C.E.). This same king's brother married the daughter of a Syrian sea captain named Ben-Anath, and in the following century one of the judges in the trial of the murderers of Ramses III bore the Semitic name Mahar-Baal.

The biblical account of the elevation and office of Joseph is unusually rich in detail. The multiplicity of titles and functions bestowed on Joseph reflects a well-known feature of the great Egyptian bureaucracy about which much is now known.

On the biblical account, Joseph assuredly penetrated the highest echelons of the Egyptian nobility and government. He reported directly to the king (41:40), a prerogative shared by several officials. He supervised the king's personal estates (45:8), a function that usually carried with it the titles "Great Steward of the Lord of the Two Lands" and "The Great Chief in the Palace." Pharaoh further put him in charge of all the land of Egypt (41:41), an office that corresponds to the title "Chief of the Entire Land." As the token of authority Pharaoh handed Joseph his signet ring (41:42). This recalls the title "Royal Seal Bearer" accorded selected high officials. In placing the gold chain about Joseph's neck (*ibid.*), the king was simply following another typically Egyptian form of investiture and conferring one of his highest distinctions. When Joseph described himself as "father to Pharaoh" (45:8) he was citing a known Egyptian title "God's [i.e., the king's] Father." Finally, as the one responsible for the storage and distribution of food as well as for the collection of tax payments on produce (41:48–49; 47:24), Joseph undoubtedly performed the functions of the high office known as "Overseer of the Granaries of Upper and Lower Egypt."

In addition to his generous distribution of honors and titles, Pharaoh had Joseph ride in the chariot of his second-in-command, while men cried before him "*Abrech!" (41:43), a word of uncertain meaning. He also gave him an Egyptian name, Zaphenath-Paneah (41:45), which means "the god speaks; he lives." This, indeed, is in conformity with the known practice of Asiatics in Egyptian service acquiring local names. The king also married his new administrator to Asenath, daughter of the high priest of On, or Heliopolis (41:45, 50). The lady's name is also explicable as good Egyptian and means "she belongs to (the goddess) Neith."

Joseph set to work in pursuance of his duties. He traveled the length and breadth of the land, organizing the establishment of store cities into which the good surpluses were garnered during the years of abundance (41:46–49). During this period he became the father of two sons, *Manasseh and *Ephraim, both of whose names signify a desire to forget the past (41:50–52).

The Reconciliation

With the onset of the cycle of famine years, Joseph saw his boyhood dreams fulfilled as his unsuspecting ten older brothers, who had arrived in Egypt to buy food, bowed low before him (42:1–6). He recognized them, but suppressed the fact, spoke harshly to them, interrogated them, accused them of spying, confined them in the guardhouse for three days, then sent them home with food, but not before he had detained Simeon, insisted on their bringing Benjamin, and had their purchase money put into the brothers' sacks of grain (42:7–26).

Under the pressure of severe famine and the importuning of his sons, Jacob agreed to let Benjamin go. Once again the brothers presented themselves before Joseph who invited them for a meal and freed Simeon. They presented Joseph with gifts, offered to repay the cost of the original purchases, and exchanged greetings. When Joseph saw Benjamin he was overcome with emotion and had to rush from the room to weep. All the brothers later dined together (Gen. 43).

Joseph once again instructed the house steward to restore the purchase money in each bag of grain and also to put his personal silver divining goblet into Benjamin's. The men left early next morning and had not gone far from the city when Joseph sent his steward after them to accuse them of the theft of his goblet. The surprised brothers protested their innocence and offered to become slaves if it be found in their possession. The steward, however, insisted that only the culprit would be enslaved, but when a search disclosed the goblet in Benjamin's sack the disconsolate brothers all started back for the city where Joseph was waiting for them. They prostrated themselves before him and resigned themselves to a fate of slavery, but Joseph, too, stressed that Benjamin alone would suffer (44:1–17).

Judah then made an impassioned plea reciting Joseph's insistence on seeing Benjamin, Jacob's reluctance to let him go, and the fatal impact upon their father that a misfortune to Benjamin would have. He offered to take upon himself his brother's punishment (44:18–34). Now Joseph could contain himself no longer. He ordered everyone else out of the room and, sobbing with emotion, revealed to his dumbfounded brothers his true identity, even as he tenderly and generously propounded the notion that his original kidnapping had proved to be an act of Providence to ensure the family's survival in the harsh years of famine. He bade them hurry back to Canaan to bring their father and families to him. He then embraced Benjamin and his other brothers (45:1–15). The news of what had occurred reached Pharaoh who sent orders supporting Joseph's invitation to his family and placed baggage wagons at their disposal, while Joseph sent expensive gifts (45:16–24).

The Migration to Egypt

The brothers returned to Canaan to tell their father the startling news. His initial incredulity soon gave way to acceptance and a strong desire to see his long-lost son (45:25–28). The patriarch set out for Beer-Sheba where he received divine reassurance and then moved toward Goshen as Joseph set out to greet him. The two met in a tearful embrace (46:29–30), after a separation of 22 years (cf. 37:2; 41:46, 53; 45:11).

Joseph arranged an audience with Pharaoh for his brothers and the king granted their request to settle in the Goshen region and even offered to appoint some of them as the superintendents of his cattle (47:1–6). Joseph then introduced his father to Pharaoh (47:7–10). The family settled in the choicest part of Egypt and Joseph sustained them throughout the next five years of famine (47:11–12).

The migration of Joseph's family from Canaan to Egypt in this fashion was not an extraordinary phenomenon in itself. This is verified by a papyrus bearing a report of an official on the eastern frontier to his superior relating how he had granted Edomite shepherd tribes permission to make use of the Nile Delta pasturage "to keep them and their flocks alive." It is clear that the official had the power to make ad hoc decisions of this type without having to refer to higher authority.

What is remarkable about the Israelite experience is that a routine family visit (45:28) has been transformed in the narrative into an event of national significance (46:3–4) transcending by far its immediate import. The Exodus from Egypt and the return to the land of Canaan henceforth became the major biblical motif.

Joseph's Agrarian Measures

The rest of the Joseph story is mainly taken up with various administrative measures wholly unrelated to the fortunes of the Israelites. Joseph secured for the crown the silver and livestock that the people possessed, as payment for rations supplied. Next, he nationalized the farmlands except for those held by the priests. He reduced the population to the status of bondmen and imposed a land tax of one-fifth of the produce of the soil (47:13–26).

As a matter of fact, the state of affairs here described as having been instituted by Joseph actually corresponds to the situation of state slavery that prevailed in Egypt following the expulsion of the Hyksos toward the end of the 16th century B.C.E. It must have come about over a long period of time which covered the life-spans of several pharaohs. The biblical narrative is probably intended to emphasize the great indebtedness of the crown to Joseph and hence the base ingratitude of the later pharaohs, "who did not know Joseph" (Ex. 1:8).

Joseph's Last Days

Jacob lived with his son in Egypt for 17 years. When he felt his end nearing, he extracted a pledge from Joseph to bury him in the ancestral vault in Canaan (Gen. 47:28–31; cf. 49:29–32). Joseph brought his two sons to be blessed by their grandfather and he witnessed their adoption by Jacob as well as the transference of the birthright from the elder, Manasseh, to the younger, Ephraim (48:1–20).

Joseph was present at his father's death (50:1; cf. 46:4). He had him embalmed and fulfilled his father's wishes, returning to Egypt after the burial (50:1–14). At this point, the brothers apparently feared that Joseph would take revenge for their cruel treatment of him in his youth. He, however, dispelled their fears by citing once again his personal theological interpretation of the kidnapping (50:15–21; cf. 45:5–8).

Joseph lived another 54 years after his father's death to see great-grandchildren by both his sons. He died at 110 – considered an ideal age, incidentally, among the Egyptians. In his last words he reiterated his faith in the ultimate fulfillment of the divine promises to the Patriarchs and he made his brothers swear that when the time came they would transfer his remains to the Promised Land. He was embalmed and placed in a coffin in Egypt (50:22–26), a tradition linking Joseph with the mummies for which Egypt was famed.

The Nature of the Narrative

Of all the Genesis narratives, those about Joseph are the longest and most detailed. They are not a collection of isolated and fragmentary incidents, but a continuous biography, novelistic in complexion, the artistic creation of a consummate storyteller even though it may have utilized variant traditions (cf. the interchange of Ishmaelites and Midianites in Gen. 37:25, 27, 28, 36). The account contains an unprecedented wealth of background material, especially relating to the mores of a non-Israelite people. From this point of view it provides greater opportunity for archaeological illumination than do the earlier Genesis stories. The Joseph stories preserve traditions of the Northern kingdom, which viewed Joseph as its eponymous ancestor.

Most striking and, in fact, unique, is the secularistic complexion of the narrative. Although there are no miraculous elements; no divine revelations experienced by Joseph, no associations with altars or cultic sites, the discourse is permeated with the consciousness of God at work, and if there is no direct intervention by Him in human affairs, no doubt is left that the unfolding of events is the directed act of Providence (Gen. 45:4–8; 50: 19–20).

Joseph in the Rest of the Bible

Outside of Genesis, the personality of Joseph receives scant attention. The Pentateuch indirectly refers to his services to the Egyptians (Ex. 1:8) and records only the fulfillment by Moses of Joseph's last wish (Gen. 50:25; Ex. 13:19). The Book of Joshua (24:32) completes this story by reporting the burial of his mortal remains in Shechem (cf. Gen. 33:19). A brief reference to the sale of Joseph into slavery is to be found in Psalm 105:17 which, in context, appears to be dependent on Genesis 45:5–8; 50:20. Another Psalms passage (81:6) may also relate to Joseph's experience in Egypt, but the exact meaning of the text is unclear and the name may be a generic term for all Israel, as in Psalms 80:2. In such cases a Northern Israelite origin for the composition may be supposed.

All other references to "Joseph" are either to the twin tribes Ephraim and Manasseh (Gen. 49:22, 26; Deut. 27:12; 33:13; Ezek. 47:13; 48:32; et al.), or to the Northern Israelite Kingdom in general (Ezek. 37:16, 19; Amos 5:15; 6:6; Ps. 78:67), otherwise referred to as the "House of Joseph" (Amos 5:6;

Obad. 18; Zech. 10:6; cf. Judg. 1:22, 23, 35; II Sam. 19:21; I Kings 11:28).

The Name

The name Joseph is explained in Genesis 30:24 as meaning "May the Lord add another son for me." As a verbal form it is probably abbreviated from a fuller name containing a divine element (cf. Josiphiah, Ezra 8:10). The name once appears in the expanded form Jehoseph (Ps. 81:6), which is frequent in post-biblical inscriptions.

[Nahum M. Sarna]

In the Aggadah

The extraordinary career of Joseph as related in Genesis provided a vast amount of material for the aggadists who utilized the biblical story to emphasize various social, religious, and political ideas. Joseph's steadfastness in the face of temptation, his filial love for his father, his loyalty to his family, and his conduct in high office became favorite object lessons in rabbinic homiletics. To some extent Joseph's adventures in Egypt were symbolic of Israel's fate among the nations and of the frequent change of fortune characterizing Jewish history. Joseph's life was accordingly compared to that of Jacob (Israel) whom he resembled in many respects (Gen. R. 84:6, et al.). Joseph's brothers were secondary to him, for his merits and learning exceeded theirs (84:5). Unlike his brothers who refused even to greet him, he would go out of his way to salute them even after he had risen to power, and he generally behaved with due modesty despite his high position. This was cited as an example to officeholders inclined to assume an attitude of arrogance (Tanḥ. B., Gen. 180; Ex. R. 1:7).

Despite Joseph's merits, both he and his doting father are taken to task for various faults which the rabbis were anxious to discourage among their disciples. Jacob is criticized for favoring Joseph over his other sons – an educationally unsound attitude (Shab. 10b) – and for his original failure to recognize the significance of Joseph's dreams (Gen. R. 84:11). Joseph's troubles were attributed to such acts as "painting his eyes, curling his hair, and walking with a mincing step" (84:7; cf. 87:3). He had also wrongly charged his brothers with serious offenses for which he was appropriately punished (87:3, et al.). Significantly, similar faults among the "disciples of the wise," including excessive pride in personal appearance, mutual slander, and lack of respect for each other are castigated in rabbinic literature (RH 26b; Yev. 62b; TJ, Pe'ah 1:1, 15d–16a). Joseph was highly praised for honoring his father and obeying him even at the risk of his life (Mekh., 2, Proem; Gen. R. 84:13). When his brothers saw him at Dothan, they intended to kill him by setting dogs at him (84:14) – a punishment deserved by slanderers (Pes. 118a), but also a midrashic device to exonerate the tribal ancestors from legal culpability, since indirect murder of this type was not punishable by law (Sanh. 9:1). Joseph's righteousness is frequently stressed by the rabbis. As a result of it he emerged unharmed from the pit into which he had been cast, although it was full of snakes and scorpions (Shab. 22a; Gen. R. 84:16). The Ishmaelites who carried him to Egypt had with them sacks filled with spices instead of their usual merchandise which had an offensive odor (Tosef., Ber. 4:4; Gen. R. 84:17, et al.).

Potiphar's wife, who tried to seduce Joseph, is depicted in the *aggadah* as the prototype of the immoral pagan woman. The story of the wiles she used to win Joseph's heart was imaginatively expanded to serve as a perfect text for sermons on sexual morality. Her depravity is emphasized with a view to warning Jewish youths against the temptations of the flesh. Not only did she use the most indecent language (cf. Gen. 39:7) – in sharp contrast to Ruth in a comparable situation (cf. Ruth 3:9) – but she plotted to murder her husband so as to be free to marry Joseph (Gen. R. 87:4–5; Ruth R. 6:1). All her seductive efforts and threats were of no avail. She even became sick and wasted away on account of her unfulfilled love; but her pleading and weeping proved equally unsuccessful (Yoma 35b; ARN[1] 16, 63; Gen. R. 87:5–6). Nevertheless some rabbis believed that Joseph had in fact been on the point of yielding to temptation, and only the timely appearance of his father's and/or mother's image had cooled his passion and prevented him from sinning (Sot. 36b; TJ, Hor. 2:5, 46d; Gen. R. 87:7; 98; 20).

The rabbis also criticized Joseph's request to the butler to intercede with Pharaoh on his behalf (Gen. 40:14). He should not have put his trust in man, and for this reason had to stay in prison another two years (Gen. R. 89:2; Tanh. B. Gen. 189). The butler, represented as the archetype of the ungrateful and vicious pagan, not only "forgot" Joseph, but also did his best to discredit him in his report to Pharaoh (Gen. R. 89:7). The angel Gabriel, however, taught Joseph the traditional 70 languages, so that he could qualify to be ruler of Egypt (Sot. 36b). His elevation to power was the reward for his virtuous life (Gen. R. 90:3, et al.). Joseph's marriage to Asenath, daughter of Poti-Phera, priest of On (Gen. 41:45), is legitimized by late Midrashim which represent Asenath as Dinah's daughter (and hence Joseph's niece) later adopted by Potiphar, who is identified with Poti-Phera (PdRE 38; Targ. Jon., Gen. 41:45 and 46:20). The possibility of Asenath's conversion from paganism is implicitly rejected. Earlier Midrashim, however, which depict Asenath as the natural daughter of Potiphar and his wife and represent Joseph as refusing to sell grain to Egyptians who would not be circumcised (Gen. R. 85:2; 90:6; 91:5), reflect the view of those who favored active proselytizing.

In contrast to the biblical account that Joseph had forgotten his "father's house" (Gen. 41:51), the rabbis maintained that he was in mourning, wearing sackcloth and fasting, and refrained from drinking wine during all the years he was separated from his family (Gen. R. 85:1; 92:5; 93:7; 98:20; Shab. 139a). The Midrash also softens the harsh treatment accorded by Joseph to his brothers, and points out that he had behaved like a brother to them when they were in his power, while they had not treated him like a brother when he was in their power (Gen. R. 91:7; et al.). Simeon, who had cast Joseph into the pit (84:16; 91:6), was only ostensibly chained by Joseph; but as soon as the other brothers had left, "he gave him to eat and drink, and bathed and anointed him" (91:8). According to one view, however, Joseph died before his brothers because he had assumed superior airs toward them (Ber. 55a; Sot. 13b.). The confrontation between Joseph and his brothers is depicted in the Midrash as a clash between warriors endowed with superhuman strength. Judah especially, representing no doubt the Jewish people, is shown to be a man of fantastic physical powers which he threatens to use not only against Joseph, but against Pharaoh and the Egyptians (Gen. R. 91:6; 92:8; 93:6–8). The anti-Egyptian trend of the midrashic narrative reflects the violent hostility between Jews and Egyptians during the first and second centuries C.E.

Joseph's order to have Jacob embalmed – an Egyptian custom not practiced among Jews – was criticized by R. Judah ha-Nasi, but other rabbis maintained that it had been done in accordance with Jacob's own instructions (Gen. R. 100:3). A similar difference of views arose regarding Joseph's embalmment, carried out, according to one opinion, by the (Egyptian) physicians, and according to another, by his brothers (100:11). The issue in the case was apparently whether non-Jews could be permitted to handle the body of an Israelite. According to the *aggadah*, Joseph's body was placed in a metal coffin which the Egyptians dropped into the Nile so that its waters should be blessed. Others maintain that he was buried in a royal sepulcher as befitted his station in life. At the time of the Exodus from Egypt, Moses miraculously raised the coffin from the Nile or royal mausoleum and took it with him. During the 40 years' wandering in the wilderness, the coffin was carried next to the *Ark of the Covenant because "This one [Joseph] fulfilled all that was written in the other" (Sot. 13a–b; Tosef., Sot. 4:7; Mekh. 2, Proem., et al.).

[Moses Aberbach]

In Islam

Yūsuf was one of *Muhammad's most beloved characters; he consecrated a whole sura (the 12th) to him ("the Sura of Joseph"), which contains "the most beautiful tale," in 111 continuous verses. The tale begins with Jacob's warning to his son not to tell his dream of the sun, the moon, and the stars to his brothers because it might arouse their jealousy. Indeed, Joseph became the object of his brothers' hatred and they availed themselves of the first opportunity to throw him into the pit. Muhammad continues in light of the Bible and the *aggadah* and he embellishes his words when he tells of Joseph's enticement by the wife of his master (see Qiṭfīr = *Potiphar), whom Muhammad knows only by the name of al-ʿAzīz ("the Mighty"; verses 30, 51). Joseph was saved from her designs because Allah was with him. His shirt, which was torn from behind, was definite proof that the woman had not protected herself from the intentions of Joseph, but that she had attacked and attempted to seize hold of him when he had fled from her presence. The Egyptian women mocked the stupid woman, and when the latter invited them to a feast, she presented each of them with a knife, together with the refreshments. She then ordered Joseph to appear before the guests, and when they looked upon him, they were so enraptured by his beauty that they cut their fingers with the knives. The tale then returns to its biblical course. Before Joseph was appointed head of the king's granaries, the woman came to Pharaoh and confessed that Joseph was one of the *al-ṣādiqīn*, "the righteous" (verse 51), and that she had sought to entice him (similarly, the chief butler refers to him (Joseph) as *al-ṣiddīq*, "the righteous one"; verse 46). According to Speyer, this was due to the influence of a Syrian legend, so that Joseph would not desire vengeance against her and her husband, who had imprisoned him. Before the brothers went to Egypt for the second time, their father advised them not to enter together, through one gate (verse 67). The latter detail is taken from the Jewish *aggadah* (Gen. R. 91:2).

In post-koranic literature the tale of Joseph and Zulayka (the name of Qiṭfīr's wife) was considerably enlarged upon. It is developed into an independent subject which undergoes a romantic adaptation in prose and poetry in the Arabic and Persian languages. It is evident that many tales which stem from Jewish and Christian legends have been incorporated in this episode.

[Haïm Z'ew Hirschberg]

In the Arts

Few biblical figures have inspired more extensive and more universal literary treatment than Joseph. He appears in most of the medieval mystery cycles, in *L'Estoire Joseph* (an Old French poem), and in the early 13th-century *Iacob and Iosep*, where the biblical account is conveyed in lively English paraphrase. At about the same period, Shaiyad Hamza wrote a Turkish poem on the theme of Joseph and Potiphar's wife (Zulayka). The theme was popular in the Islamic world, where writers based their work on the 12th sura of the Koran. Though differing in detail, the Islamic legend follows the Hebrew Bible in broad outline. The Persian poet Jāmī (Maulānā Nūreddin Abd'el-Raḥmān Jāmī) wrote his most famous romance, *Yūsuf o Zuleikhā*, toward the end of the 15th century. In several variations a poem about "Yuçuf" (written in the 13th or 14th century) was current in Muslim Spain and gave rise to later Christian adaptations (*El poema de José*). The Jews of medieval Spain also created a tradition of their own which, in *Ladino literature, was entitled the *Poema de Yosef* or *Coplas de Yosef*. A definitive form of the latter, by Abraham de Toledo, was *Coplas de Yosef ha-Ẓaddik* (1732). The story of Joseph gained fresh popularity during the Renaissance and the Reformation. By 1560 there were 12 English plays on the subject and dozens more in French, Spanish, Italian, Dutch, and German. Protestant writers especially favored a moralistic treatment of Joseph's temptation, imprisonment, and final rise to glory and power, which gave them the opportunity of composing long speeches on virtue and the reward of the righteous and the punishment of evildoers. The many other colorful episodes in Joseph's career were, however, generally ignored. Some works of the 16th century were Sixtus Birck's German drama *Joseph* (1539); *Iosephus... Fabula sacra* ... (Antwerp, 1544), a neo-Latin verse play by the Flemish Catholic Georgius Macropedius (Joris van Langhveldt); Miguel de Carvajal's Spanish *Tragedia Josephina* (Seville, 1545); and *Żywot Józefa z pokolenia* *żydowskiego* (1545), a play by the Polish Calvinist Mikołaj Rej. One of the oldest Russian poems is the *Istoriya o prekrasnom Yosife*, which was probably the basis for later works about Joseph in the Slavonic languages. The rhymed allegorical *Joseph* by the Alsatian writer Thiebolt Gart (1540), based on a Latin school play by Cornelius Crocus (1536) and first staged in Schlettstadt, was the outstanding German drama of the 16th century. The Italian *sacre rappresentazioni* of the era included Simone Martelli's *Joseph figliuolo di Jacob* (Florence, 1565).

Interest in the subject during the 17th century was more or less confined to writers in England, Holland, and Germany. The late English cycle of mystery plays known as the *Stonyhurst Pageants* (c. 1625) includes a *Pageant of Joseph*. Two other treatments of the period were Sir Francis Hubert's poem, *Egypt's Favorite: The Historie of Joseph* (London, 1631), and Sir Thomas Salisbury's versified *History of Joseph* (London, 1636). Among the Dutch Catholic Joost van den Vondel's biblical verse plays were *Josef* (1635), *Joseph in Dothan* (1640), and *Joseph in Egypten* (1640); while Hugo de Groot (Grotius), the eminent jurist and statesman, wrote *Sophomopaneas* (Eng. tr. 1652), a verse tragedy partly reflecting his own career as a diplomat in the service of Sweden. Two outstanding works by German writers were the *Histori vom keuschen Joseph* (1667) by Hans Jakob Christoffel von Grimmelshausen, later reworked as *Des vortrefflich keuschen Josephs in Egypten… Lebensbeschreibung* (1671²); and *Assenat* (1670), a baroque novel by Philipp von Zesen. The subject continued to attract literary attention during the 18th century, particularly in England, where the works which it inspired included Hannah More's *Joseph Made Known to his Brethren* (in *Sacred Dramas*, 1782). In Switzerland, Johann Jacob Bodmer published several dramatic treatments, notably the epic *Joseph und Zulika* (1753) and two tragedies, *Der erkannte Joseph* and *Der keusche Joseph* (both 1754). Three other works of the period were *Joseph reconnu par ses frères* (Paris, 1786), a sacred drama by Félicité Ducrest de Saint-Aubin, countess of Genlis; the Spanish play *El mas feliz cautiverio, y los sueños de Josef* (Madrid, 1792); and *Gedullat Yosef*, or *Milḥamah be-Shalom… be-Inyan Mekhirat Yosef* (Shklov, 1797), an early Hebrew drama by Abraham b. Aryeh Loeb Ḥayyim ha-Kohen of Mogilev.

The theme retained its popularity throughout the 19th century, when it was exploited by a number of Jewish writers. In Hebrew, Suesskind Raschkow (d. 1836) wrote the drama *Yosef ve-Asenat* (Breslau, 1817); N.S. Kalckar in Denmark was the author of *Gedullat Yosef* (1834); and the Palestine kabbalist Joseph Shabbetai Farḥi (c. 1802–1882) produced his romance *Tokpo shel Yosef* (1846). Later, the Czech half-Jew Julius *Zeyer published *Asenat* (1895), a short novel about Joseph in Egypt. In Aden, Baghdad, and Tunis, there were from the late 19th century onward, many Judeo-Arabic versions of the biblical story under such titles as *Ma'aseh Yosef ha-Ẓaddik*. Non-Jewish authors who dealt with the subject included the Serbian Milovan Vidaković (*Istorija o prekrasnom Josifje*, 1805); the prolific French dramatist Alexandre Duval, whose *Joseph* (Paris, 1807) was set to music by the composer Méhul; and the U.S. poet John Eyre (*The Story of Joseph and his Brethren*, 1854). The theme retained its vogue in England, with works headed by Charles Jeremiah Well's epic *Joseph and his Brethren* (1824), which aroused much interest in its day. One British curiosity was the Gaelic work, *Each draidh Joseiph, Mhic Jacoib* (1831). There were also two distinct, but similarly titled, Italian works in verse, *Giuseppe, figlio di Giacobbe* (Lucca, 1817; Naples, 1820); and *Lyubimets* (1872), a Russian short novel by D.L. Mordovtsev.

Some of the most significant treatments of the subject have been produced by 20th-century authors. In the U.S., Louis Napoleon Parker wrote a pageant play, *Joseph and his Brethren* (1913), which was staged successfully in both America and England, Sir Herbert Beerbohm Tree playing the title role in the British production. There were many works of note in the Old World. *Jāzeps un viņa brāļi* (1919), a play by the Latvian writer J. Rainis (Jānis Pliekšans, 1865–1929), was staged in London as *The Sons of Jacob* in 1924. French biblical dramas included Camille Renard's *Joseph vendu par ses frères; figure du Messie* (1920) and Benoît L'Hermite's four-act tragedy *Joseph, victime et sauveur* (1932). The characteristic eroticism of the Flemish writer Hubert Léon Lampo is revealed in his novel *De belofte aan Rachel* (1952). One of the greatest literary treatments of all time is that contained in Thomas *Mann's novel cycle *Joseph und seine Brueder* (1933–42; *Joseph and His Brothers*, 1934–44) begun in the year of Hitler's rise to power in Germany. This tetralogy, a subtle blend of biblical history, legend, and psychological characterization, consists of *Die Geschichten Jaakobs* (1933; *Joseph and his Brothers*, 1934), *Der junge Joseph* (1934; *Young Joseph*, 1935), *Joseph in Aegypten* (1936; *Joseph in Egypt*, 1938), and *Joseph, der Ernaehrer* (1942; *Joseph the Provider*, 1944). The subject has also formed the basis of several important works by Jewish writers of the 20th century. The three earliest were *Josef, das Kind* (1906), a verse play by Emil (Bernhard) *Cohn; *Die Josephslegende* (1914) by Hugo von *Hofmannsthal; and *Josef und seine Brueder* (1917) by Micha Josef *Berdyczewski. One of the first biblical works of the Yiddish novelist Sholem *Asch was his play *Yosef-Shpil* (1924), and two Yiddish novels of the 1930s were *Der Prints fun Mitsrayim* (1931) by Saul Saphire and *Kenaan un Mitsrayim* (193?) by Hirsch Melamed. There have also been a large number of plays and stories on the theme written for Jewish children by authors in Britain and the U.S.

IN ART. Joseph does not appear before the fifth century. He does not figure in the art of the Christian catacombs, since he was not mentioned in the prayers of the *Commendatio Animae* from which its subjects were mainly drawn. However, in the Middle Ages, Joseph was popularly regarded as the type of Jesus, and the tradition remained in vogue among Christians. Joseph was seldom presented on his own but was sometimes found among the sculptures of patriarchs and prophets surrounding the doors of medieval cathedrals. There are many cycles representing the story of Joseph. They are found in manuscripts, including the fifth/sixth-century Vienna Genesis

(Vienna State Library), and Cotton Bible (British Museum), the 13th-century St. Louis Psalter, and the 14th-century Queen Mary Psalter, and also in Hebrew manuscripts such as the Sarajevo *Haggadah*. There are cycles in ivory, such as that on the sixth-century ivory chair of Bishop Maximian (Ravenna), and in mosaic, including eighth-century mosaics in Rome and 12th-century mosaics from the cupolas of the narthex of St. Mark's Cathedral, Venice, and from the Baptistery in Florence. Among early cycles of wall paintings are eighth-century frescoes from Santa Maria Antica, Rome, 12th-century Romanesque frescoes from Saint-Savin, France, and a very detailed 14th-century cycle from Sopočani in Serbia.

During the Renaissance, the story of Joseph figured in the celebrated bronze doors made for the Baptistery in Florence by Lorenzo Ghiberti and in the frescoes in the Campo Santo, Pisa, by Benozzo Gozzoli. The theme also occurs in the frescoes of the Raphael *loggie* in the Vatican. Other 16th-century cycles include the *Storia di Giuseppe Ebreo* by Jacopo da Pontormo, medallions by the Master of the Joseph Cycle (Berlin Museum), the Chaise-Dieu tapestry (1518), and carvings on the choir stalls at Amiens. Joseph also inspired a series of murals by Philipp Veit, Freidrich Overbeck, Wilhelm Schadow, and Peter Cornelius – members of the early 19th-century German Nazarene brotherhood – for the Casa Bartholdy in Rome. They are now in the Berlin Museum. Veit contributed frescoes of Joseph and Potiphar's wife and of the fat and lean years in Egypt.

There are a number of paintings by great masters of individual episodes from the life of Joseph. In the Six Gallery in Amsterdam, there is a grisaille painting by *Rembrandt of Joseph relating his dreams to his family (Gen. 37:1–10). A painting by Murillo (Wallace Collection, London) shows Joseph sold to the Midianites by his brothers (Gen. 37:28). There are two paintings by Rembrandt of Jacob receiving the bloodstained coat of Joseph (Gen. 37:31–36), one in the Hermitage, Leningrad, and another in the collection of the Earl of Derby. In addition, there is a pen drawing by Rembrandt. The subject is also treated by Velasquez in a painting in the Escorial and by the English pre-Raphaelite painter, Ford Madox Brown, in *The Coat of Many Colors* (1866; Walker Art Gallery, Liverpool). The attempted seduction of Joseph and his subsequent denunciation by Potiphar's wife (Gen. 39) is a picturesque episode much illustrated by artists of the 16th and 17th centuries. There is a painting in the Prado by Tintoretto and several by the later Italian artists, including one by Carlo Cignani (Dresden), showing a young woman who throws herself at Joseph, while the latter reels back in virtuous horror. In northern Europe, Lucas van Leyden made an engraving on the subject, and Rembrandt painted it twice (Berlin Museum and National Gallery, Washington). Here, Potiphar's wife is shown sitting on her bed in the act of denouncing Joseph to her husband. There is a sensitive painting by Barent Fabritius, a pupil of Rembrandt (Mauritshuis, Hague), of Jacob permitting Benjamin to leave with his brethren (Gen. 43:11–15), and another by Jacopo da Pontormo of *Joseph and his Brothers in Egypt* (National Gallery, London). In a work by the French artist Paul-Gustave Doré, Joseph is seen dramatically revealing his identity to his awestruck brethren. Jacob blessing his sons (Gen. 48:1–21) is the subject of a wood engraving by Holbein and of paintings by Guercino and Rembrandt. The painting by Rembrandt (Cassel Museum, Germany) shows Joseph standing over the dying Jacob, while the latter places his hands on the heads of Joseph's children.

IN MUSIC. Joseph and his brothers make an early appearance in music in a 12th-century liturgical drama from Laon, France. The theme is found among the earliest oratorio subjects at the beginning of the 17th century. The greatest number of settings are those of Pietro Metastasio's *Giuseppe riconosciuto* (Vienna, 1733, for M. Porsile), its composers including J.A. Hasse (1741), L. Boccherini (1756), and K. Fr. Fasch (1774). Other librettos of the period were J.B. Neri's *Giuseppe che interpreta i sogni*, set by A. Caldara (1726), who had already set a libretto by A. Zeno in his opera Giuseppe (Vienna, 1722); and Handel's oratorio *Joseph and his Brethren*, to a text by James Miller (first performed at Covent Garden Theatre, London, 1744). The 19th century opens with Méhul's opera *Joseph* (1807; text by Duval), for male voices only, which has remained a classic; the century ends with two parodies: Victor Roger's *Joséphine vendue par ses soeurs* (Paris, Bouffes Parisiennes, 1886) and Edmond Diel's operetta *Madame Putiphar* (Paris, 1897). Richard Strauss's ballet *Die Josephslegende* (1914) had a libretto by Hugo von Hofmannsthal and H. Kessler. Another ballet, Werner Josten's *Joseph and his Brethren* (première in New York, 1936), was also arranged as a symphonic suite (1939). The Israel composer Erich Walter *Sternberg wrote a suite for string orchestra entitled *The Story of Joseph* (1942). Two settings are based on Thomas Mann's novel cycle: David *Diamond's *Young Joseph* for three-part women's chorus and string orchestra (1944, publ. 1947), and Hilding Rosenberg's cycle of four opera-oratorios, *Josef och hans bröder* (composed between 1945 and 1948).

[Bathja Bayer]

BIBLIOGRAPHY: W.F. Albright, in: JBL, 37 (1918), 111–43; Albright, Stone, 241–8; H.G. May, in: AJSLL, 47 (1931), 83–93; T.O. Lambdin, in: JAOS, 73 (1953), 145–55; G. von Rad, in: VT Supplement, 1 (1953), 120–7; Pritchard, Texts, 23–25, 31–32, 212, 229, 259, 414, 486, 495; J.M.A. Janssen, in: *Jaarbericht… Ex Oriente Lux*, 14 (1955), 63–72; P. Montet, *L'Egypt et la Bible* (1959); J. Vergot, *Joseph en Égypte* (1959); W.A. Ward, in: JSS, 5 (1960), 144–50; N.M. Sarna, *Understanding Genesis* (1966), 211–31. IN THE AGGADAH: Ginzberg, Legends, 2 (1946[6]), 3–184; 5 (1947[6]), 324–77; B. Heller, in: MGWJ, 70 (1926), 273–6. IN ISLAM: H.A.R. Gibb and J.H. Kramers, *Shorter Encyclopaedia of Islam* (1953), s.v. *Yūsuf b. Ya'kub*, incl. bibl.; J. Horovitz, *Die Josepherzählung* (1921); H. Speyer, *Die Biblischen Erzählungen…* (1961), 187–224. **ADD. BIBLIOGRAPHY:** R. Firestone, "Yūsuf," in: EIS[2], 11 (2002), 352–54 (incl. bibl.). IN THE ARTS: J.D. Yohannan, *Joseph and Potiphar's Wife in World Literature* (1970); L. Humphreys, in: IDBSUP, 491–93; D. Redford, *A Study of the Biblical Story of Joseph* (1970); idem, *Egypt, Canaan, and Israel in Ancient Times* (1992), 422–29; G. Coats, in: ABD, 3, 976–81; S.D. Sperling, *Original Torah* (1998), 91–102; S. Bar, *A Letter That Has Not Been Read: Dreams in the Hebrew Bible* (2001).

JOSEPH (d. 38 B.C.E.), son of *Antipater and *Cypros, brother of *Herod I. When the Parthians invaded Judea (40 B.C.E.), they forced Herod to flee, and he left his family in the care of Joseph at *Masada, where a sudden thunderstorm enabled the fortress to hold out against the siege of *Antigonus. Later Herod returned with reinforcements and set his family free. Then, in 38, he set out for Samosata to meet Antony, after forbidding Joseph to get involved in battle with Antigonus until his arrival. Disregarding this advice, Joseph took his army into the hills near Jericho to harvest grain for his soldiers and was attacked by Antigonus and killed. His death caused some unrest in Judea and was later avenged by Herod.

BIBLIOGRAPHY: Jos., Ant., 14:361, 390f., 413, 438, 448–50; Jos., Wars, 1:266, 286f., 323f.; Schuerer, Hist, 115, 118.

[Lea Roth]

JOSEPH, king of the *Khazars. As his correspondence with *Ḥisdai ibn Shaprut demonstrates, he ruled in the tenth century. In the heading of his presumed reply to Ḥisdai's letter, the Reply of Joseph, he is called "the Togarmian [i.e., Turkish] king" (cf. Gen. 10:3), and in the text of the Reply is referred to as Joseph b. Aaron b. Benjamin. His descent is traced back to *Obadiah, king of the Khazars. In the fragment known as the Cambridge Document, which was found in the Cairo *Genizah*, his father Aaron and grandfather Benjamin are also mentioned by name and the document adds (line 59) that Joseph was married to a daughter of the king of the Alans.

BIBLIOGRAPHY: Dunlop, Khazars, index; A.N. Poliak, *Kazaryah* (1951[3]), index.

[Douglas Morton Dunlop]

°**JOSEPH II** (1741–1790), king of Germany (1764–90) and Holy Roman emperor (1765–90); co-regent with his mother, *Maria Theresa, until her death in 1780. Although educated in the spirit of the Enlightenment, he nevertheless remained a practicing Roman Catholic. After the death of his father in 1765 he became emperor of the Holy Roman Empire and married his second wife Josepha of Bavaria (his first wife was Isabella of Parma, 1760–1762). Strongly influenced by the ideas of Joseph von Sonnenfels, his rule was based on a system of "benevolent despotism"; his paramount belief was in the power of the state when directed by reason and his main aims religious toleration, unrestricted trade and education, and a reduction in the power of the Church. Additionally he saw himself as emperor as first servant of the state system. These views were reflected in his policy toward the Jews, first outlined in his "*Judenreformen*" of May 1781. Intending to end the long-standing isolation of the Jews and integrate them into the general social fabric, he wished to increase their means of gaining a livelihood and enable them to aquire general education, "thus rendering them more useful to the state." This attitude was deeply connected to his vision of a centralized state, in which every individual has its function. Like many of his other ideas, such as the abolition of serfdom or new legal code, his Jewish reforms were only partially realizable and had to contend with the opposition of his provincial civil servants. Joseph abolished the most humiliating measures, the yellow *badge and the body tax (*Leibmaut* see **Leibzoll*) in 1781, and on Jan. 2, 1782, he issued the first of the Edicts of Tolerance (**Toleranzpatent*). Although enthusiastically hailed by the enlightened and well-to-do, they were considered a *gezerah* ("oppressive decree") by the broader strata of Jewry, who wished to pursue their traditional way of life. They had even more influence because under his and his mother's reign the Austrian Empire had expanded after the Polish Partition (1772–1795) and annexation of Galicia and the Bukowina with their massive Orthodox Jewish population. In several other laws Joseph II damaged the traditional fabric: in 1781 he prohibited the use of Hebrew and Yiddish in business and in communal and public records. Of profound importance for the structure of Jewish life was the abolition of rabbinical jurisdiction from 1784 onward, as well as the introduction of liability for *military service in 1787. A special law in 1787 obliged Jews to adopt German-sounding family names and personal names, which had to be chosen from a list. The majority of Jewry did not benefit from Joseph's legislation, because neither the restrictions on residence in *Vienna and other cities nor the *Familiants Laws in Bohemia and Moravia were affected; the policy of curtailing the size of the Jewish population was explicitly perpetuated. However, the founding of the German-language schools and the permission to attend universities offered new opportunities to the rising merchant class and led to the development of a Jewish intelligentsia. Joseph's decrees imposed all the duties of a citizen on the Jews but did not grant them all the rights. Nevertheless, the bulk of Jewry in Hapsburg lands was thankful for the alleviations he had introduced. In the modified form of the *Systemalpatent* of 1797, his legislation remained the basis for the status of the Jews until the revolution of 1848.

BIBLIOGRAPHY: S.K. Padover, *Revolutionary Emperor: Joseph II of Austria* (1938, 1967[2]); J. Fraenkel (ed.), *Jews of Austria* (1967), index; M. Grunwald, *Vienna* (1936), index; E. Benedikt, *Kaiser Joseph II* (1936, 1947[2]); A.F. Pribram, *Urkunden und Akten zur Geschichte der Juden in Wien*, 2 vols. (1918), index; R. Kestenberg-Gladstein, *Neuere Geschichte der Juden in den boehmischen Laendern*, 1 (1969), index; W. Mueller (ed.), *Urkundliche Beitraege…* (1903), index; H. Spiel, *Fanny von Arnstein* (Ger., 1962), index; A.Y. Brawer, *Galiẓyah vi-Yhudehah* (1956), 147–87; R. Mahler, *Divrei Yemei Yisrael*, 1 pt. 2 (1954[2]), 183–93, 207–25; S.I. Schulsohn, in: MGWJ, 72 (1928), 274–86; W. Pillich, in: *Zeitschrift fuer Geschichte der Juden*, 2 (1965), 129–35; G. Kisch, in: HJ, 19 (1957), 120–1, 136–7; K. Stillschweig, *ibid.*, 8 (1946), 1–18; L. Singer, in: JGGJČ, 5 (1933), 231–311; 6 (1934), 193–284; O. Muneles, in: *Judaica Bohemiae*, 2 (1966), 3–13; P.P. Bernard, in: *Austrian History Yearbook*, 4–5 (1968–69), 101–19. **ADD. BIBLIOGRAPHY:** J. Karniel, "Die Toleranzpolitik Kaiser Joseph II," in: JIDG, Beiheft 3 (1980), 155–77; T.V. Walzer, *Die Wiener Juden in der Zeit von der Toleranzpolitik Joseph II. bis zum Israelitengesetz 1890* (2003); K. Lohrmann, "Das oesterreichische Judentum zur Zeit Maria Theresias und Joesphs II," in: *Studia Judaica Austriaca*, 7 (1980); K. Gutkas, *Kaiser Joseph II* (1989).

[Jan Herman / Bjoern Siegel (2nd ed.)]

Kibbutz Nir David (also known as Tel Amal) was established in 1936 at the foot of Mount Gilboa. It is known as the first Jewish settlement to be built in those years in the form of a "Stockade and Watchtower" outpost. *Photo: The Central Zionist Archive, Jerusalem.*

The term Zionism first appeared at the end of the 19th century to denote the movement to reestablish the Jewish homeland in Ereẓ Israel. Over the past century, the nation of Israel has experienced one of the most miraculous transformations in human history. Nowhere is this more clearly revealed than in the vast developments in Israel's architecture and urban landscape. Offered here are some stunning before-and-after views of the growth of Israel as well as some of the faces of Israel's citizens, who hail from more than one hundred countries.

ZIONISM

Nir David in 1997. *Photo: Albatross Aerial Photography.*

TOP: En Harod was first established in 1921 as a kibbutz on the southern side of the Harod valley, near the Harod spring at the foot of Mount Gilboa. *Photo: The Central Zionist Archive, Jerusalem.*

BOTTOM: In the early years of the 21st century En Harod consists of two prospering kibbutzim, each with its own political affiliation. The split occurred in 1951 as a result of a political rift. *Photo: Albatross Aerial Photography.*

TOP: In the early 20th century the area adjacent to the Western Wall, near the Jewish Quarter of Old Jerusalem, was occupied by the small Mughrabi neighborhood, built in the middle of the 19th century. The far background is dominated by Mount Scopus, still without buildings or trees. On the far left is the Augusta Victoria compound built by German Emperor Wilhelm II. *Photo: The Central Zionist Archive, Jerusalem.*

BOTTOM: A view of the area adjacent to the Western Wall at the end of the 20th century (1997). A large plaza was built in front of the Western Wall to serve the many visitors and the pilgrims who frequent it. The Hebrew University campus is seen on Mount Scopus along the far skyline, behind the Dome of the Rock. *Photo: Albatross Aerial Photography*

Israel has brought together Jews from all over the world – as here, old men from Iraq and Yemen.
Photo: Albatross Aerial Photography.

ABOVE: The cliffs along the shoreline in the west of Herzliyyah in the early 1930s *Photo: The Central Zionist Archive, Jerusalem.*

(opposite page): Hotels, restaurants and other installations of a modern resort area line the shore of Herzliyyah in 1997. The western edge of the city is now one of the most developed tourist areas in the country. *Photo: Albatross Aerial Photography.*

TOP: The town and bay of Haifa in the late 1920s after construction there by the British authorities of a modern port and a long jetty. The large building in the foreground is the Technion, the institute of technology established in 1925 in the Jewish district of Hadar ha-Karmel. *Photo: The Central Zionist Archive, Jerusalem.*

BOTTOM: Haifa and its bay in the 1990s. The city now extends over the entire slope of Mount Carmel. The old Herzliyya neighborhood, later known as Hadar ha-Karmel, is now the core of a large city. *Photo: Albatross Aerial Photography.*

JOSEPH, pioneer family in Canadian business and Jewish life. The Canadian-Jewish branch of the Joseph family (some converted to Catholicism and others intermarried with Protestants) was founded by HENRY JOSEPH (1775–1832), a nephew of Aaron Hart, regarded as the first permanent Jewish settler in Canada. In 1790, 15-year-old Henry arrived from England and settled in Berthier, Quebec, where he entered the fur trade. He later moved to Quebec City and established a chain of successful trading posts in the interior of the country (for a time, John Jacob Astor was one of his employees). He also became known as the "father of Canada's merchant marine" because of a shipping network he set up to move goods to and from his posts. He was one of three Jews among the founders of the Bank of Montreal in 1817, Canada's first bank. Henry Joseph and his son Samuel died in the cholera epidemic of 1832.

After Henry's death, his firm passed to his son ABRAHAM (1815–1886) of Quebec City. Besides the family business, Abraham served as president of the Quebec and Dominion Boards of Trade, a director of the Banque Nationale, president of the Stadacona Bank (when it failed during the panic of 1873, he used personal funds to repay investors and depositors), and a member of the Quebec city council (he failed in a bid for the mayoralty). He was a Grand Master of the Grand Masonic Lodge of Quebec and vice consul of Belgium in Quebec City. A memorial horse trough was erected there in his memory. Abraham's son, MONTEFIORE JOSEPH (1851–1943), took over the family firm, as, in turn, did his sons and grandson after him.

Two others of Henry Joseph's sons, JACOB HENRY (1814–1907) and JESSE (1817–1904) also made their mark in the Montreal business world. Jacob Henry Joseph, who married a niece of Rebecca *Gratz, the Philadelphia pioneer of Jewish Sunday-school education, was a railway promoter and director with his brother, Jesse, organizing Canada's first railway, the Saint Lawrence and Champlain. He founded Canada's first telegraph line and was a partner in the Newfoundland Telegraph Company, president of the Montreal Elevator Company, vice president of the Montreal Board of Trade, a bank director, a real estate mogul, and a supporter of charitable and cultural institutions in Montreal.

Jesse Joseph, a life-long bachelor, studied law but eventually followed the family tradition into business. He served as president of both the Montreal Gas Company (he sold his interest in the Montreal Electric Company because he did not believe electricity had a future) and the City Passenger Railway, which formed the nucleus of Montreal's mass transit, and operated the Theatre Royale, the city's premier theater. A promoter of trade between Canada and Belgium, he was named Belgian consul in Montreal, and was one of the largest real-estate owners in the city. He was a member of the executive of the SPCA and known for giving lavish parties in the Sherbrooke Street mansion, which, after his death, became the McCord Museum of McGill University.

Like others of Canada's pre-1900 Jewish elite, the Josephs were proudly British and staunchly patriotic. Abraham Joseph belonged to the St. George's society, and his daughter-in-law, Annette Pinto Joseph, was a member of the Imperial Order Daughters of the Empire. Henry, the family patriarch, fought in the War of 1812, and his son, Abraham, fought with the Royal Volunteers during the Rebellion of 1837. The family firm boasted of having provisioned the troops in every war from 1837 to World War II and never profiteered. Family members took full part in the social life of the English-speaking community in Quebec and seemed to suffer no discrimination because of their faith.

Although Henry's brother, Judah, became a Roman Catholic (one of his descendants, Joseph Olivier Joseph, was among the organizers of the French-Canadian, nationalist Saint Jean Baptiste Society in the 1870s), and some of Henry's grandchildren intermarried, the Josephs were remarkably faithful to their Jewish roots, despite the difficulties of practicing Judaism far from any sizeable community. Henry Joseph was a traditional Jew who instructed his children in Jewish living and taught himself ritual slaughtering so that the family would have a supply of kosher meat. His daughter, Esther (1823–1898), married Abraham *de Sola, the most significant Jewish minister of 19th century Canada; his son, Jesse, was a trustee of the Spanish and Portuguese Synagogue in Montreal; and another son, GERSHOM (1820–1893), a lawyer and the first Jewish Queen's Counsel in Canada, served as president of that synagogue when his nephew, Meldola de Sola, succeeded his father, Abraham, as minister.

BIBLIOGRAPHY: M. Brown, *Jew or Juif* (1987); A. Joseph, *Heritage of a Patriarch* (1995); *Dictionary of Canadian Biography*, s.v.

[Michael Brown (2nd ed.)]

JOSEPH, British family. SIR SAMUEL GEORGE (originally "GLUCKSTEIN") JOSEPH (1888–1944) was born in London and was an officer in the British army in Salonika, Egypt, and France in World War I, being twice mentioned in dispatches. He later became chairman and managing director of Bovis, the large building contracting firm. Joseph held several positions in London municipal government before serving as sheriff of the city of London (1933–34) and was lord mayor of London from 1943 to 1944, the sixth Jew to have held this position. He was made a baronet in 1934.

His son, SIR KEITH JOSEPH (1918–1994), inherited his father's title. Educated at Harrow and Oxford, he was a captain in the British army in World War II and was mentioned in dispatches. After the war he was admitted to the bar and, from 1946 to 1960, was a fellow of All Souls College, Oxford. He also held various industrial posts before becoming a director in the family building contracting firm. In 1956 Keith Joseph entered Parliament and three years later was made parliamentary secretary of the Ministry of Housing in the Conservative government. He became minister of state at the Board of Trade in 1961 and, from 1962 to 1964, was minister of housing and local government and minister for Welsh affairs. When the Conservatives returned to power in 1970, he was appointed minister of health and social services, serving until 1974. He earned a reputation for intellectual brilliance and integrity and was one of his party's chief advocates of social welfare reforms. After the Tories lost office in 1974, Joseph was often mentioned as a potential leader of the Conservative Party. He was a founder of the influential "Think Tank," the Centre for Policy Studies, which set the intellectual stage for "Thatcherism" by its advocacy of free enterprise policies. Joseph, however, never became a serious challenger for the party's leadership: he was viewed as cold and distant and, in October 1974, made a regrettable speech advocating birth control among alleged "problem families." Instead, he became a strong supporter and advisor of Margaret Thatcher who appointed him minister for industry (1979–81). From 1981 to 1986 he was minister of education. On retiring from the government he was made a peer. Joseph was treasurer of the British Friends of The Hebrew University and in 1966 became chairman of the Research Board of the Institute of Jewish Affairs.

BIBLIOGRAPHY: ODNB online; M. Halcrow, *Keith Joseph: A Singular Mind* (1989); A. Denham and Mark Garnett, *Keith Joseph* (2001).

[Vivian D. Lipman]

JOSEPH (Yosef), DOV (Bernard; 1899–1980), Israeli politician and lawyer, member of the First to Third Knessets. Born in Montreal, Canada, as a teenager he was among the founders of Young Judea in Canada and served as its president. In 1918 he joined the *Jewish Legion, and within its framework reached Palestine. After his return to Canada Joseph studied economics and political science at McGill University in Montreal, and after that law at Lavale Univesity. He studied in London, where he became a barrister and received his Ph.D. After his studies he settled in Jerusalem, and started working as a lawyer in the office of Horace Samuel. In 1933 Joseph was involved in the preparation of a claim for civil compensation in the case of the assassination of Haim *Arlosoroff and he joined *Mapai. In 1936 Joseph was appointed legal adviser and deputy head of the *Jewish Agency's Political Department, in Jerusalem, under Moshe *Sharett. During World War II he coordinated the enlistment of volunteers for the Jewish units in the British Army. In the years 1945–46 he served as a member of the executive of the Jewish Agency and was sent to the United States on special missions. On "Black Saturday," June 29, 1946, he was among the leaders of the Jewish Agency arrested by the British and held at Latrun until November.

Towards the establishment of the State in 1948 Joseph was appointed military governor of Jerusalem, during the siege on the city. After the establishment of the State he was elected to the First Knesset on the Mapai list and remained a Knesset member until 1959, serving as minister of supply and rationing in 1949–51, in which capacity he initiated a policy of rationing. Until 1959 Joseph served in numerous ministerial posts including agriculture (1950–51), transportation (1950–51), commerce and industry (1951–52), justice (1951–52 and again 1961–66), development (1953–59), and health (1956–59). From 1956 to 1961 he served as treasurer of the Jewish Agency. After the establishment of the *Israel Labor Party in 1968 he served as head of a party committee that proposed an amendment to the Israeli electoral system.

He wrote *Nationality, Its Nature and Problems* (1929); *The White Paper on Palestine: A Criticism* (1930), *British Rule in Palestine* (1948), and *The Faithful City* (1960).

[Susan Hattis Rolef (2nd ed.)]

JOSEPH, HENRY (1838–1913), first rabbi of the Argentine Republic. Born in England, Joseph arrived in Argentina in 1860 and became a successful businessman. He was very active in organizing the first Jewish institution of the country, the Congregación Israelita de la República Argentina, in 1862. He was elected by the members of the congregation as their "rabbi," and his nomination was approved by the chief rabbi of the French Consistory, Isidor Lazare, in 1882. His election as rabbi originated principally in the need for a religious authority to register Jewish births, marriages, and deaths. Joseph's wife, a Christian, converted to Judaism immediately after his appointment, but his children married out of the Jewish faith. Joseph was very active as a religious and social leader, performed weddings, religious services, and occasionally preached in Spanish to the community of West European Jews in Buenos Aires. In the early 1880s he organized a fund to help the persecuted Jews in Russia. He also was of great help to the first group of East European Jews to arrive in Argentina in 1889.

[Victor A. Mirelman]

JOSEPH, JACOB (1848–1902), rabbi. Jacob Joseph was born in Krozhe, province of Kovno. He studied at the yeshivah of Volozhin under R. Hirsch Leib Berlin and later under R. Israel Salanter, and served the communities of Vilon, Yurburg, and Zhagovy before becoming rabbi and *Maggid* of Vilna in 1883. Although a brilliant student of Talmud, Joseph was especially known for his homiletical talents. In 1888 he arrived in the U.S. to assume the post of chief rabbi of the Orthodox congregations of Russian Jews in New York City. As he was primarily concerned with the taxed supervision of meat *kashrut*, much opposition was expressed against him from sectors of the Jewish community who rejected this supervision and objected to the imposition of a kosher meat tax. Although an invalid from 1895, Joseph founded the Bes Sefer Yeshiva (1900), which was renamed the Rabbi Jacob Joseph Yeshiva upon his death. His works include the collection of sermons, *Le-Veit Ya'akov* (1888) and a contribution to the only issue of the publication *Sefer Toledot Ya'akov Yosef be-New York* (1889). His funeral procession, said to have been attended by tens of thousands of Jews, occasioned a riot as workmen of the R. Hoe & Co. factory on the East Side pelted the procession with nuts and bolts. Many mourners were injured by the assailants and police.

His grandson LAZARUS JOSEPH (1891–1966), who was

born in New York City, was a U.S. public official. He was elected to the state senate in 1934, and became a financial adviser to Governor Herbert H. Lehman. After serving six terms, he was elected New York City controller in 1946 and remained in office until 1954. Joseph was active on behalf of the United Jewish Appeal and the Federation of Jewish Philanthropies of New York.

BIBLIOGRAPHY: A.J. Karp, in: AJHSP, 44 (1955), 129–98; *The American Hebrew*, 71 (1902), 497–9.

[Edward L. Greenstein]

JOSEPH, MORRIS (1848–1930), English Reform rabbi, preacher, and writer. The son of a London minister, Joseph served as minister (rabbi) successively at the North London Synagogue, the Liverpool Old Hebrew Congregation, and, after an interval of nearly 20 years, at the West London (Reform) Synagogue. When in 1890 the newly founded Hampstead Synagogue, a constituent of the *United Synagogue, elected him as their minister, Chief Rabbi Hermann *Adler vetoed the appointment because of Joseph's unorthodox views, in particular regarding the restoration of the sacrificial cult. This was apparently no obstacle to his teaching homiletics at Jews' College in 1891–92. His views on Reform were very moderate. He expressed them in his *Judaism as Creed and Life* (1903 and several editions to 1958), which became a widely read and popular book. Joseph also published three volumes of sermons, *Ideal in Judaism* (1893), *Message of Judaism* (1906), and *Spirit of Judaism* (1930). He also contributed to the *Jewish Quarterly Review*, the *Jewish Chronicle*, and Hasting's *Encyclopaedia of Religion and Ethics*. Joseph was active in Jewish literary societies and the Jewish Peace Society.

BIBLIOGRAPHY: JC (Apr. 25, 1930), 10–12; *West London Synagogue Magazine*, 4 (1930), 146–83; R. Apple, *The Hampstead Synagogue 1892–1967* (1967), 9, 14, 17, 18, 23–6, 35–7.

JOSEPH, NORMA BAUMEL (1944–), Canadian professor, Orthodox feminist, activist. Joseph received her B.A. from Brooklyn College in 1966 and M.A. from the City University of New York in 1968. She became associate professor in the Department of Religion at Concordia University in Montreal, where she served in various administrative positions, including director of the women and religion specialization. Her teaching and research areas include women and Judaism, Jewish law and ethics, and women and religion. Her doctoral dissertation, completed in 1995 at Concordia University, focused on the legal decisions of Rabbi Moses *Feinstein concerning the separate spheres for women in the Jewish community. The dissertation was nominated for a Governor General's Gold medal award for excellence. From the early 1970s she promoted women's greater participation in Jewish religious and communal life. Joseph appeared in, and served as consultant to the films *Half the Kingdom* (1990) and *Untying the Bonds...Jewish Divorce* (1999). A founding member of the Canadian Coalition of Jewish Women for the Get (Jewish divorce), Joseph successfully worked with the Jewish community and the Canadian Federal Government to pass a law in 1990 (Divorce Act, ch.18, 21.1) that would protect Jewish women in difficult divorce situations and aid them in their pursuit of a Jewish divorce. Following the Canadian success, Joseph helped form and presided over the International Coalition for Agunah Rights, an organization for women whose husbands refuse to consent to a Jewish divorce. Author of many publications in the field of feminism and Jewish Law, Joseph won the Leo Wasserman Prize from the American Jewish Historical Society for the best article of 1995 in the journal *American Jewish History*.

[Randal F. Schnoor (2nd ed.)]

JOSEPH, SAMUEL (1881–1959), U.S. sociologist. He was taken to the U.S. from Russia as a child. He joined the Sociology Faculty of City College, N.Y., in 1928 and became professor and chairman of the department in 1940, one of the first Jews to hold a leading academic position in American sociology. An expert on immigration problems, and especially Jewish immigration, his major publications were *Jewish Immigration to the United States from 1881 to 1910* (1914), and *History of the Baron de Hirsch Fund* (1935).

[Werner J. Cahnman]

JOSEPH, SAUL ABDALLAH (1849–1906), merchant-scholar in *China. Born in *Baghdad, he was a merchant and money changer by profession. At the age of 18, he traveled to India and China, finally settling in Hong Kong. He was an interesting example of a scholar who dwelt in an environment foreign to Judaism and yet played an active role in Hebrew literature and culture. Writing for the Hebrew newspapers *Ḥavaẓẓelet* and *Ha-Levanon*, he published articles on the Jews of China and on medieval poetry. His profound knowledge of the Bible, the Hebrew language, Arabic literature, and the Oriental way of life enabled him to understand Spanish Hebrew poetry. His principal contribution lay in pointing out the influence of Arabic poetry on the Hebrew poetry of Spain (he himself translated Arabic stanzas written in the Spanish meter). By nature hot-tempered, he wrote essays noted for their sharp controversies and lack of courtesy toward contemporary scholars. Two of his works were posthumously prepared for publication by Samuel *Krauss: *Givat Sha'ul* (1923), an extensive commentary to 138 secular poems of Judah Halevi, which were previously published by H. Brody; *Mishbeẓet Tarshish* (1926), a commentary to *Sefer ha-Tarshish* or *Ha-Anak* of Moses ibn Ezra, first published by David Guensburg in 1886. The divan of Todros *Abulafia, *Gan ha-Meshalim ve-ha-Ḥidot* ("Garden of Apologues and Saws"), which was discovered and copied by Joseph, was published in phototype by Moses *Gaster (1926).

BIBLIOGRAPHY: S. Joseph, *Givat Sha'ul*, ed. by S. Krauss (1923), xxvii–xxx (Eng. and Heb.); T. Abulafia, *Gan ha-Meshalim ve-ha-Ḥidot*, ed. by D. Yellin, 2, pt. 2 (1936), xlvii–ci.

[Yehuda Ratzaby]

JOSEPH AND ASENATH, pseudepigraphic work – the story of how Asenath, daughter of Pentephres, priest of Heliopolis, converted to the worship of the God of Israel and married Joseph. The tenuous basis of this anecdote is one verse in Genesis (41:45). The marriage of the chaste and pious Joseph to the pagan Asenath was problematic for strictly observant Jews. Targum Pseudo-Jonathan solves the problem by making Asenath the daughter of Dinah, who was raped by Shechem (Gen. 34:1–3). The author of Joseph and Asenath is clearly aware of the theory of Asenath's Jewish origin, but implicitly rejects it. He makes Asenath an Egyptian who converts to Judaism in order to marry Joseph. Joseph and Asenath is extant in Greek as well as in Slavonic, Syriac, Armenian, and Latin versions and, in common with other hagiographic texts, has passed through the hands of many editors. There appear to be one short and three long recensions. The short recension is the oldest and is witnessed to by two Greek manuscripts and the Slavonic version. The original text is Greek and most of the Hebraisms it contains are derived from the Septuagint. Joseph and Asenath should be classified among the pseudepigraphs of the Bible. It provides some interesting points of similarity with the Testaments of the Twelve *Patriarchs. Just as each of the Testaments illustrates a particular virtue, Joseph and Asenath can be held to illustrate the virtue of repentance. The book can also be compared with certain Greek and Latin romances. It contains the stock situations of ancient romantic literature, such as the exceptional beauty of the hero and heroine (1:6; 6:7), love at first sight (6:1), lovesickness (7:4), the kiss (19:3), the separation (26:1), the unscrupulous rival (24), and the hero's virginity (8:2). The author had no intention, however, of writing a frivolous romance, but rather a puritan story designed for Jewish readers, while using a literary style alien to their spirit. Joseph and Asenath presents the precise social situation of Jews and Egyptians confronting each other. One of the aims of the story is to demonstrate the mutual repulsion and attraction of these two groups. The emergence of a third group, the proselytes, is one result of these tensions. Although the author's style is restricted, the literary structure of Joseph and Asenath is sophisticated. The plot contains three elements. The first of these is the missionary story. Asenath is the prototype of the proselyte, who, through repentance, passes "from shadow to light, from error to truth, from death to life" (8:10). Then there is the *roman à clef*; the author has realized that the Egyptian name Asenath means "belonging to Neith." Many almost imperceptible details of the story can only be explained as referring to the goddess of Sais, such as, for example, the fact that the heroine is hermaphrodite (15:1). These references show an extensive knowledge of late Egyptian theology. Finally, there is the mystic element, which is more complex in structure. It contains an astrological allegory, in which Joseph represents the Sun and Asenath the Moon, their marriage being the "*hieros gamos*" of Helios and Selene. There is also the gnostic drama, Joseph representing the Savior and Asenath, Fallen Wisdom. Here, there is a foretaste of Valentinian gnosticism. The text contains a liturgy of initiation comparable in many ways to that of the mystery cults. The entry of the proselyte into the community is marked by a sacred feast. The neophyte eats "the bread of life," drinks from "the cup of immortality," and is annointed with the "unction of incorruptibility" (15:4). He is then "renewed," "reformed," and "revivified" (8:11; 15:4). Joseph and Asenath is thus seen to be valuable evidence for the "mystical Judaism," whose existence has been the subject of much controversy. The short recension of Joseph and Asenath is a Jewish version. It contains no trace of Christian modification or interpolation. The text is certainly the product of Egyptian Jewry, but is not necessarily the work of a Therapeut (Essene). The author may have been an Egyptian of the *Chora* ("region," i.e., outside of Alexandria) converted to Judaism, or, more probably, the Jewish issue of a mixed marriage. Joseph and Asenath must have been composed shortly before the Jewish revolt against Trajan. Joseph and Asenath is also of interest, since the story is repeated in the passions of Saint Barbara, Saint Christine, and Saint Irene. Joseph and Asenath is also the basis for the Persian tale *Yūsuf o Zuleikhā*. There is an English translation by E.W. Brooks, *Joseph and Asenath* (1918).

BIBLIOGRAPHY: C. Burchard, *Untersuchungen zu Joseph und Asenath* (1965); M. Philonenko, *Joseph et Aséneth* (Fr., 1968), includes bibliography.

[Marc Philonenko]

JOSEPH AND AZARIAH BEN ZECHARIAH, two commanders in the army of Judah Maccabee. When, in 165 B.C.E., Judah and his brother Jonathan went to the help of the Jews in Gilead and Galilee who were being oppressed by the gentiles, Joseph and Azariah were entrusted with the defense of the people and strictly forbidden to engage in active hostilities while Judah was absent from Judea. When the news arrived of the victories of Judah and Jonathan, Joseph and Azariah decided on their own initiative to march against Jabneh. The Syrian general Gorgias counter-attacked. The Jewish army was routed and pursued to the borders of Judea, 2,000 Jews falling in the campaign. The author of I Maccabees (5:56–62) explains this defeat by saying that Joseph and Azariah were not of the stock that had been entrusted with the salvation of Israel.

BIBLIOGRAPHY: Schuerer, Hist, 35; Klausner, Bayit Sheni, 3 (1950^2), 34.

[Edna Elazary]

JOSEPH BAR ABBA, *gaon* of *Pumbedita 814–816. Joseph was a student of Shinai *gaon* of Pumbedita and successor of Avumai (or Akhumai). In his noted epistle, *Sherira Gaon relates that, as a scholar, his contemporary Mar Rav Kemoi was a more suitable choice for the gaonate, but he did not possess the miraculous powers of Joseph b. Abba, who was very pious and advanced in years. It was believed that Elijah revealed himself to Joseph b. Abba. Sherira relates that on the day of Joseph's death the earth trembled. R. Judah *gaon*, the grandfather of Sherira, was Joseph's secretary. Only a few of his responsa have been transmitted, and it is even uncertain whether these are his or were written by other *geonim* named Joseph (e.g., *Joseph b. Ḥiyya).

BIBLIOGRAPHY: J. Mueller, *Mafte'aḥ li-Teshuvot ha-Ge'onim* (1891), 79–82; B.M. Lewin (ed.), *Iggeret Rav Sherira Ga'on* (1921), 109; Abramson, Merkazim, 10.

[Meir Havazelet]

JOSEPH BAR ḤIYYA (ninth century), *av bet din, gaon*, later *av bet din* again, and once more *gaon* of Pumbedita (828–833) during one of the most crucial periods in the history of Pumbedita and the relationship between the academies of Pumbedita and Sura and the exilarchate. In the controversy between the exilarch David b. Judah and his brother Daniel, Joseph b. Ḥiyya and Abraham b. Sherira presided jointly over the academy until peace was restored, when Joseph b. Ḥiyya volunteered to renounce the office, temporarily resuming the position of *av bet din*. The two academies were then enabled to assert their full independence: according to the decree by the caliph al-Mu'mīn the exilarch was henceforth forced to submit to the judicial authority of the two academies.

BIBLIOGRAPHY: B.M. Lewin (ed.), *Iggeret Rav Sherira Ga'on* (1921), 112; Abramson, Merkazim, 11.

[Meir Havazelet]

JOSEPH (Josse) BAR NISSAN, early liturgical poet of uncertain date. His birthplace appears repeatedly in the acrostic to his poems as Shaveh-Kiriathaim (Gen. 14:5). As in the case of Kiriath-Sepher, similarly used by Kallir, this is obviously intended as the designation of an actual but differently named town: Samuel Klein identified it with Nawe in Transjordan. Joseph's *kerovot*, preserved in numerous *genizah* fragments in Oxford, Cambridge, and elsewhere, were composed according to the triennial Palestinian cycle (see *Torah, Reading of). For this reason, among many others, he cannot be identified with the Babylonian poet Joseph al-Baradani who wrote poems in conformity with the one-year cycle. Joseph's poems are written in a highly involved style.

BIBLIOGRAPHY: I. Davidson, *Ginzei Schechter*, 3 (1928), 49, 96; M. Zulay, *Zur Liturgie der babylonischen Juden* (1933), 68, 87; idem, in: YMḤSI, 2 (1936), 219, 365; 5 (1939), 158–69; Klein, in: BJPES (1936), pt. 3, 4, 76–78; A.M. Habermann, *Ateret Renanim* (1967), 133, 163–5. **ADD. BIBLIOGRAPHY:** T. Beeri, *The "Great Cantor" of Bagdad* (Heb., 2002).

[Jefim (Hayyim) Schirmann]

JOSEPH BEN AḤMAD IBN ḤASDAI (also known as **Ibn Hasdai**; 12th century), student of medicine, born in Spain of a father who converted to Islam. Joseph emigrated to Egypt, where the vizier Ma'mūn became his patron. Joseph maintained a friendship with Ibn Bajjā (Avempace), the Spanish philosopher, with whom he continued to correspond after his departure from Spain. Among his works are (1) *Al-Sharḥ al-Ma'mūnī* (Commentary on the Oath (Kitāb al Īmān) of Hippocrates). (2) *Sharḥ al-Fuṣūl* (Commentary on the *Aphorisms* of Hippocrates). (3) *Fāwā'īd* (useful observations and extracts from the Commentary of Ali Ibn Riḍwān on the *Glaukon* of Galen). (4) *Al-Qawl ʿalā Awwal al-Ṣināʿāt al-Ṣaghīra* (Study of book one of *Mikrotechnē* of Galen).

BIBLIOGRAPHY: Steinschneider, Arab Lit, 148–9; G. Sarton, *Introduction to the History of Science*, 2 pt. 1 (1931), 229–30; H. Friedenwald, *The Jews and Medicine* (1944), 174, 633.

[Isidore Simon]

JOSEPH BEN ASHER OF CHARTRES (12th–13th centuries), liturgical poet. Joseph was the brother-in-law of Joseph b. Nathan of Etampes, and granduncle of Joseph b. Nathan Official. The latter reports in his apologetic for Judaism (*Yosef ha-Mekanne*, no. 24) that Joseph engaged in a disputation with a Christian clergyman. To the latter's question as to why God had appeared to Moses in a bramblebush, rather than in a tree, Joseph is said to have replied that it was because a cross could not be made from a bramblebush. According to Gedaliah *ibn Yaḥia, Joseph was a pupil of Jacob b. Meir *Tam and *Samuel b. Meir. His notes on the Bible are cited in a few commentaries in manuscript (Oxford, Bodleian Library, Ms. Bodl. Or. 604; Ms. Marsh. 225; Ms. Opp. 724). He is also known as the author of an elegy on the massacre at York, 1190.

BIBLIOGRAPHY: Zunz, Lit Poesie, 470, 480; Z. Kahn, in: REJ, 1 (1880), 238, 240, 246; Gross, Gal Jud, 603–5; C. Roth, in: *Mezudah*, 2 (1944), 116–21; A.M. Habermann, *Gezerot Ashkenaz ve-Ẓarefat* (1945), 152–4, 260f.

JOSEPH BEN BARUCH OF CLISSON (first half of the 13th century), French tosafist. Joseph lived in Paris and was associated with *Judah b. Isaac Sir Leon. He was one of the leaders of the 300 scholars who went to settle in Ereẓ Israel in 1211. On his way there he passed through Egypt where he met Abraham, the son of Maimonides. In Ereẓ Israel the poet and traveler Judah *Al-Ḥarizi met him and refers to him in his *Taḥkemoni* (ed. by A. Kaminka (1899), 353) with great respect. Joseph is frequently mentioned in the standard *tosafot* to several tractates under different names such as "Joseph of Jerusalem," "Joseph who has gone to the Pleasant Land" (*Ereẓ ha-Ẓevi*; Jer. 3:19), and "Joseph of Israel." A comparison of parallel passages shows that they all refer to Joseph of Clisson or Joseph b. Baruch. His rulings are mentioned in many of the works of the *rishonim*, including *Meir b. Baruch of Rothenburg. Joseph's brother Meir was also one of the emigrants to Israel, but few statements by him have been preserved. There is reason to suppose that Joseph was the teacher of Samuel b. Solomon of Paris, the teacher of Meir of Rothenburg.

BIBLIOGRAPHY: Urbach, Tosafot, 265–7; S.H. Kook, *Iyyunim u-Meḥkarim*, 2 (1963), 258–62.

[Israel Moses Ta-Shma]

JOSEPH BEN DAVID HA-YEVANI ("the Greek"; early 14th century), Hebrew grammarian and lexicographer who lived in Greece. He was the author of the unpublished work *Menorat ha-Ma'or* containing a short grammar and a lexicon which, in the solely preserved Bodleian manuscript (Neubauer Cat, 1 (1886), 525 no. 1485), goes only as far as the word **חשב**. Dukes published excerpts from the lexicon (see bibl.). The author quotes the works of Judah b. David *Ḥayyuj, Jonah *Ibn Janaḥ, *Rashi, Abraham *Ibn Ezra, David *Kimḥi, and *Naḥmanides. In his grammar he relies on *Midrash ha-Ḥokhmah* by Judah b. Solomon ha-Kohen ibn Matka of Toledo. Fuerst, Benjacob, and Rosanes confused Joseph b. David with Joseph b. Moses Kilti. Joseph b. David died before 1337.

BIBLIOGRAPHY: Dukes, in: *Literaturblatt des Orients*, 10 (1849), 705–9, 727–32, 745–7; 11 (1850), 173–6, 183–5, 215–8; M. Steinschneider, *Jewish Literature* (1857), 140, 329; W. Bacher, *Die hebraeische Sprachwissenschaft* (1892), 94 (= J. Winter and A. Wuensche, *Die juedische Literatur*, 2 (1894), 216); H. Hirschfeld, *Literary History of Hebrew Grammarians and Lexicographers* (1926), 94; Rosanes, Togarmah, 1 (1930^2), 5, 2.

[Moshe Nahum Zobel]

JOSEPH BEN ELEM, temporary high priest during the reign of *Herod the Great. Numerous talmudic sources describe how Joseph b. Elem of Sepphoris substituted "for one day" as high priest, on the Day of Atonement. Josephus also relates that when the incumbent high priest, Mattathias the son of Theophilus, was rendered unclean just before the day of the fast, his relative Joseph b. Elem was appointed to serve in his place. According to the rabbinic version, Joseph was removed immediately after the fast from all subsequent priestly service.

BIBLIOGRAPHY: Derenbourg, Hist, 160 n. 1; Graetz, in: MGWJ, 30 (1881), 51–53; Schuerer, Gesch, 2 (1907^4), 270 n. 7; S. Lieberman, *Tosefta ki-Feshutah*, 4 (1962), 723–4.

[Isaiah Gafni]

JOSEPH BEN ELIJAH OF ZASLAW (first half of 17th century), rabbi and preacher. He was author of the exegetical-moralistic works *Rekhev Eliyahu* (Cracow, 1638) and *Yesod Yosef* (Lublin, 1638). In *Rekhev Eliyahu*, which he named in honor of his father Elijah, he printed as an introduction a moralizing letter by Elijah, containing much self-criticism as a merchant-scholar. Joseph demanded sincerity and humility from his own circle of scholars: "Brethren and companions, see how all of us have gone astray through the bad trait of priding ourselves on learning loudly, openly, and publicly. Whosoever praises himself more appears the better in his own view; each one thinks himself wiser than his fellow, as if the Torah was given to him alone; only he knows how to clarify talmudic problems and teach pupils. This self-glorification is very frequent, in particular among the leaders of the people, who say 'There is none but me. Is there a teacher like me?'" (*Rekhev Eliyahu*, fol. 27b). He attacked false humility: "This evil I have seen – each and every false and boastful man likes to say as if in amazement: 'Is there any pride in me? You would not find a more humble person than myself'" (*ibid.*, fol. 22a–b). He devoted a special paragraph against bankruptcy and warned that bankrupts should not give charity or buy candles for the synagogue (*ibid.*, fol. 12b). He demanded earnest *kavvanah* in prayer. Joseph's personality and work show that, in the new era of Jewish settlement and economic activity in Poland-Lithuania, a high level of Jewish culture and exacting standards of individual and social morality had been set by the first half of the 17th century.

BIBLIOGRAPHY: H.H. Ben-Sasson, *Hagut ve-Hanhagah* (1959), index.

[Haim Hillel Ben-Sasson]

JOSEPH (Joselmann) BEN GERSHON OF ROSHEIM (c. 1478–1554), the greatest of the Jewish **shtadlanim* in Germany during the Middle Ages. According to one tradition, his family originated in Louhans, France, and he himself once added "of the Loans family" to his signature, as did his sons after him. However, it is very doubtful if he was a relative of Jacob Jehiel Loans, physician to emperor Frederick III. During the 15th century, Joseph's family lived in Endingen, in Baden. Three of his father's uncles, Elijah, Aberlin, and Marcolin, were martyred there in 1470 as a result of a *blood libel. When the Jews were expelled from Endingen his father settled in Obernai, Alsace, and fled from there in 1476 after the pillage campaigns of the Swiss mercenaries and settled in Haguenau, Alsace. Orphaned at the age of six, Joseph was brought up by his mother's family. He earned his livelihood from moneylending and commerce and settled in Mittelbergheim, near Strasbourg. In 1507 the Jews who had been expelled from Obernai appealed to him to intercede with the provincial authorities and the emperor to repeal the expulsion decree. Because of his success, he was appointed in 1510, together with R. Zadok, as *parnas u-manhig* ("leader") of the Jews of Lower Alsace. He once referred to himself in one of his appeals to the imperial diet in Speyer (1535) as *Gemeiner Judischheit Regierer im deutschen Land* ("ruler of all Jewry in German lands") and was penalized for so doing because only the emperor could be considered as the ruler of the Jews. He also signed himself *Befehlshaber der ganzen Judenschaft* ("commander of all Jewry"), and was referred to by similar titles by the emperor and government bodies.

While acting on behalf of the Jews of Mittelbergheim in 1514, Joseph first came into the presence of the emperor, Maximilian I. In 1520, in the course of his activity on behalf of the Jews of Obernai, he obtained a general letter of protection for the Jews in Germany from Emperor *Charles V at the coronation celebrations held at Aachen. During the Peasants' Revolt in 1525, he saved the Jews of Alsace – and his town of *Rosheim in particular – from the peasant bands in exchange for a gift of 80 guilders. He also intervened with King *Ferdinand I, the future emperor and brother of Charles V, on behalf of the Jews of Haguenau in 1529, and in the same year was called upon to protect the Jews of *Pezinok (Poesing) in Hungary when they were threatened by a blood libel. In 1530 he succeeded in convincing the emperor and Ferdinand I that the accusation that the Jews had spied for the Turks was false, and the emperor renewed the letter of protection. During the same year the emperor ordered Joseph to engage in a disputation with the apostate Antonius *Margarita, author of the anti-Jewish work *Der gantz juedisch Glaub* (1530). When Joseph succeeded in refuting his accusations, the apostate was expelled from Augsburg. Joseph was called upon to protect the Jews of Silesia in 1535, when the danger of a blood libel threatened the Jews of Jaegerndorf, and a year later he intervened with Elector John Frederick to avert an expulsion decree against the Jews of Saxony. Martin *Luther, whose attitude toward the Jews had already become hostile, refused to receive him and act as mediator between him and the elector. In 1539, at the Protestant convention of Frankfurt, he succeeded in proving the innocence of the martyrs of Brandenburg who had been put to death as a result of an accusation of *Host desecration. Phillip *Melanchthon himself made a declaration to the convention on this subject. In 1544, after he had complained to the emperor over a renewed blood libel in Wuerzburg, he obtained a further letter of protection for the Jews of Germany, "the most liberal and generous letter of protection ever granted to Jews" (S. Stern). During the emperor's war against the Protestant princes, the Smalkaldic League, in 1546, he interceded on behalf of the Jews, who were oppressed by both sides. In 1548 he was again compelled to appeal to the emperor with a complaint against the towns of Alsace. His intervention in favor of the Jews of *Colmar continued until 1551, when at the imperial diet in Augsburg he worked against the severe restrictions on Jewish moneylending, such as the prohibition on selling promissory notes to Christians, and the threat of expulsion from the duchies of Wuerttemberg and Bavaria. His last activities – like his earlier ones – once more concerned the Jews of Alsace, when he came to the aid of the Jews of Dangolsheim and those of Rosheim.

As well as his memorandum against the blood libel of Pezinok (1530) and the disputation with Antonius Margarita, Joseph took up the defense of Judaism in his work *Iggeret Neḥamah* (1537) against the anti-Jewish attacks of the Protestant minister M. *Bucer. The Hebrew original, which has been lost, was read on the Sabbath in the synagogues of Hesse in order to raise the morale of the Jews and strengthen their faith. In 1530 he convened a meeting of communal delegates at Augsburg in order to establish a code to regulate their moneylending and trade affairs. Similar regulations covering the relations between the Jews and the general population of Alsatian towns were proposed and carried out by him. Joseph was called to Prague in 1534 in order to mediate in the dispute between the local Jews and the *Horowitz family. One of the members of the family, Sheftel, who objected to outside intervention, even planned to assassinate him. Joseph was also opposed to the messianic movement of David *Reuveni and Solomon *Molcho. Appealing to the municipal council of Strasbourg against the anti-Jewish writings of Luther in 1543, Joseph obtained a ban on the propagation of these libelous documents within the city.

Joseph wrote several religious, ethical and historical works, which in part are still extant (see bibl.). His *Derekh ha-Kodesh*, a work of ethics and guidance for a life of sanctity and martyrdom (*Kiddush ha-Shem), written in 1531 while he was in Brabant waiting for an audience with the emperor, has been lost and only a few extracts from it were copied by R. Joseph Yospa *Hahn in his *Yosef Omeẓ*. His grandson was the kabbalistic scholar R. Elijah b. Moses *Loans.

BIBLIOGRAPHY: S. Stern, *Josel of Rosheim* (1965); S.P. Rabbinowitz, *Rabbi Yosef Ish Rosheim* (1902); M. Lehmann, *Rabbi Joselmann von Rosheim; eine historische Erzaehlung*, 2 vols. (1925); E. Scheid, *Histoire de Rabbi Joselmann de Rosheim* (1886); Krakauer, in: REJ, 16 (1888), 88–105; Stern, in: ZGJD, 3 (1889), 65–74; Bresslau, *ibid.*, 5 (1892), 307–34; L. Feilchenfeld, *Rabbi Josel von Rosheim* (1898); H. Fraenkel-Goldschmidt (ed.), *Rabbi Yosef Ish Rosheim, Sefer ha-Mikneh* (1970); M. Ginsburger, *Josel von Rosheim* (1913); JJLG, 14 (1921), 45; Y. Tishbi, in: *Sefer Assaf* (1953), 515–28. **ADD. BIBLIOGRAPHY:** H. Fraenkel-Godlschmidt (ed.), *Rabbi Yosef Ish Rosheim, Ketavim Hstoriyyim* (1996); E. Carlebach, in: *Jewish History and Jewish Memory* (1998), 40–53.

[Jacob Rothschild]

JOSEPH BEN ḤIYYA (d. 333 C.E.), Babylonian *amora* and head of the Pumbedita academy for two and a half years, after the death of *Rabbah. Joseph was a pupil of Judah b. Ezekiel. Hundreds of his sayings in *halakhah* and *aggadah* are to be found throughout the Babylonian and Jerusalem Talmuds, and a large number of his pupils transmitted statements in his name. He devoted himself particularly to the text of the Mishnah, which he would clarify by means of the *beraitot*. His knowledge was exceptionally comprehensive, his teaching was well ordered, and his halakhic decisions clear, so that he was called *Sinai*, i.e., a scholar with wide knowledge (Hor., end). He also delved into mysticism, and was one of the "masters of the merkabah" (see Merkabah *Mysticism; Ḥag. 13a). He was also distinguished in biblical exegesis and left an Aramaic translation of parts of the Bible, which is often quoted. It is not to be assumed, however, that Joseph translated the whole Bible, though the Aramaic translation of the Book of Chronicles is ascribed to him and is called "the Targum of Rav Joseph."

Despite the fact that Joseph was recommended for the position of head of the yeshivah, he deferred this honor for the 22 years that Rabbah headed the yeshivah, and during this period Joseph accepted Rabbah's authority, declining even the slightest external signs of honor or office (Ber. 64a). According to the Talmud, he had an overwhelming love of the Torah and its students and, possessing considerable wealth (he owned fields and vineyards and his wine was praised), he undertook the support of 400 of his pupils (Ket. 106a). He stressed the importance of the Torah and its students in his *aggadah* and underwent many fasts, until he received assurance from heaven that the study of Torah would not depart from his descendants during the course of three generations (BM 85a). One of the central events in his life was a severe illness which caused him "to forget his learning," and Abbaye – his pupil – re-taught him what he had forgotten (Ned. 41a; cf. Er. 10a), and this illness may have been the cause of his blindness (Kid. 31a; cf. Pes. 111 b).

Many remarkable stories of his conduct are related, and even the details of his death and burial were embellished by legends. His teachings and rulings stress concern for the plight of the poor and the improvement of social life. His aspiration to raise the importance of the academy above that of the exilarch, which would lead to the dependence of the latter upon the academies, is discernible in his aggadic dicta, and can also be seen in the tendency in his teachings toward giving increased authority to the courts of law and their decisions (see e.g., Beẓah 5a; Ket. 81b; Git. 88b; et al.). The first struggle in the conflict of the academies with the exilarch originated with Joseph. Another noteworthy detail in his *aggadah* is that he is the only one to mention conversations with *Asmodeus (Asmedai), king of the demons (Pes. 110a).

BIBLIOGRAPHY: Hyman, Toledot, 742–9; Halevy, Dorot, 2 (1923), 440ff.; Epstein, Mishnah; Judelowitz, *Ḥayyei ha-Yehudim bi-Zeman ha-Talmud: Ir Pumbedita bi-Ymei ha-Amora'im* (1939), 96–98; J.S. Zuri, *Shilton Rashut ha-Golah ve-ha-Yeshivot* (1939), 127–56, 184–9; Ḥ. Albeck, *Mavo la-Talmudim* (1969), 291–3.

[Israel Moses Ta-Shma]

JOSEPH BEN ISAAC HA-LEVI (17th century), philosophical writer. Born in Lithuania, he later settled in Prague, where he taught medieval religious philosophy to many rabbinical scholars. Ephraim Solomon of Luntschits reports that after Joseph settled in Prague, he became known as a scholar and philosopher and some of the greatest scholars of Prague came to learn from him (see S. Fuenn, *Kiryah Ne'emanah* (1915), 64). Joseph's short commentary on *Maimonides' *Guide*, under the title *Givat ha-Moreh*, was published by Yom Tov Lipmann *Heller, author of the Mishnah commentary *Tosafot Yom Tov*, with his own introduction and annotations (Prague, 1611). Joseph also wrote *Ketonet Passim* (Lublin, 1614), dealing with the basic ideas of the *Guide*.

BIBLIOGRAPHY: Zunz, Gesch, 288 no. 141, 290 no. 156; Cowley, Cat., 334; M. Steinschneider, in *Festschrift A. Berliner* (1903), 355; Fuenn, Keneset, 479.

[Samuel Abba Horodezky]

JOSEPH BEN ISRAEL (late 16th–early 17th centuries), the most prominent among the poets of the town Mashtā who molded Yemenite Jewish poetry into its religious, national, and mystic character. Joseph was the earliest member of the group and the predecessor of his younger contemporary, Shalem *Shabazi. (According to legend, he was of the same town and was the latter's relative.) His works consist of about 150 poems and *piyyutim* in Hebrew and Arabic (most of them are extant in manuscript). Their contents deal with religious subjects and are marked by sublime emotion, flowing style, and power of expression. He developed the category of poems which open with *Mi Nishkani* ("Who Has Kissed Me"). Superficially, these are sensual love poems, but in reality they are fiery allegoric religious poems characterized by supplications and "embraces" of the bride (the Jewish People) for her husband, the bridegroom (God). He wrote about 25 graceful *piyyutim* and *seliḥot*.

BIBLIOGRAPHY: A.Z. Idelsohn and H. Torczyner (eds.), *Shirei Teiman* (1930), 45–64; Kafaḥ in: *Ha-Ẓofeh* (Jan. 18, 1957).

[Yehuda Ratzaby]

JOSEPH BEN ISSACHAR BAER OF PRAGUE (end of 16th century), rabbi and author. Joseph was a pupil of Mordecai Jaffe and of Judah Loew b. Bezalel (the Maharal of Prague). He was the author of *Yosef Da'at* (Prague, 1609), a supercommentary on Rashi's commentary to the Pentateuch, in which he corrects mistakes in the text and gives illustrations for understanding it. The work also includes some notes on the biblical commentary of Jacob b. Asher. In the introduction Joseph mentions his commentary to the *Beḥinat Olam* of Jedaiah ha-Penini Bedersi, which has not been published. *Alei Ayin*, a reference work to the *Ein Ya'akov* of Jacob Ibn Ḥabib, has also been attributed to him, though this is doubtful. It is stated that Joseph used a manuscript of Rashi's commentary on the Pentateuch dating from the year 1300.

BIBLIOGRAPHY: Zunz, Gesch, 285; Ghirondi-Neppi, 144; Neubauer, Cat, nos. 3697, 5928, 6463, 5566; S. Hock, *Die Familien Prags* (1892), 210f.; Fuenn, Keneset, 498.

[Yehoshua Horowitz]

JOSEPH BEN JACOB (11th century), liturgical poet. His compositions, among which was a *kerovah* in four parts for *Ne'ilah (unpublished) as well as *ma'araviyyot* for Pesaḥ and Shavuot, were part of the French rite at a very early period. Single poems by him have been included in both the Roman and German-Polish *maḥzor*. His *ma'aravit* for the seventh evening of Passover is attributed by S.D. Luzzatto to the younger Joseph b. Jacob *Kalai.

BIBLIOGRAPHY: Zunz, Ritus, 104; Zunz, Lit Poesie, 172f.; Davidson, Oẓar, 4 (1933), 402.

[Jefim (Hayyim) Schirmann]

JOSEPH BEN JACOB BAR SATIA (tenth century), *Gaon* of *Sura. The derivation and meaning of the name Bar Satia is not clear. He was appointed *gaon* by the exilarch *David b. Zakkai, some time after 930 C.E., after the exilarch had become embroiled in a dispute with Saadiah Gaon and had deposed him as *gaon* of Sura. Even though the exilarch and Saadiah were reconciled in 937, Joseph was not entirely deposed and, on Saadiah's death in 942, he was reappointed *gaon*. Not of a very strong character, he was unable to stand up to his wealthy and influential opponent in Pumbedita, Aaron *Sargado, and the academy of Sura declined during his days. Some time after 943, Joseph left Sura and went to Basra, where he died shortly after.

BIBLIOGRAPHY: Neubauer, Chronicles, 1 (1887), 65f.; 2 (1895), 81ff.; S. Eppenstein, *Beitraege zur Geschichte und Literatur im geonaeischen Zeitalter* (1913), 125f.; B.M. Lewin (ed.), *Iggeret Rav Sherira Ga'on* (1921), 118ff.; H. Malter, *Saadia Gaon, his Life and Works* (1921), 111; Krauss, in: *Livre d'Hommage… S. Poznański* (1927), 140.

[Eliezer Bashan (Sternberg)]

JOSEPH (Jossel) BEN JOSHUA MOSES OF FRANKFURT (d. 1681), German *dayyan*. Joseph was born in Frankfurt. Until his death he served as *dayyan* in Fuerth. He was the author of *Torat Yosef* (Wilmersdorf, 1725), which contains homilies and explanations of the *Masorah and achieved considerable fame. In the preface he points out that in earlier generations people had a wide knowledge of Scripture, with the result that the meaning of the Masorah was plain to all, but that this had changed during recent generations. The aim of the book was to explain the Masorah on the Torah in accordance with the *halakhah*, as well as to explain Rashi's commentary, and to justify statements of his which had been queried by later commentators. In his preface, Joseph mentions his work on the 613 commandments, *Torat Moshe* (in manuscript), which he named after his father "who gave his life on my behalf, as is known to all my father's family in Frankfurt."

BIBLIOGRAPHY: Loewenstein, in: JJLG, 8 (1911), 117.

[Yehoshua Horowitz]

JOSEPH BEN JUSTU OF JAÉN (early 12th century), Spanish scholar. Joseph was a pupil of Isaac *Alfasi. *Zerahiah b. Isaac ha-Levi (*Ha-Ma'or*, to Alfasi Pes. ch. 2) notes that he came from "the province of Jaén" but the exact location is unknown. From a parallel passage in *Ma'or* (Av. Zar. ch. 5, fol. 31b) it may possibly be inferred that Joseph lived in North Africa for some time after the death of Alfasi. The material extant by him or about him is very scanty. It is known that Alfasi charged him with circulating his "amendments" to various *halakhot* of his large work (see *Teshuvot ha-Ge'onim* by A. Harkavy (1887), 258, no. 519), and on one occasion he is found testifying after Alfasi's death to the fact that Alfasi had changed his mind (*Ha-Ma'or*, loc. cit.). *Teshuvot ha-Ge'onim* contains a collection of his queries to Alfasi and the latter's replies, but it is not possible to determine where the collection ends or how many paragraphs it contained. Only a fragment of one of Joseph's own responsa remains preserved in a responsum of Joseph *Ibn Migash (quoted in *Shitah Mekubbeẓet* to BK 108b). Some scholars are of the opinion that the name Justu is an abbreviation of Justus (Zedekiah). It may be that Joseph is identical with Joseph b. Abraham b. Seth (Shet), a collection of whose queries to Alfasi and the latter's replies were also published in *Teshuvot ha-Ge'onim* (51 no. 83 ff.), and that Seth (שת, Shet) should read ישת (Yeshet), i.e., Justu.

BIBLIOGRAPHY: S. Shefer, *Ha-Rif u-Mishnato* (1967), 18–19.

[Israel Moses Ta-Shma]

JOSEPH BEN KALONYMUS HA-NAKDAN I (13th century), grammarian and poet from a family of grammarians and *nakdanim* in Germany. Joseph copied and vocalized many manuscripts and signed with the addition "the scribe who gives goodly words" (see Gen. 49:21). *Abraham b. Azriel, author of the *Arugat ha-Bosem*, cites him in his book on matters of language and *piyyut*. His extant *piyyutim* include the *seliḥah* he composed in memory of the martyrs of 1235 of Laudna and Bischofsheim, beginning with the words "*Ezak Ḥamas Korotai*" ("I cry for the violence that has befallen me") and a *piyyut* for Rosh Ha-Shanah, *Melekh Elyon Addir ba-Marom Adonai* ("Exalted King, God, mighty on high") found in a French festival prayer book of 1278. It is possible that he is to be identified with Jose of Heidelberg, who corrected Torah scrolls and lived in Bohemia where the aforementioned Abraham b. Azriel dwelt. Joseph's nephew was Joseph b. Kalonymus ha-Nakdan II (died after 1294). He too was a grammarian and *paytan*. He lived in Xanten and studied under his maternal grandfather, *Samson ha-Nakdan. He was much occupied in copying and vocalizing of manuscripts and composed poems for learning the correct reading and the intonations of the books of the Bible, one of which, entitled *Ta'amei Emet*, for Job, Proverbs, and Psalms, was published with the author's explanation by A. *Berliner (see bibliography).

BIBLIOGRAPHY: Davidson, Oẓar, 4 (1933), 402; Zunz, Lit Poesie, 335; A. Berliner (ed.), *Ta'amei Emet im Be'ur be-Ḥaruzim me'et ha-Nakdan Yosef bar Kalonymus* (1886); N. Bruell, *Jahrbuecher fuer Juedische Geschichte und Literatur*, 8 (1887), 118–21; J. Freimann, in: *Festschrift… Dubnow* (1930), 169–71; E. Urbach (ed.), *Arugat ha-Bosem*, 1 (1939), 281.

[Abraham David]

JOSEPH BEN MORDECAI GERSHON HA-KOHEN OF CRACOW (1510–1591), Polish halakhic authority. Joseph, who was born in Cracow, was a brother-in-law of Moses *Isserles and a member of his *bet din*. For about 50 years he served as head of a yeshivah in Cracow. He is the author of *She'erit Yosef* (Cracow, 1590), comprising responsa, expositions of the *Mordekhai* of *Mordecai b. Hillel to the orders *Nezikin* and *Mo'ed*, the tractate *Berakhot*, and the Minor Tractates, and of *Tur Ḥoshen Mishpat*. The responsa were also published separately (Fuerth, 1767). In the introduction he notes that his sons, TANḤUM (d. 1618) and AARON MOSES (d. 1616) "persuaded me to have it published." Most of his responsa deal with commercial and financial matters, in which he was especially expert. He was approached with problems from Moravia (nos. 7, 9, 40), Italy (33), and Turkey (6) and corresponded with Meir *Katzenellenbogen (no. 1) and Solomon *Luria (no. 17). The latter asked him to look into a certain ruling and express his opinion on it, and in reply Joseph wrote a complete responsum. He was inclined to be stringent, as Isserles (no. 111) testified, and when a grain of wheat was found on a salted piece of meat during Passover, he prohibited all the pieces that were in the vessel at the time (no. 46). At the end of this responsum he stressed that many "of my colleagues opposed me, saying that it was a new prohibition and one should take into account only those prohibitions imposed explicitly by our predecessors." Only after he adduced additional evidence in support of his ruling was it accepted as binding in Cracow. His individuality and independence in determining halakhic ruling is marked; for instance he opposed a ruling by Solomon Liebermann in the case of a doubtful betrothal and relied upon Katzenellenbogen, who agreed with his opinion (no. 28). He wrote glosses to and published *Sefer ha-Aguddah* (Cracow,

1571) by *Alexander Susslin ha-Kohen. In the introduction Joseph states that he found it necessary to add his glosses because of the succinct style of the work and the difficulty in understanding it. David *Gans, the author of *Ẓemaḥ David* wrote that Joseph "was adorned with four crowns: the crown of Torah, the crown of the priesthood, the crown of greatness, and the crown of a good name."

BIBLIOGRAPHY: I.M. Zunz, *Ir ha-Ẓedek* (1874), 23–26; Rabbinovicz, in: *Ha-Maggid*, 19 (1875), 311f.; H.N, Dembitzer, *Kelilat Yofi*, 1 (1888), 4b–8a; H.D. (B.) Friedberg, *Luḥot Zikkaron* (1897) 8f.; idem, *Toledot ha-Defus ha-Ivri be-Polanyah* (1950^2), 4, 6, 15; A. Siev, *Ha-Rema* (1957), 29f.

[Yehoshua Horowitz]

JOSEPH BEN MORDECAI HA-KOHEN (late 17th and early 18th century), talmudist of *Jerusalem. Joseph was a pupil of Moses b. Jonathan *Galante. From 1706 to 1718 he wandered through various European countries and, while in Venice, arranged for the printing of his own and other works. Toward the end of his life he was appointed rabbi in Ankara, Turkey.

He was the author of: *Sha'arei Yerushalayim*, a collection of religious poems and prayers in praise of Jerusalem (both his own and those of other authors), printed with the annotations of Moses Cohen (Venice, 1707); *Divrei Yosef*, homilies (*ibid.*, 1710); *Likkut Yosef*, responsa on the laws of *sheḥitah* (unpublished). Joseph further edited *Zevaḥ ha-Shelamim* of Moses Galante (Amsterdam, 1708), as well as the *Idrot ha-Kedoshot*, based on the manuscripts of the *Zohar brought by Nathan Shapiro from Jerusalem (*ibid.*, 1708), and also a work entitled *Leket ha-Omer*, containing diverse prayers according to the custom of the Jews of Corfu (*ibid.*, 1718).

BIBLIOGRAPHY: Frumkin-Rivlin, 2 (1928), 87, no. 11;4 (1930), 20; Yaari, Sheluḥei, 372f.

[Samuel Abba Horodezky]

JOSEPH (Joselein) BEN MOSES (1423–1490?), talmudist and author. Born in Hoechstaedt, Bavaria, he studied under Jacob *Weil at Augsburg, Judah *Minz at Padua, and Joseph *Colon at Mestre. His principal teacher, however, was Israel *Isserlein under whom he studied at Wiener Neustadt for 10 years, and whose statements, customs, and daily conduct he noted carefully. From these notes he wrote his work *Leket Yosher* (ed. by J. Freimann, 1903), which is a compilation of his teacher's customs, together with his responsa and halakhic decisions. He was apparently the first to base his work on the *Arba'ah Turim*, but only the sections on the *Oraḥ Ḥayyim* and *Yoreh De'ah* are extant. The language of the author is not clear, as he himself admits. He was, however, an extremely precise and conscientious compiler, regularly indicating his sources, comparing different manuscripts, and, on several occasions, pointing out that a responsum he had found was a revised version and not a true copy of the author's original statement. At times he added brief annotations from the Talmud and halakhic authorities. The work is significant also because of the many new responsa of contemporary scholars which are cited and because of its great value for the history of the Jews and scholars of Germany, whose important communities he visited.

BIBLIOGRAPHY: Joseph b. Moses, *Leket Yosher*, ed. by J. Freimann (1903), introd.; S. Eidelberg, *Jewish Life in Austria in the 15th Century* (1962), index.

[Yedidya A. Dinari]

JOSEPH BEN MOSES (Ashkenazi), DARSHAN OF PRZEMYSLANY (17th century), rabbi, preacher, and *dayyan*. He was noted for his *derashot* of admonishment. The *Councils of the Lands approved the publication of *Ketonet Passim* (Lublin, 1691) and *Ẓafenat Pa'ne'aḥ he-Ḥadash* (Frankfurt on the Oder, 1694), two collections of his sermons. Joseph is also the author of *Keter Yosef* (Berlin, 1700), a commentary on liturgy. He was suspected of Shabbatean leanings.

BIBLIOGRAPHY: I. Halpern (ed.), *Pinkas Va'ad Arba Araẓot* (1945), 209, 213f.; idem, *Yehudim-ve-Yahadut be-Mizraḥ Eiropah* (1968), 85, 95.

JOSEPH BEN MOSES OF KREMENETS (second half of the 16th century), Polish talmudist. Joseph's teachers in Cracow included Moses *Isserles, Israel ben Shalom *Shakhna, and R. Mardush in Ostrog. The influence of his teachers is seen in his *Be'urei ha-Semag* (Venice, 1605), a commentary on the section on negative precepts in the *Sefer Mitzvot Gadol* of *Moses of Coucy. He also wrote *Be'urei Rashi*, a supercommentary to Rashi's commentary on the Pentateuch (Prague, 1615), as well as *Be'urei Sha'arei Dura* (*ibid.*, 1609), on the work of that name by Isaac ben Meir *Dueren (Cracow, 1534). A halakhic decision of Joseph appears in the *Mashbit Milḥamot* about the *Mikvah* of Rovigo (Venice, 1606, 88a–89b).

BIBLIOGRAPHY: Zunz, Gesch, 286, no. 121; 290, no. 158.

[Samuel Abba Horodezky]

JOSEPH BEN MOSES OF TROYES (known as **Joseph Porat**; 12th century), French scholar of Epernay. Joseph was an older contemporary of Jacob *Tam and a principal pupil of Tam's brother, *Samuel b. Meir, during whose lifetime he wrote *tosafot*. Many scholars studied his works in order to acquaint themselves with Samuel's teachings. Tam himself, as well as *Eliezer b. Samuel of Metz, and, particularly, *Judah Sir Leon, already made use of his *tosafot* to tractate *Shabbat*. His name is frequently mentioned in the printed *tosafot*, particularly to the tractates *Berakhot* and *Shabbat*, and in the *Tosafot Yeshanim* on tractate *Yoma*, and it is possible that wherever "Joseph" is mentioned without qualification in these tractates, it is he that is being referred to. Mention is also made of his *tosafot* to *Mo'ed Katan* and *Ketubbot*. Joseph corresponded with Tam and submitted problems to him (*Sefer ha-Yashar*, section of responsa ed. by F. Rosenthal (1898), 25–28) – even before Tam had left Ramerupt in 1146 – and the latter replied in terms of great respect. Tam's pupil, Aaron, may have been Joseph's son.

BIBLIOGRAPHY: Urbach, Tosafot, index.

[Israel Moses Ta-Shma]

JOSEPH BEN MOSES PHINEHAS (1726–1801), Polish talmudic scholar and author. Joseph was a son-in-law of Ezekiel *Landau, who described him as the "unrivaled" scholar of his generation. He was renowned for his piety and is usually referred to as "Joseph the Righteous." His insistence on imposing punishment on members of his community in accordance with Jewish law brought him into conflict with the authorities, who had withdrawn this privilege from the Jewish communities.

Joseph carried on an extensive correspondence with scholars, including his father-in-law; his scholarly exchange of letters with Akiva *Eger is particularly noteworthy. A large part of his writings was destroyed by fire in Dubno, where his widow had taken up residence; the remainder was collected and published by his grandson, Samuel Schoenblum, under the title *Zikhron She'erit Yosef* (1881). Some of his decisions and novellae are quoted in the *Noda bi-Yhudah* (e.g., to EH 63, ḤM 25–28) and *Ẓiyyun le-Nefesh Ḥayyah* (1783, 1855) of his father-in-law; a number of his novellae appear in the *Beit Shemu'el Aḥaron* (1816) of his brother.

BIBLIOGRAPHY: J.A. Kamelhar, *Mofet ha-Dor* (1934[2]), 89–92, 113–5 (New York, 1966), 24, 30; J. Perles, *Geschichte der Juden in Posen* (1865), 74–75, 126; I.T. Eisenstadt and S. Wiener, *Da'at Kedoshim* (1897–98), 69; A. Heppner and J. Herzberg, *Aus Vergangenheit und Gegenwart der Juden… in den Posener Landen* (1904–14) 782–3.

[Elias Katz]

JOSEPH BEN NOAH (**Abu Ya'qub Yūsuf ibn Nūḥ**; early 11th century), Karaite scholar. According to a report by *Ibn al-Hītī, he lived in Jerusalem and was principal of an academy of 70 scholars (possibly to conform with the number of members of the *Sanhedrin). His contemporaries were *Sahl b. Maẓli'aḥ and *Japheth b. Ali, who opposed him on certain questions. Joseph b. Abraham ha-Kohen ha-Ro'eh (Abu Ya'qūb al-Baṣīr) and *Abu al-Faraj Harun ibn al-Faraj refer to him as their teacher. Judah *Hadassi, who mentions Joseph several times in *Eshkol ha-Kofer*, reports that he rejected one of the basic tenets of Karaite doctrine, deduction by analogy. Joseph's works are no longer extant. They included a commentary on the Pentateuch, which Abu al-Faraj is supposed to have summarized and which Ali ibn Suleiman used for his commentary on Deuteronomy. He also wrote a grammatical work, likewise quoted by Abu al-Faraj.

BIBLIOGRAPHY: Steinschneider, Arab Lit, 76, no. 38; Mann, Texts, 2 (1935), 33f.; Z. Ankori, *Karaites in Byzantium* (1959), index; L. Nemoy, *Karaite Anthology* (1952), 231ff., 374ff.

[Isaak Dov Ber Markon]

JOSEPH BEN PHINEHAS (d. before 928), *Baghdad businessman and banker. By 877 he was already engaged in large and far-flung business transactions, with *Aaron b. Amram as his partner. In 908 the two had financial dealings with the vizier Ibn al-Furāt, and in 911/12 they were appointed court bankers to the caliph al-Muqtadir – this was regarded as the most important post under the *Abbasid regime. There are records of their activities as court bankers until 924, and it appears that Joseph b. Phinehas retained his post until his death. He knew how to use his high office to further the cause of Babylonian Jewry in government circles. A report by R. *Nathan ha-Bavli refers to a bitter controversy between the exilarch *Ukba and the *Gaon* *Kohen Zedek (according to Mann, the exilarch's controversy was with R. Judah Gaon, the grandfather of R. *Sherira Gaon, and not with Kohen Ẓedek) about revenues from Khorasan for the academy of *Pumbedita. Joseph b. Phinehas and his son-in-law *Netira, who also held a high position in the administration, gave their support to the *gaon* and twice succeeded in having the exilarch Ukba removed from his post. Joseph's position at court was inherited by his grandsons, the sons of his son-in-law Natira who died in 916.

BIBLIOGRAPHY: Neubauer, Chronicles, 2 (1895), 78–79; W.J. Fischel, in: JRAS (1933), 339–52, 569–603; Fischel, Islam, index; Mann, in: *Tarbiz*, 5 (1933/34), 148–54, 156f.; Baron, Social, 3 (1957), 152f.; 5 (1957), 10; **ADD. BIBLIOGRAPHY:** M. Gil, *Be-Malkhut Ishma'el*, 1:651–56; M. Ben-Sasson, in: *Tarbut ve-Ḥevrah be-Toledot Yisrael bi-Ymei ha-Benayim*, dedicated to the memory of H.H. Ben-Sasson (1989), 182.

[Abraham David]

JOSEPH BEN SAMUEL BEN ISAAC HA-MASHBIR (**Rodi**; d. 1700), Karaite author and scholar. Born in Derazhnya, Volhynia, Joseph was a pupil of Nisan Kukizow and a teacher of his son Mordechai b. Nisan *Kukizow. He helped Mordechai to answer the questions on the Karaites received from the Leiden professor Jacob Trigland (incorporated in *Dod Mordechai*). About 1670 Joseph moved from Derazhnya to *Halicz, where his innovations brought the Galician Karaites into closer contact with those of the Crimea. This earned him the name "*ha-Mashbir*" ("provider of bread"; cf. Gen. 42:6). He endeavored to raise the educational level of Halicz's Karaites and established a number of regulations that were observed also by following generations of that community.

He was an author of several treatises. Most of them are known only by title: *Ner Ḥokhmah* (Ms. JTS, NY), a commentary on the prayer book that was never finished; *Porat Yosef* or *Tiferet Yosef*, a work on Hebrew grammar (Mss. Oxford, Strasbourg); *Er ve-Onah; Perush al Asarah Ikkarim* (Ms. Strasbourg); *Shever Yosef*, an exegetical work, written in the form of questions and answers.

Fourteen of his *seliḥot*, prayers, and hymns are incorporated in the Karaite prayer book.

BIBLIOGRAPHY: Fuerst, Karaeertum, 3 (1869), 86; R. Fahn, *Le-Korot ha-Kara'im be-Galiẓyah* (1910), 7–8; S. Poznański, in: ZHB, 14 (1910), 95; Mann, Texts, 2 (1935), index, 1558.

[Isaak Dov Ber Markon / Golda Akhiezer (2nd ed.)]

JOSEPH BEN SHALOM ASHKENAZI (also called **Joseph ha-Arokh**, "the tall"; early 14th century), Spanish kabbalist. According to his own testimony, he was a descendant of *Judah b. Samuel he-Ḥasid. Only two of his works have survived:

(1) a commentary on the Sefer *Yeẓirah (Mantua, 1562), erroneously published under the name of R. *Abraham b. David of Posquières. An abridged version of this commentary was published in Constantinople in 1719. The commentary is often cited in kabbalistic works and even gained Isaac *Luria's appreciation; (2) a commentary on the portion of Genesis in the *Midrash Rabbah* (in Ms.). Although Ashkenazi made use of many talmudic, philosophical, and kabbalistic sources, he cites very few of them. He did not regard the *Zohar as an authoritative work. Despite his opposition to the Aristotelians, he admired *Maimonides, and his works reveal a tendency to merge philosophy and Kabbalah. Joseph Solomon *Delmedigo of Candia stated that Ashkenazi was "a sophisticated and knowledgeable philosopher." He was opposed to mythical speculation.

Ashkenazi's Teaching

Ashkenazi's philosophical inquiry led him to the conclusion that there must be one cause for all causes which cannot be in potentiality, in change, or in motion. Ashkenazi calls this the *Illat ha-Illot* ("cause of causes") and, infrequently, *Ein-Sof ("the Infinite"). By using this causal term, he wished to emphasize the revelatory aspect, although he stressed the cause of all causes as being above the world of emanation (*Aẓilut*). Even the first *Sefirah, Keter* ("crown"), is neither identical nor coexistent with the cause of all causes despite certain resemblances between them. Thus Ashkenazi opposed a number of Spanish kabbalists who identified *Ein-Sof* with *Keter*. At a certain point, the *Ein-Sof* intended to elevate the *Sefirot* hidden within it, which served as manifestations of the concealed divinity. The *Sefirot* constitute inclusive unity and variegated activity into which man is integrated by his theurgic activity.

The principle of paradigma is valid for the entire structure of existence. The emanating element in the *Sefirot* is described in the image of male and female. And just as the microcosm was created as an amorphous mass, according to the Midrash, the macrocosm began as hylic matter "which was neither potential nor actual," and thus, preceding the *Sefirot*, there was an amorphous mass called *havayot* ("essences") or *omakim* ("depths") – a conception resembling Platonic ideas. The force of evil (*temurot*, "changes") is considered a real entity, deriving from a supernal source and dependent on good. Evil's main tasks are provocation, accusation, and punishment. In the world to come man will inevitably fulfill the *mitzvot* and evil will be abolished. Ashkenazi approved of magic as a science, but opposed those who practiced it.

According to Ashkenazi, all existence is merely a system of layers. He posits as a cosmic rule that all that exists, including the seven lower *Sefirot* (and herein lies his great innovation), will undergo transmigration (*gilgul); through transmigration, a being changes form, either rising or declining. Death is a metamorphosis and not the cessation of existence, and man, in part or as a whole, may be reincarnated into any entity in the world. Ashkenazi is the source of the idea that the Messiah is a reincarnation of Moses.

BIBLIOGRAPHY: Basilea, Solomon Aviad Sar-Shalom, *Emunat Ḥakhamim* (1888), 139; G. Scholem, in: KS, 4 (1928), 286–302; 5 (1929), 263–6; G. Vajda, in: *Tarbiz*, 27 (1958), 290–300; M. Hallamish, in: *Leshonenu la-Am*, 17 (1966), 107–12; idem, in: *Bar Ilan*, 7–8 (1970), 211–24; R.J.Z. Werblowsky, *Joseph Karo, Lawyer and Mystic* (1962), 249–51; Y.A. Vaida, in: *Archives d'histoire doctrinale et littéraire du moyen âge* (1956), 144–5.

[Moshe Hallamish]

JOSEPH BEN SHESHET IBN LATIMI (c. 1300), Hebrew poet. Joseph, who lived in Lérida (Spain), was a member of a well-known Jewish family. His best-known work is a prayer, composed in the year 1308, consisting of 1,000 words, each of which begins with the letter *alef*. Aside from this bit of ingenuity, the piece is distinguished by a highly complicated structure and a long acrostic. It is found in a number of manuscripts, as well as in an edition by Isaac Akrish, *Kovez Vikkuḥim* (Breslau, 1844). Joseph is also the author of numerous liturgical poems and elegies, which have remained unknown to most scholars in the field.

BIBLIOGRAPHY: Landshuth, Ammudei, 98; Zunz, Lit Poesie, 499; Baer, Urkunden, 1 (1929), 985; Margoliouth, Cat, 3 (1965), 163 no. 871, 241 no. 929 vi, 428 no. 1058; Davidson, Oẓar, 4 (1933), 400.

[Jefim (Hayyim) Schirmann]

JOSEPH BEN SOLOMON OF CARCASSONNE (11th century), liturgical poet. One of the first representatives of the *piyyut* in France, Joseph is already quoted by *Rashi. His *yoẓer* for the first Sabbath of Ḥanukkah (*Odekha Ki Anafta*) appears in the German-Polish and in the Roman rites, and has repeatedly been printed and commented upon. The poem is composed in the old poetic style, in strophes of three lines, with a nine-fold alphabetical acrostic. Its content is largely based on the Scroll of Antiochus, the Book of Judith, and the Books of the Maccabees (I, ch. 1 and II, chs. 6–7).

BIBLIOGRAPHY: Zunz, Lit Poesie, 123; Landshuth, Ammudei, 96; Fuenn, Keneset, 505; Gross, Gal Jud, 614f.; Elbogen, Gottesdienst, 331; Davidson, Oẓar, 4 (1933), 408; A.M. Dubarle, *Judith, forme et sens*, 1 (1966), 98f.; 2 (1966), 162f. **ADD. BIBLIOGRAPHY:** Schirmann-Fleischer, *The History of Hebrew Poetry in Christian Spain and Southern France* (1997), 426 (Heb.).

[Jefim (Hayyim) Schirmann]

JOSEPH BEN TANḤUM YERUSHALMI (b. 1262), Hebrew poet, son of the grammarian-exegete *Tanḥum b. Joseph Yerushalmi of Cairo. It seems that he spent most of his life in Egypt, though he traveled to Jerusalem, Hebron, and other cities of Palestine. At the age of 15 Joseph composed *'Arugot ha-Besamim'*, a collection of poems with *tajnīs* rhymes, distributed in 10 sections (*arugot*), in imitation of Moses ibn Ezra's *Sefer ha-'Anak*; the book was published by J. Dishon in 2005. As a means of earning a livelihood Joseph had to write poems in honor of several Jewish patrons. Many of his poems were dedicated to Maimonides' grandson David b. Abraham *Maimuni, who had befriended him. Joseph also addressed verses to David's son, Abraham, to several relatives of this family, and to many others. He celebrated the familiar events (births, circumcisions, weddings) of his sponsors and wrote elegies in case of illness. On the death of his father in 1291 he composed a lamentation in which he mentions the conquest of Acre by the Crusaders. He may have still been alive in 1330.

Beside the poems collected in the *Arugot ha-Besamim*, with Arabic glosses, other of Joseph's poems were collected in a *Divan*, divided into seven sections (*abwāb*). The extant manuscripts are all fragmentary and contain only poems of section 2 (Letters and *maqāmāt*), 4 (Eulogies and Congratulations), 5 (Love and Wine), 6 (Elegies and Dirges), 7 (Miscellaneous). He knew the most important Andalusian Hebrew poets very well and was particularly influenced by Moses *Ibn Ezra and Judah *Al-Ḥarizi; most genres of the Spanish-Hebrew poetry are represented in the *Divan*. There are poems with verses in different meters, strophic verse (*muwashshaḥ*) occasionally with Arabic endings, *maqāmāt* in which the narrator is called Aḥiṭūb b. Ḥakmoni, and plays on words (*tajnīs*). A small number of liturgical poems also appear. Although the compositions are without originality, and often even devoid of precise expression, Joseph displays a knowledge of Arabic and Hebrew literary tradition and stylistic skill and is no doubt the most representative Hebrew poet of Egypt in the 13th century. A.M. Habermann published a number of his shorter wine and love poems. Several other poems and *maqāmāt* were published by H. Brody, J. Schirmann, S.M. Stern, P. Naveh, H.V. Sheynin, J. Yahalom, and J. Dishon.

BIBLIOGRAPHY: Brody, in: *Kobez al Jad*, 9 (1893), 7–8, 17–19; Poznański, in: REJ, 40 (1900), 129–53; 41 (1900), 46–61; Mann, Texts, 1 (1931), 435–45; J. Schirmann, *Shirim Ḥadashim min ha-Genizah* (1965), index; idem, in: *Kobez al Jad*, 3 (1939), 62–64; Habermann, in: *Maḥbarot le-Sifrut*, 2 no. 2 (1942), 39–40; Ashtor, Toledot, 1 (1944), 163–6; S.M. Stern, in: *Tarbiz*, 18 (1947), 184–86; Toledano, in: *Sinai*, 42 (1958), 339–55; P. Naveh, in: *Molad*, 25 (1968), 237–44; idem, in: *Studies in Bibliography and Booklore*, 9 (1970), 57–75, V. Sheynin, in: AO, 22 (1969), 245–71. **ADD. BIBLIOGRAPHY:** Y. Ratzaby, in: *Pirkei Shirah*, 1 (1990), 77–110, 2 (1999), 53–81; J. Yahalom, in: *Sefer Yisrael Levin* (1994), 145–54; idem, in: *Pirkei Shirah*, 3 (2003), 87–98; S. Einbinder, in: *Medieval Encounters*, 1 (1995), 252–70; J. Dishon, in: *Dappim le-Meḥkar be-Sifrut*, 12 (1999/2000), 25–63; idem (ed.), *The Book of the Perfumed Flower Beds* (Heb., 2005).

[Jefim (Hayyim) Schirmann / Angel Sáenz-Badillos (2nd ed.)]

JOSEPH BEN UZZIEL, name of the grandson of *Ben Sira, according to two pseudepigraphical sources. In the first source, the Alphabet of *Ben Sira (a late-geonic work, which contains some heretical tendencies), the unknown author used the literary device of a dialogue between two or three characters, his intention being to create a satirical imitation of midrashic forms. These characters were Ben Sira, his son Uzziel, and the latter's son Joseph b. Uzziel. Probably the idea of Ben Sira's grandson originated from the author's knowledge that the historical Ben Sira had a grandson who had edited and translated his book. The second text, the *baraita* of Joseph b. Uzziel, is a short treatise found in several manuscripts, usually followed by a religious poem which might be part of the pseudepigraphical work. The *baraita* was written by one or more of the early Ḥasidei Ashkenaz, probably in the 12th century. It claims to contain revelations which the prophet Jeremiah handed to his great-grandson (Ben Sira was described as Jeremiah's daughter's son). This treatise is a commentary on *Sefer *Yeẓirah* ("Book of Creation") and contains some of the main ideas of Ashkenazi ḥasidic esoteric doctrines, in addition to some ideas unknown from any earlier source, e.g., the "Special Cherub," which shines in the east (*Shekhinah* ("Divine Presence") shines from the west), and is described as the main vehicle of divine revelation. The *baraita* of Joseph b. Uzziel served as a major source for a group of Ashkenazi ḥasidic thinkers, who wrote some numerous works based on its ideas. The most extensive of these works is the commentary on the *Sefer Yeẓirah* attributed to *Saadiah Gaon. Some quotations from a lost commentary on the *baraita* by one Avigdor ha-Ẓarefati are found in the writings of the Ḥasidei Ashkenaz. *Elhanan b. Yakar used the *baraita* extensively in his esoteric writings.

BIBLIOGRAPHY: A. Epstein, *Mi-Kadmoniyyot ha-Yehudim* (1957), 241, 248; Scholem, Mysticism, 87, 111–8; G. Scholem, *On the Kabbalah and Its Symbolism* (1965), 173ff.; Dan, in: *Molad*, 23 (1966), 490–6; idem, in: *Tarbiz*, 35 (1965/66), 349–72.

[Joseph Dan]

JOSEPH BEN ẒADDIK (late 15th century), rabbinic scholar and chronicler of Arévalo (central Spain). From 1467 to 1487 he was engaged in writing a compendium on ritual law, which he entitled *Zekher Ẓaddik*. The final chapter comprises a chronicle of significant events, with special emphasis on Jewish history, from the creation down to the author's own day; the last entry is dated 1487. This chapter was edited by Neubauer from the manuscript in the Bodleian Library. The contents agree to a considerable extent with the *Sefer ha-Kabbalah* of *Abraham b. Solomon of Torrutiel, which Baer attributes to their borrowing from common sources (see bibl.). Often faulty in its citation of names and dates, Joseph's chronicle contains a number of anachronisms and contradictions; thus, in one passage, Romulus is made a contemporary of David, with whom he allegedly signed a peace treaty, while elsewhere the date of the founding of Rome is placed more correctly in the time of Hezekiah, about 725 B.C.E. However, the chronicle does have some value for the Spanish period from the 11th to the 15th centuries, approximately from the time of *Ferdinand I to *Ferdinand and Isabella, since Joseph frequently cites non-Jewish sources and has a broader and more objective viewpoint than some of the later chroniclers, who were embittered by the final edict of expulsion in 1492.

BIBLIOGRAPHY: Y.F. Baer, *Untersuchungen ueber... Schebet Jehuda* (1923), 26f.; F. Cantera Burgos, *Libro de la Cabala* (1928), 8f., 47–64 (annotated Spanish translation of chronicle covering events from 1015 on); Neubauer, Chronicles, 1 (1887 repr. 1965), xiv; Waxman, Literature, 2 (1960²), 462f.

[Jacob Haberman]

JOSEPH (Josel) BEN ZE'EV WOLF HA-LEVI (first half of the 18th century), rabbi and author. Originally from Lissa, he served as a rabbi in Hohensalza and in Dubno. The following of his works have been printed: *Tiferet Yosef*, the first part of a supercommentary on Rashi's Bible commentary (Prague, 1725), dealing with the first three books of the Pentateuch; *Ateret Yosef*, a collection of his halakhic and aggadic novellae to the tractate *Kiddushin* (Berlin, 1746); *Sugyot ha-Shas* (Berlin, 1736–39); a collection of supplements to the 1734–39 Berlin and Frankfurt on the Oder editions of the Talmud, in which old *tosafot* to the Talmud and *tosafot* to *Horayot* and *Keritot* are quoted. This work was criticized as having been largely copied from the Frankfurt on the Main edition of the Talmud (1720–22).

BIBLIOGRAPHY: R.N.N. Rabbinovicz, *Ma'amar al Hadpasat ha-Talmud* (1952), 103, 116; O. Muneles, *Bibliographical Survey of Jewish Prague* (1952), 72, no. 240.

[Elias Katz]

JOSEPH DAVID (Joseph ben David; 1662–1736), rabbi of *Salonika. Born in Salonika, at an early age he was appointed as preacher and, on the death of Solomon *Amarillo in 1721, he was appointed *av bet din*, despite the objection of Amarillo's son Moses, who claimed the succession. In 1728 he became chief rabbi of Salonika, succeeding Joseph *Covo. He tended toward leniency in his rulings, and a considerable controversy arose when he gave a lenient punishment to a Jew who had been intimate with a married woman and had a child by her. The local rabbis protested against his ruling and demanded that the man be put to death in accordance with Jewish law. In his defense, Joseph David argued that at that time no Jewish court had the right to inflict capital punishment.

His works, which were published in Salonika, include: *Beit David* – halakhic novellae and responsa (pt. 1, 1740; pt. 2 (*Petaḥ Beit David*), 1746), and *Ẓemaḥ David* (2 pts., 1785–1811) – sermons on the Pentateuch, including a few on the prophets and hagiographa. A number of his works are still in manuscript.

BIBLIOGRAPHY: Rosanes, Togarmah, 5 (1938), 21–22; Rivkind, in: KS, 3 (1926/27), 172, no. 209; Toiber, *ibid.*, 8 (1931/32), 275–6; Wilensky, *ibid.*, 15 (1938/39), 491–3.; 16 (1939/40), 271–2; J.M. Toledano, *Oẓar Genazim* (1960), 217, nos. 28–29.

[Abraham David]

JOSEPH DELLA REINA, hero of a kabbalistic legend who attempted to bring an end to Satan's power and thus lead to the redemption. The earliest version of the story, which evolved between the 15th and 17th centuries, is recorded by *Abraham b. Eliezer ha-Levi in his treatise *Iggeret Sod ha-Ge'ullah*, written in Jerusalem in 1519. The author used terms current only in kabbalistic literature of the period of the expulsion from Spain (1492). The story is very short and dwells more on a detailed description of Satan and his hosts than on the hero and his deeds. However, its salient feature is Joseph's burning of incense before Satan; this, being tantamount to idolatry, caused Joseph's failure and undoing. Nothing about the subsequent fate of the hero is reported. Abraham used this story to explain that Joseph's crime caused the redemption, which should have occurred in 1490, to be postponed for 40 years (one generation later) to 1530, according to the author's calculations the proven year of the beginning of the redemption and the coming of the Messiah. Abraham states that Joseph undertook his task in about 1470, a conclusion attested to by various sources which show that Joseph was actually a known kabbalist in the mid-15th century, probably from the Ibn *Gabbai family. Some factual basis for the story exists, though it serves the purposes and reflects the beliefs of later generations.

The story of Joseph was known in 16th-century Safed. Moses *Cordovero and Ḥayyim *Vital mention his name in descriptions of the dangers of messianic and magical activity. Ḥayyim Vital also recalls that his teacher Isaac *Luria once recognized Joseph's soul in the body of a black dog, Joseph's punishment for his crime. However, until the mid-17th century, a full and detailed written description of Joseph's deeds and fate does not exist, although apparently such a story was repeated orally in Ereẓ Israel. Solomon Navarro (b. 1606), the author of the most complete, detailed, and artistic version, lived for a long time in Jerusalem. Sent as emissary to Italy, he married a Christian, was converted to Christianity in 1664, and was involved in the Shabbatean movement. He wrote a book predicting that the redemption would occur in 1676. Navarro claimed that in Safed he had discovered an ancient manuscript of the story, written by a surviving disciple of Joseph. It is clear, however, that he himself had written the story, using the literary and oral traditions which had developed in the 200 years following Joseph's deed. Navarro's version is the first which contains a description of Joseph's fate after his failure to bring about the redemption. He became an ally of Satan and a lover of *Lilith, and later fell in love with the wife of the king of Greece, whom Lilith had brought to his bed every night. After some time this was revealed to the king and Joseph had to commit suicide. Both Eastern and Western folkloristic motifs appear in this last part. In contrast to earlier versions, Navarro describes Joseph's mistake as accidental. The earlier moral of the story, that a man should not try to use magic to bring forth the redemption, does not emerge clearly.

In Navarro's version, the tale may be interpreted as encouragement to follow Joseph's example and as a demonstration of the dangers of such practice, an aspect which interested the Shabbatean writers. Solomon *Ayllon, a leading Shabbatean thinker after *Shabbetai Ẓevi's conversion to Islam, composed a version of the story which has been preserved in Yiddish. It reveals a more sympathetic attitude toward Joseph. The Shabbateans, naturally, noticed the similarity between Joseph, who became a servant of Satan, and their converted messiah. In the late 17th century a Shabbatean Jew who belonged to the *Doenmeh wrote a mythical biography of Shabbetai Ẓevi, using a motif found in this story to describe his messiah's struggle against the cosmic forces of evil.

Navarro's version became very popular in the 18th and 19th centuries, was translated into many languages, and is included in almost every anthology of Jewish stories. Joseph della Reina has served as the subject of many poems, short epics, ballads, and plays.

BIBLIOGRAPHY: *Sippur Devarim* (Constantinople, 1728), vols. 28–36; G. Scholem, in: *Zion* (*Me'assef*), 5 (1933), 124–30; idem, in: *Sefunot*, 9 (1965), 201; J. Dan, *ibid.*, 6 (1962), 313–26; Z. Rubashov (Shazar), *Eder ha-Yekar* (1947), 97–118.

[Joseph Dan]

JOSEPH HA-KOHEN (1496–1578), historiographer, physician, and philologist active in Italy. His parents were originally from Spain, and, after the expulsion of the Jews from that country, went to Avignon. In 1501/02 they moved to *Genoa, where Joseph received a comprehensive education, including languages, history, literature, and medicine, in which he specialized and became celebrated. With the expulsion of the Jews from Genoa in 1516, Joseph moved with his family to Novi, where he married the daughter of Abraham b. Moses ha-Kohen, one of the most prominent rabbis of Italy. Joseph subsequently moved from place to place. In 1538 he returned to Genoa, and in 1550, when the Jews were expelled from there a second time, he was invited by the inhabitants of Voltaggio to settle in this town as their physician. Seventeen years later a decree ordering the expulsion of the Jews from Voltaggio was issued, and although the townsmen obtained permission for him to stay, Joseph refused to dissociate himself from the rest of the community. Joseph did much to assist in the ransom and rehabilitation of Jewish captives brought to Italy, contributing to this from his own resources. The loss of his three sons caused him bitter grief.

Joseph's writings evince his versatility. His first historical work was *Divrei ha-Yamim le-Malkhei Ẓarefat u-le-Malkhei Beit Ottoman ha-Togar* (Sabbioneta, 1554; Amsterdam, 1733), a history of the kings of France and Turkey, which earned him the title of the "second Josephus" from the Hebraist Jacques *Basnage. The first part deals with the period from the downfall of the Roman Empire until 1520 and dwells particularly on the Crusades and events close to them. The second part deals with the period 1520–53 and contains a description of events in the author's own generation. The work is a general history and includes some events concerning the Jews, such as the exile, persecutions, and massacres. His knowledge of Latin and other languages gave him access to various sources, and his conclusions are well based and objective. A Latin summary of the first two parts of this work was printed in 1670, and an English translation in 1835–36. The third part, dealing with the period 1554–75, was first published in 1955, in Hebrew. After the publication of Samuel *Usque's *Consolaçam as tribulaçoens de Ysrael* in 1552, Joseph decided to compose a similar book in Hebrew, which appeared in 1558 under the title *Emek ha-Bakha* ("Valley of Tears"; cf. Ps. 84:7). In it he tells of the "hardships which befell us since the day of Judah's exile from its land." In the second edition he added events of his own day. A complete edition, with additions until 1605 by an unknown editor, was prepared by S.D. *Luzzatto and published in Vienna in 1852 by M. Letteris. Passages from the *Emek ha-Bakha*, which list at length the sufferings, persecutions, expulsions, and forced conversions undergone by the Jews, were read in some of the Italian communities on the Ninth of Av. The work was translated into German in 1858 and French in 1881. Other works by Joseph have been preserved in manuscript on various subjects – geographical-historical themes, linguistics and medicine. They include *Maẓiv Gevulot Amim*, a translation from the Italian version of Boemus' work *Omnium gentium mores leges et ritus*, a geography of Africa, Asia, and Europe; *Sefer ha-India* and *Sefer Fernando Cortes*, a two-part translation of Francisco López de Gómara's *Historia General de las Indias*, and *La Conquista de Mexico*, a description of the lands of South America and Mexico, and of their conquest by the Spaniards; and *Mekiẓ Nirdamim*, a translation of a medical treatise by the physician Meir *Alguadez, to which Joseph added a chapter on "remedies for the French disease." Several poems by Joseph were published at the end of *Sefer Sha'ashu'im* by Joseph b. Meir Zabara (published in New York, 1913).

BIBLIOGRAPHY: A. Kahana, *Sifrut ha-Historyah ha-Yisre'elit*, 2 (1923), 91–108; D.A. Gross (ed.), Joseph ha-Kohen, *Sefer Divrei ha-Yamim le-Malkhei Ẓarefat u-Malkhei Beit Ottoman ha-Togar* (1955), introd.; M.A. Shulwass, *Ḥayyei ba-Yehudim be-Italyah bi-Tekufat ha-Renaissance* (1955), index; M. Wiener (trans.), Joseph ha-Kohen, *Emek habacha* (1858), introd.; I. Loeb, in: REJ, 16 (1888), 28–56; 212–23; M. Steinschneider, *Die Geschichtsliteratur der Juden* (1905), 101–3; G. Musso, in: *Scritti in Memoria di L. Carpi* (1967).

[Ephraim Kupfer]

JOSEPH ḤAYYIM BEN ELIJAH AL-ḤAKAM (1833 or 1835–1909), *Baghdad rabbi. He was the son of Elijah al-Ḥakam and the father of Jacob al-Ḥakam (see *Al-Ḥakam). Born in Baghdad, he studied with his maternal uncle, David Ḥai b. Meir. In 1848 he began to study under Abdallah *Somekh. He succeeded his father (1859) as preacher, a post he held until his death. In 1869 he visited Ereẓ Israel. In 1876 Jacob Obermeier of *Vienna, who had come to Baghdad to teach French, insulted Joseph Ḥayyim. The community excommunicated him and compelled him to request the rabbi's pardon. Al-Ḥakam was renowned as a great halakhic authority who instituted many *takkanot*. He wrote some 60 works on all aspects of Torah, only a few of which have been published. He is best known for his *Ben Ish Ḥai* (1898), homilies blended with *halakhah* and Kabbalah. This work achieved immense popularity, particularly in Oriental communities, where it is studied extensively and has gone through many editions. His other published works include *Ben Yehoyada* (1898–1904), five volumes of commentaries to the aggadic portions of the Babylonian Talmud and *Rav Pe'alim* (1901–12), responsa. He wrote approximately 200 *piyyutim* and *pizmonim*, about 50 of which are incorporated in the liturgy of Baghdad Jewry; the rest are still in manuscript.

BIBLIOGRAPHY: A. Ben-Jacob, *Yehudei Bavel*, index; D.J. Sassoon, *History of Jews in Baghdad* (1969), index.

[Abraham David]

JOSEPH HA-ẒAREFATI, illuminator of the *Cervera Bible* of 1300 (see Illuminated *Bibles). Joseph ha-Ẓarefati ("the Frenchman") is one of the first Jewish artists known from medieval Europe. His colophon (fol. 449) stating: "I, Joseph ha-Ẓarefati, illustrated this book and completed it," which terminates the manuscript, is written in large anthropomorphic letters, each line framed by a colored band. Joseph's illustrations to the Bible are important as an example of early illuminated Castilian Bibles. No other extant illuminated manuscript was signed by Joseph, but the accomplishment of his work indicates an experienced artist. His style is influenced by 13th-century northern French illumination; the iconography of his illustrations is partly Castilian and partly French, but mostly his own invention. It is probable that his work influenced many artists, especially Joseph *Ibn Ḥayyim, who in 1476 used the *Cervera Bible* as a model for illustrating the *First Kennicott Bible*, where even the colophon is a direct imitation.

BIBLIOGRAPHY: Mayer, 2221, 2229, 3009 c; C. Roth, *Gleanings* (1967), 316–9; B. Narkiss, *Hebrew Illuminated Manuscripts* (1969), 15, 245, 252; Schirmann, Sefarad, 2 (1956), 417.

[Bezalel Narkiss]

JOSEPH ḤAZZAN BEN JUDAH OF TROYES (13th century), French scholar, grandson of *Baruch b. Isaac of Regensburg, author of the *Sefer ha-Terumah*. As *ḥazzan* in his town, Joseph carefully studied the customs and versions of the liturgy of that community and its synagogal customs in their various traditions, adding customs of his own. After his death, his son Menahem, who succeeded him, wrote, at the request of many, *Seder Troyes* (ed. by M. Weiss, 1905), in which he summarized all of his father's research. Joseph was one of the few scholars of Germany and France who wrote grammatical works as well: *Yedidut*, on biblical grammar, and (apparently) *Sefer Sarim Rim* (Rim being acronym of **R**abbi **J**oseph **M**i-Troyes), on Hebrew grammar. Another book of his was *Yesod ha-Ibbur* ("The Basis of Calendar Intercalation"). With the exception of a few pages of *Yesod ha-Ibbur*, these works have been lost.

BIBLIOGRAPHY: M. Weiss (ed.), *Seder Troyes* (1905), introd.; Zunz, Gesch, 84f. 112; Gross, Gal Jud, 239f.; Bruell, in: *Jahrbuecher fuer Juedische Geschichte und Literatur*, 8 (1887), 63–65; Epstein, in: MGWJ, 41 (1897), 474f.; J. Freimann, in: *Ha-Eshkol*, 6 (1909), 106.

[Ephraim Kupfer]

JOSEPH IBN SHRAGA (d. 1508–09), kabbalist. Ibn Shraga lived in Italy apparently before the expulsion. He stayed for a long time in Argenta, near Ferrara, and was the father-in-law of Joseph b. Ḥayyim *Jabez. Ibn Shraga was considered the greatest Italian kabbalist in his generation and trained many students in Kabbalah, including Moses b. Mordecai Basola (I. Sonne, *Mi-Paulo ha-Revi'i ad Pius ha-Ḥamishi* (1954), 135), Elijah Menahem b. Abba Mari *Ḥalfan in Venice, and Isaac b. Joseph Jabez (according to his introduction to *Ḥasdei ha-Shem*). He wrote a treatise on the language of the Zohar on redemption which was widely circulated after the expulsion from Spain (printed at the end of *Likkutei Shikhḥah u-Fe'ah*, 1556) and denounced by *Abraham b. Eliezer ha-Levi as a forgery in *Mashreh Kitrin*. In addition, Joseph wrote (1) a kabbalistic commentary on the prayers; (2) a commentary on the blessings (both in Brit. Mus. Alm. Coll. Ms. 140); (3) a commentary on the Torah (Alm. Coll. Ms. 140); (4) *Seder Tikkun ha-Magefah* (printed in *Moshi'a Ḥosim*, 1587); (5) polemical observations on some kabbalistic responsa by the pseudo-prophet Asher *Lemlein (A. Marx, in REJ, 61 (1911), 135–8); (6) on different kabbalistic topics (Alm. Coll. Ms. 124). In 1505 he was living in his son-in-law's house in Padua and perhaps died there.

BIBLIOGRAPHY: HB, 5 (1862), 45–46; G. Scholem, in: KS, 2 (1925), 111; 7 (1931), 149–51; 8 (1933), 262–5.

[Gershom Scholem]

JOSEPH IBN ṬABŪL (c. 1545–beginning 17th century), kabbalist and one of the foremost students of R. Isaac *Luria. He came from North Africa (*Maghreb, Ma'arav*) and was therefore called "Joseph ha-Ma'aravi." He went to Safed in its most flourishing period and joined the circle of the disciples of Luria in 1570. After Luria's death, Ibn Ṭabūl remained in Safed and began to spread his teacher's doctrines. Tension grew between him and Ḥayyim *Vital. In his old age he went to Egypt and remained there for several years. Apparently at the beginning of the 17th century he returned to Ereẓ Israel and died in Hebron. His expositions on the Lurianic system served as one of the primary sources through which it became known in kabbalistic circles. It is preserved in many manuscripts and in time it was given the name (not by the author) *Derush Ḥefẓi-Bah*, and it was even attributed to his rival Ḥayyim Vital, under whose name the book was published when included in *Simḥat Kohen* by Masʿūd ha-Kohen al-Ḥaddād (Jerusalem, 1921). In addition, several of Ibn Ṭabūl's kabbalistic works, *yiḥudim* (hymns on the unity of God), sermons, and several commentaries on different portions of the *Zohar, including on the *Idra*, have been preserved in manuscript. Toward the end of his life, the question was raised if he had the right to leave the *Musta'arabi community (to which he belonged throughout his life) in order to join the Sephardi community. His students in Kabbalah included R. Samuel ben Sid and R. *Israel Benjamin I.

BIBLIOGRAPHY: A.L. Frumkin, *Toledot Ḥakhmei Yerushalayim*, 1, p. 15; G. Scholem, in: *Zion*, 5 (1940), 148–60.

[Gershom Scholem]

JOSEPH ISSACHAR BAER BEN ELHANAN (also called **Baer Frankfurter**; c. 1642–1705), author of rabbinical and kabbalistic works. The son of the kabbalist Elhanan b. Ẓevi, Joseph Issachar Baer served in his youth as rabbi in Moravia but then withdrew to Frydek in order to devote all his time to the study of Torah. In 1677 he was living in Eibenschitz (now Ivancice). Around 1680 he was rabbi of Frankfurt on the Oder, and from 1687 to 1694 district rabbi of Kremsier (Kromeriz), where he signed with David Oppenheim the resolutions prepared by the synod there in 1694. In 1696 he left Kremsier to travel to Palestine but during his journey made lengthy stays in Nikolsburg, in Vienna (where he enjoyed the hospitality of Samson *Wertheimer), and in Venice (1700–01). Baer's published works are *Arba Ḥarashim* (Frankfurt on the Oder, 1681), an anthology of kabbalistic homilies in four parts, and *Sheloshah Sarigim* (Venice, 1701), homilies on the *haftarot. His *Mei Be'er, Matteh Oz*, and *Peraḥ Levanon* remain in manuscript.

BIBLIOGRAPHY: S. Buber, *Kiryah Nisgavah* (1903), 49; Baumgarten, in: *Gedenkbuch… David Kaufmann* (1900), 506ff.; B. Wachstein, *Die Inschriften des alten Judenfriedhofes in Wien*, 1 (1912), 281–3; H. Gold, *Die Juden und Judengemeinden Maehrens in Vergangenheit und Gegenwart* (1923), 292.

[Joseph Maier]

JOSEPH JOSKE BEN JUDAH JUDEL OF LUBLIN (1659?–1706), talmudist and kabbalist. Joseph studied with his father, who was rabbi at Lemberg and later at Kowel. He was appointed rabbi, first of Minsk, and in 1698, of Dubnow where he lived until his death. Ẓevi Hirsch *Koidonover, one of his pupils, mentions in his *Kav ha-Yashar* the kabbalistic lore he learned from him. Joseph is the author of several works dealing with ethics and moral conduct: (1) *Yesod Yosef* (Sklow, 1785); (2) *Lu'aḥ Hanhagot* (Wilhelmsdorf, 1719); (3) *Ne'imah Kedoshah*, including a Sabbath hymn (Zolkiew, 1720); and (4) *Hanhagot Yesharot* (Zhitomir, 1868).

In his *Yesod Yosef* he describes realistically the conduct of the communal leaders and exhorts the community to behave morally.

BIBLIOGRAPHY: I.T. Eisenstadt, *Da'at Kedoshim* (1897–98), 78; H.N. Maggid-Steinschneider, *Ir Vilna*, 1 (1900), 141, n. 2, 190, n. 3; Horodezky, in: *YIVO Historishe Shriftn*, 2 (1937), 1–8; B. Dinur, *Be-Mifneh ha-Dorot* (1955), 99–101, 121ff.; Zinberg, *Sifrut*, 3 (1957), 25 0–1.

[Yehoshua Horowitz]

JOSEPH MAMAN AL-MAGHRIBI (1741–1822), rabbi and emissary of *Safed. Born in *Tetuán, *Morocco, Joseph Maman later settled in Safed with his family. Ḥayyim Joseph David *Azulai, the great Safed scholar, suggested he be sent on a special mission to the Jewish communities in *Syria, *Iraq, *Turkey, and *Persia to collect funds for the victims of the great famine in Safed. He traveled to Constantinople, Kermanshah, *Hamadan, *Teheran, and *Meshed, where he met Siman Tov Melamed, who persuaded him to visit the Jews in *Bukhara, then living in isolation and ignorance. On his mission, Joseph Maman was accompanied by Mulla Daniel of Meshed, who served him as interpreter. He arrived in Bukhara in 1793 and stayed there for 30 years, completely revitalizing the communities in Bukhara and the vicinity. He established Jewish schools in Bukhara, introduced the Sephardi rite in place of the Persian, and obtained books from *Baghdad, Constantinople, and particularly from Russia. Joseph Maman can be regarded as the spiritual father of the Ḥibbat Zion movement in Central Asia which, under the impact of his personality and teachings, brought thousands of Bukharian Jews to the Holy Land.

BIBLIOGRAPHY: S. Ḥakham, *Zekher Ẓaddik* (1894), 42a–47b; Yaari, Sheluḥei, 664–5; W.J. Fischel, in: L. Jung (ed.), *Jewish Leaders* (1953), 535–47; M. Eshel, *Galleryah: Demuyyot shel Rashei Yehudei Bukharah* (1968), 17–29.

[Walter Joseph Fischel]

JOSEPH MOSES BEN JEKUTHIEL ZALMAN (d. 1781), rabbi and kabbalist. At first he served as rabbi in Drohiczyn (near Pinsk), subsequently in Pinsk itself, and from 1746 in Sambor (Galicia). In his old age he migrated to Ereẓ Israel and died in Safed. He was the author of *Maggid Mishneh*, a commentary on *Mafte'aḥ ha-Olamot*, the first part of *Mishnat Ḥasidim*, the kabbalistic treatise of Immanuel Ḥai *Ricchi (printed with the text, Zolkiew, 1745); *Kiryat Arba*, a kabbalistic commentary to the *Shema*, together with a supplement to his *Maggid Mishneh* and *Ḥillukei de-Rabbanan*, talmudic novellae (*ibid.*, 1768). His *Ḥokhmat ha-Tekhunah*, a commentary on the astronomical portions of Maimonides' Code, was published in the introduction to the *Toledot Avraham* of Abraham b. Isaac Eisenberg (1881), while his *Mareh Ofannim* on astronomy and the calculation of the new moon has remained in manuscript, as has his *Mirkevet ha-Mishneh*, talmudic novellae.

BIBLIOGRAPHY: S. Wiener, *Kohelet Moshe* (1893–1918), 505, no. 4183; B. Wachstein, *Mafte'aḥ ha-Hespedim*, 1 (1922), 25; A. Yaari, *Meḥkerei Sefer* (1958), 454.

[*Encyclopaedia Judaica* (Germany)]

JOSEPH MOSES OF SALOSITZ (c. 1735–c. 1815), ḥasidic preacher. He was active in spreading Ḥasidism in Zborov and Salositz (Zalosce) and gave clear formulation both to his own ḥasidic teachings and those of others. Following *Dov Baer, the Maggid of Mezhirech, Joseph emphasized the theory that absolute evil does not exist but that there are different levels of good. According to him "justice (*din*) in itself is mercy (*hesed*)." *Ẓimẓum* ("concentration"), the creation of the world according to justice, is the equivalent of mercy which enables those created to receive and attain the divine emanation "because man is unable to attain divine emanation and God's mercies alone." He wrote *Berit Avraham* (Brody, 1875), a lengthy commentary on the Pentateuch, and *Be'er Mayim* (Medzibezh, 1817), on the Passover *Haggadah*.

JOSEPH OF GAMALA, Jewish patriot leader in the Jewish War (66–70/73 C.E.). Together with Chares, he organized the defense of Gamala when it was besieged by Vespasian in 67 C.E. The Romans were decisively repulsed in their first attack. The town fell, as a consequence of severe famine and lack of water, after a siege lasting nearly a month. Joseph was killed when trying to cut his way through the Roman ranks.

BIBLIOGRAPHY: Jos., Wars, 4:3–10; Schuerer, Hist, 35; Klausner, Bayit Sheni, 5 (1951^2), 197.

[Edna Elazary]

JOSEPH ROSH HA-SEDER (12th century), Egyptian rabbinical scholar. There is very little biographical information about him. He was born in *Baghdad. His father, Jacob, who died before 1211, was a pupil of *Samuel b. Ali, who sent him in 1187 to visit the communities of Babylonia as an emissary of the Baghdad yeshivah. Joseph emigrated to *Egypt in middle age, leaving behind him in Babylonia an extensive library. He earned his living as a scribe and copyist, and perhaps also as a bookseller. He is unique in having worked out for himself a series of rabbinic-literary projects of very wide scope, and even took preliminary steps for their implementation. Among the *Genizah documents, there are many fragments from planned works which never got beyond their first stage. His projects included compiling a *Gemara* for those tractates which have none, by assembling the relevant passages from the rest of the Talmud; connecting the oral with the written law by assembling Midrashim according to the weekly scriptural readings; a commentary on the Pentateuch and the *haftarot* taken from previous commentators; commentaries on the Mishnah, the Talmud, the code of *Alfasi and the prayer book of *Saadiah Gaon. Some of the extant fragments have been published. In order to facilitate his work, Joseph made a collection of numerous geonic responsa according to the order of the tractates, and for the same purpose compiled several lists of books, a number of which are extant. These lists contain material valuable for the history of rabbinical literature. It is worth mentioning Joseph's peculiar habit of applying to himself various honorific titles, some of them self-devised, e.g., *Rosh be-Rabbanan* ("Chief of the Scholars").

BIBLIOGRAPHY: Assaf, in: KS, 18 (1941/42), 272–81; Abramson *ibid.*, 26 (1949/50), 72–95; Benedikt, *ibid.*, 28 (1952/53), 229ff.; Allony, *ibid.*, 38 (1962/63), 531–57; Scheiber, *ibid.*, 44 (1968/69), 546–8.

[Israel Moses Ta-Shma]

JOSEPH SAMUEL BEN ẒEVI OF CRACOW (d. 1703), rabbi and talmudist. After having served for 26 years as a member of the Cracow *bet din*, he was in 1689 appointed rabbi in Frankfurt. There he established a yeshivah and headed charitable institutions. In his approbation (*haskamah*) to Ḥayyim Krochmal's *Mekor ha-Ḥayyim* (1697), he protested against the excessive publication of rabbinic literature in Germany, accusing the writers of many such works of "writing books not for the sake of Heaven… but seeking only their own benefit and advantage." He himself wrote several works on *halakhah* and *aggadah* but refrained from publishing them. His annotations to the Talmud were published by his son Aryeh Loeb in the Frankfurt and Amsterdam editions of the Talmud (1714–21), and appeared afterward in the Vienna and Sulzbach editions. Only one of his responsa has been published (in Enoch b. Abraham's *Ḥinnukh Beit Yehudah*, 137 (Frankfurt, 1710)).

BIBLIOGRAPHY: M. Horovitz, *Frankfurter Rabbinen*, 2 (1883), 56–57; Fuenn, Keneset, 505; H.N. Dembitzer, *Kelilat Yofi*, 1 (1888), 72a, n. 8; 2 (1893), 144b–151a; R.N.N. Rabbinovicz, *Ma'amar al Hadpasat ha-Talmud*, ed. by Habermann (1952), index.

[Yehoshua Horowitz]

JOSEPH SOLOMON ZALMAN BEN MEIR (18th cent.), Hungarian rabbi and author. Joseph Solomon Zalman was born in Pressburg in 1727. At the age of 19 he married the daughter, apparently, of Ezekiel *Landau, but he separated from her after 13 years of domestic unhappiness (he refers to his wife as "more bitter than death"; *Minḥat Ani*, introd.; cf. Eccles. 7:26). His life as a whole was one of suffering. In the introduction to his book he alludes to the baseless hatred of his enemies who "deprived me of property and of lives," and to the three of his children "sweet and pure" whom he buried in his lifetime. He wandered from place to place but found no peace. He was in Prague, Frankfurt on the Main, and Fuerth, and everywhere was welcomed with respect and love by the great scholars of his time. He writes (*Minḥat Ani*, 2nd ed., p. 29b) that he did not succeed in clarifying a certain subject "because of lack of strength and brokenheartedness, for I have not yet succeeded in returning in peace to my father's house and my native land, and if I succeed in this I shall fulfill my vows." It is not known where he died or was buried. In 1780 Joseph Solomon published in Prague his *Minḥat Ani*, novellae on talmudic themes; it was republished with additions in Fuerth in 1787. On the title page he mentions his book *Kunteres Aḥaron*, on Maimonides and Abraham b. David of Posquières, that he wanted to publish. Some of his novellae were published at the end of the *Noda bi-Yhudah Mahadura Kamma* (Prague, 1801) of Ezekiel Landau and in his *Ẓiyyun le-Nefesh Ḥayyah* (*Ẓelaḥ*) to *Pesaḥim* (Prague, 1783). His son, GABRIEL ISAAC PRESSBURGER, served as secretary to Ezekiel Landau, and his son SAMUEL was a teacher in Prague and also published *Religioese Gespraeche* (1825) and *Asefat Ḥakhamim* (1846), a collection of explanations of verses in the Pentateuch in Hebrew and German. Pressburger is also mentioned in the *Noda bi-Yhudah, Mahadura Tinyana* (E.H. nos. 67 and 120).

BIBLIOGRAPHY: J.J.(L.) Greenwald (Grunwald), *Ha-Yehudim be-Ungarya* (1913), 42 no. 22; P.Z. Schwartz, *Shem ha-Gedolim me-Ereẓ Hagar*, 3 (1915), 25a no. 71.

[Naphtali Ben-Menahem]

JOSEPHSON, Swedish family which had emigrated from Prussia in the late 18th century.

JACOB AXEL JOSEPHSON (1818–1880), conductor, composer, and writer, was born in Stockholm, the son of Salomon Josephson, a merchant. He studied at Uppsala University and, from 1841 (the year in which he converted to Christianity) to 1844, held various conducting and teaching posts. A grant by the famous singer Jenny Lind enabled him to tour and study on the Continent from 1844 to 1847. After directing the Stockholm Harmonic Society for two years, he was appointed *Director musices* of Uppsala University in 1849. In the same year he founded the Uppsala Philharmonic Society, which he headed for 30 years, and in 1867, the choir of Uppsala Cathedral. From 1864 onward he lectured at the university on music history. Under his direction, the Philharmonic Society Orchestra and the cathedral choir became the foremost performing bodies in Sweden and the first to achieve there, in the 19th century, a level comparable with the major European orchestras and choirs. Josephson's writings and his publications of musical anthologies were equally influential. Among his compositions, which were mostly in the Mendelssohn-Schumann vein, the vocal works predominate, and for many of these he wrote the words himself. Some of the works for chorus and orchestra and for male chorus have remained in the Swedish repertoire until today.

[Bathja Bayer]

His brother, LUDVIG OSCAR JOSEPHSON (1832–1899), was a stage director noted for his productions of Ibsen and Strindberg. Born in Stockholm, he began his career as an actor. His talent, however, lay in directing, and from 1865 to 1868 he was administrator of the national theaters. During this time he directed Shakespeare's *Coriolanus*, Byron's *Sardanapalus*, and Meyerbeer's opera, *L'Africaine*, as well as historical plays of his own. From 1873 to 1877 he worked in Christiania (now Oslo), where he became known for his brilliant presentations of Ibsen's *Peer Gynt* and *Pretenders*. Returning to the Swedish Theater in Stockholm (1879–87), he directed plays by the world's great dramatists and staged Strindberg's first important theatrical success, *Master Olof*.

[Viveka Heyman]

His nephew, ERNST ABRAHAM JOSEPHSON (1851–1906), was a well-known painter. He was born in Stockholm. A series of tragic events contributed to his eventual mental breakdown. As long as he adhered to traditional painting and acceptable subject matter, his talent was appreciated by both the Stockholm Academy and the Paris Salon. Difficulties arose after he became a follower of Courbet and then of Manet. Josephson's robust *Spanish Blacksmiths* was roundly rejected by all conservatives when displayed at the Paris Salon, as were his vital, non-posed portraits.

In Paris, Josephson became the leader of The Opponents, a group of Swedish artists who were dissatisfied with the aesthetic backwardness of Sweden. They sought far-reaching reforms and addressed a "Letter of Opposition" to the Swedish king. Josephson soon found out that he had become too radical to please his patron, the Swedish banker Pontus Fuerstenberg, who withdrew his support, and even too uncompromising for The Opponents, who selected a more conciliatory and prudent man as their new leader.

With his patronage lost and his inheritance exhausted, Josephson had recourse only to a friend, the Swedish painter Österlind, with whom he retreated to an island off the coast of Brittany. There the two experimented with spiritualism. Josephson began to have hallucinations: he believed himself to be in communication with Holbein, Velasquez, and Rembrandt, and signed his drawings with the name of the great one under whose "dictation" he had produced it. Realizing that his colleague had become seriously ill, Österlind took him to Sweden (1888), where Josephson was confined to a mental hospital. After he had regained some of his strength and balance he returned to live in Stockholm. In a novel, August Strindberg described the invalid as sitting in a cafe and gazing "far off into space as if he were alone with dreams and visions he could not communicate."

Yet the "sick" man did communicate – through art works, including over a thousand pen-and-ink drawings and about a hundred watercolors and oils. While his "healthy" work, though excellent, was largely eclectic, the work Josephson created after his breakdown was highly original. He became a full-fledged Expressionist more than 20 years before the term was coined, and he is treated with respect and even admiration in works of general art history as one of the precursors of Expressionism. His paintings are to be found in all major museums in the Scandinavian countries. In 1964 and 1965, a Josephson exhibition toured the United States.

[Alfred Werner]

GUNNAR JOSEPHSON (1889–1972) was also born in Stockholm and was a bookseller, community director, and magistrate. From 1936 to 1962, he was chairman of the governing board of the Stockholm Jewish community and was a member of the Swedish State Committee for Refugees during the Nazi period. Josephson was involved specifically in aiding the Jewish refugees who reached Sweden. He represented Jewish interests before the Swedish authorities.

RAGNAR JOSEPHSON (1891–1966), Gunnar's brother, was also born in Stockholm. An author and historian of the fine arts, he served as professor of the history of art at the University of Lund from 1929 to 1957. In a series of monographs he wrote about both North European and other works of art, especially those from the period of the Baroque. In Lund he founded a museum for the study of the North European monumental art and its development. In 1940 he published *Konstverkets födelse* ("Birth of the Work of Art"), the subject of his main interest. He was director of the Dramatic Theater in Stockholm from 1948 to 1951 and wrote dramatic works. He also published some anthologies, including *Judiska dikter* ("Jewish Poems," 1916; new edition 1943 as *Valda judiska dikter*) and in 1961 was elected to the Swedish Academy.

ERLAND JOSEPHSON (1923–), another member of the Josephson family, was an actor and author. He was a member of the City Theater Companies of Helsingborg (1945–49) and Göteborg (1949–56) before joining the national Dramatiska Teatern, Stockholm, of which he became administrator in 1966. Although he came from an assimilated family and knew little about Jewish tradition, Josephson often dealt with the theme of antisemitism in his writings. These include the novel *En Berättelse om herr Silberstein* ("A Tale About Mr. Silberstein," 1957) and the plays *Benjamin* (1963) and *Doktor Meyers sista dagar…* ("Doctor Meyer's Last Days," 1964). He acted in some of Peter Weiss's plays, playing the Marquis de Sade in *Marat-Sade* (1964) and Mulka in *The Investigation* (1965).

[Hugo Mauritz Valentin]

BIBLIOGRAPHY: MGG, incl. bibl.; Riemann-Einstein; Riemann-Gurlitt, incl. bibl.; Grove, Dict, incl. bibl.; Baker, Biog Dict (on Jacob Axel); S.L. Millner, *Ernst Josephson* (Eng., 1948); I. Mesterton, *Vägen till försoning* (Thesis, Göteborg, 1957; on Ernst); E. Blomberg, *Ernst Josephson, hans liv* (1951); idem, *Ernst Josephsons konst* (1956); *Vision och Gestalt. Studier tillägnade Ragnar Josephson* (1958), index.

JOSEPHSON, BRIAN DAVID (1940–), British physicist. Josephson was born in Cardiff, Wales, where he was a brilliant pupil. He studied physics at Cambridge, receiving his doctorate in 1964. In 1962, at the age of only 22, he discovered the Josephson effect, showing the special characteristics of tunneling between superconductors, which led to the attainment at IBM of switching speeds up to 100 times faster than those obtained with conventional chips and incomparably greater data-processing capabilities. In the same year he was made a fellow of Trinity College, Cambridge, subsequently becoming assistant director of research and reader in physics at the university and professor in 1974. He was appointed a fellow of the Royal Society in 1970. In 1969, he received a $10,000 Research Corporation award for his outstanding contribution to science and, in 1973, was awarded the Nobel Prize for physics (jointly with Dr. Ivar Giaever and Dr. Leon Esaki), one of the youngest men ever to receive this award.

JOSEPHSON, MANUEL (c. 1729–1796), merchant and leader in the Philadelphia and New York Jewish communities. Josephson was born in Germany and emigrated to New York City. During the French and Indian War he was a sutler, and during the Revolution supplied the Congressional Army with weapons. In 1762 Josephson was named president of Congregation Shearith Israel in New York. He fled to Philadelphia during the American Revolution, remaining there permanently. Having a considerable Hebrew education, Josephson quickly rose to a position of eminence in Philadelphia, and was appointed president of Congregation Mikveh Israel in 1785. He was given the honor of extending the congratulations of four Jewish communities to George Washington on his assumption of the presidency in 1790.

BIBLIOGRAPHY: Rosenbloom, Biogr Dict 77.

[Leo Hershkowitz]

JOSEPHSON, MATTHEW (1899–1978), U.S. author and historian. Born in Brooklyn, he lived for a time in Paris. He was a member of the editorial board of the international arts magazine *Broom* (1921–24), U.S. editor of *Transition* (1928–29), and assistant editor of the *New Republic* (1931–32). After a brief period in Wall Street, Josephson returned to literature in 1930 and became known as a writer on 19th-century French literature and American economic history. His books on French literature include biographical studies such as *Zola and His Time* (1928), *Jean-Jacques Rousseau* (1931), and *Victor Hugo* (1942). He made a significant contribution to the revival of American interest in Stendhal with the study he published in 1946. Josephson's books on American history are moderately leftist in their approach, particularly in regard to the growth of industry. *The Robber Barons* (1934) dealt with the emergence of the 19th-century industrial and railroad magnates. His study of political corruption appeared in two volumes: *The Politicos, 1865–1896* (1938) and *The President Makers: 1896–1919* (1940). His other works include *Portrait of the Artist as American* (1930); *Empire of the Air* (1943), the story of an airline; *Sidney Hillman, Statesman of American Labor* (1952); *Union House, Union Bar* (1956); and *Edison* (1959), a biography. Josephson also wrote two volumes of recollections, *Life among the Surrealists* (1962) and *The Infidel in the Temple: A Memoir of the 1930's* (1967).

BIBLIOGRAPHY: S.J. Kunitz and H. Haycraft, *Twentieth Century Authors* (1942), and *First Supplement* (1955). **ADD. BIBLIOGRAPHY:** D. Shi, *Matthew Josephson, Bourgeois Bohemian* (1981).

[Hans L. Trefousse]

JOSEPHTAL, LOUIS MAURICE (1869–1929), U.S. naval officer. Born in New Rochelle, N.Y., Josephtal joined the New York naval militia in 1891 and during the Spanish-American War (1898) was an assistant paymaster. During World War I he was a captain (paymaster) at the naval militia headquarters. In 1923 he was appointed rear admiral in the supply corps and was later commander of the New York naval militia. An observant Jew, Josephtal was active in Jewish affairs and was a director of Mount Sinai Hospital for many years.

JOSEPHTHAL, GIORA (**Georg Josephsthal**; 1912–1962), Israeli social worker and labor leader. Born in Nuremberg, Germany, to an assimilated family, Josephthal joined the pioneering Zionist youth movement during the period of the Nazi rise to power. As a social worker in the Munich Jewish community, he established the Berufsumschichtung, a professional training project for Jewish youth preparing for settlement in Palestine. In 1934 he became director of the *Youth Aliyah office in Berlin and two years later secretary of the *He-Ḥalutz movement in Germany. He went to Palestine in 1938 and led the group that established kibbutz Gal-Ed in 1945. In World War II he joined the British army. After the war he began organizing the *Jewish Agency's Absorption Department and was successively director of the Absorption Department and treasurer of the Jewish Agency's executive. In 1952 he participated in the *reparations negotiations with West Germany. In 1956 he became general secretary of *Mapai and, three years later, was elected to the Fourth *Knesset and appointed minister of labor. In this capacity he continued the work of absorption through the building of housing projects and the development of technical training and an employment service. His last post was that of minister of housing and development. His wife, SENTA (1912–), was born in Fuerth, Germany, settled in Palestine in 1938, and was also a founding member of kibbutz Gal-Ed. She served in various positions in the *Histadrut and the Iḥud ha-Kevuẓot ve-ha-Kibbutzim and was a member of the Third Knesset.

BIBLIOGRAPHY: B. Halpern and S. Wurm, *The Responsible Attitude, Life and Work of Giora Josephthal* (1966); H. Laufbahn, *Ish Yoẓe el Eḥav* (1968).

JOSEPHUS FLAVIUS (c. 37–after 100 C.E.), Jewish historian and one of the chief representatives of Jewish-Hellenistic literature.

BIOGRAPHY

Early Life

Born in Jerusalem into an aristocratic priestly family belonging to the *mishmeret* of Jehoiarib, through his mother Josephus was related to the Hasmonean dynasty. Josephus relates of himself that in his youth he was so renowned for his knowledge of the Torah that high priests and leading men of the city would come to consult him on matters of *halakhah*, and he was apparently distinguished in his youth as an aggadist. At all events, he was certainly not ignorant of the Torah, as many scholars have maintained. From the age of 16 he spent three years with a certain Bannus, who appears to have been a member of one of the many contemporary sects (but not necessarily an *Essene), who lived an ascetic life in the wilderness, wore clothes made of leaves, fed on wild herbs – like John the Baptist (Matt. 3:4) – and made ablutions in the morning and evening. In 64 C.E., at the age of 26, Josephus was sent on a mission to Rome to secure the release of some priests who had been seized and delivered to Rome by the procurator *Felix to render an account to the emperor for some offense they had committed. Josephus was probably selected for this mission because of his knowledge of Greek. With the help of the Jewish actor Aliturus he obtained an introduction to the empress *Poppaea Sabina; his efforts were crowned with success and the priests were released. The visit had a profound effect on Josephus, Rome making an indelible impression on him.

As Commander of Galilee During the Jewish War

At the outbreak of the Jewish War (66 C.E.), Josephus was appointed commander of Galilee, which was probably the most important military assignment during the first stage of the war. Despite this he seems to have belonged to the moderate party that had gained control after the victory over Cestius *Gallus, and it was hoped that he would exert his influence at a critical juncture to achieve a compromise settlement. Simeon b. Gamaliel could have found no one more suitable for this purpose than Josephus, since the latter was quite capable of outwitting his rivals until an opportune moment arrived to work for peace. However, it remains uncertain whether John of Giscala was actually ousted from the leadership in Galilee on explicit instructions from Jerusalem and overall command given to Josephus by the Sanhedrin, since his account of his operations in Galilee (contained in the *Life*) is extremely vague, and gives the impression that he conceals more than he reveals. Josephus may have acted on his own responsibility when he sought to supersede John. In any case there is no justification for the theory that Josephus was never sent to Galilee but seized control there against the wishes of the Sanhedrin even before the outbreak of the revolt. In fact Josephus seems to have come to Galilee only after Cestius Gallus' defeat, which marked the beginning of the revolt.

The position of the Sanhedrin's envoy was a difficult one, since the local Galilean leaders had no wish to accept a man who had been appointed over them by the central authority in Jerusalem. Because of this there was continuous strife, and clashes took place between Josephus and John and his Galilean supporters. John failed in his attempt to induce the Sanhedrin to recall Josephus, and the conflict in Galilee persisted until the arrival of *Vespasian in the spring of 67 C.E. The country, unprepared for hostilities, was wholly unable to wage an offensive war. The cities, which Josephus claimed to have fortified, were isolated from one another and could only defend themselves singly, without any cohesion or plan. The decisive battle took place around the city of Jotapata, to which Josephus had retired and which resisted for six weeks. When the city fell on Tammuz 1, 67, Josephus fled with 40 men to a cave. There each man resolved to slay his neighbor rather than be taken captive by the enemy. Josephus artfully cast the lots, deceitfully managing to be one of the two last men left alive and then persuaded his companion to go out with him and surrender to the Romans.

Josephus' "Prophecy" Regarding Vespasian

Josephus relates that when he appeared before Vespasian he foretold the greatness in store for the Roman commander, who spared his life, binding him in chains only. This is a very surprising account, for the Talmud tells a similar story except that there the prophecy was made by R. *Johanan b. Zakkai. In fact, there is some substance in both accounts. Presumably under no circumstances would Josephus have dared so brazenly to misrepresent the truth had the story been a complete fabrication, since *The Jewish War* was written under the patronage of the emperor and its contents sanctioned by the imperial dynasty. The emperor would hardly have assented to the account had it not contained a nucleus of truth, which led him to accept the fictitious element in the story as well. The primary fabrication was that the "prophecy" was not made by Josephus when he appeared as a captive before Vespasian, who received the rebel commander as a prisoner of war punishable with death. It was apparently Vespasian's intention to have him taken to Rome and there to execute him during his triumph, as he later did to *Simeon b. Giora. Josephus was held prisoner in the Roman camp for the duration of Vespasian's campaign until the news was received of Nero's death (68 C.E.). This information undoubtedly caused a stir in Vespasian's camp too, and the ferment increased greatly when word was heard of the death of Galba (69 C.E.), who had been proclaimed emperor. The officers and troops began to entertain the idea of appointing an emperor of their own.

His Exploitation of Circumstances Surrounding Nero's Death

Josephus was determined to exploit this new state of affairs to his own advantage, shrewdly perceiving it as an opportunity for obtaining his freedom – and perhaps even more – if only he was able to make proper use of the favorable turn of events. He was fully aware of the prophecy, which was widespread in

Judea and throughout the east, that the ruler of the world was destined to come forth from Judea. An echo of it even reached the Romans. The basis of the prophecy was undoubtedly messianic, and Josephus, when mentioning it in *The Jewish War*, adds that the Zealots interpreted it as referring to the Messiah. It was then that Josephus, having decided to make use of the belief to gain his freedom, gave it added force by dilating on the prophecy. To convince the Romans, Josephus attributed to himself the qualities of a diviner, which gave great encouragement to the soldiers. It may be asserted that Josephus' "prophecy" was uttered between January 15, the date of Galba's death, and July 1, 69 C.E., the day on which Vespasian was proclaimed emperor in Alexandria, Egypt. The role played by Josephus is somewhat similar to that of Agrippa I at the time of Claudius' accession, and in both instances the intermediary was richly rewarded by the victor. Vespasian undoubtedly learned of Josephus' share in the propaganda on his behalf and, bearing it in mind, awaited coming events.

While all this was taking place in Vespasian's camp, the conquering army advanced still nearer to Jerusalem, a move made necessary by the appearance of Simeon b. Giora and his troops. The whole of Judea was now taken, except for Jerusalem and its immediate environs. The proximity of the Roman army spread the knowledge in the city of events in the enemy camp. Realizing immediately that Vespasian would become emperor, R. Johanan b. Zakkai reasoned that a new ruler, confronted as he would be with weighty problems, might be prepared to reach a peaceful solution, and would be disposed to bring this provincial war to a speedy conclusion.

In Jerusalem with Titus

When Vespasian was proclaimed emperor at Caesarea, Josephus, who was with him there, was released from his chains. From there he went to Alexandria, and when *Titus was given command of the army with orders to take Jerusalem, Josephus accompanied him. Josephus tried several times to induce the rebels to lay down their arms, but they treated him with contempt, and during one of his exhortations injured him. Nor was his position an enviable one in the Roman camp, for the Romans suspected him of being a spy and would have killed him had he not enjoyed Titus' protection. He continued to accompany Titus after the capture of Jerusalem. When Titus permitted him to remove from the ruins of Jerusalem whatever he wished, he took a *Sefer Torah*. His estate in the neighborhood of Jerusalem was confiscated by Titus and instead he received land in the valley of Jezreel.

Favored by Roman Rulers and Hated by Jews

Josephus left to settle in Rome where he was granted Roman citizenship and a pension by the emperor, who allowed him to live in his palace. He never again saw his native land. Although generally a favorite among the members of the courts of Vespasian and Titus during their lifetime, Josephus' position vis-à-vis the Jews was wretched in the extreme. Both in and outside Rome, they despised and hated him for his past and tried to harm him at every turn. After the suppression of the revolt of the *Zealots, who had escaped to Cyrene, the rebels accused him of having been the organizer, but Vespasian refused to believe them.

Inauspicious Family Life

Josephus' family life, too, was inauspicious. In all he was married four times. His first wife died during the siege. The second, whom he married on the advice of Vespasian, left him. In Alexandria he took a third wife who bore him three children, of whom one son, Hyrcanus, born in 72/73 C.E., survived. Having divorced this wife, Josephus married an aristocratic woman from Crete who bore him two sons, Justus and Simonides-Agrippa. The year of Josephus' death is unknown, but it was probably after 100 C.E.

WORKS

The Jewish War

It is very probable that Josephus' decision to become the historian of the Jewish War stemmed primarily from the fact that he was subject to the emperor's wishes and obliged to support his political aims. His history was probably the price exacted by the emperor in return for the grant of freedom and property. Fully appreciating Josephus' talents, Vespasian knew that the freedman could be of use to him in both his foreign and internal policy. After the events in the east and west of the Roman Empire, the fate of the entire state hung in the balance and Vespasian found himself obliged to warn the still powerful enemies of Rome that she could destroy any foe who intended to renew the war.

LOST ARAMAIC VERSION. In the introduction to *The Jewish War* Josephus clearly mentions that he wrote two versions of "the war of the Jews against the Romans," first "in my vernacular," that is, in Aramaic, "for the up-country barbarians." These were the Aramaic-speaking peoples in the lands of the Parthian kingdom, principally the Jews living in Babylonia, who, contrary to the rebels' hopes, had played no considerable part in the war but who were likely to flock to join the fighting should hostilities break out afresh. In this version, which unfortunately has not been preserved, Josephus undoubtedly included material not found in the extant Greek rendering. It presumably also contained factual accounts different from those in the Greek version. At the beginning of the century the German-Baltic scholar Behrends published an ancient Slavonic translation of *The Jewish War*, which he claimed was based on the original Aramaic version, a contention, however, without foundation; nor did Robert Eisler succeed in substantiating it in his great work (see bibl.).

THE EXTANT GREEK VERSION. The extant Greek version, which was adapted by Josephus from the Aramaic work, was divided into seven books by the author himself. However it seems that at first it was intended to comprise only six books, up to the destruction of Jerusalem, as attested by the title "The Capture" (ἅλωσις) given to the work in most manuscripts. The Greek version also served the internal political purpose of bolstering the dynasty which had recently acceded to the throne. Through it the emperor sought to prove to the Roman aristocracy, who despised the Sabine peasant who had risen to eminence, that although he and his sons were *homines novi* in the Roman polity their merit was by far the greater. Since Josephus' Greek rendering of *The Jewish War* was intended to serve as the new dynasty's mouthpiece in Rome, Vespasian and Titus consented to accept the text of the work from him and to sanction its contents. This approval was used by Josephus as proof that he had told the truth and only the truth.

PRINCIPLES PROFESSED BY JOSEPHUS AND DEFECTS IN THE WORK. In his introduction the author declares that he has described the war without bias. Unlike other writers, who had not been eyewitnesses of events and whose obvious intention was to flatter certain persons, he, a native of Jerusalem, had himself fought against the Romans as long as resistance was possible but afterward had become reconciled to the enemy; hence his account was credible. His undoubted aim was to give his work a pragmatic character in keeping with the theory developed by Polybius, in particular, which, rejecting historiography, espoused "truth" and "accuracy." Although Josephus advocated these principles, he cannot be said always to have applied them in practice. As well as being subject to the imperial dynasty, he had a personal interest in revealing some things and in concealing others, better passed over in silence. His own reprehensible actions are shrouded in obscurity or completely evaded. There is no hint of his incompetence on the battlefield, and instead there is boasting based on obvious lies. The Romans' methods of warfare are always portrayed as pure and unsullied. Titus and Vespasian act only under constraint for which they deserve no censure. They refrain from excessive cruelty and are anxious to save the Jews, but the "bandits" are responsible for deterioration in the situation. The Jewish people did not want war at all; it was forced on them by the "robbers." An entirely different picture of the complete participation of the whole people, both men and women, in the war is presented by the anti-Jewish Tacitus, but every historical fact likely to support this view is deliberately omitted by Josephus. In one passage only – Titus' speech to the Zealots – does he have the former voice a comment which was undoubtedly current, namely, that the Jews were always the sworn enemies of Rome. A more serious defect is his distortion of the messianic movement in Judea and its role in fanning the flames of war, doubtless an intentional perversion of the state of affairs in order to represent the Jewish War as the action of limited circles, with the aim of exculpating the nation as a whole in the eyes of the Roman administration.

ITS LITERARY AND HISTORIOGRAPHIC VALUE. These defects naturally diminish the value of Josephus' work as history and in this respect it must be treated with considerable caution. Nonetheless it must be emphasized that the excellence of the work, in both its literary and historiographic qualities, earns it an honorable place in Jewish and in general literature. Its literary skill is considerable: the descriptions are epic in the full sense of the word, scenes are plastically and impressively portrayed, the horrors and the vast spectacle of war are graphically depicted, culminating in one great panorama with the destruction of Jerusalem and the burning of the Temple. Much of *The Jewish War* derives from the author's personal observation. This is especially true of the description of the actual siege. Josephus noted everything he saw, and in addition made use of evidence obtained from those who defected to Titus' camp. These details have a documentary or semi-documentary value.

Great significance attaches also to some descriptions of the war which are almost certainly based on Roman military reports, their Roman origin being apparent in their style, which is concise, dry, and devoid of all rhetorical embellishment. Official material on the stationing of Roman garrisons throughout the kingdom can be discerned in Agrippa's great speech. In this passage, Josephus apparently used an official document made accessible to him from the imperial archives: the speech is a remarkably fervent recapitulation of official propaganda by a lackey of the lord of the Roman Empire. In addition, Josephus made use of works compiled by other writers on the Jewish War. The book is constructed in three sections, with the account of the war as the principal, central one. The first section opens with the events that preceded the revolt of the Maccabeans and continues with a description of the history of the Hasmonean and Herodian dynasties up to the outbreak of the Jewish War (bk. 1 and about half of bk. 2). The second section recounts various episodes of the war, such as the siege of *Masada and the final death agonies of the Jewish people's opposition, as well as several important details about the kingdom of the Parthians. Josephus' sources for the material in the introductory section were a work on the Hasmonean dynasty written originally in Hebrew and Nicholas of *Damascus' great work which provided him with the information on the Herodian dynasty recounted in this section.

ITS LANGUAGE AND STYLE. The Greek of *The Jewish War* is often excellent, but very probably the style was largely the result of polishing by Josephus' literary assistants. According to his own testimony his accent was defective, and his insufficient command of literary Greek is attested by his large work *Jewish Antiquities*, the language of which is poor, sometimes even labored, largely artificial, and much inferior to the clear, flowing style of *The Jewish War*. The careful attention paid to the style of this latter work probably resulted from its official character. It was, moreover, Josephus' first production, the one which would gain him a place in the literary world in Rome. Among the auspicious circumstances of the work was his comparatively youthful age when he wrote it, for he was about 40 years old when it was published, whereas he completed the *Antiquities* at the age of 56. Furthermore the *Antiquities*, unlike *The Jewish War*, was written with the aim of enlightening the non-Jewish world about the nature of Judaism, that it might understand the extent to which it was mistaken in its judgment of the Jewish people.

Jewish Antiquities

The work was the outcome both of the objective circumstances of Jewish life in the Diaspora, and of Josephus' personal conclusions drawn from his experience in Rome, where he saw the Jewish people living in a non-Jewish environment and yet preserving its character and observing its religion.

ITS PURPOSES: ENLIGHTENMENT OF THE GENTILES; PROOF OF THE ANTIQUITY OF THE JEWS. For the first time he came face to face with the gentiles' hatred of the Jews and it appeared to him that nothing but their ignorance of the religion of Israel was responsible. Feeling that if only the gentiles knew and understood the light that permeated Judaism, they would certainly forsake their capricious behavior and cease their hostility toward the Jews, Josephus drew the clear and simple conclusion: he had to teach the non-Jews a lesson in Jewish history so as to show them the error of their ways. The title, *Jewish Antiquities*, was apparently chosen by him on the analogy of *Antiquitates Romanae* by Dionysius of Halicarnassus who lived during the reign of the emperor Augustus; but it also hints at the chief aim which Josephus set himself in this work: to prove the antiquity of Jews and to dispel the slander that the Jewish nation was not an ancient one.

HELLENISTIC, AGGADIC, AND HALAKHIC ASPECTS. He recounts the biblical events, but not as they are given in the Bible. Josephus' approach is that of a Hellenistic writer who, never forgetting his audience, adapts his writing to their taste. A Hellenistic flavor is often added to the narrative, as, for example, in the story of Joseph and Potiphar's wife. The Jewish reader, too, is rewarded with aggadic statements which, taken from literary sources, embellish biblical tales. Some of Josephus' aggadic Midrashim are known from existing sources, others have not been preserved in the extant literature and Josephus is their only source. In these passages he reveals himself as an outstanding aggadist. Nor were halakhic subjects alien to him. Book 4 of his great work contains *halakhot* which are not in agreement with the existing *halakhah*, which should not be interpreted as ignorance on Josephus' part but rather as a halakhic tradition no longer extant, either because it was rejected or because it was forgotten in the course of time.

HELLENISTIC SOURCES FOR BIBLICAL NARRATIVES. In his version of the biblical narratives Josephus preserved many quotations and notices from Jewish-Hellenistic and also from general Hellenistic literature insofar as the latter touches on Jewish subjects, including such writers such as *Artapanus, *Cleodemus Malchus, Berosus, *Manetho, *Menander of Ephesus, and others. There are divergent views on the sources of Josephus' information, some maintaining that he had read the authors in the original, others that he had only an indirect acquaintance with them. In all probability the former view is correct, at least with regard to an author such as Berosus. For a recently published, new Babylonian source, a chronicle of the days of Nebuchadnezzar, reveals Josephus' accuracy on the events preceding the destruction of the First Temple, making it clear that he could only have derived his remarkably precise knowledge from Berosus' work itself. He undoubtedly also used compilations such as that of Alexander Polyhistor as an important source.

USE OF THE SEPTUAGINT FOR BIBLICAL NARRATIVES AND FOR THE PERSIAN PERIOD. There is no basis for the contention that Josephus was ignorant of Hebrew and did not read the Bible in the original. Nevertheless he used mainly the *Septuagint, in a version significantly different from the existing one, as several clear indications testify, notably the personal names found primarily in the *Antiquities*. As stated, Josephus' first work was written in Aramaic and only later, at the request of the imperial court, in Greek. His progress along the path of Hellenistic literature, so completely strange to him, was not easy. It is reasonable to assume that his original draft was in Aramaic and that assistants helped him to give it a Greek garb worthy of the name. In the course of time however there naturally came a change for the better, since there is no doubt that with his talents Josephus had ample opportunities in Rome to improve his knowledge of the language. Yet from his own evidence, referred to previously, it may be concluded that Greek remained a strange tongue to him throughout his life. Using the Septuagint apparently made it easier for him to cast the biblical narratives in a Hellenistic mold than following the Hebrew original, though the language of the Septuagint, which was the Greek spoken by the Jewish masses in Egypt and the rest of the Diaspora, was not agreeable to the fastidious Atticist taste of the public in Rome. Nevertheless, copying the biblical narratives on the basis of the Septuagint version made matters somewhat easier for him, a consideration that presumably played a part in his decision to use it. There is however not a single reference to the prophetical books in the work. This omission apparently resulted from the fact that Josephus wrote for a non-Jewish public, to whom the figure of Moses was familiar, while the Prophets were, it seems, completely unknown to the enlightened Hellenistic world.

The second section of the *Antiquities*, which begins near the end of book 11, opens with an account of the period of Persian rule in Ereẓ Israel. From this account it can be seen that few of the sources extant at present were available to Josephus. Using the Septuagint, he filled out the gaps in the Book of Esther, which he regarded as historical.

POSSIBLE SAMARITAN SOURCE FOR PERSIAN PERIOD. In addition, book 11 contains an extract from an unknown source with regard to the murder committed in the Temple in Jerusalem during the rule of the Persian governor *Bagohi, which Josephus may have taken from a Samaritan source that probably included the description of Alexander the Great's arrival in Ereẓ Israel and the foundation of the Samaritan temple on Mount Gerizim. That there is a historical background to this account of the murder can be seen from the *Elephantine papyri which mention two of the men who figure in it: Bagohi, the Persian governor, and Johanan, the high priest. Thus for the obscure Persian period, too, great importance attaches to the scanty material furnished by Josephus.

TREATMENT OF THE PTOLEMAIC PERIOD AND EVIDENCE OF JOSEPHUS' WEAKNESS AS HISTORIAN. He was however almost entirely ignorant of the rule of the Ptolemies in Ereẓ Israel, filling in the void with the Letter of *Aristeas and with the story of Joseph the Tobiad, the tax-collector, which has at least a historical background and substance (see *Tobiads). Instead of revealing his importance as a transmitter of historical information, Josephus here demonstrates his weakness as a historian. The story about Joseph the tax-collector undoubtedly refers to the time of Ptolemy III and Ptolemy IV, that is, up to the end of the third century B.C.E. Josephus however tells the story as though it took place after the conquest of Ereẓ Israel by Antiochus III, that is, after 200 B.C.E., and resolves the incongruity between the contents of the story and its insertion within the context of the Seleucid conquest by the comment, which has its origin in propaganda for the restoration of Ptolemaic rule in Ereẓ Israel, that Ereẓ Israel and the cities of *Coele-Syria were given by Antiochus III as a dowry to his daughter Cleopatra on her marriage to Ptolemy V, the king of Egypt.

Josephus' lack of awareness of the contradiction attests to his weakness as a historian. He was guilty of inaccuracy, and many passages indicate that his critical sense was not highly developed. He skims over the surface of events rather than penetrate into their inner significance. He gives scant attention to the events preceding Antiochus III's conquest of Ereẓ Israel without mentioning anything of the development in Judea on the eve of the conquest. In this respect he is far inferior to the later *Porphyry whose brilliant analysis of the historical background of the Book of Daniel is incorporated in *Jerome's commentary on that book.

THREE DOCUMENTS FROM THE PTOLEMAIC PERIOD. Josephus quotes three extremely important documents: the first is Antiochus III's proclamation in favor of the Temple in Jerusalem; the second prohibited unclean animals from being brought within the limits of the holy city; while the third decreed the transfer of 2,000 Jewish families from Babylonia to Phrygia and Lydia as military colonists, who were charged with preserving law and order in those countries, then in a state of rebellion following the revolt of Achaeus (see: *Antiochus III).

THE MACCABEAN AND HASMONEAN PERIOD. The account of the Maccabean and Hasmonean period commences in the middle of book 12. Josephus' source for this period is primarily I Maccabees, but there are indications that the history of the Hasmonean dynasty up to the death of *Salome Alexandra, or perhaps only to the end of Alexander *Yannai's reign, was copied by him from a comprehensive work written originally in Hebrew and later translated into Greek. The contention of some scholars that Nicholas of Damascus was the source of Josephus' information on Salome Alexandra is untenable.

NICHOLAS OF DAMASCUS AS SOURCE FOR HERODIAN PERIOD. Nicholas' share in Josephus' work is to be found in books 14–17, that is, from the end of the Hasmonean dynasty to the establishment of the rule of the procurators in Judea in 6 C.E. The main part of this lengthy section describes Herod's accession and his great achievements during his rule in Judea, though Josephus undoubtedly adopted a critical attitude toward Herod's rule and did not accept all Nicholas' statements about him. For example, he rejects the story of Herod's Babylonian origin, regarding it as expressive of Nicholas' flattery of Herod who wished to free himself from the disability of being a "half-Jew" and to be considered as descended from those Jews of pure descent who came back from Babylonia. Against Nicholas, Josephus declares that Herod throughout his life craved honor and that it was this craving that prompted him to squander his money with the aim of acquiring a great reputation in the Hellenistic-Roman world. Josephus regards the murder of Herod's sons as an abhorrent deed, which only a man with the soul of a murderer could perpetrate.

INFORMATION ON DIASPORA COMMUNITIES IN ROMAN TIMES. Because of his admiration for Rome, Josephus included in his work a number of documents, most of them in book 14, which testify to the favorable attitude of the Roman Empire toward the communities in the Diaspora. Although preserved in a state that is far from satisfactory, their importance is inestimable. The view put forward in the 19th century that these documents are forgeries has now been discarded. They reveal the position of the Jewish communities in Hellenistic society, the pent-up hatred of the gentile world for the Jewish religion, and the suspicions that accompanied the Jews everywhere, even to the extent of the wish to extirpate them. On the other hand they show how the Roman administration endeavored to act impartially and to protect the Jews from the attacks of the more populous nations. They also mirror the struggle of the communities for the observance of the precepts of Judaism and their loyalty to Jerusalem, as a result of which they aroused the anger of the gentiles. The documents are also important for the information they provide on the many privileges granted to the Jews by the Roman administration, first and foremost exemption from military service for religious reasons. The source from which Josephus obtained these documents is not known. He may have copied them from Nicholas of Damascus' work, but more probably they came from special collections of documents dealing with the rights granted to the Jews, which were to be found in large communities, like Alexandria, Ephesus, Rome, and great cities in the empire such as Cyrene.

The last part of the *Antiquities*, consisting of books 18–20, presents a difficulty both in its sources and the manner in which the events are recounted.

CONTROVERSIAL PASSAGE ON JESUS. One of the great riddles of the work, and perhaps of ancient history in general, is the well-known passage about Jesus of Nazareth in book 18 which scholars have not yet succeeded in elucidating. Some regarded it as a Christian forgery of the third century C.E., others still consider it as historical evidence of the activities and death of Jesus; but the passage contains statements which could not have been made by a Jew such as Josephus, as Schuerer recognized. Around the 1930s–1940s there was a change in scholarly outlook, the passage being regarded not as a forgery, but as Josephus' original statement tampered with by a Christian. The foremost proponent of this view was Robert Eisler (see bibliography) who even made an unsuccessful attempt to reconstruct the original version. For the period from the procurators to the reign of Agrippa I, Josephus apparently used material from the Roman archives and the works of other authors, but on the whole he writes as a contemporary eyewitness.

FAVORABLE ACCOUNT OF AGRIPPA I. The account of Agrippa I which occupies part of book 18 and the whole of book 19 gives the impression of a uniformity that undoubtedly proves that it had a single source. The division of the material seemed reasonable to Josephus, desirous as he was of giving an account of Agrippa's reign in relation to the events which took place in the days of the emperors Gaius Caligula and Claudius. In this part of the *Antiquities*, it is very likely that Josephus copied the work of his rival *Justus of Tiberias ("On the Crowned Kings of Judah" as it is to be translated, in contradiction to Schuerer, who understands στέμματα as meaning "pedigree"). In it Justus gave an account of the Jewish kings up to Agrippa I, apparently on the instructions of Agrippa II, who wishing to glorify the memory of his father, assigned to his secretary, Justus of Tiberias, the task of writing a work describing the activities of Agrippa I. Clearly the account had to be favorable; and indeed Agrippa I is depicted in the *Antiquities* in a decidedly complimentary light.

ACCOUNTS OF THE TWO BABYLONIAN JEWS AND OF THE ADIABENE ROYAL HOUSE. A large part of book 18 consists of the gripping story of two Babylonian Jews, the brothers Anilaeus and Asinaeus. Book 20 contains the remarkable episode of the proselytization of the royal house of *Adiabene. The two events took place in adjacent regions in which Aramaic was the vernacular. What prompted Josephus to incorporate them in his work? He apparently used the story of the two Babylonian brothers for Roman propaganda purposes aimed primarily at the Jews throughout the Roman Empire, in order that, in the days following the destruction of the Second Temple, they should not entertain any further idea of rebellion, since Rome was ultimately the empire of law and justice with which, unlike countries beyond its borders, it was possible to negotiate. The account of the proselytization of the Adiabene royal house was apparently included by Josephus in book 20 (which deals with the 22 years prior to the outbreak of the Jewish War) because of the part played by the Adiabene royal family in the final days of the Second Temple in general and in the Jewish War in particular. Josephus describes the events contained at the end of book 20 as an actual eyewitness. This book concludes with a list of the high priests from the time of Alexander the Great until the Jewish War, the source for this being, at least from the days of Herod onward, the genealogies of the priests in general and of the high priests in particular which were kept in the Temple archives. Josephus' list is far from clear: much in it is obscure, and the problems it raises have not been satisfactorily solved.

The Life

Finally, there are Josephus' last two works, the *Life* and *Against Apion*. The former was written in response to the attacks of Justus of Tiberias, who accused him of misconduct in Galilee before the arrival of Vespasian and his army, charging in particular that he belonged to the war party, was an enemy of Rome, had suppressed the peace party in Tiberias, committed acts of brigandage, and violated women. Such allegations were highly unpalatable to Josephus, in his position of access to the upper circles in Rome. Josephus' defense conceals more than it reveals, clearly evading any straightforward answers and thereby indirectly confirming Justus' accusations. The testimony of King Agrippa, intended as evidence in his favor, is so worded that it is actually tantamount to an indictment. The *Life* apparently appeared as an appendix to the *Antiquities*, which was published in 93/94 C.E., according to Josephus' own testimony. It seems that Justus' accusation became current shortly before, and Josephus took the first available opportunity to answer him. The *Life*, then, was written either in continuation of, or soon after, the *Antiquities* but before it appeared on the book market in Rome, that is, in 93/94 C.E. or, as held by Laqueur (see bibliography), together with the second edition of the *Antiquities*, between 93/94 and 100 C.E.

Against Apion

In *Against Apion* (or, *On the Antiquity of the Jews*, the original title of the work), which consists of two parts, Josephus lashes out against various antisemites and seeks to refute their accusations with logical arguments and with biting derision. The work reveals outstanding literary skill and great persuasiveness. The first part, a lengthy series of extracts from works no longer extant, in particular from the Egyptian Manetho, is especially significant since it is the only record of a whole body of literature which would otherwise have been completely unknown. This part constitutes a negative defense of the Jews, i.e., it sets out to refute the contentions of the antisemites. The purpose of the positive defense in the second part was to reveal the inner value of Judaism and its ethical superiority over Hellenism. In this part especially Josephus appears as a Jew completely committed to his people and his religion. Here the true Josephus is revealed, not the one who acted treacherously toward his comrades to save his life, but Josephus the Jew who fights his people's fight, and suffers with them.

EVALUATION OF JOSEPHUS

As a Jew

On this subject there are opposing views. By some he is regarded as a traitor who, deserting his people in their hour of need, defected to the enemy, and acting as the apologist of the Romans, distorted the facts. A more charitable view contends that he was essentially a Pharisee who acted in conformity with this outlook, had faith in the future of the Jewish people whose survival depended on submission to Rome, and sordid though the manner was in which he saved his life, he did so in order to devote himself to the highest interests of his people.

As a Writer

As for his merit as an author, it may be said that in point of literary talent Josephus ranks among the leading writers in world literature. His style is epic, his portrayals plastic, his gift of description captivates the reader alike by its fidelity and its colorful presentation. All these qualities apply to what, from the literary aspect, is his principal work, *The Jewish War*, which is marked by a complete identity between the author and his calamitous subject. The reader believes the writer as he mourns over the city, becomes an actual eyewitness as he presents the dramatic picture of the burning of the Temple or the tragic bravery of the heroes of Masada. The pathos inherent in the occasion communicates itself to the reader.

As a Historian

Not so, however, is his merit as a historian. Josephus is, of course, not to be judged according to the criteria of a modern historian. The expression "historical science" does not apply to ancient historiography, for in ancient times the historian was a writer and his craft part of general literature. This aspiration of the historian proved his misfortune, since the requirements of literature did not accord with the demands of historiography, and most often the writer prevailed over the historian. Josephus shared all the defects that characterized contemporary and earlier historians. Nonetheless, he occupies a place of prime importance also as a historian, an importance which is greatly increased because his work is the only surviving source and without it little would have been known of the history of the Second Temple nor would it have been possible to write such a history.

The historian must be grateful to the Christian Church for preserving this treasure. As early as in the first centuries the Christians eagerly translated the writings of the "Greek Livy" into Latin – *Antiquities* and *Against Apion* were translated through the efforts of Cassiodorus in the sixth century C.E. and *The Jewish War* apparently already at the end of the fourth. A distinction must be made between the accurate rendering, ascribed to Rufinus, of *The Jewish War* and the freer version known as Hegesippus or Gegesippus. The first edition of the Greek text of Josephus' writings was printed in 1544 by Frobenius and Episcopus in Basle. The new, scholarly edition, that of Niese, was begun in 1887 in Berlin. The main English editions of Josephus are *Josephus: Complete Works* (1969), translated by W. Whiston; *The Jewish War* (1959), by G.A. Williamson; and the Loeb Classical Library edition translated by H. St. John Thackeray, R. Marcus and L.H. Feldman (1926–65).

[Abraham Schalit]

In the Arts

The Jewish historian and his writings made an imprint on art and literature. In the 11th century, an East Slavonic version made Josephus' *Jewish War* a popular source of legend in the Slav lands and later influenced Russian heroic literature. The rediscovery in the 15th century of the writings of Josephus created a vogue in Western Europe for dramas about the Maccabees and the Herodians. After early translations of Josephus into Latin (1481), German (1531), French (1558), and Italian (1574), the English poet Thomas Lodge (1558–1625) produced the first complete edition in English, *The Famous and memorable workes of Josephus, a man of much honour and learning among the Jewes…* (London, 1602). While there was practically no early fiction about the Jewish historian, there were many 17th-century English dramas dealing with subjects such as *Herod and Mariamne and the fall of Jerusalem which acknowledged their indebtedness to "Josephus, the learned and famous Jew." English dramatists anxious to exploit such themes on the stage found in Josephus a convenient post-biblical authority, enabling them to circumvent Puritan objections to dramatization of the Bible. There was a renewal of interest in these subjects during the Restoration era, and Josephus' account of the destruction of Jerusalem, for example, continued to attract the attention of English playwrights well into the 19th century. In general, however, Josephus himself became significant in fiction only toward the end of the 19th century. The Jew's need to fight for equality was stressed by the Russian author Vladimir Galaktionovich *Korolenko in his tale *Skazaniye o Flore, Agrippe i Menakheme syn Yegudy* ("Tale of Florus, Agrippa, and Menahem ben Judah," in *Ocherki i Razskazy*, vol. 3, 1894[2]). Practically all of the works dealing with the theme in the 20th century were written by Jews. They include *Az áruló* ("The Traitor," 1923), a historical drama by the Hungarian author Lajos *Szabolcsi; Yehiel Yeshaia *Trunk's Yiddish short story *Yosepus Flavius fun Yerusholayim* (1930); Julius Wolffsohn's German play *Joseph ben Matthias* (1935; staged in 1934); and *Yerushalayim ve-Romi: Yosifus Flavius* (1939), a Hebrew drama by the writer Nathan *Agmon (Bistritski). The outstanding work on the subject was the German novelist Lion *Feuchtwanger's *Josephus* trilogy: *Der juedische Krieg* (1932; *Josephus*, 1932); *Die Soehne* (1935; *The Jew of Rome*, 1936); and *Der Tag wird kommen* (1941; *The Day Will Come* (U.S. ed., *Josephus and the Emperor*), 1942). After World War II, the Israel writer Shin *Shalom published his play *Me'arat Yosef* (in *Ba-Metaḥ ha-Gavoha*, 1956) and Naftali Ne'eman the Hebrew novel *Beino le-Vein Ammo* (1956–57). Josephus also appears in a number of interesting works of art. A striking first-century marble bust (found in Rome and formerly in the Carlsberg Glyptotekat, Copenhagen) has been thought to represent the Jewish historian because of its pronounced "Semitic" features. Two outstanding French manuscripts that have survived are copies of his works. The first, a late 12th-century Josephus text (Bibliothèque Nationale, Paris), contains stylized figures and elongated, convulsive forms resembling those of French Romanesque sculpture of the same period. In one illustration

Josephus is shown presenting his work to Vespasian. The emperor sits enthroned like a medieval monarch, while Josephus – complete with the notorious "Jew's hat" – is depicted in the stance of one of the four Evangelists. Assembled behind Josephus is a group of Jews also wearing the obligatory pointed headgear. The second manuscript, a masterpiece of illumination, is the French *Antiquités judaïques* with miniatures by Jean Fouquet (1415–1480; Bibliothèque Nationale). Painted toward the end of the Middle Ages, these freshly colored works betray the influence of the Italian Renaissance, although the soft landscape backgrounds are those of 15th-century France. In this work Fouquet, a master of grouping, action, and drama, interpreted biblical scenes such as David lamenting the death of Saul and Solomon building the Temple. The *Antiquities* also inspired Altichiero and Avarizi to paint a series of triumphs for the great hall of the palace at Verona (c. 1377). These later served as models for Renaissance masters seeking to evoke the glory of Rome, notably Andrea Mantegna (1431–1506), whose *Triumph of Caesar* (1484–92) is now at Hampton Court Palace, near London. Many printed editions of Josephus' works have also been illustrated by well-known artists.

BIBLIOGRAPHY: N. Bentwich, *Josephus* (1914, 1945); H. St. J. Thackeray, *Josephus, the Man and the Historian* (1929, 1967); F.J. Foakes-Jackson, *Josephus and the Jews* (1930); S. Zeitlin, *Josephus on Jesus* (1931); S. Belkin, *The Alexandrian Halakah in Apologetic Literature of the First Century* C.E. (1936); Baron, Social[2], index; W.R. Farmer, *Maccabees, Zealots, and Josephus* (1956); R.J.H. Shutt, *Studies in Josephus* (1961); G.A. Williamson, *World of Josephus* (1964); M. Duschak, *Mar Deror, Josephus Flavius und die Tradition* (1864); H. Bloch, *Die Quellen des Flavius Josephus…* (1879); J. Destinon, *Die Chronologie des Josephus* (1880); idem, *Die Quellen des Flavius Josephus* (1882); A. Schlatter, *Zur Topographie und Geschichte Palaestinas* (1893); Niese, in: *Historische Zeitschrift*, 76 (1896); 193–237; Buechler, in: REJ, 32 (1896), 179–99; 34 (1897), 69–93; Schuerer, Gesch, index; A. Schlatter, *Wie sprach Josephus von Gott?* (1910); idem, *Die hebraeischen Namen bei Josephus* (1913); idem, *Die Theologie des Judentums nach dem Bericht von Josefus* (1932); E. Norden, *Josephus und Tacitus ueber Jesus…* (1913); Hoelscher, in: Pauly-Wissowa, 18 (1916), 1934–2000, no. 2; R. Laqueur, *Der juedische Historiker Flavius Josephus* (1920); W. Weber, *Josephus und Vespasian* (1921); R. Eisler, *Jesus Basileus on Basileusas…*, 2 vols. (Ger., 1929–30); S. Rappaport, *Agada und Exegese bei Flavius Josephus* (1930); S. Pelletier, *Flavius Josèphe adaptateur de la Lettre d'Aristée* (1962); Josef b. Mattityahu, *Kadmoniyyot ha-Yehudim*, ed. by A. Schalit, 1 (1955[2]), xi–lxxxii; A. Schalit, in: *Klio*, 26 (1933), 67–95; idem, *Koenig Herodes* (1969), passim; idem, *Namenwoerterbuch zu den Schriften des Flavius Josephus* (1969). **ADD. BIBLIOGRAPHY:** U. Rappaport (ed.), *Josephus Flavius: Historian of Eretz Israel in the Hellenistic-Roman Period* (1982), extensive bibliography; T. Rajak, *Josephus* (1983); M. Broshi, "How to Recognize A Jew," in: *The Israel Museum Journal* XI (1993), 81–84; Y. Shahar, *Josephus Geographicus: The Classical Context of Geography in Josephus* (2004).

JOSHUA (Heb. יְהוֹשֻׁעַ; "YHWH is salvation"), son of Nun of the tribe of Ephraim and leader of the Israelites in the conquest and apportionment of the land of Canaan; his name was originally Hosea (Num. 13:8, 16; Deut. 32:44). Joshua, who appears in the Bible as a commander and as *Moses' attendant, led Israel against *Amalek in the battle of Rephidim (Ex. 17:9–14). He accompanied Moses during his ascent and descent of Mt. Sinai (24:13; 32:17–18), and was placed in charge of security at the tent of meeting (33:11). One of the 12 spies sent from Kadesh, Joshua, together with Caleb, opposed the negative report of the other ten (Num. 13:8; 14:6–9). Because of their trust in the Lord, they were the only two privileged to enter Canaan (14:30). Moses appointed Joshua as his successor (27:15–23; Deut. 1:38) with the duty to conquer and apportion the land among the Israelites (Num. 34:17; Deut. 31:7, 14, 23). He himself received Timnath-Serah in the hills of Ephraim as his lot (Josh. 19:50). On his death at the age of 110, he was buried there (*ibid.* 24:30; cf. Judg. 2:9, as Timnath-Heres). Joshua is portrayed in the Bible as combining the qualities of a military leader and a prophet. His major function lay in the conquest and settlement of Canaan (Deut. 3:21; 31:3–8; Josh. 13:22), but he "was filled with the spirit of wisdom because Moses had laid his hands upon him" (Num. 27:18–20; Deut. 34:9). Like Moses, he is called "servant of the Lord" (Josh. 24:29), and it is also said of him: "And the Lord spoke unto Joshua saying" (20:1) – the form of address used for Moses. He begins his farewell address to Israel: "Thus says the Lord" (24:2). The event of Mt. Ebal (Josh. 8:30–35; cf. Deut. 27) is a kind of act of prophetic leadership continued from Moses to Joshua. In his parting words of chapter 23 and those at Shechem (24), the Bible attributes to him the character of a prophet-legislator in the style of Moses (24:1–28). (For fuller details see *Joshua, Book of.)

The historical role of Joshua has been variously evaluated. There is a general consensus that the Joshua traditions in the Pentateuch are secondary. He appears to have been inserted into the spy story of Numbers 13–14; Deut. 1:34–7, which in an earlier form included only Caleb. As to his historicity E. Meyer and G. Hoelscher deny his existence as a historical reality and surmise that he is the legendary hero of a Josephite clan. Others, especially Y. Kaufmann, accept the biblical tradition in essence and view him as the historical leader of an alliance of tribes during the conquest of Canaan. Before the extensive archaeological excavations of the recent decades demonstrated that the Bible's account of the conquest of the land are unhistorical, most modern scholars did not doubt his historicity, but suggested that he was the leader of only part of the Israelite conquerors, and that he became a national hero associated with Moses only after the passage of time, when numerous stories and traditions accumulated about him. W.F. Albright, T. Meek, B. Mazar, and others held that Joshua was only the leader of the house of Joseph and that he conquered Jericho, Ai, and Beth-El, and won the battle of Gibeon. In the opinion of Alt and Noth, Joshua won only the battle of Gibeon, and following this victory he became the first judge, consolidating the tribes of Israel around their religious center in Shechem, in the center of the hills of Ephraim (Josh. 24). In the present circumstances it seems best to conclude that if there is a historical person ultimately behind the Joshua legends, he cannot be recovered.

[Yohanan Aharoni / S. David Sperling (2nd ed.)]

In the Aggadah

Joshua received the Torah from Moses (Avot 1:1). He was worthy to succeed him and to receive the gift of prophecy because of his faithful service to him both by day and night (Num. R. 12:9). That his inspiration was derived from Moses is indicated in the statement "the face of Moses was as the face of the sun, the face of Joshua as the face of the moon" (BB 75a). Joshua was designated as the "first of the conquerors" at the time of the creation of the world (Esth. R., Proem 10). The rabbis solve the moral problem that Joshua had taken by conquest a land which was occupied by another nation by maintaining that it was divinely designated for the children of Israel, and the Canaanites were merely acting as caretakers of the land until their arrival (Sifra 7:9). The identical plea was used by the Spartans to justify their right to Sparta and Messene, namely, that Heracleus conquered Sparta with his own hands and ordered it to be preserved for his descendants (Diodorus 4:33, 5). Before attacking a city Joshua issued an edict wherein was written, "Whosoever desires to go, let him go; and whosoever desires to make peace, let him make peace; and whosoever desires to make war, let him do so. The Girgashites departed, and so were given a land as good as their own … Africa [Carthage]. The Gibeonites made peace. The 31 kings waged war and were defeated" (Deut. R. 5:14; Lev. R. 17:6). Joshua's dedication of the spoils of Jericho to God was done of his own accord, Joshua reasoning that since it was captured on the holy Sabbath, then all that was taken should be holy to the Lord. Moreover, as the first city to be captured, it was to be regarded as the first of the produce, which belongs to God (Tanḥ B., Num. 42; Jos., Ant., 5:26). When the Gibeonites appealed to Joshua to save them (Josh. 10:6), his first thought was that he should not put the congregation to trouble for the sake of these proselytes, but God pointed out that Joshua himself was a descendant of proselytes (Num. R. 8:4), since he was descended from Ephraim, son of Joseph and Asenath, daughter of Poti-Phera. Joshua succeeded where Moses did not. He allotted and apportioned the land and was vouchsafed the wholehearted cooperation of the entire people which Moses had failed to achieve (Tanḥ B., Lev. 23). He was one of the three for whom the sun stood still (Ta'an. 20a). Joshua married *Rahab after she became a proselyte (Meg. 14b).

[Elimelech Epstein Halevy]

In Christianity

The similarity of the names Yehoshua and Yeshua brought about an early identification, in Christian symbolism, of Joshua as a "type" or prefiguration of Jesus. The typology is first mentioned in the Epistle to the Hebrews (4:8–9), where Joshua, who brought the children of Israel to an imperfect rest only, is contrasted with Jesus who brought his believers to the true and perfect rest. Other events of Joshua's life are similarly interpreted as prophetic anticipations of the life of Jesus. Thus Joshua fights with Amalek, the symbol of the Devil, with whom Jesus too must fight, and he leads the Israelites in battle while Moses folds his arms in the "crossed" position. According to the Church Father Irenaeus, Joshua, who leads the people into the Holy Land, succeeds Moses, the symbol of the superseded Law.

In Islam

When the people of Israel refused to enter Ereẓ Israel out of fear of the people of Anak (see Num. 13–14), they were encouraged by two men who feared Allah and who said to them: "Verily, we shall be victorious and upon God do ye rely if ye be believers" (Sura 5:23–26). The commentators explain that these two were Yūshaʿ (Joshua) ibn Nūn and Kalāb (Caleb) ibn Yūfannā (Jephunneh). Ṭabarī (*Ta'rīkh*, p. 306) mentions that there were divergences of opinion among the earlier authorities (cf. Kisā'ī, 240) as to whether the conquest of Jericho occurred during the lifetime of Moses, and that Joshua commanded the vanguard of the army in this campaign, or whether it occurred after the death of Moses, solely at the hands of Joshua. Ṭabarī (*Ta'rīkh*, p. 311), however, was familiar with the order of the events of the conquest as they are described in the Bible: Joshua conquered more than 30 towns (cf. Josh. 12). In the traditions of Ṭabarī (*Ta'rīkh*, p. 312) the tale of Joshua is connected with that of the Amalekites who were driven out of *Yemen by Shamīr, the first of the *Ḥimyar kings and the same person who was at first the viceroy of the king of Persia in Yemen. The remnants of the Canaanites, who remained after the wars of Joshua, headed by Ifrīqis, a descendant of the Ḥimyarite kings, went to Africa – which they conquered – put its king Jarjīr (or Jarjaṣ – the Girgasite) to death and settled there; these people are the *Berbers. Ibn Khaldūn, the celebrated Arabic-Maghribi historian (late 14th–early 15th century), objected to this genealogy. These confused legends are an echo of the tale of Procopius (sixth century C.E.), and of the Jewish legends – which go back to the period of the *tannaim* – on the expulsion of the Canaanites by "Joshua the Robber" to Africa, or their voluntary departure. They later appear in Arabic literature as the expulsion of the Philistines from Canaan and are connected with the Jālūt (see *Goliath).

[Haïm Z'ew Hirschberg]

In the Arts

Among writers, artists, and musicians the siege and capture of Jericho was the most popular episode in Joshua's career. In literature, Joshua drew little attention during the Middle Ages. One of the earliest works on the subject was a late Elizabethan play by the English writer S. Rowley, whose *Joshua* – though the text has not survived – is known to have been staged in 1602. The theme became more popular in the 18th century, with works beginning with García Aznar Vélez's Spanish drama *El sol obediente al hombre* (Seville, 1720?[2]). Thomas Morell's *Joshua. A Sacred Drama* (1748), enhanced by the music of Handel, was one of the oratorios on Old Testament themes which appealed to the patriotism of a British public unable to see biblical plays on the stage because of rigid censorship. There were also strong patriotic undertones to *The Conquest of Canaan* (1785), an epic poem by the theocratic U.S. writer and preacher Timothy Dwight. Dwight, one of the leading

"Connecticut wits," injected references to the American War of Independence into his allegorical account of the Israelite *The Battles of Joshua* (1843), an anonymous American ballad – generally attributed to Samuel B.H. *Judah – portraying the Israelite leader as a cruel invader. Works on the subject by two other 19th-century Jewish writers were less controversial: *Yehoshu'a; Sar Ẓeva'ot Yisrael* (1853), a Hebrew epic in ten cantos by Benjamin Kewall (1806–1880), and *Joshua* (1890; *Joshua: A Story of Biblical Times*, 1890) by the German Egyptologist Georg Moritz *Ebers, who was raised as a Christian. The subject has retained its popularity in the 20th century, and a three-act drama *Rahab* by the U.S. literary critic Richard Burton appeared in 1906. Another work of the same period was "Josuas Landtag" (composed 1906), a poem by the Prague-born Austrian writer Rainer Maria Rilke. Other works on the theme by modern writers include Tadeusz Breza's Polish novel, *Mury Jerycha* ("The Walls of Jericho," 1946); *The Seven Days of Jericho* (1944), a poem by Patrick Dickinson; a drama, *Das rote Seil* (1952), by the Swiss-German writer Gerhard Wipf; and Frank G. Slaughter's *The Scarlet Cord: a Novel of the Woman of Jericho* (1956). Among treatments by Jewish authors are Saul Saphire's Yiddish novel, *Moyshe Rabeynes Nakhfolger, Yehoshue* (1935), and Israel Isaac Taslitt's *At the Walls of Jericho* (1961). There have also been several works for Jewish children, such as Shlomo Skulsky's *Aggadot Yehoshu'a bin Nun* (1958; *Legends of Joshua*, 1961).

In art, Joshua was regarded as the type of Jesus (Yehoshu'ah = Yeshu'a), both because of his name and because of the symbolic meaning attached to his actions. The crossing of the Jordan, like the crossing of the Red Sea, was regarded as foreshadowing the baptism of Jesus and was therefore represented on baptismal fonts. Joshua also owed much of his popularity in the medieval Christian world to the miracle he performed in arresting the course of the sun in the heavens (Josh. 10:12). He was regarded as one of the Nine Worthies, and was represented in this role in sculpture, painting, and tapestries. The cycles of episodes drawn from the Book of Joshua comprise the fourth-century mosaics from the church of Santa Maria Maggiore, Rome; the tenth-century Greek *Joshua Roll* (Vatican Library); the bronze doors by Ghiberti for the Baptistery at Florence; and a series of 16th-century Brussels tapestries (Vienna Museum). In the mosaics of Santa Maria Maggiore, the scene of the crossing of the Jordan is based on the triumph over the fall of Jerusalem from the Arch of Titus. There is a statue of Joshua by Donatello at the Campanile, Florence, and scenes from his life are found in Byzantine and western manuscripts, including the 12th-century Admont Bible (British Museum); the 13th-century St. Louis Psalter (Bibliothèque Nationale, Paris), in which the priests are shown wearing the pointed hats of medieval Jewry; the 14th-century Queen Mary Psalter (British Museum); and the 16th-century *Hours of Henry II* (Bibliothèque Nationale). Similar scenes are also found in medieval frescoes and sculpture. Among other notable representations are an illustration of the fall of Jericho by Jean Fouquet (1415–1480) in his famous manuscript of Josephus (Bibliothèque Nationale); frescoes by the school of Raphael in the *loggie* of the Vatican; and a painting by Tiepolo (1696–1770; Poldi-Pezzoli Museum, Milan) showing Joshua arresting the course of the sun, a subject also treated by Italian artists of the 17th century.

IN MUSIC. Joshua has also inspired a comparatively large number of compositions. The sudden appearance of several oratorios on the subject – mainly about the fall of Jericho – beginning with G.M. Bononcini's *Il Giosuè* (1688) is no doubt directly linked with political events of the time, particularly the victories of Charles of Lorraine over the Turks at Mohács, and of Prince Eugene of Savoy and the Duke of Marlborough. Some early 18th-century works of note are M.-A. Charpentier's *Josué* (c. 1700); the oratorio-pasticcio *I trionfi di Giosuè* (1703), jointly written in Florence by more than ten composers (including Veracini and Bononcini); and other oratorios by Veracini (c. 1715), Logroscino (1743), and Hasse (1743). Handel's oratorio *Joshua* has been mentioned above. The subject was taken up by some relatively undistinguished composers in France. The only noteworthy – or notorious – example there is of slightly later date, *La Prise de Jéricho*, an opera put together from various sources (chiefly Mozart) by Lachnith and Kalkbrenner (1805). Of the very few works on the subject written during the 19th century only Moussorgsky's retains significance. His *Jesus Navin* ("Joshua, the Son of Nun"), for baritone, alto, mixed choir, and piano, is based on melodies which he heard from Jewish neighbors in St. Petersburg in about 1864. Moussorgsky first utilized some of the material in 1866 for the "Chorus of the Libyan Warriors" in his projected opera *Salammbô*. Between 1874 and 1877 he reworked and completed it as a choral scene on the battle of Gibeon, adapting the text himself from the Bible. The work was first performed and published in 1883 by Rimsky-Korsakov, who had arranged the piano accompaniment for orchestra. The opening theme of the main chorus, "Thus saith the Lord of Hosts," is engraved on Moussorgsky's tombstone. It was translated into Hebrew by Saul *Tchernichovsky for the *Lider-Zamlbuch* (1911) published by Z. Kisselgov, A. Zhitomirski, and P. Lwow for the *Society for Jewish Folk Music.

Later works about Joshua include C. Franckenstein's opera *Rahab* (première in Hamburg, 1911), Franz Waxman's oratorio *Joshua* (première in Dallas, 1959), and Ben-Zion *Orgad's *The Story of the Spies* for chorus and orchestra (1953). The Afro-American spiritual "Joshua fit de battle of Jericho" is among the most famous of its type.

[Bathja Bayer]

BIBLIOGRAPHY: IN THE BIBLE: A.Moehlenbrink, in: ZAW, 59 (1943), 14–58; T.J. Meek, *Hebrew Origins* (1950²), 1–48. For further bibliography see Book of *Joshua. IN THE AGGADAH: Ginzberg, Legends, 4 (1947⁵), 3–17; 6 (1946³), 169–80; A.A. Halevi, *Sha'arei ha-Aggadah* (1963), 68–70, 109–11. IN CHRISTIANITY: J. Daniélou, *Sacramentum Futuri* (1950), 203–17; *Dictionnaire de théologie catholique* (1925). IN ISLAM: Ṭabarī, *Tafsīr*, 10 (1327 A.H.), 112–4; Ṭabarī, *Ta'rīkh*, 1

(1357 A.H.), 306–12; ʿUmāra ibn Wathīma, *Qiṣaṣ* Vatican Library, Borgia Ms. 165; Thaʿlabi, *Qiṣaṣ* (1356 A.H.), 202–4, 207–11; Kisāʾī, *Qiṣaṣ*, ed. by I. Eisenberg (1922), 240–3; Ibn Khaldūn ʿAbd al Raḥmān, *The Muqaddimah* trans. by F. Rosenthal (1958), index s.v. *Berber*; 3 vols.; Hirschberg, Afrikah, 1 (1965), 23–25, bibl. 337, no. 38–40; H.A.R. Gibb and J.H. Kramers, *Shorter Encyclopaedia of Islam* (1953), s.v. *Yūshaʿ b. Nūn*, incl. bibl. **ADD. BIBLIOGRAPHY:** "*Yūshaʿ*," in: EIS[2], 11 (2002), 351 (incl. bibl.); J. van Seters, *In Search of History* (1997; repr. of 1983), 322–53; S.D. Sperling, in, HUCA, 58 (1987), 119–36; reprinted with comments in G. Knoppers and G. McConville (eds.), *Reconsidering Israel and Judah* (2000), 204–58; G. Ramsey, in: ABD, 3:999–1000.

JOSHUA (mid-second century C.E.), *tanna*, son of *Akiva. It is told that he stipulated in his marriage contract that his wife had to support him so that he could devote himself to study. Later, during a famine, she contested the validity of the stipulation but under the extraordinary conditions of the time the court upheld the original agreement (Tosef., Ket. 4:6). It is possible that he and his wife are also mentioned in the *Midrash Tehillim* (ed. Buber (1959), p. 302). Joshua is once mentioned as asking his father a halakhic rule (Tosef., Neg. 1:1), and it is also related that his father charged him with seven rules of behavior (Pes. 112a). Some *rishonim*, among them Rashi (Bek. 58a), identify Joshua with *Joshua b. Korḥa. It can be assumed that he perished during the persecutions at the time of *Hadrian. The Talmud mentions that Akiva mourned for the loss of his sons (MK 21b).

BIBLIOGRAPHY: Bacher, Trad, 89; Hyman, Toledot, 647.

JOSHUA, early liturgical poet of unknown period. Joshua, who apparently lived in Palestine, is mentioned by *Saadiah in his introduction to the *Iggaron*, in conjunction with Eleazar (i.e., *Kallir) and *Phinehas, as one of the first composers of *piyyutim*. Some liturgical compositions by Joshua, who bore the surname "ha-Kohen," were recently found among *Genizah* fragments. Only a few of these texts have been published. In Zulay's opinion, Joshua could have been the father of the well-known poet Johanan ha-Kohen. Joshua is not to be confused with poets of similar name of a later period.

BIBLIOGRAPHY: A. Harkavy, *Zikkaron la-Rishonim ve-gam la-Aḥaronim*, 1 no. 5 (1891), 110–2; M. Zulay, in: YMḤSI, 5 (1939), 155–7; idem, in: *Alei Ayin, S. Schocken Jubilee Volume* (1952), 89f.

[Jefim (Hayyim) Schirmann]

JOSHUA, BOOK OF, the first book of the Former Prophets, which relates the conquest of *Canaan and its early settlement from the death of *Moses to the death of *Joshua. The Book of Joshua is divided into three main sections: the conquest of the land (chs. 1–12); the division of the land among the tribes and the establishment of cities of refuge for the levites (chs. 13–21); and the final chapters, which include the negotiations with the tribes dwelling east of the Jordan and the covenant at Shechem (chs. 22–24). (See Table: Book of Joshua – Contents.)

BOOK OF JOSHUA – CONTENTS

1:1–12:24	**The Conquest of Canaan**
1:1–5:12	Crossing the Jordan.
5:13–8.35	First conquests (Jericho, Ai).
9:1–10:27	Success in south-central Canaan.
10:28–43	Southern campaign.
11:1–15	Northern campaign.
11:16–12:24	Summary of conquest.
13:1–21:43	**Allotment of the land**
13:1–6	Land still unconquered.
13:7–33	Inheritance of Transjordanian tribes.
14:1–19:51	Allotment of Canaan.
20:1–9	Cities of refuge.
21:1–43	Levitical cities.
22:1–34	**Departure of Transjordanian tribes**
23:1–24:33	**Joshua's last days**
23:1–16	Joshua's farewell address.
24:1–28	Covenant at Shechem.
24:29–31	Death and burial of Joshua.
24:32–33	Two burial traditions: Joseph's at Shechem, Eleazar's at Gibeah.

THE COMPOSITION OF THE BOOK

According to talmudic tradition, "Joshua wrote his own book" (BB 14b), although the talmudic sages found it necessary to add the qualification that Joshua's death was recorded by *Eleazar son of Aaron, and the latter's death by his son *Phinehas (BB 15a). No mention of the author is made in the book itself, and the statement that "Joshua wrote these things in a record of divine teaching" (24:26) does not refer to the book in its entirety but only to the last section concerning the covenant. Both the date and the editing of the book are subjects of controversy.

The traditional exegetes (Rashi, 15:14–16; Rashi and David Kimḥi, 19:47; Levi b. Gershom, Judg. 1:10) held that most of the book is from the time of Joshua, but mentioned additional details from a later period, which were added in subsequent generations, such as the Danites' wanderings northward (19:37) and the conquest by Caleb and Othniel (15:14–19), who also lived after the time of Joshua (Judg. 1:10–13). Abrabanel rejected this view. According to him the statement "until this day" which recurs throughout the book (Josh. 4:9; 5:9; 7:26; 8:28; 9:27; 13:13; 14:14; 15:63; 16:10) reflects a distinct lapse between the events themselves and their description in the book. An additional important proof, according to him, is provided by the mention of the Book of Jashar (10:13), which is not very early since it contains David's lament over Saul and Jonathan (II Sam. 1:18). For this reason, Abrabanel held that the author of the book was probably the prophet Samuel; "and if you desire … to agree with the words of the sages, you would have to say that Jeremiah … or Samuel collected these sayings, arranged them in a book, and added to them with God's benevolent aid" (Introduction to commentary to Former Prophets). There are significant differences between the Hebrew and

Greek texts of Joshua. Fragments of Joshua have been found at Qumran (see in Ahituv, 28–37). These demonstrate that the text of Joshua was somewhat fluid as late as the Hasmonean period and perhaps even later.

A group of scholars suggest that the Book of Joshua be considered, together with the Five Books of Moses, as part of a six-book literary creation, or Hexateuch. There is no consensus concerning the P, D, E and J sources found in the book (see *Pentateuch). Some scholars hold that not all of the conjectured Pentateuchal sources are represented here. Beatrice Goff thinks that the bulk of the J source for the story of Joshua's conquest of the land has been lost. W. Rudolph denies the existence of the E source in Joshua. A. Alt and M. Noth assume that the first part consists of stories of various origins edited about 900 B.C.E. by one editor, while the second part consists of two separate geopolitical documents, one dating from the end of the period of the Judges, the other from Josiah's time, both of which were combined and edited near the end of the pre-Exilic period. Then during the Babylonian Exile, the Deuteronomist combined these disparate sources and added a historical framework. Finally, some sections were added from the P source, while other small additions were made before the book assumed its present form. For an updated summary of scholarly opinions on Joshua see Auld in Bibliography.

Y. Kaufmann disagrees with all these theories and maintains the unity and antiquity of the Book of Joshua. He is of the opinion that the Book of Joshua correctly reflects the historical events of the conquest and early settlement of Canaan and was written soon after these events took place. The geographical chapters also belong to the period of early conquest; they are partially a realistic description and partly a utopian ideal – a plan that was only partially realized. The current consensus based on extensive excavation of biblical Israel is that the conquest is unhistorical (see *History: Beginning until the Monarchy). As such Kaufmann's views cannot be sustained. Other solutions must be sought for the differing "maps" in the book. The commentary by Ahituv is extremely helpful in identifying the many geographic sites in Joshua.

[Yohanan Aharoni / S. David Sperling (2nd ed.)]

THE CONTENT OF THE BOOK

The Conquest of the Land of *Canaan (chs. 1–12). The book introduces Joshua as continuing the work of Moses (1:1–9), beginning preparations for crossing the *Jordan, and calling upon the tribes who settled east of the Jordan to participate in the war of conquest (1:10–18). After sending the spies to *Jericho (ch. 2), the crossing of the Jordan is described (chs. 3–4). It is followed by the description of the circumcision of the people at Gibeath ha-Araloth and the Passover festival in *Gilgal (ch. 5). Then stories are told about the miraculous conquest of Jericho (ch. 6) and the destruction of *Ai, after the punishment of *Achan in the valley of Achor (ch. 7; 8:1–29); the construction of the altar on Mt. *Ebal (8:30–35); the covenant with the cities of *Gibeon (Gibeon, Chephirah, Beeroth, and Kiriath-Jearim, ch. 9); the victory over the alliance of the five *Amorite kings of the Judean hills and the lowland (Jerusalem, Hebron, Jarmuth, *Lachish, and *Eglon), and their flight from Gibeon, through Beth-Horon, to the valley of Aijalon, Azekah, and Makkedah; the conquest of Makkedah, Libnah, Lachish (despite the help of the king of Gezer), Eglon, and *Debir (ch. 10); and finally the victory at the waters of Merom over the alliance of the northern kings (*Hazor, Madon, Shimron, and Achshaph) and the capture of Hazor (11:1–15). The description of the wars concludes with a summary of the battles, the conquered areas (11:16–12:6), and a listing of the vanquished Canaanite kings.

In this section, the editor wove several battle stories into a geographical and contextual unit in order to depict a single campaign of conquest under Joshua's leadership. It would appear that this is actually a selection of stories about the conquest, as is apparent from the concluding catalog of vanquished Canaanite kings (12:9–24). This list includes the cities mentioned in the stories of the conquest, such as Jericho and Ai; the alliances of southern and northern cities; cities which do not appear in the biblical stories, such as Geder (Gerar?), Hormah, *Arad, and Adullam in the south, *Beth-El, Tappuah, Hepher, Aphek in the Sharon (according to LXX), Tirzah in the central area, and Taanach, *Megiddo, Kedesh, Jokneam, and Dor in the north; and finally the king of Goiim in Gilgal (according to the LXX in Galilee: i.e., king of the region [Heb. *galil*] of Goiim). There undoubtedly were stories about the conquest of these cities which were not handed down.

Most scholars believe that the stories of the battles originally were related to individual tribes and were only associated with Joshua, and with Israel as a whole, at a later period. Such earlier sources are preserved mainly in Judges 1 and in a few sections in the Book of Joshua, e.g., the conquest of Hebron and Debir which is attributed to Caleb and Othniel (Josh. 15:13–19; 21:12–15), to Judah (Judg. 1:10–11), and finally to Joshua and all of Israel (Josh. 10:36–39). Other cities appearing in the concluding list (ch. 12) were captured, according to Judges (1:16–17, 22–26), by individual tribes: Arad by the Kenites, Hormah by Simeon, and Beth-El by the house of Joseph. Judges 1:4ff. describes a separate campaign launched by Judah against Jerusalem via Bezek and from there to the Judean hills, which concludes with the words "and he drove out the inhabitants of the hill-country; for he could not drive out the inhabitants of the valley, because they had chariots of iron" (1:19).

Among the modern scholars, G.E. Wright prefers the tradition in the Book of Joshua because it presents a total viewpoint in comparison with the fragmentary contradictory data of Judges 1; the progress of the conquest is logical both circumstantially and topographically, and archaeological investigations, particularly in the mounds of the plains, have disclosed ruins dating from the 13th century B.C.E., i.e., the period of Joshua. However, it is impossible to deduce from the ruins of a city whether the destruction was accomplished by individual tribes or as part of a unified campaign of conquest. Nor can the ruins be dated with absolute certainty, so that one cannot rule out the possibility that some towns, such as Lachish, continued to exist until the beginning of the 12th century B.C.E. While it is clear that the editor of the Book of Joshua organized the chapters in logical topographical fashion, this does not necessarily indicate that the events themselves occurred in this same order. Other scholars, such as W.F. Albright, associate the stories of the conquest with the various waves of immigration by different tribes; in his opinion archaeological findings prove the basic historicity of the stories. While the date of Jericho's destruction has not been established with certainty, it is clear that its great decline preceded the period of Joshua. A more complicated problem has arisen in the excavation of *Ai (et-Tell); it is clear that a large city existed there in the early Canaanite period and was destroyed about 1,000 years before Joshua's time. Albright assumes that there was a confusion between the stories of Ai and Beth-El (Josh. 8:17; cf. 8:9, 12). A. Vincent conjectures that the men of *Beth-El temporarily defended themselves in the destroyed city of Ai; others doubt the identification of Ai with et-Tell – but all these are tenuous guesses. Only the destruction of Beth-El, Lachish, Eglon (Tell el-Hesi), Debir (Tell Beit Mirsim?), and Hazor can be dated approximately to the 13th century B.C.E.

Various scholars assume that some of the stories in the Book of Joshua are only etiological legends created in order to explain the existence of outstanding objects in the landscape, as is evident in the emphatic reference to the existence of these objects "unto this very day" at the end of each section, e.g., the stones in the midst of the Jordan (4:9), the house of *Rahab in Jericho (6:25), the heap of stones in the valley of *Achor (7:26), the mound of ruins known as Ai (8:2–8), the heap of stones at the conjectured gate of the city (8:29), the inferior condition of the Gibeonites (9:27), and the great stones by the mouth of the cave in Makkedah (10:27). A. Alt and M. Noth view most of these stories as purely etiological legends and believe that only the stories about the wars of Gibeon and the waters of Merom have an historical basis. The Gibeonite war was apparently associated with Joshua, since he became, in the course of time, the central figure in the stories of the conquest, a result of this decisive victory in the center of the country. In the light of archaeological excavations, one cannot doubt the conquest of the southern cities. Libnah, Lachish, Eglon, and Makkedah were neighboring cities on the plain which evidently fell to the families of Judah at the end of the 13th or the beginning of the 12th century B.C.E. Hebron and Debir were conquered at about the same time by the families of Caleb and Kenaz. The battle of the waters of Merom undoubtedly reflects an historical event, but it should be associated only with the tribes of Galilee.

The Division of the Land Among the Tribes and the Establishment of Cities of Refuge and the Cities of the Levites (chs. 13–21)

These chapters constitute the richest collection of geographical source material in the Bible. They include "the remaining land" which was not conquered by the Israelite tribes (13:1–6); a description of the portions of Reuben and Gad, whose lands lay east of the Jordan (13:7–32); and after an introduction (ch. 14), a description of the lands of Judah (ch. 15), Ephraim (ch. 16), and Manasseh (ch. 17), with introductory and closing remarks which pertain exclusively to the households of Joseph (17:1–4; 14–18). The last seven tribes are apportioned their lands by casting lots at Shiloh before the Lord (18:1–10; 19:51): Benjamin (18:11–28), Simeon (19:1–9), Zebulun (19:10–16), Issachar (19:17–23), Asher (19:24–31), Naphtali (19:32–39), and Dan (19:40–48). The catalog ends with an enumeration of the cities of refuge (ch. 20) and of the 48 cities of the Levites, which were given to them as an inheritance by the 12 tribes of Israel (ch. 21).

Most scholars now generally agree that this is a collection of geographical and administrative documents dating from various periods which were gathered together in order to describe the inheritances of the tribes. One can differentiate among the following documents:

A DESCRIPTION OF THE "REMAINING LAND" (13:1–6). The editor made use of the document in order to introduce the subject of the land which is to be inherited and divided among the tribes. In fact, this is a document completing the boundaries of the tribes and describing those regions of the land of Canaan (cf. Num. 34) which "remained" and were not settled by the Israelite tribes, e.g., all the Philistine provinces from the Egyptian border to north of Ekron; the Phoenician-Sidonian coastal area, from Misrephoth (-Maim, or reading Misrephoth-Miyyam) on the west to the Amorite border in the northern area of Lebanon; and all of Lebanon and the valley of the Lebanese from Baal-Gad at the foot of Mount Hermon to the Lebo-Hamath at the northern limit of Canaan (cf. Num. 34:8; Judg. 3:3).

THE BOUNDARIES OF THE *TRIBES. A. Alt distinguished two separate documents, different in type and in date, describing the territories of the tribes, the tribal boundaries, and the lists of towns. The boundary descriptions consist of a series of consecutive border points on the four corners of the tribal territory. M. Noth showed, through a comparison of parallel sections in the documents, that the original document only enumerated the border points, the connecting verbs between points being added at a later period. The list of boundaries includes the following sections: Judah (15:1–12), the house of Joseph (16:1–3), Ephraim (16:5–8), Manasseh (17:7–10), Benjamin (18:12–20), Zebulun (19:10–14), Asher (19:25–29), and Naphtali (19:33–34). The document therefore contains only the boundaries of seven tribes (Ephraim and Manasseh are included in the house of Joseph); the others – Simeon, Issachar, Dan, and the tribes east of the Jordan – are missing. Noth attempted to prove that the lists of towns belonging to Issachar, Reuben, and Gad are the original boundary descriptions in which the connecting verbs are missing; but there would not seem to be any basis for this theory. The descriptions vary in detail; they are more specific in the case of the southern tribes and briefer for the northern tribes. The most detailed description is that of the boundary between Judah and Benjamin in the area of Jebus (= Jerusalem; 15:8; 18:16), which ran south of the city, an integral part of the area of Benjamin.

On the basis of the detailed description of the border in the Jerusalem area, Albright and others hold that the list does not predate the time of David, who captured Jerusalem. Alt surmises that the list predates the monarchy and comprises both the actual situation and the theoretical Israelite claims to territories still held by the Canaanites (similarly to Judg. 1:27–35). S. Mowinckel, on the other hand, claims that one cannot conceive of a union of tribes, which would include both Israel and Judah, in the period of the Judges. None of these hypotheses has taken the connection between the list of tribal boundaries and the borders of the land of Canaan into consideration (Num. 34) – the southern border of Judah is none other than the southern border of Canaan (Josh. 15:2–4; Num. 34:3–5), and as the Jordan is the eastern border of Canaan, it serves as the boundary of the tribes which have no portion east of the Jordan. It therefore seems that the list did not include Judah (its northern boundary is the southern boundary of Benjamin, and its remaining – theoretical – boundaries are the borders of Canaan) and that it originated in the alliance of the six tribes of the hill-country of Ephraim and Galilee (cf. Judg. 1:27–35; 5:14–18; 6:35). These, then, are the tribes of Israel (as opposed to Judah) as they appear at the beginning of the monarchial period. It would seem that these boundaries were established by the league of tribes whose center was Shiloh (18:8; 19:51) and that the original document included detailed descriptions of the boundary points. It was the Judahite editor who shortened them to their present form. Therefore, no chronological and substantive conclusions can be drawn from the more detailed bits of boundary description.

THE TOWN LISTS. Alt was the first to identify the list of the Judean cities in chapter 15 as a list of the 12 regions of the kingdom of Judah. In his opinion the list included the Judahite cities (15:21–62), arranged in geographical groupings in the south, the lowland, the hill region, and the wilderness, together with the district of *Beth-Lehem, which is preserved only in the Septuagint (v. 59), and the towns of Benjamin (18:21–28) and of Dan (19:41–46). In view of the enlarged territory of the kingdom as reflected in this regional list, Alt dated it to the reign of Josiah. Alt's basic assumption has been accepted by many scholars, but with some modifications. F.M. Cross and G.E. Wright are opposed to the inclusion of the towns of Dan in the list; they believe that the list dates from the time of *Jehoshaphat (II Chron. 17:2) and includes the region of Beth-El, which was conquered in the time of his grandfather, *Abijah (II Chron. 13:19). However, from the days of Abijah to those of Jehoshaphat territorial changes occurred in the boundaries of Judah and Israel (I Kings 15:17–22). It therefore appears that only the southern group of Benjaminite cities (18:25–28) belongs to the list of the regions of Judah, while the northern group (18:21–24) comprises the towns of Benjamin, which belonged to the kingdom of Israel. In this form, a description of Judah does, in fact, reflect the age of Jehoshaphat or Uzziah rather than that of Josiah. The remainder of the town lists are apparently associated with the regional division of the northern kingdom of Israel as it crystallized from the time of *Solomon (I Kings 4:7–12). The absence of city lists for the tribes of Ephraim and Manasseh suggested to Alt that the lists of the cities of the tribes of Galilee are derived from a description of the Assyrian province of *Megiddo, which was formed in the days of *Tiglath-Pileser III and comprised these regions.

CITIES OF REFUGE (CH. 20). The list of the cities of refuge is associated with the ancient law of blood vengeance and the establishment of places of sanctuary for the accidental manslayer (Deut. 4:41–43; 19:1–13). Three cities of refuge were established east of the Jordan River (Bezer, Ramoth-Gilead, and Golan; cf. Deut. 4:43) and three west of the Jordan (Kedesh, Shechem, and Hebron). The formulation of the law apparently belongs to the conjectured D source with additions from the P document, but there is no evidence for the establishment of these sacred sites during the period of Josiah or the Babylonian Exile. More likely is the view of I. Lohr and Y. Kaufmann that the list is early and belongs to the period of the Judges or of the united kingdom.

The Levite Cities (ch. 21)

The list of the *levitical cities concludes the collection of geographical documents in the Book of Joshua. S. Klein and Albright have shown that the composition of the list indicates that it dates from the united kingdom. Based on the parallel version in I Chronicles 6:39–66, Albright reconstructed an original version consisting of 48 cities – four in each tribe (see Num. 35:1–8; Josh. 21:41). Alt showed that the list consists mainly of cities in the border areas and the Canaanite regions; B. Mazar suggested the identification of them as centers of administration to which levite families from Judah, loyal to the house of David, were appointed "for all the business of the Lord and for the service of the king" (I Chron. 26:30–32). It is thus understandable why the levite families were expelled from their towns in the kingdom of Israel during the reign of Jeroboam and were resettled in Judah by Rehoboam (II Chron. 11:13–14).

The Concluding Chapters (22–24)

These chapters include the negotiations with the Transjordanian tribes concerning the altar in the region of the Jordan (ch. 22), Joshua's concluding address (ch. 23), the covenant in Shechem (24:1–20), the death of Joshua and of Eleazar the Priest, and the transfer of Joseph's bones and their burial in Shechem (24:29–33).

Construction of the Altar in the Region of the Jordan

The introduction (22:1–8), which evidently belongs mainly to the supposed D source, associates the construction of the altar with the period of the return of the Transjordanian tribes from the wars of conquest in the land of Canaan. The story itself (22:9–34) belongs mainly to the P source. The Transjordanian tribes – apparently, at first only Reuben and Gad (22:25, 33, 34) – build an altar "in the forefront of the land of Canaan, in the region about the Jordan, on the side that pertains to the children of Israel" (22:11). This arouses the suspicions of the Israelites gathered at Shiloh who consequently send a delegation to Gilead. In response, the Transjordanian tribes state that it is not their intent to rebel against the Lord, but rather that the altar was constructed as a witness to the tie between them and the remaining tribes; they feared that future generations should say that they had no part in the worship of the Lord since they did not dwell in the land of Canaan. There is hardly a basis for the theory that this is a later tradition which belongs to the period of the unification of the cult. It refers rather to the fear of the Transjordanian tribes, who live outside the land of Canaan (Num. 34), and to the boundaries of the tribes (see above).

JOSHUA'S FINAL ADDRESS AND THE SIGNING OF THE COVENANT IN SHECHEM. Most scholars see a redundancy in chapters 23–24; they associate chapter 23 with the D source and the Shechem covenant (ch. 24) with an earlier source (according to some, the E document). Alt and Noth hold that the covenant of Shechem was connected from the beginning with the historical figure of Joshua, through whom the Sinai covenant was extended to include the tribes who lived in Canaan and had not originally participated in it. The covenant of Shechem is the appropriate conclusion to the Book of Joshua and the zenith of Joshua's accomplishments. It is therefore possible to assume, according to Alt, that "the victor in battle against the Canaanites, and the judge of disputes among the tribes, is also the man who, in the dawn of Israel's existence, set it upon the firm foundation of its history by uniting it about a new sanctuary of the Lord in the heart of the land."

[Yohanan Aharoni]

BIBLIOGRAPHY: COMMENTARIES: H.W. Hertzberg (Ger., 1959²); G.A. Cooke (Eng., 1913); M. Noth (Ger., 1953²); R.P. Fourmond and J. Steinmann (Fr., 1960); J.J. de Vault (Eng., 1960); Y. Kaufmann (Heb., 1964); GENERAL: O. Eissfeldt, *The Old Testament, an Introduction* (1965), 248–57 (incl. bibl.); EM, 3 (1965), 543–63 (incl. bibl.); J. Garstang, *Joshua, Judges* (1931); C. Rabin et al. (eds.), *Iyyunim be-Sefer Yehoshu'a* (1960); SPECIAL TREATMENTS: Alt, Kl Schr. 1 (1953), 176–202; Y. Kaufmann, *The Biblical Account of the Conquest of Palestine* (1953); K. Moehlenbrink, in: ZAW, 56 (1938), 238–68; S. Mowinckel, *Zur Frage nach dokumentarischen Quellen in Joshua xiii–xix* (1946); Noth, in: *F. Noetscher Festschrift* (1950), 152–67; Dornseiff, in: ZDMG, 93 (1939), 296–305; Goff, in: JBL, 53 (1934), 241–9; Wright, in: JNES, 5 (1946), 105–14; Mendenhall, in: BA, 25 (1962), 66–86; Aharoni, Land, 73–83, 174–239. **ADD. BIBLIOGRAPHY:** R. Boling, in ABD, 3, 1002–15; A.G. Auld, in: DBI, 1:625–32 (history of interpretation with extensive bibliography); W. Koopmans, *Joshua 24 as Poetic Narrative* (1990); S. Ahituv, *Joshua* (1995); M. Anbar, *Joshua and the Covenant at Shechem* (1999).

JOSHUA (Jesus), SON OF SAPPHAS, patriot leader at the outset of the first revolt against Rome. When, after the defeat of *Cestius Gallus in the late summer of 66 C.E., the Jewish defense forces were reorganized, Joshua, together with Eleazar son of Neus (Ananias?), was appointed to the command of Idumea, with *Niger the Perean serving under him. According to Josephus, Joshua was one of the "chief priests," which possibly may only mean that he belonged to one of the families from which high priests were chosen, since this name is not found in any of the lists of high priests. Nothing further is known of him.

BIBLIOGRAPHY: Jos., Wars, 2:566; Schuerer, Hist, 250; Klausner, Bayit Sheni, 5 (1951²), 163.

[Edna Elazary]

JOSHUA (Jesus), SON OF SETH, high priest during the reign of Archelaus (4 B.C.E.–6 C.E.), Herod's son. Joshua, preceded by Eleazar the son of Boethus, was the second high priest to be appointed by Archelaus, but nothing further is known of him (Jos., Ant., 17:341). His father's (or family's) name (Σεέ) is reminiscent of that of a subsequent high priest, Ananus, the son of Seth (Σεθ, Σεθι; *ibid.*, 18:26), and it is possible that both were of the same family.

BIBLIOGRAPHY: Schuerer, Gesch, 2 (1907⁴), 270, no. 9; Klausner, Bayit Sheni, 4 (1950²), 179.

[Isaiah Gafni]

JOSHUA BEN ABRAHAM MAIMUNI (1310–1355), *nagid* of Egyptian Jewry who lived in Cairo. Joshua was the third son of *Abraham b. David Maimuni. His brother Moses was probably *nagid* of Egyptian Jewry before him. He was a respected scholar, and his responsa on religious and halakhic questions are quoted by such prominent halakhic authorities of the 16th century as *David b. Solomon ibn Abi Zimra and Joseph *Caro. The majority of his extant responsa were answers to questions asked by the Jews of Yemen. Most of them deal with the subjects of prayer and ritual. Joshua's answers are generally based on the *Mishneh Torah* of his ancestor *Maimonides.

BIBLIOGRAPHY: Freimann, in: *Kobez al Jad*, 13 (1939), 75–113; Ashtor, Toledot, 1 (1944), 230f., 298–300; Goitein, in: *Tarbiz*, 34 (1964/65), 255.

[Eliyahu Ashtor]

JOSHUA BEN DAMNAI, high priest in 62–63 C.E. Joshua was appointed to succeed *Anan b. Anan after the latter had been deposed by Agrippa II at the request of Albinus, because of the execution of James, brother of Jesus (cf. Jos., Ant., 20:200–3). These were the days immediately preceding the Roman War when the anarchy which prevailed in Jerusalem began to assume major proportions. The high priesthood ceased to be a purely religious office, becoming more and more a position of power contested among influential members of the priestly families, of whom Joshua b. Damnai was one. When the high priesthood was taken from him and given to *Joshua b. Gamla, street fighting broke out between their followers (Jos., Ant., 20:213).

BIBLIOGRAPHY: Klausner, Bayit Sheni, 5 (1951²), 22–23.

[Abraham Schalit]

JOSHUA BEN ELIJAH HA-LEVI, collector and final editor of Judah Halevi's *divan* (Oxford, Bodl. Ms. No. 1971). Joshua lived, at the latest, in the 15th century, and was probably of Yemenite origin. From his Arabic preface to the Oxford *divan* (Ms. No. 1971 formerly in the possession of S.D. Luzzatto) it is learned, among other things, that three scholars, Ḥiyya al-Dayyan, David b. Maimun, and Ibn al-Kash, had preceded Joshua in collecting Judah Halevi's poems. Joshua states that he has employed for his *divan* all the previous collections, and in particular the first one, by the Maghrebi Ḥiyya, introducing the "improvements" of the two other compilations; as is usual in similar Arabic collections, he follows the alphabetical order of the rhymes, dividing the materials into three parts (monorhymed compositions, strophic poems and letters, and rhymed prose), with an Arabic introduction. Moreover, Joshua mentions his collection of Abraham Ibn Ezra's poems, which is the *divan* of Ibn Ezra now available in an edition by Egers (see bibl., Ms. Berlin, 1233). The name of the earlier collector of Ibn Ezra's *divan* is not known because the part of the Arabic preface in which Joshua must have mentioned him is missing. It is not excluded that Joshua may be identical with the author of an Arabic grammatical work of which only a small fragment has been preserved (A. Harkavy, *Zikkaron la-Rishonim ve-gam la-Aḥaronim*, 1 (1879), 114).

BIBLIOGRAPHY: S.D. Luzzatto (ed.), Judah Halevi, *Betulat Bat Yehudah* (1840), 15f.; A. Geiger, *Divan des Castiliers…* (1851), 167–75 (Ar. and Ger. translation); J. Egers, *Diwan des Abraham Ibn Ezra* (1836), 15–20 (Ar. and with Ger. translation); J.H. Schirmann, in: YMḤSI, 2 (1936), 125. **ADD. BIBLIOGRAPHY:** C.B. Starkova, in: XXV *Intern. Cong. of Orient.* (1960), 1–13; J. Yahalom and I. Benabu, in: *Tarbiz*, 54 (1985), 246–7; J. Yahalom, in: *Pe'amim*, 46–47 (1991), 55–74; idem, in: MEAH, 44:2 (1995), 23–45; E. Fleischer, in: *Asufot*, 5 (1991), 103–81; Schirmann-Fleischer, *The History of Hebrew Poetry in Muslim Spain* (1995), 81–90 (Heb.).

[Jefim (Hayyim) Schirmann / Angel Sáenz-Badillos (2nd ed.)]

JOSHUA BEN GAMLA (d. 69/70 C.E.), a high priest in the last years of the Second Temple. Joshua was married to one of the wealthiest women of Jerusalem, *Martha, daughter of Boethus (Yev. 6:4; *ibid.*, 61a; Yoma 18a and Tos. *ibid.*; Git. 56a). He is apparently to be identified with the Joshua b. Gamaliel referred to by Josephus (Ant., 20:213) as a high priest appointed by *Agrippa II. In common with the high priests at the end of the Second Temple period Joshua, too, was appointed to office because of his wealth. Although most of the others were deprecated in rabbinic literature, Joshua was singled out for praise for his establishing a universal system of education after all previous attempts failed. He evolved a system whereby "teachers of young children be appointed in each district and each town," whereas previously they were to be found only in Jerusalem. In addition he laid down sound pedagogical principles. Because of this, it was said of him: "Truly, the name of that man is blessed… since but for him the Torah would have been forgotten in Israel" (BB 21a). Some scholars deny the historicity of this story, maintaining that the establishment of the schools was wrongly attributed to Joshua by later writers. However, Klausner affirms its historical accuracy. The Mishnah also mentions an improvement made by Joshua in the Temple appurtenances. He substituted for the boxwood casket from which the lots were drawn for the scapegoat on the Day of Atonement one of gold, "and his memory was therefore kept in honor" (Yoma 3:9).

Josephus, who describes Joshua as his intimate friend (Life, 204), says he was one of the most vehement opponents of the extremist Zealots at the time of the Roman War (Wars, 4:160). He cites the speech made by Joshua (apparently son of Gamla), the high priest, to the Idumeans who had been invited by the Zealots to assist them against their enemies. He tried unsuccessfully to influence them to desist from this step (*ibid.*, 238ff.). After the Idumeans entered Jerusalem, they put him to death, together with other opponents of the Zealots (*ibid.*, 316). Josephus praises him greatly, saying of him that "he stood far above the rest" (*ibid.*, 322).

BIBLIOGRAPHY: Graetz, Hist, 2 (1893), 249, 277–8, 294–6; Schuerer, Gesch, 1 (1901⁴), 584, 618; 2 (1907⁴), 273, 494; Klausner, Bayit Sheni, 3 (1950²), 176–7; 5 (1951²), 22–24; N. Morris, *The Jewish School…* (1937), index.

[Zvi Kaplan]

JOSHUA BEN HANANIAH (first and second centuries C.E.), *tanna*, one of the five disciples of *Johanan b. Zakkai's inner circle (Avot 2:8), and the primary teacher of *Akiva. Joshua (together with *Eliezer ben Hyrcanus) served as the bridge between the earlier (pre-destruction) and later (post-destruction) periods of tannaitic tradition. Hundreds of statements in *halakhah* and *aggadah* are ascribed to him in both the Mishnah and the Tosefta, distributed fairly evenly over five of the six *sedarim*, with a slightly smaller presence of his teachings in *seder Nezikin*. In the eyes of later storytellers, the period of the *tannaim* was a heroic age, and even the slightest scrap of information about the least of the *tannaim* can develop in the later *aggadah* into a tale of epic proportions. In the case of truly significant and heroic figures, like Joshua, this process of literary expansion and elaboration is inevitable. Since the narrative traditions in which Joshua eventually played a leading role developed over a period of centuries, it is essential to distinguish between the earlier forms of these traditions, found in the tannaitic sources themselves, and later developments found only in the *Talmudim* and the amoraic Midrashim. At the same time, the tannaitic traditions themselves are not necessarily free of redactional bias, and must be critically evaluated before using them to reconstruct the life and career of Joshua.

For example, the Mishnah of *Rosh Ha-Shanah* (2:8–9) tells the story of a conflict between Joshua and *Gamaliel of Jabneh, in which Joshua reportedly challenged Gamaliel's authority to fix the Jewish calendar, and so to determine the precise dates of the Jewish holidays. (RH 2:8–9). According to this tradition, on one occasion Gamaliel, as head of the rabbinic court, accepted the testimony of two witnesses, who claimed to have seen the new moon, and on the basis of their testimony Gamaliel fixed the date for the Day of Atonement. Joshua had reason to view this testimony as suspect and unreliable and was at first unwilling to accept Gamaliel's ruling. Gamaliel, asserting his authority as *nasi*, commanded Joshua to appear before him with his "staff and money on the Day of Atonement according to your reckoning." After Akiva's attempt to persuade Joshua to accept Gamaliel's ruling in this matter failed, *Dosa b. Harkinus told Joshua: "If we question the rulings of Rabban Gamaliel's court, we would have to question the rulings of every court, all the way back to the time of Moses." The argument that the authority of the *nasi* takes precedence over all doubts – even legitimate doubts – concerning the truth of his rulings finally convinced Joshua. When Joshua appeared before Gamaliel, "Gamaliel rose and kissed Joshua on his head, saying: 'Come in peace, my master and my pupil – my master in wisdom, and my pupil, in that you accepted my words.'" On one level this tradition deals with the tension between the authority of duly constituted communal authority and the autonomy of wisdom. On another level it describes a very human drama involving arrogance and condescension, pride and submission. As one of the most prominent narratives found in the Mishnah, the story also provides a theoretical justification for the preeminent authority of R. Judah ha-Nasi himself – both personally, as grandson of Gamaliel and as inheritor of his role as *nasi*, and for the Mishnah which he redacted and in which this story appears. All of these factors no doubt influenced the way in which this story is told in Mishnah Rosh Ha-Shanah, and must be taken into account when evaluating its worth as historical evidence concerning events which reportedly occurred three generations earlier.

Another stage in the aggadic saga of the ongoing conflict between Joshua and Gamaliel is found only in later amoraic traditions (TJ, Ber. 4:1, 7c–d, Ta'an. 4:1, 77d; TB, Ber. 27b–28a). This tradition concerns a dispute – ascribed in these sources to Joshua and Gamaliel – over the question whether the evening prayer is obligatory or optional. While there is no clear evidence that Joshua and Gamaliel ever actually disagreed over this rather minor point of law, the *Talmudim* describe in detail the dramatic events surrounding this dispute, including the eventual removal of Gamaliel from the office of *nasi*. According to the Jerusalem Talmud, Gamaliel, upon discovering inadvertently that Joshua disagreed with his view on this matter, arranged for the question to be raised in public the following day, whereupon he deliberately attempted to provoke Joshua into contradicting him is front of all the sages and students. Despite repeated taunting, Joshua refused to contradict him in public, and so Gamaliel continued humiliating Joshua in public, until the sages finally were forced to depose Gamaliel, and to appoint another sage in his place. After seeing that his arrogant abuse of authority had undermined his position as *nasi*, Gamaliel decided to go around to all those whom he had offended, in order to appease them. When he arrived at Joshua's house Gamaliel was shocked to find Joshua making needles, from which labor he apparently supported himself. In response to Gamaliel's expression of surprise, Joshua exclaimed: "Woe to the generation that has you for its leader," thereby expressing his contempt for an aristocratic leadership which is so removed from the ordinary existence of the common people that it is totally unaware of the physical and economic conditions under which they must live. Before addressing the question of the historical reliability of this late tradition, it should be noted that the redactional tendencies of the amoraic continuation of this tannaitic story are totally at odds with the original story as found in Mishnah Rosh Ha-Shanah. Rather than justifying the authority of the *nasi*, the amoraic tradition shows how the irresponsible and arrogant abuse of the office of the *nasi* actually undermines the *nasi*'s very right to hold his office and to exercise its authority. This story in the Jerusalem Talmud is told from the perspective of sages who apparently feel that they have suffered mistreatment and humiliation at the hands of a leadership which, while legitimately possessing office and authority, exercises that authority in an illegitimate and unjustifiable fashion. While this *aggadah* could reflect a different historical perspective on the life and times of Joshua and Gamaliel of Jabneh, it is more likely that it is symptomatic of the problematic relations between the sages and the person and institution of the *nasi* characteristic of a far later period. The expansion and elaboration of these events in the Babylonian Talmud (Ber. 27b–28a; Bekh. 36a) are largely consistent with the redactional tendencies found in the Jerusalem Talmud. It would therefore be fair to say that any attempt to use these later amoraic traditions in order to describe the social or political tensions which may have existed among the rabbinic leadership (Joshua and Gamaliel) in the newly established center of Jabneh shortly after the destruction of the Temple would probably be misguided.

Similar care must certainly be taken when examining historical *aggadot* for which little or no evidence can be adduced from tannaitic sources. For example, as a close disciple of *Johanan b. Zakkai, Joshua reportedly plays a central role (together with Eliezer ben Hyrcanus) in the events surrounding Johanan's dramatic and fateful escape from besieged Jerusalem. According to this story, which has reached us in several different versions (TB Git. 56a, Lam. R. 1:5, 31, ARN[1] 4, ARN[2] 6), Joshua and Eliezer carried Johanan b. Zakkai out of Jerusalem in a coffin so that their master might meet with Vespasian. According to one of them (Lam. R.), Joshua and Eliezer were even sent back into the city to help bring out R. Zadok. Since, however, "in Tannaitic sources we find not the slightest reference to an escape" (Neusner, *Development of a Legend*, 228), and in fact all the traditions concerning this episode are late amoraic (TB Git. 56a, Lam. R.) or post-amoraic (ARN), it would probably be ill advised to use this or other similar "events" in order to draw historical conclusions concerning Joshua's attitude toward the Roman conquest of Judea, or toward the policies of various Jewish factions during the struggle. The same must be said about Joshua's role in the dispute over the "oven of Akhnai" (TB, BM 59b). According to this *aggadah*, Joshua boldly articulated and defended the principles of the autonomy of rabbinic legal reasoning and majority rule, in opposition to the repeated attempts of Eliezer to circumvent the decisions of an earthly court by an appeal to divine authority in the form of a heavenly voice. The tannaitic sources themselves, however, make no mention of any dramatic or supernatural events surrounding this dispute, nor is Joshua mentioned by name as playing any special role in it (cf. Kelim 5:10, Eduyot 7:7, Tosefta Eduyot 2:1; cf. TJ, MK 3:1, 81d). While no one can dispute the dramatic power and theological significance of the later versions of this story, it is also true that they almost certainly reflect the synthetic literary activity of many generations of scholars, and so cannot be used as evidence for history of the early tannaitic period or the personal biography of R. Joshua.

Various other legends developed around the figure of Rabbi Joshua, many of them also rooted to some degree in early tannaitic sources. For example, in *Avot* Johanan b. Zakkai praises Joshua, saying: "Happy is she who bore him" (Avot 2:8). A later *aggadah* reports that, when Joshua was still an infant, his mother used to bring him to the synagogue so that "his ears might become accustomed to the words of Torah" (TJ, Yev. 1:6, 3a). According to Ma'as. Sh. 5:9 Joshua was a Levite. A later tradition describes him as having actually served as a chorister in the Temple (Ar. 11b). According to the Tosefta (Sanh. 13:2) Joshua held that "pious gentiles have a share in the world to come," while Eliezer denied them any such reward. Later Midrashim ascribe to Joshua a positive attitude toward the acceptance of proselytes, while Eliezer was described as harsh and unreceptive (Gen. R. 70:5; Eccles. R. 1:8; 4; cf. TB, AZ 17a), thus paralleling somewhat the stereotypical opposition between Hillel and Shammai found in other late *aggadot*. It is reported in *Nega'im* (14:13) that the people of Alexandria once asked Joshua a certain question in *halakhah*. According to the Babylonian Talmud (Nid. 69b–70a) they asked him no fewer than 12 questions: 3 in *halakhah*, 3 in *aggadah*, 3 in practical matters, and 3 questions of *borut* (understood by Rashi as "silly questions," but interpreted by Lieberman to mean idle theoretical questions characteristic of Hellenistic rhetorical education). In line with his leading role in the Jewish community, Joshua may indeed have participated in a number of official missions. The later *aggadah* describes Joshua as having engaged on such occasions in discussions on both theological and quasi-scientific matters with eminent non-Jews, notably the emperor Hadrian and the "elders" of Athens (Bekh. 8b; cf. Ein Ya'akov ad loc.). Similarly his discussions with the Roman emperor are described in the Babylonian Talmud (Ḥul. 59b–60a) and Palestinian Midrashim (see *Hadrian in *aggadah*). Finally, according to the testimony of the Tosefta (Ḥag. 2:2, and cf. 2:6), Joshua served as the primary teacher of Akiva in matters of esoteric speculation, transmitting to him the traditions of the *merkavah* which he had received from Johanan b. Zakkai, though here also Joshua's role in this tradition expanded significantly with the passage of time (Neusner, *Development of a Legend*, 247–52).

BIBLIOGRAPHY: J. Podro, *The Last Pharisee, The Life and Times of Rabbi Joshua ben Hananiah* (1959); L. Finkelstein, *Akiba* (1962[2]), index; A. Lewisohn, in: *Bikkurim* (1864), 26–35; Bacher, Tann; Halevy, Dorot, 1, Vol. 5, 307–18; S. Lieberman, *Greek in Jewish Palestine* (1942), 16–19; Alon, *Meḥkarim*, 2 (1958), 250–2; Epstein, Tanna'im, 59–65; Z. Vilnay, *Maẓẓevot Kodesh be-Ereẓ Yisrael* (1963), 362–3; J. Neusner, *Development of a Legend: Studies on the Traditions Concerning Yohanan Ben Zakkai* (*Studia Post-Biblica*, vol. 16), (1970); S. Lieberman, in: *The Jewish Expression*, ed. J. Golden (1976), 119f.; M. Kister, in: *Tarbiz*, 67 (1998), 483–529.

[Stephen G. Wald (2nd ed.)]

JOSHUA BEN HYRCANUS (beginning of the second century C.E.), *tanna*. He is only once mentioned in the Mishnah (Sot. 5:5) expounding that Job served the Lord from love (not from fear). For this aggadic teaching he is praised by *Joshua b. Hananiah, who calls him the pupil of the pupil of *Johanan b. Zakkai, referring most probably to *Akiva (see Rashi, Sot. 27b; but see Maimonides, in his Mishnah commentary). Since this saying starts with the formula, "On that day," which often refers to the day on which *Eleazar b. Azariah was installed as a member of the Sanhedrin (Epstein, *Tannaim*, 424), it is assumed that Joshua was a member of the Sanhedrin in *Jabneh at that period.

BIBLIOGRAPHY: Hyman, Toledot, 623.

JOSHUA BEN KORḤA (middle of the second century C.E.), *tanna*. He is quoted four times in the Mishnah. In two of these cases (Ber. 2:2, Ned. 3:11) his statements have an aggadic character, and in two others (RH 4:4, San. 7:5) they are of a more halakhic nature. He is quoted dozens of times in the Tosefta and in the tannaitic midrashim, and here also his statements divide fairly evenly between *halakhah* and *aggadah*. He is often quoted together with students of Rabbi Akiva, and in one passage (Sifra, Shemini, parsh. 8:8) he discusses the impurity of drinks with R. Judah at length. He transmits two *halakhot* in the name of *Eleazar b. Azariah (Tosef., Kelim, BB 2:6; Neg. 7:3), and in the Jerusalem Talmud Rabbi Johanan relates a story connecting Joshua with *Johanan b. Nuri (TJ, Kil. 4:4, 29b). He favored compromise in legal suits, rather than the strict application of judicial rulings, since the judge is thereby able to effect both truth and peace at the same time (Tosef., Sanh. 1:3). He laid down the rule (later accepted; cf. Av. Zar. 7a and Maim. Yad, Mamrim, 1:5) that when the sages differed over a matter of law, one follows the more stringent view with regard to biblical injunctions and the more lenient view with regard to rabbinic injunctions (Tosef., Eduy. 1:5). His testimony on the situation that prevailed in Ereẓ Israel in the aftermath of the Bar Kokhba war is instructive: "Joshua b. Korḥa said: We were once sitting among the trees when the wind blew and knocked the leaves against each other. We got up and ran, saying: Woe unto us! Perhaps the cavalry will overtake us; after a time we looked back and saw that no one was there, and we sat in our places and wept, saying: Woe unto us for whom the verse has been fulfilled [Lev. 26:36]: and the sound of a driven leaf shall chase them …" (Sifra, Be-Ḥukkotai 7:4).

The later *aggadah* describes him as sitting together with the *nasi*, *Simeon b. Gamaliel, while the latter's son, *Judah ha-Nasi, sat on the ground before them (BM 84b; Mid. Ps. to 1:8). According to the Talmud, Joshua lived to an exceptionally advanced age (which he attributed to the fact that he never looked into the face of a wicked man) and blessed Judah ha-Nasi that he should attain to half his age (Meg. 28a). According to a late *aggadah* he sired a son at the age of 100 and played with him in a spirit of abandon ("as though he had become crazy"; Mid. Ps. to 92:13). In a talmudic aggadah he referred to his pupil, *Eleazar b. Simeon, as "vinegar son of wine" for serving as a police officer under the Roman government (TJ, Ma'as. 3:8, 50d; BM 83b; PdRK 92a), since, according to this tradition, Joshua was opposed to all collaboration with the Romans, even in the apprehension of criminals. In post-talmudic aggadic tradition he is described as roundly castigating the sectarians (possibly Judeo-Christians; ARN² 3) with whom, as well as with non-Jews, he engaged in disputations (see Lev. R. 4:6; et al.). An *aggadah* in the Babylonian Talmud (Shab. 152a) reports an interchange between Joshua and a certain eunuch, in which the eunuch tries to ridicule Joshua's alleged baldness (a play on Joshua's name: Korḥa = baldhead). Joshua, of course, gets the upper hand in this exchange. For other late associations between the name Korḥa and baldness, see: Arukh s.v. *qrh*; in the name of Gershom b. Judah, Rashi to Bek. 58a, and *Tosafot*, Bek. loc. cit., Pes. 112a.

BIBLIOGRAPHY: Hyman, Toledot, 648–50; Bacher, Tann; Frankel, Mishnah (19232), 187; S. Klein, in: *Leshonenu*, 1 (1929), 343; Alon, Meḥkarim, 1 (1958), 88–91.

[Moshe David Herr / Stephen G. Wald (2nd ed.)]

JOSHUA BEN LEVI (first half of the third century C.E.), Palestinian *amora* of the transition period from the *tannaim* to the *amoraim*. In his youth he was apparently in the company of Judah ha-Nasi, since Joshua mentions the customs which he followed (Shab. 46a; Yev. 60b; TJ, Meg. 1:1, 70a; et al.). He was a native of Lydda and studied under its scholars Eleazar ha-Kappar (Av. Zar. 43a; et al.), Bar Kappara (Ber. 34a; et al.), and Judah b. Pedaiah (TJ, Or. 1:3, 61b; Gen. R. 94:5). He also transmitted teachings in the names of Antigonus (TJ, Hor. 3:7, 48a) and Oshaiah (TJ, Ḥag. 3:8, 79d). He was an associate of Ḥanina b. Ḥama (TJ, Kil. 9:4, 32c), who, however, was his senior (Yoma 49a; Shab. 156a) and was in contact with Ḥiyya (Lam. R. 3:17, no. 6). According to the Babylonian Talmud, Joshua's son was a son-in-law of Judah Nesiah (Judah II; see Kid. 33b). Joshua b. Levi taught in his native town (Lam. R. *ibid.*), and occupied himself greatly with communal needs (Tanḥ. Va-Era 5). He was also active in matters affecting the community in their relations with the Roman authorities and was a member of various missions to them in Caesarea and in Rome (TJ, Ber. 5:1, 9a; Gen. R. 78:5). His sound practical common sense in these matters is evident (see TJ, Ter. 8:10, 46b). He transmitted sayings in the name of "the holy community of Jerusalem" (Yoma 69a).

Joshua was a halakhist whose opinions were widely accepted (Tos. to Meg. 27a; Tos. to Ḥul. 97a), but he was especially renowned as an aggadist (BK 55a). Talmudic tradition relates that in his *bet midrash* particular attention was devoted to *aggadah*, and it included a special scholar who was called "the arranger [*mesadder*] of the *aggadah*" (Ber. 10a). He was, however, opposed to committing the *aggadah* to writing (TJ, Shab. 16:1, 15c). He preached in praise of humility: "He whose mind is lowly is regarded by Scripture as if he had offered all the sacrifices, as it says [Ps. 51:19] 'The sacrifices of God are a broken spirit'" (Sot. 5b); he also asserted that humility is greater than all the virtues (Av. Zar. 20b). He emphasized the need for pure speech: "One should never utter a gross expression, for the Bible employs a circumlocution rather than utter a gross expression, for it is said (Gen. 7:8) 'Of every clean beast ... and of the beasts that are not clean' instead of 'every unclean beast'" (Pes. 3a). He vehemently denounced slander (Zev. 88b; Lev. R. 16:6) and even unnecessary speech: "A word is worth a *sela*, but silence is worth two" (Lev. R. 16:5).

His love of and devotion to Torah also found expression in the story that he attached himself to sufferers from *ra'atan* (an acute festering disease) and studied the Torah (see Ket. 77b). He also said: "If a man is on a journey and has no company, let him engage in the study of Torah ... if his head aches, let him occupy himself with the Torah ... if he feels pain in his throat, let him occupy himself with the Torah ... if he feels pain in his bowels, let him occupy himself with the Torah ... if he feels pain in his bones, let him occupy himself with the Torah ... if his whole body aches, let him occupy himself with the Torah" (Er. 54a). He had discussions with Christian heretics, but he refrained from cursing them despite his annoyance with their questions, because it is written (Ps. 145:9), "And His tender mercies are over all His works" (Ber. 7a; but see TJ, Shab. 14:4, 14d). He was accustomed to fast on the two successive days, the ninth and the tenth of Av "because most of the Temple was burned on that latter day" (TJ, Ta'an. 4:9, 69c). He said of himself that he had never excommunicated any man (TJ, MK 3:1, 81d). It was also said of him that by virtue of his prayers rain fell in the south of Israel (TJ, Ta'an. 3:4, 66c), and that because of his merit the rainbow was not seen during his lifetime (Ket. 77b; see also Gen. R. 35:2). He himself was a hero of the *aggadah*, which narrates that he became worthy of and achieved the revelation of Elijah (Mak. 11a; TJ, Ter. 8:10, 46b; Gen. R. 35:2).

> He once asked Elijah: "When will the Messiah come?"
> Elijah replied: "'Go and ask him himself."
> "And by what sign may I recognize him?"
> "He is sitting among the poor, who are afflicted with disease; all of them untie and retie [the bandages of their wounds] all at once, whereas he unties and rebandages each wound separately, thinking, perhaps I shall be wanted [to appear as the Messiah] and I must not be delayed."
> Joshua thereupon went to the Messiah and greeted him:
> "Peace unto thee, master and teacher!"
> To this he replied, "'Peace unto thee, son of Levi."
> "When will you come, master?"
> "Today."

He returned to Elijah … and said: "He spoke falsely to me. For he said he would come today and he has not come." Elijah rejoined: "This is what he said! [Ps. 95:7]: Today – if you would but hearken to His voice" (Sanh. 98a as adapted by J. Ibn-Shmuel, *Midreshei Ge'ullah* (1954²), 292–4, 306–8).

Joshua b. Levi had a son named Joseph (see Ḥul. 56b and Dik. Sof. ad loc.), who, according to the *aggadah*, on one occasion became ill and fell into a trance. When he recovered, his father asked him what he had seen in the upper world. The son replied: "I saw a topsy-turvy world. The upper [class] below and the lower [class] on top." "My son, you saw the world clearly," observed his father (Pes. 50a; BB 10b; however see Dik. Sof. ad loc.).

Descriptions of the future life of the righteous (Sanh. 92a), of the punishments of the wicked after death, and of Joshua b. Levi's conversations with the angel of death (Ber. 51a; Ket. 77b) served as the basis for stories about Joshua b. Levi's journeys to the Garden of Eden and Gehinnom which have been preserved in various forms (see A. Jellinek, *Beit ha-Midrash*, 2 (1938²) 48–51; M. Higger, *Halakhot ve-Aggadot* (1933), 141–50). One of them has been preserved only in a Latin translation in the work of Peter of Cluny against the Jews and apparently derives from the "Alphabet of Ben Sira." These stories contain motifs known from the legends about the journeys of Pythagoras.

Although he was an *amora*, some of Joshua b. Levi's sayings are attached to collections of tannaitic sayings. The Mishnah concludes with one of his aggadic statements: "In the world to come the Holy One will make each righteous person inherit 310 worlds." In the chapter on "The Acquisition of Torah," appended to *Avot* in the prayer book, appears his saying: "Every day a *bat kol* [heavenly voice] goes forth from Mt. Horeb proclaiming, 'Woe to mankind for contempt of the Torah … for no man is free but he who labors in the Torah. But whosoever labors in the Torah constantly shall be exalted'" (Avot 6:2).

BIBLIOGRAPHY: Hyman, Toledot, 636–46; Bacher, Pal Amor; I. Rachlin, *Bar Livai* (1906); I. Levy, *La Légende de Pythagore* (1927), 154ff., 165, 192; S. Lieberman, *Sheki'in* (1939), 34–42; Ḥ. Albeck, *Mavo la-Talmudim* (1969), 767.

[Zvi Kaplan]

JOSHUA BEN MORDECAI FALK HA-KOHEN (1799–1864), rabbi. Joshua was born in Brešć Kujawski in the district of Warsaw. In his youth he settled in Kurnik (Kornik), Poznania, and was therefore called Joshua of Kurnik. In c. 1854 he emigrated to the United States, was appointed rabbi in Newburg, New York, and also acted as an itinerant preacher. His career in the U.S. is obscure. He subsequently left the rabbinate and died in Keokuk, Iowa. His *Avnei Yehoshu'a* (New York, 1860), a commentary on *Avot*, is of special importance in that it was the first work of rabbinic learning published in the United States. In the commentary he utilizes talmudic sources and the works of Maimonides, Judah Halevi, Isaac Arama, and Joseph Albo. In the introduction he mentions his unpublished works, *Binyan Yehoshu'a*, on religious philosophy, and *Ḥomat Yehoshu'a*, on *halakhah*.

BIBLIOGRAPHY: Lebrecht, in: HB, 4 (1861), 27f.; Fuenn, Keneset, 431; E. Deinard, *Sifrut Yisrael ba-Amerikah*, 2 (1913), 1 no. 2; idem, *Kohelet Amerikah*, 2 (1926), 5, no. 4; M. Davis, *Yahadut Amerikah be-Hitpatteḥutah* (1951), 197.

[Yehoshua Horowitz]

JOSHUA BEN PERAḤYAH (second half of the second century B.C.E.), one of the **zugot* ("pairs" of scholars), together with *Nittai of Arbela. Joshua was a pupil of Yose b. Joezer of Ẓeredah and of Yose b. Johanan of Jerusalem. According to the Mishnah, he was the **nasi* (see *Sanhedrin), and in the well-known difference of opinion on **semikhah* (laying of hands upon the sacrifice) on the festival his view was "not to lay on the hands" (Ḥag. 2:2). One halakhah has been preserved in his name (but see: Lieberman, *Tosefet Rishonim*, 4, 116 top) concerning the laws on what renders food liable to become impure: "Joshua b. Peraḥyah said: wheat coming from Alexandria is impure because of their *antlia* (ἀντλια, watering device). The sages said: If so, they shall be impure for Joshua b. Peraḥyah and pure for all Israel" (Tosef., Makhsh. 3:4). One aggadic dictum is ascribed to him in the Mishnah: "Provide thyself with a teacher; get thee a companion; and judge all men charitably" (Avot 1:6).

The Babylonian Talmud (Sot. 47a and Sanh. 107b in mss. and non-censored editions) contains an *aggadah* that Joshua b. Peraḥyah was the teacher of *Jesus, and that on their return together from Alexandria, having fled there out of fear of Alexander Yannai, Joshua found Jesus guilty of sin and was responsible for his failure to repent. It would seem likely that this *aggadah* is an enlarged reworking of an earlier *aggadah* concerning *Judah b. Tabbai and one of his pupils of unknown name when they were about to return from Alexandria to Jerusalem (TJ, Ḥag. 2:2, 77d). One of the statements attributed in the Babylonian Talmud (Men. 109b) to Joshua b. Peraḥyah appears in *Avot de-Rabbi Nathan* (version 1, 10, 43; version 2, 20, 43) in the name of Judah b. Tabbai, and in TJ, Pes. 6:1 this dictum occurs in the name of Joshua b. Kabsai. The statement that Hillel the elder witnessed the preparation of the ashes of a *red heifer in the time of Joshua b. Peraḥyah (Sif. Zut. 19, 3) cannot be reconciled according to chronology, and so the mention of Joshua b. Peraḥyah (and perhaps Hillel also) in this context would seem to be anachronistic.

BIBLIOGRAPHY: Frankel, Mishnah (1923²), 35–37; Weiss, Dor, 1 (1871), 131–3; Halevy, Dorot, 1c (1922), 351–3, 468–78; Urbach, in: *Tarbiz*, 27 (1958), 170f.; L. Ginzberg, *Al Halakhah ve-Aggadah* (1960), 15f. **ADD. BIBLIOGRAPHY:** S. Lieberman, *Tosefet Rishonim*, 4 (1939), 115–116; D. Sperber, *Roman Palestine, 200–400 Money and Prices* (1974), 126–27, 247–48.

Moshe David Herr / Stephen G. Wald (2nd ed.)]

JOSHUA BEN PHABI (1st century B.C.E.), high priest. According to Josephus, Herod the Great ousted Phabi from office to replace him by *Simeon the son of Boethus, an Alexandrian, and father of Herod's wife Mariamne II. The house of Phabi (פיאבי, פואבי) was a well-known priestly family, and at least two other members, both named *Ishmael b. Phabi, served as high priests (Jos., Ant., 15:322).

BIBLIOGRAPHY: Schuerer, Gesch, 2 (1907[4]), 269 n.6.

[Isaiah Gafni]

JOSHUA BOAZ BEN SIMON BARUCH (16th century), Italian scholar and printer. One of the Spanish exiles (from Catalonia), Joshua Boaz settled in Italy and took up residence in Sabbioneta and in Sarigliano. He was the author of several talmudic reference works: (1) *Ein Mishpat*, giving the references where the laws of the Talmud can be found in the early codes – *Mishneh Torah, Sefer Mitzvot Gadol*, and *Arba'ah Turim;* (2) *Ner Mitzvah*, an enumeration of the laws cited in the *Ein Mishpat*; (3) *Torah Or*, giving source references of the biblical verses in the Talmud, which were first added to M.A. Giustiani's edition of the Babylonian Talmud (Venice, 1546/51), and have since appeared in almost every edition of the Talmud; (4) *Shiltei ha-Gibborim* on the Rif of Isaac Alfasi and the Mordekhai of *Mordecai b. Hillel (published with the *Hilkhot Alfasi*, Sabbioneta, 1554/55), containing supplementary *halakhot*, differing views and criticisms of Alfasi by the greatest posekim, as well as the talmudic novellae of Isaiah di Trani (the Younger).

It is as a result of these quotations by Joshua Boaz that the main teaching of Trani has been preserved. In his extensive introduction to the *Shiltei ha-Gibborim*, he writes that "when the pillars of the exile collapsed… as a result of which dissension increased in Israel, he decided to remedy the situation, attributing the failings to the lack of yeshivot and insufficient study of the words of the scholars." As a result he planned two halakhic works: *Sefer ha-Tamim* or *Ha-Peshutim*, to summarize all the *halakhot* on which there was no difference of opinion, and a second work, *Sefer ha-Maḥaloket*, on disputed *halakhot*, giving all the valid arguments from which the *posekim* derived their differences. Ḥ.J.D. *Azulai states that he saw *Tamim* in manuscript, and in his view the *Sefer ha-Maḥaloket* is identical with the *Shiltei ha-Gibborim* on the *Rif.* Other scholars, however, hold that the two works are not identical.

In 1553 Joshua Boaz commenced the great work of publishing the Talmud in Sabbioneta, but only succeeded in issuing tractate *Kiddushin*. He also wanted to write a *Masoret ha-Tosafot* giving the halakhic rulings of the *tosafot* according to their halakhic order, and he arranged these rulings accordingly, giving the sources for these decisions. He planned to add a halakhic index, entitled *Ḥikkur Dinim*, at the end of the Talmud which would follow the order of Maimonides' *Mishneh Torah*, enumerating the *halakhot* of the Talmud and giving their source according to the tractate and chapter. Only the part to *Bava Batra* was published (Pesaro, 1510). Joshua Boaz emphasized that it is forbidden to be satisfied merely with the decisions of the *posekim*, but reference must be made to the talmudic sources.

BIBLIOGRAPHY: Azulai, 2 (1852), 141–2; Heilprin, Dorot, 3 (1882), 33, 106; H. Strack, *Einleitung in den Talmud* (1908[4]), 151ff.; D.W. Amram, *Makers of Hebrew Books in Italy* (1909), 253; M. Mielziner, *Introduction to the Talmud* (1925[3]), 76ff.; S.M. Chones, *Toledot ha-Posekim* (1929), 579; H. Tchernowitz, *Toledot ha-Posekim*, 1 (1946), 165; R.N.N. Rabbinovicz, *Ma'amar al Hadpasat ha-Talmud*, ed. by A.M. Habermann (1952), 48–51, 55, 74–75, 103; Urbach, Tosafot, 394ff.; Ḥ.D. Friedberg, *Toledot ha-Defus ha-Ivri be-Italyah* (1956[2]), 68n. 19, 77–78.

[Yehoshua Horowitz]

JOSHUA HA-GARSI (middle of the second century C.E.), mentioned only once, indirectly, in a tannaitic source (Tosef. Makh. 3:13; TB, Bekh. 10b) by R. Jose, who transmits a *halakhah* in the name of "Onomis, the brother of Joshua the Garsi." The Babylonian Talmud relates that Joshua the Garsi was once asked a question concerning the writing of *tefillin*, which he answered by means of an *aggadah* (Shab. 108a, but cf. TJ, Meg. 1:9, 71d). According to the Babylonian Talmud (Er. 21b), Joshua attended upon *Akiva when he was sentenced by Tinneius Rufus. Stories about the deeds of Joshua and his ministrations to Akiva when the latter was in prison are also preserved in the Midrash (Lam. R. 3, Mid. Prov., ch. 9). Opinions differ on the meaning of his name. Some hold he was named for his locality Gerasa in Transjordan, one of the towns of the Decapolis; according to others his locality was Garsis (or Doris) in Galilee, near Sepphoris (cf. Jos., Wars, 3:129). A third opinion is that the name refers to his avocation, a grinder of *gerisim* ("grits").

BIBLIOGRAPHY: Hyman, Toledot, 652; S. Lieberman, *Tosefet Rishonim*, 4 (1939), 119.

[Israel Moses Ta-Shma / Stephen G. Wald (2nd ed.)]

JOSHUA HOESCHEL BEN JACOB (1595–1663), Polish rabbi, also called "**the Rebbi Reb Hoeschel**." Joshua Hoeschel was apparently born in Lublin. He studied under his father *Jacob b. Ephraim Naphtali Hirsch. Because of his many talents, his father brought him into the administration of the yeshivah which he had established in Brest-Litovsk. When in 1635 his father was appointed rabbi and *rosh yeshivah* of Lublin, Joshua Hoeschel continued to assist him there in its administration and was responsible for it after the death of his father in 1644. In 1650 he was appointed to succeed his father as rabbi of the Lublin community. On the death of Yom Tov Lipmann *Heller, rabbi of Cracow, in 1654, he was invited to succeed him and held the post until his death. As a result of the *Chmielnicki massacres of 1648–49 and the consequent impoverishment of the Jewish communities of Poland and Lithuania, as well as the pogrom in Lublin in 1656, he moved to Vienna around 1657, exerted himself with the government for the benefit of his people, and urged the wealthy Jews to intensify their assistance during this difficult period. About 1659 he returned to Poland, where he continued his educational activities and enacted various *takkanot. Among his distinguished pupils were *Shabbetai b. Meir ha-Kohen (the Shakh) and Samuel *Koidanover.

The profound acumen of Joshua Hoeschel was a byword among the Jews of Poland, and he himself became a legendary figure, many remarkable tales being told about him. His method of study was distinguished by a profound penetration into the theme and a reliance upon Rashi and **tosafot*, without allowing extensive scope for *pilpul* introduced by Jacob b. Joseph *Pollak and then customary in most Polish yeshivot. Jair Ḥayyim *Bacharach approved this method, stressing that, to the extent that he used *pilpul*, it was "on genuine difficulties." Joshua Hoeschel's great modesty prevented him from publishing his many works, and only a small part has appeared, among them: (1) *Toledot Aharon* (Lublin, 1682, named after his pupil, Aaron Klinger, who collected the material), consisting of novellae on *Bava Kamma, Bava Meẓia*, and *Bava Batra*. They were republished in an enlarged form under the title *Ḥiddushei Halakhot* (Frankfurt, 1725); (2) novellae and glosses on the *Sefer Mitzvot Gadol* of Moses of Coucy (Kopys, 1807); (3) *Ḥanukkat ha-Torah* (1880), novellae on the Bible collected by H. Ersohn. His many responsa are scattered in various collections: two of them were published in the *Ammudei Shittim le-Veit ha-Levi* (Prague, 1791; 58–66) by Levi b. David Pollack. He occupied himself to a considerable extent with the problem of permitting *agunot to remarry, but in consequence of a mistake in one such case he resolved to refrain from giving decisions on this in the future.

BIBLIOGRAPHY: Ḥ.N. Dembitzer, *Kelilat Yofi*, 2 (1893), 39–83; Kaufmann, in: MGWJ, 39 (1895), 556–8; Ḥ.D. Friedberg, *Luḥot Zikkaron* (1897), 16–18; S.B. Nissenbaum, *Le-Korot ha-Yehudim be-Lublin* (1900), 56–58; J. Loewenstein, in: *Ha-Eshkol*, 4 (1902), 182–90; Kohen-Ẓedek, in: *Ha-Yehudi*, 5 (1902), nos. 35–42, 47; Michelsohn, *ibid.*, no. 47; Ḥ. Tchernowitz, *Toledot ha-Posekim*, 3 (1947), index; N. Shemen, *Lublin* (1952), 66, 72, 78, 322, 370 (Yid.).

[Yehoshua Horowitz]

JOSHUA HOESCHEL BEN JOSEPH OF CRACOW (1578–1648), Polish rabbi. Joshua Hoeschel was born in Vilna. In his youth he studied under Samuel b. Feibush in Przemysl and then in the yeshivot of *Meir b. Gedaliah of Lublin and Joshua *Falk of Lemberg. From 1634 to 1639 he served as rabbi in the towns of Grodno, Tiktin, Przemysl, and Lemberg. At the beginning of 1640 he was appointed head of the yeshivah of Cracow in succession to Nathan *Spira, and from 1640 to 1644 he served there as rabbi in an honorary capacity. He died in Cracow. His pupils included *Shabbetai b. Meir ha-Kohen, Gershon Ulif *Ashkenazi, and Menahem Mendel *Auerbach. Halakhic problems were addressed to him from many countries. He corresponded on kabbalistic topics with his relative, the kabbalist Samson b. Pesaḥ of Ostropol. Joshua Hoeschel did not follow the method of *pilpul*; he strove toward greater independence in the domain of *halakhah* and directive ruling, stating, "according to the custom of our country anything printed in the Shulḥan Arukh may not, God forfend, be changed, any more than the law of Moses… God spare us from such a view. The judge may decide only according to the facts before him… and anyone may disagree, even with the words of the *rishonim*, if he has definite proof."

He wrote (1) *Meginnei Shelomo* (Amsterdam, 1715), on eight tractates of the Talmud, in which he defends Rashi against the difficulties raised by the tosafists; (2) the responsa *Penei Yehoshu'a* (pt. 1, *ibid.* 1715; pt. 2, 1860), on the four divisions of the Shulḥan Arukh. Other responsa were published in various collections of responsa: *Ge'onei Batra'i* (Zolkiew, 1795); *Beit Ḥadash ha-Yeshanot* (Frankfurt, 1697); *Beit Ḥadash ha-Ḥadashot* (Koretz, 1785) of Joel Sirkes; in the *Gevurat Anashim* (Dessau, 1697) of Meir Katz and his son Shabbetai, author of the *Shakh*; and elsewhere. There remain still in manuscript novellae to the Tur *Yoreh De'ah Hilkhot Sheḥitah*, and a commentary to the *Asarah Ma'amarot* of Menahem Azariah de Fano.

[Yehoshua Horowitz]

His grandson, JUDAH LOEBUSH BEN ISAAC (d. 1731?), was a talmudist. Judah was appointed rabbi in Raków at a youthful age and in 1701 became rabbi at Szydlowiec. Thereafter he was referred to as "R. Leib of Szydlowiec." In 1713, together with Benjamin Ze'ev Horowitz of Wodzislaw, he represented Cracow and the district at the session of the Council of the Four Lands in Jaroslaw, Cracow being then without a rabbi. At the end of 1713 he was appointed rabbi in Cracow. Of his six sons, one, David Schmelka, succeeded his father in Cracow, while Joshua, Isaac, and Joseph served as rabbis in Szydlowiec, Tarnow, and Pinczow, respectively.

[Samuel Abba Horodezky]

BIBLIOGRAPHY: JOSHUA: A.L. Feinstein, *Ir-Tehillah* (1886), 26, 147; Ḥ.N. Dembitzer, *Kelilat Yofi*, 2 (1893), 1a–38b; S. Buber, *Anshei Shem* (1895), 82–85; Graetz-Rabbinowitz, 8 (1899), 114, 120f.; S.M. Chones, *Toledot ha-Posekim* (1910), 375–7; Karl, in: *Arim ve-Immahot be-Yisrael*, 2 (1948), 305, 307; Ḥ. Tchernowitz, *Toledot ha-Posekim*, 3 (1947), 122, 144 n. 7, 149 n. 11, 154 n. 15, 159; Shulvass, in: *Beit Yisrael be-Polin*, 2 (1954), 19f.; Zinberg, Sifrut, 3 (1958), 191. JUDAH: J.M. Zunz, *Ir ha-Ẓedek* (1874), 159–60; Ḥ.N. Dembitzer, *Kelilat Yofi*, 2 (1893), 29b–30a; Ḥ.D. Friedberg, *Luḥot Zikkaron* (1904^2), index, s.v. *Yehudah Lebush Shidlov*; Halpern, Pinkas, 586 (index); Yaari, in: *Talpioth*, 8 (1963), 457.

JOSHUA IBN NUN (second half of the 16th century), Safed scholar, kabbalist, and *rosh yeshivah*. Joshua was one of the leaders of the Safed community. He was in charge of the local charities, and from his own considerable means supported the scholars and the poor of Safed. He became attracted to the teaching of Isaac *Luria and implored Ḥayyim Vital to reveal to him Luria's esoteric doctrines. Vital, however, refused to comply though Joshua, according to one report, humbled himself before him, following him wherever he went, even to Jerusalem and to Egypt. According to that report, which is substantially correct, Vital became ill in 1587, whereupon Joshua bribed Moses, the brother of Ḥayyim, with 50 gold pieces, to copy Luria's writing that his brother had recorded. Moses hired scribes who copied the writings in three days and from then they became available to a select coterie in Israel. Joshua endorsed many of the rulings of Yom Tov *Ẓahalon.

According to Ḥ.J.D. Azulai, some of his responsa are to be found in the responsa *Zera Anashim* (Mss.). The date of his death is usually given as 1587 but if reliance is to be placed on a recently discovered document he was no longer alive in 1585. In that case the above-mentioned incident must have occurred some years earlier than was previously thought.

BIBLIOGRAPHY: Frumkin-Rivlin, 1 (1929), 131; Rosanes, Togarmah, 3 (1938), 293; Scholem, in *Zion*, 5 (1940), 138–40; M. Benayahu, *Sefer Toledot ha-Ari* (1967), 74–76; D. Tamar, *Meḥkarim be-Toledot ha-Yehudim be-Ereẓ Yisrael u-ve-Italyah* (1970).

[David Tamar]

JOSIAH (Heb. יֹאשִׁיָּהוּ, יֹאשִׁיָּהוּ), son of Amon, king of Judah (640–609 B.C.E.). When his father was assassinated, Josiah, then only eight years old, was proclaimed king. His reign was marked by a great national revival, and the author of the Book of Kings in evaluating Josiah says: "Before him there was no king like him … nor did any like him arise after him" (II Kings 23:25; cf. II Kings 18:5 in connection with Hezekiah, the forerunner of Josiah). Josiah not only acted as the king of a completely independent Judah, but his kingdom extended northward into the erstwhile Assyrian provinces of Samaria (II Kings 23:19). Archaeological discoveries in the 1960s brought to light new facts about Josiah's expansion. Following archaeological findings in *Yavneh-Yam (cf. Naveh, in bibl.), it became quite clear that Josiah established feudal estates on the shore of Philistia. Unwalled settlements of the time of Josiah were discovered in the south and east of Gaza (Gophna, in bibl.). In the eastern part of Judah, excavations uncovered the town of En-Gedi (cf. Josh. 15:62), which had been founded at the time of Josiah as a balsam plantation of the king (Mazar and Dunayewski, in bibl.). During Josiah's reign, Jerusalem developed greatly, and it is at this time that a new wall was built on the western slopes of the city, and new quarters (Mishneh and Maktesh) were constructed which served mainly as industrial and commercial centers. Remains of buildings and walls discovered in the Jewish quarter of Old Jerusalem prove that the city expanded even more to the west. The extent of Judah's expansion in this period may be deduced from the list of Ezra 2 (= Neh. 7), where Beth-El and Jericho (previously Ephraimite cities), on the one hand, and the cities of the coastal plain Lydda and Ono, on the other, are considered part of Judah. The borders of Judah as presented in this list undoubtedly go back to the times of Josiah and remained the same until the destruction of Jerusalem. According to A. Alt (in bibl.), the lists of the cities of Judah, Simeon, Dan, and Benjamin in Joshua 15, 18, and 19 also reflect the Josianic administrative reorganization of Judah. Though one has to take into account previous organizations by *Jehoshaphat and *Hezekiah which might be reflected in these lists, there is no doubt that the final formulation of these lists was done in the Josianic period; this may be corroborated by the archaeological evidence cited above. These lists actually cover the area of Josiah's rule: Ekron, Ashdod, and Gaza in the coastal zone (Josh. 15:45–47), Beth-El and Geba al-Tell, 22 mi. (35 km.) to the north of Jerusalem (according to Mazar) in the north, En-Gedi and the other towns of Joshua 15:61–62 in the east, and the Simeonite settlements in the south. The stamped jar handles with the inscription למלך and the inscribed weights characteristic of this period may serve as a good indication of the scope of Josiah's dominion. These have been found not only in the area of the Kingdom of Judah but also in Acre, Shechem, Ashdod, Gezer, etc. This territorial expansion was accompanied by a religious upsurge, which found expression mainly in: (1) the cultic reform, including both the purification of worship (in Judah as well as in the northern areas) and the centralization of the legitimate worship in Jerusalem; (2) the publication and authorization of the "Book of the Torah" (see *Deuteronomy) discovered in the 18th year of the reign of Josiah, i.e., 622 B.C.E., which ultimately turned the book into the main vehicle of the Jewish religion (see below). These religious-spiritual enterprises, though reflecting inner developments of Israelite religion, were conditioned by contemporary political events and especially by the gradual decline of the Assyrian Empire. Assyria, which had acquiesced in Psammetichus I's disregard of its claim to suzerainty over Egypt about 655 B.C.E., was compelled by its strenuous wars in Asia Minor, and then by the enormous effort of pacifying the rebellious Babylonians and the independent peoples to the south and east of them who supported them, to relax its hold on Palestine as well.

The Reform and Its Historical Antecedents

Josiah's reform activities are given in two parallel accounts: II Kings 22–23 and II Chronicles 34–35. According to the account of Kings, the reform was motivated by the discovery of "Book of the Torah" in 622 B.C.E.; before that no reformative action had been reported. Chronicles, in contrast, tells about three stages of the reform:

(1) in the eighth year of his reign (632 B.C.E.) he started "to seek the God of David" (II Chron. 34:3);

(2) in the 12th year (628 B.C.E.) he began to extirpate objectionable cults in Judah and Jerusalem (34:3b–5), as well as in other parts of the land of Israel (34:6–7);

(3) finally, in the 18th year (622 B.C.E.), when the "Book of the Torah" was discovered, he concluded the Covenant before the Lord (34:29–33) and celebrated the Passover (35:1–18).

Each account has its problems. Scholars have observed that the story of the temple repairs in II Kings 23 is modeled on the repairs ordered by *Joash, an earlier king of Judah described in II Kings 12. In addition, the account in Kings telescopes all of Josiah's activity into one year. If that account is accurate, then pious King Josiah had been tolerating a temple "overloaded with idolatrous objects" (Japhet, 1019) for 17 years of his reign, as had the high priest Hilkiah. It strains credibility to believe that such a drastic change in Judahite religion (which included the purge of ancient native Israelite practices as well as the newer astral cults that had become popular in the eighth century), as described in II Kings, would have been inspired by the chance finding of the book. The chronology in Chronicles is more plausible, but as noted by Japhet, the Chronicler depends on the Deuteronomistic source in Kings and gives no indication that he had access to any other. For the Chronicler there was need to purge the temple because he had already attributed that to the repentance of wicked King Manasseh (II Chron. 33). The fact that this picture absolves both Josiah and Hilkiah from complicity in a polytheistic temple cult is perhaps too convenient. The contradictory accounts in II Kings and Chronicles are each motivated by the agenda of their writers. The goal of the Deuteronomists was to highlight the importance of the book. The goal of the Chronicler was to make the account in Kings plausible and to show that Josiah had always been a pious religious reformer. According to Chronicles, it was only after the completion of the reform that the book was found (II Chron. 34:8), so that its role is limited to bringing the people into a covenant to purge the land of the idolatrous practices in the former northern kingdom (II Chron. 34:33) and the celebration of the Passover.

There are good reasons for antedating Josiah's reform to the discovery of the book: (1) The reforms of the other Judahite kings, e.g., Asa, Jehoshaphat, Jehoash, and Hezekiah, were put into effect without relying upon a written book. (2) It would be inconceivable to suppose that Josiah concluded the covenant in the House of God while all the idols still stood there. The establishing or renewing of the relationship between God and the people was always preceded by the removal of the foreign gods (Gen. 35:2–4; Josh. 24:23ff.; Judg. 10:16; I Sam. 7:3–4). (3) In his account of the king's message to Huldah the prophetess (II Kings 22:13), the narrator has Josiah confess not his own sins but the sins of his ancestors, which clearly indicates that at this time (622 B.C.E.) the Judahite cult of Yahweh no longer tolerated other gods. It is the sins of Manasseh hanging over the people (cf. II Kings 21:11; 24:3; Jer. 15:4) with which he is concerned.

(4) The book was discovered in the midst of an action taken in connection with the repairs of the Temple which apparently followed the removal of the cultic objects installed by Manasseh (II Kings 23:4ff.). II Chronicles, in fact, informs us that the repairs were connected with the restoration of the Temple, or rather with its "undergirding," which had been demolished by the previous kings of Judah (II Chron. 34:11).

The Stages of the Reform

It is not known whether the purgative activities in Judah were contemporaneous with those in the northern territories (Beth-El, Samaria, and the Galilee). The presentation of the events in II Kings 23:4–20 leaves the impression that the reform had been performed step by step. The first move of Josiah was the abolition of objectionable cults from Jerusalem and the cities of Judah (23:4–14), then came the destruction of the altar of Bethel, and afterwards the destruction of the high places of the Samarian province (23:19–20). According to II Chronicles 34:6, the reform extended as far as the cities of Naphtali in Galilee. The gradual political deterioration of the Assyrian Empire adds support to the supposition of a gradual takeover of the northern territories by Josiah. A fortress unearthed at Megiddo may be Josianic.

Centralization of Cult

No exact date can be given for the centralization of the cult. Centralization of worship is the great innovation of the Book of Deuteronomy, and therefore its implementation by Josiah might be the result of the "discovery" of the book. But the way Josiah implements the centralization is not in full accord with the prescriptions of Deuteronomy. Deuteronomy 18:6–8 gives the provincial levite equal rights with the priests of the central shrine: "to serve at the altar and to share the dues," whereas, according to II Kings 23:9, the provincial priests are to share the dues with the Jerusalemite priests but are not permitted to officiate along with them (though one must admit that the levite is not necessarily to be identified with the "priest of the high place"). The contracting of the covenant and the celebration of Passover are performed, according to Kings and Chronicles, in the 18th year, so that in this case there is an established date.

The Significance of the Reform

Josiah's death probably brought an end to his reforming efforts, and in any event, the state of Judah fell in 586 B.C.E. The reform found its full implementation beginning in the Persian period, which saw the reconstruction of the temple in 520. That temple stood as the only Jewish sacrificial shrine in the Land of Israel for almost 600 years until its destruction in 70 C.E. by the Romans. Ultimately, of even greater significance for the history of Judaism was the relocation of divine revelation. Thanks to Josiah's circle, Jews began to seek God's word in the book of Torah. The pledge of the people to observe the Law "as written in the book" brought about a metamorphosis in Israelite religion. To observe the law meant that one had to study it. As a result, the Second Temple period saw the rise of scribes and scholars alongside of the temple cult as well as the gradual eclipse of prophecy. By the time of the destruction of the Second Temple other sacred books had joined the Torah to make up Holy Scripture (*kitvei ha-kodesh*; Mishnah Yad. 3:5), whose study and exposition led to the crystallization of rabbinic Judaism, which survived for almost 2,000 years.

The Death of Josiah

Assyria, weakened by her struggle with Babylon, found the Egyptians as allies. In 616 B.C.E. the Egyptians went up to the north to help the Assyrians, but to no avail. After the fall of Nineveh in 612, the Assyrian army consolidated its positions in the western part of the empire, Harran and Carchemish. This time they were assisted by the newly enthroned Egyptian king, Neco II (610–595; son of Psammetichus), who in the summer of 609 marched with a large force to help the Assyrians retake Harran from the Babylonians. Josiah went to Megiddo to meet the Pharaoh, who killed him there. According to II Chronicles 35:20–24, Josiah ignored God's word and engaged Necho in battle. But the account is suspect because: (a) it is modeled on the account of Ahab's death (I Kings 22:30, 34–37); (b) it is characteristic of the Chronicler's theology to find some sin to account for the downfall of an otherwise righteous king. II Kings 23:29–30 says only that Necho put Josiah to death as soon as he saw him and gives no account of a battle nor any motive for Necho's action. Josiah's death, especially in light of subsequent events, was considered a heavy loss for the nation, as may be learned from II Chronicles 35:24–25: "All Judah and Jerusalem held mourning rites for Josiah … and the singers have spoken of Josiah in their laments to this day and have made these a rule in Israel…"

[Moshe Weinfeld / S. David Sperlimg (2nd ed.)]

In the Aggadah

According to one opinion, Josiah was pious from infancy, and his "repentance" (II Kings 23:25) consisted in his reviewing and revising all the judgments he had given from the time he ascended the throne at the age of eight until his 18th year (Shab. 56b). According to another opinion, he is considered a perfect example of a truly repentant individual (OR 24). Because of his righteousness, his father, Amon, was permitted to enjoy the world to come (Sanh. 104a). When he opened the Torah which had been found, the first verse to meet his eyes was, "The Lord shall bring thee and thy king unto exile, unto a nation which thou hast not known" (Deut. 28:36; Yoma 52b). He sought to enlist the intercession of the prophets in his behalf. He addressed his request to the prophetess *Huldah rather than to Jeremiah since he felt that a woman would be more compassionate (Meg. 14b). When informed of the impending destruction of the Temple, Josiah hid the Holy Ark and all its appurtenances, in order to guard them against desecration at the hands of the enemy (Yoma 52b).

The king's efforts on behalf of God found little echo with the majority of the people. Though successful in preventing public idolatry, he was deceived by the people. He sent his pious sympathizers to inspect the homes of the people and was satisfied with their report that no idols were found. In reality, the recreant Israelites had fastened half an image on each wing of the doors, so that they were not recognizable when the doors were opened, but reappeared when they were closed (Lam. R. 1:53). His death was due to this godless generation. When Pharaoh, in his campaign against the Assyrians, wished to travel through the Land of Israel, Jeremiah advised the king not to deny the Egyptians passage. Josiah, innocent of the deception practiced by the people and therefore unaware that they were idol worshipers, retorted that Moses had promised that the sword would not pass through the land and therefore refused permission. In the ensuing battle no less than 300 arrows pierced the king. In his death agony he uttered no word of complaint, proclaiming, "the Lord is righteous for I have rebelled against His word" (Lam. 1:18), thus admitting his guilt in not having heeded the prophet's advice. On hearing the king's confession, Jeremiah exclaimed, "the breath of our nostrils, the anointed of the Lord" (Lam. 4:20; Ta'an. 22b).

Josiah was the only monarch since Solomon to rule over both Judah and Israel, since Jeremiah had brought the ten exiled tribes of the north back to Israel and made them subject to him (Meg. 14b). The mourning for him was profound (MK 28b), and Jeremiah perpetuated his memory in Lamentations (4:20; SOR 24).

BIBLIOGRAPHY: Alt, Kl Schr, 2 (1953), 276–88; F.M. Cross and D.N. Freedman, in: JNES, 12 (1953), 56–58; D.J. Wiseman, *Chronicles of Chaldean Kings* (1956), 13ff.; Kaufmann Y. Toledot, 1 (1960), 34–39, 81–112; Bright, Hist, 288–302; J. Naveh, in: IEJ, 10 (1960), 129–39; M. Weinfeld, in: *Oz le-David* (1964), 396–420; B. Mazar and M. Dunayewski, in: IEJ, 14 (1964), 121–30; R. Gophna, in: *Atiqot* 6 (1970), 25–30 (Heb.). IN THE AGGADAH: Ginzberg, Legends, 4 (19475), 28 1–3; 6 (19463), 376–8. **ADD. BIBLIOGRAPHY:** R. Nelson, in: W. Hallo et al. (eds.), *Scripture in Context II* (1983), 177–89; M. Cogan and H. Tadmor, *II Kings* (AB; 1988), 277–302; M. Weinfeld, *Deuteronomy 1–11* (1991), 65–84; S. Japhet, *I & II Chronicles* (1993), 1015–59; W. Dever, in: M. Cogan et al. (eds.), *Scripture and Other Artifacts Essays… P. King* (1994), 143–68, incl. bibl.; R. Althann, in: ABD, 3:1015–18; M. Cogan, in: C. Cohen et al. (eds.), *Sefer Moshe … Weinfeld Jubilee* (2004), 3–8.

JOSIAH (middle of the second century C.E.), *tanna*. His father's name is not known. He originated in Babylon and apparently taught in Huẓal (Git. 61a). He discussed law in Nisibis with *Judah b. Bathyra. At that time he was already quoting *halakhot* he heard in the name of "the Men of Jerusalem" (Sif. Num. 123; Deut. 218). Later he moved to Ereẓ Israel, where he studied under R. Ishmael (Men. 57b). He is mentioned in the Talmud about 50 times, never in the Mishnah, and once in the Tosefta (Shevu. 1:7). He is quoted very often in the *Mekhilta*, and in the *Sifrei* on Numbers, both of which belong to the school of R. Ishmael. Very frequently he appears alongside his colleague Jonathan, another of R. Ishmael's pupils, with whom Josiah often disagrees. Their disagreements as a rule depend on different methods of biblical interpretation, both variants of R. Ishmael's particular method (Yoma 57–58; Sota 24–25, et al.). A characteristic method of his is *Sares ha-Mikra ve-Doreshehu*, i.e., "transpose the order of the words [lit. "emasculate"] of the verse and then interpret it." His talmudic dicta cover a wide variety of subjects. One of his most famous rulings, which was accepted by the *posekim*, concerns heterogeneous sowing in a vineyard and so limits culpability as to make the interdiction almost nonexistent as far as the biblical law is concerned (Kid. 39a et al.). Many of his other rulings also incline to leniency. Although from Babylon, he firmly upheld the authority of the Great *Bet Din in Jerusalem as the sole body competent to intercalate the year (Mekh. Pisḥa 2). Josiah was still alive in the first age of the *amoraim* and is therefore sometimes called Josiah the Great, to distinguish him from an *amora* of the same name (Sanh. 19b). Of his few aggadic dicta, the following may be noted: "the deeds of the righteous yield fruit … the deeds of the wicked do not produce fruit, for if they produced fruit they would destroy the world" (Gen. R. 33:1); "If a good deed comes your way, do it immediately" (Mekh. Pisḥa 9).

BIBLIOGRAPHY: Bacher, Tann; Frankel, Mishnah, 154–7; Hyman, Toledot, 529–31; Neusner, Babylonia, 1 (1965), 128–35; idem, in: PAAJR, 30 (1962), 92ff.

[Harry Freedman]

JOSIAH (third century C.E.), Palestinian *amora*. Josiah was a pupil of Johanan, in whose name he transmitted teachings (TJ, Kil. 9:4, 32b; Ḥul. 128a; et al.). He also studied under Kahana (TJ, RH 1:1, 56d), who upon his death ordered that part of his legacy be given to Josiah (TJ, Sanh. 3:9, 21d; cf. Gen. R. ed. by Theodor and Ḥ. Albeck (19652) 53n. 1). He discussed halakhic problems with Eleazar b. Pedat (Sot. 19a; et al.), and some of his other colleagues were Ḥiyya b. Abba, Ammi, and Assi (TJ, Ta'an. 2:1, 65a–b). On one occasion, when preaching on a public fast day, he interpreted *hitkosheshu va-koshu* (Zeph. 2:1) as if the verb were from the root *kash*, meaning stubble, and rendering it as "let us remove our own stubble before removing the stubble of others," i.e., "let us mend our own ways before pointing out other peoples' faults" (TJ, Ta'an. 2:1, 65a–b; and cf. BM 107b). He was held in high esteem by his contemporaries. When Isaac b. Redifa came to ask a halakhic question of Jeremiah, the latter replied, "the lions are available and you enquire of the foxes! Go and ask Josiah" (TJ, Shev. 9:5, 39a). A number of *amoraim* with the name Josiah are mentioned in the Talmud, and it is possible that one of them, Josiah of Usha (Git. 33b; et al.), is the same as this Josiah.

BIBLIOGRAPHY: Heinemann, Toledot, 531f.; Frankel, Mevo, 90b, 109b; Ḥ. Albeck, *Mavo la-Talmudim* (1969), 243.

[Yitzhak Dov Gilat]

JOSIAH BEN AARON HE-ḤAVER (fl. 11th century), Palestinian *gaon*. Josiah belonged to the family of the *gaon*, *Aron b. Meir. He was the head of Yeshivat Geon Ya'akov in Jerusalem, and later in Ramleh, to which the yeshivah was transferred, presumably as a result of pressure by the Karaites. Josiah engaged in a controversy with a Karaite leader, possibly Solomon b. David b. Boaz. The exact years of his gaonate are not known; his signature appears on a document of the year 1015, and it is thought that he was active until 1020. He appointed *Ephraim b. Shemariah, head of Palestinian Jews in Egypt, as a "*ḥaver*" (a rabbinical title of honor). His letters to the Jewish community of Egypt, appealing for help, reflect the sufferings endured by the Jews of Ereẓ Israel as a result of the persecutions of the Fatimid caliph Ḥakim.

BIBLIOGRAPHY: S. Poznański, *Babylonische Geonim im nachgaonaeischen Zeitalter* (1914), 85–86, 97; idem, in: REJ, 66 (1913), 59–71; Mann, Jews, 1 (1920), 65–66, 71; 2 (1922), 49, 52f., 66–72; Mann, in: HUCA, 3 (1926), 265; Mann, Texts, 1 (1931), 314; 2 (1935), 46, 135f.; S. Assaf and L.A. Mayer (eds.), *Sefer ha-Yishuv*, 2 (1944), 57–58, 126–7; Dinur, Golah, 1 pt. 4 (1962^2), index.

[Eliezer Bashan (Sternberg)]

JOSIAH BEN JESSE (d. after 1235), *nasi* of the Jews in *Damascus during the first half of the 13th century. Judah *Al-Ḥarizi met him when he visited Damascus, about 1216, and wrote poems of praise in his honor. In these Al-Ḥarizi mentions Josiah's lineage, which could be traced to *Zerubbabel. He refers to him by the title of *Nesi Galuyyot Kol Yisrael* ("prince of the Diasporas of all Jewry"). It appears that there was a special significance to this title and that it was more than mere rhetoric, because in the ban which he issued in 1235 the title appears again. In this ban his brother, Solomon b. Jesse (d. after 1244) who lived in Fostat, is also mentioned. He is also referred to by the title of *Nesi Galuyyot Yisrael* ("prince of the Diasporas"). Hodayah b. Jesse ha-Nasi, referred to as *Nesi Nesi'ei Galuyyot Kol Yisrael* ("chief of the princes of Diasporas of all Jewry"), was also Josiah's brother. It is known that Hodayah was in Alexandria for a few years, since he came into conflict with the *dayyan* R. Joseph b. Gershon, who lived at the same time as Abraham b. Moses b. *Maimuni. One of his descendants was the *nasi* *Jesse b. Hezekiah.

BIBLIOGRAPHY: Judah Al-Ḥarizi, *Taḥkemoni*, ed. by, A. Kaminka (1899), 21–24, 355; S. Poznański, *Babylonische Geonim im nachgaonaeischen Zeitalter* (1914), 123; Simonsen, in: *Festschrift… Jacob Guttmann* (1915), 218ff.; Mann, Egypt, 1 (1920), 175f.; 2 (1922), 210, 357–9; idem, in: *Sefer… S.A. Poznański* (1927), 28f. **ADD BIBLIOGRAPHY:** M. Gil, *Be-Malkhut Ishmael*, 439–43.

[Abraham David]

JOSIAH BEN SAUL BEN ANAN (late eighth to ninth century), Karaite authority, presumed grandson of *Anan b. David, the titular founder of the sect, and son of *Saul b. Anan. His writings have not been preserved. Judah *Hadassi (in *Eshkol ha-Kofer*, 258, letter ק) refers to Josiah as a "shining light of knowledge" and reports that he ruled that, in the case of inheritance, the brothers of the deceased should have an equal share with the dead man's sons. *Elijah b. Abraham, author of *Ḥilluk ha-Kara'im ve-ha-Rabbanim*, mentions him as "Josiah, crown of the Torah"; *Aaron b. Elijah (*Gan Eden*, 144b) and Elijah *Bashyazi (*Adderet Eliyahu*, 80b) refer to him as "Prince Josiah" and quote his opinion on the preconditions necessary for entrance into matrimony. Only in the genealogical tables and the "chain of tradition" of the later Karaite authors is Josiah mentioned definitely as a grandson of Anan.

BIBLIOGRAPHY: Markon, in: *Jeschurun*, 14 (1927), 25ff.; Mann, Texts, 2 (1935), 128–30.

[Isaak Dov Ber Markon]

JOSIPHIAH (Jehosiphia) THE PROSELYTE (early 12th century), French liturgical poet. Josiphiah is quoted by *Jacob ha-Levi of Marvège and is also mentioned in *Sefer ha-Gan*, and by *Judah b. Eliezer (1313) and Moses *Rieti (15th century). Of the known eight poems which bear Josiphiah's signature, only three have been published, among them an introduction to *Illu Finu*, translated into German by S. Heller (*Die echten hebraeischen Melodien* (1908^3)) on the basis of S.D. Luzzatto's edition in *Tal Orot* (1881), 34, no. 43.

BIBLIOGRAPHY: Zunz, Lit. Poesie, 469; Dukes, in: *Oẓar Neḥmad*, 2 (1857), 101; Landshuth, Ammudei, 88; Brody (ed.), in: *Maḥzor Vitry* (1923) *(Kunteres ha-Piyyutim)*, 49 no. 83, 55 no. 95; Urbach, Tosafot, 194; Davidson, Oẓar, 4 (1933), 391. **ADD. BIBLIOGRAPHY:** E. Fleischer, *Hebrew Liturgical Poetry in the Middle Ages* (1975), 461.

[Jefim (Hayyim) Schirmann]

JOSIPOVICI, GABRIEL (1940–), English novelist, playwright, and literary critic. Born in Nice, France, Josipovici was educated at Victoria College, Cairo, and at Oxford University. From 1963 he taught at the University of Sussex where he became a professor of English Literature. In 1981 he was made the Northcliffe Lecturer at University College, London. His first novel, *The Inventory*, was published in 1968 and his outstanding work of literary criticism, *The World and the Book: A Study of Modern Fiction*, appeared in 1971. He also wrote *The Lessons of Modernism and Other Essays* (1977) and edited *The Modern English Novels. The Reader, The Writer, and the Work* (1976). As well as his acclaimed literary criticism, Josipovici published *Four Stories* (1977), a collection of short stories, and ten stage and radio plays. *Mobius the Stripper: Stories and Short Plays* (1974) contains an important selection of this work.

Josipovici is a consciously postmodernist writer who has rejected the tradition of 19th-century realism. Instead, his literary tradition is made up of Marcel *Proust, Franz *Kafka, Rainer Maria Rilke, T.S. Eliot and, more recently, Samuel Beckett, Alaine Robbe-Grillet, Jorge Luis Borges and George *Perec. All of these writers transcend a too easy identification with a national culture. Their "rootlessly self-contained" art, in the words of one critic, corresponds to Josipovici's own abstract, vulnerable, inconclusive short novels. Much of his fiction, such as *The Inventory, Words* (1971), and *Conversations in Another Room* (1984), juxtaposes the lightness and musicality of the author's dialogue with a series of haunting, unanswered questions. *Migrations*, on the other hand, lacks a narrative thread as it moves between nameless, displaced individuals who are related only by the author's recurring images.

Josipovici's disdain for fiction which is based on large historical questions means that his novels do not deal explicitly with Jewish themes. The Jewish writers which interest him the most are, therefore, those that write outside of a defined Jewish tradition – such as Saul *Bellow, Bernard *Malamud, and, of course, Kafka and Proust – and not such "insiders," in Josipovici's terms, as Isaac Bashevis *Singer and S.Y. *Agnon. It was only after the Six-Day War that Josipovici began to explore his Jewishness with considerable interest. He wrote the introduction to the English edition of Aharon *Appelfeld's *The Retreat* (1985), and he was a regular contributor to *European Judaism* and *The Jewish Quarterly.*

BIBLIOGRAPHY: J. Vinson (ed.), *Contemporary Novelists*, (1982) 356–357; *The Jewish Quarterly*, 32 (1985). **ADD. BIBLIOGRAPHY:** M. Fludermik, *Echoes and Mirrorings: Gabriel Josipovici's Creative Oeuvre* (2001).

[Bryan Cheyette]

JOSIPPON, historical narrative in Hebrew, of anonymous authorship, describing the period of the Second Temple, written in southern Italy in the tenth century. The author starts his narrative by listing the different nations and their places of settlement, based on the catalog of the descendants of Japheth mentioned in Genesis 10, and relating these to peoples of his own times. The author proceeds to recount the history of ancient Italy and the founding of Rome; he then passes to the period of the Second Temple. The book – like Josephus' *The Jewish War* – ends with the fall of Masada. A large part of the work is devoted to the wars of the Jews against the Romans.

The author states that the Hungarians, the Bulgarians, and the Pechenegs dwelt "on the great river called the Danube, i.e., Donau," and this was a geographical situation existing after 900 C.E. The author also observes that the "Ishmaelites" (i.e., Arabs) lived in Tarsus, which is in Asia Minor. Since this town was conquered by Byzantium in 965 C.E., it is clear that the book was written between these two dates. In one of the manuscripts of *Josippon* the precise date of the book is given: "and we wrote from the book, from the book of Joseph ben Gorion ha-Kohen in the year 885 from the Destruction." Since it was customary then to reckon the Destruction of the Temple from the year 68 C.E., it follows that the book was composed in 953 C.E. All signs point to the fact that the Hebrew book was written in southern Italy which, at the time, was one of the important Jewish centers. The author's place of birth was part of the Byzantine Empire, where the official language was Greek. The author, however, could not read Greek, only Latin. The main source of *Josippon* was a Latin manuscript which included 16 of the 20 books of Josephus' *Jewish Antiquities* and the Latin adaptation of *The Jewish War.* The latter was written in the second half of the fourth century C.E. and called *Hegesippus*. The author of *Josippon* also knew random facts from *The Jewish War* itself with which he was acquainted only incidentally; he knew also about the *Contra Apionem* of Josephus. The author calls Josephus "Joseph ben Gorion," although Josephus' father was called Mattathias. He was misled by the inaccurate language of the *Hegesippus*, and he identified Josephus with Joseph b. Gorion who had also been a general in the war against the Romans. The author's second important source was the Latin version of the *Apocrypha; thus he learned about the Hasmonean period from the two books of Maccabees. The remainder of his secular sources were various medieval chronicles; from these he mainly gained information concerning the gentile kingdoms. He had, of course, a certain knowledge of talmudic literature, but his main sources were Latin. Considering the period in which he lived, the author was a gifted historian, aware of his responsibilities and endowed with excellent historical insight. Fables drawn from obscure sources are only rarely found in his book, mainly in the chapters dealing with the ancient history of Italy. The author also had great literary gifts. His narrative is filled with national pride and is written in an excellent biblical Hebrew style. In the Middle Ages, the book was already called *Sefer Josippon*; this is the Jewish-Greek form for *Josephus*. In the original version found preserved in manuscripts the author speaks in the first person and defines the purpose of his writing thus: "I have collected stories from the book of Joseph b. Gorion and from the books of other authors who wrote down the deeds of our ancestors, and I compiled them in one scroll." Since the name of the author was not known, the book was ascribed, by the time of Rashi, to Josephus himself. This mistaken ascription later became explicit in an expanded and revised version of the book written not later than 1160, and edited in the 14th century by Judah Leon *Moskoni. This edition served as a basis for the Constantinople edition of 1510 which was the source for all subsequent editions. This version, too, was composed in Italy. Its author restyled the book, ascribed it to Joseph b. Gorion, and added fictitious elements, although he himself was lacking neither in Jewish nor in secular knowledge. The most famous among the passages to be found in the expanded version is a fictitious description of the crowning of Vespasian in Rome. This was written under the influence of the crowning of emperors in Rome during the Middle Ages. Today the book is known to the reader in this rewritten and popular version. Another early edition of *Josippon* is that of Mantua (c. 1480), based on a carelessly restyled, and at times even abbreviated, manuscript of the original version. In this edition, all reference to Joseph b. Gorion as author has been omitted. The original form and the true character of the book of *Josippon* can, therefore, be known only from manuscripts. Among the better known manuscripts, three are based on a manuscript that R. *Gershom b. Judah copied "in his own hand." In one of these appears the date of composition. R. Gershom probably copied *Josippon* to use as a textbook on the history of the Jews during the time of the Second Temple.

During the Middle Ages, *Josippon* served as a source of information about the period of the later books of the Bible (such as the books of Esther and Daniel) and about the whole period of the Second Temple. This is the reason that Bible and Talmud commentators frequently quoted it during the Middle Ages and at the beginning of the modern period. The book of *Josippon* attained great importance during the Middle Ages. For instance, a passage on Alexander the Great translated from it appeared in the early Russian chronicle of Nestor, without mentioning the source. The book is referred to by name, however, by the Arab scholar Ibn Ḥazm (d. 1063). The importance attached to the book stemmed from its ascription to Josephus, who had been a contemporary of events described in it.

An Arabic translation of *Josippon* by a Yemenite Jew was probably in existence already in the 11th century. From Arabic it was translated into Ethiopian (c. 1300). Translations into European languages, such as Latin, English, Czech, Polish, and Russian, were generally made from printed editions. The author of the book of *Josippon*, following his sources, mentions John the Baptist, but he refers neither to Jesus nor to the beginnings of Christianity. Brief mention of Jesus is made in the manuscript of the expanded version of *Josippon*, and a polemical story about Jesus and the beginnings of Christianity was inserted in a number of manuscripts. *Josippon*'s relationship (or lack of relationship) with Christianity interested both Muslims and Christians. From the age of humanism, leading Christian humanists discussed the question of whether the book of *Josippon* had really been composed by Josephus. The book was also known to the Karaites and, in a Samaritan chronicle written in Arabic, *Josippon*'s account of Alexander the Great's visit to Jerusalem is included; the place of the visit was changed to Mt. Gerizim. A short Hebrew narrative translated from the Greek was inserted into some versions of *Josippon*. The narrative is an abridgment of a legend about Alexander the Great, ascribed to Calisthenes, and an anonymous Greek-Byzantine chronicle on the period from Alexander to Tiberius. This important narrative has been preserved independently in one manuscript.

Two works on Josippon by Professor David Flusser were published almost simultaneously in 1978. The first is an edition based upon the original manuscript with a photostatic reproduction of selected extracts from Josippon, with an introduction (Mercaz Zalman Shazar). The second was the first volume of a critical edition, based upon all existing manuscripts and giving the text with an introduction; the second volume of the critical edition appeared in 1980, completing the work.

BIBLIOGRAPHY: *Josiphon*, ed. by H. Hominer (1967), introd. by A.J. Wertheimer; Baer, in: *Sefer Dinaburg* (1949), 178–205; Flusser, in: *Zion*, 18 (1953), 109–26; Baron, Social, 6 (1958^2), 189–96, 417–21; Toaff, in: *Annuario di studie ebraici*, 3 (1964), 41–46; idem, *Cronaca Ebraica del Sepher Yosephon* (1969); Zeitlin, in: JQR, 53 (1963), 277–97; Roth, Dark Ages, 2 (1966), 277–81; A.A. Neuman, *Landmarks and Goals* (1953), 1–57.

[David Flusser]

JOSKO (or **Jossko**; end of 15th–beginning of 16th century), wealthy Jewish merchant in Lvov. He was a customs duties collector and a banker to King Alexander of Poland (1501–06), and for many years was a purveyor of cloth and fur to the court. In 1503, as a result of Josko's intervention, the king ordered that the Jews of Lvov be permitted to trade at fairs and the town's markets, despite vigorous opposition from the townsmen. Josko assisted the community against them on several occasions.

BIBLIOGRAPHY: *Russko-yevreyskiy arkhiv*, 3 (1903), nos. 30–35, 47, 48; I. Schipper, *Studya nad stosunkami gospodarczymi Żydow w Polsce podczas średniowiecza* (1911), 201; M. Balaban, in: *Kwartalnik Historyczny*, 25 no. 2 (1911).

[Arthur Cygielman]

JOSPE, ALFRED (1909–1994), rabbi, educator, author, and editor. Jospe was born in Berlin to Josef and Rosa Jospe; his father and both his grandfathers, Israel Jospe and Selmar Cerini (Steifmann), were cantors. An active Zionist from his youth, Jospe received his doctorate in philosophy at the University of Breslau in 1932. In 1935 he married Eva Scheyer and received his rabbinic ordination from the Juedisch-Theologisches Seminar in Breslau. After serving for two years (1934–35) as district rabbi of the province of Grenzmark, he was appointed to the community rabbinate in Berlin (1936). Following **Kristallnacht* (November 9–10, 1938), Jospe was interned in the Sachsenhausen concentration camp. In March 1939 he was able to leave Germany for the United States (via England) with his wife and daughter.

Jospe's first American rabbinical position, and only pulpit, was in Morgantown, West Virginia (1939–44), where in 1940 he also assumed the responsibility for directing the Hillel Foundation at the University of West Virginia. In 1944 he became director of Hillel at Indiana University, and in 1949 joined the national leadership of Hillel in New York, becoming its director of programs and resources. Jospe and his family moved to Washington, D.C., in 1957, when B'nai B'rith (including the Hillel Foundations) moved its headquarters there from New York. In 1971 he was elected Hillel's international director, a position he held until his retirement at the end of 1974.

For most of his career Jospe was involved in educational administration, and in many respects he provided the intellectual leadership shaping the Hillel Foundations during its years of great growth, seeking to formulate an evolving "philosophy of Hillel" that would enable Hillel to meet changing student needs (especially in the "turbulent years" of the 1960s and early 1970s), while remaining faithful to abiding underlying principles.

At the same time, Jospe retained an active interest in philosophy and Jewish thought. His many publications include academic works (on Moses Mendelssohn, on *Wissenschaft des Judentums*, on the history of the German rabbinate, and on the teaching of Jewish Studies at German universities); essays in Jewish thought; anthologies he edited of thematically arranged lectures by leading thinkers and scholars, based on programs at successive national summer institutes of Hillel; and professional guides relating to Hillel as the "Jewish presence on the campus." The rapid expansion of purely academic programs in Jewish Studies in many universities began to take place during the last few years of Jospe's career. Until then, on many campuses, Hillel, besides its other functions in offering religious, cultural, and chaplaincy services, provided the only link for students with an academic (even if extracurricular) presentation of Judaism, to combat what Jospe called the "pediatric Judaism" of many alienated young Jews, whose minimal childhood exposure to Jewish education could not compete with their advanced secular education for intellectual respectability and serious commitment. A proper Jewish education should be both cognitive and affective, involving both mind and heart: "Both celebration and cerebration have a legitimate place, but not at the expense of the other."

Jospe's publications, reflecting his diverse areas of interest, include *Die Unterscheidung von Mythos und Religion bei Hermann Cohen und Ernst Cassirer in ihrer Bedeutung fuer die juedische Religionsphilosophie* (1932); *The Legacy of Maurice Pekarsky* (1965); an annotated English translation with introduction of *Jerusalem and Other Jewish Writings* of Moses Mendelssohn (1969); *Tradition and Contemporary Experience: Essays on Jewish Life and Thought* (1970); *Bridges to a Holy Time: New Worship for the Sabbath and Minor Festivals* (with Richard Levy; 1973); *Studies in Jewish Thought: An Anthology of German Jewish Scholarship* (1981). *To Leave Your Mark: Selections from the Writings of Alfred Jospe*, ed. E. Jospe and R. Jospe, was published posthumously (2000). For a complete bibliography until 1980, see *Go and Study: Essays and Studies in Honor of Alfred Jospe*, ed. R. Jospe and S. Fishman (1980).

His wife EVA (1913–) was born in Oppeln, Germany (now Opole, Poland) and pursued graduate studies in philosophy at the New School for Social Research in New York and Georgetown University in Washington, DC. She taught modern Jewish thought at Georgetown and then at George Washington University until the age of 80. Her publications and translations include Martin Buber's "Early Addresses" in *On Judaism*, ed. N. Glatzer (1967); *Reason and Hope: Selections from the Jewish Writings of Hermann Cohen* (1971; reissued 1993); *Moses Mendelssohn: Selections from His Writings* (1975); "Hermann Cohen's Judaism: A Reassessment," in: *Judaism* 25:4 (1976), 461–72; "Encounter: The Thought of Martin Buber," in: *Judaism*, 27:2 (1978), 135–47; "Moses Mendelssohn: Some Reflections on His Thought," in: *Judaism* 30:2 (1981), 169–82; Franz Rosenzweig's commentary to *Ninety-Two Poems and Hymns of Yehuda Halevi*, ed. R. Cohen (2000).

Eva and Alfred Jospe had three children: SUSANNE GREENBERG (1935–), a rabbi in West Chester, PA; NAOMI PISETZKY (1942–), a teacher in Petaḥ Tikvah; and RAPHAEL JOSPE (1947–) of the department of Jewish Philosophy at Bar-Ilan University and the Hebrew University Rothberg International School, and editor of the Jewish Philosophy division of the second edition of the *Encyclopaedia Judaica*.

Alfred Jospe's brother, ERWIN JOSPE (1907–1983), was a musician, choir director, professor of music and dean of fine arts at the University of Judaism. He edited with Joseph Jacobsen a collection of Jewish music, *Hawa Naschira: Auf! Lasst uns Singen* (1935; reissued 2001).

JOST, ISAAC MARCUS (1793–1860), German educator and historian. Jost was born in Bernburg, central Germany. He received his primary education at the Samson-Schule in Wolfenbuettel, where he became an intimate friend of Leopold Zunz. After studies at the universities in Goettingen and Berlin, he became head of a private high school in Frankfurt on the Main. The school was attended by both Jewish and Christian boys until the Prussian government prohibited this "revolutionary" project; the school then became exclusively Jewish. From 1835 onward he taught at the Philanthropin high school in Frankfurt. In 1853 he founded an orphanage for Jewish girls in Frankfurt. In conjunction with his educational activities Jost published a Pentateuch for young people (1823) and a vocalized Mishnah text (1832–34), with translation and notes; he also published a textbook of English (1843^3), a dictionary of Shakespeare (1830), and a manual of German style (1852^2).

In Frankfurt he edited (with M. Creizenach) the short-lived Hebrew journal *Zion* (1841–42), and from 1839 to 1841 the *Israelitische Annalen*. He founded, with Ludwig Philippson and others, the Institut zur Foerderung der Israelitischen Literatur, which published the *Jahrbuch fuer Geschichte der Juden und des Judentums* (4 vols., 1860–69).

A moderate supporter of the Reform movement, he helped prepare the second Rabbinical Conference at Frankfurt in 1845 and acted as its secretary. Jost, however, opposed extremist tendencies and vigorously defended the use of Hebrew in synagogue and school.

Jost was a pioneer in the field of modern Jewish historiography and his works in this field include: *Geschichte der Israeliten seit der Zeit der Maccabaeer bis auf unsere Tage* (9 vols., (1820–28)); *Neuere Geschichte der Israeliten von 1815 bis 1845* (3 vols., 1846–47); *Allgemeine Geschichte des Israelitischen Volkes* (2 vols., 1832); and *Geschichte des Judenthums und seiner Sekten* (3 vols., 1857–59). Jost wrote his work while others were still laying the foundations of the new Science of Judaism; Zunz himself shrank from writing a comprehensive history, and Graetz soon afterward wrote *Geschichte der Juden*, which exhibited far greater brilliance and scholarship. However, the adverse criticism by A. Geiger, H. Graetz, and S.D. Luzzatto tended to overlook the real merits of Jost's pioneering work with its high standard of objective scholarship. Although a rationalist who felt little sympathy with the religious view of Jewish history and who concentrated mainly on writing political history to the almost complete exclusion of cultural history, Jost anticipated later historiography by his critical approach to the sources, the individual treatment of Jewish history in different countries, and his recognition of the importance of social institutions for the understanding of history. His *Neuere Geschichte* has, in addition, great value as a contemporary record.

BIBLIOGRAPHY: J. Pascheles, *Sippurim*, 3 (1854), 141ff. includes an autobiography by Jost; H. Zirndorf, *Isaac Markus Jost und seine Freunde* (1886), includes bibliography; S.W. Baron, *History and Jewish Historians* (1964), 240ff. **ADD. BIBLIOGRAPHY:** R. Michael, *Y.M. Jost* (Heb., 1983); U. Wyrwa, in: K. Hoedl (ed.), *Historisches Bewusstsein* (2004), 99–108.

[Marcus Pyka (2nd ed.)]

JOTABAH, an island in the Gulf of Elath (Aila) inhabited by a colony of Jewish merchants. In the second half of the fifth century C.E., it was seized by a Persian adventurer called Amorkesos, who controlled the Red Sea trade from there and levied customs. The emperor Leo confirmed the position of Amorkesos in 474, but in 498 Anastasius sent an expedition under the general Aratus against him and the fortress was stormed. The community remained unmolested till the time of Justinian (527–65), who expelled the Jews. Procopius located the island 1000 stadia from Alia, a position which corresponds to that of the island of Tiran at the mouth of the gulf. A Hebrew University expedition to Tiran in 1956, however, found no evidence of a Byzantine settlement. Recently, Jezīrat el-Farʿūn, 7½ mi. (12 km.) south of Elath, which has remains of Byzantine fortifications, has been proposed as an identification.

BIBLIOGRAPHY: Abel, in: RB, 47 (1938), 511ff.; J. Aharoni and B. Rothenberg, *God's Wilderness* (1961); M. Avi-Yonah, *Geschichte der Juden im Zeitalter des Talmud …* (1962), 237.

[Michael Avi-Yonah]

JOTAPATA or **Yodefat** (Heb. יוֹדְפַת), Galilean fortress. It appears as [*Ia*]-*aṭ-bi-te* among the cities captured by Tiglath Pileser III in 732 B.C.E., together with Qana and Ruma. Four hundred of the inhabitants were deported by the Assyrians. It was possibly the home town of Haruz of Jotbah, the wife of Manasseh, king of Judah (II Kings 21:19). In the Mishnah it is described as a fortress dating from the time of Joshua (Ar. 9:6; as Yodefat). In 66 C.E., at the beginning of the Jewish War against Rome, *Josephus turned it into a strong fortress, which served as the key to his line of fortifications protecting Galilee. After the dispersal of his army, he proceeded there and withstood a siege by Vespasian and his army for 47 days (Jos., Wars, 3:141–288, 316ff.). The fortress, as described by Josephus, was built on a ridge surrounded by ravines on all sides but the north, where a suburb lying on the next ridge was also fortified.

Jotapata continued as a Jewish town after it fell to the Romans. Following the destruction of the Temple, the priestly family of Miyamin settled there. In the period of the Bar-Kokhba rebellion Jotbah was the seat of the priestly family of Miyamin; it may also be the Gopatata referred to in the midrash (Eccles. R. 108a). The Babylonian Talmud also mentions a R. Menahem of Jotapata (Zev. 110b) and it may have been the episcopal town of Jotabe from 536 C.E. The site was identified by E.G. Schultz in 1847 with Khirbet Shifat, 6 mi. (c. 10 km.) north of Sepphoris, near Mt. Azmon. The site was subsequently explored by C. Conder and H.H. Kitchener for the Palestine Exploration Fund in the 1870s.

Excavations were conducted at the site in 1992 by D. Edwards, M. Aviam, and D. Adan-Bayewitz, revealing remains dating from the Hellenistic period through to medieval times. A fortification wall from the Ptolemaic period was uncovered with three phases of construction evident. To the northwest were the remains of a ramp dating from the time of the Roman siege in 67 C.E. The finds included remains from the battle including ballista balls and iron bow and catapult arrowheads. Rubble walls built at this location seem to have been part of the Jewish preparations prior to the arrival of the Romans. An oil press, pottery kilns, and several ritual baths (*mikvaʾot*) were uncovered. The lower part of the site was reoccupied in the late first or early second centuries C.E., and there were also signs of occupation of medieval date.

[Michael Avi-Yonah / Shimon Gibson (2nd ed.)]

The modern kibbutz of Yodefat is situated north of the ancient mound. It was founded in 1961 by Israel-born youth, mostly from Haifa, unaffiliated with any countrywide settlement federation. In 1968 Yodefat had 47 inhabitants, mostly vegetarians. Fruit orchards were its main farm branch. Since then it has become a large-scale flower bulb exporter, with around 1,000 acres of land under cultivation and 369 residents in 2004.

[Efraim Orni]

BIBLIOGRAPHY: E. Forrer, *Die Provinzeinteilung des assyrischen Reiches* (1920), 61; Saarisalo, in: JPOS, 9 (1929), 39; Oehler, in: ZDPV (1905), 53ff.; Alt, in: PJB, 27 (1931), 40; Avi-Yonah, Geog; idem, *Atlas Karta li-Tekufat Bayit Sheni ve-ha-Talmud* (1966), map no. 109.

ADD. BIBLIOGRAPHY: D.R. Edwards et al., "Yodefat, 1992," in: *Israel Exploration Journal*, 45 (1995), 191–97.

JOTBATH, JOTHBATAH (Heb. יָטְבָתָה), a station of the Israelites during their wanderings in the wilderness, situated between Hor-Haggidgad and Abronah (Num. 33:33–34). It is also described as "a land of brooks of water" (Deut. 10:7). The identification of Jotbath depends on the view held of the route taken by the Israelites between Mt. Sinai and Ezion-Geber (Elath). Scholars who favor the northern route to Elath identify Jotbath with ʿAyn Ghadyān near a marsh called Sabkhat al-Ṭāba. The name ʿAyn Ghadyān is derived from the Roman Ad Dianam, which is located on the Peutinger Map 26 mi. (40 km.; erroneously given on the map as 16 mi.) north of Aila (Elath) (see also *Yotvatah). According to this map the Damascus-Elath road joined the Jerusalem-Elath road at Ad Dianam, but this, however, is disputed. Its name suggests that it contained a temple dedicated to Diana. Remains of forts from the time of the Judahite kings and of a fort and pool from the late Roman and Byzantine periods have been discovered at ʿAyn Ghadyān; a kibbutz called Yotvatah has been established there. Other scholars who maintain that the approach to Ezion-Geber was from the south place Jotbath at Wadi al-Ṭāba, which is rich in water and falls into the Read Sea 7 mi. (11 km.) south of Elath.

BIBLIOGRAPHY: Abel, Geog, 2 (1938), 216, 366; Glueck, in: AASOR, 18/19 (1939), 95; Frank, in: ZDPV, 57 (1934), 191ff., 238; EM, s.v.; J. Aharoni and B. Rothenberg, *God's Wilderness* (1961); Alt, in ZDPV, 58 (1935), 1ff.; Aharoni, in: iej, 4 (1954), 9ff.; idem, in: *Eretz Israel*, 5 (1958), 129ff.

[Michael Avi-Yonah]

JOTHAM (Heb. יוֹתָם; "YHWH is perfect"), the youngest son of *Gideon the judge. Jotham was the only one to survive the massacre conceived by his half brother *Abimelech, whose hired assassins slew 70 of the 71 sons of Gideon (Jerubbaal) "on one stone" (Judg. 9:1–6). Jotham alone survived. Perhaps the writer is punning on his name in that in Hebrew *yatom* means orphan. He escaped to Mt. Gerizim above the city of Shechem and, with sparkling irony, denounced the Shechemites for accepting Abimelech as king. Jotham relates the fable of the trees (Judg. 9:8–15) which tells how the trees once anointed one of their number king. The good trees – the olive, fig, and vine – to whom the crown was offered, refused to trade their unique capacities for honoring both God and man in return for mere power, but the fruitless bramble accepted the throne. From the subsequent verses (16–20) it is clear that the trees represent the rulers of Shechem, while Abimelech, whom they had crowned, is the bramble. The oration concludes with a curse upon both the Shechemites and Abimelech.

Jotham's fable has frequently been interpreted as a piece of anti-monarchical irony exposing the unproductive and ultimately disastrous nature of kingship. However, the fable does not denounce the institution as such nor are its details in consonance with the historical reality. Unlike the trees, the Shechemites had not taken the initiative, nor had they offered the crown to anyone; Gideon's sons had inherited their position of rulership, and no reference to the murder of the 70 brothers is to be found in the fable. Therefore Jotham's fable is probably an ancient etiology explaining how the lowly, useless thornbush became an incendiary danger to all trees, even to the mighty cedars. The trees, in their folly, gave the bramble power because the good trees had evaded their duty. But in the mouth of Jotham, the fable becomes a parable warning of the fatal danger of placing royal power in the wrong hands (Kaufmann, p. 202 in bibl.). After he delivered his oration, Jotham fled to Beer (Judg. 9:21) and is not heard of again. The subsequent downfall of Abimelech is seen as the fulfillment of the curse (9:57).

BIBLIOGRAPHY: Bright, Hist, 151–60; E.H. Maly, in: CBQ, 22 (1960), 299–305; Y. Kaufmann, *Sefer Shofetim* (1962), 199–206. **ADD. BIBLIOGRAPHY:** Y. Amit, *Judges* (1999), 165–70.

[Nahum M. Sarna and Robert G. Boling]

JOTHAM (Heb. יוֹתָם; "YHWH is perfect"; c. 758–743 B.C.E.), king of Judah; son of *Uzziah (Azariah) and Jerusha, daughter of Zadok (II Kings 15:32–33; II Chron. 27:1). Jotham became king at the age of 25 and, according to II Kings 15:33, reigned 16 years. This contradicts the statement three verses earlier that "*Hoshea son of Elah, made a conspiracy … in the twentieth year of Jotham son of Uzziah" (II Kings 15:30), indicating that Jotham reigned at least 20 years. This may be the result of a miscalculation by a late historian who did not take the coregency (below) into account (Cogan and Tadmor, 181). The concluding phrase is missing from the Lucianic recension of the Septuagint. Apparently Jotham died close to the time of his father's death. According to II Kings 15:5, he was co-regent with his father after the latter had contracted a dread skin disease (*ẓaraʿat*; traditionally but inaccurately rendered "leprosy"), and was isolated outside the city, while Jotham was "in charge of the palace" (*al ha-bayit*), and thus was actually second in rank to the king.

According to II Chronicles 27, Jotham built cities and fortresses and engaged the Ammonites in battle to defend Judah's claims in Trans-Jordan. He was successful in subjugating the Ammonites to Judah and in collecting tribute from them for three years (II Chron. 27:5). The rule of Judah in Transjordan is attested indirectly by I Chronicles 5:17, which tells of the census of the tribes of Israel in the area during the reigns of Jotham king of Judah and Jeroboam king of Israel. The notice that "the Lord began to send Rezin … and Pekah … against Judah" (II Kings 15:37) may indicate that the King of Israel and the King of Aram were responding to Jotham's expansionist moves (Cogan and Tadmor, 182–83). The prosperity of the country during his reign enabled him to undertake projects of fortification throughout the country. The general description given by the Chronicler is that Jotham continued his father's work. He fortified the wall of the Ophel in Jerusalem (II Chron. 27:3) and undertook repairs and made additions in the Temple area (*ibid.*, II Kings 15:35). The Chronicler contrasts the piety of Jotham with the impiety of his father Uzziah, whose skin disease he attributes to Uzziah's attempt to usurp priestly functions (II Chron. 26:16–21). According to Josephus, Jotham built chambers in the Temple and possibly raised the height of the building.

[*Encyclopaedia Hebraica* / S. David Sperling (2nd ed.)]

In the Aggadah

Jotham was one of the most righteous of the kings of Judah. He loyally observed the fifth commandment by being content to act as regent during his father's reign, without even aspiring to the throne. Moreover, he always gave a ruling in his father's name. Simeon b. Yoḥai referred to Jotham's piety in the statement: "I alone am able to exempt the world from judgment from the day I was born until now; were my son Eliezer with me, we could exempt it from creation until now; and were Jotham with us, we could exempt it from the creation of the world until its end" (Suk. 45b).

The difficulties presented by the conflicting scriptural datings of the reigns of Amaziah and Jotham are explained by the statement that Jotham ruled for 20 years during the illness of his father, Uzziah. The scriptural reference to the 20th year of Jotham's reign (II Kings 15:30), as against the statement that he reigned only for 16 years (II Chron. 27:1), is resolved by pointing out that because of his piety four years were deducted from Ahab's reign and added to those of Jotham (SOR 22).

BIBLIOGRAPHY: Bright, Hist, 240, 256; Aharoni, in: *Tarbiz*, 21 (1940), 94ff.; S. Yeivin, *Luḥot Kronologiyyim…* (1962); E. Auerbach, *Wueste und Gelobtes Land*, 2 (1936), 85ff.; Tadmor, in: A. Malamat (ed.), *Bi-Ymei Bayit Rishon* (1961), 158ff.; EM, S.V. (includes bibliography). AGGADAH: Ginzberg, Legends, index; I. Ḥasida, *Ishei ha-Tanakh* (1964), 197. **ADD. BIBLIOGRAPHY:** M. Cogan and H. Tadmor, *II Kings* (AB; 1988); S. Japhet, *I & II Chronicles* (1993), 889–93; J. Kuntz, in: ABD, 3:1021–22.

JOURNALISM.

Jews have played a major role in journalism since the early years of the profession. Publishers, editors, columnists, and reporters contributed to the development of political analysis, mass circulation techniques, methods of worldwide news gathering, chain journalism, and techniques that deepened the influence and impact of the written word. The overall number of Jews engaged in journalism in various countries is actually small. The significance of their contributions is readily apparent, however, in any examination of the relatively new, constantly changing and developing field of communications.

There have been Jews who distinguished themselves in journalism by their direction of some of the leading and most influential papers of the day. In the United States there were Adolph S. *Ochs and Arthur Hays *Sulzberger of *The New York Times*, Joseph *Pulitzer of the St. Louis *Post-Dispatch*, *The World*, and the *Evening World*, and Samuel *Newhouse, newspaper chain owner; in Germany, Leopold *Ullstein and Bernhard *Wolff; in Britain, Baron Paul Julius *Reuter of the news agency bearing his name, Lord *Southwood of the *Daily Herald*, and Joseph Moses Levy and his son Lord Burnham (see *Lawson family) of the *Daily Telegraph*, the newspaper which, selling at a penny and aiming at popular appeal, started the trend toward brighter newspapers. In the 1890s Rachel *Beer edited two leading London weeklies owned by her husband. The overwhelming majority of publishers and editors, however, were and are non-Jewish, notwithstanding the old canard that the world's press is controlled by Jews. Jews entered the main currents of journalism when they entered the mainstream of life in Europe. In the late 18th century, emancipation broke down the ghetto walls and Jews were able to enter a world from which they had been excluded.

Modern journalism was born after the French and American Revolutions. The freedom to think, to speak, and to write sought expression in the journals then developing, which were read by the rapidly growing educated and semi-educated population of the cities and towns. The Jew emerging from the ghetto was thus in the right place at the right time. German Jews, excluded before 1848 from the professions for which they had been trained, were disproportionately prominent in journalism during this early period and tended to advocate "radical" liberal views. His gift of adaptability permitted the Jew to act as an intermediary, the link between the event and the reader, as the journalist has often been called.

Jewish journalists were active during the 19th century in Austria, Czechoslovakia, Germany, and Hungary, and to a somewhat lesser degree in the United States, England, France, and Romania. Small numbers also worked with the general press in Scandinavia, the Baltic states, Italy, Belgium, Russia, the Netherlands, Spain, Portugal, the Balkans, and Switzerland. Involvement of the Jew in journalism in other areas of the world came later. The activities of Jewish journalists were proscribed, of course, in those countries where antisemitism was practiced officially during the 20th century. Jewish journalists and publishers who led some of Germany's most important newspaper enterprises became the special targets of the Nazis. Some were killed; others fled their homeland to practice their craft in a different land. For at least two decades the voice of Jewish journalists was stilled in Germany and for years also in countries overrun by the Germans.

In the United States, Jews became part of the developing journalism of the new land early in its history. But it took almost a century and a half for any measurable numbers of Jews to enter the profession. Jewish engagement in journalism in the United States began with Mordecai Manuel *Noah, editor of the *Enquirer* in New York. Similarly, in Europe, Jewish participation began almost with the birth of modern journalism.

The impact and influence of Jews on the general press increased markedly during the 19th and 20th centuries. Jews did not work as Jews. In Europe, talented Jewish writers turned to journalism as the best means of expressing themselves. The emancipated mind and spirit often eschewed such traditional forms of expression as poetry and fiction in favor of journalism, which had brightness and novelty. In Germany and Austria, Jewish influence in the new craft was marked by the contributions of such outstanding men as Heinrich *Heine and

Ludwig *Boerne (in the *Augsburger Zeitung*), and Karl *Marx (in the *Rheinische Zeitung*), and by the efforts of Daniel Spitzer (1835–93) and Moritz *Saphir, by the work of Theodore *Herzl, Max *Nordau, and Alfred *Polgar. David Kalisch founded *Kladderadatsch* in 1848 and made it famous as a satirical journal. His collaborator was the poet Rudolf Loewenstein.

Important publishing enterprises were begun by Rudolf *Mosse, who in 1872 founded the *Berliner Tageblatt*; Leopold *Sonnemann, who founded the *Frankfurter Zeitung* in 1856; and Leopold Ullstein, publisher, whose *Morgenpost* reached a circulation of 600,000. Herzl, Nordau, and Spitzer wrote for the *Neue Freie Presse* of Vienna, making it one of the outstanding journals of its day. Eduard Bacher was its publisher. Moritz Saphir published the witty paper *Der Humorist* (1837), and Polgar won a reputation through his contributions to *Die Weltbuehne*. Bernhard Wolff founded the Wolff Telegraphic Bureau in 1848.

This fruitful period of the 19th century was also marked by the journalistic work of Gabriel *Riesser, Johann *Jacoby, and Edward *Lasker. The primary contribution of the most famous of these was in the form of the feuilleton, a personal essay or commentary that has no precise counterpart in present-day journalism. The feuilleton was marked by a highly personal character and a well-developed style. In America only Simeon Strunsky could be said to have reflected this special skill. Several decades later the field attracted such names as Karl *Kraus, Egon Erwin *Kisch, Kurt *Tucholsky, Theodore *Wolff, who served as editor in chief of the *Berliner Tageblatt*, and Georg *Bernhard, editor in chief of the *Vossische Zeitung*. The early 20th century also saw the development of a large group of art, music, and drama critics, such as Alfred *Kerr, who produced a quantity of creative criticism which influenced and fostered the arts.

In Great Britain, first mention of a Jewish journalist is made by Oliver Goldsmith in his *Haunch of Venison* (1776). Emanuel Samuel (d. 1818) contributed to the *Morning Post* as early as 1786 and later worked in *The World*. He is the first Anglo-Jewish journalist on record, followed at the end of the century by Lewis *Goldsmith, a vigorous political writer and propagandist. The contribution of Jews was greater in publishing and organizing than in writing. Men like Ralph D. *Blumenfeld of the *Daily Express*, Lord Burnham (Levy), founder of the *Daily Telegraph*, Paul Julius Reuter, founder of Reuter's news agency, and Lord Southwood (Elias) of the *Daily Herald*, were among the builders of the modern British press. Other important names in British journalism were Sidney *Low, editor of the *St. James Gazette*, Lucien *Wolf, foreign editor of the *Daily Graphic*, Henri Georges Stephane Adolphe Opper de *Blowitz, correspondent of *The Times*, and Bernard Falk, editor of the *Sunday Dispatch*. While a number of leading columnists in the British press in recent years have been Jewish, such as *The Times'* Bernard *Levin, Jewish ownership of the British press in recent decades has been slight, with only the ill-fated period of ownership of the *Daily Mirror* by Robert *Maxwell being an exception. In the 1990s the *Daily Telegraph* was owned by the non-Jewish but strongly pro-Zionist Canadian, Conrad Black (Lord Black of Crossharbour), whose Jewish wife, Barbara Amiel, had an influential pro-Israeli column in the paper.

In France, Jewish journalists were concerned primarily with politics, although several were active in literature. Perhaps the nation's foremost journalist was Leon *Blum, who did his principal journalistic work in the period 1920 to 1939 in such papers as *L'Humanité* and *Le Populaire*. Blum, Joseph *Reinach, and Bernard *Lazare were three of France's greatest journalists at the turn of the 20th century. Other French journalists of repute were Marcel Hutin of *L'Echo de Paris* and *L'Epoque*, Pierre Lazareff, general director of *Paris Soir*, George London of *Le Journal*, Jacques Kayser of *La Dépêche de Toulouse*, Arthur Meyer of *Le Gaulois*, and Louise Weiss of *L'Europe nouvelle*.

In Italy, with its relatively small Jewish population, Jewish journalists made important contributions to the country's liberal movements. Among the most prominent were Cesare Rovighi; Angiolo *Orvieto, who with his brother Adolfo founded the Florentine weekly, *Il Marzocco*; Giacomo Dina, editor of *Opinione*; Salvatore *Barzilai, foreign editor of *La Tribuna*; and Margherita Sarfatti, literary editor of *Il Popolo d'Italia*, who became a member of Mussolini's inner circle.

In Russia and Poland where the suppression of Jews was a continuing governmental policy, several journalists of importance emerged. During the Bolshevik period, many Jewish revolutionaries engaged in newspaper work for political purposes, and Ilya *Ehrenburg won international fame as a journalist of uncommon ability. In Poland the name of Isaac Ignac *Schwarzbart stands out with those of Wilhelm Berkelhammer, Joseph Perl, and Florian Sokolow. Schwarzbart directed the most important paper in Lvov. In Scandinavia, Jews held important posts on papers in Denmark. Among the journalists were Carl *Brandes, who helped to found *Politiken*, M.A. *Goldschmidt, Moritz Nathansen, and Gottlieb Siesby. In Holland, Marcus van Blankenstein, Louis de *Jong, Eduard Elias, Joseph F. Stoppelman, and Arnold Vaz Dias were important.

Jews entered the general Hungarian press during the 1840s when newspapers appeared mainly in German. Active in liberal organs and in the production of pamphlets which preached assimilation, most of them changed their faith. In the revolution of 1848, they attained high posts in the government service. After 1867, the year of "The Compromise" (which ended Austrian domination) and the year of emancipation of Hungarian Jewry, Jews had an important part in the founding of a modern press and its technical organization. Jews worked on almost every paper (except those openly antisemitic), from the nationalist papers which preached complete assimilation for all minorities to the radical and socialist, where the Jews were in a majority. In 1910, out of 1,214 journalists in Hungary, 516 were Jews; but in 1920 their number had dropped to 358, and continued to fall. From 1938 onward Jews were ousted from editorial posts under the provisions of antisemitic legislation; only a small percentage retained their jobs. During the first hours of the German invasion in 1944, the Hungarian Nazis, using prepared lists, hunted down the Jewish journalists still at work and had them sent to the extermination camps. From 1945, during the period of the coalition administration, which was set up after World War II, Jews regained important positions, especially in the socialist and communist press; but after the rise of the communist regime they tried to conceal their Jewish identity.

Unlike the European press (primarily concerned with ideas), the press in the United States focuses its attention on information and news. It is chiefly devoted to reporting the events of the world and not to the propagation of opinions. Jews became active in journalism not long after the first papers made their appearance in the colonies (1704–30). In the first quarter of the 19th century Mordecai Noah was the editor of the *City Gazette* of Charleston, South Carolina and later the editor and publisher of the *New York Enquirer.* Noah also helped James Gordon Bennett to establish the *New York Herald* in 1835. A visionary and dreamer with a Zionist ideal long before the word itself was invented, Noah may be said to have been the first important Jewish journalist in the New World. He was among the first to attempt to enliven his paper for the benefit of the ordinary reader. As in Europe, Jewish journalists participated in all sections – in publishing, chain journalism, circulation techniques, and writing. Their overall numbers are small. Of the 1,800 dailies published in the United States at the end of the 20th century about 50 were owned by Jews, among them some of the most influential – *The New York Times, The Daily News* in New York, and the 22 papers owned by Samuel I. Newhouse.

As on the Continent, it is difficult to define the distinctive Jewish contribution. Most Jewish journalists on the staffs of the general press were entirely integrated into American newspaper routines. An early figure of importance was Edward *Rosewater, who worked during the second half of the 19th century in Nebraska as a correspondent and owner of the *Omaha Bee* (1871). The earliest papers in the New World were commonly called penny papers. They were sensational in their treatment of news, and their attitude was to influence the journalism of two outstanding American Jewish publishers, Joseph Pulitzer and Adolph Ochs, whose papers were among the most important in the nation.

Pulitzer purchased *The New York World* in 1883 after having followed an aggressive policy in earlier penny-paper journalism, both in news and editorial columns. He engaged in numerous crusades, one of the most important of which was the exposure of the mismanagement of life insurance companies in New York City. He introduced political cartoons, striking illustrations, colored pictures, and colored comics. The circulation of *The World* rose and in 1886 it claimed the largest circulation of any newspaper in the United States – 250,000. Pulitzer and William Randolph Hearst, who had purchased the *Morning Journal* in 1895, vied with each other in sensationalism. Their rivalry gave rise to the expression "yellow journalism." Pulitzer was an ardent believer in professional training, and provided a large endowment for a school of journalism, which was opened at Columbia University in 1912, as well as for the prizes in journalism and the arts that bear his name. Adolph Ochs took another road. When he became publisher of *The New York Times*, he issued a statement of purpose under a signature that is still the basic credo of the paper: "... to give the news impartially, without fear or favor, regardless of any party, sect or interest involved..." Ochs recognized that New York was beginning to tire of sensationalism and he promised to give straight news as fast as, or faster than, any other paper. He thought of *The New York Times* as a kind of public institution of which he had only temporary charge, and was fiercely determined that no individual, or favored group, would ever use it selfishly or for self-glorification. When he died he was succeeded by his son-in-law, Arthur Hays *Sulzberger, whose youngest son, Arthur Ochs Sulzberger, became publisher in 1963. His son, Arthur Sulzberger Jr., succeeded him and was publisher and chairman of the board of the New York Times Company, a publicly traded corporation, through the early years of the 21st century. The latter Sulzbergers, along with their advisers and editors, including Executive Editor A.M. *Rosenthal, played prominent roles in putting *The Times* on a sound financial footing, in uncovering government misfeasance, and in furthering the aims of a free press.

In the early 1970s *The Washington Post*, under Katharine Graham, took the lead in exposing an attempted cover-up of the break-in at Democratic Party headquarters in the Watergate office complex in Washington. That reporting, by the team of Robert Woodward and Carl *Bernstein, got Graham's personal backing and eventually resulted in the resignation in 1974 of President Richard M. Nixon in disgrace. During that period, *The New York Times* came into possession of a secret history of the war in Vietnam, which came to be known as the Pentagon Papers when it was published at great length in 1973. The Nixon administration tried to suppress publication of the historic documents and their analyses on the grounds of national security, but the United States Supreme Court upheld the right of the press to publish the information. The case was a landmark ruling against prior restraint of the press, and its champion was *The Times.*

Other important Jewish figures in American journalism include Emanuel Philip Adler who founded the Lee Syndicate, a chain of papers in the Midwest; Eugene *Meyer, former owner of *The Washington Post*; Paul Block (1877–1941), who helped to foster the growth of chain journalism; Moses *Koenigsberg, the creator of the King Features Syndicate; Walter *Annenberg, publisher of *The Philadelphia Inquirer*; J. David *Stern, owner and publisher of papers in Camden, NJ, and Philadelphia; Dorothy *Schiff, owner and publisher of *The New York Post*; Edwin S. Friendly who served on the former *Evening Sun*; Herbert Bayard *Swope of *The World*; and Harry *Golden who, in the 1950s, achieved the distinction of making his *Carolina Israelite* a weekly with general readership. After Dorothy Schiff's death, *The Post* changed hands a few times. The other major New York City newspaper, *The*

Daily News, was bought by Robert Maxwell in 1991 and then, with the paper in bankruptcy, shortly afterward by Mortimer Zuckerman, a Boston builder and the publisher of the magazine *U.S. News and World Report*. *The Post* and *News* became embroiled in a bitter advertising and circulation war in the first years of the 21st century.

Jews scored successes in two special areas of American journalism – commentary on current affairs and the "gossip" column. In the first, Walter *Lippmann, Arthur *Krock, and David *Lawrence commented on domestic and foreign affairs in some of the nation's most important journals, winning attention in world capitals. As gossip columnists, Walter Winchell, Leonard Lyons (d. 1976), Louis Sobol, and Sidney Skolsky (d. 1983) attracted a wide readership and developed an influence by their reporting on the lives of stage and screen personalities, government officials, and public and political figures. Identical twin sisters from the Middle West, Pauline Esther Friedman, writing as Abigail Van Buren, and Esther Pauline *Lederer, writing as Ann Landers, dispensed homespun advice in their newspaper columns, each appearing daily in over 1,200 newspapers and reaching 20 million readers. Each received 10,000 letters a week for help, and both sisters dispensed blunt, common-sense remedies for most of the second half of the 20th century. Other Jewish journalists were active as foreign correspondents and as writers on science, economics, politics, and sports. Among American journalists, Franklin Pierce Adams, Meyer Berger, and Ben *Hecht had especially keen eyes for the unusual. In sketching the human condition they successfully translated the stories of ordinary people into newspaper prose of high quality. As Jews assimilated into the mainstream of American life, they rose to prominent positions in journalism. Rosenthal of *The Times* was succeeded by Max *Frankel, who was succeeded by Joseph *Lelyveld. All had been star reporters and winners of the Pulitzer Prize. And Thomas L. *Friedman of *The Times* became the most influential foreign affairs columnist as well as the first reporter to win a Pulitzer for reporting on Lebanon and another for reporting from Israel. At least one Jewish American journalist lost his life, Daniel *Pearl of *The Wall Street Journal*, while affirming his faith.

The participation of Jews in Latin American journalism began at an early stage of their immigration. Since the publications for which they wrote were oriented toward the Jewish public, the newspapers, journals, and publications in general were in Yiddish during the first years, and with the immigration from Central Europe in the 1930s, also in German. However, publication in Spanish and Portuguese commenced very quickly, and these became the main languages of communication in the community framework with the decline of Yiddish.

Jews were active in general journalism in almost all the Latin American countries. Some of them achieved prominent positions and can be considered pioneers in their field. The first Jewish journalist who published in Argentina in a general daily was Enrique Lipschutz (1864–1937), who wrote in *La Prensa* from 1895. After him, many Jewish journalists and writers published in general newspapers and journals and some of them also became section editors and also chief editors. One of them was Alberto Gerchunoff (1884–1950), who was with the leading daily *La Nación* for 40 years and part of the time was its editor in chief. Other leading journalists were Bernardo Verbitsky (1907–1979) in *El Mundo* (his son Horacio Verbitsky became editor in chief of *Página 12*), Santiago Nudelman (1904–1961) editor in chief of *Crítica* from 1958, and Antonio Portnoy at *La Gaceta*. In the 1960s and 1970s one of the best-known journalists was Jacobo Timerman (1923–1999). In the 1960s he founded and directed two successful current affairs magazines, *Primera Plana* and *Confirmado*, and in 1970 the daily *La Opinión*, which tried to be a new kind of newspaper in the style of the French *Le Monde*. Timerman became known worldwide when was kidnapped by the military junta in 1977. International pressure, especially from the U.S. and Israel, led to his release in 1979. In those years of dictatorship the weekly *Nueva Presencia* (1977) was founded, which started as a Spanish offshoot of the Yiddish daily *Di Prese*. Under the editorship of Herman Schiller, it adopted an opposition stance against the repression in Argentina. This journal became one of the referents of the Argentinean Human Rights Movement, and Schiller, who participated in the organization of the Jewish Movement for Human Rights, was recognized as one of its leaders.

In the early 21st century there were many well-known Jewish journalists who published in the printed press as well as in the electronic media – radio, television, and the internet. These included José Eliaschev, Marcelo Zlotogwiazda, Ernesto Tenenbaum, Roman Lejtman, Martín Liberman, and Juan Pablo Varsky.

Jews were prominent in Chilean journalism. Ana Albala-Levy was editor of *Las Últimas Noticias* of Santiago; her husband, Robert Levy, wrote for many newspapers and journals; Max Dickmann, was literary and managing editor of *El Ateneo* of Santiago and an author of substantial reputation; and Marcos Chamudes was chief editor of the magazine *Política, Economía y Cultura* (PEC) and later of the newspaper *La Nación*.

In Brazil Jews were prominent as journalists as well as entrepreneurs in the news media. One of the most important media companies was Bloch Editores owned by Adolfo Bloch, which at its peak included 25 magazines, among them the famous weekly *Manchete*, six radio stations, and a TV network, *Rede Manchete*. Two important Jewish journalists collaborated in many stages of their career with this group. Zevi Ghivelder (1934–) worked for many years for the magazine *Manchete* and directed the news magazine on its TV network, also publishing numerous books that won national prizes. Henrique Veltman (1936–) was editor in chief of Bloch Editores publications from 1971, including the magazine *Manchete*, and was also editor in chief of the most important newspapers of Rio de Janeiro – *Ultima Hora* and *O Globo*. Both of them were much involved in Jewish community life and Zionist action. Also

Naum Sirotzky was editor in chief of *Manchete* in the 1950s. Alberto Dines (1932–), who started his career as a journalist with *Manchete* under Naum Sirotzky, became one of the most prominent and innovative in the field. As a professional who combined writing and news photography, he was editor in chief of many major newspapers, such as *Jornal do Brasil* and the *Folha de São Paulo* branch in Rio de Janeiro. Besides teaching journalism in many universities, he developed a new kind of journalistic criticism in Brazil with *Observatorio da Imprensa* on TV programs and the internet. Diane Kuperman (1949–), a journalist at *Jornal do Brasil* and director of the Instituto de Comunicação Social da Universidade Gama Filho, and Osias Wurman (1950–), a journalist at *O Globo* and *Jornal do Brasil*, were also the leaders of the Jewish Federation of Rio de Janeiro.

Samuel Wainer (1912–1980) is also considered one of the professionals responsible for a revolution in Brazilian journalism. In 1930 he started his career at *Diário de Notícias* and in 1938 he founded the monthly magazine *Diretrizes* with an agenda in politics, culture, and economic affairs. In 1971 he founded the magazine *Domingo Ilustrado* as part of Bloch Editores, and in 1973–75 was editor in chief of *Última Hora* of São Paulo. From 1977 he was a member of the editorial board of *Folha de São Paulo*.

Arnaldo Niskier (1935–) was, in addition to his more than 40 years in journalism, a teacher at the University of Rio de Janeiro State and secretary of the state for science, technology, education, and culture. He was also chairman of the Academia Brasileira de Letras.

One of the most prominent journalists in Mexico was undoubtedly Jacobo Zabludovsky (1928–). He started his career in 1946 as assistant editor of news magazines at Cadena Radio Continental. In 1950, at the very beginning of TV transmissions in Mexico, he initiated the production and direction of the first professional news magazine on Mexican television, and subsequently directed and presented many news magazines. He also directed the cinema news magazine *El Mundo en Marcha*, wrote for the newspapers *Observaciones* and *Novedades*, for the weeklies *Claridades* and *El Redondel*, and from 1959 edited the magazine *Siempre*. He held official posts in radio and television and also wrote many books on politics and the Mexican media and containing interviews with Mexican painters.

There were also important contributors to the local press like Luis Rubio, Ezra Shabot, Enrique Krauze, Hellen Krauze, and Alberto Musacchio, all of them on the daily *Reforma*, and Esther Shabot on *Excelsior*. Enrique Burak and Abraham Faitelson are sports journalists on TV.

In Canada, Jews were prominent in all facets of the journalism professions, and in ways unimaginable even 30 years ago. In 2000, the Asper family acquired the Hollinger media holdings, thereby controlling a large number of newspapers both in Canada and abroad, including the *National Post*, one of Canada's two English-language newspapers. They also own Global Television Network, Canada's second large independent television network. Another Jew, Edward Greenspon, is the editor in chief of Canada's other major national English language paper, *The Globe and Mail*. Michael Goldbloom is the current publisher of the Toronto *Star*, which is the largest mass circulation newspaper in Canada. Jews are also prominent as reporters, columnists, and feature writers in newspapers across the country, and have achieved a high profile in the electronic media. Peter C. Newman, Joe Schlesinger, William Weintraub, Barbara Frum, Simma Holt, Robert Matas, Michelle Landsberg, Rick Salutin, Ralph Benmergui, Avi Lewis, and Naomi Klein, to name only a few over the last four decades, have become journalistic icons in Canada.

In Australia, an outstanding newspaper owner and builder was Theodore *Fink. In recent decades, none of Australia's newspapers had a Jewish owner, although Michael Gawenda, a Melbourne Jew, was editor of the *Melbourne Age* from 1996 to 2004.

In South Africa, the leading weekly *The Sunday Times* was edited (1912–40) by J. Langley Levy. From 1960 the same paper was edited by Joel Mervis and its companion paper the *Sunday Express* by Meyer Albert "Johnny" Johnson from 1961. Johnson subsequently assumed the editorship of the conservative daily *The Citizen* in 1979. In 1987, the left-leaning weekly *Weekly Mail* (later *Mail & Guardian*) was founded by Irwin Manoim and Anton Harber.

[Kalman Seigel / Stewart Kampel, Richard Menkis, Harold Troper, William D. Rubinstein, David Saks, and Efraim Zadoff (2nd ed.)]

JOY, a term used to render into English a number of Hebrew words expressing a response of pleasure to persons, things, situations, and acts. Commenting on the phrase, "We will be glad and rejoice in thee," the Midrash (Song R. 1:4) notes that there are ten words used in the Bible to describe Israel's pleasurable response: "Israel is summoned by ten expressions of rejoicing, *gilah, sisah, simḥah, rinnah, piẓḥah, ẓahalah, alẓah, alizah, ḥedvah, teru'ah*." The primary root used is *smḥ*, occurring as a verb and as a noun. On the level of interpersonal relationships it covers a range from sexual enjoyment: "and have your pleasure [*u-semaḥ*] with the wife of your youth" (Prov. 5:18); to a satisfactory political arrangement: "rejoice in Abimelech and let him rejoice in you" (Judg. 9:19); and social status: "there is nothing better for a man than to be happy in what he is doing, since that is his lot" (Eccles. 3:22). This word also refers to a particular response on the part of man, as when letters and gifts were sent by the king of Babylon, "and Hezekiah was pleased [*va-yismaḥ*] with them" (Isa. 39:2). There is, too, a kind of joy which is judged negatively: "Rejoice not [i.e., have not malicious joy; *a'l tismeḥi*] against me, O mine enemy" (Micah 7:8); "because you clapped your hand and stamped your foot and rejoiced [*va-tismaḥ*] with all your disdain against the land of Israel" (Ezek. 25:6).

The Bible often warns that purely worldly pleasure brings sorrow, tears, and suffering: "Even in laughter the heart acheth; and the end of mirth is heaviness" (Prov. 14:13). Joy is, however, not an emotion experienced solely on this level. It is viewed in the Bible as a true response to divine action: "I rejoice in your saving action" (I Sam. 2:1); "Be glad and rejoice, for the Lord has done great things" (Joel 2:21). Man's presence in the Temple was considered reason for such a response: "And you shall rejoice before the Lord seven days" (Lev. 23:40); "I rejoiced when they said unto me; let us go into the house of the Lord" (Ps. 122:1). The divine commandments, too, are viewed as a source of human joy (Ps. 19:9). In addition, even nature is called upon to respond joyfully to the divine presence (I Chron. 16:31–33; Ps. 97:1). Joy is even thought of as a response which is proper to God: "Let the Lord rejoice in His works" (Ps. 104:31), and its absence is caused by human misbehavior: "Therefore the Lord shall have no joy in their young men" (Isa. 9:17).

The biblical themes were taken over by rabbinic Judaism and developed in terms of the changed and changing situations of the community. This is particularly noticeable in the period following the destruction of the Temple. The disasters of the period, reflected in extra-biblical literature as well, provided an impulse for a negative judgment on life in the world, and the rise of radical asceticism. Thus rabbinic Judaism warned against the rejection of the world, but at the same time against making the world the sole source of joy. R. Eliezer ha-Kappara viewed self-affliction, i.e., refraining from legitimate pleasure, as a sin similar to that for which the Nazirite was required to bring an atoning sacrifice (Sif. Num. 30; see *Asceticism). Some rabbis went so far as to say that, "He who has seen something pleasant and not enjoyed it will be held responsible" (Yal. Ps. 688). However, the truest source of joy was understood to lie in the performance of the divine commandments (*mitzvot*). In connection with the apparent contradiction between Ecclesiastes 8:15: "then I commended joy," and 2:2: "and of joy I said what does it accomplish?" it was taught (Shab. 30b) that the first phrase refers to the joy present in the performance of a commandment (*simḥah shel mitzvah*), while the second refers to joy which is unconnected with such an act. It must be noted, therefore, that Judaism in this period, while rejecting radical asceticism, did not endorse sensualism. Perhaps the best statement of the disciplined joy prescribed by rabbinic Judaism is found in the comment on Deuteronomy 14:2: "'For you are a people consecrated to God.' Sanctify yourselves even in that permitted you: things allowed to you, but forbidden to others, do not regard as permissible in their presence" (Sif. Deut. 104; see C. Montefiore and H. Loewe, *A Rabbinic Anthology* (1963), 202–3, 523–9). Joy was stressed in many aspects of Jewish life, especially those concerned with the observance of practical commandments. In public observances it was particularly connected with the Sabbath and certain festivals including *Purim, *Sukkot, and *Simḥat Torah – in Temple times – with the Water Drawing Festival (of which it was said that a person who had not witnessed this festival had never witnessed real joy; Suk. 5:1), and in the modern period, with Israel Independence Day. In private circles, there were many joyous occasions of which the outstanding were the circumcision, bar mitzvah, and wedding ceremonies and festivities. Matrimony was regarded as a precondition for happiness and "the man who lives without a wife lives without joy" (Yev. 62b).

While the element of joy was never totally absent from the life of the Jewish community (see I. Abrahams, *Jewish Life in the Middle Ages* (1932), passim), ascetic and restrictive attitudes and practices did hold sway during the Middle Ages.

In the pietist revival of 18th century *Ḥasidism, the emotional quality of joy was once again renewed. Thus, while eating, drinking, sleeping, and the other ordinary functions of the body are regarded by the older Jewish moralists as mere means to an end, to the Ba'al Shem Tov, Ḥasidism's founder, they are a service of God in themselves: "All pleasures are manifestations of God's attribute of love" (S. Schechter, *Studies in Judaism*, 1 (1911), 28). For the Ba'al Shem Tov "weeping is evil indeed, for man should serve God with joy. But if one weeps for joy, tears are commendable" (L.I. Newman and S. Spitz, *The hasidic Anthology* (1963), 204). More than a hundred years later, R. *Ḥanokh of Aleksandrow underscored Ḥasidism's emphasis on joy with these words: "Do you wish to know how important it is to be full of joy at all times? Moses enumerated a long series of curses (Deut. 28) and then remarked in verse 47, 'because you did not serve the Lord your God with joyfulness, and with gladness of heart'" (Newman and Spitz, 202).

Hermann Cohen (*Religion der Vernunft* (1929), 540) saw in the joy of the Sabbath "the symbol of the joy that will spread throughout humanity when all men will be free and ready to serve in the same way…" It is this joy, the joy of the messianic era, that will disclose the reality of peace as a dynamic quality of the human spirit.

[Lou H. Silberman]

JÓZEFOWICZ (also **Ezofovich**), family of financiers prominent in Lithuania during the early 16th century. Its founder, JOSEF RABCHIK (Rebi), from whom the additional name of the family Rabinkovich (Rebichkovich) derives, was the tax collector of Kiev. In 1482, after the capture of Kiev by the Tatars, he settled first in Lutsk and later in Brest-Litovsk, where he continued to engage in commerce and the leasing of the state incomes. Of his three sons, ABRAHAM JAN EZOFOVICH (c. 1450–1519), was a merchant and tax collector and successful head of the treasury (*Podskarbik Litewski*) of the grand duchy of Lithuania (1509–18). Having left Kiev with his father in about 1488, he became an apostate, converting to the Orthodox Church, and entered the service of the grand duke of Lithuania. In 1494 he was appointed commander of the fortress of Kovno. From 1496 he leased or administered customs stations and the collection of taxes in Smolensk, Polotsk, Minsk, Novogrudok, Kovno, and Vilna. Over the years he accumulated a vast fortune, in part from the income derived from gifts of land granted him by the grand duke. From 1507 he served as court banker in Lithuania for King Sigismund I, when he was granted a title of nobility. During the last years of his life, Abraham acquired, with the consent of the king, additional estates in various places, and even ownership of the town of Solec in the province of Sandomierz, in Poland. In 1519 the king still owed Abraham the sum of 12,000 zlotys. He left two sons and a daughter who became Catholics.

His brother MICHAEL EZOFOVICH (d. c. 1529), merchant, banker, and agent of King Sigismund I, was also appointed the elder (senior) of the Jews of Lithuania. Until 1519 he traded in grain, wax, textiles, furs, jewelry, and ironware in partnership with his brother Isaac. When the partnership was liquidated they owned, in addition to valuables and large amounts of money, considerable real estate in houses and lands. The apportionment of these between the brothers was confirmed by the king in 1527 upon the request of Isaac Ezofovich. Michael Ezofovich became one of the leading tax collectors and lessees of the state incomes of his time. At first he supervised the customs administration of Brest-Litovsk (1506) and the provinces of Volhynia and Podolia. Later, in conjunction with partners, he rented the state incomes in additional provinces. After the death of his brother, Abraham Jan, the king effectually appointed him over the customs administration of the whole country. He succeeded in raising the revenues by carrying out stringent controls on the roads. To strengthen his position, his headquarters and residence were established in the fortress of Brest-Litovsk. He granted loans in exchange for pledges in real estate. In 1514, by royal authorization, Michael built a bridge over the River Bug, near the town of Drohiczyn, and was granted the right to collect tolls. In 1514 he was appointed elder (senior) of the Jews of Lithuania to facilitate tax collection and impose a central leadership over the Jews of the grand duchy. The same considerations motivated the appointment of *Abraham Judaeus Bohemus and Moses *Fishel in Poland. Despite the wide powers granted to them, and their activity on behalf of the community, the appointed leadership was resented by the Jews and failed to gain their acceptance. Michael did much for the Brest-Litovsk community, which was to become the most important in Lithuania, thanks to the foundation laid by him. Of his sons are known Moses (who held rabbinical office), Abraham, Chemio, and Ducko (David?).

BIBLIOGRAPHY: *Russko-yevreyskiy arkhiv*, 1 (1882), nos. 42, 51–63, 65, 66, 68–75, 77–92, 96, 97, 103–6, 108–12, 119–21, 128, 130; S.A. Bershadski, *Litovskiye Yevrei* (1883), 358–68; idem, *Avram Ezofovich Rebichkovich...* (Rus., 1888); M. Balaban, *Skizzen und Studien zur Geschichte der Juden in Polen* (1911), 77–97; I. Schiper, *Dzieje handlu żydowskiego na ziemiach polskich* (1937), index; A.L. Feinstein, *Ir Tehillah* (1886), 21–22, 53–59, 68–69.

[Arthur Cygielman]

JUAN (Poeta), DE VALLADOLID (c. 1420–after 1470), Spanish *Marrano poet, nicknamed "el judío." As many of the 15th-century cancioneros clearly show, Juan Poeta was long a center of controversy and a butt for satire, owing to the ambiguity of his religious position. Antón de *Montoro sneered at his humble origins, while others maintained that he was "neither a Jew nor a Christian, but an excellent Marrano." He is reputed to have been an astrologer and to have enjoyed the favor of Queen Isabella. While on a voyage to the Holy Land, Juan Poeta was said to have been captured by Moslems and to have embraced Islam, for which reason he was bitterly attacked by Gómez Manrique. Like other members of his family, Juan Poeta seems to have retained or reverted to his ancestral Jewish traditions, at least after he left Spain. He was one of the group of poets associated with Alfonso V of Aragon in Naples, and a number of his poems appear in the *Cancionero* of Juan Alfonso de *Baena and in other collections of the period.

BIBLIOGRAPHY: Kayserling, Bibl. 54; Baer, Spain, 2 (1966), 301–2, 490; Levi, in: *Homenaje... Menéndez Pidál* 3 (1925), 419–39.

JUAN DE CIUDAD (15th century), Castilian Converso. In 1465 Juan and his son arrived at Huesca in Aragon, then the main center in Spain of Jewish activities for encouraging Conversos to return to Judaism. Juan approached the *ḥakham* Abraham *Bibago and his circle, and after they had become convinced of his sincerity, he and his son were circumcised in a festive ceremony. Subsequently they immigrated to Ereẓ Israel, as customary among many Conversos who regarded this as a means of atonement for adopting Christianity. In 1489 the community of Huesca was charged by the Inquisition with helping Conversos to return to Judaism, the chief indictment being responsibility for the reversion of Juan de Ciudad. The inquisitors arrested the Jews who had been present at the circumcision ceremony, including prominent members of the community such as R. Isaac *Bibago, the brother of Abraham, R. Abraham Almosnino, and others, who confessed their action under torture. At the end of that year the accused were sentenced and burned alive, except Isaac Bibago, who in return for adopting Christianity was strangled before being committed to the pyre.

BIBLIOGRAPHY: Baer, Urkunden, 2 (1936), 486ff.; Baer, Spain, 2 (1966), 297f., 384ff.

JUAN DE ESPAÑA (El Viejo; c. 1350–c. 1420), Spanish Marrano poet and controversialist. Born in Villamartín, Juan de España apparently embraced Christianity under the impact of the preaching of Vicente *Ferrer, but may also have been influenced by the arguments presented by the apostate Geronimo de Santa Fé at the Tortosa disputation (1413–14). An accomplished talmudist, Juan de España became a fervent apologist for his adopted faith and turned his rabbinic knowledge against the Jews. His experiences and opinions are contained in the *Memorial de los misterios de Christo* (1416), the original manuscript of which is in the Madrid National Library. His *Declaración del Salmo LXXII del Salterio* also bears the stamp of wide learning.

BIBLIOGRAPHY: J. Amador de Los Ríos, *Estudios Históricos, politicos y literarios sobre los judíos de España* (1848), 430–6; Roth, Marranos, 26; Baer, Spain, 2 (1966), 159, 476.

JUBAL (Heb. יוּבָל), son of Lamech and Adah; mythical culture hero, inventor of "the lyre and the pipe" (Gen. 4:21) in the seventh generation after Adam.

ADD. BIBLIOGRAPHY: N. Sarna, *JPS Torah Commentary Genesis* (1989), 37.

JUBAR (Djobar), village N.E. of *Damascus; settled by an ancient Mustarabian (Arabic-speaking) Jewish community which was frequently mentioned by early travelers, such as *Pethahiah of Regensburg (1180) and Samuel b. Samson (1211). The community owned fields, orchards, and vineyards; in addition to farming, the Jews of Jubar worked as artisans and were engaged in commerce and peddling in the nearby villages. After the expulsion of the Jews from Spain, several families settled in Jubar. At the beginning of the 16th century the village had a population of approximately 60 families. There is an ancient synagogue located on top of a cave which tradition associates with the prophet Elisha. Damascus Jews attributed special powers to the synagogue and it was customary for them to hold Sabbath prayers there. The synagogue possessed a "Tāj," or "*Keter Torah*," i.e., an illuminated Hebrew Bible on vellum, written in 1252. The place is sacred to the *Karaites also. In the 20th century Jews ceased living there, but a beadle remained in charge of the synagogue and the large cemetery. Residents of Damascus and Jewish visitors from abroad continued their pilgrimages to the synagogue and the village; according to reports, there are several deeper layers of graves and tombstones underneath the visible tombstones in the cemetery, which date back to the early Jewish settlement.

BIBLIOGRAPHY: I. Ben-Zvi, *Meḥkarim u-Mekorot* (1966), 578–81; idem, *She'ar Yashuv* (1965), 484–8.

[Abraham Haim]

JUBAYL (Djubayl, Jubail, Gebal-Byblos), a small town N. of *Beirut, *Lebanon. When Jubayl was annexed to the military province (*Jund*) of *Damascus at the beginning of the Muslim rule, there was a medium-sized Jewish community some of whose members were wealthy merchants. When the *Fatimid caliph al-Ḥākim issued (c. 1010) his decrees against the Jews and Christians, the Jews of Jubayl had their synagogue seized from them but were later authorized to rebuild it. In a document of the late 11th century, the community is mentioned as one of those visited by the messengers of the *nasi* *David b. Daniel in their attempt to gain recognition for him as exilarch. *Benjamin of Tudela found some 150 Jews in the town during the period of Genoese rule in the 12th century. Some documents concerning the Jews of Jubayl were found in the Cairo **Genizah*. After the return of the town to Muslim rule, the Jewish population decreased in numbers until it finally disappeared.

BIBLIOGRAPHY: Mann, Egypt, 1 (1920), 73; Braslawski, in: *Eretz Israel*, 1 (1951), 155–7.

[Eliyahu Ashtor]

JUBILEES, BOOK OF, pseudepigraphic work dating from the middle of the Second Temple period. It purports to be the secret revelation of the angel of the "Divine Presence" to Moses, upon his second ascent to Mount Sinai.

Names

The original title of the book seems to have been: "Book of the Divisions of the Seasons According to their Jubilees and their Weeks" (see R.H. Charles (ed.), *Fragments of a Zadokite Work* (1912), 20:1). It was later shortened to "The Jubilees" (οἱ Ἰωβηλαῖοι or τά Ἰωβηλάῖα) or "The Little Genesis" (ἡ λεπτὴ Γένεσις), but it was also given such incorrect titles as "The Testament of Moses," and "The Apocalypse of Moses." Although the original language of the book was Hebrew, all the extant versions (Latin, Ethiopic) are translations from the Greek, as is clearly evident from the exegesis of the proper names, scribal errors, etc. Several fragments, apparently in the original Hebrew, have been found in the Qumran caves.

Contents

The book is in the form of a monologue in the first person on the part of the angel of the "Divine Presence," in which he recapitulates the contents of the Bible, at the same time providing an exact date for the events and stories, calculated according to the jubilee year, the sabbatical year and the year of the sabbatical cycle, and sometimes giving even the month and the day. Occasionally he remains entirely faithful to the biblical narrative, but more often he makes changes. He adds material, deletes, gives novel and different reasons for occurrences, and also adds names of wives to those of the men mentioned in the biblical narrative. Besides the new aggadic material (only some of which is hinted at or contained in talmudic and traditional midrashic sources), the author also makes halakhic innovations. According to the author, the Commandments were written on the "tables of heaven" before they were given to man. Some of them (such as circumcision, the Sabbath, and Shavuot) are also performed by the angels, and some were also kept by the patriarchs. The reasons given for the commandments frequently differ from those found in the Bible. In contrast to the traditional view, Shavuot is said to commemorate the renewal of the covenant between God and man after the Flood (6:17); Noah and his descendants, as well as Abraham and Jacob, already observed it; Sukkot is said to have already been celebrated by the patriarch Abraham (16:21–31), and the "Eighth Day of Assembly" (Shemini Aẓeret) to have been instituted by Jacob (when he received the appellation "Israel"). The Day of Atonement was also given a "historical" etiology, it being the day that Joseph was sold (34:18–19). The hallowed position of the tribe of Levi is also explained – not as due to their zeal at the time of the transgression of the Golden Calf (Ex. 32:29 et al.), but as a reward for the action of Levi in Shechem, where they killed those guilty of immoral conduct (30:17–20; 32:1–3).

The book opposes all intimacy with gentiles (22:16; 25:5) and is extremely stringent in its interpretation of the Sabbath laws. It even opposes mandatory fighting and sexual intercourse on the Sabbath. According to it, even slaves are obligated to fulfill the commandment of dwelling in *sukkot* (16:21). Like the rabbinical *halakhah* (cf. Mishnah Rosh Ha-Shanah 1:1), the author is cognizant of four different "new years," but neither all the dates nor the significance ascribed to them are identical. His four new years are the first day of the first, the fourth, the seventh, and the tenth months. Their significance is not a function of normal agricultural life but, rather, of cosmic events which occurred at the time of the Flood (the beginning of the construction of the ark and the day when the land became dry after the Flood; the day when the mouths of the depths of the abyss of the earth were opened and the waters began to descend into them; and the day when the tops of the mountains became visible: 6:15–28). The date of Shavuot is fixed in accord with the interpretation that "the morrow of the Sabbath" (Lev. 23:16) refers to the first Sunday after Passover, so that it always fell on Sunday. It is mainly for this reason that the author ordained the use of the solar *calendar (already familiar from the Book of *Enoch and the *Dead Sea Scrolls), which contained exactly 52 weeks, each month having 30 days except for the third, the sixth, the ninth, and the twelfth months which have 31. In contrast to the *Pharisees (who also disagreed with this interpretation of "on the morrow of the Sabbath"), Jubilees maintains the literal observance of the phrase "an eye for an eye." Neither does the author believe in the Pharisaic doctrine of the resurrection of the dead, but only in the immortality of the soul (23:31) and, again in contrast to the Pharisees, he lays stress on the deterministic element in human affairs. Angels (both good and bad) rule the world, but the war between good and evil will continue until "the day of judgment." At the end of days, the author envisions a Messiah from the tribe of Judah (31:12f.) and another from the tribe of Levi.

The biblical text reflected in the work is not always identical with the Masoretic Text. Sometimes it parallels that of the Septuagint and sometimes the Samaritan text, e.g., in the calculations connected with the enumeration of the ten generations from Adam to Noah. In view of this, as well as several other points which also differ from the traditional interpretation, it is obvious that the author was not a Pharisee (nor do his *halakhot* represent any stage of "early halakhic development"). The author's views are similar to those found in the First Book of Enoch and, to a lesser extent, in the Testaments of the Twelve *Patriarchs.

Influence

Jubilees is mentioned in the literature of the community of *Qumran, and fragments of it were found in the Qumran caves. Its ideological tenets are similar to those of the community of Qumran (the immortality of the soul, the calendar, and the hegemony of Belial in the mundane sphere). In short, it was most probably one of the basic texts written and used by this sect – which was apparently early *Essene (see *Dead Sea Sect). From several details concerning events which he relates, and from the particular religious prescriptions which he stresses – for example, he "knows" that the children of Israel will abandon the ordinance of circumcision (15:33) and that the children of Israel will acquire hegemony over the Philistine cities (24:28–32; cf. I Macc. 5:68; Ex. 84) and over Idumea (38:14) – the author seems to have lived at the end of John Hyrcanus' reign (135–104 B.C.E). The book greatly influenced later midrashic literature (*Midrash Tadsheh; Pirkei de-Rabbi Eliezer; Genesis Rabbati*). It is the source of the legend found in the famous liturgical *piyyut* ("*Elleh Ezkerah*") recited on the Day of Atonement, according to which Joseph was sold by his brethren on the Day of Atonement. The book had a particularly great influence over *Beta Israel, whose ritual observances and whose calendar (particularly in respect to the date of Shavuot) are based upon it.

BIBLIOGRAPHY: R.H. Charles (ed.), *Ethiopic Version of the Hebrew Book of Jubilees* (1895); idem, Apocrypha, 2 (1913), 1–82; idem, *Book of Jubilees* (1917); A. Dillmann, in: *Jahrbuecher der Biblischen Wissenschaft*, 2 (1849), 230–56; A. Jellinek, *Ueber das Buch der Jubilaeen* (1855); Z. Frankel, in: MGWJ, 5 (1856), 311–16, 380–400; H. Roensch, *Buch der Jubilaeen* (1874); W. Singer, *Das Buch der Jubilaeen oder die Leptogenesis* (1898); E. Littmann, in: E. Kautsch (ed.), *Die Apocryphen und Pseudepigraphen des Alten Testaments*, 2 (1900), 31–119; A. Buechler, in: REJ, 82 (1926), 251–74; 89 (1930), 321–48; A. Cahana, *Ha-Sefarim ha-Ḥiẓonim*, 1 (1936), 216–313; H.H. Rowley, *The Relevance of Apocalyptic* (1944), 60–63, 84–90; G. Hoelscher, *Drei Erdkarten* (1949), 57–71; A. Epstein, *Kitvei…*, 1 (1950), 153ff.; 2 (1957), 133–9; A. Jaubert, in: VT, 3 (1953), 250–64 (Fr.); J.B. Segal, *ibid.*, 7 (1957), 290–4; O. Eissfeldt, *The Old Testament, an Introduction* (1956), 606–8 (incl. bibl.).

[Yehoshua M. Grintz]

JUDA, WALTER (1916–), U.S. inventor. Born in Berlin, Juda settled in the U.S. in 1939. He did research and development at the Harvard Chemistry Department from 1939 to 1948, including production of novel fungicides and fire-retardants for the war effort (1940–45) and a brackish water desalination prototype plant tested at the Weizmann Institute in the winter of 1947–48. He joined the division of industrial cooperation at the Massachussets Institute of Technology and co-founded Ionics Inc. In 1948 he became its executive vice president and technical director, until 1960, pioneering water desalting by electrodialysis; he also was a consultant to the Oak Ridge National Laboratory in 1951–54. Juda founded and ran the Prototech Company from 1960 to 1992, developing and producing gas electrodes (for electrolysis applications and fuel cells) and air pollution control catalysts. Prototech sold its electrochemistry business in 1990 and its catalyst businesses in 1992. From 1992, his third company, Hy9 Corporation (formerly Walter Juda Associates, Inc.), developed new hydrogen generation technology.

[Gali Rotstein (2nd ed.)]

JUDAESAPTAN, legendary kingdom in Austria. The legend, first printed in Hagen's chronicle (15th century), relates how the Jew Abraham of Theomanaria arrived in Austria 860 years after the flood and founded the kingdom of Judaesaptan with its capital, Stockerau; there he reigned for 33 years, while his sons ruled as tetrarchs in Korneuburg, Tulln, and Vienna. The 16th-century historian, Wolfgang Lazius, attempted to establish the truth of the legend (which was considered historic fact even in 1738) by interpreting Hebrew inscriptions on tombstones. Another version speaks of two men, Saunas and Juda Saptai, who established the kingdom in 1700 B.C.E. Yet another version credits them with the founding of Vienna.

One chronicle enumerates 72 Jewish princes, ruling in Austria until 200 B.C.E.

BIBLIOGRAPHY: H. Gold, *Geschichte der Juden in Wien* (1966), 1; H. Tietze, *Die Juden Wiens* (1933), 13–14; E. Scherer, *Die Rechtsverhaeltnisse der Juden in den deutsch-oesterreichischen Laendern* (1901), 112.

JUDAH (Heb. יְהוּדָה), fourth son of Jacob and Leah. The biblical explanation of the name Judah connects it with "thanksgiving" and "praise" (Heb. אוֹדֶה, *o'deh*; Gen. 29:35). However, if one compares the names Judith (Gen. 26:34) and Jahdai (I Chron. 2:47) it is clear that this explanation is a popular etymology. According to Yeivin, the name is derived from the Arabic root *whd* (Heb. *yhd*), which yields, for example, the Arabic noun *wahd*, meaning "low ground." The name originated either in the tribe's connection with the land west of the hill country of Judah (the lowland; see below), or in its original lowly social status. As to the latter, the traditional placing of Judah fourth in the first group of Leah's sons should be noted, as well as his Canaanite matrimonial connections (see below). These indicate that the tribe once had a low social status, having contained more non-Israelite elements than any other tribe. It was only subsequently that Judah acquired an honorable and leading place for itself by virtue of its size and its political activity.

Judah in the Pentateuch

Apart from the sons of Rachel (Joseph and Benjamin), Judah is one of the few of Jacob's children (see *Reuben, *Simeon) about whom the traditions of the patriarchal period speak in detail. They tell first and foremost of his marriage to the daughter of a Canaanite named Shua who bore him three sons (Gen. 38). Although they reached adolescence, two of his sons (see *Onan, *Er) had no descendants, while the third, *Shelah, had many children and grandchildren (I Chron. 4:21ff.). In connection with the childless marriages of Judah's older sons, tradition recounts the affair of *Tamar who bore Judah *Perez and *Zerah, the main ancestors of the tribe of Judah. In the *Joseph stories an important role is ascribed to Judah as spokesman for the sons of Jacob (Gen. 37:26; 43:3–5, 8–10; 44:16–34). In the first census in the wilderness (Num. 1:27; 2:4), the tribe numbered 74,600 and had the largest population of the tribes of Israel. In the second census the tribe numbered five families of 76,500 souls (26:19–22), and was again the largest. In the camping and marching arrangements, "the standard [or division] of the camp of Judah," comprising Judah, Issachar, and Zebulun, camped on the eastern side of the Tabernacle and marched at the head of the host (Num. 2:1–9; 10:14–16). (On Judah in the blessings of Jacob and Moses, see below.)

History of the Tribe

*Othniel son of Kenaz, a descendant of Judah, was regarded as the first judge (Judg. 3:4ff.), but this narrative is to be connected, it seems, with the end of the conquest and the settlement of Debir and its vicinity by the sons of Kenaz (cf. Judg. 1:11ff.; see *Cush, *Cushan Rishathaim, and the Book of *Joshua). If this passage be disregarded, no explicit mention of the tribe of Judah is to be found during the greater part of the period of the Judges. In the Song of Deborah the tribe of Judah is not mentioned, although ten of the tribes are enumerated. During this period of 200 years or more (c. 1250–1030 B.C.E.), the Judahite patriarchal families settled in the mountains, in the Shephelah, and in the pasture lands of the wilderness of Judah. It seems that they also had border skirmishes with the Philistines. At the beginning of the Philistine penetration of the coastal strip the Judahites were capable of inflicting local defeats upon them, apparently in concert with the pre-Israelite elements who dwelt in the Shephelah. The deeds of *Shamgar son of Anath, alluded to in two verses of the Book of Judges (3:31; 5:6), belong, as far as can be seen, to this stage of the struggle. However, once the Philistines were entrenched in the coastal strip and began to extend the area of their rule to the hinterland, they imposed their authority over the whole of the Shephelah and Wadi Sorek, as far as the approaches of the mountains (cf. Judg. 14–16); they also settled, as far as one can tell, in the northwestern part of the Negev (cf. "Negev of the Cherethites," I Sam. 30:14). On the other hand, it appears that in the course of time the Judahites succeeded in checking the advance of the Jebusite kingdom in the north and in depriving it of very extensive areas, until they were able to break through toward the northwest and to penetrate into the area in which the Danites first settled before their northward migration. Here they came into conflict with the Benjamites who also wanted to take possession of the Danite inheritance. This rivalry fanned the quarrels between Benjamin on one side and Judah and Ephraim on the other. At the close of the era of the judges (c. 1070 B.C.E.) it led to the fratricidal war between Benjamin and its two neighbors to the north and the south, who were also apparently joined by many units from some of the other tribes of Israel (see *Gibeah; *History; *Judges, Book of). As a result of the defeat of the Benjamites, the Israelite opposition to the Philistine invaders was weakened, and the latter now ruled over almost the entire mountain area of western Israel (c. 1050 B.C.E.).

It seems that while the Judeans were establishing themselves in western Canaan, the tribes of *Reuben, *Simeon, and *Levi were simultaneously spreading southward over the hill country of Judah. However, the Judahites, who where more numerous, did not allow them to settle in their midst. In the course of time, apparently after the Moabites had been defeated by *Ehud son of Gera, the Reubenites crossed eastward into Transjordan and settled the territory between the wadis Jabbok and Arnon, while the Simeonites and Levites were squeezed together on the periphery of Judah's territory in the northern Negev. The close tie with the tribe of Simeon is evidenced also by the fact that its inheritance was actually included within the borders of Judah.

When the Benjamites recovered from their defeat at the hands of the Judahites and took the leading position in the struggle against the domination of the Philistines, Judah par-

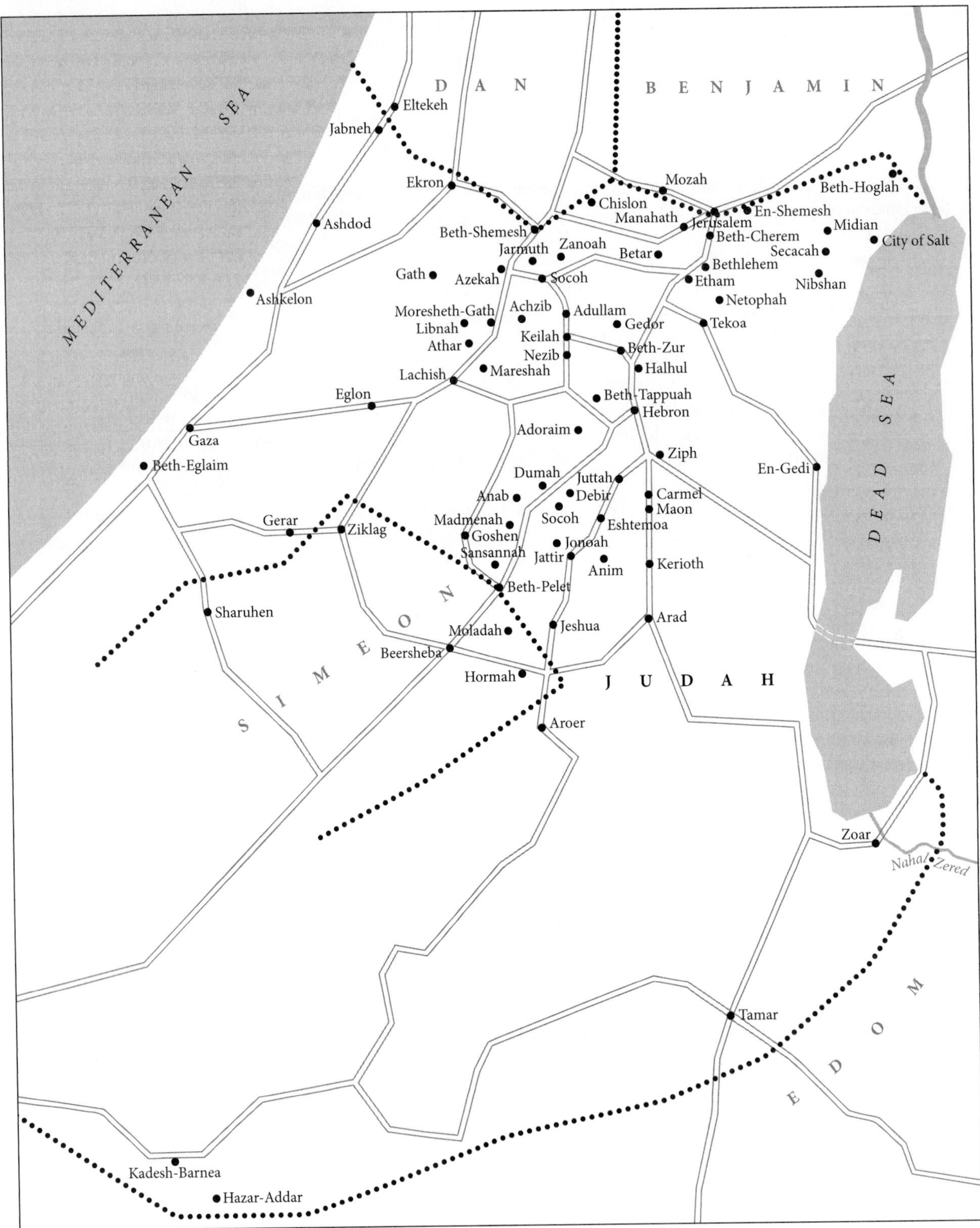

Territory of the tribe of Judah. After Y. Aharoni in Lexicon Biblicum, *Dvir, Tel Aviv, 1965.*

ticipated actively in this war. With the ascendancy of David, the main initiative passed into Judahite hands, a situation reflected in the blessing of Jacob: "The scepter shall not depart from Judah, nor the ruler's staff from between his feet" (Gen. 49:10). This blessing also extols the economic and political status of the tribe (49:8ff.). This text has apparently to be assigned to the time of the united kingdom. Since Levi's office is not mentioned it can be dated to the second half of David's reign (see *Gad, *David), but before the appointment of the Levites to their religious administrative offices (see *Levi). The blessing of Moses, on the other hand, attaches no particular importance to Judah who is alluded to being outside the circle of the other tribes of Israel (Deut. 33:7). This seems to describe the situation from the Israelite point of view in the first years of the reign of *Jeroboam son of Nebat.

Land of Judah

The use of the expression "land of Judah" (Heb. אֶרֶץ יְהוּדָה, *Ereẓ Yehudah*) is not uniform in the Bible. In Deuteronomy 34:2 it serves to indicate the southern part of the hill country west of the Jordan – in contrast to Galilee, the hill country of Ephraim, and the *Negev – and includes the whole area between the plain of the Jordan and the Mediterranean Sea. In other passages it seems to indicate only the tribal territory of Judah (cf. I Sam. 22:5; Ruth 1:7). From the dissolution of the union between Israel and Judah to the fall of the latter, "Judah" designates the kingdom of Judah (cf. I Kings 19:3 with 12:17), and after the return to Zion it signifies the province of Judah (cf. Zech. 2:4; for the political transformations of the expression, see *Israel, Names of). The territory of the tribe is delineated in Joshua 15:1–12. The southern boundary passed from the southern end of the Dead Sea in the Arabah by way of the ascent of Akrabbim, skirted the oasis of *Kadesh-Barnea, and ran with the Wadi of Egypt to the Mediterranean Sea. This line corresponds to the southern boundary of the land of Canaan (cf. Num. 34:3–5). The eastern boundary ran along the shore of the Dead Sea from its southern tip to the mouth of the Jordan. The northern boundary was so drawn as to include within Judah Beth-Hoglah and Beth-Arabah in the western plain of the Jordan. From here it ascended by way of the valley of *Achor and the ascent of Adummim to *En-Rogel, passed through the valley of Ben-Hinnom up to the northern extremity of the valley of *Rephaim, and, progressing by way of the waters of Nephtoah, extended through *Kiriath-Je'arim, Chislon, and *Beth-Shemesh to *Timnah through the Wadi *Sorek, continuing along the southern edge of the wadi until it emptied into the Mediterranean Sea. The western border was the seashore between Wadi Sorek (Wādi Rūbīn) and the Brook of Egypt (Wadi el-Arish). From the enumeration of the Judahite towns (Josh. 15:21–61), which follows the delineation of the boundaries, it would seem that the list was drawn up in the reign of King *Jehoshaphat and expanded in the wake of the conquests of King *Uzziah (Azariah). The last verse (Josh. 15:63) appears to be a gloss by a later editor made to correlate the record before him with the situation at the time of the Judges. This list of cities comprises only ten compact groups, if verses 45 to 47 are excluded. These verses are exceptional in that they do not give a complete enumeration of towns, but merely indicate city-territories (in Philistia), and the usual total at the end is missing. In the enumeration of the towns of Benjamin (Josh. 18:21–28), on the other hand, we have two further compact groups of towns (18:21–24, 25–28). Clearly these combined compact enumerations of Judahite and Benjamite towns are simply an exact marking of the twelve administrative divisions of the kingdom of Judah which included the territories of the tribes of Judah, Simeon (cf. Josh. 19:3–7 with 15:27–32), and Benjamin. Attempts have been made to assign the list to the time of Josiah or Hezekiah, but it would seem that the area described can correspond only to the situation in the time of Jehoshaphat. The area ruled by Josiah extended north of the border described in this list and included only part of the addition recorded in verses 42 to 47. In the time of Hezekiah, too, the situation differed both on the northern border and on the west. Moreover, in the Septuagint, there is an additional verse between verses 59 and 60 that enumerates another group of 11 towns in the vicinity of Jerusalem, i.e., it includes an additional administrative division, which was necessary for the economy of the country in a leap year (verse 59a). Some time after the conquests of Uzziah (apparently in the time of *Hezekiah) a later editor, it seems, added verses 45 to 47, listing the king's conquests in the lowland.

The geographical area from south to north included (1) part of the Negev region (cf. also Judg. 1:15 and parallel passages) and the region of Geshur north of it; from west to east (changing according to political circumstances) parts of the coastal plain, the *Shephelah, and the hill country of Judah, which has a Mediterranean climate; (2) and the wilderness of Judah, small areas of the Jordan plain (north of the Dead Sea), and the Arabah (south of the Dead Sea), whose climate is partly arid. The livelihood of the inhabitants of the different regions varied accordingly (rain agriculture, some irrigated agriculture, horticulture; cattle rearing, some exploitation of the natural resources).

[*Encyclopaedia Hebraica*]

In the Aggadah

Judah was honored more than all his brothers in that all descendants of Jacob are called *Yehudim* ("Jews," lit. "Judah-ites"; see *Jew; Gen. R. 98:6). His superiority was recognized by his brothers who appointed him their king (Gen. R. 84:17). Judah earned these distinctions for saving Joseph's life, for his candor in confessing his relationship with *Tamar (Gen. 38:1–27), and for his admirable traits of character. Although it was at his suggestion that *Joseph was sold rather than put to death, Judah should nevertheless have returned him to their father (Gen. R. 85:3). Indeed, his brothers later blamed him for their crime, since they claimed they would have obeyed him had he suggested it (Tanḥ. B., Gen. 181). The subsequent death of his wife and two sons (Gen. 38:7–12) was divine retribution for the suffering he caused his father by selling Joseph (Tanḥ. B., Gen. 209). Judah was sent on ahead of his father to Egypt (Gen. 46:28) to erect a *bet midrash* in Goshen so that Jacob might begin instructing his sons at once after his arrival. This honorable task was a compensation for the wrongful suspicion that he had slain Joseph which Jacob had previously harbored against him (Gen. R. 95:2).

Judah would never have sinned with Tamar, but God sent the "angel of desire" to entice him, for kings and redeemers were destined to issue from this union (Gen. R. 85:8). Judah's father, grandfather, and brothers wished to condemn Tamar, since they felt that she may have found the signet, cord, and staff (Ex. R. 30:19). At first, Judah also wanted to deny his guilt, but he was moved by Tamar's plea that he "acknowledge his Creator and hide not his eyes from her" (Gen. R. 85:11). Judah never separated himself from Tamar after this incident. Because he rescued Tamar and her two sons from death by burning, three of his descendants, Hananiah, Mishael, and Azariah, were later to be delivered from the fiery furnace (Sot. 10b). Judah was the first to institute the levirate marriage when he insisted that Onan marry Er's widow (Gen. R. 85:5).

Judah revealed his profound wisdom when he induced his father to send Benjamin to Egypt. He reasoned that it was doubtful whether Benjamin would be seized, whereas it was certain that without grain they would all die (Gen. R. 91:10). His wisdom is also displayed by his not responding to Joseph's inquiries until he fully perceived Joseph's intentions (Gen. R. 93:4). Judah also possessed remarkable physical strength. When he became angry, the hairs on his chest became so stiff that they pierced his clothes, and he could chew iron bars into dust and powder (Gen. R. 93:6). His voice traveled 400 parasangs when he shouted so that his conversation with Joseph in Egypt was heard in Ereẓ Israel (Gen. R. 93:7). Judah was the key warrior during the battles which the children of Jacob had to fight after Simeon and Levi destroyed Shechem. When the enemy warriors caught sight of Judah's lion-like face and teeth (cf. Gen. 49:9) and heard his powerful voice, they were terrified, and Judah without difficulty slew thousands of them (Midrash publ. by S. Schechter from Ms. in *Semitic Studies in Memory of A. Kohut*, 490–1; *Sefer ha-Yashar, Va-Yishlaḥ*). Judah's pledge to ban himself from the community if he did not return Benjamin to his father (Gen. 43:9) is regarded as proof that a conditional ban, even if the condition is not fulfilled, still takes effect. As a result of this vow, his bones rolled about in his coffin without rest during the 40 years the Children of Israel wandered in the wilderness. Moses finally secured rest for his remains when he prayed to God, arguing that the example of Judah's confession had induced Reuben likewise to confess his sin with Bilhah (Sot. 7b).

[Aaron Rothkoff]

BIBLIOGRAPHY: Th. J. Meek, *Hebrew Origins* (1936), 31–50, 112–20; S. Klein, *Ereẓ Yehudah* (1939); B. Maisler (Mazar), *ToledotEreẓ Yisrael* (1938), 39ff., 220ff., 278ff.; H.H. Rowley, *From Joseph to Joshua* (1948), 4–7, 44–45, 101–41 (incl. bibl.); F.N. Cross and E. Cross, in: jbl 75 (1956), 202ff.; Y. Aharoni, *Yehudah vi-Yrushalayim* (1957), 46ff.; idem, *Ereẓ Yisrael bi-Tekufat ha-Mikra* (1963); S. Yeivin, in: EM, 3 (1958), 487–508 (incl. bibl.); idem, *Meḥkarim* (1960), 178ff.; idem, in: A. Malamat (ed.), *Bi-Ymei Bayit Rishon* (1962), 54. JUDAH IN THE AGGADAH: Ginzberg, Legends, 1 (1942²), 401–11; 2 (1946⁶), 31–37, 89–94, 103–10.

JUDAH (Nesiah), *nasi* from about 230 to 270 C.E., son of Gamaliel III, and grandson of Judah ha-Nasi. During his period of office the power of the *nasi* began to decline and the struggle between him and the scholars became intensified. Judah and his brother Hillel were apparently regarded favorably (Sem. 8:4, ed. Higger), and Judah conducted his relationship with his opponents among the scholars with skill and understanding, with the aim of drawing them to him. One of his most determined opponents was *Simeon b. Lakish, who criticized him for levying taxes on scholars (BB 7b) and accepting gifts from the people (Gen. R. 78:12). On one occasion Lakish even states that "a *nasi* who sins is flogged," which incidentally was not in accordance with Roman law. As a result Lakish was compelled to flee. On the advice of Johanan, however, with whom he was intimate, Judah himself went to appease him (TJ, Sanh. 2:1). Complaints of persecution were also heard from other scholars (Yose of Oni – Gen. R., Theodor-Albeck edition, p. 950 et al.; Mani – Ta'an. 23b, et al.), all of whom openly preached against him. Although it is not certain whether the *nasi* was made responsible for the collection of taxes from the inhabitants of Judea, it is nevertheless certain that in Judah's time the office of the *nasi* was in great financial straits, and this apparently was the reason for Judah's actions, which included his appointment of unsuitable judges in exchange for money, a step which widened the rift between him and the scholars.

Judah is referred to as "a great man" (TJ, Av. Zar. 1:1). Not only did he go out of his way to appease his opponents, but he also used his authority to impose the decisions of the scholars upon the community (TJ, Ket. 9:2). He himself was a scholar and a member of a *bet din* which became known as "the permissive *bet din*" because it permitted, among other things, oil of the gentiles, which had been long prohibited (Av. Zar. 35b–37a, et al.). This permission was recognized also in Babylon. As a result he is sometimes referred to in the Mishnah as "Rabbi," the title by which his grandfather was known. Simeon b. Lakish, his great opponent, himself transmitted *halakhot* in his name, and also aggadic statements on the importance of Torah study, such as: "The world is sustained for the sake of the breath of schoolchildren," and "Every town in which there are no schoolchildren shall be destroyed" (Shab. 119). Judah's prayer for rain was answered (Ta'an. 249). When he died, it was proclaimed that "the priesthood was abolished for that day" (TJ, Ber. 3:1) to enable kohanim to participate in his funeral. His son was *Gamaliel IV. A tradition dating from the Middle Ages states that his grave was in Upper Galilee.

BIBLIOGRAPHY: Frankel, Mevo, 92–94; Alon, Meḥkarim, 2 (1958), 15–57; Z. Vilnay, *Maẓẓevot Kodesh be-Ereẓ Yisrael* (1963), 352.

[Israel Moses Ta-Shma]

JUDAH III (Judah Nesiah II), *nasi* from 290 to 320. Judah III was the son of Gamaliel IV and the grandson of Judah Nesiah. It is sometimes difficult to determine from the sources whether a reference is to Judah II or III. Judah III was a pupil of Johanan (see RH 20a). He was especially intimate with *Ammi and *Assi, who headed the academy of Tiberias after the death of Johanan. Halakhic problems raised by him with

Ammi are mentioned (Av. Zar. 33b; Beẓah 27a), and it is also related that Ammi was particularly insistent that Judah should conduct himself beyond that which was required by the strict letter of the law, as was befitting for "a prominent person" (MK 12b). These two scholars were sent by Judah to found schools for children throughout the land of Israel (TJ, Hag. 1:7, 76c). Although the status of the office of *nasi* had deteriorated greatly in his time, dignity was preserved internally and the people obeyed his directives. Judah was himself a scholar and Zera established *halakhah* from his conduct (TJ, Beẓah 1:9, 60d). He was in contact with the scholars of his time (see TJ, Shab. 6:9), and there is a suggestion of a dispute between him and Jeremiah and of a letter of appeasement sent by the latter (TJ, Meg. 3:2, 74a). It is stated that he imposed 13 fasts upon the community in a time of drought (Ta'an. 14a), and mention is made of his slave, Germanius, a member of the Gothic guard, presented to him by the government (TJ, Shab., 6:9; TJ, Yoma 8:5; et al.). During his time the Roman emperor *Diocletian stayed in Tiberias while waging war against the Persians, and the *aggadah* describes a meeting between the two at the invitation of the emperor, embellishing the account with miraculous details (TJ, Ter. 8:10, 46b–c; Gen. R. 63:8).

BIBLIOGRAPHY: Hyman, Toledot, 612–5; Alon, *Meḥkarim*, 2 (1958), 16–17.

[Israel Moses Ta-Shma]

JUDAH IV (fl. c. 385–400 C.E.), patriarch, son of *Gamaliel V. Very little is known about him, and even that little is doubtful. He seems to have been unpopular with contemporary rabbis, and when his sister Mana died, a leading Palestinian scholar refused to attend her funeral (TJ, Ber. 3:1, 6a; cf. Ta'an. 23b). Epiphanius (*Adversus Haereses*, 30:7, 3) reports, in the name of a convert called Joseph, that under the influence of his evil companions, the young patriarch had become dissipated. Under Judah IV the general decline of the patriarchate continued, although Jewish religious and judicial privileges were confirmed by Arcadius and *Honorius in 396. According to Bacher (Pal. Amor, 3 (1899), 312 f.), Judah IV is identical with the R. Judah Nesiah who asked Phinehas b. Ḥama why Boaz had demeaned himself to "lie down at the end of the heap of grain" (Ruth R. 5:15 on Ruth 3:7). This identification, however, is uncertain, since Phinehas may have been a contemporary of Judah III. Judah IV was the father of *Hillel, the patriarch who fixed the calendar.

BIBLIOGRAPHY: Graetz, Gesch, 4 (1908), 354, 449; M. Avi-Yonah, *Bi-Ymei Roma u-Byzantiyyon* (1952), 78 f., 116 f., 220; Hyman, Toledot; Baron, Social2, 2 (1952), 191 ff.

[Moses Aberbach]

JUDAH, surname of at least three colonial American families not known to be related.

New York Judahs

BARUCH JUDAH (c. 1678–1774), who was born in Breslau, founded a family appearing in New York, Newport, Rhode Island, and Richmond, Virginia, in colonial times. Baruch became a freeman of New York in 1715 or 1716. He was active in the affairs of Congregation Shearith Israel. A son, HILLEL (c 1730–1815), a *shoḥet* in Newport and a New York merchant, married Abigail, daughter of Isaac Mendes *Seixas. Three of their sons were connected with Beth Shalom Congregation in Richmond: BARUCH H. (1763–1830) as a founder, ISAAC H. (1761–1827) as *ḥazzan*, and MANUEL (1769–1834) as a trustee. SAMUEL (1728–1781), another son of the elder Baruch, was a well-known New York merchant. In 1770 he signed the Non-Importation Agreement, a boycott of British goods. His eldest child, BENJAMIN S. (1760–1831), conducted an extensive trade with the West Indies and was a founder of the New York Tontine (1786). His youngest child, WALTER JONAS (1778–1798), a student at the medical school of Columbia College, died while treating patients during a yellow fever epidemic.

Another son, NAPHTALI (1774–1855), was a New York printer, publisher, and merchant. In 1797 he published D. Levi's *Defence of the Old Testament*, against attacks by the deists Thomas Paine and Joseph Priestley. Naphtali Judah was active in Congregation Shearith Israel, serving as president and committee member, particularly in matters involving cemetery maintenance. He also established strong ties with the non-Jewish community, as a member of the Tammany Society, holding the office of sachem; as a prominent Mason; and as one of the original subscribers of New York Hospital in 1811.

The oldest child of Benjamin S. was Samuel Benjamin Helbert *Judah, the playwright. His son EMANUEL (d. 1839) achieved some reputation as an actor.

Canadian Judahs

Another family of Judahs, also originating from Breslau, was established in Canada by SAMUEL JUDAH (1725–1789). He went to Canada with Lord Amherst's army and was one of the founders of the Montreal Jewish community, establishing himself there by 1761. He and his brother-in-law Aaron *Hart of Trois Rivières, Canada, later conducted an extensive business in furs with London. He sympathized with the colonists during the Revolutionary War, lending them a considerable sum of money which was never repaid. His brother URIAH (1714–1782) became prothonotary of Trois Rivières in 1768. His son BERNARD S. (1777–1831) married Aaron Hart's daughter Catherine.

The eldest of their nine sons, SAMUEL (1799–1869), who was born in New York City, became a pioneer Middle Western lawyer and politician. He graduated from Rutgers College in 1816, studied law, and was admitted to the bar. He settled in Vincennes, Indiana, in 1818. From Vincennes he practiced law widely. He was a close friend of Henry Clay. Samuel became active in politics and was elected several times to the Indiana legislature, in 1840 serving as speaker of its house of representatives. In 1830 he was appointed U.S. attorney for the district of Indiana, serving to 1833. He was a man of culture, known for his proficiency in Greek and Latin.

Connecticut Judahs

MICHAEL JUDAH (D. 1786) was a businessman of Norwalk and Hartford, Connecticut, and New York City. He willed his property to the Jews of New York City. His descendants were not Jewish.

BIBLIOGRAPHY: Stern, Americans, 101–3; Rosenbloom, Biog Dict, 78–81; D. de Sola Pool, *Portraits Etched in Stone* (1952), index; T. and D. de Sola Pool, *An Old Faith in the New World* (1955), index; B.G. Sack, *History of the Jews in Canada* (1964), index.

[Irving I. Katz and Leo Hershkowitz]

JUDAH, SAMUEL BENJAMIN HELBERT (1799–1876?), U.S. playwright. A member of a prominent Sephardi mercantile family, Samuel Judah was born in New York City. One of the first Jews to contribute to American literature, he was successful with his earliest play, *The Mountain Torrent* (1820), which was followed by other melodramas such as *The Rose of Arragon* (1822). According to the author, it took him just four days to complete his historical drama of the American Revolutionary War, *A Tale of Lexington* which was received "with unbounded applause" when it was performed in New York on Independence Day 1822. His career as a dramatist ended, however, when he wrote *Gotham and the Gothamites* (1823), which satirized well-known New Yorkers, including his eminent fellow playwright Mordecai M. *Noah. He was sued for defamation and imprisoned but on his release took up law. Judah's later writings appeared under the pseudonym Terentius Phologombos. They included a biblical play, *The Maid of Midian*, which, probably because of its sacrilegious approach, was never performed.

BIBLIOGRAPHY: W. Dunlap, *History of the American Theatre* (1832), 409; A.H. Quinn, *History of the American Drama from the Beginning to the Civil War* (1923), 155, 197; S. Liptzin, *Jew in American Literature* (1966), 27–28. **ADD. BIBLIOGRAPHY:** L. Harap, *The Image of the Jew in American Literature* (1974), 261–63.

[Sol Liptzin]

JUDAH, SON OF ẒIPPORAI (first century), patriot. According to Josephus, Judah was a sophist of highest reputation among the Jews, an unrivalled interpreter of their ancestral laws, and educator of the youth. Taking advantage of Herod's illness (4 B.C.E.) he, together with his friend and fellow scholar Mattathias son of Margalot, persuaded their disciples to pull down the golden eagle, the symbol of Rome, which Herod had erected over the great gate of the Temple, since it was contrary to Jewish law. The two scholars, together with their disciples, were burnt alive on the command of Herod shortly before his death.

BIBLIOGRAPHY: Jos., Ant., 17:149–167; Jos., Wars, 1:648–55; Schuerer, Hist, 157; Klausner, Bayit Sheni, 4 (1950^2), 164f.; C. Roth, in: HTR, 49 (1956), 169ff.

[Edna Elazary]

JUDAH ARYEH LEIB BEN DAVID (d. 1709), rabbi and author, also called Leib Kalish. He was a grandson of Joel *Sirkes and Abraham Ḥayyim Schor, the author of *Torat Ḥayyim* (Lublin, 1624). He served as rabbi and *rosh yeshivah* in the communities of Kremsier (Moravia) and Lobsens (Posen) for 22 years, and Kalisz. In 1708 he accepted an invitation to become the rabbi of the Ashkenazi community of Amsterdam, but he died a year and a half later. He was succeeded in the rabbinate of Amsterdam by Ẓevi Hirsch b. Jacob *Ashkenazi (the Ḥakham Ẓevi). Judah Aryeh Leib was the author of *Gur Aryeh* (Amsterdam, 1733), homilies on the Pentateuch, to which was appended the *Bedek ha-Bayit*, composed by his grandfather Abraham Ḥayyim Schor. Many of Judah Aryeh Leib's aggadic novellae are mentioned in the introduction to *Shama Shelomo* (Amsterdam, 1710) by Solomon *Algazi. His responsa have remained in manuscript.

BIBLIOGRAPHY: Michael, Or, no. 991; Ḥ.N. Dembitzer, *Kelilat Yofi*, 1 (1888), 97b–99a; 2 (1893), 143a; A. Heppner and J. Herzberg, *Aus Vergangenheit und Gegenwart der Juden... in den Posener Landen* (1909), 617; I.D. Beth-Halevy, *Toledot Yehudei Kalisch* (1961), 152, 220, 230.

[Yehoshua Horowitz]

JUDAH BAR EZEKIEL (d. 299), Babylonian *amora*, founder of the academy at *Pumbedita. Judah's father was a famous *amora* and "wonder worker" (see Kid. 32a, 33b; TJ, Ta'an 1:3, 64b). Judah's brother was the *amora* Rami b. Ezekiel, who appears to have gone to Ereẓ Israel and returned to Babylonia (Ket. 21a; Kid. 32a; Ḥul. 44a, etc.). According to the Talmud "on the day R. Judah ha-Nasi passed away ... Judah [b. Ezekiel] was born," and on his deathbed Judah ha-Nasi said "today R. Judah is born in Babylonia" (Kid. 72a–b; cf. Guttmann, in: HUCA, 25 (1954), 241ff. for a discussion of the date on which this took place). Judah was a pupil first of Rav in Sura, then of R. Assi of Huẓal, and finally of *Samuel in Nehardea, and he quotes many *halakhot* in their names (see Suk. 9a; BB 139b; Yev. 17a and Rashi *ibid.*; Av. Zar. 16b and Rashi *ibid.*). Notwithstanding Judah's boundless esteem for Samuel, he once directed an admonishing remark at him (see Shab. 55a), and in several instances took issue with him (Ber. 36a). Samuel's affectionate nickname for his pupil, "Shinena" (*ibid.*; Shab. 7a, 152a) is generally taken to mean "sharp in talmudic knowledge," although some interpret it as "bigtoothed" (*Arukh*, s.v. *shen* 2). So great was Samuel's admiration for his pupil that he said of him, "he is not of woman born" (Nid. 13a).

After the destruction of Nehardea by *Papa b. Neẓer in 259, part of the academy of Nehardea moved to Pumbedita, where Judah became its head (Git. 60b and Rashi *ibid.*). Pumbedita was considered the heir to Nehardea, in that it continued the tradition of being a purely "Babylonian academy," as opposed to *Sura, where the Palestinian influence – due to Rav's way of learning – remained very strong. However, throughout the lifetime of Huna, Sura remained the main center of learning. Only after Huna passed away in 297 did Pumbedita come to the foreground, where indeed it remained for the next 800 years. The main subject of study there was the order **Nezikin* (Ber. 20a), the importance of which was emphasized by Judah (BK 30a). Judah's *halakhah* is extensively quoted in both the Babylonian and the Jerusalem Talmuds.

His main disputant is Huna, and their discussions occupy a prominent place in the Babylonian Talmud. Judah was highly esteemed by the sages of his day, among them R. Naḥman (see Kid. 70a–b), and R. Eleazar "the master from Palestine" and Ulla, who were loath to give decisions in Pumbedita (Nid. 20b). Among his prominent pupils were Kahana and Joseph (Yev. 17a), Zeira (Ber. 39a) and Abba (Ḥul. 19b).

Judah was opposed to returning from Babylonia to Ereẓ Israel before the coming of the Redeemer (Ket. 110b–111a). When Zeira and Abba decided to do this, they had to do it clandestinely without his knowledge (*ibid.*; Ber. 24b). Nevertheless his devotion to Ereẓ Israel is attested (see Ber. 43a). He was accustomed to speak Hebrew, even in daily conversations with his servant (Shab. 41a). He considered the use of Hebrew mandatory for prayer and enjoined the Aramaic-speaking Jews of Babylonia, "Never should a person plead his needs in Aramaic" (Shab. 12b; see however Sot. 33a).

Judah was noted for his saintliness and piety (Ḥag. 15b; Nid. 13a), and in consequence wonderful powers were popularly ascribed to him. For example, it is stated that in times of drought he had but to remove one shoe (an indication that he was about to undertake a fast) and rain would immediately begin to fall (see Ber. 20a; Ta'an. 24b; Sanh. 106b). Judah was distinguished by the firmness of his convictions and his not indulging anyone (MK 17a; Kid. 70a–b). The *amora* Isaac b. Judah was his son (Yev. 63b; Kid. 71b). When, according to legend, Joseph, the son of R. Joshua b. Levi, ascended to heaven and returned, and was asked by his father what he had seen, he replied, "A world upside down; the exalted below and the lowly above" (BB 10b). This statement is interpreted by geonic tradition to refer to the fact that he saw Samuel sitting at the feet of his pupil Judah, who was thus honored because he had not refrained from admonishing his master (*Arukh*, s.v. *neged* 1; Tos. to BB 10b).

BIBLIOGRAPHY: B.M. Lewin (ed.), *Iggeret R. Sherira Ga'on* (1921), 82–85; Neusner, Babylonia, 2–3 (1966–68), index; J. Heilprin, *Seder ha-Dorot*, pt. 2, *Seder Tanna'im ve-Amora'im* (Warsaw, 1905), 179–81; Frankel, Mevo, 91a; Hyman, Todedot, 542–52; Ḥ. Albeck, *Mavo la-Talmudim* (1969), 199–201.

[Zvi Kaplan]

JUDAH BAR ILAI (mid-second century C.E.), *tanna*. He is the R. Judah mentioned in the Talmud and tannaitic literature without patronymic. Judah came from Usha in Galilee (see Song R. 2:5 n. 2). He studied under his father, who was a pupil of *Eliezer b. Hyrcanus (Tosef. Zev. 2:17).

While still young Judah went to reside in Lydda, close to *Tarfon (Tosef. Meg. 2:8, Neg. 8:2), becoming one of his pupils (Ned. 6:6; Tosef., Yev. 12:15, et al.). He also studied under *Akiva (Tosef., Kel. BM 6:7, Oho. 4:2).

Judah played a central role in the establishment of the new centers of learning in Galillee after the suppression of the Bar Kokhba revolt. The sources preserve a number of contradictory *aggadot* concerning these events. According to one tradition in the Babylonian Talmud, Judah was one of the five ordained by *Judah b. Bava, at the cost of his life, during the time of the Hadrianic persecutions (Sanh. 14a). The historical authenticity of this account has been seriously and convincingly challenged (Oppenheimer, 78–79). According to another tradition he was among "the seven elders" who convened to intercalate the year in the valley of Rimmon (TJ, Ḥag. 3:1, 78c). According to a third tradition, Judah played a leading role in the convention of scholars in Usha at which the Sanhedrin was reestablished, being granted the honor of speaking first, since Usha was his home town (Song R. loc. cit.). In a later Babylonian version of this tradition, there is a "shift of venue," from Usha to Jabneh (Ber. 63b). Judah is still portrayed as the opening speaker at this convention of the Sanhedrin, but this honor is no longer explained by Judah's connection to the location, but rather by means of an obscure title: "R. Judah, the first speaker in every situation" (Oppenheimer, 80–82). This title is then explained by the Talmud as resulting from Judah's role in the events which eventually led to R. Simeon's flight from the Romans with his son, seeking refuge for years in a cave (Shab. 33b). However, there is no evidence in earlier Palestinian sources for the title "first speaker in every situation" with respect to Judah, nor does Judah play any role in the parallel Palestinian versions of the saga of R. Simeon and his son (cf. TJ, 9, 38d, Gen. R. 79:6, PdRK 11:16). As a further sign of Judah's prominent position in the eyes of later tradition, all the scholars of his generation were described as "the generation of Judah b. Ilai" (Sanh. 20a). Judah was the halakhic authority in the house of the *nasi*, *Simeon b. Gamaliel II (Men. 104a), and *Judah ha-Nasi was one of his pupils (Shevu. 13a), as was *Ishmael b. Yose (Suk. 18a).

Tannaitic literature has many statements and teachings by Judah. Long series of *mishnayot* and *halakhot*, as well as whole chapters in the Mishnah and the Tosefta, are from his Mishnah. In his Mishnah Judah had a special place for the *halakhot* of Eliezer b. Hyrcanus which he had received from his father Ilai (cf. Tosef. Zev. 2:17), and for early *halakhot* that he received from Tarfon, particularly with regard to the Temple and its service. He gave the Mishnah of Akiva as the view of an individual (Ma'as. Sh. 5:8) and recorded the disputes between Bet Shammai and Bet Hillel in accordance with a tradition which differed from that of Akiva. The Babylonian Talmud describes Judah's share in the Sifra – the halakhic Midrash to the Book of Leviticus – by the words, "an anonymous Sifra is by Judah" (Sanh. 86a). Though this statement is ascribed in the Babylonian Talmud to R. Johanan, neither its authenticity nor its accuracy can be confirmed. Rules explaining the language used by Judah have been laid down, and in the view of the *amora*, Joshua b. Levi: "Wherever Judah said 'when' or 'these words apply' in our Mishnah, his intention was only to explain the words of the scholars; but where Johanan said 'when' he introduces an explanation, while 'these words apply' indicates disagreement" (Er. 81b–82a). His tendency to generalize is also discernible in his own statement: "Collect the words of the Torah as general rules – and divide them up like the drops of dew which are small … for if a man collects them in items, they will weary him and he will not know what to do" (Sif. Deut. 306). In a dispute between Meir – or Simeon – and Judah, the *halakhah* follows Judah, but in a dispute with Yose, the *halakhah* follows Yose, but some disagree with regard to this (Er. 46b). Another rule laid down was: "Wherever Judah taught a law concerning the *eruv*, the *halakhah* follows him" (Er. 81b).

Explanations of Scripture by Judah have been preserved, which give the plain meaning; some explain difficult words, and some explain the subject matter. Judah issued a warning about the difficulty of giving an accurate Aramaic translation of the Bible: "He who translates a verse literally is a liar, and he who adds to it is a libeler" (Tosef., Meg. 4:41). In his view in several places Scripture removes anthropomorphic or offensive expressions (Mekh. Shirata, 6). His interpretations touch upon many and varied topics. His main disputant in *halakhah* is *Simeon b. Yoḥai and in *aggadah* *Nehemiah; no less than 180 disputes between Judah and Nehemiah have been preserved in both tannaitic literature and in the amoraic Midrashim, particularly in the early *Genesis Rabbah*. Their style shows them to be the product of a dialogue – at times there is not even a substantial difference of view between them – and from them it is possible to discern the aggadic exegetical method of the *tannaim*. Their disputes touch upon all the books of the Bible except Leviticus and Job.

Judah was known for his piety, so that the Talmud states that wherever it is stated, "it once happened with a certain pious man," the reference is either to Judah b. Bava or to Judah b. Ilai (BK 103b). Several of his practices were transmitted by the *amora* Judah in the name of Rav: "This was the practice of Judah b. Ilai. On the eve of the Sabbath a basin filled with hot water was brought to him. He washed his face, hands and feet, and wrapped himself in fringed linen robes, and was like an angel of the Lord of Hosts" (Shab. 25b); "On the eve of the Ninth of Av, dry bread with salt was brought to him, and he sat between the baking oven and the cooking stove and ate and drank with a pitcher of water and looked as if a dead relation were lying before him" (Ta'an. 30a–b); he used to take a myrtle twig, dance before the bride, and say: "Beautiful and graceful bride" (Ket. 17a). A memory of the impressive figure of Judah is found in the story (TJ, Pes. 10:1, 31c and parallels; and cf. Ned. 49b) of a Roman matron who, because of Judah's shining countenance, suspected him of being either a moneylender or a pig breeder – his shining face being due to his wealth – or of having drunk excessively, but he referred her to Ecclesiastes 8:1 ("A man's wisdom maketh his face to shine").

BIBLIOGRAPHY: Hyman, Toledot, 534–42; I. Konovitz, *Rabbi Yehudah bar Ilai* (1965); Frankel, Mishnah (1923), 167–73; Bacher, Tann. **ADD. BIBLIOGRAPHY:** Epstein, Tannaim, 106–25. A. Oppenheimer, in: Z. Baras, S. Safrai, M. Stern. Y. Tsafrir (eds.), *Eretz Israel from the Destruction of the Second Temple to the Moslem Conquest*, (Hebrew) (1982), 75–82.

[Zvi Kaplan / Stephen G. Wald (2nd ed.)]

JUDAH BAR SHALOM (occasionally with the addition **ha-Levi**; Tanh. B., Gen. 141; Mid. Ps. to 119:1), Palestinian *amora* of the fourth century C.E.; aggadist. Judah was apparently a pupil of the Palestinian *amora*, Yose (TJ, Dem. 6:3, 25c; Ma'as. Sh. 4:4, 55a). His aggadic sayings are scattered throughout the Talmud and the Midrashim, especially the *Tanḥuma* (Noah 13; Va-Yera 13; Va-Era 14; Tanḥ B., Gen. 88, et al.). Halakhic statements by him are found in the Jerusalem Talmud (Shab. 12:4, 13d; Er. 5:5, 22d; Shevu, 7:5, 38a). They consist mainly of amplifications, comments, and explanations of the statements of his predecessors. Of special importance are his anti-Christian polemics, in which he emphasizes the importance of the Oral Law: "Moses wished the Mishnah too to be committed to writing. God, however, foresaw that the nations of the world would translate the Torah, read it in Greek, and say: we too are Jews. So God said to him: 'Shall I write for him so many things of My law?' and as a result 'they shall be accounted as strange?' [his interpretation of Hos. 8:12]. Why was He so opposed? Because the Mishnah is God's secret. God reveals His secret only to the righteous, as it is said [Ps. 25:14]: 'The counsel of the Lord is with them that fear Him'" (Tanḥ. B, Gen. 88).

BIBLIOGRAPHY: Bacher, Pal Amor, 3; Hyman, Toledot, s.v.

[Zvi Kaplan]

JUDAH BAR SIMEON (**Sima**; late third–early fourth century C.E.), Palestinian aggadist. Judah was the son of *Simeon b. Pazzi. In the Jerusalem Talmud he is usually referred to as Judah b. Pazzi, but in the Babylonian his full name, Judah the son of Simeon b. Pazzi, is given. He studied under his father, in whose name he transmitted both *halakhah* and *aggadah*. He was a priest (TJ, Ber. 5:4, 9c) and members of his family apparently married into the house of the *nasi* (Shab. 12:3, 13c). His homilies, interpretations of Scripture, poems, and parables are quoted in the Talmud (Sanh. 100a; TJ, Ta'an. 4:8, 68c; et al.) and in the Midrashim (Gen. R. 35:3; Lev. R. 7:2, et al.). The Babylonian Talmud also quotes a *baraita* that he "learned in the [tractate] *Nezikin* of the school of Karna" (BK 47b; see Dik. Sof. *ibid.*). In his sermons he deals with the suffering of the people and pleads for its redemption. For example, interpreting the word *aḥar* ("behind") in Genesis 22:13 as meaning "after," he comments: "What is meant by 'after'? After the passage of all the generations, your children will be caught by their sins and entangled in troubles but will finally be redeemed through the horns of this ram, as its says [Zech. 9:14] 'The Lord God will blow the horn and will go with the whirlwinds of the south'" (TJ, Ta'an. 2:4, 65d). Similarly he interprets Psalms 10:12, "Arise O Lord, O God, lift up Thy hand," as "Israel said to God, 'Lord of the Universe! Troubles are about to destroy us like a man drowning in the sea; stretch out Thy hand and save us'" (Mid. Ps. 10:6).

BIBLIOGRAPHY: Bacher, Pal Amor; Hyman, Toledot, 566f.; Ḥ. Albeck, *Mayo la-Talmudim* (1969), 329f.

[Zvi Kaplan]

JUDAH BEN ASHER (1270–1349), rabbi and talmudist. Judah was born in Cologne, Germany. His father was *Asher b. Jehiel (the Rosh), in whose yeshivah he studied; *Jacob b. Asher was his brother. Because of his impaired eyesight, from which he suffered all his life, he did not succeed in compiling large works. In consequence of the violent anti-Jewish outbreaks of 1283 in Germany, Judah left his father's house and made his way to Spain, reaching Toledo in 1285 (this according to Schechter, but according to Abrahams, in 1305). When his parents reached Spain, Judah renewed his studies under his father. In 1314 he signed a *takkanah* of his father, continuing a family tradition of tithing one's income for charity, a custom that his children also undertook to observe. He married first the daughter of his elder brother, Jehiel, and after her death, Miriam, the daughter of his second brother, Solomon.

In 1321 Judah was appointed his father's successor by the Toledo community, and on the latter's death in 1327 he immediately inherited his position as head of the *bet din* and of the Toledo yeshivah, serving until his death. He conducted his rabbinical office justly and impartially and was considered authoritative in his rulings. The Castilian government took account of his judgment even in non-Jewish cases. Taking into consideration the interests of the Jewish communities in Castile, he maintained that in principle the death sentence could be imposed, but he demanded restraint from the rabbis in imposing punishments and took care to preserve the legal autonomy of Jewish communities. From his responsa he appears to have tended toward stringency. The leaders of the Toledo community attempted to compel his *bet din* to give halakhic rulings only in conformity with the rulings of Maimonides, and to depart from them only where his father Asher had ruled accordingly, in order to avoid differences of practice; Judah vehemently opposed them and threatened to resign his post, though he finally agreed to remain. Among his pupils were *Menahem b. Aaron ibn Zeraḥ, author of the *Ẓeidah la-Derekh*, and Machir, author of the *Avkat Rokhel.*

Among his' works may be mentioned *Zikhron Yehudah* (ed. by J. Rosenberg and D. Cassel, 1846), comprising 83 responsa, and *Iggeret Tokheḥah* (ed. by Schechter, see bibl.), his testament to his children, which contains ethical sayings, an account of his family history, and instruction in the method of learning; apart from its ethical value it also has great historical importance, as it gives details of the social life of the Jews in the 14th century and the mutual relationship between the rabbi and the community in Spain. Also ascribed to him are "a confession" included in the *Ẓeidah la-Derekh* (4:5, chap. 17) and a commentary to tractate *Shabbat*, the last part of which is included at the end of his volume of responsa, and the *Ḥukkat ha-Torah*, consisting of an anthology of *halakhot*. The collection *Ta'am Zekenim* (ed. by A. Ashkenazi (1854) 64b–66a) contains a responsum by Judah "on the subject of metempsychosis and the reply of Asher b. Jehiel." Two *piyyutim* in his name have been preserved.

BIBLIOGRAPHY: Michael, Or, no. 965; Graetz-Rabbinowitz, 5 (1897), 278, 282f.; Judah b. Asher, *Zikhron Yehudah* ed. by J. Rosenberg (1846), introd. by D. Cassel; Schechter, in: *Beit Talmud*, 4 (1884), 340–6, 372–7; Weiss, Dor, 5 (1904[4]), 68f., 84, 121–4; S. Assaf, *Mekorot le-Toledot ha-Ḥinnukh be-Yisrael*, 1 (1925), 25–27; I. Abrahams, *Hebrew Ethical Wills*, 2 (1926), 163–200; S.M. Chones, *Toledot ha-Posekim* (1910), 240f.; Davidson, Oẓar, 4 (1933), 391; Baer, Spain, index; Ḥ. Tchernowitz, *Toledot ha-Posekim*, 2 (1947), 191f.; Guedemann, Gesch Erz, 3 (1888), 63, 68f.; Guedemann, Quellenschr, 25–27; A. Freimann, in: JJLG, 13 (1920), 212–42; Waxman, Literature, 2 (1933), 295f.

[Yehoshua Horowitz]

JUDAH BEN BARZILLAI ("ha-Nasi"), **AL-BARGELONI** (late 11th and early 12th century), rabbi of Barcelona. Naḥmanides claimed descent from him, referring to him as "*zekeni*" ("my ancestor"). According to one statement (responsa, *Tashbeẓ*, 1:15), he was a pupil of R. *Isaac b. Reuben of Barcelona, but this is not substantiated from any other source and is open to question. The assumption that *Abraham b. Isaac of Narbonne was his pupil is unfounded, even though Abraham constantly refers to his teachings. He was a contemporary of *Abraham b. Ḥiyya, with whom he engaged in an interesting controversy on the question of postponing a wedding date for astrological reasons. Judah was strongly opposed, since he regarded it as contrary to Jewish law. Judah's works consist mostly of codes which were highly regarded in their time, but most of them were subsequently lost. Quotations from them by other authors show that they embraced all the *halakhah* which applied in practice.

His works are (1) *Sefer ha-Ittim*, dealing with Sabbath and festivals in the Jewish calendar, and of which there have been published – with many errors – only those concerning the Sabbath, with commentaries by R.J. Schorr (Cracow, 1902), and two further fragments, by J.L. Zlotnick (see bibliography); (2) *Yiḥus She'er Basar*, on marriage and personal law, known through a few quotations; (3) *Sefer ha-Din*, on civil law, of which the *Sefer ha-Shetarot* only has been published (Berlin, 1898). In 1928 S. Assaf published *Likkutei Sefer ha-Din*, a précis of the original book (*Madda'ei ha-Yahadut*, 2, 1926); (4) commentary on *Sefer Yeẓirah* (Berlin, 1885). This work is a mine of information on geonic and philosophical literature.

One important aspect of Judah's commentary on *Sefer Yeẓirah* is that in it he quotes extensively from the *Ishrūn Maqālāt* ("Twenty Tractates") of *Al-Mukammis. Since only a small portion of this work has been published, Judah's summaries are the major source of Al-Mukammis' teachings. Among Judah's own philosophical contributions were his polemics against dualistic and trinitarian doctrines (Commentary on *Sefer Yeẓirah*, 75, 175), and especially against Christian allegorism (*ibid.*, 77). Even when not polemicizing, he tried to interpret all of Scripture with a view to removing doubts about God's total spirituality. Among other philosophic doctrines he held that the revelations received by the prophets were emanations of the Divine Spirit, the first created being, to which Scripture also refers as the "glory of God" (*ibid.*, 16, 119, 174). At the end of his commentary Judah reproduced a considerable portion of one early Hebrew translation (no longer extant) of about half of *Saadiah's commentary on *Sefer Yeẓirah* (see H. Malter, *Saadiah Gaon, His Life and Works* (1921), 355–8).

The *hassagot* ("strictures") of the "Ri [ר״י] of Barcelona" on the early work, *Shimmusha Rabba*, quoted in the *Halakhot Ketannot* (laws of *tefillin*) of R. Asher b. *Jehiel are not to be attributed to Judah, but to the aforementioned Isaac, of Barcelona.

Judah based himself mainly on the *halakhot* of Isaac *Alfasi, his older contemporary, on the latter's responsa, and especially, on the geonic responsa and the *Hilkhata Gavruta* of *Samuel ha-Nagid. He also made use of the works of *Isaac b. Judah ibn Ghayyat and Isaac b. Baruch *Albalia, without mentioning them by name. Though the book was planned as a halakhic codex, the author adopted the practice of commenting extensively on the subject under discussion, thus rendering the work of great importance, both for the study of talmudic themes and for *variae lectiones*. Until the 16th century Judah's works were much used and extensively quoted but were increasingly neglected in favor of other codes, mainly because of their enormous range and prolixity. Nevertheless, many extracts and selections from his work have been published: the *Sefer ha-Eshkol* of Abraham b. Isaac of Narbonne is merely a précis of the *Ittim*, indicating its original magnitude; such too are the collections of geonic responsa, *Sha'arei Teshuvah* (Leghorn, 1869) and those published by Jacob Musafia (Lyck, 1864) which are anthologies taken from the *Ittim*. The *Sefer ha-Orah*, from the "school" of Rashi, contains many extracts from *Ittim* (S. Buber (ed.), *Sefer ha-Orah*, 1 (1905), 27). The *Temim De'im* of *Araham b. David of Posquières contains many quotations from Judah's works. Judah was in possession too of the most ancient version of *Ḥisdai ibn Shaprut's letter to the king of the Khazars, though, with the critical approach which characterizes all his works, he doubted its authenticity.

BIBLIOGRAPHY: S.J. Halberstam (ed.), *Perush Sefer Yeẓirah* (1885), ix–xxx (introd.); R.J. Schorr (ed.), *Sefer ha-Ittim* (1902), iii–xxiii (introd.); Albeck, in: *Tiferet Yisrael* (= *Festschrift... Lewy*; 1911), 104–31 (Heb. pt.); S. Albeck (ed.), *Sefer ha-Eshkol* (1935), 31–65 (introd.); Assaf, in: *Jeschurun*, 11 (1924), 13–7 (Heb. pt.); idem, in *Zion*, 7 (1941/42), 48–50; J.L. Zlotnick, in: *Sinai*, 16 (1944/45), 116–38; Z. Schwarz, in: *Festschrift... A. Schwarz* (1917).

[Israel Moses Ta-Shma]

JUDAH BEN BATHYRA, *tanna* of the second century C.E. He was apparently a student of Eliezer b. Hyrcanus and *Joshua b. Hananiah (Pes. 3:3; Eduy. 8:3; Neg. 9:3, 11:7), and an associate of *Akiva (Kelim 2:7) and Tarfon (Peah 3:6). His name is regularly associated with *Nisibis in Babylon (Tosef. Yev. 12:4; Tosef. Ket. 5:1; Sifre Num. 117), and the story is told that Simeon ben Shammua and *Johanan ha-Sandelar were on their way to Nisibis to learn Torah from Judah ben Bathyra, but when they reached the border, "tears streamed down and they tore their garments..., saying: 'Residence in the Land Israel is equivalent to the fulfillment of all the precepts of the Torah,' and they returned to the Land of Israel" (Sif. Deut. 80). His yeshivah in Nisibis is mentioned in the Talmud among the centers of study which were recommended to students as worthy of attendance (Sanh. 32b). According to the *aggadah*, Judah b. Bathyra claimed to be a descendant of the dead whom Ezekiel (ch. 37) brought to life, and that the *tefillin* left to him by his paternal grandfather came from them (Sanh. 92b). Another talmudic *aggadah* tells of a certain gentile who once boasted to Judah b. Bathyra that, despite the fact that gentiles are forbidden to eat of the paschal sacrifice, he would regularly go up to Jerusalem, and passing himself off as a Jew, eat from the "juiciest parts" of the paschal lamb. Judah b. Bathyra advised him: "When you go there, tell them to let you eat from the tail fat." Since the tail fat is not eaten, but rather burned up on the altar, his request brought suspicion upon himself, and after an investigation the gentile was exposed. The sages in Jerusalem then sent Judah a message, saying: "Peace be upon you, R. Judah b. Bathyra, for while you remain in Nisibis, your trap is set in Jerusalem" (Pes. 3b). This somewhat fanciful and anachronistic story created problems for some overly literal-minded scholars, who posited the existence of another, earlier Judah b. Bathyra, who must have lived during the time of the second Temple – also in Nisibis – despite the fact that virtually all traditions transmitted in the name of Judah b. Bathyra in talmudic literature clearly refer to the "second" Judah b. Bathyra (Margalioth), the "first" Judah b. Bathyra having left virtually no record in talmudic sources other than this story itself. Compare Mik. 4:5, where Judah b. Bathyra reports a precedent in the name of Bet Shammai, which occurred in Jerusalem during the time of the Second Temple, which has been construed by some as further "evidence" that Judah b. Bathyra himself lived during the time of the Second Temple. See also, *Tosafot* to Men. 65b.

BIBLIOGRAPHY: Frankel, Mishnah, 99–102; Halevy, Dorot, 1 pt. 5 (1923), 681–8; Hyman, Toledot. M. Margalioth, Encyclopedia, 412–415.

[Stephen G. Wald (2nd ed.)]

JUDAH BEN BAVA (second century C.E.), *tanna*, and according to the later *aggadah*, a martyr of the era of *Jabneh. A number of *halakhot* are reported in his name in the Mishnah, the Tosefta and the tannaitic Midrashim. One dealt with the case of a husband's death in order to permit his wife to remarry (Yev. 16:3, 5), and Judah was the only one of the scholars of Ereẓ Israel in his generation to permit this on the testimony of a single witness (Yev., 16:7), giving evidence that that was the halakhic decision to this effect. He also testified concerning many other *halakhot*, including some belonging to the period before the destruction of the Temple (Eduy. 6:1, 8:2). After the crushing of the Bar Kokhba revolt, Judah, as a sign of mourning, forbade the use of *foliatum* (aromatic oil of spikenard; Tosef., Sot. 15:9). The Tosefta of *Bava Kama* (8:13) states:

> "It was said of Judah that all his actions were for the sake of Heaven," except for one: he transgressed the injunction against the rearing of small cattle. The Tosefta then tells a story of a painful and protracted illness from which Judah suffered. The only remedy for the pain was to drink warm milk from a small

goat which he kept in his house. When he eventually died (apparently from this same illness), the sages determined that this was in fact his only sin. As a result of this piety the Talmud states (BK 103b): "Wherever the phrase occurs, 'It once happened to a certain pious man' [*ḥasid*], it refers either to Judah b. Bava or to Judah b. Ilai." According to another tannaitic tradition, despite the fact that he was renowned for his piety and modesty, Judah was not properly eulogized, apparently because of the troubled times (Tosef., Sot. 13:4).

According to an *aggadah* in the Babylonian Talmud, Judah's death occurred as a result of Hadrian's decrees of religious persecution, because he transgressed a Roman decree forbidding the *ordination of scholars. This tradition, ascribed to the early *amora* Rav, stated that Judah "sat between Usha and Shefaram and there ordained five scholars, namely Meir, Judah, Simeon, Yose, and Eleazar b. Shammua, and according to some, also Nehemiah. When they were surprised by the Romans, Judah said to them: 'My children, flee.' They said to him: 'What will become of thee, Rabbi?' He said: 'I lie before them like a stone which none can overturn' [i.e., let them do their will]. It was said that the enemy did not leave the spot until they had driven 300 iron spearheads into his body, making it like a sieve" (Sanh. 14a). The historical authenticity of this tradition has been seriously questioned, both because of the alternative tradition concerning the circumstances of his death (Tosef. BK 8:13), and also because of an alternative tradition concerning the ordination of Meir and Simeon by Akiva himself (cf. TJ, Sanh. 1, 19a; Oppenheimer, 78–79). According to other late *aggadot*, when the report of the execution of R. Akiva in Caesarea was received, Judah and Hananiah (Ḥanina) b. Teradyon said that his death was an omen: very soon there would be no place in Ereẓ Israel where corpses would not be found, and the city councils (see *Boule) of Judea would come to an end. Their forebodings were fulfilled (Sem. 8:9, ed. by M. Higger (1931), 154). The *aggadot* about the *ten martyrs, contrary to these earlier aggadic traditions, describe the execution of Judah as the result of a verdict given after judicial proceedings.

BIBLIOGRAPHY: Hyman, Toledot, 554f.; J. Bruell, *Mevo ha-Mishnah*, 1 (1876), 133f.; Bacher, Tann; A. Buechler, *Der galilaeische 'Am ha 'Areṣ* (1906), 305f.; Alon, Meḥkarim, 2 (1958), index. **ADD. BIBLIOGRAPHY:** A. Opperheimer, in: *Eretz Israel from the Destruction of the Second Temple to the Moslem Conquest*, (ed.) Z. Baras, S. Safrai, M. Stern. Y. Tsafrir (Heb., 1982), 78–80.

[Moshe David Herr / Stephen G. Wald (2nd ed.)]

JUDAH BEN DOSOTHEOS (Dostai; first century C.E.), *tanna*. In *Simeon b. Shetaḥ's name he transmitted the legal rule that a sentence passed by a Palestinian court over a person who later escaped abroad is not set aside for a new hearing, but in the case of a person who escaped to Palestine the sentence is set aside (Mak. 7a). In some versions, however, the reading here is Dosotheos b. Judah. The former reading is almost certainly a scribal (or printer's) error and, in all likelihood, no such first century C.E. *tanna* ever existed. On the other hand, the halakhic dictum that an "eye for an eye" (Ex. 21:24) refers only to pecuniary compensation, which is rendered in the name of Dosotheos b. Judah (BK 83b), is quoted in some manuscripts in the name of Judah b. Dosotheos.

BIBLIOGRAPHY: Hyman, Toledot, 559.

[Stephen G. Wald (2nd ed.)]

JUDAH BEN ELEAZAR (Riba; 17th century), Persian physician and philosopher, considered the greatest scholar to emerge from the Jewish community of Persia. His most valuable work is titled *Ḥovot Yehudah* ("Duties of Judah"), which was completed in 1686. He also produced works on astronomy and medicine. *Ḥovot Yehudah* deals with the fundamental principles of Jewish belief and philosophy. These are presented systematically, from a traditional religious-legal and a philosophical – or, as the author puts it, rational – perspective. The work consists of an introduction, four main parts, and an epilogue, which are further divided into 18 sections comprising a total of 50 chapters. Its four main parts correspond to the four principles of Jewish faith asserted by the author (as opposed to Maimonides' 13 principles of faith). *Ḥovot Yehudah* is written in *Judeo-Persian, apart from the epilogue, which is in Hebrew.

By virtue of his training and intellectual inclination, Riba, like *Maimonides, belonged to the school of religious scholars who chose to explain issues of belief in rational terms. His knowledge of the Torah, philosophy, and other intellectual fields of his time was comprehensive and profound. This is indicated by the large variety of texts he analyzed and expounded and by his systematic handling of a broad range of complex subjects. Thanks to his extensive, diligent study of the Persian language and literature, he had a masterful command of the language, as well as knowledge of Arabic, Hebrew, and Aramaic. Thus, Riba stands among the giants of Jewish philosophy.

We have no information concerning the life and activities of the author from other sources. Since he lived before 1686, there is no doubt that he, like the rest of the Jews of *Kashan, suffered persecutions and forced conversions. Riba made use of a wide array of sources. In addition to the Bible, the Talmud, midrashic texts, and the Zohar, all of which he quoted extensively, he also used the New Testament, the Apocrypha, and the Koran. He reveals solid knowledge of the writings of Plato, Aristotle, *Avicenna, *Averroes and al-*Ghazali, paying the most attention to Aristotle's metaphysics, against which he polemicizes. However, the work in its entirety has to do with the principles of Jewish belief, as represented by Jewish thinkers, Maimonides in particular. Special attention is given to Maimonides' *Guide*; *Shemonah Perakim* ("Eight Chapters"); *Perek Ḥelek*; and *Hilkhot Yesodei ha-Torah* in *Sefer ha-Madda* of the *Mishneh Torah*. Also much admired is Rabbi David Messer *Leon, whom Riba calls "the perfect and great rabbi, divine erudite scholar." Quotations from Leon's book, *Tehillah le-David*, may be found throughout the treatise. At times, Riba refutes Maimonides, especially with respect to his 13 principles of faith. He is not satisfied with the explanations of the great commentators, such as Rashi. He criticizes those who do not understand the basic issues of the Torah, but instead play with *sefirot* (divine emanations) and consider themselves kabbalists: "In my opinion, who is a heretic? He who has no knowledge of the rational world and the literal meaning [of the Torah] and occupies himself with the *sefirot* in his wish to be considered a divine mystic. (Concerning him) the Sages said: 'He lacks the outside keys but searches for the inner ones.' We might call him – and certain Ashkenazim with their convoluted treatises – a pious fool (*ḥasid shoteh*)" (Part I, Sec. 1/28).

In its 18 sections and epilogue, *Ḥovot Yehudah* discusses on one hand the accounts of Creation and the Divine Chariot, the nature of God, prophecy, human free will, knowledge, divine providence, the eternal nature of the Torah, immortality of the soul, reward and punishment, the messianic era and resurrection of the dead, and on the other hand, mathematics, astronomy, cosmology, medicine, music, logic, and rhetoric.

The last chapter of the work is a kind of short *summa contra gentiles*. By means of biblical exegesis, Riba attempts to show that there is no passage in the Hebrew Bible that verifies Muslim claims regarding the emergence of their Prophet. In addition, he rejects Muslim contentions that the Torah now in the hands of Jews is a forgery. However, Riba writes, he prefers not to argue with them too much, for according to their custom, anyone who does not believe as they do may be executed; he continues, "they do not hesitate to apply this practice" (*ibid.*, 70).

BIBLIOGRAPHY: A. Netzer, *Duties of Judah by Rabbi Yehudah ben Elazar* (1995); idem, "*Redifot u-Shemadot be-Toledot Yehudei Iran ba-Me'ah ha-17*," in: *Pe'amim*, 6 (1980), 32–56.

[Amnon Netzer (2nd ed.)]

JUDAH BEN ELI (**Elan**; d. 932), Karaite grammarian and liturgical poet. Although *rosh yeshivah* in Jerusalem, the city in which he died, Judah is known as "the Tiberian." He has been identified by J.L. Dukes (Dukes (ed.), *Kunteres ha-Masoret* (1850), 2) and A. Geiger (*Oẓar Neḥmad*, 2 (1857), 158) with the Eli b. Judah ha-Nazir quoted by David Kimḥi in his *Mikhlol* (Fuerth 1893 ed., 406). S. Pinsker in his *Likkutei Kadmoniyyot* (1860, 105–6) identifies him with the scholar of Jerusalem mentioned by Abraham ibn Ezra at the beginning of his *Moznayim* as the author of eight grammatical works.

Judah is best known as the author of the grammatical work *Me'or Einayim* or *Me'irat Einayim* in which he divided the Hebrew nouns into 35 classes. He also wrote *piyyutim* included in the Karaite prayer book and a dirge on the destruction of Zion containing his name in acrostic (see: Pinsker, op. cit. Supplement, 139).

BIBLIOGRAPHY: A. Gottlober, *Bikkoret le-Toledot ha-Kara'im* (1865), 170f.; N. Allony, in: *Leshonenu*, 34 (1970), 75–80; Perles, in: MGWJ, 26 (1877), 365; Kaufmann, *ibid.*, 35 (1886), 33–37; Mann, Texts, 2 (1935), 304, 1472, see *Yehudah b. 'Ilān*.

JUDAH BEN ELIEZER (known as **Yesod,** the Heb. initials of **Y**ehudah **S**afra ve-**D**ayyan; "scribe of the *bet din,*" lit. "judge") d. 1762, Lithuanian talmudist, communal worker, and philanthropist. Judah was born in Vilna where he served as communal secretary, *dayyan*, and for a while as rabbi, deputizing for his son-in-law, *Samuel b. Avigdor. He used his position and wealth for the benefit of the community and the needy, rendering valuable service in the community's struggle with the local authorities (1742). His name frequently appears in the communal records of the time. A yeshivah in Vilna was named after him. Judah attended the rabbinical conference at Mir (in 1751), where he supported Jonathan *Eybeschuetz in the latter's controversy with Jacob *Emden. He died in Vilna.

BIBLIOGRAPHY: S.J. Fuenn, *Kiryah Ne'emanah* (1915^2), 121–4; Fuenn, Keneset, 389f.; I. Klausner, in: *Zion*, 2 (1937), 137–52; *Yahadut Lita*, 1 (1960), index; 2 (1967), 53.

[Samuel Abba Horodezky]

JUDAH BEN GERIM (mid-second century C.E.), *tanna*. Ben Gerim (*Bar Giore* in Aramaic) means "the son of proselytes" (see Rashi, Shab. 33b). In Gen. R. 35:3 it is told that Judah bar Giore went, together with R. Isaac and R. Jonathan, to study with *Simeon b. Yoḥai. In the parallel version cited in the Babylonian Talmud, Judah ben Gerim went together with Jonathan b. Asmai (or Johanan b. Akhnai) to study with Simeon, and they both pleased their teacher to such an extent that he counseled his son to let himself be blessed by these students. When he asked for a blessing, they apparently cursed him, though Simeon himself managed to interpret their words in a positive light (MK 9 a–b). In sharp contrast to this idyllic description of the warm relationship between these two sages, we are told in another *aggadah* (Shab. 33b–34a) that Simeon b. Yoḥai once uttered critical remarks against the Roman authorities, and Judah b. Gerim, who overheard these remarks, repeated them to others, and thus they became known to the Roman authorities, who sentenced Simeon to death. Simeon escaped by hiding in a cave for 13 years. According to this version of the story, after emerging from his hiding place, he saw Judah in the street. Simeon then "set his eyes upon him" and Judah immediately "turned into a pile of bones." However, in the parallel versions of this story (TJ, 9, 38d, Gen. R. 79:6, PdRK 11:16) Judah ben Gerim is not mentioned at all, and it is a different character upon whom Simeon "set his eyes," and who immediately "turned into a pile of bones." S. Friedman has suggested, however, that this figure was intentionally identified as Judah b. Gerim in the tradition of the Babylonian Talmud, because of the latter's apparently harsh and cruel behavior toward Simeon and his son as described in Mo'ed Katan 9b.

BIBLIOGRAPHY: Hyman, Toledot, II, p. 559.

[Stephen G. Wald (2nd ed.)]

JUDAH BEN ḤIYYA (end of the second and beginning of the third century C.E.), *amora*. Judah and his twin brother *Hezekiah moved with their father *Ḥiyya from Babylon to

Ereẓ Israel and assisted him in his work of teaching Torah to the people (Suk. 20a). Like their father, they studied under Judah ha-Nasi (Sanh. 38b). They were called *"ha-rovim"* ("the youths," TJ, Ḥag. 3:4) and several halakhic dicta were transmitted in their name (*ibid.*; Av. Zar. 46a; Zev. 15a; et al.). Judah's father-in-law was *Yannai, who referred with respect to his son-in-law as *"Sinai"* (a profound scholar) and stood up in his presence. Judah apparently died at an early age, since it is stated that he was accustomed to visit his father-in-law every Sabbath eve, and when he failed to arrrive on one occasion his father-in-law understood that he was dead (TJ, Bik. 3:4). His aggadic sayings include: "Come and see how the dispensation of mortals is not like that of the Holy One. Among mortals, when a man administers a medicament to a fellow it may be beneficial to one limb but injurious to another, but with the Holy One, it is not so. He gave a Torah to Israel and it is a medicament of life for all the body" (Er. 54a); "Exile atones for half of man's sins" (Sanh. 37b).

[Zvi Kaplan]

JUDAH BEN ISAAC (**Judah Sir Leon of Paris**; also called **Gur Aryeh** ("lion's whelp") or **Aryeh,** after Genesis 49:9 (*Or Zaru'a*, pt. 1 no. 17; *Tosefot Yeshanim* to Yoma 8a); 1166–1224), French tosafist. Judah headed the Paris *bet ha-midrash*, which was apparently reopened on the return of Jews after the expulsion of 1192. He studied many years under his teacher *Isaac b. Samuel of Dampierre who was his relative, together with his teacher's son Elhanan. Judah was numbered among the most distinguished pupils of Isaac, in whose presence he wrote *tosafot* to various tractates and whose rulings and responsa he collected (Assaf, in *A. Marx Jubilee Volume* (Heb., 1950), 11). Much of Judah's teaching is based upon that of his teacher Isaac which he incorporated into his own works (as did Isaac's other pupils), particularly into his *tosafot*.

Of his teachings there remain only his *tosafot* to the tractates *Berakhot* (first edition in *Berakhah Meshulleshet*, 1863; a supplement to pages 2a–8b was published by Sachs in: *Sinai*, 37 (1955) 87–105), and a new edition by N. Sachs collated with additional manuscripts began to appear in Jerusalem in 1969 under the title *Ginzei Rishonim; Shitat ha-Kadmonim* (ed. M.J. Blau), *Avodah Zarah* (1969), and a fragment of *Nedarim* (J.N. Epstein, *Perushei R. Yehudah Ben Natan*, in: *Musaf le-Tarbiz*, 3 (1933) 171–80). Although this fragment is attributed in the manuscript (Montefiore, see *Kohelet Shelomo, Catalog… A.J. Halberstam*, (1890) 58 no. 323) to Judah b. Nathan, Epstein proved that it was really by Judah b. Isaac. Many of his statements can be detected in the standard *tosafot* printed with the Talmud, particularly the *Tosafot Yeshanim* to the tractate *Yoma*, which are an adaptation by his pupil *Moses of Coucy (Urbach, Tosafot, 394), *Megillah* (*ibid.*, 483f.) and *Bava Kamma* (*ibid.*, 275). It is clear that he wrote *tosafot* to other tractates since he mentions them in the aforementioned works, where he alludes to his commentaries on 12 additional tractates: *Shabbat, Pesaḥim, Beẓah, Rosh Ha-Shanah, Sukkah, Yevamot, Ketubbot, Kiddushin, Bava Kamma, Bava Batra, Ḥullin*, and *Niddah* (*ibid.*, 273 and n. 67). Those *tosafot* were known and used by scholars even at a later date, for instance by his pupils Moses of Coucy and *Isaac Or Zaru'a of Vienna, the latter's pupil Meir of Rothenburg, and even later by Aaron ha-Kohen in the *Orḥot Ḥayyim* and by Joseph Colon (*ibid.*, and n. 68, p. 274 and n. 72). In addition there are references to other *tosafot* compiled by him on *Eruvin, Yoma, Ta'anit, Nedarim, Bava Meẓia*, and *Shevu'ot* (*ibid.*, 274 and n. 73, 74). To these may be added references of his *tosafot Mo'ed Katan* (commentary of Talmid R. Jehiel of Paris to MK, 14b (in: *Kitvei Makhon Harry Fischel* (1937) and the *Mordekhai* (MK, no. 862), to *Gittin* (*ibid.*, n. 73), and to *Zevaḥim* (Tos. Ri to Av. Zar. 51). Great scholars of France and Germany of the following generation, such as Jehiel of Paris, Moses of Coucy, Isaac Or Zaru'a of Vienna, and others, were his pupils (Isaac b. Abraham was not his pupil as stated by Ḥ.J. Michael), and they faithfully transmitted his decisions and customs in their works. Only a few of his responsa have survived. Judah also apparently occupied himself with the *masorah* and there is report of a *Sefer Rabbenu Judah of Paris* (G. De Rossi, *Catalogue*… Parma, no. 721). Judah has been erroneously confused at times with Judah he-Ḥasid (b. Samuel) and this error still persists, very likely because Judah was also occasionally referred to as "He-Ḥasid" ("the pious"; see Michael Or, no. 999).

BIBLIOGRAPHY: H. Gross, in: *Magazin*, 4 (1877), 173–87; 5 (1878), 179–83; Gross, Gal Jud, 519–24; J.N. Epstein, in: *Tarbiz*, 4 (1932/33), 179–81; Urbach, Tosafot, 267–76.

[Shlomoh Zalman Havlin]

JUDAH BEN ISAAC (14th or 15th century), author of a Hebrew treatise on music. Judah ben Isaac, who was probably a native of Southern France and seems to have been connected with the Jewish cultural renaissance in 14th-century Provence, adapted his treatise from several Latin sources. The text is preserved in a manuscript in Paris (Bibliothèque Nationale, Cod. heb. 1037, fol. 22b–27b), and is one of the very few theoretical treatises known to be the work of Jews of the period living in a Christian environment; it was also published in *Yuval* (vol. 1 (1968), 1–47), with a French translation and footnotes by I. Adler.

[Claude Abravanel]

JUDAH BEN ISAAC IBN SHABBETAI (13th century), Spanish Hebrew poet. Born around 1188, presumably in Toledo (according to some scholars, in Burgos, or in a town of Aragon), he lived for some time in Toledo and Saragossa. Judah composed at the age of 20 his best-known work, the rhymed prose narrative *"Minḥat Yehudah Sone ha-Nashim"* ("The Gift of Judah the Misogynist"), which aroused a poetical polemic for and against women, continuing into the 16th century. Even Judah *Al-Ḥarizi's *"Maqāma* of Marriage" in the *Taḥkemoni* (Gate 6) is unmistakably composed under Judah's influence. He follows the Andalusian Arabic pattern of a long narrative with different episodes. The story told in "The Misogynist" is of a young man, Zeraḥ, who had to take a vow of continence at his father's deathbed but who soon fell prey to the vengeance of the offended fair sex: after having established a celibate brotherhood that preaches dissuasion from marriage and incites to divorce, he is seduced by a fair maiden, but through some hoax finds himself married to an ugly witch. When he tries to get a divorce, he almost has to face a death sentence thanks to the intrigues of the women. The fable is not directed against women, but describes the arguments of medieval misogynist discourse and has a very ambiguous attitude in respect to marriage; it may be interpreted as having a twofold aim – to warn men of female vengeance and against rash marriages. In consonance with similar ideas expressed in Latin and Romance narratives of the time, women are presented as the cause of quarrels and troubles, who will turn cosmos back into chaos. The book is dedicated to a patron by the name of Abraham Alfakhar; the work was very popular during the Middle Ages and early Renaissance, and has been preserved in many manuscripts, but the unreliable texts of both complete editions (Constantinople, 1543, and in E. Aschkenasi, *Ta'am Zekenim* (1854), v. 1a–12b) make it impossible to determine the precise date of composition. Halberstam and Davidson believe there must have been three versions: 1188, 1208, and 1225, but very likely the book was composed in 1208, and substantially modified and enlarged in 1225 or 1228. The two versions, plus a revised form of the first one, were edited by M. Huss in his dissertation (1991). In the epilogue Judah attacks a certain Ibn Samun who had accused him of plagiarism. A certain Isaac published around 1210 two short writings attacking the apparent misogynist attitude of Ibn Shabbetai: *Ezrat ha-Nashim* and *Ein Mishpat*.

Judah wrote around 1214 a second narrative in rhymed prose, called *Milḥemet ha-Ḥokhmah ve-ha-Osher* ("Strife of Wisdom and Wealth"), which apparently was dedicated to Todros b. Judah, the father of Meir *Abulafia, who acted as judge in the quarrel in question between two brothers, one of them rich and the other wise, disputing about a tiara left to them by their father (Constantinople, 1503). Judah is also the author of another rhymed prose narrative, *Divrei ha-Alah ve-ha-Niddui* ("The Curse and the Ban"), a parody, or a satirical work, in which he settles accounts with five respected Jews of Saragossa (published by Davidson in *Ha-Eshkol*, 6 (1909), 165–75). It seems that another work on history was destroyed or burned by the leaders of the community of Saragossa, and has not been preserved.

BIBLIOGRAPHY: Steinschneider, in: *Israelietische Letterbode*, 12 (1887/88), 63–65, 69–73; idem, in: HB, 13 (1873), 137; Halberstam, in: *Jeschurun* (Kobak's), 7 (1871), 33ff. (Heb. pt.); idem (ed.), *Ben ha-Melekh ve-ha-Nazir* (rev. ed. 1952), appendix; D. Kaufmann, *Gesammelte Schriften*, 3 (1915), 470–7; J. Davidson, *Parody in Jewish Literature* (1907), 7–12; J. Schirmann, *Die Hebraeischen Uebersetzungen der Maqamen des Hariri* (1930), 112f., Schirmann, Sefarad, 2 (1956), 67–86, 689; N. Wieder, in: *Metsudah*, 2 (1943), 122–31; Baer, Spain, 1 (1961), 94f., 398; Zinberg, Sifrut, 1 (1955), 186–9. **ADD. BIBLIOGRAPHY:** T. Rosen, in: *Prooftexts*, 8 (1988), 67–87; idem, *Unveiling Eve* (2003), 103–123; T. Fishman, in: *Prooftexts*, 8 (1988), 89–111; M. Huss, "*Minḥat Yehudah, Ezrat ha-Nashim, ve-Ein Mishpaṭ*," diss. (Hebrew Univ., 1991); Schirmann-Fleischer, *The History of Hebrew Poetry in Christian Spain and Southern France* (1997), 129–44 (Heb.).

[Jefim (Hayyim) Schirmann / Angel Sáenz-Badillos (2nd ed.)]

JUDAH BEN JACOB HA-KOHEN (18th century), German rabbi. Judah served as *rosh yeshivah* in Berlin and was later appointed *dayyan* in Lissa. He carried on an extensive correspondence with Ezekiel b. Judah *Landau and Ephraim Zalman *Margolioth. All his possessions were lost in the great fire that raged in Lissa in 1767, from which however he succeeded in rescuing some of his manuscripts. His writings, relating mainly to the priesthood, include a comprehensive work in the form of novellae to the order of *Kodashim*, of which only the portions to the tractates *Zevaḥim* and *Menaḥot* have been published, under the titles *Mareh Kohen* (Frankfurt, 1776) and *Minḥat Kohen* (Prague, 1775, 1778, or 1788), respectively. In these two books, Judah mentions *Mattenot Kehunnah*, his novellae to the tractate *Bekhorot*, and *Mishpat ha-Kelal*, methodological rules for the study of the Talmud.

BIBLIOGRAPHY: H.N. Dembitzer, *Kelilat Yofi*, 2 (1893), 56b; L. Lewin, *Geschichte der Juden in Lissa* (1904), 268f.; Michael, Or, no. 1004; A. Walden, *Shem ha-Gedolim he-Ḥadash*, 2 (1864), 24b no. 95.

[Elias Katz]

JUDAH BEN JOSEPH OF KAIROUAN (end of 10th and beginning of 11th century), talmudic scholar of the geonic era. Judah is referred to as *resh sidra*, **resh kallah*, and *alluf. He corresponded on halakhic problems with *Sherira and his son *Hai, *geonim* of *Pumbedita, as well as with *Samuel b. Hophni, *Gaon* of *Sura. His last extant letter is dated 1021 C.E. From Cairo **Genizah* fragments and laudatory poems written by Hai Gaon and by an anonymous poet, it is clear that he was a wealthy merchant who had considerable influence with the government. Together with Joseph b. Berechiah and Abraham b. Nathan, **nagid* of *Kairouan, Judah assisted the Jews expelled from *Fez in 979/980 following the revolt of the Beni Ziri against the *Fatimids. Judah was a patron of scholars and contributed to the Babylonian yeshivot. He opposed the *Karaites and is thought to have written a biblical commentary.

BIBLIOGRAPHY: A. Harkavy, *Zikkaron la-Rishonim ve-gam la-Aḥaronim*, 4 (1887), nos. 207, 434, 442; Mann, in: *Tarbiz*, 5 (1933/34), 301–4; Hirschberg, in: *Zion*, 23–24 (1958–59), 166–73; Goitein, *ibid.*, 27 (1962), 159–64; Abramson, in: *Sinai; Sefer Yovel* (1958), 403–17; Abramson, Merkazim, 79–82.

[Eliezer Bashan (Sternberg)]

JUDAH BEN KALONYMUS BEN MEIR (d. 1196/99), German scholar, and *dayyan* in his native Speyer. His father was a communal leader and was one of those responsible to the king regarding the collection of community taxes. His mother was the daughter of Judah, the brother of *Samuel b. Kalonymus he-Ḥasid. Judah frequently quotes *Abraham ben Samuel he-Ḥasid, the brother of *Judah he-Ḥasid. Meir b. Kalonymus, Judah's elder brother, was a well-known scholar who is often quoted by the talmudic scholars, including Judah himself, and there are grounds for thinking that David of Minzburg, the well-known *posek* and formulator of *takkanot*, was also his brother. *Ephraim of Regensburg was one of Judah's teachers, and one of his important pupils was *Eleazar b. Judah of Worms, author of the *Rokeaḥ*. Judah was in Speyer at the time of the anti-Jewish decree of 1196, and his elegy on this event was published by A.H. Habermann. Judah is known mainly for his *Seder Tanna'im ve-Amora'im*, apparently the original name of the book, the beginning of which is missing in the manuscripts. The work is an extensive and valuable talmudic lexicon of the names of the *tannaim* and *amoraim*. Statements of those scholars found in the works available to Judah are listed, sometimes in the context of the discussion where the quoted statements are found and with a comprehensive and extensive exposition, so that it reads like a commentary on the Talmud itself. The book reveals a strong critical tendency, and throughout it the author attempts to establish the correct reading by comparing parallel sources and manuscripts. Judah had a sense of historical perspective and noted many historical details which were found in the sources. The book is infused with the spirit of the *Ḥasidei Ashkenaz, and in explaining the anthropomorphisms in the *aggadah* relies upon the theory of the *Kavod* of that school. There is no doubt that Judah obtained much of his kabbalistic knowledge from Judah he-Ḥasid, even though the latter's name is only once mentioned explicitly in the book. R.N.N. Rabbinovicz, who was the first to publish part of the book (the section containing the letter *bet*), called it *Sefer Yiḥusei Tanna'im ve-Amora'im*, in order to differentiate it from the earlier work known as *Seder Tanna'im ve-Amora'im*. The letters *Bet* to *Tet* were later published by J.L. Fishman (Maimon), at first as a series in *Sinai*, and later in book form with an introduction by M.H. Katzenellenbogen (Jerusalem, 1963). The original manuscript gets only as far as the name Kruspedai, and it is not clear whether the manuscript is incomplete, or whether Judah did not complete the work. The extensive nature of the work was a hindrance to its being copied, for which reason it was hardly used by scholars until recent times. Judah also wrote other works that are no longer extant, including *Sefer ha-Agron*, which was apparently a kind of dictionary of realia on the names of the minerals, vegetables, and animals in the Talmud, and, like his first work, included many digressions; a special work on benedictions; and *tosafot* on a number of tractates. (Those to tractates *Beẓah* and *Sotah* are explicitly mentioned by him.)

BIBLIOGRAPHY: Urbach, Tosafot, 299–315; A. Epstein, in: MGWJ, 39 (1895), 398–403, 447–60, 507–13; A.M. Habermann, *Gezerot Ashkenaz ve-Ẓarefat* (1946), 60, 155–8, 162.

[Israel Moses Ta-Shma]

JUDAH BEN KALONYMUS BEN MOSES OF MAINZ (d. c. 1200), German scholar, halakhic authority, *paytan*, and kabbalist. He was the pupil of Shemariah b. Mordecai in Speyer, and of *Judah he-Ḥasid, who taught him mysticism. During the Third Crusade (1189–93) Judah braced his community to face the approaching trials and inspired them to repentance. Among his prominent pupils were his son Eleazar (who stated that he had received the mystical interpretation of the prayers and other kabbalistic knowledge from his father), *Eliezer b. Joel ha-Levi, and *Baruch b. Samuel, the author of *Sefer ha-Ḥokhmah*. His halakhic decisions are quoted in the works of the earlier authorities. He wrote *seliḥot* and *piyyutim*.

BIBLIOGRAPHY: Landshuth, Ammudei, 78; Davidson, Oẓar 4 (1933), 392; Aptowitzer, *Mavo le-Sefer Ravyah* (1938), 252, 342–3; Urbach, Tosafot, 303f., 321–4.

[Yehoshua Horowitz]

JUDAH BEN MENAHEM OF ROME (early 12th century), liturgical poet. Judah, whose son Menahem was the head of the Talmud academy in Rome, is one of the major Italian *paytanim*. His poems must have been fairly popular in the Middle Ages, since they have come down in a number of manuscripts of the Roman ritual. At present, 15 of Judah's poems are known, of which only six have appeared in print: the *Yoẓerot* for **Shabbat ha-Gadol*, *Shabbat Naḥamu*, Simḥat Torah, and Shavuot; the *ofan* for the last; and a poem for Purim. He was perhaps the compiler of *Seder Ḥibbur Berakhot*, the oldest work on the Roman rite.

BIBLIOGRAPHY: Landshuth, Ammudei, 68f.; Zunz, in: ZHB, 19 (1916), 132f.; Luzzatto, in: *Maḥzor Italyani*, 1 (1857), 23, 25, 27, introd.; Schirmann, 76f.; Davidson, in: JQR, 21 (1931), 244–6; Davidson, Oẓar, 4 (1933), 391f. **ADD. BIBLIOGRAPHY:** E. Fleischer, *Hebrew Liturgical Poetry in the Middle Ages* (1975), 445 (Heb.).

[Jefim (Hayyim) Schirmann]

JUDAH BEN MOSES HA-DARSHAN (11th century), French scholar, son of *Moses ha-Darshan, under whom he studied and whose teachings he transmitted. He apparently also studied under *Gershom b. Judah in Mainz, then returned to Narbonne where *Isaac b. Merwan ha-Levi was among his disciples, many of whom later became distinguished. He lived for some time in Toulouse, where *Menahem b. Ḥelbo was his pupil. Menahem thus served as the main channel for the transmission of the works of Moses ha-Darshan from Narbonne in the south to northern France. One saying quoted by his son Joseph has been preserved by Samuel *Ibn Jama.

BIBLIOGRAPHY: Abraham b. Azriel, *Arugat ha-Bosem*, ed. by E.E. Urbach, 4 (1963), 3–5.

[Israel Moses Ta-Shma]

JUDAH (Judel) BEN MOSES OF LUBLIN (17th century), rabbi and author. Judah was rabbi and *rosh yeshivah* of Kovel, and district rabbi and *rosh yeshivah* of Lemberg in 1652. From 1691 to 1699 he also served in Lublin, but whether as rabbi as well as head of the yeshivah is uncertain. He was regarded as one of the important rabbis of his generation, his commendations appearing in many books, and was one of the rabbis of the *Council of Four Lands. He wrote commentaries to the Shulḥan Arukh, *Oraḥ Ḥayyim* (called *Kol Yehudah*), as well as notes to *Asher b. Jehiel's Talmud commentary, which he intended to have published along with *David b. Samuel ha-Levi's *Turei Zahav*. The money he sent for this purpose was used without his knowledge to publish David ha-Levi's commentary on the Pentateuch, *Divrei David* (Dyhrenfurth, 1689). Some of his comments are quoted in the *Kav ha-Yashar* (Frankfurt, 1705) of Ẓevi Hirsch *Koidanover. He died in Dubnow. Of his sons, Joseph was rabbi in Dubnow, Ze'ev Wolf in Minsk, Aryeh Leib in Slutsk, and Moses in Posen.

BIBLIOGRAPHY: H.N. Dembitzer, *Kelilat Yofi*, 1 (1888), 68b–70a; S.B. Nissenbaum, *Le-Korot ha-Yehudim be-Lublin* (1899), 130, 135; S. Buber, *Anshei Shem* (1895), 77 no. 188; I.T. Eisenstadt and S. Wiener, *Da'at Kedoshim* (1897–98), 78; Halpern, Pinkas, 143, 214, 496.

[Itzhak Alfassi]

JUDAH BEN NAḤAMANI (Nahman; third century C.E.), Palestinian *amora*. Judah was the *meturgeman* ("interpreter"; see *amora) of *Simeon b. Lakish in the *bet ha-midrash* of Tiberias. He was also known as a preacher and preached in the *bet ha-midrash* of Johanan (TJ, Suk. 5:1, 55a). Many of his homilies are cited in the Talmud (Ḥag. 16a; Ket. 8b, et al.). On one occasion he was acting as a *meturgeman* for one who had been appointed *dayyan* by the *nasi*. Although the *dayyan* was not a scholar, Judah bent down, as it was the custom for the *meturgeman*, to listen to what the *dayyan* said to him in a low voice, and then explain and convey it to the audience audibly. The *dayyan*, however, was incapable of saying anything to him. Thereupon Judah delivered his own address, taking as his text the verse Habbakuk 2:19: "Woe unto him who sayeth unto wood: Awake! – to the dumb stone: Arise! Can this teach? Behold it is overlaid with gold and silver, and there is no breath at all in the midst of it" (Sanh. 7b), a patent allusion to the circumstances.

BIBLIOGRAPHY: Hyman, Toledot, s.v.; Ḥ. Albeck, *Mavo la-Talmudim* (1969), 245.

[Zvi Kaplan]

JUDAH BEN NATHAN (known as **Rivan**; 11th–12th centuries), tosafist. Little is known of his life. He was one of Rashi's most eminent pupils and married his daughter Miriam. R. Yom Tov of Falaise was his son, and his daughter Elvina was known for the traditions which she transmitted from her mother. R. Judah wrote extensively, mainly elaborating on Rashi's teachings, but he did not arrive at a crystallized system of study, such as is found in the *tosafot*. For this reason he is to be regarded as occupying an intermediate stage between Rashi and the *tosafot*. Judah was the author of glosses to Rashi's Talmud commentary, and of independent commentaries to most of the talmudic tractares, extensively quoted in the *tosafot* and by other *rishonim*. He made frequent use of the commentaries of the sages of Mainz as well as that of R. *Hananel b. Ḥushi'el. Most editions of the Talmud include his commentary on *Makkot* from p. 19a onward. Judah also wrote the commentary, sometimes erroneously attributed to Rashi, on chapter ten of *Sanhedrin*. A large part of his commentary on *Ketubbot* has been preserved in Bezalel *Ashkenazi's *Shitah Mekubbeẓet*. Fragments of his commentaries on the tractate *Yevamot* have been printed by A.N.Z. Roth (see Bibliography). The suggestion that the commentary on *Nazir*, generally ascribed to Rashi, is by Judah is ill-founded. Some sources mention a commentary on the Pentateuch by him.

BIBLIOGRAPHY: J.N. Epstein, *Perushei Rabbenu Yehudah bar Natan li-Khetuvot* (1933); idem, in: *Tarbiz*, 4 (1932/33), 11–34; S. Lieberman, *Sheki'in* (1939), 192ff.; Urbach, Tosafot, 36–38; A.N.Z. Roth, in: *Sefer Yovel… S.L. Mirsky* (1958), 285–312; M. Hirshler, in: *Sinai*, 63 (1968), 198–215.

[Israel Moses Ta-Shma]

JUDAH BEN NISSAN (b. early 17th century), Polish talmudic scholar. He was related by marriage to many important rabbinic personages. He held rabbinic positions in Olkusz, Sieniawa, and Tomaszow (all in Poland). The great respect for his scholarship is evidenced by his being appointed to the important rabbinate of Kalisz at the time when Abraham Abele *Gombiner was *dayyan* there. He participated in the Council of the Four Lands in 1681. Judah wrote *Beit Yehudah*, containing novellae on the more frequently studied tractates of the orders *Nashim* and *Nezikin*, as well as on *Ḥullin*. It is in two parts: the first part (Sulzbach, 1687) covers the aggadic sections of the tractates, while the second, edited by his son Abraham (Dessau, 1698), deals with the halakhic material.

BIBLIOGRAPHY: H.N. Dembitzer, *Kelilat Yofi*, 1 (1888), 82a; Lewin, in: *Festschrift… A. Harkavy* (1908), 149f.; Michael, Or, no. 1029; Weinberg, in: JJLG, 1 (1903), 123f.

[Jacob Haberman]

JUDAH BEN PEDAYA (**Padah**; early third century C.E.), Palestinian *amora*. His statements, both in *halakhah* and *aggadah*, are numerous in both Talmuds and the Midrash, but he was recognized as a master of *aggadah*. In the Babylonian Talmud he was known as Bar Pada, in the Jerusalem Talmud as Bar Pedaya, and in the Midrash by his full name. He studied under *Judah ha-Nasi or *Ḥiyya (according to an alternative reading), and he was a pupil of his uncle, *Bar Kappara. Among his disciples were *Joshua b. Levi, Johanan, *Hezekiah, and *Ilfa. His statement concerning the belated attempt of the wicked to repent on Judgment Day has become popular: "If a man has not prepared before the Sabbath, how can he eat on the Sabbath?"

BIBLIOGRAPHY: Bacher, Pal Amor; Hyman, Toledot, s.v.; H. Albeck, *Mavo la-Talmudim* (1969), 163.

JUDAH BEN SAMUEL HE-ḤASID (c. 1150–1217), main teacher of the *Ḥasidei Ashkenaz movement. Judah was one of the most prominent scholars of the Middle Ages in the fields of ethics and theology. He probably lived some time in Speyer and then moved to Regensburg (he was sometimes called "Rabbi Judah of Regensburg"). Very little of his life is known from contemporary sources. However, many legends about his life dating from 15th- and 16th-century sources have survived. In them, he is described as a mystic (whereas his brother Abraham is described as a scholar of *halakhah*) who performed many miracles in order to save the Jews from the gentiles. Judah taught and practiced extreme humility. He even forbade an author to sign a book he wrote, because his sons might take pride in their father's fame. This seems to be the reason why his works were circulated as anonymous works. Even his pupils did not quote his works by name; *Abraham b. Azriel, the author of *Arugat ha-Bosem*, used the title רי"ח, בש"ם, ניחו"ח (*Re'aḥ Bosem Niḥo'aḥ*) when he quoted him, an appellation which hints at his name by the use of *notarikon and *gematria. His descendants helped propagate his teachings. His son Moses wrote a commentary on the Pentateuch; his grandson *Eleazar b. Moses ha-Darshan wrote works in esoteric theology, and his great-grandson, Moses b. Eleazar, who was a kabbalist, tried to harmonize Ashkenazi-ḥasidic teaching with the Kabbalah. However, his most prominent pupil, whose writings popularized Judah's teachings among the Jews in Germany and elsewhere, was *Eleazar b. Judah of Worms. Even though Judah did not write in the field of *halakhah* and ritual practice, many later Ashkenazi writers depended on his teachings and practices in their works. Most of Judah's writings in esoteric theology have not survived. His major work was probably *Sefer ha-Kavod* ("Book of Divine Glory"), of which only quotations in later works have survived. He also wrote a voluminous commentary on the prayers, of which only a small part is known today. Besides these major works, a few small ones have survived: *Sod ha-Yiḥud* ("The Secret of God's Unity"); exegesis of a few *piyyutim*; and some short magical treatises. Because he did not sign his writings, some works by others have been attributed to him, e.g., Eleazar of Worms' *Sefer ha-Ḥokhmah*. In ethics, his main work was his contribution to the *Sefer Ḥasidim*, of which he was the principal author. Eleazar edited a short treatise on *teshuvah* ("repentance") which Judah wrote, and a short collection of ethical and magical paragraphs was published as *Ẓavva'at Rabbi Yehudah he-Ḥasid* ("The Will of Rabbi Judah the Pious," Cracow, 1891).

BIBLIOGRAPHY: J. Dan, *Torat ha-Sod shel Ḥasidei Ashkenaz* (1968), 50–59; idem, in: *Tarbiz*, 30 (1961), 273–289; Bruell, in: JJGL, 9 (1889), 1–71; Scholem, Mysticism, 80–118; E.E. Urbach, *Arugat ha-Bosem* 4 (1963), 73–111; J. Freimann, *Sefer Ḥasidim* (1924²), 1–15 (introd.).

[Joseph Dan]

JUDAH BEN SHAMMUA (second half of the second century C.E.), *tanna*, presumably a pupil of R. *Meir. He is not mentioned in the Mishnah, and only once in the Tosefta (Kel. BB 7:9, RH 19a) where he is quoted transmitting a ruling about the ritual cleanness of glass vessels in the name of Meir. His name is also found in the manuscript readings of the parallel text in Shab. 15b, the omission of his name in the printed editions being almost certainly a scribal (or printer's) error. An *aggadah* relates that he succeeded in his intercession with the Roman authorities in having their decree forbidding the study of Torah, Sabbath observance, and the circumcision of children repealed (RH 19a; Meg. Ta'an., 22). In this venture he was aided by a Roman matron, probably the widow of *Tineius Rufus (v. Av. Zar. 20a). In commemoration, the day on which the decrees were abrogated, Adar 28, was proclaimed a feast day. The sons of Judah b. Shammua are mentioned in the Palestinian Talmud as having possessed a great flock of sheep, of which over 300 were killed in a raid by wolves (TJ, Beẓah 1:1, 60a).

BIBLIOGRAPHY: Hyman, Toledot, s.v.; Graetz, Gesch, 4 (1904³), 169; B. Lewin, *Megillat Ta'anit* (1964), 198–9. V. Noam, *Megillat Ta'anit* (2003), 312–15.

[Stephen G. Wald (2nd ed.)]

JUDAH BEN TABBAI (first century B.C.E.), one of the **zugot*, the colleague of *Simeon b. Shetaḥ. A disciple of Joshua b. Peraḥyah and Nittai of Arbela. According to one tradition he was the *nasi* (see *Sanhedrin) and Simeon b. Shetaḥ the *av bet din*, but another tradition reverses their roles (Ḥag. 2:2; Tosef., Ḥag. 2:8; cf. TJ, Ḥag. 2:2, 77d and Sanh. 6:9, 23c; TB, Hag. 16b). According to one tradition (Tosef. Sanh. 6:6) Simeon b. Shetaḥ once criticized a halakhic decision of Judah b. Tabbai who thereafter accepted upon himself "never to make a halakhic ruling without Simeon b. Shetaḥ's consent." An attempt in the Babylonian Talmud (Ḥag. 16b) to use this tradition in order to determine which of them was *nasi* and which *av bet din* was inconclusive. Moreover, in the parallel version of this story (Mekh. Nezikin, 20), the roles of Judah b. Tabbai, and Simeon b. Shetaḥ are reversed, and S. Friedman has recently shown that the version in the Mekhilta is more original. A story is told of how Judah b. Tabbai fled from Jerusalem to Alexandria, and the people of Jerusalem wrote to Alexandria, "How long will my betrothed stay with you while I sit grieving for him," whereupon he returned (TJ, Ḥag. 2:2, 77d; cf. TJ, Sanh. 6:9, 23c). Judah's saying in *Avot* (1:8) contains advice for a judge: "Do not play the part of an advocate [or presiding judge]; while the litigants are standing before thee, let them be regarded by thee as if they were guilty; and when they leave thy presence [after] having submitted to the judgment, let them be regarded by thee as guiltless." In the well-known dispute regarding **semikhah* ("the laying on" of hands on the head of the sacrifice on the festival), Judah held that it may not be done (Ḥag. 2:2). According to a Palestinian *amora*, Judah decreed, alone or together with Simeon b. Shetaḥ, the impurity of metal vessels (TJ, Shab. 1:7, 3c; TJ, Pes. 1:6, 27d, TJ, Ket. 8:11, 32c). A *baraita* in the Babylonian Talmud, ascribes this decree to Simeon b. Shetaḥ alone (Shab. 14b).

BIBLIOGRAPHY: Frankel, Mishnah (1923²), 35–39. **ADD. BIBLIOGRAPHY:** S. Friedman, "If They Have Not Slain They Are Slain; But If They Have Slain They Are Not Slain," in: *Sidra*, 20 (2005).

[Moshe David Herr / Stephen G. Wald (2nd ed.)]

JUDAH BEN TEMA, *tanna*. He is mentioned only once in the Mishnah (Avot 5:20), and twice in the Tosefta (Er. 2:6, and Git. 5:12). It is difficult to determine his date, but from these two passages it would seem that he belonged to the last generation of *tannaim*. His saying in *Avot* 5:20 is, "Be bold as a leopard, swift as an eagle, fleet as a hart, and strong as a lion, to do the will of thy Father in heaven." The Babylonian Talmud refers to "Judah and his colleagues" as examples of "masters of the Mishnah" (Ḥag. 14a), and later tradition ascribes to him the saying: "Love Heaven, fear Heaven, quiver and rejoice with all the precepts. If you have done your fellow a slight harm, let it be regarded as a grievous one in your eyes; if you have done him a great favor, let it be regarded as slight in your eyes; but if your fellow has done you a slight favor, let it be as great in your eyes, and if he has done you great harm, let it be a slight one in your eyes" (ARN[1], 41, 133). The Babylonian Talmud (Pes. 70a) quotes a *halakhah* in the name of "ben Tema," which in the parallel tannaitic traditions (Tosef. Pes. 9:8, Zev. 8:11; Sifra, Nedava 18) is quoted in the name of "Ben Azzai."

BIBLIOGRAPHY: Frankel, Mishnah, 213; Hyman, Toledot, s.v.; J. Kanowitz, *Ma'arekhot Tanna'im*, 2 (1968), 49–51. S. Friedman, in: Y. Elman et al. (eds.), *Neti'ot Ledavid, Jubilee Volume for David Weiss Halivni* (Hebrew), (2005).

[Stephen G. Wald (2nd ed.)]

JUDAH BEN YAKAR (d. between 1201 and 1218), talmudist and kabbalist, teacher of *Naḥmanides. Judah was born in Provence, but in his youth he moved to northern France where he studied under *Isaac b. Abraham, the tosafist. Subsequently he went to Barcelona where his signature is found on a document of 1175. From other documents signed by Abraham b. Judah of Narbonne, who was apparently his son, the years of Judah's death can be established as between 1201 and 1218. Judah was also a kabbalist, having studied under *Isaac the Blind. In his lifetime Judah was famous for two large works. One – which has been completely lost – was a commentary on the Jerusalem Talmud and was one of the earliest systematic commentaries on it. It is frequently quoted by the early authorities and covered at least a large part of the orders of *Mo'ed* and *Nezikin*. His other work is the *Ma'yan Gannim*, a rational commentary on the liturgy and blessings, though the esoteric element is by no means absent. His aim in this work was to show the scriptural and rabbinic versions and sources of the prayers and to detail the various laws connected with them. The commentary was published on the basis of a number of manuscripts by S. Yerushalmi (1968). The work is frequently cited by the *rishonim*, among them Jacob ha-Kohen of Lunel and David *Abudarham. The latter quotes him literally in almost every *halakhah*, without, however, mentioning his name. Judah's main claim to fame in subsequent generations was that he was one of the teachers of Naḥmanides, who refers to him in his works. It seems that he was one of the channels through which Naḥmanides became acquainted with the literature and methods of study of the tosafists.

BIBLIOGRAPHY: Judah b. Yakar, *Perush ha-Tefillot ve-ha-Berakhot*, ed. by S. Yerushalmi (1968), introd.; D. Zomber, in: MGWJ, 9 (1860), 421–6; G. Scholem, in: *Tarbiz*, 3 (1932), 276f; C.B. Chavel, *Rabbenu Moshe b. Naḥman* (1967), 38–44.

[Israel Moses Ta-Shma]

JUDAH THE GALILEAN (d. c. 6 C.E.), considered by many scholars identical with Judah, the son of *Hezekiah who was put to death by Herod in Galilee. Judah came from Gamala in the Golan (Jos., Ant., 18:4). Immediately after the death of Herod (4 B.C.E.) Judah participated in the widespread disturbances in the country. He had put himself at the head of a band of rebels near Sepphoris and had seized control of the armory in Herod's palace in the city. According to Josephus, he had even aspired to the throne (Ant., 17:271–2; Wars, 2:56). Though the rebels were defeated, Judah apparently succeeded in escaping (Jos., Ant., 17:289ff.). Together with *Zadok the Pharisee, he was one of the founders of the "fourth philosophy," i.e., the Sicarii (Ant., 18:23–5). When Sulpicius *Quirinius, the governor of Syria, arrived in Judea in 6 C.E. to take a census, as the first step toward converting the country into a Roman province, Judah and Zadok urged the people to resist, maintaining that submitting to a census in Judea was a religious sin, the Jewish people being forbidden to acknowledge any other master but God (Jos., Wars, 2:118, 433). Judah's doctrine struck root among the embittered people, especially among the youth, and its consequences were visible in the period of the procurators, particularly in the last years before the Roman War and during the war itself.

Of his three sons, Jacob and Simeon both continued the zealot tradition and headed the rebels. Both brothers were arrested and crucified during the procuratorship of Tiberius Alexander (46–48 C.E.; Jos., Ant., 20:102). Their brother Menahem was one of the Jewish leaders in the Roman War. For the "fourth philosophy" founded by Judah the Galilean, see *Zealots and *Sicarii.

BIBLIOGRAPHY: Schuerer, Hist, index, s.v. *Judas of Galilee* and p. 226 (for his sons); Klausner, Bayit Sheni, index, s.v. *Yehudah ha-Galili*; A.H.M. Jones, *The Herods of Judaea* (1938), 163, 225, 243.

[Abraham Schalit]

JUDAH HALEVI (before 1075–1141), Hebrew poet, philosopher, and physician. Halevi was one of the most distinguished and emblematic medieval intellectuals, perhaps the most mature and representative model of Jewish culture in al-Andalus; he was deeply involved in the life of his times and, because of his prestige, he had a deep influence on future Judaism. Judah Halevi's own work constitutes his most important biographical source: his poems tell of his journeys in Spain and in other countries, of his relations with his contemporaries, of his position in society, and of his spiritual development. Many biographical particulars are also contained in his extant letters and in poems of his contemporaries, as well as in later writers (e.g., Ibn Ezra's commentary to the Pentateuch, and *Maḥberet he-Arukh* of Salomon ibn *Parḥon). Publications of letters from the Cairo *Genizah* have clarified many aspects of the last period of Judah Halevi's life. Wider acquaintance with the many manuscripts and fragments of his writings preserved in the libraries of Russia have notably helped in the last years to increase our knowledge of his person and work.

Biography

EARLY YEARS AND ADULT LIFE. Despite the traditional location of Judah Halevi's birthplace in Toledo, modern research (since Schirman's study in *Tarbiz*, 10 (1939), 237–9) prefers the town of Tudela, still under Muslim rule and close to the border of Castile, as birthplace of both Halevi and Abraham *Ibn Ezra. Judah Halevi, apparently from a wealthy and learned family, received a comprehensive education in both Hebrew and Arabic. His childhood years were spent during a peaceful period for the Jews of the region. He lived for some time in Christian territory, as confirmed by his own words in a letter and by the testimony of his contemporaries. In some manuscripts he is called "the Castilian." Some researchers have pushed forward the date of his first visit to al-Andalus. But it is very likely that he was still very young when he traveled to the Muslim South with the intention of proceeding to the large Jewish center in Granada. Among the various communities he passed through on his way were Córdoba and Lucena; it was probably in one of these places that he participated in a poetry writing contest (styled after those of the Arabs). He won the competition for imitating a complicated poem by Moses ibn Ezra, who invited Judah Halevi to his home. The two developed a close friendship and Judah Halevi seems to have spent some time in Granada, in an atmosphere of wealth and culture. There he also wrote his first important poems – primarily eulogies and poetical letters – and apparently some of his wine and love poems, which reflect his easy-going, hedonistic life during those years. Judah Halevi also became friendly with Ibn Ezra's brother, Isaac, and was in contact with other great poets in Granada, Seville, and Saragossa.

With the coming of the Almoravides from Africa and their conquest of Muslim Spain (after 1090), the position of the Jews in Andalusia deteriorated, and Judah Halevi left Granada. For the following 20 years he traveled through numerous communities. In various places he was in contact with Jewish and non-Jewish nobles and dignitaries (e.g., Joseph ibn Migash in Lucena and the vizier Meir ibn Kamniel in Seville). He spent some time in Christian Toledo, practicing medicine, apparently in the service of the king and his nobles. Like many of his fellow Jews at that time, he trusted that the status and influence of the Jewish nobles and community leaders who were close to the royal house would ensure security and peace for the Jews in the Christian lands. However, he was disillusioned by the murder in 1108 of his patron and benefactor, the nobleman Solomon ibn Ferrizuel, who had achieved a high rank in the service of Alfonso VI. Judah left Toledo apparently before the death of Alfonso VI (1109) and again began to travel. His fame continued to spread, and the circle of his friends and admirers, to whom he wrote many poems, broadened greatly. Judah Halevi also had contact with the Jewish communities in North Africa, Egypt, and Narbonne.

His financial situation was generally sound; it seems that he was only rarely dependent on gifts. Aside from his profession as a physician, he also engaged in trade, apparently with Jewish merchants in Egypt, and, in particular, with the great Jewish merchant, Abu Sa'id Ḥalfon ha-Levi of Damietta, who on one of his many travels came to Spain. Five letters of Halevi to Ḥalfon have been found in the *Genizah*, written by the poet between 1127 and 1140. Active in community affairs, too, he helped to collect money for the ransom of captives.

FRIENDSHIP WITH ABRAHAM IBN EZRA. Of all his ties with various people, Judah Halevi's friendship with Abraham ibn Ezra was especially close and long-lasting. Some scholars believe that both wandered through the various cities of Muslim Spain, and even traveled to North Africa together. They were both in North Africa, but it is not sure that they were there together. In his biblical commentaries, Abraham ibn Ezra quotes Judah Halevi numerous times in matters of grammar, exegesis, and philosophy (e.g., Ex. 9:1; 20:1; Dan. 9:2). Various traditions maintain that the two were related by blood or by marriage. According to a later tradition (*Sefer ha-Yuḥasin* of Abraham Zacuto, ed. by A. Freimann, 1925) they were cousins, while another – no doubt legendary – mentioned in Abrabanel's commentary on the Torah and in the *Shalshelet ha-Kabbalah* of Gedaliah ibn Yaḥya (Cracow, 1596), asserts that Judah Halevi gave his daughter in marriage to Abraham ibn Ezra, despite the latter's poverty. On the basis of letters from the Cairo *Genizah*, however, it may be surmised that his son-in-law was Isaac, the son of Abraham ibn Ezra, who traveled with him to Egypt.

Last Days in Ereẓ Israel

Judah Halevi's decision to emigrate to Ereẓ Israel, a gradual one, reflected the highest aspiration of his life. It resulted from a complex of circumstances: intense and realistic political thought; disillusionment with the possibility of secure Jewish existence in the Diaspora; intense longing for a positive, redeeming act; and the prevalent messianic climate, which so affected him that he once dreamt that the redemption would come in the year 4890 (1130 C.E.).

The decision was strengthened by his religious philosophy, developed at length in his book the *Kuzari* and in many of his poems. This philosophy maintained the unity which ensues from the relationship between the God of Israel, the people of Israel – to whom He chose to reveal His truth through His prophets, Ereẓ Israel – the "Gate of Heaven," the only place where prophecy is possible, and Hebrew – the language of Israel. From this it clearly followed that the ideal existence for the Jews was attainable only in their own land. Throughout the philosophical and poetic work of Judah Halevi, as in his life, one can sense the intellectual effort to make other Jews conscious of this. In his philosophical work as well as in his poetry, Judah Halevi spoke out harshly against those who deceived themselves by speaking of Zion and by praying for its redemption while their hearts were closed to it and their actions far removed from it. Judah, however, understood the problems which emigration to Ereẓ Israel posed for many people; he decided to realize his own *aliyah* – the educational act of an individual who also seeks personal redemption.

Great difficulties lay before him. The long journey by both sea and desert was perilous. He knew that he would encounter very difficult living conditions in Ereẓ Israel, which was under Crusader rule at that time. Moreover, Judah Halevi had to counter the arguments of his friends who tried to deter him; he had to overcome his attachment to his only daughter and son-in-law, to his students, his many friends and admirers; and he had to give up his high social status and the honor which he had attained in his native land. He struggled deeply with his intimate attachment to Spain, the land of "his fathers' graves": at one time he had even looked upon Spain with pride and thankfulness, as a homeland for the Jews. These indecisions, which occupied him in the last period of his life, find expression in his "Poems of Zion," in the *Kuzari* (mainly in the fifth and final part), and in the *Genizah* letters which date from the same period. On the other hand, Judah Halevi was encouraged to make the journey by his friend Ḥalfon ha-Levi, whom he met in Spain in 1139.

Important new letters and documents published by Goitein on the one hand (five of them are holographs of Judah Halevi himself), and by M. Gil and E. Fleischer (2001) on the other, have illuminated in a decisive way his last days in Egypt and his trip to Palestine. Thanks to the letters found in the *Genizah* we know that on the 24th of Elul (Sept. 8, 1140) Judah Halevi, accompanied by Isaac, the son of Abraham Ibn Ezra, among others, arrived in Alexandria. His arrival caused great excitement, and the *dayyan* Aaron ibn al-'Ammānī was his host. Several months later he went to Cairo where he stayed with Ḥalfon ha-Levi. The scenery, pleasures, the admiration and honor generally accorded him everywhere, and the friendships he enjoyed all served to prolong his stopover in Egypt. He wrote there a substantial number of poems, no fewer than 50, praising his Egyptian friends. He wanted to continue his trip to Jerusalem and began to fear that he would die before reaching his destination. His friends tried to convince him to remain in Egypt, claiming that Egypt was as important as Ereẓ Israel, since the first prophecy as well as great miracles took place there. He tried the land route from Cairo to Jerusalem, but had to return. Isaac Ibn Ezra decided to follow his own route and did not return with him to Alexandria. Judah Halevi boarded a ship at Alexandria on May 8, 1141, bound for Ereẓ Israel, but its departure was delayed by inclement weather. The ship finally set sail on May 14. The sea journey to Ashkelon or Acre took about 10 days, and it seems very likely that he actually arrived in the Holy Land. A letter by Ḥalfon informs us that Halevi died in the month of July. It seems that he succeeded spending his last month in the land of his dreams. What was denied him in life, however, the famous legend, first mentioned in *Shalshelet ha-Kabbalah*, and later by Heinrich Heine in his *Hebraeische Melodien*, has supplied. It relates that he managed to reach the city of Jerusalem, but, as he kissed its stones, a passing Arab horseman (Jerusalem, in fact, was then under the Crusaders) trampled on him just as he was reciting his elegy, "*Ẓiyyon ha-lo tishali.*"

Poetry

About 800 poems written by Judah Halevi are known, covering all the subjects commonly found in Spanish Hebrew poetry, as well as the forms and artistic patterns of secular and religious poetry.

LOVE POEMS. His love poems, which number about 80, are addressed to a deer or gazelle, or – as marriage poems – to the two together. His short poems with internal rhyme, and his girdle poems, as well as those of the *zajal* type, in which plays on sound and rhyme sometimes add a musical grace, attained great artistic perfection ("*Ḥammah be-ad reki'a ẓammah,*" "*Bi bi ha-ẓevi, bi adoni*"). Their content and form are those generally found in Arabic-Hebrew love poetry, such as the yearnings and travails of the lover, the cruelty of the beloved who delights in mocking her victims, her countenance shining from the darkness of a stormy night, and her "lethal" glances. Sometimes there is a particularly original description of feminine beauty, such as the one comparing the face surrounded by a red fall of hair to the setting of the sun which reddens the clouds of the horizon ("*Leil gilleta elai*"); sometimes the light playful spirit unites with a surprisingly graphic description. A popular vein is discernible in the clear and simple style of the epithalamia. Interpretations of Judah Halevi's love poems vary: some assert that they reflect his personal experiences, while others maintain that they are simply artistic compositions, with accepted literary themes and descriptions. Following contemporary trends, Judah Halevi also composed poems in praise of wine and its pleasures. A playfulness can also be felt in his entertaining riddles and in his various epigrams, which in the main are witty ("*Lo nikreti*").

POEMS OF EULOGY AND LAMENT. The largest number of Judah Halevi's secular poems deal with eulogy and friendship. A small portion of the approximately 180 were written for unnamed individuals but the majority for his famous contemporaries – poets, philosophers, religious scholars (e.g., Moses ibn Ezra, Judah ibn Ghayyat, Joseph ibn Ẓaddik, Joseph ibn Migash), nobles, and philanthropists. Their form is the *qaṣīda* and their language, rich and brilliant, with much embellishment. Splendid poetic descriptions, such as that of the night in the poetic eulogy composed for Solomon ibn Ghayyat ("*Ayin nedivah asher tashut ke-soḥeret*"), or that of the garden, the wine, and the party of friends in a poem in honor of Isaac ibn al-Yatom ("*Ereẓ ke-yaldah hayetah yoneket*") are attained. The opening is generally the most artistic part of the poem, whereas the eulogy itself – which for the most part comprises the content – is usually pedestrian, lacking any mark of individuality, and tending to extreme exaggeration. The frank and sensitive poems within this type were written for those people, like the Ibn Ezra family, toward whom Judah Halevi felt deep affection and admiration.

The *qaṣīda* is also the form of most of the laments (approximately 45) on the deaths of many of his friends and acquaintances. His grief is combined with pessimistic meditation on omnipotent death, and on fate which strikes arbitrarily, and with exaggerated eulogies of the deceased – all in the contemporary style. The death of close friends, however, evoked a strong personal feeling which succeeded in investing the usual motifs with originality (*"Alei zot tivkeinah"* on the death of Moses ibn Ezra and his brother Joseph). As was common in this period, Judah Halevi combined a conscious intellectual structuring of the whole poem with an expression of genuine emotion, as exemplified in particular by the lament on the murder of Solomon ibn Ferrizuel at the hands of Christian mercenaries. Here the tragedy of the individual unites with the catastrophe of the people, and perplexity with rage against Christendom, which is cursed in this poem. Stylistically the openings of the laments are unique. The poems themselves, adapted to different mourning situations, are written in strophic forms, free from the stylized contents and the representations of the classic laments. The influence of folk songs is clearly discernible in them; the ballad verse form is sometimes used, especially in dialogue between the living who stand by the grave and the deceased.

PIYYUTIM. Outstanding among the 350 *piyyutim* which Judah Halevi composed for all of the Jewish festivals is a large group, which may be entitled *"Shirei ha-Galut"* ("Poems of the Diaspora"). The realism of these poems clearly reflects the tragic events suffered by the Jewish people. Their main value, however, is to be found in the lyric fashioning of his own world by the poet, who identified deeply with the fate of his people and whose poetry afforded true expression to many others. The combination of stylistic aspects of Spanish-Hebrew poetry with the various characteristics of the ancient Hebrew style results in rare achievements of perfection and beauty. Job's lament, the cries of Lamentations and of the psalmist, and the bitter complaints of Jeremiah resound in these poems, together with the joy of the prophetic visions of redemption. By relating his personal experience, the poet particularizes the idea of suffering – heightened by imagery and descriptions drawn from ancient sources. In their rich language and imagery, in the force of their varied style, and in the magic effect of their sound patterns, these poems rank among the most outstanding Hebrew poetry of all time (e.g., *"Yonah nesatah al kanfei nesharim"*).

In discussing the problem of the "end of days," Judah Halevi uses the obscure eschatology of the Book of Daniel. He sometimes expresses depression arising from his fear at the delay of the redemption and of the danger of destruction of his people. In these *piyyutim* Judah Halevi expresses his yearning for redemption in an urgent demand for its realization and in rejoicing over its expected realization. Following an ancient midrashic motif, he allegorically expressed the pain of God's chosen and faithful people, whom He had seemingly forsaken to idolators, in terms of the anguish of a prince whose servants have captured him and whose father delays in rescuing him; in contrast God, the lover, promises to keep His covenant and assures His people of His love and the future redemption. In this section the poetry is replete with descriptions of love and spring taken from the Song of Songs. In these poems Judah Halevi takes a polemical stand against false belief; against the enticements of monks and apostates, the beloved, wounded and insulted, vows unconditional faithfulness to her lover (*"Yode'ei yegoni"*), proclaiming happiness in her pains which are but wounds of a lover (*"Me-az me'on ha-ahavah"*). He emphasizes the superiority of the Jewish religion, which alone is divinely revealed (*"Ya'alat ḥen mi-me'onah raḥakah,"* *"Yekar im ha-shabbat tagdil"*). The poems are imbued with sometimes strongly contrasting emotions: loneliness and suffering; rejoicing in the light of the past and sufferings in the darkness of the present; despair and security; lust for revenge and yearning for redemption. The strong tensions between these opposites find imagistic expression in such figures as a dove escaping the hunter (the Jewish people carried, in the past, on the wings of eagles); the degradation of the slave (the lost kingdom); the loneliness of the exiled son (the essential chosenness of the people).

PERSONAL LYRIC POETRY. Along with *piyyutim* of a national nature on such biblical and historic themes as the description of the miracles in Egypt in the poems for Passover, the miracle of Purim, the *Avodah* for the Day of Atonement, are found lyric poems expressing personal religious experiences: *yoẓerot, kerovot, reshuyyot,* and mainly *seliḥot*, which are among the greatest in Jewish religious poetry after the Psalms. Judah Halevi expresses man's reverence for God, his dread of sin, and the desperate struggle against his carnal nature. He repeatedly admonishes the soul with harsh words, instills in it the fear of judgment and death, entices it with the idea of the reward of paradise, and deters it with the threat of the fire of hell. In this conflict God, a harsh judge, is too lofty to be approached and known. On the other hand, he writes of his happiness with God, which pervades his entire being; his powerful love of and devotion to God increase the light in his soul, mitigate its fear, and protect it from the power of evil. At that time, God is revealed to the heart. Traces of contemporary philosophical views can be discerned in these poems, as well as influences of similar motifs in earlier Hebrew poetry. Exalted style is only rarely used (*"Yeḥav lashon ḥazot ishon,"* *"Elohim el mi amshilkha"*); generally the poetic tone is gentle, humble, and quiet. Some poems confront the great paradoxes of religious experience; some combine deep meditation with emotional feeling (*"Yah, anah emẓa'akha"*); others occasionally border on the mystical, as the poet ventures into areas of the ancient revelation in quest of his "lover," his God, "and no one answers."

SONGS OF ZION AND SONGS OF THE SEA. The most famous of the poetic works of Judah Halevi are the *"Shirei Ẓiyyon"* ("Poems of Zion," or Zionides), approximately 35 in number. Their originality is evident in the very topic, which was at that period an uncommon one, but even more so in their varied and beautiful artistry. Several categories of these poems can be differentiated, although they were written over several decades, and contain recurring motifs and similar tones.

(1) The poems of longing for Ereẓ Israel express the inner tension between love and pain, between the dream and

the reality, and the effort required to bridge the West and East (*"Libbi be-mizraḥ," "Yefeh nof," "Elohai, mishkenotekha yedidot"*).

(2) The poetic disputations exhibit a strong intellectual base, overpowered by personal emotion. At times the controversy is an expression of the poet's own inner uncertainties. To Judah Halevi it seemed that for many life in Spain was a kind of slavery, a pursuit of worthless enticements, and a betrayal of God. He found true freedom in servitude to God and in subservience to His will, realized by his emigration to Ereẓ Israel. Prior to his voyage, Judah Halevi lived it in his imagination and poetry, overcoming deep fears in this way; he even taught himself to anticipate happily and excitedly the dangers of the future (*"Ha-tirdof ne'arut," "Ha-yukhlu pegarim"*). It was in his poems of dispute with others – in which Judah Halevi appears a vigorous opponent – that his doctrine on Ereẓ Israel was developed and the national consciousness elevated to a hitherto unknown level. In the 12th century he was able, as a result of reasoning and clear political understanding, to argue that there is no secure place for the Jewish people except Ereẓ Israel. As for its being desolate, it was also given that way to the forefathers.

(3) Some of the poems of the voyage were actually written aboard ship; others are imaginary descriptions composed before the journey, while still others were written after it. Important descriptive poems are structurally influenced by ancient biblical poetical forms (e.g., Ps. 107:23–32). They begin with a description of the world, but the subsequent descriptions diminish in perspective: the stormy Mediterranean Sea, the weak ship at its mercy, and finally the poet himself in prayer. Following that is the final calm after the storm. The roaring of the waves dominate the rhythm and sound patterns. His prayer is identified with Jonah's, and the roaring of the sea is consciously identified with the moaning of his heart. The best of his *"Shirei Ẓiyyon"* is *"Ẓiyyon ha-lo tishali"* ("Zion, wilt thou not ask the welfare of thine prisoners?").

> How shall it be sweet to me to eat and drink while I behold
> Dogs tearing at thy lion's whelps?
> Or how can light of day be joyous to mine eyes while yet
> I see in ravens' beaks torn bodies of thine eagles.

Numerous imitations and translations of this poem have appeared. By virtue of its inclusion (according to the Ashkenazi rite) in the *kinot* for the Ninth of Av, many generations have lamented the destruction of the Temple and dreamt their dream of redemption in the words of this poem. All aspects of the poem focus on Zion. The single rhyme of all the stanzas is יִךְ, which produces a trance-like effect. Deep attachment to Ereẓ Israel alone permeates the meaning of everything in the poem. The holy qualities of the land are specified at length with a lyric feeling which imaginatively transplants the poet to places of former revelation, prophecy, monarchy, and to the graves of the forefathers. In a unique poetic outcry, he expresses his grief at its destruction and his humiliation in subjugation:

> As the deep groans and roars beneath me
> Learning from my inmost fears.

He expresses the happiness of his hope in the quiet lines which end the poem. With these lines he blesses those who will be fortunate enough to see the real redemption in the dawn.

Judah Halevi's poems were widespread in manuscript from an early period. Thousands of fragments of his poems were preserved in the *Genizah*, and also in other manuscripts collections that are kept today in Russia and many other countries. During his lifetime they were already known outside of Spain. Not long after his death his poems started to be collected in *diwānīm* by different scholars. The best known of them is the large *diwān* compiled, probably in Cairo, by Ḥiyya al-Dayyan al-Maghribī, not long after Halevi's visit to Egypt (Oxford, Bodl. Ms. 1970). Other editors tried to increase the number of poems of the *diwān*, as the Cairene compiler *Joshua ben Elijah Halevi did at least one century later, including an appendix with more compositions (Oxford, Bodl. Ms. 1971). Before him David ben Maimon and Sa'id ibn al-Kash also collected Halevi poetry.

From the beginning of printing many of Judah Halevi's *piyyutim* were included in *maḥzorim* and in collections of *piyyutim, seliḥot,* and *kinot.* From the 19th century scholars began to publish his secular and liturgical poems from manuscripts in literary journals and periodicals, e.g., A. Geiger, in *Melo Ḥofnayim* (1840); S.H. Edelman in *Ginzei Oxford* (1850); J.L. Dukes in *Oẓar Neḥmad* (1857); S.D. Luzzatto in *Tal Orot* (1881) and in *Iggeret Shadal* (1882–84). The first scholar to publish collections of Judah Halevi's poems as individual books and to publish his complete diwan was S.D. Luzzatto. He received from Oxford a copy of the manuscript of the diwan made by Joshua Elijah bar-Levi (14th century) and published the poems in it in *Betulat Bat Yehudah* (Prague, 1864). He also began to publish the entire diwan but he only managed to publish the first section of it (Lyck, 1864). Afterward many collections of Judah Halevi's poems were published, completely or in part. The following may be mentioned: A.A. Harkavy, *Rabbi Yehudah Halevi, Koveẓ Shirav u-Meliẓotav*, 2 vols. (Warsaw, 1893–94); H. Brody, *Diwan Jehudah ha-Levi*, 4 vols., of which two are annotated (Berlin, 1894–1930); S. Bernstein, *Shirei Rabbi Yehudah Halevi* popular edition (with notes and an explanation; New York, 1945); Y. Zmora, *Kol Shirei Rabbi Yehudah Halevi*, 3 vols. (Tel Aviv, 1955). A commentary on the first section of Judah Halevi's diwan was published by Abdallah Saul Joseph, *Givat Sha'ul* (Vienna, 1923), edited by S. Krauss. In the various anthologies of Hebrew poetry much space was devoted to Judah Halevi's poems, e.g., H. Brody-K. Albrecht, *Sha'ar ha-Shir* (1905); H. Brody-M. Wiener, *Mivḥar ha-Shirah ha-Ivrit* (1922, 1946[2], ed. A.M. Habermann); Ḥ. Schirmann, *Ha-Shirah ha-Ivrit bi-Sfarad u-ve-Provence*, vol. 1 (1959). A new comprehensive and critical edition of all Halevi's poems is one of the great desiderata of medieval Hebrew poetry in our days. J. Yahalom is working on it.

Part of Judah Halevi's poetry has been translated and

published either alongside the Hebrew original or by itself, e.g., by J.M. Sachs (in *Die religoese Poesie der Juden in Spanien*, 1845); by A. Geiger (*Divan des Castiliers Abu'l-Hassan Juda ha-Levi*, 1851); by Franz Rosenzweig (*Zionslieder*, 1933); into English by N. Salaman (*Selected Poems of Jehudah Halevi*, 1924), G. Levin (2002), etc.; into Dutch by S. Pinkhof (1929); Hebrew and Spanish by A. Sáenz-Badillos and J. Targarona (1994); Italian by S. de Benedetti (1871); Hungarian by J. Patai (1910).

CHARACTERISTICS OF HALEVI'S POETRY. Halevi's poetry has received countless commentaries and very different interpretations. No other medieval author has been received with the same enthusiasm by all subsequent generations. His poetry is considered one of the outstanding models of the Andalusian school. Some scholars have shown reserve about his conservative attitude, in sharp contrast, for example, to the much more liberal Ibn *Gabirol. But no one has doubted the literary and esthetic value of his poetry.

Halevi follows the conventions of the time in poems that may be considered "formalist," like most of his love or bacchic poems that are sometimes almost literal translations from Arabic; but even in these cases he has his own particular and personal style. He can also write with the most profound lyricism, expressing in a wondrous way his own aspirations or those of his people in exile. His words of friendship are not simple formulas, and his affection for his people is entirely sincere. As a poet, he feels like a prophet proclaiming the liberation of Israel.

Coming from the Christian North, as a stranger, Halevi became fully integrated in the Andalusian world with its Arabic lore, exhibiting the maximum degree of cultural adaptation. Even some of the most significant topics and images that he employs in his poetry, including the feelings of the exile and the heart's separation from the object of its affection, are taken from Arabic poets, always with the nuances imposed by a Jewish mind. But he seems to have become disenchanted with the life of al-Andalus, gradually rejecting the Andalusian-Jewish courtly cultural and social values; a consequence of this may have been the trip to Jerusalem in the last days of his life and his possible decision to abandon the writing of poetry.

Analyzing this particular situation of Halevi, R. Brann sees in the poet's contradictory attitudes toward poetry a sign of the conflicts inherent in living in two quite different worlds, in cultural ambiguity; for him, Halevi did not undergo a "conversion" in his adult years; he remained an Andalusian and compunctious Hebrew poet conflicted about the ambiguity of his literary identity. However, in the last 15 years of his life, Brann observes in Halevi a clear deviation from literary traditions and cultural conventions that produces a "culturally subversive discourse" tending to replace the dominant values of this society.

R. Scheindlin has examined the individual vision and religious experience of Halevi (in contrast to that of Ibn Gabirol) as reflected in liturgical poetry. Although both poets share the Neoplatonic psychology, they are in fact widely separated: Halevi attributes great importance to the distance between God and man, to His transcendence, introducing in his poems a climate of tranquil confidence in God and a passive acceptance of His will that seem to have their main sources in Arabic religious poetry. In a very beautiful study Scheindlin (2003) has contemplated Halevi's pilgrimage as a literary phenomenon, underlining the significance of his pervasive use of imagery involving birds. Birds can be connected with Israel, with the human soul, or with the pilgrimage itself. In particular, he frequently employs the image of the dove to represent the nation Israel, combining it many times with the words "silence" and "distance" to express the exile or the dream of redemption. When finally he focused his literary energies on the pilgrimage, the distant, silent dove served him also as an image of his search for the land of his dreams.

Halevi's poetry was not an isolated phenomenon. When he arrived in al-Andalus he met a large number of poets in all the important Jewish centers. He learned from them and became the friend of many of them. Poetry was one of the most highly esteemed activities of Andalusian society, a sign of intellectual distinction and an ideal of life. Literary meetings, competitions, proof of inventive capacity and imaginative talent, correspondence between poets, riddles, plays on words and images were usual practices among these groups of cultivated Jewish Andalusians. Judah Halevi was surrounded by the members of the Ibn Ezra family, by Joseph ibn Zaddiq, Joseph ibn Sahal, Judah and Solomon ibn Gayyat, Ibn al-Mu'alim, Levi ibn al-Tabban, and other minor poets that represented the rich life of a Golden Century close to its end.

[*Encyclopaedia Hebraica* / Angel Sáenz-Badillos (2nd ed.)]

His Philosophy

Judah Halevi was one of medieval Jewry's most influential thinkers, and his arguments for the truth of Judaism and the essential superiority of the Jewish People are invoked to this day in traditionalist circles. Although Halevi rejected Islamic Aristotelianism, which was beginning to be adopted by his fellow Jews and would soon be considered by most Jewish philosophers (such as Maimonides) as scientifically authoritative, he maintained that Judaism could be defended rationally by emphasizing its empirical basis. Hence, his rejection of the leading philosophy of the day did not mean that he was an anti-rationalist.

Halevi's thought is developed in *Kitâb al-Radd wa-'l-Dalîl fi 'l-Dîn al-Dhalîl* (*The Book of Refutation and Proof on the Despised Faith*, 1140), commonly called *The Kuzari*, after the king of the Khazars, who is portrayed as initiating a search for the correct religion after repeated dreams in which an angelic figure tells him that his intentions were pleasing to God, but his actions were not. The story is based on the historical conversion of the central Asian Khazars to Judaism in the eighth century, even though Halevi's account of the king's search for truth is purely his own literary invention. As the story is told by Halevi, the king first heard and rejected the doctrines of an Aristotelian philosopher, a Christian, and a Muslim. The philosopher presented a theory of a wholly impersonal God who does not care which actions humans choose; such a stance contradicted the evidence of the king's own dream. In contrast, both the Christian and Muslim claimed that the actions of their religion are those which are pleasing to God, but the king rejected their creeds as illogical (Christianity) and unsubstantiated (Islam).

Having had the king reject the dominant intellectual and religious doctrines of his day, Halevi then presented the king as finally inviting a Jew to hear his views. Eventually he was persuaded by a Jewish sage (the *ḥaver*) of the truth of Judaism. After the king's conversion to Judaism, described at the beginning of *Kuzari*, Book 2 (out of 5), his discussions with the *ḥaver* continued until the latter announced his departure to the Land of Israel at the end of the treatise. This dialogue provided Halevi with the framework for presenting his defense of Judaism.

SOURCES. Halevi used the Bible as the basic text for his reconstruction of Jewish history, paying only scant attention to rabbinic interpretations of the biblical narrative. His use of midrash is selective, highlighting those traditions which emphasize Jewish particularity. There is very little legal material in *The Kuzari*, but Halevi was well aware of rabbinic *halakhah*, especially compared to the Karaite practices. Certain trends in the Jewish mystical tradition, especially *merkavah* speculation, also had an impact on Halevi's ideas; in turn, his thought had a vital impact on later Kabbalah.

The Kuzari benefited greatly from an assortment of non-Jewish sources. While Halevi rejected Greek philosophy as it was developed in the Islamic world, he was very much aware of the Aristotelian system (of which he may have been enamored in his youth). His portrayals of philosophy were indebted to the works of Abû Bakr Muhammad ibn Bajja and Abû Ali al- Hussain Ibn Sînâ (*Avicenna, whose treatise on the soul is transcribed in *Kuzari* 5:12). Halevi's opposition to philosophy seems to have been inspired in part by Abû Hâmid Al-Ghazâli. He also drew from the kalamic sources used by his Jewish predecessors, such as *Saadiah Gaon and *Baḥya ibn Paquda, but he considered Kalam useful only to the extent that one is searching for a rationalistic defense of Jewish theology. Greek science, as moderated by the Islamic environment, had an impact on his thought as well. In recent years, attention has been paid to the way in which Shi'ite and Sufi concepts and terms helped frame Halevi's religious outlook, especially vis-à-vis the special status of the Jewish People.

METHOD. Halevi rejected the two regnant scientific/philosophical models of his day: Kalam and Aristotelianism. He believed that both relied on theoretical constructs rather than hard, empirical truth. Kalam arrived at the correct conclusions, such as the creation of the world and the existence and unity of God, but it was useful mainly for apologetics. Aristotelianism, in contrast, taught many incorrect doctrines, since Aristotle lacked reliable tradition when he set out to understand the world by use of his syllogistic reasoning (*qiyâs*) alone. For instance, he believed that the world is eternal; if he had known the Bible, he would have used his reason to defend the proposition that the world was created (*Kuzari* 1:67). Furthermore, philosophy can go only so far: philosophical, syllogistic knowledge of God, for instance, is possible, but it is deficient compared with immediate, unmediated experience (*dhawq*, literally "taste") of God through prophecy (*Kuzari* 4:15–17).

The Jewish tradition provided true knowledge based on the experience of the Jewish people. The reliability of the tradition is guaranteed by the large number of witnesses to the miraculous exodus from Egypt, the revelation on Mt. Sinai, and the entrance into the Land of Israel. Not only were there hundreds of thousands of observers of these events, but also the original testimony of these witnesses has been transmitted publicly over the centuries. Since, Halevi claimed, all Jews accepted the accuracy of the biblical account as having been passed down to them by previous untold generations, there is no possibility of error or falsification of the tradition. If the Bible were a fabrication, there would not be universal Jewish consent to its truth. In contrast, Christianity and Islam claimed to have been revealed to only a small number of people, and, therefore, cannot be validated. Although this historical argument for the certainty of the Jewish tradition is not totally original (it has an antecedent in the work of Saadiah Gaon), Halevi's formulation of it is probably his most significant legacy.

Once Halevi established the veracity of Judaism, he employed reason to explain its truths. Nothing in Scripture or tradition, he claimed, contradicted reason (*Kuzari* 1:67, 89). Thus, one may look for justifications of problematical doctrines (such as the superiority of the Jewish people) or historical occurrences (such as revelation). These explanations may strike the modern reader as rationally invalid, but they were based in part on medieval scientific notions or commonplace notions of the time. In any event, it is too facile to dismiss Halevi as solely a doctrinaire religious critic of philosophy; he attempted to replace Aristotelian rationalism, which to his mind was insufficient, with a form of Jewish empiricism.

SINGULARITY OF THE JEWISH PEOPLE. According to Judah Halevi, the Jewish people were capable of achieving prophecy and receiving the Torah because they are essentially different from other nations. Borrowing notions common in Shi'ite literature, Halevi argued that Adam was the original perfect human whose status was passed on biologically to a selective line of his descendants. At first, this singular distinctiveness (Arabic: *safwa*, usually translated into Hebrew as *segulah*) was confined to individuals such as Seth, Noah, Shem, Abraham, Isaac, and Jacob. With the generation of Jacob's sons, this special characteristic became universal among all Jews. As a result of their distinctiveness, the Jewish people were able to conjoin with an aspect of God called "the divine influence" or "the divine order" or "the divine faculty" (Arabic: *al-amr al-ilahi*, usually translated into Hebrew as *ha-inyan ha-elohi*) and become prophets (*Kuzari* 1:95 and other places). It is this special relationship which marks Jews off from all non-Jews; a convert to Judaism can aspire at most to a sub-prophetic level of inspiration but will never be equal to the native-born Jew (*Kuzari* 1: 27, 115; the status of the proselyte's Jewish-born progeny is not clarified in the *Kuzari*, although there is reason to think that Halevi believed they would also be inferior to other Jews). The fact that the non-Jewish king of the Khazars chose to become Jewish, despite the convert's lower status, is presented as a strong argument for the essential truth of Judaism.

Even though Jews were a persecuted minority, they actually functioned as the "heart" of humanity; without a heart, a living organism could not exist, but the heart can be very weak when other limbs are strong. Humanity could not exist without Jews, who are like a sick man who once was vibrant and can still return to his earlier state. The nations of the world are like a beautiful statue which is externally impressive but which was never truly alive (*Kuzari* 2:29–44).

THE LAND OF ISRAEL AND THE HEBREW LANGUAGE. A corollary to the theory of the superiority of the Jewish people was the concept of the superiority of the Land of Israel (usually called by the Arabic geographical term *al-sham*, namely "greater Syria") and of the Hebrew language (*Kuzari* 2). For instance, prophecy is possible only in the Land of Israel (or "for its sake"; Halevi was aware that a number of biblical prophets were not in the Land of Israel). In order to explain this geographical uniqueness, Halevi adopted a climatological theory, originally innovated by the Greeks and developed by the Arabs, which postulated that the center of the populated areas of the earth is superior to the northern and southern areas. The Land of Israel is the most perfect of all lands. This is yet another example of the use of what was considered a scientific theory to justify Jewish exclusivity.

The sad state of the Land of Israel in Halevi's own time was explained as a result of the destruction of the Temple and the dispersion of the Jews. Just as a particular piece of land might have all the natural attributes to produce a wonderful vineyard, if other factors necessary to grow grapes (e.g., rain, fertilization, weeding) are missing, the vineyard will not produce as it should. Thus, without the ongoing observance of the commandments, especially the sacrifices, the visible *Shekhinah* is no longer present; the Jewish inhabitants of the Land of Israel have temporarily lost their special status, although it remains latent in both the land and the people. Nevertheless, Jews should return to the Land of Israel, even in its unredeemed state. The *ḥaver*'s departure from Khazaria at the end of the *The Kuzari* mirrors Judah Halevi's own departure from Andalusia.

The Hebrew language has also deteriorated despite its intrinsic superiority. Although it was the language in which the world was created, the language spoken by Adam and Eve, and the language of prophecy, in the exile it has suffered the same fate as the Jewish people. It should be noted that, although Halevi wrote his poetry in Hebrew, *The Kuzari* was written in Arabic.

REASONS FOR THE COMMANDMENTS. Halevi accepted Saadiah Gaon's distinction between rational and revelational commandments, but in contrast to the Gaon, he stressed the value of the revelational commandments as distinguishing Judaism from other religions. Everyone, including a gang of thieves, can observe the basic societal norms (the rational commandments) in their own limited communities; only Jews can observe the specific commandments given in the Torah. Those religions which teach the observance of "intellectual nomoi," and not the divine commandments of the Torah, are human in origin and are merely "syllogistic" and "governmental" or "political" (*Kuzari* 1:13, 81; 2:48).

One should accept observance of the Torah as the will of God, without searching for the reasons for the revelational commandments. For those who were incapable of reaching such a level of belief, Halevi offered a number of different justifications of the commandments, including their contribution to harmony in the world and to personal harmony of the individual worshipper (*Kuzari* 2:25–65; 3:1–22). Unlike those Jewish rationalists who gave historical reasons for many of the commandments, such as the sacrifices, thereby undermining their intrinsic worth, Halevi believed that each of the commandments has its own value and fits into a way of life which, by pleasing God, results in prophecy and divine providence.

INTERRELIGIOUS POLEMIC. Halevi attacked not only Aristotelian philosophy in his *Kuzari*. He was equally opposed to Judaism's rival religions, Christianity and Islam, as well as to Karaism, a Jewish sect which challenged the truth of rabbinic Judaism. Writing at a time of Christian-Muslim warfare both in Iberia and in the Land of Israel, Halevi was sensitive to the claim that numerical, military, and economic successes were signs of the truth of a religion. Compared to both Christianity and Islam, Jews were at a distinct material disadvantage, a fact which called into question the Jewish claim of superiority and divine favor.

Halevi maintained that temporal success is not a measure of truth, and even early Christianity and Islam themselves pointed to the martyrdom of their believers as a sign of the certainty of their religions. The fact that Judaism had survived adversity for such a long time, despite the ease with which individual Jews could have escaped persecution by converting to one of the other religions, is a sign of divine providence (*Kuzari* 1:112–115). Furthermore, Judaism's competitors thrive in this world specifically since they promise their adherents great rewards without demanding a concomitant commitment to observing divine commandments. Christianity and Islam are poor imitations of the one true religion, Judaism, but, in the messianic future, their adherents will recognize the superiority of the People of Israel. In the meanwhile, they prepare the way for the coming of the Messiah (*Kuzari* 4:23).

Refutation of the Karaite interpretation of Judaism may have been one of the Halevi's motivations when he composed an early version of *The Kuzari* (the question of possible changes in Halevi's views has recently been discussed in the scholarly literature, but meanwhile no consensus on the issue has emerged and the suggestions which have been proposed are highly speculative). Halevi regarded Karaism as parallel to philosophy because its adherents used personal exertion (*idjtihâd*) and syllogistic reasoning (*qiyâs*), rather than reliable tradition, as a source of interpreting the Torah and its commandments. Despite the worthiness of their intentions, their lack of reliable legal traditions resulted in behavioral anarchy, since each Karaite interpreted the Torah as he saw fit; in like manner the philosophers' lack of reliable metaphysical traditions resulted in a form of intellectual anarchy, such as their denial of creation of the world (*Kuzari* 3:22–74).

BIBLIOGRAPHICAL NOTE. The Judaeo-Arabic original of *The Kuzari* was first published by Hartwig Hirschfeld (Leipzig, 1887) on the basis of the unique manuscript of the text. A more definitive edition was prepared by David Baneth and completed by Haggai Ben-Shammai (Jerusalem, 1977). A medieval Hebrew translation was executed by Judah ibn Tibbon and has been reprinted many times, but there is no scientific edition. Hirschfeld's edition of this translation, which took into account the Judeo-Arabic original and restored censored passages, has served as the basis of most 20th century editions of the Ibn Tibbon text, despite its problematic nature. Johannes Buxtorf the Younger published a good version of the Ibn Tibbon text, accompanied by a Latin translation (Basel, 1660).

Two modern Hebrew translations exist: Yehudah Even Shmuel (Tel Aviv, 1972; the translation is not strictly literal; for instance it blurs some of Halevi's more ethnocentric statements, among its other idiosyncrasies); and Yosef Kafih (Kiryat Ono, 1997). Hirschfeld's English translation (many editions) is superseded by a new translation being prepared by Barry S. Kogan on the basis of the original work of Lawrence V. Berman. A number of other contemporary English editions have been translated from the Hebrew and have little scholarly significance. Charles Touati's French translation from the Arabic (Louvain, 1994) is of great value. *The Kuzari* has also been translated into a number of other European languages.

[Daniel J. Lasker (2nd ed.)]

In Jewish Literature

It is as the romantic "singer of Zion," rather than as the religious philosopher, that Judah Halevi has figured in literary works written by Jews. Perhaps the most memorable of such portrayals is that by the German poet Heinrich *Heine in "Jehuda Ben Halevi," one of the *Hebraeische Melodien* contained in his late *Romanzero* (1851). In lines which reecho the Psalms and the verse of the Spanish poet himself, Heine fondly traces the early education and later career of the courtly troubadour whose heart was set on Jerusalem. Indeed, Heine wrongly credited him with the authorship of the Sabbath Eve *Lekhah Dodi hymn (both here and in "*Prinzessin Sabbat*," in *Hebraeische Melodien*). A Yiddish version of Heine's "*Jehuda Ben Halevi*" was published by Zelig I. Schneider in 1904. Later in the 19th century, Ludwig *Philippson wrote the historical novel *Rabbi Jehuda Halevi, der juedische Minister* (Yid. tr., 1895), a Hebrew version of which later appeared as "*Sefarad vi-Yrushalayim…*" (in *Ha-Asif*, 3 (1886), 481–564). The subject has retained its popularity in the 20th century with works including the U.S. writer Eisig *Silberschlag's Hebrew epic poem *Yehudah Halevi* (1925) and the Yiddish poet A. Leyeles' "*Yehudah Halevi*" (in his *Labyrinth*, 1918). In his Hebrew novel *Elleh Masei Yehudah Halevi* (1959), the Israel writer Yehudah *Burla emphasized Judah Halevi's call for the Jewish people's return to Zion.

BIBLIOGRAPHY: WORKS OF (TRANSLATIONS) AND ON JUDAH HALEVI IN ENGLISH: A. KUZARI: H. Hirschfeld (tr.), *Judah Hallevi's Kitāb al Khazari* (1906, 1931³, repr. 1945); I. Heinemann (ed. and tr.), *Kuzari: the Book of Proof and Argument* (abridged ed., 1947; repr. in: *Three Jewish Philosophers*, 1960); M. Friedlaender, in: *Semitic Studies in Memory of Alexander Kohut* (1897), 139–51; I.I. Efros, in: PAAJR, 2 (1931), 3–6; L. Nemoy, in: JQR, 26 (1935/36), 221–6; M. Buber, in: *Contemporary Jewish Record*, 8 (1945), 358–68; L. Strauss, in: PAAJR, 13 (1943), 47–96; M. Wiener, in: HUCA, 23 (1951), 669–82. B. POETRY: N. Salaman (tr.), *Selected Poems of Jehudah Halevi* (1924); A. Lucas (tr.), in: JQR, 5 (1893), 652–63; J.J. Ackerman, *Biblishe un Moderne Poemen… fun R. Yehudah Halevi* (1923), incl. Eng. transl.; N. Allony, in: JQR, 35 (1944/45), 79–83 (no. 4 by Judah Halevi); *Yehuda Halevi – Sweet Singer of Zion…* (1940), incl. selections of his poems; J. Schirmann, in: KS, 15 (1938/39), 360–7 incl. Eng.). **ADD. BIBLIOGRAPHY:** T. Carmi, *The Penguin Book of Hebrew Verse* (1981), 333–52; G. Levin (tr.), *Yehuda Halevi, Poems from the Diwan* (2002). C. WORKS ON JUDAH HALEVI IN ENGLISH: J. Schirmann, in: EB, Macropaedia, 10 (1973), 282–284; D. Druck, *Yehudah Halevi, His Life and Works* (1941); I.I. Efros, *Judah Halevi as Poet and Thinker* (1941); idem, in: PAAJR, 11 (1941), 27–41; R. Kayser, *Life and Time of Jehudah Halevi* (1949), incl. bibl., 171–4; J. Jacobs, in: *Jews' College Literary Society* (1887), 98–112; idem, *Jewish Ideals and Other Essays* (1896), 103–34; K. Magnus, *Jewish Portraits* (1897), 1–23; D. Neumark, in: *Hebrew Union College Catalogue…* (1908), 1–91; S. Baron, in: JSOS, 3 (1941), 243–72; S.S. Cohon, in: AJYB, 43 (1941),447–88; H. Keller, *Modern Hebrew Orthopedic Terminology and Jewish Medical Essays* (1931), 152–76; D. de Sola Pool, in: L. Jung (ed.), *Jewish Library* (1943²), 79–104; S. Solis-Cohen, *Judaism and Science* (1940), 170–92; H.A. Wolfson, in: PAAJR, 11 (1941), 105–63; idem, in: *Essays in Honour of J.H. Hertz…* (1942), 427–42; S. Zeitlin, in: JQR, 35 (1944), 307–13. **ADD. BIBLIOGRAPHY:** M. Saperstein, in: *Prooftexts*, 1:3 (1981), 306–11; idem, in: *AJS Review*, 26:2 (2002), 301–26; A. Hamori, in: *Journal of Semitic Studies*, 30 (1985), 75–83; J. Yahalom and I. Benabu, in: *Tarbiz*, 54 (1985), 246–47 (Heb.); R. Brann, in: *Prooftexts*, 7 (1987), 123–43; idem, in: M.R. Menocal, R.P. Scheindlin, and M. Sells (eds.), *The Literature of Al-Andalus* (2000), 265–81; S.D. Goitein, *A Mediterranean Society*, vol. 5 (1988), 448–68; R.P. Scheindlin, in: *Prooftexts*, 13 (1993), 141–62; J. Yahalom, in: *Miscelánea de Estudios Arabes y Hebraicos*, 44, 2 (1995), 23–45; idem, in: S. Reif (ed.), *The Cambridge Genizah Collections* (2002), 123–35; A. Brener, *Judah Halevi and His Circle of Hebrew Poets in Granada* (2005). D. WORKS IN OTHER LANGUAGES: Schirmann, Sefarad, 1 (1959), 425–536; 2 (1956), 684f. incl. bibl. idem, *Ḥamishah Piyyutim li-Yhudah Halevi* (1966); idem, in: *Haaretz* (May 31, 1968); I. Zmora (ed.), *Rabbi Yehudah Halevi, Meḥkarim ve-Ha'arakhot* (1950); S. Ben Shevet, in: *Tarbiz*, 25 (1955/56), 385–92; S.D. Goitein, in: PAAJR, 28 (1959), 41–56; S.B. Starkova, *Versions of Judah Halewi's Diwan According to Leningrad Fragments* (1960); Y. Levin, in: *Oẓar Yehudei Sefarad*, 7 (1964), 49–69; Y. Ratzaby, *ibid.*, 8 (1965), 11–16; S. Abramson, *Bi-Leshon Kodemim* (1965), passim; A. Scheiber, in: *Tarbiz*, 36 (1967), 1–156. **ADD. BIBLIOGRAPHY:** E. Hazan, "Poetical Elements in the Liturgical Poetry of Yehuda Halevi" (Heb., diss., 1979); idem, in: *Poesía hebrea en al-Andalus* (2002), 213–24; A. Vilsker, in: *Sovietishe Heimland*, 5 (1982), 128–36, and 6 (1983), 135–51 (Yiddish); A. Doron, *Yĕhudah ha-Leví: repercusión de su obra* (1985); E. Fleischer, in: *Kiryat Sefer*, 61 (1986–87), 893–910; idem, in: *Asupot*, 5 (1991), 139–41; idem, in: *Israel Levin Jubilee Volume*, 1, (1994), 241–76; A. Sáenz-Badillos, *Actas del VI Simposio de la Sociedad Española de Literatura General y Comparada* (1989), 123–30; idem, in: *Luces y sombras de la judería europea* (1996), 69–84; J. Yahalom, in: *Pe'amim*, 46–47 (1991) 55–74; *Yĕhudah ha-Levi. Poemas*. Critical Hebrew text with Spanish transl. A. Sáenz-Badillos & J. Targarona, lit. stud. A. Doron (1994); Schirmann-Fleischer, *The History of Hebrew Poetry in Muslim Spain* (Heb., 1995), 421–80; M. Itzhaki, *Juda Halévi: d'Espagne à Jérusalem: (1075?–1141)* (1997); M. Gil & E. Fleischer, *Yehuda ha-Levi and his Circle* (Heb., 2001); A. Schippers, in: *Poesía hebrea en al-Andalus* (2002), 173–86; R.P. Scheindlin, in: *Poesía hebrea en al-Andalus* (2002), 187–212; A. Salvatierra, in: *Poesía hebrea en al-Andalus* (2002), 225–44. AS PHILOSOPHER: Husik, Philosophy, index; Guttmann, Philosophies index; L. Strauss, *Persecution and the Art of Writing* (1952), 95–141; H.A. Wolfson, in: JQR, 32 (1941/42), 345–70; 33 (1942/43), 49–82; Heinemann, in: *Keneset*, 7 (1942), 261–79; idem, in: *Sinai*, 9 (1941), 120–34; J. Guttmann, *Dat u-Madda* (1955), 66–85; D.Z. Baneth, in: *Keneset*, 7 (1942), 311–29; Schweid, in: *Tarbiz*, 30 (1960/61), 257–72; S.B. Orbach, *Ammudei ha-Maḥashavah ha-Yisre'elit*, 1 (1953), 199–267. **ADD. BIBLIOGRAPHY:** D. Lobel, *Between Mysticism and Philosophy: Sufi Language of Religious Experience in Judah Ha-Levi's Kuzari* (2000); Shlomo Pines, in: JSAI, 2 (1980), 165–251; H, Davidson, in: REJ, 131 (1973), 351–96; and H.T. Kreisel, *Prophecy: The History of an Idea in Medieval Jewish Philosophy* (2001), 94–147; D.J. Lasker, in: JQR, 81:1–2 (July–October, 1990), 75–91; C.H. Manekin, in: B.C. Bazán et al. (eds.), *Moral and Political Philosophies in the Middle Ages* (1995), 1686–97; E.R. Wolfson, in: PAAJR, 57 (1991), 179–242; Y. Silman, *Philosopher and Prophet: Judah Halevi, the Kuzari and the Evolution and his Thought* (1995); H.A. Wolfson, *Studies in the History of Philosophy and Religion*, vol. 2 (1977), 1–119; L. Strauss, *Persecution and the Art of Writing* (1952; 1973), 95–141 (but cf. K.H. Green, in: JAAR, 61:2 (Summer, 1993), 225–73); A. Altmann, *Melilah*, 1 (1944), 1–17; I. Heinemann, in: *Zion*, 9 (1944), 147–77.

JUDAH HA-LEVI BEI-RABBI HILLEL, medieval paytan, some of whose work was recently discovered in the Cairo *Genizah*. Judah's *piyyutim* are based on customs prevailing in Ereẓ Israel, which would indicate that he lived there or in Egypt, where there was a Palestinian community. He is the only *paytan* known to have composed *piyyutim* for Tu bi-Shevat. Two of his *kerovot* for the *Shemoneh Esreh are preserved; one, published by M. Zulay (*Leket Shirim u-Fiyyutim* (1936)) contains names of trees growing in Palestine.

BIBLIOGRAPHY: M. Zulay, in: *Eretz Israel*, 4 (1956), 138–44; A.M. Habermann, *Ateret Renanim* (1967), 123.

[Menahem Zulay]

JUDAH HA-NASI (latter half of the second and beginning of the third century C.E.), patriarch of Judea and redactor of the *Mishnah. He is referred to also as "*rabbenuha-kadosh*" ("our holy teacher") or simply as "Rabbi." Judah was the son of Rabban Simeon b. *Gamaliel and the seventh (or sixth?) generation descended from Hillel (see **Nasi*), having been born, according to an aggadic tradition, "on the day that R. Akiva died" during the Hadrianic persecutions (Kid. 72b). Both his contemporaries and later generations held him in veneration, and regarded him as the savior of Israel, as much as *Simeon the Just, *Mattathias the Hasmonean, and *Mordecai and Esther (Meg. 11a). In him the sages found all the qualities which they enumerated as becoming to the righteous (Avot 6:8). They even associated his name with messianic hopes to the extent of applying to him the verse (Lam. 4:20): "The breath of our nostrils, the anointed of the Lord" (TJ, Shab. 16:1, 15c), and in his days chose for the proclamation of the new month the password: "David, King of Israel, lives and exists" (RH 25a). His wisdom, sanctity, and humility, as well as his wealth and close ties with the Roman emperor, became the subject of numerous legends. In addition to his father, his teachers included *Judah b. Ilai (TJ, BM 3:1, 9a), *Simeon b. Yoḥai (Shab. 147b), *Eleazar b. Shammua (Er. 53a), *Jacob b. Korshai (TJ, Shab. 10:5, 12c), and, apparently, R. *Meir (Shab. 13b). His mastery of the vast volume of tradition, his great application to his studies (Ket. 104a), his humility (Sot. 9:15), coupled with self-confidence, sound judgment, and a rule that was based on a strict discipline (Ket. 103b), combined to give authority to his leadership and an undisputed status to the patriarchate.

His Power in Ereẓ Israel and Relationship with Rome

Judah lived in *Bet She'arim where he had his yeshivah (Sanh. 32b) but, because of ill-health, moved toward the end of his life to *Sepphoris where the air was salubrious (Ket. 103b); according to one tradition he lived there for 17 years (TJ, Ket. 12:3, 35a). He applied himself to the strengthening of the economic position of the Jews in Ereẓ Israel, their settlement on its soil, and to shaping the country's national religious institutions. He devoted himself to spreading a knowledge of the Torah and the observance of its *mitzvot* among all sections of the people, and to maintaining the unity of the nation. His position was recognized by the Roman administration, and this, together with his wealth, enabled him to reinforce the dignity of the patriarchate and give it a quasi-royal status. Various identifications have been suggested for *Antoninus whose friendship for, and discussions with, Judah ha-Nasi form the subject of aggadic stories. These *aggadot* and conversations, which reveal a Stoic influence, were intended to demonstrate the wisdom of Judah and the superiority of the Torah. For this purpose a philosopher-emperor was chosen – probably Marcus Aurelius – who was on friendly terms with the patriarch and respected the Jewish religion. Judah ha-Nasi's contacts with the Roman authorities in the economic and political spheres probably provided the historical background to these aggadic stories, which tell that Antoninus gave him the tenancy of estates in Golan (TJ, Shev. 6:1, 36d) and that they were partners in cattle breeding (*Midrash Bereshit Rabbah*, ed. by Theodor and Albeck, 20:6, p.190). The balsam trees of his household are mentioned along with those on the emperor's estates (Bet. 43a), the reference being undoubtedly to the plantations of balsam trees at En-Gedi and Jericho which were "imperial estates." The grant of greater judicial autonomy, attested by Origen in his letter to Julius Africanus (J.P. Migne (ed.), *Patrologia Graeca*, 11 (1857), 47ff.), was presumably the result of such contacts, and it is possible that Judah ha-Nasi actually met one and perhaps two Roman emperors during their stay in Ereẓ Israel, most probably Septimius *Severus and Antoninus *Caracalla, whose good relations with the Jews are attested by the inscription of Kaẓyon near Safed dated 197–198 C.E. (S. Klein (ed.), *Sefer ha-Yishuv*, 1 (1939), 151) and also by Jerome (commentary on Dan. 11:34).

Circumspection marked Judah ha-Nasi's relations with the Roman authorities. In contrast to the Samaritans, the Jews adopted a policy of nonintervention in the civil war which broke out after the murder of Clodius in 192 C.E. between Septimius Severus and his rival Pescennius Niger. Judah was also careful not to flaunt his position outside Ereẓ Israel, as is illustrated in the following story: "Rabbi said to R. Afes: 'Write a letter in my name to our lord, the emperor Antoninus.' He arose and wrote: 'From Judah ha-Nasi to our lord, the emperor Antoninus.' [Judah] took and read it, tore it up, and wrote: 'To our lord the emperor from your servant Judah.' He [R. Afes] said to him: 'Rabbi, why do you lower your dignity?' He answered him: 'Am I, then better than my ancestor? Did he not declare [Gen. 32:5]: 'Thus shall ye say unto my lord Esau: Thus saith thy servant Jacob'?'" (Gen. R. 75:5). When he went to the Roman authorities at Acre, he refrained from taking with him "Romans," apparently soldiers stationed in his neighborhood (Gen. R. 78:15). His attitude toward the Roman Empire was a negative one, there being ascribed to him the statement that "the destroyers of the Second Temple [Rome] are destined to fall into the hand of Persia" (Yoma 10a). Despite the external splendor of the empire, he realized its faults. At the sight of a legion of fine and distinguished men, whose heads reached up to the capital of the pillars at Caesarea, his son Simeon exclaimed: "How fattened are the calves of Esau!" But Rabbi answered him: "These legions are worth nothing" (Tanḥ Va-Yeshev, 3), knowing as he did that they both raised up and murdered emperors and were a source of weakness and degeneration. Certain that God would bring an end to the Roman Empire, even as He had done to the kingdoms of Babylonia, Media, and Greece, Judah ha-Nasi referred to those who wished to hasten the advent of the redemption as "complainers, the descendants of complainers" (PdRK 130). Aware that the Jews in Ereẓ Israel were unable to influence the course of great political events which were to be left to "Him that called the generations from the beginning," Judah realized that the time was nevertheless opportune to work for the unity of the nation and its internal consolidation.

Judah's Bet Din and Its Rulings

After the destruction of the Second Temple, and especially after the Bar Kokhba revolt, the non-Jewish population increased in several parts of Ereẓ Israel. In order to ease the financial burden on the Jews, enabling them to remain on their lands, Judah ha-Nasi exempted several places from the tithes (Beth-Shean, Caesarea, Bet Guvrin, Kefar Ẓemaḥ: TJ, Dem. 2:1, 22c) by excluding them from the sanctity ascribed to Ereẓ Israel. In order that lands which had been confiscated from Jews should not remain in the possession of non-Jews, Rabbi assembled a *bet din* which decided by a vote "that if the property had been in the hands of the **sikarikon* [the occupier of confiscated property] for 12 months, whoever first purchased it acquired the title, but had to give a quarter [of the price] to the original owner" (Git. 5:6; *ibid.*, 58b). Judah ha-Nasi also attempted to permit the produce of the sabbatical year in an effort to ease the grave economic situation (TJ, Ta'an. 3:1, 66b–c). Although several of Judah ha-Nasi's regulations are given as those of his *bet din* ("Rabbi and his *bet din* decided by a vote": Oho. 18:9), the sources testify to the antagonism and even the opposition of contemporary sages (see Tosef., Oho. 18:18; Ḥul. 6b), but he subjected the *bet din* to his authority, maintaining that "the Holy One, blessed be He, left this crown to us that we may invest ourselves therewith" (TJ, Dem. 2:1, 22c and see Ḥul. 6b). Judah ha-Nasi was not assisted, as his father had been, by an *av bet din* or a *ḥakham*, but instead concentrated all authority in his own hands (TJ, Sanh. 1:3, 19a) including the supervision of the various communities and their religious and judicial institutions (Gen. R. 81:2; TJ, Yev. 12:7, 13a).

Judah ha-Nasi and his *bet din* exercised their influence not only over Galilee but also over the south, and sages of the south were close to him. He showed a special interest in the *Holy Congregation in Jerusalem, which included two sages who were on intimate terms with him – *Simeon b. Menasya and *Yose b. Meshullam (TJ, Ma'as. Sh. 2:10, 53d; Eccles. R. 9:9). The proclamation of the new month and the intercalation of the year were significant areas of the Diaspora's dependence on Ereẓ Israel as the religious center of the Jewish people. After the destruction of the Second Temple the year was intercalated in Judea (Tosef., Sanh. 2:13) but was transferred in the days of Judah ha-Nasi to Galilee (TJ, Sanh. 1:2, 18c), in order to enhance the prestige of the patriarchate, whose seat was there. He also abolished the fire signals announcing the new month and instead introduced regulations calculated to expedite both the hearing of witnesses and the dispatch of messengers (TJ, RH 2:1, 58a). At all events there is no reference to an attempt at intercalating the year in Babylonia as had been done in the preceding generation by *Hananiah, the nephew of R. Joshua (in TJ, Ned. 6:8, 40a, the name is wrongly given as Rabbi: see Ber. 63b). In his relations with the Babylonian Diaspora Judah ha-Nasi displayed the same blend of concession and strength: the *nasi* was king, with none superior to him. He was, however, prepared to show honor to the exilarch (Hor. 11a–b; TJ, Kil. 9:4, 32a). He opposed the sages of Ereẓ Israel who wished to make Babylonia as "dough" in comparison with Ereẓ Israel, that is to declare the Jews of Ereẓ Israel to be of pure descent and those of Babylonia as descended from families suspected of containing an alien element, so that if a Babylonian Jew wished to marry into an Ereẓ Israel family he would have to prove the purity of his descent. Judah ha-Nasi said: "You are putting thorns between my eyes. If you wish, R. Ḥanina b. Ḥama will join issue with you." R. Ḥanina b. Ḥama joined issue with them and said to them: "I have this tradition from R. Ishmael b. Yose who stated on his father's authority: 'All countries are as dough in comparison with Ereẓ Israel and Ereẓ Israel is as dough in comparison with Babylonia'" (Kid. 71a). Furthermore, the inclusion of Babylonian sages in his intimate circle helped to cement Judah ha-Nasi's ties with the important Babylonian Diaspora.

The Aristocracy of Learning

Judah ha-Nasi's numerous activities designed to resuscitate Jewish settlement in Ereẓ Israel are reflected in his desire to give Hebrew precedence over Aramaic, as shown by his remark: "What has the Syrian tongue to do with Ereẓ Israel? Speak either Hebrew or Greek" (BK 82b–83a). Even the maidservant of his household knew Hebrew, and it is related that the sages learned from her the meaning of rare Hebrew words (RH 26b; Meg. 18a). Judah's preference for Hebrew is shown in a *halakhah* quoted in his name: "I declare that the *Shema* is to be said only in Hebrew," thus controverting the earlier *halakhah* that it may be said in any language (Tosef., Sot. 7:7).

The patriarchate, which Judah ha-Nasi elevated to the spiritual and social leadership of the nation, was marked by a lordly manner and a regal splendor. He had guards (eunuchs – Ber. 16b) who punished recalcitrants (Eccles. R. 10:2). There was a hierarchy in the patriarch's court, sages close to him being engaged in special functions and dining at his table (Er. 73a). His wealth enabled him to give generous assistance to students. Affluent circles were attracted to his court, and support for the saying "Rabbi showed respect to rich men" (Er. 86a) can be found in the stories about the son of Bonyis and the son of Elasah (Judah ha-Nasi's wealthy son-in-law) who were not learned in the Torah (Er. 85b; TJ, MK 3:1, 81c; Ned. 51a). Judah's aristocracy of learning found expression in a bluntly negative attitude toward the unlearned. By exempting sages from the city taxes (BB 8a), he undoubtedly increased the burden of taxation on artisans and intensified the hostility between the sages and the uneducated; this hostility was mainly religious and intellectual, but was tinged with economic and class antagonism and is a conspicuous feature of the story told in the *baraita* that he opened his storehouse of food in a year of scarcity to the learned but not to the ignorant. When, however, he was told that there were scholars who refused to disclose their learning because they had no wish to benefit from the honor due to the Torah, he thereafter gave to all the needy without distinction (BB 8a). Yet his negative attitude toward the ignorant did not change, there being ascribed to him the statement: "Trouble comes to the world only on account of the unlearned" (*ibid.*).

There was opposition to several other actions of Judah ha-Nasi. Simeon b. Eleazar criticized his method of making appointments (Mid. Tan., ed. by Hoffmann, 8; and TJ, Ta'an. 4:2, 68a). Even R. Ḥiyya, one of his intimate circle, did not refrain from demonstrating opposition to Judah ha-Nasi's interference in the freedom of teaching by his decree that "pupils are not to be taught in the open public market place" (MK 16a). On one occasion, when *Judah and *Hezekiah, the sons of Ḥiyya, dined with Judah ha-Nasi and were somewhat under the effects of wine, they said: "The son of David [i.e., the Messiah] cannot come until the two ruling houses in Israel will have come to an end, namely, the exilarchate in Babylonia and the patriarchate in Ereẓ Israel" (Sanh. 38a). This remark of theirs echoes the views of the sages who belonged to pietistic circles and were ill-disposed to the domination of the patriarchate and to its affluent and regal habits.

Tradition bestowed on Rabbi the title of *Ha-Kadosh* (the Holy One), but the very form in which this is transmitted: "Why were you called our holy teacher?" (Shab. 118b) testifies to its late date. Unlike sages who were given the title of "holy" because they did not look at iconic statues or at the human figures engraved on coins (TJ, Av. Zar. 3;1, 42c), Judah ha-Nasi, since he was concerned with the needs of others (Eccles. R. 5:11) and in contact with the Roman authorities, was quite unable to act in this manner, especially in view of the statement of his uncle Ḥanina b. Gamaliel that "members of my father's household used seals with human features engraved on them" (TJ, Av. Zar. 3:1, 42c). It is very doubtful whether his preference for Greek over Aramaic, which was widely used by the people (Sot. 49b), his injunction that it is a father's duty to teach his son civics (Mekh., Pisḥa, 18), and even his statement: "Which is the right course that a man should choose for himself? That which is honorable to himself and also brings him honor from men" (Avot 2:1) were able to satisfy the pietists and activists among the sages. The reply of Eleazar b. Simeon's widow to Judah ha-Nasi's proposal of marriage, "Shall a utensil, in which holy food has been used, be used for profane purposes?" (BM 84b) reflects the opposition of the sages to the secular aspect of the sway exercised by him in his patriarchate, an opposition that also found expression in *Phinehas b. Jair's refusal to accept the patriarch's hospitality (Ḥul. 7b; and see TJ, Dem. 1:3, 22a). Whereas Judah ha-Nasi was severe with sages close to him, such as Bar Kappara and Ḥiyya, even to the extent of punishing them (MK 16a), he adopted a conciliatory attitude toward Phinehas b. Jair, as he did to the other pietists among the sages (see Shab. 152a), thus allaying tension and preventing a breach between them and himself. General esteem for Judah ha-Nasi's momentous achievements most probably played a decisive role in the attitude of the majority of the sages toward him. For at no other time did the sages exercise such a sway over all sections of the nation, and at no other period did the honor of the Torah reach such heights. At the head of the nation was one who was not only a courageous personality but also a sage whose indisputable religious and halakhic greatness is shown in his work of codifying the Mishnah, with which his name is permanently associated.

The Redaction of the Mishnah

There is no clear tradition extant regarding Judah ha-Nasi's approach and method in his redaction of the Mishnah. But from the work itself, as also from a comparison with the *beraitot* in the Tosefta, in the halakhic Midrashim, and in the Jerusalem and Babylonian Talmuds, the picture which emerges is that the Mishnah was not intended to serve as a collection of legal judgments in the accepted sense of the word, for in the main it does not constitute the definitive and decided *halakhah*, nor "a receptacle for the Oral Law," but rather a legal canon. The *amoraim* did indeed attribute to him emendations, interpolations, additions, and judgments with regard to the sources at his disposal. Not a few Mishnayot show such elaboration, while many quoted anonymously are the subject of divergent views in the *beraitot*. However, Judah ha-Nasi's redaction was not limited only to such instances but is apparent in the selection and compilation he made from the mishnaic collections of various *battei midrash* without even altering their phraseology. He apparently aimed at giving his Mishnah a variegated form and at making it representative of all the known collections of *mishnayot*, in order that it might be generally acceptable. Mention is made of the "thirteen different interpretations" of the Mishnayot, some of which Judah ha-Nasi taught to Ḥiyya (Ned. 41a), and from which he, exercising his judgment, selected and polished his Mishnah. Due to the pains he took, his compilation became the Mishnah and all the other collections – the "outside *mishnayot*," the **beraitot*. A "canon" was fixed, a standard by which the remainder of the *mishnayot* were judged. It marked the conclusion of the Mishnah, to which no new material was added as had hitherto been done to the other *mishnayot*. Instead, the new material was included in the Talmud, which was studied as a commentary on the Mishnah. Thus, although Judah ha-Nasi produced a legal codex, it did not put an end to the development of the *halakhah* but rather provided it with a solid foundation. His status and personal authority likewise helped to make his collection of *mishnayot* the basis of study and of legal decisions, second in significance and sanctity only to the Scriptures.

The admiration of Judah ha-Nasi's contemporaries for him and their appreciation of his personality found expression in Bar Kappara's announcement of his death: "The angels and the mortals took hold of the holy ark. The angels overpowered the mortals and the holy ark has been captured" (Ket. 104a; and TJ, Kil. 9:4, 32b), and in Yannai's proclamation on that day: "There is no priesthood today" (i.e., the laws pertaining to the priests were suspended for Judah ha-Nasi's funeral; TJ, Ber. 3:1, 6a); in the statement of Hillel b. Vallas that "not since the days of Moses were learning and high office combined in one person until Rabbi" (Git. 59a); and in the addendum to the Mishnah that "when Rabbi died humility and the fear of sin ceased" (Sot. 9:15; and see Maimonides' commentary ad loc.).

Many *amoraim* of the first generation were Judah's pupils: *Ḥanina b. Ḥama, *Yannai ha-Kohen, *Levi, *Rav, and also Ḥiyya, who was both his pupil and associate. On his deathbed he gave the following instructions: "My son Simeon [is to be] *ḥakham*, my son Gamaliel patriarch, Ḥanina b. Ḥama shall preside" (Ket. 103b). A comparison between this version and that in the Jerusalem Talmud (TJ, Ta'an. 4:2, 68a) shows that Judah ha-Nasi's intention was clearly to reinstate the form of group leadership which had prevailed before his time: patriarch, *av bet din*, and *ḥakham*, but that he left the right of appointment in the hands of the patriarch – his son – and not of the Sanhedrin, as had previously been the case [but cf. Goodblatt, 371–72]. Judah ha-Nasi was buried at Bet *She'arim (TJ, Kil. 9:4, 32b; TJ, Ket. 12:3, 35a: Eccles. R. 7:12; cf. Levine, 112–13). The medieval tradition that his tomb is at Sepphoris is not supported by the sources.

Tendencies in Recent Research

From about 1975 there has been a radical change in the scholarly attitude toward the talmudic *aggadah* as a source for the historical biography of the *tannaim* and the *amoraim*. Starting with J. *Neusner's later work on Johanan ben Zakkai (*Development of a Legend*) attention has shifted away from the critical analysis of talmudic traditions, in order to isolate "kernels" of historical fact which may then be used in order to reconstruct the image of a concrete historical figure, and has focused instead on the development of the talmudic legends themselves. This approach has been particularly successful with respect to figures like *Beruryah and *Elisha ben Avuya, whose very existence as historical figures is questionable at best, or like Rabban *Johanan ben Zakkai, whose historical identity lies buried in the shadowy past of the earliest tannaitic traditions, and is known to us primarily through the medium of a far later "normative tradition" consisting mostly of legend. The case of Judah ha-Nasi is exceptional, however, in that his concrete historical identity is present to us, both in the form of the Mishnah which he himself redacted, and as reflected in many contemporary reports and traditions which were recorded and redacted in or shortly after his own lifetime, sometimes by his own disciples and in his own academy. Therefore, even in the "post-Neusner" era historians have profitably continued to investigate the concrete historical role which Judah ha-Nasi played in Ereẓ Israel at the end of the second and the beginning of the third centuries, on the basis of talmudic tradition and contemporary archaeological and documentary evidence (see, for example, Levine). Nevertheless, two of Neusner's insights must be kept in mind when evaluating the historical reliability of different and often conflicting talmudic traditions. The first is that the Rabbis themselves were uninterested in talmudic biography as such, and almost never preserved continuous historical records concerning even the most significant rabbinic figures. Historical accounts – even the earliest and most "authentic" – are fragmentary, usually describing some particular episode or anecdote, and almost always reflecting some ethical, theological, or polemical agenda. The second insight derives from Neusner's synoptic studies, in which he concluded that later talmudic traditions are often literary expansions and elaborations of earlier literary sources, and therefore cannot always be considered to be independent historical sources. This second insight has been most thoroughly and rigorously developed in recent decades by S. *Friedman, who, in a series of studies on the historical *aggadot* of the Babylonian Talmud, has shown that its elaborate and colorful descriptions of events in the lives of the *tannaim* and the *amoraim* are often the product of deliberate and considered editorial revision of earlier sources. Using Friedman's method, S. Wald ("Hate and Peace") has recently analyzed an important Babylonian *aggadah* concerning Judah ha-Nasi found in BB 8a. This tradition has been used by various scholars as evidence for Judah ha-Nasi's vast wealth (Levine, 100), his establishment of an "aristocracy of learning" (see above), the kinds of taxes imposed by the Roman government on the Palestinian Jewish community (Levine, 103–4), and even as evidence for the "portrait of Judah ha-Nasi as a leader" (Meir, 226–27). Wald has shown that the first half of this tradition represents a conscious Babylonian revision of various Palestinian traditions, reflecting a particularly virulent form of consistent anti-*am-ha-arez* polemic characteristic of an important trend in post-amoraic Babylonian tradition (see Wald, *Pesaḥim III*, 211–39). The second half of this tradition – which was viewed by Levine as independent corroboration of the imposition in the time of Judah ha-Nasi of the "aurum coronarium" mentioned also in Bavli BB 143a – was shown by Wald to be a later Babylonian reworking of the earlier Babylonian tradition found further on in TB, BB 143a, whose relative originality and authenticity is confirmed by a parallel tradition found in TJ, Yoma 1:2, 39a. The second half of this tradition also reflects the same post-amoraic anti-*am-ha-arez* polemic. This example may serve as a warning against accepting the historical *aggadot* of the Babylonian Talmud at face value, even under the best of circumstances. When examined against the background of its immediate literary sources, and in the context of the ideological tendency of the family of Babylonian traditions to which it belongs, this *aggadah* is seen to reflect the ideological agenda of its redactor, who had little or no interest in the historical figure of Judah ha-Nasi or even in providing a coherent "image of Judah ha-Nasi as a leader."

BIBLIOGRAPHY: Graetz, Hist, index; S. Krauss, *Antoninus und Rabbi* (1910); Klein, in: JQR, 2 (1911–12), 545–56; idem, in: MGWJ, 78 (1934), 168f.; Frankel, Mishnah, 201–8; G. Bader, *Jewish Spiritual Heroes*, 1 (1940), 411–36; Wallach, in: JQR, 31 (1940/41), 259–86; A. Buechler, *Studies in Jewish History*, ed. by I. Brodie and J. Rabbinowitz (1956), 179–244; B. Mazar, *Beit She'arim*, 1 (1957[2]), 15–18; Ḥ. Albeck, *Mavo la-Mishnah* (1959), 99–115; Urbach, in: *Molad*, 17 (1959), 422–40; idem, in: *Divrei ha-Akademyah ha-Le'ummit ha-Yisre'elit le-Madda'im*, 2 (1965), 51–53; Alon, Toledot, 2 (1961[2]), 129–58; Epstein, Mishnah, 1 (1964[2]), 7–18; Epstein, Tanna'im, 200–30. **ADD. BIBLIOGRAPHY:** L.I. Levine, in: Z. Baras, S. Safrai, M. Stern, and Y. Tsafrir (eds.), *Eretz Israel from the Destruction of the Second Temple to the Moslem Conquest* (Heb., 1982), 94–118; A.I. Baumgarten, in: E.P. Sanders et al. (eds.), *Jewish and Christian Self-Definition*, 2 (1981), 213–25, 382–91; idem, in: *Journal for the Study of Judaism*, 12:2 (1982), 135–72; S.J.D. Cohen, in: PAAJR, 48 (1981), 62–68; D. Goodblatt, in: *Ẓion*,49 (1984), 349–74; S. Friedman, "The Historical Aggadah of the Babylonian Talmud" (Hebrew), in: S. Friedman (ed.), *Saul Lieberman Memorial Volume* (1993), 119–64; O. Meir, *Rabbi Judah the Patriarch* (Heb., 1999); S. Wald, "Hate and Peace in Rabbinic Consciousness," in: A. Bar-Levav (ed.), *War and Peace* (Heb., 2005); idem, *Pesaḥim III* (Heb., 2000), 211–39.

[*Encyclopaedia Hebraica* / Stephen G. Wald (2nd ed.)]

JUDAH HA-PARSI ("the Persian"), medieval scholar. No details are known about his personality or period. He is first mentioned by Abraham *Ibn Ezra (12th century), who states that Judah wrote a work attempting to prove that the ancient Israelites calculated the calendar according to the solar year, like the other peoples of antiquity. S. *Pinsker, and later H. *Graetz and I.H. *Weiss, identified him with the eighth-century sectarian leader *Yudghān, of Persian origin, but this identification seems highly doubtful. Some scholars consider Judah to have been a Karaite. These include S.I. Luzki, who ascribes to Judah a commentary on the Pentateuch. There is, however, no mention of Judah in Karaite literature.

BIBLIOGRAPHY: S. Pinsker, *Likkutei Kadmoniyyot* (1860), 24, 25 (first pagination); Mann, Texts, 2 (1935), 472.

[Isaak Dov Ber Markon]

JUDAH ḤASID (Segal), HA-LEVI (1660?–1700), Shabbatean preacher, born in Dubno. Of his early life nothing is known, but it is possible that he is "the ḥasid Judah Ashkenazi," who stayed in Italy in 1678 and is mentioned in the responsa of contemporaries. His affinity with the Shabbatean movement in Poland has been proved from reliable sources which have been verified by modern research. Judah was *Maggid* in Szydlowiec, Lithuania, in 1695, when the Shabbatean preacher Zadok b. Shemariah visited that town. Judah became active in preparing the people for the second appearance of *Shabbetai Ẓevi (in 1706) which was anticipated by many. An impressive preacher, he traveled throughout the communities and urged total repentance, mortifications, and fasts. In 1697, a "holy community" (*ḥavurah kedoshah*), consisting of 31 families of scholars, organized itself in order to emigrate together to Jerusalem and there await the revelation of the Messiah. Early in 1699 they left Poland for Moravia and stopped for a long time at Nikolsburg, where there were many Shabbateans. It is reported that in the spring of 1699 about ten scholars assembled there, "all believers" (i.e., Shabbateans), among them Judah, Heshel *Ẓoref, and Ḥayyim Malakh, who discussed matters pertaining to Shabbetai Ẓevi "with great joy until midnight" (Ms. Ben-Ẓvi Institute, Jerusalem). Some leaders of the group, among them Judah, left Nikolsburg and wandered through Germany and Austria in 1700, where they urged the communities to repent and to contribute toward the support of the emigrants in Ereẓ Israel. They received sympathy and support from some rabbis and wealthy men in the communities, but some opposed them and suspected Judah of being Shabbatean in secret. Emigrants from numerous circles joined the group, including some scholars, apparently mainly from circles with Shabbatean tendencies. It is reported that the number of emigrants traveling from Germany and Moravia via Turkey or Italy reached 1,300, of whom approximately 500 died en route. These numbers perhaps are exaggerated, but there is no doubt that several hundred journeyed to Jerusalem.

Judah traveled through Italy and arrived in Jerusalem on Oct. 14, 1700; he died suddenly a few days later. His death disheartened the remnants of his followers. After they had been in the country for a few years, disputes broke out among them. Some remained in Jerusalem, others returned and joined various Shabbatean groups in Poland and Germany, and others, out of disappointment, converted to Islam or to Christianity. Among the latter was Judah's nephew. Judah's group was the first organized Ashkenazi immigration to Ereẓ Israel. It left a deep impact on his contemporaries, and there are many testimonies to its appearance and customs, as well as sermons and *zemirot* by some of its members. According to tradition, Judah succeeded in buying a large plot in the Old City, on which was built 150 years later the chief synagogue of the Ashkenazi community in Jerusalem, Ḥurvat R. Yehudah he-Ḥasid.

BIBLIOGRAPHY: Z. Rubashov, in: *Reshumot-Me'assef le-Divrei Zikhronot*, 2 (1927²), 461–93 (second set of *Reshumot*); Yaari, Sheluhei, 322–3; G. Scholem, *Beit Yisrael be-Polin*, 2 (1953), 56; M. Benayahu, in: *Sefunot*, 3–4 (1960), 133–82; S. Krauss, in: *Abhandlungen zur Erinnerung an Hirsch Perez Chajes* (1933), 51–94.

[Gershom Scholem]

JUDAH LEIB BEN BARUCH (fl. 1800), talmudic scholar and kabbalist. Judah was the brother and disciple of *Shneur Zalman of Lyady, the founder of the *Chabad movement, and preacher at Yanovichi. He recorded his brother's teachings in Hebrew, including his homilies which appeared later as *Torah Or* (Kopys, 1837). Some contributions by Judah are included in the *siddur* of Shneur Zalman. After his brother's death, he corrected Shneur Zalman's Shulḥan Arukh and approved a new edition (*ibid.*, 1822). There was a three-sided dispute among the latter's son, the "middle rabbi," and *Aaron of Starosielce over who was to succeed Shneur Zalman. Judah, in a letter addressed to Aaron, supported his nephew. The "third rabbi," Menahem Mendel of Lubavich (see *Schneersohn family), included several contributions by Judah in his responsa. After Judah's death, his grandson, Ze'ev Wolf, published a tract by Judah *She'erit Yehudah*, which contains instructions for the salting of meat as well as responsa and elucidations of his brother's teachings (Vilna, 1841).

BIBLIOGRAPHY: H.M. Heilman, *Beit Rabbi* (Heb., 1965), 109f., 166f.

[Samuel Abba Horodezky]

JUDAH LEIB BEN ENOCH ZUNDEL (1645–1705), German rabbi. Judah Leib's father was rabbi of Gnesen (Gniezno), Poznania. As a result of the *Chmielnicki persecutions (1648) he fled to Germany and became rabbi of the district of Swabia, settling in Oettingen. Judah Leib succeeded him in 1675 but took up his residence in the town of Pfersee, where he remained until his death. He was the author of *Ḥinnukh Beit Yehudah* (Frankfurt, 1708), containing 145 responsa, some of which are by his father, on the four sections of the Shulḥan Arukh. It was published posthumously by his son Ḥanokh Enoch, *av bet din* of Schnaittach. Another work, *Reshit Bikkurim* (*ibid.*, 1708), sermons by Judah Leib and his father, was also published by the son. It contains homilies for festivals and Sabbaths based upon Joseph Albo's three principles of faith – the existence of God, revelation, and reward and punishment. According to his son, this work consists of excerpts from a commentary on the whole Bible which Judah Leib had intended publishing.

BIBLIOGRAPHY: Michael, Or, no. 906; J. Perles, in: MGWJ, 14 (1865), 122; S. Wiener, *Kohelet Moshe* (1904), 515, no. 4256; A. Heppner and J. Herzberg, *Aus Vergangenheit und Gegenwart der Juden in… den Posener Landen* (1909), 407.

[Yehoshua Horowitz]

JUDAH LEIB BEN HILLEL OF SCHWERSENZ (17th century), rabbi of Schwersenz (Posen). He was the author of *Ḥakham Lev* (Fuerth, 1693), a short commentary on the 613 biblical and rabbinical precepts according to the *Mishneh Torah* by Maimonides and the *Sefer Mitzvot Gadol* by *Moses b. Jacob of Coucy. A Latin translation was published (Lund, 1731) with notes by Karl Schulten. In his apologia in the introduction to *Ḥakham Lev*, the author points out that he dealt only briefly with precepts of practical application which are to be found in the Shulḥan Arukh, but at greater length with laws which have no practical application. The succinct style of the book is due to the fact that it was intended for those who wished to study daily the 613 precepts with their reasons and explanations.

BIBLIOGRAPHY: Michael, Or, no. 1009; Steinschneider, Cat Bod, 1328 no. 5714; S. Wiener, *Kohelet Moshe* (1893–1918), 500 no. 4148; A. Heppner and J. Herzberg, *Aus Vergangenheit und Gegenwart der Juden… in den Posener Landen* (1909), 977f.

[Yehoshua Horowitz]

JUDAH LOEW (Liwa, Loeb) BEN BEZALEL (known as **Der Hohe Rabbi Loew** and **MaHaRaL mi-Prag**; c. 1525–1609), rabbi, talmudist, moralist, and mathematician. Judah Loew was the scion of a noble family which hailed from Worms. His father, Bezalel b. Ḥayyim, was the brother-in-law of R. Isaac Klauber of Posen, the grandfather of Solomon *Luria. Judah Loew's older brother, Ḥayyim b. *Bezalel, and his two younger brothers, Sinai and Samson, were also scholars of repute. (According to one tradition, however, Judah was the youngest son.) His teachers are unknown. From 1553 to 1573 he was *Landesrabbiner* of Moravia in Mikulov (Nikolsburg) after which he went to Prague. There he founded a yeshivah called Die Klaus, organized circles for the study of the Mishnah, to which he attached great importance, and regulated the statutes of the *ḥevra kaddisha*, founded in 1564. He remained in Prague until 1584, and from then until 1588 served as rabbi in Moravia (according to others, in Posen), eventually returning to Prague. On the third of Adar 5352 (Feb. 16, 1592) he was granted an interview by Emperor *Rudolph II, but it is not known what its purpose was. There seems little basis for the belief that it was due to their common interest in alchemy. Shortly afterward he left Prague for Posen, where he became chief rabbi; several years later he returned to Prague, becoming its chief rabbi and remaining there until his death.

Judah Loew was revered for his piety and asceticism. He was a great scholar, whose knowledge was not confined to religious subjects, but embraced secular studies as well, particularly mathematics. He was an outstanding personality, held in the highest repute by Jews and non-Jews alike. The astronomer, Tycho Brahe, with whom he enjoyed a social relationship, is said to have arranged his audience with the emperor. Judah preferred recourse to talmudic sources rather than the use of Maimonides' code or the *Tur* for deciding cases of Jewish law (cf. *Netivot Olam, Netiv ha-Torah*, 15). He was a great educationalist whose pedagogic views are of contemporary relevance. Dissatisfied with current methods of education, he strongly criticized his contemporaries for not following the manner of education indicated in Mishnah *Avot* 5:21, which takes into consideration the age of the student and the subjects taught. The "fools nowadays," he said, "teach boys Bible with the commentary of Rashi, which they do not understand, and also Talmud, which they cannot yet grasp" (see the references in Assaf, *Mekorot*, 1 (1925), 48ff.). Furthermore, he claimed that they neglected the study of the Mishnah. He also strongly opposed *pilpul*, and although he sharply criticized Azariah de' *Rossi (*Be'er ha-Golah*, ch. 6), he favored scientific study which did not contradict the principles of Judaism. According to S.J. Rapaport, he did not engage in Kabbalah; G. Scholem, on the other hand, regards him as the forerunner of Ḥasidism in that he popularized kabbalistic ideas. His language is not kabbalistic, and this fact stands in the way of a full understanding of his teaching to the present day. He stresses that philosophy and esoteric love are diametrically opposed to one another ("two things each of which contradicts and opposes the other" – *Derekh Ḥayyim*, ch. 5) and unhesitatingly associates himself with the world of Kabbalah.

Judah Loew's works in the fields of ethics, philosophy, and homiletics are all based on the same homiletical system: exegetical and homiletical interpretation of the sayings of the rabbis of the Talmud. His whole life's work may be regarded as a new interpretation of the *aggadah*. Every chapter (and nearly every paragraph) in his many works opens with a quotation from the traditional sources, which he then goes on to interpret in his unique fashion. His close attachment to the *aggadah* may be the reason for his strong defense of oral tradition against its Italian critics, which was incorporated in his *Be'er ha-Golah*. Even his systematic work on ethics, *Netivot Olam*, which was to become one of the most popular and influential works in the field, is also based on reinterpretation of aggadic passages. Although chapters of his works may be read as a late offspring of the philosophical moralistic literature of the Spanish period, the philosophical terms which he employs do not bear their original meanings but are given new ones geared to the expression of his ideas. Some passages in his writings, as well as some of his basic views regarding the transcendent meaning of the Torah, of prayer, etc., seem to point to familiarity with Kabbalah. He never states kabbalistic ideas as such but seems to have made use of them in his interpretation of talmudic passages. The question has not been sufficiently studied, however, to permit definite conclusions. The most important questions which he tried to solve in his many works were the problem of the relationship between Israel and God, with the Torah serving as mediator between them, and the problem of the *galut*, the reasons for it, and the manner of its termination. His *Tiferet Yisrael* and *Gevurot ha-Shem* are completely devoted to these subjects, and he deals with them in his other works as well.

Judah Loew rejects the Aristotelian view, which is adumbrated mainly by Maimonides, that intellectual perfection is the supreme human goal. In his opinion the study of Torah and observance of its precepts bring man to this goal, and study of the Torah for its own sake has a metaphysical influence and brings about communion with God. The precepts, implemented by means of physical actions, are symbols whereby man comes closer to the Creator and penetrates to the secrets of the Divine; this is the true purpose of the ceremonial precepts.

He lived in an era of the revival of the sciences and displayed some familiarity with scientific studies, but the new discoveries did not influence his cosmic outlook. He knew about Copernicus but remained faithful to the rabbinic view of cosmogony, for, he said, it was received by them from Moses at Sinai who received it from God Who alone can possibly know the truth (*Netivot Olam, Netiv ha-Torah*). An echo of the discovery of America also reached his ears: "They say that recently a certain place has been found, called by them a new world, previously undiscovered" (*Neẓaḥ Yisrael*, ch. 34); in consequence he expressed the hope that the ten tribes too would one day be discovered in a country still unknown. He drew his scientific explanations, generally speaking, from Aristotle's natural philosophy which was generally accepted in the Middle Ages, and his psychological outlook was chiefly Platonic with the addition of Aristotelian and other elements. He also took from Plato the division of people into three classes: philosophers (= talmudic scholars), watchmen (= those who observe precepts), and breadwinners (= merchants). Although the spirit of the Renaissance and of humanism reached him, he remained fundamentally anchored to the outlooks common in the Middle Ages. A number of his formulations in social problems would appear to be very forward looking, but the subject has still to be investigated.

In fixing the standard for *halakhah*, he develops the view that the source of dispute in *halakhah* lies in the diversity of reality and its numerous aspects, which human intelligence cannot fully comprehend, and since human methods of understanding differ – "each one receives one aspect in accordance with his lot" (*Be'er ha-Golah*, ch. 1).

Fundamental Doctrines

NATURAL ORDER. By the terms "nature," "the natural order," "natural reality," and the like, that run like a golden thread throughout all his writings, he refers to the regular physical order of the universe. The various phenomena are connected one with another in a logical connection of cause and effect that can be rationally explained. This order, however, has no validity for the relationship between the Creator and the universe, for two reasons: (a) God created the system of regularity in nature of His own free will; (b) there exist phenomena outside the natural order which are deviations from the fixed order, i.e., the miracles. Since it is inconceivable that God should lay down laws and abrogate them, establish an order and destroy it – he assumes that in principle the natural order is only enduring and valid in this world, while in the upper world, a different order, "the discrete," exists. The miracle has its source in this upper world and occurs when this upper world temporarily penetrates and intrudes into this world. Hence even phenomena that at first sight appear as deviations are ab initio subject to special rules of their own.

THE UNIQUE NATURE OF THE JEWISH PEOPLE AND ITS STATUS. Since the time of Judah Halevi no one had stressed the unique nature of the people of Israel, its mission and its destiny, as did Judah Loew. God chose Israel per se and not because of the merits of the patriarchs. Hence it cannot be said that only when Israel fulfills the will of the Omnipresent the choice exists, but when they rebel it is annulled. This being so, the claim of Christians that the exile is proof that God has forsaken His people is similarly nullified. Cancellation of the choice would have involved a change in reality "until the world would have become different from what it was previously," and this is an impossibility. He terms the choice of Israel *beḥirah kelalit* ("general choice"), and the tie with God which constitutes the nature of the choice *devekut kelalit* ("general attachment").

Israel constitutes the "form," whereas other nations constitute the "matter." From this stem the differences in their ethical conduct and in their comprehension of divine matters. In Israel the forces of the soul prevail, among the nations – physical forces.

EXILE AND REDEMPTION. The natural order is not limited to natural phenomena, it also comprehends human relations. He holds that the exile is a "departure" (deviation) from the natural order of the world, a breakdown in the universal system of relations, in the otherwise unchangeable regularity. The exile expresses itself in three ways:

(1) uprooting from the natural locality; every nation has a country specifically its own, and separation from one's country and dwelling beyond it deleteriously affect the natural order;

(2) loss of political independence and subjection to aliens – "for the subjection of one nation to another does not accord with the proper order of reality, for it is the right of each nation to be free";

(3) the dispersion – every nation is a distinct entity and in the absence of a territorial center it loses its unity; it is not "a complete compact nation" (*Neẓaḥ Yisrael* ch. 1).

However, every departure from the natural order is but a passing phenomenon – hence the conviction of, and faith in, the messianic redemption which will inevitably come about and remedy the anomaly of the exile (see *Galut). Yet despite all his attachment to the messianic faith, he was utterly opposed to "forcing the end" (of the exile) and to the actual messianic speculations of his time. Not only the natural order but its consequences were established by the will of God, and man should not attempt to change them; the decree of God may not be nullified by force. One must pray for the redemption but not "too much," not even in a generation of religious persecution. Even to calculate the time of the redemption is forbidden; it will come in its due time. Shortly before the redemption "the degradation of Israel will be greater than it ever was," and precisely from this "absence" will the redemption emerge. The apocalyptic *aggadot* are explained allegorically by Judah Loew in such a way that the image of the personal Messiah is blurred. He explains the *aggadah* about the birth of the Messiah on the day the Temple was destroyed to the effect that "this birth is not an actual physical birth … but it means that the Messiah was born from the point of view of the messianic potentiality existing in the world."

He discusses the cosmopolitan basis of the exile. Though indeed it is fitting that the Israelite nation, which is the essence of the world, should have for its dwelling place Ereẓ Israel, which is the essence of the geographical world, nevertheless, when they were exiled from the land the whole world became their locality. In accordance with the midrashic saying "wherever Israel went into exile the Divine Presence accompanied them," he stresses that it is fitting that the Divine Presence should be with Israel in exile more than in Ereẓ Israel. In consequence he emphasizes the need for the Jewish people to work for their survival in exile by separating themselves from the nations and by observing the precepts, such as congregational prayer, practice of charity, and study of Torah.

Judah Loew was a prolific writer. His works include:

(1) *Derekh Ḥayyim*, commentary on *Avot* (Cracow, 1589);

(2) *Netivot Olam*, on ethics, the second part of *Derekh Ḥayyim* (Prague, 1596);

(3) *Tiferet Yisrael*, on the excellence of the Torah and the commandments (Prague, 1593);

(4) *Be'er ha-Golah*, on difficult talmudic passages, and, at the same time, a defense of the Talmud, the second part of *Tiferet Yisrael* (Prague, 1598);

(5) *Neẓaḥ Yisrael*, on exile, messianic redemption, and repentance (Prague, 1599);

(6) *Or Ḥadash* on *Megillat Esther* and Purim, and

(7) *Ner Mitzvah* on Ḥanukkah (Prague, 1600);

(8) *Gur Aryeh*, commentary on Rashi, including comments on Bible, Targum, and Midrash (Prague, 1578);

(9) *Gevurot ha-Shem*, on the Exodus from Egypt, the *Haggadah*, and the laws of Pesaḥ (Cracow, 1582);

(10) *Gur Aryeh*, novellae on tractates *Shabbat, Eruvin*, and *Pesaḥim* (Lvov, 1863);

(11) *Haggadah shel Pesaḥ*, with a discourse on *Shabbat ha-Gadol* (1589);

(12) *Ḥiddushei Yoreh De'ah*, novellae on *Tur Yoreh De'ah* (Amsterdam, 1775);

(13) *Sefer Perushei Maharal mi-Prag le-Aggadot ha-Shas* (1959–60);

(14) sermons, novellae, and responsa, some published and others still in manuscript. Most of the above-mentioned works have appeared in several editions.

He is unique in the history of Hebrew literature by virtue of his not having belonged to any defined school, or having been followed by disciples who subscribed to his ideas. He was a lone thinker, who developed his own philosophy as well as its method of presentation. It is ironic that he is better known to later generations for the unfounded and atypical legend that he was the creator of the famous Prague *golem* (he seems not to have dealt with magic) than for his original and profound ideas (see *Golem). Rabbi A.I. Kook used his sayings and methods extensively in his works, and a considerable revival of his ideas has taken place among 20th-century Jewish thinkers. Of his pupils, particular mention should be made of Yom Tov *Heller, Elijah *Loans, and David *Gans (the author of *Ẓemaḥ David*).

BIBLIOGRAPHY: M. Perels, *Megillat Yuḥasin* (1902²); C. Bloch, *The Golem; legends of the ghetto of Prague* (1925); A. Gottesdiener, in: *Azkarah… Kook*, 4 (1937), 253–443; M. Buber, *Bein Am le-Arẓo* (1945), 78–91; Y. Hertzberg, *Yosele ha-Golem ve-Yoẓero Maharal mi-Prag* (1947); A. Mauskopf, *Religious Philosophy of the Maharal of Prague* (1949); B.Z. Bokser, *From the World of the Cabbalah – the Philosophy of Rabbi Judah Loew of Prague* (1954); F. Thieberger, *The Great Rabbi Loew of Prague* (1954); Scholem, Shabbetai Ẓevi, 1 (1957), 51–52, 173; idem, *Zur Kabbala und ihrer Symbolik* (1960), 209–59; M.S. Kasher and J.J. Blacherowitz (eds.), *Sefer Perushei Maharal mi-Prag*, 1 (1958), 7–40 (introd.); A. Kariv (ed.), *Kitvei Maharal mi-Prag – Mivḥar* (1960), introd.; A.F. Kleinberger, *Ha-Maḥashavah ha-Pedagogit shel ha-Maharal mi-Prag* (1962); G. Vajda, in: REJ, 123 (1964), 225–33; O. Muneles (ed.), *Prague Ghetto in the Renaissance Period* (1965), 75–84; idem, in: *Judaica Bohemiae*, 5 (1969), 103–7, 117–22; A. Neher, *Le Puits de l'Exil; la théologie dialectique du Maharal de Prague* (1966); idem, in: M. Zahari and A. Tartakover (eds.), *Hagut Ivrit be-Europah* (1969), 107–17; Y. Kohen-Yashar, *Bibliografyah Shimmushit shel Kitvei ha-Maharal mi-Prag* (1967); B. Gross, *L'éternité d'Israël*, 2 vols. (1968); idem, *Le messianisme juif* (1969); T. Dreyfus, *Dieu parle aux hommes; la révélation selon le Maharal de Prague* (1969).

JUDAH MACCABEE, one of the great warriors of history, who laid the foundation of the future Hasmonean state. Judah, the third son of *Mattathias the Hasmonean, assumed leadership of the revolt against *Antiochus Epiphanes in accordance with the deathbed disposition of his father. No suggestion that has been put forward to explain the meaning of his name (Heb. מַכַּבִּי or מַקַּבִּי (Gr. Μακκαβᾶιος)) or those of the other Hasmonean brothers is satisfactory. His exceptional military talent made him the natural choice as military commander of the rebels, and the author of I Maccabees is unstinting in praise of his valor. Because of the disparity between the contending forces during the first days of the revolt, Judah's strategy was to avoid any involvement with the regular army of the Seleucids, but to attack the enemy from ambush, in order to give them a feeling of insecurity. Already at the beginning of the struggle he succeeded in defeating a small Syrian force under the command of *Apollonius, who was killed. Judah took possession of his sword which he used until his death as a symbol of vengeance. More important was his success in battle against Seron, "the commander of the Syrian army." The choice of the neighborhood of Beth-Horon as the field of battle and the coordination of the limited forces at his disposal testify to Judah's outstanding tactical skill, but his military talent was revealed in all its brilliance in the third battle, near Emmaus. This time he faced regular forces led by *Gorgias, an experienced officer. This force had not been dispatched by Antiochus, who at the time was in the northern provinces of his kingdom, but by Lysias, whom the king, on the eve of his departure for the east, had appointed as regent of the western sector of the kingdom and tutor to the young crown prince, the future Antiochus V Eupator. By forced night march, Judah succeeded in eluding Gorgias, who had intended to attack and destroy his enemy in their camp. He then made a surprise attack upon the Syrian camp near Emmaus while Gorgias was searching for him in the mountains. The Syrian commander had no alternative but to withdraw to the coast. This defeat convinced Lysias that he must prepare for a serious and prolonged war. He accordingly assembled a new and larger army and marched to meet Judah. Once again, however, the Jewish commander succeeded in overcoming the numerically superior enemy in a great battle near Beth-Zur. This victory opened up the road to Jerusalem, which Judah entered at the head of his army; he purified the defiled Temple and instituted a festival of eight days on the 25th of Kislev of the year 148 of the Seleucid era corresponding to 164 B.C.E., which became a permanent festival, *Ḥanukkah. It was the first step on the road to ultimate independence.

Hard upon these events came news that the enemies of the Jews had attacked the sparse Jewish settlements in Gilead, in Transjordan, and in Galilee. Judah immediately went to their aid. His brother, Simeon, sent to Galilee at the head of 3,000 men, successfully fulfilled his task and transplanted a substantial portion of the Jewish settlements, including women and children, to Judea. Galilee, however, does not apparently seem to have been evacuated of its Jewish population, since two generations later, when John Hyrcanus conquered it, he found it largely inhabited by Jews. A more difficult task was undertaken by Judah and his younger brother Jonathan, who were compelled to engage in fierce fighting with the Arabian tribes before they could rescue the Jews concentrated in fortified towns in Gilead. At the conclusion of the fighting in Transjordan, Judah turned against the Edomites in the south, captured and destroyed Hebron, and, after marching against the coastal land of the Philistines, returned to Judea with much booty. Judah now laid siege to the Syrian army garrison in the *Acra, the fortress of Jerusalem. In response to desperate appeals from the besieged – who included not only Syrians but also hellenized Jews – Lysias the regent, together with the young king Antiochus Eupator (Antiochus Epiphanes having died in the meantime in the east) came out to do battle at the head of a powerful army. Lysias skirted Judea as he had done in his first campaign, entering it from the south, and besieged Beth-Zur. Judah raised the siege of the Acra and went to meet Lysias, but was defeated in a battle near Bet Zekharyah and withdrew to Jerusalem. Beth-Zur was compelled to surrender and Lysias reached Jerusalem, besieging Judah on Mount Zion. The defenders found themselves in dire straits; their provisions were exhausted, it being a sabbatical year. The situation changed unexpectedly, however; news reached the Syrian camp that Philip, commander in chief of Antiochus, having been appointed regent by the monarch before his death, was about to enter Antioch and seize power. Lysias thereupon decided to propose a peaceful settlement to the Jews based on the restoration of religious freedom, i.e., the repeal of the edicts of Antiochus Epiphanes.

The order of events thus far has followed I Maccabees. According to II Maccabees, however, the order is: Judah's victory over Gorgias and Nicanor, his conquest of Jerusalem, the death of Antiochus Epiphanes, the purification of the temple, the rise to power of Antiochus Eupator, and the wars with the neighboring peoples. Only after these does II Maccabees give the details of the first campaign of Lysias, as a result of which peace was established between the Jews and the Syrians. It continues with the wars between the Jews and their neighbors, and finally relates the second campaign of Lysias against Judah and the subsequent signing of a peace treaty. With this the war for religious freedom came to an end, but it did not bring peace. In place of war against the external enemy, an internal struggle now took place between the nationalist party led by Judah and between the Hellenist party. Changes in the situation in Syria led to a strengthening of the Maccabees and a weakening of the Hellenists among the people. Demetrius I, who fled from Rome in defiance of the Roman senate, appeared on the scene in Syria. Lysias and the young Antiochus Eupator were brought captive before him and put to death. In view of the happenings in Judea and the strengthening of the nationalists, the Hellenist party turned to the new king with a request for help. The delegation was led by Alcimus, a priest who did not, however, belong to a high priestly family. He complained to Demetrius of the persecution of the Hellenist party in Judea and was granted his request to be appointed high priest under the protection of the king's army. Demetrius sent to Judea a new army led by Bacchides, and Alcimus accompanied him as high priest. The *Hassideans, taking it for granted that the religious war was over, received him cordially, but Alcimus, acting in Judea with an iron hand, had 60 of them executed. This again changed the internal situation in Judea in favor of the nationalist party. Judah wreaked havoc among the followers of Alcimus, so that after Bacchides' return to Antioch, Alcimus was again compelled to seek help from the Syrians. Demetrius dispatched a new army with *Nicanor at its head, but Nicanor's plan to seize Judah by guile failed and the war was renewed. The decisive moment came in a battle near Adasa, on the 13th Adar, 161 B.C.E., in which Nicanor was killed and his army destroyed. The annual "Day of Nicanor" was instituted to commemorate this brilliant victory.

Judah then sent a delegation to Rome headed by Eupolemus son of Johanan and Jason son of Eleazar (the fact that their names were Greek and their fathers' Hebrew is noteworthy), with the request for an alliance. The outcome of the mission was less than Judah had hoped for, the Romans committing themselves only to such obligations as were in their own interests. The letter dispatched by the senate to Demetrius, forbidding him to act in a hostile manner against the Jews, failed to exercise any influence on him, for on receipt of the news of Nicanor's defeat he dispatched a new army commanded by Bacchides. This time the Syrian forces were numerically so superior that most of Judah's men left the field of battle and advised their leader to do likewise and to await a more favorable opportunity. Despite this, Judah decided to try his fortune once more. His final battle was near Elasa (so far unidentified). The outcome was inevitable: Judah and those who remained faithful to him were killed. His body was taken by his brothers from the battlefield and buried in the family sepulcher in Modi'in. Virtually all that is known about Judah Maccabee is contained in the Books of the Maccabees (in the Apocrypha) and in Josephus, largely dependent on this source.

[Abraham Schalit]

In the Arts

As warrior hero and national liberator, Judah Maccabee has inspired many writers, and several artists and composers. In literature, however, he makes an unexpectedly late appearance, little of significance having been written before the 17th century. William Houghton's *Judas Maccabaeus*, performed in about 1601 but now lost, is thought to have been the first drama on the theme; however, the earliest surviving literary work is *El Macabeo* (Naples, 1638), a somewhat bombastic Castilian epic by the Portuguese Marrano author Miguel de *Silveyra. Two other 17th century works were *La chevalerie de Judas Macabé* by the French dramatist and tragedian Pierre du Ryer (c. 1600–1658) and the anonymous neo-Latin "melodrama" *Judas Machabaeus* (Rome, 1695). Interest in the subject only revived in the 19th century, with *Giuda Macabeo, ossia la morte di Nicanore…* (1839), an Italian "azione sacra" on which Vallicella based an oratorio. One of the best-known literary works on the theme was *Judas Maccabaeus* (1872), a five-act verse tragedy by the U.S. poet Henry Wadsworth Longfellow. In verse rising at times to a Miltonic grandeur, Longfellow shows how Antiochus, bent on forcibly hellenizing the Jews, finds a compliant tool in the high priest Jason. Act II retells the tragic Apocryphal story of Hannah ("Máhala") and her seven sons, the resolute Judah first appearing only in Act III.

A Hebrew version of Longfellow's play was published by J. Massel in 1900. Two later 19th-century interpretations of the story were *Judas Makkabaeus*, a novella by the German writer Josef Eduard Konrad Bischoff which appeared in *Der Gefangene von Kuestrin* (1885); and *The Hammer* (1890), a book by Alfred J. Church and Richmond Seeley. Several Jewish authors of the 20th century also turned to the subject. They include Jacob Benjamin Katznelson (1855–1930), who wrote the poem *Alilot Gibbor ha-Yehudim Yehudah ha-Makkabi le-Veit ha-Ḥashmona'im* (1922); the U.S. novelist Howard *Fast (*My Glorious Brothers*, 1948); the Yiddish writer Moses Schulstein, who wrote the dramatic poem "*Yehudah ha-Makkabi*" (in *A Layter tsu der Zun*, 1954); and Jacob *Fichmann, whose "*Yehudah ha-Makkabi*" is one of the heroic tales included in *Sippurim le-Mofet* (1954). Many children's plays have also been written on the theme by various Jewish authors. During World War II the Swiss-German writer Karl Boxler published his novel *Judas Makkabaeus; ein Kleinvolk kaempft um Glaube und Heimat* (1943), the subtitle of which suggests that Swiss democrats then drew a parallel between their own national hero, William Tell, and the leader of the Maccabean revolt against foreign tyranny.

In art, during the Middle Ages, Judah Maccabee was regarded as one of the heroes of the Old Testament. He figures in a tenth-century illuminated manuscript of the *Libri Maccabaeorum* (Leyden University Library); and the late medieval French artist Jean Fouquet painted an illustration of Judah triumphing over his enemies for his famous manuscript of Josephus (Bibliothèque Nationale, Paris). A painting by Rubens of Judah Maccabee praying for the dead is of special interest. In II Maccabees 12:39–48 there is an account of an episode in which Judah's troops found stolen idolatrous charms on the corpses of Jewish warriors slain on the battlefield. He therefore offered prayers and an expiatory sacrifice for these warriors who had died in a state of sin. During the Counter-Reformation the passage was used by Catholics against Protestants in order to justify the doctrine of purgatory. Accordingly, Rubens painted the scene for the Chapel of the Dead in Tournai Cathedral. This painting is now in the Nantes Museum. In the 19th century, Paul Gustave Doré executed an engraving of Judah Maccabee victoriously pursuing the shattered troops of the Syrian enemy.

In music, almost all the compositions inspired by the Hasmonean revolt are primarily concerned with Judah. The first of distinction – and still the outstanding work – was Handel's oratorio *Judas Maccabaeus*, which had its première in London in 1747. This work, with libretto by Thomas Morrell, had been written for the celebrations following the Duke of Cumberland's victory over the Scottish Jacobite rebels at the battle of Culloden (1746); and its heroic and martial spirit was set off, but in no way lessened, by the doleful and lyrical passages of the composition. The oratorio's most famous chorus is "See, the conqu'ring hero comes." Handel's *Judas Maccabaeus* was often performed in Ereẓ Israel, and the "conqu'ring hero" melody has become a Ḥanukkah song.

BIBLIOGRAPHY: Schuerer, Gesch, index; Schuerer, Hist, index; Klausner, Bayit Sheni, index; J. Wellhausen, *Israelitische und juedische Geschichte* (1897[3]). 252ff.; Niese, in: *Hermes*, 35 (1900), 268–307, 453–527; E. Meyer, *Ursprung und Anfaenge des Christentums*, 2 (1921), 205ff.; Avi-Yonah, in: *Sefer Yoḥanan Levi* (1949), 13–24; W.R. Farmer, *Maccabees, Zealots and Josephus* (1956), index; V. Tcherikover, *Hellenistic Civilization and the Jews* (1959), index; E. Bickerman, *From Ezra to the Last of the Maccabees* (1962), 112ff.; E.R. Bevan, *Jerusalem under the High Priests* (1920[2]), 69, 88–99; C.R. Conder, *Judas Maccabaeus and the Jewish War of Independence* (1879); S. Zeitlin, *The Rise and Fall of the Judaean State*, 1 (1962), index. **ADD. BIBLIOGRAPHY:** E.J. Bickerman, "The Maccabean Uprising: An Interpretation," in: J. Goldin (ed.), *The Jewish Expression* (1976), 66–86; F. Millar, "The Background to the Maccabean Revolution…," in: *Journal of Jewish Studies* 29 (1978), 1–12; D. Mendels, *The Land of Israel as a Political Concept in Hasmonean Literature* (1987); idem, *The Rise and Fall of Jewish Nationalism* (1992); D. Amit and H. Eshel, *The Days of the Hasmonean Dynasty* (1995).

JUDAISM, the religion, philosophy, and way of life of the Jews.

DEFINITION

The term Judaism is first found among the Greek-speaking Jews of the first century C.E. (*Judaismes*, see II Macc. 2:21; 8:1; 14:38; Gal. 1:13–14). Its Hebrew equivalent, *Yahadut*, found only occasionally in medieval literature (e.g., Ibn Ezra to Deut. 21:13), but used frequently in modern times, has parallels neither in the Bible (but see Esth. 8:17, *mityahadim*, "became Jews") nor in the rabbinic literature. (The term *dat Yehudit*, found in Ket. 7:6, means no more than the Jewish law, custom, or practice in a particular instance, e.g., that a married woman should not spin or have her head uncovered in the street.)

The Term "Torah"

The term generally used in the classical sources for the whole body of Jewish teaching is *Torah, "doctrine," "teaching." Thus the Talmud (Shab. 31a) tells the story of a heathen who wished to be converted to the Jewish faith but only on the understanding that he would be taught the whole of the Torah while standing on one leg. Hillel accepted him and, in response to his request, replied: "That which is hateful unto thee do not do unto thy neighbor. This is the whole of the Torah. The rest is commentary. Go and study." Presumably if the Greek-speaking Jews had told the story they would have made the prospective convert demand to be taught Judaism while standing on one leg.

Modern Distinctions Between "Judaism" and "Torah"

In modern usage the terms "Judaism" and "Torah" are virtually interchangeable, but the former has on the whole a more humanistic nuance while "Torah" calls attention to the divine, revelatory aspects. The term "secular Judaism" – used to describe the philosophy of Jews who accept specific Jewish values but who reject the Jewish religion – is not, therefore, self-contradictory as the term "secular Torah" would be. (In modern Hebrew, however, the word *torah* is also used for "doctrine" or "theory" (e.g., "the Marxist theory"), and in this sense it would also be logically possible to speak of a secular *torah*. In English transliteration the two meanings might be distinguished by using a capital *T* for the one and a small *t* for the other, but this is not possible in Hebrew which knows of no distinction between small and capital letters.)

A further difference in nuance, stemming from the first, is that "Torah" refers to the eternal, static elements in Jewish life and thought while "Judaism" refers to the more creative, dynamic elements as manifested in the varied civilizations and cultures of the Jews at the different stages of their history, such as Hellenistic Judaism, rabbinic Judaism, medieval Judaism, and, from the 19th century, Orthodox, Conservative, and Reform Judaism. (The term *Yidishkeyt* is the Yiddish equivalent of "Judaism" but has a less universalistic connotation and refers more specifically to the folk elements of the faith.)

It is usually considered to be anachronistic to refer to the biblical religion (the "religion of Israel") as "Judaism," both because there were no Jews (i.e., "those belonging to the tribe of Judah") in the formative period of the Bible, and because there are distinctive features which mark off later Judaism from the earlier forms, ideas, and worship. For all that, most Jews would recognize sufficient continuity to reject as unwarranted the description of Judaism as a completely different religion from the biblical.

THE ESSENCE OF JUDAISM

The Hebrew writer *Aḥad Ha-Am (*Al Parashat Derakhim*, 4 (Berlin ed. 1924), 42) observed that if Hillel's convert (see above) had come to him demanding to be taught the whole of the Torah while standing on one leg, he would have replied: "'Thou shalt not make unto thee a graven image, nor any manner of likeness' (Ex. 20:4). This is the whole of the Torah. The rest is commentary," i.e., that the essence of Judaism consists in the elevation of the ideal above all material or physical forms or conceptions.

Aḥad Ha-Am's was only one of the latest attempts at discovering the essence of Judaism, its main idea or ideas, its particular viewpoint, wherein it differs from other religions and philosophies. This is an extremely difficult – some would say impossible – task, since the differing civilizations, Egyptian, Canaanite, Babylonian, Persian, Greek, Roman, Christian, Muslim, with which Jews came into contact, have made their influence felt on Jews and through them on Judaism itself. It is precarious to think of Judaism in monolithic terms. Developed and adapted to changing circumstances throughout its long history, it naturally contains varying emphases as well as outright contradictions. Belief in the transmigration of souls, for example, was strongly upheld by some Jewish teachers and vehemently rejected by others. Yet the quest has rarely ceased for certain distinctive viewpoints which make Judaism what it is. Some of these must here be mentioned.

Talmudic Attempts to State Essence

In a talmudic passage (Mak. 23b–24a) it is said that God gave to Moses 613 precepts, but that later seers and prophets reduced these to certain basic principles: David to eleven (Ps. 15); Isaiah to six (Isa. 33:15–16); Micah to three (Micah 6:8); Isaiah, again, to two (Isa. 56:1); and, finally, Habakkuk to one: "The righteous shall live by his faith" (Hab. 2:4). This would make trust in God Judaism's guiding principle.

In another passage the second-century rabbis ruled at the council of Lydda that, although the other precepts of the Torah can be set aside in order to save life, martyrdom is demanded when life can only be saved by committing murder, by worshiping idols, or by offending against the laws governing forbiddden sexual relations (e.g., those against adultery and incest). The historian Heinrich Graetz (in JQR, 1 (1889), 4–13) deduces from this ruling that there are two elements in the essence of Judaism: the ethical and the religious. The ethical includes in its positive side, love of mankind, benevolence, humility, justice, holiness in thought and deed, and in its negative aspects, care against unchastity, subdual of selfishness and the beast in man. The religious element includes the prohibition of worshiping a transient being as God and insists that all idolatry is vain and must be rejected entirely. The positive side is to regard the highest Being as one and unique, to worship it as the Godhead and as the essence of all ethical perfections.

Maimonides' 13 Principles

In the 12th century, *Maimonides (commentary to the Mishnah, on Sanh., ch. Ḥelek (10)) drew up 13 principles of the Jewish faith. These are:

(1) Belief in the existence of God;

(2) Belief in God's unity;

(3) Belief that God is incorporeal;

(4) Belief that God is eternal;

(5) Belief that God alone is to be worshiped;

(6) Belief in prophecy;

(7) Belief that Moses is the greatest of the prophets;

(8) Belief that the Torah is divine;

(9) Belief that the Torah in unchanging;

(10) Belief that God knows the thoughts and deeds of men;

(11) Belief that God rewards the righteous and punishes the wicked;

(12) Belief in the coming of the *Messiah;

(13) Belief in the *resurrection of the dead.

A close examination of Maimonides' thought reveals that his principles are far more in the nature of direct response to the particular challenges that Judaism had to face in his day than conclusions arrived at by abstract investigation into the main ideas of Judaism. The third principle, for instance, is clearly directed against cruder notions of deity which were popular among some talmudists in Maimonides' day. (Maimonides' contemporary critic, *Abraham b. David of Posquières, while believing with Maimonides that God is incorporeal, refuses to treat a belief in God's corporeality as heretical since, he says, many great and good Jews do entertain such a notion because they are misled by a literal understanding of the anthropomorphic passages in Scripture and the rabbinic literature; see Maim. Yad, Teshuvah, 3:7). The seventh principle seems to be aimed against the Christian claims for Jesus and the Muslim claims for Muhammad. The ninth principle similarly serves as a rejection of the Christian and Muslim claim that Judaism had been superseded (see S. Schechter, *Studies in Judaism*, 1 (1896), 147–81).

Reactions to Maimonides

Joseph *Albo (*Sefer ha-Ikkarim*, 1:26) reduces Maimonides' principles to three basic ones – (1) Belief in God; (2) Belief that the Torah is divine; (3) Belief in reward and punishment – while Isaac *Arama (*Akedat Yiẓhak*, Gate 55) reduces them to (1) Belief in *creatio ex nihilo*; (2) Belief that the Torah is divine; (3) Belief in the hereafter. On the other hand Isaac *Abrabanel (*Rosh Amanah*, 23) is out of sympathy with the whole enterprise of trying to discover the basic principles of Judaism, in that it implies that some parts of the Torah are less significant than others. Similarly, the 16th-century teacher *David b. Solomon ibn Abi Zimra writes: "I do not agree that it is right to make any part of the perfect Torah into a 'principle' since the whole Torah is a principle from the mouth of the Almighty. Our sages say that whoever states that the whole of the Torah is from heaven with the exception of one verse is a heretic. Consequently, each precept is a principle and a basic idea. Even a light precept has a secret reason beyond our understanding. How, then, dare we suggest that this is inessential and that fundamental?" (Radbaz, Resp. no. 344; see also *Articles of Faith).

Modern Trends

In modern times two new factors have been operative in the search for the essence of Judaism, one making the task more difficult, the other more urgent. The first is the rise of the Wissenschaft des Judentums movement in the 19th century. This had as its aim the objective historical investigation into the sources and history of Judaism. Its practitioners succeeded in demonstrating the complexity of Jewish thought and the fact that it developed in response to outside stimuli, so that there could no longer be any question of seeing Judaism as a self-contained unchanging entity consistent in all its parts. The second new factor was the emancipation of the Jew and his emergence into Western society, calling for a fresh adaptation of Judaism so as to make it viable and relevant in the new situation. The historical movement had demonstrated the developing nature of Judaism and seemed, therefore, to offer encouragement to those thinkers who wished to develop the faith further in accord with the new ideals and challenges. Yet this very demonstration made it far more difficult to detect that which is permanent in Judaism when so much is seen to be fluid and subject to change. Among modern thinkers, Leo *Baeck was so convinced that the quest was not futile that his book carries the revealing title, *The Essence of Judaism* (1948[2]). Acknowledging the rich variety of forms and differing phenomena in Judaism's history, Baeck still feels able to declare: "The essence is characterized by what has been gained and preserved. And such *constancy*, such *essence*, Judaism possesses despite its many varieties and the shifting phases of its long career. In virtue of that essence they all have something in common, a unity of thought and feeling, and an inward bond."

The Concept of "Normative Judaism"

Jewish thinkers who hold that an essence of Judaism can be perceived tend to speak of "normative Judaism," with the implication that at the heart of the Jewish faith there is a hard, imperishable core, to be externally preserved, together with numerous peripheral ideas, expressed, to be sure, by great Jewish thinkers in different ages but not really essential to the faith, which could be dismissed if necessary as deviations.

Unfortunately for this line of thinking, no criteria are available for distinguishing the essential from the ephemeral, so that a strong element of subjectivity is present in this whole approach. Almost invariably the process ends in a particular thinker's embracing ideas he holds to be true and valuable, discovering these reflected in the tradition and hence belonging to the "normative," while rejecting ideas he holds to be harmful or valueless as peripheral to Judaism, even though they are found in the tradition. Nor is the statistical approach helpful. An idea occurring very frequently in the traditional sources may be rejected by some thinkers on the grounds that it is untrue or irrelevant, while one hardly mentioned in the sources may assume fresh significance in a new situation, to say nothing of the difficulties in deciding which sources are to be considered the more authoritative. The absurdities which can result from the "normative Judaism" approach can be seen when, for example, contemporary thinkers with a dislike for asceticism, who wish at the same time to speak in the name of Judaism, virtually read out of the faith ascetics such as *Baḥya ibn Paquda and Moses Ḥayyim *Luzzatto (see, for instance, Abba Hillel Silver, *Where Judaism Differed* (1957), 182–223).

Recognition of Constant Ideas

However, if due caution is exercised and no exaggerated are claims made, the idea of a normative Judaism is not without value in that it calls attention to the undeniable fact that for all the variety of moods in Judaism's history there does emerge among the faithful a kind of consensus on the main issues. It has always been recognized, for instance, after the rise of Christianity and Islam, that these two religions are incompatible with Judaism and that no Jew can consistently embrace them while remaining an adherent of Judaism. The same applies to the Far Eastern religions. This, of course, is very different from affirming that there are no points of contact between Judaism and other faiths, or no common concerns. Nor has the idea of a Judaism divorced from the peoplehood of Israel ever made much headway, even in circles in which the doctrine of Israel's chosenness is a source of embarrassment. Nor does Jewish history know of a Torah-less Judaism, even though the interpretations of what is meant by Torah differ widely. The most important work of Jewish mysticism, the Zohar, speaks of three grades or stages bound one to the other – God, the Torah, and Israel (Zohar, Lev. 73a–b). Historically considered, it is true that Judaism is an amalgam of three ideas – belief in God, God's revelation of the Torah to Israel, and Israel as the people which lives by the Torah in obedience to God. The interpretation of these ideas has varied from age to age, but the ideas themselves have remained constant.

The Development of Judaism

THE BIBLICAL PERIOD. Any account of the development of Judaism must begin with the Bible as the record of those ideas, practices, and institutions which became prominent in the faith. With regard to the biblical record, as with regard to Judaism itself, the monolithic view has yielded among modern scholars to that of development and change, so that it is unsatisfactory to speak of the faith of the Bible, as if the Bible were a unit rather than a collection of books produced over a period of many hundreds of years and stemming from diverse circles with divergent views. The opinions of biblical criticism are frequently at variance with the traditional viewpoint on such questions as to whether the biblical accounts of the lives of the patriarchs are factually accurate, or whether all the legislation attributed to Moses really goes back to the great lawgiver or was fathered by him. Nevertheless, it is possible to trace certain key ideas, which eventually assumed importance in the Bible and which were influential in shaping Judaism.

MONOTHEISM. The usual description of the biblical faith is ethical *monotheism. Whether, as a minority of scholars suggest (e.g. Y. Kaufmann), monotheism erupted spontaneously among the people in ancient Israel or whether, as the majority would have it, there can be traced a gradual progress from polytheism through henotheism to complete monotheism (see the survey and critique by H.H. Rowley, *From Moses to Qumran* (1963), 35–63), the doctrine that there is one God, Lord of the universe, is clearly taught in a large number of biblical passages (e.g., Gen. 1:1–2:3; 5:1–2; 6:1–7; 9:1–8; 11:1–9; 14:18–22; Ex. 19:5; 20:1–14; Deut. 4:15–19; 5:6–8; 10:14; 32:8; I Kings 8:27; Isa. 2:1–4; 11; 45:5–8; 66:1–2; Jer. 32:17–19; Amos 5:8; Jonah 1:9; Micah 1:2; Hab. 3:3; Zech. 8:20–23; 14:9; Mal. 1:11; Ps. 8:2–4; 33:8–11; 47:6–9; 67:2–5; 86:9; 90:1–4; 96:5; 104; 113:4–6; 115:16; 136; 139:7–18; 145; 148; Job 38; 39; 40). What later became Israel's declaration of faith – the **Shema* – is found in Deuteronomy 6:4: "Hear, O Israel: The Lord our God, the Lord is one." The probable meaning of *eḥad* ("one") in this verse is not only "not many" but also "unique." God is transcendent and different from all His creatures (S.R. Driver, ICC, *Deuteronomy* (1896²) 89–91). From the critical standpoint these passages are comparatively late, but they are present in the Bible and were consequently adopted by Judaism.

CHARACTERISTICS OF THE ONE GOD. This one God is holy (Lev. 19:2; Isa. 6:3) and demands holiness (Ex. 22:30; Lev. 19:2), righteousness, and justice from His people (Gen. 18:19; Ex. 23:2; Deut. 16:18–20) and from all mankind (Gen. 6:13; Amos 1; 2:1–3). He has compassion over all His creatures (Ps. 145:9), and man can respond to His love in love and fear of Him (Deut. 6:5; 10:20). This God, Lord of all the earth, has chosen the people of Israel, the descendants of Abraham, Isaac, and Jacob, to serve as a "nation of priests" (Ex. 19:6) and to assist in the fulfillment of His purposes (Isa. 43:10; Zech. 8:23). It is incorrect to see the biblical idea of Israel's choice in terms of the relationship between the god of a tribe and the tribe: a tribal god cannot choose; his destiny is bound up with that of his people. When the tribe is vanquished he, too, suffers defeat. In the biblical record it is the God of all the earth who chooses Israel (Heinemann, in *Sinai*, 16 (1944/45), 17–30). God has given Israel the holy land as its place of abode (Gen. 28:13; 50:24; Ex. 6:8; Deut. 26:15). The special place in which God is to be worshiped by the sacrifices is the *Temple (Deut. 12:11–14; I Kings 8).

CEREMONIAL AND ETHICAL LAWS. Prominent among the ceremonial laws are the observance of the *Sabbath (Ex. 20:8–11; 31:12–17; Lev. 25:1ff.; Deut. 5:12–15), the *New Moon feast (Num. 28:11–15; Amos 8:5; Hos. 2:13; Isa. 1:14; II Kings 4:23), and the celebration of the festivals of *Passover (Ex. 12:14–20; 23:15; Lev. 23:5–8; Deut. 16:1–8), *Shavuot (Ex. 23:16; Lev. 23:15–21), and *Sukkot (Ex. 23:16; Lev. 23:33–43). Males were to be circumcised (see *Circumcision) as a sign of the covenant made with Abraham (Gen. 17:9–27; 34:13–15; Josh. 5:2–8). The *dietary laws (Lev. 11:1–23; Deut. 14:3–21) were to be observed, as well as laws governing dress (Deut. 22:11; Num. 15:37:41; Lev. 19:27) and agriculture (Lev. 19:9–10; 23:22; Num. 18:8–32). Numerous are the laws governing human relationships and social justice (Ex. 21; 22; 23:1–9; Lev. 19; Deut. 22; 23; 24; 25).

SPIRITUAL LEADERS. The spiritual leaders of the people were of different kinds: the *priest (kohen) who served in the Temple and was the custodian of the law (Lev. 21; 22:1–25; Deut. 17:8–13); the prophet (*navi*) who brought a particular message from God to the people (Deut. 18:18; I Sam. 9:9); and the sage (*ḥakham*), the teacher of worldly wisdom and good conduct (Jer. 9:22; Eccles. 7:4–5).

MESSIANIC BELIEFS. The belief became more and more pronounced that a day would eventually dawn when God's kingdom would be established over all the earth and war would be banished (Isa. 2:1–4; 11:1–10; Micah 4:1–4; Zech. 14:9). After the destruction of the Temple and the exile of the people to Babylon, this hope became associated with that of national restoration under a Davidic ruler, later called the *Messiah, and the resurrection of the dead (Dan. 12:2).

UNIVERSALISM AND PARTICULARISM. Israel, it was taught, had been chosen to be a light unto the nations (Isa. 42:6; 49:6) and to be God's special treasure (Ex. 19:5). But both universalism and particularism are found in the Bible, with all the tensions inseparable from belief in God as Father and King of all men and belief in His special concern with Israel. This people were to lead lives of absolute faithfulness to God. The greatest sin they could, and did, commit was idolatry.

There are many prayers in the Bible but these are private and individualistic. Communal prayer was a later development (see *Prayer).

The Pre-Rabbinic Age

The period after the return from Babylon is shrouded in obscurity, but some of the main lines of development can be traced. Not later than the fifth century B.C.E. the Pentateuch had become the Torah, sacred Scripture, with the prophetic books and the books of the Hagiographa being added later on as holy writ. The process of canonization of the biblical books, other than the Pentateuch, was a lengthy one, the full acceptance of all 24 books which constitute the Hebrew Bible, taking place as late as the second century C.E. (see *Bible: Canon).

THE RISE OF ORAL TRADITION. The concept of Torah was, of course, known in the earlier biblical period, but there it referred to groups of laws taught by the priests (Lev. 6:2, 7; 7:11, 37; 13:59; 14:2; 15:32; Num. 5:29–30; 6:13, 21) or to general "teaching" or "doctrine" (Isa. 2:3). In this period, for the first time, the new idea of the Torah (i.e., the Pentateuch) as a sacred text came to the fore. The regular reading of the Torah in assembly began at this period. Out of these assemblies the synagogue and the whole system of public worship evolved. The reading of the Torah was accompanied by its exposition and its application to new situations (see Reading of the *Torah). It is commonly assumed that the notion of an Oral Law, as distinct from the Written Law, was the invention of the *Pharisees in their determination to make Judaism viable by freeing it from the bonds of a text written down in former ages. It is said, further, that the *Sadducees rejected the whole notion of an Oral Law. While it is undoubtedly true that the full development of the Oral Law idea was the work of the Pharisees, the issue must not be oversimplified. The Sadducees, too, must have had some traditions of Torah interpretation, if only because the literal reading of the Torah text cries out for further amplification. Buying and selling, for instance, are referred to in the Torah, but no indications are given there as to how the transfer of property is to be effected. There are references in the Torah to keeping the Sabbath, but hardly any indication of what is involved in Sabbath work (see *Sabbath).

PERSIAN AND GREEK INFLUENCES. The two civilizations with which the Jews came into contact at this period, first the Persian then the Greek, made their influence felt on Jewish beliefs. Under Babylonian and Persian influence there came into Jewish life and thought the notion of angels as identifiable, sentient, but not necessarily corporeal beings, each with his own name: Michael, Gabriel, Raphael and so forth (see *Angels and Angelology). The personification of the evil in the universe as Satan probably owes much to Persia, as do the beliefs in demons and the resurrection of the dead. It was probably under Greek influence that the doctrine of the immortality of the soul came into Judaism. The doctrine of the resurrection also established itself, possibly at the time of the *Hasmoneans when young men were dying for their religion, so that the older solutions to the problem of suffering, in terms of worldly recompense, became increasingly untenable. There are no doubt indications of this belief in the earlier period, but it had not at that time obtained a complete foothold in the faith. Basically, the two beliefs of resurrection and the soul's *immortality are contradictory. The one refers to a collective resurrection at the end of days, i.e., that the dead sleeping in the earth will arise from the grave, while the other refers to the state of the soul after the death of the body. When both ideas became incorporated into Judaism it was held that, when the individual died, his soul still lived on in another realm (this gave rise to all the beliefs regarding heaven and hell), while his body lay in the grave to await the physical resurrection of all the dead here on earth (see also *Garden of Eden, and *Netherworld). However, the pronounced this-wordly emphasis of the early biblical period was not abandoned completely. This life was still held to be good in itself as a gift from God. But the thought took shape that, in addition, this life was a kind of school, a time of preparation for eternal life.

ESCHATOLOGICAL ELEMENTS. Toward the end of the Second Temple period, when ominous clouds of complete national catastrophe began to gather, the eschatological note was sounded particularly loudly. Speculations were rife regarding the end of days and hope for a new era to be ushered in by direct divine intervention. The doctrine of the Messiah and the messianic age, heralded by the prophets, was seen as a hope shortly to be realized. Some groups of Jews fled into the desert, there to await the coming of the Messiah, as is evidenced by the sect of *Qumran (held by most scholars to be identical with the *Essenes).

CHALLENGES FROM OTHER RELIGIONS. From the time of Judaism's contact with Zoroastrianism, faith in the unity of God had to be defended against dualistic theories that there were two gods, one of light and goodness, the other of darkness and evil. With the rise of Christianity the challenge came from the doctrines of the incarnation and the trinity. These challenges took the place of the polytheism and idolatry of the earlier biblical period, though, of course, idolatry continued to exist in the form of the Greek and Roman gods, and made polemics and legislation against *avodah zarah* ("strange worship") all but academic.

The Rabbinic Period

Rabbinic Judaism, the heir to all these tendencies, emerged at the beginning of the present era and lasted until the year 500, but many of the ideas put forward by the great rabbis had their origin in an earlier age. In the rabbinic literature there is a fairly consistent treatment of the three ideas of God, Torah, and Israel, with much debate among the rabbis on this or that detail.

PARTICULARISTIC TENDENCIES. With regard to the doctrine of Jewish peoplehood, the greater the degradation and the more intense the feelings of national rejection, the stronger became the need for national consolation and the assurance that God still cared. All the poignancy of Israel's hope against hope is expressed in the typically rabbinic, imaginary dialogue between God and Israel, in which Israel complains that she has been forgotten by God, and God replies "My daughter, 12 constellations have I created in the firmament, and for each constellation I have created 30 hosts, and for each host I have created 30 legions, and for each legion I have created 30 cohorts, and for each cohort I have created 30 maniples, and for each maniple I have created 30 camps, and to each camp I have attached 365 thousands of myriads of stars, corresponding to the days of the solar year, and all of them I have created only for thy sake, and thou sayest that I have forgotten thee" (Ber. 32b). It can hardly be accidental that the groupings are taken from the divisions of the Roman army. The universalistic tendencies in Judaism are apt to become obscured by the particular in this period. Nevertheless, conversion to Judaism is possible. The biblical *ger* ("sojourner") had long been interpreted to mean a *proselyte to the Jewish faith, and the equal rights demanded in the Bible for the *ger* are applied. "Our rabbis taught: If at the present time a man wishes to become a convert, he is to be addressed as follows: 'What reason have you for wishing to become a convert; do you not know that Israel at the present time is persecuted and oppressed, despised, harassed, and overcome by afflictions?' If he replies 'I know and yet am unworthy,' he is accepted forthwith and is given instruction in some of the minor and some of the major commandments" (Yev. 47a).

DOMINANT VALUE OF TORAH STUDY. The study of the Torah is now the supreme religious duty, the closest approach to God, the Pharisaic form of the beatific vision (R. Travers Herford, *The Ethics of the Talmud, Sayings of the Fathers* (1962), 15). Typical is the saying in the Mishnah (Pe'ah 1:1): "These are the things whose fruits a man enjoys in this world while the capital is laid up for him in the world to come: honoring father and mother, deeds of lovingkindness, making peace between a man and his fellow; but the study of the Torah is equal to them all." When a rabbi took an unduly long time over his prayers it was not considered incongruous for his colleague to rebuke him: "They neglect eternal life [Torah study] and engage in temporal existence [prayer]" (Shab. 10a). Only such devotion to Torah study can explain the remarkable ruling in the Mishnah (BM 2:11): "If a man is called upon to seek the lost property of his father and that of his teacher, his teacher's comes first – for his father only brought him into this world but his teacher, that taught him wisdom, brings him into the world to come; but if his father was also a sage, his father's comes first. If his father and his teacher each bore a burden, he must first relieve his teacher and afterward his father. If his father and his teacher were taken captive, he must first ransom his teacher and afterward his father; but if his father was also a sage he must first ransom his father and afterward ransom his teacher." The reference to wisdom in this passage comes at the end of a long process in which wisdom no longer means, as it does in the Bible, worldly knowledge and practical philosophy but the wisdom of the Torah. Moreover, Torah is no longer the province of the priest but the heritage of all the people.

ANTHROPOMORPHISM. Anthropomorphic descriptions of God abound in the rabbinic literature but, when excessively bold, are generally qualified by the term *kivyakhol* ("as it were"). The two most popular names for God in this literature are *Ribbono shel olam* ("Lord of the universe"), used in direct speech, and *ha-Kadosh barukh Hu* ("the Holy One, blessed be He"), used in indirect speech.

THIS WORLD AND THE WORLD TO COME. The idea of this life as a preparation for eternal bliss in the hereafter looms very large in rabbinic thinking, yet the value of this life as good in itself is not overshadowed. The second-century teacher, R. Jacob, said: "Better is one hour of repentance and good deeds in this world than the whole life of the world to come; but better is one hour of bliss in the world to come than the whole life of this world" (Avot 4:17). The same teacher said (Avot 4:16): "This world is like a vestibule before the world to come: prepare thyself in the vestibule that thou mayest enter the banqueting hall." In the same vein is the saying that this world is like the eve of Sabbath and the world to come like the Sabbath. Only one who prepares adequately on the eve of the Sabbath can enjoy the delights of the Sabbath (Av. Zar. 3a). Bliss in the hereafter is not limited to Jews. The view of R. Joshua, against that of R. Eliezer, was adopted that the righteous of all nations have a share in the world to come (Tosef., Sanh. 13:2).

The Middle Ages

During the Middle Ages Judaism was confronted with the challenge of Greek philosophy in its Arabic garb. The Jews mainly affected were those of Spain and Islamic lands. The French and German Jews were more remote from the new trends, and their work is chiefly a continuation of the rabbinic modes of thinking. The impact of Greek thought demanded both a more systematic presentation of the truths of the faith and a fresh consideration of what these were in the light of the new ideas. A good deal of the conflict was in the realm of particularism. There is definite hostility in much of Greek thought to the notion of truths capable of being perceived only by a special group. Truth is universal and for all men. There is a marked tendency in medieval Jewish thought to play down Jewish particularism. This is not to say that Judaism was held to be only relatively true, but that the doctrine of Israel's chosenness had become especially difficult to comprehend philosophically. The greatest thinker of this period, Maimonides, hardly touches on the question of the chosen people and, significantly enough, does not number the doctrine among his principles of the faith. For most of the thinkers of this age a burning problem was the relationship between reason and revelation. What need is there for a special revelation of the truth if truth is universal and can be attained by man's unaided reason?

In rabbinic times, wisdom is synonymous with Torah. The tendency in medieval thought is to give wisdom its head but to incorporate this, too, under the heading of Torah. Greek physics and metaphysics thus not only become legitimate fields of study for the Jew but part of the Torah (Maim. Yad, Yesodei ha-Torah, 2:5).

LAW CODES AND BIBLICAL EXEGESIS. The great codes of Jewish law were compiled in this period, partly in response to the new demand for great systemization, partly because the laws were scattered through the voluminous talmudic literature and required to be brought together, so that the *posekim* could easily find the sources of their decisions. A further aim was to render decisions in cases of doubt.

In addition to the incorporation of secular learning into Torah, the scope of Torah studies proper was widened considerably. The *Karaites were responsible for a new flowering of biblical scholarship. The *Kabbalah was born, its devotees engaging in theosophical reflection on the biblical texts. According to the Kabbalah every detail of the precepts mirrored the supernal mysteries, and the performance of the precepts consequently had the power of influencing the higher worlds. In the writings of the later kabbalists, Judaism becomes a mystery religion, its magical powers known only to the mystical adepts.

THEOLOGICAL SPECULATIONS. Under the impact of Greek thought the emphasis in medieval Jewish thinking among the philosophers is on the impersonal aspects of the Deity. Not only is anthropomorphism rejected but the whole question of the divine attributes – of what can and cannot be said about God – receives the closest scrutiny. Baḥya ibn Paquda (*Duties of the Heart, Sha'ar ha-Yiḥud*, 10) and Maimonides (*Guide*, 1:31–60) allow only negative attributes to be used of the Deity; to say that God is wise is to say no more than that He is not ignorant. It is not to say anything about the reality of the divine nature in itself which must always remain utterly incomprehensible. In reaction to the philosophers' depersonalization of the Deity, the kabbalists, evidently under Gnostic influence, developed the doctrine of the *Sefirot*, the ten divine emanations by which the world is governed, though among the kabbalists, too, in the doctrine of *Ein Sof* ("the Limitless"), God as He is in Himself – the Neoplatonic idea of *deus absconditus* – is preserved. Indeed, from one point of view, the Kabbalah is more radical than the philosophers in that it negates all language from *Ein Sof*. The utterly impersonal ground is not mentioned in the Bible. Of it nothing can be said at all. No name can be given it except the negative one of "Nothing" (because of it, nothing can be postulated). By thus affirming both the impersonal ground and the dynamic life of the *Sefirot*, the kabbalists endeavor to satisfy the philosophical mind while catering to the popular need for the God of Abraham, Isaac, and Jacob.

The Period of Transition

The 18th century was a period of great ferment in Jewish life, the old world dying, the new not yet coming to birth. The pioneer Jewish historian *Zunz correctly sees the Jewish Middle Ages as lasting until the end of this century. The repercussions following on the adventures of the pseudo-messiah *Shabbetai Ẓevi caused Jewish leaders to retreat into the past. There was a fear of new tendencies in Jewish thought and a pronounced suspicion of mystical fervor. Yet revivalist tendencies were in the air, and not only among Jews. The century which saw the phenomenal successes of a Wesley in England, and movements addicted to what Father Ronald Knox calls "enthusiasm" in America and the European continent, also witnessed the rise of *Ḥasidism. The three towering Jewish figures of this age each represented a prominent trend important at the time and influential for the future. R. *Elijah b. Solomon, the Gaon of Vilna (1720–97), "the last great theologian of classical Rabbinism" (L. Ginzberg, *Students, Scholars and Saints* (1928), 125), spent his days and nights shut up in his study with drawn shutters and setting standards of utter devotion to Torah study in the classical sense as man's noblest pursuit. In the 16th century, Poland had become a home of Torah. The complete devotion there to talmudic studies on the part of so many was unparalleled. The Gaon was an outstanding but not untypical product of this type of hermit-like dedication. The old teaching (Avot 6:4), "This is the way of the Torah. Thou shalt eat bread with salt and thou shalt drink water by measure, and on the ground shalt thou sleep and thou shalt lead a life of suffering the while thou toilest in the Torah," became, in large measure through the Gaon's influence, the pattern for many thousands of talmudists in Russia, Poland, and Lithuania.

ḤASIDISM. It is extremely difficult to disentangle fact from legend in studying the life and work of R. *Israel Ba'al Shem Tov (d. c. 1760), but Ḥasidism, the movement he founded – with its message that simple faith is superior to scholasticism untouched with fervor, that joy is to be invoked in God's service, and that there are "holy sparks" in all things to be redeemed by a life of sanctity – spread so rapidly, despite the most powerful opposition of established rabbinic authorities, that by the end of the 18th century it had won over to its side numerous Jewish communities in Galicia, the Ukraine, Poland, and Belorussia.

MENDELSSOHN AND THE ENLIGHTENMENT. Moses *Mendelssohn (1729–86) is rightly looked upon as the pioneer in bringing the Jewish people face to face with the modern world. Religious truth, taught Mendelssohn, was universal and could be attained by the exercise of the free human reason. No special revelation was required. The Torah, for Mendelssohn, is not revealed religion but revealed legislation. The eternal truths that there is a God, that He is good, and that man's soul is immortal are revealed in all places and at all times. Mendelssohn, thus speaking as a child of the Enlightenment, succeeded in paving the way for those Jews – and they were many – who wished to eat of its fruits. But Mendelssohn was not able to explain adequately why a special revelation to Israel was necessary if the basic truths were attainable by all men.

What was the purpose of this special revealed legislation and, if it had value, why was this confined to a special group? He speaks of "a special favor" for "very special reasons," but nowhere states what these reasons were (M.A. Meyer, *The Origins of the Modern Jew* (1967), 37). Moreover his advice to his fellow Jews to comply with the customs and civil constitutions of the countries in which they lived while, at the same time, being constant to the faith of their forefathers, was easier said than done. Nevertheless no modern Jew is immune from Mendelssohn's influence, and, by the same token, opponents of any kind of modernism in the Jewish camp have laid all the ills of subsequent Jewish faithlessness at Mendelssohn's door.

With the possible exception of the Oriental communities, every Jew in the post-emancipation era, insofar as he strove to remain Jewishly committed, was a disciple of the Gaon, or the Ba'al Shem Tov, or Mendelssohn, with many Jews disciples of more than one of these great figures at the same time.

The Emancipation

The entrance of the Jew into Western society at the beginning of the 19th century presented Judaism with a direct confrontation with modern thought, without the long period of preparation and adjustment that had been available to Christendom since the Renaissance. On the practical side there were the problems connected with the new social conditions. How, for example, were Jews to participate in life in a non-Jewish environment without surrendering their distinctiveness and the claims of their ancient past? How were they to avoid being dubbed antisocial or outlandish? How were they to earn a living if they refused to work on the Sabbath? How were they to mix freely with their neighbors and keep the dietary laws? On the intellectual plane fresh challenges were being presented to the ancient faith by the new scientific viewpoints, by modern philosophy, by art, music, and literature, cultivated independently of any dogmatic considerations, and later, by the historical investigations into the Bible and Jewish origins. It was in Germany that Judaism had to bear the brunt of the new thinking, though, as evidenced by the emergence of a Russian *Haskalah movement, other Jewries were not unaffected by the revolutionary trends.

THEOLOGICAL CHALLENGES. It is not surprising that atheism and agnosticism had their unprecedented appeal for some Jews, and Christianity in one form or another for others. But among the faithful, traditional theism remained the accepted philosophy of life until more recent years, when a number of Jewish thinkers began to explore the possibility of a radical reinterpretation of theism in naturalistic terms. The main tensions, however, in post-emancipation Judaism centered on the ideas of Torah and Israel rather than God.

THE NATIONALISTIC QUESTION. With regard to Jewish peoplehood, the *Zionist movement at the end of the century posed in acute form a problem which had agitated Jewish minds from the beginning of the century – the role of nationalism in Judaism. Were the Jews merely adherents of a common religion – as it was put, Germans, Frenchmen, Englishmen of the Mosaic persuasion – or were they a nation? Was Judaism dependent for its fullest realization on residence in the Holy Land, or was it desirable that Jews be dispersed in many lands to further there the "mission of Israel" in bringing God to mankind in the purest form of teaching? These questions were being asked, and the replies varied considerably. The early Reformers deleted from the prayer book all references to national restoration. Exile was not seen as an evil to be redressed but as an essential step in the fulfillment of the divine purpose (see *Reform Judaism). The Reformers were not alone in their opposition to a nationalistic interpretation of Judaism. When political Zionism became a practical policy for Jews, many of the Orthodox opposed it as a denial of Jewish messianism according to which, it was believed, the redemption would come through direct divine intervention, not at the hands of men. There were not lacking, however, religious leaders who advocated a form of religious Zionism, claiming that, as in other spheres, the divine blessing follows on prior human effort.

With the actual establishment of the State of Israel the older attitudes became academic. With the exception of the fringe groups of the *Neturei Karta (Orthodox) and the *American Council for Judaism (Reform), the majority of Jews now accept the special role the new state has to play as a spiritual center (over and above the haven of refuge it provides), while generally acknowledging that to uncover the full implications of this concept requires a good deal of fresh thinking. Some Orthodox thinkers have taken refuge in the notion of the establishment of the State of Israel as *atḥalta di-ge'ullah* ("the beginning of the redemption"), i.e., that while complete redemption is at the hands of God through the Messiah, the present life of the State still has messianic overtones and belongs in a realm far removed from the secular. Some see this as an unsuccessful attempt literally to have the best of both worlds.

THE QUESTION OF HALAKHAH. The great divide between Orthodoxy and Reform was on the question of Jewish law (*halakhah*). According to the Orthodox position, the traditional doctrine of *Torah min ha-Shamayim* ("the Torah is from Heaven") means that both the Written and the Oral Laws were communicated by God to Moses and that, therefore, all the Pentateuchal laws, in their interpretation as found in the rabbinic literature, are binding upon Jews by divine fiat. The Sabbath, for instance, is to be kept in the manner set forth in detail in the Talmud; the dietary laws are to be observed in all their minutiae. On this view nothing in the law is trivial or unworthy or out-of-date, since every law is a direct command of God for all time. Reform Judaism rejects the idea of a permanently binding religious law. In the Reform view, the moral law alone is eternally valid, together with those religious ceremonies which are still capable of inspiring contemporary Jews to appreciate the beauty, dignity, and supreme worth of a God-orientated life. A middle of the road position was advocated by the followers of the historical school in Germany and later by the *Conservative movement in the United States. In this view, Reform is in error in rejecting the *halakhah*, but Orthodoxy is also mistaken in wedding adherence to *halakhah* to a fundamentalism which recognizes no change or development in Jewish law.

Contemporary Judaism

There are a number of groupings in contemporary Orthodox Judaism. Reform has made little headway among Sephardi or Oriental Jews, and the majority of these, if religious, are at least Orthodox, with many of their own rites and customs.

ORTHODOXY OF THE LITHUANIAN PATTERN. Among the Ashkenazim, possibly the most prominent Orthodox group is that represented by the yeshivot of the Lithuanian pattern and the rabbis educated in these institutions, most of them in Israel and the U.S. The main emphasis here is on Torah study, to the virtual exclusion of all else, and the carrying out of the detailed practical observances. In this group the stress is on intellectual comprehension, particularly of the difficult logic and reasoning of the Talmud, the most admired figure being the *lamdan*, the man proficient in these studies. Religious feeling and ethical content is provided by the *Musar movement, which succeeded in capturing the Lithuanian yeshivot at the end of the last century. Secular learning is either entirely frowned upon or treated as necessary for earning a living, and little more.

NEO-ORTHODOXY. Neo-Orthodoxy (not generally called by this name) has a far more positive attitude to secular learning, with a particular fondness for the physical sciences. In this group are the followers of the Samson Raphael *Hirsch school, which aims at combining Torah (i.e., strict adherence to *halakhah*) with *derekh ereẓ* ("the way of the earth," in this context, the values of Western civilization). In this group, too, are the majority of Orthodox synagogues in the U.S. (the rabbis mainly alumni of *Yeshiva University) and Great Britain (the rabbis mainly alumni of *Jews College).

ḤASIDISM. The Ḥasidim still owe their allegiance to various dynasties of rabbis. Ḥasidism is emotional and mystical. Most of the Ḥasidim wear a special garb, consisting of a girdle for prayer, a long black coat, and fur hat. Beards are generally worn long and earlocks (*pe'ot*) cultivated. Ritual immersion plays an important part in ḥasidic life. The best-known ḥasidic rabbis with large followings today are the Lubavitcher and the Satmarer in New York, and the Gerer, Viznitzer, and Belzer in Israel. Neo-Ḥasidism, as presented in the writings of Martin Buber, is not a movement but a mood of sympathy with some of the ḥasidic values as relevant to the spiritual predicament of Western man.

The two major world groupings of Orthodoxy, embracing members of all preceding groups, are the Zionist *Mizrachi movement and the more right-wing *Agudat Israel.

CONSERVATIVE JUDAISM. This movement is especially strong in the U.S., with its teaching center at the *Jewish Theological Seminary in New York. It is organized in the *United Synagogue of America and has sympathizers in other parts of the Jewish world. It has been said that, while contemporary Reform stresses the God idea and contemporary Orthodoxy the idea of Torah, Conservative Judaism stresses that of Israel (i.e., Jewish peoplehood). This is too much of a generalization, but it is true that an important plank in the Conservative platform is the unity of the Jewish people amid its diversity.

REFORM JUDAISM. This movement is strong in the U.S., with its teaching headquarters at the *Hebrew Union College in Cincinnati, but with followers in other parts of the Jewish world. Reform congregations are loosely organized in the World Union of Progressive Synagogues. (The term "Traditional Judaism" is used, nowadays, to denote either Orthodox or Conservative Judaism. The term "Torah-true Judaism" is used by some of the Orthodox as a synonym for Orthodoxy in order to avoid the possible pejorative implications of the latter term as suggesting reaction or obscurantism. "Liberal Judaism" is the term used in Great Britain for the Reform position, though there are in Great Britain both Liberal and Reform congregations, with the Liberals more to the left.)

There are very few Reform or Conservative congregations in the State of Israel. Orthodoxy is the official religious position in Israel, with the majority of the rabbis belonging to the old school of talmudic jurists. Here and there in recent years a number of small groups have emerged with the aim of seeking a religiously orientated outlook, but one not necessarily Orthodox.

THE INFLUENCE OF JUDAISM

Judaism's main influence on civilization has been in the sphere of religion. This influence has been especially felt by the daughter religions, Christianity and Islam. The institutions of church and mosque are direct descendants of the synagogue, with many of their forms of worship adapted from the mother faith. Words like amen and Hallelujah have become part of the religious vocabulary of a large portion of mankind. The Church uses the Bible in its worship. The Sabbath, the Psalms, the prophetic readings, the weekly sermon, are, through Judaism, the common heritage of the Christian world. The language of the Bible has helped to mold the tongues of the Western world, so that the peoples of Great Britain and the U.S., France, Germany, Spain, and Italy, speak without incongruity in the idioms of ancient Judea. The prophetic vision of a world at peace is still a potent force in human affairs despite the war-blackened pages of human history. Judaism's insistence on justice and righteousness, and the brotherhood of man founded on the Fatherhood of God, has been, in part at least, responsible for the emergence of Western democratic patterns and social reforms.

The rise of modern science was due to a number of factors, prominent among them the Greek element in Western thought. But Judaism's teachings regarding the unity of nature as the creation of the one God are not to be underestimated in their effects on early scientific thought. It is doubtful whether science could have emerged in its full boldness and confidence against a polytheistic backcloth in which each god is allotted only a portion of the world.

The concrete nature of Jewish thought, its concern with the deed, its practical application of lofty ideals, has been responsible, perhaps more than any other factor, for the emergence of ideas connected with social justice. Individual Jews have stood on both sides of the debate on the major social issues. "Yet the determination not to abandon Justice to the realm of the abstract is independent of the machinery suggested for its establishment, and in so far as any movement sets before itself the task of bringing the good things of life within the reach of the masses, it is carrying on the work of the prophets" (L. Roth, in: E.R. Bevan and C. Singer (eds.) *The Legacy of Israel* (1928²), 468).

In speaking of the influence of Judaism it is sometimes customary to refer to the contributions made by individual Jews, but this is a highly questionable procedure. Adapting a maxim of Rabbi *Kook, it can be argued that these are the contributions of Jews who were great rather than of great Jews. It is certainly a moot point to what extent the thought of a *Spinoza, a *Marx, a *Bergson, an *Einstein, or a *Freud, was nurtured by his Jewish background. Yet it would seem that some of Judaism's influence is to be detected even here in a roundabout way. It can be argued, not unconvincingly, that something of Judaism's spirit contrives to live even in the souls of those of her children who have abandoned her.

BIBLIOGRAPHY: J.B. Agus, *The Evolution of Jewish Thought* (1959); Baron, Social²; I. Epstein, *Judaism, A Historical Presentation* (1959); M. Friedlaender, *The Jewish Religion* (1913³); A. Hertzberg (ed.), *Judaism* (1961); M. Joseph, *Judaism as Creed and Life* (1958⁴); M.M. Kaplan, *Judaism as a Civilization* (1957²); K. Kohler, *Jewish Theology* (1918); Loewe, in ERE, 7 (1914), 581–609; G.F. Moore, *Judaism in the First Centuries of the Christian Era*, 2 vols. (1927); L. Roth, *Judaism, A Portrait* (1960); M. Steinberg, *Basic Judaism* (1947); Werblowsky, in: *The Concise Encyclopedia of Living Faiths* (1959), 23–50; L. Baeck, *The Essence of Judaism* (1961); M. Buber, *On Judaism* (1967). **ADDITIONAL BIBLIOGRAPHY:** R.S. Frank and W. Wollheim, *The Book of Jewish Books: a Reader's Guide to Judaism* (1986); C. Cutter and M.F. Oppenheim, *Judaica Reference Sources: a Selective, Annotated Bibliographic Guide* (1993²); R.P. Bulka, *The Coming Cataclysm: the Orthodox-Reform Rift and the Future of the Jewish People* (1984); D. Cohn-Sherbok, *Dictionary of Judaica* (1992); M.L. Raphael, *Profiles in American Judaism: the Reform, Conservative, Orthodox, and Reconstructionist Traditions in Historical Perspective* (1984); G.S. Rosenthal, *Contemporary Judaism: Patterns of Survival* (1985); J.J. Schacter (ed.), *Jewish Tradition and the Non-traditional Jew* (1992); J. Wertheimer, *A People Divided: Judaism in Contemporary America* (1993).

[Louis Jacobs]

JUDAIZERS, persons who, without being Jews, follow in whole or in part the Jewish religion or claim to be Jews. The prototype of the Judaizer was *Naaman, the minister to the king of Syria, who, after being cured by Elisha, worshiped the God of the Hebrews while continuing outwardly to follow the idolatrous state religion. During the counter-attacks at the time of Esther, it is stated that many of the terror-stricken population "acted as Jews" (מִתְיַהֲדִים), though it is difficult to tell what precisely is implied by this term. In the classical period, the principles and certain practices of Judaism exercised a powerful attraction on some segments of the general population even in Rome, who changed the tenor of their lives, becoming "God-fearers" (σεβόμενοι) who rejected pagan worship and observed the Sabbath. The obligation of submitting to circumcision was of course a deterrent for male sympathizers, who, probably more than women, contented themselves, therefore, with half-way conversion, which became recognized too in rabbinic law. With the rise of Christianity, the differentiation between the followers of the new faith and the old was sometimes not easy to impose, and the Church inveighed violently against Judaizers within the Church, who wore Jewish ritual vestments, followed some of the dietary laws, kept the seventh-day Sabbath, and observed Easter on the Passover or with Jewish rites. In the Church, over a prolonged period (for instance at the time of the Albigensian schism), the accusation of Judaizing was frequently made against dissidents. In fact, some of them, such as the "Passagi" and "Circumcisi," were, it seems, Judaizing sects in the full sense of the term. Similar accusations were common at the time of the Reformation, sometimes even within the internal polemics of the Reformers (see *Disputations and Polemics). The ambivalence of the period of the rise of Christianity was long perpetuated in North Africa, where a good part of the population seems to have been affected by Judaism both before and after the spread of Christianity among them. The "Hebrewisms" which have been discerned down to the present day in some African tribes may be a relic of this. With the rise of Puritanism in England and the North Atlantic area generally, including America, the study of the Old Testament led to a relatively wide spread of Judaizing tendencies, expressed in the demands of some extremists for the use of Hebrew in the liturgy, the modeling of the constitution on biblical prescriptions, the observance of the seventh-day Sabbath, and rigorous abstention from blood. In certain cases, as that of the followers of John *Traske in England in the first half of the 17th century, these Judaizing tendencies had as their inexorable sequel in due course the formal adoption of Judaism. The same occurred in the 18th to 19th centuries with the Sabbath-observing sects in Hungary (see *Somrei Sabat) and in Russia (see below), and recently with the proselyte community of *San Nicandro in southern Italy. At the present time, the Seventh Day Adventists, while they have adopted certain Jewish practices based on the Bible, remain a closely organized separate sect. On the other hand, it is difficult to determine whether certain other groups who claim to be Jewish, such as the Mexican Indians or some groups of the black Jews in the United States, should properly be considered Jews or Judaizers. Some of the "Old Christian" victims of the Inquisition in Spain convicted of following Old Testament rites, and therefore termed Jews, are also in this category.

[Cecil Roth]

Present-day Judaizers or Judaizing sects are mostly to be found outside Europe. On the American continent, apart from the black Jews of the United States there are the so-called "Indian" Jews in *Mexico and the Iglesia Israelita de Chile, consisting of less than one thousand people in the southern Chilean province of Cautin. Many of them joined the Zionist movement and some even settled in Israel. They originated in the early 20th century in a Christian fundamentalist sect which gradually adopted Old Testament rites and festivals. Some Protestant Sabbath-observing "Israelitas" in Peru are sometimes mistaken as Jews. In *Japan several Christian sects are deeply interested in Judaism, the Old Testament and the Hebrew language, and their members often visit Israel. In Uganda a Judaizing sect called *Bayudaya, of which only about 500 remained faithful to Judaism, was founded in the 1920s by the political and military leader Semei Kakungulu. It was recognized in 1964 by the Uganda government as a religious community under the name "The Propagation of Judaism in Uganda – Moses Synagogue."

In Russia

There were various Judaizing sects and trends in Russia from the second half of the 15th century on. Occasionally they even adopted Judaism and its precepts, in part or completely, sometimes leading to formal conversion. The emergence of Judaizers in this area stemmed from ancient Byzantine oppositional traditions to the established Church, going as far back as iconoclasm and the *disputations with Jews and encounters with them in the Kievan principality. In the 16th century and later, the Judaizers were influenced by the radical wing of the *Reformation. Long-held critical opinions simmering in the Athos monasteries influenced the many Russian pilgrims who visited them. The first open appearance of Judaizers occurred in Novgorod, the principal commercial city of northern Russia, where heretical expressions had already been known in the 14th century. An ancient Russian chronicle relates that in 1471 Prince Michael Alexandrovich of Kiev came to Novgorod with several Jewish merchants in his retinue; "The Jew Zechariah" (Skhariya Zhidovin) is stated to have "corrupted to Judaism" two clergymen, Alexis and Denis. They were joined by the Lithuanian Jews, Joseph Samuel Skorovey and Moses Khanush, thus forming the nucleus for the new sect. In 1479 Grand Prince Ivan Vasilevich (Ivan III) of Moscow visited Novgorod and invited Alexis and Denis to officiate in the Church of Moscow. There they influenced many members of the grand prince's court, among them his daughter-in-law Helena.

In 1487 Archbishop Gennadi of Novgorod denounced the "atheists," whose numbers were increasing throughout the kingdom, to the grand prince. An investigation was entrusted to Gennadi. Manuscripts of hymns and prayers which did not accord with the doctrine of the official Church were uncovered. Several members of the sect were arrested and severely tortured at Novgorod. Others fled to Moscow, where they found influential protectors. At the Church council of 1490, Gennadi called for the adoption of severe measures against the Judaizers and suggested the establishment of an *Inquisition. The grand prince rejected this project, but it was agreed that the Judaizers were to be confined to monasteries. In 1494 the metropolitan of Moscow, Zosima, was accused of being a Judaizer and deposed. The struggle against the Judaizers became rapidly enmeshed with the underground struggle between various factions of the nobility over the succession to the throne and the course of Russian policy. The Judaizers supported Dmitri, the son of Princess Helena. In 1502 Ivan III nominated his son Vasili (Basil) as his successor; a campaign of persecution against the Judaizers began, and in 1504 the leaders of the sect were condemned to be burned at the stake. The sect rapidly disappeared from the political and cultural scene in Russia.

The extent of actual Judaizing within this sect is disputed among scholars. Some rely on the few extant remains of its literature – among them numerous translations of the Bible from the traditional Hebrew text and extracts from *Millot ha-Higgayon* of "Moses the Egyptian" (Maimonides) – and stress its proximity to Judaism. Others claim that the faulty style of these translations proves that they are not the work of Russians, but of Jews, and do not prove much about the Russian sect. Adherents of the sect were certainly named "Judaizers" by its opponents, who thus sought to impugn its standing among the masses (Joseph Volotski, one of the most violent opponents of the sect, referred to its members as *zhidovo-mudrstvuyushchiye*, "Jewish wiseacres"). According to some scholars, the Judaizers were a Christian rationalist sect, which tended to reject the Church hierarchy, the religious ceremonies, and icon adulation, whilst some of them even negated belief in the Trinity. Whatever may have been the true character of this sect, the propaganda against it, which emphasized its affinity with Judaism, aroused a persisting fear of the Jews among all classes of the Russian population. The consequences were felt in the Russian attitude toward the Jews during the 16th to 18th centuries.

At the beginning of the 18th century Judaizers reappeared in Russia, but there is no proof of any link between them and the Judaizers of the 15th century. The origin of the later groups was essentially due to a profound study of the Bible. St. Dimitri of Rostov, who concerned himself with tracking down sects which deviated from the Church, mentions the sect of Sabbath observers in his work of the early 18th century. During the second half of the 18th century, sects of Judaizers and Sabbath observers appeared in the interior provinces of Russia, as well as in the Volga provinces and the northern Caucasus. Among the most prominent was the Molokan sect, which broke away from the Dukhobors. Its founder was Simeon Uklein, noted for his biblical erudition, who introduced many Jewish customs among the members of his sect. His disciple Sundukov called for greater association of the sect with the Jews; this resulted in a split within its ranks and the creation of the "Molokan Sabbath Observers."

During the early 19th century, the authorities began to persecute the Judaizers systematically. The existence of Sabbath observers was discovered in the province of Voronezh. After a series of persecutions, many of them were brought back within the fold of the ruling Church. The others were impressed into the army. According to official figures, the number of members of this sect was 3,770 in 1823. In 1805 the authorities of the province of Moscow announced the existence of Sabbath observers, and in the province of Tula about 150 persons were discovered as claiming that they had been attached to their faith from ancient times, but that they had concealed this so as not to provoke their Christian neighbors. The Judaizers succeeded particularly in the province of Saratov, where the preacher Milyukhin won over whole villages to his faith. In 1817 Milyukhin submitted a memorandum to the minister of the interior in which he complained against the persecutions of the local authorities and the Christians. He argued that his followers did not observe the Jewish laws because they had no leaders versed in the customs of Judaism. He requested that the members of the sect be authorized to establish relations with Jewish scholars. In 1820 the Council of Ministers decided to instruct the local authorities to act with lenience toward the Judaizers and to content themselves with banishing their preachers to the Caucasus, where they were to settle. The remainder were not to be attacked so long as they did not propagate their faith. In a memorandum of 1823, submitted by Count Kochubey to the Council of Ministers, he claimed that the Judaizers' sect was widespread throughout Russia and that its adherents were estimated at about 20,000 persons. It was decided to enlist all who propagated the beliefs of the sect into the army, whilst those who were unsuitable for military service were to be banished to Siberia and settled in such a way as to preclude them from any intercommunication. It was also decided to expel the Jews from all places to which the sect had spread. Another decision prohibited the issue of passports to the Judaizers, so as to restrict their movements, prevent them from meeting with Jews, or propagating their faith. In order to arouse the masses of the people against them and ostracize them, it was emphasized that they were merely members of a Jewish sect. At the same time, the Judaizers were prohibited from holding prayer meetings and carrying out circumcision, marriage, and burial ceremonies according to Jewish custom. Many members of the sect decided to accept Christianity outwardly while continuing to practice their customs clandestinely.

With the accession of *Nicholas I to the throne, the position of the Judaizers deteriorated. Those who were apprehended in the observance of Jewish customs were forced to join the army or were exiled to Siberia. Entire villages were thus depopulated and destroyed. Many of the Judaizers were expelled beyond the Caucasus Mountains, where they settled, founded flourishing villages, and spread their religion among the Russian settlers. Near Aleksandrovsk, in the Caucasus, almost all the inhabitants adhered to the Judaizers' sect. During the 1840s, the Russian government supported the settlement of members of the sect in the northern Caucasus because it regarded them as an industrious and desirable element. The expulsion of Judaizers from their former places of residence was nevertheless continued. In Siberia, large settlements of Judaizers of various categories were also established (as in the town of Zima).

With the accession of *Alexander II, the administrative pressure was alleviated and the authorities did not insist on the application of the law. Many of the Judaizers began to observe their religion openly. They were particularly numerous in the provinces of Voronezh and Saratov. In 1887 the government officially recognized the right of the members of the sect to perform marriage and burial ceremonies according to their customs. With the manifesto issued on Oct. 17, 1905, which included freedom of religion for all the citizens of Russia, all the discriminatory legislation against the Judaizers and Sabbath observers was abolished. The government even emphasized, in special circulars issued by the ministry of the interior, that the Sabbath observers were not to be regarded as Jews, and that the special laws directed against the Jews did not apply to them.

All those who came into contact with the members of the sect, even their opponents, pointed out that they were mainly industrious peasants, moral, literate, charitable, and sober in their lives. Their main divisions were (1) the Molokan Sabbath Observers, believers in the New Testament and in Jesus as Christ, but not as God. Their observance of precepts of the Jewish religion (circumcision, the Sabbath, dietary laws, and the like) stemmed from their interpretation of the evangelists; (2) the Sabbath Observers (Subbotniki), who accepted the Hebrew Bible only, but not the Talmud. They were also occasionally referred to as the "Karaite Sabbath Observers" or the "Bareheaded"; (3) the proselytes (Gery), considered themselves Jews in every religious aspect and were also known as the "Covered Heads" (because they covered their heads, according to Jewish custom, both when at prayer or in other places). The proselytes endeavored to intermingle with the Jews as much as possible. Marriage with Jews was regarded by them as an important achievement. They sent a number of their children to yeshivot. Some Jews were secretly active among them as rabbis, *shoḥatim*, and teachers. David Teitelbaum of Lithuania, who was active in the proselyte settlements during the 1880s, became particularly renowned among them. These proselytes traveled to Ereẓ Israel among the masses of Russian pilgrims, and many of their families settled there. They were especially associated with settlements in Galilee (Yesud ha-Ma'alah, Bet Gan, etc.). In Ereẓ Israel they became completely integrated within the Jewish population.

There is no information available on the lives of the Judaizers and the proselytes under the Soviet regime.

[Yehuda Slutsky]

BIBLIOGRAPHY: L.I. Newman, *Jewish Influence on Christian Reform Movements* (1925); Z. Casdai, *Ha-Mityahadim* (1930^2); R. Matthews, *English Messiahs* (1936); H.J. Schoeps, *Philosemitismus im Barock* (1952); M. Simon, *Recherches d'Histoire Judéo-Chrétienne* (1962); Roth, England, 149–50; S. Grayzel, *The Church and the Jews in the XIIIth Century* (1966^2); G. Boehm, *Nuevos antecedentes para una* *historia de los Judíos en Chile colonial* (1963), 124–6; A. Oded, in: *Ha-Mizraḥ he-Ḥadash*, no. 1–2 (1967), 92–98. IN RUSSIA: I. Berlin, in: YE, 7 (c. 1910), 577–87; S. Ettinger, in: *Zion*, 18 (1953), 156–68; Ever ha-Dani (A. Feldman), *Ha-Hityashevut ba-Galil ha-Taḥton* (1955), 163–71; S. Ettinger, in: *I.F. Baer Jubilee Volume* (1960), 228–47.

°JUDAS, Christian writer, probably at the beginning of the third century C.E., author of a work (not extant) on the "seventy weeks" prophecy in Daniel (9:24ff.). Influenced by the persecution of the Christians, he predicted the imminent coming of the Antichrist. He is mentioned in Eusebius (*Historia Ecclesiastica* 6:7).

[Jacob Petroff]

JUDE, DER, name of four periodicals in the German language. The first appeared in nine issues between 1768 and 1772 in Leipzig and was published by an apostate, Gottfried Selig, with the intention of making the Christian world familiar with Jewish ritual, religion, and habits.

The second, edited by Gabriel *Riesser, was published for two years (1832–33) with one further issue. It consisted mainly of Riesser's own articles, in which he criticized the political negotiations within various German states concerning the emancipation of the Jews. Riesser chose the name "Der Jude," which had become almost an insult, in order to rehabilitate it.

The third, a monthly (1916–24), was founded and edited by M. *Buber, who adopted the name of Riesser's periodical but pointed out that "the Jew" was meant as representative of the Jewish people, and that he demanded liberty and freedom of work for this oppressed people. The Jewish problem had again been brought to the fore during the latter years of World War I, which had also given rise to nationalist ideas. Nearly all leading personalities among German-speaking Jewry contributed to the periodical during the eight years of its publication. Buber himself published in it his most important essays in that period. After monthly publication ceased, five special issues appeared on antisemitism, education, Jewry and German nationality, Jewry and Christianity (1925–27), and on M. Buber's 50th birthday (1928).

The fourth publication of this name, a Zionist periodical, appeared in Vienna between 1934 and 1938.

BIBLIOGRAPHY: J. Feiner, *Gabriel Riessers Leben und Wirken* (1911), 33f.; M.T. Edelheim-Muehsam, in: YLBI, 1 (1956), 171; M. Rinott, *ibid.*, 7 (1962), 32–34; H. Kohn, *Martin Buber* (1961), 162ff.; A. Altmann, in: YLBI, 1 (1956), 202f. **ADD. BIBLIOGRAPHY:** E. Lappin, *Der Jude 1916–1928* (2000).

[Reuven Michael]

JUDEA, Latin form of Judah, the southern province of Ereẓ Israel during the period of Roman hegemony. Although this article deals with Judea as a Roman province, it should be pointed out that the name precedes the period. It was the natural name, in its various forms, for the area. The return to Zion, which consisted overwhelmingly of the exiles of the kingdom of Judah, settled in the territory from which they had been exiled (cf. Neh. 11:25–36), and during the Persian period the territory was called Yehud (cf. Dan. 2:25, 5:13; Ezra 5:1, 8) and the name has been found on coins and jar handles of the period. The actual name Judea occurs from the Hellenistic period. It is first used by Clearchus, a disciple of Aristotle (Jos. Apion 1:179), and *Hecateus of Abdera and *Manetho (*ibid.* 1:90) use it to define the area where the Jews of Ereẓ Israel lived. With the direct Roman rule of Ereẓ Israel, which dates from the banishment of *Archelaus to Gaul in 6 C.E., a special governor was appointed over Judea who was given the title *procurator and was responsible to the governor of Syria. The procuratorship was confined to Judea until the accession of *Agrippa I to the throne in 41. On the resumption of Roman rule after his death in 44 the procurator's rule was extended over the whole of Palestine.

Josephus (*Wars*, Wilkinson's translation, Excursus 2) gives the borders of Judea as follows: Ayanot, also called Barkai, on the north, the frontier with Arabia in the south, and on the east from the Jordan to Jaffa. "Nor is Judea cut off from seaside delights, since it has a coastal strip which stretches all the way to Ptolemais." This incomplete description can be supplemented from other references in Josephus and from the Mishnah. In the same passage Josephus states that it was divided into 11 toparchies, which he details, Jerusalem being the most important. Although Judea was primarily a political geographical term, defining one of the three districts into which Roman Palestine was divided, the other two being *Samaria in the center and *Galilee in the north, the division was a natural one, and it is often mentioned with regard to the agricultural laws. "Three countries are to be distinguished in what concerns the laws of removal-Judea, Transjordan, and Galilee" – and Judea is subdivided into "the hill country, the Shephelah and the valley" (Shev. 9:2; Tosef. Shev. 7:10). This subdivision is further expanded by the Jerusalem Talmud (TJ, Shev. 9:2, 38d) which explains that "the mountains are the Royal Mount [not identified], the Shephelah is the plain of the south, and the valley the area between Jericho and En-Gedi," while R. Johanan gives another division: "From Beth-Haran to Emmaus is the mountain country, from there to Lydda the Shephelah, and from Lydda to the sea, the valley."

BIBLIOGRAPHY: Neubauer, Géogr, 59–96; S. Klein, *Ereẓ Yehudah* (1939), 83–107; Z. Kalai, *Gevuloteha ha-Ẓefoniyyim shel Yehudah* (1960), 95–106. **ADD. BIBLIOGRAPHY:** Y. Aharoni et al., *The Carta Bible Atlas* (2002[4]), 149–50.

JUDEAN DESERT CAVES. Following the discovery of the *Dead Sea Scrolls in the *Qumran caves, frantic searches for additional documents were carried out by Bedouin in all the caves of the valleys in the area of the Dead Sea. As a result of evidence of such activities by Arab infiltrators from Jordanian territory into the territory of Israel, an expedition directed by Y. Aharoni set out to survey the area (November–December 1953). This was followed by a full-scale expedition, divided into four groups, which was undertaken jointly by the Hebrew University, the Israel Department of Antiquities, and the Israel

Exploration Society, assisted by the Israel Defense Forces. In two campaigns (March 24–April 5, 1960; March 15–27, 1961) caves were explored in the valleys between Masada and En-Gedi as far as the Jordanian border. The investigations revealed two major periods of occupation in the Judean Desert Caves – during the Chalcolithic period and as shelters at the time of the Bar Kokhba War (132–135); some had also been inhabited during the First Jewish War (66–70/73). Expedition A, directed by N. Avigad, explored the vicinity of En-Gedi, clearing burial caves from the Second Temple period (including one which contained a wooden sarcophagus inlaid with bone ornaments) and the "Cave of the Pool," which had been inhabited by refugees who had constructed a reservoir to ensure a sufficient water supply; they apparently survived and left the cave when the danger had passed. Expedition B, directed by Y. Aharoni, investigated the caves of Naḥal Ẓe'elim where they discovered several biblical texts and Greek papyri containing lists of names. They also explored the "Cave of Horror" on the southern bank of Naḥal Ḥever where some 40 fugitives took refuge at the end of the Bar Kokhba War. A Roman camp was perched above them on the cliff. In the end the besieged succumbed from lack of water; they buried their dead and made a bonfire of their possessions, apparently choosing to die rather than surrender. Expedition C, led by P. Bar-Adon, explored the "Cave of the Treasure" in the Mishmar Valley. The main finds dated to the Chalcolithic period and consisted of a cache of 429 objects, 416 of copper, six of hematite, six of ivory, and one of stone. These included 240 mace heads of metal, six of hematite, one of stone, about 20 metal chisels and axes, 80 metal wands, ten metal "crowns" ornamented with birds and gate-like structures, five sickle-shaped objects made from hippopotamus teeth, and a box of elephant tusks. These were apparently ritual articles and may represent the treasures of a temple which were hidden from or by robbers. Other finds in this cave include plant remains, among them grains of emmer, which is the "missing link" between wild emmer and durum wheat. Expedition D, under Y. Yadin, worked in the "Cave of the Letters" on the northern bank of Naḥal Ḥever. In this cave, also guarded from above by a Roman camp, Jonathan b. Bayan, one of Bar Kokhba's commanders at En-Gedi, took refuge together with his family which included a woman named Babatha. Objects found here included 19 metal vessels (a patera, jugs, and incense shovels), apparently booty from the Romans; several glass plates, a great number of keys, clothing, sandals, etc., as well as palm mats, a hunting net, and wool for working. Together with these articles were hidden 15 letters from Bar Kokhba to the commanders of En-Gedi, and an archive of 35 documents (17 in Greek; 6 in Nabatean; 3 in Aramaic; and 9 in Greek with Nabatean or Aramaic subscriptions). They are dated to 93/4–132 and represent the family and property archives of Babatha who was related by marriage to the Jonathan mentioned above. The absence of jewelry or coins in the cave together with the meticulous care with which the objects were cached suggests that the inhabitants of the cave survived and left it in the end.

Along with the finds at the Murabba'at caves these discoveries have revolutionized the conception of the Bar Kokhba War and have opened new vistas on the material and religious culture of the Chalcolithic period. By providing precisely dated material they are of great significance for the archaeology of the Roman and talmudic periods.

[Michael Avi-Yonah]

Further Exploration

The archaeological exploration of the Judean Desert, made possible following the victory of the Six-Day War, was continued in subsequent years by a joint expedition headed by Pessah Bar-Adon on behalf of the Hebrew University, the Government Department of Antiquities, and the Israel Exploration Society, and with the assistance of the Military Government. A preliminary archaeological survey of the Judean Desert, the Jericho Plain, and the Jordan Valley revealed large numbers of hitherto unknown sites which have completely changed the previous historical-archaeological picture. Additional information has been gained of the Chalcolithic period as well as settlements, a planned defense system of strongholds, and secret water supplies, belonging to the periods of the First and Second Temples, These strongholds were used to protect flocks and herds, agricultural and manufactured products as well as caravans, Among the important discoveries on the shore of the Dead Sea mention should be made of the uncovering of a large house, 20 × 45 m., consisting of a hall and two rooms, in 'Ein al-Ghuweir. In the area which served as the kitchen were found stoves, granaries, and large vessels in cavities surrounded with stones. An additional floor had been built on a layer of ashes, 10–20 cm. thick. Coins of the reigns of Herod, Archelaus, and Agrippa I were found and earthenware vessels identical with those found at *Qumran. The building seems to have served as a communal one for the Qumran sect, a supposition reinforced by the discovery of a cemetery to the north. Twenty graves were excavated which were in every respect identical with those in the cemetery of Qumran. On a potsherd in one the name Jehohanan could be deciphered.

In the area of 'Ein al-Ghuweir and 'Ein at-Turaba sites were uncovered belonging to the 8th–7th centuries B.C.E. A building was uncovered typical of the Israelite period, but unique in that it had a square chamber, divided in three by inner walls. The utensils discovered, all of the Israelite II period, were similar to those found at Tel Goren in En-Gedi, which have been ascribed to the manufacture of balsam perfume. There was evidence of more houses. A defense wall, to which were attached rooms, suggests that they were part of a general defense system extending from the stronghold of Rujm al-Baḥr to Qumran and south and west. Three such fortresses have been excavated. One of them, on which only experimental soundings had previously been made by I. Blake, has now been excavated in its entirety. It contains eight rooms with sloping walls built of large unhewn stones. The entrance, to the north, was approached by a sloping ramp. Utensils were found belonging to the Israelite II period. A small fortress was found at Rujm a-Sejra, and another fortress, 33 × 55 m., was discovered at the sources of Wadi Mezān = Wadi al-Nār. The excavations revealed a tower 7 m. high containing four rooms and two plastered water cisterns, more than 5 m. in depth. In it were found typical Herodian ashlars, and an adorned frieze or capital. Also found were fragments of plaster in red and black paint, with diagrammatic figures. The utensils found were similar to those of Qumran and coins of Alexander Yannai were also found. All these discoveries raise the interesting question of whether these settlements were founded by the *Dead Sea Sects in view of the statement of Josephus as to their simple and modest way of life. It seems probable that they settled in former estates which had been established as part of a royal network of defense and agriculture in the desert which may be ascribed to John Hyrcanus or to another ruler of the Hasmonean dynasty, and the question is how these sects fitted in with this system.

[Pessah Bar-Adon]

During the 1980s and early 1990s new surveys of caves in the Judean Desert were made by Hanan Eshel and others, and these brought to light Bar Kokhba period remains, as well as fragments of written documents. In 1993 a new project consisting of surveys and excavations was conducted within caves in the northern Judean Desert ("Operation Scroll"). The project was undertaken by the Israeli Antiquities Authority and their stated goal was to find new scrolls. This IAA survey was undertaken by a large numbers of archaeologists at the time when the first Oslo Accords were being agreed upon; as a result the timing of the survey by the IAA was heavily criticized and the survey was seen by some to be an act of opportunism. The survey was undertaken along the eastern cliffs of the Judean and Ramallah anticlines, from Wadi ed-Daliya in the north to Nahal Deregot in the south. A total of about 650 caves and sites were surveyed, and 70 were excavated. Finds were made dating from all periods from the Neolithic through Ottoman times, including numerous finds dating from the time of Bar Kokhba.

[Shimon Gibson (2nd ed.)]

BIBLIOGRAPHY: Avigad et al., in IEJ, 11 (1961), 1ff.; 12 (1962), 176ff.; Y. Yadin, *The Finds from the Bar Kokhba Period in the Cave of Letters* (1963); Aharoni et al., in *Atiqot*, 3 (1961), 148ff.; P. Bar-Adon, in: *Seker Yehudah, Shomron ve-Golan, Seker Arkheologi 1967–8* (1972); idem, in: Eretz Israel, 10, *Sefer Ha-Nasi Shazar* (1971); I. Blake, in: *Illustrated London News*, 4/3 (1967), 27–29; P. Bar-Adon: *Revue Biblique*, 79 (1972), 411–13. **ADD. BIBLIOGRAPHY:** H. Eshel and D. Amit, *Refuge Caves of the Bar Kokhba Revolt* (1998); L. Wexler (ed.), *Surveys and Excavations of Caves in the Northern Judean Desert (CNJD) – 1993*, *Atiqot*, 41, parts 1–2 (2002).

JUDENBURG, city in Styria, S. central Austria. The name Judenburg first appears between 1074 and 1087, bearing witness to Jewish settlements there in the early Middle Ages (see *Carinthia, *Graz). It may be assumed that the name was also derived from the city's ancient Latin name Idunum. The first documentary mention of Jews in Judenburg dates from 1290; a *iudex Judaeorum is recorded in 1308. There is a report of a massacre in 1312, which is probably legendary. That Jews made their living primarily as moneylenders may be deduced from several instances of financial transactions between Jews and the clergy, dating from 1329. At the beginning of the 15th century there are reports of 22 Jews, each with a fortune of 100,000 florins, and 38 with 50,000 each. In 1467 Emperor *Frederick III permitted the city to expel all Jews who did not pay taxes. After the expulsion of the Jews from the whole of Styria (1496) there was no community in Judenburg until the second half of the 19th century, when there was a small congregation (affiliated to the Graz community) with a prayer room and a cemetery. Thirteen Jews lived in the town in 1869 and 92 in 1880. The municipal arms (at least from 1488) depicted a head wearing a Jewish hat (see *dress). Under the Nazi regime this was replaced (1939) by a seal showing a city gate, but in 1958 the Jew's head was reintroduced. At the time of the 1938 *Anschluss* 16 families (42 persons) lived in Judenburg. The prayer room was closed and its contents confiscated. By February 1939 all Jews had left the city, most of them for Vienna. In 1968 three Jewish families lived in the whole district. The *ḥevra kaddisha* (founded 1887) was still in existence, but there was no community.

BIBLIOGRAPHY: J.E. Scherer, *Die Rechtsverhaeltnisse der Juden in den deutsch-oesterreichischen Laendern* (1901), 455–517, passim; A. Rosenberg, *Beitraege zur Geschichte der Juden in Steiermark* (1914), index; K. Grill, *Judenburg einst und jetzt* (1925³), 23–29; Herzog, in: *Zeitschrift fuer die Geschichte der Juden in der Tschechoslovakei*, 3 (1931/33), 172–90; Germ Jud, 1 (1963), 135–6; 2 (1968), 379–80; PK (Germanyah).

[Meir Lamed]

JUDENPFENNIGE (Ger. for "**Jews' Pennies**"), small coins issued by Rhineland Jews. When Prussia stopped issuing small change in 1808, a serious lack of coins in the lower denominations was felt in the Rhineland. To overcome these difficulties, some Jews issued copper coins in denominations of *Pfennig* and *Heller*. As these were nonofficial issues, they gave them imaginary names, such as "Atribuo," "Halbac," or "Theler." These coins were somewhat lighter than the official coins. They bear fictitious designs, such as a coat of arms, a star, a wreath, a lion, a cock, and others, and carry the dates of 1703, 1740, 1807, 1809, 1810, 1818, 1819, 1820, and 1821. In 1821, however, the Prussian mint renewed the issue of small change, thereby putting a rather abrupt end to these illegal monetary enterprises. The authorities appointed a special unit, the *Muenzpolizei* ("coin police"), whose task was to confiscate these coins and to bring to court those who produced and distributed them. It is not known where they were struck. Some Jews seem to have made immense profit by handling them. One Jew from the city of Neuss is said to have made 54,000 florins profit. One single Westphalian customs office collected about 940 kilograms of such coins.

BIBLIOGRAPHY: E. Fellner, *Die Muenzen von Frankfurt am Main*, 2 vols. (1896–1903), 624ff., 855.

[Arie Kindler]

JUDENRAT (Ger. for "Jewish Council"), a body heading a Jewish community, appointed by the German occupying authorities during World War II, which was responsible for the enforcement of Nazi orders affecting the Jews and for the administration of the affairs of the Jewish community. From its inception, Judenrat leaders faced an impossible dilemma. To the Germans, the Judenrat represented Jewish needs, and they were essentially uninterested in fulfilling or responding to Jewish needs, but the Judenrat was also an instrumentality for maintaining control of the ghetto and thus freeing German personnel for other activities. To the Jews, the function of the Judenrat was to provide for their needs, much like municipal officials, in conditions that were not conducive to fulfilling their needs. The power of the Judenrat was severely limited, fully derivative from their German masters, although it did not necessarily appear so to the Jews within the ghettos of Eastern Europe.

The Nazi leadership came to the conclusion that the existence of comprehensive councils representing all the Jewish factions of a city or state would make the execution of their anti-Jewish policies easier. Such bodies were in existence in Germany, Vienna, and Prague, but they were called by various names other than Judenrat and differed in their varying degrees of dependence on Nazi factors (principally the Gestapo). With the German occupation of Poland in September 1939, the decision to set up bodies under this name was endorsed by the central authorities, and *Heydrich sent this decision to the commanders of the *Einsatzgruppen* in a secret letter dated Sept. 21, 1939, which included the following paragraph: "In each Jewish community a council of Jewish elders is to be set up which, as far as possible, is to be composed of the remaining influential personalities and rabbis. The council is to be composed of (up to) 24 male Jews (depending upon the size of the Jewish community). It is to be made fully responsible (in the literal sense of the word) for the exact and punctual implementation of all instructions released or yet to be released."

Since Heydrich used the term Judenrat, this body came to be known as such, and in many places the head of the council was called *Judenaeltester.* According to Heydrich's document, the Judenrat was to be responsible for the transportation of Jews from small towns to large concentrations (ghettos) and their settlement there, and for arranging the entrance to and departure from the ghettos. In the course of time the functions of the Judenrat expanded in two directions. After the establishment of the ghettos they were responsible for everything that happened within them. All the institutions that had been in existence beforehand were given new tasks, and additional institutions, as they became appropriate, were created. The Judenrat quickly became the dominant body and controlled the police, court of law, fire brigade, and employment agency, and departments for economic affairs, food supplies, housing, health, social work, statistics, sanitation, burial, education, and religion. The large working staff necessary for these activities was artificially increased on the assumption that a person working for the Judenrat would not be sent to a forced labor camp or elsewhere. In 1942, as resettlement to the East, what we now know as deportation to death camps, began, it was assumed that those working for the Judenrat would be exempt. In addition, the Germans placed upon the Judenrat other duties, principally the supplying of a work force, choosing people for the work camps, and, later in 1942, choosing those to be sent to camps that were in reality death camps. It seemed at first that the Judenrat had wide authority in this extremely difficult task, but it very quickly became apparent that the Germans did not always pay attention to the decisions of the Judenrat, and at the most the Judenrat had only the opportunity to postpone the dispatch to the death camps.

Fully fledged Judenraete were not set up in all occupied areas. The Germans refrained from appointing Judenraete in France, Belgium, and Greece, apparently because they had no intention of annexing these states to Germany. Under German pressure, however, bodies representing the Jews were created there. According to Heydrich's instructions, men of standing in Jewish public affairs, most of whom were active in Jewish political parties and in religious and charitable institutions, were appointed to the Judenrat. Often many appointees were chosen arbitrarily by local officials or because they knew German. When the German-Soviet war broke out (1941), Jews were largely opposed to joining the Judenrat in the occupied cities, though many saw in it a possibility of saving Jews. The German administrators almost always coordinated the council's authority in the hands of the *Judenaeltester*, and the measure of cooperation given by the other members of the Judenrat to its decisions and activities were contingent upon the character and position of the *Judenaeltester.* Since he was the direct and often only line to the Germans, he seemed to many in the ghettos to be a ruler with great influence on the Germans, while in reality he had to accept and enforce every German decree without objection. Efforts were made to delay, block, argue, plead, postpone, and alleviate the harshness of the decrees. Sometimes these met with modest temporary success; most often the result was failure.

In every ghetto the defining moments that tested the courage and character of Judenrat leaders came when they were asked to provide lists of those to be deported. A decision had to be made. In some ghettos such as Kovno and Vilna rabbis were consulted, seeking guidance from tradition for an unprecedented situation. In Vilna, Judenrat chairman Jacob Gens proceeded with the deportation, hoping that the loss of some would protect the majority. In Lodz, Chaim Mordechai *Rumkowski felt it his duty to "preserve the Jews who remained … The part that can be saved is much larger than the part that must be given away." He confronted his critics: "You may judge me as you wish." In Sosnowiec, Moshe Merin also complied. When faced with the deportation of the children of Warsaw, Judenrat chairman Adam *Czerniakow closed the ninth book of his diary with a tragic confession of failure: "The SS wants me to kill children with my own hands." This he could not do. He swallowed a cyanide pill and the order for deportation appeared without his signature. Some saw his suicide as an act of personal integrity and public responsibility. Emanuel *Ringelblum was far more harsh: "Suicide of Czerniakow, too late, a sign of weakness – should have called for resistance – a weak man."

Other Judenrat leaders would not deliver their people. Dr. Joseph Parnas, the first Judenrat leader in Lvov, refused to deliver several thousand Jews. He was shot. Leaders of the Judenrat in Bilgoraj were also shot. On October 14, 1941, the entire Judenrat of Bereza Karuska committed suicide. The leader of the Jewish Council at Nieswiez Magalif marched to his death rather than turn Jews over. He said: "Brothers, I know that you had no trust in me. You thought I was going to betray you. In this last minute, I am with you – I and my family. We are the first ones to go to our death."

The membership of the Judenrat changed frequently. Many were incarcerated and sent to death camps even before the final liquidation of the ghettos, or were killed. This even happened to the *Judenaeltesten* who for some reason would cease to please the German authorities or when, as a matter of principle, they would not carry out German orders, knowing full well that it would cost them their lives. About 40 members of Judenraete committed suicide when they saw that they could do nothing to prevent the transportation of Jews to the death camps. Others felt that, by executing the orders of the Nazis and sending some people to the camps, they would be able to save others until the Nazis were overcome by the Allies. In the end, however, the fate of the Judenrat was the same as that of the Jewish population at large. The majority of them were deported to death camps, and of the *Judenaeltesten* in Eastern Europe (Poland, the Soviet interior, and the Baltic countries) practically none remained alive. Only in rare circumstances (Holland or Greece, for instance) did the *Judenaeltesten* receive special treatment.

From its establishment a sharp controversy about the role of the Judenrat spread among Jews. The contemporary assessment in diaries, and most especially among the leadership of the resistance, was often most harsh. Even men of unquestioned integrity, who were trusted by their communities, were shattered by their responsibility. In Kovno, the leader of the Judenrat, Dr. Elchanan Elkes, wrote dispassionately of his situation.

> We are trying to steer our battered ship in furious seas, when waves of decrees and decisions threaten to drown it every day. Through my influence I succeeded at times in easing the verdict and scattering some of the dark clouds that hung over our heads. I bore my duties with head high and upright countenance. Never did I ask for pity; never did I doubt our rights … The Germans killed, slaughtered and murdered us in complete equanimity … I saw them when they sent thousands of people – men, women, children, infants to their death – while enjoying their breakfast, and while mocking our martyrs … There is a desert inside me. My soul is scorched. I am naked and empty.

At the end of World War II a negative view of the Judenrat and its members prevailed among members of the underground and the survivors from the camps. In Israel, the Judenrat was viewed as the exemplar of Diaspora weakness, often with scorn. Over time, research has tended to show that the intentions of members of the Judenrat were often guided by a sense of communal responsibility, and that they did not really have the means to foil the methods of the Nazis, who had not only a strong army but also enjoyed the active support of many non-Jews in the local population. These were reinforced by the findings during the *Eichmann trial, and specific research conducted for the trial shed more light on the subject.

[Jozeph Michman (Melkman) / Michael Berenbaum (2nd ed.)]

Holocaust Historiography's View

The *historiography of the *Holocaust has produced two extreme views regarding the role of the Judenraete ("Jewish Councils"). One view sees them as an instrument of collaboration in the Nazi policy of extermination. Hannah *Arendt made that very argument in her work *Eichmann in Jerusalem: A Report on the Banality of Evil.* She charged that, had the Jewish people remained leaderless, they could never have been killed in such massive numbers, the German task would have been far more difficult. The other view regards them as a continuation of the Jewish communal structure of the pre-World War II period which contributed greatly to the continued existence and functioning of Jewish communal life during the Holocaust.

Both of these views stem from inadequate information and a lack of sufficient perspective immediately after the Holocaust. In recent years, however, considerable research has uncovered much new material which enables a more objective view to be taken of the Judenraete. Isaiah Trunk's work on the Judenrat presented a far more complete view of the complexity of their role, the diversity of their composition, their fate, and their decisions. Raul *Hilberg, who had been improperly identified with Arendt's view, introduced the *Warsaw Diary of Adam Czerniakow* with a long and distinguished essay on the Judenrat.

It is now possible to distinguish between the various stages of the Judenrat activities corresponding to the changes which took place in the policy of the Nazis, and, in addition, one can now investigate the differences arising from changes in personnel during the various stages of the Judenraete and their composition.

It is, of course, true that the Judenrat organizations were imposed on Jewish communities as their only central representative bodies, and that the Nazis saw in them an instrument for the realization of their policies, from persecution to total annihilation. But the Jewish leaders could not know that, at least not at the outset. Nevertheless, it now appears that the Jews were not only a passive suffering element in this process, but developed their own initiative. As a result, two aims were in direct conflict with one another – the German and the Jewish.

*Heydrich insisted that important and influential personalities be included in the Judenraete, in order to exploit their influence among the Jews on the one hand, and to discredit them in the eyes of the Jewish populace on the other hand, thus neutralizing a potentially active opposition, The Jewish communities on their part tried to include veteran and devoted leaders in the councils, in order to utilize them for the welfare of the community. This was not an easy task in Poland since many Jewish leaders fled eastward toward the Soviet Union in the face of the advancing Germany armies. There were, indeed, instances of communal workers who were reluctant to join the Judenraete. However, those who joined, whether as a result of Nazi pressure or because of the desire of the community, were most conscious of the experience which the Jews had accumulated during different periods of Diaspora history, when a similar organic framework had been enforced and had lent itself to further the interests of the community. Consequently, during the early period of the Judenraete there was some significant continuity of personnel between the Judenraete and the prewar communal institutions.

An analysis of the composition of 128 Judenraete in the Generalgouvernement (German-occupied Poland) showed that more than 80% of the personnel held similar positions of responsibility and authority in the *kehillah*, city councils, and other organizations.

The Judenraete developed a wide range of communal activities in which they applied the dual principle of fulfilling the demands of the Nazis (forced labor and financial levies) as well as the needs of the community (health, education, supervision of communal kitchens, aid to refugees and the poor). A sticking point in many ghettos was the relationship of established Jewish leadership to emerging Jewish leadership, whether it be youth groups or the resistance, self-help groups or even those who fought for memory and documentation.

During the early period of their establishment, the Judenraete regarded obedience to the Nazi demands as a means of ensuring the continued survival of their communities, even when they were faced with the tragic contradictions of this situation. Supplying the Nazis with a labor force, which often provided vital supplies to the Germans and enriched local German supervisors, should have strengthened the position of the Jews and prevented attacks on them. However, this labor force strengthened the German war potential at a time when the fate of the Jews depended upon its weakening. Rational policy considerations would have suggested that the ghettos be sustained, but Judenrat leaders did not comprehend the depth of the Nazi commitment to the "Final Solution." During the first period, the Judenraete employed every tactic and subterfuge in order to alleviate the burdens of the community: bribery, protectionism, and exploitation of conflicts between the various German authorities. It should be taken into consideration, however, that the political, social, and psychological conditions which would have made rebellions possible did not exist for the Jewish communities. The members of the Judenraete did not, and could not, know that Nazi policy was destined to reach the stage of mass extermination. Among other factors which militated against a large-scale anti-Nazi resistance movement in the Jewish communities during the early period of German occupation were: the hostile attitude of the surrounding non-Jewish population, which prevented any possibility of effective dispersion or concealment; the collective punishments inflicted by the Nazis; their threats against any budding opposition; and finally, the belief that, as the war progressed, the tide would turn and this would lead to a collapse of the German war machine.

These factors led to the strategy combining the demands of the Germans with provision for the internal needs of the community.

It would be wrong and misleading to describe the relationship between the Judenraete and the Nazis as "collaboration" in any meaningful sense of the term, as "collaboration" implies a degree of partnership, even if an unequal one; its basis is a *voluntary* agreement between the two parties. This was certainly not the case with the Judenraete and the Nazis – whose relationship was that of a murderer and his victims. The Judenraete were a passive object of pressure in the realm of German policies, and their initiative was used to strengthen the standing of the community within the official framework of Nazi authority and to promote illegal activity.

As soon as the Nazi policy of mass extermination was embarked upon, the Judenraete were no longer able to strike a balance between the demands of the Nazis and the interests of the community. It was at this point that a split occurred in the reactions of the Judenraete. An investigation reveals that 80% of the early Judenraete did not succumb to Nazi pressures. Some refused to carry out the economic decrees, others warned the Jews against imminent *aktions*, and many refused to hand Jews over for expulsion. The Nazis eliminated those who failed to implement their policies and replaced them with more acquiescing individuals who had a much weaker sense of communal responsibility.

During the later stage, in 89 communities in the Generalgouvernement area, only 40 were headed by individuals who had been associated with communal activity before World War II. The others had no such association with Jewish community life, and it is of interest to note that 23 of them were refugees, some from Germany, Austria, or Czechoslovakia. Even during this latter period, examples of self-sacrifice in the interests of the community were not lacking. However, the number of those who succumbed to Nazi pressure – putting their own personal interest before that of the community – exceeded the number of those who did not. Some of the members of the Judenraete came to the conclusion that, if the Nazis were indeed intent upon the total extermination of the Jews, it might still be possible to save a remnant by acquiescing in, and reconciling oneself to, the destruction of the rest. There was also a policy of deliberate misrepresentation and deceit on the part of the Germans, so as to prevent opposition on the part of their victims, by deluding them into the belief that they were not all being sent to their death. In addition, the members of the Judenrat, even when they had no more doubt as to the fate awaiting those transported, nevertheless harbored another hope – that the course of the war was running in favor of the Allies, and that the approaching victory would result in the liberation of at least that remnant of the Jews which had succeeded in remaining alive.

In conclusion, one can distinguish four lines of Judenrat conduct *vis-à-vis* the Nazis:

1. Limited cooperation – even in the economic and material spheres.

2. A willingness to acquiesce in Nazi demands when it was merely a question of expropriating Jewish property and of other material pressures, but a total opposition to the handing over of Jews.

3. Reluctantly agreeing to the deportation to near certain death of one part of the Jewish population in the hope that the other part might, as a result, be saved.

4. Complete submission to Nazi demands in order to safeguard the narrow interests of those concerned.

The majority of members of the Judenraete who belonged to the veteran leadership of the community chose to act according to the first two of these lines of conduct. The last two were pursued by relatively few Judenrat leaders and were characteristic of the final stages, when the leaders were men with no communal background or past association with the *kehillah*. However, it is impossible to indulge in generalizations when judging the actions of the members of the Judenraete. The fact that the framework was forcibly imposed upon the community did not necessarily transform those involved into willing tools of the Nazis. The behavior of each Judenrat must be examined separately and in relation to the different periods of their activity.

In the final analysis, the Judenraete had no influence on the frightful outcome of the Holocaust; the Nazi extermination machine was alone responsible for the tragedy, and the Jews in the occupied territories, most especially Poland, were far too powerless to prevent it.

[Aharon Weiss / Michael Berenbaum (2nd ed.)]

BIBLIOGRAPHY: P. Friedman, in: *Yad Vashem Studies*, 2 (1958), 95–112; N. Eck, *ibid.*, 6 (1961), 395–430; J. Trunk, *ibid.*, 7 (1968), 147–64; 189–92; R. Hilberg, *Destruction of the European Jews* (1961) (1985) (2004); Hannah Arendt, *Eichmann in Jerusalem* (1963), 104–10; J. Robinson, *And the Crooked Shall be Made Straight* (1965), 142–87; G. Hausner, *Justice in Jerusalem* (1966), index; P. Friedman, in: L. Blau et al. *Essays on Jewish Life and Thought* (1959), 199–230; J. Trunk, in: *Dappim le-Ḥeker ha-Sho'ah ve-ha-Meri*, 2 (1969), 119–36; idem, in: *Ha-Amidah ha-Yehudit bi-Tekufat ha-Sho'ah* (1970), 160–80; idem, *Nittuk o Reẓifut be-Va'adei ha-Kehillot ba-Tekufah ha-Naẓit* (pub. by: Ha-Ḥug li-Ydi'at Am Yisrael ba-Tefuẓot be-Veit Nesi ha-Medinah, 1 no. 3, 1966); Z.A. Bar-On, *Ha-Hanhagah: Derakheha ve-Aḥrayutah* (1970), 180–92. **ADD. BIBLIOGRAPHY:** I. Trunk, *Judenrat, The Jewish Councils in Eastern Europe under the Nazi Occupation* (1972); Y. Bauer, *Hashlakhot Meḥkar ha-Shoah al Toda'atenu ha-Historit* (1973); A. Weiss, in: *Yalkut Moreshet*, 15 (1973); R. Hilberg, S. Staron, and J. Kermisz, *The Warsaw Diary of Adam Czerniakow* (1979).

JUDENREIN (Judenfrei; Ger. for "cleansed [or free] of Jews"), National Socialist term applied in the "Final Solution of the Jewish Question." The creation of a "Germany and of German living space and ultimately of a Europe free of Jews" was the definitive aim of the National Socialist "Final Solution." In National Socialist terminology and in the Nazi policy of extermination of the Jews, the term referred to towns and regions after their entire Jewish population had been deported to the extermination camps. Especially in occupied Poland (General Government), the term *judenfrei* formed a permanent part of the unofficial and official language used by Nazi officials (see also *Nazi-deutsch). The "cleansing of Jews" was first accomplished by deporting Jews from Germany and other countries to the east. There were discussions about the shipment of Jews to reservations – the Nisko and Lublin plans – and of Jews to Madagascar, where they would be contained. Eventually, as the "Final Solution" evolved, the solution became final, namely the "cleansing of Jews" was accomplished by systematic murder.

BIBLIOGRAPHY: Jewish Historical Institute, Warsaw, *Faschismus-Ghetto-Massenmord* (Ger., 1961[2]), passim.

[Wolfgang Scheffler]

JUDEO-ARABIC. The Jewish population of North Africa is divided by language into Arabic and Berber-speaking communities, and groups speaking *Ladino (Judeo-Spanish). Arabic-speaking communities include descendants of the *megorashim* (expellees from *Spain) who were arabicized, and the majority of the *toshavim* ("residents"), the Jewish population which existed in the Maghreb before the expulsion of Jews from Spain. The date of earliest settlement and the ethnic origin of the latter group have posed historical problems which have still to be solved satisfactorily. An examination of documentary evidence reveals the existence within this group of a variety of branches, which provide different means of expression. The various so-called classical or pseudo-classical languages used by authors of the period of Spanish rule for all philosophical, scientific, or religious literature are not within the scope of this survey. The educated Jew in the Maghreb is no longer able to understand these works in their original form and knows them only in their Hebrew translations. However, an exception must be made for certain poetical works in Hispanic Arabic (which has become Zajal), and certain *muwashshaḥāt*, which formed the lyrics of the so-called Andalusian music. This poetic form remains the preserve of a very small Jewish elite, unable to read Arabic script and thus taught orally, by Muslim or Jewish teachers. There is a collection of these verses in an extremely rare edition published in *Tunis in 1886 in Hebrew and Arabic, and entitled *Sefinah Maluf.*

There is also a later type of poetry, the *qiṣṣa*, composed in a type of *koine* (i.e., a form of colloquial Arabic), which is understood by all North African communities. It is extremely popular in cultured circles, as well as among the masses. The *qiṣṣa* includes as its main genre rhymed adaptations of Bible stories or liturgical poems, songs of joy or lamentation, songs in praise of saintly men in Ereẓ Israel or North Africa, homilies on virtue, and satirical works. Folksongs sung on family occasions (funerals and celebrations) are written in a language close to colloquial speech.

Of all North African dialects, those of the Jews have best preserved the oldest characteristics of the language introduced during the early centuries of Arab rule. This conservatism has also produced a paucity of expression. When the realm of the concrete and of everyday life is abandoned for abstract concepts, it is necessary to resort to the vocabulary and morphosyntactical structure of Hebrew and Aramaic. This constitutes the heterogeneous language of preaching, talmudic instruction, circular letters, and decisions of the rabbinical courts or of the community council. The *sharḥ*, or commentary on sacred writings, such as the Bible and liturgical texts, has a special place because of its basic role in traditional education and its special linguistic rules. Beside these, there is an epistolary language and a Jewish slang called *lashon* (Heb.: "language") used to mislead strangers.

Judeo-Berber

There is no written literature, but *Berber society in general possesses an oral literature, whose basis (still scarcely investigated) consists of fables, legends, proverbs, and poetic works, generally on the theme of love and war, or else of a homiletical nature. Apart from their living dialects and folklore, which are no less rich than those of their Muslim neighbors, the Berber-speaking Jews have a traditional and religious oral literature, of which, unfortunately, very little has been preserved and recently collected. Without dealing with the controversial subject of the origin of these communities, it should be noted that Berber was one of the vernaculars of the Jewish communities of the Atlas mountains and the Moroccan Sous (and, apparently, of certain parts of *Algeria and *Tunisia). Most Jews were bilingual, speaking both Berber and Arabic, but others spoke only Berber, and until the 1950s there were a few isolated immigrants to Israel, who settled in Ashkelon, belonging to this latter group. Traditional education employed Berber as the language of interpretation and translation of sacred texts (and sometimes of the liturgy). Several biblical passages have been recorded in their Berber form, but the most important document, which is of vital importance for a knowledge of the linguistic and cultural traditions of this part of the Diaspora (which long remained unknown), is a Passover *Haggadah*. This *Haggadah* has been entirely translated into a dialect which resembles Tamazigt; the antiquity of its literary form appears to be beyond dispute.

BIBLIOGRAPHY: H. Zafrani, in: *Revue de l'Occident Musulman…*, 4 (1967), 175–88.

[Haim Zafrani]

JUDEO-ARABIC LITERATURE, written in Arabic by Jews for Jews. It is written in an idiom which is linguistically closer to the spoken form of Arabic than is the idiom used in Muslim literature. It may plausibly be assumed that, prior to the rise of Islam in the early seventh century, the Jews who lived in the Arabian peninsula spoke Arabic and belonged to the more or less cultivated class, which may have included some writers. If this is so, almost nothing of their works has survived. The one Jewish poet whose work is extant, *Samuel ibn Adiya, can be distinguished so little from his non-Jewish colleagues in theme, imagery, and style, that only history has preserved the knowledge of his Jewish identity. The writings of *Muhammad, which contain a considerable amount of biblical and midrashic material, suggest that the Torah and the Midrash were studied during the period, but concrete testimony is wanting.

The remarkable spread of Muslim domination over vast territories in Southwest Asia, North Africa, and *Spain, and the diffusion of Arabic in these areas, did not leave the Jews unaffected. It may be surmised that Arabic gradually displaced the Aramaic vernacular, initially in the larger centers, and that the Jewish population began to use it in its everyday intercourse from about the eighth century. The more inquiring Jews also began to acquire a knowledge of Arabic literature and science, which were undergoing a tremendous growth as a result of the large number of Greek, Syriac, Pahlavi, and Hindi works that had been translated into Arabic. The language became a storehouse for much of the world's knowledge and learning, and there was an upsurge of writing in Arabic on subjects which originated in other cultures. The participation of non-Arab Muslims and of other minorities in this activity was very great, and it likewise stimulated an intensive study of the imported learning among interested Jews. From the eighth century onward, there appeared in the Jewish communities under Muslim rule men who presumably received a traditional education, but who also turned their attention to the recently developed or rediscovered areas of secular studies. They took a particular interest in medicine, mathematics, astrology and astronomy, and philosophy and theology. Of equal importance with their pursuit of these studies was the influence this acquaintance with foreign lore had on their understanding of their Jewish heritage. Not only did they introduce into Jewish culture the investigation of theology, secular Hebrew prose and poetry, Hebrew grammar and lexicography, they also subjected traditional areas to the rationalism and orderliness which they acquired from their excursions into foreign fields. In the biblical commentaries of the time, in the compilations of talmudic law and the expositions on diverse topics particularly relevant to the Jewish world, a novel organization and presentation of the material can be discerned. With the exception of certain *Karaite circles around 1000 C.E., Jews wrote Arabic in Hebrew characters. In the first millennium two methods of transcription into Hebrew characters developed, one phonetic, the other mostly imitating the Arabic spelling. At the beginning of the second millennium, this second way of transcription prevailed (see J. Blau and S. Hopkins, *Zeitschrift fuer arabische Linguistik*, 1984, 9–27).

The East

Just as the Muslims of Spain for a time looked to the East for learning, and for scholars and literary personalities, so in Judeo-Arabic letters it was *Babylonia, *Palestine, and *Egypt, the ancient centers of Jewish cultural activity, which were the first to flourish. Mashallah (770–820) of Egypt was an astrologer and astronomer of note who is credited with a considerable number of works on astronomical phenomena. Māsarjawayh of *Basra (late 9th cent.) was among the first to translate medical works into Arabic, among them the *Pandect* in Syriac of the archdeacon Ahron. Māsarjawayh probably also wrote original works, since Uṣaybiʿa, the historian of medicine, states that the quotations from "the Jew" in the encyclopedic *al-Ḥāwī* by the celebrated physician al-Rāzī are taken from his writings. Isaac b. Solomon *Israeli (c. 850–950), of Egypt and, later, *Kairouan, established a reputation as a philosopher and medical scholar. His writings include *Kitāb al-Ḥudūd wa al-Rusūm* ("The Book of Definitions and Descriptions"), an explanation of logical and philosophical terms; *al-Ustuqṣāt* ("The Elements"), a treatise on the components of the physical world, based on the works of Aristotle, Hippocrates, and Galen; a study of the nature and value of different foods (*Fī Ṭabāʾī al-Aghdhiya wa-Quwāhā*); a study of the knowledge of urine and its components (*Fī Maʿrifat al-Bawl wa-Aqsāmuhu*); an introduction to the study of medicine (*al-Madkhal ilā ṣināʿat at-Ṭibb*); an introduction to logic (*al-Madkhal ilā-al-Manṭiq*); an essay regarding philosophy (*Fī Ḥikma*); and commentary on the Sefer *Yeẓirah.

*Saadiah b. Joseph Gaon (882–942) left his native Egypt and traveled through Palestine to Babylonia, where he was appointed *gaon* of the Academy of Sura. Possessing encyclopedic knowledge and capable of enormous productivity, he wrote works which include a translation of the Bible into Arabic, a long and a short commentary on the Pentateuch, and comments on and introductions to other books of the Bible. He codified the laws relating to such topics as inheritance, trusts, and oaths. In addition, he compiled a list of *hapax legomena in the Bible, which he sought to explain with the aid of rabbinic Hebrew, a Hebrew grammar, and a rhyming dictionary. In expounding the *Sefer Yeẓirah*, a theosophical tract, Saadiah attempted to interpret it as a philosophical monograph. He also wrote a theological work, the *Kitāb al-Amānāt wa-al-Iʿtiqādāt*, made great contributions to liturgy and chronology, and composed polemics against the *Karaites and other heretics. His vigorous attack on the Karaites roused their anger, and he was designated their arch-enemy. He also encountered criticism from the Rabbanite R. Mevasser ha-Levi, who raised objections to explanations of rulings in his works, either because they did not agree with tradition or because they appeared to contradict a previous statement of the author. David ibn Marwān *Al-Mukammiṣ, a contemporary of Saadiah who converted to Christianity and subsequently returned to Judaism, wrote the theological treatise, *ʿIshrūn Maqālā* ("Twenty Tracts"; S. Stroumsa's edition, 1989). The work deals with the attributes of God, and, in accordance with the Mu'tazilite view, regards them as aspects of His essence.

R. Samuel b. Hophni (d. 1013), who was a *gaon* in the Academy of Sura, devoted all his writings to the exposition of traditional Jewish lore. However, the influence of Arabic literature and theology is very evident in his works. More verbose than Saadiah, Samuel supplied commentaries on those parts of the Torah which the former did not annotate, as well as on Ecclesiastes and on some of the Later Prophets. He did not hesitate to include an excursus on any subject related to his theme, for example, his digression on dreams in general after having dealt with the dreams of Pharaoh. He produced a refutation of the doctrine held by Muslim theologians that God would void His revelation to Moses in favor of one to be revealed later. His major work, however, was on the Talmud, to which he wrote an introduction, and he compiled monographs on various topics in Jewish law, such as ritual slaughter, benedictions, partnership, and gifts. As with Saadiah, what distinguishes Samuel's writings is his systematic organization and treatment: in each case, he provides an introduction and a table of contents, and he divides his material into chapters with headings summarizing what is to be dealt with. His son-in-law, *Hai b. Sherira Gaon (939–1038), wrote both in Hebrew and in Arabic. His well-known work *Purchase and Sale* is in Arabic, as is his monograph *Oaths* and a number of other writings. Although his responsa were generally in Hebrew, they were written in Arabic when the inquiry was written in that language. Of particular interest is his glossary of difficult words in the Bible and Talmud, *al-Ḥāwī* ("The Comprehender"), which works on the basis of triliteral roots. The glossary was used in Spain and was directly consulted until at least the end of the 11th century. Of the writings of Hai's father, *Sherira b. Ḥanina Gaon, only one responsum is a manifest translation from Arabic, and although it is said that he wrote halakhic works in that language, nothing has survived. But he did use Arabic in the course of his Hebrew and Aramaic writings.

*Ḥefeẓ b. Yaẓli'aḥ (late 10th or early 11th cent.) was the author of *Sefer ha-Mizvot*, a work which enumerated and discussed in detail the 613 commandments of Jewish law (edited and translated by B. Halper, *A Volume of the Book of Precepts by Ḥefeṣ b. Yaṣli'aḥ* (Philadelphia 1915); appendices by S. Asaf, *Tarbiz* 15 (1954), and M. Zucker, *Proceedings* etc. 29 (1960–61), *Ha-Do'ar,* 23 (1963; reprinted by Zion, Tel Aviv, 1972). He began every elucidation with either "It is commanded" or "It is required," in the case of positive precepts, and "It is prohibited" in the case of negative commandments. First the biblical law is summarized, and then follows the rabbinic expansion and ramification. His work was used by scholars who read or wrote Arabic, among them *Maimonides; but since it was not translated into Hebrew, later citations are secondary. Moreover, only a relatively small part of what must have been a large work has so far come to light; from the table of contents of the extant section only an idea of the probable extent of the entire production can be formed.

The Karaites

Although they adopted an antagonistic stance toward rabbinic traditions and initially asserted every individual's right, nay duty, to make his own intensive study of the Holy Scriptures, the Karaites gradually restricted this prerogative to the learned, whose conclusions were then followed by the masses. Originating in the eighth century, the movement's earlier leaders – first as Ananites led by *Anan b. David, and in the middle of the ninth century as Karaites, led by Benjamin b. Moses *Al-Nahawendi, and afterwards by Daniel b. Moses *Al-Qūmisī – used Aramaic or Hebrew in their writings. But as Arabic came into wider use, Karaite writers began to adopt it as their means of communication. Among the more renowned was *David b. Boaz (c. 930), a descendant of the movement's founder, Anan, who translated the Pentateuch into Arabic and also wrote a commentary on it. *Salmon b. Jeroham, one of the most vitriolic opponents of Saadiah, wrote a polemic in Hebrew against the *Gaon* which, following the manner of the time, heaped abuse on him as part of the attack. His outlook was in general narrow and partisan, and he was also opposed to the pursuit of secular studies. In Arabic he composed commentaries on the Five Scrolls and also on the Psalms. Jacob *Al-Qirqisānī (c. 930) produced a large work, *al-Anwār wa al-Marāqib* ("The Lights and the Lookouts"), which is in the main an exposition of Karaite beliefs and laws and a somewhat polemical defense of them against criticism from the ranks of the Rabbanites and from fellow Karaites. In addition, the book contains a historical survey of the Jews and Karaites, as well as of heretical sects, which is highly esteemed by modern scholars, particularly for its information about the early divisions among the Karaites and the attitudes toward Anan of his immediate successors. Qirqisānī also wrote a commentary on the book of Genesis, which makes extensive use of Saadiah's interpretations. In the field of Bible study, *Japheth b. Eli ha-Levi holds a high place. He lived in Jerusalem, where the Karaites had established a community in 950–980. He translated the Bible into Arabic, much more literally and unidiomatically than Saadiah, and wrote extensive commentaries which contain a considerable amount of grammatical analysis. He tended toward making as much of the text as he could contemporary in application; this is particularly true of his explanation of Daniel. He made attacks upon Saadiah, Christianity, and Islam; and he is also credited with the authorship of a polemical tract directed against Jacob b. Ephraim, a disciple of Saadiah. His son, *Levi b. Japheth (Abu Saʿid), was likewise a writer. Levi's most important work, a book on the precepts called *Sefer ha-Mitzvot* in its Hebrew translation, was completed in 1007 and is a codification of Karaite *halakhah*. It deals with such topics as the calendar, the nazirite prayer, and civil law, and it is cited by many later Karaites. He may also have composed commentaries on the Early Prophets and on the Psalms.

David b. Abraham *Alfasi (second half of 10th cent.) compiled a dictionary of the Bible in 22 parts corresponding to the letters of the Hebrew alphabet. The various usages of a word are cited, and every entry is translated into Arabic. He refers to Onkelos and Jonathan b. Uzziel, the Aramaic versions of the Bible, and also to the Mishnah, the Talmud, the masorah, and even the Rabbanite prayerbook. He occasionally compares the vocable with Arabic, Aramaic, and mishnaic Hebrew. *Abu al-Faraj Hārūn ibn al-Faraj (c. 1000–1050), who lived in Jerusalem, wrote a grammar of Hebrew called *al-Mushtamil* ("The Encompasser"), which he completed in 1007. It consisted of seven parts and dealt with the manifold aspects of the language. He utilized his knowledge of Arabic and Aramaic for comparison and elucidation. Abu al-Faraj, when giving paradigms of the Hebrew verb, started from the infinitive and showed the difference in the use of this form in Hebrew and Arabic; he also discussed Hebrew particles and syntax. His work was known in Spain and is cited by Jonah *Ibn Janāḥ, and Moses and Abraham *Ibn Ezra. An epitome of the *Mushtamil*, which was probably intended as an appendix, also exists; this may explain why Abraham ibn Ezra speaks of the book as having eight parts. Joseph b. Abraham al-*Baṣīr (called the Seer, a euphemism for "the Blind") was a widely traveled theologian, a polyglot, and a student of Rabbanite lore. He was held in high esteem by the Karaites as a religious authority. His works include *al-Muḥtawi* ("The Compendium," or, in Hebrew, *Sefer Ne'mot*), a theological study which reveals deep Muʿtazilite influence. Consisting of 40 chapters, the book presents a Karaite adaptation of the *kalām* doctrines, as well as polemics against Christians and pagans. He also left an epitome of his major work, *al-Tamyīz*, and a book on inheritance and on ritual cleanliness, *al-Istibṣār* ("Investigation"). His pupil Joshua b. Judah Abu-l-Faraj Furqān ibn Asad (c. 1050–1080) is known as the teacher par excellence. He made an Arabic translation of the Torah together with a commentary on it, which were completed about 1050. His detailed commentary on the Decalogue is available only in the Hebrew translation, which covers only the first four commandments. He also produced *Bereshit Rabbati*, philosophic homilies on Genesis, partially translated into Hebrew. His most important work is on the precepts and is called *Sefer ha-Yashar*. Because of the comparative relaxation of the strict system of relationships (*rikkūb*) which prevailed among the Karaites, the best-known section of the book is on incestuous marriages. He defends his personal views, arguing with his Karaite predecessors and criticizing *Halakhot Gedolot* and the *Hilkhot Re'u*, compilations of Rabbanite law.

The West

The Jewish communities of North Africa and *Spain were as influenced by the Islamic-Arabic environment in which they existed as were their brethren in the East. Although the Jews in those lands (as the Muslims) were for a considerable time pupils of their coreligionists in *Iraq, Palestine, and Egypt, some of them began to write books at about the same time as the Jews in the East. Abu Sahl *Dunash ibn Tamim (10th cent.) was a grammarian, theologian, astronomer, and physician. His work on grammar, of which a small fragment may have been found, is cited by several Spanish Jewish writers. He appears to have undertaken a comparative study of the cognate Semitic languages, lexical rather than morphological; he believed Hebrew to be the mother of Semitic languages, and therefore Arabic to be only a derivative of Hebrew. In his work on astronomy he included a critique of astrology for the

Fatimid Imam Manṣūr Isma'il, and in another study on the same topic he answered the inquiries of *Hisdai ibn Shaprut. There is also mention of works on philosophy and medicine. It is not clear whether his commentary on the *Sefer Yeẓirah* is a revision and editing of Isaac *Israeli's commentary or an entirely independent study. Judah *Ibn Quraysh of Tahert in Morocco (first half of tenth century) was the physician of the emir of Fez. He knew *Eldad ha-Dāni, the self-styled traveler from a distant Jewish land, and believed in his account. His work, called *Risāla* (Epistle; ed. D. Becker, 1984), or possibly *Av va-Em* after the first vocables, is an attempt at comparative linguistics. He states that he composed it in order to rebuke his fellow Jews for neglecting the reading of the Aramaic version of the Torah, which he believed important for the knowledge of Hebrew. In the first of the three parts of the book he compares Aramaic and biblical Hebrew words in alphabetical order; in the second he does the same with Aramaic and Hebrew words in the Mishnah and the Talmud. The final section deals with Arabic and biblical Hebrew.

Talmudic studies flourished in North Africa in the 10th and 11th centuries. One scholar writing in Arabic was *Nissim b. Jacob ben Nissim of Kairouan (c. 990–1060), who headed a school in his native city. His works (a discussion and selections in S. Abramson, *Rav Nissim Ga'on*; Heb., 1965) in chronological order are: *Ha-Mafte'aḥ she-le-Manulei ha-Talmud* ("The Keys to the Locks of the Talmud"), in Arabic, which apparently covered the entire Babylonian Talmud, although only parts of it have so far come to light; comments on the Talmud in Arabic and Hebrew, of which some portions are known and more are being discovered; *Piskei Halakhot* ("Legal Decisions"), in Arabic, fragments of which have been discovered; *Megillat Setarim* ("Scroll of Secrets"), a collection of explanations on difficult passages in the Talmud and on sundry religious topics; and *al-Faraj ba'd al-Shidda* ("Relief After Distress"; in Hebrew, *Ḥibbur Yafeh me-ha-Yeshu'ah*), a book of consolation, a genre current in classical Arabic literature, made up of stories written to bring comfort, faith, and acceptance of God's judgment. This last work has appeared both in Hebrew and in its Arabic original, but it is not yet clear what the author's form and arrangement were.

Jewish works of importance written in Arabic were far more abundant in Muslim Spain than in the East. Among the men who were primarily grammarians and only incidentally biblical exegetes, two names are distinguished. The first, Judah b. David *Ḥayyuj (10th–11th cent.), a native of Fez who died in Spain, devoted two works to the geminated verbs and the verbs with weak letters in their roots. He established the principle that all Hebrew verb-roots, regardless of what happens to them in inflection, consist of three letters; and in this manner he worked out the rules which govern the classes of weak verbs. He also compiled a book of random comments on the books of the Bible, parts of which have been found and published. The second name of importance is Ḥayyuj's outstanding disciple, Jonah *Ibn Janāḥ (first half 11th cent.), who compiled a comprehensive work, *al-Tanqīḥ* ("Polishing"), consisting of a grammar and a lexicon. The former, called *al-Luma'* ("Brightness"; in Hebrew, *Ha-Rikmah*), is a presentation of the rules of Hebrew grammar and their exceptions. The lexicon, which consists of the Hebrew roots, gives their definition, together with examples from the Bible, to illustrate their secondary and tertiary meanings as well as their most common usage. He also composed three smaller works which examine and explain the classes of weak verbs. As a result of culling illustrations from the Bible, his writings contain considerable exegetical material.

Moses b. Samuel ha-Kohen ibn *Gikatilla (11th cent.) occupies a prominent place among biblical commentators who used Arabic. A native of Cordoba who lived in Saragossa, he produced commentaries on most of the books of the Bible, which unfortunately have been lost, with the exception of part of his commentary on the Book of Psalms. However, many of his views are known from extracts quoted in the writings of others, notably of his critic Judah b. Samuel *Ibn Bal'am, who condemned him for his "radical" views on the messianic prophecies. Ibn Gikatilla interpreted these prophecies as predictions of events to take place soon after they were uttered, and he also made efforts to explain miracles rationally. Another work, his short grammatical treatise on gender in Hebrew, is extant. Ibn Bal'am, Ibn Gikatilla's younger contemporary, whose exegetical work has survived, was an eclectic commentator who frequently made use of the works of others. True to the practice of the time, he mentions authors only when he disagrees with them. He charges both Saadiah and Ibn Gikatilla with violating Arabic usage in their translations, and occasionally finds fault even with his master, Ibn Janāḥ. In the field of grammar, he compiled a list of Hebrew particles and their uses, a list of homonyms with their different meanings, and a list of verbs derived from nouns. He is known to have had a remarkably good memory and a very sour disposition.

While many halakhic responsa by Spanish Jews were penned in Arabic, legal compilations were composed in Hebrew or hebraized Aramaic. Even Maimonides, who wrote most of his works in Arabic, turned to Hebrew for his *magnum opus*, the compendium of Jewish law entitled *Mishneh Torah* or *Ha-Ḥibbur*. However, as an aid to making his great compilation well-arranged and complete, he prepared in Arabic a list of the 613 commandments before embarking upon his enterprise. He provided this propaedeutic because he had his own ideas, which differed from those of his predecessors, on the nature of the laws which ought to be included in the 613. He insisted, for example, on the need to distinguish between a biblical and a rabbinic prescription and to exclude general admonitions, such as "Be ye holy." By laying down these principles of selection he hoped to establish an unchallengeable list, a hope that was not fulfilled.

Both Maimonides and his father wrote epistles in Arabic. The latter addressed a letter of comfort to the Jews in North Africa who were victims of religious persecution by the Almohads, a fanatical Muslim movement preached by Ibn Tūmart and adopted by a Berber tribe. The letter seeks to fortify the Jews with the faith that God will not forsake them and that the promises of reward to the righteous will be realized. Maimonides himself discussed the same persecution, but in a much more pragmatic fashion. His missive is in fact in response to a question asked of him by a North African crypto-Jew, who had been told by a local rabbi that his secret practice of Judaism was of no use, since he was outwardly a Muslim. Maimonides refutes the rabbi's ruling, adding, however, an analysis of the talmudic principle that certain demands made by persecutors should not be acceded to, even if the consequence is martyrdom. He exhorts Jews in the same position as the inquirer to leave the locale where the oppression exists, or, if this is too difficult, to practice Jewish law as much as possible without endangering their lives. A second letter, *Iggeret Teiman*, deals with the religious persecution in that country in 1172, which was complicated by the rise of a pseudo-Messiah who promised imminent salvation and the return to Zion. Maimonides offers consolation, and gives warning against the readiness to believe in the pseudo-Messiah out of despair. He also wrote the monograph *Resurrection*, the object of which was to refute accusations that he did not believe the dead would eventually return to life. His refutation was that, since he included this hope as one of the 13 articles of the Jewish faith, it was unnecessary to repeat it; and his failure to discuss resurrection in other appropriate places was due to the distinction between rational doctrines and those accepted on faith.

A unique volume in Arabic was composed by the celebrated poet Moses b. Jacob ibn Ezra. It is a study of the art of Hebrew, especially biblical poetry, called *Kitāb al-Muḥāḍara wa al-Mudhākara*, but it is in fact much more than that, for it also contains a brief history, and occasionally characterizations, of the literary figures who flourished in Spain, a disquisition on the composition of poetry in sleep, and an explanation of why the Arabs excel in poetic composition. The whole work is presented in the style of *adab*, a popular Arabic genre in which the author enjoyed the freedom to digress on any subject. The digression was accompanied by an occasional reminder that it was time to return to the major theme.

Religious Philosophy and Theology

These subjects were cultivated more actively in Muslim Spain than in the East; but like most other cultural activities, they flourished initially in the Levant. Ibn Mukammiṣ has been discussed above. Saadiah's *Emunot ve-De'ot*, though not blindly following Mu'tazilite thought, was nonetheless considerably influenced by it. In general he used reason to buttress the accepted articles of the Jewish faith. With the exception of *Baḥya b. Joseph ibn Paquda (11th cent.), who in the first chapter of his *Ḥovot ha-Levavot* gives a brief resume of a theological position deriving from Saadiah, the works of the other great Spanish Jewish thinkers show that they were under the influence of Plato and Aristotle, or a combination of the latter and neoplatonism. The most philosophic of the group, Solomon b. Judah ibn *Gabirol (1021–1058), was drawn to the views of the Muslim thinker Ibn Masarra (883–931), who was strongly influenced by pseudo-Empedocles and who taught the doctrine of universal matter and universal soul. Basing his philosophy on the Aristotelian principles of matter and form, Ibn Gabirol in his writings cited no passage from biblical or rabbinic sources and made no reference to the Jewish tradition. He did not treat matter and form as opposite ends of being, rather he defined matter as the substrate, common to all being, and form as the differentiating principle which gives individuality to every existent. He regarded matter and form as the universal constituent factors in every object, from the lowest species to the highest intellectual being, and he ascribed the appearance of corporeality to some quality in matter which gives it body. In Ibn Gabirol's view, since matter is the subject, it is logically prior to form, which specifies it; nevertheless, both universal matter and universal form are the sources of all being. The beginning of the world, the first cause, was God's Will, which is intermediate between Infinite God and the universe. Ibn Gabirol did not, however, define God's Will with sufficient clarity to make it plainly comprehensible, and his philosophy did not win favor among Jews. Although neglected by Jewish theologians, it was adopted by some Christian thinkers, and it subsequently exerted considerable influence on the Kabbalah.

As stated above, Baḥya ibn Paquda (11th–12th century) employed the reasoning of *kalām* to prove the existence and oneness of God. But these issues were not his primary concern, they were merely the first requirement of the correct attitude to be taken toward God.

Baḥya's real interest was in emphasizing the duties of the heart (the title of his book), the state of mind and of emotion prerequisite to the true performance of the practical religious precepts. He feels doubly impelled to undertake this task, first because among the community in general performance of ritual acts is the backbone of Judaism, and, secondly because concern with the approved manner of practice occupies the time and mind of the learned. Essentially, Baḥya preached the inward experience of faith: trust, humility, asceticism, repentance, and self-examination. His book, therefore, may be regarded as a guide which, though written about Judaism for Jews and replete with quotations from the Bible and the Talmud, actually belongs to the sphere of religion in general; and for this reason Baḥya does not hesitate to adduce proofs from outside sources. Of all the religious literature produced in the Islamic world, his work was probably the best known and most widely studied among Jews. The monograph *Ma'anī al-Nafs* ("Matters of the Soul") falsely ascribed to him, although probably dating from the same period, deals primarily with the fate and duty of the human soul from the time it separates from its source to join the body until it is once again free to return to its original home. In the course of this exposition, the author also gives his views on the emanation and creation of the world, its constituent factors, and other religious and philosophical issues.

Joseph ibn *Ẓaddik (d. 1149) wrote his *Olam Katan* (*Microcosm*) as a guide to help man gain, through introspection and self-analysis, the necessary knowledge of the world, its Maker, the human soul, and the ethical life. This short tract is not endowed with originality, following neoplatonism in its psychology, Aristotelianism in its physics, and *kalām* in its proof of the existence of God. A far better known poet and literary figure, Moses ibn Ezra, mentioned above, is the author of *Kitāb al-Ḥadīqa fī maʿnā al-majāz wa al-ḥaqīqa* ("The Garden of the Subject of Metaphor and Reality"; in Hebrew, *Arugat ha-Bosem*), a semiphilosophical study in which there is the usual discussion of God and His attributes, and man and his psychology, but in addition there is much attention given to metaphor in the Bible.

The well-known poet *Judah Halevi (1080–1141) was also the author of a philosophical work which was unique in its time among the books in this field. Its title, *Kitāb al-Ḥujja wa al-Dalīl fī Naṣr al-Dīn al-Dhalīl* ("The Book of the Argument and the Proof in Defense of the Despised Faith" (crit. ed. D.H. Banett, prepared for publication by H. Ben-Shammai, Jerusalem 1977), popularly called *Sefer ha-Kuzari*, indicates that it was produced in defense of the Jewish religion, which, the author says, was held in low esteem by the Gentiles. Although critical of philosophy, Judah Halevi is not, like the extremely orthodox, against it; in fact, in his discussion of ethics and of God's uniqueness, he concedes the correctness of the philosophic approach. However, he criticizes metaphysics on the grounds that it simply cannot attain to the ultimate truths, but nevertheless pretends that its conclusions are totally valid. Because their revelation is historically attested, the Jewish Scriptures and tradition are the only unimpeachable sources for the essential truths. The revealed source teaches that man's highest attainment is the gift of prophecy, a gift reserved for the people of Israel in Ereẓ Israel. The Jew receives this gift when he lives in full accord with the Law revealed to Moses. Halevi makes the interesting point that the essence of Judaism is not found in the prescriptions which are rational and apprehensible by human reason, but in the irrational precepts known to us only because they were revealed. He thus demonstrates that the Jewish tradition contains not only the basic truths but also the highest good. The book is written in the form of a dialogue between the author and the king of the Khazars, who wanted to learn about the Jewish faith. It is interesting, although not surprising, that this spokesman for Judaism concludes his discussion by announcing his decision to settle in Ereẓ Israel, which he in fact did, as we know from his poetry. Abraham *Ibn Daud (d. c. 1180), the compiler of an original history of the Jewish tradition, was the first Jewish thinker in Spain to attempt a fusion of the doctrines of the Jewish faith with Aristotelian philosophy (the latter, it must be remembered, was suffused with the neoplatonic system of emanations). Ibn Daud did not examine all theological issues, but he provided summaries of topics such as proofs of the existence of God, the Creation, the Revelation, immortality, and providence. His work, *Sefer ha-Emunah ha-Ramah*, was apparently disregarded in favor of Maimonides' celebrated synthesis; its Arabic original is unknown, and the two translations into Hebrew, one of them published in 1852, were both prepared in the late 14th century.

As stated above, Maimonides (1135–1204) wrote most of his works in Arabic. Of these the most celebrated is his *Guide of the Perplexed* (*Moreh Nevukhim*), a philosophical analysis of Jewish law and theology. Believing like many others that revealed truth and philosophical conclusions reach one and the same end, he proposed to establish the principles of Jewish theology according to doctrines of Aristotelian philosophy, which he accepted as the valid interpretation of the sublunar cosmic process. On this basis he discusses the person of God, the Creation, prophecy, providence, the afterlife, and the content and purpose of the revealed law. In order to anchor his philosophy in Jewish doctrine, he used proof texts from the Bible and traditional Jewish sources. The *Guide* became the most important philosophic work in the Jewish world. Its Hebrew translation had been eagerly awaited by admirers of his earlier works. Two Hebrew renderings, almost simultaneously produced, became available, one by Samuel ibn Tibbon, and the other by Judah b. Solomon *Al-Ḥarizi. The former has always been treated as the authentic and reliable version, although it was severely criticized by Shem Tov b. Joseph *Falaquera, one of the early commentators on the work. In modern times the work has been translated again into Hebrew, by Rabbi J. Kafih, and more recently by Prof. M. Schwartz, who produced a brilliant critical edition (*Maimonides: The Guide of the Perplexed*, Tel Aviv, 2002).

The *Guide*'s popularity resulted in two contrary developments. For many it became the basic text, the authoritative reconciliation between the two sources of the one truth, so that the philosophically-minded in subsequent centuries invariably took it as their point of departure for commentary, summary, or controversy. At the same time, there were scholars who were wary of the intrusion of philosophical reflection into the religious sphere, because they sensed that reconciliation meant setting up philosophy as the judge of what in religion could be maintained, and what had to be interpreted, no matter how far the interpretation carried it from its literal meaning. Even students who were not particularly interested in philosophical speculations were compelled to confront it since Maimonides introduced a number of philosophical concepts into the first of the 14 books of his legal compendium. This alignment of admirers and antagonists led to serious conflict in the 13th and 14th centuries.

Joseph b. Judah ibn *Aknin (c. 1150–1220), a contemporary and friend of Maimonides, settled in Fez after his departure from his native Spain. By his own admission he lived there as a crypto-Jew, although his energetic literary activity seems to show that his private life did not suffer any interference. Save for his commentary on *Avot*, which was originally in Hebrew, his other writings were probably all in Arabic, although there is naturally uncertainty in the case of those of his writings which are no longer extant. Of his surviving works,

Ṭibb al-Nufūs al-Salīma … ("Medicine for Healthy Souls…"), is an ethical treatise which includes a chapter on the soul and its needs and destiny. The book also contains chapters on friendship, speech and silence, keeping a secret, lying, food and drink, and asceticism. In every chapter there is an exposition, followed by relevant rabbinical sayings and epigrams culled from Arabic anthologies. The work is concluded by a chapter on persecutions, and Jewish behavior in relation to them, and a chapter on repentance. A threefold commentary on the Song of Songs, dealing with the plain meaning, the rabbinic elaboration, and a philosophical-psychological interpretation, which Joseph claimed to be an original contribution, has the distinction of providing an explanation of every word in the Scroll. He wrote an *Introduction to the Talmud* (*Mevo ha-Talmud*) and a tract on quantities and measurements in Jewish literature. An as yet undiscovered compilation, *Ḥukkim u-Mishpatim*, may have resembled the legal compendium of Maimonides, and his *Risālat al-Ibāna fī Uṣūl al-Diyāna* ("A Religious Clarification of Religious Fundamentals") was apparently theological in character.

From the 13th Century

In Judeo-Arabic literature, in both Spain and the Middle East, the 13th century marks a division between what preceded it and what followed. In Spain, Christendom's final victory over Islamic power in 1212 led to the gradual elimination of Arabic from Jewish life in favor of the Romance languages in daily intercourse, and of Hebrew in writing. During the 11th and 12th centuries, the continuous shift of the Jewish population from Andalusia to Christian territory, where Arabic had never been the dominant language, accelerated the abandonment of Arabic. However, knowledge of the language remained essential for the translation of texts on philosophy and logic, medicine, mathematics, and astronomy into Hebrew, Latin, and Spanish. It was at this time that the cultural heritage which originated in the East and was enriched during the period of Islamic ascendency was transmitted to the West. Among the authors who continued to write in Arabic, Judah b. Solomon ibn *Matkah (13th cent.), who corresponded with Emperor Frederick II of Sicily, compiled an encyclopedia of logic, physics, and metaphysics, which he translated into Hebrew under the title *Midrash ha-Ḥokhmah*. He also produced *Mishpetei ha-Kokhavim*, a digest of Ptolemy's astronomical *Almagest*. Joseph b. Isaac Israeli of Toledo (d. 1331) wrote a compendium on astronomy which was based on his father's well-known monograph, *Yesod Olam*. Samuel ibn Waqār, the personal physician of Alfonso XI of Castile, may have been the author of the medical work "Castilian Royal Medicine" (1376). Solomon b. Ya'īsh (d. 1345) composed a supercommentary on Abraham ibn Ezra's commentary to the Pentateuch, as well as a six-volume commentary on Avicenna's *Canon*, which remained the standard medical text for centuries. In the field of theology, Moses ibn Crispin Cohen, who in 1336 left his native Cordoba to settle in Toledo, composed a tract on providence and the afterlife. Joseph b. Abraham *Ibn Waqār (14th cent.), a philosopher and kabbalist, also wrote a book on theological matters, for which only a Hebrew title, *Ma'amar ha-Kolel*, is suggested by the name of one of the two extant translations. Judah b. Nissim *Malkah (14th cent.) of North Africa was a neoplatonist who wrote a tripartite work in the spirit of that philosophy; the first two sections were a commentary on the *Sefer Yeẓirah*, the former being an introduction to the theosophic booklet, *Uns al-Gharīb* ("Consolation of the Foreigner," i.e., man's soul on earth) and the latter was on the Midrash *Pirkei De-Rabbi Eliezer*.

The composition of works in Arabic by Jews was much more prevalent in the East, where Arabic continued to be used as the spoken language. However, the general reaction against foreign influences, which gradually eliminated from Muslim intellectual life the variety of interests that had attracted earlier generations, also affected Jewish literary productivity. There was a marked decline in the pursuit of secular subjects, with the exception of medicine; and studies in humanistic areas became confined to theological and ritual topics. Salāma b. Mevorakh (12th cent.), a physician and philosopher, and a student of Ephraim b. āl Zafāh (who was physician to the court), wrote *Niẓām al-Mawjūdāt* ("Arrangement of the Existents"), which was probably philosophic in character, *al-Sabab al-Mūjib li-Qillat al-Maṭar fi-Miṣr* ("The Reasons for the Paucity of Rain in Egypt"), and *fi-al-ʿIlm al-Ilāhī* ("On Theology"). Ḥibat Allah ibn al-Ḥasan b. Ephraim was possibly the head of the academy and community of Fostat, whom the traveler Benjamin of Tudela mentioned by the name of Nethanel and who wrote, among other works: *Irshād li-Maṣāliḥ Anfus al-Ajsād* ("Guide to the Well-Being of Souls and Bodies"), which treats of illnesses, cures, and hygiene; and *al-Taṣrīḥ fī Tanqīḥ al-Qānūn* ("Revelation of the Hidden in Correcting the Canon of Avicenna"). The Karaite *David b. Solomon (1161–1240), physician to Sultan al-Malik al-ʿAdil, and possibly the teacher of Ibn Abī Uṣaybiʿa, wrote a celebrated history of medicine and physicians. He compiled the 12-chapter antidotary *Akrabadhin* or *Dustūr al-Adwiya al-Murakkaba* ("Register of Compound Remedies") and *Risālat al-Mujarrabāt* ("Epistle on Experiences"). Jacob b. Isaac (al-Asad al-Maḥallī; c. 1200) was the author of *Maqāla fī Qawānīn al-Ṭibbiyya* ("Treatise on the Fundamentals of Medicine") and *Masā'il Ṭibbiyya wa-Ajwibatiha* ("Questions and Answers on Medicine"), addressed to the Samaritan author Ṣadaqa ibn Munajja in Damascus. Abu-al-Munā ibn abi Naṣr al-Kohen al-ʿAṭṭār (13th cent.) compiled a popular pharmacopoeia, *Minhāj al-Dukkān wa-Dustūr al-Aʿyān* ("Practice of the Shop and List of the Important"), which is a painstaking collection, arranged in alphabetical order, of pertinent material gleaned from diverse sources, both oral and written. It includes a moralizing first chapter addressed to his son, which in fact may be an addition written by someone else. Nuʿmān ibn abi al-Riḍā' (14th cent.) wrote a medical treatise which he considered to be a collection of glosses on the work of al-Masīḥī. There were a large number of other physicians in the Arabic-speaking Jewish communities who tended to write on religion rather than on their profession. *Abraham

b. Moses b. Maimon (1186–1237), who succeeded his father as court physician and head of the Jewish community, composed a voluminous work, *Kifāyat al-ʿĀbidīn* ("Enough for the Worshippers"), most of which has yet to be discovered. Although he was an ardent defender and great admirer of his father, Abraham's work exhibits a piety which was independent of his father. While not minimizing the importance of learning, he stressed that worship requires humility, concentration, devotion, and other qualities characteristic of pietists such as the Sufis. He also wrote a commentary on Genesis and Exodus and composed two works in answer to his father's critics, as well as responsa (still extant) in answer to religious and legal inquiries. Attributed to one of his two sons, *David b. Abraham (1212–1300), who succeeded him as *nagid*, is a commentary on the *Avot*, which enjoyed great popularity. Also attributed to David is a collection of homilies on the weekly portion of the Torah, but the authorship of both works has been rightly disputed. Like his father, David also had occasion (1290) to rise to the defense of Maimonides. Obadiah (1228–1265), David's brother, composed a *vade mecum* for his son, called *al-Maqāla al-Ḥudiyya* ("The Inclusive Treatise"), in which biblical and rabbinic passages were interpreted allegorically, in order to provide moral instruction (ed. P. Fenton).

An ardent admirer of Maimonides, *Tanḥum b. Joseph Yerushalmi (d. 1291), wrote the commentary *al-Ijaz wa al-Bayān* ("Short and Clear"), which was probably on the entire Bible and is still largely extant, although only very few of his remarks on Ezra and Nehemiah have so far been discovered. His *Commentary on the Minor Prophets* has been published by H. Shay (1991). A rationalist, entirely rejecting any mystical approach to the text, he strove to explain every facet of it with the aid of medicine, *realia*, chronology, geography, and philosophy. Of philosophy he made use on numerous occasions, particularly where the literal meaning of the text was difficult to accept. He employed allegory and included digressions on subjects such as prophecy and the allegorical method. He occasionally disagreed with the *Seder Olam*, the chronological monograph which was almost undisputed during the Middle Ages, although he sometimes assumed approximate dates in the Bible in order to explain away discrepancies. He showed an appreciation for the aesthetic quality of the Bible and also a recognition that copyists' errors may have found their way into the masoretic text. In a comprehensive introduction to his vast enterprise, Tanḥum discussed grammatical and philosophical principles at length and also dwelt on the relation between exegesis and *aggadah*. In addition, he compiled a lexicon of the Hebrew in Maimonides' Code, *al-Murshid al-Kāfī* ("The Adequate Guide"). In the introduction to this work he elaborated upon the tremendous importance of the Code, especially at a time when there was a decline in the study of the Talmud. He criticized the *Arukh*, the lexicon of *Nathan b. Jehiel of Rome (11th cent.), because it did not include all the words in the language and operated on the basis of biliteral roots. Despite his criticisms, he was in fact extremely indebted to the lexicon. Moreover, in his own lexicon he strayed from his objective. Not all the words in the Code are listed, nor are all the vocables given there taken from the Code, since he also provided explanations of a number of mishnaic terms. His tendency to go into philosophical and theological matters emerges even in this work. His son, *Joseph b. Tanḥum ha-Yerushalmi, a gifted writer of Hebrew poetry, may also have been the author of a book in Arabic on theology and philosophy, a fragment of which is extant.

*Ibn Kammuna (Saʿd b. Manṣūr; d. 1184) lived in Baghdad; toward the end of his life he was the target of attack by orthodox Muslims, who took offense at his statements about Islam in *Tanqīḥ al-Abḥāth lil-Milal al-Thalāth* ("Examination of the Inquiries into the Three Faiths"), a study of Judaism, Christianity, and Islam. The book, interesting and enlightened, opens with a general discussion of religion and prophecy and continues with sections on each of the three religions. Ibn Kammuna's method is to present the principles of each faith in a general essay, and then to list questions and objections, followed by replies of the adherents of the particular faith. The work is outstanding for its fairmindedness and objectivity, which may be the reason for the belief, now discredited, that the author was a convert to Islam. His other writings include *al-Ḥikma al-Jadīda* ("The New Science"), on logic; *Risāla* ("Epistle"), on the immortality of the soul; and *Sharḥ Talwīḥāt*, a commentary on the *Notes* of the Muslim mystic Suhrawardi (d. 1191). He also wrote on chemistry and ophthalmology.

*Israel ha-Dayyan ha-Ma'aravi (14th cent.) lived in Cairo and was judge of the Karaite community there. His works include a legal compendium known only by its Hebrew name, *Sefer Mitzvot*, a compilation of the personal and ritual laws of the Karaites. His *Shurūṭ al-Dhabāḥa* ("Requirements of Ritual Slaughter") may have been part of his original *Arabic Code*. He also wrote *Tartīb al-ʿAqā'id al-Sitta* ("Classification of the Six Articles of Faith: God, Moses, the Other Prophets, the Torah, Jerusalem, and the Final Judgment"), as well as a book on the calendar. *Samuel b. Moses al-Maghribi (15th cent.), a physician living in Cairo, compiled *al-Murshid* ("The Guide"), which was a book of laws in 12 sections; he also wrote a commentary on the Pentateuch and a history of Mount Moriah and the Temple. David b. Sa'del al-Hīti (15th cent.) composed a bibliography of Karaite scholars, which, although uncritical and sometimes unreliable, has been of service to modern scholars.

The Jews of *Yemen, who were subjected to many trials and persecutions, probably constituted the most cultivated among the Jewish communities living under Islam in the second millenium. In any case, they can boast of a larger number of literary figures than can other centers. One of the earliest, *Nethanel ibn al-Fayyūmī (d. c. 1170), was probably the head of the community and was the father of *Jacob b. Nethanel whose inquiry to Maimonides brought about the latter's *Iggeret Teiman*. Nethanel wrote *Bustān al-ʿUqūl* ("The Garden of the Intellects"), a theological study with chapters on the unity of God, man the microcosm, the worship of God, repentance, reliance on God, messianic times and the afterlife, influenced by the Isma'ilī. He quoted a good deal from extraneous sources and did not hesitate to invoke the support of the Koran and other Islamic works. *Abraham b. Solomon (1350–1400), probably of Yemen, compiled a commentary on the Prophets and probably also on the Hagiographa. His *Midrash al-Ṣiyāna* is eclectic, quoting copiously from a number of predecessors. Its chief value lies in the fact that it preserves material from works no longer extant. Several Yemenite compositions are midrashic in character, probably because there were frequent occasions in the community when a small sermon was preached at some religious ceremony. *Nethanel b. Yesha, a 14th-century scholar and preacher, composed the midrash *Nūr al-Ẓulām* ("Illumination of the Dark") in 1329. It was written in a combination of Hebrew and Arabic and made up of citations from other sources. In the 15th century *Zechariah b. Solomon ha-Rofe (Yaḥyā b. Suleiman al-Ṭabīb), a physician in Sanʿa, produced *Midrash ha-Ḥefez*, a commentary on the Pentateuch, Lamentations, and the Scroll of Esther. It, too, is eclectic and shows the author's preference for ethical and philosophical interpretations. Zechariah is also credited with a *Sharḥ* ("Commentary") to Maimonides' *Guide*. Another 15th-century author, Abu Manṣūr al-Daimari, composed in a philosophic tone the midrashic commentary on the Pentateuch, *Sirāj al-ʿUqul* ("The Light of the Intellects").

In conclusion, it is to be noted that composition of Jewish works in Arabic continued to appear until there ceased to be Jewish communities in the Arabic-speaking lands. However, it must be admitted that there is little value in these works, most of which are liturgical, exegetic, or translations of Hebrew pietistic works. The European influence, which from the end of the 19th century began to affect Arabic literature as it had affected Jewish literature in Europe a century earlier, does not seem to have played a part in the intellectual life of the Jews in the East. Nevertheless, their output of Hebrew or predominantly Hebrew poetry, rhymed prose, and religious works is of higher quality.

[Abraham Solomon Halkin]

Judeo-Arabic Culture

INTRODUCTION. We are dealing here with that particular body of Jewish religious writings of all types, written in the shadow of *Islam, usually in Arabic, but in Hebrew characters, during the period from before Saadiah Gaon until after the days of Maimonides and his son Abraham, i.e., from approximately the 8th century to the end of the 13th century. This culture is not merely a Jewish culture in Arabic language, but rather a Judeo-Islamic culture. Consequently, it is needless to point out that the Jewish writers who wrote in Arabic during this period were influenced by ideas then current in Islam, but their work should be viewed as the fruit of a period of centuries of creativity and cultural fertility shared by both religions. Similarly, the Arabic language used by the Jews in this period should not be regarded as a mere instrument employed by them, but as an integral part of the religious culture they had absorbed.

The extent to which a culture has absorbed and assimilated influences from another culture, as well as the preconditions which enabled their absorption and assimilation, is well known. The renowned Orientalist H.A.R. Gibb, who studied the influence of Islam on the European Renaissance,[1] laid down, among others, three basic theses which may constitute also a suitable starting point for a discussion of the influence of Islam on medieval Judeo-Arabic culture. These are the following:

(1) No culture absorbs influences from another culture unless the two possess certain similar and related qualities and the ground has been further prepared by similar activities.

(2) The absorption of foreign influences is a sign of the vitality of the absorbing culture or religion, but "the borrowed elements conduce to the expanding vitality of the borrowing culture only insofar as they draw their nourishment from the activities which led to their borrowing in the first place."

(3) Additional evidence of the vitality of the absorbing culture is provided if it confines this foreign influence to certain limits, thus preventing it from becoming too strong and undermining the foundations of the absorbing culture. "A living culture disregards or rejects all elements in other cultures which conflict with its own fundamental values, emotional attitudes or esthetic criteria."

There is no doubt that all this applies to the interrelationship of Judaism and Islam. The essential similarity of these two monotheistic religions which, unlike other religions, are based on law, created from the very beginning a sense of special relationship and led to extensive reciprocal borrowing. The fact that the new religion of Islam assimilated many Jewish elements at the time of its origin and during the years of its consolidation was the reason that many Jewish Sages adopted a much more lenient attitude toward it than toward other religions, and even declared explicitly that it was not to be regarded as idolatry, and differed from Christianity in essential aspects.[2] On the other hand, there is no doubt that Judaism had at least some reservations with regard to borrowing and assimilating Islamic influences. As we will see later on, these reservations were especially strong in the field of mysticism, though many Jews were strongly attracted by Sufi (Islamic mystical) teachings. It is also an established fact that much Islamic material absorbed by Jewish culture has been adapted and developed in a clearly Jewish spirit.

To be properly appreciated, at least three interesting and important viewpoints should be added, however, to these three theses:

(1) Two periods can be clearly distinguished in the interrelationship of Judaism and Islam. During the first period – the 7th and maybe also the 8th centuries – Judaism, more than any other religion and culture, left a decisive impact on Islam, a new religion in the process of consolidation. In the second period – probably from the 8th century, and in particular from the 9th century onward – Islam, which had become a rich and variegated culture, profoundly influenced Jewish culture. Consequently, the interrelationship of these two cultures may be regarded as a closed circle, a rare phenomenon in cultural relationships. Thus it is sometimes possible to trace an idea,

concept or custom that was absorbed by early Islam from Judaism, assimilated by it in a genuine Islamic spirit and, subsequently, in its Muslim guise, left its impact on Judaism. As an example, the concept of intention (*kavanah*, the devotional frame of mind which has to accompany compliance with a religious duty) was doubtless taken from Jewish – mainly Talmudic[3] – sources by Islamic thinkers, who turned it into a Ḥadith saying, allegedly of the prophet, or into a saying of the Sufi (mystic pietists). However, Islam also transformed this concept into a formula which may sometimes deprive it of its very spirit: every believer must declare, before performing a commandment, that he is about to perform it with intention, by reciting a formula: "I now intend to perform the commandment of morning prayer (or midday prayer, etc.)." Pietist Jewish circles seem (at a rather late stage) to have accepted and translated it into Hebrew.[4]

(2) The interrelationship of these two cultures – Judaism and Islam – always took place in the presence of a third religious culture, Christianity, which has strong links with both Judaism and Islam. This permanent Christian presence left its imprint on the interrelationship of these religions. Islam, for instance, regards Judaism and Christianity as belonging to the same category in many respects. They are recognized by Islam as the two earlier monotheistic religions, even though Islam claimed to have superseded and abrogated them. The "People of the Book" (*Ahl al-Kitāb*) or the "Protected People" (*Ahl al-Dhimma*), as both Jews and Christians were called, were granted freedom of worship, though many humiliating restrictions were imposed upon them.[5] The Jews, on their part, generally regarded Islam either as a counterpart of Christianity (as did Judah Halevi, for instance, in his *Kuzari*, Book IV, par. 11), or as its opposite (Maimonides, for instance, in his above-mentioned Responsa). Only seldom did they deal with Islam in a specific way unlinked to Christianity.

(3) This leads us to the central and principal feature of the relationship of Islam and Judaism (and we may now add: and Christianity) in the medieval Arab East: there was a profound religious-cultural alliance among these three positive religions in their common confrontation with the pagan cultural legacy which, in its philosophical Arabic disguise, threatened equally the existence of the three revelational religions.[6] The extent and depth of their spiritual collaboration is highly astonishing and probably has no parallel in any other period of human history. It seems that only against the special cultural background of medieval Islam could such a spiritual alliance have sprung up. The rich Arabic language, with its advanced religious and philosophical terminology, in which the scholars and thinkers of all three religions wrote, was an additional factor. One striking example may be given: it had long been noticed that the "Duties of the Heart" of Baḥya ibn Paquda contains a chapter ("The Ways of Discernment of the Creatures," *Bāb Al-I'tibār Fi-al-Makhlūkīn*) which is surprisingly similar to the book "The Wisdom of God in His Creatures" (*Al-Ḥikma fī makhlūkāt Allah*), probably written by al-Ghazālī (d. 1111), one of the greatest Muslim thinkers of all times. Some passages of these works, which praise God's creation, especially man, are literally identical, and their general contents are the same. It was long believed that Baḥya had copied al-Ghazālī. D.Z. Baneth, however, discovered a manuscript upon which both based their work, and he maintains that it was written by a Christian Arab author. Both Baḥya ibn Paquda and al-Ghazālī adapted this book, each in the spirit of his own religion, mainly by adding verses from the Torah of the Jewish Sages in the case of the former, or verses from the *Qur'ān* or sayings of the Prophet and his companions, by al-Ghazālī.

STUDYING JEWISH CULTURE IN THE SHADOW OF ISLAM. The relationship of Judaism and Islam has so far been considered, as it were, from the outside – a step which is necessary if one wishes to study the Arabic period of Jewish history or the form of Jewish culture that was created in the shadow of Islam. Only thus is it possible to obtain an overall picture of the relationship between two cultures, without which one is bound to get entangled in details, without being able to discern the general framework clearly. However, these cultures must now be considered "from within" in order to determine their characteristic and striking features.

But first an important methodological problem has to be faced. There is a widespread tendency to ascribe a phenomenon occurring in two cultures to the influence of the earlier culture on the later. A. Geiger, in the introduction to his "Was hat Mohammed aus dem Judenthum aufgenommem?" (Leipzig, 1830), and I. Goldziher already warned against this tendency with regard to the relationship of Judaism and Islam. Similar developments and phenomena in different cultures are not necessarily the result of the influence of one on the other, but may also be the fruit of equal external conditions or of the religious needs and developments of the individual believer or the community, etc.

A few examples may illustrate this point.

Both Judaism and Islam are unique in that they have a sacred oral law in addition to the Divinely given written law.[7] It is, nevertheless, questionable whether this phenomenon in Islam is necessarily the fruit of the influence of the older religion. It is true that when the Muslim oral law (*al-Sunna*) was committed to writing, the opponents of this act used arguments very similar to those of the Jewish Sages, who opposed the redaction of the oral law into a book. Nevertheless, Goldziher strongly rejects the assumption that this is a case of direct Jewish influence. An oral law is bound to appear sooner or later in a religion that possesses a written law, in order to answer new questions and needs which arise and are not solved by the written law. It is also natural that initially such a suggestion will meet with fierce opposition, but gradually the oral law will take its place alongside the written law and even overshadow it, in matters of both doctrine and practice. In Islam this is even explicitly expressed by the saying that the oral law, the *Sunna* of the Prophet, may change or even abrogate explicit statements of the *Qur'ān*. Both in Judaism and Islam it is explicitly stated that the later sayings of the oral law are as sacred and binding as the early words of the legislator. In Judaism this was formulated by Rabbi Joshua ben Levi: "Even what an outstanding student may point out to his teacher in the future was already said to Moses on Mount Sinai" (TJ, Ḥag. 1, 8); and in Islam, in the paradoxical sayings ascribed to the Prophet Muhammad, such as: "All beautiful things that are said stem from me, whether I have said them or not."[8]

Another example is the commandment of Islam to make, at least once in a lifetime, the pilgrimage to the holy places in Mecca. Abraham I. Katsh maintains that this practice was adopted from Judaism (see Ex. 23:14ff; Deut. 16:16–17).[9] Yet the assumption is unfounded. The Ḥajj was a common practice in the Arabian peninsula already in pre-Islamic times, and it was adopted by Islam, which gave it an ethiological and monotheistic interpretation, just as Judaism did with the many pagan relics it preserved.

There are, of course, many cases in which direct influence of one religion on another can be established with certainty, especially direct influence of Judaism on Islam; not only in basic concepts and ideas, biblical narratives[10] (such as the stories of the Patriarchs) and laws, but also with regard to minor details, of which two examples are given here, though the main subject of this article is the second stage of Muslim-Jewish interaction, in which Judaism was influenced by Islam.

Originally, the Islamic fast, which is now Ramadan, was held on the tenth day of the first month, from sunset to sunset, like the Jewish Day of Atonement. The change to a whole month's fast was probably the result of Muhammad's disillusion with the Jews and his wish to sever relations with Judaism. Nevertheless, an interesting example of Jewish influence is seen in the verse of the *Qur'ān*: "… and eat and drink until you distinguish between the white thread that becomes distinct to you from the black thread at dawn (or: of the dawn)" (Sura II, 187). The source of this verse is almost certainly the Mishnah Ber. 1, 1: "When is the morning prayer said? When blue can be distinguished from white." For the Jew, wrapped in his usually white prayer shawl with blue stripes, these words had a real meaning, but transferred to an entirely foreign sphere they reveal the direct influence of Judaism.[11]

To the same category belongs a passage of the story in the *Qur'ān* of Joseph (Sura XII) and its commentaries. When Potiphar's wife heard that the women were gossiping about her passion for Joseph, she invited them to a meal and gave each a knife. When Joseph entered, they were so overwhelmed by his handsomeness that they cut themselves. The knife was presumably to cut fruit which was placed before them, but the name of the fruit is not given in the *Qur'ān*. The story is also found in later Midrashim, e.g., the *Midrash ha-Gadol*, which was composed under Muslim influence of the *Qur'ān*. But the commentators state that it was the etrog, the citron, a fruit which was completely unknown in the northern Arabian peninsula. The Israelites, on the other hand, already knew this fruit, perhaps even as early as the Babylonian captivity, and they perhaps transmitted this story to Islam together with the story of Joseph.[12]

ISLAMIC INFLUENCE ON JUDAISM. We now return to the second period in the history of Jewish-Muslim relations, the long period in which Islam exerted its influence on Judaism. This investigation is still in its initial stage, even though many scholars – mainly Jewish – have dealt with it since the 19th century, and the results of their research are published in scores of books and hundreds of articles scattered through periodicals and books.

The philosophical and theological influence of Islam on Jewish thought in the Middle Ages, or on the history and way of life of the Jews in Muslim culture, is now generally recognized. The many studies of Goldziher (published mainly in REJ and MGWJ, and most of them now collected in several volumes by D. Desomogyi) have perhaps also brought about a general recognition of the fact that Muslim sources contain much material for the study of Jewish history and the religious way of life. But only few scholars, especially S.D. Goitein, G. Vajda, N. Wieder and M. Zucker, have hitherto discussed the influence of Islamic religious terminology and practice on Jewish literature and practice. S.D. Goitein's monumental *A Mediterranean Society* has become a major breakthrough in this respect as well, although its more important contributions lie, of course, in the completely new description and analysis of Jewish social and economic history under Islam in the Middle Ages.

Judeo-Arabic also has been studied so far mainly from its linguistic angle – as the counterpart of Christian-Arabic – or as an additional aspect of middle Arabic. Arabic was the main language of the Jews in speech and religious literature in all its varieties; a close examination may help to appreciate the tremendous religious influence of Islam on Jewish medieval scholars, which is more than a mere linguistic phenomenon. Scores of religious Islamic terms permeated Jewish literature, including denominations of the Torah by *Qur'ānic* terms such as *al-Kitāb, al-Shari'a, al-Maṣḥaf, al-Nūzūl, Um al-Kitāb* and even *al-Qur'ān*. Chapters of the Torah were called "Suras" (verses retained their Hebrew name, *Pasuq*, although for the plural an Arabic form was used, *Pawāsīq*). The oral law was called *Sunna* or *Fiqh*, the cantor *Imām*, Jerusalem became *Dār-a-Salām*, Abraham *Khalīl Allah*, Moses *Rasūl-Allah* like Muhammad; the Messiah was called *al-Qā'im al-Muntaẓar* like the awaited Messiah of the Shi'ites; the direction of prayer to the east was named *al-Qibla*, which is the name the Muslims gave their direction of prayer to the south towards Mecca. There are, in addition, hundreds of religious words that may be classified as mere linguistic phenomena, such as *al-Mu'minūn* (the believers); *Nawāfil* (optional prayer); *Jamā'a* (congregation, community; also minyan, the quorum of ten men required for Jewish prayer); *Bid'a* (undesirable religious innovation), etc.[13] In contrast to the west, where Jews never used their non-Hebrew names for religious purposes, Jews used their Arabic names in the synagogue, in marriage contracts, etc.

Combined Hebrew-Arabic phrases, such as *Ṣalāt al-Shaḥarit*, or *Laylat al-Pesaḥ*, and such terms as *Qādī* and

Muftī (judge) and *Fatwā* (*halakhic* responsa) were also widely used. Apart from these, Jewish literature is full of literal quotations from the *Qur'ān* and the Ḥadīth, as well as from later religious literature of Islam. Medieval translations of Arabic works into Hebrew, such as Abraham ben Ḥasdai's translation of al-Ghazālī's *Mīzān al-Amāl* ("The Scales of Justice"), also retained Qur'ānic verses and Ḥadīth sayings in the Hebrew version, but sometimes added biblical verses and sayings of the Jewish Sages.[14] The Jewish authors often changed the proper names, but seldom the quotation itself. For instance, instead of "Aisha," the wife of the Prophet Muhammad, they quoted "the Prophetess Deborah"; instead of writing "said Umar ibn Khattāb," they wrote "said Rabbi Akiva"; they replaced Abū Ḥanīfa and al-Shāfi'ī by Ravina and Rav Ashi; the expression "said the Messenger of Allah" by "said one of the Prophets" or "one of the sons of the Prophets" and "the words of al-Saḥāba" ("the Companions of the Prophets") by "the words of our Sages," etc.[15] Moreover, in the Cairo *Genizah* (see below, note 32) and other places, verses of the *Qur'ān* (especially the two last Suras) and fragments of Arabic religious literature (for instance, verses of the mystic martyr al-Ḥallāj or of al-Ghazālī's autobiography) were found in Arabic, but in Hebrew transcription, apparently for use as amulets or for study. During the Middle Ages the whole *Qur'ān* was also transcribed word for word in Hebrew characters. Unlike some scholars, who consider the use of Hebrew characters in writing Arabic proof of the fact that the spiritual assimilation of the Jews to Islamic culture was less extensive than their assimilation to modern European culture, it is maintained that the Jewish use of Arabic is much more than a mere linguistic phenomenon and had far-reaching cultural-religious repercussions. Medieval Judaism in the Arab East was not only arabicized, but in almost every sphere of life – and not only in philosophy and theology – it bore the stamp of Islam.[16]

A few examples, some better known than others, are given here. The first is taken from the field of linguistics, but its significance exceeds this field by far. The linguistic skill of the Arabs and their veneration of the Arabic language, from the dawn of their civilization (cf. pre-Islamic poetry), may be one of the reasons that the *Qur'ān*, the Word of Allah, may have been one of the best miraculous proofs of the truth of Muhammad's message (just as, according to the Ḥadīth, the previous prophets had performed their own miracles, each in conformity with the characteristics of either his people or times).[17] Hence the interesting Muslim theological doctrine, according to which the *Qur'ān* is superior to other holy writs not only from the religious, but also (and mainly) from the linguistic-stylistic viewpoint and, therefore, cannot be imitated by men.[18] This veneration of language as such was adopted by the medieval Jews (Moses ibn Ezra was one of the intermediaries) and even led to a revival of Hebrew among them to attempt to demonstrate that Hebrew was in no way inferior to the rich language of their Muslim neighbors. Even the Muslim belief that the Quraish, the tribe to which the prophet belonged, spoke a purer language than the other Arabs, had its Jewish parallel in the belief that the tribes of Yehuda and Binyamin, or the Jerusalemites, spoke the purest form of Hebrew.[18]

The second example is from the field of history. It was a strange phenomenon, alien to the spirit of the People of the Book, that some of our false messiahs, who appeared in the shadow of Islam, boasted of their illiteracy and were proud to claim that they could neither read nor write. This motif is found in Judaism only in the appearance of some later false messiahs. Again, we may have here an obvious case of Muslim influence, namely of the concept of *al-Nabī al-Ummi*, a title conferred on Muhammad on the basis of an obscure expression in the *Qur'an*, the original meaning of which was that Muhammad considered himself the prophet who was sent to all nations, but very soon it was interpreted as "the prophet who cannot read and write."[19]

This motif was transmitted to Judaism, but it is so alien to the spirit of Judaism that it justifies the assumption that it was a Muslim motif which the false messiahs needed to rally the ignorant masses of Israel behind them.

The next example belongs to an entirely different sphere. Judaism and Islam both possess a special class of literature which, to a large extent, fulfills the part that is taken in other cultures by the written law, the responsa literature. This literature consists of legal decisions given in answer to questions by individuals. These responsa (*Fatwā*, pl. *Fatāwā*, in Arabic) have the force of decisions of law, and have been collected in tens of books which, both in Judaism and Islam, serve as textbooks of legal precedents and as the basis of subsequent decisions. It is true that Roman law also knew this genre of legal literature (*Jus Respondendi*), and the assumption that the Jewish and Muslim responsa literature was derived from the Roman practice cannot be rejected out of hand.

However, with regard to Judaism and Islam, it is difficult to establish with certainty what preceded what. In general, one can state, however, that a great part of Muslim religious law developed in Iraq was influenced to a certain extent by the Jewish *halakhic* activity, which reached its zenith there under the *Geonim*. It seems, therefore, reasonable to assume, with Goitein, that the well-developed *halakhic* literature left its imprint on the early law of Islam, but, on the other hand, the possibility should be considered that the development of Jewish *halakhah* received momentum as a result of the rise and influence of Islam.[20] Moreover, it should be kept in mind that Islam had the same needs as Judaism, which led to the growth of a similar *halakhic* literature, and vice versa. The tremendous socioeconomic revolution the Jews faced under Muslim rule (their transition from a people of farmers to a people of merchants) led to the rise of laws similar to those of Islam, which is, to a considerable extent, the product of a middle-class, mercantile civilization.[21]

However this may be, the fact remains that the two religions, Judaism and Islam, seem to be the only *halakhic* religions in the world (the Muslim name for *halakhah* is *Sharī'a*, meaning the main road; and the various *halakhic* schools are called *Madhāhib*, a root also related to "going" and expressing – just like the Hebrew term **halakhah* – the idea of a "way of life"). As mentioned above, both possess a sacred oral law alongside the written law, and both have created a huge literature of religious law, chiefly by means of rational analogy. In both, this was the work of independent religious scholars (*Fuqahā*, *ʿUlamā* – in Arabic), and in both, different schools of law are all considered equally orthodox. In both, religious preoccupation with the religious law is considered a Divine precept, and both even believe that God Himself engages in the same activity together with His heavenly companions; both have similar basic principles (cf., for instance, the idea that "the power of permission is preferable," in the Babylonian Talmud, *Ber.* 60a, with the end of Sura II in the Koran) and categories to classify all human deeds and scores of identical legal details. It is, however, impossible to determine with certainty when the literary genre of Responsa first appeared, or whether it was the result of the influence of one religion on another. There are hardly any Jewish responsa from the time preceding R. Yehuda Gaon (middle of the 8th century), and in Islam there were, up to the same time, only a few "private" responsa from such individuals as Ibrāhīm al-Nakh'i of al-Kufa, who lived in the first century of the Hegira. According to those scholars who believe that this literary genre already occurs in the Talmud, and that the *geonim* only continued the work of earlier Jewish Sages, the responsa literature would have been taken over by Islam from Judaism, but the question still requires thorough research.[22] I. Goldziher, on the other hand, showed that, in some details at least, the influence of Islamic responsa literature on Judaism can be asserted with some certainty. Much of the Jewish responsa literature in Islamic countries was written in Arabic, and the questions addressed to the Sage from all over the world sometimes open with this formula: "Let our master teach us, and may the Lord give him a double reward." But why a double reward? Goldziher showed that this formula is based on a popular Ḥadīth saying, ascribed to the Prophet, which says: "If a judge rules with deliberation and his decision is right, he shall receive a double reward from the Lord."[23]

One more example of responsa literature illustrates Islamic influence on Judaism, even though this whole literary religious genre may have first started in Islam under Jewish influence. Jewish religious literature proscribes the playing of any musical instrument as a token of mourning over the destruction of the Temple. However, during the period between Saadiah Gaon and Maimonides, another strange argument for this prohibition was added: here it is linked to the immoral ways of musicians and singers (especially female singers). It seems that this reflects the general religious Muslim negative attitude to music (with the exception of the pietist Sufis, who cultivated religious music). Some Muslim scholars even forbade singers and musicians to appear as witnesses in court, since their profession made them unfit to give evidence. Jewish Sages in the same period followed this example and forbade singers to give evidence in court since they were considered transgressors.[24]

RABBI ABRAHAM, THE SON OF MAIMONIDES. This final chapter deals with the interesting topic of Rabbi Abraham, the son of Maimonides, who succeeded his father as the head of the Jewish community in Egypt (1204–37), and more generally with the influence of Muslim Sufi pietism and mysticism on Judaism. This Muslim movement and its marvelous religious literature had a tremendous impact on the Jews, who were attracted by it even more than by Arab philosophy.[25] That some Jews actually joined Sufi groups is attested by Muslim sources, as well as by Jewish letters from the *genizah*. S.D. Goitein published a heartrending letter from a poor Jewish woman to the Nagid David (probably the David II Maimonides who, in the middle of the 14th century, became one of the leaders of Egyptian Jewry), in which she implores him to help her bring her husband Basir back to her from the company of "al-Fuqarā" (the Muslim mystics; literally: the poor). Basir had forsaken his wife and children and taken up residence in a Sufi convent on a mountain near Cairo. His wife expressed her fear that he would abandon Judaism and that their three children would follow his example.[26]

Fragments of poetical and prose works of the Muslim mystics, in their original language but in Hebrew transcription, were found in the Cairo Genizah, and R. Abraham Gavison of Tlemcen in Algeria (d. 1605) says in his commentary on the Proverbs that "every educated man must be impressed by the great philosopher Abu Ḥamid al-Ghazālī," whose books are studied by many Jewish scholars.[27] Al-Ghazālī was, of course, not only one of the great Muslim thinkers, but also an outstanding Sufi pietist. Jewish writers, however, never reached the same degree of extreme ecstasy which the Muslim mystics sought, and which induced them to tear down the partitions between religions, between good and evil, and even between God and man.

The story of R. Abraham the son of Maimonides is one of the most striking episodes in the history of this influence.[28] R. Abraham (d. 1237), who had inherited the function of *Ra'īs al-Yahūd* (leader of the Jews) from his father, was not only a leader and a *halakhic* scholar (see the volume of his responsa published by C. Freiman and S.D. Goitein), but also an outstanding Sufi. He wrote a great pietist Sufi compendium named *Kifāyat al-ʿābidīn* ("The Sufficient Book for the Servants of God"), and tried to win his generation over to the Sufi way of life and to prove to them, with the help of a great many quotations from Jewish sources, that this was the true way for God-fearing men. Although opinions differ as to his sources, there is no doubt that he was deeply influenced by the world of Sufism, with which he had become closely acquainted in Egypt.[29] Rabbi Abraham argued that Islam, especially in its Sufi version, preserved many elements of the practices and teachings of the ancient Jewish Sages, which the latter had intentionally neglected with the appearance of pietist heretic circles. Among these elements were kneeling and prostration during prayer, ritual immersions, nightly prayers, etc. Early Islam adopted these ceremonies, as well as the attendant feelings of awe for the Day of Judgment and disgust at this world.

In the world of Islam all these elements were developed in a special way in the Sufi movement, and that is why they are so closely related to the ancient Jewish Sages.

R. Abraham did not, however, content himself with theoretical study alone. His conviction induced him to demand the return to the ancestral customs by imitating the Muslim surroundings, for instance in the matter of prayer. In one section of his work he suggests the removal of pillows from the synagogues and, instead, the spreading of prayer mats and carpets on the floor as in the mosques, and to the practice of prostration in prayer, like the Muslims,[30] and he praises the respectful silence in the mosques, which was in flagrant contrast to the noise and lack of devotion in the synagogues of his day. R. Abraham's suggestion, however, was not adopted, as we learn from the *genizah* documents. The members of his congregation filed a complaint against him with al-Malik al-'Ādil, the ruler, the brother and heir of Saladin, that he tried to force upon them innovations (*bid'a*) forbidden by their religion. This was in contravention of the laws of Islam, which in this respect were also applied to the non-Muslim communities under its jurisdiction. R. Abraham was compelled to apologize to the Muslim ruler and to announce that he did not intend to abuse his authority as leader of the Jewish community by introducing such religious innovations.[31]

Judeo-Arabic culture should not, therefore, be treated as a Jewish culture which merely expressed itself in Arabic, but as a common Jewish-Muslim culture cultivated by Jews who lived under the rule of Islam, spoke Arabic, and were deeply influenced not only by some spheres of Islamic civilization, such as Muslim philosophy, but by Islam as a religion in its widest sense.

Notes

1. H.A.R. Gibb, "The Influence of Islamic Culture on Medieval Europe," in: *John Rylands Library Bulletin* 38 (1955–56), 82–98, esp. 85–87.
2. See, e.g., R. Moses b. Maimon, *Responsa*, ed. and transl. from the Arabic into Hebrew by J. Blau, Jerusalem, 1957, II, 726ff (in Hebrew). This does not mean that Jewish Sages, Maimonides included, refrained from stressing the basic differences and points of dispute between Judaism and Islam.
3. Cf. *Mishnah*, Ber. 5:1, 5: "None may stand up to say the *Tefillah* save in sober mood. The pious men of old used to wait an hour before they said the *Tefillah*, that they might direct their heart towards God."
4. S.D. Goitein, *Jews and Arabs: Their Contacts through the Ages*, Schocken, N.Y. 1955, 178–79.
5. Many of those regulations were taken over by Islam from Byzantine legislation. Cf. A.S. Tritton, *The Caliphs and Their Non-Muslim Subjects* (London, 1930) and *Encyclopaedia of Islam*, v. dhimma.
6. This aspect was especially stressed by J. Guttmann in his studies. See, e.g., his *Philosophies of Judaism* (transl. by D.W. Silverman), The Jewish Publication Society of America, Phila., Pa., 1964, Ch. II, and see his article, "Religion u. Wissenschaft im mittelalterlichen u. modernen Denken," in: *Festschrift zum 50. Bestehen der Hochschule für die Wissenschaft des Judentums, Berlin*, 1922, 146–240. In spite of the feeling of alliance, as it were, there also flourished, of course, a whole genre of polemic literature, especially Islamic polemics against Judaism and Christianity, often composed by Jewish or Christian converts to Islam. Cf. M. Perlmann, "The Medieval Polemics between Judaism and Islam," in: S.D. Goitein (ed.), *Religion in a Religious Age*, Association for Jewish Studies, Ktav Publishing House, New York, 1974, 103ff., and especially the general bibliography mentioned there on 135–38. Cf. now also his ed. and transl. of *Shaykh Damanhuri on the Churches of Cairo*, University of California Press, 1975, and see Hava Lazarus-Yafeh, *Studies in Al-Ghazzali*, Jerusalem, Magnes Press, Appendix A.
7. See G. Weil, *Oral Tradition in Judaism and Islam* (Hebrew), Magnes Anniversary Book, Jerusalem, 1938, 132–42. (English summary, ibid., xxxi–xxxviii)
8. Cf. I. Goldziher, *Vorlesungen über den Islam*, Heidelberg, 1925, Ch. II, 44.
9. See A.I. Katsh, *Judaism in Islam, Biblical and Talmudic Backgrounds of the Koran and its Commentators*, New York, 1954, Sura II, 193, 137–39, and cf. my review of the Hebrew translation of this book (in Hebrew) in: *Ha-Mizrah he-Ḥadash (The New East), Quarterly of the Israel Oriental Society*, 9 (1958–59), 111–12.
10. A. Geiger's above-mentioned study was translated into English by M. Young as *Judaism and Islam*, Madras, 1848 (and reprinted by Ktav, New York, 1970, with a prolegomenon by M. Perlmann), and was followed by many studies. It should be noted here again that many of these Jewish (and Christian) stories *(Isrā'īliyyāt)* were "islamicized," as it were, and elaborated upon in special Muslim collections called *Qiṣaṣ al-Anbiyā*. Afterwards these Islamic versions of ancient biblical stories exercised clear influence on late Hebrew Midrashim, thus proving once more the "closed circle" relationship mentioned above between the two cultures. Cf. e.g., J. Heinemann, *Aggadah and Its Development* (Hebrew), Jerusalem, 1973, Ch. 12 (on the late Midrash "Pirkei de Rabbi Eliezer"). The study and translation of the various "*Qiṣaṣ al-Anbiyā*" as a literary genre of Arabic religious literature has only recently been begun.
11. G. Vajda, "Jeune Musulmane et Jeune Juif," in: HUCA, 12–13 (1938), 369. *Encyclopaedia of Islam*, v. Ramaḍān (S.D. Goitein).
12. Cf. Encyclopedia Judaica, **Etrog*." See also S.D. Goitein, *Jews and Arabs*, 193. According to Goitein, this specific Arabic version of the Joseph story may have its origins in early Persian literature, ibid., 194–95.
13. Cf. J. Blau, *The Emergence and Linguistic Background of Judeo-Arabic*, Oxford, 1965 (third revised edition, Jerusalem, 1999), 158ff (Appendix II, c). Idem, in: *Tarbiẓ*, Quarterly for Jewish Studies, 15 (1970–71), 512–14; see also the innumerable Judeo-Arabic texts, such as Saadiah Gaon's *Siddur* (Book of Prayers), his translations of the Bible into Arabic or his famous

Kitāb al-Amānāt wal-I'tiqādāt (Book of Beliefs and Opinions; transl. into English by S. Rosenblatt, Yale University Press). The same holds true for Judeo-Persian Literature. Cf. e.g., H.H. Paper, *A Judeo-Persian Pentateuch*, Jerusalem, 1972, passim. This may mean that we deal not only with Arabic linguistic influences, but with Islamic influences.

14. The Hebrew translation of the book was published with a Hebrew introduction by J. Goldenthal, Paris, 1839, with the title *Compendium Doctrinae Ethicae, auctore al-Ghazzali Tusensi, philosophe Arabum clarissimo, de arabico hebraice conversum ab Abrahamo bar Chasdai Barcinonensi (liber argumento luculentissimus et oratione dulcissimus…)*. Cf. also M. Gottstein, "Translations and Translators in the Middle Ages," in: *Gotthold E. Weil Jubilee Volume*, Jerusalem 1953, 74–80.

15. A.S. Halkin (ed. and transl. into Hebrew), Moshe b. Ya'akov ibn Ezra, *Kitāb al-Muḥadāra wal-l-Mudhākara, Liber Discussions et Commemorationis (Poetica Hebraica)*, passim, and see A.S. Yahuda (ed.), *Al-Hidāya Ilā Farā'id Al-Qulūb des Bahja ibn Jōsēf Ibn Paqudā aus Andalusien*, Leiden 1912. Introduction (German), Ch. 3.

16. See S.D. Goitein's monumental *A Mediterranean Society*, especially Vol. 2, *The Community*, University of California Press, 1971, and Vol. 3, *Daily Life and the Individual*, 1976. As for specific influences cf. also N. Wieder, *Islamic Influences on Jewish Worship* (Hebrew), Oxford, 1957, or M. Zucker, "The Problem of "Isma – Prophetic Immunity to Sin and Error in Islamic and Jewish Literatures" (Hebrew), in: *Tarbiz*, 35 (1966), 149–73 (English summary p. VII). Yet one has to be very careful, especially when dealing with details. Cf. e.g., S.D. Goitein's review of J. Blau's edition of Maimonides' *Responsa*, "Maimonides as Chief Justice," in: JQR, 49 (1958–9), 191–204, especially 198, n. 25. Nevertheless, the fact of Islamic influence on medieval Oriental Judaism is today acknowledged almost unanimously among students of Jewish history. Cf. also A.S. Halkin, "Judeo-Arabic Literature," in: L. Finkelstein (ed.) *The Jews, Their History, Culture and Religion*, Vol. 2, New York, 1960, 1116–48; G. Vajda, *Introduction à la Pensée Juive au Moyen Age*, Paris, 1947. It is interesting to discern the same acknowledgement of general influence and the same reservation with regard to specific religious influences in the study of Islamic influences on the Christian West. As against this, see, e.g., G. Makdisi's studies, for example his article "The Scholastic Method in Medieval Education…," in: *Speculum*, 49 (1974), 640–61, esp. 641, 661.

17. Cf. EIS[2] v. *i'djāz*.

18. Cf. A.S. Halkin, "The Medieval Attitude Toward Hebrew," in: A. Altmann (ed.) *Biblical and Other Studies*, Brandeis University, P.W. Lown Institute of Advanced Studies, Studies and Texts 1, Harvard University Press, 1963, and Moshe Ibn Ezra, ibid., p. 42ff, 54ff.

19. See EIS v. *Ummī*. I. Goldziher, *Vorlesungen*, ibid., Ch. 1, 27ff. Cf. also W.M. Watt, *Bell's Introduction into the Qur'ān*, Edinburgh, 1970 (Islamic Surveys 8), 33ff.

20. See J. Schacht, *An Introduction into Islamic Law*, Oxford 1964, 20–21; S.D. Goitein, *Jews and Arabs*, 59–61; idem, Introduction into Muslim Law, in: Goitein and Ben-Shemesh, *Muslim Law in Israel* (Hebrew), Jerusalem, 1957. For a different view with regard to the responsa, see A.J. Rosenthal, *Judaism and Islam*, Popular Jewish Library, 1961, 55. See also M.A. Friedman, "The Ransom Divorce, Proceedings in Medieval Jewish Practice," in: *Israel Oriental Studies*, 6 (1976), 288–307, esp. 298–99.

21. See S.D. Goitein, *Jews and Arabs*, Ch. VI, 89ff. and cf. idem, *A Mediterranean Society, Vol. 1: Economic Foundations*, University of California Press, 1967, esp. Chs. 2, 3.

22. Cf. also EIS[2], v. *Fatwā*.

23. I. Goldziher, "Über eine Formel in der jüdischen Responsa Literatur und in den Muh. Fatwas," in: ZDMG, 53 (1899), 645–52 (Jewish medieval sources trace this formula back to Isaiah 57:14).

24. Cf. B.M. Lewin (ed.), *Oẓar ha-Ge'onim*, Gittīn, Jerusalem, 1941, 10, Responsum 20. On music in Islam, see now A. Shiloh, "The Dimension of Sound," in: B. Lewis (ed.), *The World of Islam*, London, 1976, esp. 168. Cf. also EIS[2], v. *"Adl*; EIS, v. *Shāhid*; and Th. W. Juynboll, *Handbuch des Islamischen Gesetzes*, Leiden, 1910, 316.

25. Cf. e.g., G. Vajda, "La Théologie Ascetique de Bahya ibn Paquda," in: *Cahiers de la Société Asiatique*, 7 (1947); F. Rosenthal, "A Judeo-Arabic Work under Sufi influence," in: HUCA, 15 (1940), 443–84; R.J.Z. Werblowsky, "Faith, Hope and Trust: A Study in the Concept of Bitaḥon," in: *Annual of Jewish Studies*, London, 1964, 118ff.

26. S.D. Goitein, "A Jewish Addict to Sufism," in: JQR, 44 (1953), 37–49.

27. *Omer ha-Shikhḥah* (Hebrew), Livorno, 1748, 138a.

28. For a full account, see S.D. Goitein, "Abraham Maimonides and his Pietist Circle" (English), in: A. Altmann (ed.), *Jewish Medieval and Renaissance Studies*, P.W. Lown Institute of Advanced Jewish Studies, Brandeis University, Studies and Texts 4, Harvard University Press, 1967, 145–64; and the bibliography mentioned there in note 1. Cf. also idem, i.e., "A Treatise in Defense of the Pietists by Abraham Maimonides," in: JJS, 16 (1966), 105–14; *Jews and Arabs*, 182ff.; *A Mediterranean Society*, Vol. 2, 1971, 156–57, 406–7; G. Cohen, "The Soteriology of R. Abraham Maimoni," in: PAAJR, 35 (1967), 75–98; 36 (1968), 33–48. An analysis, edition, and English translation of parts of R. Abraham's *Kifāyat al- "Abīdīn* is to be found in S. Rosenblatt (ed.), *The Highways to Perfection of Abraham Maimonides*, 1, New York, 1927; 2, Baltimore, 1938.

29. Scholars are divided upon the question, and some, like G. Cohen, try to minimize Islamic influences on R. Abraham.

30. It may be important to note here that in many aspects there is a much greater affinity between a synagogue and a mosque than between the former and a church, especially a Catholic church. Cf. for example, the common prohibition of paintings and sculptures of men and animals, based on Exodus 20:4–5 and Sūra V, 91 and the commentaries thereon. (This prohibition did not hinder the rise of the fine arts, especially in Islam. Cf. K.A.C. Creswell, "The Lawfulness of Painting in Early Islam," in: *Ars Islamica*, 11 (1946), 159–66, and cf. EI-Sūra; cf. now

also the general survey of R. Ettinghausen, "Decorative Arts and Paintings: Their Character and Scope," in: J. Schacht and C.E. Bosworth (ed.): *The Legacy of Islam*, Oxford, 1974; 274ff. and the bibliography mentioned there 291–92.) Suffice it to mention here that the religious laws of both Judaism and Islam permit paintings, sculptures, etc., of people and animals, only if they are maimed or put on the earth to be trodden upon.

31. The most interesting documents concerning this affair were preserved in the Cairo Genizah (see S.D. Goitein, *A Mediterranean Society*, Vol. 1, Introduction, and idem (ed.) *Religion in a Religious Age*, 139ff.).

[Hava Lazarus-Yafeh]

BIBLIOGRAPHY: Steinschneider, Arab Lit; S. Poznanski, *Karaite Literary Opponents of Saadiah Gaon* (1908); idem, in: OLZ, 7 (1904), 257–76, 304–15, 345–59; A.S. Halkin, in: L.W. Schwarz (ed.), *Great Ages and Ideas of the Jewish People* (1956), 215–63; idem, in: L. Finkelstein (ed.), *The Jews* (1960³), 1116–45.

JUDEO-FRENCH, the Old French spoken and written by medieval French and Rhenish Jewry. It should be stated from the outset that there probably never existed a Judeo-French dialect, with specific Jewish traits. The term applies only to Jewish activities in medieval France, which had French as their vehicle. The mother tongue of the Jews in France during the Middle Ages was what is now called Old French. It was identical with the language spoken by the other inhabitants of the region with whom they lived in close contact. The Latin which they originally spoke underwent the same evolution and the same geographical diversification: thus the Jews of Normandy spoke the Norman dialect, those of Troyes that of Champagne, those of Dijon, Burgundian. They spoke it at home, in the market, at the synagogue, and at school. Rabbinical discussions were conducted in Old French, and it was sometimes even the language of prayer. The pronunciation of Hebrew was gallicized, חַיִּים being pronounced *agin*. Very few Hebrew words relating exclusively to Jewish traditional practices were used even in prayers: most were gallicized, such as *plain* for פְּשַׁט; *bonteable* for חָסִיד. The names adopted by Jews were French: *Colon* (= יוֹנָה), *Bendit* (= בָּרוּךְ), *Vives* (= חַיִּים), *Quinet* (*Jacquinet* = יַעֲקֹב), *Monet* (*Simonet* = שִׁמְעוֹן), *Belasez* (*Belle assez*), *Fleurdelis*.

The written word, however, had a different appearance, since the Jews preferred Hebrew characters, the Latin ones being too strongly identified with the Church. This transliteration had undergone its own evolution from the Latin period and obeyed its own orthographic rules. The Latin *k*, when pronounced [*tš*] in Old French, was still rendered by ק, a diacritical mark showing the new value: ק; the Latin *j*, Old French [dzh], was transcribed by י with a diacritical mark until the 13th century; and the Latin *u*, becoming the French [ü], was written יֻ. The spelling testifies to dialectal differences in keeping with, and stemming from, knowledge of the Latin characters of Old French. The best-known Old French words in Jewish texts are the (glosses) in commentaries on the Bible and Talmud. Somewhat older are the glosses in the commentaries of *Menahem b. Ḥelbo and the Pseudo-Gershom. From the 12th century onward French glosses appeared in all the rabbinic writings of French and English Jewry: biblical and talmudic commentaries, responsa, halakhic treatises, prayer books, codes of law and custom, and financial records, as well as in the margins of innumerable manuscripts. Far more important, however, are the biblical glossaries, of which only six more or less complete 13th-century examples are still extant, although there are fragments of nine more. They contain tens of thousands of Old French words rendering the Scriptures into the vernacular. Together with two complete biblical dictionaries and the fragments of two more, these testify to a continuous translation of the Bible into French as taught in Jewish schools and houses of study. Because of their traditional character, they carried a certain number of ancient Old French words which had disappeared from gentile literary usage, pointing to Normandy as the likely home of the French version. Because of a misleading impression given by the Hebrew script and a false analogy with and – not to speak of a general ignorance of the Old French dialects – a mistaken idea of a distinctive Judeo-French dialect came into being. There are, however, few reasons to doubt that Jews in France spoke and even prayed in the Old French of their Gentile surroundings. Only a few liturgical poems, written according to French literary norms, have survived, and their quality suggests a wide use of this medium in religious services and ceremonies.

French seems to have been the vernacular in Rhineland Jewries in the early Middle Ages and some Old French words were thus carried over into Yiddish, for example *chalant* (חַמִּין, literally "being warm" – *tsholent*). This also accounts for the gallicized form of the official name of certain Jewish communities: *Aspire* (Speyer), *Germèse* (Worms), *Magence* (Mainz); and in English Jewry, *Londres* (London) and *Nicol* (Lincoln).

BIBLIOGRAPHY: A. Darmesteter, *Reliques scientifiques*, 1 (1890), 103–307; D.S. Blondheim, *Les Parlers judéo-romans et la Vetus Latina* (1925); idem, *Poèmes Judéo-français du moyen âge* (1927); H. Pflaum (Peri), in: *Romania*, 59 (1933), 389–422; 60 (1934), 144; R. Lévy, *Contribution à la lexicographie française selon d'anciens textes d'origine juive* (1960). **ADD. BIBLIOGRAPHY:** M. Banitt, "Une langue-fantôme – Le judéo-français," in: *Revue de Linguistique Romane*, 27 (1963), 245–294; idem, *Le Glossaire de Bâle* (1972); idem, *Rashi Interpreter of the Biblical Letter* (1985); idem, *Le Glossaire de Leipzig* (1997); C. Aslanov, "Le français de Rabbi Joseph Kara et de Rabbi Eliézer de Beaugency d'après leurs commentaires sur Ezéchiel," in: *Revue des Études Juives*, 159:3–4 (2000), 425–46.

[Menahem Banitt / Cyril Aslanov (2nd ed.)]

JUDEO-GREEK. The Judeo-Greek language is known from medieval times onward. It contains an element of Hebrew and Aramaic origin in its vocabulary and grammar and is written in Hebrew characters. Since the 15th century there has also been an element of Turkish origin. Three examples of the Hebrew element are *Yavan* (Javan, Gen. 10:1–2, used in Hebrew for Greece=Ionia), "a Greek"; *ḥamor* (donkey), "a dunce"; *akhlantzis* (Heb. *akhlan*), "glutton." The earliest Judeo-Greek glosses are considered to be those in the *Arukh* (c. 1101), the talmudic dictionary by Rabbi *Nathan ben Jehiel of Rome. Two other early documents are a fragment of Ecclesiastes translated into Greek and a translation of Jonah containing elements foreign to the language spoken in the 13th century. A fragment of a Greek mishnaic glossary of 124 Hebrew words with their Greek equivalents has been assigned to the 10th or 11th century because of the colloquial phenomena familiar from Byzantine epigraphy; and a Hebrew manuscript of 99 words (1408 – Bibliothèque Nationale, Paris) probably dates from about 1250. A beautiful parchment manuscript of the Book of Jonah found at Candia, Crete, in which the copy's sale in 1263 is recorded, is thought to be the earliest known relic in Judeo-Greek, because the language employed is nearer to ancient Greek than that of any other relic of Byzantine literature (Oxford, Bodleian Library, 1144). Another translation of Jonah (3574, University of Bologna) occurs in a *maḥzor* written in the Corfu dialect dating from the 15th century. Another important document of this period is a fragment of a manuscript located in the National Library in Jerusalem. This includes a brief commentary on Psalms, Lamentations, and Ecclesiastes (see bibliography). The most extensive Judeo-Greek work intended for Greek-speaking Jews of the Balkan peninsula is the translation of the Constantinople Polyglot Pentateuch (1547). The total absence of Turkish words has led some scholars to conclude that the Judeo-Greek Pentateuch was written at least two centuries before the date of publication. There are some archaisms in this work, but they are exceptional. In most translations, as well as in many original works, vowels are indicated by vowel signs (in addition to the vowel letters). The sound "a" was indicated by *kamaẓ* or *pattaḥ* (often with a following *alef*); the sound "i" by *ḥirik* (followed by *yod*); "e" by *ẓeireh* (followed by *yod*); "o" by a full *ḥolam*; and "u" by a *shuruk* or *kubbuẓ*. A Judeo-Greek translation of Job (Constantinople, 1576) was the work of Moses b. Eliezer Phobian (or Pobian), who states explicitly that his aim was to facilitate the teaching of the Hebrew language. Manuscript versions of these translations are to be found in the Bodleian Library, Oxford. There are several collections of Judeo-Greek hymns, one of which – *Yanniotika Evraika Traghoudhia* (1953) – contains 16 hymns, 13 of them previously unpublished. A hymn which begins "Ενας ό Κύριος όθεός" ("The Lord, God, is One") consists of eight stanzas, each of which has a two-word Hebrew refrain: "Israel Hallelujah." A Jewish liturgical song dating from the Renaissance, *Pismon tou Purim*, occurs in two forms: the Chalcis version (ten stanzas) and the superior Oxford version (24 stanzas). The vowel points of the former can be judged only by the vocalization of the Hebrew refrain, the words of which are "Merciful living God, the true King."

The Corfu linguist Papageorgios, editor of *O Israilitis Khronoghrafos* (published in Corfu), first announced the discovery of Judeo-Greek poetry in 1881. In 1889 and in 1900, he reproduced eight stanzas of a hymn entitled "Song Sung Formerly in the Synagogue of Corfu on the Sabbath." The same collection (no. 2, p. 3) contains fragments of 70 verses from an old manuscript, inspired by Isaiah and other biblical prophets. The Karaite Elijah Afeda Beghi produced a Judeo-Greek version in 1627 of the Aramaic chapters of Daniel and Ezra still in manuscript in 1914, while for the rest of the Bible he compiled a glossary of difficult words. The Karaites continued to use Judeo-Greek even after the fall of Constantinople in 1453. Judeo-Greek continued to be spoken and written in Janina, Prevesa, Larissa, Arta, Trikkala, Volos, Chalcis, and especially in Corfu and Zante. During the Nazi occupation of Greece, some Jews communicated with each other in Judeo-Greek as a protective measure. Except for those still familiar with *Ladino, Greek Jews of the post-World War II era spoke standard Greek.

BIBLIOGRAPHY: General Works: A. Neubauer, in: JQR, 4 (1891/92), 9–19; C. Sirat, in: *Institut de Recherche et d'Histoire des Textes, Bulletin d'information*, 12 (1963), 103–12. Texts: Ph. Kukules, in: *Byzantinische Zeitschrift*, 19 (1910), 422–9; M. Schwab, in: *Revue des Études Grecques*, 24 (1911), 152–67; M. Sp. Papageorgios, *Merkwuerdige in den Synagogen von Corfu in Gebrauch befindlichen Hymnen*, 2 pt. 1 (1882), 226–32; D.C. Hesseling, in: *Byzantinische Zeitschrift*, 10 (1901), 208–17 (the Book of Jonah); L. Modona, in: REJ, 23 (1891), 134–6 (the Book of Jonah); J. Starr, in: PAAJR, 6 (1934–35), 353–67 (Judeo-Greek Glossary); D. Goldschmidt, in: KS, 33 (1957/58), 131–4 (list of texts); M. Lazare Belléli, in: *Revue des Études Grecques*, 3 (1890), 289–308; I.M. Matsa, *Yanniotika Evraika Traghoudhia* (1953). Studies: D.S. Blondheim, *Les Parlers Judéo-Romans et la Vetus Latina* (1925), Appendix B, 157–70; M. Schwab, in: France, Missions Scientifiques et Littéraires. *Nouvelles Archives*. Nouvelle Série, fascicule 10 (1913), 1–141; M. Sp. Papageorgios, in: *Annuaire Pamassou*, 5 (1901), 157–75. **ADD. BIBLIOGRAPHY:** N. De Lange, *Greek Jewish Texts from the Cairo Genizah* (1996); C. Aslanov, "The Judeo-Greek and Ladino Columns in the Constantinople Edition of the Pentateuch (1547): A Linguistic Commentary on Gn 1:1–5," in: *Revue des Études Juives*, 158:3–4 (Jul.–Dec. 1999), 385–97; G. Drettas, "Propos sur la judéité grécophone," in: S. Morag, M. Bar Asher, and M. Meyer Modena (eds.), *Vena Hebraica in Judæorum Linguis. Proceedings of the 2nd International Conference on the Hebrew and Aramaic Elements in Jewish Languages (Milan, October 23–26, 1995)* (1999).

[Rachel Dalven / Cyril Aslanov (2nd ed.)]

JUDEO-ITALIAN. Among the Jews living in central and southern Italy, a special dialect took shape from the early Middle Ages onward, particularly in Rome, which scholars have termed Judeo-Italian or Judeo-Roman (*giudeo-romanesco*). One of the several Judeo-Romance dialects which developed alongside the Romance vulgars, Judeo-Italian contains many linguistic elements common to all these dialects. With the formation of a major Jewish cultural center in Rome during the 13th–14th centuries, Judeo-Italian became a type of *koine* spoken by Jews throughout Italy, who called it *Latino* or *Volgare*. Although Jews spread its use as far as Venice and Piedmont to the north and Corfu in the Aegean to the east, the dialect retained its old, archaic form only in Rome, although here, too, it underwent modification and development over the generations. Judeo-Italian belongs to the south-central group of Italian dialects. Both written evidence and the spoken language itself show that a considerable part of the ancient Roman substratum – identical with the dialect of Rome and the surrounding areas spoken by non-Jews in the 13th century – is still recognizable in Judeo-Italian. However, together with this basic element, it is possible to detect the important influence of other central Italian dialects, such as those of the Marches, Campania, Umbria, and the Abruzzi. Judeo-Italian has also preserved still earlier elements, imported by Jews who immigrated from southern Italy and Sicily. A distinct development may be seen in the dialect's Judeo-Roman form during the 15th–16th centuries, although this became frozen after the Jews were isolated in the Roman ghetto from 1555 onward. The special linguistic peculiarities of Judeo-Italian are hard to determine because of the marked affinity of the various Italian dialects. The sole basis for its study lies in the classification and investigation of Judeo-Italian's archaic phonetic and morphological characteristics, as well as in its ancient vocabulary (which has been preserved as a result of Italian Jewry's historical mobility), such characteristics having long vanished in other Italian dialects. The various linguistic phenomena characteristic of the Jewish dialects in general are recognizable in Judeo-Italian. They include (a) the creation of words with a Hebrew root and an Italian suffix, and vice versa – *achannoso* (<*ḥen*, "charming," "comely"), *dabberare* (<*dibber*, "to speak"), *achlone* (<*akhlan*, "glutton"); (b) the creation of mixed terms, half-Hebrew and half-Italian – *mal-mazzalle* ("bad luck," cf. Yiddish *shlimazl*), *magna-torà* ("Torah eater," applied to one who reads at an excessive speed), *perdi-zemàn* ("time loser," i.e., one who wastes time); (c) the preservation of many Hebrew words, including those relating to prayer, study, and worship, which did not readily lend themselves to translation – *cavanà* (<*kavvanah*, "devotion"), *chinianne* (<*kinyan*, "betrothal contract"), *sirichoddi* (<*seliḥot*, "penitential prayers"), *bangavanodde* (>*be-avonoteinu*, "for our sins," a nickname for an unfortunate, luckless person); (d) abstention from the use of Italian words relating to Christian ritual, or a deliberate distortion of such terms – *tonghevà* (<*to'evah*, "abomination," signifying "crucifix"); (e) the coining of approved or secret terms similar to the language of the underworld – *jorbedde* (from י״ב "twelve" = "policeman," a nickname given to the policemen because of the number "12" embroidered on their uniform); (f) the use of Hebrew words in a sense differing from the accepted meaning, or the rejection of one Hebrew word in favor of a synonym – *chavèr* (<*ḥaver*, for "servant"), *beridde* (<*berit*, for "sex organ"), *ngarelle* (<*arel*, for "non-Jew"); (g) a tendency, especially in translations, to use homophones or Italian words reminiscent of identical or similar Hebrew terms.

Judeo-Italian Literature

Judeo-Italian literature may be said to include all the works intentionally written in the dialect, using Hebrew orthography and the set rules of transliteration. The outstanding original work is a Lamentation for the Ninth of Av written at the beginning of the 13th century and based on literary motifs borrowed from the Midrash. This Lamentation, one of the earliest poetic texts in Italian, possesses considerable literary value and the author was apparently influenced in his choice of style by the Italian religious poetry of his time. Other documents which have survived include a "Hymn in honor of Queen Sabbath" by Mordecai b. Judah *Dato (published by Cecil Roth, see appended bibliography). In addition, it would appear that Judeo-Italian was the language in which R. Moses *Rieti wrote his ethically oriented, 15th-century philosophical treatise, now preserved in manuscript at Leiden (MS X, 1 or, Scaliger). Because of their linguistic character, translations form the richest and most important part of Judeo-Italian literature. To facilitate study of the Bible, liturgy, grammar, philosophy, and medicine, and to assist children and women who could read Hebrew without actually knowing the language, Italian Jews translated the entire Bible, the prayer book, the Passover *Haggadah*, the Ethics of the Fathers, various hymns, and large portions of the liturgy. Other works translated were Moses b. Joseph Kimḥi's grammatical treatise *Mahalakh Shevilei ha-Da'at* (early 14th century), Maimonides' *Millot ha-Higgayon* (15th-century manuscript) and *Guide of the Perplexed* (translated by Jedidiah da Recanati, c. 1580), together with various pharmaceutical lists and selections from books on practical medicine. The Bible and the liturgical translations are notable for their conservative nature and for their establishment of a particular method of translation and unified tradition of translation, whose origins date from the era of the later Roman Empire and were crystallized during the 13th century. These Judeo-Italian translations are distinguished by their use of ancient terms long vanished from normative Italian, and by their preservation of the old Jewish exegetical tradition governing the comprehension of particular biblical nouns and expressions. However, despite the mechanical method of translation, the translators succeeded in preserving aesthetic values, both in poetic rhythm and in the lyrical power of the biblical source. Evidence of this is provided by a 13th-century Judeo-Italian version of the Song of Songs, which is the oldest Italian translation of the biblical work. Apart from isolated portions published in recent times, these translations of the Bible remain in manuscript. The liturgical translations were, however, published several times during the 16th century (Fano, 1505; Bologna, 1538; Venice, 1547; Mantua, 1561). A translation into Judeo-Italian was included in a series of Passover *Haggadot* published in Venice in the 17th–18th centuries. Pedantic adherence to the original Hebrew, shown both in the preservation of ancient vocabulary and in the Hebrew influence on the morphology and syntax of the sentence structure, is also characteristic of the translations of the philosophical and grammatical treatises. Several glossaries in Judeo-Italian have survived, composed especially for Bible study and to aid an understanding of any text written in Hebrew. Of the biblical glossaries which have been published – many remain in manuscript – the most important was the *Makrei Dardekei* of Pereẓ Trabot (Naples, 1488), a biblical dictionary with Arabic and Judeo-Italian translations of the roots. One of the most ancient and important collections of glosses is that found in the first talmudic dictionary, the *Arukh* of Rabbi *Nathan ben Jehiel of Rome (late 11th century), which contains some 600

Judeo-Italian words. There is also a multitude of Judeo-Italian glosses in Judah b. Moses b. Daniel Romano's early 14th-century edition of Maimonides' *Mishneh Torah.*

As a spoken language, Judeo-Italian has disappeared in most parts of Italy, although it continues to retain a certain degree of vigor among the Jewish working classes of Rome.

BIBLIOGRAPHY: Milano, Bibliotheca (1954), Supplemento (1964), index s.v. *Dialetti giudeo-italiani e pronunzia*; A. Milano, *Il Ghetto di Roma* (1964), index; M. Steinschneider, in: *Il Buonaroti*, 6 (1871); idem, in: MGWJ, 42 (1898), passim; 43 (1899), passim; 44 (1900), passim; D.S. Blondheim, Notes on the Italian Words in *ʿArukh Completum* (1933); C. Roth, in: RMI, 1 (1926), 37–46; G. Fiorentino, in: *Archivo Glottologico Italiano*, 29 (1937), 138–60; J. Sermoneta, in: *Romanica et Occidentalia…* (1963), 23–42; idem, in: *Scritti in memoria di L. Carpi* (1967), 59–100; idem, in: *Lessico Intellettuale Europeo* (1969). **ADD. BIBLIOGRAPHY:** A. Freedman, *Italian Texts in Hebrew Characters: Problems of Interpretation* (1972); G. Jochnowitz, "Had Gadya in Judeo-Italian and Shuadit (Judeo-Provencçal)," in: J.A. Fishman (ed.), *Readings in the Sociology of Jewish Languages* (1985), 241–45; L. Ferretti-Cuomo, "Le glosse volgari nell' ʿArukh di r. Natan ben Yeh'iel da Roma. Note di lavoro a proposito del fondo germanico," in: *Medioevo Romanzo*, 22:2 (1998), 232–83; M.Mayer-Modena, *Lexicon of the Hebrew Componant in Judeo-Italian* (2006).

[Joseph Baruch Sermoneta / Cyril Aslanov (2nd ed.)]

JUDEO-PERSIAN, a form of Persian used by Jews and written in Hebrew characters. The oldest Judeo-Persian texts are the earliest known records in the Persian language (see Judeo-Persian Literature below). These consist of the inscriptions of Tang-i Azao (Central Afghanistan, 752–53 C.E. according to W.B. Henning, in: *Bulletin of the School of Oriental and African Studies,* 20 (1957), 335–42; E.L. Rapp, in: *East and West,* 17 (1967), 51–58, suggested, with insufficient arguments, a much later date) and a fragment from a private letter found at Dandan-Uiliq in the region of Khotan (Sinkiang), which can also be dated to the eighth century. Next to be found among the dated documents are a brief inscription on a ninth-century copper tablet discovered at Quilon in southern India; a Karaite legal deed from an unknown locality (presumably in Khuzistan), dated 951 C.E.; a law report written at Ahvaz, Iran, in 1021 C.E., and a collection of funerary inscriptions dating from the late 11th to the early 13th centuries and emanating from a community at Firuzkuh in central Afghanistan. In the exegetic literature as well as in fragments of commercial and personal correspondence, the Cairo *Genizah* and certain other Oriental manuscript depositories acquired by Abraham *Firkovich for his collection (now in St. Petersburg), provide texts datable to the period before the early 13th century. Some of these texts will be enumerated and discussed below.

Many Judeo-Persian writings contain linguistic peculiarities which do not occur in Persian texts written in Arab-Persian script. These peculiarities have often been classified quite simply as "Judeo-Persian." Such a statement has little meaning, since it is evident to anybody examining Judeo-Persian literature as a whole that it has no linguistic unity. The term "Judeo-Persian" does not define a particular form of Persian distinguished from the classical language by regular characteristics. There never was a unified Persian dialect which could be said to belong specifically to the Jews of Iran. Some of the linguistic peculiarities of Judeo-Persian are purely stylistic. Translations of the Scriptures have, throughout the centuries, presented certain specific traits: a literal method of translation, word for word or even morpheme for morpheme (this being also the method used by Muslim translators of the Koran), and a systematic use of certain rare or archaic forms such as active participles in *-ā* to translate Hebrew participles and the particle *azmar* to translate אֶת. Such traits are restricted to the style peculiar to this kind of writing.

Most of the Judeo-Persian linguistic characteristics are, however, dialectal: they belong to local forms of Persian spoken in different regions of Iran. The fact that they appear practically only in Judeo-Persian texts may be explained in connection with the history of the Persian language and the conditions in which Judeo-Persian literature was produced. From the time when the Persian language extended from its original home in southwest Iran to the entire Iranian plateau, it was diversified into a large number of local variants. These dialects were restricted to colloquial usage and did not, as a rule, find their way into the literature in Arabic script, where the classical language (which became fixed and unified at an early stage) reigns, with few exceptions, supreme. On the contrary, Judeo-Persian writings, with the exception of the most literary texts, are foreign to the tradition of classical literature and escaped its normalizing influence. In particular, the old translators of and commentators on the Scriptures, who wrote merely to instruct their fellow-Jews and who did not care for aesthetic considerations, addressed them quite naturally in the current language of the locality, which may have been quite similar among Jews and non-Jews. For this reason, Judeo-Persian literature affords valuable evidence as to the history and dialectology of the Persian language. It would be helpful if we could identify the geographical origins of the different compositions in Early Judeo-Persian, but, apart from a well-defined group of documents coming from Khuzistan in South-West Iran, most fragments cannot be assigned to a definite place of origin.

Dialectal peculiarities are particularly frequent and interesting in the early texts. In the later period, from the 14th century on, the Jews generally used in writing a form of standard Persian which was practically the same as classical Persian. The differences are mainly those of script (the Hebrew alphabet being used for Judeo-Persian), orthography (Judeo-Persian tends to indicate the short vowels *u* and *i* by the letters *vav* and *yod*, contrary to the practice in Standard Persian, and they use different conventions for some of the consonants, e.g., *j* and *č*), and vocabulary (Judeo-Persian often uses Hebrew and Aramaic expressions). The writings which emerged in the 18th–19th century among the Bukharan community are however strongly marked by the local vernacular. Although the early Judeo-Persian texts have not yet been fully explored, a number of dialectal variants can be distinguished among them.

(1) Among the ancient documents, the somewhat laconic inscriptions are of limited instructive value. The Dandan-Uiliq letter, which is fragmentary and cannot be interpreted fully, is remarkable for certain archaisms, notably the use of the *ezāfe* particle (written ארי) as a relative; this usage, common in Middle Persian, does not appear in New Persian texts in Arabic script. Also noteworthy is the almost total absence of Arabic words, characteristic of a very early phase of the language.

(2) The two legal documents, one written in Khuzistan province in 951 (Mosseri Collection Ia.1), and the other, written in Hormshir in 1021 (Bodl. Ms.Heb. b.12.24), the fragment of a Karaite Book of Precepts in the British Library (Or. 8659), together with a number of still unpublished letters from the Cambridge *Genizah* collection, all display some typical features of the Khuzistan dialect: they use the *ezāfe* particle as a relative, and that particle is most often attached in writing to the following word; the word for "thing" is תיס, as in Manichaean Middle Persian, while classical New Persian has the form *čīz* for this word; they have a preposition written א or או (possibly pronounced *o*), which perpetuates the Middle Persian preposition *ō*, a preposition that no longer exists in Standard Persian; they have a passive present stem which ends with the morpheme *ih-*, spelled *-yh-* or *-h-*, before the personal endings, another Middle Persian feature; there is frequent attestation of *imāla* in Arabic words, viz. the change of long *ā* vowel to *ē* or *ī* in certain phonetic conditions, as in *klyp* for Arabic *khilāf* "difference, contrariness." In addition, the vocabulary of these texts contains a whole range of rarely attested or hitherto unknown words, some of which are only familiar from Middle Persian.

(3) Among the ancient exegetic texts, several fragments of commentaries on biblical books are preserved which display the same type of Khuzistan dialect as is attested in the texts described in the previous paragraph. One of these is a Karaite commentary on the *Nevi'im* and the *Ketuvim*, of which a number of fragments are preserved in the *Genizah* Collection of Cambridge University Library. One of these fragments was published in *Irano-Judaica* (1982), 313–22. The same type of language is also attested in an extensive grammatical commentary on the *Ketuvim* of which several fragments survive; see *Irano-Judaica* (1982), 310–12; Khan, *Early Karaite Grammatical Texts* (2000), 250–331.

(4) An extensive Karaite commentary on the book of Genesis (Firkovich I 4605), discussed by S. Shaked in: *Persian Origins* (2003), 195–219, of which a substantial fragment is preserved, seems to belong, by its linguistic features, to North-Eastern Iran. The most conspicuous grammatical element which ties it to the Tajik language is the use of an indeclinable past tense form of the type of *būdagī* "was." The same feature is also attested in Part I of the St. Petersburg commentary on Ezekiel, discussed in the following.

(5) The Ezekiel commentary (Firkovich Collection I 1682) is a curious instance of a single book written in two different dialects by several scribes. The manuscript, which represents a very large but incomplete composition, is on the whole well preserved, and is datable to the 11th century. Part 1 of the manuscript displays a north-east-Iranian type of language, as in the commentary on Genesis mentioned earlier, while Part 2 belongs to the type of language identified with Khuzistan region. The text has been studied by T.E. Gindin, and is to be published in full.

(6) A small fragment of a Judeo-Persian version of the Psalms, acquired by A. Netzer in 1973 in Zefreh, 100 km. northeast of Isfahan, displays a distinct form of the language. It is close to the Khuzistan dialect in that it has the form *kyrd* for standard Persian *kard*, the ending of the abstract noun usually in *-yh*, and the plural ending *-yh*'; but it has some divergent features. The *ezāfe* is spelled *y* and written as an independent word; an optative ending *ē* is attached to verbs, of which the form *hysty* "that it may be" is noteworthy. There are also lexical peculiarities attested in this fragment; cf. A. Netzer, *Jerusalem Studies in Arabic and Islam* 27 (2002), 419–38; S. Shaked, in: *Irano-Judaica* 6 (2006, fc.).

(7) A fragment of a book of Aramaic proverbs with a Judeo-Persian translation was published by S. Shaked, in: *Acta Iranica* 30 (1990), 230–39, and several further fragments of biblical commentaries, some of which not yet studied in detail.

(8) Further books which belong to an early layer of Judeo-Persian compositions are: the Story of Daniel (Bibliothèque Nationale Ms. Héb. 128) – not a translation of the book of Daniel, but a midrash on the Daniel theme; a translation of Isaiah, Jeremiah, and Ezekiel, also preserved in the Bibliothèque Nationale in Paris, and a translation of the Pentateuch in the Vatican. All of them exhibit the same variant of Persian. This may be illustrated by forms such as פֿרבֿיד ("fat"; classical Persian *farbih*); זיה ("to live"; classical Persian *ziy-*); דושכיזה ("virgin"; classical Persian *dūšiza*); כומאנא ("indeed"; classical Persian *hamānā*); אניז ("also"; classical Persian *nīz*); תנג ("to drink"); and a large number of words unknown in classical Persian.

(9) A translation of the Pentateuch found in a manuscript of the British Museum copied in 1319 represents a dialectal variant distinct from the preceding one (אהנג, "to drink," הניז "also"): but it is not yet possible to determine the region to which it belongs.

(10) The later literary writings (14th–18th centuries) are generally free from dialectal traits. They emanate from a milieu of highly cultured Jews who knew and appreciated the masterpieces of classical Persian literature and imitated them. To commemorate the past or record the sad events of the time in a worthy style, they could choose no better medium than classical Persian. This is the language employed by *Shāhīn and ʿImrānī at Shiraz, by Bābāy at Kashan, and even by Yūsuf Yahūdī in Bukhara. Only in their works does one come across examples of local pronunciation, and these are probably attributable to the copyist. In works of a more popular nature, such as the elegy of Mollā Hizqiyā (17th century), some colloquialisms are to be found, which are also common in the vernacular of modern Iran.

(10) The literary or exegetic texts composed in Bukhara during the 17th–19th centuries in general bear marks of their origin, such marks being more numerous in texts of a lower stylistic level. The poem *Khudāydāt* and the prose writings abound in dialectal peculiarities of the Persian of central Asia (Tajik), which naturally are completely different from those of the ancient texts of southwest Iran. Of particular importance linguistically is the book *Likkutei Dinim*, a collection of rabbinical precepts compiled in six parts by Abraham Aminof and published in Jerusalem between 1899 and 1904. For this book see in particular W. Bacher, in: ZFHB, 5 (1901), 147–54; ZDMG, 56 (1902), 729–59.

One of the characteristic traits is that of vocalization, always written in the manuscripts and printed books of Bukharan Jews in conformity with Tajik, as opposed to the Persian of Iran. Three examples are: בֵּזָר ("who renounces," Tajik *bezor*, Iranian Persian *bizâr*), רוֹז ("day" Tajik *růz*, Iranian Persian *ruz*), and לוּטף ("favor," Tajik *lutf*, Iranian Persian *lotf*). The language of these texts, which may appropriately be termed "Judeo-Tajik," is very close to the modern literary language of Tajikistan.

Judeo-Iranian Dialects

One medieval piece of evidence for a Judeo-Iranian dialect which is not Persian but cannot be identified more closely was discovered among the Cambridge *Genizah* fragments; cf. Shaked, in: *Acta Iranica*, 28 (1988), 219–35.

Along with Judeo-Persian proper, mention must be made of the Iranian dialects still in use today among certain communities in Kashan, Hamadan, Isfahan, Kerman, Yazd and Shiraz. These dialects, used exclusively in speech, are not variants of Persian but are related to the local dialects of these regions and belong to the "central" group of western Iranian dialects. A survey of Jewish dialects was undertaken by E. Yarshater, in: *Mémorial Jean de Menasce* (1974), 453–66.

The *Judeo-Tat of the Caucasus region (Daghestan and Soviet Azerbaijan), together with neighboring dialects spoken by Muslims, form a dialectal unit, possibly dating back to a time when Iranian colonies were established by the Sassanian dynasty along the frontier of the empire. All these dialects may be called "Judeo-Iranian."

There is a group of speech-forms used by Jews as a secret language. They are known as *Loterai*, a word which denotes a secret language. They are essentially a jargon in which Hebrew words and some distorted forms take the place of the more familiar Persian words. This phenomenon was discussed by Yarshater, in: *Journal of the American Oriental Society*, 97 (1977), 1–7; Lazard, in: *Journal Asiatique* (1978), 251–55; A. Netzer, in: J. Dan (ed.), *Tarbut ve-Historiyah* (1987), 22–23. The language of the Jews of Herat mentioned by Zarubin, in: *Doklady Rossijskoj Akademii Nauk* (1924), 181–83, seems also to belong to this type of speech.

JUDEO-PERSIAN LITERATURE

The Jews of Iran developed a rich and varied literature in the Persian language. They also contributed to several branches of Jewish literature in Hebrew, but this falls outside the scope of this entry. Its formal identification is based on the fact that this is a literature written by Jews, most often on themes of Jewish interest and related to the world of Jewish practice and thinking, and it is written in Hebrew characters and contains a varying number of expressions in Hebrew and Aramaic. This literature was as a rule inaccessible to non-Jews, which explains why there is no reference to the monuments of Jewish-Persian literature in the mainstream Persian literature created by Muslims. There are some towering figures of former Jews who converted to Islam and who contributed to the general literature of Islamic Iran, but what was written in Judeo-Persian remained until modern times entirely unknown and unacknowledged by Muslims.

The literature composed in Judeo-Persian should be treated under two distinct chronological periods: up to the Mongol invasion of Iran in the 1220s, and from that period up to our time. The Mongol invasions created havoc in the life of Iran in general and in particular as far as the Jewish communities of Iran are concerned. Very little of the pre-Mongol literature of Iran survived into the later period, and, on the other hand, a whole new post-Mongol literature was created from the 14th century onwards with characteristic features which did not exist before.

Judeo-Persian Literature in Its Earliest Period

We now have a substantial body of literature for the early period of Judeo-Persian, most of which derives from manuscripts which have come to light during the past decades and not all of which have yet been published. The origin of these manuscripts is the Cairo *Genizah*, scattered in various collections around the world, but most of it at the Cambridge University Library; and the Firkovich Collection acquired in various book depositories in the Middle East, presently housed in St. Petersburg. The use of Judeo-Persian was not confined to the mainland of Iran. A substantial colony of Persian-speaking Jews seems to have lived during the 10th–13th centuries in Palestine, mostly in Jerusalem, and there was a continuity of Jewish Persian presence in Cairo, where some of the Persian Jews held positions of influence. Some manuscripts which may belong to this layer of literature were acquired in Iran and are now kept in the Bibliothèque Nationale, Paris, and in private collections. The main classes of the extant remnants of this once evidently vast literature are the following:

1. Bible exegesis;
2. Hebrew grammar and lexicography;
3. *Halakhah*;
4. Midrash
5. Poetry;
6. Stories and proverbs;
7. Magic;
8. Letters and legal documents.

The literary pieces that have survived represent the creative activity of both major groups within the Jewish community of Persian-speaking Jews, Rabbanites, and Karaites. It is significant that the Cairo *Genizah*, which did not function as a library but as a place for dumping discarded pieces of writing which have lost their relevance to the owners, has usually preserved small fragments of books and a relatively large number of ephemeral writings, such as letters and legal documents, while the collections of manuscripts which derive from other sources, presumably usually synagogue libraries, often comprise larger sections of literary compositions, but their holdings contain no writings of the non-literary type, like letters.

A short survey of the compositions that have survived in the different categories follows.

1. EXEGETICAL WORKS. It is possible that Persian translations of the Bible or of certain biblical books were current among Jews even before the Islamic period. A hint in that direction is found in the Talmud (Meg. 18a), where versions of the Book Esther are mentioned in what is called "Elamite" and "Median," two languages of the Iranian region, although we do not know which precise languages are meant by these designations. Among the versions which have turned up the following, largely unpublished, may be mentioned:

1) A translation of the *Ketuvim*, of which 54 pages have survived, covering Ps. 9–40, Prov. 1–3 and Eccl. 2–5. This translation goes verse-by-verse and follows closely the Hebrew text. This is, by its language, probably a fairly late translation (14th century?)

2) Commentary of grammatical points in *Ketuvim*, written in the Khuzistani dialect of Persian. The surviving fragments make up 32 pages. The composition does not treat every verse, but only with selected themes which are always introduced by a question. The fragments deal with topics from Ruth 1–4, Song of Songs 1–5, Lamentations 2–3, Eccl. 1–2, Daniel 10–11, Nehemiah 8–9. The commentary reflects the grammatical school of the Karaites. (See S. Shaked, in: *Irano-Judaica* (1982), 310–12; Khan, *Early Karaite Grammatical Texts* (2000), 250–331).

3) An exegesis on the Book of Genesis, of which eight pages are extant;

4) A Karaite commentary on selected verses in *Nevi'im* and *Ketuvim*, Isa. 54–66, Dan. 11–12, Est. 1–5. Twenty-one pages are preserved of this composition. One section was published by S. Shaked, *Irano-Judaica* (1982), 313–22.

5) A commentary on selected questions in Ruth (chapters 1–4), each section starting with the words: *guftan-i šān* "(As to) what they said: …"

6) An extensive translation and commentary on Ezekiel, comprising 226 large pages, and treating in detail Ezek. 1–39. To be published by T.E. Gindin (see in the meantime in: idem, *Persian Origins* (2003), 14–30).

7) A Karaite commentary on Genesis, containing an extensive introduction and the beginning of the detailed commentary; a study by S. Shaked is in: *Persian Origins* (2003), 195–219.

8) A small fragment of a translation of the Psalms, possibly from the 11th century, purchased in 1973 in Zefreh (*Jerusalem Studies in Arabic and Islam*, 27 (2002), 419–438; *Irano-Judaica*, 6 (2006), fc).

9) There are, besides, eight further fragments of exegetical compositions on various books of the Bible.

2. HEBREW GRAMMAR AND LEXICOGRAPHY. Besides the grammatical commentary on the Bible (number 2 above), there are two fragments of a systematic Hebrew grammar called by the Hebrew title *qarqaʿot ha-diqduq* "the principles of grammar." This is a typically Karaite treatment of grammar, written in the Khuzistani dialect of Persian. A preliminary edition of one of the fragments of the text is in *E.Z. Melammed Festschrift* (*Hebrew*), 291–311.

Several fragments of a dictionary of the Talmud are found among the Cambridge *Genizah* texts.

3. HALAKHAH. There are a number of fragments of books dealing with legal questions. One fairly large fragment comprising 36 pages, unfortunately in a bad state of preservation, is a Karaite treatise, which contains polemics against the Rabbanites. Another fragment contains part of the introduction to a Karaite *Sefer Mitzvot* or Book of Precepts, followed by the beginning of the book and dealing with the rules for circumcision (British Library Or. 8659). It was published by D.N. MacKenzie, in: *Bulletin of the School of Oriental and African Studies*, 31 (1968), 249–69; comments by S. Shaked, in: *Israel Oriental Studies*, 1 (1971), 178–82; English translation in V.B. Moreen, *In Queen Esther's Garden* (2000), 248–55.

Another fragment in this genre seems to be a Rabbanite treatise dealing with the rules of *ʿeruv*, still unpublished.

4. MIDRASH. An extensive collection of midrashim in Hebrew by the order of the books of the Pentateuch is found in an incomplete manuscript dated 1328 C.E., written in Sambadagan, perhaps in North-East Iran, under the title *Pitron Torah*, "Exegesis on the Torah." The underlying composition has a good chance of being older, and seems to have been composed in the late 9th or early 10th century. The manuscript contains an appendix in Judeo-Persian, based on midrashic material, and probably reflecting a pre-Mongol Khuzistan type of Persian (edited E.E. Urbach, 1978, Heb.).

5. POETRY. Poetry, which becomes the most distinctive creation of Judeo-Persian in the post-Mongol period, is not yet so prominent in this early period. Still, we have one piece of popular poetry, in a dialect which is hard to place; see S. Shaked, in: *Peʿamim*, 32 (1985), 22–37. Other fragments contain portions of the liturgy for the Day of Atonement. The Adler Collection in the Jewish Theological Seminary contains a number of poetic fragments, mostly translated from Hebrew, which seem to reflect late Judeo-Persian (i.e., 14–18 century C.E.).

6. STORIES AND PROVERBS. A section of the texts in the category of early Judeo-Persian falls within the domain of folk stories, and includes a fragment of a story about King David, and two fragments of early Islamic history (one concerning the Caliph ʿUmar).

A separate section consists of a fragment of a collection of wisdom sayings in Aramaic with a translation into Judeo-Persian, published by S. Shaked, in: *Acta Iranica*, 16 (1990), 230–39.

7. MAGIC AND MEDICINE. One of the fragments in a Judeo-Iranian language (not Persian) contains magic recipes; edited by S. Shaked, in: *Acta Iranica* 28 (1988), 219–35.

Other, still unedited fragments, deal with medical questions.

8. LETTERS AND LEGAL DOCUMENTS. A large section of the Judeo-Persian find from the Cairo *Genizah* consists of private and commercial letters, written in Judeo-Persian, sometimes with phrases in Arabic expressed by the Arabic alphabet. Another group of documents belongs to the legal field, and contains court reports concerning financial and property disputes between people, usually within one family. These documents have a special value because they mostly belong to the Khuzistan dialect of Judeo-Persian, and make it possible to contrast other Judeo-Persian dialects. The oldest documents in Judeo-Persian, and in fact in Persian altogether, fall within this group: the first is a commercial letter found in Dandan Uiliq in Chinese Turkistan, which belongs to the eighth century C.E. The document is at the British Library, Or. 8212, first published by D.S. Margoliouth, in: *Journal of the Royal Asiatic Society* (1903), 737–60; Further studies and comments: C. Salemann, *Zapiski Vostočnago Otdelenja*, 16 (1904/5), 46–57; Henning in: BSOAS, 20 (1957), 341–42; idem, in: *Mitteliranisch (Handbuch der Orientalistik)* (1958), 79–80; B. Utas, in: *Orientalia Suecana*, 17 (1968), 123–36; idem, in: Moreen, *In Queen Esther's Garden* (2000), 22–25; G. Lazard, in: *Acta Iranica*, 28 (1988), 205–9 (Reprinted in: Lazard, *La formation de la langue persane* (1995), 157–61); S. Shaked, in: *Israel Oriental Studies*, 1 (1971), 182.

The second is a Karaite legal deed dated 951 C.E.; the original is in the Jacques Mosseri Collection Ia.1; it was published by S. Shaked, in: *Tarbiz*, 41 (1972), 49–58 (Heb.).

A further document is a JP law report from Ahvaz, dated 1021 C.E., first published by D.S. Margolious, in: JQR, (1899), 671–75. Further studies are J.P. Asmussen, in: *Acta Orientalia*, 19 (1965), 49–60; D.N. MacKenzie, in: *Journal of the Royal Asiatic Society* (1966), 69; S. Shaked, in: *Israel Oriental Studies*, 1 (1971), 180–82.

These fragments survived by chance, and they no doubt point to the existence of a much vaster and more varied literature, most of which has not survived.

Judeo-Persian Literature from the 14th Century to the Modern Period

From the 14th century, under the Il-Kahnids and later dynasties, a new phase of literary creativity starts for the Jews of Iran, and the works composed fall into a wide range of literary genres. There is a clear division between standard Judeo-Persian literature and the literature composed, especially in the more recent period, in Central Asia in Judeo-Tajik or Bukharan, a variety of Persian. An offshoot of Judeo-Persian literature is found in the manuscripts of the Jewish community of Kai Feng in China.

1. TRANSLATIONS OF THE BIBLE IN THE POST-MONGOL PERIOD. Judeo-Persian translations of the Pentateuch did not become known in the West before the sixteenth century. The first one printed (1546), is the work of the Persian scholar, Jacob b. Joseph *Tavus. It was thought at the time to be the oldest, and perhaps the sole literary achievement of Persian Jewry, but the manuscripts collected by the Florentine scholar Giambattista Vecchietti early in the 17th century, and the manuscripts which came to light in the 20th century, establish that Tavus' work actually represents the culmination of many centuries of Jewish Persian Bible study.

The oldest dated Judeo-Persian Pentateuch translation is in a manuscript in the British Library (Or 5446), copied by Joseph ben Moses in 1319 C.E. No place of origin is given, but the version could well be from Khurasan in north-east Iran. The manuscript is written in a clear hand, but is incomplete. It begins with Genesis 3:9 and goes to the end of the Pentateuch, with some large sections missing, among them, for example, the whole of Exodus. The initial Hebrew word is given for each verse, and this is followed by a word-by-word Persian translation of the entire verse. Often the Hebrew word is vocalized, usually in the supralinear Babylonian system, occasionally in the Tiberian vowel-points (see *Pronunciations of Hebrew). A commentary in Judeo-Persian or Hebrew, or by a combination of both, sometimes follows the translation, usually on grammatical points, with parallels adduced from the whole Bible. There are several citations from the *Mishneh Torah* of Maimonides to illustrate moral teachings. At the end of the text are two pages that contain the Hebrew verb paradigms. The translation portion of the text is clearly older than that of the commentary. A certain Abi Sa'id, whose earlier commentary influenced the work of the present author, is mentioned. An edition is available by H.H. Paper, *A Judeo-Persian Pentateuch* (Heb.) (Jerusalem, 1972).

Another important translation of the Pentateuch into Judeo-Persian is preserved in a Vatican manuscript (Vat. Pers. 61). The manuscript lacks a colophon, and its date and place of origin cannot be established. Its main interest lies in the large number of unusual Persian words and expressions which it contains. It was published in romanized transliteration by Paper, in: *Acta Orientalia*, 28 (1965), 363–140; 29 (1965/6), 75–181, 254–10; 31 (1968), 55–113.

The earliest Pentateuch version in Judeo-Persian to come to the notice of scholars was printed, as mentioned above, in Constantinople in 1546. It is the work of Jacob ben Joseph Tavus, and his version was included in the polyglot Bible done by Eleazar son of Gershon Soncino. Thomas Hyde transcribed the version from the Hebrew alphabet to Persian (Arabic) characters and published it in Walton's Bible, London (1657).

There are a very large number of other Judeo-Persian versions of biblical books, especially of the Psalms, in the period from the 14th century to the present. A brief survey of some of these versions is given in the following:

Of the Prophets, there is a lexical commentary on Samuel, called *'Amuqot Shemu'el*, in a British Library manuscript, Or. 10472(2), studied by W. Bacher in: ZDMG, 51 (1897), 392–425.

A Judeo-Persian version of Isaiah, Jeremiah, and Ezekiel exists in a manuscript of Paris. P. de Lagarde, *Persische Studien* (1884), published Isaiah and a portion of Jeremiah and Ezekiel. Two chapters from Isaiah are given by H.H. Paper, in: *Acta Iranica*, 5 (1975), 145–61.

Amos was published from a Paris manuscript by B. Hjerrild, in: *Acta Iranica*, 23 (1984), 73–112.

Joel was published from a manuscript at the Ben-Zvi Institute by H.H. Paper, in: *Essays in honor of Bernard Lewis. The Islamic world: From classical to modern times* (1989), 259–67.

Hosea was partly published by J.P. Asmussen, in: *Acta Iranica*, 4 (1975), 15–18. Another version is in a manuscript at the Ben-Zvi Institute, edited by not yet published by Dan Shapira.

Obadiah was published by J.P. Asmussen, in: *Acta Antiqua*, 25 (1977), 255–63, from a Paris manuscript.

Jonah was published from a Paris manuscript by B. Carlsen in: *Acta Iranica* (1976), 13–26.

Numerous versions of the Psalms exist; for details see A. Netzer, *Oẓar Kitvei ha-Yad* (1985), 17.

Proverbs was published by E. Mainz, in: JA, 268 (1980), 71–106, from a manuscript in Paris and by H.H. Paper, in: *Irano-Judaica* (1982), 122–47 from a manuscript of the Jewish Theological Seminary in New York.

Job was published from a manuscript in the Benayahu Collection in Jerusalem by H.H. Paper, in: *Proceedings of the Israel Academy of Sciences and Humanities*, 5 (1976), 313–65.

The Song of Songs exists in several versions. The version of the Paris Bibliothèque Nationale was edited by J.P. Asmussen and H.H. Paper, *The Song of Songs in Judeo-Persian* (1977); and by E. Mainz in: *Journal Asiatique* (1976), 9–34. Other versions have been printed in various non-scholarly publications in Jerusalem. Details are in A. Netzer, *Oẓar Kitvei ha-Yad* (1985), 18–19.

Ruth was published by E. Mainz in the same article (1976) from a manuscript of Paris.

Lamentations was published from a Paris manuscript by E. Mainz, in: *Studia Iranica*, 2 (1973), 193–202.

Ecclesiastes was published by E. Mainz, in: *Studia Iranica*, 3 (1974), 211–28, from a Paris manuscript, and by H.H. Paper, in: *Orientalia*, 42 (1973), 328–37, from a manuscript at the Jewish Theological Seminary. Part of a commentary on Ecclesiastes by Judah ben Benjamin of Kashan, from New York and Jerusalem manuscripts is given in English translation by V.B. Moreen, *In Queen Esther's Garden* (2000), 198–200.

Esther was published from a Paris manuscript by E. Mainz, in: *Journal Asiatique*, 257 (1970), 95–106.

Daniel was published from a Paris manuscript by E. Mainz, in: *Irano-Judaica* (1982), 148–79. Reference was made above to an Early Judeo-Persian version.

Although the Judeo-Persian translations originated in different Jewish communities, they show a certain uniformity in style, suggesting that there may have been contacts between the different centers of learning, with perhaps more than one school of translators that flourished in the 14th and 15th centuries. Many of the authors of the Judeo-Persian Bible translations, treatises, and lexica show a measure of familiarity with the leading biblical and rabbinical authorities of the West. Following traditional Jewish methods of Bible interpretation, these Jewish authors utilized not only Targum Onkelos, Talmud, Midrash, *Saadiah Gaon, and *Hai Gaon, but also western authorities such as *Rashi, David *Kimḥi, and Abraham *Ibn Ezra.

2. MIDRASHIM AND RELIGIOUS NARRATIVES. The Story of Daniel is a composition based on the theme of the book of Daniel, enriched with a narrative which presumably reflects a Jewish midrash not otherwise extant in the relevant literature. The language of this composition is rather old, and abounds in unusual words and expressions. It was first published by H. Zotenberg, in: *Archiv für die wissenschaftliche Erforschung des Alten Testaments*, 1 (1870), 385–427; J. Darmesteter, in: *Mélanges Renier* (1886), 405–20. The latest edition is by D. Shapira, in: *Sefunot*, NS 7 (1999), 337–66 (Heb).

Several small collections of midrashim are found in Judeo-Persian, among which mention can be made of a midrash recounting the death of Moses, and another one on the death of Aaron. A midrash on the ascension of Moses was edited by A. Netzer, in: *Irano-Judaica*, 2 (1990), 105–43; English translation in V.B. Moreen, *In Queen Esther's Garden* (2000), 189–96.

Many of these and other midrashim were translated from Hebrew or Aramaic. In a related genre, that of sermons, there are again several compilations, the most comprehensive of which is the 19th-century book called *Maṭ'ame Binyamin*, by Binyamin ben Eliyahu of Kashan, preserved in a Ben-Zvi Institute manuscript written by the author in 1823. The book *Zikhron Raḥamim* attributed to Raḥamim Melammed Ha-Kohen, published in 1962, is largely the same compilation; cf. A. Netzer (1985), 23.

There are several Judeo-Persian versions of the Tractate *Avot*, for which examples are given by W. Bacher, in ZFHB, 6 (1902), 112–18, 156–57; H.H. Paper, in: *Michigan Oriental Studies… George G. Cameron* (1976), 81–95. There is also a large versified elaboration on the themes of Avot made by 'Imrani, on which see further below. Details can be found in A. Netzer, *Oẓar Kitvei ha-Yad* (1985), 21.

There are also quite a few compilations of laws relating to everyday practices, such as the daily blessings, the laws of ritual slaughter, laws pertaining to marriage, etc.

3. PHILOSOPHY, SCIENCE, MEDICINE, MAGIC. One extensive book which belongs to this genre is *Ḥovot Yehudah*, by Judah ben Eleazar, written probably in 1686, possibly in Kashan. The book was published by Netzer, *Duties of Judah by Rabbi Yehudah ben Elazar* (Heb.) (1995). An excerpt in English

translation is in V.B. Moreen, *In Queen Esther's Garden* (2000), 255–59. The same author wrote other books, one of which is on astronomy under the title of *Taqwim Yehuda*; one deals with medicine and one is a versified moralistic treatise known as *Timthāl nāme*. A tractate against the drinking of wine is lost. Details about these books, which are still unpublished, can be found in A. Netzer, *op. cit.*, 18–21.

There is a whole range of medical books which were copied from Standard Persian to Hebrew characters, to facilitate their use by Jewish physicians or learners. A list is provided by A. Netzer, *Oẓar Kitvei ha-Yad* (1985), 48–49.

Among the other sciences, handbooks for calculating the Jewish calendar are quite numerous. The interest of the Jewish public in astronomy is indicated by the books which were copied from Standard Persian to Hebrew characters. See a list in A. Netzer, *Oẓar Kitvei ha-Yad* (1985), 49.

Several collections of amulet formulae and divinations are found among the Judeo-Persian manuscripts and scattered in the various libraries. A book of dream interpretation (*Pitron ḥalomot*) was printed in Judeo-Persian in Jerusalem in 1900/1 by Shim'on Ḥakham. The book contains also other treatises on divination, one by limb twitching (*pirkus avarim*) and another one by astronomical omens.

4. PRAYER BOOKS AND PIYUTIM. The earliest Persian synagogue ritual recorded was based on that of R. Saadiah Gaon. The Persian Jews abandoned this ritual under the influence of a Moroccan-born visitor from the Land of Israel, Joseph ben Moses Maman, toward the end of the 18th century and adopted the Sephardi prayer-book, which they are still using today. A facsimile edition of an early Persian prayer book from the E.N. Adler Collection, one of the few remnants of the original Persian ritual, was published by S. Tal, *Nusaḥ ha-Tefillah shel Yehudei Paras* (1981).

To the field of liturgy belong also the *piyyutim* or religious poetry sung in the synagogues, which was one of the major areas of artistic activity of the Jews of Iran. More details are given in the section on poetry.

5. LEXICAL WORKS. One of the earliest extant lexicographical compositions in Judeo-Persian is *'Amuqot Shemuel*, a lexicon explaining rare and difficult words in the Book of Samuel, arranged by the order of the verses. The work, preserved in a manuscript at the British Library, Or. 10482(2), is still unpublished. A study of it was made by W. Bacher, in: ZDMG, 51 (1897), 392–425.

A major lexicon of Hebrew and Aramaic words occurring in the Bible, Targum, Talmud and Midrashim is *Sefer Ha-Meliẓah* (Book of Rhetoric), also called *Egron*, written, according to a colophon, by Solomon ben Samuel in the town of Gurganj (Urganch, in today's Uzbekistan) in the year 1339 C.E. The Persian part of the lexicon reflects the vocabulary of north-east Iran, but also quotes Turkish and Arab forms. This composition has considerable importance for the study of the Jewish sources, especially the Talmud, and demonstrates a high level of learning and intellectual tradition. The book is unedited, but an extensive monograph, with numerous extracts from the text, was written by W. Bacher, *Ein hebraeisch-persisches Woerterbuch aus dem vierzehnten Jahrhundert*, Strasbourg (1900). There are six known manuscripts of this important book, four of which are described in Bacher's study. A detailed enumeration of all can be found in A. Netzer, *Oẓar Kitvei ha-Yad* (1985), 45–46.

Another important lexicographical work is *Egron* by Moses ben Aaron of Shirvan, written in 1459. This is a biblical lexicon preserved in an incomplete manuscript in the British Library, Or. 10482(1). The book is discussed by W. Bacher, *Zeitschrift fuer die alttestamentliche Wissenschaft* 16 (1896), 201–47; 17 (1897), 199–200; P. Horm, in: *Zeitschrift fuer die alttestamentliche Wissenschaft*, 17 (1897), 201–3; T. Noeldeke, in: ZDMG, 51 (1897), 669–76.

Several other lexical works, often called *Mikhlal* or *Mikhlol* or *Perush ha-Millot*, exist in manuscripts scattered in various libraries. A list can be found in A. Netzer, *Oẓar Kitvei ha-Yad* (1985), 46–48.

6. POETRY. Persian Jews found their highest literary expression in original Judeo-Persian poetry. The first known poet was the 14th-century poet Mawlānā Shāhīn, possibly of Shiraz, but this is uncertain; it is also unclear whether Shāhīn is his name or merely an attribute. He is regarded as the foremost Judeo-Persian poet. Shāhīn was imbued with a profound Jewish consciousness and keenly desired to clothe Jewish traditions in the literary ornaments of Persian poetry. He devoted himself to writing verses on biblical topics, and his greatest work, *Sefer Sharḥ Shāhīn al ha-Torah*, is a poetic paraphrase and reinterpretation of the Pentateuch.

Three major works of Shāhīn are extant: (1) the *Mūsā-Nameh* ("Moses Book," concluded in 1327 C.E.), a commentary on Exodus, Leviticus, Numbers, and Deuteronomy. (2) *Ardashīr-Nameh*, consisting of the stories of Esther and Mordecai and of Shero and Mahzad, the latter a typical Iranian love story. There is also *Ezra-Nameh*, dealing mainly with the reign of Cyrus the Great and the building of the Temple of Jerusalem. A. Netzer, *Oẓar Kitvei ha-Yad* (1985), 28, has however argued that the two last books were meant to be a single composition, since they appear following each other in the manuscripts, the former without a conclusion, while the latter without an opening text. The colophon at the end of *Ezra Nameh* gives as the date of completion 1333 C.E. (3) a *Bereshit-Nameh* (concluded in 1359), which includes the story of Joseph and Potiphar's wife, known to Muslims as Zulaykhā. In all his poetic writings, Shāhīn adopted the typical features of Persian poetry and applied the patterns, forms, technique, meter, and language of Persian classical poetry to the presentation of Israel's religious heroes and the events recorded in the biblical narrative, while using both midrashic themes and stories and Muslim ones to fill in the narrative. To Persian-speaking Jews, Shāhīn is "Mawlānā Shāhīn Shīrāzī" (our master Shāhin of Shiraz"), the founder of Judeo-Persian poetry. See on Shāhīn A. Netzer, in: *Israel Oriental Studies*, 4 (1974), 258–64; extensive excerpts from Shāhīn's compositions in English translation are incorporated in V.B. Moreen, *In Queen Esther's Garden* (2000), 26–119.

The next great poet in Judeo-Persian is *ʿImrānī, who was probably born in Isfahan in 1454 and died in Kashan after 1536. Inspired by Shāhīn, ʿImrānī chose as his field the post-Mosaic era from Joshua to the period of David and Solomon. He composed altogether some 12 poetic works. His major work, *Fatḥ-Nameh* ("The Book of the Conquest," begun in 1474), was the first composition that he wrote. He recounts in it in poetic form the events of the biblical books of Joshua, Ruth, and Samuel. He started composing it in 1474 C.E., when he was 20 years old, under the guidance of a teacher by the name of Amin al-Dawla wa-l-Din, and later under that of Judah ben Isaac. The work is unfinished. The last great work of Imrani was *Ganj-Nameh* ("The Book of the Treasures"), a free poetic paraphrase of and commentary on the mishnaic treatise *Avot*. This composition was concluded in the year 1536, when the author was above 80. This work was edited and published by D. Yeroushalmi, *The Judeo-Persian Poet 'Emrānī and his "Book of Treasure"* (1995).

In between these two major works, ʿImrani composed several other smaller poetic compositions, as well as at least two prose works. For further details about ʿImrānī see A. Netzer, in: *Israel Oriental Studies*, 4 (1974), 258–64; idem (1985), 31–33. On ʿImrānī and extracts from his works in English translation, see also V.B. Moreen, *In Queen Esther's Garden*, 119–43, 159–75.

Another early 16th-century author of this type of poetry was Yahuda b. David of Lar. *Makhzan al-Pand* ("The Treasure House of Exhortation") is one of his few extant works. Cf. W. Bacher, *Keleti Szemle* 12 (1911/2), 223–28. An extract in English translation is included in V.B. Moreen, *In Queen Esther's Garden*, 176–183.

In 1606, Khāja Bukhārāī composed a poetical work called *Dāniyāl nāma*, based on the Book of Daniel as well as the Apocrypha and midrashic literature, using the poetic conventions of the earlier Jewish poets, Shāhīn and ʿImrānī. A study of this poet by A. Netzer is in G.L Tikku (ed.), *Islam and Its Cultural Divergence* (1971), 145–64; idem, in: *Israel Oriental Studies*, 2 (1972), 305–14; idem, *Oẓar Kitvei ha-Yad* (1985), 33. Extracts in English translation are included in V.B. Moreen, *In Queen Esther's Garden* (2000), 146–58.

Aaron ben Mashiah is a 17th-century poet. He was born in Isfahan and moved later to Yazd. His composition *Shofetim Nāma* (The Book of Judges), a poetic elaboration of the biblical book of Judges up to chapter 19, was composed in 1692 and follows the pattern of Imrani's *Fatḥ Nāma*. The book contains an allusion to the bloody riots in Isfahan in which the Sabbatean emissary Mattitya Bloch was killed. Cf. A. Netzer, *Oẓar Kitvei ha-Yad* (1985), 33–34. Extracts in English translation are in V.B. Moreen, *In Queen Esther's Garden* (2000), 143–46. The poetic work of Aaron ben Mashiah was continued by Mordecai ben David, who composed a narrative poem under the title of *Ma'ase Pillegesh ba-Giva*, which recounts the events of Judges 19–21. Nothing is known of the biography of this poet.

Elisha ben Shemuel, with the poetic name Rāghib, was a poet who lived in Samark in the 17th century. One of his two poetical compositions are *Shāhzāda va ṣūfī*, based on Abraham ben Ḥisdai's Hebrew composition *Ben ha-Melekh ve ha-Nazir*, a re-working of a widespread Buddhist frame story. The other is *Ḥanukka Nāma*, recounting the events in the saga of the Maccabees, and influenced by Imrani's poetic composition with the same title.

Binyamin ben Misha'el, known under the name Amina, was born in Kashan probably in 1672 C.E. He is the author of some 40 poetic compositions, mostly rather short. One of the longer compositions is *Tafsir Akedat Yiẓḥak* (published in Jerusalem 1901/2), on the sacrifice of Isaac. Another one is *Tafsir Megillat Ester*, on the Book of Esther, and a third one is *Tafsir le-Azharot Rashbag*, on the *Azharot* liturgy. He also composed a eulogy to King Ashraf, the ruler of Afghanistan who invaded Iran and fought the Safavids in 1722. Some of Amina's poems were sung in the synagogues, including an alphabetical poem in Hebrew; cf. A. Netzer, in: *Pe'amim*, 2 (1979), 48–54. Translations of poems by Amina can be found in V.B. Moreen, *In Queen Esther's Garden* (2000).

Siman Tov Melammed, with the poetic name Tuvia, was a mystical poet born in Yazd, who lived for a time in Herat and later in Mashhad. He died in 1823 or 1828. He composed *Ḥayāt al-rūḥ*, a poem based on Baḥya Ibn Paquda's *Ḥovot ha-Levavot* and on the *Guide of the Perplexed* by Maimonides (published Jerusalem 1906/7). Another poetic composition of his is *Azharot*, written in Hebrew and Persian, where the precepts are enumerated (published Jerusalem 1895/6). A discussion of this author is by A. Netzer, *Oẓar Kitvei ha-Yad* (1985), 38; idem, in: *Pe'amim*, 79 (1999), 56–95; V.B. Moreen, *In Queen Esther's Garden* (2000), 260–67.

Two major poets composed narrative compositions dealing with the history of their time. One of them is Bābāī ben Luṭf of Kashan, who described the persecution of the Jews under the Safavids during the years 1613–1662. His book, *Kitāb-i anūsī* describes a sequence of decrees against the Jews, the killing of Jews and the confiscation of their property. A large part of his composition is devoted to the events of 1656–62, including the persecutions under Shāh ʿAbbās II. The importance of this book is derived from the fact that it gives details not only concerning the harsh measures against the Jews but also concerning the internal communal organization of the Jewish communities, including the distribution of crafts and occupations among the Jews. A study and extracts in French translation by W. Bacher are in REJ, 47 (1903), 262–82; vol. 51 (1906), 121–36, 265–79; vol. 52 (1906), 77–97, 234–71; further studies are by E. Spicehandler, in: HUCA (1975), 46:331–56; A. Netzer, in: *Pe'amim*, 6 (1980), 33–56; idem, *Oẓar Kitvei ha-Yad* (1985), 42–43. An English translation is by V.B. Moreen, *Iranian Jewry's Hour of Peril and Heroism* (1987). Further on Bābāī ben Luṭf cf. J.P. Asmussen, in: *Acta Orientalia*, 28 (1964), 243–61.

Bābāī ben Farhād, a descendant of Bābāī ben Luṭf, described the suffering of the Jews of Kashan during another difficult period in Iranian history, in which Sunni Afghan invaders got hold of large parts of Shi'ite Iran. The pressure on Jews to convert to Islam was enormous, and huge sums of money were extorted from the Jewish communities in order to finance the costly wars. Bābāī ben Farhād's composition, written in 1729/30, has the title *Kitāb-i sarguzašt-i Kāshān dar bāb-i ʿibrī va gūyīmī-ye thānī*, or "The Book of the Events of Kashan concerning the Second (Conversion) from Judaism to a Foreign Faith." The Jews of Kashan were forced converts to Islam for seven months, after which they were allowed, against payment of a high ransom, to revert to Judaism. Extracts in French translation are in W. Bacher, in: REJ, 53 (1907), 85–110. A facsimile edition is available in A. Netzer, *Sifrut Parsit-Yehudit* (1978). A short presentation is in A. Netzer, *Oẓar Kitvei ha-Yad* (1985), 43–44. An English translation is by V.B. Moreen, *Iranian Jewry during the Afghan invasion* (1990). Mashiaḥ ben Refaʾel added a supplement to Bābāī ben Farhād's poem, in which he praised the head of the Jewish community in Kashan, Abraham.

Several other minor poets who composed shorter poems in Judeo-Persian are known.

Besides the original compositions in Judeo-Persian, we have Hebrew poems which were translated into Judeo-Persian, mostly poems of a liturgical character.

7. POETRY TRANSCRIBED FROM STANDARD PERSIAN. The Jews of Iran had a taste for poetry, and they read not only the compositions of their own poets but also those of the Muslims. They deeply admired the classical Persian poetry of such writers as Firdawsī, ʿAṭṭār, Niẓāmī, ʾumar Khayyām, Rūmī, Saʿdī, Ḥāfiẓ, and Jāmī. They transcribed a large number of Persian texts into Hebrew characters. Among the various types of Persian classical poetry – romantic, lyrical, and didactic – popularized in transliteration were *Khusrow o Shirin* and *Haft Paikar* ("Seven Images") by Niẓāmī (d. 1201); some poems of the *Mathnawī* by Jalāl al-Dīn Rūmī (d. 1273); some parts of the *Gulistān* by Saʿdi (d. 1291); the *Dīwān* of Ḥāfiẓ (d. 1390); *Yūsuf o Zulaykhā* by Jāmī (1414–92); portions of the *Dīwān* of Saʾib of Isfahan (d. 1678); and others. The Jews often emulated these poets and composed works in the same style. A survey of some of the more popular Muslim compositions which circulated in Hebrew transliteration can be found in A. Netzer, *Oẓar Kitvei ha-Yad* (1985), 39–41. A discussion of some phenomena connected to this topic is by J.P. Asmussen, in: SBB, 8 (1968), 44–53; and in the same author's *Studies in Judeo-Persian literature* (1973), 60–109.

8. POPULAR STORIES. A large number of popular stories are found in the Judeo-Persian manuscripts, often embedded in the midrash-type literature mentioned earlier. A succinct summary of these compositions is found in A. Netzer, *Oẓar Kitvei ha-Yad* (1985), 49. In Israel, a concentrated effort has been made to collect orally transmitted stories by Persian Jews, and many of them have been written down in Hebrew and are preserved in the Archive of the Israeli Folkstories. Examples of publications of folktales may by quoted: two small volumes of *Maʿasiyyot Niflaʾim* ("Wonderful Tales"), which were printed by Israel Gul Shaulof and his son in Jerusalem (1911/2); a collection of Bukharan stories was published by J. Pinhasi, *Folktales from Bukhara*, ed. D. Noy, Jerusalem (1978, Heb.).

9. MINIATURES IN JUDEO-PERSIAN MANUSCRIPTS. Persian Jews took part in or sponsored the production of miniatures to illuminate manuscripts. In some of the Shāhīn and ʿImrānī manuscripts, and in those of the classical poetry in Hebrew transliteration, large colored miniatures of exceptional beauty were incorporated. It is not clear who the artists were who drew these pictures. It is quite possible that in some cases non-Jewish workshops were responsible for the execution of the illustrations in Judeo-Persian manuscripts. A study of the miniatures is by J. Gutmann, in: SBB, 8 (1968), 54–76. An illustrated catalogue of miniatures in Judeo-Persian manuscripts is provided by V.B. Moreen, *Miniature Painting in Judeo-Persian Manuscripts* (1985).

10. THE ACTIVITY OF THE BUKHARAN MEN OF LETTERS IN THE MODERN PERIOD. In Bukhara, where the Jews were not subjected to the persecution their brethren endured in Safavid Persia, there appeared Jewish poets and translators who began to create Jewish literature and poetry in their own Bukharan, or rather Judeo-Tajik, dialect. Outstanding among them was Yūsuf *al-Yahūdī (d. 1755), an exponent of the biblical narrative developed by Shāhīn and ʿImrānī. See on him W. Bacher, in: *Zeitschrift der Deutschen Morgenlaendischen Gesellschaft*, 53 (1899), 389–427. He wrote a *Mukhammas*, an ode in praise and glory of Moses; *Haft Barāderān* ("The Seven Brothers"), based on the Midrash story of the martyrdom of the seven brothers and their mother; and bilingual and trilingual hymns honoring biblical heroes. He also wrote a poetic version of *Megillat Antiochus* and his translations into the Bukharan dialect of many of the **zemirot* of Israel *Najara were incorporated into the Judeo-Persian song books still in use today. Under his inspiration there emerged a school of Bukharan Jewish poets. It included a Judeo-Persian translation and commentary, *Daniel-Nameh*, which was edited by Binyamin b. Mishaʾel, known as Amina, who published a Judeo-Persian Book of Esther in metric form and translated some poems of Solomon ibn *Gabirol, such as *Azharot* and *Yigdal*, into Judeo-Persian.

In 1793 a significant cultural and religious change was inaugurated by the arrival in Bukhara of R. Joseph Maman al-Maghribī ("the messenger from Zion"). A native of Tetuan, Morocco, who had settled in Safed, he came as the official emissary (*shaliaḥ*) of that community. During his 30-year stay, he became the spiritual leader of Bukharan Jewry and effected a radical transformation in its religious life. He established Jewish schools, introduced the Sephardi rite, and imported books from abroad, especially from Shklov, Russia. Under his leadership the Bukharan Jews reestablished contact with other Jewish communities, and integrated their religious life with that of the Jewish people as a whole.

A narrative poem recounts in Judeo-Bukharan the story of a certain cloth merchant, Khudāidāt, who refused the pressure to convert to Islam and was executed as a martyr. The poem was composed probably in the late 18th or early 19th century by an unknown author. It was first published by C. Salemann, in: *Mémoires de l'Académie Impériale des Sciences*, 7, 42, 14 (1897); and studied by W. Bacher, in: ZDMG, 52 (1898), 197–212; ZFHB, 3 (1899), 19–25. A shortened translation is in V.B. Moreen, *In Queen Esther's Garden* (2000), 238–42.

An outstanding Bukharan Jewish scholar can be credited with a major share in the promotion of Judeo-Persian literature in the modern period, Simon *Ḥakham (1843–1910). He moved in 1890 to Jerusalem, where he joined the rapidly increasing colony of Bukharan Jews. Ḥakham began his activities in Jerusalem as author, translator, editor, and publisher of Judeo-Persian works. Among his many impressive achievements was his Judeo-Tajik translation of the novel *Ahavat Ẓiyyon* by Abraham *Mapu, which appeared in 1908. The crowning glory of Shim'on Ḥakham's literary activities was, however, his translation into Judeo-Bukharan of the Bible (Pentateuch, 5 vols., 1901–02). With this work, Ḥakham entered the ranks of the great Jewish Bible translators. He published an edition of Shāhīn's *Sharḥ al ha-Torah* (3 vols., 1902–08). An edition of Shim'on Ḥakham's *Mūsā nāma* was published by H.H. Paper in Cincinnati (1986). An excerpt is translated into English by V.B. Moreen, *In Queen Esther's Garden* (2000), 200–5.

Of great interest is the collection of *dinim* or religious laws under the title *Likkutei Dinim*, compiled by Abraham Aminof and published in Jerusalem between 1899 and 1904; a study of this book was made by W. Bacher, in: ZFHB, 5 (1901), 147–54; ZDMG, 56 (1902), 729–259.

Under Soviet rule Bukharan Jewry at first enjoyed a measure of cultural autonomy, which it lost by the end of World War II. During the 1960s Yakub Chaimov wrote novels and stories in the Tajik variant of Judeo-Persian, but these were published in Uzbek or Russian and presented as the work of a Muslim. In 1959 nearly 20,000 Bukharan Jews gave the Tajik dialect as their mother tongue.

11. THE JUDEO-PERSIAN LITERARY CENTER IN JERUSALEM. Judeo-Persian literature experienced an unforeseen development in the second half of the 19th century, not in Persia but in Jerusalem. This was precipitated by a wave of immigration into Ereẓ Israel, paralleling the Ḥovevei Ẓion immigration from Russia, of Persian-speaking Jews from Bukhara, Turkestan, Afghanistan, and Persia itself. They settled in Tiberias and Safed, in Haifa and Jaffa, but most of them went to Jerusalem, where they established a colony. In Jerusalem they inaugurated a new and spectacular epoch in the history of Judeo-Persian literary activity. Their leaders were eager to help those who remained in their lands of origin and to cement stronger ties between Jerusalem and the "remnants of Israel" in the remote Persian-speaking Oriental Diaspora. They established in Jerusalem a publishing center to perpetuate the manuscripts which Persian Jews had brought with them. This led to a decisive change in the history of Judeo-Persian literature.

Although some Judeo-Persian works had previously been published in Europe, particularly in Vienna and Vilna, Jerusalem now became the main center of Judeo-Persian printing activities. Almost every field in the religious, literary, historical, and philosophical spectrum was included in its program: Bible, Bible commentaries, prayer books for every occasion, rabbinical writings, Mishnah and Zohar, medieval Jewish poetry and philosophy, *piyyutim, seliḥot, pizmonim, midrashim*, historical narratives, and anthologies of songs and stories. Even translations of non-Jewish literature, such as portions of the *Arabian Nights* and selections from Shakespeare's *Comedy of Errors*, found their way to the printer. These literary activities represented a creative effort, a cooperative endeavor of all the groups of Persian-speaking Jews who had settled in the Holy Land. Among the promoters and initiators were the above-mentioned Shim'on Ḥakham of Bukhara and Solomon Babajan Pinchasoff of Samarkand; the leading rabbis of Herat in Afghanistan; the Garjis; Mullā Mordecai b. Raphael *Aklar (Mullā Murād), the secret rabbi of the *anusim* of *Mashhad; and many leading personalities from Shiraz, Hamadan, Isfahan, and other Jewish communities who settled in Jerusalem. They converted Zion into a cultural center for Persian-speaking Jews.

A collection of liturgical poems under the title *Ge'ulat Yisra'el* was printed in Jerusalem in 1969 in Judeo-Persian; it contains several thanksgiving poems composed at the end of the Six-Day War (1967) by Shulamit Tilayoff and others. These poems are given both in Judeo-Persian and in Hebrew, demonstrating the fact that knowledge of the Bukharan dialect was dwindling among the younger members of the community.

12. MODERN JUDEO-PERSIAN. The renaissance of Judeo-Persian literature in Persia found expression in the establishment of a "Society for the Promotion of the Hebrew Language" in 1917 and in the establishment of a Judeo-Persian and Hebrew printing press in Teheran. Teheran became the seat of a Hebrew press and the center of a modern Hebrew and Jewish-Persian literature. Motivated by the endeavor to halt the decline of Jewish life, to combat assimilation and ignorance, and to implant a knowledge of Hebrew, this society published a work titled *Sefer Ḥizzuk Sefat Ever* (1918), a textbook of modern Hebrew. The author, Solomon ben Kohen-Ẓedek of Teheran, was an inspiring leader and teacher of the Jewish community and a former Persian government official. This was the first attempt of its kind in Persia. It concludes with the Hebrew and Persian texts of the Zionist anthem, *Ha-Tikvah*. The society also published the first history of the Zionist movement in the Persian language printed in Hebrew characters (1920) by Aziz ben Jonah Naim, a survey of the Zionist movement, its organizations, and its colonies in Ereẓ Israel. The numerous biblical quotations from Isaiah and the Psalms in this history indicate the strong religious and messianic character of Persian Jewry's conception of Zionism. This history

introduced in Persian Jewish literature leaders of the Zionist movement.

The same Jewish circle also published a Jewish newspaper in the Persian language, *Ha-Ge'ulah* (1920), and another, rather short-lived, periodical called *Ha-Ḥayyim*, which became the mouthpiece of the Jewish renaissance movement in Persia. These periodicals contained some poems by Bialik, first translated into Persian by Aziz ben Jonah Naim. The only other Judeo-Persian newspapers that are known were *Rushnai*, published in Samarkand, and *Raḥamim*, published in Bukhara.

The awakening of Zionism was closely connected with the revival of Judaism. The leading figure in this group, who tried to revive Jewish consciousness among the Persian Jews, was Mulla Elijahu Chayin More. The author of three important works on Jewish tradition, history, and philosophy in Judeo-Persian, *Sefer Derekh Ḥayyim* (1921), *Sefer Gedulat Mordekhai* (1924), and *Sefer Yedei Eliyahu* (1927), he exerted a great influence on his generation. Though deprived of his eyesight, blind from his early youth, this rabbi played a most important role in efforts to lead Persian Jewry toward a Jewish revival.

After the Islamic revolution of Iran (1979), the literary Jewish activity in Iran seems to have halted. A substantial Jewish-Iranian Diaspora was established in various cities in the United States, and with time a whole range of publications was established in standard Persian, in the Arab-Persian alphabet. The younger generation, while wishing to retain its double identity, Jewish and Iranian, is no longer familiar with the brand of Persian written in Hebrew characters. Among the efforts to inculcate Jewish-Iranian consciousness in the Jewish public, both in Iran and in the new Judeo-Iranian Diaspora, mention must be made of the publications of Amnon Netzer, professor of Persian at the Hebrew University in Jerusalem, who, besides writing a history of the Jews in Persian and an anthology of Judeo-Persian poetry in the Arab-Persian script, and besides contributing much to the academic study of Jewish Iranian history, also edited a few volumes of a high-level intellectual annual under the title of *Pādyāvand*.

13. HISTORY OF RESEARCH INTO JUDEO-PERSIAN LANGUAGE AND LITERATURE. *1. The major collections of Judeo-Persian manuscript.* One of the earliest manuscripts acquired for Western libraries was brought to Italy by Giambattista Vecchietti, who got in Lar in 1606 the Judeo-Persian Pentateuch version now kept at the Vatican Library.

Abraham Firkovich (1785–1874) was a Karaite scholar and collector of manuscripts, who traveled to Palestine, Syria and Egypt, and acquired valuable Judeo-Persian manuscripts, sold to the Imperial (now Public) Library of St. Petersburg.

Cambridge University Library acquired a large portion of the manuscripts in the Cairo *Genizah*, including a surprising number of manuscript fragments in Early Judeo-Persian through the efforts of S. Schechter (1847–1915).

One of the most important collectors was Elkan Nathan Adler (1861–1946), who acquired manuscripts during his travels in many lands. His collection is now housed in the library of the Jewish Theological Seminary in New York. A catalogue of his collection was published in Cambridge (1921).

The Bibliothèque Nationale in Paris houses one of the important collections of Judeo-Persian manuscripts, chiefly Bible translations (catalogues by H. Zotenberg, 1866; E. Blochet, 1905). An equally important collection is kept by the British Library, some of it deriving from the Cairo *Genizah*; the catalogue descriptions are by E. Seligsohn, in: JQR, 15 (1903), 278–310; J. Rosenwasser (1966).

Among other significant acquisitions of Judeo-Persian manuscripts, that of Ezra Spicehandler, who bought manuscripts in Iran on behalf of the Hebrew Union College in the late 1950s, should be mentioned, as well as Amnon Netzer, who collected valuable Judeo-Persian manuscripts in Iran in the 1970s and handed them over to the Ben-Zvi Institute in Jerusalem. His catalogue of the Ben-Zvi Institute J-P collection, *Otsar kitve ha-yad* (1985), may serve as a survey of Judeo-Persian literature.

2. A short history of research. One of the earliest scholars to recognize the interest and importance of the field of Judeo-Persian was Paul de Lagarde (1827–1891), who studied the Judeo-Persian Bible versions in the Bibliothèque Nationale in Paris and published the translation of Isaiah and parts of Jeremiah and Ezekiel, see Lagarde, *Persische Studien* (1884). He made the oft-quoted comment that from now on it would be impossible to claim knowledge of Persian without having gone through the body of Judeo-Persian literature.

The most important contribution to the investigation of Judeo-Persian literature was made by Wilhelm *Bacher (1850–1913) who turned much of his considerable energy and scholarly output to this field, in which he became the undisputed authority.

In the 1960s the two most prominent scholars of Judeo-Persian literature and language were H.H. Paper, who edited the two oldest complete Pentateuch manuscripts, and J.P. Asmussen, who published a long list of books and articles on various Judeo-Persian themes. At the same time Ernst Mainz published a series of Bible versions from the Paris Collections. The most important contribution to the study of Judeo-Persian dialectology is Gilbert Lazard, who emphasized the importance of Judeo-Persian for the study of the development of the Persian language, showing as he did the intermediate position of Judeo-Persian between Middle Persian and Classical Persian, while demonstrating that the early Judeo-Persian texts derived from different local dialect, which explains their divergence from the Classical Persian texts. D.N. MacKenzie studied the Karaite Book of Precepts and the problems of the Tafsir of Ezekiel from St. Petersburg. E. Yarshater devoted some studies to the spoken dialects of Persian Jews. A. Netzer made immense contribution to the study of the history of Judeo-Persian literature of the classical period by identifying the authorship of works and discovering the precise dates and places of several of the authors. He also published a number of important J-P works.

BIBLIOGRAPHY: SURVEYS, ANTHOLOGIES, CATALOGUES OF JUDEO-PERSIAN: E.N. Adler, JQR, 10 (1898), 584–626; J.P. Asmussen, *Jewish Persian Texts* (1968); W.J. Fischel, in: L. Finklestein (ed.), *The Jews, Their History, Culture and Religion*, 2 (1960[3]), 1149–90; Mizrahi, *The History of the Persian Jews and Their Poets* (Heb., 1966; V.B. Moreen, *In Queen Esther's Garden. An Anthology of Judeo-Persian literature, translated and with an introduction and notes* (Yale Judaica Series), (2000); A. Netzer, *Muntakhab-i aš'ār-i fārisī az āthār-i yahūdiyān-i īrān* (1352 Hijra, Solar); idem, the introduction to: *Oẓar Kitvei ha-Yad shel Yehude Paras be-Makhon Ben-Zvi* (Heb., 1985); J. Rosenwasser, in: *The British Museum. Handlist of Persian Manuscripts, 1895–1966* (1966), 38–44; M. Seligsohn, in: JQR, 15 (1903), 278–301; E. Spicehandler, in: *Studies in Bibliography and Booklore*, 8 (1968), 114–36. STUDIES IN LANGUAGE AND LEXICON: J.P. Asmussen, in: *Temenos*, 5 (1969), 17–21; idem, in: *K.R. Cama Oriental Institute Golden Jubilee Volume* (1969), 93–102; G. Lazard, in: SBB, 8 (1968), 77–98 (Fr.; incl. bibl.); idem, *La formation de la langue persane* (1995); E. Mainz, in: *Studia Iranica*, 6 (1977), 75–95; A. Netzer, in: J. Dan (ed.), *Tarbut ve-Historiya* (1987), 19–44; H.H. Paper, in: JAOS, 87 (1967), 227–230; 88 (1968), 483–494; idem, in: *Indo-Iranian Journal*, 10 (1967–68), 56–71; L. Paul, *Grammatical and Philological Studies on the Early Judeo-Persian Texts from the Cairo Geniza* (unpublished habilitation thesis, Göttingen 2002); idem, in: *Irano-Judaica*, 5 (2003), 96–104; idem, in: *Persian Origins* (2003), 177–194; S. Shaked, in: *Études irano-aryennes offertes à Gilbert Lazard* (1989), 315–19; idem, in: *Persian Origins* (2003), 195–219. A. EARLY JUDEO-PERSIAN: GHUR TOMB INSCRIPTIONS: G. Gnoli, *Le iscrizioni giudeo-persiane del Ġūr (Afghanistan)* (Serie Orientale Roma, 3) (1964); E.L. Rapp, *Die jüdisch-persisch-hebräischen Inschriften aus Afghanistan* (1965); idem, *Die persische-hebräischen Inschriften Afghanestans aus dem 11. bis 13. Jahrhundert* (1971); idem, in: *Jahrbuch der Vereinigung "Freunde der Universität Mainz"* (1973), 52–66; S. Shaked, in: *Studies in Judaism and Islam Presented to S.D. Goitein* (1981), 65–82; idem, in: *Irano-Judaica*, 6 (2006). TAFSIR OF EZEKIEL: T. Gindin, in: *Jerusalem Studies in Arabic and Islam* 27 (2002), 396–418; idem, in: L. Paul (ed.), *Persian Origins* (2003), 15–30; idem, *Early Judaeo-Persian: the Language of the Tafsīr of Ezekiel* (unpub. doct. diss., Hebrew University 2004); D.N. MacKenzie, in: L. Paul (ed.), *Persian Origins* (2003), 103–10; S. Shaked, in: *Studia grammatica iranica. Festschrift fuer H. Humbach* (1986), 393–405. B. LITERATURE OF THE CLASSICAL PERIOD: BIBLE TRANSLATIONS: Some major editions: P. Lagarde, *Persische Studien* (1884); H. Ethe, *Die Psalmen im hebräischen Text mit persischer Übersetzung* (1883); idem, in: *Literaturblatt für orientalische Philologie*, 1 (1883/84), 186–94; H.H. Paper, "The Vatican Judeo-Persian Pentateuch," in: *Acta Orientalia* 28 (1965), 363–140; 29 (1965/6), 75–181, 254–310; 31 (1968), 55–113; idem, *A Judeo-Persian Pentateuch*, Jerusalem (1972); idem, *Biblia Judaeo-Persica: Editio Variorum* (1973), republication with numerous corrections. STUDIES AND SURVEYS OF BIBLE VERSIONS: *General*: W. Bacher, in: *Jewish Encyclopaedia*, 7 (1906), 313–24; W.J. Fischel, in: HTR, 45 (1952), 3–45; P. Horn, in: *Indo-germanische Forschungen*, 2 (1893), 132–43; H.H. Paper, in: *Studies in Bibliography and Booklore* (1968), 99–113. *Pentateuch*: A. Kohut, *Kritische Beleuchtung der persischen Pentateuchübersetzung des Jacob b. Joseph Tavus* (1871). *Psalms*: J.P. Asmussen, in: AO, 30 (1966), 15–24; E.Z. Melammed, in: *Sefunot*, 9 (1964), 295–319; idem, *Tafsir Tehillim bi-Leshon Yehudei Paras* (1968). *Proverbs*: K.V. Zettersteen, in: ZDMG, 54 (1900), 555–59. LEXICAL WORKS: W. Bacher, *Ein hebräisch-persisches Wörterbuch aus dem vierzehnten Jahrhundert* (1899–1900); idem, in: ZDMG, 51 (1897), 392–425; idem, in: *Zeitschrift für die alttestamentliche Wissenschaft*, 16 (1896), 201–247; 17 (1897), 199–200. POETRY (SHĀHĪN, IMRĀNĪ, ETC.): J.P. Asmussen, in: *Acta Orientalia*, 28 (1965), 245–61; W. Bacher, *Zwei jüdisch-persische Dichter, Schāhīn und Imrānī* (1908); D. Blieske, *Sāhīh-e Sirāzīs Ardašir-Buch* (1966); W.J. Fischel, in: KS, vol. 9, 522–4; W.J. Fischel, in: *Mélanges d'Orientalisme à Henri Massé* (1963), 141–50; N. Mullaqandow and M. Rahimi (eds.), in: *Šarqi surkh* (1958), no. 3, 86–106; no. 4, 105–28; M. Rahimi, in: *Madanijoti Toğikiston* (1958), no. 8, 12–7, cont. in: *Šarqi surch* (1964), no. 2, 101–13; H. Striedl, in: *Forschungsberichte Marburger Kolloquium 1965* (1966), 119–33. On 'Imrani and the *Fatḥ-nāme* cf. also D. Yeroushalmi, in: *Irano-Judaica* 4 (1999), 223–250. NEW JUDEO-PERSIAN DIALECTS: *Different localities*: S. Soroudi, in: *Irano-Judaica* (1982), 204–64; idem, in: *Irano-Judaica*, 2 (1990), 167–83; A. Netzer, *Montakhab-e aš'ār-e fārsi* (1973), 56–57; V.A. Zhukovskij, *Obrazstsy persidskago narodnago tvorčestvo* (1902), 131–34. *Hamadan*: R. Abrahamian, *Dialectes des Israélites de Hamadan et d'Ispahan et dialecte de Baba Tahir*, Paris (1936); H. Sahim, in: *Irano-Judaica*, 3 (1994), 171–81. *Isfahan*: I. Kalbāsī, *Gūyeš-e kalīmiyān-e eṣfahān* (1373 HS); A. Netzer, in: *Irano-Judaica* (1982), 180–203; idem, in: *Miqqedem u-miyyam*, 4 (1991), 179–98; *Kashan*: V.A. Zhukovskij, *Materialy dlja izučenija persidskix narečij*, 2 (1922), 390–94; *Tajrish*: V.A. Zhukovskij, *Materialy dlja izučenija persidskikh narečij*, 2 (1922), 395–98; *Yazd*: H. Homayoun, in: *Yādnāme-ye Doktor Mehrdād-e Bahār*, Tehran (1998), 686–706; idem, *Gūyeš-e kalimiyān-e yazd* (2004). JUDEO-TAJIK (JEWISH BUKHARAN): *Language:* T. Nöldeke, in: ZDMG, 51 (1897), 548–53; S.A. Birnbaum, in: *Archivum Linguisticum*, 2 (1950), 60–73, 158–76; W. Sundermann, in: *Mitteilungen des Instituts für Orientforschung*, 11 (1965), 275–300. *Literature:* A. Yaari, in: *Kirjath Sepher*, 18 (1941/2), 282–97, 378–93; 19 (1942/3), 35–55, 116–39 (Heb.); W. Bacher, in: ZDMG, 53 (1899), 389–427; C. Salemann, in: *Mémoires de l'Académie Impériale des Sciences de St. Pétersbourg*, 7è série, 42:14 (1897).

[Gilbert Lazard, Walter Joseph Fischel, and Herbert H. Paper / Shaul Shaked (2nd ed.)]

JUDEO-PROVENÇAL, the name given to the various dialects spoken among the Jews of Provence. By the sixth Century C.E. Jews formed important communities in the southern area of France known as Provence. The oldest texts in Judeo-Provençal are the glosses found in the *Ittur* of *Isaac ben Abba Mari of Marseilles, written between 1170 and 1193; in the glosses found in the anonymous *Sefer ha-Shorashim* appended to the *Farḥi Bible* (Ms. Sassoon no. 368, p. 42–165); and in extracts from an anonymous 12th-century commentary on the First Prophets (Margoliouth, Cat, no. 249). Other commentaries of the 13th–14th centuries also provide examples of Provençal and Catalonian glosses transcribed in Hebrew letters. The only medieval texts still preserved in Judeo-Provençal are a fragment of the Book of Esther by the 14th-century Crescas du Caylar (published by A. Neubauer and P. Mayer in *Romania*, 21 (1892), 194–227) and a translation of the daily prayers (*siddur*), also from the 14th–15th centuries (Ms. Roth 32). These texts were composed in the vernacular for the benefit of women who could not understand the Hebrew original. A literary text written in the common language of its time, the Judeo-Provençal Esther fragment, though transcribed in Hebrew characters, contains no words or phrases of Hebrew origin. The *siddur*, however, is interspersed with Hebraisms inherent to a translation of this kind. These consist mainly of terms which cannot be easily translated, such as צבור for

מועדות, מזבח, פרוכת, בכורים, פסח, פאה, חטאת, גויה, קהל for צבאות, כהנים, ימים טובים. The Hebrew transcription is based on a system more or less common to both texts, and provides no characteristics which would point to a specifically "Jewish" pronunciation, except for some examples of metathesis (*torp* for *trop*, *pormet* for *promet*, *plubic* for *public*) and transposition (*nembres* for *menbres*), which seem to be merely transcription errors. These texts do not warrant the identification of a Judeo-Provençal language distinct from the Provençal in use at this period. They nevertheless do not exclude the possibility of a specifically Jewish dialect or speech such as was later found in the *Comtat-Venaissin.

In later times (17th and 18th centuries) the Jews in the Comtat customarily spoke Provençal, Hebrew, and French. By its phonetic and morphological elements, Judeo-Provençal differed slightly from the Provençal Rhodanien of the Gentile surroundings. Traces of this language, commonly known as *Chuadit* (or Shuadit; perhaps from the Hebrew שפה יהודית *Safah Yehudit* or simply יהודית; the term appears for the first time in a satire of 1803), or sometimes as *ebraicum vulgare* or *jargon de l'escolo*, are to be found in the satires and comedies written in Provençal by non-Jews who introduced Jewish characters using this type of speech. The oldest document of this kind dates only from the 17th century. The comedy *Harcanot et Barcanot* (published by Hirschler in 1896 and, in a second version by Pansier in 1925), entirely written in this language, is the most important specimen of the language of Provençal Jews at the end of the 18th century. Its author was probably the lawyer Bedarrides of Montpellier, who had only an indirect knowledge of the language of the Jews of Carpentras, but the principal phonetic characters were later distinguished in Carpentras by Hirschler in the second half of the 19th century. The most important phonetic changes can be seen in Table: Judeo-Provençal – Phonetics.

Judeo-provencal – phonetics

VOWELS	
l > i	plus > pius, blanc > bianc
endings: ero > èyo	tabatièro > tabatyèo
	filho > fèyo, escanbilho > escobèyo,
ilho > èyo	familho > famèyo
iso > èyo	camiso > camèyo, Aliso > Alèyo
ב > ü	katàv > kataü, ganav > ganaü, rav > raü
l > h	galino > gahino
a (final) > é in Provençalisms and Gallicisms:	apresta > apresté, douna > douné, debita > debité
CONSONANTS	
s > f	basar > bafar, cènt > fant, seḥel > fehe
ט, צ, שׂ, ת > f	perat > peraf
	mesilah > mefilah
	ẓurah > furah
	seḥel > fehel
	emet > emef
ז > v	zonah > vonah
	mamzer > mamver
כ, ח > r	ḥadash > radas
	ḥokhmah > rourmah
	ḥote > rotie
j, g (soft) > ch	ges > ches
	louja > loucha
	juge > chuche
י (yod) > ch	yehudit > chuadit
	yayin > chain
	yaḥid > chaïd

Together with this dialect, rich in Hebraisms and Gallicisms, there exists a language written in Hebrew characters which, for the most part, shares its linguistic and lexicological traits with the other Provençal dialects, thus constituting one of the literary dialects of Provence. This language is represented only in the *Obros*, Hebrew-Provençal songs in which verses in Hebrew and Provençal alternate; these were sung on Purim, on the evening before a circumcision, and at special events (critical edition by M. Lazar, 1963). The author of the major part of *Obros* was Mardochée Astruc (end of 17th cent.) who also composed a tragedy in Provençal on Queen Esther entitled *La Tragediou de la Reine Esther*. This was revived in the 18th century by *Jacob de Lunel, who edited it under this same title (The Hague, 1774; 2nd ed. by E. Sabatier, Nîmes, 1877). The language of the *Obros* is the pure Comtadin dialect of Provence transliterated into Hebrew. It is a literary form of speech coexisting with the less pure language of Judeo-Provençal. The language of the *Tragediou de la Reine Esther* is also a debased but purely Provençal dialect, such as was used in Provence in the 17th–18th centuries, and free from the characteristics peculiar to the Jewish dialects.

BIBLIOGRAPHY: Z. Szajkowski, *Dos Loshon fun di Yiden in di Arba Kehiles fun Comtat-Venaissin* (1948); R. Hirschler, in: *Calendrier à l'usage des Israélites pour l'année religieuse 5655* (1894/95), 26–32; P. Pansier, *Histoire de la langue provençale à Avignon du XIIe au XIXe siècle*, 3 (1927), 178–85; idem, in: REJ, 81 (1925), 113–45; M. Lazar, in: *Romanica et Occidentalia: études… H. Peri* [Pflaum] (1963), 290–345. **ADD. BIBLIOGRAPHY:** C. Aslanov, *Le provençal des Juifs et l'hébreu en Provence: le dictionnaire Sharshot* ha-Kesef *de Joseph Caspi* (2001); idem, "Judéo-provençal médiéval et chuadit: essai de délimitation," in: *La France latine (Revue d'Études d'Oc)*, 134 (2002), 103–22.

[Henri Guttel / Cyril Aslanov (2nd ed.)]

JUDEO-TAT (Zuhun Tati; Zuhun Juhuri), Iranian language derived from a spoken form of New Persian and heavily influenced by Azeri Turkic; traditionally spoken in Jewish communities of the eastern and northern Caucasus, known as the Mountain Jews (*dağ-çufut*; *gorskie jevrei*; *yehudim harariyim* / *qavqaziyim*). Judeo-Tat does form a dialectal unity with neighboring Tati dialects spoken in the past by a Muslim population; these "Tati" Muslim dialects of Azerbaijan and Dagestan, in turn, are to be distinguished from the so-called Southern

Tati dialects of northern* Iran. On the other hand, Judeo-Tat is close to a dialect of the New Persian type spoken, in the past, by a small Armeno-Grigorian community in northern-western Azerbaijan. During the 19th and 20th centuries, Judeo-Tat was adopted by smaller Jewish linguistic minorities of Transcaucasia and northern Caucasus (Neo-Aramaic, Kurdish, Azeri, Adyge-Circassian). The Mountain Jews migrated to Transcaucasia and the eastern and northern Caucasus from Iran during the post-Mongol and, especially, Safavid periods. There is no linguistic evidence to support the claim that they are presumably descended from Iranian military colonies established during the Sassanid period (226–641 C.E.) on the northern frontier of the empire. From the early 19th century, the Mountain Jews were established chiefly in the towns of Makhachkala / Mahaç-Qal'ah and Derbend (Darband, Dagestan), in villages situated in the Caucasian foothills of southern Dagestan and in the district of Qubba (northern Azerbaijan). In the early 21st century the Mountain Jews are to be found chiefly in well-organized communities in Israel, Qubba, Moscow, New York, and Derbend. Before 1917 only two books existed in Judeo-Tat, both translated from Hebrew ("What is Zionism?" and the Sephardi prayerbook, both printed in Vilna). During World War I a newspaper appeared, *Hed Harim*. In the Soviet period the Mountain Jews were recognized as one of the nationalities of the republic of Dagestan, and their language ("Tati") became one of the five official languages of the Dagestan Republic. In 1929, as a secularization measure, the Latin alphabet was imposed on this language in place of the Hebrew one; this was done as part of the general "Latinization politics" in the U.S.S.R.; however, by 1939 the language politics had changed and all the Latin scripts were replaced by the Cyrillic alphabet. In the Soviet period, especially in the 1920s–1960s, there were many Judeo-Tat schools, newspapers and other publications. In the 1960s, some community leaders in Soviet Dagestan (but not in Azerbaijan) promoted the politics of "Tatization," claiming non-Jewish origin of the Mountain Jews and encouraging them to register as "Tats." (There were, however, no other registered "Tats" except the Mountain Jews"). Though withering, this language is now one of the nine literary and official languages of Dagestan; in the 1959 Soviet census about 30,000 Jews declared Judeo-Tat as their mother tongue. Judeo-Tat is an endangered language, and almost all Mountain Jews now speak Russian and/or Hebrew. There are publishing activities in Israel and Russia, but this is either in Russian or in Hebrew.

BIBLIOGRAPHY: V.F. Miller, *Materialy dlya izucheniya yevreyskotatskogo yazyka; Vvedenie, teksty, slovar* (1892) / *Materials for Study of the Judeo-Tat Language. Introduction, Texts, Glossary*); *idem, Ocherk morfologii ievrejsko-tatskago narechia* (1901); *idem, Tati studies.* Part I. *Texts and Tat-Russian dictionary,* 1905); *idem, Tati Studies,* Part II. *An Attempt at a Grammar of the Tati Language* (1907); *idem,* "Tati texts," in: *The Iranian languages,* vol. 1 (Moscow-Leningrad, 1945); N.A. Anisimov, *Grammatik zuhun tati* (1932 [in Judeo-Tat]; Z. Bakhshiev et al. (eds.), *Antologiya tatskikh poetov* (1932); EIS, 4 (1934), s.v. *Tāt*; Kh. D. Avshalumov, *Folklor Tati* (1940) [in Judeo-Tat]; A. Bennigsen and M. Carrère d'Encausse, in: *Revue des études islamiques,* 23 (1955), 7–56; A.L. Griunberg, *Yazyk severo-azerbaydzhanskikh Tatov* (1963); idem, *Sistema glagoda v Tatskom yazyka* (1963), 121–49 (these two works treat *not* the Judeo-Tat, but the Muslim Tati dialects); E. Yar-Shater, *A Grammar of Southern Tati Dialects* (1969) (treats the Tati dialects of northern Iran, non-related to Judeo-Tat or to Muslim Tati dialects of Azerbaijan); M. Zand, "The Literature of the Mountain Jews of the Caucasus," in: SOJA, 15:2 (1985), 3–22; 16:1 (1986), 35–51; idem, "The Culture of the Mountain Jews of the Caucasus and the Culture of the Jews of Bukhara during the Soviet Period," in: JCSU (1973), 134–47; idem, "*Hityashevut ha-Yehudim be-Asya ha-Tikhona bi-Yemei Kedem u-vi-Yemei ha-Beinayim ha-Mukdamim,*" in: *Pe'amim,* 35 (1988), 4–23; J.M. Agarunov (Aharonov) and M.J. Agarunov (Aharonov), *Tati (Jewish)-Russian Dictionary* (1997).

[Dan Shapira (2nd ed.)]

JUDGES (Heb. שׁוֹפְטִים), **BOOK OF**, the second book in the second section of the Bible, called Prophets (*Nevi'im*). (See Table: Book of Judges – Contents.) The Book of Judges is named for the series of charismatic leaders of the period between the death of Joshua and the institution of monarchy in ancient Israel. None of them has a name that includes the divine element Yahweh. These judges were not judges in the legal sense, but heroes upon whom "rested the spirit of God" and who led single tribes or groups of tribes in military campaigns to free Israel from periodic foreign oppression.

(The Akkadian cognate *šāpiṭu* has the meaning "district governor," "high administrative official"; see CAD Š/I, 459). Their rule was temporary, and in no case did these leaders receive the allegiance of all the tribes. Only in the case of Deborah (4:4), the only female judge, is there any hint of a judicial function among the activities of a judge-savior. It should be noted that other women play significant roles, active and passive, in the narratives of Judges. One woman, *Jael, assassinates a general; an anonymous woman kills Abimelech, ruler of Shechem (Judg. 9:5–54). Samson's unnamed mother receives an annunciation before his father (Judg. 13:2–3). Clever women get what they want from a father (Akhsah; Judg. 1:12–15); a husband (Samson's Philistine wife; Judg. 14:15–18); and a lover (Delilah; Judg. 16: 4–21). A father's vow leads to the (likely) sacrifice of his daughter (Judg. 11:30–40; but see

Book of Judges – Contents

1:1–2:5	Completion of the conquest.
2:6–3:6	Introduction to the careers of the judges.
3:7–11	Othniel.
3:12–30	Ehud.
3:31	Shamgar.
4:1–5:31	Deborah and Barak (and Jael).
6:1–8:35	Gideon (Jerubbaal).
9:1–57	Abimelech.
10:1–5	Tola and Jair.
10:6–16	Introduction to later judges.
10:17–12:7	Jephthah.
12:8–15	Ibzan, Elon and Abdon.
13:1–16:31	Samson.
17:1–21:25	Migration of Dan to the north and war against the Benjamites.

Marcus). The rape of a woman leads to civil war (Judges 19–21) and the abduction of many women leads to reconciliation (Judg. 21:10–25).

The exact nature of the early history of Israel in Palestine has long been a matter of controversy among scholars. (See *History.)

Completion of the Conquest (1:1–2:5)

Though the biblical account of a unified conquest is unhistorical, it was taken as factual by the compilers of Judges. The biblical text places the events of the first chapter of Judges after the death of Joshua. Israel had had a long series of impressive victories, but several areas of the land were yet to be conquered (David Kimḥi on Judg. 1:1). Whereas the initial stage of the conquest was carried out by all Israel in a single camp under one leader, Joshua, the mopping-up operations were left to the individual tribes. The text relates the capture of several cities that had escaped the unified onslaught of the tribes. Ending the account is a listing of the cities not destroyed by the tribal operations, which were placed under tribute by Israel. Similar city lists appear in the latter half of the Book of Joshua. Medieval Jewish commentators already pointed out that their mention in Joshua is not primary. Their place in the internal historical continuum is in Judges 1, after the death of Joshua (Rashi on Josh. 15:14). It is difficult to reconstruct a chronology within the Book of Judges, because judgeships that may have been contemporaneous or overlapping are presented as though they occurred sequentially. Joshua 1–11 and Judges 1 provide two distinct accounts of the Israelite conquest of Palestine. The unified conquest idea is the product of authors, who, accustomed to the campaign methods of the Assyrian and other empires, retrojected them into their own history. The account in Judges 1, which concentrates on individual tribes, is a pro-Judahite polemic contrasting how the southern Judahites with Simeonite aid fought the Canaanites and mostly wiped them out, whereas the northern tribes at best subjected them and lived among them, thereby setting the stage for the cycles of apostasy and return (Amit, 1999). Another polemic is directed at the sanctuary at Dan, which though Yahwist, is fully equipped with a carved image and other disapproved paraphernalia (Judg. 18:14–31).The polemics against Benjamin and Saul are apparent in chapters 19–21 which close the book.

Introduction to the Careers of the Judges (2:6–3:6)

Although the present Book of Judges contains much ancient material, the final compilers indicate their temporal and geographic distance from the events by phrases such as "in those days" (18:1; 19:1; 20:28; 21:25); "to this very day" (18:12); "until the land went into exile" (19:30); and "Shiloh, which is in the land of Canaan" (21:12). There is less evidence of the work of the Deuteronomists in Judges than in other parts of the Deuteronomistic History (I Samuel–II Kings). Nonetheless, modern scholars are generally in agreement that the central core of Judges (2:6–16:31) was put into its final form by Deuteronomic editors. These editors provided a framework which joined the stories of individual judges around a common theme, the recurrent lapses into idolatry by the Israelites. The history of the period is understood as cyclical. Israel sins by chasing after false gods, and therefore God punishes the people by subjecting them to foreign oppressors. Realizing their misdeeds, the people repent of their idolatry and pray to the Lord for deliverance. The Lord sends a judge to rescue the people from the hands of the oppressors. A tranquil period follows. Some time after the death of the judge the people lapse into idolatry and the cycle begins again (3:7–9, 12, 14–15; 4:1–3; 6:1, 7). These principles, underlying the present structure of the Book of Judges, are stated and elaborated in the introduction to the careers of the judges (2:6–3:6).

Although it would be mistaken to consider the Book of Judges (and most of the rest of the Bible) as literature, the redaction is artful and there are some nice literary touches. Halpern and others detect scatological and sexual humor in the story of Ehud (Judges 3). The exchange over Samson's riddles is riddled with double entendre (Judges 14), and Delilah's henpecking of Samson (Judges 16) conforms to stereotypes modern and ancient (Prov. 19:13). The names *Cushan-Rishathaim, "Cushan-of Double Wickedness," and Gaal Ben Ebed "Loathsome, son of Slave" (Boling) are likely mutilations. There is an ancient ethnic joke about anyone from Ephraim who, when asked to say *shibboleth*, (Judg. 11:6) "said '*sibboleth*,' for he did not prepare (Heb. *yakin*) to pronounce it right," even though his life depended on it. The activities of the judges are arranged geographically from south to north.

Othniel (3:7–11)

*Othniel, the first judge mentioned in Judges, is a transitional figure between the elders who had outlived Joshua (Judg. 2:7) and the judges. As a youth, he had participated in the Conquest, capturing the city of Debir (Judg. 1:13). In chapter 3 he appears as a fighter against foreign oppression, the first of a series of charismatic leaders. Since the story of Othniel is little more than the typical framework formula of Judges, some scholars maintain that the narrative is a fiction invented to place a Judahite hero among the ranks of the judges. Others have rejected the narrative as unhistorical because of the unreal name *Cushan-Rishathaim and the improbability of a northern Aramean ruler oppressing the southern tribe of Judah. Malamat (in Bibliography) made an effort to defend the authenticity of the Othniel narrative, citing Aramean inroads into Egypt around 1200 B.C.E. The Israelites, not particularly important in themselves, were subdued during the Aramean march toward Egypt. It is the Palestine-centered biblical narrative that obscures this fact. Oded sees this story as a hidden polemic against the Saulides, which nevertheless contains a vague reminiscence of an ancient battle (extensive bibliography on Cushan in Oded).

Ehud (3:12–30)

A hero of Benjamin, *Ehud rescues his tribe and others from a long oppression by the Moabites, led by *Eglon. The assassination of Eglon (3:21) was followed by *shofar* blasts (3:27), probably a prearranged signal for Israelite troops to take the fords of the Jordan, thus preventing any Moabite retreat (Kaufmann, 1962, in bibl., 106). Some scholars have suggested that the story is compiled from two sources, citing, e.g., Ehud's "double" entrance in 3:19–20, while others have maintained that such repetitions are just a bit of sloppiness on the part of the storyteller, very common in folktales (Kraeling, in bibl.). There is much discussion about the location of Eglon's house, whether it was in Jericho, in Moab proper, or in some military camp west of the Jordan.

Shamgar (3:31)

The same *Shamgar is mentioned in the Song of Deborah as living in a time of great fear of the enemy, a fear so great that the Israelites kept off the roads lest the enemy find them (Judg. 5:6). Although it is stated that Shamgar succeeded Ehud, Ehud does not die until 4:1, which leads directly into the story of Deborah. Judges reports that "he also" saved Israel, but not how many years of peace there were under his leadership. The regular elements for the description of a judge, e.g., a theological motivation for the oppression of Israel and an indication of where he was located, are lacking. The Philistines are the enemy, despite other biblical evidence that the first real clashes with the Philistines took place later, in the period of Samuel and Eli. Finally, there is the question of Shamgar's very un-Israelite sounding name. Some scholars acknowledged the historical existence of Shamgar, because his name is mentioned in the Song of Deborah. One conjecture was to identify Shamgar as a Canaanite hero from Beth-Anath in Galilee (Albright, in bibl., 111). Another scholar explained that Shamgar was originally a Canaanite warrior so great that he was given the title "son of Anath," the goddess of war (van Selms, in bibl.). Shamgar is a foreign name, probably Hurrian, but this is not decisive, since many foreigners became part of Israel. His conquests resemble those of Samson, who did not use a regular weapon. Both Shamgar and Samson were active against the Philistines in the southwest in the period before Deborah, and the Septuagint traditions which pair them are probably correct (see chapter 13 below). In recent years arrowheads bearing the names *bin-anat* and Aramaic *bar anat,* dating from the 11th to 7th centuries, have been discovered. Following the lead of van Selms, we note that Anat was an archer. Presumably the patronymic ben-Anat was given to skilled archers but Shamgar is not so designated. But as Cross has noted, several arrowheads demonstrate that *bin-anat* was a proper name rather than a patronymic, so that Shamgar ben Anath is to be understood as Shamgar the son of Ben-Anath.

Deborah and Barak (4–5)

Israel sinned after the death of Ehud, and their punishment was enslavement to *Jabin, the king of Canaan. Because the Book of Joshua (chapter 11) attributes Jabin's defeat to Joshua, attempts at harmonization were made as early as the Middle Ages. According to Kimḥi, Jabin of Judges 4 was a descendant of the king of the same name defeated by Joshua. When Ḥazor was destroyed, the survivors of the royal family fled to Ḥarosheth-Goiim, which became the new seat of the kingship (David Kimḥi on Judg. 4:2). From this town Jabin and his general *Sisera oppressed the Israelites in the area. *Deborah sent a message to *Barak son of Abinoam of Kedesh-Naphtali, telling him to bring the men of Zebulun and Naphtali to seize Mount Tabor (Judg. 4:6; see Tur-Sinai). Barak refused to go without Deborah, and she agreed to accompany him, noting, however, that the death of Sisera would be at the hands of a woman. Sisera was leading his chariots toward the area when the Israelite forces swept down from Mount Tabor and inflicted a decisive defeat on his army at the Kishon River. Sisera sought refuge in the tent of Ḥeber the Kenite, who was allied with Jabin. *Jael, the wife of Ḥeber, took him in and killed him when he was asleep by hammering a tent peg through his temples. Barak was informed by Jael of Sisera's death.

From then on the Israelites grew stronger and stronger until they finally overwhelmed Jabin, the king of Canaan (Judg. 4:24). In the parallel poetic account of the battle with Sisera, Deborah sang her famous song (Judges 5). Most modern critics accept the Song of Deborah as one of the oldest biblical compositions, perhaps nearly contemporary with the events it describes. The prose narrative in chapter 4 is more problematic. At the root of all difficulties is the presence of Jabin, king of Canaan, who is identified with the Jabin mentioned in Joshua 11:1–9. Most explanations of the presence of Jabin revolve around the theory that two narratives were somehow fused into one. One account was of a war waged by Zebulun and Naphtali against Jabin, and the second was the war against Sisera, which is the subject of the song (Moore, in bibl., 109). The references to Jabin in Judges 4 are reminiscent of Joshua's victory in Joshua. In his attempt to make the conquest appear as a united effort, a later editor took a tale about a victory by Zebulun and Naphtali and changed it into a national battle during the days of Joshua (Burney, in bibl., 81). Any questions raised by the contradictions between Judges 4 and Judges 5 are answered by showing that these two accounts are not parallel at all, but a confusion of two distinct battles against two different enemies. Others advance the theory that Joshua 11 and the Song of Deborah do not speak of two distinct battles, but of two scenes in the same campaign. In later times, it was not known who was responsible for the great defeat, Jabin, the northern commander, or Sisera, commander of the plains forces (Batten, in bibl, 34). Given the current consensus that Joshua 11 is an unhistorical attempt to credit Joshua with victory over the northern kings, the theory is unlikely. Many scholars conceive of the prose narrative of Judges 4 as an independent formulation of the events surrounding the war with Sisera. Others see the prose account as derived from the poem. Although the two narratives are contradictory, they nonetheless complement one another, in a manner hardly unique in biblical redaction (see, e.g., the contradictory creation accounts in Genesis). One cannot avoid consulting the prose account for several important facts, including the identity of Shamgar, son of Anath, the reasons why Deborah and Barak were involved in the battle, and the function and the title of Sisera.

Gideon (6–8)

The story of the fourth major judge, *Gideon, is probably a composite of two stories (7:1–8:3; 8:4–21). Midianite raids annually terrorized the Israelite populace, and an anonymous prophet tells the people that these raids are a punishment for Israel's turning away from God. Gideon's call to judgeship was validated first by the appearance of an angel of God and second by a miracle involving wet and dry fleece. (In divination it was not uncommon to inquire more than once in order to assure the reliability of the oracle.) With a force of only 300 men he routed the camp of the Midianites with a daring night attack. Pursuit of the fleeing Midianites resulted in the death of the Midianite princes Oreb and Zeeb, and later in the blood revenge killings of Midianite kings Zebaḥ and Ẓalmunna. Kingship was offered to Gideon because of his exploits, but he declined, saying that kingship belongs only to God. Some scholars have cast doubt on the historicity of the first half of the Gideon story with its dominant theme of a national holy war. They also regarded with great skepticism the possibility of 300 men overcoming a large enemy camp. In contrast, the second incident involving the blood feud against Zebaḥ and Ẓalmunna describes the 12th-century atmosphere. It has an air of simple realism missing in the first story (McKenzie, in bibl., 130–7). Other scholars regard this approach as an oversimplification. They regard as implausible that a personal blood feud could impress itself on the national consciousness as the "day of Midian" (Isaiah 9:3). Several contemporary Israeli scholars have defended the 300-man raid as making sense from the military point of view. Rather than a miraculous fantasy, they see it as a logical recourse to a well coordinated night attack to offset the enemy's advantage in numbers and arms.

Abimelech (9)

The story of *Abimelech is a supplement to the Gideon narratives. Son of Gideon and his concubine in Shechem (8:31), Abimelech used money given him from the temple of Baal-Berith to hire men to murder his 70 half brothers from the house of Gideon. Jotham, the one surviving brother, related an old parable of the trees' electing the bramble bush to rule over them and applied it to Abimelech. He predicted a break between Abimelech and his Shechemite supporters, and a short-lived rule for Abimelech. True to his prediction, a rebellion under *Gaal soon broke out; Abimelech put it down, but in a campaign against nearby Thebeẓ, a woman threw a millstone at him from the city walls, mortally wounding him. Abimelech ordered his armor-bearer to kill him, lest it be said that a woman killed him. He reigned only three years, failing his kingly ambitions mainly because there was no outside threat for which the people might have needed a strong king (Oesterley and Robinson, in bibl., 153).

Tola and Jair (10:1–5)

These two minor judges are mentioned as having judged Israel after the death of Abimelech and before Jephthah. Some scholars have concluded from these notices, lacking the usual framework of the Book of Judges (see above), that the minor judges were judges in the legal sense, filling a central office in an amphictyonic league of the 12 tribes. The major judges were charismatic leaders and not judges, and the only reason these two separate groups were combined was the presence of Jepthah in both groups (Noth, in bibl., 101). Noth's amphictony hypothesis has generally been abandoned. Other scholars have suggested that the names of minor judges are clan names, which were inserted to bring the total number of judges to 12 (Burney, in bibl., 289–90). Conservative scholars have rejected these suggestions. In their view, the minor judges are also "saviors" and not mere adjudicators. Use of the term *wa-yaqom* (*va-yakom*, "and he arose") implies that they came to power sporadically, as did the major judges (Kaufmann, 1962, in bibl., 46–48).

Introduction to Later Judges (10:6–16)

The characteristic framework of the Book of Judges is expanded into a recapitulation of recent history, recounting the Israelites' worship of foreign gods. God rebukes the people (evidently through a prophet not mentioned), telling them that He will punish them, and challenging them to rely on their false gods to protect them on the day of His wrath. The people confess their sins and remove the false gods from their midst. This forms an introduction to the story of Jephthah.

Jephthah (10:17–12:7)

*Jephthah's reputation as a warrior in the land of Tob reached the elders of Gilead, and they asked him to be their "chief" (*qaẓin*) in a war against Ammon, who had attacked Israel. They tried to convince him to forget the shame the elders caused him when they had condoned his expulsion because of his illegitimate birth. Jephthah accepted their offer of leadership in war on the condition that he would lead the people in peacetime as well. Before going to war Jephthah began a diplomatic correspondence with Ammon, arguing that Ammon had no cause for war with Israel, since Israel had conquered the Transjordan territory from the Amorites, not from Ammon (Levi b. Gershom on Judg. 11:12). Furthermore, God had given the land to Israel as an inheritance, and for more than 300 years no counterclaims had been made (Judg. 11:26). The arguments did not convince the Ammonites. Jephthah made a solemn vow that if God would grant him victory, whatever emerged from his house to greet him on his return would be sacrificed to God as a burnt offering (11:31). Jephthah was successful in his battle, and on his return home his daughter was the first to greet him. In fulfillment of his vow Jephthah offered his daughter as a sacrifice, after she had been given time to bewail her virginity (11:29–40). Medieval Jewish commentators stress the unbinding nature of Jephthah's vow according to Jewish law, and many suggest that his daughter was not really sacrificed, but instead was condemned to eternal virginity (Marcus). One legend acknowledges the sacrifice of Jephthah's daughter, but relates that as a punishment Jephthah was buried "in the cities of Gilead" (12:7), that is, his body slowly rotted and each limb was buried in a different city (David Kimḥi on 12:7). The people of Ephraim complained to Jephthah that they were not called to join the battle. Unlike Gideon, Jephthah gathered an army to fight the Ephraimites. They captured the fords of the Jordan, and all people who attempted to cross the river and who were recognized as Ephraimites were immediately killed. The most extreme critics consider the whole story an etiological narrative designed to explain the yearly observance of the young women of Gilead (Moore, in bibl., 284). More conservative scholars see Jephthah as a historical figure, but believe some elements of the story are not original. In the diplomatic correspondence (11:12–28), Khemosh, god of Moab, rather than Milcom, god of Ammon, is mentioned, and therefore scholars have maintained that this section belongs to another story about Israelite-Moabite relations (Moore, in bibl., 283). Kaufmann suggested that out of diplomatic courtesy Jephthah did not mention Milcom. He used instead the name of the god Khemosh. The Ammonite king understood the hint: the failure of Khemosh to stop Siḥon (Num. 21:26–30) was also the beginning of the failure of Ammon (Kaufmann, 1962, in bibl., 222). More likely, we have an original story of a territorial dispute with the Moabites. According to Jephthah, Israel had held the territory for 300 years, reminiscent of the statement on the stela of King Mesha of Moab (mid-ninth century) that "the men of Gad had dwelt in Ataroth forever" (COS II, 137). The Moabite stratum of the story dates from the ninth century (Taeubler apud Amit 1999, 200). At a later date, perhaps as early as the eighth century (see Amos 1:13) or later (see Zephaniah 2:8) the reality of Ammonite and Judahite hostility was retrojected into pre-monarchic times.

Ibzan, Elon, and Abdon (12:8–15)

See above the discussion of Tola and Jair.

Samson (13–16)

*Samson did not go to war against the enemy as a judge-savior, nor did he lead tribes against a foreign oppressor or invader. He fought alone with his bare hands or with some improvised weapons. His weakness for Philistine women led him into several clashes with the Philistines and finally to his death in the temple of Dagon (16:23–31). Modern scholars have argued that the Samson stories were secular stories of a popular local hero but were given a religious cast by such details as a miraculous birth and the appearance of angels (Renan, in bibl., 282). Others have theorized that the Samson cycle was an Israelite reworking of a sun god myth. The name Samson (from the Hebrew *shemesh*, "sun") and the fact that the events took place near Beth-Shemesh suggest that the people in the area, who worshipped the sun, may have pictured the sun and its rays as the head of a warrior whose strength lay in his locks. A group of stories then grew up around the conception (Renan, *ibid.*, 283–4). Others have rejected this explanation. The name Samson, even if Canaanite in origin, is no proof of his mythical origin. Unlike mythical figures, Samson was not of divine ancestry (but see Reinhartz). Samson was, rather, a "war-Nazirite," a common phenomenon in those days. People believed that the uncut hair of the *Nazirite protected him, and this served as the basis for the legend of a divinely elected hero with superhuman strength, whose strength lay in his hair (Kaufmann, 1962, in bibl., 242, 244). That his hair is the source of his sexual virility is nicely demonstrated (Judg. 16:19) when Delilah tries to initiate sex with him (the only case in the Bible of *innah* directed by a woman toward a man). Chronologically, the Samson stories would seem to fit best before Deborah. In the Samson narrative *Dan is still in the south, but in the Song of Deborah they had already moved north. The stories about Samson were removed from their proper chronological place, because they break up the flowing pattern of Judges 2–12, but the mention of Shamgar was left before Deborah as a reminder that the beginnings of the Philistine problem were at that time (Kaufmann, 1962, in bibl., 113). The presence of the word *ḥiddah*, "riddle"(Judg. 14:12 passim), a loan from Aramaic *aḥidah* after the shift of Aramaic *dhal* to *dalet* in the Imperial Aramaic that arose in the sixth century precludes an early period for the date of composition of that chapter.

Migration of Dan to the North (17–18) and the War Against the Benjaminites (19–21)

These concluding sections have no immediate introductory statements to connect them with the rest of the book and are characterized by the recurring phrase "in those days there was no king in Israel, each man doing what was right in his own eyes" (17:6, 18:1, 19:1, 21:25). It would seem that these sections were intended to illustrate the dangers of irregular tribal rule. The potential anarchy could be prevented only by the crowning of a king. The Danites, unable to resist the pressures of the Philistines in their southern home, traveled to the north and settled there. They stole the cult objects from the personal sanctuary of a certain northerner named Micah and set them up in their new sanctuary at Laish (17–18). The war against the Benjaminites was the direct result of an abominable offense committed by the people of Gibeah. A levite traveler came to Gibeah to spend the night. The people of Gibeah, surrounding the house in which he lodged, demanded that the levite be sent out to them for homosexual acts (19:22). (One point of the story is to show that the Benjaminites of Gibeah shared the values of the ancient Sodomites. The many elements common to Judges 19 and Genesis 19 were already pointed out by Naḥmanides to Gen. 19:8.) His concubine was sent out instead and she was abused until she died. The levite cut her body into 12 pieces, sending one to each of the tribes, demanding revenge for the foul deed. An intertribal war resulted, in which Benjamin was decisively defeated. Fearing that a tribe of Israel might be wiped out, yet not wanting to break their vow against marrying Benjaminites, the Israelites resorted to several subterfuges to repopulate the tribe (21). First they attacked the city of Jabesh-Gilead, which had not participated in the campaign against Benjamin. Only young virgins were spared and given to the men of Benjamin. To acquire women for the rest of the survivors, the Benjaminites were advised to lie in wait in the vineyards of Shiloh and take for their wives the young girls who usually came there to dance in celebration for the harvest. Technically, this was no breach of the vow, since the women were taken by force. Both medieval and modern commentators have advanced several theories concerning the date of these events. The Danite migration would seem to follow directly on the Samson narratives and be dated some time before Deborah. Perhaps 18:30, in which the first priest of Dan is of the generation of Moses' grandchildren, further supports this thesis (Kaufmann, 1962, in bibl. 267). Various dates have been suggested for the concubine in the Gibeah story, including the period of Othniel, of Joshua, and before Eli, the priest, and Samuel. Some scholars cited the concerted action of the tribes against Gibeah and Benjamin as proof for the theory that, before the foundation of the monarchy, Israel was governed by an amphictyony, a tribal federation grouped around a sanctuary similar to Greek federations, but that view has been generally abandoned.

For all its theological tendentiousness, the picture presented by Judges of conditions in pre-monarchic Israel finds a good deal of archaeological support (Bloch-Smith and Nakhai, 118). In addition, despite the imposition of their own concerns by later writers, Judges has preserved literary fragments of great antiquity and affords insights into the social and religious conditions of the period between the conquest and the monarchy. The theological picture presented by the Book of Judges is that the overriding, uniting goal of conquest was no longer present. The strong loyalty to Yahweh that had characterized the generation of Joshua declined. Israelites turned to the gods of their neighbors. The present Book of Judges stresses the point that these phenomena were the prime cause of national disaster, and that only in true repentance would the nation be able to live a secure life on its land. The Christian author of Hebrews 11:32–33 cites Gideon, Barak, Samson, and Jephthah as examples of ancient worthies whose faith brought them triumph.

BIBLIOGRAPHY: COMMENTARIES: G.F. Moore, *Judges* (ICC, 1895); C.F. Burney, *Judges* (1930[2]); Y. Kaufmann, *Sefer Shofetim* (1962). GENERAL STUDIES: E. Renan, *History of the People of Israel* (1894); W.O.E. Oesterley and T.H. Robinson, *History of Israel* (1932), 112–70; Y. Kaufmann, *Biblical Account of the Conquest of Palestine* (1953); Kaufmann Y., Toledot, 2 (1960), 90–158; Noth, Hist. Isr. 164ff.; Bright, Hist, 151–60; J.L. Mc-Kenzie, *The World of the Judges* (1966); A. Malamat, in: H.H. Ben-Sasson (ed.), *Toledot Am Yisrael bi-Ymei Kedem* (1969), 70–83. SPECIALIZED STUDIES: L.W. Batten, in: JBL, 24 (1905), 31–40; E.G. Kraeling, *ibid.*, 54 (1935), 205–10; Albright, Arch Rel, 79–124; A. Malamat, in: PEQ, 85 (1953), 61–65; idem, in: JNES, 13 (1954), 231–42; J. Bright, *Early Israel in Recent History Writing* (1956); E. Danelius, in: JNES, 22 (1963); A. van Selms, in: VT, 14 (1964), 294–309; J. Liver (ed.), *Historya Ẓeva'it shel Ereẓ Yisrael...* (1965), 79–124; A. Alt, *Essays on Old Testament History and Religion* (1966), 173–237. **ADD. BIBLIOGRAPHY:** N.H. Tur-Sinai, *The Language and the Book*, 1 (1954), 409–23; S. Niditch, in: CBQ, 44 (1982), 365–78; D. Marcus, *Jephthah and His Vow* (1986); A. Reinhartz, in: JSOT, 55 (1992), 25–37; A. Brenner (ed.), *A Feminist Companion to Judges* (1993); R. Boling, in: ABD, 3, 1107–17, incl. bibl.; B. Halpern, *The Creation of History in Ancient Israel* (1998), 79–90; Y. Amit, in: VT, 60 (1990), 4–19; idem, *The Book of Judges: The Art of Editing* (1998); idem, *Judges* (1999); B. Oded, in: M. Fox (ed.), *Texts, Temples, and Traditions ... Tribute Haran* (1999), 89*–948; L. Bloch-Smith and B. Nakhai, in: NEA, 62 (1999), 62–92, 101–27; T. Beal and M. Gunn, DBI, 1:637–47 extensive bibl.; M. Brettler, *Judges* (2001); F. Cross, *Leaves from an Epigrapher's Notebook* (1993), 216–20; N. Na'aman, in: VT, 55 (2005), 47–60.

[Gershon Bacon / S. David Sperling (2nd ed.)]

JUDIN, SAMUEL (1730–1800), Russian medalist. Judin possessed extraordinary natural talent and was accepted at a very early age by the School of Engraving of the St. Petersburg (Leningrad) Mint. From 1757 to 1762 he was the principal mint engraver there. In his first year he struck the silver ruble for Peter III; the limited edition showed his Cyrilian initials ("S. Yu.") on the sleeve and is a coveted numismatic item. Judin's best-known medal is the one commemorating the Russian victory over Charles XII of Sweden at Poltava in 1709. He also engraved a group of medals, following previous models, which dealt with the life of Peter the Great. Judin collaborated with Timothy Ivanov on large portrait medals, an excellent example being their joint medal of Elizabeth I of Russia.

BIBLIOGRAPHY: Friedenberg, in: *The Numismatist*, July (1969), 895–6.

[Daniel M. Friedenberg]

JUDITH (c. 200 C.E.), the wife of R. Ḥiyya. She was the mother of twin daughters, Pazi and Tavi, and twin sons, Judah and Hezekiah. Having suffered unusually in childbirth, she disguised herself and asked her husband whether a woman was commanded by the Torah to propagate the race. On being told that she was not, she drank a sterilizing potion – a form of birth control permitted to women (Shab. 111a). Ḥiyya, however, was greatly displeased (Yev. 65b). According to another account, she claimed unsuccessfully that her father had betrothed her to another man when she was still a child, so that she was forbidden to cohabit with Ḥiyya (Kid. 12b). Judith constantly tormented her husband – so much so that he once told his nephew Rav, "May God deliver you from that which is worse than death," i.e., a bad wife (cf. Eccles. 7:26). He nevertheless used to buy her many gifts, explaining to his surprised nephew, "It is sufficient for us that they bring up our children and save us from sin" (Yev. 63a).

BIBLIOGRAPHY: Hyman, Toledot, 430, 616.

[Moses Aberbach]

JUDITH, BOOK OF, a historical narrative dating from Second Temple times, included by the Septuagint and the canon of the Catholic and Greek churches in the Bible and by the Protestants in the Apocrypha.

The story is as follows: Nebuchadnezzar, king of Assyria who reigned in Nineveh, after having defeated Arphaxad, king of Media, in the valley of Ragau, sent Holofernes, his commander in chief, on a campaign of conquest, in the course of which he overran all the countries from the border of Persia to Sidon and Tyre. When he reached the valley of Esdraelon before the narrow pass leading to Judea and Jerusalem, he found that, by order of the high priest in Jerusalem, all the passes had been occupied by the Jews living in the fortified mountain-pass towns of Bethulia and Betomesthaim. At this Holofernes summoned a council, as a result of which he ordered that Achior, the Ammonite chief, who had spoken confidently of the victorious power of Israel so long as they remained faithful to God, be sent to the Jews of Bethulia. Holofernes then laid siege to the town. After a month, when there was no water left in Bethulia and its leaders had already decided to open the gates to the enemy, there suddenly appeared a widow named Judith the daughter of Merari. She was of the tribe of Simeon and a resident of Bethulia, young and beautiful, righteous and wealthy. With the permission of the leaders of the town she went down to the camp of Holofernes who, attracted by her wisdom and beauty, invited her to a feast. When Holofernes fell asleep, overcome by wine, Judith took his dagger, cut off his head, and handing it to her maid returned with her to Bethulia. Deprived of their commander in chief by Judith's courageous deed, the panic-stricken Assyrian soldiers fled.

There are many obscure elements in the story. Its date has been assigned to the period of the return to Zion after the Babylonian Exile. At that time the kingdoms of Assyria and Media no longer existed, and hence various other theories have been advanced by scholars. Some (following Luther) have maintained that it is merely an allegory. More probably it is a historical novel written in the days of the Hasmoneans to inspire courage, its historical kernel being found in the events which took place under Artaxerxes III, when in 352 B.C.E. a Cappadocian prince named Holofernes fought against the Egyptians (Diodorus Siculus xvii, 6, 1). However, even this theory presents some difficulty, since the story contains no Greek features (and its geographic and ethnic background even conflicts with such an interpretation). On the other hand it contains definitely Persian names (Holofernes, Bagoas) and elements (such as ἀκινακῄ for "dagger"; presenting "earth and water" to the king as a sign of surrender; the appellation "the God of heaven" for God of Israel; and the royal designation, "the king of all the earth"). It has therefore been suggested that the entire book is a "Persian" production. While, according to this view, the background of the story is Darius I's war against Phraortes, the "king" of Media at the time of the return to Zion (which is mentioned in the book), it was written only at the end of the Persian period, in the wake of the great revolt of 362 B.C.E. (in the reign of Artaxerxes II) which also spread to Ereẓ Israel. Nor, according to this theory, is the most important geographical detail in the book, namely the reference to a Jewish (Simeonite) settlement on the border of the valley of Dothan, a fabrication. For a combination of various sources (Meg. Ta'an. for 25 Marḥeshvan (chap. 8); Jos., Ant. 13:275f., 379f: Wars 1:93f.; and also apparently I Macc. 5:23) shows that at the time of the return in the region of Samaria, in the neighborhood of what was known as "the cities of Nebhrakta," there was a Jewish-Simeonite settlement (which may in effect have existed as early as in the days of the First Temple and being of Semite origin: cf. II Chron. 34:6, 15:9; and also I Chron. 4:31). The supposition is that in the great revolt at the end of the reign of Artaxerxes II (404–359 B.C.E.) this region fulfilled some function.

From a literary standpoint, by virtue of its epic description, the book is one of the most finished productions of Second Temple times. A prose work, it embodies two poems, Judith's prayer before setting out for the camp of Holofernes (9) and the thanksgiving of Israel after the victory (16). Very close to the later biblical poetry, in its structure and poetic imagery, this song of thanksgiving antedates those found at Qumran. The book is also significant by reason of both the *halakhah* it contains and the religious faith it reflects. Yet it reveals no trace of sectarianism, as do the works written in the post-Hasmonean period.

As is clearly evident from its many Hebraisms, the book was originally written in Hebrew (cf., for example, the expressions: "the space of 30 days"; "all flesh," as a designation for human beings; "let not thine eye spare"; "the face of the earth"; and "smote with the edge of the sword," etc.). In the precise Greek translation there is also discernible the special Ereẓ Israel spelling (the substitution of the ע״ו verb by פ״י).

The book is extant in four principal Greek versions (A, B, Codex 58, and Codex 108), all of which derive from the Hebrew. In ancient times an abridged Aramaic translation was made, on the basis of which Jerome translated the work into Latin (this being the Vulgate version). At an early stage the Hebrew book was lost, but in one form or another (chiefly through translations and adaptations from the Latin), from the 10th–11th centuries, several abridged Hebrew versions of the work found their way back into midrashic literature.

[Yehoshua M. Grintz]

In the Arts

Judith has attracted more writers, artists, and composers than any other figure in the Apocrypha. Two of the earliest literary works were *Judith*, a fragmentary Old English epic, and a Middle High German poem of the same title dating from the 13th century. One of the first recorded plays about Judith and Holofernes was that staged at Pesaro, Italy, in 1489 by the local Jewish community. By the beginning of the 16th century, the subject was arousing fresh attention – particularly among Protestant writers, who reinterpreted it in terms of the triumph of virtue over wickedness. Martin *Luther favored the use of Old Testament material as a basis for drama, especially recommending Judith as a tragic theme. Two pioneering works of the Renaissance era were *Judita* (1521), a religious epic by the Croatian humanist Marko Marulić and the German playwright Sixtus Birck's *Judith* (1532). Another *Judith* (1551) was written by the German *Meistersinger* Hans Sachs. In Italy, where the subject was treated in an orthodox Catholic fashion, Luca (Ciarafello) de Calerio produced the drama *Giuditta e Oloferne* (Naples, 1540), and G. Francesco Alberti the tragedy *Oloferne* (1594). The subject retained its popularity throughout the 17th–19th centuries and was the subject of plays in various countries. Thus in Spain, the Marrano dramatist and preacher Felipe *Godínez wrote *Judit y Holofernes* (1620); and *Iyudif* (1674), a seven-act Russian prose drama, was one of the first biblical works to be staged in Moscow. An anonymous work of 1761, *Sefer Yehudit ve-Sefer Yehudah ha-Makkabi*, appeared at Amsterdam. Two curiosities of the 19th century, both written in *Judeo-Italian and titled *La Betulia liberata*, were a poem by Luigi Duclou (1832) and an epic by Natale Falcini (1862). An outstanding tragedy on the theme was the German dramatist Friedrich Hebbel's *Judith* (1841). In the United States, the Quaker John Greenleaf Whittier included "Judith at the Tent of Holofernes" (1829) among his biblical poems, while Thomas Bailey Aldrich dramatized his *Judith and Holofernes* (1896), and Adah Isaacs *Menken wrote her sensual story, "Judith" (in *Infelicia*, 1888). An impressive number of works about Judith have been written by authors of the 20th century. The German expressionist Georg Kaiser adopted an original approach in his comedy *Die juedische Witwe* (1911). The urge to "modernize" the subject was particularly evident in England, where Thomas Sturge Moore's *Judith* (1911; staged 1916) suggested that the heroine became the tyrant's mistress before she killed him. The *Judith* of Lascelles Abercrombie (in *Emblems of Love*, 1912) contained strong undertones of suffragette thinking, while Arnold Bennett's heroine (1919) created a furore by appearing on the stage in a revealing costume. Among the plays that appeared between the world wars were Henry *Bernstein's drama *Judith* (1922), Bartholomaeus Ponholzer's *Judith, die Heldin von Israel* (1927), and Ricardo Moritz's *Giuditta* (1938). In his psychological tragedy, *Judith* (1931), the French writer Jean Giraudoux went even further than the British by treating the whole story as a myth, transforming the heroine into a courtesan and the villain into the more likeable character.

Judith has often been portrayed by artists. For medieval Christianity, the Jewish heroine's slaying of Holofernes represented the triumph of the Virgin over the devil. It also signified the victory of *sanctimonia* (chastity and humility) over lust and pride. Judith is usually shown either with the sword in her right hand and Holofernes' head in her left, or dropping the head into a receptacle held by her servant. A dog, the symbol of fidelity, often accompanied her. In Renaissance and later painting she was sometimes shown nude. The story was treated in narrative cycles and in isolated incidents. An early cycle exists in the Bible of San Paolo fuori le Mura (Rome, ninth century). The arches over the north portal of Chartres Cathedral (13th century) depict several episodes, as does a window of the same period in La Sainte-Chapelle, Paris. The subject was found suitable for tapestry, two examples being a Tournai cycle (15th century in Brussels' Musées royaux d'art et d'histoire), and a French version (c. 1515; now in the Cathedral of Sens). In the Loggia dei Lanzi, Florence, there is an ornate sculpture of the subject by Donatello. Among the Renaissance painters, Andrea Mantegna treated the subject several times and Botticelli painted some episodes from the story of Judith that are not commonly illustrated: Judith and her maid arriving home with the head, and the discovery of the dead body of Holofernes (both in the Uffizi Gallery, Florence). There is a painting of Judith with the head by the same artist in the Rijks Museum, Amsterdam. Michelangelo included figures of Judith and her maid in his Sistine Chapel ceiling.

Several of the great Venetian artists painted Judith. There is an upright figure of the heroine delicately trampling on Holofernes' head by Giorgione (Hermitage, Leningrad). Paolo Veronese painted a very attractive Judith (Kunsthistorisches Museum, Vienna), and there is a study of her in the act of killing Holofernes by Tintoretto (Prado, Madrid). Of the later Italian artists, Caravaggio painted the same scene (Naples Museum) with a certain violence. The German Renaissance painter Lucas Cranach was particularly attracted by the subject of Judith and Holofernes and painted it several times. One version is in the Kunsthistorisches Museum, Vienna. Rubens used a dramatic chiaroscuro to portray Judith in the act of killing Holofernes (Brunswick Museum).

In Jewish musical tradition, the story of Judith is represented by the singing of the *piyyut, Mi Khamokha Addir Ayom ve-Nora* (Davidson, Oẓar, 1143) on the Sabbath of Ḥanukkah, a custom retained in several communities. The "Canticle of Judith," *Hymnum cantemus Domino* (Judith 16: 15–21), is prescribed in the Catholic Church for the *Laudes* (dawn service) on Wednesdays, and intoned to a simple psalmodic melody. Polyphonic settings of the text appear only rarely: one instance is *O bone Deus, ne projicias* by Jacobus Gallus (Handl), the text being a combination of verses from chapters 8, 14, 16, and 19 of the Apocryphal book. With the rise of the oratorio, the subject – possessing a naturally dramatic plot – came into its own and it continues to maintain its popularity. Two factors contributed to the remarkably frequent appearance of *Judith* oratorios in the second and third quarters of the 18th century: first of all, the appeal of Metastasio's libretto, *Betulia liberata* (commissioned by the emperor Charles VI of Austria, and first performed in the Imperial Chapel, Vienna, with music by Georg Reutter, in 1734); and secondly, the reign of Maria Theresa (1740–80), who was symbolized as a latter-day Judith standing up to the new Holofernes – Frederick the Great of Prussia. The regular production of operas about Judith only began toward the middle of the 19th century, by which time biblical subjects were permitted on the stage and the early romantic "horror opera" had prepared audiences for the sight of Holofernes' severed head.

The following is a selective list of compositions about Judith; all are oratorios, if not designated otherwise: Caspar Foerster, *Dialogus de Holoferne* (1667); Antonio Draghi, *La Giuditta* (1668–69); Giovanni Paolo Colonna, *Bettuglia liberata* (1690); Alessandro Scarlatti, *La Giuditta vittoriosa* (1695); Marc-Antoine Charpentier, *Judith sive Bethulia liberata* (c. 1700); Antonio Vivaldi, *Judith triumphans devicta Holofernis barbarie* (1716); Giuseppe Porsile, *Il trionfo di Giuditta* (1923); Wilhelm de Fesch, *Judith* (English libretto: London,

1733); Georg Reutter, *Betulia liberata* (first setting of Metastasio's libretto; Vienna, 1734); Joseph Anton Sehling, *Firma in Deum fiducia... in Judith Israelis Amazone* (melodrama; Prague, 1741); Niccolò Jomelli, *Betulia liberata* (Metastasio's text; Venice, 1743; the composer's first oratorio); Antonio Bernasconi, *Betulia liberata* (Metastasio's text; 1754); Giovanni Battista Martini, *In cymbalis and Hymnum novum*, two puzzle canons in his *Storia della musica*, 1 (1757), 165, 334; Ignaz Holzbauer, *Betulia liberata* (Metastasio's text; 1760); John Christopher Smith, *Judith* (scenic oratorio; 1760, not performed); Thomas Augustine Arne, *Judith* (1761, restaged 1773; first use of female choristers on the English stage); Domenico Cimarosa, *Giuditta* ("opera sacra," 1770); Florian Gassmann, *Betulia liberata* (Metastisio's text; Vienna, 1771; inaugurating the concerts of the *Tonkuenstlersozietaet*); Wolfgang Amadeus Mozart, *Betulia liberata* (Metastasio's text; 1771; see also below); Leopold Anton Koželuch, *La Giuditta* (c. 1780) and *Judith und Holofernes* (after Metastasio; as opera, c. 1779; as oratorio, 1799); Ludwig van Beethoven, three canons on "Te solo adoro" from Metastasio's libretto (1823); Samuele Levi, *Giuditta* (opera; Venice, 1844); Julius Rietz, *Judith* (ouverture and entr'actes to Hebbel's drama, 1851); Emil Naumann, *Judith* (opera, 1858); Alexander Serov, *Judith* (opera; text by the composer and three collaborators; St. Petersburg, 1863; his greatest success); Giacomo *Meyerbeer, *Judith* (operatic fragment, 1864; unpublished); Albert Franz Doppler, *Judith* (opera, 1870); Paul Hillemacher, *Judith* ("scène lyrique," 1876); Charles Lefebvre, *Judith* (opera, 1879); Cart Goetze, *Judith* (opera, 1887); Sir Hubert Parry, *Judith* (1888); George W. Chadwick, *Judith* ("lyric drama," 1901); August Reuss, *Judith* (for orchestra; "after Hebbel," 1903); Carlo Ravasenga, *Giuditta e Oloferne* (for orchestra, 1920); Max Ettinger, *Judith* (opera, 1920); Emil von Resniček, *Holofernes* (opera; libretto by the composer, based on Hebbel, 1923; the overture, in the form of an arrangement of *Kol Nidre*, was also performed and published separately); Arthur Honegger, *Judith* (opera; text by René Morax, 1926); Eugene Goossens, *Judith* (opera; text by Arnold Bennett, 1928); Gabriel Grad, *Judith and Holofernes* (opera in Hebrew; only parts published, 1931 and 1939); Carl Nathanael Berg, *Judith* (opera, 1931–35); Mordechai *Seter, *Judith* (ballet, 1963; reworked in 1967 as a "symphonic chaconne" for orchestra). Metastasio's *Betulia liberata* was translated into Hebrew by David Franco *Mendes in 1790–91 as *Teshu'at Yisrael*. It is not certain whether the translation was made for a performance with Mozart's music, since the manuscript bears only the direction *Lahakat Meshorerim* ("group of singers," i.e., chorus), and does not indicate the solos. F. Clément, in his *Dictionnaire des Opéras* (1897², 624), reports the United Hebrew Opera Company's performance in Boston of an opera titled *Judith und Holofernes* (1861), which was "sung in German, with the program printed in Hebrew." Both the performance and the program were probably in Yiddish.

[Bathja Bayer]

BIBLIOGRAPHY: Y.M. Grintz, *Sefer Yehudit* (1957), incl. bibl., 209–19; idem, in: *Molad*, 17 (1959), 564–6; A. Schalit, *Namenwoerterbuch zu Flavius Josephus* (1968), 130–3; A.M. Habermann, in: *Maḥanayim*, 52 (1961), 42–47; A.M. Dubarle, *Judith, Formes et Sens des Diverses Traditions* (1966); Y.L. Bialer, in: *Min ha-Genazim*, 2 (1969), 36–51. **IN THE ARTS:** R.E. Glaymen, *Recent Judith Drama and Its Analogues* (1930), incl. "a list... of plays based on the whole Bible": 112–34; E. Purdie, *Story of Judith in German and English Literature* (1927), incl. bibl., 1–22; M. Sommerfeld (ed.), *Judith-Dramen des 16./17. Jahrhunderts* (1933). **ADD. BIBLIOGRAPHY:** C.A. Moore, "Judith: The Case of the Pious Killer," in: *Bible Review*, 6 (1990), 26–36.

JUEDISCHE FREISCHULE (Ger.; "Jewish Free School"), private school for poor children, founded in Berlin in 1778 by Isaac Daniel *Itzig and David *Friedlaender, who were influenced by Moses Mendelssohn's ideas on education. Adjoining the school was a printing shop whose returns were to contribute to the maintenance of the school. The subjects taught comprised writing, arithmetic, accountancy, drawing, reading in German and French, and geography. Biblical Hebrew was taught only to a very limited extent, the greatest amount of time being given to commercial courses. In 1779 Friedlaender published a reader for his pupils – one of the first of its kind to be used in German Jewish schools – containing excerpts from German and Hebrew literature, the latter in German translations by Mendelssohn. Some Christians were included on the teaching staff. During the first few years there were about 80 pupils. After ten years, however, about 500 pupils had graduated from the school. Following the death of I.D. Itzig in 1806, Lazarus *Bendavid was appointed principal. He was prompted by ideological and practical considerations to accept Christian pupils, whose number increased, in the course of time, to one-third of the total. The Freischule thus became the first interdenominational school in Germany. Of the 80 pupils attending the school, in 1817, 40 were educated free of charge, and 16 were Christians. At the time of the reaction following the Napoleonic wars, the Prussian government forbade Christian children to attend Jewish schools; consequently, all non-Jewish pupils had to leave the school in 1819. In the same year the number of Jewish pupils decreased to 50 and by 1825 the school had to be closed.

In the 48 years of its existence the Freischule educated about 1,000 students, a majority of whom later took an active part in the Reform movement. The school, which had always advocated modern teaching methods, served as a model for similar schools such as the Samsonschule in *Wolfenbuettel and the Philanthropin in Frankfurt.

BIBLIOGRAPHY: M. Eliav, *Ha-Ḥinnukh ha-Yehudi be-Germanyah* (1961), 71–79. **ADD. BIBLIOGRAPHY:** I. Lohmann, *Ḥevrat Ḥinukh Ne'arim* (2001).

[Reuven Michael]

JUEDISCHE PRESSE, German weekly reflecting an Orthodox viewpoint, published in Berlin. The *Juedische Presse* was founded in 1870 on the initiative of Azriel *Hildesheimer, and edited from 1884 to 1910 by his son, Hirsch *Hildesheimer. From the first, it reflected Hildesheimer's view on the evils of **halukkah* and on the need in Jerusalem for educational reform and technical training. The paper also supported the *Ḥibbat Zion movement and colonization in Ereẓ Israel, but was critical of *Herzl and of political Zionism. In communal politics, it stood against the dogmatic secessionism (*Austritt*) of some Orthodox from the community, with its center in Frankfurt, and defended the so-called "communal Orthodoxy" which worked within the framework of the state-established congregations. In 1919 the *Juedische Presse* became the official organ of the German *Mizrachi (with a Hebrew and Yiddish supplement) but ceased publication in 1923.

BIBLIOGRAPHY: M. Eliav, in: *Sinai*, 65 (1969), 221–33.

JUEDISCHER FRAUENBUND, organization of Jewish women founded in 1904 by Sidonie Werner and Bertha *Pappenheim originally in order to combat white slavery, especially of Jewish girls from Eastern Europe. Under Pappenheim's energetic leadership the organization expanded rapidly and after 30 years of existence boasted 30,000 members in about 450 branches. Politically the organization was neutral: the women's organizations of the *Central-Verein and *B'nai B'rith were affiliated with it, whereas Orthodox and Zionist women's organizations were not. Its charitable agencies were concerned with adoption, social work, and health, and especially the Isenburg home for wayward women. In the Jewish communities the Frauenbund strove for full female suffrage in communal elections, and it received nominal representation in national and international forums. Bertha Pappenheim was succeeded by Hannah Karminski (1887–1943), who was deported and killed by the Nazis after the forced shutdown of the Juedischer Frauenbund in 1938 (refounded by Jeanette Wolff and Ruth Galinski in 1953).

BIBLIOGRAPHY: D. Edinger (ed.), *Bertha Pappenheim, Leben und Schriften* (1963); Wiener Library, *German Jewry* (1958). **ADD. BIBLIOGRAPHY:** M.A. Kaplan, "German-Jewish Feminism in the Twentieth Century," in: JSS, 38 (1976), 39–53; M.A. Kaplan, *The Jewish feminist movement in Germany – The campaigns of the Jüdischer Frauenbund 1904–1938* (1979); S.L. Tananbaum, "Jewish Feminist Organisations in Britain and Germany at the Turn of the Century," in: M. Brenner, R. Liedtke, and D. Rechter (eds.), *Two Nations* (1999), 371–92; F. Gleis and S. Werner, "Norddeutschlands Fuehrungsgestalt in der juedischen Frauenbewegung," in: G. Paul and M. Gillis-Carlebach (eds.), *Menora und Hakenkreuz* (1998), 135–140; M. Grandner, *Geschlecht, Religion und Engagement – Die jüdischen Frauenbewegungen im deutschsprachigen Raum* (2005).

JUEDISCHER KULTURBUND (Ger. "Jewish Cultural Association"), German Jewish organization founded in Berlin in May 1933 when the National Socialist regime dismissed Jewish high school teachers, artists, and authors from their positions and excluded all Jews from German cultural life. The Juedischer Kulturbund was initiated by Kurt Baumann, a young theater director, and directed by Kurt Singer, who was a physician and a musician and a director of the Berlin Opera. Singer engaged some good Jewish artists to perform and also organized a series of lectures on scientific subjects. Their existence was accepted by the Gestapo only after the words "German Jews" were eliminated from its title and their activities were under Nazi scrutiny. The Juedischer Kulturbund devoted itself to extensively spreading interest in Jewish art and culture in spite of the Nazi persecution and worked to secure continued cultural activity by providing funds from the resources of its members and through the communities themselves. Evidently the work of the Juedischer Kulturbund largely helped to maintain a closely knit Jewish population and awaken a love for the land of Israel by promoting Zionist ideas. This body also published the *Monatsblaetter des Kulturbundes deutscher Juden* from 1933 on, edited by Julius *Bab. The paper was forced to change its name to *Monatsblaetter des juedischen Kulturbundes* in 1938, after **Kristallnacht*.

From its foundation until October 1938 it organized 8,457 programs, including lectures, concerts, plays, art exhibits, and operas. Julius Bab, Joseph Rosenstock (d. 1985; musical director), Kurt Singer, Kurt Baumann, and Werner Levie (secretary general) directed the Juedischer Kulturbund's affairs. In early 1938 there were 76 branches of the Kulturbund in 100 towns, with more than 50,000 members and 1,700 artists. Membership and the scale of activities were proportionately larger outside of Berlin. Yet, in Berlin alone the membership fluctuated between 12,000 and 18,000. The choice of the programs for lectures, plays, and concerts was often very difficult and was constantly controlled by the secret police (*Gestapo), the Chamber for Arts and Culture (Reichskulturkammer), and the leadership (Gauleitung) of the Nazi Party in Berlin. The Kulturbund was itself divided over whether to present general cultural programs or those of specific Jewish content as advocated by the Zionists. For every organized performance the material had to be submitted in writing for approval by the state commissioner, *Staatskommissar* Hinkel. Hinkel told the Juedischer Kulturbund which plays and lectures could be performed and which articles and literary works could be published. After the November 1938 **Kristallnacht* pogroms, local activities were centralized and therefore better controlled by the national organization, which was disbanded in September 1941. A few of the leading organizers managed to emigrate, but the great majority of artists eventually perished in death camps. The Kulturband provided spiritual support for Jews in Germany during a time of ever more intense persecution; and for individual artists it provided both employment and an opportunity to remain creative and productive amidst the great struggle for basic survival.

BIBLIOGRAPHY: H. Freeden, in: YLBI, 1 (1956), 142–62; idem, *Juedisches Theater in Nazideutschland* (1964); B. Cohn, in: *Yad Vashem Studies*, 3 (1959), 272–5. Y. Cochavi, *Armament for Spritual Survival* (1988).

[B. Mordechai Ansbacher / Michael Berenbaum (2nd ed.)]

JUEDISCHE RUNDSCHAU, journal of the Zionist Federation in Germany. Founded in 1896 under the editorship of Heinrich *Loewe, it appeared twice weekly and was the chief rival of the anti-Zionist *Central-Vereins-Zeitung*. By 1937 the paper had a circulation of over 30,000, much of it outside

Germany. Its influence on the younger generation of Zionists was profound, especially during the Nazi period when it helped to strengthen Jewish morale. When Hitler made the wearing of the yellow patch compulsory, Robert *Weltsch's editorial article urged readers to "wear it with pride." Its last editors were Weltsch and Kurt Loewenstein. It was among the Jewish newspapers banned by the Nazis and ceased publication in 1938.

JUEDISCHER VERLAG, the first Jewish-Zionist publishing house in Western Europe. It was established in 1902 by M. *Buber; B. *Feiwel, E.M. *Lilien, L. *Motzkin, A. *Nossig, Ch. *Weizmann, and others, who constituted the core of the *Democratic Fraction. In line with the aims of the Fraction, the publishing house was to serve as an expression of the Jewish renaissance by publishing the spiritual, cultural, literary, and artistic treasures of the Jewish people over the ages as a basis for the spiritual-cultural rebirth of the Jewish people. The idea had received *Herzl's warm support at the Fifth Zionist Congress (1901). The aim of the plan was to supplement the political activities of the Zionist Organization and to serve as a bridge between Western and Eastern Jews. The first book, *Juedischer Almanach* (1902) edited by Feiwel and Lilien, included authors from both East and West and presented all types of literary works, some of them translated from Hebrew and Yiddish. The second book, *Eine juedische Hochschule* (1902), written by Buber, Feiwel, and Weizmann (translated into Hebrew in 1968 by S. Esh with a preface by S.H. Bergman), voiced for the first time the idea of establishing a Hebrew University in Jerusalem. In 1907, when the publishing house was transferred to the Zionist Organization, it was removed to Cologne; it returned to Berlin in 1911. Until 1920 it was directed by A. Eliasberg, and from 1920 on by S. *Kaznelson. The firm passed through periods of prosperity and times of crisis. It flourished especially under the direction of Kaznelson, when it became one of the greatest Jewish publishing firms in the world, maintained without external support. Among the hundreds of books published by it were the works of *Aḥad Ha-Am, Herzl, *Nordau, A.D. *Gordon, *Agnon (in Hebrew and in German), *Bialik, J.L. *Peretz, *Abramovitsh (Mendele Mokher Seforim), and *Bergelson, *Dubnow's *Weltgeschichte des Juedischen Volkes*, the five volume *Juedisches Lexikon*, L. *Goldschmidt's German translation of the Talmud in twelve volumes, Adolf *Boehm's *Die Zionistische Bewegung*, *Tur-Sinai's German translation of the Bible, the book "*Yizkor*" (dedicated to Ha-Shomer in Ereẓ Israel), *Trumpeldor's diaries, *Jabotinsky's book on the Jewish Legion, the monthly *Der Jude*, edited by Buber, etc. The distribution of some books was extraordinarily large (Dubnow's works on Jewish history and history of Ḥasidism, 100,000 copies; the *Juedisches Lexikon*, 50,000 copies; the translation of the Talmud, 100,000 copies; Herzl's works and diaries, 30,000 copies). In 1938 the firm was closed by the Gestapo and its warehouse confiscated. S Kaznelson, who had settled in Palestine, established in 1931 a daughter company, Hoẓa'ah Ivrit, in partial partnership with the Dvir Publishing Company, Ltd. After the liquidation of the Juedischer Verlag Hoẓa'ah Ivrit continued its work in Palestine. In 1958 the Juedischer Verlag was newly established in Berlin. From 1990 it was part of the German publishing house Surkamp in Frankfurt am Main.

BIBLIOGRAPHY: *Juedischer Verlag, Almanach 1902–1964* (1964). **ADD. BIBLIOGRAPHY:** S. Urban-Fahr, in: *Buchhandlungsgeschichte*, 1 (1994), 12–29; A. Schenker, *Der Juedische Verlag 1902–1938*, (2003) (see also bibliographies on pages 517–605).

[Getzel Kressel]

JUEDISCHE VOLKSPARTEI, party organized in 1919 by M. Kollenscher, H. Loewe, G. Kareski, A. Klee, and others from Zionist-oriented groups in Berlin and other large cities of Germany. The Juedische Volkspartei originated in circles influenced by Herzl's call for Zionists to enter communal politics to contest the dominance of assimilationist and conservative factions. This program was successfully carried out only after World War I by a coalition of East European Jewish immigrants (who, in a few communities, were not entitled to a communal vote as foreign citizens) and the Zionist parties. This coalition successfully agitated for the democratization of the statutes of the Jewish communities. Communal elections, formerly peaceful affairs, aroused great interest and were hotly contested. The Juedische Volkspartei achieved resounding successes in Saxony and a few larger cities after the electoral regulations of the communities had been democratized and standardized. In a coalition with the Orthodox forces they succeeded in the 1926 communal elections to overthrow the long-time Liberal dominance in Berlin. Under their leadership, new Jewish schools were opened and the social welfare institutions were strengthened. In the 1930 Berlin communal elections they had to return power to a Liberal majority despite an increase in the number of votes.

BIBLIOGRAPHY: Cahnman, in: YLBI, 4 (1959), 134ff.; M. Brenner, in: YBLBI 35 (1990), 219–43

[Michael Brenner (2nd ed.)]

JUEDISCH-LITERARISCHE GESELLSCHAFT, society for the advancement of the scientific study of Judaism, founded in Frankfurt on the Main by Orthodox Jews in 1902, the same year as the founding of the liberal Berlin *Gesellschaft zur Foerderung der Wissenschaft des Judentums. Its founding members were the rabbis Solomon Bamberger, Jonas Bondi, Isaac *Halevy, Heymann Kottek, and Moses Marx, and educator Gerson Lange. This society endeavored to show that properly oriented Jewish scholarship need not be in conflict with the tenets of traditional Judaism. Thus, it rejected such "unproven hypotheses" as the documentary theory of biblical criticism while concentrating on post-biblical studies. In pursuit of its aims it published an annual titled *Jahrbuch der juedisch-literarischen Gesellschaft* (1903–32), of which 22 volumes appeared (until 1929 edited by Jonas Bondi). It contained articles on diverse aspects of Jewish history and thought, book reviews, and a few contributions in Hebrew. In addition to the yearbook, the society published a number of scholarly and popular works, of which the following may be mentioned: I. Halevy, *Dorot ha-Rishonim* (6 vols., 1897–1939); H. Kottek, *Geschichte der Juden* (1915); and B. Lewin's critical edition of *Iggeret Rav Sherira Ga'on* (1921). It also granted subventions toward the publication of other scholarly volumes. The founding members of the society were among the most active in its scholarly ventures.

[Michael A. Meyer]

JUEDISCH-THEOLOGISCHES SEMINAR, BRESLAU, first modern rabbinical seminary in Central Europe. Founded in 1854 with the funds which Jonas Fraenkel, a prominent Breslau businessman, had willed for the purpose, the seminary became the model for similar colleges set up in Europe and the U.S. Its first head was Z. *Frankel, to the disappointment of A. *Geiger, who had conceived the idea of the seminary and won Jonas Fraenkel's support for it. The seminary also trained teachers until 1887, and this training was resumed in the 1920s and 1930s. However, the seminary's basic aim was to teach "positive historical Judaism." The "positive" stood for a faithful adherence to the practical precepts of Judaism, while "historical" permitted free inquiry into the Jewish past, including even Bible criticism, though with some self-imposed limitations.

Thus the Breslau seminary, under Frankel's guidance, took a middle position between dogmatic Orthodoxy, as represented by S.R. *Hirsch and A. *Hildesheimer's Rabbinical Seminary, and Geiger's *Lehranstalt (Hochschule) fuer die Wissenschaft des Judentums, officially an academic institution without ideology, but in fact largely a training college for Reform rabbis. Many of its graduates became rabbis in Liberal or Reform congregations, some in Orthodox ones.

After his death in 1875, Frankel was succeeded by L. Lazarus. However, when the latter died in 1879, the administrative functions were henceforth exercised by the lecturers collectively. The one who taught Talmud and rabbinics held the post of "seminary rabbi" and was alone entitled to bestow rabbinical ordination. The seminary graduated about 250 rabbis between 1854 and 1938. Many students of the college made a name for themselves in Jewish scholarship and/or public life.

The seminary issued annual reports (until 1937) containing scholarly contributions by the staff. There was a close association between the college and the *Monatsschrift fuer die Wissenschaft des Judentums. The library, based on the Saraval Collection, grew to over 30,000 volumes and contained more than 400 valuable manuscripts (see D.S. Loewinger and B.D. Weinryb, *Catalogue of Hebrew Manuscripts in the Library of the Juedisch-Theologisches Seminar in Breslau*, 1965).

The years after World War I saw considerable expansion, with teachers' and youth leaders' training courses. Modern Hebrew, too, was given a place in the curriculum. In 1931 the Prussian government approved the addition to the seminary's original name of that of Hochschule fuer juedische Theologie. Nazi rule in Germany from 1933 led to a decrease in the number of regular students, and some of the lecturers sought refuge abroad. The pogrom of November 1938 led to the sack of the seminary and the destruction of the greater part of its library. By order of the police, all teaching activities had to cease and many students were sent to the Buchenwald concentration camp. Nonetheless, some more or less clandestine work continued until February 21, 1939, when the seminary ordained (for the last time) two students.

BIBLIOGRAPHY: G. Kisch (ed.), *The Breslau Seminary, Memorial Volume* (Eng. and Ger., 1963); M. Brann, *Geschichte des juedisch-theologischen Seminars in Breslau (Festschrift zum 50-jaehrigen Jubilaeum, 1904); Festschrift zum 75-jaehrigen Bestehen des juedisch-theologischen Seminars*, 2 vols. (1929).

JUELICH, former duchy and town in Germany. During the 13th century Jews lived in the county of Juelich (from 1356 the duchy of Juelich-Berg). In the course of the 16th century the Jews of Juelich-Berg were persecuted and finally expelled in 1595; however, they were readmitted around the first quarter of the 17th century. The first privilege, granted in 1689, was renewed and approved every 16 years up to the French occupation in 1792. In 1808 the duchy of Juelich-Berg was transformed into the grand duchy of *Berg and in 1815 it was incorporated into the Prussian kingdom.

Among other documentary evidence, reference to a Jewish martyr bears witness to the fact that Jews resided in the town of Juelich in the 13th century. The names of four Jews are known from documents dating from 1324, when a community possessing a synagogue was in existence. A R. Jacob of Juelich lived c. 1300. During the *Black Death persecutions (1348–49) the Jewish community was destroyed and its property and synagogue confiscated. Among the few survivors was "Jacob son of the martyr Joel of Gulkha" (Juelich). In 1356, Margrave William IV of Juelich-Berg relinquished his claims to the property of the defunct community to the archbishop of Cologne. Later the community was restored: at the end of the 16th century there was one Jewish family in Juelich; there were three families in 1673 and 13 in 1786. In the 18th century services were held in a private house. The community of Juelich was under the jurisdiction of the **Landesrabbiner* of the duchy Juelich-Berg, with his seat in *Duesseldorf. In the 18th century he performed his rabbinic functions in both Juelich and Dueren. From 1706 to 1750 Samson Levi Froehlich served as rabbi, Judah Loeb Senever was rabbi in 1779–1821.

In 1806 there were 95 Jews in Juelich. The community reached its peak of 137 in 1910. When the Nazis seized power in 1933, there were 120 Jews in Juelich, owning a synagogue (erected 1860) and a cemetery. There were then two charitable societies and two cultural organizations. As a result of emigration the community had declined to 52 by May 17, 1939. On March 24, 1941, the last 24 Jews of Juelich were removed to Kirchberg and from there deported to the East. With those local Jews deported after reaching Holland and Belgium a total of 71 of the town's Jews perished in the Holocaust.

BIBLIOGRAPHY: Aronius, *Regensten*, 195 no. 441, 259 no. 614; Germ Jud, 1 (1963), 138–9, 2 (1968), 380–2; A. Kober, *Cologne* (Eng., 1940), index; E. Ouverleaux, in: REJ, 7 (1883), 117ff.; FJW (1932–33), 258; Salfeld, Martyrol, 24, 155; A. Wedell, *Geschichte der juedischen Gemeinde Duesseldorfs* (1888).

[Chasia Turtel]

JUJUBE. Two species of jujube grow wild in Israel: the wild jujube (*Zizyphus spina-Christi*) and the lotus jujube (*Zizyphus lotus*). The former is a tall tropical tree with dense, prickly branches (from which, according to Christian tradition, Jesus' crown of thorns was made, hence its scientific name), growing in the hot regions of Israel. The latter is a prickly desert bush, bearing small floury fruit; it grows wild in North Africa where the people make bread from it. These are "the lotus eaters" mentioned by Herodotus (*Historiae*, 4:177). Also growing in Israel is the cultivated jujube (*Zizyphus vulgaris*) which produces a large fruit with an excellent flavor. This is the *sheizaf* of rabbinic literature which is commonly grafted on to the wild jujube, called *rimin*, the two species being counted as diverse kinds (*kilayim*) according to *halakhah* (Kil. 1:4). The fruits of the wild jujube are tasty but were not highly thought of (cf. Dem. 1.1). This tree, widespread in the wadis of the Arabah and the Jordan Valley, is identified with the *ẓe'elim* (lotus trees, AV "shady trees") of Job 40:21–22 under which the *behemoth* lies near the banks of the Jordan. Near Ein Ḥaẓevah in the Arabah grows a huge wild jujube which is counted among the oldest trees in Israel.

BIBLIOGRAPHY: Loew, Flora, 3 (1924), 133–41; H.N. and A.L. Moldenke, *Plants of the Bible* (1952), 248f.; J. Feliks, *Kilei Zera'im ve-Harkavah* (1967), 103–5. **ADD. BIBLIOGRAPHY:** Feliks, Ha-Ẓome'aḥ, 152, 160.

[Jehuda Feliks]

°JULIAN THE APOSTATE (Flavius Claudius Julianus; 331–363 C.E.), Roman emperor 361–363 C.E. As a child Julian escaped the slaughter of his immediate family during the struggles for the throne after the death of his uncle Constantine the Great. Although in his youth Julian received a Christian education under the supervision of Eusebius, the bishop of Nicomedea, he later was greatly influenced by Greek philosophy and ideas. In 355 Emperor Constantius appointed Julian governor of Gaul, where he proved to be an outstanding soldier and administrator, defeating the invading German tribes, and strengthening the provincial administration. In 360 Julian's troops, ordered to join Constantius in the war against Persia in the East, mutinied and declared Julian emperor. When Constantius suddenly died the following year, Julian became the undisputed ruler over the entire Empire.

Julian saw Christianity – which within a generation had ceased to be a persecuted belief and had become the official religion persecuting others – as a sickness within the body politic, and felt deep revulsion toward it from an ethical-religious viewpoint. Although he issued an edict of universal religious toleration, he gave practical expression to his opposition to Christianity by founding a pagan cult in which he served as pontifex maximus. He established regulations governing the behavior and way of life of the pagan priests, formulated important ethical values, and forbade certain books because they were inimical to pagan religious belief. His polemics against Christianity were reinforced by the use of imperial influence – though not force – on behalf of paganism. His writings reveal his knowledge of the Bible and the New Testament. Many of the themes in his polemic *Against the Galileans* (as the Christians were known) have some relevance to Judaism, but they must be judged less in terms of his friendship to the Jews than of his hatred of Christianity. He chides Christianity for having adopted the worst aspects of paganism and Judaism, and for having broken away from Judaism; he writes that the beliefs of the Jews are identical with or only slightly different from those of other nations, with the exception of belief in one God; and on various occasions he denies the allegorical interpretation of Christianity, deriving his arguments from the Bible.

Julian discussed Jewish monotheism from two viewpoints: first, he refuted the Christian claim that Jesus, the Logos, is God, since the Bible recognizes only one God (*Against the Galileans*, 253Aff.); second, he attempted to fit Judaism into the pagan pantheon and isolate Christianity. He therefore argued that the Jews are the chosen people of their god, who is their particular national and local deity (or daemon) and watches over them, just as do other city gods and national deities "who are a kind of regent for the king" (*ibid.* 99E, 115D, 141C–D, 176A–B). However, he was not pleased with Jewish zealousness against other gods, and with the Jews' observance of the Sabbath. He compared the myths of Genesis with the Homeric epic and the Platonic cosmogony, and argued that paganism's religious tradition and view of godhood is superior to Judaism's. He found supporting evidence in the Jewish history of bondage, and the fact that the Jewish people never spawned great military leaders, philosophers, lawmakers, natural scientists, physicians, musicians, logicians, etc. in proportion to their numbers – reflecting negatively upon their religion.

Julian's attitude toward the Jews was generally defined by the needs of his polemic against the Christians. Just before Julian embarked on his Persian campaign he promised to abolish the anti-Jewish laws and to rebuild the Temple where he would join the Jews in worship (*Letter to the Community of the Jews*, no. 51, 396–8). Shortly after this he wrote that "even now the temple is being raised again" (*Letter to a Priest*, 295c). Jewish sources contain only vague hints of these activities. R. Aḥa said that the five sacred objects present in the First Temple were missing in the Second (TJ, Ta'an. 65a; *ibid.* Hor. 47c; Yoma 21b), implying that the Third Temple would be built without any of these. He also said that it would be rebuilt before the Messiah (TJ, Ma'as. Sh. 56a). Jerome reports that some Jews interpreted *sublevabuntur auxilio parvulo* (Dan. 11:34) to refer to this episode (Commentary to Daniel 717). A fuller account is found in Ammianus Marcellinus where Julian is said to have wanted to found the Temple as a memorial to his rule. He arranged for money and building materials to be provided, appointing

Alypius of Antioch, but after several attempts to build on the site he was discouraged by a fire which broke out in the ruins there (Res Gestae 23:2–3). The Church Fathers embellished the story in various ways adding that the Jews received Julian's proposal enthusiastically, coming in thousands to the Temple Mount with stones in their hands, but when the first stones were laid the Jews were threatened by earthquakes and hurricanes, and finally driven off by a heavenly fire and specter of Christ (Gregory of Nazianz, *Contra Julianum, Oratio,* no. 4, 2:149–50; Socrates, *Historia Ecclesiastica,* 3:196; Sozomenus, *Historia Ecclesiastica,* 5:214–5). Two important facts may be gathered from these sources: (1) Julian wished to rebuild the Temple to strengthen paganism against Christianity (he saw Judaism and paganism as having sacrificial rites in common); (2) he wished to refute Jesus' prophecy concerning the Temple (Luke 21:6; Matt. 24:2). Later Christian writers claimed that at Julian's decree to rebuild the Temple the Jews massacred the Christians, burning churches at Ashkelon, Damascus, Gaza, and Alexandria (Ambrose, *Epistles,* 1, no. 40:14–15; Sozomenus, *loc. cit.* 5:22). Most scholars accept rather the opposite view of Bar Hebraeus that the Christians in anger at the decree killed the Jews of Edessa (*Chronography,* 63). A Hebrew inscription quoting part of Isaiah 66:14 found on the Western Wall in 1969 has been ascribed to this period of messianic revival. Julian's works were published with an English translation by W.C. Wright under the title *The Works of the Emperor Julian* (3 vols., 1913–23).

BIBLIOGRAPHY: M. Adler, in: JQR 5 (1892/3), 591–651; Graetz, History, 2 (1956), 595–603; J. Bidez, *La Vie de l'Empereur Julien* (1930), 306ff.; P. de Labriolle, *La Réaction Païenne* (1934), 401–10; J. Vogt, *Kaiser Julian und das Judentum* (1939); J. Heinemann, in: *Zion,* 4 (1939), 269–93; M. Hak, in: *Yavneh,* 2 (1940), 118–39; Alon, *Meḥkarim,* 2 (1958), 313f.; J. Levy, *Olamot Nifgashim* (1960), 221–54 (= Zion, 6 (1941), 1–32); S. Lieberman, in: *Annuaire de l'Institut de Philologie et d'Histoire Orientales et Slaves,* 7 (1939–44), 395–446; idem, in: JQR, 36 (1945/46), 239–53; 37 (1946/47), 329–36; I. Sonne, *ibid.,* 307–28; M. Simon, *Verus Israel* (1948), 139–44 and index; A. Momigliano (ed.), *The Conflict between Paganism and Christianity in the Fourth Century* (1963); E.E. Urbach, in: *Molad,* 19 (1961), 368–74; D. Rokaḥ, in: *Ha-Ishiyyut ve-Dorah, Kovez Harza'ot she-Hushme'u ba-Kenes ha-Shemini le-Iyyun be-Historyah* (1963), 79–80. **ADD. BIBLIOGRAPHY:** S.P. Brock, "The Rebuilding of the Temple Under Julian: A New Source," in: PEQ, 108 (1976); G.W. Bowersock, *Julian the Apostate* (1978).

[David Rokeah]

°**JULIUS III (Giovanni Maria Ciocchi del Monte**; b. 1487). pope, 1550–55. Julius III showed himself comparatively favorably disposed toward the Jews by employing many Jewish physicians, by imposing a fine of 1,000 ducats on anyone who forcibly baptized Jewish children, and by placing no limit on the residence permits of the Marranos at *Ancona. Naturally he was in favor of conversion: he himself acted as godfather to Andrea del Monte (Joseph *Sarfati) and set aside certain taxes levied from the Jews for the House of *Catechumens. On the other hand, he allowed the Franciscan Cornelio de Montalcino, a Jewish convert, to be condemned to the stake. In 1550, he confirmed the constitution of the Society of Jesus. Following the denunciations of two rival printers and a number of converted Jews, Julius set up in 1553 a new commission to examine the Talmud and, on the commission's recommendation, ordained that it be publicly burned. After a new inquiry, in 1554, passages deemed anti-Christian were censored and suppressed.

BIBLIOGRAPHY: Vogelstein-Rieger, 2 (1895), 144; Milano, Italia, 596f.

[Bernhard Blumenkranz]

JULIUS ARCHELAUS (first century C.E.), a member of one of the notable families of Judea who married into the Herodian dynasty. His name indicates that he was a Roman citizen. Josephus sold him a copy of his work, *The Jewish War,* and praises him highly, describing him as well acquainted with Hellenistic learning. Agrippa I promised him his daughter Mariamne in marriage, but since she was only ten years old when Agrippa died, the marriage was not celebrated until the reign of Agrippa II. Subsequently Mariamne abandoned him for *Demetrius, a noble and wealthy Alexandrian Jew, who held the position of the *alabarch of Alexandria.

BIBLIOGRAPHY: Jos., Ant., 19:355; 20:140, 147; Jos., Apion, 1:51; Schuerer, Hist, 373 n. 38; Stern, in: *Tarbiz,* 35 (1965/66), 244f.

[Edna Elazary]

°**JULIUS CAESAR** (c. 100–44 B.C.E.), Roman leader. During the civil war between him and Pompey (49 B.C.E.), Caesar freed *Aristobulus II, the deposed ruler of Judea, planning to send him to Syria, along with troops to aid him to recover his throne. Pompey's supporters, however, succeeded in poisoning Aristobulus before he could leave Rome (cf. Dio Cassius 41:18, 1). At the same time, Hyrcanus II and Antipater, in common with the other vassal rulers in the East, remained loyal to Pompey and even sent him troops for the battle of Pharsalus (48 B.C.E.); but after Caesar's victory and his conquest of the Orient, they went over to the side of the victor. When Caesar besieged Alexandria, Hyrcanus was one of the Oriental rulers who sent him reinforcements, and Hyrcanus's letter influenced the Jews living in the "territory of Onias" to grant the invading army free passage. Upon his return to Syria, Caesar ratified Hyrcanus' appointment as high priest and granted Antipater Roman citizenship and exemption from taxes. The efforts of Aristobulus' younger son Antigonus to turn Caesar against Hyrcanus and Antipater met with failure. At the same time, Caesar nullified Gabinius' Judean settlement and even attempted to correct some of Pompey's abuses against the Jews. In a series of decrees and through decisions made by the Senate at his instigation, Caesar instituted a new administration in Judea. He permitted the reconstruction of the walls of Jerusalem, restored to Judea the port of Jaffa, and confirmed Hyrcanus and his descendants after him as high priests and ethnarchs of Judea. Hyrcanus' realm now included Judea, Jaffa, and the Jewish settlements in Galilee and Transjordan. He also ratified Hyrcanus' ownership of the Hasmonean territory in the "Great Valley of Jezreel." The annual taxation of Judea was set as 12.5% of the produce of the land, with total exemption during the sabbatical year. Extortion by the military was forbidden under any pretext. Caesar's settlement favored the continued rise of the House of Antipater. Caesar permitted Jewish organization in the Diaspora, and his tolerant attitude to Diaspora Jewry was emulated by the rulers of the provinces. Caesar's enmity toward Pompey, who had conquered Jerusalem and defiled the Holy of Holies, led to a positive attitude toward him among the Jews. His restoration of the unity of Judea, his deference toward the high priest, Hyrcanus II, and his tolerant attitude toward the Diaspora Jews increased the sympathy of the Jewish masses for him. When he was assassinated, he was mourned by the Jews more than by any other nation, and for a long time after they continued to weep over his tomb both by day and night (Suetonius, *Divus Iulius*, 84).

BIBLIOGRAPHY: Jos., Ant., 14:123–48, 156–7, 192–216, 268–70; Jos., Wars, 1:183–203, 218; Buechler, in: *Festschrift Steinschneider* (1896), 91–109; Schuerer, Gesch, 1 (1901[4]), 342ff.; O. Roth, *Rom und die Hasmonaeer* (1914), 47ff.; Momigliano, in: *Annali della Reale scuola normale superiore di Pisa* (1934), 192ff.; A. Schalit, *Koenig Herodes* (1969), index.

[Menahem Stern]

°JULIUS FLORUS (second century C.E.), author of an abridged Roman history. He mentions Pompey's capture of Jerusalem and his involvement in Jewish affairs in 63 B.C.E. He says that Pompey entered the Temple and (if the text is correct) saw there the image of an ass (*Epitomae*, 1:40, 30).

[Jacob Petroff]

°JULIUS SEVERUS (Sextus Julius Severus), Roman commander who suppressed the revolt of *Bar Kokhba. He was governor of Britain at the outbreak of the revolt and was called to Judea after *Tinneius Rufus, procurator of Judea, and Marcellus, governor of Syria, had failed to suppress it. Considered one of Hadrian's most able commanders, Julius Severus, according to Dio Cassius, avoided pitched battles and obliged the rebels to engage in a defensive war (*Historiae Romanae*, 69:13). He fought a war of attrition, attacking each fortress and citadel individually, until the whole country, with the exception of Bethar, had been conquered. Dio Cassius relates that dozens of fortresses as well as hundreds of villages were destroyed, and that over half a million people were killed, in addition to those who died of hunger and disease. Jewish sources also testify to the great carnage of the war, in which the Romans likewise suffered heavy losses. The fall of Bethar marked the end of the war. The Romans, regarding Severus' victory as one of special importance, conferred special honors on him.

BIBLIOGRAPHY: Schuerer, Gesch, 1 (1901[4]), 648f., 689f., 697f.; Groag, in: *Pauly-Wissowa*, 30 (1932), 1813–16, s.v. *Minicius*, no. 11; H. Dessau, *Inscriptiones Latinae Selectae*, 1 (1897), 231, no. 1056–57; CIL, 3 (1873), no. 2830; D. Atkinson, in: *Journal of Roman Studies*, 12 (1922), 66, no. 20; L. Petersen (ed.), *Prosopographia Imperii Romani*, 4 pt. 3 (1966[2]), 279–80, no. 576.

[Lea Roth]

JUN-BRODA, INA (1902–1983), Yugoslav poet and translator. Born in Zagreb, Ina Jun-Broda wrote stories for Jewish children. She was a leader of the left-wing women's organization and after the Nazi invasion fled to Dalmatia, where she joined the partisans. In 1947 she settled in Vienna and thereafter published poems, essays, and German translations from Serbo-Croat and Italian. Much of her work reflects her experiences during World War II. *Der Dichter in der Barbarei* (1950) contains sensitive but powerful verse inspired by her life in the occupation period and after; *Die schwarze Erde* (1958), an anthology of Yugoslav partisan poetry; and the first Serbo-Croat selection of Bertolt Brecht's poems, *Pjesme* (1961). She also produced a German version of Krleza's "Balladen des Peter Kerempuch" and commented on Croatian poetry in her "Die aelteste kroatische Dichtung," Zagreb, 1972.

BIBLIOGRAPHY: *Jevrejski almanah* (1959/60), 6–7 (Eng. summ.) and the Eventov Archives Jerusalem,

[Zdenko Lowenthal]

JUNG, LEO (1892–1987), U.S. Orthodox rabbi. Jung was born in Ungarisch-Brod (Uhersky-Brod), Moravia, son of Meir Jung who became rabbi of the London Federation of Synagogues in 1912. He pursued rabbinical studies at Hungarian yeshivot and received his rabbinical ordination first from Rabbi Mordecai Schwartz and Rabbi Avraham Kook; after World War I he returned to Berlin to receive his ordination from Rabbi David Hoffman at the Rabbinical Seminary of Berlin (1920). His secular education was at the University of London where he received his Ph.D. In 1920 he went as rabbi to Congregation Kenesseth Israel, in Cleveland, Ohio, in place of his father, who had been offered the position first.

In 1922 he became rabbi of the Jewish Center in New York, one of the most prominent Orthodox congregations in the city, where Mordecai Kaplan had been rabbi before he left Orthodoxy. He shaped the congregation into a bastion of modern Orthodoxy based on the philosophy of Torah and Derekh Eretz. Jung emerged as one of the best-known spokesmen of neo-Orthodoxy in America. He helped organize the Rabbinical Council of the Union of Orthodox Congregations, which served English-speaking rabbis, and was its president from 1928 to 1935. Together with his cross-town colleague and rival, Rabbi Joseph *Lookstein, Jung was instrumental in Americanizing the Orthodox rabbinate and in making the Orthodox synagogue prestigious for affluent Jews. He became professor of ethics at Yeshiva University in 1931 and held a similar position at Stern College for Women from 1956. During World War II he personally collected 1,200 affidavits and helped rescue some 9,000 Jews. He worked closely with Mike Tress of Ẓe'irei Agudah and with the Va'ad ha-Haẓẓalah. Active in efforts to regularize *kashrut* supervision in New York, Jung was appointed chairman of the New York State Advisory Board for Kashrut Law Enforcement in 1935. He was associated with the *American Jewish Joint Distribution Committee as chairman of its cultural committee (from 1940) and was a trustee of the *National Jewish Welfare Board from 1928. Jung was at one time identified with the Agudat Israel organization and was a member of its supreme council until 1929. He withdrew when the organization refused to cooperate in the Jewish Agency for Palestine, of whose first council he became a member.

A noted writer and editor, Jung started the Jewish Library in 1928 and edited eight volumes. His own writings numbered some 35 books. His *Harvest: Sermons, Addresses, Studies* appeared in 1956. Jung's 70th birthday was commemorated by the *Leo Jung Jubilee Volume* (edited by M.M. Kasher, 1962). His other writings included *The Path of a Pioneer: the Autobiography of Leo Jung* (1980) and *Business Ethics in Jewish Law* (1987).

Leo's brother MOSES (1891–1960) was a professor of religion. Born in Moravia, he went to the U.S. in 1922. A prolific writer, Moses Jung contributed to various Jewish publications and published several books on Jewish law, history, and education. He lectured at Columbia University from 1952. Another brother, JULIUS (1894–1975), was secretary (1925–54) and executive director (1954–59) of the Federation of Synagogues in London.

[Michael Berenbaum (2nd ed.)]

JUNGHOLZ, village in the Haut-Rhin department, E. France. There is evidence that there were Jews in Jungholz in the second half of the 15th century, but there is no further record of another settlement until the beginning of the 18th century. The community was at its height in 1784 with 215 members, but the number had fallen to 12 by 1880. At the end of the 17th century, the elders of the Jewish community of *Ribeauvillé acquired the right to bury their dead at Jungholz, in a site on the outskirts of the village. Around the end of the 18th century, this cemetery, successively and officially enlarged, served 35 communities in upper Alsace. From the 19th century, when numerous communities acquired local cemeteries, the Jungholz burial ground lost its importance. The six communities who used it erected there a memorial to their World War II dead.

BIBLIOGRAPHY: M. Ginsburger, *Der israelitische Friedhof zu Jungholz* (1904); Z. Szajkowski, *Analytical Franco-Jewish Gazetteer* (1966), 251.

[Bernhard Blumenkranz]

JUNGREIS (Jungreisz), ASHER ANSHEL (1806–1872), Hungarian rabbi. Jungreis studied under Meir Eisenstadter and Jacob Koppel Altenkundstadt (Kunstadt) of Verbo, For 40 years he served as rabbi of Csenger and gained a widespread reputation for his piety, to the extent that from all quarters people turned to him for amulets and cures from ailments. He supported widows, cared for the education and marriage of orphans, and also sent considerable sums to the Hungarian *kolel in Ereẓ Israel. After his death his children published his *Menuḥat Asher* in two parts (1876–1908), consisting of talmudic exposition and responsa. Jungreis left three sons who served in the rabbinates of various Hungarian communities. ABRAHAM HA-LEVI (d. 1904) succeeded his father in Csenger. MOSES NATHAN NATA HA-LEVI (1832–1889) was rabbi of Fehergyarmat for 27 years, and of Tiszafüred for 21. He was the author of *Torat Moshe Natan* in two parts (1896, 1923) and of *Menuḥat Moshe* (1905). SAMUEL ZE'EV HA-LEVI (d. 1909) was rabbi of Bojom for 30 years. His three sons-in-law were also rabbis: Joshua Baruch Reinitz (1823–1912), rabbi of Balkany and then Galszecs; Samuel David Segal Jungreis (1837–1894), rabbi and *rosh yeshivah* of Fehergyarmat from 1868; and Jacob Schick (d. 1915), rabbi of Miskolcz and then of Nadudvar.

BIBLIOGRAPHY: N. Ben-Menahem, *Mi-Sifrut Yisrael be-Ungaryah* (1958), 107f., 244f., 310f.; idem, in: *Sinai*, 61 (1967), 206; P.Z. Schwartz, *Shem ha-Gedolim me-Ereẓ Hagar*, 1 (1914), 17a no. 203; A. Stern, *Meliẓei Esh al Ḥodshei Kislev Tevet* (1962²), 14b no. 39.

[Naphtali Ben-Menahem]

JUNIPER. The juniper is the biblical *berosh* (Heb. בְּרוֹשׁ) or *berot* (Heb. בְּרוֹת; Song 1:17), wrongly used in modern Hebrew for the *cypress (the AV translation of *rotem* as juniper is not acceptable). *Beroshim* are frequently mentioned in the Bible, chiefly together with the cedar of Lebanon. It is a tall evergreen tree (Hos. 14:9), smaller than the cedar (Ezek. 31:8) but, like it, symbolizing strength and high stature (II Kings 19:23). It grows in the Lebanon (*ibid.*; Isa. 14:8) and on Mt. Senir, which is Hermon (Ezek. 27:5). In ancient times its choice wood, like that of the cedar, was the most important source of timber for building in the Near East (cf. Isa. 14:8). Junipers were sent by Hiram, king of Tyre, for the building of the Temple (I Kings 5:22), whose flooring, walls, and doors were faced with them (*ibid.* 6:15). From its wood the ships of Tyre were built (Ezek. 27:5). In his vision of the blossoming desert, Isaiah (41:19; 55:13) prophesied that the juniper would one day grow in the wilderness. The Semitic name *berosh* or *berot* occurs in Greek (βράθυ) and in Latin (*bratus*) as a species of lofty juniper. In the hills of Lebanon and of Hermon two species of juniper (*Juniperus drupacea* and *Juniperus excelsa*) grow wild and are called by the Arabs *berota*. Both are upright trees, up to 65 feet (20 m.) high, evergreens, whose tiny leaves are like splinters. The wood is hard and very fragrant (the "fragrance as Lebanon" (Hos. 14:7) refers to the juniper and the cypress). The Septuagint identified the biblical *berosh* with the cypress, and from there the usage passed into modern Hebrew. This identification is not acceptable, however, because the cypress does not grow wild in the hills of Lebanon and Hermon in the neighborhood of the cedar, as described in the Bible. The biblical name for the cypress is *te'ashur* or *gofer*. Nor can the juniper be identified with the *arar ba-aravah* (AV "the heath in the desert"; Jer. 17:6), since this cannot refer to the juniper growing in the Lebanon. The species *Juniperus oxycedros* grows in Upper Galilee and *Juniperus phoenicea* in the desert regions of Edom and Sinai, but it cannot be supposed that Jeremiah was referring to these distant trees. The *arar* is to be identified with the *tamarisk.

BIBLIOGRAPHY: Loew, Flora, 3 (1924), 15, 33–38; J. Feliks, *Olam ha-Ẓome'aḥ ha-Mikra'i* (1968²), 79–83. **ADD. BIBLIOGRAPHY:** Feliks, Ha-Ẓome'aḥ, 40.

[Jehuda Feliks]

°**JUNOSZA, KLEMENS** (pseudonym of **Klemens Szaniawski**; 1849–1898), Polish author. Junosza, who was born in Lublin, translated from Yiddish *Mendele Mokher Seforim's *Masoes Binyomin Hashlishi*, published as *Don Kiszot żydowski* ("A Jewish Don Quixote," 1885), as well as *Shalom Aleichem's *Briv fun Menakhem-Mendl* (*Miljony*) and a few short stories by I.L. *Peretz. Several of Junosza's original writings describe Polish-Jewish life, notably "*Łlaciarz*" ("A Patcher," i.e., a tailor who only patches clothes, first published in *Z mazurskiej ziemi* ("From the Mazurian Land," 1884); *Pająki* ("Spiders," 1894); and *Żywota i spraw Imć Pana Symchy Borucha Kaltkugla ksiąg pięrcioro* ("Five Books on the Life and Affairs of His Highness Simḥah Baruch Kaltkugel," 1895). In *Laciarz*, Junosza showed sympathy for the Jewish poor, but in *Pająki*, he castigated Jews who exploited the Polish peasants. In many of his articles, and especially in his book *Nasi Żydzi w miasteczkach i na wsiach* ("Our Jews in Townlets and Villages," 1889), Junosza discussed the Jewish problem. He defended the Jews against antisemitic attacks but, at the same time, stressed that, because of their traditional education, the Jews were not prepared or fit for productive work. Driven by extreme poverty, they often turned to the exploitation of the peasants, to usury, smuggling, and other illegal activities. The remedy, in his view, was a change in the Jewish educational system, to hasten the productive employment and assimilation of Polish Jewry.

BIBLIOGRAPHY: Rejzen, Leksikon, 3 (1928[3]), 1268–70; T. Jeske-Choiński, *Żyd w powieści polskiej* (1914), 61–68; J. Kryżanowski, *W kręgu wielkich realistów* (1962), 243–6.

[Yehuda Arye Klausner]

JURBARKAS (Ger. **Jurburg**), town in S.W. Lithuania; until the incorporation of Lithuania within Russia in 1795, the town belonged to the principality of Zamut (Zhmud; Samogitia); subsequently, until the 1917 Revolution, it was in the province of Kovno. Jews who visited Jurbarkas at the end of the 16th century are mentioned in the responsa of Meir b. Gedaliah of Lublin (Metz, 1769, 4a no. 7). Within the framework of the Lithuanian Council (see *Councils of the Lands) the community of Jurbarkas belonged to the province (*galil*) of Kaidany (Kedainiai). In 1766, 2,333 Jews were registered with the community. A wooden synagogue built in Jurbarkas during the second half of the 17th century was preserved until the Holocaust. There were 2,527 Jews registered with the community in 1847. The Jews numbered 2,350 (31% of the total population) in 1897, and 1,887 in 1923. In June–September 1941, after the occupation of the town by the Germans, some 1,000 Jews were murdered at the cemetery and outside the town.

BIBLIOGRAPHY: *Lite* (1951), 1595–97, 1849–54, index 2; M. and K. Piechotka, *Wooden Synagogues* (1959), 200; *Yahadut Lita*, 1 (1960), index.

[Yehuda Slutsky]

JURNET OF NORWICH (Hebrew name: **Eliab**; c.1130–1197), English financier. He had important dealings with the crown and with the monastery of Bury St. Edmunds. In 1184, a fine of 6,000 marks was imposed on him and he went abroad, but was permitted to return in 1186 after a payment of 2,000 marks. In the Hebrew sources he is referred to as *nadiv*, indicating that he was a patron of learning. The story that he married a Christian heiress has now been disproved. His son ISAAC OF NORWICH (c. 1170–1235/6), termed *nadiv* like his father, was an outstanding financier under Henry III and was able to survive a fine of 20,000 marks imposed on him for concealment of chattels in 1218, paid off at the rate of one mark daily. A remarkable caricature of him and his associates is preserved (see *Caricature). On his death, his son SAMUEL (before 1204–1273) succeeded to his position in the Norwich community. Substantial relics of the family mansion, which originally had a wharf attached, are still known as Isaac's Hall.

BIBLIOGRAPHY: V.D. Lipman, *Jews of Medieval Norwich* (1967), index; H.G. Richardson, *English Jewry under Angevin Kings* (1960), 32–45; Roth, England[3], index. **ADD. BIBLIOGRAPHY:** ODNB online.

[Cecil Roth]

JUSTER, GEORGE (1902–1968), Romanian painter. Born in Jassy, he devoted himself to painting, soon developing a distinctive style of his own. During World War II, he fled to the Soviet Union and spent two years in Armenia. While there his works were acquired by museums and private collections. After the war he returned to Romania and became one of the most important masters of water color. In 1956 he was awarded the title of artist emeritus. His work aimed at authentic expression rather than external likeness. Juster endowed his portraits with vigor and his landscapes and static themes with a vibrating reality. His work included many illustrations of the Romanian classics such as Eminescu, Topîrceanu. These are filled with inventive spirit, poetry and humor.

JUSTER, JEAN (c. 1886–1916), lawyer and historian. Juster, born in Piatra-Neamţ, Romania, studied in Germany and at the Sorbonne in Paris, where he was admitted to the bar in 1913. Later, he became an advocate at the Paris Court of Appeal. He died in military action. In 1913 Juster contributed a valuable study of the legal position of the Jews under the Visigothic kings to *Etudes d'histoire juridique offertes à Paul F. Girard* (2 (1912–13), 275–336). His doctoral dissertations, *Examen critique des sources relatives à la condition juridique des juifs dans l'empire romain* (1911) and *Les Droits politiques des juifs dans l'empire romain* (1912), marked the bent of his interests and became the basis of his major work, *Les juifs dans l'empire romain: leur condition juridique, économique et sociale* (2 vols., 1914). Juster's approach is a legal one, but his goal, as he explains in the preface to his work, is the study of the relations of the Jews, by way of conflict and resolution, to their environment. In this purview fall civic, communal, confessional, national, military, domestic, jurisdictional, economic, social, and sartorial relations. He does not treat "Jewish religion, Jewish morality or Jewish law" per se, but only their external effects on Jewish relations with the Roman world. The investigation of these matters, he explains, involves the utilization of varied sources, and their classification and critical evaluation. The result is an essay "on the Jews in pagan and Christian literature, a tableau of their geographical dispersion and indications of their numerical importance."

Within these limits his work has remained a model of comprehensiveness, clarity, and scholarly documentation. If he errs at all, it is in the sharpness of his judgment stemming from the juridical approach used, but even critics of his method or conclusions find his work an indispensable tool and source of suggestion. This is illustrated in his handling of the Jewish *privilegia* ("privileges"), in which he takes sharp issue with Theodor *Mommsen, who had argued that the Jewish War of 66–70 C.E. altered the status of all Jews in the empire by transforming their religion from a national cult into a *religio licita* ("licensed" or "licit religion"), and the individual synagogues into *collegia licita* ("legalized associations"). Juster denies both parts of the thesis: The *natio*, or national community, continues to be the basis of the Jewish privileges after, as before, the year 70; the synagogue never became a *collegium licitum*; it was and remained an institution *sui generis*.

BIBLIOGRAPHY: S.L. Guterman, *Religious Toleration and Persecution in Ancient Rome* (1951), index; N. Bentwich, in: JQR, 6 (1915/16), 325–36; G. La Piana, in: HTR, 20 (1927), 350ff.; Waxman, Literature, 4 (1960), 777–780.

[Simeon L. Guterman]

JUSTICE. Justice has widely been said to be the moral value which singularly characterizes Judaism both conceptually and historically. Historically, the Jewish search for justice begins with biblical statements like "Justice (Heb. *ẓedek*), justice shall ye pursue" (Deut. 16:20). On the conceptual side, justice holds a central place in the Jewish world view, and many other basic Jewish concepts revolve around the notion of justice.

God's primary attribute of action (see Attributes of *God) is justice (Heb. *mishpat*; Gen. 18:25; Ps. 9:5). His commandments to men, and especially to Israel, are essentially for the purpose of the establishment of justice in the world (see Ps. 119:137–44). Men fulfill this purpose by acting in accordance with God's laws and in other ways imitating the divine quality of justice (Deut. 13:5; Sot. 14a; Maimonides, *Guide*, 1:54, 3:54). This process of establishing justice in the world is to be completed in the messianic reign of universal justice (see Isa. 11:5ff.; Deut. R. 5:7). All history, therefore, like the Torah itself, which is its paradigm, begins and ends with justice (Ex. R. 30:19).

The two main biblical terms for justice are *ẓedek* and *ẓedakah*. They refer to both divine and human justice, as well as to "the works of justice" (Ex. 9:27; Prov. 10:25; Ps. 18:21–25). This justice is essentially synonymous with holiness (Isa. 5:16). In the Bible, furthermore, "justice" is so consistently paired with "mercy" or "grace" (*ḥesed*; Isa. 45:19; Ps. 103:17ff.), that by talmudic and later times the term *ẓedakah* has come to mean almost exclusively "charity" or "works of love" (BB 10b), and the notion of "justice" is rendered by the terms "truth" (*emet*), "trust" (*emunah*), and "integrity" (*yosher*). Throughout the literature, finally, other values, particularly peace and redemption, are consistently associated with justice, as its components or products (Hos. 12:7; Ps. 15:1; Ta'an. 6:2). Ultimately, therefore, virtually the entire spectrum of ethical values is comprised in the notion of justice.

Jewish justice is different from the classic philosophic (Greek-Western) view of this concept. In the latter, justice is generally considered under the headings of "distributive" and "retributive." These are, of course, also comprised in *ẓedakah*, but while "distributive" and "retributive" justice are essentially procedural principles (i.e., how to do things), Jewish justice is essentially substantive (i.e., what human life should be like). Substantive justice depends on an ultimate (i.e., messianic) value commitment. This is also made clear by modern thinkers, such as Hermann *Cohen, who regards the just society as the ideal society of universal human dignity and freedom (*Ethik des reinen Willens* (1904), ch. 15; *Religion der Vernunft aus den Quellen des Judentums* (1929), ch. 19), and Ch. Perelman, who in his analysis of justice writes: "…in the end one will always come up against a certain irreducible vision of the world expressing nonrational [though justifiable] values and aspirations" (Perelman, *Justice* (1967), 54). Although Perelman does not claim to be discussing a particularly Jewish concept of justice, he is aware of the Jewishness of this ethos (cf. W. Kaufmann, in: *Review of Metaphysics*, 23 (1969), 211, 224ff., 236). The substantive view of justice is concerned with the full enhancement of human and, above all, social life. Thus it suffuses all human relations and social institutions – the state (the commonplace dichotomy between individual and collective responsibility, often illustrated by the contrast between Ex. 20:5 and Ezek. 18, is transcended in the recognition of the dialectical interrelationship between the two, illustrated in Deut. 24:16 alongside Lev. 19:16 (see also Sanh. 73a), and in the contemporary involvement of the individual citizen in the collective actions of his nation), lawcourts (e.g., II Chron. 19:6; Maim. Yad, Sanhedrin, 23:8–10), economics (Lev. 19:36), and private affairs – and, indeed, the single positive ordinance encumbent also on all non-Jews is the establishment of judiciaries (Sanh. 56a).

Justice is not contrasted with love, but rather correlated with it. In rabbinic literature, Jewish philosophy, and Kabbalah, God is described as acting out of the two "attributes of lawfulness and compassion" (PR 5:11, 40:2; Maimonides, *Guide* 3:53).

The critical problem pertaining to justice is that of theodicy: if God is just and rules the world, how can the successes of evil be explained? The problem of theodicy, a recurrent theme in literature, is raised by the Psalmist and is the theme of Job. It is the subject of E. *Wiesel's story, written in the wake of the Holocaust, in which three rabbis subpoena God to a trial and find Him guilty. In the history of Jewish thought many solutions to the problem have been suggested, among them the essentially neoplatonic notion that evil is privation, i.e., that it is not something positive in itself but merely the absence of good

(*Guide* 3:18–25); the view that evil and suffering constitute trials of the just, or, in rabbinic literature, "afflictions of love," i.e., that God tests the righteous by causing them to suffer in this world; and the doctrine of reward and punishment in *Olam ha-Ba (Sanh. 90b–92a; Albo, *Sefer ha-Ikkarim*, 1:15).

The rabbis regard Moses as the ideal of strict unbending justice, in contrast to Aaron, who is the prototype of the ideal of peace, and they interpret the incident of the Golden Calf as exemplifying the problem arising from the clash of these two ideals (cf. Sanh. 6a–7b and parallels). In the same context they suggest that compromise in legal cases may constitute a denial of justice (*ibid.*).

A reply to, though not a resolution of, the problem of theodicy in our time may be attempted in two directions. (a) to protest against injustice in the tradition of Job, *Ḥoni ha-Me'aggel, and the ḥasidic leader Levi Isaac of Berdichev, which is possible only before a responsible authority, i.e., a just God; (b) to regard justice as a normative, rather than a descriptive, concept, as does Cohen, who writes that "justice maintains the tension between reality and the eternal ideal" (*Religion der Vernunft*, p. 569). According to this view, justice can be striven for and looked for only in the future – whether the future of mankind as a whole (the days of the Messiah) or of the individual – i.e., in God, whose justice in judgment is affirmed in the blessing recited in the hour of death, "blessed be the just judge."

Man is obliged to imitate God by acting on the principle of compassionate equity (Micah 6:8; Mak. 24b; BM 30b, 83a), and – at the final consummation of history – justice and mercy become identical.

ADD. BIBLIOGRAPHY: L.E. Goodman, *On Justice: An Essay in Jewish Philosophy* (1991).

[Steven S. Schwarzschild]

°**JUSTIN** (**Marcus Junian(i)us Justinus;** third century C.E.), author of the *Epitoma Historiarum Philippicarum*, an abridgment of *Pompeius Trogus' "Universal History" and the main source for that work. Justin gives a very brief, error-filled summary of Jewish history, from its biblical beginnings into the Hasmonean period.

[Jacob Petroff]

°**JUSTINIAN I**, emperor of the Eastern Roman Empire, 527–565, a virulent and consistent persecutor of all non-Orthodox Christians, heretics, pagans, and also of Jews and Judaism. Justinian's famous *Corpus Juris Civilis* and his novellae (imperial instructions on specific subjects) included legislation on the Jews which confirmed or amended that of *Theodosius II (408–450) and virtually fixed the status of the Jew in Byzantine society for the next 700 years (see *Byzantine Empire). Adding to the restrictions and disabilities imposed by Theodosius, Justinian declared that Jews could not retain heretical and pagan slaves who converted to Orthodox Christianity, and that they could give evidence only for (not against) Orthodox Christians, while they could testify either for or against heretics. Justinian's novellae concerning the Jews are the following:

NOVELLA 37 (535 C.E.), forbidding Jews and heretics in the newly conquered province of North Africa to practice their religious rites. Synagogues and the meeting places of heretics were to be confiscated and, suitably consecrated, put to ecclesiastical use. Contrary to the prevailing Christian attitude, this novella attempted to view Judaism as a heresy and may have been motivated by suspicion of Jewish support for the Vandal regime overthrown by Justinian and the belief, prevalent in North Africa, in the alleged Jewish role in spreading heresy. Although it is known that the ancient synagogue in the city of Borion was transformed into a church and the local Jewish population was forced to accept Christianity, the novella was not put into effect. However, it was a dangerous precedent, symptomatic of the deterioration of the attitude toward the Jews under Justinian.

NOVELLA 45 (537 C.E.), prohibiting Jews, Samaritans, and heretics any exemption from service on local municipal bodies (the decurionate), a service which entailed heavy financial burdens. Previously, Jews as well as gentiles could claim exemption on the grounds of holding a religious office in their own community. The few privileges enjoyed by the decurions, such as immunity from corporal punishment or exile, would not apply to Jewish decurions. It was stated that "Jews must never enjoy the fruits of office but only suffer its pains and penalties." If a Jew was found holding a higher office than a Christian, he had to pay a fine. This novella affected the western provinces for a short time.

NOVELLA 131 (545 C.E.), prohibiting sales of ecclesiastical property to Jews, Samaritans, pagans, and heretics, and declaring synagogues built on land subsequently shown to be ecclesiastical property subject to confiscation.

NOVELLA 146 (553 C.E.), supposedly in response to a Jewish request, forbids the insistence that the readings from the Pentateuch be exclusively in Hebrew from the Scrolls of the Law (Torah). They could be in Greek, Latin, or any other tongue, and the Greek could be either that of the Septuagint or the translation of *Aquila, which had rabbinic sanction. Secondly, the use of the *deuterosis*, the Mishnah, for exegesis was forbidden. Justinian argued that the *deuterosis* was not divinely inspired and could only mislead men. Rabbinic interpretations spread errors such as a denial of the existence of angels and the Last Judgment (probably a confusion with earlier *Samaritan beliefs). Just as the Byzantine emperor was the arbiter of Christian practice, Justinian also saw him as the arbiter of the only other legal religion in his dominions. The extent of Justinian's interference in the service of the synagogue is open to question, but it attempted to impose a Christian interpretation of what Judaism and its holy texts should be.

Besides the novellae, Justinian allegedly prohibited the celebration of Passover if its date fell before the date of Easter. Ereẓ Israel was the scene of several outbursts against the empire, mainly on the part of the Samaritans, whose efforts to form their own kingdom were brutally suppressed in 529. In

556 Jews joined Samaritans in an anti-Christian riot in Caesarea in which several churches were burned down. Imperial troops were eventually dispatched to subdue the rebels.

BIBLIOGRAPHY: W.G. Holmes, *Age of Justinian and Theodora*, 2 vols. (1912²); F. Schulz, *History of Roman Legal Science* (1953²); D.M. Nicol, in: *History Today*, 9 (1959), 513–21; R. Schoell and W. Kroll (eds.), *Corpus Juris Civilis*, 3 (1954), 244–5, 277–9, 663, 714–7; J. Parkes, *Conflict of the Church and the Synagogue* (1934), 245–56; Juster, Juifs, 1 (1914), 167ff., 237–8; 2 (1914), 91–92, 103–4; P. Browe, in: *Analecta Gregoriana*, 8 (1935), 101–46; G. Ferrari dalle Spade, in: *Muenchener Beitraege zur Papyrusforschung und antiken Rechtsgeschichte*, 35 (1945), 102–17 (Italian); J.A. Montgomery, *The Samaritans* (1968), 113f.; Baron, Social², 3 (1957), 4–15; M. Avi-Yonah, *Bi-Ymei Roma u-Bizantiyyon* (1952), 177–85; Hirschberg, Afrikah, 1 (1965), 31–32; H.H. Ben-Sasson (ed.), *Toledot Am Yisrael*, 2 (1969), index; B. Biondi, *Giustiniano Primo, principe e legislatore cattolico* (1936); idem, *Il diritto romano cristiano*, 3 vols. (1952–54); V. Colorni, *Gli ebrei nel sistema del diritto comune fino alla prima emancipazione* (1956); idem, in: *Labeo*, 12 (1966), 140ff.; M. Simon, *Verus Israel* (Fr., 1964²); P. Kahle, *Cairo Geniza* (1959), 39, 315; J.H. Lewy, *Olamot Nifgashim* (1960), 255ff.

[Andrew Sharf]

°**JUSTIN MARTYR** (c. 100–c. 165 C.E.), early Church Father who waged an active polemic against Jews and Judaism. Justin Martyr was born to pagan parents in Neapolis, the modern Nablus. After his conversion to Christianity he became a staunch advocate of his new faith against its major then current adversaries, Greek philosophy and Judaism. He was martyred for his faith as a Christian by the Roman authorities sometime between 163 and 167.

Justin's principal polemic against Judaism was waged in his work, *Dialogue with Trypho*. The latter is presented as a Jew who during the Bar Kokhba war fled from Jerusalem to Ephesus, where he encountered Justin, and the two engaged in a dialogue on the merits of Judaism and Christianity. All the issues then current between the two faiths are marshaled in the dialogue. Justin is the aggressive protagonist; Trypho seeks to counter Justin's arguments, but he is clearly the weaker of the opponents. Justin's goal is to convert Trypho to Christianity, and while this is not accomplished by the end of the dialogue, the reader feels that Trypho has been seeded with the Christian truth, and conversion will follow.

Some Christian scholars, and also the Jewish historian Heinrich Graetz, have identified Trypho with the *tanna* Rabbi *Tarfon. This would make the dialogue the record of a historical event. However, certain historical facts show this to be impossible. Rabbi Tarfon served in the Temple as a priest before the destruction in 70 C.E. Since 30 was the minimum age for such service, he could no longer have been active in 135 C.E. Trypho cites interpretations paralleled in the Septuagint and the New Testament, which are at variance with interpretations current in the rabbinic academies. It is clear the Trypho is a fictional character, and the entire dialogue is merely a literary format for the exposition of Justin's views.

Justin's thesis is an extension of the kind of reasoning which pervades the New Testament. In essence it makes the claim that Christianity is the authentic flowering of biblical Judaism, and that the Jews who cling to their faith in its old form are clinging to an obsolete doctrine. For doing so they are berated as blind and stubborn and insensitive, a fossil people clinging to a superseded faith. Justin expounds this position through a hermeneutical device parallel to the Midrash: a figurative interpretation of biblical texts investing them with Christian meanings. Some of these passages are direct citations from the New Testament. Thus the identification of the new covenant in Jeremiah 31:3–32 with the structure of Christian truth, in replacement of the earlier truth of Judaism (Dial. 11:3), appears in Hebrews 8:8–10, 10:16–17. But other interpretations seem to be Justin's own. Water and faith and wood (the ark) figure in the rescue of Noah, and the rescue of men from sin as mediated by Jesus is likewise effected by water (baptism) and faith and wood (the cross). The upraised hands of Moses which occasioned Israel's victory against the Amalekites (Ex. 17:8–14) are interpreted by Justin as having derived their efficacy because the sign thus formed foreshadowed the cross. The rod with which Moses performed the wonders of leading the Israelites out of Egypt, of parting the Red Sea for them, of drawing water from the rock – these and more were all made possible, according to Justin, because the rod was in truth a type of the cross (Dial. 138,9:1–2,86:1–6).

Justin does not content himself with the exposition of a Christian interpretation of the Bible. He often denounces the Jews for having crucified Jesus, and he accuses them of continuing to persecute Christians. He finds many indications that God had deemed the Jews as especially reprehensible. In repudiating the efficacy of the law as prescribed in the Bible, Justin makes the bold assertion that the law was initially given to the Jews because, as an especially unspiritual race, hardhearted, rebellious, and ungodly, they needed a more elaborate law, with many more disciplines as a means of mitigating some of their offensive qualities. For the gentiles, however, it was enough to prescribe two commandments as Jesus did, the love of God and the love of man (Dial. 93:4). Justin also makes himself into a philosopher of history and offers the theory that the defeats of the Jews in the wars against Rome, both in the year 70, and again in 135, were God's visitation of a deserved punishment, because they had sinned so grievously by crucifying Christ and rejecting his new faith. Justin gloated as he contemplated the destruction of Jerusalem and the collapse of the Jewish struggle for freedom, and he taunted Trypho with this sweeping assertion: "All this has happened to you rightly and well, For ye slew the Just One and His prophets before Him, and now ye reject, and … dishonor those who set their hopes on Him, and God Almighty and Maker of the universe who sent Him …" (Dial. 16:3–4).

Justin's invective against Jews and Judaism entered the mainstream of Christian thought and became a sinister influence which contributed not a little toward the development of what is known as Christian antisemitism.

BIBLIOGRAPHY: *Justin Martyr, The Dialogue with Trypho* (tr. A.L. Williams, 1930); L.W. Barnard, *Justin Martyr, His Life and*

Thought (1967); E.R. Goodenough, *The Theology of Justin Martyr* (1968); C.C. Martindale, *Justin the Martyr* (1921); W.A. Shotwell, *The Biblical Exegesis of Justin Martyr* (1965); B.Z. Bokser, in: JQR, 64 (1973), 7–122, 204–11.

[Ben Zion Bokser]

JUSTITZ, ALFRED (1879–1934), Czech painter and graphic artist. Justitz was born in Novā Cerekev and studied first architecture and then painting at the Academy in Prague and, from 1905, in Karlsruhe and Berlin. In 1910 he settled temporarily in Paris, where he was greatly influenced by impressionist theories of form, retaining at the same time, however, his decorative lyricism. After serving in the Austro-Hungarian army in World War I, he returned to Prague and became one of the founders of modern Czechoslovak art. In 1920 and 1921 he participated in the exhibitions of the most important avant-garde group of that time in Prague, which called itself "Tvrdošijní" ("The Stubborn Ones"). He was again in Berlin and Paris in 1922 and 1923, but in 1924 he returned to Prague, where he spent the rest of his life. His best paintings – *Men in Landscape* (1914), *Head of a Dancer* (1922), *Road between Barns* (1924), and *Three Men* (1926) – are in the Prague National Gallery.

[Avigdor Dagan]

JUSTMAN, JOSEPH (1909–), U.S. educator. Justman, who was born in Warsaw, taught at Brooklyn College from 1934, was appointed professor of education in 1950, and director of teacher education and chairman of the department in 1960. Upon his retirement, he became professor emeritus of education at Brooklyn College.

Justman spent 1956–57 in Italy, preparing *The Italian People and Their Schools* (1958). He subsequently returned several times to Rome, Florence, and Padua as visiting lecturer. His books include *Theories of Secondary Education in the United States* (1940), *College Teaching: Its Practice and Potential* (1956), *Evaluation in Modern Education* (1956), *Improving Instruction with Supervision* (with T. Briggs, 1960), and *The Effects of Ability Grouping* (with Miriam L. Goldberg, 1966). His work was mainly concerned with giving the college teacher a deeper understanding of his profession through an evaluation of educational principles, practices, and their effects on curriculum and organization.

[Ronald E. Ohl / Ruth Beloff (2nd ed.)]

JUSTMAN, MOSHE BUNEM (pseudonym: **B. Yeushzon**; 1889–1942), Yiddish journalist, humorist, and novelist. Born in Warsaw, he was educated in yeshivah and torn between admiration for ḥasidic life and the lure of modernism. He published in a broad spectrum of Yiddish periodicals, but from 1910 to 1925, his articles in the Warsaw Yiddish daily *Moment* under the pseudonym Itshele won him a large following among troubled ḥasidic youth. In 1925 he transfered his journalistic activities to the rival Warsaw daily, *Haynt*. His best novel *Inem Rebms Hoyf* ("At the Rabbi's Court," 1914) depicted the joyous fervor prevailing in Polish ḥasidic courts but also the infiltration of maskilic ideas even among the children of ḥasidic rabbis. While nostalgic for the old order, he recognized the inevitability of its decline. His other tales include *Oyf der Frisher Luft* ("Fresh Air," 1912) and *Apikorsim* ("Heretics," 1913). His articles on Jewish folklore, written over a number of years, were collected in eight volumes, *Fun Unzer Alten Oytser* ("From Our Old Treasure," 1932) and constitute his major work. Together with Menahem *Kipnis, he wrote a parody on S. *An-ski's *The Dybbuk*, which was performed on the Warsaw stage in 1921. He escaped Warsaw at the last moment and then also Vilna, settling in Ereẓ Israel in 1940. A posthumous collection of his feuilletons was published in 1988 (*Nekhtn: A Bukh Felyetonen*).

BIBLIOGRAPHY: LNYL, 4 (1961), 179–81; Zeitlin, *In a Literarisher Shtub* (1937), 161–4; M. Ravitch, *Mayn Leksikon*, 1 (1945), 113–5. **ADD. BIBLIOGRAPHY:** Y. Szeintuch, in: *Ḥulyot*, 7 (2002), 309–20.

[Shlomo Bickel / Jerold C. Frakes (2nd ed.)]

JUSTUS OF TIBERIAS, historian; a contemporary of *Josephus and his rival in describing the Jewish War (66–70/73 C.E.). The main source of knowledge of Justus – the disparaging polemic directed against him by Josephus in his *Life* – is of doubtful value, since Josephus may have falsified facts. Nevertheless two things are clear: that Justus came from a respected Tiberian family, and that "he did not lack Greek culture," as Josephus himself admits. Justus' name and that of his father (Pistus) also attest Hellenistic influence, and he was, moreover, appointed private secretary to *Agrippa II, a post which obviously demanded a thorough command of Greek. Apart from this it is difficult to find in Josephus anything further in Justus' favor. Josephus accuses him of personal turpitude, licentiousness, bribery, and theft. These accusations may be ignored. Of a more complex nature is the question of Justus' loyalties during the war. Josephus charges that Justus was the sworn enemy of the Romans and an associate of the *Zealots, doing everything in his power to draw Tiberias and Galilee into the revolt against Roman rule. In addition, Josephus states that Justus organized an attack on the Greek cities of the Decapolis, whose inhabitants were faithful allies of the Romans, adding that this attack is also mentioned in the memoirs of Vespasian. According to Josephus, Justus, while in Berytus (Beirut), was accused of treason against the Romans and would certainly have been sentenced to death but for Vespasian's friendliness to Agrippa. All this, however, does not necessarily prove that Justus was a Zealot. Possibly Agrippa explained the attack as a loyal Tiberian's vengeance against the Greeks for their bloody attacks on the Jews at the outbreak of the war.

Nevertheless, Justus was obviously no lover of Roman rule. In view of his friendship with Agrippa, Justus probably shared the views expressed by the latter in his speech to the rebels in Jerusalem (the account of which in Josephus undoubtedly has an historical basis). The gist of this was that Roman might was so decisive that it could not be overcome, and that there was therefore no sense fighting it. Agrippa himself, then, was not an admirer of Roman rule in Judea, but only reconciled to it. Justus, a devoted Tiberian concerned for the welfare of his native city, did everything in his power to ensure Agrippa's continued rule in Tiberias. This brought him into conflict with Josephus, who arrived in Galilee on behalf of the revolutionary government in Jerusalem and strove to extend his influence over the whole province. In an attempt to crush the opposition against him, Josephus imprisoned many of the city notables, including Justus and his father. Justus, however, succeeded in escaping from his prison in Tarichaeae to Berytus, and henceforth had no further direct contact with the events of the war. It was after his escape that he was appointed Agrippa's private secretary, which gave him good opportunity of hearing at first hand about the conduct of the war in Galilee, and especially about the questionable role played by Josephus. He embodied this information in a book about the war, which was for the most part an extensive account of events in Galilee before the arrival of Vespasian, and dealt particularly with the misdeeds of Josephus in Tiberias. Since Josephus published his own history of the war after 75 C.E. and Justus suppressed his reply for some 20 years (Vita, 360), it may be concluded that Justus' work was published only after the death of Domitian (96 C.E.) when Nerva ascended the throne. From the fact that Josephus begins his *Life* with a detailed description of his distinguished descent from the Hasmoneans, it may be assumed that Justus tried to derogate not only him but also his family. Justus' main purpose in writing the book was apparently to wreak belated vengeance on his rival, which he could not exact under the Flavian emperors.

It is generally believed that Justus also wrote a second book, a chronicle of the kings of Israel. Although a list which was in the possession of Photius, patriarch of Constantinople, between 858 and 868, seemed to make the description of the war merely part of the chronicle, the detailed nature of the description of the events in Galilee (as evidenced in Josephus) presupposes a separate work.

BIBLIOGRAPHY: Schuerer, Gesch, index; A. Baerwald, *Flavius Josephus in Galilaea* (Ger., 1877); Niese, in: *Historische Zeitschrift*, 76 (1896), 227ff.; H. Luther, *Josephus und Justus von Tiberias* (1910); R. Laqueur, *Der juedische Historiker Flavius Josephus* (1920), 6ff.; H. Drexler, in: *Klio*, 19 (1925), 293ff.; A. Schalit, *ibid.*, 26 (1933), 66–95; M. Stein, *Ḥayyei Yosef* (1939[3]), introd., 5–16, and notes; A. Pelletier, *Flavius Josèphe, Autobiographie* (1959), xivff.

[Abraham Schalit]

°JUVENAL (c. 50–c. 127 C.E.), the most famous Roman satirist, a rhetorician by profession. Juvenal is most bitter against those foreigners – Greeks, Syrians, and especially Jews – who have, in his opinion, brought about the decline and fall of the old Roman way of life.

In *Satire* 14:96–106, he derides those who sympathize with Judaism, reverencing the Sabbath, worshipping clouds and a heavenly divinity (cf. *Hecataeus, Varro, *Strabo, and *Petronius Arbiter), and avoiding pork. Their children, he says, go still further (so also *Tacitus, Hist. 5:5), undergoing circumcision. He also denounces these proselytes for despising Roman statutes while observing the law which Moses had handed down in a secret scroll (perhaps a reference to Judaism as a mystery, as seen by the Romans generally or as seen in *Philo, who may have been known to Juvenal through *pseudo-Longinus), hating anyone who is not one of them (so also Tacitus, loc. cit.), to the point of being unwilling to direct a non-Jew to the road that he seeks or a thirsty man to a fountain (perhaps an allusion to the baptism required of proselytes). Lewy has indicated that to show the way to wanderers and to give drink to the thirsty were basic to Juvenal's Stoic philosophy, for which reason he felt so strongly about them. He also condemns the Judaizers for showing laziness by abstaining from work on the Sabbath (so also *Seneca the Younger).

Juvenal mocks at the poverty among the Jews (3:12–16; 6:542–7), though perhaps this is a reflection merely of the Jewish tradition of charity. Synagogues in particular, he says, are the haunts of beggars (3:296). The Jews, for a very small fee, interpret dreams and tell fortunes for credulous Romans (6:542–7). Juvenal also mentions an incestuous relationship between *Agrippa II and his sister *Berenice and contemptuously speaks of the poverty and piety of the Jewish kings who observe the Sabbath with bare feet (6:156–60), perhaps referring to the belief that Jews fasted on the Sabbath (cf. Strabo, *Augustus, *Pompeius Trogus, and Petronius Arbiter), which may be an allusion to the Day of Atonement, as possibly in *Horace's "thirtieth Sabbath" (Satires 1:9, 69).

BIBLIOGRAPHY: Reinach, Textes, 290–3; J. Lewy, in: *Sefer Yoḥanan Lewy* (1949), 1–2; L.H. Feldman, in: *Transactions… of the American Philological Association*, 81 (1950), 200–8.

[Louis Harry Feldman]

Initial letter "K" for Karolus (Charlemagne), from the opening of Book 25 of Vincent of Beauvais, Speculum Historiale, *Metten, S. Germany, 1332. Munich, Bayerische Staatsbibliothek, Cod. lat. 8201c, fol. 9v.*

KA-KAS

KAATZ, SAUL (1870–1942?), rabbi and scholar. Kaatz, who was born in Schwersenz (Swarzedz), Poznania, served as rabbi at Hindenburg, Upper Silesia, from 1895. When the validity of the Nazis' anti-Jewish legislation in Upper Silesia was contested before the League of Nations in 1933 (see *Bernheim Petition), Kaatz was among those who courageously resisted the German government's intimidation. He spurned the possibility of emigration and was deported to his death with his congregation in 1942. Kaatz was an individualist and often upheld unpopular ideas against his fellows in the Orthodox rabbinate, just as he opposed, in 1897, the anti-Zionist line of the *Allgemeiner Rabbinerverband.* His published writings include *Die Scholien des Gregorius Abulfaragius Bar Hebraeus zum Weisheitsbuch des Josua ben Sira…* (1892); *Das Wesen des juedischen Religionsunterrichts* (1904); *Wesen des prophetischen Judentums* (1907); *Abraham Geigers religioeser Charakter* (1911); *Die muendliche Lehre und ihr Dogma…* (2 vols., 1922–23); *Weltschoepfungsaera und Wissenschaft* (1928); and *Sendschreiben an den Vorstand… der Vereinigung traditionell-gesetzestreuen Rabbiner Deutschlands,* in which he opposed the custom of abbreviating the name of God in non-Hebrew languages. Kaatz was a regular contributor to Wohlgemuth's *Jeschurun* and the weekly *Israelit.* He also wrote short stories (*Alter Vogel,* 1919) and a play, *Alexander der Grosse vor Jerusalem.*

KABACHNIK, MARTIN IZRAILOVICH (1908–1997), Russian organic chemist. Kabachnik was attached to the U.S.S.R. Academy of Sciences from 1939 and to the Institute of Organic Chemistry until 1954. Thereafter he was at the Institute of Elementary Organic Compounds. He was awarded the Stalin Prize in 1946, and became an academician in 1958. His field of research included tautomerism and phosphorus-containing organic insecticides.

KABAK, AARON (Aharon) ABRAHAM (1880–1944), Hebrew author. Born in Smorgon in the province of Vilna, Kabak lived in Turkey, Palestine, Germany, and France before studying in Switzerland at the universities of Geneva and Lausanne. He finally settled in Palestine in 1921. A teacher at the

Jerusalem Reḥavyah Gymnasium, he played a central role in the literary, educational, and civic life of the city.

Kabak's first novel *Levaddah* ("By Herself," 1905) was hailed as the first Zionist novel in Hebrew literature. Sarah, a young girl of the 1890s, is drawn to Zionism although all her friends are socialists. She learns that she has chosen a lonely path, demanding self-sacrifice and unflinching determination. Similarly, the hero of *Daniel Shafranov* (1912) discovers that the way of redemption is through sacrifice. The action takes place before the Russian Revolution of 1905. Daniel fails in his efforts to unite the disparate segments of Jewish life, even in the face of a pogrom mob, and commits suicide. *Ahava* ("Love," 1914) depicts the life and loves of the emigrant Russian intelligentsia in Switzerland. *Nizzaḥon* ("Victory," 1923) is set in Germany, before World War I. Zinner, a Jewish sculptor in Berlin, practices "German" art, but is won back to Judaism by a young girl from Palestine. Kabak introduced the realistic historical novel into Hebrew literature with his trilogy *Shelomo Molkho* (1928–29; 1973), each book of which deals with a crucial phase in the life of the false messiah, Solomon *Molkho.

Bein Yam u-vein Midbar ("Between the Sea and the Desert," 1933) was Kabak's first novel with a Palestinian setting. *Ba-Mishol ha-Ẓar* (1937; *The Narrow Path*, 1968) was written after Kabak's return to Orthodox Judaism, in the early 1930s. It depicts Jesus of Nazareth as a Jew whose teaching centers around the idea that man must seek the Kingdom of God in himself. The book contains vivid descriptions of the Galilean landscape. *Toledot Mishpaḥah Aḥat* ("History of One Family," 1943–45; 1998) is a series of loosely connected novels in which the author intended to trace the development of the national renaissance from its beginnings in Russia "to the heroic days of *Ḥanitah" through events that befall a single family. The three novels which he succeeded in completing before his death are set respectively in mid 19th-century Russia, Poland of the 1863 insurrection, and Odessa in the 1860s. They are *Be-Ḥalal ha-Reik* ("The Empty Space," 1943), *Be-Ẓel Eẓ ha-Teliyyah* ("In the Shadow of the Gallows," 1944), and *Sippur beli Gibborim* ("Story without Heroes," 1945, posthumous).

Of Kabak's many short stories the most noteworthy is "*Ha-Ma'pil*" ("The Trailblazer"), in which a boy sets out to force the coming of the Messiah and dies in an act of heroism (*Ha-Shilo'aḥ*, 14, 1904). Among his more important stories and novelettes are "*Ḥalom*" (*Ha-Shilo'aḥ*, 20, 1909), *Me-al ha-Migdal* (1910), *Nano* (1911), *Ha-Navi* (*Ha-Shilo'aḥ*, 38, 1921), *Kol ba-Afelah* (1927), *Ẓe'if ha-Mayyah* (in: *Sefer Klausner*, 1937). Kabak wrote two biblical dramas: *Be-Himmot Mamlakhah* (1929) and *Bat Sanballat* (in *Beitar*, 2, 1934). He was also the author of numerous critical essays, and translated works by Loti, Stendhal, Wassermann, and Merezhkovsky. He also edited several anthologies.

While critics condemned Kabak's early work as tendentious, didactic, catering to popular taste, and lacking psychological depth, their comments became more favorable after the publication of *Shelomo Molkho*. Kabak's major contribution to Hebrew literature was in the genre of the novel, which he freed of stereotyped heroes, settings, and themes, giving it modern characters, plot, dialogue, and a sense of progression. One of the first Hebrew novelists to use the wide canvas approach, Kabak had strong impact on the Hebrew reading public in general, and most particularly on its younger members. By applying European methods and forms to Jewish content, he was a decisive force in bringing the Hebrew novel into line with world literature.

BIBLIOGRAPHY: W. Weinberg, "Life and Work of Aaron Abraham Kabak" (Dissertation, Hebrew Union College, Cincinnati, 1961); Waxman, Literature, 4 (1960^2), 162–70; R. Wallenrod, *The Literature of Modern Israel* (1956), index, s.v. *Kabak, Abraham Aba*; A. Ben-Or, *Toledot ha-Sifrut ha-Ivrit ha-Ḥadasha*, 3 (1963), 159–76; Epstein et al., in: *Bitzaron*, 12 (Kabak issue, 1945), 239–338, 343–4, includes bibl. **ADD. BIBLIOGRAPHY:** W. Weinberg, "Kabak's Connections with America," in: *American Jewish Archives*, 22 (1970), 166–73; S. Werses, "*Ha-Mevaker A.A. Kabak*," in: *Moznayim*, 42 (1976), 26–37; G. Shaked, *Ha-Sipporet ha-Ivrit*, 1 (1977), 303–14; N. Tarnor, "A.A. Kabak: The Heroic Quest," in: *Jewish Book Annual*, 40 (1982), 120–26; R. Scheinfeld, "*Ha-Roman ha-Odisei shel A.A. Kabak*," in: *Meḥkarei Yerushalayim be-Sifrut Ivrit* (1986), 215–36; M. Shaked, "*Bein Teliyah le-Teḥiyah*," in: *Biẓaron*, 37–38 (1988), 58–74; S. Hauptman, *Darkhei ha-Iẓuv ha-Figurativi shel ha-Gibbor ha-Moderni bi-Yeẓirato shel A.A. Kabak* (1990).

[Werner Weinberg]

KABAKOFF, JACOB (1918–), U.S. educator and scholar. Born in New York, Kabakoff earned a diploma from the Teachers Institute of Yeshiva University in 1935 and a B.A. from the same institution in 1938. He was ordained a rabbi and awarded an M.H.L. from the Jewish Theological Seminary in 1944. He received a D.H.L. from the JTS in 1958. He served as a Conservative rabbi in Philadelphia (1944–48). From 1952 to 1968 he was dean of the Cleveland College of Jewish Studies, and then was appointed associate professor of Hebrew literature at Lehman College in New York City. A specialist in Hebrew literature in America, his *Ḥalutzei ha-Sifrut ha-Ivrit ba-Amerikah* ("Pioneers of Hebrew Literature in America," 1966) dealt with such writers as Jacob Ẓevi Sobel, Henry Gersoni, Ze'ev Schurr, Gershon Rosenzweig, and Isaac Rabinowitz. His contributions to the *Jewish Book Annual* were listed in JBA, 25 (1967/68), 418. Kabakoff served as editor of the JBA from 1977 to 1996. He also served as chairman of the editorial board of the Hebrew weekly newspaper *Hadoar* and was a member of the Rabbinical Assembly, the American Association of Jewish Studies, the World Congress of Jewish Studies, and the American Association of Professors of Hebrew. In 1988 he was acknowledged by the Habermann Institute for Literary Research with its publication of a Hebrew Festschrift entitled *Migvan: Studies in Honor of Jacob Kabakoff.* He wrote *Seekers and Stalwarts: Essays on American Hebrew Literature and Culture* (1978) and edited *Master of Hope: Selected Writings of Naphtali Herz Imber* (1985).

[Eisig Silberschlag / Ruth Beloff (2nd ed.)]

KA'B AL-AḤBĀR (**Abū Isḥāq Ka'b al-Aḥbār** or "Ka'b of-the Jewish-doctors"; also **Ka'b al-Ḥabr**, "Ka'b the former Jewish doctor"; d. ca. 654), Jewish Yemenite convert to Islam from the tribe of Ḥimyar who lived in Ḥims (Homs). He was referred to as "the owner of the two books" (*dhūl-kitābayni*, i.e., the Koran and the Bible).

Some say that he converted to Islam in Muhammad's lifetime at the hands of the latter's cousin, ʿAli ibn Abī Ṭālib, while others say that he converted at the hands of the caliph Abu Bakr. But the most widespread version has it that he converted during the caliphate of *Omar ibn al-Khattab at the hands of Muhammad's uncle al-ʿAbbas, thus becoming the latter's *mawlā* or client. He is supposed to have been one of Omar ibn al-Khattab's closest advisors. Under ʿUthmān ibn ʿAffān Kaʿb was a salaried preacher (*qāṣās*). He allegedly legitimized for ʿUthmān the borrowing of money from the treasury, on which an opponent of this caliph commented by saying: "You son of two Jewish parents, will you teach us our religion?" A polemical account associates the recent convert Kaʿb with Jewish scholars: in a meeting that took place in Jerusalem, Kaʿb resorted to a book found in Daniel's tomb in Susa in order to convince 42 Jews to embrace Islam; the then governor of Syria and Palestine, Muʿāwiya ibn Abī Sufyān, later included them among those entitled to an annual pension from the treasury.

Kaʿb's reputation as an expert in "sacred books" was an asset for the rulers who employed him to convey messages in their favor and to combat opposition movements. Supposed quotations from the "Torah" or the "Tales about Prophets," in addition to eschatological traditions, were used to indoctrinate the masses in general and the warriors in particular. Kaʿb reportedly died on his way to an expedition against Byzantium; one assumes that he was a battlefield preacher rather than a warrior.

Widespread accounts describe Kaʿb as providing Omar with the background necessary for Islamizing the Temple Mounṭ. For example, he bribed a Jewish *ḥabr* or doctor to pinpoint the rock on which Solomon had stood upon the completion of the Temple (or "the mosque"). However, in several anecdotes Kaʿb is accused of an attempted "Judaization" of nascent Islam by combining the directions of prayer of Moses and Muhammad. He argued that while praying in Jerusalem in the direction of Mecca, a Muslim had to direct himself at the same time to the Rock. Omar established the correct Muslim direction by praying toward Mecca with his back to the Rock. It was another famous Jewish convert, Abdallah ibn Salam, who confirmed that this had been the original direction before it was changed by the Jews. Omar in turn declared Abdallah more truthful than Kaʿb.

BIBLIOGRAPHY: "Kaʿb," in: Ibn ʿAsākir, *Taʾrīkh madīnat Dimashq*, ed. L. al-ʿAmrawī, 151–76; B. Chapira, "Légendes bibliques attribuées a Kaʿb el-Ahbar," in: *Revue des Études Juives*, 69 (1919), 86–107; 70 (1920), 37–43; D.J. Halperin and G.D. Newby, "Two Castrated Bulls: A Study in the Haggadah of Kaʿb al-Aḥbār," in: JASOR, 102 (1982), 631–38; M. Perlmann, "A Legendary Story of Kaʿb al-Aḥbār's Conversion to Islam," in: *The Joshua Starr Memorial Volume* (1953), 85–99; idem, "Another Kaʿb al-Aḥbār Story," in: JQR, 45 (1954), 48–58; M. Schmitz, "Kaʿb al-Aḥbār," in: EIS, 2 (1927) 582b–583b; abridged version in: EIS² 4 (1978), 316–317 (includes bibliography).

[Michael Lecker (2nd ed.)]

KAʿB AL-ASHRAF (d. 625), poet and chief opponent of Muhammad at *Medina. A member of the *Naḍīr tribe or of mixed Arab-Jewish descent (his mother was a Naḍīr), Kaʿb espoused the cause of Judaism and composed verses against Muhammad and *Islam. He went to Mecca to incite the Quraysh tribe to fight against Muhammad and later lamented its defeat. His lament and other poetry are extant. On his return to Medina, he allegedly seduced Muslim women. Anxious for his death, Muhammad ibn Maslama led Muhammad's followers into enticing Kaʿb to leave his house one night on the pretext of plotting against the Prophet; they then assassinated Kaʿb. The poet was mourned by the Naḍīr, who were expelled from Medina one year after his death. The story is recorded in the eighth-century Arab history by Muhammad ibn Isḥāq, *Sīrat Rasūl Allah* (tr. by Guillaume, *The Life of Muhammad* (1955), 364–9); EIS² 4 (1978), 315 (incl. bibliography)..

BIBLIOGRAPHY: H.Z. Hirschberg, *Yisrael be-Arav* (1946), index; W.M. Watt, *Muhammad at Medina* (1956), 209f.; EIS, 2 pt. 1 (1927), 583.

KABBALAH (Heb. קַבָּלָה; "received (doctrine)," "tradition"). Today the term Kabbalah is used for the mystic and esoteric doctrine of Judaism (see following entry). The mystical connotation is unknown in the Talmud. In the Talmud the word occurs, however, in two other and entirely different senses. The first refers to the prophets and the Hagiographa as distinct from, and in contrast to, the Pentateuch. The other, especially in its verbal form *mekubbelani* ("I have received a *kabbalah*"), is used to indicate oral traditions handed down either from teacher to disciple, or as part of a family tradition.

The Talmud points out that the proof that Nisan is the first month of the year in the civil calendar (see *New Year) is derived from "the words of *kabbalah*," the reference being to Zechariah 1:7 (RH 7a), and that the Fast of Gedaliah was instituted in the *kabbalah (ibid.* 19a). Similarly, it points out that "the words of the Torah cannot be derived from words of *kabbalah*," the "words of *kabbalah*" being respectively from the Books of Kings and Amos (BK 2b., Ḥag. 10b), and in a passage of the Midrash a man protests that he is being sentenced to flogging on the strength of a verse from the *kabbalah* (Ezra 10:3), which has not the same force as a law in the Pentateuch (Gen. R. 7:2). Mishnah *Taʿanit* 2:1, however, quotes a verse from the Book of Jonah (3:10) and continues "and in the words of *kabbalah* it says," quoting Joel 2:13. It has been suggested that in this passage the word should here be read as "*kevalah*" ("protest") instead of "*kabbalah*."

In the sense of "oral tradition," the verbal form of the word is frequently found for a tradition going back to the earliest times: "I have a *kabbalah* from R. Meʾasha, who received it from his father, who received it from the *zugot, who received it from the prophets" (Peʾah 2:6); "So I have a *kabbalah* from Rabban Johanan b. Zakkai, who heard it from his teacher, who heard it from his teacher" (Ḥag. 3b). It is also used for traditions from the outstanding early authorities Shemaiah and Avtalyon (Pes. 66a) or from Shammai the Elder (Git. 57a). Family traditions are quoted as a *kabbalah* "from my father's house" (Ber. 10a, 34b), "from my ancestors" (Shab. 119b), and to emphasize a continuous tradition "from the house of my father's father" (BM 59b; BB 110a; Sanh. 89a). From the Middle Ages the word *kabbalah* has been used for the certificate of competence issued by a rabbi for a *shoḥet*.

BIBLIOGRAPHY: W. Bacher, *Die exegetische Terminologie der juedischen Traditionsliteratur*, 1 (1905), 165f.; C. Tchernowitz, *Toledot ha-Halakhah*, 1 pts. 1–2 (1934–36), index S.V. *Kabbalah, Torah she-be-al Peh*.

KABBALAH.

This entry is arranged according to the following outline:

INTRODUCTION

General Notes

Kabbalah is the traditional and most commonly used term for the esoteric teachings of Judaism and for Jewish mysticism, especially the forms which it assumed in the Middle Ages from the 12th century onward. In its wider sense it signifies all the successive esoteric movements in Judaism that evolved from the end of the period of the Second Temple and became active factors in the history of Israel.

Kabbalah is a unique phenomenon, and should not generally be equated with what is known in the history of religion as "mysticism." It is mysticism in fact; but at the same time it is both esotericism and theosophy. In what sense it may be called mysticism depends on the definition of the term, a matter of dispute among scholars. If the term is restricted to the profound yearning for direct human communion with God through annihilation of individuality (*bittul ha-yesh* in ḥasidic terminology), then only a few manifestations of Kabbalah can be designated as such, because few kabbalists sought this goal, let alone formulated it openly as their final aim. However, Kabbalah may be considered mysticism in so far as it seeks an apprehension of God and creation whose intrinsic elements are beyond the grasp of the intellect, although this is seldom explicitly belittled or rejected by the Kabbalah. Essentially, these elements were perceived through contemplation and illumination, which is often presented in the Kabbalah as the transmission of a primeval revelation concerning the nature of the Torah and other religious matters. In essence, the Kabbalah is far removed from the rational and intellectual approach to religion. This was the case even among those kabbalists who thought that basically religion was subject to rational enquiry, or that, at least, there was some accord between the path of intellectual perception and the development of the mystical approach to the subject of creation. For some kabbalists the intellect itself became a mystical phenomenon. So we find in Kabbalah a paradoxical emphasis on the congruence between intuition and tradition. It is this emphasis, together with the historical association already hinted at in the term "kabbalah" (something handed down by tradition), that points to the basic differences between the Kabbalah and other kinds of religious mysticism which are less closely identified with a people's history. Nevertheless, there are elements common to Kabbalah and both Greek and Christian mysticism, and even historical links between them.

Like other kinds of mysticism, Kabbalah too draws upon the mystic's awareness of both the transcendence of God and His immanence within the true religious life, every facet of which is a revelation of God, although God Himself is most clearly perceived through man's introspection. This dual and apparently contradictory experience of the self-concealing and self-revealing God determines the essential sphere of mysticism, while at the same time it obstructs other religious conceptions. The second element in Kabbalah is that of theosophy, which seeks to reveal the mysteries of the hidden life of God and the relationships between the divine life on the one hand and the life of man and creation on the other. Speculations of this type occupy a large and conspicuous area in kabbalistic teaching. Sometimes their connection with the mystical plane becomes rather tenuous and is superseded by an interpretative and homiletical vein which occasionally even results in a kind of kabbalistic *pilpul*.

In its form the Kabbalah became to a large extent an esoteric doctrine. Mystical and esoteric elements coexist in Kabbalah in a highly confused fashion. By its very nature, mysticism is knowledge that cannot be communicated directly but may be expressed only through symbol and metaphor. Esoteric knowledge, however, in theory can be transmitted, but those who possess it are either forbidden to pass it on or do not wish to do so. The kabbalists stressed this esoteric aspect by imposing all kinds of limitations on the propagation of their teachings, either with regard to the age of the initiates, the ethical qualities required of them, or the number of students before whom these teachings could be expounded. Typical of this is the account of the conditions for initiates in Kabbalah found in Moses *Cordovero's *Or Ne'erav*. Often these limitations were disregarded in practice, despite the protests of many kabbalists. The printing of kabbalistic books and the influence of Kabbalah on widening circles broke down such restrictions, especially as far as the teachings on God and man were concerned. Nevertheless, there remained areas where these limitations were still more or less adhered to; for example, in the meditations on the letter-combinations (*ḥokhmat ha-ẓeruf*) and practical Kabbalah.

Many kabbalists denied the existence of any kind of historical development in the Kabbalah. They saw it as a kind of primordial revelation that was accorded to Adam or the early generations and that endured, although new revelations were made from time to time, particularly when the tradition had been either forgotten or interrupted. This notion of the nature of esoteric wisdom was expressed in apocryphal works like the Book of Enoch, was again stressed in the *Zohar, and served as the basis for the dissemination of kabbalistic teaching in *Sefer ha-Emunot* by *Shem Tov b. Shem Tov (c. 1400) and in *Avodat ha-Kodesh* by *Meir b. Gabbai (1567). It became widely accepted that the Kabbalah was the esoteric part of the Oral Law given to Moses at Sinai. Several of the genealogies of the tradition appearing in kabbalistic literature, which were intended to support the idea of the continuity of the secret tradition, are themselves faulty and misconceived, lacking in any historical value. In actual fact, some kabbalists themselves give concrete instances of the historical development of their ideas, since they regard them either as having deteriorated to some extent from the original tradition, which found its expression in the increase of kabbalistic systems, or as part of a gradual progress toward the complete revelation of the secret wisdom. Kabbalists themselves rarely attempt to attain a historical orientation, but some examples of such an approach may be found in *Emunat Ḥakhamim* by Solomon Avi'ad Sar-Shalom *Basilea (1730), and in *Divrei Soferim* by *Zadok ha-Kohen of Lublin (1913).

From the beginning of its development, the Kabbalah embraced an esotericism closely akin to the spirit of Gnosticism, one which was not restricted to instruction in the mystical path but also included ideas on cosmology, angelology, and magic. Only later, and as a result of the contact with medieval Jewish philosophy, the Kabbalah became a Jewish "mystical theology," more or less systematically elaborated. This process brought about a separation of the mystical, speculative elements from the occult and especially the magical elements, a divergence that at times was quite distinct but was never total. It is expressed in the separate usage of the terms *Kabbalah iyyunit* ("speculative Kabbalah") and *Kabbalah ma'asit* ("practical Kabbalah"), evident from the beginning of the 14th century – which was simply an imitation of *Maimonides' division of philosophy into "speculative" and "practical" in chapter 14 of his *Millot ha-Higgayon*. There is no doubt that some kabbalistic circles (including those in Jerusalem up to modern times) preserved both elements in their secret doctrine, which could be acquired by means of revelation or by way of initiation rites.

Once rabbinic Judaism had crystallized in the *halakhah*, the majority of the creative forces aroused by new religious stimuli, which neither tended nor had the power to change the outward form of a firmly established halakhic Judaism, found expression in the kabbalistic movement. Generally speaking, these forces worked internally, attempting to make of the traditional Torah and of the life led according to its dictates a more profound inner experience. The general tendency is apparent from a very early date, its purpose being to broaden the dimensions of the Torah and to transform it from the law of the people of Israel into the inner secret law of the universe, at the same time transforming the Jewish *ḥasid* or *ẓaddik* into a man with a vital role in the world. The kabbalists were the main symbolists of rabbinic Judaism. For Kabbalah, Judaism in all its aspects was a system of mystical symbols reflecting the mystery of God and the universe, and the kabbalists' aim was to discover and invent keys to the understanding of this symbolism. To this aim is due the enormous influence of the Kabbalah as a historical force, which determined the face of Judaism for many centuries, but it too can explain the perils, upheavals, and contradictions, both internal and external, which the realization of this aim brought in its wake.

Terms Used For Kabbalah

At first the word "kabbalah" did not especially denote a mystical or esoteric tradition. In the Talmud it is used for the extra-Pentateuchal parts of the Bible, and in post-talmudic literature the Oral Law is also called "kabbalah." In the writings of *Eleazar of Worms (beginning of the 13th century) esoteric traditions (concerning the names of the angels and the magical Names of God) are referred to as "kabbalah," e.g., in his *Hilkhot ha-Kisse* (in *Merkabah Shelemah*, 1921), and *Sefer ha-Shem*. In his commentary to the Sefer *Yeẓirah (c. 1130), when he is discussing the creation of the Holy Spirit, i.e., the *Shekhinah*, *Judah b. Barzillai states that the sages "used to transmit statements of this kind to their students and to sages privately, in a whisper, through kabbalah." All this demonstrates that the term "kabbalah" was not yet used for any one particular field. The new, precise usage originated in the circle of *Isaac the Blind (1200) and was adopted by all his disciples.

Kabbalah is only one of the many terms used, during a period of more than 1,500 years, to designate the mystical movement, its teaching, or its adherents. The Talmud speaks of *sitrei torah* and *razei torah* ("secrets of the Torah"), and parts of the secret tradition are called *ma'aseh bereshit* (literally, "the work of creation") and *ma'aseh merkabah* ("the work of the chariot"). At least one of the mystical groups called itself *yoredei merkabah* ("those who descend to the chariot"), an extraordinary expression whose meaning eludes us (perhaps it means those who reach down into themselves in order to perceive the chariot?). In the mystical literature from the close of the talmudic period and afterward, the terms *ba'alei ha-sod* ("masters of the mystery") and *anshei emunah* ("men of belief") already occur, and the latter also appears as early as the Slavonic Book of Enoch. In the period of the Provençal and Spanish kabbalists the Kabbalah is also called *ḥokhmah penimit* ("inner wisdom"), perhaps a phrase borrowed from Arabic, and the kabbalists are often called *maskilim* ("the understanding ones"), with reference to Daniel 12:10, or *doreshei reshumot* ("those who interpret texts"), a talmudic expression for allegorists. In the same way as the word Kabbalah came to be restricted in meaning to the mystical or esoteric tradition, so, at the beginning of the 13th century, the words *emet* ("truth"), *emunah* ("faith"), and *ḥokhmah* ("wisdom") were used to designate the mystical or inner truth. Hence the widespread use of *ḥokhmat ha-emet* ("the science of truth") and *derekh ha-emet* ("the way of truth"). There is also found the expression *ḥakhmei lev* ("the wise-hearted"), after Exodus 28:3. The kabbalists are also called *ba'alei ha-yedi'ah* ("the masters of knowledge" – Gnostics) or *ha-yode'im* ("those who know") beginning with *Naḥmanides. Naḥmanides also coined the phrase *yode'ei ḥen* ("those who know grace"), after Ecclesiastes 9:11, where *ḥen* is used as an abbreviation for *ḥokhmah nistarah* ("secret wisdom"). The author of the Zohar uses terms such as *benei meheimnuta* ("children of faith"), *benei heikhala de-malka* ("children of the king's palace"), *yade'ei ḥokhmeta* ("those who know wisdom"), *yade'ei middin* ("those who know measures"), *meḥaẓdei ḥakla* ("those who reap the field"), and *inon de-allu u-nefaku* ("those who entered and left in peace"), after *Ḥagigah* 14b. Several authors call the kabbalists *ba'alei ha-avodah* ("masters of service"), i.e., those who know the true, inner way to the service of God. In the main part of the Zohar the term Kabbalah is not mentioned, but it is used in the later strata, in the *Ra'aya Meheimna* and the *Sefer ha-Tikkunim*. From the beginning of the 14th century the name Kabbalah almost completely superseded all other designations.

THE HISTORICAL DEVELOPMENT OF THE KABBALAH

The Early Beginnings of Mysticism and Esotericism

The development of the Kabbalah has its sources in the esoteric and theosophical currents existing among the Jews of Palestine and Egypt in the era which saw the birth of Christianity. These currents are linked with the history of Hellenistic and syncretistic religion at the close of antiquity. Scholars disagree on the measure of the influence exerted by such trends, and also by Persian religion, on the early forms of Jewish mysticism. Some stress the Iranian influence on the general development of Judaism during the period of the Second Temple, and particularly on certain movements such as the Jewish apocalyptic, a view supported by many experts on the different forms of Gnosticism, like R. Reitzenstein and G. Widengren. That there was an extensive degree of Greek influence on these currents is maintained by a number of scholars, and various theories have been adduced to explain this. Many specialists in the Gnosticism of the first three centuries of the common era see it as basically a Greek or Hellenistic phenomenon, certain aspects of which appeared in Jewish circles, particularly in those sects on the fringes of rabbinic Judaism – *ha-minim*. The position of *Philo of Alexandria and his relationship with Palestinian Judaism is of special weight in these controversies. In contrast to scholars like Harry Wolfson who see Philo as fundamentally a Greek philosopher in Jewish garb, others, like Hans Lewy and Erwin Goodenough, interpret him as a theosophist or even a mystic. Philo's work, they believe, should be seen as an attempt to explain the faith of Israel in terms of Hellenistic mysticism, whose crowning glory was ecstatic rapture. In his monumental book, *Jewish Symbols in the Greco-Roman Period* (13 vols. 1953–68), Goodenough maintains that, in contrast to Palestinian Judaism which found expression in *halakhah* and *aggadah* and in the esoteric ideas which were indigenous developments, Diaspora Judaism showed little evidence of Palestinian influence. Instead, he avers, it had a specific spirituality based on a symbolism which is not rooted solely in the *halakhah*, but which is endowed with an imaginative content of a more or less mystical significance. He believes that the literary evidence, such as the writings of Philo and Hellenistic Judaism, provides extremely useful keys to an understanding of the archaeological and pictorial documentation which he has assembled in such abundance. Although considerable doubt has been cast on Goodenough's basic theories there is sufficient material in his great work to stimulate investigation into previously neglected aspects of Judaism and into evidence which has been insufficiently examined. His argument on the basically mystical significance of the pictorial symbols cannot be accepted, but he did succeed in establishing a link between certain literary evidence extant in Greek, Coptic, Armenian, and esoteric teachings prevalent in Palestinian Judaism. A similar link between Philonic ideas and the viewpoint of the *aggadah*, including the *aggadah* of the mystics, was also suggested by Yitzḥak Baer (*Zion*, 23–24 (1958/59), 33–34, 141–65). Philo's book *De Vita Contemplativa* (*About the Contemplative Life*, 1895) mentions the existence of a sectarian community of "worshipers of God," who had already formulated a definitely mystical understanding of the Torah as a living body, and this paved the way for a mystical exegesis of Scripture.

An important element common to both Alexandrian and Palestinian Judaism is the speculation on Divine Wisdom which has its scriptural roots in Proverbs 8 and Job 28. Here Wisdom is seen as an intermediary force by means of which God creates the world. This appears in the apocryphal Wisdom of Solomon (7:25) as "a breath of the power of God, and a clear effluence of the glory of the Almighty… For she is an effulgence from everlasting light, And an unspotted mirror of the working of God, And an image of His goodness" (Charles). In the Slavonic Book of Enoch God commands His Wisdom to create man. Wisdom is here the first attribute of God to be given concrete form as an emanation from the Divine Glory. In many circles this Wisdom soon became the Torah itself, the "word of God," the form of expression of the Divine Power. Such views of the mystery of Wisdom demonstrate how parallel development could take place, on the one hand through rabbinic exegesis of the words of Scripture, and on the other through the influence of Greek philosophical speculations on the Logos. It should be noted that there is no definite proof that Philo's writings had an actual direct influence on rabbinic Judaism in the post-tannaitic period, and the attempt to prove that the *Midrash ha-Ne'lam* of the Zohar is nothing but a Hellenistic Midrash (S. Belkin, in: *Sura*, 3 (1958), 25–92) is a failure. However, the fact that the Karaite *Kirkisānī (tenth century) was familiar with certain quotations drawn from Philonic writings shows that some of his ideas found their way, perhaps through Christian-Arab channels, to members of Jewish sects in the Near East. But it should not be deduced from this that there was a continuous influence up to this time, let alone up to the time of the formulation of the Kabbalah in the Middle Ages. Specific parallels between Philonic and kabbalistic exegesis should be put down to the similarity of their exegetical method, which naturally produced identical results from time to time (see S. Poznański, in REJ, 50 (1905), 10–31).

The theories concerning Persian and Greek influences tend to overlook the inner dynamism of the development taking place within Palestinian Judaism, which was in itself capable of producing movements of a mystical and esoteric nature. This kind of development can also be seen in those circles whose historical influence was crucial and decisive for the future of Judaism, e.g., among the Pharisees, the *tannaim* and *amoraim*, that is to say, at the very heart of established rabbinic Judaism. In addition, there were similar tendencies in other spheres outside the mainstream, in the various currents whose influence on subsequent Judaism is a matter of controversy: the *Essenes, the *Qumran sect (if these two are not one and the same), and the different Gnostic sects on the periphery of Judaism whose existence is attested to by the writings of the *Church Fathers. Some have sought to demonstrate the existence of mystical trends even in biblical times (Hertz,

Horodezky, Lindblom, Montefiore), but it is almost certain that the phenomena which they connected with mysticism, like prophecy and the piety of certain psalms, belong to other strands in the history of religion. Historically speaking, organized closed societies of mystics have been proved to exist only since the end of the Second Temple era; this is clearly attested to by the struggle taking place in this period between different religious forces, and by the tendency then current to delve more deeply into original religious speculation.

Apocalyptic Esotericism and Merkabah Mysticism

Chronologically speaking, it is in apocalyptic literature that we find the first appearance of ideas of a specifically mystical character, reserved for the elect. Scholars do not agree on whether the origins of this literature are to be found among the Pharisees and their disciples or among the Essenes, and it is quite possible that apocalyptic tendencies appeared in both. It is known from Josephus that the Essenes possessed literature which was both magical and angelological in content. His silence concerning their apocalyptic ideas can be understood as his desire to conceal this aspect of contemporary Judaism from his gentile readers. The discovery of the literary remains of the Qumran sect shows that such ideas found a haven among them. They possessed the original Book of Enoch, both in Hebrew and Aramaic, although it is quite likely that it was composed in the period preceding the split between the Pharisees and the members of the Qumran sect. In fact, traditions resembling those embedded in the Book of Enoch found their way into rabbinic Judaism at the time of the *tannaim* and *amoraim*, and it is impossible to determine precisely the breeding ground of this type of tradition until the problems presented by the discovery of the Qumran writings have been solved. The Book of Enoch was followed by apocalyptic writing up to the time of the *tannaim*, and, in different ways, after this period also. Esoteric knowledge in these books touched not only upon the revelation of the end of time and its awesome terrors, but also upon the structure of the hidden world and its inhabitants: heaven, the Garden of Eden, and Gehinnom, angels and evil spirits, and the fate of the souls in this hidden world. Above this are revelations concerning the Throne of Glory and its Occupant, which should apparently be identified with "the wonderful secrets" of God mentioned by the *Dead Sea Scrolls. Here a link can be established between this literature and the much later traditions concerning the *ma'aseh bereshit* and the *ma'aseh merkabah*.

It is not just the content of these ideas which is considered esoteric; their authors too hid their own individuality and their names, concealing themselves behind biblical characters like Enoch, Noah, Abraham, Moses, Baruch, Daniel, Ezra, and others. This self-concealment, which was completely successful, has made it extremely difficult for us to determine the historical and social conditions of the authors. This pseudepigraphical pattern continued within the mystical tradition in the centuries that followed. The clear tendency toward asceticism as a way of preparing for the reception of the mystical tradition, which is already attested to in the last chapter of the Book of Enoch, becomes a fundamental principle for the apocalyptics, the Essenes, and the circle of the Merkabah mystics who succeeded them. From the start, this pietist asceticism aroused active opposition entailing abuse and persecution, which later characterized practically the whole historical development of pietist tendencies (*ḥasidut*) in rabbinic Judaism.

The mysteries of the Throne constitute here a particularly exalted subject which to a large extent set the pattern for the early forms of Jewish mysticism. It did not aspire to an understanding of the true nature of God, but to a perception of the phenomenon of the Throne on its Chariot as it is described in the first chapter of Ezekiel, traditionally entitled *ma'aseh merkabah*. The mysteries of the world of the Throne, together with those of the Divine Glory which is revealed there, are the parallels in Jewish esoteric tradition to the revelations on the realm of the divine in Gnosticism. The 14th chapter of the Book of Enoch, which contains the earliest example of this kind of literary description, was the source of a long visionary tradition of describing the world of the Throne and the visionary ascent to it, which we find portrayed in the books of the Merkabah mystics. In addition to interpretations, visions, and speculations based on the *ma'aseh merkabah*, other esoteric traditions began to crystallize round the first chapter of Genesis, which was called *ma'aseh bereshit*. These two terms were subsequently used to describe those subjects dealing with these topics. Both Mishnah and Talmud (Ḥag. 2:1 and the corresponding *Gemara* in both the Babylonian and Jerusalem Talmud) show that, in the first century of the common era, esoteric traditions existed within these areas, and severe limitations were placed on public discussion of such subjects: "The story of creation should not be expounded before two persons, nor the chapter on the Chariot before one person, unless he is a sage and already has an independent understanding of the matter." Evidence concerning the involvement of *Johanan b. Zakkai and his disciples in this sort of exposition proves that this esotericism could grow in the very center of a developing rabbinic Judaism, and that consequently this Judaism had a particular esoteric aspect from its very beginning. On the other hand, it is possible that the rise of Gnostic speculations, which were not accepted by the rabbis, made many of them tread very warily and adopt a polemical attitude. Such an attitude is expressed in the continuation of the Mishnah quoted above: "Whoever ponders on four things, it were better for him if he had not come into the world: what is above, what is below, what was before time, and what will be hereafter." Here we have a prohibition against the very speculations which are characteristic of Gnosticism as it is defined in "Excerpts from the writings of [the Gnostic] Theodotus" (*Extraits de Théodote*, ed. F. Sagnard (1948), para. 78). In actual fact, this prohibition was largely ignored, as far as can be judged from the many statements of *tannaim* and *amoraim* dealing with these matters which are scattered throughout the Talmud and the Midrashim.

In an age of spiritual awakening and deep religious turmoil there arose in Judaism a number of sects with heterodox ideas resulting from a mixture of inner compulsion and outside influence. Whether Gnostic sects existed on the periphery of Judaism before the coming of Christianity is a matter of controversy (see below); but there is no doubt that *minim* ("heretics") did exist in the tannaitic period and especially in the third and fourth centuries. In this period a Jewish Gnostic sect with definite antinomian tendencies was active in Sepphoris. There were also of course intermediate groups from which members of these sects gained an extended knowledge of theological material on *ma'aseh bereshit* and *ma'aseh merkabah*, and among these should be included the Ophites (snake worshipers) who were basically Jewish rather than Christian. From this source a considerable number of esoteric traditions were transmitted to Gnostics outside Judaism, whose books, many of which have been discovered in our own time, are full of such material – found not only in Greek and Coptic texts of the second and third centuries but also in the early strata of Mandaic literature, which is written in colloquial Aramaic. Notwithstanding all the deep differences in theological approach, the growth of Merkabah mysticism among the rabbis constitutes an inner Jewish concomitant to Gnosis, and it may be termed "Jewish and rabbinic Gnosticism."

Within these circles theosophical ideas and revelations connected with them branched out in many directions, so that it is impossible to speak here of one single system. A particular mystical terminology was also established. Some of it is reflected in the sources of "normal" Midrashim, while part is confined to the literary sources of the mystics: the literature of the *heikhalot* and the *ma'aseh bereshit*. Verbs like *histakkel, ẓafah, iyyen*, and *higgi'a* have specific meanings, as do nouns like *ha-kavod, ha-kavod ha-gadol, ha-kavod ha-nistar, mara di-revuta, yoẓer bereshit, heikhalot, ḥadrei merkabah*, and others. Particularly important is the established usage of the term *Kavod* ("glory") as a name both for God when He is the object of profound mystical enquiry and also for the general area of theosophical research. This term acquires a specific meaning, distinct from its scriptural usage, as early as the Book of Tobit and the end of the Book of Enoch, and it continues to be used in this way in apocalyptic literature. In contrast, the use of the word *sod* ("mystery") in this context was relatively rare, becoming general only in the Middle Ages, whereas *raz* ("secret") is used more often in the earlier texts.

Merkabah terminology is found in a hymn-fragment in the Dead Sea Scrolls, where the angels praise "the image of the Throne of the Chariot" (Strugnell). Members of the sect combined ideas concerning the song of the angels, who stand before the Chariot, with other ideas about the names and duties of the angels, and all this is common to the sect of Qumran and to later traditions of the *ma'aseh merkabah*. From the very beginning these traditions were surrounded by an aura of particular sanctity. Talmudic *aggadah* connects exposition of the Merkabah with the descent of fire from above which surrounds the expositor. In the literature of the *heikhalot* other and more daring expressions are used to describe the emotional and ecstatic character of these experiences. Distinct from the exposition of the Merkabah which the rabbis gave while on earth below was the ecstatic contemplation of the Merkabah experienced as an ascent to the heavens, namely descent to the Merkabah, through entering *pardes* ("paradise"). This was not a matter for exposition and interpretation but of vision and personal experience. This transition, which once again connects the revelations of the Merkabah with the apocalyptic tradition, is mentioned in the Talmud alongside the exegetic traditions (Ḥag. 14b). It concerns the four sages who "entered *pardes*." Their fate demonstrates that here we are dealing with spiritual experiences which were achieved by contemplation and ecstasy. *Simeon b. Azzai "looked and died"; *Ben Zoma "looked and was smitten" (mentally); *Elisha b. Avuyah, called *aḥer* ("other"), forsook rabbinic Judaism and "cut the shoots," apparently becoming a dualistic Gnostic; R. *Akiva alone "entered in peace and left in peace," or, in another reading, "ascended in peace and descended in peace." So R. Akiva, a central figure in the world of Judaism, is also the legitimate representative of a mysticism within the boundaries of rabbinic Judaism. This is apparently why Akiva and *Ishmael, who was his companion and also his adversary in halakhic matters, served as the central pillars and chief mouthpieces in the later pseudepigraphic literature devoted to the mysteries of the Merkabah. In addition, the striking halakhic character of this literature shows that its authors were well rooted in the halakhic tradition and far from holding heterodox opinions.

In mystic circles particular conditions were laid down for the entry of those fit to be initiated into the doctrines and activities bound up with these fields. The basic teachings were communicated in a whisper (Ḥag. 13b; *Bereshit Rabbah*, Theodor-Albeck edition (1965), 19–20). The earliest conditions governing the choice of those suitable were of two types. In the *Gemara* (Ḥag. 13b) basically intellectual conditions were formulated, as well as age limits ("at life's half-way stage"); and in the beginning of *Heikhalot Rabbati* certain ethical qualities required of the initiate are enumerated. In addition to this, from the third and fourth centuries, according to Sherira Gaon (*Oẓar ha-Ge'onim* to *Ḥagigah* (1931), *Teshuvot*, no. 12, p. 8), they used external methods of appraisal based on physiognomy and chiromancy (*hakkarat panim ve-sidrei sirtutin*). *Seder Eliyahu Rabbah*, chapter 29, quotes an Aramaic *baraita* from the Merkabah mystics concerning physiognomy. A fragment of a similar *baraita*, written in Hebrew in the name of R. Ishmael, has been preserved, and there is no doubt that it was a part of Merkabah literature. Its style and content prove its early date (see G. Scholem in *Sefer Assaf* (1953), 459–95; the text itself is translated into German in *Liber Amicorum*, in honor of Professor C.J. Bleeker, 1969, 175–93).

Esoteric Literature: the *Heikhalot*, the *Ma'aseh Bereshit*, and the Literature of Magic

This literature occupies an extremely important place in the development of esotericism and mysticism. It is connected at innumerable points with traditions outside its boundaries, in the Talmuds and Midrashim, and these traditions sometimes explain each other. In addition, esoteric literature contains a wealth of material that is found nowhere else. Many scholars, including Zunz, Graetz, and P. Bloch, have tried to show that a vast distance, both in time and subject matter, separates the early Merkabah ideas from those embedded in Talmud and Midrash, and they ascribed the composition of Merkabah literature to the geonic era. Even though it is quite possible that some of the texts were not edited until this period, there is no doubt that large sections originated in talmudic times, and that the central ideas, as well as many details, go back as far as the first and second centuries. Many of the texts are short, and in various manuscripts there is a considerable amount of basic material quite devoid of any literary embellishment. (For a list of the books belonging to this literature see *Merkabah Mysticism.) Of great importance are the texts entitled *Heikhalot Rabbati*, whose main speaker is R. Ishmael; *Heikhalot Zutrati*, whose main speaker is R. Akiva; and the *Sefer Heikhalot*, which has been published under the name of the Third Book of Enoch or the Hebrew Enoch. The traditions assembled here are not all of the same kind, and they indicate different tendencies among the mystics. We find here extremely detailed descriptions of the world of the Chariot, of the ecstatic ascent to that world, and of the technique used to accomplish this ascent. As in non-Jewish Gnostic literature, there is a magical and theurgic aspect to the technique of ascent, and there are very strong connections between Merkabah literature and Hebrew and Aramaic theurgic literature from both this and the geonic period. The earliest stratum of the *heikhalot* strongly emphasizes this magical side, which in the practical application of its teachings is linked to the attainment of the "contemplation of the Chariot." It is very similar to a number of important texts preserved among the Greek magic papyri and to Gnostic literature of the *Pistis Sophia* type which originated in the second or third century C.E.

The *heikhalot* books mentioned above refer to historical figures, whose connection with the mysteries of the Chariot is attested by Talmud and Midrash. On the other hand, there also existed early sources containing traditions attributed to various *tannaim* and *amoraim*; as some of them are almost or completely unknown, there would have been no point in appending their names to pseudepigraphical writings. In the Cairo *Genizah* a few fragments of a tannaitic Midrash on the Chariot were discovered (Ms. Sassoon 522), and the short fourth-century text *Re'iyyot Yeḥezkel* belongs to the same category. It could be inferred from this that the mystics did not always try to conceal their identities, although in most cases they were inclined to do so. The ascent to the Chariot (which in the *Heikhalot Rabbati* is deliberately called "descent") comes after a number of preparatory exercises of an extremely ascetic nature. The aspirant placed his head between his knees, a physical positon which facilitates changes in consciousness and self-hypnosis. At the same time, he recited hymns of an ecstatic character, the texts of which are extant in several sources, particularly in the *Heikhalot Rabbati*. These poems, some of the earliest *piyyutim* known to us, indicate that "Chariot hymns" like these were known in Palestine as early as the third century. Some of them purport to be the songs of the holy creatures (*ḥayyot*) who bear the Throne of Glory, and whose singing is already mentioned in apocalyptic literature. The poems have their own specific style which corresponds to the spirit of "celestial liturgy," and they have a linguistic affinity with similar liturgical fragments in the writings of the Qumran sect. Almost all of them conclude with the *kedushah* ("sanctification") of Isaiah 6:3, which is used as a fixed refrain. *Isaac Nappaḥa, a third-century Palestinian *amora*, puts a similar poem in the mouth of the kine who bore the Ark of the Covenant (I Sam. 6:12), in his interpretation of "And the kine took the straight way" (*va-yisharnah*, interpreted as "they sang"; Av. Zar. 24b), for he sees a parallel between the kine who bear the ark singing and the holy creatures who bear the Throne of Glory with a glorious festive song. These hymns clearly show their authors' concept of God. He is the holy King, surrounded by "majesty, fear, and awe" in "the palaces of silence." Sovereignty, majesty, and holiness are His most striking attributes. He is not a God Who is near but a God Who is afar, far removed from the area of man's comprehension, even though His hidden glory may be revealed to man from the Throne. The Merkabah mystics occupy themselves with all the details of the upper world, which extends throughout the seven palaces in the firmament of *aravot* (the uppermost of the seven firmaments); with the angelic hosts which fill the palaces (*heikhalot*); the rivers of fire which flow down in front of the Chariot, and the bridges which cross them; the *ofan* and *ḥashmal*; and with all the other details of the Chariot. But the main purpose of the ascent is the vision of the One Who sits on the Throne, "a likeness as the appearance of a man upon it above" (Ezek. 1:26). This appearance of the Glory in the form of supernal man is the content of the most recondite part of this mysticism, called **Shi'ur Komah* ("measure of the body").

The teaching on the "measure of the body" of the Creator constitutes a great enigma. Fragments of it appear in several passages in the *ma'aseh merkabah* literature, and there is one particularly long section which has come down separately (an early *genizah* Ms. Oxford, Bodleian Library, Ms. Heb., c. 65). Such passages enumerate the fantastic measurements of parts of the head as well as some of the limbs. They also transmit "the secret names" of these limbs, all of them unintelligible letter combinations. Different versions of the numbers and the letter combinations have survived and so they cannot be relied upon, and, all in all, their purpose (whether literal or symbolic) is not clear to us. However, the verse which holds the key to the enumeration is Psalms 147:5: "Great is Our Lord, and mighty in power," which is taken to mean that the extent of the body or of the measurement of "Our Lord" is alluded to in the words *ve-rav ko'aḥ* ("and mighty in power") which in *gematria* amount to 236. This number (236 × 10,000 leagues, and, moreover, not terrestrial but celestial leagues) is the basic measurement on which all the calculations are based. It is not clear whether there is a relationship between speculations on "the greatness of the Lord of the world" and the title *mara di-revuta* ("Lord of greatness") which is one of the predications of God found in the Genesis Apocryphon (p. 2, line 4). The terms *gedullah* ("greatness"; e.g., in the phrase "*ofan* [wheel] of greatness") and *gevurah* ("might") occur as names for God in several texts of the Merkabah mystics. We should not dismiss the possibility of a continuous flow of specific ideas from the Qumran sect to the Merkabah mystics and rabbinic circles in the case of the *Shi'ur Komah* as well as in other fields. The paradox is that the vision of the *Shi'ur Komah* is actually hidden "from the sight of every creature, and concealed from the ministering angels," but "it was revealed to R. Akiva in the *ma'aseh merkabah*" (*Heikhalot Zutrati*). The mystic, therefore, grasps a secret which even the angels cannot comprehend.

The provocative anthropomorphism of these passages perplexed many rabbis, and was the object of attacks by the Karaites – so much so that even Maimonides, who at first regarded the *Shi'ur Komah* as an authoritative work requiring interpretation (in his original Ms. of his commentary to the Mishnah, Sanh. 10), later repudiated it, believing it to be a late forgery (*Teshuvot ha-Rambam* (1934), no. 117). In fact, as G. *Scholem and S. *Lieberman have demonstrated, the *Shi'ur Komah* was an early and genuine part of mystic teaching in the days of the *tanna'im*. The theory does not imply that God in Himself possesses a physical form, but only that a form of this kind may be ascribed to "the Glory," which in some passages is called *guf ha-Shekhinah* ("the body of the Divine Presence"). *Shi'ur Komah* is based on the descriptions of the beloved in Song of Songs (5:11–16), and it apparently became a part of the esoteric interpretation of this book. The early date of the *Shi'ur Komah* is attested by allusions to it in the Slavonic Book of Enoch, chapter 13 (ed. Vaillant (1952), p. 39), which still reflects the Hebrew terminology in its translation. Similarly, the Gnostic teaching of Markos (second century), on "the body of the truth" is a spiritualized Gnostic version of the *Shi'ur Komah*. Perhaps the idea of the "tunic" and garment of God also belonged to the *Shi'ur Komah*. This "tunic" is of great significance in the *ma'aseh bereshit* of the *Heikhalot Rabbati*, and echoes of this idea can be found in the rabbinic *aggadot* concerning the garment of light in which the Holy One, blessed be He, wrapped himself at the moment of creation.

The ascent and passage through the first six palaces are described at length in the *Heikhalot Rabbati*, with details of all the technical and magical means which assist the ascending spirit and save it from the dangers lying in wait for it. These dangers were given much emphasis in all Merkabah traditions. Empty visions meet the ascending soul and angels of destruction try to confound it. At the gates of all the palaces it must show the doorkeepers "the seals," which are the secret Names of God, or pictures imbued with a magical power (some of which are extant in the Gnostic *Pistis Sophia*), which protect it from attack. The dangers especially increase in number at the entrance to the sixth palace where it appears to the Merkabah mystic as if "one hundred million waves pour down, and yet there is not one drop of water there, only the splendor of the pure marble stones which pave the palace." It is to this danger in the ecstatic ascent that the words of R. Akiva refer in the story of the four who entered *pardes*: "when you come to the place of the pure marble stones, do not say 'water, water.'" The texts also mention a "fire which proceeds from his own body and consumes it." Sometimes the fire is seen as a danger (*Merkabah Shelemah* (1921), 1b) and at other times as an ecstatic experience which accompanies the entry into the first palace: "My hands were burned, and I stood without hands or feet" (Ms. Neubauer, Oxford 1531, 45b). The *pardes* which R. Akiva and his companions entered is the world of the celestial Garden of Eden or the realm of the heavenly palaces and the ascent or "rapture" is common to several Jewish apocalypses, and is mentioned by Paul (II Cor. 12:2–4) as something which needs no explanation for his readers of Jewish origin. In contrast to the dangers which attend those who, although unfit for them, indulge in these matters and in the magical science of theurgy, great emphasis is laid on the illumination which comes to the recipients of the revelations: "There was light in my heart like lightning," or "the world changed into purity around me, and my heart felt as if I had entered a new world" (*Merkabah Shelemah* 1a, 4b).

An early passage enumerating the basic subjects of the mystery of the Chariot is to be found in the Midrash to Proverbs 10, and, in a different version, in R. *Azriel's *Perush ha-Aggadot* (ed. Tishby (1945), 62). The subjects mentioned are the *ḥashmal*, the lightning, the cherub, the Throne of Glory, the bridges in the Merkabah, and the measurement of the limbs "from my toenails to the top of my head." Other subjects which are of great importance in a number of sources are not mentioned. Among these are ideas concerning the *pargod* ("curtain" or "veil") which separates the One Who sits on the Throne from the other parts of the Chariot, and upon which are embroidered the archetypes of everything that is created. There are different, highly colored traditions concerning the *pargod*. Some take it to be a curtain which prevents the ministering angels from seeing the Glory (Targ. of Job 26:9), while others hold that "the seven angels that were created first" continue their ministry inside the *pargod* (*Massekhet Heikhalot*, end of ch. 7). There was no fixed angelology, and different views, and indeed complete systems, have been preserved, ranging from those found in the Ethiopic Book of Enoch to the Hebrew Enoch found among the literature of the *heikhalot*. These ideas occupy a considerable place in the extant Merkabah literature, and, as would be expected, they reappear in various forms of a practical nature in incantations and theurgical literature. Knowledge of the names of the angels was already part of the mysticism of the Essenes, and it developed in both rabbinic and heterodox circles up to the end of the geonic period. Together with the concept of the four or seven key angels, there developed (about the end of the first or the beginning of the second century) a new doctrine concerning the angel *Metatron (*sar ha-panim*, "the prince of the Presence") – who is none other than Enoch himself after his flesh had been transformed into "flaming torches" – and the place assigned to him above all the other angels. There are some sources which contain little or no reference to this subject or to other views associated with it (e.g., concerning the angel *Sandalfon), while others like the Hebrew Enoch (ed. H. Odeberg, 1928), dwell on it at length. At the beginning of the tannaitic period speculations are found concerning the angel who bore within him the name of God Himself, the angel Yahoel, who occupies a dominant position in the Apocalypse of Abraham. Everything said here of Yahoel was transferred in another circle to Metatron, to whom the mystics assigned many other secret names, most important of which were Yahoel and "the lesser YHWH." While traditions concerning Yahoel and the lesser YHWH reappeared in different forms among the Gnostics, the subject of Metatron remained confined to Jewish circles for a long time. Metatron also took upon himself several of the duties of the angel *Michael, and from the amoraic period onward he was identified with the "prince of the world." His title *ha-na'ar* ("the boy") refers to his role as servant of God and is based on the linguistic usage of the Bible. Several extant passages of the *Shi'ur Komah* include references to Metatron and his role as servant of the Chariot.

In Merkabah literature the names of the angels easily intermingle with the secret Names of God, many of which are mentioned in the fragments of this literature still extant. Since many of these names have not been completely explained it has not yet been possible to ascertain whether they are meant to convey a specific theological idea – e.g., an emphasis on a particular aspect of God's revelation or activity – or whether they have other purposes which we cannot fathom. Fragments of *heikhalot* literature mention names like Adiriron, Zohararariel, Zavodiel, Ta'zash, Akhtriel (found also in a *baraita* emanating from this circle in Ber. 7a). The formula "the Lord, God of Israel" is very often added to the particular name, but many of the chief angels also have this added to their names (e.g., in the Hebrew Enoch) so it cannot be deduced from this whether the phrase refers to the name of an angel or to the name of God. Sometimes the same name serves to designate both God and an angel. An example of this is Azbogah ("an eightfold name") in which each pair of letters adds up, through *gematria*, to the number eight. This "eightfold" name reflects the Gnostic concept of the *ogdoas*, the eighth firmament above the seven firmaments, where the Divine Wisdom dwells. In the *Heikhalot Zutrati* it is defined as "a name of power" (*gevurah*), i.e., one of the names of the Divine Glory, while in the Hebrew Enoch chapter 18 it becomes the name of one of the angelic princes; its numerical significance is forgotten and it is subject to the customary aggadic interpretation of names. The same is true of the term *ziva rabba*, which from one angle is no more than an Aramaic translation of *ha-kavod ha-gadol* ("the great glory") found in the apocalypses and also in Samaritan sources as a description of the revealed God. But it also occurs in the lists of the mysterious names of the angel Metatron, and it is found with a similar meaning in Mandaic literature. Just as non-Jewish Gnostics sometimes used Aramaic formulae in their Greek writings, so Greek elements and Greek formulae found their way into Merkabah literature. The dialogue between the mystic and the angel Dumiel at the gate of the sixth palace in the *Heikhalot Rabbati* is conducted in Greek (J. Levy, in *Tarbiz*, 12 (1941), 163–7). One of the names of God in this literature is Totrossiah, which signifies the *tetras* of the four letters of the name YHWH. The reverse parallel to this is the name Arbatiao which is found frequently in the magic papyri of this period.

The different tendencies of Merkabah mysticism established ways of contemplating ascent to the heavens – ways which were understood in their literal sense. Their basic conception did not depend on scriptural interpretation but took on its own particular literary form. The magical element was strong in the early stages of *heikhalot* literature only, becoming weaker in later redactions. From the third century onward interpretations appear which divest the subject of the Chariot of its literal significance and introduce an ethical element. Sometimes the different palaces correspond to the ladder of ascent through the virtues (e.g., in the *Ma'aseh Merkabah*, para. 9, ed. by Scholem in *Jewish Gnosticism*... (1965), 107); and sometimes the whole topic of the Chariot completely loses its literal meaning. This kind of interpretation is especially evident in the remarkable mystic utterance of the third-century *amora* *Simeon b. Lakish: "the patriarchs are the Chariot" (Gen. Rabba, 475, 793, 983, with regard to Abraham, Isaac, and Jacob). Statements like these opened the door to the type of symbolic interpretation which flourished afterward in kabbalistic literature.

The first center for this type of mysticism was in Palestine, where a large part of *heikhalot* literature was written. Mystical ideas found their way to Babylonia at least as early as the time of *Rav, and their influence is recognizable, among other places, in the magical incantations which were inscribed on bowls to afford "protection" from evil spirits and demons, and which reflect popular Babylonian Judaism from the end of the talmudic period to the time of the *geonim*. In Babylonia, apparently, a number of magical prayers were composed, as well as treatises on magic, like the *Ḥarba de-Moshe* (ed. Gaster 1896), *Sefer ha-Malbush* (Sassoon Ms. 290, pp. 306–11), *Sefer ha-Yashar* (British Museum, Margoliouth Ms. 752, fol. 91ff.), *Sefer ha-Ma'alot, Havdalah de-R. Akiva* (Vatican Ms. 228), *Pishra de R. *Ḥanina b. Dosa* (Vatican Ms. 216, fols. 4–6), and others, some of which were written in Babylonian Aramaic. In all these the influence of Merkabah ideas was very strong. In Palestine, perhaps at the end of the talmudic period, the *Sefer ha-*Razim* was composed, which contains descriptions of the firmaments greatly influenced by *heikhalot* literature, while the "practical" part, concerning incantations, has a different style, partly adopted verbatim from Greek sources. From circles such as these emanated the magical usage of the Torah and Psalms for practical purposes (see JE III, s.v. Bibliomancy). This practice was based on the theory that essentially these books were made up from the Sacred Names of God and His angels, an idea that first appeared in the preface to the *Sefer Shimmushei Torah*; only the midrashic introduction, with the title *Ma'yan ha-Ḥokhmah*, has been printed (Jellinek, *Beit ha-Midrash*, part 1 (1938), 58–61), but the whole work is extant in manuscript. Of the same type is the *Sefer Shimmushei Tehillim*, which has been printed many times in Hebrew and also exists in manuscript in an Aramaic version.

The poetical content of the literature of the *ma'aseh merkabah* and the *ma'aseh bereshit* is striking; we have already noted the hymns sung by the *ḥayyot* and the ministering angels in praise of their Creator. Following the pattern of several of the Psalms, the view was developed that the whole of creation, according to its nature and order, was singing hymns of praise. A hymnology was established in the various versions of the **Perek Shirah*, which without any doubt derives from mystical circles in the talmudic period. Connected with this poetical element is the influence that the Merkabah mystics had on the development of specific portions of the order of prayer, particularly on the morning *kedushah* (Ph. Bloch, in MGWJ, 37, 1893), and later on the *piyyutim* which were written for these portions (*silluk, ofan, kedushah*).

Jewish Gnosis and the *Sefer Yeẓirah*

In these stages of Jewish mysticism, the descriptions of the Chariot and its world occupy a place which in non-Jewish Gnosticism is filled by the theory of the "aeons," the powers and emanations of God which fill the *pleroma*, the divine "fullness." The way in which certain *middot*, or qualities of God, like wisdom, understanding, knowledge, truth, faithfulness, righteousness, etc., became the "aeons" of the Gnostics is paralleled in the tradition of the *ma'aseh bereshit*, although it did not penetrate the basic stages of Merkabah mysticism. The ten sayings by which the world was created (Avot 5:1) became divine qualities according to Rav (Ḥag. 12a). There is also a tradition that *middot* such as these "serve before the Throne of Glory" (ARN 37), thus taking the place occupied by the *ḥayyot* and the presiding angels in the Merkabah system. The semi-mythological speculations of the Gnostics which regarded the qualities as "aeons" were not admitted into the rabbinic tradition of the Talmud or the Midrashim, but they did find a place in the more or less heterodox sects of the *minim* or *ḥizẓonim*. To what extent the growth of Gnostic tendencies within Judaism itself preceded their development in early Christianity is still the subject of scholarly controversy. Peterson, Haenchen, and Quispel, in particular, along with several experts on the Dead Sea Scrolls, have tried to prove that Jewish forms of Gnosis, which retained a belief in the unity of God and rejected any dualistic notions, came into being before the formation of Christianity and were centered particularly around the idea of primordial man (following speculation on Gen. 1:26; see *Adam Kadmon). The image of the Messiah, characteristic of the Christian Gnostics, was absent here. These scholars have interpreted several of the earliest documents of Gnostic literature as Gnostic Midrashim on cosmogony and Haenchen in particular has argued that their basic Jewish character is clearly recognizable in an analysis of the teaching of Simon Magus, apparently the leader of Samaritan Gnosis, a first-century heterodox Judaism. Even before this, M. *Friedlaender had surmised that antinomian Gnostic tendencies (which belittled the value of the Commandments) had also developed within Judaism before the rise of Christianity. Although a fair number of these ideas are based on questionable hypotheses, nevertheless there is a considerable measure of truth in them. They point to the lack of Iranian elements in the early sources of Gnosis, which have been exaggerated by most scholars of the last two generations, whose arguments rest on no less hypothetical assumptions. The theory of "two principles" could have been the result of an internal development, a mythological reaction within Judaism itself, just as easily as a reflection of Iranian influence. The apostasy of the *tanna* Elisha b. Avuyah to a Gnostic dualism of this kind is connected in the Merkabah tradition with the vision of Metatron seated on the Throne like God. Mandaic literature also contains strands of a Gnostic, monotheistic, non-Christian character, which many believe originated in a Transjordanian Jewish heterodox sect whose members emigrated to Babylonia in the first or second century. The earliest strata of the *Sefer ha-*Bahir*, which came from the East, prove the existence of definitely Gnostic views in a circle of believing Jews in Babylonia or Syria, who connected the theory of the Merkabah with that of the "aeons." These early sources are partly linked with the book **Raza Rabba*, which was known as an early work at the end of the geonic period; fragments of it can be found in the writings of the *Ḥasidei Ashkenaz. Concepts which did not originate exclusively in Jewish mysticism, like the idea of the *Shekhinah* and the hypostases of stern judgment and compassion, could easily have been interpreted according to the theory of the "aeons" and incorporated with Gnostic ideas. The "exile of the *Shekhinah*," originally an aggadic idea, was assimilated in Jewish circles at a particular stage with the Gnostic idea of the divine spark that is in exile in the terrestrial world, and also with the mystic view of the Jewish concept of the *keneset Yisrael* ("the community of Israel") as a heavenly entity that represents the historical community of Israel. In the elaboration of such motifs, Gnostic elements could be added to rabbinic theories of the Merkabah and to ideas of Jewish circles whose connection with rabbinism was weak.

THE *SEFER YEẒIRAH*. Speculation on the *ma'aseh bereshit* was given a unique form in a book, small in size but enormous in influence, that was written between the second and sixth centuries, perhaps in the third century, in a Hebrew style reflecting that of the Merkabah mystics. In early manuscripts it is called *Hilkhot Yeẓirah* ("*Halakhot* on Creation"), and later *Sefer Yeẓirah* ("Book of Creation"; uncritical edition by L. Goldschmidt, 1894). We should not dismiss out of hand the possibility that the *hilkhot yeẓirah* mentioned in *Sanhedrin* 65b and 67b could be one early version of this text. There is here an independent adaptation of the concept of the *ma'aseh bereshit* conceived in the spirit of the Pythagoreans of the talmudic period. On the one hand the book is closely connected with Jewish speculation on "Divine Wisdom," *Ḥokhmah*, and with the traditions concerning cosmogony, and on the other hand it introduces new concepts and an original plan of cosmogony far removed, for example, from the *baraita* of the work of creation. The "32 secret paths of Wisdom," by means of which God created His world, are nothing more than the "ten *Sefirot*" added to the 22 letters of the Hebrew alphabet. The *Sefirot*, a term which first appears in this text, are merely the primordial numbers of the later Pythagoreans. They are created powers, and not emanations from within the Divine. They also fulfill a decisive role in both the creation and the order of the world. When he describes their work the author uses expressions purposely taken from the description of the *ḥayyot* in the first chapter of Ezekiel. The first four *Sefirot* represent the four elements of the entire world: the spirit of God; ether – the spirit which is the world's atmosphere; water; and fire. The following six *Sefirot* represent the six dimensions of space. The *Sefirot* are described in a style full of mysterious solemnity almost without parallel in Jewish tradition. This enigmatic style enabled both philosophers and kabbalists of a later age to base their ideas mainly on the first chapter of the book, interpreting it in their own individual ways.

In the rest of the book there is no further mention of these *Sefirot*, and there follows a description of the parts that the letters play in creation. The whole work of creation was enacted through the combinations of the Hebrew letters that were inscribed on the sphere of heaven and engraved into the spirit of God. Every process in the world is a linguistic one, and the existence of every single thing depends on the combination of letters that lies hidden within it. This idea is very close to the view mentioned in *Berakhot* 55a in the name of the *amora* Rav, that there are "letters through which heaven and earth were created," and that Bezalel built the tabernacle (which, according to some, was a microcosmic symbol of the whole work of creation) through his knowledge of the combinations of these letters. Perhaps this view can be seen as the ultimate conclusion of the theory that the world was created through the Torah, which is made up of letters and which contains these combinations in some mysterious way. At this point an element common to the concepts of the *Sefer Yeẓirah* and to ideas concerning the practice of magic through the power of letters and names and their permutations clearly emerges. The author compares the division of the letters according to their phonetic origin with the division of creation into three areas: world (place), year (time), and soul (the structure of the human body). The relationship of the letters to the *Sefirot* is obscure. The whole of creation is "sealed" with combinations of the name Yaho (יהו), and the emphasis on this name in the *Sefer Yeẓirah* recalls Gnostic and magical speculations on that same name, in its Greek form Ἰάω. Through "contemplation" of the mysteries of the letters and the *Sefirot* Abraham attained a revelation of the Lord of All. Because of this conclusion the authorship of the book was attributed to Abraham, and in some manuscripts it is even entitled "The Letters of our Father Abraham." The Ḥasidim of Germany (see *Ḥasidei Ashkenaz) read the book as a manual of magic, and they connected it with traditions about the creation of the *golem* (see G. Scholem, *On the Kabbalah and its Symbolism* (1965), 165–73).

Mysticism in the Geonic Period

The mishnaic and the talmudic periods were times of irrepressible creativity in the field of mysticism and esoteric inquiry. In the geonic era (from the seventh to the 11th centuries) little that was essentially original emerged, and the various streams already mentioned continued to exist and to intermingle. The center of mystical activity shifted to Babylonia, although its continuing influence in Palestine is evident in several chapters of later midrashic literature and particularly in the Pirkei de-R. *Eliezer. The poems of Eleazar *Kallir, which are greatly influenced by *Merkabah* literature and also by the *Shi'ur Komah*, belong to the end of the earlier period or were composed between the two eras. The poet made no attempt to conceal ideas which had been transmitted through old esoteric theories. As mysticism developed in this period, in both Palestine and Babylonia, it followed the pattern of the earlier period. Apocalyptic writing continued with great momentum; examples are extant from the time of the *amoraim* almost to that of the Crusades, and they were collected in Judah Even-Shemuel's great anthology, *Midreshei Ge'ullah* (1954[2]), most of them from the geonic period. They display a marked connection with the Merkabah tradition, and several have been preserved in manuscripts of works by mystics. Simeon b. *Yoḥai appears here for the first time, side by side with R. Ishmael, as a bearer of apocalyptic tradition (in the *Nistarot de-R. Shimon b. Yoḥai*). Apocalypses were also attributed to the prophet Elijah, Zerubbabel, and Daniel.

At the other extreme there grew and flourished in these circles an angelology and a theurgy which produced a very rich literature, much of it extant from this period. Instead of, or in addition to, the contemplation of the Chariot, this presents a many-sided practical magic associated with the prince or princes of the Torah, whose names vary. Many incantations addressed to the angel Yofiel and his companions, as princes of wisdom and of Torah, are found in a large number of manuscripts of magical manuals, which continue the tradition of the earlier magical papyri. There was also a custom of conjuring up these princes particularly on the day before the Day of Atonement or even on the night of the Day of Atonement itself (see G. Scholem, in *Tarbiz*, 16 (1945), 205–9). Formulae for more mundane purposes have also been preserved in many incantations written in Babylonian Aramaic by Jewish "masters of the Name," and not always on behalf of Jewish customers. Concepts from the Merkabah mystics' circle, as well as mythological and aggadic ideas – some unknown from other sources – filtered through to groups which were far removed indeed from mysticism and much closer to magic. A demonology, extremely rich in detail, also grew up side by side with the angelology. Many examples of these (published by Montgomery, C. Gordon, and others) were found on clay bowls which were buried, according to custom, beneath the thresholds of houses. They have important parallels among the incantations transmitted through literary tradition in the fragments of the *Genizah* and in the material which found its way as far as the Ḥasidim of Germany (e.g., in the *Havdalah de-R. Akiva*). The theology and angelology of the incantations were not always explained correctly by their editors, who saw in them a heterodox theology (for an example of this see Scholem, *Jewish Gnosticism* (1965), 84–93). It was in Babylonia also, apparently, that the book *Raza Rabba* ("The Great Mystery") was composed. Attacked by the Karaites as a work of sorcery, the book does indeed contain magical material but the extant fragments show that it also has some Merkabah content, in the form of a dialogue between R. Akiva and R. Ishmael. As the angelology in these fragments has no parallel in other sources, it would seem that the work is a crystallization of an early form of a theory of the "aeons" and of speculations of a Gnostic character. The style, quite different from that of the *heikhalot*, indicates a much later stage. These fragments were published by G. Scholem in *Reshit ha-Kabbalah* (1948), 220–38.

The beginnings of new trends in this period can be discerned in three areas:

(1) The utterances employed in the creation of the world were conceived either as forces within the Chariot or as "aeons," *middot*, or hypostases. To what extent this speculation is associated with the view of the ten *Sefirot* in the *Sefer Yeẓirah* is not altogether clear. It is evident, however, that in Jewish Gnostic circles the concept of the *Shekhinah* occupied a completely new position. In the early sources "*Shekhinah*" is an expression used to denote the presence of God Himself in the world and is no more than a name for that presence; it later becomes a hypostasis distinguished from God, a distinction that first appears in the late Midrash to Proverbs (Mid. Prov. 47a: "the *Shekhinah* stood before the Holy One, blessed be He, and said to Him"). In contrast to this separation of God and His *Shekhinah*, there arose another original concept – the identification of the *Shekhinah* with *keneset Yisrael* ("the community of Israel"). In this obviously Gnostic typology, the allegories which the Midrash uses in order to describe the relationship of the Holy One, blessed be He, to the community of Israel are transmuted into this Gnostic concept of the *Shekhinah*, or "the daughter," in the eastern sources which are embedded in *Sefer ha-Bahir* (G. Scholem, *Les Origines de la Kabbale* (1966), 175–94). Gnostic interpretations of other terms, like wisdom, and of various talmudic similes in the spirit of Gnostic symbolism, can be understood as going back to the early sources of the *Sefer ha-Bahir (ibid.*, 78–107). Several of the book's similes can be understood only against an Oriental background, and Babylonia in particular, as, for example, the statements concerning the date palm and its symbolic significance. The ascent of repentance to reach the Throne of Glory is interpreted in a late Midrash (PR 185a) as an actual ascent of the repentant sinner through all the firmaments, and so the process of repentance is closely connected here with the process of ascent to the Chariot.

(2) In this period the idea of the transmigration of souls (*gilgul) also became established in various eastern circles. Accepted by Anan b. *David and his followers (up to the tenth century) – although later rejected by the Karaites – it was also adopted by those circles whose literary remains were drawn upon by the redactors of the *Sefer ha-Bahir.* For Anan (who composed a book specifically on this subject) and his followers the idea, which apparently originated among Persian sects and Islamic Mutazilites, had no mystical aspects. It is apparent, however, that the mystics' idea of transmigration drew upon other sources, for in the sources of the *Sefer ha-Bahir* it makes its appearance as a great mystery, alluded to only through allegory, and based on scriptural verses quite different from those quoted by the sect of Anan and repeated by Kirkisānī in his *Book of Lights* (pt. 3, chs. 27–28).

(3) A new element was added to the idea of the Sacred Names and angels which occupied such a prominent position in the theory of the Merkabah. This was an attempt to discover numerological links, through *gematria*, between the different types of names and scriptural verses, prayers, and other writings. The numerological "secrets," *sodot*, served two purposes. They ensured, firstly, that the names would be spelled exactly as the composers of *gematriot* received them through written or oral sources – though this system did not entirely save them from mutilation and variation, as is clearly shown by the mystical writings of the Ḥasidei Ashkenaz. Secondly, by this means they were able to give mystical meanings and "intentions" (*kavvanot*) to these names, which served as an incentive to deeper meditation, especially since many of the names lacked any significance. This process seems to be connected with a decline in the practical use of this material during preparation for the soul's ecstatic ascent to heaven. Names which originated through intense emotional excitement on the part of contemplatives and visionaries were stripped of their meaning as technical aids to ecstatic practice, and so required interpretations and meanings on a new level of *kavvanah*. All the names, of whatever kind, have therefore a contemplative content; not that ascent to the Merkabah completely disappeared at this time, for the various treatises in many manuscripts on the methods of preparation for it testify to the continuity of their practical application. However, it is clear that this element gradually became less significant. Another new factor must be added to this: the interpretation of the regular prayers in the search for *kavvanot* of this numerical type.

It is impossible to determine with any certainty from the evidence that remains where the secrets of the names and the mysteries of prayer according to this system of *gematria* first made their appearance. The new interpretations of prayer link the words of phrases of the liturgy generally with names from the Merkabah tradition and angelology. Perhaps this link was first formulated in Babylonia; but it is also possible that it grew up in Italy, where the mysteries of the Merkabah and all the associated material spread not later than the ninth century. Italian Jewish tradition, particularly in the popular forms it assumed in *Megillat *Aḥimaʿaẓ*, clearly shows that the rabbis there were well versed in matters of the Merkabah. In addition it tells of the miraculous activity of one of the Merkabah mystics who emigrated from Baghdad, namely Abu Aharon (see Aaron of *Baghdad), who performed wonders through the power of the Sacred Names during the few years that he lived in Italy. The later tradition of the Ḥasidim of Germany (12th century) maintained that these new mysteries were transmitted about the year 870 to R. Moses b. *Kalonymus in Lucca by this same Abu Aharon, the son of R. Samuel ha-Nasi of Baghdad. Afterward, R. Moses went to Germany where he laid the foundations of the mystical tradition of the Ḥasidei Ashkenaz, which grew up around this new element. The personality of Abu Aharon remains obscure in all these traditions, and the recent attempts (in several papers by Israel Weinstock) to see him as a central figure in the whole development of the Kabbalah and as author and editor of many mystical works, including the *heikhalot* literature and the *Sefer ha-Bahir*, are founded on an extreme use of *gematriot* and on dubious hypotheses (see *Tarbiz*, 32 (1963), 153–9 and 252–65, the dispute between I. Weinstock and G. Scholem, and Weinstock's reply in *Sinai*, 54 (1964), 226–59). In any event, there is no doubt that at the end of the geonic period mysticism spread to Italy, in the form of Merkabah literature and perhaps also in the form of the above-mentioned theory of names, which served as an intermediate link between the orient and the later development in Germany and France. These ideas reached Italy through various channels. The magical theurgic elements in them came to the fore, while the speculative side became weaker. This latter was represented in the main by the commentary of the physician Shabbetai *Donnolo to the *Sefer Yeẓirah* which was indisputably influenced by the commentary of Saadiah b. Joseph *Gaon to the same work. It is impossible to say to what extent theosophic writings of a Gnostic character, in Hebrew or Aramaic, also passed through these channels, but this possibility should not be denied.

From the numerous remains of mystical literature extant from the talmudic and geonic periods it can be deduced that these types of ideas and attitudes were widespread in many circles, wholly or partially restricted to initiates. Only on very rare occasions is it possible to establish with certainty the personal and social identity of these circles. There is no doubt that, apart from the individual *tannaim* and *amoraim* whose attachment to mystical study is attested by reliable evidence, there were many whose names are unknown who devoted themselves to mysticism and even made it their chief preoccupation. In addition to the rabbis that have already been mentioned, R. *Meir, R. *Isaac, R. *Levi, R. Joshua b. *Levi, R. *Hoshaiah, and R. Inyani b. Sasson (or Sisi) were also involved with mystical ideas. The identity of those who studied theurgy (who were called, in Aramaic, "users of the Name," and only from the geonic period onward "masters of the Name," *ba'alei ha-Shem*) is completely unknown, and most of them, of course, did not come from rabbinic circles. Our knowledge of the exponents of mysticism and esotericism in the geonic period is even more limited. Geonic responsa reveal that esoteric traditions did spread to the leading academies, but there is no proof that the foremost *geonim* themselves were steeped in these teachings or that they actually practiced them. The material touching on Merkabah traditions in the responsa and in the commentaries of the *geonim* (the greater part of which were assembled by B.M. Levin in *Oẓar ha-Ge'onim* to *Ḥagigah* (1931), 10–30, and in the section on commentaries 54–61) is notable for its extreme caution, and occasionally for its forbearance. The main attempt to link the theories of the *Sefer Yeẓirah* with contemporary philosophical and theological ideas was made by Saadiah Gaon, who wrote the first extensive commentary to the book. He refrained from dealing in detail with the subject matter of the Merkabah and the *Shi'ur Komah*, but at the same time he did not disown it despite the attacks of the Karaites. In several instances Sherira b. Ḥanina *Gaon and Hai *Gaon set out to discuss matters in this field, but without connecting their explanations with the philosophical ideas expressed elsewhere in their writings. Hai Gaon's opinion in his well known responsum concerning some of the Secret Names, such as the 42-and the 72-lettered Name, led others to attribute to him more detailed commentaries on these subjects, and some of these came into the possession of the Ḥasidei Ashkenaz (see J. Dan, *Torat ha-Sod shel Ḥasidut Ashkenaz*, 1968). The words that Hai Gaon addressed to the rabbis of Kairouan show that the esoteric teaching on names had an impact even on the more distant Diaspora, but they also demonstrate that there was no tradition and little textual distribution of the literature of the *heikhalot*, of which the *gaon* says "he who sees them is terrified by them." In Italy this literature did spread, particularly among the rabbis and the poets (*paytanim*), and an important section of the work of Amittai b. Shephatiah (ninth century) consists of Merkabah poems. As these traditions passed into Europe, some circles of rabbinic scholars became once more the principal but not the only exponents of mystical teaching.

Aggadot and Midrashim with angelological and esoteric tendencies were also written in this period. The *Midrash Avkir*, which was still known in Germany up to the end of the Middle Ages, contained material rich in mythical elements concerning angels and names. The remains of it which appear in the *Likkutim mi-Midrash Avkir* were collected by S. Buber in 1883. Various parts of the *Pesikta Rabbati* also reflect the ideas of the mystics. The *Midrash Konen* is made up of different elements (Jellinek, *Beit ha-Midrash*, pt. 2 (1938), 23–39, and, with a commentary, in *Sefer Nit'ei Na'amanim*, 1836); the first part contains a remarkable combination of ideas concerning the Divine Wisdom and its role in creation and the theory of the *Shekhinah*, while the rest of the work includes different versions of angelology and a version of *ma'aseh bereshit*. An element of *gematria* also appears. Judging from the Greek words in the first part, the extant text was edited in Palestine or in southern Italy. In the tradition of the Ḥasidei Ashkenaz (British Museum Ms. 752 fol. 132b) a fragment of a Midrash survives concerning the angels active during the Exodus from Egypt, which is also based to a large extent on the exegesis of *gematriot*, and it would seem that there were other Midrashim of this type whose origin is not known.

While many ideas concerning God and His manifestation are expressed or implied in the Merkabah literature, no particular concentrated attention is paid in these early stages of mysticism to the teaching about man. The emphasis of the Merkabah mystics is on the ecstatic and contemplative side, and man interested them only insofar as he received the vision and revealed it to Israel. Their speculations contain no specific ethical theory nor any new concept of the nature of man.

Ḥasidic Movements in Europe and Egypt

Religious impulses which were mystical in the sense of involving man's powerful desire for a more intimate communion with God and for a religious life connected with this developed in the Judaism of the Middle Ages in different places and by various means; not all are associated exclusively with Kabbalah. Such tendencies resulted from a fusion of internal drives with the external influence of the religious movements present in the non-Jewish environment. Since their proponents did not find the answer to all their needs in the talmudic and midrashic material which purported to bind man closer to God – although they utilized it as far as they could and also at times based far-fetched interpretations on it – they drew extensively on the literature of the Sufis, the mystics of Islam, and on the devout Christian ascetic tradition. The intermingling of these traditions with that of Judaism resulted in tendencies which were regarded as a kind of continuation of the work of the *Ḥasideans of the tannaitic period, and they stressed the value of *ḥasidut* as a way of bringing man nearer to *devekut* ("communion" with God) although this term was not yet used to designate the culmination of *ḥasidut*. Extremism in ethical and religious behavior, which in the sayings and literature of the rabbis characterized the term "*ḥasid*" ("pious") as against "*ẓaddik*" ("righteous"), became the central norm of these new tendencies. They found their classical literary expression, first and foremost, in 11th-century Spain in *Ḥovot ha-Levavot* by *Baḥya ibn Paquda which was originally written in Arabic. The material dealing with the life devoted to communion of the true "servant" – who is none other than the *ḥasid* yearning for the mystical life – is taken from Sufi sources and the author's intention was to produce an instructional manual of Jewish pietism which culminated in a mystical intent. A Hebrew translation of the *Ḥovot ha-Levavot* was made on the initiative of *Abraham b. David of Posquières and the early circle of kabbalists in Lunel. The book's great success, especially in Hebrew, shows how much it answered the religious needs of people even beyond the confines of the Kabbalah. The obvious connection with talmudic tradition, which served as the point of departure for explanations of a remarkable spiritual intent, was a distinguishing feature in works of this kind, which also clearly reveal neoplatonic philosophical elements. Such elements facilitated the creation of formulations of a mystical character, and this philosophy became one of its most powerful means of expression. Several of the poems of Solomon ibn *Gabirol, Baḥya's older contemporary, evidence this trend toward a mystical spirituality, and it is expressed particularly in the concepts of his great philosophical work, *Mekor Ḥayyim*, which is completely saturated with the spirit of neoplatonism. The extent to which his poems reflect individual mystical experiences is controversial (cf. the view of Abraham Parnes, *Mi-Bein la-Ma'arakhot* (1951), 138–61). In Spain, after a century or more, these tendencies intermingled with the emerging Kabbalah, where traces of Gabirol may be seen here and there, especially in the writings of Isaac b. *Latif.

Parallel with this was a growth of *ḥasidut* of a mystical bent in Egypt in the days of Maimonides and his son Abraham b. Moses b. *Maimon; this, however, found no echo in the Kabbalah, remaining an independent occurrence of a Jewish Sufi type which is recorded as late as the 14th or even the 15th century. No mere figure of speech, the epithet "Ḥasid" was a description of a man who followed a particular way of life, and it was appended to the names of several rabbis from the 11th century onward, in both the literary and the personal records that survived in the *Genizah*. The Egyptian trend of *ḥasidut* turned into "an ethically oriented mysticism" (S.D. Goitein), particularly in the literary productions of Abraham b. Moses b. Maimon (d. 1237). The mystical aspect of his book *Kifāyat al-ʿĀbidīn* (ed. S. Rosenblatt, 2 vols. (1927–38), with the title *The High Ways to Perfection*) is entirely based on Sufi sources and bears no evidence of any similar Jewish tradition known to the author. The circle of Ḥasidim which grew up around him stressed the esoteric aspect of their teaching (S.D. Goitein), and his son, R. Obadiah, also followed this path (G. Vajda, in JJS, 6 (1955), 213–25). A much later work of the same kind was discussed by F. Rosenthal (HUCA, 25 (1940), 433–84). What remains of this literature is all written in Arabic, which may explain why it found no place in the writings of the Spanish kabbalists, most of whom had no knowledge of the language.

An essentially similar religious movement grew up in France and Germany, beginning in the 11th century. It reached its peak in the second half of the 12th and in the 13th century, but it continued to have repercussions for a long time, particularly in the Judaism of the Ashkenazi world. This movement – known as the Ḥasidei Ashkenaz – has two aspects: the ethical and the esoteric-theosophical. On the ethical plane a new ideal developed of extreme *ḥasidut* linked to a suitable mode of life, as described particularly in the *Sefer Ḥasidim* of Judah b. Samuel *he-Ḥasid, extant in two versions, one short and the other long. Along with specific pietistic customs there grew up a particular method of repentance which, remarkable for its extremism, had a marked influence on Jewish ethical behavior. The common factor in all the ḥasidic movements of Spain, Egypt, and Germany was the violent opposition that they aroused, attested by the Ḥasidim themselves. A Ḥasidism which does not arouse opposition in the community cannot, according to their own definition, be considered a true one. Equanimity of spirit, indifference to persecution and ignominy; these are the distinguishing traits of the Ḥasid, to whichever particular circle he belongs. Although the Ḥasidei

Ashkenaz reflect to some extent the contemporary Christian asceticism, nevertheless they developed mainly within the framework of a clear talmudic tradition, and the basic principles were often identical with the principles of this tradition. All these movements had from the beginning a social significance intended "to revive the hearts." The Ḥasidei Ashkenaz did not, relatively speaking, lay great stress on the mystical element associated with the ḥasidic ideal. Despite the paradox inherent in the situation, they tried as far as possible to integrate the Ḥasid, ostensibly an unnatural phenomenon, into the general Jewish community, and to make him responsible in practice to the community. The Ḥasid who renounced his natural impulses and always acted "beyond the limit of strict justice" was the true embodiment of the fear and love of God in their purest essence. Many of these Ḥasidim attained the highest spiritual levels, and were considered to be masters of the holy spirit, or even prophets, a term applied to several men who are known for their activity in tosafist circles, e.g., R. Ezra ha-Navi ("the prophet") of Montcontour, and also to others who are otherwise completely unknown, e.g., R. Nehemiah ha-Navi and R. Troestlin ha-Navi from Erfurt. These men's attainment of such spiritual heights was connected not only with their behavior on the ethical plane but also with the distinction they achieved in the realm of esoteric theosophy. The latter was assigned an important position; in it all earlier trends were maintained, joined and mingled with new forces. Remaining the main object of enquiry, and even a practical guide toward the "ascent to heaven," the searching on the Merkabah became largely interwoven with number mysticism and the speculations based on it. In addition to the ecstatic or visionary ascent to heaven, there developed a tendency toward deep meditation, toward prayer and the mysteries of prayer, which were communicated orally. Medieval Jewish philosophy introduced a new element, mainly through Saadiah Gaon's commentary to the *Sefer Yeẓirah* (which had been translated into Hebrew as early as the 11th century), and through the early translation of his *Sefer Emunot ve-De'ot* in a style reminiscent of the *piyyutim* of the Kallir school. This was the source of the theory of the *Kavod* ("Glory"), transmitted through ḥasidic literature, which saw the Divine Glory as the first created entity, although the mystics dared speak of it only with trembling awe. Despite their distinction between God and the *Kavod*, which is also called *Shekhinah*, they continued to refer to the *Shekhinah* in terms of the talmudic and midrashic conception of it as an attribute of God. An additional factor from the 12th century onward was the influence of rabbis of the neoplatonic school, especially Abraham ibn *Ezra, and Abraham b. *Ḥiyya. Perhaps Ibn Ezra's travels to France and his personal contacts there contributed to this influence as well as his books. In all the literature they inherited from Saadiah and the Spanish rabbis, the Ḥasidim concentrated on that part that was closest to their thought, practically turning these authors into theosophists. Arriving at no unified systemization of these disparate and contradictory elements, in formulating their ideas they contented themselves with eclectic presentations. The ideas of the Merkabah and the *Shi'ur Komah* were already known in France at the beginning of the ninth century, as witnessed by the attacks on them by *Agobard, bishop of Lyons. Here and there glimpses of these traditions appear in the writings of *Rashi and the tosafists of the 12th and 13th centuries. The study of the *Sefer Yeẓirah* was looked upon as an esoteric discipline, consisting both of revelations concerning creation and the mysteries of the world, and of a profound knowledge of the mysteries of language and the Sacred Names. Traditions of this type have come down from Jacob b. Meir *Tam, Isaac of Dampièrre, Elhanan of Corbeil, and Ezra of Montcontour. The latter, claiming divine revelation, aroused messianic excitement in France and beyond in the second decade of the 13th century (Scholem, *Origines de la Kabbale*, 254–5). These traditions were given written form in France in the *Sefer ha-Ḥayyim* (Munich Ms. 107), written around 1200. However, following Ibn Ezra, its basic doctrine assimilated other theosophical elements concerning the divine attributes and their place in the *Kavod* and beneath the Throne whose similarity to the kabbalistic outlook is clear.

In all aspects, including the esoteric, the movement reached its peak in Germany, first within the widespread Kalonymus family from the 11th century on. In Worms, Speyer, and Mainz, and afterward in Regensburg, the main upholders of the tradition are known: *Samuel b. Kalonymus, *Judah b. Kalonymus of Mainz, and his son, *Eleazar of Worms; his teacher, Judah b. Samuel ha-Ḥasid (d. 1217); Judah b. Kalonymus of Speyer (author of *Sefer Yiḥusei Tanna'im ve-Amora'im*), and the descendants of Judah he-Ḥasid who were scattered throughout the German cities of the 13th century. They and their pupils gave a far-reaching popular expression to the movement, and several of them wrote books of a wide compass which embodied a major part of their traditions and ideas. In addition to the bulk of the *Sefer Ḥasidim*, Judah he-Ḥasid, the movement's central figure in Germany, wrote other books known to us only through citation in other works, particularly the *Sefer ha-Kavod*. According to J. Dan he was also the author of a large work extant in Oxford manuscript 1567. His pupil, Eleazar of Worms, included in books large and small (most of which have been preserved in manuscript) the major part of the material he had received concerning the teachings of the *ma'aseh merkabah*, the *ma'aseh bereshit*, and the doctrine of Names. They are a mixture of mythology and theology, of Midrash and speculation on one side, and of theurgy on the other. All the tendencies already mentioned above find expression in his work, existing side by side, as in his *Sodei Razayya* (considerable parts of which were published in the *Sefer *Razi'el*, and all of which is extant in B.M. Margoliouth 737) or in texts which are arranged like *halakhot*: *Hilkhot ha-Malakhim, Hilkhot ha-Kisse, Hilkhot ha-Kavod, Hilkhot ha-Nevu'ah* (printed under the title of *Sodei Razayya*, 1936), and also in many others that remain unpublished. The scope of this literature is very wide (see J. Dan in: *Zion*, 29 (1964), 168–81), and it contains some fragments of traditions of an unusual type, Gnostic in character, which apparently traveled from the east by way of Italy. The mysteries of prayer and the extensive interpretation of Scripture through number mysticism were further developed in Germany, partly through the chain of tradition of the Kalonymus family and partly through other developments which went so far that the emphasis on the search for associations by way of *gematriot* was considered by Jacob b. *Asher (Tur OḤ 113) to be the most characteristic feature of the Ḥasidei Ashkenaz. In the 13th century a very rich literature grew up, grounded on the different aspects of ḥasidic tradition but still independent of the kabbalistic literature that developed in the same period. The names of many rabbis who trod the path of ḥasidic theosophy are recorded in these sources, most of which are in manuscript. Many of their sayings were incorporated in Eleazar Hirz Treves' commentary to the liturgy (in *Siddur ha-Tefillah*, 1560), and in the *Sefer Arugat ha-Bosem* of Abraham b. *Azriel, an early 13th-century commentary on the *piyyutim* of the *maḥzor* of the Ashkenazi rite (ed. E. Urbach, 1939–63; see the introduction (vol. 4) in the section on mysticism). In this circle the *Sefer Yeẓirah* was nearly always interpreted in the manner of Saadiah and Shabbetai Donnolo, with an added tendency to see the book as a guide for both mystics and adepts of magic. The study of the book was considered successful when the mystic attained the vision of the *golem*, which was connected with a specific ritual of a remarkably ecstatic character. Only in later times did this inner experience assume more tangible forms in popular legend (Scholem, *On the Kabbalah and its Symbolism*, 173–93).

The theological views of the Ḥasidim are summarized in the *Hilkhot ha-Kavod*, and in the *Sha'arei ha-Sod ve-ha-Yiḥud ve-ha-Emunah* (*Kokhevei Yiẓḥak*, 27, 1862), and in the various versions of the *Sod ha-Yiḥud* from Judah he-Ḥasid to Moses Azriel at the end of the 13th century (Scholem, *Reshit ha-Kabbalah*, 206–9). In addition to the ḥasidic version of the concept of the *Kavod*, another view developed in a particular circle in the 11th or 12th century which is not mentioned in the writings of Judah he-Ḥasid and his school. This is the idea of *keruv meyuḥad* ("the special cherub") or *ha-keruv ha-kadosh* ("the holy cherub"). According to this view, it is not the *Kavod* pure and simple which sits upon the Throne but a specific manifestation in the shape of an angel or a cherub, to whom the mysteries of the *Shi'ur Komah* refer. In the writings of Judah ha-Ḥasid and Eleazar of Worms, and in the *Sefer ha-Ḥayyim*, there are a number of variations on the theme of the *Kavod* and various ways of presenting the idea. Sometimes a distinction is made between the revealed and the hidden *Kavod*, and so on. The special cherub appears as an emanation from the great fire of the *Shekhinah* or from the hidden *Kavod*, which has no form. In this circle the two basic divine attributes are contrasted with one another: God's "holiness," which denotes the presence of the *Shekhinah* in all things and the hidden *Kavod*, and God's "greatness" or "sovereignty," which has both appearance and size. Such an idea is somewhat reminiscent of the speculations of members of sects, such as that of Benjamin b. Moses *Nahawendi, who believed that the world was created through an angelic intermediary (a concept which also had precedents among early heterodox sects during the development of Gnosis). This idea becomes apparent among the Ḥasidim in the pseudepigraphicai text called the *Baraita of Yosef b. Uzziel*, which appears, from its language, to have been written in Europe. Joseph b. *Uzziel is taken to be the grandson of Ben Sira. The *baraita* is found in several manuscripts and was published in part by A. *Epstein (in *Ha-Ḥoker*, 2 (1894), 41–47). This idea was accepted by several rabbis, including Avigdor ha-Ẓarefati (12th century?); the author of *Pesak ha-Yir'ah ve-ha-Emunah*, which was mistakenly combined by A. *Jellinek with the *Sha'arei ha-Sod ve-ha-Yiḥud*; the anonymous author of the commentary to the *Sefer Yeẓirah*, which was apparently composed in France in the 13th century and printed under the name of Saadiah Gaon in the editions of the *Sefer Yeẓirah*; and, finally, Elḥanan b. *Yakar of London, in the first half of the 13th century (J. Dan, in *Tarbiz*, 35 (1966), 349–72). In the course of time such ideas, and particularly that of the special cherub, became combined and confused with Spanish Kabbalah, and in Germany in the 14th century several texts were composed which reflect this combination; some are still extant (British Museum Ms. 752; Adler Ms. 1161 in New York, and the commentary of Moses b. Eliezer ha-Darshan to the *Shi'ur Komah; Reshit ha-Kabbalah*, 204ff.).

Ḥasidic ideology, particularly in its French manifestations and in the form given it by Elḥanan of London, adopted the theory of the five worlds. Mentioned by Abraham b. Ḥiyya in his *Megillat ha-Megalleh* and originating among the Islamic neoplatonists in Spain, this theory enumerates in order the worlds of light, of the divine, of the intellect, of the soul, and of nature (Scholem, in MGWJ, 75 (1931), 172–90). Occasionally the writings of this circle incorporated material which originally came from Latin Christian literature, as G. Vajda demonstrated in connection with Elḥanan of London (*Archives d'histoire doctrinale du moyen-âge*, 28 (1961), 15–34). The views of the Ḥasidim were reflected to a large extent in their own special prayers, composed either in the style associated with Saadiah's concept of the *Kavod* (e.g., in the *Shir ha-Yiḥud*, a hymn which was perhaps written by Judah he-Ḥasid or even earlier), or frequently based on the Secret Names, alluded to in the acronym. Many of these have survived in the writings of Eleazar of Worms, particularly in the manuscripts of his commentary to the *Sefer Yeẓirah*. There are also prayers and poems which their authors intended to represent the songs of heavenly beings, a kind of continuation of the *heikhalot* hymns, the songs of the sacred *ḥayyot*. Generally speaking, these prayers were not accorded a fixed place in the liturgy, and they were apparently the preserve of a chosen few. At a much later time they were included in liturgical anthologies in Italy and Germany, collected by kabbalists in the Safed period, and many of them were finally published in the *Sha'arei Ẓiyyon* by Nathan *Hannover (ch. 3). Several of them were attributed in manuscript to Spanish kabbalists, e.g., Jacob b. Jacob *ha-Kohen of Segovia, who was, in fact, personally connected with the German Ḥasidim, or Solomon *Alkabeẓ (see Werblowsky, in *Sefunot* 6 (1962), 135–82).

Eleazar of Worms clearly recognized the esoteric character of those subjects that merited special study, and he enumerates with some variations the areas involved: "The mystery of the Chariot, the mystery of Creation, and the mystery of the Unity [*Sod ha-Yiḥud*, a new concept] are not to be communicated except in a fast" (*Ḥokhmat ha-Nefesh* (1876), 3c). He defines "the science of the soul," to which he devotes one of his main works, as the means and gateway to the "mystery of the Unity," which he apparently saw as the root of mystical theology. In the *Sodei Razayya* he enumerates "three kinds of mystery," those of the Chariot, Creation, and the Commandments. The question of whether the Commandments also have an esoteric purpose is also discussed in the *Sefer Ḥasidim* (ed. Wistinetzki (1891), no. 1477). This book (no. 984) mentions "the profundity of piety [*ḥasidut*], the profundity of the laws of the Creator, and the profundity of His Glory [*Kavod*]," and initiation in these subjects depends on the fulfillment of the conditions laid down in the Talmud in connection with the *ma'aseh merkabah*. The mystics (*ḥakhmei ha-ḥidot*) are "nourished" in this world on the savor of some of the mysteries that originate in the heavenly academy, most of which are treasured up for the righteous in the world to come (no. 1056). Associated with the ḥasidic affinity for mysticism was their desire to synthesize the early material, including the anthropomorphic elements, with the spiritual interpretation that denies these elements. Aroused by this compromise, Moses *Taku (writing in the early 13th century), denied the Saadian principles and defended a corporeal point of view. His attack was included in the *Sefer Ketav Tammim*, of which two extensive fragments survive (*Oẓar Neḥmad*, 3 (1860), 54–99, and *Arugat ha-Bosem*, vol. 1, 263–8). Seeing in the new tendencies "a new religion" which smacked of heresy, he also denounced the attention that the Ḥasidim paid to the mysteries of prayer, and particularly the dissemination of these mysteries in their books. By his attack he shows how widespread the ideas and literature of the Ḥasidim were in his time.

The Establishment of the Kabbalah in Provence

Contemporaneously with the growth of *ḥasidut* in France and Germany, the first historical stages of the Kabbalah emerged in southern France, although there is no doubt that there were earlier steps in its development which cannot now be discerned. These earlier stages were connected with the existence of a Jewish Gnostic tradition, associated in particular eastern circles with Merkabah mysticism. The main remnants were incorporated in the early parts of Sefer *ha-Bahir and also in a few records preserved in the writings of the Ḥasidei Ashkenaz. *Sefer ha-Bahir*, ostensibly an ancient Midrash, appeared in Provence some time between 1150 and 1200 but no earlier; it was apparently edited there from a number of treatises which came from Germany or directly from the East. An analysis of the work leaves no doubt that it was not originally written in Provence (Scholem, *Les Origines de la Kabbale*, 59–210), and to a large extent confirms the mid-13th-century kabbalistic tradition concerning the history of the book and its sources before it reached the early Provençal mystics in a mutilated form. That the book reflects opinions which were not current in Provence and Spain is quite clearly shown by the commentary to the *Sefer Yeẓirah* by Judah b. Barzillai, written in the first third of the 12th century and containing all that the author knew of the traditions of the *ma'aseh bereshit* and especially the *ma'aseh merkabah*. In his interpretations of the ten *Sefirot* of the *Sefer Yeẓirah* there is no mention of them as "aeons" or divine attributes, or as powers within the Merkabah, as they appear in the *Bahir*. His commentary is impregnated throughout with the spirit of Saadiah Gaon, quite unlike the *Bahir*, which is completely unconcerned with philosophical ideas or with any attempt to reconcile philosophy with the concepts it advances. Cast in the form of interpretations of scriptural verses, particularly passages of mythological character, the *Bahir* transforms the Merkabah tradition into a Gnostic tradition concerning the powers of God that lie within the Divine Glory (*Kavod*), whose activity at the Creation is alluded to through symbolic interpretation of the Bible and the *aggadah*. Remnants of a clearly Gnostic terminology and symbolism are preserved, albeit through a Jewish redaction, which connects the symbols with motifs already well known from the *aggadah*. This is especially so with regard to anything that impinges on *keneset Yisrael*, which is identified with the *Shekhinah*, with the *Kavod*, and with the *bat* ("daughter"), who comprises all paths of wisdom. There are indications in the writings of Eleazar of Worms that he too knew this terminology, precisely in connection with the symbolism of the *Shekhinah*. The theory of the *Sefirot* was not finally formulated in the *Sefer ha-Bahir*, and many of the book's statements were not understood, even by the early kabbalists of western Europe. The teaching of the *Bahir* is introduced as *ma'aseh merkabah*, the term "Kabbalah" not yet being used. The theory of transmigration is presented as a mystery, an idea which is self-explanatory and has no need for philosophical justification, despite the opposition of Jewish philosophers from the time of Saadiah onward.

The book *Raza Rabba* may be identified as one of the sources of the *Bahir*, but there is no doubt that there were other sources, now unknown. The earliest signs of the appearance of the Gnostic tradition, and of religious symbolism constructed upon it, are to be found in the mid-12th century and later, in the leading circle of the Provençal rabbis: Abraham b. Isaac of *Narbonne, the author of *Sefer ha-Eshkol*, his son-in-law Abraham b. David *(Rabad), the author of the "animadversions" to Maimonides' *Mishneh Torah*, and Jacob *Nazir of Lunel. Their works did not deal specifically with the subject of mysticism, but fragments of their opinions scattered here and there prove their association with kabbalistic views and with kabbalistic symbolism (*Origines de la Kabbale*, 213–63). In addition to this, according to the reliable testimony of the Spanish kabbalists, they were considered as men inspired from above, who attained "a revelation of Elijah," that is, a mystical experience of spiritual awakening, through which something novel was revealed. Since the theory of the *Sefirot* in its theosophical formulation is already contained in the *Sefer ha-Bahir*, it cannot be regarded as the basic content of these revelations; these were apparently connected with a new idea of the mystical purpose of prayer, based not on *gematriot* and secret Names but on contemplation of the *Sefirot* as a means of concentrating on the *kavvanah* ("meditation") in prayer. Within this circle Jacob Nazir belonged to a special group – called *perushim* in rabbinic parlance and "nazirites" in biblical terminology – whose members did not engage in commerce, but were supported by the communities so that they could devote all their time to the Torah. From its very nature, this group was akin to the Ḥasidim, and there is evidence that several of them led a ḥasidic life. Within this group a contemplative life could develop in which mystic aspirations could easily be aroused. The rabbis mentioned above did not share one consistent system of thought: there are several different and conflicting tendencies in their writings. The idea of the *Kavod*, in its plain Saadian meaning, was not regarded particularly as a mystery, but interpretations in the spirit of the theory of the *Sefirot* in the *Bahir* were considered to be "the great mystery." In the school of Abraham b. David, traditions of this type were transmitted orally, and mysteries relating to the profundities of the Divine were added to the new theory concerning mystical *kavvanah* during prayer.

This circle of the early kabbalists in Provence worked in a highly charged religious and cultural environment. Rabbinic culture had reached a high stage of development there, and even Maimonides considered those proficient in the *halakhah* to be great exponents of the Torah. Their minds were open to the philosophical tendencies of their age. Judah ibn *Tibbon, head of the renowned family of translators, worked in this circle, and translated for his colleagues many of the greatest philosophical books, among them works of a distinctly neoplatonic tendency. He also translated Judah Halevi's *Kuzari* from Arabic, and its profound influence derived from this circle. The early kabbalists absorbed the *Kuzari*'s ideas concerning the nature of Israel, prophecy, the Tetragrammaton, the *Sefer Yeẓirah* and its meaning, in the same way as they assimilated the writings of Abraham ibn Ezra and Abraham b. Ḥiyya, with their tendency toward neoplatonism. Jewish versions of neoplatonic theories of the Logos and the Divine Will, of emanation and of the soul, acted as a powerful stimulus. But philosophical theories concerning the Active Intellect as a cosmic force, association with which could be attained by the prophets and the select few, also penetrated these circles. The close proximity of this theory to mysticism stands out clearly in the history of medieval Islamic and Christian mysticism, and not surprisingly it acts as an important link in the chain which connects many kabbalists with the ideas of Maimonides. The influence of the asceticism of *Ḥovot ha-Levavot* has already been mentioned, and it continued to play an active role in the ethics of the Kabbalah and in its theory of mystical communion. In the last 30 years of the 12th century the Kabbalah spread beyond the circle of Abraham b. David of Posquières. The encounter between the Gnostic tradition contained in the *Bahir* and neoplatonic ideas concerning God, His emanation, and man's place in the world, was extremely fruitful, leading to the deep penetration of these ideas into earlier mystical theories. The Kabbalah, in its historical significance, can be defined as the product of the interpenetration of Jewish Gnosticism and neoplatonism.

In addition, Provence in these years was the scene of a powerful religious upheaval in the Christian world, when the Catharist sect gained control of a large part of the Languedoc, where the first centers of Kabbalah were to be found (see *Albigenses). It is not yet clear to what extent if any there was a connection between the new upsurge in Judaism in the circles of the *perushim* and the Ḥasidim, and the profound upheaval in Christianity which found expression in the Catharist movement. In their ideology there is practically nothing in common between the ideas of the kabbalists and those of the Cathari, except for the theory of transmigration, which kabbalists in fact took from the eastern sources of the *Sefer ha-Bahir.* The dualistic theology of the Cathari was clearly opposed to the Jewish view; nevertheless, it remains a possibility that there were some contacts which can no longer be discerned between the different groups, united as they were by a deep and emotional religious awakening. There is some evidence that the Jews of Provence were well aware of the existence and the beliefs of the sect as early as the first decades of the 13th century (Scholem, *Origines*, 252).

Fragments of the kabbalist tradition that was familiar to Abraham b. David and Jacob Nazir are found in the writings of the kabbalists, and the clear contradictions between them and later ideas, whether on the teaching on God or on the question of *kavvanah*, testifies to their authenticity. Abraham b. David's statement in his criticism of Maimonides (*Hilkhot Teshuvah*, 3, 7) defending those who believe in God's corporeality becomes clarified when it is seen against the background of his kabbalistic views, which distinguish the "Cause of Causes" from the Creator, who is the subject of the *Shi'ur Komah* in the early *baraita*. His interpretation of the *aggadah* in *Eruvim* 18a, that Adam was at first created with two faces, also reflects kabbalistic speculation on the divine attributes – the *Sefirot*.

Abraham b. David's son, Isaac the Blind (d. c. 1235), who lived in or near Narbonne, was the first kabbalist to devote his work entirely to mysticism. He had many disciples in Provence and Catalonia, who spread kabbalistic ideas in the form they had received them from him, and he was regarded as the central figure of the Kabbalah during his lifetime. His followers in Spain have left some record of his sayings and his habits, and a few letters and treatises written at his dictation are also extant: their style is quite different from that of any of his known disciples. Generally he couched his ideas elliptically and obscurely, and he used his own peculiar terminology. Something of his opinions can be learned from the common elements in the writings of his pupils. At all events, he is the first kabbalist whose historical personality and basic ideas clearly emerge. Entrusting his writings only to a few chosen individuals, he definitely opposed the public dissemination of the Kabbalah, seeing in this a dangerous source of misunderstanding and distortion. At the close of his life he protested in a letter to Naḥmanides and Jonah *Gerondi against popularization of this sort in Spain, in which several of his pupils were engaged (*Sefer Bialik* (1934), 143ff.). When the Spanish kabbalists of the 13th century speak simply of "the Ḥasid" they refer to Isaac the Blind. He developed a contemplative mysticism leading to communion with God through meditation on the *Sefirot* and the heavenly essences (*havayot*). The earliest instructions on detailed meditations associated with basic prayers, according to the concept of the *Sefirot* as stages in the hidden life of God, came from him. There is no doubt that he inherited some of his main ideas from his father, on whom he sometimes relied, but he had also recognized the value of the *Sefer ha-Bahir* and he built on its symbolism. His commentary to the *Sefer Yeẓirah* (established as an appendix to G. Scholem, *Ha-Kabbalah be-Provence*, 1963) is the first work to explain the book in the light of a systematic *Sefirot* theory in the spirit of the Kabbalah. At the head of the world of divine qualities he puts the "thought" (*maḥashavah*), from which emerged the divine utterances, the "words" (λόγοι) by means of which the world was created. Above the "thought" is the Hidden God, who is called for the first time by the name **Ein-Sof* ("the Infinite"; see below). Man's thought ascends through mystic meditation until it reaches, and is subsumed into, Divine "Thought." Along with the theory of the *Sefirot* he developed the concept of the mysticism of language. The speech of men is connected with divine speech, and all language, whether heavenly or human, derives from one source – the Divine Name. Profound speculations on the nature of the Torah are found in a long fragment from Isaac's commentary on the beginning of the *Midrash Konen*. The neoplatonic character of his ideas is immediately striking, and distinguishes them completely from the *Bahir*. (For an analysis of his thought, see Scholem, *Origines*…, 263–327.)

There were other circles in Provence who spread the kabbalistic tradition on the basis of material which seems partly to have reached them directly from anonymous eastern sources. On the one hand they continue the neoplatonic, speculative trend of Isaac the Blind, especially in his commentary to the *Sefer Yeẓirah*; and on the other hand they connect this trend with new ideas concerning the world of the Merkabah and the spiritual powers from which it is composed. There is a marked tendency to particularize and name these powers, and the theory of the *Sefirot* occupies only an incidental place among other attempts to delineate the world of emanation and the forces which constitute it. While Isaac the Blind and his disciples revealed their identities and refrained from writing pseudepigraphically, these circles concealed their identities as far as possible, both in Provence and in Spain, and produced a rich kabbalistic pseudepigrapha imitating the literary forms used in Merkabah literature and the *Sefer ha-Bahir*. One portion of this pseudepigraphic literature is neoplatonic and speculative in character, while another is angelological, demonological, and theurgic. This latter tendency in particular found a home in some Castilian communities, e.g., Burgos and Toledo. Among the early kabbalists of Toledo are mentioned the Ḥasid Judah ibn Ziza, Joseph ibn Mazaḥ, and Meir b. Todros *Abulafia (Scholem, *Origines*…, 414). How, and in what circumstances, the Kabbalah arrived there around the year 1200 is not known, but there is evidence linking the Provençal kabbalists with the citizens of Toledo. A reliable document from Provence mentions as sources the traditions of the Provençal teachers, Abraham b. David and his father-in-law, Ḥasidim of Germany, and Judah ibn Ziza from Toledo (*ibid.*, 241). The pseudepigraphic literature used names from the time of Moses up to the later *geonim* and the Ḥasidim of Germany. Provence was undoubtedly the place of composition of the *Sefer ha-Iyyun* ascribed to Rav Ḥamai Gaon, the *Ma'ayan ha-Ḥokhmah*, which was communicated by an angel to Moses, the *Midrash Shimon ha-Ẓaddik*, and other texts, while the home of most of the writings attributable to the circle of the *Sefer ha-Iyyun* could have been either Provence or Castile. More than 30 texts of this kind are known, most of them very short (see the list of them in *Reshit ha-Kabbalah*, Heb. ed. pp. 255–62; *Origines*…, 283–91). New interpretations of the ten *Sefirot* are found side by side with notes and expositions of the "32 paths of wisdom," the Tetragrammaton, and the 42-lettered Name of God, as well as various cosmogonic speculations. Platonic and Gnostic tendencies are interwoven in them. Knowledge of the "intellectual lights," which fill the place previously occupied by the Chariot, competes with theories of the ten *Sefirot* and of the mystical names. The authors of these works had their own solemn, abstract terminology, but the terms are given differing interpretations as they recur in various places. The order of emanation varies from time to time, and it is clear that these speculations had not yet reached their final state. There were considerable differences of opinion within this circle, and each individual author seems to have been trying to define the content of the world of emanation as it was disclosed to his vision or contemplation. Even where the theory of the *Sefirot* was accepted it underwent remarkable changes. One group of texts interprets the 13 attributes of divine mercy as the sum of the powers which fill the world of emanation, some authors adding three powers to the end of the list of *Sefirot*; while in other texts the three powers are added to the top, or are considered to be intellectual lights shining within the first *Sefirah*. This view, which stimulated many speculations as the development of the Kabbalah continued, occurs in the responsa attributed to Hai Gaon on the relationship of the ten *Sefirot* to the 13 attributes.

There are clear connections leading from Saadiah's theory of the *Kavod* and his concept of "the ether which cannot be grasped," stated in his commentary to the *Sefer Yeẓirah*, to this circle, which made use of his ideas through the early translation of the *Sefer Emunot ve-De'ot*. The circle seems to have had little use for the *Sefer ha-Bahir*. The stress on the mysticism of the lights of the intellect is near in spirit, although not in detail, with later neoplatonic literature, e.g., the "Book of the Five Substances of Pseudo-Empedocles" (from the school of

Ibn Masarra in Spain). For example, the supernal essences which are revealed, according to the *Sefer ha-Iyyun* and several other texts, from "the highest hidden mystery" or "the primeval darkness," are: primeval wisdom, wonderful light, the *ḥashmal*, the mist (*arafel*), the throne of light, the wheel (*ofan*) of greatness, the cherub, the wheels of the Chariot, the surrounding ether, the curtain, the throne of glory, the place of souls, and the outer palace of holiness. This mixture of terms from widely different fields is characteristic of the blending of sources and of a hierarchical arrangement that does not depend on the theory of the *Sefirot*, although it too is incorporated in some of the writings of this circle. A theurgic tendency also appears along with a desire to indulge in philosophical speculations on the Sacred Names. In addition to the influence of Arab neoplatonism, there are indications of some links with the Christian Platonic tradition transmitted through the *De Divisione Naturae* of John Scotus Erigena, but this question needs further research.

The Kabbalist Center of Gerona

Under the influence of the first kabbalists, their ideas spread from Provence to Spain, where they found a particular response in the rabbinic circle of Gerona, in Catalonia, between the Pyrenees Mountains and Barcelona. Here, from the beginning of the 13th century, a center of great and far-ranging importance came into being which fulfilled an essential role in the establishment of the Kabbalah in Spain and in the development of kabbalistic literature. For the first time, books were written here which, despite their emphasis on the esoteric side of Kabbalah, sought to bring its major ideas to a wider public. Sometimes allusions to these ideas are found in works which are not basically kabbalistic – e.g., works of *halakhah*, exegesis, ethics, or homiletics – but there were a number of books which were completely or largely devoted to the Kabbalah. Several letters from members of this group have survived which contain important evidence of their feelings and their participation in contemporary disputes and discussions. The main figures in this group were a mysterious individual by the (pseudonymous?) name of Ben Belimah (Scholem, *Origines*…, 413); Judah b. Yakar, Naḥmanides' teacher and for a certain time *dayyan* in Barcelona (1215), whose commentary to the liturgy (JQR, 4 (1892), 245–56) contains kabbalistic statements; *Ezra b. Solomon and *Azriel; Moses b. Naḥman (Naḥmanides); Abraham b. Isaac *Gerondi, the *ḥazzan* of the community; Jacob b. Sheshet *Gerondi; and the poet Meshullam b. Solomon *Da Piera (whose poems were collected in *Yedi'ot ha-Makhon le-Ḥeker ha-Shirah*, 4, 1938). In addition, their pupils should also be included, although many of them spread further afield to the Aragonese communities.

A personal and literary link between the kabbalists of Provence and those of Gerona may be seen in *Asher b. David, a nephew of Isaac the Blind. A number of his writings were very widely scattered in manuscript (collected by M. Ḥasidah in *Ha-Segullah* (fascicles 17–30, Jerusalem, 1933–34). In content, his writings are very similar to those of Ezra and Azriel, who were apparently among the first to write works entirely devoted to Kabbalah, composed mainly in the first third of the 13th century. Ezra wrote a commentary to the Song of Songs (which was published under Naḥmanides' name), interpreted the *aggadot* to several tractates of the Talmud wherever he was able to connect them with the Kabbalah, and summarized traditions, the greater part of which doubtless derived from the Provençal kabbalists. His younger companion, Azriel, made an independent rendering of his interpretation of the *aggadot* (ed. Tishby, 1943), wrote a commentary to the liturgy (extant in Ms.) according to the theory of the *kavvanot*, a commentary to the *Sefer Yeẓirah* published in editions of that work under the name of Naḥmanides, and two small books on the nature of God, *Be'ur Eser Sefirot* (also entitled *Sha'ar ha-Sho'el*), and *Derekh ha-Emunah ve-Derekh ha-Kefirah*. These two kabbalists also left separate "mysteries" on several subjects (e.g., "the mystery of sacrifices"), and letters on kabbalistic questions, including a long letter from Azriel to the kabbalists of Burgos (*Madda'ei ha-Yahadut*, 2 (1927), 233–40). Azriel stands out above other members of the group because of the systematic nature of his thought and the depth of his intellect. He is the only one of the group whose work is connected in style and content with the writings of the circle of the *Sefer ha-Iyyun* mentioned above. In his books, the interpenetration of neoplatonic and Gnostic elements reached their first apex. The neoplatonic element came largely from the writings of Isaac b. Solomon Israeli, some of which were undoubtedly known in Gerona (Altmann, in JJS, 7 (1956), 31–57). Jacob b. Sheshet, in his polemical work against Samuel ibn *Tibbon, *Meshiv Devarim Nekhoḥim* (ed. Vajda, 1968), combined philosophical enquiry with kabbalistic speculation. Two of his books were devoted to the latter: *Sefer ha-Emunah ve-ha-Bittaḥon*, which was later attributed to Naḥmanides and published under his name, and *Sha'ar ha-Shamayim*, a rhymed summary of kabbalistic ideas (*Oẓar Neḥmad*, 3 (1860), 133–65).

It is doubtful if these kabbalists, who were known only to a small circle and who composed no works outside the field of Kabbalah, would have had the great influence that they did if it had not been for the stature of their colleague Naḥmanides (c. 1194–1270), the highest legal and religious authority of his time in Spain. The fact that he joined the ranks of the kabbalists as a young man prepared the way for the reception of the Kabbalah in Spain, just as the personality of Abraham b. David had prepared the way in Provence. The names of these two men were a guarantee to most of their contemporaries that, despite their novelty, kabbalistic ideas did not stray from the accepted faith and the rabbinic tradition. Their undisputed conservative character protected the kabbalists from accusations of deviation from strict monotheism or even of heresy. Charges of this kind were made, provoked mainly by the wider publicity given to the earlier works of Kabbalah and to their oral propagation in a number of communities. Isaac the Blind refers to polemics between the kabbalists and their opponents in Spain, and evidence of similar arguments in Provence (between 1235 and 1245) is extant in the accusations of *Meir b.

Simeon of Narbonne, a reply to which, in defense of the Kabbalah, is included in the works of Asher b. David (see *Sefer Bialik* (1934), 141–62).

From the very beginning two opposing tendencies appear among the kabbalists, the first seeking to limit the Kabbalah to closed circles as a definitely esoteric system, and the second wishing to spread its influence among the people at large. Throughout the history of the Kabbalah right down to recent times these two tendencies have been in conflict. Parallel with this, from the time of the appearance of the Kabbalah in Gerona, two attitudes developed concerning the relationship of the bearers of rabbinic culture to the Kabbalah. The kabbalists were accepted as proponents of a conservative ideology and as public defenders of tradition and custom, but at the same time they were suspected, by a substantial number of rabbis and sages, of having non-Jewish leanings and of being innovators whose activities must be curtailed wherever possible. Most of the kabbalists themselves saw their role in terms of the preservation of tradition, and in fact their first public appearance was associated with their taking the traditionalists' side in the controversy over Maimonides' writings and the study of philosophy in the 13th century (Scholem, *Origines*…, 416–54). In these disputes the Kabbalah of the Gerona scholars seemed to be a symbolic interpretation of the world of Judaism and its way of life, based on a theosophy which taught the inner secrets of the revealed Godhead and on a rejection of rationalist interpretations of the Torah and the Commandments. Nevertheless, it cannot be ignored that the system of thought elaborated by a man like Azriel did not invalidate the philosophic teachings of his time but rather added to it a new dimension, that of theosophy, as its crowning glory.

In several of his works Naḥmanides gives room to the Kabbalah, particularly in his commentary to the Torah, where his many veiled and unexplained allusions to interpretations "according to the true way" were meant to arouse the curiosity of those readers who had never heard of that "way." He also used kabbalistic symbolism in some of his *piyyutim*. And his views on the fate of the soul after death and the nature of the world to come, expressed in *Sha'ar ha-Gemul* at the end of his halakhic work *Toledot Adam*, represent the ideas of his circle and are in contrast to Maimonides' views on this subject. His commentary to the Book of Job is based on the theory of transmigration (without mentioning the term *gilgul* itself) and on the views of his companion, Ezra, concerning the *Sefirah Ḥochmah* ("wisdom"). Naḥmanides wrote no works specifically on the Kabbalah, apart from a commentary to the first chapter of the *Sefer Yeẓirah* (KS, 6 (1930), 385–410) and a sermon on the occasion of a wedding (*He-Ḥalutz*, 12 (1887), 111–4). Since the 14th century, several books by other authors were attributed to him. In the writings of the Gerona kabbalists there is a definite, well-established symbolic framework which is related first and foremost to the theory of the *Sefirot* and to the way in which this theory interprets scriptural verses and homilies dealing with the acts of God. This symbolism served as the main basis for the development of the Kabbalah in this group, and numerous anonymous kabbalists of this and later periods made out lists and tables, mostly brief, of the order of the *Sefirot*, and of the nomenclature in Scripture and *aggadah* which fitted them. In points of detail practically every kabbalist had his own system but there was a wide measure of agreement on fundamentals (a list of such tracts in KS, 10 (1934), 498–515).

Contacts were made between the Spanish kabbalists and the Ḥasidei Ashkenaz, either through individual Ḥasidim who visited Spain or through books which were brought there, e.g., the works of Eleazar of Worms. Abraham Axelrod of Cologne, who traveled through the Spanish communities between 1260 and 1275 approximately, wrote *Keter Shem Tov* dealing with the Tetragrammaton and the theory of the *Sefirot*. It exists in various versions, one of which was published in Jellinek's *Ginzei Ḥokhmat ha-Kabbalah* (1853), while another gives the author's name as Menahem, a pupil of Eleazar of Worms. This combination of the theory of the Sacred Names and speculations using the methods of *gematria* with the theory of the *Sefirot* of the Gerona kabbalists contains, at least in a third version of the book, a powerful renewal of ecstatic tendencies, which took on the new form of "prophetic Kabbalah" (*Kelal mi-Darkhei ha-Kabbalah ha-Nevu'it*; see G. Scholem, *Kitvei Yad be-Kabbalah* (1930), 57). Other kabbalists from Castile also established contacts with one of the pupils of Eleazar of Worms who lived in Narbonne in the middle of the 13th century.

It is almost certain that an anonymous kabbalist from the Gerona circle, or one of the Provençal kabbalists, was the author of the book **Temunah* (written before 1250), which was attributed several generations later to R. Ishmael, the high priest. The style of the book is very difficult, and its contents are obscure at many points. An interpretation of the "image of God" through the shapes of the Hebrew letters, it became the basis of several other texts, composed in a similar fashion and perhaps even by the same author; e.g., interpretations of the secret 72-lettered Name of God mentioned in the mystical literature of the geonic period. The importance of the book lies in its detailed though enigmatic explanation of the theory of *shemittot* (see below), to which the Gerona kabbalists alluded without a detailed explanation. The difficult style of the *Temunah* was elucidated to some extent by an old commentary, also anonymous (published with the book itself in 1892), which was written at the end of the 13th century. *Temunah* had a distinct influence on Kabbalah up to the 16th century.

Other Currents in 13th-Century Spanish Kabbalah

The combination of theosophic-Gnostic and neoplatonic-philosophical elements, which found expression in Provence and Gerona, led to the relative, or sometimes exaggerated, dominance of one element over the other in other currents from 1230 onward. On one side there was an extreme mystical tendency, expressed in philosophical terms and creating its own symbolism which was not based on the theory or nomenclature of the *Sefirot* found among the Gerona kabbalists. Refuting some of the suppositions of the latter (e.g., the theory of transmigration), nevertheless it saw itself as the true "science of Kabbalah." Its first and most important exponent was Isaac ibn *Latif, whose books were written (perhaps in Toledo) between 1230 and 1270. "He had one foot inside [in Kabbalah], and one foot outside [in philosophy]" as Judah *Ḥayyat said of him (preface to *Minḥat Yehudah* on *Ma'arekhet ha-Elohut*). Becoming a kind of independent mystic, he drew his philosophical inspiration from the writings in both Arabic and Hebrew of the neoplatonists, and especially from Ibn Gabirol's *Mekor Ḥayyim* and the works of Abraham ibn Ezra, although at times he completely transformed their meaning. His main work, *Sha'ar ha-Shamayim* (written in 1238), was intended to be, in a speculative mystical vein, both a continuation of and a substitute for Maimonides' *Guide of the Perplexed*. Together with most of the Gerona kabbalists he accorded the highest place to the Primeval Will, seeing in it the source of all emanation. The theory of the Divine Logos, which he took from the Arabic neoplatonic tradition, became divided into the Will – which remained completely within the Divine and was identified with the Divine Word (Logos) which brought forth all things – and into the "first created thing," the Supreme Intellect that stands at the top of the hierarchy of all beings, and was presented in symbols which in other places belong to the Logos itself. But Ibn Latif is not consistent in his use of symbolism and often contradicts himself, even on important points. From the "first created thing" emanated all the other stages, called symbolically light, fire, ether, and water. Each of these is the province of one branch of wisdom: mysticism, metaphysics, astronomy, and physics. Ibn Latif created a complete and rich system of the universe, basing his views on a far-fetched allegorical interpretation of Scripture, although he was opposed to the extreme allegorists who regarded allegory as a substitute for the literal interpretation and not simply an addition to it. His ideas about prayer and true understanding have a distinctly mystical tinge, and in this respect exceed the theory of *kavvanah* and meditation prevalent among the kabbalists of Gerona. The influence of Ibn Gabirol is most noticeable in his *Ẓurat ha-Olam* (1860) which contains specific criticisms of kabbalistic theosophy. Nevertheless, Ibn Latif regards Kabbalah as superior to philosophy both in nature and efficacy, in particular because it takes hold of truth which is of a temporal nature, whereas philosophical truth is atemporal (*Rav Pe'alim* (1885), no. 39). Ibn Latif had personal ties with exponents of Kabbalah whose conceptions were completely opposed to his, and he dedicated *Ẓeror ha-Mor* to Todros *Abulafia of Toledo, one of the leaders of the Gnostic trend of Kabbalah. His books were read by kabbalists and philosophers alike, e.g., the philosopher Isaac *Albalag (Vatican Ms. 254, fol. 97b), who criticized his *Ẓurat ha-Olam*. According to Ibn Latif, the highest intellectual understanding reaches only the "back" of the Divine, whereas a picture of the "face" is disclosed only in supra-intellectual esctasy, which involves experience superior even to that of prophecy (*Ginzei ha-Melekh*, chs. 37 and 41). This perception he calls "the beatitude of supreme communion." True prayer brings the human intellect into communion with the Active Intellect "like a kiss," but from there it ascends even to union with the "first created thing"; beyond this union, achieved through words, is the union through pure thought intended to reach the First Cause, i.e., the Primeval Will, and at length to stand before God Himself (*Ẓeror ha-Mor*, ch. 5).

The second exponent of philosophic-mystical tendencies distinct from the theosophical Kabbalah of the Gerona school and aspiring toward an ecstatic "prophetic Kabbalah" was Abraham *Abulafia (1240–after 1292). The striking image of this man derives from his outstanding personality. He came into contact with a group whose technique of letter combination and number mysticism stimulated his own ecstatic experiences. At least part of his inspiration was derived directly from the German Ḥasidei Ashkenaz and perhaps also through the influence of Sufi circles, whom he met with during his travels in the east in his early years. Abulafia's teacher was the *ḥazzan* Barukh Togarmi (in Barcelona?), who, judging by his name, came from the east. From him he learned the fundamental teachings of prophetic Kabbalah to whose dissemination he devoted his life, after he had attained illumination in Barcelona in 1271. His prophetic and perhaps also his messianic claims aroused strong opposition both in Spain and in Italy, but his books were widely read from the end of the 13th century, especially those where he expounded his system of Kabbalah as a kind of guide to the upward journey from philosophical preoccupations of the Maimonidean type to prophecy and to those mystical experiences which he believed partook of the nature of prophecy. Abulafia was also a copious borrower of kabbalistic ideas whenever he found them relevant, but those aspects which were foreign to his nature he opposed even to the point of ridicule. A passionate admirer of Maimonides, he believed that his own system was merely a continuation and elaboration of the teaching of the *Guide of the Perplexed*. Unlike Maimonides, who dissociated himself from the possibility of prophecy in his time, Abulafia defended such a prospect, finding in "the way of the Names," i.e., a specific mystical technique also called "the science of combination" (*ḥokhmat ha-ẓeruf*), a means of realizing and embodying human aspirations toward prophecy.

So inspired, he himself wrote 26 prophetic books of which only one, *Sefer ha-Ot*, has survived. *Derekh ha-Sefirot* ("the way of the *Sefirot*"), he believed, is useful for beginners but is of little value compared with *Derekh ha-Shemot* ("the way of the Names"), opening up only after deep study of the *Sefer Yeẓirah* and the techniques to which it alludes. Abulafia saw his Kabbalah, therefore, as another layer added to the earlier Kabbalah, which did not contradict such major works as the *Bahir*, the *Temunah*, and the writings of Naḥmanides. His promise to expound a way which would lead to what he called "prophecy," and his practical application of kabbalist principles, found a distinct echo in Kabbalah from the 14th century onward, first in Italy and later in other countries. His great manuals (*Sefer ha-Ẓeruf, Sefer Or ha-Sekhel, Sefer Ḥayyei ha-Olam ha-Ba*, and others), which have been copied right down to recent times, are textbooks of meditation, the objects of which are the Sacred Names and the letters of the alphabet and their combinations, both comprehensible and incomprehensible. It was precisely this kind of manual which had been lacking in the usual type of kabbalistic literature, which had confined itself to symbolic descriptions, and refrained from advancing in writing techniques for mystic experience. The work of Abulafia filled this need, and the fierce criticism of him which was heard here and there did not prevent their absorption and influence. One of Abulafia's pupils wrote (perhaps in Hebron) at the end of 1294 a small book on prophetic Kabbalah, *Sha'arei Ẓedek*, which includes an important autobiographical description of his studies with his teacher, and of his mystical experiences (Scholem, *Mysticism*, 146–55).

On the other side of this twofold development of the Kabbalah was a school of kabbalists who were more attracted to Gnostic traditions, whether genuine or only apparently so, and who concentrated on the Gnostic and mythological element rather than on the philosophical. The exponents of this trend set out to find and assemble fragments of documents and oral traditions, and added to them just as much themselves, until their books became an astonishing mixture of pseudepigrapha with the authors' own commentaries. In contrast with the Kabbalah of Gerona, the pseudepigraphic element was very strong in this branch, although it is not absolutely certain that the authors of these books themselves invented the sources which they quoted. This school, which might properly be called "the Gnostic reaction," includes the brothers *Jacob and *Isaac, sons of Jacob ha-Kohen of Soria, who traveled in Spain and Provence and met their older kabbalist predecessors: Moses b. *Simeon, their pupil and successor, rabbi of Burgos; and Todros b. Joseph *Abulafia of Burgos and Toledo, one of the leaders of Castilian Jewry of his day. Their main work belongs to the second half of the 13th century. In Kabbalist circles Moses of Burgos was widely considered to be endowed with particular authority, and he was also the teacher of Isaac ibn Sahula, author of *Meshal ha-Kadmoni*. It is extraordinary that such a complete rationalist and devotee of philosophical enquiry as Isaac Albalag could see three members of this school as the true exponents of Kabbalah in his time, with Moses of Burgos at their head: "His name has spread throughout the country: Moses has received [*kibbel*] the [authentic] kabbalist tradition" (*Madda'ei ha-Yahadut*, 2 (1927), 168).

The speculative side is not altogether absent in this school, and some fragments of one of Isaac ha-Kohen's books (*ibid.*, 276–9) in particular show some relationship between him and Ibn Latif, but its true characteristics are quite different. He developed the details of the theory of the left, demonic, emanation, whose ten *Sefirot* are the exact counterparts of the Holy *Sefirot*. A similar demonic emanation is already mentioned in the writings of the *Sefer ha-Iyyun* group, and in the works of Naḥmanides, and it is possible that its origins stemmed from the east. In the evidence extant, this theory appeared in pseudepigraphic texts and its roots were mainly in Provence and Castile. From these traditions came the Zoharic theory of the *sitra aḥra* (the "other side"). There is a strong tendency here to make long lists of beings in the world below the realm of the *Sefirot* – that are given specific names – and so establish a completely new angelology. These emanations of the second rank are presented partly as "curtains" (*pargodim*) in front of the emanations of the *Sefirot*, and as "bodies" and "garments" for the inner souls, which are the *Sefirot*. This multiplicity of personified emanations and the listing of them recall similar tendencies in the later development of several Gnostic systems, and in particular the book *Pistis Sophia*. To everything in the world below there is a corresponding force in the world above, and in this way a kind of strange mythology without precedent in other sources is created. This theme runs through all the writings of Isaac b. Jacob ha-Kohen, and through some of the work of his elder brother Jacob. The novelty of the names of these forces and their description is obvious, and some of the details of the *Sefirot* and their nomenclature occasionally assume a form different from that in the Kabbalah of Gerona. In the writings of Todros Abulafia the kabbalists who are exponents of the Gnostic trend are given the specific name of *ma'amikim* ("those who delve deeply"), in order to distinguish them from the others. The Spanish kabbalists of the 14th century made an additional distinction between the Kabbalah of the Castilian kabbalists, which belonged to the Gnostic school, and that of the Catalonian kabbalists. In this circle we can observe quite clearly the growth of the magical element and the tendency to preserve theurgic traditions of which there is no trace in the Gerona school.

This new Gnostic bent did not stop the individual mystical or visionary experience. The two elements go hand in hand in the writings of Jacob ha-Kohen, who wrote the extensive *Sefer ha-Orah*, which has no link with earlier kabbalistic tradition but is based entirely on visions which "were accorded him" in heaven. The Kabbalah of these visions is completely different from the traditionalist portion of his other writings, and it is not taken up anywhere else in the history of the Kabbalah. It is based on a new form of the idea of the Logos which assumes here the image of Metatron. The theory of emanation also acquires another garb, and concern with the *Sefirot* makes way for speculations on "the holy spheres" (*ha-galgalim ha-kedoshim*) through which the power of the Emanator is invisibly dispersed until it reaches the sphere of Metatron, which is the central cosmic force. This very personal theosophy, nourished and inspired by vision, has no relationship with the theosophy of the Gerona kabbalists but it has some connection with the Ḥasidei Ashkenaz. Jacob ha-Kohen was the first Spanish kabbalist to build all his mystical teachings concerning the reasons for the Commandments and other matters on *gematriot*. Metatron, to be sure, was created, but came into being simultaneously with the emanation of the inner heavenly spheres, and the verse "Let there be light" alludes to the "formation of the light of the intellect" in the shape of Metatron. There is little doubt that Jacob ha-Kohen knew about the art of "combination" as a prerequisite for mystical perception, but had no knowledge of those mysteries derived from it through rationalist interpretation characteristic of Abraham Abulafia. *Sefer ha-Orah* has not been preserved in its entirety, but large parts of it exist in various manuscripts (Milan 62, Vatican 428, etc.). It is the most striking example of how an entirely new Kabbalah could be created side by side with the earlier Kabbalah, and it is as if each one of them speaks on a different plane. In his *Oẓar ha-Kavod* on the legends of the Talmud (1879), and in his *Sha'ar ha-Razim* on Psalm 19 (Munich Ms. 209) Todros Abulafia strove to combine the Kabbalah of Gerona with the Kabbalah of the Gnostics, but he never alluded to the revelations accorded to Jacob ha-Kohen.

THE ZOHAR. The mingling of the two trends emanating from the Gerona school and from the school of the Gnostics is to a certain extent paralleled in the main product of Spanish Kabbalah, the character of which is also determined by them. This is the *Sefer ha-Zohar*, written largely between 1280 and 1286 by Moses b. Shem Tov de *Leon, in Guadalajara, a small town northeast of Madrid. In this city there also lived two kabbalist brothers, Isaac and Meir b. Solomon ibn *Sahula, and it is in Isaac's books that the first quotations are found from the earliest stratum of the Zohar, dating from 1281 (G. Scholem, in *Tarbiz*, 3 (1932), 181–3; KS, 6 (1929), 109–18). Many kabbalists were working at this time in the small communities around Toledo, and there is evidence of mystical experience even among the unlearned. An example of this is the appearance as a prophet in Avila in 1295 of Nissim b. Abraham, an ignorant artisan, to whom an angel revealed a kabbalistic work, *Pil'ot ha-Ḥokhmah*, and who was opposed by Solomon b. Abraham *Adret (Responsa of Solomon b. Adret, no. 548). This was the community where Moses de Leon passed the last years of his life (d. 1305). The Zohar is the most important evidence for the stirring of a mythical spirit in medieval Judaism. The origin of the book, its literary and religious character, and the role that it has played in the history of Judaism, have been subjects of prolonged argument among scholars during the last 130 years, but most of it has not been based on historical and linguistic analysis. In an analysis of this kind we can establish a precise place for the Zohar in the development of Spanish Kabbalah, which has set its seal on the book. In so doing we must resist continually recurring apologetic attempts to antedate its composition by turning its late literary sources into evidence for the earlier existence of the book, or by proclaiming ancient strata in it – of whose presence there is no proof whatsoever (J.L. Zlotnik, Finkel, Reuben Margulies, Chavel, M. Kasher, and others).

The mingling of these two currents – the Kabbalah of Gerona and the Kabbalah of the "Gnostics" of Castile – became in the mind of Moses de Leon a creative encounter which determined the basic character of the Zohar. Instead of the brief allusions and interpretations of his predecessors he presents a broad canvas of interpretation and homiletics covering the whole world of Judaism as it appeared to him. He was far removed from systematic theology, and indeed there are fundamental problems of contemporary Jewish thought which do not arise in his work at all, such as the meaning of prophecy and the questions of predestination and providence; however, he reflects the actual religious situation, and expounds it through kabbalistic interpretation. In a pseudepigraph attributed to Simeon b. Yoḥai and his friends, Moses de Leon clothed his interpretation of Judaism in an archaic garb – long and short Midrashim on the Torah and the three scrolls, the books Song of Songs, Ruth, and Lamentations. The explanations in the book revolve round two axes – one consisting of the mysteries of the world of the *Sefirot* that constitute the life of the Divine, which is also reflected in many symbols in the created world; and the other of the situation of the Jew and his fate both in this world and in the world of souls. The deepening and broadening of a symbolic view of Judaism was very daring in an age when the kabbalists still preserved in some measure the esoteric character of their ideas. The appearance of what purported to be an ancient Midrash which actually reflected the basic viewpoints of the Spanish kabbalists, and successfully expressed them in an impressive literary synthesis, sparked off a number of arguments among the kabbalists of the day. However, it also served to spread knowledge of the Kabbalah and ensure its acceptance. The author's viewpoint progressed from a tendency toward philosophy and allegoric interpretation to Kabbalah and its symbolic ideas. The steps in this progress can still be recognized in the differences between the *Midrash ha-Ne'lam*, the earliest part of the Zohar, and the main body of the book. There is little doubt that the aim of the book was to attack the literal conception of Judaism and the neglect of the performance of the *mitzvot*, and this was accomplished by emphasizing the supreme value and secret meaning of every word and Commandment of the Torah. As in most great mystical texts, inner perception and the way to "communion" are connected with the preservation of the traditional framework, whose value is increased sevenfold. The mystical viewpoint served to strengthen the tradition and indeed became a conscious conservative factor. On the other hand, the author of the Zohar concentrated frequently on speculations on the profundities of the Nature of the Divinity, which other kabbalists did not dare to dwell upon, and his boldness was an important contributory factor in the renewed development of Kabbalah several generations later. When the Zohar appeared few kabbalists turned their attention to this original aspect. Instead they used the Zohar as a distinguished aid to strengthening their conservative aims. In his Hebrew books written in the years after 1286, after he had finished his major work in the Zohar, Moses de Leon himself concealed many of his more daring speculations (which the obscure Aramaic garb had suited very well). On the other hand he stressed in them the principles of *Sefirot* symbolism, with its value for the comprehension of the Torah and of prayer, and also the homiletical and moral element of the Zohar. His Hebrew books expanded, here and there, themes which were first adumbrated with some variations in the Zohar. These works have largely been preserved, and some of them were copied many times, but only one has been published (*Sefer ha-Mishkal*, also called

Sefer ha-Nefesh ha-Ḥakhamah, 1608). It is hard to say to what extent Moses de Leon expected his work in the Zohar actually to be accepted as an ancient and authoritative Midrash, or how far he intended to create a compendium of Kabbalah in a suitable literary form which would be perfectly clear to the discerning eye. Many kabbalists in the succeeding generation used similar forms and wrote imitations of the Zohar, something which they would not have dared to do in the case of genuine Midrashim, thus showing that they did not take the framework of the book too seriously. This does not detract from (indeed it may add to) the value of the Zohar from a historical point of view, whether for its own sake or for the sake of the influence that it exerted.

Moses de Leon was certainly very closely associated with another kabbalist, who began as a disciple of Abraham Abulafia himself. This was Joseph *Gikatilla, who wrote *Ginnat Egoz* in 1274 and later a number of other works under the inspiration of his first master. However, while still young he also became associated with Gnostic circles and afterward he struck up a friendship with Moses de Leon; each came under the other's influence. Turning his attention from the mysteries of letters, vowels, and names, Gikatilla embarked on a profound study of the theosophy of the *Sefirot* system, and his books provide an independent and valuable parallel to the writings of Moses de Leon. *Sha'arei Orah*, written about 1290, already shows the influence of certain parts of the Zohar, although there is no mention of it. An important summary of, and renowned introduction to, the interpretation of *Sefirot* symbolism, this book became one of the major works of Spanish Kabbalah. It is worth noting that three different streams, the Kabbalah of Gerona, the Kabbalah of the Zohar, and the Kabbalah of Abulafia, were able to meet and be reconciled in Gikatilla's mind, a very rare occurrence in this period. His *Ginnat Egoz* is the latest source, insofar as we know, utilized by the author of the Zohar.

Two works written in the 1290s or in the earliest years of the 14th century, the *Ra'aya Meheimna* and the *Sefer ha-Tikkunim*, comprise the latest strands in the zoharic literature. They are the work of an unknown kabbalist who was familiar with the major part of the Zohar and wrote his books as a kind of continuation of it (albeit with some change in literary style and framework). The books contain a new interpretation of the first chapters of Genesis and a tabulated explanation of the reasons for the Commandments. Elevating the importance of the Zohar as the final revelation of the mysteries, these two works connected its appearance with the beginning of the redemption: "Through the merits of the Zohar they will go forth from exile in mercy," i.e., without the dread pains of the redemption (Zohar 3, 124b). The author exaggeratedly blends the image of the biblical Moses with Moses the revealer of the Zohar on the eve of the final redemption. It is possible that he was very close to the circle of Moses de Leon, and perhaps he was also called Moses. These books are the first of a whole line of kabbalistic works which were written in the pseudo-Aramaic style of the Zohar and as a continuation of it. Some authors also wrote in Hebrew, adding interpretations in the name of zoharic characters but reflecting their own ideas. In this category mention should be made of *Mar'ot ha-Ẓove'ot* (Sassoon Ms. 978) by David b. Judah *he-Ḥasid, known from his other writings as a grandson of Naḥmanides (*Ohel Dawid*, 1001–06); and *Livnat ha-Sappir* (on Gen., 1914; on Lev. British Museum Ms. 767) by Joseph Angelino, written in 1325–27, and wrongly ascribed by several kabbalists to David b. Judah Ḥasid. This latter David was the first to write a quasi-commentary on and elaboration of the speculations in the *Idra Rabba* of the Zohar, called *Sefer ha-Gevul* (Jerusalem Ms., and see Scholem in KS, 4 (1928), 307–10). He also wrote a long commentary, *Or Zaru'a*, on the liturgy, and several other books (*ibid.*, 302–27).

An important pseudepigraph written at the time of the appearance of the Zohar was "The Mystery of the Names, Letters, and Vowels, and the Power of the [Magical] Operations, according to the Sages of Lunel," which is found in several manuscripts under different names (Vatican Ms. 441). Attributed to the circle of Abraham b. David, the book is actually based on the works of Gikatilla and Moses de Leon, and connects speculations on the letters, vowels, and the Sacred Names with the theory of practical Kabbalah. Its author, who gave the words of the late 13th-century kabbalists a new pseudepigraphic frame, also compiled the kabbalist anthology *Sefer ha-Ne'lam* (Paris Ms. [3]), using similar source material. An obscure figure in zoharic imitation literature is Joseph "who came from the city of Shushan" (i.e., from Hamadan in Persia). Perhaps this is a completely fictitious name concealing a Spanish kabbalist who lived about 1300 or a little later and wrote a lengthy work on the Torah section of *Terumah* and the Song of Songs, which is largely written in the style of the Zohar and develops the ideas of the zoharic *Idras* concerning the *Shi'ur Komah*. According to A. Altmann he is to be identified with the anonymous author of the *Sefer Ta'amei ha-Mitzvot*, which was used as the source of a literary plagiarism by Isaac ibn Farḥi in the 16th century (KS, 40 (1965), 405–12). At any rate, his extensive work is preserved (British Museum Ms. 464) and was widely disseminated, even in comparatively late times (G. Scholem, in *Sefer Yovel le-Aron Freimann* (1935), 51–62). The book is full of astonishing ideas not to be found in other kabbalistic texts, and the author introduces opinions which are quite foreign to the Zohar, although couched in its style. The third book in this category is the *Sefer ha-She'arim* or *She'elot la-Zaken* (Oxford Ms. 2396) from the first quarter of the 14th century. The old man (*zaken*) who replies to the questions of his disciples in none other than Moses himself. The bulk of the book is written in Hebrew and only a minor section in the zoharic style. Also a completely independent work, it relies a great deal on allusion without fully explaining its ideas.

The Kabbalah in the 14th Century up to the Expulsion from Spain

The 14th century was a period of intellectual development which produced an extremely rich literature. The Kabbalah spread through most of the communities of Spain and beyond, in particular to Italy and the East. Once the gates were opened wide through the books that revealed mystical ideas, all the preceding trends found their continuators and their interpreters; with this expansion all the different trends mingled with one another to a certain extent, and attempts were made to find a compromise between them.

The Kabbalah of Gerona was continued through the prolific literary activity of the disciples of Naḥmanides' pupils, who were taught by Solomon b. Abraham Adret (Rashba) and Isaac b. *Todros, author of a commentary to the *maḥzor* according to Kabbalah (Paris Ms. 839). Members of this school, who did not favor the prevailing pseudepigraphic style, produced many books attempting to clarify the kabbalistic passages of Naḥmanides' commentary to the Torah. An unknown author writing at the beginning of the 14th century composed *Ma'arekhet *ha-Elohut* (1558), a compendium which expounded the doctrine of Kabbalah in a terse and systematic fashion. This book was very widely read and its influence was felt as late as the 16th century. Although Solomon b. Abraham Adret was very cautious in his dealings with kabbalistic matters, he often alluded to them in his commentary to the *aggadot* (Vatican Ms. 295), and he also composed a long prayer in the kabbalistic way. His pupils, however, assigned a central place to the Kabbalah. To this school belong: Baḥya b. *Asher from Saragossa, whose commentary to the Torah contributed greatly to the dissemination of the Kabbalah and was the first kabbalist book to be printed in its entirety (1492); Joshua ibn *Shuaib from Tudela, author of the important *Derashot* (homilies) on the Torah (1523), the first book in this genre to assign a central place to the Kabbalah, and the real author of the *Be'ur Sodot ha-Ramban* ("Explanation of [the kabbalistic] secrets of Naḥmanides' Commentary"), which was printed (1875) under the name of his pupil, Meir b. Solomon Abi Sahula; Ḥayyim b. Samuel of Lerida, author of *Ẓeror ha-Ḥayyim*, which contains a kabbalistic exposition of halakhic matters (Musajoff Ms.); Shem Tov b. Abraham ibn *Gaon from Soria, who began a large-scale literary activity on the Kabbalah between 1315 and 1325, emigrated to Ereẓ Israel with his friend Elhanan b. Abraham ibn Eskira, and settled in Safed. Elhanan's *Yesod Olam* (Guenzburg Ms. 607) merges the Gerona tradition with neoplatonic philosophical Kabbalah. In the school of Solomon Adret a large amount of raw material was assembled which has been preserved in *collectanea* of considerable value (Vatican Ms. 202, Parma Mss. 68 and 1221, and others). In the same way several anonymous texts have been preserved which interpret the hidden meanings in Naḥmanides. The main storehouse for all the traditions of this school is *Me'irat Einaim* by Isaac b. Samuel of *Acre, who also dealt at length in other books with completely different aspects of the Kabbalah, under the joint influence of the Zohar and the school of Abraham Abulafia. In contrast to the attempts to seek a compromise between Kabbalah and philosophy, he insisted on the independence and supreme worth of kabbalist theosophy. Parts of the collection of revelations that were granted to him in various ways were assembled in *Oẓar ha-Ḥayyim* (Guenzburg Ms. 775), parts of which have been frequently copied. He was associated with many contemporary kabbalists, and he was the first of this circle to write an autobiography, which, however, is now lost.

Another kabbalist who migrated to Spain and became acquainted with the Kabbalah there was Joseph b. Shalom *Ashkenazi, author of an extensive commentary to the *Sefer Yeẓirah* (which has been printed in editions of the book under the name of Abraham b. David). He also wrote a commentary to the *bereshit* section of the *Midrash Genesis Rabbah* (KS, 4 (1928), 236–302). The works of David b. Judah Ḥasid develop the theory of the *Sefirot* to the extreme, assigning to everything a precise place in the world of the *Sefirot*. Joseph b. Shalom engaged in a kabbalistic critique of philosophy, but he interpreted its principles kabbalistically in a very bold way. Like most of the kabbalists of his time he was taken with the idea of the *shemittot*, which gained much ground in this period. Among the most important versions of this theory is that of *Sod ilan ha-aẓilut* by Isaac b. Jacob ha-Kohen (*Kovez al Yad*, 5, 1951). Joseph b. Shalom expounded an extreme conception of the theory of transmigration of souls, turning it into a cosmic law involving a change of form which affected every part of creation from the *Sefirah* of *Ḥochmah* down to the lowest grade of inanimate objects.

Together with the influence of the Zohar and the school of Solomon Adret the Spanish Kabbalah began to spread into Italy, particularly through the writings of Menahem *Recanati who wrote, early in the 14th century, a commentary "according to the path of truth" on the Torah (1523) and a work on the mystical reasons for the commandments (complete ed. 1963). But there was little independence in Italian Kabbalah, and for a long time it consisted of no more than compilations and interpretations, following the Zohar and the *Ma'arekhet ha-Elohut*, and, to an even greater extent than in Spain itself, the writings of Abraham Abulafia. One exception is the *Iggeret Purim* (KS, 10 (1934), 504, no. 52), whose author gives an unusual symbolic interpretation of the theory of the *Sefirot*. In Germany also there was little independent creativity in the Kabbalah. German kabbalists contented themselves with mingling the Zohar and the *Ma'arekhet* with the tradition of Ḥasidei Ashkenaz. Avigdor *Kara (d. 1439), who achieved fame there as a kabbalist (see *Sinai*, 5 (1939), 122–48), wrote *Kodesh Hillulim* on Psalm 150 (Zurich Ms. 102). In the second half of the 14th century Menahem *Ẓiyyoni of Cologne wrote *Sefer Ẓiyyoni* on the Torah, and Yom Tov Lipmann *Muehlhausen devoted part of his literary activity to the Kabbalah, e.g., *Sefer ha-Eshkol* (ed. Judah Even-Shemuel (Kaufmann), 1927). From the beginning of the 14th century the Kabbalah also spread to the East. In Persia Isaiah b. Joseph of Tabriz wrote *Ḥayyei ha-Nefesh* (1324; Jerusalem Ms. 8ø 544; part of it was published in 1891); and in Constantinople Nathan b. Moses Kilkis, who says that he studied in Spain, wrote *Even Sappir* (1368–70; Paris Ms. 727–8).

These last two books belong to the strain which attempted to combine Kabbalah and philosophy in more or less radical ways. Originating mainly among the Spanish kabbalists of the period, these attempts became quite common, and their proponents attacked the opposite tendency to emphasize the two sides' basic differences of approach. The unequivocal neoplatonic line of Ibn Latif was continued (about 1300) by *David b. Abraham ha-Lavan in his *Masoret ha-Berit*. Joseph b. Shalom, mentioned above, linked Kabbalah with Aristotelian metaphysics and with natural philosophy, showing how even abstract philosophical concepts had a mystical content. Obviously, some tended toward a more philosophical view, while others concentrated on the specifically kabbalistic side. Two of the chief exponents of these tendencies wrote in Arabic, an extremely rare occurrence in kabbalistic literature. One was Judah b. Nissim ibn *Malka from Fez, who wrote in 1365; his works have been analyzed by G. Vajda (1954), who has done a great deal of research on the relationship between Kabbalah and philosophy in this period. The other, who lived a generation earlier, was Joseph b. Abraham ibn *Waqar of Toledo. In his lengthy work entitled *al-Maqāla al-Jamī a bayna al-Falsafa wa-al-Shariʿa* ("A Synthesis of Philosophy and Kabbalah"), he set down the views of the philosophers, the kabbalists, and the astrologers, evaluated their ideas according to their relative merits, and tried to establish a basis common to them all (Vajda, *Récherches sur la philosophie et la kabbale* (1962), 115–297). His book also includes a lexicon of *Sefirot* symbolism, which was translated into Hebrew and circulated widely. The author was deeply indebted to Naḥmanides and Todros Abulafia, but he warns "that many errors have crept into" the Zohar. Ibn Waqar wrote poems on the Kabbalah (A.M. Habermann, *Shirei ha-Yiḥud ve-ha-Kavod* (1948), 99–122). His personal friend was Moses *Narboni, who was inclined basically toward philosophy; however, in the *Iggeret al Shi'ur Komah* and in other places in his writings, through a positive albeit somewhat reluctant approach to Kabbalah, Narboni tries to explain kabbalistic statements as if they were in agreement with philosophy (A. Altmann (ed.), *Jewish Medieval and Renaissance Studies*, 4 (1967), 225–88).

An attempt to weight the balance in favor of Kabbalah found expression in the criticism of the work of Judah ibn Malka attributed to Isaac of Acre (Vajda, in REJ, n.s. 15 (1956), 25–71). Samuel b. Saadiah *Motot in Guadalajara (c. 1370) also followed Ibn Waqar in his commentary to the *Sefer Yeẓirah* called *Meshovev Netivot*, and his commentary to the Torah, *Megalleh Amukot* (to Ex., Oxford Ms. 286, and Lev. to Deut., Jerusalem, National Library, Ms. 8°552). But the Zohar had a very strong influence on him. In the discussions of the philosophical kabbalists a great deal of attention was paid to the question of the relationship between the theosophic theory of the *Sefirot*, the philosophers' theory of the separate intelligences, and the neoplatonic idea of the cosmic soul. Attempts were made to explain the *Guide of the Perplexed* in a kabbalistic manner, or at least to clarify certain problems in it from the standpoint of the Kabbalah, using methods different from that of Abraham Abulafia; e.g., in the critique attributed to Joseph Gikatilla (1574; Vajda, in *Mélanges E. Gilson* (1959), 651–9), or in the *Tish'ah Perakim mi-Yiḥud* attributed to Maimonides (*Kovez al-Yad*, 5 (1950), 105–37). Following Abulafia, the urge to make a kabbalist of Maimonides was emphasized in the legend that he had a change of heart at the end of his life and turned to the Kabbalah (Scholem, in *Tarbiz*, 6 (1935), 90–98), a tale that was current from the year 1300 and appears in several versions. In this period the *Megillat Setarim* was also written, which was said to be a letter of Maimonides concerning the Kabbalah (in Z. Edelmann's collection, *Ḥemdah Genuzah* (1855), 45–52).

Totally in contrast to these tendencies toward compromise were two important phenomena which were absolutely opposed to the world of philosophy. The first is connected with the growth of meditative movements leading to contemplation, whether of the inner world of the *Sefirot* and the innumerable hidden lights concealed therein, or of the inner world of the Sacred Names which themselves conceal mystic lights. As a rule this contemplation follows the methods of prophetic Kabbalah, but by changing it and bringing it into the realm of Gnostic theosophy. The 13th-century theory of the *Sefirot* is subordinated to the contemplation of the lights of the intellect, which originated in the writings of the *Sefer ha-Iyyun* school, and produced a voluminous literature, wavering between pure inner contemplation and magic. There is no doubt that Isaac of Acre was very much inclined to this trend. Practically the whole of this literature is still concealed in manuscript form, no doubt because of the self-censorship of the kabbalists, who regarded it as the truly esoteric part of the Kabbalah. One characteristic example, however, did find its way into print, namely *Berit Menuḥah* (1648), which dates from the second half of the 14th century and was wrongly attributed to Abraham b. Isaac of *Granada. It deals at length with meditations on the inner lights sparkling from the various vocalizations of the Tetragrammaton. This literature represents a continuation of Abulafia's science of letter combination with the addition of the theory of *kavvanah* of the theosophical Kabbalah. The book *Toledot Adam* (Jerusalem Ms., Scholem, Catalogue, 58–60) also belongs to this body of writing, and parts of it were printed under the name of *Sefer ha-Malkhut* (1930). The true *Sefer ha-Malkhut*, also a treatise on letter combinations, was written about 1400 by the kabbalist David ha-Levi from Seville (printed in the collection *Ma'or va-Shemesh*, 1839). Intended as practical manuals for initiates, these books are of little interest for kabbalistic theory or philosophy.

The second phenomenon is connected with the composition of two pseudepigraphic works: *Sefer ha-Peli'ah* (1784) on the first section of the Torah and *Sefer *ha-Kanah* (1786) on the (meaning of) the Commandments. The author, who wrote between 1350 and 1390, speaks in the guise of the grandson of R. Neḥunya b. *ha-Kanah, the supposed author of the *Sefer ha-Bahir*. Actually, a large part of the first book consists of an anthology of earlier kabbalistic literature. The author, a considerable talmudist, adapted these sources and added a comparable amount to them. His main object was to prove, through the use of talmudic argument, that the *halakhah* has no literal meaning but mystical significance alone, and that the true literal meaning is mystical. With sweeping enthusiasm, these works go to greater lengths than the Zohar in their insistence that Judaism has no true meaning outside the world of the Kabbalah, thus representing the peak of kabbalistic extremism (S.A. Horodezky, *Ha-Mistorin be-Yisrael* vol. 2: *Ginzei Seter* (1952), 341–88; Baer, Spain, 1 (1961), 369–73). Clearly, in such a case there is no room for a philosophical approach. The anti-philosophical line was continued in the works of Shem Tov b. Shem Tov, who wrote two systematic books on the Kabbalah around 1400. His *Sefer ha-Emunot* (1556) demonstrates how completely the Zohar had become accepted, a century after its appearance, as the central work of Kabbalah. A large portion of the second book, whose title is unknown, is extant (British Museum Ms. 771). In this work the anti-philosophical tendency, which was perhaps influenced by contemporary events and by the persecution of 1391, is expressed quite clearly: there is no longer any room for compromise between mysticism and the demands of rationalistic thought. It cannot be affirmed, however, that this point of view dominated the Kabbalah in its entirety, for in the years that followed, up to the beginning of the 16th century, there were various moves toward reconciliation, especially noticeable among the Italian kabbalists.

In contrast with the clear direction followed by the pseudepigraphy of the *Sefer ha-Peli'ah*, there is no obvious goal in the voluminous pseudepigraphic activity of the Provençal kabbalist Moses *Botarel. He wrote a large number of books around 1400, including a long commentary to the *Sefer Yeẓirah*, filling them with fabricated quotations from the works of kabbalists and others, both historical and imaginary figures. However, his method was not at all like that of the Zohar and he also cultivated a conciliatory attitude toward philosophy, in complete contrast to Shem Tov b. Shem Tov. While the author of *Sefer ha-Peli'ah* and *Sefer ha-Kanah* put forward the Kabbalah as the only interpretation which could save Judaism from deteriorating and disintegrating, in other circles, imbued with a distinct talmudic and ethical spirit, it was regarded as a complementary element, through a stress on its moral and ascetic ideas. It is clear that the Kabbalah had already attained a firm status in the mind of the public, and quite obvious kabbalistic elements had begun to appear in the ethical literature of the 14th and 15th centuries. In this connection the *Sefer Menorat ha-Ma'or* by Israel *al-Nakawa of Toledo (d. 1391) is very important. It is a comprehensive work on Judaism with a clear halakhic standpoint. Wherever ethical questions are discussed in this book, which was intended for a wide public, statements are quoted from the Zohar (in Hebrew, under the name of *Midrash Yehi Or*) and from the other kabbalists, including specifically the *Ḥibbur ha-Adam im Ishto*, a treatise on marriage and sexuality written by an anonymous kabbalist at the end of the 13th century and later attributed to Naḥmanides (KS, 21 (1945), 179–86).

The literature of the kabbalists themselves testifies to the continuous existence in various circles of a strong opposition to Kabbalah and its claims – among halakhists, literalists, and philosophers. Beginning with the polemic of Meir b. Simeon of Narbonne (1250) this opposition continued to be expressed, either *en passant*, as was the case with Isaac Polkar and Menahem *Meiri, or in specific works; e.g., in the *Alilot Devarim* of Joseph b. Meshullam (?), who wrote in Italy in 1468 (*Oẓar Neḥmad*, 4 (1863), 179–214), and in several writings of Moses b. Samuel Ashkenazi of Candia, 1460 (in Vatican Ms. 254). Even with the expansion of the Kabbalah's influence to much wider circles these voices were not silenced, particularly not in Italy.

In Spain kabbalistic creativity diminished considerably in the 15th century. The original stimulus of the Kabbalah had already reached its fullest expression. There were many kabbalists still to be found in Spain, and the numerous manuscripts written there testify to the large numbers who were engaged in Kabbalah, but their work shows very little originality. In 1482 Joseph *Alcastiel from Jativa wrote responsa to 18 questions on various kabbalistic subjects which had been addressed to him by Judah Ḥayyat, and in them he adopts a very independent approach (*Tarbiz*, 24 (1955), 167–206). Joshua b. Samuel ibn Naḥmias in his book *Migdol Yeshu'ot* (Musajoff Ms.), Shalom b. Saadiah ibn Zaytun from Saragossa, and the pupils of Isaac *Canpanton, who occupied a central position in the Judaism of Castile in the middle of the 15th century, were among the chief exponents of Kabbalah. Many kabbalists had crossed to Italy even before the expulsion from Spain, e.g., Isaac Mar-Ḥayyim who wrote in 1491, en route for Ereẓ Israel, two long letters on problems concerning the beginning of emanation (JQR, 21 (1931), 365–75; Yael Nadav, in *Tarbiz*, 26 (1956), 440–58). Joseph ibn *Shraga (d. 1508/09) who was called in his time "the kabbalist from Argenta," and Judah Ḥayyat, the author of a long commentary, *Minḥat Yehudah*, on the *Ma'arekhet ha-Elohut* (1558), were also among the chief transmitters of Spanish Kabbalah to Italy. The book *Ohel Mo'ed* (Cambridge Ms.) was written by an unknown kabbalist before 1500 – in Italy or even still in Spain – in order to defend the Kabbalah against its detractors. Abraham b. Eliezer *ha-Levi and Joseph *Taitaẓak, too, began their kabbalistic activities while still in Spain. The migrants strengthened the Kabbalah, which acquired many adherents in Italy in the 15th century. Reuben Ẓarfati interpreted the theory of the *Sefirot*; Johanan Alemano, who united Kabbalah with philosophy, wrote a commentary to the Torah in *Einei ha-Edah* (Paris Ms.), and to the Song of Songs in *Ḥeshek Shelomo*, and he also compiled a large anthology of kabbalistic miscellanies. He also composed an unnamed work on the Kabbalah (Paris Ms. 849; KS, 5 (1929), 273–7). Only the introduction of his commentary to the Song of Songs has been published (1790). Judah b. *Jehiel Messer Leon of Mantua opposed the tendencies of the later kabbalists and defended the view that kabbalistic principles agreed with Platonic ideas (S. Assaf in *Jubilee Volume for D. Yellin* (1935), 227). This emphasis on kabbalistic Platonism undoubtedly suited the spiritual temperament of the humanists of the circle of Marsilio Ficino and Pico della *Mirandola. The poet Moses *Rieti devoted part of his long poem *Mikdash Me'at* to a rhymed discourse on kabbalistic ideas, and Elijah Ḥayyim of *Gennazano wrote an introduction to the Kabbalah entitled *Iggeret Ḥamudot* (1912).

The Kabbalah after the Expulsion from Spain and the New Center in Safed

The expulsion from Spain in 1492 produced a crucial change in the history of the Kabbalah. The profound upheaval in the Jewish consciousness caused by this catastrophe also made the Kabbalah public property. Despite the fact that the Kabbalah had spread in preceding generations, it still remained the preserve of relatively closed circles, who only occasionally emerged from their aristocratic seclusion. The aims of certain individuals like the author of the Zohar or the *Sefer ha-Peli'ah*, who intended quite consciously to create a work of historical and social importance, were not fully achieved until the 16th century. It was not until this period also that the eschatological mood prevalent among particular individuals in Spain was combined with the more basic stimuli of the Kabbalah. With the expulsion, messianism became part of the very core of Kabbalah. The earlier generations centered their thoughts on the return of man to the wellspring of his life, through the contemplation of the upper worlds, and on instruction in the method of his return through mystic communion to his original source. An ideal which could be realized in any place and at any time, this communion was not dependent on a messianic framework. Now it became combined with messianic and apocalyptic trends which laid greater stress on man's journey toward redemption than on his contemplated future return to the source of all existence in God. This combination of mysticism with messianic apocalyptic turned Kabbalah into a historic force of great dynamics. Its teachings still remained profound, abstruse, and difficult for the masses to assimilate, but its aims lent themselves easily to popularization, and many kabbalists sought to extend its influence throughout the general community. The Kabbalah penetrated many areas of popular faith and custom, overcoming the unceasing opposition of some individuals. It should be noted that the highly original development of the Kabbalah after the expulsion did not start in Italy, although that country was a center of a flourishing Jewish culture, and fruitful kabbalistic activity could be found there. The real creative force came from the new center which was established in Ereẓ Israel about 40 years after the expulsion. The religious movement which originated in Safed, and which manifested a renewal of the Kabbalah in all its intensity, is particularly important because it was the last movement in Judaism to have such a wide scope and such a decisive and continuous influence on the Diaspora as a whole, in both Europe, Asia, and North Africa. This influence was maintained even after the break-up of the Shabbatean movement, which testifies to the degree to which it had become rooted in the national consciousness.

A connection between the appearance of new aspects of the Kabbalah and its rapid dissemination, and the imminent redemption of Israel, had already been established by a few of the Spanish kabbalists, like Abulafia, the author of the *Ra'aya Meheimna*, and the author of the *Sefer ha-Peli'ah*. But it was only after the expulsion that this became a dynamic and all-embracing force. A clear indication of this is the statement of an unknown kabbalist: "The decree from above that one should not discuss kabbalistic teaching in public was meant to last for only a limited time – until 1490. We then entered the period called 'the last generation,' and then the decree was rescinded, and permission given… And from 1540 onward the most important *mitzvah* will be for all to study it in public, both old and young, since this, and nothing else, will bring about the coming of the Messiah" (quoted in Abraham *Azulai's introduction to his *Or ha-Ḥammah* on the Zohar).

The exiles mostly studied the Kabbalah in its earlier forms, but they sought to respond to the interest in the Kabbalah aroused in Italy, North Africa, and Turkey by means of systematic and complete presentations, which at this time, however, did not contain any new points of view. The main exponents of the Kabbalah were Judah Ḥayyat, in his extensive commentary to *Ma'arekhet ha-Elohut*; Abraham Saba and Joseph *Alashkar, in their commentaries to Scripture and Mishnah; Abraham Adrutiel, in an anthology of earlier traditions entitled *Avnei Zikkaron* (KS, 6 (1930), 295ff.; 7 (1931), 457ff.); and particularly Meir ibn *Gabbai, in his exhaustive presentation in *Avodat ha-Kodesh* (1568), which was perhaps the finest account of kabbalistic speculation before the resurgence of the Kabbalah in Safed. There was intensive activity along traditional lines in Italy and Turkey in particular. Among those active in Italy were Elijah Menahem Ḥalfan of Venice, Berakhiel b. Meshullam Cafman of Mantua (*Lev Adam*, 1538, in Kaufmann Ms. 218), Jacob Israel Finzi of Recanati (commentary on the liturgy, Cambridge Ms.), Abraham b. Solomon Treves ha-Ẓarfati (b. 1470) who lived in Ferrara and had "a revelation of Elijah," and Mordecai b. Jacob Rossillo (*Sha'arei Ḥayyim*, Munich Ms. 49). A panentheistic view of the relationship between God and the world was quite clearly stated in *Iggeret ha-Ẓiyyurim* by an unknown kabbalist of the first half of the 16th century in Italy (JTS Ms.). An important center was formed in Salonika, then in Turkey. Among the leaders there were Joseph *Taitaẓak, apparently the author of a large book of revelations which he had composed in the last decade before the expulsion from Spain: *Sefer ha-Meshiv*, in which the speaker is God Himself (G. Scholem, in *Sefunot*, vol. 11); Ḥayyim b. Jacob Obadiah de *Busal (*Be'er Mayim Ḥayyim*, 1546); Isaac Shani (*Me'ah She'arim*, 1543); and Isaac b. Abraham Farḥi, who circulated in his own name the anonymous *Ta'amei ha-Mitzvot*, which had actually been written about 1300. The kabbalist philosopher David b. Judah Messer Leon left Italy to work in Salonika, but his book *Magen David* (London, Jews' College, Ms. 290) on the philosophical principles of the Kabbalah was apparently written in Mantua; this work influenced several later kabbalists, including Meir ibn Gabbai and Moses Cordovero (Schechter, in REJ, 62 (1892), 118ff.; KS, 9 (1933), 258). Solomon *Alkabeẓ also began working in this circle before he went to Safed.

We also know of considerable kabbalistic activity in Morocco. Joseph Alashkar wrote most of his books in Tlemçen (*Ẓofenat Pa'neaḥ*, 1529, Jerusalem Ms. 2° 154; and several other books in the *Katalog der Handschriften … E. Carmoly*, 1876), but the main center in this area was Dra (or Dar'a), whose kabbalists were renowned. There Mordecai *Buzaglo wrote the *Ma'yenot ha-Ḥokhmah*, which was hidden by the kabbalists (Goldschmidt Ms. Copenhagen), and a commentary on the liturgy (*Malkhei Rabbanan* (1931), 86–87). This was the environment where the *Ginnat Bitan* was written, an introduction to the theory of the *Sefirot* by Isaac b. Abraham Cohen (Gaster Ms. 720). This work should not be confused with the *Ginnat ha-Bitan* which has two commentaries attributed to the Spanish kabbalists Jacob b. Todros and Shem Tov ibn Gaon (Gaster Ms. 1398), and which is, from beginning to end (as shown by E. Gottlieb), a late 16th-century forgery based on *Ma'arekhet ha-Elohut* and Judah Ḥayyat's commentary to it. The most important book produced by the Moroccan kabbalists in this period was *Ketem Paz* by Simeon ibn *Labi of Fez, the only commentary on the Zohar that was not written under the influence of the new Kabbalah of Safed. Consequently, it is frequently closer to the primary meaning of the text (the part on Genesis was printed in 1795). Several kabbalists were working in Jerusalem and Damascus. Some of them were emigrants from Spain, and some from the Musta'rabim. Among the emigrants from Portugal was Judah b. Moses *Albotini (d. 1520), who wrote an introduction to prophetic Kabbalah (*Sullam ha-Aliyyah*, see Scholem, *Kitvei Yad be-Kabbalah*, 225–30; KS, 22 (1946), 161–71), and devoted many chapters of his book *Yesod Mishneh Torah* on Maimonides to the Kabbalah (M. Benayahu in *Kovez ha-Rambam* (1955), 240–74). In Damascus, in the middle of the century, Judah Ḥaleywa, a member of a Spanish family, wrote the *Sefer ha-Kavod* (Jerusalem Ms. 8ø 3731). In the main, however, this was the center of activity of Joseph b. Abraham ibn Ẓayyaḥ, one of the rabbis of the Musta'rabim who lived for several years in Jerusalem and in 1538 wrote there *Even ha-Shoham* (G. Scholem, *Kitvei Yad be-Kabbalah*, 89–91), in 1549 *She'erit Yosef* (Ms. of the pre-War Vienna community, Schwarz catalogue 260), and also several other kabbalistic works. Noteworthy for their theoretical speculations on details of the *Sefirot* system and for their profound meditation on the mysticism of the infinite number of luminaries which shine in the *Sefirot*, his books represent the culmination of a certain approach, and at the same time reveal a strong leaning toward practical Kabbalah and matters concerning the *sitra aḥra*.

Books written by the Ashkenazim after the expulsion from Spain were mainly of the anthology type: like the *Shoshan Sodot* of Moses b. Jacob of *Kiev (partially printed 1784, and extant in its entirety in Oxford Ms. 1656); *Sefer ha-Miknah* of Joseph (Josselmann) of Rosheim (1546, Oxford Ms. 2240); and the great commentary to the liturgy by Naphtali Hirz Treves (1560). The writings of Eliezer b. Abraham Eilenburg on Kabbalah and philosophy show how different fields became intertwined in the mind of a German kabbalist who studied in Italy and traveled in several countries. Eilenburg edited the books of the original kabbalists together with additional material of his own, some of it autobiographical (Hirsch Ms. 109, Schwager and Fraenkel 39, 5–10, now in New York; A. Marx, in ZHB, 10 (1906), 175–8). The Kabbalah was established in Germany long before it found its way into Poland, where it penetrated only in the second half of the century through the work of Mattathias *Delacrut and Mordecai *Jaffe.

The printing of several classical works contributed a great deal to the dissemination of the Kabbalah, particularly in the middle of the 16th century. At first no opposition was roused – neither when Recanati's book was produced in Venice (1523) nor when several other books came out in Salonika and Constantinople – although these works did not receive the *haskamah* ("approval") of the rabbinic authorities. However, when the printing of the Zohar itself and the *Ma'arekhet ha-Elohut* (1558) was contemplated, the plan gave rise to bitter arguments among the Italian rabbis; a few of the leading kabbalists violently opposed it, saying that they were afraid that these things would fall into the hands of men who were both ignorant and unprepared and so be liable to lead people into error. The burning of the Talmud in Italy on the order of Pope Julius III (1553) played a part in this controversy, for there were those who feared that the widespread publication of kabbalistic works would in itself tend to stimulate missionary activity. Some kabbalists who at first were opposed to the idea later became the chief protagonists of the printing of the Zohar, e.g., Isaac de *Lattes, the author of a decision in favor of the printing of the Zohar, which appears at the beginning of the Mantua edition. At length, the protagonists prevailed, and the publication of other works of Kabbalah in Italy, Germany, Poland, and Turkey met with no further opposition (I. Tishby, in *Perakim* 1 (1967), 131–82; S. Assaf, in *Sinai*, 5 (1940), 360–8).

In addition to the traditional Kabbalah, during the first 40 years after the expulsion from Spain there arose a remarkable apocalyptic movement, whose leading exponents among the émigrés were active in Palestine and Italy. Abraham b. Eliezer *ha-Levi, who traveled through many countries and settled in Jerusalem about 1515, devoted most of his energies to the propagation of a kabbalistic apocalyptic which was then causing a great stir. A few years after the expulsion a book appeared which affords striking evidence of this movement; called *Kaf ha-Ketoret* (Paris Ms. 845), it is an interpretation of the Psalms as battle-hymns for the war at the end of time, and was apparently written in Italy. At this time messianic movements also sprang up among the Marranos in Spain (Y. Baer, in *Me'assef Shenati Zion*, 5 (1933), 61–77), and emerged in Italy around the kabbalist Asher *Lemlein (1502). This too was the time of the first account of the attempt of the Spanish kabbalist Joseph della *Reina to bring about the final redemption by means of practical Kabbalah (G. Scholem, *ibid.*, 4 (1933),

124–30; J. Dan, in *Sefunot*, 6, 1962, 313–26). The story subsequently went through many adaptations and was very widely publicized. The commentator Isaac *Abrabanel also turned his attention to the propagation of apocalyptic views, whose adherents fixed the date of redemption variously at 1503, 1512, 1540, and 1541. The most serious repercussion was the agitation marking the appearance of David *Reuveni and his supporter Solomon *Molcho, whose kabbalistic expositions (*Sefer ha-Mefo'ar*, 1529) were favorably received by the Salonika kabbalists. Molcho's visions and discourses were a mixture of Kabbalah and incitement to political activity for messianic purposes among the Christians. With his martyrdom (1532) he was finally established in the Jewish community as one of the "saints" of the Kabbalah. For the apocalyptists the advent of Martin *Luther was another portent, a sign of the break-up of the Church and the approach of the end of days.

After its failure as a propagandist movement, the apocalyptic awakening penetrated to deeper spiritual levels. Both Christian and Jewish apocalyptists began to perceive that on the eve of redemption light would be revealed through the disclosure of mysteries that had previously been hidden. The most profound expression of this new movement was that Ereẓ Israel became the center of Kabbalah. First Jerusalem and from 1530 onward Safed were for decades the meeting places of many kabbalists from all corners of the Diaspora; they became the leaders of the religious awakening which elevated Safed to the position of spiritual center of the nation for two generations. Here the old and the new were combined: the ancient traditions together with an aspiration to reach new heights of speculation which almost completely superseded the older forms of Kabbalah, and which in addition had a profound influence on the conduct of the kabbalistic life and on popular custom. Even such great halakhic authorities as Jacob *Berab and Joseph *Caro were deeply rooted in the Kabbalah, and there is no doubt that their messianic expectations set the scene for the great controversy over the reintroduction of ordination, which Jacob Berab wanted to organize in 1538 when Safed had already been established as a center. Sephardim, Ashkenazim, and Musta'rabim all contributed something to this movement, which attracted sympathizers from far afield and was also responsible for a great upsurge in the Diaspora, where communities far and wide accepted the supreme religious authority of the sages of Safed. The spread of a pietistic way of life was a practical expression of the movement and it prepared the ground for the colorful legends which quickly grew up around the major kabbalists of Safed. As with the beginning of Kabbalah in Provence, so here too profound rational speculations were combined with revelations which welled up from other sources, and they took the form (especially after the expulsion from Spain) of the revelations of *maggidim*: angels or sacred souls who spoke through the lips of the kabbalists or made them write down their revelations. Far from being merely a literary device, this was a specific spiritual experience, as indicated by *Sefer ha-Meshiv*, attributed to Joseph Taitaẓak, and Joseph Caro's *Maggid Mesharim* (R.J.Z. Werblowsky, *Joseph Karo, Lawyer and Mystic*, 1962). Once more, like the beginning of Kabbalah in Provence and Spain, here too there were two opposing trends of a philosophic and theoretical nature on the one hand, and of a mythical and anthropomorphic kind on the other.

The earlier forms of the Kabbalah were represented by David b. Solomon ibn *Zimra (known as Radbaz, d. 1573), first in Egypt and later in Safed: in *Magen David* (1713) on the shape of the letters; *Migdal David* (883) on the Song of Songs; *Meẓudat David* (1662) on the meaning of the Commandments; and also in his poem *Keter Malkhut*, which is a kabbalistic imitation of the famous poem of the same name by Solomon ibn Gabirol (in the collection *Or Kadmon*, 1703). In contrast, a new system was propounded by Solomon b. Moses Alkabeẓ, who emigrated to Ereẓ Israel from Salonika, and by his pupil and brother-in-law Moses b. Jacob Cordovero (known as Remak, 1522–70). In Cordovero Safed produced the chief exponent of Kabbalah and its most important thinker. Combining intensive religious thought with the power to expound and explain it, he was the main systematic theologian of the Kabbalah. His theoretical philosophy was based on that of Alkabeẓ and was completely different from the earlier Kabbalah, especially with regard to the theory of the *Sefirot*. It also developed greatly between his first major work, *Pardes Rimmonim*, written in 1548, and the second, *Elimah Rabbati*, composed 19 years later; this later work followed his long commentary on the Zohar, *Or Yakar*, which interprets the book in the light of his own system. Cordovero interprets the theory of the *Sefirot* from the standpoint of an immanent dialectic acting upon the process of emanation, which he sees as a causative process. According to his view there is a formative principle subject to a specific dialectic, which determines all the stages in the revelation of the Divine (*Ein-Sof*) through emanation. The Divine, as it reveals itself when it emerges from the depths of its own being, acts like a living organism. These and other ideas give his system quite a different appearance from that adopted in Gabbai's *Avodat ha-Kodesh*, which was written (1531) shortly before the establishment of the center at Safed, although both are based on the Zohar. It would appear that Alkabeẓ' systematic presentation was written only after the *Pardes Rimmonim* (*Likkutei Hakdamot le-Ḥokhmat ha-Kabbalah*, Oxford Ms. 1663). Cordovero was followed by his disciples, Abraham ha-Levi *Berukhim, Abraham *Galante, Samuel *Gallico, and Mordecai *Dato, who introduced his master's Kabbalah to Italy, his birthplace and the scene of his prolific kabbalistic activity. Eleazar *Azikri and Elijah de *Vidas, both students of Cordovero, wrote in Safed the two classical works on kabbalistic ethics which were destined to have a wide public among students of Torah: *Sefer Ḥaredim* and *Sefer Reshit Ḥokhmah*. Not only did they have a great influence in their own right, these books also opened the way to a whole literary genre of works on ethics and conduct in the kabbalistic manner which appeared in the 17th and 18th centuries and were widely popular. This literature did more for the mass dissemination of Kabbalah than those books dealing with Kabbalah in the narrower sense whose mystical content was comprehensible only to a few.

One book which is not dependent on Cordovero's Kabbalah, but which is saturated with the atmosphere of Safed, where the idea of transmigration held an important place, is the *Gallei Razayya* by an unknown author. Doubtfully attributed to Abraham ha-Levi Berukhim, this comprehensive book was written in 1552–53, and the most important section is devoted to the theory of the soul and its transmigrations. Especially striking is the attempt to explain the lives of the biblical heroes, in particular their more unscrupulous deeds and their relationships with foreign women, in terms of transmigration. The book is among the more original creations of the Kabbalah; only part of it has been printed (1812), although the whole work is extant (Oxford Ms. 1820). Its daring psychology became a precedent for the paradoxical approach of the Shabbateans in their interpretation of the sins of the biblical characters (G. Scholem, *Shabbetai Ẓevi*, (1967), 47–49). Curiously enough, it did not arouse any recorded opposition.

In the magnetism of his personality and the profound impression he made on all, Isaac *Luria Ashkenazi, the "Ari" (1534–72), was greater than Cordovero. The central figure of the new Kabbalah, he was the most important kabbalistic mystic after the expulsion. Although he worked in Safed during the last two or three years of his life only, he had a profound influence on the closed circle of students – some of them great scholars – who after his death propagated and interpreted various versions of his ideas and his way of life, mainly from the end of the 16th century onward. Immediately after his death a rich tapestry of legend was woven around him, in which historical fact was intermingled with fantasy (M. Benayahu, *Toledot ha-Ari*, 1967). Luria's powers as a thinker cannot be compared with those of Cordovero, with whom he studied for a short while in 1570; but his personal and historical influence went far deeper, and in the whole history of Kabbalah only the influence of the Zohar can measure up to his. Developed from speculations of a mythical character on the Zohar, in general his system depends more than was previously thought on Cordovero, although he effected a kind of remythicization of the latter's theoretical concepts. In particular Cordovero's interpretations of the ideas in the *Idra* of the Zohar, voiced in his *Elimah Rabbati*, had a marked influence on Luria, who based the details of his system to a large extent on the *Idrot*. With Luria these ideas are bound up with his preoccupation with letter combinations as a medium for meditation. A large area of his system does not lend itself to complete intellectual penetration, and in many instances it can only be reached through personal meditation. Even in his theory of creation (see below), which from its inception is associated with the extreme mysticism of language and the Holy Names in which the divine power is concentrated, we quickly arrive at the point – the details of the idea of the *tikkun ha-parẓufim* ("the restoration of the faces [of God]") – which is beyond the scope of intellectual perception. Here we are dealing with an extreme case of Gnostic reaction in the Kabbalah, which finds its expression in the placing of innumerable stages among the degrees of emanation, and the lights which sparkle in them. This Gnostic reaction, and with it the mythical tendency in the Kabbalah, reached its highest point in Luria, while at the same time its relationship with the philosophical trends of Spanish Kabbalah and of Cordovero also was at its most tenuous.

Those passages which are comprehensible, and which are related to the origin of the process of creation, are quite dissimilar from the starting-points of the neoplatonists, but they are of great importance for the history of mysticism and their historical influence was astounding. It is precisely in these sections that we find important differences in the various versions of Lurianic Kabbalah. Some concealed particular parts of these speculations, as did Moses *Jonah with regard to the whole theory of *ẓimẓum* ("contraction") in his *Kanfei Yonah*, and Ḥayyim *Vital with the problem of *berur ha-dinim*, the progressive removal of the powers of rigor and severity from the *Ein-Sof* in the process of contraction and emanation. Some added new ideas of their own, like Israel *Sarug, in his theory of the *malbush* ("garment") which is formed by the inner linguistic movement of the *Ein-Sof* and is the point of origin, preceding even the *ẓimẓum*. The original aspects of Luria's work, both in general and in particular, were both profound and extreme, and despite the fact that they were rooted in earlier ideas, they gave the Kabbalah a completely new appearance. A new terminology and a new and more complex symbolism are the outstanding features of the literature of this school. There was much originality in the ideas concerning the *ẓimẓum* which preceded the whole process of emanation and divine revelation; the dual nature of the evolution of the world through the *hitpashetut* ("egression") and *histallekut* ("regression") of the divine forces, which introduced a fundamental dialectical element into the theory of emanation (already apparent in Cordovero); the five *parẓufim* ("configurations") as the principal units of the inner world, which are simply configurations of the *Sefirot* in new arrangements, in the face of which the ten *Sefirot* lose their previous independence; the growth of the world out of the necessary catastrophe which overtook Adam; and the slow *tikkun* ("restoration") of the spiritual lights which have fallen under the domination of the *kelippot* ("shells, husks"; forces of evil). The Gnostic character of these ideas, which constitute a new mythology in Judaism, cannot be doubted. Parallel to the cosmogonic drama there exists a psychological drama, just as complex, concerning the nature of original sin and the restoration of the souls condemned to transmigration because of that sin. The theory of prayer and mystical *kavvanah* ("intent") once more becomes central to the Kabbalah, and the emphasis it receives far surpasses any previously accorded to the subject. This mysticism of prayer proved to be the most important factor in the new Kabbalah because of the steady stimulus it provided for contemplative activity. A fine balance existed in Lurianic Kabbalah between theoretical speculations and this practical activity. The messianic element is far more noticeable here than in other kabbalistic systems, for the theory of *tikkun* confirmed the interpretation of the whole meaning of Judaism as an acute messianic tension. Such tension finally broke in the Shabbatean messianic movement, whose particular historical power may be explained through the combination of messianism with Kabbalah. A messianic explosion like this was unavoidable at a time when apocalyptic tendencies could easily be resuscitated in large sections of the people because of the dominance of Lurianic Kabbalah. Not that this form of Kabbalah was distinct from other streams in its tendency to practical application or its association with magic. These two elements also existed in other systems, even in that of Cordovero. The theory of *kavvanah* in prayer and in the performance of the *mitzvot* undoubtedly contained a strong magical element intended to influence the inner self. The *yiḥudim*, exercises in meditation based on mental concentration on the combinations of Sacred Names which Luria gave to his disciples, contained such an element of magic, as did other devices for attaining the holy spirit.

Luria's disciples saw him as the Messiah, son of Joseph, who was to prepare the way for later revelation of the Messiah, son of David (D. Tamar, in *Sefunot*, 7 (1963), 169–72), but for a whole generation after his death they kept themselves in esoteric groups and did little to spread their belief among the people (G. Scholem, in *Zion*, 5 (1940), 133–60). Only occasionally did written fragments and various anthologies or summaries of Luria's teachings penetrate beyond Ereẓ Israel. In the meantime, in Ereẓ Israel itself, a complete literature of "Lurianic writings" came into being, which originated in the circles of his disciples together with their own disciples. Only a very few of these works come from Luria's own writings (KS, 19 (1943), 184–99). In addition to the disciples mentioned above, Joseph ibn *Tabul, Judah Mishan, and others also took part in this activity, but not one of them became a propagandist or was active outside Ereẓ Israel. This work began only at the end of the 16th century with the journeys of Israel Sarug to Italy and Poland (*Zion*, 5 (1940), 214–43; 9 (1954), 173), and then through a scholar who, despite his pretensions, was not one of Luria's pupils in Safed but only a disciple in the spiritual sense. Up to about 1620 the Kabbalah remained largely under the influence of the other Safed kabbalists, Cordovero in particular.

As the Kabbalah began to radiate from Safed to the Diaspora it was accompanied by great religious excitement, particularly in Turkey, Italy, and Poland. In Italy particular importance attaches to the work of Mordecai Dato, who also engaged in literary messianic propaganda around the year 1575, which many considered to be the actual year of redemption (D. Tamar, in *Sefunot*, 2 (1958), 61–88). Equally important was his pupil Menahem Azariah *Fano (d. 1623), who was regarded for many years as the most prominent kabbalist of Italy, and who produced a considerable number of works, following Cordovero first of all and then Lurianic Kabbalah in the version spread by Sarug. He and his disciples, particularly Aaron Berechiah b. Moses of *Modena (d. 1639) and Samuel b. Elisha Portaleone, made Italy into one of the most important centers of Kabbalah. Preachers in Italy and Poland began to speak of kabbalistic matters in public, and kabbalistic phraseology became public property. Some attempts were also made to explain kabbalistic ideas without using technical language. This is seen particularly in the writings of Judah Loew b. *Bezalel (Maharal of Prague) and in the *Bet Mo'ed* of Menahem Rava of Padua (1608). The spread of the Kabbalah also brought with it a mingling of popular belief and mystic speculation, which had widespread results. The new customs of the kabbalists in Safed found their way to the wider public, especially after the appearance of *Seder ha-Yom* by Moses ibn Makhir from Safed (1599). Penitential manuals based on the practice of the Safed kabbalists and new prayers and customs became widespread. In Italy, and later in other lands too, special groups were established for their propagation. Small wonder that the movement resulted also in the revival of religious poetry, rooted in the world of the Kabbalah. Beginning in Safed too, where its main exponents were Eliezer Azikri, Israel *Najara, Abraham Maimin, and Menahem *Lonzano, this poetry spread to Italy and was exemplified in the works of Mordecai Dato, Aaron Berechiah Modena, and Joseph Jedidiah *Carmi; in the years that followed it was echoed extensively. Many poets owed a major stimulus of their creativity to Kabbalah, especially the great Yemenite poet Shalom (Salim) *Shabbazi, Moses *Zacuto, and Moses Ḥayyim *Luzzatto. In their works they revealed the imaginative and poetic value of kabbalistic symbols, and many of their poems found their way into prayer books, both of the community and of individuals (G. Scholem, *Lyrik der Kabbalah?* in *Der Jude*, 6, 1921, 55–69; A. Ben-Yisrael, *Shirat ha-Ḥen*, 1918).

As long as Ḥayyim Vital, Luria's chief disciple, refused to allow his writings to be publicized – a process which did not begin in earnest until after Vital's death (1620) – detailed knowledge of Luria's system reached the Diaspora at first only through the versions of Moses Jonah and Israel Sarug. Nearly all the works of Kabbalah which were devoted to the spread of these ideas through the press in the first half of the 17th century bear the imprint of Sarug. But in his book *Shefa Tal* Shabbetai Sheftel Horowitz of Prague based his attempt to reconcile the Lurianic theory of *ẓimẓum* with the Kabbalah of Cordovero on the writings of Joseph ibn Tabul. Abraham *Herrera, a pupil of Sarug who connected the teaching of his master with neoplatonic philosophy, wrote *Puerto del Cielo*, the only kabbalistic work originally written in Spanish, which came to the knowledge of many European scholars through its translations into Hebrew (1655) and Latin (1684).

At first Lurianic ideas appeared in print in an abbreviated form only, as in the *Appiryon Shelomo* of Abraham Sasson (Venice, 1608); but in 1629–31 the two bulky volumes by Joseph Solomon *Delmedigo were published, *Ta'alumot Ḥokhmah* and *Novelot Ḥokhmah*, which also included source material from the writings of Sarug and his pupils. The latter volume also contains lengthy studies of these ideas and a number of attempts to explain them philosophically. During these years manuscripts of Vital's teachings were disseminated and in 1648 there appeared in Amsterdam the *Emek ha-Melekh* of Naphtali *Bacharach, which contained an extremely detailed presentation of Lurianic doctrine based on a mixture of the two traditions of Vital and Sarug. It had an enormous influence although it also aroused protest and criticism. It was followed by the publication of other sources which sought to interpret the new teaching; e.g., *Hatḥalat ha-Ḥokhmah* from the Sarug school, published by a Polish kabbalist, Abraham Kalmanks of Lublin, who assumed authorship of the book under the title *Ma'ayan ha-Ḥokhmah* (Amsterdam, 1652). However, the books published in the field of Kabbalah, which continued to increase in number during the 17th century, only partially reflect the great tidal waves of Kabbalah which were sweeping both East and West. From Ereẓ Israel and Egypt spread a great variety of different editions and redactions of all kinds of Lurianic teachings, which captivated those who were mystically inclined. A large amount of this output was the work of men at the center established in Jerusalem between 1630 and 1660 whose leaders, Jacob *Ẓemaḥ, Nathan b. Reuben Spiro, and Meir *Poppers, labored unstintingly both in editing Vital's writings and in composing their own works. Of these, only the books of Nathan Spiro, who spent some of his later years in Italy, were actually printed (*Tuv ha-Areẓ*, 1655, *Yayin ha-Meshummar*, 1660, and *Maẓẓat Shimmurim*, all in Venice). The way in which the Kabbalah penetrated every aspect of life can be seen not only in the long list of homiletic works of a completely kabbalistic nature and of ethical works written under its influence (especially the *Shenei Luḥot ha-Berit* of Isaiah *Horowitz), but also in the interpretations of legal and halakhic details based on kabbalistic principles. Ḥayyim b. Abraham *ha-Kohen of Aleppo was particularly distinguished in this field and his book *Mekor Ḥayyim*, with its various parts, paved the way for a new type of kabbalistic literature.

The rise of the Kabbalah and its complete dominance in many circles was accompanied by some hostile reaction. It is true, of course, that the support given to the Kabbalah by men of renowned rabbinic authority prevented vituperative attacks and, in particular, open charges of heresy, but many intellectuals of a more conservative nature were suspicious of the Kabbalah and some even expressed their hostility openly in their books. Among these should be mentioned Elijah *Delmedigo in his *Beḥinat ha-Dat*, and Mordecai Corcos in a special work now lost. A bitter attack on the Kabbalah was launched by Moses b. Samuel Ashkenazi of Candia (c. 1460) in a number of writings preserved in Vatican Ms. 254. An anonymous work, *Ohel Mo'ed* (of the Spanish expulsion period; Jerusalem Ms.), was written in answer to the rabbis who belittled and mocked the Kabbalah. As the Kabbalah spread more widely in the community Leone (Judah Aryeh) *Modena of Venice (about 1625) wrote the classical polemical work against it, *Ari Nohem*, but he did not dare to publish it in his lifetime (ed. N. Libowitz, 1929). However, his book became widely known in manuscript and provoked many reactions. Solomon Delmedigo also criticized the Kabbalah severely in his *Iggeret Aḥuz*, which was also circulated in manuscript only (published by Abraham *Geiger in *Melo Chofnajim*, Berlin, 1840).

In its continued advance, the Kabbalah reached Poland from the second half of the 16th century (see the mass of material in Dembitzer, *Kelilat Yofi*, 2 (1888), 5–10, 117–26). Public enthusiasm reached such proportions that "he who raises objections to the science of the Kabbalah" was considered "liable to excommunication" (R. Joel *Sirkes in a responsum). At first Cordovero's approach was in the forefront, but from the beginning of the 17th century Luria's Kabbalah began to dominate. Nevertheless, before 1648, the actual systematic ideas of the Kabbalah had little influence, as far as can be judged from the writings of Aryeh Loeb Priluk (commentaries to the Zohar), Abraham Kohen Rappaport of Ostrog (in his homilies at the end of the collection of responsa *Eitan ha-Ezraḥi*), Nathan b. Solomon Spira of Cracow (*Sefer Megalleh Amukot*, 1637), Abraham Chajes (in *Holekh Tamim*, Cracow, 1634), and others. Here also the writings of the Sarug school were the first to be circulated; apparently the visit of Sarug himself to Poland shortly after 1600, which is convincingly documented, also left its mark. Great stress was laid here on the war against the power of the *sitra aḥra* crystallized in the *kelippot*, which was divorced from its association with the Lurianic idea of *tikkun* and treated as a basic principle in its own right. The tendency to personify these powers in various demonological forms is featured particularly in the work of Samson b. Pesaḥ *Ostropoler, who after his death (in the *Chmielnicki massacres of 1648) was considered one of the greatest Polish kabbalists. The attempt to create a complete demonological mythology gave this particular stream of Kabbalah a unique character. To some extent it was based on writings falsely ascribed to Isaac Luria, but really composed in Poland (see REJ, 143 (1953), 37–39).

The Kabbalah in Later Times

A generation after Lurianic Kabbalah had become widely established, the messianic tension embodied within it burst out into the Shabbatean movement. Although there were, of course, various local factors involved in the extent to which people's minds were open to the announcement of the Messiah's coming, nevertheless the growing dominance of the Kabbalah in the popular consciousness of the time, and particularly among the fervently religious, must be seen as the general background which made the movement possible and fixed its mode of expression. The profound upheaval which the messianic experience brought in its wake opened the way for great changes in the world of traditional Kabbalah – or in the Kabbalah that the generations preceding Shabbateanism considered to be traditional. When large groups of people continued to hold fast to their faith in the messianic claim of Shabbetai *Ẓevi even after his apostasy, two factors combined to create an abnormal and audacious Shabbatean Kabbalah which was regarded as heretical by the more conservative kabbalists: (1) the idea that the beginning of redemption made it already possible to see the changes that redemption would effect in the structure of the worlds, and that the mystery of creation could be unravelled in terms of visionary revelations which had not been possible before; and (2) the need to fix the place of the Messiah in this process and to justify in this way the personal career of Shabbetai Ẓevi despite all its contradictions. Consequently it is clear that the whole Shabbatean Kabbalah was new, full of daring ideas which had great powers of attraction. Whatever essential originality later Kabbalah contains is derived mainly from the Kabbalah of the Shabbateans, whose principal ideas were the creation of Nathan of *Gaza (d. 1680), Shabbetai's prophet, and of Abraham Miguel *Cardozo (d. 1706). Although their books were not printed, they were frequently copied, and the influence of their ideas on those who were secret adherents of Shabbateanism is easily recognizable, even in several works that did in fact reach the press. The fact that some of the greatest rabbis were to be counted among the concealed Shabbatean faithful meant that there was a twilight area in their printed writings. This new Kabbalah showed its strength mainly in the period from 1670 to 1730.

By contrast, originality in the work of the kabbalists who remained outside the Shabbatean camp was limited. Continuators rather than original thinkers, they concentrated their efforts in two directions: (1) to continue the way that had emerged through the development of the Kabbalah from the Zohar to Isaac Luria; to examine and interpret the words of the earlier authorities; and generally to act as if nothing had happened and as if the Shabbatean explosion had never taken place; and (2) to limit the spread of the Kabbalah among the populace, because of the dangerous consequences they feared Shabbateanism had had for traditional Judaism; and to restore the Kabbalah to its former position, not as a social force but as an esoteric teaching restricted to a privileged few. Hence the predominantly conservative character of the Kabbalah from 1700 onward. Careful not to burn themselves on the hot coals of messianism, its adherents emphasized rather the aspects of meditation, of praying with *kavvanah*, of theosophy, and of moral teaching in the spirit of Kabbalah. New revelations were suspect. Differences of approach began to crystallize particularly around the question of how exactly the teachings of Isaac Luria should be understood as they had been formulated in the different schools of his disciples or of their disciples. Here there was room for quite striking differences of opinion. There were even some kabbalists who, secretly influenced by Shabbateanism, drew a clear boundary between the traditional Lurianic Kabbalah and the area of new revelations and researches which remained closed to outsiders. It was as if there were no point of contact between these two areas, and they were able to remain side by side within the same domain. This was the case, for example, with Jacob Koppel Lifschuetz (one of the secret Shabbateans) in his *Sha'arei Gan Eden* (Koretz, 1803) and, in a different way, with Moses Ḥayyim Luzzatto (d. 1747), who tried to make a distinction between his systematic studies of Lurianic Kabbalah (in *Pitḥei Ḥokhmah* and *Addir ba-Marom*, etc.) and the studies based on the revelations granted to him through his **maggid*.

Most of those who were considered the foremost kabbalists devoted themselves to cultivating the Lurianic tradition, sometimes attempting to combine it with Cordovero's system. The enormous literary output, of which only a fraction has been printed, reflects this state of affairs. In addition to this, selections or anthologies were made, most outstanding of which was the *Yalkut Reuveni* by Reuben *Hoeshke, arranged in two parts, the first according to subject matter (Prague, 1660) and the second following the order of the Torah (Wilmersdorf, 1681). This collection of the aggadic output of the kabbalists had a wide circulation. Anthologies of this type were composed mainly by the Sephardi rabbis up to recent times, mostly with the addition of their own interpretations; e.g., the valuable *Midrash Talpiyyot* of Elijah ha-Kohen ha-Itamari (Smyrna, 1736).

Apart from works of Kabbalah in the precise sense of involvement in, and presentation of, its ideas, a more popular Kabbalah began to spread from the end of the 17th century. Emphasizing mainly the basic ethical foundation and teaching concerning the soul, this popular Kabbalah chose a few isolated ideas from other kabbalistic teachings and embroidered them with general aggadic homilies. The influence of these books was no less than that of the works of technical Kabbalah. Literature of this kind was initiated by great preachers like Bezalel b. Solomon of Slutsk, Aaron Samuel Kaidanover (*Koidanover), and his son Ẓevi Hirsch, author of *Kav ha-Yashar*, and Berechiah Berakh Spira of Poland. Among the Sephardim were Ḥayyim ha-Kohen of Aleppo in his *Torat Ḥakham*, Elijah ha-Kohen ha-Itamari of Smyrna, Ḥayyim ibn *Attar of Morocco in *Or ha-Ḥayyim*, and Mordecai Moses Sasson of Baghdad. Commentaries in this vein on midrashic literature also circulated; e.g., *Nezer ha-Kodesh* by Jehiel Mikhal b. Uzziel (on Gen. R., 1719) and *Zikkukin de-Nura* by Samuel b. Moses Heida (on *Tanna de-Vei Eliyahu*, Prague, 1676). Under the influence of the Kabbalah, the *Midrashei ha-Peli'ah* were composed in Poland in the 17th century. These extremely paradoxical and mystifying sayings, often couched in an early midrashic style, can be understood only through a mixture of kabbalistic allusion and ingenuity. According to Abraham, the son of the Gaon of Vilna (in *Rav Pe'alim*, 97), a collection of this type, *Midrash Peli'ah*, was printed in Venice in the 17th century. Other such collections are known from the 19th century.

In this period there were important kabbalistic centers in Morocco where a very rich literature was produced, although most of it remained in manuscript. The Kabbalah was dominant in other North African countries and the emphasis was mainly on Lurianic Kabbalah in all its ramifications. A mixture of all the systems is evident among the kabbalists of Yemen and Kurdistan, where the Kabbalah struck very deep roots, particularly from the 17th century onward. The most prominent Yemenite kabbalists, both from Sana, were the poet Shalom b. Joseph Shabbazi (17th century), to whom has been attributed the *Midrash Ḥemdat Yamin* on the Torah, and Joseph Ẓalaḥ (d. 1806), author of the commentary *Eẓ Ḥayyim* on the liturgy according to the Yemeni rite (*Tikhlal*, Jerusalem, 1894). The Hariri family of kabbalists was active in *Ruwandiz in Kurdistan in the 17th and 18th centuries, and most of their writings are extant in manuscript. Later centers were formed in Aleppo and Baghdad, whose kabbalists were renowned in their own lands. In all these countries, and also in Italy, religious poetry of a kabbalistic nature developed and spread widely. The main later poets were Moses Zacuto, Benjamin b. Eliezer ha-Kohen, and Moses Ḥayyim Luzzatto in Italy, Jacob b. Ẓur in Morocco (*Et le-Khol Ḥefez*, Alexandria, 1893), Solomon Molcho (the second) in Salonika and Jerusalem (d. 1788), and Mordecai Abadi in Aleppo.

In contrast to these regional centers, a special position was occupied by the new center established in Jerusalem in the middle of the 18th century, headed by the Yemenite kabbalist Shalom Mizraḥi *Sharabi (ha-Reshash; d. 1777), the most important kabbalist throughout the Orient and North Africa. He was thought to be inspired from on high and in this respect equalled only by Isaac Luria himself. In his personality and in the yeshivah Bet El which continued his tradition for nearly 200 years in the Old City of Jerusalem (it was destroyed in an earthquake in 1927), a twofold approach crystallized: (1) a definite, almost exclusive, concentration on Lurianic Kabbalah based on the writings of Vital, particularly his *Shemonah She'arim*, and the adoption of the doctrine of *kavvanot* and mystical contemplation during prayer as being central to Kabbalah in both its theoretical and practical aspects; (2) a complete break with activity on the social level and a shift toward the esotericism of a spiritual elite, who embody the exclusive, pietist life. There are obvious points of similarity between this later form of Kabbalah and the type of Muslim mysticism (Sufism) prevailing in those lands from which Bet El drew its adherents. Sharabi himself wrote a prayer book (printed in Jerusalem in 1911) with detailed elaborations of the *kavvanot*, outnumbering even those transmitted in the *Sha'ar ha-Kavvanot* in the name of Luria. The training of the members of this circle, popularly known as the *Mekhavvenim*, required them to spend many years on the spiritual mastering of these *kavvanot*, which every member was duty-bound to copy in their entirety. From the first two generations after Bet El was founded a number of *shetarei hitkasherut* ("bills of association") still exist, in which the signatories pledged themselves to a life of complete spiritual partnership both in this world and in the world to come. Apart from Sharabi, the leaders of the group in the first generation were Yom Tov *Algazi (1727–1802), Ḥayyim Joseph David *Azulai, and Ḥayyim della Rosa (d. 1786). As in the case of the writings of Isaac Luria, Sharabi's books also gave rise to an abundant exegetical and textual literature. (For a detailed list of the Bet El kabbalists see Frumkin, *Toledot Ḥakhmei Yerushalayim*, 3 (1930), 47–54, 107–21.) The supreme authority of this circle as the true center of Kabbalah was quickly established throughout all Islamic countries and its position was very strong. Many kabbalistic legends were woven around Sharabi. The last of the chief mainstays of Bet El were Mas'ud Kohen Alḥadad (d. 1927), Ben-Zion Ḥazan (1877–1951), and Ovadiah Hadayah (1891–1969).

Only a few chosen individuals, naturally, went to the center at Bet El. Among those leaders of Kabbalah who remained in their own countries in the East, particular mention should be made of Abraham *Azulai of Marrakesh (d. 1741), Abraham Tobiana of Algiers (d. 1793), Shalom *Buzaglo of Marrakesh (d. 1780), Joseph Sadboon of Tunis (18th century), and Jacob Abi-Ḥasira (d. 1880); Sasson b. Mordecai Shandookh (1747–1830) and Joseph Ḥayyim b. *Elijah (d. 1909) were the main kabbalists of Baghdad. Several of the Turkish and Moroccan kabbalists of the 18th century were wavering with regard to Shabbateanism, like Gedaliah Ḥayon of Jerusalem, Meir *Bikayam of Smyrna, and David di Medina of Aleppo. The classic work to emerge from the kabbalists of these circles, who clung to all the minutiae of the tradition but at the same time did not sever their links with Shabbateanism, was **Ḥemdat Yamim*, by an anonymous author (Smyrna, 1731–32), which was enormously influential in the East.

The later development of the Kabbalah in Poland did not lead to the establishment of a center like Bet El, but a center of a slightly similar type existed between 1740 and the beginning of the 19th century in the *Klaus (*kloiyz*) at Brody. In this era the *Yoshevei ha-Klaus* ("the Sages of the Klaus") constituted an organized institution of kabbalists who worked together and were consulted as men of particular authority. At the head of this group were Ḥayyim b. Menahem Zanzer (d. 1783), and Moses b. Hillel Ostrer (from Ostrog; d. 1785). When the new ḥasidic movement developed in Podolia and became an additional and independent stage in the growth of Jewish mysticism and of the wider popularization of the kabbalistic message, the kabbalists of the Klaus remained outside it and indeed stood aloof from it. In this center, too, great emphasis was laid on profound study of Lurianic Kabbalah. The only link between the two centers was provided by Abraham Gershon of *Kutow (Kuty), the brother-in-law of Israel b. *Eliezer, the Ba'al Shem Tov, who was at first a member of the Klaus at Brody, and who went to Ereẓ Israel and in his later years joined the kabbalists of Bet El, or at least was close to them in spirit. Many of the kabbalistic works published in Poland in the 18th century received the official approval of the Klaus group; but even before the establishment of this center the study of Kabbalah flourished in many places in Poland, as well as in Germany and other Hapsburg lands.

At this time many kabbalists came in particular from Lithuania, like Judah Leib Pohovitzer at the end of the 17th century, and Israel *Jaffe, the author of *Or Yisrael* (1701). In the 18th century the foremost Lithuanian kabbalists were Aryeh Leib *Epstein of Grodno (d. 1775) and R. Elijah, the Gaon of Vilna, whose approach set the pattern for most 19th-century Lithuanian kabbalists. Especially notable among the latter were Isaac Eisik (Ḥaver) *Wildmann, author of *Pitḥei She'arim*, and Solomon *Eliashov (1841–1924), who wrote *Leshem Shevo ve-Aḥlamah*; both works are systematic discourses on Lurianic Kabbalah. Many kabbalistic works appeared in Poland and

Germany from the end of the 17th century, and just as many ethical treatises based on kabbalistic principles. Attempts at systematization occur in *Va-Yakhel Moshe* by Moses b. Menahem *Graf of Prague (Dessau 1699) and several books by Eliezer Fischel b. Isaac of *Strzyzów. Literature which based its religious fervor on the power of "revelation from above" was generally suspected, not without reason, of Shabbatean tendencies, but books of this genre did exist within the more conservative Kabbalah, e.g., *Sefer Berit Olam* by Isaac b. Jacob Ashkenazi (vol. 1 Vilna, 1820, vol. 2 Jerusalem, 1937). The development in Poland in the 18th century was linked to a great extent with the influence of Italian kabbalists, and particularly with the *Shomer Emunim* of Joseph *Ergas and the *Mishnat Ḥasidim* and *Yosher Levav* of Immanuel Ḥai *Ricchi, which presented different approaches to an understanding of Lurianic teaching. The kabbalistic revelations of Moses David *Valle of Modena (d. 1777) remained a closed book, but copies of the writings of Moses Ḥayyim Luzzatto reached the Lithuanian kabbalists, and some of them were known to the early Ḥasidim, on whom they made a great impression. Ergas was followed by Baruch b. Abraham of *Kosov in his various introductions to the Kabbalah, which remained unpublished until some 100 years after his death. An orthodox systematic presentation was made by the kabbalist Jacob Meir Spielmann of Bucharest in *Tal Orot* (Lvov, 1876–83). Attempts were made once again to link Kabbalah with philosophic studies, as in the *Ma'amar Efsharit ha-Tiv'it* by Naphtali Hirsch *Goslar, the early writings of Solomon *Maimon (see A. Geiger, JZWL, 4, 1866, 192–6), which remained in manuscript, and particularly the *Sefer ha-Berit* of Phinehas Elijah Horowitz of Vilna (Bruenn, 1897) and the *Imrei Binah* by Isaac *Satanow, one of the first *maskilim* in Berlin.

In contrast to these attempts at a deeper study of Kabbalah, the ḥasidic movement broadened the canvas and strove to make kabbalistic ideas more and more popular, often by means of a new and more literal interpretation of its principles (see *Ḥasidism). In this movement Jewish mysticism proved to be once again a living force and a social phenomenon. In the *Chabad branch of Ḥasidism an original form of Kabbalah was created, which had a clear psychological objective and produced a variegated literature; but in the ḥasidic camp too there were currents that went back to a study of Lurianic Kabbalah. This Kabbalah flourished anew for a century, particularly in the school of Ẓevi Hirsch of *Zhidachov (Zydaczów; d. 1831) which produced a rich kabbalistic literature. The heads of this school were Isaac Eizik Jehiel of *Komarno (d. 1874), Isaac Eizik of Zhidachov (d. 1873), and Joseph Meir Weiss of *Spinka (1838–1909).

At the beginning of the nationalist ferment of the 19th century two kabbalists were active – Elijah *Guttmacher in Graetz (1796–1874) and Judah *Alkalai in Belgrade (1798–1878); the latter's Zionist writings are suffused with the spirit of Kabbalah. In Central and Western Europe the influence of the Kabbalah swiftly declined, particularly after the conflict between Jacob *Emden and Jonathan *Eybeschuetz concerning the latter's association with Shabbateanism. Nathan *Adler in Frankfurt gathered around himself a circle which had kabbalistic tendencies, and his pupil, Seckel Loeb *Wormser, "the Baal Shem of Michelstadt" (d. 1847), was for some time removed by the government from the rabbinate of his city, "because of his superstitious kabbalistic faith" – apparently as the result of intrigue by the *maskilim*. While Phinehas Katzenelenbogen, the rabbi of Boskovice in the middle of the 18th century, was cataloging the kabbalistic dreams and experiences of his family (Oxford Ms. 2315), and in the circle of Nathan Adler, as in the circles of the later Frankists in Offenbach, claims to prophetic dreams were made, the rabbis were withdrawing further and further from any manifestation of a mystical tendency or a leaning toward the Kabbalah. When Elhanan Hillel Wechsler (d. 1894) published his dreams concerning the holocaust which was about to befall German Jewry (1881), the leading Orthodox rabbis tried to prevent him from doing so, and his kabbalistic leanings led to his being persecuted. The last book by a German kabbalist to be printed was *Torei Zahav* by Hirz Abraham Scheyer of Mainz (d. 1822) published in Mainz in 1875. However, various kinds of kabbalistic literature continued to be written in Eastern Europe and the Near East up to the time of the Holocaust, and in Israel until the present. The transformation of kabbalistic ideas into the forms of modern thought may be seen in the writings of such 20th-century thinkers as R. Abraham Isaac *Kook (*Orot ha-Kodesh, Arpilei Tohar, Reish Millin*); in the Hebrew books of Hillel *Zeitlin; and in the German writings of Isaac Bernays (*Der Bibel'sche Orient*, 1821) and Oscar *Goldberg (*Die Wirklichkeit der Hebraeer*, Berlin, 1925).

The fervent assault on the Kabbalah by the Haskalah movement in the 19th century limited its deep influence in Eastern Europe to a marked degree; but it succeeded hardly at all in lessening the influence of the Kabbalah in Oriental countries, where the life of the Jewish community was deeply affected by it until recent times. An exception was the anti-kabbalistic movement in the Yemen known as *Dor De'ah* ("Doerde"). Headed by Yiḥya *Kafaḥ (Kafiḥ) of Sana (d. 1931), it caused much strife among the Jews of Yemen. Apart from the accusatory and defamatory writings from 1914 onward, there appeared in connection with this controversy the *Milḥamot ha-Shem* of Kafaḥ and the reply of the Yemeni rabbis, *Emunat ha-Shem* (Jerusalem 1931 and 1938). This voluminous defense was actually written by an 18-year-old scholar, Joseph Jacob Zubiri.

THE BASIC IDEAS OF KABBALAH

As is apparent from the preceding account, the Kabbalah is not a single system with basic principles which can be explained in a simple and straightforward fashion, but consists rather of a multiplicity of different approaches, widely separated from one another and sometimes completely contradictory. Nevertheless, from the date of the appearance of the *Sefer ha-Bahir* the Kabbalah possessed a common range of symbols and ideas which its followers accepted as a mystical tradition, although they differed from one another in their interpretation of the precise meaning of these symbols, of the philosophical implications inherent in them, and also of the speculative contexts through which it became possible to regard this common framework as a kind of mystical theology of Judaism. But even within this system two stages must be differentiated:

(1) the range of symbols of the early Kabbalah up to and including the Safed period, i.e., the theory of the *Sefirot* as it crystallized in Gerona, in the various parts of the Zohar, and in the works of kabbalists up to Cordovero; and

(2) the range of symbols created by Lurianic Kabbalah, which in the main dominated kabbalistic thinking since the 17th century until recent times. The Lurianic system goes beyond the doctrine of the *Sefirot*, although it makes a wide and emphatic use of its principles, and is based on the symbolism of the *parẓufim*.

In addition to this, two basic tendencies can be discerned in kabbalistic teaching. One has a strongly mystical direction expressed in images and symbols whose inner proximity to the realm of myth is often very striking. The character of the other is speculative, an attempt to give a more or less defined ideational meaning to the symbols. To a large extent this outlook presents kabbalistic speculation as a continuation of philosophy, a kind of additional layer superimposed upon it through a combination of the powers of rational thought and meditative contemplation. The speculative expositions of kabbalistic teaching largely depended on the ideas of neoplatonic and Aristotelian philosophy, as they were known in the Middle Ages, and were couched in the terminology customary to these fields. Hence the cosmology of the Kabbalah is borrowed from them and is not at all original, being expressed in the common medieval doctrine of the separate intellects and the spheres. Its real originality lies in the problems that transcend this cosmology. Like Jewish philosophy, the speculative Kabbalah moved between two great heritages, the Bible and talmudic Judaism on the one hand, and Greek philosophy in its different forms on the other. The original and additional feature, however, was the new religious impulse which sought to integrate itself into these traditions and to illuminate them from within.

God and Creation

All kabbalistic systems have their origin in a fundamental distinction regarding the problem of the Divine. In the abstract, it is possible to think of God either as God Himself with reference to His own nature alone or as God in His relation to His creation. However, all kabbalists agree that no religious knowledge of God, even of the most exalted kind, can be gained except through contemplation of the relationship of God to creation. God in Himself, the absolute Essence, lies beyond any speculative or even ecstatic comprehension. The attitude of the Kabbalah toward God may be defined as a mystical agnosticism, formulated in a more or less extreme way and close to the standpoint of neoplatonism. In order to express this unknowable aspect of the Divine the early kabbalists of Provence and Spain coined the term *Ein-Sof* ("Infinite"). This expression cannot be traced to a translation of a Latin or Arabic philosophical term. Rather it is a hypostatization which, in contexts dealing with the infinity of God or with His thought that "extends without end" (*le-ein sof* or *ad le-ein sof*), treats the adverbial relation as if it were a noun and uses this as a technical term. *Ein-Sof* first appears in this sense in the writings of Isaac the Blind and his disciples, particularly in the works of Azriel of Gerona, and later in the Zohar, the *Ma'arekhet ha-Elohut*, and writings of that period. While the kabbalists were still aware of the origin of the term they did not use it with the definite article, but treated it as a proper noun; it was only from 1300 onward that they began to speak of *ha-Ein-Sof* as well, and generally identify it with other common epithets for the Divine. This later usage, which spread through all the literature, indicates a distinct personal and theistic concept in contrast to the vacillation between an idea of this type and a neutral impersonal concept of *Ein-Sof* found in some of the earlier sources. At first it was not clear whether the term *Ein-Sof* referred to "Him who has no end" or to "that which has no end." This latter, neutral aspect was emphasized by stressing that *Ein-Sof* should not be qualified by any of the attributes or personal epithets of God found in Scripture, nor should such eulogies as *Barukh Hu* or *Yitbarakh* (found only in the later literature) be added to it. In fact, however, there were various attitudes to the nature of *Ein-Sof* from the very beginning; Azriel, for example, tended toward an impersonal interpretation of the term, while Asher b. David employed it in a distinctly personal and theistic way.

Ein-Sof is the absolute perfection in which there are no distinctions and no differentiations, and according to some even no volition. It does not reveal itself in a way that makes knowledge of its nature possible, and it is not accessible even to the innermost thought (*hirhur ha-lev*) of the contemplative. Only through the finite nature of every existing thing, through the actual existence of creation itself, is it possible to deduce the existence of *Ein-Sof* as the first infinite cause. The author of the *Ma'arekhet ha-Elohut* put forward the extreme thesis (not without arousing the opposition of more cautious kabbalists) that the whole biblical revelation, and the Oral Law as well, contained no reference to *Ein-Sof*, and that only the mystics had received some hint of it. Hence the author of this treatise, followed by several other writers, was led to the daring conclusion that only the revealed God can in reality be called "God," and not the hidden "*deus absconditus*," who cannot be an object of religious thought. When ideas of this kind returned in a later period in Shabbatean and quasi-Shabbatean Kabbalah, between 1670 and 1740, they were considered heretical.

Other terms or images signifying the domain of the hidden God that lies beyond any impulse toward creation occur in the writings of the Gerona kabbalists and in the literature of the speculative school. Examples of these terms are *Mah she-ein ha-maḥashavah masseget* ("that which thought cannot attain" – sometimes used also to describe the first emanation), *ha-or ha-mit'allem* ("the concealed light"), *seter ha-ta'alumah* ("the concealment of secrecy"), *yitron* ("superfluity" – apparently a translation of the neoplatonic term *hyperousia*), *ha-aḥdut ha-shavah* ("indistinguishable unity," in the sense of a unity in which all opposites are equal and in which there is no differentiation), or even simply *ha-mahut* ("the essence"). The factor common to all these terms is that *Ein-Sof* and its synonyms are above or beyond thought. A certain wavering between the personal and the neutral approach to the concept of *Ein Sof* can also be seen in the main part of the Zohar, while in the later stratum, in the *Ra'aya Meheimna* and the *Tikkunim*, a personal concept is paramount. *Ein-Sof* is often identified with the Aristotelian "cause of all causes," and, through the kabbalistic use of neoplatonic idiom, with the "root of all roots." While all the definitions above have a common negative element, occasionally in the Zohar there is a remarkable positive designation which gives the name *Ein-Sof* to the nine lights of thought that shine from the Divine Thought, thus bringing *Ein-Sof* out of its concealment and down to the more humble level of emanation (the contrast between the two concepts emerges through comparison between various passages, e.g., 1, 21a, and 2, 239a with 2, 226a). In later development of Lurianic Kabbalah, however, in distinct opposition to the view of the earlier kabbalists, several differentiations were made even within *Ein-Sof*. In Kabbalah, therefore, *Ein-Sof* is absolute reality, and there was no question as to its spiritual and transcendental nature. This was so even though the lack of clarity in some of the expressions used by the kabbalists in speaking of the relationship of the revealed God to His creation gives the impression that the very substance of God Himself is also immanent within creation (see below on Kabbalah and pantheism). In all kabbalistic systems, light-symbolism is very commonly used with regard to *Ein-Sof*, although it is emphasized that this use is merely hyperbolical, and in later Kabbalah a clear distinction was sometimes made between *Ein-Sof* and "the light of *Ein-Sof*." In the popular Kabbalah which finds expression in ethical writings and ḥasidic literature, *Ein-Sof* is merely a synonym for the traditional God of religion, a linguistic usage far removed from that of the classical Kabbalah, where there is evidence of the sharp distinction between *Ein-Sof* and the revealed Divine Creator. This can be seen not only in the formulations of the early kabbalists (e.g., Isaac of Acre in his commentary to the *Sefer Yeẓirah*, in: KS 31 (1956), 391) but also among the later ones; Barukh Kosover (c. 1770) writes: "*Ein-Sof* is not His proper name, but a word which signifies his complete concealment, and our sacred tongue has no word like these two to signify his concealment. And it is not right to say '*Ein-Sof*, blessed be He' or 'may He be blessed' because He cannot be blessed by our lips" (*Ammud ha-Avodah*, 1863, 211d).

The whole problem of creation, even in its most recondite aspects, is bound up with the revelation of the hidden God and His outward movement – even though "there is nothing outside Him" (Azriel), for in the last resort "all comes from the One, and all returns to the One," according to the neoplatonic formula adopted by the early kabbalists. In kabbalistic teaching the transition of *Ein-Sof* to "manifestation," or to what might be called "God the Creator," is connected with the question of the first emanation and its definition. Although there were widely differing views on the nature of the first step from concealment to manifestation, all stressed that any account of this process was not an objective description of a process in *Ein-Sof*; it was no more than could be conjectured from the perspective of created beings and was expressed through their ideas, which in reality cannot be applied to God at all. Therefore, descriptions of these processes have only a symbolic or, at best, an approximate value. Nevertheless, side by side with this thesis, there is detailed speculation which frequently claims objective reality for the processes it describes. This is one of the paradoxes inherent in Kabbalah, as in other attempts to explain the world in a mystical fashion.

The decision to emerge from concealment into manifestation and creation is not in any sense a process which is a necessary consequence of the essence of *Ein-Sof*; it is a free decision which remains a constant and impenetrable mystery (Cordovero, at the beginning of *Elimah*). Therefore, in the view of most kabbalists, the question of the ultimate motivation of creation is not a legitimate one, and the assertion found in many books that God wished to reveal the measure of His goodness is there simply as an expedient that is never systematically developed. These first outward steps, as a result of which Divinity becomes accessible to the contemplative probings of the kabbalist, take place within God Himself and do not "leave the category of the Divine" (Cordovero). Here the Kabbalah departs from all rationalistic presentations of creation and assumes the character of a "theosophic" doctrine, that is, one concerned with the inner life and processes of God Himself. A distinction in the stages of such processes in the unity of the Godhead can be made only by human abstraction, but in reality they are bound together and unified in a manner beyond all human understanding. The basic differences in the various kabbalistic systems are already apparent with regard to the first step, and since such ideas were presented in obscure and figurative fashion in the classical literature, such as the *Bahir* and the Zohar, exponents of widely differing opinions were all able to look to them for authority. The first problem, which from the start elicited different answers, was whether the first step was one toward the outer world at all, or rather a step inward, a withdrawal of *Ein-Sof* into the depths of itself. Early kabbalists and Cordovero adopted the former view, which led them to a theory of emanation close to the neoplatonic although not absolutely identical with it. But Lurianic Kabbalah, which took the latter position, speaks not only of a return of created things to their source in God but also of a return (*regressus*) of God into the depths of Himself preceding creation, a process identifiable with that of emanation only by means of interpreting it as a mere figure of speech. Such an interpretation did, in fact, appear before long (see the section on Lurianic Kabbalah). The concepts which occur most frequently in the description of this first step mainly concern will, thought, *Ayin* ("absolute Nothingness"), and the inner radiation of *Ein-Sof* in the supernal lights called "splendors" (*ẓaḥẓaḥot*), which are higher than any other emanation.

WILL. If *Ein-Sof* is denied any attributes then it must be separated from the Divine Will, however exalted the latter is and however clearly connected with its possessor, which is *Ein-Sof*. The kabbalists of Gerona frequently speak of the hidden God working through the Primal Will, which is, as it were, encompassed by Him and united with Him. This, the highest of emanations, which is either emanated from His essence, or concealed within His power, constitutes the ultimate level to which thought can penetrate. Mention is made of "the infinite Will" (*ha-raẓon ad ein-sof*), "infinite exaltation" (*ha-rom ad ein-sof*) or "that which thought cannot ever attain," and the reference is to that unity of action between *Ein-Sof* and its first emanation, which is bound to and returns constantly to its source. In some works, e.g., Azriel's *Perush ha-Aggadot*, there is hardly any mention of *Ein-Sof* at all; instead, the Primal Will appears in expressions which are generally connected with *Ein-Sof* itself. Was this Will co-eternal with *Ein-Sof* itself, or did it originate only at the time of its emanation, so that it is possible to think of a situation in which *Ein-Sof* existed without Will, i.e., volition to create or be manifested? Several of the kabbalists of Gerona and their followers tended to believe that the Primal Will was eternal, and thus they fixed the beginning of the process of emanation at the second step or *Sefirah*, which was consequently called *reshit* ("beginning"), identified with the Divine Wisdom of God (see below). Most of the statements in the main part of the Zohar follow this view. What is called "the infinite Will," in the sense of the unity of *Ein-Sof* with the Will and their joint manifestation in the first *Sefirah*, is given the figurative name *Attika Kaddisha* ("the Holy Ancient One") in the Zohar. Also, in those passages which speak of *Ein-Sof* and the beginning of emanation, this beginning (*reshit*) is always related to the second *Sefirah*, there being no mention that what preceded it also came into being in time and had not been eternally emanated. Therefore in some cases the first emanation is seen as only an external aspect of *Ein-Sof*: "It is called *Ein-Sof* internally and *Keter Elyon* externally" (*Tikkunei Zohar*, end of *Tikkun* 22). However, this ordering occurs only in those passages which discuss the process in detail; in those dealing with the process of emanation in general there is no differentiation between the status of the first *Sefirah* and that of the other *Sefirot*. As the Kabbalah developed in Spain the tendency prevailed to make a clear distinction between *Ein-Sof* and the first emanation, which now began to be considered neither eternal nor pre-existent. Among the kabbalists of Safed, indeed, the contrary view was considered almost heretical, since it made possible the identification of *Ein-Sof* with the first *Sefirah*. In fact this identification is actually found in several early kabbalistic sources, and the anonymous author of *Sefer ha-Shem*, mistakenly attributed to Moses de Leon (c. 1325, printed in *Heikhal ha-Shem*, Venice, 1601, 4b), criticizes the Zohar because of it, saying it is contrary to "the view of the greatest kabbalists" and an error made possible only by the false assumption that the *Ein-Sof* and first emanation are one.

The early kabbalists, particularly Azriel of Gerona and Asher b. David, considered the Divine Will as that aspect of the Divine Essence which alone was active in creation, and was implanted there by the power of *Ein-Sof*. Communion with the Supreme Will was the final aim of prayer, for it was "the source of all life," including emanation itself. Does this specific concept of the Will as the supreme Divine Power, which, according to the Gerona kabbalists and the Zohar, takes precedence even over Divine Thought and pure intellect, contain traces of the indirect influence of Solomon ibn Gabirol's central idea in *Mekor Ḥayyim*? A historical connection seems clearly apparent in the teachings of Isaac ibn Latif (fl. 1230–60), who apparently lived in Toledo and could have read Gabirol's book in the Arabic original. His theory is a mixture of Gabirol's ideas and those of the first generations of Spanish Kabbalah. His view of the Will can be found mainly in his *Ginzei ha-Melekh* and *Ẓurat ha-Olam*. "The primordial Will" (*ha-ḥefeẓ ha-kadmon*) is not completely identical with God, but is a garment "clinging to the substance of the wearer on all sides." It was "the first thing to be emanated from the true pre-existent Being" in a continuing process which had no real beginning. Above matter and form, this Will unites the two in their first union, thus bringing into being what Ibn Latif calls "the first created thing" (*ha-nivra ha-rishon*). His description of the details of the processes that take place below the level of the Will differs from that of the other kabbalists; it was not accepted nor did it have any influence on the theory of emanation as it was formulated in later Kabbalah. As the tendency to all but identify *Ein-Sof* with the first *Sefirah* became less and less pronounced, so the distinction between Ein-Sof and the Will was emphasized to a correspondingly greater degree, although the question as to whether the Will was created or eternal continued to be surrounded by controversy, or was consciously obscured.

THOUGHT. Another concept basic to the whole problem of the first manifestation of *Ein-Sof* is that of "Thought" (*maḥashavah*). In the *Sefer ha-Bahir* and the writings of Isaac the Blind no special status is accorded to the Will, whose place is taken by "the Thought which has no end or finality," and which exists as the highest state, from which all else has emanated, without being designated as an emanation itself. Accordingly, the first source of all emanation is sometimes also called "pure Thought" – a domain impenetrable to merely human thought. According to this theory, the whole creative process depends on an intellectual rather than a volitional act, and the history of Kabbalah is marked by a struggle between these two views of creation. The essential identity of Will and Thought was insisted on by Ibn Latif alone. For most kabbalists, that Thought which thinks only itself and has no other content was demoted to a level below that of Will and became identified with the Divine Wisdom, which proceeded to contemplate not only itself but the whole plan of creation and the paradigma of all the universe. Therefore, the Gerona kabbalists and the author of the Zohar speak of "the Will of Thought," i.e., the Will which activates Thought, and not vice versa. The highest aspect of *ḥokhmah* ("Wisdom"), which the Gerona kabbalists speak of a great deal, is called *haskel* (from Jer. 9:23), a term denoting divine understanding, the activity of the *sekhel* ("divine intellect"), whatever the content of this might be, and not, as with *ḥokhmah*, its crystallization into a system of thought. The concept of *haskel* took the place of Will among those who were disinclined to accept the theory or were perplexed by it, particularly in the school of Isaac the Blind.

NOTHINGNESS. More daring is the concept of the first step in the manifestation of *Ein-Sof* as *ayin* or *afisah* ("nothing," "nothingness"). Essentially, this nothingness is the barrier confronting the human intellectual faculty when it reaches the limits of its capacity. In other words, it is a subjective statement affirming that here is a realm which no created being can intellectually comprehend, and which, therefore, can only be defined as "nothingness." This idea is associated also with its opposite concept, namely, that since in reality there is no differentiation in God's first step toward manifestation, this step cannot be defined in any qualitative manner and can thus only be described as "nothingness." *Ein-Sof* which turns toward creation manifests itself, therefore, as *ayin ha-gamur* ("complete nothingness"), or, in another version: "God Who is called *Ein-Sof* in respect of Himself is called *Ayin* in respect of His first self-revelation." This daring symbolism is associated with most mystical theories concerning an understanding of the Divine, and its particular importance is seen in the radical transformation of the doctrine of *creatio ex nihilo* into a mystical theory stating the precise opposite of what appears to be the literal meaning of the phrase. From this point of view it makes no difference whether *Ein-Sof* itself is the true *ayin* or whether this *ayin* is the first emanation of *Ein-Sof*. From either angle, the monotheistic theory of *creatio ex nihilo* loses its original meaning and is completely reversed by the esoteric content of the formula. Since the early kabbalists allowed no interruption in the stream of emanation from the first *Sefirah* to its consolidation in the worlds familiar to medieval cosmology, *creatio ex nihilo* may be interpreted as creation from within God Himself. This view, however, remained a secret belief and was concealed behind the use of the orthodox formula; even an authoritative kabbalist like Naḥmanides was able to speak in his commentary to the Torah of *creatio ex nihilo* in its literal sense as the free creation of the primeval matter from which everything was made, while simultaneously implying, as shown by his use of the word *ayin* in his commentary to Job 28:12 and by kabbalistic allusions in his commentary to Genesis 1, that the true mystical meaning of the text is the emergence of all things from the absolute nothingness of God. Basing their speculations on the commentary to the *Sefer Yeẓirah* by Joseph Ashkenazi (attributed in the printed editions to Abraham b. David), kabbalists who held an undoubted theistic view tried to rescue the original significance of the formula by defining the first *Sefirah* as the first effect, which is absolutely separated from its cause, as if the transition from cause to effect involved a great leap from *Ein-Sof* to *ayin*, a view which conformed with the traditional theological picture. However, in order to escape the inner logic of the early theory, a few later kabbalists, from the 16th century onward, tried to add a new act of *creatio ex nihilo* after the emanation of the *Sefirot* or at each stage of emanation and creation. Doubts of this kind did not exist in Spanish Kabbalah, nor in the works of Cordovero, although in the *Elimah Rabbati* he found it hard to decide between a symbolic and a literal interpretation of the formula. David b. Abraham ha-Lavan in *Masoret ha-Berit* (end of 13th century) defined the *ayin* ("nothingness") as "having more being than any other being in the world, but since it is simple, and all other simple things are complex when compared with its simplicity, so in comparison it is called 'nothing'" (*Kovez al-Yad*, new series, i, 1936, 31). We also find the figurative use of the term *imkei ha-ayin* ("the depths of nothingness"), and it is said (*ibid.*) that "if all the powers returned to nothingness, the Primeval One who is the cause of all would remain in equal oneness in the depths of nothingness."

THE THREE LIGHTS. Another idea connected with the transition from the Emanator to the emanated originated in a responsum (early 13th century) attributed to Hai Gaon, and subsequently aroused a great deal of speculation (see *Origines*…, 367–75). There it is stated that, above all emanated powers, there exist in "the root of all roots" three hidden lights which have no beginning, "for they are the name and essence of the root of all roots and are beyond the grasp of thought." As the "primeval inner light" spreads throughout the hidden root two other lights are kindled, called *or meẓuḥẓaḥ* and *or ẓaḥ* ("sparkling light"). It is stressed that these three lights constitute one essence and one root which is "infinitely hidden" (*ne'lam ad le-ein sof*), forming a kind of kabbalistic trinity that precedes the emanation of the ten *Sefirot*. However, it is not sufficiently clear whether the reference is to three lights between the Emanator and the first emanation, or to three lights irradiating one another within the substance of the Emanator itself – both possibilities can be supported. In the terminology of the Kabbalah these three lights are called *ẓaḥẓaḥot* ("splendors"), and they are thought of as the roots of the three upper *Sefirot* which emanate from them (see Cordovero, *Pardes Rimmonim*, ch. 11). The need to posit this strange trinity is explained by the urge to make the ten *Sefirot* conform with the 13 attributes predicated of God. It is hardly surprising that Christians later found an allusion to their own doctrine of the trinity in this theory, although it contains none of the personal hypostases characteristic of the Christian trinity. In any case, the hypothesis of the *ẓaḥẓaḥot* led to further complication in the theory of emanation and to the predication of roots in the essence of *Ein-Sof* to everything that was emanated. In the generation following the publication of the Zohar, David b. Judah Ḥasid, in his *Mare'ot ha-Ẓove'ot*, mentions ten *ẓaḥẓaḥot* placed between *Ein-Sof* and the emanation of the *Sefirot*.

Emanation and the Concept of the *Sefirot*

Scholars have long been engaged in a controversy over whether or not the Kabbalah teaches emanation as the emergence of all things from within God Himself. In this controversy there is considerable conceptual confusion. Like several scholars before him, A. Frank interpreted the Kabbalah as a pure emanatist system, which he considered identical with a clearly pantheistic approach. He therefore thought of emanation as an actual going-forth of the substance of God and not simply of the power of the Emanator. He based his interpretation on the Zohar, and especially on later Lurianic teaching, although neither of these two sources contains any reference to a direct theory of substantive emanation. In contrast to Frank, D.H. Joel set out to prove that the Zohar and early Kabbalah in general contained nothing of the theory of emanation, which Joel believed first appeared in the writings of "the modern commentators" of the 16th century, where it was the result of faulty interpretation. In his opinion there is no significant difference between "the pure theology" of Jewish medieval thinkers, and "the true Kabbalah," the very foundation of which is the idea of the free creation of primeval substance *ex nihilo* in the literal meaning of the term. There is no doubt that Joel and Frank were equally mistaken, and that both were at fault in interpreting the basic content of Lurianic Kabbalah in pantheistic terms. Inasmuch as early Kabbalah needed a theoretical foundation it was largely influenced by neoplatonism; and although it proposed a definite process of emanation – the theory of the emanation of *Sefirot* – this was a kind of activity which took place within the Divine itself. The God who manifests Himself in His *Sefirot* is the very same God of traditional religious belief, and consequently, despite all the complexities such an idea involves, the emanation of the *Sefirot* is a process within God Himself. The hidden God in the aspect of *Ein-Sof* and the God manifested in the emanation of *Sefirot* are one and the same, viewed from two different angles. There is therefore a clear distinction between the stages of emanation in the neoplatonic systems, which are not conceived as processes within the Godhead, and the kabbalistic approach. In Kabbalah, emanation as an intermediate stage between God and creation was reassigned to the Divine, and the problem of the continuation of this process outside the Godhead gave rise to various interpretations. At first there was no need to conclude that worlds below the level of the *Sefirot*, and the corporeal world itself, were also emanated from the *Sefirot*. Perhaps intentionally, the kabbalists dealt with this point in a highly obscure fashion, frequently leaving open the way to the most diverse interpretations. God's actions outside the realm of the *Sefirot* of emanation led to the emergence of created beings separated from the *Sefirot* by an abyss, although few kabbalists maintained unambiguously that the process of emanation came to an absolute end with the final *Sefirah* and that what followed constituted a completely new beginning. The early kabbalists agreed that all creatures below the *Sefirot* had an existence of their own outside the Divine, and were distinguished from it in their independent existence since their state was that of created beings, although they had their archetypes in the *Sefirot*. Even given the belief that from the point of view of God they have their root in His being, nevertheless they are in themselves separated from His essence and possess a nature of their own. Distinctions of this kind are common to the Kabbalah and to other mystical theologies, like those of medieval Islam and Christianity, but they were generally neglected in most kabbalistic discussions of emanation, with all the consequent unclarity that this entailed. Particularly in a number of important books which do not attempt to build their doctrines on a firm theoretical foundation, such as the *Bahir*, the Zohar, and the works of Isaac b. Jacob ha-Kohen, the authors often use highly ambiguous terms and speak of "creation" even when they mean "emanation." This ambiguity can be explained in the light of the history of the Kabbalah, which was at first concerned with the description of a religious and contemplative experience and not with questions of purely theoretical systematization. In addition, the developing Kabbalah was heir to a strong, mythically inclined Gnostic heritage of speculation on the aeons (whose nature was also subject to many theoretical interpretations). Thus, when their figurative and symbolic language was put to a logical test, sources like the above were accorded many different theological and analytical interpretations.

As the Kabbalah developed in Provence and Spain and the Gnostic tradition was confronted with neoplatonism, a host of short tracts were written in which it was attempted to give an independent description of the processes of emanation. Most of these works belong to the circle of the *Sefer ha-Iyyun* (see above). They show quite clearly that, aside from the theory of the *Sefirot*, there were other approaches to a description of the spiritual world, such as in terms of a world of powers (*koḥot*), lights, or divine intellects, which were sometimes given identical names but which were ordered each time in quite different ways. Obviously these were the first gropings toward the establishment of a definitive order in the degrees and stages of emanation. However, as they did not correspond with the symbolism that had been constructed in a more or less unified fashion from the time of Isaac the Blind up to the Zohar, they were almost completely disregarded.

Unlike these first hesitant steps, the theory of the *Sefirot* ultimately became the backbone of Spanish kabbalistic teaching and of that basic system of mystical symbolism which had such important repercussions on the kabbalists' view of the meaning of Judaism. Right from the beginning, ideas concerning emanation were closely bound up with a theory of language. On the one hand, much is written about the manifestation of the power of *Ein-Sof* through various stages of emanation which are called *Sefirot* and are no more than the various attributes of God or descriptions and epithets which can be applied to Him – that is, about a continuous process of emanation. Yet at the same time this very process was described as a kind of revelation of the various Names peculiar to God in His capacity of Creator. The God who manifests Himself is the God who expresses Himself. The God who "called" His powers to reveal themselves named them, and, it could be said, called Himself also, by appropriate names. The process by which the power of emanation manifests itself from concealment into revelation is paralleled by the manifestation of divine speech from its inner essence in thought, through sound that as yet cannot be heard, into the articulation of speech. Through the influence of the *Sefer Yeẓirah*, which speaks of "the ten *Sefirot* of *belimah*," the number of the stages of emanation was fixed at ten, although in this early work the term refers only to the ideal numbers which contain the forces of creation. In kabbalistic usage, on the other hand, it signifies the ten powers that constitute the manifestations and emanations of God. Since the *Sefirot* are intermediary states between the first Emanator and all things that exist apart from God, they also represent the roots of all existence in God the Creator.

That many themes are united, or sometimes simply commingled, in this concept is demonstrated by the profusion of terms used to describe it. The term *Sefirah* is not connected with the Greek σφαῖρα ("spheres"), but as early as the *Sefer ha-Bahir* it is related to the Hebrew *sappir* ("sapphire"), for it is the radiance of God which is like that of the sapphire. The term is not used at all in the main part of the Zohar, appearing only in the later stratum, but other kabbalists too employed a wealth of synonyms. The *Sefirot* are also called *ma'amarot* and *dibburim* ("sayings"), *shemot* ("names"), *orot* ("lights"), *koḥot* ("powers"), *ketarim* ("crowns"; since they are "the celestial crowns of the Holy King"), *middot* in the sense of qualities, *madregot* ("stages"), *levushim* ("garments"), *marot* ("mirrors"), *neti'ot* ("shoots"), *mekorot* ("sources"), *yamim elyonim* or *yemei kedem* ("supernal or primordial days"), *sitrin* (i.e., "aspects" found mainly in the Zohar), *ha-panim ha-penimiyyot* ("the inner faces of God"). (A long list of other designations for the *Sefirot* can be found in Herrera, *Sha'ar ha-Shamayim*, 7:4.) Terms like "the limbs of the King" or "the limbs of the *Shi'ur Komah*," the mystical image of God, allude to the symbolism of the supernal man, also called *ha-adam ha-gadol*, or primordial man. Sometimes the term is used for one specific *Sefirah*, but often it denotes the whole world of emanation. The term *ha-adam ha-kadmon* ("primordial man") occurs for the first time in *Sod Yedi'at ha-Meẓi'ut*, a treatise from the *Sefer ha-Iyyun* circle. These different motifs of the *Sefirot*, which express themselves in this proliferation of names, tend to vary both with the specific context and with the overall inclinations of the kabbalist making use of them.

No agreed canonical definition exists. The conceptual connection between the *ma'amarim* or the *ketarim*, as the *Sefirot* were called in the *Sefer ha-Bahir*, and the intermediate substances between the infinite and the finite, the one and the many, of neoplatonism, originated mainly in the work of Azriel, who was determined to divest the idea of the *Sefirot* of its Gnostic character. His definitions, which appear in *Perush Eser Sefirot* and *Derekh ha-Emunah ve-Derekh ha-Kefirah*, and those of his companion Asher b. David, were largely instrumental in fixing the concept of the *Sefirot* in Spanish Kabbalah, although the tendency to portray them as Gnostic aeons did not entirely disappear. According to Azriel, things were created in a specific order, since creation was intentional, not accidental. This order, which determines all the process of creation and of generation and decay, is known as *Sefirot*, "the active power of each existing thing numerically definable." Since all created things come into being through the agency of the *Sefirot*, the latter contain the root of all change, although they all emanate from the one principle, *Ein-Sof*, "outside of which there is nothing." In terms of their origin in *Ein-Sof* the *Sefirot* are not differentiated, but in respect of their activity within the finite realm of creation they are. Existing alongside these Platonic definitions is the theosophic conception of the *Sefirot* as forces of the divine essence or nature, through which absolute being reveals itself; they therefore constitute the inner foundation and the root of every created being in a way which is generally not specifically defined, but not necessarily as "intermediaries" in the philosophical sense. The contrast with the neoplatonic pattern is very definitely expressed in a doctrine, common to all kabbalists of every age (even to Azriel), concerning the dynamic of these powers. Although there is a specific hierarchy in the order of the *Sefirot*, it is not ontologically determined: all are equally close to their source in the Emanator (this is already so in the *Sefer ha-Bahir*). It is possible for them to join together in mystical unions, and some of them move up and down within the framework of the hidden life of God (both Gnostic motifs), which does not fit the Platonic point of view. In other words, within a conceptual Platonic system a theosophic understanding of God came to the fore.

The nature or essence of these *Sefirot*, that is the relationship of the manifested world of the Divine to the created world and to the hidden being of the Emanator, was a widely disputed subject. Were the *Sefirot* identical with God or not, and, if not, wherein lay the difference? At first this question did not arise, and the imagery used to describe the *Sefirot* and their activity was not aimed at a precise definition. The description of the *Sefirot* as vessels for the activity of God, the Emanator, which occurs, for example, as early as Asher b. David, does not contradict the idea that in essence they are equated with God. The term *ko'aḥ* ("force," "power," "potency"), which is common in kabbalistic literature, does not always indicate a precise distinction between "force" and "essence" in the Aristotelian sense. It is also used to refer to the independent existence of "potencies," hypostases which are emanated from their source, without any preceding indication of whether this emanation is an expansion of the latter's essence or only of its radiation that was previously concealed in potentiality and now is activated. In purely figurative descriptions of the world of the *Sefirot* these philosophical distinctions did not come to the forefront, but once questions of this sort were raised it was impossible to evade them.

Most of the early kabbalists were more inclined to accept the view that the *Sefirot* were actually identical with God's substance or essence. This is stated in many documents from the 13th century, and stressed later in the school of R. Solomon b. Adret, and particularly in the *Ma'arekhet ha-Elohut*, which was followed in the 16th century by David Messer Leon, Meir ibn Gabbai, and Joseph Caro. According to this view, the *Sefirot* do not constitute "intermediary beings" but are God Himself. "The Emanation is the Divinity," while *Ein-Sof* cannot be subject to religious investigation, which can conceive of God only in His external aspect. The main part of the Zohar also tends largely toward this opinion, expressing it emphatically in the interchangeable identity of God with His Names or His Powers: "He is They, and They are He" (Zohar, 3, 11b, 70a). In the latter stratum, however, in the *Ra'aya Meheimna* and the *Tikkunim*, and subsequently in the *Ta'amei ha-Mitzvot* of Menahem Recanati, the *Sefirot* are seen not as the essence of God but only as vessels or tools: although they are indeed neither separated from Him nor situated outside Him like the tools of a human artisan, nevertheless they are no more than means and instruments which He uses in His work. Recanati states that most of the kabbalists of his time disagreed with this view. In the writings of Joseph Ashkenazi (Pseudo-Ravad) this theory is developed to the extreme where the *Sefirot*, being intermediaries, pray to God Himself and are actually unable to perceive the nature of their Emanator, a view which was first presented in the writings of Moses of Burgos and subsequently appeared in many kabbalistic works. Cordovero tried to reconcile these two opposing views and to accord a certain measure of truth to each one. Just as in all organic life the soul (the essence) cannot be distinguished from the body (the vessels) except *in abstracto* and in fact they cannot be separated at all when they are working together, so it may be said of God that He works, so to speak, as a living organism, and thus the *Sefirot* have two aspects, one as "essence," and the other as "vessels." Dominating this theosophic organism is a metabiological principle of measure and form called *kav ha-middah* (according to specific statements in the Zohar which use this term to express the nature of the activity of the first *Sefirah*). From this point of view the *Sefirot* are both identical with the essence of God and also separated from Him (see *Pardes Rimmonim*, ch. 4). In later Kabbalah this view became paramount.

The *Sefirot* emanate from *Ein-Sof* in succession – "as if one candle were lit from another without the Emanator being diminished in any way" – and in a specific order. Nevertheless, in contrast to the neoplatonic concept in which the intermediaries stand completely outside the domain of the "One," they do not thereby leave the divine domain. This influx is given the name *hamshakhah* ("drawing out"), that is to say, the entity which is emanated is drawn out from its source, like light from the sun or water from a well. According to Naḥmanides (in his commentary to Num. 11: 17) and his school, the second term, *aẓilut*, expresses the particular position of this emanation. The term is understood as deriving from *eẓel* ("near by," or "with"), for even the things that are emanated remain "by Him," and act as potencies manifesting the unity of the Emanator. Naḥmanides' anti-emanatist interpretation of the term *aẓilut* was apparently intended only for the uninitiated, for in his esoteric writings he also uses the term *hamshakhah* (in his commentary to the *Sefer Yeẓirah*). Generally speaking, stress is laid on the fact that the God who expresses Himself in the emanation of the *Sefirot* is greater than the totality of the *Sefirot* through which He works and by means of which He passes from unity to plurality. The personality of God finds expression precisely through His manifestation in the *Sefirot*. It is therefore surprising that, in those circles close to Naḥmanides, the nature of the Emanator which remained concealed beyond all emanation was thought to be a closely guarded tradition. Naḥmanides himself refers to it as "the hidden matter at the top of the *Keter*," at the head of the first *Sefirah*, a designation which deprives it of any personal quality (commentary to the *Sefer Yeẓirah*). As noted above, however, some of his contemporary kabbalists, like Abraham of Cologne (1260–70) in *Keter Shem Tov*, completely rejected this idea by denying an impersonal aspect to God and by identifying *Ein-Sof* with the first *Sefirah*.

Deriving *aẓilut* from *eẓel* does not necessarily imply that the process of emanation is eternal: it simply signifies the contrast between two domains – the *olam ha-yiḥud* ("the world of unification") and the *olam ha-perud* ("the world of separation"). Emanation is the world of unification, not of the static unity of *Ein-Sof* but of the process which occurs in God, who is Himself unified in the dynamic unity of His powers ("like the flame linked to a burning of coal"). In contrast to this, "the world of separation" refers to the domain which results from the act of creation, whose theosophic inner nature is expressed in the emanation of the *Sefirot*. But this process of emanation of the *Sefirot* is not a temporal one, nor does it necessitate any change in God Himself; it is simply the emergence from potentiality into actuality of that which was concealed within the power of the Creator.

However, opinion differed on the question of emanation and time. Azriel taught that the first *Sefirah* was always within the potentiality of *Ein-Sof*, but that other *Sefirot* were emanated only in the intellectual sense and had a beginning in time; there were also *Sefirot* that were emanated only "now, near to the creation of the world." Others maintained that the concept of time had no application to the process of emanation, while Cordovero held that this process occurred within "non-temporal time," a dimension of time which involved as yet no differentiation into past, present, and future. A dimension of this type was also important in the thinking of the later neoplatonists, who spoke of *sempiternitas*. This supermundane concept of time was defined "as the twinkling of an eye, without any interval" between the various acts which were part of emanation (so in *Emek ha-Melekh* and *Va-Yakhel Moshe* by Moses Graf). Joseph Solomon Delmedigo in *Navelot Ḥokhmah*, and Jonathan Eybeschuetz in *Shem Olam*, also posited the coeternity of the *Sefirot*, but generally speaking this idea aroused a great deal of opposition. As early as the 13th century the counter-doctrine was formulated that "the essences existed but emanation came into being" (*Origines*..., 295). If the essences preceded emanation then they must of necessity have existed in the will or thought of *Ein-Sof*, but they were made manifest by an act which had something of the nature of new creativity although not in the usual sense of creativity in time.

In the literature of the Kabbalah the unity of God in His *Sefirot* and the appearance of plurality within the One are expressed through a great number of images which continually recur. They are compared to a candle flickering in the midst of ten mirrors set one within the other, each of a different color. The light is reflected differently in each, although it is the same single light. The daring image of the *Sefirot* as garments is extremely common. According to the Midrash *(Pesikta de-Rav Kahana)*, at the creation of the world God clothed Himself in ten garments, and these are identified in the Kabbalah with the *Sefirot*, although in the latter text no distinction is made between the garment and the body – "it is like the garment of the grasshopper whose clothing is part of itself," an image taken from the Midrash *Genesis Rabbah*. The garments enable man to look at the light, which without them would be blinding. By first growing used to looking at one garment man can look progressively further to the next and the next, and in this way the *Sefirot* serve as rungs on the ladder of ascent toward the perception of God (Asher b. David, *Perush Shem ha-Meforash*).

The doctrine of the *Sefirot* was the main tenet clearly dividing Kabbalah from Jewish philosophy. The subject matter of philosophy – the doctrine of divine attributes and in particular "the attributes of action" as distinct from "the essential attributes" – was transformed in Kabbalah into the theosophic conception of a Godhead that was divided into realms or "planes" which, in the eyes of the beholder at least, existed as lights, potencies, and intelligences, each of unlimited richness and profundity, whose content man could study and seek to penetrate. Each one was like "a world unto itself," although it was also reflected in the totality of all the others. As early as the beginning of the 13th century, after the appearance of the *Sefer ha-Bahir*, the view was propounded that there were dynamic processes not only between the *Sefirot* but also within each separate *Sefirah*. This tendency toward an increasingly more complex doctrine of the *Sefirot* was the most distinctive characteristic of the development of kabbalistic theory. The number ten provided the framework for the growth of a seemingly endless multiplicity of lights and processes. In the circle of the *Sefer ha-Iyyun*, where this development began, we find an enumeration of the names of the intellectual lights and powers, which only partially fit the traditional symbolism of the *Sefirot* (see below) and sometimes diverge widely from it. The writings of "the Gnostic circle" in Castile expanded the framework of emanation and added potencies bearing personal names which gave a unique coloring to the world of the *Sefirot* and to all that existed outside it. This tendency was continued by the author of the Zohar, whose descriptions of the first acts of creation, and particularly those in the *Idra Rabba* and the *Idra Zuta* concerning the configurations of the forces of emanation (called *Attika Kaddisha, Arikh Anpin* and *Ze'eir Anpin*), are very different from the original simple concept of the *Sefirot*. Here is the beginning of the anatomical and physiological symbolism of the *Shi'ur Komah* – a description of the image of God based on analogy with human structure – which shook the very foundations of the *Sefirot* doctrine and introduced into it new differentiations and combinations. An additional complexity resulted when the theory of the *Sefirot* was combined with prophetic Kabbalah and "the science of combination" of the school of Abraham Abulafia. Every different combination of letters and vowels could be seen in the radiance of that intellectual light which appears under certain circumstances in the meditations of the mystic. Whole books, like the *Berit Menuḥah* (second half of the 14th century), *Toledot Adam* (see *Kitvei Yad ba-Kabbalah*, 58–60; printed in part in Casablanca in 1930 in *Sefer ha-Malkhut*), and *Avnei Shoham* by Joseph ibn Sayyaḥ (*ibid.*, 89–91), reflect this view. These complexities in the doctrine of the *Sefirot* reached their most extreme expression in Cordovero's *Elimah Rabbati* and, finally, in the Lurianic theory of the *parẓufim* (see below).

The *Sefirot*, both individually and collectively, subsume the archetype of every created thing outside the world of emanation. Just as they are contained within the Godhead, so they impregnate every being outside it. Thus, the limitation of their number to ten necessarily involves the supposition that each one is composed of a large number of such archetypes.

Details of the Doctrine of the Sefirot and Their Symbolism

Both theosophical and theological approaches are equally evident in kabbalistic speculation about the *Sefirot* in general and their relationship to the Emanator in particular. When it comes to the sequential development of the *Sefirot*, on the other hand, and to the individual function of each, especially from the second *Sefirah* onward, a strong Gnostic and mythic element begins to predominate. The kabbalists continuously stressed the subjective nature of their descriptions: "everything is from the perspective of those who receive" *(Ma'arekhet ha-Elohut)*; "all this is said only from our view, and it is all relative to our knowledge" (Zohar 2, 176a). However, this did not prevent them from indulging in the most detailed descriptions, as if they were speaking after all of an actual reality and objective occurrences. The progressive movement of the hidden life of God, which is expressed in a particular structural form, established the rhythm for the development of the created worlds outside the world of emanation, so that these first innermost structures recur in all the secondary domains. Hence there is basic justification for a single comprehensive symbolic system. An inner existence that defies characterization or description because it is beyond our perception can only be expressed symbolically. The words of both the Written and the Oral Law do not describe mundane matters and events alone, situated in history and concerned with the relations between Israel and its God, but also, when interpreted mystically, they speak of the interaction between the Emanator and the emanated, between the different *Sefirot* themselves, and between the *Sefirot* and the activities of men through Torah and prayer. What in the literal sense is called the story of creation is really a mystical allusion to the process which occurs within the world of emanation itelf and therefore can be expressed only symbolically. General speaking, such symbolism interested the kabbalists far more than all the theoretical speculation on the nature of the *Sefirot*, and the greater part of kabbalistic literature deals with this aspect and its detailed application. Most of the commentaries to the Torah, to Psalms, and to the *aggadot*, as well as the voluminous literature on the reasons for the Commandments (*ta'amei ha-mitzvot*), are based on this approach. As noted above, however, none of this symbolism has any bearing on *Ein-Sof*, although there were nevertheless kabbalists who did attribute to the latter specific expressions in Scripture or in the *Sefer Yeẓirah*.

The common order of the *Sefirot* and the names most generally used for them are (1) *Keter Elyon* ("supreme crown") or simply *Keter*; (2) *Ḥokhmah* ("wisdom"); (3) *Binah* ("intelligence"); (4) *Gedullah* ("greatness") or *Ḥesed* ("love"); (5) *Gevurah* ("power") or *Din* ("judgment"); (6) *Tiferet* ("beauty") or *Raḥamim* ("compassion"); (7) *Neẓaḥ* ("lasting endurance"); (8) *Hod* ("majesty"); (9) *Ẓaddik* ("righteous one") or *Yesod Olam* ("foundation of the world"); (10) *Malkhut* ("kingdom") or *Atarah* ("diadem"). This terminology was greatly influenced by the verse in 1 Chronicles 29: 11, which was interpreted as applying to the order of the *Sefirot*. Although the *Sefirot* are emanated successively from above to below, each one revealing an additional stage in the divine process, they also have a formalized structure. Three such groupings are most commonly found. In their totality the *Sefirot* make up "the tree of emanation" or "the tree of the *Sefirot*," which from the 14th century onward is depicted by a detailed diagram which lists the basic symbols appropriate to each *Sefirah*. The cosmic tree grows from its root, the first *Sefirah*, and spreads out through those *Sefirot* which constitute its trunk to those which make up its main branches or crown. This image is first found in the *Sefer ha-Bahir*: "All the divine powers of the Holy One, blessed be He, rest one upon the other, and are like a tree." However, in the *Bahir* the tree starts to grow by being watered with the waters of Wisdom, and apparently it includes only those *Sefirot* from *Binah* downward. Alongside this picture we have the more common image of the *Sefirot* in the form of a man. While the tree grows with its top down, this human form has its head properly on top, and is occasionally referred to as the "reversed tree." The first *Sefirot* represent the head, and, in the Zohar, the three cavities of the brain; the fourth and the fifth, the arms; the sixth, the torso; the seventh and eighth, the legs; the ninth, the sexual organ; and the tenth refers either to the all-embracing totality of the image, or (as in the *Bahir*) to the female as companion to the male, since both together are needed to constitute a perfect man. In kabbalistic literature this symbolism of primal Man in all its details is called *Shi'ur Komah*. The most common pattern is the following:

	Keter	
Binah		*Ḥokhmah*
Gevurah		*Gedullah*
	Tiferet	
Hod		*Neẓaḥ*
	Yesod	
	Malkhut	

Sometimes the three *Sefirot, Keter, Ḥokhmah*, and *Binah*, are not depicted in a triangle, but in a straight line, one below the other. On the whole, however, the overall structure is built out of triangles.

From the end of the 13th century onward a complementary *Sefirah*, called *Da'at* ("knowledge"), appears between *Ḥokhmah* and *Binah*, a kind of harmonizing of the two that was not considered a separate *Sefirah* but rather "the external aspect of *Keter*." This addition arose from the desire to see each group of three *Sefirot* as a unit comprising opposing attributes and as a synthesis which finally resolved them. This was not, however, the original motivation of the pattern. In the *Sefer ha-Bahir*, and in several early texts of the 13th century, the *Sefirah Yesod* was thought of as the seventh, preceding *Neẓaḥ* and *Hod*, and only in Gerona was it finally assigned to the ninth place. On the model of the neoplatonic hierarchy, according to which the transition from the one to the many was accomplished through the stages of intellect, universal soul, and nature, many kabbalists, Azriel in particular, thought of the *Sefirot* as also comprising these stages (although they still remained within the domain of deity). *Keter, Ḥokhmah*, and *Binah* were "the intellectual" (*ha-muskal*); *Gedullah, Gevurah*, and *Tiferet* were "the psychic" (*ha-murgash*); *Neẓaḥ, Hod*, and *Yesod* were "the natural" (*ha-mutba*). Apparently it was intended that these three stages should be understood as the sources of the independent realms of intellect, soul, and nature, which were fully activated and developed only at a lower level.

Since the *Sefirot* were conceived of as the progressive manifestation of the Names of God, a set of equivalences between the latter and the names of the *Sefirot* was established:

	Ehyeh	
YHWH (vocalized as *Elohim*)		*Yah*
Elohim		*El*
	YHWH	
Elohim Ẓeva'ot		YHWH *Ẓeva'ot*
	El Ḥai or *Shaddai*	
	Adonai	

According to the Kabbalah these are "the ten names which must not be erased" mentioned in the Talmud, and compared with them all other names are mere epithets. The Zohar distinguishes *Shaddai* as the name particularly related to the *Sefirah Yesod*, while Joseph Gikatilla associates this *Sefirah* with *El Ḥai*.

The division of the Sefirot was also determined by other criteria. Sometimes they were divided into five and five, i.e., the five upper *Sefirot* corresponding to the five lower, an equal balance between the hidden and the revealed being maintained. On the basis of the statement in the *Pirkei de-R. Eliezer* "with ten sayings was the world created, and they were summarized in three," they were also divided into seven and three. In this case there was a differentiation between three hidden *Sefirot* and "the seven *Sefirot* of the building," which are also the seven primordial days of creation. Six of these were also equated with the six sides of space in the *Sefer Yeẓirah*. How these six were complemented by a seventh was never decisively established. Some thought that the seventh was the sacred palace which stood in the center, as in the *Sefer Yeẓirah*. Others considered it to be represented by Divine Thought, while for others it was a symbolic Sabbath. The correlation of the "*Sefirot* of the building" with the days of creation became extremely complex. Many kabbalists, including the author of the main part of the Zohar, could not agree on the automatic association of each *Sefirah* with one particular day, and they regarded creation, which from the mystical viewpoint was the completion of "the building" of emanation, as having been already completed by the fourth day. They were particularly perplexed by the problem of the Sabbath, which many interpreted as a symbol of *Yesod*, since it paralleled the original seventh place of this *Sefirah*, while many others saw in it an allusion to the last *Sefirah*, especially since the powers came to an end there. Just as each day performed an act specific to it, apart from the seventh, so each *Sefirah* performed its own specific activities by which it was characterized, except for the last *Sefirah*, which had no such active force, but comprised the totality of all the *Sefirot* or the specific principle that received and united the active forces without adding anything particular of its own. On the contrary it is this absence of activity and the tenth *Sefirah's* function as an all-inclusive entity which constitute its uniqueness. The division of the *Sefirot* into three lines or columns was especially important: the right hand column includes *Ḥokhmah, Gedullah*, and *Neẓaḥ*; the left hand column includes *Binah, Gevurah*, and *Hod*; and the central column passes from *Keter* through *Tiferet* and *Yesod* to *Malkhut*.

All of these groupings testify to the kabbalists' belief that there was a definite structure to the *Sefirot*, no matter how great the possibilities may have been. In contrast to them all is yet another arrangement which presents the *Sefirot* either as adjoining arcs of a single circle surrounding the central Emanator, or as ten concentric spheres (called "circles") with the power of emanation diminishing as it moves further away from the center. This latter concept is related to the medieval cosmological picture of a universe of ten spheres, which could be imagined in terms of the outward gyration of these spiritual circles. The circular concept appears especially from the 14th century onward (Pseudo – Ravad to the *Sefer Yeẓirah*, 1, 2). In Lurianic Kabbalah every one of these diagrammatic arrangements, circular or linear, is accorded a specific place in the plan of emanation.

When we come to deal with the symbolism of the *Sefirot* we must distinguish between the general symbolic systems appertaining to the processes of emanation as a whole and the symbolism related to each individual *Sefirah* or to a particular combination of *Sefirot*. The overall symbolic systems are based on both mathematical and organic imagery. In the system depending on mathematical concepts, which is sometimes linked with images of light and rivers, the first *Sefirah* is nothingness, zero, and the second is the manifestation of the primordial point, which at this stage has no size but contains within it the possibility of measurement and expansion. Since it is intermediate between nothingness and being, it is called *hatḥalat ha-yeshut* ("the beginning of being"). And since it is a central point it expands into a circle in the third *Sefirah*, or it builds around itself a "palace" which is the third *Sefirah*. When this point is represented as a source welling up from the depths of nothingness, the third *Sefirah* becomes the river that flows out from the source and divides into different streams following the structure of emanation until all its tributaries flow into "the great sea" of the last *Sefirah*. This first point is established by an act of the Divine Will, taking its first step toward creation. In the Zohar the appearance of the supernal point (which is called *reshit*, "beginning," the first word of the Bible) is preceded by a number of acts that take place between *Ein-Sof* and the first *Sefirah* or within the first *Sefirah*. As well as being nothingness (*ayin*) and the will of God, this *Sefirah* is also the primordial ether (*avir kadmon*) which surrounds *Ein-Sof* like an eternal aura. From the mystery of *Ein-Sof* a flame is kindled, and inside the flame a hidden well comes into being. The primordial point shines forth in being when the well breaks through the ether (1, 15a). It is as if all the possible symbols were assembled together within this description.

The organic symbolism equates the primordial point with the seed sown in the womb of "the supernal mother," who is *Binah*. "The palace" is the womb which is brought to fruition through the fertilization of the semen and gives birth to the children, who are the emanations. In another organic image *Binah* is compared to the roots of a tree which is watered by *Ḥokhmah* and branches out into seven *Sefirot*. In another symbolic pattern – very common in the 13th century and particularly in the Zohar – the first three *Sefirot* represent the progress from will to thought and thence to intellect, where the general content of wisdom or thought is more precisely individuated. The identification of the following *Sefirot* as love, justice, and mercy links this doctrine with the aggadic concept of the divine attributes. References to male and female appear not only in the symbolism of father and mother, son and daughter (*Ḥokhmah* and *Binah*, *Tiferet* and *Malkhut*) but also in the striking use of sexual imagery which is a particular characteristic of the Zohar and Lurianic Kabbalah. The use of such images is especially prominent in the description of the relationships between *Tiferet* and *Yesod* on the one hand and *Malkhut* on the other. Many kabbalists did their utmost to minimize the impact of this symbolism, which afforded much scope for mythical images and daring interpretations.

A general symbolism of a different type is related to the stages in the manifestation of the personal, individual identity of God. The first *Sefirah* contains only "He"; sometimes this "He" is hidden and no mention is made of Him because of His extreme self-concealment, as, for example, within the verb *bara* ("He created") at the beginning of the Bible. Thus *bereshit bara Elohim* (usually "in the beginning God created") is interpreted mystically to refer to the first three *Sefirot*: through the medium of *Ḥokhmah* (called *reshit*), the first *Sefirah* – the force hidden within the third person singular of the word bara – produced by an act of emanation the third *Sefirah* (*Binah*), which is also called *Elohim. Elohim* ("God") is thus not the subject but the object of the sentence. This daring interpretation is common to almost all 13th-century kabbalists. But as His manifestation continues, God becomes "Thou," whom man is now able to address directly, and this "Thou" is related to *Tiferet* or to the totality of the *Sefirot* in *Malkhut*. However, God reaches His complete individuation through His manifestation in *Malkhut*, where He is called "I." This conception is summed up in the common statement that through the process of emanation "Nothingness changes into I" (*Ayin le-Ani*). The three letters or elements which make up *Ayin* ("Nothingness") – *alef, yod, nun* – are also contained in *Ani*, that is in both the beginning and the end of the process, but like the forces which they denote they are combined in a different way. In a similar fashion the name YHWH denotes just one *Sefirah* (*Tiferet*) but also contains within it all the fundamental stages of emanation: the spike at the top of the *yod* represents the source of all in *Ayin*, the *yod* itself is *Ḥokhmah*, the first *heh* is *Binah*, the *vav* is *Tiferet* or, because of the numerical value of the letter *vav*, the totality of the six *Sefirot* and the final *heh* is *Malkhut*. Since the latter comprises the other *Sefirot* and has no independent power, it cannot be assigned a letter of its own but only that *heh*, which has already appeared at the beginning of the emanation of the structure of the *Sefirot* and whose manifestation has reached its final development at the end of the process. The other names of God in the Bible are also interpreted in a similar fashion, their letters alluding to an inner progress in the process of emanation.

Emanation in its totality is the "Celestial Chariot" and individual components are "parts of the Chariot" which are interpreted in particular in the commentaries on the Chariot by Jacob Kohen of Soria, Moses de Leon, and Joseph Gikatilla. Biblical figures are also connected with this. "The patriarchs are the Chariot" (*Genesis Rabbah*), for Abraham represents the attribute of abundant love (*Ḥesed*), Isaac the attribute of strict justice (*Din*), and Jacob the attribute of mercy (*Raḥamim*), which is a combination of the other two. These three, together with King David, the founder of the kingship (*Malkhut*) of Israel, constitute the "four legs of the Throne" in the Chariot. And when Moses and Aaron are added, as representing the sources of prophecy in *Neẓaḥ* and *Hod*, and then Joseph – according to the talmudic picture of him as Joseph the righteous, keeper of the covenant, who resists the temptations of the sexual instinct – we have the seven *Sefirot* portraying the heroes of the Bible, who are called the "seven shepherds" or guests (*ushpizin*). This kind of symbolism conveys the moral content of the *Sefirot* as specific ethical attributes. The righteous, each of whom is inspired by a characteristic moral quality, embody the rule of the divine attributes in the world.

In addition to this ethical symbolism we find several cosmological systems. The four elements, the four winds, and even the four metals (gold, silver, copper, and lead) are indications of *Gedullah, Gevurah, Tiferet*, and *Malkhut*; the sun and the moon of *Tiferet* or *Yesod* and *Malkhut*. The moon, which receives its light from the sun and has no light of its own, and which waxes and wanes according to a fixed cycle, occupies an important place in the very rich symbolism of the last *Sefirah*. However, the most important of these symbols are the *Keneset Yisrael* ("the community of Israel") and the *Shekhinah* ("the Divine Presence"). The Kingdom of Heaven, which is realized in time in the historical *Keneset Yisrael*, represents therefore the latter's meta-historical aspect as well. The supernal *Keneset Yisrael* is the mother (*matrona*), the bride, and also the daughter of the "king," and they appear in countless midrashic parables on the relationship between God and the Jewish people. In her capacity as bride (*kallah*) she is also, by a mystical etymology, "the consummation of all" (*kelulah mi ha-kol*). She is the receptive aspect of "the holy union" of "king" and "queen." Other of her features are to be seen in the symbols of her as freedom, the Torah, and the trees in the Garden of Eden. The *Sefirah Binah* is the "supernal Jubilee," in which everything emerges into freedom and returns to its source, and therefore *Binah* is also called *Teshuvah* ("return"). But the last *Sefirah* is the *shemittah*, the seventh year when the earth rests and is renewed. The Written Law is woven from the name YHWH, and alludes to an emanation which already has some manifestation but has yet to be fully articulated. The Oral Law, which gives a detailed interpretation of the ways of the Written Law and of its application to life, is embodied in *Keneset Yisrael*, both in heaven and on earth. And similarly with regard to the trees: the Tree of Life is the *Sefirah Yesod* (though later on it is mainly *Tiferet*), while the Tree of Knowledge is a symbol of *Malkhut*, or of the Oral Law. In the early *aggadah* the *Shekhinah* is a synonym for God, indicating His presence, His "dwelling" in the world, or in any specified place. In the Kabbalah, on the other hand, from the *Sefer ha-Bahir* onward, it becomes the last attribute through which the Creator acts in the lower world. It is "the end of thought," whose progressive unfolding demonstrates God's hidden life. From its source at "the beginning of thought" in *Ḥokhmah* ("wisdom"), the thought of creation pursues its task through all the worlds, following the laws of the process of the *Sefirot* themselves. The emphasis placed on the female principle in the symbolism of the last *Sefirah* heightens the mythical language of these descriptions. Appearing from above as "the end of thought," the last *Sefirah* is for man the door or gate through which he can begin the ascent up the ladder of perception of the Divine Mystery.

The symbols mentioned so far form only part of a rich symbolism which drew on material from every sphere. Often there are differences in the details of its presentation, and there was a certain amount of freedom in the way given symbols were connected to a given *Sefirah*, but as far as basic motifs were concerned there was a great degree of agreement. Yet works explaining the attributes of the *Sefirot* were written from the time of the Gerona kabbalists onward, and the differences between them should not be minimized. Even in the Zohar itself there are many variations within a more or less firmly established framework. Such differences can also be seen between the symbolism of Moses de Leon and that of Joseph Gikatilla. The best sources for an understanding of this symbolism are: *Sha'arei Orah* and *Sha'arei Ẓedek* by Gikatilla; *Shekel ha-Kodesh* by Moses de Leon; *Sefer ha-Shem* written by another, unidentified Moses; *Sod Ilan ha-Aẓilut* by R. Isaac (*Koveẓ al-Yad*, 68, 5, 1951, 65–102); *Ma'arekhet ha-Elohut*, chs. 3–7; *Sefer ha-Shorashim* by Joseph ibn Wakkar (translation of the section on symbolism from his Arabic work; found separately in many Mss.); *Sha'ar Arkhei ha-Kinuyim* in *Pardes Rimmonim* by Cordovero, ch. 22; *Sefat Emet* by Menahem Azariah Fano (Lobatschov 1898); *Arkhei ha-Kinuyim* by Jehiel Heilprin (Dyhrenfurth 1806); *Kehillat Ya'akov* by Jacob Ẓevi Jolles (Lemberg 1870) and the second part entitled *Yashresh Ya'akov* (Brooklyn, about 1961). The attributes of the *Sefirot* according to Lurianic Kabbalah are described in detail in *Me'orot Natan* by Meir Poppers (text) and Nathan Nata Mannheim (notes) (Frankfurt 1709); *Regal Yesharah* by Ẓevi Elimelech Spira (Lemberg 1858); *Emet le-Ya'akov* by Jacob Shealtiel Niño (Leghorn 1843); and *Or Einayim* by Eliezer Ẓevi Safrin (Part 1 Premysl 1882, Part 2 Lemberg 1886).

From the 13th century onward we find the idea that each *Sefirah* comprises all others successively in an infinite reflection of the *Sefirot* within themselves. This formal method of describing the rich dynamic that exists within each *Sefirah* was also expressed in other ways. So, for example, we read of the 620 "pillars of light" in *Keter*, of the 32 "ways" in *Ḥokhmah*, of the 50 "gates" of *Binah*, of the 72 "bridges" in *Ḥesed*, and so on (in the *Tefillat ha-Yiḥud* ascribed to R. Neḥunya b. ha-Kanah), and of forces which are called by magical names whose meaning cannot be communicated but which denote the various concentrations of power that can be differentiated in emanation. As early as Moses of Burgos and Joseph Gikatilla it is stressed that from each *Sefirah* are suspended worlds of its own that do not form part of the hierarchical order of the worlds that follow the world of emanation. In other words, the total power of each *Sefirah* cannot be expressed simply with reference to the known creation. There are aspects that have other purposes: hidden worlds of love, of justice, and so on. In the Zohar descriptions of this type occur only in relation to the world of *Keter* (*Arikh Anpin*, lit. "the long face," properly "the long-suffering God") and the world of *Tiferet* (*Ze'eir Anpin*, lit. "the short face," properly "the impatient One") and take the form of a description of the anatomy of the "the white head," written with an extreme tendency to anthropomorphism. Parts of this "head" symbolize the ways in which God acts: the brow refers to His acts of grace, the eye to His providence, the ear to His acceptance of prayer, the beard to the 13 facets of mercy, and so on. An allegorization of the theological concepts in the doctrine of the attributes, a symbolism which views its own imagery as an accurate allusion to that which is beyond all imagining, and an attempt to reconcile the apparently incompatible doctrines of the *Sefirot* and the earlier *Shi'ur Komah* – all meet in these symbols of the *Idrot* of the Zohar. The author never states openly that his descriptions entail a positing of "*Sefirot* within *Sefirot*" (which are mentioned in the main part of the Zohar and also in the Hebrew writings of Moses de Leon, but only incidentally and without any detail). Apparently he saw no need to offer any speculative theory to justify his use of corporeal images, so difficult to probe rationally in any detail. His world was symbolic rather than conceptual. However, the kabbalists from the beginning of the 14th century did give such "revelations" a theoretical interpretation, starting with the *Sefer ha-Gevul* (based on the *Idra Rabba* in the Zohar) by David b. Judah he-Ḥasid and ending with Cordovero's *Elimah Rabbati* and his commentary to the Zohar. A similar doctrine is also evident in the writings of Joseph b. Shalom Ashkenazi. In their meditations on these internal reflections of the *Sefirot* within one another some kabbalists, such as Joseph ibn Sayyaḥ, went as far as to describe in detail the play of lights inside the *Sefirot* to the fourth "degree," as, for example, the "*Tiferet* which is in *Gedullah* which is in *Binah* which is in *Keter*." Cordovero too went further along this path than most kabbalists.

In Cordovero's teachings this theory of *Sefirot* within *Sefirot* is connected with another – that of the *beḥinot*, the infinite number of aspects which can be differentiated within each *Sefirah* and whose main purpose is to explain how each *Sefirah* is connected with both the preceding and the following ones. According to Cordovero, there are, in the main, six of these aspects in each *Sefirah*:

(1) its concealed aspect before its manifestation in the *Sefirah* which emanates it;

(2) the aspect in which it is manifested and apparent in the emanating *Sefirah*;

(3) the aspect in which it materializes in its correct spiritual location, that is to say, as an independent *Sefirah* in its own right;

(4) the aspect which enables the *Sefirah* above it to instill within it the power to emanate further *Sefirot*;

(5) the aspect by which it gains the power to emanate the *Sefirot* hidden within it to their manifested existence within its own essence; and

(6) the aspect by which the following *Sefirah* is emanated to its own place, at which point the cycle begins again.

This complete array of *beḥinot* is seen as causal relationship, each *beḥinah* causing the awakening and the manifestation of the following *beḥinah* (*Pardes Rimmonim*, ch. 5, 5). But there are many other "aspects" in the *Sefirot* as well and their discovery depends on the perspective of their investigator. Each *Sefirah* "descends into itself," and the process of this descent is infinite in its internal reflections. At the same time, however, it is also finite, in that it begets or brings into being from within itself another *Sefirah*. This concept necessitates the premise that the roots of emanation have a concealed "aspect" in *Ein-Sof* itself, and Cordovero interprets the three *ẓaḥẓaḥot* mentioned above as the three hidden *beḥinot* of *Keter* in *Ein-Sof*. He is thus forced to demolish the natural boundary between *Ein-Sof* and the first *Sefirah*, despite his clear desire to establish such a natural division. He therefore postulates that the *beḥinot* of *Keter* within *Keter* within *Keter* and so on, although they potentially continue *ad infinitum*, do not in fact reach an identity with the essence of the Emanator, so that the propinquity of *Ein-Sof* and *Keter* remains asymptotic. All this, of course, is stated from the point of view of created beings for even the supernal awakening of "aspects" of the Will within the Will within the Will and so on does not reveal *Ein-Sof*, and it is this differential which comprises the leap from the essence of the Emanator to that of the emanated. On the other hand, the differential gap closes when it is regarded from the point of view of the Emanator Himself. Cordovero's doctrine of the *beḥinot* shows how closely he approached a clearly dialectic mode of thought within the framework of kabbalistic ideas. With Cordovero the *Sefirot* are more than emanations which manifest the attributes of the Emanator, though they are this too. They actually become the structural elements of all beings, even of the self-manifesting God Himself. The implied contradiction between the processes of emanation and structuralism was never fully resolved by Cordovero himself, and it appears even in the systematic presentation of his ideas in *Shefa Tal* by Shabbetai Sheftel Horowitz. In such works as *Elimah Rabbati* and *Shefa Tal* zoharic Kabbalah undergoes an extremely profound speculative transformation in which as far as possible theosophy dispenses with its mythical foundations. Nevertheless, it is evident than this speculative trend does not turn Kabbalah into philosophy, and that the acknowledgment of a hidden life within the deity – the process of the emanation of the *Sefirot* – depends finally on mystical intuition, for by it alone can this domain be understood. In the Zohar this intuition is called "fleeting vision [of the eternal]" (*istakluta le-fum sha'ata*; 2, 74b; ZH 38c), and this is the element that the prophet and the kabbalist have in common (1, 97a and b).

In addition to the process of emanation which takes place between the *Sefirot*, there are two symbolistic modes of expressing the way in which each *Sefirah* radiates upon the others:

(1) Reflected light. This is based on the premise that, in addition to the direct light which spreads from one *Sefirah* to the next, there is a light which is reflected back from the lower *Sefirot* to the upper. Thus the *Sefirah* can be seen as both a medium for the transference of the light from above to below, and as a mirror serving to reflect the light back to its source. This reflected light can re-ascend from any *Sefirah*, particularly from the last one, back up to the first, and it acts on its return path as an additional stimulus that causes the differentiation of still further *beḥinot* in each *Sefirah*. Reflected light, according to Cordovero (*Pardes* 15), fulfills a great task in the consolidation of the potencies and *beḥinot* of judgment (*din*) in each *Sefirah*, for it functions through a process of restrictive contraction rather than free expansion. Only marginally based on early Kabbalah – e.g., the statements in the Zohar on the relationships among the first three *Sefirot* – this doctrine was developed by Solomon Alkabez and Cordovero alone and it formed an important factor in their dialectical reasoning.

(2) Channels. This is based on the premise that specific *Sefirot* stand in particular relationships of radiation with other *Sefirot* (though not necessarily with all of them). The face of one *Sefirah* turns toward another and consequently there develops between them a "channel" (*ẓinnor*) of influence which is not identical with actual emanation. Such channels are paths of reciprocal influence between different *Sefirot*. This process is not a one-way influx from cause to effect; it also operates from effect to cause, dialectically turning the effect into a cause.

It is not clear to what extent there is any identity between the symbols of reflected light and channels nor, if there is none at all, what their relationship is. Any interruption in the return influx from below to above is called a "breaking of the channels" (*shevirat ha-ẓinnorot*; Gikatilla, *Sha'arei Orah*), an idea which serves to explain the relations between the lower and upper worlds on the occasion of sin and divine disapproval. These channels are alluded to by the Gerona kabbalists, Gikatilla, Joseph of Hamadan (if this is the real name of the author of *Shushan ha-Birah*, a commentary to Song of Songs and to the *parashah Terumah* in British Museum Ms. Margoliouth 464), as well as other kabbalists of the 14th and 15th centuries, and the doctrine is presented in detail in chapter 7 of *Pardes Rimmonim*.

Earlier Worlds, Lower Worlds, and Cosmic Cycles (the Doctrine of the *shemittot*)

The emergence of God from the depths of Himself into creation, which constitutes the foundation of the doctrine of the *Sefirot*, was not always understood as a single, uninterrupted, straightforward process. In other views of the process of emanation and creation, a vital role was played by the midrashic legend concerning the worlds which were created and destroyed before the creation of our present world. An important variation of this idea lies at the root of a doctrine of the *Idrot* in the Zohar, in which the *Midrash* and other similar *aggadot* are connected with a description of how God entered into the form of the *Adam Kadmon* or Primeval Man, or into the different configurations of this form. Here we have a motif whose origin is in no way consistent with the classical formulation of the *Sefirot* doctrine, as can be easily seen from its reversed treatment of the male-female principle. Unlike in classical tradition, the male principle is considered here to be the principle of *din* or strict judgment which needs softening and "sweetening" by the female principle. A creation dominated solely by the forces of judgment could not survive. The exact nature of such earlier, unsuccessful creations, however – called in the

Zohar "the Kings of Edom" or "the Primeval Kings" (*malkhei Edom* or *malkin Kadma'in*) – is not made plain. It was only when the form of Primeval Man was fashioned perfectly, with a harmonious balance between the male and the female forces, that creation was able to sustain itself. This balance is called in the Zohar *matkela* ("the scales"), and only through its power did our world come into being. The biblical list of the kings of Edom (Gen. 35:31ff.) was interpreted in the light of this doctrine, for Edom was understood to represent the principle of judgment.

The author of the Zohar also expressed this doctrine in other ways. The worlds which preceded ours and were destroyed were like the sparks that scatter and die away when the forger strikes the iron with his hammer. This doctrine, in a completely new version, acquired a central place in Lurianic Kabbalah, while still other kabbalists tried to divest it of its literal meaning because of its theological difficulties. Cordovero's interpretation related it to the emanation of the *Sefirot* themselves, and to the dialectical process within each *Sefirah* – an interpretation quite out of keeping with the original idea. Other kabbalists of the Zohar period, such as Isaac ha-Kohen of Soria, expressed similar ideas, which they connected with the development of a "left-sided" emanation, that is, of an emanation of the forces of evil. The common element in all these doctrines is the supposition that during the first steps toward emanation certain abortive developments took place that had no direct effect on the actual creation of the present worlds, although remnants of these destroyed worlds did not entirely disappear and something of them still hovers disruptively among us.

Spanish Kabbalah concentrated its thinking on the emanation and structure of the *Sefirot*, a subject which is not dealt with at all in the writings of the philosophers. As regards the continuity of this process below the level of the last *Sefirah*, the kabbalists were in the main deeply influenced by medieval philosophical cosmology. Most kabbalists agreed that there was no essential break in the continuity of the influx of emanation which led to the development of additional areas of creation as well, such as the world of the intellect, the world of the spheres, and the lower world. But they maintained that whatever preceded these secondary stages was part of the divine domain, which they symbolically portrayed as a series of events in the world of emanation, whereas from this point on, the outward movement departed from the realm of the Godhead and was thought of as a creation distinct from the divine unity. This fundamental distinction between "the world of unity" of the *Sefirot* and "the world of separate intelligences" that was below them was made as early as the beginning of the 13th century. When the philosophers spoke of "separate intelligences," however, which they identify with the angels, they thought of them as immaterial beings representing pure form, whereas in kabbalistic language the term refers rather to a separation from the sefirotic unity of the divine domain.

As the Kabbalah developed, the world of the Merkabah (see above) described in the *heikhalot* literature became quite clearly distinguished from the world of the divine above it. The former was now often called "the domain of the Throne," and a rich angelology developed around it which was only partly identical with the earlier angelology of the Merkabah literature. In the main body of the Zohar there are detailed descriptions of the inhabitants of the seven "palaces" which spread out below the *Sefirah Malkhut* and are the products of its emanative influx, and which have little in common with the *heikhalot* of earlier literature. No fixed hierarchical order had been established in earlier Kabbalah for the world of the angels, and the writings of various 13th- and 14th-century kabbalists contain quite different angelological systems. Such systems occupy an important place in the works of Isaac ha-Kohen, his brother Jacob, and their pupil Moses of Burgos, all of whom spoke in detail of secondary emanations which served as garments for the *Sefirot* and were situated even higher than the most prominent angels in the traditional angelology, such as Michael, Raphael, Gabriel, and so on. Other systems occur in the *Tikkunei Zohar*, in the *Sod Darkhei ha-Nekuddot ve-ha-Otiyyot* attributed to the school of Abraham b. David of Posquières, in the books of David b. Judah ha-Ḥasid, and in the *Sefer Toledot Adam*. Sometimes a distinction was made between the Merkabah as a symbol of the world of the *Sefirot* themselves, and the *merkevat ha-mishneh*, or "second chariot," which represented the domain that came after the *Sefirah Malkhut*, and was itself divided into ten *Sefirot* of its own. Everything below the last *Sefirah* is subject to time and is called *beri'ah* ("creation") since it is outside (*le-var*) the Godhead.

The general scheme of a world of the Godhead and the *Sefirot*, and of the intelligences and the spheres, did not prevent many kabbalists, such as the author of the Zohar and Gikatilla, from supposing the existence of a very large number of secondary worlds within each one of these primary worlds. This expansion of an originally narrower cosmological framework is analogous to similar motifs in Indian thought, although there is no need to try to establish a direct historical link between the two. Every stage in the process of creation is crystallized in a specific world where the creative power of the Creator achieves the perfect expression of one of its many aspects. At the same time, we can trace the development of a unified doctrine of a series of worlds from above to below forming one basic vector along which creation passes from its primeval point to its finalization in the material world (see G. Scholem, *Tarbiz*, 2–3, 1931–32). The outcome of this development, in which Jewish, Aristotelean, and neoplatonic principles were all mingled together, was a new doctrine of four basic *worlds, called *olam ha-aẓilut* (the world of emanation – the ten *Sefirot*), *olam ha-beriah* (the world of creation – the Throne and the Chariot), *olam ha-yeẓirah* (the world of formation – sometimes the world of the angels centered around Metatron), and *olam ha-asiyyah* (the world of making – which sometimes includes both the whole system of the spheres and the terrestrial world, and sometimes the terrestrial world only). This arrangement, although without the nomenclature of "worlds," is already mentioned in the later strata of the Zohar, particularly in the *Tikkunei Zohar*. It appears in the form of four actual worlds in the *Massekhet *Aẓilut*, from the beginning of the 14th century. Isaac of Acre also made frequent use of this arrangement and gave it, for the first time, the abbreviated name *abiya* (*aẓilut, beri'ah, yeẓirah, asiyyah*). However, the doctrine was not fully developed until the 16th century when the kabbalists of Safed went into the details even of the worlds of *beri'ah* and *yeẓirah*, particularly Cordovero and the school of Isaac Luria. In the *Tikkunei Zohar* the world of *asiyyah* was understood as the domain of the material world and of evil spirits, while according to the *Massekhet Aẓilut* it included the whole range of creation from the angels (known as *ofannim*) through the ten spheres to the world of matter. According to Lurianic Kabbalah, all the worlds, including the world of *asiyyah*, were originally spiritual, but through the "breaking of the vessels" the world of *assiyyah*, after its descent from its earlier position, was commingled with the *kelippot* or impure "husks," which in principle should have remained completely separate, thus producing a world of matter that contained nothing spiritual. The ten *Sefirot* are active in all four worlds according to their adaptation to each one, so that it is possible to speak of the *Sefirot* of the world of *beri'ah*, the *Sefirot* of the world of *yeẓirah* and so on. Some concomitant of the *Sefirot* may be seen in the lower world also. Even the image of *Adam Kadmon* is reflected in each of these worlds (*adam di-veriyah, adam de-aẓilut*, etc., as in the writings of Moses de Leon, in the *Ra'aya Meheimna* and the *Tikkunim*). Even the terrestrial world of nature may be called *adam gadol* ("the great man"; macroanthropos). In another kabbalistic view dating to the period of the expulsion from Spain, nature is defined as *ẓel Shaddai*, that is, the shadow of the Divine Name.

Beginning in the 13th century, and especially from the 15th and 16th centuries, the kabbalists tried to make pictorial representations of the structure of creation as it progressed from *Ein-Sof* downward. Such diagrams were generally called *ilanot* ("trees"), and the obvious differences between them reflect divergences among the various doctrines and schemes of symbolism. Drawings of this kind are found in a large number of manuscripts. A detailed pictorial representation of the Lurianic system, called *ilan ha-gadol* ("the great tree"), which was made by Meir Poppers, has been published, first in the form of a long scroll (Warsaw 1864) and later as a book (Warsaw 1893).

These speculations were accorded a unique form in the doctrine of the *shemittot* or cosmic cycles which was based on a fixed periodicity in creation. Although dependent on aggadic motifs, this doctrine displays some relationship with similar non-Jewish systems, whose influence on Jewish authors can be traced in Muslim countries and in Spain, particularly in the writings of Abraham bar Ḥiyya. In his *Megillat ha-Megalleh*, he speaks of unnamed "philosophers" who believed in a long, even infinite series of cyclical creations. Some of them, he said, maintained that the world would last for 49,000 years, that each of the seven planets would rule for 7,000 years, and that God would then destroy the world and restore it to chaos in the 50th millenium, only to subsequently recreate it once again. These were astrological ideas drawn from Arabic and Greek sources, which could easily be assimilated to certain views expressed in the *aggadah*, such as the statement of Rav Katina (Sanh. 97a) that the world would last for 6,000 years and be destroyed in the seventh millenium, in which a parallel is drawn between the days of creation and those of the world, seen as a great cosmic week, at the end of which it "rests" and is destroyed. The earlier kabbalists related these ideas to their own doctrine of emanation. Their new teaching concerning the cycles of creation, which was widely referred to and even summarized in the Kabbalah of Gerona, was fully articulated, although in a highly cryptic style, in the *Sefer ha-Temunah*, which was written about 1250. The main point of this doctrine is that it is the *Sefirot* and not the stars that determine the progress and span of the world. The first three *Sefirot* remain concealed and do not activate "worlds" outside themselves – or at least not worlds that we can recognize as such. From the *Sefirah Binah*, also called "the mother of the worlds," the seven apprehendable and outgoing *Sefirot* are emanated. Each one of these *Sefirot* has a special role in one creation-cycle, which comes under its dominion and is influenced by its specific nature. Each such cosmic cycle, bound to one of the *Sefirot*, is called a *shemittah* or sabbatical year – a term taken from Deuteronomy 15 – and has an active life of 6,000 years. In the seventh millenium, which is the *shemittah* period, the Sabbath-day of the cycle, the sefirotic forces cease to function and the world returns to chaos. Subsequently, the world is renewed through the power of the following *Sefirah*, and is active for a new cycle. At the end of all the *shemittot* there is the "great jubilee," when not only all the lower worlds but the seven supporting *Sefirot* themselves are reabsorbed into *Binah*. The basic unit of world history is therefore the 50,000-year jubilee, which is subdivided as described above. The details of this doctrine in the *Sefer Temunah* are complicated by the fact that, according to the author, the *Sefirah Yesod*, which is also called *Shabbat*, does not activate a manifest *shemittah* of its own. Rather, its *shemittah* remains concealed and works through the power of the other cosmic cycles. Nor is there explicit mention here of any new cycle of creation after the jubilee. According to the kabbalists of Gerona, the laws in the Torah concerning the sabbatical and the jubilee years refer to this mystery of recurrent creation.

An even more radical doctrine came into being in the 13th century, according to which the world-process lasts for no less than 18,000 jubilees (Baḥya b. Asher, on the Torah portion *Be-Ha'alotekha*). Moreover, the actual chronology of these calculations is not to be taken literally, because the *Sefer ha-Temunah* teaches that in the seventh millenium there sets in a gradual and progressive retardation in the movement of the stars and the spheres, so that the measurements of time change and become longer in geometrical progression. Fifty thousand "years" therefore becomes a much longer period. Hence other kabbalists, and Isaac of Acre in particular, arrived at truly astronomical figures for the total duration of the world. Some kabbalists taught that after each "great jubilee" a new creation would begin *ex nihilo*, a view which passed from Baḥya b. Asher to Isaac Abrabanel, and from him to his son Judah, who mentioned it in his famous Italian work, *Dialoghi di Amore*. These views were also accepted much later by the author of *Gallei Razaya* (1552), and even by Manasseh Ben Israel. No kabbalist posited an infinite number of jubilees. In contrast to such enormous vistas, others maintained that we do not know what will follow the jubilee and that investigation of the subject is forbidden.

There were also divergent views on the question of which *shemittah* in the jubilee period we are living in now. Generally speaking, the accepted position was that of the *Sefer ha-Temunah*, namely, that we are now in the *shemittah* of judgment, dominated by the *Sefirah Gevurah*, and the principle of strict justice. Consequently, this must have been preceded by the *shemittah* of *Ḥesed* or lovingkindness, which is described as a kind of "golden age," akin to that of Greek mythology. According to another view (for example, that of the *Livnat ha-Sappir* by Joseph Angelino), we are in the last *shemittah* of the present jubilee period. Each *shemittah* experiences a revelation of the Torah, which is simply the complete articulation of the Divine Name or Tetragrammaton, but comprehension of it, that is, the combination of its letters, differs in every *shemittah*. Therefore, in the previous *shemittah* the Torah was read completely differently and did not contain the prohibitions which are the product of the power of judgment; similarly, it will be read differently in the *shemittot* to come. The *Sefer ha-Temunah* and other sources contain descriptions of the final *shemittot* which are of a distinctly utopian character. In their view, some souls from the previous *shemittah* still exist in our own, which is governed by a universal law of transmigration that includes the animal kingdom as well. As the power of judgment is mitigated in subsequent *shemittot*, so laws and customs will be relaxed also. This doctrine allowed tremendous play to the power of the imagination, which was particularly exploited by Isaac of Acre. It should be noted that in itself the premise that one and the same Torah could be revealed in a different form in each *shemittah* did not at the time arouse any open opposition, and was even extended by some who maintained that the Torah was read differently in each of the millions of worlds involved in the complex of creation – a view first expressed in Gikatilla's *Sha'arei Ẓedek* (see *Tarbiz*, 39, 1970, 382–3). One of the most extreme manifestations of this belief was the theory that in the present *shemittah* one of the letters of the alphabet is missing and will be revealed only in the future, thus the reading of the Torah will obviously be absolutely transformed.

The influence of the *Sefer ha-Temunah* and the doctrine of the *shemittot* was extremely strong and it still had its champions as late as the 17th century. However, the author of the Zohar ignored it completely, apparently out of some fundamental disagreement, although he too held that there was a great jubilee lasting 50,000 years in the world. As the Zohar became increasingly recognized as the authoritative and chief source for later Kabbalah, this silence on the subject strengthened opposition to the doctrine. Joseph ibn Zayyaḥ, Cordovero, and Isaac Luria rejected it as a mistaken or unnecessary hypothesis, at least in the version found in the *Sefer ha-Temunah*, and as a result of their influence it more or less disappeared from later kabbalistic literature. However, Mordecai Jaffe, a contemporary of Isaac Luria, was still teaching at the end of the 16th century that sequences of *shemittot* existed, even within the limits of historical time. The *shemitah* of *Din* ("judgment") began precisely at the time of the giving of the Torah, while everything that preceded it still belonged to the end of the *shemittah* of *Ḥesed* ("lovingkindness"). Its visionary utopianism and its mystical theory concerning the changing manifestations of the essence of the Torah were without doubt among the main reasons why the doctrine of *shemittot* was accepted so widely in kabbalistic circles. The disciples of Shabbetai Ẓevi made much of it, stressing its inherently antinomian implications.

The Problem of Evil

The question of the origin and nature of evil was one of the principal motivating forces behind kabbalistic speculation. In the importance attached to it lies one of the basic differences between kabbalistic doctrine and Jewish philosophy, which gave little original thought to the problem of evil. Various kabbalistic solutions were proffered. The *Ma'arekhet ha-Elohut* reveals the influence of the conventional neoplatonist position that evil has no objective reality and is merely relative. Man is unable to receive all the influx from the *Sefirot*, and it is this inadequacy which is the origin of evil, which has therefore only a negative reality. The determining factor is the estrangement of created things from their source of emanation, a separation which leads to manifestations of what appears to us to be the power of evil. But the latter has no metaphysical reality, and it is doubtful whether the author of the *Ma'arekhet ha-Elohut* and his disciples believed in the existence of a separate domain of evil outside the structure of the *Sefirot*. On the other hand, we already find in the *Sefer ha-Bahir* a categorization of the *Sefirah Gevurah*, as "the left hand of the Holy One blessed be He," and as "an attribute whose name is evil" and which has many offshoots in the forces of judgment, the constricting and limiting powers in the universe. As early as Isaac the Blind this led to the conclusion that there must of necessity be a positive root of evil and death, which was balanced within the unity of the Godhead by the root of goodness and life. During the process of differentiation of these forces below the *Sefirot*, however, evil became substantified as a separate manifestation. Hence the doctrine gradually developed which saw the source of evil in the superabundant growth of the power of judgment, which was made possible by the substantification and separation of the attribute of judgment from its customary union with the attribute of lovingkindness. Pure judgment, untempered by any mitigating admixture, produced from within itself the *sitra aḥra* ("the other side"), just as a vessel which is filled to overflowing spills its superfluous liquid on the ground. This *sitra aḥra*, the domain of dark emanations and demonic powers, is henceforth no longer an organic part of the World of Holiness and the *Sefirot*. Though it emerged from one of the attributes of God, it cannot be an essential part of Him. This view became dominant in the Kabbalah through the writings of the Gerona kabbalists and the Zohar.

According to the "Gnostics" of Castile and, in a different version, the Zohar also, there exists a complete hierarchy of the "emanation of the left," which is the power of uncleanness that is active in creation. However, this objective reality lasts only as long as it continues to receive fresh strength from the *Sefirah Gevurah*, which is in the holy order of the *Sefirot*, and in particular, only as long as man revives and fortifies it through his own sinful deeds. According to the Zohar, this *sitra aḥra* has ten *Sefirot* of its own, and a similar view, albeit with several variations and the addition of certain mythical elements, is expressed in the writings of Isaac ha-Kohen and in *Ammud ha-Semoli* by his pupil, Moses of Burgos. Isaac ha-Kohen taught that the first worlds that were destroyed were three dark emanations, which perished because of the overly concentrated power of strict judgment that they contained. The force of evil in this world, he argues, does not come from the *Sefirah Gevurah* but is a continuation of the *Sefirah Binah* that was substantified in the destructive potencies corresponding to the seven constructive *Sefirot* of creation. These two forces battle with one another from the beginning of creation itself.

In the Zohar too it is implied that the evil in the universe originated from the leftovers of worlds that were destroyed. The power of evil is compared to the bark (*kelippah*) of the tree of emanation, a symbol which originated with Azriel of Gerona (see Altmann, JJS, 9, 1958, 73–81) and became quite common from the Zohar onward. Some kabbalists called the totality of the emanation of the left "the outer tree" (*ha-ilan ha-ḥizon*). Another association, found in the Gerona kabbalists, and following them in the Zohar as well, is with "the mystery of the Tree of Knowledge." The Tree of Life and the Tree of Knowledge were bound together in perfect harmony until Adam came and separated them, thereby giving substance to evil, which had been contained within the Tree of Knowledge of Good and Evil and was now materialized in the evil instinct (*yeẓer ha-ra*). It was Adam therefore who activated the potential evil concealed within the Tree of Knowledge by separating the two trees and also by separating the Tree of Knowledge from its fruit, which was now detached from its source. This event is called metaphorically "the cutting of the shoots" (*kiẓẓuẓ ha-neti'ot*) and is the archetype of all the great sins mentioned in the Bible, whose common denominator was the introduction of division into the divine unity. The essence of Adam's sin was that it introduced "separation above and below" into what should have been united, a separation of which every sin is fundamentally a repetition – apart, that is, from sins involving magic and sorcery, which according to the kabbalists join together what should have remained separate. In actual fact, this view too tends to stress the separation of the power of judgment contained within the Tree of Knowledge from the power of lovingkindness contained within the Tree of Life. The latter pours out its influence unstintingly, while the former is a restrictive force with a tendency to become autonomous. This it can do either as the result of man's actions or of a metaphysical process in the upper worlds.

Both these views appear concurrently in kabbalistic literature without any clear distinction being drawn between them. The cosmic evil stemming from the inner dialectic of the emanating process is not differentiated here from the moral evil produced by human action. The Zohar tries to bridge these two realms by positing that the disposition toward moral corruption, toward evil in the guise of human temptation, derives from the cosmic evil which is in the domain of the *sitra aḥra* (3, 163a). The basic difference between the Zohar and the writings of the Gnostics in Castile was that the latter indulged in exaggerated personifications of the powers in this domain, resorting on occasion to earlier demonological beliefs and calling the potencies of "the emanation of the left" by proper names, whereas the author of the Zohar generally kept to more impersonal categories, with the exception of the figures of *Samael – the kabbalistic equivalent of Satan – and his mate *Lilith, to whom he assigned a central role in the realm of evil. Another departure from this rule is his detailed description of the "palaces of impurity" with their guardians in his commentary on Exodus 38–40 (2, 262–9), which follows a parallel description of the "palaces of holiness."

In the symbolism of the Zohar concerning the *sitra aḥra*, a number of different themes confront and occasionally even conflict with one another. The *kelippot* ("shells" or "husks" of evil) are sometimes understood neoplatonically as the last links of the chain of emanation where all turns to darkness, as "the end of days" in the language of the Zohar. At other times they are defined simply as intermediaries between the upper and lower worlds, in which light they are not necessarily seen as evil. Indeed, every mediating principle is a "shell" from the perspective of that which is above it but a "mind" from the point of view of that which is below (Zohar, 1, 19b). In other descriptions the domain of evil is delineated as the natural waste product of an organic process and is compared to bad blood, a bitter branch on the tree of emanation, foul waters (2, 167b), the dross which remains after gold has been refined (*ḥittukhei ha-zahav*), or the dregs from good wine. Such descriptions of the *sitra aḥra* in the Zohar are particularly rich in mythical images. The identification of evil with physical matter, though it occurs occasionally in the Zohar and in other kabbalistic books, never became an official doctrine of either. The equivocation of medieval philosophy between the Aristotelian and Platonic-emanatist concepts of matter is equally strongly felt in the Kabbalah, although the problem of how matter is emanated is referred to only infrequently. Generally speaking, the question of the nature of matter is not central in the Kabbalah, where the major interest was rather the question of how the Divine was reflected in matter. Occasional discussions of the nature of matter from a neoplatonic viewpoint can already be found in the literature of the *Sefer ha-Iyyun* circle. Cordovero, in his *Sefer Elimah*, explains the emanation of matter from spirit by means of a dialectic treatment of the concept of form that was common in medieval philosophy.

According to the Zohar there is a spark of holiness even in the domain of "the other side," whether from an emanation of the last *Sefirah* or as an indirect result of man's sin, for just as the fulfillment of a commandment strengthens the side of holiness, so a sinful act revitalizes the *sitra aḥra*. The realms of good and evil are to an extent commingled, and man's mission is to separate them. In contrast to this view which acknowledges the metaphysical existence of evil, an alternative approach has found its basic expression in Gikatilla, who defined evil as an entity which was not in its rightful place: "every act of God, when it is in the place accorded to it at creation, is good; but if it turns and leaves its place, it is evil." These two views – that of the Zohar, which accords evil actual existence as the fire of God's anger and justice, and that of Gikatilla, which attributes to it only a potential existence that nothing can activate save the deeds of men – occur throughout kabbalistic literature without any victory of one over the other. Even in the different versions of Lurianic doctrine the two are perpetually in conflict. (On the problem of evil in Lurianic Kabbalah, see below.)

A new and final development in regard to the problem of evil occurred in the doctrine of the Shabbateans, as formulated particularly in the writings of Nathan of Gaza. According to him, there were from the very beginning two lights in *Ein-Sof*: "the light which contained thought" and "the light which did not contain thought." The first had in it from the very beginning the thought of creating worlds, while in the latter there was no such thought, its whole essence striving toward remaining concealed and resting within itself without emerging from the mystery of *Ein-Sof*. The first light was entirely active and the second light entirely passive and immersed in the depths of itself. When the thought of creation arose in the first light, it contracted to make room for this creation, but the thought-less light which had no share in creation remained in its place. Since it had no other purpose but to rest in itself, it passively resisted the structure of emanation which the light containing thought had built in the vacuum created by its own contraction. This resistence turned the light without thought into the ultimate source of evil in the work of creation. The idea of a dualism between matter and form as being at the root of good and evil here assumes a most original pattern: the root of evil is a principle within *Ein-Sof* itself, which holds itself aloof from creation and seeks to prevent the forms of the light which contains thought from being actualized, not because it is evil by nature but only because its whole desire is that nothing should exist apart from *Ein-Sof*. It refuses to receive within itself the light that contains thought, and consequently it strives to frustrate and destroy whatever is constructed by that light. Evil is therefore the outcome of a dialectic between two aspects of the light of *Ein-Sof* itself. Its activity arises from its opposition to change. The approximation of this idea to the neoplatonic view of matter as the basis of evil is obvious. The struggle between the two lights is renewed at every stage of creation, nor will it come to an end until the time of final redemption, when the light that contains thought will penetrate through and through the light without thought and delineate therein its holy forms. The *sitra aḥra* of the Zohar is no more than the totality of the structure which the light without thought is forced to produce as a result of this struggle. As the process of creation goes on, the struggle becomes sharper, because the light of thought wants by its very nature to penetrate all the space that has been vacated by its contraction and to leave nothing untouched in that formless, primordial realm that Nathan calls *golem* (the formless *hyle*). The premise that the principles of both good and evil exist together in the supreme mind of God and that there is no other possible logical solution to the problem of evil in a monotheistic system was shared by Leibnitz, who approached the problem similarly some 50 years later in his *Théodicée*.

Although there is no doubt that most kabbalists held that evil did have a real existence at various levels, even though it functioned through negation, they were divided in their views concerning the eschatological problem of how it would finally be terminated both in the world and in man. Would the power of evil be totally destroyed in the time to come? Would it perhaps survive, but without any possibility of influencing the redeemed world once good and evil, which had become intermingled, had now been finally separated? Or would evil perhaps be transformed into good once more? The view that in the future world, whenever that would be, all things would return to their original, holy state, had eminent advocates from the days of the Gerona kabbalists onward. Naḥmanides spoke of "the return of all things to their true essence" – a concept drawn perhaps from Christian eschatology and the doctrine of *apokatastis* – and he meant by this the reascent of every created being to its source in emanation which would no longer leave room for the continued existence of the kingdom of evil in creation or of the power of the evil instinct in man. It would appear, indeed, that this return was connected in his view with the great jubilee, according to the doctrine of the *shemittot*. Such a position accepted the reality of evil within the different *shemittot*, in each *shemittah* according to its specific nature.

Generally speaking, kabbalistic arguments about the ultimate fate of evil limited themselves to the time of the redemption and the final day of judgment. The dominant view was that the power of evil would be destroyed and disappear, since there would be no longer any justification for its continued existence. However, others held that the evil domain would survive as the place of eternal punishment for the wicked. A certain vacillation between these two beliefs is found in both the Zohar and Lurianic Kabbalah. On the whole, the Zohar emphasizes that the power of the *kelippot* will be terminated and "broken" in the time to come, and in a number of places it states quite plainly that the *sitra aḥra* "will pass from the world" and the light of holiness will shine "without hindrance." Gikatilla states, on the other hand, that in the time to come "God will take the attribute of misfortune [i.e., the power of evil] to a place where it will not be able to be malignant" (*Sha'arei Orah*, ch. 4). Those who upheld the doctrine that evil would once more become good claimed that Samael himself would repent and be transformed into an angel of holiness, which would automatically cause the disappearance of the kingdom of the *sitra aḥra*. This view is expressed in the book *Kaf ha-Ketoret* (1500), and particularly in the *Asarah Ma'amarot* of Menahem Azariah Fano, but is opposed in the writings of Vital, who took a less liberal position. A powerful symbolic statement of Samael's future return to sanctity, and one particularly common from the 17th century onward, was the view that his name would be changed, the letter *mem*, signifying death (*mavet*), dropping out to leave Sa'el, one of the 72 holy Names of God.

The Doctrine of Creation in Lurianic Kabbalah

The one factor common to all kabbalistic doctrines of emanation and creation before Isaac Luria was their belief in an inner, uni-directional development that led from the stirring of *Ein-Sof* toward creation by means of more or less continuous stages. This process was prone to assume more complex forms and to go beyond the general doctrine of the ten *Sefirot*, to delve into the inner dynamic of the *Sefirot* themselves, or to describe the world of emanation through other symbolic systems, such as that of the mutually evolving, mutually conjoining Names of God. But the basic theme always remained the same: the progressive manifestation of *Ein-Sof* as articulated through the processes of emanation and creation. Even the classic formulation of this doctrine in the books of Cordovero, with all its dialectic complexity, does not diverge from this basic line. In contrast to this, we find a crucial turning-point in Lurianic cosmogony, whose extremely dramatic conception introduced far-reaching changes in the structure of kabbalistic thought. The details of this system are extremely complex even where they are clearly expounded, as for example, with regard to the principal acts of the creation-drama, to say nothing of its many obscurities that mystical meditation alone can perhaps comprehend. Lurianic doctrine created an enormous chasm between *Ein-Sof* and the world of emanation, which in previous kabbalistic teachings had been closely bound together, and then proceeded to fill it with divine acts of which the earlier Kabbalah had known nothing, although they can often be better understood against the background of older motifs. The principal accounts of the stages of creation found in the different versions of Lurianic doctrine given in the writings of his disciples and their pupils (on these sources, see the article on Luria) are basically similar, but they vary in emphasis and in the speculative interpretations they give to the significance of the main acts of creation. It may indeed be said that with Isaac Luria a new period of kabbalistic speculation was inaugurated which must be distinguished from earlier Kabbalah in all respects.

This new Kabbalah was based on three main doctrines, which determined its character: *ẓimẓum*; "the breaking of the vessels"; and *tikkun*.

ẒIMẒUM ("CONTRACTION"). The basic source of this doctrine is found in an early fragment from the circle of the *Sefer ha-Iyyun* (a preface to a commentary on "the 32 paths of wisdom" in the Florence Ms.) which speaks of an act of divine contraction that preceded emanations: "How did He produce and create this world? Like a man who gathers in and contracts (*meẓamẓem*) his breath [Shem Tov b. Shem Tov has, "and contracts Himself"], so that the smaller might contain the larger, so He contracted His light into a hand's breadth, according to His own measure, and the world was left in darkness, and in that darkness He cut boulders and hewed rocks." Here the reference is to the creation of *Keter*, which was thought to evolve from an act of contraction that left room for that darkness which alone was *Keter*. This was also in fact Naḥmanides' view in his commentary to the *Sefer Yeẓirah*, but not until Luria was the idea elevated to a basic cosmological principle.

The main originality of this Lurianic doctrine lay in the notion that the first act of *Ein-Sof* was not one of revelation and emanation, but, on the contrary, was one of concealment and limitation. The symbols employed here indicate an extremely naturalistic point of departure for understanding the beginning of creation and their very audacity made them highly problematic. Not surprisingly, therefore, important points of Luria's doctrine, which was preserved in its original wording in Luria's own literary remains and in Joseph ibn Tabul's version, were either obliterated (as in Vital's *Eẓ Ḥayyim*) or completely suppressed (as in *Kanfei Yonah* by R. Moses Jonah). The starting point of this theory is the idea that the very essence of *Ein-Sof* leaves no space whatsoever for creation, for it is impossible to imagine an area which is not already God, since this would constitute a limitation of His infinity. (This problem was not a source of concern to either the Zohar or Cordovero.) Consequently, an act of creation is possible only through "the entry of God into Himself," that is, through an act of *ẓimẓum* whereby He contracts Himself and so makes it possible for something which is not *Ein-Sof* to exist. Some part of the Godhead, therefore, retreats and leaves room, so to speak, for the creative processes to come into play. Such a retreat must precede any emanation.

Unlike the midrashic use of the word (*meẓamẓem*), which speaks of God contracting Himself into the Holy of Holies in the abode of the cherubs, kabbalistic contraction has quite the reverse significance: it is not the concentration of God's power *in* a place, but its removal *from* a place. The place from which He retreats is merely "a point" in comparison with His infinity, but it comprises from our point of view all levels of existence, both spiritual and corporeal. This place is primordial space, and it is called *tehiru*, a term taken from the Zohar (1, 15a). Luria also answers the question of how this *ẓimẓum* actually took place. Before *ẓimẓum* all the forces of God were stored within His infinite Self and equitably balanced without any separation between them. Hence, even the forces of *Din* ("judgment") were stored there but were not distinguishable as such. When the primal intention to create came into being, *Ein-Sof* gathered together the roots of *Din*, which had been previously concealed within him, into one place, from which the power of mercy had departed. In this way the power of *Din* became concentrated. *Ẓimẓum* therefore was an act of judgment and self-limitation, and the process thus initiated was intended to continue by means of a progressive extraction and catharsis of the power of *Din* that was left in primordial space, where it was intermingled in a confused fashion with the remnants of the light of *Ein-Sof* that had remained behind even after *ẓimẓum*, like the drops of oil that remain in a vessel after it has been emptied. This residue was called *reshimu*. Into this inchoate mixture, which is the hylic aspect of the future universe, there descends from the primordial, space-encompassing *Ein-Sof* a *yod*, the first letter of the Tetragrammaton, which contains a "cosmic measure" or *kav ha-middah*, that is, the power of formation and organization. This power may be seen as belonging to the attribute of mercy (*Raḥamim*).

Creation, therefore, is conceived of as a double activity of the emanating *Ein-Sof* following on *ẓimẓum*: the Emanator acts both as a receptive substratum in the light of the *reshimu*, and as a form-giving force which descends from the essence of *Ein-Sof* to bring order and structure to the original confusion. Thus, both the subject and object of the process of creation have their origin in God but were differentiated from each other in the *ẓimẓum*. This process is expressed in the creation of "vessels" (*kelim*) in which the divine essence that remained in primordial space is precipitated out: at first this takes place still hylically, in the vessel called "primordial air" (*avir kadmon*), but subsequently it assumes a clearer form in the vessel called "primordial man" (*Adam Kadmon*) that is created by a raising and lowering of the "cosmic measure," which serves as a permanent connection between *Ein-Sof* and the primordial space of *ẓimẓum*.

This version of the doctrine of *ẓimẓum* was obscured to a great extent by Vital, although occasional allusions to it remain scattered here and there in his works. At the beginning of his *Eẓ Ḥayyim*, however, there is a much simpler account. Without mentioning either the gathering out of the roots of *Din* or the *reshimu*, he describes a process whereby as a result of the act of divine contraction an empty vacuum was formed in the midst of *Ein-Sof*, into which emanated a ray of light that filled this space with ten *Sefirot*. Since the *ẓimẓum* took place equally on all sides, the resulting vacuum was circular or spherical in shape. The light which entered it in a straight line after the *ẓimẓum* has, therefore, two aspects from the start: it arranges itself both in concentric circles and in a unilinear structure, which is the form of "the primordial man that preceded every first thing." The form of a circle and of a man are henceforth the two directions in which every created thing develops. Just as the first movement in creation was in reality composed of two movements – the ascent of *Ein-Sof* into the depths of itself and its partial descent into the space of *ẓimẓum* – so this double rhythm is a necessarily recurring feature of every stage in the universal process. This process works through the double beat of the alternately expanding movement of *Ein-Sof* and its desire to return to itself, *hitpashtut* ("egression") and *histalkut* ("regression"), as the kabbalists call it. Every movement of regression toward the source has something of a new *ẓimẓum* about it. This double-facedness in the process of emanation is typical of the dialectical tendency of Lurianic Kabbalah. Every stage in the development of the emanating light has not only a circular and linear aspect but also the modes of both an "inner light" within the vessels that are produced and a "surrounding light," as well as the modes of *aẓmut ve-kelim* ("substance and vessels"), and "direct light and reflected light," that are taken from the teachings of Cordovero. Luria's special interest in the structure of the spiritual worlds and their emergence through dialectical processes is also expressed in the distinction he makes between the structural "totality" (*kelalut*) of the forces of emanation and the structural "individuality" (*peratut*) of each, that is, the isolated articulation in itself of each such power that is active in a given overall structure.

Our earliest sources for the doctrine of *ẓimẓum* clearly show that Luria did not differentiate between the substance of *Ein-Sof* and its light, in both of which *ẓimẓum* occurred. Such a distinction was made only when problems arose concerning the harmonization of this doctrine with the idea of God's immutability. This desire for consistency had two consequences:

(1) a differentiation between the substance of *Ein-Sof* and its light (i.e., its will), which made it possible to argue that the *ẓimẓum* occurred only in the latter and not in its "possessor"; and

(2) the insistence that the concept of *ẓimẓum* was not to be taken literally, being only figurative and based on a human perspective. These two beliefs were particularly stressed in the school of Israel Sarug, whose teachings on the subject were based on a combination of Ibn Tabul's redaction of Lurianic doctrine with that of Moses Jonah in his *Kanfei Yonah*, which makes no mention of *ẓimẓum* but speaks only of an emanation of one primal point comprising all the *Sefirot* without going into the details of how the latter came into being. To this Sarug added original ideas of his own which had a great influence on later Kabbalah; a summary of them can be found in his book *Limmudei Aẓilut*. According to him, the *ẓimẓum* was preceded by processes of a more internal nature within *Ein-Sof* itself. In the beginning *Ein-Sof* took pleasure in its own autarchic self-sufficiency, and this "pleasure" produced a kind of "shaking" which was the movement of *Ein-Sof* within itself. Next, this movement "from itself to itself" aroused the root of *Din*, which was still indistinguishably combined with *Raḥamim*. As a result of this "shaking," "primordial points" were "engraved" in the power of *Din*, thus becoming the first forms to leave their markings in the essence of *Ein-Sof*. The contours

of this "engraving" were those of the primordial space, that was to come into being as the end-product of this process. As the light of *Ein-Sof* outside this "engraving" acted upon the points within it, the latter were activated from their potential state and the primordial Torah, the ideal world woven in the substance of *Ein-Sof* itself, was born. This Torah, the linguistic movement of *Ein-Sof* within itself, is called a *malbush* ("garment"), though in fact it is inseparable from the divine substance and is woven within it "like the grasshopper whose clothing is part of itself," to use the language of the Midrash. Sarug described the structure of this "garment" in great detail. Its length was made up of the alphabets of the *Sefer Yeẓirah* and had 231 "gates" (i.e., possible combinations of the 22 letters of the Hebrew alphabet in the progression אב, אג, אד etc.), which form the archistructure of divine thought. Its breadth was composed of an elaboration of the Tetragrammaton according to the numerical value of the four possible spellings of the fully written names of its letters, viz., the "name" 45 (יוד, הא, יאו, הא), the "name" 52 (יוד, הה, וו, הה), the "name" 72 (יוד, הי, ויו, הי), and the "name" 63 (הי, יוד, הי, ואו), which were the "threads" of the "weave" that were originally situated in the hem of the garment. This primordial Torah contained potentially all that could possibly be revealed through the Torah to be given on earth. In effect, it was a kabbalistic version of the Platonic world of ideas. The size of this garment was twice the area necessary for the creation of all the worlds. After it had been woven, it was folded in two: half of it ascended and its letters stood behind the letters of the other half. The "names" 45 and 52 were arranged behind the "names" 72 and 63, and consequently the last *yod* of the "name" 63 was left without a partner in the folded garment. This folding constituted a contraction (*ẓimẓum*) of the garment to half its area, and with the removal of half of it from its previous place, something was created in *Ein-Sof* that no longer partook of its substance. All that remained in this primordial square was the unmatched *yod*, which now assumed the dynamic task of transferring the light of *Ein-Sof*, which spread in circles, to the area produced by the act of *ẓimẓum*, as in the version of Ibn Tabul. The empty area created by the folding of the garment is not an actual vacuum but is merely deprived of the garment or of the light of its substance. Yet the hidden law of the whole of creation that is inscribed within the "engraving" of *Ein-Sof* is henceforward active and expresses itself throughout all subsequent processes through the power invested in this one intruding *yod*. Made manifest in the vacated space are both the residue (*reshimu*) of the remaining light of its essence and some of the light of *Ein-Sof* itself, which acts as the soul that sustains all and without which all would return to *Ein-Sof* as before. This soul too contracts to a point, which is none other than the *anima mundi* of the philosophers. Moreover, the various movements of the *ẓimẓum*, and the ascents and descents of this *yod*, produce still other points in space that constitute the primordial "world of points" (*olam ha-nekudot*), which at this stage still has no definite structure and in which the divine lights exist in an atomized state. According to Sarug, not one but many contractions occur in the place of the *reshimu*, and even more so thereafter. Elsewhere he states that there are two kinds of *reshimu*, one of the divine substance and one of the folded garment, and that only the second is articulated in the world of the points. Only upon the return of the *yod*, which ascends to *Ein-Sof* and re-descends from it, is that supernal light created in the primordial space which is known as the *tehiru* or primal matter of every being.

The dialectical confusion apparent in Sarug's presentations bears witness to the uncertainty and excitement caused by the new idea of the *ẓimẓum*. The importance of the power of *Din* in those acts which led to its embodiment in primal matter is obliterated to a much greater extent in Sarug's presentation than in that of Ibn Tabul, though it does not disappear altogether. The contradiction inherent in the opposing conceptions of the vacated primordial space, now as a square and now a sphere created by the activity of the emanating *yod*, posed an additional problem in Sarug's work that was not found elsewhere and that had no consistent solution. In any case, extreme naturalistic descriptions in these accounts were qualified by the stress laid on their symbolic character.

One of the most interesting of the further speculative attempts to explain the theories of *ẓimẓum*, which continued to be made for more than 200 years, is the daring interpretation of Shabbetai Sheftel Horowitz in his *Shefa Tal*. Horowitz tried to revise the doctrine of *ẓimẓum* once again and to regard it as merely a symbolic account of the emanation of the *Sefirah Keter*. Following Sarug's presentation, although without mentioning the *malbush* ("garment"), he attempted to equate the different stages in *ẓimẓum* with what he considered to be the parallel stages in the emanation of *Keter* in Cordovero's teachings. The emergence of the *tehiru* was no longer produced by the *ẓimẓum* itself but by the emanation of the light of *Ein-Sof* from within the essence of *Ein-Sof* itself. Only within this emanated *tehiru* did a contraction take place of the light of *Ein-Sof*, a residue of which mingled with some of the emanated substance to form the *reshimu*. Thus, the soul came into being as a supernal point in the *Sefirah Keter*. This transformation of the *ẓimẓum* into a second divine act following an original act of emanation made the doctrine once more compatible with Cordovero, who had also acknowledged the existence of a *ẓimẓum* within the chain of emanations, in which the power of the Creator became inevitably restricted in a progressive manner. Thus, Horowitz's interpretation removed the paradoxical thrust which was inherent in the doctrine of *ẓimẓum* from its very conception.

From the 17th century onward kabbalistic opinion was divided on the doctrine of *ẓimẓum*. Was it to be taken literally? Or was it to be understood symbolically as an occurrence in the depths of the Divine, which the human mind could only describe in figurative language? The question was a bone of contention in the many arguments that took place between the kabbalists and the more philosophically inclined who found kabbalistic speculation distasteful, for all that the concept of *ẓimẓum* was in fact very close to ideas that later developed in modern idealist philosophies, such as those of Schelling and Whitehead. As a result of the exposition of the doctrine given by the author of *Emek ha-Melekh*, many kabbalists were inclined to take the *ẓimẓum* literally, a view that became especially popular among the Shabbateans, whose entire creed made a non-literal interpretation impossible. This position was clearly expressed in the writings of Nathan of Gaza and Nehemiah Ḥayon. It was Ḥayon's determined defense of the literalist interpretation, in fact, that prompted Joseph Ergas to stress even more keenly Abraham Herrera's view that the *ẓimẓum* doctrine was symbolic. This dispute, which was also bound up with the anthropomorphistic doctrine of the Shabbateans in general, broke out in 1714 and was summed up by Ergas in his *Shomer Emunim* (1736), which is our main source for that fundamental reinterpretation that restored Lurianic doctrine to its Cordoveroan starting-point. By then the Shabbatean side of the argument was no longer a factor, so that the literalist position was defended again, even in the camp of the orthodox kabbalists, whose chief spokesman was Immanuel Hai Ricchi in his *Yosher Levav* (1737). Ergas' system, on the other hand, was expanded in the *Amud ha-Avodah* by Baruch Kosover (written about 1763, but not printed until 1854). Ergas greatly influenced ḥasidic literature, especially the Ḥabad teachings of Shneur Zalman of Lyady and his pupil Aaron ha-Levi of Staroselye, who devoted a profound dialectical discussion to the subject in his *Avodat ha-Levi*. In his *Tanya* Shneur Zalman maintained that the Gaon of Vilna mistakenly took *ẓimẓum* literally, but it is an open question if he was justified in interpreting the Gaon's teachings in this way. Aaron ha-Levi's system is based on the premise of a double *ẓimẓum*. The first *ẓimẓum*, also called *beki'ah* ("piercing"), is a contraction in the substance of *Ein-Sof* which renders possible the appearance of the Infinite in general and which is completely beyond our understanding. It leads to a revelation of the light of *Ein-Sof*, but it is so unfathomable that there is not the slightest mention of it in Ḥayyim Vital's *Eẓ Ḥayyim*. It is only after this *beki'ah*, which is conceived of as a "leap" from absolute *Ein-Sof* to relative *Ein-Sof*, that the second contraction occurs, whereby the Infinite light of *Ein-Sof* is made to appear finite. In fact, however, the finite has no existence at all and is made possible only through the emission of a line or a ray from the Infinite. The cathartic concept of *ẓimẓum* mentioned above was developed independently in the writings of Moses Ḥayyim Luzzatto, who believed the crux of *ẓimẓum* to lie in the fact that the Creator "overcomes, as it were, His innate law of goodness in creation, so that His creatures should not be made perfect, even seen from their own point of view, let alone seen from that of God." The metaphysical root of evil is inherent in the very privation that the act of *ẓimẓum* involves, and the whole development of created beings depends on their being given an opportunity to perfect themselves according to their merits and to separate the power of evil from the power of good.

In sum, we can say that those kabbalists who wrote with one eye on the philosophers tended to stress the non-literal nature of *ẓimẓum*, whereas those kabbalists who had little use for Aristotelian philosophy to begin with presented the doctrine literally and unadorned. Nor should we overlook the close connection in the view of many kabbalists between *ẓimẓum* and the existence of the hylic matter which served as the basis for creation as a whole. Even Ḥayyim Vital himself defined the Infinite as the Nothing, which became manifest in *Keter* only through *ẓimẓum*, the hylic matter in the whole of creation (*Eẓ Ḥayyim*, ch. 42, para. 1). Others connected the existence of the *hyle* with the *reshimu*, the primordial space, or the primordial air which was made manifest through *ẓimẓum*. A special discussion of the subject occurs in Eliakim b. Abraham Hart's *Ẓuf Novelot* (London, 1799), summarizing the far longer elaboration in *Novelot Ḥokhmah* by Joseph Solomon Delmedigo (1631).

THE BREAKING OF THE VESSELS. The point in *Ein-Sof* that was vacated in the act of *ẓimẓum* was subsequently filled with a proliferation of worlds and ontological events, each one of which tends in Lurianic Kabbalah to become the subject of a description whose complexity verges on the extreme. Moreover, these descriptions themselves vary widely in the different redactions of Ibn Tabul, Moses Jonah, and Ḥayyim Vital, and highly contradictory versions of them can even be found in several of Vital's own works. Israel Sarug's attempts to make a unified whole out of this confusion only added still further to it. Nevertheless, in each of these many presentations the same broad outlines appear. Isaac Luria's main preoccupation, it would appear, was to trace the further development of the vessels that received the light of emanation which shone into the primordial space after the act of *ẓimẓum*. In the actual emergence of these vessels a part was played both by the lights that were located in the *tehiru* after the *ẓimẓum* and by the new lights that entered with the ray. The purpose of this process was the selecting out of the forces of *Din* that had collected, a catharsis that could have been attained either by eliminating these forces from the system entirely or else by integrating them within it by first "softening" and purifying them – two conflicting approaches which we frequently encounter side by side. In either case, however, in order to further those processes that were a necessary prelude to the complex hierarchy of creation, a progressive differentiation was called for in the vessels themselves, without which the emanating streams would have been unable to regulate themselves and function properly. To this end, the various conjunctions of the first emanating lights as they collided with each other resulted in the creation of the vessels, which "crystallized out," as it were, from certain modes that these lights contained.

All the Lurianic redactions agree that the ray of light that comes from *Ein-Sof* in order to organize the *reshimu* and the forces of *Din* that have filled the primordial space functions in two opposing fashions which inform all the developments in this space from beginning to end. These are the two aspects of "circle and line" (*iggul ve-yosher*). Practically speaking, a point can expand evenly in one of two ways, circularly or linearly, and herein is expressed a basic duality that runs through the process of creation. The more harmonious of the two forms, which partakes of the perfection of *Ein-Sof*, is the circle; the latter conforms naturally to the spherical space of the *ẓimẓum*, while the straight ray of light goes forth to seek its ultimate structure in the form of man, who represents the ideal aspect of *yosher* ("straightness"). Thus, while the circle is the natural form, the line is the willed form that is directed toward the figure of man. Moreover, because the line of light comes directly from *Ein-Sof*, it is of a higher degree than the circle, whose shape is a reflection of the *ẓimẓum*. The former, according to Isaac Luria, comprehends the principle of the *ru'aḥ*, the latter the principle of the *nefesh* or natural perfection. Essentially, this doctrine is a restatement of the Pythagorean geometrical symbolism that dominated natural philosophy until the 17th century. Every act of emanation, therefore, contains these two aspects, and should one be missing various disruptions or unexpected developments will take place. All purposeful, teleological movements are basically those of the line, while to the circle belong all processes dominated by natural, immanent necessity.

The first form that emanation assumes after the *ẓimẓum* is that of the *Adam Kadmon* ("primordial man"), which in the Lurianic system stands for a realm above the four worlds of *aẓilut*, *beri'ah*, *yeẓirah*, and *asiyyah* with which pre-Lurianic Kabbalah began. Isaac Luria did, it is true, seek to support this belief with a number of citations from the Zohar and the *Tikkunim*, but in fact it represented a completely new departure. Though he and his disciples maintained that many of the processes that take place in the *Adam Kadmon* are mysteries beyond human knowledge, they nevertheless discussed in great detail the manner in which the forces of emanation were organized after the *ẓimẓum* in this form. Throughout their treatment of this figure and of the supernal lights that radiated from it, the double dialectical movement mentioned above remains dominant. Thus, the ten *Sefirot* first took shape in the *Adam Kadmon* in the form of concentric circles, of which the outermost, the circle of *Keter*, remained in close contact with the surrounding *Ein-Sof*. This was the *nefesh* of the *Adam Kadmon*. Next the ten *Sefirot* rearranged themselves as a line, in the form of a man and his limbs, though of course this must be understood in the purely spiritual sense of the incorporeal supernal lights. This was the *ru'aḥ* of the *Adam Kadmon*. The higher aspects of the *nefesh*, known as *neshamah, ḥayyah*, and *yeḥidah*, are also rooted in the upper *Sefirot* in their linear configurations. All of these lights possess vessels which are still so subtle and "pure" that they can hardly be considered vessels at all. The promotion of the *Adam Kadmon* to the rank of the first being to emerge after the *ẓimẓum* accounts for the strong anthropomorphic coloring that accompanies all descriptions of the process of emanation in the Lurianic system. The *Adam Kadmon* serves as a kind of intermediary link between *Ein-Sof*, the light of whose substance continues to be active in him, and the hierarchy of worlds still to come. In comparison with the latter, indeed, the *Adam Kadmon* himself could well be, and sometimes was, called *Ein-Sof*.

From the head of the *Adam Kadmon* tremendous lights shone forth and aligned themselves in rich and complex patterns. Some assumed the form of letters while others took on still other aspects of the Torah or the Holy Tongue, such as the cantillations (*te'amim*), the vowel points, or the scribal affixes (*tagim*), which too are components of Holy Writ. Thus, two essentially different symbolisms – that of light, and that of language and writing – are here joined. Every constellation of light has its particular linguistic expression, though the latter is not directed toward the lower worlds but rather inward toward its own hidden being. These lights combine to form "names" whose concealed potencies become active and are made manifest through concealed "configurations" (*millu'im*) where each letter is fully written out by name in the alphabet. This primordial world from the lights of *Adam Kadmon's* forehead, which issued from the spot where the phylactery-of-the-head is laid. The lights issuing from the *Adam Kadmon's* ears, nose, and mouth, however, expanded linearly only, nor did their *Sefirot* have special vessels, since they were at first joined together in a common vessel in accord with the "collectivity" that was their structural nature. Vital called this sphere *olam ha-akudim*, meaning a world where the *Sefirot* were not yet differentiated (lit. bound together). The function assigned to these lights in the drama of creation was never clearly defined. The lights of the eyes, on the other hand, were differentiated into every *Sefirah*. In theory these lights should have issued from the navel, but the place of their appearance was deflected by a medium acting within the *Adam Kadmon* and referred to as *parsa* (apparently a reference to the diaphragm). This displacement is described as the result of another *ẓimẓum* within the lights themselves. Having changed their path, these lights issued from the eyes both linearly and circularly, and each of their *Sefirot* commanded a vessel of its own. Vital calls these separated lights "the world of dots" (*olam ha-nikuddim*), but in other Lurianic writings they are grouped together with the light of the *tehiru* and referred to as "the world of points" (*olam ha-nekuddot*) or "the world of chaos" (*olam ha-tohu*) – the latter because at this stage the lights of the *Sefirot* had not yet attained a stable structural arrangement. All the lights of these *Sefirot* were given vessels, themselves made of thicker light, in which to arrange themselves and function.

At this point, however, there occurred what is known in Lurianic Kabbalah as "the breaking of the vessels" or "the death of the kings." The vessels assigned to the upper three *Sefirot* managed to contain the light that flowed into them, but the light struck the six *Sefirot* from *Ḥesed* to *Yesod* all at once and so was too strong to be held by the individual vessels; one after another they broke, the pieces scattering and falling. The vessel of the last *Sefirah, Malkhut*, also cracked but not to the same degree. Some of the light that had been in the vessels retraced its path to its source, but the rest was hurled down with the vessels themselves, and from their shards the *kelippot*, the dark forces of the *sitra aḥra*, took on substance. These shards are also the source of gross matter. The irresistible pressure of the light in the vessels also caused every rank of worlds to descend from the place that had been assigned to it. The entire world process as we now know it, therefore, is at variance with its originally intended order and position. Nothing, neither the lights nor the vessels, remained in its proper place, and this development – called after a phrase borrowed from the *Idrot* of the Zohar, "the death of the primordial kings" – was nothing less than a cosmic catastrophe. At the same time, the breaking of the vessels, which corresponds to the destruction of the first, unsuccessful worlds in earlier Kabbalah, was not understood in Lurianic writings to be an anarchic or chaotic process; rather, it too took place in accord with certain clear internal laws that were elaborated extensively. Similarly, the emergence of the *kelippot* as the root of evil was described as a process following fixed rules and involving only the shards of those vessels that had been struck by the first sparks of light. These lights remained "captured" among the *kelippot*, which are nourished by them; they, in fact, provide the life-force for the entire world of *kelippot*, which in one degree or another interpenetrated the whole hierarchy of worlds once the vessels had been broken. The broken vessels too, of course, were subjected to the process of *tikkun* or restoration which began immediately after the disaster, but their "dross" was unaffected, and from this waste matter, which can be compared to the necessary by-products of any organic process, the *kelippot*, in their strict sense as the powers of evil, emerged. The catastrophic aspects of the breaking of the vessels were especially stressed in the simplified versions of the story that appeared in popular kabbalistic literature which described the entire process in highly mythical imagery.

Widely differing explanations for the breaking of the vessels were offered in Lurianic writings. Some commentators were content to attribute it to the weak and atomized inner structure of "the world of points," whose isolated, unorganized parts were too unstable to prevent the occurrence. Another explanation was that since the first emanations of the points were all circular rather than partly linear, an inevitable imbalance was created. In some texts it is stated that only the "branches" of the points went forth from *Adam Kadmon* while the "roots" remained within him, and that the former lacked the power by themselves to withstand the pressure of the light. All of these explanations are based on the premise that the unsound structure of the world of points was at fault, and view the breaking of the vessels as a mishap in the existence of the life-process of the Godhead. (See Tishby, *Torat ha-ra ve-ha-kelippah be-kabbalat ha-Ari*, 39–45.) Other explanations which seem to derive from Isaac Luria himself actually seek to justify this unsound structure by viewing it as a reaction to the roots of *Din* and the *kelippot* that were from the start present in the emanation. According to this view, the main design of the emanative process was to bring about a catharsis of these harsh elements and of the waste matter in the divine system. The presence of the roots of the *kelippot* in the emanation was the true inner reason for the breaking of the vessels. This cathartic explanation is frequently associated with the teleological view that the vessels were broken in order to pave the way for reward and punishment in the lower worlds that were due to emerge as the last phase of the creation. Differently stressed versions of such explications can be found in Moses Jonah, Vital, and Ibn Tabul. The cathartic and teleological explanations represent basically different approaches and well illustrate the tension in Lurianic Kabbalah between mythic and theological modes of thought. Later kabbalists ruled that the teleological explanation was indeed the literally correct one but that the cathartic explanation represented the mystical truth (Meir Bikayam, *Me'orei Or*, 1752, 15c). In the Lurianic school of Israel Sarug an additional, organic analogy was offered: the world of points was like a sown field whose seeds could not bear fruit until they had first split open and rotted.

TIKKUN. The breaking of the vessels marks a dramatic turning-point in the relations between the *Adam Kadmon* and all that develops beneath him. All the subsequent processes of creation come about to restore this primal fault. In its imaginative boldness, the belief that such an event could take place within a realm that, according to all opinions, was still part of the self-manifesting Godhead can be compared only to the doctrine of the *ẓimẓum* itself. Indeed, it was even suggested that the *ẓimẓum* too represented a kind of primordial "breakage" within *Ein-Sof*. The laws by which the process of cosmic restoration and reintegration (*tikkun*) works itself out constitute the largest part of Lurianic Kabbalah, for they touch on all the realms of creation, including the "anthropological" and "psychological" ones. The details of the doctrine of *tikkun* are extremely complex and seem to have been intentionally designed as a challenge to mystical contemplation. The most crucial element in this doctrine is the concept that the chief medium of *tikkun*, that is, of the restoration of the universe to its original design in the mind of its Creator, is the light that issued from *Adam Kadmon's* forehead to reorganize the disorderly confusion that resulted from the breaking of the vessels. The main support of these lights comes from the linear *Sefirot* of "the world of points," which did not undergo any breakage and henceforward have the task of encouraging the formation of balanced and stable structures in the future realms of creation. These new structures are called *parẓufim*, that is, configurations or *gestalten*, and each comprises an organic pattern of hierarchies of *Sefirot* with its own dynamic laws.

These *parẓufim* (literally, "faces" or "physiognomies") now take the place of the *Sefirot* as the principal manifestations of *Adam Kadmon*. In each of them newly emanated forces are bonded together with others that were damaged in the breaking of the vessels; thus, each *parẓuf* represents a specific stage in the process of catharsis and reconstruction. The *Sefirah Keter* is now re-formed as the *parẓuf* of *Arikh Anpin* (literally, "the long-faced one," i.e., "the indulgent one" or "forbearing one," a phrase borrowed from the Zohar, where it appears as an Aramaic translation of the biblical *erekh-appayin*, "long-suffering"), or *Attika* ("the ancient one"), which are sometimes treated as two separate aspects of the same *parẓuf*. The *Sefirot Ḥokhmah* and *Binah* now become the *parẓufim* of

Abba and *Imma* ("father and mother"), which function in a dual capacity: they exist as a medium for the reindividuation and redifferentiation of all the emanated beings into transmitters and receivers of influx, and they also serve as the supreme archetype for that procreative "coupling" (*zivvug*) which, in its metaphorical aspect of "face-to-face contemplation" (*histakkelut panim-be-fanim*), is the common root of all intellectual and erotic unions. This "coupling" is aroused by the re-ascent of the 288 sparks that had been in the broken vessels and returned to the bowels of *Binah*, where they play the role of animating and quickening forces within a structure whose function is primarily receptive. Without such assisting forces, which are referred to as "female waters" (*mayim nukbin*), there can be neither "coupling" nor unification even in the world of *aẓilut*. From the union of *Abba* and *Imma* a new *parẓuf* is born, known as *Ze'eir Anpin* (literally, "the short-faced one," i.e., "the impatient" or "unindulgent one"), which is comprised of the six lower *Sefirot*, from *Gevurah* to *Yesod*. Here we have the center for the cathartic processes that take place in all the *parẓufim* in order to mitigate the harsh powers of *Din*; their ultimate success depends on a long, almost endless series of developments. The self-manifestation of *Ein-Sof* in the created worlds takes place largely through this *parẓuf*, which undergoes an embryonic development in the depths of *Imma*, followed by "birth," "suckling," and the progressive emergence of the formative powers known as "immaturity" (*katnut*) and "maturity" (*gadluṭ*). The latter in turn are reinvigorated through a second "conception" by means of new powers that join them from other *parẓufim*. The structural unity of *Ze'eir Anpin* is assured by the workings of a principle called *ẓelem* ("image," after the verse in Gen. 1:27), which involves the activity of certain lights that help serve as a constituent element in all the *parẓufim* but are especially centered in *Ze'eir Anpin*. The last and tenth *Sefirah, Malkhut*, is also converted into a *parẓuf*, which is named *Nukba de-Ze'eir*, "the female of *Ze'eir*," and represents the latter's complementary feminine aspect. The main source of this boldly anthropomorphic symbolism is in the *Idrot* of the Zohar, but in its development in the Lurianic Kabbalah it took a radical turn. Isaac Luria himself undoubtedly viewed the *parẓufim* as power centers through which the creative dynamism of the Godhead was able to function and assume form. The various names, configurations, and sub-configurations that accompany these symbolic descriptions were probably intended to mute this almost provocatively conspicuous anthropomorphism to some extent. Over and above the five *parẓufim* just mentioned, whose inner dialectic is extensively explained in Ḥayyim Vital's *Eẓ Ḥayyim*, there are still other, secondary *parẓufim* that constitute the articulation of certain powers in the *Ze'eir Anpin* and its feminine *Nukba*, such as *Yisrael Sava, Tevunah, Raḥel*, and *Leah*. Indeed, in Isaac Luria's richly associative thought, practically every biblical personage was immediately transformed into a metaphysical figure from which sprang new hypostases and *parẓufim*. An outstanding example of this tendency can be found in chapter 32 of the *Eẓ Ḥayyim*, where all that happened to the "generation of the desert" is construed as representing processes in the *parẓufim* of the three upper *Sefirot* of the *Ze'eir Anpin* and its female counterpart.

The five principal *parẓufim* of *Abba, Imma, Arikh Anpin, Ze'eir Anpin*, and *Nukba de-Ze'eir* constitute the figure of the *Adam Kadmon* as it evolves in the first stages of *tikkun*, which is quite different from the figure of *Adam Kadmon* that existed before the breaking of the vessels. These *parẓufim* also comprise "the world of balance" (*olam ha-matkela*), which is identical with the world of *aẓilut* of earlier Kabbalah. From this world, though not its substance, an influx of spiritual light descends downward to the lower worlds of *beri'ah, yeẓirah*, and *asiyyah*. At the bottom of each world is a "curtain" which serves to filter out the sefirotic substance that properly corresponds to the nature of that world and to let all else pass on through a secondary reflex which in turn becomes the substance of a subsequent stage. The basic structure of the world of *aẓilut* repeats itself with certain modifications in the three lower worlds. The *tikkun*, however, has not yet been completed. As a result of the breaking of the vessels, none of the worlds is located in its proper place. Each one of them stands a rank lower than it should be, the original place of the world beneath it. In consequence, the world of *asiyyah*, which in essence is also a spiritual world (like the Ideal Nature of the neoplatonists), has descended and commingled with the lowest part of the realm of the *kelippot* and with the physical matter that is dominant there.

The main concern of Lurianic Kabbalah, as has been mentioned, is with the details of the process of *tikkun* and the developments that take place in the *parẓufim* of the different worlds, in the "*adam* of *aẓilut*," the "*adam* of *beri'ah*," etc. (Over three-quarters of the *Eẓ Ḥayyim* is devoted to this subject.) The crucial point in the various Lurianic discussions of these developments is that although the *tikkun* of the broken vessels has almost been completed by the supernal lights and the processes stemming from their activity, certain concluding actions have been reserved for man. These are the ultimate aim of creation, and the completion of *tikkun*, which is synonymous with the redemption, depends on man's performing them. Herein lies the close connection between the doctrine of *tikkun* and the religious and contemplative activity of man, which must struggle with and overcome not only the historic exile of the Jewish people but also the mystic exile of the *Shekhinah*, which was caused by the breaking of the vessels.

The object of this human activity, which is designed to complete the world of *tikkun*, is the restoration of the world of *asiyyah* to its spiritual place, its complete separation from the world of the *kelippot*, and the achievement of a permanent, blissful state of communion between every creature and God which the *kelippot* will be unable to disrupt or prevent. Of crucial importance here is the Lurianic distinction between the inward and outward aspects of the supernal lights and the worlds of creation themselves: the *tikkun* of the outward aspects of the worlds is not up to man at all, whose mission is solely concerned with certain aspects of inwardness. In the

Lurianic system the hierarchical rank of the inward is always lower than that of the outward, but precisely because of this it is within reach of the truly spiritual, inward individual, to some extent at least. Should the latter perform his task properly, the "female waters" that enable the supernal couplings to take place will be aroused, and the work of outward *tikkun* will be completed by the supernal lights that have remained concealed in the *parzuf* of *Attika* and are due to reveal themselves only at some future time. At the very least, human activity in accordance with the Torah can prepare the way for the *tikkun* of the lower worlds.

The Gnostic character of this cosmogony cannot be denied, though the detailed manner in which it is worked out is drawn entirely from internal Jewish sources. Typically Gnostic, for example, are the depiction of the creation as a cosmic drama centered around a profoundly fateful crisis within the inner workings of the Godhead itself, and the search for a path of cosmic restoration, of a purging of the evil from the good, wherein man is assigned a central role. The fact that such an unrecognized Gnostic theology was able to dominate the mainstream of Jewish religious thought for a period of at least two centuries must surely be considered one of the greatest paradoxes in the entire history of Judaism. At the same time, side by side with this Gnostic outlook, we find a most astonishing tendency to a mode of contemplative thought that can be called "dialectic" in the strictest sense of the term as used by Hegel. This tendency is especially prominent in attempts to present formal explanations of such doctrines as that of the *ẓimẓum*, the breaking of the vessels, or the formation of the *parẓufim*.

In addition to the Lurianic texts mentioned above, the basic tenets of Lurianic Kabbalah are systematically and originally presented in the following works: *Ma'amar Adam de-Aẓilut* by Moses Praeger, in his *Va-Yakhel Moshe* (Dessau, 1699); Joseph Solomon Delmedigo's *Novelot Ḥokhmah* (Basle, actually Hanau, 1631); *Kelaḥ* [138] *Pitḥei Ḥokhmah* by Moses Ḥayyim Luzzatto (Koretz, 1785); Jacob Meir Spielmann's *Tal Orot* (Lvov, 1876–83); Isaac Eisik Ḥaver's (see Wildman) *Pitḥei She'arim* (1888); Solomon Eliashov's *Leshem Shevo ve-Aḥlamah* (1912–48); and Judah Leib Ashlag's *Talmud Eser ha-Sefirot* (1955–67). Well-known expositions of Lurianic Kabbalah by Abraham Herrera and Joseph Ergas were greatly influenced by their tendency to reconcile or at least to correlate the Lurianic system with the teachings of Cordovero, as can be seen in Ergas' allegorization of the Lurianic doctrine of *ẓimẓum*.

The Kabbalah and Pantheism

The question of whether, and to what degree, the Kabbalah leads to pantheistic conclusions has occupied many of its investigators from the appearance in 1699 of J.G. Wachter's study attempting to show that the pantheistic system of Spinoza derived from kabbalistic sources, particularly from the writings of Abraham Herrera. Much depends here, of course, on the definition of a concept which has been employed in widely different meanings. A teaching can be considered pantheistic when it insists that "God is everything" and that "everything is God," yet we must distinguish between occasional formulas which have this kind of pantheistic coloring and the exact place assigned them within the framework of a systematic theology. Such formulas are found extensively in Christian and Muslim mysticism as well, yet their actual content does not always conform to their outward pantheistic appearance. This is equally true of many similar utterances in kabbalistic literature, especially those which occur in expositions of kabbalistic thought deliberately intended for popular consumption, as in a great deal of ḥasidic writing. On the other hand, the opposite phenomenon may occur as well, and here and there we find explicitly theistic formulas that belie their inner pantheistic or near-pantheistic content. All depends on the internal context of a given system of thought. Apparent theistic tendencies can serve to conceal actually pantheistic views, while general formulas can more often than not be variously interpreted and do not therefore prove a great deal. Examples of this are Azriel's pronouncement that "nothing is outside" *Ein-Sof*, Meir ibn Gabbai's declaration that "everything is in Him and He is in everything," or the recurring insistence in the Zohar that God "is everything" and that everything is unified in Him, "as is known to the mystics" (2, 85b). Such statements can also be found in orthodox theistic systems of thought, where they serve to underline the belief that nothing could exist without a first, divine cause and that the latter, since it is the cause of all, includes and comprehends within itself whatever it has caused. In this respect God can be said to be present and immanent in all that He has caused, and were He to discontinue His presence all caused existence would thereby be annihilated. The neoplatonic principle that every effect is included in its cause greatly influenced such formulations in the Kabbalah without casting them in a necessarily pantheistic mold.

Strictly speaking, however, the problem of pantheism does occur in connection with a number of specific questions that greatly preoccupied kabbalistic speculation and to which pantheistic doctrines were at least able to offer unambiguous answers. Such questions were:

(1) Is there a unity of substance between the Emanator and the emanated? Does the actual substance of God go forth into all or only the radiated potency of that substance?

(2) If there is a unity of substance between *Ein-Sof* and the *Sefirot*, is there also such a unity between *Ein-Sof* and created beings?

(3) Is God the soul of the world or identical with the world?

(4) Does God exist in created beings (or, in the language of the philosophers, is He immanent in them), or even in them alone?

Wherever we find positive answers to these questions there is good reason to assume that we are dealing with pantheism, and wherever we do not, we can assume the converse.

The majority of kabbalists from Isaac the Blind on rejected the notion that God's substance manifests itself in the world of emanation and insisted, as did most medieval neoplatonists, that God's power alone, as opposed to his substance, goes forth in the emanative process. Some of the earliest kabbalists, however, in particular the author of the *Ma'arekhet ha-Elohut*, did believe the emanated *Sefirot* to be of one substance with the emanating *Ein-Sof*. Only in the realms below the *Sefirot*, they held, was the divine potency alone active as the cause of beings that were separate from the Godhead. On the whole, we find that this school of thought had clearly theistic tendencies. Isaac b. Samuel Mar Ḥayyim (1491) distinguished between an "emanation of essence," which is the beaming forth of the *Sefirot* within the substance of *Ein-Sof*, and an "emanation of influx," which is the potency of the Emanator as it manifests itself in accordance with the receptive capacity of the given medium. Those kabbalists who identified *Ein-Sof* with the *Sefirah Keter* were obliged to consider the *Sefirot* as consubstantial with *Ein-Sof*. Yet those who held this view also explicitly denied that there could be any oneness of substance between God and the separate intellects, much less between God and other created beings. Such, for instance, was the opinion of Joseph Gikatilla in his commentary on the *Guide of the Perplexed*. Even he, however, did not restrain himself from declaring that "He fills all and He is all." Many other kabbalists, on the other hand, denied the consubstantiality of God with the emanated world, in which they professed to see only His emanating potency. In carrying on the thought of Cordovero (see below), the disciples of his school emphasized the separate substance of the emanated as opposed to the substance of the Emanator whose "garment" the former was.

The author of the Zohar was not especially concerned with this problem and was content to dispose of it with conceptually vague formulations which were open to conflicting interpretations, but in Moses de Leon's Hebrew works there is a more discernible tendency to stress the unity of all beings in a continuous chain of being. There are no qualitative jumps in the links of this chain, and God's true essence is "above and below, in heaven and on earth, and there is no existence besides Him" (*Sefer ha-Rimmon*). In the theophany at Mount Sinai God revealed all the worlds to the children of Israel, who saw that there was nothing in them that was not His manifest glory and essence. Implied here is the suggestion that every being has a secondary existence of its own apart from the Godhead but that this disappears before the penetrating gaze of the mystic which uncovers the unity of essence behind it. The pantheistic tendencies in this line of thought are cloaked in theistic figures of speech, a device characteristic of a number of kabbalists. On the one hand such writers describe *Ein-Sof* in personalistic terms and stress its absolute transcendence over everything, even the *Sefirot*, which have no apprehension of it, while on the other hand they make much of its "clothing itself" in the latter, and through them in the lower worlds as well. There is also a certain ambiguity in their double interpretation of the *creatio ex nihilo*, sometimes insisting that it be taken literally, which would of course rule out any pantheistic approach, and sometimes explaining it symbolically, rejecting a simple literalism in order to leave the door open to the possibility that all being has it place, at least partially, in the divine reality. The true nothingness from which all was created manifests itself in the transition from *Ein-Sof* to the first *Sefirah*, nor is there in reality any jump or discontinuity in the structure of being. The creation from nothingness is a manifestation of the divine wisdom where human thought reaches its limit, or of that nothingness which is the first emanation, *Keter*. In those systems where *Ein-Sof* was identified with the *Keter*, it was *Ein-Sof* itself that became the Divine Nothingness in which all has its source. Such views left room for the belief that God, who is one with *Ein-Sof*, comprehends much more than what proceeds from Him in the emanative and creative processes but that He encompasses the latter within Himself as well. All is comprehended within the Godhead but not everything is identical with it. In the early 19th century the term "panentheism" was coined to distinguish such a view from pure pantheism. There is no doubt that the term could apply to a number of well-known kabbalists, who were able to argue – with some measure of justice – that a similar position is already implied in the statement in the Midrash (Gen. R. 68) that "The Holy One blessed be He is the place of the world but the world is not His place." The panentheist view offered a clear compromise between pure theism and pure pantheism and left room for a personalistic depiction of the Godhead.

It is evident, therefore, that while not a single kabbalist school of thought ever claimed that God has no existence apart from created beings, the position most commonly held was that He was nevertheless to be found within them in variously definable ways. Hence, too, the neoplatonic assertion frequently encountered in kabbalistic literature that God is "the soul of souls," a claim which is not entirely free of pantheistic nuances although it lends itself to other interpretations as well. This phrase was already favored by the Zohar, but it must be observed that "soul" (*neshamah*) in its precise sense often does not imply in such writings an actual inherence in or existence contingent on the body but rather a higher mode of being. The *neshamah* proper does not descend to the lower worlds at all but radiates downward to the mode that we call man's "soul." Such, for instance, was the opinion of Isaac Luria. Other kabbalists, on the other hand, especially Moses de Leon, considered the human soul "a part of God above" (Job 31:2), not just in a figurative sense, as it was generally understood to be, but quite literally. Thus, their thought was based on the assumption that there is something in the soul consubstantial with God. It was this same assumption that led Moses de Leon in his *Mishkan ha-Edut* (see *Midrash Talpiot* (1860), 113c) to challenge the view that the punishment of the souls of the damned in hell is eternal, for how is it possible that God should inflict such suffering on Himself? This opinion is also indirectly hinted at in the Zohar, where it is stated that that highest part of the soul (*nefesh*) that is called *neshamah* is incapable of sinning and departs from the sinner at the moment that a sin is committed. Shabbetai Sheftel Horowitz was in agreement with this view and conceded only a quantitative distinction between the soul and the substance of God, a position that, because of its pantheistic implications, was challenged, especially by Manasseh Ben Israel in his *Nishmat Ḥayyim* (1652).

In contrast to the main part of the Zohar, its later strata (the *Ra'aya Meheimna* and the *Tikkunim*) have a markedly theistic flavor. Here too, however, it is especially stressed that if God stands apart from the world He is also within it ("He is outside as much as He is inside"), and that He "fills all and causes all" without this immanence precluding a personalistic and theistic view of Him. Such formulations in the Zohar became extremely popular among later kabbalists and in the writings of Ḥasidism, where they were used to bridge theistic and panentheistic opinions abounding in these texts. Kabbalistic works written between 1300 and 1500 tended on the whole to obscure the problem, as can be seen in the writings of the disciples of Solomon b. Adret and in the *Sefer ha-Peliah*. Similarly, popular kabbalistic texts written at the time of the expulsion from Spain show a marked preference for decidedly theistic formulations (Abraham b. Eliezer ha-Levi, Judah Ḥayyat, Abraham b. Solomon Ardutiel), which in rare cases only conceal a different content between the lines.

A detailed discussion of the problematics of pantheism can be found in the writings of Cordovero, whose own panentheistic outlook was more carefully worked out than that of any other kabbalist, especially in his *Sefer Elimah* and *Shi'ur Komah*. His presentation of the question is extremely subtle and has nothing in common with that "Spinozist" approach which, in its more vulgar sense, a number of authors have sought to attribute to him. Cordovero understood full well that the salient point of the whole theory of emanation was the transition from *Ein-Sof* to the *Sefirah Keter* and he devoted great effort to its solution. The *Sefirot*, he argues, owe the source of their existence to *Ein-Sof*, but this existence is "hidden" in the same sense that the spark of fire is hidden in the rock until it is struck with metal. Moreover, this aspect of their existence is incomparably more rarified than their existence once they have been emanated to their respective places, for in their emanated existence they assume a totally new guise. Even in their ultimate, "hidden" mode of existence, however, when they are comprehended in the substance of *Ein-Sof* and united with it perfectly, they are nevertheless not truly identical with this substance, which apprehends them while remaining unapprehended by them. This being the case, should it be said that the first change in their ontological status takes place in their hidden existence or not until their manifest one? Cordovero avoided giving an unequivocal answer to this question, while at the same time developing the theory that even the highest aspects of the *Keter*, which he called "the *Keter* of the *Keter*," "the *Keter* of the *Keter* of the *Keter*," and so forth, approach the substance of *Ein-Sof* asymptotically until the human intellect can no longer distinguish them. Nevertheless they retain an identity distinct from it, so that there is a kind of leap between *Ein-Sof* and their hidden existence within it that continually approaches to infinity. The existence of these inward stages is considered by Cordovero to represent an entirely new departure within the Godhead, and the coming into being of this hidden existence, or "Will of Wills" as he calls it, is what consitutes the act of creation from nothingness in its literal sense. The initial awakening of the Divine Will in this chain of wills (*re'utin*) is, he argues, the one occasion on which true creation from nothingness takes place, a view whose paradoxical nature testifies to the manner in which he felt torn between the theistic and the pantheistic approach. From the divine point of view God comprehends all, inasmuch as He encompasses the "wills" both by virtue of being their cause and of embracing them in His essence, but from the human point of view all of these subsequent stages comprise a secondary reality existing separately from *Ein-Sof* and contingent on it, so that they cannot possibly share a true identity with the substance of the Emanator. Even at the highest levels this substance clothes itself in "vessels" which are by their very nature secondary and preceded by a state of privation (*he'eder*).

In all of these processes, therefore, it is necessary to distinguish between the substance of the Emanator, which clothes itself in vessels, and the substance of the emanated. Though this distinction is somewhat obscured in the *Pardes Rimmonim*, it is emphasized in the *Sefer Elimah*, where Cordovero asserts that while in the act of emanation the divine substance goes forth into vessels, these vessels (*kelim*) or garments (*levushim*) assume an increasingly less refined existence as the process continues downward. And yet behind these infinite garments there is not a single link in the chain where the substance of *Ein-Sof* does not remain present and immanent. Even from the viewpoint of the human condition it is potentially possible to contemplatively "undress" these garments and reveal "the processions of the substance" (*tahalukhei ha-ezem*) which clothe themselves in them. Such a moment of revelation is the supreme happiness to which the mystic can attain in his lifetime. Yet again, this immanence of *Ein-Sof* in everything is not identical with the specific existence of the vessels: "The products of causation as they descend do not share one substance with their cause but rather… are diminished from their cause as they descend until the lowest [level of] existence." Only as they reascend toward their cause are they reunified with it, until they reach the Supreme Cause of all, which is the *Keter*, where there is no longer any distinction between the agent and the products of its action, for they adhere to it as far as is in any way possible and are truly united to *Ein-Sof*, "where there is no cause or caused but everything is cause" (*Elimah*, 18c). The single most definitive statement in Cordovero's treatment of the problem can be classed as panentheistic: "God is all that exists, but not all that exists is God" (*Elimah*, 24d). To be sure, this reascent toward first causes must be taken as applying to the culminating process of all creation in its return to the bosom of the Emanator rather than to the mystical experience of the individual. Moreover, in many passages Cordovero further dilutes the concept by warning against misunderstanding: the caused beings themselves will not be reabsorbed into the substance of *Ein-Sof* but only their "spirituality" once their separate garments have been cast off. What has been forever sundered from the Godhead cannot be redeified.

Lurianic Kabbalah tended on the whole to avoid even the panentheistic formulations of Cordovero and to adopt an openly theistic position. The doctrine of the *ẓimẓum*, by stressing the discontinuity between *Ein-Sof* and the world of emanation, heightened this proclivity even more. Granting even that something of the divine substance goes forth into the *Adam Kadmon* and even into the *parẓufim* that emanate from him, clothing itself in them, this process comes to a definite end with the emanated *Sefirot* in the first world of *aẓilut*. Beneath them stretches a "curtain" which prevents the divine substance from finding garments for itself in the worlds of *beri'ah, yeẓirah*, and *asiyyah* as well. Of course it is possible to speak of a radiation of *Ein-Sof* into all the worlds, *asiyyah* included, but not of its substance being immanent in them. On the other hand, though such theistic arguments dominate most of the writings of Ḥayyim Vital and Ibn Tabul, even here there are occasional statements that are closer to Cordovero's position. Indeed, the doctrine that every higher principle "clothes itself" in a lower one, which in the final analysis is a doctrine of divine immanence, was sometimes carried to extremes. Above all the kabbalist was expected to understand "how all the worlds share a single mode of being as garments of *Ein-Sof*, so that *Ein-Sof* clothes itself in them and surrounds [*sovev*] them and nothing goes beyond it. Everything can be seen under one aspect and all the worlds are bound to the Emanator," although caution decrees that "it would be inadvisable to reveal more of this matter" (*Sha'ar ha-Hakdamot*, Hakdamah 4). Others, such as Ibn Tabul, emphasized that only God's "inner light" (*ha-or ha-penimi*) was filtered out by the "curtains," whereas His "comprehensive light" (*ha-or ha-mekif*) was not curtained off at all. Inasmuch as the latter comprises the main part of the divine substance that goes forth into the world of emanation, a door was here opened once again for a return to the panentheistic views of Cordovero.

Whether the light of *Ein-Sof* that goes forth into the vacuum of the *ẓimẓum* and clothes itself in vessels can be considered part of the Godhead even though it does not partake of the latter's substance remained an open question which most Lurianic kabbalists emphatically answered in the affirmative. The Lurianists held that without question the world of *aẓilut* with its inner dynamic processes belonged to the Godhead. Nevertheless, many of them denied that there was a unity of substance between the manifestations of the Godhead in *aẓilut* and the substantive properties of *Ein-Sof*. Even the highest circle of the *Sefirot* of the *Adam Kadmon*, they argued, was closer to the lowliest worm than to *Ein-Sof*. Such analogies bear witness to a continual equivocation between two inherently conflicting points of view. One radical solution to this ambivalence was the strict theistic doctrine of Moses Ḥayyim Luzzatto, who insisted that *aẓilut* could be called a "world" (*olam*) in the figurative sense only, because in it the Godhead manifested itself directly, whereas all the other worlds were created by a free act of God from literal nothingness. No statement to the effect that these lower worlds had evolved or developed out of the world of *aẓilut* was to be taken literally, for at most it could mean that they had been patterned after *aẓilut*. "We must not think that there can be any bond [*hitkashrut*] between what is created and the Creator." It would appear that Luzzatto had an especially firm grasp of the built-in contradiction between the doctrine of emanation and that of a paradigmatic creation, in the clash between which lay the crux of the problem of pantheism in the Kabbalah. Generally speaking, most kabbalistic texts that were written for the benefit of a wider audience, such as Ḥayyim Vital's *Sha'arei Kedushah*, were theistic on the surface, sometimes concealing beneath it the germs of a different, essentially panentheistic interpretation. These germs, such as the Lurianic doctrines of the creative ray, the residue or *reshimu*, the primordial space of the *ẓimẓum*, the unity of the chain of being, and so forth, nourished panentheistic tendencies which subsequently came to the fore once more in a number of the classic texts of Ḥasidism.

Man and His Soul (Psychology and Anthropology of the Kabbalah)

Over and above disagreements on specific details that tend to reflect different stages in the Kabbalah's historical development, there exists a basic consensus among kabbalists on man's essential nature. The fundamental doctrine of a hidden life of the Godhead which through a dynamism of its own determines the life of creation as a whole had inevitable implications as regards the human condition, in which the same theosophic process, though with certain significant differences, was thought to repeat itself. At opposite poles, both man and God encompass within their being the entire cosmos. However, whereas God contains all by virtue of being its Creator and Initiator in whom everything is rooted and all potency is hidden, man's role is to complete this process by being the agent through whom all the powers of creation are fully activated and made manifest. What exists seminally in God unfolds and develops in man. The key formulations of this outlook can already be found in the Kabbalah of Gerona and in the Zohar. Man is the perfecting agent in the structure of the cosmos; like all the other created beings, only even more so, he is composed of all ten *Sefirot* and "of all spiritual things," that is, of the supernal principles that constitute the attributes of the Godhead. If the forces of the *Sefirot* are reflected in him, he is also the "transformer" who through his own life and deeds amplifies these forces to their highest level of manifestation and redirects them to their original source. To use the neoplatonic formula, the process of creation involves the departure of all from the One and its return to the One, and the crucial turning-point in this cycle takes place within man, at the moment he begins to develop an awareness of his own true essence and yearns to retrace the path from the multiplicity of his nature to the Oneness from which he originated. The essential correspondence or parallelism between the inward aspects of man, God, and creation introduces a mutual interplay among them that was frequently dramatized in the Kabbalah by means of anthropomorphic symbols, though the latter are nearly always accompanied by warnings that they are only to be understood "as if." If the *Sefirot* in which God reveals Himself assume the form of man, making him a microcosm in himself – a doctrine which found universal acceptance among the kabbalists – then man on earth is obviously capable of exerting an influence upon the macrocosm and upon primordial man above. Indeed it is this which bestows on him the enormous importance that the kabbalists went to great lengths to describe. Because he and he alone has been granted the gift of free will, it lies in his power to either advance or disrupt through his actions the unity of what takes place in the upper and lower worlds. His essence is unfathomably profound; he is "a face within a face, an existence within an existence, and a form within a form" (Ezra of Gerona). Even man's physical structure corresponds to that of the *Sefirot*, so that we find Ezra of Gerona's description of the last *Sefirah* as "the form [*temunah*] that includes all forms" applied in the Zohar to man himself, who is called "the likeness [*deyokna*] that includes all likenesses." Such speculations about man's essence were most pithily expressed in various statements about Adam before his fall. Though his original harmony was disrupted by his sin, his principal mission remained to bring about a *tikkun* or restoration of this world and to connect the lower with the upper, thereby "crowning" creation by setting the Creator upon His throne and perfecting His reign over all His handiwork.

Man's essence has a spiritual nature for which his body serves only as an outer cloak. One widespread belief was that prior to Adam's sin his body too was spiritual, a kind of ethereal garment which became corporealized only after his fall. (In support of this view, the statement in Gen. 3:21 that God made "garments of skin," *kotnot o'r*, for Adam and Eve after their expulsion from Eden, was taken as meaning that previously they had worn "garments of light," *kotnot 'or*.) Had it not been for Adam's sin, the supreme divine will would have continued to work unfragmentedly in Adam and Eve and all their descendants, and all of creation would have functioned in perfect harmony, transmitting the divine influx downward from above and upward from below, so that there would have been no separation between the Creator and His creation that adhered to Him. This uninterrupted communion, which is the goal of creation, was broken off at the time of Adam's sin when his lower will was parted from the divine will by his own free volition. It was then that his individuality, whose origin lay in his separation from God with its attendant proliferation of multiplicity, was born. What had been intended to be nothing more than a series of periodic fluctuations within a single harmonic system now turned into an opposition of extremes that found their expression in the fierce polarization of good and evil. It is the concrete destiny of the human race, and of the Jew as the principal bearer of this mission and the recipient of God's revelation through the Torah, to overcome this polarization from within the human condition created by the first sin.

It is at this point that the problem of man in the world and the problem of evil in the world are interlaced. The sin which gave evil an active existence lies in mankind's failure to achieve his primal purpose, a failure which occurred again and again in history. It is the function of good in the world, whose tools are the Torah and its commandments, to bridge the abyss of separation that was formed by man's sin and to restore all existence to its original harmony and unity. The final goal, in other words, is the reunification of the divine and the human wills. It is likely that this kabbalistic doctrine of the corruption of the world through man's first sin originated as a result of direct contact with Christian beliefs, although it is also possible that these Christian ideas were derived from the same sources from which homologous *aggadot* in the Midrash took their inspiration. There can be no doubt that the kabbalists accepted the doctrine that the entire creation was fundamentally flawed by man's sin, after which the *sitra aḥra* or "other side" achieved a dominion over man which will not be finally abolished until the ultimate redemption in which all things will revert to their original state. The crucial Christian element, however, is lacking here, for unlike the Christian dogma of original sin, the Kabbalah does not reject the idea that every man has the power to overcome this state of corruption, to the extent that he too is affected by it, by means of his own powers and with the help of divine aid prior to and independently of the final redemption. Speculations of this sort concerning the essence of sin as a disruption of the primordial order of things, the effects of which as it were reach up to and include the world of the *Sefirot* themselves, and concerning the means to achieve a *tikkun* whereby creation will be restored to its former grandeur, assumed a central place in the kabbalistic doctrine of man. This teaching developed out of purely religious motifs that only incidentally became motivated in the course of time with certain psychological motifs as well. Judah Halevi's metaphor in the *Kuzari* of Israel constituting the heart of the nations was taken over by the author of the Zohar and the kabbalists of Gerona, who spoke of the Jewish people as being "the heart of the cosmic tree" [*lev ha-ilan*], a symbol borrowed from the *Sefer ha-Bahir*. Within this basic context, a fuller understanding of Israel's mission depends on the kabbalistic teachings on the structure of man's soul.

The kabbalists adopted the psychological doctrines of neoplatonism and tried to adapt them to the language of Jewish tradition. The Zohar occasionally mentions the three faculties or dispositions of a unified human soul as they are spoken of in the philosophy of Aristotle, but generally the Zohar refers to three essentially different parts of the soul that form a sequence from lower to higher and are designated by the Hebrew terms *nefesh*, *ru'ah*, and *neshamah*. True, here too a unity was posited among these parts, but for the most part it remained problematic. The *nefesh* or first element is to be found in every man, for it enters him at the moment of birth and is the source of his animal vitality (*ḥiyyut*) and of the totality of his psychophysical functions. Whatever is necessary for the well-being of these functions is already contained in it and it is equally the property of all human beings. The two other parts of the soul, on the other hand, are postnatal increments that are found only in the man who has awakened spiritually and made a special effort to develop his intellectual powers and religious sensibilites. The *ru'aḥ* or *anima* is aroused at an unspecified time when a man succeeds in rising above his purely vitalistic side. But it is the highest of the three parts of the soul, the *neshamah* or *spiritus*, which is the most important of all. It is aroused in a man when he occupies himself with the Torah and its commandments, and it opens his higher powers of apprehension, especially his ability to mystically apprehend the Godhead and the secrets of the universe. Thus, it is the intuitive power that connects mankind with its Creator. It is only in the most general terms, however, that this tripartite division was adopted by all the various kabbalistic schools of thought. The terminology indeed remains the same, but the meanings and interpretations assigned to it differ widely in detail.

The fundamental division of the soul into three parts and the use of the terms *nefesh*, *ru'aḥ*, and *neshamah* (*naran* in the kabbalistic acronym) to describe them came from such Jewish neoplatonists as Abraham ibn Ezra and Abraham bar Ḥiyya, but in the course of the Kabbalah's development in the 13th century the philosophical content of these categories became considerably blurred and yielded to occultistic associations under whose influence the strictly defined concepts of neoplatonic psychology took on fantastic and mythic dimensions. This process can be clearly traced in the classic texts of early Kabbalah. Already for the kabbalists of Gerona, though they still retained the original identification of the *neshamah* with the rational soul of the philosophers, the rational faculty of the soul was merged with the intuitive and mystic. Only the *neshamah*, they held, which was like a divine spark in man, was emanated directly from the Godhead itself rather than evolved from the separate intellects like the *ru'aḥ* or from the four elements like the *nefesh*. There is still an echo here of the philosophical division of the soul into its animal or vital, vegetative, and rational faculties and of the association of the soul's origin with the world of the intellects, and particularly of the active intellect, as in the philosophy of Isaac Israeli. Within this system man's *nefesh* is still a common denominator between him and the animal world, while only the rational *neshamah*, whose origin is in the world of the *Sefirot*, and more precisely in the *Sefirah Binah*, truly deserves to be called the human soul, for it is a divine spark, one that was created from nothingness, to be sure, but from a nothingness that belongs nonetheless to the realm of the Godhead itself. Some of the kabbalists of Gerona even held that the source of the *neshamah* was in the *Sefirah* of Divine Wisdom or *Ḥokhmah*, a difference of opinion which bore on the question of the heights to which man's mystical cognition could attain.

The different strata of the Zohar reflect the varying psychological doctrines toward which its author leaned at different times. In the *Midrash ha-Ne'elam* there is still a clear debt to the psychology of the school of Maimonides with its doctrine of the "acquired intellect" which is activated in man through his pursuit of the Torah and its commandments and which alone has the power to bestow on him immortality of the soul. Together with this, however, we find the characteristic Aristotelian division of the soul, though minus the identification with the *nefesh, ru'aḥ*, and *neshamah*, and in connection with a number of functions that are peculiar to Moses de Leon alone. Thus, for instance, we find a distinction between the "speaking soul" (*ha-nefesh ha-medabberet*) and the "rational soul" (*ha-nefesh ha-sikhlit*), the latter alone possessing the supernal power which can bring man to perfection and which is identical with the true soul or *neshamah*. In effect the faculty called *nefesh* embraces all three forces, the animal, the vegetative, and the cognitive (*medabber*), which comprise the psycho-physical totality of man. The *neshamah*, in contrast, is a power concerned exclusively with mystical cognition, while the *ru'aḥ* represents an intermediate stage that involves the ethical power to distinguish between good and evil. The *neshamah* itself, on the other hand, by virtue of being "a part of God above," is capable of performing good only. It is impossible to speak here of a consistent approach: purely religious motifs alternate freely with philosphical ones, a confusion that extends to the relationship between intellectual awareness and the *neshamah* itself. In some instances the author, who expresses his views through the mouths of various rabbinic sages, even abandons the tripartite division of the soul entirely in favor of a twofold distinction between the vital soul (*ha-nefesh ha-ḥayyah*) and the *neshamah*. In the main corpus of the Zohar these divergent opinions are consolidated into a unified position of sorts in which religious motifs predominate over traditional philosophical and psychological ones. Here a fundamental contradiction emerges between the belief that the soul is universally the same for all mankind and another, double standard according to which the soul of the Jew and the soul of the gentile are dissimilar. The kabbalists of Gerona knew only of the former doctrine, that is, of the soul that is universally shared by all the descendants of Adam, and it is in the main body of the Zohar that we read for the first time of a twofold though corresponding division of souls into non-Jewish and Jewish. The first group has its source in the "other side" or *sitra aḥra*, the second in the "holy side" or *sitra di-kedusha*. Interest in the Zohar is almost entirely confined to the psychic structure of the Jew. In the later Kabbalah, particularly in the works of Ḥayyim Vital, this duality between the "divine soul" (*ha-nefesh ah-elohut*) and the "natural soul" (*ha-nefesh ha-tiv'it*) is given enormous emphasis.

An important problem for the Kabbalah was the different sources of the different parts of the soul in the different worlds of emanation. According to the *Midrash ha-Ne'elam* even the highest *neshamah* emanates only from the Throne of Glory, that is, from a realm beneath that of the *Sefirot* though above that of the intellects. It is thus considered to be something created, though a creation of the highest order. In the main corpus of the Zohar this view is abandoned and each part of the soul is assigned a root in the world of the *Sefirot*: the *nefesh* originates in the *Sefirah Malkhut*, the *ru'aḥ* in the *Sefirah Tiferet*, and the *neshamah* in the *Sefirah Binah*. The descent of the supernal *neshamah* is brought about by the "holy union" of the "king" (*melekh*) and the "queen" (*matronita*), who are synonymous with the *Sefirot Tiferet* (or *Yesod*) and *Malkhut*. In its root every soul is a composite of male and female, and only in the course of their descent do the souls separate into masculine souls and feminine souls. The symbolism used to describe the descent of the souls from the world of emanation has a strongly mythical flavor. Especially prominent are the symbols of the tree of souls on which each soul blooms, and of the river which carries the souls downward from their supernal source. In both symbolisms the *Sefirah Yesod* is considered to be a halfway station through which all the souls must pass before entering the "treasure-house of souls" (*oẓar ha-neshamot*), which is located in the celestial paradise (*gan-eden shel ma'lah*), where they live in bliss until they are called to descend still further and assume a human form. Many differences in detail exist among the various accounts of this process, but all the kabbalists agree as to the preexistence of the soul, especially in the latter's more strictly defined sense. Undisputed too is the belief that the soul originates on a plane higher than that of the angels, a doctrine that is referred to repeatedly in discussions of the human condition, for if man is capable of plunging to indescribable depths of depravity, he also has the capacity, when he fulfills his true destiny, of rising even above the angelic realm. No angel has that potential power to restore the worlds to a state of *tikkun* which has been granted to man.

In addition to the three parts of the soul that were collectively referred to by the acronym *naran*, kabbalists after the Zohar came to speak of two more additional, higher parts of the soul which they called *ḥayyah* and *yeḥidah* and which were considered to represent the sublimest levels of intuitive apprehension and to be within the grasp only of a few chosen individuals. In Lurianic Kabbalah these five parts of the soul (*naran-ḥai* in acronym) became associated with the five *parẓufim* of *Adam Kadmon* in each of the worlds of *aẓilut, beri'ah, yeẓirah*, and *asiyyah*, so that a tremendous multiplicity of potential soul-ranks was created in accordance with the particular world of emanation and *parẓuf* from which a given soul stemmed. The soul having its source in the *yeḥidah* of the *Sefirah Keter* of the world of *aẓilut* was believed to be that of the Messiah. Unlike the masses of souls which are subject to the general laws of transmigration, such high-ranking souls were thought to remain concealed among the supernal lights until their time arrived and not to enter the cycle of reincarnation at all.

From the Zohar and through the works of the disciples of Isaac Luria mention is made of an aspect of man that is referred to in the Kabbalah as the *ẓelem* (the "image," on the basis of Gen. 1:26, "Let us make man in our image, after our likeness") and which is not identical with any of the parts of the soul referred to above. The *ẓelem* is the principle of individuality with which every single human being is endowed, the spiritual configuration or essence that is unique to him and to him alone. Two notions are combined in this concept, one relating to the idea of human individuation and the other to man's ethereal garment or ethereal body which serves as an intermediary between his material body and his soul. Because of their spiritual nature, the *neshamah* and *nefesh* are unable to form a direct bond with the body, and it is the *ẓelem* which serves as the "catalyst" between them. It is also the garment with which the souls clothe themselves in the celestial paradise before descending to the lower world and which they don once again after their reascent following physical death; during their sojourn on earth it is hidden within man's psycho-physical system and is discernible only to the intellectual eye of the kabbalist. The source of this belief is undoubtedly the similar doctrine held by the later neoplatonists concerning the ethereal body that exists in every man and that reveals itself to the mystical experience of those endowed with the gift of vision. Unlike the soul, the *ẓelem* grows and develops in accordance with the biological processes of its possessor. The kabbalists made use of a play on words to draw a parallel between a man's *ẓelem* and his shadow (*ẓel*). The Zohar apparently considers the shadow to be a projection of the inner *ẓelem*, a belief that brought with it various popular magical superstitions that were widespread in Europe during the Middle Ages. Supposedly the *ẓelem* was the repository of the years a man lived and it departed with the approach of his death. According to another view, the *ẓelem* was woven as a garment for the soul from a man's good deeds and served as a kind of supernal appearance that protected and clothed him after his death. An ancient belief concerning such an ethereal body, whose source lies in Persian religion and which reached the author of the Zohar through later legends to become associated in his mind with various occultist ideas, was that the *ẓelem* was actually a man's true self. In Lurianic Kabbalah the *nefesh*, *ru'aḥ*, and *neshamah* were each assigned a *ẓelem* of their own which made it possible for them to function in the human body. Without the *ẓelem* the soul would burn the body up with its fierce radiance.

Moses de Leon, in his Hebrew writings, connects Maimonides' teaching that man's mission in this world is the full realization of his intellectual power with the doctrines of the Kabbalah. In his *Ha-Nefesh ha-Ḥakhamah* (1290), De Leon writes: "The purpose of the soul in entering the body is to exhibit its powers and abilities in the world… And when it descends to this world, it receives power and influx to guide this vile world and to undergo a *tikkun* above and below, for it is of high rank, [being] composed of all things, and were it not composed in a mystic manner of what is above and below, it would not be complete… And when it is in this world, it perfects itself and completes itself from this lower world… And then it is in a state of perfection, which was not the case in the beginning before its descent."

According to an even earlier belief, which is already present in the *heikhalot* literature, all the souls are initially woven into a curtain (*pargod*) that hangs before the Throne of Glory, and this symbol of "the curtain of souls" was both adopted and adapted by a number of classic kabbalistic texts. The entire past history and future destiny of each single soul is recorded in this curtain. The *pargod* is not just a mystical fabric composed of spiritual ether which contains or is capable of receiving a record of each man's life and works; it is in addition the abode of all those souls that have returned from below to their native land. The souls of the wicked will find no place in it.

The kabbalistic doctrine of man and his soul dealt at great length with such eschatological problems as the fate of the soul after death, and its ascent up a river of fire, which resembles a kind of purgatory, to the terrestrial paradise and from there to the still sublimer pleasures of the celestial paradise and the realm referred to by the early kabbalists as "eternal life" (*ẓeror ha-ḥayyim*), which is sometimes synonymous with the celestial paradise and sometimes taken to refer to one of the *Sefirot* themselves, to which the soul returns to partake of the life of the Godhead. Human life on earth, therefore, must be seen in the broad context of the soul's life before birth and after death; hence the great interest of the Kabbalah in descriptions of heaven and hell such as those that we find in extensive and imaginative detail in the works of the kabbalists of Gerona or the Zohar, which inaugurated a long and influential tradition that flourished especially in the more popularly oriented literature of the Kabbalah until recent generations. Much use was made here of beliefs that were already to be found in the *aggadah*, particularly in a number of small, late Midrashim, and which were reinterpreted in the light of kabbalistic symbolism and embellished with further details. Many obvious parallels exist between such material and similar eschatological motifs in Christianity and Islam. None of these teachings was ever given a definitive or authoritative form, thus enabling them to preserve a great deal of imaginative freedom in which folkloristic and mystic elements came together. The kabbalists of the 13th century in particular, among them the author of the Zohar, were attracted to such speculations and devoted considerable attention to such questions as the garments of the souls in paradise, the nature of their perceptions, the expansion of their consciousness in the apprehension of the divine, and the unification of the highest level of the *neshamah* with God.

Generally speaking, however, the kabbalists were wary about speaking of an actual mystic union of the soul with God and preferred to talk in terms of a spiritual communion (*devekut*) and no more. In his commentary on the letters of the Hebrew alphabet, Jacob b. Jacob Kohen (1270) speaks of mystic union without defining its nature. Moses de Leon mentions a supreme but temporary condition in which the soul finds itself standing before God in a state of contemplation and ultimate bliss without any garment between it and Him, though as a rule it must don a garment of ether or light even in the celestial paradise. Descriptions of the soul's union with God in terms of a divine nuptial are rare in the Kabbalah, though there are occasional examples, such as commentaries on the Song of Songs interpreting it as a conjugal dialogue between God and the soul. Even here, however, the love that is described is that between a father and daughter rather than of an erotic nature nor is anything said about the dissolution of the soul in the substance of God but merely about its temporary rapture in His presence. Only in the writings and poetry of the kabbalists of Safed is there an obviously strong erotic overtone. Whether later schools of kabbalistic thought tended to the extreme mystical position, such as that found in Ḥabad Ḥasidism, which holds that the soul loses its selfhood entirely in God, remains open to question. The author of the Zohar (2, 253a) writes of the souls passing before God in the "room of love" from which the new souls depart to descend, but not in terms of conjugal imagery. On the contrary, the outcome of this divine "reception" is that God makes the soul swear to fulfill its earthly mission and attain to the "knowledge of the mysteries of the faith" which will purify it for its return to its homeland. By means of its awakening through the Torah and its commandments it gains new strength and helps complete the mystical figure of the *Keneset Yisrael* or Community of Israel, which is one with the *Shekhinah*. Only a few rare souls, such as those of Enoch and Elijah, ever achieve a permanent communion (*devekut*) with God; among the other biblical heroes of righteousness there are infinite degrees and differences of rank. Nor does a single fate await the different parts of the soul after death. The *nefesh* remains for a while in the grave, brooding over the body; the *ru'aḥ* ascends to the terrestrial paradise in accordance with its merits; and the *neshamah* flies directly back to its native home. Punishment and retribution are the lot of the *nefesh* and *ru'aḥ* alone. According to Moses de Leon, once in a cosmic jubilee the soul ascends from its communion with the *Shekhinah* to the hidden, celestial paradise in the world of the divine mind, that is, to the *Sefirah Ḥokhmah*.

The teachings of the Kabbalah concerning the soul are inextricably connected with the doctrine of transmigration, a basic kabbalistic principle that frequently came into conflict with other beliefs, such as that in the reward and punishment that are meted out to man in heaven and hell. (For further details, see *Gilgul.) In the course of the development of the Kabbalah the idea of transmigration was radically expanded from that of a punishment restricted to certain sins to that of a general law encompassing all the souls of Israel, and, in a later stage, the souls of all human beings and even, in its most radical form, of all creation from the angels to unsentient things. Thus, transmigration ceased to be considered merely a punishment and came also to be viewed as an opportunity for the soul to fulfill its mission and make up for its failures in previous transmigrations.

In comparison with the Zohar, the teachings of the Lurianic Kabbalah in regard to man's psychic structure are far more complex, concerning both the source of soul and man's inner make-up. In the works of Ḥayyim Vital there is also a discrepancy between his presentation of the subject in books meant for popular consumption, such as his *Sha'arei Kedushah*, and in his more esoteric writings. In the former work Vital distinguishes clearly between three "quarries" (*maḥẓevim*): the quarry of the *Sefirot*, which is all divinity, the quarry of the souls, and the quarry of the angels, who are not themselves divine. His explanation of the coming-into-being of the souls through the emanative process in his *Eẓ Ḥayyim*, on the other hand, is far more complex and largely parallels his outline of the development of the lights that manifest the divine existence in the worlds of *aẓilut* and *beri'ah*. Just as the supernal lights in the *parẓufim* of *aẓilut* develop through conjunctions and "couplings" (*zivvugim*) of the *parẓufim*, so are the souls born through corresponding processes. Within the *Sefirah Malkhut* of each *parẓuf* are concealed souls in a potential state that ascend to the highest modes of that *parẓuf* and are actualized as a result of the "unions" of the *Sefirot*. At the outset these souls exist only in the state of "female waters" (*mayim nukbin*); that is, they are passive potencies that possess the power of active arousal but still lack harmony and form, for their supernal source lies in those 288 sparks of light that fell into the *kelippot* at the time of the breaking of the vessels. Only through additional "couplings" of the *parẓuf* of *Ze'eir Anpin* with its female counterpart or *nukba* do they receive the actual structure of souls. With each new arousal of the "female waters" in these *parẓufim*, new opportunities arise for the creation of souls. Such a process occurs in all four worlds of emanation, the possible variations in modes of souls being practically infinite. Each of these souls recapitulates in miniature the structure of the worlds through which it passed in the process of being created, so that when it descends to enter a body in this world it will be able to work toward the latter's *tikkun* and uplifting and, to some extent, toward the uplifting of the higher worlds as well. On the other hand, a number of Lurianic texts stress the view that in substance the souls as such remain above and do not enter into bodies at all but rather radiate sparks of themselves that can be called souls (*neshamot*) by analogy only. The true soul hovers over a man, whether from near or afar, and maintains an immediate magic tie with its spark below. Popular expositions of these doctrines were always much simpler than their original elucidations, which tended to have a strong Gnostic flavor.

The soul of Adam was composed of all the worlds and was destined to uplift and reintegrate all the sparks of holiness that were left in the *kelippot*. Its garment was of spiritual ether and it contained within it all of the souls of the human race in perfect condition. It had 613 limbs, one for each of the commandments in the Torah, the spiritual aspect of which it was Adam's mission to uplift. Each of these limbs formed a complete *parẓuf* in itself known as a "great root" (*shoresh gadol*), which in turn contained 613 or, according to other versions, up to 600,000 "small roots." Each "small root," which was also referred to as a "great soul" (*neshamah gedolah*), concealed within it 600,000 sparks or individual souls. These sparks too were apt to fission still further, but there remained a special affinity and power of attraction between all the sparks that descended from a common root. Each of these sparks formed a complete structure or *komah* in itself. Had Adam fulfilled his mission through the spiritual works of which he was capable, which called for contemplative action and deep meditation, the living chain between God and creation would have been closed and the power of evil, the *kelippah*, would have undergone that complete separation from holiness that, according to Luria, was the aim of the entire creative process. Thus, Adam had within him the fully developed powers of the *Adam Kadmon* in all his *parẓufim* and the depth of his fall when he sinned was equal to the great height of his cosmic rank beforehand (see below). Instead of uplifting everything, however, he caused it to fall even further. The world of *asiyyah*, which had previously stood firmly on its own base, was now immersed in the realm of the *kelippot* and subjected to their domination. Where the *Adam Kadmon* had stood a satanic creature now rose up, the *Adam Beliyya'al* who gained power over man. As a result of the admixture of the world of *asiyyah* with the *kelippah*, Adam assumed a material body and all his psycho-physical functions were corporealized. Moreover, his soul shattered and its unity was smashed to pieces. In it were elements of high rank known as "upper light" (*zihara ila'ah*) which refused to participate in Adam's sin and departed for above; these will not return to this world again until the time of the redemption. Other souls remained in Adam even after his spiritual stature was diminished from cosmic to mundane dimensions; these were the holy souls that did not fall into the clutches of the *kelippot*, and among them were the souls of Cain and Abel, which entered their bodies through direct hereditary transmission rather than through the process of transmigration. The bulk of the souls that were in Adam, however, fell from him and were subjugated by the *kelippot*; it is these souls that must achieve their *tikkun* through the cycle of transmigration, stage after stage. In a manner of speaking, Adam's fall when he sinned was a repetition of the catastrophe of the breaking of the vessels. The Lurianic Kabbalah went to great lengths to play up the dramatic elements in Adam's sin and its consequences. The inner history of the Jewish people and the entire world was identified with the recurrent reincarnations through which the heroes of the Bible struggled to achieve *tikkun*. Among these heroes were both "original souls" (*neshamot mekoriyyot*), which embraced a great and powerful psychic collectivity and were capable of great powers of *tikkun* whereby the whole world stood to benefit, and other, private souls which could achieve a *tikkun* only for themselves. Souls descending from a single "root" comprised "families" who had special relations of affinity and were especially able to help each other. Now and then, though only very rarely, some of the upper souls that had not even been contained in the soul of Adam might descend to earth in order to take part in some great mission of *tikkun*. A complete innovation in Lurianic Kabbalah was the stress laid on the high rank of the souls of Cain and Abel, and particularly of the former. These two sons of Adam were taken to symbolize the forces of *gevurot* and *ḥasadim*, that is, the restrictive and outgoing powers of creation. Though the outgoing power of *ḥesed* is at present greater than the restrictive power of *gevurah* and *din*, this order will be reversed in the state of *tikkun*. Paradoxically, therefore, many of the great figures of Jewish history are represented as stemming from the root of Cain, and as the messianic time approaches, according to Isaac Luria, the number of such souls will increase. Ḥayyim Vital himself believed that he was of the root of Cain.

The nature of Adam's sin itself was never authoritatively defined in kabbalistic literature and highly differing views of it can be found. The problem of the first sin is closely connected with the problem of evil discussed above. According to the Spanish Kabbalah, the crux of the sin lay in "the cutting of the shoots" (*kiẓẓuẓ ha-netiyyot*), that is, in the separation of one of the *Sefirot* from the others and the making of it an object of a special cult. The *Sefirah* that Adam set apart was *Malkhut*, which he "isolated from the rest." In the *Ma'arekhet Elohut*, nearly all the major sins mentioned in the Bible are defined as different phases of "the cutting of shoots," or as repetitions of Adam's sin which prevented the realization of the unity between the Creator and His creation. Such were the drunkenness of Noah, the building of the Tower of Babel, Moses' sin in the desert, and above all the sin of the golden calf, which destroyed everything that had been accomplished in the great *tikkun* that took place during the theophany at Mount Sinai. In the final analysis, even the destruction of the Temple and the exile of the Jewish people were the results of misinformed meditations that brought division into the emanated worlds. Such sins wreaked havoc above and below, or, in the symbolism of the Zohar, caused division between the "king" (*melekh*) and the "queen" (*matronita*) or *Shekhinah*. The exile of the *Shekhinah* from her husband was the main metaphysical outcome of these sins. The good deeds of the biblical heroes, on the other hand, especially those of the patriarchs Abraham, Isaac, and Jacob, came to set this fundamental fault in creation aright and to serve as a paradigm for those who came after. It is noteworthy that the author of the Zohar himself was reticent in his remarks on the nature of Adam's sin. The author of the *Tikkunei ha-Zohar* was less circumspect. Adam's sin, he held, took place above all in the divine mind itself, that is, in the first or second *Sefirah*, from which it caused God's departure; indeed, it was Adam's sin alone that caused God to become transcendent (*Tikkun* 69). As far as the effect of the first sin is concerned, we find two conflicting lines of thought:

(1) Whereas previously good and evil had been mixed together, the sin separated evil out as a distinct reality in its own right (as in Meir ibn Gabbai's *Avodat ha-Kodesh*);

(2) Good and evil were originally separate, but the sin caused them to become mixed together (such was Gikatilla's position, and in general, that of the Lurianic Kabbalah).

In the tradition of earlier teachings, such as those in the *Ma'arekhet ha-Elohut* and the *Sefer ha-Peli'ah*, Lurianic Kabbalah also occasionally explained the first sin as a "technical" mishap, though one with grave consequences, in the procedure of *tikkun*. This occurred because Adam was in a hurry to complete the *tikkun* before its appointed time, which was to have been on the first Sabbath of creation, starting late on the afternoon of the sixth day. The tendency in such explanations is to emphasize that essentially the greatest biblical sinners meant to do good but erred in their choice of means.

The principal instrument for repairing the primal fault, both in the metaphysical aspect of completing the *tikkun* of the broken vessels and in relation to Adam's sin which disrupted the channels of communication between the lower and upper worlds, is human engagement in holiness through Torah and prayer. This activity consists of deeds, which restore the world in its outward aspects, and of mystical meditations, which affect it inwardly. Both have profound mystical dimensions. In the act of revelation God spoke and continues to speak to man, while in the act of prayer it is man who speaks to God. This dialogue is based on the inner structure of the worlds, on which each human action has an effect of which man himself is not always aware. The actions of the man who is conscious of their significance, however, have the greatest effect and help speed the ultimate *tikkun*. Because the world became corporealized as a result of the first sin, the great majority of the commandments in the Torah acquired a material meaning, because every instrument must be adjusted to the end it is meant to serve. Yet this does not detract from the inward spiritual dimension that each commandment possesses, whose collective purpose is the restoration and perfection of the true stature of man in all 613 of the limbs of his soul. (For further details, see Reasons for *Commandments.) The same Torah which prescribes a practical way of life for human beings in the light of revelation simultaneously provides an esoteric guide for the mystic in his struggle to commune with God. Evident in such an approach is the conservative character of the Kabbalah as a factor working to defend and deepen Jewish values. Observance of the Torah was sanctified as the way to abolish division in the world, and every man was called upon to play his part in this task in accordance with the rank of his soul and the role that was allotted him. The spiritual light that shines in every commandment connects the individual with the root of his soul and with the supernal lights in general. Thus, a mission was entrusted to the collective body of the souls of Israel which could not easily be carried out and involved many descents and reascents before all obstacles could be overcome, but which in the final analysis had a clear and urgent purpose: the *tikkun* and redemption of the world.

Exile and Redemption

It therefore follows that the historical exile of the Jewish people also has its spiritual causation in various disturbances and faults in the cosmic harmony for which it serves as a concrete and concentrated symbol. The situation of the spiritual worlds at the time of the exile was completely different from that ideal state in which they were supposed to exist according to the divine plan and in which they will find themselves at the time of redemption. In one form or another this belief recurs throughout the development of the Kabbalah. The kabbalists of Gerona held that for as long as the exile continues the *Sefirot* do not function normally; as they are withdrawn toward the source of their original emanation, Israel lacks the power to adhere to them truly by means of the Divine Spirit, which has also departed for above. Only through individual effort can the mystic, and he alone, still attain to a state of *devekut*. In some texts we are told that only the five lower *Sefirot* continue to lead an emanated existence below, whereas the upper *Sefirot* remain above. When the Jewish people still lived in its own land, on the other hand, the divine influx descended from above to below and reascended from below to above all the way to the highest *Keter*. The letters of the Tetragrammaton, which contain all the emanated worlds, are never united for the duration of the exile, especially the final *vav* and *he*, which are the *Sefirot Tiferet* and *Malkhut*, and which were already parted at the time of Adam's first sin, when the exile in its cosmic sense began. Since then there has been no constant unity between the "king" and "queen," and this will be restored only in the future when the queen, who is the *Shekhinah* and the *Sefirah Malkhut*, reascends to be rejoined with the *Sefirah Tiferet*. Similarly, only in messianic times will man return to that paradisical state in which "he did of his own nature that which it was right to do, nor was his will divided against itself" (Naḥmanides on Deut. 30:6). It was in these same Spanish circles that there first arose the belief in the mystical nature of the Messiah, who was supposedly a harmony of all the levels of creation from the most rarified to the most gross, so that he possessed "a divine power, and an angelic power, and a human power, and a vegetative power, and an animal power" (Azriel in his Epistle to Burgos). The Messiah will be created through the special activity of *Malkhut*, and this origin will serve to elevate his powers of apprehension above those of the angels. The Zohar too takes the position that the crux of the redemption works itself out in the continuing conjunction of *Tiferet* and *Malkhut*, and that redemption of Israel is one with the redemption of God Himself from His mystic exile. The source of this belief is talmudic and can be found in both the Palestinian Talmud, *Sukkah* 4, 3 and in the *Midrash Va-Yikra Rabbah*, sect. 9, 3: "The salvation of the Holy One blessed be He is the salvation of Israel." At the time of the redemption "all the worlds will be in a single conjunction [*be-zivvug eḥad*]," and in the year of the grand jubilee *Malkhut* will be joined not only with *Tiferet* but with *Binah* as well. In the *Ra'aya Meheimna* and the *Tikkunei Zohar* we find the idea that whereas during the period of the exile the world is in thrall to the Tree of Knowledge of Good and Evil, in which the realms of good and evil struggle between themselves so that there are both holiness and impurity, permitted acts and forbidden acts, sacred and profane, in the time of the redemption dominion will pass to the Tree of Life and all will be as before Adam's sin. The utopian motifs in the messianic idea are given their ultimate expression in these works and in those composed under their influence. The future aboliton of the commandments mentioned in the Talmud (Nid. 61b) was taken by the kabbalists to refer to the complete spiritualization of the commandments that would take place under the dominion of the Tree of Life. The details of this vision tended to vary greatly according to the homiletic powers of the particular kabbalist who embraced it.

In Lurianic Kabbalah too the exile of Israel is connected with Adam's sin, the outcome of which was the scattering of the holy sparks, both of the *Shekhinah* and of Adam's soul. When the sparks became diffused even further in Adam's descendants, the mission of gathering them and raising them up, that is, of preparing the way for redemption, was awarded to Israel. The exile is not, therefore, merely a punishment and a trial but is a mission as well. The Messiah will not come until the good in the universe has been completely winnowed out from the evil, for in Vital's words "the ingathering of the exiles itself means the gathering of all the sparks that were in exile." The exile may be compared to a garden that has been abandoned by its gardener so that weeds have sprung all over it (*Eẓ Ḥayyim*, ch. 42, para. 4). The *tikkun* progresses in predetermined stages from one generation to the next and all the transmigrations of souls serve this purpose. As the exile draws to an end, the *tikkun* of the human structure of the *Sefirot* reaches the "feet" (*akevayim*); thus, the souls that go forth in "the footsteps of the Messiah" are unusually obdurate and resistant to *tikkun*, from whence stem the special ordeals that will occur on the eve of the redemption.

Opinions varied as to whether the Messiah's soul too entered the cycle of transmigration: some kabbalists held that his soul had also been incarnated in Adam and in David (according to other views, in Moses as well), while others contended (a view first found in the *Sefer ha-Bahir*) that it was not subject to the law of transmigration. According to the Lurianic Kabbalah, each of the *parẓufim* of the *Adam Kadmon* had a female counterpart (*nukba*) except for the *parẓuf* of *Arikh Anpin*, which was instrumental in creating the world through a process of autogeny (*zivvug minnei u-vei*), that is, of "coupling" with itself. At the time of the redemption, however, it will be able to "couple" through the pairing of its *Yesod* with its *nukba* (the waxing *Sefirah Malkhut*), and the offspring of this act will be the most hidden root of the soul of the Messiah Son of David, which is its *yeḥidah*. The descent of this soul depends on the state of *tikkun* prevailing in the different worlds, for in every generation there is one righteous man who has the disposition to receive it if only the age is worthy. The soul of the Messiah Son of Joseph, on the other hand, who is the harbinger of the Messiah Son of David, is part of the regular cycle of transmigration. The redemption will not come all at once but will rather manifest itself in stages, some of which will be inwardly hidden in the spiritual worlds and others of which will be more apparent. The final redemption will come only when not a single spark of holiness is left among the *kelippot*. In the writings of Luria's school different views can be found on whether the Messiah himself has an active role to play in the process of redemption through his unique ability to raise up certain last sparks that are beyond the power of anyone else. This question assumed particular importance in the development of the Shabbatean movement. In the course of the redemption certain hitherto concealed lights from the *parẓuf* of *Attika* will manifest themselves and alter the structure of creation. In the final analysis, national and even nationalistic motifs blend with cosmic ones in the Lurianic Kabbalah to form a single great myth of exile and redemption.

The Torah and Its Significance

The role of the Torah in the Kabbalah as an instrument and a way of life in the service of a universal *tikkun* has already been discussed. The central position of the Torah in the Kabbalah, however, goes far beyond such definitions. The kabbalistic attitude to the Pentateuch, and in a somewhat lesser degree to the Bible as a whole, was a natural corollary of the overall kabbalistic belief in the symbolic character of all earthly phenomena. There was literally nothing, the kabbalists held, which in addition to its exterior aspect did not also possess an interior aspect in which there existed a hidden, inner reality on various levels. The kabbalists applied this view of the "transparency" of all things to the Torah as well, but inasmuch as the latter was the unique product of divine revelation, they also considered it the one object which could be apprehended by man in its absolute state in a world where all other things were relative. Regarded from this point of view in its quality as the direct word of God and thus unparalleled by any other book in the world, the Torah became for the kabbalists the object of an original mystical way of meditation. This is not to say that they sought to deny the concrete, historical events on which it was based, but simply that what interested them most was something quite different, namely, the conducting of a profound inquiry into its absolute nature and character. Only rarely did they discuss the relationship among the three parts of the Bible, the Pentateuch, the Prophets, and the Hagiographa, and for the most part their attention was concentrated almost exclusively on the Torah in its strict sense of the Five Books of Moses. The Zohar (3, 35a) actually attempts in one place to assert the absolute superiority of these books and their students over the Prophets and the Hagiographa and their students, yet only in the context of commenting on the talmudic statement that "the sage is preferable to the prophet." In his *Ginnat Egoz* (1612, 34dff.), Joseph Gikatilla also sought to attach a kabbalistic interpretation to the tripartite division of the Bible. On the whole, however, where kabbalistic commentaries do exist on the Prophets and the later writings (and especially on the Book of Psalms), their approach to these texts is essentially no different from that of the commentaries on the Torah.

The classic formulations of this approach appear as early as the 13th century, nor do later and bolder restatements of them, even in the Lurianic school, add anything fundamentally new. A large part of the literature of the Kabbalah consists of commentaries on the Pentateuch, the Five Scrolls, and the Book of Psalms, and the Zohar itself was largely written as a commentary on the Pentateuch, Ruth, and the Song of Songs. Books such as the commentaries on the Pentateuch by Menahem Recanati, Baḥya b. Asher, and Menahem Ẓiyyoni became classic kabbalistic texts. Noteworthy too is the fact that there are practically no kabbalistic commentaries to speak of on entire books of the Prophets or on the Book of Job and the Book of Daniel. Only a few, isolated exegeses of fragments of these texts tend to recur regularly in connection with certain mystical interpretations. The only known kabbalistic commentary ever to have been composed on the entire Bible is the 16th-century *Minḥat Yehudah*, written in Morocco, large sections of which have been preserved in various manuscripts. Outside the Pentateuch, the Song of Songs alone was made the subject of a large number of kabbalistic commentaries, beginning with Ezra of Gerona's and continuing down to several written in recent generations.

The main basis of the Kabbalistic attitude toward the Torah is, as was mentioned above, the fundamental kabbalistic belief in the correspondence between creation and revelation. The divine emanation can be described both in terms of symbols drawn from the doctrine of *Sefirot* and of the emanated, supernal lights, and of symbols drawn from the sphere of language and composed of letters and names. In the latter case, the process of creation can be symbolized as the word of God, the development of the fundamentals of divine speech, and as such it is not essentially different from the divine processes articulated in the Torah, the inwardness of which reveals the same supreme laws that determine the hierarchy of creation. In essence, the Torah contains in a concentrated form all that was allowed to develop more expansively in the creation itself. Strictly speaking, the Torah does not so much mean anything specific, though it in fact means many different things on many different levels, as it articulates a universe of being. God reveals Himself in it as Himself rather than as a medium of communication in the limited human sense. This limited, human meaning of the Torah is only its most external aspect. The true essence of the Torah, on the other hand, is defined in the Kabbalah according to three basic principles: the Torah is the complete mystical name of God; the Torah is a living organism; and the divine speech is infinitely significant, and no finite human speech can ever exhaust it.

THE TORAH AS THE MYSTICAL NAME OF GOD. Underlying this principle is an originally magical belief which was transformed into a mystical one. Such a magical belief in the structure of the Torah can already be found in the *Midrash Tehillim* (on Ps. 3): "Had the chapters of the Torah been given in their correct order, anyone who read them would have been enabled to raise the dead and work miracles; therefore, the Torah's [true] order has been hidden and is known [only] to God." The magical uses of the Torah are discussed in the book *Shimmushei Torah*, which dates at the very latest from the geonic period, and in which it is related that together with the accepted reading of the Torah, Moses received yet another reading composed of Holy Names possessing magical significance. To read the Torah "according to the names" (Naḥmanides' introduction to his commentary on the Pentateuch) does not, therefore, have any concrete human meaning but rather one that is completely esoteric: far from having to do with historical narrations and commandments, the Torah thus read is solely concerned with concentrations of the divine power in various combinations of the letters of God's Holy Names. From the magical belief that the Torah was composed of God's Holy Names, it was but a short step to the mystical belief that the entire Torah was in fact nothing else than the Great Name of God Himself. In it God expressed His own being insofar as this being pertained to creation and insofar as it was able to manifest itself through creation. Thus, the divine energy chose to articulate itself in the form of the letters of the Torah as they express themselves in God's Name. On the one hand this Name comprises the divine potency; on the other hand it comprehends within it the totality of the concealed laws of creation. Obviously, such an assumption about the Torah did not refer to the physical text written on parchment but rather to the Torah in its pre-existential state in which it served as an instrument of the creation. In this sense, the creation of the Torah itself was simply a recapitulation of the process by which the *Sefirot* and the individual aspects of the Divine Names were emanated from the substance of *Ein-Sof*. Nor is the Torah separate from this substance, for it represents the inner life of God. In its earliest and most hidden existence it is called "the primordial Torah," which is occasionally identified with the *Sefirah Ḥokhmah*. Thereafter it develops in two manifestations, that of the Written Torah and that of the Oral Torah, which exist mystically in the *Sefirot Tiferet* and *Malkhut*, while on earth they exist concretely and are geared to the needs of man.

The relationship between the Torah as the all-comprehensive Name of God and the Ineffable Name or Tetragrammaton was defined by Joseph Gikatilla in his *Sha'arei Orah*: "The entire Torah is like a commentary on the [Ineffable] Name of God." In what way is it essentially an explication of the Ineffable Name? In that it is a single "fabric" woven out of the epithets of God in which the Ineffable Name unfolds. Thus, the Torah is a structure the whole of which is built on one fundamental principle, namely, the Ineffable Name. It can be compared to the mystic body of the Godhead, and God Himself is the soul of its letters. This view evolved among the kabbalists of Gerona, and can be found in the Zohar and in contemporaneous works.

THE TORAH AS A LIVING ORGANISM. The weaving of the Torah from the Ineffable Name suggests the analogy that the Torah is a living texture, a live body in the formulation of both Azriel of Gerona and the Zohar. The Torah "is like an entire building; just as one man has many organs with different functions, so among the different chapters of the Torah some seem important in their outward appearance and some unimportant," yet in actual fact all are bound together in a single organic pattern. Just as man's unified nature is divided up among the various organs of his body, so the living cell of God's Name, which is *the* subject of revelation, grows into the earthly Torah that men possess. Down to the last, seemingly insignificant detail of the masoretic text, the Torah has been passed on with the understanding that it is a living structure from which not even one letter can be excised without seriously harming the entire body. The Torah is like a human body that has a head, torso, heart, mouth, and so forth, or else it can be compared to the Tree of Life, which has a root, trunk, branches, leaves, bark, and pith, though none is distinct from another in essence and all form a single great unity. (According to Philo of Alexandria, a similar conception of the Torah as a living organism inspired the sect of Therapeutes, as it did to a certain extent his own biblical commentaries, without there of course being any demonstrable historical filiation between such sources and the Kabbalah.) This organic approach was well able to explain the apparent stylistic discrepancies in the Bible, which was part narrative (and sometimes even seemingly superfluous narrative), part law and commandment, part poetry, and part even raw statistic. Behind all these different styles stood the mystic unity of the great Name of God. Such outward appearances were simply the garments of the hidden inwardness that clothed itself in them, and "Woe is he who looks only at the garments!" Connected with this is the view that the Torah is revealed in a different form in each of the worlds of creation, starting with its primordial manifestation as a garment for *Ein-Sof* and ending with the Torah as it is read on earth – a view that was especially promulgated by the school of Israel Sarug (see above). There is a "Torah of *aẓilut*," a "Torah of *beri'ah*," and so forth, each one reflecting the particular function of the mystical structure of a given phase of creation. In each of these phases there is a relativization of the Torah's absolute essence, which is in itself unaffected by these changes, great though they be. Similarly, as was explained above, the single Torah appears in different forms in the different *shemmitot* or cosmic cycles of creation.

THE INFINITE SIGNIFICANCE OF THE DIVINE SPEECH. A direct consequence of this belief was the principle that the content of the Torah possessed infinite meaning, which revealed itself differently at different levels and according to the capacity of its contemplator. The unfathomable profundity of the divine speech could not possibly be exhausted at any one level alone, an axiom that applied as well to the concrete, historical Torah revealed by God in the theophany at Mount Sinai. From the outset this Torah possessed the two aspects mentioned above, a literal reading formed by its letters that combined to make words of the Hebrew language, and a mystical reading composed of the divine Names of God. But this was not all. "Many lights shine forth from each word and each letter," a view that was summed up in the well-known statement (itself an epigrammatic rendering of a passage in the *Otiyyot de-Rabbi Akiva*) that "the Torah has 70 faces." The conventional four categories by which the Torah was said to be interpretable, the literal (*peshat*), the allegorical (*remez*), the hermeneutical or homiletical (*derash*), and the mystical (*sod*), served only as a general framework for a multiplicity of individual readings, a thesis which from the 16th century on was expressed in the widespread belief that the number of possible readings of the Torah was equal to the number of the 600,000 children of Israel who were present at Mount Sinai – in other words, that each single Jew approached the Torah by a path that he alone could follow. These four categories were first collectively given the acronym *pardes* (literally, "garden") by Moses de Leon. Basically, this "garden of the Torah" was understood as follows. The *peshat* or literal meaning did not embrace only the historical and factual content of the Torah but also the authoritative Oral Law of rabbinic tradition. The *derash* or hermeneutical meaning was the path of ethical and aggadic commentary. The *remez* or allegorical meaning comprised the body of philosophical truths that the Torah contained. The *sod* or mystical meaning was the totality of possible kabbalistic commentaries which interpreted the words of the Torah as references to events in the world of the *Sefirot* or to the relationship to this world of the biblical heroes. The *peshat*, therefore, which was taken to include the corpus of talmudic law as well, was only the Torah's outermost aspect, the "husk" that first met the eye of the reader. The other layers revealed themselves only to that more penetrating and latitudinous power of insight which was able to discover in the Torah general truths that were in no way dependent on their immediate literal context. Only on the level of *sod* did the Torah become a body of mystical symbols which unveiled the hidden life-processes of the Godhead and their connections with human life. This fourfold exegetical division was apparently influenced by the earlier yet similar categories of Christian tradition. Literal, aggadic, and philosophical-allegorical commentaries had previously been known to Jewish tradition as well, and Joseph ibn Aknin's long commentary on the Song of Songs, for example, which was composed early in the 13th century, combined all three of these approaches. Baḥya b. Asher was the first biblical commentator (1291) to introduce a kabbalistic aspect into his textual explications as well, though he did not use the acronym *pardes* and referred to the philosophical reading of the Torah as "the way of the intellect." Explication on the level of *sod*, of course, had limitless possibilities, a classic illustration of which is Nathan Spira's *Megalleh Amukkot* (1637), in which Moses' prayer to God in Deuteronomy 3:23ff. is explained in 252 different ways. In the main corpus of the Zohar, where use of the term "Kabbalah" is studiously avoided, such mystical interpretations are referred to as "mysteries of the faith" (*raza de-meheimnuta*), that is, exegesis based on esoteric beliefs. The author of the Zohar, whose belief in the primacy of kabbalistic interpretation was extreme, actually expressed the opinion (3, 152a) that had the Torah simply been intended as a series of literal narratives, he and his contemporaries would have been able to compose a better book! Occasionally kabbalistic interpretations would deliberately choose to stress certain words or verses that seemed insignificant on the surface and to attribute to them profound symbolic importance, as can be seen in the Zohar's commentary on the list of the kings of Edom in Genesis 36 or on the deeds Benaiah the son of Jehoiada related in II Samuel 23.

Since the Torah was considered to be essentially composed of letters that were nothing less than configurations of the divine light, and since it was agreed that it assumed different forms in the celestial and terrestrial worlds, the question arose of how it would appear in paradise or in a future age. Certainly its present reading had been affected by the corporealization of its letters that took place at the time of Adam's sin. The answer given to this conundrum by the kabbalists of Safed was that the Torah contained the same letters prior to Adam's sin but in a different sequence that corresponded to the condition of the worlds at that time. Thus, it did not include the same prohibitions or laws that we read in it now, for it was adjusted in its entirety to Adam's state before his fall. Similarly, in future ages the Torah will cast off its garments and will again appear in a purely spiritual form whose letters will assume new spiritual meanings. In its primordial existence, the Torah already contained all the combinational possibilities that might manifest themselves in it in accordance with men's deeds and the needs of the world. Had it not been for Adam's sin, its letters would have combined to form a completely different narrative. In messianic times to come, therefore, God will reveal new combinations of letters that will yield an entirely new content. Indeed, this is the "new Torah" alluded to in the Midrash in its commentary on Isaiah 51:4, "For instruction shall go forth from Me." Such beliefs continued to be widespread even in ḥasidic literature.

The most radical form that this view took was associated with the talmudic *aggadah* according to which prior to the creation of the world the whole of the Torah was written in black fire on white fire. As early as the beginning of the 13th century the daring notion was expressed that in reality the white fire comprised the true text of the Torah, whereas the text that appeared in black fire was merely the mystical Oral Law. Hence it follows that the true Written Law has become entirely invisible to human perception and is presently concealed in the white parchment of the Torah scroll, the black letters of which are nothing more than a commentary on this vanished text. In the time of the Messiah the letters of this "white Torah" will be revealed. This belief is referred to in a number of the classic texts of Ḥasidism as well.

The Mystic Way

DEVEKUT. Life in the framework of Judaism, through the study of Torah and prayer, offered the kabbalist a way of both active and passive integration in the great divine hierarchy of creation. Within this hierarchy, the task of the Kabbalah is to help guide the soul back to its native home in the Godhead. For each single Sefirah there is a corresponding ethical attribute in human behavior, and he who achieves this on earth is integrated into the mystic life and the harmonic world of the Sefirot. Cordovero's *Tomer Devorah* is dedicated to this subject. The kabbalists unanimously agreed on the supreme rank attainable by the soul at the end of its mystic path, namely, that of *devekut*, mystical cleaving to God. In turn, there might be different ranks of *devekut* itself, such as "equanimity" (*hishtavvut*, the indifference of the soul to praise or blame), "solitude" (*hitbodedut*, being alone with God), "the holy spirit," and "prophecy." Such is the ladder of *devekut* according to Isaac of Acre. In contrast, a running debate surrounded the question of what was the highest quality preparatory to such *devekut*, the love of God or the fear of God. This argument recurs throughout the literature of the Kabbalah with inconclusive results, and continued into the later *musar* literature that was composed under kabbalistic influence. Many kabbalists considered the worship of God in "pure, sublime fear," which was quite another thing from the fear of punishment, to be an even higher attainment than the worship of Him in love. In the Zohar this "fear" is employed as one of the epithets of the highest Sefirah, thus giving it supreme status. Elijah de Vidas, on the other hand, in his *Reshit Ḥokhmah*, defended the primacy of love. In effect, both of these virtues lead to *devekut*.

The early Kabbalah of Provence already sought to define *devekut* both as a process by which man cleaves to his Creator and as an ultimate goal of the mystic way. According to Isaac the Blind: "The principal task of the mystics [*ha-maskilim*] and of they who contemplate on His Name is [expressed in the commandment] 'And ye shall cleave unto Him' [Deut. 13:5]. And this is a central principle of the Torah, and of prayer, and of [reciting] the blessings, to harmonize one's thought with one's faith as though it cleaved to [the worlds] above, to conjoin God in His letters, and to link [*likhol*] the ten *Sefirot* in Him as a flame is joined to a coal, articulating his epithets aloud and conjoining Him mentally in His true structure." In a more general sense, Naḥmanides, in his commentary on Deuteronomy 11:22, defines *devekut* as the state of mind in which "You constantly remember God and His love, nor do you remove your thought from Him… to the point that when [such a person] speaks with someone else, his heart is not with them at all but is still before God. And indeed it may be true of those who attain this rank, that their soul is granted immortal life [*ẓerurah bi-ẓeror ha-ḥayyim*] even in their lifetime, for they are themselves a dwelling place for the *Shekhinah*." Whoever cleaves in this way to his Creator becomes eligible to receive the holy spirit (Naḥmanides, *Sha'ar ha-Gemul*). Inasmuch as human thought derives from the rational soul in the world of *aẓilut* it has the ability to return to its source there, "And when it reaches its source, it cleaves to the celestial light from which it derives and the two become one" (Meir ibn Gabbai). In his commentary on Job 36:7, Naḥmanides refers to *devekut* as the spiritual level that characterizes the true *ḥasid*, and in fact Baḥya ibn Pakuda's definition of *ḥasidut* in his *Ḥovot ha-Levavot* (8, 10) is very similar to Azriel of Gerona's definition of *devekut* in his *Sha'ar ha-Kavvanah*, for both speak in almost identical terms of the effacement of the human will in the divine will or of the encounter and conformity of the two wills together. On the other hand, kabbalistic descriptions of *devekut* also tend to resemble the common definitions of prophecy and its various levels. In his Epistle to Burgos, Azriel of Gerona speaks of the way to prophecy as being also the way to *devekut*, while in his *Perush ha-Aggadot* (ed. Tishby, 40), he virtually equates the two.

Devekut results in a sense of beatitude and intimate union, yet it does not entirely eliminate the distance between the creature and its Creator, a distinction that most kabbalists, like most Ḥasidim, were careful not to obscure by claiming that there could be a complete unification of the soul and God. In the thought of Isaac of Acre, the concept of *devekut* takes on a semi-contemplative, semi-ecstatic character. (See E. Gottlieb, *Papers of the Fourth World Congress of Jewish Studies*, 1969, Vol. 2, 327–34.) Here and there ecstatic nuances can be found in the conceptions of *devekut* of other kabbalists. (See Y. Tishby, *Mishnat ha-Zohar* 2, 247–68; G. Scholem, *Review of Religion* 14, (1950), 115–39.)

PRAYER, *KAVVANAH*, AND MEDITATION. The main path traveled by the mystic was of course associated in the kabbalistic consciousness with the practical observance of the commandments, yet the two were not intrinsically connected, for essentially the mystic way involved the ascent of the soul to a state of ecstatic rapture through a process of concentrated thought and meditation. Above all, in the Kabbalah it is prayer that serves as the principal realm for this ascent. Prayer is unlike the practical commandments, each of which demands a certain well-defined action, the performance of which does not leave much room for meditation and mystical immersion. True, every commandment has its mystical aspect whose observance creates a bond between the world of man and the world of the *Sefirot*, but the full force of spirituality can express itself far better in prayer. The mystical intention or *kavvanah* that accompanies every commandment is in effect a concentration of thought upon the kabbalistic significance of the action at the time that it is performed; prayer, on the other hand, stands independent of any outward action and can easily be transformed into a comprehensive exercise in inward meditation. The tradition of mystical prayer accompanied by a system of meditative *kavvanot* that focused on each prayer's kabbalistic content developed as a central feature of the Kabbalah from its first appearance among the Ḥasidei Ashkenaz and the kabbalists of Provence and on through the Lurianic Kabbalah and the latter's last vestiges in modern times. The greatest kabbalists were all great masters of prayer, nor would it be easy to imagine the Kabbalah's speculative development without such permanent roots in the experience of mystical prayer. In its kabbalistic guise, the concept of *kavvanah* was given new content far beyond that bestowed on it in earlier rabbinic and halakhic literature. (See Enelow, *Jewish Studies in Honor of Kaufmann Kohler* (Berlin, 1913), 82–107; G. Scholem, MGWJ 78, 1934, 492–518.)

Kabbalistic doctrine sought a way out of the dilemma, which the kabbalists themselves were aware of, that was posed by the theologically unacceptable notion that prayer could somehow change or influence the will of God. The Kabbalah regarded prayer as the ascent of man to the upper worlds, a spiritual peregrination among the supernal realms that sought to integrate itself into their hierarchical structure and to contribute its share toward restoring what had been flawed there. Its field of activity in kabbalistic thought is entirely in the inward worlds and in the connections between them. Using the traditional liturgical text in a symbolic way, prayer repeats the hidden processes of the universe which, as was explained above, can themselves be regarded as essentially linguistic in nature. The ontological hierarchy of the spiritual worlds reveals itself to the kabbalist in the time of prayer as one of the many Names of God. This unveiling of a divine "Name" through the power of the "word" is what constitutes the mystical activity of the individual in prayer, who meditates or focuses his *kavvanah* upon the particular name that belongs to the spiritual realm through which his prayer is passing. In early Kabbalah, it is the name of the appropriate *Sefirah* on which the mystic concentrates when reciting the prayers and into which he is, as it were, absorbed, but in later Kabbalah, and especially in the Lurianic school, this is replaced by one of the mystical Names of God. Thus, while prayer has an aspect of "inward magic" by which it is empowered to help order and restore the upper worlds, it has no outwardly magical efficacy. Such "inward magic" is distinguished from sorcery in that its meditations or *kavvanot* are not meant to be pronounced. The Divine Names are not called upon, as they are in ordinary operational magic, but are aroused through meditative activity directed toward them. The individual in prayer pauses over each word and fully gauges the *kavvanah* that belongs to it. The actual text of the prayer, therefore, serves as a kind of a banister onto which the kabbalist holds as he makes his not unhazardous ascent, groping his way by the words. The *kavvanot*, in other words, transform the words of the prayer into holy names that serve as landmarks on the upward climb.

The practical application of mystical *meditation in the Kabbalah, therefore, is connected mainly, if not exclusively, with the moment of prayer. In terms of Jewish tradition, the principal innovation in this approach lay in the fact that it shifted the emphasis from group prayer to individual mystical prayer without in any way destroying the basic liturgical framework itself. Indeed, in their effort to preserve this framework, the first generations of kabbalists largely refrained from composing original prayers of their own that would reflect their beliefs directly. Only from the 16th century onward, and especially under the influence of the Lurianic school, were large numbers of kabbalistic prayers added to the old. The short meditations of the early kabbalists were now replaced by increasingly lengthy and involved *kavvanot* whose execution led to a considerable lengthening of the service. The system of *kavvanot* reached its maximum development in the school of the Yemenite kabbalist Shalom Sharabi, where prayer required an entire congregation of mystical meditators who were capable of great psychical exertion. Several such groups are actually known to have existed. According to Azriel of Gerona, he who meditates mystically in his prayer "drives away all obstacles and impediments and reduces every word to its 'nothingness.'" To achieve this goal is in a sense to open a reservoir whose waters, which are the divine influx, pour down on the praying individual. Because he has properly prepared himself for these supernal forces, however, he is not overwhelmed and drowned by them. Having completed his upward ascent, he now descends once again with the aid of fixed *kavvanot*, and in this manner unites the upper and the lower worlds. An excellent example of this circle of ascent and descent can be found in the *kavvanot* to the *Shema*.

In contrast to the contemplative character of prayer in the Kabbalah of Gerona and the Zohar, Lurianic Kabbalah emphasized its more active side. Every prayer was now directed not only toward the symbolic ascent of him who prays, but also toward the upraising of the sparks of light that belonged to his soul. "From the day the world was created until the end of time, no one prayer resembles another." Despite the fact that there is a common collectivity to all the *kavvanot*, each one has its completely individual nature, and every moment of prayer is different and demands its own *kavvanah*. In this way, the personal element in prayer came to be highly stressed. Not even all the *kavvanot* listed in the writings devoted to them exhausted the totality of possibilities, just as a musical score cannot possibly contain the personal interpretation that the musician brings to it in the act of performance. In answer to the question in the Talmud, "From whence can it be known that God Himself prays?" the Kabbalah replied that through mystical prayer man was drawn upward or absorbed into the hidden, dynamic life of the Godhead, so that in the act of his praying God prayed too. On the other hand, the theory can also be found in kabbalistic literature that prayer is like an arrow shot upward by its reciter with the bow of *kavvanah*. In yet another analogy from the Lurianic school, which had a great impact on ḥasidic literature, the process of *kavvanah* is defined in terms of the drawing downward of the spiritual divine light into the letters and words of the prayer book, so that this light can then reascend to the highest rank (*Ḥesed le-Avraham*, 2, par. 44). In the opinion of the Zohar (2, 215b), the individual passes through four phases in his prayer: he accomplishes the *tikkun* of himself, the *tikkun* of this lower world, the *tikkun* of the upper world, and, finally, the *tikkun* of the Divine Name. Similarly, the morning service as a whole was interpreted as representing a symbolic progression, at the end of which the reciter was ready to risk all for God, whether by yielding to a near-ecstatic rapture or by wrestling with the *sitra aḥra* in order to rescue the imprisoned holiness from its grasp. In Lurianic prayer a special place was reserved for *yiḥudim* ("acts of unification"), which were meditations on one of the letter combinations of the Tetragrammaton, or on configurations of such names with different vocalizations, such as Isaac Luria was in the habit of giving to his disciples, to each "in accordance with the root of his soul." As employed in such individual *yiḥudim*, the *kavvanot* were detached from the regular liturgy and became independent instruments for uplifting the soul. They also were sometimes used as a method of communing with other souls, particularly with the souls of departed *ẓaddikim*.

A wide kabbalistic literature was devoted to the path of prayer and to mystical interpretations of the traditional liturgy. Such interpretations were less commentaries in the ordinary sense than systematic handbooks for mystical meditation in prayer. Among the best known of these are Azriel of Gerona's *Perush ha-Tefillot* (extant in many Mss.); Menahem Recanati's *Perush ha-Tefillot* (1544); David b. Judah he-Ḥasid's *Or Zaru'a* (see Marmorstein in MGWJ 71 (1927), 39ff.) and a commentary by an anonymous author (c.1300), the long introduction to which has been published (*Kovez Madda'i le-Zekher Moshe Shor*, 1945, 113–26). Among such books written in the 16th century were Meir ibn Gabbai's *Tola'at Ya'akov* (1560); Jacob Israel Finzi's *Perush ha-Tefillot* (in Cambridge Ms.); and Moses Cordovero's *Tefillah le-Moshe* (1892). The rise of Lurianic Kabbalah led to an enormous outpouring of books of *kavvanot* and mystical prayers. The most detailed among them are Ḥayyim Vital's *Sha'ar ha-Kavvanot* and *Pri Ez Ḥayyim*, and Emmanuel Ḥai Ricchi's summary *Mishnat Ḥasidim* (1727). As early as Vital's circle the practice developed of compiling special prayer books with the corresponding *kavvanot*, and many copies of these circulated in manuscript under the title *Siddur ha-Ari* ("The Prayer Book of Isaac Luria"). A number of such prayer books were published, among them *Sha'arei Raḥamim* (Salonika, 1741); *Ḥesed le-Avraham* (Smyrna, 1764); Aryeh Loeb Epstein's *Mishnat Gur Aryeh* (Koenigsberg, 1765); the *Siddur ha-Ari* of the kabbalists of the Brody *Klaus* (Zolkiew, 1781); and the kabbalistic prayer books of Asher Margoliot (Lvov, 1788), Shabbetai Rashkover (1794), and Jacob Koppel Lipshitz, whose *Kol Ya'akov* (1804) is full of Shabbatean influence. The acme of such books was the prayer book of Shalom Sharabi, the bulk of which was published in Jerusalem in a long series of volumes beginning in 1910. To this day there are groups in Jerusalem who pray according to Sharabi's *kavvanot*, although the spiritual practice of this can take many years to master. Other guides to prayer from this period are Isaiah Horowitz's *Siddur ha-Shelah* (Amsterdam, 1717); Solomon Rocca's *Kavvanat Shelomo* (Venice, 1670); Moses Albaz's *Heikhal ha-Kodesh* (Amsterdam, 1653); and Ḥayyim Vital's son Samuel's *Ḥemdat Yisrael* (1901). In his *Sha'ar Ru'aḥ ha-Kodesh* (with commentary, 1874), Ḥayyim Vital discusses the *yiḥudim*. Numerous kabbalist prayer books were compiled for various specific occasions, a genre that began with Nathan Hannover's *Sha'arei Ẓiyyon* (1662).

ECSTASY. Beside the mystical meditation of prayer, a number of other mystical "disciplines" developed in Kabbalah. (On the ecstatic ascents of the Merkabah mystics, see above.) From the beginning of the geonic period there is a text called *Sefer ha-Malbush* describing a half-magical, half-mystical practice of "putting on the Name" (*levishat ha-Shem*), whose history apparently goes back even further. Of central importance in this context is the "prophetic Kabbalah" of Abraham Abulafia, in which an earlier tradition of systematic instruction based on "the science of combination," *ḥokhmat ha-ẓeruf* (a play on the double meaning of the word in *ẓeruf ha-otiot*, "the combination of letters," and *ẓeruf ha-levavot*, "the purification of hearts"), was refashioned. This mystical discipline made use of the letters of the alphabet, and especially of the Tetragrammaton and the other Names of God, for the purpose of training in meditation. By immersing himself in various combinations of letters and names, the kabbalist emptied his mind of all natural forms that might prevent his concentrating on divine matters. In this way he freed his soul of its natural restraints and opened it to the divine influx, with whose aid he might even attain to prophecy. The disciplines of *kavvanah* and letter combination became linked together toward the end of the 13th century and from then on mutually influenced each other. The Lurianic *kavvanot* were especially heavily influenced by *ḥokhmat ha-ẓeruf*. The doctrine of the *Sefirot* was also absorbed by these disciplines, though Abulafia himself regarded it as a less advanced and less valuable system than "the science of combination" as the latter was expounded in his books.

In the further course of the development of the Kabbalah, many kabbalists continued to regard such disciplines as the most esoteric side of Kabbalah and were reluctant to discuss them in their books. Abulafia himself described quite explicitly, and in a seemingly objective manner, just what were the obstacles and dangers, as well as the rewards, that such mystical experience could bring. He drew a clear parallel between "the science of combination" and music, which too could conduct the soul to a state of the highest rapture by the combination of sounds. The techniques of "prophetic Kabbalah" that were used to aid the ascent of the soul, such as breathing exercises, the repetition of Divine Names, and meditations on colors, bear a marked resemblance to those of both Indian Yoga and Muslim Sufism. The subject sees flashes of light and feels as though he were divinely "anointed." In certain stages he lives through a personal identification with an inner spiritual mentor or *guru* who is revealed to him and who is really Metatron, the prince of God's countenance, or in some cases, the subject's own true self. The climactic stage of this spiritual education is the power of prophecy. At this point Abulafia's Kabbalah coincides with the discipline of *kavvanot* developed by the kabbalists of Gerona, which was also intended to train its practitioner so that "whoever has mastered it ascends to the level of prophecy."

Here and there mention is made in the Kabbalah of various other occult phenomena, but on the whole there is a clear-cut tendency to avoid discussing such things, just as most kabbalists refrained from recording their personal experiences in the autobiographical form that was extremely common in the mystical literature of both Christianity and Islam. Descriptions exist of the mystical sensation of the subtle ether or "aura," called also "the ether of the *ẓelem*," by which man is surrounded, of mystical visions of the primordial letters in the heavens (Zohar, 2, 130b), and of invisible holy books that could be read only with the inward senses (KS 4, 319). In a number of places prophecy is defined as the experience wherein a man "sees the form of his own self standing before him and relating the future to him" (MTJM, 142). One anonymous disciple of Abulafia actually composed a memoir about his experiences with *ḥokhmat ha-ẓeruf* (MTJM, 147–55). Generally speaking, however, the autobiographical confession was strictly disapproved of by most kabbalists. In the Zohar, a description of mystical ecstasy occurs only once, and that in a highly circumspect account of the experience of the high priest in the Holy of Holies on the Day of Atonement (3, 67a, and in the *Zohar Ḥadash*, 19a). Even in those writings that essentially continue the tradition of Abulafia, there is little of the latter's ecstatic extravagance, and ecstasy itself is moderated into *devekut*. Not until the golden period of the ḥasidic movement in the late 18th century, particularly in the circle of the Maggid of Mezhirech, are descriptions of ecstatic abandon once again encountered in the literature of Judaism. Several books or sections of books that dealt openly and at length with the procedure to be followed for the attainment of ecstasy and the holy spirit, such as Judah Albotini's *Sulam ha-Aliyah* (c. 1500) and the last part of Ḥayyim Vital's *Sha'arei Kedushah*, called *Ma'amar Hitbodedut*, "On Solitary Meditation" (Ginzburg Ms. 691, British Museum 749), were suppressed in their day and preserved only in manuscript. The only such book to have been actually published was the *Berit Menuḥah* (Amsterdam, 1648), the work of an anonymous 14th-century author that has been mistakenly attributed to Abraham of Granada. This book, which contains lengthy descriptions of visions of the supernal lights attained by meditating on various vocalizations of the Tetragrammaton with the aid of a symbolic system unparalleled elsewhere in the Kabbalah, borders on the frontier between "speculative Kabbalah" (*kabbalah iyyunit*), whose primary interest was in the inner spiritual guidance of the individual, and "practical Kabbalah" (*kabbalah ma'asit*), which was concerned above all with magical activity.

Practical Kabbalah

The disciplines discussed in the preceding section, though they deal with practical instructions for the spiritual life, do not belong to the realm of "practical Kabbalah" in the kabbalistic sense of the term, which refers rather to a different set of preoccupations. For the most part, the realm of practical Kabbalah is that of purely motivated or "white" magic, especially as practiced through the medium of the sacred, esoteric Names of God and the angels, the manipulation of which may affect the physical no less than the spiritual world. Such magical operations are not considered impossible in the Kabbalah, or even categorically forbidden, though numerous kabbalistic writings do stress the prohibitions against them. In any case, only the most perfectly virtuous individuals are permitted to perform them, and even then never for their private advantage, but only in times of emergency and public need. Whoever else seeks to perform such acts does so at his own grave physical and spiritual peril. Such warnings were generally observed in the breach, however, as is demonstrated by the extensive literature of practical Kabbalah that has survived. In actual practice, moreover, the boundary between physical magic and the purely inward "magic" of letter combination and *kavvanot* was not always clear-cut and could easily be crossed in either direction. Many early scholarly investigators of the Kabbalah did not often distinguish clearly between the two concepts and frequently used the term "practical Kabbalah" to refer to the Lurianic school as opposed to Cordovero and the Zohar. This confusion can be traced as far back as Pico della Mirandola, who considered the Kabbalah of Abulafia to belong to the "practical" variety. Abulafia himself, however, was well aware of the distinction and in many of his books he fiercely attacked the "masters of names" (*ba'alei shemot*) who defiled themselves with magical practices. The anonymous author of a text once attributed to Maimonides (*Megillat Setarim*, published in *Ḥemdah Genuzah* 1 (1856), 45–52), who himself belonged to the Abulafian school, differentiates between three kinds of Kabbalah, "rabbinic Kabbalah," "prophetic Kabbalah," and "practical Kabbalah." The latter is identified with theurgy, the magical use of Sacred Names, which is not at all the same thing as the meditation on such names. Before the term "practical Kabbalah" came into use, the concept was expressed in Hebrew by the phrase *ḥokhmat ha-shimmush*, which was a translation of the technical Greek term (*praxis*) used to denote magical activity. The Spanish kabbalists made a clear distinction between traditions that had come down to them from "masters of the doctrine of the *Sefirot*" (*ba'alei ha-sefirot*) and those that derived from magicians or "masters of the names." Also known to them were certain magical practices that were referred to as "great theurgy" (*shimmusha rabba*) and "little theurgy" (*shimmusha zutta*; see *Tarbiz*, 16 (1945), 196–209). Unlike Abulafia, however, Gikatilla, Isaac ha-Kohen, and Moses de Leon all mention such "masters of the name" and their expositions without holding them up to reproach. From the 15th century on the semantic division into "speculative" and "practical" Kabbalah became prevalent, though it was not necessarily meant to be prejudicial to the latter. On the whole, however, general summaries of kabbalistic doctrine rarely referred to its "practical" side except accidentally, such as in Cordovero's angelology *Derishot be-Inyanei ha-Mal'akhim* (at the end of R. Margaliot's *Malakhei Elyon*, 1945).

Historically speaking, most of the contents of practical Kabbalah considerably predate those of speculative Kabbalah and are not dependent on them. In effect, what came to be considered practical Kabbalah constituted an agglomeration of all the magical practices that developed in Judaism from the talmudic period down through the Middle Ages. The doctrine of the *Sefirot* hardly ever played a decisive role in these practices, despite occasional attempts from the late 13th century on to integrate the two. The bulk of such magical material to have been preserved is found in the writings of the Ḥasidei Ashkenaz, which for the most part were removed from the theological influences of Kabbalism, both in texts that were especially written on the subject, such as Eliezer of Worms' *Sefer ha-Shem*, and in collected anthologies. Most earlier theurgical and magical works, such as the *Ḥarba de-Moshe* or the *Sefer ha-Razim* (see above), were eventually assimilated into practical Kabbalah. Various ideas and practices connected with the figure of the *golem* also took their place in practical Kabbalah through a combination of features drawn from the *Sefer Yeẓirah* and a number of magical traditions. The ostensible lines drawn by the kabbalists to set the boundaries of permissible magic were frequently overstepped and obscured, with the consequent appearance in practical Kabbalah of a good deal of "black" magic – that is, magic that was meant to harm others or that employed "the unholy names" (*shemot ha-tum'ah*, Sanh. 91a) of various dark, demonic powers, and magic used for personal gain. The open disavowal of practical Kabbalah by most kabbalists, to the extent that it was not simply an empty formality, was for the most part in reaction to practices like these. Such black magic embraced a wide realm of *demonology and various forms of sorcery that were designed to disrupt the natural order of things and to create illicit connections between things that were meant to be kept separate. Activity of this sort was considered a rebellion of man against God and a hubristic attempt to set himself up in God's place. According to the Zohar (1, 36b), the source of such practices was "the leaves of the Tree of Knowledge," and they had existed among men since the expulsion from the Garden of Eden. Alongside this view, there continued the ancient tradition, first found in the Book of Enoch, that the rebellious angels who had fallen from heaven were the original instructors of the magic arts to mankind. To this day, the Zohar relates (3, 208a, 212a–b), the sorcerers journey to "the mountains of darkness," which are the abode of the rebel angels Aza and Azael, to study under their auspices. The biblical archetype of the sorcerer is Balaam. Such black magic is called in the Kabbalah "apocryphal science" (*ḥokhmah ḥiẓonah*) or "the science of the Orientals" (*ḥokhmah benei kedem*, on the basis of 1 Kings 5:10), and though a theoretical knowledge of it is permitted – several kabbalistic books in fact treat of it at length – its practice is strictly forbidden. The sorcerer draws forth the spirit of impurity from the *kelippot* and mixes the clean and the unclean together. In the *Tikkunei Zohar* the manipulation of such forces is considered justifiable under certain circumstances, inasmuch as the *sitra aḥra* must be fought with its own weapons.

The opposition of the speculative kabbalists to black magic was unable to prevent a conglomeration of all kinds of magical prescriptions in the literature of practical Kabbalah. Often the white-magical practices of amulets and protective charms can be found side by side with the invocation of demons, incantations, and formulas for private gain (e.g., magical shortcuts, the discovery of hidden treasure, impregnability in the face of one's enemies, etc.), and even sexual magic and necromancy. The international character of magical tradition is evident in such collections, into which many originally non-Jewish elements entered, such as Arab demonology and German and Slavic witchcraft. It was this indiscriminate mixture that was responsible for the rather gross image of practical Kabbalah that existed in the Jewish popular mind and eventually reached the Christian world too, where the theoretical kabbalistic distinction between forbidden and permitted magical practices was of course overlooked completely. The widespread medieval conception of the Jew as a powerful sorcerer was nourished to no small extent by the practical kabbalistic sources that fostered this confusion. As early as the geonic period the title *ba'al shem* or "master of the name" signified a master of practical Kabbalah who was an expert at issuing amulets for various purposes, invoking angels or devils, and exorcising evil spirits (see *Dibbuk) who had entered a human body. On the whole such figures were clearly identified with white magic in the popular mind, as opposed to sorcerers, witches, and wizards.

Among earlier kabbalistic works that are especially rich in material taken from practical Kabbalah are the Zohar, the writings of Joseph b. Shalom Ashkenazi and Menahem Ẓiyyoni, and the *Berit Menuḥah*, while in the post-Lurianic period the *Emek ha-Melekh* is outstanding in this respect. Magical prayers attributed to some of the leading *tannaim* and *amoraim* were already composed long before the development of speculative Kabbalah, and indeed magical material that has been preserved from the geonic age contains many similarities to magical Greek papyri that have been discovered in Egypt. Contemporaneous with such sources are various magical reworkings of the *shemoneh esreh* prayer, such as the *Tefillat Eliyahu* (Cambridge Ms. 505), which was already known to Isaac the Blind, or the maledictory version of the same prayer, quoted from the archives of Menahem Recanati in the complete manuscript of *Shoshan Sodot*. Almost all such compositions have been preserved in manuscript only, except for occasional borrowings from them in more popular anthologies. Among the most important known manuscripts of practical Kabbalah with its characteristic mixture of elements are Sassoon Ms. 290; British Museum Ms. 752; Cincinnati Ms. 35; and Schocken Ms. 102. Literature of this sort was extremely widespread, however, and hundreds of additional manuscripts also exist. Noteworthy also are the anonymous *Sefer ha-Ḥeshek* (*Festschrift fuer Aron Freimann* (1935), 51–54) and *Shulḥan ha-Sekhel* (in Sassoon Ms.), and Joseph ibn Ẓayyah's *She'erit Yosef* (1549, formerly in the Jewish Library of Vienna). In none of these books, however, is there any serious attempt at a systematic exposition of the subject. In many popular anthologies, which were widely circulated, both practical Kabbalah and folk medicine were combined together.

Other prominent works of practical Kabbalah include Joel Ba'al Shem's *Toledot Adam* (1720) and *Mif'alot Elohim* (1727); *Derekh ha-Yashar* (Cracow, 1646); Ẓevi Chotsh's *Derekh Yesharah* (Fuerth, 1697); *Ta'alumot Ḥokhmah* (Venice, 1667); Zechariah Plongian's *Sefer ha-Zekhirah* (Hamburg, 1709); Abraham Ḥammawi's anthologies *He'aḥ Nafshenu* (1870), *Devek me-Aḥ* (1874), *Abi'ah Ḥidot* (1877), *Lidrosh Elohim* (1879), and *Nifla'im Ma'asekha* (1881); and Ḥayyim Palache's *Refu'ah ve-Ḥayyim* (1874). A great deal of valuable material from the realm of practical Kabbalah can be found in *Mitteilungen der Gesellschaft fuer juedische Volkskunde* (1898–1929), and *Jahrbuecher fuer juedische Volkskunde*, 1–2 (1923–24). Ḥayyim Vital too compiled an anthology of practical Kabbalah mixed with alchemical material (Ms. in the Musayof Collection, Jerusalem). His son Samuel composed an alphabetical lexicon of practical Kabbalah called *Ta'alumot Ḥokhmah*, which has been lost. Moses Zacuto's comprehensive lexicon *Shorshei ha-Shemot*, on the other hand, has been preserved in many manuscript copies (selections from it were published in French by M. Schwab, 1899). Clear proof exists of several books on the subject of practical Kabbalah written by some outstanding kabbalists, but these have not been preserved. Among the great masters of practical Kabbalah in the eyes of kabbalistic tradition itself were figures like Judah Ḥasid, Joseph Gikatilla, Isaac of Acre, Joseph della Reyna, Samson of Ostropol, and Joel Ba'al Shem Tov.

To the realm of practical Kabbalah also belong the many traditions concerning the existence of a special archangelic alphabet, the earliest of which was "the alphabet of Metatron." Other such alphabets or *kolmosin* ("[angelic] pens") were attributed to Michael, Gabriel, Raphael, etc. Several of these alphabets that have come down to us resemble cuneiform writing, while some clearly derive from early Hebrew or Samaritan script. In kabbalistic literature they are known as "eye writing" (*ketav einayim*), because their letters are always composed of lines and small circles that resemble eyes. Under exceptional circumstances, as when writing the Tetragrammaton or the Divine Names Shaddai and Elohim, these alphabets were occasionally used even in a text otherwise written in ordinary Hebrew characters. Such magical letters, which were mainly used in amulets, are the descendants of the magical characters that are found in theurgic Greek and Aramaic from the first centuries C.E. In all likelihood their originators imitated cuneiform writing that could still be seen in their surroundings, but which had become indecipherable and had therefore assumed magical properties in their eyes.

The well-known medieval book, *Clavicula Salomonis* ("Solomon's Key"), was not originally Jewish at all, and it was only in the 17th century that a Hebrew edition was brought out, a mélange of Jewish, Christian, and Arab elements in which the kabbalistic component was practically nil. By the same token, *The Book of the Sacred Magic of Abra-Melin* (London, 1898), which purported to be an English translation of a Hebrew work written in the 15th century by a certain "Abraham the Jew of Worms" and was widely regarded in European occultist circles as being a classical text of practical Kabbalah, was not in fact written by a Jew, although its anonymous 16th-century author had an uncommon command of Hebrew. The book was originally written in German and the Hebrew manuscript of it found in Oxford (Neubauer 2051) is simply a translation. Indeed, the book circulated in various editions in several languages. It shows the partial influence of Jewish ideas but does not have any strict parallel in kabbalistic literature.

The relationship of the Kabbalah to other "occult sciences" such as astrology, alchemy, physiognomy, and chiromancy was slight. Astrology and alchemy play at most a marginal role in kabbalistic thought. At the same time, practical Kabbalah did manifest an interest in the magical induction of the pneumatic powers of the stars through the agency of specific charms. This use of astrological talismans, which clearly derived from Arabic and Latin sources, is first encountered in the *Sefer ha-Levanah* (London, 1912), cited by Naḥmanides. Another text of astrological magic is the Hebrew translation of the *Picatrix, Takhlit he-Ḥakham* (Arabic original and German translation, 1933 and 1962). This genre of magical book is also referred to in the Zohar (1, 99b), and several tracts on the subject have been preserved in manuscripts of practical Kabbalah. A number of kabbalistic works dealing with the preparation of magical rings combine astrological motifs with others taken from "the science of combination." A book in this vein that claims to have been divinely revealed has been preserved in Sassoon Ms. 290. *The Sefer ha-Tamar*, which has been attributed to Abu Aflaḥ (ed. G. Scholem, 1927), was preserved in practical kabbalistic circles but did not derive from them, having its source rather in Arabic astrological magic. Interestingly, kabbalistic attitudes toward astrological magic were highly ambivalent, and some leading kabbalists, such as Cordovero, actually approved of it.

Alchemy too had relatively little influence on the Kabbalah (G. Scholem, in: MGWJ, 69 (1925), 13–30, 95–110; *ibid.*, 70 (1926), 202–9). Indeed, there was a basic symbolic divergence between the two from the start, for while the alchemist considered gold to be the symbol of perfection, for the kabbalists gold, which symbolized *Din*, had a lower rank than silver, which symbolized *Ḥesed*. Nevertheless, efforts were made to harmonize the two systems and allusions to this can already be found in the Zohar. Joseph Taitaẓak, who lived at the time of the Spanish expulsion, declared the identity of alchemy with the divine wisdom of the Kabbalah (*Ẓefunot* 11 (1971), 86–87). In 17th-century Italy a kabbalistic alchemical text called *Esh Meẓaref* was composed in Hebrew, but the original has been lost; some parts have been preserved in the Latin in Knorr von Rosenroth's *Kabbala Denudata* (Eng. London, 1714, and in a new edition, 1894). Ḥayyim Vital spent two years of his youth studying alchemy exclusively and composed a book on alchemical practices which he publicly repented of in old age. No kabbalistic reworkings of physiognomy are known, but there are several treatments of *chiromancy, especially in the Zohar and in traditions of the Lurianic school. Some kabbalists believed that the lines of the hand and the forehead contained clues to a man's previous reincarnations.

The practice of practical Kabbalah raised certain problems concerning occult phenomena (see also preceding section). A number of these come under the category of *giluy eynayim*, whereby a man might be granted a vision of something that, generally speaking, only the rare mystic was permitted to see. Such visions included a glimpse of the "sapphiric ether" (*ha-avir ha-sappiri*) that surrounds all men and in which their movements are recorded, "the book in which all one's deeds are expressly written down" (especially in the works of Menaḥem Azariah Fano). The concept of the *ẓelem* was often associated with this ether, according to Lurianic sources, as was that of the angelic "eye-writing," and invisible letters that spelled out the secret nature of each man's thoughts and deeds which hovered over every head and might be perceived by initiates. Sometimes, especially during the performance of certain commandments such as circumcision, the initiate might also be granted a vision of the Tetragrammaton in the form of fiery letters that "appear and disappear in the twinkling of an eye." A *mohel* who was also a kabbalist could tell by the hue of this fire what the fortune of the newborn child would be (*Emek ha-Melekh*, 175b). The *aggadah* about the rays of light that shone from Moses' forehead (*Midrash Shemot Rabba*, 47) fathered the kabbalistic notion of a special halo that circled above the head of every righteous man (*Sefer Ḥasidim*, par. 370). This belief became widespread, although the halo was sometimes considered to appear only shortly before the *ẓaddik's* death. Visions of angels were explained in a similar fashion: the angel's form was imprinted in an invisible ether that was not the same as ordinary air, and could be seen by a select few, not because they were prophets but because God had opened their eyes as a reward for having purified their corporeal bodies (Cordovero in his *Derushei Mal'akhim*). Sorcerers who saw demons constituted an analogous phenomenon. Automatic writing is mentioned in a number of sources. Thus, Joseph b. Todros Abulafia, for example, composed a kabbalistic tract under the influence of "the writing name" (*Kerem Ḥemed*, 8, 105). Such "names" that facilitated the process of writing are referred to in a number of practical kabbalistic manuscripts. In describing a "revelation" that was granted to him, Joseph Taitaẓak speaks of "the mystic secret of writing with no hand." The anthology *Shoshan Sodot* (Oxford Ms., par. 147) mentions the practice of automatic writing, "making marks [*ḥakikah*] by the pen," as a method of answering vexing or difficult questions. A number of other spiritualistic phenomena, both spontaneous and deliberately induced, are also mentioned in various sources, among them the "levitating table," which was particularly widespread in Germany from the 16th century on. According to one eyewitness report, the ceremony was accompanied by a recital of Divine Names taken from practical Kabbalah and the singing of psalms and hymns (Wagenseil, *Sota*, 1674, 530). An acquaintance of Wagenseil's told him (*ibid.*, 1196) of how he had seen some yeshivah students from Wuerzburg who had studied in Fuerth lift such a table with the aid of Divine Names. Specific instructions for table levitation have been preserved in a number of kabbalistic manuscripts (e.g., Jerusalem 1070 8ø, p. 220). The use of divining rods is also known in such literature, from the 15th century on at the latest (Y. Perles, *Festschrift fuer H. Graetz* (1887), 32–34; see also Eliahu Kohen ha-Itamari, *Midrash Talpiot*, under *devarim nifla'im*).

Certain magical names or *shemot* were prescribed for certain special activities. The *shem ha-garsi* was invoked in the study of Talmud or any rabbinic text (*girsa*); the *shem ha-doresh* was invoked by the preacher (*darshan*). There was a "name of the sword" (*shem ha-ḥerev*), a "name of ogdoad" (*shem ha-sheminiyut*), and a "name of the wing" (*shem hakanaf*). Some of these invocations were borrowed from non-Jewish sources, as for example, the name "Parakletos Jesus b. Pandera" that a preacher recommended for use in synagogue (*Hebr. Bibl.*, 6 (1863), 121; G. Scholem, *Kitvei Yad be-Kabbalah* (1930), 63).

THE WIDER INFLUENCES OF AND RESEARCH ON THE KABBALAH

The Influence of the Kabbalah on Judaism

Though it has been evaluated differently by different observers, the influence of the Kabbalah has been great, for it has been one of the most powerful forces ever to affect the inner development of Judaism, both horizontally and in depth. Jewish historians of the 19th century, while conceding the Kabbalah's significant role, considered it to have been overwhelmingly negative and even catastrophic, but the appraisal of 20th-century Jewish historiography has been far more positive, no doubt due in part to profound changes in the course of Jewish history itself since the beginnings of the Zionist revival. There has been a new readiness in recent decades to acknowledge the wealth of rich symbolism and imagery that the kabbalistic imagination added to Jewish life, as well as to recognize the contributing role of the Kabbalah in strengthening the inner life of collective Jewry and the individual Jew. This reappraisal has made itself felt especially in the last two generations, both in literature and historical studies. Indeed, at times it has assumed panegyric proportions, as in the works of S.A. Horodezky, which have done little to further a fruitful discussion of the religious motives that found their expression in the Kabbalah with results that were sometimes problematic.

As was pointed out at the beginning of this exposition, the Kabbalah represented a theological attempt, open to only a relative few, whose object was to find room for an essentially mystical world-outlook within the framework of traditional Judaism without altering the latter's fundamental principles and behavioral norms. To what extent if at all this attempt was successful remains open to debate, but there can be no doubt that it achieved one very important result, namely, that for the three-hundred-year period roughly from 1500 to 1800 (at the most conservative estimate) the Kabbalah was widely considered to be *the* true Jewish theology, compared with which all other approaches were able at best to lead an isolated and attenuated existence. In the course of this period an open polemical attack on the Kabbalah was practically unheard of, and characteristically, when such an attack appeared, it was almost always in the guise of a rebuke addressed to the later kabbalists for having misrepresented and corporealized the pure philosophy of their predecessors, rather than an open criticism of the Kabbalah itself. Examples of this tactic, which was dictated by necessity, can be found in the anonymous polemic written in Posen in the middle of the 16th century (see

P. Bloch, MGWJ 47, 1903, 153ff., 263ff.) and in Jacob Francis of Mantua's anti-kabbalistic poems from the middle of the 17th century. When Mordecai Corcos, on the other hand, wished to publish a book openly opposed to the Kabbalah itself in Venice in 1672, he was prevented from doing so by the Italian rabbinical authorities.

In the area of *halakhah*, which determined the framework of Jewish life in accordance with the laws of the Torah, the influence of the Kabbalah was limited though by no means unimportant. As early as the 13th century there began a tendency to interpret the *halakhah* in kabbalistic terms without actually seeking to effect halakhic rulings or discussions by this means. In the main such kabbalistic interpretations touched on the mystical reasons for the commandments. At times there was an undeniable tension between the kabbalists and the strict halakhists, which in some cases expressed itself partly in kabbalistic outbursts rooted both in the natural feeling of superiority, which, whether justified or not, is frequently found in mystics and spiritualists (as in the case of Abraham Abulafia), and partly in the lack of a certain religious intensity, that kabbalists believed characterized the outlook of some leading halakhists. The attacks on cut-and-dried legalism that can be found in Baḥya ibn Paquda's *Ḥovot ha-Levavot* and in the *Sefer Ḥasidim* clearly reflect an attitude that did not exist only in the imagination of the mystics and was responsible for the fierce polemical assaults of the authors of the *Ra'aya Meheimna* and the *Sefer ha-Peli'ah* against the "talmudists," that is, the halakhists. Popular witticisms directed against such scholars, such as the ironic reading of the word *ḥamor* ("donkey") as an acronym for the phrase *ḥakham mufla ve-rav rabanan* ("a great scholar and a rabbi of rabbis"; see Judah Barzilai's *Perush Sefer Yeẓirah*, 161), have their echoes in the *Ra'aya Meheimna* (3, 275b), whose author does not shrink from the pejorative expression *ḥamor de-matnitin* ("mishnaic donkey"), and in the mystical homily 127b, in a passage belonging to the *Tikkunei Zohar* that refers to the Mishnah in a double-entendre as "the burial place of Moses." Other similar discourses, such as the exegesis (*ibid.*) relating the verse in Exodus 1:4, "And they made their lives bitter with hard service," to talmudic studies, or the angry descriptions of rabbinic scholars in the *Sefer ha-Peliah*, reveal a good deal of resentment. On the other hand, there is no historical basis for the picture drawn by Graetz of an openly anti-talmudic campaign waged by the kabbalists, who in reality insisted in their own writings on a scrupulous observance of halakhic law, albeit of course from a mystical perspective. At the same time, however, true antinomian tendencies could easily spring from the Kabbalah when it joined forces with messianism, as happened in the case of the Shabbatean movement.

A trend toward actually ruling on moot halakhic questions by treating them according to kabbalistic principles first appears in the mid-14th century, in the *Sefer ha-Peliah* and especially in discussions of the commandments in the *Sefer ha-Kanah*. Dating from the same period or shortly after are a number of similarly minded rabbinic responsa that have been attributed to Joseph Gikatilla (first published in the *Festschrift* for Jacob Freimann (1937) 163–70). Yet this school of thought remained in the minority, and most kabbalists, to the extent that they were also leading authorities on the *halakhah*, such as David b. Zimra, Joseph Caro, Solomon Luria, Mordecai Jaffe, and Ḥayyim Joseph Azulai, deliberately refrained from adopting halakhic positions that conflicted with talmudic law. The accepted rule among them was that decisions were only to be made on the basis of the Zohar when no clear talmudic guideline could be found (*Beit Yosef le-Oraḥ Ḥayyim*, par. 141). The entire question of whether halakhic rulings could ever be made on the basis of the Zohar or other kabbalistic texts led to considerable controversy. No less accomplished a kabbalist than David b. Zimra declared that, apart from the Zohar itself, it was forbidden to cite a kabbalistic work in opposition to even an isolated halakhic authority. A differing view was expressed by Benjamin Aaron Selnik, a disciple of Moses Isserles, in his volume of responsa, *Mas'at Binyamin* (1633): "If all the [halakhic] writers since the closing of the Talmud were placed in one pan of the scales, and the author of the Zohar in the other, the latter would outweigh them all." The laws and regulations that could be gleaned from the Zohar were collected by Issachar Baer b. Pethahiah of Kremnitz in his *Yesh Sakhar* (Prague, 1609). Joseph Solomon Delmedigo (1629) assembled a large amount of material dealing with the attitudes of the halakhic authorities to various kabbalistic innovations (*Maẓref le-Ḥokhmah* (1865), 66–82). The tremendous growth of new customs influenced by Lurianic Kabbalah led a number of kabbalists to seek to elevate Isaac Luria himself to a halakhically authoritative status. Even Ḥayyim Joseph David Azulai, who generally accepted as authoritative the halakhic opinions of Joseph Caro, wrote that Isaac Luria's interpretations of *halakhah* took precedence over Caro's Shulḥan Arukh (*Shiyurei Berakhah* on *Oraḥ Ḥayyim*). The tendency to refer to kabbalistic sources in the course of halakhic discussions was much more prominent in the post-Lurianic period among the Sephardim than among the Ashkenazim. The influence of the Kabbalah was particularly felt in connection with observances involving prayer, the Sabbath, and holidays, and was much less pronounced in more purely legal matters. It was common practice to comment on halakhic fine points from a kabbalistic perspective without actually claiming for the latter any halakhic authority. Outstanding examples of this are the *Mekor Ḥayyim* (1878–79) of Ḥayyim ha-Kohen of Aleppo, a disciple of Ḥayyim Vital, and Jacob Ḥayyim b. Isaac Baruch's *Kaf ha-Ḥayyim* (1912–29), a compilation of all the kabbalistic matter connected with the *Oraḥ Ḥayyim* of the Shulḥan Arukh.

In the realm of *aggadah*, the Kabbalah was unrestricted, and many kabbalists made use of this opportunity not only to compose far-reaching interpretations of the early *aggadot* of the Midrash, in which they saw the key to many of their mystic doctrines, but also to create a rich new body of aggadic legend bearing a strongly mythic character. In general, they were more at home in aggadic expression than in systematic exposition, and it is to this "kabbalization" of the *aggadah* that much of the enormous attraction of the Zohar must be credited. As for the fresh aggadic material created by the kabbalists themselves, it largely consisted of a mystical dramatization of the epos of creation and of the interaction of upper and lower worlds in the lives of the biblical heroes. The latter are portrayed as acting against a broad cosmic background, drawing sustenance from supernal powers and affecting them in turn by their deeds. The classic anthology of nearly 500 years of this kabbalistic *aggadah* is Reuben Hoeshke of Prague's *Yalkut Re'uveni*, a first edition of which (Prague, 1660) was organized topically, while its second, enlarged version (Wilmersdorf, 1681), which was modeled after the early midrashic anthology, *Yalkut Shimoni*, was arranged as a commentary on the Torah. Another comprehensive collection of both exoteric and esoteric *aggadot* on the period from the first week of creation to Adam's sin is Nahum Breiner's *Yalkut Naḥmani* (1937).

The main influence of Kabbalah on Jewish life must be sought in the three areas of prayer, custom, and ethics. Here the Kabbalah had practically unlimited freedom to exert its influence, which expressed itself in the creation of a broad body of literature that was directed at every Jewish home. From the middle of the 17th century onward, kabbalistic motifs entered the everyday prayer book and inspired special liturgies intended for a variety of specific occasions and rituals, many of which were in essence kabbalistic creations. This development began in Italy with books by Aaron Berechiah Modena and Moses Zacuto, and above all, with the appearance of Nathan Hannover's *Sha'arei Ẓiyyon* (Prague, 1662), one of the most influential and widely circulated of all kabbalistic works. In this volume the Lurianic doctrines of man's mission on earth, his connections with the powers of the upper worlds, the transmigrations of his soul, and his striving to achieve *tikkun* were woven into prayers that could be appreciated and understood by everyone, or that at least could arouse everyone's imagination and emotions. Such liturgies reached the furthest corners of the Diaspora and continued to be popular among Jews in Muslim countries long after they were excised from the prayer book by the Jewish communities of Central Europe as a consequence of the decline of the Kabbalah there in the 19th century. Sizable anthologies of highly emotional prayers composed under kabbalistic inspiration were published mainly in Leghorn, Venice, Constantinople, and Salonika. Especially important in this realm were the activities of Judah Samuel Ashkenazi, Abraham Anakawa, and above all, Abraham Hammawi (or Hamoj), who published a series of such books in Leghorn for the Jews of North Africa (*Bet Oved, Bet El, Bet ha-Kaporet, Bet ha-Beḥirot, Bet Av, Bet Din, Bet ha-Sho'evah, Bet Menuḥah*). The liturgical anthology *Oẓar ha-Tefillot* (1914) reflects the last lingering kabbalistic influences on the prayers of Eastern European Jewry.

Popular customs and popular faith were also highly affected by the spread of the Kabbalah. Many kabbalistic concepts were absorbed at the level of folk beliefs, such as the doctrine of man's first sin as the cause of a disruption in the upper worlds, the belief in transmigration of souls, the kabbalistic teachings about the Messiah, or the demonology of the later Kabbalah. Throughout the Diaspora, the number of folk customs whose origins were kabbalistic was enormous; many were taken directly from the Zohar, and many others from Lurianic tradition, the observances of which were compiled in the middle of the 17th century by Jacob Ẓemaḥ in his *Shulḥan Arukh ha-Ari* and *Naggid u-Meẓavveh*. A more recent guide to Lurianic customs was the compilation *Ta'amei ha-Minhagim* (1911–12). Such customs came on the whole to fulfill four mystical functions: the establishment of a harmony between the restrictive forces of *Din* and the outgoing forces of *Raḥamim*; to bring about or to symbolize the mystical "sacred marriage" (*ha-zivvug ha-kadosh*) between God and His *Shekhinah*; the redemption of the *Shekhinah* from its exile amid the forces of the *sitra aḥra*; the protection of oneself against the forces of the *sitra aḥra* and the battle to overcome them. Human action on earth assists or arouses events in the upper worlds, an interplay that has both its symbolic and its magical side. Indeed, in this conception of religious ceremony as a vehicle for the workings of divine forces, a very real danger existed that an essentially mystical perspective might be transformed in practice into an essentially magical one. Undeniably, the social effects of the Kabbalah on popular Jewish custom and ceremony were characterized by this ambivalence. Alongside the tendency to greater religious inwardness and insight was the tendency to a complete demonization of all life. The conspicuous growth of this latter trend at the expense of the former was undoubtedly one of the factors which, by reducing Kabbalah to the level of popular superstition, ultimately helped eliminate it as a serious historical force. (See G. Scholem, The *Kabbalah and its Symbolism* (1965), 118–57.)

Among kabbalistic customs that became particularly widespread were the holding of midnight vigils for the exile of the *Shekhinah*, the treating of the eve of the new moon as "a little Day of Atonement," and the holding of dusk-to-dawn vigils, which were dedicated to both ordinary and mystical study, on the nights of Pentecost, Hoshanah Rabba, and the seventh day of Passover. All such ceremonies and their accompanying liturgies and texts were referred to as *tikkunim* (e.g., "the *tikkun* of midnight" for the exile of the *Shekhinah*, etc.). A special atmosphere of solemn celebration surrounded the Sabbath, which was thoroughly pervaded with kabbalistic ideas about man's role in the unification of the upper worlds. Under the symbolic aspect of "the marriage of King and Queen," the Sabbath was enriched by a wealth of new customs that originated in Safed, such as the singing of the mystical hymn *Lekhah Dodi* and the recital of the Song of Songs and Chapter 31 of Proverbs ("A woman of valor who can find?"), all of which were intended as meditations on the *Shekhinah* in her aspect as God's mystical bride. Mystical and demonic motifs became particularly interwined in the area of sexual life, to which an entire literature was devoted, starting with the *Iggeret ha-Kodesh*, later mistakenly ascribed to Naḥmanides (see G. Scholem, in: KS 21 (1944), 179–86; and Monford Harris, in: HUCA 33 (1962), 197–220) and continuing up to Naḥman of

Bratslav's *Tikkun ha-Kelali*. Connected with these motifs were also a number of common burial customs, such as the circling of corpses and the forbidding of sons to attend their fathers' funerals. Similar ideas were behind the fast days in the months of Tevet and Shevat for "the *tikkun* of the *shovevim*," that is, of the demonic offspring of nocturnal emission.

This penetration of kabbalistic customs and beliefs, which left no corner of Jewish life untouched, is especially well documented in two highly influential books: Isaiah Horowitz's *Shenei Luḥot ha-Berit* (1648), which was accorded a particularly prominent place among Ashkenazi Jewry, and the anonymous *Ḥemdat Yamim* (1731), which was written by a moderate Shabbatean in the early 18th century. The latter book was circulated at first in Poland as well, but once its Shabbatean character came under attack its influence became largely restricted to the Sephardi world, where it fostered an entire literature of breviaries and study texts for special occasions. Despite the bulkiness of such works, their expressive power and rich contents made them classics of their kind. Noteworthy among more recent examples of this literature is Mordecai Moses Sassoon of Baghdad's *Davar be-Itto* (1862–94). A custom that became particularly widespread among the Sephardim was that of reciting the Zohar aloud, paying no attention to its contents, simply as "salutary for the soul."

Most of the popular ethical works of *musar* literature, especially the more prominent of them, bear the stamp of kabbalistic influences from the 1570s until the beginning of the 19th century, and even until the latter's end in the Sephardi world. The pioneer works in this respect were Eliezer Azikri's *Sefer Ḥaredim* (Venice, 1601), and Elijah de Vidas' *Reshit Ḥokhmah* (Venice, 1579), a comprehensive and exhaustive volume on all ethical aspects of Jewish life which served as a link between the motifs of medieval aggadic and *musar* literature and the new world of popular Kabbalah. Contemporaneous homiletic literature, much of which was also devoted to ethical instruction, also contains strong kabbalistic elements, which were further reinforced by the spread of Lurianic beliefs. The Lurianic doctrines of *tikkun*, the transmigration of souls, and the struggle with the *sitra aḥra* were subjected to especially intensive popular treatment. Such exhortative works as Ḥayyim Vital's *Sha'arei Kedushah* (Constantinople, 1734), Ẓevi Hirsch Koidanover's *Kav ha-Yashar* (Frankfurt, 1705), Elijah ha-Kohen's *Shevet Musar* (Constantinople, 1712), and many others down to the *Nefesh ha-Ḥayyim* of Ḥayyim of Volozhin, a disciple of the Gaon of Vilna, manifest indebtedness to kabbalistic sources on every page. Even the crowning masterpiece of this type of ethical literature, Moses Ḥayyim Luzzatto's *Mesillat Yesharim* (Amsterdam, 1740), was basically inspired by a conception of the ethical education of the Jew as a stage on the way to mystical communion with God, despite its restricted use of kabbalistic citations and symbols. Similar works of ethical exhortation composed in Poland in the middle of the 18th century are highly charged with attitudes and ideas that clearly served as a prelude to the beginnings of Ḥasidism. Examples of such books are Moses b. Jacob of Satanov's *Mishmeret ha-Kodesh* (Zolkiew, 1746), the *Bet Pereẓ* (Zolkiew, 1759) of Pereẓ b. Moses who was a kabbalist of the Brody *Klaus*, and Simḥah of Zalosicz's *Lev Simḥah* and *Neti'ah shel Simḥah* (Zolkiew, 1757 and 1763). In the 20th century the deep influence of kabbalistic *musar* literature can still be felt in the works of R. Abraham Kook. Similarly, in the mid-19th century, we find R. Judah Alkalai of Belgrade, one of the earliest heralds of Zionism, still totally immersed in the ethical world of the Kabbalah (see his collected writings in Hebrew, Jerusalem, 1944).

The Christian Kabbalah

From the late 15th century onward, in certain Christian circles of a mystical and theosophical persuasion a movement began to evolve with the object of harmonizing kabbalistic doctrines with Christianity, and, above all, of demonstrating that the true hidden meaning of the teachings of the Kabbalah points in a Christian direction. Naturally, such views did not meet with a friendly reception from the kabbalists themselves, who expressed nothing but derision for the misunderstandings and distortions of kabbalistic doctrine of which Christian Kabbalah was full; but the latter undeniably succeeded in arousing lively interest and debate among spiritualistic circles in the West until at least the middle of the 18th century. Historically, Christian Kabbalah sprang from two sources. The first was the christological speculations of a number of Jewish converts who are known to us from the end of the 13th century until the period of the Spanish expulsion (G. Scholem, in *Essays Presented to Leo Baeck* (1954), 158–93), such as Abner of *Burgos (Yiẓḥak Baer, *Tarbiẓ* 27 (1958), 152–63), and Paul de Heredia, who pseudepigraphically composed several texts of Christian Kabbalah entitled *Iggeret ha-Sodot* and *Galei Rezaya* in the name of Judah ha-Nasi and other *tannaim*. Another such tract put out by Jewish converts in Spain toward the end of the 15th century, and written in imitation of the styles of the *aggadah* and the Zohar, circulated widely in Italy. Such compositions had little effect on serious Christian spiritualists, nor was their clearly tendentious missionary purpose calculated to win readers. Another matter entirely, however, was the Christian speculation about the Kabbalah that first developed around the Platonic Academy endowed by the Medicis in Florence and was pursued in close connection with the new horizons opened up by the Renaissance in general. These Florentine circles believed that they had discovered in the Kabbalah an original divine revelation to mankind that had been lost and would now be restored, and with the aid of which it was possible not only to understand the teachings of Pythagoras, Plato, and the Orphics, all of whom they greatly admired, but also the secrets of the Catholic faith. The founder of this Christian school of Kabbalah was the renowned Florentine prodigy Giovanni Pico della *Mirandola (1463–94), who had long passages of kabbalistic literature translated for him into Latin by the very learned convert Samuel b. Nissim Abulfaraj, later Raymond Moncada, also known as Flavius *Mithridates, Pico began his kabbalistic studies in 1486, and when he displayed his 900 famous theses for public debate in Rome he included among them 47 propositions taken directly from kabbalistic sources, the majority from Recanati's commentary on the Torah, and 72 more propositions that represented his own conclusions from his kabbalistic research. These theses, especially the daring claim that "no science can better convince us of the divinity of Jesus Christ than magic and the Kabbalah," first brought the Kabbalah to the attention of many Christians. The ecclesiastical authorities fiercely rejected this and other of Pico's propositions, and there ensued the first real debate on the subject of the Kabbalah ever to take place in humanistic and clerical circles. Pico himself believed that he could prove the dogmas of the Trinity and the Incarnation on the basis of kabbalistic axioms. The sudden discovery of an esoteric Jewish tradition that had hitherto been completely unknown caused a sensation in the Christian intellectual world, and Pico's subsequent writings on the Kabbalah helped to further increase the interest of Christian Platonists in these newly uncovered sources, particularly in Italy, Germany, and France. Under Pico's influence the great Christian Hebraist Johannes *Reuchlin (1455–1522) also took up the study of Kabbalah and published two Latin books on the subject, the first ever to be written by a non-Jew, *De Verbo Mirifico* ("On the Miracle-working Name," 1494) and *De Arte Cabalistica* ("On the Science of the Kabbalah," 1517). The years between these two dates also witnessed the appearance of a number of works by the learned convert Paul Ricius, the private physician of Emperor Maximilian, who took Pico's and Reuchlin's conclusions and added to them through an original synthesis of kabbalistic and Christian sources. Reuchlin's own main contribution was his association of the dogma of the Incarnation with a series of bold speculations on the kabbalistic doctrine of the Divine Names of God. Human history, Reuchlin argued, could be divided into three periods. In the first or natural period, God revealed Himself to the patriarchs through the three-lettered name of Shaddai (שדי). In the period of the Toráh He revealed Himself to Moses through the four-lettered name of the Tetragrammaton. But in the period of grace and redemption He revealed Himself through five letters, namely, the Tetragrammaton with the addition of the letter *shin*, signifying the Logos, thus spelling Yehoshua or Jesus. In the name of Jesus, which is the true Miraculous Name, the formerly forbidden name of God now became pronounceable. In Reuchlin's schematic arrangement, which was able to draw for support on the common abbreviation for Jesus in medieval manuscripts, JHS, Jewish beliefs in three world ages (Chaos, Torah, Messiah) blended with the tripartite Christian division of the millennialist school of Joachim of Fiore into a reign of the Father, a reign of the Son, and a reign of the Holy Ghost.

Pico's and Reuchlin's writings, which placed the Kabbalah in the context of some of the leading intellectual developments of the time, attracted wide attention. They led on the one hand to considerable interest in the doctrine of Divine Names and in practical Kabbalah, and on the other hand to further speculative attempts to achieve a synthesis between kabbalistic motifs and Christian theology. The place of honor accorded to practical Kabbalah in Cornelius Agrippa of Nettesheim's great compendium *De Occulta Philosophia* (1531), which was a widely read summary of all the occult sciences of the day, was largely responsible for the mistaken association of the Kabbalah in the Christian world with numerology and witchcraft. Several Christian kabbalists of the mid-16th century made a considerable effort to master the sources of the Kabbalah more deeply, both in Hebrew and in Latin translations prepared for them, thus widening the basis for their attempts to discover common ground between the Kabbalah and Christianity. Among the most prominent of these figures were Cardinal Egidio da *Viterbo (1465–1532), whose *Scechina* (ed. F. Secret, 1959) and "On the Hebrew Letters" were influenced by ideas in the Zohar and the *Sefer ha-Temunah*, and the Franciscan Francesco *Giorgio of Venice (1460–1540), the author of two large and at the time widely read books, *De Harmonia Mundi* (1525) and *Problemata* (1536), in which the Kabbalah assumed a central place and manuscript material from the Zohar was used extensively for the first time in a Christian work. The admiration of these Christian authors for the Kabbalah aroused an angry reaction in some quarters, which accused them of disseminating the view that any Jewish kabbalist could boast of being a better Christian than an orthodox Catholic. A more original mystical thinker who was also better acquainted with the Jewish sources was the renowned Frenchman Guillaume *Postel (1510–1581), one of the outstanding personalities of the Renaissance. Postel translated the Zohar and the *Sefer Yeẓirah* into Latin even before they had been printed in the original, and accompanied his translation with a lengthy theosophic exposition of his own views. In 1548 he published a kabbalistic commentary in Latin translation on the mystical significance of the *menorah*, and later a Hebrew edition as well. These authors had many connections in Jewish circles.

During this period, Christian Kabbalah was primarily concerned with the development of certain religious and philosophical ideas for their own sake rather than with the desire to evangelize among Jews, though this latter activity was occasionally stressed to justify a pursuit that was otherwise suspect in many eyes. One of the most dedicated of such Christian kabbalists was Johann Albrecht *Widmanstetter (Widmanstadius; 1506–1557), whose enthusiasm for the Kabbalah led him to collect many kabbalistic manuscripts that are extant in Munich. Many of his contemporaries, however, remained content to speculate in the realm of Christian Kabbalah without any firsthand knowledge of the sources. Indeed, in the course of time the knowledge of Jewish sources diminished among the Christian kabbalists, and consequently the Jewish element in their books became progressively slighter, its place being taken by esoteric Christian speculations whose connections with Jewish motifs were remote. The Lurianic revival in Safed had no effect on these circles. Their commitment to missionary work increased, yet the number of Jewish converts to Christianity from kabbalistic motives, or of those who claimed such motives retrospectively, remained disproportionately small among the numbers of converts in general. There is no clear evidence in the writings of such Christian theosophists to indicate whether or not they believed the Jewish kabbalists to be hidden or unconscious Christians at heart. In any event, Christian Kabbalah occupied an honored place both in the 16th century, primarily in Italy and France, and in the 17th century, when its center moved to Germany and England.

In the 17th century Christian Kabbalah received two great impetuses, one being the theosophical writings of Jacob Boehme, and the other Christian Knorr von *Rosenroth's vast kabbalistic compendium *Kabbala Denudata* (1677–84), which for the first time made available to interested Christian readers, most of whom were undoubtedly mystically inclined themselves, not only important sections of the Zohar but sizable excerpts from Lurianic Kabbalah as well. In this work and in the writings of the Jesuit scholar Athanasius Kircher the parallel is drawn for the first time between the kabbalistic doctrine of *Adam Kadmon* and the concept of Jesus as primordial man in Christian theology. This analogy is pressed particularly in the essay entitled *Adumbratio Kabbalae Christianae* which appears at the end of the *Kabbala Denudata* (Fr. trans., Paris, 1899), and from which the very term Christian Kabbalah was taken over by many writers. Its anonymous author was in fact the well-known Dutch theosophist, Franciscus Mercurius van Helmont, all of whose works are shot through with kabbalistic ideas. It was Van Helmont who served as the link between the Kabbalah and the Cambridge Platonists led by Henry More and Ralph Cudworth, who made use of kabbalistic motifs for their own original speculative purposes, more especially. Somewhat earlier, students (as well as opponents) of Jacob Boehme had discovered the inner affinity between his own theosophical system and that of the Kabbalah, though there would seem to be no historical connection between them, and in certain circles, particularly in Germany, Holland, and England, Christian Kabbalah henceforward assumed a Boehmian guise. In 1673 a large chart was erected in front of a Protestant church in Teinach (southern Germany), which had as its purpose the presentation of a kind of visual summary of this school of Christian Kabbalah. Several different interpretations were given to it. As early as the late 16th century a pronounced trend had emerged toward the permeation of Christian Kabbalah with alchemical symbolism, thus giving it an oddly original character in its final stages of development in the 17th and 18th centuries. This mélange of elements typifies the works of Heinrich Khunrat, *Amphitheatrum Sapientiae Aeternae* (1609), Blaise de *Vigenère, *Traité du Feu* (1617), Abraham von Frankenberg, Robert Fludd (1574–1637), and Thomas Vaughan (1622–1666), and reaches its apogee in Georg von Welling's *Opus Mago-Cabbalisticum* (1735) and the many books of F.C. Oetinger (1702–1782), whose influence is discernible in the works of such great figures of German idealist philosophy as Hegel and Schelling. In yet another form this mixture reappears in the theosophical systems of the Freemasons in the second half of the 18th century. A late phase of Christian Kabbalah is represented by Martines de Pasqually (1727–1774) in his *Traité de la réintégration des êtres*, which greatly influenced theosophical currents in France. The author's disciple was the well-known mystic Louis Claude de St. Martin. Pasqually himself was suspected during his lifetime of being a secret Jew, and modern scholarship has in fact established that he was of Marrano ancestry. The sources of his intellectual indebtedness, however, have still to be clarified. The crowning and final achievement of Christian Kabbalah was Franz Josef Molitor's (1779–1861) comprehensive *Philosophie der Geschichte oder Ueber die Tradition*, which combined profound speculation in a Christian kabbalistic vein with highly suggestive research into the ideas of the Kabbalah itself. Molitor too still clung to a fundamentally christological view of the Kabbalah, whose historical evolution he completely failed to understand, yet at the same time he revealed an essential grasp of kabbalistic doctrine and an insight into the world of the Kabbalah far superior to that of most Jewish scholars of his time.

Scholarship and the Kabbalah

As implied above, the beginnings of scholarly investigation of the Kabbalah were bound up with the interests of Christian Kabbalah and its missionary zeal. A number of Christian kabbalists were led to study the literature of the Kabbalah first hand, one of the first being Reuchlin, who resorted primarily to the works of Gikatilla and to a large collection of early kabbalistic writings that has been preserved in Halberstamm Ms. 444 (in the Jewish Theological Seminary in New York). Though a significant number of kabbalistic works had been translated by the middle of the 16th century, only a few of these translations, such as one of Gikatilla's *Sha'arei Orah* (1516), had been published, while the majority remained in manuscript where they did little to stimulate further research. In addition, the theological presuppositions of the Christian kabbalists ruled out any historical, to say nothing of critical, perspective on their part. A crucial turning-point was the publication of Knorr von Rosenroth's *Kabbala Denudata*, despite its many erroneous translations which were further compounded in the retranslation of some of its parts into English and French (see MGWJ 75 (1932), 444–8). The appearance of this book aroused the interest of several scholars who had not previously had any attachment to Christian Kabbalah. Completely at variance with the latter's premises was Johann Georg Wachter's study of Spinozistic tendencies in Judaism, *Der Spinozismus im Juedenthumb* [sic!] (Amsterdam, 1699), which was the first work to interpret the theology of the Kabbalah pantheistically and to argue that the kabbalists were not disguised Christians but rather disguised atheists. Wachter's book greatly influenced discussions on the subject throughout the 18th century. Early in the 18th century J.P. Buddeus proposed the theory of a close connection between the early Gnostics and the Kabbalah in his "Introduction to the History of the Philosophy of the Jews" (in Latin, Halle, 1720), which was largely devoted to the Kabbalah. J.K. Schramm too, in his "Introduction to the Dialectics of the Kabbalists" (Braunschweig, 1703) sought to discuss the subject in scientific and philosophical terms, while G. Sommer's *Specimen Theologiae Soharicae* (Gotha, 1734) presented an anthology of all the passages from the Zohar that were in the author's opinion close to Christian doctrine. A particularly valuable though now totally forgotten book was Hermann von der Hardt's *Aenigmata Judaeorum Religiosissima* (Helmstadt, 1705), which dealt with practical Kabbalah. J.P. Kleuker published a study in 1786 in which he argued the case for a decisive Persian influence on the kabbalistic doctrine of emanation. Common to all these early scholars was the belief that the Kabbalah was in essence not Jewish at all, but rather Christian, Greek, or Persian.

Scholarly investigation of the Kabbalah by Jews also first served a tendentious purpose, namely, to polemicize against what was felt to be the Kabbalah's undue influence on Jewish life. The first critical work to be written in this vein was Jacob Emden's highly influential *Mitpaḥat Sefarim* (Altona, 1768), which grew out of the author's battle with Shabbateanism and was intended to weaken the authority of the Zohar by proving that many of its passages were late interpolations. In the 19th century also most Jewish scholarship on the Kabbalah bore a polemical character primarily aimed against kabbalistic influences as they appeared in Ḥasidism. For the most part such scholars too considered the Kabbalah to have been an essentially foreign presence in Jewish life. At the time, indeed, Kabbalah was still a kind of stepdaughter in the field of Jewish scholarship whose actual literary sources were studied by only a few. Even from this limited perspective, however, important contributions to the investigation of the Kabbalah were made by Samuel David Luzzatto, Adolphe Franck, H.D. Joel, Senior Sachs, Aaron Jellinek, Isaac Mieses, Graetz, Ignatz Stern, and M. Steinschneider. The works of the single Jewish scholar of this period to devote in-depth studies to the Zohar and other important kabbalistic texts, Eliakim Milsahagi (Samiler), remained almost completely unpublished and were eventually forgotten and largely lost. All that has been preserved of them is his analysis of the Zohar (Jerusalem Ms. 4° 121), and the *Sefer Raziel*. Works on the Kabbalah during the Haskalah period are almost all practically worthless, such as the many tracts and books of Solomon Rubin. Exceptions are David Kahana's studies of Lurianic Kabbalah, which despite their polemic tendentiousness have some historical value. The only two scholars of the age to approach the Kabbalah out of a fundamental sympathy and even affinity for its teachings were the Christian P.J. Molitor and the Jew Elijah Benamozegh. The many books written on the subject in the 19th and 20th centuries by various theosophists and mystics lacked any basic knowledge of the sources and very rarely contributed to the field, while at times they even hindered the development of a historical approach. Similarly, the activities of French and English occultists contributed nothing and only served to create considerable confusion between the teachings of the Kabbalah and their own totally unrelated inventions. To this category of supreme charlatanism belong the many and widely read books of Eliphas Levi (actually Alphonse Louis Constant; 1810–1875), Papus (Gérard Encausse; 1868–1916), and Frater Perdurabo (Aleister Crowley; 1875–1946), all of whom had an infinitesimal knowledge of Kabbalah that did not prevent them from drawing freely on their imaginations instead. The comprehensive works of A.E. Waite, S. Karppe, and P. Vulliaud, on the other hand, were mere compilations made from secondhand sources.

The profoundly altered approach to Jewish history that followed in the wake of the Zionist revival and the movement for national rebirth led, particularly after World War I, to a renewal of interest in the Kabbalah as a vital expression of Jewish existence. A new attempt was made to understand, independently of all polemic or apologetic positions, the genesis, development, historical role, and social and intellectual influence of the Kabbalah within the total context of the internal and external forces that have determined the shape of Jewish history. The pioneers of this new approach were S.A. Horodezky, Ernst Mueller, and G. Scholem. In the years following 1925 an international center for kabbalistic research came to reside in the Hebrew University of Jerusalem. Among the foremost representatives of the school of historical criticism that developed there were G. Scholem, Y. Tishby, E. Gottlieb, and J. Ben-Shlomo. Elsewhere important contributions to kabbalistic scholarship were made too, particularly by G. Vajda, A. Altmann, and François Secret. With the development of new perspectives in recent years, scholarly investigation of the Kabbalah is only now emerging from its infancy. Ahead of it lies a great deal of room for fruitful expansion that will yet take in kabbalistic literature in the whole of its richness and its many implications with regard to the life of the Jewish people.

BIBLIOGRAPHY: For editions of English translations of individual works, see the respective articles. BIBLIOGRAPHY AND SOURCES: Wolf, Bibliotheca, 2 (1721), 1191–1247; 4 (1733), 734ff.; Steinschneider, Cat Bod; idem, *Die hebraeischen Handschriften der K. Hof- und Staatsbibliothek in Muenchen* (1897); Neubauer, Cat, 537ff.; Margoliouth, Cat, 3 (1909), 1–155; S. Spector, *Jewish Mysticism: an Annotated Bibliography on the Kabbalah in English* (1984); G. Scholem, *Bibliographia Kabbalistica* (1927); idem, *Kitvei Yad be-Kabbala ha-Nimẓa'im be-Bet ha-Sefarim ha-Le'umi ve-ha-Universita'i bi-Yrushalayim* (1930); Shunami, Bibl, 739–48; C. Knorr von Rosenroth, *Kabbalah Denudata*, 2 vols. (1677–84; Eng. tr. by S.L. Mac-Gregor Mathers, 1887, repr. 1962). GENERAL: Scholem, Mysticism; idem, *Perakim le-Toledot Sifrut ha-Kabbalah* (1931); idem, *Von der Mystischen Gestalt der Gottheit* (1962); idem, *Ursprung und Anfaenge der Kabbala* (1962; *Les origines de la Kabbale*, 1966); idem, *On the Kabbalah and its Symbolism* (1965); D. Kahane, *Toledot ha-Mekubalim, ha-Shabbeta'im ve-ha-Ḥasidim*, 2 vols. (1913); M.D.G. Langer, *Die Erotik der Kabbala* (1923); P. Villiaud, *La Kabbale juive*, 2 vols. (1923); S.A. Horodezky, *Ha-Mistorin be-Yisrael*, 3 vols. (1931–52); idem, *Yahadut ha-Sekhel ve-Yahadut ha-Regesh*, 2 vols. (1947); idem, *Kivshono shel Olam* (1950); Ḥayyim ben Shelomo Araki, *Sefer Emunat ha-Shem* (1937); H. Sérouya, *La Kabbale: ses origines, sa psychologie mystique, sa metaphysique* (1947); L. Schaya, *L'homme et l'absolu selon la Kabbale* (1958); H. Zeitlin, *Be-Fardes ha-Ḥasidut ve-ha-Kabbalah* (1960); A. Safran, *La Cabale* (1960); G. Vajda, *Recherches sur la philosophie et la Kabbale dans la pensée juive du moyen-âge* (1962); Dinur, Golah, 2, pt. 4

(1969), 275–435; I. Weinstock, *Be-Ma'aglei ha-Nigleh ve-ha-Nistar* (1969); I. Tishby, *Le-Berur Netivei ha-Hagshamah ve-ha-Hafshatah ba-Kabbalah*, in: *Alei Ayin* (1948–52), 147–55; L. Baeck, *Jewish Mysticism*, in: JJS, 2 (1950), 3–16. EARLY BEGINNINGS: N.I. Weinstein, *Zur Genesis der Agada*, 2 (1901); M. Friedlaender, *Die Religioesen Bewegungen innerhalb des Judentums im Zeitalter Jesu* (1905); E. Bischoff, *Babylonisch-Astrales im Weltbilde des Thalmud und Midrasch* (1907); J. Abelson, *Immanence of God in Rabbinical Literature* (1912); W. Schencke, *Die Chokma (Sophia) in der juedischen Hypostasenspekulation* (1913); B.J. Bamberger, *Fallen Angels* (1952); H.J. Franken, *Mystical Communion with JHWH in the Book of Psalms* (1954); C.L. Montefiore, *Mystic Passages in the Psalms*, in: JQR, 1 (1889), 143–61; D. Castelli, *Gli antecedenti della Cabbala nella Bibbia e nella letteratura talmudica*, in: *Actes du XLLM^e Congrès des Orientalistes*, 3 (1899), 57–109; G.F. Moore, *Intermediaries in Jewish Theology*, in: HTR, 15 (1922), 41–85; J. Hertz, *Mystic Currents in Ancient Israel*, in: *Jews at the Close of the Bible Age* (1926), 126–56; J. Lindblom, *Die Religion der Propheten und die Mystik* in: ZAW, 57 (1939), 65–74; R. Marcus, *On Biblical Hypostases of Wisdom*, in: HUCA, 23 (1950–51), 157–71; I. Efros, *Holiness and Glory in the Bible*, in: JQR, 41 (1950/51), 363–77; I.F. Baer, *Le-Berurah shel Torat Aḥarit ha-Yamim bi-Yemei ha-Bayit ha-Sheni*, in: *Zion*, 23–24 (1958/59), 3–34, 141–65. APOCALYPTIC ESOTERICISM AND MERKABAH MYSTICISM: M.D. Hoffmann, *Toledot Elisha ben Avuya* (1880); H. Kraus, *Begriff und Form der Haeresie nach Talmud und Midrasch* (1896); A. Jellinek, *Elischa ben Abuja-Acher* (1891); M. Buttenwieser, *Outline of the Neo-Hebraic Apocalyptic Literature* (1901); H. Bietenhard, *Die himmlische Welt im Urchristentum und Spaetjudentum* (1951); J. Maier, *Vom Kultus zur Gnosis* (1964); M.J. Ben-Gorion, *Erekh "Aḥer,"* in: *Ha-Goren*, 8 (1912), 76–83; V. Aptowitzer, *Bet ha-Mikdash shel Ma'alah al Pi ha-Aggadah*, in: *Tarbiz*, 2 (1931), 137–85; A. Buechler, *Die Erloesung Elisa b. Abujahs aus dem Hoellenfeuer*, in: MGWJ, 76 (1932), 412–56; H. Hirschberg, *Once Again – the Minim*, in: JBL, 67 (1948), 305–18; A. Neher, *Le Voyage Mystique des Quatre* in: RHR, 140 (1951), 59–82; J. Strugnell, *The Angelic Liturgy at Qumran 4Q, Serek Sirot 'Olat Hassabbat*, in: suppl. to VT, 7 (1960), 318–45; W.C. van Unnik, *Die juedische Komponente in der Entstehung der Gnosis*, in: *Vigiliae Christianae*, 15 (1961), 65–82; E. Haenchen, *Gab es eine vorchristliche Gnosis*, in: *Gott und Mensch* (1965), 265ff.; E.E. Urbach, *Ha-Masorot al Torat ha-Sod bi-Tekufat ha-Tanna'im*, in: *Meḥkarim… G. Scholem* (1967), 1–28. ESOTERIC LITERATURE: B. Jacob, *Im Namen Gottes* (1903); J.A. Montgomery, *Aramaic Incantation Texts from Nippur* (1913); A. Ravenna, *I sette santuari (Hekhalot)* (1964); G. Scholem, *Jewish Gnosticism, Merkabah Mysticism and Talmudic Tradition* (1965^2); C. Gordon, *Five Papers on Magical Bowls and Incantations (Jewish and Mandaean)*, in: *Archiv Orientální*, 6 (1934), 319–34, 466–74; 9 (1937), 84–106; 18 (1949), 336–41; 20 (1951), 306–15; A.I. Altmann, *Gnostic Themes in Rabbinic Cosmology*, in: *Essays… J.H. Hertz* (1943), 19–32; idem, *A Note on the Rabbinic Doctrine of Creation*, in: JJS, 7 (1956), 195–206; E.R. Goodenough, *A Jewish-Gnostic Amulet of the Roman Period*, in: *Greek and Byzantine Studies* (1958), 71–81; B.Z. Bokser, *The Thread of Blue*, in: PAAJR, 31 (1963), 1–32; J. Maier, in: *Kairos*, 5 (1963), 18–40 (Ger.); N. Séd, *Une cosmologie juive du haut moyen-âge. La Berayta du Ma'aseh Beresit*, in: REJ, 3 (1964), 259–305; 4 (1965), 23–123; idem, *Les Hymnes sur le Paradis de Saint Ephrem et les Traditions juives*, in: *Le Muséon*, 81 (1968), 455–501; R. Loewe, *The Divine Garment and Shi'ur Qomah*, in: HTR, 58 (1965), 153–60; I. Gruenwald, *Piyyutei Yannai ve-Sifrut ha-Merkavah*, in: *Tarbiz*, 36 (1967), 257–77. JEWISH GNOSIS AND THE SEFER YEZIRAH: H. Graetz, *Gnosticismus und Judenthum* (1846); M. Friedlaender, *Ben Dosa und seine Zeit* (1872); idem, *Der vorchristliche juedische Gnosticismus* (1898); A. Epstein, *Recherches sur le Séfer Yecira*, in: REJ, 28 (1894), 94–108; 29 (1894), 61–78; P. Mordell, *The Origin of Letters and Numerals According to the Sefer Yetzirah*, in: JQR, 2 (1911/12); 3 (1912/13); A.M. Habermann, *Avanim le-Ḥeker Sefer Yeẓirah*, in: *Sinai*, 20 (1946), 241–65; G. Vajda, *Le commentaire kairouanais sur le 'Livre de la Création,'* in: REJ, 107 (1947), 5–62; 110 (1949/50), 67–92; 112 (1953), 5–33; idem, *Nouveaux fragments arabes du commentaire de Dunash b. Tamim sur le 'Livre de la Création,'* in: REJ, 113 (1954), idem, *Notes et Mélanges*, in: REJ, 122 (1963), 149–66; idem, *Sa'adya Commentateur du 'Livre de la Création.'* in: *Ecole pratique des Hautes Etudes*, Section des Sciences Religieuses, *Extrait de l'Annuaire 1959–60* (1960), 1–35; idem, *Les Lettres et les Sons de la Langue Arabe d'après Abu Hatim Al-Razi*, in: *Arabica* 15 (1961), 113–30; K. Schubert, *Der gegenwaertige Stand der Erforschung der in Palaestina neu gefundenen hebraeischen Handschriften, 25: Der Sektenkanon von En Fescha und die Anfaenge der juedischen Gnosis*, in: *Theologische Literaturzeitung*, 8/9 (1953), 496–506; G. Quispel, *Christliche Gnosis und juedische Heterodoxie*, in: *Evangelische Theologie* (1954), 1–11; S. Loewenstamm, *Mah le-Ma'alah u-Mah le-Matah, Mah le-Fanim u-Mah le-Aḥor*, in: *Sefer ha-Yovel le-Yeḥezkel Kauffmann* (1960), 112–22; S. Morag, *Sheva Kefulot Begad Kafrat*, in: *Sefer Tur-Sinai* (1960), 207–42; J. Neusner, *Masa al Ma'aseh Merkavah*, in: *Ha-Ashnav* (1961); M. Smith, *Observations on Hekhalot Rabbati*, in: Brandeis University, *Studies and Texts*, 1 (1963), 142–60; P. Merlan, *Zur Zahlenlehre im Platonismus (Neuplatonismus) und im Sefer Yezira*, in: *Journal of the History of Philosophy*, 3 (1965), 167–81; N. Sèd, *Le Memar samaritain, Le Séfer Yesira et les trente-deux sentiers de la Sagesse*, in: RHR, 170 (1966), 159–84. GEONIC PERIOD: E.E. Hildesheimer, *Mystik und Agada im Urteile der Gaonen R. Scherira und R. Hai* (1931); I. Weinstock, *Oẓar Razim Kadmon ve-Gilgulav* in: *Shanah be-Shanah 5723* (1962), 345–58; idem, *Demut Aharon ha-Bavli bi-Megillat Aḥima'aẓ; ibid., 5724* (1963), 242–65; idem, *Gilluy Izavon ha-Sodot shel Abu Aharon ha-Bavli*, in: *Tarbiz*, 32 (1962/63), 153–9; idem, *Oẓar ha-Sodot shel Abu Aharon – Dimyon o Meẓi'ut*, in: *Sinai*, 54 (1963), 226–59; G. Scholem, *Ha-Im nitgallah Izavon ha-Sodot shel Abu Aharon ha-Bavli?*, in: *Tarbiz*, 32 (1963), 252–65. ḤASIDIC MOVEMENTS IN EUROPE AND EGYPT: J. Freimann, *Mavo le-Sefer Ḥasidim* (1924); J. Dan, *Torat ha-Sod shel Ḥasidut Ashkenaz* (1968); idem, *Sefer ha-Hokhmah le-R. Elazar mi-Worms u-Mashma'uto le-Toledot Toratah ve-Sifrutah shel Ḥasidut Ashkenaz*, in: *Zion*, 29 (1964), 167–81; idem, *Sefer ha-Navon*, in: *Koveẓ al Yad*, 16 (1966), 201–23; idem, *Beginnings of Jewish Mysticism in Europe*, in: Roth, Dark Ages, 282–90, 455–6; idem, *Ḥug ha-Kruv ha-Meyuḥad bi-Tenu'at Ḥasidut Ashkenaz*, in: *Tarbiz*, 35 (1966), 349–72; idem, *Ḥokhmath Ha-'Egoz, Its Origin and Development*, in: JJS, 17 (1966), 73–82; A. Epstein, *Lekorot ha-Kabbalah ha-Ashkenazit*, in: *Ha-Ḥoker*, 2 (1894), 37–48; idem, *R. Shemu'el he-Ḥasid ben R. Kalonimus ha-Zaken*, in: *Ha-Goren*, 4 (1903), 81–101; G. Vajda, *The Mystical Doctrine of Rabbi Obadyah, Grandson of Moses Maimonides*, in: JJS, 6 (1955), 213–25; idem, *Perusho ha-Rishon shel Rabbi Elḥanan Yiẓḥak ben Yakar mi-London le-Sefer Yeẓirah*, in: *Koveẓ al Yad*, 16 (1966), 147–97; A.I. Altmann, *Eleazar of Worms' Ḥokhmath ha-'Egoz*, in: JJS, 11 (1960), 101–13; A. Rubin, *Concept of Repentance Among the Ḥasidey Ashkenaz*, in: JJS, 16 (1965), 161–76; R. Edelmann, *Das 'Buch der Frommen' Als Ausdruck des Volkstuemlichen Geisteslebens der deutschen Juden im Mittelalter*, in: *Miscellanea Mediaevalia* (1966), 55–71; S.D. Goitein, *A Treatise in Defence of the Pietists by Abraham Maimonides*, in: JJS, 17 (1966), 105–14; idem, *Abraham Maimonides and his Pietist Circle*, in: *Jewish Medieval and Renaissance Studies* (1967), 145–64; I.F. Baer, *Shenei Perakim shel Torat ha-Hashgaḥah be-Sefer Ḥasidim*, in: *Meḥkarim… G. Scholem* (1967), 47–62. KABBALAH IN PROVENCE: G. Scholem, *Te'udah Ḥadashah le-Toledot Reshit ha-Kabbalah*, in: *Sefer Bialik* (1934), 141–62; H. Wirshubsky, *Akdamot le-Bikoret ha-*

Nusaḥ shel Perush Sefer Yezirah le-R. Yiẓḥak Sagi-Nahor, in: *Tarbiz*, 27 (1958), 257–64. IN GERONA: G. Scholem, *Ursprung und Anfaenge der Kabbala* (1962), 324–419; G. Vajda, *Le commentaire d'Ezra de Gérone sur le cantique des cantiques* (1969); I. Tishby, *Kitvei ha-Mekubbalim R. Ezra ve-R. Azriel mi-Gerona*, in: *Sinai*, 16 (1945), 159–78; idem, *Ha-Mekubbalim R. Ezra ve-R. Azriel u-Mekomam be-Ḥug Gerona* in: *Zion*, 9 (1944), 178–85; A.I. Altmann, *The Motif of the 'Shells,' in 'Azriel of Gerona,'* in: JJS, 9 (1958), 73–80; G. Sed-Rajna, *De quelques commentaires Kabbalistiques sur le rituel dans les manuscrits de la Bibliothèque National de Paris*, in: REJ, 124 (1965), 307–51. OTHER CURRENTS – THE ZOHAR: D.H. Joel, *Midrash ha-Zohar: Die Religionsphilosophie des Zohar* (1849); A. Jellinek, *Moses ben Schem-Tob de Leon und sein Verhaeltnis zum Sohar* (1851); S. Karppe, *Etude sur les origines et la nature du Zohar* (1901); A.E. Waite, *The Secret Doctrine in Israel. A Study of the Zohar and its Connections* (1913); G. Scholem, *Kabbalot R. Ya'akov ve-R. Yiẓḥak Kohen* (1927); idem, *Ha-Kabbala shel Sefer ha-Temunah ve-shel Abraham Abulafia* (1965); idem, *Le-Ḥeker Kabbalat R. Yiẓḥak ben Ya'akov ha-Kohen*, in: *Tarbiz*, 2 (1931), 188–217, 415–42; 3 (1932), 33–66, 258–86; 4 (1933), 54–77, 207–25; 5 (1934), 50–60, 180–98, 305–28; A. Bension, *The Zohar in Moslem and Christian Spain* (1932); I. Tishby, *Mishnat ha-Zohar*, 1 (1949, 1957[2], with F. Lachower); 2 (1961); Baer, Spain, 1 (1961), ch. 6; idem, *Ha-Reka ha-Histori shel ha-"Raya Meheimna."* in: *Zion*, 5 (1940); E. Gottlieb, *Ha-Kabbalah be-Kitvei Rabbenu Baḥya ben Asher* (1970); K. Preis, *Die Medizin in der Kabbala*, in: MGWJ, 35 (1928); G. Vajda, *Le traité pseudo-Maimonidien – Neuf chapitres sur l'unité du Dieu*, in: *Archives d'Histoire Doctrinale et Litteraire du Moyen Age* (1954), 83–98; J. Finkel, *The Alexandrian Tradition and the Midrash ha-Ne'elam*, in: *Leo Jung Jubilee Volume* (1962), 77–103; S.A. Heller-Wilensky, *Li-she'elat Meḥabro shel Sefer Sha'ar ha-Shamayim ha-Meyuḥas le-Avraham ibn Ezra*, in: *Tarbiz*, 32 (1963), 277–95; A.I. Altmann, *Li-She'elat Ba'aluto shel Sefer Ta'amei ha-Mitzvot ha-Meyuḥas le-R. Yiẓḥak ibn Farḥi*, in: KS, 40 (1965), 256–412; idem, *Midrash al Pi Derekh ha-Kabbalah ha-Penimit al Bereshit 24*, in: *Sefer ha-Yovel Tiferet Yisrael… Brodie* (1966), 57–65; M.C. Weiler, *Iyyunim ba-Terminologiyah ha-Kabbalit shel R. Yosef Gikatilla ve-Yaḥaso la-Rambam*, in: HUCA, 32 (1966), 13–44; I. Gruenwald, *Shenei Shirim shel ha-Mekubal Yosef Gikatilla*, in: *Tarbiz*, 36 (1967), 73–89. 14th CENTURY: G. Scholem, *Seridei Sifro shel R. Shem Tov ibn Gaon al Yesodot Torat ha-Sefirot*, in: KS, 8 (1931/32), 397–408, 534–42; 9 (1932/33), 126–33; idem, *Perusho shel R. Yiẓḥak de-min Ako le-Perek Rishon shel Sefer Yeẓirah*, in: KS, 31 (1955/56), 379–96; idem, *Li-Yedi'at ha-Kabbalah bi-Sefarad Erev ha-Gerush* in: *Tarbiz*, 24 (1954/55), 167–206; G. Vajda, *Les observations critiques d'Isaac d'Acco sur les ouvrages de Juda ben Nissim ibn Malka*, in: REJ, 115 (1956), 25–71; idem, *Un chapitre de l'histoire du conflict entre la-Kabbale et la Philosophie. La polemique anti-intellectualiste de Joseph ben Shalom Ashkenazi de Catalogne, in: Archives d'Histoire Doctrinale et Litteraire du Moyen Age* (1957), 45–144; idem, *Deux chapitres du 'Guide des Egares' repenses par un Kabbaliste*, in: *Mélanges' Etienne Gilson* (1959), 651–9; idem, *Recherches sur la synthese philosophico – kabbalistique de Samuel ibn Motot*, in: *Archives d'Histoire Doctrinale et Litteraire du Moyen Age* (1961), 29–63; D.S. Lewinger, *R. Shemtov b. Abraham b. Gaon*, in: *Sefunot*, 7 (1963), 9–29. AFTER THE EXPULSION FROM SPAIN – THE NEW CENTER IN SAFED: P. Bloch, *Die Kabbalah auf ihrem Hoehepunkt und ihre Meister* (1905); A. Ben-Israel, *Alumot* (1952); Moses Cordovero, *Palm Tree of Deborah*, tr. by L. Jacobs (1960); R.J.Z. Werblowsky, *Joseph Karo, Lawyer and Mystic* (1962); M. Benayahu, *Toledot ha-Ari* (1967); idem, *R. Yehudah b. R. Mosheh Botini ve-Sifro 'Yesod Mishneh Torah,"* in: *Sinai* (1955), 240–74; idem, *Hanhagot Mekubalei Ẓefat be-Meron*, in: *Sefunot*, 6 (1962), 11–40; D. Tamar, *Meḥkarim be-Toledot ha-Yehudim be-Erez Yisrael u-ve-Italyah* (1970); S. Assaf, *La-Pulmus al Hadpasat Sifrei ha-Kabbalah*, in: *Sinai*, 5 (1939/40), 360–5; G. Scholem, *Shtar ha-Hitkashrut shel Talmidei ha-Ari*, in: *Zion*, 5 (1940), 133–60; idem, *Yisrael Sarug – Talmid ha-Ari?*; *ibid.*, 214–41; J. Dan, *"R. Yosef Karo – Ba'al Halakha u-Mistikan" le-R.J.Z. Werblowsky*, in: *Tarbiz*, 33 (1964), 89–96. LATER TIMES: M. Wiener, *Die Lyrik der Kabbalah: eine Anthologie* (1920); A. Bension, *Sar Shalom Sharabi* (1930); Y. Kafah, *Sefer Milḥamot ha-Shem* (1931); F. Lachower, *Al Gevul ha-Yashan ve-ha-Ḥadash* (1951); S. Ratner, *Le-Or ha-Kabbalah* (1962); H. Weiner, *Nine and One Half Mystics; the Kabbala Today* (1969); E. Tcherikower, *Di Komune fun Yerushalayimer Mekubolim 'Ahavas Sholom' in Mitn dem 18ten Yorhundert*, in: *Historishe Shriften fun* YIVO, 2 (1937), 115–39; I. Gruenwald, *Le-Toledot ha-Mekubalim be-Ungaryah* in: *Sinai*, 24 (1949), 2–22; G. Scholem, *Zur Literatur der letzten Kabbalisten in Deutschland*, in: *Siegfried Moses zum 75. Geburtstag* (1962), 359–76. LURIANIC KABBALAH: I. Tishby, *Torat ha-Ra ve-ha-Kelippah be-Kabbalat ha-Ari* (1942); S.A. Horodezky, *Torat ha-Kabbalah shel Rabbi Yiẓḥak Ashkenazi ve-Rabbi Ḥayyim Vital* (1947); L.I. Krakovsky, *Kabbalah: The Light of Redemption* (1950); J. von Kempski, *Ẓimẓum: Die Schoepfung aus dem Nichts*, in: *Merkur*, 14 (1960), 1107–26. KABBALAH AND PANTHEISM: M.S. Freystadt, *Philosophia cabbalistica et Pantheismus* (1832); J. Ben-Shlomo, *Torat ha-Elohut shel R. Moshe Cordovero* (1965). MAN AND HIS SOUL: M.D.G. Langer, *Die Erotik der Kabbala* (1923). EXILE AND REDEMPTION: G. Scholem, *The Messianic Idea in Judaism and Other Essays* (1971); I. Klausner, *'Kol Mevaser' le-Rabbi Yehudah Alkalay*, in: *Shivat Ẓiyyon*, 2 (1953), 42–62; H.H. Ben-Sasson, in: *Sefer Yovel le-Yiẓḥak Baer* (1960), 216–27. THE TORAH AND ITS SIGNIFICANCE: G. Scholem, *The Meaning of the Torah in Jewish Mysticism*, in: *On the Kabbalah and its Symbolism* (1965), 32–86; E. Lipiner, *Idiyalogiya fun Yidishn Alef-Beis* (1967). THE MYSTIC WAY: Dov Baer of Lubavitch, *Tract on Ecstasy*, tr. by L. Jacobs (1963); A.J. Heschel, *Al Ru'aḥ ha-Kodesh bi-Yemei ha-Beinayim*, in: *Sefer ha-Yovel… A. Marx* (1950), 175–208; G. Vajda, *Continence, mariage et vie mystique selon la doctrine du Judaïsme*, in: *Mystique et Continence, Études Carmélitaines* (1952), 82–92; R.J.Z. Werblowsky, *Tikkun Tefillot le-Rabbi Shelomoh ha-Levi ibn Alkabets*, in: *Sefunot*, 6 (1962), 137–82. PRACTICAL KABBALAH: G. Brecher, *Das Transcendentale, Magie und magische Heilarten im Talmud* (1850); D. Joel, *Der Aberglaube und die Stellung des Judenthums zu demselben*, 2 vols. (1881–83); L. Blau, *Das altjuedische Zauberwesen* (1898); J. Guenzig, *Die Wundermaenner im juedischen Volke* (1921); J. Trachtenberg, *Jewish Magic and Superstition* (1939); T. Schrire, *Hebrew Amulets: Their Decipherment and Interpretation* (1966); J. Dan, *Sippurim Dimonologiyim mi-Kitvei R. Yehuda he-Ḥasid*, in: *Tarbiz*, 30 (1961), 273–89; idem, *Sarei Kos ve-Sarei Bohen*, *ibid.*, 32 (1963), 359–69; I. Shahar, *The Feuchtwanger Collection of Jewish Tradition and Art* (Heb., 1971), 227–305 (amulets). INFLUENCE OF KABBALAH ON JUDAISM: G. Scholem, *On the Kabbalah and its Symbolism* (1965), 118–57; I. Weinstock, *Be-Ma'aglei ha-Nigleh ve-ha-Nistar* (1969), 249–69; I.D. Wilhelm, *Sidrei Tikkunim*, in: *Alei Ayin* (1948–52), 125–46; J. Avida, *Ha-Malakhim ha-Memunim al ha-Shofer ha-Ma'alim et ha-Teki'ot*, in: *Sinai*, 33 (1953), 3–23; M. Benayahu, *Hanhagot Mekubalei Ẓefat be-Meron*, in: *Sefunot*, 6 (1962), 11–40; Y. Yaari, *Toledot ha-Hillula be-Meron*, in: *Tarbiz*, 31 (1962), 72–101. CHRISTIAN KABBALAH: Johannes Pistorius, *Artis Cabalisticae Scriptores*, 1 (Basel, 1587); Johann Steudner, *Juedische* ABC *Schul vom Geheimnuss dess dreyeiningen wahren Gottes…* (Augsburg, 1665); F.C. Oetinger, *Denkmal der Lehrtafel der Prinzessin Antonia* (Tuebingen, 1763); D. Saurat, *Literature and Occult Tradition: Studies in Philosophical Poetry* (1930); E. Anagnine, *G. Pico della Mirandola: sincretismo religioso-filosofico 1463–1494* (1937); J.L. Blau, *The Christian Interpretation of the Cabala in the Renaissance* (1944); F. Secret, *Le Zohar chez les Kab-*

balistes chrétiens de la Renaissance (1958); idem, *Les Kabbalistes chrétiens de la Renaissance* (1964); idem, in: *Bibliothèque d'Humanisme et Renaissance*, 17 (1955), 292–5; 20 (1958), 547–55; idem, *Les debuts du kabbalisme chrétien en Espagne et son histoire à la Renaissance*, in: *Sefarad*, 17 (1957), 36–48; idem, *Le symbolisme de la kabbale chrétienne dans la 'Scechina' de Egidio da Viterbo*, in: *Archivo di Filosofia* (1958), 131–54; idem, *Pedro Ciruelo: Critique de la Kabbale et de son usage par les Chrétiens*, in: *Sefarad*, 19 (1959), 48–77; idem, in: *Rinascimento*, 11 (1960), 169–92; 14 (1963), 251–68; idem, *L'hermeneutique de G. Postel*, in: *Archivo di Filosofia* (1963), 91–117; idem, *Le soleil chez les Kabbalistes chrétiens*, in: *Le Soleil à la Renaissance* (1965), 213–40; idem, *Nouvelles précisions sur Flavius Mithridates maître de pic de la Mirandole et traducteur de commentaires de Kabbale*, in: *L'opera e il pensiero di G. Pico della Mirandola*, 2 (1965), 169–87; idem, *"L' Ensis Pauli" de Paulus de Heredia*, in: *Sefarad*, 26 (1966), 79–102, 253–71; idem, *La Revelacion de Saint Pablo*, in: *Sefarad*, 28 (1968), 45–67; idem, *Guillaume Postel et son Interprétation du Candélabre de Moyse* (1966); G. Postel, *Apologies et Retractions* (1972); E. Benz, *Die Christliche Kabbala: Ein Stiefkind der Theologie* (1958); C. Wirszubski, *Sermo de passione Domini* (1963); idem, *Giovanni Pico's Companion to Kabbalistic Symbolism*, in: *Studies... G. Scholem* (1967), 353–62; idem, in: *Journal of the Warburg and Courtauld Institutes*, 32 (1969), 177–99; idem, *Mors Osculi, Poetic Theology and Kabbala in Renaissance Thought*, in: *Proceedings of the Israel Academy of Sciences and Humanities* (1971); M. Brod, *Johannes Reuchlin und sein Kampf* (1965); G. Scholem, *Zur Geschichte der Anfaenge der Christlichen Kabbala*, in: *Essays... Leo Baeck* (1954), 158–93; R.J.Z. Werblowsky, *Milton and the Conjectura Cabbalistica*, in: *Journal of the Warburg and Courtauld Institutes*, 18 (1955), 90–113; W.A. Schulze, *Schelling und die Kabbala*, in: *Judaica*, 13 (1957), 65–98, 143–70, 210, 232; idem, *Der Einfluss der Kabbala auf die Cambridger Platoniker Cudworth und More, ibid.*, 23 (1967), 75–126, 136–60, 193–240; I. Sonne, *Mekomah shel ha-Kabbalah bi-Fe'ulat ha-Hassatah shel ha-Kenesiyah ba-Me'ah ha-Sheva-Esreh*, in: *Bitzaron*, 36 (1957), 7–12, 57–66; I.F. Baer, *Torat ha-Kabbalah be-Mishnato ha-Kristologit shel Avner mi-Burgos*, in: *Tarbiz*, 27 (1958), 278–89; R.T. Llewellyn, *Jacob Boehmes Kosmogonie in ihrer Beziehung zur Kabbala*, in: *Antaios*, 5 (1963), 237–50; F. Haeussermann, in: *Blaetter fuer Wuertembergische Kirchengeschichte*, 66–67 (1966/67), 65–153; 68–69 (1968/69), 207–346. RESEARCH ON THE KABBALAH: G. Scholem, *Die Erforschung der Kabbala von Reuchlin bis zur Gegenwart* (1969); G. Kressel, *Kitvei Elyakim ha-Milzahagi*, in: KS, 17 (1940), 87–94; G. Vajda, *Les origines et le développement de la Kabbale juive d'après quelques travaux récents*, in: RHR (1948), 120–67; idem, *Recherches récentes sur l'ésotérisme juif (1947–1953; 1954–1962)*, in: RHR (1955), 69–92; (1963), 191–212.

[Gershom Scholem]

KABBALAH IN THE LATE 20TH CENTURY

During and after World War II, numerous kabbalistic and ḥasidic centers were destroyed or weakened as a result of the Holocaust and the relocation of the Jewish communities of the Middle East and North Africa. However, powerful new centers were soon established, mostly in Israel and the United States. As a result, kabbalistic literature was written, published, and studied on a scale totally unknown even during its previous "Golden Ages," such as the 13th and 16th centuries. This quantitative expansion accelerated the appearance of new forms of kabbalistic creativity. Thus, 20th-century Kabbalah often markedly diverged from its classical roots and acquired a distinctive modern (and even post-modern) character. This can be best appreciated by considering several themes, which shall be enumerated after a brief presentation of central schools and figures.

Central Schools and Figures

THE ḤASIDIC WORLD. Large parts of the ḥasidic world were destroyed during the Holocaust. One example of a unique ḥasidic group devoted to intense mystical practice which was almost totally destroyed was the circle of Kalonymus Kalman Shapira (1889–1943) in Warsaw. The post-Holocaust recovery of the various ḥasidic schools was one of the most striking quantitative developments in the history of Kabbalah in the 20th century. The most influential ḥasidic school was that of *Chabad-Lubavitch. Under the leadership of its last rebbes, Joseph Isaac (1880–1950) and Menahem Mendel *Schneersohn (1902–1994), who operated from New York, Lubavitch expanded into a worldwide network, which utilized sophisticated technology to propagate its mystical and messianic doctrine (on the latter, see below). The late 20th century also saw the expansion of Braslav ḥasidism (which follows the leadership of Naḥman of Braslav) from a small sect into a diverse popular movement. Leaders of various branches of this school included Israel Odesser (1905?–1994), Eliezer Berland (1937–) and Jacob Meir Schecter (1931–). Numerous secular Israeli cultural figures went through a process of "return" and joined one of these branches. In the United States, the teachings of Naḥman of Braslav were popularized by the kabbalistic writer Aryeh *Kaplan (1934–1983), who was also one of the pioneers of the "return" movement.

THE NON-ḤASIDIC ULTRA-ORTHODOX. One of the most striking developments of 20th-century Kabbalah was the "kabbalization" of the non-ḥasidic Ultra-Orthodox world and especially the *Musar (Ethics) movement. The founders of this school, such as Israel *Salanter (1809–1883), were initially reserved towards the study of Kabbalah, preferring to focus on the transformation of everyday behavior and feeling. However, during the course of the 20th century, Musar thinkers such as Judah Leib Bloch (1860–1930) of Telz Yeshivah, Isaac *Hutner (1906–1980) of New York, and Shelomo Wolbe (1915–2005) of Israel often resorted to mystical doctrines in developing its psychological theory and praxis.

THE ORIENTAL JEWISH WORLD. During the first part of the 20th century, Oriental (Sephardi) kabbalists continued to engage in traditional kabbalistic practice in the Near East and North Africa. The most prominent among these included Joseph Ḥayyim of Baghdad (1834–1909) and his student Judah Petaya (1859–1942). In the middle of the century, the displacement of Oriental Jews from these centers significantly disrupted these activities. However, as a response to its social and cultural marginalization in its new home in Israel, the Oriental world enjoyed a marked resurgence during the course of the last two decades of the century. This included the establishment of numerous "Yeshivot for Kabbalists" as well as the expansion of existing institutions, such as Bet El, Aḥvat Shalom, and Ha-Ḥayyim ve-ha-Shalom. One of the most prominent amongst the leaders of these yeshivot was Ovadiah Haddayah (1891–1969), who incorporated kabbalistic doctrines in his halakhic (legal) writing and public discourses. These influential kabbalists also included figures with a more magical orientation, such as Israel Abu-Hatzeira (1889–1984), who acquired a mass following as well as a marked effect on political and economic life in Israel. The most prominent of contemporary Oriental kabbalists are R. Isaac Kadoorie (1904?–2006) and Jacob Moses Hillel, himself an opponent of magical practices.

RELIGIOUS ZIONISM. Another major development was the rise of the messianic branch of Religious Zionism. This group is led by the followers of the first chief rabbi of Palestine, Abraham Isaac *Kook (1865–1935), whose writings reflect intense mystical practice and thought. This is most apparent in his diaries (*Shemonah Kevaẓim*, published 1999), which were previously censored by his followers, partly in order to obscure this aspect of his thought. His heirs included David Cohen (1887–1972), who further developed the mystical aspects of his thought, as well as Jacob Meir Harlap (1883–1951), and Ẓevi Judah *Kook (1891–1982) who emphasized the nationalistic elements of his doctrine. The most prominent contemporary leader of this school is Ẓevi Israel Tau (1938–) of the Har ha-Mor Yeshivah. Various aspects of the nationalistic interpretation of Kabbalah offered by Rabbi Kook and his disciples will be discussed below at length.

NON-JEWISH KABBALAH. Another central development was the proliferation of kabbalistic literature in the non-Jewish world. One result of this change was the flourishing of Christian interpretations of Kabbalah, as well as various "New Age" renderings of kabbalistic thought (see below). Another was the "marketing" of popular versions of Kabbalah to the non-Jewish world by some of the followers of Judah Leib Ashlag (1885–1954). Towards the end of the century, the Internet, as well as popular entertainment figures such as Madonna, played a prominent role in these processes. At the same time, more academic figures, such as the philosopher Jacques *Derrida (1930–2004) and the writer and theorist Umberto Eco (1932–), were also substantially influenced by kabbalistic ideas and images.

The Ideology of Dissemination

A distinct characteristic of 20th-century Kabbalah was the abandonment of earlier strictures placed on the study and propagation of kabbalistic literature, which was traditionally regarded as esoteric lore. This reservation was replaced by an ideology of mass dissemination of kabblistic doctrines. The propagation of Kabbalah was to be accomplished through modern and popular interpretations designed to translate often obscure texts into accessible forms. Numerous 20th-century kabbalists regarded the spread of Kabbalah as an expression of the imminence, or even advent, of the messianic epoch – and sometimes even as the means of bringing it about.

Two of the figures mentioned above developed an elaborate ideological rationale for the dissemination of Kabbalah. Abraham Isaac Kook wrote that he was vouchsafed a prophetic revelation which legitimated the overriding of the talmudic prohibition against the revelation of mysteries. Furthermore, he saw the creation of a "popular literature" based on Kabbalah as a means towards the return of prophecy. Kook predicted that "the chosen will become multitudes"; in other words, that his small circle will eventually become a mass movement guided by this literature.

Judah Leib Ashlag expressed his belief in the rendering of Kabbalah into popular terms through a large-scale project of translation and interpretation of canonical kabbalistic texts (as in his "Ha-Sulam" series on the Zohar). Interpretation centered on a psychological re-reading of key kabbalistic concepts, to be described below. Ashlag's heirs, and especially Philip *Berg (b. 1929, a breakaway student of Ashlag's disciple R. Judah Brandwein (1904–1969)), utilized aggressive marketing and sophisticated technology in order to transform Ashlag's ideology into a global mass "product."

At the same time, the new ideology of dissemination was not unopposed. Various kabbalists, including members of Rabbi Kook's circle and some adherents of the Musar school, insisted on the continuing restriction of the study of Kabbalah to the select few. This internal opposition was joined by certain Orthodox Jewish figures, such as Yeshayahu *Leibovitz (1903–1994), whose internalization of modern rationalism led them to descry the Kabbalah itself.

National Mysticism

The 20th century was marked by the proliferation of nationalistic interpretations of Kabbalah. These provided substantial support for the Zionist movement, and especially its more chauvinistic branches, such as the *Gush Emunim movement, which established numerous settlements in the territories occupied in 1967.

The concept of power played a key role in this discourse. While the Ultra-Orthodox branch of Jewry maintained the split between earthly and supernal power that originated after the destruction of the Second Temple, Religious Zionism sought to merge these domains. The latter attempt is nowhere more apparent than in the mystical vision of Abraham Isaac Kook. Kook saw the return of the Jews to embodied and seemingly mundane forms of empowerment as an expression of the power of the divine, rather than as its denial (as claimed by the Ultra-Orthodox). Furthermore, in his vision, the manifestation of Jewish power through the return to the Land of Israel would theurgically enhance the power of the divine domain. In one passage, Kook wrote that "our state, the state of Israel" is "the foundation of God's throne in the world."

However, Kook's message was far from unequivocal. In another passage, written in response to the horrors of World War I, he envisioned the postponemet of the establishment of the state until such time that it would be possible to forgo the "barbarity" of violence and war. This complexity, though reflected in the works of one of his close students, David Cohen, was not maintained when the Kookist school became transformed into a mass movement. Kook's son, Ẓevi Judah, transformed his father's mystical reflections into an ideological platform, which was galvanized by the 1967 war and the occupation of the ancestral territories of Judea and Samaria (the West Bank). Ẓevi Judah and his students unequivocally taught that the political and military might of Israel is "one" with the power of God.

Nationalistic interpretations of the kabbalistic teachings on divine power may also be found in other streams of 20th century Jewish mysticism – most notably in the messianic thought of the last Rebbe of Lubavitch. One of his disciples, the kabbalist Isaac Ginsburg (1944–), composed a kabbalistic treatise detailing the theurgical benefits of the massacre committed in Hebron by Baruch Goldstein in 1995! Other nationalistic interpreters of Kabbalah included Ẓevi Ribek (1910–1995), whose work *Al Ketz ha-Tikkun* contains a detailed theosophical explanation of the fall of the Soviet Bloc and the Israeli-Arab conflict, and the French teacher Judah Leon Ashkenazi (1922–1996).

Psychological Interpretations

Alongside the proliferation of nationalistic interpretations, some 20th-century kabbalists offered an extensive psychological reinterpretation of classical kabbalistic symbols and ideas. The most prominent of these is the elaborate system constructed by Judah Leib Ashlag. Ashlag redefined the main concern of the canonical texts of Kabbalah as the struggle between two psychological forces – the "will to receive," or the egoistical impulse, and "the will to bestow" – the altruistic impulse. The essentially universalistic nature of this proposal ensured the smooth reception of Ashlagian doctrine in broad non-Jewish circles after his death.

As in the case of the nationalistic interpretation, the psychological reading includes a theurgical dimension: According to Ashlag, the highest form of giving is that of granting God pleasure by performing His will on earth. By doing so, Man imitates God's own generous bestowal of pleasure on Man. Actually, the greatest gift that God bestows on Man is the ability to give back to Him. Thus, one should only accept God's good with the intention of fulfilling the divine desire to give, and thus dialectically, receiving becomes giving. For Ashlag, the observance of Jewish law, and especially its social aspects, can be seen as training in overcoming one's innate egotistical tendencies and developing the capacity to give.

However, in this doctrine, the heart of Judaism is the Kabbalah, rather than the Law, for it is the former lore which uncovers the true intent of the Law, and most effectively leads to psychic transformation. While rationalistic cognition merely perpetuates the logic of self-interest, transcending rationality through mysticism enables a shift to a different order of being, which is characterized by pure generosity.

Here, psychology leads into social psychology: According to Ashlag, the elect or *ẓaddikim* (righteous) are those who manifest the power of giving, as well as possessing access to the trans-rational. Therefore the ordinary individual should train to overcome his egotism by setting aside his own reason and accepting the directives of mystical leaders, such as Ashlag himself. This social doctrine was especially developed by some of Ashlag's successors, such as his son Baruch Ashlag (1907–1991), and Baruch's own heir, Michael Leitman, who expressed its social implications through their centralized leadership of the Bnei Baruch sect.

In one text (published in the collection *Ha-Ummah*), Ashlag's teachings on altruism are translated into an affinity to Socialism, which he found to express this ideal over and above other political systems. However, Ashlag warned that the perversion of Socialism in the Soviet Union was a sign that the implementation of this ideal in actual practice was premature and required the development of purer forms of altruism, which would overcome class warfare. In his vision, these would be cultivated by the study and practice of Kabbalah.

Besides Ashlag, several other figures in contemporary Kabbalah (such as Isaac Ginsburg) offered psychological renderings of its teachings. In the non-Jewish world such universalistic approaches were quite popular, as evidenced by the Jungian interpretation given to the Kabbalah by "Zeev Ben Shimeon Halevi" (Warren Kenton) in his *Kabbalah and Psychology*, as well as numerous "New Age" renderings of kabbalistic ideas. However, the influence of modern and postmodern psychology has penetrated into the most Orthodox of circles.

A striking example is that of the Musar (Ethics) movement. As mentioned above, its proponents initially insisted that their focus was on human failings and potential rather than divine realms. However, in the course of its development in the yeshivot of Eastern Europe, the Musar school increasingly turned to Kabbalah in order to embellish its elaborate psychological doctrine. The results of this shift could be later seen in the works of major Musar teachers of the late 20th century, such as Shelomo Wolbe and Chaim Friedlander (1923–1986).

Sacred Space and Sacred Persons

During the 20th century, the pivotal event of return to the Land of Israel intensified kabbalistic discourse on sacred space. On the one hand, certain kabbalists greatly enhanced the role of the land within their mystical schema. At times, however, the growing importance of the chosen person, or *ẓaddik*, supplanted the centrality of sacred space. In other words, the body of the saint was regarded as the true sacred space in certain kabbalistic texts.

Already in classical Kabbalah, one can find two basic models of sacred space; as an actual geographical location, and as an internal experiential state or site of consciousness. In general, Rabbi Kook and his followers developed the first model, and in fact reached new heights of valorization of the Land of Israel. For instance, Jacob Moses Harlap wrote (in his *Mei Marom*) that the Land of Israel is destined to reveal itself as identical with the Infinite, or the highest level of divinity! In general, the leaders of the Kookian school saw themselves as the new prophets, whose higher inspiration was enhanced by the return to the Land, and the resultant renewal of the spirit of the Jewish nation.

However, in the previously censored diaries of Abraham Isaac Kook himself, one can discern a different theme, which echoes the second, more internal model. He wrote of Moses as an archetype of the spiritual leader whose level transcends that of the actual land, as his vision entails the transformation of the entire world into sacred space. Certain textual parallels disclose that R. Kook saw himself as a leader of this type (or *higher ẓaddik*), and thus as equivalent to the "higher Land of Israel."

This tendency is far more readily apparent in 20th century Ḥasidism. During his last years, Menahem Mendel Schneersohn of Lubavitch rather openly affirmed the faith expressed by his followers that he was in fact the Messiah. In the voluminous messianic literature composed by the Rebbe and his faithful, it is stated that the redemption would begin at the residence of the Rebbe in New York City, as the dwelling place of the "leader of the generation" is the true sacred space.

As in the case of Rabbi Kook, the spiritual leader is one who can transform the entire world into sacred space. However, while Rabbi Kook felt that this leader should naturally commence this messianic project in the land of Israel, the Lubavitcher Rebbe took this model one step further: he developed an even stronger messianic doctrine, in which the leader is charged with redeeming the Diaspora, and is thus absolved or even prevented from entering Israel prior to his coronation as "the King, the Messiah."

Braslav Ḥasidism developed a further variant on this model. For these ḥasidim, the true sacred space is R. Naḥman's grave in Uman, Ukraine. During the late 20th century, this became a site for mass pilgrimage. As in the case of Lubavitch, the residence of the saint was seen as the true sacred space. In this case, however, it is his grave rather than his home. From a broader perspective, the displacement of concrete sacred space can be attributed to the decline of concrete location in an age of globalization. This process facilitated the creation of "transnational" sacred sites, such as Uman or the Rebbe's house in Brooklyn.

The Loosening of the Link to *Halakhah* (Jewish Law)

A final theme to be considered is that of the loosening of the connection between contemporary Kabbalah and normative Jewish practice (*halakhah*) during the 20th century, and especially its last decades. Although this process partly reflected the expansion of Kabbalah beyond the boundaries of the Orthodox and indeed the Jewish world, it was paralleled by developments within Orthodox circles.

The decoupling of Kabbalah and *halakhah* can be located already in the censored writings of Rabbi Kook – the first chief rabbi of Palestine! In part, this expresses his self-image as a "higher *ẓaddik*." For Kook, such saints are not bound by the rules of rote halakhic observance, as they should remain free of all bondage, including that of the Law. Furthermore, Kook expressed sympathy for the non-halakhic conduct of the secular Zionists. In his view, this reflected the exalted level of their souls, which should not be judged by legalistic standards.

Rabbi Kook's openness towards transgression of the law is closely related to his prophetic self-perception. Traditionally, a prophet is empowered to authorize a temporary transgression of the *halakhah*, and Rabbi Kook definitely regarded himself as such a figure. However, in one previously censored passage, he expresses the fear that he actually may have been a false prophet. This self-doubt may have led him to moderate the public expression of his radical views.

Another movement in which a looser connection to the law was readily apparent was the "Neo-Ḥasidism" of the late 20th century. Both in Israel and North America, figures such as Shlomo *Carlebach (1925–1994) anchored their avoidance of strict adherence to the *halakhah* in an updated interpretation of ḥasidic thought. One of the central sources for this move was the radical corpus composed by Mordecai Joseph Leiner (1801–1854), the Izbicher Rebbe. Neo-Hasidism delved into the works of this earlier figure, who espoused transcendence of the letter of the law in favor of deeper spiritual intuitions.

As in the case of sacred space, the displacement of halakhic norms owes much to the rise of the figure of the saint. As we have seen in the case of Rabbi Kook, spiritual virtuosi are seen as transcending mundane norms. Here developments in Jewish mysticism reflected more global phenomena. These included the marginal place of the *Shari'a* (Islamic law) in Western Sufism, the antinomian behavior of certain Christian mystics (such as Thomas Merton, 1915–1968), and the extreme conduct of American Buddhist leaders such as Chogyam Trungpa (1939–1987).

Contemporary Kabbalah and Classical Kabbalah

The proliferation of Jewish mysticism in the late 20th century was part of a more global phenomena – that of the "New Age" movement. Empirical sociological studies of this movement showed that to a marked extent "New Age" spirituality increasingly displaced traditional forms of religious practice.

This was also the case for Kabbalah: While the core of most branches of classical Kabbalah was the idea and practice of influencing the divine realm through observance of Jewish law, in almost all 20th century schools, this theurgical goal gave way to focus on the human realm, whether from a national or psychological point of view. The radical implications of this shift were noticed and critiqued already at the beginning of the century, by more traditionally oriented kabbalists such as Solomon Eliashiv (1841–1928), the author of the "Leshem Shevo ve-Aḥlamah" series.

While in earlier periods the kabbalistic endeavor was subsumed to normative religious pursuits, over the course of the century the propagation of the Kabbalah became a goal in itself. Thus, the halakhic restrictions placed on the dissemination of this lore, together with the notion of esotericism, were the first "victims" of this radical change. At the same time, the authority of halakhic experts was increasingly undermined by that of the prophet, saint, or would-be Messiah.

An interesting sociological expression of the new centrality of the Kabbalah was the establishment of rural communities dedicated to the propagation of kabbalistic doctrine and the intensification of kabbalistic practice, such as the Or ha-Ganuz community of followers of Judah Leib Ashlag (in Galilee), or the Bat Ayin settlement in the West Bank, which was established by followers of Isaac Ginsburg.

The rise of magic was another important result of this cultural change. Though this was also part of a more global phenomenon, it had distinct manifestations within the kabbalistic world. Classical kabbalists usually frowned on "practical," or magical, applications of their teachings, or saw them as secondary to the theurgical task. Yet late 20th century kabbalists, from the Oriental world to Philip Berg's popular version, increasingly stressed the benefits of kabbalistic practice for marital, economic, and political success! This dramatic shift reflected not only the more global tendency towards weakening of rationalistic beliefs in this period, but also the essentially pragmatic, and often commercial, nature of late 20th century Kabbalah.

Another marked move away from more classical kabbalistic practice pertains to the role of women. One of the most revolutionary characteristics of late 20th century Kabbalah was the emergence of female mystical teachers, perhaps for the first time in the history of Jewish mysticism. These included the Israeli medium and mystic Yemima Avital (1929–1999), as well as American and Israel neo-ḥasidic teachers.

BIBLIOGRAPHY: PRIMARY SOURCES: Y.L. Ashlag, *In the Shadow of the Ladder: Introductions to Kabbalah* (2003), idem, *Ten Luminous Emanations* (1973), Z. Ben Shimon Halevi, *Kabbalah and Psychology* (1986), Y. Ginsburgh, *Transforming Darkness into Light: Kabbalah and Psychology* (2002), A.I. Kook, *The Lights of Penitence, The Moral Principles, Lights of Holiness, Essays, Letters and Poems* (1978), T.Y. Kook, *Torat Eretz Yisrael: The Teachings of ha-Rav Tzvi Yehudah* (1991), K.K. Shapira, *Conscious Community: a Guide to Inner Work* (1996). STUDIES: Y. Bilu, "The Making of Modern Saints: Manufactured Charisma and the Abu-Hatseiras of Israel," in: *American Ethnologist*, 19 (1992), 672–87, R. Elior, "The Lubavitch Messianic Resurgence: the Historical and Mystical Background," in: P. Schafer and M.R. Cohen (eds.), *Towards the Millenium: Messianic Expectations from the Bible to Waco* (1998), 383–408, J. Garb, "Rabbi Kook and His Sources: from Kabbalistic Historiosophy to National Mysticism," in: M. Sharon (ed.), *Studies in Modern Religions, Religious Movements and the Babhi-Bahai Faiths* (2004), 77–96, idem, "*Yeḥide ha-Segulot Yihiyu la-'adarim*": *Iyunim be-Kabbalat ha-Me'ah ha-Esrim* (2005), W. Hanegraaff, *New Age Religion and WesternCulture: Esotericism in the Mirror of Secular Thought* (1998), D. Hansel, "The Origin in the Thought of Rabbi Yehuda Ashlag: Simsum of God or Simsum of the World." in: *Kabbalah*, 7 (2002), 37–46, P. Heelas et al, *The Spiritual Revolution*: (2005), B. Huss, "Lo lishol kol she'elot: Gershom Scholem ve-Ḥeker ha-Mistikah ha-Yehudit Bat Yameinu," in: *Pe'amim*, 94–95 (2003), 57–72, B. Ish Shalom and S. Rosenberg (eds.), *The World of Rav Kook's Thought* (1991), L. Kaplan (ed.), *Rabbi Abraham Isaac Kook and Jewish Spirituality* (1995), S. Magid, "Rainbow Hasidism in America: The Maturation of Jewish Renewal," *The Reconstructionist*, 68 (2004), 34–60, A. Ravitzky, *Messianism, Zionism and Jewish Religious Radicalism* (1997).

[Jonathan Garb (2nd ed.)]

KABBALAH STUDIES

The present survey of scholarship in the field of Jewish mysticism attempts to point to the main lines of development in the generation following 1973. However, in order to better understand them we shall first briefly survey the fundamental phases of previous scholarship, periodize them, and then delineate the most important areas in which scholarship developed in the last decades.

Kabbalah Studies in the 20th Century: Three Main Stages from 1923 to 1998

The most influential event for future studies of Jewish mysticism was the arrival of Gershom *Scholem in the Land of Israel in 1923 and the foundation, through his scholarship and teaching, of the Jerusalem school of studies in Jewish mysticism. In that same year his first book, his doctoral thesis on the book of *Bahir*, was published. This is a convenient starting point that neatly lends itself to a threefold division of the following 75 years into three phases of scholarship of roughly equal length which may be described as the creative, the reproductive, and the critical. This threefold scheme applies mainly to developments in the study of Kabbalah in Israel rather than abroad.

1923–1948: THE CREATIVE PERIOD. This phase spans the period between Scholem's arrival in Israel and the establishment of the State of Israel. It is characterized by the intensive production of a wide-ranging series of studies, written and published in three languages, Hebrew, English, and German, mostly by Gershom Scholem. It is in this period that a clear outline for an historical understanding of Jewish mysticism emerged. The many articles of Scholem in *Kiryat Sefer, Tarbiz,* and *Zion* represented a comprehensive and mature exposition of Scholem's insights, and those of his followers. This is obvious in two major books written toward the end of the creative period: *Major Trends in Jewish Mysticism*, originally delivered as a series of lectures in New York in 1939 and published in Jerusalem in 1941; and *Reshit ha-Kabbalah* ("Beginning of Kabbalah"), published in Hebrew in 1948. The two books complement one other, as Scholem himself once noted, covering all the main phases of Jewish mystical literatures. This is not the place to survey in detail Scholem's enormous influence on the historiography and phenomenology of Kabbalah, as this has been done several times by various writers. It should be pointed out that as creative as this period indeed was, it did not lack critical attitudes, especially toward Kabbalah scholarship in previous generations. During this phase, two other scholars were active in this field in Israel, both Scholem's students, who contributed significant studies. The most eminent was Isaiah *Tishby, who wrote an analysis of the Lurianic Kabbalah and printed a critical edition of an early kabbalistic text, and Chaim *Wirszubski, who wrote the first in-depth analyses of Shabbatean theosophy.

1948–1973: THE REPRODUCTIVE PERIOD. This phase saw the publication of still more studies of Jewish mysticism in Israel or by Israeli scholars abroad, most of which consolidated the findings and articulated in greater detail many of the theories first brought forth during the creative period. The most conspicuous evidence of the reproductive impulse is the fact that many of the chapters of Scholem's *Major Trends* become in this period full-fledged books. Thus, for example, Scholem himself contributed two books, one dealing with the first chapter, the *Hekhalot* literature, and his famous monograph on Sabbatai Sevi (*Shabbetai Ẓevi), first published in Hebrew in 1957 and then, in a much more elaborate English version, in 1973. Likewise, Tishby published in 1949 and 1961 his two volumes of *Mishnat ha-Zohar* paralleling in a way Scholem's two chapters on the Zohar in *Major Trends*. Joseph Dan published in 1968 his monograph on the esoteric theology of *Ḥasidei Ashkenaz and in the same year Rivka Schatz-Uffenheimer published her book on mystical, basically quietist aspects of Beshtian Ḥasidism. In fact, the single chapter in *Major Trends* which was not elaborated into a full-fledged monograph is that on Abraham *Abulafia, whose kabbalistic thought had to wait much longer for exposition. In fact, we may speak of a process of specialization, as each of the scholars mentioned above, with the exception of Scholem, analyzed only some part of the spectrum of mystical literature that had already been surveyed by the master. Though each of the students was destined to broaden his knowledge and studies to other fields, none of them offered an original picture of the whole field, based on his or her readings. Leaving aside for the moment *Major Trends*, another main contribution of Scholem's, which appeared in 1962, *Ursprung und Anfaenge der Kabbala*, is an expansion of the much shorter version published in 1948 as *Reshit ha-Kabbalah*.

The term reproductive does not intend solely to point to the external correspondences between the chapters in *Major Trends* and the subsequent monographs, including Scholem's own. The turning to details was in itself a sound development from the point of view of determining what was more important and what less. However, reproduction means much more the historical, phenomenological, and methodological continuity between Scholem's studies and those of his followers. If, for Scholem himself, the original thinker and writer, such continuity and elaboration is natural, it is much less so for other scholars. Little had been done to test Scholem's broad phenomenological and historical theories. With the major exception of the assaults of Baruch *Kurtzweil, who was an outsider from the point of view of Kabbalah scholarship, and an audacious critique of Scholem's *Sabbatai Sevi* by R.J. Zwi *Werblowsky, who was destined to retreat from his arguments and devote many years and much talent to translating the very book he so sharply criticized into an impeccable English, no methodological debates took place in the Scholemian school. In fact, the points made in these two critiques were never accepted, not even with qualifications, by Scholem or any member of his school. The single significant divergence to be noted between Scholem and his most important follower, Isaiah Tishby, has to do with the polemic concerning the interpretation of Ḥasidism in messianic or non-messianic terms: While Tishby, who developed Ben-Zion *Dinur's thesis about the messianic message of Ḥasidism, adduced more material from kabbalistic Lurianic sources contemporary with early Ḥasidism in order to make the point only roughly advanced by the historian, Scholem remained convinced that his, basically Buberian understanding of the role of messianism in early Ḥasidism, is the correct explanation for the emergence of this movement.

In this period, an excellent and isolated monograph was written by Werblowsky on the 16th-century paragon of Jewish culture, R. Joseph *Caro, which significantly differed from the main methodological line in Scholem's school. Another senior member of the inner circle of the Scholemian school, Joseph ben Shlomo, published in 1965 his analysis of R. Moses *Cordovero's theology, written from a much more philosophical point of view than the more common historical-philological products of his colleagues.

Another significant phenomenon commencing precisely in 1948 and remaining constant during the whole reproductive period is Scholem's attendance at the Eranos conferences in Ascona, Switzerland. In a long series of lectures delivered there and published in several languages, Scholem took on a number of the main concepts of Kabbalah. These lectures may be regarded as the most important contribution to the study of Kabbalah in this period, as it adopted a far more phenomenological than historical approach. However, though these lectures contributed tremendously to the explication of Scholem's phenomenology, most of the theories advanced in those expositions had already been adumbrated, and sometimes even fully explicated, in the studies he produced during the creative phase.

There are indications in Scholem that modern historical events were regarded as being useful in opening up the possibility of understanding the past, including the symbols of Kabbalah. The existential matrix of modern scholars was sometimes conceived of as serving as powerful filters. Thus, for example, we read in an essay by Scholem written toward the end of World War II: "In a generation that has witnessed a terrible crisis in Jewish history, the ideas of these medieval Jewish esoterics no longer seem so strange. We see with other eyes, and the obscure symbols strike us as worth clarifying."

The phrase "other eyes" presupposes that prior to the crisis brought on by the terrible news concerning the Holocaust, one could not indeed understand properly the "obscure symbols." The history of the Jews, or more concretely their experience in recent times, is capable, therefore, of producing a new understanding of kabbalistic symbolism. This retrospective reading of kabbalistic symbolism also assumes the potential relevance of kabbalistic symbols for events which might take place hundreds years later. A certain isomorphism makes possible an understanding of the earlier by the later, namely of medieval Kabbalah by modern scholars of Kabbalah, and vice versa. The experience of exile and redemption shared by kabbalists and by scholars of Kabbalah creates the epistemological circle. This is the systemic basis of what Scholem designated as the "productive" scholarship of Kabbalah, and its relevance for understanding history. Indeed, in another essay, Scholem returns to the affinity between the expulsion of the Jews from Spain and the Holocaust: "From a historical point of view, Luria's myth constitutes a response to the expulsion of the Jews from Spain, an event which more than any other in Jewish history down to the catastrophe of our time gave urgency to the question: why the exile of the Jews and what is their vocation in the world?"

The nexus between the Lurianic myth and the expulsion is hardly a matter of history. It is, if at all, a matter of psychology, of systemic restructuring of a complex theosophical lore: If the historical event that inspired the emergence of the Lurianic myth is unparalleled except by the recent catastrophe, is not the understanding of kabbalistic symbolism both easier and acutely relevant in the aftermath of the modern Holocaust? Is not scholarship an attempt to answer metaphysical questions about the meaning of national destiny and national vocation? The basic presupposition of Scholem and Tishby assumes a privileged historical and psychological status enjoyed by a certain academic school, which facilitates a proper understanding, hardly accessible to earlier scholars who did not endure the travails of historical catastrophes.

Isaiah Tishby, the other great scholar in Scholem's school, juxtaposes the negative attitude of 19th century scholars to Kabbalah to that of 20th century scholars, writing as follows:

> ... especially those of the last generation who were expelled from Paradise into the great desolation and are wandering on the paths of life, divided and perplexed, without a compass and without a way ... reality revealed itself in its demonic, threatening face. The age of anxiety, which the kabbalists and those like them apprehended in their time and in other times returned again, an age of disintegration and breakdown of values. The crisis of values ... did not pass over the small Jewish world at all. We were standing, feeble and ill and without solid values. Our generation, as human beings and as Jews, as individuals and as a community, is pushed toward the chasm and before us there is a parting of the ways: to roll down the slope of nihilism or to be spiritually elevated and discover the existing values hidden within the external shattered reality. It is possible that a profound study of the wisdom of Kabbalah, and especially the meaning of the symbolistic approach for the values of Judaism, will illumine our eyes and help us in the search for the exit from the great perplexity.

Both Scholem and Tishby suffered from the consequences of the catastrophe and they spoke about it in a very direct manner. Scholem's brother, Werner, was killed by the Nazis in Buchenwald early in the war, and his best friend, Walter *Benjamin, committed suicide in 1940. To him he dedicated his *Major Trends in Jewish Mysticism*, and the dedication ends with the sentence: "Died at Port Bou (Spain) on his way into freedom." Those deaths must have been terrible personal losses. Worse blows were part of Tishby's experience while in Israel. He dedicated his first book – an M.A. thesis written under Scholem's guidance earlier in 1939 – *The Doctrine of Evil and Shells in Lurianic Kabbalah*, published in 1942 – "To Father and Mother, who are imprisoned in the kingdom of Satan, and are waiting for imminent redemption," but in the second edition, published in 1962, another dedication was added, "To the Memory of Father and Mother, who were imprisoned in the kingdom of Satan, and waited for imminent redemption." Tishby was originally from Transylvania, Romania, from where he made *aliyah* to the Land of Israel; his parents remained in the Diaspora and perished toward the end of World War II. Never before had scholars in Jewish studies to deal with situations where redemption and freedom were not abstract concepts or cherished beliefs but matters of life and death, namely, the death of their closest relatives and friends. However, the tribulations of the Holocaust were not the end of his suffering. Tishby's most important scholarly achievement, *Mishnat ha-Zohar*, whose first volume, co-authored by F. Lachover, was published in 1949, had the following dedication: "My work on *Mishnat ha-Zohar* is dedicated to the memory of my brother Shmuel, blessed be his memory, one of the survivors of the Nazi hell, who fell in the war for the defense of the homeland."

Therefore, two of the most important studies on the nature of Kabbalah are explicitly dedicated to persons who lost their lives in fateful struggles for survival. The personal tragedy and the national one are mentioned explicitly by the scholars of Kabbalah. This is also the case with the scholarly oeuvre of Mendel Piekarz, a leading scholar of Ḥasidism, who suffered terrible family loss in the Holocaust. To a certain extent, his expositions of Ḥasidism also contain implicit and explicit criticism related to the role played by ḥasidic leaders during the Holocaust.

The terrible events of World War II were at least one of the main reasons for the strong focus on exile and redemption, and theories of evil, in the overall vision of the nature of Kabbalah and Ḥasidism. Not that these subjects are absent in numerous kabbalistic sources; nor are they negligible. It would seem that a variety of messianic ideas was as important for the kabbalists as they were for many traditional Jews, but their transformation by scholars into the main clue for understanding Kabbalah represents an overemphasis whose existential background has been briefly surveyed above.

In different ways, the scholarship of Kabbalah in this period advanced in a manner that resonates with the main concerns deriving from the two major events in the history of modern Jewry: the optimistic and the somewhat messianically oriented aspects of Zionism, on the one hand, and the pessimism generated by the Holocaust, which demanded answers to the perennial question of the meaning of Jewish tragic experiences, on the other. Like Martin *Buber at the beginning of the 20th century, who looked for spiritual alternatives in Ḥasidism, Scholem's school preferred Kabbalah, understood as reflecting antinomian and paradoxical tendencies, as the spiritual alternative. In other words, far from being detached scholars, as they are sometimes portrayed, both Scholem and Tishby looked to their academic subject-matter as a possible source of spiritual inspiration. From this point of view, they continued the spiritual experiments which non-traditional alternatives underwent in non-religious Zionism, started by Buber. However, they did so in the extraordinarily terrible circumstances of the Holocaust and under the spell of the exuberant impetus created by Zionism and the establishment of the State of Israel. All the vicissitudes of exile and the hopes for redemption were epitomized in the experience of the two representative scholars of the creative period, whose basic phenomenology reflects the dichotomy that informed the history of the Jewish nation. Scholarship of Kabbalah in the first generation of scholars active in Israel was not only a revival of old lore, a cold and distanced analysis of neglected ideas of old forgotten masters, but also a mirror for expressing deep personal and national quandaries. Studying Kabbalah certainly was, for both Scholem and Tishby, a total vocation that demanded infinite dedication and forms of sacrifices which we can hardly understand today in a period of abundance in universities, of unparalleled mobility, and speedy circulation of information. In the much greater propensity to criticism characteristic of the third period, however, the particular circumstances that shaped the achievements of the founding scholars should not be overlooked. By pointing out the importance of the historical circumstances that served as the background of modern studies of Kabbalah in Israel, and the impact of these circumstances on the structure of these studies, the achievements of those scholars are put in bold relief and seen as as outstanding.

The first main reservations about Scholem's theories come from historians, even from some who were influenced by Scholem. In the writings of Yitzhak F. *Baer, there are indications that some kabbalistic ideas are earlier than supposed. Jacob Katz doubted whether Scholem's suggested nexus between Shabbateanism and Reform in the 19th century was indeed plausible, while much earlier Azriel Shohat doubted the affinities seen by Scholem between the dissemination of Lurianic Kabbalah and the emergence of Shabbateanism. More vehemently and much later, Shmuel Ettinger criticized the historical method applied by Scholem's school to the study of Ḥasidism. However, as critical as some of their views were, they never touched the overall historical scheme of Scholem, and even less his phenomenology of religion. The first detailed and penetrating critique of a major tenet of Scholem's school came in 1978 with the publication of Mendel Piekarz's book on the beginnings of Ḥasidism. The book represents a major departure from the explication predominant in Scholem's school, based on the linkage between Ḥasidism and Shabbateanism. In its stead Piekarz pointed to the existence of what were regarded as radical views in the ethical-mystical literature that either preceded or were contemporary with the first generation of ḥasidic masters.

It is in this period that some of the studies of Shlomo Pines, an illustrious historian of philosophy, dealing with Jewish mysticism were published. They deal with an ancient Jewish theology that had interesting parallels in early Kabbalah, with the emergence of some of the main concepts of *Sefer Yeẓirah*, with views associated with the town of Ismailiyyah and reflecting on the thought of *Sefer ha-Bahir*, with kabbalistic views in *Sefer ha-Temunah*, 35 with the history of the magical concept of *ruḥaniyyut* – which had profound reverberations in Kabbalah, in Ḥasidism, and even among certain Jewish intellectuals of the early 20th century Germany – and with the Arabic origin of the concept of the angelic mentor known as Maggid. Pines put his unequalled knowledge of Arabic sources into the service of the scholarship of Jewish mysticism, pointing the way to solutions to questions concerning the sources of certain kabbalistic ideas in Islamic thought. Two major contributions of Pines to our general understanding of Kabbalah may be summarized as follows: (a) the possibility that ancient Jewish theologies hitherto not addressed by Kabbalah scholarship contributed to the emergence of the medieval kabbalistic theosophies; (b) the possibility that Arabic sources were significant catalysts for kabbalistic ideas, especially in the case of astro-magic.

1973–1998: THE PERIOD OF CRITICISM. In this period the critical attitude becomes much more prominent among scholars of Kabbalah. This does not mean that both creative and reproductive aspects are absent in the scholarship of the period.

There is good reason to choose the year 1973 as a significant turning point: in this year Werblowsky's English translation of Scholem's *Sabbatai Sevi* was published, which represents the last major formulation of the most important contribution of Scholem's historiography that introduced additional material. By then, in 1974, Scholem's last comprehensive summary of his oeuvre, his items in the *Encyclopaedia Judaica*, had been published as a separate book under the title *Kabbalah*. It is in the autumn of 1973, that one of the main scholars in Scholem's school, Ephraim Gottlieb, passed away.

In general terms, in the immediately following years a group of younger scholars in Israel began to emerge: Yehudah Liebes, Mordekhai Pachter, Moshe Hallamish, Rachel Elior, Amos Goldreich, Mikhal Kushnir-Oron, Bracha Sack, Assi Farber-Ginnat, Yoram Jacobson, Hava Tirosh-Rotschild, and Moshe Idel. Students of Alexander Altmann and George Vajda also entered the study of Jewish mysticism, such as Arthur I. Green, Daniel C. Matt, and Lawrence Fine.

The most important event that contributed to a shift in the direction of research among younger scholars in Israel was the Yom Kippur War. The profound restructuring of the Israeli worldview also changed the course of study in certain domains of Jewish studies, including Kabbalah, in subtle ways. The most important change is the more general and diffuse feeling that concepts that were conceived of as permanent and around which the national, political, or ideological agenda was organized were inadequate. In the military-political realm the term used in modern Hebrew for "concept" is *konẓepẓiyah*, which represents unexamined presuppositions that guide major areas of thought and behavior. There is no need to dwell on the consequences of such a *konẓepẓiyah* on the military-political plane, or on the turmoil created in the wake of the Yom Kippur War on the intellectual plane. The more critical examination of the findings and theories of the founders of Kabbalah studies since that time reflects an upheaval which, though much more general and diffuse, is less evident in other fields of Judaica. The single most important shift is the modification of the earlier emphasis on the importance of *gnosticism as a historical source of medieval Kabbalah and the marginalization of the phenomenological affinities between the two types of literature.

New Developments in the Study of Jewish Mysticism since 1973

In the last generation, the volume of studies published on the subject of Jewish mysticism increased in a dramatic manner. Even if we ignore the more widespread trend of vulgarization and popularization of Kabbalah, which scholars themselves sometimes contribute to, and limit our survey to the more scholarly publications, we still see a huge increase in the number of published studies. This new harvest of studies differs in many cases from the earlier ones in a variety of ways: more and more studies are written in other languages than Hebrew, they address in many cases new topics, they also adopt methodologies other than the philological-historical one and sometimes offer different answers to questions that were answered in the previous generations of scholars. Some of these changes are the result of the greater diversification of the intellectual centers in which Jewish mysticism is studied. It is only after 1973 that we may speak of the significant expansion of the study of Jewish mysticism in centers other than Israel, especially the United States, France, Germany, Great Britain, and Italy. There are many signs of the establishment of Jewish mysticism as an independent field of research, with positions in universities, a growing number of students on all levels, the inevitable emergence of internal debates in the field as well as the emergence and development of specialized journals where topics related to Jewish mysticism are regularly discussed. This is part of both the renewed interest in Jewish mysticism in general and of the much greater resources the academic world has placed at the disposal of scholars in this field. In the limited space of this survey it is impossible to encompass all the variety of developments.

First and foremost, we should emphasize the expansion of study of topics that were the subject of intense earlier study. This does not mean that there are no new and important contributions in areas like Hekhalot literature, early Kabbalah, the origins of Kabbalah, the book of *Bahir*, *Naḥmanides, the *Zohar, Abraham Abulafia, Safedian Kabbalah, or Shabbateanism. Moreover, many of the new developments are quite recent, and represent ongoing processes initiated by young scholars, and we lack the necessary perspective to evaluate them properly.

There are six main topics, some relatively new in the scholarship of Jewish mysticism, in which major developments have been made in the last generation: emphasis on the experiential nature of Jewish mysticism, the relationship between Jewish mysticism and *halakhah*, the relation between magic and Jewish mysticism, a variety of discussions of hermeneutics in Jewish mysticism, the history of Kabbalah in the Renaissance and Christian Kabbalah, and more recently the attitude to sex and femininity in Jewish mysticism. All six topics represent the dialogue between scholars of Jewish mysticism and modern developments in the history of religion in general, and are less related to the historical aspects of Jewish mysticism that were at the center of most of the earlier studies of this lore. To be sure, all of them were touched upon in one way or another also earlier, but in the last generation they were put in much more bolder relief than previously, not only because more has been written about them but also because they were regarded as more important than earlier scholars assumed.

The more experiential nature of Jewish mysticism has been addressed in scholarship in different ways: the special emphasis on the importance of ecstasy, of mystical experiences, of *unio mystica*, of techniques and paths to reach such experiences. The interest in the writings of Abraham Abulafia, Isaac of Acre, and Ḥayyim *Vital, where these topics are dealt with, as well as in concepts like *hitbodedut*, namely isolation and mental concentration, *devekut* (union and communion with God), prophecy, and *hitpashtut mi-gashmiyyut*, namely divestment of corporeality and ascent of the soul, is much more pronounced. Especially in the studies of Yehudah Liebes, the affinities between the personal and the systemic aspects of the writings of some mystics, like Isaac *Luria and Shabbatai Ẓevi, have been emphasized. Most of the extant material which was until now found only in manuscripts has been published and analyzed.

Another major field of research that developed in the 1980s is the the relationship between Kabbalah and *halakhah*. A small but but basic series of studies on this subject has charted the most important developments in the long history of the relationship between Jewish mysticism and *halakhah*. The first major contribution is Jacob Katz's monograph on the subject, followed by Israel M. *Ta-Shma's book on the *Zohar* and his study of Joseph Caro, Moshe Hallamish's numerous studies dealing especially with Jewish liturgy and Kabbalah, Robert *Bonfil's study of Menahem Azariah of Fano, and Moshe Halbertal's analyses of Naḥmanides's halakhic thought. The manifold affinities between the two religious aspects of Judaism now underlie scholarship more than the earlier emphasis on the antinomian and paradoxical approaches that were deemed to characterize Jewish mysticism.

A topic that draws more and more attention is the role played by magic, and sometimes also astrology, in the general economy of Jewish mysticism. This is especially evident in the material related to the Hekhalot literature, to the Kabbalah during the Renaissance in Italy, to Safedian Kabbalah, and 18th century Ḥasidism.

The second half of the 20th century represents a linguistic turn in general philosophy, and its repercussions are evident also in the scholarship of Jewish mysticism. A series of studies dealing with Jewish mystical theories of the origin and nature of language, interpretation, the status of the text – mainly that of the Torah – and more general hermeneutical questions like the role of the reader and interpreter and the nature of the kabbalistic symbols, moved much closer to the center of scholarly interest than earlier. At the same time, the impact of Scholem's scholarship and that of others on main figures in modern thought like Harold *Bloom, Jacques Derrida, Umberto Eco, and George *Steiner can be detected.

A field having great potential which began to become more and more prominent is the history of Kabbalah in Italy and the emergence and development of the Christian Kabbalah. The prominence of the Italian Kabbalah has been placed in relief in studies by Ephraim Gottlieb, Moshe Idel, Fabrizio Lelli, David Ruderman, and Hava Tirosh-Samuelson. Thanks to the innovative studies of Chaim Wirszubski, and more recently the publications of Brian Copenhaven and Giulio Busi, Giovanni Pico della Mirandola's and Johann Reuchlin's kabbalistic sources have been charted. Allison Coudert has contributed important studies to the impact of Jewish Kabbalah on 17th-century European thought.

The reluctance to resort to psychological explanations to understand Jewish mysticism, so evident in pre-1973 scholarship, changed dramatically afterwards. Under the impact of Freudian psychoanalysis in its various guises, and somewhat less so also Jungianism, new interpretations of Jewish mysticism have been advanced. Subjects like the appearance of the mandala during the mystical experience, the issue of Kabbalah as phallocentric, androgyny, the status of feminine elements within kabbalistic thought, the theories of eroticism found in Jewish mysticism, can be found in the studies of Daniel Abrams, David Halperin, Moshe Idel, Yehudah Liebes, and in a more comprehensive and sophisticated manner in those of Elliot R. Wolfson. The impact of feminist scholarship on the understanding of Kabbalah can also be seen from time to time in the choice of the subjects addressed by scholars in recent decades.

Methodologically speaking, we should also mention the greater effort efforts to offer more phenomenological descriptions of Jewish mysticism, evident in the writings of Yehudah Liebes, who emphasizes the important role of myths, Moshe Idel, who proposed theories of the models informing the major developments of Jewish mysticism, Elliot R. Wolfson, who describes Jewish mysticism as phallocentric, Haviva Pedaya's categorizations of mystical experiences, and Jonathan Garb, who put into relief the importance of concepts of power in many mystical literatures in Judaism.

To be sure, expansions of the subjects and phases of the study of Jewish mysticism as delineated above continued steadily also after 1973. The number of collections of Scholem's articles in different forms and translations, as well as studies on his thought, proliferated, as the bibliography below demonstrates. Nevertheless, the one field in Jewish mysticism which flourished more than any other is modern Ḥasidism. In addition to monographs and numerous articles dealing with the history of Ḥasidism, a plethora of studies dealing with its mystical aspects, its approach to story-telling, to magic, to messianism, to the topic of interiorization, ecstasy, and psychologization, or to the sources of Ḥasidism have been published in the last generation. Many monographs dedicated to individual ḥasidic masters and schools put scholarship on a surer track than the earlier generalizations about the nature of Ḥasidism. Unlike the earlier debates between Buber and Scholem, or between Tishby and Scholem, scholarship in more recent years now emphasizes much more the particularity of each form rather than the global picture of this mystical movement. This is evident in the many studies and monographs dedicated to the Besht himself, to R. Naḥman of Braslav, and to the Chabad school. Also important are the critical editions of important ḥasidic texts, especially by Gedaliah Nigal, and the reprinting of almost the entire corpus of ḥasidic writings in two series of books, mainly in the United States.

From Martin Buber to Scholem's school, Ḥasidism has been studied mainly as a mystical movement. However, in a series of monographs, Mendel Piekarz has described the social aspects of the ḥasidic movement, denying the main role of mystical elements.

There has also been increasing study of the Kabbalah of Naḥmanides and of R. *Elijah, the Gaon of Vilna, known as ha-Gra, and of his students, on the one hand, and the development of Kabbalah in North Africa, on the other.

The bibliographical survey compiled below is, for the most part, arranged according to the principal topics mentioned above, and is by definition incomplete.

BIBLIOGRAPHY:

General Studies on Jewish Mysticism

A. Altmann, *Faces of Judaism* (Heb., 1983);
J. Dan, *Jewish Mysticism and Jewish Ethics* (1986);
idem, *On Sanctity* (Heb., 1997);
idem, *Jewish Mysticism*, vol. 1: Late Antiquity (1998);
idem, *Jewish Mysticism*. vol. 2: The Middle Ages (1998);
L. Fine (ed.), *Essential Papers on Kabbalah* (1995);
M. Fishbane, *The Kiss of God, Spiritual and Mystical Death in Judaism* (1994);
J. Garb, *Manifestations of Power in Jewish Mysticism From Rabbinic to Safedian Kabbalah* (Heb., 2004);
E. Ginsburg, *The Sabbath in the Classical Kabbalah* (1989);
E. Gottlieb, *Studies in the Kabbalah Literature*, ed. J. Hacker (Heb., 1976);
A. Green (ed.), *Jewish Spirituality* (1986/1987), 2 volumes;
A. Green, *Keter, The Crown of God in Early Jewish Mysticism* (1997);
I. Gruenwald, "Jewish Mysticism's Transition from Sefer Yesira to the Bahir," in: J. Dan (ed.), *The Beginnings of the Jewish Mysticism in Medieval Europe* (Heb., 1987), 15–54;

idem, *Apocalyptic and Merkavah Mysticism* (1980);
M. Halbertal, *Concealment and Revelation: The Secret and its Boundaries in Medieval Jewish Tradition* (Heb., 2001);
D. Halperin, *The Faces of the Chariot* (1988);
J. Hecker, *Mystical Bodies, Mystical Meals, Eating and Embodiment in Medieval Kabbalah* (2005);
M. Idel – M. Ostow (eds.), *Jewish Mystical Leaders and Leadership* (1998);
M. Idel, *Kabbalah: New Perspectives* (1988);
idem, *Messianic Mystics* (1998);
idem, "On Binary 'Beginnings' in Kabbalah-Scholarship," in: *Aporematha, Kritische Studien zur Philologiegechichte*, vol. 5 (2001), 313–37;
idem, "On the Theologization of Kabbalah in Modern Scholarship," in: Y. Schwartz and V. Krech (eds.), *Religious Apologetics – Philosophical Argumentation*, (2004), 123–74;
Y. Liebes, *Studies in Jewish Myth and Jewish Messianism* (1993);
idem, "New Trends in Kabbala Research," in: *Pe'amim*, vol. 50 (1992), 150–70 (Heb.);
idem, "Shlomo Pines and Kabbala Research," in: M. Idel, W.Z. Harvey, E. Schweid (eds.), *Shlomo Pines Jubilee Volume*, Part 2 (1990);
idem, *Jerusalem Studies in Jewish Thought*, vol. 9, 16–22 (Heb.);
C. Mopsik, *Chemins de la cabale* (2004);
P. Schaefer, *The Hidden and the Manifest God* (1992);
M. Pachter, *Roots of Faith and Devequt* (2004);
N. Sed, *La mystique cosmologique juive* (1981);
S. Sharot, *Messianism, Mysticism, and Magic, A Sociological Analysis of Jewish Religious Movements* (1982);
I. Tishby, *Studies in Kabbalah and Its Branches*, (Heb., 1982–1993), 3 vols.;
idem, *The Wisdom of the Zohar, An Anthology of Texts*, tr. D. Goldstein (1991), 3 vols.;
E.R. Wolfson, *Along the Path* (1995);
idem, *Through a Speculum that Shines, Vision and Imagination in Medieval Jewish Mysticism* (1994).

Recent Collections of Scholem's Studies and Studies on Scholem

E. Liebes (ed.), *Devils, Demons and Souls, Essays on Demonology*, (2004);
Kabbalah (1974);
On the Possibility of Jewish Mysticism in Our Time and Other Essays, ed. A. Shapira, tr. J. Chipman (1997);
On the Mystical Shape of the Godhead (1991);
G. Scholem, *Studies in Kabbalah* I, eds. J. ben Shlomo and M. Idel (1998);
Origins of the Kabbalah, tr. A. Arkush, ed. R.J. Zwi Werblowsky (1987);
On Jews and Judaism in Crisis, ed. Werner J. Dannhauser (1976);
D. Biale, *Gershom Scholem, Kabbalah and Counter-History* (1979);
H. Bloom (ed.), *Gershom Scholem* (1987);
J. Dan, *Gershom Scholem and the Mystical Dimension of Jewish History* (1988);
A. Funkenstein, "Gershom Scholem: Charisma, Kairos and the Messianic Dialectic," in: *History and Memory*, 4 (1992), 123–39;
P. Mendes-Flohr, *Gershom Scholem, The Man and His Work* (1994);
N. Rotenstreich, "Symbolism and Transcendence: On Some Philosophical Aspects of Gershom Scholem's Opus," in: *Review of Metaphysics*, vol. 31 (1977/78), 604–14;
P. Schaefer and J. Dan (eds.), *Gershom Scholem's Major Trends in Jewish Mysticism, 50 Years After* (1993);

Experiential Aspects of Jewish Mysticism

S. Brody, "Human Hands Dwell in Heavenly Heights": Contemplative Ascent and Theurgic Power in Thirteenth Century Kabbalah," in: *Mystics of the Book: Themes, Topics & Typology*, ed. R.A. Herrera (1992), 123–58;
J. Dan, *The Heart and the Fountain, An Anthology of Jewish Mystical Experiences* (2002);
M. Hellner-Eshed, *A River Issues Forth from Eden, On the Language of Mystical Experience in the Zohar* (Heb., 2005);
M. Idel, *Ascensions on High In Jewish Mysticism* (2005);
idem, *Enchanted Chains: Techniques and Rituals in Jewish Mysticism* (2005);
idem, "Universalization and Integration: Two Conceptions of Mystical Union in Jewish Mysticism," in: *Mystical Union and Monotheistic Faith, An Ecumenical Dialogue*, eds. M. Idel and B. McGinn (1989), 27–58, 157–61, 195–203;
idem, "*Unio Mystica*" as a Criterion: "Hegelian" Phenomenologies of Jewish Mysticism," in: S. Chase (ed.), *Doors of Understanding, Conversations in Global Spirituality in Honor of Ewert Cousins* (1997), 305–33;
idem, *Studies in Ecstatic Kabbalah* (1988);
Natan ben Sa'adyah Har'ar, Le Porte della Giustizia, a Cura di Moshe Idel (2001);
L. Jacobs, *Jewish Mystical Testimonies* (1987);
H. Pedaya, *Vision and Speech: Models of Revelatory Experiences in Jewish Mysticism* (Heb., 2002);
E.R. Wolfson, *Through a Speculum that Shines, Vision and Imagination in Medieval Jewish Mysticism* (1994).

Jewish Mysticism and Magic

J.H. Chajes, *Between Worlds, Dybbuks, Exorcists, and Modern Judaism* (2003);
M. Goldish (ed.), *Spirit Possession in Judaism* (2003);
I. Gruenwald, "On Writing, and Written and the Divine Name – Magic, Spirituality and Mysticism," in: Michal Oron and Amos Goldreich (eds.), *Massu'ot, Studies in Kabbalistic Literature and Jewish Philosophy in Memory of Prof. Ephraim Gottlieb* (Heb., 1994), 75–98;
M. Idel, "Between Magic of Names and Kabbalah of Names, The Critique of Abraham Abulafia," in: *Mahanayyim*, 14 (2003), 79–95 (Heb.);

idem, "On Prophecy and Magic in Sabbateanism," in: *Kabbalah*, vol. 8 (2003), 7–50;
idem, "Astral Dreams in Judaism: Twelfth to Fourteenth Centuries," in: D. Shulman and G.G. Stroumsa (eds.), *Dream Cultures, Explorations in the Comparative History of Dreaming* (1999), 235–50;
idem, *Golem; Jewish Magical and Mystical Traditions on the Artificial Anthropoid* (1990);
idem, "Golems and God: Mimesis and Confrontation," in: O. Krueger, R. Sarioender, A. Deschner (eds.), *Mythen der Kreativitaet*, (2003), 224–68;
idem, "Hermeticism and Judaism," in: I. Merkel and A. Debus (eds.), *Hermeticism and the Renaissance* (1988), 59–76.
idem, "Inquiries in the Doctrine of *Sefer ha-Meshiv*," in: *Sefunot*, 7 (ed. J. Hacker, 1983), 185–266 (Heb.);
idem, "On Judaism, Jewish Mysticism and Magic," in: P. Schaefer and H. Kippenberg (eds.), *Envisioning Magic* (1997), 195–214;
idem; "The Magical and Theurgical Interpretation of Music in Jewish Texts: Renaissance to Hasidism," in: *Yuval*, 4 (1982), 33–63 (Heb.);
idem, "Hermeticism and Kabbalah," in: P. Lucentini, I. Parri, V.P. Compagni (eds.), *Hermeticism from Late Antiquity to Humanism* (2004), 389–408;
ISWM, "Jewish Magic from the Renaissance Period to Early Hasidism," in: J. Neusner, E.S. Frerichs, P.V. McCracken Flesher (eds.), *Religion, Science and Magic, In Concert and In Conflict* (1989), 82–117;
idem, "The Magical and Neoplatonic Interpretations of Kabbalah in the Renaissance," in B.D. Cooperman (ed.), *Jewish Thought in the Sixteenth Century* (1983), 186–242, reprinted in ed. D.B. Ruderman, *Essential Papers on Jewish Culture in Renaissance and Baroque Italy* (1992), 107–69;
R. Kiener, "Astrology in Jewish Mysticism from Sefer Yezira to the Zohar," in: J. Dan (ed.), *The Beginnings of the Jewish Mysticism in Medieval Europe* (1987), 1–42;
G. Nigal, *Magic, Mysticism and Hasidism* (Heb., 1992);
M. Oron (ed.), *Samuel Falk, The Baal Shem of London* (Heb., 2002);
S. Pines, "Le Sefer ha-Tamar et les *maggidim* des Kabbalistes," in: G. Nahon and Ch. Touati (eds.), *Hommages à Georges Vajda* (1980), 333–63;
P. Schaefer, *Hekhalot Studien* (1988);
M.D. Swartz, *Scholastic Magic* (1996).

Kabbalah in Italy and Christian Kabbalah

A. Altmann, "Beyond the Realm of Philosophy: R. Elijah Hayyim ben Benjamin of Gennazano," in: M. Idel, W.Z. Harvey, E. Schweid (eds.), *Shlomo Pines Jubilee Volume* (Heb., 1988), I:61–102;
K. Bland, "Elijah del Medigo's Averroistic Response to the Kabbalahs of the Fifteenth-Century Jewry and Pico della Mirandola," in: *Jewish Thought and Philosophy*, 1 (1991), 23–53;
The Great Parchment. Flavius Mithridates' Latin Translation, The Hebrew Text, and an English Version, edited by Giulio Busi with Simonetta M. Bondoni and Saverio Campanini (2004);
A.P. Coudert, *The Impact of the Kabbalah in the Seventeenth Century, The Life and Thought of Francis Mercury van Helmont (1614–1698)* (1999);
A. Coudert, *Leibniz and the Kabbalah* (1995).
J. Dan (ed.), *The Christian Kabbalah, Jewish Mystical Books and Their Christian Interpreters* (1997);
H.J. Hames, *The Art of Coversion, Christianity & Kabbalah in the Thirteenth Century* (2000);
M. Idel, "Between the View of *Sefirot* as Essence and Instruments in Renaissance Period," in: *Italia*, vol. 3 (1982), 89–111 (Heb.);
idem, "Particularism and Universalism in Kabbalah, 1480–1650," in: D.B. Ruderman (ed.), *Essential Papers on Jewish Culture in Renaissance and Baroque Italy* (1992), 324–44;
idem, "*Prisca Theologia* in Marsilio Ficino and in Some Jewish Treatments," in: M.J.B. Allen and V. Rees (eds.), with M. Davies, *Marsilio Ficino, His Theology, His Philosophy, His Legacy* (2001), 137–58;
E. Kanarfogel, "Mysticism and Asceticism in Italian Rabbinic Literature of the Thirteenth Century," in: *Kabbalah*, vol. 6 (2001), 135–60;
E. Kupfer, "The Visions of the Rabbi Asher ben Rav Meir also Called Lemlin Reutlingen," in: *Kovez al Yad*, vol. 8 (1976), 387–423 (Heb.);
D. Ruderman, *Kabbalah, Magic, and Science, The Cultural Universe of a Sixteenth-Century Jewish Physician* (1988);
D.R. Ruderman, *The World of a Renaissance Jew: The Life and Thought of Abraham ben Mordecai Farissol* (1981);
D.B. Ruderman, *Kabbalah, Magic, and Science, The Cultural Universe of a Sixteenth-Century Jewish Physician* (1989);
H. Tirosh-Rotschild, *Between Worlds, The Life and Thought of Rabbi David ben Judah Messer Leon* (1991);
C.Wirszubski, *Pico della Mirandola's Encounter with Jewish Mysticism* (1988);
idem, *Between the Lines, Kabbalah, Christian Kabbalah and Sabbateanism* (1990);
F.A. Yates, *The Occult Philosophy in the Elizabethan Age* (1979);
K. Burmistrov and M. Endel, "The Place of Kabbalah in the Doctrine of Russian Freemansons," in: *Aries*, vol. 4 (2004), 27–67.

Halakhah and Kabbalah

R. Bonfil, "Halakhah, Kabbalah, and Society: Some Insights into Rabbi Menahem Azariah da Fano's Inner World," in: I. Twersky and B. Septimus (eds.), *Jewish Thought in the Seventeenth Century* (1987), 39–61;
M. Halbertal, "Custom and the History of the Halakhah in Nahmanides' Thought," in: *Zion*, 67:1 (2002), 25–56 (Heb.);
M. Hallamish, *Kabbalah, in Liturgy, Halakhah and Customs* (Heb., 2000);

J. Katz, *Halakhah and Kabbalah* (Heb., 1984);
I.M. Ta-Shma, *Ha-Nigle She-Banistar, The Halakhic Residue in the Zohar,* (Heb., 2001[2]).

Major Critical Editions and Translations

D. Abrams, "Critical and Post-Critical Textual Scholarship of Jewish Mystical Literature: Notes on the History and Development of Modern Editing Techniques," in: *Kabbalah,* 1 (1996), 17–71;
idem, *R. Asher ben David, His Complete Works and Studies in his Kabbalistic Thought* (1996);
idem, *The Book Bahir* (1994);
Seymour J. Cohen (ed.), *The Holy Letter, A Study in Jewish Sexual Morality* (1993);
Adam Afterman (ed.), *The Intention of Prayers in Early Ecstatic Kabbalah* (Heb., 2004);
M.S. Cohen, *The Shi'ur Qomah: Texts and Recensions* (1985);
A. Goldreich (ed.), *R. Yizhaq of Acre's Me'irat 'Einayyim*, a critical edition with preface and commentary (1984);
I. Gruenwald, "A Preliminary Critical Edition of Sefer Yeẓira," in: *Israel Oriental Studies,* 1 (1971), 132–77;
G. Sed-Rajna, *R. Azriel de Gerone, Commentaire sur la liturgie quotidienne* (1974);
Rabbi Ezra ben Solomon of Gerona, *Commentary on Song of Songs and Other Kabbalistic Commentaries*, selected, translated and annotated by S. Brody (1999);
Jewish Mystical Autobiographies, tr. and introduction Morris Faierstein (1999),
Judah ben Nissim ibn Malka, *Judaeo-Arabic Commentary on the Pirkey Rabbi Eli'ezer* with a Hebrew Translation and Supercommentary by Isaac b. Samuel of Acco, ed. P.B. Fenton (1991);
R. Yehudah ibn Malka, *Kitab Uns we-Tafsir,* ed. G. Vajda (1974);
D. Ch. Matt, *The Book of Mirrors: Sefer Mar'ot ha-Zove'ot* by R. David ben Yehudah he-Hasid (1982);
P. Schaefer, *Synopse zur Hekhalot-Literatur* (1981);
J. Gikatilla, *Gates of Light, Sha'arei 'Orah,* tr. A. Weinstein (1994);
E. Wolfson (ed.), *The Book of the Pomegranate, R. Moses de Leon's Sefer ha-Rimmon* (1988).

Monographs on Individual Books and Kabbalists

L. Fine, *Physician of the Soul, Healer of the Cosmos, Isaac Luria and His Kabbalistic Fellowship* (2003);
R. Goetschel, *R. Meir Ibn Gabbai; Le Discours de la Kabbale espagnole* (1981);
K. Herrmann, *Massekhet Hekhalot* (1994);
B. Huss, *Sockets of Fine Gold, The Kabbalah of Rabbi Shim'on ibn* Lavi (Heb., 2000);
M. Idel, *R. Menahem Recanati, the Kabbalist* (Heb., 1998);
Y. Jacobson, *Along the Paths of Exile and Redemption, The Doctrine of Redemption of Rabbi Mordecai Dato* (Heb., 1996);
Y. Liebes, *Ars Poetica in Sefer Yetzirah* (Heb., 2000);
F. Lelli (ed.), *Elijjah Hayyim ben Binyamin da Genazzano, La lettera preziosa* (2002);
H. Pedaya, *Name and Sanctuary in the Teaching of R. Isaac the Blind* (Heb., 2001);
M. Verman, *The Book of Contemplation, Medieval Jewish Mystical Sources* (1992).

Language, Hermeneutics, and Jewish Mysticism

H. Bloom, *Kabbalah and Criticism* (1984);
A. Elqayam, "Between Referrentionalism and Performativism, Two Approaches to the Understanding of the Symbol in *Sefer Ma'arekhet ha-'Elohut,*" in: *Daat,* 24 (1990), 29–37 (Heb.);
Umberto Eco, *The Search for the Perfect Language*, tr. James Fentress (1995);
B. Huss, "*NISAN* – The Wife of the Infinite: The Mystical Hermeneutics of R. Isaac of Acre," in: *Kabbalah,* 5 (2000), 155–81;
idem, "*Sefer ha-Zohar* as a Canonical, Sacred and Holy Text Changing Perspectives in the Book of Splendor Between the Thirteenth and Eighteenth Centuries," in: *Journal of Jewish Thought and Philosophy,* 7 (1998), 257–307;
idem, "Rabbi Joseph Gikatilia's Definition of Symbolism and Its Influence on Kabbalistic Literature," in: JSJT, 12 (1996), 157–76 (Heb.);
M. Idel, *Absorbing Perfections: Kabbalah and Interpretation* (2002);
idem, "The Infant Experiment: The Search for the First Language," in: Allison Coudert (ed.), *The Language of Adam, Die Sprache Adams* (1999), 57–80;
idem, "The Function of Symbols in G. Scholem," in: *Jewish Studies,* 38 (1998), 43–72 (Heb.);
idem, "Kabbalah, Hierogliphicity and Hieroglyphs," in: *Kabbalah,* 11 (2004), 11–47;
idem, "On Talismatic Language in Jewish Mysticism," in: *Diogenes,* 43:2 (1995(, 23–41;
idem, "The Concept of the Torah in Heikhalot Literature and Its Metamorphoses in Kabbalah," in: *Jerusalem Studies in Jewish Thought,* 1 (1981), 23–84 (Heb.);
A. Kilcher, *Die Sprachtheorie der Kabbala als Aestetisches Paradigma* (1998);
Y. Liebes, "Myth vs. Symbol in the Zohar and Lurianic Kabbalah," in: L. Fine (ed.), *Essential Papers on Kabbalah* (1995), 212–42;
B. Rojtman, *Feu Noir sur Feu Blanc: Essai sur l'Hermeneutique Juive* (1986);
E.R. Wolfson, "Divine Suffering and the Hermeneutics of Reading," in: R. Gibbs and E.R. Wolfson (eds.), *Suffering Religion* (2002), 101–62;
idem, "Left Contained in the Right: A Study in Zoharic Hermeneutics," in: *AJS Review,* 11:1 (1986), 27–52;
idem, "Beautiful Maiden Without Eyes: Peshat and Sod in Zoharic Hermeneutics," in M. Fishbane (ed.), *The Midrashic Imagination* (1993), 155–202;
E.R. Wolfson, "Female Imaging of the Torah: From Literary Metaphor to Religious Symbol," in: *From Ancient Israel to Modern Judaism: Intellect in Quest of Understanding: Essays in Honor of Marvin Fox* (1989), 271–307;

Gender, Sex, Eros, and Femininity in Jewish Mysticism

D. Abrams, *Sexual Symbolism and Merkavah Speculation in Medieval Germany* (1997);

idem, *The Female Body of God in Kabbalistic Literature* (Heb., 2004);

D. Biale, *Eros and the Jews* (1992);

A. Elqayam, "To Know the Messiah: The Dialectics of the Sexual Discourse in the Messianic Thought of Nathan of Gaza," in: *Tarbiz*, 65 (1996), 637–70 (Heb.);

T. Fishman, "A Kabbalistic Perspective on Gender-Specific Commandments: On the Interplay of Symbols and Society," in: *AJS Review*, 17:2 (1992), 199–245;

P. Giller, "Love and Upheaval in the Zohar's *Sabba de-Mishpatim*," in: *Jewish Thought and Philosophy*, 5 (1997), 1–30;

A.Y. Green, *Shekhinah, the Virgin and the Song of Songs* (Heb., 2003);

M. Idel, *Kabbalah and Eros* (2005);

Y. Jacobson, "The Aspect of the "Feminine" in the Lurianic Kabbalah," in: P. Schaefer and J. Dan (eds.), *Gershom Scholem's Major Trends in Jewish Mysticism, 50 Years After* (1993), 239–55;

Y. Liebes, "Zohar and Eros," in: *Alppayyim*, 9 (1994), 67–119 (Heb.);

Mortimer Ostow (ed.), *Ultimate Intimacy, The Psychodynamics of Jewish Mysticism* (1995);

C. Mopsik, *Lettre sur la saintete, traduction et commentaire* (1986);

idem, *Sex of the Soul* (2005);

M. Rotenberg, *The Yetzer, A Kabbalistic Perspective on Eroticism and Human Sexuality* (1997);

P. Schaefer, *Mirror of His Beauty* (2002);

E.R. Wolfson, *Circle in the Square, Studies in the Use of Gender in Kabbalistic Symbolism* (1995);

idem, *Language, Eros, Being: Kabbalistic Hermeneutics and Poetic Imagination* (2005);

idem, "Coronation of the Sabbath Bride: Kabbalistic Myth and the Ritual of Androgynation," in: *Journal of Jewish Thought and Philosophy*, 6 (1997), 301–43.

Origins of Jewish Mysticism

R. Elior, *The Three Temples, The Emergence of Jewish Mysticism* (2005);

S. Pines, "God, the Divine Glory, and the Angels according to a 2nd Century Theology," in: J. Dan (ed.), *The Beginnings of Jewish Mysticism in Medieval Europe* (1987), 1–14 (Heb.);

idem, "Points of Similarity between the Exposition of the Doctrine of the *Sefirot* in the *Sefer Yezira* and a Text of the Pseudo-Clementine Homilies: The Implications of this Resemblance," in: *Proceedings of the Israel Academy of Sciences and Humanities*, 7:3 (1989), 63–142;

M. Idel, "On the Problem of the Study of the Source of the Book of Bahir," in: J. Dan (ed.),*The Beginning of Jewish Mysticism* (1987), 55–72 (Heb.);

idem, "About Theosophy at the Beginning of Kabbalah," in: Z. Gries, Ch. Kreisel, B. Huss (eds.), *Shefa' Tal, Studies in Jewish Thought and Culture presented to Bracha Sack* (2004), 131–58 (Heb.);

E.R. Wolfson, "The Theosophy of Sabbetai Donnolo, with Special Emphasis on the Doctrine of *Sefirot* in His *Sefer Hakhmoni*," in: *Jewish History*, 6 (1992), 281–316.

Safedian Kabbalah

J. Avivi, "The Writings of Rabbi Isaac Luria in Italy before 1620," in: *Alei Sefer* 11 (1984), 91–134 (Heb.);

K. Bland, "Neoplatonic and Gnostic Themes in R. Moses Cordovero's Doctrine of Evil," in: *Bulletin of the Institute of Jewish Studies*, 3 (1975), 103–28;

M. Benayahu, *Yosef Behiri* (Heb., 1991), 523–85;

idem, "*Shitrei Hikasherut shel Mekubbalei Ẓefat u-Miẓrayim*," in: *Assufot*, 9 (1995), 133–34;

G. Bos, "Hayyim Vital's Practical Kabbalah and Alchemy – A 17th Century Book of Secrets," in: *Journal of Jewish Thought and Philosophy*, 4 (1994), 55–112;

M. Idel, "R. Yehudah Hallewah and his Composition *Ẓafenat Pa'aneaḥ*," in: *Shalem*, 4 (1984), 119–48;

R. Elior, "R. Joseph Karo, and R. Israel Ba'al Shem Tov – Mystical Metamorphosis, Kabbalistic Inspiration and Spiritual Internalization," in: *Tarbiz*, 65 (1996), 671–709 (Heb.);

idem, "Messianic Expectations and the Spiritualization of Religious Life in the Sixteenth Century" in: *Revue des etudes juives*, 145 (1986), 35–49;

J. Garb, "The Kabbalah of Rabbi Joseph Ibn Sayyah as a Source for the Understanding of Safedian Kabbalah," in: *Kabbalah*, 4 (1999), 255–313 (Heb.);

M. Idel, "On Mobility, Individuals and Groups: Prolegomenon for a Sociological Approach to Sixteenth-Century Kabbalah," in: *Kabbalah*, 3 (1998), 145–76;

idem, "Italy in Safed, Safed in Italy; toward an interactive history of sixteenth-century Kabbalah," in: D. Ruderman and G. Veltri (eds.), *Cultural Intermediaries* (2004), 239–69;

R. Meroz, "The Brotherhood of Rabbi Moshe ben Makkir and its Regulations," in: *Pe'amim*, 31 (1987), 40–61 (Heb.);

idem, "R. Israel Sarug, the Student of Luria? – A Reconsideration of the Question," in: *Daat*, 28 (1992), 41–50 (Heb.);

idem, "Faithful Transmission versus Innovation: Luria and his Disciples," in P. Schaefer and J. Dan (eds.), *Gershom Scholem's Major Trends in Jewish Mysticism, 50 Years After* (1993), 257–75;

idem, "The School of Sarug, A New History," in: *Shalem*, ed. J. Hacker, 7 (2001), 151–93 (Heb.);

M. Pachter, *From Safed's Hidden Treasuries* (Heb., 1994);

B. Sack, The *Kabbalah of Rabbi Moshe Cordovero* (Heb., 1995).

Naḥmanides

D. Abrams, "Orality in the Kabbalistic School of Nahmanides: Preserving and Interpreting Esoteric Traditions and Texts," in: *Jewish Studies Quarterly*, 2 (1995), 85–102;

H. Pedaya, *Nahmanides, Cyclical Time and Holy Text* (2003);

M. Idel, "*Nishmat 'Eloha, The Divinity of the Soul in Nahmanides and His School*," in: S. Arzy, M. Fachler, B. Kahana

(eds.), *Life as a Midrash: Perspectives in Jewish Philosophy* (Heb., 2004), 338–82;
idem, "Nahmanides: Kabbalah, Halakhah and Spiritual Leadership," in: M. Idel and M. Ostow (eds.), *Jewish Mystical Leaders and Leadership* (1998), 15–96;
D. Novak, *The Theology of Nahmanides Systematically Presented* (1992);
C. Henoch, *Nachmanides: Philosopher and Mystic* (Heb., 1976).

Shabbateanism
Y. Barnai, "Christian Messianism and the Portuguese Marranos: The Emergence of Sabbateanism in Smyrna," in: *Jewish History*, 7 (1993), 119–26;
idem, "The Outbreak of Sabbateanism – The Eastern European Factor," in: *Journal for Jewish Thought and Philosophy*, 4 (1994), 171–83;
idem, *Sabbateanism – Social Perspectives* (Heb., 2000), 20–29;
S. Berti, "A World Apart? Gershom Scholem and Contemporary Readings of 17th century Christian Relations," in: *Jewish Studies Quarterly*, 3 (1996), 212–14;
R. Elior, ed., *The Sabbatean Movement and Its Aftermath: Messianism, Sabbateanism, Frankism*, 2 vols. (Heb., 2001);
A. Elqayam, "Sabbatai Sevi's Manuscript Copy of the Zohar," in: *Kabbalah*, 3 (1998), 345–87 (Heb.);
M. Goldish, *The Sabbatean Prophets* (2004);
M. Idel, "Saturn and Sabbatai Tzevi: A New Approach to Sabbateanism," in: P. Schaefer and M. Cohen (eds.), *Toward the Millennium, Messianic Expectations from the Bible to Waco* (1998), 173–202;
Y. Liebes, *On Sabbateaism and its Kabbalah, Collected Essays* (Heb., 1995);
E.R. Wolfson, "Construction of the *Shekhinah* in the Messianic Theosophy of Abraham Cardoso," in: *Kabbalah*, 3 (1998), 11–143.

Kabbalah in North Africa
M. Benayahu, "R. Abraham ben Musa and his Son," in: *Michael*, 5 (1978), 40–133 (Heb.);
R. Elior, "The Kabbalists of Dra," in: *Pe'amim*, 24 (1985), 36–73 (Heb.);
H. Goldberg, "The Zohar in Southern Morocco: A Study in Ethnography of Texts," in: *History of Religion*, 29 (1990), 249–51;
P.B. Fenton (Yosef Yinon), "Rabbi Makhluf Amsalem – A Morrocan Alchemist and Kabbalist," in: *Pe'amim*, 55 (1993), 92–123 (Heb.);
M. Hallamish, *The Kabbalah in North Africa, An Historical and Cultural Survey* (Heb., 2001);
M. Idel, "The Beginning of Kabbalah in North Africa? – A Forgotten Document by R. Yehudah ben Nissim ibn Malka," in: *Pe'amim*, vol. 43 (1990), 4–15 (Heb.);
idem, "The Kabbalah in Morocco; a survey," in: V. Man (ed.), *Morocco; Jews and Art in a Muslim Land* (2000), 105–24;
D. Manor, *Exile and Redemption in Moroccan Jewish Philosophy* (Heb., 1988);
idem, "Kabbalah in the Homilies of R. Joseph Adhan," in: *Pe'amim*, 15 (1983), 67–81 (Heb.);
idem, "R. Hayyim ben Attar in Hasidic Tradition," in: *Pe'amim*, 20 (1984), 88–110 (Heb.);
E. Moyal, *The Shabbetaian Movement in Morocco – Its History and Sources* (Heb., 1984);
A. Stahl, "Ritual Reading of the Zohar," in: *Pe'amim*, 5 (1980), 77–86 (Heb.);
H. Zafrani, *Kabbale, vie mystique et magie* (1986).

Mystical and Related Studies in Ḥasidism
A. Brill, *Thinking God, The Mysticism of Rabbi Zadok of Lublin* (2002).
M. Altschuler, *The Messianic Secret of Hasidism* (Heb., 2002);
J. Dan, *Jewish Mysticism*, vol. 3 *The Modern Times* (1999);
idem, *The Hasidic Story – Its History and Development* (Heb., 1975);
R. Elior "The Affinity between Kabbalah and Hasidism – Continuity or Changes," in: *Ninth World Congress of Jewish Studies Division C* (1986), 107–14 (Heb.);
idem, *The Paradoxical Ascent to God*, tr. Jeffrey Green (1993);
idem, *The Theory of Divinity of Hasidut Habad, Second Generation* (Heb., 1982);
Y. Elstein, *The Ecstasy Story in Hasidic Literature* (Heb., 1998);
I. Etkes, *The Besht, Magician, Mystic and Leader* (2004);
A. Green, *Tormented Master A Life of Rabbi Nahman of Bratslav* (1979);
idem, *Menahem Nahum of Chernobyl, Upright Practices, The Light of the Eyes* (1982);
idem, *Devotion and Commandment, The Faith of Abraham in the Hasidic Imagination* (1989);
Z. Gries, *Conduct Literature (Regimen Vitae), Its History and Place in the Life of the Beshtian Hasidism* (Heb., 1989);
idem, *The Book in Early Hasidism* (Heb., 1992);
M. Idel, *Hasidism: Between Ecstasy and Magic* (1995);
L. Jacobs, *Hasidic Prayer* (1978);
M. Krassen, *Uniter of Heaven and Earth, Rabbi Meshullam Feibush of Zbarazh and the Rise of Hasidism in Eastern Galicia* (1998);
N. Loewenthal, *Communicating the Infinite: The Emergence of the Habad School* (1990);
S. Magid, *Hasidism on the Margin, Reconciliation, Antinomianism and Messianism in Izbica/Radzin Hasidism* (2003);
R. Margolin, *The Human Temple, Religious Interiorization and the Inner Life in Early Hasidism* (Heb., 2004);
Z. Mark, *Mysticism and Madness in the Work of R. Nahman of Bratslav* (Heb., 2003);
H. Pedaya, "The Baal Shem Tov, Rabbi Jacob Joseph of Polonoye and the Great Maggid," in: *Daat*, 45 (2000), 25–73 (Heb.);
idem, "The Mystical Experience and the Religious World in Hasidism," in: *Daat*, 55 (2005), 73–108 (Heb.);
M. Piekarz, *Ideological Trends of Hasidism in Poland During the Interwar Period and the Holocaust* (1990);

idem, *Studies in Braslav Hasidism* (Heb., 1995);
idem, *The Beginning of Hasidism – Ideological Trends in Derush and Musar Literature* (Heb., 1978);
idem, "The Devekuth as Reflecting the Socio-Religious Character of the Hasidic Movement," in: *Daat*, 24 (1990), 127–44 (Heb.);
A. Rapoport-Albert, "God and the Zaddik as the Two Focal Points of Hasidic Worship," in: *History of Religions*, 18 (1979), 296–325;
idem, "The Hasidic Movement," in: *Zion*, 55 (1990), 183–245 (Heb.);
idem (ed.), *Hasidism Reappraised* (1996);
A. Rubinstein (ed.), *Studies in Hasidism* (Heb., 1977);
I. Tourov, "Hasidism and Christianity of the Eastern Territory of the Polish-Lithuanian Commonwealth: Possible Contacts and Mutual Influences," in: *Kabbalah*, 10 (2004), 73–105;
J. Weiss, *Studies in Eastern European Jewish Mysticism* (1985).

[Moshe Idel (2nd ed.)]

KABBALAT SHABBAT (Heb. קַבָּלַת שַׁבָּת; "Reception of the Sabbath"), term designating the inauguration of the Sabbath in general and, in a more specifically liturgical sense, that part of the Friday evening service which precedes the regular evening prayer and solemnly welcomes the Sabbath. The inauguration begins considerably before nightfall "so as to add from the weekday to the holy day" (Yoma 81b). Much care is traditionally lavished on preparing for the Sabbath. All housework that is forbidden on the Sabbath, e.g. cooking, is completed beforehand (cf. Shab. 2:7; Shab. 119a). Before the Sabbath, some people used to read the weekly Torah section, twice in the original Hebrew texts and once in the Aramaic (Targum) version. It is customary to bathe before the beginning of the Sabbath and to put on festive clothes. The Talmud (Shab. 119a) tells that R. Ḥanina used to put on his Sabbath clothes and stand at sunset of Sabbath eve and exclaim: "Come and let us go forth to welcome the Queen Sabbath" and R. Yannai used to don his festive robes at that time and exclaim, "Come, O bride! Come, O bride!" These stories served as the main motif for the Sabbath hymn *"Lekhah Dodi" of Solomon b. Moses ha-Levi *Alkabeẓ and formed the basis of the custom of the kabbalists of Safed, who welcomed the Sabbath by going into the fields on Fridays at sunset to recite special prayers and hymns in honor of the Sabbath amid nature. In traditional synagogues this prayer is recited no later than half an hour after sunset. It opens with Psalm 29 (in the Ashkenazi and some other rites with the six Psalms 95–99 and 29 corresponding to the six days of creation or the six weekdays). The hymn "Lekhah Dodi" is then sung, followed by Psalms 92 and 93. In some rituals the evening service is preceded by the recital of the *Song of Songs in honor of the Bride (or Queen) Sabbath. In many traditional rituals the hymn *"Anna be-Kho'aḥ" is said before the "Lekhah Dodi" (or Psalm 121). Chapter 2 of Mishnah *Shabbat* (*Ba-Meh Madlikin*) is recited in some rites before the main evening prayer, in other rites following it. In the Yemenite ritual special *piyyutim* are also inserted before the evening prayer on those Sabbaths which coincide with the New Moon as well as for Sabbaths in the *Omer period. The major deviations from the regular evening service are the elimination of the petitions of the *Amidah* and the substitution of blessings in honor of the Sabbath.

In modern Israel special *Kabbalat Shabbat* ceremonies are held on Friday at noontime in schools and kindergartens, and before supper in some kibbutzim, where they consist of lighting the Sabbath candles, reciting poetry, and singing songs in honor of the weekly day of rest. In the United States, many Reform and Conservative synagogues have introduced the late Friday evening service, which starts after the end of the business day in order to enable a greater number of the congregants to participate. The central feature of the service is the rabbi's sermon; after the service an *Oneg Shabbat* (Sabbath Reception) is usually held.

BIBLIOGRAPHY: Elbogen, Gottesdienst, 107–12; Idelsohn, Liturgy, 128ff.

[Meir Ydit]

KAʿB BEN ASAD (d. 627), chief of the Jewish tribe of *Qurayẓa in Medina. When Kaʿb saw the tragic fate awaiting his tribe as a result of their defeat by Muhammad's forces and their betrayal by their Arab allies, he offered three suggestions to his council: conversion to Islam; that the men kill their wives and children to save them from slavery and dishonor, but that they continue to fight; and that they unexpectedly attack Muhammad's forces on the Sabbath, thus desecrating the holy day. Each suggestion was rejected. He was put to death along with the rest of his tribe in 627, after refusing to accept Islam. Kaʿb is the subject of Tchernichowsky's poem "*Ha-Aḥaron li-Venei Kurayta*" ("The Last of the Banu Qurayẓa").

BIBLIOGRAPHY: H.Z. Hirschberg, *Yisrael be-Arav* (1946), 145f.; M. Ibn Ishaq, *Life of Muhammad*, tr. by A. Guillaume (1955), 461, 464f.

KABĪR, ABRAHAM ṢĀLIḤ AL- (1885–), Iraqi official. Born in *Baghdad, al-Kabīr received a legal education and was at first employed in various banks, later joining the Iraqi treasury service; he held important and responsible positions, especially at the time when Ezekiel *Sassoon was finance minister. Al-Kabīr also played an active role in Jewish communal life, and in 1946 testified before the Anglo-American Commission of Inquiry on the discrimination practiced against Jews by the Iraqi authorities. He settled in London in the 1960s.

Abraham Ṣāliḥ's brother, JOSEPH, also born in Baghdad, was a lawyer and communal worker. Al-Kabīr was at first employed in the Iraqi Ministry of Justice, but from 1925 he maintained a private law practice. From the early 1930s he lectured at the Baghdad School of Law on private international law and comparative law. He published his lectures in two books (in Arabic). As a member of the general council of the Jewish community of Baghdad from 1932, he was among the critics of the community's administration by its president Sasson *Kadoorie and published a pamphlet on this subject (Baghdad, 1944). In 1935–36, he represented the Jews of Baghdad in the Iraqi Parliament.

[Hayyim J. Cohen]

KABRI (Heb. כַּבְרִי), kibbutz bordering on Acre Plain and the hills of Upper Galilee in Israel, affiliated to Ha-Kibbutz ha-Me'uḥad. It was founded in 1949 by settlers from *Bet Arabah who were forced to abandon their settlement north of the Dead Sea in the *War of Independence (1948). In 1968 Kabri, with 560 inhabitants, engaged in mixed farming. In 2002 its population numbered 728, with the economy based on the manufacture of aluminum and plastic products and a few farming branches such as fruit plantations and cattle. Large-scale excavations in 1986–93 revealed settlement on the site from the Neolithic period and enormous growth in the Middle Bronze II period (2000–1550 B.C.E.). By the end of the Bronze Age (1200 B.C.E.) the site was deserted. In Roman and Byzantine times, Kabri (*Kabritha) was a flourishing center (Tos. Shev. 4:11). Numerous ashlars and mosaic floors remain from this era, some of which were reused in the houses of the Arab village which was abandoned in 1948. Porous limestone beneath a stratum of impervious heavy soil resulted in the formation of four copious springs whose fresh waters were led a distance of about 7 mi. (12 km.) to Acre by the aqueduct built in 1800 by the governor Aḥmad al-Jazzār. Under British Mandatory rule, a British-owned plant bottled the "Kabri water." In the spring of 1948, *Haganah soldiers on their way to reinforce the isolated kibbutz of *Yeḥi'am further east were caught at Kabri in an ambush, and 46 men fell; a memorial has been set up there. A government fruit-tree nursery, a Jewish National Fund (JNF) forest-tree nursery, and the JNF regional administration were located at Kabri.

WEBSITE: www.cabri.org.il.

[Efram Orni / Shaked Gilboa (2nd ed.)]

KABRITHA, a village in the territory of Ptolemais (Acre). In the talmudic lists describing the area held by those who returned from Babylonian exile, it is located on the border between the "wall of Acre" to the north and the "spring of Ga'aton" to the south (Sif. 51; Tosef. Shev. 4:11; TJ, Shev. 6:1, 36c, et al.). Some scholars have looked for it at Khirbat Qabārṣa to the south of Nahariyyah and near the outlet of Naḥal Ga'aton, but as this position is too close to the sea and is also west of the coastal road which marked the theoretical boundary of the Holy Land, the identification with *Kabri to the northwest of Nahariyyah is preferable.

BIBLIOGRAPHY: Dalman, in: PJB, 19 (1923), 22 n. 3; Press, Ereẓ 3 (1952), 467. **ADD. BIBLIOGRAPHY:** Y. Tsafrir, L. Di Segni, and J. Green, *Tabula Imperii Romani. Iudaea – Palaestina. Maps and Gazetteer* (1994), 159, s.v.

[Michael Avi-Yonah]

KACH, Israeli party established by Rabbi Meir *Kahane in 1971, as an outpost of the Jewish Defense League in the United States. Kach advocated that the *halakhah* should become the law of the State of Israel in Greater Israel, and proposed that the state's Arab inhabitants be given the option of becoming citizens after a security check, on condition that they would agree to serve in the defense forces and undertake other civilian duties, and accept the status of *ger toshav* (non-Jewish resident), or emigrating from the country. In the elections to the Eighth, Ninth and Tenth Knessets Kach ran but did not pass the 1% qualifying threshold. An attempt to disqualify the party from running in the elections to the Tenth Knesset failed. In that election campaign Kach advocated that the Arabs be expelled from the country, to prevent their becoming a majority. It also advocated that the Camp David Accords and the Egyptian-Israeli Peace Treaty be abrogated, that the Israeli response to acts of terror should be counterterror, and that the mosques be removed from the Temple Mount. Kach was disqualified by the Central Elections Committee from running in the Eleventh Knesset elections. However, the High Court of Justice ruled that the disqualification was illegal. In these elections Kach finally passed the qualifying threshold, and Kahane entered the Knesset. In the Knesset Kahane presented several bills that were rejected by the Knesset Presidium, headed by Knesset Speaker Shlomo *Hillel, since they were viewed as racist. On July 31, 1985, both Basic Law: the Knesset and the Election Law were amended to enable the Central Elections Committee to disqualify lists that incite to racism and deny the democratic character of the State of Israel. On this basis Kach was disqualified from running in the elections to the Twelfth Kensset.

Following the murder of Kahane in November 1990 in New York by an Egyptian assassin, Kach split into two movements. "Kahane Ḥai," which was headed by his son Binyamin Ze`ev, who was killed in a terrorist attack in Samaria in December 2000, and Ko'aḥ, which soon assumed the name Kach, headed by Kahane's former assistant Baruch Marzel, who lives in Tel Rumeida in Hebron.

Following the massacre by Baruch Goldstein in the Cave of Machpelah on February 24, 1994 – which was welcomed by Kach – the movement was declared illegal, but it has since continued to exist underground, with its members participating in demonstrations, clashing with the police, and attacking Palestinians and Palestinian property. After the Government approved the plan for disengagement from the Gaza Strip and the dismantlement of settlements, Kach advocated violent resistance to the removal of settlements, while verbally and physically attacking ministers. Among its activists are Marzel, No'am Federman, Tiran Pollack, and Itamar Ben-Gvir, who have frequently been detained by the police.

[Susan Hattis Rolef (2nd ed.)]

KACYZNE (Katsizne), ALTER (1885–1941), Yiddish poet and essayist. Born in Vilna, he was a professional photographer and also wrote poetry, fiction, drama, and essays. His earliest short stories were written in Russian and published by S. *An-Ski, one of whose literary executors he was; he also completed An-Ski's fragmentary drama *Tog un Nakht* ("Day and Night"), which was frequently performed on Yiddish, Polish, and German stages in the 1920s. Under the influence of I.L. *Peretz and modern Polish poets, Kacyzne wrote his first mystical drama, which was not favorably received. He aroused greater attention with his folk ballads and with semi-mystical, semi-realistic short stories, such as "Kranke Perl" ("Sick Pearl" in *Arabeskn*, 1922). His drama *Dukus* ("The Duke," 1926), whose hero was a legendary Vilna aristocrat who embraced Judaism, was first staged in Warsaw with Abraham *Morewski in the leading role and then often performed in Yiddish theaters worldwide. His less popular historical drama *Hordes* ("Herod," 1926) was generally held to be of greater literary value. His two-volume novel *Shtarke un Shvakhe* ("Strong and Weak"), dealing with Polish-Jewish intellectuals during World War I, was published posthumously in Argentina in 1954. Fleeing the Germans in 1941, he tried to escape to Tarnopol, but was seized by Ukrainian collaborators and beaten to death. His daughter Shulamit Reale published the first volume of his collected works in 1967.

BIBLIOGRAPHY: Rejzen, Leksikon, 4 (1929), 531–6; Ravitch, in: A. Kacyzne: *Shtarke un Shvakhe* (1954), introduction. **ADD. BIBLIOGRAPHY:** LNYL, 8 (1981), 117–19; N. Mayzl, *Forgeyer un Mitsaytler* (1946), 361–71; A. Goldberg, *Undzere Dramaturgn* (1961), 333–54; D. Sadan, in: *Avnei Miftan*, 3 (1972), 188–1; Y. Rapoport, *Mehus fun Dikhtung* (1963), 294–300; Sh. Belis, *Portretn un Problemen* (1964), 68–73.

[Melech Ravitch]

KACZÉR (originally **Katz**), **ILLÉS** (1887–1980), Hungarian author and journalist. Born in Szatmár, Kaczér began his career in provincial journalism before starting to write for Budapest newspapers. He made his name as a novelist and playwright, and his dramas enjoyed considerable success in Hungary during the 1920s. By this time, however, as a result of the revolution of 1918–19, he had left the country and gone to live first in Vienna and later in Berlin, Romania, and Czechoslovakia. In 1938 he moved to London but in 1959, at which time he was already established as a contributor of stories and essays to the Hungarian-language newspaper *Uj Kelet*, made his home in Israel. Kaćzer was noted for his powerful treatment of Jewish themes, ranging from biblical times to the era of social and religious family conflict in the 19th and 20th centuries. His works include the novel *Khafrit, az egyiptomi asszony* (1916); the play *Megjött a Messiás* (1921); *Ikongo nem hal meg* (1936); *Fear Not, My Servant Jacob* (1947); and *The Siege of Jericho* (1949), originally published in London as *The Siege*, 2 vols; and *Három a csillag* (1956).

BIBLIOGRAPHY: *Magyar Zsidó Lexikon* (1929), 445; *Magyar Irodalmi Lexikon*, 1 (1963), 565.

[Baruch Yaron]

KACZERGINSKY, SZMERKE (1908–1954), Yiddish writer. Born in Vilna (Lithuania), Kaczerginsky joined the literary group *Yung Vilne in 1929, contributing poems and stories to its publications. He worked as a printer and was active in underground communist movements, for which activity he was frequently arrested. During the German occupation he was one of several Yiddish intellectuals (including *Abraham Sutzkever) forced to select the most important holdings of the *YIVO Institute to be shipped to Germany (unchosen material was slated to be destroyed). This *Papir Brigade* smuggled both books to be hidden in the Vilna ghetto and weapons to the partisans. Kaczerginsky escaped the ghetto before its liquidation and joined the partisans. After liberation Kaczerginsky returned to Vilna, where he helped dig up the hidden materials and ship them to the new YIVO headquarters in New York. Discouraged by Soviet control, he left for Poland and then Paris. In May 1950 he settled in Argentina, where he became a leading figure in Yiddish cultural life. While returning from a lecture tour he was killed in an airplane crash. Kaczerginsky's writings are notable for their simplicity and power. His most important work chronicles, in verse, prose, and drama, the Vilna ghetto and the Jewish partisan movement. Among his books are: *Khurbn Vilne* ("The Destruction of Vilna," 1947) and *Ikh Bin Geven a Partizan* ("I Was a Partisan," 1952); in his travels after the war he collected *Lider fun di Getos un Lagern* ("Songs of the Ghettos and Concentration Camps," 1948).

BIBLIOGRAPHY: E. Schulman: *Yung Vilne* (1946), 17–20; *Shmerke Katsherginski Ondenk-Bukh* (1955), incl. bibl. **ADD. BIBLIOGRAPHY:** LNYL, 8 (1981), 48–50.

[Elias Schulman / Faith Jones (2nd ed.)]

KADAN (Czech **Kadaň**; Ger. **Kaaden**), town in N.W. Bohemia, Czech Republic. Jews are first mentioned in Kadan in 1339 and 1341. Between 1465 and 1517, seven Jews were formally granted citizenship. However, after the town had bought its freedom from the local lord, the Jews were expelled in 1520. After receiving permission from Frederick II, one Jewish family settled in Kadan in 1624; more followed (mainly from *Udlice) in spite of protests by the townsmen. This new community was expelled in 1650 after the execution of a visiting Jew on charges of killing a Christian child. The body of the child was preserved in a special altar in the church (which was burned down in 1810). There were ten Jewish families in the town in 1724 and nine in 1798. More lived there from the middle of the 19th century, totaling 118 in the district in 1869 and 219 in 1881. The congregation, founded in 1874, was approved in 1884 and legally became a community in 1893. From 409 in 1910, the number of Jews fell to 116 (1.5% of the total population) in 1930. The community was dispersed at the time of the Nazi occupation of the Sudeten area and the synagogue was set on fire on Nov. 10, 1938. Most of the Jews who remained in the Protectorate were sent to the death camps.

BIBLIOGRAPHY: J. Hoffmann, in: H. Gold (ed.), *Juden und Judengemeinden Boehmens…* (1934), 223–45; Germ Jud, 2 (1968), 384.

[Jan Herman]

KÁDAR, JÁN (1918–1979), film director. Born in Budapest, Kádar was imprisoned in a Hungarian labor camp during World War II. Later he worked for the Czech state film studios, and with Elmar Klos made *Death Is Called Engelchen*, which won acclaim. He became known in the West for the film *The Shop on Main Street* (1965), which starred Ida Kaminska and won an Academy Award. Kádar was linked with the writers and artists involved in the liberal movement in Czechoslovakia in 1968. In 1969 he directed the American film of Bernard *Malamud's story, *Angel Levine*.

KADARI, SHRAGA (1907–1982), Hebrew author. Born in Lvov, he went in 1927 to Ereẓ Israel, where he worked as an agricultural laborer, and later was one of the founders of *Kefar Pines. In 1936 he joined the staff of the cultural department of the *Va'ad Le'ummi. After the establishment of the State of Israel he became an official of the Ministry of Social Welfare. His stories and articles appeared in many newspapers and journals (particularly the dailies *Davar* and *Ha-Ẓofeh*). He published several books, including *Mi-Martef ha-Olam* (1936), *Asonah shel Alinah* (1939), *Einayim Aẓumot* (1945), *Eẓ ha-Ahavah* (1956), *Mi Yitten Boker* (1960, a novel), *Megillat Korekh ha-Sefarim* (1962), *Veha-Boker le-Darko Oleh* (a novel, 1981), and *Shezufei ha-Leḥi ha-Aḥat* (1967, a collection of stories).

BIBLIOGRAPHY: J. Lichtenbaum, *Bi-Teḥumah shel Sifrut* (1962), 121–5; J. Churgin, in: *Ha-Ḥinnukh*, 4 (1962), 454–8; A. Cohen, *Soferim Ivriyyim Benei Zemannenu* (1964), 80–83. **ADD. BIBLIOGRAPHY:** A. Sharvit, "*Hilkhei Nefesh u-Markhei Lashon: Iyyun bi-Yeẓirat Shraga Kadari*," in: *Yerushalayim* 13:1–2 (1979), 111–18; A. Sharvit, "*Yeẓirat Shraga Kadari be-Hebet Nossaf*," in: *Haẓofeh* (1983), 6; A. Lipshitz, "*Li-Demutam shel Shenei Mesaperim: Yehudah Ya'ari ve-Shraga Kadari*," in: *Biẓaron*, 5:17–18 (1983), 123–27; G. Shaked, *Ha-Sipporet ha-Ivrit*, 3 (1988), 158–64.

[Getzel Kressel]

KADDARI, MENACHEM ZEVI (1925–), Hebrew scholar and linguist. Born in Mezoekoevesd (Hungary), Kaddari studied philosophy and Semitic languages at the Pazmany-Peter University of Budapest and Jewish bibliography, Bible, and Jewish philosophy at the Rabbinical Seminary (1945–46). He immigrated to Israel in 1947 and continued his academic training in Hebrew, Bible, Jewish philosophy, and Kabbalah at the Hebrew University of Jerusalem (1947–50). In 1953 he submitted his Ph.D. thesis on *Grammar of the Aramaic Language of the Zohar* (published in 1971). Teaching at Bar-Ilan University from 1961, he was appointed full professor in 1970, where he also served as dean of the Faculty of Humanities (1967–70) and rector of the University (1971–74). He also taught at several universities abroad, among them UCLA (1967), the University of Leeds, U.K. (1978), and the University of Witwatersrand, Johannesburg (1979–81). Kaddari was elected a member of the Hebrew Academy in 1973 and its vice president in 1994. He received the Israel Prize in 1999. Kaddari's major fields of research are Aramaic, Hebrew syntax, biblical and rabbinic Hebrew, and, mainly, modern Hebrew. Among his major works are *Oẓar Leshon ha-Mikrah: Konkordansi'ah Mele'ah u-Millon Ivri ve-Angli*, letters י–ת, initiated by Y. Blau and S. Loewenstamm, with whom he had already collaborated in the publication of vol. 3 (letters ז–ט), and *Taḥbir ve-Semantikah ba-Ivrit shel-le-aḥar ha-Mikra: Iyyunim ba-Di'akhroni'ah shel ha-Lashon ha-Ivrit*, 2 vols. (1991, 1995). A full list of Kaddari's works and scientific publications appeared in *Meḥkarim ba-Lashon ha-Ivrit ha-Attikah ve-ha-Ḥadashah li-Khevod Menachem Zevi Kaddari* (ed. S. Sharvit, 1999, 413–24).

During World War II, Kaddari was active in the clandestine pioneering Zionist movement in Hungary (1943–46) and a member of the joint secretariat of the *ma'pilim* (*"illegal" immigration) camps in Cyprus (1946–47). During Israel's War of Independence, he fought in the Haganah in *Gush Etzyon (*Massu'ot Yitzḥak) and Jerusalem.

[Aharon Maman (2nd ed.)]

KADDISH (Aram. קַדִּישׁ; "holy"), a doxology, most of it in Aramaic, recited with congregational responses at the close of individual sections of the public service and at the conclusion of the service itself. There are four main types of *Kaddish*:

(a) THE WHOLE (OR COMPLETE) KADDISH, the text of which is as follows:

> Glorified and sanctified be God's great name throughout the world which He has created according to His will. May He establish His kingdom in your lifetime and during your days, and within the life of the entire house of Israel, speedily and soon; and say, Amen.

The congregational response, which is repeated by the **sheli'aḥ ẓibbur* is

> May His great name be blessed forever and to all eternity.
> Blessed and praised, glorified and exalted, extolled and honored, adored and lauded be the name of the Holy One, blessed be He, beyond all the blessings and hymns, praises and consolations that are ever spoken in the world; and say Amen.
> May the prayers and supplications of the whole house of Israel be accepted by their Father in heaven; and say, Amen.
> May there be abundant peace from heaven and life, for us and for all Israel; and say, Amen.
> He who creates peace in His high places, may He create peace for us and for all Israel; and say Amen.

It is recited by the *sheli'aḥ ẓibbur* after each **Amidah* (virtually concluding the whole service), except in the morning service when it comes after the prayer *U-Va le-Ẓiyyon*.

(b) THE "HALF" KADDISH consists of the above text with the exception of the concluding passage, from "May the prayers and supplications ..." until the end of the prayer. It is also recited by the *sheli'aḥ ẓibbur* and functions as a link between the sections of each service. In the morning service, the "Half" *Kaddish* is recited after the psalms (**Pesukei de-Zimra*), the *Amidah* (or the **Taḥanun*, when that is said), and the Reading of the Law. In the afternoon service, it is recited before the *Amidah*; in the evening service before *Ve-Hu Raḥum* (when the special psalms before it are recited) and before the *Amidah*. It is also recited before the **Musaf* service.

(c) THE KADDISH DE-RABBANAN ("the scholars' *Kaddish*") consists of the whole *Kaddish* with "May the prayers and supplications ...," however, replaced by, "[We pray] for Israel, for our teachers and their disciples and the disciples of their disciples, and for all who study the Torah, here and everywhere. May they have abundant peace, loving-kindness, ample sustenance and salvation from their Father Who is in heaven; and say, Amen." The prayer then continues with the passage "May there be abundant peace from Heaven ..." It is recited by mourners after communal study and in the synagogue, particularly after the reading of **Ba-Meh Madlikin* (Shab. 2) on Friday nights, after the early morning service, and after **Ein Ke-Elohenu*.

(d) THE MOURNERS' KADDISH contains the full text of the whole *Kaddish* with the exception of the line "May the prayers and supplications ..." It is recited by the close relatives of the deceased (see: *Mourning) after the **Aleinu*, at the end of each service, and may be repeated after the reading of additional psalms.

All four forms of the *Kaddish* are recited standing, facing Jerusalem. In some communities, the whole congregation stands, in others only the mourners. If one stands at the beginning of the *Kaddish*, however, one should not sit down before the response "May His great name be blessed ..." When the *Kaddish* is recited at the burial service, an addition, stressing the eschatological aspect of the *Kaddish*, is made to the opening paragraph. It is also added to the *Kaddish* recited at the celebration marking the conclusion of the study of a Talmud tractate (*Siyyum*).

The *Kaddish* is characterized by an abundance of praise and glorification of God and an expression of hope for the speedy establishment of His kingdom on earth. The brief reference to the latter ("May He establish His kingdom") in the usual Ashkenazi version is expanded by the Sephardim with *ve-Yaẓmaḥ purkaneih ve-karev meshiḥeih* ("May He make His salvation closer and bring His Messiah near"). The congregational response "May His great name be blessed for ever and to all eternity" is the kernel of the prayer (Sifre to Deut. 32:3). The verse is akin to Daniel 2:20 (in Aramaic), to Job 1:21, and to Psalm 113:2 (in Hebrew), and to the eulogy "Blessed be the name of His glorious kingdom for ever and ever," which was recited in the Temple (Yoma 3:8). According to R. Joshua b. Levi, "joining loudly and in unison in [this] congregational response ..." has the power of influencing the heavenly decree in one's favor (Shab. 119b; cf. Mid. Prov. 10).

The simple form in which the eschatological pleas are phrased and the lack of allusion to the destruction of the Temple indicate the antiquity of the *Kaddish* prayer. The opening phrase, "Magnified and sanctified be His great name in the world ..." (whose origin is Ezek. 38:23), shows affinities to the "Lord's Prayer" (Matt. 6:9–13); similar phrases were apparently used in a variety of public and private prayers (e.g., that of thanksgiving for rain, cited in TJ, Ta'an. 1:3, 64b). The *Kaddish* prayer was not originally part of the synagogue service. The Talmud (Sot. 49a, and Rashi ad loc.) specifically records that it first served as a concluding prayer to the public aggadic discourse which was also conducted in Aramaic. The *Kaddish de-Rabbanan* testifies to this connection. Special verses were even inserted into the *Kaddish de-Rabbanan*, for the *nasi*, *resh galuta*, and the heads of the academies (cf. Schechter in *Gedenkbuch D. Kaufmann* (1900), Hebr. part 52–4), or, as in Yemen, for such distinguished scholars as Maimonides (Letter of Naḥmanides to the French Rabbis, in *Kovez Teshuvot ha-Rambam*, Leipzig edition (1859), 9a).

The *Kaddish* is mentioned as part of the prescribed synagogue daily prayers for the first time in tractate *Soferim* (c. sixth century C.E.). By geonic times, it had become a statutory synagogue prayer requiring the presence of ten adult males. The name *Kaddish* is first mentioned in *Soferim* 10:7, and the explanatory passage beginning "Blessed and praised ... etc." (which is recited in Hebrew) was added for non-Aramaic speakers. The plea for the acceptance of the prayer ("May the prayers and supplications ... etc."), the prayer for the welfare of the supplicants ("May there be abundant peace from heaven ..."), and the concluding passage ("He who creates peace ... etc.," cf. Job 25:2), were all later additions.

The German and Italian text, quoted above, is derived from *Seder Rav *Amram* (ed. by D. Hedegard, 1951) but exhibits local variations. In the Yemenite rite, the phrase *le-ella u-le-ella* ("much beyond all praises") is repeated all the year round, and not only during the *ten days of penitence. In Jerusalem and Safed the word *kaddisha* is added in the *Kaddish de-Rabbanan* ending "in this holy place and everywhere," and according to the *Maḥzor Romanyah*, several additions were made to the passage "May the prayers and supplication ..." On the other hand, the final invitation to the congregation to respond "*amen*" (i.e., *ve-imru*, "and say") is neither in the *Seder Rav Amram* nor in other old manuscripts.

The practice of mourners reciting the *Kaddish* seems to have originated during the 13th century, at the time of severe persecutions in Germany by the Crusaders. No reference is made to it in the *Maḥzor Vitry* (the comment on page 74 is a later interpolation). According to a late *aggadah* (originating in *Seder Eliyahu Zuta*), R. *Akiva rescued a soul from punishment in hell by urging the latter's sons to recite the verse "May His great name be blessed ..." The idea was already earlier expressed in *Sanhedrin* 104a. The mourner's *Kaddish*, now recited for 11 and not the full 12 months of the mourning period (according to the Sh. Ar., YD 376:4, the longer period implies a disrespectful view of the parents' piety), is also recited on the **yahrzeit*. It has been suggested that the *Kaddish* became the mourner's prayer because of the mention of the resurrection of the dead in the messianic passage at the beginning. (The phrase, however, no longer occurs in most versions today.) The *Kaddish* is not properly "a prayer for the soul of the departed," but an expression of the *ẓidduk ha-din* ("justification of judgment") by the bereaved, conforming to the spirit of the maxim: "Man is obliged to give praise for the evil [that befalls him] even as he gives praise for the good" (Ber. 9:5). However, the prayer is popularly thought to be a "prayer for the dead" to the extent that a son, in Yiddish, is often called "a *Kaddish*," and a man is said to have died "without leaving a *Kaddish*."

Musical Rendition

The various forms and functions of the *Kaddish* in the service are matched by a variety of musical configurations. Melodies range from simple *parlando* recitatives to elaborate solo productions, from light tunes in the popular taste to most solemn and impressive compositions. Salamone de *Rossi even set the entire text for three- and five-part chorus (*Ha-Shirim asher li-Shelomo*, Venice, 1623, nos. 1 and 16). Nevertheless, some guiding principles may be ascertained from the multiplicity of *Kaddish* tunes. In the Ashkenazi rite, the *Kaddish* before the *Amidah* (especially in the *Musaf* prayer) is distinguished by a striving for sublime melodic expression (see *Music, Jewish, Ex. 30; and **Mi-Sinai Niggunim*, Ex. 1, nos. 3, 7, 9); its music is sometimes identical with that of the following *Avot* benediction. The Sephardim emphasize rather the *Kaddish* preceding *Barekhu*, by means of elaborate coloraturas (Idelsohn, Melodien, 2 (1922), 97, no. 50; 4 (1930), 137, no. 32; 195, no. 220), or by melodic identity with the said benediction. In the Ashkenazi synagogues, certain liturgical situations evoke *Kaddish* melodies of a definite character or form. The *Kaddish* which closes the *Musaf* prayer is preferably sung to a lively and gay tune, sometimes in a dancelike manner (earliest example notated by Benedetto Marcello in his *Estro Poetico-Armonico*, Venice, 1724–27). During festivals the *Kaddish* over the Torah scroll and that before the evening *Amidah* are "labeled" with musical motives characteristic of the feast in question. On Simḥat Torah, which closes the cycle of holidays, the characteristic motives of all the festivals are assembled in the "Year-*Kaddish*."

A Kaddish *melody sung before* Barekhu *in the Sephardi morning service on Rosh Ha-Shanah.* Barekhu *is sung to the same melody. From O. Cahby (ed.),* Liturgie Sephardi *no 65, 1959. Courtesy World Sephardi Federation, London.*

The particular tunes anchored in local traditions are also worth mentioning, such as the so-called *Trommel* ("drumming") *Kaddish* which used to be sung in Frankfurt on the Main on "Purim Vinz" – the 20th of Adar, commemorating that day in 1616 when, after the *Fettmilch persecution, the Jews were brought back into the town "with trumpets and drums" as described in Elhanan Helen's *Megillat Vinz* (see F. Ogutsch, *Der Frankfurter Kantor*, 1930, 103, no. 319). The famous "*Kaddish*" of R. *Levi Isaac of Berdichev, *A Din-Toyre mit Got*, is a kind of introduction to the liturgical *Kaddish*, in which Levi Isaac addresses and rebukes God in an extended "prose poem" whose melody comprises elements of the High Holiday liturgy (see Idelsohn, Melodien, 10 (1932), XII, 29, no. 104). Leonard Bernstein's *Kaddish* (his Symphony no. 3, 1963) for narrator, choir, and orchestra is also a kind of "lawsuit with God" centering on the *Kaddish* and is thus a descendant of Levi Isaac's song.

[Hanoch Avenary]

Women and *Kaddish*

Responsa literature, historical sources, and contemporary testimony indicate that at least since the 17th century some women have recited the mourner's *Kaddish*, both at home during *shiva* and at daily services in the synagogue. Saying *Kaddish* at the grave during the funeral was also a customary practice among devout women in certain communities. The earliest known responsum in which the issue of women and *Kaddish* is discussed appears in the late 17th-century work of R. Jair Hayyim Ben Moses Samson *Bacharach, known as the *Ḥavvat Yair.* Based on a particular set of circumstances in Amsterdam, R. Bacharach's responsum, which became known as "the Amsterdam case," concludes that women may recite *Kaddish*, but the nuances of the responsum are used by various rabbis in different ways. Among those who restrict the Amsterdam case, arguing variously for limitations on women's expression of grief through public recitation of *Kaddish*, are the *Be'er Heitev*, *Gesher ha-Ḥayyim*, *Mishpetei Uziel*, *Matteh Ephraim*, and *Aseh Lekha Rav.* R. Israel Meir *Lau, former Ashkenazi chief rabbi in Israel, and Reuven Fink in the U.S. are adamant in their opposition to women's saying *Kaddish.*

While R. Bacharach, who realized that he was transforming social practice, also articulated caution, those who restrict his opinion project a general fear of women's entering the public religious sphere. This apprehension is absent in the vocal minority of decisors who offer lenient interpretations of the Amsterdam case, often adding specific details relevant to changed social circumstances. Examples are found in the writings of R. Joseph B. *Soloveitchik, R. Aaron *Soloveitchik, R. Moshe Leib Blair, and R. Yehuda Herzl Henkin.

In 1916, Henrietta *Szold expressed her conviction that it was never intended by Jewish law and custom that women should be exempt from positive commandments if they were able to perform them, writing, "And of the *Kaddish* I feel sure this is particularly true" (letter to Haym Peretz, in *Four Centuries of Jewish Women's Spirituality*, ed. E. Umansky and D. Ashton (1992), 164–65).

Among Modern Orthodox women at the beginning of the 21st century, the recitation of *Kaddish* is widespread. In Reform, Reconstructionist, and most Conservative practice, women recite the mourner's *Kaddish* as a matter of course and are also counted among the ten persons required to constitute the *minyan* required for communal worship. In recent years, several women have written personal testimonies about reciting *Kaddish* in Orthodox settings. These include E.M. Broner (*Mornings and Mourning: A Kaddish Journal* (1994)) and Sara Reguer and Deborah E. Lipstadt (in essays anthologized in *On Being a Jewish Feminist*, ed. S. Heschel (1983; rep. 1995), 177–81, 207–9).

[Rochelle L. Millen (2nd ed.)]

BIBLIOGRAPHY: D. de Sola Pool, *The Old Jewish-Aramaic Prayer, the Kaddish* (1909); Karel, in: *Ha-Shilo'aḥ*, 35 (1918), 36–49, 426–30, 521–7; Elbogen, Gottesdienst, 92–98; Abrahams, Companion, xxxixf., lxxxviiif.; Idelsohn, Liturgy, 84–88; J. Heinemann, *Ha-Tefillot bi-Tekufat ha-Tanna'im ve-ha-Amora'im* (1966²), index, 189, s.v.; Heinemann, in: JSS, 5 (1960), 264–80. **ADD. BIBLIOGRAPHY:** R.L. Millen, *Women, Birth, and Death in Jewish Law and Practice* (2004); D. Golinkin, *Halakhah for Our Time: A Conservative Approach to Jewish Law* (1991); idem (ed.), *Responsa of the Va'ad Halakhah of the Rabbinical Assembly of Israel*, vol. 3 (1997); W. Jacob (ed.), *American Reform Responsa: Collected Responsa of the Central Conference of American Rabbis, 1889–1983* (1983).

KADELBURG, LAVOSLAV (1910–1995), lawyer. Kadelburg was born in Vinkovci, Croatia, and completed his secondary education there. He participated in the local Herut youth organization (1925–30) and studied law and economics. He was appointed attorney general in the High Court of the Serbian Republic; later he acted as judge in the same court, retiring in 1966. In the following years acted as judge in International Arbitration Tribunals.

Before the Nazi invasion of Yugoslavia in April 1941, he was mobilized as a reserve officer of the Royal Yugoslav Army; he was interned in POW camps in Germany throughout WWII. Upon his return, Kadelburg developed close contacts with the new regime that took over the country under Tito's leadership and became involved again in Jewish affairs. Along with Dr. Albert *Vajs (Weiss), he helped in rehabilitating the few survivors of the Holocaust and in restoring Jewish life. On Vajs's death, he carried on as the president of the renewed Federation of Jewish Communities in Belgrade. He held that position for many years and was considered the mainstay of Jewry in that area. He was also a member of the Executive of the World Jewish Congress.

Commanding several languages, he was a widely respected figure in European Jewish assemblies, where his advice was often sought.

[Zvi Loker (2nd ed.)]

KADESH (Heb. קָדֵשׁ), name of several places in Ereẓ Israel and Syria to which a sacred character is attributed.

(1) Kadesh, Kadesh-Barnea (Heb. קָדֵשׁ, קָדֵשׁ בַּרְנֵעַ), an important oasis situated on the southern border of Canaan (Num. 34:4; Josh. 15:3; Ezek. 47:19; 48:28) in the wilderness of Zin (Num. 20:1; 27:14; 33:36; Deut. 32:51) – part of the wilderness of Paran (Num. 20:16) – at a distance of an eleven days' journey from Mt. Horeb (Deut. 1:2). Kadesh is alternatively called En-Mishpat ("spring of judgment"; Gen. 14:7) and the "waters of Meribah" ("strife," Num. 20:13, 24; 27:14; Deut. 32:51), names which indicate its special role as a sacred place of judgment and assembly for the desert tribes.

Kadesh-Barnea appears in the stories of Abraham (Gen. 16:14; 20:1) and in the description of the expedition of Chedorlaomer and his allies; Kadesh-Barnea, here called En-Mishpat, is said to have been inhabited by Amalekites (Gen. 14:7). During the Exodus it served as an assembly point for the Israelite tribes in the desert (Deut. 1:46). Some scholars regard it as the first amphictyonic center of the Israelites. From Kadesh-Barnea spies were sent to explore Canaan (Num. 13:26); the attempt was made to penetrate into Canaan which was prevented by Arad and Hormah (Num. 14:40–45; 21:1; 33:36–40); messengers were sent to the king of Edom; and from here the Israelites started out on their eastward march to Transjordan (Num. 20:14ff.; 33:36ff.; Deut. 1:46ff.; Judg. 11:16ff.). Biblical tradition associates Kadesh-Barnea with the family of Moses in particular: here Moses drew water abundantly from the rock; here he and Aaron were punished for their lack of faith by being denied entrance into the land of Canaan (Num. 20:2ff.); here his sister Miriam died and was buried (Num. 20:1); and Aaron died nearby at mount Hor (Num. 20:22–29; 33:37–39). Kadesh-Barnea has been identified with the group of springs 46 mi. (75 km.) south of Beer-Sheba and 15 mi. (25 km.) south of Niẓẓanah. The name is preserved at the southernmost spring ʿAyn Qudays, but ʿAyn al-Qudayrāt to the north of it is of much greater importance being a rich spring which waters a fertile plain. In its vicinity a large fortress from the time of the Judahite kings was discovered. Most scholars therefore identify Kadesh-Barnea with the larger spring; the entire group of springs may have originally been called Kadesh-Barnea and the name survived at the southern one despite its lesser importance. During the Sinai campaign a large Israelite fortress was discovered also above ʿAyn Qudays as well as numerous remains in the whole region from the Middle Bronze I (c. 2000 B.C.E.) and Israelite periods.

Large-scale excavations in 1976 and 1982 uncovered three superimposed fortresses on the site. The first was dated to the 11th century, the second to around the time of Hezekiah and measured 65 ft. × 195 ft. (20 × 60 m.) with six rectangular towers and a moat and glacis on three sides, and the third to the seventh century, probably destroyed by Nebuchadnezzar. Inscriptions indicate that the inhabitants of the fortress probably spoke Hebrew.

(2) Kedesh in Galilee (Heb. קֶדֶשׁ בַּגָּלִיל), one of the principal cities in Upper Galilee in the Canaanite and Israelite pe-

riods. In the opinion of some scholars, it is mentioned in the list of cities conquered by Thutmosis III (c. 1468 B.C.E.) and depicted on a relief of Seti I (c. 1300 B.C.E.); others, however, argue that these references are to Kadesh on the Orontes. In the Bible, "Kedesh in Galilee in the hill country of Naphtali" appears in the list of defeated Canaanite kings (Josh. 12:22), as a city of refuge (Josh. 20:7) and a levitical city (Josh. 21:32; I Chron. 6:61), and as one of the fortified cities of the tribe of Naphtali (Josh. 19:37). It was conquered by Tiglath-Pileser III in his expedition in 733/2 B.C.E. (II Kings 15:29) but continued to exist in the Second Temple period eventually becoming a Hellenistic city in the territory of Tyre. Near Kedesh, Jonathan the Hasmonean defeated the army of Demetrius II (I Macc. 11:63–73; Jos., Ant. 13:154). It is identified with Tell Qadis, a large tell overlooking the fertile plateau west of the Ḥuleh, and containing remains and fortifications from the Canaanite, Israelite, and later periods. A Roman temple was partially excavated in 1981–84, dedicated under Hadrian in 117/8 C.E.

(3) Kedesh-Naphtali (Heb. קֶדֶשׁ־נַפְתָּלִי), the birthplace of Barak, son of Abinoam, located in Galilee in the territory of the tribe of Naphtali (Judg. 4:6, 9–11). It is generally identified with Kedesh (2) but this seems unsound for the following reasons:

(a) Kedesh Upper Galilee is far from Mt. Tabor in the vicinity of which Deborah's battle with the Canaanite kings took place;

(b) "Elon-Bezaanannim, which is by Kedesh" (Judg. 4:11) is also known from the border description of Naphtali where it is situated between the Tabor and the Jordan (Josh. 19:33).

Kedesh-Naphtali should therefore be sought east of Mount Tabor and in this area Khirbat al-Kadīsh near Poriyyah which contains extensive remains from the early Israelite period has been proposed as the location of the site.

(4) Kadesh on the Orontes, a major city in the Canaanite period on the Orontes River, identified with Tell Nabī Mind south of Lake Homs. Together with Megiddo, Kadesh headed the coalition of Canaanite kings against Thutmosis III in their great battle in c. 1468 B.C.E. Although confined with the other defeated kings within the walls of Megiddo, the king of Kadesh succeeded in escaping the Egyptian siege and Kadesh was conquered only during Thutmosis' sixth campaign, in his eighth year. In the 14th century B.C.E. the city came under Hittite influence, as indicated by the *El-Amarna letters. It was conquered at the beginning of the 13th century by Seti I as shown in a stele discovered by Pézard in his excavations at Kadesh. A relief depicting Seti's conquest may be preserved in the Karnak temple in Egypt but some scholars interpret it as referring to Kadesh in Galilee. During the reign of Ramses II, a famous battle between the Egyptians and the Hittites (c. 1280 B.C.E.) took place near Kadesh; it actually terminated in a defeat for the Egyptians and Kadesh remained in the possession of the Hittites. According to the peace treaty concluded after the battle, the border between the two kingdoms in the Lebanon al-Biqʿa was moved south of Kadesh. Further information on the city is lacking. It was apparently destroyed in the invasion of the Sea Peoples at the beginning of the 12th century B.C.E. and its place was taken over in the Israelite period by Riblah on the Orontes south of Kadesh. The border of Lebo-Hamath in the Bible corresponds to the Egyptian border south of Kadesh.

Excavations from 1975 reveal a settlement at the site in the sixth millennium B.C.E. and then reoccupation in the third millennium. The settlement was apparently destroyed around 1600 B.C.E. and reestablished by the time mentioned in the sources, i.e., 1468.

BIBLIOGRAPHY: (1) B. Rothenberg and J. Aharoni, *Tagliyyot Sinai* (1958); H.C. Trumbull, *Kadesh-Barnea* (1884): C.L. Woolley and T.E. Lawrence, *The Wilderness of Zin* (1915); Glueck, in: AASOR, 15 (1935), 118ff.; Phythian-Adams, in: PEFAS, 67 (1935), 69ff.; 114ff.; de Vaux and Savignac, in: RB, 47 (1938), 89ff. (2) J. Aharoni, *Hitnaḥalut Shivtei Yisrael ba-Galil ha-Elyon* (1957), index; Avi-Yonah, Land, index; Albright, in: BASOR, 19 (1928), 12; 35 (1929), 9; J. Garstang, *Joshua-Judges* (1931), 390–91. (3) Press, in: BJPES, 1, pt. 3 (1933/34), 26ff.; J. Aharoni, op. cit., index; Kolshari, in: BIES, 27 (1963), 165ff. (4); M. Péyard, *Qadesh Mission à Tell Nebi Mend…* (1931); Du Buisson, in: *Mélanges Maspéro*, 1 (1938), 919ff.; Gardiner, in: *Onomastica*, 2 (1947), index; Aharoni, Land, index.

[Yohanan Aharoni]

KADIMAH (Heb. קָדִימָה; "Forward"), semi-urban settlement in central Israel. Kadimah was founded as a moshav in 1933. It was initially based almost exclusively on citrus groves, but suffered from the citrus crisis during World War II. After 1948 an immigrant camp (*ma'barah*) was established there and replaced later by permanent housing. In 1950 it received municipal council status. In 1969 Kadimah had 3,920 inhabitants, jumping to 9,130 in 2002 with an annual growth rate of 4.6%. Its municipal area, extending over 5 sq. mi. (13 sq. km.), included Ilanot ("Trees"), the national forest tree research station affiliated to the Agricultural Research Institute of Reḥovot. In 2003 Kadimah was united with the nearby settlement of *Zoran, and the two became known as Kadimah-Zoran.

[Efram Orni / Shaked Gilboa (2nd ed.)]

KADIMAH, the first Jewish national students' association, established in Vienna in 1882. The founders and leaders of the *Akademischer Verein Kadimah* were Ruben *Bierer, a physician from Lemberg and the oldest of the group, Moritz Tobias *Schnirer, a student of medicine from Bucharest, and Nathan *Birnbaum. Under the impression of the Russian pogroms, they were united in the conviction that only "the struggle against assimilation and the fostering of Jewish peoplehood are a barrier against the destruction of Judaism." The three decided to found a Jewish students' association at Vienna University that would be "a center for the cultivation and dissemination of the national idea and a workshop for the development of Jewish leadership for the future." The group was greatly influenced by the Hebrew writer *Pereẓ Smolenskin, who was then living in Vienna and editing the nationalist monthly *Ha-Shaḥar.* He became friendly with the group and named it "Kadimah," with the double meaning *kedmah* – eastward, i.e., to Ereẓ Israel – and *kidmah* – forward. In autumn

1882 the association was founded in Bierer's house in Vienna, although the governmental permit for the organization was issued only in March 1883. Because of the watchful eye of the Vienna police, the aim of the association was defined as "cultivation of Jewish literature and scholarship to the exclusion of any political tendency." In secret, however, every new member was requested to adopt a credo of three points: struggle against assimilation, Jewish nationhood, and the settlement of the land of Israel as a means toward Jewish independence. At the first official meeting (May 5, 1883) Schnirer was elected to head the association and P. Smolenskin and J.L. *Pinsker, who inspired the association, were elected as honorary members.

Already in its first year the group established its own library and reading room, housing German and Hebrew books, and regularly organized talks on Jewish nationalist topics. The publication of the group, *Selbst-Emancipation!* (renamed the *Juedische Volkszeitung* in 1894), was edited by N. Birnbaum and named after Pinsker's pamphlet *Autoemancipation!* (1882), which was of great influence on its members.

The first act of the association was to paste posters in German and Hebrew on the walls of Vienna University that proclaimed loudly the message of Jewish nationhood. This step was a daring one, since the majority of the Jewish students as well as the Viennese Jewish bourgeoisie opposed Kadimah's program. The association was exposed to attacks, but many young people from both Eastern and Western Europe joined it. From its beginnings Kadimah adopted customs of traditional German student associations, like regular beer drinking (*Kneipen*) and assemblies (*Kommers*), and in the early 1890s even changed into a "dueling fraternity." By then Kadimah had become a central institution of Jewish national activity and an educational framework for many who later became associates of *Herzl. Following the example of Kadimah, Jewish-nationalist associations and student fraternities were founded all over Europe.

BIBLIOGRAPHY: *Festschrift zur Feier des 100. Semesters der akademischen Verbindung Kadimah* (1933); O. Abeles, in: *Die Welt*, 5 (1913), 145–7. **ADD. BIBLIOGRAPHY:** Nahum Sokolow, *Hibbath Zion* (1934), pp. 380ff; G. Kressel, *Shivat Ẓiyyon*, 4 (1956), 55–59; H.P. Freidenreich, in: *Columbia Essays in International Affairs*, 5 (1970) 119–136.; M.L. Rozenblit, in: YLBI, 27 (1982), 171–186; J.H. Schoeps, in: YLBI, 27 (1982), 155–170; idem, in: N. Leser (ed.), *Theodor Herzl und das Wien des Fin de Siècle* (1987), 113–137.

[Getzel Kressel / Mirjam Triendl (2nd ed.)]

KADISHMAN, MENASHE (1932–), Israeli painter and sculptor. Kadishman was born in Tel Aviv, the son of Russian pioneers. When he was 15 his father died and he had to give up his education, leave school, and help his mother. During his army service Kadishman served as a shepherd at kibbutz Ma'yan Barukh. This experience made an indelible impression on him that was later expressed in his art. In 1959 Kadishman followed Itzhak *Danziger's advice and went to London to study sculpture in the St. Martin School of Art. During the 13 years that he spent in London he refined his Minimalist Conceptual style. Most of his sculptures from that period were made from steel or aluminum and some of them included glass, too. The common theme in these sculptures was tension. The forms assembled in the sculptures created a strange posture that was contrary to the laws of nature. The ability of the sculptures to stand without falling constituted their formal power. Kadishman installed some of these sculptures in Israel on his return to his homeland (*Rising*, 1974, Habimah Square, Tel Aviv).

In 1978 Kadishman represented Israel in the Venice Biennial. He created an unforgettable performance in a sheep pen. Kadishman stood, as a shepherd, in the middle of the Israeli pavilion and painted the backs of the sheep blue. The smell of the pavilion and the bleating sounds attracted the curious, integrating conceptual art and biblical imagery.

The sheep motif returned in Kadishman's art in different kinds of media. Over time it became a ram and in 1983 the whole scene expanded to become the Sacrifice of Isaac. The inspiration for this subject was his son's military service in Lebanon. In the paintings and the sculptures that deal with the biblical scene Abraham appears as a secondary figure while the ram's image increases in significance (*Sacrifice of Isaac*, 1982–85, Jewish Museum, New York).

Another series of sculptures deal with birth. The mother and infant are described as silhouettes in exaggerated postures of pain. Toward the end of the 1990s the single motif of a screaming head was left in the sculptures. In a very impressive installation Kadishman placed hundreds of heads on the floor under the title *Shalekhet – Fallen Leaves* (1997–99, Julie M. Gallery, Tel Aviv). The reference to the famous painting of Edward Munch as well as the Holocaust symbolism was unmistakable. The romantic title was provocative, since the work had such a different meaning.

In 1995 Kadishman received the Israel Prize.

BIBLIOGRAPHY: Suermondt Ludwig Museum, Aachen, *Menashe Kadishman – Shalechet Heads and Sacrifices* (1999); The Jewish Museum, New York, *Sacrifice of Isaac* (1985).

[Ronit Steinberg (2nd ed.)]

KADMAN (formerly **Kaufman**), **GURIT** (1897–1987), Israeli folk-dance teacher. Gurit Kadman, who was born in Leipzig, Germany, settled in Ereẓ Israel in 1920 and for 18 years taught dancing and gymnastics in schools and kibbutzim. Through her initiative, the first folk-dance festival was held in kibbutz *Daliyyah in 1944 and the folk-dancing movement grew in popularity under her aegis, demonstrating the evolution, under various influences, toward a national style. She was awarded the Israel Prize in 1981 for dance. In her book, *Am Roked* (1968; *The New Folkdances of Israel*, 1968), she maintained that subtle changes had taken place over the decades; some of the dance movements introduced by early immigrants from Poland, Romania, Russia, and Yemen were becoming more restrained and Oriental, and in some of the later creations she detected an Eastern Mediterranean quality reminiscent of Greek and Bulgarian characteristics.

[Yohanan Boehm]

KADOORIE (Heb. כַּדּוּרִי), Israel agricultural school at the northern foot of Mt. Tabor in Lower Galilee, founded in 1933 and named for Sir Elly Silas *Kadoorie whose contribution to the Palestine Mandate government made possible the establishment of the Jewish school and a similar school for Arabs at *Tūl Karm. During the Arab riots of 1936–39, the *Haganah organized Kadoorie's pupils for self-defense, and during World War II, the nucleus of the *Palmaḥ was formed there, making the school a Palmaḥ training and organizational center. In agricultural education Kadoorie emphasized branches of hill farming.

[Efraim Orni]

KADOORIE, family with large business interests in the Far East, known for its philanthropy. The founder of the family, ṢĀLIḤ KADOORIE (d. 1876), was a well-known philanthropist in *Baghdad. His sons, SIR ELLIS (1865–1922) and SIR ELLY SILAS (1867–1944), were born in Baghdad. At the end of the 19th century they settled in *Hong Kong, developing their business in *Shanghai and other cities. Sir Ellis endowed a chair in physics at Hong Kong University and bequeathed funds for the building of two agricultural schools for Jews and Arabs in Mesopotamia. He also contributed generously to the Anglo-Jewish Association for education. He and his brother also established schools in Baghdad and Bombay. Sir Elly, an active Zionist from 1900, was president of the Palestine Foundation Fund in Shanghai and established agricultural schools in Palestine, as well as contributing a large sum toward the construction of the Hebrew University. In Baghdad in 1911 he established a school in honor of his wife Laura Kadoorie, as well as a girls' sewing school in 1922, also named after her; he set up an ophthalmic hospital in 1924 which was named after his mother Rima, with a trust for its maintenance. In 1935 he built a training school for the blind and in 1926 a club for women. In both *Basra and Mosul he founded separate schools for boys and girls, as well as a girls' sewing school. In 1934 he established in Kirkuk a school for boys and two schools for girls. He was knighted in 1926. His sons, BARON LAWRENCE (see next entry) (1899–1993) and SIR HORACE (1902–1995), continued their father's widespread business activities in Hong Kong. In 1951 they established the Kadoorie Agricultural Aid Loan Fund, which has assisted over 300,000 Chinese refugees. They also gave substantial support to the small Hong Kong Jewish community. A knighthood was conferred on Lawrence in the 1974 New Year Honours List for his manifold civic and philanthropic services in Hong Kong, and in the 1981 Queen's Birthday Honours he was made a life peer.

BIBLIOGRAPHY: Simmonds, in: *Le Judaïsme Sephardi* (Jan. 1965), 1274, 1276 (Eng.); A. Ben-Jacob, *Yehudei Bavel* (1965), 179–81.

[Rudolph Loewenthal]

KADOORIE, LAWRENCE, BARON (1899–1993), Hong Kong businessman and communal leader. Kadoorie was descended from prominent Sephardi business families in Hong Kong and Britain; his mother was a *Mocatta. His father built up a substantial business presence in Hong Kong as a banker and company financier, and, in particular, as head of China Power and Light, a major firm on the island and the mainland. Kadoorie was educated at Clifton College in England and then in Shanghai, where the family owned significant property. Kadoorie and his family were interned by the Japanese during World War II. After losing his mainland holdings following the Communist takeover in 1949, Kadoorie focused exclusively on Hong Kong. As head of Sir Elly Kadoorie & Sons, he was one of the most influential businessmen in the colony, holding 14 chairmanships in local companies and serving on Hong Kong's legislative and executive councils. He was knighted in 1974 and received a life peerage on the recommendation of Hong Kong's governor in 1981, possibly the last senior honor to be conferred on a British colonial figure. Shortly before receiving his title, Kadoorie's firm had placed an order worth £600 million with British companies, the largest order in Hong Kong's history. When he died, his fortune was estimated by *Fortune* magazine at $3.3 billion. Baron Kadoorie was closely associated with Jewish and Sephardi causes and charities.

BIBLIOGRAPHY: ODNB online.

[William D. Rubinstein (2nd ed.)]

KADOORIE, SASSON (1885–1971), *Baghdad rabbi and community leader. Born in Baghdad, Kadoorie was educated at the rabbinical seminary there and later appointed head of the rabbinical court of the community. He was chief rabbi of Baghdad from 1927 to 1929. Before being appointed to this post, he supported Zionist institutions such as the *Jewish National Fund, but later he rejected *Zionism, to the anger of his congregation. Despite the fact that the Iraqi government supported him, the community forced him to resign. In 1932 he became chairman of the community and served in this capacity until 1949, when the members of the community again compelled him to resign, suspecting him of helping the authorities to suppress the Jewish national movement in Iraq. Together with Menahem and Ezra *Daniel, Kadoorie advocated opposition to Zionism in order to prevent the persecution of Iraqi Jewry by the Muslim population. In 1953 he resumed office as community chairman and also became again chief rabbi of the community.

BIBLIOGRAPHY: H.J. Cohen, *Ha-Pe'ilut ha-Ẓiyyonit be-Iraq* (1969), index.

[Haim J. Cohen]

KADUSHIN, MAX (1895–1980), U.S. rabbinic scholar. Kadushin was born in Minsk, Russia, and immigrated with his family to Seattle, Washington in 1897. He earned his B.A. at New York University (1916). He was ordained by the Jewish Theological Seminary of America in 1920, where he also received his D.H.L. in 1932. Kadushin held pulpits in New York City (Temple Israel, 1921–26) and left to seek distance from his mentor, Rabbi Mordecai Kaplan, in Chicago (Humboldt Blvd. Temple, 1926–31). A Reconstructionist at the time, Kadushin established the Midwest Council of the Society for the

Advancement of Judaism. Despite his success in the pulpit, he was drawn to the university and became the Hillel Foundation director at the University of Wisconsin (1931–42). He resigned and moved to New York in 1942, where he taught at the Hebrew High School of Greater New York (1942–52) and then had a series of pulpits, each of short duration. He later taught at the Academy for Higher Jewish Learning in New York, an interdenominational rabbinical school, of which he was also dean (from 1958). In 1960, he received a coveted academic appointment to the faculty of JTS, where he taught ethics and rabbinic thought. Kadushin's scholarly interest was the explication of talmudic thought. Basing his observations on the latest rabbinic texts and historical investigations, Kadushin explained the unique character of the rabbinic mind. Rather than being random and disorganized, Kadushin believed that the rabbis' thought-world was made up primarily of value concepts, which were expressed in such noun forms as *berakhah* ("blessing"), *ẓedakah* ("charity), and *derekh ereẓ* ("proper behavior," "ethics"). Kadushin believed that four rabbinic concepts play a dominant role in integrating the entire complex of concepts: *Middat ha-Din* (God's justice), *Middat Raḥamim* (God's love of mercy), Torah, and Israel. In addition, rabbinic thought reflects certain "emphatic trends," i.e., love, the individual, universality, and the experience of God, which Kadushin calls "normal mysticism." His major works are *The Theology of Seder Eliahu; A Study in Organic Thinking* (1932); *Organic Thinking: A Study in Rabbinic Thought* (1938); *The Rabbinic Mind* (1952, 1965); *Worship and Ethics: A Study in Rabbinic Judaism* (1964). His wife EVELYN GARFIEL was a psychologist and author. She taught at the universities of Chicago and Wisconsin and wrote *The Service of the Heart* (1958) on the prayer book. Together they created one of the first Hebrew-speaking homes in America.

BIBLIOGRAPHY: T. Steinberg, "Max Kadushin, Scholar of Rabbinic Judaism: A Study of His Life, Work, and Theory of Valuational Thought" (Ph.D. dissertation NYU, 1980).

[Michael Berenbaum (2nd ed.)]

KAEL, PAULINE (1919–2001), U.S. film critic. Probably the most influential film critic of her time, Kael, who was born in Petaluma, Calif., did not write movie criticism until she was 35. She reviewed movies for *The New Yorker* magazine from 1968 to 1979 and, after working in the film industry, again from 1980 to 1991. Enchanting her fans and infuriating her foes, she was rarely dull and often sharp and funny, with an intellectual bent. She was outspoken, sometimes to a fault, promoting her favorite films (*Last Tango in Paris*), actors and directors and dismissing some sacred cows. Always provocative, her writing style bred a legion of acolytes, known as Paulettes. Kael's appetite for movies began in childhood as the daughter of immigrants from Poland. Her father was a gentleman farmer and moviegoer, and her own trips to see films began early. Among her early favorites were the *Marx Brothers comedies *Monkey Business* of 1931 and *Duck Soup* of 1933. In 1936 she enrolled at the University of California at Berkeley, where she majored in philosophy. However, she went to New York with a friend, the poet Robert Horan, for about three years. She returned to California, tried writing plays and helped make experimental films. Married and divorced three times, she supported herself and her daughter by writing advertising copy, clerking in a bookstore, and working as a cook, a seamstress, and a textbook writer. In 1953, while she was in a coffee shop in the San Francisco area, the editor of *City Lights* magazine asked her and a friend with whom she was arguing about a movie to review the Charlie Chaplin film *Limelight*. The friend turned in nothing. Kael's review called the film "slimelight," and a career was born. Kael began being published in magazines like *Sight and Sound* and *Partisan Review*, and her criticism was broadcast on a Berkeley listener-supported radio station. While managing an art theater, she wrote funny, feisty reviews for the programs and she began lecturing on film at universities in San Francisco and Los Angeles. She was 46 when her essays in *Partisan Review* led to an offer to publish her first book, *I Lost It at the Movies*, a collection of her articles and broadcasts. It became a bestseller. In it she praised movies like Jean Renoir's *Grand Illusion*, Vittorio de Sica's *Shoeshine*, and Martin Ritt's *Hud*. She attacked other critics, derided materialistic movie magnates, and attacked the pretensions of Alan Resnais's *Last Year at Marienbad*, calling it "the snow job in the ice palace." In 1968 she was invited to review for *The New Yorker*. Her first review was virtually the only rave that *Bonnie and Clyde* received in New York, but it compelled other critics to reconsider their assessments. Her favorite actors included Marlon Brando, Nicolas Cage, Sean Connery, Paul Newman, Diane Keaton, Anjelica Huston, Jessica Lange, and Debra Winger. She championed films of the 1970s like Francis Ford Coppola's *Godfather* and *Godfather, Part II*, and Martin Scorsese's *Mean Streets* and *Taxi Driver*. Her reviews and essays were assembled in a series of books whose double-entendre titles suggested the intimacy of her love affair with movies: *Kiss Kiss Bang Bang, Going Steady, Deeper into Movies, Reeling, When the Lights Go Down, Movie Love, Hooked* and *For Keeps*. In 1991, at 71, after 22 years at the magazine, Kael retired from regular reviewing.

[Stewart Kampel (2nd ed.)]

KAEMPF, SAUL ISAAC (1818–1892), rabbi and Orientalist. Kaempf, who was born at Lissa (Leszno), Poznania, was a disciple of Akiva *Eger there. He later studied at the University of Halle where he was a student of *Gesenius. In 1845 he became a preacher in Prague and in 1858 professor of Semitics at the University of Prague. His works include the two-volume *Nichtandalusische Poesie andalusischer Dichter aus dem 11., 12. und 13. Jahrhundert* (2 vols., 1858), an important pioneering contribution to the study of Hebrew poetry; a biography of R. Akiva Eger with a eulogy at his death (1838); *Mamtik Sod* (1861), a defense of Z. *Frankel's *Darkhei ha-Mishnah* against S.R. *Hirsch (1861); popular German translations of the *maḥzor* (1854) and of the *siddur* (1874), both following the rite of his temple in Prague (1874); *Das Ruehmen Moab's, oder* *die Inschrift auf dem Denkmal Mesa's* (1870); and collections of sermons and poetry.

BIBLIOGRAPHY: Zeitlin, Bibliotheca, 163ff.; M. Reines, *Dor ve-Ḥakhamav*, 1 (1890); I. Davidson, in: PAAJR, 1 (1930), 43–44.

[Jacob Hirsch Haberman]

KAF (Heb. כַּף; ך, כ), the eleventh letter of the Hebrew alphabet; its numerical value is 20. In the Proto-Sinaitic and early Proto-Canaanite inscriptions the *kaf* was drawn as a pictograph of the palm of the hand and hence its name. In the later Proto-Canaanite and in the early Phoenician scripts the letter was represented by three fingers meeting at a common base. From the late tenth century B.C.E. and onward a down-stroke was added. The *kaf* developed in the various branches the following variations: (Phoenician); (Hebrew); and (Aramaic). From the fourth century B.C.E. Aramaic script the *kaf* (as well as *mem, nun, pe,* and *ẓadi*) in medial position began to bend its downstroke to the left, toward the next letter within the word, and the long downstroke was used only in the final forms. The distinction, which survived also in Syriac and Nabatean, is clear in the Jewish script: כ (medial), ך (final).

The Greek *kappa* – the ancestor of the Latin "K" – developed from the ninth-century Phoenician *kaf.* See *Alphabet, Hebrew.

[Joseph Naveh]

KAFAḤ (Kafih), YIḤYE BEN SOLOMON (1850–1932), Yemenite scholar. Kafaḥ was orphaned as a child and was brought up by his grandfather. Though a goldsmith by trade, he dedicated most of his life to study and teaching. He excelled in *halakhah* and many of the responsa of the *bet din* of San'a which were sent to inquirers from Yemen and other parts of the world were written by him. He studied the works of medieval Jewish scholars and Haskalah literature while his preoccupation with secular studies and languages (Arabic and Turkish) and his connections with scholars outside Yemen rendered him unique among his Yemenite contemporaries. Especially worthy of mention is his correspondence with A.I. *Kook and Hillel *Zeitlin concerning matters of Kabbalah. His study of philosophy and Haskalah literature and his contact and discussions with intellectuals and scholars such as Joseph Halevy and Eduard Glaser constituted a turning point in his mode of thought. The Young Turk revolution was also a factor in arousing Kafaḥ's desire for reform, and he sought to introduce reforms in the social life of the Jews in all areas: in the way of thought, methods of education, prayer and study, in customs and superstitions (occult medicine, amulets, charms, etc.). For this purpose he set up the movement of Darda'im (a combination of Dor De'ah, after the learning and intellectualism which characterize the movement, and the name of one of the four ancient sages, Darda, who is mentioned in I Kings 5:11 [4:31]). This movement, which developed before World War I, was a microcosm of the Enlightenment of 18th-century European Jewry, which it resembled in its aspiration for learning and reform in Jewish life. It led to a certain intellectual revival, but provoked a storm in the life of the community. Kafaḥ wrote *Sefer Milḥamot ha-Shem* (1931), which sought to prove that the Kabbalah harms the true unity of God. In his *bet midrash* he directed the study of Torah in a new spirit, away from the study of homiletics, allegories, and mystical interpretation and toward the simple meaning of the Torah and the study of philosophic speculation. His method of teaching developed a sense of reflection and criticism. In his time the writings of Maimonides were again fully studied. Previously Yemenite Jewry only studied the *Mishneh Torah,* but from this time Maimonides' other (Arabic) works were also studied, as were other classics, including the *Kuzari* of Judah Halevi and *Ḥovot ha-Levavot* of Baḥya ibn Paquda. Kafaḥ was also interested in the writings of the *rishonim,* both of Yemenite origin and others whose works reached Yemen. He spent considerable time searching for manuscripts, copying them, and preserving them.

[Yehuda Ratzaby]

In Jerusalem in 1914 the pamphlet *Amal u-Re'ut Ruaḥ ve-Ḥaramot u-Teshuvatam* was published, including the excommunication of Kafaḥ by the Jerusalem rabbis and his reply. The pamphlet characterizes the energetic struggle of the movement against the Zohar and kabbalistic literature. Defending the Kabbalah, Yemenite rabbis answered it in *Emunat ha-Shem* (1937).

BIBLIOGRAPHY: *Shevut Teiman* (1945), 166–231; Yishayahu, in: *Harel* (1962), 255–8; S. Koraḥ, *Iggeret Bokhim* (1963).

KAFAḤ (Kafih, קאפח), YOSEF (1917–2000), Israeli rabbi and scholar, grandson of Yiḥye *Kafaḥ, who was born in *San'a, *Yemen, first became a gold-and silversmith there and also owned a textile business. In 1943 he emigrated to Palestine and worked as a gold- and silversmith in Tel Aviv. Eventually, he gave up his trade and settled in Jerusalem where he enrolled in the Merkaz ha-Rav yeshivah. In 1950 Kafaḥ was appointed a member of the *bet din* of Tel Aviv and a year later of that of Jerusalem.

Encouraged by M. Berlin (*Bar-Ilan), Kafaḥ began to publish research in Yemenite Jewish literature and translated important works, written in Arabic, into Hebrew, including an edition of Maimonides' commentary on the Mishnah containing the Arabic text with a new Hebrew translation and notes (1963–68), and a three-volume edition (1963–68), consisting only of the translation. His scholarly editions of Arabic texts with Hebrew translation include: the Yemenite Nethanel b. Isaiah's commentary on the Pentateuch, *Me'or ha-Afelah* (1957); Saadiah's translation and commentary on Psalms (n.d.); Nethanel b. (or al-) Fayyumi's *Gan ha-Sekhalim* (1954, "Garden of Intellects"); and a collection of various translators and commentators on the Five Scrolls (1962); Saadiah's *Emunot ve-De'ot* (1970); Maimonides' *Book of Precepts,* his *Guide,* and his epistles to the Yemen and on resurrection with a concordance of biblical references in all his writings (all in 1971). He also edited a commentary by Saadiah on the Pentateuch (1963) and on Psalms (1966); Isaac Alfasi's *Halakhot* on *Ḥullin* (1960); Abraham b. David of Posquières' *She'elot u-Teshuvot* ("Responsa," 1964) and his ritual treatise *Ba'alei ha-Nefesh*, with Zerahiah ha-Levi's strictures *Sela ha-Maḥaloket* (1964); the responsa of Abraham b. Isaac (of Narbonne; 1962), and those of Yom Tov b. Abraham (Ritva; 1959). He translated Nathan b. Abraham's commentary on the Mishnah from the Arabic (1955). In the field of liturgy he edited a *siddur, Shivat Ẓiyyon* (1952), and a Passover *Haggadah* according to the Yemenite rite with commentaries translated from the Arabic (1952). An important contribution to the history of Yemenite religious culture and folklore is Kafaḥ's *Halikhot Teiman* (1961). He received the Israel Prize in 1969 for his translation of Maimonides' commentary on the Mishnah. His translation of Maimonides' *Guide for the Perplexed* appeared in 1972 along with his translation of Ibn Pakuda's *Ḥovot ha-Levavot*. Kafaḥ went on to write a total of 83 books and 182 articles. His collected writings, *Rav Yosef Kafaḥ: Ketavim*, appeared in three volumes in 1989. His *magnum opus* was a 23-volume edition of Maimonides' *Mishneh Torah*. Kafaḥ's edition contains a corrected text according to Yemenite manuscripts, as well as cross-references to all of Maimonides' other work and Kafaḥ's own concise commentary. Despite his contribution in translating and publishing the works of Saadiah Gaon and the relatively large corpus of medieval Yemenite philosophical works, the center of Kafaḥ's intellectual universe was Maimonides. Kafaḥ never founded or taught in a yeshivah. Aside from his work as a rabbinical judge, he was the rabbi of a synagogue in Jerusalem where he gave both daily and weekly classes, many of which were devoted to the study of Maimonides. These classes were attended both by his congregants and by many others.

In 1969, Kafaḥ was appointed to the Rabbinical Council of the Israeli Chief Rabbinate. He became a member of the Rabbinical High Court in 1970. Throughout his life, he received numerous prizes. Aside from the 1969 Israel Prize, he received the Rav Kook Prize from the Municipality of Tel Aviv-Yaffo twice, in 1964 and 1986. He received the Bialik Prize in 1973, the Katz Prize in 1986, and the Yiẓhak Ben-Zvi Prize in 1994 for his work on Yemenite Jewish communities. In 1997 he received an honorary doctorate from Bar-Ilan University. When asked why he never entered politics, Kafaḥ answered that instead of trying to understand ministers and MKs, he would rather devote himself to understanding the commentaries on the *Mishneh Torah*. He retired from the Rabbinical Court in 1988 at the age of 70 and from the Rabbinical Council in 1997.

Known as a very precise person, who was always on time and never long-winded in speech or in print, Kafaḥ was a unique rabbinic figure. His legacy includes historical works alongside the traditional rabbinic commentaries and halakhic responsa. At the same time, contrary to current trends, Kafaḥ viewed the scientific and medical statements made in talmudic and medieval Jewish literature within their historical context. If these statements contradicted modern science, then they were to be discarded. Kafaḥ contended that these statements were actually the opinions of the non-Jewish scientists of those eras and therefore had no lasting authority. On the other hand, Kafaḥ is quick to point out that this proves that these ancient Jewish sages did study science, thus teaching us the great value in studying science today. Kafaḥ viewed scientific knowledge as necessary for forming firm religious convictions that are the essence of Jewish belief.

BIBLIOGRAPHY: Kressel, Leksikon, 2 (1967), 725–6. **ADD. BIBLIOGRAPHY:** A. Levi-Kafaḥ, *Holekh Tamim* (2003); R. Cohen, *Ẓafnat Pane'aḥ: Bibliografyah Mele'ah shel ha-Rav Yosef Kafaḥ* (2001); Z. Amar and H. Sari (eds.), *Sefer Zikaron le-Rav Yosef Kafaḥ* (2001); Y.Ẓ. Langermann in: *Aleph*, 1 (2000) 333–40.

[Alexander Carlebach / David Derovan (2nd ed.)]

KAFKA, BRUNO ALEXANDER (1881–1931), Czechoslovak jurist. Born in Prague, Kafka was the son of a lawyer and a cousin of Franz *Kafka. He became a professor of law at the German University of Prague in 1918 and was the author of several works on civil and family law, including *Die eheliche Guetergemeinschaft* (1906) and *System des buergerlichen Rechtes* (1920). He also served on the commission for the reform of the Czechoslovakian code of civil law as an expert on family law. He was dean of the faculty of law on several occasions and was elected rector of the University of Prague in 1931, but died before taking office. Kafka entered politics in 1917 and became editor of *Bohemia*, the oldest German-language newspaper in Czechoslovakia. He sat in the Czechoslovakian parliament as a representative of the German Democratic Liberal Party, of which he was a founder. It advocated cooperation among the various national groups in the Republic and secured the cooperation of leading industrialists and intellectuals. Kafka converted to Catholicism.

[Yehuda Gera]

KAFKA, FRANTIŠEK (1909–1991), Czech author. His novel *Krutá léta* ("The Cruel Years," 1958), notable for its combination of poetic fantasy and reality, vividly describes the Lodz ghetto during the Nazi era. He also adapted for broadcasting his namesake Franz Kafka's *Letters to Milena*.

[Avigdor Dagan]

KAFKA, FRANZ (1883–1924), Czech-born German novelist, whose work has had an enormous impact on western art and literature. Kafka, who was born and raised in Prague, studied law at the German University there. He worked in a law office and then for an insurance company, writing only in his spare time. A tyrannical father greatly affected Kafka's psychological development. He never married, but three women played an important part in his life. The first was Felice Bauer, known only as F. or F.B. from Kafka's Diaries until she sold his letters to her to Schocken in 1955; they were finally published in 1967 as *Briefe an Felice* (*Letters to Felice*, 1973). Kafka met her in 1912 and they were engaged twice before Kafka finally broke off their tortured relationship in 1916. Representing for Kafka the "real" world, the world of home and family, she could not overcome the pull of Kafka's other world, the world of his literary imagination. The second woman was the journalist Milena Jesenska, wife of the Jewish intellectual Ernst Pollak, with whom he maintained a close relationship from 1920; the last was Dora Dymant, a Polish Jewess who nursed him in his last illness. During his lifetime, Kafka published some collections of sketches and stories: *Betrachtung* (1913); *Das Urteil* (1916); *Die Verwandlung* (1916; *The Metamorphosis*, 1937); *In der Strafkolonie* (1919; *The Penal Colony*, 1948); and *Ein Landarzt* (1919; *The Country Doctor*, 1945). Kafka suffered from migraine and insomnia for years. In 1917 his illness was diagnosed as tuberculosis, and he spent much of the rest of his life in a sanatorium. He deposited his manuscripts with his close friend and eventual biographer, Max *Brod, and when he was dying left instructions that they were to be burnt. Brod, however, was fully aware of the importance of Kafka's work, and succeeded in getting it published. Kafka's most famous novels are *Der Prozess* (1925; *The Trial*, 1937); *Das Schloss* (1926; *The Castle*, 1930); and *Amerika* (1927; *America*, 1938). Between 1925 and 1937 Brod published Kafka's collected works, together with his *Tagebuecher und Briefe*.

The action in most of Kafka's books is centered in the hero's unremitting search for identity. The nature of this identity is never revealed and can only be vaguely conjectured from the obstacles placed in the hero's path and his failure to reach his goal. The story generally begins with an event outside normal everyday experience: "Someone must have been telling lies about Joseph K. for without his having done anything wrong, he was arrested one fine morning." This is the opening of *The Trial*, a sentence which, in its sheer simplicity, foreshadows the nightmare quality of the novel. The hero never knows what he is accused of, never discovers the nature of his tribunal, and is either unconscious of any guilt, or only too conscious of it. *The Trial* has a tragic finale, but in the other novels there is no ending at all. *The Castle* is even more obscure: no goal is ever reached, the castle can never be entered.

Few writers are as difficult to interpret as Kafka. Some critics see in his works a mirror of his own life; others are psychoanalytical, stressing his relationship with his father. There are those who explain the alienation of his heroes from their environment in terms of the Jew's isolation in the world. Most interpreters, however, sense in his works a symbolic representation of the religious plight of contemporary man. Even these interpretations range from nihilistic existentialism to a positive faith in divine salvation. The latter view is that of Max Brod. However, Kafka must be regarded primarily as a creative artist, not as a prophet or a philosopher. Through his imaginative writing, he tried to elevate his own existential situation into the realm of what he himself called "the true, the pure, the indestructible." His prose is unusually lucid, with a melodic range that lifts it to the heights of poetry. His narration is full of surprises, sudden shifts of perspective, and contradictions whose humor only accentuates the grimness of a particular situation.

In common with most assimilated Prague Jews, Kafka was at first only vaguely conscious of his Jewish heritage, but learned about Zionism from Max Brod and Hugo *Bergman. He heard about Jewish life in Eastern Europe from Isaac Loewy, an actor in a Yiddish theatrical troupe with whom he struck up a friendship. Through the writer Georg Langer, he became interested in *Ḥasidism. He studied Hebrew, attended lectures at the Hochschule fuer die Wissenschaft des Judentums in Berlin and, when he came to know Dora Dymant, toyed with the idea of settling in Palestine with her. This progress toward a deeper understanding and appreciation of Judaism corresponds to Kafka's search for his ideal of genuineness and his intense longing for a pure life.

Kafka's novels have been translated into many languages, including Hebrew. They have been adapted for plays, operas, and movies. The Theater of the Absurd is unthinkable without Kafka, and "Kafkaesque" has become an international word to describe the feeling of being trapped in a maze of grotesque happenings. In the introduction to the collection of unpublished stories and fragments issued in 1931 as *Beim Bau der chinesischen Mauer* ("The Building of the Chinese Wall"), Kafka is eulogized as "a master-stylist and a master of the short story, a novelist to be compared only with the very greatest, and an inexorable molder and interpreter of our time." It was not, however, until 1964 that the Czech Communist government thought fit to rehabilitate this "decadent" genius.

BIBLIOGRAPHY: KAFKA LITERATURE: R. Hemmerle, *Franz Kafka, eine Bibliographie* (1958); H. Järv, *Kafka-Literatur* (1961), contains about 5,000 titles. STUDIES BY MAX BROD, THE PRINCIPAL AUTHORITY ON KAFKA: *Franz Kafka, a Biography* (1947); *Franz Kafka's Glauben und Lehre* (1948); *Franz Kafka als wegweisende Gestalt* (1951); *Verzweiflung und Erloesung im Werk Franz Kafkas* (1959); *Der Prager Kreis* (1966); in: *Jewish Quarterly*, 6:1 (1958), 12–14. WORKS BY OTHER CRITICS: J. Starobinski, in: E.J. Finbert (ed.), *Aspects du Génie d'Israël* (1950), 287–92; A. Flores and H. Swander, *Franz Kafka Today* (1958), includes bibliography; F. Weltsch, *Franz Kafka, Datiyyut ve-Humor be-Ḥayyav u-vi-Yẓirato* (1959); W. Emrich, *Franz Kafka* (Eng., 1968); Binder, in: YLBI, 12 (1967), 135–48; M. Greenberg, *The Terror of Art: Kafka and Modern Literature* (1968); J. Urzidil, *There Goes Kafka* (1969). **ADD. BIBLIOGRAPHY:** E. Canetti, *Der andere Prozess* (1969; *Kafka's Other Trial: The Letters to Felice* (1974)); E. Pavel, *The Nightmare of Reason: A Life of Franz Kafka* (1984); N. Murray, *Kafka* (2004).

[Felix Weltsch]

KAFR KAMĀ, the larger of the two Muslim-Circassian villages in Israel, in eastern Lower Galilee, 3 mi. (4½ km.) northeast of Kefar Tavor. The second Circassian village is al-Rīḥāniyya, located in Upper Galilee. Kafr Kamā was founded toward the end of the 19th century on the remains of an earlier settlement which had existed from the Roman to the Early Arab period. The Circassian founding settlers, who abandoned their Caucasian homeland in 1878 when it was occupied by czarist Russia, were granted asylum in the Turkish Empire. During the Israeli *War of Independence (1948), the inhabitants of Kafr Kamā were not inimical toward their Jewish neighbors, and good economic relations subsequently developed. Farming includes field crops and livestock. In 1950 Kafr Kamā received municipal council status. Its population rose from 1,330 in 1968 to 2,710 in 2002, occupying an area of 4 sq. mi. (10 sq. km.)

[Efraim Orni]

KAFR QĀSIM, Muslim-Arab village on the southwestern rim of the Samarian Hills, Israel, northeast of Petaḥ Tikvah. The longest bridge in Israel is located nearby as part of Route 6, the Trans-Israel Highway. In 1968 Kafr Qāsim had 3,720 inhabitants, rising to 15,700 in 2002, on an area of 3.5 sq. mi. (9.2 sq. km.). Its farming was based on field and garden crops and fruit orchards. Income in the village was about half the national average. On the eve of the *Sinai Campaign (1956), the literal execution of a curfew order resulted in the shooting of 47 people, including women and children, by Israel border police. The military personnel responsible were tried and convicted of murder. The court also decided that obedience to an order from above (the defense counsel's argument) does not excuse military personnel from responsibility in the execution of crimes. During the trial, a public board, headed by the mayor of Petaḥ Tikvah, Pinḥas Rashish (d. 1978), was set up to determine compensation to the families of the victims and decided to pay out IL500,000 in reparations. At the end of 1957, a reconciliation ceremony (*sulḥa*) was held between the families of the victims and a representative of the Jewish community (Avraham *Shapira).

[Efraim Orni]

KAGAN, ELIE (1928–1999), French photographer. Kagan was born in Paris to parents who had emigrated from Russia and Poland and worked in the garment industry. His father disappeared during the German occupation while he himself was hidden in the countryside. A member of the French Communist Party during his youth, he tried his hand at various jobs until he became a professional photographer in 1957. His most famous photographs are those he made during the repression of the FLN-organized Algerian demonstration in Paris on October 17, 1961. He was the only photographer to capture the faces of many who were not to survive the day. Probably the outstanding photojournalist on the French political scene in the 1960s and 1970s, with a clear leftist orientation, he displayed a measure of the humor and irreverence typical of the period. A partner of Serge and Beate *Klarsfeld in their campaign against Nazis who had committed crimes in France and their French accomplices, he expressed his solidarity with the State of Israel, which ran counter to the position of the far left. In 1969 he published *Le Reporter engagé: trente ans d'instantanés* (with Patrick Rotman), also including images of artists he had befriended. In 2001, Jean-Luc Einaudi published posthumously his *17 octobre 1961*. The collection of his photographs, deposited in the BDIC library in Nanterre, was used in 2004 for an exhibition on Michel Foucault as a political activist.

[Philippe Boukara (2nd ed.)]

KAGAN, HELENA (1889–1978), physician and social worker. Kagan was born in Turkestan and received her medical education in Switzerland. In 1916 she founded the first children's hospital in Jerusalem, and from 1923 until 1943 was medical director of the Spafford Baby Home for Arab Children in the Old City of Jerusalem. After the establishment of the State she was associated with the Bikkur Ḥolim and Hadassah hospitals, and was prominently associated with WIZO and the Hebrew University. In 1958 she was awarded the Freedom of the City of Jerusalem for her outstanding services and in 1975 was awarded the Israel Prize.

KAGAN, JOSEPH, BARON (1915–1995), British businessman. Born Juozapas Kaganas in Lithuania, Kagan, with most of his family, managed to survive World War II in hiding near the Kaunas (Kovno) ghetto. Kagan migrated to Britain after the war to join his father (who lived to be 109), who had emigrated there in 1940 and established a successful textile business. In 1951 Kagan founded the enterprise for which he became well known, Gannex raincoats, made from waterproof nylon. In Bradford, Kagan became acquainted with Harold *Wilson, who had been born nearby and adopted the wearing of Gannex raincoats as his trademark. The coats enjoyed a fad throughout Britain in the 1950s and early 1960s, being worn as well by royalty. When Wilson became prime minister in 1964, Kagan became a close but unofficial advisor on industrial policy and technological innovation. It is also said that Kagan paid a monthly consultancy fee to Wilson before he became prime minister and financially assisted other members of Wilson's entourage. Kagan was knighted by Wilson in 1970 and received a life peerage from him in 1976.

In 1978 Kagan became the subject of national controversy when, charged with theft and fraud (in matters unrelated to his relationship with Harold Wilson), he fled to Israel. Kagan was forced to return to England, where he was fined £375,000 and served ten months in prison. He was stripped of his knighthood by the Queen but allowed to remain a peer. From 1982 he again became a frequent speaker in the House of Lords.

BIBLIOGRAPHY: ODNB online.

[William D. Rubinstein (2nd ed.)]

KAGAN, SOLOMON ROBERT (1889–1955), U.S. medical historian. Kagan was born in Orany, Lithuania, of a prominent rabbinic family. He was ordained as a rabbi but turned to medicine. He emigrated to the United States in 1922 and practiced in Boston. He was the author of many books including *Researches in Hebrew Literature* (2 vols. 1929–30), *American Jewish Physicians of Note* (1942), *Jewish Contributions to Medicine in America* (1934), *Leaders of Medicine* (1941), *The Modern Medical World* (1945), *Fielding H. Garrison; a biography* (1948), and *Jewish Medicine* (1952).

[Fred Rosner]

KAGANOVICH, LAZAR MOISEYEVICH (1893–1991), Soviet politician. Born in Kiev province, Kaganovich joined the Communist Party in 1911 and became a member of the Kiev committee of the party in 1914. In 1915 he was arrested and restricted to residence in Kabana, his native village, but left illegally and for the following two years lived in various parts of Russia under false names. Kaganovich took an active part in the October Revolution in the Red Army, where he headed the Saratov war organization, and later in Belorussia, where he played a major role in taking Gomel. During the Civil War (1917–20) he served on the All-Russian Committee for building up the Red Army. He rose rapidly in the Party hierarchy. In 1924 he became a member of the Communist Party's Central Committee and from 1925 to 1928 was first secretary of the party organization in the Ukraine. Between 1930 and 1935 he was secretary of the Moscow party committee, headed the reconstruction of the capital, and managed the construction of the Moscow underground, which was named after him until 1957. In 1930 he became a member of the Politburo, the nine-man committee controlling the party. In 1932 he was in the Politburo for organizing terror in the party, and he took part in the execution of it. At the 17th party congress in 1934 he reported on "organizational questions" and was elected chairman of the party control commission.

Kaganovich organized the industrialization of the Moscow region. He was subsequently appointed commissar for communications and commissar for heavy industry. From 1938 he served also as vice chairmen of the Council of Commissars of the Union. During World War II he was a member of the State Defense Committee. In 1947 he was again secretary of the party in Ukraine, and from March 1953 first vice chairman of the Council of Ministers of the Union. Kaganovich's subservience to Stalin was made abundantly clear in his pamphlet *Stalin vedyot nas k pobede komunizma* ("Stalin leads us to the victory of Communism") printed in 1950 in half a million copies. For a number of years he was the only Jew to occupy a top position in the Soviet leadership. In 1957, as a member of the "anti-Party group" of Molotov, Malenkov, and Shepilov, he was expelled from the Central Committee and dismissed from all government posts. In the years 1957–61 he was director of a metallurgical factory in the Ural area. And in 1961 he was expelled from the party and pensioned. Regarding Jewish matters, he was not only estranged from Zionism and the Bund, but he was also against the Yevsektsiya. While visiting the Jewish State Theater in the 1930s, he called to show real Jewish heroes like the Maccabeans and Bar-Kokhba. It is not clear what his role was in the Crimean Affair, and rumors say that he was in favor of a Jewish republic there.

BIBLIOGRAPHY: *Bolshaya Sovetskaya Entsiklopediya*, 19 (1953[2]), 282–3; *Current Biography Yearbook 1955* (1956), 315–7.

[Shmuel Spector (2nd ed.)]

KAGANOWSKI, EFRAIM (1893–1958), Yiddish writer. Deeply influenced by Chekhov and Maupassant, his many stories of his native Warsaw, which appeared in the best Yiddish journals, had an international vogue and were collected in the jubilee edition *Shriftn* ("Works," 1951) and *Poylishe Yorn* ("Polish Years," 1956). The title of his earliest group of short stories, *Meydlekh* ("Girls"), marked the importance of the erotic theme in his works, but even more important was the specifically Jewish cultural richness that emerged from his portraits of Warsaw Jewry. Upon the German invasion of Warsaw, he found refuge in Soviet Russia, being repatriated to Poland in 1946. His last years were spent in Paris. Among his story collections are *Tiren-Fenster* ("Doors-Windows," 1921), *Leyb un Lebn* ("Body and Soul," 1928), *Figurn* ("Figures," 1937), and a novel, *A Shtot oyf der Volge* ("A City on the Volga," 1961).

BIBLIOGRAPHY: Rejzen, Leksikon, 3 (1929), 370–3; M. Ravitch, *Mayn Leksikon*, 1 (1945), 212–4. **ADD. BIBLIOGRAPHY:** LNYL, 8 (1981), 7–9; Y. Botoshansky, *Portretn fun Yidishe Shrayber* (1933), 55–66; Y.Y. Trunk, *Di Yidishe Proze in Poyln* (1949), 150–51; N. Mayzl, *Noente un Eygene* (1957), 283–94; Y. Hofer, *Mit Yenem un Mit Zikh* (1964), 183–211; Y. Shpigl, *Geshtaltn un Profiln* (1971), 155–63.

[Melech Ravitch]

KAGE, JOSEPH (1912–1996), Canadian Jewish educator, communal worker, and author. Kage was born in Minsk, Belarus, emigrating to Canada in his youth. He acquired an extensive university education, culminating in a doctorate in history at the University of Montreal. He worked in Jewish education and later in social work with the Jewish Family Services of Montreal. In 1947, he began working for Canada's Jewish Immigrant Aid Society, where he ultimately became national executive director and national executive vice president until his retirement in 1983. In this role, he became an authority on issues of Canadian immigration policy and was chair of the Canadian governmental Advisory Board on Immigrant Adjustment. He was active in numerous civic and Jewish community organizations, and was chair of the Canadian Jewish Congress National Conference on Yiddish and Yiddish culture as well as president of Montreal's Jewish Public Library.

He published *With Faith and Thanksgiving: The Story of Two Hundred Years of Jewish Immigration and Immigrant Aid Efforts in Canada* (1962) and *Chapter One: Sketches of Canadian Life Under the French Regime* (1964), which was published bilingually in English and in French.

BIBLIOGRAPHY: I. Robinson, *Canadian Jewish Studies* 1998, 81–87.

[Ira Robinson (2nd ed.)]

KAHAN, BARUCH MORDECAI (pseudonym **P. Virgily**; 1883–1936), Bundist, born in Mogilev, Belorussia. His father Isaac, a wealthy Ḥasid, was the brother of Mordecai b. Hillel *Hacohen. Kahan, who studied in a yeshivah, joined the *Bund in Gomel, Belorussia, at the age of 18, becoming a professional revolutionary. In 1905 he helped to lead Jewish self-defense during the pogrom in Zhitomir and was one of the leaders during the revolution in *Lodz. He served as a reporter for the Bundist press. In the wake of a religious crisis, he returned to religion for a short time and worked as a simple laborer. He rejoined the Bund during World War I and in 1917 became a member of the Petrograd Soviet Workers' and Soldiers' Council. Between the two world wars he lived in Vilna, was active in ORT and YIVO and in Jewish education, and represented the Bund on the communal and municipal councils.

BIBLIOGRAPHY: LNYL, 4 (1961), 312–4; I.S. Hertz (ed.), *Doyres Bundistn* (1956), 391–401.

[Moshe Mishkinsky]

KAHAN, LOUIS (1905–2002), Australian portraitist. Kahan, who was born in Vienna, originally studied tailoring and dress design. He showed a talent for portraiture and this was fostered during World War II, when as a member of the French Foreign Legion, he painted regimental murals and portraits. When the Americans landed in North Africa, Kahan became a war artist, sketching wounded soldiers of the Allied armies. After the war he was appointed staff artist to the French newspaper *Le Figaro*. He immigrated to Australia in 1951 and settled in Melbourne, where he sketched famous personalities for the literary magazine *Meanjin*, and for the weekend literary section of the *Age* newspaper. In 1981 he published *Australian Writers: The Face of Literature*. Kahan is represented in the National Gallery of each of the six states of Australia.

ADD. BIBLIOGRAPHY: L. Klepac, *Louis Kahan* (1990).

[Shmuel Gorr]

KAHAN, SALOMON (1896–1965), Yiddish essayist and musicologist. Born in Bialystok, he was educated in Warsaw and Berlin and immigrated to Mexico City in 1921 where he was professor of the history of modern civilization at the Mexican National Teachers' College (1925–39). He served as music critic for Mexican dailies and, between 1936 and 1964, published five volumes of critical and impressionistic articles on music, written in Spanish. He was editor of *Der Veg* (Mexico City, 1945–48), and managing editor of *Tribuna Israelita* (1953–65). He played an important role in the cultural life of Mexico's Jewish community and collected his many essays on literature, music, and important Jewish and Mexican personalities in five Yiddish volumes, of which the most significant was his *Literarishe un Zhurnalistishe Fartseykhnungen* ("Literary and Journalistic Sketches," 1961). He published an abridged Spanish translation of *Graetz's *History of the Jews* under the title *Historia del pueblo de Israel*. His son, José Kahan, achieved renown as a concert pianist.

BIBLIOGRAPHY: J. Glatstein, *Mit Mayne Fartogbikher* (1963), 413–8. **ADD. BIBLIOGRAPHY:** LNYL, 8 (1981), 22–23; Y. Rapoport, *Fragmentn fun a Lebn* (1967), 79–86.

[Sol Liptzin]

KAHANA, name of several Babylonian *amoraim*. The first two of these *amoraim*, Kahana (1) and Kahana (2), were both disciples of Rav, and certain traditions relating to these two scholars have become conflated in the Babylonian Talmud. As a result it is necessary to trace the development of these traditions in order to determine which originally related to Kahana (1) and which to Kahana (2).

(1) The first Kahana, together with his companion *Assi, were already prominent scholars when Rav returned from Ereẓ Israel to Babylonia (c. 219 C.E.) but they immediately joined his academy (Sanh. 36b; Naz. 19a) and became his disciples (TJ, Suk. 1:1, 52a). Rav held them in very high esteem (Shab. 146b; Naz. 19a) and because of their profound erudition he was sometimes unable to answer their questions (Suk. 6b; Beẓah 6a, 37b; et al.). Kahana later emigrated to Palestine where he joined some of the last of the *tannaim* such as *Simeon son of *Judah ha-Nasi (Zev. 59a), Judah and Hezekiah the sons of Ḥiyya (BK 10b), and *Oshaiah (TJ, Ḥag. 1:14, 57c). Among his pupils were *Eleazar b. Pedat (TJ, Kil. 1:7, 27b; MK 3:8, 83d), and *Zeiri (BM 60b). Rav's advice to Kahana: "flay carcasses in the marketplace and earn wages and do not say 'I am a priest and a great man and it is beneath my dignity'" (Pes. 113a) may indicate that Kahana lived in poverty. A Palestinian *aggadah* describes a meeting between Kahana (1) and *Johanan and *Simeon b. Lakish, two of the most prominent Palestinian *amoraim* (TJ, RH 4:1, 59b; PdRK, 345; Lev. R. 29, 684–5). This tradition is of special interest because certain elements of this story were later combined in the Babylonian Talmud with other narrative elements concerning events relating to Kahana (2) (see below). We are told in the Jerusalem Talmud (and in the parallel texts) that Johanan and Simeon b. Lakish were once sitting and studying together, when they encountered a difficulty concerning a certain *halakhah*. At that moment Kahana was passing by, so Johanan and Simeon b. Lakish said: "Behold, here is a great scholar (thus in TJ; in PdRK, Lev. R.: "a master of the teachings"); let us ask him." They asked Kahana, and he replied with an authoritative answer which they apparently accepted. From this story it is clear that (this) Kahana was already recognized as a mature and respected scholar, to whom both Johanan and Simeon b. Lakish felt comfortable turning to in order to resolve the problem which arose in their study together. There can therefore be no doubt that the Kahana mentioned in this tradition is the elder Kahana (see below).

(2) The second Kahana was also one of Rav's pupils, and used to read the weekly Bible portion at Rav's academy (Shab. 152a). He also stood in close contact with *Samuel and transmitted *halakhot* from both teachers (Ber. 14b; Ket. 101a, et al.). According to a well-known *aggadah* in the Babylonian Talmud (BK 117a), Kahana (2) was forced to escape from Babylonia after impulsively killing a person who had threatened to denounce a fellow-Jew to the Persian authorities – by "tearing out his windpipe." Rav advised him to flee to Ereẓ Israel, but made him swear that he would sit passively in R. Johanan's academy and refrain from asking any difficult questions for a period of seven years, apparently in order not to embarrass R. Johanan with his superior scholarship. Kahana's reputation as a brilliant scholar preceded him, and R. Johanan, unaware of the oath which Kahana had taken, prepared his lesson for the next day with care, anticipating that Kahana might cause him some difficulties. Placed in the first row from which he would be able to engage the master directly, Kahana nevertheless remained silent. Considered by those present to be incapable of serious scholarly debate, he was progressively demoted, until he was seated in the seventh and final row. At this point, R.

Johanan mocked Kahana, saying that "the lion who has arrived from Babylonia has turned out to be no more than a fox." After hearing this remark, Kahana held himself absolved of his oath, and began asking questions, which R. Johanan was unable to answer. Quickly regaining his position in the first row, Kahana continued raising objections. For each unanswered question they removed one cushion from under R. Johanan until all seven cushions had been removed and he was sitting on the floor. At this point, R. Johanan made an effort to get a good look at this "lion who arrived from Babylonia," and saw that his mouth was distorted. R. Johanan, unaware that Kahana had a split lip, thought that Kahana was laughing at him and became upset at him, as a result of which Kahaha died. After his students informed R. Johanan of his unfortunate mistake, Johanan went to the cave in which Kahana's body was being kept. The mouth of the cave was, however, blocked by a snake with its tail in its mouth. At first Johanan demanded that the snake grant him entrance to the cave, so that "the master may go in to his pupil." The snake did not respond. He then asked permission to enter the cave so that "one friend may visit another." Still the snake did not respond. Finally he asked permission to enter the cave so that "the pupil may go in to his master." Only then did the snake grant him entrance to the cave. Johanan offered to restore Kahana to life, but the latter apparently refused. R. Johanan then put to him "all the uncertainties that he had, and he solved them for him." R. Johanan concluded by conceding that the Torah of Ereẓ Israel was in fact derivative of the more incisive and original Torah of Babylonia.

After paring away the many supernatural and obviously legendary elements from this tale, the resulting "historical kernel" of this story has in the past been accepted by scholars as providing reliable historical information concerning the life and career of Kahana (2). In 1982 D. Sperber seriously challenged the historical authenticity of this tale as a whole, writing that its author "demonstrates ignorance of Palestinian chronology, of the structure of the Palestinian academy, and, on the other hand, he possesses a knowledge of Persian, of Sasanian folk-literature, courtly practice, and of the structure of the Babylonian academy" (Sperber, 93–94). In addition, the tendency of the entire story is polemical, "asserting Babylonian authority and ascendancy in learning" in opposition to the similar claims put forward by the yeshivot of Ereẓ Israel (98). In Sperber's view such a polemic must reflect a very late, certainly post-amoraic stage in the development of the Babylonian talmudic tradition. Some twenty years later, S. Friedman published a detailed analysis of this *aggadah*, revealing its literary sources, both in Palestinian and in other parallel Babylonian traditions, and explaining the way in which these sources were combined and reworked by the late Babylonian editor of this story. Particularly relevant here is the Palestinian version brought by Friedman of the events surrounding Kahana's encounter with R. Johanan. The Jerusalem Talmud tells us (Ber. 2:8, 5c): "Kahana was a tall lad. When he came up here (i.e., to Ereẓ Israel), a certain rogue saw him, and asked: What do you hear all the way up there in the sky?" Kahana then impulsively replied: "[I heard that] your death sentence has been sealed." In fact the rogue died. After the same thing happened a second time, Kahana was struck with remorse and said to himself: "I came to do good, and I ended up sinning." Racked with doubts he considered leaving Ereẓ Israel and returning to Babylonia. He then went to see R. Johanan and posed him the following enigmatic question: "If one's mother despises you, but your father's second wife treats you well, where should you go?" R. Johanan responded that he should return to the house of his father's second wife. Kahana took this response to mean that he should return to Bavel, and again impulsively set off home without asking permission or taking his leave from R. Johanan. The description of Kahana (2) in this story is one of an impulsive and indecisive youth, lacking in self-confidence – inexperienced and clearly subordinate to R. Johanan in all respects. Friedman concluded that the first part of the Babylonian *aggadah* "appears to be a radical reworking of a Palestinian account concerning the *second* Rav Kahana, who causes death with a lack of self restraint," and the third part of the Babylonian *aggadah* "is a Babylonian expansion of the [Palestinian] tradition that R. Johanan revered the *first* Rav Kahana, and turned to him concerning perplexing questions" (Friedman, 258). Therefore the two Palestinian traditions cited above, which clearly distinguish between these two *amoraim*, must provide the starting point for any historical description of their lives and careers, and not the Babylonian tradition, which conflates the two – in all likelihood intentionally, as Sperber has made clear (cf. Pes. 49a, and Rashi to BK 117a).

(3) Another *amora* who lived in the second half of the third century C.E., was one of the prominent students of *Huna (MK 13b), the head of the academy of *Sura from 250 C.E., and of *Judah b. Ezekiel of *Pumbedita (Ḥul. 19b). He appears to have visited Ereẓ Israel for a short while (BB 41b), after which he returned to Babylonia. Among his pupils were *Joseph b. Ḥiyya (Yev. 17a, 102a), *Rabbah b. Naḥamani (Yev. 102a), *Abba (Shab. 38a), and Isaac (RH 3b–4a). He may, however, be identical with the second Kahana.

(4) A pupil of Rabbah b. Naḥamani in Pumbedita (Sanh. 41b; Shevu. 36b), early part of the fourth century C.E. He knew the whole Mishnah order by heart at the age of 18 years (Shab. 63a). Among his associates were Aḥa b. Huna, Rama b. Ḥama, and *Safra whom he accompanied on a journey to Ereẓ Israel (Pes. 52b), remaining there for some time. There he joined a new circle of scholars, *Ḥiyya b. Abba (TJ, RH 2:6, 58b), Zera (TJ, Bik. 2:1, 64d) and *Jacob b. Aḥa with whom he collaborated in the fixing of the calendar (TJ, RH 2:6, 58b). Most probably it is this Kahana whom the Talmud refers to as an extremely handsome person (BM 84a; BB 58a). According to the *aggadah* he was compelled to sell baskets in the marketplace because of his poverty. On one occasion a Roman woman persuaded him to follow her, but he managed to escape from her home by jumping from the roof. The prophet Elijah rescued him and richly rewarded him (Kid. 40a).

(5) A pupil of Rava (Ket. 63a; BK 41b). Ḥanan of Nehardea was his colleague (Kid. 81b; Nid. 66b). He taught at the academy of Pure Nahara (Ḥul. 95b; BB 22a, 88a; et al.). Among his distinguished pupils was *Ashi, the redactor of the Babylonian Talmud (Ber. 39a, 42a; Ket. 69a; et al.). His sons were very wealthy (Me'il. 19a).

(6) *Amora* who died c. 414 C.E. He succeeded Rafram b. Papa as the head of the academy of Pumbedita from 396 until his death (*Iggeret R. Sherira Ga'on*, ed. Lewin, 90; cf. Halevy, *Dorot*, ii, 518, note 144). As a Kohen he once accepted a garment instead of silver coins for the ceremony of *Pidyon ha-Ben* (Kid. 8a; see also Tos. ad loc.). It is not always possible to distinguish between this Kahana and Kahana (2).

BIBLIOGRAPHY: Hyman, Toledot, 846–9; Ḥ. Albeck, *Mavo ha-Talmudim* (1969), 174–5, 203. D. Sperber, in: S Shaked (ed.), *Irano-Judaica* (1982), 83–100; S. Friedman, in: P. Schäfer (ed.), *The Talmud Yerushalmi and Graeco-Roman Culture III* (2002), 247–71.

[Stephen G. Wald (2nd ed.)]

KAHANA, ABRAHAM (1874–1946), biblical scholar and historian. Kahana, who was born in Skomorochy, Russia, was self-educated and started writing on Jewish subjects at an early date. In 1923 he emigrated to Palestine where he engaged in teaching and also served as librarian at the Sha'ar Zion library in Tel Aviv. From 1903 onward, he edited the Hebrew Bible, with a critical commentary and introductions (*Perush Madda'i*), he himself being responsible for Genesis, Exodus, Numbers, Job, Proverbs, Ecclesiastes, Ezra, and Nehemiah. The project, with which H.P. *Chajes, A. *Kaminka, S. *Krauss, F. Perles, M.L. Margolis, and others were associated, was, however, not completed. Kahana also edited the two-volume *Apocrypha (1936–37), which went through many reprints. He translated part of the Greek text into Hebrew, added commentary and introductions to each book, and took care of a considerable number of the apocryphal and pseudepigraphical books himself. Kahana wrote the introduction to D. Ginzburg's edition of the Mantua version of *Josippon (1896–1913). His historical writings include: *Korot ha-Yehudim be-Roma* (1901, 1914[2]; "History of the Jews in Rome") based on the works of A. *Berliner and that of H. *Vogelstein and P. *Rieger; a biography in Hebrew of M.Ḥ. *Luzzatto (1898); an edition of Leone de *Modena's autobiography (1912); and an edition of the travel diary of David *Reuveni (1922). Kahana also published a two-volume historical anthology, *Sifrut ha-Historyah ha-Yisre'elit* (1922–23), and an anthology on Ḥasidism, *Sefer ha-Ḥasidut* (1922). His interest in the ḥasidic movement is also shown by his biography of Israel b. Eliezer Ba'al Shem Tov (1900) and his edition of *Sippurei Ma'asiyyot shel R. Naḥman mi-Bratslav* (1922). Kahana's contribution to linguistics consisted of a Hebrew grammar (1931), a translation into Hebrew of S.D. Luzzatto's grammar (1899, repr. 1944), and a Russian-Hebrew dictionary (1907, 1919[4]).

BIBLIOGRAPHY: Alon, Meḥkarim, 2 (1958), 137ff.; Kressel, Leksikon, 2 (1967), 132–3.

KAHANA, ABRAHAM ARYEH LEIB BEN SHALOM SHAKHNA (also called **Loeb Scheines**; d. 1788), rabbi and author. Born in Horodenka, Galicia, where his father was rabbi, Kahana is not to be confused with his great-uncle, Abraham b. Shalom Shakhna Kahana, who was rabbi in Brody, Ostrog, and Dubno. Kahana himself was rabbi in Berdichev and Polonnoye (south Russia). He wrote novellae to the first three and to the fifth orders of the Babylonian Talmud under the title *Or ha-Ne'erav*, which was published with annotations, *Divrei Shelomo*, by his son Solomon Zalman (Ostrog, 1824). His homilies and a Bible commentary entitled *Divrei Ḥemed* and *Zer Zahav*, respectively, remain unpublished.

BIBLIOGRAPHY: Fuenn, Keneset, 34; M.M. Biber, *Mazkeret li-Gedolei Ostroha* (1907), 84n.; S. Wiener, *Kohelet Moshe* (1893–1918), 55 no. 439.

[Joseph Elijah Heller]

KAHANA, AHARON (1905–1967), Israeli painter. Kahana was born in Stuttgart, Germany. As soon as he began painting as a child he discovered abstraction. He studied art at the Stuttgart Academy of Art from 1922 to 1925. After he finished his studies he traveled to Berlin and Paris to learn more about the history of art and the modern art of his time. In 1934 he immigrated to Ereẓ Israel and settled in Ramat Gan. In his first decade in Israel, his style became Realistic. Only in 1943 did he return to abstraction. This was in keeping with the ideas of a new group of artists, New Horizons, that Kahana helped found. From 1962 Kahana painted in a very personal Pop Art style. He died suddenly of a heart attack in Paris during the Six-Day War.

Kahana was known for the unique art style he developed in the beginning of the 1950s. It was a mixture of Modernist forms, usually geometric, presenting very remarkable defining lines together with an archaic conceptual and biblical content. This style was suitable for wall decoration in public spaces in the young country, and using ceramic technique Kahana indeed decorated such walls (*Sacrifice of Isaac*, Hebrew University, Givat Ram).

During his last years he worked in a completely opposite style. The lines became soft and liquid, the figures were brimming with intensity, and the rhythm expressed vitality. The content of these drawings was more personal, showing nude figures and women's bodies.

Kahana's house in Ramat Gan was made into a museum of ceramic art in his memory.

[Ronit Steinberg (2nd ed.)]

KAHANA (Kogan), DAVID (1838–1915), scholar. Kahana, who was born in Odessa, published his first article in *Ha-Meliẓ* in 1866. He became known through his monographs on kabbalists, Shabbateans, and Ḥasidim which were first published in *Ha-Shaḥar* (1874–75; later in *Keneset Yisrael* 1886, and *Ha-Shilo'aḥ*, 1897, 1899, 1909), and then in book form. His main work in this field is concentrated in his two-volume *Toledot ha-Mekubbalim, ha-Shabbeta'im ve-ha-Ḥasidim* (1913; 1926[2]).

In the field of Bible studies he published (1) *Or Ḥadash* (1880) on Psalm 68; (2) *Meḥkerei Kohelet ben David* (1881), an introduction to the Book of Ecclesiastes, with a commentary to Psalm 119 as an appendix; (3) *Devar Ester* (1881), introduction and commentary to the Book of Esther; (4) *Masoret Seyag la-Mikra* (1882), a defense of the masorah; (5) *Mavo le-Parshat Bilam u-Devar Atono* (1883); and (6) *Toledot Shelomo* (1883), on Solomon and Solomonic literature.

Kahana also wrote numerous studies on other periods of Jewish history, in particular a number of articles on medieval grammarians and poets published in *Ha-Shilo'aḥ*. Noteworthy among his other works are (1) *Le-Toledot R. Sa'adyah Ga'on* (1892); (2) *Rosh Petanim* (1883), on *Eisenmenger; (3) *Ma'asei Even Reshef* (1884), on the forgeries of *Firkovich; (4) *Ḥokhmat Yehudah* (1892), Jewish-Christian polemics on religion; (5) "On Lilienthal and the Russian Haskalah Movement" (*Ha-Shilo'aḥ*, 1912). Kahana also edited the Hebrew original of Ben Sira, *Ḥokhmat ben Sira* (1912; first published in *Ha-Shilo'aḥ*), together with the only Hebrew commentary on the book existing at that time; the collected poems, with introductions and notes, of Dunash b. Labrat (1894), Solomon Sharvit ha-Zahav (1894), and Abraham ibn Ezra (1894); and *Megillat Sefer* (1897), an autobiography of Jacob *Emden, based on manuscripts in Oxford. He died in Odessa.

BIBLIOGRAPHY: N. Sokolow (ed.), *Sefer Zikkaron le-Soferei Ereẓ Yisrael ha-Ḥayyim Ittanu ka-Yom…* (1889), 199; *Lu'aḥ Aḥi'asaf*, 2 (1895), 269–71; J. Klausner, *Yoẓerim u-Vonim*, 1 (1944[2]), 46–56; G. Scholem, *Bibliographia Kabbalistica* (1933), 80–82.

[*Encyclopaedia Judaica* (Germany)]

KAHANA, JACOB BEN ABRAHAM (d. 1826), rabbinical scholar in Vilna. His father was rabbi at Brestowitz in the province of Grodno. Supported by his father-in-law, Issachar Baer, the brother of *Elijah of Vilna and one of the prominent rabbis of that town, he devoted himself to study. On the death of his father-in-law, he was appointed by the communal leaders of Vilna as trustee of the local charities. He is the author of a commentary in three parts on tractate *Eruvin*: on the tractate in the Babylonian Talmud, the *Tosefta*, and the Jerusalem Talmud respectively. Each section has a different title but the whole work was given the general title *Ge'on Ya'akov*. It was published, together with Joseph Padua's two-page pamphlet *Zikhron Yosef* (1863), by Raphael Nathan Neta *Rabbinovicz, who wrote a lengthy introduction containing a biography of the author. Kahana occupied no rabbinical position, but was held in the highest esteem.

BIBLIOGRAPHY: R.N.N. Rabbinovicz, in: J. Kahana, *Ge'on Ya'akov* (1863), introd.; S.J. Fuenn, *Kiryah Ne'emanah* (1915[2]), 239f.; L. Ginzberg, *Perushim ve-Ḥiddushim ba-Yerushalmi*, 1 (1941), IX (Eng. introd.), 128f. (Heb. introd.).

[Itzhak Alfassi]

KAHANA, JEHIEL ẒEVI BEN JOSEPH MORDECAI (first half of 19th century), member of a family of Hungarian rabbis. He was a grandson of Judah b. Joseph ha-Kohen, who was a brother of Aryeh Leib b. Joseph ha-Kohen *Heller, author of the *Keẓot ha-Ḥoshen*. Kahana served as *dayyan* in Sziget, and all three of his sons were well-known *dayyanim* in Hungary. The first, ḤAYYIM ARYEH (d. 1917), served as *dayyan* of Máramarossziget (Sighet). He was the author of *Divrei Ge'onim* (1870), containing 113 principles and themes in civil law. The work is in alphabetical order, collected from various responsa and books. In his introduction the author stresses that it was not his purpose "to give practical rulings of the law… and I only intend to stimulate these scholarly teachers who know the law thoroughly." The second son, JOSEPH MORDECAI (d. 1896), served as *dayyan* of Teczo, Hungary, and was the author of *Divrei Ẓaddikim* (2 parts, 1874–76), an alphabetical work on the reasons for the precepts and customs. In his introduction he stresses that the purpose of the work was to show "that Jewish customs are binding as law." The disregard of a good custom is tantamount to disregarding the commands of the Lord and His Torah. The third son, JACOB GEDALIAH, was the author of *Rimzei Torah ve-Alfa Beta* (1876), a commentary on Genesis, also giving the reasons for different customs in alphabetical order.

BIBLIOGRAPHY: P.Z. Schwartz, *Shem ha-Gedolim me-Ereẓ Hagar*, 1 (1913), 35a no. 45, 42b 99/2, 3 (1915), 12b no. 9, 13a no. 23, 35a no. 8; N. Ben-Menahem, in: *Sinai*, 17 (1945), 340–3; 25 (1949), 207f.; J.J. Greenwald (Grunwald), *Maẓẓevet Kodesh* (1952), 21, 43, 48.

[Yehoshua Horowitz]

KAHANA, KALMAN (1910–1991), leader of the *Po'alei Agudat Israel movement. Born in Brody, Galicia, Kahana studied at the Berlin rabbinical seminary and the universities of Berlin and Wuerzburg. He was one of the founders of the Agudat Israel youth movement in Germany and moved to Palestine in 1938 with a group of young Orthodox settlers, joining the Po'alei Agudat Israel movement. Kahana was a founder of kibbutz *Ḥafeẓ Ḥayyim (1944) and a member of the *Knesset from its establishment in 1949. He was deputy minister of education (1962–69). He became president of the Po'alei Agudat Israel movement. Kahana published several studies in rabbinics and wrote on Maimonides.

[Menachem Friedman]

In later years Kahana occupied himself with the *halakhah* pertaining to the agricultural laws which apply in Israel. In 1976 he published *Miẓvot ha-Areẓ* and in 1980 tractate *Shevi'it* according to both the Babylonian and Jerusalem Talmuds with the notes and commentary of Elijah, Gaon of Vilna, and as an appendix his own commentary to the Mishnah and the Tosefta to the order *Zeraim*.

KAHANA (Kagan), KOPPEL (1895–1978), rabbinical scholar and authority on Jewish, Roman, and English law. Kahana, who was born in Eisiskes, Lithuania, studied at Lithuanian yeshivot and served as rabbi in Bialowieza and Rozanai, Poland. Before World War II, he went to Cambridge, where he studied law. From 1946 to 1968 he was lecturer in Talmud and codes at Jews' College, London, which before then had trained few rabbis. The new Rabbinical Diploma Course, introduced by the principal, Isidore *Epstein and conducted by Kahana, attracted to the college also some of its former students, raising a new generation of Anglo-Jewish rabbis, who were inspired by his teaching. Among his published writings are: *Three Great Systems of Jurisprudence* (1955), a comparative study of Jewish, Roman, and English Law; *The Case for Jewish Civil Law in the Jewish State* (1960); and *The Theory of Marriage in Jewish Law* (1966). Under the name of K. Kagan, he contributed articles to some of the leading American and English law reviews. Kahana represented the rare type of Lithuanian *Gaon*, who was acquainted with modern legal studies and whose contributions in this field were considerable.

KAHANA, NAḤMAN (1861–1904), Hungarian rabbi. Kahana, the son-in-law of Joseph Meir *Weiss, was rabbi of Szaploncza. He became particularly well-known because of his *Orḥot Ḥayyim* (2 pts., 1898; 1962[2]), on the Shulḥan Arukh *Oraḥ Ḥayyim*, which for a long time was regarded as an indispensable reference work for every rabbi. It included the important glosses of Shalom Mordecai ha-Kohen Schwadron and Elijah David *Rabinowitz-Teomim. The author made use of more than 800 works of responsa and codes, assembling the material logically in a clear style. In the new edition glosses from the author's private copy, and by Solomon Zalman Ehrenreich, Ephraim Weinberger, and others were added. He also arranged the publication of the *Divrei Ge'onim* (1901) of his father, Ḥayyim Aryeh ha-Kohen, and of the *Likkutei Torah ve-ha-Shas* on Deuteronomy (1892) by Isaac Eichenstein of Zhidachov.

BIBLIOGRAPHY: P.Z. Schwartz, *Shem ha-Gedolim me-Ereẓ Hagar*, 2 (1914), 20a; A. Stern, *Meliẓei Eshal Ḥodesh Tammuz* (1931), 66b; N. Ben-Menahem, *Mi-Sifrut Yisrael be-Hungaryah* (1958), 130–2, 245, 302.

[Naphtali Ben-Menahem]

KAHANA, SOLOMON DAVID (1869–1953), Polish rabbi. Born in Yanova, province of Kovno, Kahana studied at the yeshivah of Volozhin and the *kolel of Kovno. He was ordained by R. Isaac Elhanan *Spektor. He collaborated with and later succeeded his father-in-law, R. Samuel Zanvil *Klepfish, as a member of the Warsaw rabbinate, where he was much in demand as an arbiter in business disputes. In matters of ritual law he took a lenient view. After World War I he took an active part in rehabilitation and relief, and in particular established a special department in Warsaw to deal with problems of war *agunot* (see *agunah), forming a network of information bureaus in the larger cities of Europe for this purpose. The information gathered about missing husbands made possible the remarriage of thousands of *agunot*. He was among the founders and a member of the presidium of the Agudat ha-Rabbanim of Poland, created after Poland's independence was restored in 1919. After the Nazi invasion of Poland in September 1939, he managed to escape to Ereẓ Israel. He was appointed rabbi of the Old City of Jerusalem and took up residence in the historic courtyard which 200 years earlier had been occupied by R. Ḥayyim b. *Attar. After the Holocaust he organized an *agunot* department on behalf of the Chief Rabbinate. With the outbreak of Arab disturbances in 1947 he was evacuated, with the help of the Belgian consul, to the new city of Jerusalem, where he lived until his death. With the exception of some responsa published in the compilations of other rabbis, his literary output was lost during his two forced evacuations. His son, Shmuel Zanwil Kahana (1905–), served as director general of the Ministry of Religions in Israel.

BIBLIOGRAPHY: EẒD, 3 (1965), 42–45; D. Plinker, in: *Arim ve-Immahot be-Yisrael*, 3 (1948), 2–3 (introd. by Kahana), 160.

[Jacob Goldman]

KAHANA-CARMON, AMALIA (1926–), Israeli writer. Amalia Kahana-Carmon was born in kibbutz En-Ḥarod but lived in Tel Aviv since childhood. She served in the Negev Brigade during the War of Independence and took part in the capture of Beersheba. After studying at the Hebrew University in Jerusalem, she stayed for seven years in England and Switzerland, and then returned to Tel Aviv, where she worked for many years as a librarian. Chronologically she belongs to the group of writers who began writing in the 1940s and subsequently became known as the "Palmaḥ generation," but her work differs basically from theirs: though it does echo the events of the pre-State period and War of Independence and later periods, she makes no attempts to deal with external reality and social themes as such. Others consider her as a member of the experimental "New Wave." Her prose is intrinsically lyrical, concentrating on the characters' inner responses. The events depicted are usually minor ones, the characters mainly described during an attempt to break out of their closed world, generally in order to reach another person. These attempts mostly fail, and the stories end with characters withdrawing into themselves again, resigned and somewhat changed. A contact that is established is frequently described as miraculous and blessed.

The lyrical nature of her prose is a reflection of her major themes: most of her characters are represented while reflecting on events rather than creating them, discovering their inability to break out and effect a change. Amalia Kahana-Carmon's style is remarkable for its capacity to represent the inner world of her characters, with all the subtle changes that take place there. Critics have praised her stylized impressionistic diction, her way of portraying in a refined poetic manner melodramatic moments as well as trivial daily matters. One of the first self-aware feminine voices in Hebrew prose, author of a series of articles in which she criticized the discrimination against women as writers and readers in a male-dominated, male-oriented Hebrew literature, Kahana-Carmon's oeuvre has become the subject of research and interpretation among scholars in the fields of Gender Studies and Feminist Theory. Her works include a collection of 17 short stories, *Bi-Khefifah Aḥat* ("Under One Roof," 1966); the novel *Ve-Yareaḥ be-*

Emek Ayalon ("And the Moon in the Valley of Ayalon," 1971); a collection of three novellas, *Sadot Magnetiyyim* ("Magnetic Fields," 1977); stories collected as *Himurim Gevohim* ("High Stakes," 1980); *Lema'alah be-Montifer* ("Up in Montifer," 1984); novellas and stories. The novel *Liviti Otah ba-Derekh Le-Veitah* ("I Escorted Her on the Way Home," 1991) depicts the relationship between Me'irah, a well-known middle-aged Ashkenazi actress, and an Oriental Israeli from a development town, twenty years her junior. *Kan Nagur* ("Here We'll Live," 1996), is composed of five novellas: Two of these depict the life of three students in Jerusalem under the British Mandate; "*Lev ha-Kayiẓ, Lev ha-Or*" portrays the life of a family from the point of view of a child, while "*Mi-Mar'ot Gesher ha-Barvaz ha-Yarok*" is a historic novella, focusing on the notion of captivity and personal freedom.

Kahana-Carmon received many major awards, including the Bialik Prize and the prestigious Israel Prize for literature (2000). Although much admired in Israel, very few of her works have been translated into other languages, mainly due to her own objection: "Despite interest from various publishers all over the world, I have not yet found the translator who is capable of transporting my words into another language," she said in an interview. The novel *Liviti Otah ba-Derekh Le-Veitah* was translated into Italian and Chinese, a few stories appeared in German anthologies of Hebrew literature. The story "Bridal Veil" appeared in G. Abramson (ed.), *Oxford Book of Hebrew Short Stories* (1996) as well as in R. Domb (ed.), *New Women's Writing from Israel* (1996). Further information regarding translation is available at the ITHL website at www.ithl.org.il

BIBLIOGRAPHY: G. Shaked, *Gal Ḥadash be-Sipporet ha-Ivrit* (1971), 168–79; idem, in: *Moznayim*, 2 (July, 1971), 121–30; S. Grodzensky, in: *Davar* (July 30, 1971); N. Calderon, in: *Siman Keriah*, 1 (Sept. 1972), 321–6; R. Litvin, in: *La-Merḥav* (Oct. 3, and 10, 1969); A. Balaban, *Ha-Kadosh ve-ha-Drakon: Iyyun bi-Yẓirot Amalia Kahana-Karmon* (1979). **ADD. BIBLIOGRAPHY:** L. Yudkin, "Kahana-Carmon and the Plot Unspoken," in: *Modern Hebrew Literature*, 2:4 (1976), 30–42; W. Bargad, "A.K.C. and the Novel of Consciousness," in: *Prooftexts*, 1:2 (1981), 172–184; H. Herzig, *A. Kahana-Karmon* (1983); L. Rattok, *Amalia Kahana-Karmon: Monografiyyah* (1986); E. Fuchs, "A.K.C. and Contemporary Hebrew Women's Fiction," in: *Signs*, 13:2 (1988), 299–310; S. Grober, "*First Axioms*," in: *Modern Hebrew Literature*, 13:3–4 (1988), 10–14; H. Hever, "Minority Discourse of a National Majority," in: *Prooftexts*, 10:1 (1990), 129–147; L. Rattok, *Ha-Kol ha-Aḥer* (1994), 287f.; W. Bargad, "Elements of Style in the Fiction of A. Kahana-Carmon," in: *Hebrew Annual Review*, 2 (1978), 1–10; P. Shirav: *Ketivah Lo Tamah* (1998); Y.S. Feldman, *No Room of Their Own: Gender and Nation in Israeli Women's Fiction* (1999); R.A. Jones, *Self and Place in "The White Light" by A. Kahana-Carmon*, in: *Textual Practice*, 16:1 (2002), 93–110.

[Abraham Balaban / Anat Feinberg (2nd ed.)]

KAHAN COMMISSION, commission set up by the Israeli government on Sept. 28, 1982, to investigate "the atrocities committed by a unit of Lebanon forces against the civilian population in the Sabra and Shatilla camps" adjacent to Beirut between Sept. 16 and 18. The members were Justice Yitzhak Kahan, president of the Supreme Court; and General (reserve) Yona Efrat.

The commission held 60 meetings and examined 58 witnesses. It also had available a number of official documents provided by the relevant government departments. The public at large, both in Israel and abroad, were invited to appear and present evidence. The commission was assisted in its work by a specially appointed professional unit. For reasons of security, many sessions were held *in camera* and part of the evidence was withheld from publication. Nine individuals (including the Israeli prime minister, the foreign minister, the defense minister, the chief of General Staff, and other military commanders) were specifically notified of their right to appear and be heard because of the harm that might accrue to them, and they all took the opportunity to do so.

The commission spent considerable time investigating the events preceding the killings, the intense divisions and hostilities – religious, ethnic and political – in the Lebanese population, the military and political relations existing between Israel and the Christian Phalange forces (as well as, in the south, with the Free Lebanese Army under Major Saad Haddad), and the differing evaluations made by the two intelligence arms, the Mossad and Army Intelligence, of the stability and battle behavior of these forces.

The commission found that the premature departure of the Multinational Force from Beirut induced the Israeli army to enter the city and rid it of terrorists, in the course of which it was decided to allow the Phalange to enter the camps, a step intended to involve them more closely in clearing the area. The forward Israeli army observation post close to the camps was, however, so sited that it was difficult or impossible to observe what was happening inside the camps. Israeli units advancing on the camps were halted by heavy gunfire and suffered considerable casualties.

The commission examined in depth the information available to the Israeli authorities, military and political, the meetings held with the Phalange commanders, and the warnings given not to harm the civilian population. Much of what transpired was not apparently recorded or minuted, and the faulty recollection of the persons involved led, in the view of the commission, to inconsistencies in the evidence. In addition, radio communication between the Phalange in the camps and their liaison officer in the forward post, which were overheard by the Israelis there and should have aroused concern about what was taking place, were either dismissed or ignored and certainly not reported to the upper military and political levels. The Israeli cabinet's attention was drawn to events only after a journalist had reported to a minister information he had heard from an Israeli officer or officers at the forward post. The minister informed the foreign minister, but recollection of the parties was confused. Equally disputed were the oral reports made by the chief of General Staff to the defense minister. No report reached the prime minister until he learned of the events from a British broadcast on September 18 after the Phalange had finally left the camps.

The commission could not establish precisely the number of people killed. Non-Israeli sources put it between 328 and 460. The International Red Cross indicated they included over 100 Lebanese and over 300 Palestinians, most of them males; women and children victims numbered 35. The commission noted the difficulty of distinguishing between those who fell in military action and those who were simply slain.

The report held that direct responsibility lay with the Phalange. The victims were all found in the camps which the Phalange alone had entered; no other forces were present or had means of entry. The Phalange were notorious for their extreme hostility to the Palestinians for their acts against Lebanese Christians during the civil war that had raged since 1975. The assassination of Bashir Jemayel, the Phalange leader, two days earlier, had also inflamed passions.

No evidence was produced to implicate the forces of Haddad. Nor was the IDF present in the camps throughout the three vital days, and the Phalange were refused the artillery and tank support they asked for.

In the opinion of the commission, the manner in which the decisions were reached at the political level and the handling of intelligence gave cause for concern. The decision of the minister of defense and the military command to allow entry to the Phalange was made without proper consideration as to its implementation and without thought for the likely consequences. The decision was not passed on in a timely manner to the political element or to other military elements that should have been informed. Nor were reports of what was happening that filtered through passed on or fully passed on, and then only after some delay that prevented appropriate orders to be issued or action to be taken. The commission was clear as to the steps to be taken to remedy the deficiencies disclosed. In addition to internal review by the military themselves, it recommended investigation by a ministerially appointed team of experts to establish the responsibility of those concerned.

Regarding the indirect responsibility of the nine persons who were notified of the jeopardy they were in, the commission came to the following conclusions: Prime Minister Menaḥem Begin, preoccupied as he was with other matters of state, was entitled to rely on the optimistic reports he received from the minister of defense and the chief of General Staff. Under the circumstances, however, he should have given thought to all the possibilities, especially those raised by other members of the government, but he seems to have distanced himself from the matter.

Although no clear warning was received from Intelligence by Minister of Defense Ariel Sharon, his disregard of the obvious dangers and his failure to order that suitable safeguards be taken could not be justified, especially in view of the very active role he played in the Lebanon War. The commission thought he should draw the necessary personal conclusions; if necessary, the prime minister should exercise his constitutional right to remove him from office.

Foreign Minister Yiẓḥak Shamir, although informed by his deputy minister (with whom he was not on good terms) of what was happening, did not show any special interest or attempt to investigate the matter or take it up with the minister of defense.

The Chief of Staff General Raphael Eitan knew from his past experience with Phalange that they could not be relied upon. His view that they were a disciplined force was entirely baseless, and he made no proper provision to control their actions; his belief that the Phalange would report fully was naive, especially in view of what he heard from the local Israeli commanders. Since he was soon due to retire, the commission made no recommendation in his regard.

The head of Military Intelligence, General Yehoshua Saguy, could not be believed when he said that he received no information about the plan to let the Phalange into the camps. He was present at all relevant meetings but acted with complete indifference. His awareness that his organization took second place to the Mossad in the deliberations did not justify his complete inactivity. It was recommended that he should cease to act.

The head of the Mossad did not initially know, nor should he have known, of the decision about the Phalange but, having learned of it, he failed in his duty to evaluate the situation, especially in the light of his close association with Phalange.

General Amir Drori, head of the Northern Command, had no explicit information. He relied on the chief of General Staff and acted correctly with understanding and responsibility, although he should have warned the CGS.

Brigadier Amos Yaron of the local command was severely criticized for the absence of critical oversight of events. He was content with taking Phalange promises at their face value. He did not act firmly though he knew that the behavior of the Phalange left much to be desired. He did not keep the chief of General Staff fully informed and made no suggestions as to how to proceed. It was recommended that he should not fill a position of command for at least three years.

Finally, the personal assistant of the minister of defense was exonerated, having, it seems, done what was to be expected from him.

[Peter Elman (2nd ed.)]

KAHANE, ARTHUR (1872–1932), German author and editor. Kahane, who was born and educated in Vienna, became literary adviser to the Deutsches Theater in Berlin, under the direction of Max *Reinhardt, in 1905. He also edited the theater's journal, *Blaetter des deutschen Theaters* (later combined with *Das junge Deutschland*). Kahane's novels and essays reveal an extremely individualistic philosophy. In his two lyrical works, *Clemens und seine Maedchen* (1918) and *Willkommen und Abschied* (1919), he contrasts the modern age of materialism and brutality with an earlier era of love and tenderness. In *Das Judenbuch* (1931) Kahane declared: "I love the Jews and my own Jewish character"; but he believed that the Jews were destined to be restless forever. "Ahasver" (i.e., the *Wandering Jew), he contended, "will always remain the true symbol of our immortal people." Other works by Kahane deal with his experiences in the theater. He left the Jewish community when he was 19 years old.

ADD. BIBLIOGRAPHY: T. Betz, in: W. Killy (ed.), *Literatur Lexikon*, 6 (1990), 186–87.

[Rudolf Kayser]

KAHANE, ISAAK (Yitzḥak Ze'ev; 1904–1963), rabbinic scholar. Kahane was born in Munkacs, Hungary, and studied at talmudic schools in his hometown, where he was ordained. He continued his studies at the Jewish Theological Seminary of Breslau and the University of Prague. Subsequently he became rabbi of Pohorelice (Pohrlitz), Moravia, serving until his emigration to Palestine in 1939. In Jerusalem he was associated with several religious research institutions, chiefly Mosad ha-Rav Kook. During the last years of his life, he taught rabbinic literature at Bar-Ilan University. Kahane's major field of research was rabbinic responsa literature. In numerous studies he organized and analyzed a variety of topics and problems discussed in rabbinic responsa and also abstracted material of historical or linguistic interest from them. Among his works are *Shemittat Kesafim* (1945), on the cancellation of debts in the sabbatical year; *Le-Takkanat Agunot* (1946), on the *agunah* ("deserted wife") problem; *Sefer ha-Agunot* (1954), a voluminous collection of source material on the *agunah* question; and *Teshuvot, Pesakim u-Minhagim* (3 vols., 1957–62), responsa, rulings, and customs of Rabbi Meir of Rothenburg, systematically arranged and annotated. His contributions to Hebrew scholarly periodicals and publications include: "Military Service in Rabbinic Responsa" (*Sinai*, 1948); "Changes in the Value of Currency in Jewish Law" (*ibid.*, 1949); "Medicine in Post-Talmudic Halakhic Literature" (*ibid.*, 1950) and "Synagogue Art in Halakhic Literature" (*Beit ha-Keneset*, 1955). He also wrote on the history of the Jews of Moravia, including a monograph on the Jewish community of Nikolsburg (in J.L. Maimon (ed.), *Arim ve-Immahot be-Yisrael*, 4 (1950), 210–313).

BIBLIOGRAPHY: T. Preschel, in: *Aresheth*, 4 (1966), 511–7.

[Tovia Preschel]

KAHANE, MEIR (1932–1990), religious activist. Born in Brooklyn, New York, he was as a youth a member of the *Betar youth movement and was often imprisoned for his acts of violence. He was ordained as an Orthodox rabbi and graduated in law from New York University. In 1960, he founded the Jewish Defense League whose activities included self-defense of the Jewish community of Brooklyn threatened with urban violence and harassment of Soviet activities in New York as a protest against the treatment of Jews in Russia. In 1971 he moved to Israel and in 1976 founded the extremist nationalist *Kach movement, advocating the removal of Arabs from Israel. Kahane served as a member of the Knesset on its behalf, 1981–1985. His party was eventually disbarred for its racism and advocacy of violence. Kahane was assassinated while addressing a meeting in New York. An Egyptian-born Arab was acquitted of the murder on technicalities but in 1995 was sentenced to a long term of imprisonment for his involvement in Muslim fundamentalist terror in New York.

KAHANEMAN, JOSEPH (popularly known as the "**Ponevezher Rav**"; 1888–1969), rabbi and yeshivah head, founder of the talmudic educational complex in *Bene Berak, Israel. As a young man, Kahaneman studied in the yeshivah of Telz. The *rosh ha-yeshivah*, Eliezer *Gordon, had a lifelong influence on Kahaneman. For ever after, whenever Kahaneman made reference to "*der rov*," he meant Rabbi Gordon. After Telz, he spent a short time in the *musar* yeshivah of Navarodok. From there he went to join the *kolel* of the Ḥafez Ḥayyim in Radin. It was there that Kahaneman became close with Rabbi Elḥanan *Wasserman and Rabbi Ḥayyim *Soloveitchik of Brisk. In 1910 he married the daughter of another famous Lithuanian rabbi, Aryeh Leib Rubin. In 1916 he was appointed head of the yeshivah of Grodno, where his outstanding organizing abilities soon became evident. Possessed of a dynamic and winning personality, he devoted himself not only to the development of the yeshivah, but also to the establishment of similar centers of learning throughout Lithuania, among them a preparatory yeshivah in Ponevezh. On the death of Isaac Rabinowitz, the rabbi of Ponevezh, in 1919, Kahaneman was appointed his successor. He opened a yeshivah which after the attainment of Lithuania's independence became one of the largest in the country. In addition to his preoccupation with the yeshivah, in which he lectured twice a week, and whose material needs he personally looked after, Kahaneman was active in many spheres of communal endeavor. He was a leader of *Agudat Israel and an elected member of the Lithuanian parliament. He established a Talmud Torah attended by 400 children and a preparatory yeshivah to serve as a feeder for the main institution.

Kahaneman was on a mission abroad when World War II broke out. In 1940 he settled in Ereẓ Israel and from there directed efforts, in vain, toward the rescue of Lithuanian Jewry from the Nazis. Most of his family perished in the Holocaust. Thereafter, he devoted himself to reestablishing in Ereẓ Israel a network of Torah institutions. In 1943 he established Batei Avot, an orphanage for refugee children. At the end of 1944 he laid the foundation of the Ponevezh Yeshivah in Bene Berak with seven students. Over the years, he traveled throughout the Jewish world to enlist financial support for his ambitious venture. The result was Kiryat Ponevezh, where more than 1,000 students have studied and which has included hostels for children and adults, a large library, and a memorial to Lithuanian Jewry. He instituted the *yarḥei kallah*, an annual summer refresher course in talmudic studies for adults. All this, he stated, he did "with 21 fingers," those of his hands and feet and the finger of God. In later years, he established a branch yeshivah in the development town of Ashdod. He was widely revered among all sections of the population. Kahaneman was among those approached by Israeli Prime Minister David Ben-Gurion to answer the question, "Who is a Jew?"

In his answer, Kahaneman wrote, "I see the vision of the return to Zion in our generation as the revelation of the light of divine providence, which strengthens our hand and accompanies us through the evil waters that have risen against us … I see miracles every moment, every hour! I am sure that His Honor [i.e., Ben-Gurion] sees the thing as I do, for who like the ship's captain standing at the wheel of the ship sees these miracles." Kahaneman also viewed the Six-Day War as a miracle. The Ponevezh Yeshivah in Bene Berak and its sister institution in Ashdod have thrived along with the communities Kahaneman built around them. In 1989 and again in 2003, collections of Kahaneman's writings and lectures were published, *Kovez Shi'urim ve-Ḥidushei Torah* and *Sefer Divrei ha-Rav*, respectively.

BIBLIOGRAPHY: A. Avnon (ed.), *Ishim be-Yisrael* (1966), 154; D. Lipez et al. (eds.), *Sefer Yahadut Lita* (1960), index; S. Kol, *Eḥad be-Doro*, 2 vols. (1970). **ADD. BIBLIOGRAPHY:** A. Sorasky, *Ha-Rav mi-Ponevezh*, 3 vols. (1999); Y. Schwartz, *Ha-Rav mi-Ponevezh* (1997).

[Mordechai Hacohen / David Derovan (2nd ed.)]

KAHANOV, MOSES NEHEMIAH (1817–1883), Jerusalem talmudist. He was born in Belorussia but after his marriage at the age of 15, settled in Petrovice where at the age of 18 he was appointed assistant to the local rabbi. Some years later, he became rabbi of Khaslavich, a city noted for its scholars. In 1864 he set out for Jerusalem. On his arrival, after a journey of six months, he was appointed head of the Ez Ḥayyim yeshivah, the most important in Jerusalem, remaining in this position until his death. Kahanov was remarkably progressive for his time and environment. He appealed for the founding of industrial enterprises, a daring proposal for that time. He even consented to the proposal of Sir Moses *Montefiore to introduce the teaching of the vernacular, Arabic, in his yeshivah, but was obliged to abandon the proposal in the face of pressure from extremist elements. One of the first of the old *yishuv* to speak only Hebrew, he was also one of those who encouraged settlement outside the walls of the Old City of Jerusalem, building a house for himself in Naḥlat Shivah.

Among his publications were *Erez Ḥefez* (1884), on laws of *terumah* and tithes; *Ḥukkot Olam* (1886), on mixed species (*kilayim); *Mei Menuḥot* (c. 1860) on the laws of the sabbath, to which was appended *Palgei Mayim*, giving rules for those traveling by ship on the sabbath; and *Netivot ha-Shalom* on the Shulḥan Arukh (pt. 1 (1858, 1875²), pt. 2 (1861)). He applied himself particularly to the question of the application of the laws of the sabbatical year which had become of practical importance with the establishment of the Jewish agricultural colonies, and in this connection published *Shenat ha-Sheva* (1881). The eulogies he delivered on the deaths of Baron Asher Rothschild and Sir Moses Montefiore were published. His *Sha'alu Shelom Yerushalayim* (1867) on the state of Jerusalem and its citizens was published three times. His will was published in 1968 (*Siftei Yeshenim*, Jerusalem) together with a responsum on Jerusalem and a brief biography.

BIBLIOGRAPHY: Frumkin-Rivlin, 3 (1929), 270f.; Bath Yehudah, in: EZD, 3 (1965), 45–52.

[Itzhak Alfassi]

KAHANOVITCH, ISRAEL ISAAC (1872–1945), Canadian rabbi and communal leader in Winnipeg. Born in Grodno, Poland, Kahanovitch studied at the yeshivot in Grodno and Slobodka, Lithuania. He received his *semikhah* at age 20 from the leading halakhic authority, Rabbi Jehiel Michal Epstein, author of the *Arukh ha-Shulḥan*. In the wake of the 1905 pogroms, Kahanovitch moved to North America. For one year he served as rabbi in Scranton, Pennsylvania, and then moved to Winnipeg, where he lived out the rest of his life.

On the strength of his rabbinic learning, his speaking ability, and extraordinary energy, Kahanovitch was widely recognized as the rabbinic authority of Winnipeg, and he exercised influence across western Canada. A passionate advocate for Jewish education, he established groups for Talmud study and was actively involved in the creation and support of the Winnipeg Hebrew Free School first established in 1907 and in the construction of a proper building to house the school. Although a Mizrachi Zionist at heart, Kahanovitch participated in communal functions with secular Zionists. He served on the National Executive of the Zionist Organization of Canada and regularly attended the Zionist congresses in Canada. He also looked to strengthen Jewish communal bonding by supporting the Canadian Jewish Congress (CJC) at the national level, both in its first incarnation at the end of World War I and when it was revamped in the 1930s to counteract the bitter antisemitism and restrictive immigration policies of Depression-era Canada. He was elected a delegate to the first CJC meeting in Montreal by an overwhelming majority. At the local level, shortly after his arrival he was the prime mover behind the establishment of the United Hebrew Charities in Winnipeg and hoped in vain for a *kehillah*-type organization.

Kahanovich was appreciated by those in smaller Jewish communities across western Canada who struggled to sustain local Jewish community life and institutions. At a time when travel was often difficult and rabbinic authorities few and far between, Kahanovich supported the creation of a Jewish school in Regina, attended a teachers' conference in Saskatoon, and traveled to tiny Melville in Saskatchewan to dedicate a new synagogue, to name just a few of his activities outside of Winnipeg

While highly regarded, Kahanovich's authority on matters of supervision of kosher slaughtering did not go unchallenged. His most serious challenger was Rabbi I.D. Gorodsky who also held a rabbinic position in Winnipeg between 1911 and 1919. But Kahanovitch remained a beloved figure among Jews, religious and secular, in Winnipeg and across western Canada. In 1927 a number of communal leaders established a special committee to raise money to increase Kahanovich's salary, when a rumor circulated that he was going to leave Winnipeg. His funeral in 1945 was attended by a crowd of about 5,000, about one-third of the total adult Jewish community of Winnipeg.

BIBLIOGRAPHY: A.D. Hart, *The Jew in Canada* (1926), 154; M.S. Stern, in: *The Rabbi I.I. Kahanovitch Memorial Volume* (1984), 93–114.

[Richard Menkis (2nd ed.)]

KĀHINA (feminine form of the Ar. *Kāhin*, "soothsayer," sometimes incorrectly thought to be derived from Cohen), the surname given by the Arabs to the *Berber queen of the mountainous Aurès region in southeast Algeria. According to Arabic authors, the powerful Jerawa tribe of Berber converts to Judaism, to which Kāhina belonged, was led by her during the final resistance to the Arab invasion. She defeated the armies of Ḥasān ibn al Nuʿmān and took prisoners, one of whom, Khālid b. Yazīd, she kept and adopted. Allegedly, Khālid betrayed Kāhina who died in combat (698 or 702). The Arabs then poured into Africa and invaded Spain with Berber troops. Arab authors' accounts of Kāhina are partly legendary, but they nevertheless contain some historical facts such as the historical personage of the Queen of the Aurès. Her opposition to the Muslim Arabs was not religiously inspired; some authorities deny that she was Jewish. The history of Kāhina remains controversial.

BIBLIOGRAPHY: Basset, in: EIS², s.v. *al-Kāhina*; N. Slouschz, *Etude sur l'Histoire des Juifs et du Judaïsme au Maroc*, 1 (1905), 66; 2 (1906), 11–18; idem, *Travels in North Africa* (1927), 309–16; G. Marçais, *La Berbèrie Musulmane* (1946), 34–35; E.F. Gauthier, *Le Passé de l'Afrique du Nord* (1952), 225, 267, 270–80; A. Julien, *Histoire de l'Afrique du Nord*, 2 (1952²), 21–22; Hirschberg, in: *Tarbiz*, 26 (1956/57), 370–83; idem, Afrikah, index.

[David Corcos]

°KAHLE, PAUL ERNST (1875–1965), Orientalist, masoretic scholar, and minister. Kahle, who was born in Hohenstein (East Prussia), served for five years as a pastor in Cairo. He then taught at the universities of Halle, Giessen, and Bonn, and from 1923 was director of the Oriental Institute at Bonn. Under his guidance, many of his students devoted themselves to the study of the **Genizah*, especially the early history of **piyyut*. Many of his students, including M. *Zulay, settled in Israel and became prominent in Jewish scholarship. In 1924 Kahle wrote an opinion defending the Talmud against the libels of the notorious antisemite, T. Fritsch. Because of his and his wife's pro-Jewish activities following Kristallnacht, the family had to seek refuge in England (Oxford) in 1938. Kahle continued his work at Oxford University. He received two doctorates: his philosophy thesis was published as *Textkritische und Lexikalische Bemerkungen zum samaritanischen Pentateuchtargum* (1898), while his theology thesis was published as *Der masoretische Text des Alten Testaments nach der Ueberlieferung der babylonischen Juden* (1902, repr. 1966). Masoretic studies were the dominating interest of his life. His first major work in this field was *Masoreten des Ostens* (1913, repr. 1966), and the two-part *Masoreten des Westens* (1927–30, repr. 1967). This research led him from the popular text of Jacob ben Ḥayyim's *Second Rabbinic Bible* (1524/25) to the Aaron ben Asher texts of the 11th century. Due to Kahle's research, one of these texts, the Leningrad Codex B 19a, supplanted the former as basis for Kittel's *Biblia Hebraica* (1937³ and later), and was later used for its successor, *Biblia Hebraica Stuttgartensia* (1969ff.). Kahle's main source of evidence for his study of the masorah were the fragments from the Cairo *Genizah*, in which his interest was aroused by Solomon Schechter. With the aid of the fragments he was able to make a pioneering contribution to the understanding of the emergence and development of the masoretic text. Using the *Genizah* material as his main source of evidence, he developed his thesis regarding Hebrew vocalization in which he contended that the two centers of rabbinic learning, Babylon and Palestine, each created both a simple and a complete system of vocalization, which ultimately emerged into the official Tiberian vocalization which is an integral part of the Ben Asher text and masorah.

This, and much else, is to be found in Kahle's *Cairo Geniza* (1947, enlarged 1959²). Basically, to Kahle, all textual transmission was a matter of emergence from earlier traditions. The Targums of the Torah and the Prophets were originally free, random renderings and were later edited in Babylon as Targums Onkelos and Jonathan and transferred to Palestine as official renderings, c. 1000 C.E. The Septuagint, which originally had only the Torah, with its authorized form advocated in the Letter of *Aristeas, emerged as a full version only in and for the Christian Church. It was composed from a variety of Targum-like Greek renderings. This hypothesis was stretched to include all known versions. Opposition to Kahle's view was widespread, and it is possible that his attempt to make his hypothesis so universally applicable shows that it has a fundamental weakness, but his text remains important as a parallel to the Aleppo text of the Hebrew University Bible project.

Kahle's two-volume *Volkserzaehlungen aus Palaestina* (with H. Schmidt, 1918–30) deals with Ereẓ Israel. He also wrote a series of articles on Muslim holy places in Palestine (in PJB, vols. 6–8, 1910–12), and studies of the Dead Sea Scrolls (*Die hebraeischen Handschriften aus der Hoehle* (1951)). On the occasion of his 60th birthday, Kahle was honored by a festschrift (*Studien zur Geschichte und Kultur des Nahen und Fernen Ostens* (1935), with bibliography), and on his 80th birthday by a collection of his minor studies (*Opera Minora* (1956), again with bibliography). A memorial volume, *In memoriam Paul Kahle*, edited by M. Black and G. Fohrer, appeared in 1968.

BIBLIOGRAPHY: M. Zulay, in: *Molad*, 4 (1949–50), 355–7; *Recent Progress in Biblical Scholarship* (1965). **ADD. BIBLIOGRAPHY:** M. Black, "Paul Ernst Kahle (1875–1965)," in: *Proceedings of the British Academy*, 51 (1965/66), 485–95; *Biographisches-Bibliographisches Kirchenlexikon*, vol. 3 (1997), 943–45; *International Biographical Dictionary of Central European Émigrés 1933–1945*, vol. 2 (1999), 581–82.

[B.J. Roberts / Bjoern Siegel (2nd ed.)]

KAHLER, ERICH (1885–1970), historian and philosopher. Born in Prague, raised in Vienna, educated at the universities of Berlin, Munich, Heidelberg, and Vienna, he settled in

Munich after obtaining his doctorate in Vienna (1908) with his dissertation *Recht und Moral* (published 1911). His study, *Das Geschlecht Hapsburg* (1919), was followed by *Der Beruf der Wissenschaft* (1920), a polemic directed against Max Weber's *Wissenschaft als Beruf.* A publisher to whom he submitted the manuscript of his major work, *Der deutsche Charakter in der Geschichte Europas*, denounced him to the Nazis in 1933, but he had already escaped to Vienna, afterwards to Czechoslovakia, and then to Switzerland, where the book appeared in 1937 and aroused much attention. In 1938 he found a permanent refuge in Princeton. His public lectures and seminars at American universities, primarily at Cornell from 1947 to 1955, resulted in seven scholarly volumes. A book of tributes to him by John Berryman, G.A. Borgese, Hermann Broch, Albert Einstein, Rudolf Kassner, Thomas Mann, Wolfgang Pauli, and others appeared in 1951.

Kahler's approach to history was characterized by Hermann Broch as moral anthropology. This approach was apparent in his study of the Hapsburgs, which considered the royal family as a historical organism with common psychological traits throughout six centuries. In his sociological and historical study *Israel unter den Völkern* (1936) he found a common Jewish type persisting down the millennia from its tribal origin until the twentieth century. In *Der deutsche Charakter in der Geschichte Europas*, he presented the Germans as a specific historic organism, its evolution and its impact upon Europe. Its ideas continued to occupy Kahler's thinking and formed the basis for *The Germans* published in 1974. In it, the material was presented not topically, as in the earlier volume, but rather chronologically, from the confrontation of the German tribes with the Roman Empire until the Nazi assumption of power and the catastrophe of World War II.

Kahler's most important work, *Man the Measure* (1943), was subtitled *A New Approach to History.* It studied the human species as an organism whose historical changes were grafted on to an enduring psychic structure. It emphasized the evolution and transformation of human consciousness.

The Tower and the Abyss (1957) may be regarded as a sequel to *Man the Measure.* As an inquiry into the transformation of the individual, it stresses the evolutionary forces that converged to bring about the disruption, disintegration, and fragmentation of the contemporary individual personality from without and from within. Kahler sees the present as a state of transition from an individual form of existence to a supra-individual form, whose character is still obscure. The work concludes with Kahler's own vision of a possible Utopia, which will permit the reintegration of fragmented Man in free communities.

Kahler's essays were collected in the German volume *Die Verantwortung des Geistes* (1952) and in the English volumes *Out of the Labyrinth* (1947), *The Disintegration of Form in the Arts* (1968), and *The Inward Turn of the Narrative* (1973).

BIBLIOGRAPHY: S. Liptzin, *Germany's Stepchildren* (1944), 275–81.

[Sol Liptzin (2nd ed.)]

KAHN, ALBERT (1860–1940), French philanthropist. Born in Marmoutier (Alsace) to a family of merchants, Kahn settled in Paris in 1876 and found a job at the Banque Goudchaux. However, he displayed such genius in the field of finance that he soon became a partner in the bank and founded his own bank in 1898. He built his fortune by investing in the diamond and gold mining projects developed by Cecil Rhodes in South Africa in the 1880s and 1890s. A confirmed bachelor, Kahn devoted his energy and his financial resources to the promotion of utopian concepts of peace and harmony in the world through better mutual understanding among the different civilizations and social forces. In 1898, he created the Autour du monde ("Around the World") fellowships to encourage young French intellectuals to travel and discover other parts of the world. The project was later extended to candidates from many other countries. His Archives de la Planète, created in 1912, sent photographers to various parts of the world and accumulated a wealth of rare animated images and photographs both of daily life and of specific events. In the same year, he sponsored the creation in the Collège de France, by Jean Brunhes, of a Human Geography cathedra.

From 1920, Albert Kahn endowed various French institutions of higher learning (notably the École Normale Supérieure in Paris) with documentation centers. He encouraged discussion of the social and human problems in a spirit of goodwill in the Autour du monde forum (1906) and the Comité national d'études sociales et politiques (1916), which published much material. A friend of Henri *Bergson since the time of their youth, he supported the activities of the League of Nations in the field of intellectual cooperation. His connections were particularly close with Japan and were reflected in the Japanese garden in his mansion in Boulogne Billancourt (near Paris), combined with an Alsatian-style garden reminding him of his youth. Kahn was ruined by the economic crisis of the 1930s, and most of his public activities were curtailed. His garden remains open to the public at large, and from the 1990s, mainly through Japanese sponsorship, his films and photographs have been digitized and are available to visitors together with thematic exhibitions.

[Philippe Boukara (2nd ed.)]

KAHN, ALBERT (1869–1942), U.S. industrial architect. Kahn was born in Rhaunen, Germany, and was taken to the United States in 1881. He was trained in Detroit and specialized in factory design. He was engaged by Henry Ford as one of his principal architects. He also designed assembly plants for other leading automobile companies. His outstanding buildings include the General Motors Building in Detroit (1901) and the Ohio Steel Foundry Company Building (1940). In 1930 the Soviet government engaged him to design a series of factories in the Volga region, and members of his staff helped supervise the construction of industrial plants for the second 5-year plan. He built two Reform synagogues in Detroit for the Beth-El congregation of which he was a member, both in the classical style.

BIBLIOGRAPHY: R. Wischnitzer, *Synagogue Architecture in the United States* (1955); J.M. Fitch, *American Building*, 1 (1966[2]), index; J. Burchard and A. Bush-Brown, *Architecture of America* (1961), index.

KAHN, ALEXANDER (1881–1962), U.S. lawyer and newspaper executive. Kahn, who was born in Smolensk, Russia, was taken to the U.S. in 1893. He was an active member of the Socialist literary club that took part in the founding of the *Jewish Daily Forward* (1897) and became general counsel to the Forward Association, the nonprofit organization established to run the paper. In 1939 he became the paper's general manager. Kahn, a founder and vice president of the New York State Liberal Party, was an unsuccessful candidate for public office on that ticket as well as on the American Socialist Party and American Labor Party tickets on several occasions during his career. Extremely active in Jewish affairs, he was a founder and vice chairman of the American Jewish Joint Distribution Committee. He was also a founder of the liberal weekly magazine, the *New Leader.*

KAHN, ALFRED JOSEPH (1919–), U.S. educator and social planner. Born in New York City, Kahn received his B.S.S. from the City College of New York (1939), his Master's of Social Work from Columbia University School of Social Work (1946), and his Ph.D. in Social Welfare from Columbia University (1952). It was the first doctorate given at Columbia's School of Social Work.

He was with the U.S. Army Air Force from 1942 to 1946. After serving as a psychiatric social worker with the Jewish Board of Guardians in New York City (1946–47), he began teaching at the Columbia University School of Social Work and in 1954 was appointed a full professor. His special areas of expertise included delinquency, services for children, mental health, and social policy and planning. After his retirement from teaching, he became professor emeritus, special research scholar, and special lecturer at the Columbia University School of Social Work.

Kahn was a consultant to a number of social agencies and foundations. His writings show his special interest in social planning. These include *A Court for Children* (1953), *Planning Community Services for Children in Trouble* (1963), *Neighborhood Information Centers* (1965), and *Day Care as a Social Instrument* (1966, with Anna Mayer). His companion volumes *Theory and Practice of Social Planning* and *Studies in Social Policy and Planning*, published in 1969, are basic texts in this field. He was editor of *Issues in American Social Work* (1959). Kahn's recommendations have been incorporated in a number of social programs to meet the problems of the young.

Kahn served as consultant to federal, state, and local agencies; to voluntary organizations; and foundations concerned with the planning of social services, income maintenance, child welfare-related programs, international collaboration, and social policy. He was national chairman for the Division of Practice and Knowledge of the National Association of Social Workers and served for two terms on the NASW Board.

Kahn completed several overseas assignments for the Department of Health Education and Welfare, the State Department, private foundations, the UN, and various foreign governments. He received a Lifetime Achievement Award from the Council on Social Work Education (1990), the National Association of Social Workers (1996), and the Social Welfare Policy and Policy Practice Group (2001). In 2002, the Alfred J. Kahn Doctoral Fellowship was established at the Columbia University School of Social Work. Some of Kahn's later works, which he co-authored with Sheila Kamerman, include *Not for the Poor Alone* (1981), *Helping America's Families* (1982), *Maternity Policies and Working Women* (1983), *The Responsive Workplace* (1987), *Mothers Alone* (1988), *Child Support* (1988), and *Starting Right* (1995).

[Ruth Beloff (2nd ed.)]

KAHN, BERNARD (1876–1955), organization executive. Born in Oscarsham, Sweden, Kahn studied in Germany, where he became involved in Jewish communal affairs. In 1904 he was appointed secretary-general of the *Hilfsverein der Deutschen Juden, a position he held until 1921 and from which he helped direct the large flow of Jewish emigration in those years from Germany and Central Europe to the United States. In 1921 he became director of the refugee department of the *American Jewish Joint Distribution Committee (JDC), whose main European office was in Paris, and in 1924 overall European director of the JDC, as well as managing director of its subsidiary, the American Joint Reconstruction Foundation. Kahn held these positions until 1939, a period during which the Joint was called on to perform enormous tasks in the fields of resettlement, medical and financial help, and education and vocational training, particularly among the ravaged Jewish communities of Eastern Europe, to which he frequently traveled. His own special interest was in the Reconstruction Foundation, which created a large network of cooperative Jewish loan societies that provided a credit and banking structure for Jews who were being progressively shut out of economic life in various Central and Eastern European countries. His knowledge of finance also led him to play active roles in the Central Bank for Cooperative Investment in Palestine, the Palestine Economic Corporation, and Keren Hayesod. With the outbreak of World War II in 1939, Kahn emigrated to the U.S. He served as honorary chairman of the JDC European Council from 1939 to 1950 and as vice chairman of the JDC from 1950 until his death.

[Hillel Halkin]

KAHN, DOROTHY C. (1893–1955), U.S. social worker. Dorothy Kahn, who was born in Seattle, Washington, began her career as a caseworker for the Jewish Social Service Bureau, Chicago (1915–18). She subsequently held several important posts in the social work field, including: executive director of both the Jewish Social Service Bureau of Baltimore (1919–28), and the Philadelphia County Board of Assistance (1932–38); faculty member at the Pennsylvania School of Social Work (1930–45); director of the department of economic adjustment and family service of the National Refugee Service, Inc. (1941–43); and chairman of the subcommittee on unemployment relief of the President's Committee on Social Security during World War II. From 1951 to 1954 she headed the social services section of the UN's Department of Social Affairs. As such, she represented the UN at social work and child welfare conferences at Madras and Bombay, India (1952), and advised the Israel government on social welfare administration.

KAHN, ELY JACQUES (1884–1972), U.S. architect, born in New York. He studied at Columbia University and in Paris. Kahn was an outstandingly versatile and successful New York architect in the period between the two world wars. He built houses, country clubs, office blocks, department stores, hospitals, factories, and other buildings and was also a designer in the applied arts. At the same time, he lectured on design and architecture. His buildings of Jewish interest are the Mount Sinai Hospital, New York, and the offices of the Jewish Federation for the Support of Philanthropic Societies of New York City. Kahn held that each new architectural problem demanded a fresh solution, free from the "heavy and deadly practice" of copying the architecture of the past. Although he built many skyscrapers in the manner of the period, some of his works, such as his country clubs, were built in a historical style despite his scruples. He also maintained that architectural beauty consists in proportions and material rather than in ornamentation. He wrote *Design in Art and Industry* (1935).

BIBLIOGRAPHY: A.T. North (ed.), *Ely Jacques Kahn* (Eng., 1931).

KAHN, ERICH ITOR (1905–1956), composer and pianist. Born in Germany, Kahn spent some time in France and then settled in the United States. He was a distinguished performer of chamber music. As a composer, he was influenced by the *Schoenberg school, and he also made frequent use of ḥasidic material. Among his important compositions are: *Rhapsodie Hassidique*, for mixed chorus (1938); *Ciaccona dei tempi di guerra*, for piano (1943); *Nenia Judaeis Qui Hac Aetate Perierunt*, for cello and piano (1943); *Actus Tragicus* for ten solo instruments (1946); and *Three Madrigals for Mixed Choir* (1956). He died after a road accident.

KAHN, FLORENCE PRAG (1866–1948), U.S, congresswoman. Elected in 1924 to the United States House of Representatives for the first of six two-year terms, Kahn in her first speech before the House observed that since Moses had conducted the world's first census, she was especially qualified to address the reapportionment issue. Kahn, a Republican from San Francisco, California, the first Jewish congresswomen, chose to introduce herself to her colleagues as a Jew.

Kahn's Polish parents reached San Francisco during the Gold Rush. Her father was a 49er, while her mother arrived in 1852. Florence, born in Salt Lake City (where her parents lived briefly) grew up in a family and city where a Jewish woman had examples of success. In cosmopolitan San Francisco, Jews worked with non-Jews and faced relatively little antisemitism.

Educated in San Francisco's public and Jewish schools, Kahn earned a degree at the University of California at Berkeley in 1887. She became the first Berkeley graduate to teach in the San Francisco public school system. In 1899 Florence Prag married San Francisco Congressman Julius Kahn; he served in the House until 1924 except one term when he failed to win re-election.

In Washington, Florence served as her husband's secretary and observer for his local district, regularly sitting in the gallery of the House. Starting in 1919 she wrote columns for the *San Francisco Chronicle* which discussed a wide range of political issues.

After her husband's death in 1924, Kahn ran successfully for his seat in Congress. While her husband had been ill, she had been the de facto representative. The first piece of legislation Kahn introduced was a bill to reimburse Indians for land that had been taken from them in the treaties of 1851 and 1852. The bill was defeated. However, eventually California's native peoples received some compensation.

Kahn also helped her district's Chinese citizens. She supported an amendment providing citizenship for Chinese women married to American-born Chinese men, noting that the existing law deprived Chinese men and women of family life. In 1930 Congress changed the law to allow Chinese women who had married before the 1924 immigration legislation to enter the country. She also supported an amendment that passed on citizenship to children of American-born women residing outside the United States, the law already gave men this right.

Often receiving endorsements from both Republicans and Democrats, Kahn was the first woman appointed to the Committee on Military Affairs. She also served on the Appropriations Committee and co-authored legislation that obtained federal support for California's military installations and the building of the Oakland-Bay Bridge which connected Oakland to San Francisco.

For Kahn, citizenship rights for men and women, the Republican Party, and a confident Jewish identity were the core of her life and politics. She only voted against her party when Republicans supported prohibition and movie censorship, two issues that had a financial impact on her district. Known as a forceful, shrewd, and witty politician, Kahn's credo was "[t]here is no sex in citizenship, and there should be none in politics."

BIBLIOGRAPHY: D.G. Dalin, "Jewish and Non-Partisan Republicanism in San Francisco, 1911–1963," in: *American Jewish History*, 68 (June 1979), 492–516; D. Gelfand, "Gentlewomen of the House," in: *American Mercury*, 18 (October 1929), 151–60; H. Hansen, "Woman Enters Politics: San Francisco's Pioneer Congresswoman, Florence Prag Kahn" (M.A. thesis, San Francisco State University,

1969); A.F. Kahn and G. Matthews, "120 Years of Women's Activism," in: A.F. Kahn and M. Dollinger (eds.), *California Jews* (2003); Kahn Collection, Western Jewish History Center, Judah Magnes Museum, Berkeley, California; F.P. Keyes, "The Lady from California," in: *Delineator*, 118 (February 1931); A.R. Longworth, "What Are the Women Up To?" in: *Ladies Home Journal*, 51 (March 1934); G. Matthews, "'There is No Sex in Citizenship': the Career of Congresswoman Florence Prag Kahn," in: M. Gustafson, K. Miller, and E.I. Perry (eds.), *We Have Come to Stay: American Women and Political Parties, 1880–1960* (1999).

[Ava F. Kahn (2nd ed.)]

KAHN, FRANZ (1895–1944), Zionist leader in Czechoslovakia. Born in Pilsen, Bohemia, Kahn joined the Zionist youth movement *Blau-Weiss when he was still in high school. He was severely wounded in World War I, losing his left arm. After the war he completed his studies in law. In 1921 he was appointed secretary-general of the Czechoslovak Zionist Federation and a member of its administrative committee, subsequently becoming deputy chairman of the federation. As director of the bureau of the Zionist Congress, Kahn was responsible for the organization of most *Zionist Congresses between the two world wars. Seeing Zionism as a safeguard for the survival of the Jewish people and a continuous aspiration toward the reform of Jewish society, Kahn devoted himself to the creation of an organizational framework for such a Zionist society. When Nazi Germany occupied Czechoslovakia, he viewed the future of Jewry with great pessimism. He did not believe that Jewish lives could be saved by making them useful to the oppressor, though he did not oppose the attempt. Considering it his duty to keep control over the activities of the Jewish institutions, without any self-deception, on the very day of the occupation he decided to remain behind. Later, in *Theresienstadt, he was mainly concerned in keeping contact with the pioneering youth movements, who saw him as the embodiment of the Jewish and human conscience. In 1944, at a meeting marking the 40th anniversary of Herzl's death, he addressed thousands of camp inmates. Summarizing Zionist teachings for the last time, he concluded his address with the call "The people of Israel lives." In October 1944 Kahn and his wife, along with many other militant Zionists, were taken to Auschwitz to perish in the gas chambers.

BIBLIOGRAPHY: *Theresienstadt* (Heb., 1947); Ch. Yahil, *Devarim al ha-Ẓiyyonut ha-Czechoslovakit* (1967).

[Chaim Yahil]

KAHN, GUSTAVE (1859–1936), French poet and author. Kahn, who was born in Metz, was one of the outstanding poets of the Symbolist movement and, with Jules Laforgue, is considered the inventor of *vers libre* (free verse), which uses mixed rhythms, especially of common speech. His *Premiers poèmes* (1897) included "Les palais nomades" (1887), "Chansons d'amant" (1891), and "Le Domaine de fée" (1895). An admirer of Baudelaire and Verlaine, Kahn was also an art critic, and he sponsored the review *Vogue*. He published essays on French painters, including "François Boucher" (1905), "Jean-Honoré Fragonard" (1907), and "Fantin-Latour" (1926). Kahn also wrote a work of criticism entitled *Symbolistes et décadents* (1902), and a few novels. Though generally remote from Jewish communal affairs, he became an enthusiastic advocate of the Zionist cause, which was, in his opinion, a romantic, heroic, and mystical form of Judaism. These sympathies inspired his *Contes juifs* (1926), *Vieil Orient, Orient neuf* (1928), *Images bibliques* (1929), and *Terre d'Israël* (1933). For many years Kahn edited the *Menorah*, a French Zionist periodical and, after his death, his manuscripts were deposited at the Jewish National and University Library in Jerusalem.

BIBLIOGRAPHY: *Univers Israélite* (Sept. 11, 1936); H. Talvart and J. Place, *Bibliographie des auteurs modernes de langue française*, 10 (1950), 213–23; J.C. Ireson, *Oeuvre poétique de Gustave Kahn* (1962).

[Moshe Catane]

KAHN, JEAN (1929–), French Jewish leader. Kahn was born in Strasbourg where he attended school and the university law school. He received his doctorate in law for a thesis on "Marriage in Jewish and Roman Law." Kahn qualified as a lawyer in 1953 but gave up his practice to enter the family textile business. He was early involved in communal affairs and from 1969 to 1990 was president of the Strasbourg Jewish Community. Active in the World Jewish Congress from 1979, he became president of its European Commission in 1979 and president of the European Jewish Congress in 1991. In 1983, Kahn was elected vice president of CRIF (the French Jewish Representative Council) and in 1989, by a 75% vote, he became its president. He has been involved in various major problems facing the European Jewish community, especially in view of the recrudescence of antisemitism. He was active in the efforts to transfer the Carmelite convent from Auschwitz, in the protests against the desecration of Jewish graves in the Carpentras cemetery, and in the struggle against France's National Front Party, including a crucial intervention in having the parliamentary immunity of its leader, Jean-Marie le Pen, lifted so he could face charges before the European Parliament. In 1991 he became president of the Bas-Rhin Consistoire. He has been awarded the Legion of Honor and other honors.

[Gideon Kouts]

KAHN, JULIUS (1861–1924), U.S. congressman. Kahn, who was born in Kuppenheim, Germany, was taken to the U.S. in 1866. After following a career as an actor for ten years, Kahn became a lawyer (1894). He served one term in the California State Assembly. From 1899 to 1903 he was Republican congressman from California's Fourth District (representing part of San Francisco). Reelected in 1905, he served in the House until his death. Kahn, a strong advocate of universal military training and naval preparedness, was ranking Republican member of the House Military Affairs Committee during World War I. As such, he helped to steer through Congress President Wilson's World War program, particularly the administration's conscription bill which was opposed by the majority of Democratic committee members. In 1921 Kahn became chairman of the House Military Affairs Committee and took charge of legislation for reorganizing the army on a peacetime basis. He was the first member of Congress to advocate that candidates be obliged to publish their primary campaign expenses and contributions. He was an active opponent of Zionism. Kahn was one of the founders of the Jewish Educational Society in San Francisco (1897). His widow, FLORENCE PRAG KAHN (1868–1948), was appointed to his House seat on his death. She served in the House until 1937.

BIBLIOGRAPHY: H. Schneiderman, in: AJYB, 27 (1925), 238–45.

[Robert E. Levinson]

KAHN, LÉON (1851–1900), French historian and publicist. Born in Paris, Kahn became secretary-general of the Paris *Consistory in 1895. He was active in many Jewish associations in Paris; for a time he edited *Univers Israélite* and collaborated on the yearbook of the *Archives Israélites*. A specialist on the history of the Jews of Paris, he wrote a book, *Les Juifs de Paris pendant la revolution* (1899), and a number of studies on that subject, based on archival material.

[Georges Weill]

KAHN, LOUIS (1895–1967), French general and naval engineer. Born in Versailles, Kahn commanded a battery in World War I and was wounded twice. After the war, he graduated as a maritime engineer and helped construct the first modern French cruisers. Head of the technical department of the Air Force Ministry between 1928 and 1938, he discovered a new method of cartographic projection, well-known to air navigators as the "transcontinental orthodromic itineraries." He also participated in the design of modern aircraft carriers. In 1940 Kahn was dismissed from the French Navy by the Vichy government (see *France: Holocaust Period). He escaped to London where, as director of naval construction with the Free French, he introduced new techniques of submarine warfare. After the liberation, Kahn was put in charge of the reconstruction of industrial equipment and was responsible for coordinating the operations of refloating 1,400,000 tons of scuttled ships to reestablish navigation. In 1950 he was appointed secretary-general of the armed forces by Jules *Moch, then minister of national defense. Parallel to his military and naval career, Kahn always took an active part in Jewish cultural and communal affairs. He presided over the "Chema Israel" Jewish cultural association from 1925, and, after the liberation, drew up with Edmond *Fleg the manifesto of the Alliance Israélite *Universelle. From 1963, Kahn was president of the Central *Consistory of French Jews, deputy president of Alliance Israélite, and vice president of *Ort.

[Emmanuel Beeri]

KAHN, LOUIS I. (1901–1974), U.S. architect. Born on the island of Osel (Saaremaa), Estonia, he was taken to the U.S. in 1905. After traveling in Europe he worked with Paul Cret, an academic architect, and later became an expert in city planning. During World War II he designed a number of housing projects with associates, and later became resident architect of the American Academy in Rome, design critic at Yale, and professor of architecture at the University of Pennsylvania.

His first building of importance was the Yale Art Gallery, New Haven (1952–55). In his Community Center of Trenton (1956–59), the cross-axial plan reveals the influence of the Beaux-Arts tradition. Here and in the Yale Art Gallery Kahn revived the use of the column as a means of defining space. The Richards Medical Research Building, University of Pennsylvania (1958–60), was a spectacular construction which placed Kahn at the forefront of international architecture. The horizontal buildings are surmounted by thrusting vertical towerlike ducts, the purpose of which is to allow toxic atmospheres to escape from the laboratories. By this means Kahn created a flamboyantly picturesque skyline out of a functional need.

Kahn later designed many synagogues. The exterior of his design for Congregation Mikveh Israel, Philadelphia (1963) is very austere and resembles a fortress. It features a series of massive, repetitive, round stone blocks. The rounded walls of the interior are broken up by arched openings which let in the light. Emphasis is placed on the area of space rising above the congregation. His notebooks and drawings were published in 1962.

BIBLIOGRAPHY: *L'architecture d'aujourd'hui* (special issue in honor of Louis I. Kahn), 142 (Feb.–March 1969), 1–99 (Eng.); I. McCallum, *Architecture U.S.A.* (1959), 83–88; Bush-Brown, in: *Horizon*, 5 (Sept. 1962), 57–63; V.J. Scully, *Louis I. Kahn* (Eng., 1962).

KAHN, MADELINE (Madeline Gail Wolfson; 1942–1999), U.S. actress. Born in Boston, Massachusetts, Kahn began acting in school productions during high school, first at a boarding school in Pennsylvania and then at Martin Van Buren High School in Queens, New York, where she earned a drama scholarship to Hofstra University. She graduated from Hofstra in 1964 and began auditioning for professional roles, landing her first part as a chorus girl in a City Center revival of *Kiss Me Kate* (1965). Kahn's first starring role on Broadway came three years later playing Cunegonde, the female lead in Leonard Bernstein's *Candide* (1968). Kahn made her film debut the same year in the comic mock-Swedish short film *The Dove*, but her first major film appearance was four years later, playing Ryan O'Neal's uptight fiancé in Peter Bogdanovich's *What's Up, Doc?* (1972). In 1973, Kahn received an Oscar nomination for Best Supporting Actress for another role opposite Ryan O'Neal in a second Bogdanovich film, *Paper Moon*, but the award eventually went to her fellow co-star in the film, Ryan O'Neal's 11-year-old daughter Tatum. The following year, Kahn delivered her unforgettable performance as saloon singer Lili Von Shtupp in Mel Brooks' irreverent comedy *Blazing Saddles*, for which she received her second Oscar nomination for Best Supporting Actress in two years. Kahn continued to work with Brooks in two subsequent films that further cemented her reputation as one of Hollywood's best comedic actresses, *Young Frankenstein* (1974) and *High Anxiety* (1977). On the stage, Kahn was nominated for three Tony Awards before winning the Best Actress Tony in 1993 for the role of Gorgeous in Wendy Wasserstein's *The Sisters Rosenzweig*, the tale of three sisters, all accomplished assimilated Jewish women approaching middle-age, who gather to celebrate a birthday. Later Kahn played a major role on the television show *Cosby* (1996–99) and provided the voice of the Gypsy Moth in the animated Pixar film *A Bug's Life* (1998), before succumbing to ovarian cancer in 1999 at the age of 57.

[Walter Driver (2nd ed.)]

KAHN, OTTO HERMANN (1867–1934), U.S. banker, arts patron, and philanthropist. Kahn, who was born in Mannheim, Germany, was the son of Bernhard Kahn, a banker and arts patron. Otto Kahn began his banking career at a small bank in Karlsruhe. After service with a German elite cavalry regiment, he joined the Deutsche Bank. From 1888 to 1893 he worked at the bank's London branch, and became its assistant manager. In 1893 Kahn accepted a position with the New York banking house of *Speyer & Co. Three years later he married Addie, the daughter of Abraham Wolff, a partner in *Kuhn, Loeb & Co., and joined that firm in 1897. His financial aptitude attracted the attention of the world's financial leaders, and at the age of 30 he was considered a leading banking authority. Kahn opposed inflationary policies and excessive government intervention in economic affairs. During World War I, he advocated the establishment of a war finance board to cope with the complex situation. After the war, he opposed both the Versailles Peace Treaty and the League of Nations, and urged the cancellation of all foreign war debts provided that European governments curb their militaristic tendencies and limit armaments production. Kahn endowed and subsidized art schools, orchestras, universities, museums, galleries, opera projects, and theatrical productions, including *Habimah, Yiddish productions, and Max *Reinhardt's United States tour in 1928, and contributed prizes for black artists in New York. From 1903 to 1917 he served as chairman of the board of the Metropolitan Opera and from 1917 to 1931 was its president. He was instrumental in bringing Toscanini to New York. In recognition of his many public services, he was decorated by several foreign governments. His Jewish interest concentrated on the Federation of Jewish Philanthropies of New York of which he was a founder. Kahn's works include *Right Above Race* (1918); *Our Economic and Other Problems* (1920); and *Of Many Things* (1926).

BIBLIOGRAPHY: J. Matz, *Many Lives of Otto Kahn* (1963).

[Joachim O. Ronall]

KAHN, RICHARD FERDINAND, LORD (1905–1989), British economist. Kahn, son of Augustus Kahn (1868–1944), a well-known educator and communal worker, was a disciple of the economist J.M. Keynes, whom he succeeded as bursar of King's College, Cambridge. Born in London, Kahn was educated at St. Paul's and Cambridge and became a fellow of King's College, Cambridge, in 1930. In 1951 he was appointed professor of economics at Cambridge. He was the author of the "multiplier theory," which deals with the ability to save and invest as against the propensity to consume. Kahn was extremely influential in the origins of Keynes' celebrated General Theory (1936) and was the originator of several of its crucial concepts. An authority on investment and international trade, Kahn was a member of several government committees, a part-time member of the National Coal Board (1967), and an adviser to banking firms. In 1955 he was appointed to the research and planning division of the United Nations Economic Commission for Europe. He was created a life peer in 1965. Among his writings are "The Relation of Home Investment to Unemployment" (*Economic Journal*, 1931), and *Payments Arrangements among the Developing Countries for Trade Expansion* (1966). In early and later life Kahn was an observant Orthodox Jew.

ADD. BIBLIOGRAPHY: ODNB online.

[John M. Shaftesley]

KAHN, ROBERT I. (1910–), U.S. rabbi and community leader. Born in Des Moines, Kahn was a graduate of the University of Cincinnati (1932) and ordained by the Hebrew Union College (1935). He then became an assistant rabbi to Congregation Beth Israel in Houston. Kahn served in the infantry during World War II in New Guinea and the Philippines and then returned to Houston as rabbi of Congregation Emmanu-El. Kahn preached and lectured all over the United States, in person and over radio and television. In a national "Back to God" telecast, he shared the camera with Billy Graham.

In his community, Kahn served on the boards of several social agencies such as Red Cross, Boy Scouts, Travelers Aid, Mental Health, Muscular Dystrophy, Houston Metropolitan Ministries, and United Fund. He was a member of B'nai B'rith, of which he was a past president, the Masons, and Shriners. He was president of the Houston Rotary Club in 1967–68, the largest rotary club in the world, and was district governor from 1978 to 1979. He was grand chaplain of the grand lodge of Texas.

He was honored by the Boy Scouts of America with the Silver Beaver and Ner Tamid Awards; by the Freedoms Foundation with a George Washington Medal; by the French government for service to veterans; by the Masonic Order with the 33rd degree; and by the State of Israel with the Prime Minister's Medal for Israel Bonds. A forest has been planted in his honor in Israel.

Among his writings are *Lessons for Life* (1963); *The Ten Commandments for Today* (1964); *May the Words of My Mouth* (1984); and the *Letter and the Spirit* (1972).

In Houston he taught at St. Thomas University and at St. Mary's University and was a guest lecturer on Judaism at universities and colleges throughout the Southwest. Upon his retirement in 1978 he returned to Hebrew Union College to teach liturgy, in keeping with his work as chair of the committee that published the new Reform Prayer Book *Gates of Prayer* in 1975.

BIBLIOGRAPHY: K. Olitzky, L.J. Sussman, and M.H. Stern, *Reform Judaism in America: A Biographical Dictionary and Sourcebook* (1993).

[Michael Berenbaum (2nd ed.)]

KAHN, ROGER (1927–), U.S. sportswriter. Born and raised in Brooklyn, N.Y., Kahn worked at the *New York Herald Tribune* in the early 1950s covering the Brooklyn Dodgers. He was named sports editor at *Newsweek* in 1956, and editor at large at the *Saturday Evening Post* from 1963 to 1969 as well as writing freelance magazine essays for *Esquire, Sports Illustrated, Time,* and other publications. His most famous work among 17 books was the 1972 bestseller *The Boys of Summer,* an account of the Dodger teams of the 1950s and how the players aged 20 years later. He also wrote *How The Weather Was* (1973); *A Season in the Sun* (1977); *Good Enough to Dream* (1985), chronicling the Class A Utica Blue Sox baseball team in the summer of 1983; *Joe & Marilyn: A Memory of Love* (1986); the controversial *Pete Rose: My Story* (1989); *The Era: 1947–1957, When the Yankees, the Giants, and the Dodgers Ruled the World* (1993); *Games We Used to Play* (1994); *Memories of Summer: When Baseball Was an Art and Writing about It a Game* (1997); *Flame of Pure Fire: Jack Dempsey and the Roaring '20s* (1999); *Head Game: Baseball Seen From the Pitcher's Mound* (2000); and *October Men: Reggie Jackson, George Steinbrenner, Billy Martin, and the Yankees' Miraculous Finish in 1978* (2003). Kahn also wrote two non-sports books, *The Passionate People: What It Means to Be a Jew in America* (1968) and *The Battle for Morningside Heights: Why Students Rebel* (1970), and two novels, *But Not to Keep* (1979) and *The Seventh Game* (1982).

[Elli Wohlgelernter (2nd ed.)]

KAHN, ZADOC (**Zadig**; 1839–1905), chief rabbi of France. Born in Mommenheim, Alsace, Kahn was the son of a village peddler. His mother was the daughter of Rabbi Isaac Weyl (Reb Eisik) of Wintzheim, whose father, Jacob Meyer, was a member of the Sanhedrin convened by Napoleon I, and chief rabbi of the Lower Rhine department. Kahn was educated in a yeshivah at Strasbourg and from 1856 at the Ecole Rabbinique in Metz (later in Paris), from which he graduated in 1862. He then became director of the Talmud Torah, a preparatory school of the Ecole. In 1866 Kahn became assistant to Chief Rabbi Isidore Lazare of Paris, whom he succeeded in 1868. Kahn's appointment over many candidates was determined by his excellent thesis, *L'Esclavage selon la Bible et le Talmud* (1867). In 1889 Kahn was appointed chief rabbi of France. His position both as chief rabbi of Paris and chief rabbi of France was marked by a series of critical events in the history of French and world Jewry. After the death of Adolphe *Crémieux in 1880, French Jewry had no recognized secular leader, and institutions and individuals turned to Kahn for advice and leadership. His freedom of action was often limited by the attitude of the official Franco-Jewish leaders, so that Kahn never really became one of the great Jewish leaders who developed out of the period. French Jewry lost its most active communities during his tenure of office, when Alsace-Lorraine was annexed by Germany. The years 1881–82 witnessed the beginning of a mass emigration of East European Jews, some of whom turned to France. But Kahn was unable to influence this important event, as policy was dictated by the *Alliance Israélite Universelle and the Paris charity administration, which tried to limit the immigration. The plan for the first project on Jewish colonization in Argentina was addressed to Kahn and he forwarded it to Baron Maurice de *Hirsch.

From the establishment of *Ḥibbat Zion, Kahn was the head of the movement in France, directing it from Paris. He was also responsible for putting the leaders of Ḥibbat Zion in contact with Baron Edmund de *Rothschild. His activities in Ḥibbat Zion were for the most part disapproved of by the leaders of French Jewry. He was very involved with the practical problems of settlement in Ereẓ Israel, as all the reports coming from Ereẓ Israel and movement functionaries passed directly or indirectly through his hands. Kahn witnessed the birth of the Zionist Movement and sympathized with *Herzl, but officially he adopted the view that French Jews must in all aspects of their lives be faithful citizens of France alone and must therefore reject the idea of a Jewish state in Palestine. He was one of the first Jewish leaders to suspect that Alfred Dreyfus was the victim of an antisemitic campaign, but during the *Dreyfus Affair he was unable to persuade Franco-Jewish leaders to adopt a policy of self-defense instead of remaining silent. Kahn called a few meetings for the purpose of drafting a new policy, but they were unsuccessful, and the defense of Dreyfus was left in the hands of Jewish individuals and non-Jews. The same conservative attitude prevailed in response to the violent antisemitic campaign in Algeria. In 1880 Kahn was more successful in helping to create the *Société des Études *Juives, of which he was president and whose publication, **Revue des Etudes Juives*, became one of the leading scholarly periodicals for the study of Judaism. He was also the editor of a French Bible translation known as the "Bible of the Rabbinate," and of the *Bible de la Jeunesse* (both 1899). In addition, he assisted Isidore *Singer in preparing the *Jewish Encyclopaedia.* Kahn published a few volumes of his sermons. He was the last official chief rabbi of France. Shortly after his death the law of the Separation of the Church and the State was adopted and the Jewish Consistories were reorganized as nongovernmental religious bodies. Before his death Kahn tried to prepare the Consistories for such an event and took part in drafting the bylaws of the new nonofficial Consistories.

BIBLIOGRAPHY: J. Weill, *Zadok Kahn* (Fr. 1912); idem, in: REJ, 105 (1940), 3–9; E.M. Levy, in: *Cahiers de l'AIU*, 94 (1956), 15–19.

KAHNEMAN, DANIEL (1934–), Israeli-American scientist, psychology professor, and researcher; joint winner of the 2002 Nobel Prize in economic sciences. Kahneman was born in Tel Aviv (while his mother was visiting Palestine; his Lithuanian-born parents usually resided in Paris). He held dual

Israeli and United States citizenship. Kahneman studied at the Hebrew University in Jerusalem, receiving a B.A. in psychology and mathematics, and earned a Ph.D. in psychology at the University of California. Kahneman began his academic career lecturing psychology at the Hebrew University in 1961. He held a variety of positions, from visiting scientist to professor of psychology at several institutions throughout the United States, Canada, and England. From 1993 Kahneman was the Eugene Higgins Professor of Psychology and professor of public affairs at the Woodrow Wilson School of Public and International Affairs at Princeton University.

While Daniel Kahneman is not an economist, his work earned him half of the 2002 Nobel Prize in economic sciences, "for having integrated insights from psychological research into economic science, especially concerning human judgment and decision-making under uncertainty." Among Kahneman's recognitions in the field of psychology are the Hilgard Award for Lifetime Contribution to General Psychology, the Warren Medal of the Society of Experimental Psychologists, and a variety of other fellowships, recognitions and honorary degrees. His extensive work with colleague Amos Tversky (who died in 1996) was recognized in 2003 when the two were awarded the Grawemeyer Award for Psychology.

The focus of Kahneman's work is the study of various aspects of experienced utility, or the measure of the utility of outcomes. His theories in behavior finance combine economics and cognitive science to decipher human risk management behaviors. His main findings demonstrate how human decisions may contradict what is predicted by standard economic theory. His work has inspired a new generation of study using cognitive psychology and human motivation in economics and finance. Kahneman's work with Tversky challenges the traditional economic thought that people make rational decisions motivated by self-interest, including rational financial decisions. According to Kahneman and Tversky's studies, people's economic behavior is more psychologically and emotionally motivated.

In an autobiography Kahneman wrote for the Nobel award, he tells of his beginning interest in the field of psychology, describing an incident in France where he, as a child in either 1941 or 1942, was out past the 6 P.M. curfew that Jews were forced to adhere to. He had turned his brown sweater with the required Star of David inside out to hide the symbol, and he found himself face to face with a German soldier on an empty street. The soldier called to him, speaking in excited German, hugged him and showed him a picture of a young boy, and even gave him some money. Kahneman writes that he walked home convinced that his mother was right when she had told him that "people were endlessly complicated and interesting."

Kahneman's published works include articles in the *American Economic Review, Journal of Risk and Uncertainty, Journal of Environmental Economics and Management, Journal of Economic Perspectives,* and other scholarly and association journals.

[Lisa DeShantz-Cook (2nd ed.)]

KAHNSHTAM, AHARON (1859–1921), Hebrew and Yiddish educator. Born in Plock, Poland, Kahnshtam studied law but decided to devote his time to the study and practice of education. In 1895 he was invited to direct a *talmud torah* in Lodz. His ambition was to modernize Jewish schools and to train competent teachers. A gifted teacher, Kahnshtam partially realized his dream in Lodz where, after working diligently, he succeeded in making the *talmud torah* a model school. He organized summer camps in Lodz for culturally deprived children where they were taught such subjects as farming and carpentry. In 1898, Kahnshtam was invited to head the school of the Society for the Diffusion of Culture in St. Petersburg. Kahnshtam served in this post for nine years, and when the Society decided to establish a teachers training school in Grodno, Kahnshtam was appointed director. This school attracted many highly intelligent young Jews, among them writers and scholars, who were devoted to Zionism, Hebrew reform, and Jewish education. During World War I, because of the Grodno school's proximity to the front lines, it was moved to Kharkov in 1915–16. However, in the new location the school's existence was precarious because of the decline in the number of students, the decision to make the study of Yiddish mandatory, and the political upheaval of February 1917. Kahnshtam became the theoretician and an organizer of the *Tarbut Society, which in the postwar period developed a network of modern schools in Eastern Europe. In 1918–19 he became the director of the Tarbut Society's teachers' school in Kiev, but the school functioned only for a very short time.

BIBLIOGRAPHY: M.A. Beigel et al. (eds.), *Rishonim* (1936), esp. 3–39.

[Judah Pilch]

KAHNWEILER, DANIEL-HENRY (1884–1979), German art patron, art dealer, and writer. Kahnweiler was born in Mannheim, Germany. Following his father's profession he volunteered at the Paris Stock Exchange, but soon developed a passion for contemporary art. After a short time working in London he decided to open a gallery of contemporary art in Paris in 1907, sponsored by his family. While recruiting his artists, especially the circle of Montparnasse, he met Pablo Picasso and George Braque and became their principal agent, but he also supported the cubist painters Fernand Léger and Juan Gris. A famous portrait by Picasso of 1910 (Art Institute of Chicago) reveals the dominant role of Kahnweiler in the promotion of Cubism at that time. In 1909 Kahnweiler started his career as a publisher with *L'Enchanteur pourrisant* written by Guillaume Apollinaire with woodcarvings by André Derain. In 1914, Kahnweiler fled to Rome to escape German military service. Shortly after he moved in with a friend in Berne, where he began to write his first art book, *The Path to Cubism*, published in 1920. In 1920 he returned to Paris and together with André Simon launched the Galerie Simon. He tried to retrieve his art collection, which had been confiscated by the French government, and with the help of his brother Gustave and the art dealer Alfred Flechtheim was able to redeem part of his former property. At the time Picasso and Juan Gris fell out with Kahnweiler when he tried to become their exclusive agent. Picasso was reconciled with him only after World War II, which Kahnweiler and his wife survived in hiding near Limoges. However, his gallery in Paris continued to exist under the name of Galerie Louise Leiris, his non-Jewish sister-in-law. Until his death in 1979 Kahnweiler organized more than 80 exhibitions of works by Braque, Picasso, Klee, Masson, Léger, and Gris. Moreover, he was the author of many books which were seminal to the popularization of contemporary art in general and cubist art in particular.

BIBLIOGRAPHY: Assouline, *L'Homme de l'art: Daniel-Henry Kahnweiler* (1988); B. Aldor, *Daniel-Henry Kahnweiler, Kunsthaendler Verleger Schriftsteller* (1986).

[Philipp Zschommler (2nd ed.)]

KAIFENG (formerly **P'ien-liang**), capital of Honan province, central China. Jews arrived in Kaifeng probably before 1127 from India or Persia. They were an ethnic unit of approximately 1,000 in all. It is believed that their daily language was New Persian and presumably they were experts in the production of cotton fabrics, in dyeing them, or printing patterns on them. This industry was well developed in India, but China with its rapidly increasing population was just introducing cotton, in order to meet the acute silk shortage. The first Kaifeng synagogue was constructed in 1163. It was restored in 1279 and after being destroyed in a disastrous flood was rebuilt again through the efforts of *Chao Ying-ch'en, a mandarin of Jewish descent, in 1653, when the sacred scrolls were also restored. Thereafter the community fell into rapid decay, most likely as a result of its complete isolation from other centers of Jewish life. By the middle of the 19th century the Jews of Kaifeng preserved only a rudimentary knowledge of Judaism and only the ruins of the former synagogue were left.

The first news concerning the presence of Jews in China reached Europe when Matteo Ricci, the Italian Jesuit missionary, informed his superior in Rome about the visit that the Kaifeng Jew *Ai T'ien of Kaifeng had paid him in 1605. Ai informed Ricci in detail about the status of his community which led Ricci to reach the conclusion that they were of Jewish descent. Other important records are four Chinese stone inscriptions of the Kaifeng Jewish community on three steles, dating from 1489, 1512, 1663, and 1679. Rubbings have been preserved of Chinese inscriptions on wooden tablets formerly in the Kaifeng synagogue. The Hebrew Union College in Cincinnati has in its possession a genealogical register in Chinese and Hebrew of the Kaifeng community (1660–70), as well as a large collection of prayer books obtained from Kaifeng by Christian missionaries in 1850–51. A unique scroll of the Book of Esther (in the Roth collection), with Chinese illuminations by three different artists, is believed to have probably come from the same source. Several outstanding members of the Kaifeng community, who became officials or military officers, are mentioned in provincial Chinese gazetteers. Gradually, however, the Jewish community adopted Chinese customs and surnames: Ai, Chang, Chao, Chin, Chou, Huang, Li, Mu, Nieh, Pai, Tso, and Yen. At the end of World War II, about 200 or 250 traceable descendants of the original Kaifeng Jewish community still survived. Descendants of some of these families can still be traced locally, but all have intermarried with local Chinese including Muslims, and they more or less have lost their Jewish identity. Nonetheless the Jewish world still has great interest in the remnants of the community.

[Rudolf Loewenthal]

Further Information

In 1957 a Canadian Jewish visitor to Kaifeng was told by a local Communist cadre that of 2,000 individuals in the city known to be of Jewish extraction 700 still acknowledged their Judaic descent. The figures, the validity of which is not otherwise confirmed, seem to have been derived from the census of minority (non-Han) peoples taken by the Chinese government in 1953. In 1980 there appeared *Juifs de Chine* by J. Dehergne and D.D. Leslie, a collection of letters preserved in various Jesuit archives, several of which had never previously been published, which provide new information on the Jews of Kaifeng.

BIBLIOGRAPHY: R. Loewenthal, *Jews in China: A bibliography* (1939); idem, *Jews in China: An annotated bibliography* (1940); idem, *Early Jews in China: A supplementary bibliography* (1946); Shunami, Bibl, nos. 2202–11; W.C. White, *Chinese Jews* (1966²), incl. bibl.; Leslie, in: *Abr-Nahrain*, 4 (1963–64), 20–49; 5 (1964–65), 1–28; 6 (1965–66), 1–52; 8 (1968–9), 1–35, incl. bibl. **ADD. BIBLIOGRAPHY:** M. Pollak, *Mandarins, Jews, and Missionaries: The Jewish Experience in the Chinese Empire* (1980); J. Goldstein (ed.), *The Jews of China: Historical and Comparative Perspectives* (1999).

KAIROUAN (Qairuwān) Tunisian town situated 77 mi. (125 km.) S. of *Tunis. Kairouan was founded in 670 by ʿUqba ibn Nāfiʿ, the Arab conqueror of North Africa. For about four centuries it was the government center and the capital of the *Aghlabids, the *Fatimids (until 969), and the *Zirid emirs, and the meeting place of commerce of East and West. It is possible, though not certain, that Jews settled in the town from the time of its establishment. In about 690 the *Umayyad caliph ʿAbd al-Malik ibn Marwān had 1,000 Copt families transferred from *Egypt to Kairouan. Some traditions have it that these families were Jewish. The fact remains that Jewish life prospered there. The community became the leading Jewish economic and cultural center in North Africa during the Middle Ages. The detailed extant information on this community begins with the ninth century. Studies of documents from the Cairo **Genizah* have shed light on the Jewish society of Kairouan about which some aspects were previously known from rabbinical literature, especially responsa by Babylonian *geonim*. An important correspondence was maintained between the Jews of Kairouan and the Babylonian academies.

The academy of Kairouan was well-known throughout the Jewish world. Its heads, known as *resh kallah*, were outstanding scholars. When Natronai b. Ḥavivai (c. 775) was not accepted as exilarch in Babylonia, he is said to have gone for some time to the Maghreb, i.e., Kairouan. In the tenth century (c. 920) another exilarch, Mar Ukba, also settled in Kairouan, after being compelled to leave Baghdad. In 880 the mysterious Jewish traveler *Eldad ha-Dani, who claimed to belong to the lost Ten Tribes of Israel, also went to Kairouan. His presence and his knowledge aroused discussions among the rabbis of Kairouan, who also addressed themselves to this subject in correspondence with Ẓemaḥ Gaon of *Sura. The medical writer and philosopher, Isaac *Israeli, went to Kairouan from Egypt, and died there in 932 or 942. From 904 he was the private physician of Ziyādat-Allah III (903–909), the last Aghlabid sovereign, and later held the same position in the service of ʿUbayd Allah al-Mahdī (910–934), the founder of the Fatimid dynasty in Tunisia. His numerous students included the astronomer and physician *Dunash ibn Tamim, who was born in Kairouan at the beginning of the tenth century and spent his entire life as the private physician to the Fatimid caliphs.

Toward the end of the tenth century the arrival of *Ḥushi'el b. Elhanan in Kairouan marked a turning point in the study of *halakhah*. R. Ḥushi'el, like many other Jews, went to Kairouan from *Italy. The actual population which made up the Jewish community was varied in origin. In addition to numerous names which were obviously of *Berber origin, such as Labrat, Sighmar, and Masnut, documents from the Cairo *Genizah* have furnished many names of families of foreign origin which were established in Kairouan. These include Andalusi (of Spanish origin), Fasi (of *Fez), Taherti (of Tahert (now Tiaret) in southwestern *Algeria), and Siqili (of Sicily).

Kairouan scholars were in contact with Palestine where in fact there were many immigrants of North African origin. The *gaon* of the Palestinian academy at the beginning of the 11th century, Solomon b. Judah, who was originally from Fez, maintained contact with Kairouan. R. Ḥushi'el introduced a new method of study in his academy which did not rely upon the opinions of the Babylonian scholars. Moreover, the academy of R. Ḥushi'el asserted itself in a stronger fashion than was generally the case for such academies. This resulted in the intellectual and spiritual independence of the school of Kairouan, which was accentuated to an even greater degree when R. Ḥushi'el was succeeded by his son R. *Hananel, one of the great medieval Jewish scholars. However, other rabbis, such as *Jacob b. Nissim ibn Shahin, the head of a second academy in Kairouan and representative of the Babylonian academies, continued to correspond with the *Pumbedita *geonim* R. Sherira and his son R. Hai. From the end of the first half of the 11th century R. *Nissim, the son of R. Jacob, held a prominent position in Kairouan as a result of his vast erudition and his connections. He was the teacher of the Spanish poet Solomon ibn *Gabirol and his daughter married *Joseph, the son of *Samuel ha-Nagid of Granada. R. Nissim succeeded his friend Hananel b. Ḥushi'el as representative of the Babylonian academies in Kairouan. His writings are a valuable source for the history of the Jews of North Africa, as well as being important in the field of *halakhah*. R. Nissim witnessed the destruction of his community when the town was sacked in 1057 by Arabs who invaded North Africa from Egypt.

This invasion considerably impoverished the area occupied by present-day *Libya and Tunisia. It marked the end of Kairouan as a Jewish intellectual center; one finds its Jewish inhabitants scattered in Egypt and Sicily. The town itself never regained its former prosperity. The last **nagid* of Kairouan left for Egypt, where he was followed by large numbers of Tunisian Jews. The Jews of Cairo had to collect contributions in order to provide him with a livelihood. There is much documentary evidence to show the extraordinary prosperity of the community during the period which preceded its ruin. Its worldwide contacts, from *Spain in the West to *India in the East, were particularly active and intensive. The Jews, like the other inhabitants of the town, were spoiled by a life of wealth, and had extravagant tastes so that, for example, they desired expensive and richly colored cloths of Persian origin. They were also fond of perfumes and music. Their business firms were represented in many centers of commerce. These large firms were headed by families with numerous branches; they were noted for their activity and wealth. Typical examples include the following: the Ibn Sighmar family, which in addition to its economic importance and great influence at the court furnished Kairouan with at least four generations of *dayyanim*; the Berechiah family, which was made up of scholars and community leaders; the Majjani family, which played a prominent role in world commerce; and many other families.

The most important personalities of Kairouan during the first half of the 11th century included the first *nagid* of the Jewish community, Abu Isḥāq Abraham ibn ʿAta, who was not only exceedingly wealthy, concerned with the welfare of others, and a scholar, but also a general in the army of the Zirids. The second *nagid* of Kairouan was Jacob b. Amram, whose power and generosity were lauded by the *geonim* of Palestine.

When Tunisia was conquered by the *Almohads in 1160, there is no mention of the Jews of Kairouan. From then until 1881, when Tunisia became a French protectorate, Kairouan, a holy city of *Islam, remained strictly out of bounds for all non-Muslims. From 1881, French civil servants were sent to Kairouan. Shortly afterwards Jewish shopkeepers settled there with their families and two synagogues were founded. The small community had its own *shoḥeṭ* and *ḥazzan*. In 1936 there were 348 Jews in Kairouan. They suffered hardships during the German occupation (see *Tunisia: Holocaust period) when many fled. Some subsequently returned, and in 1946 there were 275 Jews in Kairouan. These, however, left – some for the bigger cities, some to other countries – and by the late 1960s no Jews remained in Kairouan.

BIBLIOGRAPHY: G. Marçais, *Tunis et Kairouan* (1937); Hirschberg, Afrikah, index; R. Brunschvig, *Berbérie Orientale Sous les Ḥafsides*, 1 (1940), 357–77, 396ff.; S. D, Goitein, in *Etudes d'Orientalisme dédiées à… Lévi-Provençal*, 2 (1962), 559–79; idem, *A Mediterranean Society* (1967), index s.v. *Qayrawān*; A.N. Chouraqui, *Between East and West* (1968), index. **ADD. BIBLIOGRAPHY:** *"Al-kayrawan,"* in: EIS² s.v., 4 (1978), 824–32) (includes bibliography); M. Ben-Sasson, *Ẓemīḥat ha-Kehīllah ha-Yehudīt be-Arẓōt ha-Islam: Qairawān 800–1057* (1996), includes bibliography.

[David Corcos]

KAISER, ALOIS (1840–1908), *ḥazzan* and composer. Born in Hungary, Kaiser sang as a boy with Salomon *Sulzer. From 1859 to 1863 he was *ḥazzan* in Vienna, then went to Prague and three years later to the U.S. where he officiated until his death at the Oheb Shalom Congregation in Baltimore. Kaiser's intention in his compositions and arrangements was to provide music for the American synagogue, based on the traditional melodies but stripped of all "unnecessary ornamentation." With William Sparger he was responsible for the first edition of the *Union Hymnal* (1897) for the Conference of American Rabbis and edited *A Collection of the Principal Melodies of the Synagogue from the Earliest to the Present* (1893).

KAISERSLAUTERN, city in Germany. The first documentary evidence for the existence of a Jewish community dates from 1242, but it is probably somewhat older. The community suffered during the *Black Death persecution of 1348–49. The Jews lived on a *Judengasse* and the community possessed both a cemetery and a synagogue, built by those who returned after the Black Death persecutions. Between 1383 and 1388 the Jews were expelled "forever," but during the 17th and 18th centuries a few *Schutzjuden* ("protected Jews") were tolerated. The community was reestablished after emancipation was granted during French rule (1797–1814). From 1828 it had a rabbi. A synagogue, built in 1823, was rebuilt in 1848, and a Reform synagogue was dedicated in 1886 (the massive neo-Gothic structure was sold and dismantled before November 1938). A cemetery was consecrated in 1858. In 1840 the community totaled 118 persons, and 716 (2.72% of the total) in 1880. The number remained stable until Nazi persecution reduced it to 395 in 1937 and 85 in 1939. Of the 74 remaining, 48 were deported to *Gurs on Oct. 22, 1940. In 1951 a synagogue was consecrated and in 1965 a community center serving about 150 Jews in the town and neighborhood was opened.

BIBLIOGRAPHY: Germ Jud, 1 (1963), 139–40; 2 (1968), 384–5; M. Weinberg, *Geschichte der Oberpfalz*, 3 (1909); H. Friedel, in: *Pfaelzer Heimat* (1965), 16, 41ff.; S. Baron, in: *Bayerischeisraelitische Gemeindezeitung*, 12 (1936), 310–2.

KĀKHYA (Kiāhya), Turkish version of the Persian *ketkhudā*, meaning majordomo or intendant (also: head of a guild). Many Jews served the sultans, viziers, and pashas as commissioners of revenue, superintendents of the mint, and farmers of tolls and customs. More important, they held monopolies on certain exported and imported goods. The *kākhya* appears as the official intercessor for the Jewish community with the Turkish authorities in 16th-century documents and responsa. From a responsum of R. Elijah *Mizraḥi (no. 15), chief *dayyan* of Constantinople, it appears that while serving as official spokesman for Constantinople, *Kākhya* Shaltiel accepted bribes. In 1518 representatives of the various congregations in the city complained to Mizraḥi, and at the end of the year, in their presence and with their consent, he deprived the *kākhya* and his sons of all rights which they hitherto had enjoyed. In 1520 the judgment was reversed and Shaltiel was restored with the promise to act in a public capacity only with the permission of persons appointed by the congregations. The term *kākhya* also designates a representative of the Greek Orthodox and Armenian *millets and of the provincial tax farmers, each protecting the interests of his constituency at the Sublime Porte. Later on the *kākhya* appears as a minister in *Syria, or as representative of the pasha in *Palestine and *Egypt.

BIBLIOGRAPHY: C.F.C. de Volney, *Travels through Syria and Egypt*, 2 (1787), 27; A. Galanté (ed.), *Documents officiels turcs* (1931), 134, 251; W. Foster (ed.), *Travels of John Sanderson in the Levant* (1931); H.A.R. Gibb and H. Bowen, *Islamic Society and the West*, 1 pt. 2 (1957), index; ʿAbd al-Raḥmān Jabartī, *ʿAjāʾib al-Āthār fī al-Tarājim wa-al-Akhbār*, 1 (1290 H), 94, 109; Rosanes, Togarmah, 1 (1930), 73f. **ADD. BIBLIOGRAPHY:** EIS², 4 (1978), 893–94, s.v. Ketkhudā (incl. bibl.).

[Haïm Z'ew Hirschberg]

KALAI, JOSEPH B. JACOB (13th century), liturgical poet. Probably a native of Southern Europe (perhaps Greece or Sicily), the poet, whose surname קלעי is of Arabic origin, signs his name in addition as *ḥazzan, payyat* ("poet"), and כרפאן or בן כרפאן. For the latter, neither Zunz, who renders it κορυφαῖος ("precentor"), nor S. Krauss, who prefers "of Corfu," provides a satisfactory explanation. His compositions were adopted chiefly in the *Maḥzor Romania* (Greek rite). Single poems were in use in Rome, Tripoli, Kaffa, and among the Karaites. Zunz (see bibl.) lists 23 poems by Kalai. His compositions include *yoẓerot, ḥatanu, taḥanun*, and *tokhaḥot*; two dialogues, one between Haman and Ahasuerus and the other between the Sabbath and the New Moon, deserve special mention.

BIBLIOGRAPHY: A Berliner, *Aus meiner Bibliothek* (1898), supplement, xxiiif.; Davidson, Oẓar, 4 (1933), 406f., s.v. *Yosef Kalai*; A.M. Habermann (ed.), *Ateret Renanim* (1967), 50f., no. 28; S. Krauss, *Studien zur byzantinisch-juedischen Geschichte* (1914), 83, 102, 139; Landshuth, Ammudei, 90; I.D. Markon, in: *Festschrift... A. Harkavy* (1908), 459 (Heb. pt.); M. Steinschneider, in: JQR, 11 (1898/99), 129 no. 292, 605 no. 663; Zunz, Lit Poesie, 339–41 and additions, 20f.

[Jefim (Hayyim) Schirmann]

KALAI (Kali), MORDECAI BEN SOLOMON (1556–1647), Salonikan talmudist. The family name derives from Calatayud in Spain. Kalai was born in Salonika, and studied under Aaron ben Ḥason and Aaron Sason. His manuscripts were destroyed in the great fire in Salonika in 1625, but he resumed writing. He was known as a capable communal leader, being active in the ransoming of captives and other charitable and benevolent activities. Among his many disciples who later served as rabbis in the cities of Peloponnesus were Daniel *Estrosa and David *Conforte. Kalai's responsa were included in the *Mekor Barukh* (Smyrna, 1659) of his brother Baruch, published by the latter's son. Kalai is quoted by many of his contemporaries, including Joshua Handali, Ḥayyim *Shabbetai (Maharḥash), and Judah Lerma, and by Solomon *Levi and Joseph of *Trani in their responsa. Mordecai's brother, BARUCH (d. 1597), who also studied under Aaron ben Ḥason, was rabbi of Siderocapsa, near Salonika. *Mekor Barukh* contains 61 responsa which consist of halakhic discussions with his teacher, and with Solomon Levi the Elder, in addition to those with his brother. He also wrote *Arba Shitot*, on four tractates of the Talmud, and left an unpublished volume of sermons on Sabbaths and festivals.

BIBLIOGRAPHY: Conforte, Kore, index; I.S. Emmanuel, *Maẓevot Saloniki*, 1:1 (1963), 296f.; M.D. Gaon, *Yehudei ha-Mizraḥ be-Ereẓ Yisrael*, 2 (1938), 627, 749; Rosanes, Togarmah, 3 (1938), 172–4, 194.

[Simon Marcus]

KALAI, SAMUEL BEN JOSEPH (d. 1754), Karaite scholar of Chufut-Qaleh, Crimea. He was the head of the study-house in Chufut-Qaleh. After his demise Simḥah Isaac *Luzki occupied his place.

He wrote *Me'il Shemu'el* (which survived in several mss. in St. Petersburg, NY, Oxford, and Cambridge), a supercommentary on *Sefer ha-Mivḥar* by *Aaron b. Joseph; the work remained unfinished and was later edited by S.I. Luzki.

BIBLIOGRAPHY: J. Fuerst, Karaeerthum, 2 (1865), 241; J. Mann, *Texts*, 2 (1935), 1326–27, 1429; A. Neubauer, *Aus der Peterburger Bibliothek* (1866), 49; 142.

[Isaak Dov Ber Markon]

KALAI (Kal'i), SAMUEL BEN MOSES (16th century), Turkish rabbi. Kalai may have been born in Corfu. He was a son-in-law of Benjamin ibn Mattathias, author of *Binyamin Ze'ev*. At first he lived in Salonika and subsequently in Arta. In consequence of a dispute he left the town and stayed for a time in Trikkala, but later returned to Arta where he served as rabbi. In about 1560 he was appointed rabbi of Vidin in Bulgaria. He was compelled to leave Vidin because of a dispute that broke out between him and other rabbis as a result of his prohibiting the use of a certain cheese. He was among the signatories of the ban against the David (Da'ud), who had opposed Don Joseph *Nasi. In his old age Kalai settled in Salonika where he served as rabbi of the Keianah community. He was regarded as the talmudic authority for the whole country and problems were addressed to him from various Balkan towns. He was the author of the responsa *Mishpetei Shemu'el* (Venice, 1599).

BIBLIOGRAPHY: Rosanes, Togarmah, 1 (1930[2]), 158; 2 (1937–38[2]), 112f.; M.D. Gaon, *Yehudei ha-Mizraḥ be-Ereẓ Yisrael*, 2 (1938), 627 n.1.

[Simon Marcus]

KALĀM, meaning *ʿilm al-kalām* (the science of *Kalām*), is one of the branches of Islamic religious science. The common use of the word *kalām* is word, words, or speech. The *Koran is called *kalām Allāh*, i.e., the speech of God, and so, it was suggested, *ʿilm al-kalām* is "the science of the word [of God]." The exponent of *Kalām* is called *mutakallim* (lit. speaker, pl. *mutakallimūn*). The Hebrew designation *ha-medabberīm* and the Latin *loquentes* are equivalent to *mutakallimūn*.

The term *Kalām*, which represents the use of dialectics in theology, probably has antecedents in Greek (as derived from *logos* or *dialexis*) and Syriac (as derived from both *mamlā*, i.e. *dialexis* and *mamlūt allāhūtā*, i.e., theology). *Kalām* is usually translated as "theology," although this rendering is inaccurate, and it is best to use "speculative theology." The theological arena in Sunnite *Islam consisted not only of the Muʿtazilite *mutakallimūn*, who used logical argumentation, in order to prove some of the principles of religion (= *ʾuṣūl al-dīn*), but mainly of traditionalist theologians, who were, and still are, the central trend of Islam. While *Kalām* gives precedence to human reason (= *ʿaḳl*) in the process of perceiving God and the world, Islamic traditional theology declares to draw its authority solely from divine revelation and tradition (= *naḳl*) and the teachings of the ancestors (= *salaf*) of the Muslim community. It should be noted, that even the Muʿtazilite *mutakallimūn* could not be considered pure rationalists, because they rely to some extent upon divine revelation.

Kalām is commonly identified with two rival schools in Sunnite Islam: the *Muʿtazila*, flourished as two separate schools in *Baṣra and *Baghdād from the first half of the 8th century until the middle of the 11th century, and the *Ashʿariyya*, founded in Baṣra in the first half of the 10th century. The eponym of the *Ashʿariyya*, Abū al-Ḥasan al-Ashʿarī (d. 935) was a former Muʿtazilite, who used the rationalistic tools of the *Muʿtazila* in order to defend the doctrines of traditional Islam and to defeat the *Muʿtazila*. Another important theological school is the *Māturīdiyya-Ḥanafiyya*, probably founded in central Asia in the 11th century.

The beginning of *Kalām* is by all means connected to the Arab conquests of *Iraq and *Persia in the 7th century, when the relatively young Muslim community came into contact with Hellenistic philosophical thought, both Christian and non-Christian, and with other religious doctrines, mainly Mazdaean and Manichaean. Public debates with holders of well-established faiths increased the need to use various rationalistic tools in order to defend Islamic doctrines and articles of faith (*ʿaḳīda* pl. *ʿaḳāʾid*), whose origins are to be found in the Koran and *Ḥadīth* (= prophetic traditions), and to uproot what was perceived as heretical concepts (= *zandaḳa*), infiltrated into Islamic thought. According to al-Tahānawī (d. circa 1745): "[*ʿilm al-kalām*] is the science, which enables one to assert the authenticity of religious beliefs and [discredit] others by giving proofs and dispelling doubts" (*al-Kashshāf*, vol. 1, p. 22).

The *mutakallimūn* comprehended their occupation as two-fold: on the one hand, *Kalām* is a process of a pure intellectual speculation in search of the ultimate truth, that is "to grasp the unity of God, and study the essence of God and His attributes" (al-Ghazālī, *Iḥyāʾ ʿulūm al-dīn*, vol. 1, p. 25); on the other hand, *Kalām* is a system of defense and attack. Defeating the adversary by using various dialectical instruments is the main feature of *Kalām*. Alongside the use of analogy (= *ḳiyās*), one of the prominent methods of *Kalām* is *ilzām*, which means forcing the adversary to admit heretical or absurd views, drawn from his own set of arguments.

Most of the activity of the *mutakallimūn* was in the inner circles of Islam, mainly against Sunnite traditionalist theologians. Nevertheless, the boundaries between the two groups were never definite. Although traditionalist scholars prohibited practicing *Kalām* and debating with *mutakallimūn*, *Kalām*'s methods had a huge impact upon them. For example, Ibn Taymiyya (d. 1328), who belonged to the ultra-traditionalist Ḥanbalite movement, used Muʿtazilite theses and argumentations in his dispute with the Ashʿarites about predestination and free will.

Another group challenged by *Kalām* and labeled as heretics were the Muslim philosophers, in spite of the resemblance between *Kalām*'s areas of interest and that of *falsafa* (= Muslim philosophy). The most elaborate endeavor in that direction is *Tahāfut al-Falāsifa* (= The Incoherence of the Philosophers) by the Ashʿarite theologian *al-Ghazālī (d. 1111). The philosophers, on their part, attacked *ʿilm al-kalām* and refuted its tenets and methods, as reflected in Ibn Rushd's (= Averroes, d. 1198) *Tahāfut al- Tahāfut* (= The Incoherence of the Incoherence).

Main Themes in Kalām

All *Kalām* manuals, after introducing the sources of knowledge of God and the world, viz. human reason and divine revelation, prove the existence of God and the creation of the world by using the proof from accidents, which is based on the doctrine of atoms. According to this doctrine, reality is made up of indivisible atoms with concomitant accidents, which exist only for an instant. Therefore, in every instant God is creating the world anew; there are no intermediate causes. This Islamic occasionalism allows for creation from nothing.

A point of dispute between the *Muʿtazila* and the *Ashʿariyya* is the denial of anthropomorphism (= *tashbīh*). This theme is derived from numerous Qurʾānic verses, which ascribe human properties to God. The *Muʿtazila* denied the figurative interpretation and applied allegorical interpretation to these verses. The *Ashʿariyya* for their part used the doctrine of *bi-lā kayfa*, which means believing the Qurʾānic formulae without trying to explain them.

The question of the unity of God (= *tawḥīd*), which is actually a cluster of problems, such as proving the existence of God, proving the creation of the world and explaining divine attributes, set out numerous points of dispute between the *Muʿtazila* and the *Ashʿariyya*. In the question of divine attributes (= *ṣifāt*), for example, the *Muʿtazila* denied their real existence, while the *Ashʿariyya* stressed their independent status.

The *Muʿtazila* asserted man's free will, while stating that man creates his own good and bad actions, due to the power God grants him beforehand, and therefore he is liable to reward and punishment. The *Ashʿariyya*, on the other hand, emphasized that God, as a creator of all things, creates all human actions. Man's responsibility over his actions is maintained by using the doctrine of *kasb* (lit. acquisition), according to which, when God creates man's acts he also creates in him the ability to "acquire" them. Designed to provide for man's responsibility for his actions, this doctrine is not far removed, if at all, from complete determinism.

The *Kalām* manuals discuss in length various topics regarding theodicy, eschatology and the status of prophecy. A major issue concerns the created or uncreated character of the Koran, and whether it exists as a divine attribute from all eternity.

Shiʿite Islam embraced Muʿtazilite theses as part of its doctrine from the 9th century, so in a sense they are current to some extent even nowadays. The Ashʿarite manuals are being studied in Sunnite *madrasas* (= religious boarding schools) alongside the works of the traditionalists.

[Livnat Holtzman (2nd ed.)]

Influence on Jewish Philosophy

The influence of *Kalām*, in its Muʿtazilite version only, on Jewish thinkers, both *Karaite and Rabbanite, during the Middle Ages was considerable. The earliest Jewish philosopher who was also influenced by *Kalām* was David ibn Marwan al-*Mukammis (first half of ninth century), who may have received it from his Christian teachers. It also had a great impact on *Saadiah Gaon. Muʿtazilite influence is visible from the very opening of Saadiah's *Book of Doctrines and Beliefs*, which begins with a demonstration of the createdness of the world and proceeds to deduce from this the existence of a creator. The very structure of Saadiah's theological masterpiece follows the order of the five Muʿtazilite theses previously mentioned. Most of his proofs of the noneternity of the world are derived from the *Kalām*, except that Saadiah did not hold the theory of atomism. Saadiah uses *Kalām* arguments, as well, in proving the unity of God, and his doctrine of attributes is similar to that of the Muʿtazilah. In treating the commandments, Saadiah distinguishes between rational and revealed commandments, thus sharing the Muʿtazilite distinction. In positing a future world in which children and animals will find reward for suffering in this world, Saadiah merely repeats a doctrine based on the Muʿtazilite sense of justice. In general, one may say that through Saadiah the Muʿtazilite *Kalām* exercised enormous influence on Jewish thought throughout the Middle Ages. *Samuel b. Hophni (d. 1013) followed closely the Muʿtazilite system in its Basran version. His son in law *Hai Gaon, did so to a lesser extent. Traces of the speculation of the *Kalām* are to be found in *Baḥya ibn Paquda and Joseph ibn Ẓaddik's proofs of creation. *Maimonides expounded and refuted kalamic doctrine in detail in the *Guide of the Perplexed* (1:73–76), although he did mention that his own point of view resembles the *Kalām* in certain respects (*ibid.*, 2: 19). The influence of *Kalām* on Karaite thinkers was very pronounced. Its earliest attestations are found in the formulation of normative beliefs by al-*Qumisi (late 9th century). It had become accepted by most medieval Karaite thinkers. Joseph b. Abraham ha-Kohen *al-Baṣīr wrote theological works that follow closely the Basran Muʿtazilah both in structure and in contents, and so did his disciple *Jeshua ben Judah. They even accepted the doctrine of atoms. As late as the 14th century, *Aaron ben Elijah the Younger of Nicomedia defended the *Kalām* outlook in his *Eẓ Ḥayyim*, which was intended to be the Karaite counterpart of Maimonides' *Guide*.

[Lawrence V. Berman / Haggai Ben-Shammai (2nd ed.)]

BIBLIOGRAPHY: H. Corbin, Histoire de la philosophie islamique (1964), 152–78; M. Fakhry, Islamic Occasionalism… (1958); L. Gardet and G.C. Anawati, Introduction à la théologie musulmane (1948), 21–93; G. Vajda, Introduction à la pensée juive du moyen âge (1947), 23–37, 45–65; Guttmann, Philosophies, 61–84, index. **ADD. BIBLIOGRAPHY:** PRIMARY SOURCES: ʿAbd al-Jabbār ibn Aḥmad al-Asadabādī, *Al-Mughnī fī abwāb al-tawḥīd wa'l-ʿadl* (1960–69); Al-Ashʿarī, Abū al-Ḥasan, *Al-Ibāna ʿan uṣūl al-diyāna* (n.d.); Al-Baghdādī, Abū Manṣūr, *Uṣūl al-dīn* (1928); Al-Bāḳillānī, Abū Bakr, *Kitāb al-tamhīd* (1957); Al-Ghazālī, Abū Ḥāmid Muḥammad b. Aḥmad, *Iḥyāʾ ʿulūm al-dīn* (1998); Ibn Taymiyya, Abū al-ʿAbbās Aḥmad, *Minhāj al-sunna al-nabawiyya fī naḳḍ kalām al-shīʿa al-ḳadariyya* (1986) Al-Jurjānī, ʿAli b. Muḥammad, *Kitāb al-taʿrīfāt* (1978); Al-Māturīdī, Abū Manṣūr, *Kitāb al-tawḥīd* (1970); al-Tahānawī, Muḥammad Aʿlā ibn ʿAlī, *Mawsūʿat kashshāf iṣṭilaḥāt al-funūn* (1996). SECONDARY SOURCES: B. Abrahamov, "Ibn Taymiyya on the Agreement of Reason with Tradition," in: *The Muslim World*, 82:3–4 (1992), 256–72; idem, *Islamic Theology – Traditionalism and Rationalism* (1998); idem, "Necessary Knowledge in Islamic Theology," in: *British Journal of Middle Eastern Studies*, 20 (1988), 20–32; G.C. Anawati, "*Kalām*," in: *The Encyclopaedia of Religion*, vol. 8, 231–42; R. Arnaldez "Apories sur le prédestination et le libre arbitre dans le Commentaire de Rāzī," in: *Melanges de l'Institut dominicain d'études orientales du Caire*, 6 (1959–60), 123–36; R. Brunschvig "Devoir et pouvoir," in *Studia Islamica*, 20 (1964), 5–46; M.A. Cook, "The Origins of *Kalām*," in: *Bulletin of the School of Oriental and African Studies*, 43 (1980), 32–43; J. van Ess, *Theologie und Gesellschaft im 2. und 3. Jahrhundert Hidschra: eine Geschichte des religioesen Denkens im fruehen Islam* (1990); idem, *Zwischen Hadith und Theologie. Studien zur Entstehung praedestinatianischer Ueberlieferung* (1975); idem, "The Logical Structure of Islamic Theology," in: G.E. von Grunebaum (ed.), *Logic in Classical Islamic Culture* (1970), 21–50; R.M. Frank, "*Kalām* and Philosophy, A Perspective from One Problem," in: P. Morewedge (ed.), *Islamic Philosophical Theology* (1979), 71–95; L. Gardet, "ʿIlm al-Kalām," in: *Encyclopaedia of Islam*², vol. 3, 1141–50; L. Gardet and G.C. Anawati, *Introduction à la théologie musulmane* (1948), 21–93; L. Gardet, *Les grands problèmes de la théologie musulmane: Dieu et la destinée de l'homme* (1967); D. Gimaret, *Théories de l'acte humain en théologie musulmane* (1980); G.F. Hourani, *Reason and Tradition in Islamic Ethics* (1985); D.B. Macdonald, "Kalām," in: H.A.R. Gibb and J.H. Kramers (eds.), *Shorter Encyclopaedia of Islam* (1995), 210–14; W. Madelung, "The Late Muʿtazila and Determinism: the Philosophers' Trap," in: *Yad-nama in memoria di Alessandro Bausani*, vol. 1 (1991), 245–57; idem, "The Origins of the Controversy Concerning the Creation of the Koran," in: *Orientalia Hispanica*, 1 (1974), 504–25; M.E. Marmura. (ed.), *Islamic Theology and Philosophy: Studies in Honor of G.F. Hourani* (1984); S.H. Nasr and O.Leaman (eds.), *History of Islamic Philosophy* (1996); E.L. Ormsby, *Theodicy in Islamic Thought* (1984); M.S. Seale, *Muslim Theology* (1964); J.M. Pessagno, "*Irāda, ikhtiyār, qudra, kasb*: The View of Abū Manṣūr Al-Māturīdī," in: *Journal of the American Oriental Society*, 104:1 (1984), 177–99; J.R.T.M. Peters, *God's Created Speech* (1976); Sh. Pines, "A Note on an Early Meaning of the Term *Mutakallim*," in: *Israel Oriental Studies*, 1 (1971), 224–40; idem, *Studies in Islamic Atomism* (1997); G. Vajda, *Introduction à la pensée juive du moyen âge* (1947), 23–37, 45–65; W.M. Watt, *The Formative Period of Islamic Thought* (1973); idem, *Free Will and Predestination in Early Islam* (1948); idem, *Islamic Creeds – A Selection* (1994); A.J. Wensinck, *The Muslim Creed* (1965); H.A. Wolfson, *The Philosophy of the Kalam* (1976). INFLUENCE ON JEWISH PHILOSOPHY: H. Ben-Shammai, in: D.H. Frank and O. Leaman (eds.), *History of Jewish Philosophy* (1997), 114–15; idem, in: *Jerusalem Studies in Arabic and Islam*, 6 (1985), 243–98; H. Davidson, *Proofs for Eternity, Creation and the Existence of God in Medieval Islamic and Jewish Philosophy* (1987); M. Schwarz, in: *Maimonidean Studies*, 2 (1991), 159–209; C. Sirat, *A History of Jewish Philosophy in the Middle Ages* (1985); G. Vajda (ed. and tr.), *Al Kitāb al-Muḥtawī par Yūsuf al-Baṣīr* (1985); H.A. Wolfson, *The Philosophy of the Kalam* (1976); idem, *Repercussions of the Kalam in Jewish Philosophy* (1979).

KALARASH (Rom. **Călăraşi**, formerly also **Tuzora**), town in Bessarabia, Moldova. Jews began to settle there in the first half of the 19th century. They numbered 4,593 in 1897, forming 89% of the population. Most were engaged in trade, primarily in agricultural produce, and some in agriculture. Most of the Jews were ḥasidim and spoke Yiddish. The wave of pogroms in Russia in October 1905 also hit Kalarash, where 60 Jews were killed, 300 were injured, and over 200 houses were burned down. After Bessarabia passed to Romania in 1918, communal life flourished in Kalarash. The community had welfare organizations and educational institutions, including a hospital (founded in 1890), a *talmud torah*, a library, and a loan and savings fund. In 1930 the Jewish population numbered 3,631 (76% of the total population). Israel *Giladi was born in Kalarash. Zionist organizations were also active.

[Eliyahu Feldman]

Holocaust Period and After

When World War II broke out, some of the community managed to escape from Kalarash, apparently to the Soviet Union. Those caught on the way were either killed on the spot or deported to Transnistria. In July 1941 Romanian troops assembled all the remaining Jews in Kalarash and took them to a forest not far from the city, where a deep ditch had been prepared. Some 250 Jews were thrown into the ditch and killed. This action had been ordered by the commander of the gendarmerie legion in the Lăpuşna district, Lieut. Col. Nicolai Caracas. The local Kalarash gendarmerie commander also took part in the slaughter and looted Jewish property. In 1970 the Jewish population was estimated at about 750. The only synagogue was closed down by the authorities in 1961 and converted into a public library. The baking of matzah was stopped in 1962. In 1964 seven Jews were arrested for economic crimes allegedly committed 20 years earlier.

BIBLIOGRAPHY: *Judenpogrome in Russland*, 2 (1909), 97–102; P. Cowen, *Memories of an American Jew* (1932), 212–24; Y. Yakir, in: *Eynikeyt* (Dec. 3, 1946). **ADD. BIBLIOGRAPHY:** *Sefer Kalarasch* (1966).

[Jean Ancel]

KALB, BERNARD (1922–), U.S. journalist. Born in New York, the son of immigrants from Poland and Russia, Kalb graduated from the City College of New York in 1942. He then spent two years in the Army, mostly on an Army newspaper in the remote Aleutian Islands. His editor was Sgt. Dashiell Hammett, the detective story writer. After the war, Kalb got a job with *The New York Times*, first as a writer for its radio station and then as a reporter in New York City and at the United Nations bureau. On his first overseas assignment, he accompanied Adm. Richard E. Byrd on a mission to Antarctica in late 1955 and early 1956. Later, he was sent to Indonesia and served there until 1961, covering the chaotic rule of President Sukarno. In 1962 Kalb opened a CBS News bureau in Hong Kong and worked there until 1970. Returning to the United States, Kalb was posted to Washington, where he covered the State Department for eight years, traveling constantly with secretaries of state, until 1984, when he became the department's spokesman, with the title of assistant secretary of state for public affairs. It was the first time a journalist who covered the State Department had been named as its spokesman. Kalb worked there first for CBS News and after 1980 for NBC News. At the time of his appointment, Kalb's younger brother, Marvin, was chief diplomatic correspondent for NBC News. As a television correspondent, he accompanied President Nixon on the opening trip to China in 1972. As State Department spokesman, Kalb was with the U.S. delegation when President Reagan held his first summit with Mikhail Gorbachev in Geneva in November 1985. In 1986, when he read about the Reagan Administration's reported effort to deceive news organizations, Kalb resigned from the State Department. Kalb then became the founding anchor and a panelist on the weekly CNN program *Reliable Sources*, which turned a critical eye on the media in a weekly series that ran for 10 years. He was co-author with his brother of two books: *Kissinger* (1974), about the former secretary of state, and *The Last Ambassador* (1975), a novel about the collapse of Saigon.

[Stewart Kampel (2nd ed.)]

KALB, MARVIN (1930–), U.S. journalist. Born in New York City, Kalb graduated from the City College of New York. He earned a master's degree from Harvard and was completing studies for a doctorate in Russian history when he left in 1956 to accept a State Department appointment in Moscow. Kalb made his mark as a broadcast journalist, serving over a 30-year period as chief diplomatic correspondent for CBS News and NBC News and as moderator of the long-running *Meet the Press*. Among his many honors were two Peabody awards, the DuPont Prize from Columbia University, and more than half a dozen Overseas Press Club awards. Kalb was the first director of the Joan Shorenstein Center on the Press, Politics and Public Policy at Harvard, serving for 12 years. He also taught and lectured as the Edward R. Murrow Professor on Press and Politics. He left to be executive director of the institute's office in Washington, D.C., where he frequently led seminars addressing critical issues facing the business and practice of journalism. Kalb was also the host of a number of television series for the Public Broadcasting System, including *Vox Populi*, a four-part series on citizen attitudes toward government. He authored or co-authored seven nonfiction books, including *Kissinger* (1974), *Roots of Involvement*, *The Nixon Memo* (1994), and *One Scandalous Story* (2001), which dissects Washington journalism in the breaking of the Monica Lewinsky scandal, as well as two best-selling novels.

[Stewart Kampel (2nd ed.)]

KALDOR, NICHOLAS, BARON (1908–1986), British economist. Born in Budapest as Miklos Kaldor, he was educated there and then studied at the London School of Economics, where he taught economics from 1932. At the end of World War II, Kaldor worked for the United States government as chief of the economic planning staff of the Strategic Bombing Survey and from 1947 to 1949 was director of the research and planning division of the Economic Commission for Europe. In 1952 he became a lecturer at Cambridge University, where he was appointed professor of economics in 1966. Kaldor acted as adviser on taxation and fiscal matters to various governments and from 1964 to 1970 was special adviser to the chancellor of the exchequer of the Labour government on employment, development, and fiscal policy. Kaldor's numerous publications advocate an extension of state control and high taxation as the prerequisite for faster economic growth. He edited *Essays on Economic Policy* (1964) and contributed essays to *National and International Measures for Full Employment* (1950), an economic report to the United Nations. Kaldor's lecture, *Accumulation and Economic Growth*, was published in *The Theory of Capital* (1961), a major work of the International Economic Association. Kaldor's emphasis on the role of the manufacturing industry in the growth process was of considerable influence on the Labour government of 1964–70, but his impact waned with the rise of monetarism. He was awarded a life peerage in 1974.

ADD. BIBLIOGRAPHY: ODNB online.

[Joachim O. Ronall]

KALECKI, MICHAL (1899–1970), Polish economist. Born in Lodz and educated at Cambridge and Oxford, Kalecki worked for the United Nations Economic Department from 1947 to 1954. In 1957 he joined the Polish State Planning Commission where he was instrumental in preparing Poland's first 20-Year Plan (1959). He taught in Warsaw from 1961 to 1968 when, under pressure exerted by the Polish authorities, he resigned and ceased teaching. His studies on business cycles, inspired by Karl *Marx and Rosa *Luxemburg, anticipated much of Keynes' *General Theory of Employment, Interest and Money* (1936), and his work on war economics and full employment ensured him an eminent place, particularly among English-speaking economists. He was a member of the Polish Academy of Sciences. Outstanding among his more than 200 publications are *Essays in the Theory of Economic Fluctuations* (1939); *Studies in Economic Dynamics* (1943); *Theory of Economic Dynamics* (1954, 1965^2); and *Zarys teorii wzrostu gospodarki socjalistycznej* ("Outline of the Theory of Development in a Socialist Economy", 1963).

BIBLIOGRAPHY: *Problems of Economic Dynamics and Planning* (1966).

[Joachim O. Ronall]

KALEF, YEHOSHUA (1875–1943), Bulgarian Zionist leader. Born in Plovdiv (Philippopolis) to a large and influential family, Kalef was educated in Alliance Israélite schools and later completed his law studies in Sofia and in Brussels. With the appearance of *Herzl, Kalef joined *Z.H.Belkowsky in his Zionist work. He began by publishing the Zionist newspaper *Kol ha-Am* ("Voice of the People") in Bulgarian (1896) and together with K. *Herbst translated Herzl's *Judenstaat* into Bulgarian (1896). He participated in the First Zionist Congress (1897) and thereafter fought for Zionist leadership in the Jewish communities, the crystallization of a Zionist consciousness among Bulgarian Jewry, and the domination of Jewish national ideology and of the Hebrew language in Jewish schools. Kalef was a member of the Bulgarian government's delegation to the Paris Peace Conference after World War I. In 1920 he was elected chairman of the Jewish Consistory and later also president of the Zionist Organization in Bulgaria. Afterward, he moved to Alsace and then to Paris, where he lived out his life. In 1961 his remains were reinterred in Bet Ḥanan, a moshav of Bulgarian immigrants in Israel.

BIBLIOGRAPHY: EG, 10 (1967), 611–3, and index; *Haaretz* (Sept. 18, 1961).

[Getzel Kressel]

KALÉKO, MASCHA, pseudonym of **Golda Malka Kaléko**; 1907–1975), German lyrical poet. Mascha Kaleko was born in Chrzanów (Poland), but grew up in Frankfurt, Marburg and Berlin. Escaping the poverty of the Berlin *Scheunenviertel*, she started to work at a young age as a shorthand typist and married the Hebraist Saul Kaléko. In 1938 she emigrated with her son and second husband, the musicologist and composer Chemjo *Vinaver, to New York. In 1959 she left the U.S. and settled with her family in Jerusalem. After the death of her son (1968) and her husband (1973) she lived in isolation until she died during a trip to Europe, in Zurich.

Between 1929 and 1933 Mascha Kaléko regularly published poems in newspapers, like the *Vossische Zeitung*, the *Berliner Tagblatt*, and the *Welt am Montag*. Her first book of verse, *Das Lyrische Stenogrammheft. Verse fuer den Alltag* (1933), though seemingly influenced by Erich Kaestner's "Gebrauchslyrik" (lyrics for everyday use) with its cynical yet neo-romantic tone, nevertheless reveals a very personal style with a specific Berlinesque flavor. Her extraordinary sense of humor and a gift for playing on words kept her work fresh over the years, and her *Kleines Lesebuch fuer Grosse Gereimtes und Ungereimtes*, after it had been confiscated at the printer's in 1935, was published together with her first book after the war in many editions.

Kaleko's third volume, *Verse fuer Zeitgenossen* (published in the U.S. in 1945 and in Germany in 1958), reflects many facets in the life of the Jewish exiles, such as material and psychological misery, loneliness, and the difficulties of acculturation in the new country. Her denunciation of the Nazi tyrants – in a poem dedicated to the victims of Hitler's annihilation camps – concluded: "But you, who taught me hate, I hate the worst."

Mascha Kaléko later expanded her scope to include children's books and epigrams. After her death numerous collections of unpublished poems were printed, including *In meinen Traeumen laeutet es Sturm. Gedichte und Epigramme aus dem Nachlass* (1980) and *Heute ist morgen schon gestern. Gedichte aus dem Nachlass* (1980).

ADD. BIBLIOGRAPHY: A. Frankenstein, in: *Emuna*, 10, suppl. 1 (1975), 40–44; I.A. Wellershoff, *Vertreibung aus dem "Kleinen Glück." Das lyrische Werk von Masha Kaléko* (1982); G. Zoch-Westphal, *Aus den sechs Leben der Mascha Kaléko* (1987); B. Schmeichel-Falkenberg, in: *Deutschsprachige Exillyrik von 1933 bis zur Nachkriegszeit*, ed. by Jörg Thunecke (1998), 199–215; A. Nolte, *Mir ist zuweilen so als ob das Herz in mir zerbrach: Leben und Werk Mascha Kalékos im Spiegel ihrer sprichwörtlichen Dichtung* (2003).

[Erich Gottgetreu /Mirjam Triendl (2nd ed.)]

KALFA, ISAAK BEN JOSEPH (d. 1801), Karaite scholar, *hazzan*, and teacher of Torah from *Chufut-Qaleh. He was a head of a study house where he taught both Karaite and Rabbanite treatises. One of his disciples was *Isaac ben Solomon, who became one of the last prominent scholars of the Crimea and who established the calendar reform (1779), which was supported by most scholars in Crimea and some other Karaite communities. Kalfa wrote a book on ritual slaughter and about the 10 principles of the Karaite faith, *Ziz Nezer ha-Kodesh* and a number of liturgical poems, some of which were included in Karaite *siddurim*. He corresponded with the Karaite community in Jerusalem and sent donations there.

BIBLIOGRAPHY: G. Akhiezer, in: M. Polliack (ed.), *Karaite Judaism* (2003), 742; Mann, Texts, 2 (1935), index, 1552.

[Golda Akhiezer (2nd ed.)]

KALIB, SHOLOM (1929–), *ḥazzan* and musicologist. Kalib was born in Dallas, Texas, and studied cantorial music with his father Morris Kalib. He also studied in Chicago with the *ḥazzanim* Todros Greenberg and Joshua Lind, both of whose cantorial compositions he later edited. He studied at Northwestern University and received a doctorate in music. In 1969 he was appointed professor of music at Eastern Michigan University and from 1977 was *ḥazzan* in Flint, Michigan. Kalib composed music for Sabbath and High Holiday services and wrote ḥasidic melodies. His *Days of Awe*, a concert rendition of the High Holiday service, was recorded with the Beth Abraham Youth Chorale conducted by Jerome B. Kopmar. His magnum opus as a musicologist is his five-volume *Musical Tradition of the Eastern European Synagogue*, which makes available a single, definitive resource for the vast musical, cultural, and historic legacy of the Eastern European synagogue.

[Akiva Zimmerman / Raymond Goldstein (2nd ed.)]

KALICH, BERTHA (1875–1939), U.S. actress born in Poland. She was the first outstanding Yiddish actress to win recognition on the English-speaking stage. Bertha Kalich trained for opera in Lemberg and later appeared in the Bucharest National Theater. Offered a leading role in *La Dame Blanche* at the Romanian Imperial Theater in 1894, she learned Romanian in three months and received an ovation for her performance.

She reached New York in 1895 and appeared in Yiddish repertory which included Ibsen's *Doll's House* and Tolstoy's *Kreutzer Sonata.* Her performance in Sardou's *Fedora* in English in 1905 led to a contract with Harrison Grey Fiske, who engaged her to appear in Maeterlinck's *Monna Vanna.* She remained under his management until 1910, and then acted for Lee Shubert in *Sappho* (1912) and *Rachel* (1913), and repeated in English some of her Yiddish successes, such as *The Riddle Woman* (1918) and *Magda* (1926).

[David S. Lifson]

KALICHSTEIN, JOSEPH (1946–), Israeli pianist. Born in Tel Aviv, Kalichstein studied with Prof. Sher at the Ḥolon Conservatory. In 1962, he moved to the U.S. to study with Edward Steuermann and Ilona Kabos at the Juilliard School in New York. Kalichstein won the Young Concert Artists Award (1967) and the Leventritt Award in 1969. His extraordinary technique, coupled with a superb musical sensibility, made him a favorite with leading conductors and orchestras in the U.S., Europe, Japan, Australia, and Latin America. Kalichstein toured widely in a trio with the violinist Jaime Laredo and the cellist Sharon Robinson from 1976. Together with the Guarneri Quartet they presented Brahms' complete works for piano and strings in New York in 1983 to celebrate the 150th anniversary of the composer's birth. Their rapport, intimacy, and sense of communication earned the trio tremendous acclaim.

ADD. BIBLIOGRAPHY: Grove online.

[Uri Toeplitz and Yohanan Boehm / Naama Ramot (2nd ed.)]

KALIK, MIKHAIL (Moshe; 1927–), Russian film director. The son of an actor, Kalik graduated in 1949 from the art history faculty of the State Institute of Cinematography in Moscow. From 1951 to 1954 he was imprisoned in a "corrective-labor" camp, having been sentenced for "Jewish bourgeois nationalism." After graduating from the Institute's directing faculty in 1958, he became one of the representatives of the so-called "poetic cinema," a significant aspect of the new wave in Soviet art in the early 1960s. Together with B. Rytsarev he made the film *Yunost' nashikh otsov* ("Youth of Our Fathers," 1958), adapted from the novel *Razgrom* ("The Rout") by Fadeyev in which the appearance of the Jewish hero Levinson was stressed, and *Ataman Kodr* ("The Cossack Leader Kodr," 1959). Kalik included scenes with Jewish characters in his films *Kolbel'naya* ("Cradle Song," 1960), and *Chelovek idet za solntsem* ("Man Goes Beyond the Sun," 1962). In his film *Do svidaniya, mal'chiki* ("Goodbye, Boys," 1965), Kalik partially relied on his personal experience to depict the tragic fate of his generation. One of the film's three heroes, a Jewish youth, is arrested during the Doctors' Plot and perishes in prison. Despite his successes and prizes, he was not allowed to make films on Jewish themes, for example, about *Korczak. His television film *Tsena* ("The Price," 1969), based on the play by Arthur *Miller, was shown with the name of Kalik omitted from the credits several years after he immigrated to Israel in 1971 after a long struggle.

In Israel Kalik directed *Three Men and a Girl* (1975) based on short stories by Gorky, several short films, and a video-documentary about the country, which was shown at the entrance to the Israeli pavilion at the Moscow International Book Fair in 1987. In 1991 he made the autobiographical *And the Wind Returneth.*

[E. Kapitaikin / *The Shorter Jewish Encylopaedia in Russian*]

KALIKOW, PETER S. (1943–), U.S. real-estate executive, civic official. Born in New York City and a graduate of Hofstra University, Kalikow began his career in real estate in 1967 with the family's 75-year-old company. He became president of H.J. Kalikow & Co. in 1973. The company, with his father at the helm, had concentrated on building middle-class housing in the borough of Queens. Following his father's death in 1982, he assumed responsibility for all Kalikow holdings, which included vast swaths of Manhattan residential and commercial buildings. He brought it into the big-time business of office and cooperative apartment development in Manhattan. Branching out, Kalikow in 1988 bought the *New York Post*, the oldest daily newspaper in the United States, from Rupert Murdoch, for about $37.6 million (he later sold the paper back to Murdoch). But in 1991, Kalikow, once one of the wealthiest individuals in the United States, filed for personal bankruptcy protection. Burdened by debt taken on to expand his empire, Kalikow was forced to put up some of his property partnerships and other businesses as collateral during a wide-ranging reorganization. At the time Kalikow and his companies had more than $1 billion in debt, some of which he defaulted on.

In 1994 Kalikow was appointed to the board of the Metropolitan Transportation Authority, an agency that oversees New York's subways, bridges and tunnels, and commuter railroads, by Gov. Mario M. Cuomo, and served for a little more than a year. Gov. George E. Pataki appointed him to be vice chairman of the MTA in 1999 and he became chairman in 2001. The organization provides mass transit to nearly 8 million riders each weekday and moves nearly 300 million vehicles through bridges and tunnels a year.

Kalikow was involved in numerous real estate, health, and philanthropic activities. In 1982 he was awarded the Peace Medal, the State of Israel's highest civilian award, for his many years in aiding Israel's development. In 1987 he was honored by the American Jewish Committee and in 1989 the Anti-Defamation League awarded him and his wife its first annual Jacob K. Javits award for outstanding accomplishment. He was a member of the board of trustees of New York's Museum of Jewish Heritage: A Living Memorial to the Holocaust and served on the board of the Jewish National Fund.

In 1995 he received the Jerusalem 3000 Award from the State of Israel Bonds for his chairmanship of the real-estate division for eight years.

[Stewart Kampel (2nd ed.)]

KALILA AND DIMNA, a cycle of fables which originated in *India in the third century C.E. and were collected and compiled in Kashmir. In the course of centuries the cycle has gone through numerous changes, especially as a result of having been translated into many languages: Persian, Arabic, Hebrew, Syriac, Ethiopian, Malay, Mongolian, Greek, and many European languages. Most of the translators also acted as adaptors and added material of their own. The story was greatly expanded and revised in the seventh century when Abdallah ibn al-Muqaffaʿ translated it into Arabic from the Persian adaptation, i.e., from Pahlavi. In the 12th century this Arabic translation was the basis for the story's translation and adaptation into Hebrew by an author about whom nothing is known except his name, Joel. In the 13th century the poet *Jacob b. Eleazar not only translated the story into Hebrew, but also adapted it into rhymed rhetoric. Since the original source has been lost, these medieval Hebrew translations are of great importance in studying the textual changes in the story during succeeding generations. The apostate *John of Capua's 13th-century Latin translation of the story (*Directorium Vitae*), from which most European translations have been made, was executed in accordance with Joel's Hebrew translation. In 1881 both Hebrew translations, which had over centuries become deficient because of copying errors, were published in Paris, Joel's work being accompanied by Joseph Derenbourg's French translation. A new Hebrew translation from the Arabic was made by Abraham *Elmaleh and appeared in Tel Aviv in 1927.

In both content and form the story resembles other books that have come down from Indian sources, i.e., stories whose bare outlines had been fleshed out by the addition of new material or the substitution of new stories for old ones. *Kalila and Dimna* comprises a collection of moral fables and fables about birds and animals, Kalila and Dimna being the names of two foxes. The story, in outline, tells of a physician named Barzoyeh, who, at the behest of the king of *Persia, sought plants whose juice would not only bring health to the sick but immortality as well. Ultimately, the physician learns that such "plants" are really symbols for the books of wisdom which help man achieve perpetual life. Barzoyeh told the king of his discovery and the king ordered "all those books to be collected from every native and every traveler, and to be brought to the king's treasury." It is said that from these collected wisdom books, *Kalila and Dimna*, the essence of wisdom and morality, was compiled. The major part of the book is constituted by the king's queries and the replies of the philosopher Sindbar, or in Jacob b. Eleazar's translation, *Dod Ḥokhmah* (lit. "lover of wisdom," the Hebrew equivalent of philosopher). Some editions of the book including, apparently, the Hebrew translations, were accompanied by pictures.

BIBLIOGRAPHY: J. Derenbourg, *Deux Versions Hébraïques du Livre de Kalîâ et Dimnâh* (1881); Schirmann, Sefarad, 2 (1960²), 209–37, 690–1; Zinberg, Sifrut, 1 (1955), 208–13.

[Abraham Meir Habermann]

KALININDORF (until 1927, **Bolshaya Seidemenukha**, from the Heb. שְׂדֵה מְנוּחָה), Jewish settlement in Ukraine; one of the first four Jewish agricultural colonies to be founded in the province of Kherson in 1807. After several decades of hardship caused by droughts and the distant attitude of Russian clerks nominated to help and supervise, the settlement became a Jewish village whose inhabitants engaged in agriculture. In 1897 there were 1,786 Jewish inhabitants (81% of the population), most of them farmers with a few being artisans. From 1924 there was an influx of settlers into the vicinity and many lived temporarily in the settlement. By 1926 there were 2,400 Jews (89.3% of the population) living in the locality, and by 1939 the numbers had dropped to 1,879 (of a total 3,126). On March 22, 1927, Kalinindorf became the center of the first autonomous Jewish region in the Soviet Union. It had 11 county councils, eight of them Jewish, and 49 settlements, 39 of them Jewish. In 1927 there were in the region 15,833 Jews (87% of the total population), with the figures dropping to 7,717 (40% of the total) in 1939. The main cause was the severe crisis during the process of collectivization (1930–32), and many of the settlers left. In 1932 it comprised over 72,000 hectares of land. The largest villages were then the settlements of Kalinindorf (population 902), *Bobrovy Kut (832), Lvova (702), and Sterndorf (formerly called Malaya Seidemenukha, 503 inhabitants). During the 1920s a Jewish elementary school operated, enlarged later to a junior high, and in the 1930s there were a Jewish agricultural high school and a teachers' college. About 2,000 (in 1932), almost all Jewish children of the region, attended Jewish schools. During the 1930s a daily, *Kolvirt Emes*, was published in the area. Kalinindorf was occupied by the Germans on August 27, 1941. Some Jews succeeded in escaping. On September 17, 1,423 Jews were killed. A few days later Jews from neighboring villages, like Shterendorf and Judendorf, were brought there and murdered. More than 4,100 Jews were killed in the region during the Nazi occupation. After World War II Kalinindorf was rehabilitated, but most of its inhabitants were non-Jews; it was renamed Kalininskoye and the Jewish Autonomous Region was abolished.

BIBLIOGRAPHY: J. Lezman, *Fun Seydemenukhe biz Kalinindorf* (1932); I. Sudarski, *Kalinindorfer Rayon* (1932); E. Gordon, *In di Yidishe Kolvirth* (1940), 21–29; O. Heller, *Die Untergang des Judentums* (1931), 298–300; *Ḥakla'im Yehudim be-Arvot Rusyah* (1965).

[Yehuda Slutsky / Shmuel Spector (2nd ed.)]

KALINKOVICHI, townlet in Polesye district, Belarus. In 1811 there were 108 Jews, and in 1897 their number grew to 1,341. All inhabitants of the town were then Jews. Many of them traded in flour, and others worked in crafts. The invalid Jewish author Joseph Ḥayyim Dorozhka (1869–1919), who lived in Kalinkovichi, was the leading spirit behind an attempt made during 1911–12 to introduce Hebrew as the spoken language of the town. For this purpose, a network of Hebrew schools was established. The townlet suffered heavily at the end of the Civil War (1920). In March 1920 the Polish soldiers staged a pogrom, and on November 10, 1920, Balakhovich's gang killed 32 Jews. At that time many Jews from the surrounding district flocked to the town. The 3,106 Jews living in Kalinkovichi in 1926 constituted about half of the total population, and in 1939 it reached 3,386 Jews (out of a total population of 9,799). From 1923 there was a Yiddish school, with 397 pupils enrolled in 1930. Classes for adult studies were also available at this time. Shlome *Simon, who was born there, described the town in *Vortslen* (1956) and *Tsvaygn* (1960). The Jewish Soviet poet Zalman Telesin was also a native of Kalinkovichi. The Germans occupied Kalinkovichi on August 22, 1941. Many Jews had fled before. On September 22, 1941, the remaining 700 were murdered by the Nazis. The last synagogue was closed down in 1960, after 10 of the 20 "aldermen" responsible for its upkeep were compelled to sign a letter accusing the Jews of organizing illegal activity within the synagogue.

BIBLIOGRAPHY: Z. Baharow, in: *He-Avar*, 16 (1969), 245–52; Z. Epstein, *Y.Ḥ. Dorozhka* (Heb., 1934).

[Yehuda Slutsky / Shmuel Spector (2nd ed.)]

KALIR, AVRAHAM (1903–1985), Israeli industrialist. Born in Bukovina, he immigrated to Israel in 1934, where he devoted himself to the development of the textile industry. Kalir is a pioneer in developing industrial projects in new development areas in the country, introducing modern technological methods. He distinguished himself in developing human relations in his enterprises and programs of technological training and instruction. In 1962 he became the chairman of the Israel Manufacturers Association, serving on its board for 20 years. In 1976 he was awarded the Industrial Prize by the Manufacturers Association. He was also active in security and defense matters prior to the establishment of the State of Israel and after that time contributed to the development of cultural and educational institutions. In 1961 he was one of the founders of the Beit Tzvi school for stage arts, named after his son Tzvi Kalir, who died during the War of Independence. Subsequently he served on the boards of directors of Bank Leumi and the Dead Sea Works. He also served on the boards of the Technion, the Hebrew University, and ORT. In 1978 he was named director of Bank Leumi's special fund for social projects. He was awarded the Israel Prize in 1977 for achievements in industry and social activities. In 1985 he was selected as one of the torchbearers in Israel's Independence Day ceremonies, representing industrialists.

[Shaked Gilboa (2nd ed.)]

KALISCH, DAVID (1820–1872), German playwright and humorist. Kalisch was born in Breslau. After a brief business career, he visited Paris in 1844 and there associated with a group of poets and socialists, among them Heinrich *Heine, Georg Herwegh, and Karl Marx. When his funds were exhausted he returned to Germany and in 1846 started writing comic sketches and farces for various theaters, first in Leipzig and later in Berlin. The couplets of his comedy *Einmal Hunderttausend Taler* (1847) became extremely popular. In 1848 Kalisch founded the humorous and satirical weekly *Kladderadatsch* and edited it together with Ernst Dohm and Rudolf Löwenstein. This periodical spread his fame quickly throughout the German-speaking world. His successful farces and light comedies, some of which he wrote in collaboration with other playwrights, were popular on the Berlin stage for many years. His humorous writings were collected in *Berliner Volksbuehne*, 4 vols. (1864), and *Lustige Werke*, 3 vols. (1870).

BIBLIOGRAPHY: M. Ring, *David Kalisch* (Ger., 1873). **ADD. BIBLIOGRAPHY:** R. Freydank, *Theater in Berlin* (1988), 270–84; H.P. Bayerdörfer, in: R. Schöwerling (ed.), *Die fuerstliche Bibliothek Corvey*, (1992), 294–318.

[Sol Liptzin / Noam Zadoff (2nd ed.)]

KALISCH, MARKUS MORITZ (1825–1885), Hebraist and biblical commentator. Kalish was born in Treptow, Pomerania and studied at the Berlin University, where he graduated in 1848, and the Rabbinical College of Berlin. He was active in the struggle for freedom in Europe which resulted in the *emeute* of 1848 and as a result had to leave Germany; he settled in England, where he remained until his death. He was appointed secretary to Chief Rabbi N.M. *Adler, holding the post from 1848 to 1853, after which he served as tutor and literary adviser to the Rothschild family, a post in which he was able to devote himself to biblical scholarship and Hebrew grammar. He contemplated writing a comprehensive commentary on the Pentateuch, giving a resumé of Jewish and Christian scholarship to date, but completed only the first three volumes, Exodus (1885), Genesis (1858), and Leviticus (Part 1, 1867; Part 2, 1872), in the last of which he anticipated *Wellhausen to a considerable extent. Other publications were a Hebrew grammar in two parts and Bible studies on the book of Jonah (1876) and on the prophecies of Balaam (1877). In 1880 there appeared his last work *Path and Goal: A Discussion on the Elements of Civilization and the Conditions of Happiness*, consisting of an attempt to combine the views of the representatives of the main religions.

BIBLIOGRAPHY: *Jewish Chronicle* (August 28, 1885); *The Times* (August 31, 1885); S. Morais, *Eminent Israelites* (1880), 170–173; A. Rofe, *The Book of Balaam* (1979), 42–45. **ADD BIBLIOGRAPHY:** ODNB online.

KALISCHER, JUDAH LEIB BEN MOSES (d. 1822), *av bet din* in Lissa. The head of the yeshivah of Lissa for many years, Kalischer was referred to as "the sharp sword" on account of his profound acumen in the study of the Talmud. He was the author of *Ha-Yad ha-Ḥazakah* (Breslau, 1820), novellae and casuistic discussions on 27 sections in talmudic law dealing with *ḥazakah ("presumption"). In the work he stresses that "I have come to understand and learn, but not to give decisions." His glosses to the Talmud have remained in manuscript. Kalischer was on friendly terms with Akiva *Eger. Kalischer had five sons, of whom one, ABRAHAM MOSES (d. 1812), was a son-in-law of Akiva Eger and served as rabbi of Schneidemuehl, dying there at an early age. One of his novellae is quoted at the end of the *Ha-Yad ha-Ḥazakah*.

BIBLIOGRAPHY: Fuenn, Keneset, 419; L. Lewin, *Geschichte der Juden in Lissa* (1904), 278–82.

[Josef Horovitz]

KALISCHER, ẒEVI HIRSCH (1795–1874), rabbi and harbinger of the Zionist idea. Born in Lissa (Leszno), Posen district, Kalischer studied under the great scholars of his day, Jacob of Lissa (Lorberbaum) and Akiva Eger. In 1824 he settled in Thorn, where he lived until his death, rejecting invitations from many communities to serve as their rabbi. Even in Thorn he served only as unpaid acting rabbi and lived off the meager income supplied by his wife's small business. He published books on *halakhah* (*Even Boḥan; Moznayim la-Mishpat*, 1843–55) and on religious philosophy (*Emunah Yesharah*, 1843), and contributed to the Hebrew press for many years. (Before the existence of a regular Hebrew press, his articles were published in German translation in the German-Jewish press.) His major activity, however, throughout his life, was advocating the idea of mass settlement of European Jewry in Ereẓ Israel. In his discussions with members of the Reform movement on the observance of religious precepts, the belief in the coming of the Messiah, the *mitzvot* connected with Ereẓ Israel, etc., Kalischer revealed not only his strong attachment to religious tradition but also his preoccupation with the problems of the day.

As early as his meeting with Anschel *Rothschild in 1836, Kalischer revealed his opinion that the redemption of Israel would not come, as had been believed for generations, through a miracle, that "suddenly God would come down from the heavens or suddenly send His messiah," but rather that salvation would be brought about by human endeavor. He stressed the idea that the natural redemption would serve as the first and main stage before the miraculous redemption at the end of days. This was a revolutionary departure from over 1,000 years of Jewish thinking about redemption. His system initially included the observance of the *mitzvot* connected with Ereẓ Israel, especially those of sacrifice, as basic steps toward the future redemption, but at a later stage he disregarded this element in his ideology. Indeed, he wrote to Rothschild detailing the halakhic issues involved in renewing the practice of sacrifice on the Temple Mount. Shortly thereafter, Kalischer corresponded at length with his former teacher Akiba *Eger about the sanctity of the Temple Mount, the problems regarding the laws of purity and the genealogies of the priests. Unfortunately for Kalischer, Eger, who opposed Kalischer's ideas, died in 1837 before they could come to a resolution. Following Judah *Alkalai, he based his doctrine on the talmudic saying "It [the coming of the Messiah] depends solely on the return [to God]" (Sanh. 97b), interpreting the word "return" as return to Ereẓ Israel. He based this interpretation on *Tikkunei Zohar*. Thus he introduced an active human element into the concept of the redemption of the Jewish people, in opposition to most of the Orthodox rabbis of the time, who objected to this interpretation and its practical implications. His urge to gather supporters for the return to Ereẓ Israel was reinforced by the various national movements in Europe, which were specifically cited by Kalischer. Pointing to the struggles of European nations to achieve independence, Kalischer chastised his fellow Jews for being the only people without such an aspiration. He was particularly critical of the Reform Jews who tried to emulate the gentile lifestyle. Kalischer urged them to emulate gentile nationalism as well by returning to the Jewish homeland, Ereẓ Israel. Kalischer was a realist. He was aware that only a catastrophic event or the very slow process of education would change the attitudes of Europe's Jews. However, he felt that the mid-nineteenth century was ripe for this change, for there were enough wealthy Jewish leaders who could influence the European political leadership without begging for their mercy and good will. After Rothschild gave a noncommittal response, Kalischer approached Moses *Montefiore. Unfortunately, his correspondence with Montefiore has not survived. Nevertheless, the result was the same lukewarm response that did not produce any practical results.

Practical activities for the settlement in Ereẓ Israel did not come into being until 1860, when Ḥayyim *Lorje established the first society for this purpose in Frankfurt on the Oder and Kalischer supported it. The society quickly attracted many of the leaders of the European Jewish community. Among them were Albert *Cohen, R. Joseph Blumenthal of Paris, R. Nathan *Adler of London, S.J. *Finn of Vilna, R. Judah *Alkalai and Dov Meisels, chief rabbi of Budapest. The society did not last long, basically because of the eccentric personality of its leader, but it did manage to publish Kalischer's book *Derishat Ẓiyyon* (1862), which for many years served as the basic book to explain the idea of the return to Ereẓ Israel to Orthodox groups (the book came out in a number of editions, was translated into German, and portions of it were translated into English and other languages). In the book, Kalischer expounded at length his theory that redemption would come in two stages: the natural one, return to Ereẓ Israel and labor – particularly agricultural – in the country, and the supernatural one to follow. The first stage would invigorate the *yishuv* and put it on a healthy economic foundation instead of its dependence upon donations from abroad (*ḥalukkah*). In his program he did not ignore the unstable security situation (this argument was used against him mainly by the rabbis in Ereẓ Israel), and he devoted one paragraph especially to the necessity of appointing guards trained for war and police duty. He also envisioned the establishment of an agricultural school for the younger generation. The book had a great influence on, inter alia, Moses *Hess, who included portions of it in German translation in his book *Rome and Jerusalem*. Even though the society founded by Lorje collapsed, it left Kalischer with numerous contacts and key friendships. One was with Rabbi Joseph Natank of Hungary, who became a loyal and assiduous worker on Kalischer's behalf. From the time Kalischer published *Derishat Ẓiyyon*, his life was devoted to traveling through Europe in order to enlist the support of Jewish groups for his idea. He tried to win leading Jewish personalities over to his plan. He also published sermonizing articles in many Hebrew newspapers and journals. At the same time he continued his writing in the field of *halakhah* as well as his struggle against those who, in his opinion, undermined the foundations of religious tradition. He also found himself disputing with the rabbis who objected to his ideas on religious grounds, and especially with the rabbis in Ereẓ Israel, who also brought up the argument that conditions, especially of security, in Ereẓ Israel were not yet ripe for beginning agricultural settlement. Their vigorous opposition was also based on theological objections to Kalischer's view of redemption. At the same time, they feared that mass settlement would lead to the lessening of their authority. Kalischer stood his ground even before the great rabbis of his time. He distinguished between philanthropy on behalf of Ereẓ Israel, in which German Orthodox rabbis were active, and settlement activity of redeeming value in the future. Thus he adopted a critical attitude toward the building of houses in Jerusalem at the beginning of the 1860s (the "*Battei Maḥaseh*" in the Old City), as he saw this project as a private endeavor and not promoting the "main objective." He believed that only agriculture on a large scale could serve as a stable solution for both the *yishuv* and the victims of persecution in Europe. Kalischer saw a small beginning of his ideal realized toward the end of his life when the agricultural school was opened at Mikveh Israel (1870) and even thought of settling there at the invitation of the school's director, Charles *Netter, to supervise the observance of the *mitzvot* connected with Ereẓ Israel, but his desire was not realized. His son Ze'ev Wolf continued Kalischer's activity and, at his initiative, a tract of land near Rachel's tomb was purchased from the funds in Kalischer's estate. A selection of his Zionist writings was published together with an introduction by G. Kressel (1943). All his Zionist writings were collected with an introduction by I. Klausner (1947). Both collections have full bibliographies.

In practical terms, there was little difference between Kalischer's plans and those of Herzl: A Jewish state based on agriculture, with its own police and army. So why did Kalischer fail to start a mass Zionist movement? Kalischer was a bit of an anomaly. East European Orthodox Jews thought that his messianic ideas were too modern and were thus afraid that they might lead to assimilation. West European Jews saw him as an East European rabbi who spoke and wrote using a talmudic and rabbinic idiom that was foreign to them.

BIBLIOGRAPHY: J. Katz, in: L. Jung, *Guardians of Our Heritage 1724–1953* (1958), 207–28; N. Sokolow, *Hibbath Zion* (Eng., 1935), index; A. Hertzberg, *The Zionist Idea* (1960), 108–14; A.I. Bromberg, *Ha-Rav Ẓ.H. Kalischer* (1960). **ADD. BIBLIOGRAPHY:** J.E. Myers, *Seeking Zion: Modernity and Messianic Activism in the Writings of Tsevi Hirsch Kalisher* (2003); Y. Asaf, "*Reshit Hitgavveshutah shel Ortodoksiyah Le'ummit ba-Me'ah ha-19: Ha-Mikreh shel ha-Rav Ẓevi Hirsch Kalischer*" (Dissertation, 2002); S.N. Lehman-Wilzig, in: *Tradition*, 16:1 (1976) 56–76; I. Klausner, in: *In the Dispersion*, 5–6 (1966), 281–89; M.N. Penkower, in: *Judaism*, 33:3 (1984), 289–95; Y. Salmon, in: *Danzig, Between East and West: Aspects of Modern Jewish History* (1985), 123–37; idem, in: *Ereẓ Yisrael be-Hagut ha-Yehudit be-Et ha-Ḥadashah* (1998), 424–46; D. Koliv, in: *Ge'ulah u-Medinah: Ge'ulat Yisrael – Ḥazon u-Meẓi'ut* (1979), 293–303; M. Hildesheimer, in: *Sefer Avi'ad: Koveẓ Ma'amarim u-Meḥkarim le-Zekher Yeshayahu Wolfsberg-Avi'ad* (1986), 195–214; M.S. Samet, in: *Cathedra*, 33 (1985), 54–56; A.H. Shishah, in: *ibid.*, 38 (1986), 195–200; J. Ticker in: *Working Papers in Yiddish and East European Studies*, 15 (1975); E. Segel, *Jewish Free Press* (March 30, 2000), 14–15; http://www.wzo.org.il/en/resources/view.asp?id=1338&subject=70.

[Getzel Kressel / David Derovan (2nd ed.)]

KALISZ (Ger. **Kalisch; Kalish**), city in Poznan province, W. Poland; it had the most ancient community in Poland. The first Jews to arrive there, in the last third of the 12th century, were minters. They served Mieszko III the Oldster, prince of Great Poland (1127–1202), and his descendants. A large group of Jews from the Rhineland and other parts of Germany arrived in Kalisz by way of Silesia in the middle of the 13th century and received protection from the ruler. They established a settlement in the city of Kalisz, and engaged in financial activity and commerce. They were among the initiators of the Statute of Kalisz issued by *Boleslav V the Pious in 1264, which they apparently helped to draft. In 1287 the elders of the community (*judei seniores Kalisienses*) bought a plot of land from the owner, Rupinus, on which a cemetery was established. In the middle of the 14th century there existed a "Jewish street" in the city which was the center of varied financial activities. At the time of the *Black Death in 1349 the Jews in Kalisz suffered from persecutions. In 1358 the heads of the community obtained permission from King *Casimir III the Great to establish a synagogue; its erection was begun immediately, and it remained standing until 1857 when it was destroyed by fire. In 1364 the head of the Kalisz community, Falk, obtained Casimir's ratification of the charter of privileges for the Jews of Poland.

Apart from *moneylending, during the 15th and 16th centuries the Jews of Kalisz engaged in commerce with Cracow and Breslau, and in crafts including goldsmithing, tailoring, and butchery. The Jewish quarter was extended, and the community grew with the addition of immigrants and refugees from Bohemia (1542), Hungary, and Germany. During the 15th century many Jews in Kalisz moved to new settlements in other towns in Poland. At the beginning of the 16th century the Kalisz community was headed by a *kahal* administered by three to five *parnasim*.

Anti-Jewish disorders broke out in Kalisz in 1542 owing to the Jewish commercial competition with the townsmen. A *Host libel involving the Jews in Kalisz occurred in 1557. In 1565 the Kalisz community applied to the king for justice with a claim against the municipality for damages and desecration of the synagogue which had occurred during a mob outbreak that year. At the end of the 16th century wealthy Jews of Kalisz engaged in extensive commercial activities at the fairs of Lublin, Cracow, and Poznan, and also with towns in Silesia. In 1580–81, they conveyed through the local customs station approximately 4,500 hides, 13,500 kg. wool, 4,000 kg. wax, and 70 kg. pepper, among other merchandise. Apart from this elite there existed a poorer stratum of Jews in Kalisz; in 1579 about one-third of the Jews of the city had not paid their taxes because they were in financial straits.

The Kalisz community was severely affected by the cataclysm in Poland in the middle of the 17th century. Hundreds of Jewish refugees from south and east Poland passed through Kalisz in 1648–49 escaping from the *Chmielnicki massacres. In 1659, toward the end of the war between Sweden and Poland, hundreds of Jews were killed in Kalisz and the Jewish quarter was razed by the troops of S. *Czarniecki. The Kalisz community was rehabilitated within a short time through the prompt assistance given it by the Jews of Poznan, *Leszno, and *Krotoszyn. By 1670 it was able to give asylum to refugees from Vienna. King John III Sobieski ratified the privileges of the Jews of Kalisz in 1676, and in 1678 the Sejm (diet) granted them tax reliefs to assist them to overcome a severe financial crisis. In the last third of the 17th century many Jews of Kalisz did business at the fairs of Breslau and *Leipzig, exporting furs and hides, and importing costly cloth, metal ware, and precious stones. Apart from commerce, the Jews of Kalisz also engaged in crafts as tailors, furriers, goldsmiths, saddlers, smiths, engravers, bakers, and butchers. From 1672 Jewish craftsmen were obliged to join crafts associations.

During a fire which broke out in Kalisz in 1706, 45 Jews perished, and two years later 450 Jews lost their lives in a plague in the town. Many Jews became ruined after these calamities and the financial crisis, and in 1713 the community was obliged to borrow money from Christians in order to aid the needy. The position of the Jews in Kalisz became even more serious when Christian merchants in the 1720s organized themselves in a confraternity one of whose main objectives was to oppose Jewish commerce. The economic position of the Jews in Kalisz improved only in the second half of the 18th century due to their success in dealing in grain, cattle, sheep, wool, and cloth, and in the production and sale of alcoholic liquor. In 1761 the community arrived at an agreement with the municipal authorities by which the Jewish population was exempted from the duty of supporting soldiers in exchange for an annual payment of 1,200 zlotys. Following a *blood libel incited by extreme Catholic circles in 1763, four Jews were sentenced to death. There were 809 Jews who paid the poll tax in Kalisz in 1765. In 1786 among 207 craftsmen 101 were Jews.

In the second half of the 17th century Kalisz was an important spiritual center of Polish Jewry. The first rabbi known by name, Solomon Zalman b. Jeremiah Jacob, officiated there from 1639 to 1643. Israel b. Nathan Shapira (R. Israel ha-Darshan) who served as rabbi in the second half of the 17th century, established an important yeshivah there. He was followed until 1696 by *Judah b. Nissan, author of *Beit Yehudah*. From 1656 to 1683 Abraham Abele *Gombiner, author of *Magen Avraham*, served as *dayyan* there.

Within the framework of the *Councils of the Four Lands the communities of Kalisz, Poznan, Leszno (Lissa), and Krotoszyn, were the most important in the province of *Great Poland. In the second half of the 17th century the Kalisz community obtained the leadership of the provincial council, continuing to hold it until 1714 when the treasury of the council was transferred to the Leszno community. Representatives of the Kalisz community frequently served as *parnasim* of the Councils of Four Lands at the end of the 17th century and the beginning of the 18th. In 1737 the province of Poznan-Kalisz had the third-largest Jewish population in the kingdom of Poland (after the provinces of "Russia" and *Sandomierz-Krakow), and was responsible for 16% of the sum that the Jews of Poland were obliged to pay to the royal treasury.

When Kalisz was under Prussian rule (1793–1806), many Jews found employment in the expanding commerce and crafts, as well as in supplying the army. The number of Jews in the town had increased to 2,113 (c. 30% of the total population) in 1804. The struggle of the townsmen against the Jews now intensified, particularly after Kalisz was incorporated within Congress Poland in 1815. In 1827, under pressure by the local authorities, the government ordered that the Jews of Kalisz should reside in a separate quarter (*rewir*) which existed until 1862 and was severely overcrowded. In addition, until this year Jews from other places were prohibited, under the czarist regulations concerning residence of Jews in the border zones, from settling in Kalisz to the border with Prussia. The Jewish population numbered 3,463 (29% of the total) in 1827, and 4,352 (36%) in 1857. In 1854 only 23 Jews had houses outside the Jewish quarter.

From the 1840s Jewish economic activity became more extensive. Up to 1861 Jewish merchants and contractors developed enterprises for wool weaving and tanning, and also traded in cotton, wool, and wine. After the economic standstill resulting from the Polish uprising (1863–64) came to an end, and following the opening of the railway (1871), Jews with capital opened factories for soap, candles, and liqueurs, and in the 1870s began to develop the lace industry in Kalisz which soon became celebrated on the Russian and Chinese markets. Toward the end of the 19th century and the beginning of the 20th, Jewish manufacturers established modern textile works and knitting factories for mass-produced socks, as well as a toy factory (for dolls). The Jewish population in Kalisz numbered 7,580 (32% of the total) in 1897, and 14,318 (36%) in 1908; among the 67 factories in Kalisz that year, 32 were Jewish-owned. A Jewish hospital was founded in Kalisz in 1836 by the industrialist L. Mamroth, on the initiative of the physician Michael Morgenstern, which continued to exist until 1939. A Jewish school with Russian as the language of instruction was founded in Kalisz in 1875, in which 150 pupils were registered that year. In 1878 anti-Jewish riots occurred in the town, provoked by religious fanatics in which many peasants took part;

13 Jews were killed and damage caused to Jewish property in the city amounted to 200,000 rubles. From 1881 on, the Russian authorities organized frequent expulsions from Kalisz of Jews who were German or Austrian citizens. By the beginning of the 20th century there was a large stratum of Jewish workers in Kalisz, who in 1909 numbered over 3,000, including apprentices and hired workers employed in workshops. Toward the end of the 19th century and beginning of the 20th century *Ḥasidism gained influence in Orthodox circles in Kalisz, especially the Hasidim of Gur (*Gora Kalwaria), Kotsk (see Menahem Mendel of *Kotsk), and *Warka. Progressive circles established their own synagogue in 1911. Among rabbis of Kalisz in the 19th and 20th centuries were Solomon b. Akiva *Eger (1835–40), Elijah Ragoler (1840–50), Ẓevi Hirsch *Chajes (1851–55), Meir b. Isaac *Auerbach (1855–60), Hayyim Eleazar Waks (1862–81), Samson Ornstein (1881–1902), and Ezekiel Lipschuetz (until 1932).

When the German army occupied Kalisz in August 1914, the soldiers — as a result of deliberate incitement without any military justification — set fire to about 150 Jewish houses in the center of the city. Thirty-three Jewish residents of Kalisz lost their lives in this action, and many fled from the city. Later, schools were established, including a Tahkemoni school directed by Jacob Shalom Engel, and a national religious school for girls, Havazelet.

After the establishment of Polish rule, members of the *Endecja party in Kalisz organized a pogrom there in March 1919 in which two Jews lost their lives. In order to defend themselves against antisemitic agitation, Jewish youth and workers there organized *self-defense groups at the end of 1919 and in 1920. The Jewish population of Kalisz numbered 15,566 (35% of the total) in 1921, and 19,248 in 1931. During the interwar period all the Jewish parties were active in the city, as well as trade associations of workers in the lace factories, to which both Jews and Poles belonged, and of garment workers, leather workers, porters, and others. In the municipal elections held in 1927, 11 Jews were elected among 34 members of the council. A Jewish secondary school was opened in 1916. There were three Yiddish schools in Kalisz in the 1920s and 1930s (belonging to CYSHO), founded by workers' parties. Periodicals published in Kalisz included a weekly of Zionist orientation, *Di Kalisher Vokh*, founded in 1919 and edited by M. Abramowitz, and an independent weekly, *Kalisher Lebn*, founded in 1927 by Dr. Fogelson, which continued as *Dos Naye Lebn* under the editorship of A. Mamelok until 1938. Between 1929 and 1937 *Agudat Israel published a weekly, *Kalisher Vokh*, under the editorship of Rabbi Littman. In the 1930s there were two synagogues and about 35 prayer-houses in Kalisz.

Antisemitic propaganda increased in Kalisz under the leadership of the Endecja party from 1933, and many attempts were made to impose an economic *boycott on Jewish businessmen and artisans there.

[Arthur Cygielman]

Holocaust Period

In 1939 there were over 20,000 Jews living in Kalisz (almost 50% of the total population). The Germans occupied Kalisz on Sept. 6, 1939. Jews were seized by the Germans in the streets for slave labor, and were subjected to confiscation of property. Measures were introduced imposing a curfew, and the wearing of the yellow *badge. The beards and earlocks of Orthodox Jews were cut off, Polish antisemites taking part in these activities with particular zeal. Over a short time about 20% of the local Jews managed to escape while 10,000 others were evicted from their homes in an *Aktion* on Nov. 20, 1939, to make room for Baltic *Volksdeutsche*. The evicted families were at first lodged in warehouses, but during the first two weeks of December were deported to the Lublin district of the General Government. Following the deportation several thousand additional Jews managed to escape from Kalisz and dispersed over many parts of Poland, including nearly 7,000 who found refuge in the *Warsaw ghetto (1940). The Germans established a labor camp in the nearby village of Kozminka where 1,300 able-bodied Jews were employed. By Jan. 1, 1940, 612 Jews remained in Kalisz, some of them craftsmen. In October 1940 the Germans murdered all those chronically ill in a nearby forest.

The Jewish community of Kalisz, reduced to some 400 able-bodied young people, was housed in three buildings, in which workshops were established. Some Jews were forced to dismantle the tombstones from the Jewish cemetery to be used for pavements. By the end of 1941, 200 Jews, including some children, were sent to the death camp at *Chelmno. A few months later the remaining Jews were sent to *Lodz ghetto, where the few Jews still in the Kozminka work camps were sent. Kalisz thus became **judenrein*.

The Jewish community numbered nearly 300 in 1946 after some of the survivors returned, but all eventually left. Several memorial books for the Kalisz community were published in Israel: *Sefer Kalish* (2 vols., Heb. and Yid., 1964–67); *The Kalish Book* (1968); and *Toledot Yehudei Kalish* (1961, by Y.D. Beit-Halevi).

[Danuta Dombrowska]

BIBLIOGRAPHY: Warsaw, Archiwum Glowne Akt Dawnych, *Komisja wojewósztwa Kaliskiego*, no. 50; *ibid.*, *Komisja rządowa do spraw wewnętrznych i duchowych*, vol. 2–4, nos. 1124–26; *ibid.*, *Księgi Kancelarskie*, no. 25, pp. 287–305; *ibid.*, *Ostrzeszków, Inscriptiones religioses*, vol. 55, no. 22 (= CAHJP, ḤM 2/1068, 2194–96, 703/1, 2/703/2 respectively); Lodz, Wojewódzkie Archiwum Państwowe, *Kancelaria gubernium Kaliskiego*, vol. 3, nos. 276–8, 343, 1499; *Rada opiekuńcza gubernium Kaliskiego*, nos. 88, 100, 129, 157, 172, 234; vol. 8, nos. 270–4 (= CAHJP, ḤM 7529, 7534 a–1, 8202a–c, respectively); Poznan, Wojewódzkie Archiwum Państwowe, *Kalisz*, nos. 47, 49 (= CAHJP, ḤM 2445); M. Bersohn, *Dyplomataryusz, dotyczący Żydów Polsce* (1910), nos. 96, 127, 161–2, 231, 250, 282, 358; R. Mahler, *Yidn in Amolikn Poyln in Likht fun Tsifern* (1958), index; B. Wasiutyński, *Ludność żydowska w Polsce w wiekach XIX I XX* (1930), 6, 10, 12, 26, 49, 50, 71, 176, 180, 185, 200, 210, 214; *Osiemnaście wieków Kalisza, studia i materialy…*, 2 vols. (1960); R. Rybasrski, *Handel i polityka handlowa Polski w XVI stuleciu*, 1 (1928), 35, 141–3, 157–9, 224–5; J. Caro, *Vortraege und Essays*

(1906), 124–5; M. Gumowski, in: BŻIH, 41 (1962), 10; A. Chodyński, *Dawne ustawy miasta Kalisza* (1875), 91–96; L. Lewin, *Beitraege zur Geschichte der Juden in Kalisch* (1909) = *Festschrift… A. Harkavy* (1908), 141–76; idem, *Die Landessynode der grosspolnischen Judenschaft* (1926), 42, 55, 59, 95, 104, 106, 116; I. Schiper, *Dzieje handlu żydowskiego na ziemiach polskich* (1937), index; F. Kuper and T. Lewicki, *Źródła hebrajskie do dziejów słowian* (1956), 152, 155; Y.D. Beit-Halevi, *Toledot Yehudei Kalish* (1961); *Sefer Kalish*, 2 vols. (1964–67); D. Dabrowska, *Kronika getta Lodzkiego*, vols. 1–2 (1965–1966), passim; idem, in: BŻIH, no. 13–14 (1955).

KALLAH (Heb. כַּלָּה; "bride"), one of the minor tractates appended to the end of the fourth order, *Nezikin*, in the printed texts of the Babylonian Talmud. There are two separate versions of the tractate. The shorter one consists of a single chapter while the larger version contains ten chapters and is known as *Kallah Rabbati*. Originally only the shorter tractate was known and it was published in the printed edition of the Talmud and the *Maḥzor Vitry*. The manuscript of the longer version was first published by Naḥman Coronel (Vienna, 1864), and subsequently printed in the *Romm (Vilna) edition of the Talmud. In three places the Babylonian Talmud cites the same passage, which mentions a tractate *Kallah* (Shab. 114a; Ta'an. 10b; Kid. 49b). It is related that a person is considered a disciple of the wise when he can answer any question of *halakhah* connected with his studies "even though it is on a subject dealt with in the *Kallah* tractate." Scholars are uncertain as to the exact meaning of this phrase. Some hold that the allusion is to this tractate, while others explain that the reference is to the semiannual assemblies of the Babylonian scholars which were termed *kallah* and at which a designated tractate was studied.

The smaller tractate of *Kallah* discusses the subject of betrothal, marriage, chastity, and moral purity both in thought and action. The subject matter of this treatise is culled from **beraitot* contained in the Babylonian Talmud. Its authorship was generally attributed to Yehudai Gaon (eighth century), but M. Higger concludes that the original *Kallah* was compiled by a disciple of *Eliezer b. Hyrcanus and that a later compiler added to it (intro. to M. Higger's edition of *Kallah*, 13).

The larger tractate of *Kallah Rabbati* resembles the format of the Talmud, consisting of *beraitot* and *Gemara*. According to N. Friedmann (*Seder Eliyahu Zuta*, introd. p. 15), it emanated from the school of *Rava in Maḥoza (Babylonia, third century). A. Aptowitzer, however, held that the author was Rava, a disciple of Yehudai Gaon (REJ 57 (1909), 239–48). Of the ten chapters comprising *Kallah Rabbati* only the first two discuss betrothal and marriage and they form a commentary to the shorter version of *Kallah*. Except for chapter 8, the remaining chapters form an amplification of *Derekh Ereẓ Rabbah* and *Derekh Ereẓ Zuta*. Chapter 8 is closely related to "the chapter on the acquisition of the Torah" or "the *baraita* of R. Meir" appended to *Pirkei Avot*. Much aggadic material is contained in this tractate, including the interesting stories of Akiva and the spirit of a deceased man (ch. 2); the four sages and the philosopher (ch. 7); Simeon b. Antipatros and his guests (ch. 9); and Akiva and the Athenian (ch. 10). A critical edition of the texts of *Kallah* and *Kallah Rabbati* was published by M. Higger in 1936. An English translation of these tractates was issued by Soncino Press in 1965.

KALLAH, MONTHS OF, a term for the months of Elul and Adar when, during the talmudic and geonic eras, large gatherings assembled to study Torah in the Babylonian academies. Many conjectures have been made about the etymology of the word *kallah*, but they are all doubtful (see Krauss, in *Tarbiz*, 20 (1949), 123ff. and bibliography). The custom of the institution of the *kallah* apparently began in Babylon in the third century. It is related that Rabbah b. Nahamani, head of the Pumbedita academy (end of the third and beginning of the fourth centuries), was calumniated to the government for hindering 12,000 people from paying their tax to the king during the two months of the *kallah*, since they refrained from work during this period (BM 86a). Rav Ashi stated that the gentiles of Mata Meḥasya, near Sura, were obdurate, since they saw the glory of the Torah twice a year, in the months of Adar and Elul, and yet remained unconverted (Ber. 17b). Besides the *benei kallah* (the "members of the *kallah*") who participated in the studies during the whole day, many of the ordinary people would come just for the public sermon and were called *benei pirkei* (Ket. 62a). The students devoted themselves diligently to their studies during the *kallah* months. Bibi b. Abbaye had not the time even to go over the weekly Bible portion "twice in Hebrew and once in the Targum," and would complete the reading on the eve of the Day of Atonement (Ber. 8b in Ms. readings and He-Arukh s.v. כל). Rav Naḥman (end of the third century) gave instructions that litigants who were members of the *kallah* were not to be summoned to appear before the courts during the *kallah* so as not to interrupt their studies (BK 113a). The Talmud mentions two heads of *kallah* by name: *Naḥman b. Isaac was the head of the *kallah* and Adda b. Abba used to "go over the discourse" with him every day before he went in to expound it in the *kallah* (BB 22a). It is said of Abbahu that he was one of the heads of the *kallah* of Refram (Ḥul. 49a). It is therefore evident that several heads of *kallah* served in that office during one *kallah* period.

During each *kallah* month the studies were one specific tractate, the "*kallah* tractate," which the head of the academy announced at the end of the previous *kallah*, so that each participant could study it during the months intervening between one *kallah* and the next. During the *kallah* month, the head of the academy would give a discourse on that tractate and reply to the queries of the students, and then one of the scholars among those sitting in the first row, "the heads of the *kallah*," would discuss the topic with the hearers until it was explained and clarified to all. In the last week of the *kallah* month the head of the academy would test and examine the permanent members of the academy, and if "he saw that one of them had not organized his studies … he would diminish his stipend, rebuke him, and reprimand him … as a result they applied themselves and occupied themselves well with their studies in order not to come to grief in a halakhic matter before him" (Neubauer, 2 (1895), 87–88).

These descriptions, and others known from R. Nathan ha-Bavli, describe mainly the arrangements in the academies in the geonic era, but they had their source at the beginning of the talmudic era and continued unchanged in Babylonia for centuries. According to one tradition (*ibid.*) the month of Adar was used for the clarification of the written queries which reached the Babylonian academies. During this month the queries which reached the heads of the academy from the communities in the Diaspora were brought out, and the scholars of the academy examined them together, finally arriving at the practical *halakhah*. After "the truth had become clear to them," the scribe committed the result to writing, and at the end of the month the head of the academy signed them and sent the replies to the inquirers. It is clear from other geonic sources, however, that during the rest of the year, too, replies were sent in answer to questions (S. Assaf, *Tekufat ha-Ge'onim ve-Sifrutah* (1955), 256–60). The institution of *kallah* months was unknown in Ereẓ Israel, and is mentioned neither in the Jerusalem Talmud, nor in any *baraita*. The phrase "and even in the *kallah* tractate" in the *beraitot* of tractates *Ta'anit* (10b) and *Kiddushin* (49b) was added in accordance with the custom of the time among the Babylonians (see the Mss. and the parallels in the Tosefta and the Jerusalem Talmud). Rashi explains the expression "tractate *kallah*" as referring to tractate *Kallah Rabbati* or to the festival *halakhot* on which they were accustomed to discourse before the festival (Shab. 114a; et al.). But the correct meaning is that given by Hai Gaon (*Sefer ha-Ittim*, 246–8) and others, that the months of Adar and Elul are meant (see also the supplement to the Tanḥuma, No'ah 3). In modern Israel a modified form of the *kallah* month was instituted by Rabbi J. Kahaneman at the Ponevezh yeshivah in Bene-Berak, and it spread to other centers.

BIBLIOGRAPHY: Neubauer, Chronicles, 2 (1895), 77–78; S. Schechter, *Saadyana* (1903), 118; Epstein, in: JQR, 12 (1921/22), 369ff.; Lauterbach, in: *Hebrew Union College Jubilee Volume* (1925), 211–22; Krauss, in: *Ha-Shilo'aḥ*, 43 (1924/25), 65–71; idem, in: *Livre d'Hommage à la mémoire… S. Poznański* (1927), 143–6 (Ger.); idem, in: *Tarbiz*, 20 (1948/49), 123–32; Hildesheimer, in: *Emet le-Ya'akov. Sefer Yovel… Y. Freimann* (1937), 58–71 (Heb. pt.); Assaf, Ge'onim, 256–60; S.K. Mirsky (ed.), *She'iltot de Rav Aḥai Ga'on* (1959), 8–10 (introd.); Ḥ. Albeck; *Mavo la-Talmudim* (1969), 12ff., 601–4; K.F. Tcorsh, *Keter Efrayim* (1967), 272–326.

[Yitzhak Dov Gilat]

KALLEN, HORACE MEYER (1882–1974), U.S. philosopher and educator. Kallen was born in Berenstadt, Silesia, Germany, the son of a rabbi, and was taken to the United States in 1887. Early in his career he taught at Harvard University (1908–11), Clark College (1910), and the University of Wisconsin (1911–18). He was one of the founders of the New School for Social Research in New York City and taught there 1919–52, serving as dean of the graduate faculty of political and social science, 1944–46. From 1952 to 1965 he was research professor there, and in 1965 he began teaching at Long Island University. Kallen was an active member of the Jewish community, working at such organizations as the American Jewish Congress, the American Association for Jewish education, of which he was vice president, and *YIVO. He served on many government committees, e.g., the Presidential Commission on Higher Education and the New York City Commission on Intergroup Relations (1961), and was active in such organizations as the International League for the Rights of Man and the Society for the Scientific Study of Religion. Kallen's philosophy has been characterized as Hebraism, aesthetic pragmatism, humanism, cultural pluralism, and cooperative individualism. Among its distinctive features is the stress on the variety of men and things in nature and society. Chance and individuality are primary in nature; law and group characteristics are secondary. Against the ancient Greek stress on fixity and eternity, Kallen's philosophy affirms the importance of time, change, becoming, and futurity. As a Hebraist he rejected predestination in any form. He believed in freedom of the will and in each individual's responsibility for his actions. Kallen's cultural pluralism affirms that each ethnic and cultural group in the United States has a special contribution to make to the variety and richness of American culture and, thus, provided a rationale for those Jews who wish to preserve their Jewish cultural identity in the American melting pot. He argued strongly for 60 years that the Jewish people need a homeland in Palestine to protect them against persecution and to enhance their Jewish cultural heritage. He also championed the ideal of a world in which all varieties of peoples and cultures will be able to live together, each one the equal of the others in its right to life, liberty, and the pursuit of happiness. According to Kallen, the goal of modern education and society is the creation of free men in an expanding free society. He warned that such a free society can be preserved only if moral conviction is accompanied by military strength. In the economic sphere he urged consumers' cooperatives as a protection against business exploitation. Kallen's aesthetics were concerned with the relations between beauty, use, and freedom in the context of each individual's experience. All ideas, values, deeds, tools, and methods are to be tested by their contribution to the satisfactions of human beings.

Although Kallen's philosophy was addressed to all mankind, he always affirmed his debt to the positive values of his Jewish inheritance. By affirming his integrity as a Jew he vindicated the integrity of the Jew as a man and thinker. His insistence on the link between thought and action led him into active participation in the extension of democracy at home and abroad, especially in relation to civil liberties and minority rights. Kallen's writings include, among many others, *The Book of Job as a Greek Tragedy* (1918); *Zionism and World Politics* (1921); *Judaism at Bay* (1932); *Individualism: An American Way of Life* (1933); *The Decline and Rise of the Consumer* (1936); *Art and Freedom* (2 vols., 1942); *The Education of Free Men* (1949); *Of Them Which Say They Are Jews* (1954), edited by J. Pilch, a collection of Kallen's essays on the Jewish struggle for survival; *Utopians at Bay* (1958) on his impressions of Israel; and *Liberty, Laughter and Tears* (1968).

BIBLIOGRAPHY: S. Hook and M.R. Konvitz (eds.), *Freedom and Experience; Essays Presented to Horace M. Kallen* (1947), includes bibliography; S. Ratner (ed.), *Vision and Action; Essays in Honor of Horace M. Kallen* (1953), includes bibliography; A. Hertzberg, *The Zionist Idea* (1960), 524–33.

[Sidney Ratner]

KALLENBACH, HERMANN (1871–1945), South African architect and intimate of *Gandhi. Kallenbach was born in East Prussia and studied architecture in Stuttgart and Munich. In 1896 he went to South Africa, where he practiced as an architect. In 1904 he met Mohandas Gandhi, who was then working in South Africa. He became his intimate friend and dedicated devotee. Abandoning the life of a wealthy, sport-loving bachelor, he adopted the vegetarian diet and simple lifestyle of Gandhi. In Gandhi's words, they became "soulmates" and, for a time, shared Kallenbach's home. Together with another Jew, H.S.L. Polak, Kallenbach was associated with Gandhi throughout the *Satyagraha* (non-violent resistance) struggle which lasted in South Africa until 1914.

In 1910 Kallenbach purchased a farm near Johannesburg as a commune for the families of Indian resisters who had been imprisoned. It was named Tolstoy Farm and Kallenbach joined Gandhi there. During the great *Satyagraha* march of Indians in 1913, he risked his personal safety to confront hostile whites in defense of the Indians. In November 1913 he was imprisoned together with Gandhi. Upon their release they both went to England. Kallenbach planned to accompany Gandhi to India, but with the outbreak of World War I, he was detained in England because of his German citizenship. After the war he returned to South Africa, where he resumed his work as an architect, but continued to correspond with Gandhi.

The rise of Nazism shocked Kallenbach into a rediscovery of his Jewish roots. He became a convinced Zionist, served on the Executive of the South African Zionist Federation, and planned to settle in Ereẓ Israel. At the request of Moshe Shertok (Sharett), Kallenbach visited Gandhi in May 1937 to enlist his sympathy and support for Zionism. In private conversations he gained the sympathy of Gandhi and his promise to take an interest in the Zionist cause. In his public statements, however, Gandhi continued to maintain a position unsympathetic to Zionism. Although disagreeing with Gandhi over Zionism and also in his (Kallenbach's) conviction that Hitler had to be resisted by violence, Kallenbach's deep friendship with Gandhi continued, and he visited him again in 1939. When Kallenbach died in 1945 he left a portion of his considerable estate for South African Indians, but the bulk was left for the benefit of Zionism. His large collection of books went to the Hebrew University, and his cremated remains were buried at Deganyah.

ADD. BIBLIOGRAPHY: I. Sarid and C. Bartolf, *Hermann Kallenbach – Mahatma Gandhi's Jewish Friend in South Africa: A Concise Biography* (1997).

[Gideon Shimoni]

KALLIR, ELEAZAR (Heb. אֶלְעָזָר בִּירְבִּי קַלִּיר, and קִילִיר; instead of אֶלְעָזָר, also the Palestinian form לְעָזָר), the greatest and most prolific of the early *paytanim*, and one of the most influential liturgical poets. He apparently lived in Ereẓ Israel and resided in Tiberias.

Works

Kallir wrote *piyyutim* for all the main festivals (sometimes more than one for the same festival), for the special Sabbaths, for weekdays of festive character, and for the fasts. The structures of his *yoẓer, kerovah, shivatah,* and *hoshana* poems, of his elegies, prayers for dew, and prayers for rain, which he often took from his predecessors and developed, have remained classic models. Poems written in his style are even called *Kalliri* after him. Kallir in his poetic writings drew on the didactic *aggadah*, thus preserving some otherwise forgotten aggadic traditions. Closely following the midrashic original in content, Kallir's poetic originality is expressed in his linguistic inventiveness. Probably the most audacious coiner of neologisms in Hebrew, Kallir was however very selective in his language and despite complicated poetic forms composed of intricate acrostics, interpolated with biblical verses, various types of rhyme, and auditory images, he rarely coined a word which did not fit the text. The new words, the many midrashic allusions, and the numerous errors in the extant texts of Kallir gave an aura of obscurity to Kallir's works, and thus commentaries to Kallir were written as early as the 11th century and perhaps even earlier; one of them is attributed to Rashi (cf. L. Ginzberg, and S. Klein, see bibl.). Kallir's *piyyutim* were widely known in the Orient, the Balkans, Italy, France, Germany, and Eastern Europe, and more than 200 are extant in various rites. The fact that more of his *piyyutim*, previously unknown, were found in the *Genizah* implies an even greater popularity than presumed. Several of these were published. A complete collection of Kallir's work, however, has not yet appeared.

Biography

Biographical facts about Kallir are shrouded in mystery. His name, country of birth, and when he lived are still unknown and can only be speculated upon. The assumption that *Natronai b. Hilai, *Gaon* of Sura in 857, mentions Kallir's poems is doubtful. *Saadiah b. Joseph Gaon quotes Kallir as one of the old *paytanim* (see bibl., A. Harkavy). According to a late (12th-century) source, Kallir was killed by his teacher *Yannai (see bibl., S.J. Rapoport and I. Davidson) who apparently was jealous of him. There is evidence that as early as the tenth century Kallir had already become a subject for legends.

Derivation of his Name

An old tradition derives the name Kallir (קַלִּיר) from *kalura* (Gr. κολλύρα), a cake that Jewish boys were given when they started school (*Arukh ha-Shalem* of *Nathan b. Jehiel, ed. by Kohut, s.v. קלר). Another interpretation holds that the name was derived from the poet's or his father's hometown: Cagliari in Sardinia, Calais, Cologne, Kallirrhoe in Transjordan (A. Jellinek, S. Cassel), or Edessa in Syria, whose Greek name has a phonetic resemblance to Kallir (F. Perles). J. Derenbourg assumes that Kallir may perhaps be a Latin nickname (*celer*, "the fast one") which would have been attached to the real name of Kallir's father, Jacob (alluding to Hosea 12:13, "And Jacob fled into the field of Aram"); S. Shullam claims to have found the acrostic בְּרַבִּי יַעֲקֹב *be-Rabbi Ya'akov*. J. Perles holds Kallir to be Cyril (Gr. Κύριλλος), a name popular in the Byzantine Empire. W. Heidenheim assumes that the hometown given in many acrostics as קִרְיַת סֵפֶר (*Kiryat Sefer*) could be identified with the biblical place in Ereẓ Israel of the same name (Kiriath-Sepher; Jos. 15:15). S.J. Rapoport read סְפָר (*sefar*) and interpreted it as "coastal town," associating it with Cagliari, Bari, or Ostia. Others, in a similar interpretation, suggested Civitas Portas, the former port of Rome (Derenbourg); Constantinople (S. Krauss); Civita di Penna in the Abruzzi (I.S. Reggio); while Luzzatto first suggested Bocherville in Normandy, Speyer in Germany, and later, cities in Babylonia: first Pumbedita and afterward nearby Sippar; L. Zunz suggested Lettere in southern Italy, later Antioch and Hama in Syria because of ספר; Bruell thought of the Phoenician town Byblos. S. Cassel read in the acrostic in Kallir's prayer for rain קִרְיַת שֶׁפֶר *Kiryat Shefer* ("fairtown") and identified it with Kallirrhoe in Palestine (from the Greek "fair," "beautiful"). According to S. Eppenstein the town meant is Tiberias, the place of Masoretic biblical studies since the seventh century. R. Solomon b. Abraham Adret believed him to be the *tanna* *Eleazar b. Arakh (Resp. Rashba no. 449); while the tosafists identified him with the *tanna* *Eleazar b. Simeon (Ḥag. 13a).

Dates

The conjectures as to when Kallir lived cover several centuries (from the second to the tenth or eleventh). As early as the 12th century he was thought to have been a *tanna* (see above). Rapoport tried to place him around 970, but this had to be antedated by a century after M.H. Landauer's discovery of Saadiah's *Yeẓirah* commentary. According to Zunz the earliest acceptable date is the first half of the ninth century. Some modern scholars believe Kallir to have lived about 750 at the latest, a date deduced from a statement by al-Kirkisānī, a younger contemporary of Saadiah's (see bibl., A. Harkavy), according to whom the *paytan* Yannai was a source for the founder of Karaism. Yannai, therefore, must have lived at least during the same period, if not earlier, and his pupil, Kallir, a generation later. Other scholars assume him to have lived no later than the sixth or the early seventh century, i.e., before the Arab conquest of Ereẓ Israel in 635, since in his poems he laments the suffering inflicted and the destruction wrought by Edom (i.e., the Christians) only, and does not mention Ishmael (i.e., the Arabs).

From a linguistic point of view it would also seem that Kallir lived in Ereẓ Israel at the end of the sixth century. Kallir's language, considered by later medieval grammarians as ungrammatical, is a product of the poet's conception of the grammatical structure of the Hebrew language. Abraham *Ibn Ezra (commentary to Eccles. 5:1) denounced the style of Kallir, a criticism which centuries later influenced the *maskilim* in their disparagement of the *paytan*. Many of Kallir's *piyyutim* are interlaced with Hebrew folk language. Like the Palestinian *piyyut*, Kallir's works are an organic continuation of ancient Hebrew while the Hebrew poetry of Spain is a revival of the biblical language.

Published Works

Many of Kallir's liturgical poems were published in different prayer books, *maḥzorim*, and also by various scholars. Those liturgical poems published until 1933 are listed by I. Davidson, in: *Oẓar ha-Shirah ve-ha-Piyyut*, pt. 4 (1933), 367. Since then many more have been published: I.M. Elbogen, in *Jewish Studies in Memory of G.A. Kohut* (1935), 159–77; idem, in *Sefer ha-Yovel… S. Krauss* (1936), 307, 309–10; idem, in: *Sefer Klausner* (1937), 235–9; E. Fleischer, in: *Tarbiz* 36 (1967), 119–28, 139–40, 147f., 350–7; 38 (1969), 264–5, 271–2, 276–9; idem, in: *Sinai*, 62 (1967/68), 13–40, 142–51, 155–8; 63 (1968), 32–49; 64 (1968/69), 184; 65 (1969), 34–35; 66 (1969/70), 225–6); idem, in: *Ha-Sifrut*, 2 (1969/70), 202–4, 208–18, 229, 231–6; A.M. Habermann, in: YMḤSI, 5 (1939), 52–56, 76–77, 104); idem, in: *Tarbiz*, 14 (1943), 53ff. 59–65, 143; 15 (1944), 216; J. Marcus, *Ginzei Shirah u-Fiyyut* (1933), 11–66; idem, in: *Horeb*, 1 (1934), 21–31, 151–66; 2 (1935), 6–16; A. Marmorstein, in: JQR (15 (1924/25), 418 (see a note of S. Abramson, in: *Tarbiz*, 15 (1944), 50); A. Murtonen and G.J. Orman, *Materials for a Non-Masoretic Hebrew Grammar*, 1 (1958), 52–60 (Heb. part); A. Scheiber, in: *Ginzei Kaufmann*, 1 (1949), 3–35; idem, in: *Alexander Marx Jubilee Volume* (1950), 545–6 (Eng. part); idem, in: HUCA, 23, pt. 2 (1950/51), 355–68; S. Spiegel, in: YMḤSI, 5 (1939), 269–91; S. Wieder, in: *Ginzei Kaufmann*, 1 (1949), 89–92; M. Zulay, in: *Lu'aḥ ha-Areẓ* (1944/45), 5; idem, in: *Sinai*, 17 (1945), 289–90; 32 (1952/53), 52–54; idem, *Mivḥar ha-Shirim* (1948?), 9–11, 13; idem, in: *Melilah*, 5 (1955), 70–74.

BIBLIOGRAPHY: S.J. Rapoport, in: *Bikkurei ha-Ittim*, 10 (1829), 95–123; 11 (1830), 92–102; idem, in: *Kerem Ḥemed*, 6 (1841), 10–40, passim; L. Zunz, *ibid.*, 4–10; Zunz, Lit. Poesie, 29–64; Landshuth, Ammudei, 27–44; P.F. Franke, in: *Jubelschrift… L. Zunz* (1884), 160–71 (Ger. part), 201–17 (Heb. part); J. Derenbourg, in: *Mélanges Renier* (1886), 429–41; A.E. Harkavy, *Zikkaron la-Rishonim…* 5 (1891), 109–10; M. Sachs, *Die religioese Poesie der Juden in Spanien* (1901), index; S. Klein, *Beitraege zur Geographie und Geschichte Galilaeas* (1902), 95, 97–108; Elbogen, Gottesdienst, 310–9, 561; idem, *Studien zur Geschichte des juedischen Gottesdienstes* (1902), index; idem, in: HUCA, 3 (1926), 215–24; 4 (1922), 405–31; idem, in: *Ẓiyyunim, Koveẓ le-Zikhrono shel J.N. Simḥoni* (1929), 83–87; S. Eppenstein, *Beitraege zur Geschichte und Literatur im geonaeischen Zeitalter* (1913), 35–40; B. Halper, *Post-Biblical Hebrew Literature*, 1 (1921), 21–24; 2 (1921), 45–48; L. Ginzberg, *Ginzei Schechter*, 1 (1928), 246–97; A.M. Habermann, in: *Mizraḥ u-Ma'arav*, 4 (1929/30), 250–1; idem, in: *Tarbiz*, 7 (1935/36), 186–216; A.I. Schechter, *Studies in Jewish Liturgy* (1930), index; I. Davidson, in: JQR, 21 (1930/31), 252ff.; idem, in: HUCA, 12–13 (1937/38), 3–8; M. Zulay, in: KS, 10 (1934), 480–4; idem, in: *Ginzei Kaufmann*, 1 (1949), 36–41; H. Brody, in: *Kobeẓ al-Jad*, 11 (1936), 1–23; A. Mirsky, in: *Tarbiz*, 17 (1945/46), 168–73; idem, in: KS, 35 (1959/60), 237–9; idem, *Reshit ha-Piyyut* (1965), 86–99; idem, in: *Sinai*, 65 (1969), 177–87; J. Schirmann, in: JQR, 44 (1953/54), 145–6; idem, in: *Divrei ha-Akad-*

emyah ha-Le'ummit ha-Yisre'elit le-Madda'im, 3 (1969/70), 28–36, 45–54; S. Bernstein, in: *Sefer Yovel… S. Federbush* (1960), 105–16; idem, in: *Sura*, 4 (1964), 478–516; S. Abramson, in: *Sinai*, 54 (1963/64), 31–32; E. Fleischer, *ibid.*, 65 (1969), 31–37, 167; idem, in: *Tarbiz*, 39 (1969/70), 24–27.

[*Encyclopaedia Judaica* (Germany)]

KALLIR, ELEAZAR BEN ELEAZAR (1728–1801), rabbi. Kallir's father died before his birth, and he was therefore given his father's name. In 1759 he was appointed rabbi of Zabludow, and from there proceeded to Berlin where he lectured in the college of the wealthy Moses b. Isaac Levy. He was appointed rabbi of Rechnitz and head of its large yeshivah in 1768, and in 1781 rabbi of Kolin near Prague. Kallir was highly regarded by his contemporaries. *Azulai says, "he has the reputation of being sharpwitted and erudite," while Baruch Jeiteles states that "after the death of Ezekiel *Landau, he was the sole remaining authority in the country." His first work, *Or Ḥadash*, on the Pentateuch, was an appendix to the *Kotnot Or* of his grandfather, Meir *Eisenstadt, which he published under the title *Me'orei Esh* (Fuerth, 1766). Under the same title he subsequently published commentaries on tractate *Pesaḥim* (Frankfurt on the Oder, 1771, and often republished) and on *Kiddushin* (Vienna, 1799); he also wrote *Ḥavvot Ya'ir he-Ḥadash* (Prague, 1792), sermons and eulogies; *Ḥeker Halakhah* (Vienna, 1838), responsa. His books met with a wide acceptance and are quoted by his contemporaries. Other works remain in manuscript. His son Alexander Susskind was a well-known philanthropist.

BIBLIOGRAPHY: J.J. (L.) Greenwald (Grunwald), *Lifnei Shetei Me'ot Shanah, O Toledot ha-Rav Eleazar Kallir u-Zemanno* (1952).

[Itzhak Alfassi]

KALLIR (Kallier), MEIER (d. 1875), banker and politician in Brody (Galicia; now Ukraine). Son of Alexander Kallir, an émigré from Germany, Meier managed the banking business established by his father. He served as chairman of the Board of Commerce and Trade several times and in 1853 as deputy mayor of Brody. In 1848 he was elected to the Galician *Landtag* (Diet), and served as a deputy once more from 1861 to 1867. Together with two other Jewish deputies Kallir introduced the proposal for the emancipation of the Jews in 1861. Also active in the Jewish community of Brody, he supported agricultural settlement of the Galician Jews on the plains, publishing an appeal entitled *Galizyah Kol Titten*. However, since Orthodox Jewry opposed it, the project was never realized. Meier's son NATHAN VON KALLIR (1821–1886), also a deputy in the Galician *Landtag* (1870–73), was a noted philanthropist.

BIBLIOGRAPHY: Ph. Friedman, *Die galizischen Juden im Kampfe um ihre Gleichberechtigung* (1929), index; M. Balaban, *Dzieje Żydów w galicyi i w Rzeczypospolitej Krakowskiej* (1916), index; M. Weissberg, in: MGWJ, 57 (1913), 741.

[Benjamin Lubelski]

KALLO, YIZḤAK ISAAC (of Taub, 1751–1821), rabbi and ḥasidic *admor* in Hungary. According to legend his talents were recognized by *Aryeh Leib Sarahs and the latter sent him to be educated by Samuel Shmelke *Horowitz of Nikolsburg, who was his teacher in Talmud as well as in Ḥasidism. He also studied for some time under *Elimelech of Lyzhansk. In 1781 he became rabbi of Kallo and district, where he resided for 40 years, and became known for his learning and piety. Yizḥak Isaac was the first ḥasidic leader to live permanently in Hungary and helped to further the spread of the ḥasidic movement there. His contemporaries esteemed both his talmudic learning and ḥasidic teachings, but he left no works in writing. Possessed of great musical talent, he wrote songs in Yiddish and Hungarian and composed many melodies, some of them adaptations of Hungarian folk songs. Some of his grandsons were ḥasidic leaders in Kallo and other places.

BIBLIOGRAPHY: N. Ben-Menahem, in: Y.L. Ha-Cohen Maimon (ed.), *Sefer Yovel… I. Elfenbein* (1963), 20–32; idem, in: *Sinai*, 55 (1964), 344–6; L. Szilágyi-Windt, *A kállói cadik* (1959).

[Adin Steinsaltz]

KÁLMÁN, EMMERICH (Imre; 1882–1953), composer. Born in Siófok, Hungary, Kálmán studied at the Budapest Academy with Hans Koessler, while also taking his law degree. Until 1908 he worked in a law office, acted as a music critic, and composed several serious works. The success of the cabaret songs which he had written under a pseudonym drew him to the field of operetta. The first of his 21 works in this genre was *Tatárjárás* (1909), produced in Vienna as *Ein Herbstmanoever* (1909) and in the same year in New York as *The Gay Hussars*. Kálmán settled in Vienna, where he remained until 1936. In 1938 he went to Switzerland, then to France, and in 1940 to the United States. Returning to Europe in 1949 he was feted in Paris and in major German-speaking cities. He returned briefly to New York where he finished his last operetta, *Arizona Lady* (1954). The most famous of Kálmán's operettas are *Der Zigeunerprimas* (1912); *Die Bajadere* (1921); *Circus Princess* (1926); and the two world-wide successes – *Gypsy Princess* (1915), produced in the U.S. as *Riviera Girl*, and *The Countess Maritza* (1924). The latter, as well as most of his other works, were based on the melodic idiom of urban Hungarian folk and entertainment music, including the gypsy element. Kálmán's operettas – orchestrated by himself – have been appreciated for their melodic richness, which ranges from sentimental pathos to dashing gaiety. Together with Franz Lehár, Leo *Fall, and Oskar *Straus, Kálmán represents the third and last phase of the European operetta. His son Charles (1929–) was also a composer.

BIBLIOGRAPHY: V. Kálmán, *Gruess' mir die suessen, die reizenden Frauen. Mein Leben mit Emmerich Kalman* (1966); MGG, incl. bibl.; Riemann-Gurlitt, incl. bibl.; Grove, Dict; Baker, Biog Dict, incl. bibl.

[Bathja Bayer]

KALMAN, MAIRA (1950–), U.S. author, illustrator, designer. Born in Tel Aviv, Kalman immigrated to New York in 1954. She met her husband, Tibor, at New York University, where both were English students. While nurturing an ambition to write short stories, she helped her husband found M&Co, the quirky design firm. In 1987 she published her first book, *Stay Up Late* (1987), illustrating David Byrne's lyrics with an array of colorful primitive-looking characters. A year later she published *Hey Willy, See the Pyramids* (1988), a sarcastic, witty book abounding in non sequiturs and naïve drawings. Her major protagonist, a dog named Max, won children's hearts and book awards. She also wrote and illustrated *Chicken Soup, Boots; Next Stop Grand Central* (1999), based on murals she created for New York's Grand Central Terminal, and *What Pete Ate From A–Z* (2001), a culinary biography of her mutt Pete. After her husband's death in 1999, she continued their work with *(un)Fashion* (2000), a book about the way the non-Westernized world attires itself, and *Colors* (2002), an anthology of his work as editor of that magazine. She has written and illustrated a dozen children's books and runs M&Co as an entrepreneurial producer of paperweights, clocks, and "art" products. She also produced window displays for Sony and clothes mannequins for Pucci. Her book *Fireboat: The Heroic Adventures of the John J. Harvey* (2002), about the decommissioned boat that fought fires at the World Trade Center attack on 9/11, reveals a growing interest in fusing real life and art into an entertaining though poignant form of social commentary. Kalman endeared herself to countless readers with her illustration that appeared on the cover of *The New Yorker* magazine on December 8, 2001. It showed a simple pastel map, a flat, bird's-eye view of New York City drawn in pen and wash with the city's neighborhoods Afghanistanicized: Lubavistan, Kvetchnya, Irate, Feh, Fattushis, Fuhgeddaboutitstan, etc. The map became almost as famous as the one Saul *Steinberg drew for the *New Yorker* cover of March 29, 1976, showing his *View of the World from Ninth Avenue.*

[Stewart Kampel (2nd ed.)]

KALMAN, TIBOR (1949–1999), U.S. graphic designer. A native of Budapest, Hungary, Kalman moved with his family in 1957 to Poughkeepsie, N.Y., after the unsuccessful Hungarian uprising. He spent a year at New York University, where he joined Students for a Democratic Society, and traveled to Cuba to pick cotton with the Venceremos Brigade, which took middle-class Americans to help support the Cuban regime. When he returned to the United States in 1971, Kalman did window displays for the Student Book Exchange at NYU, which was owned by Leonard Riggio, who later bought Barnes & Noble and made Kalman its first creative director. Kalman designed the bookstore's first shopping bag, featuring an antique woodcut of a scribe. The design was still in use decades later. In 1979 Kalman was hired as the creative director of the discount department store E.J. Korvettes ("Eight Jewish Korean War Veterans"). Unhappy, he established M&Co in his Greenwich Village apartment in 1980. The enigmatic name was typical of Kalman's wit: it gave an aura of mystery and confused his more traditional clientele, who wanted to know what the M stood for. His wife, Maira *Kalman, then a children's book author and illustrator, had the nickname M. Kalman's transformation into a progressive design impresario came when M&Co designed an album for the rock group Talking Heads that featured four digitally manipulated photographs of the group's members and a title with upside-down letters. From that point on, the firm received attention in the design trade press for pushing beyond the conventions of design and typography. A number of cutting-edge designs produced by M&Co were sold at the Museum of Modern Art in New York for years. Kalman moved on to editing and being the creative director for the magazines *Art Forum* and *Interview.* He made a splash as editor in chief of *Colors*, the Italian and English magazine published by the Italian clothing company Benetton, an assignment that forced him to move his family to Rome. *Colors* focused on sociocultural issues like racism, AIDS, and sports. An issue devoted to racism had a featured titled "How to Change Your Race" and examined cosmetic means of altering hair, features, and skin color. Another feature was a collection of manipulated photographs showing famous people racially transformed. Kalman returned to New York in 1997 to battle cancer. In the last months of his life, Kalman designed the exhibition *Tiborocity*, which consisted of "neighborhoods" representing different aspects of his work as well as the protest posters and graphics that influenced him in the 1960s and 1970s. He told friends he intended the retrospective, which was shown at the San Francisco Museum of Modern Art, to be his last testament.

[Stewart Kampel (2nd ed.)]

KALMAN OF WORMS (d. 1560), Polish rabbi. Kalman is the first known rabbi of Lemberg and one of the leading Polish talmudic scholars of his time. He is known mainly from references in the works of contemporary rabbis. Joseph Katz of Cracow (the brother-in-law of Moses *Isserles) on one occasion enlisted his support and states: "The elder scholar… Kalman of Worms agreed with my decision…" (responsa *She'erit Yosef* (Cracow, 1590), no. 1). A responsum by Kalman himself, dated 1558 and signed "Kalman Wermeisa," appears in the responsa of Moses Isserles (responsum no. 15). It is possible he is the Kalman referred to in a responsum from Meir *Katzenellenbogen of Padua (in responsa *Maharshal* [S. Luria] (Lemberg, 1859), 38a, no. 37). Both David Gans and Jehiel Heilprin, in *Ẓemaḥ David* and *Seder ha-Dorot* respectively, mention Kalman of Worms among the foremost scholars of the first half of the 16th century.

BIBLIOGRAPHY: Ḥ.N. Dembitzer, *Kelilat Yofi*, 1 (1888), 37a–b; S. Buber, *Anshei Shem* (1895), 200f., no. 498.

[Alexander Tobias]

KALMANOVITCH, ZELIG (1881–1944), Yiddish writer, philologist, and translator. Born in Goldingen, Latvia, in 1929, he settled in Vilna, where he joined the *YIVO Institute and became editor of its journal *YIVO Bleter.* Kalmanovitch published studies on Yiddish philology, the influence of Hebrew on Yiddish syntax (1906, 1907), and on the Yiddish dialect spoken in Courland (1926). He translated into Yiddish Josephus' *Jewish Wars* (1914), Dubnow's *History of the Jews* (1909–10), and H.G. Wells' *Outline of History* (1930). During the Nazi occupation he was forced to select the books to be shipped to Germany. In the Vilna ghetto Kalmanovitch kept a diary in Hebrew. It is written in a spirit of resignation; he expresses the hope that, by carrying out the orders of the Nazis, some lives might be spared. With the liquidation of the Vilna ghetto in September 1943, he was deported to an extermination camp in Estonia where he died the following winter. His ghetto diary was published in an English translation in the YIVO *Annual of Jewish Social Science*, 8 (1951) and in a Yiddish translation in the YIVO *Bleter*, 35 (1951) and New Series, 3 (1997), 43–113.

BIBLIOGRAPHY: Rejzen, Leksikon, 3 (1929), 693–6; S. Kaczerginski, *Khurbn Vilne* (1947), 208–10: M. Dworzecki, *Yerushalayim de-Lita in Kamf un Umkum* (1948). **ADD. BIBLIOGRAPHY:** Y. Mark, in: *Di Goldene Keyt*, 93 (1977), 127–43.

[Elias Schulman / Gennady Estraikh (2nd ed.)]

KALMANOWITZ, ABRAHAM (1891–1964), rabbi and *rosh yeshivah*. Born in Delyatis, Belorussia, he received his education at the yeshivot of Zavahil, Eisiskes, Slobodka, and Telz, and was ordained by the rabbis Raphael Shapiro of Volozhin, Elijah Baruch Komai of Mir, Moses Mordecai *Epstein of Slobodka, and Eliezer Rabinowitz of Minsk. At the unusually young age of 22, Kalmanowitz was chosen as the rabbi of Rakov (1913), where he later established an advanced yeshivah (1916). During the Bolshevik Revolution he aided Jews who had been arrested by the Bolsheviks and was consequently arrested and imprisoned in Minsk. Kalmanowitz served as a member of the Mo'eẓet Gedolei ha-Torah of *Agudat Israel and was among the founders of the Va'ad ha-Yeshivot in Vilna. He assisted R. Ḥayyim Ozer *Grodzinski in organizing the Ateret Ẓevi *kolel* in Vilna which later moved to Otwock. In 1926, Kalmanowitz was elected president of the Mir yeshivah. In 1929 he became the rabbi of Tiktin (Tykocin) and also established a yeshivah there.

After the outbreak of World War II, Kalmanowitz accompanied the Mir yeshivah to Vilna, where it sought refuge. In 1940 he succeeded in emigrating to the United States and there devoted himself to rescuing European rabbis, heads of yeshivot, and their students. Kalmanowitz arranged for the transfer of the Mir yeshivah to Kobe, Japan, and later Shanghai, where Kalmanowitz made himself responsible for its upkeep for the duration of the war. In 1945 he arranged for its transfer to the United States and Ereẓ Israel, and in 1946 he reopened the Mir yeshivah in Brooklyn, New York, with the new arrivals serving as the nucleus. American-born youngsters were gradually attracted to the new school and it became a leading American yeshivah. Later, Kalmanowitz was active in the Oẓar ha-Torah, which aided Jewish education in Morocco, Algeria, and Tunisia, bringing youngsters from these countries to the United States to study in a special division of the Mir yeshivah.

BIBLIOGRAPHY: O. Rand (ed.), *Toledot Anshei Shem* (1950), 117f.

[Aaron Rothkoff]

KALMS, SIR (Harold) STANLEY, BARON (1931–), British businessman, communal leader, and figure in the Conservative Party. Born in London in 1931, Kalms was chairman of the Dixon Group from 1948 to 2002, which he developed from a single photographic shop into one of the biggest and best known of British high street retail chains, specializing in electronic equipment, especially televisions and stereos, computers, and household appliances. Dixons also owned a number of other well-known British retail chains in the same field, such as Currys and PCWorld. Within the Anglo-Jewish community Kalms became well known as the author of the "Kalms Report" of 1992, entitled *A Time For Change*, which recommended a sweeping reorganization of the financial bases of the mainstream United Synagogue. He was also the founder of the Stanley Kalms Foundation to encourage Orthodox Jewish education. In addition, Kalms was an influential figure in the administrative organization of the Conservative Party, serving from 2001 as the Party's treasurer. He was knighted in 1996 and received a life peerage in 2004.

[William D. Rubinstein (2nd ed.)]

KALNITSKY, GEORGE (1917–), U.S. biochemist, born in Brooklyn, New York City. He worked at the University of Chicago and the U.S. Office of Scientific Research and Development before joining the University of Iowa College of Medicine (1946), where he became professor (1957). His main research field was bacterial and mammalian metabolism. He made major contributions to clarifying the intermediate steps in the citric acid (Krebs) cycle for generating energy from the oxidation of glucose. He also contributed to understanding the chemistry of enzyme action. He was active in Jewish communal affairs.

[Michael Denman (2nd ed.)]

KALONYMUS, one of the most eminent Jewish families in Germany which flourished from the 9th to the 13th century, especially in the cities near the Rhine. Among its members were numerous rabbis, preachers, poets, teachers, authors, moralists, and theologians, and most of the prominent communal leaders of this period came from its ranks. The origins of the family go back to eighth-century Italy, although the name Kalonymus appears in talmudic literature. The father of Onkelos, the great translator of the Bible, was, according to *Avodah Zarah* 11a, called Kalonymus, although other sources refer to him by a different name, e.g., Kolonikos (Git. 56b). While Kalonymus is the name of many medieval Jewish families, its appearance does not always indicate a connection with the family described here.

Two major events stand out in the family's history: the migration of the family from southern Italy to Germany in the ninth century, and their leadership of the Jews in Germany during the Crusades, especially during the massacres of 1096 (the year of the First Crusade) and the subsequent upheaval of the 12th and 13th centuries. The Kalonymus family tree, despite many attempts, has not been accurately described. The family had many branches, with the same names frequently recurring in different cities and different generations, so that it is very easy to confuse them. The best and most complete tradition regarding the history of the family is given in a small polemical work written probably around 1220 by *Eleazar b. Judah (b. Kalonymus) of Worms, the author of the *Rokeaḥ*. Eleazar's aim in his polemic was to prove that the version of the prayers recited by himself and his circle was the true one, as opposed to the various changes introduced by rabbis in France and England. He gave a list of his family and teachers in order to demonstrate the antiquity and reliability of his version, which was printed by Joseph *Delmedigo in his *Maẓref le-Ḥokhmah*. The list also appears in other manuscripts and has been discussed at length by many scholars, especially H. Gross and A. Neubauer. The Paris manuscript, no. 772, p. 60a, gives the following version:

> "I, Eleazar ha-Katan, received the true version of the prayers from my father and teacher, Rabbi Judah, son of Rabbi Kalonymus, son of Moses, son of Rabbi Judah, son of Rabbi Kalonymus, son of Rabbi Moses, son of Rabbi Kalonymus, son of Judah.
>
> "And I also received it from *Judah he-Ḥasid, as he received it from his father, Rabbi *Samuel he-Ḥasid, as he received it from Rabbi Eleazar he-Ḥazzan of Speyer; for when Rabbi Kalonymus died, his son Rabbi Samuel he-Ḥasid was only a boy, so he gave (transmitted) it to Rabbi Eleazar he-Ḥazzan of Speyer, and when he, Rabbi Samuel he-Ḥasid, grew up, he received [the secrets] from him, as was ordered by Rabbi Kalonymus the Elder.
>
> "And Rabbi Kalonymus the Elder received [the tradition] from his father, Rabbi Isaac; and Rabbi Isaac received [it] from his father, Rabbi Eleazar the Great, son of Rabbi Isaac, son of Rabbi Joshua, son of Rabbi Abun, the Rabbi Abun who was the grandfather of Rabbi Simeon the Great, of Mainz.
>
> "And Rabbi Eleazar the Great was a student of Rabbi Simeon the Great. For Rabbi Isaac, the father of Rabbi Simeon the Great, and Rabbi Joshua, the grandfather of Rabbi Eleazar the Great, were brothers. This is why Rabbi Simeon was like a father to him, for when Rabbi Isaac died his son Rabbi Eleazar the Great was just a small boy, and he grew up in his house and he taught him the Torah, And he was [with] Rabbi Gershom, Me'or ha-Golah.
>
> "Rabbi Judah ha-Kohen also transmitted his [knowledge] to Rabbi Eleazar the Great. This was Rabbi Judah ha-Kohen who wrote the book of laws; he was the father of Rabbi Abraham ha-Kohen, and Rabbi Abraham ha-Kohen was the father of Rabbi Meir ha-Kohen, who was the father of Rabbi Eleazar ha-Kohen he-Ḥasid. Rabbi Eleazar ha-Kohen he-Ḥasid was the father of Rabbi Jacob ha-Kohen he-Ḥasid, the young one.
>
> "They all received the secret of the true version of the prayers, teacher from his teacher, up to Abu Aaron, the son of Rabbi Samuel ha-Nasi, who came from Babylonia because of a misadventure, and had to wander from place to place [as a punishment], until he came to the country of Lombardy, to a city named Lucca, where he found Rabbi Moses [son of Kalonymus], who wrote the *piyyut, Eimat Norotekha*, and he [Abu Aaron] transmitted to him all his secrets. And he was Rabbi Moses, son of Kalonymus, son of Rabbi Judah. He was the first who left Lombardy, he and his sons, Rabbi Kalonymus and Rabbi Jekuthiel, and his relation Rabbi Ithiel, and other important persons; for the king Charles brought them with him from the country of Lombardy, and settled them in Mainz, and there they multiplied and flourished very much; until God's fury hit all the holy communities in the year 1096. And then we were all lost, all perished, except very few who were left from our kinsmen. [Rabbi Kalonymus] the Elder who transmitted [the Torah] to Rabbi Eleazar he-Ḥazzan of Speyer, as we have written above, and Rabbi Eleazar he-Ḥazzan transmitted it to Rabbi Judah he-Ḥasid, and from him I, the small one, received the secrets of the prayers and other secrets."

This list is as close to a Kalonymus family tree as exists today, though many more members of the family are known from other sources (see below). It is evident that the family originally flourished in southern Italy, from where some of its members were moved by one of the Carolingian emperors to the Rhine cities in Germany. There was some controversy among scholars as to the identity of this ruler; some texts explicitly named Charlemagne as the king responsible for the move, but this seems to be a later emendation to the text. It is now accepted that it must have been Charles the Bald, who lived in the second half of the ninth century.

It should be noted that Eleazar of Worms stresses the fact that the family received "secrets" orally from the Babylonian scholar, Aaron son of Samuel. Generally, the Jewish communities in southern Italy were under the influence of the center of learning in Palestine, and not in Babylonia. It seems, therefore, that the traditions transmitted from generation to generation within the Babylonian and Palestinian elements of the family were fused together into one whole which gave the members of the family stature and importance among the scholars in Germany. No clear connection has been established between the Kalonymus family and another family which received secret traditions from Abu Aaron, and which is described in the *Megillat *Aḥimaaẓ* as an Italian family of the 8th to the 11th centuries.

The Kalonymus family provided the Jews in Germany with leaders of the communities, as attested by the chronicles describing the massacres of the crusaders from 1096 to the middle of the 13th century (see A.M. Habermann, *Gezerot Ashkenaz ve-Ẓarefat*, 1945). Their leadership extended to cultural fields as well. It is probable that more than a dozen prominent *paytanim*, who wrote of the sufferings of German Jewry during this period, belonged to this family. Many of the most prominent halakhists and talmudic scholars of the time were also members of the Kalonymus family. The *Ḥasidei Ashkenaz were led and directed by members of the family, who formulated their esoteric theology, and created their code of ethical, pious behavior – *Sefer *Ḥasidim*. Furthermore, the political and cultural life of the Jews in Germany between the 9th and 13th centuries was dominated by the family.

Among the prominent members of the Kalonymus family in Italy and Germany were KALONYMUS OF LUCCA, a *paytan*, who lived in Italy probably in the ninth century; *MOSES BEN KALONYMUS, a *paytan*, who lived in Italy but who moved to Mainz, and influenced the early *paytanim* in Germany, especially *SIMEON BEN ISAAC; KALONYMUS BEN JUDAH HA-BAḤUR (the Younger), a *paytan* in Mainz at the end of the 11th century and the beginning of the 12th, who witnessed the persecutions of 1096 and who wrote of them in many liturgical poems; KALONYMUS BEN MOSES OF LUCCA, a talmudic scholar, halakhist, and author of many responsa, who probably also emigrated to Mainz; KALONYMUS BEN MESHULLAM HA-PARNAS, the leader of the Mainz community during the persecutions of 1096, who was martyred with his whole community; KALONYMUS BEN ISAAC HA-ZAKEN (the Elder), a communal leader and halakhist, and the founder of the branch of the Kalonymus family which most influenced German Jewry during the 12th and 13th centuries; his son *SAMUEL BEN KALONYMUS HE-ḤASID, the founder of the Ḥasidei Ashkenaz, author of a part of *Sefer Ḥasidim* and other works; Samuel's son, *JUDAH B. SAMUEL HE-ḤASID, who was the principal leader of the Ḥasidei Ashkenaz and the author of *Sefer Ḥasidim*. Other descendants of Kalonymus ha-Zaken were *JUDAH B. KALONYMUS B. MEIR OF SPEYER, author of the monumental talmudic lexicon, *Seder Yiḥusei Tanna'im ve-Amora'im*; and *JUDAH B. KALONYMUS B. MOSES OF MAINZ, a talmudic scholar and a poet, who was the father of *Eleazar of Worms. Eleazar's children were murdered by the crusaders, probably terminating his family line. The descendants of Judah b. Samuel he-Ḥasid, however, carried on for at least three more generations, giving rise to such scholars as MOSES ZALTMAN, son of Judah, who wrote a commentary on the Torah; *Eleazar b. Moses ha-Darshan, author of mystical and theological works; and MOSES B. ELEAZAR, great-grandson of Judah he-Ḥasid. KALONYMUS BEN GERSHON, a halakhist, also flourished in the 13th century. Among other *paytanim* of the Kalonymus family were *Meshullam ben Moses of the 11th century; MOSES BEN MESHULLAM OF LUCCA (probably the ninth century); KALONYMUS BEN MESHULLAM OF MAINZ, c. 1000; and notably *Meshullam b. Kalonymus of Rome of the tenth century, a *paytan* and halakhist who had contact with Gershom b. Judah, Me'or ha-Golah.

The name Kalonymus appears also among some families in Provence, where several great scholars and writers bear that name, for example the 13th-century writers Kalonymus ha-Nasi of Beaucaire and Kalonymus ben Kalonymus of Arles, author of *Even Boḥan*. However, it is not known whether the Provençal rabbis of this name were connected with the Italian-German family.

BIBLIOGRAPHY: Zunz, Gesch, 104ff.; Landshuth, Ammudei, passim; S. Buber (ed.), *Shibbolei ha-Leket* (1887), introd.; Graetz, Gesch, 5 (1895³), n. 12, 383–94; M. Guedemann, *Ha-Torah ve-ha-Ḥayyim be-Arẓot ha-Ma'arav*, 1 (1896; repr. 1968); J.A. Kamelhar, *Ḥasidim ha-Rishonim* (1917); J. Freimann, *Mavo le-Sefer Ḥasidim* (1924); J. Kamelhar, *Rabbenu Eleazar mi-Germeiza* (1930); Germ Jud; A. Aptowitzer, *Mavo le-Sefer Ravyah* (1938), 308ff.; A.M. Habermann, *Piyyutei Rabbi Shimon ben-Rabbi Yiẓḥak ve-Rabbi Moshe ben-Rabbi Kalonymus* (1938); idem, *Gezerot Ashkenaz ve-Ẓarefat* (1945); idem, *Shirei ha-Yiḥud ve-ha-Kavod* (1948); idem, *Sefer Zekhirah le-Rabbi Efrayim ben Ya'akov* (1970); B. Klar (ed.), *Megillat Aḥima'aẓ* (1944); G. Scholem, *Reshit ha-Kabbalah* (1948), 195–238; A. Epstein, *Kitvei* …, 1 (1950), 245–68; idem, *Mi-Kadmoniyyot ha-Yehudim* (1957), 211ff.; Urbach, Tosafot, 164f., 301f.; idem (ed.), *Arugat ha-Bosem*, 4 (1963), passim; Baron, Social², 4 (1957), 46, 103f., 145, 273; 5 (1957), 60f.; J.L. Maimon, *Sefer Yiḥusei Tanna'im ve-Amora'im me'et Rabbi Yehudah be-Rabbi Kalonymus mi-Speyer* (1963); Roth, Dark Ages, index; J. Dan, *Torat ha-Sod shel Ḥasidei Ashkenaz* (1968), 14ff., 50–51; I. Perles, in: MGWJ, 25 (1876), 372ff.; idem, in: *Jubelschrift… H. Graetz* (1887), 17ff.; A. Neubauer, in: REJ, 23 (1891), 230–7; idem, in: JQR, 6 (1893/94), 348–54; D. Kaufmann, *ibid.*, 4 (1892), 20–22; H. Gross, in: MGWJ, 49 (1905), 692–700; M. Szulwas, in: *Alummah*, 1 (1936), 152–3; A.J. Bruck, in: HJ, 9 (1947), 159–77; A.J. Zuckerman, in: PAAJR, 33 (1965), 51ff.; M. Grabois, in: *Tarbiz*, 36 (1967), 49ff. **ADD. BIBLIOGRAPHY:** K.R. Stow, in: *Cross Cultural Convergences in the Crusader Period* (1995), 319–34.

[Joseph Dan]

KALONYMUS BEN KALONYMUS (Ben Meir ha-Nasi; 1286–after 1328), author and translator. Probably born in Arles (Provence), Kalonymus pursued his studies in Salonica and devoted himself from his youth to the translation of Arabic scientific works into Hebrew. His first translation, Ibn Ridwan's *Principles of Medicine*, is believed to have been lost during the expulsion of the Jews from the territories directly under the rule of the king of France in 1306. During the years 1307–17 he lived in Arles (he was in Avignon in 1314), and in 1318 he stayed again for a time in Salonica. He later entered the service of Robert d'Anjou "the Wise" (1277–1343), king of Naples and count of Provence, for whom he is said to have made translations from Arabic and Hebrew into Latin. Probably in about 1319–21, Kalonymus traveled to Rome, where he frequented the circle to which the poet *Immanuel of Rome and the philosopher Judah b. Moses (among others) belonged. Whether, as some surmise, he was the representative sent by the Jews of Rome to the papal court at Avignon in 1321 remains uncertain. When Kalonymus was recalled to Arles, the Rome community addressed to the Jews of Arles a letter composed by the poet Immanuel explaining why it was desirable for Kalonymus to remain in Rome (*Maḥberot Immanuel*, no. 23). However, Kalonymus subsequently made his way home and from there went to Catalonia, but returned to Provence after 1322. In 1324 he was again in Naples and in 1328 he was still busy in Arles working on the Latin translation of Averroes for the King.

The works of Kalonymus comprise a polemic epistle against Joseph *Kaspi (1318; ed. Perles, Munich 1879) written in Provence; *Massekhet Purim*, a parody for the festival of Purim, composed in Rome; this work, in the guise of a talmudic tractate in four chapters, has gone through many editions (Pesaro 1513, c. 1520; Venice 1552, etc.); a fragment on mathematics (Munich MS 290); *Iggeret Musar*, an ethical work written for his son, published by I. Sonne in *Kovez al Yad*, 1 (1936), 93–110; *Iggeret ha-Hitnaẓẓelut ha-Katan*, published by J. Schatzmiller in *Sefunot*, 10 (1966), 9–52. One of his best-known works is *Even Boḥan*, a satire in rhymed prose, composed c. 1322 in Barcelona, on the moral and religious abuses prevailing among the author's contemporaries (Naples 1489; Venice 1546; Tel Aviv, ed. A.M. Habermann, 1956). He dedicated it to 10 notable Catalan Jews who had helped him during his stay in Catalonia. As T. Rosen has commented, Kalonymus includes in his *Even Boḥan*, among others things, the case of a man who asks God to turn him into a female – something that is unique in Jewish literature. It can be seen as a critique of the Jewish view on the life of men and women. The author describes also with humor many aspects of the life of the Jewish communities of his time, the celebration of Jewish festivals, and many kinds of social types (rich people, physicians, astronomers, grammarians, experts in masorah, poets, talmudists, etc.), criticizing their habits in a way that is sometimes picturesque, sometimes even grotesque.

He also translated works on philosophy, natural sciences, medicine, mathematics, and astronomy by other writers (more than 30), including 10 works by Averroes, the *Centiloquium* attributed to Ptolemy, with the commentary of Abu Jaffar Ahmed ben Yussuf; the *Sphere and Cylinder* of Archimedes (two translations, one of which has been lost); Galen's *De clysteriis et colica* and *De Phebotomia*, the *Compendium of Arithmetic* by Nicomachus of Gerasa; the *Principles of Medicine* by Ibn Ridwan (second translation; the first was lost in 1306); the treatise *Cylinder and Cone* of Ibn Samkh; the *Figura sector* of Thabit b. Kurras, the *Hypotheses* of Ptolemy and "Iggeret Ba'alei Ḥayyim," from the 21st treatise of the *Encyclopedia of the Sincere Brethren* (Mantua 1557, etc.). Only one of Kalonymus' translations into Latin is known, namely the *Destructio destructionis* of Averroes (part printed, Venice 1497; Venice 1508). Other works and translations have been incorrectly attributed to Kalonymus.

E. Fleischer sees in the work of Kalonymus, with all his bitter criticism and his satiric humor, but at the same time with his philosophic and scientific knowledge and his literary virtues, the last brilliant representative of the culture of Provence, inspired by the Sephardi tradition.

BIBLIOGRAPHY: J. Chotzner, in: JQR, 13 (1901), 128–46, A.M. Habermann (ed.), *Even Boḥan* (1956), 163–87 (incl. bibl.). **ADD. BIBLIOGRAPHY:** Schirmann-Fleischer, *The History of Hebrew Poetry in Christian Spain and Southern France* (1997), 514–41 (Heb.); T. Rosen, in: *Prooftexts*, 20 (2000), 87–110; idem, *Unveiling Eve* (2003), 168–86.

[Umberto (Moses David) Cassuto / Angel Sáenz-Badillos (2nd ed.)]

°KALTENBRUNNER, ERNST (1903–1946), Nazi lawyer, SS leader, chief of the Reichssicherheitshauptamt (*RSHA). Born in Ried im Innkreis, Austria, he attended school in Linz and was trained as a lawyer in Prague. He was an attorney. He joined the Nazis in 1932 and was imprisoned in Austria for his Nazi activities. After the Anschluss he was appointed undersecretary of state for public security in Ostmark (Nazi-renamed Austria) and was responsible for the Central Office for Jewish Emigration headed by Adolf *Eichmann. On January 30, 1943 he succeeded *Heydrich, who was assassinated the previous May, as chief of the RSHA and served in this assignment until the collapse of Nazi Germany. Kaltenbrunner, who was a boyhood friend of Eichmann and became his superior, was largely responsible for the implementation of the annihilation policy against the Jews. He was previously responsible in part for the *Euthanasia program. A member of *Hitler's inner circle, he not only opposed *Himmler's efforts to seek peace with the West, but also sabotaged Himmler's order given in the last phase of the war to prevent the further murder of Jews. He was tried as a major war criminal by the International Military Tribunal in *Nuremberg, where he downplayed his role and knowledge, and was hanged on October 16, 1946.

BIBLIOGRAPHY: E. Davidson, *Trials of the Germans* (1966), index; G. Reitlinger, *SS: Alibi of a Nation 1922–1945* (1956), index; idem, *Final Solution* (1953), index; G.M. Gilbert, *Nuremberg Diary* (1947), index; IMT, *Trial of the Major War Criminals*, 24 (1949), index; P.R. Black, *Ernst Kaltenbrunner: Ideological Soldier of the Third Reich* (1984).

[Yehuda Reshef]

KALUSH (Pol. **Kalusz**), city in Ivano-Frankovsk (Stanislavov) district in southwestern Ukraine, formerly within Poland; in 1772 it passed to Austria, reverting to Poland in 1919, and was within the U.S.S.R. from 1939 to 1991 when Ukraine gained independence. The salt mines in the area around Kalush became noted as early as the 15th century, and were leased on occasion by Jews during the following century; they were the main source of livelihood in the 19th century. An organized Jewish community existed in the city by 1650. According to the census of 1765, there were 1,087 Jews in Kalush who paid poll tax. They owned about 130 buildings in the city. The great synagogue was completed in 1825. In 1880 there lived in Kalush 4,266 Jews, representing 59% of the total population. Apart from salt, they controlled trade in lumber, grain, hides, and clothing. The community numbered 4,363 in 1910, about half the total population, and maintained six synagogues and charitable and religious institutions. During World War I the town suffered, mostly from Russian troops, leaving 200 widows, 400 orphans, and about 250 Jewish homes in the center of the city destroyed, along with the community's archives and records. In the fall of 1918 the region came under independent Ukrainian rule. A Jewish local council was set up and a Jewish militia organized to defend the community against pogroms. When Kalush reverted to independent Poland, the Jewish council and prewar communal organizations were disbanded and a government-appointed Jewish community council established. In 1921 there lived in Kalush 3,121 Jews, representing 47% of its total population. During the period between the two world wars, a Hebrew school (200 pupils in 1938), a *talmud torah*, a *Beth Jacob school, and various welfare associations were established. The community numbered approximately 6,000 in 1938, about one-third of the total population in Kalush.

[Arthur Cygielman]

Holocaust Period

During the period of Soviet occupation (1939–41), the Jewish community in Kalush underwent many changes: independent political activity was prohibited, and the community institutions, political parties, and youth movements were disbanded. Trade and industry were nationalized. After the German occupation of Kalush at the beginning of July 1941, the Jews and their property were attacked. In October 1941 several hundred Jews were murdered. Other *Aktionen* took place in March–April 1942, and the victims were sent to the *Belzec death camp, where they perished. On Sept. 15–17, 1942, the ghetto was destroyed and the city was declared *Judenrein*. The few remaining Jews in Kalush were transferred to *Stanislav and subsequently perished. The community was not reconstituted after the war.

[Aharon Weiss]

BIBLIOGRAPHY: *Almanach gmin żydowskich* (1939), index; B. Wasiutynski, *Ludnosé żydowska w Polsce w wiekach XIX i XX* (1930), 122; I. Schiper, *Dzieje handlu zydowskiego na ziemiachi polskich*, 1939, index; R. Mahler, *Yidn in Amolikn Poyln in Likht fun Tsifern* (1958), index.

KALUSZYN, town in Warszawa province, E. central Poland. Jews lived there almost from the date of its foundation and always formed the majority of the population. There was an organized Jewish community from the beginning of the 17th century which established educational and cultural institutions. The most notable rabbi of the community was Meir Shalom Rabinowicz (1896–1902). Mordecai Mottel Mikhelson, one of the wealthiest merchants of the town during the 19th century, assumed the role of *shtadlan*. The community numbered 1,455 (80% of the total population) in 1827; 6,419 (76%) in 1897; 5,033 (82%) in 1921; 7,256 (82%) in 1931; and approximately 6,500 on the eve of the Holocaust. Jewish economic activity included industrial enterprises, such as pottery, flour mills, the weaving of prayer shawls, the fur trade which employed many Jewish workers, and crafts, notably tailoring and carpentry. The community administration elected in 1924 was composed of six members for *Agudat Israel, five for *Mizrachi, and one Zionist.

[Shimshon Leib Kirshenboim]

Holocaust Period

The German Army entered Kaluszyn on Sept. 11, 1939, after a heavy bombardment and conflagrations that killed around 1,000 Jews. Some 4,000 Jews were then confined 15–20 to a room in the part of the town still standing. In summer 1940 a ghetto was established, including also 1,000 Jewish refugees. On November 25, 1942, around 3,000 were deported to the *Treblinka death camp where they were exterminated. Another group of Jews from Minsk Mazowiecki was then deported to the Kaluszyn ghetto and in December 1942 also sent to Treblinka. The Jewish community was not reconstituted after the war.

[Stefan Krakowski]

BIBLIOGRAPHY: T. Brustin-Berenstein, in: BŻIH, no. 1 (1952), 83–125, passim.

KALVARIJA (Pol. **Kalwaria**; Rus. **Kalvariya**), town in S.E. Lithuania. Jews who had settled there, including several families of weavers, received a grant of privilege in 1713 to engage in commerce and crafts independently of the guilds, and permission to build a synagogue. A new synagogue was built in 1803. The community numbered 1,055 poll tax payers in 1766 and 6,508 persons (over 80% of the population) in 1856. During the 1860s many Jews in Kalvarija immigrated to the United States, and by 1897 the community had decreased to 3,581 (37%). Isaac Slonimer, author of *Emek Yehoshu'a*, and Mordecai Klaczko (also called Mordecai Melzer), author of *Tekhelet Mordekhai*, served as rabbis in Kalvarija. Other prominent scholars and communal workers included Baer Ratner and Isaac Meir Margoliot. During World War I there was a further decline in the Jewish population when, owing to the war and a fire which broke out in 1915, many Jews moved to towns in Russia and Lithuania. Their numbers had decreased to 1,233 by 1923 (27%). The gradual nationalization of the agricultural import trade, from which Jews largely derived their livelihood, led to further emigration, and by 1939 only 1,000 Jews remained in Kalvarija. During the period of Lithuanian independence (1918–40) the community had five synagogues and three Jewish schools, a loan bank, and communal and cultural institutions.

Following the outbreak of World War II Jewish refugees from nearby Polish towns arrived in Kalvarija where they were warmly received by the community. After the Germans occupied Kalvarija on June 22, 1941, the Jews were brought to the Marijampole barracks on August 30 with thousands of other Jews from the area and murdered.

BIBLIOGRAPHY: *Yahadut Lita*, 3 (1967), 348–50; Y. Metz, in: Life, 1 (Yid., 1951), 1499–1512.

[Dov Levin]

KAMELHAR, JEKUTHIEL ARYEH BEN GERSHON (1871–1937), Galician rabbi and author. Kamelhar was born in Kolaczyce, Galicia. During his youth, his parents moved to Tarnow, where he received a thorough talmudic education, and in 1897 took up residence in Rzeszow. In 1906 he was appointed head of the yeshivah Or Torah in the town of Stanislav, Eastern Galicia. At the outbreak of World War I he went to Vienna as a refugee, returning to Rzeszow after the war. In 1926 he accepted an appointment as rabbi of the congregation Reisha-Kurtshin in New York. In 1933 he emigrated to Ereẓ Israel, and lived in Jerusalem for the rest of his life. He wrote a number of biographies of rabbis: *Mofet ha-Dor* (1903), on Ezekiel *Landau; *Em le-Binah* (1909), a life of Ẓevi Hirsch of Romanov; *Ḥasidim ha-Rishonim* (1917), on *Samuel he-Ḥasid and his son *Judah he-Ḥasid; *Dor De'ah* (1933–35; new ed. under the title *Arba Tekufot ba-Ḥasidut ha-Beshtit*), biographies of the leaders of the modern ḥasidic movements; and another work of the same name (1935), which contains a survey of the activities of great talmudists and a methodology of their systems. His talmudic works are *Boker Yizraḥ* (1896), on the order of service for the blessing of the sun at the beginning of its cycle; a commentary on *Rosh ha-Shanah* attributed to Maimonides (1906, 1955[2], published by his son Moses); *Ḥedvata di-Shemateta* in 2 parts (1912–13), whose purpose was "to resolve doubts and problems in *halakhah* by means of authoritative sources and examples from the Babylonian and Jerusalem Talmuds." He wrote *Ha-Talmud u-Madda'ei ha-Te-*

vel (1928), comprising a kind of methodology of the Talmud, and appended to it *Netivot ha-Talmud*, on tractate *Berakhot* of the Babylonian and Jerusalem Talmuds, giving general rules and principles derived from the *Gemara*, Rashi, and *tosafot* of the tractate. Among his other works was *Ma'amar ha-Avodah ve-Ishei Yisrael* (1935–36), a blueprint for the renewal of the Temple service in Jerusalem. Kamelhar was also the editor of *Ohel Mo'ed* – a talmudic periodical that appeared between the years 1898 and 1901. A complete bio-bibliography of the works of Kamelhar in the possession of the Jewish National and University Library, including unpublished manuscripts, incomplete works, projects and notes, has been published by Binyamin (Tel Aviv, 1978).

BIBLIOGRAPHY: Y.A. Kamelhar, *Ahavat ha-Kadmonim* (1938), introd.; H. Malachowsky, *Kitvei Hillel… Malachowsky*, 7 (1939), 150–4; M. Kamelhar (ed.), *Perush La-Rambam al Massekhet Rosh Ha-Shanah im Ḥiddushim u-Mekorot me'et Y.A. Kamelhar* (1955^2), 151f.; idem, in: *Rzeszów Jews Memorial Book* (1967), 95–99.

[Yehoshua Horowitz]

KAMENETSKY, YAAKOV (1891–1986), U.S. rabbi and scholar. A leader of modern Orthodox Jewry for more than a half-century, Kamenetsky was born in Kalushkave, a small Lithuanian village near Minsk. He studied under Torah luminaries at the Slobodka yeshivah, including Rabbi Moshe Mordechai Epstein and Rabbi Nosson Zvi Finkel (the *Sabba* of Slobodka), who nurtured the brilliant student's education and his interest in **musar* (spiritual self-improvement). By 18, Kamenetsky had become a renowned Torah scholar who had earned rabbinical ordination by several esteemed Lithuanian rabbis.

In 1919, Kamenetsky married Etta Heller, daughter of the *mashgi'aḥ* of the Slobodka yeshivah and continued to study at the Kollel Bet Yisroel in Slobodka. He accepted his first rabbinic position in 1926 at Zitavian, near Kovno, Lithuania, serving as communal rabbi until 1937. However, harsh Communist rule led Kamenetsky to immigrate to Seattle, Washington, in 1937 to accept a temporary position at Congregation Bikur Cholim. Later that same year, Kamenetsky moved to Toronto, where he served as rabbi of Congregation Toras Emes and as headmaster of a small yeshivah.

In 1946, Kamenetsky joined the faculty of Mesivta Torah Vo-Da'ath in Brooklyn, New York. Within two years, he headed the yeshivah (together with Rabbi Gedalya Schorr) following the passing of the dean, Rabbi Shraga Feivel Mendlowitz. Under Kamenetsky's energetic and inspiring leadership, the Mesivta Torah Vo-Da'ath added a high school, a post-high school seminary, and a *kolel* institute. Through these efforts, Kaminetsky helped fuel the unprecedented surge in Torah education in the U.S. in the post-Holocaust era. By the 1960s, Kaminetsky was widely regarded as one of the leading Torah scholars in the U.S. He served on the presidium of the Council of Torah Sages of the Agudath Israel of America (*Moetzet Gedolei HaTorah*) and as chairman of the Advisory Board of Torah U'Mesorah (National Society of Hebrew Day Schools).

Unlike many other Orthodox rabbis of his generation, Kaminetsky read and admired some works of classic secular literature. Such secular reading was controversial, as some feared the further secularizing influences on European and American Orthodox youth, many of whom were already shedding their religious lifestyles.

Kamenetsky retired to Monsey, New York, in 1968, where he continued to teach Talmud classes from his home, provide personal counseling and halakhic advice to those who sought it. He also wrote articles for the journals *Jewish Observer* and *Ha-Pardes*. He died at the age of 95.

His son, Nathan, a brilliant Talmudist, published a biography of his father, *The Making of a Gadol*. Respectful and insightful as it was, the book was banned because of the climate of Ḥaredi Judaism in the early 20th century. Published in a limited edition of 1,000, the book is now rare and offered at auction at many times its original publication price. It seems that the ban has only excited the interest of would-be readers. The book will be reissued without the offending passages.

BIBLIOGRAPHY: M. Sherman, *Orthodox Judaism in America* (1996); N. Kamenetsky, *The Making of a Gadol* (2002); D. Rachelson, "Rabbi Yaakov Kamenetsky," at: www.eilatgordonlivitan.com.

[Judy Gruen (2nd ed.)]

KAMENETS-PODOLSKI, city in Khmelnitski district (until the 1950s district capital), in Ukraine; under the rule of Lithuania from the 14th century, and after the union with Poland (1569) under Poland-Lithuania (but for the short though important and formative interval of Ottoman rule there, 1672–99); it passed to Russia in 1795, and from then until the 1917 Revolution was capital of the province of Podolia. For a long time the municipality of Kamenets-Podolski prevented attempts of Jews to settle in this important trading and communications center in southeast Poland-Lithuania. In 1447 Jews were prohibited from staying there for more than three days. In 1598 King Sigismund III prohibited Jews from settling in the city and suburbs and from engaging in trade there; their visits were again restricted to three days only. During the *Chmielnicki uprising, many Jews sought refuge in the fortified city which withstood attacks by the Cossacks in 1648 and 1652. Subsequently King John II Casimir permitted Jews to reside there, and they apparently continued to live in Kamenets-Podolski despite repeated prohibitions in 1654, 1665, and 1670. Under Ottoman rule Jewish settlement was permitted and grew to a considerable size.

After the city's return to Poland in 1699, the Christian citizens resumed their opposition to Jewish settlement. In 1737 the city council submitted a request to the state and Church authorities to banish the Jews from the city, maintaining that they had no right to settle there, and were competing with the Christian inhabitants and impoverishing them. King Augustus III expelled the Jews from Kamenets-Podolski in 1750. Their houses passed to the town council and the synagogue was demolished. The expelled Jews settled in the suburbs and in nearby villages, which were under jurisdiction of Polish noblemen, and developed extensive trading activity there which led to additional complaints on the part of the citizens. In 1725 the Council of Four Lands met in Kamenets-Podolski.

In 1757 a public disputation was held by the Church in Kamenets-Podolski – enjoined by the local bishop – between the representatives of Podolian Jewry and Jacob *Frank and his supporters. After it took place the Talmud was publicly burned in the city on the bishop's orders (see *Disputations; *Talmud, Burning of).

After Kamenets-Podolski passed to Russia, Czar Paul I confirmed in 1797 the right of Jews to reside there. At that time 24 Jews belonging to merchant guilds and 1,367 Jewish inhabitants were registered in the tax-assessment books of the city. Two years later, in 1799, 29 merchants and 2,617 Jewish inhabitants were registered. In 1832 the Christians in Kamenets-Podolski petitioned the government to expel the Jews from the city, basing themselves upon their ancient privileges. The petition was rejected but in 1833 the government restricted the right of the Jews to build shops and new houses, or to acquire houses, to two suburbs of the city only in order to prevent them from residing in the city itself. The restriction was rescinded in 1859. The community numbered 4,629 in 1847, 16,211 (40% of the total population) in 1897, and they were busy in small industry, trade, and artisanship. Rabbis who served in the city were Pinkhas of Koretz, David Wahrman, a disciple of R. Levi Isaac from Berdichev, S.Y. Abramovitsh (Mendele Mokher Sforim), and Menakhem Poznanski; the poets Aharon Ashman and Avraham Rosen were active for various periods. In 1910 there were 22,279 Jews. Four private schools and modernized *ḥadarim* were operating, and later also two Hebrew schools and a library. All major Jewish parties were active there.

After 1918, during the civil war, the Jews in Kamenets-Podolski suffered severely and 200 Jews were killed there in pogroms by Petlyura's gangs in July 1919. After the establishment of the Soviet regime, many wealthy Jews fled across the frontier and the economy of the Jewish population was ruined. Jewish cultural and communal life was entirely suppressed after a protracted struggle with the *Yevsektsiya. In 1922 ORT opened vocational schools to train Jewish youth in crafts. By 1926 only 12,774 Jews remained (29.9% of the total population), and by 1939 they numbered 13,796. In the 1920s 76 families left to settle in Crimea, and 80 to settle in Birobidzhan. Three Yiddish schools and two teachers' colleges opened there, but only one school was active in 1938.

Holocaust Period

The Germans entered the town on July 11, 1941. A ghetto was established on July 20, and by the end of the month 11,000 Jews were brought in from Hungary as well as from Czechoslovakia and Poland. From August 25 through 28, 23,600 Jews were killed. Laborers with skills, from town and from neighboring settlements, were concentrated in a labor camp within the ghetto. In January 1942, 4,000 were murdered and much later 500 children (aged 4–8) were executed; 2,500 were killed in January 1943 and another 2,000 in February. In 1979 about 1,800 Jews lived in Kamenets-Podolski; most of them left in the 1990s for Israel or the West.

BIBLIOGRAPHY: M. Balaban, *Le-Toledot ha-Tenu'ah ha-Frankistit* (1934), 137–51; A. Gumener, *A Kapitl Ukraine* (1921); *Kaminits-Podolsk u-Sevivatah* (1965).

[Yehuda Slutsky / Shmuel Spector (2nd ed.)]

KAMENETZKY, ABRAHAM SHALOM (1874–1943), Polish scholar. Kamenetzky, born in Slonim, studied Oriental languages at German and Swiss universities. Until 1914 he was on the staff of the *Yevreyskaya Entsiklopediya* and lectured at the St. Petersburg Institute of Jewish Studies. After World War I he was in charge of the library attached to the Warsaw Tlomackie Synagogue. During the Nazi occupation of Poland he was in Lodz, where he worked in the ghetto archives. He died in the ghetto. Kamenetzky's publications in Hebrew, Yiddish, German, and French appeared in various periodicals. He produced an illustrated geography of Ereẓ Israel, *Geografyah Meẓuyyeret shel Ereẓ Yisrael* (1920 and subsequent editions), and coedited a shortened Hebrew version of Graetz's *Geschichte der Juden*, called *Divrei Yemei Yisrael* (6 vols., 1929–30), of which he translated parts three and four.

KAMENEV, LEV (pseudonym for **Lev Borisovich Rosenfeld**; 1883–1936), Soviet state and party activist. He was born in Moscow to a father who was an engineer and a Russian mother. Kamenev joined the Social Democratic Party in 1901, while studying law at Moscow University, and in 1903 the Bolshevik faction. Until 1914 he worked in the foreign press of the party, and returned to Russia to head the editorial board of *Pravda*. In 1915 he was exiled to Siberia and returned to Petersburg after the February 1917 revolution; he headed the Bolshevik Party until Lenin's return. He was against armed uprising and for a coalition with socialist parties, which countered Lenin's ideas. As a protest he resigned from the Central Committee of the party, and was restored only in mid-1918. In the years 1919–26 he was a member of the Politburo, and at the same time chairman of the Moscow Town Council, and chairman of the Council of the People's Commissars. In 1926 he was Commissar of Trade, and chief editor of Lenin's writings. In 1927 he was ambassador to Italy.

In 1922–24 he was, together with Zinovyev and Stalin, involved in a struggle with *Trotsky for the leadership of the party. In 1925 he headed together with Zinovyev the new opposition, and in 1926 he joined Trotsky. For that he was banished in 1927 from the Central Committee and the party. In 1928 he admitted his "mistakes," and was reinstated in the party, but given second-rate jobs. In 1932 he was again banished from the party and exiled to the Urals. He was freed but arrested again in December 1934, after the assassination of S. Kirov, and sentenced to five years' imprisonment. In July 1935 Stalin organized a closed trial, and only due to M. Gorki's intervention was he not executed but sentenced to ten years in prison. In August 1936 in the first show trial he was accused together with Zinovyev and others of conterrevolution, terror, and espionage, and under physical and psychological pressure he admitted his guilt and was shot, according to an official announcement on August 25, 1936.

In the 1920s he promoted the Habimah theater, helped Prof. Shor of the Moscow Conservatory to immigrate to Ereẓ Israel, and was active in reducing the arrest of Zionists to expulsion from the Soviet Union.

[Shmuel Spector (2nd ed.)]

KAMENKA, ẒEVI HIRSCH OF (d. 1781), founder of a ḥasidic dynasty in Kamenka, Ukraine. Kamenka was one of seven brothers who were disciples and admirers of *Israel b. Eliezer, the Ba'al Shem Tov, and were active in furthering his influence. The eldest brother was SAMUEL (THE ELDER) OF KAMENKA (d. 1831?). A grandson of Ẓevi Hirsch, SAMUEL II OF KAMENKA, was a ḥasidic *admor, a disciple of *Baruch of Medzhibezh and *Abraham Joshua Heschel of Apta, and an outstanding disciple and colleague of *Levi Isaac of Berdichev. His grandson, ABRAHAM DAVID of Miropolye, a noted scholar and *admor* of many Ḥasidim, continued the dynasty. David's son, SAMUEL III, author of *Shem mi-Shemu'el*, succeeded to his father's position and moved to the United States.

The book *Shenei ha-Me'orot* (Kishinev, 1896) includes some of the sayings of Ẓevi Hirsch and his brothers, and of Samuel II of Kamenka.

[Adin Steinsaltz]

KAMENKA-BUGSKAYA (Pol. **Kamionka Strumiłowa**), city in Tarnopol district, Ukraine. The earliest information on Jewish settlement dates from 1456. An agreement reached between the burghers and the Jews, granting the latter rights of residence and free trade, was confirmed by King Sigismund III Vasa in 1589. Jews traded in grain, cattle, fish, and lumber. At the end of the 17th century the bishop of Lvov permitted the community to erect a wooden synagogue. The walls of this fine building were covered with paintings (done in 1730) mainly depicting animal figures. In 1662 there were 16 Jewish and 90 Christian houses in the town. At the beginning of the 18th century Ḥayyim b. Isaac *Reiẓes served as rabbi of the community, which was under the jurisdiction of the regional *kahal* of the province of "Russia." In 1719 and 1736 the Jews paid poll taxes of 786 and 400 zlotys respectively. Of the 522 Jews in the city in 1765, 79 were innkeepers. The community numbered 2,922 (48% of the total population) in 1880, 3,164 (43.3%) in 1900, and 2,685 (41%) in 1921. The drop in their number resulted from devastation by a large fire during WWI. From 1924 until 1939 there was a supplementary Hebrew school with about 200 pupils. In 1931 the Jewish population numbered 3,283; before September 1939 it had reached 4,000.

[*Encyclopaedia Judaica* (Germany)]

Holocaust Period

The Jewish community changed greatly during the Soviet period of 1939–41, when community institutions were dissolved and any independent political activity was forbidden. The traditional Jewish economy was also hurt. Jews tried to integrate into the new activities by organizing themselves into craftsmen's cooperatives and entering the municipal and civil service. On June 28, 1941, the city was occupied by the Germans, and the next day they murdered 200 Jews. On July 2, the Ukrainians, instigated by the Germans, carried out a pogrom, killing a few hundred Jews. On November 10, 1941, another 500 Jews were killed near the city. In the summer of 1942 a census was taken of the Jewish population; workers were given special permits, while of the others some 1,500 persons were deported to *Belzec death camp (Sept. 15, 1942). On Sept. 21, 1942, 600 persons were put to death in Zabuze (area beyond the River Bug), where Jews from *Busk, Cholojow, and Radziechow (Radekhou) were also murdered. On Oct. 28, 1942, another group was deported to Belzec, thereby completing the murder of most of the community. In November 1941 a forced-labor camp was set up in which Jews from the entire neighborhood were concentrated. On July 10, 1943, more than 5,000 Jews were murdered there.

[Aharon Weiss]

BIBLIOGRAPHY: M. Baliński and T. Lipiński, *Starożytna Polska*, 2 (1845), index; A. Breier, M. Eisler, and M. Grunwald, *Holzsynagogen in Polen* (1934), 16, 35, 40, 44, 47, 48, 52, 62; G. Loukomsky, *Jewish Art in European Synagogues* (1947), 37, 39, 41, 64; B. Wasiutyński, *Ludnośe żydowska w Polsce w XIX i XX wiekach* (1930), 98, 108, 120; I. Schiper, *Dzieje handlu żydowskiego na ziemiach polskich* (1937), index.

KAMENSZAIN, TOBIAS (1918–2000), lawyer and leader of the Argentinean Jewish community. Kamenszain was born in Ostrow, Poland. In 1928 his family emigrated to Buenos Aires. In addition to studying at a state school he attended the Hebrew school of the Zionist Federation (General Zionists). He joined Ha-Shomer ha-Ẓa'ir as a teenager and in 1939 began his university studies, which he completed in 1946. He also joined the Right Po'alei Zion Party and was close to one of its leaders, Moshe Kostrinsky-*Kitron. In 1946 he married Eva Staif, a graduate in biochemistry. Her family was very active in Jewish life, and her father, Moshe Staif, was one of the founders of the Zionist Bialik School in Buenos Aires. Eva was much involved in Jewish education and for many years directed the ORT school. In 1947 Kamenszain was elected to the central committee of Right Po'alei Zion and became secretary of *Keren Kayemet with Isaac Kaplan as chairman. Subsequently he was secretary of *Keren Hayesod. When Yitzhak Harkavi made *aliyah*, Kamenszain was elected secretary general of Po'alei Zion. In 1960 and 1966 Kamenszain was elected chairman of AMIA-Ashkenazi Community of Buenos Aires. In 1966 he was also elected chairman of the Vaad Hakehilot – the federation of all the Jewish communities of Argentina. Among other positions, in the 1960s and 1970s he headed the board of Hamidrasha Haivrit (high school for Jewish studies and seminar for secondary school teachers) and in the 1990s the Keren Kayemet of Argentina.

[Efraim Zadoff (2nd ed.)]

KAMHI, JAK V. (1925–), Turkish industrialist. Born in Istanbul, Kamhi graduated as an engineer from Yıldız Technical University, becoming chairman of the board of the Profilo Group of companies. He was an adviser to the prime ministry of Turkey for Turkey-EU and Turkey-U.S. relations. He was the founding chairman of the Quincentennial Foundation, which was established in 1989 with the purpose of celebrating the arrival of the Sephardim exiled in 1492 to the Ottoman lands; and he lobbied on behalf of the Turkish Republic, especially in the U.S., where Turkey was severely criticized for denying the Armenian genocide and for the infringement of human rights. He was given several awards, including the High Service Award from the Turkish Ministry of Foreign Affairs, the Légion d'Honneur, and the rank of commander in the National Order of Merit from the president of the French Republic and the commander of the Order of Spanish Civil Merit from the king of Spain.

[Rifat Bali (2nd ed.)]

KAMHI, LEON (1898–1943), commercial agent and Zionist activist. Kamhi was born and lived in Bitola (Monastir) in the Yugoslav part of Macedonia, also known as Vardar Macedonia. He received his education in the Alliance school and intended to pursue studies in Paris, but family problems prevented him and he had to start earning a living without delay. Working hard, he soon became an independent businessman. From his youth on, he was a Zionist leader and organizer. He was influential also in the affairs of the Kehillah, helping in financing the participation of Macedonian Jewish youth in the Zionist summer camps, mostly held in the Julian Alps, in faraway Slovenia. He founded or managed Zionist groups in other towns of the region, such as Stip and the provincial capital, Skopje. He represented Macedonian Jewry in all countywide forums and gatherings, maintaining intimate ties with Jewish leaders in Zagreb, the Zionist center, as well as in Belgrade, the seat of the Federation of Jewish Communities. His assistance in promoting *aliyah* to Palestine was essential, including the sending of unmarried young girls or arranging for them fictional marriages to assure the fullest use of the very scarce available certificates (immigration affidavits) apportioned by the British, allocated through the services of the Jewish Agency for Palestine and its representatives in Zagreb.

Kamhi planned to emigrate himself and corresponded on this matter with his friends already residing in Palestine during the years 1934 to 1936, postponing the implementation of his plan time and again for personal and/or communal reasons.

He was the uncontested leader of Macedonian Jewry, eventually sharing their tragic fate in March 1943, when the Bulgarian fascists, cruel and willing collaborators with the Nazis, arrested all 7,000 Jews, mistreating them and handing them over to the Germans in the Bulgarian town of Lom, from where they were deported, in four transports, to their death in Treblinka.

[Zvi Loker (2nd ed.)]

KAMINER, ISAAC (1834–1901), Hebrew writer. Born in Lewkiow in the Ukraine, he was drawn into the Haskalah movement in his youth, and taught at the government school for Jews in Zhitomir (1854–59). Later he completed medical school at the University of Kiev and was a physician in that town till the end of the 1870s. During that period he inclined toward socialism and joined the circles of A.S. *Liebermann and Judah Loeb *Levin (Yehalel).

Kaminer wrote verse satires for the Hebrew socialist papers *Ha-Emet* and *Asefat Ḥakhamim* (among them his best poem *Shir ha-Yiḥud la-Matbe'a*), but he disagreed with the assimilationist tendencies prevalent in socialist circles. Only two works were published separately in his lifetime, *Kinot mi-Sidduram shel Benei Dan* (1878), and *Seder Kapparot le-Va'al Takse* (1878). Kaminer criticized not only the Ḥasidim and those clinging to old notions but also supporters of the Haskalah and the rich community leaders. In a series of poems, *Maskil el Dal*, he described, in a favorable light, folk figures like the peddler and the destitute rabbis. In some of his verse he strongly defended the use of the Hebrew language and lamented the younger generation's alienation from "Jewish nationality." After the pogroms of the 1880s he joined the Ḥibbat Zion movement and from then on his verse was dedicated to the cause of Jewish nationalism and the settlement of Palestine. The board of Ḥovevei Zion published his selected poems posthumously (1905), edited by *Aḥad Ha-Am and J.H. Rawnitzky. The selection was drastically edited. Kaminer's works have little artistic value but they had an influence upon the readers of his day.

BIBLIOGRAPHY: J.H. Rawnitzky, *Dor ve-Soferav* (1926), 143–59; Klausner, Sifrut, 6 (1950^2), 208–42; Waxman, Literature, 3 (1960), 263–4.

[Yehuda Slutsky]

KAMINETSKY, JOSEPH (1911–1999), director of Torah Umesorah. Kaminetsky attended public school for one year, when his father realized that this would not do. He sold their home so he his son could attend Yeshiva Chaim Berlin in Brownsville, Brooklyn, New York. The boy then attended Talmudical Academy High School on the Lower East Side and was a student in the first freshman class of Yeshiva University. He graduated magna cum laude in 1932.

While working toward his doctoral degree in education at the Teacher's College at Columbia University, he was the founding principal of the after-school learning program of the Jewish Center Synagogue in Manhattan. Later, he was the congregation's assistant rabbi under Rabbi Leo Jung. After earning his degree, Rabbi Kaminetsky was appointed executive director of Manhattan Day School.

In 1946, he was handpicked by Rabbi Shraga Feivel Mendlowitz, founder of Torah Umesorah, the National Association for Hebrew Day Schools, to be its educational director, and then two years later, its national director. Upon his retirement, 36 years later, he was appointed director emeritus. Dr. Joe, as he was affectionately known, served Torah Umesorah for 41 years.

Kaminetsky was the key figure in the explosive growth of Orthodox day schools in the United States and Canada since World War II. When he began his tenure at Torah Umesorah, his goal was that every town or city with a Jewish population of at least 5,000 would establish a Jewish day school. As Kaminetsky put it in his memoirs, *Memorable Encounters*, his job was to create "a national bureau of 'doers' who could help communities establish all-day Jewish schools of their own."

Dr. Hillel Goldberg of the National Council of Synagogue Youth, recalls that in the post-Holocaust 1940s, there was almost no American Jew who had all of Kaminetsky's qualifications to become executive director of Torah Umesorah.

Goldberg wrote that

> Dr. Kaminetsky could sell Jewish education, not just because he believed in it, understood it, or cared. He did not found scores of Jewish day schools on these qualities alone. Still less, on these qualities alone did he persuade others to give up potentially lucrative careers to found hundreds more day schools. The secret… *his* secret? Dr. Joseph Kaminetsky convinced you that *you* were building the school, *you* were the leader, *you* were the doer, *you* were making the sacrifice, *you* had the abilities, *you* were making the difference.

Today there are well over 600 yeshivah day schools in the United States and Canada with over 170,000 students.

Marvin Schick wrote of Rabbi Kaminetsky as an educator who bridged three worlds.

> Torah Umesorah represented a coming together in common cause of a remarkable group of Roshei Yeshiva, lay leaders and staff. The Roshei Yeshiva set the over-all policy and decided difficult questions. Led by Rav Aharon Kotler, the transcendent Torah leader of American Orthodoxy in the post-Holocaust years, their involvement in day schools was remarkable in view of their personal histories and the character of the institutions which they headed. Their Torah Umesorah activities entailed, in a certain way, a measure of compromise, for they were sanctioning schools whose standards were at times more than a notch below what they ordinarily would be willing to accept. Yet they all knew that the building of Torah in America required nurturing.

In the mid-1950s, most lay leaders were Modern Orthodox, while the *roshei yeshivah*, generally, were also the leaders of the more stringent Agudath Israel. As Shick says, "There were strains, some serious, in the tripartite arrangement. Dr. Joe served as the mediator between the yeshivish world of Torah Umesorah leadership and the Modern Orthodox community."

In his memoirs, Dr. Kaminetsky wrote

> Although I felt sympathetic to the ideals of both the pure yeshivish and Modern Orthodox worlds, I was typed as a "modern" by some of the Torah Umesorah kehillah… In truth, in those early years, I did indeed find myself living ideologically in two worlds: the Modern Orthodox milieu of Yeshiva University and the more traditional yeshiva world of my early Brownsville days and of Torah Umesorah… I was criticized now and then by… religiously conservative people who objected to any hint of ideological flexibility on the day-school initiative – while at the same time, many of my former friends at Yeshiva called me a "black-hatter." Yet the L-rd was good to me and enabled me to maintain a careful equilibrium between the two worlds and to work with both for the sake of Torah.

[Jeanette Friedman (2nd ed.)]

KAMINKA, ARMAND (**Aaron**; 1866–1950), rabbi and scholar. Kaminka, who was born in Berdichev, studied at the universities of Berlin and Paris as well as at the orthodox Rabbinerseminar in Berlin and the Lehranstalt fuer die Wissenschaft des Judentums in Berlin. His first appointment was as rabbi at Frankfurt on the Oder, then as preacher at the Reform temple in Prague (1893–97). After serving as chief rabbi of Esseg (Osyek), Slavonia (1897–1900), he moved to Vienna where he became secretary of the Israelitische Allianz (whose history he described in *Haolam*, 35 (1948), nos. 1–11). In 1903 Kaminka was sent by the Israelitische Allianz to Kishinev to investigate the pogrom that had taken place there that April. He also taught Talmud, philosophy, and history at the *bet ha-midrash* of I.H. Weiss (1901–04), as well as at the community's religious teachers' training college. In 1924 Kaminka founded Maimonides College (for the spreading of Jewish knowledge among Viennese Jewry), and from 1926 lectured on Talmud and Jewish philosophy at the University of Vienna. With the annexation of Austria by Hitler in 1938, Kaminka settled in Palestine.

As secretary of the Allianz, Kaminka was involved in relief work for the victims of persecution in Romania and Russia to the end of World War I. He had been active from youth in the Ḥibbat Zion movement and was long associated with Theodor *Herzl, who considered Kaminka a suitable intermediary between himself and the Russian Ḥovevei Zion. Kaminka took part in the first Zionist Congress (1897), where he gave the official address on Jewish settlement in Palestine. Because of his interest in "practical Zionism," he eventually fell out with Herzl.

Kaminka was a poet and translator. His translations into Hebrew from classical literature include: Marcus Aurelius' *Meditations* (1923); Aristotle's *De Anima* (1949); Seneca's *Epistulae Morales* (1940–42), *Dialogues* (1943–45), and *Naturales Quaestiones* (1946); and a two-volume selection of tragedies by Aeschylus, Sophocles, and Euripides (*Tragedyot Nivḥarot…*, 1940–48). Kaminka's own poetry as well as some of his translations were published in several collections. He also wrote a drama, *Shever Beit Aḥav* ("Downfall of the House of Ahab," 1941).

In his writings on the Bible, Kaminka generally adopted a conservative line, strongly rejecting the theories of the Bible criticism and arguing for the unity of Isaiah and for the pre-Exilic origin of much of Psalms and Song of Songs. Kaminka also published numerous studies on the talmudic literature. Here, in contrast to his biblical research, he adopted a very critical view denying the historicity of many talmudic statements. He also began to publish a critical edition of the *She'iltot de-R. Aḥai Ga'on* (1908), a subject to which he returned in several articles, claiming that the work is of a rhetorical and nonhalakhic nature. Kaminka also prepared an edition of Al-Ḥarizi's *Taḥkemoni* (1899), with introduction and notes. In the field of Apocrypha, he translated the so-called IV Ezra from Latin into Hebrew as *Ḥazonot Asir She'alti'el* (1936), with notes and introduction. He also turned his attention to the early translators in his *Studien zur Septuaginta* (1928). In this study he tries to prove that the Septuagint did not have a textually different Hebrew version as its basis. Some of his scholarly articles were republished in *Meḥkarim ba-Mikra u-va-Talmud…* (2 vols., 1938–51), and *Kitvei Bikkoret Historit* (1944).

BIBLIOGRAPHY: *Festschrift Armand Kaminka…* (Ger. and Heb., 1937), includes bibliography; M. Zucker, in: *Hadoar*, 29 (1950), 820–1, 840–1; Th. Herzl, *Complete Diaries…*, ed. by R. Patai, 5 (1960), index; Aḥad Ha-Am, *Iggerot…*, 6 vols. (1956–60²), index; Ḥ.N. Bialik, *Iggerot…*, 5 vols. (1938–39), index; I. Klausner, *Ha-Tenu'ah le-Ẓiyyon be-Rusyah…* (1962), index; A. Freud, in: *Zeitschrift fuer die Geschichte der Juden*, 3 (1966), 222–3.

[Tobias Grill (2nd ed.)]

KAMINSKI or **KAMINSKA**, family of Yiddish actors. ABRAHAM ISAAC KAMINSKI (1867–1918) organized his own theatrical company in Warsaw at the age of 20 and also toured the smaller towns. When the Russian ban on Yiddish theater was lifted in 1908, he also toured in Russia. Among the plays he staged were several of his own and translations of Gorki (*The Lower Depths*), Schiller (*Die Raeuber*), and Molière (*Le Malade imaginaire*). Shortly before World War I he founded the Kaminski Theater in Warsaw.

His wife ESTHER RACHEL KAMINSKA (née Halpern; 1870–1925) won fame in her husband's company. When she appeared in St. Petersburg in 1905, she was hailed as "the Yiddish Duse." Her repertoire included plays by Ibsen, Dumas, and Sudermann, but she was considered at her best in portrayals of the mother roles of Jacob *Gordin She toured the U.S. in 1909–11, and played in London and Paris in 1913.

IDA KAMINSKA (1899–1980), their daughter, started her career as a child in her father's company and became its leading figure. Her first husband was Martin Sigmund *Turkow; her second Meir Melman (1899–1978), a leading actor.

On the invasion of Poland in 1939, the family fled into the Soviet-occupied zone and later into Central Asia. When she returned to Poland after World War II, she resumed activity in Lodz. In Warsaw she earned for her company the status of the "Jewish State Theater," with which she toured Israel, North and South America, and later western Europe. She also achieved fame in films. Her role in the film *The Shop on Main Street* (1967) was widely acclaimed. She left Poland in 1968 as a result of the antisemitic campaign in the country when the emigration of many of the country's remaining Jews deprived her of her audience. After emigrating to the United States, where she starred in *Glueckel von Hameln*, Kaminska settled in Israel in 1975 with her actor-husband Meir Melman, and joined the newly formed Yiddish Theater in Tel Aviv.

Another member of the family, JOSEPH KAMINSKI (1903–1972), son of Abraham and Esther Rachel, studied music in Berlin and Vienna, settled in Palestine in 1937, and became first violinist in the Israel Philharmonic Orchestra. He composed works for orchestra, chamber groups, and solo instruments.

ADD. BIBLIOGRAPHY: Y. Turkov-Grudberg, *Yidddish Teater in Poylen* (1951), 34.ff.

[Joseph Leftwich]

KAMNIEL, ABU AL-HASAN MEIR IBN, physician in Seville who was invited by the Almoravide ruler Ali b. Yūsuf ibn Tāshfin (1106–43) to serve at his court in *Marrakesh. Ibn Kamniel was a friend of *Judah Halevi, who dedicated some of his poems to him. At the court in Marrakesh he met Solomon ibn al-Muʿallim, also a physician and poet, and a friend of Judah Halevi and Abraham *Ibn Ezra, who both praised Ibn al-Muʿallim in their poems. According to Ibn *Aknin, Ibn al-Muʿallim expounded verses to the ruler from Song of Songs according to their plain meaning, thereby arousing Ibn Kamniel's anger. At the time these Jewish physicians met in Marrakesh, which was the capital of the Almoravide empire and Ibn Tāshfin's residence, it was generally not permitted for Jews to live in the city. Therefore, Ibn Tāshfin's invitation to the two Jewish physicians from Spain to serve at his court must have been with good reason, particularly when his policies were not friendly toward Jews. It is known that there were competent Arab physicians in North Africa at the time. In sending for the Jewish physicians Ibn Tāshfin may have desired to establish a medical school in Marrakesh which could compete with that in Fez. Be that as it may, these physicians seem to have built the nucleus for a small Jewish community in Marrakesh which was destroyed by the *Almohads in the middle of the 12th century.

BIBLIOGRAPHY: Hirschberg, Afrikah, 1 (1965), 264, 386 n. 83 (includes bibliography); Dinur, Golah, 2 pt. 1 (19652), 335 no. 14; M. Maimonides, *Treatise on Asthma*, ed. by S. Muntner (1963), 43.

[Haïm Z'ew Hirschberg]

KAMPELMAN, MAX M. (1920–), U.S. lawyer and diplomat. Born in New York, Kampelman received his undergraduate and legal education at New York University, and his M.A. and Ph.D. in political science at the University of Minnesota. He taught political science at the University of Minnesota (1946–48) and at Bennington College (1948–50). He came under the influence of Senator Hubert H. Humphrey and served as his legislative counsel (1949–55). He then joined the law firm of Fried, Frank, Harris, Shriver and Kampelman, in Washington, D.C. He served as director and as chairman of the executive committee of the District of Columbia National Bank (1962–66). He was a creator and moderator of the popular television program *Washington Week in Review* (1967–70) and chairman of the Washington public broadcasting radio and television stations (1963–70).

Kampelman has had an active career as a major American diplomat, serving in several important and delicate negotiations. He has served as senior adviser to the U.S. delegation to the United Nations. From 1980 to 1983, by appointment of President Carter and then of President Reagan, he was ambassador and head of the U.S. delegation to the Conference on Security and Cooperation in Europe (under the Final Act signed in Helsinki in 1975). Then he was appointed by President Reagan as ambassador and head of the Delegation on Negotiations on Nuclear and Space Arms.

Kampelman has a long and distinguished record of public and philanthropic service. By appointment of the president of the United States, he was chairman of the board of trustees of the Woodrow Wilson International Center for Scholars (1979–81), and continued as a member of the board of trustees. He was chairman of Freedom House (1983–85). He has served on the board of directors of Georgetown University, on the board of advisers of the Kennedy Institute of Ethics, on the board of trustees of the Law Center Foundation of New York University, on the board of trustees of the U.S. Council for International Business, as vice president of the Helen Dwight Reid Educational Foundation, vice chairman of the Coalition for a Democratic Majority, a member of the executive committee of the Committee on the Present Danger, and a member of the board of directors of the Atlantic Council of the United States. He was chairman of the Board of Governors of the United Nations Association (1989–93) and served as vice chairman of the United States Institute of Peace (1992–2001).

Kampelman has been actively identified with many Jewish and Israeli interests. He is honorary chairman of the Jerusalem Foundation and honorary governor of the Hebrew University of Jerusalem. He has served as honorary vice chairman of the B'nai B'rith Anti-Defamation League; as a member of the board of governors of Tel Aviv University and of the University of Haifa; as chairman of the National Advisory Committee of the American Jewish Committee; as a member of the board of directors of HIAS; as vice president of the Jewish Publication Society; on the board of trustees of the America-Israel Cultural Foundation and of the American Friends of the Israel Conservatory of Music; and on the board of trustees of the American Histadrut Cultural Exchange Institute.

In 1989 he received the Presidential Citizens Medal; in 1999 he was awarded the Presidential Medal of Freedom; and in 2000, he was among those who received the first Library of Congress Living Legend award. Kampelman is the author of many articles and pamphlets on public affairs, American foreign policy, and Jewish subjects. He also wrote *The Communist Party vs. the* CIO (1957) and *Entering New Worlds: The Memoirs of a Private Man in Public Life* (1991).

[Milton Ridvas Konvitz / Ruth Beloff (2nd ed.)]

KAMSON, YA'AKOV (Jacob) DAVID (1907–1980), Hebrew poet. Born in Vorna, Lithuania, Kamson immigrated to Palestine in 1926, living first in Jerusalem and later in Ashkelon. While in Germany he began publishing his poems in the German-Jewish press, and later contributed to most Hebrew periodicals. His works include *Yerushalayim* (1950), a collection of poems on the theme of Jerusalem, and books of poetry and stories for children. He was an editor of the album about Lithuanian Jewry, *Yahadut Lita* (1959). He also wrote in Yiddish. For a list of English translations of his poetry see Goell, Bibliography, 30f.

BIBLIOGRAPHY: U. Ofek, *Gan ha-Ḥaruzim* (1961), 97; G. Bergson, *Sheloshah Dorot be-Sifrut ha-Yeladim ha-Ivrit* (1966), 165f.

[Getzel Kressel]

KAMẒA AND BAR KAMẒA, figures in one of the *aggadot* dealing with the events which led to the destruction of the Second Temple (Git. 55b–56a; cf. Lam. R. 4:2 no. 3). The passage opens with the statement, "Because of Kamẓa and Bar Kamẓa Jerusalem was destroyed," and states that a certain man instructed his servant to invite his friend Kamẓa to a feast. By mistake the servant extended the invitation to a certain Bar Kamẓa, his master's personal enemy. Bar Kamẓa was ordered to leave, but offered increasing sums of money to be allowed to stay and avoid the humiliation of being thrown out. His host remained obdurate. Bar Kamẓa was compelled to leave. Furious with the rabbis who witnessed the scene and did not speak up on his behalf Bar Kamẓa went to the emperor and informed him that the Jews were planning a revolt, the proof being that they would refuse to accept his sacrifice. The emperor sent a sacrifice through Bar Kamẓa, who inflicted a blemish on it which would disqualify it according to Jewish law but not according to Roman law. The sages were inclined to overlook this blemish and offer up the sacrifice so as not to offend the Romans. A certain *Zechariah b. Avkilus, however, objected strongly on the grounds that "people will think that blemished animals may be offered for sacrifice." To a proposal that Bar Kamẓa be put to death to prevent him from informing the emperor, Zechariah b. Avkilus objected, maintaining that "people will think that the penalty for inflicting a blemish on sacrificial animals is death."

There may well be a grain of historical truth in this legend. Josephus states that Eleazar, son of Hananiah the high priest, and a leader of zealots, sought to abolish sacrifices of non-Jews in the Temple, and maintains that this was the signal for the outbreak of the Roman War, since it meant the abolition of daily sacrifice for the emperor (Wars, 2:409ff.), constituting an act of rebellion. In the story one can detect an echo of the factional dissensions that ravaged Jerusalem in the years preceding the destruction of the Temple. It should be associated with similar popular sayings from talmudic literature, e.g., "Why was the Second Temple destroyed…? Because of baseless hatred" (Yoma 9b).

Some scholars see a resemblance between the name Kamẓa and Bar Kamẓa and the name Compsus b. Compsus mentioned by Josephus (Life, 33). Compsus was a member of the aristocratic party in Tiberias and among the supporters of the Romans. Support for the theory is found in the fact that the legend is attributed to Johanan who taught in Tiberias, which might well have been the scene of the story.

BIBLIOGRAPHY: Derenbourg, Hist, 266–7; A.A. Halevi, *Sha'arei ha-Aggadah* (1963), 203ff.

[A'hron Oppenheimer]

KANAH, Cana (Heb. קָנָה).

(1) City in the territory of Asher (Josh. 19:28), mentioned in Egyptian lists of cities conquered by Seti I and Thutmosis III (no. 26); now Kanah, 6 miles (10 km.) southeast of Tyre.

(2) Town in Galilee captured by Tiglath-Pileser III in 732 B.C.E. According to John 2, a marriage feast at Cana was the scene of Jesus' miracle of changing water into wine; there also he performed a miracle of healing (John 4:46ff.). Josephus made it his headquarters early in 67 C.E. during the Jewish War (Life, 86). After the destruction of the Temple, Kanah was settled by priests of the Eliashib family. Identified since the Middle Ages with Kafr Kannā, the site is now more likely placed at Khirbat Kannā, 5 miles (8 km.) north of Sepphoris.

(3) River separating the territories of Manasseh and Ephraim (Josh. 17:9); now Wadi Kannā, a tributary of the Yarkon.

BIBLIOGRAPHY: G.H. Dalman, *Sacred Sites and Ways* (1934), 113; Press, Ereẓ, s.v.

[Michael Avi-Yonah]

KANAH AND PELIYAH, BOOKS OF, two of the most important compositions of pre-Safedian *Kabbalah. The former is a lengthy commentary on the commandments, the latter a commentary on the first chapters of Genesis. Though different from the literary point of view, the two books have been confused by many kabbalists, the title *Kanah* being attributed to both. Written by the same kabbalist, they were attributed to members of the family of the famous tannaitic figure R. *Neḥunyah ben ha-Kanah, to whom some other kabbalistic writing had been attributed previously. The author introduces three generations of this family, who discuss and exchange among themselves kabbalistic ideas. The main assumption of the author is the superiority of Kabbalah, which contains the most important clues for understanding Judaism.

For many years the books were thought to have been composed in Spain, but findings of Kushnir-Oron and Ta-Shma established the Byzantine background of the books, presumably at the end of the 14th century. A study of the sources demonstrates that the anonymous kabbalist drew on a huge variety of kabbalistic sources starting from early Kabbalah, the book of the Zohar, prophetic Kabbalah, R. Joseph Gikatilla, R. Menahem Recanati, and R. Joseph b. Shalom Ashkenazi. Especially important is the impact of *Sefer ha-Temunah* and the kabbalistic thought in writings from its circle, plausibly produced in mid-14th century Byzantium. Also the appropriation of Heikhalot poems, late Midrashim, and Ashkenazi sources is detectable. Many of these sources were copied verbatim or with slight changes and interpolations. Despite the highly eclectic nature of these books, the recasting of the sources in a dialogue form, which uses many parables, was helpful in introducing the variety of ideas appropriated by the author to wider and variegated audiences. Together with writings from the *Temunah* circle, the books of *Kanah* and *Peliyah* are cornerstones of Byzantine Kabbalah as a divergent school from the Spanish center of Kabbalah, and contributed a special blend of views which underscore transmigration and cosmic cycles (*shemittot*), surmising that the present eon is one of stern judgment, and show special interest in Hebrew letters and divine names.

The books contain ideas stemming from earlier sources which deviate from the consensus of the main kabbalistic schools in Spain. On the other hand, they express critical attitudes toward students of *Halakhah*, depicted as immersed in the study of Jewish law, but enjoying a good life instead of fasting and preaching to the Jews about their plight in exile. The style of admonition and the frequent appearance of Elijah, who teaches supernal secrets, permeate the two compositions and had an impact on later writings. Because of the recurring concern with messianism and eschatology – again following earlier kabbalistic sources – the books have been seen as a very reliable source because of their mooted early date. The computation of the year of arrival of the Messiah as 1490 evoked special interest after the expulsion of the Jews from Spain.

The impact of the books on the further development of Kabbalah has been quite substantial. They were canonized already at the beginning of the 16th century, and their influence is discernible among Spanish kabbalists who were expelled from Spain and others. The most important names in this context are Johanan *Alemanno, *Moses of Kiev, Solomon *Molcho, Joseph *Caro, Solomon ha-Levi *Alkabez, Meir ibn Gabbai, Moses *Cordovero, David ibn Zimra, *Shabbetai Ẓevi and other Shabbatean figures, and some in early Ḥasidism. Some of its more radical ideas contributed to the rejection of the books by other kabbalists, like R. Isaac *Luria.

Sefer ha-Kanah was published in part in 1617 in Prague, in 1730 in Wilharsdorf, in 1786 in Poritsk, and in 1894 in Cracow, and in 1974 in Jerusalem. *Sefer ha-Peliyah* was published twice, in 1784 in Koretz and in 1884 in Premislany.

BIBLIOGRAPHY: M. Benayahu, *The Sabbatean Movement in Greece* (Heb., 1971–1977), 350–354; T. Fishman, "A Kabbalistic Perspective on Gender-Specific Commandments: On the Interplay of Symbols and Society," in: *AJS Review*, 17:2 (1992), 199–245; M. Oron, "The Introduction to Sefer ha-Peliyah," in: *Kovez al-Yad Jubilee Volume*, 2 (1989), 273–95; M. Kushnir-Oron, "The Sefer Ha-Peli'ah and Sefer Ha-Kanah: Their Kabbalistic Principles, Social and Religious Criticism and Literary Composition" (Heb., Ph. D. Thesis, Hebrew University, Jerusalem, 1980); S.A. Horodezky, *Ha-Mistorin be-Yisrael*, 4 (1952), 341–88, M. Idel, "Saturn and Sabbatai Tzevi: A New Approach to Sabbateanism," in: P. Schaefer and M. Cohen, *Toward the Millennium, Messianic Expectations from the Bible to Waco* (1998), 173–202; I. Ta-Shma, "Where Have the Books Kanah and Peliyah Been Composed?" in: *Sefer Jacob Katz* (1980), 56–63 (Heb.).

[Moshe Idel (2nd ed.)

KANDEL, ERIC RICHARD (1929–), neurophysiologist and Nobel laureate in physiology and medicine. Kandel was born in Vienna, Austria, and emigrated to the U.S. in April

1939 after a childhood experience of Nazi occupation which determined his life-long interest in behavior. After attending the Yeshiva of Flatbush elementary school, followed by Erasmus Hall High School, he majored in European history at Harvard before entering New York University Medical School with the initial intention of pursuing a career in psychiatry. An elective course at Columbia University with Harry Grundfest reinforced his decision to become a scientist. After graduation (1956) he joined the National Institutes of Health (NIH), Bethesda (1957–60), and trained in clinical psychiatry at Harvard Medical School (1960–65), a period which included a seminal year as a postdoctoral fellow with Ladislav Tauc in Paris. He formed a neurophysiology group at New York University (1965–72). In 1972 he moved to Columbia University College of Physicians and Surgeons as founding director of the Center for Neurobiology and Behavior, where he became professor (1983), senior investigator of the Howard Hughes Medical Institute (1984), and director of the Kavli Institute for Brain Sciences (2004). His research has centered on the biological basis of memory and its implications for normal and abnormal behavior. He was among the first to devise experimental methods for establishing the physiological and molecular basis of a crucial function of the brain. He worked initially on the relatively simple giant marine snail *Aplysia* and later on the hippocampus, the memory center, in mice, convinced that only simple systems would give insight into the formidable challenge of understanding consciousness and related brain function in humans. He ended previous fruitless speculation by establishing that memory involves the connections between nerve cells and patterns of protein synthesis in these cells. He was awarded the Nobel Prize (2000) jointly with Arvid Carlsson and Paul Greegard. His other honors include membership in the U.S. Academy of Sciences (1974), the Lasker Award (1983), the Gairdner Award (1987), the Harvey Prize of the Haifa Technion (1993), and the Wolf Prize (1999). His publications include (with J. Schwartz and T. Jessell) the standard textbook *Principles of Neural Science*.

[Michael Denman (2nd ed.)]

KANDEL, ISAAC LEON (1881–1965), U.S. educator, an internationally known specialist on comparative education. Kandel was born in Romania, and went to university in Manchester, England, and at Columbia University, New York. From 1914 to 1923 he was a research specialist for the Carnegie Foundation for the Advancement of Teaching and produced significant monographs, including one on the examination system in the United States. From 1923 to 1947, he was professor of education at Teachers College of Columbia University and editor of its *Educational Yearbook of the International Institute*. From 1944 to 1949 he edited *Universities Quarterly*, and from 1946 to 1953, *School and Society*. In 1948–50, Kandel was professor of American studies at the University of Manchester, England. Kandel contributed to the fields of educational history, educational theory, and comparative and international education. His most important work was *Comparative Education* (1933), and his other books include *History of Secondary Education* (1930), *Conflicting Theories of Education* (1938), *Intellectual Cooperation: National and International* (1944), *The New Era in Education* (1955), and *American Education in the Twentieth Century* (1957). Of great significance was his pioneering study, *The Making of Nazis* (1935), in which he documented the theory and practice of Nazi education and warned of its dangers. Kandel's work is distinguished by vigorous opposition to extremism in progressive education, his advocacy of international cooperation in culture and education, and his application of a precise, multilingual approach to educational research. Kandel was a member of the advisory board of the American Friends of the Hebrew University, the editorial council of *Jewish Social Studies*, and of the Institute for Religious and Social Studies (Jewish Theological Seminary of America). He was coauthor of an article on Jewish education in Monroe's *Cyclopedia for Education*. He taught for a period at the Jewish Institute of Religion in New York.

BIBLIOGRAPHY: L.A. Cremin, *Isaac Leon Kandel* (1966); W.W. Brickman, in: *Educational Forum*, 15 (1950–51), 398–412; R.G. Templeton, *Isaac L. Kandel's Contribution to the Theory of American Education* (1956).

[William W. Brickman]

KANDLEIN OF REGENSBURG (14th century), community leader first mentioned in the records of Regensburg in 1351. Kandlein was a widow whose relatives, including her brother, son, and son-in-law, were the most prominent moneylenders in that city. The family, originally from Graz, also payed the highest taxes. Kandlein was one of the appointed leaders of the Regensburg Jewish community and was usually mentioned first in the listings of the important Jews. This group set the taxes for local Jews and regulated which Jews should be allowed to settle in Regensburg and what they should pay for the privilege. In July 1356, the Regensburg council gave Kandlein and others permission to live in Regensburg for two further years and all rights to sing in their synagogue and to their graveyard. Kandlein was murdered sometime before August 1365 during a robbery of her home.

BIBLIOGRAPHY: E. Taitz, S. Henry, and C.I. Tallan, "Kandlein of Regensburg," in: *The JPS Guide to Jewish Women, 600 B.C.E.–1900 C.E.* (2003), 79–80; F. Bastian and J. Wideman (eds.), *Monumenta Boica Regensburger Urkundbuch*, vol. 2, *Urkunden der Stadt 1351–1378* (1956).

[Cheryl Tallan (2nd ed.)]

KANE, BOB (1916–1998), U.S. comic book creator. Born in New York City with the surname Cahn, he attended Cooper Union and the Art Students League before entering the comics field. His first strips, *Peter Pupp* and *Hiram Hick*, were published in 1936. In 1938, while he was drawing adventure strips for National Comics, a comic book hero named Superman appeared. Kane's boss asked him and his high-school classmate, Bill Finger, then a shoe salesman, to come up with a Supercompetitor. They developed *Batman*, which came out in May 1939 in *Detective Comics*, the successor to National. Batman the Caped Crusader was not as strong as Superman, but he was much more agile, a better dresser, and had more sophisticated technological contraptions. He lived in the Batcave with his "ward," Robin the Boy Wonder, drove the Batmobile, which had a crime laboratory and a closed-circuit television in the back, and owned a Batplane. In creating Batman, really a man named Bruce Wayne, a wealthy socialite, Kane said he drew on a number of sources: a 1920s movie, *The Mark of Zorro*, a radio show called *The Shadow*, and a 1930 movie called *The Bat Whispers*. As Batman's popularity increased – there was a television series, Batman movies, toys, and costumes – over the years, Kane did less and less of the drawing. Although his name appeared on the strip until 1964, the work was done mostly by other artists. According to a recollection-tribute by Jerry Robinson, who was a writer during the creation of Batman, Kane and Finger, like himself and the creators of Superman, came from middle-class Jewish families beset by the Depression. Bruce Wayne, he wrote, "is rich, handsome and equipped with a butler, the Batmobile and an array of seductive women. That, of course, represented our ultimate fantasy." The fantasy proved to be universal. Batman was soon speaking Greek, Arabic, and Japanese, among other languages. In 1966 Kane turned to children's television cartoons and in his last years he devoted himself to Batman paintings and lithographs for collectors.

[Stewart Kampel (2nd ed.)]

KANE, CAROL (1952–), U.S. actress. Born in Cleveland, Ohio, Kane traveled extensively as a child, living with her parents in Paris and Haiti before settling with them in New York. She attended the Professional Children's School in New York City until the age of 14, when she began acting professionally in theater roles in New York and around the Northeast. Kane's first significant film roles were in *Carnal Knowledge* (1971) and *The Last Detail* (1973), and she played a memorable role as a bank teller-hostage in *Dog Day Afternoon* (1975). Later that year, Kane received an Oscar nomination for her portrayal of Gitl, a young Jewish bride in Joan Micklin Silver's *Hester Street*, a tale of immigrant life on New York's lower East Side circa 1896. In 1977, Kane played the role of Woody Allen's first wife in *Annie Hall* and Gene Wilder's girlfriend in *The World's Greatest Lover*. Two years later, she received acclaim for her role as babysitter Jill Johnson in *When A Stranger Calls* (1979). Despite her success in film, however, Kane is perhaps best known for her role as the ditzy nonsense-speaking immigrant Simka on the television show *Taxi*. Kane's performance as Simka, who eventually married Andy *Kaufman's character on the show, Latka, won her Emmy Awards in 1982 and 1983. Subsequently, Kane appeared in a myriad of films and television shows while continuing to perform in the theater. Among these appearances, Kane's other notable credits include the TV series *Brooklyn Bridge* (1991) and the films *Racing with the Moon* (1984), *The Princess Bride* (1987), *Ishtar* (1987), *Scrooged* (1988), *The Lemon Sisters* (1990), *Addams Family Values* (1993), *Even Cowgirls Get the Blues* (1994), *Office Killer* (1997), *Jawbreaker* (1999), *My First Mister* (2001), and *Confessions of a Teenage Drama Queen* (2004).

[Walter Driver (2nd ed.)]

KANE, GIL (1926–2000), U.S. comic book artist. Born in Latvia and named Eli Katz, he immigrated to New York with his family when he was three. Kane dropped out of high school at 15 to seek work penciling comic books, the first stage of the process. Some artists would go over his lines in ink, others would add words, and some would add color. His first job was at MLJ, publishers of *Archie* comics. Just before entering the army in 1944, Kane took a job with DC Comics. He returned there after the war to work at the dawn of a new medium and gradually became recognized as one of the greatest comic book artists. His breakthrough came in 1959 when he drew an early follow-up to DC's *Flash*, a feature that had been a hit in the 1940s. He then revamped the characters Green Lantern and Atom and infused them with a vibrant new life. He represented an integral part of the resuscitation of superheroes in the 1960s, an era known as the "silver age" of comic books. He gave dynamic new interpretations to the Hulk, Captain Marvel, and Spider-Man. Kane drew tens of thousands of pages of superheroes for DC and Marvel Comics as well as for dozens of other companies.

[Stewart Kampel (2nd ed.)]

KANE, IRVING (1908–1988), U.S. attorney, businessman, and communal leader. Kane was born in Kiev, Russia, and went to America in 1913 with his parents, who settled first in Hoboken, New Jersey, and then moved to Cleveland, Ohio, in 1917. Kane worked in a Cleveland law firm until 1937, when he established his own firm. President of the Hospital Specialty Co. of Cleveland from 1941 to 1962, he owned and operated Irving Kane Associates, a consulting firm for business and finance. Kane first entered communal service as chairman of the Jewish Community Relations Committee of Cleveland in 1947. He served with both Jewish and non-Jewish organizations in various capacities, among them as chairman of the National Community Relations Advisory Council (1949–53), vice president of the American Jewish Congress (1956–58), and president of the Council of Jewish Federations and Welfare Funds (1959–62). He was a member of the campaign cabinet of the United Jewish Appeal from 1961. In 1964, Kane was one of the 29 high-profile guarantors of the newly formed *Cleveland Jewish News*, as well as one of the attorneys involved in negotiating the deal to create the English-language community Jewish newspaper. He also served as chairman of the American Israel Public Affairs Committee.

[Hillel Halkin / Ruth Beloff (2nd ed.)]

KANEE, SOL (1909–), Canadian philanthropist, lawyer, and businessman; Jewish community official. Kanee was born into an immigrant family in the small Saskatchewan farm community of Melville. He graduated with a B.A. from the University of Manitoba in 1929 before going on to complete a degree in law at the University of Saskatchewan in 1932. He was admitted to the Saskatchewan Bar in 1933. Kanee returned to Melville to begin practicing law but with the outbreak of war in Europe he enlisted in the Canadian Army. From 1940 to 1945 he served in the Royal Canadian Artillery, retiring with the rank of major. Rather than return to Melville, Kanee settled in Winnipeg, where he combined law and business. He became president of Loo Line Mills and director of the Kanee Grain Company. In 1956 he was appointed director of the Bank of Canada and served on its board for 17 years, the longest anyone had ever sat as a director. He was also director of the Federal Business Development Bank, which offered financial services to support the long-term growth of businesses in all sectors of the Canadian economy.

Active in both Jewish and non-Jewish community life, Kanee supported a number of community organizations and service groups in Winnipeg. Long an officer of the Canadian Jewish Congress, he served as chairman of the National Executive of the Canadian Jewish Congress and president of the organization between 1971 and 1974. He was also chair of the University of Manitoba board of governors where an annual lecture series has been named in his honor. In addition, Kanee held executive volunteer positions with the World Jewish Congress, the United Way of Greater Winnipeg, the Royal Winnipeg Ballet, and the Canadian National Millers Association, among other organizations. A lifelong Liberal Party supporter and Israel advocate, he was close to leading Canadian and Israeli political figures. His record of community service was recognized when Winnipeg's Jewish nursing home was renamed in honor of the Kanee family and, among his many awards, Sol Kanee was inducted into the Order of Canada in 2000.

[Judith E. Szapor (2nd ed.)]

KANETI, SELIM (1934–1992), professor of civil and tax law. Born in Istanbul, Kaneti graduated from the Faculty of Law of Istanbul University. In 1968 he was an associate professor and in 1972 became a professor of civil law. In 1984 he was appointed president of the Finance and Economy Department of the Faculty of Law of Istanbul University and president of the Tax Law Department. He was also deputy director of the Center for Comparative Research and Application of Law in the Law Faculty. From 1957 he was a member of the Istanbul Bar Association and worked as a lawyer. He was president of the Secular Council of Turkey's Chief Rabbinate between 1989 and 1992. He wrote *Akdin İfa Edilmediği Def'i* (1962); *İsviçre Federal Mahkemesi Borçlar Hukuku Kararları Özel Borç İlişkileri* (1969); *Hukuki İşlemlerin Çevrilmesi (Tahvili)* (1972); *Sınırlı Ayni Haklar* (1972); *Medeni Hukuk Sorunları* (1976); *Aile Hukuku* (1985); and *Vergi Hukuku* (1989).

[Rifat Bali (2nd ed.)]

KANEV, port on the Dnieper River in Kiev district, Ukraine. Jewish settlement began in the end of the 17th century or the beginning of the 18th. From 98 (including the surrounding villages) in 1765, the Jewish population grew to 1,635 in 1847 and 2,682 (30% of the total population) in 1897. On the eve of WWI most of the petty trade in town was in Jewish hands, all groceries and textile shops as well as others. On November 6, 1917, local hoodlums ransacked many Jewish properties; this happened again in the beginning of autumn 1919 by General *Denikin's soldiers. The number of Jews in 1926 was 1,305 (17.2%), and it dropped to 487 in 1939 (total population 8,020). In the 1920s there was a two-grade school with 59 pupils. Kanev was occupied by the Germans on August 16, 1941. The Jews who remained were herded into one building under horrible conditions and robbed of all their property. After two months they were taken to Korsun and murdered in November 1941 together with the local Jews. Kanev was liberated on February 3, 1944.

[Shmuel Spector (2nd ed.)]

KANEV, ISAAC (1896–1980), specialist in social insurance. Born in the Crimea, Kanev studied science and economics at the University of Simferopol. He immigrated to Ereẓ Israel in 1919 and took part in the defense of Tel Ḥai, where he was wounded. After working as an agricultural laborer he was appointed to the executive of Kuppat Ḥolim in 1923, and henceforth devoted himself entirely to the field of social insurance, completing his studies in Vienna and London, after which he was made responsible for social health research at Kuppat Ḥolim. In 1947 he founded the Institute for Social Research of the Histadrut and on the establishment of the state was appointed to work out a scheme for social insurance and social services, the results of which he published in 1950. He served in the First Knesset as a representative of *Mapai. In 1957 he was appointed by the government to work out a scheme for comprehensive health insurance. From 1928 he was a member of the executive of the International Social Security Association, of which he was vice president from 1955 to 1964, and in 1958 lectured at a United Nations seminar on the social and demographic problems of the Mediterranean countries. He published a large number of works on social insurance and was awarded the Israel Prize for social sciences in 1962.

[Shaked Gilboa (2nd ed.)]

KANIEVSKY, JACOB ISRAEL (**"the Steipler"**; 1899–1985), rabbi. Kanievsky was born in Hornistopol from which his appelation "the Steipler" was derived. From an early age he studied at the yeshivah of Gomel, which was directed by the "elder of Novogrudok," Joseph Yozel *Hurvitz. Kanievsky soon became known as the *illui* ("genius") from Stopol. At the end of his teens he was pressed into service in the Russian army.

In 1925 his first book, *Sha'arei Tevunah*, was published. After the Ḥazon Ish, Avraham Yeshayahu *Karelitz, read the work, he offered his sister Miriam in marriage to Kanievsky and the two were married. Emigrating to Palestine in 1934 – about a year and a half after his brother-in-law had settled in Bene-Berak – Kanievsky was appointed the head of Bet Yosef-Novohardok yeshivah in Bene-Berak. Karelitz was once asked was there any man in his generation for whom one could recite the blessing "blessed is He for having shared His wisdom with His reverers," and the reply of the Ḥazon Ish was, "the Steipler."

Kanievsky was the author of nearly 30 books and devoted much time to writing, teaching, and dealing with the vast public which constantly streamed to his home seeking spiritual guidance. Religious and nonreligious alike sought his counsel, and Jews from many communities looked to him for guidance. Some 200,000 people from all over Israel attended his funeral.

KANIN, FAY MITCHELL (1917–), screenwriter and leader in the U.S. film and television industries. Born in New York City to Bessie (Kaiser) and David Mitchell, Kanin grew up in Elmira, N.Y., where as a teenager she won the New York State Spelling Championship. Kanin attended Elmira College on a scholarship and received a B.A. from the University of Southern California after the family moved to Los Angeles.

Kanin got her start in film as a script reader at RKO Studios, where she met her future husband, Michael Kanin (1910–1993), who was writing his first screenplay. Fay and Michael, who married in 1940, raised two sons while collaborating for 20 years on dozens of scripts for film, theater, radio, and television. Their dramatic version of the Japanese film *Rashoman* (1957) continues to be performed. Michael Kanin's brother, Garson *Kanin, and his wife, Ruth Gordon, were a similar husband-and-wife team. Fay Kanin also wrote independently. Her play, *Goodbye, My Fancy*, about a congresswoman, was a Broadway success in 1949. Many of Fay Kanin's scripts present characters who reflect her own values as an educated, independent, career woman. They focus on the importance of personal integrity, academic freedom, and individual accomplishment. One of her most important scripts, *Friendly Fire* (1979), which starred Carol Burnett, won an Emmy for its moving depiction of an Iowa couple who lost their son in Vietnam. She also won an Emmy for *Tell Me Where it Hurts* (1974). Kanin, who was nominated with her husband for an Academy Award for writing *Teacher's Pet* (1958), was also nominated for a Tony Award for Best Book (Musical) for *Grind* in 1985.

Kanin served for over 25 years in various leadership roles in the film industry, including governor of the Academy of Motion Picture Arts and Sciences, representing the writers branch; president of the Academy Foundation, the educational and cultural arm of the Academy; and chair of the National Film Preservation Board of the Library of Congress. She was an officer of the Writers Guild Foundation and a member of the board of directors of the American Film Institute. From 1979 to 1983, Kanin was president of the Academy of Motion Picture Arts and Sciences for four consecutive terms, the only woman elected to that office since Bette Davis's brief stint as president in 1941.

BIBLIOGRAPHY: H. Reisen. "Kanin, Fay," in: P.E. Hyman and D.D. Moore (eds.) *Jewish Women in America*, vol. 1 (1997), 718–19.

[Sharon Pucker Rivo (2nd ed.)]

KANIN, GARSON (1912–1999), U.S. playwright and director. Kanin, born in Rochester, New York, became a Hollywood director for Samuel Goldwyn at 25. He directed John Barrymore in *A Great Man Votes* (1939) and Ginger Rogers in both *Bachelor Mother* (1939) and *Tom, Dick and Harry* (1941). After army service during World War II, Kanin was co-director, with Sir Carol Reed, of *The True Story* (1945). The film was about the Allied victory, and it won the Academy Award for Best Documentary.

Plays Kanin wrote that were performed on Broadway include *The Smile of the World* (1949), *Rat Race* (1950), *The Live Wire* (1950), *A Gift of Time* (1962), and *Come on Strong* (1962). He wrote and directed the Broadway hits *Born Yesterday* (1946) and *Do Re Mi* (based on his novella, 1960; Tony nominations for Best Musical and Best Director). He also directed such Broadway productions as *The Rugged Path* (1945), *Years Ago* (1947), *The Leading Lady* (1948), *The Diary of Anne Frank* (1955, Tony nomination for Best Director), *A Hole in the Head* (1957), *Sunday in New York* (1962), and *Funny Girl* (1964). He produced and directed *A Very Rich Woman* (1965), written and acted by his author-actress wife Ruth Gordon.

In the realm of cinema, Kanin and Gordon co-authored such films as *A Double Life* (1947, Oscar nomination for Best Screenplay), *Adam's Rib* (1949, Oscar nomination for Best Screenplay), *The Marrying Kind* (1952), *Pat and Mike* (1952, Oscar nomination for Best Screenplay), and *It Should Happen to You* (1954). In 1969 he wrote and directed the films *Where It's At* (based on his novel) and *Some Kind of a Nut*. In 1979 the couple co-wrote the TV movie *Hardhat and Legs*. In 1980, Kanin's novel *Movieola* (1979) was adapted into three separate made-for-TV movies: *This Year's Blonde; The Scarlett O'Hara War*; and *The Silent Lovers*.

Ruth Gordon died in 1985; Kanin married actress Marian Seldes in 1990. He was the brother of screenwriter Michael Kanin (1910–1993).

Among Garson Kanin's published works are *Remembering Mr. Maugham* (1966), *Cast of Characters: Stories of Hollywood* (1969), *Tracy and Hepburn: An Intimate Memoir* (1971), the novel *A Thousand Summers* (1973), *Hollywood* (1974), the novels *One Hell of an Actor* (1977) and *Smash* (1980), *Together Again: Stories of the Great Hollywood Teams* (1981), and the novel *Cordelia* (1982).

[Ruth Beloff (2nd ed.)]

KANIUK, YORAM (1930–), Israeli writer. Kaniuk, who was born in Tel Aviv, fought in the War of Independence, during which he was wounded, spent the 1950s as journalist and painter in New York, and in 1961 settled down in Tel Aviv. One of the country's most prolific writers, his oeuvre sets up a mirror to the changes within Israeli society while taking issue with the so-called Zionist narrative. Kaniuk's disillusioned, critical voice is reminiscent of that of Y.H. *Brenner, a writer whom he greatly admires and with whom he shares a thematic and expressive affinity.

His works, commingling autobiographical elements with collective concerns, revolve around three major themes: the Arab/Palestinian-Israeli conflict and in particular the War of Independence, the Holocaust, and the attitude of the New Jew, the Israeli, to Diaspora tradition.

The protagonist of Kaniuk's first novel, *Ha-Yored le-Ma'alah* (which appeared in an English translation as *The Acrophile* in 1961, two years before it was published in Hebrew!) is an Israeli living abroad, as it were an uprooted Sabra, who is tormented by guilt feelings for having killed an Arab boy during the war, preferring life in total isolation rather than to return to his native country. A similar theme, clearly inspired by the personal experience of Kaniuk in the U.S., is treated in the novel *Sus-Eẓ* (1974; *Rocking Horse*, 1977). The moral dilemma, present in several works of other writers of his generation, underlies many of Kaniuk's novels, including *Bitto* (1987; *His Daughter*, 1988) and *Aravi Tov* (1984; *Confessions of a Good Arab*, 1987), the latter being a compelling and deliberately provocative Arab-Jewish family saga, which "is out to fracture the badly set bone that deforms the Middle East" (*The Los Angeles Times*). While his second novel, *Ḥimmo Melekh Yerushalayim* (1965; *Himmo King of Jerusalem*, 1969), describes the dramatic relationship between a severely wounded Israeli soldier and the nurse who attends to his needs in an old monastery in Jerusalem during the War of Independence, the third novel, *Adam Ben Kelev* (1968; *Adam Resurrected*, 1969; 1971) marks a new thematic and stylistic direction in Kaniuk's prose. In this novel as well as in *Ha-Yehudi ha-Aḥaron* (1982; *The Last Jew*, 2005), Kaniuk confronts the ever-open scars of Holocaust survivors and their traumatized life. In expressionistic style, harsh, gruesome, and provocative, Kaniuk tells the pathetic-grotesque story of Adam Stein, once a well-known clown in Europe, who survived the death camp because he entertained victims on their way to the gas chamber. Stein arrives in Israel but suffers a nervous breakdown. A patient at a rehabilitation and therapy institute, he presides over a demented kingdom which includes distraught persons, like Jenny, who provides him with medical and sexual services, and a "dog," who slowly shows feeling and finally can even speak. The novel, which has been translated into fourteen languages, was also successfully staged and is undoubtedly one of the most original and powerful Hebrew novels about the Holocaust. *The Last Jew*, one of Kaniuk's most ambitious works, attempting to present a historic panorama of Jewish fate in the 20th century, is the tragic-grotesque story of Ebenezer Schneurson, who believes he is the "last Jew." Confronting the Holocaust and the incurable wounds of the survivors prompted Kaniuk also to look closer at the relations between Germans and Jews. In *Post Mortem* (1992), an impressive, albeit disturbing portrait of his parents, Kaniuk does not hide his ambivalent emotions toward Germany and its culture. It was the father, Moshe Kaniuk, for many years director of the Tel Aviv Museum, who imbued his son with a passion for the German language and its culture. Kaniuk recounts how he, a boy in Tel Aviv of the 1930s, wished to rid himself of the ubiquitous Sabra attributes and resemble the children of the German Templars. One of the most successful Israeli authors in Germany, Kaniuk visited that country many times and published in 2002 (first in German, two years later in Hebrew!) his impressions of a haunted and haunting country.

Other prose works by Kaniuk examine the Zionist Myth and its realization, as in *Afar ve-Teshukah* ("Soil and Desires," 1975) or *Ha-Sippur al Dodah Shlomẓiyon ha-Gedolah* (1976; *Aunt Schlomzion the Great*, 1978); tell of the passionate, obsessive love of a 60-year-old film producer for a much younger woman ("Another Love Story," 1996); relate an imaginary, humorous encounter with Queen Elizabeth (*Ha-Malkah va-Ani*; "The Queen and I," 2001); or recollect personal moments, both turbulent and inspiring, in New York of the 1950s (*Ḥayyim al Neyar Zekhukhit*, "I Did It My Way," 2003). In 2005 Kaniuk published *Ha-Ne'ederet mi-Naḥal Zin*, a sophisticated thriller in which he examines the corrosion of values in Israeli society. Kaniuk also wrote books for young readers, such as *Wasserman* (1988), and a biographical novel about the commander of the famous ship *Exodus* (1999). Kaniuk won the Prix de Droits de l'Homme in Paris (1997), and he received the Bialik Prize (1999). In 2000 he was awarded the prestigious Prix Mediterranée Etranger.

Kaniuk's books have been translated into twenty languages, and a list is available at the ITHL website at www.ithl.org.il

BIBLIOGRAPHY: A. Feinberg, "The Story of Great Aunt Schlomzion," in: *Modern Hebrew Literature*, 1:3–4 (1975), 73–75; A. Feinberg, "'Afar u-Teshukah," in: *Moznayim*, 42 (1976), 149–150; H. Barzel, "*Derekh ha-Sippur shel Y. Kaniuk*," in: *Alei Siaḥ*, 7–8 (1980), 172–190; G. Moked, "*Ha-Toda'ah ve-ha-Eimah shel Y. Kaniuk*," in: *Yedioth Aharonoth* (June 19, 1981); J. Green, "Ambitions and Obsessions," in: *Modern Hebrew Literature*, 9:3–4 (1984); O. Bartana, "*Anatomiyyah shel Melankholiyyah Yehudit*," in: *Akhshav* 49 (1984), 303–308; H. Daniel, "Die israelische Tragödie, Bekenntnisse eines guten Araber," in: *Allgemeine juedische Wochenzeitung* (May 5, 1989); W. Hinck, "Adam Hundesohn," in: *Frankfurter Allgemeine Zeitung* (February 10, 1990); G. Dachs, "Der letzte Jude," in: *Die Zeit*, 17 (April 19, 1991); R. Jütte, "Der letzte Jude," in: *Allgemeine juedische Wochenzeitung*, 47:29 (July 16, 1992); R. Ben-Shahar, "*Al Leshon ha-Roman 'Bitto' shel Y. Kaniuk*," in: *Lashon ve-Ivrit*, 4 (1999), 36–45; H. Halperin, "*Ha-Im Immo shel Yoram Kaniuk Yoda'at Levashel? Ha-Ḥomarim ha-Biografiyim bi-Yẓirot Kaniuk*," in: *Moznayim* 69:5 (1995), 13–17; H. Zmiri, "*Ha-Tekst ke-Sheder shel Idiologiyyah ve-Tikshoret*," in: *Moznayim*: 71:4, 27–32; G. Kaynar, "The Holocaust Experience through Theatrical Profanation," in: C. Schumacher (ed.), *Staging the Holocaust* (1998), 53–69; J. Lushizki, "*Kalat ha-Met*," in: *Mabbatim fiktiviyyim al Kolno'a Yisraeli* (1998), 247–260; G. Shaked, "*Reshut ha-Ze'akah*," in: *Akhshav*, 65 (1998), 66–92; G. Shaked, *Ha-Sipporet ha-Ivrit*, 5 (1998), 183–205; L. Haber, "Fact and Fiction by Yoram Kaniuk," in: *Midstream*, 46:8 (2000), 33–35; G. Morahg, "*Mekorot Musmakhim*," in: *Meḥkarei Yerushalayim be-Sifrut Ivrit*, 18 (2001), 341–357; D. Juette, "*Yoram Kaniuks Der Letzte Berliner*," in: *Mitteilungsblatt*, 178:12 (2002), 12; Y. Orian, "*Yoman Mas'a be-Moledet ha-Naẓim*," in: *Maariv* (May 28, 2004); M. Azaryahu, "*Ha-Emet ve-ha-Elbon*," in: *Haaretz Sefarim* (June 9, 2004); D. Juette, "*Die Queen, ihr Liebhaber und ich*," in: *Stuttgarter Zeitung* (September 3, 2004).

[Anat Feinberg (2nd ed.)]

KANN, JACOBUS HENRICUS (1872–1945), banker; founder of the Zionist Organization in Holland. Born in The Hague, from 1891 Kann was the owner and manager of his family's bank, Lissa & Kann – one of the largest banks in Holland (established in 1805) and for three generations that of the Dutch royal family. Herzl's *Der Judenstaat* made a great impression on Kann, who was not at all involved in Jewish public life until then. He participated as an observer in the First Zionist Congress (1897) and later became Herzl's aide, especially in matters of banking. He and David *Wolffsohn were among the founders of the *Jewish Colonial Trust, despite his earlier hesitation about the financial effectiveness of the bank. He established the Zionist Organization in Holland, becoming its leader and representative at the Zionist General Council (then called Greater Actions Committee; 1897–1905). At the Seventh Zionist Congress (1905) he was elected to the Zionist Executive (the "Smaller Actions Committee"), reduced to three members, Kann, Wolffsohn, and Otto *Warburg, at the Eighth Zionist Congress (1907). Throughout, he was an enthusiastic fighter for Herzl's political Zionism as opposed to "practical" Zionism, which the Zionist organization introduced during his term of office in the executive. When the opposition to Wolffsohn was victorious at the Tenth Congress (1911), Kann also resigned, but he continued to manage the financial institutions (the Jewish Colonial Trust and the Anglo-Palestine Bank). The plot of the "Aḥuzzat Bayit" suburb near Jaffa, purchased by an association of settlers in Ereẓ Israel and from which Tel Aviv developed, was registered under his name. Impressions of his visit to *Ereẓ Israel* in 1907, published in his *Ereẓ Israel* (Dutch, 1908; German, 1909; French, 1910), included a demand for Jewish autonomous home rule in Ereẓ Israel. This demand aroused sharp criticism from V. *Jabotinsky, then head of the Zionist press in Constantinople, who claimed that Kann's statement was causing political harm to Zionism in the Ottoman capital. When Wolffsohn rejected his argument, Jabotinsky resigned and left Constantinople. From 1911, Kann remained in the Zionist opposition. He did not participate in the Zionist Congresses after World War I. Nevertheless, he moved to Palestine in 1923 as the consul-general of Holland (until 1927). He returned to Holland in 1931, working on behalf of different projects in Palestine (among them the establishment of the Jewish National Library on Mt. Scopus, using the resources of the Wolffsohn Fund, etc.). After the 1929 riots in Palestine, Kann published a pamphlet in English (1930) in which he criticized the actions of the Zionist Executive in economic matters and in Arab-Jewish relations. When Holland was occupied by the Germans in World War II, he was dismissed from the bank and eventually deported to *Theresienstadt, where he died shortly before the liberation.

BIBLIOGRAPHY: N. Sokolow, *History of Zionism*, 2 (1919), index; A. Boehm, *Die Zionistische Bewegung*, 1 (1935), index; T. Herzl, *Complete Diaries*, ed. and tr. by R. Patai (1960), index; J. Simon, in: *Haaretz* (March 11, 1945).

[Getzel Kressel]

KANN, MOSES (d. 1761), head of the yeshivah in Frankfurt on the Main. Born of a wealthy and influential family which had resided in Frankfurt from 1530, Moses was a leading authority in his day. His first wife was a daughter of the famous Court Jew Samson *Wertheimer, who collaborated with Moses in enabling J.L. Frankfurter, the rabbi of Frankfurt, to publish a new edition of the Talmud (Amsterdam-Frankfurt, 1714–22). When the Talmud was confiscated following the denunciations of the apostate Paul Christian, Moses appealed to the elector of Mainz; the confiscation order was finally rescinded in 1753. Moses' second wife was a daughter of the Court Jew Behrend *Lehmann. The talmudic scholar Jacob Joshua *Falk owed his appointment to the rabbinate of Frankfurt largely to Moses' influence.

Moses and his brother BEER LOEB ISAAC doubled the sum of 10,000 thalers, which their father had bequeathed for the support of scholars, and presented it to the community in 1736. In 1749 David Meyer Kulp initiated a revolt against Beer Loeb Isaac's long and unpopular oligarchic rule over the community. The bone of contention was the control of the communal treasury. Frankfurt Jewry divided into opposing factions, disturbances broke out, and troops had to be called in. Beer Loeb Isaac was supported by the city council, while Kulp appealed to the emperor. An investigation absolved Beer Loeb Isaac of charges of embezzlement. Both contenders were impoverished by the continued litigation; the power of the Kann family was broken and constitutional reforms were introduced in the community. Beer Loeb Isaac died in 1754; his son, LAZARUS BEER ISAAC, settled in The Hague about a year later. Lazarus' son, HIRSCHEL (1772–1819), founded the firm of Lissa & Kann, which his son, ELEAZAR (1810–90), made into a leading banking house. Eleazar's grandson, Jacobus Henricus *Kann, also a banker, was a well-known philanthropist and Zionist.

BIBLIOGRAPHY: I. Kracauer, *Geschichte der Juden in Frankfurt...*, 2 vols. (1925–27), index s.v. *Kann, Baer*; M. Horovitz, *Frankfurter Rabbinen...*, 4 vols. (1882–85), passim; Th. Stevens, in: *Studia Rosenthaliana*, 4 (1970), 43–95; A. Dietz, *Stammbuch der Frankfurter Juden* (1907); H. Schnee, *Die Hoffinanz und der moderne Staat*, 6 (1967), 244–9.

KANN, PETER R. (1947–), U.S. publisher. A native of Princeton, N.J. Kann graduated from Harvard University with a bachelor's degree in journalism. Joining the San Francisco bureau of *The Wall Street Journal* in 1963, Kann became a staff reporter the following year and worked in the Pittsburgh and Los Angeles news bureaus. In 1967 Kann became the *Journal*'s first resident reporter in Vietnam. From 1969 to 1975 he continued to cover the Vietnam War, as well as other events across Asia, as a roving reporter based in Hong Kong. In 1972 he was awarded a Pulitzer Prize for distinguished reporting on international affairs for his coverage of the 1971 India-Pakistan war. In 1976 Kann was named the first publisher and editor of *The Asian Wall Street Journal*, headquartered in Hong Kong. After 12 years in Asia, Kann returned to the United States in 1979, and the following year he was named associate publisher of the *Journal* and a vice president of Dow Jones & Company, publisher of the *Journal*. Later that year he became chief operating officer of Dow Jones. He became chief executive officer in January 1991 and chairman in July 1991. During his tenure, the *Wall Street Journal* grew significantly as readers sought more business information. Kann also presided over the expansion of the *Journal* from five days to six days when it added a feature-oriented Saturday edition in 2005. Kann's wife, Karen Elliott House, who received a Pulitzer Prize for international reporting in 1984 for her coverage of the Middle East, became publisher of *The Wall Street Journal* in 2002.

[Stewart Kampel (2nd ed.)]

KANNEGISER, LEONID AKIMOVICH (1873–1918). Russian poet who assassinated M.S. Uritsky, the chairman of the Petrograd Secret Police, the Cheka. Kannegiser's grandfather, a physician, attained the status of nobility while his father was a famous engineer. Both were involved in Jewish communal life. Kannegiser was born in St. Petersburg. From 1915 to 1917 he studied at the Petrograd Polytechnical Institute, then joined the Union of Jewish polytechnic students. After the February Revolution of 1917 he entered the military academy and was elected chairman of the socialist cadets. His attitude toward the October Revolution was positive but after the conclusion of the Brest-Litovsk peace treaty he began to be highly critical of the Bolsheviks. The assassination of Uritsky and the attempt on the life of Lenin on the same day (August 30, 1918) served as a pretext for the Soviet authorities to declare their "red terror." Kannegiser was executed by the Cheka in Petrograd soon after.

From childhood Kannegiser had written poetry. He was close to the Acmeists (see O. *Mandelstamm). Jewish motifs appear in his poetry (e.g. in "Yevreyskoe venchanie"; "Jewish Betrothal"). The anthology *Leonid Kannegiser* containing several of his surviving lyric poems with memoirs of him by M. *Aldanov and others appeared in Paris in 1928. A major part of Kannegiser's literary heritage is preserved in the closed files of the Central Government Archives of Literature and Art in Moscow.

[*The Shorter Jewish Encylopaedia in Russian*]

KANNER, LEO (1894–1981), U.S. child psychiatrist. Kanner, who was born in Klekotow, Austria, emigrated to the U.S. in 1924. In 1928 he began his connection with Johns Hopkins University, where he was appointed associate professor of psychiatry in 1948 and professor of child psychiatry in 1957. He was chairman of the child psychiatry section of the American Psychiatric Association in 1942–43.

Kanner may well be considered the father of American child psychiatry. Coming as he did from the tradition of psychobiologically oriented psychiatry, he gave proportionate attention, when describing the basis of behavior, to constitutional, biological, environmental, psychological, and situational aspects of the child's life. For more than two decades his *Child Psychiatry* (1935, 1957[3]) was the basic textbook in this field, and it has left its impact upon child psychiatry in the United States and Europe alike. He is particularly well known for his original description of "early infantile autism," or what is now called "Kanner's autism" – a severe behavioral disorder which is apparent from early infancy. He wrote the introduction to *Modern Perspective in International Child Psychiatry* (ed. by J.C. Howells, 1969).

[Joseph Marcus]

KANOVICH, GRIGORY (pseudonym of **Yakov Semenovich**; 1929–), Soviet prose writer, poet, and dramatist. Kanovich, who wrote in Russian and Lithuanian, was born in the town of Ionava near Kaunas or, according to another source, in Kaunas itself, into the family of an observant Jewish tailor. In 1953 he graduated from Vilnius University. His first writings were published in 1949. He wrote collections of poetry in Russian: *Dobroye utro* ("Good Morning," 1955) and *Vesenniy grom* ("Spring Thunder," 1960); of literary epigrams and parodies in Lithuanian (*"With a Joyful Eye,"* 1964; *Naked Ones on Olympus*, 1981); 30 plays and film scenarios (some co-authored) on contemporary themes; and he translated literary prose from Lithuanian into Russian.

Kanovich's Russian prose works are almost all devoted to the life of Lithuanian Jewry. The theme of the moral quest of a Jewish boy from a Lithuanian shtetl in his long stories "Ya smotryu na zvezdy" ("I Gaze at the Stars," 1959) and "Lichnaya zhizn"' ("Private Life," 1967) is developed in his trilogy *Svechi na vetru* ("Candles in the Wind") consisting of the novels: *Ptitsy nad kladbishchem* ("Birds over the Cemetery," 1974), *Blagoslovi i list'ya i ogon'* ("Bless Both the Leaves and the Fire," 1977), *Kolybel'naya snezhnoy babe* ("Lullaby for a Snowman," 1979, translated into Hebrew in 1983). The trilogy, the action of which takes place between 1937 and 1943, recreates the traditional world and spirituality of East European Jewry. The events, even those on the most massive scale such as the Holocaust, are presented through the eyes of a youth and, as he develops, of a young man; in its structure the novel in places resembles a lyrical diary. An epic, philosophic element predominates in Kanovich's cycle of novels devoted to Jewish shtetl life of the end of the 19th and early 20th centuries – *Slëzy i molitvy durakov* ("Tears and Prayers of Fools," 1983); *I net rabam raya* ("There's No Heaven for Slaves," 1985), *Kozlenok za dva grosha* ("A Kid for Two Pennies"). The ethnic character of the novels (the heroes' way of thinking, reminiscent of Talmudic dialectics, and their way of speaking) and the problems they raise (the aspiration of the Jewish masses for national self-preservation, the feeling of responsibility for the ethical and ethnic essence of the people, the tendency of part of the Jewish intelligentsia to reject its identity for the sake of career, and assimilation) brought these works popularity among Soviet Jews. Kanovich visited Israel in 1980 and settled there in 1993.

[*The Shorter Jewish Encylopaedia in Russian*]

KANOVITZ, HOWARD (1929–), U.S. painter. Kanovitz was born at Fall River, Mass., and studied at Providence College, Rhode Island (1947–49), and Rhode Island School of Design (1949–51). He taught at Brooklyn College and Pratt Institute, New York City, until 1964, when he moved to London. Kanovitz achieved international prominence with the development of "*Photo-Realism*" in the late 1960s and the exhibition under that title of American painters and sculptors, which toured Europe in 1973. Kanovitz's work tends to be more complex than that of the meticulous imitators of reality; he often works in collage or three-dimensional forms. In an interview in the German magazine *Kunst* (4th quarter, 1971), he explained: "There is nothing in my work that isn't real, yet there is nothing real in my work but paint, canvas, and stretcher. There is much, though, that seems to be real, and this resemblance is the way of cooling off my anxious vision.… The point for me is to find that stage in the painting of images that brings objects to a state of relaxed relationship to other objects, no matter how absurd, and all this should take place logically and with good sense." His first one-man exhibition was at the Stable Gallery, New York, in 1962, since when he held numerous exhibitions in America, including the Jewish Museum, New York, in 1964.

[Charles Samuel Spencer]

KANSAS, midwestern state in the central United States. The population in 2001 numbered 2,692,000, with a Jewish population of 14,000, the bulk of the Jews living in the greater Kansas City area. Wichita has some 1,300 Jews. The first Jewish settlers began arriving soon after Kansas Territory was established in 1854. Two early arrivals were August *Bondi and Theodore Wiener, who were members of John Brown's Free-Soil army and also fought in the Civil War. The state's first Jewish cemetery was the Mt. Zion Cemetery Association, founded in Leavenworth in 1857. That city was also the site of the state's earliest congregation, B'nai Jeshurun, which was formed in 1859. An Orthodox congregation, Beth Jacob, was organized much later. The second congregation to be formed in Kansas was Emanu-El, of Wichita, in 1885. The first rabbi, Bernard Cantor, was killed in 1920 while serving as a representative of the Joint Distribution Committee in the Ukraine. An Orthodox congregation, Ahavath Achim, was organized in 1913. The I. Goldsmith Memorial Library, containing the largest collection of Judaica in Kansas, was located in Wichita. It was named after Ike Goldsmith, who opened the city's first bookstore and was one of the founders of Temple Emanu-El. There were many unsuccessful Jewish agricultural colonies, the most important of which was Beersheba, established in 1882 by Isaac Mayer Wise. Other colonies, such as Lasker, Montefiore, Gilead, Touro, Leeser, and Hebron also failed. The settlers returned to the East, moved on to Colorado, or joined other settlements. By 1890 Kansas contained six Jewish congregations, with a membership of 486. Between that date and 1905 only one more was formed, Ohev Shalom in Kansas City. In 1917 the Jewish Community Center of Kansas City, Kansas first opened its doors. In 1924 Congregation Beth Shalom was organized in Topeka, and the city of Hutchinson later built a Jewish center. Many Jews were scattered among the smaller Kansas communities, where often there was not a sufficient number to organize a congregation. There are old Jewish cemeteries in Atchinson, Fort Scott, and Eudora, indicating that these towns once had Jewish communities, which have since disappeared. The Mid-Kansas Jewish Federation was created in 1935 to unify the Jewish population of south-central Kansas. In 1959 came the establishment of The Jewish Community Foundation of Kansas City, Kansas, which provides education and charitable contributions as well as caring for urgent economic needs of the community. The *Kansas City Jewish Chronicle* was founded in 1920 to provide the Jews of Kansas City, Kansas, and Missouri with news on their community. In recent years the Jewish population of Kansas has greatly diminished, mainly because young people attend colleges in areas of larger Jewish population, and do not return to Kansas. Still, both major universities in the state, the University of Kansas and Kansas State University, maintain Hillel houses that help their student populations to live a Jewish life on campus and offer courses in Jewish Studies. Several Kansas Jews have distinguished themselves in public life, such as Adolph Gluck, mayor of Dodge City; Sol Kohn, mayor of Wichita; and B.I. Litovich, president of the Kansas Bar Association. Kansas Jews are served by Topeka-Lawrence Jewish Federation and the Mid-Kansas Jewish Welfare Federation. Dan *Glickman was a U.S. congressman representing Wichita and later the first Jewish secretary of agriculture. Senator Arlen *Spector of Pennsylvania was born in Kansas and was a descendant of Jewish farmers.

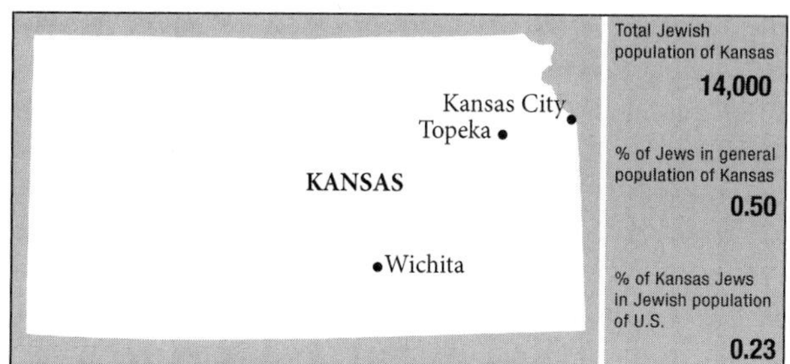

Jewish population of Kansas, 2001.

[Helen Kragness-Romanishan / Ben Paul (2nd ed.)]

KANSAS CITY, Missouri commercial and industrial center on the Missouri River opposite Kansas City, Kansas; Jewish population totaled approximately 19,000 or 1.1 percent of the total city population which is listed as 2,692,000 (2005).

As early as 1839 several Jews had found their way to the settlement of Wyandotte, Missouri, which was not renamed "Kansas City" until 1889. Among the earliest Jewish residents were Herman and Benjamin Ganz, Henry Miller, and Lewis Hammerslough. During the Civil War, 12 Jews served in the local home guard and another, Lieutenant Colonel Reuben E. Hershfield, was commander of nearby Fort Leavenworth.

Kansas City, MO, is part of the greater Kansas City area, which incorporates Kansas City, Kansas, as well as their surrounding suburbs. The first Jewish organization in Kansas City was a burial society founded in 1864. Three years later a local chapter of B'nai B'rith was formed. The first synagogue, Bnai Jehudah, was established in 1870 as a Reform congregation. An Orthodox congregation, Keneseth Israel, was organized in 1878; a decade later its more liberal wing split off to become Congregation Beth Sholom. Bnai Jehudah opened the city's first Sunday school in the 1880s and Keneseth Israel founded a *talmud torah* in 1901. As the Jewish population of Kansas City grew, other institutions were not long in following. The city's first Jewish social group, the Progress Club, was established in 1881. In 1895 a chapter of the Council of Jewish Women was formed and in 1901 The Jewish Family and Children Services was established to aid in resettlement and counseling. In 1913 the first Hadassah group came into being after a visit by Henrietta Szold. A branch of the Workmen's Circle was created in 1904. A Jewish Home for the Aged was opened in 1912 and a Jewish Community Center and YMHA-YWHA in 1917. The Kansas City United Jewish Charities, chartered in 1901, established the Jewish Educational Institute in 1907 and a health center, the Alfred Benjamin Dispensary, in 1919. While the UJC was extending its services, newcomers developed other agencies which provided help in ways often more acceptable to their recipients, such as the Hebrew Ladies Relief, the Hebrew Free Loan Society, the Jewish Orphans' Home, and the Wayfarers' Lodge. Zionism had its supporters in Kansas City from the time of the first Zionist Congress in 1897, and several Zionist groups were formed shortly after. The 1920s witnessed the continued growth of institutional life. The weekly *Kansas City Jewish Chronicle* has been reporting on Jewish activity in the area since it began publication in 1920. In 1926 the Jewish Memorial Association was formed and soon after it received a bequest of $200,000 for the erection of a hospital with a *kasher* kitchen. The building, first called Menorah Hospital and later the Menorah Medical Center, was dedicated in 1931.

The economic crisis of the 1930s posed a severe economic threat to Kansas City's Jewish institutions, and in 1933 the situation became so bad that the Jewish Community Center was almost forced to close its doors. To meet this challenge, several leaders of the community evolved a plan for setting up a federation and conducting a campaign for immediate needs. The joint drive was a success and since then the federation has continued to minister to the community's financial wants. The trend toward consolidation continued into the late 1930s and 1940s. In 1939 the Rabbinical Association was organized by Samuel S. Mayerberg and Gershon Hadas and in 1945 all community organizations were joined together into a council combined with the federation. In 1968 Kansas City had seven congregations: Bnai Jehudah, Beth El (est. 1958), and the New Reform Congregation (est. 1967) were Reform; Ohev Sholom (est. 1930), Beth Israel-Abraham (est. 1958), and Kehilath Israel (est. 1959) were Orthodox; and Beth Shalom in the Overland Park suburb was Conservative. In addition to congregational schools, a Jewish day school, the Hebrew Academy, was founded in 1966. Adult Jewish education, formerly offered through the School of Jewish Studies (1946–56), was under the joint direction of the Jewish Community Center and the congregations in 1968.

In that same year, in the social services field, the United Jewish Charities, which was renamed the Jewish Family and Children's Service in 1960, continued to offer a wide variety of programs. The Jewish Vocational Service, helped into existence in 1950 by the Federation and Council for the initial purpose of finding jobs for newcomers, was largely occupied with guidance for young people. The Menorah Medical Center, enlarged in 1951 and again in 1960 and 1963, had a capacity of 335 beds. In 1966 the Jewish Educational Program was founded to help assist the Jewish community of Kansas better to understand their heritage.

Jews have played important roles in almost every phase of Kansas City's growth. The settlers, who often began as peddlers, soon moved into retail business and later became wholesale merchants. A goodly number became manufacturers and developed such enterprises as the important center for the manufacture of women's garments. Jews have been prominent dealers in grain and flour, cattle and hides, meatpacking and produce, insurance and real estate, and, in recent years, securities and banking. Civic and political participation by Jews has been significant for many years. Several Jews were on the board of trade as early as 1869. From 1904 to approximately 1934 Jewish aldermen and councilmen sat continuously on the city council. From 1932 to 1937 Rabbi Mayerberg assumed a leading part in spearheading the long, bitter, and ultimately successful campaign against the city's corrupt, machine-dominated government. After World War II, Richard H. Koenigsdorf was city counselor and then circuit judge. Kenneth Krakauer and Bert Berkley were presidents of the chamber of commerce, Irving Fane served on the police board and Richard L. Berkley was Republican county chairman. Early in 1948, when Jewish settlements in Palestine were under heavy Arab attack, several residents of Kansas City called upon Eddie *Jacobson, a fellow townsman and a close friend of President Truman, to persuade Truman to grant an audience to Chaim Weizmann, a mission which he successfully carried out.

In 1968 it was estimated that approximately 60 percent of the Jewish population was self-employed, approximately 20 percent were employed by others, and another 20 percent were in the professions. This relative isolation of Jewish economic achievement had its social counterpart in the generally small amount of intermingling with non-Jews. The major downtown social club began accepting Jewish members only in 1967. Other clubs still retained an informal practice of exclusion. The two Jewish country clubs, on the other hand, were almost totally devoid of non-Jews. Yet, the rate of intermarriage had steadily increased while the size of the Jewish population had remained practically unchanged from 1948 to 1968. Today many of the Jews in the Greater Kansas City area have moved out of the city center and into suburbs such as Overland Park, Kansas. With a general population of over 160,000 (2004 estimate), Overland Park has become the new center of the Jewish community in Greater Kansas City. Several Jewish institutions have moved into Overland Park in recent decades, including the Jewish Historical Society and Temple Bnai Jehudah. This is part of a larger trend across the country, as Jewish populations in many metropolitan areas move steadily from the heart of the city and into more residential suburban communities.

[Gershon Hadas / Ben Paul (2nd ed.)]

In the early 21st century the Kansas City metropolitan area contained 12 synagogues, 7 Jewish cemeteries, and several new organizations devoted to Jewish life. The Midwest Center for Holocaust Education was founded in 1993 in Overland Park, with an endowment of $2.4 million. The Kansas City community also sponsors the Village Shalom senior living community, located in the heart of the city. Although small in numbers, the Jewish community of Kansas City works hard to maintain its identity and ensure that its members receive a strong Jewish education.

BIBLIOGRAPHY: L.A. Campbell, *Campbell's Gazetteer of Missouri* (1875), 715; *American Israelite* (1900), no. 28; *The Reform Advocate* (March 28, 1908); Sachs, in: *Missouri Historical Review*, 60 (April 1966), 350–60.

°KANT, IMMANUEL (1724–1804), German philosopher. Born in Koenigsberg, East Prussia, Kant studied at the university in that city, where in 1755 he began to teach as a Privatdozent. In 1770 he was appointed to the chair of logic and metaphysics. His major work, the *Critique of Pure Reason*, in which he lay down the foundations of his critical philosophy, appeared in 1781. In 1783 he published the *Prolegomena to Every Future Metaphysic* in an effort to explain more clearly the main arguments of the *Critique*. The *Critique of Practical Reason* and the *Critique of Judgment* were published in 1790, *Religion Within the Limits of Reason Alone* in 1793, and the *Foundation of the Metaphysics of Morals* in 1797.

Attitude Toward Religion

Kant's statement in the *Critique of Pure Reason*, "I have found it necessary to deny *knowledge* in order to make room for *faith*" (*Critique of Pure Reason*, BXXX) succinctly expresses his attitude to religion, revealing both its critical and constructive aspects. His critical analysis of pure reason leads Kant to limit the scope of theoretical, demonstrative knowledge to the phenomenal world, i.e., to the world of sense perception, thereby denying the possibility of metaphysics, and consequently the validity of the traditional proofs for the existence of God – the ontological, cosmological, and teleological arguments (*ibid.*, B811–25). But while Kant maintains that God, as a supersensuous being, cannot be an object of demonstrative knowledge, he does not claim that God does not exist, or that He is beyond the reach of reason as such. Indeed – and this is the constructive aspect of Kant's philosophy – he claims that reason must postulate the existence of God. In the realm of scientific knowledge the need for a "regulative principle of the systematic unity of the manifold of empirical knowledge…" leads reason to postulate the existence of God. It is, however, mainly in the realm of ethics that the burden of establishing the existence of God lies. God comes into the picture here not as the giver of the moral law, for this would destroy the autonomy of the moral law which is fundamental to Kant's ethical theory, but as the "necessary condition for the possibility of the *summum bonum*," i.e., for the "distribution of happiness in exact proportion to morality" (*Critique of Practical Reason* (tr.) Beck (1956), 129). The existence of God is postulated in order to fulfill a fundamental requirement of the moral law, namely, that the virtuous man is worthy to be happy (*ibid.*, 135). True religion, in contrast to clericalism, is, therefore, ethical religion in which the kingdom of God is nothing else than the ethical commonwealth (*Religion Within the Limits of Reason Alone* (1960), 90ff.).

View of Judaism

Kant believes that Christianity, because of its idealized, spiritualized ethical teachings based on pure love, approaches this ideal of ethical religion more than any other historical religion. In contrast, following *Spinoza, he views Judaism as a mere national-political entity, contending that it fails to satisfy the essential criteria of religion in that it fails to inculcate the inner appropriation of morals, demanding only external obedience to statutes and laws. Interpreting Jewish messianism as nothing more than a national-political experience, Kant maintains that Judaism is concerned only with things of this world, and lacks any formulation of the concept of immortality.

Kant's negative view of Judaism, however, in no way interfered with his congenial relations with the Jewish community or with individual Jews, such as Moses *Mendelssohn. Nor did it deter many emancipated Jews from becoming attracted to Kantian philosophy. In Kant's lifetime Markus *Herz, Lazarus *Bendavid, and Solomon *Maimon were among his staunch supporters, and later, in the neo-Kantian revival, Hermann *Cohen and Ernst *Cassirer were numbered among his ardent followers. Kant also exercised an appreciable influence on Moritz *Lazarus, and a less pronounced, though significant, influence on Solomon *Formstecher, Solomon *Steinheim, and Franz *Rosenzweig.

Kant and Liberal Judaism

Kant's influence on Jewish philosophers may result from the basic affinity between his philosophic formulation of religion and the orientation of modern liberal Judaism (see *Reform Judaism). The exponents of liberal Judaism, regarding religion as essentially a system of ethics, found in Kant a philosophical formulation of religion which articulated their own conceptions of Judaism. The similarity between Kant and Judaism goes even deeper than the linking of religion with ethics. It is reflected in the structuring of the ethical system itself. The structure of Kant's ethics parallels that of biblical ethics with its source-consequences pattern and the central categories of "duty" and the "right" and not the Greek model with its means-end pattern and the categories of the "good" and "happiness." Yet it is at this point of closest similarity that basic differences emerge. For Kant the ethical source is reason. Thus religion is ultimately grounded in reason; it is "religion within the limits of reason alone," and, as such, is ahistorical, universal, and available to every individual by virtue of his inherent rational capacity. For classical Judaism, on the other hand, the ethical source is God. Ethics is grounded not in reason but in the will of God, a will which expresses itself not in timeless continuity but at a specific moment in time through revelation. While for Kant, religion is grounded in ethics, in Judaism it is ethics which is grounded in religion. Hence, notwithstanding the similarities between Kant and Judaism, the two formulations of religion move in radically different "worlds," making the attempt of adopting Kant as an authentic philosophic expression for Judaism problematic.

It is interesting to note that it was precisely in those aspects where he differed most from Judaism that Kant proved most congenial to his Jewish followers. This is understandable insofar as his followers were emancipated Jews for whom religion in its historical, particularistic manifestation, and its mystical, supernaturalistic, or ritualistic dimension was unacceptable. To be acceptable religion had to be thoroughly rationalized, ethicized, and universalized. These people gave up the attempt to find in Kant a philosophic formulation capable of authentically expressing Judaism, but sought rather to interpret Judaism in such a way that it would conform to Kant's formulation of religion. Kant's philosophic formulation became the norm and ideal. Indeed, for many of his followers the merit of Judaism lay precisely in being, as they thought, malleable to such a transformation.

Moritz Lazarus and Hermann Cohen

This can be seen in a particularly striking manner in the writings of Moritz *Lazarus and Hermann *Cohen. In his *Ethik des Judentums* (2 vols., 1898–1911; vol. 1 tr. into Eng. under the title *The Ethics of Judaism*, 1900) Lazarus, although he somewhat reinterprets the Kantian ethical imperative, follows Kant completely in giving priority to ethics over religion, and the autonomy of ethics is fully safeguarded (*Ethics of Judaism*, 1 (1900), no. 104). Ethics is not the content or expression of religion, rather religion is one of the subdivisions or expressions of ethics. Thus God is subjected to the ethical. He commands the ethical because it is ethical: "Moral laws, then, are not laws because they are written; they are written because they are laws" (*ibid.*, 1 (1900), no. 85).

In Hermann Cohen's earlier writings there is a strong Kantian influence. The autonomy of ethics is never compromised. Religion, with its central idea of God, is established only on the basis of, and to the extent of, the requirements of ethical considerations. In his *Ethik des reinen Willens* (1904) he maintains that ethics require God as an idea, a hypothesis guaranteeing the existence of nature for the realization of the infinite ethical goal.

BIBLIOGRAPHY: Guttmann, Philosophies, index; idem, *Kant und das Judentum* (1908); *Encyclopedia of Philosophy* (1967); A. Lewkowitz, in: *Festschrift… des juedish-theologischen Seminars*, 1 (Breslau, 1929), 215ff., 226; M. Wiener, *Juedische Religion im Zeitalter der Emanzipation* (1933); S.H. Bergmann, *Hogim u-Ma'aminim* (1959), index; N. Rotenstreich, *Jewish Philosophy in Modern Times: From Mendelssohn to Rosenweig* (1968), index; S. Pines, in: *Scripta Hierosolymitana*, 20 (1968), 3–54; S. Axinn, in: JQR, 59 (1968), 9–23; E.L. Fackenheim, in: *Commentary*, 36 (1963), 460–7.

[Manfred H. Vogel]

KANTOR, JACOB ROBERT (1888–1984), U.S. psychologist. Born in Harrisburg, Pennsylvania, Kantor spent most of his teaching and research years at Indiana University. His major fields were behavior theory, language and logic, physiological psychology, and the history of psychology and related sciences. In 1937 he founded, and for decades contributed to, the journal *The Psychological Record*. Kantor was an important early spokesman in the U.S. for the view that the proper goal of psychology in its every aspect is to become an objective natural science of behavior, rather than a subjective or mentalistic discipline. In his writings, Kantor used the term "interbehavior" to emphasize certain theses: (1) that the variables which control behavior are physical, continuous, and instant; (2) that the physical consequences of behavior themselves become part of the complex of determiners of ensuing behavior; and (3) that behavior is an ever-changing stream, so that concepts of "stimulus" and "response" as static events do not provide analytic categories that are suitable starting points for behavior theory.

Following his retirement from Indiana University in 1959, Kantor served as visiting professor at New York University (1952–63) and at the University of Maryland (1963–64). He lectured often at universities and professional societies in the U.S. and, beginning in 1974, often lectured and gave seminars at universities in Mexico.

Among Kantor's major works are *Principles of Psychology*, 2 vols. (1924, 1926), *An Objective Psychology of Grammar* (1935), *Psychology and Logic*, 2 vols. (1945–50), *Problems of Physiological Psychology* (1947), *The Logic of Modern Science* (1953), *Interbehavioral Psychology* (1958, 1959[2]), *The Scientific Evolution of Psychology*, 2 vols. (1963, 1969), *Psychological Linguistics* (1977), *Cultural Psychology* (1982), *Tragedy and the Event Continuum* (1983), and *Psychological Comments and Queries* (1984).

BIBLIOGRAPHY: N. Smith, *Greek and Interbehavioral Psychology: Selected and Revised Papers of Noel Smith* (1993); N. Smith, et al., *Reassessment in Psychology: The Interbehavioral Alternative* (1983).

[William N. Schoenfeld / Ruth Beloff (2nd ed.)]

KANTOR, JUDAH LEIB (1849–1915), founder of the first Hebrew daily newspaper. Born in Vilna, he became a devotee of the Haskalah in his youth, graduated from the Government Rabbinical Seminary in Zhitomir, and also studied medicine in Berlin. After editing **Ha-Ẓefirah* in Berlin (1874–75) and the Russian weekly *Russki Yevrey* (The Russian Jew, 1879–84), he founded the Hebrew daily **Ha-Yom* in 1886, a bold publication venture for the time. As a supplement to *Ha-Yom*, for which he wrote most of the articles under various pseudonyms, Kantor issued a scientific-literary monthly, *Ben-Ammi* (of which four issues appeared).

At first *Ha-Yom* was successful, but competition with the established papers, **Ha-Meliẓ* and *Ha-Ẓefirah*, which also became dailies under its influence, led to its demise. The failure of Kantor's literary projects was partly caused by his negative attitude to the Ḥibbat Zion movement, which alienated the only circles who regarded Hebrew and Hebrew literature as a vital national need. From 1888 to 1890 Kantor was one of the editors of *Ha-Meliẓ*; he also edited the Yiddish weekly, *Dos Yidishe Folksblat*.

Kantor was a representative of the last generation of *maskilim* in Hebrew literature who believed that Haskalah held the cure for all Jewry's ills and were unable to accept the nationalist and Zionist movements. In his last years he served as an official rabbi in Libau (1890–1904), Vilna (1905–08), and Riga (1909–15).

BIBLIOGRAPHY: Torch, in: *Moznayim*, 20 (1945), 91–99, 219–26, includes bibliography; N. Sokolow, Ishim (1958), 153–91; Waxman, Literature, 4 (1960[2]), 441f., 448f., 608.

[Yehuda Slutsky]

KANTOR, MICHAEL ("Mickey"; 1939–), U.S. lawyer and lobbyist. Kantor was U.S. representative to the World Trade Organization (WTO) and then as secretary of commerce in the Clinton administration served as a staunch advocate of free trade and a tireless foe of restrictive trade barriers abroad. The scion of Nashville-based furniture retailers, Kantor attended Vanderbilt University, where he became a star shortstop for the baseball squad. Graduating in 1961, Kantor served four years as a lieutenant in the U.S. Navy, later studying law at Georgetown University Law Center, where he graduated in 1968. In 1972, he worked as a staff coordinator for vice presidential candidate R. Sargent Shriver during George McGovern's unsuccessful bid for office. After representing migrant farm groups as an anti-poverty lawyer and founding the Los Angeles Conservation Corps in 1973, Kantor managed Senator (D-California) Alan Cranston's reelection. In 1976, Kantor joined the Los Angeles lobbying firm of Manatt, Phelps, Phillips & Kantor, where he represented entertainment industry clients such as the U.S. National Cable Television Association as well as companies such as Occidental Petroleum, Lockheed, Philip Morris, and General Electric. Kantor specialized in securing market access and growing foreign markets through trade, direct investment, joint ventures, and strategic business alliances. Failure to repeat his success in ensuing political campaigns did not prevent Kantor, a friend of Hillary Clinton and an apt fundraiser and political dealmaker, from helping Bill Clinton secure the Democratic Party nomination and the presidency in 1992. Named to the Clinton transition team, Kantor became U.S. representative to the WTO in January 1993, a position he held until 1996, when he took over as commerce secretary after the death of Ron Brown in an airplane crash. Kantor left the Cabinet in 1997, involving himself in Clinton's efforts to fend off impeachment. That year, Kantor joined Mayer, Brown, Rowe & Maw, LLP, a Washington-based legal firm specializing in global project finance, and Morgan & Stanley Co. Inc. as a senior advisor. After a year's hiatus from politics, he lobbied on behalf of the American wheat industry and other major clients.

Described as "gruff," "prodigiously tempered," and possessing the "tact of a pit bull," Kantor traumatized the international community, alternately charming and browbeating counterparts and governments from Canada and Mexico to China and Japan. During negotiations with Japan on behalf of American automakers, Kantor presented his opposite number, Ryutaro Hashimoto, a kendo martial-arts sword symbolizing courage, honesty, integrity, and patience. Hashimoto, who would become Japan's prime minister, is reputed to have feared that Kantor might use it on him, declaring that "He's scarier than my wife when I come home drunk." As Clinton's trade enforcer, however, Kantor proved unusually successful, negotiating hundreds of trade agreements that generated close to $100 billion in contracts for U.S. businesses. Kantor's achievements were offset by several personal tragedies, including the loss of his wife in a passenger-jet crash in 1978, and of a 17-year-old son in a car accident ten years later. He has two grown children and a nine-year-old daughter by his second wife, former NBC reporter Heidi Schulman.

[Sheldon Teitelbaum (2nd ed.)]

KANTOROVICH, LEONID (1912–1986), Soviet mathematician and economist, joint winner of the Nobel award for economics in 1975. A member of the Soviet Academy from 1958, he was also a winner of the Stalin (1949) and Lenin (1965) Prizes. He was a professor at Leningrad University in 1934–60. However, his position was weakened during the last years of Stalin's life, and his methods were criticized as "bourgeois science." His applications of mathematical methods to economic planning were not favored by the Soviet leadership. However after 1953, he was again recognized and became a professor at Leningrad University, and at the Moscow Institute for Management of the People's Economy, apart from teaching in the Novosibirsk Mathematics Institute. The Nobel award called him "the leading representative of the mathematics school in Soviet research" and noted that in his book *The Best Use of Economic Resources*, he analyzed conditions for efficiency in an economy as a whole and demonstrated the connection between allocation of resources and the process of economic growth. He contended that a deficient Soviet investment policy has failed to achieve optimum economic growth.

KANTOROWICH, ROY (1917–1996), South African architect and town planner. Born in South Africa, the son of a Transvaal pioneer, Kantorowich won an international reputation for town planning. In Israel, he was responsible for the master design and detailed plans for the town of *Ashkelon. In South Africa he planned a number of large-scale civic and industrial projects. These included the foreshore development scheme in Cape Town, the design for the Transvaal steel center of Vanderbijlpark, a central redevelopment scheme for Pretoria (with the British expert Lord Holford), and plans for several smaller towns. He prepared the winning design (with Jack Barnett) for the civic center in the new Orange Free State goldfields town of Welkom. He acted as consultant town planner for the city of Port Elizabeth and, with Lord Holford, advised on the replanning of central Durban.

Kantorowich was president of the South African Institute of Town Planners in 1960. From 1961 he held the chair of town and country planning at the University of Manchester, England.

[Louis Hotz]

KANTOROWICZ, ERNST HARTWIG (1895–1963), German medieval historian. Born and educated in Prussia, he joined the army in World War I and was wounded at Verdun. At Heidelberg, Kantorowicz carried out research in ancient and then in medieval history and produced his first and most famous book *Kaiser Friedrich der Zweite* (2 vols., 1927), which combined deep historical insight with literary skill and imagination. Critics who termed his interpretation a *Mythenschau* were silenced by *Kaiser Friedrich der Zweite: Ergaenzungsband* (1931). The book ran through several editions and was translated into English (*Frederick the Second*, 1931) and into Italian. In 1930, Kantorowicz was appointed professor of medieval history at Frankfurt. Dismissed by Nazi pressure in 1934, he went to Oxford as a lecturer and from there to the U.S. to the University of California (Berkeley) from 1940 to 1949, and after 1951 as professor at the Institute for Advanced Study at Princeton. In America, Kantorowicz studied the nature of theocratic kingship as revealed in patristic, liturgical, and archaeological sources. He created a new area of studies, political theology, in *Laudes regiae* (1946, 1958^2), in *The King's Two Bodies* (1957), and in many papers which were later collected in his *Selected Studies* (1965).

BIBLIOGRAPHY: Y. Malkiel in: *Romance Philology*, 18 (1964), 1–15; F. Baethgen, in: *Deutsches Archiv fuer Erforschung des Mittelalters*, 21 (1965), 1–17 (incl. bibl.).

[Helene Wieruszowski]

KANTOROWICZ, HERMANN (1877–1940), German jurist. Born in Posen, Kantorowicz became assistant lecturer at the University of Freiburg in 1908 and professor extraordinary in 1913. In 1923 he was made a member of the German parliamentary commission investigating the origins of World War I and the war debt question, and in 1929 was appointed full professor of jurisprudence and criminal law at the University of Kiel. He was removed from his post by the Nazis in 1933 and immigrated to the United States, where he taught at Columbia and New York universities. In 1935 he settled in England, where he lectured and conducted legal research at the universities of London, Oxford, and Cambridge.

Kantorowicz was an authority on jurisprudence and legal history. He was the author of numerous works on jurisprudence, including *Kampf um die Rechtswissenschaft* (1906); *Rechtwissenschaft und Soziologie* (1911); *Der Geist der englischen Politik* (1929; *The Spirit of British Policy*, 1931) and *Dictatorships* (1935). In his last work, *Studies in the Glossators of the Roman Law* (1938), he examined the development of Roman law in the Middle Ages.

BIBLIOGRAPHY: K. Muscheler, *Herman Kantorowicz* (Freiburger Rechtsgeschichtliche Abhandlungen, Neue Folge Vol. 6), 1984; S. Silberg, "Hermann Kantorowicz und die Freirechtsbewegung" (Dissertation; 2004); D. Ibbentson, "Hermann Kantorowicz and Walter Ullmann," in: J. Beatson, R. Zimmermann (eds.), *Jurists Uprooted – German-speaking Émigré Lawyers in Twentieth-Century Britain* (2004), 269–98.

[B. Mordechai Ansbacher]

KANTROWITZ, ADRIAN (1918–), U.S. cardiovascular surgeon born in New York City. He graduated as an M.D. from Western Reserve University (1943). After training in cardiovascular physiology, he became director of surgical services at Maimonides Medical Center in Brooklyn and professor of surgery at New York State University (1964–70), and chairman of the department of surgery at Sinai Hospital, Detroit (1970). He was also director of the biotechnology company LVAD of Detroit. He was a pioneer in bioengineering relating to the heart and cardiovascular surgery. He devised a plastic heart valve, a heart-lung machine, an internal pacemaker, the first partial mechanical heart implanted in humans, a machine recording blood loss during open heart surgery, devices to aid the failing heart ventricle to pump blood more effectively, and techniques for taking films inside the living heart. He carried out the world's second heart transplant (1967). His bioelectronic techniques have also been used to control bladder function in paraplegics. He won the Max Berg Award (1966).

[Michael Denman (2nd ed.)]

KANTROWITZ, ARTHUR (1913–), U.S. physicist and aerodynamicist. Kantrowitz, who was born in New York, worked with the National Advisory Council on Aeronautics from 1935–46, and for the next ten years was professor of aeronautical engineering and engineering physics at Cornell University. From 1956 he was director of the Avco-Everett Research and Laboratories and of Avco Corporation. His numerous scientific papers have been concerned with supersonic axial flow compressors, the effect of molecular vibrations on gas dynamics, magnetohydrodynamic generators, shock tube studies, shock waves in the interplanetary plasma, and the re-entry of space vehicles into the earth's atmosphere. He invented the high-intensity molecular beam which has been instrumental in several Nobel Prize-winning research projects. Kantrowitz also worked in medical engineering in the development of cardiac-assist devices.

[Samuel Aaron Miller]

KAPLAN, ABRAHAM (1918–1993), U.S. philosopher. Born in Odessa, Ukraine, Kaplan was the son of a rabbi and the youngest of eight children. The Kaplan family immigrated to the United States in 1923. Kaplan graduated high school in Duluth at the age of 14. He won five national debating awards at Duluth Junior College and the College of St. Thomas. He studied philosophy at the University of Chicago under Rudolf Carnap and visiting lecturer Bertrand Russell, with whom he became close friends.

Kaplan received his Ph.D. from the University of California in 1942, and taught philosophy there for many years. He taught in many other universities including Harvard, Columbia, and the University of Michigan and in 1966 was named by *Time* Magazine as one of the ten great teachers of America. He was director of the East-West Center in Hawaii and was chairman of the Israeli Philosophical Society. In 1972 Kaplan moved to Israel to join the Haifa University as dean of the philosophy-sociology department. The Haifa University, which had just been established, was seeking renowned Jewish professors to join the university's faculty. Kaplan was the only professor to oblige, fulfilling his and the Zionist aspirations of his wife, Iona.

Kaplan's philosophical interests were broad in scope, including ethics, aesthetics, political theory, and methodology of the social sciences, as well as Oriental philosophy and philosophy of religion, including Ḥasidic thought. He wrote *Power and Society* (with W.H.D. Lasswell, 1950); *The New World of Philosophy* (1962); *American Ethics and Public Policy* (1963); *Conduct of Inquiry* (1964); *Love... and Death* (1973) and *In Pursuit of Wisdom* (1977). He also published about a hundred articles in professional journals and became associate editor of *Philosophy East and West* in 1951. Kaplan's motto was "Interest in everything." As Kaplan said of himself: "I am by training a positivist, by inclination a pragmatist, in temperament a mystic, in practice a democrat; my faith Jewish, educated by Catholics, a habitual Protestant; born in Europe, raised in the Midwest, hardened in the East, softened in California and living in Israel."

[Eyal Diskin (2nd ed.)]

KAPLAN, ALEXANDER SENDER BEN ZERAH HAKOHEN (d. 1884), Lithuanian rabbi. Few biographical details are known about him. Kaplan served first as *dayyan* in Wilkomierz (Ukmerge), but was later appointed rabbi of Kupishki (Kupiskis) in the district of Ponevezh (Panevezys), where he served for 40 years. He is best known for his *Shalmei Nedarim* (1881), a comprehensive commentary on tractate *Nedarim. He regarded the compilation of a commentary on tractate *Nedarim* as of prime importance, because many errors had crept into it through the fault of the printers. Already in the previous generations this had resulted in *haggahot* being added to it by both Isaiah *Berlin-Pick and Samuel Straschun. Appended to the volume is *Millu'im li-Shelamim* containing a letter from Elijah David Rabinowitz-Teomim on a halakhic problem submitted to Kaplan, and his reply. Another responsum by Rabinowitz-Teomim to Kaplan is mentioned in the *Shalmei Nedarim* (p. 470). Kaplan's notes on the Talmud remain in manuscript.

BIBLIOGRAPHY: D. Kamzon et al., *Yahadut Lita, Temunot ve-Ẓiyyunim* (1959), 95, 237; *Yahadut Lita*, 3 (1967), 305, 343.

[Yehoshua Horowitz]

KAPLAN, ANATOLI LVOVICH (1902–1980), Russian draftsman and lithographer. Kaplan studied at the Leningrad Academy from 1921 to 1927 and then he worked as a stage designer for ten years. He became a member of the Union of Soviet Artists in 1939 and his work was regularly shown in Russia. In 1941 he was commissioned to arrange the Jewish exhibit in the Leningrad Ethnological Museum. Kaplan started doing lithographs in 1937. His prints are inspired by Jewish tradition and Russian folklore. An emphasis on decorative elements imbues many of his works with a fairy tale quality. Kaplan drew illustrations to *Shalom Aleichem's *Kasrilovka* (1937–41), *The Bewitched Tailor* (1953–57); and *Tevye the Milkman* (1957–61). The series "Views of Leningrad" (1946), executed during the days of the blockade, were acquired by many Russian museums. He also created lithographs for *Song of Songs* (1958–60), *Yiddish Folk Songs* (1959–60), and *The Little Goat* (1958). Kaplan, even at this late date, caught the atmosphere of the Jewish shtetl with simplicity and humor and succeeded in conveying the poetic mood of the literary sources.

BIBLIOGRAPHY: *Kaplan* (catalog of the Bezalel National Museum Jerusalem, 1962).

[Elisheva Cohen]

KAPLAN, ARYEH (1934–1982), U.S. scholar and author. Kaplan was a teacher of Judaism who had profound influence on the Teshuvah movement of the late 1950s and 1960s. He was a foremost figure in the Jewish meditation movement, a thinker and writer whose translations, commentaries, and essays inspired thousands of young Jews to a deeper connection with the Jewish religious tradition.

Born in the Bronx, Kaplan came from a family whose origins were in Salonika, Greece. He was educated in the Torah Voda'ath and Mir yeshivot in Brooklyn. Subsequently, he was ordained by Rabbi Eliezer Yehuda Finkel of the Mir Yeshivah in Jerusalem. Trained as a scientist (he was for a time the assistant of world-renowned physicist J. Robert Oppenheimer), he chose instead to devote his life to the teaching of Judaism.

Kaplan's writing career began in the early 1970s with booklets of the Young Israel Intercollegiate Hashkafa Series. Other booklets dealing with the fundaments of Jewish observance were published by the Orthodox Union, and its youth wing, National Conference of Synagogue Youth (NCSY). He also wrote anti-missionary works, which were combined into the volume *The Real Messiah* (1976).

Kaplan was a pioneer in the study and teaching of Breslov Ḥasidism. On the initiative of Rabbi Zvi Aryeh Rosenfeld, who was the leading English-speaking Breslover teacher in the U.S., he made the first reliable translation into English of Rebbe Nachman's writings.

He translated into English and wrote notes and introductions to classic works on the great classics of Jewish Mysticism, the *Bahir* ("Book of Illumination," 1989) and *Sefer Yeẓirah* (1997), which he elucidates in terms of traditional Kabbalistic doctrine, providing details of esoteric practice not ordinarily discussed in printed form. He also wrote three works on Jewish meditation.

In his works *Meditation and the Bible* (1989) and *Jewish Meditation* (1995) he considers meditation in relation to current Jewish practices through the prism of biblical texts and kabbalistic commentaries upon them.

His capacity for work was extraordinary as reflected in his more than 50 published books. His works ranged over a wide variety of subjects including Ḥasidism, Kabbalah, and *Aggadah*.

[Shalom Freedman (2nd ed.)]

KAPLAN, CHAIM ARON (1880–1942), educator and diarist of the Holocaust. Kaplan was born in Gorodishche, Belorussia. He received a talmudical education at the famous yeshivah of Mir and later studied at the Government Pedagogical Institute in Vilna. In 1902 he settled in Warsaw, where he founded a pioneering elementary Hebrew school, of which he was principal for 40 years. The school was known as "the Sixth Grade Grammar Elementary School of Ch. A. Kaplan." Kaplan was an exponent of the direct method of language teaching, in which Hebrew was taught as a spoken language, using the Sephardi pronunciation. Stubbornly following this system, despite strong opposition from exponents of traditional methods, he published several Hebrew textbooks advocating his method. An ardent Hebraist, he participated actively in the Society for Jewish Writers and Journalists in Warsaw, and contributed to many Hebrew and Yiddish periodicals.

Kaplan visited the United States in 1921. In 1936 he visited Ereẓ Israel, intending to settle there in order to be with his two children who had emigrated there earlier, but was unable to obtain a position and returned to Warsaw. In 1937, Kaplan published a book in Hebrew called *Pezurai*, a collection of essays and articles on the Hebrew language and Jewish education that he had published during the 40 years of teaching. He also wrote Hebrew grammar and children's textbooks on Jewish history and customs.

Kaplan's Judaism seems to have been based on national and historic allegiance, rather than on traditional observance. Something of an introvert, he made books his friends and the walls of the academies his companions. At times he felt that his ambition to be independent was a primary obstacle to him in attaining leadership in the Warsaw community, and for that reason he was unable to develop his full talents and intellectual abilities. On the other hand, the fact that he was a respected member of the community gave him comfort and satisfaction.

Kaplan began a personal diary as early as 1933. This trained him for the mission he undertook at the beginning of World War II, to devote all his efforts to preserving a record for posterity. No diarist, of course, can be fully objective, even in a less tormented time than Kaplan's. Yet his intention of objectivity is carried out with remarkable tenacity, and with increasing dedication in the face of hardship, as the dreadful events increased his own physical and emotional suffering and his anguish at the mounting tragedy around him. It is significant that, although he had suffered from diabetes since 1928, there is no mention of this illness in his diary dealing with the war years. The diary has been preserved in toto, having been smuggled out of the Warsaw Ghetto before its total destruction. Kaplan himself was largely responsible for the miracle of its preservation. In 1942, when he knew that the Nazi noose was around his neck, he gave it to a Jewish friend named Rubinsztejn, who was working daily at forced labor outside the ghetto, returning each evening. Rubinsztejn smuggled the notebooks out one by one, handing them over to a Pole.

Kaplan's Hebrew script is clear and beautiful, with no erasures, a remarkable feat in view of the almost impossible conditions under which it was written. At the worst moments, on the brink of destruction, Kaplan sustained himself with the hope that the diary would be saved. His own future worried him little; the fate of his chronicle was his main concern. This concern increased in proportion with the daily atrocities of the Nazis. During the most tragic days, in the midst of frenzied flight from one place to another, he felt himself obligated to quicken the pace of his work. He wrote several times a day in order to include every detail of the horror surrounding him. It was not easy to "catch with the pen the knife which cuts down ceaselessly without a drop of pity," but he continued to record events with amazing regularity. Thus he writes in his last entry (August 4, 1942) during the Great Aktion that began on July 23 and lasted until September, "If the hunters do not stop, and if I am caught, I am afraid my work will be in vain. I am constantly bothered by the thought: If my life ends, what will become of my diary?"

The diary records the daily events and experiences of the author and the ghetto community. The heart of a pained, dedicated educator is revealed when he describes the yearning of the children for a bit of nature, the sight of a tree, or a blade of grass. A smile – the laughter of the condemned – illuminates his description of the bringing of the gypsies to the ghetto, for the gypsies, too, according to the Nazi ideology, were of inferior race.

The diarist has an eye for detail as well for major trends. He is concerned with politics as well as with philosophy. Since the diary was his constant companion, Kaplan poured into it a great deal of his intellectual life – his thoughts, his information, and all the conversations he had with his friends. He is not detached from the scene; indeed, he apparently sought out all possible first-hand information and his descriptions deal with the mood of the time, the hour of occurrence. Many seeming contradictions are really the hourly changes of those fantastic times, with the result that at times he condemns the leaders of the Jewish community and at times praises them. He had no use for Adam *Czerniakow, the president of the *Judenrat whom he accused of usurping power at a time when the Warsaw Jewish community was powerless to elect a leader. Yet when Czerniakow committed suicide because he could no longer bring himself to deliver Jews to the Nazis, Kaplan wrote a noble eulogy of him, commenting: "His end proves conclusively that he worked and strove for the good of his people, though not everything that was done in his name was praiseworthy. Czerniakow earned immortality in a single instant." The diary has been translated into English, German, French, Danish, and Japanese.

BIBLIOGRAPHY: A.I. Katsh, *Scroll of Agony, The Warsaw Diary of Chaim A. Kaplan* (1965); idem, *The Warsaw Diary of Chaim A. Kaplan* (1973); idem, Hebrew ed. (1947), 60; E. Ringelblum, *Notes of the Warsaw Ghetto* (Yiddish, 1952), 339–40; Ch. A. Kaplan, *Pezurai* (1937); idem, *Hebrew Grammar* (1924); B. Mark, *Yiddish Book* (1952), 339–40.

[Abraham I. Katsh]

KAPLAN, ELIEZER (1891–1952), Israeli financial leader and politician, member of the First and Second Knessets. Born in Minsk in White Russia, as a child he studied in a *ḥeder* and later on in a Russian gymnasium. Kaplan received a diploma in construction engineering from the Higher School for Technology in Moscow in 1917. In 1915 he joined the Socialist Zionists, and in 1918 Ẓe'irei Zion, becoming a member of its Central Committee and representing it on the Zionist Central Committee. In the course of World War I Kaplan was active in helping Jewish refugees and at the end of the war was a member of the Jewish delegation from Russia that participated in the *Comité des Délégations Juives, which represented the Jewish people at the peace negotiations at Versailles in 1919. In 1920 Kaplan was one of the initiators of the union between part of Ẓe'irei Zion and Ha-Po'el ha-Ẓair, that came to be known as Ha-Hitaḥadut ha-Olamit, and whose program was "pioneering and labor in Eretz Yisrael and popular socialism." He represented the Hitaḥadut at the London Zionist Conference in 1920 and was elected to the Zionist Executive.

Kaplan immigrated to Palestine in 1920, but was immediately sent to run the office of Ẓe'irei Zion–Ha-Po'el ha-Ẓa'ir in Berlin. He returned to Palestine in 1923 and served as a member of the executive of the Public Works Department in the *Histadrut, that was later renamed Solel Boneh, and became a member of the Histadrut Executive. In 1923–25 he ran the technical department in the Tel Aviv municipality, and in 1925–33 was a member of the Tel Aviv Council. He was also a member of the Ha-Po'el ha-Ẓa'ir Central Committee, and was one of the initiators of the union between Ha-Po'el ha-Ẓa'ir with Aḥdut ha-Avodah in 1930, and the foundation of *Mapai, becoming a member of its Central Committee. Within Mapai he was considered a moderate. In 1933–48 Kaplan served as the treasurer of the *Jewish Agency and was a member of its Executive; in 1943–48 he also served as head of its Settlement Department. As treasurer he managed to attain loans abroad and made great efforts to introduce strict supervision over expenditure. He was among the initiators and implementers of all the major Zionist economic enterprises of the period. In those years he supported Chaim *Weizmann on the issue of moderation in the struggle against the British authorities, and opposed David *Ben-Gurion's activist line. During the transitional period toward the establishment of the State of Israel, he directed the financial affairs of Minhelet ha-Am (the People's Administration) and was appointed minister of finance in the Interim Government after the establishment of the State. Kaplan laid the foundations for the financial and fiscal policy of the State of Israel, and helped shape its policy toward the various branches of the economy, being particularly interested in the development of agriculture. In 1949 he obtained the first loan from the U.S. Ex-Im Bank. He also contributed to the organization of the Israel Bonds drive in the U.S. Kaplan served as minister of finance until June 1952, and resigned as a result of poor health, serving as deputy prime minister until his death in July. He published several books on the economy of Israel.

BIBLIOGRAPHY: J. Shapira (ed.), *Eliezer Kaplan – Ḥazon u-Ma'as* (1973).

[Susan Hattis Rolef (2nd ed.)]

KAPLAN, ISAAC (1878–1976), leader of Jewish farmers in Argentina and veteran Zionist. Born in Svisloch, Belorussia, in 1895 Kaplan arrived in Argentina with his family and went directly to Colonia Clara in Entre Ríos, one of the colonies of the Jewish Colonization Association. Together with Miguel Sajaroff and Noé Yarcho, Kaplan was among the most enthusiastic promoters of the cooperative movement among the colonists through his work in the Fondo Communal of Clara, founded in 1904. Kaplan advocated the doctrines of the Fondo Communal, which began as an institution to help the colonists and later developed into a cooperative, in articles in *Colono Cooperador* (the Jewish settlers' monthly paper), which he headed from 1921 to 1947. He also held executive positions in the Federación Agraria Israelita Argentina, founded in 1925, and was an active participant in various national and provincial agrarian congresses. He promoted the passage of various laws in the Argentinian parliament for the welfare of all colonists and was appointed to serve on several projects by the secretary of agriculture. He was also one of the founders of the Zionist organizations in the Jewish colonies and held leading positions in the major Jewish institutions in Buenos Aires (e.g., the Federación Sionista Argentina, over which he presided for eight years; the JNF; Keren Hayesod; and DAIA).

[Victor A. Mirelman]

KAPLAN, JACOB (1895–1994), French rabbi and author. Born in Paris, Kaplan served with distinction in World War I and later graduated from the Sorbonne (1919) and the Séminaire Israélite de France (1921). He held rabbinical posts in Mulhouse, Alsace (1922), and in Paris (1929). During the German occupation he worked with the resistance movement.

He served briefly as interim chief rabbi of France (1944) and later became chief rabbi of Paris (1950). He participated in the creation of the Jewish-Christian friendship movement (1948) and in 1953 negotiated the return to their family of the *Finaly children. He was appointed to the post of chief rabbi of France in 1955. He retired as chief rabbi of France at the end of 1980 and was appointed honorary chief rabbi. Kaplan openly proclaimed French Jewry's solidarity with the State of Israel during the period of the Six-Day War and after, when French official policy was hostile to Israel. Apart from his Jewish scholarship, Kaplan was also a lecturer at l'Institut d'Etudes Politiques and a member of the Académie des Sciences Morales et Politiques in Paris (1967). His published works include *Le Judaïsme et la justice sociale* (1937), *Racisme et Judaïsme* (1940), *French Jewry under the Occupation* (1945–46), *Le Judaïsme dans la société contemporaine* (1948), *Témoignages sur Israël* (1949), *Les Temps d'Epreuve* (1952), and *Notice sur la vie et les travaux de Georges Duhamel* (1968).

[Lucien Lazare]

KAPLAN, JOHANNA (1942–), U.S. author and teacher. Born in New York City, Kaplan became a teacher of emotionally disturbed children in the New York City school system and at Mt. Sinai Hospital. At the same time, she developed an interest in writing and following the publication of a collection of short stories and a novel was recognized as a significant talent among the younger generation of Jewish writers.

Her short stories collection, *Other People's Lives* (1975), revealed her sensitive development of character and dialogue, a talent exploited to the full in her first novel *O My America!* (1980). *O My America!* describes the life of a famous radical, Ezra Slavin, as told after his death by one of his children. The book follows Slavin's early years on the Lower East Side, his intellectual rise, and his attempted dissociation from his Jewish roots. As it unfolds, the novel also surveys several generations of the Jewish experience in America.

Johanna Kaplan also contributed book reviews to the *New York Times* and other journals.

[Susan Strul]

KAPLAN, JOSEPH (1902–1991), geophysicist. Kaplan was born in Tapolcza, Austro-Hungary, and moved with his family to Baltimore at the age of eight. He received his B.Sc. in chemistry in 1924 and his Ph.D. in physics in 1927 at Johns Hopkins University, Baltimore, after which he was a research fellow at Princeton University before moving to the University of California at Los Angeles (UCLA) in 1928. He remained at UCLA for the rest of his life. At UCLA he was a full professor from 1940, chairman of the Department of Physics (1939–44), and director of the Institute of Geophysics (1946–47). Kaplan's laboratory work simulated the atomic and molecular reactions which occur in the earth's upper atmosphere. His subsequent work characterized the physical nature of nitrogen in the upper atmosphere and the atmospheric bands of oxygen which contribute to the light of the night sky. With colleagues he founded the science of "aeronomy," which studies the physics of the planetary atmosphere. Kaplan was an enthusiastic undergraduate and graduate teacher. He also contributed to the World War II program training U.S. Army Air Force weather officers. He was an outstanding contributor to international organizations concerned with geophysics, including the presidency of the International Union of Geodesy and Geophysics (1963). His many honors included membership in the U.S. National Academy of Sciences (elected 1957). He was an honorary member of the Board of Governors of the Hebrew University of Jerusalem and a member of the Board of Governors of the Weizmann Institute of Science.

[Michael Denman (2nd ed.)]

KAPLAN, LOUIS LIONEL (1902–2001), U.S. educator. Kaplan was born in Slonim, Russia, was taken to the U.S. in 1909, and educated in New York. From 1930, he served as executive director of the Baltimore Board of Jewish Education. He was president of the Baltimore Hebrew College, now *Baltimore Hebrew University, from 1930 to 1970. He was president of the National Council for Jewish Education (1939–41); and from 1940, he was a member of the board of governors of *Dropsie College, Philadelphia. He was also a member of the Board of Regents of the University of Maryland from 1952. He wrote *A New Approach to the Teaching of the Torah* (1942) and edited Hebrew texts and readers. Kaplan viewed Jewish education as an instrument for helping the individual, through a study of the unique Judaic religious-historical tradition, to find his place in the larger society of which he is a part.

From 1975 to 1981, he served as an interim rabbi at the Beth Am Synagogue in Baltimore.

With Theodor Schuchat, Kaplan wrote *Justice, Not Charity: A Biography of Harry Greenstein* (1967).

Baltimore Hebrew University has established the Louis L. Kaplan Prize in Hebrew Literature; and the University of Maryland awards the Louis L. Kaplan Scholarship to its most outstanding undergraduate student leaders.

ADD. BIBLIOGRAPHY: J. Fruchtman (ed.), *A Life in Jewish Education: Essays in Honor of Louis L. Kaplan* (1997).

[Leon H. Spotts / Ruth Beloff (2nd ed.)]

KAPLAN, MORDECAI MENAHEM (1881–1983), rabbi, philosopher, educator, activist, and founder of the *Reconstructionist school of thought. Kaplan was born in Svencian, Lithuania. His father, Israel Kaplan, was a talmudic scholar who immigrated to the United States in 1888, where he was joined a year later by his wife, Anna, and their two children, Sophie and Mordecai. Kaplan's early education was strictly Orthodox, but by the time he reached secondary school, he had been attracted to heterodox opinions, particularly regarding the critical approach to the Bible. After his ordination from the *Jewish Theological Seminary of America, he became the minister and superintendent of education of Kehilath Jeshurun, a noted Orthodox synagogue in New York City. It was only in 1908, when he was granted traditional ordination by

Rabbi Isaac Jacob *Reines, that the synagogue was prepared to honor the title of rabbi that had been conferred upon him by the Seminary. Meanwhile Kaplan had become uncomfortable at Kehilath Jeshurun, because by then he realized that he could no longer serve an Orthodox congregation in good conscience.

In 1909, Solomon *Schechter invited Kaplan to become the principal of the newly established Teachers Institute of the Jewish Theological Seminary. Shortly thereafter, he also began to teach homiletics as well as Midrash in the Seminary's rabbinical department. Later on, he began to teach philosophies of religion as well. For over 50 years, Kaplan influenced the thinking of Conservative rabbis. He spoke to their existential spiritual problems in light of contemporary philosophical and sociological developments and, in his view, the breakdown of traditional theology. Even those who disagreed with his views appreciated his direct approach. They were impressed by his emphasis on intellectual honesty in confronting the challenges posed by modern thought to traditional Jewish beliefs and practices. In his approach to Midrash and philosophies of religion, Kaplan combined scientific scholarship with creative application of the texts to contemporary problems. Kaplan's Reconstructionist philosophy influenced not only his own immediate students, but through them and through his extensive writings and public lectures over several decades, the American Jewish community at large. Many of his ideas, such as Judaism as a civilization (and not merely a religion or nationality), bat mitzvah, egalitarian involvement of women in synagogue and communal life, the synagogue as a Jewish center and not merely a place of worship, and living as Jews in a multicultural society, eventually came to be accepted as commonplace and implemented in all but strictly Orthodox segments of the community.

Kaplan was undoubtedly a product of his times. But he was also a cultural innovator. All advances in human thought are generated by seminal minds working on the knowledge they have acquired from equally creative thinkers. Early in his career, Kaplan became a devotee of the scientific and historical study of the Bible. He was the leading educator to confront rabbis, teachers, and laity with the changes in Jewish thought that had become necessary once the Bible had been exposed to modern techniques of examination and interpretation. But far from denigrating the genius of the biblical text, Kaplan taught his students to regard it as an indispensable source for an understanding of Jewish peoplehood and Jewish civilization.

Kaplan was a voracious reader. References in his published writings and in his Diaries are a veritable catalogue of the outstanding thinkers of ancient, medieval and modern times. Nonetheless, it can be said that for the most part, Kaplan's ideas were part of the Zeitgeist but not carbon copies of the thought of the men and women he quoted.

Kaplan did not live in an ivory tower. Although he produced studies on M.H. *Luzzatto and Hermann *Cohen, he was not primarily interested in academic scholarship. Instead, he focused on teaching future rabbis and educators to reinterpret Judaism and to make Jewish identity meaningful under modern circumstances. This was also the focus of many of his sermons and cross-continental lectures. He was heavily involved in communal efforts to improve Jewish education and was one of the founders of the New York Kehillah. He became the first rabbi of the Jewish Center, when it opened in 1918. Due to ideological conflicts with the Center's lay leadership, he resigned his position and, in 1922, organized the Society for the Advancement of Judaism. In 1935, he and his colleagues published the first issue of *The Reconstructionist.* A few years later, he participated in the founding of the Jewish Reconstructionist Foundation.

Kaplan was frequently called upon to participate in Zionist affairs. In 1925, when the Hebrew University of Jerusalem was officially opened, the American Zionist Organization sent Kaplan to Jerusalem as its official representative. His associations with Weizmann, Brandeis, Magnes, Ben-Gurion and other prominent figures constitute interesting chapters in Zionist history. In addition, Kaplan was very active in various aspects of Jewish social work and communal organization. He traveled the length and breadth of America to spread his ideas.

Kaplan's Philosophy of Judaism

In formulating his philosophy of Judaism, Kaplan drew upon classic rabbinic sources, as well as Jewish and non-Jewish philosophers, including the thinkers of the Haskalah, and the findings of the physical and human sciences. He defined Judaism as an "evolving religious civilization," attempting thereby to aid in the adjustment of world Jewry to the social and intellectual conditions of the 20th century. He maintained that as a civilization, the Jewish people possesses all the characteristics of land, language, political structure, culture, and other characteristics associated with that designation.

While Kaplan was always an ardent Zionist, he was equally convinced that the creative survival of the Jewish people in the free Diaspora was both possible and necessary. Although Jews had been forced for many centuries to live in exile, they had become a transterritorial people by choice. As long as Jews are free, they will live wherever they choose. And so, Kaplan thought, it is highly unlikely that the "ingathering of the exiles" will ever be fully implemented. Therefore, he never ceased to prod his people to formulate a new covenant, which would proclaim the centrality of Ereẓ Israel in their transterritorial identity and state the historical and cultural elements of their unity and identity.

Jewish civilization, Kaplan argued, expresses its genius best in its historical religion. Religion entails clarifying the purposes and values of human existence, wrestling with God, whom Kaplan conceived in impersonal terms, and maintaining the vitality of the rituals of home, synagogue, and community. However, because Judaism is a civilization, the secular elements of culture are as essential as Jewish religion. These elements curb the frequent tendency of religion to foster rigidity, uniformity, and excessive worship of the past. For Kaplan,

Jewish religion should embrace all that pertains to the Jewish people's search for a meaningful existence for itself.

By "evolving," Kaplan means that Judaism should be considered from a pragmatic, historical point of view, rather than a metaphysical or revelational one. All concepts and rituals should be measured by their usefulness in sustaining individual and communal growth. The focus of Jewish life has to be the Jewish people, its needs and its response to challenge, rather than reliance on "revealed" texts or metaphysical constructions. Kaplan argued that the Jewish people will not and should not rely on a static theory of Judaism. After responsible study, each Jew must contribute his own understanding to solving the perplexities of life. Tradition must guide but not dictate. Kaplan fully embraced the pluralism inherent in his conception. He understood that his own naturalistic approach can be only an option. Henceforth, Jews will have to learn the art of compromise and how to orchestrate their differences with mutual respect.

Kaplan developed a concept of "sancta" by which he meant that civilizations differ from one another not so much ideationally in their ideas and values, which they claim are universally applicable, as they do existentially in the particular ways they express those ideas and values. For example, Kaplan designated as sancta texts, ritual and folk practices, festivals, or symbols which are regarded as sacred, namely as of special significance and as evoking respect and awe. The sancta of a civilization are continually subject to "revaluation," by which they are given new meaning, much as the term "democracy" was differently understood in ancient Athens from the way it is currently interpreted in the United States, or in totalitarian "people's democratic republics." Similarly, "God" and "Torah" were valued in different ways by Moses, Ezra, Hillel, and Maimonides. The ancient sancta of Judaism need to be subject to functional interpretation, by which Kaplan meant that we must understand how concepts and practices functioned in the lives of Jews over the centuries and how they might function today. Specifically, with regard to God, Kaplan argued that a functional interpretation of the theistic belief leads to an impersonal concept of God as cosmic process and not as a personal being. Like such nouns as parent, teacher, or president, God denotes function and not substance.

The most controversial aspect of Kaplan's thought is this pragmatic theology. Early in his career, he rejected the traditional notion of a personal God who intervenes in human affairs. Kaplan chose to emphasize the divine aspects of the universe and the creative forces that are embodied in our attempt to become fully human. His theology is complex and multilayered. He explicitly rejected the terms naturalism and humanism to characterize his thought but rather looked to what he called transnaturalism, a realm beyond but not apart from the natural, where we find the reality of the divine.

In arguing that ideas of God are correlatives of ideas of man and the cosmos and therefore bear an organic relationship to man's understanding of himself and the world, Kaplan has been criticized for what is claimed to be his excessive reliance on human reason as expressed in the latest scientific theories of his day.

Nonetheless, it is noteworthy that some of the criticisms of Kaplan have only heightened the cogency of much of his thought. In defense of his theology, he exemplified intellectual modesty by pointing out that pluralism in this discipline was an ineluctable outcome of the uncertainties that seem to inhere in all efforts to plumb the depths of cosmic reality.

Kaplan was a strong supporter of the equality of women in Jewish life. He inaugurated the first bat mitzvah ceremony in 1922, when he called his daughter, Judith (*Eisenstein), to read from the Torah. He publicly advocated that Jewish rituals be reconstructed to include greater equality for women. Though his ideas were advanced for his time, he never attempted to revise the liturgy to be gender sensitive. But his call for reading the Bible as an inspired but man-made document, his demand for the equality of women, his insistence on adjusting liturgy to contemporary beliefs – these and other hallmarks of his philosophy are now generally accepted in all but strictly Orthodox ranks. One persistent criticism has related to what is mistakenly held to be Kaplan's failure to appreciate the primacy of emotion in worship. Kaplan, however, argued that emotion is purer when worshippers believe in the truth of the content of their prayers.

No understanding of Kaplan can be complete without reference to his Diaries, which are contained in 27 volumes of 300 handwritten pages each. The Diaries are an unmatched collection of autobiographical data, historical source material, philosophical reflection, literary criticism, sketches of innumerable persons, and reflections on life. The originals are housed in the library of the Jewish Theological Seminary of America.

On Denominationalism

For many years, Mordecai Kaplan sought to keep his philosophy of Judaism within the bounds of a school of thought. He resisted the pressure of some of his supporters to leave the Jewish Theological Seminary and accept the invitation of Rabbi Stephen S. *Wise to join the faculty of the Jewish Institute of Religion (founded in 1922), a move which might well have been the precursor of a new Jewish denomination. In 1927, Kaplan finally did resign his JTS position and accepted Wise's proposal. Although some of Kaplan's Seminary colleagues might have been pleased with this step, many students and alumni were not. Kaplan bowed to their pressure, withdrew his resignation, and remained at the Seminary until he retired in 1963. Despite his dissatisfaction with the Seminary, Kaplan believed that a new denomination would further fragment the American Jewish community. He advocated that Reconstructionism be conceived as a school of thought that could operate within all the streams in the American Jewish community. By the late 1940s, however, a number of laymen in synagogues throughout the United States decided to organize an independent federation of Reconstructionist synagogues. Kaplan was unable to forestall this development.

Meanwhile, some of Kaplan's primary supporters, including Rabbis Ira *Eisenstein (his son-in-law), Solomon *Goldman, Max *Kadushin, Milton *Steinberg, Joshua Loth *Liebman, and Edward *Israel urged him at various times to establish a new rabbinical school. In 1963, Kaplan retired from the Seminary at the age of 82. Within a short time, his supporters, led by Eisenstein, set up the Reconstructionist Rabbinical College, which is now located in Wyncote, Pennsylvania. Kaplan taught willingly at the College for a year or so. In addition to the slow growth of the Reconstructionist movement, which by the beginning of the 21st century included over a 100 congregations and havurot, increasing numbers of graduates of the Reconstructionist Rabbinical College and a successful summer camp, Kaplan's school of thought continues to permeate and to challenge other Jewish movements, especially the Reform, Conservative and modern Orthodox.

Literary Output

Although he began to publish books at what might be considered an advanced age, Kaplan was a prolific writer. His first and major work, *Judaism as a Civilization*, was first published in 1934, when Kaplan was 53. Other writings include *A New Approach to the Jewish Problem* (1924); the translation and editing of *Mesillat Yesharim*, by Moses Ḥayyim Luzzatto (1937); *The Meaning of God in Modern Jewish Religion* (1937); *The New Haggadah for the Pesah Seder* (1941); *The Faith of America* (ed. with Paul Williams, 1951); *Ha-Emunah ve-ha-Musar* (1954); *The Future of the American Jew* (1949); *A New Zionism* (1955); *Questions Jews Ask* (1956); *Judaism Without Supernaturalism* (1958); *The Greater Judaism in the Making* (1960); *Higher Jewish Learning* (1963); *The Purpose and Meaning of Jewish Existence* (1964); *Not So Random Thoughts* (1966); *The Religion of Ethical Nationhood* (1970); *If Not Now, When?* (with Arthur A. Cohen, 1973). Over the years, Kaplan was also the dominant figure in the production of the *siddurim, maḥzorim*, and other liturgical material of the Reconstructionist movement. Three of the above volumes have been translated into Hebrew: *The Meaning of God in Modern Jewish Religion, A New Zionism,* and *The Religion of Ethical Nationhood. Ha-Emunah ve-ha-Musar* appeared only in Hebrew. A full bibliography of over 400 items can be found in *The American Judaism of Mordecai Kaplan*, ed. by Emanuel S. Goldsmith, Mel Scult, and Robert Seltzer (1990).

BIBLIOGRAPHY: E.S. Goldsmith and M. Scult (eds.), *Dynamic Judaism: The Essential Writings of Mordecai M. Kaplan* (1985); E.S. Goldsmith, M.Scult and R.M. Seltzer (eds.), *The American Judaism of Mordecai M. Kaplan* (1990); M. Scult, *Judaism Faces the Twentieth Century: A Biography of Mordecai M. Kaplan* (1993); D. Breslauer, *Mordecai Kaplan's Thought in a Post-Modern Age* (1994); J.S. Gurock and J.J. Schacter, *A Modern Heretic and a Traditional Community* (1997); J.J. Cohen, *Guides for an Age of Confusion* (1998); M. Scult (ed.), *Communings of the Spirit: The Journals of Mordecai M. Kaplan* [1913–1934] (2001).

[Jack Cohen, Mel Scult, and Raphael Jospe (2nd ed.)]

KAPLAN, PESAḤ (1870–1943), Hebrew and Yiddish journalist. Born in Stawiski, Poland, Kaplan lived in Bialystok from 1888 and was active in Zionist circles, writing regularly in the Hebrew press. He also published a series of popular works and children's books in Hebrew. Later he moved away from Zionism, wrote in Yiddish, and served as journalist and editor of Yiddish periodicals. He was a member of the *Judenrat in the Bialystok ghetto and perished in the Holocaust. Two diaries which he kept in the ghetto (on the Bialystok Judenrat, and on the expulsion of the Jews of Bialystok) are preserved in the archives of *Yad Vashem in Jerusalem.

BIBLIOGRAPHY: Kressel, Leksikon, 2 (1967), 288f.

[Getzel Kressel]

KAPLAN, ROBERT P. (**Bob**; 1936–), Canadian politician, lawyer, businessman. Kaplan was born in Toronto. He earned a B.A. (1958) and LL.B. (1961) from the University of Toronto, during which time he was awarded a number of academic prizes and wrote for the University's student newspaper and for the *Toronto Telegram*. Called to the Ontario Bar in 1963, he practiced corporate and tax law with several prominent firms. In 1968 he entered national politics, working on Pierre Elliott Trudeau's successful campaign for leadership of the Liberal Party. In the federal election that same year, Kaplan was elected to the House of Commons for Toronto's Don Mills riding. He lost his seat in the election of 1972 but was re-elected in 1974 in the heavily Jewish York Centre riding and held the seat until he retired from electoral politics in 1993.

In 1980 Trudeau appointed Kaplan to the cabinet post as solicitor general, responsible for Canadian law enforcement and for national security. He also held the post during the short-lived administration of Trudeau's successor, John Turner. Among Kaplan's contributions as solicitor general was overseeing a reorganization of the Royal Canadian Mounted Police and establishing the Canadian Security Intelligence Service. He also implemented the Young Offenders Act (1982), dealing with youth accountability for criminal actions, and reformed the Correctional Services of Canada. When the Liberals lost the 1984 federal election, Kaplan was personally re-elected in York Centre and became the Liberal opposition's justice critic.

Kaplan is best remembered in the Canadian Jewish community for his attempts to persuade a reluctant Liberal government to take action against war criminals living in Canada. The government, under Trudeau's influence, however, was wary of inciting inter-ethnic passions and refused to take action, despite strong lobbying by Jewish leaders. Nevertheless, Kaplan was able to extradite a Nazi war criminal, Helmut Rauca, to West Germany in 1982, where he was imprisoned.

Kaplan was honored with numerous awards, including the Order de la Pléiade for his service to francophonie in Canada. From 1994, he was honorary consul general of Kazakhstan in Canada and fostered relations and business contacts between that country and Canada. Kaplan was a member of committees at the University of Toronto, the Alliance Française in Toronto, the Canadian Jewish Congress, and B'nai

B'rith Canada. He sat on boards of a number of publicly traded companies and was a trustee of H&R REIT, one of Canada's largest real estate investment trusts, and a director of TV Niagara and European Goldfields.

[Frank Bialystok (2nd ed.)]

KAPLAN, SENDER MEYER (1914–1992), journalist and Zionist activist; honorary consul of Israel in Cuba. He was the son of Rabbi Zvi Kaplan, the spiritual leader of the Ashkenazi congregation Adath Israel in Havana (1929–31) and later of Knesset Israel (1931–41), Sender Kaplan emigrated from Poland to Cuba with his family at the age of 15. After serving a short time as an apprentice to a watchmaker, he began to work at the Yiddish periodical *Havaner Lebn*, serving as its editor from 1935 until it was closed down in 1960. *Havaner Lebn*, which was published twice a week, was the main Jewish periodical in Cuba, and Kaplan had a central role in shaping Jewish public opinion. An outstanding Zionist leader, he was the president of the Unión Sionista de Cuba in 1940–43. When JNF leader Nathan Bistritzky began to organize the Comité Cubano Pro Palestina Hebrea (the Cuban Committee for a Jewish Palestine) Kaplan served as the link with Cuban politicians and intellectuals. Thanks to his great devotion to the Zionist cause and to his close contacts in government circles, Kaplan was appointed honorary consul when the Consulate of Israel was opened in Havana (1952). In 1954 the Israeli ambassador in Mexico presented his credentials to President Batista, and Kaplan remained the only diplomatic representative of Israel residing in Havana until the Castro revolution. In 1961 Kaplan emigrated to Miami, where he continued to serve the Zionist cause. He worked as director of the Latin Department of the Jewish Federations of Greater Miami. He devoted the later years of his life to writing the history of the Jews of Cuba, but was unable to complete the work.

[Margalit Bejarano (2nd ed.)]

KAPLANSKY, KALMEN (1912–1997), Canadian labor leader and human rights advocate. Kaplansky was born in Bialystok, Poland, and, while still in his teens immigrated alone to Canada in 1929. He settled into Montreal's downtown Jewish immigrant community. A typesetter and linotype operator, during the Depression Kaplansky rose through the ranks of the labor movement. He was a delegate of Montreal Typographical Union 176 to the Trades and Labour Congress of Canada and, soon after, to the merged Canadian Labour Congress. In 1939, he helped organize the Jewish Labour Committee (JLC) in Canada, an offshoot of the American labor organization founded in 1933.

Kaplansky became the Canadian group's national director in 1946. Under his leadership the JLC was instrumental in forging the 1946 alliance of Jewish clothing manufacturers and labor leaders who convinced the federal government to open Canada's door to several thousand clothing workers from the Displaced Persons' camps in Europe. The JLC was also a key player in the tripartite committee of labor, manufactures, and government responsible for selecting tailors in Europe for Canadian immigration.

A champion of human rights, Kaplansky was incensed by the discriminatory employment restrictions common in Canada, and organized the Joint Labour Committees Against Racial and Religious Discrimination, later known as the Labour Committees for Human Rights. He also convinced the Trades and Labour Congress of Canada and the Canadian Congress of Labour to establish parallel committees. Together they actively lobbied the Ontario government for legislation barring discrimination and, in large part, were responsible for the passing of the Ontario Fair Employment Practices Act in 1951 (subsequently used as a model for virtually all provincial and federal codes that followed), the Ontario Fair Accommodations Act in 1954, and, ultimately, the Ontario Human Rights Code. Kaplansky also pioneered efforts to eradicate discrimination against blacks and native peoples in Canada. He was involved in the Canadian Jewish Historical Society and twice ran for public office as a Co-Operative Commonwealth Federation (CCF) candidate.

Remembered as a humble, unpretentious man, loyal to his roots, Kaplansky was the recipient of many awards and commendations, including the Order of Canada, the nation's highest civilian award.

[Frank Bialystok (2nd ed.)]

KAPLANSKY, SHELOMO (1884–1950), Zionist labor leader. Born in Bialystok (then Russia), Kaplansky trained as an engineer and joined the Zionist labor movement at an early age. He lived in Vienna between 1903 and 1912, founded the *Po'alei Zion movement in Austria, and edited its journal *Der Juedische Arbeiter*, which appeared in German and Yiddish. He was a founder of the World Union of Po'alei Zion and was instrumental in having it accepted as a member of the Socialist International. He devised the idea of the Ereẓ Israel Workers' Fund (Kuppat Po'alei Ereẓ Yisrael) which was founded in 1910 by the World Union of Po'alei Zion to foster cooperative settlements and enterprises in Ereẓ Israel. He went to Ereẓ Israel in 1912 to settle there, but between 1913 and 1919 he was secretary of the *Jewish National Fund head office at The Hague. He was a member and chairman of the finance and economics committee of the Zionist Executive in London between 1919 and 1921. Kaplansky, who belonged to the moderate socialist trend, supported the participation of Po'alei Zion in the World Zionist Organization and all its institutions. At the 1920 World Conference of Po'alei Zion in Vienna he preferred the movement's split, repudiating its pro-Communist faction (the Left Po'alei Zion). Between 1927 and 1929 he was a member of the Zionist Executive in Jerusalem and the director of its Settlement Department. From 1929 until 1931 he lived in London as an emissary of the Zionist labor movement to the British Labour Party, which was then in power. From 1932 until his death, Kaplansky was director of the Haifa *Technion. During the debate over the partition of Palestine in 1937 he opposed the scheme, preferring the idea of a binational state in the whole of Palestine. As a result, he left the *Mapai Party in 1944 and later joined *Mapam. Some of his many articles and pamphlets in Russian, German, English, Hebrew, and Yiddish are collected in *Ḥazon ve-Hagshamah* ("Vision and Fulfillment," 1950).

BIBLIOGRAPHY: Z. Shazar, *Or Ishim*, 2 (1964^2), 159–68; A. Granott, *Dor Tekumah* (1963), 321–4; M. Singer, *Shelomo Kaplansky*, 2 vols. (1971).

KAPO, prisoner in charge of a group of inmates in Nazi concentration camps. The derivation of the word is not clear; according to one view the name is Italian (*capo* = "boss"); according to others it is an abbreviation of *Kameradschaftpolizei* and would then have originated among the prisoners themselves. Similarly, it is not possible to ascertain when this unofficial term first came into use. The appointment of Kapos was made by the SS who guarded the camps; but the authority to appoint Kapos was never explicitly defined. It was the Kapo's task to carry out the orders of the SS and to ensure absolute control over the prisoners. The Kapo was not an expert like the "chief worker" (*Vorarbeiter*) but just a strong man. For the most part, Kapos were in charge of work gangs, but there were also Kapos for the hospitals or the kitchens. Certain camps even had a hierarchy: Oberkapo, Kapo, Unterkapo. Initially, Kapos were appointed from the ranks of ethnic German prisoners convicted on criminal charges. These criminals enjoyed extra privileges of great importance under camp conditions: better food, clothing, and housing. In return, many of them tyrannized the prisoners with a cruelty equal to that of the SS, motivated both by the desire to curry favor among the SS as well as by sadistic inclinations. In the course of time, the political prisoners in many camps succeeded in ousting some of the criminals and having them replaced by Kapos from their own ranks. Jews were appointed Kapos only in those camps which were all Jewish. Some Kapos exercised their power humanely and sensitively and worked to assist their fellow prisoners. Others mimicked the oppressive behavior of the SS and may have indeed internalized their values. Thus, the term Kapo became synonymous with a cruel and egocentric person who oppresses, tortures, and exploits others.

BIBLIOGRAPHY: E. Kogon, *Theory and Practice of Hell* (1950), passim; E.A. Cohen, *Human Behavior in Concentration Camp* (1953), index; D. Gaussen, *Le Kapo* (1965); O. Wormser-Migot, *Le Système concentrationnaire nazi 1933–1945* (1968), index.

[Jozeph Michman (Melkman)]

KAPOSI (Kohn), MORITZ (1837–1902), dermatologist. Born in Kaposvar, Hungary, he became assistant to Ferdinand Hebra at the dermatological hospital, Vienna, in 1879, and the collaboration with the famous pathologist proved most fruitful. Kaposi completed Hebra's studies on the anatomical-pathological aspects of dermatology by new findings in chemistry and bacteriology. Together they were the first to describe several diseases. In 1875 Kaposi, a convert to Christianity, was appointed professor of dermatology at Vienna University. Kaposi was an outstanding diagnostician and teacher as well as a prolific author. He wrote *Pathologie und Therapie der Hautkrankheiten* (1879) and *Handatlas der Hautkrankheiten* (1898–1900) which included the most complete descriptions and illustrations of skin diseases at that time. He was the first to describe multiple idiopathic hemorrhagic sarcoma, called Kaposi's sarcoma, and *xeroderma pigmentosum*, called Kaposi's disease. He wrote many articles in the field of dermatology and syphilology.

BIBLIOGRAPHY: *Biographisches Lexikon der hervorragenden Aerzte*, 3 (1931), s.v.; S.R. Kagan, *Jewish Medicine* (1952), 414–5.

[Suessmann Muntner]

KAPOSVAR (Hung. **Kaposvár**), city in S.W. Hungary. In 1784 there were 15 Jews living in the town. The numbers increased to 95 in 1840; 1,078 in 1869; 3,505 in 1920; and 2,341 in 1941. A Jewish elementary school functioned from 1840 until the Holocaust. The synagogue was erected in 1862. Like those in all the surrounding communities the Jews of Kaposvar were inclined toward *assimilation. In 1860 A. Freystaedtler, a Jew, leased an estate from Count Esterházy and endeavored to employ Jews. At the beginning of the 20th century, many banks were owned by Jews, as well as several large factories and flour mills. A Jew served as deputy mayor for 20 years. Anti-Jewish attacks were made in 1848. The antisemite G. *Istóczy and some noblemen who had been dispossessed of their estates were responsible for anti-Jewish outbreaks in the town. Rabbis of the community included A. Ehrental (1852–54) and S. Kuttna (1853–71).

Holocaust Period

In 1940 all Jewish men were moved to a labor camp and after the German invasion in March 1944 around 6,000 Jews including refugees were concentrated in a ghetto around the synagogue in May. On July 4 all were deported to *Auschwitz. After the liberation of the town (December 1944) by the Red Army, Jewish men from the surrounding labor camps began to return to Kaposvar. Only about 200 of those deported from Kaposvar survived. There were 450 Jews living in the town in 1945 and 574 in 1949. After the revolution of 1956, many of them left the country, and by 1959 only 261 Jews remained in Kaposvar.

[Baruch Yaron]

KAPPAROT (Heb. כַּפָּרוֹת, plural of the Heb. כַּפָּרָה, *kapparah*; "expiation"), custom in which the sins of a person are symbolically transferred to a fowl. The custom is practiced in certain Orthodox circles on the day before the *Day of Atonement (in some congregations also on the day before *Rosh Ha-Shanah or on *Hoshana Rabba). Psalms 107:10, 14, 17–21, and Job 33:23–24 are recited; then a cock (for a male) or a hen (for a female) is swung around the head three times while the following is pronounced: "This is my substitute, my vicarious offering, my atonement; this cock (or hen) shall meet death, but I shall find a long and pleasant life of peace." The fowl is thought to take on any misfortune which might otherwise befall a person in punishment of his sins. After the ceremony, it is customary to donate the fowl to the poor, except for the intestines which are thrown to the birds. Some rabbis recommended that money, equivalent to the fowl's value, be given instead.

This custom is nowhere mentioned in the Talmud. It appears first in the writings of the *geonim* of the 9th century, who explain that a cock is used in the rite because the word *gever* means both "man" and "cock"; the latter can, therefore, substitute for the former.

In Babylonia, other animals were used, especially the ram since Abraham offered a ram in lieu of his son Isaac (see: *Akedah and Gen. 22:13), or plants, e.g., beans, peas, (cf. Rashi, Shab. 81b). After the destruction of the Temple, no animals used in sacrificial rites could serve similar purposes outside the Temple (Magen Abraham to Sh. Ar., OḤ 605) and therefore cocks or hens were employed in the *kapparot* rite because they were not used in the Temple sacrificial cult. R. Solomon b. Abraham *Adret strongly opposed *kapparot* because it was similar to the biblical atonement rites (see *Azazel; cf. Lev. 16:5–22); he also considered the *kapparah* ritual to be a heathen superstition ("*Darkhei Emori*," responsa ed. Lemberg (1811) pt. 1, no. 395). This opinion was shared by *Naḥmanides and Joseph *Caro who called the *kapparot* "a stupid custom" (OḤ 605). The kabbalists (Isaac *Luria, Isaiah *Horowitz), however, invested the custom with mystical interpretations. These appealed strongly to the masses, and it became very popular when the rabbis acquiesced to it. Isserles made it a compulsory rite and enjoined for it many ceremonials similar to those of the sacrificial cult; e.g., the laying of the hands upon the animal, its immediate slaughter after the ceremony, prayers of confession, etc.

If a cock, or hen, cannot be obtained, other animals, fish or geese, may be used instead. A white cock or hen was especially desirable (based on Isa. 1:18, and Yoma 6:8). Some authorities, e.g., Joel Sirkes, forbade the use of a white cock on the grounds that it was a pagan rite (cf. Bayit Ḥadash, to Tur., OḤ 605, and Av. Zar. 1:5 and 14a). *Kapparot* is not practiced with a fowl at all in some traditional and many modern congregations. Money is substituted for a cock and the formula is changed accordingly ("this coin shall go to charity but we…," etc.). In Yiddish and popular Hebrew parlance the word *kapparot* may also refer to a financial or material loss, a regretted waste, or a vain effort.

BIBLIOGRAPHY: J.Z. Lauterbach, *Rabbinic Essays* (1951), 354–76; idem, in: *Jewish Studies… G.A. Kohut* (1935), 413–22; Eisenstein, Yisrael, 5 (1911), 289–90; H. Schauss, *Guide to Jewish Holy Days* (1968[5]), 149ff., 164ff.; S.Y. Agnon, *Days of Awe* (1965[2]), 147–50.

KAPPER, SIEGFRIED or **VÍTĚZSLAV** (1821–1879), Czech poet and the first Jew to publish in Czech. Born and educated in Prague, Kapper graduated in medicine from the University of Vienna and spent some time as a physician, but he devoted his life mainly to writing. Like Moritz *Hartmann, the German revolutionary who became his brother-in-law, he belonged to the "Young Bohemia" circle and took an interest in Slavic culture. From 1839 Kapper was a contributor to *Ost und West*, and the following year he began translating Czech poems into German. In 1841 he moved to Vienna, where he met Václav Bolemír Nebeský, who urged him to devote himself to Czech and Slavic affairs. Accordingly, in 1843, Kapper began a press campaign, and a year later published his *Slavische Melodien*, some of which were later set to music. In his *České listy* ("Czech Epistles," 1846), Kapper criticized the Austrian regime's treatment of the Czechs and called for the restoration of their national and civic rights. In the same book he expressed his hopes for the cultural assimilation of Czech Jewry. Both the form and the ideology of the poems were completely rejected by the eminent nationalist critic, Karel Havliček-Borovský, and as a result Kapper temporarily abandoned writing in Czech. It was at this period that he published three of the earliest "ghetto" stories in the German language (1845–49). During the 1848 Revolution Kapper was medical officer of the academic legion. The revolution inspired a volume of political poems, *Befreite Lieder* (1848–49). He then became a parliamentary reporter, but returned to medical practice in 1867.

Kapper's works include *Suedslavische Wanderungen* (1851; *A Visit to Belgrade*, 1854); the epic poem *Fuerst Lazar* (1851), which was his major literary achievement; *Christen und Tuerken* (1854); *Boehmische Baeder* (1857); and several volumes of Czech and German translations of Serbian, Montenegrin, and Bulgarian folk songs, in which field he became an acknowledged authority. Though estranged from traditional Jewish life, Kapper developed ideas of a Czech-Jewish symbiosis which greatly impressed the younger generation of Czech Jewry, and the first Czech-Jewish students' organization was named in his honor.

BIBLIOGRAPHY: Schatzky, in: *Freedom and Reason; Studies… M.R. Cohen* (1951), 423–7; *Jews of Czechoslovakia*, 1 (1968), index; G. Kisch, *In Search of Freedom* (1949); J. Krejčí, *Siegfried Kapper* (Cz., 1919); O. Donath, *Židé a židovství v české literatuře 19. a 20. století*, 2 (1930), index; idem, in: JGGJČ, 6 (1934), 323–442; P. Eisner, in: *Věstník židovské obce náboženské v Praze*, 11 (1949), 266; J. Vyskočil, in: *Judaica Bohemiae*, 3 (1967), 37–39 (Ger.); A. Hofman, *Die Prager Zeitschrift "Ost und West"* (1957), index. **ADD. BIBLIOGRAPHY:** *Lexikon české literatury*, 2/II (1985); A. Mikulášek et al., *Literatura s hvězdou Davidovou*, vol. 1 (1998).

[Avigdor Dagan]

KAPUZATO, MOSES HA-YEVANI (fl. second half of 15th century), rabbi in Salonika. Moses was the author of a commentary on the Pentateuch in which he takes issue with Abraham ibn Ezra, Maimonides, and in particular with Karaite exposition. He was the author of the poem – a *reshut* for Passover: "*Imrei Higyonai Ashir ve-Azamer la-Adonai*" included in the Romaniot *maḥzor* and the Kaffa and Aleppo rites. He was a trenchant opponent of the Karaites, who reacted violently to his criticism. He sharply criticized Aaron b. Joseph, author of the *Sefer ha-Mivḥar* and the Karaites Abraham *Bali, the physician, author of the *Iggeret ha-Issur Ner shel Shabbat*, and Caleb Abba *Afendopulo answered his criticisms. He was especially attacked by Elijah *Bashyazi in his *Aderet Eliyahu* for daring to speak against Aaron b. Joseph, against the Karaite scholars, and for following in the wake of Mordecai *Comtino. Moses is also mentioned by Karaites of later generations, such as Joseph Bagi (end of 15th and beginning of 16th centuries) in his *Iggeret Kiryah Ne'emanah.*

BIBLIOGRAPHY: Zunz, Lit Poesie, 509; J. Fuerst, *Geschichte des Karaeerthums*, 2 (1865), 297, 303; A. Berliner, *Aus Meiner Bibliothek* (1898), XXVI; Markon, in: *Festschrift... A. Harkavy*, (1908), Heb. pt., 463; Davidson, Oẓar, 1 (1924), 270, no. 5922; Rosanes, Togarmah, 1 (1930^2), 32f.

[Simon Marcus]

KARA (Cara), AVIGDOR BEN ISAAC (d. 1439), rabbi, kabbalist, and poet. Kara was of German origin. It is uncertain whether the name Kara indicates, as some think, that he was a descendant of Joseph *Kara, or whether it is a reference to his expert knowledge of Scripture (*Mikra*). His father, Isaac Kara, met a martyr's death. About 1389 Kara was appointed *dayyan* in Prague. He and Yom Tov Lipmann *Muelhausen were among the most important rabbis of Prague of the age. Kara is the author of the elegy *Et Kol ha-Tela'ah asher Meẓa'atnu* to commemorate the sufferings which overtook the Jews of Prague on the last day of Passover 1389, as a result of an accusation that they had desecrated the Host. This elegy is recited by the Jews of Prague during the *Minḥah* service on the Day of Atonement. Like his colleague Yom Tov Lipmann Muelhausen he became famous for his polemics with Christians. According to the tradition of Jacob *Moellin, which is not to be accepted as true, he was a favorite of Wenceslaus IV, king of Bohemia, and played an important role in his court. It may be assumed, however, that he had discussions with high Christian dignitaries on theological matters, and it appears that John Huss and his colleagues and disciples were influenced in no small degree by his views. The Hussite sect, founded by Huss, opposed the authority of the Church and many of its principles. Probably due to this the Jews were persecuted by the Catholics in the war that broke out between the Hussites and Catholics. Huss even made use of a poem by Kara on the unity of God, beginning *Eḥad Yaḥid u-Meyuḥad*, which has been published in the *Birkat ha-Mazon* (Amsterdam, 1722).

Kara was also known as a kabbalist, and was one of the first to cause the spread of the Spanish and German Kabbalah in his land. Moses *Cordovero and Menahem Azariah da *Fano wrongly attributed to him the authorship of **Kanah*, a kabbalistic work on the reasons for the precepts, and *Peli'ah*, a commentary on the first six chapters of Genesis. His kabbalistic compositions are still in manuscript, including: *Kodesh Hillulim*, a kabbalistic commentary on Psalm 150; and a biblical commentary based on *gematriot*. He appears also to have composed the kabbalistic work *Sefer ha-Emet*. He was known as a *paytan* and some of his *piyyutim* have been published in various places while others are still in manuscript. Some of his responsa have also been preserved. MENAHEM BEN JACOB KARA, who wrote commentaries on various philosophical works, including Maimonides' *Guide of the Perplexed*, may have been his half brother. He is regarded as the originator of the movement whose aim was to find common ground between the Kabbalah of Eastern Europe and the doctrines of the Spanish scholars, particularly Maimonides. *Abraham b. Avigdor, a 16th-century rabbi of Prague, was his descendant.

BIBLIOGRAPHY: Scholem, Mysticism, 371, 400; A. Marcus, *Der Chassidismus* (1901), 244–61; Horodezky, in: *Ha-Tekufah*, 10 (1921), 283–329; J. Kaufmann, *R. Yom Tov Lipmann Muehlhausen* (Heb., 1927), 10–12; Kestenberg, in: JGGJČ, 8 (1936), 1–25; Luzzatto, in: G. Polack (ed.), *Halikhot Kedem* (1847), 79ff.; Graetz-Rabbinowitz, 6 (1898), 58, 75, 139; S. Bernfeld, *Sefer ha-Dema'ot*, 2 (1924), 159–64; Davidson, Oẓar, 4 (1933), 347; Kamelhar, in: *Sinai*, 5 (1939), 122–48; Scholem, Shabbetai Ẓevi, 1 (1957), 93f.

[Abraham David]

KARA, JOSEPH (before c. 1060–70), Bible commentator from the north of France. The surname "Kara" (presumably Bible commentator) is an indication of Joseph's major occupation. The assumption that his surname means "teacher" is supported by his popular style and his frequent use of words in French (**la-az*), probably reflecting the fact that his commentaries are based on oral teaching.

His father, Simeon, was apparently also a scholar, but S.J. Rapoport's ascription to him of the authorship of *Yalkut Shimoni* has been shown by A. Epstein to be without foundation (see bibl.). Joseph studied under his paternal uncle, *Menahem b. Ḥelbo, and was also a student and colleague of Rashi. Rashi obviously knew Kara, who was about 25 years his junior, since he mentions him (cf. Rashi on Is. 10:24 and 64:3) and quotes some of his interpretations; at least in one case he states that Kara told him an explanation of Menaḥem b. Ḥelbo. Recent scholarship asserts that there is no evidence that Kara studied under Rashi. There is evidence that the latter occasionally accepted his biblical exegesis, and Samuel b. Meir calls Kara "our colleague" (Commentary on Gen. 37:13). Kara was the first to copy and edit Rashi's commentary. In the process he added his own remarks, some of which were approved by Rashi and many of them were integrated into the standard Rashi commentary. Some 100 such notes were compiled by A. *Berliner in his *Pletath Soferim*. Kara lived mainly in Troyes and for a period in Worms and is known to have taken part in theological discussions with Christians.

He wrote commentaries on most of the books of the Bible (possibly all), most of which remained in manuscript until recent times. Recently, fragments of his commentary on the Pentateuch have been discovered in the Italian *genizah*. Until recently, this commentary was only known from the many quotations in later works, some even incorporated in Rashi's commentary. The main characteristic of his biblical commentaries is the intention (cf. his remarks on I. Sam. 1:17; Judg. 5:4) of interpreting Scripture according to the *peshat* ("literal meaning"). Now and then, however, he deviates from this course and explains the text according to the *derash* ("homiletical interpretation"; e.g., Jer. 2:3), especially where the text presents difficulties, and he sometimes gives *derash* together with the *peshat*. Nevertheless, there is still no explanation for the distinction he makes between homiletic explanations that "the ear may hear," i.e., which are plausible (*aggadah ha-nishma'at la-ozen*, on Job 26:13) and those which are only meant to "make the Law great and glorious," such as his commentary on I Sam. 1:17. Though Kara relied heavily upon Rashi's commentary, at times even quoting it verbatim, he sometimes vigorously refutes his interpretations, stating of I Kings 7:33, for example: "This is a distortion of the words of the Living God, which causes all Israel to go astray." Other characteristics of Kara's approach are: indication of the connection between different scriptural verses; exegesis in accordance with the cantillation; differentiation between the language of the Mishnah and that of the Talmud and the Midrash; extensive use of Targum, including the Palestinian Targum, and frequent use of French and German **la'azim*; etymology of biblical words based on similar usage, roots, and sounds; pointing out words or phrases that are meaningless in context but allude to events or ideas that appear later on in the text; and literary analysis. In some places Kara's text differs from the accepted one (Josh. 9:4; Jer. 25:13). Kara was well aware of some problems concerning the biblical text and its transmission. Sometimes, as on Joshua 9:4, he cites two different versions of the text, and at least once (on Jer. 25:13) he states that a certain interpretation would be acceptable "provided a fitting version can be found in some accurate book." Kara's commentaries on the Former Prophets, the Megillot (except Song of Songs), Job, and most of the Latter Prophets are now at our disposal. Since Kara considered his works as amplifications of Rashi's commentaries, he often mentions, or even quotes, Rashi without referring to him. Some of Kara's commentaries (on Ezekiel, for example), seem to have been edited by his pupils.

Kara was one of the first to participate in a unique phenomenon that occurred in French biblical exegesis at the end of the 11th century and the beginning of the 12th century: The sudden appearance of biblical commentary based on strict *peshat*, the explicit meaning of the text. This new trend dissipated by the end of the 12th century. This new trend is seen as an attempt to refute Christian interpretation of the Hebrew Bible. A close reading of Kara's commentaries and those of Rashbam (*Samuel ben Meir, Rashi's grandson) reveals a very strong anti-Christian polemic. Contemporary Jewish polemical works quote extensively from Kara's work to refute the Christian attempts to use the Hebrew Bible (Old Testament) as proof for their theology. Even Kara's occasional use of Midrash can be ascribed to this general purpose. Given heavy Christian censorship of Jewish books, Kara was careful to hide his polemical intentions.

In addition to his biblical commentary, Kara also commented extensively on the *piyyutim*, exerting a great influence in this field on his successors who often referred to him simply as "the commentator," by virtue of his ability to penetrate into their literal meaning and the beauty and simplicity of his style. He wrote commentaries on all *piyyutim* recited in his time on festivals and special Sabbaths, and on *kinot* and *hoshanot*. There is hardly a manuscript commentary on the liturgy which does not quote him. Many of his commentaries are also to be found in printed editions, in which however, they are often abridged and quoted anonymously. Kara received many of his explanations of the *piyyutim* from scholars in southern and northern France, Germany, and Rome, including Rashi, Menahem b. Ḥelbo, and Kalonymus b. Shabbetai of Rome. Although the *aggadah* is an important source for the *piyyutim*, and Kara paid great attention to it in his commentaries, here too he extracted from the Midrash only what was essential to an understanding of the text, avoiding all extraneous matter. He explained the language and the literary aspects of the *piyyutim*, but did not concern himself with historical background. In his liturgical commentaries he made much use of his Bible commentary and laid down general principles of *piyyut*.

Berliner suggested that Kara was the author of the commentary on *Genesis Rabbah*, generally attributed to Rashi. Epstein, however, proved that it only contains additions by Kara and that the original commentary is not his.

BIBLIOGRAPHY: M. Littmann, *Joseph b. Simeon Kara als Schrifterklaerer* (1877); S. Poznański (ed.), *Perush al Yeḥezkel u-Terei Asar le-R. Eli'ezer mi-Belganẓi* (1913), p. xxiii–xxxix; to the bibliography given on p. xxiii n. 2 there should now be added: A. Epstein, *Mi-Kadmoniyyot ha-Yehudim*, 2 (1957), 328–36, (= *Ha-Ḥoker*, 1 (1891), 29–35); Kristianpoller, in: *Sefer ha-Yovel… S. Krauss* (1936), 110ff., incl. editions of texts; Abraham b. Azriel, *Arugat ha-Bosem*, ed. by E.E. Urbach, 4 (1963), 13–23 and see 276 (index); J. Gad, *Asarah Me'orot ha-Gedolim* (1952), 110–47; idem, *Ḥamishah Me'orot ha-Gedolim* (1952), 7–38, 101–56; Joseph Bekhor Shor, *Perush al ha-Torah*, ed. by J. Gad, 3 (1959), 87–128; A. Berliner, *Pletah Soferim* (1872), Hebr. text 12–25; idem, *Rashi al ha-Torah* (1905 = Jerusalem 5722), x; S. Eppenstein (ed.), *Perushei Rabbi Joseph Kara li-Nevi'im Rishonim* (1972); idem, ibid., Introduction, 7–24; M. Ahrend, in: *Sefer ha-Zikkaron le-A. Tweg* (1979); M. Ahrend, *Le commentaire sur Job de Rabbi Yoseph Qara* (1978). **ADD. BIBLIOGRAPHY:** A. Grossman, in: *Zion* 51:1 (1987), 29–60; idem, in: *Tarbut u-Ḥevrah be-Toldot Yisra'el be-Yemei ha-Beinayim: Kovez Ma'amarim le-Zikhro shel Ḥayyim Hillel Ben-Sasson* (1989), 269–301; idem, in: *Ha-Genizah ha-Italkit* (1998), 39–51; Y. Nevo, in: *Sinai*, 105 (2002), 231–44; Y. Raḥman, in: *Bet Mikra* (1990), 272–77; H. Mack, in: *Tarbiz*, 63:4 (1994), 533–53; S. Jafet, in: *The Midrashic Imagination* (1993), 98–130; K.A. Fudeman, in: JQR, 93:3–4 (2003), 397–414; M. Ahrend, in: *Le'elah*, 24 (1987), 30–33; G. Brin, *Meḥkarim be-Ferusho shel Rav Yosef Kara* (1990).

[Avraham Grossman and Moshe-Max Arend / David Derovan (2nd ed.)]

KARA, MENAHEM BEN JACOB, *dayyan* and scribe in Prague at the beginning of the 15th century. Kara refers to Avigdor b. Isaac *Kara as "my brother" and he may in fact have been his half-brother from the same mother. If, however, he is to be identified, as some suggest, with the Menahem who signed a power of attorney in 1413, together with Avigdor and Yom Tov Lipman *Muelhausen (two *dayyanim* in Prague), it must be assumed that the word means "relative" and not "brother." He wrote commentaries on various parts of the Bible, and studied philosophical literature. The following known works by Kara are in manuscript: a commentary on Maimonides' *Guide of the Perplexed*, a commentary on Al-Ghazālī's *Kavvanot ha-Pilosofim*, and on the *Mareh Elohim* of Enoch Al-Kostantin. It is maintained by some that he aspired to bring the pietists and *kabbalists of Eastern Europe closer to the Torah teaching of the Sephardim, and in particular to the teaching of Maimonides. Kara was one of the Prague scholars attracted to philosophical speculation who exercised a considerable influence on subsequent generations.

BIBLIOGRAPHY: Zunz, Gesch, 165; K. Lieben, *Gal Ed* (1856), Ger. pt. 2, Heb. pt. xlv; Weiss, Dor, 5 (1904[4]), 263; Neubauer, Cat, no. 1649; J. Kaufmann, *R. Yom Tov Lipman Muehlhausen* (Heb., 1927), 10; O. Muneles and M. Vilimková, *Starý židovský hřbitov v Praze* (1955), 105; Gottesdiener, in: *Azkarah… A.I. Kook*, 4 (1937), 260f.

[Yehoshua Horowitz]

KARÁCSONY, BENÖ (**Bernát Klaermann**; 1888–1944), Hungarian author. Karácsony, who lived in Kolozsvár (Cluj), was a leading social writer in Transylvania during the era of Romanian control. Though not class-conscious, he often satirized middle-class failings in works such as *Új élet kapujában* ("At the Gates of a New Life," 1932) and *A napos oldalon* ("On the Sunny Side," 1940). *A megnyugvásösvényein* ("For me, Tranquility") appeared in 1946. He died in Auschwitz.

KARACZEWSKI, ḤANINA (1877–1926), music teacher and composer. Born in Petrovka, Bessarabia, he went in 1899 to Warsaw where for a time he conducted a military band. In 1908 he went to Palestine and taught music at various schools in Tel Aviv, chiefly at the Herzlia Gymnasium where he remained for 18 years. Here he instituted a choir and an orchestra. Many of his pupils became music educators and choral conductors. He also organized an adult choir of 200 voices whose most memorable appearance was at the cornerstone-laying ceremony of the Hebrew University in 1925. Karaczewski and A.Z. *Idelsohn were considered the "music teachers of the National Renaissance." Only a few of Karaczewski's songs and arrangements were published during his lifetime, but a collection of his works, *Ẓelilei Ḥanina* (1927), appeared after his death. Three of his songs entered the permanent "corpus" of Palestinian-Israel folk songs: the song for Lag ba-Omer, *Ha-Ya'arah be-Keshet va-Ḥeẓ* ("To the Forest with Bow and Arrow"), with words by Samuel Leib *Gordon; *El Rosh ha-Har* ("To the Peak of the Mountain"), with words by Levin *Kipnis; and one of the most beautiful songs inspired by Lake Kinneret, *Al Sefat Yam Kinneret* ("On the Shore of Lake Kinneret"), with words by Jacob *Fichmann.

BIBLIOGRAPHY: *Ha-Gimnasyah ha-Ivrit Herẓiliyyah Zekher la-Ḥaver… Ḥanina Karaczewski* (1927).

[Bathja Bayer]

KARAITES (Heb. קָרָאִים, בְּנֵי מִקְרָא, בַּעֲלֵי מִקְרָא, *Qara'im, Benei Miqra, Ba'alei Miqra*; Ar. *Qarā'iyyūn*), Jewish sect which came into being toward the middle of the ninth century. (See Map: Karaite Settlement). Its doctrine is characterized primarily by its denial of the talmudic-rabbinic tradition. This article is arranged according to the following outline:

Name; Relation to Biblical Tradition

Scholars have had different opinions as to the exact vocalization of the name: Whether it is *qara'im* (sing. *qara'*), or *qera'im* (sing. *qera'i*). The common sing. form *qara'i*, seems to be secondary. The accepted meaning of the name of the sect – Kara'im, Ba'alei ha-Mikra ("people of the Scriptures") – is assumed to imply the main characteristic of the sect: the recognition of the Scriptures as the sole and direct source of law, to the exclusion of the Oral Law as it is embodied in the talmudic-rabbinic tradition. At the early stage of the group's history the name may have indicated their concentrated occupation with the text of the Hebrew Bible. At that stage their activity was perhaps connected to the Massoretes. Indeed, the famous authority on Massorah, Aharon ben Asher (who was responsible for the Massoretic element of the Aleppo Codex), was most probably a Karaite. There is, however, another interpretation of the name Kara'im, defining it as "callers" or "propagandists," in the sense of the Arabic word *du'āt* by which the Shi'ite Muslim sect designated propagandists on behalf of 'Ali. Since a religion based on revelation cannot tolerate the complete exclusion of tradition, either in principle or in practice, the Karaite demand for a return to Scripture, and a rejection of any tradition as the authoritative interpretation of Scripture, should be taken as a theoretical watchword, directed not against all tradition, but specifically against the rabbinical tra-

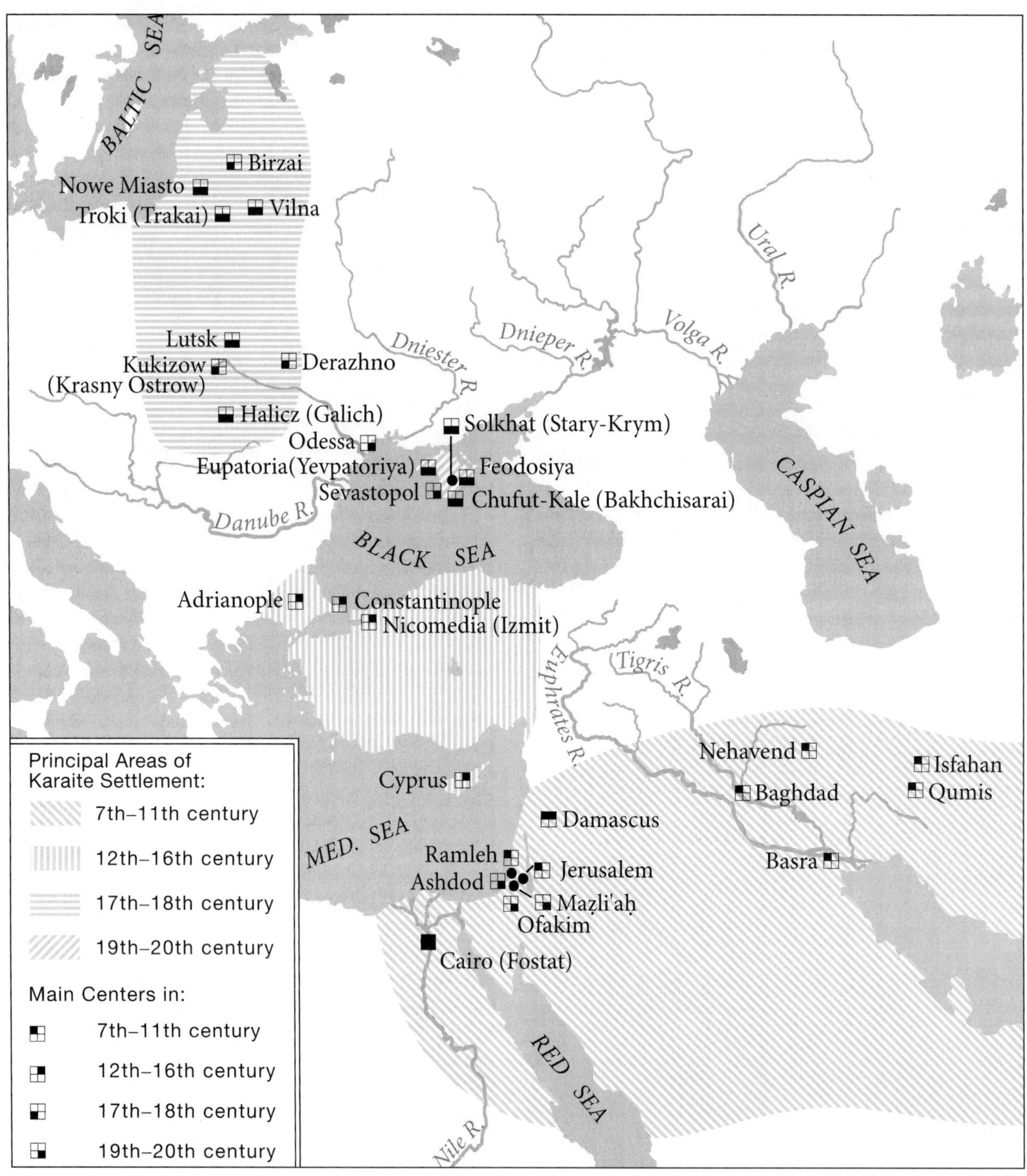

Principal areas of Karaite settlement and main centers, 7th–20th centuries.

dition. As a matter of fact, the Karaites also developed a tradition of their own, described by them as *sevel ha-yerushah* ("burden of inheritance"), consisting of doctrines and usages which, although not found in the Bible, were accepted as binding by the entire community (the *qibbuẓ* or *ʿedah*, corresponding to the Muslim term *ijmāʿ*, "consensus"). According to the Karaite view, a large number of these had come down from the Jews who had returned from the Babylonian exile (those designated as the "good figs," Jer. 24:5). The Karaite alternative tradition has developed over the centuries, and in some areas has come quite close to rabbinic tradition.

Karaism and the Dead Sea Scrolls

The discovery of the documents of the Dead Sea Sect has given rise to much speculation as to the possible influence of that sect and its literature upon the early schismatics who later merged into the Karaite sect. Assuming, with the overwhelming majority of students of the Dead Sea Scrolls, that they date from about the time of Jesus and that the Dead Sea sectarians went out of existence by the second century C.E., the problem may be considered under several aspects. The chronological aspect demands an explanation of the gap of some seven hundred years between the disappearance of the Dead Sea sectarians and the rise of the early Karaite schismatics. To account for it, several ancient notices of the finding of Jewish manuscripts in caves (by Origen, c. 217 C.E., Timotheus, c. 800 C.E., and by al-*Kirkisānī, c. 937 C.E.) are cited. Origen records the discovery of a Greek biblical manuscript and does not identify the contents of the other manuscripts found with it. al-Kirkisānī describes the manuscripts found in a cave as belonging to the literature of the pre-Christian sect of the Magharians, whose books, with two exceptions, he dismisses as "merely… idle tales." The testimony of Timotheus, Nestorian catholicos of Elam (south-western Iran), is perhaps more substantial. He tells of a letter that reached him from Jerusalem, reporting on scrolls found in a cave near Jericho that contained Hebrew texts resembling the Psalms. He requested that Jerusalem send him copies, but we do not know whether his request was ever fulfilled. A different case is the fragments of the so-called Damascus Document (medieval copies of which had been discovered in the Cairo *Genizah*) which were found among the Dead Sea documents. This provides substantial evidence that some Dead Sea documents did surface in the early Middle Ages. It can be argued, though, that this indicates only that the Damascus Document was known in Jewish circles, not necessarily Karaite alone, in Cairo early in the second millennium C.E. Nowhere in early Karaite literature so far known is there mention of the discovery of pre-Karaite documents confirming the righteousness of the Karaite teachings.

With respect to links between Dead Sea sects and the Karaites, there are several considerations for and against the theory that there was a connection of some kind between the two groups. A number of close parallels between Dead Sea and Karaite doctrines have been pointed out – for example, the emphasis on searching Scripture for right guidance, the implied rejection of oral tradition, the pressing and impatient messianism with its concomitant search in Scripture for hidden forecasts of the "end," when the Messiah will come to redeem Israel, and the tendency to regard biblical events not as accounts of past happenings but as prognostications of present-day situations. The similarity is not only in doctrines but also in terminology. Added to all this is, of course, the common conviction that this is the true Mosaic faith, and that those who believe otherwise are misled into error. In addition they have in common the ritual rigor, with respect to the laws of purity and Sabbath. These similarities must be weighed against an at least equally substantial series of dissimilarities, which cannot be reconciled with historical Karaism: the dualism of the Dead Sea Sect which divided the world into two opposing camps of good and evil ("light and darkness") subject to a predestined and immutable fate, and the rigid and absolute monastic hierarchy. Recent studies have suggested that there are significant parallels between Second Temple period controversies, including especially the Qumranites, and medieval controversies between Karaites and Rabbanites. In addition, the discussion of this question should differentiate between various pre-cursors of Karaism or its sub-groups. Some of those, like Mishawayh al-ʿUkbari, show perhaps more affinity to the Dead Sea Scrolls. The conclusion that may be drawn from all these considerations would therefore be the following: There is, at the present state of knowledge of the literature of both sects, no tangible evidence that the early Karaites had any direct contact with the Dead Sea writings, though some of them may have reached them. If they were influenced by them to any recognizable extent, this influence had little effect in the long run.

Historical Development

EMERGENCE OF THE SECT. The name "Karaites" was not applied to the sect until the ninth century; the precursor of the sect was known as "Ananites," from the name of its founder, *ʿAnan b. David. The sect appears to have come into being as the result of a combination of factors: the amalgamation of various heterodox trends in Babylonian-Persian Jewry, which clashed with the efforts of the heads of the Babylonian yeshivot to consolidate their position as the exclusive and central authority of Jewish law; the tremendous religious, political, and economic fermentation in the entire East, resulting from the Arab conquests and the collision of Islam with world religions. The Karaite sect absorbed both such Jewish sects as the Isawites (adherents of *Abu ʿIsā al-Iṣfahānī) and *Yudghanites, who were influenced by East-Islamic tendencies, and other anti-traditional movements.

The Karaites themselves, however, trace their origin to the first split among the Jewish people, at the time of *Jeroboam; the true law had subsequently been preserved by the descendants of Ẓadok, who had discovered a portion of the truth. The process of this discovery of the truth was then continued by the exilarch ʿAnan (thus al-Kirkisānī and others). The unhistorical, fanciful, and biased Karaite sources also influenced the reports of Arab authors. Rabbanite sources, on the other hand, give their own one-sided version of the emergence of the Karaite schism, ascribing it exclusively to ʿAnan's personal ambition and the injury his pride suffered when his younger brother Hananiah was elected exilarch.

The absorption by ʿAnan's movement of many elements of an older, extra-talmudic tradition was pointed out particularly by A. Geiger and R. Mahler. As a matter of fact, ʿAnan's system included many laws that are quoted from old rabbinic authorities in the Mishna, the Talmud and other tannaitic and targumic sources but were not accepted (e.g., the *lex talionis*, i.e., the literal interpretation of "an eye for an eye" principle in the criminal law). Anan cannot, however, be described as a "reformer" of Judaism in the modern sense; far from easing the "yoke" of traditional law, he made it more difficult to bear:

he did not recognize the minimum quantities (*shi'urim*) of forbidden foods fixed by the rabbis; he introduced more complicated regulations for the circumcision ceremony; he added to the number of fast days; he interpreted the prohibition of work on the Sabbath in stricter terms; etc. He was particularly severe with regard to the laws on marriage between relatives, ritual cleanliness, and relations with non-Jews. In his interpretation of Scripture, he made use of the 13 hermeneutic principles of R. *Ishmael b. Elisha, adding to them the principle of analogy (*hekkesh*, Ar. *qiyās*; the latter, perhaps, under the influence of Abu Ḥanīfah, the founder of the Ḥanafite school of Muslim jurisprudence).

The dictum quoted in Anan's name by *Japheth b. Ẏeli (commentary on Zech. 5:8), "Search well in the Torah and do not rely on my opinion," is composed of two clauses: the first in Aramaic, and the second in Hebrew. The second clause, though, is not found in the oldest MS of Japheth's commentary and seems to reflect a somewhat later development. The first half was possibly designed to uphold the Holy Scriptures as the sole source of the law through a process of thorough investigation; notwithstanding, the fragments of Anan's Book of Precepts contain several references to the definitive authority of Anan's own interpretations of Biblical verses. In the wake of Anan's activity, numerous groups and parties were formed, mainly in the eastern parts of the Caliphate. Some of them shared the designation "Karaites," and soon, as related by Kirkisānī, it became impossible to find two Karaites who held the same opinions on all religious issues. Anan's adherents, in the stricter sense, called themselves Ananites (Arabic *ʿanāniyya*, sometimes applied by Muslim authors to Karaites in general) and remained few in number (in Iraq, Syria and Spain). They seem to have disappeared some time during the 11th century. Anan's descendants, who, like Anan before them, were given the honorific title of *nasi* ("prince") by their contemporaries, lived first in Jerusalem, and then, from the early 11th century, for the most part in Egypt. The names of his son, *Saul b. Anan, and his grandson, Josiah b. Saul b. Anan, are known from the prayer for the dead in the Karaite Sabbath and festival liturgy; neither seems to have had any role in the further development of the sect. Saul is also mentioned in *Sefer ha-Kabbalah*, by Abraham ibn Daud, and Josiah in *Eshkol ha-Kofer*, by Judah Hadassi, and in *Gan Eden*, by Aaron b. Elijah the Younger of Nicomedia. Karaite traditions about Anan's emigration to Jerusalem and his settlement there refer possibly to his great-grandson, whose name was Anan.

As the non-Rabbanite, proto-Karaite movement did not recognize any single leader, it was not long before many groups arose in its midst, in opposition to the Ananites. Thus, in the first half of the ninth century, the ʿUkbarites, whose founder was *Ishmael of ʿUkbara, came into being in ʿUkbara, near Baghdad, at the time of the caliph al-Muʿtaṣim (833–842). Ishmael was violently opposed to Anan, "often denouncing him as a fool and an ass." Nothing of Ishmael's writing has been preserved, and the little known about him and his school derives almost exclusively from the reports of al-Kirkisānī, at whose time (second half of the tenth century) the group was probably no longer in existence. In his teaching, Ishmael rejects, *inter alia*, the masoretic variants (*keri* and *ketiv*, the reading of certain words in the Bible in a manner that differs from their spelling).

The same town, ʿUkbara, was also the place of origin of another group, founded in the second half of the ninth century by Mīshawayh al-ʿukbarī. Characteristic of this sect is the principle that in all disputed matters (such as the day of the New Year Festival and the determination of the new moon), the Rabbanite practice was to be followed ("all coins are counterfeit, so one might as well use the one at hand," i.e., observe the holidays with the "whole," the Rabbanites). Among Mīshawayh's innovations is his opinion that the day, in the religious sense, begins at sunrise and comes to an end at the following sunrise (whereas according to the Rabbanites, and most other Jewish groups and movements, the day commences and ends at sunset). Another proto-Karaite sect was founded by a contemporary of Mīshawayh, Mūsā (Moses) al-Zaʿfarānī, a resident of Tiflis (Tbilisi, Georgia); also known as Abu ʿImrān *al-Tiflīsī, he was probably a native of Zaʿfarān, a district of Baghdad. The report by al-Kirkisānī (perhaps the earliest mention of Jewish settlement in the Caucasus) states that al-Tiflīsī was a disciple of Ishmael of ʿUkbara, and the author of a treatise sanctioning the consumption of meat (whereas many sects, including the earliest Karaite authorities, regarded the eating of meat as prohibited as long as Zion was in ruins and Israel in exile). Mūsā was also mentioned by the Karaite authors Japheth b. Eli (10th century) and Judah Hadassi, and by *Saadiah Gaon; the latter, in his commentary on the Pentateuch, cites the opinion held by al-Tiflīsī and his supporters that the new month always commences at the moment when the new moon first makes its appearance, so that the day of the new moon is already a part of the new month (commentary to Gen. 1:14–18). Another sect, closely related to that of al-Tiflīsī and its contemporary, was created at Ramleh in Ereẓ Israel by *Mālik al-Ramlī. According to al-Kirkisānī, Mālik declared on oath on the Temple site in Jerusalem that chickens had been sacrificed at the Temple altar; by this oath, Mālik sought to strengthen his view – as reported by the Karaite author *Jacob b. *Reuben in his commentary on Leviticus – that the *torim* mentioned in Leviticus 1:14, which were used as Temple sacrifices, were chickens, thereby contradicting Anan and his successors, who translated the term *dukhifat* ("the hoopoe") in Leviticus 11:19, as hen, and accordingly classified the chicken as an impure, prohibited bird.

It follows that in the 9th century and the beginning of the 10th, the Karaite movement was a conglomeration of various anti-Rabbanite groups, some of which had sprung up after Anan's death. Al-Kirkisānī gives a vivid description of the countless differences on questions of religious ritual obtaining among the various Karaite groups, some of which still existed in al-Kirkisānī's time. In order to counter the Rabbanite arguments in polemics with the Karaites, based upon these heterogeneous views, al-Kirkisānī concludes his description with a characteristic observation: the Karaite readers of his work, he states, had no reason for concern, for in this respect there was a great difference between them and the Rabbanites: "They [i.e., the Rabbanites] believe that their laws and regulations have been transmitted by the prophets; if that was the case, there ought not to exist any differences of opinion among, them and the fact that such differences of opinion do exist refutes their presumptuous belief. We, on the other hand, arrive at our views by our reason, and reason can lead to various results."

The many sects which had come upon the proto-Karaite or early Karaite scene after Anan disappeared as fast as they had sprung up, without leaving any noticeable trace upon the movement. By their gradual self-liquidation, however, they prepared the ground for the consolidation of a well-defined, uniform doctrine which has subsisted to this very day as Karaism. The outstanding representative of the new movement in the ninth century was Benjamin b. Moses *Nahāwendī (from Nehavend, Persia; c. 830–860), who laid the groundwork for the new development of Karaite doctrine and was also the first Karaite writer to employ, according to some sources, the term *Kara'im* (*Benei Mikra*). Rabbanite scholars, such as Saadiah Gaon and Judah Halevi, regard Anan and Benjamin as the fathers and founders of the Karaite sect; Arabic and Karaite authors also refer to Karaites as *Aṣḥāb ʿAnān wa-Binyāmīn* (i.e., followers of Anan and Benjamin). The Karaites themselves put Benjamin almost on the same level as Anan, and in the memorial prayer (*zikhronot*) Benjamin's name follows immediately upon those of Anan, Saul, and Josiah. It was Benjamin, in particular, who turned the free and independent individual study of the Scriptures into a basic principle of Karaism. In theory it became possible for Karaism to tolerate differing interpretations of the Bible. Benjamin also differed from Anan in making no special efforts to maintain a hostile attitude to the Rabbanites and stress a fundamental opposition to them. He sought to base each law upon the Bible (without differentiating between the Pentateuch, the Prophets, and the Hagiographa) and freely borrowed from the Rabbanites (although he declared such regulations as not binding upon Karaites). Furthermore, he advised his coreligionists to adopt the Rabbanite view in cases where the Bible did not provide a clear prescription. Benjamin is also the first Karaite to whom Karaite sources ascribe statements concerning dogmas and religious philosophy. Seeking to remove all taint of anthropomorphism from the conception of God, he embraced in his exegesis of the Bible ideas that are reminiscent of *Philo's theory of the Logos (which he may have known in Arabic translation or by the way of the *Maghāriyya* – the cave dweller – sect, mentioned by al-Kirkisānī; see also *Sects, Minor). Accordingly, the creator of the world, its builder, and its guide, was an angel created by God to represent His will; it was this angel who performed the miracles, revealed the Law, etc., and it is to this angel that the anthropomorphic passages in the Bible refer.

*Daniel b. Moses al-Qūmisī, who lived toward the end of the ninth century, seems to have been the first eminent Karaite scholar to settle in Jerusalem. He was the first to make the "mourning in Zion" a basic tenet and a hallmark of Karaism. In an epistle ascribed to him he fervently urged Karaites in the Diaspora to immigrate to Ereẓ Israel. In the same epistle he also expounded his particular positions on halakhic issues and, perhaps for the first time in Jewish history, proposed a set of normative, binding beliefs ("articles of faith"). He opposed Benjamin's method of Bible exegesis and denied the existence of angels, interpreting the term *malakhim* as natural forces employed by God to serve as His emissaries (cf. Psalms 78:49; 104:4). Opposing also Benjamin's leaning toward Rabbinic *halakhah*, he called for strict adherence to the literal sense of the Scriptures. This may also explain his fight against Anan, whom he had at first revered as "first among the sages" ("*rosh ha-maskilim*"), only to denounce him later as "first among the fools" ("*rosh ha-kesilim*"). Yet in his commentaries there are cases of alternative and homiletic interpretations. It may be assumed that it was his attitude to Anan that caused al-Qūmisī's exclusion from the Karaite memorial prayer, in spite of the great respect in which he was held by later Karaite writers. al-Qūmisī wrote commentaries on several books of the Bible, but of his commentaries only the one on Minor Prophets survived almost complete. He also taught that, in case of doubt, the more rigorous interpretation of the law should be accepted.

CONSOLIDATION: LATE NINTH TO 12TH CENTURIES. In the tenth century, when Karaism was already fairly consolidated, the movement adopted an aggressive attitude, designed to spread its doctrine. This was also the golden age of Karaite literature (with most of the Karaite works of this period being written in Arabic). Karaite attempts to gain mass support for their beliefs among the Rabbanites (which, however, seem to have attracted only a few converts of no particular distinction) brought forth, on both sides, an apologetic and polemic literature. There were in this period (ninth and tenth centuries) a considerable number of outstanding Karaite theologians, religious teachers, grammarians, lexicographers, and biblical exegetes. Rejection of secular sciences, which Anan had advocated, was not followed by all Karaites. Some Karaite scholars became active participants in the flourishing Arabic culture. Others (e.g. al-Qūmisī, Salmon ben Yerūḥim) prohibited any engagement in "foreign" books and sciences as leading to heresy. In view of the special significance attached by Karaism to the study of the Bible, the Karaites dedicated themselves with great zeal to massoretic and grammatical exegetic studies and must have had a stimulating influence upon Rabbanite scholars. The view of Jewish historians (such as J. Fuerst, S. Pinsker, H. Graetz) that some of the first and most appreciated Jewish massoretes and grammarians (notably Aharon ben Asher), and biblical exegetes had been Karaites, has been discussed again in recent research and probably proven correct.

Karaite missionary activity, while hardly successful, forced the Rabbanites to take note of their existence and combat them. The first prominent Rabbanite to attack the

Karaites was Saadiah Gaon, who at the age of 23 wrote a book (in Hebrew [rhymed] and Arabic versions) attacking Anan. On both sides the battle was waged with great ardor and often with a lack of objectivity; it remained in the main a war of words, but occasionally degenerated into physical violence, or resorted to harsh social measures (excommunication) or intervention by the Muslim authorities. The main targets of Karaite attacks were the anthropomorphisms of the *aggadah* and of Jewish mystical literature and the Rabbanite claims to divine origin of the Oral Law. Karaite literature flourished in most of the areas under Muslim rule – in Egypt, North Africa, and particularly in Ereẓ Israel, in addition to Babylonia and Persia, where Karaism had come into being.

The greatest Karaite mind of the tenth century was Abu Yūsuf Yaʿqūb al-Kirkisānī, whose work on religious law, *Kitāb al-Anwār wa-al-Marāqib*, particularly its opening chapter, represents one of the foremost sources for the history of the Karaite sect. *David b. Boaz, a descendant of Anan, attained great repute as a biblical commentator, and is also said to have composed a work (in Arabic) on the basic doctrines of religion. In the second half of the tenth century, David b. Abraham *Alfasi, a native of Fez (Morocco) who emigrated to Ereẓ Israel, became known as a lexicographer and biblical exegete. At the end of the century *Japheth b. Eli in Jerusalem translated the entire Hebrew Bible into Arabic and added his extensive commentary, becoming the most important Karaite Bible commentator. Japheth's son, Levi b. *Japheth, in addition to Bible commentary, also wrote an important book of precepts (extensive fragments of the Arabic original and the medieval Hebrew translation survived). One of the most active opponents of Rabbanism, and especially of Saadiah Gaon, was *Salmon b. Yeruḥim (mid-tenth century). In a similar vein was the work of *Sahl b. Maṣliaḥ ha-Kohen, a skillful and eloquent Karaite missionary who wrote a commentary on the Pentateuch and was a religious teacher; his Hebrew introduction to his Arabic-language book of precepts contains important information on the Karaite community in Jerusalem.

At that time Jerusalem was the outstanding spiritual centers of Karaism. Among the scholars residing there at the end of the tenth century was *Joseph b. Noah, who gained fame as the head of a religious academy, biblical commentator, and Hebrew grammarian. His pupil, *Abu al-Faraj Hārūn (Aaron b. Jeshua), who lived in the first half of the 11th century, was also a noted grammarian ("the grammarian of Jerusalem"), lexicographer, and biblical exegete. A contemporary scholar was *Nissi b. Noah, a resident of Persia, author of a philosophical commentary on the Ten Commandments. The outstanding Karaite theologian and religious philosopher of the 11th century was Joseph b. Abraham ha-Kohen ha-Ro'eh *al-Baṣīr (Heb. "ha-Ro'eh," euphemistically for "the Blind"), who had also been a disciple of Joseph b. Noah. Al-Baṣīr's religious philosophy was decisively influenced by the teachings of *Kalām; he denounced the extremist interpretations of forbidden marriages (the so-called *rikkuv* theory). His pupil *Jeshua b. Judah (Arabic name: Abu al-Faraj Furqān ibn Asad), the most prolific Karaite writer in the 11th century, became known as a religious teacher and philosopher, as well as a translator of the Bible and an exegete (in the latter capacity he earned the admiration of Abraham *Ibn Ezra). Like his teacher, Jeshua was also an adherent of the philosophy of Kalām, and his opposition to the extension of the categories of forbidden marriages was even greater, and more decisive, than that of Joseph. Jeshua was the last important Karaite scholar in Ereẓ Israel. At the end of the 11th century Karaite literary and scientific work in Ereẓ Israel came to an abrupt end as the result of the First Crusade (1099). When the invading army, under Godfrey of Bouillon, took Jerusalem, some of the members of the Karaite community, with the Rabbanites, were driven into a synagogue and burned alive, while others were taken prisoners and ransomed expensively later. This marked the destruction of the first Karaite community in Jerusalem. Like the Rabbanites, the Karaites returned to Jerusalem after the city had come again under Muslim rule. In the 15th and 16th centuries the community had grown, and for some time even gained control over Samuel's tomb (al-Nabī Samwīl), which had become a very popular site of pilgrimage for Jews and Muslims alike. In 1642, according to the report of the Jewish traveler *Samuel b. David, there were only 27 Karaites living in Jerusalem. In the beginning of the 18th century the Karaites had to leave their residence in Jerusalem for a while, because they had been unable to pay their debts to Rabbanite Jews. In 1744 Samuel ben Abraham, a descendant of a Jerusalemite family, returned with several families from Damascus to the city and renewed the Karaite presence in the Old City. The ever-shrinking community endured until 1948. After 1967 a number of Karaites of Egyptian origin settled in Jerusalem. They maintain the synagogue that is said to have been established by Anan, the old Karaite courtyard in the Old City, and the cemetery in Abu Tor started by Samuel ben Abraham in the 18th century.

12TH TO 16TH CENTURIES: BYZANTIUM AND TURKEY. The decline of Karaism in the East began in the 12th century. No original writer of any significance came to the fore there after the first half of that century, even in the field of religious law. The only exception was in Egypt, where the Karaite communities (mainly in Cairo and Alexandria) still numbered members who possessed considerable financial means and had good political connections, or belonged to the intellectual or professional elite. When *Maimonides took up residence in Cairo their influence, social and religious, decreased, as well as their public standing. Notwithstanding, the Karaite community in Egypt remained the largest in the Islamic east until modern times. Also living in Egypt at this period was Moses b. Abraham *Darʿī, the outstanding Karaite poet of his time. Other Karaite writers who lived in Egypt (mainly in Cairo) in the 12th to 15th centuries, such as *Japheth al-Barqamānī, Japheth ibn Ñaghīr, *Israel ha-Ma'aravi, and *Samuel b. Moses *al-Maghribī, played no independent role in the further development of Karaism. But the Karaites in Egypt, and to a lesser extent in Syria, Erez Israel, Iraq, and Persia continued to collect and study the writings of the Golden Age and to produce new copies. This may explain the very large book collections amassed in Karaite synagogues in these centers.

At the end of the 11th century, the center of Karaite intellectual activity shifted to Europe. This was largely the work of the many European disciples of Jeshua b. Judah, who, upon returning to their homes from Jerusalem, acted as the emissaries of Karaite doctrine. One such propagator of Karaism was Sīdī ibn *al-Tarās, who was active in Spain in strengthening the Karaite, or Ananite presence (which had been there already for about two centuries), and whose wife continued his missionary work after his death. According to the description of Abraham ibn Da'ud in his *Sefer ha-Kabbalah*, after a short while the Castilian government, influenced by the Rabbanites, turned against the Karaites and extirpated the movement in Spain. However, the concentrated polemic of several Spanish writers in the 12th century (e.g., Abraham ibn Da'ud, Judah Ha-Levi, Abraham Ibn Ezra) against Karaism seems to testify that in that time the Karaites were still considered a threat to the Rabbanite hegemony.

In the Byzantine Empire, on the other hand, Karaism succeeded in gaining a firm foothold. A massive Karaite literature of translation came into being here, produced mainly by former disciples of Jeshua b. Judah who, for the most part, were residents of Constantinople. The most eminent among them was *Tobias b. Moses ha-Avel (known as "ha-Oved" [the worshiper] and also as "ha-Maʿtik" [the translator]) whose major work was the translation of the Arabic writings of Jeshua, as well as of Joseph b. Abraham al-Baṣīr. He also wrote a commentary on the Pentateuch, *Ozar Neḥmad*, based primarily upon the works of David b. Boaz and Japheth b. Ali. The only other name to be preserved is that of *Jacob b. Simeon, one of the most prominent Karaite translators of this period. To this period belongs also the work on Hebrew linguistics entitled *Me'or ʿAyin*, by an anonymous author. It seems to have been based on Arabic works of the Golden Age. It survived in a single MS, copied in 1208 (published by M. Zislin, 1990). Prominent religious scholars and biblical exegetes active in Byzantium in the 12th century were Jacob b. Reuben, author of a Bible commentary, *Sefer ha-Osher*, which consists largely of excerpts from Hebrew translations of works of earlier Karaite authors, especially those of Japheth b. Ali (part of the commentary on the Prophets and the entire commentary on the Writings was printed at the end of the edition of *Mivḥar Yesharim* by Aaron ben Joseph, 1836); Aaron b. Judah *Kusdini (from Constantinople), of whose works there survives only a responsum on marriage laws; and Judah b. Elijah *Hadassi, author of *Eshkol ha-Kofer*, an encyclopedic summary of Karaite theology, one of the most important works of Karaite literature and, undoubtedly, the outstanding Karaite work in Hebrew. Most Byzantine Karaite translations and original works of that period contain a considerable number of Greek glosses, or other phrases, which constitute very important evidence of early Medieval Judeo-Greek.

In the second half of the 13th century, Karaism in the Byzantine Empire entered a period of spiritual florescence. It was in this period that *Aaron b. Joseph ha-Rofe ("Aaron the Elder"), one of the most important Karaite biblical exegetes, was active; highly revered by his coreligionists, he was given the title of "ha-Kadosh" ("the Saint"), most probably for his work in arranging the hitherto unstable Karaite liturgy into an organized ritual, valid to this day. His commentary on the Bible, *Sefer ha-Mivḥar*, is regarded as the classic Karaite work in Bible exegesis; it shows the influence of Abraham ibn Ezra's commentary. *Aaron b. Elijah of Nicomedia ("the Last Aaron"), a codifier, biblical exegete, and religious philosopher who lived in the first half of the 14th century, was regarded by the Karaites as the "Karaite Maimonides"; he was the author of *Gan Eden*, a systematic code of Karaite law and belief, corresponding in its significance for Karaism to the *Turim* by R. *Jacob b. Asher; of *Keter Torah*, a Bible commentary which has enjoyed, for many centuries now, a status and prestige comparable to that of Rashi's commentary among Rabbanites; and of *Ez Ḥayyim*, which attempts to refute the Aristotelian views of Maimonides by a religious philosophy, which, while familiar with Aristotelian terminology and concepts, is basically committed to Muʿtazilite Kalām. To the same century belongs *Moses b. Samuel of Damascus, a native of Safed in Erez Israel who moved to Damascus and obtained an appointment as manager of the emir's private estates. In 1354 he was compelled, under threat of execution for allegedly blaspheming Islam, to become a Muslim and to accompany the emir on a pilgrimage to Mecca. What he saw of the pilgrimage rites moved him to flee to Egypt, where he found a kindlier superior in the vizier's office, and he returned to Judaism. Among his poetical works is a description of his forced conversion and pilgrimage.

The conquest of the Byzantine Empire by the Turks in 1453 was followed by a change in the relationship between Rabbanite and Karaite Jews. Some Jews expelled from Spain in 1492 were granted asylum in Turkey, where they were well treated, especially during the reign of *Suleiman the Magnificent. Jewish intellectual life rose to new heights. Jewish schools, synagogues, and printing presses were established, and Jewish scholars no longer confined themselves exclusively to talmudic studies, devoting themselves also to secular sciences – physics, astronomy, mathematics, and medicine. In the 15th and 16th centuries a rapprochement took place between the Karaite and Rabbanite Jews; Rabbanite scholars guided Karaites in the study of Jewish literature and secular sciences, and some, such as *Shemariah b. Elijah Ikriti, Mordecai b. Eliezer *Comtino, and Elijah b. Abraham *Mizraḥi, even accepted Karaites as their students. One of the Karaite students of Comtino was Elijah b. Moses *Bashyazi, the most celebrated Karaite scholar of his time, whom the Karaites regard as "the final decider" *(ha-posek ha-aḥaron)*. His code of law, *Adderet Eliyahu*, became the Karaite counterpart of the rabbinic Shulḥan Arukh. His pupil and brother-in-law, Caleb b. Elijah *Afendopolo, adapted *Adderet Eliyahu* and completed it; a versatile scholar, he himself also composed works on theological and liturgical themes and on secular subjects (mathematics, astronomy, law, philosophy), as well as religious and secular poems, some of which contain references to the expulsion from Spain and from Lithuania and Kiev (1495). A great-grandson of Elijah Bashyazi, Moses b. Elijah *Bashyazi, was the last outstanding Karaite author of this period, and his death also ended the Byzantine chapter in Karaite history (end of the 16th century). His works contain important Arabic quotations from the writings of the earliest Karaite authors, which he had discovered in manuscript in the course of his travels, especially in Egypt. The Byzantine-Turkish Karaite communities, similar to their brethren in Babylonia, Persia, and Egypt, gradually fell into a state of decline, and the center shifted once again to another area.

17TH TO 18TH CENTURIES: KARAITES IN CRIMEA AND LITHUANIA. In the 17th and 18th centuries, Karaite activity shifted to the Crimea and Lithuania, and Karaites in these areas assumed leadership of the sect. The existence of individual Karaites in the Crimea is traced back to the 12th century; *Pethahiah of Regensburg mentions meeting several sectarians among the Turkish nomads occupying parts of southern Russia, who observed the Sabbath in the dark and regarded even the cutting of bread as prohibited on that day. In the 13th century, at the time of the Tatar "Golden Horde," a considerable number of Karaites settled in the Crimea, mainly from the Byzantine Empire, perhaps also from Persia. At the end of the 14th century, according to a Karaite tradition, Grand Duke Witold of Lithuania, after defeating the Tatars (1392), carried a large group of Tatar prisoners, including some Karaite families, to *Troki (near Vilna), *Lutsk, and *Halicz, and settled them there. It seems more probable that the Karaites were brought or invited by Witold to Troki to help him develop the economy, rather than as prisoners, and that Karaites arrived in Lutsk and Halicz from Troki or somewhere else, early in the 15th century. From there the Karaites spread to other towns in Lithuania, Volhynia, and Podolia. Polish-Lithuanian Karaites continued to speak "Tatar" (actually a few different Turkish dialects) and translated the prayers into their language.

East European Karaites established firm contacts with their Byzantine coreligionists. Thus, letters have been preserved which were exchanged between the Karaites in Lutsk and Troki, and Elijah Bashyazi in Constantinople; the latter also had Lithuanian Karaites among his pupils. The Karaites living in the Crimea under Tatar rule were unable to engage in any intellectual and scientific activities; but their brethren in Lithuania benefited from their contact with the Rabbanite Jews in that area, which in the second half of the 16th century entered a period of spiritual renaissance. The first important Karaite author in Lithuania was Isaac b. Abraham *Troki (1533–1594), who wrote an anti-Christian treatise, *Ḥizzuk Emunah* (first published, with Latin translation, by Wagenseil in his work *Tela ignea Satanae*, in 1681). The final compilation of the book was the work of Isaac Troki's pupil, Joseph b. Mordecai *Malinovski, who also wrote several works of his own. Joseph's brother, Zephaniah Malinovski, wrote a treatise on the calendar. A contemporary of the Malinovski brothers, *Zerah b. Nathan of Troki, was well versed in both the natural sciences and rabbinic literature; in his letters to Joseph *Delmedigo, he raised 70 questions, mainly of mathematical-astronomical content, and this prompted Delmedigo to write *Elim* and *Iggeret Aḥuz*. At the time of the *Chmielnicki massacres in 1648, the Karaites, for the most part, suffered the same fate as the Rabbanite Jews; in general the relations between the two groups were quite good in this period. One effect of the persecution of the Jews and Karaites was to arouse interest in the Karaite sect among Christian scholars; another was the creation of an apologetic historiography on the part of Lithuanian Karaites. Among the Christian works on the Karaites that appeared in this period were *Epistola de Karaitarum rebus in Lithuania* (1691), by Gustav Peringer, a professor at Upsala; *Diatribe de Secta Karaeorum* (1703), by Jacob Trigland in Holland; and *Notitia Karaeorum* (1721), by Johann Christoph Wolf of Hamburg. Around 1700, at the request of two Swedish scholars, the Karaite scholar *Solomon b. Aaron Troki wrote a treatise on Karaism and its major differences with Rabbanite Judaism, under the title of *Appiryon Asah Lo*. The same author also composed polemics against Rabbanite Judaism and Christianity. In 1699, Mordecai b. Nisan *Kukizow wrote two treatises on Karaism; one, entitled *Dod Mordekhai*, was written in reply to inquiries submitted to him by Trigland, while the second, a smaller work, entitled *Levush Mordekhai*, sought to answer questions posed by King Charles XII of Sweden. In writing *Dod Mordekhai*, Mordecai b. Nisan was assisted by *Joseph b. Samuel ha-Mashbir, a relative; the latter also wrote many other works, including *Porat Yosef*, a valuable book on grammar. Born in Lithuania, Joseph became *ḥakham* of Halicz, Galicia, in about 1700 (thereby starting a dynasty of *ḥakhamim* and *ḥazzanim*) and was instrumental in raising the cultural standard of the Karaites in the area.

In the second half of the 18th century, the Crimean Karaites also entered upon a period of literary and scientific activity, profiting from a close connection with Lithuanian Karaites and the immigration of a group of Karaite scholars from Lutsk (Volhynia). Hitherto Crimean Karaites, who maintained fairly large communities in four major cities of the peninsula and were living under favorable economic conditions, had suffered from a lack of religious leaders and teachers (*ḥakhamim*, *ḥazzanim*, and *melammedim*). Outstanding among the group from Lutsk was Simḥah Isaac b. Moses *Luzki, a prolific author, who settled in *Chufut-Kale in 1750. Two of his numerous works appeared in print in the 18th and 19th centuries: *Or ha-Ḥayyim*, a philosophical commentary on *Eẓ Ḥayyim* by Aaron b. Elijah of Nicomedia (together with the text, Eupatoria, 1847) and *Oraḥ Ẓaddikim*, a history of Karaism with an apologist tendency, which also contains the first attempt at a Karaite bibliography (together with *Dod Mordekhai* by Mordecai b. Nisan Kukizow, Vienna, 1830). Several other works have appeared in recent years.

UNDER RUSSIAN RULE: LEGAL SEPARATION FROM RABBANITES. A new epoch in the history of the Karaites was opened by the incorporation of Lithuania and Crimea (1793 and 1783, respectively) into Russia. Until then, the external history of the Karaites had been similar, and parallel, to that of the Rabbanite Jews; both considered each other as Jews and regarded even the most violent polemics between them as an internal Jewish quarrel. Wherever the Karaites had taken up residence, they had been treated as Jews. For example, a decree issued by Grand Duke Witold in 1388 describes the Karaites of Troki as "Judaei Trocenses" and grants them the same special legal status as that accorded to Jews of Brest-Litovsk and other Lithuanian communities. The decree was reconfirmed by King Sigismund I of Poland in 1507, for both Karaite and Rabbanite Jews in Lithuania. In 1495, Grand Duke Alexander expelled both Jews and Karaites from Lithuania, and both were admitted into Poland by his brother, King John Albert. John's successor, Alexander, in turn permitted the return of both Jews and Karaites to Lithuania. During the Chmielnicki persecutions, hardly any difference was made between the two groups. In Lithuania, Poland, and Volhynia, the state taxes payable by Jews and Karaites had to be remitted in a lump sum; the Karaites would hand their taxes over to the Rabbanite Jews, and these would add their own taxes and transmit the whole sum to the government. Under the Tatar khans and the Ottoman Turks, Rabbanite Jews and Karaites in the Crimea also had the same legal status. It was only at the end of the 18th century, when Russia conquered the Crimea, that a difference in status was made between Rabbanite Jews and Karaites under the law. In 1795, Empress Catherine II relieved the Karaites of the double tax imposed upon the Jews, and also permitted them to acquire land. Thus the 1795 law created a wall of separation between Jews and Karaites, each group enjoying civil rights to a different degree (although legislative decrees continued to refer to Karaites as "Jews").

Inequality before the law of the two groups was further expanded in 1827, when the Crimean Karaites, like the Crimean Tatars, were exempted from the general military draft law enacted by Czar Nicholas I, a privilege that was not extended to the Jews. In 1828, exemption from military service was also granted to the Karaites of Lithuania and Volhynia. In their attempts to improve their legal status, Russian Karaite leaders had at first refrained from resorting to attacks upon Rabbanite Jews; this policy was changed in 1835, when the Karaites, in appeals and memoranda to the Russian government, began to stress their fundamental difference from other Jews, namely their refusal to accept the validity of the Talmud. They also claimed to possess qualities which distinguished them from other Jews: that, contrary to the Rabbanites, they were industrious people, honest in their behavior and loyal to the throne. In 1835 they succeeded in having the Rabbanite Jews of Troki expelled from the town, on the basis of ancient Lithuanian privileges which granted them the sole right of settlement there. They also achieved a change in their official designation; instead of "Jews-Karaites" they first came to be called "Russian Karaites of the Old Testament Faith," and eventually simply "Karaites." The special legal status accorded to Karaites, as compared with the other Jews, was also influenced by the difference in their social and economic situation. Whereas the Jews in the Crimea were mainly peddlers and artisans, the Karaites were wealthy landowners, deriving their income from tobacco plantations, orchards, and salt mines, and maintaining good relations with the authorities. In 1840 the Karaites were put on an equal footing with the Muslims, and were granted an independent church statute. Two dioceses were established, each headed by a *ḥakham*, with residences at *Feodosiya (Crimea) and Troki respectively; the *ḥakhamim* were laymen, elected by delegates from all Karaite communities. Each community also elected its *ḥazzan*, who performed religious functions and served as an assistant to the *ḥakham*. Finally, in 1863, the Karaites were given rights equal to those of the native Russian population.

The last Karaite spiritual leader under Tatar rule was Benjamin b. Samuel *Aga (d. 1824), who continued to hold his post – albeit unofficially – under Russian rule. A contemporary, Isaac b. *Solomon of Chufut-Kale, attempted to introduce a reform of the Karaite calendar and wrote a treatise on the subject, *Or ha-Levanah* (1872); he was also the author of *Iggeret Pinnat Yikrat* (1834, 1872), a treatise on the Karaite dogmas, and composed liturgical poems. Simḥah *Babovich, the first Karaite *ḥakham* to be recognized as such by the Russian government, played a major role in the political history of Russian Karaism and in the drafting of its statute as an autonomous congregation. In 1827 he was a member of the two-man delegation of Crimean Karaites (the other member being the Karaite scholar Joseph Solomon b. Moses *Luzki), which succeeded in persuading the Russian government in St. Petersburg to exempt Karaites from military service. Luzki wrote many works dealing with *halakhah*, the most important of which was a commentary on *Sefer ha-Mivḥar* by Aaron b. Joseph, published under the title *Ṭirat Kesef* (1835). Luzki's views were opposed by David b. Mordecai *Kukizow (1777–1855), a great-grandson of Mordecai b. Nisan, who was the author of *Ẓemaḥ David*, a theological work (1897). Mordecai b. Joseph *Sultansky, a versatile writer, composed works on theology, history, and grammar; one of his pupils was the *ḥakham* and writer Solomon b. Abraham *Beim.

The most eminent Karaite scholar of the 19th century, however, and the most active champion of the Karaite struggle for civil rights, was Abraham b. Samuel *Firkovich (1787–1874) whose advent upon the scene opened a new chapter in Karaite historiography. Notwithstanding the numerous forgeries, tendentious quasi-discoveries, and unfounded hypotheses which mar Firkovich's writings (later to be refuted by Jewish scholars), Karaite historical studies, as well as Jewish studies, undoubtedly owe him a great debt of gratitude. During his travels in the Crimea, the Caucasus, Ereẓ Israel, Syria, and Egypt, he discovered many works of Rabbanite and Karaite literature which had been presumed lost. His collection of valuable Jewish manuscripts is the largest in the world of its kind. After his death his heirs sold it to the then Imperial Library, presently Russian National Library in St. Petersburg. Firkovich was the last Karaite writer of any importance; after his death, Karaite learning declined. Mention should be made, however, of several authors who exerted influence on Karaite spiritual life, writing in Hebrew, Tatar, and Russian: Samuel Pigit, *ḥazzan* in Yekaterinoslav (1849 – 1911), who composed homilies and poems in Hebrew (*Iggeret Niddeḥei Shemuel*, 1894) and a book of sermons in Tatar (*Davar Davur*, 1904); Elijah *Kazaz of Eupatoria (1832–1912), author of a Hebrew textbook, in Tatar (*Regel ha-Yeladim*) and translator of French philosophical works into Hebrew (Janet, Vigouroux, and others); Isaac Sinani, author of a biased history of Karaism, in Russian (2 vols, 1888–89); and Judah *Kukizow who wrote several works in Russian.

NUMBERS OF KARAITES. Toward the end of the 19th century the number of Karaites did not increase significantly. In 1783, when the Crimea was conquered by the Russians, there were 2,400 Karaites in Russia; according to official figures, their number (including all areas of former Poland and Lithuania) had grown to 9,725 in 1879, 12,894 in 1897, and 12,907 in 1910. In 1932 the number of Karaites in Russia (mainly in the Crimea) was estimated at 10,000. In 1910 a Karaite synod, held in Eupatoria, made an attempt to relax the Karaite marriage laws, which, however, was unsuccessful, as it was opposed by Karaite clerics in Troki, Constantinople, and Cairo. In 1911 Karaite students at the University of Moscow sought to inaugurate a Karaite renaissance and founded a Karaite monthly, in Russian, named *Karaimskaya Zhizn*; it had to close down before the year was over. In 1913–14 a Russian-language Karaite periodical, *Karaimskoye Slovo*, was published in Vienna, and in 1924 a Polish-language periodical, *Myśl Karaimska*, was founded, also in Vienna, which contained scholarly articles and reports on Karaite life.

In 1932 the number of Karaites outside Russia, in Poland (Halicz, Troki, Vilna), Constantinople, Jerusalem, Cairo, and Hit (on the Euphrates), was estimated at 2,000 (but this number seems to low, considering the fact that in 1877 their number in Egypt alone was recorded at 2,000). The total number of Karaites in the world was approximately 12,000. After World War I Vilna became a new center of Karaite life, and it was there that attempts were made at a reorganization of the Karaite sect. In 1932, the Polish Ministry of Culture and Education gave its provisional approval to the election of Serayah *Shapshal, a former senior Russian official, as *ḥakham* of Troki and spiritual leader of the Polish Karaites. On Jan. 9, 1939, the German Ministry of the Interior expressly stipulated that the Karaites did not belong to the Jewish religious community; their "racial psychology" was considered non-Jewish. This decision was subsequently applied to France. In Eastern Europe the Nazi *Einsatzgruppen* during World War II received orders to spare the Karaites, who enjoyed favorable treatment and were given positions of trust and authority with the German occupation authorities. On Oct. 6, 1942, the ruling of Jan. 9, 1939, was extended to the Crimea and the Ukraine, where the majority of Karaites lived. The Karaite question continued to be debated by the German authorities who queried the Rabbanite scholars Zelig *Kalmanovitch, Meir S. *Balaban, and Itzhak *Schipper on the origin of the Karaites. In order to save them, all three gave the opinion that the Karaites were not of Jewish origin. The behavior of the Karaites during the Holocaust period vacillated between indifference to the Jewish cause and some cases of actual collaboration with the Germans. No adequate study, however, has been made on this subject. In the Arab countries, on the other hand, the persecution of Jews which followed upon the establishment of the State of Israel caused the Karaites in Egypt and Iraq to settle in Israel, where they were welcomed and enabled to settle in compact groups, and were given government assistance in establishing themselves economically and in providing for their religious and educational needs.

CONTEMPORARY KARAITE LIFE. The Karaites came to Israel essentially in two waves: following the Suez Canal crisis (Operation Kadesh) in 1956 and in 1962. They first settled mainly in the Ramleh area and from there spread to other areas. Presently they live mostly in the following areas: Ashdod (the largest community), Ramleh district (the seat of the "World Center" and the central library and archives), Bat-Yam, Kiryat Gat, Ofakim, Rannen, Beersheba, and Acre. From the 1970s, the Karaite community in Israel has grown in numbers and has seen the consolidation of its institutions. According to their own estimate there are 30,000 Karaites in Israel. The actual number is probably lower. The major force behind this Karaite strengthening was Chief Rabbi Haim Hallevi of Ashdod. For many years, Hallevi had been acting chief rabbi of the Israeli Karaites, becoming chief rabbi in title, as well as in fact, with the death of Chief Rabbi David ben Moses Yerushalmi, in 1987. (Yerushalmi became chief rabbi in 1976, having succeeded the late Shelomo ben Shabbetai Nono.) Since 1991 Elijah Marzouk from Ofakim has been chief rabbi of the Karaites in Israel. In addition to the chief rabbi, Israel's Karaites are served by 15 other rabbis and a larger number of *hazzanim*. Some of the rabbis function also as ritual slaughterers and circumcisers. There are additional slaughterers and circumcisers, although Rabbanite practitioners are often called in. Many books for their use have been published recently, including a complete prayer book, Bashyazi's *Adderet Eliyahu*, and Aaron ben Elijah's *Keter Torah*.

The majority of Israeli Karaites are of Egyptian origin. A small number came from Hit (Iraq). After the breakup of the Soviet Union an unknown number of Karaites emigrated from there to Israel. Not all of them identify as Karaites. Israeli Karaites have had difficulty maintaining their religious customs and their independent identity since immigrating to Israel, mostly in the 1950s. There are two basic problems. On the one hand, they have encountered many of the same phenomena of secularization as have confronted other traditional Jewish groups from Islamic countries. On the other hand, there are strong forces of assimilation into the general Rabbanite Jewish community. For instance, since the Karaite holidays do not always coincide with those of most Israeli Jews, demands of work, army, and school make it difficult for many Karaites to continue their own customs. While Ḥanukkah is not considered a religious holiday by Karaites, it is often observed anyway as an Israeli national holiday. Though Karaism has its own laws of ritual slaughter, many Karaites are satisfied with the meat produced under Rabbanite supervision, which is more easily available. Some Karaites try to avoid any possibility of stigmatization by severing their ties with the Karaite community completely.

The Karaite leadership in Israel has tried to maintain the loyalty of their faithful by promoting various religious, cultural, and educational activities. Children participate in after school classes (there are no independent Karaite public schools) and summer camps. It is still too early to determine how successful these measures are. Some of the questions of Karaite assimilation and acculturation have been investigated by Emanuela Trevisan Semi, especially in her *Gli ebrei caraiti tra etnia e religione*, 1984 (which also deals with non-Israeli Karaites), and by Sumi E. Colligan in her dissertation, *Religion, Nationalism, and Ethnicity in Israel: The Case of the Karaite Jews*, 1980.

Although the Karaites are not fully recognized by Israeli law as a separate community, due to a decision by the Supreme Court (1995) their separate *bet din* is binding on members of the community in matters of marriage and divorce. According to Karaite legal usage in recent times, they disapprove of intermarriage with the rest of the Jewish population. According to the current usage in Rabbinic courts in Israel, the Karaites are permitted to intermarry with the rest of the Jewish population on condition that the Karaite member of the couple is willing formally to accept Rabbanism. Not all Rabbanite rabbis, however, are prepared to accept such intermarriages because of the problems of *mamzerut* (see **mamzer*). Karaites maintain de facto, but not de jure, authority over intra-Karaite marriage and uncontested divorce. These issues are discussed by Michael Corinaldi in his *The Personal Status of the Karaites in Israel*, 1984; Y. Shapira, in: *Meḥkerei Mishpat*, 19:1 (2002), 285–361 (both Heb.).

In 1983, the Karaite Jews of America were incorporated as a religious organization. Karaites claim that there are at least 1,200, and perhaps as many as 10,000, Karaite Jews of Egyptian origin in the United States, most of whom live in the San Francisco Bay Area of California. The Karaites in that region conduct services, either in private homes or monthly at a Conservative synagogue in Foster City. Other small concentrations of American Karaites are found in the New York and Chicago areas. There appears to be strong evidence of Americanization of this community.

The Karaites of Turkey are grouped particularly in Istanbul, but their deep religious attachment has led many to Israel in order to find Karaite mates to marry. Those who marry non-Karaite Jews or partners from other communities are automatically segregated from the community and constitute a loss for the Istanbul community, which numbers 50–60 families.

In recent years, many young Karaites have studied medicine, while others have tended towards craftsmanship such as jewelry. In some cases the jewelry artisanship is handed down from father to son and practiced in the Covered Bazaar in Istanbul. One Covered Bazaar street is called "The Street of the Karaites." Similarly, an important business center of Istanbul has retained its name – "Karaköy."

Following the destruction by fire of the great Karaite Synagogue, the Karaites have been using the Hasky Karaite Synagogue. This is the last available and usable Karaite sanctuary. Because their dwellings (Moda, Şişli, Nişantaşl, Gayrettepe, etc.) are far away from the synagogue, Karaites are not able to attend as frequently as previously. The synagogue, led by Yusuf Sadik, never witnesses three generations attending together. Only during rare religious holidays do a few Karaites, usually elderly, come to pray. Nevertheless, the Karaites continue to survive and strive to maintain their numbers.

There are still a few Karaites in Cairo, mostly older people who look after the Karaite synagogue and precious manuscripts.

In 1970, 4,571 Karaites were reported to be in the Soviet Union. Following the breakup of the Soviet bloc and the Soviet Union, some awakening of Karaite identity and activity took place in these countries. According to a report by Mourad El-Qodsi (resident of Rochester, N.Y., originally from Egypt), who visited the Karaite communities of Eastern Europe in 1991, the overall number of Karaites there was approximately 1,400, with 800 of them living in the Crimea, and the rest in Poland (in Warsaw, Gdansk and Wroclaw), Lithuania (in Vilna, Poniewiez and Troki), Halicz (Ukraine) and Moscow. In Russia there appeared a "Karaite National Movement," which also attempted to achieve an autonomous political status for Russian Karaites. Similar attempts have been made by Crimean Karaites. The majority of the latter also developed the ideas of Seraya *Shapshal to unprecedented extremes, severing all links to Judaism (which was also accepted in Western Europe by Simon *Szyszman), and tracing their ethnic origin to Mongol-Turkic roots and their religion to Turkish pagan practices and the cult of the Turkic deity Tengri. Most of the minority of Crimean Karaites who did not share this line emigrated to Israel, as did Karaites from other eastern European communities, which brought a further decrease in their numbers.

Scholarship on Karaism and the Karaites

The Israeli Karaite community has been active in editing previously unpublished Karaite works or reissuing unavailable classics. These works included among others Aaron ben Elijah's *Keter Torah* and *Gan Eden* (both reissued, 1972), Isaac Troki's *Hizzuk Emunah* (1975), Caleb Afendopolo's *Patshegen Ketav ha-Dat* (1977). All these were semi-critical editions. A major Karaite project of publishing semi-critical editions of tens of works by medieval and early modern Karaite authors has been undertaken in recent years by the Institute Tif'eret Yosef headed by Rabbi Yosef Algamil. The latter also published a multi-volume work on Karaite history and life. The first two volumes discuss in general the history of Karaism and Karaites, and the third volume is devoted to the Karaite community of Egypt. While characterized by a partisan Karaite interpretation of Karaite origins and history, these books contain much material about Karaism unavailable elsewhere. The personal accounts of Karaite communities and the many illustrations are especially important. Another recent one-sided exposition of Karaism is by the Paris-based Polish Karaite Simon *Szyszman, *Le Karaïsme*, 1980 (German tr. *Das Karäertum*, 1983). Szyszman has also begun a journal entitled *Bulletin d'Études Karaïtes*.

Leon *Nemoy continued to publish in the 1970s until the early 1990s on the subject almost 60 years after his first article on Kirkisani. His many publications during these years, ranging from early Karaism (and Kirkisani studies) to contemporary Karaism, have contributed greatly to Karaite studies. In honor of Nemoy's eightieth birthday, two Festschriften were published (*Studies in Judaica, Karaitica, and Islamica*, 1983, and *Jewish Quarterly Review* 73:2, October 1982), both with articles about many aspects of Karaism.

Georges *Vajda (d. 1981), in addition to his many publications in all fields of Jewish and Islamic thought, took special interest in early Karaite philosophy, law, and exegesis (see below).

The one question of Karaite studies which continues to intrigue scholars more than any other is the issue of Karaite origins and the possible relation between medieval sectarianism and Jewish groups of the Second Temple period. The issue, simply put, is whether Karaism was founded in the eighth century by *Anan ben David, or whether Anan merely reorganized and consolidated non-Rabbinic groups which had existed for hundreds of years. The discovery in 1947 of the *Dead Sea Scrolls, with certain obvious parallels to Karaite literature, occasioned a flurry of research comparing the ancient scrolls with medieval writings. While more and more parallels have been adduced between apocryphal and Qumranian literature, on the one hand, and Karaism, on the other, there is yet no decisive proof that an organic connection can be shown between Second Temple groups and Karaites. N. Wieder's *The Judean Scrolls and Karaism* appeared in 2005 in a revised expanded edition. A recent comprehensive contribution on the subject is Y. Erder, *The Karaite Mourners of Zion and the Qumran Scrolls*, (2004, Heb.). The latter work is representative of a revival of Karaite studies, especially in Israel, since the early 1970s. Studies have addressed a wide range of subjects related to Karaites and Karaism. Most scholars no longer accept the simplistic Rabbanite view of Karaism as a schismatic heresy begun by a single disgruntled individual, Anan. Some of the scholars who have addressed themselves recently to these issues are Haggai Ben-Shammai, Daniel Lasker, Yoram Erder, and Moshe Gil (who has also published *The Tustaris, Family and Sect*, 1981, about a sub-group of Karaites).

A large scale survey of "the state of the art" of Karaite studies is Meira Polliack (ed.), *Karaite Judaism: A Guide to Its History and Literary Sources*, (2003).

Research in Karaite exegesis and religious thought in recent decades included Georges Vajda, *Deux commentaires karaïtes sur l'Ecclésiaste* (1971) and his edition of Joseph *al-Baṣīr's *Kitāb al-Muĺtawī* (edited by David R. Blumenthal). The book includes an edition of the original Arabic text and French translations or paraphrases, accompanied by extensive commentaries showing al-Baṣīr's dependence on contemporary Muslim Kalām, especially the works of ʿAbd al-Jabbār. Uriel Simon, *Four Approaches to the Book of Psalms*, 1982, based his discussion of the Karaite approach upon the opinions of Salmon and Japheth. Haggai Ben-Shammai presented Japheth's (and Kirkisani's) philosophy in his dissertation, *The Doctrines of Religious Thought of Abû Yûsuf Yaʿqûb al-Qirqisânî and Yefet ben ʿElî*, 1977. Moshe Sokolow's dissertation, *The Commentary of Yefet ben Ali on Deuteronomy* XXXII, 1974, provides an Arabic edition and Hebrew translation of part of Japheth's Torah commentary. Mention should be made of the studies of Bruno Chiesa, notably Bruno Chiesa and Wilfrid Lockwood, *Yaʿqub al-Qirqisani on Jewish Sects and Christianity* (1984). Mention should be made also of Daniel Franks contributions: his Ph.D. thesis "The religious philosophy of the Karaite Aaron ben Elijah: the problem of divine justice" (1991), and *Search Scripture Well: Karaite Exegetes and the Origins of the Jewish Bible Commentary in the Islamic East* (2004).

In the area of Karaite Arabic Bible translations, M. Polliack dedicated a monograph to *The Karaite Tradition of Arabic Bible Translation* (1997). Further, in the area of exegesis and linguistics, mention should be made of the works of Geoffrey Khan, who published *The Early Karaite Tradition of Hebrew grammatical thought: including a critical edition, translation and analysis of the Diqduq of ʿAbu Yaʿqub Yusuf ibn Nuh on the Hagiographa* (2000) as well as the grammatical compendium of Abu ʾl-Faraj Hārūn, *al-Kitāb al-Kāfī* (together with M. Angeles Gallego, J. Olszowy-Schlanger, 2003), and the studies of Aharon Maman.

Haggai ben-Shammai's and David Sklare's publications concerning early Karaite authors and their philosophies (Daniel ben Moses *al-Qūmisī, Kirkisani, Japheth ben Ali, *Jeshua ben Judah) have also shown the Kalamic milieu of these Karaite thinkers. Daniel J. Lasker's studies of late Karaite philosophy (Judah *Hadassi, *Aaron ben Elijah, Elijah *Bashyazi) have challenged the widely held assumption that Karaites invariably remained loyal to the early Karaite Kalamic thought. In fact, Aaron ben Elijah was greatly influenced by Aristotelianism, and Bashyazi was a follower of Maimonides. Mention should also be made of Sarah Stroumsa's dissertation edition of David *al-Mukammis' *ʿIshrūn Maqāla*, 1983, though it is unclear if the latter was indeed a Karaite.

Two large scale projects of Karaite studies have been undertaken at the Ben-Zvi Institute for the Study of Jewish

Communities in the East: (a) The most comprehensive bibliography ever compiled on Karaites and Karaism, including texts and studies, was prepared by B. Walfish (containing over 7,000 entries) and is scheduled to appear in 2006. (b) In the Center for the Study of Judeo-Arabic Culture and Literature, the cataloguing of the Judeo-Arabic manuscripts of the Firkovich Collection (over 9,000 items) has been under way. So far several thousand manuscripts have been catalogued and two printed catalogues have appeared, of manuscripts of writings by al-Baṣīr (1997), and of Japheth ben Eli's commentary on Genesis (2000).

Karaite ethnomusicology has been investigated extensively by Jehoash Hirshberg, who has compared the changes that have taken place in Egyptian Karaite musical traditions in Israel and in the United States. Rachel Kollender has specialized in Karaite liturgical music. Both authors have noted the role music has played in preserving Karaite identity.

The fate of Karaites during the Holocaust has been discussed recently by Warren P. Green and Shmuel Spector. All evidence seems to point to the conclusion that, while individual groups of Karaites were murdered, generally the Nazis regarded European Karaites as a Tataric group similar to other Crimeans.

Other scholars who have been engaged in Karaite research include the late Alexander Scheiber, Philip E. Miller, Giuliano Tamami, William Brinner, and Jonathan Shunari.

A major desideratum of Karaite studies is an intensified effort towards the publication of critical editions of Karaite texts, many of which remain either in manuscript or in inferior printed editions.

[Daniel J. Lasker and Eli Citonne / Haggai Ben-Shammai (2nd ed.)]

Karaite Doctrine

PRINCIPLES OF HERMENEUTICS AND LEGAL THOUGHT. In principle, the Bible in its entirety is the sole source of Karaite creed and law. All religious precepts must derive directly from the Bible, based upon the literal meaning of the text, the customary use of the words and the context. Tradition is accepted, provided it is indispensable for the application of precepts contained in the text, for the clarification of ambiguities, or to make up for deficiencies in the concrete details of precepts; it must not be at variance, explicit or implicit, with any Biblical statement, and it must have the general consensus of the (Karaite) community; even so, however, its role remains restricted and subordinate. Certain rabbinic laws are accepted, not as valid components of the Oral Law transmitted by the Rabbanites, but as clarifying prescriptions, indicated in the text and reinforced by custom and tradition (*sevel ha-yerushah*, "yoke of inheritance"; *haʿakah*. "transmission"). For the rest, every scholar must study Scripture for himself, and, if urged to do so by his own knowledge and conscience, alter earlier opinions. Thus, Karaite doctrine is characterized, on the one hand, by rigidity and immutability of tradition, and, on the other hand, by an absence of restrictions on individual understanding of the Scriptures.

In the initial period of the development of Karaism (ninth century), it was the individualist trend that predominated, resulting in an almost anarchic state of affairs. This situation in Karaism of an infinite variety of opinions, as it existed until the middle of the tenth century, is reported on by al-Kirkisānī, who also attempts to explain and justify it by the principle of a free conception of Scriptures based on human reason (see above). Eventually, Karaite doctrine underwent a process of systemization and unification and an alternative tradition(s) to the Rabbanite one (as was Anan's tradition in the beginning); in its essentials, this process was developed at the time of Judah Hadassi (middle of the 12th century), achieving its final form at the time of Elijah Bashyazi (end of 15th century).

The following principles were established as norms for the determination of the law:

(1) the literal meaning of the biblical text (*ketav, mishma*, Arabic *samʿ*);

(2) the consensus of the community (*ʿedah, kibbuẓ*, Arabic *ijmāʿ*);

(3) the conclusions derived from Scripture by the method of logical analogy (*hekkesh*, Arabic *qiyās*);

(4) knowledge based on human reason and intelligence (*ḥokhmat ha-daʿat*, Arabic *ʿaql*); this latter principle, however, was not universally accepted by Karaite scholars. The principle of logical analogy was applied in its broadest sense and encompassed inference based upon analogy of words (*gezerah shavah*), upon induction (*hekkesh ha-ḥippus*), and upon analogy of notions (e.g., in respect of the prohibition of *kil'ayim*, and others). Judah Hadassi established not less than 80 different hermeneutical rules, including those applied by the Talmud (*Eshkol ha-Kofer*, nos. 114, 168–73). The hermeneutical rules most widely applied (especially with regard to marriage laws and degrees of consanguinity) are:

(1) analogous interpretation of juxtaposed words and passages (*semukhin*);

(2) inferences drawn a fortiori (*kal va-ḥomer*);

(3) interpreting a general principle on the basis of individual examples (*kelal u-ferat*; *perat u-khelal*; *kelal u-ferat u-khelal*), as well as all kinds of subsumption under a general principle (*binyan av*, etc.);

(4) extensive interpretation of a notion (*hagbarah*);

(5) a variety of rules for the interpretation of special words and grammatical peculiarities (e.g., the hermeneutical interpretation of the particles *et* and *kol* in the expansive sense, and of *akh*, *rak*, and *min* in the restrictive sense).

CREED. Apart from its fundamental stand on the Oral Law, Karaite creed does not differ in its essentials from that of Rabbanite Judaism. In its early stages normative beliefs had been formulated already by Daniel al-Qumisi, and reflect Kalam-oriented theology. Later creeds in Arabic and Hebrew were also based on the same principles. A list of ten articles of faith was formulated by Judah Hadassi (mid-12th century). In the late Middle Ages the philosophical foundation of Karaite creed was established in *Ez Ḥayyim*, the work of Aaron b. Elijah of Nicomedia, which the Karaites recognized as authoritative. Elijah Bashyazi and his pupil Caleb Afendopolo formulated the philosophy of the Karaite creed in ten principles (which are somewhat different from those of Hadassi):

(1) God created the whole physical and spiritual world in time, out of nothing;

(2) He is a creator who Himself was not created;

(3) He is formless, One in every respect, incomparable to anything, incorporeal, unique, and absolutely unitary;

(4) He sent our teacher Moses (this presumes belief in the Prophets);

(5) He sent us the Torah through Moses which contains the perfect truth (which cannot be complemented or altered by any other law, specifically not by the Oral Law recognized by the Rabbanites);

(6) every believer must learn to know the Torah in its original language and with its proper meaning (*mikra* and *perush*);

(7) God also revealed Himself to the other Prophets (although their gift of prophecy was less than that of Moses);

(8) God will resurrect the dead on the day of judgment;

(9) God rewards every man according to his way of life and his actions (individual providence, freedom of will, immortality of the soul, and just reward in the hereafter);

(10) God does not despise those living in exile; on the contrary, He desires to purify them through their sufferings, and they may hope for His help every day and for redemption by Him through the Messiah of the seed of David. (In some earlier Karaite creeds, e.g., Hadassi, the doctrine of the Messiah is omitted.)

LAW. Unlike Rabbanite Judaism, Karaism has no fixed number of commandments (of commission or omission). Karaite legal doctrine does not, of course, even approach rabbinic Judaism in its multi-faceted development. The calendar (including Sabbath and holidays), laws of marriage, dietary laws, and precepts on ritual purity have received the most intensive treatment in Karaism, usually in a strictly literal sense and with a tendency toward greater severity.

CALENDAR AND HOLIDAYS. The calendar was the subject by which the Karaites distinguished themselves from the Rabbanites. It was also the subject of much dispute among the Karaites. In principle the calculation of the Karaite calendar was based on lunar observation, and observation of the barley for the purpose of intercalation. By the middle of the 19th century the use of mathematical calculation, in addition to visual observation of the new moon, was accepted, following the lead of *Isaac ben Solomon, at least by the majority of the Crimean Karaites. Like the Rabbanite calendar, the Karaite calendar is based on the calculation of the new moon. Karaites also recognize the 19-year cycle with seven leap months of 29 days each; determination of the beginning of the month, however, in addition to being based upon the calculation of the moment of the appearance of the new moon (*molad*) and its location in accordance with special tables, also depends upon direct observation of the new moon. Thus, if direct lunar observation is made on the eve of the 30th day of the month, the following day becomes the day of the new moon; otherwise, the 31st day becomes the day of the new moon and the preceding month is determined to have had 30 days. The month of Nisan is regarded as the first month of the calendar year. In practice, however, following the tables of Bashyazi, the calendar is calculated in advance, by approximation (*haqrava*), as though the new moon was observed. In Israel, in order to emphasize this "approximation," observations are conducted in advance, in the spring, and accordingly the calendar of the following year (starting in the month of Tishri) is printed. Rabbi Samuel Magdi has been trying for several years to introduce mathematical calculation in principle, so far without success.

In determining the date of the holy days, Karaites deviate from Rabbanite usage in the following manner: the New Year Festival may begin on any day of the week (contrary to the Rabbanite rule, which provides for the postponement of the day of the New Year in three specific cases); as a result, the Karaite Day of Atonement does not always coincide with the Rabbanite; Passover and Sukkot (Feast of Tabernacles) are observed everywhere in the world for seven days only; the Feast of Weeks (Shavuot) falls on the 50th day following the Saturday of the Passover week (in accordance with the literal interpretation of Lev. 23:11, which the Talmud interprets in a different manner), and is therefore always on a Sunday; Ḥanukkah is not recognized, but Purim is, although the Fast of Esther is not; the Fast of Gedaliah is observed on the 24th of Tishri (as it was by the exiles returning from Babylon). Other fast days, with the exception of the Tenth of Tevet, are also observed on dates that differ from the rabbinic fast days (Karaites relate the fast days to the destruction of the First Temple, not the Second Temple).

Special rules apply to the sanctification of the Sabbath. Prohibition of work extends, beyond the 39 actions proscribed by Rabbanite Judaism, to any action not forming part of the prayer service or not absolutely necessary for nourishment or the satisfaction of other physical human needs. The earlier Karaite teachers (up to Jeshua b. Judah), like the *Samaritans and the *Beta Israel, prohibited the kindling of lights on Friday for use on the Sabbath (see *Eshkol ha-Kofer*, no. 146), and even taught that a light already lit had to be extinguished on the Sabbath; Jeshua b. Judah and his successors, however, taught that light on the Sabbath was permitted as an indispensable need and for the joy of the Sabbath (see *Adderet Eliyahu*, 1835, 31a). To this day, however, Karaites are either "friends of light" or "enemies of light," depending on whether or not they use artificial light on the Sabbath. Sexual intercourse is also prohibited on the Sabbath, and Karaites also oppose a number of alleviations of Sabbath precepts sanctioned by the rabbis.

CIRCUMCISION AND DIETARY LAWS. Certain rabbinical precepts pertaining to circumcision (*peri'ah* and *meẓiẓah*) are rejected by the Karaites. They also differ on the detailed regulations of ritual slaughter and therefore regard the meat of animals slaughtered according to Rabbanite regulations as prohibited. An important difference is the rejection of the "minimal quantities" (*shi'urim*) fixed by the Talmud in connection with dietary laws and the laws of purity. The prohibition contained in the Bible (Ex. 23:19; 34:26; Deut. 14:21) of boiling "a kid in its mother's milk" is also accepted by the Karaites as forbidding the consumption of the meat of cattle (not of fowl) with milk or butter; they do not, however, accept the additional restrictions enacted by the rabbis. They also strictly prohibit the consumption of the meat of an animal taken alive from the womb of its slaughtered mother (*ben pequʿah*). Karaites permit the consumption of the meat of those animals only that are enumerated in the Bible, and reject the criteria for permitted mammals and birds as formulated in the Talmud. Many Karaite scholars hold that, ever since the destruction of the Temple, any consumption of meat is prohibited.

MARRIAGE LAWS AND LAWS ON RITUAL PURITY. Karaite laws on marriage and the prohibited degrees of consanguinity are of special severity. In the early period, even the farthest removed degree of consanguinity was regarded as prohibited, with the result that by the 11th century the Karaite community was running the danger of extinction. The Karaite scholars of that period established the so-called *rikkuv* theory. Historically it was based on the adoption of Anan's views on this subject in their entirety. Exegetically and logically it was based on the assumption that man and wife form a unity of flesh (according to Gen. 2:24), from which it follows that persons related by marriage are also blood relations (*she'er*). In arriving at this conclusion, they made use not only of direct analogy (*hekkesh*) but also of derivative analogy (*hekkesh ha-hekkesh*), of the second, or even a higher degree. In this manner, the most distant relatives came to be included in the biblical term *she'er.*

This extreme theory of incest was rejected by Joseph b. Abraham ha-Kohen ha-Ro'eh al-Baṣīr and his pupil Jeshua b. Judah and was replaced by a less stringent law consisting of a set of six regulations (five, according to Joseph ha-Ro'eh). The reforms were not accepted by all Karaites immediately, and the debates about it continued for several centuries. The first regulation states that, according to the Bible and tradition, "blood relatives" (*she'er*) for a man are father and mother, brother and sister and their blood relatives; i.e., the father's or the mother's sister, the son's daughter and the daughter's daughter (in accordance with Lev. 18:10, 12, 13) and – by analogy – the brother's daughter and the sister's daughter. The corresponding relatives are regarded as prohibited for a woman (this is the second regulation). The third regulation prohibits the wife's blood relatives (based on Lev. 18:17). The fourth prohibits blood relatives of the wife's blood relatives. The fifth forbids marriage between two blood relatives and two blood relatives, e.g., two brothers marrying a mother and her daughter, respectively, or two sisters a father and his son, respectively (based on Lev. 18:11). The sixth regulation prohibits marriage between two blood relatives and two blood relatives once removed (thus Jeshua b. Judah, on the basis of an extensive interpretation of Lev. 18:14). Furthermore, any prohibition applying to one person also applies to all his blood relatives in the ascending and descending line, ad infinitum (but only to a limited degree as far as lateral lines are concerned).

In respect of ritual impurity, especially the impurity of the menstruation period (*niddah*), Karaite regulations are far stricter than the ones fixed by the rabbis. Notwithstanding, Karaite women are not required to immerse in a *mikveh*. Instead, they are required to pour water on the body with a vessel, from the head over the back, downwards. Rabbanite women in 12th century Egypt adapted this custom, causing Maimonides to stage a public campaign against it, which resulted in the promulgation of specific regulations reiterating the obligation of Jewish women to immerse in a *mikveh.*

LITURGY, ẒIẒIT, AND TEFILLIN. Karaite liturgy – which originally consisted solely of biblical psalmody – has the least similarity with its Rabbanite counterpart. There are two prayer services a day, mornings and evenings; on the Sabbath and holy days the *Musaf* prayer and other non-obligatory prayers are added. Originally, the *Ma'amadot* (prayers referring to the Temple sacrifices) formed the main basis of the Karaite rite. A prayer may be short or long, but must consist of seven parts (*shevaḥim, hoda'ah, vidduy, bakkashah, teḥinnah, ẓe'akah, keri'ah*) and the confession of faith. The prayers consist mainly of passages from the Bible (with the emphasis on Psalms) and partly also of prayer-poems, unknown to the Rabbanite rite. The *Shema* prayer is included in the Karaite rite, but the *Shemoneh-Esreh* (daily prayer consisting of 18 benedictions, and their equivalents for Sabbath and holidays, consisting of seven benedictions) is not known. The yearly cycle of weekly reading-portions from the Torah is almost identical with that of the Rabbanites. Until the end of the Middle Ages they used to begin the cycle in the spring, but changed it later, to begin in the fall, after Sukkot. The *haftarot* selection used by the Karaites differs from the Rabbanite one. During the prayer service, Karaites wear *ẓiẓit* (a fringed garment), the *ẓiẓit* including a light-blue thread. The biblical prescriptions concerning *mezuzah* and *tefillin* are regarded by the Karaites as having a figurative and symbolic meaning, and they reject the rabbinical regulations based upon them.

[Joseph Elijah Heller / Leon Nemoy]

Attempts at Reconciliation between Karaism and Rabbanism

The basic disagreement between the Karaites and the Rabbanites over the authority of the post-biblical oral tradition, and the unshakable conviction of the Karaites that their teaching represented the pure original Mosaic faith, free of Rabbanite distortion and corruption, made attempts at reconciliation anything but hopeful. The finality of Saadiah's proscription of the Karaites as complete heretics, and the resultant extreme bitterness of his Karaite opponents, made any rapprochement impossible in the tenth century, while the Karaite propensity to repeat over and over again the dicta of their great scholars of the golden age extended this bitterness into later centuries. At the same time, in 11th–12th centuries Egypt, relations seem to have been much improved, as is attested, among others, by several marriage contracts between members of the highest social layers, in which one party was Rabbanite and the other Karaite. Eventually, however, feelings calmed down on both sides. No less an authority than Elijah Bashyazi quotes his predecessors approvingly to the effect that "most of the Mishnah and the Talmud comprise genuine utterances of our fathers, and... our people are obligated to study the Mishnah and the Talmud." On the Rabbanite side Maimonides states his view that the Karaites "should be treated with respect, honor, kindness, and humility, as long as they... do not... slander the authorities of the Mishnah and the Talmud. They may be associated with, and one may enter their homes, circumcise their children, bury their dead, and comfort their mourners." Two medieval efforts to heal the breach are noteworthy. The first, an Arabic tract on the differences between the two camps, was composed some time before 1284 by Saʿd ibn Kammūna, a Rabbanite physician and philosopher in Iraq. He cites the mutual accusations proffered by each side against the other, and offers his own replies to them, silently implying that both sides have sinned against each other and that the ancient split has long lost its pertinence. Half a century later, an Italian Rabbanite scholar who settled on the island of Crete, Shemariah b. Elijah of Negropont, surnamed Ikriti (the Cretan), wrote on the same theme, calling upon both camps to come together, "so that all Israel might once more become one union of brethren." The fact that in the 16th century Egyptian rabbis contested the agreement between Sephardi codifiers (Shulḥan Arukh) and Ashkenazi ones (Rabbi Moses Isserles) on the prohibition of mixed marriages, because of possible *mamzerut* (see **mamzer*), testifies to the correct relations between the two communities in Egypt at the time.

In modern times, the policy of the Karaite leaders in Russia and Poland in the 19th and 20th centuries, in completely dissociating themselves from their Rabbanite cousins, in order to escape the crushing disabilities and persecutions imposed on Jews there, led to a quiet but profound estrangement, although scholars in both camps continued to maintain an amicable dialogue in the course of their research into Karaite history and literature. (On the situation in Israel, see above.)

Karaite Printing

Unlike the Rabbanites, who produced a flood of Jewish printed books from the 1470s to the present day, the Karaites ignored the printing press down to the 18th century, and the very few Karaite books printed earlier were the work of Rabbanite printers. The earliest Karaite printed work is an edition of the liturgy, set up in 1528/29 by Rabbanite typesetters at the press of Daniel Bomberg in Venice. The next Karaite book to come off the press, Bashyazi's *Adderet Eliyahu*, was produced Constantinople in 1530/31 by Gershom b. Moses, a member of the great Rabbanite family of master printers, the Soncinos. Two more works, Aaron the Elder's *Kelil Yofi* and Judah Fuki's *Shaʿar Yehudah*, were published in 1581 and 1582, respectively, likewise at Constantinople, by unnamed, but no doubt Rabbanite, printers. In the 17th century only one Karaite work, Joseph Malinovski's *Ha-Elef Lekha*, was published, at Amsterdam in 1643 by the press of *Manasseh b. Israel.

The first Karaite printers were the brothers Afdah (Afidah) and Shabbetai Yeraqa, who issued a few sample sheets of the liturgy in Constantinople, in 1733, under the auspices of the Crimean Karaite leader Isaac Sinani. They then moved to Chufut-Kale, in the Crimea, and there produced in 1734 a larger sample of their work, an edition of the *haftarot*. This was followed by an edition of the entire liturgy in 1737 and a booklet of benedictions in 1741; an edition of the Rabbanite liturgy according to the rite of Feodosiya and Karasubazar (in the Crimea) was also issued in 1735. The press apparently went out of business soon after 1741, although why Isaac Sinani, who lived on until 1756, permitted it to expire, is not known. In 1804, several years after the Crimea was annexed to Russia, a new Karaite press was organized, likewise at Chufut-Kale, and between 1804 and 1806 it produced four works – revised editions of the liturgy and the benedictions, and two tracts on the calendar. Then it too went out of existence, and the few Karaite books printed later came from non-Karaite presses in Vienna and Ortākoy (near Constantinople). The first more or less successful Karaite press was established in 1833 in Eupatoria and published some important texts. (See above, the section "Scholarship on Karaism and the Karaites").

The reason for this paucity of Karaite printing can only be conjectured. Presumably it was their traditional rigid conservatism and dislike of innovations, however beneficial, and the small demand for books, which made printing for the Karaite market an unprofitable undertaking.

[Leon Nemoy]

Musical Tradition

The musical tradition of the Karaite community has been mainly determined by two factors: their ethnic-historical heterogeneity, and their religious-conceptual homogeneity. It is reasonable to assume that the Karaites were not completely isolated from their surroundings, and that it ought to be possible to find traces of Byzantine, Sephardi, Tatar, Slavic, and Arabic traditions in their music. However, the only living tradition in Karaite music today is the one derived mainly from Egypt, which is almost entirely centered in Israel. This tradition finds expression in the recitation of prayers, partic-

Example 1

Example 2

Example 1. Ekra be-Shir ve-Zimrah, *hymn for the* ḥatan *Simḥat Torah (*Sefer Mo'adim, *part 2, p. 252). Recorded in Israel and transcribed by S. Hofman.*

Example 2. Ashreikhem Yisrael, *hymn for the Simḥat Torah (*Sefer Mo'adim, *part 2, p. 250). Recorded in Israel and transcribed by S. Hofman.*

Example 3. Haftarah *reading, Isaiah 62:1, Recorded in Israel and transcribed by S. Hofman.*

Example 4. Karati be-Koli. Piyyut *(*Siddur Mekuẓẓar, *p. 141). Melody by David Ḥusni. Recorded in Israel and transcribed by S. Hofman.*

Example 3

Example 4

ularly on Sabbaths, festivals, and life-cycle celebrations, and in the reading of the Torah and *haftarot*. The four volumes of the *Siddur ha-Tefillot ke-Minhag ha-Yehudim ha-Kara'im* ("Prayer Books of the Karaite Ritual") are richly endowed with psalms, *piyyutim*, and songs by Karaite poets, such as Samuel ha-Ḥazzan, Mordecai of Troki, Moses ha-Levi ha-Katan of the Sages of Kedar, and also by Rabbanite poets like *Judah Halevi and Judah al-Ḥarizi, who were greatly esteemed by the Karaites. These *piyyutim* are recited by the Karaites in an animated intonation somewhat resembling both cantillation and singing. In the prayer books there are many musical directions, such as ברון גרון בהלל שיר וזמרה "with note of throat in praising song and chant." Based on a center tone, the Karaite prayers are generally recited in a fairly flat melodic curve, which ranges from a second to a third, and almost never exceeds the range of a fourth. On festivals, especially Simḥat Torah, the chants are far richer, both melodically and rhythmically. An example is the *piyyut Ekra be-shir ve-zimrah*, in which the range is a fifth and the *maqām is *nihāwand*. The *piyyut* is recited alternately by the cantor and the congregation, the congregation repeating the refrain, while the cantor sings the several stanzas with improvised rhythmic variants. However, a *piyyut* such as *Ashreikhem Yisrael*, which is also in *maqām nihāwand*, has the range of a seventh, and is somewhat dance-like in style. The Karaites read the Torah in *maqām sīkāh* (similar to the Rabbanite Near Eastern communities), even though their reading is not always faithful to the *maqām*. They distinguish 21 cantillation accents, ignoring the *shalshelet, merkha kefulah, telisha ketannah, yare'aḥ ben yomo*, and *munnaḥ le-garmei*. While the *etnaḥ* lacks a clear melodic motive and tends to be expressed as a descending speech intonation, the *pazer gadol* ranges through a seventh, and the *revi'a* an octave (with about 20 notes). In the cantillation of the *haftarah*, the Karaites observe only eight accents. The reader ignores the remaining accents, "drawing" the other parts of the text into the eight motives. The outstanding characteristic of the reading of the *haftarah* is the frequency of actual motives amid a kind of dramatic recitation. The melodically richest songs are those sung at weddings and circumcisions. However, the loftiest musical expression is found in the songs of an artistic character, such as *Karati be-koli*, whose melody is attributed to David Ḥusni, a Karaite musician who lived and worked in Egypt during the first half of the 20th century. This song, in *maqām rāst* and in the ABA form, is common among the Karaites and enjoys special popularity. Section B of the song is in the Arab *mawāl* style. Although among the Egyptian Karaites it is still possible to find a musician who plays the *qānūn*, violin, drum, or even, nowadays, the accordion, the community as a whole does not like instrumental music. As with the cultures of all other communities in the Israel melting pot, the future of the Karaite tradition now hangs in a precarious balance.

[Shlomo Hofman]

BIBLIOGRAPHY: R. Mahler, *Kara'im* (Yid., 1947, Heb., 1949); L. Nemoy, *Karaite Anthology* (1952); idem, in: JQR, 50 (1959/60), 277–9; 51 (1960/61), 332–40; idem, in; PAAJR, 36 (1968), 102–65; Z. Ankori, *Karaites in Byzantium* (1959), includes extensive bibliography, 461–84; idem, in: PAAJR, 24 (1955), 1–38; 25 (1956), 157–82; idem, in: *Essays on Jewish Life and Thought… in Honor of S.W. Baron* (1959), 1–38; idem, in: *Tarbiz*, 29 (1959/60), 195–202; 30 (1960/61), 186–208; Mann, Texts; R. Fahn, *Legenden der Karaiten* (1921); idem, *Kitvei Reuven Fahn*, 1 (1929); P. Grajewsky, *Me-Ḥayyei ha-Kara'im bi-Yrushalayim* (1922); S. Assaf, in: *Tarbiz*, 4 (1932/33), 35–53, 193–206; idem, *Be-Oholei Ya'akov* (1943), 181–222; Z. Cahn, *The Halakah of the Karaites* (1936); idem, *The Rise of the Karaite Sect* (1937); Baron, Social, index; I. Ben Zvi, in: KS, 32 (1956/57), 366–74; idem, *Meḥkarim u-Mekorot* (1966), 267–78; P.S. Goldberg, *Karaite Liturgy and its Relation to Synagogue* (1957); N. Allony, in: KS, 36 (1960/61), 390–8; idem, in: HUCA, 35 (1964), 1–35 (Heb. pt.); A. Loewenstamm, in: *Sefunot*, 8 (1964), 165–204; Dinur, Golah, 4 (1962), index, 601; M. Corenaldi, in: *Mahalakhim*, 1 (1969), 7–18; E. Feldmann, in: *Tarbiz*, 38 (1968/69), 61–74; J. Rosenthal, in: *Sefer ha-Yovel… Ḥ. Albeck* (1963), 425–42 (= *Meḥkarim u-Mekorot*, 1 (1967), 234–52); idem, in: KS, 36 (1963/64), 59–63; C. Roth, in: *Yerushalayim*, 4 (1953), 138–40; P. Friedman, in: M. Beloff (ed.), *On the Track of Tyranny* (1960), 97–123; Ẓ. Harkavy, in: *Gesher*, 15 (1969), no. 4 107–9, incl. bibl.; Ch. Burchard, *Bibliographie zu den Handschriften vom Toten Meer*, Berlin, 1957–65 (continued periodically in the *Revue de Qumran*, 1/1958 onward); N. Wieder, *The Judean Scrolls and Karaism*, 1962 (cf. JQR, 82/1963, 222ff.); R. Kashani, *Kara'im, Korot, Masorot, Minhagim* ("Karaites, Their History, Traditions and Customs," Jerusalem, 1978). MUSICAL TRADITION: S. Hofman, in: *Leshonenu*, 22 (1948), mus. examples between pages 264–5; idem, in: *Abstracts Fifth World Congress of Jewish Studies* (1969), div. 4, 26–27. For later studies, see "Scholarship on Karaism and the Karaites" above.

KARAN, DONNA (1948–), U.S. fashion designer. Karan (born Donna Faske) was raised in the Forest Hills neighborhood of Queens, N.Y., to parents already immersed in the fashion business. Her father, Gabby Faske, who died when she was 3, was a custom tailor in New York City. Her mother, Helen, was a showroom model and sales representative. Karan – who got her surname from her first husband, Mark Karan – would become one of the best-known businesswomen in the U.S., head of a publicly owned company, her name on everything from apparel to accessories, from fragrances to furnishings. She designed her first collection while still in high school and staged her first fashion show while an undergraduate at Parsons School of Design in New York City. In 1968, she dropped out of school to become an assistant to Anne *Klein, a popular women's sportswear designer known for skirts, blouses, sweaters, and jackets that could easily be mixed and matched. Klein, who had become Karan's mentor, unexpectedly died of cancer in 1974. The 26-year-old Karan, who had given birth to a daughter only two days earlier, took over the line with co-designer Louis Dell'Olio and built it into a highly successful business.

In 1984, Karan, who had been divorced a year earlier, launched Donna Karan Co., her own business, in partnership with her second husband, sculptor Stephan Weiss, and Takihyo, a Japanese company that owned the Anne Klein firm. Her approach to dressing was geared more to practicality than to "fashion." Just as Klein had promulgated a wardrobe of interchangeable parts, so did Karan. She identified with urban women who worked for a living and did not necessarily look like runway models or wealthy matrons, and they identified with her. Her design concept was based on a handful of interchangeable items that created a complete wardrobe able to flow from day to evening, and from weekday to weekend. It was distinguished by its use of black cashmere, leather, stretch fabrics and molded fabrics, and silhouettes that wrapped and sculpted the body. In short, clothes that were comfortable, flattering, and easy to organize. Karan called the jacket the foundation of a woman's wardrobe, and advocated versatile blazers that were equally appropriate for home, business, or leisure. She took the concept a step further in 1985, when she launched DKNY, a subsidiary label that was a less expensive version of the Donna Karan collection. With its nod to city life, DKNY emphasized bodysuits and active sportswear, often accompanied by loose, easy garments. Karan also returned to school at that time, earning a B.F.A. from Parsons in 1987. By the early 1990s, she had branched into men's wear and introduced a fragrance and a skin-care line. In 1996, the company made a heavily anticipated public offering, becoming one of the few firms on the New York Stock Exchange to be headed by a woman. It opened its first DKNY store in 1996, on New York's Madison Avenue. Karan's husband, Stephan, died in 2001, the same year her company was acquired by LVMH Möet Hennessy Louis Vuitton, a Paris-based fashion conglomerate, for $243 million. Karan remained as artistic director, in control of all creative aspects. By 2004, the company – since renamed Donna Karan International – boasted 70 company-owned and licensed Donna Karan Collection and DKNY stores worldwide, including units in London, Manchester, and Tokyo. In 2004, it generated some $1.4 billion in retail sales and employed 1,600 workers.

Karan was named Designer of the Year by the Council of Fashion Designers of America in 1985, 1990, and 1996, and men's wear Designer of the Year in 1992. The Fragrance Foundation saluted her for Best Fragrance of the Year in 1993.

That same year, she was honored for humanitarian efforts by the Design Industries Foundation for AIDS. In 1996, she won a Fashion Critics Award from Parsons. Karan was named Intimate Apparel Designer of the Year in 1999 and in 2003 she became the first American designer to receive a Superstar Award from Fashion Group International. She was presented with a Lifetime Achievement Award from the CFDA in 2004, the same year she got an honorary doctorate from Parsons. As a board member of the CFDA, Karan headed its Seventh on Sale fundraiser for AIDS awareness and education. She was a co-chair of New York's annual "Kids for Kids" events for the Elizabeth Glaser Pediatric AIDS Foundation, and co-chaired an annual flea market and barbecue to benefit Ovarian Cancer research. In 1999, she and her husband established the Karan Weiss Foundation to benefit children's causes, medical research, and the arts.

BIBLIOGRAPHY: *New York Times Magazine* (May 4, 1986).

[Mort Sheinman (2nd ed.)]

KARASU, ALBERT (1885–1982), journalist. Karasu was born in Salonica. After studying political science in Switzerland, in 1918 he established the French language newspaper *Le Journal d'Orient*. In 1922–23 he covered the Lausanne Treaty negotiations. The newspaper was closed down in 1971.

BIBLIOGRAPHY: N. Benbanaste, *Örneklerle Türk Musevi Basınının Tarihçesi* (1988); S. Kaneti, "La disparition du dernier quotidien de langue française à Istanbul: *Le Journal D'Orient*," in: *Presse Turque et Presse de Turquie Actes Des Colloques d'Istanbul* (1988), 65–69.

[Rifat Bali (2nd ed.)]

KARASUBAZAR (from 1945 **Belogorsk**), city in Crimea oblast, Ukraine, the main community of the Crimean Jews (Krimchaks). In 1595, Selameth-Girey Khan granted the Jews of Karasubazar a privilege according them far-reaching concessions with regard to taxes and customs duties. This privilege was confirmed many times by the succeeding khans (for the last time in 1728). A collection of ancient *Sifrei Torah* and manuscripts was removed from the Karasubazar synagogue in 1839 by Abraham *Firkovich without the consent of the community; he later handed them over to the Imperial Library in St. Petersburg. From 1,969 in 1847 the number of Jews in the town increased to 3,144 by 1897 (total population 13,000), the overwhelming majority of them Krimchaks, who spoke the Tatar language among themselves and prayed according to the Crimean rite (*minhag Kaffa*). There were also 47 Karaites living in the town. From 1866 to 1899 R. Ḥayyim Hezekiah *Medini, chief rabbi of the Crimean Jews, had his seat in Karasubazar. He was able to use his considerable influence to raise the religious and spiritual standards of his communities. The Jews of Karasubazar engaged in crafts, market gardening, and petty trade. During the Civil War, the community decreased in numbers as a result of famine and disease. In 1939 the number of Jews dropped to 429. In 1932 there were in the environs three Jewish farm settlements with 149 families. The Germans occupied Karasubazar on November 1, 1941. On December 10 they killed 76 Jews, and on January 17, 1942, using mobile vans, they gassed 468 Krinchak Jews from the town and surrounding settlements. The few remaining Jews (probably needed artisans) were shot later.

BIBLIOGRAPHY: A. Harkavy, *Altjuedische Denkmaeler aus der Krim* (1876); A. Harkavy and H.L. Strack, *Catalog der hebraeischen Bibelhandschriften der... Bibliothek in St. Petersburg* (1866); V.D. Smirnov, *Krymskoye khanstvo pod verkhovenstvom Ottomanskoy Porty* (1897); *Zapiski Odesskago obschestva istorii i drevnosti*, 14 (1866), 103; *Regesty i nodpisi*, 1 (1899), 397; 2 (1899), 93; O. Lerner, *Yevrei v Novorossiskom kraye* (1901), 141–7.

[Yehuda Slutsky / Shmuel Spector (2nd ed.)]

KARAVAN, DANI (1930–), Israeli painter, sculptor, and architect. Karavan was born in Tel Aviv when it was still full of orchards and plantations. One of his first artistic memories is of the sand dunes where, as a boy, he first sculpted forms in play. These sand structures, which involve building and digging, can be seen to anticipate his mature style. Karavan studied art in the Bezalel Academy of Art and Design in Jerusalem under Mordecai *Ardon. He remained a kibbutz member until 1950 for ideological reasons. This orientation could be seen later in his public art. Karavan continued his art studies in Florence, where he learned fresco techniques at the Accademia Della Belle Arti. In 1960–73 he created stage sets for Israeli theaters and for Israeli ballets. This can be seen as the beginning of his spatial work.

Karavan was known for his environmental sculptures and installations. He won the Israel Prize in 1977. While he moved between Tel Aviv, Paris, and Florence his works were shown all over the world.

Karavan's artistic language contained a limited number of forms. The basic form was taken from the architectural world. The dome, the pyramid, and the stair were integral components of his art. The location of these forms in the environment and in a sculptural space created a link between them. In spite of the repetitive style, each work looked different because the artist created a clear connection between the work and the chosen environment. Karavan emphasized the difference between sculptures, for example, by the selection of the material. In the desert near Beersheba he used bare concrete, in Jerusalem he used chiseled stone, and in Tel Aviv he used white concrete. (*Negev Monument*, 1963–68, Beersheba; *Environment Sculpture*, 1980, Givat Ram, Jerusalem; *White Square*, 1977–88, Tel Aviv). Another material used as a popular symbol in Karavan's works was the olive tree that grew between walls or above them. In some works the tree grew upside down. The sea also became a part of his works, especially in his impressive *Passages*, *The Memorial to Walter Benjamin* (1994, Portbou, Spain).

Karavan's most famous piece of art in Israel is the wall relief in the Knesset Assembly Hall, in Jerusalem (*Jerusalem City of Peace*, 1966). The location of the wall behind the speaker's podium made it a component of the visual forms that constitute the Israeli collective identity. One of Karavan's largest permanent works is three kilometers long. (*Exe Majeur*, 1980–86, Cergy Pontoise, France).

BIBLIOGRAPHY: Tel Aviv Museum, *Dani Karavan Passages* (1997); Institut Valenciá d'art Modern, *Dani Karavan* (2002).

[Ronit Steinberg (2nd ed.)]

KAR-BEN/LERNER, U.S. publisher. Kar-Ben Publishing, a division of Lerner Publishing Group, is the largest publisher of Jewish children's books in North America. Founded in 1975 by Judyth Groner and Madeline Wikler, the imprint's first title was a self-published children's *Haggadah*, which had more than 2 million copies in print in the early 21st century. Over the next 27 years the company published more than 200 books for children and their families, the creative work of 60 authors and illustrators. In 2003, Groner and Wikler received the Sydney Taylor Body of Work Award from the Association of Jewish Libraries in recognition of their contribution to Jewish children's literature by creating Kar-Ben.

Kar-Ben's titles include such subjects as Jewish holidays, Bible, crafts, cooking, folktales, Holocaust, life-cycle events, and contemporary stories. Kar-Ben, which was purchased by Lerner Publishing Group in 2001, publishes 12–15 new titles a year, and celebrated its 30th anniversary in 2005.

Established in 1959, Lerner Publishing Group is based in Minneapolis, Minnesota. With more than 2,500 titles in print, Lerner Publishing Group is one of the largest independent educational children's book publishers in North America. Its titles include biographies, social studies, science, geography, sports, picture books, activity books, multicultural issues, and fiction. Company founder Harry J. Lerner also helped establish the Minnesota Book Publishers' Roundtable, the Minnesota Center for Book Arts, and the Jewish Historical Society of the Upper Midwest. He served as chief executive officer of Lerner Publishing Group; his son, Adam Lerner, became publisher and president.

[Joanna Sussman (2nd ed.)]

KARDINER, ABRAM (1891–1981), U.S. psychoanalyst. Born and educated in New York City, Kardiner studied with *Freud from 1921 to 1922. In 1949 he was appointed clinical professor of psychiatry at Columbia University and in 1955 director of the psychoanalytic clinic. He conducted joint seminars at Columbia University on the interplay of individual personality and culture in diverse societies. Various patterns of child rearing, the biography of adult behavior, and institutional structure were subjected to psychodynamic analysis. Inferences about the personality produced in the culture were drawn and checked by actual psychological tests. The findings were documented in Kardiner's *The Individual and His Society* (1939) and his *Psychological Frontiers of Society* (1945).

Kardiner, and those following his lead, believed it possible to elicit a "basic personality structure" – a set of trends entering into the characters of all individuals reared in the same culture. This structure was the product of "primary institutions" such as child training methods in dealing with aggression and sex and the family organization. The basic personality expressed itself unconsciously in secondary institutions such as folklore, art, and religion. It was from these cultural institutions, therefore, that the basic personality expected in the culture could be inferred.

Kardiner's theoretical procedure involved analyses of the social frustration of adult neurotics and "normal" individuals within the Western culture. From his conclusions he established how groups in any culture would react to similar social frustration.

Kardiner was one of the founders of the Association for Psychoanalytic Medicine (APM) and of the Columbia University Center for Psychoanalytic Training and Research. In recognition of his role as a renowned pioneer in the application of psychoanalysis to the study of culture, the APM established the Abram Kardiner Lectureship on Psychoanalysis and Culture in 1978.

BIBLIOGRAPHY: Kardiner co-authored with Lionel Ovesey *Mark of Oppression* (1951), which explored the impact of social pressures on the African-American personality. Other works by Kardiner include *The Traumatic Neuroses of War* (1941), *Sex and Morality* (1954), *They Studied Man* (1961), and *My Analysis with Freud: Reminiscences* (1977). **ADD. BIBLIOGRAPHY:** W. Manson, *The Psychodynamics of Culture: Abram Kardiner and Neo-Freudian Anthropology* (1988).

[Ephraim Fischoff and Louis Miller / Ruth Beloff (2nd ed.)]

KARDOS, ALBERT (1861–1945), literary scholar and historian. Headmaster of the Debrecen Jewish high school, Kardos was an expert on 16th-century Hungarian literature. Even in his eighties, victimized by the Nazis, he continued his literary work. Two important products of his research were *A XVI század lírai költészete* ("Lyric Poetry of the 16th Century," 1883) and a history of Hungarian literature (1892). He died after deportation.

KARDOS, LÁSZLÓ (1898–1987), Hungarian literary scholar and translator. Kardos became a teacher at the Jewish high school in his native Debrecen. After World War II he worked in the Hungarian Ministry of Education until 1950, when he was appointed professor of world literature at Budapest University. Kardos made his name as a skilled translator from many languages. In addition to Greek and Latin authors he translated English, French, German, Czech, Polish, Romanian, and Russian classics into Hungarian. His literary sensitivity enabled him to translate even from languages which he did not know fluently. With the help of expert assistants he produced, for example, an anthology of Hebrew poetry, *Héber költők antológiaja* (1942). Kardos also edited a Hungarian periodical devoted to world literature, *Nagyvilág*. His works include *Ay huszonegyéves Ady Endre* (1922), *Karinthy, Frigyes* (1946), *Válogatott műforditások* (1953), and *Toth Árpád* (1955).

BIBLIOGRAPHY: *Magyar Irodalmi Lexikon*, 1 (1963), 583; M. Szabolcsi (ed.), *A magyar irodalom története 1919 – töl napjainkig*, 6 (1966), 65–67.

[Baruch Yaron]

KAREH, SOLOMON (**Soleiman**; 1804–1885), chief rabbi in San'a (Yemen). Kareh was an eminent scholar of Torah and Kabbalah. Upon the death of his father, R. Joseph, he was elected to succeed him as *av bet din*. After some years he was elevated to the position of chief rabbi of Yemenite Jewry, which he occupied for 40 years. His period was one of disorder and rebellions, when much suffering was endured by the community of San'a. In 1859, the year of Jacob *Saphir's visit to Yemen, he fled from San'a out of fear of the authorities and took refuge in Ḳaryat al-Ḳābil. With the Turkish occupation in 1872, he returned to the capital and the new Turkish governor appointed him *ḥakham bashi*. Under Turkish rule, he was given ceremonial honors, and by the authority of his office and his personal influence he protected his coreligionists from the authorities and succeeded in nullifying persecutory decrees which threatened his community.

BIBLIOGRAPHY: J. Saphir, *Massa Teiman*, ed. by A. Yaari (1951), 115f., 124, 186, 188, 218; A. Koraḥ, *Sa'arat Teiman* (1954), 31, 46.

[Yehuda Ratzaby]

KAREL, RUDOLPH (1880–1945), composer. Born in Pilsen, Czechoslovakia, Karel was the last pupil of Dvorak. He taught for a time in Russia, and returned to Prague in 1920, where he taught at the Prague Conservatory from 1923 to 1941. In 1943 he was arrested and died at the *Theresienstadt concentration camp. His compositions include stage works, four symphonies, and chamber music.

KARELITZ, AVRAHAM YESHAYAHU (1878–1953), outstanding talmudic scholar and one of the most prominent halakhic authorities of the 20th century, known from his work as the "Ḥazon Ish." Karelitz received his education from his father, head of the *bet din* at Kossow; from an early age he manifested unusual talent and diligence. He devoted his life to the study of the Torah, although also learning such sciences as astronomy, anatomy, mathematics, and botany, since he felt that knowledge of them was necessary for a full understanding of various aspects of Jewish law and practice. After his marriage he continued to lead an extremely modest life, his wife providing for their needs while he spent day and night in study. His first work, on *Oraḥ Ḥayyim* and other parts of the Shulḥan Arukh, was published anonymously in Vilna in 1911 under the title *Ḥazon Ish*, the name by which Karelitz became almost exclusively known. It created a deep impression in the rabbinic world because of its vast knowledge and extreme profundity. He went on to write and publish dozens of volumes on numerous tractates of the Talmud, every section of the Shulḥan Arukh, the *Mishneh Torah* of Maimonides, and various specific halakhic topics. His collected letters were published in three volumes in 1990. When he moved to Vilna about 1920, he came to the notice of R. Ḥayyim Ozer Grodzinski who, henceforth, used to consult him in all religious and communal matters. Even though he lived in relative anonymity, his reputation for saintliness and knowledge was known and people from all walks of life would frequent his home, for scholarly discussions or to seek advice on religious, business or personal problems, or simply to receive his blessing. When in 1933 he settled in Ereẓ Israel, his house in Bene-Berak became the address for thousands who sought his guidance. Karelitz was an example of a personality, holding no official position, who nevertheless became a recognized worldwide authority on all matters relating to Jewish law and life. He did not head any yeshivah, yet he was teacher and guide to thousands of students. He was not a communal leader, yet he exerted an enormous influence on the life and institutions of religious Jewry. He did not publish many responsa, but became the supreme authority on *halakhah*. On one occasion, he was consulted by David Ben-Gurion, the prime minister of Israel, on the question of conscription of young women into the Israel army. He was a lover of Zion, yet did not adhere to the official Zionist movement. He was neither a Ḥasid nor an extremist, but was intimate with both these groups. He considered man's duty in life to be the constant and meticulous study of Jewish law aiming at the attainment of a maximum degree of perfection in religious observance. Although essentially a talmudic scholar, he applied himself to practical problems, devoting much effort to the strengthening of religious life and institutions. His rulings on the use of the milking machine on Sabbath (to overcome the prohibition of milking in the usual way) and on cultivation by hydroponics during the sabbatical year (when he challenged the validity of the permission to cultivate the land given by the chief rabbinate) are two illustrations of his practical approach. He wrote over 40 books which are models of lucidity and are written in a simple style.

Karelitz's theology was an attempt to adjust Maimonidean rationalism to a more Lithuanian, "mitnaggedic" set of values that corresponds to the tenets of *halakhah*. According to Karelitz, divine wisdom was transmitted directly to man by God through prophecy until the time of the Sages. Beginning with them, all that man could do was to reveal the hidden truths using his intellect. "There is no wisdom in our world unless it is delivered through the soul of a living wise man." Thus, the goal of Jewish life is to be a living wise man, i.e., a *talmid ḥakham*. The Ḥazon Ish also asserted that trust in God does not mean that God will always do what is best for the individual. Rather we can trust that God will always do what He thinks best.

Karelitz's theology stemmed from the world of *halakhah*. Even Jewish ethics are based on concrete laws, not on abstract principles. Indeed, Karelitz taught that the practice of *halakhah* trains a person in the right values.

Since the Ḥazon Ish did not study in any of the standard Lithuanian *yeshivot*, he developed his own method of Talmud study and halakhic decision-making. He rejected the cold analytical approach of Brisk and instead, integrated a human dimension into his interpretation. He maintained that the sages did not rely on abstract concepts. Rather, they often took into account social or psychological considerations. Contrary to Brisker thinking, where the Torah is the divine "word" detached from earthly reality, Karelitz grounded his interpretations in the real world. Thus, halakhic definitions should be based on the "natural senses" without involving scientific methods or social conventions. His approach was not a systematic methodology. As a result he could be contradictory. On the one hand he rejected critical readings of the talmudic text, yet on occasion he himself amended the text. He regarded the medieval and renaissance sages (the *rishonim*) as the main interpreters of the Talmud, yet he often disagreed with their comments. For the Ḥazon Ish, it was the individual scholar's own perusal and personal encounter with the text that was significant. Such an encounter was not limited to the words of the text, but also included the spirit of the text.

While he lived in an ultra-Orthodox world in Bene Berak, Karelitz did not follow the *ḥaredi* mainstream; he forged his own path. He had a tendency to be overly strict (*maḥmir*) in his halakhic rulings. He was not at all politically involved and criticized the religious Zionist camp for becoming politically involved, thus subjecting religious values to the interests of the Zionist enterprise. He rejected all public commemorations of the Holocaust.

Karelitz's efforts in the social sphere were aimed at building a strong *ḥaredi* community through the building of more yeshivot, more synagogues, and more *mikva'ot*. By 1942 he had gained a wide reputation in rabbinic circles because of his participation in halakhic debates. By 1948 he was already recognized as the foremost arbiter of *halakhah* in Israel. The Ḥazon Ish did not intend to create a revolutionary new *ḥaredi* society in Israel, but his teachings, his strongly held views, and his very life served as the foundation for the thriving ultra-Orthodox community in today's modern Israel.

BIBLIOGRAPHY: K. Kahana, *Ha-Ish ve-Ḥazono* (1964); O. Feuchtwanger, *Righteous Lives* (1965), 28–31; Jung (ed.), *Men of the Spirit* (1964), 147–69; A. Sorasky, *Ḥazon Ish* (Eng. translation by M. Karelenstein, 1973). **ADD. BIBLIOGRAPHY:** B. Brown, in: *Dinei Yisrael*, 20–21 (2001), 123–237; idem., "*Ha-Ḥazon Ish: Halakhah, Emunah ve-Ḥevrah bi-Fesakav ha-Boletim be-Ereẓ Israel*" (Dissertation) (2003); idem, in: *Ereẓ Israel be-Hagut ha-Yehudit be-Me'ah ha-Esrim* (2004) 71–103; M.Z. Neriah, *Re'iyyah ve-Ḥazon* (1982); N. Gutel, in: *Ha-Ma'ayan*, 38:1 (1997), 19–32; A. Shlosberg in: *ibid.*, 26:3 (1986), 10–25; S.Z. Havlin, in: *Sefer Beit Vaad* (2003), 13–35; A. Ben-Porath, in: *Shema'atin*, 139 (2000), 145–157; M. Friedman, in: *Masa el ha-Halakhah: Iyyunim Bein-Teḥumiyyim be-Olam ha-Ḥok ha-Yehudi* (2003), 196–218; A.H. Goldberg, in: *Shevilin*, 31–32 (1979), 71–81; B. Efrati, in: *Ḥinukh ha-Adam Ve-Yi'udo* (1978), 397–408. HAGIOGRAPHICAL BIOGRAPHIES: S. Finkelman, *The Chazon Ish: The Life and Ideals of Rabbi Avraham Yeshayah Karelitz* (1989); Z. Yavrov, *Sefer Ma'aseh Ish: Toldot Ḥayav ve-Hanhagotav shel Rabbi Avraham Yeshayahu Karelitz* (1999); R. Halprin, *Bi-Meḥiẓat ha-Ḥazon Ish* (1991); H.E. Kolitz, *ha-Ḥozeh mi-Lita: Perakim be-Hayyei ha-Ḥazon Ish* (1990).

[Mordechai Hacohen / David Derovan (2nd ed.)]

KARET (Heb. כָּרֵת; "Extirpation"), a punishment at the hands of heaven mentioned in the Bible as the penalty for a considerable number of sins committed deliberately such as: idolatry, desecration of the Sabbath, the eating of leaven on Passover, incest and adultery; and for some forbidden foods. No previous warning need be given in these cases. The *halakhah* explains *karet* as premature death (Sifra, *Emor*, 14:4), and a *baraita* (MK 28a; TJ, Bik. 2:1, 64b) more explicitly as: "death at the age of 50," but some *amoraim* hold that it refers to "death between the ages of 50 and 60." The word *karet* is also used to indicate the degree of severity of a transgression, and serves as a "standard" for many other *halakhot*. The Mishnah (Ker. 1:1) enumerates the 36 transgressions mentioned in the Torah for which the penalty is *karet*, and lays down (*ibid.*, 1:2) that only where there is *karet* for the deliberate act is there a sin-offering for the act committed inadvertently. Since the punishment is divine, and the fact that it is deliberate is known only to God, it does not require witnesses or previous warning. The *halakhah* also lays it down that only the offspring of a union for which the penalty is *karet* have the status of **mamzerim* (Yev. 4:13).

There is a dispute between *tannaim* whether or not the penalty of *karet* exempts the transgressor from *flogging, which is the automatic punishment for most prohibitions of the Torah of which one is guilty after having been duly warned (Mak. 13a–b); according to the view that it does not exempt from flagellation, the flagellation itself exempts from *karet* (Mak. 23a–b). Repentance however has the effect of annulling *karet* (*ibid.*), and, with the exception of Neḥunya b. Ha-Kanah, all agree that *karet* does not absolve the guilty person from civil claims arising out of his action (Ket. 30a).

Every attempt toward a general rationale of this punishment involves serious halakhic and philosophical difficulties, and the problem greatly exercised the early authorities; although the *halakhah* itself makes a distinction between *karet* and "death by the hand of heaven" (MK 28a), the difference between them is not clear. Some *rishonim* hold that "natural" death takes place at the age of 60 (or later), when the *karet* period has ended, and that "death by the hand of heaven" has no fixed time, save that one's span of life is curtailed. Others hold, in accordance with the Jerusalem Talmud (Bik. 2:1), that *karet* comes at the age of 50, "death by the hand of heaven" at 60, and natural death between 60 and 70. The connection between the punishment of "*ariri*" and *karet* and the real nature of the former is also not clear. In the Bible the punishments of *karet* and *ariri* are frequently found together. Some *rishonim* hold that the minor children of a sinner are also punished through the father's *karet*, and in their view this also constitutes the difference between *karet* and "death by the hand of heaven" (Rashi, Ket. 30b, et al.). Others, however, differ (Tos. to Shab. 25a). With regard to *karet* in the case of the old, it is laid down that the punishment lies in the manner of death, since "one dying in either one, two, or three days has suffered *karet*."

The punishment of *karet* raised difficulties in the theory of reward and punishment current among medieval scholars, and constituted part of the polemic around Maimonides and his views on this subject. Basing himself upon the statement (Sanh. 90b): "*Hikkaret tikkaret: 'hikkaret'* in this world, '*tikkaret*' in the world to come," Maimonides (Yad, Teshuvah 8:1) lays down that: "The punishment of the wicked is that they are not vouchsafed this life [of the world to come], but they suffer *karet* and die… and this is the *karet* written in the Torah…" This constitutes a maximal punishment, since ordinary sinners, after being punished in *Gehinnom according to their sin, live again in the world to come (*ibid.* 8:3, 5). In the opinion of *Naḥmanides (in the *Sha'ar ha-Gemul*), the soul can never perish and be annihilated and he therefore holds that those liable to *karet* are also punished in the world to come according to their sin, and he divides sinners into three categories: those who have been guilty only once of a transgression involving the penalty of *karet*; those whose wicked deeds exceed their good in addition to this transgression; and lastly the blasphemers and idolaters. Only the last are punished both by *karet* of the body and of the soul in this world and in the next (Comm. to Lev. 18:29 and in *Sha'ar ha-Gemul*). *Karet* of the soul, according to Naḥmanides, does not mean absolute perishing; it means only a degradation, in a way of metamorphosis, and absolute negation of spiritual pleasures awaiting the souls of the righteous.

In the opinion of some *Karaites *karet* was death at the hand of man (*Eshkol ha-Kofer*, no. 267), and this too seems to have been the view of Philo and of Josephus (Ant. 3:12, 1).

BIBLIOGRAPHY: G.F. Moore, *Judaism*, 3 vols. (1927–30), index, s.v. *Extirpation*; Ḥ. Albeck, *Shishah Sidrei Mishnah*, 5 (1959), 243ff.; E.E. Urbach, *Ḥazal* (1969), index.

[Israel Moses Ta-Shma]

KARFF, MONA MAY (1912–1998), seven-time winner of the U.S. women's chess championship and one of the first four Americans to be named an international woman master by the International Chess Federation (1950). Born in Bessarabia, Karff learned chess from her father, Aviv Ratner, a Zionist who later became a real estate magnate in Israel. Karff, an intensely private person who was always mysterious about her background, came to the United States in the 1930s. She was married briefly to a cousin, Abe Karff, a Boston lawyer. Between 1938, when she won her first national title at the second U.S. women's championship, to 1974, when she achieved her seventh national championship, Karff was in the forefront of women's chess in the United States. Less consistently successful in top international competitions, she placed sixth representing Palestine in the women's world championships in Stockholm in 1937 and came in fifth representing the United States at the 1939 world championships in Buenos Aires. Karff, who remained involved in the world of competitive chess throughout her life, had a long-term romantic relationship with Dr. Edward Lasker (d. 1981), a five-time winner of the U.S. Chess Open.

BIBLIOGRAPHY: M. Oehlert, "Karff, M. May," in: P.E. Hyman and D.D. Moore (eds.), *Jewish Women in America*, vol. 1 (1997), 723; *New York Times*, Obituary (Jan. 18, 1998).

[Judith R. Baskin (2nd ed.)]

KARFUNKEL, AARON BEN JUDAH LEIB HA-KOHEN (d. 1816), rabbi and author. Karfunkel was born in Kalisz after his father had died, and his mother died in childbirth. As a result he was brought up in the home of his brother, Israel. According to his own statement he served as rabbi in different Polish communities, for example in Lask as *av bet din* – though his name is not mentioned in the list of rabbis of the Lask burial society – and in Daspirshi (a community otherwise unknown). He complains bitterly about his economic position in these communities, stating that he faced starvation until he was compelled to leave his wife and children, who were maintained by his father-in-law. In 1801 he was appointed rabbi of Nachod in Bohemia and in 1807 as deputy to Levin Saul Frankel, whom he later succeeded as regional rabbi of Silesia. Karfunkel was the author of the *Sheiltot Avyah* (being the acronym from his given names), notes and novellae on the Talmud in the form of responsa to questions which he himself posed. The work comprises 12 parts, each of which is named after one of the stones of the *ephod. Two parts only, *Nofekh* and *Bareket*, were published (Berlin, 1806), with one commentary entitled *Millu'at Even*, and another entitled *Meshu'aḥ Milḥamah* on difficulties in the views of the *rishonim*. His other works, *Avnei Zikkaron*, responsa, and *Ẓanif Tahor*, on the Book of Ecclesiastes, are still in manuscript in the British Museum. He also wrote the introduction to the constitution of the Nachod burial society and rabbinate.

BIBLIOGRAPHY: A. Karfunkel, *Sheiltot Avyah* (Berlin, 1806), introd.; Fuenn, Keneset, 86f.; D. Weinryb, in: *Tarbiz*, 9 (1938), 97 n.; M. Brann, in: *Jubelschrift… H. Graetz* (1887), 266, 277.

[Itzhak Alfassi]

KARGAU, MENAHEM MENDEL BEN NAPHTALI HIRSCH (1772–1842), German rabbi and author. Kargau was born in Prostibor (Bohemia) and studied under Nathan *Adler and Phinehas *Horowitz in Frankfurt, Ezekiel *Landau in Prague, Joseph Yoske in Posen, and Herz Scheuer in Mainz. For some time he engaged in commerce in Paris, later returning to Germany and settling in Fuerth, where he devoted himself to the study of Talmud. He became friendly with Abraham Benjamin Wolf *Hamburg, in whose works *Simlat Binyamin* (Fuerth, 1841) and *Sha'ar ha-Zekenim* (*ibid.*, 1830), many of his halakhic statements are quoted. Kargau wrote hymns and poems, including a hymn in Hebrew to celebrate Napoleon's coronation (*Shir u-Mizmor* (Paris, 1805) with a free translation into French by Michel Berr). In 1840 he commemorated Moses *Montefiore's return from Damascus in another Hebrew hymn. Kargau died in Fuerth. His commentary on Shulḥan Arukh, *Yoreh De'ah*, 201 (dealing with the laws of the *mikveh*) together with 41 of his halakhic responsa, was published after his death by his pupil Jonah Rosenbaum and by Asher Anschel Stern, later chief rabbi of Hamburg, under the title *Giddulei Tohorah* (Fuerth, 1845).

BIBLIOGRAPHY: S.M. Chones, *Toledot ha-Posekim* (1910), 135; D. Hoffmann, *Der Schulchan-Aruch* (1894[2]), 39; Loewenstein, in: JJLG, 6 (1909), 212–4, 230–3; 8 (1911), 118f., 204–6.

[Joseph Elijah Heller]

KARINTHY, FERENC (1921–1992), Hungarian author and playwright. Raised as a non-Jew, Karinthy neither denied nor emphasized his Jewish roots but does not deal with Jewish subjects in his writings. His *Budapesti tavasz* ("Springtime in Budapest," 1953), while bowing to the requirements of the era, gives nevertheless a vivid picture of postwar Budapest.

[Eva Kondor]

KARIV, AVRAHAM YIẒḤAK (1900–1976), Hebrew literary critic, poet, and translator. Born in Slobodka, he made his way to the Ukraine and Crimea during World War I and entered the Tarbut Teachers' Seminary in Odessa, where he studied under Bialik and Klausner. In 1923 he went to Moscow and completed his studies in mathematics and physics. In 1934 he went to Palestine, where, after a short period of teaching, he took up editorial posts. Kariv began his literary career while studying in Odessa, and his first poems were warmly received by Bialik. In the ensuing years, until his arrival in Palestine, his poetry was published in Hebrew journals that appeared in Soviet Russia and elsewhere. After he settled in Palestine, he became a regular contributor to the Hebrew press, with essays and articles of literary criticism becoming his major endeavor and overshadowing his poetry. He wrote scathing criticism of the works of classic modern Hebrew authors, such as *Mendele Mokher Seforim, J.L. *Gordon, D. *Frischmann, J.Ḥ. *Brenner, and others. His collection of essays *Adabberah va-Yirvaḥ Li* (1961) made a deep impression with its reevaluation of prevalent negative attitudes toward Jewish life in the Diaspora. The writers of the Haskalah, he claimed, accepted the false premises of an antisemitic European culture and overlooked the moral grandeur of Jewish life in Eastern Europe. He published several collections of essays, a volume of poetry, *Kol u-Vat Kol* (1962), a book on the Bible, *Shivat Ammudei ha-Tanakh* (1968), and numerous translations from Russian and Yiddish literature. For English translations see Goell, Bibliography, 920–1.

BIBLIOGRAPHY: H. Bavli, *Ruḥot Nifgashot* (1958), 206–13; I. Cohen, *Sha'ar Soferim* (1962), 332–45; S. Zemach, *Massa u-Vikkoret* (1954), 297–300; Kressel, Leksikon, 2 (1967), 800–1.

[Getzel Kressel]

KARIYAH, AL- (Qarʿiyya, al-), a Jewish sect which existed in *Egypt (near Cairo) until the middle of the 19th century. David Alfasi in his *Agron* (s.v. *kar*) maintains that they were descendants of the sons of Kareah (Jer. 40:8ff.), who led a remnant of the Judeans into Egypt after the murder of Gedaliah. Another, more likely, explanation is that of Judah *Hadassi in his *Eshkol ha-Kofer* and *Kirkisānī in his *Kitāb al-Anwār* (chapter 9) which derives the name from the Arabic *qarʿ* (cf. the talmudic קרא), meaning "pumpkin, gourd," since the sect, for reasons of ritual purity, used only vessels made of pumpkin shells. These writers report that the al-Kariyah would not employ hired labor and rested on Sunday. Kirkisānī quotes David al-Mukammis, who regards them as a pre-Christian sect later influenced by Christianity. Harkavy is inclined to agree with this theory, as they may have been one of the many Essene sects in Hellenistic Egypt; this would explain their ascetic life and opposition to hired labor. If Sunday rest was not adopted by them later under Christian influence, there may be some confusion due to the strictness of Sabbath observance which the al-Kariyah extended to the festivals as well. This is reported by Hadassi, who does not mention Sunday rest at all.

BIBLIOGRAPHY: S. Pinsker, *Likkutei Kadmoniyyot* 1 (1860), 166; A.E. Harkavy, in: Graetz-Rabbinowitz, 3 (1894), 500f.

KARKAR (Qarqar), city on the Orontes, S. of Hamath and within its territory, now Khirbat Qarqur (the name signifies "flat (valley-earth) formation" (cf. Heb. קרקור, Judg. 8:10; Akk. *Qaqqaru*; cf. also קרקע). Karkar is famous as the site of a battle between Shalmaneser III of Assyria and a coalition of kings who came to the aid of Irḫuleni king of Hamath. It is described on the monolith of Shalmaneser III found at Kurkh, some 20 miles south of Diyarbakir in Turkey (now in the British Museum), and mentioned in his various other inscriptions. The Assyrian king gives a detailed description of the forces of the 12 kings allied against him. The list, arranged in three groups – chariots, cavalry, and foot soldiers – is as follows (Monolith from Kurkh, col. 2, lines 90ff.):

> 1,200 chariots; 1,200 riding horses [i.e., cavalrymen]; 20,000 [foot-]soldiers of Adad-idri [Hadadezer = "Ben-Hadad II"] from Damascus [Imērišu]; 700 chariots; 700 riding horses [i.e., cavalrymen]; 10,000 [foot-] soldiers of Irḫuleni [Erḫuleni] from Hamath [Amatai(a/u)]; 2,000 chariots; 10,000 [foot-] soldiers of Ahab the Israelite [Aḫabbu (māt) Sir-ʾi-la-aii(u/a),

Sir'ilajj(u/a)]; 500 [foot-] soldiers from Gu [bal] [Gebal, Byblos; not: Guaiia, Que; see Tadmor, in bibl.]; 1,000 [foot-]soldiers from Egypt [Muṣrajj(u/a); not the northern land of Muṣri; see Tadmor, in bibl.]; 10 chariots; 10,000 [foot-]soldiers from Arqa [= (māt) Er-qa-na-ta-aiiu/a; cf. ha-ʿArqi, Gen. 10:17]; 200 [foot-]soldiers of Mattan-Baʿal [Ma-ti-nu Ba-aḫ-li] of Arvad [Armadajju/a]; 200 [foot-]soldiers of the State of Usnû [Usanatajju/a]; 30 chariots; 10,000 [foot-]soldiers of Aduna-Baʿal [Adōni-Baʿal] from Shiānu (cf. ha-Sini, Gen. 10:17); 1,000 camel [-soldiers?] [*gammalū*] of Gindibu' the Arabean [(māt) Arbajju/a];... (erased) 100/1,000 [foot-]soldiers of Ba'asa (Baasa) son of Ruḫubi [Ben Rehob, i.e., the Beth-Rehobite] the Ammonite [or, far better: "from the mount of Amanah" ((har ha)-Amanah, Song 4:8); cf. Aram Beth Rehob, II Sam. 10:6; see *Aram].

The battle was joined in the sixth year of Shalmaneser III (853 B.C.E.). The inscription thus supplies the first extra-biblical confirmation of biblical chronology. The fact of *Ahab's participation in the battle of Karkar (side by side with his inveterate foes, the Arameans of Damascus, but see Ahab; *Ben-Hadad) is not mentioned in the Bible. The coalition was established to counter the growing Assyrian menace; although Shalmaneser gives a glowing account of the slaughter he wrought and of the capture of Karkar, the fact is that the battle ended in a stalemate and the Assyrian advance was halted (see *Jehu; *Mesopotamia, History). The great number of Ahab's chariots finds corroboration in the redating of the stables found at Megiddo (strata IV–V) to the period of Ahab instead of Solomon (see Yadin and Malamat in bibl.).

BIBLIOGRAPHY: GENERAL: Y. Yadin, in: IEJ, 8 (1958), 80–86; idem, in: BA, 23 (1960), 62–68; W.W. Hallo, *ibid.*, 37ff.; H. Tadmor, in: IEJ, 11 (1961), 143–50; A. Malamat, in: J. Liver (ed.), *Historyah Ẓeva'it shel Ereẓ Israel...* (1965), 246ff.; Bright, Hist., 223–4. TEXTS: G. Smith, in: H.C. Rawlinson (ed.), *The Cuneiform Inscriptions of Western Asia*, 3 (1870), pls. 7–8; Luckenbill, Records, 1 (1925), 594–611; Pritchard, Texts, 278ff.; E. Michel, in: *Die Welt des Orients* (1952), 454ff. CHRONOLOGY: E.R. Thiele, *The Mysterious Numbers of the Hebrew Kings* (1965^2), 50–51.

[Michael Avi-Yonah and Pinhas Artzi]

KARLE, JEROME (1918–), U.S. physicist and Nobel Laureate. He was born in New York City and educated at Abraham Lincoln High School before graduating with a B.S. from City College, New York (1933), an M.A. in biology from Harvard (1938), and a Ph.D. in chemistry from the University of Michigan. After working on the Manhattan Project at the University of Chicago (1944), he joined the Naval Research Laboratory, Washington (1946) as head of the Electron Diffraction Section (1946–68) and subsequently as chief scientist in the Laboratory for the Structure of Matter. He was also professor at the University of Maryland (1951–70). His research interests are crystallography and the structure of a broad range of macromolecules. Karle won the Nobel Prize in chemistry (1985) jointly with Herbert *Hauptman for his contributions to determining the structure of complex molecules by mathematical analysis of crystallographic observations. His later work analyzed the application of quantum crystallography to analyzing organic molecules. He served as chairman of the National Research Council (1973–75) and president of the International Union of Crystallography (1981–84). He was a member of the U.S. National Academy of Sciences. He had a special interest in social issues of scientific research and ecological problems. He worked collaboratively with Isabella Lugoski, whom he married in 1942.

[Michael Denman (2nd ed.)]

KARLIN, a dynasty of *ẓaddikim* (family name **Perlov**), named after the town of Karlin. Its founder was AARON BEN JACOB, referred to in ḥasidic circles as "Aaron the Great" (1736–1772), the pioneer of Ḥasidism in Lithuania. He was a disciple of *Dov Baer the Maggid of Mezhirech. During the lifetime of his teacher, in the early 1760s, he founded the first ḥasidic *minyan in Karlin, from where he spread Ḥasidism throughout Lithuania. In contemporary sources "Karliner" became a synonym for "Ḥasid" in Lithuania. The spread of "Karliner" *minyanim* there was one of the causes of the campaign against Ḥasidism; in Karlin's sister town, *Pinsk, it was directed against Aaron personally. Aaron's activity showed his concern with social problems. He helped to enforce the *takkanot* issued in 1769 at Nesvizh, abolishing an unusual and heavy tax affecting the poor, using his personal authority and imposing a *ḥerem*. His *azharot* ("Warnings"), a letter, and a testament have been preserved (in manuscript). Inclined toward asceticism, Aaron fasted frequently and even demanded of his disciples: "seclusion, one day every week in a special room, spent in fasting, repentance, and study of the Torah." But he warned against extremes in such practices. In his *azharot* he cautioned "to beware of pride and anger, even if over the observance of a precept, and all the more so over disputes." He instructed his Ḥasidim to study the Mishnah daily and to be versed in the Bible. He regarded melancholy as "the lowest abyss," while joy stems from sanctity. The Jew who does not rejoice in being a Jew is ungrateful to Heaven. Aaron composed a hymn for Sabbath: *Yah ekhsof no'am Shabbat* ("Oh God, I yearn for the Sabbath's delight"), which is included in several *siddurim* and is sung every Sabbath by the Ḥasidim of Karlin and those related to them. The Ḥasidim of Karlin have about 20 melodies for this hymn, one having become renowned as *Ha-Niggun ha-Kadosh*. Aaron was succeeded by his disciple Solomon (see below) but the leadership later returned to Aaron's son, ASHER (d. 1826), a disciple of Solomon; before 1784 he went from Karlin with his teacher to Lodomeria (Vladimir-Volynskiy). Asher studied a short while under *Baruch of Medzibezh and Israel of *Kozienice, and was for a short time rabbi in Zelechow (Poland). He then settled in the townlet of *Stolin, near Karlin. Henceforward the Karlin Ḥasidim also became known as the Ḥasidim of Stolin. Asher supported *Abraham of Kalisk in opposition to *Shneur Zalman of Lyady. He was among leading Karlinists who were imprisoned in 1798. Subsequently he returned to Karlin. In his *Divrei Torah* he stresses the human and religious value of productive work, and teaches that a man "should not be lazy in any occupation, lest his [religious] study should also be performed in laziness." He criticized Jews who exploited the labor of non-Jewish workers.

He was succeeded by his son, AARON THE SECOND (d. 1872), under whose leadership Karlin Ḥasidism reached the height of its influence in Polesie and in Volhynia. Groups of Karlin Ḥasidim settled in Tiberias and Jerusalem, supported from the center in Karlin. It was Aaron's custom to write "Words of Encouragement" to his Ḥasidim before Passover, which were particularly important as a solace during the oppressive reign of Czar Nicholas I. The celebrated Karlin ḥasidic melodies were composed during his leadership. In his *Beit Aharon* (1875) he emphasizes sincerity. He taught that "prayers should be followed by study… every day. God does not count the pages but the hours." He advised that "repentance comes essentially out of joy and delight." Regular daily life should also be considered Divine Worship, as both lead to the attainment of perfection, as a result of which redemption and the messianic era can be brought closer. Aaron also left Karlin before 1864 for Stolin, where he remained until his death. He died in the townlet of Mlinow, Volhynia, while on a journey, and was buried there.

He was succeeded by his son, ASHER THE SECOND (d. 1873), who emphasized the value of ritual immersion "which purifies the body and promotes sanctity." He was buried in Drohobycz (Drogobych), Galicia. Asher left a four-year-old son named ISRAEL; he was immediately recognized by Karlin Ḥasidim as successor to the leadership and hence known as the "Yenuka mi-Stolin" ("Babe of Stolin"). However, he also retained the loyalty of the thousands of his followers when grown up as well as gaining respect among the *Mitnaggedim* thanks to his devoted and able leadership. In his two testaments – to his family and to his Ḥasidim – he recommended study also of "language… and secular studies which are necessary"; he stressed the necessity of care for "the education of girls, because the foundation of Judaism depends on this." His son MOSES became rabbi of Stolin. A second son, ABRAHAM ELIMELECH, settled in Karlin as rabbi, a third JOHANAN (d. 1955), in Lutsk, Volhynia, and a fourth, JACOB, became rabbi of the Karlin Ḥasidim in the United States. Moses and Abraham Elimelech founded yeshivot and maintained contacts with Ereẓ Israel. Both perished with their followers in the Holocaust. Johanan went to Ereẓ Israel after the Holocaust; from there he emigrated to the United States where he died. In 1957 his body was taken to Tiberias for burial. He left a small grandson, and those of his Ḥasidim who have remained loyal to the dynasty undertook his education as its continuator, while a small number chose the *ẓaddik* of *Lelov as their leader. SOLOMON BEN MEIR HA-LEVI OF KARLIN (1738–1792), ḥasidic *ẓaddik*, a disciple of Dov Baer, Maggid of Mezhirech, and of Aaron the Great of Karlin, headed the Karlin Ḥasidim after Aaron's death in 1772 (see above). He left no written works, but many of his sayings have been quoted and tales about him have been recorded. Almost all the subsequent *ẓaddikim* in Lithuania were his disciples or the disciples of his disciples.

BIBLIOGRAPHY: Dubnow, Ḥasidut, index; W.Z. Rabinowitsch, *Lithuanian Ḥasidim* (1970), index; idem, in: YIVOA, 5 (1950), 123–51; I. Halpern, *Yehudim ve-Yahadut be-Mizraḥ Eiropah* (1968), 333–9; idem, in: *Zion*, 22 (1957), 86–92; M. Nadav, *ibid.*, 34 (1969), 98–108; M. Buber, *Tales of the Hasidim*, 1 (1968^4), 195–202, 273–285; 2, 145–173; J.M. Kleinboim, *Shema Shelomo* (1956^2).

[Wolf Zeev Rabinowitsch]

KARLINER, BARUCH (c. 1810–1871 or 1879), *ḥazzan*. Taking his name from the Russian town of Karlin where he first became a *ḥazzan*, Karliner also served other communities including Pinsk and Brisk. He had neither a particularly tuneful voice nor any musical knowledge, but would compose "when the spirit came upon him," even if this occurred during a part of the service which was not usually sung. His choir was accustomed to his sudden digressions from the rehearsed repertoire and when these occurred would continue to accompany him in his own style. His compositions, notable for their power and bold modulations, were written down by members of his choir and had a great influence on the following generations of *ḥazzanim*.

KARLSRUHE, city in Germany, formerly capital of *Baden. Jews settled there shortly after its foundation in 1715. By 1725 the community had a synagogue, bathhouse, infirmary, and cemetery. Nathan Uri Kahn served as rabbi of Karlsruhe from 1720 until his death in 1749. According to the 1752 Jewry ordinance Jews were forbidden to leave the city on Sundays and Christian holidays, or to go out of their houses during church services; but they were exempted from service by court summonses on Sabbaths. They could sell wine only in inns owned by Jews and graze their cattle, not on the commons, but on the wayside only. Business records had to be kept in German. The community officials, including two to three unmarried teachers, were exempted from tax. They exercised civic jurisdiction and could commit members of the community to the municipal prison for Jews. A *ḥevra kaddisha* was founded in 1726; the cemetery, also used by Jews of other towns, was enlarged in 1756 and 1794. There were nine Jewish families living in Karlsruhe in 1720, 50 in 1733, 80 in 1770, and 502 persons in 1802. Nethanel *Weil, who became chief rabbi of the two Baden margravates (1750–69), was succeeded by his son Jedidiah (Tiah) Weil (1770–1815).

Nethanel Weil's commentary on *Asheri, Korban Netanel* (on tractates *Mo'ed* and *Nashim*), was printed in 1755 in Karlsruhe by L.J. Held, a successor to old and well-known Augsburg printers. His successors, F.W. Lotter and M. Macklott, continued publishing Hebrew works, including some by Jonathan *Eybeschuetz (printed 1762–82) and the *Torat Shabbat* of Jacob *Weil (1839). The firm continued printing until 1899, mainly liturgical items, Judeo-German circulars, and popular stories. D.R. Marx, licensed in 1814, printed in 1836 a Hebrew Bible (1845^2), edited on behalf of the Jewish authorities (*Oberrat*) by a group of rabbis, among them Jacob *Ettlinger. Altogether some 60 Hebrew books were printed in Karlsruhe.

Karlsruhe was the seat of the central council (*Oberrat*) of Baden Jewry, according to the articles of the 1809 edict which granted them partial emancipation. Asher Loew, a participant in the Paris *Sanhedrin, was appointed rabbi of Baden and Karlsruhe in 1809; he was succeeded in 1837 by Elias Willstaedter. A new synagogue with organ was consecrated in 1875; the Orthodox faction seceded in 1878 and built its own synagogue in 1881.

From the 1820s Jews were permitted to practice law and medicine. After attaining complete emancipation in 1862, Jews were elected to the city council and the Baden parliament, and from 1890 were appointed judges.

The Jewish population numbered 670 in 1815, 1,080 in 1862 (3.6% of the total), 2,200 in 1892, 3,058 in 1913 (2.73%), 3,386 in 1925 (2.37%), 3,199 in June 1933 (2.01%), and 1,368 in May 1939. The Jews in Karlsruhe suffered from persecution during the *Hep! Hep! riots in 1819. Anti-Jewish demonstrations took place in 1843 and 1848, and in the 1880s the antisemitic movement of Adolf *Stoecker had its repercussions in Karlsruhe. The community maintained a variety of cultural and educational institutions. A *Lehrhaus* (school for adults) was founded in 1928.

During the first years of the Nazi regime the community continued to function and particularly to prepare Jews for emigration. An agricultural training school was founded and a biweekly newspaper (founded as a bulletin in 1840) was published. On Oct. 22, 1938, all male Polish Jews living in Karlsruhe were deported to Poland. The synagogues were destroyed on *Kristallnacht*, November 1938; most of the men were arrested and sent to *Dachau concentration camp, but were released after they had furnished proof that they intended to emigrate. In October 1940, 895 Jews were expelled and interned by the French Vichy authorities in *Gurs in southern France, most of whom were deported from there to *Auschwitz in November 1942. The 429 remaining Jews and non-Aryans were deported to the east between 1941 and 1944. There were 90 Jews living in Karlsruhe in May 1945, 63 in 1946, and 246 in 1968. An organized community was formed in 1945, and the Baden Central Jewish Council was reorganized in 1948. A new synagogue was consecrated in 1971. The Jewish community numbered 323 in 1989 and around 800 in 2004 after the immigration of Jews from the former Soviet Union.

BIBLIOGRAPHY: E. Biberfeld, in: ZHB, 1 (1896/97), 90–96, 148–52; 2 (1897), 28–33, 60–64, 101–4, 129–31, 176–81; 3 (1899), 25–29, 50–53; S. Seeligman, *ibid.*, 5 (1901), 61–64, 90–92; E. Biberfeld, *Die hebraeischen Druckereien zu Karlsruhe i. B.* (1898); L. Loewenstein, *Nathaniel Weil, Oberlandesrabbiner in Karlsruhe* (1898); A. Lewin, *Geschichte der badischen Juden* (1909), 1–10, 76ff., 264–7, and passim; B. Rosenthal, *Heimatgeschichte der badischen Juden* (1927); idem, in: MGWJ, 71 (1927), 207–220; *Gedenkbuch zum hundertfuenfunzwanzigjaehrigen Bestehen des Oberrats der Israeliten Badens* (1934); N. Stein, in: YLBI, 1 (1955), 177–90; H. Maor, *Ueber den Wiederaufbau der juedischen Gemeinden in Deutschland seit 1945* (1961), 29, 59, 99; K. Schilling (ed.), *Monumenta Judaica-Handbuch* (1963), index; P. Sauer, *Dokumente ueber die Verfolgung der juedischen Buerger in Baden-Wuerttemberg*, 2 vols., (1966), index; H. Schnee, *Die Hoffinanz und der moderne Staat*, 4 (1963), 43–85; G. Taddey and F. Hundsnurscher, *Die juedischen Gemeinden in Baden* (1968); E. Kotlowsky, in: *Zeitschrift fuer Geschichte der Juden*, 6 (1969), 44–53. **ADD. BIBLIOGRAPHY:** J. Stude, *Geschichte der Juden im Landkreis Karlsruhe* (1990); J. Werner, *Hakenkreuz und Judenstern. Das Schicksal der Karlsruher Juden im Dritten Reich*, Veroeffentlichungen des Karlsruher Stadtarchivs, vol. 9 (1990^2); H. Schmitt, (ed.), *Juden in Karlsruhe. Beitraege zu ihrer Geschichte bis zur nationalsozialistischen Machtergreifung*, Veroeffentlichungen des Karlsruher Stadtarchivs, vol. 8 (1990^2); J. Paulus, "Die juedische Gemeinde Karlsruhe," in: *Juden in Baden 1809–1984. 175 Jahre Oberrat der Israeliten Badens* (1984), 227–33. **WEBSITE:** http://jg-karlsruhe.bei.t-online.de/.

[Toni Oelsner]

KÁRMÁN (formerly **Kleinman**), **MÓR** (1843–1915), Hungarian educator. Born at Szeged, he was probably the first Jew to take his doctorate at the University of Budapest (1866), where he became a lecturer in pedagogy, ethics, and psychology in 1872, and professor in 1909. In 1869 he was sent to Leipzig by the minister of religion and education, Baron Joseph Eötvös, to study methods of training teachers for secondary schools. There, he was entrusted with the writing of a curriculum for the training of teachers at the model elementary school and later served as director of education at the model secondary school in Budapest. He reorganized and expanded the national secondary school system. According to Kármán, religious education was a sound basis for morals and ethics. When, in 1873, the Hungarian government decided to underwrite the teaching of religion in public schools, Kármán was asked to administer the Jewish educational needs in the public schools. He edited a Hungarian educational journal, and participated in the publishing of school textbooks. Apart from his own scholarly contributions, Kármán translated numerous works into Hungarian. He devoted much of his energies to Jewish affairs, and issued the appeal which led to the foundation of IMIT – the Jewish-Hungarian Literary Society.

BIBLIOGRAPHY: A. Moskovits, *Jewish Education in Hungary (1848–1948)* (1964), 306–7.

[Shnayer Z. Leiman]

KÁRMÁN, THEODORE VON (1881–1963), aerodynamicist. Von Kármán was born in Hungary and studied in Budapest and Goettingen. During World War I he was a lieutenant in the Austro-Hungarian aviation corps. He invented a helicopter with two counter-rotating propellers, a type never developed by industry. After the war he became a consultant to many airplane companies. He first toured the U.S. in 1926 under the auspices of the Guggenheim Fund and settled permanently in 1930 as head of the Guggenheim Aeronautical Laboratory at the California Institute of Technology. Von Kármán published many papers on aerodynamics, hydrodynamics, elasticity, strength of materials, and vibration phenomena. "Karman Vortex Trail" and "Karman Similarity Theory of Turbulence" are now standard terms in scientific literature. The *Collected Works of Theodore von Kármán* was published in four volumes (1956). The development of high speed aircraft owes much to the influence of Von Kármán. He investigated (1938) the possibility of using supersonic wind tunnels in ballistic research. He formed the Aerojet Engineering Corporation to manufacture rockets after unsuccessful attempts to interest American industry in this venture. During World War II he was in charge of all jet propulsion research in the U.S. Von Kármán was chairman of the U.S. Air Force's scientific advisory board (1944) and of the Aeronautical Research and Development Committee of the North Atlantic Treaty Organization (1951).

BIBLIOGRAPHY: Dryden, in: *National Academy of Sciences Biographical Memoirs*, 38 (1965), 345–84.

[Barry Spain]

KARMAZIN, MEL (1943–), U.S. media executive. Melvin Alan Karmazin was born and grew up in Long Island City, Queens, New York. His mother worked in a factory while his father drove a taxi. During high school Karmazin was a typist at an advertising agency in Manhattan. He attended Pace University at night while working as an advertising salesman by day. His first job at the Columbia Broadcasting System was selling ads for the radio division. In the late 1960s, when his commission exceeded $70,000, his boss objected to his earnings, so Karmazin left to work for the giant broadcasting company Metromedia. At Metromedia from 1970 to 1981, Karmazin was general manager of WNEW-AM and FM, two well-known stations in New York City. One disc jockey who worked there at the time wrote that Karmazin "had no interest in music, news, sports, books, theater. It mattered not what a station proffered, only how it profited." That attitude served Karmazin well in broadcasting. In 1981 he was hired to run Infinity Broadcasting, an owner of radio stations. Over the next 15 years, by dint of tight operating control and a string of shrewd acquisitions, he built Infinity into one of the largest radio networks in the nation. His most brilliant managerial stroke came in the late 1980s when he hired Howard Stern, a foul-mouthed talk-show host who had been fired by another station. Stern began earning millions for himself and for the station. Karmazin took Infinity public in 1992 for $17.50 a share, then sold it in 1996, when it owned 44 radio stations, to CBS for $170 a share, securing his reputation on Wall Street. In 1996, using a business strategy that became his trademark, Karmazin approached CBS, which had merged with Westinghouse in 1995, and proposed that Infinity buy the company. Instead, CBS acquired Infinity for $4.9 billion, and Karmazin came aboard to run the combined radio operations of Infinity, Westinghouse, and CBS along with its outdoor advertising business. Intent on making his stamp on the company, Karmazin was instrumental in persuading Westinghouse to dump its industrial manufacturing assets and to refashion the company under the CBS name. The chairman and chief executive of CBS named Karmazin head of CBS's station division and in October 1998 Karmazin forced his superior's resignation. He became chief executive in 1999. One of his first acts at CBS was to buy broadcast rights for National Football League games from 1998 to 2006 for $4 billion. He also invested $30 million to $50 million in an early morning show, but that project was unsuccessful. In 2000 Karmazin became the chief operating officer of Viacom-CBS, one of the world's largest producers of news and entertainment and became the presumptive heir to Sumner M. *Redstone, Viacom's chief executive, who was then 76 years old. Karmazin's relationship with Redstone was testy. He refused to conform to Redstone's more traditional conception of an entertainment mogul. Karmazin kept a close eye on expenses, a discipline anathema to many in entertainment. And Karmazin did not like the high-risk, potentially high-reward game of making blockbuster movies. For him the entertainment business was about controlling costs, selling ads, and watching pennies, not laying daring bets or dating starlets. In 2004, when he decided that he would not be succeeding the crusty octogenarian Redstone, Karmazin resigned as Viacom's president and chief operating officer, giving up his stewardship of CBS, MTV, Paramount, Simon & Schuster, and Infinity Broadcasting. He left with a severance agreement worth $30 million. Later that year, Karmazin took the reins of Sirius Satellite Radio as chief executive. The announcement came a month after Sirius had signed Howard Stern to bring his show to the satellite airwaves from commercial radio.

[Stewart Kampel (2nd ed.)]

KARMEL, ILONA (1925–2000), Holocaust survivor and author. Born in Cracow, Poland, to Hirsch and Mita (Rosenbaum) Karmel, Ilona Karmel was taken to the Cracow ghetto in November 1942. Later that year, Karmel, her mother, and her older sister, Henryka, were deported to the nearby slave labor camp in Plaszow. In 1943, they were transported to Starzysko Kamienna, a labor camp near Leipzig, and then to the Buchenwald concentration camp. Karmel attributes her own and her sister's survival to their mother's pro-active protection at critical moments. In the final days of the war, a German military vehicle ran over Karmel and her mother, apparently deliberately. Karmel's mother died from her injuries, and Karmel's legs were crushed so severely that she spent two years convalescing in a Swedish hospital.

While in the camps, the Karmel sisters composed poetry on stolen paper. In 1947, they published a volume of these poems, *Spiew za Drutami* ("Song Behind the Wire"), depicting the inner life of slave laborers and their struggle against dehumanization. In Sweden, Karmel studied English by correspondence course and began writing fiction in English. Upon reaching New York in 1948, Karmel enrolled in Hunter College and continued writing. One story, "Fru Holm," was awarded the 1950 prize for college fiction by *Mademoiselle* magazine. Karmel transferred to Radcliffe College, graduating with honors in 1952 under the mentorship of the poet Archibald MacLeish. Her first novel, *Stephania* (1953) emerged from her experiences in the Swedish hospital.

Karmel's masterpiece, *An Estate of Memory* (1969), was the product of a 10-year immersion in wartime memories. Set within a labor camp resembling Starzysko, the novel depicts the physical and psychological pressures on four women who form a surrogate family. Three of the women dedicate themselves to sustaining the secret pregnancy of the fourth. The novel explores their moral struggles and fear of degenerating. One character reflects, "Two kinds of evil ... were at work here. The first came from outside ... lurking in hunger, in typhus and the bitter dust. The other evil was new. It came from within" (121).

Karmel, who remained close to her sister, Henia Karmel-Wolfe, also a novelist, married physicist Francis Zucker, who had immigrated to the U.S. from Germany in 1938. The couple lived in Belmont, Massachusetts, taking frequent trips to Germany for Zucker's work. Karmel taught creative writing at the Massachusetts Institute of Technology, where she received the Dean's Award for Distinguished Service in 1994. M.I.T. further recognized Karmel by establishing the Ilona Karmel Writing Prizes to mark her retirement in 1995. Karmel died from leukemia.

[Sara Horowitz (2nd ed.)]

KARMI (Crémieux), French rabbinic family of the 18th century, consisting of Mordecai and Solomon Ḥayyim, the sons of Abraham, a learned merchant, and Moses, son of Solomon Ḥayyim and son-in-law of Mordecai. MORDECAI KARMI (1749–1825) was born in Carpentras. When Ḥ.J.D. Azulai was there in 1777 as an emissary of the Ereẓ Israel community, he became friendly with the Karmi family. Toward the end of his life Mordecai served as rabbi in Aix-en-Provence. He is the same Mordecai Crémieux who financed the edition of *Seder ha-Tamid*, the first prayer book of daily and Sabbath prayers according to the Provençal rite. He wrote *Ma'amar Mordekhai*, in two parts (Leghorn, 1784–86), an extensive commentary on the Shulḥan Arukh, *Oraḥ Ḥayyim*. At the beginning of the work there is a poem by the author's father in honor of his son and prefaces by his brother Solomon Ḥayyim and Solomon's son Moses. The work also contains *hassagot* ("criticisms") on Azulai's *Birkei Yosef*. This gave rise to a sharp rejoinder by Azulai in his *Maḥazik Berakhah* (Leghorn, 1785), in which he remarked that it was not fitting that he should reply and was doing so only out of fear that his silence would be taken as a justification of Karmi's strictures. Karmi again replied in a special work entitled *Divrei Mordekhai* (Leghorn, 1787). His brother SOLOMON ḤAYYIM was born in the middle of the 18th century in Carpentras, where he served as rabbi after the death of his father. At the age of 18 he compiled *Ḥeshek Shelomo*, a supercommentary on Rashi's commentary to the Pentateuch. Solomon Ḥayyim's son MOSES (1766–1837) was born in Carpentras, but in 1790, together with his father and his uncle, moved to Aix, where he was appointed rabbi. He wrote *Ho'il Moshe Be'er*, a supercommentary in 12 volumes to Abraham ibn Ezra's commentary to some of the books of the Pentateuch and to Proverbs, Job, and the Five *Scrolls (only vols. 1–6 and 12 were printed; Aix, 1833–36). He also published, under the same title, a commentary to the prayer book according to the Provençal rite (six volumes, Aix, 1829–35).

BIBLIOGRAPHY: Ghirondi-Neppi, 241–3; Gross, Gal Jud, 263; M. Benayahu, *R. Ḥayyim Yosef David Azulai* (1959), 118–21, 367–78; Roth, in: *Journal of Jewish Bibliography*, 1 (1939), 103 f.; S. Wiener, *Kehillat Moshe*, 1 (1918), 359–62.

[Yehoshua Horowitz]

KARMI, DOV (1905–1962), Israel architect. Karmi was born in Russia and went to Palestine in 1921. He studied art in Jerusalem and architecture in Ghent. He began work as an independent architect in the early 1930s, mainly in Tel Aviv. Karmi belonged to the first generation of architects of the new Jewish settlement in Ereẓ Israel. He occupied an important place in the creation of a modern architectural style for the country and in creating prototypes, especially in domestic and commercial building styles. He was one of a group of architects who developed a unique Bauhaus style for Tel Aviv, later recognized by UNESCO as a world heritage site. He emphasized simplicity and functionalism. Karmi designed and built many public buildings and offices, including the Histadrut building in Tel Aviv, the Sherman (Administration) Building and the Wise Auditorium of the Hebrew University in Jerusalem, the El Al Building in Tel Aviv, the two buildings of the Tel Aviv Cameri Theater, and, together with Z. *Rechter, Tel Aviv's Heikhal ha-Tarbut (Mann Auditorium). In 1957 he was awarded the Israel Prize for architecture.

[Abraham Erlik / Shaked Gilboa (2nd ed.)]

KARMI'EL (Heb. כַּרְמִיאֵל; "Vineyard of God," alluding to the Bet ha-Kerem Valley and neighboring Majd al-Kurūm), town in Israel, 14 mi. (22 km.) E. of Acre. Its construction as a development town, in connection with the Central Galilee Development Project, began in 1963, and the first inhabitants arrived in 1964. In 1969, Karmi'el had 1,740 inhabitants, comprised of about 40% veteran Israelis, 40% immigrants from Eastern Europe (mainly Romania), and 20% immigrants from North Africa and North and South America. Anticipated to serve as an urban center for existing Arab villages of a fairly wide periphery and Jewish villages to be founded in the area, Karmi'el hardly exercised these functions in its initial years. On the other hand, its economic development was satisfactory, with 75% of its manpower employed in local industrial enterprises and workshops. In 1984 Karmi'el received municipal status. By the mid-1990s its population had risen to approximately 30,800, further increasing to 42,400 in 2002, including 17,000 new immigrants. Commensurate with its population increase, Karmi'el underwent vast expansion, with seven new neighborhoods created and a municipal area extending over 10 sq. mi. (26 sq. km.). ORT's Braude College of Engineering, with approximately 3,500 students, is located in the city. Every summer Karmi'el hosts an international folk dancing festival.

BIBLIOGRAPHY: E. Spiegel, *New Towns in Israel* (Eng. and Germ., 1966), 173–8. **WEBSITE:** www.karmiel.muni.il.

[Efraim Orni /Shaked Gilboa (2nd ed.)]

KARMINSKI, HANNAH (1897–1942), German social worker. Born in Berlin, she taught at a Jewish kindergarten. After moving to Frankfurt, she took charge of a club for young girls. Here she met famous Jewish personalities who had a decisive influence on her future development. She made the acquaintance of Franz *Rosenzweig and Bertha *Pappenheim who persuaded her to work for the Juedische Frauenbund ("Jewish Women's Organization"). Hannah Karminski was appointed secretary general of this organization, which developed rapidly under her leadership. From 1924 she edited the Frauenbund's monthly journal, *Die Blaetter des juedischen Frauenbundes*. When Hitler's Gestapo ordered the organization to terminate its activities, Hannah Karminski became a leading figure in the work of the *Reichsvertretung (later Reichsvereinigung) der Juden in Deutschland, a body set up by the Nazis to represent the Jewish community and to manage its affairs. Hannah Karminski continued working until 1942 under incredibly difficult conditions. She was arrested while seriously ill and died on the way to a concentration camp in the East.

BIBLIOGRAPHY: E.G. Loewenthal, *Bewaehrung im Untergang* (1965), 89–93. **ADD. BIBLIOGRAPHY:** G. Maierhof, "Bleiben oder Gehen – Die Diskussion um Auswanderung im jüdischen Frauenbund in den Jahren 1933 bis 1938," in: *Exil – Emigration*, 32 (1997), 8–14.

[Giora Lotan]

KARMINSKI, SIR SEYMOUR EDWARD (1902–1974), English judge. Born in London, Karminski was admitted to the bar in 1925 and specialized in divorce cases. During World War II he served in the Royal Navy, becoming lieutenant commander in 1943. In 1945 he was made a king's counsel and in 1951 was appointed judge of the divorce division of the High Court of Justice. He was senior judge of the divorce division for several years until his promotion to lord justice of appeal in 1969. Karminski was an active figure in the Jewish community as chairman of the London Jewish Board of Guardians (later the Jewish Welfare Board). He was a prominent member of the West London Reform Synagogue. In 1967 Karminski became a member of the privy council.

[Israel Finestein]

KARMIYYAH (Heb. כַּרְמִיָּה), kibbutz in the southern Coastal Plain of Israel, near the Gaza Strip, about 5 mi. (9 km.) S.W. of Ashkelon, affiliated to Ha-Kibbutz ha-Arẓi Ha-Shomer ha-Ẓa'ir. It was founded in 1950 by a group of pioneers from France and Tunisia. Newcomers from Argentina later made up the majority of the members. Field crops, citrus groves, and dairy cattle constituted the principal farm branches. The kibbutz also started up a textile and leather factory. In 2002 the population was 326. Nearby is the Shikmah Dam, a pilot water storage plant where winter floodwaters of Naḥal Shikmah are filtered through porous sand dunes and stored underground. Thus protected from evaporation losses, they are recovered through wells for use in summer. The name Karmiyyah, which is derived from the Hebrew *kerem* ("vineyard"), also refers to the Hebrew form of Adolphe *Crémieux's name.

[Efraim Orni]

KARMON, ISRAEL (1915–1982), cantor and opera administrator. Karmon was a native of Vilna where he sang in the choir of the Vilna Great Synagogue with the cantor Gershon Sirota. He immigrated to Palestine in 1936 and studied at the Hebrew University, Jerusalem, in the department of fine arts. He was a cantor in Tel Aviv and also administrator of the Israel National Opera Company. From 1954 until his death in 1982 he was cantor of the Jewish community in Basle. He appeared in concerts in Europe and made records of cantorial music.

[Akiva Zimmerman (2nd ed.)]

KARNAIM (Heb. קַרְנַיִם), city of Bashan, associated with *Ashteroth in Genesis 14:5; in the Book of Jubilees, it is mentioned as one of the cities of the *Rephaim (29:11). Amos probably alludes to the capture of Karnaim by Jeroboam II (6:13). After the destruction of Ashteroth by Tiglath-Pileser, Karnaim became the capital of Bashan and gave its name to the Assyrian district of Qarnini. Judah Maccabee conquered the city in his campaign to Gilead (I Macc. 5:43; the Karnion mentioned in II Macc. 12:21 seems to be a different locality). It appears in Midrash *Ruth Rabbah* 2:10 as Kiryanos (קרינוס). Eusebius identifies Karnaim with the village of Karnaia in Arabia, "where the house of Job is shown" (Onom. 112:3ff.). This would place the ancient site at Sheikh Saʿad in Bashan, 3¾ mi. (6 km.) south of Nawā, where neo-Hittite sculpture and a stele of Ramses II (known locally as "Job's Stone") have been found.

BIBLIOGRAPHY: Albright, in: BASOR, 19 (1925), 14–15; E. Schumacher, *Across the Jordan* (1886), 187–8; Abel, Geog, 2 (1938), 413–4; Aharoni, Land, index.

[Michael Avi-Yonah]

KARNEI SHOMRON (Heb. קרני שומרון), urban community in Samaria. The settlement is located 13 mi. (20 km.) east of *Kefar Sava, in the Samarian foothills, and occupies an area of 3 sq. mi. (7.5 sq. km.). Karnei Shomron was founded in 1977 by a group of young families. The first settlers lived in temporary houses, until their permanent homes were built. The town received municipal council status in 1991. In 2002 its population was 6,100, including 200 immigrant families from English-speaking countries. An industrial zone near the settlement houses workshops. During the second Intifada, the settlement was attacked by terrorists: a women was killed in 2001 and three teenagers in 2002.

[Shaked Gilboa (2nd ed.)]

KARNI (Volovelski), YEHUDA (1884–1949), Hebrew poet. Born in Pinsk, his first Hebrew poem was printed in *Ha-Ẓefirah* when he was 12. In 1921 he settled in Palestine and from 1923 until his death was on the editorial board of the daily *Haaretz*.

Karni's early poetry, influenced by *Bialik and *Tchernichowsky, was individualistic, romantic, and abstract. His settling in Palestine brought about a radical change in his creative spirit. He was one of the first Hebrew poets who abandoned the Ashkenazi accentuation and shifted to the new Sephardi accent thus bringing his diction closer to rhythms of spoken Hebrew. His poetry became more concrete, reflecting the new landscape and his personal struggle for identity against the backdrop of the complex political, cultural, and economic issues which agitated the small Jewish community of mandatory Palestine. Particularly distinctive is his volume *Shirei Yerushalayim* (1948). Jerusalem in this volume looms as the eternal symbol of the people and its destiny. Although he encounters a city in apparently hopeless stagnation and decay, he senses the deeper, historical levels of consciousness of eternal Jerusalem. At the same time, he captures the concrete beauty of the Jerusalem landscape. In his last years Karni lamented the victims of the Holocaust. The poet's characteristics as moralist, lamenter, and artist were also evident in the articles and essays that appeared almost daily in *Haaretz* for 25 years. His other poetic works include *She'arim* (1923), *Bi-She'arayikh Moledet* (1935), *Shir ve-Dema* (1948), *Bimah Ketannah*, selected poetry and prose (1951), *Yalkut Shirim shel Yehuda Karni*, with introduction by Y. Ogen (1966). A collection of his poems (*Shirim*) with an introduction by Dan Miron appeared in 1992. A list of his works translated into English appears in Goell, Bibliography, 31, 100.

BIBLIOGRAPHY: S. Halkin, *Arai va-Keva* (1942), 113–23, 190; B.I. Michali, *Leyad ha-Ovnayim* (1959), 55–72; J. Keshet, *Maskiyyot* (1953), 183–204; R. Wallenrod, *The Literature of Modern Israel* (1956), index. **ADD. BIBLIOGRAPHY:** S. Abramsky, "'*Me-al Har ha-Ẓofim' be-Mikhlol Shirat Yehuda Karni*," in: *Alon la-Moreh le-Sifrut*, 14 (1993), 110–17; N. Bacharach, "*Diyyun bi-Shenei Shirim al Yerushalayim (Amichai ve-Karni)*," in: *Alon la-Moreh le-Sifrut*, 17 (1998), 58–67.

[Yitzhak Ogen]

KARNIOL, ALTER YEHIEL (1855–1929), *ḥazzan*. Born in 1855 in Dzialoszyce, Kielce province, Poland, he sang with several *ḥazzanim* in Hungary and then officiated in various congregations. In 1886 he was appointed *ḥazzan* for life by the congregation of Pecs, in Hungary, but resigned after seven years to go to the Ohab Zedek synagogue of New York. In 1898 he returned to Russia as *ḥazzan* of the Great Synagogue of Odessa. He refused then an invitation to join the Odessa Opera. When the pogroms broke out in 1905 he returned to the United States and was ultimately re-engaged as *ḥazzan* of Ohab Zedek. Karniol was noted for the extraordinary quality of his tenor which could also reach to the bass register. His style, intensely emotional, is conveyed only imperfectly in the recordings which he made in the U.S.

BIBLIOGRAPHY: Jewish Ministers Cantors' Association of America, *Di Geshikhte fun Khazones* (1924), 181–2; E. Zaludkowski, *Kultur Treger fun der Yidishe Liturgie* (1930), 330–1; H.H. Harris, *Toledot ha-Neginah ve-ha-Ḥazzanut be-Yisrael* (1950), 450–1.

[Joshua Leib Ne'eman]

KARP, ABRAHAM J. (1921–2003), U.S. Conservative rabbi and scholar. Karp, who was born in Amidur, Poland, was taken to the United States in 1930. He was educated at Yeshiva University (B.A. 1942) and the Jewish Theological Seminary, where he was ordained in 1945. For a time he served as assistant director of the Seminary College and director of the Metropolitan New York Region of the United Synagogue of America. He then held pulpits in Swampscott, Mass. (1948–1951), and Kansas City, Mo. (1951–1956) working with Gerson Hadas. From 1956 he was rabbi of Temple Beth El of Rochester, N.Y. He was also active in the Rabbinical Assembly serving as a member of the Cabinet, the Executive Council and on the editorial committee of the Joint Prayer Book Commission and of *Conservative Judaism*. While serving at Beth El, Karp became well known as an important scholar of American Judaism. He was a visiting professor at Dartmouth College (1967) and at the Hebrew University in Jerusalem; he taught American Jewish history at the Jewish Theological Seminary (1967–71, 1976). He left his rabbinic duties in 1972 and was the Philip Bernstein Professor of Jewish Studies at the University of Rochester retiring in 1991.

Karp served as president of the American Jewish Historical Society from 1972 to 1975, receiving the society's Lee M. Friedman Medal for distinguished service, and was named fellow of the Jewish Academy of Arts and Science in 1984.

Karp was what one admirer called the "greatest grassroots collector of Judaica in modern history." Rarely spending more than five or ten dollars he combed flea markets and basements, dumpsters and library sales. In the end he amassed a collection of some 3,500 items of Americana Judaica which he gave to the Jewish Theological Seminary in 1990. Prof. Arthur Kiron, curator of Judaica Collections at the University of Pennsylvania Library, called Karp's Americana material "perhaps the finest private collection of its kind ever assembled." In addition to books and manuscripts, the collection included ritual and ceremonial objects, paintings, synagogue records, newspapers, and diaries.

Karp is the author of *New York Chooses a Chief Rabbi* (1955), *Jewish Way of Life* (1962), and *History of the United Synagogue of America* (1964), all of which appeared in issues of the *Publication of the American Jewish Historical Society; Conservative Judaism – The Heritage of Solomon Schechter* (1963); and edited *Jewish Experience in America* (5 vols., 1969). He assisted in the Library of Congress's major exhibition of its Judaic treasures and wrote *From the Ends of the Earth: Judaic Treasures of the Library of Congress* (1991). He also wrote, *Jewish Perceptions of America: From Melting Pot to Mosaic* (1976), *Jewish Continuity in America: Creative Survival in a Free Society* (1998) and *To Give Life: UJA in the Shaping of the American Jewish Community* (1981).

[Jack Reimer / Michael Berenbaum (2nd ed.)]

KARP, MAX and **SOPHIE**, Yiddish actors. Max Karp (1856–1898) joined A. *Goldfaden's company in Odessa. In 1883 he went to London where he married Sophie (Sarah) Goldstein, also a member of the Goldfaden company, the first professional Yiddish actress. After appearances in England, the Karps went to New York in 1888, and appeared in operettas and melodramas. Karp organized the Schiller Dramatic Society (1890). A collection of his poetry was published under the title *Fun Oriental Teater.* Sophie Karp popularized Hurwitz and Sandler's song, "Eli, Eli."

KARPEL, HERMAN (1864–1942), French trade unionist. Karpel emigrated from Russia to France and in 1896 was cofounder of the cap-makers' union, the first Jewish trade union in France. Until 1914 Karpel played an active part in the Jewish labor movement in France. At the height of the *Dreyfus Affair in 1898, Karpel published a pamphlet entitled: *"Le Proletariat Juif. Lettre des ouvriers Juifs de Paris au Parti Socialiste Français,"* which was an appeal by French Jewish workers to their non-Jewish comrades to join the fight against antisemitism. The pamphlet also pointed out the danger of ignoring antisemitism and the mistake in the belief that the Jewish people consisted entirely of capitalists.

BIBLIOGRAPHY: Z. Szajkowski, *Etyudn tsu der Geshikhte fun Ayngevandertn Yidishn Yishuv in Frankraykh*, 2 vols. (1936–37), index; idem, *Di Profesyonele Bavegung Tsvishn di Yidishe Arbeter in Frankraykh biz 1914* (1937); E. Tcherikower and Z. Szajkowski, in: *Yidn in Frankraykh*, 2 (1942), 163–92.

KARPELES, GUSTAV (Gershon; 1848–1909), literary historian. Karpeles, who was born in Einwanowitz, Moravia, devoted himself to literary research in German and Jewish literature. One of his first studies was a biographical sketch, published anonymously, of Azriel *Hildesheimer (1870). In 1870 he became editor of the weekly *Juedische Presse*, founded by the latter, and at the same time of the German literary journal *Auf der Hoehe*. Karpeles edited the literary supplement of the *Breslauer Zeitung* and from 1878 to 1883 the influential *Westermanns Monatshefte*. In 1890 he became editor of the *Allgemeine Zeitung des Judentums*, and in 1898 editor of the *Jahrbuch fuer juedische Geschichte und Literatur.* This publication was a sequel to the founding of the Berlin Verein fuer juedische Geschichte und Literatur, by Karpeles, in association with others, an example soon followed by many other communities in Germany. These were eventually united, under his leadership, into the Verband der Vereine fuer juedische Geschichte und Literatur (1893). Karpeles published five books on *Heine, and four editions of his work. His writings include *Goethe in Polen* (1890), *Allgemeine Geschichte der Literatur*... (2 vols., 1891), and *Litterarisches Wanderbuch* (1898). His most important contribution to Jewish scholarship was the two-volume *Geschichte der juedischen Literatur* (1886, 1920–21^3; partial tr. *History of Jewish Literature*, n.d.). Smaller works in this field are his *Die Frauen der juedischen Literatur* (1871); *Zionsharfe*, a German anthology of medieval Hebrew poetry (1889); and *Sechs Vortraege ueber die Geschichte der Juden* (1896; *A Sketch of Jewish History*, 1897). Also in English appeared *Jews and Judaism in the 19th Century* (1905). Karpeles was not an original or profound scholar, but he did much to popularize Jewish literature and history.

BIBLIOGRAPHY: K. Kohler, *Living Faith* (1948), 227ff. (= AJHSP, 19 (1910), 184–9); G. Kisch (ed.), *The Breslau Seminary* (1963), 422 (incl. bibl.); M. Levin, in: JJGL, 13 (1910), 1ff.; Waxman, Literature, 3 (1960), 618–21.

[Sol Liptzin]

KARPF, MAURICE JOSEPH (1891–1964), U.S. psychologist, social worker, and marriage counselor. Karpf, who was born in Austria, was brought to the U.S. as a boy, and studied sociology and psychology at Columbia University. After being employed as a psychologist in the Chicago school system (1912–14, 1916–18), he was superintendent of the Jewish Social Service Bureau, Chicago (1919–25), director and president of the faculty of the graduate school of Jewish Social Work in New York (1924–42), and executive director of the Federation of Jewish Welfare Organizations in Los Angeles (1942–47). Active in Jewish affairs, he served as president of the National Conference of Jewish Welfare (1930–32), chairman of the International Conference of Jewish Social Work (1932–35), and non-Zionist member of the Executive of the Jewish Agency for Palestine (1930–45). His works include: *The Scientific Basis of Social Work* (1931) and *Jewish Community Organization in the United States* (1938).

BIBLIOGRAPHY: M.H. Neumeyer, in: *American Sociological Review*, 29 (1964), 753.

KARPINOVITSH, AVROM (1918–2004), Yiddish writer. Born in Vilna, he studied at the Vilna Realgymnasium where his teachers included the poet M. *Kulbak and the literary historian Max *Erik. He left Vilna in 1937 for Birobidjan, returning in 1944. Intercepted by the British in 1947 as an illegal immigrant to Palestine, he was interned in Cyprus, reached Israel in 1949, and settled in Tel Aviv, where he became the administrator of the Israel Philharmonic Orchestra. Throughout his career his writing remained focused on the life of Vilna's Jews. His collections *Af Vilner Gasn* ("On Vilna Streets," 1981), *Vilne, Mayn Vilne* ("Vilna, My Vilna," 1993), *Geven, Geven Amol Vilne* ("Once, Once There Was Vilna," 1997), among others, recapture the atmosphere of prewar Vilna Jewish society – not the city of high culture but the colorful Jewish underworld. He evokes its characters with humor, affection, and humanity, in an expressive Lithuanian Yiddish. His friend, poet Avrom *Sutskever, said that apart from Chaim *Grade no one could write about Vilna as well as Karpinovitsh. A passionate supporter of Yiddish culture, he co-edited the second *Almanakh fun di Yidishe Shrayber in Yisroel* (1967) and was a frequent contributor to the quarterly *Di Goldene Keyt* and the newspaper *Letste Nayes*.

BIBLIOGRAPHY: M. Ravitch, *Mayn Leksikon*, 3 (1958), 366f. **ADD. BIBLIOGRAPHY:** H. Beer, in: *Jewish Writers of the Twentieth Century* (2003), 274–5; S. Bickel, *Shrayber fun Mayn Dor*, 3 (1970), 346–51; A. Golumb, in: *Di Goldene Keyt*, 60 (1967), 256ff.; A. Karpinovitsh, in: *Di Pen* (Feb. 1995), 33–6 (interview).

[Israel Ch. Biletzky / Heather Valencia (2nd ed.)]

KARPLUS, HEINRICH (1905–1988), Israeli pathologist and founder of forensic medicine in Israel. Born in Vienna, he was the son of Johan Paul Karplus, known Viennese experimental neurophysiologist. Karplus graduated from the medical faculty of Vienna in 1930 and was a pupil of the Jewish pathologist Jakob Erdheim. He established the Institute of Pathology at the Hadassah Tel Aviv Municipal Hospital and directed it from 1936 to 1945, and became involved in forensic medicine. Trained in forensic medicine at Stockholm University (1945–49), he returned to Israel as advisor to the IDF and director of the department of pathology of the newly established Tel Hashomer army hospital. He established and directed the National Leopold Greenberg Institute of Forensic Medicine in Abu-Kabir from 1955 to 1974. He was known for his academic independence and uncompromising adherence to truth and moral principles. He initiated the first regional Traumatology CPC conferences in 1966 which improved the care of patients with multiple injuries. He was professor of forensic medicine at the Hebrew University of Jerusalem and at Tel Aviv University, and educated generations of physicians, lawyers, and criminologists. After his retirement he devoted himself to the study of ethics and the history of medicine.

[Bracha Rager (2nd ed.)]

KARS (originally **Karpeles**), **JIŘÍ** (1882–1945), painter and graphic artist. Kars was born into a German family in Kralupy, Bohemia. After travels in Spain and Portugal he settled in Paris in 1907. After the Nazi occupation in 1940, he escaped to Switzerland. Kars experimented in formalistic constructivism, but after 1918 turned to figurative paintings of classical composition. His work was characterized by deep lyricism and intense sorrow, occasionally overcome by explosions of brilliant color. His life work was honored by one of the first large-scale postwar exhibitions held in Prague. Shortly afterward, Kars fell victim to a depression resulting from his war experiences and committed suicide.

BIBLIOGRAPHY: Thieme-Becker, 19 (1936), s.v.; Roth, Art, 661; *Příruční slovník naučný* 2 (1963), s.v.

[Avigdor Dagan]

KARSEN, FRITZ (1885–1951), educator. Born in Breslau, Germany, Karsen began his educational career in Berlin as a secondary school teacher. In 1920, at the national school conference he presented the Einheitsschule (unified primary school) idea, which aimed at the mixing of social classes. His major achievement during this period was the organization and direction, 1921–33, of a school complex (from kindergarten through secondary school), the Karl Marx School in Berlin-Neukoelln. He introduced various new procedures in these schools, such as individualized instruction, pupil government, and activity method. Karsen undertook study trips to the U.S. and the U.S.S.R. His plans for an elaboration of his school organization to include young people aged 18 to 19 were halted by the advent of the Nazis. In 1933 Karsen left Germany and settled permanently in New York, where he served as professor of German at City College and professor of education at Brooklyn College. From 1946 to 1948, Karsen served as higher education specialist in the U.S. military government in Germany. The recognition of his educational work in Germany was commemorated by the establishment of the Fritz Karsen School in Berlin. Karsen's main writings include *Die Schule der werdenden Gesellschaft* (1921), *Deutsche Versuchsschulen der Gegenwart und ihre Probleme* (1923), and *Die neue Schulen in Deutschland* (1924), which he edited. He died in Guayaquil (Ecuador).

BIBLIOGRAPHY: A. Ehrentreich, in: *Bildung und Erziehung*, 5 (Jan. 1952), 22–28. **ADD. BIBLIOGRAPHY:** G. Radde, *Fritz Karsen – Ein Berliner Schulreformer in der Weimarer Zeit* (1973); J.P. Eickhoff, *Fritz Karsen – Ein Wegbereiter der modernen Erlebnispädagogik* (1997); J.J. Choi, *Reformpädagogik als Utopie – Der Einheitsschulgedanke bei Paulo Oestreich und Fritz Karsen* (2004).

[William W. Brickman]

KARSKI, JAN (1914–2000), member of the Polish underground in World War II; Righteous Among the Nations. Born Jan Kozielewski, before the war Karski studied law and diplomatic sciences at Jan Kazimierz University in Lwow (Lvov), and in late 1939, after the German occupation, he joined the Polish underground. Because of his knowledge of languages and foreign countries, he served as a courier between the government-in-exile and the underground. In this capacity, he made several secret trips to France and England. On the eve of one of these trips, in the summer of 1942, he was asked to meet two Jewish leaders of the Warsaw ghetto (Menachem Kirschenbaum and Leon Feiner) to transmit a message to the Polish government-in-exile in London concerning the extermination of the Jewish population then taking place. They spelled out to him the utter hopelessness of their predicament – this was the end of the Jewish people on Polish soil. As they told him: "You other Poles are fortunate. You are suffering too. Many of you will die, but at least your nation goes on living. After the war Poland will be resurrected. Your cities will be rebuilt and your wounds will slowly heal. From this ocean of tears, pain, rage, and humiliation your country will emerge again but the Polish Jews will no longer exist. We will be dead. Hitler will lose his war against the human, the just, and the good, but he will win his war against the Polish Jews. No – it will not be a victory; the Jewish people will be murdered." They urged Karski to call upon the Jewish leaders in the free world to stage a hunger strike in front of the offices of the English and American authorities, to move them to action. Fearing that his report on the fate of the Jews would be received with skepticism, Karski asked to be smuggled inside the Warsaw ghetto to be able to say that his report was based on what he saw with his own eyes. Still not satisfied with this, Karski asked to be smuggled into one of the camps. Dressed as one of the Latvian camp guards, Karski again witnessed, from a safe distance, the brutality which accompanied the unloading of Jews from the deportation wagons. Later, in London, he met the Bund representative Samuel *Zygelbojm, to whom Karski relayed the appeal by the Warsaw ghetto to Jewish leaders. Zygelbojm, who later committed suicide, felt that this approach would not produce any results. Shaken but resolved to carry the message of Polish Jewry to the United States, Karski arrived there in 1943 and personally reported to President *Roosevelt and other high American officials. Roosevelt listened attentively to the relation of events inside Poland, but when it came to the Jewish part, Karski felt that what he said fell on deaf ears. Karski emphasized: "The Jewish leaders are totally helpless. The Poles can save only individuals, they cannot stop extermination. Only the powerful Allied leaders can do that." Roosevelt closed the 90-minute meeting with assurances that the Poles had a friend in the White House; that those guilty would be punished, and that justice and freedom would prevail. Karski also met with American Jewish leader and Supreme Court justice Felix *Frankfurter. When Karski finished, Frankfurter said: "I am unable to believe you." Karski continued to address audiences, and plead for the rescue of the Jews. His book *Story of a Secret State* became a Book-of-the-Month Club selection. But frustration soon set in, as he realized that all he was getting was applause, not action. Settling in the United States, he earned a doctorate from Georgetown University, where he taught political science. After a long period of silence, he was persuaded by Elie *Wiesel in 1980 to speak up again, and subsequently appeared in public on numerous occasions. He was especially pained at the silence of the world's leaders about the massacre of the Jews. "All those great individuals, presidents, ambassadors, cardinals, who said they were shocked; they lied. They knew or didn't want to know. This shocked me." In 1982, on a visit to Yad Vashem, he was declared a Righteous Among the Nations.

BIBLIOGRAPHY: Yad Vashem Archives M31–934; J. Karski, *Story of a Secret State* (1944), 321ff.; T. Wood and S. Jankowski, *Karski* (1996); M. Paldiel, *Saving the Jews* (2000), 40–44; I. Gutman (ed.), *Encyclopedia of the Righteous Among the Nations: Poland*, Vol. 1 (2004), 337–38.

[Mordecai Paldiel (2nd ed.)]

KARTELL-CONVENT DER VERBINDUNGEN DEUTSCHER STUDENTEN JUEDISCHEN GLAUBENS (KC), an umbrella organization of German Jewish student fraternities, founded in 1896. Fraternities of Jewish students were established (the first founded in Breslau, Oct. 23, 1886) in reaction to the mounting wave of antisemitism and the exclusion of Jews from German student fraternities. They adopted from their German counterparts not only the student rituals but also dress, manners, and all their activities. In this way they attempted to establish their equality by outdrinking and outfighting them. Special emphasis was put on Jewish honor in the face of antisemitism, especially the question of "*Satisfaktionsfaehigkeit*," the right and capability of a Jew to be considered an opponent in a duel. The critical attitude of the KC toward the Jewish nationalist movement and political Zionism led students with differing views, particularly those from Eastern Europe, to found their own organizations, first the two branches of Bund Juedischer Corporationen and the Kartell Zionistischer Verbindungen, later amalgamating into the *Kartell Juedischer Verbindungen (KJV), which focused on the enhancement of Jewish consciousness and Jewish nationalism. Many prominent figures were members of the KC, such as Ludwig *Hollaender, leader of the *Central-Verein. The KC was an association of fraternities at numerous German universities such as Heidelberg, Berlin, Munich, Freiburg, Leipzig, Frankfurt, and others. Membership of the KC increased from 836 in 1913 to approximately 2,100 in 1933. The KC published the *KC-Blaetter* from 1910 until 1933, when Hitler assumed power and the fraternities were dissolved. Its alumni, the so-called *Alte Herren* ("Old Boys"), were organized in separate organizations which continued to exist outside Germany after World War II.

BIBLIOGRAPHY: Wiener Library, *German Jewry*… (1958), index; Asch and Philippson, in: YLBI, 3 (1958), 122–39; A. Asch, *Geschichte des KC (Kartellverband juedischer Studenten) im Lichte der deutschen kulturellen und politischen Entwicklung* (1964); *Kartell-Convent Jahrbuch* (1906–); H. Berlak, *Kartell Convent der Verbindungen deutscher Studenten juedischen Glaubens*… (1927). **ADD. BIBLIOGRAPHY:** K.H. Pickus, *Constructing Modern Identities. Jewish University Students in Germany 1815–1914* (1999); M. Ruerup, "Juedische Studentenverbindungen im Kaiserreich. Organisationen zur Abwehr des Antisemitismus auf 'studentische Art,'" in: *Jahrbuch fuer Antisemitismusforschung*, 10 (2000), 113–137; T. Schindler, *Studentischer Antisemitismus und juedische Studentenverbindungen 1880–1933*, (1988); L. Swartout, "Culture Wars. Protestant, Catholic and Jewish Students at German Universities, 1890–1914," in: M. Geyer and H. Lehmnann (eds.), *Religion und Nation* (2004).

[Miriam Ruerup (2nd ed.)]

KARTELL JUEDISCHER VERBINDUNGEN (KJV), an umbrella organization of Jewish university student fraternities in Germany. It was a fusion of two groups. One of them, the Bund juedischer Corporationen (BJC), was formed in 1901 and was composed of the Jewish student fraternity, Verein Juedischer Studenten (VJST), founded in Berlin in 1895, and similar groups in Leipzig, Breslau and Munich. In the following years the BJC established new groups in Strasbourg, Freiburg, Koenigsberg. Marburg, Bonn, Heidelberg, and Frankfurt. The BJC formulated its aims as follows: "… to function as the meeting center of all Jewish students who consciously feel themselves Jews and are willing to collaborate in the development of living Judaism." The second group, Kartell Zionistischer Verbindungen (KZV), was formed in 1906 by Hasmonaea, the first explicitly Zionist students' fraternity (founded in Berlin in 1902), and Jordania (Munich, 1905). A year later the Ivria (Freiburg i. Br.) joined the association. Gradually the BJC adopted an increasingly Zionist program. Thus in July 1914 both groups united in the KJV, which was dedicated to educate its members to strive for "national unity of the Jewish community" and for a "renewal in Ereẓ-Israel."

After World War I the Zionist orientation dominated the organization: the German students' habits such as fencing and beer drinking were no longer compulsory but only optional, differing from university to university. Instead more emphasis was put on *ḥaluẓiyyut* – whose aims were settling in Palestine and studying Hebrew. One group within the KJV was dissatisfied with this development and after a central convention (Kartelltag) of the KJV in 1919 established the Bund Zionistischer Korporationen (BZK), consisting primarily of the *Alte*

Herren ("Old Boys") and university students in Berlin, Breslau, and Frankfurt, insisting on purely Zionist work. The BZK rejoined the KJV in 1929, however, when the latter officially adopted the *Basle Program as the basis of its activities. In the 1920s the KJV had a short period of cooperation with the *Blau-Weiss; fusion between the two groups was only temporary. Already in 1924 the KJV established a branch in Palestine. The KJV was active until 1933, when Hitler assumed power. By that time the organization had some 2,000 members, of whom over 1,200 so-called *Alte Herren* had entered professional life after their university studies. The Alte Herren were organized into 14 district associations and conducted local Zionist activities. By 1933 the KJV had branches at 20 German universities. Its organs were *Der juedische Student* (Berlin, 1902–33), and *Der juedische Wille* (1918–20, revived in 1933, and existed till 1937 as continuation of *Der juedische Student*). The KJV groups in Palestine, operating in Jerusalem, Tel Aviv, and Haifa, continued to meet for the next few decades. But the KJV itself was not reactivated after World War II.

BIBLIOGRAPHY: S. Kanowitz, *Zionistische Jugendbewegung* (1927). **ADD. BIBLIOGRAPHY:** W. Gross, "The Zionist Students' Movement," in: LBI-YB, 4 (1959), 143–164; Z. Rosenkranz, "'Der Zionismus des Dreinschlagens.' Die Rituale der nationaljuedischen und zionistischen Studenten im ausgehenden Kaiserreich," in: *Menora. Jahrbuch fuer deutsch-juedische Geschichte* (1992), 63–84; M. Ruerup, "Gefundene Heimat? Palaestinafahrten national-juedischer deutscher Studentenverbindungen 1913/1914," in: *Leipziger Beitraege zur juedischen Geschichte und Kultur*, 2 (2004), 167–189; M. Zimmermann, "Jewish Nationalism and Zionism in German-Jewish Students' Organisations," in: LBI-YB, 27 (1982), 129–153.

[Oskar K. Rabinowicz / Miriam Ruerup (2nd ed.)]

KARU (Krupnik), BARUCH (1899–1972), Hebrew writer, journalist, editor, and translator. Born in Chernevtsy (Podolia), Karu lived in Warsaw until World War I. He spent the war years in Berne, and subsequently settled in Berlin where he served on the editorial board of the German *Encyclopaedia Judaica* and the Hebrew encyclopedia *Eshkol*. In 1932 he moved to Tel Aviv, where he joined the staff of the daily newspaper **Haaretz*. From 1942 until his retirement in 1962 he served on the editorial board of the daily *Ha-Boker*. He first began publishing in **Ha-Shiloaḥ* in 1911 and contributed articles regularly on literature, science, and other topics to the Hebrew press. His many publications include a talmudic dictionary *Millon Shimmushi la-Talmud* (1927), a literary encyclopedia *Enẓiklopedyah le-Sifrut Yisre'elit u-Khelalit* (1942–61), an Aramaic dictionary, *Millon ha-Aramit ha-Ḥayyah ba-Ivrit she-bi-Khetav u-ve-Dibbur* (1967), and many translations into Hebrew.

BIBLIOGRAPHY: M. Mevorakh, *Deyokna'ot Soferim* (1956), 171; A. Cohen, *Soferim Ivriyyim Benei Zemannenu* (1964), 361–3; Kressel, Leksikon, 2 (1967), 794–5.

[Getzel Kressel]

KASABI, JOSEPH BEN NISSIM (17th century), Turkish rabbi. Kasabi was a pupil of Joseph *Trani and was regarded as one of the outstanding halakhists of Constantinople. Problems were addressed to him from Bosnia, Belgrade, Salonika, Bucharest, and elsewhere, and among his halakhic correspondents were Abraham *Rosanes, Moses *Benveniste, and Jacob *Alfandari. Kasabi migrated to Adrianople but subsequently returned to Constantinople. Most of his sermons were lost in the great fire of 1669. Some of his halakhic rulings are cited in the *Penei Moshe* of Moses Benveniste, some in the *Dat ve-Din* of his pupil, Eliezer ibn Shangi, and others in his own *Rav Yosef* which was published by his grandson Moses Kasabi, together with the *Muẓẓal me-Esh* of Jacob and Ḥayyim Alfandari.

BIBLIOGRAPHY: Azulai, 1 (1852), 42a, no. 170; Fuenn, Keneset, 504; Rosanes, Togarmah, 4 (1935), 8–9; Steinschneider, in: JQR, 11 (1898/99), 607; Wolf, Bibliotheca, 3 (1727), 424 no. 967c.

[Simon Marcus]

KASDAN, LAWRENCE EDWARD (1949–), U.S. director, screenwriter, producer. A University of Michigan graduate with a master's degree in education, Kasdan originally worked as an advertising copywriter and submitted his screenplays on the side. In 1976 he sold his first screenplay, *The Bodyguard*, but it was not produced until 1992. His big break came when Steven Spielberg took notice of his 1980 screenplay *Continental Divide* and introduced him to George Lucas. He joined Leigh Brackett to co-write *The Empire Strikes Back* (1980). Spielberg then recruited him to write the first Indiana Jones movie, *Raiders of the Lost Ark* (1981). Kasdan returned to the world of lightsabers in 1983 to pen *Return of the Jedi* (1983) with Lucas. Kasdan stepped behind the camera for the first time in 1981 with his directorial debut of *Body Heat*, which he also wrote. *The Big Chill* (1983) was written, produced, and directed by Kasdan and earned his first Academy Award nomination for Best Original Screenplay. In 1985, he acted in the first of a handful of small roles, portraying the detective #2 in John Landis' *Into the Night*. Kasdan wrote, produced, and directed *The Accidental Tourist* (1988), which was nominated for an Academy Award for Best Picture. He and his wife, Meg Kasdan, co-wrote the Academy Award nominee for Best Original Screenplay *Grand Canyon* (1991), and he directed and produced the movie as well. In 1992, *The Bodyguard* was finally brought to life, but with Kevin Costner as the lead, not Steve McQueen, as Kasdan had originally imagined. It was a huge box-office hit. Other well-known Kasdan projects include *Wyatt Earp* (1994), *Mumford* (1999), and *Dreamcatcher* (2003), based on Stephen King's novel. Kasdan has two sons, Jacob and Jonathan Kasdan, both of whom have followed in their father's footsteps by screenwriting, directing, producing, and acting.

[Susannah Howland (2nd ed.)]

KASEJOVICE (Ger. **Kassowitz, Kasselowitz**), small town in S.E. Bohemia, Czech Republic. One Jewish family is mentioned in Kasejovice in 1570. By the 17th century there was a small community and a cemetery was consecrated in 1669. That same year a conference of notables confirmed the statutes of the Boehmische *Landesjudenschaft in Kasejovice. The community comprised 24 families in 1721, but a synagogue was not built until 1818. Only 28 Jews lived in Kasejovice in 1930. In 1942 all the Jews in the town were deported to the Nazi extermination camps, and the synagogue furniture was sent to the Central Jewish Museum in Prague. The community was not reestablished after World War II, and the synagogue building was used as a local museum. Kasejovice was the first community in which Filip *Bondy preached in Czech.

BIBLIOGRAPHY: B. Mandl, in: JGGJČ, 3 (1931), 275–82; J. Kára, in: H. Gold (ed.), *Juden und Judengemeinden Boehmens* (1934), 261–4.

[Jan Herman]

KASHAN, city in the central part of Iran. Its industrious people made Kashan prosperous, which also benefited the Jewish inhabitants. The beginning of Jewish settlement in Kashan is unknown but the dialect spoken by the Jews points to their antiquity. The earliest reference to the existence of a Jewish community in Kashan may be found in the colophon of a book of prose written in the year 1805; however, there is no doubt that their earliest presence far predated the 15th century. We know that Kashan was a flourishing city before the *Mongol invasion (early 13th century) and, although seriously damaged during the invasion, seems to have been rebuilt. Unlike many cities and towns across Persia populated by Sunni Muslims, Kashan was for the most part Shi'ite. As a result, it did not suffer from the establishment of the Shi'ite Safavid dynasty in the early 16th century, as did other Sunni cities and towns.

However, despite the beauty and prosperity of Kashan, its Jews suffered persecutions. There were several waves of forced conversion in the city. We know of these events from the account by *Babai ibn Lutf, who described the suffering of the Persian Jews between the years just before 1613 and early in 1662. The reign of Shah *Abbas II was particularly hard. From the beginning of 1657 to the beginning of 1662, Jews throughout the country (including 7,000 Jews of Kashan) were forced to convert to Islam. After seven years of apostasy, the Jews of Kashan were allowed to return to Judaism, thanks to the intervention of a Shi'ite priest, learned Sufi, and great poet Mohammad ibn Morteżā Mohsen Fayz (d. 1680), as well as substantial payments to the ruling authorities in Kashan and *Isfahan and a change in local municipal government. According to *Babai ben Farhād, Jews of Kashan suffered persecutions around 1730.

Kashan is reputed for its Jewish poets and scholars such as Judah ben Eleazar, Babai ibn Lutf, Babai ibn Farhād, Samuel Pir Ahmad, Sarmad the Sufi (who later embraced Islam), *Amina, and others. The missionary Stern was twice in Kashan, in 1850 and 1852. He wrote that there lived in Kashan 150 Jewish families in the midst of 30,000 Muslim inhabitants and, due to the prosperity of the town the general condition of the Jews in Kashan was much better than those of Isfahan. On the other hand, *Benjamin II, who was in Kashan about the same time as Stern, claimed that 180 Jewish families lived there in fear. According to Castleman the Jewish community of Kashan consisted of 100 families and most of them were poor. Neumark (1884), who did not visit Kashan, heard that the "plague of Bahaism which afflicted the Jews of Hamadan infected also the Kashani Jews."

According to BAIU (1906) there lived in Kashan 2,000 Jews in 130 houses among 50,000 Muslim inhabitants. A Jewish school was founded in Kashan in 1910 by a local philanthropist named Jekutiel. There were 1,380 Jews living in Kashan in 1943 (*'Ālam-e Yahud*, pp. 379, 472–73). Many of these Jews left Kashan to live in Teheran, London, and Israel. Lord David Alliance, a native of Kashan (b. 1932), who immigrated to London at the age of 17, became one of the greatest textile industrialists in England. At the end of the 20th century, Kashan, which once was called "the Little Jerusalem," ceased to be a dwelling place of Jews.

BIBLIOGRAPHY: *Ālam-e Yahud*, 22 (Jan. 15, 1946) and 28 (Mar. 12, 1946); Benjamin II, *Eight Years in Asia and Africa from 1846 to 1855* (1863); BAIU = *Bulletin de l'Alliance Israélite Universelle*, Paris; Y.F. Castleman, *Massa'ot Shali'aḥ Ẓefat be-Arẓot ha-Mizraḥ* (1942); V.B. Moreen, *Iranian Jewry during the Afghan Invasion* (1990); A. Netzer, "*Redifot u-Shemadot be-Toledot Yehudei Iran ba-Me'ah ha-17*," in: *Pe'amim*, 6 (1980), 32–56; E. Neumark, *Massa be-Ereẓ ha-Kedem*, ed. A. Ya'ari (1947).

[Amnon Netzer (2nd ed.)]

KASHANI, ELIEZER (1923–1947), Jew executed by the British in Palestine. Kashani was born in Petaḥ Tikvah to a poor family with many children. In his youth he was a member of the Maccabi sports organization in which he distinguished himself. Arrested on suspicion of belonging to the underground movement, he was exiled to Eritrea, and in the internment camp joined IẒL. On his release and return to Ereẓ Israel, he became active in the movement, was arrested together with Drezner and Alkaḥi, sentenced to death, and hanged with them.

BIBLIOGRAPHY: Y. Nedava, *Olei-ha-Gardom* (1966); Y. Gurion, *Ha-Nizzaḥon Olei Gardom* (1971).

KASHDAN, ISAAC (1905–1985), U.S. chess master. Born in New York, Kashdan spent 1929–32 in Europe and established himself there with Salo *Flohr as a likely successor to world champion Alexander Alekhine. Although he was one of the strongest players in the world in the early 1930s, Kashdan could not support his family with his chess career, so he became an insurance agent and administrator to earn a living.

Kashdan was a member of the men's U.S. chess team in the 1928, 1930, 1931, 1933, and 1937 Chess Olympiads. He won three gold and one silver medal and 52 games overall, losing only five. He had many notable achievements in non-Olympic tournaments as well. In 1930 he won first prizes in the tournaments in Berlin, Stockholm, and Gyor. He placed second in New York in 1931, and tied for fourth the same year. In 1932 he tied for second in Pasadena, tied for first prize in Mexico City, and tied for second in Hastings. He tied for first place in the 1942 U.S. Championship but lost the playoff against Samuel *Reshevsky. After the war, Kashdan maintained his ties to chess by organizing and directing tournaments. In 1933, he and Al Horowitz and Fred Reinfeld co-founded the monthly *Chess Review*, which he edited for a year. In 1969 the magazine merged with *Chess Life* to become *Chess Life and Review*. From 1955 to 1982 Kashdan served as editor of the chess column of the *Los Angeles Times*.

In 1950 he was awarded the IM (International Master) title; in 1954 the GM (Grand Master) title; and in 1960 the IA (International Arbiter) title. Kashdan edited two books: *First Piatigorsky Cup* (1965) and *Second Piatigorsky Cup* (1968).

[Ruth Beloff (2nd ed.)]

KASHER, or **KOSHER** (Heb. כָּשֵׁר), term originally used in the Bible in the sense of "fit" or "proper" (e.g., Esth. 8:5; Eccles. 10:10; 11:6), and later in rabbinic literature exclusively for objects that are ritually correct and faultless. Most often it denotes food that is permitted in contrast to that which is non-kasher, or **terefah*. It is also used to indicate that scrolls of the Torah, *tefillin*, and *mezuzot* are properly written, that *ẓiẓit* are correctly spun, and that a *mikveh* is properly constructed. Witnesses competent to testify in accordance with talmudic jurisprudence are also described as *kasher*. Recently, this word has been used popularly in Anglo-Saxon countries to indicate that which is proper and within the law.

KASHER, MENAHEM (1895–1983), rabbi and halakhist, distinguished for his research in talmudic and rabbinic literature. Kasher, born in Warsaw, studied under the greatest Polish rabbis of his time, and was primarily influenced in his method of study by Abraham Bornstein. He was ordained by Meir Dan *Plotzki in 1915 and went to Ereẓ Israel in 1925 as an emissary of Abraham Mordecai Alter, the head of the ḥasidic Gur dynasty, on whose behalf he founded in Jerusalem the yeshivah Sefat Emet, which he directed and managed for two years. Despite his communal work and his religious activity, Kasher never held any official appointment, and his reputation derives mainly from his literary work. This consists for the most part of varied anthologies, encyclopedic in character, which he not only initiated and wrote, but also took the responsibility for financing. His *Torah Shelemah* is an encyclopedia of the Talmud and Midrash, in which all relevant material in the oral law, both published and in manuscript, is collected according to the Scriptural verse to which it applies together with notes, expositions, and supplements. Thirty-three volumes, covering Genesis–Leviticus 24:23 had been published by 1981 (the first volume appeared in 1927). For this work, Kasher was awarded the Israel Prize in 1962. *Gemara Shelemah* (1960) deals with the first nine pages of the tractate *Pesaḥim*, with variant readings from all the known manuscripts and with all the relevant comments of the *rishonim*, together with notes and expositions by Barukh Naeh edited by Kasher – the beginning of a long-term project toward a scientific edition of the entire Talmud. *Haggadah Shelemah* (1956^3) comprises the Passover *Haggadah* with variant readings, notes, and expositions, to which are added a selection of relevant homiletic comments. *Sarei ha-Elef* (1959) consists of a list of Hebrew books whose authors lived between 500 and 1500, edited and arranged in conjunction with J. Mandelbaum. These compilations are basic reference works for all research in talmudic and rabbinic literature. In 1950 Kasher founded, in Jerusalem and in New York, the Torah Shelemah Institute for research and publication.

In 1956 Kasher discovered an extensive collection of writings by Joseph *Rozin, author of *Ẓafenat Pa'ne'aḥ*. In order to edit and publish this material he founded, together with the *Yeshiva University in New York, the Ẓafenat Pa'ne'aḥ Institute, which by 1970 had issued 12 volumes. Aside from these projects, Kasher published many works on varied subjects: *Mefa'ne'aḥ Ẓefunot* (1959), elucidating the halakhic terms and concepts used by Rozin in the above-mentioned book; *Sefer ha-Rambam ve-ha-Mekhilta de-Rabbi Shimon b. Yoḥai* (1943), clarifications of the sources of Maimonides; *Shabbat Bereshit ve-Shabbat Sinai*, in *Talpiyoth*, 1 (1944), and *Ha-Shabbat u-Mizraḥ ha-Olam*, in *Ha-Pardes*, 28 (1954), elucidations of the problem of the International Date Line prompted by the dilemma of the Jewish war refugees in Japan; a small collection of responsa by Rashi (1925); *Targum Yerushalmi ha-Shalem* from a Rome manuscript, and others. Kasher also devoted himself to the clarification of contemporary halakhic problems, and to comparisons of the views of the sages with modern concepts. These appear mostly in the annual publication *No'am* (1958–) which Kasher founded and which he edited. The halakhic aspects of such problems as artificial insemination and autopsies are dealt with in this publication. Kasher also wrote an extensive article to prove the antiquity of the Zohar, and published many articles on the importance of manuscripts for a complete and correct understanding of the Talmud. He instituted an *eruv for Manhattan in New York which gave rise to considerable controversy. In 1968 there appeared his *Ha-Tekufah ha-Gedolah* in which he maintained that the establishment of the State of Israel is the beginning of the Redemption foretold by the prophets, and its development its progressive realization. A hitherto unknown work on a similar theme by R. Hillel Shklover, a disciple of Elijah Gaon of Vilna, is appended to the work with a commentary by Kasher.

[Israel Moses Ta-Shma]

His son Shimon (1914–1968) was a Hebrew poet and writer. He was born in Warsaw and went to Palestine with his family in 1925. His first poems were published in the literary journal *Gilyonot*. His poetry (which included a number of deeply religious poems), stories, and articles appeared in various publications. His volumes of poetry included: *Sullamot la-Rom* ("Ladders Heavenward," 1938), *La-Boker Rinnah* ("Song to the Morning," 1941), *Karmelit* (1949), and *Ha-Kol Ẓafui* ("All Is Foreseen," 1964).

[Getzel Kressel]

KASHMIR, region in S. central Asia. The association of Kashmir with Jews was first alluded to by the 11th-century Muslim scholar Al-Bīrūnī in his "India-Book": "In former times the inhabitants of Kashmir used to allow one or two foreigners to enter their country, particularly Jews, but at present they do not allow any Hindus whom they do not know personally to enter, much less other people." In the time of the Moghul emperor Akbar (1556–1605), the question of the association of Jews with Kashmir and the Jewish descent of the Kashmiris was raised by the Jesuit Monserrate, who regarded the old inhabitants of this region as Jews by race and custom in view of their appearance, physique, style of dress, and manner of conducting trade. As early as the 17th century François Bernier, the scholar and traveler, who was in India from 1656 to 1668, was asked by Melchissedec Thevenot (1620–1692), a traveler and publisher, to discover if Jews had long been resident in Kashmir. Bernier reported that Jews had once lived here, but that they had converted to Islam. Nonetheless, as he put it:

> There are many signs of Judaism to be found in this country. On entering the kingdom after crossing the Pire-penjale mountains the inhabitants in the frontier villages struck me as resembling Jews. Their countenance and manner and that indescribable peculiarity which enables a traveler to distinguish the inhabitants of different nations all seemed to belong to that ancient people. You are not to ascribe what I say to mere fancy, the *Jewish* appearance of these villagers having been remarked by our Jesuit Fathers, and by several other Europeans, long before I visited Kashmir. A second sign is the prevalence of the name of Mousa, which means Moses, among the inhabitants of this city, notwithstanding they are Mahometans. A third is the tradition that Solomon visited this country and that it was he who opened a passage for the waters by cutting the mountain of Baramoulé. A fourth, the belief that Moses died in the city of Kashmir, and that his tomb is within a league of it. And a fifth may be found in the generally received opinion that the small and extremely ancient edifice seen on one of the high hills was built by Solomon; and it is therefore called the *throne of Solomon* to this day.

The claim to be of Israelite extraction is still widespread among Kashmiris, who point to the similarity of place names which appear to reflect biblical names like Mamre, Pisgah, and Mt. Nevo. The Internet is not deficient in web pages which purport to show historical connections between India and the Jews, India and Jesus (who is said to have gone there), the identical nature of Hebrew and Sanskrit, and so forth.

BIBLIOGRAPHY: F. Bernier, *Travels in the Moghul Empire, 1656–58*, ed. by A. Constable (1891). **ADD. BIBLIOGRAPHY:** T. Parfitt, *The Lost Tribes of Israel: The History of a Myth* (2002).

[Walter Joseph Fischel / Tudor Parfitt (2nd ed.)]

KASKEL (originally **Kaskele**), 17th-century family of German Court Jews and bankers, who went from Poland and settled in Dresden, Saxony, during one of the Polish-Saxonian unions. They became court bankers to the royal house of Saxony and Poland, bankers to the government, and founders of the Dresdner Bank, one of Germany's leading commercial banks. The first prominent member of the family was JACOB KASKELE (d. 1778), who in 1772 was appointed court agent. Several of his eight children, too, served as court agents in Warsaw and Dresden. One member of the family became a commissioned officer in the Austrian army in 1813. MICHAEL KASKEL (b. 1775) continued the family's banking business; he also acted as a purveyor to the Saxonian army and the mint, in addition to wider-ranging trading activities.

Michael's son KARL (1798–1874) acquired citizenship in Dresden in 1830, rose to be privy councilor, consul general for Sweden and Norway, and in 1867 obtained Austrian nobility. He converted to Christianity. At the initiative of Eugen Gutmann, Karl Kaskel in cooperation with the Rothschilds of Frankfurt, Oppenheims of Cologne, and Bleichroeder of Berlin, incorporated his banking firm and formed the Dresdner Bank.

BIBLIOGRAPHY: *Aus der Geschichte der Dresdner Bank* (1969); J.F. Kaskel, in: *Zeitschrift fuer Unternehmensgeschichte*, 28 (1983), 159–87; C. Buergelt, in: *Der alte juedische Friedhof in Dresden* (2002), 196–201.

[Joachim O. Ronall]

KASOVSKY, CHAYIM YEHOSHUA (1873–1960), Israeli rabbinical scholar. Kasovsky received his early education at the Ez̦ Ḥayyim Talmud Torah in Jerusalem where his father Abraham Abele Kasovsky was an instructor. At the age of 20, he was contributing articles to various periodicals on such subjects as Hebrew language and grammar, geometry, and talmudic themes.

Kasovsky's reputation rests upon the concordances which he compiled of the Mishnah, the Tosefta, Targum Onkelos, and the Babylonian Talmud (the last of which he was unable to complete). He undertook this task alone and under difficult conditions. He finally evolved a scheme which served as the "key" to the compilation of the concordances. Unable to afford a publisher, Kasovsky acquired a primitive press and set and printed the first volume of the concordance of the Mishnah himself. Its appearance in 1914 caused a sensation in the scholarly world. A committee was established to provide the necessary means to enable Kasovsky to continue his work: the four-volume *Oz̦ar Leshon ha-Mishnah* (1957–60); the six-volume Tosefta concordance (1933–61); and the four-volume Onkelos (1933–40). Kasovsky's works subsequently became indispensable to all scholars in those fields. His Talmud concordance (1954–) consisted of 24 volumes by 1970, up to the letter *Mem*. After his death, his youngest son Benjamin continued the work (from vol. 10, 1962). His oldest son, Moshe, prepared a concordance of the Jerusalem Talmud under the auspices of the Israel Academy for Sciences and Humanities and the Jewish Theological Seminary of America. Kasovsky was active in the religious Zionist movement.

[Mordechai Hacohen]

The continuation of the *Talmudic Concordance* of Kasovsky by his son Benjamin, mentioned in the original article, reached volume 39 up to the letter ש, before Benjamin's death in 1978. In 1981 the concordance was completed with the publication of volume 40. The remainder of the concordance of the names in the Talmud of which 3 volumes have appeared, from Abba to Othniel (א to ע), has yet to be published.

Benjamin also published a concordance to the *Mekhilta* (4 vols., 5725–6), the *Sifra* (4 vols., 5726–9), and the *Sifrei* (5 vols., 5731–5).

BIBLIOGRAPHY: Y. Werfel (Raphael), in: *Sinai*, 12 (1943), 3–9; Y. Raphael, *Rishonim ve-Aḥaronim* (1957), 421ff.; I. Goldschlag, in: *Shanah be-Shanah 5721* (1960), 366–8; *Aresheth*, 3 (1961), 430–2.

KASPAROV, GARY (1963–), Russian chess master. Kasparov, whose father was Jewish and whose mother was an Armenian, was born in Baku. He was taught the basic rules of chess by his father, Kim Vainstein, an engineer who was killed in an accident (1970) when Kasparov was seven years of age. As his career in chess developed, he adopted his mother's maiden name – apparently at the behest of the Soviet authorities. After his exceptionally great talent for chess was discovered he was taught intensively by the former world champion Mikhail *Botvinnik, who clearly understood the great potential which Kasparov had in the field of chess. His career was meteoric: in 1980 he earned the title of grand master and won the World Junior Chess Championship; in 1981 he became chess champion of the Soviet Union. His path to the world championship was paved by his victory in the Moscow interdistrict competition. He then won matches against the grand masters Alexander Blaiavsky and Viktor Korchnoi as well as defeating former world champion Vasili Smislov. The height of his achievement came after three dramatic duels against his immediate predecessor as holder of the world title, the Russian Anatoly Karpov. The first duel was called to a halt at the end of 1984 after 48 games because of the physical and mental fatigue of Karpov. Kasparov did not refrain from accusing FIDE (the World Chess Federation) and the Russian chess establishment of trying to aid his opponent. In the second battle, which was limited to 24 games and which ended in November 1985, Kasparov was the victor, the result being 13:11. He thus became the youngest person ever to hold the title of world champion. In the rematch which took place in London and Leningrad in 1986 Kasparov retained the title of world champion by a score of 12.5:11.5. As world champion he also played against – and defeated – some of the greatest players in the West, including among them Olaf Anderson of Sweden, Jan Timmam of the Netherlands, and Anthony Miles of Great Britain.

Kasparov's style of playing is deep, original, and devious. He tends to make bold moves and take chances to assume the offensive role. Kasparov puts great weight on the psychological aspects of the game and particularly on the ability to rebound after losses. He applied this in the 1986 match with Karpov after suffering three losses in a row. In 1990 he defeated Karpov again in the final meeting of a 24-game contest. He won 4, lost 3, and drew 17. In 1993 he retained his title, defeating Nigel Short of Britain.

Kasparov battled computer chess programs. In February 1966 IBM's Deep Blue defeated Kasparov in one game – the first time a computer had bested a world champion – using normal time controls, but Kasparov won the match by gaining 3 wins and playing to 2 draws. In November 2003 he played against the X3D Fritz computer program using a virtual board, 3D glasses, and a speech recognition system in a four-game match. The first game ended in a draw, XD3 won the second, Kasparov the third, and the final game ended in a draw.

Kasparov wrote a number of books which deal with the theory of openings of games and an analysis of a selection of his games.

[Yisrael Shrenzel]

KASPI, ANDRÉ (1937–), French historian teaching the history of North America at the Sorbonne. Kaspi was born in Béziers (Hérault). Among his books are *L'indépendance américaine* (1976), *Le Watergate* (1983), *La guerre de Sécession* (1992), *Kennedy, les mille jours d'un président* (1993), *Les Américains: Les États-Unis de 1607 à nos jours* (2 vols., 1998), and *La peine de mort aux États-Unis* (2003). His two doctoral dissertations were published as *La mission de Jean Monnet à Alger, mars-octobre 1943* (1969) and *Le concours américain à la France, 1917–1918* (1976). In addition to his work on American civilization, Kaspi is a pioneer of Jewish historiography in France. In the 1970s he founded the first seminar on the Holocaust and the history of the Vichy government and published several books on these topics: *La Deuxième Guerre mondiale, chronologie commentée* (1990); *Les Juifs pendant l'Occupation* (1991); and *La libération de la France* (1994); as well as a biography, *Jules Isaac ou la passion de la vérité* (2002).

[Anne Grynberg (2nd ed.)]

KASPI, JOSEPH BEN ABBA MARI IBN (En Bonafoux del'Argentière; 1279–1340?), philosopher, biblical commentator, and grammarian. Motivated by an intense desire for wisdom and knowledge, and being a wealthy man, Kaspi spent most of his days traveling from one country to another, living successively in Arles, Tarascon, Aragon, Catalonia, and on the island of Majorca. Because of his admiration for *Maimonides, he left for Egypt in 1314 in order to hear explanations on the latter's *Guide of the Perplexed* from the author's grandchildren. He was, however, disappointed in his expectations and came to realize that the grandchildren of Maimonides were indeed "all righteous, but they did not occupy themselves with the study of the sciences." When he heard that the *Guide* was being studied in the Muslim philosophical schools of Fez, he left for that town (in 1332) in order to observe their method of study. At the time of the *Pastoureaux (Shepherds' Persecutions, 1320), he was in mortal danger and his life was saved only by great fortune.

Kaspi was a prolific writer. He began to write his works when 17 years old and composed over 30 books during his lifetime. These books dealt with a variety of subjects: logic, linguistics, ethics, theology, biblical exegesis, and super-commentaries to Abraham Ibn Ezra and Maimonides. Despite their variety, all have essentially the same purpose: to demonstrate that a correct understanding of Scripture accords with the conclusions of philosophy. In his philosophic system he followed *Aristotle and *Averroes. On more than one occasion, however, he expressed contradictory opinions. Kaspi rejected the viewpoint that Maimonides had supposedly refuted the theory of the eternity of the world. He raised the importance of reason to the level of God, "because reason is God and God is reason." In spite of these ideas which border on heresy, Kaspi wrote that "after our God, blessed be He, we have no need for Plato, Aristotle, and their ilk, even if they dispute this fact."

At the same time, since the true meaning of Scripture, the opinions of the Greek philosophers and the views of Maimonides are identical regarding the creation of the world, Kaspi did not affirm the traditional belief in creation. On the other hand, since he was not only a philosopher, and his Bible commentary dealt with the plain or literal meaning (*peshat*) of Scripture, he was influenced to a great extent by the exegetical approach of Abraham ibn Ezra. Accordingly, he declared that "all the words of the Torah and the Bible are in my opinion to be accepted in their plain meaning, like the books on logic and nature of Aristotle" and, in his view, there was not "in the wonders of the prophets any action which departed from nature." He defines his aim as "not to be a fool who believes in everything, but only in that which can be verified by proof… and not to be of the second unthinking category which disbelieves from the start of its inquiry," since "certain things must be accepted by tradition, because they cannot be proven."

This complicated method adopted by Kaspi aroused violent criticism against him on the part of Jewish scholars. In referring to his first work, *Sefer ha-Sod* ("Book of the Secret"), his critics not only attacked his unorthodox opinions, but also accused him of inconsistency: "At times he is meticulous with groats and, on other occasions, he disregards golden coins." They also protested against his abuse of the masses, whom he had referred to as "animals," and accused him of having insulted the Jewish people. Kaspi was very offended by his critics and wrote of them with bitterness: "I know that if I had murdered and taken possession of ten guilders and presented them with these, they would have said that there is no man on earth like me for honesty and righteousness." He severely criticized "the great of our people." With sharp irony, he described them as "idling away all their days with unfounded arguments and lengthy discussions on the laws of uncleanliness and purity which no longer apply." With the same scorn he wrote of the wealthy, whose "body is fat and whose neck is thick" and the whole of their wisdom lies in that they know how to "lend and extract [their] debts."

Kaspi's anger did not silence his opponents, and 150 years after his death Jewish scholars still differed over the evaluation of his personality and his works. Simeon b. Ẓemaḥ *Duran and Isaac *Abrabanel considered him a dangerous heretic. On the other hand, Johanan Alemanno and Moses *Rieti praised his works and considered him among the most illustrious Jewish scholars.

Kaspi attempted to educate his children toward perfect virtues. He accustomed them to "meditate after every meal, morning and evening, on the ethics of the philosophers." Before one of his journeys, he wrote the work *Ha-Musar* ("Ethics") for his son Solomon, "lest the wind of God carries me off to a distant land or death overtake me… and perhaps these ethics will serve for [his son's] understanding and the instruction of many of the inhabitants of the country." In this work, which includes the fundamentals of his faith, he teaches his son that "truth should neither be cowardly nor bashful." This work also serves as a testament, since in it Kaspi hands down to his son a detailed program and guide of his system of learning: "and if he will act in this way, he will be a man who will combine wisdom with understanding."

Kaspi was the first to declare of the return of Israel to its country and the establishment of the Jewish state: "it becomes every intelligent person to believe in this by logic and reason, so that the promises of the Scriptures will not be required at all." After a comprehensive political survey of the changes and events of his time, he reached the conclusion that the return of Israel to its country could, without any difficulty, find its place within the framework of normal political events.

Kaspi's Works

Many of the titles of Kaspi's works include the word *kesef* ("silver"), a play on his name.

1. *Adnei Kesef* or *Sefer ha-Mashal*, commentary on the Prophetic books, ed. I.H. Last, pt. I, London 1911; pt. II, London 1912. The text is also being published anew in *Mikra'ot Gedolot 'Haketer'*, ed. Menachem Hacohen, Jerusalem 1992ff.
2. *Amudei Kesef*, exoteric commentary on *The Guide of the Perplexed*, in: *Amudei Kesef u-Maskiyyot Kesef*, ed. S.A. Werbloner, Frankfurt a/M 1848.
3. Commentaries on the book of Job (two versions), in: *Asarah Kelei Kesef*, ed. I.H. Last, vol. I, Presburg 1903.
4. Commentaries on the book of Proverbs (two versions), in: *Asarah Kelei Kesef*, ed. I.H. Last, vol. I, Presburg 1903.
5. Commentary on Ibn Janaḥ's *Sefer ha-Rikmah*, lost.
6. Commentary on Maimonides' *Milot ha-Higayyon*, Ms. Vatican 429.
7. Commentary on the Song of Songs, in: *Asarah Kelei Kesef*, ed. I.H. Last, vol. I, Presburg 1903.
8. *Gelilei Kesef*, commentary on the book of Esther, in: *Asarah Kelei Kesef*, ed. I.H. Last, vol. II, Presburg 1903.
9. *Gevi'a ha-Kesef*, treatise on esoteric topics in the book of Genesis, with English translation, ed. B.E. Herring, New York 1982.
10. *Ḥagorat Kesef*, commentary on the books of Ezra, Nehemiah, and Chronicles, in: *Asarah Kelei Kesef*, ed. I.H. Last, vol. II, Presburg 1903.
11. *Ḥaẓoẓerot Kesef*, commentary on the book of Ecclesiastes, in: *Asarah Kelei Kesef*, ed. I.H. Last, vol. I, Presburg 1903.
12. *Kappot Kesef*, commentaries on the books of Ruth and Lamentations, in: *Asarah Kelei Kesef*, ed. I.H. Last, vol. II, Presburg 1903.

13. *Ke'arot Kesef,* commentary on the book of Daniel, lost.

14. *Kesef Sigim,* 110 questions on the Bible, lost.

15. *Kevuẓat Kesef* (two versions): Version A, in: *Asarah Kelei Kesef,* ed. I.H. Last, vol. I, Presburg 1903; Version B, in E. Renan, *Les écrivains juifs français du XIVe siècle,* Paris 1983, pp. 131–201.

16. *Kippurei Kesef,* critique of earlier Bible commentaries, lost.

17. *Maskiyyot Kesef,* esoteric commentary on *The Guide of the Perplexed,* in: *Amudei Kesef u-Maskiyyot Kesef,* ed. S.A. Werbloner, Frankfurt a/M 1848.

18. *Menorat Kesef,* in: *Asarah Kelei Kesef,* ed. I.H. Last, vol. II, Presburg 1903.

19. *Mezamerot Kesef,* commentary on the book of Psalms, lost.

20. *Maẓref la-Kesef,* systematic commentary on the Torah, ed. I.H. Last, Krakow 1906.

21. *Mitot Kesef,* treatise on the intentions of the Bible, lost.

22. *Mizrak la-Kesef,* treatise on Creation, lost.

23. *Parashat Kesef,* supercommentary on Ibn Ezra, unpublished, Ms. Vatican 151.

24. *Retukot Kesef,* principles of linguistics, Ms. Rome-Angelica 60.

25. *Sharshot Kesef,* dictionary of Hebrew roots, Ms. Rome-Angelica. Part published by I.H. Last, *JQR* 1907, pp. 651–687.

26. *Shulḥan Kesef,* five exegetical and theological essays, ed. H. Kasher, Jerusalem 1996.

27. *Tam ha-Kesef,* eight theological essays, ed. I.H. Last, London 1913.

28. *Terumat Kesef,* brief treatise on ethics and politics, Ms. Wien 161. Part published by E.Z. Berman, *The Hebrew Versions of the Fourth Book of Averroes' Middle Commentary on the Nicomedean Ethics,* Jerusalem 1981 (Hebrew).

29. *Tirat Kesef* or *Sefer ha-Sod,* brief commentary on the Torah, ed. I.H. Last, Presburg 1905.

30. *Yoreh De'ah,* ethical treatise, with English translation, in: I. Abrahams (ed.), *Hebrew Ethical wills,* Philadelphia 1926, vol. I, pp. 127–161.

31. *Ẓeror ha-Kesef,* Brief treatise on logic, unpublished, Ms. Vatican 183. Part published by S. Rosenberg in *Iyyun,* 32 (1984), pp. 275–295.

BIBLIOGRAPHY: B. Mesch, *Studies in Joseph Ibn Kaspi* (1975); Pines, in: *Iyyun,* 14 (1963), 289–317; Bacher, in: MGWJ, 56 (1912), 199–217, 324–33, 449–57; 57 (1913), 559–66; Renan, Ecrivains, 131–206; M. Steinschneider, *Gesammelte Schriften,* 1 (1925), 89–137; Waxman, Literature (1960), index s.v. *Joseph Ibn Kaspi*; J. Guttmann, *Philosophies of Judaism* (1964), 196–7; J. Rosenthal, *Meḥkarim u-Mekorot,* 1 (1967), 140, 149, 286, 404–5; I. Zinberg, *Di Geshikhte fun Literatur bay Yidn,* 4 (1943), 151–65, 414. **ADD. BIBLIOGRAPHY:** C. Aslanov, "De la lexicographie hébraïque à la sémantique générale; la pensée sémantique de Caspi d'après le 'Sefer Sarsot ha-Kesef,'" in: *Helmantica,* 154 (2000), idem, "How Much Arabic Did Joseph Kaspi Know? in: *Aleph,* 2 (2002), 259–69; idem, "L'aristotélisme medieval au service du commentaire littéral; le cas de Joseph Caspi," in: REJ, 161 (2002), 123–37; W. Bacher, "Joseph Ibn Kaspi als Bibelerklarer," in: *Festschrift zu Herman Cohens siebzigsten geburstag* (1912), 119–35; Dimant, "Exegesis, Philosophy and Language in the Writing of Joseph Ibn Caspi" (diss., Ann Arbor, 1979); R. Eisen, "Joseph Ibn Kaspi on the Secret Meaning of the Scroll of Esther," in: REJ, 160 (2001), 379–408; B. Finkelscherer, "Die Sprachwissenschaft des Joseph Ibn Kaspi," in: *Breslau* (1930); R. Goetschel, "Le Sacrifice d'Isaak dans le 'Gebia Kesef' de Joseph Ibn Kaspi," in: *Pardes,* 22 (1996), 69–82; B. Herring, *Joseph ibn Kaspi's Gevia' Kesef* (1982); H. Kasher, "Joseph Ibn Kaspi's Aristotelian Interpretation, and Fundamentalist Interpretation of the book of Job," in: *Daat,* 20 (1988), 117–26 (Heb.); idem, "Linguistic Solutions to Theological Problems in the Works of Joseph Ibn Kaspi," in: M. Hallamish and A. Kasher (ed.), *Religion and Language* (1981), 91–96; H. Kasher, "On the Book of Esther as an Allegory in the Works of Joseph Ibn Kaspi, A Response to R. Eisen," in: REJ, 161 (2002), 459–64; H. Kasher (ed.), *Shulḥan Kesef* (Heb., 1996), intro., 11–53; B. Mesch, "Principles of Judaism in Maimonides and Joseph Ibn Kaspi," in: *Mystics, Philosophers, and Politicians* (1982), 85–98; S. Pines, "The Resurrection of the Jewish State according to Ibn Caspi and Spinoza," in: *Iyyun,* 14 (1963) 289–317 (Heb.); E. Renan, *Les écrivains juifs français des XIV siècle* (1893), 131–201; S. Rosenberg, "Logic, Language and Exegesis of the Bible in the Works of Joseph Ibn Kaspi," in: M. Hallamish and A. Kasher (eds.), *Religion and Language* (1981), 104–13; S. Rosenberg, "Joseph Ibn Kaspi: Sefer ha-Hata'a (Sophistical Refutation)," in: *Iyyun,* 32 (1983), 275–95 (Heb.); H. Stroudze, "Les deux commentaires d'ibn Kaspi sur les Proverbes," in: REJ, 52 (1962), 71–76; I. Twersky, "Joseph Ibn Kaspi – Portrait of a Medieval Jewish Intellectual," in: I. Twersky (ed.), *Studies in Medieval Jewish History and Literature* (1979), 231–57.

[Ephraim Kupfer / Hannah Kasher (2nd ed.)]

KASPI, NETHANEL BEN NEHEMIAH (15th century), author of religious-philosophical works. Kaspi was a disciple of Frat Maimon (Solomon b. Menahem). He composed the following works: (1) commentary on the *Kuzari,* completed in 1424, for which he made use of the Hebrew translations by Judah ibn Tibbon and Judah Cardinal; (2) commentary on the anonymous philosophical work *Ru'aḥ Ḥen*; (3) commentary on Maimonides' *Shemonah Perakim.* All three commentaries appear to be primarily a record of Frat Maimon's oral explanations. All three are contained in a Parma manuscript (no. 395), copied by Abraham Farissol in Ferrara in 1520. (4) *Lekutot* ("selections"), consisting of comments on passages in the Pentateuch, and polemical remarks against Christianity including, in the main, the arguments used by French rabbis in their debates with Christians, such as may be found in the writings of Joseph b. Nathan ha-Mekanne. Kaspi also copied works, among them *Levi b. Gershom's commentary on the Pentateuch, in Avignon in 1429. He also copied *Alfasi's *Halakhot* (in 1454) and other rabbinical works.

BIBLIOGRAPHY: Steinschneider, Uebersetzungen, 404, 427; Renan, Ecrivains, 235, 409ff., 266; Gross, Gal Jud, 10, 69–70, 89, 390.

[Bernard Suler]

KASRILS, RONNIE (1938–), South African resistance leader and politician. Kasrils was a member of the banned South African Communist Party (SACP) and was active in the armed wing of the African National Congress, Umkhonto we Sizwe (MK), from its creation. He was in MK's Natal regional command and personally carried out acts of sabotage and organized a major operation to provide it with dynamite. In 1962, he received a five-year banning order and narrowly escaped arrest under new security legislation. He remained on the run from the security police until October 1963, when he went abroad for military training. After several years in the ANC office in Dar es Salaam, Kasrils moved to London, where he worked with other exiled South African activists like Joe Slovo in establishing underground MK units in South Africa. In 1977, he held various senior positions within the resistance movements in Southern Africa, including Angola, Mozambique, and Zambia. He was chief of military intelligence in 1983–88 and was a coopted member of the ANC National Executive Committee from 1987. He was also a member of the SACP Central Committee and Politburo. With the onset of the reform process, he returned to South Africa in 1990. Following the transition to nonracial democracy in 1994, he served terms as deputy minister of defense (1994–99) and minister of water affairs and forestry (1999–2004). During the latter period, he took the lead in promoting local Jewish opposition to the policies of the State of Israel. He was appointed minister of intelligence in 2004. He wrote an autobiography called *Armed and Dangerous; My Undercover Struggle Against Apartheid* (1993).

[David Saks (2nd ed.)]

KASSEL, city in Germany, former capital of the state of *Hesse-Kassel. A record of 1293 maintains that a Jewess had been in possession of some property in Kassel at an earlier date. A Jews' street was in existence in 1318. During the *Black Death persecutions (1348–49) the Jews suffered, but some managed to escape and were living in Frankfurt (1360) and Erfurt. By 1398 there was an organized community, with a synagogue and cemetery in Kassel. The Jews' street is mentioned again in 1455 and 1486 and the "Jews' well" may date from this period. In 1513 Master Falke contributed to the construction of a local bridge; in 1520 he paid the rent for the cemetery, as did his widow in 1526. Landgrave Philip of Hesse expelled the Jews from Hesse-Kassel in 1524. However, in 1530 he admitted Michel Jud of Derenburg as court agent for ten years, and in 1532 issued a Jewry toleration law, amplified in 1539. Though restrictive and ordering Jews to attend Christian sermons, it was less severe than the extreme anti-Jewish proposals of the Reformation theologian Martin *Butzer. Only a few Jews were allowed in Kassel in the period, namely a physician and several silk knitters; in 1602 the *Court Jew Hayum was admitted as mint master.

During the Thirty Years' War the Jews were compelled to leave Kassel. However the Court Jew Benedict Goldschmidt received a residence privilege in 1635, extended in 1647 to include his two sons. From 1650 to 1715 private services were held in the Goldschmidts' house, led by the rabbi of the nearby village of Brettenhausen (later part of Kassel), where a cemetery was acquired in 1621. In 1714 a synagogue building was erected and enlarged in 1755; the community had grown by then to approximately 200 persons. A *Memorbuch was begun in 1720, and a *ḥevra kaddisha* founded in 1773. In 1772 the rabbinate was tranferred from Witzenhausen, seat of the yeshivah, to Kassel.

In 1577 Landgrave William the Wise had initiated Hesse-Kassel Jewry assemblies, first held in Kassel. The *kehillah* Hebrew constitution papers, begun in 1633, and a *pinkas* (records and decisions) were ordered to be translated into German in 1734–40. Hesse-Kassel Jewry was under the civic jurisdiction of the *Fulda rabbinate until 1625, and that of *Friedberg until 1656.

From 1807 to 1813 Kassel was the capital of the short-lived kingdom of Westphalia. The emancipation law of 1808 granted civil rights to Jews and made possible the influx of Jews from other areas. A *consistory headed by Israel *Jacobson introduced synagogue and educational reforms. The government of the reestablished principality of Hesse-Kassel issued a more restrictive Jewry ordinance in 1823, which remained in force until 1866, when Kassel came under Prussian rule and Prussian emancipation laws prevailed. In 1836–39 a new synagogue was built, accommodating around 1,000 persons. An Orthodox faction separated after 1872 and built its own synagogue in 1898. The main synagogue was rebuilt in 1890–1907. The Hesse-Kassel yeshivah was transferred to Kassel as a teachers' seminary and elementary school. The community had a library of Judaica and Hebraica, and in the *Landesmuseum* a display of ceremonial objects as well as arts and crafts, which was restored after 1945. It also possessed an orphanage and an old age home. In 1905, 2,445 Jews lived in Kassel, 2,750 (1.62% of the total) in 1925, and 2,301 (1.31%) in June 1933.

On November 7, 1938, two days before the start of Kristallnacht, the main synagogue was set on fire, but the local firemen extinguished the blaze, something that they were explicitly instructed not to do on *Kristallnacht*. Two days later, the Liberal synagogue was burned down and the Orthodox synagogue destroyed, and a completed manuscript of the second volume of the history of the Jews in Kassel, prepared under community auspices, was destroyed, as later were all records on emigration and deportation. Three hundred Jews including the rabbi were sent to Buchenwald and 560 Jews emigrated over the next year. As to the remaining Jews, 470 were deported to Riga in 1941, 99 to Majdanek in 1942, and 323 to Theresienstadt that year. In 1945–46, 200 Jews (mainly Displaced Persons) lived in Kassel, 102 in 1955, 73 in 1959, and 106 in 1970. With municipal aid a synagogue with a community center was built in 1965. The Jewish community numbered about 1,220 in 2004 after the immigration of Jews from the former Soviet Union in the 1990s. Since the synagogue became too small it was pulled down and the architect Alfred Jacoby designed a new one with a community center, which was consecrated in 2000. It was financed by the Jewish community of Kassel, the Association of Jewish Communities in Hesse, the Federal state (Land) of Hesse, and the city of Kassel.

BIBLIOGRAPHY: R. Hallo et al., *Geschichte der juedischen Gemeinde Kassel* (1931); Baron, Community, 1 (1942), 341–3; H. Maor, *Ueber den Wiederaufbau der juedischen Gemeinden in Deutschland seit 1945* (1961), 61, 79; Germ Jud, 2 (1968), 390; S. Steinberg, in: ZGJD, 2 (1930), 242–6; L. Munk, in: *Hermann Cohen Festschrift*, 337–88; idem, in: MGWJ, 41 (1897), 505–22; F. Lazarus, *ibid.*, 58 (1914), 81–96, 178–208, 326–58, 454–82, 542–61; 78 (1934), 587–607; A. Cohn, *Beitraege zur Geschichte der Juden in Hesse-Kassel* (1933); L. Horwitz, *Die Kasseler Synagoge und ihr Erbauer* (1907); H. Schnee, *Die Hoffinanz und der moderne Staat*, 2 (1954), 315–52; S. Stern, *The Court Jew* (1950), index. **ADD. BIBLIOGRAPHY:** I. Kraeling, (ed.), *Juden in Kassel 1808–1933. Eine Dokumentation anlaesslich des 100. Geburtstages von Frank Rosenzweig* (1986); E. Hass, A. Link, K.H. Wegner (eds.), *Synagogen in Kassel. Zur Austellung im Stadtmuseum Kassel* (Schriften des Stadtmuseums Kassel, vol. 9), (2000).

[Toni Oelsner]

KASSEL, DAVID (pseudonym of **Dovid Kisel**; 1881–1935), Yiddish writer. Born in Minsk, he was influenced by the *Bund, in whose publications his first poems appeared. After marrying the poet Sarah Reisen, sister of Abraham *Reisen, he settled in Warsaw and attracted attention with his short stories and novels, *In Dorf* ("In the Village," 1912); *Unter a Vaysn Forhang* ("Behind a White Curtain," 1922), and *On an Oysveg* ("No Way Out," 1922). He also wrote a series of popular textbooks, prose anthologies, and translations of Tolstoy, Lermontov, and Jules Verne. His autobiographical novella *Moysheles Kinderyorn* ("Moyshele's Childhood," 1921) was a pioneering work in Yiddish children's literature.

BIBLIOGRAPHY: A. Reisen, *Epizodn fun Mayn Lebn*, 2 vols. (1929), passim; Rejzen, Leksikon, 3 (1929), 482–8; J.S. Hertz (ed.), *Doyres Bundistn*, 1 (1956), 420–2. **ADD. BIBLIOGRAPHY:** LNYL, 8 (1981), 84–7; Sh. Niger, *Shmuesn vegn Bikher* (1922), 295–303.

[Moshe Starkman]

KASSIL, LEV ABRAMOVICH (1905–1970), Soviet Russian author. Probably the most important Soviet writer for juveniles since the beginning of the 1930s, Kassil is known to tens of millions of young Russians for his novels about adolescents. *Konduit* ("Conduit," 1930) and *Shvambraniya* (1933; *The Land of Shvambraniya*, 1935) describe the author's own childhood in a pre-revolutionary town on the Volga. *Vratar respubliki* ("The Goal-Keeper of the Republic"; 1939), *Cheremysh, brat geroya* (1938; *Brother of a Hero*, 1968), and *Khod beloy korolevy* ("The Gambit of the White Queen"; 1958) are about Soviet sportsmen. *Dorogiye moi malchiski* ("My Dear Kids"; 1944) shows children engaged in doing physical work during World War II, and *Ulitsa mladshego syna* ("The Street of the Younger Son"; 1949) describes the adventures of those youngsters who participated in the anti-Nazi underground. Kassil's works contain few Jewish themes or protagonists. One of the exceptions is his autobiographical *Shvambraniya*, which includes a scene in which Kassil, angry at the nasty antisemitic passages in Gogol's *Taras Bulba*, refuses to read the classic aloud in school. The scene was omitted from postwar editions of the book.

[Maurice Friedberg]

KASTEIN, JOSEF (pen name of **Julius Katzenstein**, 1890–1946), German writer and biographer. Kastein was born in Bremen to an assimilated family. He was an ardent Zionist from a young age and took part in the Tenth Zionist Congress in Basel. Kastein abandoned his legal career during the 1920s and devoted himself to Jewish historical studies. In 1927 he left Germany and settled in Switzerland, where he worked as a writer. He immigrated to Palestine in 1935 and lived in Tel Aviv for the rest of his life. Beginning with his well-known *Eine Geschichte der Juden* (1931; *History and Destiny of the Jews*, 1933), Kastein published a steady stream of original presentations of both the broad sweep of Jewish history and of particular historical figures and themes. His monographs include *Sabbatai Zewi, der Messias von Ismir* (1930; *The Messiah of Ismir*, 1931), *Uriel da Costa* (1932), *Suesskind von Trimberg* (1934), *Theodor Herzl* (1935), *Herodes* (1936), and *Jeremias* (1938). Among other works that appeared before the outbreak of World War II were *Jews in Germany* (1934; *Juden in Deutschland*, 1935), first published in English; *Das Geschichterlebnis des Juden* (1936), an indictment of Jewish assimilationism; and *Jerusalem; die Geschichte eines Landes* (1937). Though without pretensions to original scholarship, Kastein's books were written in a passionate style, expressing the author's faith in the mission and destiny of the Jewish people. Two works of a different type were the early verse collection *Logos und Pan* (1918) and *Eine palaestinensische Novelle* (1942). Toward the end of his life Kastein also wrote a collection of Hebrew essays, which appeared posthumously as *Middot va-Arakhim* (1947).

BIBLIOGRAPHY: E. Carlebach, *Sefer ha-Demuyyot* (1959), 286–300. **ADD. BIBLIOGRAPHY:** A. Dreyer, in: *Bremisches Jahrbuch*, 58 (1980), 93–144; idem, in: BLBI, 60 (1981), 21–50; idem, in: BLBI, 66 (1983), 23–51; idem, in: BLBI, 71 (1985), 35–56 (bibliography).

[Rudolf Kayser / Noam Zadoff (2nd ed.)]

KASTORIA (**Castoria**), town and area of Macedonia, Greece, W. of Salonika. There was a Jewish settlement in the Kastoria fortress town during the reign of Justinian (527–565). In the 11th century, the community was headed by Tobias b. Eliezer, the author of *Lekaḥ Tov*. One of his disciples was Meir of Kastoria, author of *Me'or Einayim*, a midrashic exegesis on the Torah. In the 11th century, many Jewish refugees settled in the city, in particular Jews from Hungary who escaped the pillage of the Crusaders. Noteworthy was the 14th century *Ḥakham* Leon Judah ben Moses Moskoni, who wrote on the Torah commentary of Rabbi Avraham Ibn Ezra, and the *paytan* David ben Eliezer, who composed the *Maḥzor Kastoria*. When the Ottomans conquered the city in 1385, the Jewish community was known as a Greek-speaking Romaniot culture. After the conquest of Constantinople in 1453, most of the Jews of Kastoria moved to the capital and formed a congregation in the Balat Quarter. In the 16th century Jewish refugees from Spain settled here, but most of the town's Jews came from Apulia, southern Italy. A Sicilian congregation was also formed in the 16th century. Despite the numerous Jewish immigrants from Apulia and Sicily, the Italian Jews after a generation assimilated into the Sephardi culture and lost their special Italian customs. From the 16th century onward, the Jewish merchants were active in the fur trade, and eventually gained a worldwide reputation in this field. There were also Jewish peddlers, artisans, and tax collectors. In the mid-17th century, there was an active Shabbatean following, including Rabbi Shemayah ben Moses Mayo, who in the end remained loyal to Jewish law. *Nathan of Gaza, the main disciple of the false messiah *Shabbetai Ẓevi spent time in Kastoria and wrote his work *Sefer ha-Beri'ah* there. Ali Pasha, governor of the region from 1788 to 1822, imposed oppressive taxes on the Jewish population of Kastoria. In 1828, the synagogue that was built in the mid-18th century was destroyed, and in 1830, in its place, the Aragon Synagogue was donated by the famous local philanthropist Isaac Beḥor Moses Rousso, nicknamed "Senor Shako." The Castorian Jewish community, whether in Castoria, Israel, or the U.S., has continually commemorated the annual date of the passing of this renowned 19th century benefactor. At the beginning of the 19th century the local rabbi was Moses Isaac ha-Levi, the author of *Ma'aseh Moshe*, a halakhic and aggadic index to the Talmud. A Jewish school was established in 1873. The community suffered blood libels in 1879 and 1908. The Spanish-Jewish dialect used by Kastoria Jews was of a special character. Beginning with the first decade of the 20th century, at the end of the Ottoman period, emigration from Kastoria to New York ensued. The city was annexed to Greece in 1912–13 after the Balkan Wars and Monastir Jews migrated to Castoria after World War I. In 1928 the Jewish community numbered 900. In the 1920s and 1930s, the youth of the community had an active Judeo-Spanish theater group. In the 1930s, graduates of the local AJJ (Agudat Jeunes Juives) youth movement founded by the Jewish school principal Jacob Jak Ashkenazi formed the nucleus of the *garin*, the agricultural settlement group, that in 1937 established Moshav Ẓur Moshe, one of the *Stockade and Watchtower settlements erected overnight in Ereẓ Israel to evade the British prohibition against forming new Jewish settlements. In late March 1944, 763 Jews from Kastoria were arrested and deported to Auschwitz. In 1948 there were 35 Jews living in the town, and by 1965 their number had dwindled to 22.

BIBLIOGRAPHY: M. Molho, *Histoire des Israélites de Castoria* (1938). **ADD. BIBLIOGRAPHY:** B. Rivlin, "Kastoria," in: *Pinkas Kehillot Yavan* (1999), 372–81.

[Simon Marcus / Yitzchak Kerem (2nd ed.)]

KASZTNER, REZSŐ RUDOLF (**Israel**; 1906–1957), journalist, lawyer, and a leader of the Zionist movement in Romania and Hungary. Born in Cluj, Transylvania (then part of Romania), Kasztner studied law. From 1925 to 1940 he worked on the Hungarian-language Zionist daily *Uj Kelet* in Cluj, and served as its political correspondent in *Bucharest from 1929 to 1931. During this period he was also the secretary of the parliamentary faction of the National Jewish Party. A leader of Aviva-Barissia, a Zionist youth movement (which eventually joined up with Ha-Iḥud ha-Olami), he edited its periodical *No'ar* (in Hungarian) from 1926 to 1928. After Transylvania was annexed by Hungary (1940), *Uj Kelet* was closed down by the authorities; Kasztner then moved to *Budapest (1942), and joined the local *Keren Hayesod office. He was also active in the national headquarters of Ha-Iḥud ha-Olami, and from 1943 to 1945 was deputy chairman of the small Hungarian Zionist Organization. As soon as he arrived in Budapest, Kasztner joined the Zionists' organized rescue efforts on behalf of the Jewish refugees from *Poland and Slovakia (see *Czechoslovakia). First in charge of semi-clandestine political work and later head of the rescue operations, Kasztner conducted negotiations with the Hungarian authorities and political leaders, including members of the opposition. He also maintained contact with the Hungarian military intelligence and the German intelligence (called Abwehr) which had come to Hungary even before its occupation by the Germans. After the German occupation of Hungary (March 19, 1944), rescue operations were stepped up and the Zionist contacts also came to include the officers of RSHA (Reich Security Main Office) who, headed by Adolf *Eichmann, arrived in Hungary to apply the "Final Solution" (see *Holocaust, General Survey). Kasztner conducted the rescue work jointly with Joel *Brand, who initially served as the main contact with the Germans. As a relatively unknown "foreigner" he could not have been effective with Hungarian politicians and officials so his area of contacts was with the Germans. The very idea of negotiating with the Germans was controversial both during the war and afterwards. The Nazis were imposing "The Final Solution;" they were clearly the enemy bent on destruction. Yet, they also were the only address if rescue was to be effectuated. The prime subject under discussion with the various German offices was the "*Blut fuer Ware*" ("Blood for Goods") plan by which Germany would receive quantities of supplies for the German war effort from neutral countries with the help of international Jewish bodies in exchange for the survival of the Jewish population and their transfer from German-occupied territories to safety abroad, especially to Palestine. By 1944, the German military situation was clearly deteriorating and their purposes were hardly humanitarian, but if they could improve their military situation, then the partial postponement of the murder of Jews in one sector of operation – postponement not cancellation – was a price they might be willing to pay. In connection with this plan Kasztner became the chief contact with Eichmann in place of Joel Brand, whom Eichmann had sent to Istanbul to open negotiations with Jewish leaders abroad. In the period of Aug. 21, 1944–April 1945 he visited Germany a number of times, and also went five times to Switzerland, in order to meet representatives of the *American Jewish Joint Distribution Committee and the *Jewish Agency on the rescue plan, and particularly to arrange its financing by Jewish organizations. These activities resulted in the Germans' transfer to Switzerland of two transports, first of 318 and later of 1,368 Jews from *Bergen-Belsen, most of them of Hungarian and Transylvanian origin (on Aug. 18 and Dec. 6, 1944). Among the people on the Kaszner train were the Satmar Rebbe, Joel

*Teitelbaum, and his entourage – saved by a Zionist – along with members of Kasztner's own family and wealthy Jews whose support was essential to financing the operation. This was later to be a source of controversy. Kasztner's negotiations with the Germans were also designed to ensure the survival of the Jews in the Budapest ghetto.

The postwar situation of Kasztner put him at the center of a storm. After the war Kasztner settled in Israel and was given a government post, becoming active in the *Mapai Party. He edited Mapai's Hungarian-language weekly *A Jövó* and subsequently rejoined the editorial staff of *Uj Kelet*, reestablished in Tel Aviv in 1948. In 1953, an old Jew Malkiel Gruenwald of Jerusalem published a mimeographed leaflet in which he accused Kasztner of having collaborated with the German Nazis thereby hastening the destruction of Hungarian Jewry. He also alleged that at the Nuremberg trial of Kurt Becher, an SS officer, Kasztner had testified on his behalf and thereby helped in acquitting a war criminal. In view of the fact that the person being slandered was a government official, the Israel attorney general issued a writ of indictment against Gruenwald. The trial was a media sensation. A brilliant young right-wing attorney, Shmuel *Tamir, turned the defense of Gruenwald into an indictment of Kasztner and in turn of the Israeli government and the Zionist movement.

On June 22, 1955, the judge, Benjamin Halevy, who later was one of the judges at the Eichmann trial, gave his decision in the case, in which he accepted most of Gruenwald's accusations and in a sharply worded judgment accused Kasztner of "selling his soul to Satan." Halevy said that only the accusation that Kasztner has personally profited remained unproven and thus found for the plaintiff but awarded him a pittance. The Israel Cabinet instructed the attorney general to lodge an appeal, a decision which caused a cabinet crisis when the *General Zionists refused to support the government on a nonconfidence motion. The Kasztner case thus became a major issue in the election campaign of 1955. The appeal, however, was submitted and on Jan. 17, 1958, the Supreme Court overturned the lower court's decision, finding Gruenwald guilty on most points of the slander charge and thereby clearing Kasztner's name. Kasztner himself was no longer alive; on March 3, 1957, a young man from Tel Aviv, Ze'ev Eckstein, influenced by the political atmosphere created by the lower court's verdict, shot Kasztner in the street. He succumbed nine days later. The story of Kasztner served as the model for a novel by Robert St. John, *The Man who Played God* (1962). It is a featured part of both right-wing and post-Zionist critiques of Zionist activities during the Holocaust.

The accusations against Kasztner include the argument that he should have informed Hungarian Jews of the "Final Solution." He had been privy to the Vr'ba-Wetzler report and "knew" that Jews were being killed in massive numbers. Hungarian Jews should have been warned of their fate, that he had favored privileged rather than ordinary Jews in his rescue efforts, and that he saved his own family at the expense of others. His negotiations with the Germans were by their very nature unequal; they had power, he did not. They could open the gates; he could not, at least not without their approval. So his situation was compromised from the start. Kasztner defenders argue on his behalf that information about the "Final Solution" was available to Hungarian Jews from many sources, but such information was not accepted as credible and therefore could not serve as a basis for action. Furthermore, the support of wealthy Jews was essential to financing the rescue operation. Without their participation for humanitarian or self-interested reasons no possible rescue could have been achieved, and the rescue of his family was quite natural. Even in death, the controversy endures. It remains the subject of books, journalistic pieces, and even television shows and films. Kasztner remains a useful target for those who wish to attack the Zionist establishment of the Yishuv and the early years of statehood, and his circumstances reveal the utter powerlessness of Jews under German occupation once the "Final Solution" was German policy. Hero or villain or both, the debate over Kasztner will endure though quite often the discussion has less to do with him than with contemporary issues.

BIBLIOGRAPHY: A. Weissberg, *Desperate Mission* (1958); A. Biss, *Der Stopp der Endloesung* (1966); E. Landau (ed.), *Der Kastner Bericht* (1961); Israel Supreme Court, *Piskei Din*, 12 (1958), 2017–317; Jerusalem District Court, Case 124/53, *Ha-Yo'eẓ ha-Mishpati Neged Malki'el Gruenwald* (1957). **ADD. BIBLIOGRAPHY:** Y. Bauer, *Jews for Sale: Nazi-German Negotiations, 1933–45* (1994). T. Segev, *The Seventh Million: The Israelis and the Holocaust* (1993).

[Yehouda Marton / Michael Berenbaum (2nd ed.)]

ABBREVIATIONS

GENERAL ABBREVIATIONS

This list contains abbreviations used in the Encyclopaedia (apart from the standard ones, such as geographical abbreviations, points of compass, etc.). For names of organizations, institutions, etc., in abbreviation, see Index. For bibliographical abbreviations of books and authors in Rabbinical literature, see following lists.

*	Cross reference; i.e., an article is to be found under the word(s) immediately following the asterisk (*).
°	Before the title of an entry, indicates a non-Jew (post-biblical times).
‡	Indicates reconstructed forms.
>	The word following this sign is derived from the preceding one.
<	The word preceding this sign is derived from the following one.

ad loc.	*ad locum*, "at the place"; used in quotations of commentaries.
A.H.	*Anno Hegirae*, "in the year of Hegira," i.e., according to the Muslim calendar.
Akk.	Addadian.
A.M.	*anno mundi*, "in the year (from the creation) of the world."
anon.	anonymous.
Ar.	Arabic.
Aram.	Aramaic.
Ass.	Assyrian.
b.	born; *ben, bar.*
Bab.	Babylonian.
B.C.E.	Before Common Era (= B.C.).
bibl.	bibliography.
Bul.	Bulgarian.
c., ca.	Circa.
C.E.	Common Era (= A.D.).
cf.	*confer*, "compare."
ch., chs.	chapter, chapters.
comp.	compiler, compiled by.
Cz.	Czech.
D	according to the documentary theory, the Deuteronomy document.
d.	died.
Dan.	Danish.
diss., dissert,	dissertation, thesis.
Du.	Dutch.
E.	according to the documentary theory, the Elohist document (i.e., using Elohim as the name of God) of the first five (or six) books of the Bible.
ed.	editor, edited, edition.
eds.	editors.
e.g.	*exempli gratia*, "for example."
Eng.	English.
et al.	*et alibi*, "and elsewhere"; or *et alii*, "and others"; "others."
f., ff.	and following page(s).
fig.	figure.
fl.	flourished.
fol., fols	folio(s).
Fr.	French.
Ger.	German.
Gr.	Greek.
Heb.	Hebrew.
Hg., Hung	Hungarian.
ibid	*Ibidem*, "in the same place."
incl. bibl.	includes bibliography.
introd.	introduction.
It.	Italian.
J	according to the documentary theory, the Jahwist document (i.e., using YHWH as the name of God) of the first five (or six) books of the Bible.
Lat.	Latin.
lit.	literally.
Lith.	Lithuanian.
loc. cit.	*loco citato*, "in the [already] cited place."
Ms., Mss.	Manuscript(s).
n.	note.
n.d.	no date (of publication).
no., nos	number(s).
Nov.	Novellae (Heb. *Ḥiddushim*).
n.p.	place of publication unknown.
op. cit.	*opere citato*, "in the previously mentioned work."
P.	according to the documentary theory, the Priestly document of the first five (or six) books of the Bible.
p., pp.	page(s).
Pers.	Persian.
pl., pls.	plate(s).
Pol.	Polish.
Port.	Potuguese.
pt., pts.	part(s).
publ.	published.
R.	Rabbi or Rav (before names); in Midrash (after an abbreviation) – *Rabbah*.
r.	recto, the first side of a manuscript page.
Resp.	Responsa (Latin "answers," Hebrew *She'elot u-Teshuvot* or *Teshuvot*), collections of rabbinic decisions.
rev.	revised.

Rom.	Romanian.
Rus(s).	Russian.
Slov.	Slovak.
Sp.	Spanish.
s.v.	*sub verbo, sub voce*, "under the (key) word."
Sum	Sumerian.
summ.	Summary.
suppl.	supplement.
Swed.	Swedish.
tr., trans(l).	translator, translated, translation.
Turk.	Turkish.
Ukr.	Ukrainian.
v., vv.	*verso*. The second side of a manuscript page; also verse(s).
Yid.	Yiddish.

ABBREVIATIONS USED IN RABBINICAL LITERATURE

Adderet Eliyahu, Karaite treatise by Elijah b. Moses *Bashyazi.

Admat Kodesh, Resp. by Nissim Ḥayyim Moses b. Joseph |Mizraḥi.

Aguddah, Sefer ha-, Nov. by *Alexander Suslin ha-Kohen.

Ahavat Ḥesed, compilation by *Israel Meir ha-Kohen.

Aliyyot de-Rabbenu Yonah, Nov. by *Jonah b. Avraham Gerondi.

Arukh ha-Shulḥan, codification by Jehiel Michel *Epstein.

Asayin (= positive precepts), subdivision of: (1) *Maimonides, *Sefer ha-Mitzvot;* (2) *Moses b. Jacob of Coucy, *Semag.*

Asefat Dinim, subdivision of *Sedei Ḥemed* by Ḥayyim Hezekiah *Medini, an encyclopaedia of precepts and responsa.

Asheri = *Asher b. Jehiel.

Aeret Ḥakhamim, by Baruch *Frankel-Teomim; pt, 1: Resp. to Sh. Ar.; pt2: Nov. to Talmud.

Ateret Zahav, subdivision of the *Levush*, a codification by Mordecai b. Abraham (Levush) *Jaffe; *Ateret Zahav* parallels Tur. YD.

Ateret Ẓevi, Comm. To Sh. Ar. by Ẓevi Hirsch b. Azriel.

Avir Ya'akov, Resp. by Jacob Avigdor.

Avkat Rokhel, Resp. by Joseph b. Ephraim *Caro.

Avnei Millu'im, Comm. to Sh. Ar., EH, by *Aryeh Loeb b. Joseph ha-Kohen.

Avnei Nezer, Resp. on Sh. Ar. by Abraham b. Ze'ev Nahum Bornstein of *Sochaczew.

Avodat Massa, Compilation of Tax Law by Yoasha Abraham Judah.

Azei ha-Levanon, Resp. by Judah Leib *Zirelson.

Ba'al ha-Tanya – *Shneur Zalman of Lyady.

Ba'ei Ḥayyei, Resp. by Ḥayyim b. Israel *Benveniste.

Ba'er Heitev, Comm. To Sh. Ar. The parts on OḤ and EH are by Judah b. Simeon *Ashkenazi, the parts on YD AND ḤM by *Zechariah Mendel b. Aryeh Leib. Printed in most editions of Sh. Ar.

Baḥ = Joel *Sirkes.

Baḥ, usual abbreviation for *Bayit Ḥadash*, a commentary on Tur by Joel *Sirkes; printed in most editions of Tur.

Bayit Ḥadash, see *Baḥ*.

Berab = Jacob Berab, also called Ri Berav.

Bedek ha-Bayit, by Joseph b. Ephraim *Caro, additions to his *Beit Yosef* (a comm. to Tur). Printed sometimes inside *Beit Yosef*, in smaller type. Appears in most editions of Tur.

Be'er ha-Golah, Commentary to Sh. Ar. By Moses b. Naphtali Hirsch *Rivkes; printed in most editions of Sh. Ar.

Be'er Mayim, Resp. by Raphael b. Abraham Manasseh Jacob.

Be'er Mayim Ḥayyim, Resp. by Samuel b. Ḥayyim *Vital.

Be'er Yiẓḥak, Resp. by Isaac Elhanan *Spector.

Beit ha-Beḥirah, Comm. to Talmud by Menahem b. Solomon *Meiri.

Beit Me'ir, Nov. on Sh. Ar. by Meir b. Judah Leib Posner.

Beit Shelomo, Resp. by Solomon b. Aaron Ḥason (the younger).

Beit Shemu'el, Comm. to Sh. Ar., EH, by *Samuel b. Uri Shraga Phoebus.

Beit Ya'akov, by Jacob b. Jacob Moses *Lorberbaum; pt.1: Nov. to Ket.; pt.2: Comm. to EH.

Beit Yisrael, collective name for the commentaries *Derishah, Perishah*, and *Be'urim* by Joshua b. Alexander ha-Kohen *Falk. See under the names of the commentaries.

Beit Yiẓḥak, Resp. by Isaac *Schmelkes.

Beit Yosef: (1) Comm. on Tur by Joseph b. Ephraim *Caro; printed in most editions of Tur; (2) Resp. by the same.

Ben Yehudah, Resp. by Abraham b. Judah Litsch (ליטש) Rosenbaum.

Bertinoro, Standard commentary to Mishnah by Obadiah *Bertinoro. Printed in most editions of the Mishnah.

[Be'urei] Ha-Gra, Comm. to Bible, Talmud, and Sh. Ar. By *Elijah b. Solomon Zalmon (Gaon of Vilna); printed in major editions of the mentioned works.

Be'urim, Glosses to Isserles *Darkhei Moshe* (a comm. on Tur) by Joshua b. Alexander ha-Kohen *Falk; printed in many editions of Tur.

Binyamin Ze'ev, Resp. by *Benjamin Ze'ev b. Mattathias of Arta.

Birkei Yosef, Nov. by Ḥayyim Joseph David *Azulai.

Ha-Buẓ ve-ha-Argaman, subdivision of the *Levush* (a codification by Mordecai b. Abraham (Levush) *Jaffe); *Ha-Buẓ ve-ha-Argaman* parallels Tur, EH.

Comm. = Commentary

Da'at Kohen, Resp. by Abraham Isaac ha-Kohen. *Kook.

Darkhei Moshe, Comm. on Tur Moses b. Israel *Isserles; printed in most editions of Tur.

Darkhei No'am, Resp. by *Mordecai b. Judah ha-Levi.

Darkhei Teshuvah, Nov. by Ẓevi *Shapiro; printed in the major editions of Sh. Ar.

De'ah ve-Haskel, Resp. by Obadiah Hadaya (see *Yaskil Avdi).*

Derashot Ran, Sermons by *Nissim b. Reuben Gerondi.
Derekh Ḥayyim, Comm. to *Avot* by *Judah Loew (Lob., Liwa) b. Bezalel (Maharal) of Prague.
Derishah, by Joshua b. Alexander ha-Kohen *Falk; additions to his *Perishah* (comm. on Tur); printed in many editions of Tur.
Derushei ha-Ẓelaḥ, Sermons, by Ezekiel b. Judah Halevi *Landau.
Devar Avraham, Resp. by Abraham *Shapira.
Devar Shemu'el, Resp. by Samuel *Aboab.
Devar Yehoshu'a, Resp. by Joshua Menahem b. Isaac Aryeh Ehrenberg.
Dikdukei Soferim, variae lections of the talmudic text by Raphael Nathan*Rabbinowicz.
Divrei Emet, Resp. by Isaac Bekhor David.
Divrei Ge'onim, Digest of responsa by Ḥayyim Aryeh b. Jeḥiel Ẓevi *Kahana.
Divrei Ḥamudot, Comm. on *Piskei ha-Rosh* by Yom Tov Lipmann b. Nathan ha-Levi *Heller; printed in major editions of the Talmud.
Divrei Ḥayyim several works by Ḥayyim *Halberstamm; if quoted alone refers to his Responsa.
Divrei Malkhi'el, Resp. by Malchiel Tenebaum.
Divrei Rivot, Resp. by Isaac b. Samuel *Adarbi.
Divrei Shemu'el, Resp. by Samuel Raphael Arditi.

Edut be-Ya'akov, Resp. by Jacob b. Abraham *Boton.
Edut bi-Yhosef, Resp. by Joseph b. Isaac *Almosnino.
Ein Ya'akov, Digest of talmudic *aggadot* by Jacob (Ibn) *Habib.
Ein Yiẓḥak, Resp. by Isaac Elhanan *Spector.
Ephraim of Lentshitz = Solomon *Luntschitz.
Erekh Leḥem, Nov. and glosses to Sh. Ar. by Jacob b. Abraham *Castro.
Eshkol, Sefer ha-, Digest of *halakhot* by *Abraham b. Isaac of Narbonne.
Et Sofer, Treatise on Law Court documents by Abraham b. Mordecai *Ankawa, in the 2nd vol. of his Resp. *Kerem Ḥamar.*
Etan ha-Ezraḥi, Resp. by Abraham b. Israel Jehiel (Shrenzl) *Rapaport.
Even ha-Ezel, Nov. to Maimonides' *Yad Ḥazakah* by Isser Zalman *Meltzer.
Even ha-Ezer, also called *Raban* of *Ẓafenat Pa'ne'aḥ,* rabbinical work with varied contents by *Eliezer b. Nathan of Mainz; not identical with the subdivision of Tur, Shulḥan Arukh, etc.
Ezrat Yehudah, Resp. by *Isaar Judah b. Nechemiah of Brisk.

Gan Eden, Karaite treatise by *Aaron b. Elijah of Nicomedia.
Gersonides = *Levi b. Gershom, also called Leo Hebraecus, or Ralbag.
Ginnat Veradim, Resp. by *Abraham b. Mordecai ha-Levi.

Haggahot, another name for *Rema.*
Haggahot Asheri, glosses to *Piskei ha-Rosh* by *Israel of Krems; printed in most Talmud editions.
Haggahot Maimuniyyot, Comm,. to Maimonides' Yad Ḥazakah by *Meir ha-Kohen; printed in most eds. of Yad.
Haggahot Mordekhai, glosses to *Mordekhai* by Samuel *Schlettstadt; printed in most editions of the Talmud after *Mordekhai.*
Haggahot ha-Rashash on Tosafot, annotations of Samuel *Strashun on the Tosafot (printed in major editions of the Talmud).
Ha-Gra = *Elijah b. Solomon Zalman (Gaon of Vilna).
Ha-Gra, Commentaries on Bible, Talmud, and Sh. Ar. respectively, by *Elijah b. Solomon Zalman (Gaon of Vilna); printed in major editions of the mentioned works.
Hai Gaon, Comm. = his comm. on Mishnah.
Ḥakham Ẓevi, Resp. by Ẓevi Hirsch b. Jacob *Ashkenazi.
Halakhot = Rif, *Halakhot.* Compilation and abstract of the Talmud by Isaac b. Jacob ha-Kohen *Alfasi; printed in most editions of the Talmud.
Halakhot Gedolot, compilation of *halakhot* from the Geonic period, arranged acc. to the Talmud. Here cited acc. to ed. Warsaw (1874). Author probably *Simeon Kayyara of Basra.
Halakhot Pesukot le-Rav Yehudai Ga'on compilation of *halakhot.*
Halakhot Pesukot min ha-Ge'onim, compilation of *halakhot* from the geonic period by different authors.
Ḥananel, Comm. to Talmud by *Hananel b. Ḥushi'el; printed in some editions of the Talmud.
Harei Besamim, Resp. by Aryeh Leib b. Isaac *Horowitz.
Ḥassidim, Sefer, Ethical maxims by *Judah b. Samuel he-Ḥasid.
Hassagot Rabad on Rif, Glosses on Rif, *Halakhot,* by *Abraham b. David of Posquières.
Hassagot Rabad [on Yad], Glosses on Maimonides, *Yad Ḥazakah,* by *Abraham b. David of Posquières.
Hassagot Ramban, Glosses by Naḥmanides on Maimonides' *Sefer ha-Mitzvot;* usually printed together with *Sefer ha-Mitzvot.*
Ḥatam Sofer = Moses *Sofer.
Ḥavvot Ya'ir, Resp. and varia by Jair Ḥayyim *Bacharach
Ḥayyim Or Zaru'a = *Ḥayyim (Eliezer) b. Isaac.
Ḥazon Ish = Abraham Isaiah *Karelitz.
Ḥazon Ish, Nov. by Abraham Isaiah *Karelitz
Ḥedvat Ya'akov, Resp. by Aryeh Judah Jacob b. David Dov Meisels (article under his father's name).
Heikhal Yiẓḥak, Resp. by Isaac ha-Levi *Herzog.
Ḥelkat Meḥokek, Comm. to Sh. Ar., by Moses b. Isaac Judah *Lima.
Ḥelkat Ya'akov, Resp. by Mordecai Jacob Breisch.
Ḥemdah Genuzah, , Resp. from the geonic period by different authors.
Ḥemdat Shelomo, Resp. by Solomon Zalman *Lipschitz.
Ḥida = Ḥayyim Joseph David *Azulai.
Ḥiddushei Halakhot ve-Aggadot, Nov. by Samuel Eliezer b. Judah ha-Levi *Edels.
Ḥikekei Lev, Resp. by Ḥayyim *Palaggi.
Ḥikrei Lev, Nov. to Sh. Ar. by Joseph Raphael b. Ḥayyim Joseph Ḥazzan (see article *Ḥazzan Family).
Hil. = Hilkhot … (e.g. *Hilkhot Shabbat).*
Ḥinnukh, Sefer ha-, List and explanation of precepts attributed (probably erroneously) to Aaron ha-Levi of Barcelona (see article *Ha-Ḥinnukh).*
Ḥok Ya'akov, Comm. to Hil. Pesaḥ in Sh. Ar., OḤ, by Jacob b. Joseph *Reicher.
Ḥokhmat Sehlomo (1), Glosses to Talmud, *Rashi* and Tosafot by Solomon b. Jehiel "Maharshal") *Luria; printed in many editions of the Talmud.
Ḥokhmat Sehlomo (2), Glosses and Nov. to Sh. Ar. by Solomon b. Judah Aaron *Kluger printed in many editions of Sh. Ar.
Ḥur, subdivision of the *Levush,* a codification by Mordecai b. Abraham (Levush) *Jaffe; *Hur* (or *Levush ha-Hur)* parallels Tur, OḤ, 242–697.
Ḥut ha-Meshullash, fourth part of the *Tashbeẓ* (Resp.), by Simeon b. Zemaḥ *Duran.

Ibn Ezra, Comm. to the Bible by Abraham *Ibn Ezra; printed in the major editions of the Bible *("Mikra'ot Gedolot").*
Imrei Yosher, Resp. by Meir b. Aaron Judah *Arik.
Ir Shushan, Subdivision of the *Levush,* a codification by Mordecai b. Abraham (Levush) *Jaffe; *Ir Shushan* parallels Tur, ḤM.
Israel of Bruna = Israel b. Ḥayyim *Bruna.
Ittur. Treatise on precepts by *Isaac b. Abba Mari of Marseilles.

Jacob Be Rab = *Be Rab.
Jacob b. Jacob Moses of Lissa = Jacob b. Jacob Moses *Lorberbaum.
Judah B. Simeon = Judah b. Simeon *Ashkenazi.
Judah Minz = Judah b. Eliezer ha-Levi *Minz.

Kappei Aharon, Resp. by Aaron Azriel.
Kehillat Ya'akov, Talmudic methodology, definitions etc. by Israel Jacob b. Yom Tov *Algazi.
Kelei Ḥemdah, Nov. and *pilpulim* by Meir Dan *Plotzki of Ostrova, arranged acc. to the Torah.
Keli Yakar, Annotations to the Torah by Solomon *Luntschitz.
Keneh Ḥokhmah, Sermons by Judah Loeb *Pochwitzer.
Keneset ha-Gedolah, Digest of *halakhot* by Ḥayyim b. Israel *Benveniste; subdivided into annotations to *Beit Yosef* and annotations to Tur.
Keneset Yisrael, Resp. by Ezekiel b. Abraham Katzenellenbogen (see article *Katzenellenbogen Family).
Kerem Ḥamar, Resp. and varia by Abraham b. Mordecai *Ankawa.
Kerem Shelmo. Resp. by Solomon b. Joseph *Amarillo.
Keritut, [Sefer], Methodology of the Talmud by *Samson b. Isaac of Chinon.
Kesef ha-Kedoshim, Comm. to Sh. Ar., ḤM, by Abraham *Wahrmann; printed in major editions of Sh. Ar.
Kesef Mishneh, Comm. to Maimonides, *Yad Ḥazakah,* by Joseph b. Ephraim *Caro; printed in most editions of *Yad Ḥazakah.*
Kezot ha-Ḥoshen, Comm. to Sh. Ar., ḤM, by *Aryeh Loeb b. Joseph ha-Kohen; printed in major editions of Sh. Ar.
Kol Bo [*Sefer*], Anonymous collection of ritual rules; also called *Sefer ha-Likkutim.*
Kol Mevasser, Resp. by Meshullam *Rath.
Korban Aharon, Comm. to *Sifra* by Aaron b. Abraham *Ibn Ḥayyim; pt. 1 is called: *Middot Aharon.*
Korban Edah, Comm. to Jer. Talmud by David *Fraenkel; with additions: *Shiyyurei Korban;* printed in most editions of Jer. Talmud.
Kunteres ha-Kelalim, subdivision of *Sedei Ḥemed,* an encyclopaedia of precepts and responsa by Ḥayyim Hezekiah *Medini.
Kunteres ha-Semikhah, a treatise by *Levi b. Ḥabib; printed at the end of his responsa.
Kunteres Tikkun Olam, part of *Mispat Shalom* (Nov. by Shalom Mordecai b. Moses *Schwadron).

Lavin (negative precepts), subdivision of: (1) *Maimonides, *Sefer ha-Mitzvot;* (2) *Moses b. Jacob of Coucy, *Semag.*
Leḥem Mishneh, Comm. to Maimonides, *Yad Ḥazakah,* by Abraham [Ḥiyya] b. Moses *Boton; printed in most editions of *Yad Ḥazakah.*
Leḥem Rav, Resp. by Abraham [Ḥiyya] b. Moses *Boton.
Leket Yosher, Resp and varia by Israel b. Pethahiah *Isserlein, collected by *Joseph (Joselein) b. Moses.
Leo Hebraeus = *Levi b. Gershom, also called Ralbag or Gersonides.
Levush = Mordecai b. Abraham *Jaffe.
Levush [Malkhut], Codification by Mordecai b. Abraham (Levush) *Jaffe, with subdivisions: [*Levush ha-] Tekhelet* (parallels Tur OḤ 1–241); [*Levush ha-] Ḥur* (parallels Tur OḤ 242–697); [*Levush*] *Ateret Zahav* (parallels Tur YD); [*Levush ha-Buẓ ve-ha-Argaman* (parallels Tur EH); [*Levush] Ir Shushan* (parallels Tur ḤM); under the name *Levush* the author wrote also other works.
Li-Leshonot ha-Rambam, fifth part (nos. 1374–1700) of Resp. by *David b. Solomon ibn Abi Zimra (Radbaz).
Likkutim, Sefer ha-, another name for [*Sefer*] *Kol Bo.*

Ma'adanei Yom Tov, Comm. on *Piskei ha-Rosh* by Yom Tov Lipmann b. Nathan ha-Levi *Heller; printed in many editions of the Talmud.
Mabit = Moses b. Joseph *Trani.
Magen Avot, Comm. to *Avot* by Simeon b. Ẓemaḥ *Duran.
Magen Avraham, Comm. to Sh. Ar., OḤ, by Abraham Abele b. Ḥayyim ha-Levi *Gombiner; printed in many editions of Sh. Ar., OḤ.
Maggid Mishneh, Comm. to Maimonides, *Yad Ḥazakah,* by *Vidal Yom Tov of Tolosa; printed in most editions of the *Yad Ḥazakah.*
Maḥaneh Efrayim, Resp. and Nov., arranged acc. to Maimonides' *Yad Ḥazakah* , by Ephraim b. Aaron *Navon.
Maharai = Israel b. Pethahiah *Isserlein.
Maharal of Prague = *Judah Loew (Lob, Liwa), b. Bezalel.
Maharalbaḥ = *Levi b. Ḥabib.
Maharam Alashkar = Moses b. Isaac *Alashkar.
Maharam Alshekh = Moses b. Ḥayyim *Alashekh.
Maharam Mintz = Moses *Mintz.
Maharam of Lublin = *Meir b. Gedaliah of Lublin.
Maharam of Padua = Meir *Katzenellenbogen.
Maharam of Rothenburg = *Meir b. Baruch of Rothenburg.
Maharam Shik = Moses b. Joseph Schick.
Maharash Engel = Samuel b. Ze'ev Wolf Engel.
Maharashdam = Samuel b. Moses *Medina.
Maharḥash = Ḥayyim (ben) Shabbetai.
Mahari Basan = Jehiel b. Ḥayyim Basan.
Mahari b. Lev = Joseph ibn Lev.
Mahari'az = Jekuthiel Asher Zalman Ensil Zusmir.
Maharibal = *Joseph ibn Lev.
Mahariḥ = Jacob (Israel) *Ḥagiz.
Maharik = Joseph b. Solomon *Colon.
Maharikash = Jacob b. Abraham *Castro.
Maharil = Jacob b. Moses *Moellin.
Maharimat = Joseph b. Moses di Trani (not identical with the Maharit).
Maharit = Joseph b. Moses *Trani.
Maharitaẓ = Yom Tov b. Akiva Ẓahalon. (See article *Ẓahalon Family).
Maharsha = Samuel Eliezer b. Judah ha-Levi *Edels.
Maharshag = Simeon b. Judah Gruenfeld.
Maharshak = Samson b. Isaac of Chinon.
Maharshakh = *Solomon b. Abraham.
Maharshal = Solomon b. Jeḥiel *Luria.
Mahasham = Shalom Mordecai b. Moses *Sschwadron.
Maharyu = Jacob b. Judah *Weil.
Maḥazeh Avraham, Resp. by Abraham Nebagen v. Meir ha-Levi Steinberg.
Maḥazik Berakhah, Nov. by Ḥayyim Joseph David *Azulai.

*Maimonides = Moses b. Maimon, or Rambam.
*Malbim = Meir Loeb b. Jehiel Michael.
Malbim = Malbim's comm. to the Bible; printed in the major editions.
Malbushei Yom Tov, Nov. on *Levush*, OḤ, by Yom Tov Lipmann b. Nathan ha-Levi *Heller.
Mappah, another name for *Rema.*
Mareh ha-Panim, Comm. to Jer. Talmud by Moses b. Simeon *Margolies; printed in most editions of Jer. Talmud.
Margaliyyot ha-Yam, Nov. by Reuben *Margoliot.
Masat Binyamin, Resp. by Benjamin Aaron b. Abraham *Slonik
Mashbir, Ha- = *Joseph Samuel b. Isaac Rodi.
Massa Ḥayyim, Tax *halakhot* by Ḥayyim *Palaggi, with the subdivisions *Missim ve-Arnomiyyot* and *Torat ha-Minhagot.*
Massa Melekh, Compilation of Tax Law by Joseph b. Isaac *Ibn Ezra with concluding part *Ne'ilat She'arim.*
Matteh Asher, Resp. by Asher b. Emanuel Shalem.
Matteh Shimon, Digest of Resp. and Nov. to Tur and *Beit Yosef,* ḤM, by Mordecai Simeon b. Solomon.
Matteh Yosef, Resp. by Joseph b. Moses ha-Levi Nazir (see article under his father's name).
Mayim Amukkim, Resp. by Elijah b. Abraham *Mizraḥi.
Mayim Ḥayyim, Resp. by Ḥayyim b. Dov Beresh Rapaport.
Mayim Rabbim, , Resp. by Raphael *Meldola.
Me-Emek ha-Bakha, , Resp. by Simeon b. Jekuthiel Ephrati.
Me'irat Einayim, usual abbreviation: *Sma* (from: *Sefer Me'irat Einayim*); comm. to Sh. Ar. By Joshua b. Alexander ha-Kohen *Falk; printed in most editions of the Sh. Ar.
Melammed le-Ho'il, Resp. by David Ẓevi *Hoffmann.
Meisharim, [*Sefer*], Rabbinical treatise by *Jeroham b. Meshullam.
Meshiv Davar, Resp. by Naphtali Ẓevi Judah *Berlin.
Mi-Gei ha-Haregah, Resp. by Simeon b. Jekuthiel Ephrati.
Mi-Ma'amakim, Resp. by Ephraim Oshry.
Middot Aharon, first part of *Korban Aharon,* a comm. to *Sifra* by Aaron b. Abraham *Ibn Ḥayyim.
Migdal Oz, Comm. to Maimonides, *Yad Ḥazakah,* by *Ibn Gaon Shem Tov b. Abraham; printed in most editions of the *Yad Ḥazakah.*
Mikhtam le-David, Resp. by David Samuel b. Jacob *Pardo.
Mikkaḥ ve-ha-Mimkar, Sefer ha-, Rabbinical treatise by *Hai Gaon.
Milḥamot ha-Shem, Glosses to Rif, *Halakhot,* by *Naḥmanides.
Minḥat Ḥinnukh, Comm. to *Sefer ha-Ḥinnukh,* by Joseph b. Moses *Babad.
Minḥat Yiẓḥak, Resp. by Isaac Jacob b. Joseph Judah Weiss.
Misgeret ha-Shulḥan, Comm. to Sh. Ar., ḤM, by Benjamin Ze'ev Wolf b. Shabbetai; printed in most editions of Sh. Ar.
Mishkenot ha-Ro'im, Halakhot in alphabetical order by Uzziel Alshekh.
Mishnah Berurah, Comm. to Sh. Ar., OḤ, by *Israel Meir ha-Kohen.
Mishneh le-Melekh, Comm. to Maimonides, *Yad Ḥazakah,* by Judah *Rosanes; printed in most editions of *Yad Ḥazakah.*
Mishpat ha-Kohanim, Nov. to Sh. Ar., ḤM, by Jacob Moses *Lorberbaum, part of his *Netivot ha-Mishpat;* printed in major editions of Sh. Ar.
Mishpat Kohen, Resp. by Abraham Isaac ha-Kohen *Kook.
Mishpat Shalom, Nov. by Shalom Mordecai b. Moses *Schwadron; contains: *Kunteres Tikkun Olam.*
Mishpat u-Ẓedakah be-Ya'akov, Resp. by Jacob b. Reuben *Ibn Ẓur.
Mishpat ha-Urim, Comm. to Sh. Ar., ḤM by Jacob b. Jacob Moses *Lorberbaum, part of his *Netivot ha-Mishpat*; printed in major editons of Sh. Ar.
Mishpat Ẓedek, Resp. by *Melammed Meir b. Shem Tov.
Mishpatim Yesharim, Resp. by Raphael b. Mordecai *Berdugo.
Mishpetei Shemu'el, Resp. by Samuel b. Moses *Kalai (Kal'i).
Mishpetei ha-Tanna'im, Kunteres, Nov on *Levush,* OḤ by Yom Tov Lipmann b. Nathan ha-Levi *Heller.
Mishpetei Uzzi'el (Uziel), Resp. by Ben-Zion Meir Hai *Ouziel.
Missim ve-Arnoniyyot, Tax *halakhot* by Ḥayyim *Palaggi, a subdivision of his work *Massa Ḥayyim* on the same subject.
Mitzvot, Sefer ha-, Elucidation of precepts by *Maimonides; subdivided into *Lavin* (negative precepts) and *Asayin* (positive precepts).
Mitzvot Gadol, Sefer, Elucidation of precepts by *Moses b. Jacob of Coucy, subdivided into *Lavin* (negative precepts) and *Asayin* (positive precepts); the usual abbreviation is *Semag.*
Mitzvot Katan, Sefer, Elucidation of precepts by *Isaac b. Joseph of Corbeil; the usual, abbreviation is *Semak.*
Mo'adim u-Zemannim, Rabbinical treatises by Moses Sternbuch.
Modigliano, Joseph Samuel = *Joseph Samuel b. Isaac, Rodi (Ha-Mashbir).
Mordekhai (Mordecai), halakhic compilation by *Mordecai b. Hillel; printed in most editions of the Talmud after the texts.
Moses b. Maimon = *Maimonides, also called Rambam.
Moses b. Naḥman = Naḥmanides, also called Ramban.
Muram = Isaiah Menahem b. Isaac (from: Morenu R. Mendel).

Naḥal Yiẓḥak, Comm. on Sh. Ar., ḤM, by Isaac Elhanan *Spector.
Naḥalah li-Yhoshu'a, Resp. by Joshua Ẓunẓin.
Naḥalat Shivah, collection of legal forms by *Samuel b. David Moses ha-Levi.
*Naḥmanides = Moses b. Naḥman, also called Ramban.
Naẓiv = Naphtali Ẓevi Judah *Berlin.
Ne'eman Shemu'el, Resp. by Samuel Isaac *Modigilano.
Ne'ilat She'arim, concluding part of *Massa Melekh* (a work on Tax Law) by Joseph b. Isaac *Ibn Ezra, containing an exposition of customary law and subdivided into *Minhagei Issur* and *Minhagei Mamon.*
Ner Ma'aravi, Resp. by Jacob b. Malka.
Netivot ha-Mishpat, by Jacob b. Jacob Moses *Lorberbaum; subdivided into *Mishpat ha-Kohanim,* Nov. to Sh. Ar., ḤM, and *Mishpat ha-Urim,* a comm. on the same; printed in major editions of Sh. Ar.
Netivot Olam, Saying of the Sages by *Judah Loew (Lob, Liwa) b. Bezalel.
Nimmukei Menaḥem of Merseburg, Tax *halakhot* by the same, printed at the end of Resp. Maharyu.
Nimmukei Yosef, Comm. to Rif. *Halakhot,* by Joseph *Ḥabib (Ḥabiba); printed in many editions of the Talmud.
Noda bi-Yhudah, Resp. by Ezekiel b. Judah ha-Levi *Landau; there is a first collection *(Mahadura Kamma)* and a second collection *(Mahadura Tinyana).*
Nov. = Novellae, Ḥiddushim.

Ohel Moshe (1), Notes to Talmud, *Midrash Rabbah,* Yad, *Sifrei* and to several Resp., by Eleazar *Horowitz.

Ohel Moshe (2), Resp. by Moses Jonah Zweig.
Oholei Tam. Resp. by *Tam ibn Yaḥya Jacob b. David; printed in the rabbinical collection *Tummat Yesharim.*
Oholei Ya'akov, Resp. by Jacob de *Castro.
Or ha-Me'ir Resp by Judah Meir b. Jacob Samson Shapiro.
Or Same'aḥ, Comm. to Maimonides, *Yad Ḥazakah,* by *Meir Simḥah ha-Kohen of Dvinsk; printed in many editions of the *Yad Ḥazakah.*
Or Zaru'a [the father] = *Isaac b. Moses of Vienna.
Or Zaru'a [the son] = *Ḥayyim (Eliezer) b. Isaac.
Or Zaru'a, Nov. by *Isaac b. Moses of Vienna.
Orah, Sefer ha-, Compilation of ritual precepts by *Rashi.
Oraḥ la-Ẓaddik, Resp. by Abraham Ḥayyim Rodrigues.
Oẓar ha-Posekim, Digest of Responsa.

Paḥad Yiẓḥak, Rabbinical encyclopaedia by Isaac *Lampronti.
Panim Me'irot, Resp. by Meir b. Isaac *Eisenstadt.
Parashat Mordekhai, Resp. by Mordecai b. Abraham Naphtali *Banet.
Pe'at ha-Sadeh la-Dinim and Pe'at ha-Sadeh la-Kelalim, subdivisions of the *Sedei Ḥemed,* an encyclopaedia of precepts and responsa, by Ḥayyim Hezekaih *Medini.
Penei Moshe (1), Resp. by Moses *Benveniste.
Penei Moshe (2), Comm. to Jer. Talmud by Moses b. Simeon *Margolies; printed in most editions of the Jer. Talmud.
Penei Moshe (3), Comm. on the aggadic passages of 18 treatises of the Bab. and Jer. Talmud, by Moses b. Isaiah Katz.
Penei Yehoshu'a, Nov. by Jacob Joshua b. Ẓevi Hirsch *Falk.
Peri Ḥadash, Comm. on Sh. Ar. By Hezekiah da *Silva.
Perishah, Comm. on Tur by Joshua b. Alexander ha-Kohen *Falk; printed in major edition of Tur; forms together with *Derishah* and *Be'urim* (by the same author) the *Beit Yisrael.*
Pesakim u-Khetavim, 2nd part of the *Terumat ha-Deshen* by Israel b. Pethahiah *Isserlein' also called *Piskei Maharai.*
Pilpula Ḥarifta, Comm. to *Piskei ha-Rosh, Seder Nezikin,* by Yom Tov Lipmann b. Nathan ha-Levi *Heller; printed in major editions of the Talmud.
Piskei Maharai, see *Terumat ha-Deshen,* 2nd part; also called *Pesakim u-Khetavim.*
Piskei ha-Rosh, a compilation of *halakhot,* arranged on the Talmud, by *Asher b. Jehiel (Rosh); printed in major Talmud editions.
Pitḥei Teshuvah, Comm. to Sh. Ar. by Abraham Hirsch b. Jacob *Eisenstadt; printed in major editions of the Sh. Ar.

Rabad = *Abraham b. David of Posquières (Rabad III.).
Raban = *Eliezer b. Nathan of Mainz.
Raban, also called *Ẓafenat Pa'ne'aḥ* or *Even ha-Ezer,* see under the last name.
Rabi Abad = *Abraham b. Isaac of Narbonne.
Radad = David Dov. b. Aryeh Judah Jacob *Meisels.
Radam = Dov Berush b. Isaac Meisels.
Radbaz = *David b Solomon ibn Abi Ziumra.
Radbaz, Comm. to Maimonides, *Yad Ḥazakah,* by *David b. Solomon ibn Abi Zimra.
Ralbag = *Levi b. Gershom, also called Gersonides, or Leo Hebraeus.
Ralbag, Bible comm. by *Levi b. Gershon.
Rama [da Fano] = Menaḥem Azariah *Fano.
Ramah = Meir b. Todros [ha-Levi] *Abulafia.
Ramam = *Menaham of Merseburg.
Rambam = *Maimonides; real name: Moses b. Maimon.
Ramban = *Naḥmanides; real name Moses b. Naḥman.
Ramban, Comm. to Torah by *Naḥmanides; printed in major editions. ("Mikra'ot Gedolot").
Ran = *Nissim b. Reuben Gerondi.
Ran of Rif, Comm. on Rif, *Halakhot,* by Nissim b. Reuben Gerondi.
Ranaḥ = *Elijah b. Ḥayyim.
Rash = *Samson b. Abraham of Sens.
Rash, Comm. to Mishnah, by *Samson b. Abraham of Sens; printed in major Talmud editions.
Rashash = Samuel *Strashun.
Rashba = Solomon b. Abraham *Adret.
Rashba, Resp., see also; *Sefer Teshuvot ha-Rashba ha-Meyuḥasot le-ha-Ramban,* by Solomon b. Abraham *Adret.
Rashbad = Samuel b. David.
Rashbam = *Samuel b. Meir.
Rashbam = Comm. on Bible and Talmud by *Samuel b. Meir; printed in major editions of Bible and most editions of Talmud.
Rashbash = Solomon b. Simeon *Duran.
*Rashi = Solomon b. Isaac of Troyes.
Rashi, Comm. on Bible and Talmud by *Rashi; printed in almost all Bible and Talmud editions.
Raviah = Eliezer b. Joel ha-Levi.
Redak = David *Kimḥi.
Redak, Comm. to Bible by David *Kimḥi.
Redakh = *David b. Ḥayyim ha-Kohen of Corfu.
Re'em = Elijah b. Abraham *Mizraḥi.
Rema = Moses b. Israel *Isserles.
Rema, Glosses to Sh. Ar. by Moses b. Israel *Isserles; printed in almost all editions of the Sh. Ar. inside the text in Rashi type; also called *Mappah* or *Haggahot.*
Remek = Moses Kimḥi.
Remakh = Moses ha-Kohen mi-Lunel.
Reshakh = *Solomon b. Abraham; also called Maharshakh.
Resp. = Responsa, *She'elot u-Teshuvot.*
Ri Berav = *Berab.
Ri Escapa = Joseph b. Saul *Escapa.
Ri Migash = Joseph b. Meir ha-Levi *Ibn Migash.
Riba = Isaac b. Asher ha-Levi; Riba II (Riba ha-Baḥur) = his grandson with the same name.
Ribam = Isaac b. Mordecai (or: Isaac b. Meir).
Ribash = *Isaac b. Sheshet Perfet (or: Barfat).
Rid= *Isaiah b. Mali di Trani the Elder.
Ridbaz = Jacob David b. Ze'ev *Willowski.
Rif = Isaac b. Jacob ha-Kohen *Alfasi.
Rif, *Halakhot,* Compilation and abstract of the Talmud by Isaac b. Jacob ha-Kohen *Alfasi.
Ritba = Yom Tov b. Abraham *Ishbili.
Riẓbam = Isaac b. Mordecai.
Rosh = *Asher b. Jehiel, also called Asheri.
Rosh Mashbir, Resp. by *Joseph Samuel b. Isaac, Rodi.

Sedei Ḥemed, Encyclopaedia of precepts and responsa by Ḥayyim Ḥezekiah *Medini; subdivisions: *Asefat Dinim, Kunteres ha-Kelalim, Pe'at ha-Sadeh la-Dinim, Pe'at ha-Sadeh la-Kelalim.*
Semag, Usual abbreviation of *Sefer Mitzvot Gadol,* elucidation of precepts by *Moses b. Jacob of Coucy; subdivided into *Lavin* (negative precepts) *Asayin* (positive precepts).
Semak, Usual abbreviation of *Sefer Mitzvot Katan,* elucidation of precepts by *Isaac b. Joseph of Corbeil.

Sh. Ar. = *Shulḥan Arukh,* code by Joseph b. Ephraim *Caro.
Sha'ar Mishpat, Comm. to Sh. Ar., ḤM. By Israel Isser b. Ze'ev Wolf.
Sha'arei Shevu'ot, Treatise on the law of oaths by *David b. Saadiah; usually printed together with Rif, *Halakhot;* also called: *She'arim of R. Alfasi.*
Sha'arei Teshuvah, Collection of resp. from Geonic period, by different authors.
Sha'arei Uzzi'el, Rabbinical treatise by Ben-Zion Meir Ha *Ouziel.
Sha'arei Ẓedek, Collection of resp. from Geonic period, by different authors.
Shadal [or Shedal] = Samuel David *Luzzatto.
Shai la-Moreh, Resp. by Shabbetai Jonah.
Shakh, Usual abbreviation of *Siftei Kohen,* a comm. to Sh. Ar., YD and ḤM by *Shabbetai b. Meir ha-Kohen; printed in most editions of Sh. Ar.
Sha'ot-de-Rabbanan, Resp. by *Solomon b. Judah ha-Kohen.
She'arim of R. Alfasi see *Sha'arei Shevu'ot.*
Shedal, see Shadal.
She'elot u-Teshuvot ha-Ge'onim, Collection of resp. by different authors.
She'erit Yisrael, Resp. by Israel Ze'ev Mintzberg.
She'erit Yosef, Resp. by *Joseph b. Mordecai Gershon ha-Kohen.
She'ilat Yaveẓ, Resp. by Jacob *Emden (Yaveẓ).
She'iltot, Compilation arranged acc. to the Torah by *Aḥa (Aḥai) of Shabḥa.
Shem Aryeh, Resp. by Aryeh Leib *Lipschutz.
Shemesh Ẓedakah, Resp. by Samson *Morpurgo.
Shenei ha-Me'orot ha-Gedolim, Resp. by Elijah *Covo.
Shetarot, Sefer ha-, Collection of legal forms by *Judah b. Barzillai al-Bargeloni.
Shevut Ya'akov, Resp. by Jacob b. Joseph Reicher.
Shibbolei ha-Leket Compilation on ritual by Zedekiah b. Avraham *Anav.
Shiltei Gibborim, Comm. to Rif, *Halakhot,* by *Joshua Boaz b. Simeon; printed in major editions of the Talmud.
Shittah Mekubbeẓet, Compilation of talmudical commentaries by Bezalel *Ashkenazi.
Shivat Ẓiyyon, Resp. by Samuel b. Ezekiel *Landau.
Shiyyurei Korban, by David *Fraenkel; additions to his comm. to Jer. Talmud *Korban Edah;* both printed in most editions of Jer. Talmud.
Sho'el u-Meshiv, Resp. by Joseph Saul ha-Levi *Nathanson.
Sh[ulḥan] Ar[ukh] [of Ba'al ha-Tanyal], Code by *Shneur Zalman of Lyady; not identical with the code by Joseph Caro.
Siftei Kohen, Comm. to Sh. Ar., YD and ḤM by *Shabbetai b. Meir ha-Kohen; printed in most editions of Sh. Ar.; usual abbreviation: *Shakh.*
Simḥat Yom Tov, Resp. by Tom Tov b. Jacob *Algazi.
Simlah Ḥadashah, Treatise on *Sheḥitah* by Alexander Sender b. Ephraim Zalman *Schor; see also *Tevu'ot Shor.*
Simeon b. Ẓemaḥ = Simeon b. Ẓemaḥ *Duran.
Sma, Comm. to Sh. Ar. by Joshua b. Alexander ha-Kohen *Falk; the full title is: *Sefer Me'irat Einayim;* printed in most editions of Sh. Ar.
Solomon b. Isaac ha-Levi = Solomon b. Isaac *Levy.
Solomon b. Isaac of Troyes = *Rashi.

Tal Orot, Rabbinical work with various contents, by Joseph ibn Gioia.
Tam, Rabbenu = *Tam Jacob b. Meir.
Tashbaẓ = Samson b. Zadok.
Tashbeẓ = Simeon b. Zemaḥ *Duran, sometimes also abbreviation for Samson b. Zadok, usually known as Tashbaẓ.
Tashbeẓ [Sefer ha-], Resp. by Simeon b. Ẓemaḥ *Duran; the fourth part of this work is called: *Ḥut ha-Meshullash.*
Taz, Usual abbreviation of *Turei Zahav,* comm., to Sh. Ar. by *David b. Samnuel ha-Levi; printed in most editions of Sh. Ar.
(Ha)-Tekhelet, subdivision of the *Levush* (a codification by Mordecai b. Abraham (Levush) *Jaffe); *Ha-Tekhelet* parallels Tur, OḤ 1-241.
Terumat ha-Deshen, by Israel b. Pethahiah *Isserlein; subdivided into a part containing responsa, and a second part called *Pesakim u-Khetavim* or *Piskei Maharai.*
Terumot, Sefer ha-, Compilation of *halakhot* by Samuel b. Isaac *Sardi.
Teshuvot Ba'alei ha-Tosafot, Collection of responsa by the Tosafists.
Teshjvot Ge'onei Mizraḥ u-Ma'aav, Collection of responsa.
Teshuvot ha-Geonim, Collection of responsa from Geonic period.
Teshuvot Ḥakhmei Provinẓyah, Collection of responsa by different Provencal authors.
Teshuvot Ḥakhmei Ẓarefat ve-Loter, Collection of responsa by different French authors.
Teshuvot Maimuniyyot, Resp. pertaining to Maimonides' *Yad Ḥazakah;* printed in major editions of this work after the text; authorship uncertain.
Tevu'ot Shor, by Alexander Sender b. Ephraim Zalman *Schor, a comm. to his *Simlah Ḥadashah,* a work on *Sheḥitah.*
Tiferet Ẓevi, Resp. by Ẓevi Hirsch of the "AHW" Communities (Altona, Hamburg, Wandsbeck).
Tiktin, Judah b. Simeon = Judah b. Simeon *Ashkenazi.
Toledot Adam ve-Ḥavvah, Codification by *Jeroham b. Meshullam.
Torat Emet, Resp. by Aaron b. Joseph *Sasson.
Torat Ḥayyim, , Resp. by Ḥayyim (ben) Shabbetai.
Torat ha-Minhagot, subdivision of the *Massa Ḥayyim* (a work on tax law) by Ḥayyim *Palaggi, containing an exposition of customary law.
Tosafot Rid, Explanations to the Talmud and decisions by *Isaiah b. Mali di Trani the Elder.
Tosefot Yom Tov, comm. to Mishnah by Yom Tov Lipmann b. Nathan ha-Levi *Heller; printed in most editions of the Mishnah.
Tummim, subdivision of the comm. to Sh. Ar., ḤM, *Urim ve-Tummim* by Jonathan *Eybeschuetz; printed in the major editions of Sh. Ar.
Tur, usual abbreviation for the *Arba'ah Turim* of *Jacob b. Asher.
Turei Zahav, Comm. to Sh. Ar. by *David b. Samuel ha-Levi; printed in most editions of Sh. Ar.; usual abbreviation: *Taz.*

Urim, subdivision of the following.
Urim ve-Tummim, Comm. to Sh. Ar., ḤM, by Jonathan *Eybeschuetz; printed in the major editions of Sh. Ar.; subdivided in places into *Urim* and *Tummim.*

Vikku'aḥ Mayim Ḥayyim, Polemics against Isserles and Caro by Ḥayyim b. Bezalel.

Yad Malakhi, Methodological treatise by *Malachi b. Jacob ha-Kohen.

Yad Ramah, Nov. by Meir b. Todros [ha-Levi] *Abulafia.
Yakhin u-Vo'az, Resp. by Ẓemaḥ b. Solomon *Duran.
Yam ha-Gadol, Resp. by Jacob Moses *Toledano.
Yam shel Shelomo, Compilation arranged acc. to Talmud by Solomon b. Jehiel (Maharshal) *Luria.
Yashar, Sefer ha-, by *Tam, Jacob b. Meir (Rabbenu Tam); 1st pt.: Resp.; 2nd pt.: Nov.
Yaskil Avdi, Resp. by Obadiah Hadaya (printed together with his Resp. *De'ah ve-Haskel).*
Yavez = Jacob *Emden.
Yehudah Ya'aleh, Resp. by Judah b. Israel *Aszod.
Yekar Tiferet, Comm. to Maimonides' *Yad Ḥazakah,*by David b. Solomon ibn Zimra, printed in most editions of *Yad Ḥazakah.*
Yere'im [*ha-Shalem*], [*Sefer*], Treatise on precepts by *Eliezer b. Samuel of Metz.
Yeshu'ot Ya'akov, Resp. by Jacob Meshullam b. Mordecai Ze'ev *Ornstein.
Yiẓhak Rei'aḥ, Resp. by Isaac b. Samuel Abendanan (see article *Abendanam Family).
Ẓafenat Pa'ne'aḥ (1), also called *Raban* or *Even ha-Ezer,* see under the last name.
Ẓafenat Pa'ne'aḥ (2), Resp. by Joseph *Rozin.
Zayit Ra'anan, Resp. by Moses Judah Leib b. Benjamin Auerbach.
Ẓeidah la-Derekh, Codification by *Menahem b. Aaron ibn Zerah.
Ẓedakah u-Mishpat, Resp. by Ẓedakah b. Saadiah Huẓin.
Zekan Aharon, Resp. by Elijah b. Benjamin ha-Levi.
Zekher Ẓaddik, Sermons by Eliezer *Katzenellenbogen.
Ẓemaḥ Ẓedek (1) Resp. by Menaham Mendel Shneersohn (see under *Shneersohn Family).
Zera Avraham, Resp. by Abraham b. David *Yiẓḥaki.
Zera Emet Resp. by *Ishmael b. Abaham Isaac ha-Kohen.
Ẓevi la-Ẓaddik, Resp. by Ẓevi Elimelech b. David Shapira.
Zikhron Yehudah, Resp. by *Judah b. Asher
Zikhron Yosef, Resp. by Joseph b. Menahem *Steinhardt.
Zikhronot, Sefer ha-, Sermons on several precepts by Samuel *Aboab.
Zikkaron la-Rishonim . . ., by Albert (Abraham Elijah) *Harkavy; contains in vol. 1 pt. 4 (1887) a collection of Geonic responsa.
Ẓiẓ Eliezer, Resp. by Eliezer Judah b. Jacob Gedaliah Waldenberg.

BIBLIOGRAPHICAL ABBREVIATIONS

Bibliographies in English and other languages have been extensively updated, with English translations cited where available. In order to help the reader, the language of books or articles is given where not obvious from titles of books or names of periodicals. Titles of books and periodicals in languages with alphabets other than Latin, are given in transliteration, even where there is a title page in English. Titles of articles in periodicals are not given. Names of Hebrew and Yiddish periodicals well known in English-speaking countries or in Israel under their masthead in Latin characters are given in this form, even when contrary to transliteration rules. Names of authors writing in languages with non-Latin alphabets are given in their Latin alphabet form wherever known; otherwise the names are transliterated. Initials are generally not given for authors of articles in periodicals, except to avoid confusion. Non-abbreviated book titles and names of periodicals are printed in *italics.* Abbreviations are given in the list below.

AASOR	*Annual of the American School of Oriental Research* (1919ff.).
AB	*Analecta Biblica* (1952ff.).
Abel, Géog	F.-M. Abel, *Géographie de la Palestine,* 2 vols. (1933-38).
ABR	*Australian Biblical Review* (1951ff.).
Abr.	Philo, *De Abrahamo.*
Abrahams, Companion	I. Abrahams, *Companion to the Authorised Daily Prayer Book* (rev. ed. 1922).
Abramson, Merkazim	S. Abramson, *Ba-Merkazim u-va-Tefuẓot bi-Tekufat ha-Ge'onim* (1965).
Acts	Acts of the Apostles (New Testament).
ACUM	*Who is who in ACUM [Aguddat Kompozitorim u-Meḥabbrim].*
ADAJ	*Annual of the Department of Antiquities, Jordan* (1951ff.).
Adam	Adam and Eve (Pseudepigrapha).
ADB	*Allgemeine Deutsche Biographie,* 56 vols. (1875–1912).
Add. Esth.	The Addition to Esther (Apocrypha).
Adler, Prat Mus	1. Adler, *La pratique musicale savante dans quelques communautés juives en Europe au XVIIe et XVIIIe siècles,* 2 vols. (1966).
Adler-Davis	H.M. Adler and A. Davis (ed. and tr.), *Service of the Synagogue, a New Edition of the Festival Prayers with an English Translation in Prose and Verse,* 6 vols. (1905–06).
Aet.	Philo, *De Aeternitate Mundi.*
AFO	*Archiv fuer Orientforschung* (first two volumes under the name *Archiv fuer Keilschriftforschung)* (1923ff.).
Ag. Ber	*Aggadat Bereshit* (ed. Buber, 1902).
Agr.	Philo, *De Agricultura.*
Ag. Sam.	*Aggadat Samuel.*
Ag. Song	*Aggadat Shir ha-Shirim* (Schechter ed., 1896).
Aharoni, Ereẓ	Y. Aharoni, *Ereẓ Yisrael bi-Tekufat ha-Mikra: Geografyah Historit* (1962).
Aharoni, Land	Y. Aharoni, *Land of the Bible* (1966).

Ahikar — Ahikar (Pseudepigrapha).
AI — *Archives Israélites de France* (1840–1936).
AJA — *American Jewish Archives* (1948ff.).
AJHSP — *American Jewish Historical Society – Publications* (after vol. 50 = AJHSQ).
AJHSQ — *American Jewish Historical (*Society) *Quarterly* (before vol. 50 =AJHSP).
AJSLL — *American Journal of Semitic Languages and Literature* (1884–95 under the title *Hebraica,* since 1942 JNES).
AJYB — *American Jewish Year Book* (1899ff.).
AKM — Abhandlungen fuer die Kunde des Morgenlandes (series).
Albright, Arch — W.F. Albright, *Archaeology of Palestine* (rev. ed. 1960).
Albright, Arch Bib — W.F. Albright, *Archaeology of Palestine and the Bible* (1935[3]).
Albright, Arch Rel — W.F. Albright, *Archaeology and the Religion of Israel* (1953[3]).
Albright, Stone — W.F. Albright, *From the Stone Age to Christianity* (1957[2]).
Alon, Meḥkarim — G. Alon, *Meḥkarim be-Toledot Yisrael bi-Ymei Bayit Sheni u-vi-Tekufat ha-Mishnah ve-ha Talmud,* 2 vols. (1957–58).
Alon, Toledot — G. Alon, *Toledot ha-Yehudim be-Ereẓ Yisrael bi-Tekufat ha-Mishnah ve-ha-Talmud,* I (1958[3]), (1961[2]).
ALOR — Alter Orient (series).
Alt, Kl Schr — A. Alt, *Kleine Schriften zur Geschichte des Volkes Israel,* 3 vols. (1953–59).
Alt, Landnahme — A. Alt, *Landnahme der Israeliten in Palaestina* (1925); also in Alt, Kl Schr, 1 (1953), 89–125.
Ant. — Josephus, *Jewish Antiquities* (Loeb Classics ed.).
AO — *Acta Orientalia* (1922ff.).
AOR — *Analecta Orientalia* (1931ff.).
AOS — American Oriental Series.
Apion — Josephus, *Against Apion* (Loeb Classics ed.).
Aq. — Aquila's Greek translation of the Bible.
Ar. — *Arakhin* (talmudic tractate).
Artist. — Letter of Aristeas (Pseudepigrapha).
ARN[1] — *Avot de-Rabbi Nathan,* version (1) ed. Schechter, 1887.
ARN[2] — *Avot de-Rabbi Nathan,* version (2) ed. Schechter, 1945[2].
Aronius, Regesten — I. Aronius, *Regesten zur Geschichte der Juden im fraenkischen und deutschen Reiche bis zum Jahre 1273* (1902).
ARW — *Archiv fuer Religionswissenschaft* (1898–1941/42).
AS — *Assyrological Studies* (1931ff.).
Ashtor, Korot — E. Ashtor (Strauss), *Korot ha-Yehudim bi-Sefarad ha-Muslemit,* 1(1966[2]), 2(1966).
Ashtor, Toledot — E. Ashtor (Strauss), *Toledot ha-Yehudim be-Miẓrayim ve-Suryah Taḥat Shilton ha-Mamlukim,* 3 vols. (1944–70).
Assaf, Ge'onim — S. Assaf, *Tekufat ha-Ge'onim ve-Sifrutah* (1955).
Assaf, Mekorot — S. Assaf, *Mekorot le-Toledot ha-Ḥinnukh be-Yisrael,* 4 vols. (1925–43).
Ass. Mos. — Assumption of Moses (Pseudepigrapha).
ATA — Alttestamentliche Abhandlungen (series).
ATANT — Abhandlungen zur Theologie des Alten und Neuen Testaments (series).
AUJW — *Allgemeine unabhaengige juedische Wochenzeitung* (till 1966 = AWJD).
AV — Authorized Version of the Bible.
Avad. — *Avadim* (post-talmudic tractate).
Avi-Yonah, Geog — M. Avi-Yonah, *Geografyah Historit shel Ereẓ Yisrael* (1962[3]).
Avi-Yonah, Land — M. Avi-Yonah, *The Holy Land from the Persian to the Arab conquest (536 B.C. to A.D. 640)* (1960).
Avot — *Avot* (talmudic tractate).
Av. Zar. — *Avodah Zarah* (talmudic tractate).
AWJD — *Allgemeine Wochenzeitung der Juden in Deutschland* (since 1967 = AUJW).
AZDJ — *Allgemeine Zeitung des Judentums.*
Azulai — Ḥ.Y.D. Azulai, *Shem ha-Gedolim,* ed. by I.E. Benjacob, 2 pts. (1852) (and other editions).

BA — *Biblical Archaeologist* (1938ff.).
Bacher, Bab Amor — W. Bacher, *Agada der babylonischen Amoraeer* (1913[2]).
Bacher, Pal Amor — W. Bacher, *Agada der palaestinensischen Amoraeer* (Heb. ed. *Aggadat Amora'ei Ereẓ Yisrael),* 2 vols. (1892–99).
Bacher, Tann — W. Bacher, *Agada der Tannaiten* (Heb. ed. *Aggadot ha-Tanna'im,* vol. 1, pt. 1 and 2 (1903); vol. 2 (1890).
Bacher, Trad — W. Bacher, *Tradition und Tradenten in den Schulen Palaestinas und Babyloniens* (1914).
Baer, Spain — Yitzhak (Fritz) Baer, *History of the Jews in Christian Spain,* 2 vols. (1961–66).
Baer, Studien — Yitzhak (Fritz) Baer, *Studien zur Geschichte der Juden im Koenigreich Aragonien waehrend des 13. und 14. Jahrhunderts* (1913).
Baer, Toledot — Yitzhak (Fritz) Baer, *Toledot ha-Yehudim bi-Sefarad ha-Noẓerit mi-Teḥillatan shel ha-Kehillot ad ha-Gerush,* 2 vols. (1959[2]).
Baer, Urkunden — Yitzhak (Fritz) Baer, *Die Juden im christlichen Spanien,* 2 vols. (1929–36).
Baer S., Seder — S.I. Baer, *Seder Avodat Yisrael* (1868 and reprints*).*
BAIU — *Bulletin de l'Alliance Israélite Universelle* (1861–1913*).*
Baker, Biog Dict — *Baker's Biographical Dictionary of Musicians,* revised by N. Slonimsky (1958[5]; with Supplement 1965).
I Bar. — I Baruch (Apocrypha).
II Bar. — II Baruch (Pseudepigrapha).
III Bar. — III Baruch (Pseudepigrapha).
BAR — *Biblical Archaeology Review.*
Baron, Community — S.W. Baron, *The Jewish Community, its History and Structure to the American Revolution,* 3 vols. (1942).

Baron, Social	S.W. Baron, *Social and Religious History of the Jews,* 3 vols. (1937); enlarged, 1-2(1952²), 3-14 (1957–69).
Barthélemy-Milik	D. Barthélemy and J.T. Milik, *Dead Sea Scrolls: Discoveries in the Judean Desert,* vol. 1 *Qumram Cave* I (1955).
BASOR	*Bulletin of the American School of Oriental Research.*
Bauer-Leander	H. Bauer and P. Leander, *Grammatik des Biblisch-Aramaeischen* (1927; repr. 1962).
BB	(1) *Bava Batra* (talmudic tractate). (2) *Biblische Beitraege* (1943ff.).
BBB	Bonner biblische Beitraege (series).
BBLA	*Beitraege zur biblischen Landes- und Altertumskunde* (until 1949–ZDPV).
BBSAJ	*Bulletin,* British School of Archaeology, Jerusalem (1922–25; after 1927 included in PEFQS).
BDASI	*Alon* (since 1948) or *Hadashot Arkheʾologiyyot* (since 1961), bulletin of the Department of Antiquities of the State of Israel.
Begrich, Chronologie	J. Begrich, *Chronologie der Koenige von Israel und Juda* (1929).
Bek.	*Bekhorot* (talmudic tractate).
Bel	Bel and the Dragon (Apocrypha).
Benjacob, Oẓar	I.E. Benjacob, *Oẓar ha-Sefarim* (1880; repr. 1956).
Ben Sira	see Ecclus.
Ben-Yehuda, Millon	E. Ben-Yedhuda, *Millon ha-Lashon ha-Ivrit,* 16 vols (1908–59; repr. in 8 vols., 1959).
Benzinger, Archaeologie	I. Benzinger, *Hebraeische Archaeologie* (1927³).
Ben Zvi, Eretz Israel	I. Ben-Zvi, *Eretz Israel under Ottoman Rule* (1960; offprint from L. Finkelstein (ed.), *The Jews, their History, Culture and Religion* (vol. 1).
Ben Zvi, Ereẓ Israel	I. Ben-Zvi, *Ereẓ Israel bi-Ymei ha-Shilton ha-Ottomani (1955).*
Ber.	*Berakhot* (talmudic tractate).
Beẓah	*Beẓah* (talmudic tractate).
BIES	Bulletin of the Israel Exploration Society, see below BJPES.
Bik.	*Bikkurim* (talmudic tractate).
BJCE	Bibliography of Jewish Communities in Europe, catalog at General Archives for the History of the Jewish People, Jerusalem.
BJPES	Bulletin of the Jewish Palestine Exploration Society – English name of the Hebrew periodical known as: 1. *Yediʿot ha-Ḥevrah ha-Ivrit la-Ḥakirat Ereẓ Yisrael va-Attikoteha* (1933–1954); 2. *Yediʿot ha-Ḥevrah la-Ḥakirat Ereẓ Yisrael va-Attikoteha* (1954–1962); 3. *Yediʿot ba-Ḥakirat Ereẓ Yisrael va-Attikoteha* (1962ff.).
BJRL	*Bulletin of the John Rylands Library* (1914ff.).
BK	*Bava Kamma* (talmudic tractate).
BLBI	*Bulletin of the Leo Baeck Institute* (1957ff.).
BM	(1) *Bava Meẓia* (talmudic tractate). (2) *Beit Mikra* (1955/56ff.). (3) British Museum.
BO	*Bibbia e Oriente* (1959ff.).
Bondy-Dworský	G. Bondy and F. Dworský, *Regesten zur Geschichte der Juden in Boehmen, Maehren und Schlesien von 906 bis 1620,* 2 vols. (1906).
BOR	*Bibliotheca Orientalis* (1943ff.).
Borée, Ortsnamen	W. Borée *Die alten Ortsnamen Palaestinas* (1930).
Bousset, Religion	W. Bousset, *Die Religion des Judentums im neutestamentlichen Zeitalter* (1906²).
Bousset-Gressmann	W. Bousset, *Die Religion des Judentums im spaethellenistischen Zeitalter* (1966³).
BR	*Biblical Review* (1916–25).
BRCI	*Bulletin of the Research Council of Israel* (1951/52–1954/55; then divided).
BRE	*Biblical Research* (1956ff.).
BRF	*Bulletin of the Rabinowitz Fund for the Exploration of Ancient Synagogues* (1949ff.).
Briggs, Psalms	Ch. A. and E.G. Briggs, *Critical and Exegetical Commentary on the Book of Psalms,* 2 vols. (ICC, 1906–07).
Bright, Hist	J. Bright, *A History of Israel* (1959).
Brockelmann, Arab Lit	K. Brockelmann, *Geschichte der arabischen Literatur,* 2 vols. 1898–1902), supplement, 3 vols. (1937–42).
Bruell, Jahrbuecher	*Jahrbuecher fuer juedische Geschichte und Litteratur,* ed. by N. Bruell, Frankfurt (1874–90).
Brugmans-Frank	H. Brugmans and A. Frank (eds.), *Geschiedenis der Joden in Nederland* (1940).
BTS	*Bible et Terre Sainte* (1958ff.).
Bull, Index	S. Bull, *Index to Biographies of Contemporary Composers* (1964).
BW	*Biblical World* (1882–1920).
BWANT	*Beitraege zur Wissenschaft vom Alten und Neuen Testament* (1926ff.).
BZ	*Biblische Zeitschrift* (1903ff.).
BZAW	*Beihefte zur Zeitschrift fuer die alttestamentliche Wissenschaft,* supplement to ZAW (1896ff.).
BŻIH	*Biuletyn Zydowskiego Instytutu Historycznego* (1950ff.).
CAB	*Cahiers d'archéologie biblique* (1953ff.).
CAD	*The* [*Chicago*] *Assyrian Dictionary* (1956ff.).
CAH	*Cambridge Ancient History,* 12 vols. (1923–39)
CAH²	*Cambridge Ancient History,* second edition, 14 vols. (1962–2005).
Calwer, Lexikon	*Calwer, Bibellexikon.*
Cant.	Canticles, usually given as Song (= Song of Songs).

Cantera-Millás, Inscripciones — F. Cantera and J.M. Millás, *Las Inscripciones Hebraicas de España* (1956).
CBQ — *Catholic Biblical Quarterly* (1939ff.).
CCARY — Central Conference of American Rabbis, *Yearbook* (1890/91ff.).
CD — *Damascus Document* from the Cairo *Genizah* (published by S. Schechter, *Fragments of a Zadokite Work*, 1910).
Charles, Apocrypha — R.H. Charles, *Apocrypha and Pseudepigrapha . . .*, 2 vols. (1913; repr. 1963–66).
Cher. — Philo, *De Cherubim.*
I (or II) Chron. — Chronicles, book I and II (Bible).
CIG — *Corpus Inscriptionum Graecarum.*
CIJ — *Corpus Inscriptionum Judaicarum,* 2 vols. (1936–52).
CIL — *Corpus Inscriptionum Latinarum.*
CIS — *Corpus Inscriptionum Semiticarum* (1881ff.).
C.J. — Codex Justinianus.
Clermont-Ganneau, Arch — Ch. Clermont-Ganneau, *Archaeological Researches in Palestine*, 2 vols. (1896–99).
CNFI — *Christian News from Israel* (1949ff.).
Cod. Just. — Codex Justinianus.
Cod. Theod. — Codex Theodosinanus.
Col. — Epistle to the Colosssians (New Testament).
Conder, Survey — Palestine Exploration Fund, *Survey of Eastern Palestine*, vol. 1, pt. I (1889) = C.R. Conder, *Memoirs of the . . . Survey.*
Conder-Kitchener — Palestine Exploration Fund, *Survey of Western Palestine*, vol. 1, pts. 1-3 (1881–83) = C.R. Conder and H.H. Kitchener, *Memoirs.*
Conf. — Philo, *De Confusione Linguarum.*
Conforte, Kore — D. Conforte, *Kore ha-Dorot* (1842²).
Cong. — Philo, *De Congressu Quaerendae Eruditionis Gratia.*
Cont. — Philo, *De Vita Contemplativa.*
I (or II) Cor. — Epistles to the Corinthians (New Testament).
Cowley, Aramic — A. Cowley, *Aramaic Papyri of the Fifth Century B.C.* (1923).
Colwey, Cat — A.E. Cowley, *A Concise Catalogue of the Hebrew Printed Books in the Bodleian Library* (1929).
CRB — *Cahiers de la Revue Biblique* (1964ff.).
Crowfoot-Kenyon — J.W. Crowfoot, K.M. Kenyon and E.L. Sukenik, *Buildings of Samaria* (1942).
C.T. — Codex Theodosianus.

DAB — *Dictionary of American Biography* (1928–58).
Daiches, Jews — S. Daiches, *Jews in Babylonia* (1910).
Dalman, Arbeit — G. Dalman, *Arbeit und Sitte in Palaestina*, 7 vols.in 8 (1928–42 repr. 1964).
Dan — Daniel (Bible).
Davidson, Oẓar — I. Davidson, *Oẓar ha-Shirah ve-ha-Piyyut*, 4 vols. (1924–33); Supplement in: HUCA, 12–13 (1937/38), 715–823.
DB — J. Hastings, *Dictionary of the Bible,* 4 vols. (1963²).
DBI — F.G. Vigoureaux et al. (eds.), *Dictionnaire de la Bible,* 5 vols. in 10 (1912); Supplement, 8 vols. (1928–66)
Decal. — Philo, *De Decalogo.*
Dem. — *Demai* (talmudic tractate).
DER — *Derekh Ereẓ Rabbah* (post-talmudic tractate).
Derenbourg, Hist — J. Derenbourg *Essai sur l'histoire et la géographie de la Palestine* (1867).
Det. — Philo, *Quod deterius potiori insidiari solet.*
Deus — Philo, *Quod Deus immutabilis sit.*
Deut. — Deuteronomy (Bible).
Deut. R. — *Deuteronomy Rabbah.*
DEZ — *Derekh Ereẓ Zuta* (post-talmudic tractate).
DHGE — *Dictionnaire d'histoire et de géographie ecclésiastiques,* ed. by A. Baudrillart et al., 17 vols (1912–68).
Dik. Sof — *Dikdukei Soferim,* variae lections of the talmudic text by Raphael Nathan Rabbinovitz (16 vols., 1867–97).
Dinur, Golah — B. Dinur (Dinaburg), *Yisrael ba-Golah,* 2 vols. in 7 (1959–68) = vols. 5 and 6 of his *Toledot Yisrael,* second series.
Dinur, Haganah — B. Dinur (ed.), *Sefer Toledot ha-Haganah* (1954ff.).
Diringer, Iscr — D. Diringer, *Iscrizioni antico-ebraiche palestinesi* (1934).
Discoveries — *Discoveries in the Judean Desert* (1955ff.).
DNB — *Dictionary of National Biography,* 66 vols. (1921–222) with Supplements.
Dubnow, Divrei — S. Dubnow, *Divrei Yemei Am Olam,* 11 vols (1923–38 and further editions).
Dubnow, Ḥasidut — S. Dubnow, *Toledot ha-Ḥasidut* (1960²).
Dubnow, Hist — S. Dubnow, *History of the Jews* (1967).
Dubnow, Hist Russ — S. Dubnow, *History of the Jews in Russia and Poland,* 3 vols. (1916 20).
Dubnow, Outline — S. Dubnow, *An Outline of Jewish History,* 3 vols. (1925–29).
Dubnow, Weltgesch — S. Dubnow, *Weltgeschichte des juedischen Volkes* 10 vols. (1925–29).
Dukes, Poesie — L. Dukes, *Zur Kenntnis der neuhebraeischen religioesen Poesie* (1842).
Dunlop, Khazars — D. H. Dunlop, *History of the Jewish Khazars* (1954).

EA — El Amarna Letters (edited by J.A. Knudtzon), *Die El-Amarna Tafel,* 2 vols. (1907 14).
EB — *Encyclopaedia Britannica.*
EBI — *Estudios biblicos* (1941ff.).
EBIB — T.K. Cheyne and J.S. Black, *Encyclopaedia Biblica,* 4 vols. (1899–1903).
Ebr. — Philo, *De Ebrietate.*
Eccles. — Ecclesiastes (Bible).
Eccles. R. — *Ecclesiastes Rabbah.*
Ecclus. — Ecclesiasticus or Wisdom of Ben Sira (or Sirach; Apocrypha).
Eduy. — *Eduyyot* (mishanic tractate).

Abbreviation	Meaning
EG	*Enziklopedyah shel Galuyyot* (1953ff.).
EH	*Even ha-Ezer.*
EHA	*Enziklopedyah la-Ḥafirot Arkheologiyyot be-Ereẓ Yisrael,* 2 vols. (1970).
EI	*Enzyklopaedie des Islams,* 4 vols. (1905–14). Supplement vol. (1938).
EIS	*Encyclopaedia of Islam,* 4 vols. (1913–36; repr. 1954–68).
EIS^{2}	*Encyclopaedia of Islam, second edition (1960–2000).*
Eisenstein, Dinim	J.D. Eisenstein, *Oẓar Dinim u-Minhagim* (1917; several reprints).
Eisenstein, Yisrael	J.D. Eisenstein, *Oẓar Yisrael* (10 vols, 1907–13; repr. with several additions 1951).
EIV	*Enziklopedyah Ivrit* (1949ff.).
EJ	*Encyclopaedia Judaica* (German, A-L only), 10 vols. (1928–34).
EJC	*Enciclopedia Judaica Castellana,* 10 vols. (1948–51).
Elbogen, Century	I Elbogen, *A Century of Jewish Life* (1960^{2}).
Elbogen, Gottesdienst	I Elbogen, *Der juedische Gottesdienst ...* (1931^{3}, repr. 1962).
Elon, Mafte'aḥ	M. Elon (ed.), *Mafte'aḥ ha-She'elot ve-ha-Teshuvot ha-Rosh* (1965).
EM	*Enziklopedyah Mikra'it* (1950ff.).
I (or II) En.	I and II Enoch (Pseudepigrapha).
EncRel	*Encyclopedia of Religion,* 15 vols. (1987, 2005^{2}).
Eph.	Epistle to the Ephesians (New Testament).
Ephros, Cant	G. Ephros, *Cantorial Anthology,* 5 vols. (1929–57).
Ep. Jer.	Epistle of Jeremy (Apocrypha).
Epstein, Amora'im	J N. Epstein, *Mevo'ot le-Sifrut ha-Amora'im* (1962).
Epstein, Marriage	L M. Epstein, *Marriage Laws in the Bible and the Talmud* (1942).
Epstein, Mishnah	J. N. Epstein, *Mavo le-Nusaḥ ha-Mishnah,* 2 vols. (1964^{2}).
Epstein, Tanna'im	J. N. Epstein, *Mavo le-Sifruth ha-Tanna'im.* (1947).
ER	*Ecumenical Review.*
Er.	*Eruvin* (talmudic tractate).
ERE	*Encyclopaedia of Religion and Ethics,* 13 vols. (1908–26); reprinted.
ErIsr	*Eretz-Israel,* Israel Exploration Society.
I Esd.	I Esdras (Apocrypha) (= III Ezra).
II Esd.	II Esdras (Apocrypha) (= IV Ezra).
ESE	*Ephemeris fuer semitische Epigraphik,* ed. by M. Lidzbarski.
ESN	*Encyclopaedia Sefaradica Neerlandica,* 2 pts. (1949).
ESS	*Encyclopaedia of the Social Sciences,* 15 vols. (1930–35); reprinted in 8 vols. (1948–49).
Esth.	Esther (Bible).
Est. R.	*Esther Rabbah.*
ET	*Enziklopedyah Talmudit* (1947ff.).
Eusebius, Onom.	E. Klostermann (ed.), *Das Onomastikon* (1904), Greek with Hieronymus' Latin translation.
Ex.	Exodus (Bible).
Ex. R.	*Exodus Rabbah.*
Exs	Philo, *De Exsecrationibus.*
EẒD	*Enziklopeday shel ha-Ẓiyyonut ha-Datit* (1951ff.).
Ezek.	Ezekiel (Bible).
Ezra	Ezra (Bible).
III Ezra	III Ezra (Pseudepigrapha).
IV Ezra	IV Ezra (Pseudepigrapha).
Feliks, Ha-Ẓome'aḥ	*J. Feliks, Ha-Ẓome'aḥ ve-ha-Ḥai ba-Mishnah* (1983).
Finkelstein, Middle Ages	L. Finkelstein, *Jewish Self-Government in the Middle Ages* (1924).
Fischel, Islam	W.J. Fischel, *Jews in the Economic and Political Life of Mediaeval Islam* (1937; reprint with introduction "The Court Jew in the Islamic World," 1969).
FJW	*Fuehrer durch die juedische Gemeindeverwaltung und Wohlfahrtspflege in Deutschland* (1927/28).
Frankel, Mevo	Z. Frankel, *Mevo ha-Yerushalmi* (1870; reprint 1967).
Frankel, Mishnah	Z. Frankel, *Darkhei ha-Mishnah* (1959^{2}; reprint 1959^{2}).
Frazer, Folk-Lore	J.G. Frazer, *Folk-Lore in the Old Testament,* 3 vols. (1918–19).
Frey, Corpus	J.-B. Frey, *Corpus Inscriptionum Iudaicarum,* 2 vols. (1936–52).
Friedmann, Lebensbilder	A. Friedmann, *Lebensbilder beruehmter Kantoren,* 3 vols. (1918–27).
FRLT	*Forschungen zur Religion und Literatur des Alten und Neuen Testaments* (series) (1950ff.).
Frumkin-Rivlin	A.L. Frumkin and E. Rivlin, *Toledot Ḥakhmei Yerushalayim,* 3 vols. (1928–30), Supplement vol. (1930).
Fuenn, Keneset	S.J. Fuenn, *Keneset Yisrael,* 4 vols. (1887–90).
Fuerst, Bibliotheca	J. Fuerst, *Bibliotheca Judaica,* 2 vols. (1863; repr. 1960).
Fuerst, Karaeertum	J. Fuerst, *Geschichte des Karaeertums,* 3 vols. (1862–69).
Fug.	Philo, *De Fuga et Inventione.*
Gal.	Epistle to the Galatians (New Testament).
Galling, Reallexikon	K. Galling, *Biblisches Reallexikon* (1937).
Gardiner, Onomastica	A.H. Gardiner, *Ancient Egyptian Onomastica,* 3 vols. (1947).
Geiger, Mikra	A. Geiger, *Ha-Mikra ve-Targumav,* tr. by J.L. Baruch (1949).
Geiger, Urschrift	A. Geiger, *Urschrift und Uebersetzungen der Bibel* 1928^{2}).
Gen.	Genesis (Bible).
Gen. R.	*Genesis Rabbah.*
Ger.	*Gerim* (post-talmudic tractate).
Germ Jud	M. Brann, I. Elbogen, A. Freimann, and H. Tykocinski (eds.), *Germania Judaica,* vol. 1 (1917; repr. 1934 and 1963); vol. 2, in 2 pts. (1917–68), ed. by Z. Avneri.

GHAT — *Goettinger Handkommentar zum Alten Testament* (1917–22).
Ghirondi-Neppi — M.S. Ghirondi and G.H. Neppi, *Toledot Gedolei Yisrael u-Ge'onei Italyah ... u-Ve'urim al Sefer Zekher Ẓaddikim li-Verakhah* . . .(1853), index in ZHB, 17 (1914), 171–83.
Gig. — Philo, *De Gigantibus.*
Ginzberg, Legends — L. Ginzberg, *Legends of the Jews,* 7 vols. (1909–38; and many reprints).
Git. — *Gittin* (talmudic tractate).
Glueck, Explorations — N. Glueck, *Explorations in Eastern Palestine,* 2 vols. (1951).
Goell, Bibliography — Y. Goell, *Bibliography of Modern Hebrew Literature in English Translation* (1968).
Goodenough, Symbols — E.R. Goodenough, *Jewish Symbols in the Greco-Roman Period,* 13 vols. (1953–68).
Gordon, Textbook — C.H. Gordon, *Ugaritic Textbook* (1965; repr. 1967).
Graetz, Gesch — H. Graetz, *Geschichte der Juden* (last edition 1874–1908).
Graetz, Hist — H. Graetz, *History of the Jews,* 6 vols. (1891–1902).
Graetz, Psalmen — H. Graetz, *Kritischer Commentar zu den Psalmen,* 2 vols. in 1 (1882–83).
Graetz, Rabbinowitz — H. Graetz, *Divrei Yemei Yisrael,* tr. by S.P. Rabbinowitz. (1928 1929²).
Gray, Names — G.B. Gray, *Studies in Hebrew Proper Names* (1896).
Gressmann, Bilder — H. Gressmann, *Altorientalische Bilder zum Alten Testament* (1927²).
Gressmann, Texte — H. Gressmann, *Altorientalische Texte zum Alten Testament* (1926²).
Gross, Gal Jud — H. Gross, *Gallia Judaica* (1897; repr. with add. 1969).
Grove, Dict — *Grove's Dictionary of Music and Musicians,* ed. by E. Blum 9 vols. (1954⁵) and suppl. (1961⁵).
Guedemann, Gesch Erz — M. Guedemann, *Geschichte des Erziehungswesens und der Cultur der abendlaendischen Juden,* 3 vols. (1880–88).
Guedemann, Quellenschr — M. Guedemann, *Quellenschriften zur Geschichte des Unterrichts und der Erziehung bei den deutschen Juden* (1873, 1891).
Guide — Maimonides, *Guide of the Perplexed.*
Gulak, Oẓar — A. Gulak, *Oẓar ha-Shetarot ha-Nehugim be-Yisrael* (1926).
Gulak, Yesodei — A. Gulak, *Yesodei ha-Mishpat ha-Ivri, Seder Dinei Mamonot be-Yisrael, al pi Mekorot ha-Talmud ve-ha-Posekim,* 4 vols. (1922; repr. 1967).
Guttmann, Mafte'aḥ — M. Guttmann, *Mafte'aḥ ha-Talmud,* 3 vols. (1906–30).
Guttmann, Philosophies — J. Guttmann, *Philosophies of Judaism* (1964).
Hab. — *Habakkuk* (Bible).
Ḥag. — *Ḥagigah* (talmudic tractate).
Haggai — *Haggai* (Bible).
Ḥal. — *Ḥallah* (talmudic tractate).
Halevy, Dorot — I. Halevy, *Dorot ha-Rishonim,* 6 vols. (1897–1939).
Halpern, Pinkas — I. Halpern (Halperin), *Pinkas Va'ad Arba Araẓot* (1945).
Hananel-Eškenazi — A. Hananel and Eškenazi (eds.), *Fontes Hebraici ad res oeconomicas socialesque terrarum balcanicarum saeculo XVI pertinentes,* 2 vols, (1958–60; in Bulgarian).
HB — *Hebraeische Bibliographie* (1858–82).
Heb. — Epistle to the Hebrews (New Testament).
Heilprin, Dorot — J. Heilprin (Heilperin), *Seder ha-Dorot,* 3 vols. (1882; repr. 1956).
Her. — Philo, *Quis Rerum Divinarum Heres.*
Hertz, Prayer — J.H. Hertz (ed.), *Authorised Daily Prayer Book* (rev. ed. 1948; repr. 1963).
Herzog, Instit — I. Herzog, *The Main Institutions of Jewish Law,* 2 vols. (1936–39; repr. 1967).
Herzog-Hauck — J.J. Herzog and A. Hauch (eds.), *Real-encyklopaedie fuer protestantische Theologie* (1896–1913³).
HḤY — *Ha-Ẓofeh le-Ḥokhmat Yisrael* (first four volumes under the title *Ha-Ẓofeh me-Ereẓ Hagar)* (1910/11–13).
Hirschberg, Afrikah — H.Z. Hirschberg, *Toledot ha-Yehudim be-Afrikah ha-Zofonit,* 2 vols. (1965).
HJ — *Historia Judaica* (1938–61).
HL — *Das Heilige Land* (1857ff.)
ḤM — *Ḥoshen Mishpat.*
Hommel, Ueberliefer. — F. Hommel, *Die altisraelitische Ueberlieferung in inschriftlicher Beleuchtung* (1897).
Hor. — *Horayot* (talmudic tractate).
Horodezky, Ḥasidut — S.A. Horodezky, *Ha-Ḥasidut ve-ha-Ḥasidim,* 4 vols. (1923).
Horowitz, Ereẓ Yis — I.W. Horowitz, *Ereẓ Yisrael u-Shekhenoteha* (1923).
Hos. — Hosea (Bible).
HTR — *Harvard Theological Review* (1908ff.).
HUCA — *Hebrew Union College Annual* (1904; 1924ff.)
Ḥul. — *Ḥullin* (talmudic tractate).
Husik, Philosophy — I. Husik, *History of Medieval Jewish Philosophy* (1932²).
Hyman, Toledot — A. Hyman, *Toledot Tanna'im ve-Amora'im* (1910; repr. 1964).
Ibn Daud, Tradition — Abraham Ibn Daud, *Sefer ha-Qabbalah – The Book of Tradition,* ed. and tr. By G.D. Cohen (1967).
ICC — International Critical Commentary on the Holy Scriptures of the Old and New Testaments (series, 1908ff.).
IDB — *Interpreter's Dictionary of the Bible,* 4 vols. (1962).
Idelsohn, Litugy — A. Z. Idelsohn, *Jewish Liturgy and its Development* (1932; paperback repr. 1967)
Idelsohn, Melodien — A. Z. Idelsohn, *Hebraeisch-orientalischer Melodienschatz,* 10 vols. (1914 32).
Idelsohn, Music — A. Z. Idelsohn, *Jewish Music in its Historical Development* (1929; paperback repr. 1967).

IEJ	*Israel Exploration Journal* (1950ff.).
IESS	*International Encyclopedia of the Social Sciences* (various eds.).
IG	*Inscriptiones Graecae,* ed. by the Prussian Academy.
IGYB	*Israel Government Year Book* (1949/ 50ff.).
ILR	*Israel Law Review* (1966ff.).
IMIT	*Izraelita Magyar Irodalmi Társulat Évkönyv* (1895 1948).
IMT	International Military Tribunal.
INB	*Israel Numismatic Bulletin* (1962–63).
INJ	*Israel Numismatic Journal* (1963ff.).
Ios	Philo, *De Iosepho.*
Isa.	Isaiah (Bible).
ITHL	Institute for the Translation of Hebrew Literature.
IZBG	*Internationale Zeitschriftenschau fuer Bibelwissenschaft und Grenzgebiete* (1951ff.).
JA	*Journal asiatique* (1822ff.).
James	Epistle of James (New Testament).
JAOS	*Journal of the American Oriental Society* (c. 1850ff.)
Jastrow, Dict	M. Jastrow, *Dictionary of the Targumim, the Talmud Babli and Yerushalmi, and the Midrashic literature,* 2 vols. (1886 1902 and reprints).
JBA	*Jewish Book Annual* (19242ff.).
JBL	*Journal of Biblical Literature* (1881ff.).
JBR	*Journal of Bible and Religion* (1933ff.).
JC	*Jewish Chronicle* (1841ff.).
JCS	*Journal of Cuneiform Studies* (1947ff.).
JE	*Jewish Encyclopedia,* 12 vols. (1901–05 several reprints).
Jer.	Jeremiah (Bible).
Jeremias, Alte Test	A. Jeremias, *Das Alte Testament im Lichte des alten Orients* 1930[4]).
JGGJČ	*Jahrbuch der Gesellschaft fuer Geschichte der Juden in der Čechoslovakischen Republik* (1929–38).
JHSEM	Jewish Historical Society of England, *Miscellanies* (1925ff.).
JHSET	Jewish Historical Society of England, *Transactions* (1893ff.).
JJGL	*Jahrbuch fuer juedische Geschichte und Literatur* (Berlin) (1898–1938).
JJLG	*Jahrbuch der juedische-literarischen Gesellschaft* (Frankfurt) (1903–32).
JJS	*Journal of Jewish Studies* (1948ff.).
JJSO	*Jewish Journal of Sociology* (1959ff.).
JJV	*Jahrbuch fuer juedische Volkskunde* (1898–1924).
JL	*Juedisches Lexikon,* 5 vols. (1927–30).
JMES	*Journal of the Middle East Society* (1947ff.).
JNES	*Journal of Near Eastern Studies* (continuation of AJSLL) (1942ff.).
J.N.U.L.	Jewish National and University Library.
Job	Job (Bible).
Joel	Joel (Bible).
John	Gospel according to John (New Testament).
I, II and III John	Epistles of John (New Testament).
Jos., Ant	Josephus, *Jewish Antiquities* (Loeb Classics ed.).
Jos. Apion	Josephus, *Against Apion* (Loeb Classics ed.).
Jos., index	*Josephus Works,* Loeb Classics ed., index of names.
Jos., Life	Josephus, *Life* (ed. Loeb Classics).
Jos, Wars	Josephus, *The Jewish Wars* (Loeb Classics ed.).
Josh.	Joshua (Bible).
JPESB	Jewish Palestine Exploration Society Bulletin, see BJPES.
JPESJ	Jewish Palestine Exploration Society Journal – Eng. Title of the Hebrew periodical *Kovez ha-Ḥevrah ha-Ivrit la-Ḥakirat Erez Yisrael va-Attikoteha.*
JPOS	*Journal of the Palestine Oriental Society* (1920–48).
JPS	Jewish Publication Society of America, *The Torah* (1962, 1967[2]); *The Holy Scriptures* (1917).
JQR	*Jewish Quarterly Review* (1889ff.).
JR	*Journal of Religion* (1921ff.).
JRAS	*Journal of the Royal Asiatic Society* (1838ff.).
JHR	*Journal of Religious History* (1960/61ff.).
JSOS	*Jewish Social Studies* (1939ff.).
JSS	*Journal of Semitic Studies* (1956ff.).
JTS	*Journal of Theological Studies* (1900ff.).
JTSA	Jewish Theological Seminary of America (also abbreviated as JTS).
Jub.	Jubilees (Pseudepigrapha).
Judg.	Judges (Bible).
Judith	Book of Judith (Apocrypha).
Juster, Juifs	J. Juster, *Les Juifs dans l'Empire Romain,* 2 vols. (1914).
JYB	*Jewish Year Book* (1896ff.).
JZWL	*Juedische Zeitschift fuer Wissenschaft und Leben* (1862–75).
Kal.	*Kallah* (post-talmudic tractate).
Kal. R.	*Kallah Rabbati* (post-talmudic tractate).
Katz, England	*The Jews in the History of England, 1485-1850 (1994).*
Kaufmann, Schriften	D. Kaufmann, *Gesammelte Schriften,* 3 vols. (1908 15).
Kaufmann Y., Religion	Y. Kaufmann, *The Religion of Israel* (1960), abridged tr. of his *Toledot.*
Kaufmann Y., Toledot	Y. Kaufmann, *Toledot ha-Emunah ha-Yisre'elit,* 4 vols. (1937 57).
KAWJ	*Korrespondenzblatt des Vereins zur Gruendung und Erhaltung der Akademie fuer die Wissenschaft des Judentums* (1920 30).
Kayserling, Bibl	M. Kayserling, *Biblioteca Española-Portugueza-Judaica* (1880; repr. 1961).
Kelim	*Kelim* (mishnaic tractate).
Ker.	*Keritot* (talmudic tractate).
Ket.	*Ketubbot* (talmudic tractate).

Kid. — *Kiddushim* (talmudic tractate).
Kil. — *Kilayim* (talmudic tractate).
Kin. — *Kinnim* (mishnaic tractate).
Kisch, Germany — G. Kisch, *Jews in Medieval Germany* (1949).
Kittel, Gesch — R. Kittel, *Geschichte des Volkes Israel,* 3 vols. (1922–28).
Klausner, Bayit Sheni — J. Klausner, *Historyah shel ha-Bayit ha-Sheni,* 5 vols. (1950/512).
Klausner, Sifrut — J. Klausner, *Historyah shel haSifrut ha-Ivrit ha-Ḥadashah,* 6 vols. (1952–582).
Klein, corpus — S. Klein (ed.), *Juedisch-palaestinisches Corpus Inscriptionum* (1920).
Koehler-Baumgartner — L. Koehler and W. Baumgartner, *Lexicon in Veteris Testamenti libros* (1953).
Kohut, Arukh — H.J.A. Kohut (ed.), *Sefer he-Arukh ha-Shalem,* by Nathan b. Jehiel of Rome, 8 vols. (1876–92; Supplement by S. Krauss et al., 1936; repr. 1955).
Krauss, Tal Arch — S. Krauss, *Talmudische Archaeologie,* 3 vols. (1910–12; repr. 1966).
Kressel, Leksikon — G. Kressel, *Leksikon ha-Sifrut ha-Ivrit ba-Dorot ha-Aḥaronim,* 2 vols. (1965–67).
KS — *Kirjath Sepher* (1923/4ff.).
Kut. — *Kuttim* (post-talmudic tractate).

LA — Studium Biblicum Franciscanum, *Liber Annuus* (1951ff.).
L.A. — Philo, *Legum allegoriae.*
Lachower, Sifrut — F. Lachower, *Toledot ha-Sifrut ha-Ivrit ha-Ḥadashah,* 4 vols. (1947–48; several reprints).
Lam. — Lamentations (Bible).
Lam. R. — *Lamentations Rabbah.*
Landshuth, Ammudei — L. Landshuth, *Ammudei ha-Avodah* (1857–62; repr. with index, 1965).
Legat. — Philo, *De Legatione ad Caium.*
Lehmann, Nova Bibl — R.P. Lehmann, *Nova Bibliotheca Anglo-Judaica* (1961).
Lev. — Leviticus (Bible).
Lev. R. — *Leviticus Rabbah.*
Levy, Antologia — I. Levy, *Antologia de liturgia judeo-española* (1965ff.).
Levy J., Chald Targ — J. Levy, *Chaldaeisches Woerterbuch ueber die Targumim,* 2 vols. (1967–68; repr. 1959).
Levy J., Nuehebr Tal — J. Levy, *Neuhebraeisches und chaldaeisches Woerterbuch ueber die Talmudim . . .,* 4 vols. (1875–89; repr. 1963).
Lewin, Oẓar — Lewin, *Oẓar ha-Ge'onim,* 12 vols. (1928–43).
Lewysohn, Zool — L. Lewysohn, *Zoologie des Talmuds* (1858).
Lidzbarski, Handbuch — M. Lidzbarski, *Handbuch der nordsemitischen Epigraphik,* 2 vols (1898).
Life — Josephus, *Life* (Loeb Classis ed.).
LNYL — *Leksikon fun der Nayer Yidisher Literatur* (1956ff.).
Loew, Flora — I. Loew, *Die Flora der Juden,* 4 vols. (1924 34; repr. 1967).
LSI — *Laws of the State of Israel* (1948ff.).
Luckenbill, Records — D.D. Luckenbill, *Ancient Records of Assyria and Babylonia,* 2 vols. (1926).
Luke — Gospel according to Luke (New Testament)
LXX — Septuagint (Greek translation of the Bible).

Ma'as. — *Ma'aserot* (talmudic tractate).
Ma'as. Sh. — *Ma'ase Sheni* (talmudic tractate).
I, II, III, and IVMacc. — Maccabees, I, II, III (Apocrypha), IV (Pseudepigrapha).
Maimonides, Guide — Maimonides, *Guide of the Perplexed.*
Maim., Yad — Maimonides, *Mishneh Torah (Yad Ḥazakah).*
Maisler, Untersuchungen — B. Maisler (Mazar), *Untersuchungen zur alten Geschichte und Ethnographie Syriens und Palaestinas,* 1 (1930).
Mak. — *Makkot* (talmudic tractate).
Makhsh. — *Makhshrin* (mishnaic tractate).
Mal. — Malachi (Bible).
Mann, Egypt — J. Mann, *Jews in Egypt in Palestine under the Fatimid Caliphs,* 2 vols. (1920–22).
Mann, Texts — J. Mann, *Texts and Studies,* 2 vols (1931–35).
Mansi — G.D. Mansi, *Sacrorum Conciliorum nova et amplissima collectio,* 53 vols. in 60 (1901–27; repr. 1960).
Margalioth, Gedolei — M. Margalioth, *Enẓiklopedyah le-Toledot Gedolei Yisrael,* 4 vols. (1946–50).
Margalioth, Ḥakhmei — M. Margalioth, *Enẓiklopedyah le-Ḥakhmei ha-Talmud ve-ha-Ge'onim,* 2 vols. (1945).
Margalioth, Cat — G. Margalioth, *Catalogue of the Hebrew and Samaritan Manuscripts in the British Museum,* 4 vols. (1899–1935).
Mark — Gospel according to Mark (New Testament).
Mart. Isa. — Martyrdom of Isaiah (Pseudepigrapha).
Mas. — Masorah.
Matt. — Gospel according to Matthew (New Testament).
Mayer, Art — L.A. Mayer, *Bibliography of Jewish Art* (1967).
MB — *Wochenzeitung* (formerly *Mitteilungsblatt*) *des Irgun Olej Merkas Europa* (1933ff.).
MEAH — *Miscelánea de estudios drabes y hebraicos* (1952ff.).
Meg. — Megillah (talmudic tractate).
Meg. Ta'an. — *Megillat Ta'anit* (in HUCA, 8 9 (1931–32), 318–51).
Me'il — *Me'ilah* (mishnaic tractate).
MEJ — *Middle East Journal* (1947ff.).
Mehk. — *Mekhilta de-R. Ishmael.*
Mekh. SbY — *Mekhilta de-R. Simeon bar Yoḥai.*
Men. — *Menaḥot* (talmudic tractate).
MER — *Middle East Record* (1960ff.).
Meyer, Gesch — E. Meyer, *Geschichte des Alterums,* 5 vols. in 9 (1925–58).
Meyer, Ursp — E. Meyer, *Urspring und Anfaenge des Christentums* (1921).
Mez. — *Mezuzah* (post-talmudic tractate).
MGADJ — *Mitteilungen des Gesamtarchivs der deutschen Juden* (1909–12).
MGG — *Die Musik in Geschichte und Gegenwart,* 14 vols. (1949–68).

MGG[2] *Die Musik in Geschichte und Gegenwart, 2nd edition (1994)*
MGH *Monumenta Germaniae Historica* (1826ff.).
MGJV *Mitteilungen der Gesellschaft fuer juedische Volkskunde* (1898–1929); title varies, see also JJV.
MGWJ *Monatsschrift fuer Geschichte und Wissenschaft des Judentums* (1851–1939).
MHJ *Monumenta Hungariae Judaica,* 11 vols. (1903–67).
Michael, Or H.Ḥ. Michael, *Or ha-Ḥayyim: Ḥakhmei Yisrael ve-Sifreihem,* ed. by S.Z. Ḥ. Halberstam and N. Ben-Menahem (1965[2]).
Mid. *Middot* (mishnaic tractate).
Mid. Ag. *Midrash Aggadah.*
Mid. Hag. *Midrash ha-Gadol.*
Mid. Job. *Midrash Job.*
Mid. Jonah *Midrash Jonah.*
Mid. Lek. Tov *Midrash Lekaḥ Tov.*
Mid. Prov. *Midrash Proverbs.*
Mid. Ps. *Midrash Tehillim* (Eng tr. *The Midrash on Psalms* (JPS, 1959).
Mid. Sam. *Midrash Samuel.*
Mid. Song *Midrash Shir ha-Shirim.*
Mid. Tan. *Midrash Tanna'im* on Deuteronomy.
Miége, Maroc J.L. Miège, *Le Maroc et l'Europe,* 3 vols. (1961 62).
Mig. Philo, *De Migratione Abrahami.*
Mik. *Mikva'ot* (mishnaic tractate).
Milano, Bibliotheca A. Milano, *Bibliotheca Historica Italo-Judaica* (1954); supplement for 1954–63 (1964); supplement for 1964–66 in RMI, 32 (1966).
Milano, Italia A. Milano, *Storia degli Ebrei in Italia* (1963).
MIO *Mitteilungen des Instituts fuer Orientforschung* 1953ff.).
Mish. Mishnah.
MJ *Le Monde Juif* (1946ff.).
MJC see Neubauer, Chronicles.
MK *Mo'ed Katan* (talmudic tractate).
MNDPV *Mitteilungen und Nachrichten des deutschen Palaestinavereins* (1895–1912).
Mortara, Indice M. Mortara, *Indice Alfabetico dei Rabbini e Scrittori Israeliti ... in Italia ...* (1886).
Mos Philo, *De Vita Mosis.*
Moscati, Epig S, Moscati, *Epigrafia ebraica antica* 1935–1950 (1951).
MT Masoretic Text of the Bible.
Mueller, Musiker [E.H. Mueller], *Deutisches Musiker-Lexikon* (1929)
Munk, Mélanges S. Munk, *Mélanges de philosophie juive et arabe* (1859; repr. 1955).
Mut. Philo, *De Mutatione Nominum.*
MWJ *Magazin fuer die Wissenshaft des Judentums* (18745 93).

Nah. Nahum (Bible).
Naz. *Nazir* (talmudic tractate).
NDB *Neue Deutsche Biographie* (1953ff.).
Ned. *Nedarim* (talmudic tractate).
Neg. *Nega'im* (mishnaic tractate).
Neh. Nehemiah (Bible).
NG[2] *New Grove Dictionary of Music and Musicians* (2001).
Nuebauer, Cat A. Neubauer, *Catalogue of the Hebrew Manuscripts in the Bodleian Library ...,* 2 vols. (1886–1906).
Neubauer, Chronicles A. Neubauer, *Mediaeval Jewish Chronicles,* 2 vols. (Heb., 1887–95; repr. 1965), Eng. title of *Seder ha-Ḥakhamim ve-Korot ha-Yamim.*
Neubauer, Géogr A. Neubauer, *La géographie du Talmud* (1868).
Neuman, Spain A.A. Neuman, *The Jews in Spain, their Social, Political, and Cultural Life During the Middle Ages,* 2 vols. (1942).
Neusner, Babylonia J. Neusner, *History of the Jews in Babylonia,* 5 vols. 1965–70), 2nd revised printing 1969ff.).
Nid. *Niddah* (talmudic tractate).
Noah Fragment of Book of Noah (Pseudepigrapha).
Noth, Hist Isr M. Noth, *History of Israel* (1958).
Noth, Personennamen M. Noth, *Die israelitischen Personennamen. ...* (1928).
Noth, Ueberlief M. Noth, *Ueberlieferungsgeschichte des Pentateuchs* (1949).
Noth, Welt M. Noth, *Die Welt des Alten Testaments* (1957[3]).
Nowack, Lehrbuch W. Nowack, *Lehrbuch der hebraeischen Archaeologie,* 2 vols (1894).
NT New Testament.
Num. Numbers (Bible).
Num R. *Numbers Rabbah.*

Obad. Obadiah (Bible).
ODNB online *Oxford Dictionary of National Biography.*
OḤ *Oraḥ Ḥayyim.*
Oho. *Oholot* (mishnaic tractate).
Olmstead H.T. Olmstead, *History of Palestine and Syria* (1931; repr. 1965).
OLZ *Orientalistische Literaturzeitung* (1898ff.)
Onom. Eusebius, *Onomasticon.*
Op. Philo, *De Opificio Mundi.*
OPD *Osef Piskei Din shel ha-Rabbanut ha-Rashit le-Ereẓ Yisrael, Bet ha-Din ha-Gadol le-Irurim* (1950).
Or. *Orlah* (talmudic tractate).
Or. Sibyll. Sibylline Oracles (Pseudepigrapha).
OS *L'Orient Syrien* (1956ff.)
OTS *Oudtestamentische Studien* (1942ff.).

PAAJR *Proceedings of the American Academy for Jewish Research* (1930ff.)
Pap 4QS[e] A papyrus exemplar of IQS.
Par. *Parah* (mishnaic tractate).
Pauly-Wissowa A.F. Pauly, *Realencyklopaedie der klassichen Alertumswissenschaft,* ed. by G. Wissowa et al. (1864ff.)

Abbreviation	Meaning
PD	*Piskei Din shel Bet ha-Mishpat ha-Elyon le-Yisrael* (1948ff.)
PDR	*Piskei Din shel Battei ha-Din ha-Rabbaniyyim be-Yisrael.*
PdRE	*Pirkei de-R. Eliezer* (Eng. tr. 1916. (1965^{2}).
PdRK	*Pesikta de-Rav Kahana.*
Pe'ah	*Pe'ah* (talmudic tractate).
Peake, Commentary	A.J. Peake (ed.), *Commentary on the Bible* (1919; rev. 1962).
Pedersen, Israel	J. Pedersen, *Israel, Its Life and Culture,* 4 vols. in 2 (1926–40).
PEFQS	*Palestine Exploration Fund Quarterly Statement* (1869–1937; since 1938–PEQ).
PEQ	*Palestine Exploration Quarterly* (until 1937 PEFQS; after 1927 includes BBSAJ).
Perles, Beitaege	J. Perles, *Beitraege zur rabbinischen Sprach- und Alterthumskunde* (1893).
Pes.	*Pesaḥim* (talmudic tractate).
Pesh.	Peshitta (Syriac translation of the Bible).
Pesher Hab.	Commentary to Habakkuk from Qumran; see 1Qp Hab.
I and II Pet.	Epistles of Peter (New Testament).
Pfeiffer, Introd	R.H. Pfeiffer, *Introduction to the Old Testament* (1948).
PG	J.P. Migne (ed.), *Patrologia Graeca,* 161 vols. (1866–86).
Phil.	Epistle to the Philippians (New Testament).
Philem.	Epistle to the Philemon (New Testament).
PIASH	*Proceedings of the Israel Academy of Sciences and Humanities* (1963/7ff.).
PJB	*Palaestinajahrbuch des deutschen evangelischen Institutes fuer Altertumswissenschaft,* Jerusalem (1905–1933).
PK	*Pinkas ha-Kehillot,* encyclopedia of Jewish communities, published in over 30 volumes by Yad Vashem from 1970 and arranged by countries, regions and localities. For 3-vol. English edition see Spector, *Jewish Life.*
PL	J.P. Migne (ed.), *Patrologia Latina* 221 vols. (1844–64).
Plant	Philo, *De Plantatione.*
PO	R. Graffin and F. Nau (eds.), *Patrologia Orientalis* (1903ff.)
Pool, Prayer	D. de Sola Pool, *Traditional Prayer Book for Sabbath and Festivals* (1960).
Post	Philo, *De Posteritate Caini.*
PR	*Pesikta Rabbati.*
Praem.	Philo, *De Praemiis et Poenis.*
Prawer, Ẓalbanim	J. Prawer, *Toledot Mamlekhet ha-Ẓalbanim be-Ereẓ Yisrael,* 2 vols. (1963).
Press, Ereẓ	I. Press, *Ereẓ-Yisrael, Enẓiklopedyah Topografit-Historit,* 4 vols. (1951–55).
Pritchard, Pictures	J.B. Pritchard (ed.), *Ancient Near East in Pictures* (1954, 1970).
Pritchard, Texts	J.B. Pritchard (ed.), *Ancient Near East Texts* ... (1970^{3}).
Pr. Man.	Prayer of Manasses (Apocrypha).
Prob.	Philo, *Quod Omnis Probus Liber Sit.*
Prov.	Proverbs (Bible).
PS	*Palestinsky Sbornik* (Russ. (1881 1916, 1954ff).
Ps.	Psalms (Bible).
PSBA	*Proceedings of the Society of Biblical Archaeology* (1878–1918).
Ps. of Sol	Psalms of Solomon (Pseudepigrapha).
IQ Apoc	The *Genesis Apocryphon* from Qumran, cave one, ed. by N. Avigad and Y. Yadin (1956).
6QD	*Damascus Document* or *Sefer Berit Dammesk* from Qumran, cave six, ed. by M. Baillet, in RB, 63 (1956), 513–23 (see also CD).
QDAP	*Quarterly of the Department of Antiquities in Palestine* (1932ff.).
4QDeut. 32	Manuscript of Deuteronomy 32 from Qumran, cave four (ed. by P.W. Skehan, in BASOR, 136 (1954), 12–15).
4QEx^{a}	Exodus manuscript in Jewish script from Qumran, cave four.
4QEx$^{\alpha}$	Exodus manuscript in Paleo-Hebrew script from Qumran, cave four (partially ed. by P.W. Skehan, in JBL, 74 (1955), 182–7).
4QFlor	*Florilegium,* a miscellany from Qumran, cave four (ed. by J.M. Allegro, in JBL, 75 (1956), 176–77 and 77 (1958), 350–54).).
QGJD	*Quellen zur Geschichte der Juden in Deutschland* 1888–98).
IQH	*Thanksgiving Psalms* of *Hodayot* from Qumran, cave one (ed. by E.L. Sukenik and N. Avigad, *Oẓar ha-Megillot ha-Genuzot* (1954).
IQIs^{a}	Scroll of Isaiah from Qumran, cave one (ed. by N. Burrows et al., *Dead Sea Scrolls* ..., 1 (1950).
IQIs^{b}	Scroll of Isaiah from Qumran, cave one (ed. E.L. Sukenik and N. Avigad, *Oẓar ha-Megillot ha-Genuzot* (1954).
IQM	The *War Scroll* or *Serekh ha-Milḥamah* (ed. by E.L. Sukenik and N. Avigad, *Oẓar ha-Megillot ha-Genuzot* (1954).
4QpNah	Commentary on Nahum from Qumran, cave four (partially ed. by J.M. Allegro, in JBL, 75 (1956), 89–95).
IQphyl	Phylacteries *(tefillin)* from Qumran, cave one (ed. by Y. Yadin, in *Eretz Israel,* 9 (1969), 60–85).
4Q Prayer of Nabonidus	A document from Qumran, cave four, belonging to a lost Daniel literature (ed. by J.T. Milik, in RB, 63 (1956), 407–15).
IQS	*Manual of Discipline* or *Serekh ha-Yaḥad* from Qumran, cave one (ed. by M. Burrows et al., *Dead Sea Scrolls* ..., 2, pt. 2 (1951).

IQS[a]	The *Rule of the Congregation or Serekh ha-Edah* from Qumran, cave one (ed. by Burrows et al., *Dead Sea Scrolls* ..., 1 (1950), under the abbreviation IQ28a).
IQS[b]	*Blessings* or *Divrei Berakhot* from Qumran, cave one (ed. by Burrows et al., *Dead Sea Scrolls* ..., 1 (1950), under the abbreviation IQ28b).
4QSam[a]	Manuscript of I and II Samuel from Qumran, cave four (partially ed. by F.M. Cross, in BASOR, 132 (1953), 15–26).
4QSam[b]	Manuscript of I and II Samuel from Qumran, cave four (partially ed. by F.M. Cross, in JBL, 74 (1955), 147–72).
4QTestimonia	Sheet of Testimony from Qumran, cave four (ed. by J.M. Allegro, in JBL, 75 (1956), 174–87).).
4QT.Levi	*Testament of Levi* from Qumran, cave four (partially ed. by J.T. Milik, in RB, 62 (1955), 398–406).
Rabinovitz, Dik Sof	See Dik Sof.
RB	*Revue biblique* (1892ff.)
RBI	*Recherches bibliques* (1954ff.)
RCB	*Revista de cultura biblica* (São Paulo) (1957ff.)
Régné, Cat	J. Régné, *Catalogue des actes . . . des rois d'Aragon, concernant les Juifs* (1213–1327), in: REJ, vols. 60 70, 73, 75–78 (1910–24).
Reinach, Textes	T. Reinach, *Textes d'auteurs Grecs et Romains relatifs au Judaïsme* (1895; repr. 1963).
REJ	*Revue des études juives* (1880ff.).
Rejzen, Leksikon	Z. Rejzen, *Leksikon fun der Yidisher Literature,* 4 vols. (1927–29).
Renan, Ecrivains	A. Neubauer and E. Renan, *Les écrivains juifs français ...* (1893).
Renan, Rabbins	A. Neubauer and E. Renan, *Les rabbins français* (1877).
RES	*Revue des étude sémitiques et Babyloniaca* (1934–45).
Rev.	Revelation (New Testament).
RGG[3]	*Die Religion in Geschichte und Gegenwart,* 7 vols. (1957–65[3]).
RH	*Rosh Ha-Shanah* (talmudic tractate).
RHJE	*Revue de l'histoire juive en Egypte* (1947ff.).
RHMH	*Revue d'histoire de la médecine hébraïque* (1948ff.).
RHPR	*Revue d'histoire et de philosophie religieuses* (1921ff.).
RHR	*Revue d'histoire des religions* (1880ff.).
RI	*Rivista Israelitica* (1904–12).
Riemann-Einstein	*Hugo Riemanns Musiklexikon,* ed. by A. Einstein (1929[11]).
Riemann-Gurlitt	*Hugo Riemanns Musiklexikon,* ed. by W. Gurlitt (1959–67[12]), Personenteil.
Rigg-Jenkinson, Exchequer	J.M. Rigg, H. Jenkinson and H.G. Richardson (eds.), *Calendar of the Pleas Rolls of the Exchequer of the Jews,* 4 vols. (1905–1970); cf. in each instance also J.M. Rigg (ed.), *Select Pleas* ... (1902).
RMI	*Rassegna Mensile di Israel* (1925ff.).
Rom.	Epistle to the Romans (New Testament).
Rosanes, Togarmah	S.A. Rosanes, *Divrei Yemei Yisrael be-Togarmah,* 6 vols. (1907–45), and in 3 vols. (1930–38[2]).
Rosenbloom, Biogr Dict	J.R. Rosenbloom, *Biographical Dictionary of Early American Jews* (1960).
Roth, Art	C. Roth, *Jewish Art* (1961).
Roth, Dark Ages	C. Roth (ed.), *World History of the Jewish People,* second series, vol. 2, *Dark Ages* (1966).
Roth, England	C. Roth, *History of the Jews in England* (1964[3]).
Roth, Italy	C. Roth, *History of the Jews in Italy* (1946).
Roth, Mag Bibl	C. Roth, *Magna Bibliotheca Anglo-Judaica* (1937).
Roth, Marranos	C. Roth, *History of the Marranos* (2nd rev. ed 1959; reprint 1966).
Rowley, Old Test	H.H. Rowley, *Old Testament and Modern Study* (1951; repr. 1961).
RS	*Revue sémitiques d'épigraphie et d'histoire ancienne* (1893/94ff.).
RSO	*Rivista degli studi orientali* (1907ff.).
RSV	Revised Standard Version of the Bible.
Rubinstein, Australia I	*H.L. Rubinstein, The Jews in Australia, A Thematic History, Vol. I (1991).*
Rubinstein, Australia II	*W.D. Rubinstein, The Jews in Australia, A Thematic History, Vol. II (1991).*
Ruth	Ruth (Bible).
Ruth R.	*Ruth Rabbah.*
RV	Revised Version of the Bible.
Sac.	Philo, *De Sacrificiis Abelis et Caini.*
Salfeld, Martyrol	S. Salfeld, *Martyrologium des Nuernberger Memorbuches* (1898).
I and II Sam.	Samuel, book I and II (Bible).
Sanh.	*Sanhedrin* (talmudic tractate).
SBA	Society of Biblical Archaeology.
SBB	*Studies in Bibliography and Booklore* (1953ff.).
SBE	*Semana Biblica Española.*
SBT	*Studies in Biblical Theology* (1951ff.).
SBU	*Svenkst Bibliskt Uppslogsvesk,* 2 vols. (1962–63[2]).
Schirmann, Italyah	J.Ḥ. Schirmann, *Ha-Shirah ha-Ivrit be-Italyah* (1934).
Schirmann, Sefarad	J.Ḥ. Schirmann, *Ha-Shirah ha-Ivrit bi-Sefarad u-vi-Provence,* 2 vols. (1954–56).
Scholem, Mysticism	G. Scholem, *Major Trends in Jewish Mysticism* (rev. ed. 1946; paperback ed. with additional bibliography 1961).
Scholem, Shabbetai Ẓevi	G. Scholem, *Shabbetai Ẓevi ve-ha-Tenu'ah ha-Shabbeta'it bi-Ymei Ḥayyav,* 2 vols. (1967).
Schrader, Keilinschr	E. Schrader, *Keilinschriften und das Alte Testament* (1903[3]).
Schuerer, Gesch	E. Schuerer, *Geschichte des juedischen Volkes im Zeitalter Jesu Christi,* 3 vols. and index-vol. (1901–11[4]).

Schuerer, Hist	E. Schuerer, *History of the Jewish People in the Time of Jesus*, ed. by N.N. Glatzer, abridged paperback edition (1961).
Set. T.	*Sefer Torah* (post-talmudic tractate).
Sem.	*Semaḥot* (post-talmudic tractate).
Sendrey, Music	A. Sendrey, *Bibliography of Jewish Music* (1951).
SER	*Seder Eliyahu Rabbah.*
SEZ	*Seder Eliyahu Zuta.*
Shab	*Shabbat* (talmudic tractate).
Sh. Ar.	J. Caro Shulḥan Arukh. OḤ – *Oraḥ Ḥayyim* YD – *Yoreh De'ah* EH – *Even ha-Ezer* ḤM – *Ḥoshen Mishpat.*
Shek.	*Shekalim* (talmudic tractate).
Shev.	*Shevi'it* (talmudic tractate).
Shevu.	*Shevu'ot* (talmudic tractate).
Shunami, Bibl	S. Shunami, *Bibliography of Jewish Bibliographies* (1965[2]).
Sif.	*Sifrei Deuteronomy.*
Sif. Num.	*Sifrei Numbers.*
Sifra	*Sifra* on Leviticus.
Sif. Zut.	*Sifrei Zuta.*
SIHM	Sources inédites de l'histoire du Maroc (series).
Silverman, Prayer	M. Silverman (ed.), *Sabbath and Festival Prayer Book* (1946).
Singer, Prayer	S. Singer *Authorised Daily Prayer Book* (1943[17]).
Sob.	Philo, *De Sobrietate.*
Sof.	*Soferim* (post-talmudic tractate).
Som.	Philo, *De Somniis.*
Song	Song of Songs (Bible).
Song. Ch.	Song of the Three Children (Apocrypha).
Song R.	*Song of Songs Rabbah.*
SOR	*Seder Olam Rabbah.*
Sot.	*Sotah* (talmudic tractate).
SOZ	*Seder Olam Zuta.*
Spec.	Philo, *De Specialibus Legibus.*
Spector, Jewish Life	*S. Spector (ed.), Encyclopedia of Jewish Life Before and After the Holocaust (2001).*
Steinschneider, Arab lit	M. Steinschneider, *Die arabische Literatur der Juden* (1902).
Steinschneider, Cat Bod	M. Steinschneider, *Catalogus Librorum Hebraeorum in Bibliotheca Bodleiana,* 3 vols. (1852–60; reprints 1931 and 1964).
Steinschneider, Hanbuch	M. Steinschneider, *Bibliographisches Handbuch ueber die . . . Literatur fuer hebraeische Sprachkunde* (1859; repr. with additions 1937).
Steinschneider, Uebersetzungen	M. Steinschneider, *Die hebraeischen Uebersetzungen des Mittelalters* (1893).
Stern, Americans	M.H. Stern, *Americans of Jewish Descent* (1960).
van Straalen, Cat	S. van Straalen, *Catalogue of Hebrew Books in the British Museum Acquired During the Years 1868–1892* (1894).
Suárez Fernández, Docmentos	L. Suárez Fernández, *Documentos acerca de la expulsion de los Judios de España* (1964).
Suk.	*Sukkah* (talmudic tractate).
Sus.	Susanna (Apocrypha).
SY	*Sefer Yeẓirah.*
Sym.	Symmachus' Greek translation of the Bible.
SZNG	*Studien zur neueren Geschichte.*
Ta'an.	*Ta'anit* (talmudic tractate).
Tam.	*Tamid* (mishnaic tractate).
Tanḥ.	*Tanḥuma.*
Tanḥ. B.	*Tanḥuma.* Buber ed (1885).
Targ. Jon	Targum Jonathan (Aramaic version of the Prophets).
Targ. Onk.	Targum Onkelos (Aramaic version of the Pentateuch).
Targ. Yer.	Targum Yerushalmi.
TB	Babylonian Talmud or Talmud Bavli.
Tcherikover, Corpus	V. Tcherikover, A. Fuks, and M. Stern, *Corpus Papyrorum Judaicorum,* 3 vols. (1957–60).
Tef.	*Tefillin* (post-talmudic tractate).
Tem.	*Temurah* (mishnaic tractate).
Ter.	*Terumah* (talmudic tractate).
Test. Patr.	Testament of the Twelve Patriarchs (Pseudepigrapha). Ash. – Asher Ben. – Benjamin Dan – Dan Gad – Gad Iss. – Issachar Joseph – Joseph Judah – Judah Levi – Levi Naph. – Naphtali Reu. – Reuben Sim. – Simeon Zeb. – Zebulun.
I and II	Epistle to the Thessalonians (New Testament).
Thieme-Becker	U. Thieme and F. Becker (eds.), *Allgemeines Lexikon der bildenden Kuenstler von der Antike bis zur Gegenwart,* 37 vols. (1907–50).
Tidhar	D. Tidhar (ed.), *Enẓiklopedyah la-Ḥalutẓei ha-Yishuv u-Vonav* (1947ff.).
I and II Timothy	Epistles to Timothy (New Testament).
Tit.	Epistle to Titus (New Testament).
TJ	Jerusalem Talmud or Talmud Yerushalmi.
Tob.	Tobit (Apocrypha).
Toh.	*Tohorot* (mishnaic tractate).
Torczyner, Bundeslade	H. Torczyner, *Die Bundeslade und die Anfaenge der Religion Israels* (1930[3]).
Tos.	*Tosafot.*
Tosef.	Tosefta.
Tristram, Nat Hist	H.B. Tristram, *Natural History of the Bible* (1877[5]).
Tristram, Survey	Palestine Exploration Fund, *Survey of Western Palestine,* vol. 4 (1884) = *Fauna and Flora* by H.B. Tristram.
TS	*Terra Santa* (1943ff.).

TSBA	*Transactions of the Society of Biblical Archaeology* (1872–93).
TY	*Tevul Yom* (mishnaic tractate).
UBSB	United Bible Society, *Bulletin.*
UJE	*Universal Jewish Encyclopedia*, 10 vols. (1939–43).
Uk.	*Ukẓin* (mishnaic tractate).
Urbach, Tosafot	E.E. Urbach, *Ba'alei ha-Tosafot* (1957^{2}).
de Vaux, Anc Isr	R. de Vaux, *Ancient Israel: its Life and Institutions* (1961; paperback 1965).
de Vaux, Instit	R. de Vaux, *Institutions de l'Ancien Testament,* 2 vols. (1958 60).
Virt.	Philo, *De Virtutibus.*
Vogelstein, Chronology	M. Volgelstein, *Biblical Chronology (1944).*
Vogelstein-Rieger	H. Vogelstein and P. Rieger, *Geschichte der Juden in Rom,* 2 vols. (1895–96).
VT	*Vetus Testamentum* (1951ff.).
VTS	*Vetus Testamentum* Supplements (1953ff.).
Vulg.	Vulgate (Latin translation of the Bible).
Wars	Josephus, *The Jewish Wars.*
Watzinger, Denkmaeler	K. Watzinger, *Denkmaeler Palaestinas,* 2 vols. (1933–35).
Waxman, Literature	M. Waxman, *History of Jewish Literature,* 5 vols. (1960^{2}).
Weiss, Dor	I.H. Weiss, *Dor, Dor ve-Doreshav,* 5 vols. (1904^{4}).
Wellhausen, Proleg	J. Wellhausen, *Prolegomena zur Geschichte Israels* (1927^{6}).
WI	*Die Welt des Islams* (1913ff.).
Winniger, Biog	S. Wininger, *Grosse juedische National-Biographie ...,* 7 vols. (1925–36).
Wisd.	Wisdom of Solomon (Apocrypha)
WLB	*Wiener Library Bulletin* (1958ff.).
Wolf, Bibliotheca	J.C. Wolf, *Bibliotheca Hebraea*, 4 vols. (1715–33).
Wright, Bible	G.E. Wright, *Westminster Historical Atlas to the Bible* (1945).
Wright, Atlas	G.E. Wright, *The Bible and the Ancient Near East* (1961).
WWWJ	*Who's Who in the World Jewry* (New York, 1955, 1965^{2}).
WZJT	*Wissenschaftliche Zeitschrift fuer juedische Theologie* (1835–37).
WZKM	*Wiener Zeitschrift fuer die Kunde des Morgenlandes* (1887ff.).
Yaari, Sheluḥei	A. Yaari, *Sheluḥei Ereẓ Yisrael* (1951).
Yad	Maimonides, *Mishneh Torah (Yad Ḥazakah).*
Yad	*Yadayim* (mishnaic tractate).
Yal.	*Yalkut Shimoni.*
Yal. Mak.	*Yalkut Makhiri.*
Yal. Reub.	*Yalkut Reubeni.*
YD	*Yoreh De'ah.*
YE	*Yevreyskaya Entsiklopediya,* 14 vols. (c. 1910).
Yev.	*Yevamot* (talmudic tractate).
YIVOA	*YIVO Annual of Jewish Social Studies* (1946ff.).
YLBI	*Year Book of the Leo Baeck Institute* (1956ff.).
YMḤEY	See BJPES.
YMḤSI	*Yedi'ot ha-Makhon le-Ḥeker ha-Shirah ha-Ivrit* (1935/36ff.).
YMMY	*Yedi'ot ha-Makhon le-Madda'ei ha-Yahadut* (1924/25ff.).
Yoma	*Yoma* (talmudic tractate).
ZA	*Zeitschrift fuer Assyriologie* (1886/87ff.).
Zav.	*Zavim* (mishnaic tractate).
ZAW	*Zeitschrift fuer die alttestamentliche Wissenschaft und die Kunde des nachbiblishchen Judentums* (1881ff.).
ZAWB	*Beihefte* (supplements) to ZAW.
ZDMG	*Zeitschrift der Deutschen Morgenlaendischen Gesellschaft* (1846ff.).
ZDPV	*Zeitschrift des Deutschen Palaestina-Vereins* (1878–1949; from 1949 = BBLA).
Zech.	Zechariah (Bible).
Zedner, Cat	J. Zedner, *Catalogue of Hebrew Books in the Library of the British Museum* (1867; repr. 1964).
Zeitlin, Bibliotheca	W. Zeitlin, *Bibliotheca Hebraica Post-Mendelssohniana* (1891–95).
Zeph.	Zephaniah (Bible).
Zev.	*Zevaḥim* (talmudic tractate).
ZGGJT	*Zeitschrift der Gesellschaft fuer die Geschichte der Juden in der Tschechoslowakei* (1930–38).
ZGJD	*Zeitschrift fuer die Geschichte der Juden in Deutschland* (1887–92).
ZHB	*Zeitschrift fuer hebraeische Bibliographie* (1896–1920).
Zinberg, Sifrut	I. Zinberg, *Toledot Sifrut Yisrael,* 6 vols. (1955–60).
Ẓiẓ.	*Ẓiẓit* (post-talmudic tractate).
ZNW	*Zeitschrift fuer die neutestamentliche Wissenschaft* (1901ff.).
ZS	*Zeitschrift fuer Semitistik und verwandte Gebiete* (1922ff.).
Zunz, Gesch	L. Zunz, *Zur Geschichte und Literatur* (1845).
Zunz, Gesch	L. Zunz, *Literaturgeschichte der synagogalen Poesie* (1865; Supplement, 1867; repr. 1966).
Zunz, Poesie	L. Zunz, *Synogogale Posie des Mittelalters,* ed. by Freimann (1920^{2}; repr. 1967).
Zunz, Ritus	L. Zunz, *Ritus des synagogalen Gottesdienstes* (1859; repr. 1967).
Zunz, Schr	L. Zunz, *Gesammelte Schriften,* 3 vols. (1875–76).
Zunz, Vortraege	L. Zunz, *Gottesdienstliche vortraege der Juden ...* 1892^{2}; repr. 1966).
Zunz-Albeck, Derashot	L. Zunz, *Ha-Derashot be-Yisrael,* Heb. Tr. of Zunz Vortraege by H. Albeck (1954^{2}).

TRANSLITERATION RULES

HEBREW AND SEMITIC LANGUAGES:

	General	*Scientific*
א	not transliterated[1]	ʾ
בּ	b	b
ב	v	v, b̲
גּ	g	g
ג		ḡ
דּ	d	d
ד		d̲
ה	h	h
ו	v – when not a vowel	w
ז	z	z
ח	ḥ	ḥ
ט	t	ṭ, t
י	y – when vowel and at end of words – i	y
כּ	k	k
כ, ך	kh	kh, ḵ
ל	l	ḻ
מ, ם	m	m
נ, ן	n	n
ס	s	s
ע	not transliterated[1]	ʿ
פּ	p	p
פ, ף	f	p, f, ph
צ, ץ	ẓ	ṣ, ẓ
ק	k	q, k
ר	r	r
שׁ	sh[2]	š
שׂ	s	ś, s
תּ	t	t
ת		ṯ
ג׳	dzh, J	ğ
ז׳	zh, J	ž
צ׳	ch	č
◌ָ		å, o, ȯ (short) â, ā (long)
◌ַ	a	a
◌ֲ		a, ^{a}
◌ֵ		e, ẹ, ē
◌ֶ	e	æ, ä, ę
◌ֱ		œ, ĕ, ^{e}
◌ְ	only *sheva na* is transliterated	ə, ĕ, e; only *sheva na* transliterated
◌ִ ◌ִי	i	i
◌ֹ וֹ	o	o, o, o
◌ֻ וּ	u	u, ŭ û, ū
◌ֵי	ei; biblical e	
‡		reconstructed forms of words

1. The letters א and ע are not transliterated.
   An apostrophe (') between vowels indicates that they do not form a diphthong and are to be pronounced separately.
2. *Dagesh ḥazak* (forte) is indicated by doubling of the letter, except for the letter שׁ.
3. Names. Biblical names and biblical place names are rendered according to the Bible translation of the Jewish Publication Society of America. Post-biblical Hebrew names are transliterated; contemporary names are transliterated or rendered as used by the person. Place names are transliterated or rendered by the accepted spelling. Names and some words with an accepted English form are usually not transliterated.

YIDDISH

א	not transliterated
אַ	a
אָ	o
ב	b
בֿ	v
ג	g
ד	d
ה	h
ו, וּ	u
וו	v
וי	oy
ז	z
זש	zh
ח	kh
ט	t
טש	tsh, ch
י	(consonant) y (vowel) i
יִ	i
יי	ey
ײַ	ay
כּ	k
כ, ך	kh
ל	l
מ, ם	m
נ, ן	n
ס	s
ע	e
פּ	p
פֿ, ף	f
צ, ץ	ts
ק	k
ר	r
ש	sh
שׂ	s
תּ	t
ת	s

1. Yiddish transliteration rendered according to U. Weinreich's Modern *English-Yiddish Yiddish-English* Dictionary.
2. Hebrew words in Yiddish are usually transliterated according to standard Yiddish pronunciation, e.g., חזנות = *khazones*.

LADINO

Ladino and Judeo-Spanish words written in Hebrew characters are transliterated phonetically, following the General Rules of Hebrew transliteration (see above) whenever the accepted spelling in Latin characters could not be ascertained.

ARABIC

ء ا	a[1]	ض	ḍ
ب	b	ط	ṭ
ت	t	ظ	ẓ
ث	th	ع	c
ج	j	غ	gh
ح	ḥ	ف	f
خ	kh	ق	q
د	d	ك	k
ذ	dh	ل	l
ر	r	م	m
ز	z	ن	n
س	s	ه	h
ش	sh	و	w
ص	ṣ	ي	y
ـَ	a	ـَا ى	ā
ـِ	i	ـِي	ī
ـُ	u	ـُو	ū
ـَو	aw	ـِيّ	iyy[2]
ـَي	ay	ـُوّ	uww[2]

1. not indicated when initial
2. see note (f)

a) The EJ follows the *Columbia Lippincott Gazetteer* and the *Times Atlas* in transliteration of Arabic place names. Sites that appear in neither are transliterated according to the table above, and subject to the following notes.

b) The EJ follows the *Columbia Encyclopedia* in transliteration of Arabic names. Personal names that do not therein appear are transliterated according to the table above and subject to the following notes (e.g., Ali rather than ʿAlī, Suleiman rather than Sulayman).

c) The EJ follows the *Webster's Third International Dictionary, Unabridged* in transliteration of Arabic terms that have been integrated into the English language.

d) The term "Abu" will thus appear, usually in disregard of inflection.

e) Nunnation (end vowels, *tanwīn*) are dropped in transliteration.

f) Gemination (*tashdīd*) is indicated by the doubling of the geminated letter, unless an end letter, in which case the gemination is dropped.

g) The definitive article *al-* will always be thus transliterated, unless subject to one of the modifying notes (e.g., El-Arish rather than al-ʿArīsh; modification according to note (a)).

h) The Arabic transliteration disregards the Sun Letters (the antero-palatals (*al-Ḥurūf al-Shamsiyya*).

i) The *tā-marbūṭa* (o) is omitted in transliteration, unless in construct-stage (e.g., *Khirba* but *Khirbat Mishmish*).

These modifying notes may lead to various inconsistencies in the Arabic transliteration, but this policy has deliberately been adopted to gain smoother reading of Arabic terms and names.

GREEK

Ancient Greek	*Modern Greek*	*Greek Letters*
a	a	*Α; α; ᾳ*
b	v	*Β; β*
g	gh; g	*Γ; γ*
d	dh	*Δ; δ*
e	e	*Ε; ε*
z	z	*Ζ; ζ*
e; e	i	*Η; η; ῃ*
th	th	*Θ; θ*
i	i	*Ι; ι*
k	k; ky	*Κ; κ*
l	l	*Λ; λ*
m	m	*Μ; μ*
n	n	*Ν; ν*
x	x	*Ξ; ξ*
o	o	*Ο; ο*
p	p	*Π; π*
r; rh	r	*Ρ; ρ; ῥ*
s	s	*Σ; σ; ς*
t	t	*Τ; τ*
u; y	i	*Υ; υ*
ph	f	*Φ; φ*
ch	kh	*Χ; χ*
ps	ps	*Ψ; ψ*
o; ō	o	*Ω; ω; ῳ*
ai	e	*αι*
ei	i	*ει*
oi	i	*οι*
ui	i	*υι*
ou	ou	*ου*
eu	ev	*ευ*
eu; ēu	iv	*ηυ*
–	j	*τζ*
nt	d; nd	*ντ*
mp	b; mb	*μπ*
ngk	g	*γκ*
ng	ng	*νγ*
h	–	ʽ
–	–	ʼ
w	–	*Ϝ*

RUSSIAN

А	A
Б	B
В	V
Г	G
Д	D
Е	E, Ye[1]
Ё	Yo, O[2]
Ж	Zh
З	Z
И	I
Й	Y[3]
К	K
Л	L
М	M
Н	N
О	O
П	P
Р	R
С	S
Т	T
У	U
Ф	F
Х	Kh
Ц	Ts
Ч	Ch
Ш	Sh
Щ	Shch
Ъ	omitted; see note [1]
Ы	Y
Ь	omitted; see note [1]
Э	E
Ю	Yu
Я	Ya

1. Ye at the beginning of a word; after all vowels except ***Ы***; and after **Ъ** and **Ь**.
2. O after ***Ч***, ***Ш*** and ***Щ***.
3. Omitted after ***Ы***, and in names of people after ***И***.

A. Many first names have an accepted English or quasi-English form which has been preferred to transliteration.
B. Place names have been given according to the *Columbia Lippincott Gazeteer*.
C. Pre-revolutionary spelling has been ignored.
D. Other languages using the Cyrillic alphabet (e.g., Bulgarian, Ukrainian), inasmuch as they appear, have been phonetically transliterated in conformity with the principles of this table.

GLOSSARY

Asterisked terms have separate entries in the Encyclopaedia.

Actions Committee, early name of the Zionist General Council, the supreme institution of the World Zionist Organization in the interim between Congresses. The Zionist Executive's name was then the "Small Actions Committee."

*__Adar__, twelfth month of the Jewish religious year, sixth of the civil, approximating to February–March.

*__Aggadah__, name given to those sections of Talmud and Midrash containing homiletic expositions of the Bible, stories, legends, folklore, anecdotes, or maxims. In contradistinction to **halakhah*.

*__Agunah__, woman unable to remarry according to Jewish law, because of desertion by her husband or inability to accept presumption of death.

*__Aharonim__, later rabbinic authorities. In contradistinction to **rishonim* ("early ones").

Ahavah, liturgical poem inserted in the second benediction of the morning prayer *(*Ahavah Rabbah)* of the festivals and/or special Sabbaths.

Aktion (Ger.), operation involving the mass assembly, deportation, and murder of Jews by the Nazis during the *Holocaust.

*__Aliyah__, (1) being called to Reading of the Law in synagogue; (2) immigration to Ereẓ Israel; (3) one of the waves of immigration to Ereẓ Israel from the early 1880s.

*__Amidah__, main prayer recited at all services; also known as *Shemoneh Esreh* and *Tefillah*.

*__Amora__ (pl. **amoraim**), title given to the Jewish scholars in Ereẓ Israel and Babylonia in the third to sixth centuries who were responsible for the **Gemara*.

Aravah, the *willow; one of the *Four Species used on *Sukkot ("festival of Tabernacles") together with the **etrog*, *hadas*, and **lulav*.

*__Arvit__, evening prayer.

Asarah be-Tevet, fast on the 10th of Tevet commemorating the commencement of the siege of Jerusalem by Nebuchadnezzar.

Asefat ha-Nivḥarim, representative assembly elected by Jews in Palestine during the period of the British Mandate (1920–48).

*__Ashkenaz__, name applied generally in medieval rabbinical literature to Germany.

*__Ashkenazi__ (pl. **Ashkenazim**), German or West-, Central-, or East-European Jew(s), as contrasted with *Sephardi(m).

*__Av__, fifth month of the Jewish religious year, eleventh of the civil, approximating to July–August.

*__Av bet din__, vice president of the supreme court (*bet din ha-gadol*) in Jerusalem during the Second Temple period; later, title given to communal rabbis as heads of the religious courts (see **bet din*).

*__Badḥan__, jester, particularly at traditional Jewish weddings in Eastern Europe.

*__Bakkashah__ (Heb. "supplication"), type of petitionary prayer, mainly recited in the Sephardi rite on Rosh Ha-Shanah and the Day of Atonement.

Bar, "son of . . . "; frequently appearing in personal names.

*__Baraita__ (pl. **beraitot**), statement of **tanna* not found in *Mishnah.

*__Bar mitzvah__, ceremony marking the initiation of a boy at the age of 13 into the Jewish religious community.

Ben, "son of . . . ", frequently appearing in personal names.

Berakhah (pl. **berakhot**), *benediction, blessing; formula of praise and thanksgiving.

*__Bet din__ (pl. **battei din**), rabbinic court of law.

*__Bet ha-midrash__, school for higher rabbinic learning; often attached to or serving as a synagogue.

*__Bilu__, first modern movement for pioneering and agricultural settlement in Ereẓ Israel, founded in 1882 at Kharkov, Russia.

*__Bund__, Jewish socialist party founded in Vilna in 1897, supporting Jewish national rights; Yiddishist, and anti-Zionist.

Cohen (pl. **Cohanim**), see Kohen.

*__Conservative Judaism__, trend in Judaism developed in the United States in the 20th century which, while opposing extreme changes in traditional observances, permits certain modifications of *halakhah* in response to the changing needs of the Jewish people.

*__Consistory__ (Fr. *consistoire*), governing body of a Jewish communal district in France and certain other countries.

*__Converso(s)__, term applied in Spain and Portugal to converted Jew(s), and sometimes more loosely to their descendants.

*__Crypto-Jew__, term applied to a person who although observing outwardly Christianity (or some other religion) was at heart a Jew and maintained Jewish observances as far as possible (see Converso; Marrano; Neofiti; New Christian; Jadīd al-Islām).

*__Dayyan__, member of rabbinic court.

Decisor, equivalent to the Hebrew *posek* (pl. **posekim*), the rabbi who gives the decision (*halakhah*) in Jewish law or practice.

*__Devekut__, "devotion"; attachment or adhesion to God; communion with God.

*__Diaspora__, Jews living in the "dispersion" outside Ereẓ Israel; area of Jewish settlement outside Ereẓ Israel.

Din, a law (both secular and religious), legal decision, or lawsuit.

Divan, diwan, collection of poems, especially in Hebrew, Arabic, or Persian.

Dunam, unit of land area (1,000 sq. m., c. ¼ acre), used in Israel.

Einsatzgruppen, mobile units of Nazi S.S. and S.D.; in U.S.S.R. and Serbia, mobile killing units.

*__Ein-Sof__, "without end"; "the infinite"; hidden, impersonal aspect of God; also used as a Divine Name.

*__Elul__, sixth month of the Jewish religious calendar, 12th of the civil, precedes the High Holiday season in the fall.

Endloesung, see *Final Solution.

*__Ereẓ Israel__, Land of Israel; Palestine.

*__Eruv__, technical term for rabbinical provision permitting the alleviation of certain restrictions.

*__Etrog__, citron; one of the *Four Species used on *Sukkot together with the **lulav*, *hadas*, and *aravah*.

Even ha-Ezer, see Shulḥan Arukh.

*__Exilarch__, lay head of Jewish community in Babylonia (see also *resh galuta*), and elsewhere.

*__Final Solution__ (Ger. *Endloesung*), in Nazi terminology, the Nazi-planned mass murder and total annihilation of the Jews.

*__Gabbai__, official of a Jewish congregation; originally a charity collector.

*__Galut__, "exile"; the condition of the Jewish people in dispersion.

*Gaon (pl. geonim), head of academy in post-talmudic period, especially in Babylonia.

Gaonate, office of *gaon.

*Gemara, traditions, discussions, and rulings of the *amoraim*, commenting on and supplementing the *Mishnah, and forming part of the Babylonian and Palestinian Talmuds (see Talmud).

*Gematria, interpretation of Hebrew word according to the numerical value of its letters.

General Government, territory in Poland administered by a German civilian governor-general with headquarters in Cracow after the German occupation in World War II.

*Genizah, depository for sacred books. The best known was discovered in the synagogue of Fostat (old Cairo).

Get, bill of *divorce.

*Ge'ullah, hymn inserted after the *Shema* into the benediction of the morning prayer of the festivals and special Sabbaths.

*Gilgul, metempsychosis; transmigration of souls.

*Golem, automaton, especially in human form, created by magical means and endowed with life.

*Ḥabad, initials of *ḥokhmah, binah, da'at*: "wisdom, understanding, knowledge"; ḥasidic movement founded in Belorussia by *Shneur Zalman of Lyady.

Hadas, *myrtle; one of the *Four Species used on Sukkot together with the *etrog*, *lulav*, and *aravah*.

*Haftarah (pl. haftarot), designation of the portion from the prophetical books of the Bible recited after the synagogue reading from the Pentateuch on Sabbaths and holidays.

*Haganah, clandestine Jewish organization for armed self-defense in Ereẓ Israel under the British Mandate, which eventually evolved into a people's militia and became the basis for the Israel army.

*Haggadah, ritual recited in the home on *Passover eve at seder table.

Haham, title of chief rabbi of the Spanish and Portuguese congregations in London, England.

*Hakham, title of rabbi of *Sephardi congregation.

*Hakham bashi, title in the 15th century and modern times of the chief rabbi in the Ottoman Empire, residing in Constantinople (Istanbul), also applied to principal rabbis in provincial towns.

Hakhsharah ("preparation"), organized training in the Diaspora of pioneers for agricultural settlement in Ereẓ Israel.

*Halakhah (pl. halakhot), an accepted decision in rabbinic law. Also refers to those parts of the *Talmud concerned with legal matters. In contradistinction to *aggadah*.

Ḥaliẓah, biblically prescribed ceremony (Deut. 25:9–10) performed when a man refuses to marry his brother's childless widow, enabling her to remarry.

*Hallel, term referring to Psalms 113-18 in liturgical use.

*Ḥalukkah, system of financing the maintenance of Jewish communities in the holy cities of Ereẓ Israel by collections made abroad, mainly in the pre-Zionist era (see *kolel*).

Ḥalutz (pl. ḥalutzim), pioneer, especially in agriculture, in Ereẓ Israel.

Ḥalutziyyut, pioneering.

*Ḥanukkah, eight-day celebration commemorating the victory of *Judah Maccabee over the Syrian king *Antiochus Epiphanes and the subsequent rededication of the Temple.

Ḥasid, adherent of *Ḥasidism.

*Ḥasidei Ashkenaz, medieval pietist movement among the Jews of Germany.

*Ḥasidism, (1) religious revivalist movement of popular mysticism among Jews of Germany in the Middle Ages; (2) religious movement founded by *Israel ben Eliezer Ba'al Shem Tov in the first half of the 18th century.

*Haskalah, "enlightenment"; movement for spreading modern European culture among Jews c. 1750–1880. See *maskil*.

*Havdalah, ceremony marking the end of Sabbath or festival.

*Ḥazzan, precentor who intones the liturgy and leads the prayers in synagogue; in earlier times a synagogue official.

*Ḥeder (lit. "room"), school for teaching children Jewish religious observance.

Heikhalot, "palaces"; tradition in Jewish mysticism centering on mystical journeys through the heavenly spheres and palaces to the Divine Chariot (see Merkabah).

*Ḥerem, excommunication, imposed by rabbinical authorities for purposes of religious and/or communal discipline; originally, in biblical times, that which is separated from common use either because it was an abomination or because it was consecrated to God.

Ḥeshvan, see Marḥeshvan.

*Ḥevra kaddisha, title applied to charitable confraternity (*ḥevrah*), now generally limited to associations for burial of the dead.

*Ḥibbat Zion, see Ḥovevei Zion.

*Histadrut (abbr. For Heb. **Ha-Histadrut ha-Kelalit shel ha-Ovedim ha-Ivriyyim be-Ereẓ Israel**). Ereẓ Israel Jewish Labor Federation, founded in 1920; subsequently renamed Histadrut ha-Ovedim be-Ereẓ Israel.

*Holocaust, the organized mass persecution and annihilation of European Jewry by the Nazis (1933–1945).

*Hoshana Rabba, the seventh day of *Sukkot on which special observances are held.

Ḥoshen Mishpat, see Shulḥan Arukh.

Ḥovevei Zion, federation of *Ḥibbat Zion, early (pre-*Herzl) Zionist movement in Russia.

Illui, outstanding scholar or genius, especially a young prodigy in talmudic learning.

*Iyyar, second month of the Jewish religious year, eighth of the civil, approximating to April-May.

I.Ẓ.L. (initials of Heb. ***Irgun Ẓeva'i Le'ummi**; "National Military Organization"), underground Jewish organization in Ereẓ Israel founded in 1931, which engaged from 1937 in retaliatory acts against Arab attacks and later against the British mandatory authorities.

*Jadīd al-Islām (Ar.), a person practicing the Jewish religion in secret although outwardly observing Islām.

*Jewish Legion, Jewish units in British army during World War I.

*Jihād (Ar.), in Muslim religious law, holy war waged against infidels.

*Judenrat (Ger. "Jewish council"), council set up in Jewish communities and ghettos under the Nazis to execute their instructions.

*Judenrein (Ger. "clean of Jews"), in Nazi terminology the condition of a locality from which all Jews had been eliminated.

*Kabbalah, the Jewish mystical tradition:
Kabbala iyyunit, speculative Kabbalah;
Kabbala ma'asit, practical Kabbalah;
Kabbala nevu'it, prophetic Kabbalah.

Kabbalist, student of Kabbalah.

*Kaddish, liturgical doxology.

Kahal, Jewish congregation; among Ashkenazim, *kehillah*.

*__Kalām__ (Ar.), science of Muslim theology; adherents of the Kalām are called *mutakallimūn*.

*__Karaite__, member of a Jewish sect originating in the eighth century which rejected rabbinic (*Rabbanite) Judaism and claimed to accept only Scripture as authoritative.

*__Kasher__, ritually permissible food.

Kashrut, Jewish *dietary laws.

*__Kavvanah__, "intention"; term denoting the spiritual concentration accompanying prayer and the performance of ritual or of a commandment.

*__Kedushah__, main addition to the third blessing in the reader's repetition of the *Amidah* in which the public responds to the precentor's introduction.

Kefar, village; first part of name of many settlements in Israel.

Kehillah, congregation; see *kahal*.

Kelippah (pl. **kelippot**), "husk(s)"; mystical term denoting force(s) of evil.

*__Keneset Yisrael__, comprehensive communal organization of the Jews in Palestine during the British Mandate.

Keri, variants in the masoretic (*masorah) text of the Bible between the spelling (*ketiv*) and its pronunciation (*keri*).

*__Kerovah__ (collective plural (corrupted) from **kerovez̧**), poem(s) incorporated into the **Amidah*.

Ketiv, see *keri*.

*__Ketubbah__, marriage contract, stipulating husband's obligations to wife.

Kevuz̧ah, small commune of pioneers constituting an agricultural settlement in Erez̧ Israel (evolved later into *kibbutz).

*__Kibbutz__ (pl. **kibbutzim**), larger-size commune constituting a settlement in Erez̧ Israel based mainly on agriculture but engaging also in industry.

*__Kiddush__, prayer of sanctification, recited over wine or bread on eve of Sabbaths and festivals.

*__Kiddush ha-Shem__, term connoting martyrdom or act of strict integrity in support of Judaic principles.

*__Kinah__ (pl. **kinot**), lamentation dirge(s) for the Ninth of Av and other fast days.

*__Kislev__, ninth month of the Jewish religious year, third of the civil, approximating to November-December.

Klaus, name given in Central and Eastern Europe to an institution, usually with synagogue attached, where *Talmud was studied perpetually by adults; applied by Ḥasidim to their synagogue ("*kloyz*").

*__Knesset__, parliament of the State of Israel.

K(c)ohen (pl. **K(c)ohanim**), Jew(s) of priestly (Aaronide) descent.

*__Kolel__, (1) community in Erez̧ Israel of persons from a particular country or locality, often supported by their fellow countrymen in the Diaspora; (2) institution for higher Torah study.

Kosher, see *kasher*.

*__Kristallnacht__ (Ger. "crystal night," meaning "night of broken glass"), organized destruction of synagogues, Jewish houses, and shops, accompanied by mass arrests of Jews, which took place in Germany and Austria under the Nazis on the night of Nov. 9–10, 1938.

*__Lag ba-Omer__, 33rd (Heb. **lag**) day of the **Omer* period falling on the 18th of *Iyyar; a semi-holiday.

Leḥi (abbr. For Heb. *__Loḥamei Ḥerut Israel__, "Fighters for the Freedom of Israel"), radically anti-British armed underground organization in Palestine, founded in 1940 by dissidents from *I.Z.L.

Levir, husband's brother.

*__Levirate marriage__ (Heb. *yibbum*), marriage of childless widow (*yevamah*) by brother (*yavam*) of the deceased husband (in accordance with Deut. 25:5); release from such an obligation is effected through *ḥaliz̧ah*.

LHY, see Leḥi.

*__Lulav__, palm branch; one of the *Four Species used on *Sukkot together with the **etrog*, *hadas*, and *aravah*.

*__Ma'aravot__, hymns inserted into the evening prayer of the three festivals, Passover, Shavuot, and Sukkot.

Ma'ariv, evening prayer; also called **arvit*.

*__Ma'barah__, transition camp; temporary settlement for newcomers in Israel during the period of mass immigration following 1948.

*__Maftir__, reader of the concluding portion of the Pentateuchal section on Sabbaths and holidays in synagogue; reader of the portion of the prophetical books of the Bible (**haftarah*).

*__Maggid__, popular preacher.

*__Maḥzor__ (pl. **maḥzorim**), festival prayer book.

*__Mamzer__, bastard; according to Jewish law, the offspring of an incestuous relationship.

*__Mandate, Palestine__, responsibility for the administration of Palestine conferred on Britain by the League of Nations in 1922; mandatory government: the British administration of Palestine.

*__Maqāma__ (Ar. pl. **maqamāt**), poetic form (rhymed prose) which, in its classical arrangement, has rigid rules of form and content.

*__Marḥeshvan__, popularly called Ḥeshvan; eighth month of the Jewish religious year, second of the civil, approximating to October–November.

*__Marrano(s)__, descendant(s) of Jew(s) in Spain and Portugal whose ancestors had been converted to Christianity under pressure but who secretly observed Jewish rituals.

Maskil (pl. **maskilim**), adherent of *Haskalah ("Enlightenment") movement.

*__Masorah__, body of traditions regarding the correct spelling, writing, and reading of the Hebrew Bible.

Masorete, scholar of the masoretic tradition.

Masoretic, in accordance with the masorah.

Meliz̧ah, in Middle Ages, elegant style; modern usage, florid style using biblical or talmudic phraseology.

Mellah, *Jewish quarter in North African towns.

*__Menorah__, candelabrum; seven-branched oil lamp used in the Tabernacle and Temple; also eight-branched candelabrum used on *Ḥanukkah.

Me'orah, hymn inserted into the first benediction of the morning prayer (*Yoz̧er ha-Me'orot*).

*__Merkabah__, *merkavah*, "chariot"; mystical discipline associated with Ezekiel's vision of the Divine Throne-Chariot (Ezek. 1).

Meshullaḥ, emissary sent to conduct propaganda or raise funds for rabbinical academies or charitable institutions.

*__Mezuzah__ (pl. **mezuzot**), parchment scroll with selected Torah verses placed in container and affixed to gates and doorposts of houses occupied by Jews.

*__Midrash__, method of interpreting Scripture to elucidate legal points (*Midrash Halakhah*) or to bring out lessons by stories or homiletics (*Midrash Aggadah*). Also the name for a collection of such rabbinic interpretations.

*__Mikveh__, ritual bath.

*__Minhag__ (pl. **minhagim**), ritual custom(s); synagogal rite(s); especially of a specific sector of Jewry.

*__Minḥah__, afternoon prayer; originally meal offering in Temple.

*__Minyan__, group of ten male adult Jews, the minimum required for communal prayer.

*__Mishnah__, earliest codification of Jewish Oral Law.

Mishnah (pl. **mishnayot**), subdivision of tractates of the Mishnah.

Mitnagged (pl. ***Mitnaggedim**), originally, opponents of *Ḥasidism in Eastern Europe.

*__Mitzvah__, biblical or rabbinic injunction; applied also to good or charitable deeds.

Mohel, official performing circumcisions.

*__Moshav__, smallholders' cooperative agricultural settlement in Israel, see moshav ovedim.

Moshavah, earliest type of Jewish village in modern Ereẓ Israel in which farming is conducted on individual farms mostly on privately owned land.

Moshav ovedim ("workers' moshav"), agricultural village in Israel whose inhabitants possess individual homes and holdings but cooperate in the purchase of equipment, sale of produce, mutual aid, etc.

*__Moshav shittufi__ ("collective moshav"), agricultural village in Israel whose members possess individual homesteads but where the agriculture and economy are conducted as a collective unit.

Mostegab (Ar.), poem with biblical verse at beginning of each stanza.

*__Muqaddam__ (Ar., pl. **muqaddamūn**), "leader," "head of the community."

*__Musaf__, additional service on Sabbath and festivals; originally the additional sacrifice offered in the Temple.

Musar, traditional ethical literature.

*__Musar movement__, ethical movement developing in the latter part of the 19th century among Orthodox Jewish groups in Lithuania; founded by R. Israel *Lipkin (Salanter).

*__Nagid__ (pl. **negidim**), title applied in Muslim (and some Christian) countries in the Middle Ages to a leader recognized by the state as head of the Jewish community.

Nakdan (pl. **nakdanim**), "punctuator"; scholar of the 9th to 14th centuries who provided biblical manuscripts with masoretic apparatus, vowels, and accents.

*__Nasi__ (pl. **nesi'im**), talmudic term for president of the Sanhedrin, who was also the spiritual head and later, political representative of the Jewish people; from second century a descendant of Hillel recognized by the Roman authorities as patriarch of the Jews. Now applied to the president of the State of Israel.

*__Negev__, the southern, mostly arid, area of Israel.

*__Ne'ilah__, concluding service on the *Day of Atonement.

Neofiti, term applied in southern Italy to converts to Christianity from Judaism and their descendants who were suspected of maintaining secret allegiance to Judaism.

*__Neology; Neolog; Neologism__, trend of *Reform Judaism in Hungary forming separate congregations after 1868.

*__Nevelah__ (lit. "carcass"), meat forbidden by the *dietary laws on account of the absence of, or defect in, the act of **sheḥitah* (ritual slaughter).

*__New Christians__, term applied especially in Spain and Portugal to converts from Judaism (and from Islam) and their descendants; "Half New Christian" designated a person one of whose parents was of full Jewish blood.

*__Niddah__ ("menstruous woman"), woman during the period of menstruation.

*__Nisan__, first month of the Jewish religious year, seventh of the civil, approximating to March-April.

Niẓoẓot, "sparks"; mystical term for sparks of the holy light imprisoned in all matter.

Nosaḥ (**nusaḥ**) "version"; (1) textual variant; (2) term applied to distinguish the various prayer rites, e.g., *nosaḥ Ashkenaz*; (3) the accepted tradition of synagogue melody.

*__Notarikon__, method of abbreviating Hebrew works or phrases by acronym.

Novella(e) (Heb. **ḥiddush (im)*), commentary on talmudic and later rabbinic subjects that derives new facts or principles from the implications of the text.

*__Nuremberg Laws__, Nazi laws excluding Jews from German citizenship, and imposing other restrictions.

Ofan, hymns inserted into a passage of the morning prayer.

*__Omer__, first sheaf cut during the barley harvest, offered in the Temple on the second day of Passover.

Omer, Counting of (Heb. *Sefirat ha-Omer*), 49 days counted from the day on which the *omer* was first offered in the Temple (according to the rabbis the 16th of Nisan, i.e., the second day of Passover) until the festival of Shavuot; now a period of semi-mourning.

Oraḥ Ḥayyim, see Shulḥan Arukh.

*__Orthodoxy__ (Orthodox Judaism), modern term for the strictly traditional sector of Jewry.

*__Pale of Settlement__, 25 provinces of czarist Russia where Jews were permitted permanent residence.

*__Palmaḥ__ (abbr. for Heb. *peluggot maḥaẓ*; "shock companies"), striking arm of the *Haganah.

*__Pardes__, medieval biblical exegesis giving the literal, allegorical, homiletical, and esoteric interpretations.

*__Parnas__, chief synagogue functionary, originally vested with both religious and administrative functions; subsequently an elected lay leader.

Partition plan(s), proposals for dividing Ereẓ Israel into autonomous areas.

Paytan, composer of **piyyut* (liturgical poetry).

*__Peel Commission__, British Royal Commission appointed by the British government in 1936 to inquire into the Palestine problem and make recommendations for its solution.

Pesaḥ, *Passover.

*__Pilpul__, in talmudic and rabbinic literature, a sharp dialectic used particularly by talmudists in Poland from the 16th century.

*__Pinkas__, community register or minute-book.

*__Piyyut__, (pl. **piyyutim**), Hebrew liturgical poetry.

*__Pizmon__, poem with refrain.

Posek (pl. ***posekim**), decisor; codifier or rabbinic scholar who pronounces decisions in disputes and on questions of Jewish law.

*__Prosbul__, legal method of overcoming the cancelation of debts with the advent of the *sabbatical year.

*__Purim__, festival held on Adar 14 or 15 in commemoration of the delivery of the Jews of Persia in the time of *Esther.

Rabban, honorific title higher than that of rabbi, applied to heads of the *Sanhedrin in mishnaic times.

*__Rabbanite__, adherent of rabbinic Judaism. In contradistinction to *Karaite.

Reb, rebbe, Yiddish form for rabbi, applied generally to a teacher or ḥasidic rabbi.

*__Reconstructionism__, trend in Jewish thought originating in the United States.

*__Reform Judaism__, trend in Judaism advocating modification of *Orthodoxy in conformity with the exigencies of contemporary life and thought.

Resh galuta, lay head of Babylonian Jewry (see exilarch).

Responsum (pl. ***responsa**), written opinion (*teshuvah*) given to question (*she'elah*) on aspects of Jewish law by qualified authorities; pl. collection of such queries and opinions in book form (*she'elot u-teshuvot*).

***Rishonim**, older rabbinical authorities. Distinguished from later authorities (**aharonim*).

***Rishon le-Zion**, title given to Sephardi chief rabbi of Ereẓ Israel.

***Rosh Ha-Shanah**, two-day holiday (one day in biblical and early mishnaic times) at the beginning of the month of *Tishri (September–October), traditionally the New Year.

Rosh Hodesh, *New Moon, marking the beginning of the Hebrew month.

Rosh Yeshivah, see *Yeshivah.

***R.S.H.A.** (initials of Ger. *Reichssicherheitshauptamt*: "Reich Security Main Office"), the central security department of the German Reich, formed in 1939, and combining the security police (Gestapo and Kripo) and the S.D.

***Sanhedrin**, the assembly of ordained scholars which functioned both as a supreme court and as a legislature before 70 C.E. In modern times the name was given to the body of representative Jews convoked by Napoleon in 1807.

***Savora** (pl. **savoraim**), name given to the Babylonian scholars of the period between the **amoraim* and the **geonim*, approximately 500–700 C.E.

S.D. (initials of Ger. *Sicherheitsdienst*: "security service"), security service of the *S.S. formed in 1932 as the sole intelligence organization of the Nazi party.

Seder, ceremony observed in the Jewish home on the first night of Passover (outside Ereẓ Israel first two nights), when the *Haggadah is recited.

***Sefer Torah**, manuscript scroll of the Pentateuch for public reading in synagogue.

***Sefirot, the ten**, the ten "Numbers"; mystical term denoting the ten spheres or emanations through which the Divine manifests itself; elements of the world; dimensions, primordial numbers.

Selektion (Ger.), (1) in ghettos and other Jewish settlements, the drawing up by Nazis of lists of deportees; (2) separation of incoming victims to concentration camps into two categories – those destined for immediate killing and those to be sent for forced labor.

Seliḥah (pl. ***seliḥot**), penitential prayer.

***Semikhah**, ordination conferring the title "rabbi" and permission to give decisions in matters of ritual and law.

Sephardi (pl. ***Sephardim**), Jew(s) of Spain and Portugal and their descendants, wherever resident, as contrasted with *Ashkenazi(m).

Shabbatean, adherent of the pseudo-messiah *Shabbetai Ẓevi (17th century).

Shaddai, name of God found frequently in the Bible and commonly translated "Almighty."

***Shaḥarit**, morning service.

Shali'aḥ (pl. **sheliḥim**), in Jewish law, messenger, agent; in modern times, an emissary from Ereẓ Israel to Jewish communities or organizations abroad for the purpose of fund-raising, organizing pioneer immigrants, education, etc.

Shalmonit, poetic meter introduced by the liturgical poet *Solomon ha-Bavli.

***Shammash**, synagogue beadle.

***Shavuot**, Pentecost; Festival of Weeks; second of the three annual pilgrim festivals, commemorating the receiving of the Torah at Mt. Sinai.

***Sheḥitah**, ritual slaughtering of animals.

***Shekhinah**, Divine Presence.

Shelishit, poem with three-line stanzas.

***Sheluḥei Ereẓ Israel** (or **shadarim**), emissaries from Ereẓ Israel.

***Shema** ([Yisrael]; "hear… [O Israel]," Deut. 6:4), Judaism's confession of faith, proclaiming the absolute unity of God.

Shemini Aẓeret, final festal day (in the Diaspora, final two days) at the conclusion of *Sukkot.

Shemittah, *Sabbatical year.

Sheniyyah, poem with two-line stanzas.

***Shephelah**, southern part of the coastal plain of Ereẓ Israel.

***Shevat**, eleventh month of the Jewish religious year, fifth of the civil, approximating to January–February.

***Shi'ur Komah**, Hebrew mystical work (c. eighth century) containing a physical description of God's dimensions; term denoting enormous spacial measurement used in speculations concerning the body of the **Shekhinah*.

Shivah, the "seven days" of *mourning following burial of a relative.

***Shofar**, horn of the ram (or any other ritually clean animal excepting the cow) sounded for the memorial blowing on *Rosh Ha-Shanah, and other occasions.

Shoḥet, person qualified to perform **sheḥitah*.

Shomer, *Ha-Shomer, organization of Jewish workers in Ereẓ Israel founded in 1909 to defend Jewish settlements.

***Shtadlan**, Jewish representative or negotiator with access to dignitaries of state, active at royal courts, etc.

***Shtetl**, Jewish small-town community in Eastern Europe.

***Shulḥan Arukh**, Joseph *Caro's code of Jewish law in four parts:
Oraḥ Ḥayyim, laws relating to prayers, Sabbath, festivals, and fasts;
Yoreh De'ah, dietary laws, etc;
Even ha-Ezer, laws dealing with women, marriage, etc;
Ḥoshen Mishpat, civil, criminal law, court procedure, etc.

Siddur, among Ashkenazim, the volume containing the daily prayers (in distinction to the **maḥzor* containing those for the festivals).

***Simḥat Torah**, holiday marking the completion in the synagogue of the annual cycle of reading the Pentateuch; in Ereẓ Israel observed on Shemini Aẓeret (outside Ereẓ Israel on the following day).

***Sinai Campaign**, brief campaign in October–November 1956 when Israel army reacted to Egyptian terrorist attacks and blockade by occupying the Sinai peninsula.

Sitra aḥra, "the other side" (of God); left side; the demoniac and satanic powers.

***Sivan**, third month of the Jewish religious year, ninth of the civil, approximating to May–June.

***Six-Day War**, rapid war in June 1967 when Israel reacted to Arab threats and blockade by defeating the Egyptian, Jordanian, and Syrian armies.

***S.S.** (initials of Ger. *Schutzstaffel*: "protection detachment"), Nazi formation established in 1925 which later became the "elite" organization of the Nazi Party and carried out central tasks in the "Final Solution."

***Status quo ante** community, community in Hungary retaining the status it had held before the convention of the General Jewish Congress there in 1868 and the resultant split in Hungarian Jewry.

*__Sukkah__, booth or tabernacle erected for *Sukkot when, for seven days, religious Jews "dwell" or at least eat in the *sukkah* (Lev. 23:42).

*__Sukkot__, festival of Tabernacles; last of the three pilgrim festivals, beginning on the 15th of Tishri.

Sūra (Ar.), chapter of the Koran.

Ta'anit Esther (Fast of *Esther), fast on the 13th of Adar, the day preceding Purim.

Takkanah (pl. ***takkanot**), regulation supplementing the law of the Torah; regulations governing the internal life of communities and congregations.

*__Tallit (gadol)__, four-cornered prayer shawl with fringes (*ẓiẓit*) at each corner.

*__Tallit katan__, garment with fringes (*ẓiẓit*) appended, worn by observant male Jews under their outer garments.

*__Talmud__, "teaching"; compendium of discussion on the Mishnah by generations of scholars and jurists in many academies over a period of several centuries. The Jerusalem (or Palestinian) Talmud mainly contains the discussions of the Palestinian sages. The Babylonian Talmud incorporates the parallel discussion in the Babylonian academies.

Talmud torah, term generally applied to Jewish religious (and ultimately to talmudic) study; also to traditional Jewish religious public schools.

*__Tammuz__, fourth month of the Jewish religious year, tenth of the civil, approximating to June-July.

Tanna (pl. ***tannaim**), rabbinic teacher of mishnaic period.

*__Targum__, Aramaic translation of the Bible.

*__Tefillin__, phylacteries, small leather cases containing passages from Scripture and affixed on the forehead and arm by male Jews during the recital of morning prayers.

Tell (Ar. "mound," "hillock"), ancient mound in the Middle East composed of remains of successive settlements.

*__Terefah__, food that is not **kasher*, owing to a defect on the animal.

*__Territorialism__, 20th century movement supporting the creation of an autonomous territory for Jewish mass-settlement outside Ereẓ Israel.

*__Tevet__, tenth month of the Jewish religious year, fourth of the civil, approximating to December–January.

Tikkun ("restitution," "reintegration"), (1) order of service for certain occasions, mostly recited at night; (2) mystical term denoting restoration of the right order and true unity after the spiritual "catastrophe" which occurred in the cosmos.

Tishah be-Av, Ninth of *Av, fast day commemorating the destruction of the First and Second Temples.

*__Tishri__, seventh month of the Jewish religious year, first of the civil, approximating to September–October.

Tokheḥah, reproof sections of the Pentateuch (Lev. 26 and Deut. 28); poem of reproof.

*__Torah__, Pentateuch or the Pentateuchal scroll for reading in synagogue; entire body of traditional Jewish teaching and literature.

Tosafist, talmudic glossator, mainly French (12–14th centuries), bringing additions to the commentary by *Rashi.

*__Tosafot__, glosses supplied by tosafist.

*__Tosefta__, a collection of teachings and traditions of the *tannaim*, closely related to the Mishnah.

Tradent, person who hands down a talmudic statement on the name of his teacher or other earlier authority.

*__Tu bi-Shevat__, the 15th day of Shevat, the New Year for Trees; date marking a dividing line for fruit tithing; in modern Israel celebrated as arbor day.

*__Uganda Scheme__, plan suggested by the British government in 1903 to establish an autonomous Jewish settlement area in East Africa.

*__Va'ad Le'ummi__, national council of the Jewish community in Ereẓ Israel during the period of the British *Mandate.

*__Wannsee Conference__, Nazi conference held on Jan. 20, 1942, at which the planned annihilation of European Jewry was endorsed.

Waqf (Ar.), (1) a Muslim charitable pious foundation; (2) state lands and other property passed to the Muslim community for public welfare.

*__War of Independence__, war of 1947–49 when the Jews of Israel fought off Arab invading armies and ensured the establishment of the new State.

*__White Paper(s)__, report(s) issued by British government, frequently statements of policy, as issued in connection with Palestine during the *Mandate period.

*__Wissenschaft des Judentums__ (Ger. "Science of Judaism"), movement in Europe beginning in the 19th century for scientific study of Jewish history, religion, and literature.

*__Yad Vashem__, Israel official authority for commemorating the *Holocaust in the Nazi era and Jewish resistance and heroism at that time.

Yeshivah (pl. ***yeshivot**), Jewish traditional academy devoted primarily to study of rabbinic literature; *rosh yeshivah*, head of the yeshivah.

YHWH, the letters of the holy name of God, the Tetragrammaton.

Yibbum, see levirate marriage.

Yiḥud, "union"; mystical term for intention which causes the union of God with the **Shekhinah*.

Yishuv, settlement; more specifically, the Jewish community of Ereẓ Israel in the pre-State period. The pre-Zionist community is generally designated the "old yishuv" and the community evolving from 1880, the "new yishuv."

Yom Kippur, Yom ha-Kippurim, *Day of Atonement, solemn fast day observed on the 10th of Tishri.

Yoreh De'ah, see Shulḥan Arukh.

Yoẓer, hymns inserted in the first benediction (*Yoẓer Or*) of the morning **Shema*.

*__Ẓaddik__, person outstanding for his faith and piety; especially a ḥasidic rabbi or leader.

Ẓimẓum, "contraction"; mystical term denoting the process whereby God withdraws or contracts within Himself so leaving a primordial vacuum in which creation can take place; primordial exile or self-limitation of God.

*__Zionist Commission (1918)__, commission appointed in 1918 by the British government to advise the British military authorities in Palestine on the implementation of the *Balfour Declaration.

Ẓyyonei Zion, the organized opposition to Herzl in connection with the *Uganda Scheme.

*__Ẓiẓit__, fringes attached to the **tallit* and **tallit katan*.

*__Zohar__, mystical commentary on the Pentateuch; main textbook of *Kabbalah.

Zulat, hymn inserted after the **Shema* in the morning service.

ISBN-13: 978-0-02-865939-8
ISBN-10: 0-02-865939-2